T0011362

The
Merriam-
Webster
Thesaurus

The Merriam-Webster Thesaurus

Merriam-Webster, Incorporated

Springfield, Massachusetts

A GENUINE MERRIAM-WEBSTER

The name *Webster* alone is no guarantee of excellence. It is used by a number of publishers and may serve mainly to mislead an unwary buyer.

Merriam-Webster™ is the name you should look for when you consider the purchase of dictionaries or other fine reference books. It carries the reputation of a company that has been publishing since 1831 and is your assurance of quality and authority.

PREFACE

This new edition of *The Merriam-Webster Thesaurus* is specially designed for those who want to enlarge their vocabularies and learn more about the rich variety of the English language. We hope and expect that users will readily turn to a dictionary whenever they need a better understanding of the meaning of any word used in the thesaurus.

In creating this thesaurus, the editors have drawn on years of experience with a thesaurus format that is at once easy to use and broad in its scope. We believe that this thesaurus will prove to be helpful to the user in the selection of the right word, as well as highly useful as a vocabulary builder. Rather than using the more traditional approach of presenting long, undifferentiated lists of words, we present an alphabetical ordering of entries. These entries consist of lists of words that are centered on a specific—and specified—meaning. Main entries consist of lists of synonyms and related words, as well as antonyms and near antonyms whenever applicable. Phrases and idioms that function as synonyms are occasionally offered as well.

The purpose of the differentiated lists is to accommodate the various purposes for which a thesaurus is used. People use a thesaurus generally because they are dissatisfied with the word they already have in mind. They want a different word. The question is: how different?

If users of this thesaurus are trying to avoid a boring repetition of the same word, or are seeking to vary and enrich their vocabulary, then they will wish to select from the list of synonyms a word that shares the same basic meaning as the one they already have but differs from it in suggestion and tone. If they are seeking a word that is different from but still related to what they already have, then they will want to scan the lists of related words for a rewarding journey through the variety of possibilities that English offers.

If users are seeking a word that is to some degree opposite in meaning to what they have, then they will want to consult the lists of antonyms or near antonyms. By specifying the meaning under consideration, and by making distinctions between words that are truly synonymous and those that are only somewhat synonymous, we hope that we have given users the guidance they desire. We believe that this system minimizes the need to guess.

What makes this thesaurus unique is the content of the separate entries for each and every word appearing in the lists of synonyms. Since a user's search for the right word may start anywhere, the thesaurus is arranged so that any member of a synonym group can serve as the starting point. An entry for a listed synonym consists of a restatement of the meaning common to all the members of the group. A user who happens to use a particular synonym as a starting point can follow the cross-reference to the main entry for the complete listing of synonyms, related words, and any antonyms or near antonyms.

The thesaurus format is intended to encourage and facilitate users in finding the right word, which results in writing of greater precision and clarity. The word *thesaurus* literally means "treasury" in Latin, and we hope that the treasure trove of words contained in these pages will enhance the user's interest in and appreciation of the English language. We urge all users to read carefully the following sections entitled Introduction and

Explanatory Notes in order to make the most of what the book has to offer. The Introduction contains an informative discussion of what distinguishes a synonym from a related word, an antonym from a near antonym. The Explanatory Notes section explains in detail the organization of the thesaurus and discusses the differences between the two basic types of entries. Study of this section is especially important.

The Merriam-Webster Thesaurus was edited by Serenity H. Carr, who worked on *Merriam-Webster's Intermediate Thesaurus*, upon which much of this new edition of *The Merriam-Webster Thesaurus* is based. Credit for editing also goes to Em Vezina and Linda Wood, whose work on *Merriam-Webster's School Thesaurus* informed many of the revisions made to this book. The entire project was supervised by Em Vezina, who also handled the task of cross-reference. Daniel Brandon and Anne E. McDonald handled data entry and data-file processing and contributed essential technical assistance in a number of other ways. Susan L. Brady and Faith de Castro served as editors in charge of production, guiding the book through its typesetting stages. Proofreaders included Sarah Carragher, Carin A. Helfer, Diana M. Jones, Michael D. Metivier, and Emily D. Villanueva.

INTRODUCTION

Synonyms

The English language contains a wealth of words, and perhaps no other language has as many synonyms. A carefully chosen synonym can add variety and precision to the work of any writer, whether that writer is a professional or a student.

So, just what are synonyms? Put simply, synonyms are words that mean the same thing. Words that are only somewhat similar in meaning—but do not mean the same thing—are not true synonyms. They are merely related words, and they belong in a different category. In this thesaurus a word is only classified as a synonym if it shares at least one basic meaning with another word.

Here's an example of how we arrived at the basic meaning shared by a group of words. The word *fort* is defined in *The Merriam-Webster Dictionary* as "a fortified place." Since a person using *fort* as the starting point in their search for the right word is probably dissatisfied with that term, the word they are seeking will most likely come under a broader or more basic meaning. We can phrase that more basic meaning as: "a structure or place from which one can resist attack." The list of synonyms for *fort*—*bastion, castle, citadel, fastness, fortification, fortress, hold, stronghold*—can all be said to share this basic meaning. None of these words share identically worded definitions, but they do have in common a basic meaning that allows them to be regarded as synonyms.

If a word is more limited in scope than the basic meaning given at a main entry, then it cannot be regarded as a synonym for that word group. Hence, the words *battlement* and *bulwark* are entered only as related words at *fort*, as they refer to specific kinds of defensive structures.

Related Words

Often thesaurus users are not looking for something that means exactly the same as the word they already have in mind. To help in this situation, *The Merriam-Webster Thesaurus* includes lists of words whose meanings are close to the group of synonyms and are likely to be of interest to the user. These related words do not qualify as synonyms because they have meanings that differ from the basic meaning shared by that group of synonyms. For example, the word *funny* has the meaning of "causing or intended to cause laughter." A person who is making "funny faces" is causing, or at least trying to cause, others to laugh. *Witty*, although closely related to *funny*, has a slightly different meaning: "given to or marked by mature intelligent humor." A witty person is someone who has a habit of making clever remarks that display a grown-up sense of humor. Because of the close relationship between *funny* and *witty*, some of the words listed as synonyms at *witty* are given as related words at *funny*. Thesaurus users are encouraged to go from one related entry to another when searching for just the right word for their purpose.

Some words are not true synonyms of anything, but because they are so fundamentally useful, they have been included in this thesaurus among the lists of related words and in places where they are likely to be most helpful. For example, the word *ballast*, which refers to any type of "heavy material used to stabilize a ship," is too narrow in meaning to have any synonyms of its own. It is related to the more general term *load*, however, and so, fittingly, it is included as a related word at the entry for the noun *load*.

Antonyms

An antonym is a word whose meaning is directly opposite to another word's meaning. The notion of negation is fundamental to this thesaurus's concept of an antonym. An antonym has a meaning that completely cancels out another word's meaning. *Short* and *tall* are complete opposites. Something cannot be both short and tall at the same time, and both words suggest about the same degree of deviation from the norm or average for height. *Good* and *evil* are another pair of exact opposites. Logically, something cannot be both *good* and *evil* in the same way and at the same time.

Words that are only opposite in some aspect of their meaning cannot be said to be true antonyms. For example, *sad,* which means "causing unhappiness," is not a true antonym of *funny,* which means "causing or intended to cause laughter." The opposite of unhappiness is happiness, and there are things that make people happy without generating laughter. Similarly, *hurt,* which means "to feel or cause physical pain," is not an antonym of *heal,* which means "to restore to a healthy condition." The exact opposite of "to feel or cause physical pain" would be "to feel or cause physical pleasure." *Hurt* and *heal* are certainly contrary words, but they differ in their focus and in what they suggest. Pairs of words like *hurt* and *heal* are better regarded as near antonyms.

In this thesaurus, pairs of true antonyms generally fall into three basic classes: (1) words that are mutually exclusive and have no middle ground between them, as *dead* and *alive,* or *perfect* and *imperfect;* (2) words that are on opposite ends of some spectrum, as *maximum* and *minimum,* or *huge* and *tiny;* (3) words that in effect reverse or undo one another, as *assemble* and *disassemble,* or *prove* and *disprove.*

Near Antonyms

Near antonyms are words that do not qualify as antonyms under the strict definition used for this thesaurus but which are clearly in marked contrast with the members of a synonym group. Just as a user may not be seeking a word that is exactly synonymous with another, they may not be seeking a word that is exactly opposite. The user may simply want a word that lies somewhere on the opposite side of the spectrum of meaning. *Afraid* is not so exactly opposite to *courageous* as *cowardly* is, but *afraid* and *courageous* certainly have significantly contrasting meanings and can be considered near antonyms of each other.

Phrases

This thesaurus also includes phrases that, taken as a whole, are synonymous with individual words. Some of these are fixed phrases that contain a word that is entered in the dictionary at its own alphabetical place but is never, or almost never, used except in a fixed phrase. For example, *in jeopardy* appears as a synonymous phrase at *liable* because someone who is liable (that is, "exposed") to something dangerous or undesirable is a person "in jeopardy." The word *jeopardy* is normally used with this meaning only in the phrase *in jeopardy.*

Idioms constitute the other major class of word combinations that are entered under the heading of phrases. Idioms are phrases that have a figurative meaning that is different from the literal meaning of the individual components of the phrase pieced together. For example, the phrase *make good* is virtually meaningless if one attempts to piece together the literal meanings of *make* and *good.* As a fixed phrase, however, *make good* means "to reach a desired level of accomplishment" and is a synonym of *succeed.*

Choosing the Right Word—Using Your Dictionary

Deciding which word in a thesaurus entry is best for your purposes is not always easy. The basic meaning shared by the members of a synonym group cannot tell you everything you need to know in order to choose the word that best suits your needs.

Something that is "very pleasing to look at" can be described as *attractive, beauteous, beautiful, comely, cute, fair, gorgeous, handsome, knockout, lovely, pretty, ravishing, sightly, stunning,* or *taking,* but which word is best for describing a sunset? A city? Should you use *knockout* to describe a cathedral or *ravishing* for a sports car?

If you decide that you still have not found the right word after reviewing the synonyms, then you have the list of related words to consider:

> *rel* alluring, appealing, charming, cunning, delightful, engaging, fascinating, glamorous (*also* glamourous), prepossessing; elegant, exquisite, glorious, magnificent, resplendent, splendid, statuesque, sublime, superb; flawless, perfect, radiant; dainty, delicate . . .

Now you have 38 words that mean the same thing or nearly the same thing as *beautiful*. Here's where you need a good dictionary. You can consult the dictionary to get a precise definition of any word in the lists, and perhaps an example of its use. You should always use this thesaurus along with a good dictionary.

Every user of *The Merriam-Webster Thesaurus* is encouraged to read the following information because a thorough understanding of the *Thesaurus*'s scope, philosophy, and structure is essential to its effective use.

SCOPE OF THE MERRIAM-WEBSTER THESAURUS

This thesaurus is intended to be a tool for the conscientious writer who is seeking the precisely right word. It is therefore centered on the general vocabulary of the English language. It is this part of the language that is rich with words that have special nuances, distinctive connotations, and varying degrees of formality. As a consequence, the user generally will not find words that belong to science, technology, or other specialized fields. Obsolete and extremely rare terms have also been omitted, as these would do little to help the writer seeking genuinely useful words. Lastly, words that have been labeled as *vulgar, obscene, disparaging, offensive,* or *nonstandard* in Merriam-Webster's online dictionary, *Merriam-Webster.com,* have been disregarded.

ENTRY ORDER

The boldface word or phrase at the beginning of a thesaurus entry is called a **headword.** Headwords appear in alphabetical order for ease of use. Alphabetization is by first letter, then second letter, and so on, regardless of any spaces or hyphens that may separate those letters:

make *vb*
make–believe *adj*
make out *vb*
make over *vb*
Maker *n*
makeshift *adj*

When a headword contains a numeral, the numeral is alphabetized as though it were a spelled-out word:

anywise *adv*
A1 *adj*
apace *adv*

Homographs are words that are spelled exactly the same but are different parts of speech or have entirely different etymologies (word origins). Homographs that are different parts of speech are simply entered as separate headwords:

bat *n* 1 a hard strike with a part of the body or an instrument
bat *vb* 1 to deliver a blow to (someone or something) . . .

bear *n* 1 a dull, unpleasant, or difficult piece of work
bear *vb* 1 to bring forth from the womb

If two or more homographs are the same part of speech, they are entered as separate headwords and are grouped together and numbered:

¹**list** *n* a record of a series of items (as names or titles) usually arranged according to some system
²**list** *n* the act of positioning or an instance of being positioned at an angle
³**list** *n* a long narrow piece of material
¹**list** *vb* 1 to make a list of
²**list** *vb* to set or cause to be at an angle

As discussed below under the heading "Some Notes about Verbs," verbs that are customarily used in combination with a preposition or an adverb appear as headwords in this thesaurus in either of two ways: with the verb followed by the preposition or adverb in parentheses, or with both the verb and its companion preposition or adverb. Simple verbs are listed first, followed by verbs with parenthetical prepositions or adverbs, which are in turn followed by the boldface verb-adverb or verb-preposition combinations:

talk *vb*
talk (into) *vb*
talk (to) *vb*

talkative *adj*
talk down (to) *vb*
talker *n*
talk over *vb*

When headwords are compound words, a closed compound (one without a space or hyphen) is entered before a hyphenated compound, and a hyphenated compound is entered before an open compound (one with an intervening space):

nosedive *n*
nose–dive *vb*

open–air *adj*
open air *n*

PLURAL NOUNS

Some nouns are always pluralized or are pluralized when they are used with certain meanings. When a thesaurus entry for a noun includes no senses that are used in the singular, the plural form is given as the headword:

leavings *n pl* a remaining group or portion — see REMAINDER 1

When a noun is often or usually, but not always, used in the plural form, the singular form is used for the headword, and the plural follows, introduced by the label *often* or *usually*:

shallow *n, usually* **shallows** *pl* a place where a body of water (as a sea or river) is shallow — see SHOAL

When such a noun appears in a list of synonyms, related words, etc., it is shown as a plural form with parentheses around the final *s* or *es*:

shoal *n* a place where a body of water (as a sea or river) is shallow ⟨The *shoals* of Nantucket Island are famous as the final resting place of many ill-fated ships.⟩
syn ford, shallow(s)

When a noun is used in the singular form in one sense and in the plural form in another, the singular form is given as the headword. The plural form is indicated at the appropriate sense or senses:

provision *n* **1** something upon which the carrying out of an agreement or offer depends — see CONDITION 2
2 provisions *pl* substances intended to be eaten — see FOOD 1

VARIANTS

An alternate spelling or form of a headword is called a **variant**. Variants are shown in boldface type immediately after the headword and are introduced by *or* or *also*. The label *or* means that the variant is as common, or nearly as common, as the headword. As long as the variants are equally common, the headword is the spelling that comes first alphabetically.

OK *or* **okay** *vb*
theater *or* **theatre** *n*

However, if one of the spellings is used slightly more frequently than the other, the more common one is shown first even if it does not fall first alphabetically:

goody *or* **goodie** *n*

A variant that is introduced by the label *also* is considerably less common than the headword:

among *also* **amongst** *prep*
facade *also* **façade** *n*
naught *also* **nought** *n*

When two variants are separated from the headword by *also* but from each other by *or*, it means that both variants are considerably less common than the headword:

bogey *also* **bogie** *or* **bogy** *n*

Variants are also shown in the word lists within the entries:

zero *n* **1** the numerical symbol 0 or the absence of number or quantity represented by it ⟨Anything multiplied by *zero* comes out to *zero.*⟩
syn aught, cipher, goose egg, naught (*also* nought), nil, nothing, oh, zilch, zip

CAPITALIZATION

When an entry word is capitalized in ordinary writing, it is entered in this thesaurus with a capital letter. Other entries begin with a lowercase letter.

Almighty *n* the being worshipped as the creator and ruler of the universe — see DEITY 2

Some words have special meanings when capitalized that they do not have without a capital letter. This thesaurus shows the use of the capital with such entries by putting the label *cap* at the appropriate sense.

pandemonium *n* **1** a state of noisy, confused activity — see COMMOTION
2 *cap* the place of punishment for the wicked after death — see HELL 1

PARTS OF SPEECH

Every headword is followed by one of the following abbreviated part-of-speech labels: *adj* (adjective), *adv* (adverb), *conj* (conjunction), *interj* (interjection), *n* (noun), *prep* (preposition), *pron* (pronoun), or *vb* (verb). Plural nouns are followed by the *n pl* label.

KINDS OF ENTRIES

This thesaurus consists of two types of entries: **main entries** and **cross entries**. Each main entry provides a full treatment of a group of synonyms and is located at the alphabetical place of one of the most important words in the group. The cross entries, which are shorter than the main entries, can be found at the alphabetical place of each of the synonyms listed at the main entries. Every headword with its part-of-speech label is followed by either one or more main entries, one or more cross entries, or a combination of the two. If there is more than one meaning treated at a given headword, all the main entries will come first, followed by all the cross entries, and each will begin with a boldface sense number.

A main entry always includes a statement of the core meaning shared by the members of a synonym group. It is by this means that the user knows in what sense the members of the group are being treated as synonyms. This statement of shared meaning is followed by a verbal illustration for the headword. The illustration is followed by a list of synonyms as well as such related words, phrases, near antonyms, and antonyms as may exist for that meaning.

famous *adj* **1** widely known ⟨a book about some of the most *famous* people of the last century⟩
syn celebrated, famed, noted, notorious, prominent, renowned, star, visible, well-known

rel fabled, fabulous, legendary; infamous; distinguished, eminent, exceptional, great, illustrious, leading, notable, noteworthy, outstanding, preeminent, prestigious, remarkable, supereminent, superior; important, significant; acknowledged, recognized, respected; favorite, popular, preferred
near insignificant, unimportant; inconspicuous; undistinguished, unexceptional; unpopular
ant anonymous, nameless, obscure, uncelebrated, unknown, unsung

Every word in the list of synonyms at each main entry is entered at its own alphabetical place as a cross entry. The statement of shared meaning that appears at the main entry will be shown at the cross entry as well. This is done so that the user who is looking at the cross entry will know whether the main entry treats the sense that they are interested in. The cross entry does not repeat the synonyms, related words, phrases, near antonyms, or antonyms given at the main entry. Instead, at the end of the cross entry, there is a reference that points the user to the appropriate main entry:

celebrated *adj* widely known — see FAMOUS 1
fade *vb* **1** to cease to be visible — see DISAPPEAR
2 to make white or whiter by removing color — see WHITEN
3 to lose bodily strength or vigor — see WEAKEN 2

CROSS-REFERENCES

A **cross-reference** is a direction at the end of a cross entry that tells the user where the main entry for that particular shared meaning is located. If there is more than one sense at the headword referred to in the cross-reference, the cross-reference will include the relevant sense number. If there is more than one numbered homograph for a headword, the cross-reference will include the correct homograph number as well:

pain *vb* to feel or cause physical pain —
see HURT 1
ranking *n* **1** a scheme of rank or order —
see ³SCALE 1

Cross-references are always between words having the same part of speech. In the above example, for instance, the cross-reference is to the first sense of the third homograph for the noun *scale,* which is of course the same part of speech as *ranking:*

³scale *n* **1** a scheme of rank or order ⟨a student who scored very highly on a standard intelligence *scale*⟩
syn graduation, ladder, ordering, ranking

SPECIAL USAGE LABELS

Occasionally words in this thesaurus will bear italicized usage labels. The following labels indicate that a word is limited to regional use: *British, Midland, Scottish, Southern,* and *West.* All of these designations may be used in combination with one another (as *Southern & Midland*) or qualified by the word *chiefly.* Three other labels that have been used for this thesaurus are *dialect, slang,* and *archaic.* The label *dialect* indicates that a word occurs in several regional varieties of American or British English and that the pattern of its usage is too complicated to be concisely labeled. The stylistic label *slang* indicates that the word is used most appropriately in very informal contexts. The temporal label *archaic* indicates that the word is nowadays used only in special contexts, such as poetry or historical fiction:

cop *vb, slang*
creek *n* . . . **2** *chiefly British*

kirk *n, chiefly Scottish*
plumb *adv* . . . **2** *chiefly dialect*

When a headword has multiple senses and a usage label applies to one or more of them but not to all of them, the label will come after the appropriate sense numbers:

jack *n* **1** *slang* something (as pieces of stamped metal or printed paper) customarily and legally used as a medium of exchange, a measure of value, or a means of payment — see MONEY
2 a piece of cloth with a special design that is used as an emblem or for signaling — see FLAG 1

In the word lists at main entries, special usage labels appear in square brackets immediately after the words to which they apply:

car *n* a self-propelled passenger vehicle on four wheels . . .
syn auto, automobile, machine, motor, motorcar, motor vehicle, wheels [*slang*]

SHARED MEANINGS

Every entry contains a statement of the meaning shared by members of a synonym group. This shared meaning is the "thing" that is referred to when we say that two or more words "mean the same thing" and thus qualify as synonyms. The statement of shared meaning follows the part-of-speech label in single-sense entries and the sense number in multisense entries.

Sometimes there are parenthetical elements within these statements of shared meaning, as in the following entry:

payment *n* . . .
2 something (as money) that is given or received in return for goods or services ⟨Our *payment* for all the work we did barely covered our expenses.⟩ ⟨We finally mailed our last car *payment* last week.⟩

syn compensation, consideration, pay, recompense, remittance, remuneration, requital

The parenthetical element is intended to suggest the usual range of application of a group of words, but it should not be interpreted as a strict limitation of a word's application.

SOME NOTES ABOUT VERBS

Verbs that have a given meaning only when they are followed by a particular word appear as headwords in this thesaurus in one of several ways. Sometimes both the verb and the following adverb or preposition are shown in boldface:

burn out *vb* to use up all the physical energy of

Sometimes the verb is shown followed by an adverb, preposition, or other word in parentheses:

comply (with) *vb* **1** to act according to the commands of
knock (about) *vb* to move about from place to place aimlessly
leg (it) *vb* to go on foot

And sometimes both styles are combined:

hold off (on) *vb* to assign to a later time

If there are two words inside the parentheses and they are separated by *or,* then either word can be used with the verb:

fit (in *or* into) *vb* to put among or between others

A verb that has a parenthesized element when shown as a headword has that same parenthesized element when the verb appears in a word list. Users who encounter such a verb in a list should remember that the complete verb combination must be used for it to match the shared meaning of its synonym group:

obey *vb* to act according to the commands of . . .
    syn adhere (to), comply (with), conform (to), follow, mind, observe

When the statement of shared meaning calls for a direct object, all of the members of a synonym group will take a direct object. If the statement of shared meaning does not call for a direct object, then none of the synonyms will take an object. One frequent clue that the members of a word group take an object is the fact that the statement of shared meaning ends with a preposition:

constitute *vb* **1** to be all the substance of ⟨Nine players *constitute* a baseball team.⟩

Not all verbs requiring an object are worded this way, however, so the user may need to study the verbal illustration to determine the need for a direct object.

VERBAL ILLUSTRATIONS

Every main entry word in this thesaurus is illustrated with an example of its typical use. This **verbal illustration** appears after the statement of shared meaning and is set off by angle brackets. The word being illustrated is italicized in each verbal illustration.

fight *vb* **1** to oppose (someone) in physical conflict ⟨a proud people who have fiercely *fought* all invaders of their homeland⟩
high *adj* **1** extending to a great distance upward ⟨Mount Everest is the *highest* mountain in the world.⟩

SYNONYMS USED IN DEFINING

The central word in a dictionary definition is known as the defining term, and every definition has to have one. Likewise, each statement of shared meaning in this thesaurus includes a defining term. For example, in the entry for the word **gadget**, the noun *device* is the defining term. If *device* had not been used as the defining term, it could have been included with good justification in the list of synonyms. However, since it was in fact used as the defining term, *device* was omitted from the list in accordance with our practice of not using a word both as a defining term and as a synonym at the same main entry.

gadget *n* an interesting and often novel device with a practical use ⟨She tried out a new *gadget* for weeding the garden.⟩
syn appliance, contraption, contrivance, gimmick, gizmo (*also* gismo), jigger

Synonym lists are introduced by the abbreviation **syn.**

RELATED WORDS

The cornerstone of every entry in this thesaurus is the list of synonyms. For the vast majority of main entries, an often generous supply of related words is provided to supplement the synonyms. The lists of related words are meant to suggest to the user an array of paths that might be taken in search of the precisely right word. The number of related words often exceeds that of the synonyms because related words do not have to match the synonyms' shared meaning; they need only relate to some aspect of that statement of shared meaning. Where appropriate, related words are divided into subgroups which are separated by semicolons. Words within each subgroup are usually closer in meaning to each other than to members of neighboring subgroups. The subgroups are generally presented in order of most relevant to least relevant. Related word lists are introduced by the abbreviation **rel.**

conceited *adj* having too high an opinion of oneself ⟨a *conceited* basketball player who was always too busy even to sign autographs⟩
syn assured, complacent, consequential, egoistic (*also* egoistical), egotistic (*or* egotistical), important, overweening, pompous, prideful, proud, self-conceited, self-important, self-satisfied, smug, stuck-up, vain, vainglorious
rel blusterous, blustery, boastful, bombastic, braggart, bragging, braggy, cocky, swaggering; arrogant, cavalier, disdainful, haughty, high-hat, lofty, lordly, masterful, self-assertive, supercilious, superior, toplofty (*also* toploftical), uppish, uppity; domineering, high-handed, imperious; highfalutin (*also* hifalutin), holier-than-thou, pretentious; overconfident, presuming, presumptuous; confident, self-assured, self-confident; self-adulatory, self-congratulatory, self-contented, self-gratulatory; self-applauding, self-dramatizing, self-glorifying, self-promoting; self-affected, self-centered, self-engrossed, selfish; condescending, patronizing

PHRASES

The heading **phrases** is reserved for expressions that, taken as a whole, are synonymous with their entry's synonym group. These expressions are shown in a list of their own but do not have their own cross entries. These ex-

pressions are often colorful figures of speech that add interest and variety to one's writing, but the writer is advised to look up unfamiliar expressions in a dictionary before attempting to use them.

NEAR ANTONYMS

Just as related words are not exact synonyms, near antonyms are not exact antonyms. Not every synonym group will have near antonyms, but in general they are more plentiful than exact antonyms. As is the case with related words, near antonyms are typically divided into subgroups separated by semicolons. And as with related words, near antonyms are generally

listed in order of relevancy. Near antonym lists are introduced by the abbreviation **near ant.**

maintenance *n* the act or activity of keeping something in an existing and usually satisfactory condition ⟨I was hired to perform basic *maintenance* until the property could be sold.⟩
syn conservation, conserving, preservation, preserving, upkeep

rel support, sustaining; care, custody, guardianship; defense, guarding, protection, safeguarding, safekeeping
near ant dereliction, disregard, ignor-

ing, inattention, neglect, negligence; damage, demolition, destruction, harm, hurt, injury, ruin, ruination

ANTONYMS

The words in a main entry's antonym list are exactly opposite in meaning to the headword and its list of synonyms. A true antonym is a word whose meaning completely cancels another word's meaning. True antonyms do not exist for many words in this thesaurus. There are no words that completely cancel out the shared meaning at *car*: "a self-propelled passenger vehicle on four wheels." There is no word in English that essentially means "not a car." A word like *truck* may be used in contradistinction to *car*, but *truck* and *car* are not antonyms. In this thesaurus words listed as antonyms are given their own cross entries only if they appear as synonyms at some other entry. The word *torrid* has its own cross entry; the cross-reference is to *hot* 1, where the word is a synonym, and not to *cold* 1, where it is an antonym.

At most main entries all of the members of an antonym list are synonyms of each other. At some entries, however, while all the listed antonyms are opposite

in meaning to the synonym group, they are not opposite in exactly the same way. Antonym lists are introduced by the abbreviation *ant*.

> **colorful** *adj* marked by a variety of usually vivid colors ⟨the *colorful* markings on butterflies⟩
> *syn* motley, multicolored, polychromatic, polychrome, varicolored, varied, variegated . . .
> *ant* colorless; monochromatic, self-colored, solid

The opposite meaning of "marked by a variety of usually vivid colors" is "not marked by a variety of usually vivid colors." All of the words in the antonym list fit that meaning. The word *colorless* means "lacking an addition of color." The other antonyms, *monochromatic, self-colored,* and *solid,* mean "having or consisting of a single color" and so, of course, are not synonyms of *colorless.* Antonyms that are not synonymous with each other are separated by semicolons.

THE WORD LIST LABEL KEY

This thesaurus uses the following abbreviations for word list labels:

syn synonym(s) *rel* related words
ant antonym(s) *near ant* near antonym(s)

These abbreviations are specified in the **word list label key**, located in the bottom left corner of every page spread.

A NOTE ABOUT THE LISTS: WORD DUPLICATION

In this thesaurus no word will appear in more than one list at any single main entry. The general vocabulary of the English language has a plethora of words with more than one sense. One sense of a multisense word in *The Merriam-Webster Dictionary* might be exactly synonymous with a thesaurus entry's statement of shared meaning. Another sense of that same multisense word might be properly regarded as being no more than closely related to it. To avoid confusion, this thesaurus enters such words only in the entry's synonym list and not in the list of related

words as well. For example, the much-used word *nice* is in the synonym list at *pleasant,* where the shared meaning is "giving pleasure or contentment to the mind or senses." *Nice* can also be found in the synonym list at *amiable,* where the shared meaning is "having an easygoing and pleasing manner especially in social situations." Since *amiable* is in the list of related words at *pleasant,* one might expect to find *nice* there as well. But finding the same word at two places in the same entry would be confusing for many users, so *nice* is included only in the list of synonyms.

Sometimes multisense words have meanings that are opposite to one another—or nearly so. For example, *The Merriam-Webster Dictionary* defines one sense of *nervy* as "showing calm courage," or the equivalent of "fearless," and another sense of the word as "excitable, nervous." Thus, at the thesaurus entry for *nervous*, where the shared meaning for the first given sense is "feeling or showing uncomfortable feelings of uncertainty," *nervy* appears alongside of *jittery, jumpy, tense, uneasy, uptight* and several other synonyms. The list of near antonyms for this same sense of *nervous* includes *confident, self-assured, self-confident,* and *sure. Nervy* might well have been added to the list, in light of the fact that it has a sense meaning "showing calm courage." *Nervy* was omitted from the list of near antonyms to avoid unnecessary confusion.

GUIDE WORDS

Guide words are boldface words that are placed at the top of each page spread. They are there to indicate the alphabetical range of entries on that spread, thereby facilitating the user's search for entries. The first guide word is the headword of the first entry beginning on that page spread, and the second guide word is the headword of that page spread's final entry.

aback *adv* without warning — see UN-AWARES

abaft *adv* near, toward, or in the stern of a ship or the tail of an aircraft — see AFT

abaft *prep* at, to, or toward the rear of — see BEHIND 1

abandon *n* carefree freedom from constraint ⟨She added spices to the stew with complete *abandon*.⟩

syn abandonment, ease, lightheartedness, naturalness, spontaneity, spontaneousness, unrestraint

rel ardor, enthusiasm, exuberance, fervor, spirit, warmth, zeal, zealotry, zealousness; carelessness, heedlessness, impulsiveness, indiscretion, insouciance, recklessness, thoughtlessness; unself-consciousness; casualness, offhandedness; excess, indulgence, licentiousness, permissiveness, wantonness, wildness; blank check, free hand

near ant embarrassment, reserve, reticence, self-consciousness, uneasiness; inhibition, repression, self-restraint, suppression; carefulness, discreetness, discretion, heedfulness; discipline, self-control, self-denial, self-discipline, willpower

ant deny

abandon *vb* 1 to give (oneself) over to something especially unrestrainedly ⟨more than ready to *abandon* himself to a life of complete idleness for the duration of his vacation⟩

syn deliver, give up, indulge, surrender, yield

rel overdo, overindulge; bask, luxuriate, revel, roll, wallow

near ant abstain (from), eschew, forbear, forgo (*also* forego), refrain (from); check, inhibit, restrain

ant deny

2 to cause to remain behind — see LEAVE 1

3 to put an end to (something planned or previously agreed to) — see CANCEL 1

4 to stop doing (something) permanently — see QUIT 2

abandoned *adj* 1 left unoccupied or unused ⟨She consciously avoided walking past the *abandoned* house, with its broken windows and sagging porch.⟩

syn derelict, deserted, desolate, disused, forgotten, forsaken, rejected, vacant, vacated, void

rel ignored, neglected, unattended, untended; castaway, cast-off, discarded, jettisoned, junked, refuse, waste; godforsaken, miserable, shabby, wretched; empty, idle

near ant reclaimed, recovered, redeemed, rescued, retrieved, salvaged, saved; reconditioned, rehabbed, rehabilitated, restored; repeopled

2 showing no signs of being under control — see RAMPANT 1

abandonment *n* 1 carefree freedom from constraint — see ABANDON

2 the act of abandoning — see DERELICTION 1

3 the act of putting an end to something

planned or previously agreed to — see CANCELLATION

abase *vb* 1 to lower in character, dignity, or quality — see DEBASE 1

2 to reduce to a lower standing in one's own eyes or in others' eyes — see HUMBLE

abash *vb* to throw into a state of self-conscious distress — see EMBARRASS 1

abashment *n* the emotional state of being made self-consciously uncomfortable — see EMBARRASSMENT 1

abate *vb* 1 to grow less in scope or intensity especially gradually — see DECREASE 2

2 to make smaller in amount, volume, or extent — see DECREASE 1

3 to put an end to by formal action — see ABOLISH 1

4 to take away (an amount or number) from a total — see SUBTRACT

abatement *n* 1 something that is or may be subtracted — see DEDUCTION 1

2 the amount by which something is lessened — see DECREASE

abbey *n* a residence for men under religious vows — see MONASTERY

abbreviate *vb* to make less in extent or duration — see SHORTEN

abbreviation *n* a shortened version of a written work — see ABRIDGMENT

abdicate *vb* to give up (as a position of authority) formally ⟨The revolutionary government forced Nicholas II to *abdicate* the Russian throne.⟩

syn cede, relinquish, renounce, resign, step down (from), surrender

rel abjure, deny, disavow, disclaim, disown, waive; forsake, give up, hand over, yield; abandon, desert, quit, vacate

near ant appropriate, arrogate, assume, claim, confiscate; seize, take over, usurp, wrest; defend, guard, protect, safeguard, secure

abdomen *n* the part of the body between the chest and the pelvis — see STOMACH 1

abduct *vb* to carry away (as a person) forcibly or unlawfully — see KIDNAP

aberrant *adj* 1 being out of the ordinary — see EXCEPTIONAL 1

2 departing from some accepted standard of what is normal — see DEVIANT

aberration *n* something that is different from what is ordinary or expected — see ANOMALY 1

abet *vb* 1 to bring (something volatile or intense) into being — see INCITE 1

2 to provide (someone) with what is useful or necessary to achieve an end — see HELP 1

abetment *n* an act or instance of helping — see HELP 1

abettor *also* **abetter** *n* 1 one associated with another in wrongdoing — see ACCOMPLICE

2 someone associated with another to give assistance or moral support — see ALLY

abeyance *n* a state of temporary inactivity ⟨Our weekend plans were held in *abeyance* until we could get a weather forecast.⟩

syn doldrums, dormancy, holding pattern, latency, moratorium, quiescence, suspense, suspension

rel inaction, inertia, inertness, motionlessness; impasse, standstill; coma, hibernation, hypnosis, repose, rest, sleep, slumber; recess, recession, remission; idleness, layoff

near ant recommencement, renewal, resumption, resuscitation

ant continuance, continuation

abhor *vb* to dislike strongly — see HATE

abhorrence *n* **1** something or someone that is hated — see HATE 2

2 a very strong dislike — see HATE 1

abhorrent *adj* **1** causing intense displeasure, disgust, or resentment — see OFFENSIVE 1

2 feeling or showing open dislike for someone or something regarded as undeserving of respect or concern — see CONTEMPTUOUS 1

abidance *n* **1** the following of a custom, rule, or law — see OBSERVANCE 1

2 uninterrupted or lasting existence — see CONTINUATION

abide *vb* **1** to continue to be in a place for a significant amount of time — see ¹STAY 1

2 to have a home — see LIVE 1

3 to put up with (something painful or difficult) — see BEAR 2

4 to remain indefinitely in existence or in the same state — see CONTINUE 1

abiding *adj* having an existence or validity that does not change or diminish ⟨I have an *abiding* interest in animal welfare—it's not just a phase I'm going through.⟩

syn ageless, continuing, dateless, enduring, eternal, everlasting, immortal, imperishable, lasting, ongoing, perennial, perpetual, timeless, undying

rel ceaseless, endless, permanent; changeless, constant, stable, stationary, steady, unchanging, unvarying

near ant antiquated, archaic, dated, obsolete, outdated, outmoded, out-of-date, outworn, passé

ability *n* the physical or mental power to do something ⟨As a result of the accident the once-vigorous athlete lost the *ability* to walk.⟩

syn capability, capacity, competence, competency, faculty

rel aptitude, aptness, endowment, equipment, facility, gift, knack, talent; address, adroitness, deftness, dexterity, hand, skill; gray matter, instinct, intelligence, ken, reason, understanding; might, potency, staying power; adequacy, effectiveness, effectualness, fitness, form, influence, resourcefulness, usefulness; means, resources, wherewithal

near ant helplessness, impotence, paralysis, powerlessness, weakness; defectiveness, deficiency, inadequacy, ineffectiveness, ineffectuality, inefficaciousness, inefficacy, uselessness; debilitation, disablement, impairment, incapacitation

ant disability, inability, incapability, incapableness, incapacity, incompetence, ineptitude, ineptness

abjure *vb* **1** to solemnly or formally reject or go back on (as something formerly adhered to) ⟨The woman *abjured* some longheld beliefs when she converted to another religion.⟩

syn recant, renege, renounce, repeal, repudiate, retract, take back, unsay, withdraw

rel contradict, deny, disavow, disclaim, disown, gainsay, negate, negative; abandon, bolt, forsake, give up, relinquish, spurn, surrender; disagree (with), disprove, dispute, rebut, refute; back down, back off, backtrack; disallow, recall, revoke

near ant acknowledge, admit, affirm, assert, avow, claim, contend, declare, maintain, proclaim, profess, state, vouch, vow; back, confirm, defend, endorse (*also* indorse), espouse, maintain, support, uphold; accept, adopt, embrace

ant adhere (to)

2 to resist the temptation of — see FORBEAR

ablaze *adj* **1** being on fire ⟨The entire block was *ablaze* by the time firefighters arrived.⟩

syn afire, aflame, blazing, burning, combusting, fiery, flaming, ignited, inflamed (*also* enflamed), kindled

rel aglow, flickering, glowing, live, smoldering (*or* smouldering); broiling, hot, piping hot, red-hot, roasting, scalding, scorching, searing, sizzling; burned (*or* burnt), charred, incinerated, scorched, seared, singed

near ant choked, damped, dead, doused (*also* dowsed), extinguished, quenched, smothered, snuffed (out), stamped (out), suffocated

2 filled with much light — see BRIGHT 2

able *adj* having the required skills for an acceptable level of performance — see COMPETENT 1

able–bodied *adj* enjoying health and vigor — see HEALTHY 1

ably *adv* in a skillful or expert manner — see WELL 3

abnormal *adj* **1** being out of the ordinary — see EXCEPTIONAL 1

2 departing from some accepted standard of what is normal — see DEVIANT

abnormality *n* **1** a person, thing, or event that is far from normal — see FREAK 1

2 something that is different from what is ordinary or expected — see ANOMALY 1

abode *n* the place where one lives — see HOME 1

abolish *vb* **1** to put an end to by formal action ⟨The U.S. *abolished* slavery by constitutional amendment on December 6, 1865.⟩

syn abate, abrogate, annul, avoid, cancel, dissolve, invalidate, negate, null, nullify, quash, repeal, rescind, vacate, void

rel countermand, override, overrule, overturn, veto; abort, call, call off, drop, recall, retract, reverse, revoke, suspend, withdraw; ban, enjoin, forbid, outlaw, prohibit; disallow, dismiss, reject; annihilate, break down, eliminate, eradicate, liquidate, remove, throw out, write off

phrases do away with, set aside

near ant enact, lay down, legislate; establish,

---

found, institute; formalize, legalize, legitimate, legitimize, validate; pass, ratify; allow, approve, authorize, clear, endorse (*also* indorse), permit, sanction, warrant; command, decree, mandate, order, prescribe

2 to destroy all traces of — see ANNIHILATE 1

abominable *adj* causing intense displeasure, disgust, or resentment — see OFFENSIVE 1

abominate *vb* to dislike strongly — see HATE

abomination *n* **1** something or someone that is hated — see HATE 2

2 a very strong dislike — see HATE 1

aboriginal *adj* belonging to a particular place by birth or origin — see NATIVE 1

aboriginal *n* a member of the first people to inhabit a region — see ABORIGINE

aborigine *n* a member of the first people to inhabit a region ⟨The *aborigines* had no immunity against the raft of diseases brought by the invaders.⟩

syn aboriginal

near ant alien, foreigner

ant nonnative

abort *vb* to put an end to (something planned or previously agreed to) — see CANCEL 1

abortion *n* the act of putting an end to something planned or previously agreed to — see CANCELLATION

abortive *adj* producing no results — see FUTILE

abound *vb* to be copiously supplied ⟨a city that *abounds* with art museums and private galleries⟩

syn brim, bristle, bulge, burst, bustle, buzz, crawl, hum, overflow, swarm, teem

near ant lack, need, want

abounding *adj* possessing or covered with great numbers or amounts of something specified — see RIFE

about *adv* **1** on all sides or in every direction — see AROUND 1

2 toward the opposite direction — see AROUND 2

3 very close to but not completely — see ALMOST

about *prep* **1** having to do with ⟨a poignant story *about* a young man who goes off to war⟩

syn apropos, apropos of, concerning, of, on, regarding, respecting, touching, toward (*or* towards)

rel over

phrases in regard to, in respect to, in view of, with regard to, with respect to

2 close to — see AROUND 1

3 in random positions within the boundaries of — see AROUND 2

above *adv* to or in a higher place ⟨We eventually got used to the planes constantly flying *above*.⟩

syn aloft, over, overhead

rel skyward, upward (*or* upwards)

near ant underneath

ant below, beneath, under

above *n* a dwelling place of perfect happiness for the soul after death — see HEAVEN 1

above *prep* higher than ⟨One minute our kite was *above* the telephone wires; the next minute it was tangled in them.⟩

syn over

rel atop

near ant underneath

ant below, beneath, under

abracadabra *n* **1** a spoken word or set of words believed to have magic power — see SPELL 1

2 unintelligible or meaningless talk — see GIBBERISH 1

abrade *vb* **1** to damage or diminish by continued friction ⟨Ropes *abraded* by the rocks were a huge danger to the climbers.⟩

syn chafe, erode, fray, frazzle, fret, gall, rasp, rub, wear

rel file, grate, graze, grind, nibble, sandblast, sandpaper, scour, scrape, scuff, shave; reduce, rub out, wear out, wipe (away); bite, break down, break up, chew, corrode, decompose, disintegrate, dissolve, eat; hone, sharpen, whet

2 to make sore by continued rubbing — see CHAFE 1

3 to damage by rubbing against a sharp or rough surface — see SCRAPE 2

abrasion *n* an area of skin roughened or worn away by harsh rubbing against another surface ⟨walked away from the accident with only minor *abrasions*⟩

syn bruise, graze, scrape

rel bedsore, gall

abreast *adj* having information especially as a result of study or experience — see FAMILIAR 2

abridge *vb* to make less in extent or duration — see SHORTEN

abridgment *or* **abridgement** *n* a shortened version of a written work ⟨This Italian-English pocket dictionary is an *abridgment* of the hardback edition.⟩

syn abbreviation, condensation, digest

rel abstract, brief, capsule, outline, overview, précis, recap, recapitulation, résumé (*or* resume *also* resumé), review, sketch, sum, summarization, summary, summation, survey, syllabus, synopsis, wrap-up

near ant amplification, elaboration, enlargement, expansion

abrogate *vb* to put an end to by formal action — see ABOLISH 1

abrupt *adj* **1** being or characterized by direct, brief, and potentially rude speech or manner — see BLUNT 1

2 having an incline approaching the perpendicular — see STEEP 1

3 not expected — see UNEXPECTED

abruptly *adv* with great suddenness — see SHORT

abscond *vb* to get free from a dangerous or confining situation — see ESCAPE 1

absence *n* **1** a state of being without something necessary, desirable, or useful — see NEED 1

2 the fact or state of being absent — see LACK 1

absent *adj* **1** not at a certain place ⟨Three students were *absent* because of the flu.⟩

syn away, missing, out

rel AWOL, truant; departed, gone, retired; abroad, vacationing

near ant accompanying, attending, participating

ant here, in, present

2 not present or in evidence ⟨The city's

usual stir of activity was conspicuously *absent* due to the report of an escaped lion from the zoo.⟩

syn lacking, missing, nonexistent, wanting

rel dead, departed, extinct, lost, perished, vanished; defunct, done, expired, finished, lapsed, obsolete, over, passé; inadequate, insufficient, rare, scarce, sparse, uncommon

near ant active, alive, animate, living, thriving; current, going, prevailing, uncanceled; common, prevalent; apparent, conspicuous, evident, obvious, plain

ant existent, present

3 lost in thought and unaware of one's surroundings or actions — see ABSENTMINDED 1

absent *prep* not having — see WITHOUT 1

absentminded *adj* **1** lost in thought and unaware of one's surroundings or actions ⟨I was so *absentminded* I lost track of the time.⟩

syn absent, abstracted, distracted, preoccupied

rel absorbed, daydreaming, dreaming, dreamy, engrossed, faraway, intent, pensive, rapt; heedless, inattentive, insensible, oblivious, unaware, unconscious, unheeding, unknowing, unmindful, unthinking, unwary, unwitting, vacant; befogged, befuddled, bewildered, confused, dazed, flighty, foggy, forgetful, forgetting, hazy, muddled, scatterbrained, unfocused (*also* unfocussed)

near ant alive, attentive, aware, conscious, engaged, heedful, mindful, observant, observing, open-eyed, sharp, vigilant, wary, watchful, wide-awake; clearheaded

ant alert

2 inclined to forget what one has learned or to do what one should — see FORGETFUL

absolute *adj* **1** exercising power or authority without interference by others ⟨an *absolute* monarchy⟩

syn arbitrary, autocratic (*also* autocratical), despotic, dictatorial, tyrannical (*also* tyrannic), tyrannous

rel authoritarian, jackbooted, oppressive, totalitarian; antidemocratic, antirepublican; high-handed; domineering, imperious, masterful; all-powerful, almighty, omnipotent; autonomous, self-governing, self-ruling, sovereign (*also* sovran); unconditional, unlimited

near ant circumscribed, restrained, restricted; constitutional, lawful; democratic, republican

ant limited

2 having no exceptions or restrictions ⟨Ironing is an *absolute* bore.⟩ ⟨I want the *absolute* truth.⟩

syn all-out, arrant, blank, categorical (*also* categoric), clean, complete, consummate, dead, deadly, definite, downright, dreadful, fair, flat, out-and-out, outright, perfect, plumb, profound, pure, rank, regular, sheer, simple, stark, thorough, thoroughgoing, total, unadulterated, unalloyed, unconditional, unmitigated, unqualified, utter, very

rel authentic, classic, genuine, real, veritable; constant, endless, eternal, perpetual, undying, unremitting; extreme, unrestricted; confirmed, habitual, hopeless, inveterate; extraordinary, frightful, horrible, huge, main, superlative, supreme, surpassing, terrible, terrific

near ant doubtful, dubious, equivocal, qualified, questionable, restricted, uncertain

3 being entirely without fault or flaw — see PERFECT 1

4 free from added matter — see PURE 1

5 serving to put an end to all debate or questioning — see CONCLUSIVE 1

absolution *n* release from the guilt or penalty of an offense — see PARDON

absolve *vb* to free from a charge of wrongdoing — see EXCULPATE

absorb *vb* **1** to take in (something liquid) through small openings ⟨Most of the spilled water was *absorbed* by the tablecloth.⟩

syn drink, imbibe, soak (up), sponge, suck (up), take up

rel gulp, guzzle, quaff, sip, slurp, swallow, swig, swill

2 to hold the attention of — see ENGAGE 1

3 to make a part of a body or system — see EMBODY 1

4 to make complete use of — see DEPLETE 1

5 to put up with (something painful or difficult) — see BEAR 1

absorbed *adj* having the mind fixed on something — see ATTENTIVE 1

absorbent *also* **absorbant** *adj* able to soak up liquids especially readily ⟨highly *absorbent* material that really good for wiping off automobiles⟩

syn bibulous, spongy, thirsty

rel osmotic

ant nonabsorbent

absorbing *adj* holding the attention or provoking interest — see INTERESTING

absorption *n* a focusing of the mind on something — see ATTENTION 1

abstain (from) *vb* to resist the temptation of — see FORBEAR

abstemious *adj* given to or marked by restraint in the satisfaction of one's appetites ⟨Being *abstemious* diners, they avoid restaurants with all-you-can-eat buffets.⟩

syn abstinent, continent, sober, temperate

rel ascetic (*also* ascetical), austere; disciplined, self-controlled, self-disciplined

near ant gluttonous, greedy, rapacious, voracious; self-pleasing, sensual

abstinent *adj* given to or marked by restraint in the satisfaction of one's appetites — see ABSTEMIOUS

abstract *adj* **1** dealing with or expressing a quality or idea ⟨The book deals with *abstract* matters such as honesty and integrity on the job.⟩

syn conceptual, ideal, metaphysical, theoretical (*also* theoretic)

rel conjectural, hypothetical, speculative; cosmic (*also* cosmical), intellectual, mental, spiritual; ethereal, immaterial, incorporeal, insubstantial, nonmaterial, nonphysical, unsubstantial; impalpable, imperceptible, insensible, intangible; impractical, romantic, unreal, utopian, visionary *near ant* material, physical; appreciable, detectable, discernible (*also* discernable), noticeable, observable, palpable, perceptible, sensible, substantial, tangible, visible; defined, definite, distinct; actual, factual, real

ant concrete, nonabstract

2 using elements of form (as color, line, or texture) with little or no attempt at creating a realistic picture ⟨Cubism is a style of *abstract* art in which natural forms are broken up into geometric shapes.⟩

syn nonobjective, nonrealistic

rel expressionist, expressionistic, impressionist, impressionistic; symbolist, symbolistic

near ant lifelike, natural

ant figurative, nonabstract, objective, realistic

abstract *n* **1** a short statement of the main points — see SUMMARY

2 a visible representation of something abstract (as a quality) — see EMBODIMENT

abstract *vb* **1** to draw the attention or mind to something else — see DISTRACT 1

2 to make into a short statement of the main points (as of a report) — see SUMMARIZE

abstracted *adj* lost in thought and unaware of one's surroundings or actions — see ABSENTMINDED 1

abstruse *adj* difficult for one of ordinary knowledge or intelligence to understand — see PROFOUND 1

absurd *adj* **1** conceived or made without regard for reason or reality — see FANTASTIC 1

2 showing or marked by a lack of good sense or judgment — see FOOLISH 1

3 so foolish or pointless as to be worthy of scornful laughter — see RIDICULOUS 1

absurdity *n* **1** a foolish act or idea — see FOLLY 1

2 lack of good sense or judgment — see FOOLISHNESS 1

abundance *n* **1** a considerable amount — see LOT 2

2 an amount or supply more than sufficient to meet one's needs — see PLENTY 1

abundant *adj* **1** being more than enough without being excessive — see PLENTIFUL

2 possessing or covered with great numbers or amounts of something specified — see RIFE

abuse *n* **1** harsh insulting language ⟨Hometown fans hurled *abuse* at the visiting team.⟩

syn fulmination, invective, vitriol, vituperation

rel blasphemy, curse; epithet, insult, putdown, slur; expletive, swearword; aspersion, bad-mouthing, belittlement, disparagement, revilement, vilification; castigation, chastisement, criticism, excoriation, opprobrium, rebuke, reprimand, reproof; broadside, diatribe, harangue, polemic, tirade

near ant acclaim, applause, commendation, praise; compliments, congratulations, endearments, felicitations; adulation, blarney, flattery, overpraise, soft soap

2 incorrect or improper use — see MISUSE

abuse *vb* **1** to inflict physical or emotional harm upon ⟨adopted a dog that had been *abused*⟩

syn bully, ill-treat, ill-use, maltreat, manhandle, mishandle, mistreat, misuse

rel molest, outrage, violate; harm, hurt, injure, oppress, persecute, torment, torture; burn, victimize, wrong; beat (up), mess (up), rough (up), work (over)

phrases take apart

near ant care (for), cherish, foster, nurture; baby, cater (to), coddle, favor, gratify, humor, indulge, mollycoddle, pamper, spoil

2 to criticize harshly and usually publicly — see ATTACK 2

3 to put to a bad or improper use — see MISAPPLY

4 to take unfair advantage of — see EXPLOIT 1

abusive *adj* marked by harsh insulting language ⟨He invariably launches *abusive* attacks against anyone who dares to challenge him.⟩

syn invective, opprobrious, scurrilous, truculent

rel affronting, insulting, offending, offensive, outrageous, outraging; coarse, crude, dirty, filthy, foul, foulmouthed, gross, indecent, nasty, obscene, potty-mouthed, vulgar; contemptuous, disdainful, scornful; defamatory, libelous (*or* libellous), scandalous, slanderous; maligning, traducing, vilifying; hateful, malevolent, malicious, spiteful; immoderate, intemperate, unbridled, unrestrained

near ant moderate, temperate; deferential, respectful; civil, courteous, gracious, mannerly, polite; discreet, judicious, tempered; laudatory, praiseful

abut *vb* to be adjacent to — see ADJOIN 1

abutting *adj* having a border in common — see ADJACENT

abysmal *adj* extending far downward — see DEEP 1

abyss *n* an immeasurable depth or space ⟨Looking down at the dark ocean from the ship's rail, the cruise passenger felt as though he was staring into an *abyss*.⟩

syn chasm, deep, gulf, ocean

rel cleft, crevasse, crevice, fissure; cavern, hole, hollow, pit; breadth, expanse, extent, reach, spread, stretch; emptiness, vacancy, vacuum, void

academic *also* **academical** *adj* **1** of or relating to schooling or learning especially at an advanced level ⟨"If you spent more time in *academic* pursuits and less time in social ones, you could easily make good grades," the dean told Valerie.⟩

syn educational, intellectual, scholarly, scholastic

rel bookish, nerdy, pedantic, professorial, tweedy; curricular; educative, instructive; collegiate, graduate, postgraduate

near ant extracurricular

ant nonacademic, noneducational, unacademic, unscholarly

2 existing only as an assumption or speculation — see THEORETICAL 1

academy *n* a place or establishment for teaching and learning — see SCHOOL

accede *vb* to give or express one's approval (as to a proposal) ⟨The teacher finally *acceded* to their pleas for more time to complete the project.⟩

syn acquiesce, agree, assent, come round, consent

rel adopt, embrace, espouse; abide, bear (with), endure, stand, suffer, tolerate; stomach, swallow, take; bow, knuckle under, relent, submit, succumb, yield

near ant rebuff, refuse, reject, scorn, spurn; deny, gainsay

ant dissent

accelerate *vb* **1** to become greater in extent, volume, amount, or number — see INCREASE 2

2 to cause to move or proceed fast or faster — see HURRY 1

3 to make greater in size, amount, or number — see INCREASE 1

accent *n* a special notice or importance given to something — see EMPHASIS 1

accent *vb* to indicate the importance of by centering attention on — see EMPHASIZE 1

accentuate *vb* **1** to indicate the importance of by centering attention on — see EMPHASIZE 1

2 to make markedly greater in measure or degree — see INTENSIFY

3 to make more apparent — see EMPHASIZE 2

accentuation *n* a special notice or importance given to something — see EMPHASIS 1

accept *vb* **1** to agree to receive whether willingly or reluctantly — see TAKE 2

2 to have a favorable opinion of — see APPROVE (OF)

3 to regard as right or true — see BELIEVE 1

4 to take to or upon oneself — see ASSUME 1

5 to put up with (something painful or difficult) — see BEAR 2

acceptability *n* the quality or state of meeting one's needs adequately — see SUFFICIENCY

acceptable *adj* of a level of quality that meets one's needs or standards — see ADEQUATE

acceptably *adv* in a satisfactory way — see WELL 1

access *n* **1** a sudden experiencing of a physical or mental disorder — see ATTACK 2

2 the means or right of entering or participating in — see ENTRANCE 1

access *vb* to go or come in or into — see ENTER 1

accessible *adj* **1** being within the financial means of most people ⟨a store offering stylish clothes at *accessible* prices⟩

syn affordable, popular

rel budget, cheap, discount, inexpensive, low; moderate, modest, reasonable

near ant costly, dear, expensive, high

2 possible to get — see AVAILABLE 1

3 situated within easy reach — see CONVENIENT

accessory *adj* available to supply something extra when needed — see AUXILIARY

accessory *also* **accessary** *n* **1** something that is necessary in itself but adds to

the convenience or performance of the main piece of equipment ⟨We bought a new car with lots of high-tech *accessories.*⟩

syn accoutrement (*or* accouterment), adapter (*also* adaptor); adjunct, appendage, appliance, attachment, option

rel accompaniment, additive, complement, supplement; auxiliary, subsidiary; amenity, extra, filler, frill, incidental, luxury, nonessential, nonnecessity; appurtenances, bells and whistles, equipment, furnishings, paraphernalia, trappings; adornment, decoration, embellishment, enhancement, ornament, trim, trimming

near ant essential, necessity, requirement, requisite

2 one associated with another in wrongdoing — see ACCOMPLICE

accident *n* **1** a chance and usually sudden event bringing loss or injury ⟨She was involved in a minor *accident* on her way home from work.⟩

syn casualty, mischance, mishap

rel calamity, cataclysm, catastrophe, deathblow, disaster, tragedy; bummer, knock, misadventure, misfortune; collision, crack-up, crash, smashup, wreck

near ant boon, bonanza, godsend, miracle, strike, windfall; fortune, luck, serendipity

2 the uncertain course of events — see CHANCE 1

accidental *adj* happening by chance ⟨Finding the gold was all the more remarkable because its discovery was entirely *accidental*.⟩

syn casual, chance, fluky (*also* flukey), fortuitous, inadvertent, incidental, unintended, unintentional, unplanned, unpremeditated, unwitting

rel coincidental; freak, odd; aimless, arbitrary, desultory, haphazard, random; uncertain, unexpected, unforeseeable, unforeseen; coerced, forced, involuntary; unconscious, unprompted

near ant certain, destined, expected, fixed, foreordained, foreseeable, foreseen, inevitable, predestined, predetermined, predictable, preordained, prescribed, sure; conscious, freewill, knowing, unforced, voluntary, volunteer, willful (*or* wilful)

ant calculated, deliberate, intended, intentional, premeditated, premeditative, set

2 not being a vital part of or belonging to something — see EXTRINSIC

acclaim *n* public acknowledgment or admiration for an achievement — see GLORY 1

acclaim *vb* to declare enthusiastic approval of ⟨She has long been *acclaimed* by the critics for her realistic acting.⟩

syn accredit, applaud, cheer, crack up, hail, laud, praise, salute, tout

rel bravo, clap, rise (to); ballyhoo; approve, commend, endorse (*also* indorse), favor, recommend, root (for), support; celebrate, eulogize, extol (*also* extoll), glorify, magnify, sing; adulate, belaud, flatter, overpraise; deify, idolize

phrases doff one's hat to (*or* doff one's cap to)

near ant belittle, disparage, put down;

---

blame, censure, reprehend, reprobate; admonish, chide, criticize, rebuke, reprimand, reproach, reprove; castigate, excoriate, keelhaul, lambaste (*or* lambast), skewer, vilify

ant knock, pan, slam

acclamation *n* enthusiastic and usually public expression of approval — see APPLAUSE 1

acclimate *vb* to change (something) so as to make it suitable for a new use or situation — see ADAPT

acclimatize *vb* to change (something) so as to make it suitable for a new use or situation — see ADAPT

accolade *n* 1 a formal expression of praise — see ENCOMIUM

2 public acknowledgment or admiration for an achievement — see GLORY 1

3 something given in recognition of achievement — see AWARD 1

accommodate *vb* 1 to make or have room for ⟨The back seat *accommodates* three people comfortably.⟩

syn fit, hold, take

rel carry, contain, seat; enclose (*also* inclose), encompass, enfold; harbor, house

2 to bring to a state free of conflicts, inconsistencies, or differences — see HARMONIZE 2

3 to change (something) so as to make it suitable for a new use or situation — see ADAPT

4 to do a service or favor for — see OBLIGE 1

5 to provide with living quarters or shelter — see HOUSE 1

accommodating *adj* willing to do a favor ⟨an *accommodating* waiter who readily honored our request to make substitutions in our order⟩

syn accommodative, friendly, indulgent, obliging

rel helpful, solicitous; considerate, thoughtful; agreeable, amenable, complaisant, gracious; lenient, permissive

accommodation *n* 1 *usually* accommodations *pl* a place to sleep and related amenities for the temporary use of a tourist or traveler ⟨a resort offering a wide range of *accommodations*⟩

syn lodging

rel berth, shelter; crash pad

2 the act or practice of each side giving up something in order to reach an agreement — see CONCESSION 1

3 something that adds to one's ease of living — see COMFORT 2

accommodative *adj* willing to do a favor — see ACCOMMODATING

accompaniment *n* something that is found along with something else ⟨The sound of crickets was the perfect *accompaniment* to our summer evenings on the porch.⟩

syn attendant, companion, concomitant, corollary

rel accessory (*also* accessary), adjunct, appendage; complement, supplement; counterpart, fellow, mate; consequence, follow-up; fixings, trimmings

accompany *vb* 1 to go along with in order to provide assistance, protection, or companionship ⟨Children using the pool must be *accompanied* by a parent at all times.⟩

syn attend, chaperone (*or* chaperon), companion, company, convoy, escort, see, squire

rel walk; associate, consort, pal (around), team (up); defend, guard, protect; bring, conduct, guide, lead, pilot, steer, usher; follow, shadow, tag, tag along, tail; hang (around), hover (over)

near ant abandon, desert, ditch, dump, forsake

2 to occur or exist at the same time — see COINCIDE 1

accompanying *adj* present at the same time and place — see COINCIDENT 1

accomplice *n* one associated with another in wrongdoing ⟨The thief and his *accomplices* were eventually caught and brought to justice.⟩

syn abettor (*also* abetter), accessory (*also* accessary), cohort, confederate

rel collaborationist, collaborator, informant, informer; evidence, state's evidence; companion, comrade, crony, henchman, partner; conspirator, plotter, traitor; gangster, mobster, racketeer

accomplish *vb* to carry through (as a process) to completion — see PERFORM 1

accomplished *adj* 1 having or showing a taste for the fine arts and gracious living — see CULTIVATED

2 having or showing exceptional knowledge, experience, or skill in a field of endeavor — see PROFICIENT

3 not capable of being challenged or proved wrong — see IRREFUTABLE

accomplishment *n* 1 a successful result brought about by hard work ⟨Our biggest *accomplishment* this week was finishing the living room makeover.⟩

syn achievement, acquirement, attainment, baby, coup, success, triumph

rel blockbuster, hit, jackpot, megahit, miracle, smash, winner; conquest, gain, victory, win; skill; deed, feat, performance; arrival, completion, consummation, culmination, execution, fruition, fulfillment (*or* fulfilment), implementation, realization

phrases a feather in one's cap

near ant botch, mess, muddle, shambles; bummer, bust, catastrophe, debacle (*also* débâcle), disaster, dud, failure, fiasco, fizzle, flop, washout; disappointment, letdown, loss, setback

2 the doing of an action — see COMMISSION 2

3 the state of being actual or complete — see FRUITION

4 a high level of taste and enlightenment as a result of extensive intellectual training and exposure to the arts — see CULTURE 1

accord *n* 1 a formal agreement between two or more nations or peoples — see TREATY

2 a state of consistency — see CONFORMITY 1

3 an arrangement about action to be taken — see AGREEMENT 2

4 the state of being of one opinion about something — see AGREEMENT 1

5 the act or power of making one's own choices or decisions — see FREE WILL

accord *vb* **1** to be in agreement on every point — see CHECK 1

2 to give the ownership or benefit of (something) formally or publicly — see CONFER 1

accordance *n* a state of consistency — see CONFORMITY 1

accordingly *adv* for this or that reason — see THEREFORE

account *n* **1** a relating of events usually in the order in which they happened ⟨Newspaper reporters must strive to provide an accurate *account* of what happened.⟩
syn chronicle, commentary (*usually* commentaries), history, narration, narrative, record, report, story
rel deposition, documentation, testament, testimony, witness; annals, blog, journal, log, logbook, memoir; anecdote, tale, yarn; saga; recital, recitation; case history, case study

2 a presentation of an artistic work (as a piece of music) from a particular point of view ⟨The pianist gave an *account* of the sonata that revealed a very mature understanding of the work.⟩
syn interpretation, performance, reading
rel reworking, variation

3 a record of goods sold or services performed together with the costs due — see ¹BILL 1

4 a sum of money set aside for a particular purpose — see FUND 1

5 the capacity for being useful for some purpose — see USE 2

6 the relative usefulness or importance of something as judged by specific qualities — see WORTH 1

7 a careful weighing of the reasons for or against something — see CONSIDERATION 1

8 a feeling of great approval and liking — see ADMIRATION 1

9 a person who buys a product or uses a service from a business — see CUSTOMER 1

10 a statement given to explain a belief or act — see REASON 1

11 something (as a belief) that serves as the basis for another thing — see REASON 2

12 the quality or state of being important — see IMPORTANCE

account *vb* to think of in a particular way — see CONSIDER 1

account (for) *vb* to give the reason for or cause of — see EXPLAIN 2

accountable *adj* being the one who must meet an obligation or suffer the consequences for failing to do so — see RESPONSIBLE 1

accoutre *or* **accouter** *vb* to provide (someone) with what is needed for a task or activity — see FURNISH 1

accoutrement *or* **accouterment** *n* **1** something that is not necessary in itself but adds to the convenience or performance of the main piece of equipment — see ACCESSORY 1

2 accoutrements *or* accouterments *pl* items needed for the performance of a task or activity — see EQUIPMENT

accredit *vb* **1** to explain (something) as being the result of something else — see CREDIT 1

2 to give official or legal power to — see AUTHORIZE 1

3 to declare enthusiastic approval of — see ACCLAIM

4 to give official acceptance of as satisfactory — see APPROVE

accreditation *n* the granting of power to perform various acts or duties — see COMMISSION 1

accretion *n* a mass or quantity that has piled up or that has been gathered over a period of time — see ACCUMULATION 1

2 something added (as by growth) — see INCREASE 1

accrual *n* something added (as by growth) — see INCREASE 1

accumulate *vb* **1** to become greater in extent, volume, amount, or number — see INCREASE 1

2 to bring together in one body or place — see GATHER 1

3 to gradually form into a layer, pile, or mass — see COLLECT 2

accumulating *n* the act or process of becoming greater in number — see MULTIPLICATION

accumulation *n* **1** a mass or quantity that has piled up or that has been gathered over a period of time ⟨a vast *accumulation* of evidence about the dangers of smoking⟩
syn accretion, assemblage, collection, gathering
rel agglomerate, assortment, conglomerate, conglomeration, hodgepodge, hotchpotch, jumble, medley, mélange, mishmash, mix, mixture, motley, potpourri; agglomeration, clutter, hash, heap, litter, mass, pile; aggregate, aggregation, sum, totality; backlog, cache, fund, hoard, inventory, kitty, nest egg, reserve, stock, stockpile, store, supply

2 the act or process of becoming greater in number — see MULTIPLICATION

accuracy *n* the quality or state of being very accurate — see PRECISION

accurate *adj* **1** being in agreement with the truth or a fact or a standard — see CORRECT 1

2 following an original exactly — see FAITHFUL 2

3 meeting the highest standard of accuracy — see PRECISE 1

accuse *vb* to make a claim of wrongdoing against ⟨She was *accused* of lying on the employment application.⟩
syn charge, impeach, incriminate, indict
rel blame, call (on), castigate, censure, condemn, criticize, damn, denounce, fault, impugn, reproach, reprobate; chide, rebuke, reprove, tax; appeal, arraign, book, cite, summon; sue, try; frame, implicate, inculpate, inform (against), name, report; recriminate, retaliate
near ant advocate, champion, defend; excuse, forgive, justify, pardon, remit, shrive
ant absolve, acquit, clear, exculpate, exonerate, vindicate

accustom *vb* to impart knowledge of a new thing or situation to — see ACQUAINT 1

accustomed *adj* being in the habit or

custom ⟨Josh was not *accustomed* to eating so late.⟩
syn given, habituated, used, wont
rel apt, inclined, liable, likely, prone; hardened, inured; experienced, practiced (*or* practised), seasoned, veteran; addicted, hooked
near ant unapt, unlikely; averse, disinclined, opposed; inexperienced, new, unseasoned; disaccustomed, weaned
ant unaccustomed, unused, unwonted

ace *adj* having or showing exceptional knowledge, experience, or skill in a field of endeavor — see PROFICIENT

ace *n* **1** a person with a high level of knowledge or skill in a field — see EXPERT
2 a very small amount — see PARTICLE 1
3 a very small distance or degree — see HAIR 1

ache *n* a sharp unpleasant sensation usually felt in some specific part of the body — see PAIN 1

ache *vb* to feel or cause physical pain — see HURT 1

ache (for) *vb* **1** to have sympathy for — see PITY
2 to have an earnest wish to own or enjoy — see DESIRE 1

achievable *adj* capable of being done or carried out — see POSSIBLE 1

achieve *vb* **1** to obtain (as a goal) through effort ⟨finally *achieved* stardom⟩
syn attain, bag, gain, hit, log, make, notch (up), rack up, score, win
rel acquire, capture, carry, draw, garner, get, land, make, obtain, procure, realize, secure; amount (to), approach, equal, match, measure up (to), meet, rival, tie, touch; beat, excel, outdo, surpass, top
near ant fall short (of), miss; fail (at); lose
2 to carry through (as a process) to completion — see PERFORM 1

achievement *n* **1** a successful result brought about by hard work — see ACCOMPLISHMENT 1
2 the doing of an action — see COMMISSION 2
3 the state of being actual or complete — see FRUITION

Achilles' heel *n* a vulnerable point ⟨This year, the team's *Achilles' heel* is pitching.⟩
syn back, chink, underbelly
rel downfall, ruin

aching *adj* **1** causing or feeling bodily pain — see PAINFUL 1
2 expressing or suggesting mourning — see MOURNFUL 1

achy *adj* causing or feeling bodily pain — see PAINFUL 1

acid *adj* **1** causing or characterized by the one of the basic taste sensations that is produced chiefly by acids — see SOUR 1
2 having or showing a habitually bad temper — see ILL-TEMPERED
3 marked by the use of wit that is intended to cause hurt feelings — see SARCASTIC

acidic *adj* **1** causing or characterized by the one of the basic taste sensations that is produced chiefly by acids — see SOUR 1
2 marked by the use of wit that is intended to cause hurt feelings — see SARCASTIC

acidity *n* **1** a harsh or sharp quality — see EDGE 1

2 biting sharpness of feeling or expression — see ACRIMONY 1

acidness *n* **1** a harsh or sharp quality — see EDGE 1
2 biting sharpness of feeling or expression — see ACRIMONY 1

acknowledge *vb* to accept the truth or existence of (something) usually reluctantly — see ADMIT 1

acknowledgment *or* **acknowledgement** *n* **1** a formal recognition of an achievement or praiseworthy deed — see COMMENDATION 1
2 an open declaration of something (as a fault or the commission of an offense) about oneself — see CONFESSION

acme *n* **1** the highest part or point — see HEIGHT 1
2 the most perfect type or example — see QUINTESSENCE 1

acoustic *or* **acoustical** *adj* of, relating to, or experienced through the sense of hearing — see AUDITORY

acquaint *vb* **1** to impart knowledge of a new thing or situation to ⟨Mr. King spent the first week of the summer internship *acquainting* everyone with the new computers.⟩
syn accustom, familiarize, initiate, introduce, orient, orientate
rel wont; apprise, brief, clue (in), fill in, inform; educate, enlighten, ground, instruct, school, train, verse; expose, present, subject; advise, tell, tip (off), warn, wise (up); reacquaint
2 to give information to — see ENLIGHTEN 1
3 to make (one person) known (to another) socially — see INTRODUCE 1

acquaintance *n* knowledge gained by personal experience ⟨Tiffany's *acquaintance* with goats is limited to a long-ago visit to a petting zoo when she was three.⟩
syn cognizance, familiarity
rel association, experience, exposure, intimacy, involvement; initiation, introduction; awareness, comprehension, conception, inkling, notion, understanding; education, enlightenment, grounding, information, instruction, learning, schooling, training
near ant callowness, greenness, ignorance, inexperience
ant unfamiliarity

acquainted *adj* having information especially as a result of study or experience — see FAMILIAR 2

acquiesce *vb* to give or express one's approval (as to a proposal) — see ACCEDE

acquiescence *n* a readiness or willingness to yield to the wishes of others — see COMPLIANCE 1

acquiescent *adj* receiving or enduring without offering resistance — see PASSIVE

acquirable *adj* possible to get — see AVAILABLE 1

acquire *vb* **1** to come to have gradually — see DEVELOP 2
2 to receive as return for effort — see EARN 1

acquirement *n* a successful result brought about by hard work — see ACCOMPLISHMENT 1

acquisitive *adj* having or marked by an eager and often selfish desire especially for material possessions — see GREEDY 1

acquisitiveness *n* an intense selfish desire for wealth or possessions — see GREED

acquit *vb* **1** to free from a charge of wrongdoing — see EXCULPATE

2 to manage the actions of (oneself) in a particular way — see BEHAVE

acquittal *n* a setting free from a charge of wrongdoing ⟨confidently predicted that his client's trial would result in a full *acquittal*⟩
syn clearing, exculpation, exoneration, vindication
rel absolution, condonation, forgiveness, pardon, remission; atonement, expiation
near ant accusation, arraignment, impeachment, incrimination, indictment; castigation, censure, condemnation, denunciation
ant conviction

acrid *adj* **1** having or showing deep-seated resentment — see BITTER 1

2 marked by the use of wit that is intended to cause hurt feelings — see SARCASTIC

acridness *n* **1** a harsh or sharp quality — see EDGE 1

2 biting sharpness of feeling or expression — see ACRIMONY 1

acrimonious *adj* having or showing deep-seated resentment — see BITTER 1

acrimoniousness *n* a harsh or sharp quality — see EDGE 1

acrimony *n* **1** biting sharpness of feeling or expression ⟨She responded with such *acrimony* that she never brought the subject up again.⟩
syn acidity, acidness, acridness, asperity, bile, bitterness, cattiness, tartness, virulence, vitriol
rel gruffness, harshness, hostility, relentlessness, severity, sternness, vehemence; crossness, discourteousness, iciness, impoliteness, incivility, nastiness, rudeness, sourness, surliness, ungraciousness; anger, animosity, gall, jaundice, malevolence, malice, rancor, scorn, spite, spleen, venom, vindictiveness; jealousy, pique, resentment, sour grapes
near ant civility, cordiality, courtesy, diplomacy, geniality, graciousness, kindness, politeness, tactfulness; compassion, softness, sweetness, sympathy, warmth; oiliness, smoothness, suaveness, suavity, unctuousness, urbanity

2 a harsh or sharp quality — see EDGE 1

acrobat *n* **1** one who performs feats of physical strength, balance, and agility on special apparatus ⟨a child who is a natural *acrobat* with a superb sense of balance⟩
syn gymnast
rel exerciser, tumbler; contortionist, equilibrist; aerialist, ropedancer, ropewalker, trampoliner, trampolinist, trapeze artist, trapezist

2 a person who dexterously and expediently changes or adopts opinions ⟨a political *acrobat* whose opinion on any issue is whatever will get the most votes⟩
syn opportunist, temporizer

rel self-seeker; conniver, machinator, plotter, schemer

across *adv* from one side to the other of an intervening space — see OVER 1

across *prep* **1** to the opposite side of ⟨We rowed *across* the lake.⟩
syn athwart, over, through
rel around, round; beyond, past

2 in random positions within the boundaries of — see AROUND 2

act *n* **1** a performance regularly presented by an individual or group ⟨In his nightclub *act* he impersonates a veritable galaxy of movie stars.⟩
syn bit, number, routine, turn

2 a display of emotion or behavior that is insincere or intended to deceive — see MASQUERADE

3 a rule of conduct or action laid down by a governing authority and especially a legislature — see LAW 1

4 something done by someone — see ACTION 1

act *vb* **1** to present a portrayal or performance of ⟨A local student *acted* the part of Tiny Tim in our theater company's production of *A Christmas Carol*.⟩
syn do, impersonate, interpret, perform, play, portray
rel depict, dramatize, render, represent; act out, enact, pantomime, playact, roleplay, take on; overact, overplay, underplay; ape, clown, ham, imitate, masquerade, mime, mimic, pose (as); star (in); coact, costar

2 to produce a desired effect ⟨The painkiller *acted* surprisingly quickly.⟩
syn operate, perform, take, work
rel behave, react, respond; affect, influence, sway; pan out, redound, result
phrases take effect, take hold
near ant backfire; fizzle

3 to give the impression of being — see SEEM

4 to have a certain purpose — see FUNCTION

5 to present a false appearance of — see FEIGN

6 to pretend to be (what one is not) in appearance or behavior — see IMPERSONATE 1

act (toward) *vb* to behave toward in a stated way — see TREAT 1

acting *adj* serving in a position for the time being ⟨She will serve as *acting* president of the university until a permanent replacement can be found.⟩
syn interim, provisional, temporary
rel alternate, backup, make-do, makeshift, proxy, stopgap, substitute
ant long-term, permanent

action *n* **1** something done by someone ⟨Judge people by their *actions*, not by their words.⟩
syn act, deed, doing, exploit, feat, thing
rel accomplishment, achievement, attainment; adventure, experience; emprise, enterprise, initiative, undertaking; handiwork, performance, work; stunt, trick; activity, dealing; maneuver, measure, move, operation, procedure, proceeding, step, tactic; coaction

2 the unfolding of events in a dramatic or

---

syn synonym(s)   *rel* related words
ant antonym(s)   *near ant* near antonym(s)

literary work ⟨The mystery writer displays a sure hand in managing the novel's complicated but never incoherent *action.*⟩

syn plot, story

rel subplot; arc, development; design, outline, plan, scheme; argument, subject, theme

3 a court case for enforcing a right or claim — see LAWSUIT

4 active fighting during the course of a war — see COMBAT 1

5 actions *pl* the way or manner in which one conducts oneself — see BEHAVIOR

6 readiness to engage in daring or difficult activity — see ENTERPRISE 2

action figure *n* a small figure often of a human being used especially as a child's plaything — see DOLL 1

activate *vb* to cause to function ⟨The thermostat is set to *activate* the heating system only when the temperature drops below 65 degrees.⟩

syn actuate, crank (up), drive, move, run, set off, spark, start, touch off, trigger, turn on

rel kick over, turn over; charge, electrify, energize, fire, fuel, generate, power, push; discharge, launch, release, switch, trip; reactivate; arouse, excite, kick-start, stimulate, vitalize; ignite, incite, instigate, provoke, quicken, stir up; accelerate, speed (up), step up

near ant arrest, brake, check, cut off, draw up, halt, jam, stall, stick, stop; decelerate, repress, slow, stunt, suppress

ant cut, cut out, deactivate, kill, shut off, turn off

active *adj* **1** being in effective operation ⟨The abandoned factory had not been *active* for years.⟩

syn alive, functional, functioning, going, live, living, on, operating, operational, operative, running, working

rel effective, effectual; employable, operable, usable (*also* useable), viable, workable; performing, producing, productive, serving, useful, yielding; astir, bustling, busy, dynamic, flourishing, humming, roaring, thriving

phrases in commission (*or* into commission), in force, in gear, on line

near ant deactivated, decommissioned; ineffective, ineffectual, useless; inoperable, unusable, unworkable; arrested, asleep, dormant, fallow, idle, inert, lifeless, nonproductive, quiescent, sleepy, stagnating, unproductive, vegetating

ant broken, dead, inactive, inoperative, nonactivated, nonfunctional, nonfunctioning, nonoperating, nonoperational, nonoperative

2 having much high-spirited energy and movement — see LIVELY 1

3 involved in often constant activity — see BUSY 1

activity *n* energetic movement of the body for the sake of physical fitness — see EXERCISE 1

actor *n* **1** one who acts professionally (as in a play, movie, or television show) ⟨My sister went to drama school to become an *actor.*⟩

syn impersonator, mummer, player, trouper

rel barnstormer, enactor, entertainer, performer; actress, starlet; lead, leading lady, leading man, star; coactor, costar; extra, spear-carrier, walk-on; monologuist (*or* monologist); prima donna, scene-stealer; double, understudy; comedian; tragedian, tragedienne; ham, imitator, impressionist, mime, mimic, pantomime, pantomimist, poser; buffoon, clown, harlequin, stooge, zany

ant nonactor

2 one who takes part in something — see PARTICIPANT

act out *vb* to behave badly — see MISBEHAVE

actual *adj* existing in fact and not merely as a possibility ⟨The *actual* outcome of the election was quite different from what everybody had expected.⟩

syn concrete, effective, existent, factual, genuine, real, true, very

rel attested, authenticated, confirmed, demonstrated, established, proven, substantiated, valid, validated, verified; incontestable, incontrovertible, indisputable, indubitable, inescapable, irrefutable, undeniable, unquestionable; believable, convincing, literal, realistic, unmistakable, verifiable; authentic, bona fide, real-life, real-world; absolute, certain, final, hard, objective, palpable, positive, substantial, tangible; authoritative

near ant alleged, assumed, reputed, supposed; conceived, envisaged, envisioned, imagined, pictured, visualized; chimerical (*also* chimeric), fabled, fanciful, fictional, fictitious, illusory, legendary; fabricated, fake, imaginary, invented, made-up, make-believe, pretend, romantic; abstract, symbolic, unreal; virtual

ant conjectural, hypothetical, ideal, inexistent, nonexistent, platonic, possible, potential, suppositional, theoretical (*also* theoretic)

actuality *n* **1** the fact of being or of being real — see EXISTENCE

2 the quality of being actual — see FACT 1

3 the state of being actual or complete — see FRUITION

4 something that actually exists — see FACT 2

actualize *vb* to come into existence — see BEGIN 2

actually *adv* **1** to tell the truth ⟨*Actually*, I'd rather spend the evening at home.⟩

syn admittedly, frankly, honestly, indeed, really, truly, truthfully, verily

rel absolutely, certainly, indisputably, indubitably, realistically, undoubtedly, unquestionably, veritably

phrases as a matter of fact, in actuality, in fact, in point of fact, in reality, in truth, to be sure

2 in actual fact — see VERY 2

actuate *vb* **1** to cause to function — see ACTIVATE

2 to set or keep in motion — see MOVE 2

act up *vb* **1** to behave badly — see MISBEHAVE

2 to engage in attention-getting playful or boisterous behavior — see CUT UP

acuity *n* the state or quality of being able to sense slight impressions or differences

⟨a worrisome deterioration in the *acuity* of his hearing over the years⟩

syn acuteness, delicacy, keenness, perceptiveness, sensitiveness, sensitivity, sharpness

rel hyperacuity, hypersensitiveness, hypersensitivity, oversensitiveness, oversensitivity, supersensitivity; accuracy, exactitude, exactness, fineness

acumen *n* exceptional discernment and judgment especially in practical matters ⟨She had the business *acumen* to know that the market for sportswear was becoming oversaturated.⟩

syn astuteness, caginess (*also* cageyness), canniness, foxiness, hardheadedness, intelligence, keenness, sharpness, shrewdness, wit

rel discernment, insight, perception, perceptiveness, perceptivity, sagaciousness, sagacity, sageness, sapience, wisdom; artfulness, artifice, craft, craftiness, cunning, deviousness, guile, slickness, slyness, sneakiness, subtleness, subtlety, wiliness; brain(s), gray matter, intellect, reason, sense

near ant artlessness, greenness, guilelessness, ingenuousness, innocence, naïveté (*also* naivete *or* naïveté), simpleness, simplicity, unsophistication, unworldliness; brainlessness, density, doltishness, dopiness, dumbness, fatuity, foolishness, halfwittedness, mindlessness, oafishness, obtuseness, senselessness, slowness, stupidity, vacuity, witlessness

acute *adj* **1** able to sense slight impressions or differences ⟨Dogs, with their *acute* sense of smell, are used for finding toxic substances undetectable by humans.⟩

syn delicate, fine, keen, perceptive, quick, sensitive, sharp

rel accurate, clear, discerning, good, piercing, precise, receptive, sensible, subtle; hair-trigger, hyperacute, hypersensitive, oversensitive, supersensitive

near ant bad, deadened, dimmed, dull, dulled, fading; dead, insensible, insensitive, numb; imprecise, inaccurate

2 needing immediate attention ⟨famine caused by an *acute* shortage of grain⟩

syn burning, compelling, critical, crying, dire, imperative, imperious, instant, pressing, urgent

rel demanding, extreme, immediate, insistent, intense; crucial, grave, life-and-death (*also* life-or-death), serious, severe, vital; dangerous, explosive, hazardous, perilous, precarious, unstable

near ant incidental, low-pressure, minor, negligible, trivial, unimportant; nonthreatening, safe, stable

ant noncritical, nonurgent

3 extreme in degree, power, or effect — see INTENSE 1

acuteness *n* **1** a harsh or sharp quality — see EDGE 1

2 the state or quality of being able to sense slight impressions or differences — see ACUITY

ad *n* a published statement informing the public of a matter of general interest — see ANNOUNCEMENT

adage *n* an often stated observation regarding something from common experience — see SAYING

adamant *adj* sticking to an opinion, purpose, or course of action in spite of reason, arguments, or persuasion — see OBSTINATE

adapt *vb* to change (something) so as to make it suitable for a new use or situation ⟨It always takes freshmen a little while to *adapt* themselves to high school.⟩

syn acclimate, acclimatize, accommodate, adjust, condition, conform, doctor, edit, fashion, fit, put, shape, suit, tailor

rel readapt, readjust; customize, gear, match, model, pattern; correct, harmonize, square, tune; establish, root, settle; acquaint, familiarize, orient, orientate; equip, prepare, prime, rehearse; harden, inure, season, toughen; alter, convert, make over, modify, recast, reclaim, recycle, redesign, redevelop, redo, reengineer, refashion, refigure, refit, refocus, reinvent, rejigger, remake, remodel, revamp, revise, rework, transform; accustom, condition, naturalize; ready, season; bend; fiddle (with), fine-tune, phase, register, regulate, rig

near ant misadjust

adaptable *adj* **1** able to do many different kinds of things — see VERSATILE

2 capable of being readily changed — see FLEXIBLE 1

adapter *also* **adaptor** *n* something that is not necessary in itself but adds to the convenience or performance of the main piece of equipment — see ACCESSORY 1

add *vb* **1** to join (something) to a mass, quantity, or number so as to bring about an overall increase ⟨The band recently *added* a saxophonist and a keyboard player to its ranks.⟩ ⟨Add another cup of flour to the mixture.⟩

syn adjoin, annex, append, tack (on)

rel affix, attach, fasten, fix, graft, hitch, tag, tie; infuse, inject, insert, introduce; aggrandize, amplify, augment, beef (up), boost, compound, enlarge, escalate, expand, extend, increase, multiply, raise, swell; elongate, lengthen, prolong, protract; enhance, heighten, intensify, magnify; complement, supplement, supply; enforce, strengthen; maximize

near ant detach, disconnect, disjoin, separate, unfasten; amputate, cut, excise, lop (off), sever; contract, decrease, diminish, lessen, lower, reduce; abbreviate, abridge, curtail, shorten; compress, condense, constrict, cut back, retrench

ant abate, bate, deduct, knock off, remove, subtract, take off

2 to combine (numbers) into a single sum ⟨When she *added* all the phone charges herself, she discovered an error in her bill.⟩

syn cast (up), foot (up), sum, total

rel calculate, cipher, compute, figure, reckon, table, tabulate, tally, work out; divide, multiply, subtract; count, enumerate, number, tell; recompute, refigure

phrases put together

---

syn synonym(s)   *rel* related words
ant antonym(s)   *near ant* near antonym(s)

add (to) *vb* to make greater in size, amount, or number — see INCREASE 1

added *adj* resulting in an increase in amount or number — see ADDITIONAL

addendum *n* 1 a part added at the end of a book or periodical ⟨There's an *addendum* from the author to explain certain stylistic choices that she made.⟩
syn supplement
rel coda, epilogue (*also* epilog), postlude; conclusion, ending, finale; accompaniment, addition, complement, postscript; follow-up, sequel
ant foreword, introduction, preface, prologue (*also* prolog)
2 something added (as by growth) — see INCREASE 1

addict *n* 1 a person who regularly uses drugs especially illegally ⟨an inspiring story about *addicts* who seek help and manage to kick their habit⟩
syn user
2 a person with a strong and habitual liking for something — see FAN

addition *n* 1 a smaller structure added to a main building — see ANNEX
2 something added (as by growth) — see INCREASE 1
3 the act or process of becoming greater in number — see MULTIPLICATION

additional *adj* resulting in an increase in amount or number ⟨There turned out to be *additional* reasons for her unauthorized absence.⟩
syn added, another, else, farther, fresh, further, more, other
rel accessory, adjunct, collateral, extraneous, peripheral, side, supplemental, supplementary; new; excess, extra, plus, spare, surplus; complementary, contributory
near ant fewer, less

additionally *adv* in addition to what has been said — see MORE 1

additive *adj* produced by a series of additions of identical or similar things — see CUMULATIVE

addle *vb* to throw into a state of mental uncertainty — see CONFUSE 1

addled *adj* 1 having undergone organic breakdown — see ROTTEN 1
2 suffering from mental confusion — see DIZZY 2

address *n* 1 a usually formal discourse delivered to an audience — see SPEECH 1
2 the way or manner in which one conducts oneself — see BEHAVIOR

address *vb* 1 to deal with (something) usually skillfully or efficiently — see HANDLE 1
2 to occupy (oneself) diligently or with close attention — see APPLY 2
3 to transmit information or requests to — see CONTACT

adduce *vb* to give as an example — see QUOTE 1

add up (to) *vb* 1 to be the same in meaning or effect — see AMOUNT (TO) 2
2 to have a total of — see AMOUNT (TO) 1

adept *adj* having or showing exceptional knowledge, experience, or skill in a field of endeavor — see PROFICIENT

adept *n* a person with a high level of knowledge or skill in a field — see EXPERT

adeptly *adv* in a skillful or expert manner — see WELL 3

adeptness *n* subtle or imaginative ability in inventing, devising, or executing something — see SKILL 1

adequacy *n* the quality or state of meeting one's needs adequately — see SUFFICIENCY

adequate *adj* of a level of quality that meets one's needs or standards ⟨This old computer is probably *adequate* if you just want to do some word processing.⟩
syn acceptable, all right, decent, fine, good, OK (*or* okay), passable, respectable, satisfactory, serviceable, tolerable
rel agreeable, bearable, endurable, sufferable; average, fair, indifferent, mediocre, middling, minimal; common, ordinary, run-of-the-mill, run-of-the-mine (*or* run-of-mine), second-rate, so-so; standard, unexceptional; appropriate, correct, due, fitting, meet, proper, right, seemly, suitable, useful, worthy; gratifying, satisfying
phrases up to snuff
near ant disagreeable, disreputable, improper, indecent, objectionable, unfit, unsuitable, unworthy, useless, wrong; bad, cheap, defective, faulty, imperfect, incomplete, lamentable, pitiful, shoddy; dissatisfying; insufficient, meager (*or* meagre), mean, niggardly, poor, scanty, shabby, short, skimpy, spare, stingy; insufferable, intolerable, unbearable, unendurable; atrocious, execrable, miserable, vile, wretched; exceptional, exquisite, extreme, fancy, first-class, high-grade, matchless, maximized, maximum, optimal, optimum, peerless, preeminent, premium, special, supreme, unmatched, unparalleled; A1, bang-up, banner, capital, classic, crackerjack, dandy, divine, fabulous, fine, first-rate, grand, great, heavenly, jim-dandy, keen, marvelous (*or* marvellous), mean, neat, nifty, noble, par excellence, prime, sensational, splendid, stellar, sterling, superb, superior, superlative, supernal, swell, terrific, tip-top, top, top-notch, unsurpassed, wonderful
ant deficient, inadequate, insufficient, lacking, unacceptable, unsatisfactory, wanting

adequately *adv* 1 in a satisfactory way — see WELL 1
2 in or to a degree or quantity that meets one's requirements or satisfaction — see ENOUGH 1

adhere *vb* to hold to something firmly as if by adhesion — see STICK 1

adhere (to) *vb* 1 to give steadfast support to ⟨Our coach *adheres to* the belief that we can win this game if we just have a positive attitude.⟩
syn abide by, hew (to), keep (to), stand by, stick (to *or* with)
rel cleave (to); advocate, back, champion, confirm, defend, endorse (*also* indorse), espouse, support, uphold; accept, adopt, cherish, cultivate, embrace, follow, foster, heed; bolster, boost, buttress, enforce
phrases abide by, hold to, live up to
near ant abandon, desert, forsake, give up, relinquish, spurn, surrender; recall, recant, reconsider, renege, renounce, re-

tract, revoke, take back, unsay, withdraw; disagree (with), disprove, dispute, rebut, refute; contradict, deny, disavow, disclaim, disown, gainsay, negate, negative, repudiate; back down, back off, backtrack
ant defect (from)

2 to act according to the commands of — see OBEY

adherence *n* **1** a physical sticking to as if by glue — see ADHESION 1

2 the following of a custom, rule, or law — see OBSERVANCE 1

adherent *adj* tending to adhere to objects upon contact — see STICKY 1

adherent *n* one who follows the opinions or teachings of another — see FOLLOWER 1

adhesion *n* **1** a physical sticking to as if by glue ⟨discourages the use of photo albums that keep the pictures in place by *adhesion* to the pages⟩
syn adherence, bonding, cling
rel clumping, cohesion; adhesiveness, attachment, cohesiveness, tenacity; cementing, gluing (*also* glueing)
ant unsticking

2 adherence to something to which one is bound by a pledge or duty — see FIDELITY

adhesive *adj* tending to adhere to objects upon contact — see STICKY 1

adhesive *n* a substance used to stick things together — see GLUE

adieu *n* an expression of good wishes at parting — see GOOD-BYE

adipose *adj* containing animal fat especially in unusual amounts — see FATTY

adjacent *adj* having a border in common ⟨Their house is *adjacent* to a wooded park.⟩
syn abutting, adjoining, bordering, contiguous, flanking, flush, fringing, joining, juxtaposed, neighboring, skirting, touching, verging
rel approximate, close, closest, immediate, near, nearby, nearest, next-door, nigh; attached, communicating, connected, connecting, interconnecting, joined, linked, united; bounding, circumjacent, embracing, encircling, enclosing (*also* inclosing), fencing, rimming, surrounding; peripheral, tangent, tangential; encompassing
near ant apart, detached, disconnected, discrete, free-standing, isolate, isolated, removed, separate, single, unattached, unconnected, unlinked; away, distant, far, faraway, far-off, farthest, remote; discontinuous, noncontinuous; broken up, disjoined, dissevered, dissociated, disunited, divided, divorced, parted, ramified, resolved, severed, split, sundered, uncoupled, unyoked
ant nonadjacent, noncontiguous

adjoin *vb* **1** to be adjacent to ⟨The bedroom of their apartment *adjoins* their neighbor's living room.⟩
syn abut, border (on), flank, fringe, join, neighbor, skirt, touch, verge (on)
rel attach (to), communicate (with), connect (with), link (with); bound, embrace, encircle, enclose (*also* inclose), fence, line,

margin, rim, surround; contact, converge, meet

2 to join (something) to a mass, quantity, or number so as to bring about an overall increase — see ADD 1

adjoining *adj* having a border in common — see ADJACENT

adjourn *vb* to bring to a formal close for a period of time ⟨The meeting was *adjourned* by the chairperson until further notice.⟩
syn recess, suspend
rel break off, disband, discontinue, disperse, intermit, interrupt; defer, hold off, postpone, put off, reserve, shelve, table; dissolve, end, halt, stop, terminate; break up, close, conclude, wind up, wrap up; abort, call, call off, drop, recall, repeal, rescind, revoke; abrogate, annul, invalidate, negate, nullify, quash, void
near ant inaugurate, launch, open; carry on, continue, draw out, extend, proceed, prolong; renew, reopen, resume; assemble, call, convene, convoke, muster, rally, summon

adjudge *vb* to give an opinion about (something at issue or in dispute) — see JUDGE 1

adjudicate *vb* to give an opinion about (something at issue or in dispute) — see JUDGE 1

adjunct *n* **1** a person who helps a more skilled person — see HELPER

2 something that is not necessary in itself but adds to the convenience or performance of the main piece of equipment — see ACCESSORY 1

adjure *vb* **1** to give advice to — see ADVISE 1

2 to issue orders to (someone) by right of authority — see COMMAND 1

adjust *vb* to change (something) so as to make it suitable for a new use or situation — see ADAPT

adjustable *adj* capable of being readily changed — see FLEXIBLE 1

adjutant *n* a person who helps a more skilled person — see HELPER

ad-lib *adj* made or done without previous thought or preparation — see EXTEMPORANEOUS

ad-lib *vb* to perform, make, or do without preparation — see IMPROVISE

administer *vb* **1** to give out (something) to appropriate individuals ⟨The principal *administers* discipline fairly when students break the rules.⟩
syn allocate, apportion, deal (out), dispense, distribute, mete (out), parcel (out), portion, prorate
rel admeasure, allot, allow, appropriate, assign, dish out, divide, divvy (up), dollop (out), lot, measure (out), part, proportion, ration, redistribute, set, share (out), split; bestow, disburse, furnish, issue, provide, share, supply; circulate, disperse, disseminate, scatter, spread; chip in, contribute, donate, pledge; reallocate, reapportion
near ant decline, deny, deprive (of), disallow, refuse, reject, withhold; pinch, skimp, stint
ant misallocate

2 to carry out effectively — see ENFORCE

3 to look after and make decisions about — see CONDUCT 1

---

syn synonym(s) *rel* related words
ant antonym(s) *near ant* near antonym(s)

administration *n* 1 lawful control over the affairs of a political unit (as a nation) — see RULE 2

2 the act or activity of looking after and making decisions about something — see CONDUCT 1

administrative *adj* suited for or relating to the directing of things — see EXECUTIVE

administrator *n* a person who manages or directs something — see EXECUTIVE

admirable *adj* deserving of high regard or great approval ⟨It's *admirable* the way she helps her elderly neighbor with chores and errands every Saturday.⟩

syn applaudable, commendable, creditable, laudable, meritorious, praiseworthy

rel deserving, worthy; awesome, distinctive, distinguished, excellent, honorable, impressive, noteworthy, noticeable, outstanding, redoubtable, reputable, respectable; precious, valuable; delightful, enjoyable, pleasing, satisfying, ethical, good, high-minded, moral, noble, principled

near ant base, contemptible, deplorable, despicable, detestable, dirty, infamous, lousy, nasty, notorious, pitiable, pitiful, scabby, scummy, scurvy, sorry, unlikable, unworthy, vile, worthless, wretched; disgraceful, dishonorable, disreputable, ignominious, low, mean, scandalous, seamy, shady, shameful, shocking, sordid, unethical, unsavory

ant censurable, discreditable, illaudable, reprehensible

admiration *n* 1 a feeling of great approval and liking ⟨She won *admiration* for her courage.⟩

syn account, appreciation, esteem, estimation, favor, regard, respect

rel appetite, fancy, fondness, like, love, partiality, preference, relish, shine, taste, use; acclamation, adoration, adulation, approbation, deference, homage, honor, idolatry, infatuation, lionization, praise, reverence, veneration, worship; delight, enjoyment; amazement, awe, wonder, wonderment; enthusiasm, interest, passion; bias, prejudice; affection, attachment, devotion, passion

near ant condemnation, disapproval, disdain, opprobrium, scorn; disappointment, discontent, disenchantment, disgruntlement, disillusionment, displeasure, indignation, unhappiness; aversion, contempt, disfavor, disgust, disinclination, dislike, disliking, disregard, distaste; hate, hatred, loathing, nausea, repugnance, repulsion, revulsion; abomination, antipathy; deprecation, displeasure, dissatisfaction

ant disfavor

2 the rapt attention and deep emotion caused by the sight of something extraordinary — see WONDER 2

admire *vb* to think very highly or favorably of ⟨I *admire* the way you handled such a touchy situation.⟩

syn appreciate, consider, esteem, regard, respect

rel acclaim, accredit, applaud, approve, commend, compliment, credit, praise; delight (in), enjoy, relish, revel (in), savor (*also* savour); dig, fancy, favor, groove (on), like, love; adore, adulate, canonize, deify, dote (on), hallow, idolize, revere, reverence, venerate, worship; cherish, love, prize, treasure, value

phrases set store by (*or* on)

near ant abhor, abominate, despise, detest, execrate, hate, loathe; condemn, decry, deplore, disapprove, discount, discountenance, disdain, disfavor, dislike, dismiss, disregard, scorn, vilify

admiring *adj* expressing approval — see FAVORABLE 1

admissible *adj* that may be permitted — see PERMISSIBLE

admission *n* 1 an open declaration of something (as a fault or the commission of an offense) about oneself — see CONFESSION

2 the means or right of entering or participating in — see ENTRANCE 1

admit *vb* 1 to accept the truth or existence of (something) usually reluctantly ⟨The host of the talk show eventually *admitted* that she hadn't actually read the book.⟩ ⟨You can't bring yourself to *admit* your mistakes.⟩

syn acknowledge, agree, allow, concede, confess, grant, own (up to)

rel disburden, unburden, unload; affirm, avow, confirm, profess; accept, recognize, yield; announce, break, broadcast, communicate, declare, disclose, divulge, impart, proclaim, publish, reveal, spill, tell, unveil; betray, blab, expose, give away, inform, leak, rat, squeal; talk, tattle, tip (off), warn, wise (up)

phrases come clean (about)

near ant disallow, disavow, disclaim, disown; contradict, dispute, gainsay, negate, negative; rebut, refute, reject, repudiate; conceal, cover (up), hide, obscure, veil; kid (oneself)

ant deny

2 to offer entrance (as to a place, school, or privilege) to ⟨She was *admitted* to Harvard.⟩

syn enter, take

rel entertain, welcome; fellowship; confirm, ratify

near ant decline, disallow, disapprove, dismiss, refuse, reject; blackball, blacklist, ostracize; banish, deport, exile, expel, oust, throw out

ant ban, bar

3 to make an acknowledgment of something unpleasant as true or valid — see CONFESS 1

admittance *n* the means or right of entering or participating in — see ENTRANCE 1

admittedly *adv* to tell the truth — see ACTUALLY 1

admixture *n* a distinct entity formed by the combining of two or more different things — see BLEND

admonish *vb* 1 to criticize (someone) so as to correct a fault — see REBUKE 1

2 to give advice to — see ADVISE 1

admonishing *adj* serving as or offering a warning — see CAUTIONARY

admonishment *n* 1 an opinion suggesting a wise or proper course of action — see ADVICE

2 the act or an instance of telling beforehand of danger or risk — see WARNING 1

admonition *n* **1** an opinion suggesting a wise or proper course of action — see ADVICE

2 the act or an instance of telling beforehand of danger or risk — see WARNING 1

admonitory *adj* serving as or offering a warning — see CAUTIONARY

ado *n* a state of noisy, confused activity — see COMMOTION

adolescent *adj* **1** being in the early stage of life, growth, or development — see YOUNG

2 having or showing the annoying qualities (as silliness) associated with children — see CHILDISH

3 lacking in adult experience or maturity — see CALLOW

adopt *vb* to take for one's own use (something originated by another) ⟨We *adopted* some of the local customs.⟩

syn borrow, embrace, espouse, take on, take up

rel domesticate, naturalize; appropriate, arrogate, take over, usurp; absorb, assimilate, incorporate, quote; cherish, prize, treasure; cultivate, follow, heed, honor; use, utilize; bring up, foster, nurture, raise, rear; affect, assume, copy, imitate, pretend, put on, simulate

phrases pick up on

near ant abandon, forsake, give up, relinquish, surrender; reject, renounce, repudiate, spurn; discard, jettison, junk, throw away, throw out

adorable *adj* having qualities that tend to make one loved — see LOVABLE

adore *vb* **1** to feel passion, devotion, or tenderness for — see LOVE 2

2 to love or admire too much — see IDOLIZE

3 to offer honor or respect to (someone) as a divine power — see WORSHIP 1

4 to take pleasure in — see ENJOY 1

adoring *adj* **1** feeling or showing love — see LOVING 1

2 reflecting great admiration or devotion — see WORSHIPFUL

adorn *vb* to make more attractive by adding something that is beautiful or becoming — see DECORATE

adorning *adj* serving to add beauty — see DECORATIVE

adornment *n* something that decorates or beautifies — see DECORATION 1

adroit *adj* accomplished with trained ability — see SKILLFUL 1

adroitly *adv* in a skillful or expert manner — see WELL 3

adroitness *n* **1** mental skill or quickness — see DEXTERITY 1

2 subtle or imaginative ability in inventing, devising, or executing something — see SKILL 1

adulate *vb* **1** to love or admire too much — see IDOLIZE

2 to praise too much — see FLATTER 1

adulation *n* **1** excessive admiration of or devotion to a person — see WORSHIP

2 excessive praise — see FLATTERY

adulatory *adj* **1** overly or insincerely flattering — see FULSOME 1

2 reflecting great admiration or devotion — see WORSHIPFUL

adult *adj* **1** relating to or typical of adults; displaying proper maturity ⟨an *adult* reaction to the issue⟩

syn grown-up, mature

near ant childish, infantile, kiddish

ant adolescent, immature

2 fully grown or developed — see MATURE 1

adult *n* a fully grown person ⟨At the beach, the *adults* sat under broad umbrellas while the children splashed in the water.⟩

syn grown-up

rel middle-ager; ancient, elder, gaffer, graybeard, oldster, old-timer, senior, senior citizen

near ant child, cub, kid, moppet, tad, toddler, tot; baby, infant; adolescent, juvenile, minor, youngster, youth; preteen, preteenager, teen, teenager, teener, teenybopper, tween

adulterant *n* something that is or that makes impure — see IMPURITY 1

adulterate *adj* containing foreign or lower-grade substances — see IMPURE 1

adulterate *vb* to alter (something) for the worse with the addition of foreign or lower-grade substances ⟨The company was fined for *adulterating* its "all beef" frankfurters with cereal.⟩

syn cut, dilute, extend, lace, sophisticate, thin, weaken

rel load; befoul, contaminate, corrupt, defile, dirty, envenom, foul, infect, poison, pollute, soil, spoil, sully, taint; cheapen, debase, degrade; manipulate, misrepresent, tamper (with); counterfeit, fake, falsify, fudge; doctor, spike; moderate, qualify, temper

near ant fertilize, lard; augment, supplement; decontaminate, purify; clarify, clean, cleanse, distill (*also* distil); filter, flush, leach, pasteurize, purge, refine; better, enhance, improve; compact, concentrate, condense

ant enrich, fortify, richen, strengthen

adulterated *adj* containing foreign or lower-grade substances — see IMPURE 1

adultery *n* a sexual encounter or relationship between a married person and someone other than their spouse ⟨accusations of *adultery*⟩

syn infidelity, unfaithfulness

rel promiscuity; disloyalty, faithlessness, falseness, inconstancy, perfidiousness, perfidy, treachery; affair (*also* affaire), fling, love, love affair, romance; intrigue; attachment, infatuation; entanglement, flirtation; liaison, passion

near ant allegiance, constancy, dedication, devotedness, devotion, fealty, loyalty, steadfastness

ant faithfulness, fidelity

adulthood *n* the state of being fully grown or developed — see MATURITY

advance *n* **1** forward movement in time or place ⟨During her long convalescence, the housebound woman was barely aware of the *advance* of the seasons.⟩

syn advancement, furtherance, going, headway, march, onrush, passage, process, procession, progress, progression

---

syn synonym(s)   *rel* related words
ant antonym(s)   *near ant* near antonym(s)

rel current, drift, flow, flux, stream, way; advent, approach, arrival, coming, nearing; bound, jump, leap, step, stride; impetus, momentum

near ant ebb, reflux; retraction, return, reversal, reverse

ant recess, recession, regress, regression, retreat, retrogression

2 an instance of notable progress in the development of knowledge, technology, or skill ⟨Under her new teacher, the aspiring violinist has made noticeable *advances* in her technique in just a few weeks.⟩

syn advancement, breakthrough, enhancement, improvement, refinement

rel quantum leap; amelioration, boost, heightening, increase, melioration, strengthening, upgrade, uplift, upswing, uptrend, upturn; betterment, development, elaboration, evolution, expansion, gestation, growth, maturation, perfection, ripening; civilization, edification, education, enlightenment; renascence, revival, innovation, invention

near ant breakdown, collapse, crash; hindrance, impediment, stumbling block; decadence, decay, decline, decrease, degeneration, descent, deterioration, diminishment, downgrade, ebbing, failing, flagging, languishment, lapse, lessening, reduction, sinking, slowing, weakening, worsening; detriment, disablement, drawback, glitch, impairment, shortcoming

ant setback

advance *vb* **1** to give to another for temporary use with the understanding that it or a like thing will be returned — see LEND

2 to help the growth or development of — see FOSTER 1

3 to move forward along a course — see GO 1

4 to move higher in rank or position — see PROMOTE 1

5 to set before the mind for consideration — see PROPOSE 1

6 to move closer to — see COME 1

advanced *adj* being far along in development ⟨An *advanced* civilization, among the first anywhere to use the plow, developed on the banks of the Nile River thousands of years ago.⟩

syn developed, evolved, forward, high, higher, improved, late, progressive, refined

rel precocious; full-blown, full-fledged, full-scale; aged, mature, matured, perfected, ripe, ripened; civilized, educated, enhanced, enlightened; contemporary, current, latest, leading-edge, mod, modern, new, newest, newfangled, new-fashioned, novel, now, present-day, recent, space-age, supermodern, ultramodern, up-to-date; avant

near ant green, immature, underdeveloped, undersized (*also* undersize), underweight, unripe, unripened; uncivilized, uneducated; early, embryonic, germinal, primeval, primordial; antediluvian, antiquated, antique, dated, fusty, hoary, musty, Neanderthal (*or* Neandertal), obsolete, old, oldfangled, old-fashioned, old-time, out-of-date, outworn, passé, past

ant backward, low, lower, nonprogressive, primitive, rude, rudimentary, undeveloped

advancement *n* **1** a raising or a state of being raised to a higher rank or position ⟨The young man's rapid *advancement* in the company came as no surprise to those who knew him.⟩

syn ascent, creation, elevation, preference, preferment, promotion, rise, upgrade

rel aggrandizement, ennoblement, exaltation, glorification, magnification

near ant deposition, dethronement, discharge, dismissal, expulsion, impeachment, ouster, overthrow, removal, suspension, unmaking, unseating; downfall, fall

ant abasement, comedown, degradation, downgrade, reduction

2 an instance of notable progress in the development of knowledge, technology, or skill — see ADVANCE 2

3 forward movement in time or place — see ADVANCE 1

advantage *n* **1** the more favorable condition or position in a competition ⟨Your experience volunteering at the hospital will put you at an *advantage* when you're applying for a job there.⟩

syn better, bulge, drop, edge, jump, pull, stead, upper hand, vantage

rel allowance, head start, lead, margin, odds, start; ascendancy (*also* ascendency), command, dominance, mastery, predominance, superiority, supremacy, transcendence, transcendency; precedence, preference, prerogative, privilege, seniority; break, foothold, opportunity; benefit, blessing, boon, felicity, godsend, manna, windfall

near ant detriment, stranglehold; disparity, imbalance, inequality, unevenness; disability, failing, impairment, shortcoming; bar, catch, check, clog, crimp, embarrassment, hindrance, hitch, hurdle, impediment, interference, let, manacle, obstacle, obstruction, rub, shackle, stop, trammel; lurch, setback

ant disadvantage, drawback, handicap, liability, minus, penalty, strike

2 a thing that helps — see HELP 2

advantage *vb* to provide with something useful or desirable — see BENEFIT

advantageous *adj* promoting or contributing to personal or social well-being — see BENEFICIAL

advent *n* the act of coming upon a scene — see ARRIVAL

adventure *n* **1** an exciting or noteworthy event that one experiences firsthand ⟨Our quiet hike turned into quite an *adventure* when we encountered a bear and her cub.⟩

syn experience, exploit, happening, time

rel escapade, lark, ploy; act, action, deed, doing, feat; episode, occasion; baptism, ordeal, test, trial, tribulation; enterprise, risk, venture; expedition, exploration, mission, performance, quest, stunt

near ant bore, bummer, bust, downer, drag

2 a risky undertaking — see GAMBLE

adventure *vb* **1** to place in danger — see ENDANGER

2 to take a chance on — see RISK 1

adventuresome *adj* inclined or willing to take risks — see BOLD 1

adventurous *adj* inclined or willing to take risks — see BOLD 1

adversary *adj* marked by opposition or ill will — see HOSTILE 1

adversary *n* **1** one that is hostile toward another — see ENEMY

2 one that takes a position opposite another in a competition or conflict — see OPPONENT 1

adverse *adj* **1** opposed to one's interests ⟨All the *adverse* publicity really caused the movie star's popularity to suffer.⟩

syn counter, disadvantageous, hostile, inimical, negative, prejudicial, unfavorable, unfriendly, unsympathetic, untoward

rel bad, baleful, baneful, evil; damaging, deleterious, destructive, detrimental, fatal, harmful, hurtful, ill, injurious, lethal, malignant, murderous, noxious, pernicious, poisonous, ruinous, threatening, troublesome, unhealthy, wounding; dangerous, hazardous, imperiling (*or* imperilling), jeopardizing, perilous, risky, unsafe; defamatory, offensive, scathing, slanderous; antagonistic, antipathetic, inhospitable, intolerant, uncongenial, uncooperative; competing, conflicting, counteracting, countering, opposing, resistant, resisting

near ant beneficial, good, helpful, propitious, useful; harmless, innocent, innocuous, inoffensive, nondestructive, nonfatal, nonlethal, nonthreatening; unresistant; tolerant, understanding; affable, agreeable, amiable, amicable, benign, benignant, complying, congenial, cordial, friendly, hospitable

ant advantageous, favorable, friendly, positive, supportive, sympathetic, well-disposed

2 causing or capable of causing harm — see HARMFUL

adversity *n* **1** bad luck or an example of this — see MISFORTUNE

2 something that is a cause for suffering or special effort especially in the attainment of a goal — see DIFFICULTY 1

advert (to) *vb* to make reference to or speak about briefly but specifically — see MENTION 1

advertise *vb* to make known openly or publicly — see ANNOUNCE

advertisement *n* a published statement informing the public of a matter of general interest — see ANNOUNCEMENT

advice *n* an opinion suggesting a wise or proper course of action ⟨We got some good *advice* from the vet about dealing with our dog's habit of chasing cars.⟩

syn admonishment, admonition, counsel, guidance, input

rel recommendation, suggestion; hint, pointer, tip; feedback, information; answer, solution; advisement, consideration, thought; alarm (*also* alarum), alert, caution, cautioning, expostulation, forewarning, remonstrance, remonstration, urging, warning; judgment (*or* judgement), observation, verdict; assistance, briefing, coach-

ing, direction, instruction, mentoring, priming, prompting, teaching, tutoring; interference, kibitzing (*also* kibbitzing), meddling; moralizing, pontificating, preaching; exhortation, lecture, lesson, sermon, speech

advisable *adj* suitable for bringing about a desired result under the circumstances — see EXPEDIENT

advise *vb* **1** to give advice to ⟨a popular guidance counselor who has been *advising* students about their college plans for two decades⟩

syn adjure, admonish, counsel

rel alert, caution, forewarn, warn; brief, clue (in), fill in, inform, tell, wise (up); coach, direct, guide, instruct, lead, mentor, shepherd, show, teach, tutor; pilot, steer; acquaint, apprise, familiarize; convince, encourage, induce, persuade, talk (into); beg, exhort, implore, prevail (upon), urge; propose, recommend, suggest

2 to put (something) forward as one's choice for a wise or proper course of action ⟨She *advised* calling ahead for a reservation at the new restaurant.⟩

syn counsel, recommend, suggest

rel advocate, back, champion, espouse, favor, support; exhort, urge; advance, offer, propose, submit

3 to exchange viewpoints or seek advice for the purpose of finding a solution to a problem — see CONFER 2

4 to give information to — see ENLIGHTEN 1

5 to give notice to beforehand especially of danger or risk — see WARN

advised *adj* decided on as a result of careful thought — see DELIBERATE 1

advisedly *adv* with full awareness of what one is doing — see INTENTIONALLY

advisement *n* a careful weighing of the reasons for or against something — see CONSIDERATION 1

adviser *or* **advisor** *n* a person who gives advice especially professionally — see CONSULTANT

advocate *n* **1** a person who actively supports or favors a cause — see EXPONENT 1

2 a person whose profession is to conduct lawsuits for clients or to advise about legal rights and obligations — see LAWYER

advocate *vb* to promote the interests or cause of — see SUPPORT 1

aegis *also* **egis** *n* **1** means or method of defending — see DEFENSE 1

2 the financial support and general guidance for an undertaking — see AUSPICE 1

aesthetic *also* **esthetic** *or* **aesthetical** *or* **esthetical** *adj* very pleasing to look at — see BEAUTIFUL 1

affability *n* the state or quality of having a pleasant or agreeable manner in socializing with others — see AMIABILITY 1

affable *adj* **1** having a relaxed, casual manner — see EASYGOING 1

2 having an easygoing and pleasing manner especially in social situations — see AMIABLE

3 showing a natural kindness and courtesy especially in social situations — see GRACIOUS 1

---

syn synonym(s) *rel* related words
ant antonym(s) *near ant* near antonym(s)

affair *n* **1** *also* **affaire** a brief romantic relationship ⟨an *affair* between two singles spending the summer at the same beach resort⟩
syn fling, love, love affair, romance
rel intrigue, liaison; dalliance, hanky-panky; attachment, infatuation; entanglement, flirtation; idyll (*also* idyl), passion; calf-love, puppy love
2 a social gathering — see PARTY 1
3 something produced by physical or intellectual effort — see PRODUCT 1
4 something that happens — see EVENT 1
5 something to be dealt with — see MATTER 2

¹**affect** *vb* **1** to act upon (a person or a person's feelings) so as to cause a response ⟨Their son claims that scary movies don't *affect* him in the least.⟩
syn impact, impress, influence, move, reach, strike, sway, tell (on), touch
rel carry away, dazzle, enrapture, enthrall (*or* enthral); entrance, ravish, transport; bias, color; inspire, stir; engage, interest, involve, penetrate, pierce; afflict, agitate, bother, concern, discomfort, discompose, disquiet, distress, disturb, fluster, harry, perturb, pester, plague, smite, strain, stress, trouble, try, upset, worry, wring; allure, attract, bewitch, captivate, charm, enchant, fascinate
phrases get to
near ant bore, jade, pall, tire, weary; underwhelm
2 to be the business or affair of — see CONCERN 2

²**affect** *vb* to present a false appearance of — see FEIGN
affectation *n* the quality or state of appearing or trying to appear more important or more valuable than is the case — see PRETENSE 1
affected *adj* **1** lacking in natural or spontaneous quality — see ARTIFICIAL 1
2 self-consciously trying to present an appearance of grandeur or importance — see PRETENTIOUS 1
3 having a liking or affection — see FOND 1
affectedness *n* the quality or state of appearing or trying to appear more important or more valuable than is the case — see PRETENSE 1
affecting *adj* having the power to affect the feelings or sympathies — see MOVING
affection *n* **1** a feeling of strong or constant regard for and dedication to someone — see LOVE 1
2 a habitual attraction to some activity or thing — see INCLINATION 1
affectionate *adj* feeling or showing love — see LOVING 1
affianced *adj* pledged in marriage — see ENGAGED 1
affiliate *n* a local unit of an organization — see CHAPTER 1
affiliated *adj* having a close connection like that between family members — see RELATED
affiliation *n* the state of having shared interests or efforts (as in social or business matters) — see ASSOCIATION 1
affinity *n* **1** a habitual attraction to some activity or thing — see INCLINATION 1

2 the fact or state of having something in common — see CONNECTION 1
affirm *vb* **1** to state as a fact usually forcefully — see CLAIM 1
2 to state clearly and strongly — see ASSERT 1
affirmation *n* a solemn and often public declaration of the truth or existence of something — see PROTESTATION
affix *vb* to cause (something) to hold to another — see FASTEN 1
afflict *vb* to cause persistent suffering to ⟨The South was *afflicted* by a severe drought.⟩ ⟨He's been *afflicted* by nightmares ever since the accident.⟩
syn agonize, anguish, bedevil, beset, besiege, curse, harrow, persecute, plague, rack, torment, torture
rel assail, attack; badger, dog, hound, pursue, ride; aggravate, agitate, annoy, bother, bug, chafe, distress, disturb, exasperate, gall, get, grate, gripe, hagride, harry, irk, irritate, molest, nettle, peeve, pester, pique, put out, rasp, rile, vex; discomfort, discompose, disquiet, fluster, grieve, perturb, strain, stress, trouble, try, upset, worry; crush, oppress, overpower, overwhelm, smite, strike, tyrannize, victimize; hurt, pain, pang, prick, smart, stab, sting, wring; martyr
near ant abet, aid, assist, help; deliver, release, relieve, reprieve; comfort, console, content, quiet, solace, soothe, succor
afflicting *adj* hard to accept or bear especially emotionally — see BITTER 2
affliction *n* **1** a state of great suffering of body or mind — see DISTRESS 1
2 deep sadness especially for the loss of someone or something loved — see SORROW
3 a source of harm or misfortune — see BANE 1
4 a source of persistent emotional distress — see DEMON 2
5 something that causes loss or pain — see INJURY 1
affluent *adj* having goods, property, or money in abundance — see RICH 1
afford *vb* to have enough money for ⟨We can't *afford* new clothes this month.⟩
syn go, swing
rel cover; expend, finance, outlay, pay (for), spring (for); pick up, purchase, take; acquire, get, obtain, procure, secure; bid, offer; bankroll, endow, subsidize, underwrite
affordable *adj* **1** being within the financial means of most people — see ACCESSIBLE 1
2 costing little — see CHEAP 1
affront *n* an act or expression showing scorn and usually intended to hurt another's feelings — see INSULT
affront *vb* to cause hurt feelings or deep resentment in — see INSULT
aficionado *also* **afficionado** *n* a person with a strong and habitual liking for something — see FAN
afield *adv* off the desired or intended path or course — see WRONG
afire *adj* being on fire — see ABLAZE 1
aflame *adj* being on fire — see ABLAZE 1
aflutter *adj* feeling or showing uncomfortable feelings of uncertainty — see NERVOUS 1

afoot *adj* being in progress or development — see ONGOING 1

afraid *adj* filled with fear or dread ⟨Melissa is *afraid* of flying, so she takes a train from Boston to visit her brother in Chicago.⟩

syn aghast, alarmed, fearful, frightened, horrified, hysterical, scared, scary, shocked, spooked, terrified, terrorized

rel chicken, fainthearted, fearsome, shrinking, shy, timid, timorous, tremulant, tremulous; agitated, anxious, disconcerted, disquieted, disturbed, jittery, jumpy, nervous, panicked, panicky, panic-stricken, perturbed, skittish, uneasy, upset, worried; phobic; appalled, dismayed, startled; cowed, daunted, intimidated, unnerved; coward, cowardly, craven, lily-livered; careful, cautious, heedful, prudent, unadventurous, wary

near ant adventuresome, adventurous, audacious, bold, daredevil, daring, dashing, gutsy, plucky, spirited, spunky, venturesome, venturous; brave, courageous, gallant, hardy, heroic (*also* heroical), intrepid, lionhearted, manful, stalwart, stout, stouthearted, valiant, valorous; assured, collected, composed, confident, cool, sanguine, sure, unperturbed; dauntless, resolute, undaunted

ant fearless, unafraid

afresh *adv* yet another time — see AGAIN 1

aft *adj* being at or in the part of something opposite the front part — see BACK

aft *adv* near, toward, or in the stern of a ship or the tail of an aircraft ⟨After transferring the controls to the copilot, the captain went *aft* to see what the disturbance was.⟩

syn abaft, astern

rel after, back, backward (*or* backwards), behind, rearward (*also* rearwards)

near ant ahead, before

ant forward

after *adj* 1 being at or in the part of something opposite the front part — see BACK

2 being, occurring, or carried out at a time after something else — see SUBSEQUENT

after *adv* following in time or place ⟨Upon seeing *The Nutcracker* for the first time, and for a long time *after*, Irma wanted to play the part of the Mouse King.⟩

syn afterward (*or* afterwards), later, subsequently, thereafter

rel hereafter; presently, since, soon, then, thereupon; hereinbelow, infra

near ant heretofore, theretofore

ant ahead, antecedently, anteriorly, before, beforehand, previously

after *prep* subsequent to in time or order ⟨The brass band came right *after* the mayor in the parade.⟩

syn behind, below, following, next to, past

rel since

near ant toward (*or* towards)

ant ahead of, before, ere, of, previous to, prior to, to

aftereffect *n* a condition or occurrence traceable to a cause — see EFFECT 1

---

syn synonym(s)   *rel* related words
ant antonym(s)   *near ant* near antonym(s)

---

afterlife *n* 1 a later period of one's life — see AGE 3

2 unending existence after death — see ETERNITY 2

aftermath *n* a condition or occurrence traceable to a cause — see EFFECT 1

afterward *or* **afterwards** *adv* following in time or place — see AFTER

again *adv* 1 yet another time ⟨Now I have to mop the floor *again* because you didn't wipe your feet.⟩

syn afresh, anew, over

rel always, consistently, constantly, continuously, endlessly, ever, evermore, forever, incessantly, invariably, perpetually, unfailingly; continually, frequently, oft, often, oftentimes (*or* ofttimes); recurrently, repeatedly; freshly, newly

near ant ne'er, never; infrequently, little, rarely, seldom, unusually; intermittently, occasionally, periodically, sometimes, sporadically

ant nevermore

2 in addition to what has been said — see MORE 1

3 just the opposite being true — see CONTRARIWISE

against *prep* in or into contact with ⟨He leaned *against* the fence and it collapsed.⟩ ⟨unwittingly rubbed his leg *against* some poison ivy⟩

syn on, upon

rel alongside, next, next to; upside

agape *adj* having or showing signs of eagerly awaiting something — see EXPECTANT 1

age *n* 1 an extent of time associated with a particular person or thing ⟨The Bronze *Age* marks the beginning of the use of metal by ancient peoples.⟩

syn day, epoch, era, period, time

rel cycle, generation, year; bit, space, span, spell, stretch, while; date

2 a long or seemingly long period of time ⟨It took *ages* for the clerk to ring up three items.⟩

syn eon (*or* aeon), cycle, eternity, forever, long, moon

rel infinity; lifetime

near ant flash, instant, jiffy, minute, moment, second, shake, split second, trice, twinkle, twinkling, wink; microsecond, nanosecond

3 a later period of one's life ⟨stoically endures all of the aches and pains that come with *age*⟩

syn afterlife, evening

rel sunset, twilight; anecdotage; golden years, oldness, seniority; adulthood, majority, maturity, middle, middle age, midlife, ripeness

near ant youth

ant springtime

age *vb* to become mature — see MATURE

aged *adj* 1 being of advanced years and especially past middle age — see ELDERLY

2 dating or surviving from the distant past — see ANCIENT 1

ageless *adj* having an existence or validity that does not change or diminish — see ABIDING

agency *n* 1 a large unit of a governmental,

business, or educational organization — see DIVISION 2

2 something used to achieve an end — see AGENT 1

agenda *n* a listing of things to be presented or considered (as at a concert or play) — see PROGRAM 1

agent *n* **1** something used to achieve an end ⟨The whitening *agent* in the detergent is chlorine bleach.⟩ ⟨They see themselves as *agents* of social change.⟩

syn agency, instrument, instrumentality, machinery, means, medium, organ, vehicle

rel determinant, expedient, factor, influence, ingredient, mechanism, tool; weapon; activator, animator, catalyst, driver, energizer, executor, generator, impetus, incentive, inspiration, instigation, instigator, launcher, mover, power, stimulus, trigger; antecedent, cause, occasion, reason; subagency, subagent

2 a person who acts or does business for another ⟨The sports *agent* negotiated a record-breaking contract for the baseball player.⟩

syn attorney, commissary, delegate, deputy, envoy, factor, procurator, proxy, rep, representative

rel ambassador, diplomat, diplomatist, emissary, foreign minister, legate, plenipotentiary; alternate, backup, pinch hitter, relief, replacement, stand-in, sub, substitute, surrogate, understudy; informer, operative, spy; distributor, manager; arbiter, arbitrator, conciliator, go-between, intercessor, intermediary, interposer, liaison, mediator, middleman, peacemaker; mouthpiece, point man, point person, prophet, speaker, spokesman, spokesperson

3 a person sent on a mission to represent another — see AMBASSADOR

4 a person who tries secretly to obtain information for one country in the territory of another usually unfriendly country — see SPY

age–old *adj* dating or surviving from the distant past — see ANCIENT 1

agglomerate *n* an unorganized collection or mixture of various things — see MISCELLANY 1

agglomerate *vb* to form into a round compact mass — see WAD

agglomeration *n* an unorganized collection or mixture of various things — see MISCELLANY 1

aggrandize *vb* **1** to assign a high status or value to — see EXALT 1

2 to make greater in size, amount, or number — see INCREASE 1

aggravate *vb* to disturb the peace of mind of (someone) especially by repeated disagreeable acts — see IRRITATE 1

aggravating *adj* causing annoyance — see ANNOYING

aggravation *n* **1** something that is a source of irritation — see ANNOYANCE 3

2 the act of making unwelcome intrusions upon another — see ANNOYANCE 1

3 the feeling of impatience or anger caused by another's repeated disagreeable acts — see ANNOYANCE 2

aggregate *n* a complete amount of something — see WHOLE

aggregate *vb* to have a total of — see AMOUNT (TO) 1

aggression *n* **1** an inclination to fight or quarrel — see BELLIGERENCE

2 the act or action of setting upon with force or violence — see ATTACK 1

aggressive *adj* **1** having or showing a bold forcefulness in the pursuit of a goal ⟨If you don't take a more *aggressive* approach to this yard pretty soon, the weeds are going to take over completely.⟩

syn ambitious, assertive, enterprising, fierce, go-getting, high-pressure, in-your-face, militant, self-assertive

rel argumentative, bellicose, belligerent, combative, contentious, discordant, disputatious, gladiatorial, militant, pugnacious, quarrelsome, trigger-happy, truculent, warlike; hyperaggressive, overambitious; dynamic, energetic, enterprising, gung ho, hustling, strenuous, vigorous; emphatic, obtrusive; adventuresome, adventurous, daring, dashing, emboldened, gutsy, venturesome, venturous; audacious, bold, brash, brassy, cheeky, cocksure, cocky, confident, determined, forward, impudent, insolent, overconfident, presumptuous, unapologetic, unsubdued, unyielding; bare-knuckle (*also* bare-knuckled *or* bare-knuckles), scrappy

near ant easygoing, laid-back, relaxed; acquiescent, amenable, compliant, deferential, docile, resigned, submissive, tractable, yielding; cowering, cringing, groveling (*or* grovelling), shrinking; bashful, demure, diffident, humble, lowly, meek, mild, modest, mousy (*or* mousey), overmodest, passive, quiet, reserved, retiring, shy, subdued, timid, unobtrusive; obsequious, subservient

ant ambitionless, low-pressure, nonassertive, unaggressive, unambitious, unassertive, unenterprising

2 feeling or displaying eagerness to fight — see BELLIGERENT

3 marked by or uttered with forcefulness — see EMPHATIC 1

aggressiveness *n* **1** readiness to engage in daring or difficult activity — see ENTERPRISE 2

2 the quality or state of being forceful (as in expression) — see VEHEMENCE 1

3 an inclination to fight or quarrel — see BELLIGERENCE

aggressor *n* one that starts armed conflict against another especially without reasonable cause ⟨These pocket-size states had formed an alliance to deter potential *aggressors*.⟩

syn invader, raider

rel initiator, instigator; ambusher, forayer, pillager, plunderer; hawk, jingo, militant, militarist, warmonger; belligerent, cobelligerent, combatant

near ant defender; dove, pacifist, peacemaker; nonbelligerent

aggrieved *adj* having a feeling that one has been wronged or thwarted in one's ambitions — see DISCONTENTED

aghast *adj* filled with fear or dread — see AFRAID

agile *adj* moving easily — see GRACEFUL 1

agility *n* ease and grace in physical activity — see DEXTERITY 2

aging *or* **ageing** *adj* being of advanced years and especially past middle age — see ELDERLY

agitate *vb* 1 to cause (as a liquid) to move about in a circle especially repeatedly — see STIR 1

2 to trouble the mind of; to make uneasy — see DISTURB 1

3 to make a series of small irregular or violent movements — see SHAKE 1

4 to talk about (an issue) usually from various points of view and for the purpose of arriving at a decision or opinion — see DISCUSS

agitated *adj* 1 being in a state of increased activity or agitation — see FEVERISH 1

2 feeling overwhelming fear or worry — see FRANTIC 1

agitating *adj* marked by or causing agitation or uncomfortable feelings — see NERVOUS 2

agitation *n* 1 a state of wildly excited activity or emotion — see FRENZY

2 an uneasy state of mind usually over the possibility of an anticipated misfortune or trouble — see ANXIETY 1

agitator *n* a person who stirs up public feelings especially of discontent ⟨a political *agitator*⟩

syn demagogue (*also* demagog), exciter, firebrand, fomenter, incendiary, inciter, instigator, rabble-rouser

rel demonstrator, marcher, objector, picketer, protester (*or* protestor); advocate, apostle, booster, champion, exponent, persuader, promoter, proponent, reformer, reformist, supporter; alarmist, extremist, insurgent, insurrectionist, radical, rebel, revolter, revolutionary, revolutionist, subversive, troublemaker; prodder, prompter, provoker; agent provocateur

near ant peacemaker, reconciler, uniter

aglow *adj* being or being an outward sign of good feelings (as of love, confidence, or happiness) — see RADIANT 1

agog *adj* 1 having or showing signs of eagerly awaiting something — see EXPECTANT 1

2 showing urgent desire or interest — see EAGER

agonize *vb* 1 to cause persistent suffering to — see AFFLICT

2 to feel deep sadness or mental pain — see GRIEVE

agonizing *adj* 1 hard to accept or bear especially emotionally — see BITTER 2

2 intensely or unbearably painful — see EXCRUCIATING 1

agonizingly *adv* with feelings of bitterness or grief — see HARD 2

agony *n* 1 a situation or state that causes great suffering and unhappiness — see HELL 2

2 a state of great suffering of body or mind — see DISTRESS 1

3 a sudden intense expression of strong feeling — see OUTBURST 1

---

agrarian *adj* engaged in or concerned with agriculture — see AGRICULTURAL

agree *vb* 1 to have or come to the same opinion or point of view ⟨My husband and I *agree* on just about every aspect of childrearing.⟩

syn coincide, concur

rel accede (to), accept, acquiesce, assent (to), comply (with), consent (to), go (by); affiliate, ally, associate, unite; collaborate, cooperate, get along, get on

phrases see eye to eye

near ant clash, collide, conflict; bicker, counter, dispute, dissent, diverge, fall out, object, oppose, protest, quarrel, resist, rival; dissociate, separate, split

ant differ, disagree

2 to come to an arrangement as to a course of action ⟨Since we couldn't *agree*, we tossed a coin to decide the matter.⟩

syn bargain, contract, covenant

rel come around, come round; underwrite; arrange, settle

phrases come to terms, strike a bargain

near ant differ, dissent; cancel, renege, revoke; argue, contest, dispute, object

ant disagree

3 to accept the truth or existence of (something) usually reluctantly — see ADMIT 1

4 to be in agreement on every point — see CHECK 1

5 to form a pleasing relationship — see HARMONIZE 1

6 to give or express one's approval (as to a proposal) — see ACCEDE

agreeable *adj* 1 being to one's liking — see SATISFACTORY 1

2 giving pleasure or contentment to the mind or senses — see PLEASANT 1

3 having an easygoing and pleasing manner especially in social situations — see AMIABLE

4 having or marked by agreement in feeling or action — see HARMONIOUS 3

agreeableness *n* the state or quality of having a pleasant or agreeable manner in socializing with others — see AMIABILITY 1

agreeably *adv* in a pleasing way — see WELL 5

agreement *n* 1 the state of being of one opinion about something ⟨We were in *agreement* about one thing at least: that we'd never worked so hard in all our lives.⟩

syn accord, concurrence, consensus, unanimity, unison

rel adhesion, assent, consent; acceptance, acquiescence, concession, embrace, embracement; approbation, approval, favor; alliance, collaboration, collusion; complicity, conspiracy; compliance, concert, concertedness, concord, concordance, conformity, consonance, harmony, oneness, solidarity, understanding, union; empathy, rapport, sympathy

phrases meeting of minds

near ant discord, dissension (*also* dissention); dissent, opposition, resistance; disapprobation, disapproval, disfavor

ant conflict, disagreement

2 an arrangement about action to be taken ⟨We finally reached an *agreement* regarding a fair division of the housework.⟩

syn accord, bargain, compact, contract, convention, covenant, deal, disposition, pact, settlement, understanding

rel charter, treaty; binder, pledge, promise; alliance, association, entente, entente cordiale, league, partnership; acceptance, approval, assent, concurrence, consent, OK (*or* okay)

3 a state of consistency — see CONFORMITY 1

agricultural *adj* engaged in or concerned with agriculture ⟨He grew up in an *agricultural* community and farming was still in his blood.⟩

syn agrarian, farming

rel agronomic; bucolic, pastoral, pastoralist; garden; country, rural, rustic (*also* rustical)

near ant metro, metropolitan, urban; industrial, industrialized

ant nonagricultural

agriculture *n* the science or occupation of cultivating the soil, producing crops, and raising livestock ⟨The forest was cut down, and the land given over to *agriculture*.⟩

syn farming, husbandry

rel cultivation, culture, farmwork, gardening, horticulture, tillage; animal husbandry, mixed farming, pastoralism; sharecropping

agriculturist *or* **agriculturalist** *n* a person who cultivates the land and grows crops on it — see FARMER

agronomist *n* a person who cultivates the land and grows crops on it — see FARMER

aground *adj* resting on the shore or bottom of a body of water ⟨The villagers came to stare at the foreign ship that was *aground* on their beach and at the strangely dressed sailors on board.⟩

syn beached, grounded, stranded

rel landed

ah *interj* how surprising, doubtful, or unbelievable — see NO

aha *interj* how surprising, doubtful, or unbelievable — see NO

ahead *adv* 1 so as to precede something in order of time ⟨Call *ahead* for reservations.⟩

syn before, beforehand, previously

rel early, prematurely; first, first off, now; presently, shortly, soon

phrases in advance

near ant behind, next, subsequently

ant after, afterward (*or* afterwards), later

2 toward a point ahead in space or time — see ONWARD 1

3 toward or at a point lying in advance in space or time — see ALONG

ahead of *prep* 1 earlier than — see BEFORE 1

2 preceding in space — see BEFORE 2

aid *n* 1 a person who helps a more skilled person — see HELPER

2 a thing that helps — see HELP 2

3 an act or instance of helping — see HELP 1

aid *vb* to provide (someone) with what is useful or necessary to achieve an end — see HELP 1

aide *n* a person who helps a more skilled person — see HELPER

ail *n* an abnormal state that disrupts a plant's or animal's normal bodily functioning — see DISEASE

ail *vb* to trouble the mind of; to make uneasy — see DISTURB 1

ailing *adj* 1 chronically or repeatedly suffering from poor health — see SICKLY 1

2 temporarily suffering from a disorder of the body — see SICK 1

ailment *n* an abnormal state that disrupts a plant's or animal's normal bodily functioning — see DISEASE

aim *n* something that one hopes or intends to accomplish — see GOAL

aim *vb* 1 to point or turn (something) toward a target or goal ⟨The new system is *aimed* at reducing costs.⟩

syn bend, cast, direct, head, hold, level, pinpoint, set, train

rel sight; bear, face; concentrate, focus; incline, orient, steer

near ant avert, curve, deflect, detour, divert, rechannel, shunt, sidetrack

2 to have in mind as a purpose or goal — see INTEND 1

aimless *adj* lacking a definite plan, purpose, or pattern — see RANDOM

aimlessly *adv* without definite aim, direction, rule, or method — see HIT OR MISS

air *n* 1 a rhythmic series of musical tones arranged to give a pleasing effect — see MELODY

2 a slight or gentle movement of air — see BREEZE 1

3 a special quality or impression associated with something — see AURA 1

4 **airs** *pl* a display of emotion or behavior that is insincere or intended to deceive — see MASQUERADE

air *vb* to make known (as an idea, emotion, or opinion) — see EXPRESS 1

airdrome *n* a place from which aircraft operate that usually has paved runways and a terminal — see AIRPORT

airfield *n* a place from which aircraft operate that usually has paved runways and a terminal — see AIRPORT

airman *n* one who flies or is qualified to fly an aircraft or spacecraft — see PILOT

airplane *n* a vehicle for traveling through the air that has fixed wings for lift ⟨She joined the military to learn to fly an *airplane*.⟩

syn plane

rel airbus, airliner, air taxi, liner; aircraft, air-cushion vehicle, airframe, airship; jet, jetliner, superjet, supersonic, supersonic transport, trijet, turbojet, turboprop; aerospace plane, rocket plane; bomber, fighter, jump jet, torpedo bomber, torpedo plane, warplane; amphibian, seaplane; biplane, lightplane

airport *n* a place from which aircraft operate that usually has paved runways and a terminal ⟨The *airport* nearest us has plane service on only one major airline⟩

syn airdrome, airfield, field

rel air base, air park, helipad, heliport, jetport; airstrip, landing field, landing strip, runway; launchpad, pad

airy *adj* 1 resembling air in lightness ⟨The bakery's lemon pies are famous for their *airy* meringues.⟩

syn ethereal, fluffy, gossamer, gossamery, light

rel dainty, delicate, downy, feathery, flimsy, gauzelike, gauzy, insubstantial, tender, wispy; buoyant, lighter-than-air, lightweight, rarefied, unsubstantial, weightless; pillowy

near ant firm, solid, substantial; bulky, burdensome, cumbersome, hefty, hulking, lumpish, ponderous, unwieldy, weighty

ant heavy, leaden

2 open to the free circulation of air ⟨a pleasant, *airy* room⟩

syn breezy

rel atmosphered, vented

near ant close, stifling, suffocating

ant breathless, stuffy, unventilated

3 located at a greater height than average or usual — see HIGH 3

4 having much high-spirited energy and movement — see LIVELY 1

5 satisfying or pleasing because of fineness or mildness — see DELICATE 1

akin *adj* **1** having a close connection like that between family members — see RELATED

2 having qualities in common — see ALIKE

alacritous *adj* having or showing the ability to respond without delay or hesitation — see QUICK 1

alacrity *n* cheerful readiness to do something ⟨Having just acquired his driver's license that morning, he agreed with *alacrity* to drive his cousin to the airport.⟩

syn amenability, goodwill, willingness

rel celerity, quickness, rapidity, speed, speediness, swiftness; dispatch, promptitude, promptness; ardor, avidity, eagerness, enthusiasm, exuberance, fervor, keenness, relish, zeal, zest; agreeableness, geniality, good-naturedness, heartiness, warmth; open-mindedness, receptiveness, receptivity, responsiveness

near ant leisureliness, pokiness, slowness, sluggishness; apathy, disinterestedness, halfheartedness, indifference, lukewarmness, perfunctoriness; delay, dilatoriness, doubt, equivocation, hesitance, hesitancy, hesitation, reluctance, reservation, reticence, uncertainty, vacillation; disinclination, indisposition, recalcitrance, resistance, unwillingness; antipathy, averseness, aversion

à la mode *also* **a la mode** *adj* being in the latest or current fashion — see STYLISH

alarm *also* **alarum** *n* **1** suspicion or fear of future harm or misfortune — see APPREHENSION 1

2 the act or an instance of telling beforehand of danger or risk — see WARNING 1

3 the emotion experienced in the presence or threat of danger — see FEAR 1

alarm *also* **alarum** *vb* **1** to strike with fear — see FRIGHTEN

2 to trouble the mind of; to make uneasy — see DISTURB 1

alarmed *adj* filled with fear or dread — see AFRAID

alarming *adj* causing fear — see FEARFUL 1

albeit *conj* in spite of the fact that — see ALTHOUGH

album *n* a collection of writings — see ANTHOLOGY

alcohol *n* a distilled beverage that can make a person drunk ⟨After his daughter was born, the man never again touched *alcohol*.⟩

syn drink, intoxicant, liquor, moonshine, spirits

ant nonintoxicant

alcoholic *n* a person who makes a habit of getting drunk — see DRUNK

alcove *n* a hollowed-out space in a wall — see NICHE 1

alert *adj* **1** paying close attention usually for the purpose of anticipating approaching danger or opportunity ⟨She needed to stay *alert* throughout the train ride so as not to miss her stop.⟩

syn attentive, awake, observant, openeyed, vigilant, watchful, wide-awake

rel alive, aware, conscious, sensitive; cognizant, heedful, keen, mindful, observing, regardful, sharp, sharp-eyed; hyperalert, hypervigilant, sleepless, wakeful; careful, cautious, wary; prepared, ready

phrases on guard, on one's toes, on the alert, on the ball, on tiptoe

near ant absent, absentminded, absorbed, abstracted, daydreaming, dazed, distracted, dreaming, dreamy, engrossed, faraway, insensible, oblivious, preoccupied; sleeping, unaware, unconscious, unknowing, unwitting; careless, heedless, inattentive, unheeding, unmindful, unthinking, unwary; unprepared, unready

ant asleep

2 having or showing a close attentiveness to avoiding danger or trouble — see CAREFUL 1

3 having or showing quickness of mind — see INTELLIGENT 1

4 having or showing the ability to respond without delay or hesitation — see QUICK 1

alert *n* **1** the act or an instance of telling beforehand of danger or risk — see WARNING 1

2 the state of being constantly attentive and responsive to signs of opportunity, activity, or danger — see VIGILANCE

alert *vb* to give notice to beforehand especially of danger or risk — see WARN

alertness *n* **1** a close attentiveness to avoiding danger — see CAUTION 1

2 the state of being constantly attentive and responsive to signs of opportunity, activity, or danger — see VIGILANCE

alias *n* **1** a descriptive or familiar name given instead of or in addition to the one belonging to an individual — see NICKNAME

2 a fictitious or assumed name — see PSEUDONYM

alibi *n* an explanation that frees one from fault or blame — see EXCUSE

alien *adj* **1** being, relating to, or characteristic of a country other than one's own — see FOREIGN 1

2 not being a vital part of or belonging to something — see EXTRINSIC

alienate *vb* **1** to cause to change from friendly or loving to unfriendly or uncaring — see ESTRANGE

---

syn synonym(s)　　*rel* related words
ant antonym(s)　　*near ant* near antonym(s)

2 to give over the legal possession or ownership of — see TRANSFER 1

alienation *n* the loss of friendship or affection — see ESTRANGEMENT

alight *adj* filled with much light — see BRIGHT 2

alight *vb* **1** to come to rest after descending from the air ⟨A flock of eight swans circled above, then *alighted* on the pond.⟩
syn land, light, perch, roost, settle, touch down
rel belly-land, crash-land
near ant arise, ascend, climb, rise; float, fly, glide, plane, soar, wing; hang, hover
ant blast off, take off

2 to come down from something (as a vehicle) ⟨As she *alighted* from the train, she momentarily lost her footing.⟩
syn descend, disembark, light
rel deplane, detrain
near ant board, climb (aboard), mount; enplane (*also* emplane), entrain
ant embark

alike *adj* having qualities in common ⟨All the houses in the neighborhood are *alike* in that they all have a one-car garage and a fenced-in backyard.⟩
syn akin, analogous, comparable, correspondent, corresponding, like, matching, parallel, resembling, similar, such, suchlike
rel commensurate, proportionate; tantamount, virtual; allied, kin, kindred, relatable, related; approaching, approximating, close, coextensive, coincident, conformable, conforming, consistent, consonant, duplicate, equal, equivalent, identical, indistinguishable, me-too, redundant, same, selfsame, synonymous, twin; entire, homogeneous, homogenous, unchanging, uniform, unvaried, unvarying
phrases on the order of
near ant disparate, distinct, distinguishable, nonequivalent, noninterchangeable; variable, varied, varying; imprecise, inaccurate, inexact; unconnected, unrelated
ant different, dissimilar, diverse, unakin, unlike

alike *adv* in like manner — see ALSO 1

alikeness *n* the quality or state of having many qualities in common — see SIMILARITY 1

alive *adj* **1** having or showing life ⟨After crashing into the plate glass window the little bird was not only still *alive*, it seemed merely dazed.⟩
syn animate, breathing, live, living, quick
rel active, animated, dynamic, lively, thriving, vibrant, vigorous, vital, vivacious; current, existent, existing, extant, going, prevailing, surviving; resurrected
near ant dying, fading, moribund; stillborn; reposing, resting; ghostlike, ghostly, ghosty, zombielike; absent, extinct, fallen, finished, gone, lapsed, lost, nonexistent, perished, terminated, vanished; barren, desert
ant asleep, breathless, cold, dead, deceased, defunct, departed, expired, lifeless, nonliving

2 marked by much life, movement, or activity ⟨The mall was *alive* with holiday shoppers.⟩
syn animated, astir, brisk, bustling, busy, buzzing, flourishing, happening, humming, lively, rousing, stirring, thriving, vibrant
rel abounding, crowded, overflowing, populous, swarming, teeming, thronging
ant asleep, dead, inactive, lifeless, sleepy

3 being in effective operation — see ACTIVE 1

4 having being at the present time — see EXTANT 1

5 having specified facts or feelings actively impressed on the mind — see CONSCIOUS 1

all *adj* not divided or scattered among several areas of interest or concern — see WHOLE 1

all *adv* **1** to a full extent or degree — see FULLY 1

2 for each one — see APIECE

all *pron* every person — see EVERYBODY

Allah *n* the being worshipped as the creator and ruler of the universe — see DEITY 2

all–around *also* **all–round** *adj* **1** not limited or specialized in application or purpose — see GENERAL 4

2 relating to the main elements and not to specific details — see GENERAL 2

3 able to do many different kinds of things — see VERSATILE

all around *adv* with everyone or everything taken into account at the same time ⟨*All around*, she's our best athlete.⟩
syn altogether, collectively, inclusively, overall, together
rel broadly, generally, liberally, loosely; all over, completely, comprehensively, encyclopedically, entirely, exhaustively, fully, thoroughly, totally, wholly
phrases across the board, all in all, in the aggregate, on the whole
near ant minutely; literally, restrictedly, strictly; alone, categorically, distinctly, exclusively, fractionally, individually, separately, singly, singularly, solely, solitarily

allay *vb* to make more bearable or less severe — see HELP 2

all but *adv* very close to but not completely — see ALMOST

allege *vb* to state as a fact usually forcefully — see CLAIM 1

allegiance *n* adherence to something to which one is bound by a pledge or duty — see FIDELITY

allegory *n* a story intended to teach a basic truth or moral about life ⟨Dr. Seuss's story "The Sneetches" is telling *allegory* about tolerance for people's differences.⟩
syn fable, parable
rel beast fable, bestiary; morality play; legend, myth, mythology, narrative, tale

allergic *adj* having a natural dislike for something — see ANTIPATHETIC 1

allergy *n* a strong feeling of not liking or approving — see DISLIKE 1

alleviate *vb* to make more bearable or less severe — see HELP 2

alleviation *n* reduction of or freedom from pain — see EASE 1

alliance *n* **1** a formal agreement between two or more nations or peoples — see TREATY

2 an association of persons, parties, or states for mutual assistance and protection — see CONFEDERACY

3 the state of having shared interests or efforts (as in social or business matters) — see ASSOCIATION 1

allied *adj* having a close connection like that between family members — see RELATED

all–important *adj* impossible to do without — see ESSENTIAL 1

allocate *vb* **1** to give as a share or portion — see ALLOT

2 to give out (something) to appropriate individuals — see ADMINISTER 1

3 to keep or intend for a special purpose — see DEVOTE 1

allocation *n* **1** a sum of money allotted for a specific use by official or formal action — see APPROPRIATION 1

2 the act or process of giving out something to each member of a group — see DISTRIBUTION 1

allot *vb* to give as a share or portion ⟨Each speaker was *allotted* five minutes to present his or her opinion in the debate.⟩

syn allocate, allow, apportion, assign, distribute, lot, ration

rel admeasure, administer, deal, dispense, divide, measure, mete (out), meter, parcel (out), part, portion, prorate, share (out), split; accord, award, give, grant; earmark, reserve; chip in, contribute, donate; reallocate, reapportion, reassign, redistribute

near ant deny, deprive (of); keep, retain, stint, withhold; appropriate, arrogate, confiscate

allotment *n* **1** a sum of money allotted for a specific use by official or formal action — see APPROPRIATION 1

2 something belonging to, due to, or contributed by an individual member of a group — see SHARE 1

3 the act or process of giving out something to each member of a group — see DISTRIBUTION 1

all–out *adj* **1** having no exceptions or restrictions — see ABSOLUTE 2

2 trying all possibilities — see EXHAUSTIVE 1

all out *adv* with all power or resources being used — see FULL BLAST

all over *adv* **1** in every place or in all places — see EVERYWHERE

2 to a full extent or degree — see FULLY 1

allow *vb* **1** to give permission for or to approve of ⟨Flash photography is not *allowed* inside the museum.⟩

syn have, permit, suffer

rel authorize, commission, license (*also* licence); accede (to), acquiesce, agree (to), assent (to), consent (to), OK (*or* okay), warrant; accord, concede, grant, sanction, vouchsafe; admit, brook, condone, countenance, endure, support, tolerate

phrases stand for

near ant hinder, impede, obstruct; censure, deny, disallow, disapprove, interdict, refuse, reject, revoke, suppress, withhold; deplore, discountenance, disfavor, dislike,

frown (at *or* on), grudge; check, curb, keep, repress, restrain

ant ban, enjoin, forbid, prohibit, proscribe, veto

2 to give permission to ⟨a boarding school that does not *allow* students to go on weekend trips without written permission⟩

syn leave, let, permit

rel authorize, commission, empower, license (*also* licence); approve, endorse (*also* indorse), sanction; free, liberate, release; cater (to), give in (to), humor, indulge

near ant deter, discourage; bar, block, constrain, curb, frustrate, hold back, impede, inhibit, obstruct, prevent

ant enjoin, forbid, prohibit

3 to fail to prevent (some behavior on someone's part) especially from neglect or indifference ⟨Only a lazy gardener would *allow* the weeds to grow that high.⟩

syn let, permit, suffer, tolerate

rel brush (aside *or* off), condone, disregard, ignore, overlook, shrug off, wink (at); excuse, forgive, pardon; brook, cater (to), give in (to), humor, indulge

phrases put up with

near ant forbid, prohibit; curb, deter, discourage, frustrate, hold back, impede, inhibit, interfere (with)

ant bar, block, constrain, prevent

4 to accept the truth or existence of (something) usually reluctantly — see ADMIT 1

5 to give as a share or portion — see ALLOT

6 to make able or possible — see ENABLE 1

7 to make a statement of one's opinion — see REMARK 1

allowable *adj* that may be permitted — see PERMISSIBLE

allowance *n* **1** something belonging to, due to, or contributed by an individual member of a group — see SHARE 1

2 the approval by someone in authority for the doing of something — see PERMISSION

alloyed *adj* containing foreign or lower-grade substances — see IMPURE 1

all–powerful *adj* having unlimited power or authority — see OMNIPOTENT

all–purpose *adj* not limited or specialized in application or purpose — see GENERAL 4

all right *adj* **1** being to one's liking — see SATISFACTORY 1

2 not exposed to the threat of loss or injury — see SAFE 1

3 of a level of quality that meets one's needs or standards — see ADEQUATE

4 conforming to a high standard of morality or virtue — see GOOD 2

all right *adv* **1** in a satisfactory way — see WELL 1

2 used to express agreement — see YES

3 without any question — see INDEED 1

allude *vb* to convey an idea indirectly — see HINT

allure *n* the power of irresistible attraction — see CHARM 2

allure *vb* **1** to attract or delight as if by magic — see CHARM 1

---

2 to lead away from a usual or proper course by offering some pleasure or advantage — see LURE

allurement *n* **1** something that persuades one to perform an action for pleasure or gain — see LURE 1

2 the act or pressure of giving in to a desire especially when ill-advised — see TEMPTATION 1

alluring *adj* having an often mysterious or magical power to attract — see FASCINATING 1

ally *n* someone associated with another to give assistance or moral support ⟨In trying to convince his parents to send him to soccer camp, the youngster had a strong *ally* in his coach.⟩

syn abettor (*also* abetter), backer, confederate, supporter, sympathizer

rel empathizer, well-wisher; accessory (*also* accessary), accomplice, coalitionist, collaborationist, collaborator; adjunct, assistant, coadjutor, helper; associate, cohort, colleague, fellow, partner; buddy, chum, companion, comrade, confidant, crony, familiar, friend, intimate, mate, pal

near ant belittler, detractor; adversary, enemy, foe, opponent

ally *vb* to form or enter into an association that furthers the interests of its members ⟨The area's small grape growers have *allied* and formed a cooperative that will help them get the best prices.⟩

syn associate, band (together), club, coalesce, cohere, confederate, conjoin, cooperate, federate, league, unite

rel cabal, collaborate, gang up, hang together, team (up); incorporate, organize, unionize; affiliate; amalgamate, combine, conglomerate, consolidate, converge, group, join, merge; knot, link, tie, wed

phrases close ranks, pull together

near ant detach, disengage, dissolve, disunite, divorce, part, segregate, separate, sever, split, sunder; alienate, estrange, fall out

ant break up, disband

almighty *adj* **1** extreme in degree, power, or effect — see INTENSE 1

2 having unlimited power or authority — see OMNIPOTENT

almighty *adv* to a great degree — see VERY 1

Almighty *n* the being worshipped as the creator and ruler of the universe — see DEITY 2

almost *adj* being such only when compared to something else — see COMPARATIVE

almost *adv* very close to but not completely ⟨We were *almost* finished with dinner when an unexpected visitor showed up.⟩ ⟨There were *almost* enough seats for everybody on the bus.⟩

syn about, all but, fairly, more or less, most, much, near, nearly, next to, nigh, practically, virtually, well-nigh

rel appreciably, by and large, chiefly, largely, mainly, mostly; kind of, partially, partly, somewhat; approximately, around, roughly

phrases as good as, just about, pretty much, within an inch of

near ant absolutely, altogether, completely, entirely, fully, plain, quite, thoroughly; totally, utterly, well, wholly; barely, hardly, scarcely

alms *n pl* a gift of money or its equivalent to a charity, humanitarian cause, or public institution — see CONTRIBUTION

almsgiving *n* the giving of necessities and especially money to the needy — see CHARITY 1

aloft *adv* to or in a higher place — see ABOVE

alone *adj* **1** not being in the company of others ⟨No one realized the boy was *alone* in his room so they all left for the movies without him.⟩

syn lone, lonely, lonesome, single, solitary, solo, unaccompanied

rel unattended, unchaperoned; forlorn, friendless; cloistered, disassociated, hermetic (*also* hermetical), insulated, isolate, isolated, remote, retired, secluded, withdrawn; quarantined, segregated, separated, sequestered; separate, unattached, unconnected, unlinked; detached, disconnected, disjointed, dissociated, disunited, divided; abandoned, adrift, deserted, desolate, forgotten, forsaken, lorn, neglected

phrases on one's own

near ant attended, chaperoned, escorted; adjacent, adjoining, communicating, contiguous, neighboring, next-door; attached, connected, coupled, linked

ant accompanied

2 being the one or ones of a class with no other members — see ONLY 2

alone *adv* **1** without aid or support ⟨Completely new to the big city, she nevertheless managed to find her way home *alone*.⟩

syn independently, single-handedly, singly, solely, unaided, unassisted

rel individually, separately; solo

phrases by one's own bootstraps, on one's own, on one's own hook, on one's own initiative

near ant collectively, conjointly, cooperatively, hand in hand, jointly, mutually; together; en masse

2 for nothing other than — see SOLELY 1

along *adv* toward or at a point lying in advance in space or time ⟨Traffic was inching *along* at a snail's pace.⟩ ⟨Work on the project is moving right *along*.⟩

syn ahead, forth, forward, forwards, on, onward (*also* onwards)

rel before

near ant back, backward (*or* backwards), behind, rearward (*also* rearwards)

aloof *adj* having or showing a lack of friendliness or interest in others — see COOL 1

aloud *adv* with one's normal voice speaking the words ⟨The mischievous teacher likes to call on the sleepiest-looking students to read *aloud* from the textbook.⟩

syn audibly, out, out loud

rel verbally, vocally; discernibly, distinctly, distinguishably, perceptibly, plainly; blatantly, bloody murder, boisterously, clamorously, loudly, lustily, mightily, noisily, resonantly, resoundingly, stridently, thunderously, uproariously, vociferously *near ant* faintly, feebly, low, noiselessly, quietly, softly

ant inaudibly, silently, soundlessly, voicelessly

alp *n* an elevation of land higher than a hill — see MOUNTAIN 1

alpha *n* the point at which something begins — see BEGINNING 1

alright *adj* **1** being to one's liking — see SATISFACTORY 1

2 not exposed to the threat of loss or injury — see SAFE 1

alright *adv* **1** in a satisfactory way — see WELL 1

2 used to express agreement — see YES

3 without any question — see INDEED 1

also *adv* **1** in like manner ⟨We stayed at a historic London hotel, the same establishment that had *also* welcomed our grandparents many years ago.⟩

syn alike, correspondingly, likewise, similarly, so

rel equally, equivalently, identically

phrases as well

near ant conversely, inversely, oppositely, vice versa; diversely, unequally, variously

ant differently, dissimilarly, otherwise

2 in addition to what has been said — see MORE 1

alter *vb* **1** to make different in some way — see CHANGE 1

2 to remove the sex organs of — see NEUTER

alterable *adj* capable of being readily changed — see FLEXIBLE 1

alteration *n* the act, process, or result of making different — see CHANGE 1

altercation *n* an often noisy or angry expression of differing opinions — see ARGUMENT 1

alter ego *n* **1** a person who has a strong liking for and trust in another — see FRIEND 1

2 something or someone that strongly resembles another — see IMAGE 1

alternative *n* the power, right, or opportunity to choose — see CHOICE 1

although *also* **altho** *conj* in spite of the fact that ⟨*Although* I've been to his house several times, I still can't remember how to get there.⟩

syn albeit, as, howbeit, notwithstanding, though, when, whereas, while

rel but

altitude *n* **1** the distance of something or someone from bottom to top — see HEIGHT 3

2 *usually* **altitudes** *pl* an area of high ground — see HEIGHT 4

altogether *adv* **1** for the most part — see CHIEFLY

2 to a full extent or degree — see FULLY 1

3 with everyone or everything taken into account at the same time — see ALL AROUND

altruistic *adj* having or showing a concern for the welfare of others — see CHARITABLE 1

always *adv* **1** on every relevant occasion ⟨Although we never intend more than an afternoon visit, she *always* insists we stay for dinner.⟩

syn aye (*also* ay), consistently, constantly, continually, ever, forever, incessantly, invariably, perpetually, unfailingly

rel commonly, frequently, oft, often, oftentimes (*or* ofttimes), recurrently, repeatedly; continuously, steadily, uninterruptedly, unremittingly; dependably, generally, habitually, normally, ordinarily, regularly, routinely, typically, usually; inevitably; eternally, everlastingly

phrases at every turn

near ant intermittently, occasionally, periodically, sometimes, sporadically; infrequently, rarely, seldom, unusually; variously

ant ne'er, never

2 whatever else is done or is the case ⟨You can *always* take a cab if the buses aren't running.⟩

syn anyhow, anyway

phrases at all events, at any rate, at least, in any case, in any event

3 for all time — see EVER 1

amain *adv* with great effort or determination — see HARD 1

amalgam *n* a distinct entity formed by the combining of two or more different things — see BLEND

amalgamate *vb* to turn into a single mass or entity that is more or less the same throughout — see BLEND 1

amalgamated *adj* made from the joining of two or more parts or elements — see COMPOSITE

amalgamation *n* a distinct entity formed by the combining of two or more different things — see BLEND

amass *vb* **1** to bring together in one body or place — see GATHER 1

2 to gradually form into a layer, pile, or mass — see COLLECT 1

amateur *adj* lacking or showing a lack of expert skill — see AMATEURISH

amateur *n* **1** a person who regularly or occasionally engages in an activity as a pastime rather than as a profession ⟨an *amateur* photographer who has won a number of photo contests⟩

syn dabbler, dilettante, nonprofessional, potterer, putterer

rel generalist, general practitioner, jack-of-all-trades; aficionado (*also* afficionado), buff, devotee, enthusiast, fan

ant authority, expert, pro, professional, specialist

2 a person who lacks experience and competence in an art or science ⟨a homemade doghouse that looked like it was built by an *amateur* who hadn't mastered basic carpentry⟩

syn hack, inexpert

rel beginner, freshman, greenhorn, kid, learner, neophyte, newcomer, novice, rookie, tenderfoot, tyro

near ant maestro, virtuoso, whiz, wizard; old hand, old-timer, vet, veteran

ant ace, adept, crackerjack (*also* crackajack), craftsman, expert, hand, master, past master, shark, sharp

amateurish *adj* lacking or showing a lack of expert skill ⟨That's an *amateurish* wall-

---

syn synonym(s)   *rel* related words
ant antonym(s)   *near ant* near antonym(s)

papering job—the pattern doesn't match at the seams.⟩

syn amateur, dilettante, inexperienced, inexpert, nonprofessional, unprofessional, unskilled, unskillful

rel curbstone, uninitiated, unprepared, unqualified, unschooled, untaught, untrained, untutored; awkward, clumsy, heavy-handed; crude, defective, faulty, flawed, primitive, unfinished, unpolished; beginning, entry-level, fresh, green, new, raw, unseasoned, untested, untried, would-be; incapable, incompetent, talentless, unfit, ungifted, untalented; avocational, nonprofessional

near ant able, accomplished, capable, competent, dexterous (*also* dextrous), gifted, handsome, proficient, skilled, skillful, talented; experienced, practiced (*also* practised), seasoned, veteran; educated, fitted, initiated, knowledgeable, prepared, qualified, schooled, taught, trained, tutored, versed; all-around (*also* all-round), ambidextrous, versatile, well-rounded; finished, polished, slick

ant ace, adept, consummate, crackerjack, expert, master, masterful, masterly, professional, virtuosic, virtuoso

amatory *adj* of, relating to, exciting, or expressing sexual attraction or desire — see EROTIC

amaze *vb* to make a strong impression on (someone) with something unexpected — see SURPRISE 1

amazed *adj* **1** affected with sudden and great wonder or surprise — see THUNDERSTRUCK

2 filled with amazement or wonder — see OPENMOUTHED

amazement *n* **1** the rapt attention and deep emotion caused by the sight of something extraordinary — see WONDER 2

2 the state of being strongly impressed by something unexpected or unusual — see SURPRISE 1

amazing *adj* **1** causing a strong emotional reaction because of unexpectedness — see SURPRISING 1

2 causing wonder or astonishment — see MARVELOUS 1

ambassador *n* a person sent on a mission to represent another ⟨a beloved entertainer who has often been sent abroad by the president as his country's goodwill *ambassador*⟩

syn agent, delegate, emissary, envoy, legate, minister, representative

rel ambassadress; attaché, chargé d'affaires, consul, deputy, diplomat, foreign minister, proxy; apostle, evangelist, missionary; courier, messenger; mouthpiece, spokesperson

ambiguity *n* the quality or state of having a veiled or uncertain meaning — see OBSCURITY 1

ambiguous *adj* having an often intentionally veiled or uncertain meaning — see OBSCURE 1

ambiguousness *n* the quality or state of having a veiled or uncertain meaning — see OBSCURITY 1

ambition *n* **1** eager desire for personal advancement ⟨"Talent without *ambition* will

not make you a star," the singer's voice coach liked to remind her.⟩

syn aspiration, go-getting

rel determination, diligence, drive, energy, enterprise, go, hustle, industry, initiative, motivation, push; aggression, competitiveness, killer instinct; opportunism, overambitiousness, pretentiousness, pushiness; assertiveness, daring, spirit; ardor, avidity, eagerness, keenness, passion; avarice, greed, hunger

near ant apathy, halfheartedness, indifference, unconcern; idleness, indolence, inertia, laziness, shiftlessness, sloth

2 readiness to engage in daring or difficult activity — see ENTERPRISE 2

3 something that one hopes or intends to accomplish — see GOAL

ambitious *adj* **1** having a strong desire for personal advancement ⟨an *ambitious* child actor and his even more ambitious mother, who will do anything to get him in commercials⟩

syn aspiring, go-getting, hard-driving, self-seeking

rel determined, diligent, driving, dynamic, enterprising, gung ho, hungry, hustling, industrious, motivated, scrappy, venturesome, venturous; animated, lively, spirited; ardent, avid, eager, energetic, impassioned, keen, raring, vigorous; aggressive, assertive, high-flying, opportunistic, overambitious, pretentious, self-assertive; competing, competitive, rival, rivalrous

near ant apathetic, disinterested, indifferent, uneager, unenthusiastic, unexcited, uninterested; casual, easygoing, lackadaisical, lazyish; fainthearted, lukewarm, tepid; lazy, lethargic, listless, shiftless, sluggish, spiritless; unaggressive, unassertive

ant ambitionless, unambitious

2 having or showing a bold forcefulness in the pursuit of a goal — see AGGRESSIVE 1

ambrosial *adj* **1** having a pleasant smell — see FRAGRANT

2 very pleasing to the sense of taste — see DELICIOUS 1

ambush *n* **1** a setup in which hidden attackers lie in wait ⟨Revolutionaries laid in *ambush* for the king along the route his carriage would travel.⟩

syn surprise (*also* surprize), trap

rel assault, attack, charge, sally; capture, entrapment, mousetrap, snare; hunting, stalking

2 a device or scheme for capturing another by surprise — see TRAP 1

ambush *vb* to lie in wait for and attack by surprise ⟨The king's enemies planned to *ambush* the royal coach on the way to Paris and capture the king.⟩

syn surprise (*also* surprize), waylay

rel assail, assault, attack, storm, strike; jump, mug, pounce (on), tackle; charge, sally; capture, ensnare, entrap, mousetrap, net, snare, trap; hunt, prey (on *or* upon), stalk

ameliorate *vb* to make better — see IMPROVE

amenability *n* **1** a desire or disposition to please — see COMPLAISANCE

2 cheerful readiness to do something — see ALACRITY

amenable *adj* **1** having a desire or inclination (as for a specified course of action) — see WILLING 1

2 readily giving in to the command or authority of another — see OBEDIENT

3 being the one who must meet an obligation or suffer the consequences for failing to do so — see RESPONSIBLE 1

amend *vb* **1** to make better — see IMPROVE

2 to remove errors, defects, deficiencies, or deviations from — see CORRECT 1

3 to change one's behavior or character for the better — see REFORM 2

amendment *n* a change designed to correct or improve a written work — see CORRECTION 1

amenity *n* **1** an act or utterance that is a customary show of good manners — see CIVILITY 1

2 something adding to pleasure or comfort but not absolutely necessary — see LUXURY 1

3 something that adds to one's ease of living — see COMFORT 2

4 the state or quality of having a pleasant or agreeable manner in socializing with others — see AMIABILITY 1

amiability *n* **1** the state or quality of having a pleasant or agreeable manner in socializing with others ⟨The waitress's *amiability* is what makes eating at the diner so much fun.⟩

syn affability, agreeableness, amenity, amiableness, geniality, good-naturedness, good-temperedness, graciousness, niceness, personableness, pleasantness, sweetness

rel amenability, complaisance, mellowness, sweetness and light; amicability, amicableness, amity, cordiality, friendliness; gentleness, kindliness, kindness; cheerfulness, cheeriness, sunniness; civility, considerateness, consideration, courteousness, courtesy, politeness, thoughtfulness; attractiveness, delightfulness, enjoyableness, likability, likableness, pleasingness

near ant boorishness, discourtesy, impoliteness, incivility, rudeness, ungraciousness; cantankerousness, churlishness, crankiness, fussiness, grouchiness, grumpiness, irascibility, irritability, peevishness, petulance, testiness; contentiousness, contrariness, orneriness, querulousness; hostility, unfriendliness; sourness

ant disagreeableness, unpleasantness

2 a desire or disposition to please — see COMPLAISANCE

amiable *adj* having an easygoing and pleasing manner especially in social situations ⟨The owner of the inn is an *amiable*, talkative woman who treats guests like family.⟩

syn affable, agreeable, genial, good-natured, good-tempered, gracious, mellow, nice, pleasant, sweet, well-disposed

rel amicable, cordial, friendly, neighborly; benign, gentle, kind; cheerful, cheery, sunny; companionable, conversable, sociable; civil, considerate, courteous, polite, thoughtful; accommodating, amenable, obliging; attractive, delightful, enjoyable, likable (*or* likeable)

near ant boorish, discourteous, ill-mannered, impolite, inconsiderate, rude, surly, uncivil, unkind, unmannerly, unsociable; bearish, cantankerous, choleric, churlish, crabby, cranky, dyspeptic, fussy, grouchy, grumpy, ill-humored, irascible, irritable, peevish, petulant, quick-tempered, snappish, testy, touchy; argumentative, contentious, contrary, ornery, querulous; unappealing, unattractive; sour, vinegary

ant disagreeable, ill-natured, ill-tempered, unamiable, ungenial, ungracious, unpleasant

amiableness *n* the state or quality of having a pleasant or agreeable manner in socializing with others — see AMIABILITY 1

amicable *adj* **1** having or marked by agreement in feeling or action — see HARMONIOUS 3

2 having or showing kindly feeling and sincere interest — see FRIENDLY 1

amid *or* **amidst** *prep* **1** in or into the middle of — see AMONG

2 in the course of — see DURING

amiss *adj* **1** having a fault — see FAULTY

2 not appropriate for a particular occasion or situation — see INAPPROPRIATE

amiss *adv* **1** in a mistaken or inappropriate way — see WRONGLY

2 off the desired or intended path or course — see WRONG

amity *n* kindly concern, interest, or support — see GOODWILL 1

ammunition *n* means or method of defending — see DEFENSE 1

amnesty *n* release from the guilt or penalty of an offense — see PARDON

amok *or* **amuck** *adv* in a confused and reckless manner — see HELTER-SKELTER 1

among *also* **amongst** *prep* in or into the middle of ⟨A gull landed *among* the burgers-and-fries eaters at the outdoor snack bar, clearly looking for handouts.⟩

syn amid (*or* amidst), mid, midst, through

rel between, betwixt

phrases in the thick of

near ant from, out of

amorous *adj* of, relating to, exciting, or expressing sexual attraction or desire — see EROTIC

amorphous *adj* having no definite or recognizable form — see FORMLESS 1

amount *n* a given or particular mass or aggregate of matter ⟨We'll need a large *amount* of food to feed the whole hockey team.⟩

syn measure, quantity, volume

rel coefficient, degree; body, portion; many, number

amount (to) *vb* **1** to have a total of ⟨The expenses of the trip *amounted* to nearly double what we'd budgeted for.⟩

syn add up (to), aggregate, come (to), number, sum (to *or* into), total

rel average, equal, measure, reach; compose, comprise, constitute, make up

phrases clock in at

2 to be the same in meaning or effect ⟨It makes no difference whether you're going to the game or the movies, for it *amounts*

---

syn synonym(s)   *rel* related words
ant antonym(s)   *near ant* near antonym(s)

to the same thing—that you can't baby-sit.⟩

syn add up (to), come (to), correspond (to), emulate, equal

rel approach, match, measure (up), meet, rival, touch; connote, denote, express, import, mean, signify, smack (of), spell, suggest

ample *adj* **1** being more than enough without being excessive — see PLENTIFUL

2 more than adequate or average in capacity — see SPACIOUS

amplify *vb* **1** to express more fully and in greater detail — see EXPAND 1

2 to make greater in size, amount, or number — see INCREASE 1

3 to make markedly greater in measure or degree — see INTENSIFY

amplitude *n* an area over which activity, capacity, or influence extends — see RANGE 2

amply *adv* in a generous manner — see WELL 2

amulet *n* something worn or kept to bring good luck or keep away evil — see CHARM 1

amuse *vb* to cause (someone) to pass the time agreeably occupied ⟨The older girl *amused* her four-year-old sister at the family reunion by showing her off to all the relatives.⟩

syn disport, divert, entertain, regale, solace

rel absorb, busy, distract, engage, engross, immerse, interest, involve, occupy; beguile, bewitch, captivate, charm, delight, enchant, enthrall (*or* enthral), fascinate, grip, hypnotize, intrigue, mesmerize; coddle, gratify, humor, indulge, mollycoddle, pamper, please, pleasure, spoil; appease, comfort, conciliate, console, content, mollify, oblige, pacify, placate, propitiate, soothe

near ant bore, jade; drain, enervate, exhaust, fatigue, tire, wear, wear out, weary; aggravate, annoy, bother, bug, chafe, disturb, exasperate, fret, gall, grate, harry, irk, nettle, peeve, perturb, pester, pique, upset, vex

amusement *n* the act or activity of providing pleasure or amusement especially for the public — see ENTERTAINMENT 1

amusing *adj* providing amusement or enjoyment — see FUN

analgesic *n* something (as a drug) that relieves pain — see PAINKILLER

analogous *adj* having qualities in common — see ALIKE

analysis *n* **1** the separation and identification of the parts of a whole ⟨Researchers took the sample to the lab for *analysis*.⟩

syn anatomizing, assay, breakdown, dissection

rel assessment, diagnosis, evaluation, examination, inspection, investigation, muster, scrutiny; arrangement, assortment, cataloging (*or* cataloguing), categorization, classification, codification, indexing; enumeration, inventory, itemization, tabulation; division, reduction, segmentation, separation, subdivision

near ant agglomeration, aggregation, amalgamation, assimilation, coalescence,

conglomeration, consolidation, integration, unification

2 a series of explanations or observations on something (as an event) — see COMMENTARY 1

analytic *or* **analytical** *adj* according to the rules of logic — see LOGICAL 1

analyze *vb* to identify and examine the basic elements or parts of (something) especially for discovering interrelationships ⟨We'll *analyze* the park's ecosystem before deciding whether snowmobiling should be allowed.⟩

syn anatomize, assay, break down, cut, dissect

rel assess, diagnose, evaluate, examine, inspect, investigate, scrutinize; arrange, assort, catalog (*or* catalogue), categorize, classify, codify, diagram, enumerate, index, order, schematize, sort, tabulate; divide, reduce, segment, separate, subdivide

near ant agglomerate, aggregate, amalgamate, assimilate, coalesce, conglomerate, consolidate, integrate, synthesize, unify

anarchic *also* **anarchical** *adj* not restrained by or under the control of legal authority — see LAWLESS 1

anarchy *n* a state in which there is widespread wrongdoing and disregard for rules and authority ⟨the *anarchy* that the country experienced after the dictator drained the treasury and fled the country⟩

syn lawlessness, misrule

rel anarchism; commotion, tumult, uproar; chaos, confusion, disarray, disorder, disorganization; disruption, disturbance, havoc, riot, strife, turbulence, turmoil, unrest, upheaval; mutiny, rebellion, revolution, uprising; criminality, outlawry

near ant law, law-abidingness, lawfulness, legality, legitimacy, rule; calmness, harmony, order, orderliness, peace, peaceableness, peacefulness, quiet, tranquillity (*or* tranquility)

anathema *n* **1** a prayer that harm will come to someone — see CURSE 1

2 something or someone that is hated — see HATE 2

anatomize *vb* to identify and examine the basic elements or parts of (something) especially for discovering interrelationships — see ANALYZE

anatomizing *n* the separation and identification of the parts of a whole — see ANALYSIS 1

ancestor *n* **1** a person who is several generations earlier in an individual's line of descent ⟨Bridie's Irish *ancestors* immigrated to the United States in the 19th century during the Great Potato Famine.⟩

syn father, forebear (*also* forbear), forefather, grandfather

rel ancestress, foremother, grandmother, matriarch; patriarch; ancestry, antecedents, roots

near ant children, family, issue, lineage, offspring, posterity, progeny, seed, stock; daughter, heir, inheritor, scion, son, successor

ant descendant (*also* descendent)

2 something belonging to an earlier time from which something else was later developed ⟨Pinball machines—the *ancestors* of today's video games—go back to the 19th century.⟩

syn antecedent, archetype, daddy, foregoer, forerunner, precursor, predecessor, prototype

rel model, original; originator, sire; father, mother

near ant by-product, derivative, offshoot, outgrowth, spin-off; daughter, son

ant descendant (*also* descendent)

ancestry *n* the line of ancestors from whom a person is descended ⟨She traced her Khmer *ancestry* as far back as the 16th century.⟩

syn birth, blood, bloodline, breeding, descent, extraction, family tree, genealogy, line, lineage, origin, parentage, pedigree, stock, strain

rel heredity, succession; family, house; kin, kindred, relations, relatives; race

near ant offspring; child, heir, inheritor, son, successor

ant issue, posterity, progeny, seed

anchor *n* **1** one who reads and introduces news reports on a news program — see ANCHORPERSON

2 something or someone to which one looks for support — see DEPENDENCE 2

anchor *vb* **1** to put securely in place or in a desired position — see FASTEN 2

2 to stop at or near a place along the shore — see LAND 1

anchorage *n* a part of a body of water protected and deep enough to be a place of safety for ships — see HARBOR 1

anchorperson *n* one who reads and introduces news reports on a news program ⟨The new *anchorperson* did an admirable job of dealing with the late-breaking news story.⟩

syn anchor

rel anchorman, anchorwoman, coanchor; broadcaster, commentator, telecaster; correspondent, foreign correspondent, journalist, newshound, newsie, newsman, newswoman, reporter, stringer

ancient *adj* **1** dating or surviving from the distant past ⟨Rome's *ancient* ruins remain carefully preserved even in the midst of the bustle of the modern city.⟩

syn aged, age-old, antediluvian, antique, dateless, hoar, hoary, immemorial, old, venerable

rel aging (*or* ageing), mature; antiquated, archaic, dated, fusty, geriatric, medieval (*also* mediaeval), moldy, obsolete, outmoded, out-of-date, passé; old-fashioned, old-time, old-world, retro; durable, enduring, lasting, long-lived, permanent; ageless, hallowed, time-honored, timeless, time-tested, traditional, tried, tried-and-true; classic, classical; prehistoric (*also* prehistorical), primeval, primordial

near ant fresh, vernal, young, youthful; contemporary, current, latest, mod, novel, present-day, ultramodern; untested, untried; brand-new, unused, unworn

ant modern, new, recent

2 being of advanced years and especially past middle age — see ELDERLY

3 relating to or occurring near the beginning of a process, series, or time period — see EARLY 1

ancient *n* a person of advanced years — see SENIOR CITIZEN

anecdote *n* a brief account of something interesting that happened especially to one personally — see STORY 2

anesthetic *n* something (as a drug) that relieves pain — see PAINKILLER

anew *adv* yet another time — see AGAIN 1

angel *n* **1** an innocent or gentle person — see LAMB

2 one that announces or indicates the later arrival of another — see FORERUNNER 1

3 one that helps another with gifts or money — see BENEFACTOR

anger *n* an intense emotional state of displeasure with someone or something ⟨The patient managed to stifle his *anger* when the receptionist put him on hold for the third time.⟩

syn angriness, furor, fury, indignation, irateness, ire, mad, madness, outrage, rage, spleen, wrath, wrathfulness

rel aggravation, annoyance, exasperation, irritation, vexation; acrimoniousness, acrimony, animosity, antagonism, antipathy, bile, bitterness, contempt, embitterment, enmity, grudge, hostility, rancor; envy, jaundice, jealousy, pique, resentment; malevolence, malice, spite, vengefulness, venom, vindictiveness, virulence, vitriol; belligerence, contentiousness, contrariness, crankiness, disputatiousness, hotheadedness, irascibility, irritability, orneriness, pugnaciousness, pugnacity, querulousness; blowup, flare, flare-up, outburst; chafe, dander, dudgeon, huff, pet, rise, ruffle, temper; air rage, road rage; delirium, heat, passion, warmth

phrases slow burn

near ant calmness, forbearance, patience

ant delight, pleasure

anger *vb* to make angry ⟨It's virtually impossible to *anger* Mrs. Peterson—she's the most easygoing person I've ever known.⟩

syn enrage, incense, inflame (*also* enflame), infuriate, ire, madden, outrage, rankle, rile, roil

rel affront, aggravate, annoy, cross, exasperate, get, huff, irritate, nettle, offend, peeve, pique, provoke, put out, ruffle, vex; antagonize, embitter, envenom

phrases get one's goat, rub the wrong way

near ant allay, assuage, relieve; comfort, console, soothe; appease, conciliate, mollify, pacify, placate; calm, lull, quiet, settle; beguile, bewitch, captivate, charm, disarm, enchant

ant delight, gratify, please

angered *adj* feeling or showing anger — see ANGRY

angle *n* **1** a certain way in which something appears or may be regarded — see ASPECT 1

2 a way of looking at or thinking about something — see PERSPECTIVE 1

3 something that curves or is curved — see BEND 1

angle *vb* to set or cause to be at an angle — see LEAN 1

angling *n* the act of positioning or an in-

---

syn synonym(s)   **rel** related words
ant antonym(s)   **near ant** near antonym(s)

stance of being positioned at an angle — see TILT

angriness *n* an intense emotional state of displeasure with someone or something — see ANGER

angry *adj* feeling or showing anger ⟨There's no reason to get *angry* just because your team lost.⟩

syn angered, apoplectic, choleric, enraged, foaming, fuming, furious, hot, incensed, indignant, inflamed (*also* enflamed), infuriate, infuriated, irate, ireful, livid, mad, outraged, rabid, rankled, riled, roiled, sore, steaming, wrathful, wroth

rel ranting, raving, stormy; bristling, bristly, burning, cross, passionate, seething, sizzling, smoldering (*or* smouldering), worked up, wrought (up); acrid, acrimonious, antagonistic, antipathetic, bitter, embittered, inimical, malevolent, piqued, rancorous, resentful, spiteful, vengeful, vindictive, virulent; antisocial, cold, cool, disagreeable, disapproving, distant, frigid, icy, ill-tempered, sorehead (*or* soreheaded), sulky, unfriendly, unpleasant; bearish, cantankerous, churlish, crabby, cranky, dyspeptic, fretful, fussy, grouchy, grumpy, ill-humored, irascible, irritable, peevish, perturbed, petulant, put out, quick-tempered, snappish, testy, touchy; argumentative, belligerent, contentious, contrary, disputatious, ornery, pugnacious, quarrelsome, querulous

phrases bent out of shape, blue in the face, fit to be tied, hopping mad, hot under the collar, in a fume, in a huff, in a pet

near ant accepting, accommodating, obliging; agreeable, amenable, complaisant; amicable, cordial, friendly; content, happy, satisfied; empathetic, sympathetic, tolerant, understanding; calm, pacific, peaceable, placid, serene, tranquil, unembittered; affable, amiable, easygoing, genial, good-natured, good-tempered, kind, pleasant, sweet

ant delighted, pleased

anguish *n* **1** a state of great suffering of body or mind — see DISTRESS 1

2 deep sadness especially for the loss of someone or something loved — see SORROW

anguish *vb* **1** to cause persistent suffering to — see AFFLICT

2 to feel deep sadness or mental pain — see GRIEVE

anguished *adj* expressing or suggesting mourning — see MOURNFUL 1

animal *adj* of or relating to the human body — see PHYSICAL 1

animal *n* one of the lower animals as distinguished from human beings ⟨We saw a lot of *animals* at the wildlife refuge.⟩

syn beast, brute, creature, critter

rel biped, quadruped; carnivore, herbivore, insectivore; invertebrate, vertebrate; domestic animal, pet; livestock, stock

animate *adj* **1** having much high-spirited energy and movement — see LIVELY 1

2 having or showing life — see ALIVE 1

animate *vb* to give life, vigor, or spirit to ⟨Mr. Clark *animates* history for his sixth graders by frequently showing up for class dressed like some famous historical figure.⟩

syn brace, energize, enliven, fire, invigorate, jazz (up), liven (up), pep (up), quicken, spike, stimulate, vitalize, vivify, zip (up)

rel arouse, awake, awaken, raise, rouse, stir, wake (up); activate, actuate, drive, impel, motivate, motive, move, propel; charge, electrify, galvanize; excite, ferment, foment, incite, inflame (*also* enflame), instigate, kindle, provoke, spark, trigger, turn on, whip (up); abet, boost, buoy, cheer, embolden, fortify, hearten, infuse, inspire, lift, rally, steel, strengthen; reactivate, reanimate, reawake, reawaken, recreate, reenergize, refresh, refreshen, regenerate, reinvigorate, rejuvenate, rekindle, renew, restimulate, resurrect, resuscitate, revitalize, revive

near ant burn out, debilitate, do in, drain, enervate, enfeeble, exhaust, fatigue, kayo, sap, tucker (out), undermine, wash out, weaken, wear, wear out, weary; check, curb, inhibit, jade, quell, quench, repress, restrain, slow, still, stunt, suppress; daunt, demoralize, discourage, dishearten, dispirit

ant damp, dampen, deaden, dull, kill

animated *adj* **1** having much high-spirited energy and movement — see LIVELY 1

2 marked by much life, movement, or activity — see ALIVE 2

animatedly *adv* in a quick and spirited manner — see GAILY 2

animately *adv* in a quick and spirited manner — see GAILY 2

animation *n* the quality or state of having abundant or intense activity — see VITALITY 1

animosity *n* a deep-seated ill will — see ENMITY

annals *n pl* an account of important events in the order in which they happened — see HISTORY 1

annex *n* a smaller structure added to a main building ⟨a new *annex* that will serve as the permanent home for the school library⟩

syn addition, extension, penthouse

rel arm, ell, wing

annex *vb* to join (something) to a mass, quantity, or number so as to bring about an overall increase — see ADD 1

annihilate *vb* **1** to destroy all traces of ⟨The landlord hired an exterminator to *annihilate* the ant infestation.⟩

syn abolish, black out, blot out, cancel, clean (up), efface, eradicate, expunge, exterminate, extirpate, liquidate, obliterate, root (out), rub out, snuff (out), stamp (out), wipe out

rel decimate, demolish, destroy, devastate, ravage; dismantle, flatten, mow (down), raze, tear down; ruin, total, waste, wreck; blast, blow up, dash, smash; atomize, consume, devour, dissolve, fragment, powder, pulverize, shatter, splinter; doom, finish, kill, kill off, terminate, zap; cancel, cut, discard, ditch, eject, excise, expel, jettison, oust, throw out

near ant conserve, preserve, protect, save; build, construct, create, fabricate, fashion, forge, form, frame, make, manufacture, shape; fix, mend, patch, rebuild, recondition, reconstruct, renew, renovate, repair, restore, revamp

2 to bring to a complete end the physical soundness, existence, or usefulness of — see DESTROY 1

3 to defeat by a large margin — see WHIP 2

annihilation *n* the state or fact of being rendered nonexistent, physically unsound, or useless — see DESTRUCTION 1

announce *vb* to make known openly or publicly ⟨The excited couple *announced* to everyone within hearing distance that they were expecting.⟩

syn advertise, blare, blaze, broadcast, declare, enunciate, flash, give out, herald, placard, post, proclaim, promulgate, publicize, publish, release, sound, trumpet

rel bark, call (off *or* out), cry; bill, billboard, bulletin; knell, ring, toll; blurb, feature, pitch, plug, promote, puff; disseminate, spread; disclose, divulge, introduce, manifest, report, reveal, show; advise, apprise, hand down, inform, notify; communicate, impart, intimate

phrases beat the drum (for *or* about), run with

near ant conceal, hush (up), silence, suppress, withhold; recall, recant, retract, revoke

announcement *n* a published statement informing the public of a matter of general interest ⟨An *announcement* was in today's paper regarding the merger of the two banks.⟩

syn ad, advertisement, bulletin, communiqué, notice, notification, posting, release

rel broadside, brochure, circular, fly sheet, handbill, handout; bill, billboard, placard, playbill, poster, show bill, sign; broadcast, cablecast, newscast, telecast; advertising, billing, blurb, commercial, message, pitch, plugola, spot, word; communication, dispatch, report; annunciation, declaration, edict, proclamation, promulgation, pronouncement; ballyhoo, boost, buildup, campaign, plug, promo, promotion, propaganda, publicity

annoy *vb* to disturb the peace of mind of (someone) especially by repeated disagreeable acts — see IRRITATE 1

annoyance *n* **1** the act of making unwelcome intrusions upon another ⟨They have an unlisted number in the hopes that it will reduce the constant *annoyance* by telemarketers.⟩

syn aggravation, bedevilment, bugging, disturbance, harassment, harrying, pestering, teasing, vexation

rel molestation, offense (*or* offence), persecution, provocation, torment, torture; devilment, devilry, mischief

2 the feeling of impatience or anger caused by another's repeated disagreeable acts ⟨Carlene made known her *annoyance* at having to pick up her sister's dirty clothes.⟩

syn aggravation, bother, exasperation, frustration, grief, irritation, vexation

rel agitation, discomfort, displeasure, distress, disturbance, upset; irritability, irritableness, peeve, perturbation, pet, pique, resentment, snappishness, trouble; anger, angriness, chafe, dander, dudgeon, gall, huff, indignation, irateness, ire, outrage, umbrage

near ant delight, pleasure

3 something that is a source of irritation ⟨flashing ads, visual clutter, and other *annoyances* that are the price for free information on the Internet⟩

syn aggravation, bother, bugbear, exasperation, frustration, hassle, headache, inconvenience, irk, irritant, nuisance, peeve, pest, rub, ruffle, thorn, trial, vexation

rel discomfort, fleabite, pinprick; affront, insult, offense (*or* offence); upset, worry; affliction, albatross, burden, cross, curse, menace, millstone, plague, sore; anxiety, plight, predicament, tribulation, trouble; pet peeve, problem; annoyer, disturber, mischief, offender; pandora's box

near ant delight, joy, pleasure

4 one who is obnoxiously annoying — see NUISANCE 1

annoyer *n* one who is obnoxiously annoying — see NUISANCE 1

annoying *adj* causing annoyance ⟨My brother has the *annoying* habit of eating all the pickles and leaving a jar full of pickle juice in the refrigerator.⟩

syn aggravating, bothersome, chafing, disturbing, exasperating, frustrating, galling, irksome, irritating, maddening, nettling, peeving, pestiferous, pestilent, pesty, rankling, riling, vexatious, vexing

rel burdensome, discomforting, displeasing, disquieting, distressing, importune, inconveniencing; angering, enraging, infuriating; brattish, bratty, mischievous, offensive, troublesome, upsetting; distractive, painful, stressful, tiresome, troubling, trying, worrisome; biting, grating, jangling, jarring, spiny, thorny

near ant delightful, pleasing

annuity *n* a sum of money allotted for a specific use by official or formal action — see APPROPRIATION 1

annul *vb* **1** to balance with an equal force so as to make ineffective — see OFFSET

2 to put an end to by formal action — see ABOLISH 1

anoint *vb* to rub an oily or sticky substance over — see SMEAR 1

anomalous *adj* **1** being out of the ordinary — see EXCEPTIONAL 1

2 departing from some accepted standard of what is normal — see DEVIANT

anomaly *n* **1** something that is different from what is ordinary or expected ⟨Her C grade is an *anomaly*, as she's never made anything except A's and B's before.⟩

syn aberration, abnormality, oddity, oddment, rarity

rel curiosity, peculiarity, singularity; accident, phenomenon, quirk, vagary; distortion, mutation, variation; difference, disparity, inconsistence, inconsistency; error, mistake; contradiction, paradox

near ant norm, ordinary, usual

2 a person, thing, or event that is far from normal — see FREAK 1

anon *adv* at or within a short time — see SHORTLY 2

---

syn synonym(s) *rel* related words
ant antonym(s) *near ant* near antonym(s)

anonymity *n* the quality or state of being mostly or completely unknown — see OBSCURITY 2

anonymous *adj* 1 known but not named — see CERTAIN 1

2 not named or identified by a name — see NAMELESS 1

another *adj* resulting in an increase in amount or number — see ADDITIONAL

answer *n* 1 something spoken or written in reaction especially to a question ⟨the standard *answer* of "Fine, thank you" when asked, "How are you?"⟩

syn comeback, rejoinder, reply, response, retort, return

rel back talk, banter, repartee; acknowledgment (*or* acknowledgement), comment, communication, correspondence, feedback, non sequitur, observation, reaction, remark; defense, explanation, justification, plea, rebuttal, refutation

near ant challenge, charge, cross-examination, grilling, interrogation, interrogatory, quiz; poll, questionnaire, survey

ant inquiry, query, question

2 something attained by mental effort and especially by computation ⟨The *answers* to the odd-numbered problems are at the back of the book.⟩

syn result, solution

rel conclusion, determination, explanation, finding; clue, key

3 action or behavior that is done in return to other action or behavior — see REACTION

answer *vb* 1 to speak or write in reaction to a question or to another reaction ⟨He didn't *answer* right away when the teacher asked for his thoughts.⟩

syn rejoin, reply, respond, retort, return, riposte

rel acknowledge, comment, communicate, correspond, react, remark; counter, defend, deny, explain, field, rebut, refute

near ant challenge, cross-examine, examine, grill, interrogate, pump, quiz; poll, query, survey

ant ask, inquire, question

2 to be in agreement on every point — see CHECK 1

3 to do what is required by the terms of — see FULFILL 1

4 to find an answer for through reasoning — see SOLVE

answerable *adj* 1 being the one who must meet an obligation or suffer the consequences for failing to do so — see RESPONSIBLE 1

2 capable of having the reason for or cause of determined — see SOLVABLE

antagonism *n* a deep-seated ill will — see ENMITY

antagonist *n* 1 one that is hostile toward another — see ENEMY

2 one that takes a position opposite another in a competition or conflict — see OPPONENT 1

antagonistic *adj* marked by opposition or ill will — see HOSTILE 1

antagonize *vb* to implant bitter feelings in — see EMBITTER

antecedent *adj* going before another in time or order — see PREVIOUS

antecedent *n* 1 someone or something responsible for a result — see CAUSE 1

2 something belonging to an earlier time from which something else was later developed — see ANCESTOR 2

antedate *vb* to go or come before in time — see PRECEDE

antediluvian *adj* dating or surviving from the distant past — see ANCIENT 1

antediluvian *n* a person with old-fashioned ideas — see FOGY

anterior *adj* 1 being at or in the forward part or surface of something — see FRONT

2 going before another in time or order — see PREVIOUS

anthem *n* a religious song — see HYMN 1

anthology *n* a collection of writings ⟨an *anthology* of American short stories⟩

syn album, compilation, miscellany

rel almanac, digest, garland, symposium; casebook, sourcebook; archives, library, miscellanea

antic *adj* 1 causing or intended to cause laughter — see FUNNY 1

2 given to good-natured joking or teasing — see PLAYFUL

antic *n* a playful or mischievous act intended as a joke — see PRANK

anticipate *vb* 1 to believe in the future occurrence of (something) — see EXPECT

2 to realize or know about beforehand — see FORESEE

anticipated *adj* being in accordance with the prescribed, normal, or logical course of events — see DUE 2

anticipatory *adj* having or showing signs of eagerly awaiting something — see EXPECTANT 1

antipathetic *adj* 1 having a natural dislike for something ⟨a series of adventure books that turned boys who had been *antipathetic* to reading into avid readers⟩

syn allergic, averse

rel afraid, disinclined, loath (*also* loth *or* loathe), reluctant, unwilling; antagonistic, hostile, intolerant, negative, opposed, opposing, resistant, resisting, uncongenial, unfriendly, unsympathetic; disgusted, nauseated, repelled, repulsed, revolted, shocked, squeamish, turned off

phrases down on

near ant friendly, sympathetic, tolerant, understanding; admiring, appreciative, charmed, delighted, fond, pleased, tickled

2 marked by opposition or ill will — see HOSTILE 1

antipathy *n* 1 a deep-seated ill will — see ENMITY

2 something or someone that is hated — see HATE 2

antipodal *adj* being as different as possible — see OPPOSITE

antipode *n* something that is as different as possible from something else — see OPPOSITE

antipodean *adj* being as different as possible — see OPPOSITE

antiquated *adj* having passed its time of use or usefulness — see OBSOLETE

antique *adj* 1 dating or surviving from the distant past — see ANCIENT 1

2 pleasantly reminiscent of an earlier time — see OLD-FASHIONED 1

antique *n* something belonging to or surviving from an earlier period ⟨Their house is filled with rare *antiques*, including a collection of 19th-century dolls.⟩
syn relic
rel artifact, fossil; antiquities; ruins; hangover, remains, remnant, trace, vestige

antisocial *adj* having or showing a lack of friendliness or interest in others — see COOL 1

antithesis *n* something that is as different as possible from something else — see OPPOSITE

antithetical *adj* being as different as possible — see OPPOSITE

anxiety *n* 1 an uneasy state of mind usually over the possibility of an anticipated misfortune or trouble ⟨Dorothy's *anxiety* about her brother's operation kept her awake all night.⟩
syn agitation, anxiousness, apprehension, apprehensiveness, care, concern, disquiet, fear, nervousness, solicitude, sweat, uneasiness, worry
rel strain, stress, tension; alarm (*also* alarum), anguish, consternation, desperateness, desperation, discomfort, discomposure, dismay, distraction, distress, disturbance, edginess, hand-wringing, jitters, jumpiness, panic, tremor; angst, fearfulness, torment, upset, vexation; cold feet, doubt, dread, foreboding, incertitude, misgiving, presentiment, suspense, uncertainty; compunction, qualm, scruple
near ant calm, calmness, content, contentment, ease, easiness, peace, peacefulness, placidity, placidness, quiet, quietude, sereneness, serenity, tranquillity (*or* tranquility); comfort, consolation, relief, solace
ant unconcern
2 the emotion experienced in the presence or threat of danger — see FEAR 1

anxious *adj* 1 feeling or showing uncomfortable feelings of uncertainty — see NERVOUS 1
2 marked by or causing agitation or uncomfortable feelings — see NERVOUS 2
3 showing urgent desire or interest — see EAGER

anxiousness *n* an uneasy state of mind usually over the possibility of an anticipated misfortune or trouble — see ANXIETY 1

any *adj* being one of a group — see EACH

anyhow *adv* 1 in spite of everything — see REGARDLESS
2 without definite aim, direction, rule, or method — see HIT OR MISS
3 whatever else is done or is the case — see ALWAYS 2

anymore *adv* at the present time — see NOW 1

anyway *adv* 1 in spite of everything — see REGARDLESS
2 without definite aim, direction, rule, or method — see HIT OR MISS
3 whatever else is done or is the case — see ALWAYS 2

anywise *adv* 1 in any way or respect — see AT ALL

2 without definite aim, direction, rule, or method — see HIT OR MISS

A1 *adj* of the very best kind — see EXCELLENT

apace *adv* with great speed — see FAST 1

apart *adv* into parts or pieces ⟨The fancy new adjustable rake came *apart* the first time I tried to use it.⟩
syn asunder, piecemeal
phrases to pieces
ant together

apartment *n* 1 a room or set of rooms in a private house or a block used as a separate dwelling place ⟨a spacious six-room *apartment* that occupies the entire upper floor of a two-family house⟩
syn digs, lodgings, suite, tenement
rel condo, condominium, duplex, duplex apartment, efficiency, efficiency apartment, floor-through, garden apartment, penthouse, railroad flat, salon, studio, studio apartment, triplex, walk-up; gallery, wing; apartment building, apartment house, tenement house
2 an area within a building that has been set apart from surrounding space by a wall — see ROOM 2

apathetic *adj* 1 having or showing a lack of interest or concern — see INDIFFERENT 1
2 not feeling or showing emotion — see IMPASSIVE 1

apathy *n* 1 a lack of emotion or emotional expressiveness ⟨People have shown a surprising *apathy* toward these problems.⟩
syn impassivity, insensibility, numbness, phlegm
rel bloodlessness, callosity, callousness, coolness, halfheartedness, hard-heartedness, hardness, heartlessness, imperturbability, insensitivity, obduracy; blankness, deadness, emptiness, vacancy; aloofness, detachment, indifference, unconcern; stiffness, woodenness
near ant compassion, empathy, pity, sympathy; receptiveness, receptivity, responsiveness, sensitivity; solicitude, understanding, warmth; hand-wringing, histrionics, hysteria, hysterics, melodrama; vehemence
ant emotion, feeling, sensibility
2 lack of interest or concern — see INDIFFERENCE

ape *vb* to use (someone or something) as the model for one's speech, mannerisms, or behavior — see IMITATE 1

aper *n* a person who adopts the appearance or behavior of another especially in an obvious way — see COPYCAT

aperture *n* a place in a surface allowing passage into or through a thing — see HOLE 1

apex *n* 1 the highest part or point — see HEIGHT 1
2 the last and usually sharp or tapering part of something long and narrow — see POINT 2

aphorism *n* an often stated observation regarding something from common experience — see SAYING

apiece *adv* for each one ⟨When you figure that they usually sell for six dollars *apiece*, you're getting quite a bargain.⟩
syn all, each, per, per capita

---

syn synonym(s)   *rel* related words
ant antonym(s)   *near ant* near antonym(s)

rel apart, discretely, independently, individually, respectively, separately, singly
phrases a pop, a shot, a throw
near ant aggregately, altogether, collectively, together

apish *adj* using or marked by the use of something else as a basis or model — see IMITATIVE 1

aplomb *n* 1 evenness of emotions or temper — see EQUANIMITY
2 great faith in oneself or one's abilities — see CONFIDENCE 1

apologetic *adj* feeling sorrow for a wrong that one has done — see CONTRITE

apoplectic *adj* feeling or showing anger — see ANGRY

apostate *n* 1 a person who abandons a cause or organization usually without right — see RENEGADE
2 one who betrays a trust or an allegiance — see TRAITOR

apostle *n* a person who actively supports or favors a cause — see EXPONENT 1

apothecary *n* 1 a person who prepares drugs according to a doctor's prescription — see DRUGGIST
2 a retail store where medicines and miscellaneous articles are sold — see DRUGSTORE

appall *also* **appal** *vb* to cause an unpleasant surprise for — see SHOCK 1

appalling *adj* 1 causing intense displeasure, disgust, or resentment — see OFFENSIVE 1
2 extremely disturbing or repellent — see HORRIBLE 1

apparatus *n* items needed for the performance of a task or activity — see EQUIPMENT

apparel *n* covering for the human body — see CLOTHING

apparel *vb* to outfit with clothes and especially fine or special clothes — see CLOTHE 1

apparent *adj* 1 appearing to be true on the basis of evidence that may or may not be confirmed ⟨At the start of the investigation, the *apparent* cause of the accident was mechanical failure.⟩
syn assumed, evident, ostensible, presumed, reputed, seeming, supposed
rel demonstrable, external, outward, superficial, visible; conceivable, plausible, possible, supposable; likely, probable; clear, distinct, manifest, obvious, plain; deceptive, delusive, delusory, illusive, illusory, imaginary; misleading, specious; fake, faked, feigned, phony (*also* phoney), pretended, pseudo, put-on; alleged, claimed, professed, purported, so-called
near ant inapparent; implausible, impossible, improbable, inconceivable, unlikely; actual, authenticated, confirmed, corroborated, established, genuine, real, substantiated, sure, valid, validated, verified
2 capable of being seen — see VISIBLE 1
3 not subject to misinterpretation or more than one interpretation — see CLEAR 2

apparently *adv* to all outward appearances ⟨*Apparently*, her husband didn't know the cake was for the raffle, since he helped himself to a piece.⟩
syn evidently, ostensibly, presumably, seemingly, supposedly

rel externally, outwardly, visibly; believably, credibly; likely, presumedly, probably; conceivably, maybe, mayhap, perchance, perhaps, possibly, professedly, supposably; allegedly, purportedly, reportedly, reputedly; distinctly, manifestly, obviously, plainly, self-evidently, assuredly, surely
phrases on the surface
near ant implausibly, impossibly, improbably, incredibly

apparition *n* the soul of a dead person thought of especially as appearing to living people — see GHOST 1

appeal *n* 1 an earnest request — see PLEA 1
2 the power of irresistible attraction — see CHARM 2

appeal (to) *vb* to make a request to (someone) in an earnest or urgent manner — see BEG

appealing *adj* having an often mysterious or magical power to attract — see FASCINATING 1

appear *vb* 1 to come into view ⟨A police car *appeared* just as I ran a red light.⟩
syn come out, materialize, show, show up, turn up, unfold
rel reappear, resurface; bulk, loom; arrive, come; dawn, debut; arise, blossom, bob (up), break, break out, crop (up), emerge, erupt, issue, outcrop, rise, shoot (up), spring (up), surface; happen, occur; reappear, rematerialize
near ant depart, leave, retire, withdraw
ant clear, disappear, dissolve, evanesce, evaporate, fade, go (away), melt (away), vanish
2 to give the impression of being — see SEEM
3 to come into existence — see BEGIN 2
4 to get to a destination — see COME 2

appearance *n* 1 the outward form of someone or something especially as indicative of a quality ⟨the dignified *appearance* of this world leader⟩ ⟨the college's manicured lawns and well-groomed *appearance* in general⟩
syn aspect, dress, figure, garb, look, mien, outside, presence
rel air, bearing, behavior, comportment, demeanor, deportment, manner, poise, pose; carriage, posture, stance; cast, shape, turn; color, coloring, complexion; countenance, face, features, physiognomy, visage
phrases cut of one's jib
2 outward and often deceptive indication ⟨Can't you at least give the *appearance* of listening to what I say?⟩
syn face, guise, name, outward, seeming, semblance, show
rel air, effect, impression; hint, implication, resemblance, suggestion; affectation, demonstration, display, fiction, image, imitation, imposture, likeness, make-believe (*also* make-belief), pose, pretense (*or* pretence), representation, simulation; cloak, disguise, exterior, facade (*also* façade), front, gloss, mask, masquerade, shape, shell, surface, veneer
phrases first blush
3 the act of coming upon a scene — see ARRIVAL

appease *vb* to lessen the anger or agitation of — see PACIFY 1

appeasing *adj* tending to lessen or avoid conflict or hostility — see PACIFIC 1

appellation *n* a word or combination of words by which a person or thing is regularly known — see NAME 1

append *vb* to join (something) to a mass, quantity, or number so as to bring about an overall increase — see ADD 1

appendage *n* something that is not necessarily in itself but adds to the convenience or performance of the main piece of equipment — see ACCESSORY 1

appertain *vb* 1 to be the property of a person or group of persons — see BELONG 1

2 to have a relation or connection — see APPLY 1

appetite *n* 1 a need or desire for food — see HUNGER 1

2 a strong wish for something — see DESIRE 1

3 positive regard for something — see LIKING

4 urgent desire or interest — see EAGERNESS

appetizing *adj* very pleasing to the sense of taste — see DELICIOUS 1

applaud *vb* to declare enthusiastic approval of — see ACCLAIM

applaudable *adj* deserving of high regard or great approval — see ADMIRABLE

applauding *adj* expressing approval — see FAVORABLE 1

applause *n* 1 enthusiastic and usually public expression of approval ⟨A design for a statue of the college's founder has received nothing but *applause* from students and faculty alike.⟩

syn acclamation, cheer, cheering, ovation, plaudit(s), rave(s)

rel clapping; bravo, hail, hurrah (*also* hooray *or* hoorah), hosanna; acclaim, accolade, citation, commendation, compliment, encomium, eulogy, homage, paean, panegyric, salutation, tribute; praise

near ant boo, hiss, hoot, jeer, raspberry, smirk, sneer, snicker, snigger, snort, whistle; gibe (*or* jibe), put-down, taunt

ant booing, hissing

2 public acknowledgment or admiration for an achievement — see GLORY 1

appliance *n* 1 an interesting and often novel device with a practical use — see GADGET

2 something that is not necessary in itself but adds to the convenience or performance of the main piece of equipment — see ACCESSORY 1

applicability *n* the fact or state of being pertinent — see PERTINENCE

applicable *adj* 1 capable of being put to use or account — see PRACTICAL 1

2 having to do with the matter at hand — see PERTINENT

3 meeting the requirements of a purpose or situation — see FIT 1

applicant *n* one who seeks an office, honor, position, or award — see CANDIDATE

application *n* the act or practice of em-

ploying something for a particular purpose — see USE 1

apply *vb* 1 to have a relation or connection ⟨Does your rule about calling home *apply* to me as well?⟩

syn appertain, bear, pertain, refer, relate

rel affect, concern, interest, involve, touch; associate, connect, couple, interrelate, link, tie in; deal (with), treat

phrases have to do with

2 to occupy (oneself) diligently or with close attention ⟨Sam *applied* himself to writing thank-you letters to everyone who'd helped sponsor him for the charity walk.⟩

syn address, bend, buckle, devote, give

rel readdress, reapply; knuckle down, set (to), settle (down); busy, commit, concern, engage, involve; exert, exhaust, put out, spend, strain, stress, tax, trouble, wear out; carry on, pitch in, plunge (in); grind, hump, hustle, peg (away), plod, plow, plug (away), work

phrases get cracking, get one's act together, get with it, turn one's hand (*or* turn a hand)

near ant dally, dawdle, dillydally, fiddle (around), idle, monkey (around), play, potter (around), putter (around), trifle

3 to put a layer of on a surface — see SPREAD 2

4 to put into action or service — see USE 1

5 to bring to bear especially forcefully or effectively — see EXERT

6 to carry out effectively — see ENFORCE

appoint *vb* 1 to decide upon (the time or date for an event) usually from a position of authority ⟨At the *appointed* hour we were in our places.⟩

syn designate, fix, name, set

rel adopt, assign, choose, determine, establish, opt (for), pick, pin (down), prefer, select, settle, single (out), specify; arrange, coordinate, orchestrate; advertise, announce, declare, publish

2 to pick (someone) by one's authority for a specific position or duty ⟨He was *appointed* to the council on national security.⟩

syn assign, attach, commission, constitute, designate, detail, name, place

rel authorize, delegate, deputize; anoint, consecrate, create, inaugurate, induct, install, instate, institute, invest, make, ordain; crown, enthrone, throne; choose, destine, draft, elect, handpick, select, single (out), vote (in)

near ant blackball, depose, dethrone, displace, eject, evict, oust, overthrow, remove, throw out, uncrown, unmake, unseat

ant discharge, dismiss, expel, fire

appointment *n* 1 the state or fact of being chosen for a position or duty ⟨His *appointment* to the Board of Health came as a surprise.⟩

syn assignment, commission, designation

rel billet, gig, job, office, place, position, situation, spot, station; authorization, delegation, deputation; placement, ranking; anointing, anointment, induction, installation, installment (*also* instalment), instat-

---

ing, investiture, investment, ordination; choice, choosing, destination, election, nomination, picking, selection, singling (out)

near ant blackball, rejection; deposition; dethronement, ejection, eviction, ouster, overthrow, removal

ant discharge, dismissal, dismission, expulsion, firing

2 an agreement to be present at a specified time and place — see ENGAGEMENT 2

3 an assignment at which one regularly works for pay — see JOB 1

4 appointments *pl* the movable articles (such as tables and chairs) in a room — see FURNITURE

apportion *vb* **1** to give as a share or portion — see ALLOT

2 to give out (something) to appropriate individuals — see ADMINISTER 1

apportionment *n* the act or process of giving out something to each member of a group — see DISTRIBUTION 1

apposite *adj* having to do with the matter at hand — see PERTINENT

appraisal *n* **1** an opinion on the nature, character, or quality of something — see ESTIMATION 1

2 the act of placing a value on the nature, character, or quality of something — see ESTIMATE 1

appraise *vb* to make an approximate or tentative judgment regarding — see ESTIMATE 1

appraisement *n* **1** an opinion on the nature, character, or quality of something — see ESTIMATION 1

2 the act of placing a value on the nature, character, or quality of something — see ESTIMATE 1

appreciable *adj* able to be perceived by a sense or by the mind — see PERCEPTIBLE

appreciate *vb* **1** to become greater in extent, volume, amount, or number — see INCREASE 1

2 to hold dear — see LOVE 1

3 to have a clear idea of — see COMPREHEND 1

4 to think very highly or favorably of — see ADMIRE

appreciation *n* **1** a feeling of great approval and liking — see ADMIRATION 1

2 acknowledgment of having received something good from another — see THANKS

3 the knowledge gained from the process of coming to know or understand something — see COMPREHENSION

appreciative *adj* **1** expressing approval — see FAVORABLE 1

2 feeling or expressing gratitude — see GRATEFUL 1

appreciativeness *n* acknowledgment of having received something good from another — see THANKS

apprehend *vb* **1** to have a clear idea of — see COMPREHEND 1

2 to take or keep under one's control by authority of law — see ARREST 1

apprehended *adj* taken and held prisoner — see CAPTIVE

apprehension *n* **1** suspicion or fear of future harm or misfortune ⟨The hikers entered the dark cave with a great deal of *apprehension.*⟩

syn alarm (*also* alarum), apprehensiveness, dread, foreboding, misgiving

rel agitation, anxiety, anxiousness, concern, disquiet, distress, disturbance, fearfulness, uneasiness; scruple, worry; doubt, incertitude, mistrust, suspiciousness, uncertainty, wariness; defeatism, pessimism; foreknowledge, premonition, presage, presentiment

near ant excitement, hope, hopefulness; confidence, optimism, sanguinity

2 the act of taking into one's control by authority of law — see ARREST 1

3 an uneasy state of mind usually over the possibility of an anticipated misfortune or trouble — see ANXIETY 1

4 the knowledge gained from the process of coming to know or understand something — see COMPREHENSION

apprehensiveness *n* **1** an uneasy state of mind usually over the possibility of an anticipated misfortune or trouble — see ANXIETY 1

2 suspicion or fear of future harm or misfortune — see APPREHENSION 1

apprentice *n* **1** a person who helps a more skilled person — see HELPER

2 a person who is just starting out in a field of activity — see BEGINNER

apprise *vb* to give information to — see ENLIGHTEN 1

approach *n* **1** an established course for traveling from one place to another — see PASSAGE 1

2 the means or procedure for doing something — see METHOD

approach *vb* **1** to come near or nearer ⟨The parade's *approaching*! I can hear the band playing!⟩

syn close, draw on, near, nigh

rel arrive, attain, come, gain, hit, land, make, reach, show up, turn up, waltz (up); creep up, sneak up; adjoin, border, touch, verge

near ant clear out, depart, exit, go, leave, light out, quit, remove, run away, shove (off), take off, walk out

ant back (up *or* away), recede, retire, retreat, withdraw

2 to move closer to — see COME 1

3 to come near or nearer to in character or quality — see APPROXIMATE

approaching *adj* being soon to appear or take place — see FORTHCOMING 1

approbation *n* an acceptance of something as satisfactory — see APPROVAL

appropriate *adj* meeting the requirements of a purpose or situation — see FIT 1

appropriate *vb* **1** to take or make use of under a guise of authority but without actual right ⟨Archaeologists wrongfully *appropriated* artifacts excavated at ancient sites for their museums.⟩

syn arrogate, commandeer, convert, expropriate, pirate, preempt, press, seize, take over, usurp

rel annex, attach, claim, confiscate, impound, repossess, sequester; assume, collar, grab, grasp, snatch, steal, wrench, wrest; despoil, loot, pillage; encroach, infringe, invade, occupy, preoccupy, trespass; embezzle, misapply, misappropriate, misuse

2 to take (something) without right and with an intent to keep — see STEAL 1

appropriately *adv* in a manner suitable for the occasion or purpose — see PROPERLY

appropriateness *n* the quality or state of being especially suitable or fitting ⟨Visitors remarked on the *appropriateness* of window boxes on the cottage, noting they gave it a quaint, cheerful look.⟩

syn aptness, felicitousness, felicity, fitness, fittingness, propriety, rightness, seemliness, suitability, suitableness

rel agreeableness, compatibility, congruity, harmoniousness; applicability, bearing, connection, justifiability, materiality, pertinence, relevance, relevancy, validity; acceptability, adequacy, adequateness, convenience, satisfactoriness, serviceableness, usefulness

near ant disagreeableness, incompatibility, incongruence, incongruity, incongruousness, inexpedience, inexpediency, inharmoniousness, unbecomingness; inapplicability, irrelevance, irrelevancy; meaninglessness, pointlessness

ant impropriety, inappositeness, inappropriateness, inaptness, infelicity, unfitness, unsuitability, wrongness

appropriation *n* **1** a sum of money allotted for a specific use by official or formal action ⟨The National Park Service received an increased *appropriation* for wildlife management.⟩

syn allocation, allotment, annuity, grant, subsidy

rel aid, assistance, block grant, grant-in-aid, set-aside; foreign aid, relief, state aid; advance, allowance, benefit, bequest, endowment, fund, legacy, stipend, trust, trust fund

2 the unlawful taking or withholding of something from the rightful owner under a guise of authority ⟨the insurgents' *appropriation* of the building for their headquarters⟩

syn seizure

rel annexation, assumption, attachment, confiscation, grab, repossession, sequestration; embezzlement, misapplication, misappropriation, misuse, theft; despoilment, looting, pillaging; encroachment, infringement, piracy, invasion, occupation, preoccupancy, trespass; dispossession, ejection, stripping

approval *n* an acceptance of something as satisfactory ⟨Does this poster I made for the recital meet with your *approval*?⟩

syn approbation, blessing, favor, imprimatur, OK (*or* okay)

rel backing, cachet, endorsement (*also* indorsement), finalization, formalization, nod, ratification, sanction, support, thumbs-up, vote; benediction, goodwill; acceptance, agreement, assent, concurrence, consent; countenance, liking, satisfaction

phrases clean bill of health, pat on the back

near ant refusal, rejection, repudiation; dislike, dissatisfaction; censure, condemnation, criticism, denunciation, deprecation, depreciation, disparagement, opprobrium, reprehension, reproach, reprobation

ant disapprobation, disapproval, disfavor

approve *vb* to give official acceptance of as satisfactory ⟨As soon as the pond project was *approved*, the bulldozers were at the site.⟩

syn accredit, authorize, clear, confirm, finalize, formalize, OK (*or* okay), ratify, sanction, warrant

rel accept, acknowledge, affirm; certify, endorse (*also* indorse), validate; bless, canonize, sanctify; initial, rubber-stamp, sign, sign off (on); allow, enable, legalize, license (*also* licence), pass, permit; reapprove

near ant ban, enjoin, forbid, interdict, prohibit, proscribe; disregard, ignore, neglect, overlook; rebuff, rebut, refuse, spurn

ant decline, deny, disallow, disapprove, negative, reject, turn down, veto

approve (of) *vb* to have a favorable opinion of ⟨We don't *approve of* people who stand in the "12 items or less" lane with 13 items.⟩

syn accept, care (for), countenance, favor, OK (*or* okay), subscribe (to)

rel acclaim, applaud, laud, praise, salute; back (up), concur (in), stand by, support, sustain, uphold; bear, endure, tolerate; assent (to), consent (to); commend, recommend; enjoy, like

phrases go for, hold with, take kindly to

near ant blacklist, censure, condemn, criticize, damn, denounce, deprecate, depreciate, disparage, reprehend, reprobate; dislike, mind; detest, hate, loathe; dissent (from), object (to), oppose

ant disapprove (of), discountenance, disfavor

approving *adj* expressing approval — see FAVORABLE 1

approximate *adj* **1** being such only when compared to something else — see COMPARATIVE

2 not precisely correct — see INEXACT 1

approximate *vb* to come near or nearer to in character or quality ⟨Rob's violin performance last night didn't even *approximate* what he's really capable of when he's not feeling sick.⟩

syn approach, compare (with), measure up (to), stack up (against *or* with)

rel add up (to), amount (to), come (to); duplicate, equal, match; mirror, parallel, reflect; border (on), verge (on)

phrases hold a candle to

apropos *adj* having to do with the matter at hand — see PERTINENT

apropos *prep* having to do with — see ABOUT 1

apropos of *prep* having to do with — see ABOUT 1

apt *adj* **1** having a tendency to be or act in a certain way — see PRONE 1

2 meeting the requirements of a purpose or situation — see FIT 1

aptitude *n* **1** a habitual attraction to some activity or thing — see INCLINATION 1

---

syn synonym(s)   **rel** related words
ant antonym(s)   **near ant** near antonym(s)

2 a special and usually inborn ability — see TALENT

aptness *n* **1** an established pattern of behavior — see TENDENCY 1

2 the quality or state of being especially suitable or fitting — see APPROPRIATENESS

aquatic *adj* living, lying, or occurring below the surface of the water — see UNDERWATER

aqueduct *n* an open man-made passageway for water — see CHANNEL 1

arbiter *n* a person who impartially decides or resolves a dispute or controversy — see JUDGE 1

arbitrary *adj* **1** having or showing a tendency to force one's will on others without any regard to fairness or necessity ⟨an *arbitrary* piano teacher who makes all her students do the same exercises over and over again⟩

syn dictatorial, high-handed, imperious, peremptory, willful (*or* wilful)

rel arrogant, commanding, demanding, dominant, domineering, haughty, imperative, lordly, masterful, overbearing, presumptuous; authoritarian, autocratic (*also* autocratical), despotic, totalitarian, tyrannical (*also* tyrannic), tyrannous; capricious, changeable, erratic, inconsistent, mercurial, whimsical; biased, inequitable, partisan, prejudiced, unequal, unfair, unjust, unrealistic, unreasonable; unconscionable, unethical, unprincipled, unscrupulous

near ant balanced, disinterested, dispassionate, equal, equitable, evenhanded, fair, impartial, just, nonpartisan, objective; rational, reasonable, understanding, unbiased, unprejudiced; ethical, honorable, irreproachable, law-abiding, moral, principled, unimpeachable

2 lacking a definite plan, purpose, or pattern — see RANDOM

3 exercising power or authority without interference by others — see ABSOLUTE 1

arbitrate *vb* to give an opinion about (something at issue or in dispute) — see JUDGE 1

arbitrator *n* a person who impartially decides or resolves a dispute or controversy — see JUDGE 1

arc *n* something that curves or is curved — see BEND 1

arc *vb* to turn away from a straight line or course — see CURVE 1

arch *adj* **1** coming before all others in importance — see FOREMOST 1

2 tending to or exhibiting reckless playfulness — see MISCHIEVOUS 1

arch *n* something that curves or is curved — see BEND 1

arch *vb* **1** to cause to turn away from a straight line — see BEND 1

2 to turn away from a straight line or course — see CURVE 1

archaic *adj* having passed its time of use or usefulness — see OBSOLETE 1

archetypal *also* **archetypical** *adj* **1** constituting, serving as, or worthy of being a pattern to be imitated — see MODEL

2 having or showing the qualities associated with the members of a particular group or kind — see TYPICAL 1

archetype *n* **1** something belonging to an earlier time from which something else was later developed — see ANCESTOR 2

2 something from which copies are made — see ORIGINAL

archive *n* a place where books, periodicals, and records are kept for use but not for sale — see LIBRARY 1

arctic *adj* **1** having a low or subnormal temperature — see COLD 1

2 lacking in friendliness or warmth of feeling — see COLD 2

ardent *adj* **1** having or expressing great depth of feeling — see FERVENT 1

2 showing urgent desire or interest — see EAGER

3 having a notably high temperature — see HOT 1

ardor *n* **1** depth of feeling ⟨candidates for citizenship reciting the oath of allegiance to the United States with all the *ardor* that they could muster⟩

syn emotion, enthusiasm, fervency, fervidness, fervor, fire, heat, intensity, passion, vehemence, violence, warmth

rel emotionalism, emotionality, histrionics, mawkishness, melodrama, sappiness, sentimentality; eagerness, earnestness, excitement, keenness, zest; fanaticism, fever, hot-bloodedness, infatuation, mania, obsession, zeal; compassion, responsiveness, sentiment, sympathy; torridity, torridness

near ant aloofness, calmness, collectedness, composure, detachedness, reserve, reservedness, reticence, taciturnity; apathy, indifference, stoicism, stoniness, unconcern; stiffness, woodenness; chilliness, coolness, frigidity, frigidness

ant impassivity, insensibility, insensibleness, insensitiveness, insensitivity

2 urgent desire or interest — see EAGERNESS

3 intense sexual desire — see LUST 1

arduous *adj* **1** requiring considerable physical or mental effort — see HARD 2

2 requiring much time, effort, or careful attention — see DEMANDING 1

arduously *adv* with great effort or determination — see HARD 1

area *n* **1** a part or portion having no fixed boundaries — see REGION 1

2 a region of activity, knowledge, or influence — see FIELD 2

arena *n* **1** a large room or building for enclosed public gatherings — see HALL 3

2 a region of activity, knowledge, or influence — see FIELD 2

argot *n* the special terms or expressions of a particular group or field — see TERMINOLOGY

argue *vb* **1** to state (something) as a reason in support of or against something under consideration ⟨I *argued* that a bake sale would make a lot less money than a car wash.⟩

syn assert, contend, maintain, plead, reason

rel adduce, cite, mention; claim, insist; affirm, aver, avouch, avow; advance, give, offer, propose, submit; advise, counsel, recommend, suggest, urge; convince, persuade; advocate, champion, defend, enforce, espouse, support; explain, justify, rationalize; consider, debate, discuss; confute, counter, disprove, rebut, refute

2 to express different opinions about something often angrily ⟨They started *arguing* about money.⟩

syn bicker, brawl, dispute, fall out, fight, hassle, jar, quarrel, quibble, row, scrap, spat, squabble, tiff, wrangle

rel challenge, dare, defy; clash, contend, contest, tangle; cavil, fuss, nitpick; consider, debate, discuss; kick, object, protest

phrases bandy words, butt heads, lock horns, mix it up

near ant coexist, get along; accept, agree, assent, concur, consent

3 to cause (someone) to agree with a belief or course of action by using arguments or earnest requests — see PERSUADE

4 to talk about (an issue) usually from various points of view and for the purpose of arriving at a decision or opinion — see DISCUSS

5 to give evidence or testimony to the truth or factualness of — see CONFIRM 1

arguer *n* a person who takes part in a dispute — see DISPUTANT

argument *n* **1** an often noisy or angry expression of differing opinions ⟨They settled an *argument* that started in class.⟩

syn altercation, bicker, brawl, controversy, cross fire, disagreement, dispute, falling-out, fight, hassle, misunderstanding, quarrel, row, scrap, spat, squabble, tiff, wrangle

rel clash, run-in, skirmish, tangle, tussle; feud, vendetta; attack, contention, dissension (*also* dissention); debate, difference, disputation; fuss, objection, protest, protestation; fisticuffs, fracas, fray, free-for-all, melee (*also* mêlée); catfight

2 a statement given to explain a belief or act — see REASON 1

3 an exchange of views for the purpose of exploring a subject or deciding an issue — see DISCUSSION 1

4 an idea or opinion that is put forth in a discussion or debate — see CONTENTION 1

argumentative *adj* **1** given to arguing ⟨He's too *argumentative* to be part of a project in which teamwork is critical.⟩

syn contentious, disputatious, quarrelsome, scrappy

rel aggressive, bellicose, belligerent, combative, gladiatorial, militant, pugnacious, truculent, warlike; fractious, surly; balky, contrary, ornery, perverse, restive, wayward; disobedient, froward, insubordinate, intractable, recalcitrant, refractory; hardheaded, headstrong, mulish, obdurate, obstinate, pigheaded, resistant, self-willed, stubborn, unbending, uncompromising, uncooperative, unreasonable, unyielding, willful (*or* wilful); acidic, bearish, bilious, cantankerous, captious, choleric, crabby, cranky, cross, disagreeable, dyspeptic, fretful, grouchy, grumpy, ill-humored, ill-natured, ill-tempered, irascible, irritable, peevish, pettish, petulant, querulous, rude, snappish, snappy, splenetic, testy, touchy, waspish; battling, fighting, warring; controversial

near ant affable, amiable, amicable, benevolent, cordial, easygoing, friendly, genial, good-natured, good-tempered, gracious, ingratiating, pleasant, sociable; acquiescent, agreeable, amenable, complaisant, compliant, complying, conciliatory, cooperative, obliging, docile, obedient, submissive, tractable; pacific, peaceable, peaceful

2 feeling or displaying eagerness to fight — see BELLIGERENT

arid *adj* **1** causing weariness, restlessness, or lack of interest — see BORING

2 marked by little or no precipitation or humidity — see DRY 1

arise *vb* **1** to leave one's bed ⟨The travelers *arose* before dawn and were on their way as the sun came up.⟩

syn get up, rise, turn out, uprise

rel arouse, awake, awaken, bestir, stir, wake

near ant catnap, doze, drop off, lie up, nap, nod, rest, sleep, slumber, snooze; bunk, perch, roost, settle; couch, flop (down), lie (down), recline

ant bed (down), retire, turn in

2 to come to one's attention especially gradually or unexpectedly ⟨Note in your report any problems that *arise* while you are conducting the experiment.⟩

syn crop (up), emerge, materialize, spring (up), surface

rel appear, come out, show up, turn up; chance, come, come about, fall out, go (on), go off, hap, happen, occur, pass, transpire; interfere, interpose, intervene, intrude

3 to come into existence — see BEGIN 2

4 to move or extend upward — see ASCEND

aristocracy *n* **1** the highest class in a society ⟨At one time in China only the *aristocracy* could own land.⟩

syn elite, gentility, gentry, nobility, upper class, upper crust

rel A-list, beautiful people, café society, Four Hundred (*or* 400), glitterati, jet set, society; carriage trade, plutocracy

near ant commoners; (the) crowd, (the) masses, peasantry, peonage, (the) people, plebeians, (the) populace, (the) public, rank and file; bourgeoisie, middle class, working class; dregs, (the) herd, (the) mob, rabble, rabblement, riffraff, scum, trash

ant proletarians, proletariat

2 individuals carefully selected as being the best of a class — see ELITE 1

aristocratic *adj* of high birth, rank, or station — see NOBLE 1

arithmetic *n* the act or process of performing mathematical operations to find a value — see CALCULATION

¹arm *n* a portable weapon from which a shot is discharged by gunpowder — see GUN 1

²arm *n* **1** a large unit of a governmental, business, or educational organization — see DIVISION 2

2 a part of a body of water that extends beyond the general shoreline — see GULF 1

3 an area of land that juts out into a body of water — see ²CAPE

---

syn synonym(s)   **rel** related words
ant antonym(s)   **near ant** near antonym(s)

4 the right or means to command or control others — see POWER 1

armada *n* a group of vehicles traveling together or under one management — see FLEET

armed forces *n pl* the combined army, air force, and navy of a nation ⟨Our nation's *armed forces* are stationed throughout the world.⟩
syn colors, military, service, troops
rel GIs (*or* GI's), men-at-arms, rank and file, servicemen, servicewomen, soldiers, soldiery; force; militia, reserves; armor, defense
near ant civilians, noncombatants

armistice *n* a temporary stopping of fighting — see TRUCE

armor *n* **1** means or method of defending — see DEFENSE 1
2 something that encloses another thing especially to protect it — see ¹CASE 1

armory *n* a place where military arms are stored ⟨The soldier was sent to the *armory* for a new weapon.⟩
syn arsenal, depot, dump, magazine
rel fort, fortress, stronghold; repository, storehouse, warehouse

army *n* **1** a large body of men and women organized for land warfare ⟨In 218 B.C., Hannibal crossed the Alps with an intimidating *army* of people and, most famously, a number of elephants.⟩
syn array, battalion, host, legion
rel militia, national guard, standing army; infantry, ranks, regulars, soldiers, troopers, troops
2 a great number of persons or creatures massed together — see CROWD 1
3 a group of people working together on a task — see GANG 1

aroma *n* **1** a sweet or pleasant smell — see FRAGRANCE
2 the quality of a thing that makes it perceptible to the sense organs in the nose — see SMELL 1
3 a special quality or impression associated with something — see AURA 1

aromatic *adj* having a pleasant smell — see FRAGRANT

around *adj* having being at the present time — see EXTANT 1

around *adv* **1** on all sides or in every direction ⟨He looked *around*.⟩ ⟨Butterflies were flying all *around*.⟩
syn about, round
rel all over, everyplace, everywhere; abroad, hereabouts (*or* hereabout); around, here and there
2 toward the opposite direction ⟨She turned *around* and saw him.⟩
syn about, back, backward (*or* backwards), round
rel behind, down, downward (*or* downwards), rearward (*also* rearwards); obversely, reversely; across, athwart, counter, counterclockwise
near ant clockwise, deasil
3 at, within, or to a short distance or time — see NEAR 1
4 from beginning to end — see THROUGH 1

around *prep* **1** close to ⟨I wouldn't stand *around* those rocks—there could be snakes under them!⟩
syn about, by, near, next to, nigh
rel alongside, beside; across, along, at; circa; toward (*or* towards)
phrases next door to
2 in random positions within the boundaries of ⟨Huge, strangely shaped rocks were scattered *around* the canyon floor.⟩
syn about, across, over, round, through, throughout
rel on

arouse *vb* **1** to cause to stop sleeping — see WAKE 1
2 to cease to be asleep — see WAKE 2
3 to rouse to strong feeling or action — see PROVOKE 1

arrange *vb* **1** to come to an agreement or decision concerning the details of ⟨*Arrange* a time for the meeting.⟩ ⟨*Arrange* money matters for your trip.⟩
syn decide, fix, set, settle
rel contract, pledge, promise; blueprint, calculate, chart, concert, design, draft, frame, intrigue, lay out, maneuver, map (out), plan, program (*also* programme), schematize, scheme, shape, square away, work out; choose, conclude, determine, figure, opt, resolve; affirm, approve, authorize, clear, confirm, OK (*or* okay), sanction, warrant; close, complete, end, finalize, finish, round (off *or* out), wind up, wrap up; bargain, deal, dicker, haggle, horse-trade, negotiate
phrases dispose of
near ant abort, call, call off, drop, recall, repeal, rescind, revoke; differ (over), disagree (with); counter, debate, object, oppose, protest, resist; contest, dispute
2 to put into a particular arrangement — see ORDER 1
3 to bring about through discussion and compromise — see NEGOTIATE 1
4 to work out the details of (something) in advance — see PLAN 1

arrangement *n* **1** a method worked out in advance for achieving some objective — see PLAN 1
2 the way in which something is sized, arranged, or organized — see FORMAT 1
3 the way in which the elements of something (as a work of art) are arranged — see COMPOSITION 3
4 the way objects in space or events in time are arranged or follow one another — see ORDER 1

arrant *adj* having no exceptions or restrictions — see ABSOLUTE 2

array *n* **1** a number of things considered as a unit — see GROUP 1
2 a usually small number of persons considered as a unit — see GROUP 2
3 dressy clothing — see FINERY
4 the way objects in space or events in time are arranged or follow one another — see ORDER 1
5 a large body of men and women organized for land warfare — see ARMY 1

array *vb* **1** to make more attractive by adding something that is beautiful or becoming — see DECORATE
2 to outfit with clothes and especially fine or special clothes — see CLOTHE 1
3 to put into a particular arrangement — see ORDER 1

arrest *n* **1** the act of taking into one's control by authority of law ⟨There were only two *arrests* during the massive protest.⟩
syn apprehension, bust [*slang*], collar, pinch
rel raid; house arrest; capture, entrapment, seizure; captivity, confinement, enchainment, hold, immurement, imprisonment, incarceration, restraint; rearrest; remand
near ant emancipation, liberation, release
ant discharge
2 the stopping of a process or activity — see END 1

arrest *vb* **1** to take or keep under one's control by authority of law ⟨The inept robber was promptly *arrested* by the off-duty policeman he had tried to hold up.⟩
syn apprehend, bust [*slang*], collar, nab, nail, pick up, pinch, restrain, seize
rel bag, capture, catch, get, grab, grapple, hook, land, snap (up), snare, snatch, trap; commit, confine, detain, hold, immure, imprison, incarcerate, intern, jail, jug, lock (up); bind, enchain, fetter, handcuff, manacle, shackle, trammel; rearrest; remand
near ant emancipate, free, liberate, loose, loosen, release, spring; unbind, unchain
ant discharge
2 to bring (something) to a standstill — see ¹HALT 1
3 to hold the attention of as if by a spell — see ENTHRALL 1

arrested *adj* taken and held prisoner — see CAPTIVE

arresting *adj* **1** holding the attention or provoking interest — see INTERESTING
2 likely to attract attention — see NOTICEABLE

arrival *n* the act of coming upon a scene ⟨Spring's late *arrival* meant we were still skiing in mid-April.⟩ ⟨The groom blamed his belated *arrival* for the wedding on a huge traffic snarl.⟩
syn advent, appearance, coming
rel approach, entrance, ingress; beginning, birth, commencement, dawn, dawning, debut (*also* début), genesis, inception, morning, onset, start
near ant dissipation, dissolution, evaporation, fadeaway, fading, melting, passing, vanishing; clearing out, egress, leaving, retirement, retreat, withdrawal; emigration, evacuation, exodus
ant decamping, decampment, departing, departure, disappearance, exit, exiting, farewell, going, leave-taking, parting, quitting

arrive *vb* **1** to get to a destination — see COME 2
2 to reach a desired level of accomplishment — see SUCCEED 2

arrogance *n* an exaggerated sense of one's importance that shows itself in the making of excessive or unjustified claims ⟨In his *arrogance* the president of the club made all the arrangements for the annual banquet without consulting the members.⟩
syn assumption, consequence, haughtiness, huffiness, imperiousness, loftiness, lordliness, masterfulness, pompousness, presumptuousness, pretense (*or* pretence), pretension, pretentiousness, self-importance, superciliousness, superiority
rel authoritativeness, bossiness, dominance, high-handedness; condescension, disdain, scorn; chest-thumping, self-assertion, snobbery, snobbishness, snobbism, snootiness; cheek, cheekiness, impertinence, impudence, sauciness; boastfulness, bombast, bravado, strut, swagger, triumphalism, vaingloriousness, vainglory; cockiness, complacence, conceit, egoism, egotism, pride, pridefulness, self-assumption, self-centeredness, self-complacency, self-conceit, self-content, self-contentment, self-opinion, self-partiality, self-satisfaction, smugness, vanity; superiority complex
near ant bashfulness, demureness, retiringness, shyness; diffidence, self-distrust, self-doubt, timidity, timidness; lowliness, meekness, mousiness, passiveness, passivity, submissiveness; quietness, reserve, reservedness
ant humility, modesty, unassumingness, unpretentiousness

arrogant *adj* having a feeling of superiority that shows itself in an overbearing attitude ⟨The *arrogant* young lawyer elbowed his way to the head of the line of customers, declaring that he was too busy to wait like everybody else.⟩
syn cavalier, haughty, highfalutin (*also* hifalutin), high-handed, high-hat, imperious, important, lofty, lordly, masterful, overweening, peremptory, pompous, presuming, presumptuous, pretentious, self-assertive, supercilious, superior, uppish, uppity
rel authoritarian, bossy, dominant, dominating, domineering, pontificating; condescending, disdainful, patronizing; impertinent, impudent, saucy; blusterous, blustery, boastful, bombastic, braggart, bragging, braggy, cocky, swaggering, vain, vainglorious; complacent, conceited, egocentric, egoistic (*also* egoistical), egotistic (*or* egotistical), prideful, proud, self-affected, self-applauding, self-centered, self-complacent, self-conceited, self-pleased, self-satisfied, smug, stuck-up; self-flattering, self-promoting; brash, forward, uninhibited, unreserved; extroverted (*also* extraverted), immodest
near ant bashful, cowering, cringing, demure, diffident, introverted, mousy (*or* mousey), overmodest, self-critical, self-doubting, sheepish, shrinking, shy, subdued, timid; acquiescent, compliant, deferential, meek, passive, submissive, unaggressive, unassertive, unassuming, unobtrusive, yielding; quiet, reserved, retiring
ant humble, lowly, modest, unarrogant, unpretentious

arrogate *vb* to take or make use of under a guise of authority but without actual right — see APPROPRIATE 1

arsenal *n* a place where military arms are stored — see ARMORY

arsonist *n* a person who deliberately and

unlawfully sets fire to a building or other property ⟨They finally caught the *arsonist*, but only after he'd set fire to four barns.⟩

syn firebug, incendiary

rel pyromaniac; flamer, igniter (*also* ignitor), immolator, inflamer

art *n* **1** an occupation requiring skillful use of the hands — see CRAFT 1

2 subtle or imaginative ability in inventing, devising, or executing something — see SKILL 1

artery *n* a passage cleared for public vehicular travel — see WAY 1

artful *adj* **1** clever at attaining one's ends by indirect and often deceptive means ⟨The *artful* lawyer got the witness to admit he had been lying.⟩

syn beguiling, cagey (*also* cagy), crafty, cunning, cute, designing, devious, foxy, guileful, shrewd, slick, sly, subtle, tricky, wily

rel astute, facile, glib, sharp; crooked, deceitful, deceptive, dishonest, fraudulent, knavish, Machiavellian, oblique, serpentine, shady, shifty, slippery, sneaky, treacherous, underhand, underhanded, unscrupulous; backhanded, double-dealing, hypocritical, insincere, left-handed, mealy, mealymouthed, smooth-tongued, two-faced; circuitous, circular, roundabout; clandestine, concealed, covert, furtive, hugger-mugger, secret, stealthy, surreptitious, undercover; calculating, plotting

near ant obvious, open, patent, plain, public, unconcealed; aboveboard, candid, direct, forthright, frank, honest, natural, outspoken, plainspoken, real, simple, sincere, straightforward, unaffected, unpretending, unpretentious, unvarnished; childlike, impressionable, simpleminded, unsophisticated, unworldly; unforced, unstudied; trustful, trusting

ant artless, guileless, ingenuous, innocent, undesigning

2 showing a noteworthy use of the imagination and creativity especially in inventing — see CLEVER 1

3 accomplished with trained ability — see SKILLFUL 1

artfulness *n* **1** skill in achieving one's ends through indirect, subtle, or underhanded means — see CUNNING 1

2 subtle or imaginative ability in inventing, devising, or executing something — see SKILL 1

article *n* a short piece of writing typically expressing a point of view — see ESSAY 1

articulate *adj* able to express oneself clearly and well ⟨The television crew covering the science fair were looking for photogenic and *articulate* students to explain their projects on the air.⟩

syn eloquent, fluent, well-spoken

rel facile, glib, smooth-tongued, voluble; expressive, outspoken, verbal, vocal; blabby, chatty, garrulous, loquacious, talkative, verbose

near ant faltering, halting, hesitant, maundering, mumbling, muttering, sputtering, stammering, stumbling, stuttering; mute, speechless, tongueless, tongue-tied, voiceless

ant inarticulate, ineloquent

articulate *vb* **1** to utter clearly and distinctly ⟨She uses a very measured tone and *articulates* every syllable when speaking in public.⟩

syn enunciate

rel express, pronounce, say, speak, talk, tell, utter, verbalize, vocalize, voice; speak out, speak up

near ant falter, grunt, halt, hesitate, maunder, splutter, sputter, stammer, stumble, stutter; mouth, mumble, murmur, mutter, whisper; breathe, drawl, gasp

2 to convey in appropriate or telling terms — see PHRASE

3 to express (a thought or emotion) in words — see SAY 1

articulateness *n* the art or power of speaking or writing in a forceful and convincing way — see ELOQUENCE

articulation *n* **1** an act, process, or means of putting something into words — see EXPRESSION 1

2 the clear and accurate pronunciation of words especially in public speaking — see DICTION 1

artifice *n* **1** a clever often underhanded means to achieve an end — see TRICK 1

2 skill in achieving one's ends through indirect, subtle, or underhanded means — see CUNNING 1

3 subtle or imaginative ability in inventing, devising, or executing something — see SKILL 1

4 the inclination or practice of misleading others through lies or trickery — see DECEIT 1

5 the use of clever underhanded actions to achieve an end — see TRICKERY

artificer *n* a person whose occupation requires skill with the hands — see ARTISAN

artificial *adj* **1** lacking in natural or spontaneous quality ⟨Their *artificial* smiles did not make us feel welcome.⟩

syn affected, assumed, bogus, contrived, factitious, fake, false, feigned, forced, mechanical, mock, phony (*also* phoney), plastic, pretended, pseudo, put-on, sham, simulated, strained, unnatural

rel automatic, canned, concocted, fabricated, labored, manufactured, pat, unauthentic, unreal, unrealistic; double-dealing, empty, facile, hollow, hypocritical, insincere, left-handed, mealy, mealymouthed, two-faced, unctuous; histrionic, melodramatic, overacted, overdone, theatrical (*also* theatric); cute, cutesy, genteel, goody-goody, mincing, overrefined, simpering; conventional, formal, impersonal, inflexible, rigid, stiff, stylized, wooden; artful, calculated, conscious, cultivated, deliberate, premeditated, studied

near ant authentic, bona fide, real, realistic, right, true; honest, ingenuous, sincere, unpretending; easy, effortless, smooth; extemporaneous, impromptu, impulsive, instinctive, unconscious, unprompted, unrehearsed, unstudied

ant artless, genuine, natural, spontaneous, unaffected, uncontrived, unforced

2 not being or expressing what one appears to be or express — see INSINCERE

3 being such in appearance only and made

with or manufactured from usually cheaper materials — see IMITATION

4 produced by humans rather than natural processes — see SYNTHETIC 1

artillery *n* large firearms (as cannons or rockets) ⟨The enemy attacked with heavy *artillery*.⟩

syn guns, ordnance

rel ammunition, armament, arms, munitions, weaponry, weapons

artisan *n* a person whose occupation requires skill with the hands ⟨We visited a re-created 19th-century New England village that features an array of *artisans*—a cooper, a carpenter, a blacksmith, a potter, a glassblower.⟩

syn artificer, craftsman, handicrafter, tradesman

rel craftswoman; artist, maker; journeyman, master; operative, shaper, smith, technician, wright; workman

artist *n* a person with a high level of knowledge or skill in a field — see EXPERT

artistic *adj* of or relating to the fine arts — see CULTURAL

artistry *n* subtle or imaginative ability in inventing, devising, or executing something — see SKILL 1

artless *adj* **1** free from any intent to deceive or impress others — see GUILELESS

2 hastily or roughly constructed — see RUDE 1

artlessly *adv* without any attempt to impress by deception or exaggeration — see NATURALLY 3

artlessness *n* the quality or state of being simple and sincere — see NAÏVETÉ 1

as *conj* **1** at or during the time that — see WHEN 1

2 for the reason that — see SINCE

3 in spite of the fact that — see ALTHOUGH

4 the way it would be or one would do if — see AS IF

ascend *vb* to move or extend upward ⟨The path *ascended* so steeply at one point that we had to scramble up on our hands and knees.⟩

syn arise, aspire, climb, lift, mount, rise, soar, thrust, up, uprise, upturn

rel surge, tower; boost, elevate, raise, uplift, upraise; balloon, blast off, take off, zoom; crest, scale, surmount, top; cant, incline, lean, list, recline, slant, slope, tilt, tip

near ant dive, nose-dive, plummet, sink, slide

ant decline, descend, dip, drop, fall (off), plunge

ascendancy *also* **ascendency** *n* controlling power or influence over others — see SUPREMACY 1

ascension *n* the act or an instance of rising or climbing up — see ASCENT 1

ascent *n* **1** the act or an instance of rising or climbing up ⟨Our plane broke through some heavy low clouds during its *ascent* and leveled off once we were above them.⟩

syn ascension, climb, rise, rising, soar

rel boost, hike, increase, raise; elevation, hoist, levitation, raising, takeoff; heave, thrust, upheaval, uplifting, upraising, up-

surge, upsweep, upswing, uptrend, upturn, upwelling

near ant plop, plummeting, sinking; decline, decrease, down; comedown, downfall, downgrade

ant descent, dip, dive, drop, fall, nosedive, plunge

2 an upward slope ⟨We'd reached the final *ascent* of the trail to the summit.⟩

syn hill, rise, upgrade, uphill, uprise

rel cant, diagonal, grade, gradient, inclination, incline, lean, pitch, rake, tilt; climb, hump, mound, ridge, swell

near ant basin, depression, hollow

ant declension, decline, descent, dip, downgrade, fall, hang, hanging

3 a raising or a state of being raised to a higher rank or position — see ADVANCEMENT 1

ascertain *vb* **1** to come to an awareness of — see DISCOVER 1

2 to come upon after searching, study, or effort — see FIND 1

ascribe *vb* to explain (something) as being the result of something else — see CREDIT 1

aseptic *adj* free from filth, infection, or dangers to health — see SANITARY

ashamed *adj* suffering from or expressive of a feeling of responsibility for wrongdoing — see GUILTY

ashen *adj* lacking a healthy skin color — see PALE 2

ashes *n pl* the portion or bits of something left over or behind after it has been destroyed — see REMAINS 1

ashy *adj* lacking a healthy skin color — see PALE 2

aside from *prep* not including — see EXCEPT

as if *conj* the way it would be or one would do if ⟨She looked *as if* she wanted to ask one more question before we left.⟩

syn as, as though, like

asinine *adj* showing or marked by a lack of good sense or judgment — see FOOLISH 1

asininity *n* **1** a foolish act or idea — see FOLLY 1

2 lack of good sense or judgment — see FOOLISHNESS 1

ask *vb* **1** to put a question or questions to ⟨My coworkers *asked* me all about my trip to Machu Picchu.⟩

syn grill, inquire (of), interrogate, query, question, quiz

rel besiege, bombard, cross-examine, cross-question, examine, pump; poll, survey

near ant rejoin, retort; comment, observe, remark; avoid, duck

ant answer, reply, respond

2 to make a request of ⟨*Ask* the salesclerk for assistance.⟩

syn request, solicit

rel appeal (to), beg, beseech, conjure, entreat, implore, importune, invite, petition, plead (to), pray, supplicate; demand, enjoin, exact, press, require

phrases call on (*or* upon)

near ant coerce, compel, constrain, force, oblige, require

3 to set or receive as a price — see CHARGE 1

---

syn synonym(s)   *rel* related words
ant antonym(s)   *near ant* near antonym(s)

4 to request the presence or participation of — see INVITE 1

ask (for) *vb* 1 to make a request for ⟨Don't be afraid to *ask for* help if you need it.⟩

syn call (for), desire, plead (for), quest, request, seek, solicit, sue (for)

rel apply (for), beg (for), claim, clamor (for), importune, urge, wish (for); demand, enjoin, exact, insist (on), petition (for), press (for), require, requisition; invite

2 to act so as to make (something) more likely — see COURT 1

3 to give a request or demand for — see ORDER 2

askance *also* **askant** *adv* with distrust ⟨We looked *askance* at the dealer's assertion that the car had never been in an accident.⟩

syn distrustfully, doubtfully, doubtingly, dubiously, mistrustfully, sideways, skeptically, suspiciously

rel hesitantly, hesitatingly, incredulously, questioningly, quizzically, unbelievingly; guardedly, warily; captiously, critically, cynically, deprecatingly, disapprovingly, disparagingly, negatively, reproachfully, reprovingly, unfavorably; anxiously, apprehensively, uncomfortably, uneasily

phrases with a grain of salt

near ant favorably; confidently, sanguinely; credulously, uncritically, unquestioningly

ant trustfully, trustingly

askew *adj* inclined or twisted to one side — see AWRY

aslant *adj* inclined or twisted to one side — see AWRY

asleep *adj* 1 being in a state of suspended consciousness ⟨I was sound *asleep* when the phone rang.⟩

syn dormant, dozing, napping, resting, sleeping, slumbering

rel drowsy, nodding, sleepy, slumberous (*or* slumbrous), somnolent; dreaming, reposing; hypnotized, mesmerized; semiconscious; sleepwalking, somnambulant

phrases at rest

near ant aware, conscious, sleepless; aroused, astir, awakened, roused, up, wakened; reawakened, revived

ant awake, sleepless, wakeful, wide-awake

2 lacking in sensation or feeling — see NUMB 1

aspect *n* 1 a certain way in which something appears or may be regarded ⟨Depending on what *aspect* of college life you consider most important, there are several colleges which might be good for you.⟩

syn angle, facet, hand, phase, side

rel air, appearance, character, color, complexion, condition, face, look, semblance, shape, state, visage; period, stage, step; outlook, perspective, position, posture, shoes, slant, stance, standpoint, view, viewpoint; interpretation, reading, translation; article, case, component, count, detail, dimension, element, factor, instance, item, matter, part, particular, point, regard, respect

2 the outward form of someone or something especially as indicative of a quality — see APPEARANCE 1

3 the state or fact of facing a particular direction — see EXPOSURE 2

asperity *n* 1 a harsh or sharp quality — see EDGE 1

2 biting sharpness of feeling or expression — see ACRIMONY 1

3 something that is a cause for suffering or special effort especially in the attainment of a goal — see DIFFICULTY 1

asperse *vb* to make untrue and harmful statements about — see SLANDER

aspersing *n* the making of false statements that damage another's reputation — see SLANDER

aspirant *n* one who seeks an office, honor, position, or award — see CANDIDATE

aspiration *n* 1 eager desire for personal advancement — see AMBITION 1

2 something that one hopes or intends to accomplish — see GOAL

aspire *vb* 1 to have in mind as a purpose or goal — see INTEND 1

2 to move or extend upward — see ASCEND

aspiring *adj* having a strong desire for personal advancement — see AMBITIOUS 1

ass *n* a sturdy and patient domestic mammal that is used especially to carry things — see DONKEY 1

assail *vb* 1 to criticize harshly and usually publicly — see ATTACK 2

2 to take sudden, violent action against — see ATTACK 1

assassin *n* a person who kills another person ⟨shot down by an unknown *assassin*⟩

syn cutthroat, homicide, killer, murderer

rel bravo, hit man, triggerman; butcher, executioner, massacrer, slaughterer, slayer; murderess

assault *n* the act or action of setting upon with force or violence — see ATTACK 1

assault *vb* to take sudden, violent action against — see ATTACK 1

assay *n* the separation and identification of the parts of a whole — see ANALYSIS 1

assay *vb* 1 to identify and examine the basic elements or parts of (something) especially for discovering interrelationships — see ANALYZE

2 to make an effort to do — see ATTEMPT

assemblage *n* 1 a body of people come together in one place — see GATHERING 1

2 a mass or quantity that has piled up or that has been gathered over a period of time — see ACCUMULATION 1

3 a number of things considered as a unit — see GROUP 1

4 an organized group of objects acquired and maintained for study, exhibition, or personal pleasure — see COLLECTION 1

assemble *vb* 1 to come together into one body or place ⟨The graduates were told to *assemble* in the cafeteria an hour before the ceremony.⟩

syn cluster, collect, concentrate, conglomerate, congregate, convene, converge, forgather (*or* foregather), gather, meet, rendezvous

rel affiliate, ally, associate, band (together), caucus, club, collaborate, confederate, conjoin, consolidate, consort, cooperate, couple, federate, gang up, join, merge, unite; reassemble, reconvene, regather, remeet

phrases get together

near ant depart, leave, take off; disjoin, dissociate, disunite

ant break up, disband, disperse, split (up)

2 to form by putting together parts or materials — see BUILD

3 to bring together in assembly by or as if by command — see CONVOKE

4 to bring together in one body or place — see GATHER 1

assembly *n* **1** a body of people come together in one place — see GATHERING 1

2 a body of persons gathered for religious worship — see CONGREGATION 1

3 a coming together of a number of persons for a specified purpose — see MEETING 1

assent *vb* to give or express one's approval (as to a proposal) — see ACCEDE

assert *vb* **1** to state clearly and strongly ⟨a superpatriot who is never afraid to *assert* her allegiance to flag and country⟩

syn affirm, aver, avouch, avow, declare, guarantee, lay down, profess

rel advance, advertise, boost, plug, promote, publicize; announce, blaze, call, proclaim, pronounce, say; accent, accentuate, emphasize, stress, underline, underscore; advocate, champion, defend, espouse, support, uphold; assure, convince, persuade; explain, justify, rationalize; reaffirm, reassert

near ant minimize, understate; disregard, ignore, neglect, overlook

2 to state (something) as a reason in support of or against something under consideration — see ARGUE 1

3 to state as a fact usually forcefully — see CLAIM 1

assertion *n* **1** a solemn and often public declaration of the truth or existence of something — see PROTESTATION

2 an idea or opinion that is put forth in a discussion or debate — see CONTENTION 1

assertive *adj* **1** having or showing a bold forcefulness in the pursuit of a goal — see AGGRESSIVE 1

2 marked by or uttered with forcefulness — see EMPHATIC 1

assertiveness *n* the quality or state of being forceful (as in expression) — see VEHEMENCE 1

assess *vb* **1** to establish or apply as a charge or penalty — see IMPOSE

2 to make an approximate or tentative judgment regarding — see ESTIMATE 1

assessment *n* **1** a charge usually of money collected by the government from people or businesses for public use — see TAX

2 an opinion on the nature, character, or quality of something — see ESTIMATION 1

3 the act of placing a value on the nature, character, or quality of something — see ESTIMATE 1

assiduity *n* attentive and persistent effort — see DILIGENCE

assiduous *adj* involved in often constant activity — see BUSY 1

---

assiduously *adv* with great effort or determination — see HARD 1

assiduousness *n* attentive and persistent effort — see DILIGENCE

assign *vb* **1** to give a task, duty, or responsibility to — see ENTRUST 1

2 to give as a share or portion — see ALLOT

3 to give over the legal possession or ownership of — see TRANSFER 1

4 to pick (someone) by one's authority for a specific position or duty — see APPOINT 2

assignment *n* **1** a piece of work that needs to be done regularly — see CHORE 1

2 a specific task with which a person or group is charged — see MISSION

3 something assigned to be read or studied — see LESSON

4 the state or fact of being chosen for a position or duty — see APPOINTMENT 1

assimilate *vb* **1** to describe as similar — see COMPARE 1

2 to have a clear idea of — see COMPREHEND 1

3 to make a part of a body or system — see EMBODY 1

assist *n* an act or instance of helping — see HELP 1

assist *vb* to provide (someone) with what is useful or necessary to achieve an end — see HELP 1

assistance *n* an act or instance of helping — see HELP 1

assistant *n* a person who helps a more skilled person — see HELPER

associate *n* **1** a person frequently seen in the company of another ⟨A number of his *associates* were members of organized crime, so he was a person of interest to the FBI.⟩

syn cohort, companion, compatriot, comrade, crony, fellow, hobnobber, mate

rel colleague, coworker, equal, peer, workmate; accomplice, affiliate, ally, collaborator, confederate, half, partner; buddy, chum, confidant, familiar, friend, hearty, intimate, pal; countryman; classmate, housemate, messmate, playfellow, playmate, roommate (*also* roomie), schoolmate, shipmate, teammate; attendant, escort; hanger-on, leech, parasite

2 a fellow worker — see COLLEAGUE

associate *vb* to come or be together as friends ⟨a couple who joined the nature club in order to *associate* with like-minded people⟩

syn chum, company, consort, fraternize, hobnob, pal (around), run, sort, travel

rel affiliate, ally, attach, band, bond, club, collaborate, confederate, conjoin, connect, cooperate, couple, gang, get along, get on, group, interrelate, join, knot, league, link, mingle, mix, rally, relate, side, socialize, team, tie, wed; befriend, friend

phrases be friends with, fall in with, keep company (with), rub elbows (with) *or* rub shoulders (with), take up with

near ant avoid, cold-shoulder, shun, snub; alienate, estrange; break up, disband, disperse, split (up); disjoin, dissociate, disunite, divorce, sever, split, sunder

---

2 to think of (something) in combination ⟨She still *associates* that place with the carefree days of her youth.⟩

syn connect, correlate, identify, link, relate

rel compare, equate, liken; group, join, lump (together), tie (together)

near ant contrast, differentiate, discriminate, distinguish, separate, set off

3 to come together to form a single unit — see UNITE 1

4 to form or enter into an association that furthers the interests of its members — see ALLY

5 to take part in social activities — see SOCIALIZE

association *n* **1** the state of having shared interests or efforts (as in social or business matters) ⟨The public television station is producing the series in *association* with a foundation for the arts.⟩

syn affiliation, alliance, collaboration, confederation, connection, cooperation, hookup, liaison, linkup, partnership, relation, relationship, tie-up, union

rel business, dealings, interaction; exchange, interconnection, interrelation, mutualism, reciprocity, symbiosis; integration, unification; affinity, attachment, closeness, intimacy, rapport, sympathy; kinship, oneness, solidarity, togetherness, unity; companionship, company, fellowship; bed, cahoots, league

near ant breakup, dissolution, disunion; division, parting, separation, severance, split; alienation, divorce, estrangement

ant disaffiliation, dissociation

2 a group of persons formally joined together for some common interest ⟨All *associations* meeting on town property must be registered with and approved by the registrar's office.⟩

syn board, brotherhood, chamber, club, college, congress, council, fellowship, fraternity, guild (*also* gild), institute, institution, league, order, organization, society, sodality

rel collective, commune, community, cooperative; alliance, bloc, camp, coalition, partnership; body, cadre, group; circle, clan, clique, coterie, junta, lot, set; crew, outfit, party, squad, team; branch, chapter, local; faithful, fold, membership; sisterhood, sorority; cabal, confederacy, conspiracy; band, gang, ring; cartel, combine, syndicate

3 the fact or state of having something in common — see CONNECTION 1

assort *vb* **1** to arrange or assign according to type — see CLASSIFY 1

2 to form a pleasing relationship — see HARMONIZE 1

assorted *adj* consisting of many things of different sorts — see MISCELLANEOUS

assortment *n* **1** an unorganized collection or mixture of various things — see MISCELLANY 1

2 the quality or state of being composed of many different elements or types — see VARIETY 1

assuage *vb* **1** to make more bearable or less severe — see HELP 2

2 to put a complete end to (a physical need or desire) — see SATISFY 1

3 to lessen the anger or agitation of — see PACIFY 1

assume *vb* **1** to take to or upon oneself ⟨We promised to *assume* responsibility for any damage to the flower beds caused by the volleyball game in the backyard.⟩

syn accept, bear, shoulder, take over, undertake

rel adopt, embrace, take up; advocate, back, champion, endorse (*also* indorse), espouse, stand by, support, uphold; accede, acquiesce, agree, assent, consent; reaccept, reassume

near ant abjure, recant, renounce, retract, take back, unsay, withdraw; decline, refuse, reject, spurn, turn down; abstain (from), forbear, refrain (from); avoid, bypass, detour; abandon, forsake, give up, relinquish, surrender; back down, back off, backtrack

ant disavow, disclaim, disown, repudiate

2 to take as true or as a fact without actual proof ⟨Everyone *assumed*, wrongly, that someone else was bringing dessert.⟩

syn postulate, premise, presume, presuppose, say, suppose

rel accept, believe, credit, swallow; conclude, deduce, gather, infer, judge, take; conjecture, figure, guess, surmise, suspect, think; conceive, dream, fancy, imagine, perceive, preconceive; speculate, theorize; affirm, allege, assert, aver, avouch, avow, claim, contend, declare, insist, maintain, profess

phrases take for granted

near ant challenge, disagree (with), disbelieve, discount, discredit, dispute, distrust, doubt, mistrust, question, wonder (about); deny, disavow, disclaim, disown, reject, repudiate; belie, confute, disprove, rebut, refute

3 to form an opinion from little or no evidence — see GUESS 1

4 to present a false appearance of — see FEIGN

5 to provide with a paying job — see EMPLOY 1

assumed *adj* **1** appearing to be true on the basis of evidence that may or may not be confirmed — see APPARENT 1

2 lacking in natural or spontaneous quality — see ARTIFICIAL 1

assumption *n* **1** something taken as being true or factual and used as a starting point for a course of action or reasoning ⟨Your argument is faulty because it's based on erroneous *assumptions*.⟩

syn given, postulate, premise (*also* premiss), presumption, presupposition, supposition

rel hypothesis, proposition, theory, thesis; axiom, truism, verity; belief, canon, doctrine, dogma, gospel, law; precept, principle, rule, standard, tenet; basis, foundation, ground; conclusion, deduction, inference; affirmation, assertion, avouchment, declaration

2 an exaggerated sense of one's importance that shows itself in the making of excessive or unjustified claims — see ARROGANCE

assurance *n* **1** a state of mind in which one is free from doubt — see CONFIDENCE 2

2 great faith in oneself or one's abilities — see CONFIDENCE 1

assure *vb* **1** to ease the grief or distress of — see COMFORT

2 to make sure, certain, or safe — see ENSURE

assured *adj* **1** having or showing a mind free from doubt — see CERTAIN 2

2 having or showing great faith in oneself or one's abilities — see CONFIDENT 1

3 having too high an opinion of oneself — see CONCEITED

assuredly *adv* without any question — see INDEED 1

assuredness *n* a state of mind in which one is free from doubt — see CONFIDENCE 2

astern *adv* near, toward, or in the stern of a ship or the tail of an aircraft — see AFT

as though *conj* the way it would be or one would do if — see AS IF

astir *adj* marked by much life, movement, or activity — see ALIVE 2

astonish *vb* to make a strong impression on (someone) with something unexpected — see SURPRISE 1

astonished *adj* **1** affected with sudden and great wonder or surprise — see THUNDERSTRUCK

2 filled with amazement or wonder — see OPENMOUTHED

astonishing *adj* **1** causing a strong emotional reaction because of unexpectedness — see SURPRISING 1

2 causing wonder or astonishment — see MARVELOUS 1

astonishment *n* **1** the rapt attention and deep emotion caused by the sight of something extraordinary — see WONDER 2

2 the state of being strongly impressed by something unexpected or unusual — see SURPRISE 2

astound *vb* to make a strong impression on (someone) with something unexpected — see SURPRISE 1

astounded *adj* **1** affected with sudden and great wonder or surprise — see THUNDERSTRUCK

2 filled with amazement or wonder — see OPENMOUTHED

astounding *adj* **1** causing a strong emotional reaction because of unexpectedness — see SURPRISING 1

2 causing wonder or astonishment — see MARVELOUS 1

astral *adj* **1** of or relating to the stars — see STELLAR 1

2 standing above others in rank, importance, or achievement — see EMINENT

astray *adv* off the desired or intended path or course — see WRONG

astronomical *also* **astronomic** *adj* unusually large — see HUGE

astronomically *adv* to a large extent or degree — see GREATLY 2

astute *adj* having or showing a practical cleverness or judgment — see SHREWD 1

astuteness *n* exceptional discernment and judgment especially in practical matters — see ACUMEN

asunder *adv* into parts or pieces — see APART

as well as *prep* in addition to — see BESIDES 1

asylum *n* **1** a place where mentally ill people are cared for — see INSTITUTION 2

2 something (as a building) that offers cover from the weather or protection from danger — see SHELTER

at all *adv* in any way or respect ⟨wasn't *at all* pleased with the way the family portrait came out⟩

syn anywise, ever, half

rel somehow, someway (*also* someways); remotely

athirst *adj* showing urgent desire or interest — see EAGER

athwart *adv* **1** from one side to the other of an intervening space — see OVER 1

2 in a line or direction running from corner to corner — see CROSSWISE

athwart *prep* to the opposite side of — see ACROSS 1

atmosphere *n* **1** a special quality or impression associated with something — see AURA 1

2 the circumstances, conditions, or objects by which one is surrounded — see ENVIRONMENT

atom *n* a very small piece — see BIT 1

atomic *adj* very small in size — see TINY

atomize *vb* to reduce to fine particles — see POWDER

atone (for) *vb* to make up for (an offense) — see EXPIATE

atrocious *adj* **1** extremely disturbing or repellent — see HORRIBLE 1

2 extremely unsatisfactory — see WRETCHED 1

3 having or showing the desire to inflict severe pain and suffering on others — see CRUEL 1

atrociousness *n* **1** the quality of inspiring intense dread or dismay — see HORROR 1

2 the state or quality of being utterly evil — see ENORMITY 1

3 disposition to willfully inflict pain and suffering on others — see CRUELTY

atrocity *n* **1** the quality of inspiring intense dread or dismay — see HORROR 1

2 the state or quality of being utterly evil — see ENORMITY 1

3 disposition to willfully inflict pain and suffering on others — see CRUELTY

attach *vb* **1** to cause (something) to hold to another — see FASTEN 1

2 to pick (someone) by one's authority for a specific position or duty — see APPOINT 2

3 to take ownership or control of (something) by right of one's authority — see CONFISCATE

attached *adj* having a liking or affection — see FOND 1

attachment *n* **1** a feeling of strong or constant regard for and dedication to someone — see LOVE 1

2 something that is not necessary in itself but adds to the convenience or performance of the main piece of equipment — see ACCESSORY 1

3 adherence to something to which one is bound by a pledge or duty — see FIDELITY

---

syn synonym(s)   *rel* related words
ant antonym(s)   *near ant* near antonym(s)

attack *n* **1** the act or action of setting upon with force or violence ⟨The USS Constitution was nicknamed "Old Ironsides" after its oaken hull successfully withstood a British *attack*.⟩

syn aggression, assault, attempt, blitz, blitzkrieg, charge, descent, offense (*or* offence), offensive, onset, onslaught, raid, rush, strike

rel ambush; counteraggression, counterattack, counteroffensive; sally, sortie; envelopment, flanking; breakthrough, foray, incursion, invasion; pillage, ravage, sack; air raid, bombardment, bombing; siege, storm; barrage, cannonade, fusillade, hail, salvo, volley

near ant defense, defensive, guard, shield; opposition, resistance; protection, security, shelter

2 a sudden experiencing of a physical or mental disorder ⟨Malaria is characterized by periodic *attacks* of chills and fever.⟩

syn access, bout, case, fit, seizure, siege, spell, turn

rel recurrence, relapse; brainstorm, convulsion, pang, paroxysm, spasm, throe; agitation, frenzy; breakdown, collapse, prostration

near ant arrest, relief, remission

attack *vb* **1** to take sudden, violent action against ⟨Our dog unexpectedly *attacked* the mailman.⟩

syn assail, assault, beset, charge, descend (on *or* upon), jump (on), pounce (on *or* upon), raid, rush, storm, strike

rel bum-rush, gang up (on), mob, swarm; mug, rob; ambush, surprise (*also* surprize); waylay; blitz, bomb, bombard; barrage, cannon, cannonade; bang away (at), batter, buffet, plaster; beleaguer, besiege, press; harry, loot, pillage, plunder, ravage, sack; foray, invade, overrun; envelop, flank

phrases beat up on, fly at, go at, light into, pitch into, round on, set at, set upon, tear into

near ant cover, defend, guard, protect, secure, shield

2 to criticize harshly and usually publicly ⟨The mayor and all his aides were *attacked* mercilessly in the press when the scandal erupted.⟩

syn abuse, assail, bash, belabor, blast, castigate, excoriate, jump (on), lambaste (*or* lambast), savage, scathe, slam, vituperate

rel berate, harangue, harry, revile, scold, whip; blaspheme, curse, execrate, imprecate; profane; affront, insult, slur; asperse, bad-mouth, belittle, blackguard, disparage, put down; libel, slander, traduce, vilify; chastise, chide, criticize, lace (into), rebuke, reprimand, reproof; fulminate, lash (out)

phrases beat up on, light into, sail into, tie into

near ant acclaim, commend, compliment, hail, laud, praise

3 to start work on energetically ⟨Courtney *attacked* the huge mess in her room with determination and enthusiasm.⟩

syn tackle

rel address, approach, face; buckle (down to), concentrate (on), focus (on), knuckle down (to), zero (in on); pitch in, plunge (in), settle (down); pursue, take up, undertake

phrases go at, have at, light into, pitch into, sail into, tear into

near ant avoid, evade, shun; dally, dawdle, dillydally, fiddle (around), fool, idle, lag, mess, monkey (around), play, poke, potter (around), putter (around), trifle

attain *vb* **1** to obtain (as a goal) through effort — see ACHIEVE 1

2 to receive as return for effort — see EARN 1

attainable *adj* **1** capable of being done or carried out — see POSSIBLE 1

2 possible to get — see AVAILABLE 1

attainment *n* **1** a successful result brought about by hard work — see ACCOMPLISHMENT 1

2 the state of being actual or complete — see FRUITION

attempt *n* **1** an effort to do or accomplish something ⟨It took several *attempts* before we made good ice cream with an old-fashioned hand-cranked ice cream freezer.⟩

syn bid, crack, endeavor, essay, fling, go, offer, pass, shot, stab, trial, try, whack, whirl

rel striving, struggle, throes, undertaking; trial and error

2 the act or action of setting upon with force or violence — see ATTACK 1

attempt *vb* to make an effort to do ⟨After *attempting*—and failing—to start the lawn mower on my own, I finally succeeded with a neighbor's help.⟩ ⟨Don't even *attempt* walking on your broken foot.⟩

syn assay, endeavor, essay, seek, strive, try

rel fight, strain, struggle, toil, trouble, work; aim, aspire, hope; assume, take up, undertake

phrases have a go at, shoot at (*or* shoot for), try one's hand (at)

near ant drop, give up, quit

attend *vb* **1** to go along with in order to provide assistance, protection, or companionship — see ACCOMPANY 1

2 to pay attention especially through the act of hearing — see LISTEN

3 to take charge of especially on behalf of another — see ²TEND 1

4 to occur or exist at the same time — see COINCIDE 1

attendant *adj* **1** coming as a result — see RESULTANT

2 present at the same time and place — see COINCIDENT 1

attendant *n* **1** one that accompanies another for protection, guidance, or as a courtesy — see ESCORT

2 something that is found along with something else — see ACCOMPANIMENT

attending *adj* **1** being within the confines of a specified place — see PRESENT 2

2 present at the same time and place — see COINCIDENT 1

attention *n* **1** a focusing of the mind on something ⟨I need your full *attention* right now.⟩

syn absorption, concentration, engrossment, enthrallment, immersion

rel fixation, obsession, preoccupation;

alertness, application, awareness, consideration, heedfulness, intentness, raptness, regard; contemplation, meditation, pondering, rumination

near ant absence, absentmindedness, abstractedness, detachment, distraction, obliviousness, remoteness, unawareness, unconsciousness, withdrawal; indifference, mindlessness, unconcern; befuddlement, bewilderment, confusion

ant inattention

2 a state of being aware ⟨Several parents brought to the committee's *attention* the deteriorating condition of the playground.⟩

syn awareness, cognizance, ear, eye, heed, knowledge, note, notice, observance, observation

rel hyperawareness, hyperconsciousness; advisement, care, concern, consideration, regard, watch; apprehension, discernment, grasp, mind, perception, recognition, thought, understanding

near ant disregard, neglect, obliviousness, unawareness

3 an act or utterance that is a customary show of good manners — see CIVILITY 1

attentive *adj* **1** having the mind fixed on something ⟨Susan became particularly *attentive* when the sportscaster turned to women's tennis, her favorite sport.⟩

syn absorbed, deep, engrossed, enthralled, focused (*also* focussed), immersed, intent, observant, rapt

rel engaged, interested, intrigued, involved; hypnotized, mesmerized; alert, alive, conscious, open-eyed, watchful, wide-awake

phrases all ears

near ant daydreaming, dreamy, faraway, foggy, hazy, lost, oblivious, preoccupied, remote; apathetic, disinterested, uninterested

ant absent, absentminded, abstracted, distracted, inattentive, inobservant, unabsorbed, unfocused (*also* unfocussed)

2 given to or made with heedful anticipation of the needs and happiness of others — see THOUGHTFUL 1

3 paying close attention usually for the purpose of anticipating approaching danger or opportunity — see ALERT 1

attentiveness *n* the state of being constantly attentive and responsive to signs of opportunity, activity, or danger — see VIGILANCE

attest *vb* **1** to declare (something) to be true or genuine — see CERTIFY 1

2 to make a solemn declaration under oath for the purpose of establishing a fact — see TESTIFY

3 to give evidence or testimony to the truth or factualness of — see CONFIRM 1

attestation *n* something presented in support of the truth or accuracy of a claim — see PROOF

attire *n* covering for the human body — see CLOTHING

attire *vb* to outfit with clothes and especially fine or special clothes — see CLOTHE 1

attorney *n* **1** a person who acts or does business for another — see AGENT 2

2 a person whose profession is to conduct lawsuits for clients or to advise about legal rights and obligations — see LAWYER

attraction *n* something that attracts interest — see MAGNET

attractive *adj* **1** having an often mysterious or magical power to attract — see FASCINATING 1

2 very pleasing to look at — see BEAUTIFUL 1

attractiveness *n* **1** the power of irresistible attraction — see CHARM 2

2 the qualities in a person or thing that as a whole give pleasure to the senses — see BEAUTY 1

attribute *n* something that sets apart an individual from others of the same kind — see CHARACTERISTIC

attribute *vb* **1** to explain (something) as being the result of something else — see CREDIT 1

2 to give the reason for or cause of — see EXPLAIN 2

attrition *n* a gradual weakening, loss, or destruction — see CORROSION

atypical *adj* **1** being out of the ordinary — see EXCEPTIONAL 1

2 departing from some accepted standard of what is normal — see DEVIANT

audacious *adj* **1** displaying or marked by rude boldness — see NERVY 1

2 foolishly adventurous or bold — see FOOLHARDY 1

3 inclined or willing to take risks — see BOLD 1

audacity *n* shameless boldness — see EFFRONTERY

audibly *adv* with one's normal voice speaking the words — see ALOUD

audit *n* a close look at or over someone or something in order to judge condition — see INSPECTION

audit *vb* to look over closely (as for judging quality or condition) — see INSPECT

auditorium *n* a large room or building for enclosed public gatherings — see HALL 3

auditory *adj* of, relating to, or experienced through the sense of hearing ⟨I have a bad *auditory* memory—unless I see a word in writing, and not just hear it, I forget it easily.⟩

syn acoustic (*or* acoustical), aural, auricular

rel audiovisual; audible, clear, discernible (*also* discernable), distinct, distinguishable, heard, perceptible

near ant faint, feeble, imperceptible, inaudible, indistinct, indistinguishable; low, noiseless, quiet, silent, soft, soundless

ant nonauditory

aught *n* the numerical symbol 0 or the absence of number or quantity represented by it — see ZERO 1

augment *vb* to make greater in size, amount, or number — see INCREASE 1

augmentation *n* something added (as by growth) — see INCREASE 1

augur *n* one who predicts future events or developments — see PROPHET 1

augur *vb* **1** to show signs of a favorable or successful outcome — see BODE

---

syn synonym(s)   *rel* related words
ant antonym(s)   *near ant* near antonym(s)

2 to tell of or describe beforehand — see FORETELL

auguring *n* a declaration that something will happen in the future — see PREDICTION

augury *n* **1** a declaration that something will happen in the future — see PREDICTION

2 something believed to be a sign or warning of a future event — see OMEN

august *adj* **1** having or showing a formal and serious or reserved manner — see DIGNIFIED

2 large and impressive in size, grandeur, extent, or conception — see GRAND 1

augustness *n* **1** a dignified bearing or appearance befitting someone of royal status — see MAJESTY 1

2 impressiveness of beauty on a large scale — see MAGNIFICENCE

auld lang syne *n* the events or experience of former times — see PAST

aura *n* **1** a special quality or impression associated with something ⟨The monastery perched high on a mountaintop had an *aura* of unreality and mystery about it.⟩

syn air, aroma, atmosphere, climate, flavor, mood, note, odor, smell, temper, vibration(s)

rel mystique, romance; feel, feeling, sensation, sense, spirit; attribute, character, characteristic, image, mark, notion, peculiarity, picture, property, trait; color, illusion, overtone, semblance, suggestion, tone

2 a spiritual force that is held to emanate from or give animation to living beings — see ENERGY 1

aural *adj* of, relating to, or experienced through the sense of hearing — see AUDITORY

au revoir *n* an expression of good wishes at parting — see GOOD-BYE

auricular *adj* of, relating to, or experienced through the sense of hearing — see AUDITORY

auspice *n* **1** **auspices** *pl* the financial support and general guidance for an undertaking ⟨a program for innovators that is under the *auspices* of a national corporation⟩

syn aegis (*also* egis), backing

rel bankrolling, endowment, financing, funding, subsidy; encouragement, fosterage; aid, assistance, help

2 something believed to be a sign or warning of a future event — see OMEN

auspicious *adj* **1** having qualities which inspire hope — see HOPEFUL 1

2 pointing toward a happy outcome — see FAVORABLE 2

austere *adj* **1** given to exacting standards of discipline and self-restraint — see SEVERE 1

2 harsh and threatening in manner or appearance — see GRIM 1

authentic *adj* **1** being exactly as appears or as claimed ⟨The signature on the old document was determined to be *authentic*.⟩

syn bona fide, genuine, honest, real, right, true

rel actual, historical, original; lawful, legal, legitimate; identifiable, recognizable, verifiable; proven, validated, verified; incontestable, incontrovertible, indisputable, indubitable, irrefutable, undeniable, undoubted, unmistakable, unquestionable; veritable, very; accurate, correct, proper; pure, unadulterated, unalloyed

phrases for real

near ant artificial, factitious, imitation, man-made, simulated, synthetic, unnatural; concocted, fabricated, manufactured; deceptive, delusive, delusory, misleading

ant bogus, counterfeit, fake, false, mock, phony (*also* phoney), pseudo, sham, spurious, supposititious, suppositious, unauthentic, unreal

2 following an original exactly — see FAITHFUL 2

authentically *adv* in actual fact — see VERY 2

authenticate *vb* **1** to declare (something) to be true or genuine — see CERTIFY 1

2 to give evidence or testimony to the truth or factualness of — see CONFIRM 1

author *n* **1** a person who creates a written work ⟨a brilliant novel by a first-time *author*⟩

syn pen, penman, scribe, writer

rel auteur, belletrist (*also* belle-lettrist), wordsmith; coauthor, coscenarist, cowriter; ghostwriter, hack, hatchet man, scribbler, wordmonger; biographer, hagiographer; autobiographer, memoirist, memorialist; fabulist, fictioneer, fictionist, novelist, romancer, storyteller; essayist, pamphleteer, satirist; dramatist, playwright, scenarist, screenwriter, scriptwriter; bard, poet, rhymer, versifier; blogger, columnist, journalist, newspaperman, reporter, sportswriter

ant nonauthor

2 a person who establishes a whole new field of endeavor — see FATHER 2

3 *cap* the being worshipped as the creator and ruler of the universe — see DEITY 2

author *vb* to compose and set down on paper the words of — see WRITE 1

authoritarian *adj* **1** fond of ordering people around — see BOSSY

2 given to exacting standards of discipline and self-restraint — see SEVERE 1

authoritative *adj* **1** being the most accurate and apparently thorough — see DEFINITIVE 1

2 having power over the minds or behavior of others — see INFLUENTIAL 1

3 fond of ordering people around — see BOSSY

authority *n* **1** a person with a high level of knowledge or skill in a field — see EXPERT

2 lawful control over the affairs of a political unit (as a nation) — see RULE 2

3 the power to direct the thinking or behavior of others usually indirectly — see INFLUENCE 1

4 the right or means to command or control others — see POWER 1

5 something (as a belief) that serves as the basis for another thing — see REASON 2

6 something mentioned in a text as providing related and especially supporting information — see REFERENCE 1

7 the capacity to persuade — see COGEN-CY 1

authorization *n* 1 the approval by someone in authority for the doing of something — see PERMISSION

2 the granting of power to perform various acts or duties — see COMMISSION 1

3 the right to act or move freely — see FREEDOM 2

authorize *vb* 1 to give official or legal power to ⟨Only the school nurse is *authorized* to give any necessary shots.⟩

syn accredit, certify, commission, empower, enable, invest, license (*also* licence), qualify, vest, warrant

rel approve, clear, credential, endorse (*also* indorse), OK (*or* okay), sanction; affirm, confirm, validate; inaugurate, induct, initiate, install, instate, swear in; allow, let, permit; enfranchise, entitle, privilege

near ant ban, bar, block, constrain, deny, disallow, disbar, discourage, disenfranchise, disfranchise, exclude, hinder, hold back, impede, inhibit, obstruct, prevent, shut out, stop; enjoin, forbid, interdict, outlaw, prohibit, proscribe, veto

ant disqualify

2 to give a right to — see ENTITLE 1

3 to give official acceptance of as satisfactory — see APPROVE

authorized *adj* ordered or allowed by those in authority — see OFFICIAL

auto *n* a self-propelled passenger vehicle on four wheels — see CAR

autocracy *n* a system of government in which the ruler has unlimited power — see DESPOTISM

autocrat *n* one who rules over a people with a sole, supreme, and usually hereditary authority — see MONARCH 1

autocratic *also* **autocratical** *adj* 1 exercising power or authority without interference by others — see ABSOLUTE 1

2 fond of ordering people around — see BOSSY

autograph *vb* to write one's name on (as a document) — see SIGN

automated *adj* designed to replace or decrease human labor and especially physical labor — see LABORSAVING

automatic *adj* 1 done instantly and without conscious thought or decision ⟨Carl's *automatic* use of the brakes narrowly averted a collision.⟩

syn instinctive, instinctual, involuntary, mechanical, robotic, spontaneous

rel conditioned, natural, Pavlovian, reactive, reflex, simple, subliminal, unconscious, unforced, visceral; blind, inadvertent, unintended, unintentional, unwilling, unwitting; abrupt, quick, ready, sudden; ad-lib, extemporaneous, extempore, impromptu, improvised, offhand, offhanded, snap, spur-of-the-moment, unconsidered, unplanned, unpremeditated, unprepared, unprompted, unreasoned, unrehearsed, unstudied; casual, chance, chancy, haphazard, hasty, hit-or-miss, impetuous, impulsive, mindless, random, rash

near ant calculated, conscious, cultivated, deliberate, designed, intended, intentional, predetermined, prepared, projected, refined, rehearsed, volitional, voluntary, willful (*or* wilful); advised, aforethought, careful, considered, foresighted, forethoughtful, measured, meticulous, reasoned, studied, thoughtful

ant nonmechanical

2 designed to replace or decrease human labor and especially physical labor — see LABORSAVING

automobile *n* a self-propelled passenger vehicle on four wheels — see CAR

automobile *vb* to travel by a motorized vehicle — see DRIVE 2

automobilist *n* a person who travels by automobile — see MOTORIST

autonomous *adj* not being under the rule or control of another — see FREE 1

autonomy *n* 1 the act or power of making one's own choices or decisions — see FREE WILL

2 the state of being free from the control or power of another — see FREEDOM 1

autopsy *n* examination of a dead body especially to find out the cause of death ⟨The *autopsy* revealed an advanced stage of cancer.⟩

syn postmortem, postmortem examination

rel dissection

near ant biopsy, vivisection

auxiliary *adj* available to supply something extra when needed ⟨The auditorium has an *auxiliary* cooling system used only on particularly sweltering days.⟩

syn accessory, peripheral, supplemental, supplementary

rel backup, makeshift, substitute; added, additional, another, further; complementary, contributory; adjuvant, assistant, assisting, helping, supportive; secondary, subordinate, subservient, subsidiary; dispensable, excess, nonessential, superfluous, surplus, unessential

near ant basic, fundamental, primary, prime; all-important, essential, imperative, indispensable, integral, necessary, needed, needful, required, requisite, vital

ant chief, main, principal

avail *n* the capacity for being useful for some purpose — see USE 2

avail *vb* to provide with something useful or desirable — see BENEFIT

available *adj* 1 possible to get ⟨The nursery's orchids are *available* by mail order only.⟩ ⟨Fare information is readily *available* on the website.⟩

syn accessible, acquirable, attainable, obtainable, procurable

rel getatable, reachable; appropriable, purchasable, rentable; furnished, provided, supplied; common, omnipresent, prevalent, ubiquitous, universal, widespread; free, free-for-all, open, public, unrestricted

phrases at the ready, on hand, on file, on tap

near ant limited, off-limits, restricted; deficient, lacking, missing, rare, scarce, uncommon

ant inaccessible, unattainable, unavailable, unobtainable

---

syn synonym(s)   **rel** related words

ant antonym(s)   **near ant** near antonym(s)

2 capable of or suitable for being used for a particular purpose — see USABLE 1

avarice *n* an intense selfish desire for wealth or possessions — see GREED

avaricious *adj* having or marked by an eager and often selfish desire especially for material possessions — see GREEDY 1

avariciousness *n* an intense selfish desire for wealth or possessions — see GREED

avenge *vb* to punish in kind the wrongdoer responsible for ⟨a play about a prince who struggles to *avenge* his father's death⟩
syn redress, requite, retaliate, revenge
rel castigate, fix, get, penalize, punish, scourge; chasten, chastise, correct, discipline; right; compensate, pay (back), recompense, repay
phrases get even (for)
near ant absolve, condone, excuse, forgive, pardon, remit

avenger *n* one who inflicts punishment in return for an injury or offense — see NEMESIS 1

avenue *n* **1** a passage cleared for public vehicular travel — see WAY 1
2 an established course for traveling from one place to another — see PASSAGE 1

aver *vb* **1** to state as a fact usually forcefully — see CLAIM 1
2 to state clearly and strongly — see ASSERT 1

average *adj* **1** being about midway between extremes of amount or size — see MIDDLE 2
2 being of the type that is encountered in the normal course of events — see ORDINARY 1
3 having or showing the qualities associated with the members of a particular group or kind — see TYPICAL 1

average *n* what is typical of a group, class, or series ⟨My cat's a cut above the *average* when it comes to being a finicky eater.⟩
syn norm, normal, par, standard
rel golden mean, mean, median, middle; commonplace, ordinary, rule, run, status quo, usual; exemplar, representative
near ant abnormality, anomaly, rarity

averse *adj* having a natural dislike for something — see ANTIPATHETIC 1

averseness *n* a strong feeling of not liking or approving — see DISLIKE 1

aversion *n* **1** a dislike so strong as to cause stomach upset or queasiness — see DISGUST
2 a strong feeling of not liking or approving — see DISLIKE 1
3 something or someone that is hated — see HATE 2

avert *vb* to keep from happening by taking action in advance — see PREVENT

averting *n* the act or practice of keeping something from happening — see PREVENTION

aviator *n* one who flies or is qualified to fly an aircraft or spacecraft — see PILOT

avid *adj* **1** having or marked by an eager and often selfish desire especially for material possessions — see GREEDY 1
2 showing urgent desire or interest — see EAGER

avidity *n* **1** an intense selfish desire for wealth or possessions — see GREED

2 urgent desire or interest — see EAGERNESS

avoid *vb* **1** to get or keep away from (as a responsibility) through cleverness or trickery — see ESCAPE 2
2 to put an end to by formal action — see ABOLISH 1

avoidance *n* the act or a means of getting or keeping away from something undesirable — see ESCAPE 2

avoirdupois *n* the amount that something weighs — see WEIGHT 1

avouch *vb* **1** to declare (something) to be true or genuine — see CERTIFY 1
2 to state as a fact usually forcefully — see CLAIM 1
3 to state clearly and strongly — see ASSERT 1

avouchment *n* a solemn and often public declaration of the truth or existence of something — see PROTESTATION

avow *vb* **1** to state as a fact usually forcefully — see CLAIM 1
2 to state clearly and strongly — see ASSERT 1

avowal *n* **1** a solemn and often public declaration of the truth or existence of something — see PROTESTATION
2 an open declaration of something (as a fault or the commission of an offense) about oneself — see CONFESSION

await *vb* **1** to believe in the future occurrence of (something) — see EXPECT
2 to remain in place in readiness or expectation of something — see WAIT

awaited *adj* being in accordance with the prescribed, normal, or logical course of events — see DUE 2

awake *adj* **1** not sleeping or able to sleep — see WAKEFUL
2 paying close attention usually for the purpose of anticipating approaching danger or opportunity — see ALERT 1

awake *vb* **1** to cause to stop sleeping — see WAKE 1
2 to cease to be asleep — see WAKE 2

awaken *vb* **1** to cause to stop sleeping — see WAKE 1
2 to cease to be asleep — see WAKE 2

award *n* **1** something given in recognition of achievement ⟨Faye received the highest *award* in the 16 and under category for her poem.⟩
syn accolade, decoration, distinction, honor, plume, premium, prize
rel badge, crown, cup, laurel, medal, order, plaque, plate, ribbon; applause, bravo, encomium, eulogy, homage, paean, panegyric, plaudit, tribute; citation, commendation, compliment, honorable mention
2 a position arrived at after consideration — see DECISION 1

award *vb* **1** to give something as a token of gratitude or admiration for a service or achievement — see REWARD
2 to give the ownership or benefit of (something) formally or publicly — see CONFER 1

aware *adj* having specified facts or feelings actively impressed on the mind — see CONSCIOUS 1

awareness *n* a state of being aware — see ATTENTION 2

awash *adj* **1** containing, covered with, or thoroughly penetrated by water — see WET 1

2 possessing or covered with great numbers or amounts of something specified — see RIFE

away *adj* **1** not close in time or space — see DISTANT 1

2 not at a certain place — see ABSENT 1

away *adv* from this or that place ⟨Don't walk *away* while I'm still talking to you.⟩

syn down, hence, off, out

rel apart, elsewhere; abroad, afield, astray

awe *n* the rapt attention and deep emotion caused by the sight of something extraordinary — see WONDER 2

awed *adj* filled with amazement or wonder — see OPENMOUTHED

awesome *adj* **1** causing wonder or astonishment — see MARVELOUS 1

2 of the very best kind — see EXCELLENT

awestruck *also* **awestricken** *adj* **1** affected with sudden and great wonder or surprise — see THUNDERSTRUCK

2 filled with amazement or wonder — see OPENMOUTHED

awful *adj* **1** causing intense displeasure, disgust, or resentment — see OFFENSIVE 1

2 causing wonder or astonishment — see MARVELOUS 1

3 extremely disturbing or repellent — see HORRIBLE 1

4 extremely unsatisfactory — see WRETCHED 1

awful *adv* to a great degree — see VERY 1

awfully *adv* to a great degree — see VERY 1

awfulness *n* the quality of inspiring intense dread or dismay — see HORROR 1

awkward *adj* **1** lacking social grace and assurance ⟨preteens feeling *awkward* at their first formal dance⟩

syn clumsy, gauche, graceless, inelegant, rustic (*also* rustical), stiff, stilted, uncomfortable, uneasy, ungraceful, wooden

rel angular, gawky, lubberly, ungainly; boorish, clownish, uncouth; abashed, discomfited, discomforted, discomposed, disconcerted, discountenanced, embarrassed; self-conscious; agitated, chagrined, dismayed, disquieted, distressed, disturbed, fazed, flustered, jittery, jumpy, mortified, nervous, perturbed, rattled, unsettled, upset; diffident, insecure, meek, modest, self-doubting, timid, unassertive, unassuming, unpretentious

near ant assured, calm, collected, composed, confident, cool, placid, poised, secure, self-assured, self-confident, self-possessed, serene, tranquil, undisturbed, unperturbed

ant graceful, suave, urbane

2 showing or marked by a lack of skill and tact (as in dealing with a situation) ⟨The *awkward* handling of the seating arrange-

ments at the wedding reception resulted in many hurt feelings.⟩

syn botched, bungling, clumsy, fumbled, inept, inexpert, maladroit

rel amateur, amateurish, crude, green, incompetent, ineffectual, inefficient, inexperienced, unpolished, unprofessional, unskilled, unskillful; careless, sloppy, tacky, tactless; ill-advised, ineffective, ineffectual, misdirected, misguided

near ant able, accomplished, adept, capable, clever, competent, consummate, crackerjack, expert, masterful, masterly, polished, professional, proficient, skilled, skillful, talented; diplomatic, easy, effortless, gracious, smooth, tactful

ant adroit, deft, dexterous (*also* dextrous), facile

3 causing embarrassment ⟨the *awkward* situation of having to listen as your host and hostess quarrel loudly in the next room⟩

syn discomfiting, disconcerting, disturbing, embarrassing, flustering, uncomfortable

rel confusing, difficult, disagreeable, impossible, inconvenient, intolerable, troublesome, unpleasant, unwieldy; unsettling; debasing, degrading, demeaning, humbling, humiliating, mortifying

near ant agreeable, comfortable, convenient, pleasing

4 causing difficulty, discomfort, or annoyance — see INCONVENIENT 1

5 difficult to use or operate especially because of size, weight, or design — see CUMBERSOME

6 having or showing an inability to move in a graceful manner — see CLUMSY 2

7 lacking or showing a lack of nimbleness in using one's hands — see CLUMSY 1

awning *n* a raised covering over something for decoration or protection — see CANOPY

awry *adj* inclined or twisted to one side ⟨The shutters that still remained on the run-down old house were all *awry*.⟩

syn askew, aslant, cockeyed, crazy, crooked, listing, lopsided, oblique, pitched, skewed, slanted, slanting, slantwise, tilted, tipping, uneven

rel asymmetrical (*or* asymmetric), unbalanced, unsymmetrical; contorted, disordered, distorted, irregular

phrases out of plumb (*or* off plumb)

near ant ordered, orderly, regular, uniform; balanced, symmetrical (*or* symmetric)

ant even, level, straight

awry *adv* off the desired or intended path or course — see WRONG

¹aye *also* **ay** *adv* **1** on every relevant occasion — see ALWAYS 1

2 for all time — see EVER 1

²aye *also* **ay** *adv* used to express agreement — see YES

---

syn synonym(s)   *rel* related words
ant antonym(s)   *near ant* near antonym(s)

babble *n* unintelligible or meaningless talk — see GIBBERISH 1

babble *vb* 1 to speak rapidly, inarticulately, and usually unintelligibly ⟨in such a rush to tell us the news that she just *babbled*⟩

syn chat, chatter, drivel, drool, gabble, gibber, jabber, prattle, sputter

rel blabber, blither, gab, jaw, patter, prate, rattle, run on; tittle-tattle, troll, yak (*also* yack); maunder, mouth, mumble, murmur, mutter; stammer, stutter; screech, shout, shriek

near ant articulate, enunciate, pronounce

2 to engage in casual or rambling conversation — see CHAT 1

babbler *n* a person who talks constantly — see CHATTERBOX

babe *n* 1 a person who is just starting out in a field of activity — see BEGINNER

2 a recently born person — see BABY 1

babel *n* 1 a place of uproar or confusion — see MADHOUSE

2 loud, confused, and usually inharmonious sound — see NOISE 1

babushka *n* a scarf worn on the head — see BANDANNA

baby *n* 1 a recently born person ⟨The *baby* is just learning to sit up, so be careful.⟩

syn babe, child, infant, newborn

rel cherub; foundling, preemie (*also* premie); bantling, kid, kiddo, moppet, toddler, tot; boy, nipper, tad; juvenile, minor, youngster, youth; brat, imp, squirt, urchin, whippersnapper; girl, hoyden, tomboy

near ant adult, grown-up; elder, graybeard, oldster, old-timer, senior, senior citizen

2 a successful result brought about by hard work — see ACCOMPLISHMENT 1

3 a person who makes frequent complaints usually about little things — see CRYBABY

baby *vb* to treat with great or excessive care ⟨He *babied* his car, faithfully washing it every week.⟩

syn coddle, dandle, indulge, mollycoddle, nurse, pamper, spoil

rel cater (to), humor; content, delight, gladden, gratify, mother, oblige, please, satisfy; mollify, pacify, placate, soothe

near ant control, discipline, restrain; oppress; neglect, overlook, slight; molest, outrage, violate; harm, hurt, injure, oppress, persecute, torment, torture, victimize

ant abuse, ill-treat, ill-use, maltreat, manhandle, mishandle, mistreat, misuse

babyish *adj* having or showing the annoying qualities (as silliness) associated with children — see CHILDISH

babysitter *n* a person employed to care for a young child or children — see NURSE

back *adj* being at or in the part of something opposite the front part ⟨She carried all the presents in the *back* door, as the children were playing in the front yard.⟩

syn aft, after, hind, hinder, hindmost, posterior, rear, rearward

rel dorsal

near ant ventral

ant anterior, forward, front

back *adv* 1 toward the opposite direction — see AROUND 2

2 toward the rear — see BACKWARD 1

back *n* 1 a behind part or surface — see REAR 1

2 a vulnerable point — see ACHILLES' HEEL

back *vb* 1 to promote the interests or cause of — see SUPPORT 1

2 to provide (someone) with what is useful or necessary to achieve an end — see HELP 1

3 to provide evidence or information for (as a claim or idea) — see SUPPORT 4

back away *vb* to move back or away (as from something difficult, dangerous, or disagreeable) — see RETREAT 1

backbone *n* 1 a column of bones supporting the trunk of a vertebrate animal — see SPINE

2 the strength of mind that enables a person to endure pain or hardship — see FORTITUDE

back down *vb* to break a promise or agreement — see RENEGE 1

backdrop *n* the physical conditions or features that form the setting against which something is viewed — see BACKGROUND 1

backer *n* 1 a person who actively supports or favors a cause — see EXPONENT 1

2 a person who takes the responsibility for some other person or thing — see SPONSOR

3 someone associated with another to give assistance or moral support — see ALLY

backfire *vb* to have the reverse of the desired or expected effect ⟨My plan to throw her a surprise party *backfired* when she ended up planning a getaway for her birthday.⟩

syn boomerang

rel collapse, flop, flunk, fold, wash out; flounder, struggle; decline, slip, slump, wane

near ant succeed; flourish, prosper, thrive

background *n* 1 the physical conditions or features that form the setting against which something is viewed ⟨They got married on a mountain top with the sunset as *background*.⟩

syn backdrop, ground

rel scene, scenery, set, stage; environment, milieu, setting, surroundings

near ant foreground; center, focal point, focus, heart

2 the place and time in which the action for a portion of a dramatic work (as a movie) is set — see SCENE 1

backhanded *adj* not being or expressing what one appears to be or express — see INSINCERE

backing *n* 1 an act or instance of helping — see HELP 1

2 the financial support and general guidance for an undertaking — see AUSPICE 1

back of *prep* at, to, or toward the rear of — see BEHIND 1

back off *vb* to break a promise or agreement — see RENEGE 1

backpack *n* a soft-sided case designed for carrying belongings especially on the back — see PACK 1

backside *n* the part of the body upon which someone sits — see BUTTOCKS

backslider *n* a person who has sunk below the normal moral standard — see DEGENERATE

back talk *n* disrespectful or argumentative talk given in response to a command or request ⟨His mother sent him to his room because of his constant *back talk*.⟩
 syn cheek, impertinence, impudence, insolence, mouth, sass, sauce
 rel comeback, rejoinder, retort, riposte, wisecrack; cuteness, discourtesy, disrespect, guff, impoliteness, nonsense, rudeness, tactlessness; audacity, boldness, brazenness; coarseness, crassness, vulgarity; abruptness, bluffness, brusqueness, crossness, curtness, gruffness, surliness
 near ant civility, cordiality, courtesy, diplomacy, politeness, tactfulness; consideration, gallantry, gentility, graciousness, smoothness, suaveness, suavity; deference, respect; affability

backup *n* 1 a crowded mass (as of cars) that impedes or blocks movement — see JAM 1
2 a person or thing that takes the place of another — see SUBSTITUTE

backward *adj* 1 directed, turned, or done toward the back ⟨A *backward* turn on ice skates is hard to learn because you can't see where you're going.⟩
 syn rearward, retrograde
 rel reverse, reversed; aft, after, hind, posterior, rear; astern, sternforemost
 near ant forward
2 not comfortable around people — see SHY 2

backward *or* **backwards** *adv* 1 toward the rear ⟨Looking *backward*, we could see the town receding in the distance.⟩
 syn back, rearward (*also* rearwards)
 rel astern, sternforemost; counterclockwise, left-handed, left-handedly, retrograde, reversely
 near ant before
 ant ahead, along, forth, forward, forwards, on, onward (*also* onwards)
2 toward the opposite direction — see AROUND 2

backwater *n* a rural region that forms the edge of the settled or developed part of a country — see FRONTIER 2

backwoods *n pl* a rural region that forms the edge of the settled or developed part of a country — see FRONTIER 2

bad *adj* 1 falling short of a standard ⟨A *bad* first attempt at making pie resulted in a soggy, inedible mess.⟩
 syn bush, crummy (*also* crumby), deficient, dissatisfactory, ill, inferior, lame, lousy, off, paltry, poor, punk, sour, substandard, unacceptable, unsatisfactory, wanting, wretched, wrong

rel abysmal, atrocious, awful, brutal, deplorable, detestable, disastrous, dreadful, execrable, horrendous, horrible, pathetic, stinky, terrible, unspeakable; defective, faulty, flawed; egregious, flagrant, gross; bum, cheesy, coarse, common, crappy [*slang*], cut-rate, junky, lesser, low-grade, mediocre, miserable, reprehensible, rotten, rubbishy, second-rate, shoddy, sleazy, trashy; abominable, odious, vile; useless, valueless, worthless; inadequate, insufficient, lacking, meager (*or* meagre), mean, niggardly, scanty, shabby, short, skimp, skimpy, spare, stingy; miscreant, scurrilous, villainous; counterfeit, fake, phony (*also* phoney); sham
 phrases below par (*or* under par)
 near ant classic, classical; A1, bang-up, banner, capital, choice, crackerjack, dandy, divine, excellent, exceptional, fabulous, fine, first-class, first-rate, grand, great, heavenly, high-test, jim-dandy, keen, marvelous (*or* marvellous), mean, neat, nifty, noble, par excellence, perfect, premium, prime, sensational, slick, splendid, stellar, sterling, superb, superior, superlative, supernal, swell, terrific, tip-top, top, top-notch, unsurpassed, wonderful; better, exceptional, fancy, high-grade, special, sufficient; average, fair, mediocre, middling, minimal, so-so, unexceptional; suitable, useful, worthy; gratifying, satisfying
 ant acceptable, adequate, all right, decent, fine, OK (*or* okay), passable, respectable, satisfactory, standard, tolerable
2 not conforming to a high moral standard; morally unacceptable ⟨Stealing is just plain *bad*.⟩
 syn dark, evil, immoral, iniquitous, nefarious, rotten, sinful, unethical, unlawful, unrighteous, unsavory, vicious, vile, villainous, wicked, wrong
 rel base, contemptible, despicable, dirty, disreputable, evil-minded, ignoble, ill, low, mean, snide, sordid; atrocious, cruel, infamous, nasty; blamable, blameworthy, censurable, objectionable, obscene, offensive, reprehensible; corrupt, debased, debauched, degenerate, depraved, dissolute, libertine, loose, perverted, reprobate, sick, unhealthy; defiling, noxious, pernicious, ugly, ungodly, unwholesome; banned, barred, condemned, discouraged, forbidden, illegal, interdicted, outlawed, prohibited, proscribed, unauthorized, unclean; disallowed; execrable, lousy, miserable, wretched; errant, erring, fallen, unprincipled, unscrupulous; improper, incorrect, indecent, indecorous, naughty, unbecoming, unseemly, vulgar; dishonest, dishonorable
 near ant elevated, high, high-minded, law-abiding, legitimate, lofty, noble, principled, reputable, scrupulous; allowed, authorized, legal, licensed, permissible, permitted; approved, endorsed (*also* indorsed), sanctioned; abetted, encouraged, promoted, supported; clean, correct, decent, decorous, exemplary, proper, seemly; blameless, commendable, creditable, guiltless, legitimate; chaste, immaculate, incorruptible, inno-

---

syn synonym(s)   *rel* related words
ant antonym(s)   *near ant* near antonym(s)

cent, inoffensive, irreproachable, perfect, pure, spotless, uncorrupted, unerring, unfallen, unobjectionable, venerable, wholesome; esteemed, respected, upstanding, worthy

ant decent, ethical, good, honest, honorable, just, moral, right, righteous, sublime, upright, virtuous

3 causing or capable of causing harm — see HARMFUL

4 engaging in or marked by childish misbehavior — see NAUGHTY

5 feeling unhappiness — see SAD 1

6 having a fault — see FAULTY

7 having undergone organic breakdown — see ROTTEN 1

8 not giving pleasure to the mind or senses — see UNPLEASANT

9 of low quality — see CHEAP 2

10 temporarily suffering from a disorder of the body — see SICK 1

11 having no legal or binding force — see NULL 1

bad *adv* in an unsatisfactory way — see BADLY 1

bad *n* that which is morally unacceptable — see EVIL

badly *adv* **1** in an unsatisfactory way ⟨I'm afraid you performed quite *badly* in our last rehearsal.⟩

syn bad, deficiently, inadequately, poorly, unacceptably, unsatisfactorily, wretchedly

rel abysmally, atrociously, awfully, damnably, deplorably, detestably, disastrously, dreadfully, execrably, horrendously, horribly, horrifically, rottenly, terribly; unbearably; inappropriately, incorrectly, indecently, reprehensibly, unsuitably; vulgarly; naughtily; egregiously, flagrantly, grossly; miserably, shoddily, sleazily, trashily, unspeakably; abominably, odiously, vilely; inferiorly, insufficiently, meagerly, meanly, niggardly, scantily, scantly, shabbily, skimpily, sparely, stingily

near ant appropriately, congruously, correctly, decorously, felicitously, fittingly, meetly, rightly, seemly, suitably; exactly, faithfully, ideally, precisely; satisfyingly

ant acceptably, adequately, all right, fine, good, nicely, OK (*or* okay), passably, satisfactorily, so-so, tolerably, well

2 to a great degree — see VERY 1

bad–mouth *vb* to express scornfully one's low opinion of — see DECRY 1

badness *n* the state or quality of being utterly evil — see ENORMITY 1

baffle *vb* **1** to prevent from achieving a goal — see FRUSTRATE 1

2 to throw into a state of mental uncertainty — see CONFUSE 1

bafflement *n* a state of mental uncertainty — see CONFUSION 1

bag *n* **1** a container made of a flexible material (as paper or plastic) ⟨She carries her towel and other supplies to the beach in a bright, colorful *bag* slung over her arm.⟩

syn poke [*chiefly Southern & Midland*], pouch, sack

rel carryall, portmanteau, traveling bag; bundle, pack, package, packet, parcel; backpack, barracks bag, duffel bag, haversack, knapsack, rucksack, satchel, tote;

handbag, pocketbook, purse, tote bag; ditty bag, flight bag, garment bag, kit bag, shopping bag, work bag

2 a container for carrying money and small personal items — see PURSE

bag *vb* **1** to extend outward beyond a usual point — see BULGE 1

2 to take physical control or possession of (something) suddenly or forcibly — see CATCH 1

3 to give up (a job or office) — see QUIT 1

4 to obtain (as a goal) through effort — see ACHIEVE 1

5 to receive as return for effort — see EARN 1

bail out *vb* **1** to leave a place often for another — see GO 2

2 to remove from danger or harm — see SAVE 2

bait *n* **1** something used to attract animals to a hook or into a trap ⟨Cheese is the traditional *bait* for trapping mice.⟩

syn decoy, lure

rel ambush, net, trap; hook, snare, troll; plug, scent, spinner, stool pigeon; appeal, attraction, call, draw, incentive, pull; enticement, seducement, seduction, temptation; entanglement, entrapment

near ant repellent (*also* repellant)

2 something that persuades one to perform an action for pleasure or gain — see LURE 1

bait *vb* **1** to attack repeatedly with mean put-downs or insults — see TEASE 2

2 to lead away from a usual or proper course by offering some pleasure or advantage — see LURE

baiter *n* **1** a person who causes repeated emotional pain, distress, or annoyance to another — see TORMENTOR

2 one that tries to get a person to give in to a desire — see TEMPTER

balance *n* **1** a condition in which opposing forces are equal to one another ⟨In order to determine the weight of that beaker, you need to get the two pans of the scale in perfect *balance*.⟩

syn counterpoise, equilibrium, equipoise, poise

rel counterbalance, offset; firmness, fixedness, security, stability, steadiness

near ant changeability, inconstancy, insecurity, instability, mutability, precariousness, shakiness, unsteadiness, volatility

ant disequilibration, disequilibrium, imbalance, nonequilibrium, unbalance

2 a balanced, pleasing, or suitable arrangement of parts — see HARMONY 1

3 a device for measuring weight — see ¹SCALE

4 a force or influence that makes an opposing force ineffective or less effective — see COUNTERBALANCE

5 a remaining group or portion — see REMAINDER 1

balance *vb* **1** to make equal in amount, degree, or status — see EQUALIZE

2 to show uncertainty about the right course of action — see HESITATE

3 to give what is owed for — see PAY 2

balanced *adj* **1** having full use of one's mind and control over one's actions — see SANE

2 having the parts agreeably related — see HARMONIOUS 2

bald *adj* 1 lacking a usual or natural covering — see NAKED 2

2 free from all additions or embellishment — see PLAIN 1

3 not subject to misinterpretation or more than one interpretation — see CLEAR 2

baleful *adj* 1 being or showing a sign of evil or calamity to come — see OMINOUS

2 causing or capable of causing harm — see HARMFUL

3 likely to cause or capable of causing death — see DEADLY 1

balk *n* something that makes movement or progress difficult — see ENCUMBRANCE

balk *vb* to prevent from achieving a goal — see FRUSTRATE 1

balky *adj* given to resisting authority or another's control — see DISOBEDIENT

¹**ball** *n* 1 a more or less round body or mass ⟨the little rubber *ball* used in racquetball⟩ ⟨a *ball* of string⟩

syn globe, orb, sphere

rel globule; ellipse, loop, oval, spheroid; circle, ring, round; chunk, clump, gob, hunk, lump, nugget, wad

near ant block, rectangle, square

2 a usually round or cone-shaped little piece of lead made to be fired from a firearm — see BULLET

²**ball** *n* a social gathering for dancing — see DANCE

ball *vb* to form into a round compact mass — see WAD

ballad *n* a short musical composition for the human voice often with instrumental accompaniment — see SONG 1

balloon *vb* 1 to become greater in extent, volume, amount, or number — see INCREASE 2

2 to extend outward beyond a usual point — see BULGE 1

ballot *n* 1 a piece of paper indicating a person's preferences in an election ⟨We collected all of the *ballots* from the students voting for class president.⟩

syn vote

rel aye (*also* ay), yea; nay, no; blackball; referendum; ticket; absentee ballot, Australian ballot, secret ballot, short ballot, write-in

2 the right to formally express one's position or will in an election — see VOTE 1

ballyhoo *n* 1 a state of noisy, confused activity — see COMMOTION

2 information released to the media that is designed to gain public attention or support for a person, business, or cause — see PUBLICITY

ballyhoo *vb* 1 to praise or publicize lavishly and often excessively — see TOUT 1

2 to provide publicity for — see PUBLICIZE 1

balminess *n* lack of good sense or judgment — see FOOLISHNESS 1

balmy *adj* 1 marked by temperatures that are neither too high nor too low — see CLEMENT 1

2 not harsh or stern especially in nature or effect — see GENTLE 1

3 showing or marked by a lack of good sense or judgment — see FOOLISH 1

balustrade *n* a protective barrier consisting of a horizontal bar and its supports — see RAILING

ban *n* 1 a prayer that harm will come to someone — see CURSE 1

2 an order that something not be done or used — see PROHIBITION 2

ban *vb* 1 to order not to do or use or to be done or used — see FORBID

2 to prevent the participation, consideration, or inclusion of — see EXCLUDE

banal *adj* 1 lacking in qualities that make for spirit and character — see WISHY-WASHY 1

2 used or heard so often as to be dull — see STALE 1

banality *n* an idea or expression that has been used by many people — see COMMONPLACE

¹**band** *n* 1 a circular strip — see ¹RING 2

2 something that physically prevents free movement — see BOND 1

3 a line or long narrow section differing in color from the background — see ¹STRIPE 1

²**band** *n* 1 a usually large group of musicians playing together ⟨the school's marching *band*⟩ ⟨a boy *band*⟩

syn orchestra, philharmonic, symphony, symphony orchestra

rel brass band, chamber orchestra; brasses, strings, woodwinds; combo, ensemble, group; company, troupe; duo, octet, quartet (*also* quartette), quintet, septet, sextet, trio

2 a group of people working together on a task — see GANG 1

3 a usually small number of persons considered as a unit — see GROUP 2

4 a number of things considered as a unit — see GROUP 1

band *vb* 1 to encircle or bind with or as if with a belt — see GIRD 1

2 to gather into a tight mass by means of a line or cord — see TIE 1

3 to make stripes on — see STRIPE

band (together) *vb* 1 to participate or assist in a joint effort to accomplish an end — see COOPERATE 1

2 to form or enter into an association that furthers the interests of its members — see ALLY

bandage *vb* to cover with a bandage ⟨Her mother always *bandages* her scraped knees very carefully.⟩

syn bind, dress, swathe

rel attend, care (for), doctor, medicate, minister (to), nurse, treat; cure, heal, mend, rehabilitate, remedy

near ant unbandage

bandanna *or* **bandana** *n* a scarf worn on the head ⟨She uses her colorful print *bandanna* to keep the hair out of her eyes.⟩

syn babushka, do-rag, handkerchief, kerchief, mantilla

rel shawl

bandwagon *n* a series of activities undertaken to achieve a goal — see CAMPAIGN

bandy *vb* to talk about (an issue) usually from various points of view and for the purpose of arriving at a decision or opinion — see DISCUSS

---

syn synonym(s)   *rel* related words
ant antonym(s)   *near ant* near antonyms(s)

bane n 1 a source of harm or misfortune ⟨Regarding the new laborsaving machinery as a *bane*, the 19th-century Luddites went about destroying it in protest.⟩
syn affliction, curse, nemesis, scourge
rel hex, jinx; danger, hazard, menace, peril, risk, threat, trouble; booby trap, catch, pitfall, snag
near ant advantage, aid, assistance, gift, help, relief, support; comfort, consolation, solace; delight, joy, pleasure; armor, defense, guard, protection, safeguard, safety, security, shield
ant benefit, blessing, boon, felicity, godsend, good, manna, windfall
2 a substance that by chemical action can kill or injure a living thing — see POISON
baneful adj causing or capable of causing harm — see HARMFUL
bang adv without delay — see IMMEDIATELY
bang n 1 a hard strike with a part of the body or an instrument — see ¹BLOW
2 a loud explosive sound — see CLAP 1
3 a pleasurably intense stimulation of the feelings — see THRILL
bang vb 1 to come into usually forceful contact with something — see HIT 2
2 to deliver a blow to (someone or something) usually in a strong vigorous manner — see HIT 1
3 to shove into a closed position with force and noise — see SLAM 1
bangle n an ornament worn on a chain around the neck or wrist — see PENDANT
bang–up adj of the very best kind — see EXCELLENT
banish vb 1 to force to leave a country ⟨In the old days, criminals were sometimes *banished* to distant lands.⟩
syn deport, displace, exile, expatriate, transport
rel dismiss, eject, eliminate, evict, exclude, expel, expulse, oust, run out, throw out; excommunicate, ostracize, reject, repudiate, spurn
near ant naturalize, repatriate; accept, admit, take in; entertain, harbor, house, shelter
2 to drive or force out — see EJECT 1
banishment n the forced removal from a homeland — see EXILE 1
banister also **bannister** n a protective barrier consisting of a horizontal bar and its supports — see RAILING
¹bank n 1 a number of things considered as a unit — see GROUP 1
2 a series of people or things arranged side by side — see ¹ROW 1
²bank n a pile or ridge of granular matter (as sand or snow) ⟨a *bank* of dirt that the construction workers left behind⟩
syn drift, drift, mound
rel snowbank, snowdrift; embankment, sandbar; heap, hill, mass, mountain, stack, tuft
bank vb 1 to form into a pile or ridge of earth — see MOUND 1
2 to put into an account — see DEPOSIT 1
bankroll n available money — see FUND 2
bankroll vb to provide money for — see FINANCE 1
bankrupt adj utterly lacking in something

needed, wanted, or expected — see DEVOID 1
bankrupt vb to cause to lose one's fortune and become unable to pay one's debts — see RUIN 1
banned adj that may not be permitted — see IMPERMISSIBLE
banner adj of the very best kind — see EXCELLENT
banner n 1 a piece of cloth with a special design that is used as an emblem or for signaling — see FLAG 1
2 an attention-getting word or phrase used to publicize something (as a campaign or product) — see SLOGAN
banning n the act of ordering that something not be done or used — see PROHIBITION 1
banquet n a large fancy meal often accompanied by ceremony or entertainment — see FEAST 1
banquet vb to entertain with a fancy meal — see FEAST 1
bantam adj of a size that is less than average — see SMALL 1
banter n good-natured teasing or exchanging of clever remarks ⟨Members of the panel were known for their brilliant and witty *banter*.⟩
syn chaff, give-and-take, jesting, joshing, raillery, repartee
rel barb, crack, dig, gag, jest, joke, laugh, pleasantry, quip, sally, waggery, wisecrack, witticism; drollness, facetiousness, funniness, hilariousness, humorousness, richness; fooling, kidding, mocking, razzing, ribbing, ridiculing; humor, wit, wordplay; nothings; chatter, chitchat, gossip, small talk
banter vb to make jokes — see JOKE 1
bantering adj marked by or expressive of mild or good-natured teasing — see QUIZZICAL
baptism n the process or an instance of being formally placed in an office or organization — see INSTALLATION 1
baptize vb 1 to give a name to — see NAME 1
2 to put into an office or welcome into an organization with special ceremonies — see INSTALL 1
bar n 1 a straight piece (as of wood or metal) that is longer than it is wide ⟨All of the prison's windows are partially covered with steel *bars*.⟩
syn billet, rod
rel arbor, beam, board, crossbar, crossbeam, girder; band, strip; bloom, ingot, slab, stick
2 a line or long narrow section differing in color from the background — see ¹STRIPE 1
3 a pile or ridge of granular matter (as sand or snow) — see ²BANK
4 a place of business where alcoholic beverages are sold to be consumed on the premises — see BARROOM
5 an assembly of persons for the administration of justice — see COURT 3
6 something that makes movement or progress difficult — see ENCUMBRANCE
7 something set up as an example against which others of the same type are compared — see STANDARD 1

bar *prep* not including — see EXCEPT

bar *vb* **1** to make stripes on — see STRIPE

2 to order not to do or use or to be done or used — see FORBID

3 to prevent the participation, consideration, or inclusion of — see EXCLUDE

4 to disallow entry into (a place) by means of a physical barrier at the entry point — see CLOSE (OFF)

barb *n* an act or expression showing scorn and usually intended to hurt another's feelings — see INSULT

barbarian *adj* not civilized — see UNCIVILIZED

barbarian *n* an uncivilized person — see HEATHEN 2

barbaric *adj* **1** having or showing the desire to inflict severe pain and suffering on others — see CRUEL 1

2 not civilized — see UNCIVILIZED

barbarity *n* disposition to willfully inflict pain and suffering on others — see CRUELTY

barbarous *adj* **1** having or showing the desire to inflict severe pain and suffering on others — see CRUEL 1

2 not civilized — see UNCIVILIZED

bard *n* a person who writes poetry — see POET

bardic *adj* having qualities suggestive of poetry — see POETIC

bare *adj* **1** being this and no more — see MERE

2 free from all additions or embellishment — see PLAIN 1

3 lacking a usual or natural covering — see NAKED 2

4 lacking or shed of clothing — see NAKED 1

5 lacking contents that could or should be present — see EMPTY 1

6 utterly lacking in something needed, wanted, or expected — see DEVOID 1

bare *vb* to make known (as information previously kept secret) — see REVEAL 1

barefaced *adj* not subject to misinterpretation or more than one interpretation — see CLEAR 2

barely *adv* by a very small margin — see JUST 2

bareness *n* the quality or state of being empty — see VACANCY 2

barf *vb* to discharge the contents of the stomach through the mouth — see VOMIT

bargain *n* **1** something bought or offered for sale at a desirable price ⟨Those shoes were a *bargain* because the store was going out of business.⟩

syn buy, deal, steal

rel clearance, closeout, markdown; bonus, freebie (*or* freebee), gift, giveaway, premium, present; boon, windfall

near ant overcharge, rip-off, soaking; markup, surcharge; extravagance, luxury

2 an arrangement about action to be taken — see AGREEMENT 2

bargain *vb* **1** to talk over or dispute the terms of a purchase ⟨They *bargained* with the car salesman for half an hour before settling on a price.⟩

syn deal, dicker, haggle, horse-trade, negotiate, palter

rel argue, bicker, clash, fight, hassle, quarrel, quibble, squabble, wrangle; comparison shop, shop (around); barter, exchange, trade; hawk, peddle; buy, purchase

phrases cut a deal, wheel and deal

2 to come to an arrangement as to a course of action — see AGREE 2

3 to bring about through discussion and compromise — see NEGOTIATE 1

barge *vb* to move heavily or clumsily — see LUMBER 1

¹bark *vb* to remove the natural covering of — see PEEL

²bark *vb* to speak sharply or irritably — see SNAP 1

bark *n* a boat equipped with one or more sails — see SAILBOAT

baron *n* a person of rank, power, or influence in a particular field — see MAGNATE

baronial *adj* large and impressive in size, grandeur, extent, or conception — see GRAND 1

barrage *n* a rapid or overwhelming outpouring of many things at once ⟨The teacher's rapid-fire *barrage* of homework assignments went by too fast for me to write them all down.⟩

syn blitz, blitzkrieg, bombardment, cannonade, flurry, fusillade, hail, salvo, shower, storm, volley

rel broadside, earful; avalanche, burst, cataclysm, cataract, deluge, discharge, engulfment, flood, flood tide, flush, gush, inundation, outburst, outflow, outpouring, overflow, rash, spate, surge, torrent; current, river, stream, tide; excess, glut, overabundance, overage, overkill, overmuch, oversupply, superabundance, superfluity, surfeit, surplus

near ant dribble, drip, trickle

barrage *vb* to attack with a rapid or overwhelming outpouring of many things at once — see BOMBARD 2

barred *adj* **1** having stripes — see STRIPED

2 that may not be permitted — see IMPERMISSIBLE

barrel *n* **1** a considerable amount — see LOT 2

2 a metal container in the shape of a cylinder — see CAN 1

3 an enclosed wooden vessel for holding beverages — see CASK

barrel *vb* to proceed or move quickly — see HURRY 2

barren *adj* producing inferior or only a small amount of vegetation ⟨If the fields aren't allowed to lie idle once every few years, they will become *barren*.⟩

syn dead, desolate, impoverished, infertile, poor, stark, unproductive, waste

rel bleak, inhospitable, lifeless; uncultivable, untillable; bankrupted, consumed, debilitated, depleted, diminished, drained, dried-up, enfeebled, exhausted, expended, lessened, reduced, spent, used up; arid, desert, droughty, dry, rainless, sere (*also* sear); thirsty, waterless; baked, dehydrated, parched, sunbaked

near ant arable, tillable; green, sylvan, verdant

---

ant fertile, fruitful, lush, luxuriant, productive, rich

2 not able to produce fruit or offspring — see STERILE 1

3 producing no results — see FUTILE

4 utterly lacking in something needed, wanted, or expected — see DEVOID 1

barren *n* land that is uninhabited or not fit for crops — see WASTELAND

barricade *n* a physical object that blocks the way — see BARRIER

barricade *vb* to disallow entry into (a place) by means of a physical barrier at the entry point — see CLOSE (OFF)

barrier *n* a physical object that blocks the way 〈There was a big *barrier* plastered with signs saying "Keep Out" around the trash compactor.〉

syn barricade, fence, hedge, wall

rel bar, pale, paling; block, chain, clog, crimp, deterrent, drag, embarrassment, encumbrance, handicap, hindrance, hurdle, impediment, inhibition, interference, let, obstacle, obstruction, roadblock, stop, stumbling block, trammel; fetter, hobble, manacle, shackle(s); constraint, curb, restraint, snag; buffer, bulwark, bumper, cushion, dam, fender, pad, rampart

near ant door, doorway, entrance, entry, entryway, gate, portal; break, gap, pass

barring *n* the act of ordering that something not be done or used — see PROHIBITION 1

barring *prep* not including — see EXCEPT

barroom *n* a place of business where alcoholic beverages are sold to be consumed on the premises 〈*barrooms* closed down during Prohibition〉

syn bar, pub, saloon, tavern

rel brewpub, cabaret, nightclub, speakeasy, sports bar

barter *n* a giving or taking of one thing of value in return for another — see EXCHANGE 1

base *adj* not following or in accordance with standards of honor and decency — see IGNOBLE 2

base *n* **1** an immaterial thing upon which something else rests 〈the firm belief that complete trust is the *base* of any successful marriage〉

syn basis, bedrock, bottom, cornerstone, footing, foundation, ground, groundwork, keystone, root, underpinning, warp

rel anchorage, bed, brace, bulwark, buttress, framework, mount, shore, stay, substratum, substructure, support; assumption, justification, premise (*also* premiss), presumption, presupposition, rationale, supposition, theory, thesis, warrant; backbone, center, core, cornerstone, eye, focus, heart, hub, keystone, nucleus, seat; essence, quintessence, soul, touchstone

2 a place from which an advance (as for military operations) is made 〈The army's *base* of attack was kept top secret.〉

syn bridgehead, foothold

rel staging area, staging ground; beachhead, camp, center, footing, front, headquarters, installation, station; airbase; bastion, fastness, fortress, stronghold; battlefront, field; toehold

3 a thing or place that is of greatest importance to an activity or interest — see CENTER 1

4 the lowest part, place, or point — see BOTTOM 3

5 the place from which a commander runs operations — see COMMAND 3

base *vb* to find a basis 〈She *based* her argument on careful research.〉

syn ground, hang, predicate, rest

rel establish, found; assume, postulate, premise, presume, presuppose, suppose

baseborn *adj* belonging to the class of people of low social or economic rank — see IGNOBLE 1

basement *n* **1** a room or set of rooms below the surface of the ground — see CELLAR

2 the lowest part, place, or point — see BOTTOM 3

bash *n* **1** a hard strike with a part of the body or an instrument — see ¹BLOW

2 a social gathering — see PARTY 1

bash *vb* **1** to come into usually forceful contact with something — see HIT 2

2 to deliver a blow to (someone or something) usually in a strong vigorous manner — see HIT 1

3 to strike repeatedly — see BEAT 1

4 to criticize harshly and usually publicly — see ATTACK 2

bashful *adj* not comfortable around people — see SHY 1

basic *adj* of or relating to the simplest facts or theories of a subject — see ELEMENTARY

basically *adv* for the most part — see CHIEFLY

basics *n pl* general or basic truths on which other truths or theories can be based — see PRINCIPLES 1

basis *n* an immaterial thing upon which something else rests — see BASE 1

bask *vb* to refrain from labor or exertion — see REST 1

bass *adj* having a low musical pitch or range — see DEEP 2

bastion *n* a structure or place from which one can resist attack — see FORT

bat *n* **1** a hard strike with a part of the body or an instrument — see ¹BLOW

2 a heavy rigid stick used as a weapon or for punishment — see CLUB 1

bat *vb* **1** to deliver a blow to (someone or something) usually in a strong vigorous manner — see HIT 1

2 to strike repeatedly — see BEAT 1

3 to move about from place to place aimlessly — see WANDER 1

batch *n* **1** a number of things considered as a unit — see GROUP 1

2 a usually small number of persons considered as a unit — see GROUP 2

bath *n* **1** a great flow of water or of something that overwhelms — see FLOOD

2 a room furnished with a fixture for flushing body waste — see TOILET

bathe *vb* **1** to flow along or against — see WASH 1

2 to make wet — see WET

3 to supply with light — see ILLUMINATE 1

bathed *adj* containing, covered with, or thoroughly penetrated by water — see WET 1

bathroom *n* a room furnished with a fixture for flushing body waste — see TOILET

battalion *n* a large body of men and women organized for land warfare — see ARMY 1

batter *vb* 1 to strike repeatedly — see BEAT 1

2 to use bombs or artillery against — see BOMBARD 1

battery *n* 1 a number of things considered as a unit — see GROUP 1

2 a usually small number of persons considered as a unit — see GROUP 2

battle *n* 1 a forceful effort to reach a goal or objective — see STRUGGLE 1

2 a physical dispute between opposing individuals or groups — see FIGHT 1

3 active fighting during the course of a war — see COMBAT 1

4 an earnest effort for superiority or victory over another — see CONTEST 1

battle *vb* 1 to engage in a contest — see COMPETE

2 to enter into contest or conflict with — see ENGAGE 2

3 to oppose (someone) in physical conflict — see FIGHT 1

4 to strive to reduce or eliminate — see FIGHT 2

bauble *n* a small object displayed for its attractiveness or interest — see KNICK-KNACK

bawdiness *n* the quality or state of being obscene — see OBSCENITY

bawdy *adj* 1 depicting or referring to sexual matters in a way that is unacceptable in polite society — see OBSCENE 1

2 hinting at or intended to call to mind matters regarded as indecent — see SUGGESTIVE 1

bawl *vb* 1 to shed tears often while making meaningless sounds as a sign of pain or distress — see CRY 1

2 to speak so as to be heard at a distance — see CALL 1

bawl out *vb* to criticize (someone) severely or angrily especially for personal failings — see SCOLD

¹**bay** *n* one of the parts into which an enclosed space is divided — see COMPARTMENT

²**bay** *n* a part of a body of water that extends beyond the general shoreline — see GULF 1

bay *vb* 1 to speak so as to be heard at a distance — see CALL 1

2 to make a long loud mournful sound — see HOWL 1

bazaar *n* an establishment where goods are sold to consumers — see SHOP 1

be *vb* 1 to have life ⟨stories that begin with the familiar line "once upon a time there *was* a beautiful maiden"⟩

syn breathe, exist, live, subsist

rel abide, continue, endure, hold on, hold up, keep (on), kick, last, lead, persist, rule, run on, survive; move; flourish, prosper, thrive

near ant disappear, evaporate, vanish; cease, desist, discontinue, end, quit, stop;

abate, die (down), ebb, let up, moderate, subside, wane

ant depart, die, expire, pass away, perish, succumb

2 to occupy a place or location — see STAND 1

3 to take or have a certain position within a group arranged in vertical classes — see RANK 1

4 to take place — see HAPPEN

be (to) *vb* to behave toward in a stated way — see TREAT 1

beach *n* the usually sandy or gravelly land bordering a body of water ⟨She loves walking along the *beach*, looking for shells that the waves cast up.⟩

syn sand(s), strand

rel seaboard, seacoast, seashore, seaside; coast, coastland, coastline, shore, shoreline; oceanfront, shorefront, waterfront; bank, riverbank, riverfront, riverside; esplanade

beached *adj* resting on the shore or bottom of a body of water — see AGROUND

beacon *n* something that provides illumination — see LIGHT 2

beacon *vb* to supply with light — see ILLUMINATE 1

beak *n* 1 the jaws of a bird together with their hornlike covering ⟨The bird cracked the walnut shell with its *beak* and ate the nut.⟩

syn bill, nib

rel mouth; muzzle; mandible, maw, maxilla

2 the part of the face bearing the nostrils and nasal cavity — see NOSE 1

beam *n* a narrow sharply defined line of light radiating from an object — see SHAFT 1

beam *vb* 1 to emit rays of light — see SHINE 1

2 to express an emotion (as amusement) by curving the lips upward — see SMILE 1

beaming *adj* 1 giving off or reflecting much light — see BRIGHT 1

2 having or being an outward sign of good feelings (as of love, confidence, or happiness) — see RADIANT 1

bear *n* 1 a dull, unpleasant, or difficult piece of work — see CHORE 2

2 an irritable and complaining person — see GROUCH 1

bear *vb* 1 to bring forth from the womb ⟨Fortunately, she turned out to be able to *bear* children after all.⟩

syn deliver, drop, have, mother, produce

rel labor; breed, multiply, propagate, reproduce, spawn; beget, father, generate, get, sire; calve, kid, kindle, kitten, litter, pup, whelp

phrases give birth to

near ant abort, lose, miscarry

2 to put up with (something painful or difficult) ⟨I can't *bear* the thought of losing a loved one.⟩

syn abide, absorb, accept, brook, countenance, endure, go, hack, handle, meet, pocket, stand, stick out, stomach, support, sustain, sweat out, take, tolerate

rel allow, permit, suffer, swallow; reconcile (to); acquiesce, agree (with *or* to), assent (to), capitulate, consent (to), respect, submit (to), yield (to)

---

syn synonym(s)   *rel* related words
ant antonym(s)   *near ant* near antonym(s)

phrases live with, lump (it), stand for, tough out (it)

near ant decline, dismiss, refuse, reject, repudiate, spurn, turn down; combat, contest, fight, oppose, resist; avoid, bypass, circumvent, dodge, elude, escape, evade, miss; abstain (from), forbear, refrain (from)

3 to have a relation or connection — see APPLY 1

4 to go on a specified course or in a certain direction — see HEAD 1

5 to hold up or serve as a foundation for — see SUPPORT 3

6 to keep in one's mind or heart — see HARBOR 1

7 to manage the actions of (oneself) in a particular way — see BEHAVE

8 to support and take from one place to another — see CARRY 1

9 to take to or upon oneself — see ASSUME 1

10 to wear or have on one's person — see CARRY 2

11 to be positioned along a certain course or in a certain direction — see RUN 3

12 to have as a requirement — see NEED 1

13 to have within — see CONTAIN 1

14 to occupy a place or location — see STAND 1

15 to produce as revenue — see YIELD 2

bear (down on) *vb* to push steadily against with some force — see ²PRESS 1

bearable *adj* capable of being endured ⟨The pain from a sprained ankle is annoying but *bearable*.⟩
syn endurable, sufferable, supportable, sustainable, tolerable
rel livable (*also* liveable), survivable; acceptable, adequate, admissible, allowable, permissible, reasonable, satisfactory
near ant agonizing, appalling, awful, bad, cruel, dire, dreadful, excruciating, frightful, ghastly, grisly, gruesome (*also* grewsome), harrowing, harsh, hideous, horrendous, horrible, horrid, horrifying, lurid, macabre, monstrous, nasty, nightmarish, painful, rotten, shocking, terrible, tormenting, torturous, unfortunate, vicious, vile, wretched; unacceptable; acute, extreme, intense, piercing; abhorrent, deplorable, distasteful, loathsome, nauseating, obnoxious, offensive, repugnant, repulsive, revolting, sickening; abominable, evil, foul, heinous, noxious, odious, unspeakable
ant insufferable, insupportable, intolerable, unbearable, unendurable, unsupportable

beard *vb* to oppose (something hostile or dangerous) with firmness or courage — see FACE 2

bearing *n* **1** the fact or state of being pertinent — see PERTINENCE

2 the fact or state of having something in common — see CONNECTION 1

3 the way or manner in which one conducts oneself — see BEHAVIOR

bearish *adj* **1** expecting or expecting the worst — see PESSIMISTIC 1

2 having or showing a habitually bad temper — see ILL-TEMPERED

bear out *vb* to give evidence or testimony to the truth or factualness of — see CONFIRM 1

beast *n* **1** a mean, evil, or unprincipled person — see VILLAIN

2 a person whose behavior is offensive to others — see JERK 1

3 one of the lower animals as distinguished from human beings — see ANIMAL

4 a dull, unpleasant, or difficult piece of work — see CHORE 2

beastly *adv* to a great degree — see VERY 1

beat *adj* depleted in strength, energy, or freshness — see WEARY 1

beat *n* **1** a hard strike with a part of the body or an instrument — see ¹BLOW

2 a rhythmic expanding and contracting — see PULSATION

3 the recurrent pattern formed by a series of sounds having a regular rise and fall in intensity — see RHYTHM

4 a very small space of time — see INSTANT

beat *vb* **1** to strike repeatedly ⟨He *beat* the dusty rug with a stick.⟩
syn bash, bat, batter, belabor, belt, birch, bludgeon, buffet, club, drub, flog, hammer, hide, lace, lash, lick, maul, mess (up), paddle, pelt, pommel, pound, pummel, rough (up), slate, slog, switch, tan, thrash, thump, wallop, whale, whip
rel assail, assault, attack, beset, box, bust, chop, clobber, clout, crack, cudgel, cuff, descend (on *or* upon), hit, jump (on), knock, lam, paste, pounce (on *or* upon), punch, raid, rush, slam, slap, smack, smash, sock, spank, storm, swat, swipe, thwack, whack; cane, cowhide, flagellate, horsewhip, leather, pistol-whip, rawhide, scourge, strap; gore, lacerate, wound; maim, mangle, mutilate
phrases beat up on

2 to achieve a victory over ⟨She always *beats* everyone at checkers, but she's not as good at chess.⟩
syn best, conquer, defeat, dispatch, get, get around, lick, master, overbear, overcome, overmatch, prevail (over), skunk, subdue, surmount, take, trim, triumph (over), upend, win (against), worst
rel sweep; edge (out); annihilate, blow out, bomb, break, bury, clobber, cream, crush, drub, finish, flatten, overwhelm, rout, skin, slaughter, smoke [*slang*], snow under, thrash, trounce, upset, wallop, wax [*slang*], whip; cap, excel, flourish, score, succeed; knock off, overpower, overthrow, subjugate, unseat, vanquish; ace (out), better, eclipse, exceed, excel, outdistance, outdo, outfight, outshine, outstrip, overtop, surpass, top, transcend
phrases get the better of, knock for a loop
near ant fall, give up, go down, go under; collapse, fail, flop, flunk, fold, wash out
ant lose (to)

3 to be greater, better, or stronger than — see SURPASS 1

4 to expand and contract in a rhythmic manner — see PULSATE

5 to move or cause to move with a striking motion — see FLAP

6 to prevent from achieving a goal — see FRUSTRATE 1

7 to shape with a hammer — see HAMMER 1

8 to shine with a bright harsh light — see GLARE 1

9 to strike or cause to strike lightly and usually rhythmically — see ¹TAP

10 to throw into a state of mental uncertainty — see CONFUSE 1

11 to avoid having to comply with (something) especially through cleverness — see CIRCUMVENT 1

12 to reduce to fine particles — see POWDER

13 to rob by the use of trickery or threats — see FLEECE

beater *n* one that defeats an enemy or opponent — see VICTOR 1

beating *n* **1** a rhythmic expanding and contracting — see PULSATION

2 failure to win a contest — see DEFEAT 1

beau *n* **1** a male romantic companion — see BOYFRIEND

2 a man interested in his clothing and personal appearance — see DANDY 1

beau ideal *n* **1** someone of such unequaled perfection as to deserve imitation — see IDEAL 1

2 the most perfect type or example — see QUINTESSENCE 1

beauteous *adj* very pleasing to look at — see BEAUTIFUL 1

beauteousness *n* the qualities in a person or thing that as a whole give pleasure to the senses — see BEAUTY 1

beautiful *adj* **1** very pleasing to look at ⟨a *beautiful* arrangement of flowers⟩

syn aesthetic (*also* esthetic *or* aesthetical *or* esthetical), attractive, beauteous, comely, cute, fair, fetching, good, goodly, gorgeous, handsome, knockout, lovely, pretty, ravishing, seemly, sightly, stunning, taking

rel alluring, appealing, charming, cunning, delightful, engaging, fascinating, glamorous (*also* glamourous), prepossessing; elegant, exquisite, glorious, magnificent, resplendent, splendid, statuesque, sublime, superb; flawless, perfect, radiant; dainty, delicate; personable, pleasant, presentable; prettyish; desirable, dishy, dollish, foxy, pulchritudinous, seductive; hunky; arresting, eye-catching, flamboyant, flashy, glossy, showstopping, showy, slick, snazzy, splashy, striking; photogenic, telegenic

near ant abhorrent, abominable, bad, disagreeable, dreadful, foul, frightful, ghastly, horrible, loathsome, nasty, nauseating, objectionable, offensive, repellent (*also* repellant), repugnant, repulsive, revolting, shocking, sickening, terrible, vile; unappealing, unappetizing, unimposing, unpleasant, unprepossessing; frumpish, frumpy, unbecoming, unshapely

ant grotesque, hideous, homely, ill-favored, plain, ugly, unaesthetic, unattractive, unbeautiful, uncute, unhandsome, unlovely, unpleasing, unpretty, unsightly

2 of the finest kind — see EXCELLENT

beautifulness *n* the qualities in a person

or thing that as a whole give pleasure to the senses — see BEAUTY 1

beautify *vb* to make more attractive by adding something that is beautiful or becoming — see DECORATE

beautifying *adj* serving to add beauty — see DECORATIVE

beauty *n* **1** the qualities in a person or thing that as a whole give pleasure to the senses ⟨The *beauty* of the landscape was enough to take your breath away.⟩

syn attractiveness, beauteousness, beautifulness, comeliness, cuteness, fairness, gorgeousness, handsomeness, looks, loveliness, prettiness, sightliness

rel allure, appeal, attraction, fascination, glamour (*also* glamor); charm, delightfulness, elegance, exquisiteness, gloriousness, radiance, radiancy, resplendence, sublimeness, sublimity, superbness; foxiness, lusciousness, nubility, pulchritude, seductiveness, sex appeal, sexiness, shapeliness, tastiness; flawlessness, perfection; daintiness, delicacy; flamboyance, flashiness, glossiness, showiness, slickness, splashiness

near ant disagreeableness, dreadfulness, foulness, ghastliness, horribleness, loathsomeness, nastiness, offensiveness, repellency, repulsiveness, terribleness, vileness; blemish, flaw, imperfection

ant grotesqueness, hideousness, homeliness, plainness, ugliness, unattractiveness, unbecomingness, unloveliness, unsightliness

2 a lovely woman ⟨Grandmother was a *beauty* in her younger days.⟩

syn enchantress, goddess, honey, knockout, queen, stunner

rel belle, charmer; cover girl; cutie-pie, dish, doll, pretty; coquette, femme fatale, siren, temptress

3 something very good of its kind — see JIM-DANDY

because *conj* for the reason that — see SINCE

because of *prep* as the result of ⟨I was late for work *because of* the snowstorm, which made driving a nightmare.⟩

syn due to, owing to, through, with

phrases on account of

beckon *vb* to direct or notify by a movement or gesture — see MOTION

becloud *vb* **1** to make (something) unclear to the understanding — see CONFUSE 2

2 to make dark, dim, or indistinct — see CLOUD 1

beclouded *adj* **1** covered over by clouds — see OVERCAST

2 filled with or dimmed by fine particles (as of dust or water) in suspension — see HAZY 1

become *vb* to eventually have as a state or quality ⟨Many people *became* sick with the flu.⟩ ⟨With the arrival of autumn the days *become* crisper and breezier.⟩

syn come, get, go, grow, run, turn, wax

rel alter, change, metamorphose, modify, mutate, transfigure, transform

near ant abide, be, continue, linger, remain, stay

becoming *adj* meeting the requirements of a purpose or situation — see FIT 1

---

syn synonym(s)   *rel* related words

ant antonym(s)   *near ant* near antonym(s)

bed *n* **1** a place set aside for sleeping ⟨The sofa in the living room will be your *bed* for the night.⟩

syn bunk, pad, rack, sack

rel bedstead, futon, mattress, pallet; bunk bed, cot, couch, daybed, feather bed, four-poster, hammock, Murphy bed, shake-down, sleigh bed, sofa, sofa bed, studio couch, trundle bed, water bed; bassinet, cradle, crib

2 the surface upon which a body of water lies — see BOTTOM 2

3 a natural periodic loss of consciousness during which the body restores itself — see SLEEP 1

bed *vb* **1** to go to one's bed in order to sleep ⟨The campers all *bedded* down for the night around 9:00 p.m.⟩

syn crash [*slang*], retire, turn in

rel bunk, perch, roost, settle; doze, drop off, nap, nod, sleep, slumber, snooze; couch, lie (down), recline

phrases hit the hay (*or* sack)

near ant arouse, awake, awaken, rouse, wake, waken; bestir, stir; reawake, re-awaken; shift, stir

ant arise, get up, rise, uprise

2 to set solidly in or as if in surrounding matter — see ENTRENCH

bedaub *vb* to rub an oily or sticky substance over — see SMEAR 1

bedazzle *vb* **1** to hold the attention of as if by a spell — see ENTHRALL 1

2 to overpower with light — see DAZZLE

bedazzling *adj* giving off or reflecting much light — see BRIGHT 1

bedeck *vb* **1** to make more attractive by adding something that is beautiful or becoming — see DECORATE

2 to outfit with clothes and especially fine or special clothes — see CLOTHE 1

bedevil *vb* to cause persistent suffering to — see AFFLICT

bedevilment *n* the act of making unwelcome intrusions upon another — see ANNOYANCE 1

bedim *vb* to make dark, dim, or indistinct — see CLOUD 1

bedizen *vb* to make more attractive by adding something that is beautiful or becoming — see DECORATE

bedizened *adj* elaborately and often excessively decorated — see ORNATE 1

bedlam *n* **1** a place where mentally ill people are cared for — see INSTITUTION 2

2 a place of uproar or confusion — see MADHOUSE

bedraggled *adj* **1** containing, covered with, or thoroughly penetrated by water — see WET 1

2 not clean — see DIRTY 1

bedrock *n* an immaterial thing upon which something else rests — see BASE 1

bedspread *n* a decorative cloth used as a top covering for a bed — see COUNTERPANE

beef *n* **1** an expression of dissatisfaction, pain, or resentment — see COMPLAINT 1

2 muscular strength — see MUSCLE 1

beef *vb* to express dissatisfaction, pain, or resentment usually tiresomely — see COMPLAIN

beef (up) *vb* **1** to increase the ability of (as a muscle) to exert physical force — see STRENGTHEN 1

2 to make markedly greater in measure or degree — see INTENSIFY

beefy *adj* strongly and heavily built — see ¹HUSKY 1

beer belly *n* an enlarged or bulging abdomen — see POTBELLY

beetle *vb* to extend outward beyond a usual point — see BULGE 1

befall *vb* to take place — see HAPPEN

befit *vb* to be fitting or proper — see DO 1

befitting *adj* **1** following the established traditions of refined society and good taste — see PROPER 1

2 meeting the requirements of a purpose or situation — see FIT 1

befog *vb* **1** to make (something) unclear to the understanding — see CONFUSE 2

2 to make dark, dim, or indistinct — see CLOUD 1

3 to throw into a state of mental uncertainty — see CONFUSE 1

befogged *adj* **1** filled with or dimmed by fine particles (as of dust or water) in suspension — see HAZY 1

2 suffering from mental confusion — see DIZZY 2

before *adv* so as to precede something in order of time — see AHEAD 1

before *prep* **1** earlier than ⟨Since I'm a faster runner, I got there *before* him.⟩

syn ahead of, ere, of, previous to, prior to, to

rel till, until, up to

phrases in advance of

near ant next, next to, since

ant after, following

2 preceding in space ⟨The children always insisted on running *before* their parents.⟩

syn ahead of

rel against

phrases in advance of, in front of

ant after, following

beforehand *adv* **1** before the usual or expected time — see EARLY

2 so as to precede something in order of time — see AHEAD 1

befoul *vb* **1** to make dirty — see DIRTY

2 to make unfit for use by the addition of something harmful or undesirable — see CONTAMINATE

befuddle *vb* to throw into a state of mental uncertainty — see CONFUSE 1

befuddled *adj* suffering from mental confusion — see DIZZY 2

befuddlement *n* a state of mental uncertainty — see CONFUSION 1

beg *vb* to make a request to (someone) in an earnest or urgent manner ⟨She *begged* her children to be safe.⟩

syn appeal (to), beseech, besiege, entreat, implore, importune, petition, plead (to), pray, solicit, supplicate

rel cadge, mooch, sponge; ask, desire, request, sue; claim, coerce, command, compel, demand, force, insist, require; freeload

phrases call on (*or* upon)

near ant hint, imply, intimate, suggest; appease, conciliate, gratify, mollify, oblige, pacify, placate, please, satisfy; comfort, console, content, quiet

beget *vb* **1** to be the cause of (a situation, action, or state of mind) — see EFFECT

2 to become the father of — see FATHER

begetter *n* a person who establishes a whole new field of endeavor — see FATHER 2

beggar *n* a person who lives by public begging ⟨the pitiful *beggars* who roamed the streets⟩

syn mendicant, panhandler

rel bohemian, bum, drifter, hobo, tramp, vagabond, vagrant; guttersnipe, urchin, waif; miserable, pauper; cadger, hanger-on, leech, moocher, parasite, schnorrer, sponge; dependent; derelict, idler

beggared *adj* lacking money or material possessions — see POOR 1

beggary *n* the state of lacking sufficient money or material possessions — see POVERTY 1

begin *vb* **1** to take the first step in (a process or course of action) ⟨She *began* walking to work for exercise.⟩

syn commence, embark (on *or* upon), enter (into *or* upon), get off, kick off, launch, open, start, strike (into)

rel create, generate, inaugurate, initiate, innovate, invent, originate; adopt, embrace, take on, take up; establish, father, found, institute, organize, pioneer, set up; spawn; get around (to), get down (to), get round (to)

phrases get going, get to, set about

near ant cease, desist, discontinue, halt, knock off, lay off, quit, stop; close, complete; abandon, forsake, leave; abolish, demolish, destroy, exterminate, extinguish, phase out

ant conclude, end, finish, terminate

2 to come into existence ⟨The storm *began* late in the day and lasted all night.⟩

syn actualize, appear, arise, break, commence, dawn, engender, form, materialize, originate, set in, spring, start

rel be, breathe, exist, live, subsist; arrive, emerge; coalesce, cohere, shape (up); continue, endure, last, persist, survive

near ant conclude, desist, discontinue, finish, halt, quit, terminate; disappear, dissolve, evaporate, vanish; depart, die, expire, pass away, perish

ant cease, end, stop

3 to be responsible for the creation and early operation or use of — see FOUND

beginner *n* a person who is just starting out in a field of activity ⟨Although our son is only a *beginner* at swimming, he is making excellent progress.⟩

syn apprentice, babe, colt, cub, fledgling, freshman, greenhorn, neophyte, newbie, newcomer, novice, punk, recruit, rookie, tenderfoot, tyro

rel amateur, dabbler, dilettante; learner, student, trainee; candidate, entrant, probationer

near ant expert, master, pro, professional

ant old hand, old-timer, vet, veteran

beginning *adj* **1** coming before the main part or item usually to introduce or prepare for what follows — see PRELIMINARY

2 of or relating to the simplest facts or theories of a subject — see ELEMENTARY

beginning *n* the point at which something begins ⟨The actual *beginning* of the universe is still under debate, with some scientists continuing to uphold the big bang theory.⟩

syn alpha, birth, commencement, dawn, genesis, inception, incipiency, launch, morning, onset, outset, start, threshold

rel drawing board, first base, ground zero, square one; creation, founding, inauguration, initiation, institution, origination; cradle, origin, root, source, spring, well; dawning, opening; advent, appearance, arrival, debut (*also* début), emergence; childhood, infancy, youth

near ant cessation, closing, closure, completion, finale, finish, period, stop, termination, windup

ant close, conclusion, end, ending, omega

begone *vb* to leave a place often for another — see GO 2

begrime *vb* to make dirty — see DIRTY

beguile *vb* **1** to attract or delight as if by magic — see CHARM 1

2 to cause to believe what is untrue — see DECEIVE

3 to lead away from a usual or proper course by offering some pleasure or advantage — see LURE

beguiling *adj* **1** clever at attaining one's ends by indirect and often deceptive means — see ARTFUL 1

2 tending or having power to deceive — see DECEPTIVE 1

behave *vb* to manage the actions of (oneself) in a particular way ⟨If the children *behave* themselves properly, they'll get extra time at recess.⟩

syn acquit, bear, carry, comport, conduct, demean, deport, quit

rel check, collect, compose, constrain, contain, control, curb, handle, inhibit, quiet, repress, restrain; moderate, modulate, temper; act, impersonate, play

near ant act up, carry on, cut up, misbehave, misconduct

behavior *n* the way or manner in which one conducts oneself ⟨Usually the enfant terrible, he's promising to be on his best *behavior* for the party.⟩

syn actions, address, bearing, comportment, conduct, demeanor, deportment

rel etiquette, form, manners, mores, proprieties; p's and q's; amenity, civility, courtesy, decorum, politeness; air, carriage, poise, pose, posture, presence; aspect, look, mien; formality, protocol, rules; custom, habit, pattern, practice (*also* practise), trick, wont; convention, fashion, form, mode, style; affectation, attribute, characteristic, mark, trait; distinctiveness, oddity, peculiarity, singularity, strangeness, uniqueness, weirdness

behead *vb* to cut off the head of — see DECAPITATE

behemoth *n* something that is unusually large and powerful — see GIANT

behest *n* a statement of what to do that must be obeyed by those concerned — see COMMAND 1

behind *adj* not arriving, occurring, or set-

---

tled at the due, usual, or proper time —
see LATE 1

behind *n* the part of the body upon which
someone sits — see BUTTOCKS

behind *prep* **1** at, to, or toward the rear of
⟨She preferred to be *behind* the lead hikers, who were always too much in a rush
to enjoy the scenery.⟩
syn abaft, back of
phrases in back of
near ant ahead of
ant before

2 subsequent to in time or order — see
AFTER

behindhand *adj* not arriving, occurring,
or settled at the due, usual, or proper time
— see LATE 1

behold *vb* **1** to have a clear idea of — see
COMPREHEND 1

2 to make note of (something) through the
use of one's eyes — see SEE 1

beholden *adj* being under obligation for a
favor or gift ⟨Not wanting to be *beholden*
to anyone, he insisted on paying his own
way.⟩
syn indebted, obligated, obliged
rel appreciative, grateful, thankful

being *n* **1** a member of the human race —
see HUMAN

2 one that has a real and independent existence — see ENTITY

3 the quality or qualities that make a thing
what it is — see ESSENCE 1

belabor *vb* **1** to criticize harshly and usually publicly — see ATTACK 2

2 to strike repeatedly — see BEAT 1

belated *adj* not arriving, occurring, or
settled at the due, usual, or proper time —
see LATE 1

belatedness *n* the quality or state of being late — see LATENESS

belch *vb* to violently throw out or off
(something from within) — see ERUPT 1

beleaguer *vb* to surround (as a fortified
place) with armed forces for the purpose
of capturing or preventing commerce and
communication — see BESIEGE 1

belie *vb* **1** to give a misleading impression
of ⟨His bright smile *belied* his actual
mood, which was really one of great sadness.⟩
syn misrepresent
rel contradict; camouflage, cloak, conceal,
counterfeit, disguise, hide, mask, obscure;
color, deceive, distort, falsify, garble, mislead, misrender, misreport, twist; dissemble, feign, pretend
near ant bare, demonstrate, disclose, discover, evince, exhibit, expose, reveal;
flaunt, parade, show off
ant betray, represent

2 to prove to be false — see DISPROVE

3 to keep secret or shut off from view —
see ¹HIDE 2

belief *n* **1** mental conviction of the truth of
some statement or the reality of some be-
ing or phenomenon ⟨a *belief* in UFO's led
him to relentlessly scan the nighttime
skies⟩
syn credence, credit, faith
rel axiom, law, precept, principle, tenet;
assurance, certainty, certitude, conviction, positiveness, sureness; confidence,

dependence (*also* dependance), reliance,
trust; hope; doctrine, dogma, philosophy;
fanaticism, insistence
phrases article of faith
near ant distrust, mistrust, skepticism,
suspicion, uncertainty
ant disbelief, discredit, doubt, nonbelief,
unbelief

2 an idea that is believed to be true or
valid without positive knowledge — see
OPINION 1

believable *adj* worthy of being accepted
as true or reasonable ⟨She had a *believable*
excuse for missing the deadline.⟩
syn credible, creditable, likely, plausible,
probable
rel cogent, compelling, conclusive, convincing, decisive, effective, forceful, persuasive, satisfying, strong, telling; acceptable, cogitable, conceivable, imaginable,
possible, practical, reasonable; dependable, reliable, trustworthy; sophistic (*or*
sophistical), specious
near ant absurd, doubtful, dubious, fantastic (*also* fantastical), flimsy, outlandish,
preposterous, questionable, ridiculous;
impossible, inconceivable, unimaginable,
unthinkable; skeptical, suspect, suspicious, uncertain, unsure; hopeless, unworkable, useless
ant far-fetched, implausible, improbable,
incredible, unbelievable, unlikely, unplau-
sible

believe *vb* **1** to regard as right or true
⟨Only the most naive car buyer would
have *believed* the salesman's claim that the
dealership was actually losing money on
the deal.⟩
syn accept, buy, credit, swallow, take, trust
rel account, accredit, understand; assume,
presume, suppose; conclude, deduce, infer
phrases set store by (*or* on)
near ant distrust, doubt, mistrust, question, suspect; challenge, dispute
ant disbelieve, discredit, reject

2 to have as an opinion ⟨Despite the horrors she witnessed and endured, Anne
Frank steadfastly *believed* that "people are
really good at heart."⟩
syn conceive, consider, deem, esteem,
feel, figure, guess, hold, imagine, judge,
reckon [*chiefly dialect*], suppose, think
rel regard, view; accept, perceive; depend,
rely, trust; assume, presume, presuppose;
surmise; conclude, deduce, infer
near ant distrust, doubt, mistrust, question, suspect; disbelieve, discredit, reject

belittle *vb* to express scornfully one's low
opinion of — see DECRY 1

belittlement *n* the act of making a person
or a thing seem little or unimportant —
see DEPRECIATION

belittling *adj* intended to make a person or
thing seem of little importance or value —
see DEROGATORY

bellicose *adj* feeling or displaying eagerness to fight — see BELLIGERENT

bellicosity *n* an inclination to fight or
quarrel — see BELLIGERENCE

belligerence *n* an inclination to fight or
quarrel ⟨The dominant male lion was able
to withstand the *belligerence* of younger
challengers.⟩

syn aggression, aggressiveness, bellicosity, combativeness, contentiousness, defiance, disputatiousness, fight, militancy, pugnacity, scrappiness, truculence

rel antagonism, fierceness, hostility, hyperaggressiveness, unfriendliness; imperialism, jingoism, militarism; acidity, biliousness, captiousness, crankiness, crossness, disagreeableness, fractiousness, fretfulness, grouchiness, grumpiness, huffiness, irascibility, irritability, irritableness, orneriness, peevishness, pettishness, petulance, querulousness, rudeness, surliness, testiness, waspishness

phrases chip on one's shoulder

near ant antiaggression, anti-imperialism, antimilitarism; affability, amiability, amicability, benevolence, cordiality, friendliness, geniality, graciousness, pleasantness, sociability; gentleness, kindliness, mildness; amenability, complaisance, placability

ant nonaggression, pacifism

belligerent *adj* feeling or displaying eagerness to fight ⟨The player became quite *belligerent* and was thrown out of the game.⟩

syn aggressive, argumentative, bellicose, combative, contentious, discordant, disputatious, gladiatorial, militant, pugnacious, quarrelsome, scrappy, truculent, warlike

rel antagonistic, fierce, hostile, hot-tempered; acidic, bearish, bilious, bristly, choleric, crabby, cranky, cross, disagreeable, dyspeptic, fractious, fretful, grouchy, grumpy, ill-humored, ill-natured, ill-tempered, irascible, irritable, ornery, peevish, pettish, petulant, prickly, querulous, rude, snappish, snappy, surly, testy, touchy, ugly, waspish; savage, vicious; battling, fighting, warring

phrases on the warpath

near ant anti-imperialist, antimilitarist, unwarlike; affable, amiable, amicable, benevolent, complaisant, conciliatory, cordial, easygoing, friendly, genial, good-natured, good-tempered, gracious, ingratiating, kindhearted, obliging, pleasant, sociable; calm, quiet, relaxed, serene, tranquil, benign, gentle, kindly, mild

ant nonaggressive, nonbelligerent, pacific, peaceable, peaceful, unbelligerent, uncombative, uncontentious

bellow *vb* 1 to make a long loud deep noise or cry — see ROAR 1

2 to speak so as to be heard at a distance — see CALL 1

belly *n* 1 a need or desire for food — see HUNGER 1

2 an enlarged or bulging abdomen — see POTBELLY

3 the part of the body between the chest and the pelvis — see STOMACH 1

4 the seat of one's deepest thoughts and emotions — see CORE 1

belly *vb* 1 to extend outward beyond a usual point — see BULGE 1

2 to move slowly with the body close to the ground — see CRAWL 1

bellyache *n* abdominal pain especially when focused in the digestive organs — see STOMACHACHE

bellyache *vb* to express dissatisfaction, pain, or resentment usually tiresomely — see COMPLAIN

bellyacher *n* 1 a person who makes frequent complaints usually about little things — see CRYBABY

2 an irritable and complaining person — see GROUCH 1

belong *vb* 1 to have or be in a usual or proper place ⟨Your shoes *belong* in the closet, not in the middle of the living room where people will trip on them.⟩

syn go

rel place, stay; fit (in)

2 to be the property of a person or group of persons ⟨Those textbooks *belong* to the school system and not to the students.⟩

syn appertain, pertain

rel have, hold, own, possess

beloved *adj* granted special treatment or attention — see DARLING 1

beloved *n* a person with whom one is in love — see SWEETHEART

below *adv* 1 in or to a lower place ⟨The skipper climbed *below* to fix the engine.⟩

syn beneath, under, underneath

rel beside, near, nearby

near ant aloft, overhead

ant up

2 toward or in a lower position — see DOWN 1

below *prep* 1 in a lower position than ⟨For the photo she sat *below* everyone else, on the floor actually.⟩

syn beneath, under

rel underneath

ant above, over

2 subsequent to in time or order — see AFTER

¹**belt** *n* 1 a hard strike with a part of the body or an instrument — see ¹BLOW

2 the portion of a serving of a beverage that is swallowed at one time — see DRINK 2

²**belt** *n* 1 a strip of flexible material (as leather) worn around the waist ⟨a drugstore cowboy who loves his fancily decorated *belt*⟩

syn cummerbund (*also* cumberbund), girdle, sash

rel band, waistband; circle, loop, ribbon, ring; baldric, bandolier (*or* bandoleer), Sam Browne belt

2 a broad geographical area — see REGION 2

belt *vb* 1 to deliver a blow to (someone or something) usually in a strong vigorous manner — see HIT 1

2 to encircle or bind with or as if with a belt — see GIRD 1

3 to strike repeatedly — see BEAT 1

4 to proceed or move quickly — see HURRY 2

bemoan *vb* 1 to feel or express sorrow for — see LAMENT 1

2 to feel sorry or dissatisfied about — see REGRET

bemoaning *adj* expressing or suggesting mourning — see MOURNFUL 1

bemuse *vb* 1 to hold the attention of — see ENGAGE 1

2 to throw into a state of mental uncertainty — see CONFUSE 1

bench *n* 1 a public official having author-

ity to decide questions of law — see
JUDGE 2

2 an assembly of persons for the administration of justice — see COURT 3

benchmark *n* something set up as an example against which others of the same type are compared — see STANDARD 1

bend *n* **1** something that curves or is curved ⟨It's hard to see around that *bend* in the road, so be careful.⟩

syn angle, arc, arch, bow, crook, curvature, curve, turn, wind

rel warp; circle, ring, ringlet, round; coil, curl, curlicue (*also* curlycue); buckle, flexure, fold, loop, spiral, swirl, twist, winding; incurvature, reflection; decline, inclination, incline, slope; corner, turnoff; dogleg, hairpin

2 the act of positioning or an instance of being positioned at an angle — see TILT

bend *vb* **1** to cause to turn away from a straight line ⟨She *bent* the blade of the knife when she got it jammed in the drawer.⟩

syn arch, bow, crook, curve, hook, swerve

rel arc, round; incurvate, incurve, inflect, reflect; deflect, divert; entwine, swirl, turn, twine, twist, veer, warp; coil, curl, enroll (*also* enrol), loop, spiral; dent, dimple; meander, wave, weave, wind; decline, incline, slope

ant straighten, unbend, uncurl

2 to occupy (oneself) diligently or with close attention — see APPLY 2

3 to point or turn (something) toward a target or goal — see AIM 1

4 to turn away from a straight line or course — see CURVE 1

5 to change so much as to create a wrong impression or alter the meaning of — see GARBLE

6 to cause (something) to hold to another — see FASTEN 1

bending *adj* marked by a long series of irregular curves — see CROOKED 1

beneath *adv* in or to a lower place — see BELOW 1

beneath *prep* in a lower position than — see BELOW 1

benediction *n* **1** a prayer calling for divine care, protection, or favor — see BLESSING 1

2 something that provides happiness or does good for a person or thing — see BLESSING 2

benefaction *n* a gift of money or its equivalent to a charity, humanitarian cause, or public institution — see CONTRIBUTION

benefactor *n* one that helps another with gifts or money ⟨An anonymous *benefactor* gave the school a dozen new computers.⟩

syn angel, donator, donor, patron

rel benefactress, patroness; philanthropist; altruist, bestower, contributor, giver; helper, subscriber, supporter; guardian angel, protector, savior (*or* saviour)

near ant beneficiary, donee, giftee, recipient

beneficence *n* a gift of money or its equivalent to a charity, humanitarian cause, or public institution — see CONTRIBUTION

beneficent *adj* **1** having or marked by sympathy and consideration for others — see HUMANE 1

2 having or showing a concern for the welfare of others — see CHARITABLE 1

3 promoting or contributing to personal or social well-being — see BENEFICIAL

beneficial *adj* promoting or contributing to personal or social well-being ⟨Tutoring can often be as *beneficial* and rewarding for the tutor as for the student receiving the help.⟩

syn advantageous, beneficent, benignant, favorable, friendly, good, helpful, kindly, profitable, salutary

rel gratifying, rewarding, satisfying; auspicious, promising, propitious; advisable, desirable, healthful, healthy, salubrious, salutiferous, wholesome; gainful, lucrative, remunerative; ameliorative, amelioratory, bettering, constructive, supportive

near ant damaging, deleterious, harmful, injurious

ant bad, disadvantageous, unfavorable, unfriendly, unhelpful, unprofitable

benefit *n* **1** a thing that helps — see HELP 2

2 something that provides happiness or does good for a person or thing — see BLESSING 2

benefit *vb* to provide with something useful or desirable ⟨His summer internship *benefited* him in two ways: by giving him some tuition funds and by offering vital work experience.⟩

syn advantage, avail, help, profit, serve

rel succeed, work (for); aid, assist; better, improve; content, delight, gladden, gratify, please, satisfy; bless

near ant hinder, impede; damage, harm, hurt, impair, injure; afflict, distress, upset

benevolence *n* **1** an act of kind assistance — see FAVOR 1

2 kindly concern, interest, or support — see GOODWILL 1

benevolent *adj* **1** having or marked by sympathy and consideration for others — see HUMANE 1

2 having or showing a concern for the welfare of others — see CHARITABLE 1

benighted *adj* lacking in education or the knowledge gained from books — see IGNORANT 1

benign *adj* **1** not causing or being capable of causing injury or hurt — see HARMLESS

2 not harsh or stern especially in nature or effect — see GENTLE 1

benignant *adj* **1** having or marked by sympathy and consideration for others — see HUMANE 1

2 promoting or contributing to personal or social well-being — see BENEFICIAL

bent *n* **1** a habitual attraction to some activity or thing — see INCLINATION 1

2 a special and usually inborn ability — see TALENT

bent (on *or* upon) *adj* fully committed to achieving a goal — see DETERMINED 1

benumb *vb* to reduce or weaken in strength or feeling — see DULL 1

benumbed *adj* lacking in sensation or feeling — see NUMB 1

bequeath *vb* to give by means of a will — see LEAVE 2

bequest *n* something that is or may be inherited — see INHERITANCE

berate *vb* to criticize (someone) severely

or angrily especially for personal failings — see SCOLD

bereaved *adj* suffering the death of a loved one ⟨The grief of the *bereaved* parents seemed to be without limit.⟩

syn bereft

rel orphaned, widowed; distressed, grieving, melancholy, miserable, mournful, mourning, sad, sorrowing, suffering, unhappy, upset; bemoaning, crying, lamenting, wailing, weeping

bereft *adj* **1** suffering the death of a loved one — see BEREAVED

2 utterly lacking in something needed, wanted, or expected — see DEVOID 1

berserk *adv* in a confused and reckless manner — see HELTER-SKELTER

berth *n* an assignment at which one regularly works for pay — see JOB 1

beseech *vb* to make a request to (someone) in an earnest or urgent manner — see BEG

beseeching *adj* asking humbly — see SUPPLIANT

beset *vb* **1** to cause persistent suffering to — see AFFLICT

2 to take sudden, violent action against — see ATTACK 1

besetting *adj* caused by or suggestive of an irresistible urge — see COMPULSIVE

beside *prep* **1** in addition to — see BESIDES 1

2 not including — see EXCEPT

besides *adv* in addition to what has been said — see MORE 1

besides *prep* **1** in addition to ⟨*Besides* me, there are five people working on this project.⟩

syn as well as, beside, beyond, over and above

rel plus; including

phrases along with, at that, together with

near ant except (*also* excepting); less, minus, wanting

2 not including — see EXCEPT

besiege *vb* **1** to surround (as a fortified place) with armed forces for the purpose of capturing or preventing commerce and communication ⟨Armies *besieged* the castle for six months before it finally fell.⟩

syn beleaguer, blockade, invest

rel barricade, block, cut off, dam, encircle; assail, assault, attack, beset; confine, insulate, isolate, quarantine

phrases lay siege to

near ant emancipate, free, liberate, release, rescue

2 to cause persistent suffering to — see AFFLICT

3 to make a request to (someone) in an earnest or urgent manner — see BEG

besmear *vb* to rub an oily or sticky substance over — see SMEAR 1

besmirch *vb* to make dirty — see DIRTY

besmirched *adj* not clean — see DIRTY 1

bespatter *vb* to wet or soil by striking with something liquid or mushy — see SPLASH 2

bespeak *vb* **1** to arrange to have something (as a hotel room) held for one's future use — see RESERVE 1

2 to make known (something abstract) through outward signs — see SHOW 2

3 to serve as a sign or symptom of — see INDICATE 1

best *n* **1** dressy clothing — see FINERY

2 individuals carefully selected as being the best of a class — see ELITE 1

best *vb* to achieve a victory over — see BEAT 2

bestow *vb* **1** to make a present of — see GIVE 1

2 to provide with living quarters or shelter — see HOUSE 1

bestrew *vb* to cover by or as if by scattering something over or on — see SCATTER 2

bet *n* **1** the money or thing risked on the outcome of an uncertain event ⟨He offered the *bet* of a free lunch if her team won the World Series.⟩

syn stake, wager

rel collateral; handle, jackpot, kitty, pool, pot

2 a person or thing that is chosen — see CHOICE 2

bet *vb* to risk (something) on the outcome of an uncertain event ⟨I foolishly *bet* a month's allowance on the World Series.⟩

syn gamble, go, lay, play, put, stake, wager

rel bid, offer; adventure, chance, hazard, speculate, venture; endanger, imperil, jeopardize

bête noire *n* **1** something or someone that causes fear or dread especially without reason — see BOGEY 1

2 something or someone that is hated — see HATE 2

betide *vb* to take place — see HAPPEN

betoken *vb* to serve as a sign or symptom of — see INDICATE 1

betray *vb* **1** to be unfaithful or disloyal to ⟨Childhood friends of movie stars often *betray* them by telling their secrets to the supermarket tabloids.⟩

syn cross, double-cross, sell (out)

rel give away; inform (on), rat (on), snitch (on), tell (on), turn in

phrases go back on, stab in the back

near ant defend, guard, protect, safeguard, save, shield

ant stand by

2 to make known (something abstract) through outward signs — see SHOW 2

3 to lead away from a usual or proper course by offering some pleasure or advantage — see LURE

betrayal *n* the act or fact of violating the trust or confidence of another ⟨the terrible *betrayal* of having her best friend reveal her confidences to others⟩

syn business, disloyalty, double cross, faithlessness, falseness, falsity, infidelity, perfidy, sellout, treachery, treason, unfaithfulness

rel abandonment, desertion; deceit, double-dealing, duplicity, guile, two-facedness; fraud, informing, lying, snitching, talebearing, trickery

near ant dependability, reliability, trustworthiness; defense, protection, safeguard, shield

ant allegiance, devotion, faithfulness, fealty, fidelity, loyalty, staunchness, steadfastness

---

syn synonym(s)   *rel* related words
ant antonym(s)   *near ant* near antonym(s)

betrayer *n* **1** a person who provides information about another's wrongdoing — see INFORMER

2 one who betrays a trust or an allegiance — see TRAITOR

betrothal *n* the act or state of being engaged to be married — see ENGAGEMENT 1

betrothed *adj* pledged in marriage — see ENGAGED 1

betrothed *n* the person to whom one is engaged to be married ⟨He gazed lovingly at his *betrothed* throughout the dinner.⟩

syn fiancé, fiancée, intended

rel admirer, beau, beloved, boyfriend, darling, dear, favorite, fellow, flame, girlfriend, honey, love, lover, steady, swain, sweet, sweetheart, sweetie pie, valentine; bride

better *adv* to a greater or higher extent — see MORE 2

better *n* **1** one who is above another in rank, station, or office — see SUPERIOR

2 the more favorable condition or position in a competition — see ADVANTAGE 1

better *vb* **1** to be greater, better, or stronger than — see SURPASS 1

2 to make better — see IMPROVE

better half *n* the person to whom another is married — see SPOUSE

bettor *or* **better** *n* one that bets (as on the outcome of a contest or sports event) ⟨Thousands of *bettors* were at the racetrack last weekend.⟩

syn gambler, wagerer

rel high roller, piker; dicer; bluffer, sharper, speculator; bookmaker, handicapper, oddsmaker, tipster

beverage *n* a liquid suitable for drinking — see DRINK 1

bewail *vb* to feel or express sorrow for — see LAMENT 1

bewailing *adj* expressing or suggesting mourning — see MOURNFUL 1

beware (of) *vb* to be cautious of or on guard against ⟨*Beware of* that parrot because it bites!⟩

syn guard (against), mind, watch out (for)

rel attend, heed, mark, note, notice; behold, discern, observe, perceive, see, watch

phrases be on the lookout for, keep one's eyes open for (*or* keep one's eyes peeled for)

near ant discount, disregard, ignore, miss, overlook

bewilder *vb* to throw into a state of mental uncertainty — see CONFUSE 1

bewildered *adj* suffering from mental confusion — see DIZZY 2

bewilderment *n* a state of mental uncertainty — see CONFUSION 1

bewitch *vb* **1** to cast a spell on ⟨a Wiccan who believes that it is indeed possible to *bewitch* someone⟩

syn charm, enchant, hex, overlook, spell

rel curse, jinx, possess, voodoo; attract, beguile, captivate, fascinate, mesmerize, spellbind; entice, lure, seduce, tempt

near ant bless

2 to attract or delight as if by magic — see CHARM 1

bewitched *adj* being or appearing to be under a magic spell — see ENCHANTED

bewitching *adj* having an often mysterious or magical power to attract — see FASCINATING 1

bewitchment *n* **1** a spoken word or set of words believed to have magic power — see SPELL 1

2 the power to control natural forces through supernatural means — see MAGIC 1

beyond *adv* at or to a greater distance or more advanced point — see FARTHER

beyond *n* unending existence after death — see ETERNITY 2

beyond *prep* **1** on or to the farther side of ⟨The arrow flew *beyond* the fence and into the woods.⟩

syn over, past

rel outside

phrases on the far side of

near ant inside

2 out of the reach or sphere of ⟨Letting you have the day off is *beyond* my authority.⟩

syn outside, outside of, without

rel except (*also* excepting)

near ant inside

ant within

3 in addition to — see BESIDES 1

bias *adv* in a line or direction running from corner to corner — see CROSSWISE

bias *n* **1** an attitude that always favors one way of feeling or acting especially without considering any other possibilities ⟨He has a powerful *bias* towards sentimentality, which comes through even in his grittier stories.⟩

syn favor, one-sidedness, partiality, partisanship, ply, prejudice

rel chauvinism, cronyism, favoritism, nepotism; self-opinionatedness, self-partiality; bent, inclination, leaning, penchant, predilection, predisposition, proclivity, propensity, tendency; preconception, prejudgment, prepossession; bigotry, partisanship

near ant calm, detachment, indifference; aversion, dislike, distaste, hate

ant impartiality, neutrality, objectivity, open-mindedness, unbiasedness

2 a habitual attraction to some activity or thing — see INCLINATION 1

bias *vb* to cause to have often negative opinions formed without sufficient knowledge — see PREJUDICE

biased *adj* inclined to favor one side over another — see PARTIAL 1

Bible *n* a book made up of the writings accepted by Christians as coming from God ⟨She received a lovely *Bible* as a First Communion gift.⟩

syn Book, Good Book, Holy Writ, Scripture

bibulous *adj* able to soak up liquids especially readily — see ABSORBENT

bicker *n* an often noisy or angry expression of differing opinions — see ARGUMENT 1

bicker *vb* to express different opinions about something often angrily — see ARGUE 2

bickerer *n* a person who takes part in a dispute — see DISPUTANT

bid *n* an effort to do or accomplish something — see ATTEMPT 1

bid *vb* **1** to issue orders to (someone) by right of authority — see COMMAND 1

2 to request the presence or participation of — see INVITE 1

bide *vb* **1** to remain indefinitely in existence or in the same state — see CONTINUE 1

2 to remain in place in readiness or expectation of something — see WAIT

big *adj* **1** having great meaning or lasting effect — see IMPORTANT 1

2 of a size greater than average of its kind — see LARGE

3 having, characterized by, or arising from a dignified and generous nature — see NOBLE 2

4 having an abundance of some characteristic quality (as flavor) — see FULL-BODIED

5 coming before all others in importance — see FOREMOST 1

6 enjoying widespread favor or approval — see POPULAR 1

7 containing unborn young within the body — see PREGNANT 1

big *n* one of high position or importance within a group — see BIG SHOT

bight *n* a part of a body of water that extends beyond the general shoreline — see GULF 1

big leaguer *n* one of high position or importance within a group — see BIG SHOT

bigness *n* the quality or state of being large in size — see LARGENESS

bigot *n* one who stubbornly or intolerantly adheres to his or her own opinions and prejudices ⟨an incorrigible *bigot* who hasn't entertained a new thought in years⟩
syn partisan (*also* partizan), sectarian
rel fanatic, purist; nationalist; racialist, racist, supremacist; chauvinist, sexist
near ant freethinker, latitudinarian

bigoted *adj* unwilling to grant other people social rights or to accept other viewpoints — see INTOLERANT 2

big shot *n* one of high position or importance within a group ⟨a meeting at which all of the *big shots* in the company were present⟩
syn big, big leaguer, bigwig, heavy, kingpin, nabob, wheel
rel baron, czar (*also* tsar *or* tzar), king, magnate, mogul, prince, tycoon; VIP
near ant inferior, subordinate, underling; mediocrity, obscurity
ant lightweight, nobody, nonentity, nothing, shrimp, twerp, whippersnapper, zero, zilch

bigwig *n* one of high position or importance within a group — see BIG SHOT

bile *n* biting sharpness of feeling or expression — see ACRIMONY 1

¹bill *n* **1** a record of goods sold or services performed together with the costs due ⟨Why is the electric *bill* so high this month?⟩
syn account, check, invoice, statement, tab
rel receipt, reckoning; document, ledger, record; charge, cost, expense, fee, price, rate, toll; score, tally

2 a piece of printed paper used as money

in the United States ⟨The $5 *bill* has a picture of Abraham Lincoln on the front.⟩
syn greenback, note
rel paper money, scrip; buck, smacker [*slang*]; C-note, fifty, five, one, ten, tenner, twenty, two; cash, chips, currency, dough, legal tender, lucre, money, pelf; check, draft, money order

3 a sheet bearing an announcement for posting in a public place — see POSTER

4 the amount owed at a bar or restaurant or the slip of paper stating the amount — see CHECK 1

5 a rule of conduct or action laid down by a governing authority and especially a legislature — see LAW 1

²bill *n* **1** the jaws of a bird together with their hornlike covering — see BEAK 1

2 the projecting front part of a hat or cap — see VISOR

¹billet *n* a straight piece (as of wood or metal) that is longer than it is wide — see BAR 1

²billet *n* an assignment at which one regularly works for pay — see JOB 1

billet *vb* to provide with living quarters or shelter — see HOUSE 1

billow *n* a moving ridge on the surface of water — see WAVE

billow *vb* to extend outward beyond a usual point — see BULGE 1

billy *n* a heavy rigid stick used as a weapon or for punishment — see CLUB 1

billy club *n* a heavy rigid stick used as a weapon or for punishment — see CLUB 1

bin *n* a covered rectangular container for storing or transporting things — see CHEST

binary *adj* consisting of two members or parts that are usually joined — see DOUBLE 1

bind *n* **1** a difficult, puzzling, or embarrassing situation from which there is no easy escape — see PREDICAMENT

2 something that physically prevents free movement — see BOND 1

bind *vb* **1** to confine or restrain with or as if with chains ⟨The prisoner was *bound* by the wrists.⟩
syn chain, enchain, fetter, handcuff, manacle, shackle, trammel
rel bit, hobble, hog-tie, iron, lash, secure, tie, truss; attach, fasten, join, link; confine, constrain, curb, hamper, hinder, impede; limit, restrict; entangle, tangle
near ant emancipate, free, liberate, loose, release, rescue; undo, unfasten, untangle, untie; detach, disengage
ant unbind, unfetter, unshackle

2 to cover with a bandage — see BANDAGE

3 to gather into a tight mass by means of a line or cord — see TIE 1

binge *n* **1** a time or instance of carefree fun — see FLING 1

2 a social gathering — see PARTY 1

binge *vb* to take part in drunken revelry — see CAROUSE

biography *n* a history of a person's life ⟨An unauthorized *biography* of the actor gave him some serious headaches.⟩
syn life, memoir
rel autobiography; hagiography; psychobi-

---

syn synonym(s)   *rel* related words
ant antonym(s)   *near ant* near antonym(s)

ography; tell-all; chronicle, history, past, story; character sketch, profile

bipartite *adj* consisting of two members or parts that are usually joined — see DOUBLE 1

birch *vb* 1 to strike repeatedly with something long and thin or flexible — see WHIP 1
2 to strike repeatedly — see BEAT 1

bird *n* a member of the human race — see HUMAN

birdman *n* one who flies or is qualified to fly an aircraft or spacecraft — see PILOT

bird's-eye *adj* relating to the main elements and not to specific details — see GENERAL 1

birth *adj* being such by blood and not by adoption or marriage — see NATURAL 1

birth *n* 1 the act or instance of being born ⟨Almost from *birth*, he showed all the marks of future greatness.⟩
syn nativity
rel creation, genesis, origination, rise; accouchement, bearing, childbearing, labor, parturition; begetting, breeding, fathering, generation, mothering, parenting, reproduction, siring, spawning; fatherhood, maternity, motherhood, parenthood, paternity
near ant abortion, miscarriage; stillbirth
2 the line of ancestors from whom a person is descended — see ANCESTRY
3 the point at which something begins — see BEGINNING

birthplace *n* a place of origin ⟨Montgomery, Alabama, is considered the *birthplace* of the civil rights movement.⟩
syn cradle, home, motherland
rel hometown; country, nativity, old country, roots

birthright *n* 1 something that is or may be inherited — see INHERITANCE
2 something to which one has a just claim — see RIGHT 1

bisect *vb* to divide by passing through or across — see INTERSECT

bit *n* 1 a very small piece ⟨She left only a *bit* of the broccoli on her plate.⟩
syn atom, crumb, dribble, fleck, flyspeck, grain, granule, molecule, morsel, mote, nubbin, nugget, particle, patch, scrap, scruple, snip, snippet, speck, tittle
rel ace, dab, dash, driblet, drop, iota, jot, lick, minim, mite, modicum, nutshell, ounce, pinch, shred, smidgen (*also* smidgeon *or* smidgin *or* smidge), spot, strain, streak, suspicion, taste, touch, trace, whisper, whit; bite, mouthful, nibble, tidbit (*also* titbit); fragment, part, portion, section; chip, flake, shard, shiver, sliver, splinter; clipping, paring, shaving; smithereens
near ant chunk, gob, hunk, lump, slab; abundance, barrel, bucket, bushel, deal, heaps, loads, mass, mountain, peck, pile, pot, profusion, quantity, raft, scads, stack, volume, wad, wealth
2 a broken or irregular part of something that often remains incomplete — see FRAGMENT
3 a very small amount — see PARTICLE 1
4 an indefinite but usually short period of time — see WHILE 1
5 a performance regularly presented by an individual or group — see ACT 1

6 something that is pleasing to eat because it is rare or a luxury — see DELICACY 1

bite *n* 1 a harsh or sharp quality — see EDGE 1
2 a small piece or quantity of food — see MORSEL 1
3 an uncomfortable degree of coolness — see CHILL

bite (at) *vb* to consume or wear away gradually — see EAT 2

bite (on) *vb* to crush or grind with the teeth ⟨She tends to *bite on* her pencils when she thinks hard.⟩
syn champ, chew, chomp (on), crunch (on), gnaw (on), masticate, nibble
rel ruminate; munch, nosh, snack; consume, eat, ingest, swallow; bolt, devour, gobble (up *or* down), gorge, gulp, scarf, scoff, snack, wolf; nip, pick (at); gum, mumble
phrases sink one's teeth into

biting *adj* 1 causing intense discomfort to one's skin — see CUTTING 1
2 marked by the use of wit that is intended to cause hurt feelings — see SARCASTIC

bitter *adj* 1 having or showing deep-seated resentment ⟨a *bitter* attitude about always having to work on Saturday⟩
syn acrid, acrimonious, embittered, hard, rancorous, resentful, sore
rel disaffected, discontented, disgruntled, malcontent; contemptuous, cynical, disdainful, misanthropic, scornful; angry, cruel, harsh, mad, rough, savage, vehement, vicious, virulent; acid, caustic, cutting, mordant, sarcastic, trenchant
near ant caring, forgiving, gentle, kind, kindhearted, loving, sweet, sympathetic, tender, warm, warmhearted
ant unbitter
2 hard to accept or bear especially emotionally ⟨Discovering that he had been cut from the crew team was a *bitter* disappointment.⟩
syn afflicting, agonizing, cruel, excruciating, galling, grievous, harrowing, harsh, heartrending, hurtful, painful, tormenting, torturous
rel insufferable, insupportable, intolerable, unacceptable, unbearable, unendurable, unsupportable; appalling, awful, bad, dire, dreadful, ghastly, horrible, miserable, nasty, rotten, severe, terrible, vile, wretched; acute, extreme, intense, piercing
near ant bearable, endurable, supportable, sustainable, tolerable; livable (*also* liveable), sufferable, survivable; acceptable, allowable, reasonable
ant gratifying, pleasing, sweet
3 causing intense discomfort to one's skin — see CUTTING 1
4 difficult to endure — see HARSH 1
5 having a low or subnormal temperature — see COLD 1
6 uncomfortably cool — see CHILLY 1
7 expressing or suggesting mourning — see MOURNFUL 1
8 not giving pleasure to the mind or senses — see UNPLEASANT

bitterly *adv* with feelings of bitterness or grief — see HARD 2

bitterness *n* 1 a deep-seated ill will — see ENMITY

2 a harsh or sharp quality — see EDGE 1

3 an uncomfortable degree of coolness — see CHILL

4 biting sharpness of feeling or expression — see ACRIMONY 1

bitty *adj* very small in size — see TINY

bivouac *n* a place where a group of people live for a short time in tents or cabins — see CAMP 1

bivouac *vb* 1 to live in a camp or the outdoors — see CAMP (OUT)

2 to provide with living quarters or shelter — see HOUSE 1

bizarre *adj* 1 conceived or made without regard for reason or reality — see FANTASTIC 1

2 different from the ordinary in a way that causes curiosity or suspicion — see ODD 2

blab *vb* 1 to engage in casual or rambling conversation — see CHAT 1

2 to relate sometimes questionable or secret information of a personal nature — see GOSSIP

blabber *n* 1 a person who talks constantly — see CHATTERBOX

2 unintelligible or meaningless talk — see GIBBERISH

blabbermouth *n* a person who talks constantly — see CHATTERBOX

blabby *adj* fond of talking or conversation — see TALKATIVE

black *adj* 1 having the color of soot or coal ⟨a little *black* Scottish terrier⟩

syn ebony, pitch-black, pitch-dark, pitchy, raven, sable

rel dark, dusky, inky; blackish

near ant bright, brilliant, light, pale, palish

ant white

2 causing or marked by an atmosphere lacking in cheer — see GLOOMY 1

3 being without light or without much light — see DARK 1

4 not clean — see DIRTY 1

black *n* a time or place of little or no light — see DARK 1

blackball *vb* to reject by or as if by a vote — see NEGATIVE 1

blacken *vb* 1 to make dirty — see DIRTY

2 to make untrue and harmful statements about — see SLANDER

3 to make dark, dim, or indistinct — see CLOUD 1

4 to grow dark — see DARKEN 2

blackened *adj* not clean — see DIRTY 1

blackening *n* the making of false statements that damage another's reputation — see SLANDER

blackmailer *n* a person who gets money from another by using force or threats — see RACKETEER

blackness *n* a time or place of little or no light — see DARK 1

blackout *n* a temporary state of unconsciousness — see FAINT

black out *vb* 1 to destroy all traces of — see ANNIHILATE 1

2 to grow dark — see DARKEN 2

3 to lose consciousness — see FAINT

blade *n* 1 a hand weapon with a length of metal sharpened on one or both sides and usually tapered to a sharp point — see SWORD

2 an instrument with a metal length that has a sharp edge for cutting — see KNIFE

blahs *n pl* the state of being bored — see BOREDOM

blamable *adj* deserving reproach or blame — see BLAMEWORTHY

blame *n* 1 responsibility for wrongdoing or failure ⟨willingly accepted the *blame* for not seeing that the kitchen was properly cleaned⟩

syn culpability, fault, guilt, rap

rel blameworthiness, complicity, guiltiness, sinfulness; accusation, censure, condemnation, denunciation, finger-pointing, reproach; regret, remorse, self-reproach, shame

ant blamelessness, faultlessness, guiltlessness, innocence

2 the state of being held as the cause of something that needs to be set right — see RESPONSIBILITY 1

blame *vb* to express one's unfavorable opinion of the worth or quality of — see CRITICIZE

blameless *adj* free from guilt or blame — see INNOCENT 2

blamelessness *n* the quality or state of being free from guilt or blame — see INNOCENCE 1

blameworthy *adj* deserving reproach or blame ⟨We were all equally *blameworthy*, whether we had openly approved the free-speech restrictions or simply kept quiet about them.⟩

syn blamable, censurable, culpable, reprehensible, reproachable

rel bad, guilty, sinful, wicked; foolish, irresponsible, reckless; chargeable, disciplinable, impeachable, indictable, punishable; criminal, illegal, illicit, unlawful; illegitimate, improper, wrongful

phrases at fault

near ant flawless, perfect, pure; guiltless, innocent

ant blameless, faultless, impeccable, irreproachable

blanch *vb* to make white or whiter by removing color — see WHITEN

blanched *adj* lacking a healthy skin color — see PALE 2

bland *adj* not harsh or stern especially in nature or effect — see GENTLE 1

blandish *vb* to get (someone) to do something by gentle urging, special attention, or flattery — see COAX

blank *adj* 1 not expressing any emotion ⟨The teacher knew no one was paying attention when she looked out and saw all those *blank* faces.⟩

syn deadpan, empty, expressionless, impassive, inexpressive, numb, stolid, vacant

rel dull, vacuous, vague, vapid; enigmatic (*also* enigmatical), impenetrable, inscrutable, mysterious; motionless, static, still, wooden; reserved, restrained, reticent, taciturn; aloof, apathetic, cold, cool, detached, indifferent, phlegmatic, unresponsive

near ant engaged, interested, responsive; active, alive, animated, bright, busy, dynamic, effervescent, energetic, expansive,

---

syn synonym(s)   *rel* related words

ant antonym(s)   *near ant* near antonym(s)

exuberant, lively, vivacious; eloquent, revealing, revelatory; emotional, melodramatic, theatrical (*also* theatric), unreserved, unrestrained

ant demonstrative, expressive

2 lacking contents that could or should be present — see EMPTY 1

3 having no exceptions or restrictions — see ABSOLUTE 2

blank *n* **1** a piece of paper with information written or to be written on it — see FORM 2

2 empty space — see VACANCY 1

blanket *adj* belonging or relating to the whole — see GENERAL 1

blanket *n* something that covers or conceals like a piece of cloth — see CLOAK 1

blanket *vb* **1** to form a layer over — see COVER 2

2 to keep secret or shut off from view — see ¹HIDE 2

3 to cause to cease burning — see EXTINGUISH 1

blankness *n* empty space — see VACANCY 1

blare *n* loud, confused, and usually inharmonious sound — see NOISE 1

blare *vb* to make known openly or publicly — see ANNOUNCE

blaring *adj* marked by a high volume of sound — see LOUD 1

blarney *n* **1** excessive praise — see FLATTERY

2 language, behavior, or ideas that are absurd and contrary to good sense — see NONSENSE 1

blarney *vb* **1** to get (someone) to do something by gentle urging, special attention, or flattery — see COAX

2 to praise too much — see FLATTER 1

blaspheme *vb* to use offensive or indecent language — see SWEAR 1

blasphemous *adj* not showing proper reverence for the holy or sacred — see IRREVERENT

blasphemy *n* an act of great disrespect shown to God or to sacred ideas, people, or things ⟨In the 17th century the Quakers were persecuted for beliefs and practices that older churches regarded as *blasphemies*.⟩

syn defilement, desecration, impiety, irreverence, sacrilege

rel cursing, swearing; affront, insult; violation; corruption, debasement, pollution; sin, trespass

near ant consecration, purification, sanctification; reverence, veneration

ant adoration, glorification, worship

blast *n* **1** a loud explosive sound — see CLAP 1

2 a sudden brief rush of wind — see GUST 1

3 the act or an instance of exploding — see EXPLOSION 1

4 a social gathering — see PARTY 1

blast *vb* **1** to cause to break open or into pieces by or as if by an explosive ⟨The highway engineers will have to *blast* that hill in order to put a road through here.⟩

syn blow, blow up, burst, demolish, explode, pop, shatter, smash

rel annihilate, decimate, destroy; ruin, wreck; detonate, discharge; fragment, splinter

near ant collapse, implode

2 to cause (a projectile) to be driven forward with force — see SHOOT 1

3 to cause a weapon to release a missile with great force — see SHOOT 2

4 to criticize harshly and usually publicly — see ATTACK 2

5 to proceed or move quickly — see HURRY 2

blasting *adj* marked by a high volume of sound — see LOUD 1

blasting *n* a directed propelling of a missile by a firearm or artillery piece — see SHOT 1

blatant *adj* **1** engaging in or marked by loud and insistent cries especially of protest — see VOCIFEROUS

2 very noticeable especially for being incorrect or bad — see EGREGIOUS

blaze *n* **1** a sudden intense expression of strong feeling — see OUTBURST 1

2 the steady giving off of the form of radiation that makes vision possible — see LIGHT 1

¹**blaze** *vb* to make known openly or publicly — see ANNOUNCE

²**blaze** *vb* **1** to be on fire especially brightly — see BURN 1

2 to shine with a bright harsh light — see GLARE 1

3 to proceed or move quickly — see HURRY 2

blazing *adj* **1** being on fire — see ABLAZE 1

2 having or expressing great depth of feeling — see FERVENT 1

bleach *vb* to make white or whiter by removing color — see WHITEN

bleak *adj* **1** causing or marked by an atmosphere lacking in cheer — see GLOOMY 1

2 marked by wet and windy conditions — see FOUL 1

3 uncomfortably cool — see CHILLY 1

bleakness *n* an uncomfortable degree of coolness — see CHILL

bleary *adj* **1** depleted in strength, energy, or freshness — see WEARY 1

2 not seen or understood clearly — see FAINT 1

bleed *vb* **1** to feel deep sadness or mental pain — see GRIEVE

2 to flow forth slowly through small openings — see EXUDE

3 to remove (liquid) gradually or completely — see DRAIN 1

4 to rob by the use of trickery or threats — see FLEECE

bleed (for) *vb* to have sympathy for — see PITY

blemish *n* something that spoils the appearance or completeness of a thing ⟨The first mirror had a *blemish* on its surface, so we took it back to the store.⟩

syn blotch, defect, deformity, disfigurement, excrescence, fault, flaw, imperfection, mar, mark, pockmark, scar

rel abnormality, distortion, irregularity, malformation; bug, glitch; blot, blur, spot, stain, taint; damage, defacement, impairment, injury; failing, weakness

near ant adornment, decoration, embellishment, enhancement, ornament

blemish *vb* **1** to affect slightly with something morally bad or undesirable — see TAINT 1

2 to reduce the soundness, effectiveness, or perfection of — see DAMAGE 1

¹**blench** *vb* to draw back in fear, pain, or disgust — see FLINCH

²**blench** *vb* to make white or whiter by removing color — see WHITEN

blend *n* a distinct entity formed by the combining of two or more different things ⟨That fabric is a cotton and polyester *blend*, so it shouldn't shrink as much as pure cotton.⟩

syn admixture, amalgam, amalgamation, combination, composite, compound, fusion, intermixture, meld, mix, mixture

rel half-and-half; absorption, blending, coalescence, coalition, commingling, commixture, homogenization, immingling, immixture, integration, interfusion, intermingling, mergence, merging, mingling; assortment, hash, hodgepodge, hotchpotch, jumble, medley, mélange, mishmash, motley, patchwork, potpourri, variety; accumulation, aggregation, conglomeration

near ant component, constituent, element, ingredient

blend *vb* **1** to turn into a single mass or entity that is more or less the same throughout ⟨*Blend* the ingredients for the brownies very thoroughly to eliminate lumps in the batter.⟩

syn amalgamate, combine, commingle, composite, concrete, fuse, homogenize, incorporate, integrate, intermingle, intermix, meld, merge, mingle, mix

rel add, admix, beat (in), cut in, fold, stir, toss; coalesce, compound, emulsify; conjoin, join, knit, link, unite; intertwine, interweave, weave

near ant cleave, disjoin, disunite, divide, divorce, part, rupture, sever, sunder; disperse, dissolve, scatter; detach, disengage, split

ant break down, break up, separate, unmix

2 to form a pleasing relationship — see HARMONIZE 1

bless *vb* **1** to make holy through prayers or ritual ⟨The priest *blessed* the water.⟩

syn consecrate, hallow, sanctify

rel baptize, canonize, spiritualize; chasten, cleanse, purify; expurgate; commit, dedicate, devote; reconsecrate

near ant defile, desecrate, profane; dirty, foul, pollute, soil, taint, violate; blaspheme, curse, cuss, damn, execrate; condemn, damn, punish

2 to proclaim the glory of — see PRAISE 1

3 to furnish freely or naturally with some power, quality, or attribute — see ENDOW 1

blessed *also* **blest** *adj* **1** of, relating to, or being God — see HOLY 3

2 set apart or worthy of veneration by association with God — see HOLY 2

3 giving pleasure or contentment to the mind or senses — see PLEASANT 1

blessedness *n* **1** a feeling or state of well-being and contentment — see HAPPINESS 1

2 the quality or state of being spiritually pure or virtuous — see HOLINESS

blessing *n* **1** a prayer calling for divine care, protection, or favor ⟨said a *blessing* before the meal⟩

syn benediction

rel Godspeed; appeal, entreaty, grace, intercession, orison, petition, plea, prayer, supplication; sanctification

phrases laying on of hands

ant anathema, curse, execration, imprecation, malediction

2 something that provides happiness or does good for a person or thing ⟨Winning the lottery shortly after being laid off was an unexpected *blessing*.⟩

syn benediction, benefit, boon, felicity, godsend, good, manna, windfall

rel grace, mercy; favor, kindness; advantage, aid, assistance, gift, help, relief, support; comfort, consolation, solace; bonus, extra, lagniappe; delight, joy, pleasure

near ant hex, jinx; bother, irritant, nuisance, pest; disadvantage; cross, misery, trial, tribulation

ant affliction, bane, curse, evil, plague, scourge

3 an acceptance of something as satisfactory — see APPROVAL

4 the act of making something holy through religious ritual — see CONSECRATION

blind *adj* lacking the power of sight ⟨Our old *blind* cat kept walking into walls and furniture.⟩

syn eyeless, sightless, stone-blind

rel blinded, blindfold, blindfolded, unsighted; gravel-blind, purblind

near ant observant, observing, seeing; clear-sighted; gimlet-eyed, lynx-eyed, sharp-eyed

ant sighted

blind *vb* to overpower with light — see DAZZLE

blink *vb* **1** to shine with light at regular intervals ⟨You must stop at a *blinking* red light.⟩

syn flash, twinkle, wink

rel flare, flicker, glance, glimmer, glint, glisten, glister, glitter, scintillate, shimmer, spark, sparkle

2 to rapidly open and close one's eyes — see WINK 1

3 to cease resistance (as to another's arguments, demands, or control) — see YIELD 3

4 to look long and hard in wonder or surprise — see GAPE

bliss *n* **1** a dwelling place of perfect happiness for the soul after death — see HEAVEN 1

2 a feeling or state of well-being and contentment — see HAPPINESS 1

blissful *adj* experiencing pleasure, satisfaction, or delight — see GLAD 1

blissfulness *n* a feeling or state of well-being and contentment — see HAPPINESS 1

blistering *adj* **1** extreme in degree, power, or effect — see INTENSE 1

2 moving, proceeding, or acting with great speed — see FAST 1

blithe *adj* **1** having or showing a good mood or disposition — see CHEERFUL 1

2 having or showing freedom from worries or troubles — see CAREFREE

blithesome *adj* **1** having or showing a

---

syn synonym(s)   *rel* related words
ant antonym(s)   *near ant* near antonym(s)

good mood or disposition — see CHEERFUL 1

2 indicative of or marked by high spirits or good humor — see MERRY

blitz *n* **1** a rapid or overwhelming outpouring of many things at once — see BARRAGE

2 the act or action of setting upon with force or violence — see ATTACK 1

3 a series of activities undertaken to achieve a goal — see CAMPAIGN

blitz *vb* to use bombs or artillery against — see BOMBARD 1

blitzkrieg *n* **1** a rapid or overwhelming outpouring of many things at once — see BARRAGE

2 the act or action of setting upon with force or violence — see ATTACK 1

blitzkrieg *vb* to use bombs or artillery against — see BOMBARD 1

blob *n* **1** a small uneven mass — see LUMP 1

2 the quantity of fluid that falls naturally in one rounded mass — see DROP 1

bloc *n* **1** a group of people acting together within a larger group — see FACTION

2 an association of persons, parties, or states for mutual assistance and protection — see CONFEDERACY

block *n* **1** a number of things considered as a unit — see GROUP 1

2 something that makes movement or progress difficult — see ENCUMBRANCE

3 *slang* the upper or front part of the body that contains the brain, the major sense organs, and the mouth — see HEAD 1

4 a group of people acting together within a larger group — see FACTION

5 an association of persons, parties, or states for mutual assistance and protection — see CONFEDERACY

block *vb* **1** to close up so that no empty spaces remain — see FILL 2

2 to prevent passage through by filling with something — see CLOG 1

blockade *n* the cutting off of an area by military means to stop the flow of people or supplies ⟨It was the *blockade* of all the enemy's major ports that finally won the war.⟩

syn investment, siege

rel counterblockade; containment; encirclement, encompassment; confinement, insulation, isolation, quarantine, seclusion, segregation, sequestration; incarceration, internment

blockade *vb* **1** to disallow entry into (a place) by means of a physical barrier at the entry point — see CLOSE (OFF)

2 to surround (as a fortified place) with armed forces for the purpose of capturing or preventing commerce and communication — see BESIEGE 1

blockbuster *n* **1** a person or thing that is successful — see HIT 1

2 something that is unusually large and powerful — see GIANT

blockhead *n* a stupid person — see IDIOT

blond *or* **blonde** *adj* of a pale yellow or yellowish brown color ⟨The little boy's *blond* hair darkened to brown as he grew older.⟩

syn fair, flaxen, golden, sandy, straw, tawny

rel ash-blond (*or* ash-blonde), blondish,

strawberry blonde (*or* strawberry blond), towheaded; gold, light, white

near ant black-a-vised, brown, dark, olive, swart; black, ebony, raven

blood *n* **1** a group of persons who come from the same ancestor — see FAMILY 1

2 the line of ancestors from whom a person is descended — see ANCESTRY

3 the seat of one's deepest thoughts and emotions — see CORE 1

4 the taking of another person's life — see HOMICIDE 1

bloodline *n* the line of ancestors from whom a person is descended — see ANCESTRY

bloodstained *adj* smeared or stained with blood — see BLOODY 1

bloodthirsty *adj* eager for or marked by the shedding of blood, extreme violence, or killing ⟨The Goths were feared as wild and *bloodthirsty*.⟩

syn bloody, homicidal, murdering, murderous, sanguinary, sanguine

rel barbaric, barbarous, brutal, cold-blooded, cruel, heartless, inhumane, sadistic, savage, vicious, wanton; antagonistic, ferocious, fierce, gladiatorial, hostile; aggressive, assertive, bellicose, belligerent, combative, contentious, discordant, pugnacious, quarrelsome, scrappy, truculent, violent; merciless, pitiless, ruthless; bloodstained, fell, gory, grim; despiteful, hateful, malevolent, malicious, malign, malignant, mean, nasty, spiteful

near ant appeasing, conciliatory, disarming, mollifying, pacific, pacifying, peaceable, peaceful, peacemaking, placating, placative, propitiatory; unaggressive, unassertive; benign, benignant, compassionate, good-hearted, humane, kind, kind-hearted, sympathetic, tenderhearted; tender, warm, warmhearted; clement, lenient, merciful; affable, amiable, amicable, benevolent, gentle, kindly; submissive, surrendering, yielding

bloody *adj* **1** smeared or stained with blood ⟨After the fall, her elbow was all *bloody*.⟩

syn bloodstained, gory

rel bloodred, carmine, crimson, incarnadine, red, reddish, ruby, sanguine, sanguineous; sanguinary

2 eager for or marked by the shedding of blood, extreme violence, or killing — see BLOODTHIRSTY

bloody *vb* to reduce the soundness, effectiveness, or perfection of — see DAMAGE 1

bloom *n* **1** a state or time of great activity, thriving, or achievement ⟨a handsome young man in the full *bloom* of youth⟩

syn blossom, flower, flush, heyday, high noon, prime

rel Indian summer; blooming, blossoming, efflorescence, flowering; acme, apex, climax, meridian, peak, pinnacle, summit, zenith; glory, grandeur, splendor; silver age; comeback, recovery, revival

near ant decay, decline, downfall; bottom; shriveling (*or* shrivelling), wilting, withering

2 a rosy appearance (of the cheeks) ⟨After a snowball fight, she came inside with a *bloom* on her cheeks.⟩

syn blush, color, flush

rel brightness, brilliance, glow; pinkness, reddishness, redness, rosiness, ruddiness, sanguineness

near ant paleness, pallidness, pallor, pastiness, wanness, whiteness; greenishness, greenness, sallowness

3 the usually showy plant part that produces seeds — see FLOWER 1

bloom *vb* **1** to produce flowers 〈Forsythias only *bloom* at the beginning of spring.〉

syn blossom, blow, flower, unfold

rel leave; open

near ant dry up, fade, shrivel, wilt, wither; die, drop, expire, perish

2 to develop a rosy facial color (as from excitement or embarrassment) — see BLUSH

blooming *adj* having a healthy reddish skin tone — see RUDDY

blossom *n* **1** a state or time of great activity, thriving, or achievement — see BLOOM 1

2 the usually showy plant part that produces seeds — see FLOWER 1

blossom *vb* to produce flowers — see BLOOM 1

blot *n* a mark of guilt or disgrace — see STAIN 1

blotch *n* **1** a small area that is different (as in color) from the main part — see SPOT 1

2 something that spoils the appearance or completeness of a thing — see BLEMISH

blotch *vb* to mark with small spots especially unevenly — see SPOT 1

blotched *adj* having blotches of two or more colors — see PIED

blot out *vb* **1** to destroy all traces of — see ANNIHILATE 1

2 to keep secret or shut off from view — see ¹HIDE 2

¹blow *n* a hard strike with a part of the body or an instrument 〈He was dizzy for the rest of the day after the *blow* to his head.〉

syn bang, bash, bat, beat, belt, bop, box, buffet, bust, chop, clap, clip, clout, crack, cuff, dab, hack, hit, hook, knock, lash, lick, pelt, plump, poke, pound, punch, rap, slam, slap, slug, smack, smash, sock, spank, stinger, stripe, stroke, swat, swipe, switch, thud, thump, thwack, wallop, whack

rel counter, counterblow, counterstroke; body blow, hand, kick, knee, left, one-two, rabbit punch, right, right-hander, roundhouse, shiver, sidewinder, sucker punch, swing, uppercut; cruncher, kayo, knockdown, knockout, KO; battering, beating, bludgeoning, clobbering, cudgeling (*or* cudgelling), drubbing, hammering, lambasting, licking, pasting, pounding, pummeling (*also* pummelling), thrashing; flogging, whip, whipping

²blow *n* a sudden brief rush of wind — see GUST 1

¹blow *vb* **1** to breathe hard, quickly, or with difficulty — see GASP

2 to use up carelessly — see WASTE 1

3 to break open or into pieces because of internal pressure — see EXPLODE 1

4 to cause to break open or into pieces by or as if by an explosive — see BLAST 1

5 to proceed or move quickly — see HURRY 2

6 to make or do (something) in a clumsy or unskillful way — see BOTCH

7 to praise or express pride in one's own possessions, qualities, or accomplishments often to excess — see BOAST 1

²blow *vb* to produce flowers — see BLOOM 1

blow (out) *vb* to let or force out of the lungs — see EXHALE 1

blowout *n* a social gathering — see PARTY 1

blowup *n* **1** an outburst or display of excited anger — see TANTRUM

2 the act or an instance of exploding — see EXPLOSION 1

blow up *vb* **1** to become very angry 〈She *blew up* at everybody after a very long and very bad day.〉

syn flare (up)

rel anger, fulminate, rage, rant, rave, snap, snarl, sputter, storm, tee off, vent, vituperate; bristle, burn, foam, fume, glare, glower, seethe, sizzle, smolder (*or* smoulder), steam, warm; burst, explode, flare (out), flash, inflame (*also* enflame), madden

phrases blow a gasket, blow one's cool, blow one's stack, blow one's top, fly into a rage, fly off the handle, forget oneself, go ballistic, have a fit, hit the ceiling, hit the roof, lose one's cool, lose one's temper

near ant chill out [*slang*], cool (off *or* down), relax; hush, quiet (down)

ant calm (down), simmer down

2 to break open or into pieces usually because of internal pressure — see EXPLODE 1

3 to cause to break open or into pieces by or as if by an explosive — see BLAST 1

blowy *adj* marked by strong wind or more wind than usual — see ¹WINDY 1

blubber *vb* to shed tears often while making meaningless sounds as a sign of pain or distress — see CRY 1

bludgeon *n* a heavy rigid stick used as a weapon or for punishment — see CLUB 1

bludgeon *vb* **1** to deliver a blow to (someone or something) usually in a strong vigorous manner — see HIT 1

2 to strike repeatedly — see BEAT 1

blue *adj* **1** depicting or referring to sexual matters in a way that is unacceptable in polite society — see OBSCENE 1

2 feeling unhappiness — see SAD 1

blue *n* **1** the expanse of air surrounding the earth — see SKY 1

2 the whole body of salt water that covers nearly three-fourths of the earth — see OCEAN 1

blueprint *n* a method worked out in advance for achieving some objective — see PLAN 1

blueprint *vb* to work out the details of (something) in advance — see PLAN 1

blues *n pl* a state or spell of low spirits — see SADNESS

bluff *adj* being or characterized by direct, brief, and potentially rude speech or manner — see BLUNT 1

bluff *n* a steep wall of rock, earth, or ice — see CLIFF

bluff *vb* to cause to believe what is untrue — see DECEIVE

---

syn synonym(s)　　*rel* related words

ant antonym(s)　　*near ant* near antonym(s)

2 to present a false appearance of — see FEIGN

blunder *n* an unintentional departure from truth or accuracy — see ERROR 1

blunder *vb* **1** to make a mistake — see ERR 1

2 to proceed or act clumsily or ineffectually — see FLOUNDER 1

blunt *adj* **1** being or characterized by direct, brief, and potentially rude speech or manner ⟨He values honesty and is quite *blunt* about telling people what he thinks.⟩

syn abrupt, bluff, brusque (*also* brusk), crusty, curt, downright, short, snippy, unceremonious

rel gruff, rough, snappish; candid, direct, forthright, foursquare, frank, free-spoken, open, outspoken, plain, plainspoken, point-blank, straightforward; artless, discourteous, disrespectful, impertinent, impolite, inconsiderate, insensitive, rude, tactless; brief, closemouthed, laconic, reserved, reticent, terse, tight-lipped; earnest, honest, sincere; coarse, crass, crude, low, uncouth, vulgar

near ant civil, considerate, courteous, diplomatic, gracious, polite, politic, smooth, suave, tactful; loquacious, talkative, voluble; long-winded, prolix, verbose; courtly, cultivated, gallant, genteel, polished, refined

ant circuitous, mealymouthed

2 lacking sharpness of edge or point — see DULL 1

blunt *vb* to reduce or weaken in strength or feeling — see DULL 1

blunted *adj* lacking sharpness of edge or point — see DULL 1

blur *vb* **1** to make (something) unclear to the understanding — see CONFUSE 2

2 to make dark, dim, or indistinct — see CLOUD 1

blurry *adj* not seen or understood clearly — see FAINT 1

blurt (out) *vb* to utter with a sudden burst of strong feeling — see EXCLAIM

blush *n* a rosy appearance (of the cheeks) — see BLOOM 2

blush *vb* to develop a rosy facial color (as from excitement or embarrassment) ⟨She *blushed* when she realized she had mistaken his name.⟩

syn bloom, color, crimson, flush, glow, redden

rel incarnadine, rouge, ruddle; abash, chagrin, discomfit, disconcert, embarrass, faze, humiliate, mortify

phrases turn color

bluster *n* **1** boastful speech or writing — see BOMBAST 1

2 loud, confused, and usually inharmonious sound — see NOISE 1

3 a state of noisy, confused activity — see COMMOTION

bluster *vb* to talk loudly and wildly — see RANT

blustery *adj* marked by strong wind or more wind than usual — see ¹WINDY 1

board *n* **1** a group of persons formally joined together for some common interest — see ASSOCIATION 2

2 a leg-mounted piece of furniture with a broad flat top designed for the serving of food — see TABLE 1

board *vb* **1** to provide food or meals for — see FEED 1

2 to provide with living quarters or shelter — see HOUSE 1

boarder *n* one who rents a room or apartment in another's house — see TENANT 1

boast *n* an asset that brings praise or renown — see GLORY 2

boast *vb* **1** to praise or express pride in one's own possessions, qualities, or accomplishments often to excess ⟨He *boasted* about his latest killing in real estate so I thought he should be the one to pay for dinner.⟩

syn blow, brag, crow, swagger

rel bluster, harangue, puff; pride; gush; exult, glory, rejoice; brandish, display, exhibit, expose, flaunt, glorify, parade, show off; magnify, maximize

phrases blow smoke

near ant belittle, deprecate, diminish, discount, laugh off, minimize, play down, pooh-pooh (*also* pooh), shrug off; bemoan, lament, mourn, regret

2 to have within — see CONTAIN 1

boaster *n* someone who boasts — see BRAGGART

boat *n* **1** a small buoyant structure for travel on water ⟨Paddling the little *boat* across the lake is great exercise.⟩

syn bottom, craft, vessel, watercraft

rel catboat, ketch, sailboat, schooner, yacht; canoe, catamaran, ᵈhow, dinghy, dink, dory, dugout, flatboat, garvey, gig, johnboat, kayak, outrigger, paddleboat, pontoon, pram, punt, raft, rowboat, sampan, scow, scull, shallop, shell, skiff, surfboat, umiak, wherry; cruiser, inboard, motorboat, outboard, powerboat; houseboat, riverboat; auxiliary, bumboat, cutter, jolly boat, launch, lifeboat, longboat, tender, yawl; barge, hoy, keelboat; towboat, tug, tugboat; ferry, ferryboat, gondola, taxi, water taxi; banker, hooker, lugger, scalloper, seiner, shrimper, trawler, whaleboat, whaler, workboat; cockleshell, tub; airboat, air-cushion vehicle, hovercraft; hydrofoil, hydroplane; assault boat, PT boat, torpedo boat

2 a large craft for travel by water — see SHIP

boat *vb* to travel on water in a vessel — see SAIL 1

boatload *n* a considerable amount — see LOT 2

¹bob *vb* to make (something) shorter or smaller with the use of a cutting instrument — see CLIP 1

²bob *vb* **1** to make short up-and-down movements — see NOD

2 to deliver a blow to (someone or something) usually in a strong vigorous manner — see HIT 1

bobble *n* an unintentional departure from truth or accuracy — see ERROR 1

bobble *vb* **1** to make or do (something) in a clumsy or unskillful way — see BOTCH

2 to make short up-and-down movements — see NOD

bode *vb* to show signs of a favorable or successful outcome ⟨Her natural gift for reading *boded* well for her future in school.⟩

syn augur, forebode (*also* forbode), promise

rel forecast, foretell, predict, presage, prognosticate, prophesy; forewarn, warn; anticipate, divine, foreknow, foresee; betoken, foreshadow, harbinger, portend, prefigure, presignify; indicate, signify; allude, connote, hint, imply, insinuate, intimate, suggest

phrases bid fair

bodiless *adj* not composed of matter — see IMMATERIAL 1

bodily *adj* of or relating to the human body — see PHYSICAL 1

boding *n* something believed to be a sign or warning of a future event — see OMEN

body *vb* to represent in visible form — see EMBODY 2

body *n* **1** the main or greater part of something as distinguished from its subordinate parts ⟨The *body* of the novel was quite good, even if the beginning was a bit slow.⟩

syn bulk, chief, core, generality, main, mass, staple, weight

rel majority; aggregate, amount, sum, total, totality, whole; bottom, essence, essentiality, marrow, meat, nature, pith, quintessence, root, soul, stuff, substance; center, heart, hub, middle, nucleus, nut, seat; affair, argument, burden, crux, focus, gist, nub, pitch, point, purport; matter, motif, subject, text, theme, topic

near ant accessory (*also* accessary), adjunct, appendage, extension, offshoot; component, constituent, element, ingredient; division, part, piece, section, segment; angle, aspect, facet, feature, quality, side

2 a distinct and separate portion of matter ⟨To the early explorers the Atlantic was a gigantic and forbidding *body* of water.⟩

syn mass

rel aggregate, amount, bulk, quantity, volume; item, object, thing; material, stuff, substance; totality, whole

3 a group of people acting together within a larger group — see FACTION

4 a group of people sharing a common interest and relating together socially — see GANG 1

5 a member of the human race — see HUMAN

6 a usually small number of persons considered as a unit — see GROUP 2

bog *n* spongy land saturated or partially covered with water — see SWAMP

bog (down) *vb* to place in conflict or difficulties — see EMBROIL

bogey *also* **bogie** *or* **bogy** *n* **1** something or someone that causes fear or dread especially without reason ⟨Parallel parking has long been a *bogey* for many new drivers.⟩

syn bête noire, bugaboo, bugbear, dread, hobgoblin, ogre

rel apparition, ghost, phantasm (*also* fantasm), phantom, poltergeist, shade, specter (*or* spectre), spirit, spook, wraith; banshee, bogeyman (*also* bogyman), demon (*or* daemon), devil, fiend, ghoul, imp, incubus; fright, horrible, horror, monster, monstrosity, terror; bane, curse, enemy,

plague, scourge, torment; abomination, anathema

2 the soul of a dead person thought of especially as appearing to living people — see GHOST 1

bogus *adj* **1** being such in appearance only and made with or manufactured from usually cheaper materials — see IMITATION

2 being such in appearance only and made or manufactured with the intention of committing fraud — see COUNTERFEIT 1

3 lacking in natural or spontaneous quality — see ARTIFICIAL 1

bohemian *n* a person who does not conform to generally accepted standards or customs — see NONCONFORMIST 1

boil *vb* **1** to be excited or emotionally stirred up with anger ⟨The crowd *boiled* at the speaker's ranting.⟩

syn burn, foam, fume, rage, rankle, seethe, sizzle, steam, storm

rel fulminate, rant, rave; smolder (*or* smoulder); bristle, flare (up), inflame (*also* enflame); chafe, fret, stew; agitate, convulse, roil, shake

phrases see red

2 to cook in a liquid heated to the point that it gives off steam ⟨*Boil* the potatoes until they are tender before you try to mash them.⟩

syn coddle, parboil, poach, simmer, stew

rel scald; braise, fricassee, pressure-cook, smother, steam; reboil

3 to be in a state of violent rolling motion — see SEETHE 1

boisterous *adj* being rough or noisy in a high-spirited way ⟨The fans at the baseball game became particularly *boisterous* after the home run.⟩

syn knockabout, rambunctious, raucous, rollicking, rowdy

rel carnival, carnivalesque, raffish, raucous, riotous, rowdyish, ruffianly; stormy, tempestuous, turbulent, violent; headstrong, intractable, obstreperous, recalcitrant, uncontrollable, uncontrolled, undisciplined, ungovernable, uninhibited, unmanageable, unreserved, unrestrained, unruly, wild, willful (*or* wilful); bubbly, buoyant, effervescent, exuberant, high-spirited, impassioned, lively, sprightly, vivacious; clamorous, loudmouthed, noisy, openmouthed, strident, vociferous; howling, screaming, yelling

phrases wild and woolly

near ant sedate, sober, solemn, somber (*or* sombre), staid; decorous, dignified, proper, seemly; calm, hushed, noiseless, peaceful, placid, quiet, restrained, serene, silent, soundless, tranquil; collected, composed, constrained, controlled, imperturbable, inhibited, self-controlled, unflappable, unruffled; moderate, reasonable, subdued, temperate; impassive, phlegmatic, stoic (*or* stoical), stolid; depressed; aloof, detached, indifferent

ant orderly

bold *adj* **1** inclined or willing to take risks ⟨Our youngest brother was the *boldest* one in the family, instantly taking to everything from skiing to skateboarding.⟩

syn adventuresome, adventurous, audacious, daring, dashing, emboldened, enterprising, gutsy, hardy, nerved, nervy, venturesome, venturous

rel brash, daredevil, foolhardy, heedless, hotheaded, impetuous, imprudent, impulsive, incautious, madcap, overbold, overconfident, rash, reckless, thoughtless, wild; brave, courageous, dauntless, fearless, gallant, greathearted, heroic (also heroical), intrepid, lionhearted, stalwart, stout, stouthearted, swashbuckling, unafraid, undaunted, valiant, valorous; gritty, plucky, spirited, spunky; hasty, headlong, precipitate; absurd, asinine, balmy, brainless, foolish, half-witted, harebrained, scatterbrained, silly, wacky (also whacky), witless; unnecessary; dumb, idiotic (also idiotical), moronic, stupid; irrational, unreasonable

near ant chickenhearted, coward, cowardly, craven, lily-livered, milk-livered, milky, shy, timid, timorous; careful, cautious, heedful, prudent, wary; overcareful, overcautious; affrighted, afraid, alarmed, fainthearted, fearful, frightened, horrified, scared, shocked, spooked, startled, terrified, terrorized; unnerved; calm, cool, levelheaded, rational, reasonable, sage, sane, sensible, sound, wise; appalled, concerned, dismayed, upset, worried

ant unadventurous, unenterprising

2 displaying or marked by rude boldness — see NERVY 1

3 likely to attract attention — see NOTICEABLE

4 showing a lack of proper social reserve or modesty — see PRESUMPTUOUS 1

5 having an incline approaching the perpendicular — see STEEP 1

6 feeling or displaying no fear by temperament — see BRAVE 1

bold–faced adj displaying or marked by rude boldness — see NERVY 1

bolster vb **1** to hold up or serve as a foundation for — see SUPPORT 3

2 to provide evidence or information for (as a claim or idea) — see SUPPORT 4

bolt vb **1** to move suddenly and sharply (as in surprise) — see START 1

2 to proceed or move quickly — see HURRY 2

3 to hasten away from something dangerous or frightening — see RUN 2

4 to utter with a sudden burst of strong feeling — see EXCLAIM

5 to swallow or eat greedily — see GOBBLE

bomb n something that has failed — see FAILURE 1

bomb vb **1** to attack with a rapid or overwhelming outpouring of many things at once — see BOMBARD 2

2 to be unsuccessful — see FAIL 2

3 to defeat by a large margin — see WHIP 2

4 to use bombs or artillery against — see BOMBARD 1

bombard vb **1** to use bombs or artillery against 〈The Allies bombarded Germany for a great many months during World War II.〉
syn batter, blitz, blitzkrieg, bomb, cannonade, shell
rel rake, strafe; assail, assault, attack, devastate, hit, pound, ravage, strike

2 to attack with a rapid or overwhelming

outpouring of many things at once 〈Reporters bombarded the company spokesman with sharp questions.〉
syn barrage, bomb
rel examine, grill, interrogate, pump, query, question, quiz; debrief; cross-examine; annoy, hound, pester; flood, inundate

bombardment n a rapid or overwhelming outpouring of many things at once — see BARRAGE

bombast n **1** boastful speech or writing 〈We had little interest in being subjected to the speaker's bombast.〉
syn bluster, brag, braggadocio, gas, grandiloquence, hot air, rant
rel oratory, rhapsody, rhetoric; turgidity, wind; bloviation, verbosity, windiness; babble, blab, chatter, drivel, gabble, gibber, gibberish, jabber, prattle; jawing, patter, prating, yammering; egotism, self-conceit, self-importance, swagger

2 language that is impressive-sounding but not meaningful or sincere — see RHETORIC 1

bombastic adj marked by the use of impressive-sounding but mostly meaningless words and phrases — see RHETORICAL 1

bombshell n something that makes a strong impression because it is so unexpected — see SURPRISE 1

bona fide adj being exactly as appears or as claimed — see AUTHENTIC 1

bond n **1** something that physically prevents free movement 〈Before they could release the captive, they had to undo a number of bonds.〉
syn band, bind, bracelet, chain, cuff(s), fetter, handcuff(s), irons, ligature, manacle(s), shackle
rel captivity, confinement, constraint, curb, enchainment, hindrance, immurement, imprisonment, incarceration, restraint, restriction; entanglement, net, trammel, trap; collar, straitjacket (also straightjacket); fastener, hobble, hold, hold-down, holding, tie

2 a uniting or binding force or influence 〈The bond of love between them was so strong that even death could not break it.〉
syn cement, cord, knot, ligature, link, tie
rel attachment, connection, fastening, hookup, joint, linkage, linkup, tie-up, union, yoke; affection, fondness, sympathy; fetter, handcuff, manacle, shackle, trammel; constraint, curb, hampering, limit, limitation, restraint, restriction

near ant detaching, disengaging, parting, separation; unbinding, unfastening, unfettering, untying (or untieing); emancipation, freedom, liberation, release

3 a formal agreement to fulfill an obligation — see GUARANTEE 1

4 a substance used to stick things together — see GLUE

bond vb to form a close personal relationship — see COMMUNE

bondage n the state of being enslaved — see SLAVERY

bonding n a physical sticking to as if by glue — see ADHESION 1

bone adv to a great degree — see VERY 1

bone n **1** a habitual attraction to some activity or thing — see INCLINATION 1

2 bones *pl* a small cube marked on each side with one to six spots and usually played in pairs in various games — see DIE

3 *usually* **bones** *pl* the seat of one's deepest thoughts and emotions — see CORE 1

4 bones *pl* a dead body — see CORPSE

bone (up) *vb* to use the mind to acquire knowledge — see STUDY 1

bonus *n* something given in addition to what is ordinarily expected or owed ⟨This job offers a nice yearly *bonus* in addition to the salary.⟩

syn dividend, extra, gratuity, gravy, lagniappe, perquisite, tip

rel pension; bestowal, presentation; benefaction, beneficence, benevolence, bounty, charity, generosity, largesse (*also* largess), philanthropy; contribution, donation, gift, offering, present; grant, subsidy; boon, manna, windfall; favor, freebie (*or* freebee), giveaway, premium; award, prize, reward; fringe benefit, icing

bon voyage *n* an expression of good wishes at parting — see GOOD-BYE

boo *n* a vocal sound made to express scorn or disapproval — see CATCALL

booby *n* a person who lacks good sense or judgment — see FOOL 1

booby trap *n* **1** a usually concealed explosive device designed to go off when disturbed ⟨Luckily, the bomb squad didn't find any *booby traps*.⟩

syn mine

rel land mine; torpedo; bomb, explosive; hazard, pitfall, snare, trap; ambush, net, web

2 a danger or difficulty that is hidden or not easily recognized — see PITFALL 1

book *n* **1** a set of printed sheets of paper bound together between covers and forming a work of fiction or nonfiction ⟨I bought another new *book* yesterday, and I can't wait to read it.⟩

syn tome, volume

rel hardback, hardcover, paper, paperback, paperbound, pocket book, pocket edition, softback, softcover, trade book, trade edition; folio, quarto; guidebook, handbook, how-to, manual; catalog (*or* catalogue), cyclopedia (*also* cyclopaedia), dictionary, encyclopedia; monograph, primer, text, textbook, tract, treatise; novel, novelette, pulp; album, almanac, anthology, casebook, chapbook, nonbook, omnibus, picture book

2 *cap* a book made up of the writings accepted by Christians as coming from God — see BIBLE

3 information not generally available to the public — see DOPE

book *vb* to arrange to have something (as a hotel room) held for one's future use — see RESERVE 1

bookish *adj* suggestive of the vocabulary used in books ⟨"Fealty" is a *bookish* synonym for "loyalty."⟩

syn erudite, learned, literary

rel academic (*also* academical), donnish, inkhorn, pedantic, scholastic; belletristic (*also* belle-lettristic); highbrow, intellectual; educated, schooled; elevated, eloquent, formal, high-flown, lofty, majestic, stately, towering; bombastic, declamatory, florid, flowery, grandiloquent, highfalutin (*also* hifalutin), pompous, stilted

near ant chatty, conversational; familiar, informal; slangy; illiterate

ant colloquial, nonliterary, unbookish

booklet *n* a short printed publication with no cover or with a paper cover — see PAMPHLET

bookworm *n* a person devoted to intellectual or academic pursuits — see NERD 1

boom *n* a loud explosive sound — see CLAP 1

boom *vb* **1** to become greater in extent, volume, amount, or number — see INCREASE 2

2 to make a long loud deep noise or cry — see ROAR 1

boomerang *vb* to have the reverse of the desired or expected effect — see BACKFIRE

booming *adj* **1** marked by a high volume of sound — see LOUD 1

2 marked by vigorous growth and well-being especially economically — see PROSPEROUS 1

boon *adj* likely to seek or enjoy the company of others — see CONVIVIAL

boon *n* **1** a thing that helps — see HELP 2

2 an act of kind assistance — see FAVOR 1

3 something granted as a special favor — see PRIVILEGE

4 something that provides happiness or does good for a person or thing — see BLESSING 2

boondocks *n pl* the open rural area outside of big towns and cities — see COUNTRY 2

boor *n* a person whose behavior is offensive to others — see JERK 1

boorish *adj* having or showing crudely insensitive or impolite manners — see CLOWNISH

boost *n* **1** an act or instance of helping — see HELP 1

2 something added (as by growth) — see INCREASE 1

3 something that arouses action or activity — see IMPULSE 1

boost *vb* **1** to lift with effort — see HEAVE 1

2 to make greater in size, amount, or number — see INCREASE 1

3 to make markedly greater in measure or degree — see INTENSIFY

4 to move from a lower to a higher place or position — see RAISE 1

booster *n* a person who actively supports or favors a cause — see EXPONENT 1

boot (out) *vb* to drive or force out — see EJECT 1

bootleg *n* illegally produced liquor — see MOONSHINE 1

bootless *adj* producing no results — see FUTILE

booty *n* valuables stolen or taken by force — see LOOT

bop *n* a hard strike with a part of the body or an instrument — see ¹BLOW

bop *vb* to deliver a blow to (someone or something) usually in a strong vigorous manner — see HIT 1

---

border *n* **1** the line or relatively narrow space that marks the outer limit of something ⟨a rug with a fancily embroidered *border*⟩

syn bound, boundary, brim, circumference, compass, confines, edge, end, frame, fringe, hem, margin, perimeter, periphery, rim, skirt, skirting, verge

rel ambit; crest, curb, cusp; ceiling, maximum; demarcation, extent, limitation, measure, mere, restriction, termination; borderland, frontier, march, outskirts, pale, selvage; lap; shore

near ant center, core, heart; inner, inside, interior, middle, within

2 a region along the dividing line between two countries — see FRONTIER 1

border *vb* to serve as a border for ⟨That velvet *bordered* the sleeves on this shirt, until it fell off.⟩

syn bound, edge, frame, fringe, margin, rim, skirt

rel hem, trim; circumscribe, define, delineate, demarcate, outline, silhouette, sketch, trace; circle, compass, encircle, enclose (*also* inclose), girdle, girth, loop, ring, round, surround, wall; check, confine, control, curb, limit, restrain, restrict

border (on) *vb* **1** to come very close to being ⟨That comment *borders on* insubordination, and you should be more careful in the future.⟩

syn verge (on)

rel approach, near; appear, look, resemble, seem, suggest; approximate, compare (with), measure up (to), stack up (against *or* with)

2 to be adjacent to — see ADJOIN 1

bordering *adj* having a border in common — see ADJACENT

borderland *n* a region along the dividing line between two countries — see FRONTIER 1

¹**bore** *vb* **1** to make a hole or series of holes in — see PERFORATE

2 to force one's way — see ²PRESS 4

²**bore** *vb* to make weary and restless by being dull or monotonous ⟨The professor's lifeless and unimaginative teaching style *bored* the students.⟩

syn jade, tire, weary

rel pall; burn out, do in, drain, enervate, exhaust, fatigue, tucker (out), wash out, wear, wear out; debilitate, disable, enfeeble; demoralize, discourage, dishearten, dispirit

phrases put to sleep

near ant activate, animate, energize, enliven, excite, galvanize, invigorate, stimulate, strengthen, vitalize; amuse, entertain; allure, attract, beguile, bewitch, captivate, charm, enchant, hypnotize, mesmerize; monopolize, preoccupy; busy, immerse, involve, occupy; rally, rouse, stir

ant absorb, busy, engage, engross, enthrall (*or* enthral), fascinate, grip, interest, intrigue

bore *n* someone or something boring — see DRAG 1

bored *adj* having one's patience, interest, or pleasure exhausted — see WEARY 2

boredom *n* the state of being bored ⟨She spent that whole meeting in a state of complete *boredom*, waiting for lunch.⟩

syn blahs, doldrums, ennui, listlessness, restlessness, tedium, weariness

rel cheerlessness, dispiritedness, joylessness, melancholy; languor, lassitude, lifelessness, torpidity; dullness (*also* dulness), monotonousness, monotony, sameness; apathy, indifference, unconcern

near ant beguilement, bewitchment, captivation, enchantment, fascination; absorption, engagement, engrossment, immersion, involvement; animation, excitement, invigoration, stimulation; amusement, entertainment; diversion, relief

boring *adj* causing weariness, restlessness, or lack of interest ⟨I wish this book weren't so *boring*; I keep falling asleep whenever I try to read it.⟩

syn arid, colorless, drab, dreary, dry, dull, dusty, flat, heavy, humdrum, jading, leaden, monochromatic, monotonous, numbing, old, pedestrian, ponderous, slow, stale, stodgy, stuffy, stupid, tame, tedious, tiresome, tiring, uninteresting, wearisome, weary, wearying

rel aseptic, barren, blah, dullish, pleasureless, prosaic, prosy, soggy, spiritless; blank, gray (*also* grey), pallid, pedantic, sterile, suspenseless, undramatic, uneventful, unexciting, unimaginative, uninspiring, unnewsworthy, unrewarding, unsensational, unspectacular; annoying, bothersome, irksome, irritating; longsome; palling; draining, enervating, exhausting, fatiguing, wearing; debilitating, enfeebling; demoralizing, discouraging, disheartening, dispiriting; common, commonplace, ordinary, tepid, unexceptional, unsurprising, vapid; cumbersome, lumbering, plodding, poky (*or* pokey)

near ant amazing, astonishing, astounding, awesome, eye-opening, fabulous, marvelous (*or* marvellous), sensational, surprising, wonderful, wondrous; animating, breathtaking, electrifying, energizing, enlivening, exciting, exhilarating, galvanizing, hair-raising, inspiring, invigorating, rip-roaring, rousing, stimulating, stirring, thrilling; amusing, diverting, entertaining; moving, poignant, touching; alluring, attracting, attractive, beguiling, bewitching, captivating, charming, enchanting, enthralling, entrancing, fascinating; mesmerizing, spellbinding; suspenseful; arresting, provocative, tantalizing

ant absorbing, engaging, engrossing, gripping, interesting, intriguing, involving, riveting

born *adj* **1** being such from birth or by nature — see NATURAL 1

2 belonging to a particular place by birth or origin — see NATIVE 1

borrow *vb* to take for one's own use (something originated by another) — see ADOPT

bosom *adj* closely acquainted — see FAMILIAR 1

bosom *n* the seat of one's deepest thoughts and emotions — see CORE 1

bosom *vb* to surround or cover closely — see ENFOLD 1

boss *n* the person (as an employer or supervisor) who tells people and especially workers what to do ⟨Every morning the *boss* hands out a list of top-priority tasks.⟩

syn captain, chief, foreman, head, kingpin, leader, master, taskmaster

rel directress, mistress; administrator, commander, director, executive, general, governor, hierarch, higher-up; leadman, manager, overseer, principal, skipper, standard-bearer, steward, straw boss, superintendent, superior, supervisor; dominator, overlord, potentate, ruler, sovereign (*also* sovran); figurehead; baron, czar (*also* tsar *or* tzar); king, magnate, mogul, president, prince; bigwig, top dog, top gun; cohead, coleader; employer; micromanager; subchief, subdirector; bellwether

near ant dependent, inferior, junior, secondary, subject, subordinate, underling

boss *vb* 1 to be in charge of ⟨She *bossed* that project for years, until she was promoted again.⟩

syn captain, handle, head, overlook, oversee, superintend, supervise

rel administer, command, control, direct, guide, manage, order, run, shepherd, show, steer; monitor, preside (over); govern, rule

phrases call the shots (of), call the tune (for), ride herd on, watch over

2 to exercise authority or power over — see GOVERN 1

3 to serve as leader of — see LEAD 2

boss (around) *vb* to issue orders to (someone) by right of authority — see COMMAND 1

bossy *adj* fond of ordering people around ⟨I don't want to work with him because he's so *bossy* and always runs roughshod over me.⟩

syn authoritarian, authoritative, autocratic (*also* autocratical), despotic, dictatorial, domineering, imperious, masterful, overbearing, peremptory, tyrannical (*also* tyrannic), tyrannous

rel arrogant, assumptive, disdainful, fastuous, haughty, highfalutin (*also* hifalutin), high-hat, important, lofty, lordly, overweening, presuming, presumptuous, pretentious, proud, supercilious, superior, toplofty (*also* toploftical), uppish, uppity; commanding, controlling, dictating, regimental; arbitrary, high-handed, imperial; directorial; aggressive, assertive, self-assertive; imperative; conceited, pompous, vain; all-powerful, almighty, omnipotent; firm, stern

near ant humble, meek, modest, unassuming; amenable, docile, obedient, tractable; indecisive, irresolute; acquiescent, compliant, passive, resigned, submissive, yielding

botch *vb* to make or do (something) in a clumsy or unskillful way ⟨The first time we tried to make a cake, we *botched* the job completely.⟩

syn blow, bobble, bungle, butcher, dub, flub, fluff, foozle, foul up, fumble, louse up, mangle, mess (up), muff, murder, screw up

rel blunder, muddle, piffle; blemish, damage, flaw, harm, hurt, impair, injure, mar, mutilate, ruin, spoil, vitiate; destroy, wreck; mishandle, mismanage

near ant ameliorate, better, enhance, help,

improve, meliorate, rectify, refine, reform, remedy; doctor, fix, patch, recondition, renovate, repair, revamp

botched *adj* showing or marked by a lack of skill and tact (as in dealing with a situation) — see AWKWARD 2

bother *n* 1 a state of noisy, confused activity — see COMMOTION

2 one who is obnoxiously annoying — see NUISANCE 1

3 something that is a source of irritation — see ANNOYANCE 3

4 the feeling of impatience or anger caused by another's repeated disagreeable acts — see ANNOYANCE 2

bother *vb* 1 to thrust oneself upon (another) without invitation ⟨I am never going to get this work done if people don't stop wandering into the room and *bothering* me!⟩

syn bug, chivy (*or* chivvy), disturb, intrude (upon), pester

rel inconvenience, trouble; aggravate, annoy, bedevil, chafe, devil, dog, dun, exasperate, fret, gall, get, grate, hassle, irk, irritate, nettle, peeve, persecute, pique, put out, rankle, rasp, rile, roil, torment, vex, worry; beleaguer, beset, besiege; distress, plague; afflict, provoke; anger, antagonize, enrage, incense, inflame (*also* enflame), infuriate, madden, outrage; agitate, perturb; butt in, cut in (on), obtrude; encroach, infringe, invade, trespass

near ant disregard, forget, ignore, leave, slight; appease, conciliate, disarm, mollify, oblige, placate; delight, gladden, gratify, please, satisfy; comfort, console, content

2 to disturb the peace of mind of (someone) especially by repeated disagreeable acts — see IRRITATE 1

3 to experience concern or anxiety — see WORRY 1

4 to trouble the mind of; to make uneasy — see DISTURB 1

bothersome *adj* causing annoyance — see ANNOYING

bottleneck *n* a crowded mass (as of cars) that impedes or blocks movement — see JAM 1

bottom *adj* of, relating to, or located at the bottom ⟨was sitting on the *bottom* step of the stairway⟩

syn low

rel below, lower, low-grade, lowly, nether, under; lowered, low-lying, sunken

near ant higher, loftier, upper; elevated, escalated, heightened, jacked (up), lifted, raised, uplifted, upraised

ant highest, loftiest, top, topmost, upmost, uppermost

bottom *n* 1 the side or part facing downward from something ⟨That side of the shelf is supposed to be the *bottom*, so turn it over before you assemble the bookcase.⟩

syn underbelly, underbody, underpart, underside, undersurface

rel belly, sole, toe; base, floor, foot, ground, seat, underpinning; undercarriage

near ant acme, apex, climax, crest, crown, culmination, height, high-water mark, meridian, peak, pinnacle, roof, summit; cusp, head, point, tip, tip-top, zenith

ant face, top

2 the surface upon which a body of water

---

syn synonym(s)   *rel* related words
ant antonym(s)   *near ant* near antonym(s)

box 87

lies ⟨My missing fishing pole is probably lying on the *bottom* of the lake.⟩
syn bed, floor
rel riverbed; base, basement, foundation, ground
near ant surface
3 the lowest part, place, or point ⟨sliding all the way to the *bottom* of the snow-covered slope⟩
syn base, basement, foot, rock bottom
rel basis, bed, bedrock, foundation, ground, groundwork, keystone, seat, underpinning; depth, nadir, zero
near ant acme, apex, climax, crest, culmination, height, meridian, peak, pinnacle, summit, tip, tip-top, zenith
ant head, top, vertex
4 the part of the body upon which someone sits — see BUTTOCKS
5 a small buoyant structure for travel on water — see BOAT 1
6 an immaterial thing upon which something else rests — see BASE 1
bottomless *adj* **1** being or seeming to be without limits — see INFINITE
2 extending far downward — see DEEP 1
bough *n* a major outgrowth from the main stem of a woody plant — see BRANCH 1
boulevard *n* a passage cleared for public vehicular travel — see WAY 1
bounce *n* active strength of body or mind — see VIGOR 1
bounce *vb* **1** to drive or force out — see EJECT 1
2 to strike and fly off at an angle — see GLANCE 1
3 to let go from office, service, or employment — see DISMISS 1
4 to set before the mind for consideration — see PROPOSE 1
5 to move with a light springing step — see SKIP 1
bounce (back) *vb* to regain a former or normal state — see RECOVER 2
bouncing *adj* **1** enjoying health and vigor — see HEALTHY 1
2 having much high-spirited energy and movement — see LIVELY 1
¹**bound** *n* **1** a real or imaginary point beyond which a person or thing cannot go — see LIMIT 1
2 the line or relatively narrow space that marks the outer limit of something — see BORDER 1
²**bound** *n* an act of leaping into the air — see LEAP 1
¹**bound** *vb* **1** to mark the limits of — see LIMIT 2
2 to serve as a border for — see BORDER
²**bound** *vb* **1** to move with a light springing step — see SKIP 1
2 to propel oneself upward or forward into the air — see JUMP 1
bound *adj* fully committed to achieving a goal — see DETERMINED 1
boundary *n* **1** a real or imaginary point beyond which a person or thing cannot go — see LIMIT 1
2 the line or relatively narrow space that marks the outer limit of something — see BORDER 1
bounded *adj* having distinct or certain limits — see LIMITED 1

boundless *adj* being or seeming to be without limits — see INFINITE
bounteous *adj* **1** being more than enough without being excessive — see PLENTIFUL
2 giving or sharing in abundance and without hesitation — see GENEROUS 1
bountiful *adj* **1** being more than enough without being excessive — see PLENTIFUL
2 giving or sharing in abundance and without hesitation — see GENEROUS 1
bountifully *adv* in a generous manner — see WELL 2
bountifulness *n* the quality or state of being generous — see LIBERALITY
bounty *n* **1** something offered or given in return for a service performed — see REWARD
2 the quality or state of being generous — see LIBERALITY
3 the total amount collected or obtained especially at one time — see HAUL 1
bouquet *n* **1** a bunch of flowers ⟨I bought my wife a nice *bouquet* for her birthday.⟩
syn nosegay, posy
rel boutonniere, corsage; arrangement; garland, lei
2 a sweet or pleasant smell — see FRAGRANCE
3 an admiring personal remark — see COMPLIMENT 1
bout *n* **1** a competitive encounter between individuals or groups carried on for amusement, exercise, or in pursuit of a prize — see GAME 1
2 a sudden experiencing of a physical or mental disorder — see ATTACK 2
¹**bow** *vb* **1** to cease resistance (as to another's arguments, demands, or control) — see YIELD 3
2 to give up and cease resistance (as to a liking, temptation, or habit) — see YIELD 1
²**bow** *vb* **1** to turn away from a straight line or course — see CURVE 1
2 to cause to turn away from a straight line — see BEND 1
bow *n* something that curves or is curved — see BEND 1
bowed *adj* **1** bending downward or forward — see NODDING
2 directed down — see DOWNCAST 1
bowing *adj* bending downward or forward — see NODDING
bowl *n* a large usually roofless building for sporting events with tiers of seats for spectators — see STADIUM
bowl *vb* **1** to move or proceed smoothly and readily — see FLOW 2
2 to proceed or move quickly — see HURRY 2
bowl (down or **over)** *vb* to strike (someone) so forcefully as to cause a fall — see FELL 1
bowled over *adj* affected with sudden and great wonder or surprise — see THUNDERSTRUCK
¹**box** *n* **1** a covered rectangular container for storing or transporting things — see CHEST
2 a boxlike container for holding a dead body — see COFFIN
²**box** *n* a hard strike with a part of the body or an instrument — see ¹BLOW

box *vb* to deliver a blow to (someone or something) usually in a strong vigorous manner — see HIT 1

boxer *n* one that engages in the sport of fighting with the fists ⟨That *boxer* is quite famous for being the youngest heavyweight champion ever.⟩

syn fighter, prizefighter, pugilist

rel slugger; bantamweight, cruiserweight, featherweight, flyweight, light heavyweight, lightweight, middleweight, superheavyweight, welterweight

boy *n* 1 a male person who has not yet reached adulthood ⟨A giggling little *boy* ran by.⟩

syn lad, laddie, nipper, shaver, sonny, stripling, tad, youth

rel adolescent, juvenile, kid, kiddo, minor, moppet, teenager, tween, youngster; brat, gamin, guttersnipe, imp, squirt, urchin, whippersnapper; schoolboy; toddler, tot

2 a male romantic companion — see BOYFRIEND

boyfriend *n* a male romantic companion ⟨her *boyfriend* always brings her flowers for Valentine's Day⟩

syn beau, boy, fellow, man, old man, swain

rel admirer, crush, steady; suitor, wooer; beloved, darling, dear, favorite, flame, honey, love, lover, significant other, soul mate, squeeze [*slang*], sweet, sweetheart, sweetie pie, valentine; fancy man, gigolo; date, escort; husband; fiancé, intended

brace *n* 1 a structure that holds up or serves as a foundation for something else — see SUPPORT 1

2 two things of the same or similar kind that match or are considered together — see PAIR

brace *vb* 1 to give life, vigor, or spirit to — see ANIMATE

2 to hold up or serve as a foundation for — see SUPPORT 3

3 to prepare (oneself) mentally or emotionally — see FORTIFY 1

bracelet *n* something that physically prevents free movement — see BOND 1

bracing *adj* having a renewing effect on the state of the body or mind — see TONIC 1

bracket *n* one of the units into which a whole is divided on the basis of a common characteristic — see CLASS 2

bracket *vb* to describe as similar — see COMPARE 1

brackish *adj* 1 disagreeable or disgusting to the sense of taste — see DISTASTEFUL 1

2 of, relating to, or containing salt — see SALTY 1

brag *n* 1 boastful speech or writing — see BOMBAST 1

2 someone who boasts — see BRAGGART

brag *vb* to praise or express pride in one's own possessions, qualities, or accomplishments often to excess — see BOAST 1

braggadocio *n* boastful speech or writing — see BOMBAST 1

braggart *n* someone who boasts ⟨a *braggart* who was always talking about how much money he made⟩

syn boaster, brag, bragger, swaggerer

rel blusterer; self-advertiser, self-dramatizer, self-promoter

bragger *n* someone who boasts — see BRAGGART

braid *n* a length of something formed of three or more strands woven together ⟨Until she was 15, she had a *braid* that reached to her knees.⟩

syn lace, lacing, plait, plat

rel cornrow, deadlock, pigtail, queue; braiding

braid *vb* to form into a braid ⟨They taught each other how to *braid* yarn into bracelets.⟩

syn plait, plat, pleat

rel interlace, interweave, weave

brain *n* 1 a very smart person — see GENIUS 1

2 *often* **brains** *pl* the ability to learn and understand or to deal with problems — see INTELLIGENCE 1

3 the part of a person that feels, thinks, perceives, wills, and especially reasons — see MIND 1

brainless *adj* 1 not having or showing an ability to absorb ideas readily — see STUPID 1

2 showing or marked by a lack of good sense or judgment — see FOOLISH 1

brainlessness *n* 1 lack of good sense and judgment — see FOOLISHNESS 1

2 the quality or state of lacking intelligence or quickness of mind — see STUPIDITY 1

brainstorm *vb* to engage in an exchange of information or ideas — see COMMUNICATE 2

brainy *adj* having or showing quickness of mind — see INTELLIGENT 1

brake *n* a thick patch of shrubbery, small trees, or underbrush — see THICKET

brake *vb* to cause to move or proceed at a less rapid pace — see SLOW

braking *n* a usually gradual decrease in the pace or level of activity of something — see SLOWDOWN

brambly *adj* having leaves or branches which are likely to cause a scratch — see SCRATCHY 1

branch *n* 1 a major outgrowth from the main stem of a woody plant ⟨I loved climbing among the *branches* of that old tree.⟩

syn bough, limb

rel branchlet, offshoot, outgrowth, shoot, spur; spray, sprig

2 a local unit of an organization — see CHAPTER 1

3 a large unit of a governmental, business, or educational organization — see DIVISION 2

branch *vb* to extend outwards from or as if from a central point — see RADIATE 1

branch (out) *vb* to go or move in different directions from a central point — see SEPARATE 2

brand *n* 1 a device (as a word) identifying the maker of a piece of merchandise and legally reserved for the exclusive use of that person or company — see TRADEMARK 1

2 a mark of guilt or disgrace — see STAIN 1

---

syn synonym(s)   *rel* related words
ant antonym(s)   *near ant* near antonym(s)

3 a hand weapon with a length of metal sharpened on one or both sides and usually tapered to a sharp point — see SWORD

brand *vb* to produce a vivid impression of — see ENGRAVE 2

brand–new *adj* **1** being in an original and unused or unspoiled state — see FRESH 1
2 recently made and never used before — see NEW 3

brash *adj* **1** displaying or marked by rude boldness — see NERVY 1
2 foolishly adventurous or bold — see FOOLHARDY 1
3 showing poor judgment especially in personal relationships or social situations — see INDISCREET

brashness *n* shameless boldness — see EFFRONTERY

brass *n* shameless boldness — see EFFRONTERY

brassiness *n* shameless boldness — see EFFRONTERY

brassy *adj* displaying or marked by rude boldness — see NERVY 1

brave *adj* **1** feeling or displaying no fear by temperament ⟨Despite considerable risk to their own safety, the *brave* team of rescuers rushed into the collapsed building.⟩
syn bold, courageous, dauntless, doughty, fearless, gallant, greathearted, gutsy, heroic (*also* heroical), intrepid, lionhearted, manful, stalwart, stout, stouthearted, undaunted, valiant, valorous
rel determined, firm, game, gamy (*or* gamey), gritty, plucky, resolute, Spartan, undeterred, undismayed, unflinching, unswerving; mettlesome, spirited, spunky; adventuresome, adventurous, audacious, daring, dashing, hardy, venturesome, venturous; foolish, half-witted; brash, brazen, daredevil, foolhardy, heedless, hotheaded, impetuous, imprudent, impulsive, incautious, madcap, overbold, overconfident, rash, reckless, thoughtless, wild; hasty, headlong, precipitate; comforted, emboldened, encouraged, heartened, reassured, unafraid
near ant diffident, mousy (*or* mousey), scary, shy, skittish, timid; anxious, nervous; careful, cautious, heedful, prudent, unadventurous; afraid, agitated, disconcerted, disquieted, disturbed, frightened, horrified, panicked, panic-stricken, perturbed, scared, shocked, spooked, startled, terrified, terrorized, unnerved, upset; appalled, concerned, dismayed, worried; unmanly, weak, wimpy
ant chicken, chickenhearted, chicken-livered, coward, cowardly, craven, dastardly, fainthearted, fearful, lily-livered, nerveless, spineless, spiritless, timorous, uncourageous, ungallant, unheroic, weakhearted, yellow
2 of the very best kind — see EXCELLENT

brave *vb* to oppose (something hostile or dangerous) with firmness or courage — see FACE 2

bravery *n* **1** dressy clothing — see FINERY
2 strength of mind to carry on in spite of danger — see COURAGE

brawl *n* **1** a rough and often noisy fight usually involving several people ⟨They were thrown out of the party after starting a *brawl*.⟩

syn fracas, fray, free-for-all, melee (*also* mêlée), row, ruckus, ruction
rel battle, clash, combat, conflict, contest, fisticuffs, handgrips, hassle, scrap, scrimmage, scuffle, skirmish, struggle, tussle; horseplay, roughhousing; altercation, argument, dispute, kickup, quarrel, spat, squabble, tiff, wrangle
2 an often noisy or angry expression of differing opinions — see ARGUMENT 1

brawl *vb* to express different opinions about something often angrily — see ARGUE 2

brawn *n* muscular strength — see MUSCLE 1

brawny *adj* **1** having muscles capable of exerting great physical force — see STRONG 1
2 marked by a well-developed musculature — see MUSCULAR 1
3 strongly and heavily built — see ¹HUSKY 1

brazen *adj* displaying or marked by rude boldness — see NERVY 1

brazen *vb* to oppose (something hostile or dangerous) with firmness or courage — see FACE 2

brazenness *n* shameless boldness — see EFFRONTERY

breach *n* **1** a failure to uphold the requirements of law, duty, or obligation ⟨Failure to deliver on time was a *breach* of the contract.⟩
syn infraction, infringement, transgression, trespass, violation
rel misconduct, misdemeanor, misfeasance, misprision, offense (*or* offence), sin, wrong; disregard, forgetting, ignoring, nonobservance, overlooking; delinquency, dereliction, neglect; encroachment, intrusion, invasion
near ant respecting, upholding
ant noninfringement, observance
2 a breaking of a moral or legal code — see OFFENSE 1
3 an open space in a barrier (as a wall or hedge) — see GAP 1

breach *vb* to fail to keep — see VIOLATE 1

bread *n* **1** *slang* something (as pieces of stamped metal or printed paper) customarily and legally used as a medium of exchange, a measure of value, or a means of payment — see MONEY
2 substances intended to be eaten — see FOOD

breadbasket *n*, *slang* the part of the body between the chest and the pelvis — see STOMACH 1

breadth *n* **1** a wide space or area — see EXPANSE
2 an area over which activity, capacity, or influence extends — see RANGE 2

break *n* **1** a momentary halt in an activity — see PAUSE 1
2 a period during which the usual routine of school or work is suspended — see VACATION
3 an open space in a barrier (as a wall or hedge) — see GAP 1
4 a favorable combination of circumstances, time, and place — see OPPORTUNITY
5 the act or an instance of getting free from danger or confinement — see ESCAPE 1

break vb 1 to cause to separate into pieces usually suddenly or forcibly ⟨I hated telling her that I had *broken* her favorite glass vase.⟩
syn break up, bust, dismember, disrupt, fracture, fragment, rive
rel atomize, crush, grind, powder, pulverize, reduce; blast, blow up, burst, detonate, explode; crack, pop, shatter, shiver, smash; chip, sliver, splinter, split; implode; destroy, ruin, wreck
near ant doctor, fix, heal, mend, patch, rebuild, recondition, reconstruct, renovate, repair
2 to bring (as an action or operation) to an immediate end — see STOP 1
3 to bring to a lower grade or rank — see DEMOTE
4 to change (as a secret message) from code into ordinary language — see DECODE 1
5 to come to a temporary halt in one's activity — see PAUSE
6 to cut into and turn over the sod of (a piece of land) using a bladed implement — see PLOW 1
7 to fail to keep — see VIOLATE 1
8 to find an answer for through reasoning — see SOLVE
9 to reduce the soundness, effectiveness, or perfection of — see DAMAGE 1
10 to stop functioning — see FAIL 1
11 to hasten away from something dangerous or frightening — see RUN 2
12 to use up all the physical energy of — see EXHAUST 1
13 to become known — see GET OUT 1
14 to cause to lose one's fortune and become unable to pay one's debts — see RUIN 1
15 to come into existence — see BEGIN 2
16 to depart abruptly from a straight line or course — see SWERVE 1
17 to diminish the price or value of — see DEPRECIATE 1
18 to go beyond the limit of — see EXCEED 1
19 to penetrate the surface (as of water) from below — see BROACH 1
breakable adj easily broken — see FRAGILE 1
breakdown n 1 a mental or nervous collapse ⟨If you don't ease your workload, you're going to have a *breakdown*.⟩
syn crack-up
rel frazzle, freak-out, meltdown; alarm (*also* alarum), anxiety, apprehension, disquiet; excitability, nervousness; disturbance; agitation, discomposure, perturbation; basket case
near ant aplomb, calmness, composure, coolness, imperturbability, placidity, self-possession, sereneness, serenity, tranquillity (*or* tranquility)
2 the process by which dead organic matter separates into simpler substances — see CORRUPTION 1
3 the separation and identification of the parts of a whole — see ANALYSIS 1
break down vb 1 to arrange or assign according to type — see CLASSIFY 1

2 to go through decomposition — see DECAY 1
3 to identify and examine the basic elements or parts of (something) especially for discovering interrelationships — see ANALYZE
4 to stop functioning — see FAIL 1
5 to yield to mental or emotional stress — see CRACK 2
6 to take apart — see DISASSEMBLE 1
7 to cause to break with violence and much noise — see SMASH 1
break in vb 1 to enter a house or building by force usually with illegal intent ⟨The burglars *broke in* by smashing a window.⟩
syn burglarize
rel invade, trespass; hold up, loot, plunder, rip off, rob, stick up; ransack, rifle; despoil, devastate, maraud, pillage, ravage, sack
2 to cause a disruption in a conversation or discussion — see INTERRUPT
breakneck adj moving, proceeding, or acting with great speed — see FAST 1
break off vb 1 to bring (as an action or operation) to an immediate end — see STOP 1
2 to come to an end — see CEASE 1
break out vb to develop suddenly and violently — see ERUPT 2
breakthrough n an instance of notable progress in the development of knowledge, technology, or skill — see ADVANCE 2
breakup n the act or process of a whole separating into two or more parts or pieces — see SEPARATION 1
break up vb 1 to cease to exist or cause to cease to exist as a group or organization — see DISBAND 1
2 to come to an end — see CEASE 1
3 to set or force apart — see SEPARATE 1
4 to yield to mental or emotional stress — see CRACK 2
5 to bring (as an action or operation) to an immediate end — see STOP 1
6 to cause to separate into pieces usually suddenly or forcibly — see BREAK 1
7 to show mirth with an explosive vocal sound — see LAUGH 1
breast n the seat of one's deepest thoughts and emotions — see CORE 1
breast vb to oppose (something hostile or dangerous) with firmness or courage — see FACE 2
breath n 1 a momentary halt in an activity — see PAUSE 1
2 a slight or gentle movement of air — see BREEZE 1
3 an almost imperceptible sign of something — see HINT 2
breathe vb 1 to inhale and exhale air ⟨Sometimes it gets so hot in here that it's hard to even *breathe*.⟩
syn respire
rel blow (out), draw, expire, inbreathe, inspire; gasp, huff, pant, puff, suspire, wheeze; sniff, snore, snort, snuffle, whiff
near ant asphyxiate, choke, gag, smother, suffocate; garrote (*or* garotte), stifle, strangle, throttle
2 to have life — see BE 1
breathe (out) vb to let or force out of the lungs — see EXHALE 1

---

syn synonym(s) *rel* related words
ant antonym(s) *near ant* near antonym(s)

breather *n* a momentary halt in an activity — see PAUSE 1

breathing *adj* having or showing life — see ALIVE 1

breathless *adj* 1 lacking fresh air — see STUFFY 1

2 moving, proceeding, or acting with great speed — see FAST 1

3 no longer living — see DEAD 1

breathtaking *adj* causing great emotional or mental stimulation — see EXCITING 1

breech *n* 1 the part of the body upon which someone sits — see BUTTOCKS

2 **breeches** *pl* an outer garment covering each leg separately from waist to ankle — see PANTS

breed *n* a number of persons or things that are grouped together because they have something in common — see SORT 1

breed *vb* 1 to bring forth offspring — see PROCREATE

2 to bring to maturity through care and education — see BRING UP 1

3 to be the cause of (a situation, action, or state of mind) — see EFFECT

4 to engage in sexual intercourse — see COPULATE

5 to set permanently in the consciousness or mind-set — see IMPLANT 1

breeding *n* the line of ancestors from whom a person is descended — see ANCESTRY

breeze *n* 1 a slight or gentle movement of air ⟨A warm spring *breeze* ruffled our hair.⟩
syn air, breath, puff, waft, zephyr
rel current, draft, whiff; sea breeze; blast, blow, flurry, gale, headwind, northeaster, norther, northwester, southeaster, southwester, tailwind, westerly, wind; squall, tempest, tornado, windstorm; airflow
near ant calm

2 something that is easy to do — see CINCH

breeze *vb* 1 to move or proceed smoothly and readily — see FLOW 2

2 to proceed or move quickly — see HURRY 2

breezy *adj* 1 having a relaxed, casual manner — see EASYGOING 1

2 marked by strong wind or more wind than usual — see ¹WINDY 1

3 open to the free circulation of air — see AIRY 2

brevity *n* 1 the condition of being short ⟨the *brevity* of youth⟩
syn briefness, conciseness, shortness
rel abbreviation, abridgment (*or* abridgement), compression, condensation, contraction, curtailment; decreasing, diminishing, lessening, reducing, shortening, shrinking; abruptness, brusqueness, curtness; compendiousness, crispness, laconism, pithiness, succinctness, tautness, terseness; littleness, minuteness, smallness, tininess
near ant extensiveness; elongating, elongation, extending, extension, prolongation, prolonging, protraction; stretching; expansion, growth, spread; diffuseness, long-windedness, prolixity, talkativeness, talkiness, verboseness, volubility, wordiness; bigness, bulkiness, greatness, heftiness, largeness

ant lengthiness

2 the quality or state of being marked by or using only few words to convey much meaning — see SUCCINCTNESS

brew *vb* 1 to bring (something volatile or intense) into being — see INCITE 1

2 to be about to happen — see LOOM

bribable *adj* open to improper influence and especially bribery — see VENAL

bribe *n* something given or promised in order to improperly influence a person's conduct or decision ⟨That judge refused a huge *bribe* to dismiss the charges against the wealthy defendant.⟩
syn fix, sop
rel kickback, payoff; slush fund; incentive, incitement, instigation, motivation, provocation, spur, stimulation, stimulus; boost, encouragement, goad, inducement; allurement, bait, enticement, lure, seduction, temptation, turn-on; flattery, persuasion; decoy, snare, trap

bribe *vb* to influence someone with a bribe ⟨*bribed* the inspectors to look the other way⟩
syn buy, corrupt, have, pay off, square
rel fix, tamper (with); abase, debase, debauch, defile, degrade, demean, deprave, dishonor, pervert, poison, profane, subvert, taint, warp; allure, bait, beguile, entice, lead on, lure, seduce, tempt; motivate, provoke, spur, stimulate; goad, induce; flatter, persuade; snare, trap
phrases get at, grease the hand of (*or* grease the palm of), oil the hand of (*or* oil the palm of)

bridal *n* a ceremony in which two people are united in matrimony — see WEDDING

bridgehead *n* a place from which an advance (as for military operations) is made — see BASE 2

bridle *vb* to keep from exceeding a desirable degree or level (as of expression) — see CONTROL 1

brief *adj* 1 marked by the use of few words to convey much information or meaning — see CONCISE

2 not lasting for a considerable time — see SHORT 2

3 lasting only for a short time — see MOMENTARY

brief *n* 1 a short statement of the main points — see SUMMARY

2 a specific task with which a person or group is charged — see MISSION

brief *vb* to give information to — see ENLIGHTEN 1

briefly *adv* in a few words — see SHORTLY 1

briefness *n* 1 the condition of being short — see BREVITY 1

2 the quality or state of being marked by or using only few words to convey much meaning — see SUCCINCTNESS

brig *n* a place of confinement for persons held in lawful custody — see JAIL

bright *adj* 1 giving off or reflecting much light ⟨In the desert the sun was so *bright* that it hurt my eyes.⟩ ⟨The moon is *bright* tonight.⟩
syn beaming, bedazzling, brilliant, clear, dazzling, effulgent, glowing, incandescent, lambent, lucent, lucid, luminous, lustrous, radiant, refulgent, shining, shiny, splendid

rel ablaze, ardent, blazing, burning, combusting, fiery, flaming, red-hot; agleam, aglitter, blinding, coruscant, flashing, flickering, glancing, glaring, gleaming, glimmering, glinting, glistening, glistering, glittering, scintillant, scintillating, shimmering, shimmery, sparkling, sunny, twinkling, winking; burnished, polished, shined; superbright, ultrabright

near ant blackened, dark, darkened, darkish, darkling, darksome, dimmed, dusky, gloomy, murky, obscure, obscured, pitch-black, pitch-dark, somber (*or* sombre), tenebrous; cloudy, shadowlike, shadowy, shady; gray (*also* grey), leaden, pale, palish
ant dim, dull, lackluster, unbright, unbrilliant

2 filled with much light ⟨The display windows of department stores are especially *bright* during the holidays.⟩
syn ablaze, alight, brightened, illuminated, illumined, light, lightsome
rel floodlit (*also* floodlighted), highlighted, spotlighted (*or* spotlit); ignited, kindled; moonlit, shiny, sunlit, sunny, sunshiny
near ant gloomy, somber (*or* sombre); cloudy, murky, obscured, shadowlike, shadowy; gray (*also* grey), leaden, pale; lightproof
ant blackened, dark, darkened, darkish, darkling, dimmed, dusky, pitch-black, pitch-dark, tenebrous

3 having or showing a good mood or disposition — see CHEERFUL 1

4 having or showing quickness of mind — see INTELLIGENT 1

5 having qualities which inspire hope — see HOPEFUL 1

6 pointing toward a happy outcome — see FAVORABLE 2

7 serving to lift one's spirits — see CHEERFUL 2

8 standing above others in rank, importance, or achievement — see EMINENT

9 having or being an outward sign of good feelings (as of love, confidence, or happiness) — see RADIANT 1

10 not stormy or cloudy — see FAIR 1

brighten *vb* to become glad or hopeful — see CHEER (UP) 1

brightened *adj* filled with much light — see BRIGHT 2

brightness *n* the quality or state of having or giving off light — see BRILLIANCE 1

brilliance *n* **1** the quality or state of having or giving off light ⟨The *brilliance* of the lights was so intense that I couldn't keep my eyes open for a time.⟩
syn brightness, brilliancy, candor, dazzle, effulgence, illumination, lightness, luminosity, luster (*or* lustre), radiance, refulgence, splendor
rel blaze, flare, flash, flicker, light; fluorescence, incandescence, luminescence; burnish, gloss, polish, sheen, shine, shininess; fire, flame, glare, glow; flash, gleam, glimmer, glint, glisten, glitter, scintillation, shimmer, sparkle, twinkle
near ant dimness, gloominess, somberness; cloudiness, haziness, murkiness, ob-

scureness, obscurity; colorlessness, grayness, lackluster, paleness, shadiness, shadowiness
ant blackness, dark, darkness, dullness (*also* dulness), duskiness

2 impressiveness of beauty on a large scale — see MAGNIFICENCE

brilliancy *n* the quality or state of having or giving off light — see BRILLIANCE 1

brilliant *adj* **1** giving off or reflecting much light — see BRIGHT 1

2 having or showing quickness of mind — see INTELLIGENT 1

3 likely to attract attention — see NOTICEABLE

brilliant *n* a usually valuable stone cut and polished for ornament — see GEM 1

brim *n* **1** the line or relatively narrow space that marks the outer limit of something — see BORDER 1

2 the projecting front part of a hat or cap — see VISOR

brim *vb* **1** to be copiously supplied — see ABOUND

2 to put into (something) as much as can be held or contained — see FILL 1

brimful *adj* containing or seeming to contain the greatest quantity or number possible — see FULL 1

brimming *adj* containing or seeming to contain the greatest quantity or number possible — see FULL 1

brine *n* the whole body of salt water that covers nearly three-fourths of the earth — see OCEAN 1

bring *vb* **1** to be the cause of (a situation, action, or state of mind) — see EFFECT

2 to cause (someone) to agree with a belief or course of action by using arguments or earnest requests — see PERSUADE

3 to have a price of — see COST

bring about *vb* to be the cause of (a situation, action, or state of mind) — see EFFECT

bring up *vb* **1** to bring to maturity through care and education ⟨It takes an immense commitment and a lot of love to *bring up* a child.⟩
syn breed, foster, nourish, nurse, raise, rear
rel father, mother; attend, care (for), cradle, cultivate, mind, minister (to), nurture, watch; discipline, educate, instruct, mentor, school, teach, train, tutor; edify, enlighten, indoctrinate; feed, provide (for), supply; advance, forward, further, promote; prepare; direct, guide, lead, shepherd, show
near ant abuse, ill-treat, ill-use, maltreat, mishandle, mistreat; ignore, neglect; harm, hurt, injure

2 to present or bring forward for discussion — see INTRODUCE 2

3 to bring (something) to a standstill — see ¹HALT 1

brininess *n* the quality or state of being salty — see SALTINESS

briny *adj* of, relating to, or containing salt — see SALTY 1

brisk *adj* **1** having much high-spirited energy and movement — see LIVELY 1

2 moving, proceeding, or acting with great speed — see FAST 1

3 marked by much life, movement, or activity — see ALIVE 2

briskly *adv* with great speed — see FAST 1

briskness *n* the quality or state of having abundant or intense activity — see VITALITY 1

bristle *n* a thin, flexible structure that resembles a hair — see HAIR 2

bristle *vb* 1 to be copiously supplied — see ABOUND

2 to express one's anger usually violently — see RAGE 1

bristly *adj* covered with or as if with hair — see HAIRY 1

britches *n pl* an outer garment covering each leg separately from waist to ankle — see PANTS

brittle *adj* 1 having a texture that readily breaks into little pieces under pressure — see CRISP 1

2 lacking in friendliness or warmth of feeling — see COLD 1

broach *vb* 1 to penetrate the surface (as of water) from below ⟨The immense whale *broaching* was a magnificent sight.⟩
syn break, surface
rel emerge, rise
near ant dive, drop, drown, founder, plunge, sink, submerge, submerse

2 to present or bring forward for discussion — see INTRODUCE 2

broad *adj* 1 having a greater than usual measure across — see WIDE 1

2 having considerable extent — see EXTENSIVE

3 not subject to misinterpretation or more than one interpretation — see CLEAR 2

4 relating to the main elements and not to specific details — see GENERAL 2

broadcast *vb* 1 to cause to be known over a considerable area or by many people — see SPREAD 1

2 to make known openly or publicly — see ANNOUNCE

broadly *adv* to a large extent or degree — see GREATLY 2

broad-minded *adj* 1 not bound by traditional ways or beliefs — see LIBERAL 1

2 willing to consider new or different ideas — see OPEN-MINDED 1

broadside *adv* with one side faced forward — see SIDEWAYS 1

brochure *n* a short printed publication with no cover or with a paper cover — see PAMPHLET

broiling *adj* having a notably high temperature — see HOT 1

broke *adj* lacking money or material possessions — see POOR 1

broken *adj* 1 having an uneven edge or outline — see RAGGED 1

2 not having a level or smooth surface — see UNEVEN 1

brokenhearted *adj* feeling unhappiness — see SAD 1

brood *vb* to cover and warm eggs as the young initiate develop — see SET 1

brook *n* a natural body of running water smaller than a river — see CREEK 1

brook *vb* to put up with (something painful or difficult) — see BEAR 2

brooklet *n* a natural body of running water smaller than a river — see CREEK 1

brotherhood *n* 1 a group of persons formally joined together for some common interest — see ASSOCIATION 2

2 the body of people in a profession or field of activity — see CORPS

3 the feeling of closeness and friendship that exists between companions — see COMPANIONSHIP

4 kindly concern, interest, or support — see GOODWILL 1

brotherly *adj* of, relating to, or befitting brothers — see FRATERNAL

browbeat *vb* to make timid or fearful by or as if by threats — see INTIMIDATE

brownie *n* an imaginary being usually having a small human form and magical powers — see FAIRY

browse *vb* 1 to feed on grass or herbs — see ¹GRAZE

2 to take a quick or hasty look — see GLANCE 2

bruise *n* 1 a bodily injury in which small blood vessels are broken but the overlying skin is not — see CONTUSION

2 an area of skin roughened or worn away by harsh rubbing against another surface — see ABRASION

bruit (about) *vb* to make (as a piece of information) the subject of common talk without any authority or confirmation of accuracy — see RUMOR

brush *n* a brief clash between enemies or rivals — see ENCOUNTER

¹**brush** *vb* to move or proceed smoothly and readily — see FLOW 2

²**brush** *vb* to pass lightly across or touch gently especially in passing ⟨Spiderwebs *brushed* her cheek as she walked through the basement.⟩
syn graze, kiss, nudge, shave, skim
rel bump, contact, scrape, sideswipe, strike, sweep, swipe, touch; bounce, carom, glance, rebound, ricochet; skip; caress, cuddle, fondle, love, pat, pet, stroke; miss, skirt
near ant bang, bash, bump, clash, collide, crash, hit, impact, impinge, knock, punch, ram, slam, slap, smack, smash, swipe, thud, thwack, whack

brush (aside *or* **off)** *vb* to dismiss as of little importance — see EXCUSE 1

brush–off *n* treatment that is deliberately unfriendly — see COLD SHOULDER

brushwood *n* a thick patch of shrubbery, small trees, or underbrush — see THICKET

brusque *also* **brusk** *adj* being or characterized by direct, brief, and potentially rude speech or manner — see BLUNT 1

brutal *adj* 1 difficult to endure — see HARSH 1

2 having or showing the desire to inflict severe pain and suffering on others — see CRUEL 1

brutality *n* disposition to willfully inflict pain and suffering on others — see CRUELTY

brute *adj* having or showing the desire to inflict severe pain and suffering on others — see CRUEL 1

brute *n* 1 one of the lower animals as distinguished from human beings — see ANIMAL

2 a mean, evil, or unprincipled person — see VILLAIN

bubble *vb* to flow in a broken irregular stream — see GURGLE

bubbly *adj* joyously unrestrained — see EXUBERANT

buccaneer *n* someone who engages in robbery of ships at sea — see PIRATE

buck *n* 1 a man extremely interested in his clothing and personal appearance — see DANDY 1

2 an adult male human being — see MAN 1

3 **bucks** *pl* something (as pieces of stamped metal or printed paper) customarily and legally used as a medium of exchange, a measure of value, or a means of payment — see MONEY

buck *vb* 1 to move or cause to move with a sharp quick motion — see JERK 1

2 to refuse to give in to — see RESIST

3 to shift possession of (something) from one person to another — see PASS 1

buckaroo *also* **buckeroo** *n* a hired hand who tends cattle or horses at a ranch or on the range — see COWBOY

bucket *n* 1 a considerable amount — see LOT 2

2 a round container that is open at the top and outfitted with a handle — see PAIL

bucket *vb* to lift out with something that holds liquid — see DIP 1

buckle *vb* 1 to fall down or in as a result of physical pressure — see COLLAPSE 1

2 to occupy (oneself) diligently or with close attention — see APPLY 2

bucolic *adj* of, relating to, associated with, or typical of open areas with few buildings or people — see RURAL

buddy *n* a person who has a strong liking for and trust in another — see FRIEND 1

budge *vb* 1 to cease resistance (as to another's arguments, demands, or control) — see YIELD 3

2 to change one's position — see MOVE 3

3 to change the place or position of — see MOVE 1

budget *adj* costing little — see CHEAP 1

budget *n* 1 a sum of money set aside for a particular purpose — see FUND 1

2 the number of individuals or amount of something available at any given time — see SUPPLY

budget *vb* to work out the details of (something) in advance — see PLAN 1

buff *n* a person with a strong and habitual liking for something — see FAN

buff *vb* 1 to make smooth by friction — see GRIND 1

2 to make smooth or glossy usually by repeatedly applying surface pressure — see POLISH 1

buffed *adj* having a shiny surface or finish — see GLOSSY

buffer *n* 1 one who works with opposing sides in order to bring about an agreement — see MEDIATOR

2 something that serves as a protective barrier — see CUSHION

buffer *vb* to lessen the shock of — see CUSHION

¹**buffet** *n* a hard strike with a part of the body or an instrument — see ¹BLOW

²**buffet** *n* a storage case typically having doors and shelves — see CABINET

buffet *vb* to strike repeatedly — see BEAT 1

buffoon *n* a comically dressed performer (as at a circus) who entertains with playful tricks and ridiculous behavior — see CLOWN 1

bug *n* 1 a person with a strong and habitual liking for something — see FAN

2 an abnormal state that disrupts a plant's or animal's normal bodily functioning — see DISEASE

bug *vb* 1 to disturb the peace of mind of (someone) especially by repeated disagreeable acts — see IRRITATE 1

2 to thrust oneself upon (another) without invitation — see BOTHER 1

bugaboo *n* something or someone that causes fear or dread especially without reason — see BOGEY 1

bugbear *n* 1 something or someone that causes fear or dread especially without reason — see BOGEY 1

2 something that is a source of irritation — see ANNOYANCE 3

bugging *n* the act of making unwelcome intrusions upon another — see ANNOYANCE 1

build *n* the type of body that a person has — see PHYSIQUE

build *vb* to form by putting together parts or materials ⟨He spent hours *building* a model airplane from a kit.⟩

syn assemble, construct, erect, fabricate, make, make up, piece, put up, raise, rear, set up

rel carpenter, fashion, forge, frame, hammer, handcraft, manufacture, produce, shape; prefabricate; begin, create, generate, inaugurate, initiate, innovate, invent, originate; constitute, establish, father, found, institute, organize; conceive, concoct, contrive, cook (up), design, devise, imagine, think (up); reassemble, rebuild, reconstruct, redevelop, retrofit; jerrybuild, rig (up), throw up; combine, unite

phrases put together

near ant demolish, destroy, devastate, flatten, level, pulverize, raze, ruin, ruinate, shatter, smash, wreck; blow up, explode; detach, disengage; disconnect, disjoin, disunite, divide, separate

ant demount, disassemble, dismantle, dismember, knock down, strike, take down, tear down

building *n* something built as a dwelling, shelter, or place for human activity ⟨English class will be in that big stone *building* over there.⟩

syn edifice, structure

rel construction, erection; bungalow, cabin, chalet, cottage, house, lodge; hovel, hut, shack, shanty, shed; castle, château, estate, hall, manor, mansion, palace, pile, villa; skyscraper, tower

building block *n* one of the parts that make up a whole — see ELEMENT 1

bulge *n* 1 a part that sticks out from the general mass of something ⟨several *bulges* in the old vinyl flooring⟩

syn bunch, jut, overhang, projection, protrusion, protuberance, swell

rel blob, bump, dilatation, hump, knob,

---

syn synonym(s)   *rel* related words   *ant* antonym(s)   *near ant* near antonym(s) knot, knurl, lump, nub, obtrusion, puff, snag, swelling; block, piece, portion, section; enlargement, escalation, expansion, increase; hill, mound

near ant crater, hole, well; basin, bowl, dip, valley; furrow, groove, trench, trough; dimple, gouge, impression, notch, pocket

ant cavity, concave, concavity, dent, depression, dint, hollow, indentation, pit, recess

2 the more favorable condition or position in a competition — see ADVANTAGE 1

bulge *vb* **1** to extend outward beyond a usual point ⟨The sides of the returning camper's suitcase *bulged* with a month's worth of dirty laundry.⟩

syn bag, balloon, beetle, belly, billow, bunch, jut, overhang, poke, pouch, pout, project, protrude, stand out, start, stick out, swell

rel blow up, inflate; dilate, distend, expand; mushroom, snowball; elongate, extend, lengthen, stretch

near ant compress, condense, constrict, contract, shrink

2 to be copiously supplied — see ABOUND 1

bulk *n* **1** the largest part or quantity of something — see MAJORITY 1

2 the main or greater part of something as distinguished from its subordinate parts — see BODY 1

3 the total amount of measurable space or surface occupied by something — see ¹SIZE

bulkiness *n* the quality or state of being large in size — see LARGENESS

bulky *adj* of a size greater than average of its kind — see LARGE

¹**bull** *n* an order publicly issued by an authority — see EDICT 1

²**bull** *n, slang* language, behavior, or ideas that are absurd and contrary to good sense — see NONSENSE 1

bull *vb* to force one's way — see ²PRESS 4

bulldoze *vb* **1** to force one's way — see ²PRESS 4

2 to make timid or fearful by or as if by threats — see INTIMIDATE

bullet *n* a usually round or cone-shaped little piece of lead made to be fired from a firearm ⟨fired a *bullet*⟩

syn ball, pellet

rel ammunition, cap, cartridge, charge, dumdum, gunshot, lead, load, missile, pop, projectile, round, shell, shot, slug

near ant blank

bulletin *n* **1** a publication that appears at regular intervals — see JOURNAL

2 a published statement informing the public of a matter of general interest — see ANNOUNCEMENT

bullheadedness *n* a steadfast adherence to an opinion, purpose, or course of action in spite of reasons, arguments, or persuasion — see OBSTINACY

bully *adj* of the very best kind — see EXCELLENT

bully *n* a person who teases, threatens, or hurts more vulnerable persons ⟨The school has a procedure for reporting problems with *bullies*.⟩

syn hector, intimidator

rel antagonist, enemy; abuser, baiter, giber (*or* jiber), harrier, heckler, mocker,

needler, oppressor, persecutor, ridiculer, taunter, tease, teaser, torturer; goon, mug, rough, roughneck, rowdy, ruffian, tough, toughie (*also* toughy)

bully *vb* **1** to inflict physical or emotional harm upon — see ABUSE 1

2 to make timid or fearful by or as if by threats — see INTIMIDATE

bulwark *vb* to drive danger or attack away from — see DEFEND 1

bum *adj* of low quality — see CHEAP 2

¹**bum** *n* the part of the body upon which someone sits — see BUTTOCKS

²**bum** *n* a homeless wanderer who may beg or steal for a living — see TRAMP

bum *vb* to spend time doing nothing — see IDLE

bum (out) *vb* to make sad — see DEPRESS 1

bummer *n* **1** something (as a situation or event) that is depressing — see DOWNER

2 something that disappoints — see DISAPPOINTMENT 2

3 something that has failed — see FAILURE 3

bump *n* **1** a small rounded mass of swollen tissue ⟨That's a nasty *bump* on your arm where you hit the table.⟩

syn knot, lump, node, nodule, swelling

rel growth, tumor, wart; hump, hunch; bruise, contusion; blister, boil; blob, chunk, clod, clump, gob, gobbet, hunk, knob, nub, nubble, nugget, wad

2 the act or an instance of bringing to a lower grade or rank ⟨The *bump* in rank was punishment for insubordination.⟩

syn reduction

rel disrating, downgrade; dismissal, firing, layoff, sacking; abasement, debasement, humiliation

3 a forceful coming together of two things — see IMPACT 1

bump *vb* to come into usually forceful contact with something — see HIT 2

bumper *adj* **1** of the very best kind — see EXCELLENT

2 unusually large — see HUGE

bumper *n* something that serves as a protective barrier — see CUSHION

bumpkin *n* an awkward or simple person especially from a small town or the country — see HICK

bumpy *adj* **1** marked by a series of sharp quick motions — see JERKY 1

2 not having a level or smooth surface — see UNEVEN 1

bunch *n* **1** a group of people sharing a common interest and relating together socially — see GANG 2

2 a number of things considered as a unit — see GROUP 1

3 a usually small number of persons considered as a unit — see GROUP 2

4 a part that sticks out from the general mass of something — see BULGE 1

5 a considerable amount — see LOT 2

bunch *vb* **1** to extend outward beyond a usual point — see BULGE 1

2 to gather into a closely packed group — see ²PRESS 3

bundle *n* **1** a considerable amount — see LOT 2

2 a wrapped or sealed case containing an item or set of items — see PACKAGE 1

3 a very large amount of money — see
FORTUNE 2

bundle vb 1 to cause to move or proceed
fast or faster — see HURRY 1

2 to proceed or move quickly — see HUR-
RY 2

bung vb to close up so that no empty spaces remain — see FILL 1

bungle vb to make or do (something) in a
clumsy or unskillful way — see BOTCH

bungling adj showing or marked by a lack
of skill and tact (as in dealing with a situation) — see AWKWARD 2

¹**bunk** n a place set aside for sleeping — see
BED 1

²**bunk** n language, behavior, or ideas that
are absurd and contrary to good sense —
see NONSENSE 1

bunk vb to provide with living quarters or
shelter — see HOUSE 1

buoy (up) vb to fill with courage or
strength of purpose — see ENCOURAGE 1

buoyant adj 1 having or showing a good
mood or disposition — see CHEERFUL 1

2 joyously unrestrained — see EXUBERANT

¹**burden** n 1 a mass or quantity of something taken up and carried, conveyed, or
transported — see LOAD 1

2 something one must do because of prior
agreement — see OBLIGATION 1

²**burden** n a part of a song or hymn that is
repeated every so often — see CHORUS 2

burden vb 1 to place a weight or burden
on — see LOAD 1

2 to make sad — see DEPRESS 1

burdensome adj 1 difficult to endure —
see HARSH 1

2 requiring much time, effort, or careful
attention — see DEMANDING 1

bureau n a large unit of a governmental,
business, or educational organization —
see DIVISION 1

bureaucrat n a worker in a government
agency ⟨left the private sector and became
a government *bureaucrat*⟩

syn functionary, public servant

rel clerk, officeholder, official, officiary;
employee (*also* employe), hand, hireling,
jobholder, underling, worker

burg n a thickly settled, highly populated
area — see CITY

burgeon *also* **bourgeon** vb 1 to become
greater in extent, volume, amount, or
number — see INCREASE 2

2 to grow vigorously — see THRIVE 1

burgher n a person who lives in a town on
a permanent basis ⟨The university provides job's for many of the local *burghers*.⟩

syn citizen, townie (*or* towny), villager

rel townswoman; cliff dweller, denizen,
dweller, habitant, inhabitant, national, native, occupant, resident, resider, subject;
town, townsfolk, townspeople; suburbanite, urbanite

near ant alien, foreigner, guest, nonnative,
tourist, transient, visitor; gownsman

ant noncitizen

burglarize vb 1 to enter a house or building by force usually with illegal intent —
see BREAK IN 1

2 to remove valuables from (a place) unlawfully — see ROB

burial n 1 the act or ceremony of putting a
dead body in its final resting place ⟨The
children wanted to give the dead bird a
proper *burial* in the backyard.⟩

syn burying, entombing, entombment, interment, interring, sepulture

rel embalmment, funeral; immurement,
inurnment; reburial, reinterment

near ant cremation

ant disinterment, exhumation, unearthing

2 a final resting place for a dead person —
see GRAVE 1

burlesque n a work that imitates and exaggerates another work for comic effect
— see PARODY 1

burlesque vb to copy or exaggerate
(someone or something) in order to make
fun of — see MIMIC 1

burly adj strongly and heavily built — see
¹HUSKY 1

burn vb 1 to be on fire especially brightly
⟨All evening long we just sat there, contentedly watching the campfire *burn*.⟩

syn blaze, combust, flame, glow

rel catch; fire, ignite, kindle; flare (up),
light (up); flicker, gutter, waver; bake,
char, cook, melt, roast, scorch; smolder
(*or* smoulder), spark, sputter; beam,
brighten, radiate; beat (down), flash, glare,
gleam, glimmer, glint, glisten, glitter, scintillate, shimmer, shine, sparkle, twinkle

phrases go up in flames

2 to set (something) on fire ⟨It is not a good
idea to try to *burn* old papers in the sink.⟩

syn fire, ignite, inflame (*also* enflame),
kindle, light

rel immolate; char, scorch; bake, cook;
ash, cremate, incinerate, kiln; set off;
brighten, illuminate, illumine, irradiate,
lighten, radiate; scald, scathe, sear; reig-
nite, rekindle, relight; bank, stoke

near ant choke, smother, suffocate; stamp
(out); blacken, darken, dim, dull, obscure

ant douse (*also* dowse), extinguish, put
out, quench, snuff (out)

3 to be excited or emotionally stirred up
with anger — see BOIL 1

4 to shine with a bright harsh light — see
GLARE 1

5 to cause to believe what is untrue — see
DECEIVE

6 to make complete use of — see DEPLETE 1

burnable adj capable of catching or being
set on fire — see COMBUSTIBLE

burned–out *or* **burnt–out** adj depleted in
strength, energy, or freshness — see WEA-
RY 1

burning adj 1 being on fire — see ABLAZE 1

2 having a notably high temperature —
see HOT 1

3 having or expressing great depth of feeling — see FERVENT 1

4 needing immediate attention — see
ACUTE 2

burnish n brightness created by light reflected from a surface — see SHINE 1

burnish vb to make smooth or glossy usually by repeatedly applying surface pressure — see POLISH 1

burnished adj having a shiny surface or
finish — see GLOSSY

---

syn synonym(s)   **rel** related words
ant antonym(s)   **near ant** near antonym(s)

burnout *n* a complete depletion of energy or strength — see FATIGUE

burn out *vb* to use up all the physical energy of — see EXHAUST 1

burro *n* a sturdy and patient domestic mammal that is used especially to carry things — see DONKEY 1

burrow *n* the shelter or resting place of a wild animal — see DEN 1

burst *n* 1 a sudden and usually temporary growth of activity — see OUTBREAK 1

2 a sudden intense expression of strong feeling — see OUTBURST 1

3 the act or an instance of exploding — see EXPLOSION 1

burst *vb* 1 to break open or into pieces usually because of internal pressure — see EXPLODE 1

2 to cause to break open or into pieces by or as if by an explosive — see BLAST 1

3 to be copiously supplied — see ABOUND

burst (forth) *vb* to develop suddenly and violently — see ERUPT 2

bursting *adj* containing or seeming to contain the greatest quantity or number possible — see FULL 1

bursting *n* the act or an instance of exploding — see EXPLOSION 1

bury *vb* 1 to place (a dead body) in the earth, a tomb, or the sea ⟨He died on Tuesday and was *buried* on Friday.⟩

syn entomb, inter, lay

rel immure, inurn; enshrine; conceal, cover, ensconce, hide; obscure, shade, shield; cloak, curtain, enshroud, shroud; rebury, reinter; coffin

near ant burn, cremate; bare, disclose, discover, display, exhibit, expose, reveal, show; uncoffin

ant disinter, exhume, unearth

2 to put into a hiding place — see ¹HIDE 1

3 to defeat by a large margin — see WHIP 2

burying *n* the act or ceremony of putting a dead body in its final resting place — see BURIAL 1

bush *adj* falling short of a standard — see BAD 1

bush *n* a rural region that forms the edge of the settled or developed part of a country — see FRONTIER 2

bushed *adj* depleted in strength, energy, or freshness — see WEARY 1

bushel *n* a considerable amount — see LOT 2

business *n* 1 transactions or economic support provided by customers ⟨Only places that are equal opportunity employers will get my *business*.⟩

syn custom

rel marketplace, trade, traffic; free trade; affairs, dealings, horse-trading; merchandising, retailing, wholesaling

2 a commercial or industrial activity or organization — see ENTERPRISE 1

3 something to be dealt with — see MATTER 2

4 the buying and selling of goods especially on a large scale and between different places — see COMMERCE 1

5 the action for which a person or thing is specially fitted or used or for which a thing exists — see ROLE

6 a region of activity, knowledge, or influence — see FIELD 2

7 a specific task with which a person or group is charged — see MISSION

8 the act or fact of violating the trust or confidence of another — see BETRAYAL

bust *n* 1 a hard strike with a part of the body or an instrument — see ¹BLOW

2 something that has failed — see FAILURE 3

3 *slang* the act of taking into one's control by authority of law — see ARREST 1

bust *vb* 1 to bring to a lower grade or rank — see DEMOTE

2 to cause to lose one's fortune and become unable to pay one's debts — see RUIN 1

3 to cause to separate into pieces usually suddenly or forcibly — see BREAK 1

4 to deliver a blow to (someone or something) usually in a strong vigorous manner — see HIT 1

5 *slang* to take or keep under one's control by authority of law — see ARREST 1

6 to use up all the physical energy of — see EXHAUST 1

bustle *n* a state of noisy, confused activity — see COMMOTION

bustle *vb* 1 to be copiously supplied — see ABOUND

2 to proceed or move quickly — see HURRY 2

bustling *adj* 1 involved in often constant activity — see BUSY 1

2 marked by much life, movement, or activity — see ALIVE 2

busy *adj* 1 involved in often constant activity ⟨The deadline is in two days, so everyone at work has been extremely *busy*.⟩

syn active, assiduous, bustling, diligent, employed, engaged, industrious, laborious, occupied, sedulous, working

rel knee-deep, swamped; animated, astir, buzzing, flourishing, happening, humming, lively, thriving, vibrant; absorbed, concentrating, engrossed, focused (*also* focussed), immersed, intent, preoccupied; alive, functional, functioning, going, living, operating, operational, operative, running; energetic, vigorous; hardworking; indefatigable, tireless, untiring

near ant free; asleep, dormant, latent, lifeless, quiescent, sleepy; inert, passive; dead, dull, slow; inoperative, nonoperating

ant idle, inactive, unbusy, unoccupied

2 marked by much life, movement, or activity — see ALIVE 2

3 thrusting oneself where one is not welcome or invited — see INTRUSIVE

busy *vb* to hold the attention of — see ENGAGE 1

busybody *n* a person who meddles in the affairs of others ⟨That *busybody* across the street is always telling me how to tend to my own garden.⟩

syn interferer, interloper, intruder, kibitzer (*also* kibbitzer), meddler

rel gaper, gawker, gazer, peeper, peeping Tom, prier (*also* pryer), rubberneck, rubbernecker, snoop, snooper, spy; blabber, discloser, gossip, prattler, revealer, teller; betrayer, talebearer, tattler, tattletale, telltale; snake, sneak; informant, informer, snitcher, squealer, stool pigeon

but *adv* nothing more than — see JUST 3

but *conj* if it were not for the fact that — see EXCEPT

but *prep* not including — see EXCEPT

butcher *n* someone who bungles an effort ⟨The newest intern on the campaign is a *butcher* when it comes to writing press releases.⟩
syn screwup
rel incompetent, muddler
near ant ace, adept, crackerjack (*also* crackajack), expert, maestro, master, virtuoso, wizard

butcher *vb* 1 to kill on a large scale — see MASSACRE
2 to make or do (something) in a clumsy or unskillful way — see BOTCH

butchery *n* the killing of a large number of people — see MASSACRE

¹**butt** *n* the part of the body upon which someone sits — see BUTTOCKS

²**butt** *n* 1 a person or thing that is made fun of — see LAUGHINGSTOCK
2 a person or thing that is the object of abuse, criticism, or ridicule — see TARGET 1

³**butt** *n* an enclosed wooden vessel for holding beverages — see CASK

butterflies *n pl* a sense of panic or extreme nervousness — see JITTERS

butt in *vb* to interest oneself in what is not one's concern — see INTERFERE

buttocks *n pl* the part of the body upon which someone sits ⟨She slipped in the mud puddle and hit the ground square on her *buttocks*.⟩
syn backside, behind, bottom, breech, bum, butt, can, cheeks, fanny, hams, haunches, posterior, rear, rump, seat, tail
rel beam, stern

buttress *n* 1 something or someone to which one looks for support — see DEPENDENCE 2
2 a structure that holds up or serves as a foundation for something else — see SUPPORT 1

buttress *vb* 1 to hold up or serve as a foundation for — see SUPPORT 3
2 to provide evidence or information for (as a claim or idea) — see SUPPORT 4

buy *n* something bought or offered for sale at a desirable price — see BARGAIN 1

buy *vb* 1 to get possession of (something) by giving money in exchange for ⟨I really want to *buy* that new book, but I don't have enough money right now.⟩
syn pick up, purchase, take
rel acquire, gain, garner, get, obtain, procure, secure, win; finance, pay (for), spring (for); barter (for), deal (for), dicker (over), exchange (for), haggle (for), negotiate (about), trade (for); bargain (with), chaffer (with), horse-trade (with),

palter (with); bid, offer; rebuy, repurchase
near ant deal (in), market, merchandise (*also* merchandize), retail, sell, vend
2 to influence someone with a bribe — see BRIBE
3 to regard as right or true — see BELIEVE 1

buzz *n* 1 a communication by telephone — see CALL 3
2 a monotonous sound like that of an insect in motion — see HUM
3 information or opinion that is widely disseminated without any authority or confirmation of accuracy — see RUMOR

buzz *vb* 1 to be copiously supplied — see ABOUND
2 to proceed or move quickly — see HURRY 2
3 to fly, turn, or move rapidly with a fluttering or vibratory sound — see WHIR

buzzing *adj* marked by much life, movement, or activity — see ALIVE 2

by *adv* at, within, or to a short distance or time — see NEAR 1

by *prep* 1 along the way of ⟨went *by* the woods to get to the summer cottage⟩
syn through, via
rel across, along, alongside, beyond, near, nearby, over; below, beneath, under, underneath; outside, past; throughout
phrases by way of
2 using the means or agency of ⟨We tried to convince them *by* reason.⟩
syn in, per, through, via, with
phrases by dint of, by means of, by virtue of (*or* in)
3 close to — see AROUND 1
4 in the course of — see DURING

by-and-by *n* time that is to come — see FUTURE 1

by and large *adv* for the most part — see CHIEFLY

bygone *adj* no longer existing — see EXTINCT

bylaw *n* a statement spelling out the proper procedure or conduct for an activity — see RULE 1

bypass *vb* 1 to avoid by going around — see DETOUR 1
2 to fail to give proper attention to — see NEGLECT 1
3 to avoid having to comply with (something) especially through cleverness — see CIRCUMVENT 1

by-product *n* something that naturally develops or is developed from something else — see DERIVATIVE

byword *n* 1 an often stated observation regarding something from common experience — see SAYING
2 the most perfect type or example — see QUINTESSENCE 1

---

syn synonym(s)   *rel* related words
ant antonym(s)   *near ant* near antonym(s)

cab *n* an automobile that carries passengers for a fare usually determined by the distance traveled — see TAXICAB

cabal *n* a group involved in secret or criminal activities — see ¹RING 1

cabaret *n* a bar or restaurant offering special nighttime entertainment (as music, dancing, or comedy acts) — see NIGHTCLUB

cabin *n* **1** a small, simply constructed, and often temporary dwelling — see SHACK
2 an often small house for recreational or seasonal use — see COTTAGE
3 one of the parts into which an enclosed space is divided — see COMPARTMENT

cabinet *n* a storage case typically having doors and shelves ⟨The most precious knickknacks were kept in a *cabinet* with glass doors.⟩
syn buffet, closet, console, cupboard, hutch, locker, press, sideboard
rel bookcase, breakfront, chest, china closet, secretary, showcase, vitrine; dresser, pie safe; armoire, clothespress, wardrobe

cabinetwork *n* the movable articles (such as tables and chairs) in a room — see FURNITURE

cable *n* a length of braided, flexible material that is used for tying or connecting things — see CORD 1

cache *n* **1** a collection of things kept available for future use or need — see STORE 1
2 a supply stored up and often hidden away — see HOARD 1

cache *vb* **1** to put (something of future use or value) in a safe or secret place — see HOARD
2 to put into a hiding place — see ¹HIDE 1

caching *n* the placing of something out of sight — see CONCEALMENT 1

cackle *n* **1** an explosive sound that is a sign of amusement — see LAUGH 1
2 friendly, informal conversation or an instance of this — see CHAT 1

cackle *vb* **1** to engage in casual or rambling conversation — see CHAT 1
2 to show mirth with an explosive vocal sound — see LAUGH 1

cackler *n* a person who talks constantly — see CHATTERBOX

cacophonous *adj* marked by or producing a harsh combination of sounds — see DISSONANT

cacophony *n* loud, confused, and usually inharmonious sound — see NOISE 1

cad *n* a person whose behavior is offensive to others — see JERK 1

cadaver *n* a dead body — see CORPSE

cadaverous *adj* **1** lacking a healthy skin color — see PALE 2
2 suffering extreme weight loss as a result of hunger or disease — see EMACIATED

caddy *n* a covered rectangular container for storing or transporting things — see CHEST

cadence *n* the recurrent pattern formed by a series of sounds having a regular rise and fall in intensity — see RHYTHM

cadenced *adj* marked by or occurring with a noticeable regularity in the rise and fall of sound — see RHYTHMIC

café *also* **cafe** *n* **1** a bar or restaurant offering special nighttime entertainment (as music, dancing, or comedy acts) — see NIGHTCLUB
2 a public establishment where meals are served to paying customers for consumption on the premises — see RESTAURANT

cage *n* an enclosure with an open framework for keeping animals ⟨He regularly changed the bedding in his hamster's *cage*.⟩
syn coop, corral, hutch, pen, pound
rel kennel, run; stockade; cote, dovecote (*also* dovecot), henhouse; fold, sheepfold; pigpen; aquarium, terrarium; live-box; fence

cage *vb* to close or shut in by or as if by barriers — see ENCLOSE 1

cagey *also* **cagy** *adj* **1** clever at attaining one's ends by indirect and often deceptive means — see ARTFUL 1
2 slow to begin or proceed with a course of action because of doubts or uncertainty — see HESITANT

caginess *also* **cageyness** *n* **1** exceptional discernment and judgment especially in practical matters — see ACUMEN
2 skill in achieving one's ends through indirect, subtle, or underhanded means — see CUNNING 1

cajole *vb* to get (someone) to do something by gentle urging, special attention, or flattery — see COAX

cake *n* **1** a small usually rounded mass of minced food that has been fried ⟨The rich, tender *cakes* of crabmeat had been lightly fried.⟩
syn croquette, cutlet, fritter, patty (*also* pattie)
rel stick
2 something that is easy to do — see CINCH

cake *vb* to cover with a hardened layer — see ENCRUST

calamitous *adj* **1** bringing about ruin or misfortune — see FATAL 1
2 causing or tending to cause destruction — see DESTRUCTIVE 1

calamity *n* a sudden violent event that brings about great loss or destruction — see DISASTER 1

calculate *vb* **1** to determine (a value) by doing the necessary mathematical operations ⟨The family has been *calculating* what a week at the beach resort would end up costing.⟩
syn cipher, compute, figure, reckon, work out
rel add up, average, sum, tally, total; add, divide, multiply, subtract; deduct, factor (in *or* into *or* out), figure in; figure out, solve (for); count, itemize, number; calibrate, gauge (*also* gage), measure, scale; appraise, assess, estimate, evaluate, rate, value; recalculate, recompute, refigure
2 to decide the size, amount, number, or

distance of (something) without actual measurement — see ESTIMATE 2

3 to work out the details of (something) in advance — see PLAN 1

4 to have in mind as a purpose or goal — see INTEND 1

5 to place reliance or trust — see DEPEND 2

calculated *adj* decided on as a result of careful thought — see DELIBERATE 1

calculation *n* the act or process of performing mathematical operations to find a value ⟨By my *calculation*, it should take me a month to save up for the weekend getaway.⟩

syn arithmetic, ciphering, computation, figures, figuring, number crunching, numbers, reckoning

rel addition, division, multiplication, subtraction; calibration, measurement, mensuration; appraisal, assessment, estimation, evaluation, valuation

calendar *n* a listing of things to be presented or considered (as at a concert or play) — see PROGRAM 1

caliber *or* **calibre** *n* degree of excellence — see QUALITY 1

call *n* **1** a natural vocal sound made by an animal ⟨a ranger who could immediately identify the *call* of every creature in the forest⟩

syn cry, note

rel bark, bay, bellow, bray, cackle, calling, caw, cheep, chirp, cluck, coo, crake, croak, crow, grunt, honk, hoot, howl, low, meow (*also* miaow), mew, moo, neigh, oink, peep, quack, roar, screech, squall, squawk, squeak, squeal, trumpet, tu-whit tu-whoo, twitter, whinny, yelp, yip, yowl

2 a coming to see another briefly for social or business reasons ⟨We paid a *call* on the new neighbors the day after they moved in.⟩

syn visit, visitation

rel stopover; get-together, meeting, rendezvous, tryst

3 a communication by telephone ⟨Give me a *call* as soon as you arrive, so I'll know you got there safely.⟩

syn buzz, ring

rel callback, cold call, conference call, message, toll call, voice mail

4 an act or instance of asking for information — see QUESTION 2

5 an entitlement to something — see CLAIM 1

6 a position arrived at after consideration — see DECISION 1

7 the state of being sought after especially for purchase — see DEMAND 2

call *vb* **1** to speak so as to be heard at a distance ⟨We could hear someone *calling* for help from the other side of the wall.⟩

syn bawl, bay, bellow, cry, holler, roar, shout, sound off, thunder, vociferate, yell

rel crow, whoop; scream, screech, shriek, shrill, squeak, squeal; howl, wail, yowl; hail; speak out, speak up

near ant breathe, mumble, murmur, mutter, whisper

2 to make a telephone call to ⟨Use this cell phone to *call* me if there's an emergency.⟩

syn dial, phone, telephone

rel beep, buzz; call in; cold-call

3 to make a brief visit ⟨The hospital posts the hours during which friends and relatives may *call*.⟩

syn come by, pop (in), stop (by *or* in), visit

rel barge (in); look up, see; bop (into), happen (by); frequent, haunt, resort (to)

4 to put an end to (something planned or previously agreed to) — see CANCEL 1

5 to think of in a particular way — see CONSIDER 1

6 to utter one's distinctive animal sound — see CRY 2

7 to bring together in assembly by or as if by command — see CONVOKE

8 to decide the size, amount, number, or distance of (something) without actual measurement — see ESTIMATE 2

9 to demand or request the presence or service of — see SUMMON 1

10 to give a name to — see NAME 1

11 to request the doing of by virtue of one's authority — see COMMAND 2

12 to tell of or describe beforehand — see FORETELL

call (for) *vb* **1** to ask for (something) earnestly or with authority — see DEMAND 1

2 to make a request for — see ASK (FOR)

call (on *or* upon) *vb* to make a social call upon — see VISIT 1

caller *n* a person who visits another — see GUEST 1

calligraphy *n* writing done by hand — see HANDWRITING 2

calling *n* **1** the act of putting an end to something planned or previously agreed to — see CANCELLATION

2 the activity by which one regularly makes a living — see OCCUPATION

calling off *n* the act of putting an end to something planned or previously agreed to — see CANCELLATION

call off *vb* **1** to draw the attention or mind to something else — see DISTRACT 1

2 to put an end to (something planned or previously agreed to) — see CANCEL 1

callous *adj* having or showing a lack of sympathy or tender feelings — see HARD 1

callow *adj* lacking in adult experience or maturity ⟨a story about a *callow* youth who learns the value of hard work and self-reliance⟩

syn adolescent, green, immature, inexperienced, juvenile, puerile, raw, unfledged, unformed, unripe, unripened

rel babyish, childish, infantile, infantilized, infantine; boyish, girlish, kiddish, young, youngish, youthful; ingenuous, innocent, naive (*or* naïve), tender; unknowing, unseasoned, unsophisticated, untrained, untried

phrases wet behind the ears

near ant advanced, precocious; knowing, savvy, sophisticated, worldly, worldly-wise

ant adult, experienced, grown-up, mature, ripe

calm *adj* **1** free from storms or physical disturbance ⟨After a stormy night of high winds and driving rains, the day dawned on a *calm* sea.⟩

syn halcyon, hushed, peaceful, placid,

---

syn synonym(s)　*rel* related words
ant antonym(s)　*near ant* near antonym(s)

quiet, serene, still, stilly, tranquil, untroubled

rel balmy, clement, equable, gentle, mild, moderate, temperate; clear, cloudless, fair, rainless, sunny, sunshiny, windless

near ant blizzardy (*also* blizzardly), blustery, squally, windy; extreme, foul, intemperate, nasty, severe

ant agitated, angry, inclement, restless, rough, stormy, tempestuous, turbulent, unquiet, unsettled

2 free from emotional or mental agitation ⟨Bystanders tried to help the injured person remain *calm* while they waited for the ambulance to arrive.⟩

syn collected, composed, cool, coolheaded, equal, level, limpid, peaceful, placid, sedate, self-possessed, serene, smooth, tranquil, undisturbed, unperturbed, unruffled, unshaken, untroubled, unworried

rel even, even-keeled, steady, well-adjusted, well-balanced; imperturbable, nerveless, unflappable, unshakable; centered, disciplined, equable, self-contained, self-controlled; affable, breezy, devil-may-care, easygoing, happy-go-lucky, laid-back, loosey-goosey, mellow; carefree, nonchalant, unconcerned; assured, confident, self-assured; aloof, detached, dispassionate, indifferent; bovine, impassive, phlegmatic, sober, stolid; relaxed, relieved, tranquilized (*also* tranquillized)

phrases at peace

near ant anxious, distressed, uneasy, unquiet, unsettled, worried; jittery, jumpy, nervous, restless, skittish, tense; highstrung, unstable, uptight

ant agitated, discomposed, disturbed, flustered, perturbed, unglued, unstrung, upset

3 free from disturbing noise or uproar — see QUIET 1

calm *n* **1** a state of freedom from storm or disturbance ⟨Vacationing city dwellers who are tired of the hustle and bustle enjoy the *calm* of the secluded mountain village.⟩

syn calmness, hush, peace, peacefulness, placidity, quiet, quietness, quietude, repose, restfulness, sereneness, serenity, still, stillness, tranquillity (*or* tranquility)

rel lull, pause, respite; silence; mildness, soothingness; comity, concord, harmony; casualness, easygoingness, informality, laid-backness, relaxedness

near ant clamor, din, noise, racket

ant bustle, commotion, hubbub, hurly-burly, pandemonium, tumult, turmoil, unrest, uproar

2 freedom from disquieting or oppressive thoughts or emotions — see PEACE 2

calm *vb* **1** to free from distress or disturbance ⟨The president's reassuring words did much to *calm* the public during the national emergency.⟩

syn compose, lull, quiet, settle, soothe, still, tranquilize (*also* tranquillize)

rel appease, conciliate, hush, mollify, pacify, placate; allay, alleviate, assuage, ease, lay, mitigate, quell, relax, relieve, solace; narcotize, sedate, stupefy

near ant aggravate, heighten, intensify; arouse, excite, foment, incite, rouse, stir (up), work up

ant agitate, discompose, disquiet, disturb, key (up), perturb, upset, vex

2 to gain emotional or mental control of — see COLLECT 1

calm (down) *vb* to become still and orderly — see QUIET 1

calming *adj* tending to calm the emotions and relieve stress — see SOOTHING 1

calmness *n* **1** a state of freedom from storm or disturbance — see CALM 1

2 evenness of emotions or temper — see EQUANIMITY

3 freedom from disquieting or oppressive thoughts or emotions — see PEACE 2

camaraderie *n* the feeling of closeness and friendship that exists between companions — see COMPANIONSHIP

camouflage *n* clothing put on to hide one's true identity or imitate someone or something else — see DISGUISE 1

camouflage *vb* to change the dress or looks of so as to conceal true identity — see DISGUISE 1

camp *n* **1** a place where a group of people live for a short time in tents or cabins ⟨Red Cross workers arrived at the refugee *camp*.⟩

syn bivouac, campground, campsite, encampment

rel colony, plantation, settlement; jungle, shantytown; concentration camp, prison camp; barracks, cantonment, installation, post

2 a small, simply constructed, and often temporary dwelling — see SHACK

3 an often small house for recreational or seasonal use — see COTTAGE

camp *vb* to provide with living quarters or shelter — see HOUSE 1

camp (out) *vb* to live in a camp or the outdoors ⟨Rather than stay in motels, my family usually *camps out* when we're on vacation.⟩

syn bivouac, encamp

rel sleep out, tent; bed (down); backpack, caravan

phrases rough it

campaign *n* a series of activities undertaken to achieve a goal ⟨an all-out *campaign* to bring a minor league baseball team to the city⟩

syn bandwagon, blitz, cause, crusade, drive, movement, push

rel assault, attack, maneuver, march, offensive; action, bid, enterprise, initiative, mission, project, undertaking

campaigner *n* one who seeks an office, honor, position, or award — see CANDIDATE

camper *n* a motor vehicle that specially equipped for living while traveling ⟨The family loaded up the *camper* and headed off for the tour of several national parks.⟩

syn caravan, motor home, recreational vehicle, RV, trailer

rel house trailer, mobile home; coach, van

campground *n* a place where a group of people live for a short time in tents or cabins — see CAMP 1

campsite *n* a place where a group of people live for a short time in tents or cabins — see CAMP 1

can *n* **1** a metal container in the shape of a

cylinder ⟨The shelter stores huge *cans* of water for an emergency.⟩

syn barrel, canister (*also* cannister), drum, tin

rel bucket, pail; tin can

2 the part of the body upon which someone sits — see BUTTOCKS

can *vb* 1 *slang* to bring (as an action or operation) to an immediate end — see STOP 1

2 to let go from office, service, or employment — see DISMISS 1

canal *n* an open man-made passageway for water — see CHANNEL 1

cancel *vb* 1 to put an end to (something planned or previously agreed to) ⟨Please call to *cancel* your appointment with the dentist if you can't make it.⟩

syn abandon, abort, call, call off, drop, recall, repeal, rescind, revoke, scrap, scrub

rel abrogate, annul, invalidate, nullify, void, write off; recant, retract, take back, withdraw; countermand, reverse; break off, discontinue, end, halt, stop, terminate; hold back, interrupt, suspend; give up, relinquish, surrender

near ant engage, pledge, promise; begin, commence, initiate, start; take on, take up, undertake

ant continue, keep

2 to put an end to by formal action — see ABOLISH 1

3 to show (something written) to be no longer valid by drawing a cross over or a line through it — see X (OUT)

4 to destroy all traces of — see ANNIHILATE 1

cancel (out) *vb* to balance with an equal force so as to make ineffective — see OFFSET

canceler *or* **canceller** *n* a force or influence that makes an opposing force ineffective or less effective — see COUNTERBALANCE

cancellation *also* **cancelation** *n* the act of putting an end to something planned or previously agreed to ⟨Bad weather forced the *cancellation* of dozens of flights.⟩

syn abandonment, abortion, calling, calling off, dropping, recall, repeal, rescission, revocation

rel neutralization, voidance; ending, halting, stopping, termination; giving up, relinquishment, surrender; reversal, rollback

near ant beginning, commencement, initiation; engagement, undertaking

ant continuation

candid *adj* 1 free in expressing one's true feelings and opinions — see FRANK

2 marked by justice, honesty, and freedom from bias — see FAIR 2

candidate *n* one who seeks an office, honor, position, or award ⟨Each *candidate* for town council was allowed to speak at the candidates' forum.⟩

syn applicant, aspirant, campaigner, contender, expectant, hopeful, prospect, seeker

rel competitor, contestant, entrant, entry,

favorite, qualifier; dark horse, spoiler, stalking horse; crown prince, favorite son; claimant, pretender

near ant incumbent, officeholder; awardee, honoree, inductee; dropout

ant noncandidate

candidness *n* the free expression of one's true feelings and opinions — see CANDOR 1

candor *n* 1 the free expression of one's true feelings and opinions ⟨an interview in which the members of the rock band speak with *candor* about their recent squabbling⟩

syn candidness, directness, forthrightness, frankness, honesty, openheartedness, openness, outspokenness, plainness, straightforwardness

rel earnestness, sincerity, sobriety; artlessness, genuineness, naïveté (*also* naivete *or* naiveté); simplicity, unsophistication; communicativeness, freedom, license (*or* licence), unrestrainedness, unrestraint

near ant circuitousness, evasiveness, secretiveness; inhibition, reserve, restraint, reticence, shyness; diplomacy, tact

ant dissembling, dissimulation, indirection

2 the quality or state of having or giving off light — see BRILLIANCE 1

cane *n* a heavy rigid stick used as a weapon or for punishment — see CLUB 1

canine *n* a domestic mammal that is related to the wolves and foxes — see DOG 1

canister *also* **cannister** *n* a metal container in the shape of a cylinder — see CAN 1

canned *adj* using or marked by the use of something else as a basis or model — see IMITATIVE 1

canniness *n* 1 exceptional discernment and judgment especially in practical matters — see ACUMEN

2 skill in achieving one's ends through indirect, subtle, or underhanded means — see CUNNING 1

cannonade *n* a rapid or overwhelming outpouring of many things at once — see BARRAGE

cannonade *vb* to use bombs or artillery against — see BOMBARD 1

canny *adj* having or showing a practical cleverness or judgment — see SHREWD 1

canon *n* 1 a statement or body of statements concerning faith or morals proclaimed by a church — see DOCTRINE 1

2 a record of a series of items (as names or titles) usually arranged according to some system — see ¹LIST

3 a collection or system of rules of conduct — see CODE

canonize *vb* 1 to love or admire too much — see IDOLIZE

2 to assign a high status or value to — see EXALT 1

canopy *n* a raised covering over something for decoration or protection ⟨Trees line both sides of the garden path, with their foliage forming a leafy *canopy* for walkers.⟩

syn awning, ceiling, cover, roof, tent

rel marquee; arbor, pergola; screen, shade, shelter, shield, sunshade, umbrella; canvas (*also* canvass), fly

¹**cant** *n* the degree to which something rises

up from a position level with the horizon
— see SLANT 1

²**cant** *n* **1** the pretending of having virtues,
principles, or beliefs that one in fact does
not have — see HYPOCRISY

2 the special terms or expressions of a particular group or field — see TERMINOLO-
GY

cant *adj* running in a slanting direction —
see DIAGONAL

cant *vb* to set or cause to be at an angle —
see LEAN 1

cantankerous *adj* having or showing a
habitually bad temper — see ILL-TEM-
PERED

canted *adj* running in a slanting direction
— see DIAGONAL

canticle *n* a religious song — see HYMN 1

canvas *also* **canvass** *n* a picture created
with oil paint — see PAINTING

canvass *also* **canvas** *vb* **1** to go around
and approach (people) with a request for
opinions or information ⟨We *canvassed*
people all over town, asking if they would
be interested in participating in a recycling program.⟩

syn poll, solicit, survey

rel interrogate, question; feel (out), sound
(out)

near ant report

2 to talk about (an issue) usually from
various points of view and for the purpose
of arriving at a decision or opinion — see
DISCUSS

canyon *also* **cañon** *n* a narrow opening
between hillsides or mountains that can be
used for passage ⟨As the scouts made their
way through the *canyon*, they marveled at
the sheer walls of rock on both sides.⟩

syn defile, flume, gap, gorge, gulch, gulf,
notch, pass, ravine

rel abyss, chasm, cleft, crevasse, crevice,
fissure; dale, dell, glen, hollow, shut-in,
vale, valley; basin, floodplain, kettle; arroyo, coulee, draw, gully (*also* gulley), gutter, trench, trough

¹**cap** *n* a small mass containing medicine to
be taken orally — see PILL 1

²**cap** *n* **1** a covering for the head usually
having a shaped crown — see HAT

2 a piece placed over an open container to
hold in, protect, or conceal its contents —
see COVER 1

3 a real or imaginary point beyond which
a person or thing cannot go — see LIMIT 1

cap *vb* to set bounds or an upper limit for
— see LIMIT 1

cap (off) *vb* to bring to a triumphant conclusion — see CROWN

capability *n* **1** a skill, an ability, or knowledge that makes a person able to do a particular job — see QUALIFICATION 1

2 the physical or mental power to do
something — see ABILITY

3 something that can develop or become
actual — see POTENTIAL

capable *adj* having the required skills for
an acceptable level of performance — see
COMPETENT 1

capably *adv* in a skillful or expert manner
— see WELL 3

capacious *adj* more than adequate or average in capacity — see SPACIOUS

capacity *n* **1** the largest number or
amount that something can hold ⟨The
seating *capacity* of the school auditorium
is 800 people.⟩

syn complement, volume

rel burden, fill, load, measure; area, room,
space, stowage

2 an assignment at which one regularly
works for pay — see JOB 1

3 the action for which a person or thing is
specially fitted or used or for which a
thing exists — see ROLE

4 the physical or mental power to do
something — see ABILITY

caparison *n* **1** dressy clothing — see FIN-
ERY

2 something that decorates or beautifies
— see DECORATION 1

caparison *vb* **1** to outfit with clothes and
especially fine or special clothes — see
CLOTHE 1

2 to make more attractive by adding
something that is beautiful or becoming
— see DECORATE

¹**cape** *n* a sleeveless garment worn so as to
hang over the shoulders, arms, and back
⟨The mysterious figure wrapped his *cape*
tightly around his shoulders.⟩

syn cloak, frock, mantle

rel burnoose (*or* burnous), capelet, capu-
chin, cowl, domino, joseph, manta, mante-
let, mantilla, poncho, roquelaure, tippet;
serape (*or* sarape), shawl, stole, wrap

²**cape** *n* an area of land that juts out into a
body of water ⟨Residents fled the *cape* as
the hurricane roared up the coast.⟩

syn arm, headland, peninsula, point,
promontory, spit

rel breakwater, jetty

caper *n* a playful or mischievous act intended as a joke — see PRANK

caper *vb* to play and run about happily —
see FROLIC 1

capital *adj* **1** coming before all others in
importance — see FOREMOST 1

2 of the very best kind — see EXCELLENT

capital *n* **1** a thing or place that is of greatest importance to an activity or interest —
see CENTER 1

2 the total of one's money and property —
see WEALTH 1

capitalize *vb* to provide money for — see
FINANCE 1

capitalize (on) *vb* to take unfair advantage of — see EXPLOIT 1

capitol *n* the building in which a state legislature meets ⟨The legislators were called
to the *capitol* for an emergency session.⟩

syn statehouse

rel meetinghouse; chamber, hall; house,
senate

capitulate *vb* **1** to cease resistance (as to
another's arguments, demands, or control)
— see YIELD 3

2 to yield to the control or power of enemy forces — see FALL 2

capitulating *n* the usually forced yielding
of one's person or possessions to the control of another — see SURRENDER

capitulation *n* the usually forced yielding
of one's person or possessions to the control of another — see SURRENDER

caprice *n* **1** a sudden impulsive and apparently unmotivated idea or action — see WHIM

2 an inclination to sudden illogical changes of mind, ideas, or actions — see WHIMSICALITY

capricious *adj* **1** likely to change frequently, suddenly, or unexpectedly — see FICKLE 1

2 prone to sudden illogical changes of mind, ideas, or actions — see WHIMSICAL

capriciousness *n* an inclination to sudden illogical changes of mind, ideas, or actions — see WHIMSICALITY

capsize *vb* to turn on one's side or upside down ⟨A huge wave out of nowhere caused our little sailboat to *capsize*.⟩
syn overturn, turn over, upset
rel invert, overset, overthrow, pitchpole, topple, upend; careen, heel, lean, list, tilt, tip; collapse, fall, founder, give
phrases turn turtle
near ant straighten (up); erect, raise
ant right

capsule *adj* marked by the use of few words to convey much information or meaning — see CONCISE

capsule *n* **1** a small mass containing medicine to be taken orally — see PILL 1

2 something that encloses another thing especially to protect it — see ¹CASE 1

capsule *vb* to reduce in size or volume by or as if by pressing parts or members together — see COMPRESS 1

captain *n* **1** a person in overall command of a ship ⟨The *captain* is responsible for everything that happens to the ship in the course of a voyage.⟩
syn commander, skipper
rel sea captain; master, pilot; commanding officer; admiral, commodore, vice admiral; mate, officer
near ant crew, crewman, crewmate

2 one in official command especially of a military force or base — see COMMANDER 1

3 the person (as an employer or supervisor) who tells people and especially workers what to do — see BOSS

4 a person of rank, power, or influence in a particular field — see MAGNATE

captain *vb* **1** to be in charge of — see BOSS 1

2 to exercise authority or power over — see GOVERN 1

3 to serve as leader of — see LEAD 2

caption *n* **1** an explanation or description accompanying a pictorial illustration ⟨For the school yearbook, funny *captions* were written for snapshots showing a typical day at school.⟩
syn legend
rel key; closed-captioning, subtitle, translation; motto, slogan

2 a word or series of words often in larger letters placed at the beginning of a passage or at the top of a page in order to introduce or categorize — see HEADING

captious *adj* given to making or expressing unfavorable judgments about things — see CRITICAL 1

captivate *vb* to attract or delight as if by magic — see CHARM 1

captivating *adj* having an often mysterious or magical power to attract — see FASCINATING 1

captivation *n* the power of irresistible attraction — see CHARM 2

captive *adj* taken and held prisoner ⟨The *captive* soldiers were treated humanely by the guards.⟩
syn apprehended, arrested, captured, caught, imprisoned, incarcerated, interned, jailed
rel bound, enslaved, indentured; ensnared, trapped; abducted, kidnapped (*also* kidnaped); subdued, subjugated; occupied
phrases behind bars
near ant unconfined, unrestrained; delivered, emancipated, enfranchised, freed, liberated, paroled, released
ant free

captive *n* one that has been taken and held in confinement ⟨The *captives* in the concentration camp had devised a daring plan of escape.⟩
syn capture, internee, prisoner
rel coprisoner; convict, jailbird; arrestee; abductee, kidnappee (*or* kidnapee)
near ant custodian, guard, guardian, jailer (*also* jailor), keeper, marshal (*also* marshall), warden; abductor, kidnapper (*also* kidnaper)
ant captor

captivity *n* the act of confining or the state of being confined — see INTERNMENT

capture *n* one that has been taken and held in confinement — see CAPTIVE

capture *vb* **1** to receive as return for effort — see EARN 1

2 to take physical control or possession of (something) suddenly or forcibly — see CATCH 1

captured *adj* taken and held prisoner — see CAPTIVE

car *n* a self-propelled passenger vehicle on four wheels ⟨every teenager's dream of getting a driver's license and a first *car*⟩
syn auto, automobile, machine, motor, motorcar, motor vehicle, wheels [*slang*]
rel coach, jitney, microbus, minibus, minivan, omnibus, van; convertible, fastback, hardtop, hatchback, notchback, ragtop, sports car, sport-utility vehicle, station wagon, SUV, town car, wagon, woody (*or* woodie); compact, coupe (*or* coupé), intermediate, limousine, mini, minicar, sedan, subcompact, V-8; gas-guzzler, land yacht; muscle car, stock car, turbocar; beater, crate, flivver, junker; cream puff; phaeton, roadster, tin lizzie, touring car; hybrid

caravan *n* **1** a group of vehicles traveling together or under one management — see FLEET

2 a motor vehicle that is specially equipped for living while traveling — see CAMPER

carbon copy *n* **1** something or someone that strongly resembles another — see IMAGE 1

2 something that is made to look exactly like something else — see COPY

carcass *n* a dead body — see CORPSE

card *n* **1** a list of foods served at or available for a meal — see MENU 1

---

syn synonym(s)   **rel** related words
ant antonym(s)   **near ant** near antonym(s)

2 a person (as a writer) noted for or specializing in humor — see HUMORIST

cardinal *adj* coming before all others in importance — see FOREMOST 1

care *n* **1** strict attentiveness to what one is doing ⟨Reading the report with more *care* the second time, she detected several errors.⟩

syn carefulness, closeness, conscientiousness, heed, heedfulness, meticulousness, pains, scrupulousness

rel advertence, advertency, attention, concentration, focus, observance, observation; alertness, vigilance, watchfulness; dutifulness, punctiliousness, responsibility; bother, effort, painstaking, trouble; exactness, particularity, precision

near ant inadvertence, inadvertency, inattention, inobservance

ant heedlessness, inattentiveness, negligence

2 attention accompanied by protectiveness and responsibility ⟨That's an extremely valuable violin, so handle it with *care*.⟩

syn solicitude

rel concern, considerateness, consideration, kindness, thoughtfulness; babying, coddling, pampering

near ant inconsiderateness, inconsideration, thoughtlessness, unconcern, unkindness

ant carelessness

3 a close attentiveness to avoiding danger — see CAUTION 1

4 an uneasy state of mind usually over the possibility of an anticipated misfortune or trouble — see ANXIETY 1

5 responsibility for the safety and well-being of someone or something — see CUSTODY

6 the duty or function of watching or guarding for the sake of proper direction or control — see SUPERVISION 1

7 the act or activity of looking after and making decisions about something — see CONDUCT 1

care *vb* to have an interest or concern for ⟨a teacher who *cares* what happens to her students long after they leave her classroom⟩

syn mind, watch

rel attend, heed, regard; note, notice, observe; empathize (with), feel (for), sympathize (with)

near ant disregard, ignore, overlook

care (for) *vb* **1** to take charge of especially on behalf of another — see ²TEND 1

2 to attend to the needs and comforts of — see NURSE 1

3 to have a favorable opinion of — see APPROVE (OF)

4 to wish to have — see LIKE 1

5 to show partiality toward — see PREFER 1

careen *vb* **1** to make a series of unsteady side-to-side motions — see ROCK 1

2 to move forward while swaying from side to side — see STAGGER 1

3 to proceed or move quickly — see HURRY 2

career *vb* to proceed or move quickly — see HURRY 1

carefree *adj* having or showing freedom from worries or troubles ⟨passengers on a luxury cruise ship enjoying a *carefree* vacation⟩ ⟨*carefree* college students on spring break⟩

syn blithe, debonair, devil-may-care, happy-go-lucky, insouciant, lighthearted, lightsome, unconcerned

rel blasé (*also* blase), breezy, cavalier, nonchalant; casual, easygoing, informal, laid-back, low-pressure, relaxed, unfussy

near ant earnest, grave, serious, serious-minded, somber (*or* sombre); careful, cautious, heedful, wary; anxious, concerned, upset, worried; long-suffering, overburdened, sorrowful

ant careworn

careful *adj* **1** having or showing a close attentiveness to avoiding danger or trouble ⟨*Careful* drivers slow down on slick or icy roadways.⟩

syn alert, cautious, circumspect, conservative, gingerly, guarded, heedful, safe, wary

rel advertent, attentive, awake, observant, regardful, vigilant, watchful; hypercautious; foresighted, foresightful, forethoughtful, provident, thoughtful; cagey (*also* cagy), calculating, canny, shrewd; deliberate, slow; ultracareful, ultracautious

near ant bold, brash, impetuous, rash, reckless, venturesome; asleep, inattentive, regardless; inconsiderate, thoughtless; lax, neglectful, negligent, remiss; imprudent, indiscreet, injudicious; absentminded, forgetful; inadvertent, unintentional, unplanned

ant careless, heedless, incautious, unguarded, unmindful, unsafe, unwary

2 taking, showing, or involving great care and effort — see PAINSTAKING

carefulness *n* **1** a close attentiveness to avoiding danger — see CAUTION 1

2 strict attentiveness to what one is doing — see CARE 1

careless *adj* **1** not paying or showing close attention especially for the purpose of avoiding trouble ⟨a *careless* reporter who often doesn't get his facts straight⟩ ⟨a *careless* mistake that caused the plane to crash⟩

syn heedless, incautious, mindless, unguarded, unsafe, unwary

rel bold, impetuous, rash, reckless; inattentive, regardless; blithe, inconsiderate, thoughtless; absentminded, forgetful, unmindful; lax, neglectful, negligent, remiss; slipshod; imprudent, indiscreet, injudicious; inadvertent, unintentional, unplanned

near ant attentive, observant, vigilant, watchful; foresighted, forethoughtful, provident; calculating, shrewd; considerate, thoughtful; ultracareful, ultracautious

ant alert, cautious, circumspect, gingerly, guarded, heedful, safe, wary

2 failing to give proper care and attention — see NEGLIGENT

carelessness *n* failure to take the care that a cautious person usually takes — see NEGLIGENCE 1

caress *vb* to touch or handle in a tender or loving manner — see FONDLE

caretaker *n* a person who takes care of a property sometimes for an absent owner — see CUSTODIAN 1

cargo *n* a mass or quantity of something taken up and carried, conveyed, or transported — see LOAD 1

caricature *n* **1** a poor, insincere, or insulting imitation of something — see MOCKERY 1

2 a work that imitates and exaggerates another work for comic effect — see PARODY 1

3 the representation of something in terms that go beyond the facts — see EXAGGERATION

caricature *vb* to copy or exaggerate (someone or something) in order to make fun of — see MIMIC 1

carnage *n* the killing of a large number of people — see MASSACRE

carnal *adj* **1** having to do with life on earth especially as opposed to that in heaven — see EARTHLY

2 of or relating to the human body — see PHYSICAL 1

3 pleasing to the physical senses — see SENSUAL

carnival *n* a time or program of special events and entertainment in honor of something — see FESTIVAL

carol *n* a religious song — see HYMN 1

carol *vb* **1** to produce musical sounds with the voice — see SING 1

2 to proclaim the glory of — see PRAISE 1

caroler *or* **caroller** *n* one who sings — see SINGER

carom *vb* to strike and fly off at an angle — see GLANCE 1

carouse *vb* to take part in drunken revelry ⟨a night of feasting and *carousing*⟩

syn binge, wassail

rel drink, guzzle

carp *n* an expression of dissatisfaction, pain, or resentment — see COMPLAINT 1

carp *vb* **1** to express dissatisfaction, pain, or resentment usually tiresomely — see COMPLAIN

2 to make often peevish criticisms or objections about matters that are minor, unimportant, or irrelevant — see QUIBBLE 1

carper *n* a person given to harsh judgments and to finding faults — see CRITIC 1

carpet *vb* to form a layer over — see COVER 2

carping *adj* given to making or expressing unfavorable judgments about things — see CRITICAL 1

carriage *n* **1** a horse-drawn wheeled vehicle for carrying passengers ⟨a museum with a large collection of beautiful, old *carriages*⟩

syn equipage, rig

rel buckboard, cab, cabriolet, carryall, chaise, chariot, coach, coupé (*or* coupe), dogcart, four-in-hand, gig, go-cart, hackney (*or* hackney coach), hansom (*or* hansom cab), jaunting car, landau, phaeton, post chaise, roadster, rockaway, stage, stagecoach, stanhope, surrey, tandem, trap, troika, victoria; turnout

2 a general way of holding the body — see POSTURE 1

carry *vb* **1** to support and take from one place to another ⟨Each camper must be able to *carry* his or her own backpack.⟩

syn bear, cart, convey, ferry, haul, lug, pack, tote, transport

rel deliver, hand over, transfer; forward, send, ship, transmit; bring, fetch, take; move, remove, shift

2 to wear or have on one's person ⟨I always *carry* a camera with me so as to never miss a great shot.⟩

syn bear, pack

rel flaunt, show off, sport; display, exhibit, parade, show

3 to bring before the public in performance or exhibition — see PRESENT 1

4 to have as part of a whole — see INCLUDE 1

5 to hold up or serve as a foundation for — see SUPPORT 1

6 to receive as return for effort — see EARN 1

7 to manage the actions of (oneself) in a particular way — see BEHAVE

carryall *n* a bag carried by hand and designed to hold a traveler's clothing and personal articles — see TRAVELING BAG

carry away *vb* to fill with overwhelming emotion (as wonder or delight) — see ENTRANCE

carry on *vb* **1** to behave badly — see MISBEHAVE

2 to continue despite difficulties, opposition, or discouragement — see PERSEVERE

3 to look after and make decisions about — see CONDUCT 1

carry out *vb* to carry through (as a process) to completion — see PERFORM 1

cart *n* a wheeled usually horse-drawn vehicle used for hauling ⟨a *cart* piled up with hay⟩

syn wagon, wain

rel dray, jolt-wagon [*Midland*], oxcart, spring wagon, wagonette; barrow, hand truck, pushcart, tram, truck, wheelbarrow

cart *vb* to support and take from one place to another — see CARRY 1

cartel *n* a number of businesses or enterprises united for commercial advantage ⟨a *cartel* of oil-producing nations that controls production and influences prices⟩

syn combination, combine, syndicate, trust

rel chain, conglomerate, megacorporation; association, guild (*also* gild), organization, partnership, pool, union; big business

cartoon *n* **1** a picture using lines to represent the chief features of an object or scene — see DRAWING

2 a series of drawings that tell a story or part of a story — see COMIC STRIP

3 a poor, insincere, or insulting imitation of something — see MOCKERY 1

carve *vb* to create a three-dimensional representation of (something) using solid material — see SCULPT

cascade *n* a fall of water usually from a great height — see WATERFALL

¹case *n* **1** something that encloses another thing especially to protect it ⟨Those binoculars come with their own *case*.⟩

syn armor, capsule, casing, cocoon, cover,

covering, housing, hull, husk, jacket, pod, sheath, shell

rel cartridge, cassette (*also* casette); bark; carapace, house, mail, panoply, plate, plating, shield; cuticle, hide, skin; envelope, package, wrapper; backing, coating, coverture, facing

2 a covered rectangular container for storing or transporting things — see CHEST

²**case** *n* 1 an individual awaiting or under medical care and treatment — see PATIENT

2 one of a group or collection that shows what the whole is like — see EXAMPLE

3 something that actually exists — see FACT 2

4 a statement given to explain a belief or act — see REASON 1

5 a sudden experiencing of a physical or mental disorder — see ATTACK 2

6 something that might happen — see EVENT 2

7 something that requires thought and skill for resolution — see PROBLEM 1

cash *n* something (as pieces of stamped metal or printed paper) customarily and legally used as a medium of exchange, a measure of value, or a means of payment — see MONEY

cashier *vb* 1 to let go from office, service, or employment — see DISMISS 1

2 to get rid of as useless or unwanted — see DISCARD

cash in (on) *vb* to take unfair advantage of — see EXPLOIT 1

casing *n* something that encloses another thing especially to protect it — see ¹CASE 1

cask *n* an enclosed wooden vessel for holding beverages ⟨*casks* of wine that had been in the castle for many years⟩

syn barrel, butt, hogshead, keg, pipe, puncheon

rel cistern, tub, vat; can, drum

casket *n* 1 a boxlike container for holding a dead body — see COFFIN

2 a covered rectangular container for storing or transporting things — see CHEST

cast *n* 1 a declaration that something will happen in the future — see PREDICTION

2 a property that becomes apparent when light falls on an object and by which things that are identical in form can be distinguished — see COLOR 1

3 an instance of looking especially briefly — see LOOK 2

4 facial appearance regarded as an indication of mood or feeling — see LOOK 1

5 the outward appearance of something as distinguished from its substance — see FORM 1

cast *vb* 1 to throw or give off — see EMIT 1

2 to point or turn (something) toward a target or goal — see AIM 1

3 to put (something) into proper and usually carefully worked out written form — see COMPOSE 1

4 to send through the air especially with a quick forward motion of the arm — see THROW 1

cast (off) *vb* to get rid of as useless or unwanted — see DISCARD

cast (up) *vb* to combine (numbers) into a single sum — see ADD 2

cast about (for) *vb* to go in search of — see SEEK 1

cast around (for) *vb* to go in search of — see SEEK 1

castaway *n* one who is cast out or rejected by society — see OUTCAST

caste *n* one of the segments of society into which people are grouped — see CLASS 1

castigate *vb* 1 to criticize (someone) severely or angrily especially for personal failings — see SCOLD

2 to criticize harshly and usually publicly — see ATTACK 1

3 to inflict a penalty on for a fault or crime — see PUNISH

castigating *adj* inflicting, involving, or serving as punishment — see PUNITIVE

castigation *n* suffering, loss, or hardship imposed in response to a crime or offense — see PUNISHMENT

castigator *n* 1 a person given to harsh judgments and to finding faults — see CRITIC 1

2 one who inflicts punishment in return for an injury or offense — see NEMESIS 1

castle *n* 1 a structure or place from which one can resist attack — see FORT

2 a large impressive residence — see MANSION

castoff *n* one who is cast out or rejected by society — see OUTCAST

casual *adj* 1 not designed to be worn only on special occasions ⟨a restaurant where people in *casual* clothes are always welcome⟩

syn everyday, informal, workaday

rel relaxed, sporty; dressed down; shabby, sloppy, slovenly, unkempt

near ant best; dressed up; chic, elegant, fashionable, smart, stylish; neat, tidy, trim; semiformal

ant dressy, formal, noncasual

2 happening by chance — see ACCIDENTAL 1

3 having or showing a lack of interest or concern — see INDIFFERENT 1

4 lacking in steadiness or regularity of occurrence — see FITFUL

casualness *n* lack of interest or concern — see INDIFFERENCE

casualty *n* 1 a person or thing harmed, lost, or destroyed ⟨The old tree was a *casualty* of the storm.⟩

syn fatality, loss, prey, victim

rel loser, underdog; martyr, sacrifice; collateral damage; murderee

near ant gainer, victor, winner; harmer, injurer; assassin, killer, murderer

2 a chance and usually sudden event bringing loss or injury — see ACCIDENT 1

cat *n* a small domestic animal known for catching mice ⟨The family's *cat* did an exemplary job of keeping the house and yard free of all rodents.⟩

syn feline, house cat, kitty, puss, pussy

rel mouser; kit, kitten; alley cat, tabby; gib, tomcat

cataclysm *n* 1 a great flow of water or of something that overwhelms — see FLOOD

2 a sudden violent event that brings about great loss or destruction — see DISASTER 1

3 a violent disturbance (as of the political or social order) — see CONVULSION

cataclysmal or **cataclysmic** adj 1 bringing about ruin or misfortune — see FATAL 1

2 causing or tending to cause destruction — see DESTRUCTIVE 1

3 marked by sudden or violent disturbance — see CONVULSIVE 1

catacomb n, usually **catacombs** pl an underground burial chamber — see CRYPT

catalog or **catalogue** n a record of a series of items (as names or titles) usually arranged according to some system — see ¹LIST

catalog or **catalogue** vb to put (someone or something) on a list — see ¹LIST 2

catamount n a large tawny cat of the wild — see COUGAR

catapult vb to send through the air especially with a quick forward motion of the arm — see THROW 1

cataract n 1 a fall of water usually from a great height — see WATERFALL

2 a great flow of water or of something that overwhelms — see FLOOD

catastrophe n 1 a sudden violent event that brings about great loss or destruction — see DISASTER 1

2 something that has failed — see FAILURE 3

catastrophic adj bringing about ruin or misfortune — see FATAL 1

catcall n a vocal sound made to express scorn or disapproval ⟨The band's sloppy playing produced only *catcalls* from the crowd.⟩

syn boo, hiss, hoot, jeer, raspberry, snort
rel smirk, sneer, snicker, snigger; gibe (or jibe), put-down, taunt; whistle
near ant applause, clapping
ant cheer

catch n 1 a danger or difficulty that is hidden or not easily recognized — see PITFALL 1

2 someone or something unusually desirable — see PRIZE 1

3 the total amount collected or obtained especially at one time — see HAUL 1

catch vb 1 to take physical control or possession of (something) suddenly or forcibly ⟨We tried to *catch* the kitten before she could sneak out the door.⟩

syn bag, capture, collar, cop [*slang*], corral, get, grab, grapple, hook, land, nab, nail, net, rap, seize, snag, snap (up), snare, snatch, trap
rel glove, halter, lasso, rope; apprehend, arrest, detain; bay, corner; clasp, clutch, fasten (on), fist, grasp, grip, hold, latch (on or onto), secure; rend, wrest; enmesh (*also* immesh), ensnare, entangle, entrap, mesh; abduct, kidnap, spirit (away or off)
phrases take hold (of)
near ant discharge, free, liberate, release; drop, loosen, unhand
ant miss

2 to become affected with (a disease or disorder) — see CONTRACT 1

3 to bring (something) to a standstill — see ¹HALT 1

4 to put securely in place or in a desired position — see FASTEN 2

5 to have a clear idea of — see COMPREHEND 1

6 to cause to believe what is untrue — see DECEIVE

7 to come upon face-to-face or as if face-to-face — see MEET 1

8 to make note of (something) through the use of one's eyes — see SEE 1

9 to move fast enough to get even with — see OVERTAKE

catching adj 1 capable of being passed by physical contact from one person to another — see CONTAGIOUS 1

2 exciting a similar feeling or reaction in others — see CONTAGIOUS 2

catch on (to) vb 1 to come to an awareness of — see DISCOVER 1

2 to have a clear idea of — see COMPREHEND 1

catch up (with) vb to move fast enough to get even with — see OVERTAKE

catchy adj 1 likely to attract attention — see NOTICEABLE

2 requiring exceptional skill or caution in performance or handling — see TRICKY 1

3 lacking in steadiness or regularity of occurrence — see FITFUL

categorical also **categoric** adj having no exceptions or restrictions — see ABSOLUTE 2

categorize vb to arrange or assign according to type — see CLASSIFY 1

category n one of the units into which a whole is divided on the basis of a common characteristic — see CLASS 2

cater vb to provide food or meals for — see FEED 1

cater (to) vb to give in to (a desire) — see INDULGE 1

catnap n a short sleep — see ¹NAP

catnap vb 1 to be in a state of sleep — see SLEEP 1

2 to sleep lightly or briefly — see NAP 1

catnapping n a natural periodic loss of consciousness during which the body restores itself — see SLEEP 1

cattily adv in a mean or spiteful manner — see NASTILY

cattiness n 1 biting sharpness of feeling or expression — see ACRIMONY 1

2 the desire to cause pain for the satisfaction of doing harm — see MALICE

catty adj having or showing a desire to cause someone pain or suffering for the sheer enjoyment of it — see HATEFUL

caught adj taken and held prisoner — see CAPTIVE

cause n 1 someone or something responsible for a result ⟨the much-debated *causes* of the American Civil War⟩

syn antecedent, occasion, reason
rel consideration, determinant, factor; alpha and omega, be-all and end-all; impetus, incentive, inspiration, instigation, stimulus; mother, origin, root, source, spring
near ant ramification; denouement (*also* dénouement), repercussion; conclusion, end; by-product, side effect (*also* side reaction)
ant aftereffect, aftermath, consequence, corollary, development, effect, fate, fruit, issue, outcome, outgrowth, product, result, resultant, sequel, sequence, upshot

---

syn synonym(s)   *rel* related words
ant antonym(s)   *near ant* near antonym(s)

2 a series of activities undertaken to achieve a goal — see CAMPAIGN

cause *vb* to be the cause of (a situation, action, or state of mind) — see EFFECT

caustic *adj* marked by the use of wit that is intended to cause hurt feelings — see SARCASTIC

caution *n* **1** a close attentiveness to avoiding danger ⟨the extreme *caution* with which the zookeeper handled the snake⟩
    syn alertness, care, carefulness, cautiousness, chariness, circumspection, heedfulness, prudence, wariness
    rel attentiveness, observance, vigilance, watchfulness; foresight, foresightedness, providence; calculation, canniness, deliberateness, deliberation, shrewdness; precaution, safeguard
    near ant abruptness, hastiness, impetuousness, precipitousness, rashness, suddenness; inconsiderateness, inconsideration, thoughtlessness
    ant brashness, carelessness, heedlessness, incautiousness, recklessness, unwariness
2 something extraordinary or surprising — see WONDER 1
3 something that tells of approaching danger or risk — see WARNING 2
4 the act or an instance of telling beforehand of danger or risk — see WARNING 1

caution *vb* to give notice to beforehand especially of danger or risk — see WARN

cautionary *adj* serving as or offering a warning ⟨The story of King Midas is a *cautionary* tale about the perils of wishing for something—you just might get it.⟩
    syn admonishing, admonitory, cautioning, exemplary, premonitory, warning
    rel didactic, moralistic, moralizing; advisory, counseling (*or* counselling); punishing, punitive

cautioning *adj* serving as or offering a warning — see CAUTIONARY

cautious *adj* having or showing a close attentiveness to avoiding danger or trouble — see CAREFUL 1

cautiousness *n* a close attentiveness to avoiding danger — see CAUTION 1

cavalcade *n* **1** a group of vehicles traveling together or under one management — see FLEET
2 a staged presentation often with music that consists of a procession of narrated or enacted scenes — see PAGEANT

cavalier *adj* having a feeling of superiority that shows itself in an overbearing attitude — see ARROGANT

cavalier *n* an honorable and courteous man ⟨a novel about dashing *cavaliers* and gracious ladies⟩
    syn gentleman
    rel Galahad, knight, prince; beau, Beau Brummell, blade, blood, buck, dandy, dude, fop, gallant; captivator, charmer, ladies' man (*also* lady's man), smoothy (*or* smoothie); aristocrat, patrician, swell

cave *n* a naturally formed underground chamber with an opening to the surface ⟨The *cave* is actually a series of large chambers on five levels.⟩
    syn cavern, grot, grotto
    rel abyss, chasm, gulf, hollow; crawlway, gallery, subway, tunnel; excavation, mine,

pit, shaft, well; bunker, dugout, foxhole; burrow, covert, den, hole, lair, lodge, shelter

cave (in) *vb* **1** to fall down or in as a result of physical pressure — see COLLAPSE 1
2 to give up and cease resistance (as to a liking, temptation, or habit) — see YIELD 1

cavern *n* a naturally formed underground chamber with an opening to the surface — see CAVE

cavil *vb* to make often peevish criticisms or objections about matters that are minor, unimportant, or irrelevant — see QUIBBLE 1

caviler *or* **caviller** *n* a person given to harsh judgments and to finding faults — see CRITIC 1

caviling *or* **cavilling** *adj* given to making or expressing unfavorable judgments about things — see CRITICAL 1

cavity *n* a sunken area forming a separate space — see HOLE 2

cavort *vb* to play and run about happily — see FROLIC 1

cease *n* the stopping of a process or activity — see END 1

cease *vb* **1** to come to an end ⟨The rain finally *ceased*, and we were able to continue the baseball game.⟩
    syn break off, break up, close, conclude, determine, die, discontinue, elapse, end, expire, finish, go, halt, lapse, leave off, let up, pass, quit, stop, terminate, wind up
    rel desist (from), lay off (of), refrain (from); knock off; break down, conk (out), cut out, stall; pause, stay, suspend; abate, peter (out)
    phrases bite the dust
    near ant draw out, extend, prolong, protract
    ant continue, hang on, persist
2 to bring (as an action or operation) to an immediate end — see STOP 1

cease–fire *n* a temporary stopping of fighting — see TRUCE

ceaseless *adj* **1** going on and on without any interruptions — see CONTINUOUS
2 lasting forever — see EVERLASTING 1

ceaselessness *n* uninterrupted or lasting existence — see CONTINUATION

cede *vb* **1** to give (something) over to the control or possession of another usually under duress — see SURRENDER 1
2 to give over the legal possession or ownership of — see TRANSFER 1
3 to give up (as a position of authority) formally — see ABDICATE

ceiling *n* **1** a real or imaginary point beyond which a person or thing cannot go — see LIMIT 1
2 a raised covering over something for decoration or protection — see CANOPY

celebrant *n* one who engages in merrymaking especially in honor of a special occasion ⟨All of the *celebrants* at the birthday party received a favor to take home.⟩
    syn celebrator, merrymaker, reveler (*or* reveller), roisterer
    rel bacchanal, binger, carouser, wassailer; cutup, skylarker; noisemaker
    ant killjoy, party pooper

celebrate *vb* **1** to proclaim the glory of — see PRAISE 1

2 to mark with an appropriate practice, rite, or ceremony — see KEEP 1

celebrated *adj* widely known — see FAMOUS 1

celebration *n* a time or program of special events and entertainment in honor of something — see FESTIVAL

celebrator *n* one who engages in merry-making especially in honor of a special occasion — see CELEBRANT

celebrity *n* **1** a person who is widely known and usually much talked about ⟨*Celebrities* from sports and entertainment attended the opening ceremonies of the Olympic Games.⟩
syn figure, icon (*also* ikon), light, luminary, name, notable, notoriety, personage, personality, somebody, standout, star, superstar, VIP
rel favorite, heartthrob, hero; demigod, dignitary, eminence, immortal, monument, pillar, worthy; baron, big shot, bigwig, kahuna, magnate, mogul, nabob, panjandrum
near ant lightweight, mediocrity
ant nobody, noncelebrity
2 the fact or state of being known to the public — see FAME 1

celerity *n* a high rate of movement or performance — see SPEED 1

celestial *adj* of, relating to, or suggesting heaven ⟨Movie scenes depicting life after death are usually accompanied by *celestial* music.⟩
syn ethereal, heavenly, supernal
rel supernatural, unearthly, unworldly; angelic (*or* angelical), beatific, blissful; Olympian, paradisiacal (*or* paradisiac), utopian; cosmic (*also* cosmical), stellar
near ant earthly, mundane, terrestrial, worldly; anti-utopian, dystopian
ant hellish

cell *n* **1** an area within a building that has been set apart from surrounding space by a wall — see ROOM 2
2 one of the parts into which an enclosed space is divided — see COMPARTMENT
3 a local unit of an organization — see CHAPTER 1

cellar *n* a room or set of rooms below the surface of the ground ⟨An amazing array of interesting things were found in the *cellar* of the old house.⟩
syn basement
rel cellarage; bunker, crawlway, foundation, hold, vault; cyclone cellar, storm cellar

cement *n* **1** a substance used to stick things together — see GLUE
2 a uniting or binding force or influence — see BOND 2

cemetery *n* a piece of land used for burying the dead ⟨Many of the soldiers who died in the battle are buried in a *cemetery* nearby.⟩
syn graveyard, potter's field
rel catacombs, churchyard; crypt, grave, mausoleum, sepulture, tomb, vault

censor *vb* to remove objectionable parts from ⟨The producers were told that they

would have to *censor* their movie if they wanted a PG rating.⟩
syn clean (up), expurgate
rel cleanse, purge, purify; abbreviate, edit, shorten; bleep, blip, cut (out), delete, excise, expunge, gut, x (out); black out, repress, silence, suppress; censure, condemn, denounce; examine, review, screen, scrutinize
near ant approve, authorize, sanction

censurable *adj* **1** deserving reproach or blame — see BLAMEWORTHY
2 provoking or likely to provoke protest — see OBJECTIONABLE

censure *n* an often public or formal expression of disapproval ⟨a rare *censure* of a senator by the full United States Senate for misconduct⟩
syn condemnation, denunciation, excoriation, rebuke, reprimand, reproach, reproof, stricture
rel admonishment, admonition, castigation, chastisement, damnation, punishment, remonstrance; business, devil, dressing-down, lash, lecture, lesson, rap, scolding, talking-to, tongue-lashing; belittlement, criticism, deprecation, depreciation, disparagement, pan
near ant acclamation, honor, tribute; encomium, eulogy, panegyric, plaudit(s), praise; approval, blessing, sanction
ant citation, commendation, endorsement (*also* indorsement)

censure *vb* **1** to express public or formal disapproval of ⟨a vote to *censure* the President for conduct that was unbecoming to his office⟩
syn condemn, denounce, rebuke, reprimand, reproach, reprove
rel admonish, chastise; castigate, punish; bawl out, berate, chew out, cut up, dress down, flay, gibbet, jaw, keelhaul, lambaste (*or* lambast), lecture, rail (at *or* against), rate, scold, score, tell off, upbraid; belittle, criticize, deprecate, depreciate, disparage
phrases bring to account, call to account
near ant acclaim, applause, hail, honor; eulogize, laud, praise; approve, bless, sanction
ant cite, commend, endorse (*also* indorse)
2 to declare to be morally wrong or evil — see CONDEMN 1
3 to express one's unfavorable opinion of the worth or quality of — see CRITICIZE

censurer *n* a person given to harsh judgments and to finding faults — see CRITIC 1

center *n* **1** a thing or place that is of greatest importance to an activity or interest ⟨a stretch of coastline that has long been the area's *center* of tourism⟩
syn base, capital, central, core, cynosure, eye, focus, ground zero, heart, hub, locus, mecca, nucleus, seat
rel headquarters; happy hunting ground, hive, hot spot, playground, playland; nub, pith; deep, thick; essence, quintessence, soul; attraction, lodestone (*also* loadstone), magnet
phrases where it's at
2 an area or point that is an equal distance from all points along an edge or outer surface ⟨the *center* of the earth⟩
syn core, middle, midpoint, midst

---

syn synonym(s)   **rel** related words
ant antonym(s)   **near ant** near antonym(s)

rel inside, interior

ant perimeter, periphery

center *vb* **1** to bring (something) to a central point or under a single control — see CENTRALIZE

2 to fix (as one's attention) steadily toward a central objective — see CONCENTRATE 2

central *adj* **1** coming before all others in importance — see FOREMOST 1

2 occupying a position equally distant from the ends or extremes — see MIDDLE 1

3 avoiding major social change or extreme political ideas — see MODERATE 2

central *n* a thing or place that is of greatest importance to an activity or interest — see CENTER 1

centralize *vb* to bring (something) to a central point or under a single control ⟨The company decided to *centralize* all of its operations at its Ohio plant.⟩

syn center, compact, concentrate, consolidate, unify, unite

rel coordinate, harmonize, integrate, orchestrate; blend, coalesce, combine, fuse, incorporate, merge, reduce; conjoin, join, link; assemble, collect, colligate, gather; reunify, reunite

near ant segregate, separate

ant decentralize, deconcentrate, spread (out)

cerebral *adj* **1** much given to learning and thinking — see INTELLECTUAL 1

2 of or relating to the mind — see MENTAL 1

cerebrum *n* the part of a person that feels, thinks, perceives, wills, and especially reasons — see MIND 1

ceremonial *adj* following or agreeing with established form, custom, or rules — see FORMAL 1

ceremonial *n* an oft-repeated action or series of actions performed in accordance with tradition or a set of rules — see RITE

ceremonious *adj* **1** marked by or showing careful attention to set forms and details ⟨A century ago everyday life was much more *ceremonious* than today.⟩

syn correct, decorous, formal, proper, punctilious, starchy, stiff, stilted

rel sober, solemn, stately; chivalrous, courtly, gallant; genteel, polished, refined; civil, courteous, polite, red-carpet

near ant improper, indecorous, unmannerly; discourteous, impolite, rude

ant casual, easygoing, informal, laid-back, unceremonious

2 following or agreeing with established form, custom, or rules — see FORMAL 1

ceremony *n* an oft-repeated action or series of actions performed in accordance with tradition or a set of rules — see RITE

certain *adj* **1** known but not named ⟨A *certain* person told me that today is your birthday.⟩

syn anonymous, given, one, some, unidentified, unnamed, unspecified

rel particular, specific

near ant known, named, specified

2 having or showing a mind free from doubt ⟨I'm *certain* that they'll arrive on time.⟩

syn assured, clear, cocksure, confident, doubtless, implicit, positive, sanguine, sure

rel self-assured, self-conceited, self-confident; decisive, resolute, unfaltering, unhesitating, unquestioning, unwavering

near ant hesitant, indecisive, vacillating, wavering; diffident, unassuming

ant doubtful, dubious, uncertain, unsure

3 having been established and usually not subject to change — see FIXED 1

4 impossible to avoid or evade — see INEVITABLE

5 not likely to fail — see INFALLIBLE 2

6 not capable of being challenged or proved wrong — see IRREFUTABLE

certainly *adv* without any question — see INDEED 1

certainty *n* a state of mind in which one is free from doubt — see CONFIDENCE 2

certificate *n* a written or printed paper giving information about or proof of something ⟨A *certificate* will be awarded to each person who completes the course in lifesaving.⟩

syn document, instrument

rel credentials; diploma, parchment; record; warrant, writ; warranty; coupon

certify *vb* **1** to declare (something) to be true or genuine ⟨Experts *certified* the letter as indeed having been written by Abraham Lincoln.⟩

syn attest, authenticate, avouch, testify (to), vouch (for), witness

rel guarantee, warrant; affirm, assert, aver, avow, profess, vow

2 to give official or legal power to — see AUTHORIZE 1

3 to give evidence or testimony to the truth or factualness of — see CONFIRM 1

certitude *n* a state of mind in which one is free from doubt — see CONFIDENCE 2

cessation *n* the stopping of a process or activity — see END 1

chafe *vb* **1** to make sore by continued rubbing ⟨ill-fitting boots that had badly *chafed* my heels⟩

syn abrade, excoriate, fret, gall, irritate

rel graze, scrape, scratch; burn, inflame (*also* enflame); flay, peel, skin

2 to damage or diminish by continued friction — see ABRADE 1

3 to disturb the peace of mind of (someone) especially by repeated disagreeable acts — see IRRITATE 1

¹chaff *n* discarded or useless material — see GARBAGE

²chaff *n* good-natured teasing or exchanging of clever remarks — see BANTER

chaff *vb* **1** to make fun of in a good-natured way — see TEASE 1

2 to make jokes — see JOKE 1

chaffing *adj* marked by or expressive of mild or good-natured teasing — see QUIZZICAL

chafing *adj* causing annoyance — see ANNOYING

chain *n* **1** a series of things linked together ⟨the *chain* of events that led the American colonies to seek independence from Great Britain⟩

syn concatenation, progression, sequence, string, train

rel chain reaction; belt, circle, cycle, vicious circle (*also* vicious cycle); continuum, gamut, gauntlet (*also* gantlet), scale, spectrum; flow, river, stream; file, line, queue, range, row, succession

2 something that makes movement or progress difficult — see ENCUMBRANCE

3 something that physically prevents free movement — see BOND 1

chain vb **1** to confine or restrain with or as if with chains — see BIND 1

2 to put or bring together so as to form a new and longer whole — see CONNECT 1

chair n **1** a person in charge of a meeting ⟨All questions and comments should be directed to the *chair*.⟩

syn chairman, chairperson, moderator, president, speaker

rel chairwoman; cochair, cochairman, co-chairperson, cochairwoman, copresident

2 the place of leadership or command — see HEAD 1

chairman n a person in charge of a meeting — see CHAIR 1

chairperson n a person in charge of a meeting — see CHAIR 1

chalet n an often small house for recreational or seasonal use — see COTTAGE

challenge n **1** a feeling or declaration of disapproval or dissent — see OBJECTION

2 something that requires thought and skill for resolution — see PROBLEM 1

challenge vb **1** to demand proof of the truth or rightness of ⟨Don't hesitate to *challenge* any statement that generalizes about people.⟩

syn contest, dispute, impeach, query, question

rel doubt, mistrust; kick (about), object (to); protest; combat, fight, oppose, resist

phrases call in question (or call into question)

near ant back, defend, support; advocate, champion, promote; abide, endure, stomach, tolerate

ant accept, believe, embrace, swallow

2 to invite (someone) to take part in a contest or to perform a feat ⟨I *challenge* you to swim to the other side of the pond.⟩

syn dare, defy, stump

rel beard, brave, brazen, breast, confront, face, outbrave

3 to have as a requirement — see NEED 1

challenged adj deprived of the power to perform one or more natural bodily activities — see DISABLED

challenger n one who strives for the same thing as another — see COMPETITOR

challenging adj **1** requiring considerable physical or mental effort — see HARD 2

2 requiring much time, effort, or careful attention — see DEMANDING 1

chamber n **1** an area within a building that has been set apart from surrounding space by a wall — see ROOM 1

2 one of the parts into which an enclosed space is divided — see COMPARTMENT

3 a group of persons formally joined together for some common interest — see ASSOCIATION 2

chamber vb to provide with living quarters or shelter — see HOUSE 1

champ n the person who comes in first in a competition — see CHAMPION 1

champ vb to crush or grind with the teeth — see BITE (ON)

champion n **1** the person who comes in first in a competition ⟨the *champion* of the national spelling bee⟩

syn champ, victor, winner

rel cochampion, cowinner; placer; finalist, quarterfinalist, semifinalist; medalist (or medallist), prizewinner; star, superstar; world-beater

near ant loser

2 a person who actively supports or favors a cause — see EXPONENT 1

champion vb to promote the interests or cause of — see SUPPORT 1

championship n the position occupied by the one who comes in first in a competition — see CROWN 2

chance adj happening by chance — see ACCIDENTAL 1

chance n **1** the uncertain course of events ⟨Rather than leave everything to *chance*, let's plan how we're going to spend our time in New York City.⟩

syn accident, circumstance, hazard, luck

rel fortuitousness, fortuity, haphazardry, randomness, uncertainty; happenchance, happenstance; destiny, doom, fate, fortune, lot; danger, peril, risk

near ant intent, intention, purpose; design, outline, plan, scheme

2 a favorable combination of circumstances, time, and place — see OPPORTUNITY

3 a measure of how often an event will occur instead of another — see PROBABILITY 2

4 a risky undertaking — see GAMBLE

chance vb **1** to take a chance on — see RISK 1

2 to take place — see HAPPEN

chance (upon) vb **1** to come upon face-to-face or as if face-to-face — see MEET 1

2 to come upon unexpectedly or by chance — see HAPPEN (ON or UPON)

change n **1** the act, process, or result of making different ⟨The positive *change* in our students' attitude toward people who are somehow different was a long and gradual process.⟩

syn alteration, difference, modification, redoing, refashioning, remaking, remodeling, revamping, review, revise, revision, reworking, variation

rel amendment, correction, rectification, reform; conversion, deformation, distortion, metamorphosis, mutation, transfiguration, transformation; oscillation, shift; displacement, replacement, substitution; modulation, regulation, tweak; redesign, redo; about-face, reversal

ant fixation, stabilization

2 the frequent and usually sudden passing from one condition to another — see FLUX 1

3 something (as pieces of stamped metal or printed paper) customarily and legally used as a medium of exchange, a measure of value, or a means of payment — see MONEY

change vb **1** to make different in some way ⟨We've *changed* the look of our living room so it's more fashionable.⟩

syn alter, make over, modify, recast, redo, refashion, remake, remodel, revamp, revise, rework, vary

---

syn synonym(s)   *rel* related words
ant antonym(s)   *near ant* near antonym(s)

rel deform, metamorphose, mutate; regenerate, revolutionize, transfigure, transform; commute, convert, exchange; rejigger, retool

ant fix, freeze, set, stabilize

2 to pass from one form, state, or level to another ⟨The weather in New England is constantly *changing*.⟩

syn fluctuate, mutate, shift, snap, vary

rel metamorphose, morph; better, improve; deteriorate, worsen; turn around; seesaw, teeter, vacillate, waver

ant stabilize

3 to give up (something) and take something else in return ⟨Would you mind *changing* your seat so my friends can sit together?⟩

syn commute, exchange, shift, substitute, swap, switch, trade

rel interchange; displace, replace, supersede; cede, hand over, surrender, yield

changeable *adj* **1** capable of being readily changed — see FLEXIBLE 1

2 likely to change frequently, suddenly, or unexpectedly — see FICKLE 1

changeful *adj* likely to change frequently, suddenly, or unexpectedly — see FICKLE 1

changeless *adj* not undergoing a change in condition — see CONSTANT 1

changelessness *n* the state of continuing without change — see CONSTANCY 1

changeover *n* a change in form, appearance, or use — see CONVERSION 1

changing *adj* not staying constant — see UNEVEN 2

channel *n* **1** an open man-made passageway for water ⟨Water was drained from the swamp through a specially constructed *channel*.⟩

syn aqueduct, canal, conduit, course, flume, raceway, watercourse, waterway

rel millrace, millstream; floodway, sluice, sluiceway, spillway; swash, tideway, torrent; gutter, trough; river, rivulet, stream

2 a narrow body of water between two land masses ⟨the world record for swimming the *channel* between France and Great Britain⟩

syn narrows, sound, strait

rel arm, bay, gulf, inlet; roads, roadstead; reach, stretch

3 a direct way of passing along information or supplies — see PIPELINE 1

4 a long hollow cylinder for carrying a substance (as a liquid or gas) — see PIPE 1

channel *vb* to cause to move to a central point or along a restricted pathway ⟨an athletic youth who *channeled* all of his energy into sports⟩

syn channelize, conduct, direct, funnel, pipe, siphon (*also* syphon)

rel carry, convey, transmit; concentrate, consolidate, focus

channelize *vb* to cause to move to a central point or along a restricted pathway — see CHANNEL

chant *vb* **1** to utter in musical or drawn out tones ⟨The frustrated crowd at the rock concert started to *chant*, "We want the show to start!"⟩

syn intone, sing

rel bellow, belt, roar; chime, chorus

2 to produce musical sounds with the voice — see SING 1

chaos *n* a state in which everything is out of order ⟨The boy's room is in such *chaos* that it looks as though a tornado had struck.⟩

syn confusion, disarrangement, disarray, disorder, disorganization, free-for-all, havoc, hell, jumble, mess, messiness, muddle, muss, shambles, tumble, welter

rel anarchy, lawlessness, misrule, riot; knot, snarl, tangle; labyrinth, maze, web; maelstrom, storm; bollix, clutter, litter, mishmash, shuffle; hodgepodge, medley, miscellany, morass, motley

near ant method, pattern, plan, system

ant order, orderliness

chaotic *adj* lacking in order, neatness, and often cleanliness — see MESSY

chaparral *n* a thick patch of shrubbery, small trees, or underbrush — see THICKET

chaperone *or* **chaperon** *vb* to go along with in order to provide assistance, protection, or companionship — see ACCOMPANY 1

chapter *n* **1** a local unit of an organization ⟨Our *chapter* was well represented at the Jaycees' national convention.⟩

syn affiliate, branch, cell, council, local

rel arm, division, wing; offshoot, subchapter; lodge, post

2 an individual part of a process, series, or ranking — see DEGREE 1

char *vb* to burn on the surface — see SCORCH 1

character *n* **1** a written or printed mark that is meant to convey information to the reader ⟨The pictorial *characters* of the ancient Egyptians had long been a mystery.⟩

syn icon (*also* ikon), sign, symbol

rel cipher, letter, numeral; hieroglyph, ideogram, pictogram, pictograph; rune

2 a person of odd or whimsical habits — see ECCENTRIC

3 conduct that conforms to an accepted standard of right and wrong — see MORALITY 1

4 overall quality as seen or judged by people in general — see REPUTATION

5 something that sets apart an individual from others of the same kind — see CHARACTERISTIC

6 the set of qualities that make a person different from other people — see INDIVIDUALITY 1

7 the set of qualities that makes a person, a group of people, or a thing different from others — see NATURE 1

8 a member of the human race — see HUMAN

character *vb* to point out the chief quality or qualities of an individual or group — see CHARACTERIZE 1

characteristic *adj* **1** serving to identify as belonging to an individual or group ⟨the *characteristic* taste of licorice⟩

syn classic, discriminating, distinct, distinctive, distinguishing, identifying, individual, peculiar, proper, symptomatic, typical

rel idiosyncratic; identifiable, pronounced, unmistakable; general, generic; common, normal, regular, usual; especial, particular, special, specific; archetypal (*also* archetypical), model, paradigmatic *ant* atypical, nontypical, uncharacteristic, untypical

2 having or showing the qualities associated with the members of a particular group or kind — see TYPICAL 1

characteristic *n* something that sets apart an individual from others of the same kind ⟨the ability to speak and other *characteristics* that distinguish human beings from other animals⟩

syn attribute, character, criterion, feature, hallmark, mark, marker, note, particularity, peculiarity, point, property, quality, specific, stamp, touch, trait

rel badge, indication, sign; emblem, symbol, token; charm, grace; excellence, merit, virtue; eccentricity, idiosyncrasy, oddity, quirk; individuality, singularity, uniqueness

characterize *vb* **1** to point out the chief quality or qualities of an individual or group ⟨How would you *characterize* the mission of this environmental organization?⟩

syn character, define, depict, describe, portray, represent

rel categorize, classify, pigeonhole; type; color, identify, indicate, name, specify; distinguish, individualize, mark, particularize, stamp

2 to be an important feature of ⟨A target-shaped rash *characterizes* Lyme disease.⟩

syn distinguish, mark

rel differentiate; customize, individualize, particularize

characterless *adj* lacking strength of will or character — see WEAK 2

charade *n* a display of emotion or behavior that is insincere or intended to deceive — see MASQUERADE

charge *n* **1** a formal claim of criminal wrongdoing against a person ⟨*charges* of burglary that have yet to be proved⟩

syn complaint, count, indictment, rap

rel accusation, allegation, plea; crimination; counteraccusation, countercharge; arraignment, impeachment; implication; censure, condemnation, denunciation; incrimination, recrimination

2 a specific task with which a person or group is charged — see MISSION

3 a statement of what to do that must be obeyed by those concerned — see COMMAND 1

4 something one must do because of prior agreement — see OBLIGATION 1

5 the act or action of setting upon with force or violence — see ATTACK 1

6 the amount of money that is demanded as payment for something — see PRICE 1

7 the duty or function of watching or guarding for the sake of proper direction or control — see SUPERVISION 1

8 a payment made in the course of achieving a result — see EXPENSE

9 a pleasurably intense stimulation of the feelings — see THRILL

10 the act or activity of looking after and making decisions about something — see CONDUCT 1

charge *vb* **1** to set or receive as a price ⟨Any shop would *charge* $100 to repair that thing.⟩

syn ask, command, demand

rel overcharge, undercharge; bring, fetch, sell (for); discount, mark down, mark up; assess, bill, invoice; price, value

2 to establish or apply as a charge or penalty — see IMPOSE

3 to give a task, duty, or responsibility to — see ENTRUST 1

4 to issue orders to (someone) by right of authority — see COMMAND 1

5 to make a claim of wrongdoing against — see ACCUSE

6 to put into (something) as much as can be held or contained — see FILL 1

7 to take sudden, violent action against — see ATTACK 1

8 to cause a pleasurable stimulation of the feelings of — see THRILL

charged *adj* **1** causing great emotional or mental stimulation — see EXCITING 1

2 having or expressing great depth of feeling — see FERVENT 1

3 serving or likely to arouse a strong reaction — see PROVOCATIVE

chariness *n* a close attentiveness to avoiding danger — see CAUTION 1

charisma *n* the power of irresistible attraction — see CHARM 2

charitable *adj* **1** having or showing a concern for the welfare of others ⟨a *charitable* couple who have donated a sizable chunk of their fortune to the local university⟩

syn altruistic, beneficent, benevolent, good, humanitarian, philanthropic (*also* philanthropical)

rel selfless, self-sacrificing; bounteous, bountiful, free, freehanded, generous, greathearted, handsome, liberal, magnanimous, munificent, openhanded, openhearted, unselfish, unsparing; compassionate, humane, kind, kindhearted; social-minded

near ant self-seeking; cheap, closefisted, niggardly, parsimonious, stingy, tight, tightfisted; pitiless, unfeeling; self-obsessed

ant self-centered, selfish

2 giving or sharing in abundance and without hesitation — see GENEROUS 1

3 tolerant and kind in the judgment of and expectations for others — see INDULGENT 1

charity *n* **1** the giving of necessities and especially money to the needy ⟨After amassing a fortune in the computer industry, the brothers devoted themselves to *charity*.⟩

syn almsgiving, dole, philanthropy

rel altruism, do-gooding, do-goodism, humanism, humanitarianism; beneficence, benevolence, goodwill; alms, benefaction, contribution, donation; relief, welfare; endowment, fund, grant, subsidy

2 a gift of money or its equivalent to a charity, humanitarian cause, or public institution — see CONTRIBUTION

3 kind, gentle, or compassionate treatment especially towards someone who is undeserving of it — see MERCY 1

4 the capacity for feeling for another's unhappiness or misfortune — see HEART 1

5 kindly concern, interest, or support — see GOODWILL 1

---

syn synonym(s)   *rel* related words
ant antonym(s)   *near ant* near antonym(s)

charlatan *n* one who makes false claims of identity or expertise — see IMPOSTOR

charley horse *n* a painful sudden tightening of a muscle — see ¹CRAMP

charm *n* **1** something worn or kept to bring good luck or keep away evil ⟨an old cap that I use as a *charm* for whenever I play softball⟩
syn amulet, fetish (*also* fetich), mascot, mojo, phylactery, talisman
rel gris-gris (*also* grigri), philter, toadstone; emblem, symbol, token
near ant curse, hex, spell
ant jinx
2 the power of irresistible attraction ⟨a young singer with the kind of *charm* that turns a performer into a star⟩
syn allure, appeal, attractiveness, captivation, charisma, enchantment, fascination, glamour (*also* glamor), magic, magnetism, seductiveness, witchery
rel allurement, attraction, call, lure, seduction; agreeableness, darlingness, delightfulness, niceness, pleasantness, pleasingness, sweetness
near ant disagreeableness, distastefulness, obnoxiousness, offensiveness, unpleasantness
ant repulsion, repulsiveness
3 a spoken word or set of words believed to have magic power — see SPELL 1
4 an ornament worn on a chain around the neck or wrist — see PENDANT

charm *vb* to attract or delight as if by magic ⟨a quaint seaside village that *charms* all who visit it⟩
syn allure, beguile, bewitch, captivate, enchant, fascinate, kill, magnetize, wile
rel disarm, draw, entice, lure, pull, seduce, tempt; delight, gratify, please; arrest, enrapture, enthrall (*or* enthral), entrance; appeal (to), interest, intrigue; beckon, court, invite, solicit, woo
near ant disgust, offend, repel, revolt; annoy, displease, irk; bore, tire, weary
2 to cast a spell on — see BEWITCH 1

charmed *adj* being or appearing to be under a magic spell — see ENCHANTED

charming *adj* having an often mysterious or magical power to attract — see FASCINATING 1

chart *n* an illustration of certain features of a geographical area — see MAP

chart *vb* **1** to give an oral or written account of in some detail — see TELL 1
2 to work out the details of (something) in advance — see PLAN 1

charter *vb* to take or get the temporary use of (something) for a set sum — see HIRE 1

charwoman *n* a person hired to perform household or personal services — see MAID 1

chase *n* **1** an animal that is hunted or killed — see PREY 1
2 the act of going after or in the tracks of another — see PURSUIT

chase *vb* **1** to drive or force out — see EJECT 1
2 to go after or on the track of — see FOLLOW 2
3 to seek out (game) for food or sport — see HUNT 1
4 to proceed or move quickly — see HURRY 2

chasing *n* the act of going after or in the tracks of another — see PURSUIT

chasm *n* an immeasurable depth or space — see ABYSS

chaste *adj* **1** free from any trace of the coarse or indecent ⟨As one would expect, the minister's small talk is always *chaste*, even though he likes a joke as much as the next person.⟩
syn clean, decent, immaculate, modest, pure, virgin, virginal
rel lily-white, spotless, stainless, unblemished, undefiled, unsoiled, unspotted, unstained, unsullied, untainted, untarnished; decorous, proper, seemly; cultivated, refined, tasteful; harmless, innocent, innocuous, inoffensive
near ant blemished, defiled, soiled, spotted, stained, sullied, tainted, tarnished; improper, indecorous, ribald, unseemly; crude, tacky, tasteless, unrefined
ant coarse, dirty, filthy, immodest, impure, indecent, obscene, smutty, unchaste, unclean, vulgar
2 free from dirt or stain — see CLEAN 1

chastely *adv* with purity of thought and deed — see PURELY 1

chasten *vb* **1** to inflict a penalty on for a fault or crime — see PUNISH
2 to reduce to a lower standing in one's own eyes or in others' eyes — see HUMBLE

chasteness *n* the quality or state of being morally pure — see CHASTITY

chastening *adj* inflicting, involving, or serving as punishment — see PUNITIVE

chastise *vb* **1** to criticize (someone) severely or angrily especially for personal failings — see SCOLD
2 to inflict a penalty on for a fault or crime — see PUNISH

chastisement *n* suffering, loss, or hardship imposed in response to a crime or offense — see PUNISHMENT

chastiser *n* one who inflicts punishment in return for an injury or offense — see NEMESIS 1

chastising *adj* inflicting, involving, or serving as punishment — see PUNITIVE

chastity *n* the quality or state of being morally pure ⟨a saint who is often held up as a model of *chastity*⟩
syn chasteness, innocence, modesty, purity
rel goodness, righteousness, virtue, virtuousness; morality, probity, rectitude; decency, decorum, propriety, seemliness
near ant badness, evil, sinfulness, unrighteousness, wickedness; impropriety, indecency, vulgarity
ant immodesty, impurity, unchasteness, unchastity

chat *n* **1** friendly, informal conversation or an instance of this ⟨short *chats* between parents and teachers during the school's open house⟩
syn cackle, chatter, chitchat, gab, gabfest, gossip, jaw, palaver, patter, rap, schmooze, small talk, table talk, talk, tête-à-tête
rel colloquy, conference, discourse, parley, symposium; debate, dialogue (*also* dialog), exchange, give-and-take; crosstalk, happy talk; yak (*also* yack), yammer
2 talking or a talk between two or more people — see CONVERSATION

chat *vb* **1** to engage in casual or rambling conversation ⟨The coffeehouse became the favored place to meet friends and *chat* for hours.⟩
syn babble, blab, cackle, chatter, converse, gab, gabble, gas, jabber, jaw, palaver, patter, prate, prattle, rap, rattle, run on, schmooze (*or* shmooze), talk, twitter, visit
rel gossip, tattle; descant, discuss, expatiate; yak (*also* yack), yammer
phrases blow smoke, chew the fat (*also* chew the rag), shoot the breeze, talk a blue streak
2 to speak rapidly, inarticulately, and usually unintelligibly — see BABBLE 1

chat (with) *vb* to communicate with by means of spoken words — see TALK (TO)

château *n* a large impressive residence — see MANSION

chattel *n* **chattels** *pl* transportable items that one owns — see POSSESSION 2

chatter *n* **1** friendly, informal conversation or an instance of this — see CHAT 1
2 loud, confused, and usually inharmonious sound — see NOISE 1

chatter *vb* **1** to engage in casual or rambling conversation — see CHAT 1
2 to speak rapidly, inarticulately, and usually unintelligibly — see BABBLE 1

chatterbox *n* a person who talks constantly ⟨My seat companion was a *chatterbox* who never once took a breath during the whole trip.⟩
syn babbler, blabber, blabbermouth, cackler, chatterer, conversationalist, gabbler, jabberer, prattler, talker, windbag
rel gossip, talebearer, tattler, tattletale; blatherer, blatherskite; converser, discourser

chatterer *n* a person who talks constantly — see CHATTERBOX

chatty *adj* **1** having the style and content of everyday conversation ⟨a time when campers were expected to write a *chatty* letter to their folks every week⟩
syn colloquial, conversational, gossipy, newsy
rel casual, familiar, informal, intimate, tell-all; digressive, discursive, rambling; communicative, expansive, garrulous, talkative
near ant ceremonious, dignified, elevated, formal, solemn, stately
ant bookish, literary
2 fond of talking or conversation — see TALKATIVE

chauvinism *n* excessive favoritism towards one's own country ⟨Their ingrained *chauvinism* has blinded them to their country's faults.⟩
syn jingoism, nationalism
rel loyalty, patriotism; nativism, xenophobia
near ant internationalism

chauvinist *adj* having or showing excessive favoritism towards one's own country — see NATIONALIST 1

chauvinist *n* one who shows excessive favoritism towards his or her country — see NATIONALIST

cheap *adj* **1** costing little ⟨E-mail is so popular because it's a *cheap* way to send messages.⟩
syn affordable, budget, cut-rate, inexpensive, low, popular, reasonable
rel cheapish, moderate; discount, discounted, fire-sale, lowered, reduced; wholesale; valueless, worthless; supercheap, ultra-cheap
near ant increased; exorbitant, extravagant, overpriced, prohibitive, prohibitory, steep, stiff, superexpensive, unreasonable; luxurious
ant costly, dear, deluxe, expensive, high, precious, premium, valuable
2 of low quality ⟨a *cheap* sweater that started to unravel almost as soon as I bought it⟩
syn bad, bum, cheesy, coarse, common, cut-rate, execrable, inferior, junky, lousy, low-grade, mediocre, miserable, poor, rotten, rubbishy, second-rate, shoddy, sleazy, terrible, trashy, trumpery, wretched
rel useless, valueless, worthless; indifferent, lackluster, second-class; flashy, garish, gaudy, glitzy, kitsch, kitschy, meretricious, ostentatious, showy, splashy, swank (*or* swanky), tawdry; seedy, shabby, tacky; counterfeit, fake, phony (*also* phoney), sham; supercheap, ultracheap
near ant elegant, handsome, tasteful; polished, refined
ant excellent, fine, first-class, first-rate, good, high-grade, superior, top-notch
3 giving or sharing as little as possible — see STINGY 1
4 arousing or deserving of one's loathing and disgust — see CONTEMPTIBLE 1
5 involving minimal difficulty or effort — see EASY 1

cheapen *vb* **1** to diminish the price or value of — see DEPRECIATE 1
2 to lower in character, dignity, or quality — see DEBASE 1
3 to reduce to a lower standing in one's own eyes or in others' eyes — see HUMBLE

cheapness *n* the quality or practice of being overly sparing with money — see PARSIMONY 1

cheapskate *n* a mean grasping person who is usually stingy with money — see MISER

cheat *n* a dishonest person who uses clever means to cheat others out of something of value — see TRICKSTER 1

cheat *vb* **1** to use dishonest methods to achieve a goal ⟨Students who *cheat* on tests end up never knowing anything.⟩
syn finagle, fudge
rel crib; color, distort, falsify, misinterpret, misrepresent, misstate, pervert, twist, warp; doctor, fake, tamper (with); elaborate, embellish, embroider, exaggerate, magnify, pad, stretch; dodge, evade, hedge
2 to fall short in satisfying the expectation or hope of — see DISAPPOINT
3 to rob by the use of trickery or threats — see FLEECE

cheater *n* a dishonest person who uses clever means to cheat others out of something of value — see TRICKSTER 1

check *n* **1** the amount owed at a bar or restaurant or the slip of paper stating the amount ⟨Diners at that restaurant often

---

syn synonym(s)   *rel* related words
ant antonym(s)   *near ant* near antonym(s)

look shocked when they receive the check.⟩

syn bill, tab

rel invoice, receipt; account, reckoning, record, statement; charge, cost, damage, expense, fee, figure; score, tally

2 a close look at or over someone or something in order to judge condition — see INSPECTION

3 a record of goods sold or services performed together with the costs due — see ¹BILL 1

4 a small sheet of plastic, paper, or paperboard showing that the bearer has a claim to something (as admittance) — see TICKET 1

5 something that limits one's freedom of action or choice — see RESTRICTION 1

6 an irregular usually narrow break in a surface created by pressure — see CRACK 1

7 the stopping of a process or activity — see END 1

check vb **1** to be in agreement on every point ⟨Their story of what happened checks with the report of the eyewitness.⟩

syn accord, agree, answer, cohere, coincide, comport, conform, correspond, dovetail, fit, go, harmonize, jibe, sort, square, tally

rel equal, match, parallel; align (also aline), line up, register

phrases fall in with

near ant contradict, dispute, gainsay; negate, nullify; clash, conflict, jar

ant differ (from), disagree (with)

2 to bring (something) to a standstill — see ¹HALT 1

3 to keep from exceeding a desirable degree or level (as of expression) — see CONTROL 1

check (out) vb to look over closely (as for judging quality or condition) — see INSPECT

checklist n a record of a series of items (as names or titles) usually arranged according to some system — see ¹LIST

checkmate vb to prevent from achieving a goal — see FRUSTRATE 1

checkup n a close look at or over someone or something in order to judge condition — see INSPECTION

cheek n **1** disrespectful or argumentative talk given in response to a command or request — see BACK TALK

2 shameless boldness — see EFFRONTERY

3 cheeks pl the part of the body upon which someone sits — see BUTTOCKS

cheekiness n shameless boldness — see EFFRONTERY

cheeky adj displaying or marked by rude boldness — see NERVY 1

cheep vb to make a short sharp sound like a small bird — see CHIRP

cheer n **1** a mood characterized by high spirits and amusement and often accompanied by laughter — see MIRTH

2 a feeling of ease from grief or trouble — see COMFORT 1

3 a state of mind dominated by a particular emotion — see MOOD 1

4 enthusiastic and usually public expression of approval — see APPLAUSE 1

cheer vb **1** to declare enthusiastic approval of — see ACCLAIM

2 to ease the grief or distress of — see COMFORT

cheer (up) vb **1** to become glad or hopeful ⟨Cheer up—things are bound to get better!⟩

syn brighten, lighten, look up, perk (up)

rel rejoice; liven (up), revive; beam, glow, radiate, sparkle; encourage, gladden, hearten

near ant despair, despond; brood, fret, mope

ant darken, sadden

2 to fill with courage or strength of purpose — see ENCOURAGE 1

cheerful adj **1** having or showing a good mood or disposition ⟨a cheerful person who is always fun to work with and a pleasure to be around⟩

syn blithe, blithesome, bright, buoyant, cheery, chipper, gladsome, lightsome, sunny, upbeat, winsome

rel hopeful, optimistic, rosy, sanguine; animated, chirpy, jaunty, lilting, lively, perky, sprightful, sprightly, vivacious; carefree, careless, cavalier, devil-may-care, easygoing, happy-go-lucky, insouciant, lighthearted, unconcerned; boon, gleeful, jocund, jolly, jovial, merry, mirthful; blissful, delighted, glad, gratified, happy, joyful, joyous, pleased, satisfied, tickled; beaming, grinning, laughing, smiling

near ant joyless, sad, unhappy, unsatisfied; dull, lethargic, listless, sluggish, torpid; blue, brokenhearted, crestfallen, dejected, depressed, despondent, disconsolate, disheartened, down, downcast, downhearted, droopy, forlorn, hangdog, inconsolable, low, low-spirited, melancholy, mirthless, sorrowful

ant dour, gloomy, glum, morose, saturnine, sulky, sullen

2 serving to lift one's spirits ⟨a hospital with sunny, cheerful rooms that are designed to make a patient's stay as pleasant as possible⟩

syn bright, cheering, cheery, glad

rel gladdening, heartening, heartwarming; gleaming, radiant, sparkling

near ant discouraging, disheartening; colorless, drab, dull, lackluster, lusterless; desolate, dispiriting

ant bleak, cheerless, dark, depressing, dismal, dreary, gloomy, gray (also grey)

cheerfully adv in a cheerful or happy manner — see GAILY 1

cheerfulness n a mood characterized by high spirits and amusement and often accompanied by laughter — see MIRTH

cheerily adv in a cheerful or happy manner — see GAILY 1

cheeriness n a mood characterized by high spirits and amusement and often accompanied by laughter — see MIRTH

cheering adj **1** making one feel good inside — see HEARTWARMING

2 serving to lift one's spirits — see CHEERFUL 2

cheering n enthusiastic and usually public expression of approval — see APPLAUSE 1

cheerless adj causing or marked by an atmosphere lacking in cheer — see GLOOMY 1

cheery adj **1** having or showing a good mood or disposition — see CHEERFUL 1

2 serving to lift one's spirits — see CHEERFUL 2

cheesy adj **1** marked by an obvious lack of style or good taste — see ¹TACKY 1

2 of low quality — see CHEAP 2

chef n a person who prepares food by some manner of heating — see COOK

cherish vb **1** to feel passion, devotion, or tenderness for — see LOVE 2

2 to hold dear — see LOVE 1

3 to keep in one's mind or heart — see HARBOR 1

cherished adj granted special treatment or attention — see DARLING 1

chest n a covered rectangular container for storing or transporting things ⟨a *chest* containing almost every tool that the home do-it-yourselfer is likely to need⟩

syn bin, box, caddy, case, casket, locker, trunk

rel carton, crate; footlocker, locker, sea chest; coffer, lockbox, safe, safe-deposit box, strongbox; coffin; compartment, vault; canteen; caisson, hope chest; bandbox, hatbox, jewel box, snuffbox

chew vb to crush or grind with the teeth — see BITE (ON)

chew out vb to criticize (someone) severely or angrily especially for personal failings — see SCOLD

chew over vb to give serious and careful thought to — see PONDER

chewy adj not easily chewed — see TOUGH 1

chic adj being in the latest or current fashion — see STYLISH

chicanery n the use of clever underhanded actions to achieve an end — see TRICKERY

chick n a young person who is between infancy and adulthood — see CHILD 1

chicken adj having or showing a shameful lack of courage — see COWARDLY

chicken n a person who shows a shameful lack of courage in the face of danger — see COWARD

chickenhearted adj having or showing a shameful lack of courage — see COWARDLY

chide vb to criticize (someone) so as to correct a fault — see REBUKE 1

chief adj **1** coming before all others in importance — see FOREMOST 1

2 highest in rank or authority — see HEAD

chief n **1** the main or greater part of something as distinguished from its subordinate parts — see BODY 1

2 the person (as an employer or supervisor) who tells people and especially workers what to do — see BOSS

chiefly adv for the most part ⟨Our video collection consists *chiefly* of comedies, but we have a few horror movies.⟩

syn altogether, basically, by and large, generally, largely, mainly, mostly, overall, predominantly, primarily, principally, substantially

rel about, more or less, most, much, near, nearly, next to, nigh, practically, some, virtually, well-nigh; broadly, roughly; commonly, frequently, generally, normal-

ly, ordinarily, typically, usually; incompletely, partially, partly, rather, somewhat

phrases in general, on the whole

near ant completely, entirely, fully, perfectly, thoroughly, totally, wholly; barely, hardly, just, marginally, minimally, scarcely; absolutely, categorically, unqualifiedly

child n **1** a young person who is between infancy and adulthood ⟨an imaginative animated film that appeals to adults as well as to *children*⟩

syn chick, cub, juvenile, kid, kiddo, moppet, squirt, whelp, youngster, youth

rel adolescent, minor; kindergartner (*also* kindergartener); preschooler, rug rat [*slang*], schoolboy, schoolchild, schoolgirl, schoolkid; babe, baby, bantling, infant, nestling, newborn, toddler, tot, weanling; brat, devil, hellion, imp, monkey, rapscallion, rascal, rogue, urchin, whippersnapper; cherub; preteen, preteenager, subteen, teen, teenager, teener, teenybopper; tween; lad, nipper, shaver, stripling, tad; bobby-soxer, hoyden, tomboy

near ant middle-ager; ancient, elder, golden-ager, oldster, old-timer, senior, senior citizen

ant adult, grown-up

2 a recently born person — see BABY 1

3 a condition or occurrence traceable to a cause — see EFFECT 1

childbearing n the act or process of giving birth to children — see CHILDBIRTH

childbirth n the act or process of giving birth to children ⟨women who choose to undergo *childbirth* without the use of anesthetics and other drugs⟩

syn childbearing, delivery, labor, parturition, travail

rel birth pang, contraction, pains; pregnancy; abortion, miscarriage; cesarean section (*or* caesarean section), natural childbirth; childbed, confinement, lying-in

childhood n the state or time of being a child ⟨Enjoy your *childhood*—it won't last forever!⟩

syn youth

rel boyhood, girlhood, toddlerhood; juvenescence; immaturity, juvenility; babyhood, infancy

near ant majority; middle age, midlife; sunset

ant adulthood

childish adj having or showing the annoying qualities (as silliness) associated with children ⟨You almost spoiled the ceremony for everyone with your *childish* giggling.⟩

syn adolescent, babyish, immature, infantile, juvenile, kiddish, puerile

rel boyish, brattish, bratty, girlie (*or* girly), girlish; childlike, innocent, naive (*or* naïve), simple, simplistic, unsophisticated

near ant unchildlike; cosmopolitan, experienced, knowing, smart, sophisticated, worldly, worldly-wise

ant adult, grown-up, mature

child's play n **1** something of little importance — see TRIFLE

2 something that is easy to do — see CINCH

chill adj **1** lacking in friendliness or warmth of feeling — see COLD 2

2 uncomfortably cool — see CHILLY 1

---

syn synonym(s)   *rel* related words
ant antonym(s)   *near ant* near antonym(s)

3 having a low or subnormal temperature — see COLD 1

4 causing or marked by an atmosphere lacking in cheer — see GLOOMY 1

chill *n* an uncomfortable degree of coolness ⟨There's a *chill* in the air, so you'd better wear a sweater.⟩

syn bite, bitterness, bleakness, chilliness, nip, rawness, sharpness

rel briskness, crispness; frigidity, frigidness, frostiness, gelidity, iciness, wintriness; cold, freeze, snap

near ant balminess, warmness, warmth; heat, hotness, sultriness

chill *vb* **1** to cause to lose heat — see COOL

2 to get rid of nervous tension or anxiety — see RELAX 1

3 to lessen the courage or confidence of — see DISCOURAGE 1

4 to spend time doing nothing — see IDLE

chilliness *n* an uncomfortable degree of coolness — see CHILL

chilling *adj* uncomfortably cool — see CHILLY 1

chill out *vb, slang* **1** to become still and orderly — see QUIET 1

2 to get rid of nervous tension or anxiety — see RELAX 1

chilly *adj* **1** uncomfortably cool ⟨those *chilly* nights when a warm fire can be especially comforting⟩

syn bitter, bleak, chill, chilling, nipping, nippy, raw, sharp

rel bracing, brisk, crisp, invigorating, rigorous, snappy; arctic, bitter, cold, coolish, freezing, frigid, frosty, glacial, ice-cold, icy, numbing, polar, shivery, wintry (*also* wintery); subfreezing, subzero; frosted, frozen, iced, refrigerated, unheated

near ant balmy, warm; lukewarm, tepid; heated, warmed

2 lacking in friendliness or warmth of feeling — see COLD 2

3 having a low or subnormal temperature — see COLD 1

chime *n* **1** *usually* **chimes** *pl* a series of short high ringing sounds — see TINKLE

2 peaceful coexistence — see HARMONY 2

chime *vb* **1** to form a pleasing relationship — see HARMONIZE 1

2 to make the clear sound heard when metal vibrates — see ²RING

3 to say or state again — see REPEAT 1

chime in *vb* **1** to cause a disruption in a conversation or discussion — see INTERRUPT

2 to form a pleasing relationship — see HARMONIZE 1

chimera *n* a conception or image created by the imagination having no objective reality — see FANTASY 1

chimerical *also* **chimeric** *adj* not real and existing only in the imagination — see IMAGINARY

chine *n* a column of bones supporting the trunk of a vertebrate animal — see SPINE

chink *n* **1** a vulnerable point — see ACHILLES' HEEL

2 an irregular usually narrow break in a surface created by pressure — see CRACK 1

chink *vb* to make a repeated sharp light ringing sound — see JINGLE

chip *n* **1** a small flat piece separated from a whole ⟨Wood *chips* were spread over the ground between the plants.⟩

syn flake, sliver, splint, splinter

rel bit, disk (*or* disc), fragment, part, particle, portion, scrap, section, shard; flinders, shiver, smithereens; shred, tatter; clipping, paring, shave, shaving, snippet; sheet, slice

near ant chunk, hunk, lump, slab

2 a V-shaped cut usually on an edge or a surface — see NOTCH 1

3 chips *pl* something (as pieces of stamped metal or printed paper) customarily and legally used as a medium of exchange, a measure of value, or a means of payment — see MONEY

chip in *vb* to make a donation as part of a group effort — see CONTRIBUTE 1

chipper *adj* having or showing a good mood or disposition — see CHEERFUL 1

chirp *vb* to make a short sharp sound like a small bird ⟨The sparrows were *chirping* up a storm in the backyard.⟩

syn cheep, chirrup, peep, pip, pipe, tweet, twitter

rel cackle, chatter, jabber; sing, trill, warble

chirr *n* a monotonous sound like that of an insect in motion — see HUM

chirrup *vb* to make a short sharp sound like a small bird — see CHIRP

chisel *vb* to rob by the use of trickery or threats — see FLEECE

chitchat *n* friendly, informal conversation or an instance of this — see CHAT 1

chivalrous *adj* having, characterized by, or arising from a dignified and generous nature — see NOBLE 2

chivy *or* **chivvy** *vb* to thrust oneself upon (another) without invitation — see BOTHER 1

chock–full *or* **chockful** *adj* containing or seeming to contain the greatest quantity or number possible — see FULL 1

choice *adj* **1** having qualities that appeal to a refined taste ⟨*choice* chocolates for which chocolate lovers are willing to pay extra⟩

syn dainty, delicate, elegant, exquisite, fine, rare, select

rel bijou, jewellike; better, exceptional, fancy, high-grade, special; elite, exclusive; classic, excellent, fabulous, first-class, first-rate, grand, great, marvelous (*or* marvellous), noble, outstanding, par excellence, premium, prime, sensational, splendid, stellar, sterling, superb, superior, superlative, supernal, terrific, tip-top, top, top-notch, unsurpassed, wonderful; ultrarare; exclusive, upscale

near ant coarse, gross, kitsch, kitschy, lowbrow, raffish, rough, tasteless, uncultivated, uncultured, unpolished, unrefined, vulgar; commercial, mass-produced, popular; common, ordinary; average, lesser, mediocre, run-of-the-mill, run-of-the-mine (*or* run-of-mine), second-class, second-rate; deficient, inferior, low-grade, substandard, unacceptable, unsatisfactory, wanting

2 of the very best kind — see EXCELLENT

3 singled out from a number or group as more to one's liking — see SELECT 1

choice *n* **1** the power, right, or opportunity to choose ⟨You have no *choice*: you have to go to the conference.⟩
syn alternative, discretion, election, liberty, option, pick, preference, selection, volition, way
rel determination, free will; will; say, voice, vote; inclination, liking, partiality, penchant, predilection, proclivity, propensity, tendency; discernment, judgment (*or* judgement), perspicacity
near ant coercion, duress, force; duty, obligation; Hobson's choice
2 a person or thing that is chosen ⟨my *choice* for best song of all time⟩
syn bet, chosen, pick, selection
rel favorite, like, liking, preference; elective, option; appointment, designation, nomination; candidate; preselection
ant rejectee
3 individuals carefully selected as being the best of a class — see ELITE 1
4 the act or power of making one's own choices or decisions — see FREE WILL
5 the act or process of selecting — see SELECTION 1
choir *n* an organized group of singers — see CHORUS 1
choke *vb* **1** to keep (someone) from breathing by exerting pressure on the windpipe ⟨Let go of my throat—you're *choking* me!⟩
syn garrote (*or* garotte), strangle, suffocate, throttle
rel asphyxiate, smother, stifle
near ant restore, resuscitate, revive
2 to experience complete or partial blockage of the windpipe ⟨the recommended procedure for helping someone who is *choking*⟩
syn gag, suffocate
rel heave, retch, throw up, vomit; asphyxiate, smother, stifle
near ant breathe, respire; expire, inspire
3 to be or cause to be killed by lack of breathable air — see SMOTHER 1
4 to prevent passage through by filling with something — see CLOG 1
choke (back) *vb* to refrain from openly showing or uttering — see SUPPRESS 2
choker *n* an ornamental chain or string (as of beads) worn around the neck — see NECKLACE
choleric *adj* **1** easily irritated or annoyed — see IRRITABLE
2 feeling or showing anger — see ANGRY
chomp (on) *vb* to crush or grind with the teeth — see BITE (ON)
choose *vb* **1** to decide to accept (someone or something) from a group of possibilities ⟨*Choose* a computer that best suits your needs.⟩
syn cull, elect, handpick, name, opt (for), pick, prefer, select, single (out), take
rel preselect; appoint, designate, fix, mark, set, tab, tap; accept, adopt, embrace, espouse; settle (on *or* upon)
near ant disapprove, negative, repudiate, spurn; discard, jettison, throw away, throw out

ant decline, refuse, reject, turn down
2 to see fit ⟨You can wear whatever you *choose* to the party.⟩
syn like, please, want, will, wish
rel ache (for), covet, crave, desire, die (for), fancy, hanker (for), hunger (for), itch (for), long (for), lust (for *or* after), pant (after), pine (for), repine (for), sigh (for), thirst (for), yearn (for); decide, determine, resolve
3 to come to a judgment about after discussion or consideration — see DECIDE 1
chooser *n* someone with the right or responsibility for making a selection — see SELECTOR
choosing *n* the act or process of selecting — see SELECTION 1
choosy *or* **choosey** *adj* **1** hard to please — see FINICKY
2 tending to select carefully — see SELECTIVE
chop *n* a hard strike with a part of the body or an instrument — see ¹BLOW
chop *vb* to cut into small pieces ⟨*Chop* the onions before adding them to the pot.⟩
syn dice, hash, mince
rel chip, grate, grind, kibble, mash; puree (*or* purée), slice; butcher, carve, dissect
chop (down) *vb* to bring down by cutting — see FELL 2
choppy *adj* **1** lacking in steadiness or regularity of occurrence — see FITFUL
2 marked by a series of sharp quick motions — see JERKY 1
3 not clearly or logically connected — see INCOHERENT 1
chorale *n* **1** a religious song — see HYMN 1
2 an organized group of singers — see CHORUS 1
chore *n* **1** a piece of work that needs to be done regularly ⟨Everyone in this household is expected to do weekly *chores*.⟩
syn assignment, duty, job, task
rel endeavor, enterprise, project, stint, undertaking; care, charge, commission, responsibility; function, mission, office, operation, post; errand; round, route
2 a dull, unpleasant, or difficult piece of work ⟨Cleaning everything out of the attic was a real *chore*.⟩
syn bear, beast, headache, job, killer, labor
rel drudgery, grind, heavy lifting; effort, strain, sweat; burden, load, weight; bother, nuisance, trouble
near ant breeze, child's play, cinch, duck soup, kid stuff, setup, snap
chortle *n* an explosive sound that is a sign of amusement — see LAUGH 1
chortle *vb* to show mirth with an explosive vocal sound — see LAUGH 1
chorus *n* **1** an organized group of singers ⟨the annual Spring program presented by the school's *chorus*⟩
syn choir, chorale, consort, glee club
rel ensemble; minstrelsy
2 a part of a song or hymn that is repeated every so often ⟨The whole audience joined in for the *chorus*.⟩
syn burden, refrain
rel repeat, response
chosen *adj* singled out from a number or group as more to one's liking — see SELECT 1

---

syn synonym(s)   *rel* related words
ant antonym(s)   *near ant* near antonym(s)

chosen *n* a person or thing that is chosen — see CHOICE 2

chow *n* **1** food eaten or prepared for eating at one time — see MEAL

2 substances intended to be eaten — see FOOD

christen *vb* to give a name to — see NAME 1

Christian name *n* a name that is placed before one's family name — see FORENAME

Christmastide *n* the season celebrating Christmas — see YULETIDE

Christmastime *n* the season celebrating Christmas — see YULETIDE

chronic *adj* being such by habit and not likely to change — see HABITUAL 1

chronicle *n* **1** a relating of events usually in the order in which they happened — see ACCOUNT 1

2 an account of important events in the order in which they happened — see HISTORY 1

chronicle *vb* to give an oral or written account of in some detail — see TELL 1

chronicler *n* a student or writer of history — see HISTORIAN

chronometer *n* a device to measure time — see TIMEPIECE

chubbiness *n* the condition of having an excess of body fat — see CORPULENCE

chubby *adj* having an excess of body fat — see FAT 1

chuck *n, chiefly West* substances intended to be eaten — see FOOD

chuck *vb* **1** to get rid of as useless or unwanted — see DISCARD

2 to give up (a job or office) — see QUIT 1

3 to send through the air especially with a quick forward motion of the arm — see THROW 1

chuckle *n* an explosive sound that is a sign of amusement — see LAUGH 1

chuckle *vb* to show mirth with an explosive vocal sound — see LAUGH 1

chum *n* a person who has a strong liking for and trust in another — see FRIEND 1

chum *vb* to come or be together as friends — see ASSOCIATE 1

chumminess *n* the state of being in a very personal or private relationship — see FAMILIARITY 1

chummy *adj* **1** closely acquainted — see FAMILIAR 1

2 having or showing kindly feeling and sincere interest — see FRIENDLY 1

chump *n* one who is easily deceived or cheated — see ¹DUPE

chunk *n* **1** a considerable amount — see LOT 2

2 a small uneven mass — see LUMP 1

chunky *adj* **1** having small pieces or lumps spread throughout ⟨*Chunky* peanut butter adds an interesting layer of texture when paired with jelly.⟩

syn clumpy, curdy, lumpy, nubbly, nubby

rel ropy (*also* ropey), thick, viscous; knobbed, knobbly, knobby, lumpish; clabbered, clotted, coagulated, congealed, curdled, gelled, thickened; broken, bumpy, coarse, irregular, jagged, knotted, knotty, pebbly

ant smooth

2 being compact and broad in build and often short in stature — see STOCKY

3 having or being of relatively great depth or extent from one surface to its opposite — see THICK 1

church *n* **1** a building for public worship and especially Christian worship ⟨a city that is noted for its many historic *churches*⟩

syn kirk [*chiefly Scottish*], tabernacle, temple

rel abbey, bethel, chapel, minster, mission, oratory, sanctuary, shrine; meetinghouse; mosque, pagoda, shul, synagogue (*also* synagog)

2 a body of persons gathered for religious worship — see CONGREGATION 1

churchly *adj* of or relating to a church — see ECCLESIASTICAL

churl *n* **1** an awkward or simple person especially from a small town or the country — see HICK

2 a person whose behavior is offensive to others — see JERK 1

churlish *adj* having or showing crudely insensitive or impolite manners — see CLOWNISH

churn *vb* **1** to be in a state of violent rolling motion — see SEETHE 1

2 to cause (as a liquid) to move about in a circle especially repeatedly — see STIR 1

chutzpah *also* **chutzpa** *or* **hutzpah** *or* **hutzpa** *n* shameless boldness — see EFFRONTERY

cinch *n* something that is easy to do ⟨The clear instructions made setting up the audiovisual system a *cinch*.⟩

syn breeze, cake, child's play, duck soup, picnic, pushover, snap

rel no-brainer, nothing; sitting duck; gimme, laugher, walkaway

phrases piece of cake, walk in the park

near ant brainteaser, poser, stumper, toughie (*also* toughy); bother, nuisance, trouble

ant bear, beast, chore, headache, horror show, killer, murder, pain, sticky wicket, stinker [*slang*]

cinch *vb* to make sure, certain, or safe — see ENSURE

cinema *n* **1** the art or business of making a movie — see MOVIE 2

2 a building or part of a building where movies are shown — see THEATER 1

cipher *n* **1** the numerical symbol 0 or the absence of number or quantity represented by it — see ZERO 1

2 a person of no importance or influence — see NOBODY

cipher *vb* to determine (a value) by doing the necessary mathematical operations — see CALCULATE 1

ciphering *n* the act or process of performing mathematical operations to find a value — see CALCULATION

circle *n* **1** something with a perfectly round circumference ⟨A *circle* of columns surrounds the memorial to the fallen heroes.⟩

syn ring, round

rel circlet, ringlet; ellipse, loop, oval; ball, globe, orb, sphere

2 a circular strip — see ¹RING 2

3 a group of people sharing a common interest and relating together socially — see GANG 2

4 a series of events or actions that repeat themselves regularly and in the same order — see CYCLE 1

5 a region of activity, knowledge, or influence — see FIELD 2

circle *vb* **1** to form a circle around — see SURROUND

2 to travel completely around — see ENCIRCLE 1

circuitous *adj* **1** not straightforward or direct — see INDIRECT

2 using or containing more words than necessary to express an idea — see WORDY 1

circular *adj* not straightforward or direct — see INDIRECT

circular *n* a short printed publication with no cover or with a paper cover — see PAMPHLET

circulate *vb* **1** to cause to be known over a considerable area or by many people — see SPREAD 1

2 to make (a piece of information) the subject of common talk without any authority or confirmation of accuracy — see RUMOR

3 to become known — see GET OUT 1

circumference *n* **1** the distance around a round body ⟨the *circumference* of the earth at the equator⟩

syn girth

rel ambit, compass; waistline; equator; diameter, radius; perimeter, periphery

2 the line or relatively narrow space that marks the outer limit of something — see BORDER 1

circumlocution *n* **1** deliberate evasion in speech ⟨Rather than answering the question directly, he resorted to *circumlocution*, which made her suspect that he was hiding something.⟩

syn equivocation, shuffle

rel quibbling; ambiguity, ambiguousness, equivocalness, murkiness, nebulousness, obscureness, obscurity, opacity

near ant candor, directness, forthrightness, frankness, openheartedness, openness, plainness, plumpness, straightforwardness

2 the use of too many words to express an idea — see VERBIAGE 1

circumlocutory *adj* using or containing more words than necessary to express an idea — see WORDY 1

circumnavigate *vb* **1** to travel completely around — see ENCIRCLE 1

2 to avoid by going around — see DETOUR 1

circumscribe *vb* **1** to set bounds or an upper limit for — see LIMIT 1

2 to mark the limits of — see LIMIT 2

circumscribed *adj* having distinct or certain limits — see LIMITED 1

circumspect *adj* having or showing a close attentiveness to avoiding danger or trouble — see CAREFUL 1

circumspection *n* a close attentiveness to avoiding danger — see CAUTION 1

circumstance *n* **1** a state or end that seemingly has been decided beforehand — see FATE 1

2 something that happens — see EVENT 1

3 the uncertain course of events — see CHANCE 1

circumstantial *adj* including many small descriptive features — see DETAILED 1

circumvent *vb* **1** to avoid having to comply with (something) especially through cleverness ⟨employees who try to *circumvent* the company's dress code⟩

syn beat, bypass, dodge, get around, sidestep, skirt

rel avoid, duck, elude, end-run, escape, eschew, evade, outflank, shake, shirk, shun; disobey, disregard, flout, ignore; avert, deflect, divert, obviate, parry, prevent, ward (off)

near ant accede (to), acquiesce (to), assent (to); accept, court, embrace, pursue, seek, welcome; catch, contract, incur

ant comply (with), follow, keep, obey, observe

2 to avoid by going around — see DETOUR 1

3 to travel completely around — see ENCIRCLE 1

circus *n* **1** a large usually roofless building for sporting events with tiers of seats for spectators — see STADIUM

2 a place of uproar or confusion — see MADHOUSE

citadel *n* a structure or place from which one can resist attack — see FORT

citation *n* **1** a formal expression of praise — see ENCOMIUM

2 a formal recognition of an achievement or praiseworthy deed — see COMMENDATION 1

3 a passage referred to, repeated, or offered as an example — see QUOTATION

cite *vb* **1** to give as an example — see QUOTE 1

2 to make reference to or speak about briefly but specifically — see MENTION 1

citify *vb* to accustom to the ways of the city ⟨We've become so *citified* that many people have no idea where their food comes from.⟩

syn urbanize

rel civilize, cultivate

citizen *n* **1** a person who owes allegiance to a government and is protected by it ⟨conscientious *citizens* who regard voting as a duty as well as a right⟩

syn national, subject

rel compatriot, countryman; inhabitant, native, nonimmigrant, resident

near ant foreigner, stranger; immigrant, nonnative

ant alien, noncitizen

2 a person who lives in a town on a permanent basis — see BURGHER

city *n* a thickly settled, highly populated area ⟨commuters who drive every day between their homes in the suburbs and their jobs in the *city*⟩

syn burg, megalopolis, metropolis, municipality, town

rel borough; urban sprawl; exurb, suburb, suburbia; central city, edge city, garden city; core city, downtown, inner city, midtown

civil *adj* **1** of or relating to a nation — see NATIONAL

2 showing consideration, courtesy, and good manners — see POLITE 1

---

syn synonym(s)   *rel* related words
ant antonym(s)   *near ant* near antonym(s)

civility *n* **1** an act or utterance that is a customary show of good manners ⟨After the usual *civilities*, the buyer and seller got down to business.⟩

syn amenity, attention, courtesy, formality, gesture, pleasantry, politeness

rel honors; ceremony, observance, rite, ritual; decorum, etiquette, form, manners, mores, proprieties; addresses, devoirs, greetings, regards, respects; favor, grace, kindliness, kindness; protocol, rules

2 speech or behavior that is a sign of good manners — see POLITENESS 1

civilization *n* **1** the way people live at a particular time and place ⟨a documentary on the advanced *civilization* created by the Mayas over a thousand years ago⟩

syn culture, life, lifestyle, society

rel customs, manners, mores, values; folklore, heritage, legacy, tradition; subculture, subsociety

2 a high level of taste and enlightenment as a result of extensive intellectual training and exposure to the arts — see CULTURE 1

civilized *adj* having or showing a taste for the fine arts and gracious living — see CULTIVATED

clack *vb* to make a series of short sharp noises — see RATTLE 1

claim *n* **1** an entitlement to something ⟨I'm announcing my *claim* to that last slice of pizza.⟩

syn call, pretense (*or* pretence), pretension, right

rel birthright, prerogative, title; favor, privilege; refusal

near ant disclaimer, quitclaim, release, waiver

2 a legal right to participation in the advantages, profits, and responsibility of something — see INTEREST 1

3 a solemn and often public declaration of the truth or existence of something — see PROTESTATION

4 something that someone insists upon having — see DEMAND 1

claim *vb* **1** to state as a fact usually forcefully ⟨people who *claim* that they have been kidnapped by aliens from other worlds⟩

syn affirm, allege, assert, aver, avouch, avow, contend, declare, insist, maintain, profess, protest, purport, warrant

rel announce, broadcast, proclaim; argue, rationalize, reason; confirm, justify, vindicate; defend, persevere, support, uphold; reaffirm, reassert

phrases put forth

near ant abandon; disavow, disclaim, disown, negate, negative, reject, repudiate; challenge, dispute, question; confute, disprove, rebut, refute; contradict, counter

ant deny, gainsay

2 to ask for (something) earnestly or with authority — see DEMAND 1

3 to deprive of life — see KILL 1

4 to have as a requirement — see NEED 1

clairvoyance *n* the power of seeing or knowing about things that are not present to the senses ⟨People who claim to have *clairvoyance* are sometimes asked to help locate missing persons.⟩

syn extrasensory perception, sixth sense

rel foreknowledge, foresight, prescience; precognition; telepathy; parapsychology

clamber *vb* to move (as up or over something) often with the help of the hands in holding or pulling — see CLIMB 1

clamor *n* **1** a violent shouting ⟨A *clamor* arose from the crowd as the prisoner was brought forward.⟩

syn howl, hubbub, hue and cry, hullabaloo, noise, outcry, roar, tumult, uproar

rel clangor, din, racket; outburst, protest

near ant mumble, mumbling, murmur, murmuring, rumble, rumbling

2 loud, confused, and usually inharmonious sound — see NOISE 1

clamor (for) *vb* to ask for (something) earnestly or with authority — see DEMAND 1

clamorous *adj* **1** engaging in or marked by loud and insistent cries especially of protest — see VOCIFEROUS

2 full of or characterized by the presence of noise — see NOISY 2

3 marked by a high volume of sound — see LOUD 1

clamp *vb* to put securely in place or in a desired position — see FASTEN 2

clamp down (on) *vb* to put a stop to (something) by the use of force — see QUELL 1

clam up *vb* to stop talking — see SHUT UP 1

clan *n* **1** a group of people sharing a common interest and relating together socially — see GANG 2

2 a group of persons who come from the same ancestor — see FAMILY 1

clandestine *adj* undertaken or done so as to escape being observed or known by others — see SECRET 1

clang *n* the loud sound made when metal strikes metal ⟨The horseshoe hit the stake with a satisfying *clang*.⟩

syn clangor, clank, clash

rel chime, ding-dong, knell, peal, ping, plink, ring, tintinnabulation; chink, clink, clinkety-clank, jingle, rattle, tinkle, twang; clap, clip-clop, clop, crack, crash, crunch; clump, clunk, thump

clangor *n* **1** loud, confused, and usually inharmonious sound — see NOISE 1

2 the loud sound made when metal strikes metal — see CLANG

clangorous *adj* **1** full of or characterized by the presence of noise — see NOISY 2

2 making loud, confused, and usually unharmonious sounds — see NOISY 1

3 marked by a high volume of sound — see LOUD 1

clank *n* the loud sound made when metal strikes metal — see CLANG

clannish *adj* bound together by feelings of very close association — see CLOSE-KNIT

clap *n* **1** a loud explosive sound ⟨a *clap* of thunder that woke the whole house up⟩

syn bang, blast, boom, crack, crash, pop, report, slam, smash, snap, thunderclap, thwack, whack

rel thunk; clang, clangor, clank, clash; knock, rap, tap; blare, clamor, howl, hubbub, hue and cry, hullabaloo, outcry, roar, tumult, uproar

2 a hard strike with a part of the body or an instrument — see ¹BLOW

clap *vb* to deliver a blow to (someone or something) usually in a strong vigorous manner — see HIT 1

claptrap *n* language, behavior, or ideas that are absurd and contrary to good sense — see NONSENSE 1

clarification *n* a statement that makes something clear — see EXPLANATION 1

clarify *vb* **1** to remove usually visible impurities from ⟨*Clarify* the melted butter by skimming off the milky bits.⟩
syn clear, distill (*also* distil), filter, fine, purify
rel process, rectify, refine; clean, cleanse, decontaminate, purge, wash; extract, leach; bolt, screen, sieve, sift; disinfect, sanitize
near ant cloud, dull, muddy; contaminate, dirty, soil; defile, pollute, taint; begrime, besmirch, foul, sully
2 to make plain or understandable — see EXPLAIN 1

clarity *n* **1** the state or quality of being easily seen through ⟨mountain streams with water of incredible *clarity*⟩
syn clearness, limpidity, limpidness, transparency
rel brightness, brilliance, effulgence, luminosity; resolution, sharpness; apparentness, observability, visibility
near ant fogginess, haziness, milkiness, mistiness, murkiness
ant cloudiness, opacity, turbidity, turbidness
2 clearness of expression — see SIMPLICITY 2

clash *n* **1** a physical dispute between opposing individuals or groups — see FIGHT 1
2 the loud sound made when metal strikes metal — see CLANG

clash *vb* to be out of harmony or agreement usually noticeably ⟨The colors of your shirt and pants *clash*.⟩
syn collide, conflict, discord, jar
rel battle, combat, engage, fight, war (against); chafe, gall, grate; differ, disagree, dissent
near ant agree, assent, coincide, concur, correspond
ant accord, blend, conform (to *or* with), fit, harmonize, match

clash (with) *vb* to oppose (someone) in physical conflict — see FIGHT 1

clashing *adj* not being in agreement or harmony — see INCONSISTENT 1

clasp *n* the act or manner of holding — see HOLD 1

clasp *vb* **1** to put one's arms around and press tightly — see EMBRACE 1
2 to reach for and take hold of by embracing with the fingers or arms — see TAKE 1

class *n* **1** one of the segments of society into which people are grouped ⟨a politician who appeals to people of every *class*⟩
syn caste, estate, folk, gentry, order, stratum
rel bracket, echelon, grade, layer; level; place, position, rank, standing, status; food chain, grouping, stratification; clan, family, fraternity, people, race, tribe; subcaste
2 one of the units into which a whole is

divided on the basis of a common characteristic ⟨a *class* of wireless devices that can be used for Internet access as well as personal communication⟩
syn bracket, category, classification, division, family, grade, group, kind, league, order, rank(s), rubric, set, species, type
rel description, feather, ilk, kidney, like, manner, nature, sort; branch, section, speciality, specialty, subclass, subdivision, subgroup, subspecies, variety; breed, race; generation; heading, label, title
3 a number of persons or things that are grouped together because they have something in common — see SORT 1
4 a series of lectures on a subject — see COURSE 2
5 degree of excellence — see QUALITY 1
6 dignified or restrained beauty of form, appearance, or style — see ELEGANCE
7 high position within society — see RANK 2

class *vb* to arrange or assign according to type — see CLASSIFY 1

classic *adj* **1** constituting, serving as, or worthy of being a pattern to be imitated — see MODEL
2 of the very best kind — see EXCELLENT
3 serving to identify as belonging to an individual or group — see CHARACTERISTIC 1
4 being the most accurate and apparently thorough — see DEFINITIVE 1

classic *n* **1** someone of such unequaled perfection as to deserve imitation — see IDEAL 1
2 something (as a work of art) that is a great achievement and often its creator's greatest achievement — see MASTERPIECE
3 the most perfect type or example — see QUINTESSENCE 1

classical *adj* **1** based on customs usually handed down from a previous generation — see TRADITIONAL 1
2 being the most accurate and apparently thorough — see DEFINITIVE 1

classification *n* one of the units into which a whole is divided on the basis of a common characteristic — see CLASS 2

classify *vb* **1** to arrange or assign according to type ⟨*Classify* the baseball cards in your collection on the basis of rarity.⟩
syn assort, break down, categorize, class, codify, compartment, digest, distinguish, distribute, grade, group, peg, place, range, rank, separate, sort, type
rel array, dispose, draw up, marshal (*also* marshall), order, organize, systematize; alphabetize, catalog (*or* catalogue), file, index, list, refer; pigeonhole, shelve; identify, recognize; cull, screen, set, sieve, sift, winnow; clump, cluster; recategorize, reclassify, regroup; subcategorize
near ant confuse, disarrange, jumble, lump, mix (up), scramble; misclassify, missort, mistype
2 to put into a particular arrangement — see ORDER 1

classless *adj* having or showing crudely insensitive or impolite manners — see CLOWNISH

classy *adj* having or showing elegance — see ELEGANT 1

clatter *n* a state of noisy, confused activity — see COMMOTION

clatter *vb* to make a series of short sharp noises — see RATTLE 1

clattering *adj* full of or characterized by the presence of noise — see NOISY 2

clattery *adj* full of or characterized by the presence of noise — see NOISY 2

clean *adj* 1 free from dirt or stain ⟨Although the soccer team always starts out with *clean* uniforms, they don't stay that way for long.⟩
syn chaste, fair, immaculate, pristine, spick-and-span (*or* spic-and-span), spotless, stainless, unsoiled, unstained, unsullied
rel pure, taintless, undefiled, unpolluted, untainted, wholesome; germfree, hygienic, sanitary, sterile; abluted, bleached, cleansed, purified, scrubbed, washed, whitened; milky, snowy, white; flawless, unblemished; bright, shiny, sparkling
near ant dingy, greasy, grimy, mucky, muddy, unwashed; defiled, germy, polluted, tainted, unsterile, unsterilized; blackened, discolored
ant besmirched, dirty, filthy, foul, grubby, smirched, soiled, spotted, stained, sullied, unclean, uncleaned
2 following or according to the rules — see FAIR 3
3 free from any trace of the coarse or indecent — see CHASTE 1
4 trying all possibilities — see EXHAUSTIVE 1
5 having no exceptions or restrictions — see ABSOLUTE 2
6 lacking contents that could or should be present — see EMPTY 1

clean *adv* 1 according to the rules or the law — see FAIRLY 2
2 to a full extent or degree — see FULLY 1

clean *vb* 1 to remove the dirt from ⟨We *cleaned* the clothes before donating them to charity.⟩
syn cleanse, turn out
rel decontaminate, purge, purify; disinfect, sanitize; brush, comb, dry-clean, dust, mop, muck (out), rinse, scour, scrub, shampoo, sponge, swab, vacuum, wash, wipe; brighten, deodorize, freshen; pick up, straighten (up), tidy, unclutter; neaten, trim
near ant begrime, muddy; defile, pollute, taint; blacken, discolor
ant besmirch, dirty, foul, soil, spot, stain, sully
2 to take the internal organs out of — see GUT

clean (up) *vb* 1 to make a place neat and orderly by removing extraneous stuff ⟨You're expected to *clean up* after you use the workroom.⟩
syn pick up
rel houseclean, housekeep; clean (off), clean (up), police (up), straighten (up), turn out, unclutter; arrange, order
phrases clean house, set straight
near ant clutter, disarrange, mess (up)
2 to remove objectionable parts from — see CENSOR
3 to destroy all traces of — see ANNIHILATE 1

cleaner *n* a substance used for cleaning ⟨a kitchen shelf loaded with household *cleaners*⟩

syn cleanser, detergent, soap
rel disinfectant, purifier, solvent; scrub, shampoo

cleanse *vb* 1 to free from moral guilt or blemish especially ceremonially — see PURIFY 1
2 to remove the dirt from — see CLEAN 1

cleanser *n* a substance used for cleaning — see CLEANER

cleansing *n* the act or fact of freeing from sin or moral guilt — see PURIFICATION

clear *adj* 1 easily seen through ⟨the *clear* glass walls of the aquarium's giant ocean tank⟩
syn crystalline, limpid, liquid, lucent, pellucid, transparent
rel colorless, uncolored; lucid, semitranslucent, semitransparent, sheer, translucent
near ant dark, glazed, tinted; filmy, foggy, hazy, misty, nebulous, smoky (*also* smokey); dense, muddy, murky, turbid
ant cloudy, opaque
2 not subject to misinterpretation or more than one interpretation ⟨The meaning of her broad smile was *clear* to the whole class.⟩
syn apparent, bald, barefaced, broad, clear-cut, decided, distinct, evident, lucid, luminous, manifest, obvious, open-and-shut, palpable, patent, pellucid, perspicuous, plain, straightforward, transparent, unambiguous, unequivocal, unmistakable
rel digestible, knowable; self-explanatory; clean-cut, simple, tidy, uncomplicated; overt, undisguised; appreciable, perceptible, recognizable, sensible, tangible; discernible (*also* discernable), noticeable, observable, visible; black-and-white, explicit, trenchant, well-defined; clean, decipherable, fair, readable; accessible, coherent, intelligible
near ant incomprehensible, unfathomable, unintelligible, unknowable; impalpable, imperceptible, inappreciable, indiscernible, insensible; cloudy, gauzy, gray (*also* grey), hazy, imprecise, indefinite, indeterminate, misty, murky, nebulous, noncommittal, sketchy, slippery, subtle, vague
ant ambiguous, clouded, cryptic, dark, enigmatic (*also* enigmatical), equivocal, indistinct, mysterious, nonobvious, obfuscated, obscure, unapparent, unclarified, unclear, unclouded
3 having or showing a mind free from doubt — see CERTAIN 2
4 not stormy or cloudy — see FAIR 1
5 serving to put an end to all debate or questioning — see CONCLUSIVE 1
6 allowing passage without obstruction — see OPEN 1
7 free from guilt or blame — see INNOCENT 2
8 giving off or reflecting much light — see BRIGHT 1

clear *vb* 1 to rid the surface of (as an area) from things in the way ⟨The early settlers worked hard to *clear* the land for crops.⟩
syn free, open, unblock
rel ease, facilitate, loosen (up), smooth, unchoke, unclog, unstop; unclutter; strip
near ant clog, close, dam, obstruct, plug, stop; clutter (up)
ant block

2 to set (a person or thing) free of something that encumbers — see RID

3 to give what is owed for — see PAY 2

4 to remove the contents of — see EMPTY

5 to remove usually visible impurities from — see CLARIFY 1

6 to set free from entanglement or difficulty — see EXTRICATE

7 to make passage through (something) possible by removing obstructions — see OPEN 2

8 to free from a charge of wrongdoing — see EXCULPATE

9 to give official acceptance of as satisfactory — see APPROVE

10 to take away from a place or position — see REMOVE 2

11 to give information to — see ENLIGHTEN 1

12 to receive after charges and deductions have been made — see ²NET

clear (up) *vb* to make plain or understandable — see EXPLAIN 1

clearance *n* the approval by someone in authority for the doing of something — see PERMISSION

clear–cut *adj* **1** not subject to misinterpretation or more than one interpretation — see CLEAR 2

2 so clearly expressed as to leave no doubt about the meaning — see EXPLICIT

cleared *adj* allowing passage without obstruction — see OPEN 1

clearheaded *adj* **1** having full use of one's mind and control over one's actions — see SANE

2 not having one's mind affected by alcohol — see SOBER 1

clearing *n* **1** a setting free from a charge of wrongdoing — see ACQUITTAL

2 a small area of usually open land — see FIELD 1

clearness *n* the state or quality of being easily seen through — see CLARITY 1

clear out *vb* **1** to cause (members of a group) to move widely apart — see SCATTER 1

2 to get free from a dangerous or confining situation — see ESCAPE 1

3 to leave a place often for another — see GO 2

clear–sighted *adj* **1** having or showing a practical cleverness or judgment — see SHREWD 1

2 having unusually keen vision — see SHARP-EYED

cleave *vb* to hold to something firmly as if by adhesion — see STICK 1

cleft *n* an irregular usually narrow break in a surface created by pressure — see CRACK 1

clemency *n* kind, gentle, or compassionate treatment especially towards someone who is undeserving of it — see MERCY 1

clement *adj* **1** marked by temperatures that are neither too high nor too low ⟨Hawaii is known for its delightfully *clement* climate.⟩
syn balmy, equable, genial, gentle, mild, moderate, soft, temperate

rel clear, cloudless, fair, rainless, sunny, sunshiny; calm, halcyon, peaceful, placid, tranquil; delightful, fine, pleasant
near ant blustering, blustery, breezy, gusty, rough, squally, stormy, windy; misty, rainy, showery; bleak, cloudy, dismal, foggy, gloomy, gray (*also* grey), hazy, overcast; bitter, dirty, foul, nasty, raw
ant harsh, inclement, intemperate, severe

2 tolerant and kind in the judgment of and expectations for others — see INDULGENT 1

clench *n* the act or manner of holding — see HOLD 1

clench *vb* to have or keep in one's hands — see HOLD 1

clerical *adj* of, relating to, or characteristic of the clergy ⟨*clerical* duties such as providing spiritual counseling⟩
syn ministerial, pastoral, priestly, sacerdotal
rel evangelical (*also* evangelic), missionary; apostolic, canonical, diaconal, diocesan, episcopal, papal, patriarchal; churchly, ecclesiastic, ecclesiastical; divine, holy, religious, sacramental; conventual, mendicant, monastic; rabbinic (*or* rabbinical)
ant lay, nonclerical, secular, temporal

clerk *n* **1** an official whose job is to keep records ⟨You'll need to get a copy of your birth certificate from the office of the town *clerk*.⟩
syn register, registrar, scribe, secretary
rel archivist, bookkeeper, recorder, reporter, transcriptionist; annalist, chronicler, documenter, historian

2 a person employed to sell goods or services especially in a store — see SALESPERSON

clever *adj* **1** showing a noteworthy use of the imagination and creativity especially in inventing ⟨an inventor who was constantly coming up with *clever* devices for doing everyday chores⟩
syn artful, creative, imaginative, ingenious, innovative, inventive
rel adventurous, fresh, groundbreaking, novel, original, visionary; cleverish, gadgety, gimmicky; convenient, handy, neat, nifty, practical, useful; complex, sophisticated; adroit, deft, dexterous (*also* dextrous), expert, handsome, tricky; brainy, intelligent, sharp, smart
near ant dull, pedantic, pedestrian, stodgy; assembly-line, canned, cookie-cutter, derivative, hackneyed, unoriginal; impractical, useless
ant uncreative, unimaginative

2 having or showing quickness of mind — see INTELLIGENT 1

3 skillful with the hands — see DEXTEROUS 1

4 given to or marked by mature intelligent humor — see WITTY

5 having the skill and imagination to create new things — see CREATIVE 1

cleverness *n* **1** mental skill or quickness — see DEXTERITY 1

2 subtle or imaginative ability in inventing, devising, or executing something — see SKILL 1

3 the skill and imagination to create new things — see CREATIVITY 1

cliché *also* **cliche** *adj* used or heard so often as to be dull — see STALE 1

---

syn synonym(s)   *rel* related words
ant antonym(s)   *near ant* near antonym(s)

cliché also **cliche** *n* an idea or expression that has been used by many people — see COMMONPLACE

click *vb* **1** to form a close personal relationship — see COMMUNE

2 to turn out as planned or desired — see SUCCEED 1

client *n* a person who buys a product or uses a service from a business — see CUSTOMER 1

cliff *n* a steep wall of rock, earth, or ice ⟨The *cliff* rises 200 feet from the island's south shore.⟩

syn bluff, crag, escarpment, palisade, precipice, scar, scarp

rel butte, hogback, tor; bulwark, embankment; pitch

climate *n* **1** a special quality or impression associated with something — see AURA 1

2 the circumstances, conditions, or objects by which one is surrounded — see ENVIRONMENT

climax *n* **1** a point in a chain of events at which an important change (as in one's fortunes) occurs — see TURNING POINT

2 the highest part or point — see HEIGHT 1

climax *vb* to bring to a triumphant conclusion — see CROWN

climb *n* the act or an instance of rising or climbing up — see ASCENT 1

climb *vb* **1** to move (as up or over something) often with the help of the hands in holding or pulling ⟨Visitors should use caution when *climbing* over the wet rocks along the shore.⟩

syn clamber, scrabble, scramble, swarm

rel shimmy, shin, shinny, skin; ascend, free-climb, get up, mount, scale, summit, surmount; claw, sprawl, struggle

2 to move or extend upward — see ASCEND

3 to become greater in extent, volume, amount, or number — see INCREASE 1

clinch *vb* to make final, definite, or beyond change ⟨The rain *clinched* the matter: we would have the party indoors.⟩

syn decide, determine, nail, settle

rel demonstrate, establish, nail (down), prove, show; affirm, assure, ensure, insure, secure; define, specify, state, stipulate; clarify, clear (up), illuminate; conclude, end, finish

near ant confuse, muddle, muddy, unsettle

clincher *n* something (as a fact or argument) that is decisive or overwhelming ⟨The fact that the resort had tennis courts was the *clincher* in our deciding to stay there.⟩

syn crusher, topper

rel deathblow, knockout; determinant, factor

phrases ace in the hole

cling *n* a physical sticking to as if by glue — see ADHESION 1

cling *vb* to hold to something firmly as if by adhesion — see STICK 1

cling (to) *vb* **1** to give steadfast support to — see ADHERE (TO) 1

2 to have or keep in one's hands — see HOLD 1

clink *vb* to make a repeated sharp light ringing sound — see JINGLE

clip *n* a hard strike with a part of the body or an instrument — see 1BLOW

clip *vb* **1** to make (something) shorter or smaller with the use of a cutting instrument ⟨a mother who's sad to see her little boy's curls *clipped* for the first time⟩

syn bob, crop, cut, cut back, dock, lop (off), nip, pare, poll, prune, shave, shear, snip, trim

rel skive, whittle; manicure, mow; pinch, stump; curtail, shorten

near ant elongate, extend, lengthen

2 to deliver a blow to (someone or something) usually in a strong vigorous manner — see HIT 1

clique *n* a group of people sharing a common interest and relating together socially — see GANG 2

cliquey *adj* bound together by feelings of very close association — see CLOSE-KNIT

cloak *n* **1** something that covers or conceals like a piece of cloth ⟨the *cloak* of mystery that surrounds the royal family⟩

syn blanket, cope, cover, covering, curtain, hood, mantle, mask, pall, robe, shroud, veil, wraps

rel blind, concealer, screen, shield; fig leaf, Trojan horse; camouflage, disguise, facade (also façade), face, mask, veneer; gloss, varnish

2 a sleeveless garment worn so as to hang over the shoulders, arms, and back — see 1CAPE

cloak *vb* **1** to change the dress or looks of so as to conceal true identity — see DISGUISE 1

2 to keep secret or shut off from view — see 1HIDE 2

clobber *vb* **1** to deliver a blow to (someone or something) usually in a strong vigorous manner — see HIT 1

2 to defeat by a large margin — see WHIP 2

clock *n* a device to measure time — see TIMEPIECE

clock *vb* to deliver a blow to (someone or something) usually in a strong vigorous manner — see HIT 1

clod *n* **1** a big clumsy often slow-witted person — see OAF 1

2 a small uneven mass — see LUMP 1

3 the loose surface material in which plants naturally grow — see DIRT 1

cloddish *adj* having or showing crudely insensitive or impolite manners — see CLOWNISH

clodhopper *n* **1** an awkward or simple person especially from a small town or the country — see HICK

2 a big clumsy often slow-witted person — see OAF 1

clog *n* something that makes movement or progress difficult — see ENCUMBRANCE

clog *vb* **1** to prevent passage through by filling with something ⟨the discovery that a ton of hair was *clogging* the drain in the tub⟩

syn block, choke, clot, congest, dam, jam, obstruct, occlude, plug (up), stop (up), stuff

rel bung, cork, stopper, stopple; fill, pack; fur, silt; flood, glut, inundate, overwhelm, swamp

near ant excavate, hollow (out), scoop (out); empty, lighten

ant clear, free, open (up), unblock, un-clog, unstop

2 to create difficulty for the work or activity of — see HAMPER

cloister *n* a residence for men under religious vows — see MONASTERY

cloistered *adj* screened or sequestered from view — see SECLUDED

¹**close** *n* an open space wholly or partly enclosed (as by buildings or walls) — see COURT 2

²**close** *n* **1** the stopping of a process or activity — see END 1

2 the last part of a process or action — see FINALE

close *adj* **1** having little space between items or parts ⟨The soldiers marched in *close* formation against the enemy.⟩

syn compact, crowded, dense, jam-packed, packed, thick, tight

rel crammed, jammed, overcrowded; massed, pressed, squeezed; airtight, snug; compacted, compressed, condensed, congested; firm, hard, solid; impenetrable, impermeable, impervious

near ant commodious, roomy, spacious

ant airy, loose, open, uncrowded

2 not being distant in time, space, or significance ⟨My birthday is *close* to Thanksgiving.⟩ ⟨a shopping mall that is very *close* to the highway⟩ ⟨These words are *close* synonyms.⟩

syn immediate, near, nearby, neighboring, next-door, nigh

rel abutting, adjacent, adjoining, bordering, contiguous; approaching, coming, forthcoming, oncoming, upcoming; accessible, convenient, handy; close-in, hand-to-hand

phrases at hand, to hand

near ant divorced, removed, separated

ant away, deep, distant, far, faraway, far-off, remote

3 showing little difference in the standing of the competitors ⟨The election results were so *close* that the votes had to be recounted.⟩

syn hairbreadth, narrow, neck and neck, nip and tuck, tight

rel crowded

4 closely acquainted — see FAMILIAR 1

5 given to keeping one's activities hidden from public observation or knowledge — see SECRETIVE

6 giving or sharing as little as possible — see STINGY 1

7 lacking fresh air — see STUFFY 1

8 meeting the highest standard of accuracy — see PRECISE 1

close *adv* at, within, or to a short distance or time — see NEAR 1

close *vb* **1** to position (something) so as to prevent passage through an opening ⟨Be sure to *close* the gate when you leave.⟩

syn shut

rel bar, batten (down), bolt, chain, fasten, latch, lock; plug, seal, stopper; secure; bang, clap, slam

near ant unbar, unbolt, unchain, unfasten, unlatch, unlock, unseal

---

syn synonym(s)   *rel* related words
ant antonym(s)   *near ant* near antonym(s)

---

ant open

2 to stop the operations of ⟨The merchant will *close* the store if business doesn't improve.⟩

syn shut

rel phase out, turn off; extinguish, quell, suppress; gag, muzzle, silence; fail, fold

near ant build, expand

ant open, start

3 to bring (an event) to a natural or appropriate stopping point ⟨We'll *close* the assembly with the singing of our national anthem.⟩

syn complete, conclude, end, finish, round (off *or* out), terminate, wind up, wrap up

rel climax, crown; consummate, perfect; halt, stop, suspend

phrases ring down the curtain (on)

ant begin, commence, inaugurate, open, start

4 to come to an end — see CEASE 1

5 to come near or nearer — see APPROACH 1

close (off) *vb* to disallow entry into (a place) by means of a physical barrier at the entry point ⟨Museum officials *closed off* the west wing after the fire.⟩

syn bar, barricade, blockade, guard

rel curtain (off), screen (off); dike, fence, gate, hedge; bolt, lock; obstruct

near ant reopen, unblock, unbolt

ant open, unbar

closefisted *adj* giving or sharing as little as possible — see STINGY 1

close-knit *adj* bound together by feelings of very close association ⟨a *close-knit* family that constantly keeps in touch⟩

syn clannish, cliquey

rel bosom, chummy, close, familiar, friendly, intimate, pally, palsy, thick, tight; exclusive; incestuous; forbidding, inhospitable, unfriendly

near ant receptive, welcoming

closely *adv* to a close degree — see NEAR 2

closemouthed *adj* **1** given to keeping one's activities hidden from public observation or knowledge — see SECRETIVE

2 tending not to speak frequently (as by habit or inclination) — see SILENT 2

closeness *n* **1** the practice or habit of keeping secrets or keeping one's affairs secret — see SECRECY

2 the quality or practice of being overly sparing with money — see PARSIMONY 1

3 the quality or state of being very accurate — see PRECISION

4 the state of being in a very personal or private relationship — see FAMILIARITY 1

5 the state or condition of being near — see PROXIMITY

6 strict attentiveness to what one is doing — see CARE 1

closer *adj* being the less far of two — see NEAR 1

closet *n* **1** a built-in space for storage behind a door ⟨a broom *closet* for the vacuum, carpet sweeper, ironing board, etc.⟩

syn cupboard, press

rel larder; cloakroom, coatroom, wardrobe

2 an area within a building that has been set apart from surrounding space by a wall — see ROOM 2

3 a storage case typically having doors and shelves — see CABINET

closet *vb* to close or shut in by or as if by barriers — see ENCLOSE 1

closing *adj* following all others of the same kind in order or time — see LAST 1

closing *n* the last part of a process or action — see FINALE

closure *n* the stopping of a process or activity — see END 1

clot *n* **1** a number of things considered as a unit — see GROUP 1

2 a small uneven mass — see LUMP 1

clot *vb* **1** to prevent passage through by filling with something — see CLOG 1

2 to turn from a liquid into a substance resembling jelly — see COAGULATE

cloth *n* a woven or knitted material (as of cotton or nylon) ⟨Cotton canvas was the *cloth* traditionally used for a ship's sails.⟩
syn fabric, textile
rel fiber, thread, yarn

clothe *vb* **1** to outfit with clothes and especially fine or special clothes ⟨They liked to *clothe* the twins in identical outfits.⟩
syn apparel, array, attire, bedeck, caparison, costume, dress, dress up, garb, garment, get up, gown, invest, rig (out), robe, suit
rel cloak, frock, jacket, mantle, vest; swaddle, swathe, wrap; accoutre (*or* accouter), equip, furnish, outfit, tailor, uniform; dress down, underdress
near ant denude, uncover, undrape, unveil
ant disarray, disrobe, strip, unclothe, undress

2 to convey in appropriate or telling terms — see PHRASE

clothes *n pl* covering for the human body — see CLOTHING

clothing *n* covering for the human body ⟨a store that sells both men's and women's *clothing*⟩
syn apparel, attire, clothes, dress, duds, garments, gear, raiment, rig, threads, togs, wear
rel wardrobe; array, bravery, caparison, finery, gaiety (*also* gayety), glad rags, pretties, regalia, trim; frippery; tatters; costume, ensemble, frock, garb, getup, guise, livery, outfit; civvies (*also* civies), mufti; couture, ready-to-wear, tailoring; activewear, loungewear, outerwear, playwear, sportswear; nightclothes, sleepwear, smallclothes, underclothes, underwear; haberdashery, menswear

cloud *n* an overspreading element that produces an atmosphere of gloom ⟨All day we were under a *cloud* until we heard the good news.⟩
syn darkness, pall, shadow
rel fog, haze, mist, murk; midnight; night; mantle, shroud, veil

cloud *vb* **1** to make dark, dim, or indistinct ⟨the diner's dark interior, *clouded* with smoke and grease⟩
syn becloud, bedim, befog, blacken, blur, darken, dim, fog, haze, mist, obscure, overcast, overcloud, overshadow, shadow, shroud
rel adumbrate, blot out, conceal, eclipse, hide, obliterate, screen, shade; camouflage, cloak, cover, curtain, disguise, mask, veil
near ant expose, reveal, uncover, unveil
ant brighten, illuminate, illumine, light (up), lighten

2 to make (something) unclear to the understanding — see CONFUSE 2

cloudburst *n* a steady falling of water from the sky in significant quantity — see RAIN 1

clouded *adj* **1** covered over by clouds — see OVERCAST

2 filled with or dimmed by fine particles (as of dust or water) in suspension — see HAZY 1

cloudless *adj* not stormy or cloudy — see FAIR 1

cloudy *adj* **1** having visible particles in liquid suspension ⟨The water coming out of the faucet was unusually *cloudy*.⟩
syn muddy, roiled, turbid
rel dingy, filmy, hazy, scummy, unfiltered; inky, muddied, muddled, murky, puddled, sludgy; opaque
near ant clarified, filtered, purified; colorless, transparent, uncolored
ant clear, crystalline

2 covered over by clouds — see OVERCAST

3 filled with or dimmed by fine particles (as of dust or water) in suspension — see HAZY 1

4 causing or marked by an atmosphere lacking in cheer — see GLOOMY 1

clout *n* **1** a hard strike with a part of the body or an instrument — see ¹BLOW

2 the power to direct the thinking or behavior of others usually indirectly — see INFLUENCE 1

clout *vb* to deliver a blow to (someone or something) usually in a strong vigorous manner — see HIT 1

clown *n* **1** a comically dressed performer (as at a circus) who entertains with playful tricks and ridiculous behavior ⟨a *clown* wearing big floppy shoes and a red wig⟩
syn buffoon, harlequin, zany
rel cutup, madcap; fool, jester, motley, scaramouch (*or* scaramouche); mime, mimic, mummer, pantaloon; comedian, comedienne, comic, droll, gagman, gagster, humorist, joker, jokester, merry-andrew, second banana, top banana, wag, wit

2 a person whose behavior is offensive to others — see JERK 1

clown (around) *vb* to engage in attention-getting playful or boisterous behavior — see CUT UP

clowning *n* wildly playful or mischievous behavior — see HORSEPLAY

clownish *adj* having or showing crudely insensitive or impolite manners ⟨the *clownish* antics of some of the teenagers at the wedding reception⟩
syn boorish, churlish, classless, cloddish, loutish, uncouth
rel coarse, ill-bred, uncultivated, unpolished, unrefined, unsophisticated; tasteless, vulgar; beastly; doltish, oafish, stupid; discourteous, impolite, mannerless, rude, uncivil, ungracious, unmannerly; awkward, ungainly
near ant couth, cultivated, polished, refined, sophisticated, well-bred; classy,

courtly, genteel, gentlemanly, ladylike; civil, courteous, polite

club *n* **1** a heavy rigid stick used as a weapon or for punishment ⟨They pretended to be knights with wooden swords and *clubs*.⟩

syn bat, billy, billy club, bludgeon, cane, cudgel, nightstick, rod, shillelagh (*also* shillalah), staff, truncheon

rel knobkerrie, mace; birch, crabstick, hickory, rattan, stave, switch; beetle, gavel, hammer, mallet, maul, sledgehammer; crook, crosier (*or* crozier), walking stick

2 the meeting place of an organization ⟨The Elks gather at their *club* every Monday evening.⟩

syn clubhouse, lodge

rel den, hangout, haunt, hideaway, hideout, lair; camp, headquarters; hall, house, meetinghouse

3 a group of persons formally joined together for some common interest — see ASSOCIATION 2

4 a bar or restaurant offering special nighttime entertainment (as music, dancing, or comedy acts) — see NIGHTCLUB

club *vb* **1** to form or enter into an association that furthers the interests of its members — see ALLY

2 to strike repeatedly — see BEAT 1

clubhouse *n* the meeting place of an organization — see CLUB 2

clue *n* a slight or indirect pointing to something (as a solution or explanation) — see HINT 1

clue (in) *vb* to give information to — see ENLIGHTEN 1

clump *n* **1** a number of things considered as a unit — see GROUP 1

2 a small uneven mass — see LUMP 1

clump *vb* to move heavily or clumsily — see LUMBER 1

clumpy *adj* having small pieces or lumps spread throughout — see CHUNKY 1

clumsy *adj* **1** lacking or showing a lack of nimbleness in using one's hands ⟨Diamond cutting is no job for a *clumsy* person.⟩

syn awkward, graceless, heavy-handed, left-handed, maladroit, unhandy

rel bunglesome, bungling, gauche, inept, inexpert, unskilled, unskillful

phrases all thumbs

near ant expert, masterly, skilled, skillful; coordinated

ant deft, dexterous (*also* dextrous), handy, sure-handed

2 having or showing an inability to move in a graceful manner ⟨a *clumsy* bow⟩ ⟨*clumsy* on the dance floor⟩

syn awkward, gawky, graceless, ungainly

rel galumphing, lubberly, lumbering, lumpish, shambling, shuffling, unsteady, wobbly (*also* wabbly)

near ant light, light-footed (*also* light-foot), lissome (*also* lissom), lithe, nimble, sure-footed

ant coordinated, graceful

3 lacking social grace and assurance — see AWKWARD 3

4 showing or marked by a lack of skill and tact (as in dealing with a situation) — see AWKWARD 2

5 difficult to use or operate especially because of size, weight, or design — see CUMBERSOME

6 hastily or roughly constructed — see RUDE 1

cluster *n* **1** a number of things considered as a unit — see GROUP 1

2 a usually small number of persons considered as a unit — see GROUP 2

cluster *vb* **1** to come together into one body or place — see ASSEMBLE 1

2 to gather into a closely packed group — see ²PRESS 3

¹clutch *n* **1** a number of things considered as a unit — see GROUP 1

2 a usually small number of persons considered as a unit — see GROUP 2

²clutch *n* **1** a time or state of affairs requiring prompt or decisive action — see EMERGENCY

2 the right or means to command or control others — see POWER 1

clutch *vb* to have or keep in one's hands — see HOLD 1

clutter *n* an unorganized collection or mixture of various things — see MISCELLANY 1

cluttered *adj* lacking in order, neatness, and often cleanliness — see MESSY

coach *n* a person who trains performers or athletes ⟨a *coach* who is highly respected by all of the baseball players⟩

syn trainer

rel handler, manager; instructor, teacher, tutor; driller, drillmaster; adviser (*also* advisor), counselor (*or* counsellor), guide, mentor

coach *vb* to give advice and instruction to (someone) regarding the course or process to be followed — see GUIDE 1

coadjutor *n* a person who helps a more skilled person — see HELPER

coagulate *vb* to turn from a liquid into a substance resembling jelly ⟨The blood *coagulated*, and a scab formed on the wound.⟩

syn clot, congeal, gel, jell, jelly, set

rel cake, concrete, firm (up), fix, freeze, harden, solidify; condense, thicken; clump, curd, curdle, gum, lump (up)

near ant liquefy (*also* liquify), melt, thaw

coalesce *vb* **1** to come together to form a single unit — see UNITE 1

2 to form or enter into an association that furthers the interests of its members — see ALLY

coalition *n* **1** a group of people acting together within a larger group — see FACTION

2 an association of persons, parties, or states for mutual assistance and protection — see CONFEDERACY

coarse *adj* **1** made up of large particles ⟨*Coarse* rock salt was sprinkled on the icy walkway.⟩

syn grainy, granular, granulated

rel unfiltered, unrefined; earthy, gravelly, gritty, sandy; pebbly, rocky, stony (*also* stoney); coarse-grained, cracked, kibbled, lumpy, mealy

near ant buttery, smooth, velvety; filtered,

---

refined; close-grained, ground, micronized, milled, mulled, pestled, pulverized, reduced, triturated

ant dusty, fine, floury, powdery, superfine, ultrafine

2 lacking in refinement or good taste ⟨They were disgusted by his *coarse* manners.⟩

syn common, crass, crude, gross, ill-bred, insensible, low, lowbred, lowbrow, raffish, rough, roughneck, rude, rugged, tasteless, uncouth, uncultivated, uncultured, unpolished, unrefined, vulgar

rel boorish, churlish, cloddish, clownish, loutish, ungentlemanly; clumsy, lubberly, lumpish, oafish; inconsiderate, insensitive, thoughtless; countrified (*also* countryfied), provincial, rustic (*also* rustical), unsophisticated; graceless, inelegant, tacky; animallike, barbaric, barbarous, uncivilized; mannerless, unmannerly

near ant aristocratic, courtly, patrician; elegant, graceful, restrained; considerate, gracious, sensitive, thoughtful; citified, sophisticated, urbane

ant civilized, cultivated, cultured, genteel, polished, refined, smooth, tasteful, ultrarefined, well-bred

3 depicting or referring to sexual matters in a way that is unacceptable in polite society — see OBSCENE 1

4 harsh and dry in sound — see HOARSE

5 not having a level or smooth surface — see UNEVEN 1

6 of low quality — see CHEAP 2

coarseness *n* **1** the quality or state of being obscene — see OBSCENITY

2 the quality or state of lacking refinement or good taste — see VULGARITY 1

coast *vb* to move or proceed smoothly and readily — see FLOW 2

coat *n* the hairy covering of a mammal especially when fine, soft, and thick — see FUR 1

coat *vb* to form a layer over — see COVER 2

coax *vb* to get (someone) to do something by gentle urging, special attention, or flattery ⟨Trying to *coax* their father into taking them on a ski trip, the kids mentioned what a great skier he is.⟩

syn blandish, blarney, cajole, palaver, soft-soap, wheedle

rel adulate, flatter, overpraise; charm, woo; beg, beseech, importune, urge; beguile, cozen, finagle, wangle, wile; entice, lure, seduce, tempt

near ant bug, nag, pester, tease; browbeat, bulldoze, bully, cow, intimidate; coerce, compel, constrain, demand, force, make, oblige, require

¹**cock** *n* a fixture for controlling the flow of a liquid — see FAUCET

²**cock** *n* a quantity of things thrown or stacked on one another — see ¹PILE 1

³**cock** *n* the act of positioning or an instance of being positioned at an angle — see TILT

cock *vb* to set or cause to be at an angle — see LEAN 1

cockeyed *adj* **1** inclined or twisted to one side — see AWRY

2 showing or marked by a lack of good sense or judgment — see FOOLISH 1

cocksure *adj* **1** displaying or marked by rude boldness — see NERVY 1

2 having or showing a mind free from doubt — see CERTAIN 2

cocky *adj* displaying or marked by rude boldness — see NERVY 1

cocoon *n* **1** something that encloses another thing especially to protect it — see ¹CASE 1

2 something that serves as a protective barrier — see CUSHION

cocoon *vb* to surround or cover closely — see ENFOLD 1

coddle *vb* **1** to cook in a liquid heated to the point that it gives off steam — see BOIL 2

2 to treat with great or excessive care — see BABY

code *n* a collection or system of rules of conduct ⟨Hammurabi was an ancient king of Babylon with a famous *code* of laws⟩ ⟨the tax *code*⟩

syn canon, constitution, decalogue, law

rel discipline, establishment; common law, legislation

codger *n* a person of odd or whimsical habits — see ECCENTRIC

codify *vb* **1** to arrange or assign according to type — see CLASSIFY 1

2 to put into a particular arrangement — see ORDER 1

coequal *adj* resembling another in every respect — see SAME 1

coequal *n* one that is equal to another in status, achievement, or value — see EQUAL

coerce *vb* to cause (a person) to give in to pressure — see FORCE

coerced *adj* not made or done willingly or by choice — see INVOLUNTARY 1

coercion *n* the use of power to impose one's will on another — see FORCE 2

coeval *adj* existing or occurring at the same period of time — see CONTEMPORARY 1

coeval *n* a person who lives at the same time or is about the same age as another — see CONTEMPORARY

coexist *vb* to occur or exist at the same time — see COINCIDE 1

coexistence *n* the occurrence or existence of several things at once — see CONCURRENCE 1

coexistent *adj* **1** existing or occurring at the same period of time — see CONTEMPORARY 1

2 present at the same time and place — see COINCIDENT 1

coexisting *adj* **1** existing or occurring at the same period of time — see CONTEMPORARY 1

2 present at the same time and place — see COINCIDENT 1

coextensive *adj* **1** occupying the same space ⟨South Dakota's Todd County is *coextensive* with the main Rosebud Sioux Reservation.⟩

syn coincident

rel allover, overlaying, superimposed, superposed, underlying; conjoining, crisscrossing, intersecting, overlapping; coaxial, concurrent, convergent; conjunctional

near ant nonconcurrent, noncongruent

2 existing or occurring at the same period of time — see CONTEMPORARY 1

coffer *n* **1** a specially reinforced container to keep valuables safe — see SAFE

2 coffers *pl* available money — see FUND 2

coffin *n* a boxlike container for holding a dead body ⟨*Coffins* are said to be the preferred sleeping places of vampires.⟩

syn box, casket, pall

rel charnel (*also* charnel house), crypt, sepulture, tomb, vault; urn; body bag

cogency *n* **1** the capacity to persuade ⟨the *cogency* of Thomas Paine's celebrated case for American independence⟩

syn authority, conclusiveness, effectiveness, force, forcefulness, persuasion, persuasiveness

rel impact, might, power, punch, strength, weight; believability, credibility, soundness, validity; authoritativeness, definitiveness; influence, sway; appeal, seductiveness

near ant invalidity, shakiness, unsoundness; feebleness, powerlessness, weakness

ant inconclusiveness, ineffectiveness, ineffectuality, ineffectualness

2 the quality of an utterance that provokes interest and produces an effect — see ¹PUNCH 1

cogent *adj* having the power to persuade ⟨The results of the DNA fingerprinting were the most *cogent* evidence for acquittal.⟩

syn compelling, conclusive, convincing, decisive, effective, forceful, persuasive, satisfying, strong, telling

rel authoritative, definitive; sound, valid, well-founded; important, significant, weighty; material, pertinent, relevant

near ant groundless, invalid, shaky, unfounded, unsound; inconsequential, insignificant, unimportant; immaterial, irrelevant; feeble, weak

ant inconclusive, indecisive, ineffective, unconvincing, unpersuasive

cogitate *vb* to give serious and careful thought to — see PONDER

cognizance *n* **1** a state of being aware — see ATTENTION 2

2 knowledge gained by personal experience — see ACQUAINTANCE

cognizant *adj* having specified facts or feelings actively impressed on the mind — see CONSCIOUS 1

cognomen *n* **1** a descriptive or familiar name given instead of or in addition to the one belonging to an individual — see NICKNAME

2 a word or combination of words by which a person or thing is regularly known — see NAME 1

cohere *vb* **1** to be in agreement on every point — see CHECK 1

2 to form or enter into an association that furthers the interests of its members — see ALLY

coherence *n* a balanced, pleasing, or suitable arrangement of parts — see HARMONY 1

coherent *adj* **1** according to the rules of logic — see LOGICAL 1

---

syn synonym(s)   *rel* related words
ant antonym(s)   *near ant* near antonym(s)

---

2 not having or showing any apparent conflict — see CONSISTENT

cohort *n* **1** a person frequently seen in the company of another — see ASSOCIATE 1

2 one associated with another in wrongdoing — see ACCOMPLICE

coil *vb* to follow a circular or spiral course — see WIND 1

coiling *adj* turning around an axis like the thread of a screw — see SPIRAL

coinage *n* something (as a device) created for the first time through the use of the imagination — see INVENTION 1

coincide *vb* **1** to occur or exist at the same time ⟨The heaviest snowfall of the season *coincided* with the start of our weeklong ski vacation.⟩

syn accompany, attend, coexist, concur

rel chance, hap, happen, transpire

near ant antedate, precede, predate; follow, succeed

2 to be in agreement on every point — see CHECK 1

3 to have or come to the same opinion or point of view — see AGREE 1

coincidence *n* the occurrence or existence of several things at once — see CONCURRENCE 1

coincident *adj* **1** present at the same time and place ⟨Scientists had no explanation for the *coincident* phenomena.⟩

syn accompanying, attendant, attending, coexistent, coexisting, coincidental, concomitant, concurrent

rel contemporaneous, contemporary, simultaneous, synchronous; associated, collateral, connected, linked, related; consequent, resultant, resulting; ensuing, following, subsequent; accidental, casual, chance, fluky (*also* flukey), fortuitous, freak, incident, incidental

near ant unassociated, unconnected, unrelated

2 occupying the same space — see COEXTENSIVE 1

3 existing or occurring at the same period of time — see CONTEMPORARY 1

coincidental *adj* **1** existing or occurring at the same period of time — see CONTEMPORARY 1

2 present at the same time and place — see COINCIDENT 1

coincidentally *adv* at one and the same time — see TOGETHER 1

coincidently *adv* at one and the same time — see TOGETHER 1

coitus *n* sexual union involving penetration of the vagina by the penis — see SEXUAL INTERCOURSE

cold *adj* **1** having a low or subnormal temperature ⟨the *cold* climate of the Yukon⟩ ⟨an unusually *cold* spring that was followed by a sweltering summer⟩

syn arctic, bitter, chill, chilly, cool, coolish, freezing, frigid, frosty, glacial, icecold, icy, nipping, nippy, numbing, polar, shivery, snappy, wintry (*also* wintery)

rel cryogenic, subfreezing, subzero, ultracold; cutting, keen, penetrating, piercing, sharp; bracing, brisk, crisp, invigorating, rigorous; chilled, cooled, frosted, frozen, iced, refrigerated, unheated

near ant lukewarm, tepid; heated, overheated, reheated, warmed; snug, toasty, warm; feverish, flushed, inflamed (*also* enflamed); equatorial, muggy, steamy, summery, tropical

ant ardent, blazing, broiling, burning, fervent, fervid, fiery, glowing, hot, igneous, molten, piping hot, red-hot, roasting, scalding, scorching, searing, seething, sizzling, sultry, sweltering, torrid, warming

2 lacking in friendliness or warmth of feeling ⟨The prisoners got only a *cold* stare when they tried to befriend the guard.⟩

syn arctic, brittle, chill, chilly, cold-blooded, cool, frigid, frosty, frozen, glacial, icy, unfriendly, unsympathetic, wintry (*also* wintery)

rel bloodless, coldhearted, heartless, kindless, pitiless, uncaring, unfeeling; reserved, soulless, undemonstrative, unemotional, unresponsive; apathetic, indifferent, unenthusiastic, uninterested; aloof, detached, dispassionate, impersonal, standoffish; antisocial, unsociable, unsocial

near ant compassionate, kind, kindhearted; demonstrative, emotional, expressive; eager, enthusiastic, passionate

ant cordial, friendly, genial, happy, hearty, sympathetic, warm, warm-blooded, warmhearted

3 having or showing a lack of friendliness or interest in others — see COOL 1

4 having lost consciousness — see UNCONSCIOUS 1

5 causing or marked by an atmosphere lacking in cheer — see GLOOMY 1

6 no longer living — see DEAD 1

cold *n* a weather condition marked by low temperatures ⟨The *cold* will stay with us for another day, then temperatures should rise.⟩

syn freeze, snap

rel cold front; frost; bite, chill, chilliness, chillness, frigidness, nip, wintriness

near ant dog days; torridity, torridness

ant heat, heat wave

cold-blooded *adj* **1** having or showing a lack of sympathy or tender feelings — see HARD 1

2 lacking in friendliness or warmth of feeling — see COLD 2

3 not feeling or showing emotion — see IMPASSIVE 1

4 *or* coldblood being offspring produced by parents of different races, breeds, species, or genera — see MIXED 1

cold-shoulder *vb* to deliberately ignore or treat rudely — see SNUB 1

cold shoulder *n* treatment that is deliberately unfriendly ⟨At the party the two former friends consciously gave each other the *cold shoulder*.⟩

syn brush-off, rebuff, repulse, silent treatment, snub

rel dismissal, kiss-off, rejection; banishment, blackball, ostracism

near ant acceptance, embrace, welcome; glad hand, welcome mat

ant open arms

coliseum *n* a large usually roofless building for sporting events with tiers of seats for spectators — see STADIUM

collaborate *vb* to participate or assist in a joint effort to accomplish an end — see COOPERATE 1

collaboration *n* **1** the state of having shared interests or efforts (as in social or business matters) — see ASSOCIATION 1

2 the work and activity of a number of persons who individually contribute toward the efficiency of the whole — see TEAMWORK

collapse *n* **1** a complete depletion of energy or strength — see FATIGUE

2 a falling short of one's goals — see FAILURE 2

collapse *vb* **1** to fall down or in as a result of physical pressure ⟨The motel balcony *collapsed* under the weight of so many people.⟩

syn buckle, cave (in), crumple, founder, give, go, implode, tumble, yield

rel deflate, flatten, melt; break, break down, conk (out), crash, die, fail, give out, stall; burst, shatter, smash, splinter, split; crack, crumble, pop, snap

phrases give way

near ant inflate, rise, swell

2 to be unsuccessful — see FAIL 2

3 to reduce in size or volume by or as if by pressing parts or members together — see COMPRESS 1

collar *n* **1** an ornamental chain or string (as of beads) worn around the neck — see NECKLACE

2 the act of taking into one's control by authority of law — see ARREST 1

collar *vb* **1** to take or keep under one's control by authority of law — see ARREST 1

2 to take physical control or possession of (something) suddenly or forcibly — see CATCH 1

colleague *n* a fellow worker ⟨On her first day at work her *colleagues* went out of their way to make her feel welcome.⟩

syn associate, coworker

rel equal, fellow, peer; accomplice, ally, cohort, collaborator, confederate, copartner, half, partner; buddy, chum, companion, comrade, crony, pal; compatriot, countryman

collect *vb* **1** to gain emotional or mental control of ⟨Applicants should *collect* their thoughts while waiting to be interviewed.⟩

syn calm, compose, contain, control, recollect, settle

rel hold back, restrain; rally, recover; lull, quiet, soothe, still, tranquilize (*also* tranquillize)

2 to gradually form into a layer, pile, or mass ⟨Dust has been *collecting* under my bed for years.⟩

syn accumulate, amass, concentrate, conglomerate, gather, mass, pile (up)

rel clump, lump; bank, drift, ridge

near ant disperse, dissipate, scatter

3 to bring together from several sources into a single volume or list — see COMPILE

4 to bring together in one body or place — see GATHER 1

5 to come together into one body or place — see ASSEMBLE 1

collected *adj* free from emotional or mental agitation — see CALM 2

collectedness *n* evenness of emotions or temper — see EQUANIMITY

collection *n* **1** an organized group of objects acquired and maintained for study, exhibition, or personal pleasure ⟨His stamp *collection* has become quite valuable.⟩

syn assemblage, library

rel assortment, kaleidoscope, miscellanea, treasure, trove; arsenal, cache, hoard, repertory, reserve, stock, stockpile, store, supply; accumulation, assembly, gathering

near ant bric-a-brac, clutter, heap, jumble, litter, pile, ragbag

2 a mass or quantity that has piled up or that has been gathered over a period of time — see ACCUMULATION 1

3 a number of things considered as a unit — see GROUP 1

collective *adj* used or done by a number of people as a group ⟨The cleanup of the neighborhood park was a *collective* effort for which many people should be thanked.⟩

syn combined, common, communal, concerted, conjoint, cooperative, joint, multiple, mutual, pooled, public, shared, united

rel bilateral, consensual, reciprocal, symbiotic, synergic, synergistic, two-way; mass, popular; general, generic, universal

near ant personal, private; independent, separate, several; esoteric, particular, special, specialized

ant exclusive, individual, one-man, one-sided, one-way, single, sole, solitary, unilateral

collectively *adv* with everyone or everything taken into account at the same time — see ALL AROUND

college *n* a group of persons formally joined together for some common interest — see ASSOCIATION 2

collide *vb* 1 to be out of harmony or agreement usually noticeably — see CLASH

2 to come into usually forceful contact with something — see HIT 2

collision *n* 1 a forceful coming together of two things — see IMPACT 1

2 the violent coming together of two bodies into destructive contact — see CRASH 1

colloquial *adj* 1 used in or suitable for speech and not formal writing ⟨The new coworker's rudeness soon began—to use a *colloquial* expression—to rub me the wrong way.⟩

syn conversational, informal, nonliterary, unliterary, vernacular, vulgar

rel dialectal, dialectical (*also* dialectic), nonstandard, regional; incorrect, nongrammatical, substandard, uneducated, unlearned; slang, slangy

near ant standard, undialectical; correct, educated, genteel, grammatical, proper

ant bookish, formal, learned, literary

2 having the style and content of everyday conversation — see CHATTY 1

colloquy *n* 1 a meeting featuring a group discussion — see FORUM 1

2 an exchange of views for the purpose of exploring a subject or deciding an issue — see DISCUSSION 1

3 talking or a talk between two or more people — see CONVERSATION

collusion *n* a secret agreement or cooperation between two parties for an illegal or dishonest purpose ⟨There was *collusion* between the two companies to fix prices.⟩

syn complicity, connivance, conspiracy

rel chicanery, foul play, skulduggery (*or* skullduggery); double-dealing, duplicity; frame-up, setup; conspiration, intrigue, plot, scheme

colonist *n* a person who settles in a new region — see FRONTIERSMAN

colonizer *n* a person who settles in a new region — see FRONTIERSMAN

colony *n* 1 a settlement in a new country or region ⟨the early history of New York City when it was a Dutch *colony*⟩

syn plantation

rel camp, diaspora, exclave, habitation, outpost, post; dependency, mandate, possession, protectorate, territory

2 a group of people with a common interest living in one place — see COMMUNITY 2

color *n* 1 a property that becomes apparent when light falls on an object and by which things that are identical in form can be distinguished ⟨a shirt that is available in every *color* of the rainbow⟩

syn cast, hue, shade, tincture, tinge, tint, tone

rel overtone, undertone; primary color, secondary color, tertiary color; brightness, chroma, chromaticity, contrast, lightness, saturation, value; coloration, coloring, colorway, pigmentation

near ant achromatism

2 a substance used to color other materials — see PIGMENT

3 the hue or appearance of the skin and especially of the face — see COMPLEXION 1

4 colors *pl* a piece of cloth with a special design that is used as an emblem or for signaling — see FLAG 1

5 a rosy appearance (of the cheeks) — see BLOOM 2

6 colors *pl* the combined army, air force, and navy of a nation — see ARMED FORCES

7 colors *pl* the set of qualities that makes a person, a group of people, or a thing different from others — see NATURE 1

color *vb* 1 to give color or a different color to ⟨She went to a stylist to have her hair *colored*.⟩

syn dye, paint, pigment, stain, tincture, tinge, tint

rel brighten, lighten; darken, embrown, tone (down); checker, dapple, daub, fleck, marble, mottle, pattern, polychrome, speck, speckle, streak, striate, stripe, variegate

near ant blanch, bleach, whiten

ant decolorize

2 to add to the interest of by including made-up details — see EMBROIDER

3 to change so much as to create a wrong impression or alter the meaning of — see GARBLE

4 to develop a rosy facial color (as from excitement or embarrassment) — see BLUSH

colorful *adj* marked by a variety of usually vivid colors ⟨the *colorful* markings on butterflies⟩

syn motley, multicolored, polychromatic, polychrome, varicolored, varied, variegated

---

rel brave, bright, brilliant, vibrant; flashy, garish, gaudy, loud, showy, splashy; checkered, dotted, patterned, plaid, plaided, striped; dappled (*also* dapple), marbled, mottled, parti-color (*or* parti-colored), piebald, pied, pinto; flecked, speckled, spotted; barred, brindled (*or* brindle), streaked, striated; bichrome, bicolored (*or* bicolor), dichromatic, trichromatic, tricolor (*or* tricolored), two-tone, two-toned

near ant achromatic; bleached, decolorized, faded, washed-out; dull, faint, gray (*also* grey), neutral, pale, pallid, unbrilliant

ant colorless; monochromatic, self-colored, solid

coloring *n* 1 a substance used to color other materials — see PIGMENT

2 the hue or appearance of the skin and especially of the face — see COMPLEXION 1

3 the representation of something in terms that go beyond the facts — see EXAGGERATION

colorless *adj* 1 lacking an addition of color ⟨Since we can't decide what color to paint the doghouse, our latest home project remains *colorless* for the time being.⟩

syn uncolored, undyed, unpainted, unstained, white

rel clear, limpid, liquid, lucent, pellucid, transparent; bleached, faded, palish, washed-out; dull, faint, gray (*also* grey), neutral, pale, pallid; snow-white, snowy, whited

near ant colorful, multicolored, polychromatic, polychrome, varicolored, variegated

ant colorized, dyed, hued, painted, pigmented, stained, tinct, tinctured, tinged, tinted

2 causing weariness, restlessness, or lack of interest — see BORING

colossal *adj* unusually large — see HUGE

colossally *adv* 1 to a great degree — see VERY 1

2 to a large extent or degree — see GREATLY 2

colosseum *n* a large usually roofless building for sporting events with tiers of seats for spectators — see STADIUM

colossus *n* something that is unusually large and powerful — see GIANT

colt *n* a person who is just starting out in a field of activity — see BEGINNER

coltish *adj* given to good-natured joking or teasing — see PLAYFUL

column *n* 1 a series of persons or things arranged one behind another — see LINE 1

2 an upright shaft that supports an overhead structure — see PILLAR 1

comb *vb* to look through (as a place) carefully or thoroughly in an effort to find or discover something — see SEARCH 1

combat *n* 1 active fighting during the course of a war ⟨a soldier who served throughout the war without actually seeing *combat*⟩

syn action, battle, field

rel attack, fire, firefight, pitched battle, single combat; hostilities, operations, warfare; duty, service

2 a physical dispute between opposing individuals or groups — see FIGHT 1

3 an earnest effort for superiority or victory over another — see CONTEST 1

combat *vb* 1 to oppose (someone) in physical conflict — see FIGHT 1

2 to strive to reduce or eliminate — see FIGHT 2

combative *adj* feeling or displaying eagerness to fight — see BELLIGERENT

combativeness *n* an inclination to fight or quarrel — see BELLIGERENCE

combination *n* 1 a distinct entity formed by the combining of two or more different things — see BLEND

2 the act or an instance of joining two or more things into one — see UNION 1

3 a number of businesses or enterprises united for commercial advantage — see CARTEL

4 an association of persons, parties, or states for mutual assistance and protection — see CONFEDERACY

combine *n* 1 a number of businesses or enterprises united for commercial advantage — see CARTEL

2 an association of persons, parties, or states for mutual assistance and protection — see CONFEDERACY

combine *vb* 1 to come together to form a single unit — see UNITE 1

2 to turn into a single mass or entity that is more or less the same throughout — see BLEND 1

combined *adj* used or done by a number of people as a group — see COLLECTIVE

combining *n* the act or an instance of joining two or more things into one — see UNION 1

combust *vb* to be on fire especially brightly — see BURN 1

combustible *adj* capable of catching or being set on fire ⟨Don't store oily rags and other *combustible* materials in a hot attic.⟩

syn burnable, fiery, flammable, ignitable (*also* ignitible), inflammable, touchy

rel explosive, incendiary

near ant nonexplosive

ant fireproof, incombustible, nonburnable, noncombustible, nonflammable, noninflammable, unburnable

combusting *adj* being on fire — see ABLAZE 1

come *vb* 1 to move closer to ⟨*Come* here and sit by the fire.⟩

syn advance, approach, near, nigh

rel enter, pop (in)

near ant depart, exit, leave

ant go, recede (from), retreat, withdraw

2 to get to a destination ⟨When do you think they'll *come*?⟩

syn appear, arrive, land, show up, turn up

rel fetch, hit, make, reach; touch down; debark, disembark; barge (in), blow in, breeze (in), burst (in *or* into), waltz (in); check in, clock (in)

near ant clock (out); flee

ant go, leave

3 to eventually have as a state or quality — see BECOME

4 to take place — see HAPPEN

5 to move forward along a course — see GO 1

come (to) *vb* 1 to have a total of — see AMOUNT (TO) 1

2 to be the same in meaning or effect — see AMOUNT (TO) 2

3 to enter the mind of — see OCCUR (TO)

come about vb to take place — see HAPPEN

come along vb to move forward along a course — see GO 1

come around vb to gain consciousness again — see COME TO

comeback n **1** a quick witty response — see RETORT 1

2 something spoken or written in reaction especially to a question — see ANSWER 1

3 the process or period of gradually regaining one's health and strength — see CONVALESCENCE

come by vb **1** to make a brief visit — see CALL 3

2 to receive as return for effort — see EARN 1

comedian n a person (as a writer) noted for or specializing in humor — see HUMORIST

comedown n a loss of status ⟨After a rapid rise to stardom, the rock band's *comedown* was just as quick.⟩

syn decline, demise, descent, down, downfall, fall

rel breakdown, burnout, collapse, crash, meltdown, ruin; defeat, disappointment, reversal, setback; bottom; abasement, disgrace, humiliation

near ant advance, headway, progress; flower, heyday, prime

ant aggrandizement, ascent, exaltation, rise, up

come down (with) vb to become affected with (a disease or disorder) — see CONTRACT 1

comedy n **1** humorous entertainment ⟨presented a night of *comedy*⟩

syn farce, humor, slapstick

rel high comedy, low comedy; burlesque, parody, satire; banter, persiflage, wit; foolery, fun, horseplay, knockabout, monkeyshine(s), shenanigan(s)

2 the amusing quality or element in something — see HUMOR 1

comeliness n the qualities in a person or thing that as a whole give pleasure to the senses — see BEAUTY 1

comely adj very pleasing to look at — see BEAUTIFUL 1

come out vb **1** to come to be ⟨In the end everything *came out* OK.⟩

syn fall out, pan out, prove, turn out

rel develop, emerge, evolve, germinate, play out, work out

2 to come into view — see APPEAR 1

3 to become known — see GET OUT 1

come round vb **1** to gain consciousness again — see COME TO

2 to give or express one's approval (as to a proposal) — see ACCEDE

come to vb to gain consciousness again ⟨After being in a coma for months, the patient quite unexpectedly *came to*.⟩

syn come around, come round, revive

rel pull through, rally, recover; awake, awaken, wake up

near ant black out, faint, pass out

---

comfort n **1** a feeling of ease from grief or trouble ⟨The mourners found *comfort* in their pastor's words.⟩

syn cheer, consolation, relief, solace

rel encouragement, inspiration, uplift; assurance; alleviation, assuagement, mitigation; contentment, gladness, happiness; commiseration, empathy, sympathy; aid, assistance, help, succor

near ant cold comfort; anguish, distress, heartache, heartbreak, torment, torture

2 something that adds to one's ease of living ⟨a family campground with all the *comforts* of home⟩

syn accommodation, amenity, convenience, luxury, nicety

rel bonus, extra; benefit, help, service; delight, indulgence, joy, pleasure

ant burden, millstone, weight

3 reduction of or freedom from pain — see EASE 1

4 something adding to pleasure or comfort but not absolutely necessary — see LUXURY 1

comfort vb to ease the grief or distress of ⟨The teacher did his best to *comfort* the distraught child.⟩

syn assure, cheer, console, reassure, solace, soothe

rel commiserate, condole, empathize, sympathize; boost, buoy (up), elevate, lift, uplift; allay, alleviate, assuage, relieve; calm, quiet, relax, tranquilize (*also* tranquillize)

near ant demoralize, discourage, dishearten; fret, upset, worry; aggravate, intensify, worsen; annoy, irk, irritate; pester

ant distress, torment, torture, trouble

comfortable adj **1** providing physical comfort ⟨a large, overstuffed chair that is very *comfortable*⟩

syn cozy, cushy, easy, snug, soft

rel easeful, relaxing, reposeful, restful; genial, hospitable, inviting, pleasant; commodious, roomy, spacious; homelike, homey (*also* homy), intimate

near ant hard, harsh, severe; inhospitable, uninviting, unpleasant

ant uncomfortable

2 enjoying physical comfort ⟨Make yourself *comfortable* in the living room while I fix us some snacks.⟩

syn cozy, relaxed, snug

rel toasty, warm; content, contented, pleased, satisfied; easeful, peaceful, resting; easygoing, laid-back; undisturbed, unperturbed, untroubled

phrases at ease, at home

near ant discontented, displeased, dissatisfied; agitated, disturbed, perturbed, troubled

ant uncomfortable

3 being more than enough without being excessive — see PLENTIFUL

comforting adj **1** making one feel good inside — see HEARTWARMING

2 tending to calm the emotions and relieve stress — see SOOTHING 1

comforting n the giving of hope and strength in times of grief, distress, or suffering — see CONSOLATION 1

comfortless adj **1** causing discomfort — see UNCOMFORTABLE 1

---

syn synonym(s)   **rel** related words
ant antonym(s)   **near ant** near antonym(s)

2 causing or marked by an atmosphere lacking in cheer — see GLOOMY 1

comic *adj* causing or intended to cause laughter — see FUNNY 1

comic *n* 1 a person (as a writer) noted for or specializing in humor — see HUMORIST

2 a series of drawings that tell a story or part of a story — see COMIC STRIP

3 the amusing quality or element in something — see HUMOR 1

comical *adj* 1 causing or intended to cause laughter — see FUNNY 1

2 so foolish or pointless as to be worthy of scornful laughter — see RIDICULOUS 1

comic strip *n* a series of drawings that tell a story or part of a story ⟨a *comic strip* that is beloved by both children and adults⟩

syn cartoon, comic, funny, strip

rel comic book, funny paper(s), graphic novel; animated cartoon, animation; caricature

coming *adj* 1 being about to appear or take place — see FORTHCOMING 1

2 being the one that comes immediately after another — see NEXT

3 of a time after the present — see FUTURE

coming *n* the act of coming upon a scene — see ARRIVAL

comity *n* peaceful coexistence — see HARMONY 2

command *n* 1 a statement of what to do that must be obeyed by those concerned ⟨The captain's *commands* were followed without question.⟩

syn behest, charge, commandment, decree, dictate, direction, directive, do, edict, imperative, instruction, order, word

rel demand, requirement; mandate; countermand, counterorder; law, precept, prescript, rule; ordinance, regulation, statute

near ant appeal, entreaty, petition, plea, urging; proposal, recommendation, suggestion

2 a highly developed skill in or knowledge of something ⟨a *command* of French that is the result of a year spent in France as an exchange student⟩

syn mastership, mastery, proficiency

rel virtuosity; facility, hang; fluency; experience, expertise, know-how, practice (*also* practise), skill(s); acquaintance, familiarity, intimacy

near ant incompetence; ignorance, illiteracy, unfamiliarity

3 the place from which a commander runs operations ⟨The general set up his *command* in the old port city.⟩

syn base, headquarters

rel home, seat

4 a place from which authority is exercised — see SEAT 1

5 the right or means to command or control others — see POWER 1

6 all that can be seen from a certain point — see VIEW 1

command *vb* 1 to issue orders to (someone) by right of authority ⟨The general *commanded* his troops with Caesar-like imperiousness.⟩

syn adjure, bid, boss (around), charge, direct, enjoin, instruct, order, tell

rel ask, petition, request; beg, beseech, entreat; advise, counsel, warn; appoint, assign, authorize, commission; oversee, superintend, supervise; conduct, control, lead, manage; coerce, compel, constrain, force, oblige, require

near ant comply (with), follow, keep, observe

ant obey

2 to request the doing of by virtue of one's authority ⟨The governor has *commanded* that all state flags be flown at half-mast.⟩

syn call, decree, dictate, direct, mandate, order

rel ask, petition, request; demand, require

phrases call for

near ant cancel, countermand, rescind

3 to ask for (something) earnestly or with authority — see DEMAND 1

4 to exercise authority or power over — see GOVERN 1

5 to keep, control, or experience as one's own — see HAVE 1

6 to look down on — see OVERLOOK 1

7 to serve as leader of — see LEAD 2

8 to set or receive as a price — see CHARGE 1

commandant *n* one in official command especially of a military force or base — see COMMANDER 1

commandeer *vb* 1 to take control of (a vehicle) by force ⟨The soldiers *commandeered* civilian vehicles to transport the injured.⟩

syn hijack (*also* highjack)

rel carjack, skyjack; appropriate, confiscate, expropriate, seize

2 to take or make use of under a guise of authority but without actual right — see APPROPRIATE 1

commander *n* 1 one in official command especially of a military force or base ⟨a surrender of the fort by the *commander* without a single shot having been fired⟩

syn captain, commandant, commanding officer

rel commissioned officer, field officer

phrases commander in chief

2 a person in overall command of a ship — see CAPTAIN 1

commanding *adj* 1 highest in rank or authority — see HEAD

2 likely to attract attention — see NOTICEABLE

commanding officer *n* one in official command especially of a military force or base — see COMMANDER 1

commandment *n* a statement of what to do that must be obeyed by those concerned — see COMMAND 1

commemorate *vb* 1 to be a memorial of ⟨A stone obelisk *commemorates* the Battle of Bunker Hill.⟩

syn memorialize

rel celebrate, keep, observe, remember; enshrine, exalt, glorify, honor; bless, consecrate, sanctify, solemnize

near ant disgrace, dishonor

2 to mark with an appropriate practice, rite, or ceremony — see KEEP 1

commemorating *adj* serving to preserve the memory of a person, thing, or an event — see COMMEMORATIVE

commemorative *adj* serving to preserve

the memory of a person, thing, or an event ⟨*commemorative* stamps for the stars of American popular music⟩

syn commemorating, memorial, memorializing

rel dedicatory; canonizing, enshrining, exalting, glorifying

commemorative *n* something that serves to keep alive the memory of a person or event — see MEMORIAL

commence *vb* **1** to take the first step in (a process or course of action) — see BEGIN 1
2 to come into existence — see BEGIN 2

commencement *n* the point at which something begins — see BEGINNING

commend *vb* to put (something) into the possession or safekeeping of another — see GIVE 2

commendable *adj* deserving of high regard or great approval — see ADMIRABLE

commendation *n* **1** a formal recognition of an achievement or praiseworthy deed ⟨a firefighter who has been awarded several *commendations* for bravery⟩

syn acknowledgment (*or* acknowledgement), citation, mention

rel decoration, medal, ribbon; accolade, award, honor, prize, tribute; dedication
2 a formal expression of praise — see ENCOMIUM

commendatory *adj* expressing approval — see FAVORABLE 1

commensurate *adj* corresponding in size, amount, extent, or degree — see PROPORTIONAL

comment *n* **1** a briefly expressed opinion — see REMARK
2 comments *pl* a series of explanations or observations on something (as an event) — see COMMENTARY 1

comment *vb* to make a statement of one's opinion — see REMARK 1

commentary *n* **1** a series of explanations or observations on something (as an event) ⟨The TV anchors provided a running *commentary* on the parade.⟩

syn analysis, comment, exposition

rel annotation, explication; note, observation, remark; report, review, write-up
2 *usually* **commentaries** *pl* a relating of events usually in the order in which they happened — see ACCOUNT 1

commerce *n* **1** the buying and selling of goods especially on a large scale and between different places ⟨a government agency in charge of regulating interstate *commerce*⟩

syn business, marketplace, trade, traffic

rel free trade; black market, gray market; dealings, horse-trading; e-tail, merchandising, retailing, wholesaling; bartering
2 doings between individuals or groups — see RELATION 1

commercial *adj* fit or likely to be sold especially on a large scale ⟨the *commercial* fare produced by the Hollywood movie studios⟩

syn marketable, salable (*or* saleable)

rel mass-produced, wholesale

ant noncommercial, nonsalable, uncommercial, unmarketable, unsalable

commingle *vb* to turn into a single mass or entity that is more or less the same throughout — see BLEND 1

commiserate (with) *vb* to have sympathy for — see PITY

commiseration *n* **1** sorrow or the capacity to feel sorrow for another's suffering or misfortune — see SYMPATHY 1
2 the capacity for feeling for another's unhappiness or misfortune — see HEART 1

commissary *n* a person who acts or does business for another — see AGENT 2

commission *n* **1** the granting of power to perform various acts or duties ⟨President Jefferson's *commission* to Lewis and Clark to explore the Louisiana Territory⟩

syn accreditation, authorization, delegation, license (*or* licence), mandate

rel commendation, consignment, entrustment; facilitation, fostering, promotion; commanding, directing, ordering
2 the doing of an action ⟨A single burglar was responsible for the *commission* of all the break-ins.⟩

syn accomplishment, achievement, discharge, enactment, execution, fulfillment (*or* fulfilment), implementation, performance, perpetration, pursuance

rel dispatch, expedition; administration, direction, handling, management; application, operation, practice (*also* practise)

ant nonfulfillment, nonperformance
3 a select group of persons assigned to consider or take action on some matter — see COMMITTEE
4 the state or fact of being chosen for a position or duty — see APPOINTMENT 1

commission *vb* **1** to appoint as one's representative — see DELEGATE 1
2 to give official or legal power to — see AUTHORIZE 1
3 to give a task, duty, or responsibility to — see ENTRUST 1
4 to pick (someone) by one's authority for a specific position or duty — see APPOINT 2

commit *vb* **1** to carry through (as a process) to completion — see PERFORM 1
2 to obligate by prior agreement — see PLEDGE 1
3 to put (something) into the possession or safekeeping of another — see GIVE 2
4 to put in or as if in prison — see IMPRISON

commitment *n* **1** adherence to something to which one is bound by a pledge or duty — see FIDELITY
2 something one must do because of prior agreement — see OBLIGATION 1

committee *n* a select group of persons assigned to consider or take action on some matter ⟨a *committee* in charge of planning the organization's annual holiday party⟩

syn commission, panel

rel standing committee, steering committee; subcommittee; delegation, mission; assembly, body, congress, convocation, council, synod

commodious *adj* more than adequate or average in capacity — see SPACIOUS

common *adj* **1** often observed or encountered ⟨Horse ranches are a *common* sight in that part of the state.⟩

syn commonplace, everyday, familiar, fre-

---

syn synonym(s)	*rel* related words
ant antonym(s)	*near ant* near antonym(s)

quent, household, ordinary, routine, ubiquitous, usual

rel normal, regular, standard; mandatory, obligatory; general, universal; ceaseless, constant, continual, continuous, incessant, unceasing; endemic, popular, prevailing, prevalent, rampant, perennial, recurrent, repeated

phrases a dime a dozen

near ant aberrant, abnormal, irregular, unnatural; intermittent, occasional, sporadic

ant extraordinary, infrequent, rare, seldom, uncommon, unfamiliar, unusual

2 being of the type that is encountered in the normal course of events — see ORDINARY 1

3 belonging or relating to the whole — see GENERAL 1

4 belonging to the class of people of low social or economic rank — see IGNOBLE 1

5 held by or applicable to a majority of the people — see GENERAL 3

6 used or done by a number of people as a group — see COLLECTIVE

7 of average to below average quality — see MEDIOCRE 1

8 of low quality — see CHEAP 2

9 lacking in refinement or good taste — see COARSE 2

commoners *n pl* the body of the community as contrasted with the elite — see MASS 1

commonly *adv* according to the usual course of things — see NATURALLY 2

commonness *n* **1** the fact or state of happening often — see FREQUENCY

2 the quality or state of lacking refinement or good taste — see VULGARITY 1

commonplace *adj* **1** being of the type that is encountered in the normal course of events — see ORDINARY 1

2 often observed or encountered — see COMMON 1

3 used or heard so often as to be dull — see STALE 1

commonplace *n* an idea or expression that has been used by many people ⟨the familiar summertime *commonplace* that "It's not the heat, it's the humidity"⟩

syn banality, cliché (*also* cliche), homily, platitude, shibboleth, truism

rel conventional wisdom, party line, routine; inanity; generality, generalization, simplification; adage, proverb, saw, saying; old wives' tale, stereotype

near ant profundity

commonsense *adj* based on sound reasoning or information — see GOOD 1

common sense *n* the ability to make intelligent decisions especially in everyday matters ⟨*Common sense* should tell you to go to the doctor if you're really hurt.⟩

syn discreetness, discretion, horse sense, levelheadedness, policy, prudence, sense, sensibleness, wisdom, wit

rel street smarts; farsightedness, forehandedness, foresight, foresightedness, forethoughtfulness, judgment (*or* judgement); brains, gray matter, intelligence; logicality, logicalness, practicality, rationality, rationalness; discernment, discrimination, insight, sagacity, sapience; acumen, astuteness, clearheadedness, keenness, penetration, perspicacity, shrewdness; care, caution, circumspection, premeditation

near ant shortsightedness; brainlessness, foolishness, half-wittedness, idiocy, senselessness, stupidity; carelessness, heedlessness; unreasonableness

ant imprudence, indiscretion

commonwealth *n* a body of people composed of one or more nationalities usually with its own territory and government — see NATION

commotion *n* a state of noisy, confused activity ⟨the *commotion* created when the nation's top pop band arrived in town⟩

syn ado, ballyhoo, bluster, bother, bustle, clatter, disturbance, fun, furor, furore, fuss, helter-skelter, hubbub, hullabaloo, hurly-burly, pandemonium, pother, row, ruckus, ruction, rumpus, shindy, squall, stew, stir, storm, to-do, tumult, turmoil, uproar, welter, whirl, williwaw

rel cacophony, clamor, din, howl, hue and cry, noise, outcry, racket, roar; disorder, unrest, upheaval; eruption, flare-up; flurry, flutter, outbreak, outburst; brawl, fracas, fray, hassle, melee (*also* mêlée), scuffle; dither, fever, fret, lather, tizzy

near ant calm, hush, peace, quiet, quietude, rest, stillness, tranquility (*or* tranquillity); order, orderliness

communal *adj* used or done by a number of people as a group — see COLLECTIVE

commune *vb* to form a close personal relationship ⟨After a week in the wilderness, the scouts were really starting to *commune* with nature.⟩

syn bond, click, relate

rel befriend; empathize, identify, sympathize

phrases hit it off

communicable *adj* capable of being passed by physical contact from one person to another — see CONTAGIOUS 1

communicate *vb* **1** to cause (something) to pass from one to another ⟨The infected cook unknowingly *communicated* the disease to hundreds of people.⟩

syn conduct, convey, give, impart, spread, transfer, transfuse, transmit

rel deliver, hand over, surrender, turn over; broadcast, diffuse, disseminate, propagate; hand down, hand on; contaminate, infect, poison

near ant catch, come down (with), contract

2 to engage in an exchange of information or ideas ⟨For decades the two medical centers have been *communicating* about cancer research.⟩

syn brainstorm, intercommunicate

rel correspond; converse, talk; message; bond, commune, relate; accost, approach, board, contact

3 to make known (something abstract) through outward signs — see SHOW 2

communicate (with) *vb* to transmit information or requests to — see CONTACT

communication *n* **1** a piece of conveyed information ⟨the latest *communication* from the crew of the space station⟩

syn dispatch, message

rel bulletin, communiqué, report; memo,

memorandum, notice; epistle, letter, missive, note; electronic mail, e-mail, voice mail; intelligence, news, tidings, word; command, directive, instruction, order

2 the state or fact of being able to exchange information regarding one's current situation — see TOUCH 1

communion *n* a friendly relationship marked by ready communication and mutual understanding — see RAPPORT

communiqué *n* a published statement informing the public of a matter of general interest — see ANNOUNCEMENT

community *n* **1** the people living in a particular area ⟨The whole *community* rallied to the aid of the family who had lost its home.⟩
syn neighborhood
rel city, commune, town; denizens, dwellers, inhabitants, residents; citizenry, culture, people, populace, public, society

2 a group of people with a common interest living in one place ⟨a picturesque seacoast village that is known for its sizable *community* of artists⟩
syn colony
rel circle, clique, coterie, set, society; band, company, troop; clan, family

3 a group of people sharing a common interest and relating together socially — see GANG 2

4 the body of people in a profession or field of activity — see CORPS

5 the quality or state of having many qualities in common — see SIMILARITY 1

6 the feeling of closeness and friendship that exists between companions — see COMPANIONSHIP

commutation *n* a giving or taking of one thing of value in return for another — see EXCHANGE 1

commute *vb* to give up (something) and take something else in return — see CHANGE 3

compact *adj* **1** having a consistency that does not easily yield to pressure — see FIRM 1

2 having little space between items or parts — see CLOSE 1

3 marked by the use of few words to convey much information or meaning — see CONCISE

compact *n* **1** a formal agreement between two or more nations or peoples — see TREATY

2 an arrangement about action to be taken — see AGREEMENT 2

compact *vb* **1** to bring (something) to a central point or under a single control — see CENTRALIZE

2 to reduce in size or volume by or as if by pressing parts or members together — see COMPRESS 1

compacting *n* the act or process of reducing the size or volume of something by or as if by pressing — see COMPRESSION

compactly *adv* in a few words — see SHORTLY 1

compactness *n* the quality or state of being marked by or using only few words to

convey much meaning — see SUCCINCTNESS

compadre *n* a person who has a strong liking for and trust in another — see FRIEND 1

companion *n* **1** a person frequently seen in the company of another — see ASSOCIATE 1

2 one that accompanies another for protection, guidance, or as a courtesy — see ESCORT

3 either of a pair matched in one or more qualities — see MATE 1

4 something that is found along with something else — see ACCOMPANIMENT

companion *vb* to go along with in order to provide assistance, protection, or companionship — see ACCOMPANY 1

companionable *adj* **1** having or showing kindly feeling and sincere interest — see FRIENDLY 1

2 likely to seek or enjoy the company of others — see CONVIVIAL

companionship *n* the feeling of closeness and friendship that exists between companions ⟨The widow's pet cats provided her with *companionship*.⟩
syn brotherhood, camaraderie, community, company, comradeship, fellowship, society
rel amity, benevolence, cordiality, friendliness, friendship, goodwill, kindliness; civility, comity, concord, harmony, rapport; charity, generosity; affinity, compassion, empathy, sympathy; chumminess, familiarity, inseparability, intimacy, nearness; affection, devotion, fondness, love
near ant forlornness, loneliness, lonesomeness

company *n* **1** an organized group of stage performers ⟨a city that is fortunate enough to have two thriving stage *companies*⟩
syn troop, troupe
rel stock company; cast, dramatis personae, ensemble

2 a group of people working together on a task — see GANG 1

3 a commercial or industrial activity or organization — see ENTERPRISE 1

4 the feeling of closeness and friendship that exists between companions — see COMPANIONSHIP

5 a position within view — see PRESENCE 1

company *vb* **1** to come or be together as friends — see ASSOCIATE 1

2 to go along with in order to provide assistance, protection, or companionship — see ACCOMPANY 1

comparable *adj* having qualities in common — see ALIKE

comparative *adj* being such only when compared to something else ⟨If you consider the multimillionaire's yearly income, we're living in *comparative* poverty.⟩
syn almost, approximate, near, relative
rel alike, comparable, similar; equal, equivalent
near ant genuine, real, true
ant absolute, complete, downright, out-and-out, outright, perfect, pure, unqualified

compare *vb* **1** to describe as similar ⟨reviews that *compared* the adventure movie to a thrilling ride on a roller coaster〉

syn assimilate, bracket, equate, liken

rel associate, connect, couple, link; allude, refer, relate; equal, match, parallel

ant contrast

2 to regard or represent as equal or comparable — see EQUATE 1

compare (with) *vb* to come near or nearer to in character or quality — see APPROXIMATE

compartment *n* one of the parts into which an enclosed space is divided 〈a backpack with many handy *compartments* for storing your electronics〉

syn bay, cabin, cell, chamber, cubicle

rel cubbyhole, pigeonhole; alcove, niche, nook, recess; cabinet, drawer, locker; cavity, hole, hollow; booth, box, crib, loge, stall; bunker, crypt, vault

compartment *vb* to arrange or assign according to type — see CLASSIFY 1

compass *n* **1** a guiding or motivating purpose or principle 〈a young go-getter who lost his moral *compass* in the course of his quest for fame and fortune〉

syn cynosure, direction, focus

rel benchmark, criterion, grade, mark, measure, par, standard, touchstone, yardstick; aim, ambition, aspiration, dream, goal, intention, object, objective, purpose, target

2 an area over which activity, capacity, or influence extends — see RANGE 2

3 the line or relatively narrow space that marks the outer limit of something — see BORDER 1

compass *vb* **1** to carry through (as a process) to completion — see PERFORM 1

2 to travel completely around — see ENCIRCLE 1

3 to form a circle around — see SURROUND

4 to have a clear idea of — see COMPREHEND

compassion *n* **1** sorrow or the capacity to feel sorrow for another's suffering or misfortune — see SYMPATHY 1

2 the capacity for feeling for another's unhappiness or misfortune — see HEART 1

compassionate *adj* **1** having or marked by sympathy and consideration for others — see HUMANE 1

2 having or showing the capacity for sharing the feelings of another — see SYMPATHETIC 1

compatibility *n* peaceful coexistence — see HARMONY 2

compatible *adj* **1** having or marked by agreement in feeling or action — see HARMONIOUS 3

2 not having or showing any apparent conflict — see CONSISTENT

compatriot *n* **1** a person living in or originally from the same country as another 〈an appeal to all of his *compatriots* to come to their country's aid in its hour of need〉

syn countryman

rel countrywoman; nationalist, patriot; citizen, national, subject; aborigine, native; resident

near ant alien, foreigner, immigrant, outsider

2 a person frequently seen in the company of another — see ASSOCIATE 1

compel *vb* to cause (a person) to give in to pressure — see FORCE

compelling *adj* **1** having the power to persuade — see COGENT

2 needing immediate attention — see ACUTE 2

compendious *adj* **1** covering everything or all important points — see ENCYCLOPEDIC

2 marked by the use of few words to convey much information or meaning — see CONCISE

compensate *vb* **1** to provide (someone) with a just payment for loss or injury 〈You'll have to *compensate* the neighbors for cutting down their tree.〉

syn indemnify, recompense, recoup, remunerate, requite, satisfy

rel refund, reimburse, repay; redress, remedy, repair; discharge, pay, quit

2 to give (someone) the sum of money owed for goods or services received — see PAY 1

compensate (for) *vb* to balance with an equal force so as to make ineffective — see OFFSET

compensation *n* **1** payment to another for a loss or injury 〈a warehouse worker who received a large *compensation* for his injury while on the job〉

syn damages, indemnification, indemnity, quittance, recompense, recoupment, redress, remuneration, reparation, reprisal(s), requital, restitution, satisfaction

rel amends, atonement, expiation; refund, reimbursement, repayment; settlement; punishment, retaliation

2 something (as money) that is given or received in return for goods or services — see PAYMENT 2

3 the act of offering money in exchange for goods or services — see PAYMENT 1

compete *vb* to engage in a contest 〈prizefighters *competing* for the world heavyweight championship〉

syn battle, contend, face off, fight, race, rival, vie

rel challenge, engage, play; jockey, maneuver; try out; train, work

competence *n* the physical or mental power to do something — see ABILITY

competency *n* the physical or mental power to do something — see ABILITY

competent *adj* **1** having the required skills for an acceptable level of performance 〈Any *competent* mechanic should be able to fix that.〉

syn able, capable, equal, fit, good, qualified, suitable

rel accomplished, ace, adept, experienced, expert, master, masterful, masterly, practiced (*also* practised), proficient, seasoned, skilled, skillful, veteran; overqualified; prepared, schooled, trained; apt, ready, willing; all-around (*also* all-round), protean, versatile

phrases on the ball

near ant inexperienced, inexpert, unseasoned, unskilled, unskillful; unprepared, unschooled, untrained; beginning, green, new, raw, untested, untried *ant* incompetent, inept, poor, unfit, un-qualified

2 being what is called for by accepted standards of right and wrong — see JUST 1

competently *adv* in a skillful or expert manner — see WELL 3

competition *n* **1** a competitive encounter between individuals or groups carried on for amusement, exercise, or in pursuit of a prize — see GAME 1

2 one who strives for the same thing as another — see COMPETITOR

3 an earnest effort for superiority or victory over another — see CONTEST 1

competitor *n* one who strives for the same thing as another ⟨The *competitors* for this prestigious science award come from the best high schools in the country.⟩

syn challenger, competition, contender, contestant, rival

rel archrival; finalist, semifinalist; also-ran, entrant, entry, player; adversary, antagonist, opponent

ant noncompetitor

compilation *n* a collection of writings — see ANTHOLOGY

compile *vb* to bring together from several sources into a single volume or list ⟨*compiled* the best short stories ever written into one fat book⟩

syn collect

rel edit, recompile, redact, redraft, reedit, revamp, revise, rework; accumulate, amass, assemble, collate, gather, group

complacence *n* **1** an often unjustified feeling of being pleased with oneself or with one's situation or achievements ⟨the *complacence* of some of the rich kids at the exclusive private school⟩

syn complacency, conceit, conceitedness, ego, egotism, pompousness, pride, pridefulness, self-admiration, self-conceit, self-esteem, self-importance, self-satisfaction, smugness, vaingloriousness, vainglory, vainness, vanity

rel assurance, confidence, self-assurance, self-confidence; self-righteousness; arrogance, disdainfulness, haughtiness, imperiousness, lordliness, self-assertion, snobbishness, superciliousness, superiority; hubris, overconfidence, presumption; pretense (*or* pretence), pretension, pretentiousness; egoism, self-centeredness, selfishness; self-pride, self-respect

near ant diffidence, self-doubt; self-disgust, self-hate, self-loathing; altruism, unselfishness; bashfulness, demureness, shyness, timidity, timidness; passiveness, passivity

ant humbleness, humility, modesty

2 lack of interest or concern — see INDIFFERENCE

complacency *n* an often unjustified feeling of being pleased with oneself or with one's situation or achievements — see COMPLACENCE 1

complacent *adj* **1** having or showing a lack of interest or concern — see INDIFFERENT 1

2 having too high an opinion of oneself — see CONCEITED

---

syn synonym(s)   *rel* related words
ant antonym(s)   *near ant* near antonym(s)

complain *vb* to express dissatisfaction, pain, or resentment usually tiresomely ⟨the time-honored tradition of new recruits *complaining* about the food in the mess hall⟩

syn beef, bellyache, carp, crab, croak, fuss, gripe, grouch, grouse, growl, grumble, grump, holler, kick, moan, murmur, mutter, nag, scream, squawk, squeal, wail, whimper, whine, yammer, yowl

rel object (to), protest, quarrel (with); cavil, quibble; fret, stew, worry; blubber, cry, sob; bemoan, bewail, deplore, lament

phrases kick up a fuss

near ant accept, bear, countenance, endure, take, tolerate; applaud, cheer, commend

ant crow, delight, rejoice

complainant *n* the person in a legal proceeding who makes a charge of wrongdoing against another ⟨The *complainant* charged that the defendant had broken the ironclad contract that both had signed.⟩

syn plaintiff

rel accuser, litigant, party, suitor; appellant, petitioner, pleader

near ant accused

ant defendant

complainer *n* **1** a person who makes frequent complaints usually about little things — see CRYBABY

2 an irritable and complaining person — see GROUCH 1

complaint *n* **1** an expression of dissatisfaction, pain, or resentment ⟨a warning that if there were any more *complaints*, we were turning around and not going to the beach after all⟩

syn beef, carp, fuss, grievance, gripe, grouch, grouse, grumble, holler, lament, moan, murmur, plaint, squawk, wail, whimper, whine, yammer

rel challenge, demur, expostulation, kick, objection, protest, quibble, remonstrance, stink

near ant commendation, compliment, plaudit; acclaim, applause, praise; approval, endorsement (*also* indorsement), sanction

2 a feeling or declaration of disapproval or dissent — see OBJECTION

3 a formal claim of criminal wrongdoing against a person — see CHARGE 1

4 an abnormal state that disrupts a plant's or animal's normal bodily functioning — see DISEASE

complaisance *n* a desire or disposition to please ⟨took advantage of their *complaisance* to get what she wanted⟩

syn amenability, amiability, good-naturedness

rel affability, amicability, amicableness, congeniality, cordiality, friendliness, geniality, sociability; agreeableness, graciousness, pleasantness; kindheartedness, kindliness, warmheartedness; acquiescence, compliance, docility, passivity, submissiveness

near ant disagreeableness, sullenness, surliness, ungraciousness; disobedience, intractability, recalcitrance

complement *n* **1** something that serves to complete or make up for a deficiency in something else ⟨With his practicality and her refreshing enthusiasm, they are perfect *complements* to each other.⟩

syn supplement

rel addendum, addition; adjunct, annex, appendage, extension; accessory (*also* accessary), accompaniment, appliance, attachment; additive, filler

2 the largest number or amount that something can hold — see CAPACITY 1

complement *vb* to serve as a completing element to ⟨This silk handkerchief will *complement* your suit very nicely and give it a bit of dash.⟩

syn complete, round (off *or* out)

rel finish (off), flesh (out); adorn, beautify, decorate, embellish; better, enhance, improve; constitute, form, make up; enrich, perfect

complementary *adj* related to each other in such a way that one completes the other ⟨The *complementary* contributions of the decorating and cleanup committees were essential to the success of the school dance.⟩

syn reciprocal, supplemental, supplementary

rel cooperative, mutual, symbiotic; collective, combined, common, communal, conjoint, joint, shared, united

ant noncomplementary, nonreciprocal

complete *adj* **1** not lacking any part or member that properly belongs to it ⟨a *complete* deck of cards⟩

syn comprehensive, entire, full, grand, intact, integral, perfect, plenary, total, whole

rel unabridged, uncut, undiminished; all-out, exhaustive, extensive, maximal; full-blooded, full-blown, full-bore, full-fledged, full-on, full-out, full-scale

near ant abbreviated, abridged, cut, diminished, reduced

ant imperfect, incomplete, partial

2 brought or having come to an end ⟨Your education is never *complete*—there's always something more to learn.⟩

syn completed, concluded, done, down, ended, finished, over, terminated, through, up

rel accomplished, achieved, attained, compassed, realized; dead, defunct, extinct, obsolete; expired

phrases out of hand, out of the way

ant continuing, undone, incomplete, ongoing, uncompleted, unfinished

3 covering everything or all important points — see ENCYCLOPEDIC

4 having no exceptions or restrictions — see ABSOLUTE 1

5 trying all possibilities — see EXHAUSTIVE 1

6 having or showing exceptional knowledge, experience, or skill in a field of endeavor — see PROFICIENT

complete *vb* **1** to bring (something) to a state where nothing remains to be done — see FINISH 1

2 to serve as a completing element to — see COMPLEMENT

3 to bring (an event) to a natural or appropriate stopping point — see CLOSE 3

4 to do what is required by the terms of — see FULFILL 1

completed *adj* brought or having come to an end — see COMPLETE 2

completely *adv* **1** to a full extent or degree — see FULLY 1

2 with attention to all aspects or details — see THOROUGHLY 1

complex *adj* **1** having many parts or aspects that are usually interrelated ⟨This camera is a *complex* instrument that requires careful handling.⟩ ⟨*complex* issues regarding free speech and school discipline⟩

syn complicated, convoluted, elaborate, intricate, involved, knotty, labyrinthine, sophisticated

rel overcomplex, overcomplicated; composite, compound, heterogeneous, mixed, multibranched, multifaceted, multifarious, multipart, varied; challenging, difficult, tough; impenetrable, incomprehensible, inexplicable, Kafkaesque, unfathomable, unintelligible

near ant oversimplified, simplified, simplistic; homogeneous, uniform, unvaried

ant noncomplex, noncomplicated, plain, simple, uncomplicated

2 made or done with great care or with much detail — see ELABORATE 1

complex *n* **1** a structure that is designed and built for a particular purpose — see FACILITY

2 something made up of many interdependent or related parts — see SYSTEM 1

complex *vb* to make complex or difficult — see COMPLICATE

complexion *n* **1** the hue or appearance of the skin and especially of the face ⟨a sunscreen for people with very light *complexions*⟩

syn color, coloring

rel shade, tint, tone; features, lineaments, looks; countenance, face, visage

2 the set of qualities that makes a person, a group of people, or a thing different from others — see NATURE 1

complexity *n* **1** the state or quality of having many interrelated parts or aspects ⟨The *complexity* of the company's computer system is such that a full-time repairman is needed.⟩

syn complicatedness, complication, elaborateness, intricacy, involution, sophistication

rel diversity, heterogeneousness; incomprehensibility, inexplicability

near ant simplification; homogeneity, uniformity

ant plainness, simpleness, simplicity

2 something that makes a situation more complicated or difficult — see COMPLICATION 1

compliance *n* **1** a readiness or willingness to yield to the wishes of others ⟨a strong-willed pop star who is not known for her *compliance*⟩

syn acquiescence, compliancy, deference, docility, obedience, submissiveness

rel amenability, amiability, complaisance, good-naturedness; obsequiousness, servility, subservience, subserviency; conformity; cooperativeness, receptiveness, receptivity; humoring, indulgence; acceptance, assent, consent; capitulation, submission, surrender; affability, amicability, congeniality, cordiality, friendliness, geniality, sociability

near ant animosity, antipathy, enmity, hostility, ill will

ant defiance, disobedience, intractability, recalcitrance

2 a bending to the authority or control of another — see OBEDIENCE 1

3 the following of a custom, rule, or law — see OBSERVANCE 1

compliancy *n* a readiness or willingness to yield to the wishes of others — see COMPLIANCE 1

compliant *adj* readily giving in to the command or authority of another — see OBEDIENT

complicate *vb* to make complex or difficult ⟨The need to go to both a PTA conference and condo board meeting really *complicates* tonight's schedule.⟩

syn complex, embarrass, entangle, perplex, sophisticate

rel develop, elaborate, expand; intensify, magnify; confound, confuse, mess (up), mix (up), muddle; snarl, tangle

near ant abbreviate, cut, shorten; ease, facilitate; disentangle, straighten (out), unravel, untangle; oversimplify

ant simplify, streamline

complicated *adj* **1** having many parts or aspects that are usually interrelated — see COMPLEX 1

2 made or done with great care or with much detail — see ELABORATE 1

complicatedness *n* the state or quality of having many interrelated parts or aspects — see COMPLEXITY 1

complication *n* **1** something that makes a situation more complicated or difficult ⟨The food allergies of the guests were just another *complication* for the couple trying to plan their wedding reception.⟩

syn complexity, difficulty, intricacy

rel aftereffect, ramification, side effect (*also* side reaction); subtlety, technicality; annoyance, bother, headache, inconvenience, matter, trouble

phrases fly in the ointment

2 an abnormal state that disrupts a plant's or animal's normal bodily functioning — see DISEASE

3 the state or quality of having many interrelated parts or aspects — see COMPLEXITY 1

complicity *n* a secret agreement or cooperation between two parties for an illegal or dishonest purpose — see COLLUSION

compliment *n* **1** an admiring personal remark ⟨someone who does not know how to accept a *compliment* graciously⟩

syn bouquet

rel accolade, citation, commendation, encomium, eulogy, homage, paean, panegyric, salutation, tribute, valentine

near ant affront, barb, dart, dig, epithet, insult, put-down, slight, slur

2 compliments *pl* best wishes ⟨Please extend our *compliments* to the chef for a great meal.⟩

syn congratulations, felicitations, greetings, regards, respects

rel approval, benediction, blessing, endorsement (*also* indorsement); acknowledgment (*or* acknowledgement), citation, commendation; adulation, flattery, praise; well-wishing

near ant dig, gibe (*or* jibe), insult, putdown, taunt

compliment *vb* to express to (someone) admiration for his or her success or good fortune — see CONGRATULATE

complimentary *adj* **1** expressing approval — see FAVORABLE 1

2 not costing or charging anything — see FREE 4

comply (with) *vb* **1** to act according to the commands of — see OBEY

2 to do what is required by the terms of — see FULFILL 1

component *n* one of the parts that make up a whole — see ELEMENT 1

comport *vb* **1** to be in agreement on every point — see CHECK 1

2 to manage the actions of (oneself) in a particular way — see BEHAVE

comportment *n* the way or manner in which one conducts oneself — see BEHAVIOR

compose *vb* **1** to put (something) into proper and usually carefully worked out written form ⟨*composed* a statement on this hot-button issue that managed to satisfy absolutely no one⟩

syn cast, craft, draft, draw up, formulate, frame, prepare

rel fabricate, fashion, form, sculpture, shape; couch, express, phrase, state, verbalize, word; author, indite, pen, write; conceive, concoct, devise; build, construct, make; assemble, compound, piece (together); redraft, reformulate, reframe

phrases put together

2 to be all the substance of — see CONSTITUTE 1

3 to free from distress or disturbance — see CALM 1

4 to gain emotional or mental control of — see COLLECT 1

composed *adj* free from emotional or mental agitation — see CALM 2

composer *n* a person who writes musical compositions ⟨a versatile *composer* whose works include operas, symphonies, concertos, and sonatas⟩

syn musician

rel cocomposer; songwriter, tunesmith; symphonist; arranger, orchestrator (*also* orchestrater); scorer; librettist, lyricist, lyrist

composite *adj* made from the joining of two or more parts or elements ⟨The movie's special effects included the use of many *composite* photographs.⟩

syn amalgamated, compound

rel blended, combined, commingled, mingled, mixed; coalescent, fused, integrated; interlaced, intermixed, intertwined, interwoven; cut-and-paste

near ant uncombined, unmixed

ant noncompound, simple

composite *n* a distinct entity formed by the combining of two or more different things — see BLEND

---

syn synonym(s)   *rel* related words
ant antonym(s)   *near ant* near antonym(s)

composite *vb* to turn into a single mass or entity that is more or less the same throughout — see BLEND 1

composition *n* **1** a literary, musical, or artistic production ⟨The *compositions* of Michelangelo include the dome of St. Peter's, the ceiling of the Sistine Chapel, and his monumental statue of David.⟩
syn number, opus, piece, work
rel classic, magnum opus, masterpiece, pièce de résistance, showpiece; model, outline, sketch
2 a short piece of writing done as a school exercise ⟨a teacher who is fond of having her class write *compositions*⟩
syn paper, theme
rel article, essay, story
3 the way in which the elements of something (as a work of art) are arranged ⟨Student photographers learn the importance of *composition* in creating striking images.⟩
syn arrangement, configuration, design, form, format, getup, layout, makeup, pattern
rel motif, theme
4 a short piece of writing typically expressing a point of view — see ESSAY 1

composure *n* evenness of emotions or temper — see EQUANIMITY

compound *adj* made from the joining of two or more parts or elements — see COMPOSITE

compound *n* a distinct entity formed by the combining of two or more different things — see BLEND

compound *vb* **1** to make greater in size, amount, or number — see INCREASE 1
2 to put or bring together so as to form a new and longer whole — see CONNECT 1

comprehend *vb* **1** to have a clear idea of ⟨the age at which children can *comprehend* the difference between right and wrong⟩
syn appreciate, apprehend, assimilate, behold, catch, catch on (to), compass, conceive, decipher, decode, dig, discern, get, grasp, know, make, make out, perceive, recognize, register, savvy, see, seize, sense, tumble (to), understand
rel absorb, digest, take in; realize; fathom, penetrate, pierce
phrases pick up on
near ant misapprehend, misconceive, misconstrue, misinterpret, misread, mistake, misunderstand
ant miss
2 to have a practical understanding of — see KNOW 1
3 to have as part of a whole — see INCLUDE 1

comprehension *n* the knowledge gained from the process of coming to know or understand something ⟨the president's *comprehension* of the situation⟩
syn appreciation, apprehension, grasp, grip, hold, perception, understanding
rel absorption, assimilation, digestion, uptake; conception, visualization; awareness, enlightenment, realization
near ant misapprehension, miscomprehension, misinterpretation, misperception, misunderstanding
ant noncomprehension

comprehensive *adj* **1** covering everything or all important points — see ENCYCLOPEDIC
2 not lacking any part or member that properly belongs to it — see COMPLETE 1
3 trying all possibilities — see EXHAUSTIVE 1

comprehensively *adv* with attention to all aspects or details — see THOROUGHLY 1

compress *vb* **1** to reduce in size or volume by or as if by pressing parts or members together ⟨a science textbook that *compresses* a lot of information about anatomy into a few short chapters⟩
syn capsule, collapse, compact, condense, constrict, contract, squeeze
rel cram, crowd, jam, jam-pack, pack; abbreviate, abridge, curtail, shorten; downsize, shrink; concentrate, consolidate; simplify, streamline; decrease, diminish, lessen
near ant dilate, disperse, dissipate, scatter; distend, inflate, swell
ant expand, open, outspread, outstretch
2 to become smaller in size or volume through the drawing together of particles of matter — see CONTRACT 2

compression *n* the act or process of reducing the size or volume of something by or as if by pressing ⟨The *compression* of a long, complicated story into a two-hour movie is never easy.⟩
syn compacting, condensation, constriction, contraction, squeeze, squeezing
rel abbreviation, abridgment (*or* abridgement), curtailment, shortening; concentration, consolidation; simplification, streamlining; decreasing, diminishment, lessening
near ant dilation, dispersion, dissipation, scattering; distension (*or* distention), swelling
ant decompression, expansion

comprise *vb* **1** to be made up of ⟨The mall *comprises* three department stores and 80 smaller shops selling specialized goods.⟩
syn consist (of), contain, muster
rel comprehend, embrace, encompass, entail, include, involve, take in; assimilate, embody, incorporate
2 to be all the substance of — see CONSTITUTE 1

compromise *n* the act or practice of each side giving up something in order to reach an agreement — see CONCESSION 1

compromise *vb* **1** to place in danger — see ENDANGER
2 to reduce the soundness, effectiveness, or perfection of — see DAMAGE 1

compulsion *n* the use of power to impose one's will on another — see FORCE 2

compulsive *adj* caused by or suggestive of an irresistible urge ⟨His *compulsive* clowning around can sometimes be annoying.⟩
syn besetting, impulsive, obsessive
rel irrepressible, uncontrollable; automatic, instinctive, involuntary, reflex, spontaneous; conditioned, mechanical; unconscious, unthinking, unwitting; capricious, unpredictable, whimsical
near ant unforced, voluntary, willful (*or* wilful); controllable, manageable, resistible

compulsory adj forcing one's compliance or participation by or as if by law — see MANDATORY

compunction n an uneasy feeling about the rightness of what one is doing or going to do — see QUALM

computation n the act or process of performing mathematical operations to find a value — see CALCULATION

compute vb to determine (a value) by doing the necessary mathematical operations — see CALCULATE 1

comrade n 1 a person frequently seen in the company of another — see ASSOCIATE 1
2 a person who has a strong liking for and trust in another — see FRIEND 1

comradeship n the feeling of closeness and friendship that exists between companions — see COMPANIONSHIP 1

¹**con** n a person convicted as a criminal and serving a prison sentence — see CONVICT

²**con** n an instance of the use of dishonest methods to acquire something of value — see FRAUD 1

¹**con** vb 1 to commit to memory — see MEMORIZE
2 to look over closely (as for judging quality or condition) — see INSPECT

²**con** vb 1 to rob by the use of trickery or threats — see FLEECE
2 to cause to believe what is untrue — see DECEIVE

concatenate vb 1 to put or bring together so as to form a new and longer whole — see CONNECT 1
2 to put together into a series by means of or as if by means of a thread — see THREAD 2

concatenation n a series of things linked together — see CHAIN 1

concave adj curved inward — see HOLLOW

concavity n a sunken area forming a separate space — see HOLE 2

conceal vb 1 to put into a hiding place — see ¹HIDE 1
2 to keep secret or shut off from view — see ¹HIDE 1

concealment n 1 the placing of something out of sight ⟨Your choice of the oven for the *concealment* of the money was unwise.⟩
syn caching, hiding, secretion, stashing
rel burial, burying, entombment, interment, interring
near ant disinterment, unearthing
ant display, exhibition, exposure, parading, showing
2 a place where a person goes to hide or to avoid others — see HIDEOUT

concede vb 1 to accept the truth or existence of (something) usually reluctantly — see ADMIT 1
2 to cease resistance (as to another's arguments, demands, or control) — see YIELD 3

conceit n 1 an elaborate or fanciful way of expressing something ⟨the *conceit* that the crowd at the outdoor rock concert was a vast sea of people waving to the beat of the music⟩

syn metaphor
rel device; analogy, circumlocution, code word, crank, dead metaphor, euphemism, simile; mixed metaphor
phrases figure of speech
2 a conception or image created by the imagination and having no objective reality — see FANTASY 1
3 an often unjustified feeling of being pleased with oneself or with one's situation or achievements — see COMPLACENCE 1

conceited adj having too high an opinion of oneself or image ⟨a *conceited* basketball player who was always too busy even to sign autographs⟩
syn assured, complacent, consequential, egoistic (*also* egoistical), egotistic (*or* egotistical), important, overweening, pompous, prideful, proud, self-conceited, self-important, self-satisfied, smug, stuck-up, vain, vainglorious
rel blusterous, blustery, boastful, bombastic, braggart, bragging, braggy, cocky, swaggering; arrogant, cavalier, disdainful, haughty, high-hat, lofty, lordly, masterful, self-assertive, supercilious, superior, toplofty (*also* toploftical), uppish, uppity; domineering, high-handed, imperious; highfalutin (*also* hifalutin), holier-than-thou, pretentious; overconfident, presuming, presumptuous; confident, self-assured, self-confident; self-adulatory, self-congratulatory, self-contented, self-gratulatory; self-applauding, self-dramatizing, self-glorifying; self-promoting; self-affected, self-centered, self-engrossed, selfish; condescending, patronizing
near ant diffident, self-critical, self-distrustful, self-doubting, self-reproachful, self-reproving; meek, timid, unassertive; down-to-earth, unarrogant, unassuming, unpretentious; bashful, demure, introverted, mousy (*or* mousey), overmodest, retiring, sheepish, shrinking, shy
ant egoless, humble, modest, uncomplacent

conceitedness n an often unjustified feeling of being pleased with oneself or with one's situation or achievements — see COMPLACENCE 1

conceivably adv it is possible — see PERHAPS

conceive vb 1 to form a mental picture of — see IMAGINE 1
2 to have a clear idea of — see COMPREHEND 1
3 to have as an opinion — see BELIEVE 2

concentrate vb 1 to increase the amount of (a substance in a mixture) by removing other substances ⟨Prolonged boiling is required to *concentrate* the sap when making maple syrup.⟩
syn concentrate
rel clarify, clean, cleanse, distill (*also* distil), flush, leach, purge, purify, refine; decoct, reduce; compact, harden, solidify; deepen, enhance, heighten, intensify; evaporate, extract, remove; enrich, fortify, richen, strengthen; reconcentrate, recondense
near ant adulterate, cut, thin, weaken
ant dilute, water (down)
2 to fix (as one's attention) steadily toward

---

syn synonym(s) *rel* related words
ant antonym(s) *near ant* near antonym(s)

a central objective ⟨a president who will try to *concentrate* public attention on the problems of inner cities⟩

syn center, fasten, focus, rivet, train

rel aim, direct, home (in on), hone in (on), level, nail, point, set, zero (in on); attend, heed, mind; fixate (on), obsess (over); refocus

3 to bring (something) to a central point or under a single control — see CENTRALIZE

4 to bring together in one body or place — see GATHER 1

5 to come together into one body or place — see ASSEMBLE 1

6 to gradually form into a layer, pile, or mass — see COLLECT 2

concentrated *adj* **1** having an abundance of some characteristic quality (as flavor) — see FULL-BODIED

2 not divided or scattered among several areas of interest or concern — see WHOLE 1

concentration *n* a focusing of the mind on something — see ATTENTION 1

concept *n* **1** an idea or statement about all of the members of a group or all the instances of a situation — see GENERALIZATION

2 something imagined or pictured in the mind — see IDEA 1

conception *n* **1** an idea or statement about all of the members of a group or all the instances of a situation — see GENERALIZATION

2 something imagined or pictured in the mind — see IDEA 1

conceptual *adj* dealing with or expressing a quality or idea — see ABSTRACT 1

concern *n* **1** a commercial or industrial activity or organization — see ENTERPRISE 1

2 an uneasy state of mind usually over the possibility of an anticipated misfortune or trouble — see ANXIETY 1

concern *vb* **1** to have (something) as a subject matter ⟨The book *concerns* the voyages of Arctic explorer Matthew Henson.⟩

syn cover, deal (with), pertain (to), treat (of)

rel appertain (to), bear (on *or* upon), refer (to), relate (to); advert (to), allude (to), cite, glance (upon), instance, mention, name, note, notice, quote, specify, touch (upon); offer, present; contain, embrace, encompass, entail, include, incorporate

phrases have to do with

near ant exclude, omit; disregard, forget, ignore, neglect, overlook, overpass, pass over, slight, slur (over); brush (aside *or* off), reject, shrug off

2 to be the business or affair of ⟨the problems of air and water pollution that *concern* all of us⟩

syn affect, involve, touch

rel appertain (to), apply (to), bear (on), pertain (to), refer (to), relate (to); embroil, ensnare, entangle, implicate

3 to trouble the mind of; to make uneasy — see DISTURB 1

concerning *prep* having to do with — see ABOUT 1

concert *n* an entertainment featuring singing or the playing of musical instruments

⟨During the summer various groups give *concerts* on the town green.⟩

syn musicale

rel performance, presentation; recital, symphony; hootenanny, jam, jam session, sing, songfest; festival, fete (*or* fête), shindig

concert *vb* **1** to bring about through discussion and compromise — see NEGOTIATE 1

2 to participate or assist in a joint effort to accomplish an end — see COOPERATE 1

concerted *adj* used or done by a number of people as a group — see COLLECTIVE

concession *n* **1** the act or practice of each side giving up something in order to reach an agreement ⟨When trying to get a raise in your salary, it's good to know the art of *concession*.⟩

syn accommodation, compromise, give-and-take, negotiation

rel haggle, horse trade; accord, arrangement, bargain, concurrence, consensus, deal, understanding; agreement, settlement; mediation, treaty

2 an open declaration of something (as a fault or the commission of an offense) about oneself — see CONFESSION

3 something granted as a special favor — see PRIVILEGE

conciliate *vb* **1** to bring to a state free of conflicts, inconsistencies, or differences — see HARMONIZE 2

2 to lessen the anger or agitation of — see PACIFY 1

conciliating *adj* tending to lessen or avoid conflict or hostility — see PACIFIC 1

conciliator *n* one who works with opposing sides in order to bring about an agreement — see MEDIATOR

conciliatory *adj* tending to lessen or avoid conflict or hostility — see PACIFIC 1

concise *adj* marked by the use of few words to convey much information or meaning ⟨a *concise* article on violence in the media that manages to say more than most books on the subject⟩

syn brief, capsule, compact, compendious, crisp, curt, epigrammatic, laconic, pithy, succinct, summary, terse

rel abrupt, blunt, brusque (*also* brusk), short, snippety, snippy; abbreviated, abridged, condensed, curtailed, shortened; meaty, substantial; meaningful, significant; well-turned

near ant redundant, repetitious, tautological, tautologous; enlarged, expanded, supplemented; embellished, embroidered

ant circuitous, circumlocutory, diffuse, long-winded, prolix, rambling, verbose, windy, wordy

concisely *adv* in a few words — see SHORTLY 1

conciseness *n* **1** the condition of being short — see BREVITY 1

2 the quality or state of being marked by or using only few words to convey much meaning — see SUCCINCTNESS

conclude *vb* **1** to bring (an event) to a natural or appropriate stopping point — see CLOSE 3

2 to come to an end — see CEASE 1

3 to bring about through discussion and compromise — see NEGOTIATE 1

148   concluded

4 to come to a judgment about after discussion or consideration — see DECIDE 1

5 to form an opinion or reach a conclusion through reasoning and information — see INFER 1

concluded *adj* brought or having come to an end — see COMPLETE 2

concluding *adj* following all others of the same kind in order or time — see LAST 1

conclusion *n* **1** an opinion arrived at through a process of reasoning ⟨the detective's *conclusion* that the perpetrator had to be left-handed⟩
syn consequence, deduction, determination, induction, inference
rel decision, deliverance, diagnosis, judgment (*or* judgement), resolution, ruling, verdict; conjecture, guess, surmise; assumption, presumption, supposition

2 a position arrived at after consideration — see DECISION 1

3 a condition or occurrence traceable to a cause — see EFFECT 1

4 the last part of a process or action — see FINALE

5 the stopping of a process or activity — see END 1

conclusive *adj* **1** serving to put an end to all debate or questioning ⟨The archeological discovery was *conclusive* proof that the Vikings had indeed settled in North America around 1000 A.D.⟩
syn absolute, clear, decisive, definitive, last
rel determinate, determinative, incontestable, incontrovertible, indisputable, indubitable, irrefutable, unanswerable, undebatable, undeniable, undisputable, unquestionable; unchallenged, uncontested, undisputed; unambiguous, unequivocal; certain, definite, positive, sure; cogent, compelling, convincing, persuasive, telling
near ant debatable, disputable, doubtable, doubtful, moot, problematic (*also* problematical), questionable, refutable; ambiguous, equivocal; debated, disputed
ant inconclusive, indecisive, unclear

2 having the power to persuade — see COGENT

conclusiveness *n* the capacity to persuade — see COGENCY 1

concoct *vb* to create or think of by clever use of the imagination — see INVENT

concoction *n* something (as a device) created for the first time through the use of the imagination — see INVENTION 1

concomitant *adj* present at the same time and place — see COINCIDENT 1

concomitant *n* something that is found along with something else — see ACCOMPANIMENT

concord *n* peaceful coexistence — see HARMONY 2

concordant *adj* not having or showing any apparent conflict — see CONSISTENT

concourse *n* a typically long narrow way connecting parts of a building — see HALL 2

concrete *adj* **1** existing in fact and not merely as a possibility — see ACTUAL

2 relating to or composed of matter — see MATERIAL 1

3 of a particular or exact sort — see EXPRESS 1

concrete *vb* **1** to become physically firm or solid — see HARDEN 1

2 to turn into a single mass or entity that is more or less the same throughout — see BLEND 1

concur *vb* **1** to have or come to the same opinion or point of view — see AGREE 1

2 to occur or exist at the same time — see COINCIDE 1

3 to participate or assist in a joint effort to accomplish an end — see COOPERATE 1

concurrence *n* **1** the occurrence or existence of several things at once ⟨The *concurrence* of my birthday and the concert by my favorite band made my preference for a birthday present pretty obvious.⟩
syn coexistence, coincidence
rel development, happening, occurrence; contemporaneousness, simultaneousness, synchronism, synchrony
near ant asynchrony (*or* asynchronism)

2 the state of being of one opinion about something — see AGREEMENT 1

3 the approval by someone in authority for the doing of something — see PERMISSION

concurrent *adj* **1** existing or occurring at the same period of time — see CONTEMPORARY 1

2 present at the same time and place — see COINCIDENT 1

concurrently *adv* at one and the same time — see TOGETHER 1

concussion *n* **1** a forceful coming together of two things — see IMPACT 1

2 the violent coming together of two bodies into destructive contact — see CRASH 1

condemn *vb* **1** to declare to be morally wrong or evil ⟨Their policies and practices were *condemned* as harmful.⟩
syn censure, damn, decry, denounce, execrate, reprehend, reprobate
rel attack, blame, blast, criticize, dis (*also* diss) [*slang*], dispraise, fault, knock, pan, slam; belittle, deprecate, disparage; blacklist, excommunicate, ostracize; castigate, chastise, rebuke, reprimand, reproach; admonish, chide, reprove; berate, lambaste (*or* lambast), rake, scold, upbraid, vituperate; curse, imprecate; abhor, abominate, detest, hate, loathe, revile
near ant approve, endorse (*also* indorse), sanction; eulogize, exalt, extol (*also* extoll), glorify, laud, praise; acclaim, applaud, commend, hail, salute, tout; consecrate, hallow, sanctify; honor, revere, venerate
ant bless

2 to express one's unfavorable opinion of the worth or quality of — see CRITICIZE

3 to express public or formal disapproval of — see CENSURE 1

4 to find or pronounce guilty — see CONVICT

5 to impose a judicial punishment on — see SENTENCE

condemnation *n* an often public or formal expression of disapproval — see CENSURE

---

syn synonym(s)   *rel* related words
ant antonym(s)   *near ant* near antonym(s)

condensation *n* **1** a shortened version of a written work — see ABRIDGMENT

2 the act or process of reducing the size or volume of something by or as if by pressing — see COMPRESSION

condense *vb* **1** to become smaller in size or volume through the drawing together of particles of matter — see CONTRACT 2

2 to reduce in size or volume by or as if by pressing parts or members together — see COMPRESS 1

3 to increase the amount of (a substance in a mixture) by removing other substances — see CONCENTRATE 1

condescend *vb* **1** to descend to a level that is beneath one's dignity ⟨I will not *condescend* to name-calling.⟩

syn deign, stoop

rel abase, debase, degrade, demean, discredit, disgrace, dishonor, humble, humiliate, lower, shame

near ant rise

2 to assume or treat with an air of superiority ⟨wealthy people who tended to *condescend* to their poor relations⟩

syn lord (it over), patronize, talk down (to)

rel cold-shoulder, cut, high-hat, slight, snub; queen (it over)

condiment *n* something used to enhance the flavor of cooked or prepared food ⟨The cafeteria's self-serve table has a full array of *condiments*.⟩

syn seasoning

rel herb, savory, spice; relish, sauce; flavoring

condition *n* **1** a state of being or fitness ⟨a car that was 10 years old but still in good *condition*⟩

syn estate, fettle, form, health, keeping, kilter, order, repair, shape, trim

rel practice (*also* practise); pass, phase, stage; footing, picture, posture, scene, situation, status; rank, standing

near ant disorder, disrepair

2 something upon which the carrying out of an agreement or offer depends ⟨You'll get a bonus with the *condition* that we meet our sales forecast.⟩

syn contingency, provision, proviso, qualification, reservation, stipulation

rel strings, terms; precondition, prerequisite, requirement, requisite; limitation, modification, restriction; exemption; demand, essential, must, necessity, need

3 an abnormal state that disrupts a plant's or animal's normal bodily functioning — see DISEASE

4 something necessary, indispensable, or unavoidable — see ESSENTIAL 1

5 something that limits one's freedom of action or choice — see RESTRICTION 1

condition *vb* **1** to bring to a proper or desired state of fitness ⟨the length of time that it takes for runners to *condition* their bodies for a marathon⟩

syn season, train

rel fit, prepare, ready; acclimate, acclimatize, accommodate, adapt, adjust, break in, orient, orientate, shape; accustom, familiarize, naturalize; fortify, harden, inure, season, steel, strengthen, toughen

ant decondition

2 to change (something) so as to make it suitable for a new use or situation — see ADAPT

conditional *adj* determined by something else — see DEPENDENT 1

conditioning *n* energetic movement of the body for the sake of physical fitness — see EXERCISE 1

condole (with) *vb* to have sympathy for — see PITY

condone *vb* to dismiss as of little importance — see EXCUSE 1

conduct *n* **1** the act or activity of looking after and making decisions about something ⟨The President left the *conduct* of foreign affairs to the secretary of state.⟩

syn administration, care, charge, control, direction, governance, government, guidance, handling, management, operation, oversight, regulation, running, stewardship, superintendence, superintendency, supervision

rel generalship, leadership, rulership; agency; aegis (*also* egis), custody, guardianship, keeping, lap, protection, safekeeping, trust, tutelage, ward; engineering, logistics, machination, manipulation; coadministration, codirection, comanagement

2 the way or manner in which one conducts oneself — see BEHAVIOR

conduct *vb* **1** to look after and make decisions about ⟨The company's president continues to *conduct* the everyday affairs of the software firm he founded many years ago.⟩

syn administer, carry on, control, direct, govern, guide, handle, keep, manage, operate, overlook, oversee, preside (over), regulate, run, steward, superintend, supervise, tend

rel care (for), mind, watch; lead, pilot, steer; guard, protect, safeguard; micromanage, stage-manage; codirect, comanage

phrases watch over

2 to cause to move to a central point or along a restricted pathway — see CHANNEL

3 to manage the actions of (oneself) in a particular way — see BEHAVE

4 to point out the way for (someone) especially from a position in front — see LEAD 1

5 to cause (something) to pass from one to another — see COMMUNICATE 1

conduit *n* **1** a long hollow cylinder for carrying a substance (as a liquid or gas) — see PIPE 1

2 an open man-made passageway for water — see CHANNEL 1

confection *n* a food having a high sugar content — see SWEET 1

confederacy *n* an association of persons, parties, or states for mutual assistance and protection ⟨a *confederacy* of several small nations who had promised to come to one another's aid if any were attacked⟩

syn alliance, bloc, block, coalition, combination, combine, confederation, federation, league, union

rel cabal, conspiracy, junto; cartel, syndicate, trust; faction, front, fusion, side, wing; association, group, organization;

affiliation, cooperative, partnership; conference

confederate *n* **1** one associated with another in wrongdoing — see ACCOMPLICE

2 someone associated with another to give assistance or moral support — see ALLY

confederate *vb* to form or enter into an association that furthers the interests of its members — see ALLY

confederation *n* **1** an association of persons, parties, or states for mutual assistance and protection — see CONFEDERACY

2 the state of having shared interests or efforts (as in social or business matters) — see ASSOCIATION 1

confer *vb* **1** to give the ownership or benefit of (something) formally or publicly ⟨The British monarch continues to *confer* knighthood on those who are outstanding in their fields of endeavor.⟩

syn accord, award, grant, vest

rel bestow, contribute, donate, give, present, show; furnish, provide, supply; extend, offer, proffer; allocate, appropriate, assign; appoint, designate, dub, fix, name, set

near ant abort, call, call off, drop, recall, repeal, rescind, revoke; abrogate, annul, invalidate, nullify, void, write off; recant, retract, take back; withdraw

2 to exchange viewpoints or seek advice for the purpose of finding a solution to a problem ⟨My parents are going to *confer* with a financial adviser about saving for their retirement.⟩

syn advise, consult, counsel, parley, treat

rel argue, bandy, bat (around), chew over, debate, deliberate, discuss, dispute, hash (over), moot, palaver, talk, talk over, ventilate; rehash; coach, guide, tutor; recommend, suggest; direct, refer (to)

conference *n* **1** a body of people come together in one place — see GATHERING 1

2 a meeting featuring a group discussion — see FORUM 1

3 an exchange of views for the purpose of exploring a subject or deciding an issue — see DISCUSSION 1

confess *vb* **1** to make an acknowledgment of something unpleasant as true or valid ⟨The thief *confessed* to dozens of robberies.⟩

syn admit

rel blab, talk, tattle; babble, spill

near ant clam up, hush, quiet (down), shut up

2 to accept the truth or existence of (something) usually reluctantly — see ADMIT 1

confession *n* an open declaration of something (as a fault or the commission of an offense) about oneself ⟨a *confession* that he had been lying all along⟩

syn acknowledgment (*or* acknowledgement), admission, avowal, concession

rel self-accusation, self-betrayal, self-revelation; self-incrimination, self-recrimination, self-reproach; affirmation, assertion, avouchment, claim, confirmation, declaration, insistence, profession; allowance; hand-wringing; betrayal, disclosure, divulgence, giveaway, revelation; announcement, declaration, proclamation, pronouncement; blame, fault, responsibility; contriteness, contrition, penitence, regret, remorse, remorsefulness, repentance, rue

near ant denial, disallowance, disclaimer, recantation, rejection, renouncement, repudiation

ant disavowal, nonadmission

confidant *n* a person who has a strong liking for and trust in another — see FRIEND 1

confidence *n* **1** great faith in oneself or one's abilities ⟨a lifelong *confidence* that enabled her to achieve great things despite powerful obstacles⟩

syn aplomb, assurance, self-assurance, self-confidence, self-esteem

rel cockiness, complacence, complacency, conceit, conceitedness, ego, egoism, egotism, hubris, overconfidence, pompousness, pride, pridefulness, self-admiration, self-applause, self-assumption, self-complacency, self-conceit, self-consequence, self-content, self-contentment, self-glorification, self-importance, self-opinion, self-partiality, self-satisfaction, smugness, vaingloriousness, vainglory, vanity; calmness, composure, coolness, equanimity; self-poise, self-possession

near ant apprehension, doubt, misgiving

ant diffidence, insecurity, self-distrust, self-doubt

2 a state of mind in which one is free from doubt ⟨the *confidence* with which the game show contestant answered every question⟩

syn assurance, assuredness, certainty, certitude, conviction, face, positiveness, satisfaction, sureness, surety

rel decisiveness, determination, firmness, purposefulness, resoluteness, resolution, resolve

near ant hesitancy, hesitation, indecisiveness, irresolution; disbelief, incredulity, unbelief; anxiety, concern, misgiving; distrust, mistrust, suspicion

ant doubt, incertitude, nonconfidence, uncertainty

3 firm belief in the integrity, ability, effectiveness, or genuineness of someone or something — see TRUST 1

4 information shared only with another or with a select few — see SECRET 1

confident *adj* **1** having or showing great faith in oneself or one's abilities ⟨You'll need to be *confident*—even in the face of rejection—if you want to pursue a career in show business.⟩

syn assured, secure, self-assured, self-confident

rel collected, composed, cool, coolheaded, poised, self-possessed, serene, tranquil, unperturbed, unshaken; hopeful, optimistic, rosy, sanguine, upbeat; complacent, conceited, egoistic (*also* egoistical), egotistic (*or* egotistical), important, overweening, pompous, prideful, proud, self-affected, self-applauding, self-centered, self-complacent, self-conceited, self-contented, self-important, self-pleased, self-satisfied; self-promoting, smug, stuck-up, vain,

conformity 151

vainglorious; imperturbable, nerveless, unflappable, unself-conscious, unshakable;
disciplined, self-collected, self-contained,
self-controlled, self-poised; self-reliant, self-
sufficient
near ant meek, timid, unassertive; humble, modest, unassuming, unpretentious;
jittery, jumpy, nervous; bashful, demure,
mousy (*or* mousey); overmodest, quiet,
reserved, shy; self-critical, self-reproachful, self-reproving
ant diffident, insecure, self-distrustful,
self-doubting
2 having or showing a mind free from
doubt — see CERTAIN 2
confidential *adj* not known or meant to
be known by the general populace — see
PRIVATE 1
confiding *adj* having or showing trust in
another — see TRUSTING 1
configuration *n* **1** the arrangement of
parts that gives something its basic form
— see FRAME 1
2 the way in which something is sized, arranged, or organized — see FORMAT 1
3 the way in which the elements of something (as a work of art) are arranged —
see COMPOSITION 3
4 the outward appearance of something as
distinguished from its substance — see
FORM 1
confine *vb* **1** to set bounds or an upper
limit for — see LIMIT 1
2 to put in or as if in prison — see IMPRISON
confinement *n* **1** the act of confining or
the state of being confined — see INTERN-
MENT
2 the act or practice of keeping something
(as an activity) within certain boundaries
— see RESTRICTION 2
confines *n pl* **1** a real or imaginary point
beyond which a person or thing cannot go
— see LIMIT 1
2 the line or relatively narrow space that
marks the outer limit of something — see
BORDER 1
3 an area over which activity, capacity, or
influence extends — see RANGE 2
confirm *vb* **1** to give evidence or testimony
to the truth or factualness of ⟨several eye-
witnesses who can *confirm* the defendant's
account of what happened⟩
syn argue, attest, authenticate, bear out,
certify, corroborate, substantiate, support,
validate, verify, vindicate
rel avouch, back (up), testify (to), vouch
(for), witness; guarantee, warrant; affirm,
assert, aver, avow, declare, profess; demonstrate, document, establish, prove
near ant contradict, gainsay; deny, disavow, disclaim; challenge, contest, dispute, question
ant disprove, rebut, refute
2 to give official acceptance of as satisfactory — see APPROVE
confirmable *adj* capable of being proven
as true or real — see VERIFIABLE
confirmation *n* evidence presented in
support of the truth or accuracy of a claim
— see PROOF
confirmatory *adj* serving to give support
to the truth or factualness of something —
see CORROBORATIVE

confirmed *adj* **1** being such by habit and
not likely to change — see HABITUAL 1
2 firmly established over time — see IN-
VETERATE 1
confirming *adj* serving to give support to
the truth or factualness of something —
see CORROBORATIVE
confiscate *vb* to take ownership or control of (something) by right of one's authority ⟨Anything that might be used as a
weapon will be *confiscated* by the security
guards.⟩
syn attach, expropriate, sequester
rel garnishee; appropriate, arrogate, preempt, usurp; commandeer, seize, take
over
near ant cede, deliver, forfeit, give up,
hand over, release, relinquish, render, surrender, turn over, yield
conflagration *n* **1** a destructive burning
— see FIRE 1
2 a state of armed violent struggle between states, nations, or groups — see
WAR 1
conflict *n* **1** a lack of agreement or harmony — see DISCORD
2 a physical dispute between opposing individuals or groups — see FIGHT 1
3 a state of armed violent struggle between states, nations, or groups — see
WAR 1
4 an earnest effort for superiority or victory over another — see CONTEST 1
conflict *vb* to be out of harmony or agreement usually noticeably — see CLASH
conflicting *adj* not being in agreement or
harmony — see INCONSISTENT 1
confluence *n* the coming together of two
or more things to the same point — see
CONVERGENCE
conform *vb* **1** to be in agreement on every
point — see CHECK 1
2 to form a pleasing relationship — see
HARMONIZE 1
3 to bring to a state free of conflicts, inconsistencies, or differences — see HAR-
MONIZE 2
4 to change (something) so as to make it
suitable for a new use or situation — see
ADAPT
conform (to) *vb* to act according to the
commands of — see OBEY
conformable *adj* readily giving in to the
command or authority of another — see
OBEDIENT
conformable (to) *adj* not having or showing any apparent conflict — see CONSIS-
TENT
conformation *n* **1** the outward appearance of something as distinguished from
its substance — see FORM 1
2 the way in which something is sized, arranged, or organized — see FORMAT 1
conformity *n* **1** a state of consistency ⟨The
simple lifestyle of the Amish is in *conformity* with their ascetic religious beliefs.⟩
syn accord, accordance, agreement, congruity, consonance, harmony, tune
rel compatibility; assimilation, integration; oneness, solidarity, togetherness; affinity, empathy, sympathy
near ant contrast, discrepancy, disparateness, disparity, dissimilarity, distinction,

distinctiveness, distinctness, diverseness, diversity, unlikeness; deviance, divergence; discord, discordance, dissension (*also* dissention), dissent, dissidence, disunity, friction, strife; variability, variance; incompatibility

ant conflict, disagreement, incongruence, incongruity, incongruousness

2 the following of a custom, rule, or law — see OBSERVANCE 1

confound *vb* **1** to throw into a state of mental uncertainty — see CONFUSE 1

2 to throw into a state of self-conscious distress — see EMBARRASS 1

3 to fail to differentiate (a thing) from something similar or related — see CONFUSE 3

4 to prove to be false — see DISPROVE

confront *vb* to oppose (something hostile or dangerous) with firmness or courage — see FACE 2

confrontation *n* an earnest effort for superiority or victory over another — see CONTEST 1

confuse *vb* **1** to throw into a state of mental uncertainty ⟨The similar-sounding words "censure" and "censor" often *confuse* people.⟩

syn addle, baffle, beat, befog, befuddle, bemuse, bewilder, confound, discombobulate, disorient, fox, get, maze, muddle, muddy, mystify, perplex, puzzle, vex

rel stick, stump; abash, discomfit, disconcert, discountenance, embarrass, faze, fluster, mortify, nonplus, rattle; agitate, bother, chagrin, discomfort, discompose, dismay, disquiet, distress, disturb, perturb, stun, unhinge, unsettle, upset; beguile, cozen, deceive, delude, dupe, fool, gull, hoax, hoodwink, humbug, misguide, mislead, snow, string along, take in, trick

phrases blow one's mind, go to one's head

near ant assure, reassure, satisfy; enlighten, inform

2 to make (something) unclear to the understanding ⟨Stop *confusing* the issue with irrelevant facts!⟩

syn becloud, befog, blur, cloud, fog, muddy

rel complicate, perplex, sophisticate; entangle, snarl, tangle; disarrange, disarray, discompose, dishevel, disorder, disrupt, disturb, jumble, mess (up), mix (up), muddle, scramble, shuffle, tousle, upset

near ant simplify, streamline; disentangle, straighten (out), undo, unravel, unscramble, untangle; decipher, decode; analyze, break down

ant clarify, clear (up), illuminate

3 to fail to differentiate (a thing) from something similar or related ⟨A lot of people *confuse* popular fame with enduring achievement.⟩

syn confound, mistake, mix (up)

rel lump (together); misapply, miscall, misidentify, misname

ant difference, differentiate, discriminate, distinguish, separate

4 to throw into a state of self-conscious distress — see EMBARRASS 1

5 to undo the proper order or arrangement of — see DISORDER

confused *adj* **1** lacking in order, neatness, and often cleanliness — see MESSY

2 suffering from mental confusion — see DIZZY 2

confusion *n* **1** a state of mental uncertainty ⟨The farmer's driving directions to the fairground just left us in total *confusion*.⟩

syn bafflement, befuddlement, bewilderment, distraction, fog, muddle, mystification, perplexity, puzzlement, tangle, whirl

rel abashment, discomfiture, disconcertment, embarrassment, mortification; agitation, chagrin, discomfort, dismay, disquiet, distress, disturbance, perturbation, upset; bother, commotion, dither, flurry, fluster, fuss, stew, turmoil

near ant assurance, certainty, certitude, confidence, conviction, positiveness, sureness

2 a state in which everything is out of order — see CHAOS

3 the emotional state of being made self-consciously uncomfortable — see EMBARRASSMENT 1

confutation *n* something (as an argument) that serves to disprove ⟨He crafted an elegant *confutation* to the argument that animals do not feel pain.⟩

syn disproof, rebuttal, refutation

rel counterargument, counterevidence

near ant attestation, confirmation, corroboration, documentation, evidence, substantiation, testament, testimony, validation, witness; authentication, identification, manifestation, verification

ant proof

confute *vb* to prove to be false — see DISPROVE

congeal *vb* **1** to become physically firm or solid — see HARDEN 1

2 to turn from a liquid into a substance resembling jelly — see COAGULATE

congenial *adj* **1** giving pleasure or contentment to the mind or senses — see PLEASANT 1

2 having or marked by agreement in feeling or action — see HARMONIOUS 3

congenital *adj* being such from birth or by nature — see NATURAL 1

congest *vb* to prevent passage through by filling with something — see CLOG 1

conglomerate *n* a group of businesses or enterprises under one control ⟨The huge media *conglomerate* owns TV and radio stations, a cable company, and a movie studio.⟩

syn empire

rel cartel, combination, combine, syndicate, trust; chain; association, corporation, organization, pool

conglomerate *vb* **1** to come together into one body or place — see ASSEMBLE 1

2 to gradually form into a layer, pile, or mass — see COLLECT 2

congratulate *vb* to express to (someone) admiration for his or her success or good fortune ⟨Let me be the first to *congratulate* you on winning the award.⟩

syn compliment, felicitate, hug

rel applaud, cheer, commend, hail, salute; extol (*also* extoll), glorify, laud, praise

---

syn synonym(s)   *rel* related words
ant antonym(s)   *near ant* near antonym(s)

near ant bad-mouth, belittle, cry down, decry, deprecate, depreciate, diminish, discount, disparage, minimize, put down, write off; jeer, mock, ridicule, taunt, tease

congratulations *n pl* best wishes — see COMPLIMENT 2

congregate *vb* **1** to bring together in one body or place — see GATHER 1
2 to come together into one body or place — see ASSEMBLE 1

congregation *n* **1** a body of persons gathered for religious worship ⟨The whole *congregation* began to sing with great fervor.⟩
syn assembly, church
rel flock, laity, parish; communion, confession, denomination, fold, sect; clergy, cloth
2 a body of people come together in one place — see GATHERING 1

congress *n* **1** the highest lawmaking body of a political unit ⟨The national emergency required a special session of *congress*.⟩
syn parliament
rel assembly, chamber, council, diet, house, legislative, legislature; general assembly, legislative assembly
2 a coming together of a number of persons for a specified purpose — see MEETING 1
3 a group of persons formally joined together for some common interest — see ASSOCIATION 2

congruity *n* **1** a point which two or more things share in common — see SIMILARITY 2
2 a state of consistency — see CONFORMITY 1

congruous *adj* **1** having the parts agreeably related — see HARMONIOUS 2
2 not having or showing any apparent conflict — see CONSISTENT

congruously *adv* in a manner suitable for the occasion or purpose — see PROPERLY

conjectural *adj* existing only as an assumption or speculation — see THEORETICAL 1

conjecture *n* an opinion or judgment based on little or no evidence ⟨the many *conjectures* about the true identity of Jack the Ripper⟩
syn guess, shot, supposition, surmise
rel hypothesis, hypothetical, theory, thesis; dead reckoning, guessing, guesswork, speculation; hunch, intuition; belief, faith
phrases shot in the dark

conjecture *vb* **1** to decide the size, amount, number, or distance of (something) without actual measurement — see ESTIMATE 2
2 to form an opinion from little or no evidence — see GUESS 1

conjoin *vb* **1** to come together to form a single unit — see UNITE 1
2 to form or enter into an association that furthers the interests of its members — see ALLY
3 to participate or assist in a joint effort to accomplish an end — see COOPERATE 1

conjoint *adj* used or done by a number of people as a group — see COLLECTIVE

conjointly *adv* in or by combined action or effort — see TOGETHER 2

conjugal *adj* of or relating to marriage — see MARITAL

conjugate *vb* **1** to come together to form a single unit — see UNITE 1
2 to put or bring together so as to form a new and longer whole — see CONNECT 1

conjunction *n* the coming together of two or more things to the same point — see CONVERGENCE

conjuration *n* a spoken word or set of words believed to have magic power — see SPELL 1

conjure (up) *vb* **1** to form a mental picture of — see IMAGINE 1
2 to call into being through the use of one's inner resources or powers — see SUMMON 2

conjurer *or* **conjuror** *n* a person skilled in using supernatural forces — see MAGICIAN 1
2 one who practices tricks and illusions for entertainment — see MAGICIAN 2

conjuring *n* **1** the power to control natural forces through supernatural means — see MAGIC 1
2 the art or skill of performing tricks or illusions for entertainment — see MAGIC 2

conk (out) *vb* **1** to lose consciousness — see FAINT
2 to stop functioning — see FAIL 1
3 to stop living — see DIE 1

connect *vb* **1** to put or bring together so as to form a new and longer whole ⟨Connect all the hoses so they'll reach the garden.⟩
syn chain, compound, concatenate, conjugate, couple, hitch, hook, interconnect, join, link, yoke
rel articulate, dovetail, integrate, interlock, intermesh; cord, string, wire; cement, coalesce, combine, fuse, unite, weld
near ant detach, disengage, divide, part, split; cleave, rupture, sever, sunder
ant disconnect, disjoin, disjoint, dissever, disunite, separate, unchain, uncouple, unhitch, unlink, unyoke
2 to come together to form a single unit — see UNITE 1
3 to think of (something) in combination — see ASSOCIATE 2

connecting *n* the act or an instance of joining two or more things into one — see UNION 1

connection *n* **1** the fact or state of having something in common ⟨the endless debate about the *connection* between class size and test scores⟩
syn affinity, association, bearing, kinship, liaison, linkage, relation, relationship
rel correlation, interrelation; materiality, pertinence, relevance; bond, link, tie; affiliation, alliance, union; identicalness, sameness; alikeness, community, likeness, resemblance, similarity; accordance, agreement, conformity, congruity, correspondence
near ant variability, variance; incompatibility, incongruence, incongruity, incongruousness
2 a place where two or more things are united — see JOINT 1
3 an acquaintance who has influence especially in the business or political world — see CONTACT 1

4 the act or an instance of joining two or more things into one — see UNION 1

5 the fact or state of being pertinent — see PERTINENCE

6 the state of having shared interests or efforts (as in social or business matters) — see ASSOCIATION 1

7 an assignment at which one regularly works for pay — see JOB 1

connivance *n* a secret agreement or cooperation between two parties for an illegal or dishonest purpose — see COLLUSION

connive *vb* **1** to secretly sympathize with or pretend ignorance of something improper or unlawful ⟨The principal *connived* at all the school absences that were recorded on the day of the city's celebration of its Super Bowl victory.⟩

syn wink

rel brush (aside *or* off), condone, disregard, excuse, forgive, gloss (over), gloze (over), ignore, overlook, pardon, pass over, shrug off, tolerate

near ant disapprove (of); deny, disallow, refuse

2 to engage in a secret plan to accomplish evil or unlawful ends — see PLOT

connoisseur *n* a person with a high level of knowledge or skill in a field — see EXPERT

connubial *adj* of or relating to marriage — see MARITAL

conquer *vb* **1** to bring under one's control by force of arms ⟨Before his final defeat, Napoléon had managed to *conquer* much of Europe.⟩

syn dominate, overpower, pacify, subdue, subject, subjugate, subordinate, vanquish

rel annihilate, beat, clobber, crush, defeat, drub, lick, mow (down), overcome, prevail (over), reduce, rout, skunk, smash, thrash, triumph (over), trounce, wallop, whip; enslave; break, clamp down (on), crack down (on), put down, quash, quell, repress, silence, smother, snuff (out), squash, squelch, suppress

near ant discharge, emancipate, enfranchise, free, liberate, manumit, release, spring, unbind, uncage, unchain, unfetter

2 to achieve a victory over — see BEAT 2

3 to achieve victory (as in a contest) — see WIN 1

conqueror *n* one that defeats an enemy or opponent — see VICTOR 1

conquest *n* the act or process of bringing someone or something under one's control ⟨the *conquest* of much of North and South America by the Spanish during the 16th century⟩

syn dominating, domination, overpowering, subduing, subjecting, subjection, subjugating, subjugation, vanquishing

rel triumph, victory, win, winning; beating, defeat, drubbing, licking, shellacking, trimming, trouncing, whipping; enslavement

near ant emancipation, enfranchisement, freeing, liberation, manumission, release

conscientious *adj* **1** guided by or in accordance with one's sense of right and

wrong ⟨Operated on the belief that most people are *conscientious*, the unattended farm stand has a price list and a money drawer for customers to leave payment for their purchases.⟩

syn ethical, honest, honorable, just, moral, principled, scrupulous

rel decent, good, righteous, right-minded, straight, upright, virtuous; dutiful, observant, respectful; overconscientious; reliable, responsible, solid, tried-and-true, true, trustworthy, trusty; esteemed, law-abiding, reputable, respected, upstanding, worthy

near ant bad, evil, evil-minded, immoral, indecent, sinful, unrighteous, wicked; unreliable, untrustworthy; corrupt, debased, debauched, degenerate, depraved, dissolute, perverted, reprobate; atrocious, infamous, villainous; base, low, mean, vicious, vile; iniquitous, nefarious

ant cutthroat, dishonest, dishonorable, immoral, unconscionable, unethical, unjust, unprincipled, unscrupulous

2 taking, showing, or involving great care and effort — see PAINSTAKING

conscientiousness *n* strict attentiveness to what one is doing — see CARE 1

conscious *adj* **1** having specified facts or feelings actively impressed on the mind ⟨*conscious* of the fact that my hands were sweating the whole time that I was making my presentation⟩

syn alive, aware, cognizant, mindful, sensible, sentient, witting

rel alert, attentive, careful, cautious, heedful, observant, open-eyed, regardful, safe, vigilant, wary, watchful, wide-awake; hyperaware, hyperconscious

near ant careless, heedless, inattentive, incautious, mindless, unguarded, unheeding, unwary

ant insensible, oblivious, unaware, unconscious, unmindful, unwitting

2 made, given, or done with full awareness of what one is doing — see INTENTIONAL

consciously *adv* with full awareness of what one is doing — see INTENTIONALLY

conscript *n* a person forced or required to enroll in military service ⟨As the war continued, the body of enlisted soldiers was supplemented by an increasing number of *conscripts*.⟩

syn draftee, inductee

rel levy; recruit, rookie

near ant enlistee, volunteer

conscript *vb* to pick especially for required military service — see DRAFT 1

consecrate *vb* to set apart or worthy of veneration by association with God — see HOLY 2

consecrate *vb* **1** to keep or intend for a special purpose — see DEVOTE 1

2 to make holy through prayers or ritual — see BLESS 1

consecrated *adj* set apart or worthy of veneration by association with God — see HOLY 2

consecration *n* the act of making something holy through religious ritual ⟨the *consecration* of the temple⟩

syn blessing, hallowing, sanctification

rel purification; dedication; adoration,

glorification, reverence, veneration, worship

near ant debasement, defilement, desecration, impiety, irreverence, sacrilege

consecutive *adj* following one after another without others coming in between ⟨The team's winning streak has lasted for seven *consecutive* games.⟩

syn sequential, straight, succeeding, successional, successive

rel serial; constant, continuous, uninterrupted; ensuing, following, later, next, posterior, subsequent

near ant in series

ant inconsecutive, nonconsecutive, nonsequential

consensus *n* the state of being of one opinion about something — see AGREEMENT 1

consent *n* the approval by someone in authority for the doing of something — see PERMISSION

consent *vb* to give or express one's approval (as to a proposal) — see ACCEDE

consequence *n* 1 a condition or occurrence traceable to a cause — see EFFECT 1

2 the quality or state of being important — see IMPORTANCE

3 an exaggerated sense of one's importance that shows itself in the making of excessive or unjustified claims — see ARROGANCE

4 an opinion arrived at through a process of reasoning — see CONCLUSION 1

consequent *adj* 1 according to the rules of logic — see LOGICAL 1

2 coming as a result — see RESULTANT

consequential *adj* 1 coming as a result — see RESULTANT

2 having great meaning or lasting effect — see IMPORTANT 1

3 having too high an opinion of oneself — see CONCEITED

consequently *adv* for this or that reason — see THEREFORE

conservation *n* 1 the careful maintaining and protection of something valuable especially in its natural or original state ⟨Everyone has a duty to aid in the *conservation* of our nation's wilderness areas.⟩

syn preservation

rel care, maintenance, upkeep; salvation, saving; defense, guardianship, guarding, keeping, protection, safeguarding, safekeeping; economy, husbandry, management

near ant dereliction, ignoring, neglect, squandering, waste; destruction, ruin; damage, harm, hurt, injury

2 the act or activity of keeping something in an existing and usually satisfactory condition — see MAINTENANCE

conservative *adj* 1 tending to favor established ideas, conditions, or institutions ⟨*Conservative* baseball fans consider the new ballpark too modern-looking and plain dull.⟩

syn hidebound, old-fashioned, orthodox, reactionary, traditional, unprogressive

rel conventional, square; devoted, faithful, loyal, staunch (*also* stanch), steadfast, steady, true, true-blue; neoconservative, Tory, ultraright, ultrarightist; dowdy, fogyish (*or* fogeyish), fuddy-duddy, ossified,

set, stodgy; right, right-wing; antiliberal, antimodern, antiprogressive, antireform, antirevolutionary

near ant anticonventional, antiestablishment, antitraditional, extremist, radical, revolutionary; nonconformist; advanced, contemporary, modern; lefty, radical, ultraleft, ultraleftist, ultraprogressive, ultraradical

ant broad-minded, large-minded, liberal, nonconservative, nonconventional, nonorthodox, nontraditional, open-minded, progressive, unconventional, unorthodox

2 not excessively showy — see QUIET 2

3 having or showing a close attentiveness to avoiding danger or trouble — see CAREFUL 1

conservative *n* a person whose political beliefs are centered on keeping things the way they are ⟨proposed legislation that was opposed by *conservatives* throughout the state⟩

syn reactionary, rightist, Tory

rel right, right-wing; conformist; neocon, neoconservative; diehard, standpatter; fuddy-duddy, square

near ant extremist, radical, red, revolutionary, revolutionist; reformer, reformist

ant leftist, left-winger, lefty, liberal, progressive

conservatory *n* a glass-enclosed building for growing plants ⟨The college's *conservatory* is entirely devoted to cultivating and displaying orchids.⟩

syn greenhouse, hothouse

rel cold frame, hot bed; botanical garden (*also* botanic garden)

conserve *vb* 1 to avoid the wasteful or destructive use of ⟨the need to *conserve* oil and other finite fossil fuels⟩

syn husband

rel economize, save, scrimp, skimp; preserve, protect, save; hoard, lay up

near ant clean (out), consume, deplete, drain, exhaust, expend, impoverish, spend, use up

ant blow, dissipate, fritter (away), lavish, misspend, run through, squander, throw away, waste

2 to keep in good condition — see MAINTAIN 1

conserving *n* the act or activity of keeping something in an existing and usually satisfactory condition — see MAINTENANCE

consider *vb* 1 to think of in a particular way ⟨I *consider* him a very good friend.⟩

syn account, call, count, esteem, hold, rate, reckon, regard, set down, view

rel conceive, deem, feel, sense, think; conceive, fancy, imagine; allow (for), provide (for), regard

phrases take for

2 to give serious and careful thought to — see PONDER

3 to have as an opinion — see BELIEVE 2

4 to think very highly or favorably of — see ADMIRE

considerable *adj* 1 sufficiently large in size, amount, or number to merit attention ⟨the *considerable* number of auto accidents that resulted from the surprise snowstorm⟩

syn good, goodly, handsome, healthy, largish, major, respectable, significant, sizable (*or* sizeable), substantial, tidy
rel big, bulky, hefty, hulking, outsize (*also* outsized), oversize (*or* oversized), voluminous; astronomical (*also* astronomic), bumper, colossal, elephantine, enormous, gigantic, great, herculean, huge, immense, jumbo, king-size (*or* king-sized), mammoth, massive, monstrous, monumental, prodigious, titanic, tremendous, whopping
near ant measly, minute, paltry, petty, picayune, picayunish, piddling, puny, trifling, trivial, unimportant; meager (*or* meagre), slight; little, small, tiny, undersized (*also* undersize), bitty, diminutive, miniature, pint-size (*or* pint-sized), pocket, pocket-size (*also* pocket-sized), pygmy, smallish
ant inconsequential, inconsiderable, insignificant, insubstantial, negligible, nominal
2 of a size greater than average of its kind — see LARGE
considerably *adv* to a large extent or degree — see GREATLY 2
considerate *adj* **1** given to or made with heedful anticipation of the needs and happiness of others — see THOUGHTFUL 1
2 having or showing a close attentiveness to avoiding danger or trouble — see CAREFUL 1
considerately *adv* with good reason or courtesy — see WELL 4
consideration *n* **1** a careful weighing of the reasons for or against something ⟨After much *consideration* we decided to make an offer on the house.⟩
syn account, advisement, debate, deliberation, reflection, study, thought
rel contemplation, meditation, pondering, rumination; agonizing, hesitation, indecision; premeditation
ant short shrift
2 something (as money) that is given or received in return for goods or services — see PAYMENT 2
considered *adj* decided on as a result of careful thought — see DELIBERATE 1
consign *vb* **1** to cause to go or be taken from one place to another — see SEND
2 to put (something) into the possession or safekeeping of another — see GIVE 2
consist (of) *vb* to be made up of — see COMPRISE 1
consistency *n* the degree to which a fluid can resist flowing ⟨Beat the egg whites until they take on the *consistency* of whipped cream.⟩
syn density, thickness, viscosity
rel compactness, firmness, solidity; ropiness, stickiness
consistent *adj* not having or showing any apparent conflict ⟨The clothes you wear to work must be *consistent* with the company's dress code.⟩
syn coherent, compatible, concordant, conformable (to), congruous, consonant, correspondent (with *or* to), harmonious, nonconflicting
rel self-consistent; appropriate, befitting,

---

felicitous, fit, fitting, meet, proper, right, suitable
phrases of a piece
near ant improper, inappropriate, inapt, infelicitous, unsuitable
ant conflicting, conflictive, incompatible, incongruous, inconsistent, inharmonious, noncompatible
consistently *adv* on every relevant occasion — see ALWAYS 1
consolation *n* **1** the giving of hope and strength in times of grief, distress, or suffering ⟨the *consolation* of the grieving family by their friends⟩
syn comforting, consoling, solace, solacing
rel commiseration, compassion, condolence, feeling, sympathy; counseling (*or* counselling); humanity, kindheartedness, kindliness, kindness, mercy, pity
2 a feeling of ease from grief or trouble — see COMFORT 1
console *n* a storage case typically having doors and shelves — see CABINET
console *vb* to ease the grief or distress of — see COMFORT
consolidate *vb* **1** to bring (something) to a central point or under a single control — see CENTRALIZE
2 to make markedly greater in measure or degree — see INTENSIFY
consolidation *n* the act or an instance of joining two or more things into one — see UNION 1
consoling *n* the giving of hope and strength in times of grief, distress, or suffering — see CONSOLATION 1
consonance *n* **1** a balanced, pleasing, or suitable arrangement of parts — see HARMONY 1
2 a state of consistency — see CONFORMITY 1
consonant *adj* **1** having the parts agreeably related — see HARMONIOUS 2
2 not having or showing any apparent conflict — see CONSISTENT
¹**consort** *n* **1** a usually small number of persons considered as a unit — see GROUP 2
2 an organized group of singers — see CHORUS 1
²**consort** *n* the person to whom another is married — see SPOUSE
consort *vb* **1** to come or be together as friends — see ASSOCIATE 1
2 to form a pleasing relationship — see HARMONIZE 2
conspicuous *adj* **1** likely to attract attention — see NOTICEABLE
2 very noticeable especially for being incorrect or short — see EGREGIOUS
conspiracy *n* **1** a group involved in secret or criminal activities — see ¹RING 1
2 a secret agreement or cooperation between two parties for an illegal or dishonest purpose — see COLLUSION
3 a secret plan for accomplishing evil or unlawful ends — see PLOT 1
conspire *vb* **1** to engage in a secret plan to accomplish evil or unlawful ends — see PLOT
2 to participate or assist in a joint effort to accomplish an end — see COOPERATE 1
constabulary *n* a body of officers of the law — see POLICE 2

---

syn synonym(s)   *rel* related words
ant antonym(s)   *near ant* near antonym(s)

constancy *n* **1** the state of continuing without change ⟨There's the mistaken notion that there is *constancy* in language—words do indeed change their meanings over time.⟩

syn changelessness, fixedness, immutability, invariability, stability, steadiness, unchangeableness

rel consistency, regularity, sameness, uniformity; durability, enduringness, lastingness, permanence

near ant inconsistence, inconsistency, irregularity, unevenness

ant capriciousness, changeability, changeableness, fickleness, instability, mutability, unpredictability, unsteadiness, variability, variableness, volatileness, volatility **2** adherence to something to which one is bound by a pledge or duty — see FIDELITY **3** the strength of mind that enables a person to endure pain or hardship — see FORTITUDE

constant *adj* **1** not undergoing a change in condition ⟨Change is the only *constant* thing in the world of fashion.⟩

syn changeless, stable, stationary, steady, unchanging, unvarying

rel fast, fixed, hard-and-fast, immutable, inflexible, invariable, unalterable, unchangeable; established, set, settled; ceaseless, continuing, durable, enduring, lasting, permanent

phrases on an even keel (*also* on even keel)

near ant adaptable, alterable, changeable, flexible, mutable, variable; ephemeral, evanescent, fleeting, momentary, transient, transitory; phantasmagoric (*or* phantasmagorical)

ant capricious, changeful, changing, fickle, fluctuating, fluid, inconstant, mercurial, skittish, uncertain, unpredictable, unsettled, unstable, unsteady, varying, volatile **2** appearing or occurring repeatedly from time to time — see REGULAR 1 **3** firm in one's allegiance to someone or something — see FAITHFUL 1

constantly *adv* **1** many times — see OFTEN **2** on every relevant occasion — see ALWAYS 1

constituent *n* one of the parts that make up a whole — see ELEMENT 1

constitute *vb* **1** to be all the substance of ⟨Nine players *constitute* a baseball team.⟩

syn compose, comprise, form, make up

rel embody, epitomize, incarnate, incorporate, integrate, materialize, personify, substantiate; complement, complete, supplement; fill (out), flesh (out) **2** to be responsible for the creation and early operation or use of — see FOUND **3** to pick (someone) by one's authority for a specific position or duty — see APPOINT 2 **4** to put into effect through legislative or authoritative action — see ENACT

constitution *n* **1** the set of qualities that makes a person, a group of people, or a thing different from others — see NATURE 1 **2** the type of body that a person has — see PHYSIQUE **3** a collection or system of rules of conduct — see CODE

4 a rule of conduct or action laid down by a governing authority and especially a legislature — see LAW 1

constitutional *adj* being a part of the innermost nature of a person or thing — see INHERENT

constitutional *n* a relaxed journey on foot for exercise or pleasure — see WALK 1

constitutionally *adv* by natural character or ability — see NATURALLY 1

constrain *vb* **1** to cause (a person) to give in to pressure — see FORCE **2** to keep from exceeding a desirable degree or level (as of expression) — see CONTROL 1

constraint *n* **1** the checking of one's true feelings and impulses when dealing with others ⟨In civilized society people do not just say or do whatever they feel like—they exercise some *constraint*.⟩

syn discipline, discretion, inhibition, repression, reserve, restraint, self-control, self-restraint, suppression

rel command, control, mastery, possession; self-censorship, self-containment, self-denial, self-discipline, self-government, will, willpower; composure, self-poise, self-possession; aloofness, detachedness, distance; bashfulness, modesty, shyness; reticence, silence, taciturnity

near ant self-abandonment; unrestrainedness; gratification, indulgence, overindulgence, self-indulgence; candor, frankness

ant disinhibition, incontinence **2** something that limits one's freedom of action or choice — see RESTRICTION 1 **3** the use of power to impose one's will on another — see FORCE 2

constrict *vb* **1** to become smaller in size or volume through the drawing together of particles of matter — see CONTRACT 2 **2** to reduce in size or volume by or as if by pressing parts or members together — see COMPRESS 1

constriction *n* the act or process of reducing the size or volume of something by or as if by pressing — see COMPRESSION

construct *vb* **1** to create or think of by clever use of the imagination — see INVENT **2** to form by putting together parts or materials — see BUILD

construction *n* **1** something put together by arranging or connecting an array of parts ⟨The swing set turned out to be a more complicated *construction* than the "some assembly required" warning suggested.⟩

syn structure

rel arrangement, assembly; configuration, frame, framework, shell, skeleton **2** a statement that makes something clear — see EXPLANATION 1

constructive *adj* having a role in deciding something's final form — see FORMATIVE

construe *vb* to make plain or understandable — see EXPLAIN 1

consult *n* an exchange of views for the purpose of exploring a subject or deciding an issue — see DISCUSSION 1

consult *vb* **1** to exchange viewpoints or seek advice for the purpose of finding a solution to a problem — see CONFER 2

2 to use or seek out as a source of aid, relief, or advantage — see RESORT (TO) 1

consultant *n* a person who gives advice especially professionally ⟨a *consultant* in public relations to a number of large corporations⟩
syn adviser (*also* advisor), counsel, counselor (*or* counsellor)
rel authority, expert, pro, professional, specialist; confidant; cabinet, kitchen cabinet; sounding board
near ant counselee

consume *vb* **1** to destroy all trace of ⟨Massive fires had *consumed* hundreds of square miles of forest.⟩
syn devour, eat (up)
rel gut; deplete, drain, exhaust, expend, spend, use up; annihilate, decimate, demolish, desolate, devastate, do in, pulverize, raze, ruin, shatter, smash, tear down, waste, wreck; annihilate, blot out, eradicate, exterminate, extinguish, extirpate, obliterate, remove, rub out, stamp (out), wipe out
near ant conserve, preserve, protect, save; build, construct, erect, put up, raise
2 to make complete use of — see DEPLETE 1
3 to take in as food — see EAT 1

consummate *adj* **1** having or showing exceptional knowledge, experience, or skill in a field of endeavor — see PROFICIENT
2 having no exceptions or restrictions — see ABSOLUTE 2
3 of the greatest or highest degree or quantity — see ULTIMATE 1

consummate *vb* to bring (something) to a state where nothing remains to be done — see FINISH 1

consummation *n* **1** the last part of a process or action — see FINALE
2 the state of being actual or complete — see FRUITION

contact *n* **1** an acquaintance who has influence especially in the business or political world ⟨an intern who got her summer job in the governor's office through *contacts*⟩
syn connection
rel in, insider; big shot, bigwig, somebody, VIP; arbiter, arbitrator, conciliator, go-between, intercessor, intermediary, interposer, mediator, middleman; peacemaker
2 the state or fact of being able to exchange information regarding one's current situation — see TOUCH 1

contact *vb* to transmit information or requests to ⟨You can *contact* me at this number.⟩
syn address, communicate (with), get, reach
rel get through (to); acquaint, advise, apprise, brief, clue, enlighten, familiarize, fill in, inform, instruct, notify, tell, wise (up); buzz, call, phone, telephone; keep up (with)
phrases get hold of, get in touch with (*or* keep in touch with), touch base (with)

contagious *adj* **1** capable of being passed by physical contact from one person to another ⟨chicken pox, measles, German measles, and other *contagious* diseases⟩

syn catching, communicable, pestilent, transmittable
rel infectious, infective
near ant noninfectious
ant noncommunicable
2 exciting a similar feeling or reaction in others ⟨The enthusiasm of the new club members was *contagious*.⟩
syn catching, infectious, spreading
rel palpable, perceptible, tangible; irresistible (*also* irresistable), overpowering, overwhelming; disarming, endearing, fetching, inviting, winning, winsome

contain *vb* **1** to have within ⟨The top drawer of the cabinet *contains* my stamp collection.⟩
syn bear, boast, hold
rel accommodate, fit, take; case, encase, enclose (*also* inclose), encompass; harbor, house, lodge, shelter
2 to have as part of a whole — see INCLUDE 1
3 to be made up of — see COMPRISE 1
4 to gain emotional or mental control of — see COLLECT 1
5 to keep from exceeding a desirable degree or level (as of expression) — see CONTROL 1

container *n* something into which a liquid or smaller objects can be put for storage or transportation ⟨Save the plastic *containers* from the deli for other uses.⟩
syn holder, receptacle, vessel
rel carrier; cartridge; basket, bin, box, caddy, carton, case, casket, crate, handbasket, locker, trunk; bag, hamper, pocket, sack; warmer; basin, bottle, bowl, bucket, can, jar, jug, keg, kettle, kit, pack, pail, pitcher, pot, tub, vat

contaminant *n* something that is or that makes impure — see IMPURITY 1

contaminate *vb* to make unfit for use by the addition of something harmful or undesirable ⟨a supply of drinking water that was *contaminated* by a toxic waste dump⟩
syn befoul, defile, foul, poison, pollute, taint
rel infect; begrime, besmirch, blacken, dirty, foul up, grime, mire, muddy, smirch, smudge, soil, stain, sully; corrupt, rot, spoil; adulterate, doctor; dilute
near ant clarify, clean, cleanse, clear, distill (*also* distil), purge; filter; disinfect, sanitize, sterilize
ant decontaminate, purify

contaminated *adj* containing foreign or lower-grade substances — see IMPURE 1

contemplate *vb* **1** to give serious and careful thought to — see PONDER
2 to have in mind as a purpose or goal — see INTEND 1

contemplation *n* long or deep thinking about spiritual matters ⟨the decision to enter a monastery and to spend one's life in prayer and *contemplation*⟩
syn meditation
rel brown study, daydreaming, navel-gazing, reflection, retrospection, reverie, study, trance, woolgathering; deliberation, pondering, rumination

contemplative *adj* given to or marked by long, quiet thinking ⟨a *contemplative* person who likes to go on solitary walks⟩ ⟨the

contemplative life of the monks at the abbey⟩
syn meditative, melancholy, pensive, reflective, ruminant, thoughtful
rel introspective, retrospective, self-reflective; earnest, grave, sedate, serious, serious-minded, severe, sober, solemn, somber (*or* sombre), weighty; philosophical (*also* philosophic); analytic (*or* analytical), logical, rational; deliberate, purposeful; absentminded, abstracted, preoccupied
near ant featherbrained, flighty, flippant, frivolous, goofy, harebrained, light-headed, scatterbrained; brainless, mindless, silly, thoughtless, unthinking
ant unreflective
contemporaneous *adj* existing or occurring at the same period of time — see CONTEMPORARY 1
contemporaneously *adv* at one and the same time — see TOGETHER 1
contemporary *adj* 1 existing or occurring at the same period of time ⟨the absurd notion that early cave dwellers were *contemporary* with the dinosaurs⟩
syn coeval, coexistent, coexisting, coextensive, coincident, coincidental, concurrent, contemporaneous; simultaneous, synchronous
rel accompanying, attendant, attending, concomitant, incident
ant asynchronous, noncontemporary, nonsimultaneous, nonsynchronous
2 being or involving the latest methods, concepts, information, or styles — see MODERN
contemporary *n* a person who lives at the same time or is about the same age as another ⟨Abraham Lincoln and Charles Darwin were exact *contemporaries*, actually being born on the same day in 1809.⟩
syn coeval
rel accompaniment, companion, concomitant; coordinate, counterpart, equal, equivalent, match, peer, rival
contempt *n* open dislike for someone or something considered unworthy of one's concern or respect ⟨my undying *contempt* for people who abuse animals⟩
syn despite, despitefulness, disdain, scorn
rel abhorrence, abomination, execration, hate, hatred, loathing, lovelessness; cattiness, hatefulness, invidiousness, malevolence, malice, maliciousness, malignancy, malignity, meanness, spite, spitefulness; aversion, disgust, distaste, horror, odium, repugnance, repulsion, revulsion; animosity, antagonism, antipathy, bitterness, enmity, gall, grudge, hostility, jealousy, pique, resentment; bile, jaundice, rancor, spleen, venom, vindictiveness, virulence, vitriol; aspersion, belittlement, deprecation, depreciation, detraction, diminishment, disparagement, derision, mockery, ridicule; abuse, invective, vituperation; censure, condemnation, denunciation
near ant acceptance, tolerance; adoration, adulation, deference, deification, glorification, idolatry, idolization, lionization, reverence, veneration, worship; affection, fancy, fondness, liking, love
ant admiration, esteem, estimation, favor, regard, respect
contemptible *adj* 1 arousing or deserving

of one's loathing and disgust, ⟨the *contemptible* thieves who stole the clothing intended for needy children⟩
syn cheap, deplorable, despicable, dirty, grubby, lame, lousy, mean, nasty, paltry, pitiable, pitiful, scabby, scummy, scurvy, sneaking, sorry, wretched
rel abhorrent, abominable, condemnable, detestable, execrable, hateful, loathsome, odious; reptilian, repugnant, repulsive, revolting, revulsive; discreditable, disgraceful, dishonorable, disreputable, ignominious, shameful; base, ignoble, low, shabby, sordid, squalid, vile; blamable, censurable, reprehensible, reproachable; cowardly, craven, dastardly; unethical, unprincipled, unscrupulous
near ant high-minded, honest, honorable, noble, principled, redoubtable, reputable, right-minded, scrupulous, upright; ethical, good, moral, right, righteous, virtuous
ant admirable, commendable, creditable, laudable, meritorious, praiseworthy
2 deserving pitying scorn (as for inadequacy) — see PITIFUL 1
3 not following or in accordance with standards of honor and decency — see IGNOBLE 2
contemptuous *adj* 1 feeling or showing open dislike for someone or something regarded as undeserving of respect or concern ⟨loutish tourists who are *contemptuous* of the ways and traditions of their host countries⟩
syn abhorrent, disdainful, scornful
rel bold-faced, brash, brassy, brazen, cheeky, cocky, discourteous, disrespectful, fresh, impertinent, impudent, insolent, sassy, saucy; arrogant, cavalier, highfalutin (*also* hifalutin), high-handed, high-hat, pretentious, uppish, uppity; haughty, lofty, lordly, prideful, sniffish, supercilious; pompous, self-important, superior; catty, cruel, despiteful, hateful, malevolent, malicious, malign, malignant, mean, nasty, spiteful
near ant deferential, regardful, respectful; accepting, tolerant; courteous, polite
ant admiring, applauding, appreciative, approving
2 intended to make a person or thing seem of little importance or value — see DEROGATORY
contend *vb* 1 to engage in a contest — see COMPETE
2 to state (something) as a reason in support of or against something under consideration — see ARGUE 1
3 to state as a fact usually forcefully — see CLAIM 1
contend (with) *vb* 1 to deal with (something) usually skillfully or efficiently — see HANDLE 1
2 to strive to reduce or eliminate — see FIGHT 2
contender *n* 1 one who seeks an office, honor, position, or award — see CANDIDATE
2 one who strives for the same thing as another — see COMPETITOR
content *adj* feeling that one's needs or desires have been met ⟨Are you *content* with your present salary?⟩

syn contented, gratified, happy, pleased, satisfied

rel blissful, delighted, glad, joyful, joyous, jubilant, rejoicing, tickled; ecstatic, elated, enraptured, euphoric, overjoyed, rapturous, thrilled; appeased, mollified, pacified, placated

near ant disaffected, disgruntled, displeased, unsatisfied; aggrieved, anguished, brokenhearted, dejected, depressed, despondent, disconsolate, discouraged, disheartened, dispirited, downcast, downhearted

ant discontent, discontented, displeased, dissatisfied, malcontent, malcontented, unhappy

¹**content** *n* **1** a major object of interest or concern (as in a discussion or artistic composition) — see MATTER 1
2 the amount of something (as subject matter) included — see COVERAGE
3 the idea that is conveyed or intended to be conveyed to the mind by language, symbol, or action — see MEANING 1
²**content** *n* the feeling experienced when one's wishes are met — see PLEASURE 1
content *vb* to give satisfaction to — see PLEASE 1
contented *adj* feeling that one's needs or desires have been met — see CONTENT
contentedness *n* the feeling experienced when one's wishes are met — see PLEASURE 1
contention *n* **1** an idea or opinion that is put forth in a discussion or debate ⟨My *contention* is that today's lower batting averages are the result of better pitching.⟩
syn argument, assertion, thesis
rel conjecture, guess, hunch, hypothesis, speculation, surmise, theory; proposal, proposition; assumption, presupposition, supposition; position, stand; case, explanation, rationale, reason
2 an earnest effort for superiority or victory over another — see CONTEST 1
contentious *adj* **1** feeling or displaying eagerness to fight — see BELLIGERENT
2 given to arguing — see ARGUMENTATIVE 1
contentiousness *n* an inclination to fight or quarrel — see BELLIGERENCE
contentment *n* the feeling experienced when one's wishes are met — see PLEASURE 1
contest *n* **1** an earnest effort for superiority or victory over another ⟨the eternal *contest* between the forces of good and the forces of evil⟩
syn battle, combat, competition, conflict, confrontation, contention, duel, face-off, grapple, match, rivalry, strife, struggle, sweepstakes (*also* sweep-stake), tug-of-war, war, warfare
rel horse race; showdown; clash, collision, discord, friction; argument, controversy, debate, disagreement, disputation, dispute, dissension (*also* dissention), quarrel, row, wrangle
near ant concord, harmony, peace
2 a competitive encounter between indi-

viduals or groups carried on for amusement, exercise, or in pursuit of a prize — see GAME 1
3 a physical dispute between opposing individuals or groups — see FIGHT 1
contest *vb* to demand proof of the truth or rightness of — see CHALLENGE 1
contestant *n* one who strives for the same thing as another — see COMPETITOR
contiguity *n* the state or condition of being near — see PROXIMITY
contiguous *adj* having a border in common — see ADJACENT
continent *adj* given to or marked by restraint in the satisfaction of one's appetites — see ABSTEMIOUS
continent *n* one of the great divisions of land on the globe or the main part of such a division — see MAINLAND
contingency *n* **1** something that might happen — see EVENT 2
2 something upon which the carrying out of an agreement or offer depends — see CONDITION 2
contingent *n* **1** a body of persons chosen as representatives of a larger group ⟨The local Scout troop traditionally sends a large *contingent* to the jamboree.⟩
syn delegation
rel embassy, legation, mission; band, company, crew, detachment, gang, outfit, party, squad, team
2 something that might happen — see EVENT 2
contingent (on *or* **upon)** *adj* determined by something else — see DEPENDENT 2
continual *adj* **1** going on and on without any interruptions — see CONTINUOUS
2 occurring or appearing at intervals — see INTERMITTENT 1
continually *adv* **1** many times — see OFTEN
2 on every relevant occasion — see ALWAYS 1
continuance *n* **1** the period during which something exists, lasts, or is in progress — see DURATION 1
2 uninterrupted or lasting existence — see CONTINUATION
continuation *n* uninterrupted or lasting existence ⟨The *continuation* of high unemployment has cost the government much support.⟩
syn abidance, ceaselessness, continuance, durability, duration, endurance, persistence, subsistence
rel drawing out, elongation, extension, lengthening, prolongation, prolonging, stretching; enduringness, permanence; survival
near ant abridgment (*or* abridgement), curtailment, cutback, shortening
ant cessation, close, discontinuance, discontinuity, end, ending, expiration, finish, stoppage, surcease, termination
continue *vb* **1** to remain indefinitely in existence or in the same state ⟨The heavy snow *continued* throughout the night.⟩
syn abide, bide, endure, hold on, hold up, keep up, last, persist, remain, run on
rel linger, stay, stick around, tarry; carry through, prevail, survive
near ant abate, die (down), ebb, let up, moderate, subside, wane

---

syn synonym(s) **rel** related words
ant antonym(s) **near ant** near antonym(s)

ant cease, close, conclude, desist, die, discontinue, end, expire, finish, lapse, leave off, pass, quit, stop, terminate, wind up

2 to begin again or return to after an interruption — see RESUME

continuing *adj* **1** going on and on without any interruptions — see CONTINUOUS

2 having an existence or validity that does not change or diminish — see ABIDING

continuous *adj* going on and on without any interruptions ⟨The batteries provide enough power for up to five hours of *continuous* use.⟩

syn ceaseless, continual, continuing, incessant, perpetual, running, unbroken, unceasing, uninterrupted, unremitting

rel dateless, deathless, endless, eternal, everlasting, immortal, interminable, permanent, undying, unending; changeless, constant, stable, steady, unchanging, unvarying; durable, enduring, lasting, persistent; imperishable, indestructible

near ant intermittent, periodic, periodical, recurrent, recurring; alternate, alternating, cyclic (*or* cyclical), rhythmic (*or* rhythmical), seasonal, serial; erratic, fitful, irregular, occasional, spasmodic, sporadic, spotty, unsteady

ant discontinuous, noncontinuous

contort *vb* to twist (something) out of a natural or normal shape or condition ⟨The acrobat is able to *contort* his body so that it almost looks like a pretzel.⟩

syn deform, distort, screw, squinch, torture, warp

rel deface, disfigure; wrench, wrest, wring; coil, curl, loop, spiral, twine, wind, wreathe

near ant straighten, unbend, uncurl

contortion *n* the twisting of something out of its natural or normal shape or condition ⟨The comedian is renowned for his seemingly endless variety of facial *contortions*.⟩

syn deformation, distortion, screwing, squinching, torturing, warping

rel defacement, deformity, disfigurement; malformation

contour *n* a line that traces the outer limits of an object or surface — see OUTLINE 1

contract *n* **1** a formal agreement to fulfill an obligation — see GUARANTEE 1

2 an arrangement about action to be taken — see AGREEMENT 2

contract *vb* **1** to become affected with (a disease or disorder) ⟨Before vaccines were developed, people lived in fear of *contracting* polio.⟩

syn catch, come down (with), get, sicken (with), take

rel break out (with); die (from), succumb (to); fail, languish, sink, waste (away), weaken, wilt, wither, worsen

near ant gain, heal, mend, recoup, recover, recuperate, snap back; rally, rebound, recover (from), shake (off)

2 to become smaller in size or volume through the drawing together of particles of matter ⟨Metal *contracts* at low temperatures.⟩

syn compress, condense, constrict, shrink

rel collapse, deflate, flatten; dry up, shrivel, wilt, wither; abate, decrease, diminish, dwindle, lessen; recede, retreat, withdraw

near ant accumulate, grow, increase; balloon, inflate, puff (up)

ant balloon, expand, snowball, swell

3 to reduce in size or volume by or as if by pressing parts or members together — see COMPRESS 1

4 to come to an arrangement as to a course of action — see AGREE 2

contraction *n* the act or process of reducing the size or volume of something by or as if by pressing — see COMPRESSION

contradict *vb* **1** to make an assertion that is contrary to one made by (another) ⟨No matter what I say, you always have to *contradict* me!⟩

syn disagree (with), gainsay

rel challenge, contest, dispute, question; confute, rebut, refute; cross, fight, oppose, resist

near ant confirm, corroborate, substantiate, verify; attest, authenticate, avouch, certify, testify (to), vouch (for), witness

ant concur (with)

2 to declare not to be true — see DENY 1

contradiction *n* **1** someone or something with qualities or features that seem to conflict with one another ⟨A professional organizer for others with a messy house of his own, he was a living *contradiction*.⟩

syn incongruity, paradox

rel conundrum, enigma, mystery, mystification, puzzle, puzzlement, riddle

2 a refusal to confirm the truth of a statement — see DENIAL 2

contradictory *adj* being as different as possible — see OPPOSITE

contraption *n* an interesting and often novel device with a practical use — see GADGET

contrariness *n* refusal to obey — see DISOBEDIENCE

contrariwise *adv* just the opposite being true ⟨The runner is hardly a novice; *contrariwise*, this is his fifth racing event this year.⟩

syn again, conversely

phrases if anything, on the contrary, to the contrary

near ant even, indeed, nay, true, truly, verily, yea

contrary *adj* **1** being as different as possible — see OPPOSITE

2 engaging in or marked by childish misbehavior — see NAUGHTY

3 given to resisting authority or another's control — see DISOBEDIENT

contrary *n* something that is as different as possible from something else — see OPPOSITE

contrast *n* the quality or state of being different — see DIFFERENCE 1

contrast *vb* to be unlike; to not be the same — see DIFFER 1

contribute *vb* **1** to make a donation as part of a group effort ⟨Would you like to *contribute* to the Thanksgiving fund for needy families?⟩

syn chip in, kick in, pitch in

rel bestow, donate, give, present; award, confer, dole (out); endow; afford, furnish, provide

2 to make a present of — see GIVE 1

contribution *n* a gift of money or its

equivalent to a charity, humanitarian cause, or public institution ⟨*Contributions* for the victims of the earthquake began pouring in.⟩

syn alms, benefaction, beneficence, charity, donation, philanthropy

rel offering, tithe; bequest, endowment, legacy; aid, assistance, dole, handout, relief; welfare; grant, subsidy; benevolence, bestowal, largesse (*also* largess), present, presentation

contrite *adj* feeling sorrow for a wrong that one has done ⟨Being *contrite* is not enough to spare you a detention if you're caught skipping class.⟩

syn apologetic, penitent, regretful, remorseful, repentant, rueful, sorry

rel ashamed, shamefaced, sheepish; dolorous, grieving, lugubrious, mournful, plaintive, sorrowful, wailing, weeping, woeful

near ant cruel, merciless, pitiless, ruthless, unmerciful; shameless, unashamed

ant impenitent, remorseless, unapologetic, unrepentant

contriteness *n* a feeling of responsibility for wrongdoing — see GUILT 1

contrition *n* a feeling of responsibility for wrongdoing — see GUILT 1

contrivance *n* **1** an interesting and often novel device with a practical use — see GADGET

2 something (as a device) created for the first time through the use of the imagination — see INVENTION 1

3 the ability to form mental images of things that either are not physically present or have never been conceived or created by others — see IMAGINATION 1

contrive *vb* **1** to create or think of by clever use of the imagination — see INVENT

2 to engage in a secret plan to accomplish evil or unlawful ends — see PLOT

3 to plan out usually with subtle skill or care — see ENGINEER

contrived *adj* lacking in natural or spontaneous quality — see ARTIFICIAL 1

contriver *n* one who creates or introduces something new — see INVENTOR

control *n* **1** a mechanism for adjusting the operation of a device, machine, or system ⟨The *controls* for the player are well marked.⟩

syn regulator

rel actuator; button, dial, key, knob, lever, push button, selector, switch

2 the ability to direct the course of something ⟨After the tail fell off, the plane went out of the pilot's *control*.⟩ ⟨firefighters keeping *control* of the blaze⟩

syn grasp, hand(s)

rel clutch, grip, hold, mastery; arm, command, dominion, helm, sway; authority, domination, jurisdiction, might, power; administration, direction, governance, government, guidance, management, operation, oversight, regulation, running, superintendence, supervision

near ant helplessness, weakness; impotence, impotency, powerlessness

3 the act or activity of looking after and

making decisions about something — see CONDUCT 1

4 the fact or state of having (something) at one's disposal — see POSSESSION 1

5 the right or means to command or control others — see POWER 1

control *vb* **1** to keep from exceeding a desirable degree or level (as of expression) ⟨You must learn to *control* your temper.⟩

syn bridle, check, constrain, contain, curb, govern, hold, inhibit, keep, measure, regulate, rein (in), restrain, rule, tame

rel bottle (up), choke (back), hold back, mince, muffle, pocket, repress, sink, smother, squelch, stifle, strangle, suppress, swallow; arrest, interrupt, stop; block, hamper, handcuff, hinder, impede, obstruct; gag, muzzle, silence

near ant liberate, loose, loosen, unleash; air, express, take out, vent

ant lose

2 to gain emotional or mental control of — see COLLECT 1

3 to exercise authority or power over — see GOVERN 1

4 to look after and make decisions about — see CONDUCT 1

controversy *n* **1** an often noisy or angry expression of differing opinions — see ARGUMENT 1

2 variance of opinion on a matter — see DISAGREEMENT 1

contusion *n* a bodily injury in which small blood vessels are broken but the overlying skin is not ⟨suffered multiple *contusions* as a result of a car accident⟩

syn bruise

rel abrasion, bump, lump, scrape, scratch; black eye; discoloration

conundrum *n* something hard to understand or explain — see MYSTERY

convalesce *vb* to become healthy and strong again after illness or weakness ⟨the long months that the soldier spent in the hospital slowly *convalescing*⟩

syn gain, heal, mend, rally, recoup, recover, recuperate, snap back

rel come around, come round, come to, improve, pick up, revive; cheer (up), perk (up); pull through, survive; recruit

near ant ail, collapse, sicken; decline, degenerate, deteriorate, fade, fail, languish, sink, waste (away), weaken, wilt, wither, worsen; regress, relapse

convalescence *n* the process or period of gradually regaining one's health and strength ⟨Her release from the hospital was followed by a long *convalescence* at home.⟩

syn comeback, healing, mending, rally, recovery, recuperation, rehabilitation, snapback

rel resuscitation, revival; survival

near ant decline, degeneration, deterioration, fading, failing, languishing, sinking, wasting (away), weakening, wilting, withering, worsening; regression, relapse

convene *vb* **1** to bring together in assembly by or as if by command — see CONVOKE

2 to come together into one body or place — see ASSEMBLE 1

convenience *n* something that adds to one's ease of living — see COMFORT 2

convenient *adj* situated within easy reach

---

syn synonym(s)   *rel* related words

ant antonym(s)   *near ant* near antonym(s)

⟨The shopping mall is *convenient* to all of the area's major highways.⟩
syn accessible, handy, reachable
rel close, near, nearby, nigh; abutting, adjacent, adjoining; approachable, attainable, getatable, obtainable; ultraconvenient
phrases at hand, to hand
near ant away, distant, far, faraway, far-off, remote, removed; unapproachable, unattainable, unavailable, unobtainable
ant inaccessible, inconvenient, unhandy, unreachable, untouchable
convention *n* 1 a coming together of a number of persons for a specified purpose — see MEETING 1
2 a formal agreement between two or more nations or peoples — see TREATY
3 an arrangement about action to be taken — see AGREEMENT 2
4 an inherited or established way of thinking, feeling, or doing — see TRADITION 1
conventional *adj* 1 accepted, used, or practiced by most people — see CURRENT 1
2 based on customs usually handed down from a previous generation — see TRADITIONAL 1
3 following or agreeing with established form, custom, or rules — see FORMAL 1
converge *vb* to come together into one body or place — see ASSEMBLE 1
convergence *n* the coming together of two or more things to the same point ⟨the *convergence* of the city's major arteries on a single rotary⟩
syn confluence, conjunction, meeting
rel combination, combining, connecting, connection, consolidation, coupling, joining, junction, juncture, linking, merging, unification, union
ant divergence
conversant *adj* having information especially as a result of study or experience — see FAMILIAR 1
conversation *n* talking or a talk between two or more people ⟨Thomas Jefferson was celebrated for his brilliant, wide-ranging *conversations* with a host of friends and acquaintances.⟩
syn chat, colloquy, converse, dialogue (*also* dialog), discourse, discussion, exchange
rel banter, chaff, cross fire, give-and-take, persiflage, raillery, repartee; conference, parley; babble, chatter, chitchat, gabfest, gossip, palaver, prate, prattle, rap, small talk, table talk; roundtable, symposium; debate, deliberation
conversational *adj* 1 fond of talking or conversation — see TALKATIVE
2 having the style and content of everyday conversation — see CHATTY 1
3 used in or suitable for speech and not formal writing — see COLLOQUIAL 1
conversationalist *n* a person who talks constantly — see CHATTERBOX
converse *n* talking or a talk between two or more people — see CONVERSATION
converse *vb* to engage in casual or rambling conversation — see CHAT 1
converse (with) *vb* to communicate with by means of spoken words — see TALK (TO)

conversely *adv* just the opposite being true — see CONTRARIWISE
conversion *n* 1 a change in form, appearance, or use ⟨The *conversion* of the spare bedroom into a home office was easily accomplished.⟩
syn changeover, metamorphosis, transfiguration, transformation
rel shift, transition; alteration, modification; accommodation, adaptation, conformation; reconstruction, reconversion, redo, redoing, refashioning, reformation, remaking, remodeling, revamping, revision, reworking, variation; deformation, disfigurement, distortion, mutation, transmutation; displacement, replacement, substitution, supplantation
2 the act of reasoning or pleading with someone to accept a belief or course of action — see PERSUASION 1
convert *n* 1 a person who has recently been persuaded to join a religious sect ⟨The *converts* were the most vocal and fervent worshippers in the church.⟩
syn neophyte, proselyte
rel regenerate; newcomer, novice, recruit; catechumen
2 one who follows the opinions or teachings of another — see FOLLOWER 1
convert *vb* 1 to persuade to change to one's religious faith ⟨young missionaries who go door-to-door trying to *convert* people⟩
syn proselyte, proselytize
rel missionize; brainwash, influence, sway; propagate
near ant secularize; dissuade
2 to change in form, appearance, or use ⟨The old factory was *converted* into an apartment building.⟩
syn make over, metamorphose, transfigure, transform
rel adjust, alter, recast; redesign, redo, reengineer, refashion, regenerate, remake, remodel, revamp, revise, rework, vary; deform, disfigure, distort, mutate, transmogrify; displace, replace, substitute, supplant
3 to cause (someone) to agree with a belief or course of action by using arguments or earnest requests — see PERSUADE
4 to take or make use of under a guise of authority but without actual right — see APPROPRIATE 1
convey *vb* 1 to cause (something) to pass from one to another — see COMMUNICATE 1
2 to support and take from one place to another — see CARRY 1
3 to give over the legal possession or ownership of — see TRANSFER 1
conveyance *n* something used to carry goods or passengers ⟨The covered wagon was the major *conveyance* that transported settlers and their belongings across the frontier.⟩
syn transport, transportation, vehicle
rel carrier, hauler, mover
convict *n* a person convicted as a criminal and serving a prison sentence ⟨a warning that the three escaped *convicts* were armed and dangerous⟩
syn con, jailbird

rel lifer, trusty; parolee, probationer; captive, capture, inmate, internee, prisoner

convict *vb* to find or pronounce guilty 〈The accused was tried and *convicted*.〉
syn condemn
rel accuse, arraign, charge, impeach, indict; censure, damn, denounce, rebuke, reprimand, reproach, reprove; admonish, castigate, chastise; penalize, punish, sentence
near ant cite, commend, endorse (*also* indorse); approve, bless, sanction
ant absolve, acquit, clear, exculpate, exonerate, vindicate

conviction *n* **1** a state of mind in which one is free from doubt — see CONFIDENCE 2
2 an idea that is believed to be true or valid without positive knowledge — see OPINION 1

convince *vb* to cause (someone) to agree with a belief or course of action by using arguments or earnest requests — see PERSUADE

convincing *adj* having the power to persuade — see COGENT

convincing *n* the act of reasoning or pleading with someone to accept a belief or course of action — see PERSUASION 1

convivial *adj* likely to seek or enjoy the company of others 〈The hiking club attracts a wide range of *convivial* people who share a love of the outdoors.〉
syn boon, companionable, extroverted (*also* extraverted), gregarious, outgoing, sociable, social
rel cordial, forthcoming, friendly, hospitable; affable, genial, gracious; agreeable, amiable, congenial, kindly, neighborly; animated, jaunty, jolly, jovial, lively, peppy, perky, pert, spirited, sprightful, sprightly, vivacious; communicative, expansive, garrulous, talkative; bright, buoyant, cheerful, chipper, effervescent, upbeat; bubbly, exuberant, high-spirited; colonial
near ant misanthropic; aloof, cold, cool, detached, distant, frosty, remote, reserved, standoffish; mum, mute, reticent, silent, taciturn
ant antisocial, insociable, introverted, nongregarious, reclusive, unsociable, unsocial

conviviality *n* **1** joyful or festive activity — see MERRYMAKING
2 the quality or state of being social — see SOCIABILITY

convocation *n* **1** a body of people come together in one place — see GATHERING 1
2 a coming together of a number of persons for a specified purpose — see MEETING 1

convoke *vb* to bring together in assembly by or as if by command 〈They *convoked* a meeting of the delegates.〉
syn assemble, call, convene, muster, summon
rel rally; call in, call out, call up, knell; amass, collect, gather, group, round up; reassemble, reconvene
near ant break up, dissolve

---

syn synonym(s)   *rel* related words
ant antonym(s)   *near ant* near antonym(s)

convoluted *adj* having many parts or aspects that are usually interrelated — see COMPLEX 1

convoy *vb* to go along with in order to provide assistance, protection, or companionship — see ACCOMPANY 1

convulse *vb* to make a series of small irregular or violent movements — see SHAKE 1

convulsion *n* a violent disturbance (as of the political or social order) 〈The Russian Revolution was one of the major *convulsions* of the 20th century.〉
syn cataclysm, earthquake, paroxysm, storm, tempest, tumult, upheaval, uproar
rel insurgency, insurrection, mutiny, overthrow, overturn, rebellion, revolt, revolution, subversion, unrest, uprising, upset; fit, seizure, spasm; eruption, flare-up, outbreak, outburst; bluster, bustle, coil, commotion, furor, furore, fuss, hubbub, hullabaloo, hurly-burly, pandemonium, rout, row, ruckus, ruction, rumpus, shindy, squall, stew, stir, to-do, turmoil, welter, williwaw; quaking, rocking, shaking, trembling

convulsive *adj* **1** marked by sudden or violent disturbance 〈The assassination of Martin Luther King was one of the most *convulsive* events of the 1960s.〉
syn cataclysmal (*or* cataclysmic), stormy, tempestuous, tumultuous, turbulent
rel fitful, spasmodic, sporadic; boisterous, clamorous, furious, noisy, riotous
near ant calm, peaceful, placid, serene, tranquil, undisturbed, unperturbed, unshaken, untroubled
2 marked by bursts of destructive force or intense activity — see VIOLENT 1

cook *n* a person who prepares food by some manner of heating 〈the hearty meals prepared by the *cook* at summer camp〉
syn chef, cook
rel baker; barbecuer, griller

cook *vb* **1** to change so much as to create a wrong impression or alter the meaning of — see GARBLE
2 to take place — see HAPPEN

cook (up) *vb* to create or think of by clever use of the imagination — see INVENT

cooker *n* **1** an appliance that prepares food for consumption by heating it 〈a portable gas-fired *cooker* that's perfect for camping trips〉
syn cookstove, range
rel broiler, fryer (*also* frier), microwave, microwave oven, oven, roaster, rotisserie, stove, toaster, toaster oven
2 a person who prepares food by some manner of heating — see COOK

cookery *n* the art or style of preparing food (as in a specified region) 〈an introduction to Mexican *cookery*〉
syn cooking, cuisine
rel haute cuisine; gastronomy

cooking *n* the art or style of preparing food (as in a specified region) — see COOKERY

cookstove *n* an appliance that prepares food for consumption by heating it — see COOKER 1

cool *adj* **1** having or showing a lack of

friendliness or interest in others ⟨Locals were *cool* towards tourists.⟩ ⟨The star's *cool* manner daunted her fans.⟩

syn aloof, antisocial, cold, detached, distant, dry, frosty, remote, standoffish, unbending, unsociable

rel indrawn, introverted, nongregarious, reclusive, reserved, unsocial, withdrawn; misanthropic; apathetic, hard, indifferent, unconcerned; clinical, dispassionate, impersonal, professional; disinterested, incurious, uninterested; reticent, silent, taciturn, uncommunicative; diffident, shy, timid; cliquey

near ant boon, companionable, convivial, extroverted (*also* extraverted), gregarious, outgoing; communicative, expansive, garrulous, talkative; affable, genial, gracious, hospitable; agreeable, amiable, congenial, kindly, neighborly

ant cordial, friendly, sociable, social, warm

2 free from emotional or mental agitation — see CALM 2

3 having a low or subnormal temperature — see COLD 1

4 lacking in friendliness or warmth of feeling — see COLD 2

5 *slang* being in the latest or current fashion — see STYLISH

6 *slang* of the very best kind — see EXCELLENT

cool *n* **1** the absence of emotional involvement ⟨The judge's customary *cool* stood him in good stead during the sensational trial.⟩

syn detachment

rel equitability, equitableness, fairness; disinterestedness, impartiality, objectivity, unbiasedness; balance, rationality, rationalness, reasonability, reasonableness; calm, calmness, peace, peacefulness, placidity, quiet, quietness, quietude, repose, restfulness, sereneness, serenity, tranquillity (*or* tranquility); reserve, undemonstrativeness, unresponsiveness; apathy, indifference

near ant emotionalism; bias, favor, onesidedness, partiality, partisanship, prejudice

2 the quality or state of being fashionable ⟨I envy you your *cool*.⟩

syn coolness, fashionableness, hip, modishness

rel chic, chicness, dapperness, elegance, poshness, smartness, style, swank, swankiness; class, grace, gracefulness, majesty, stateliness; artfulness, polish, sophistication, taste, tastefulness

near ant flashiness, garishness, gaudiness, gracelessness, grotesqueness, tackiness, tastelessness, tawdriness

ant unfashionableness

3 evenness of emotions or temper — see EQUANIMITY

cool *vb* to cause to lose heat ⟨*Cool* your drinks in the icy mountain stream.⟩

syn chill, refrigerate

rel air-condition; freeze, frost, quick-freeze, supercool; ventilate

near ant bake, boil, steam; heat-treat, temper; microwave

ant heat, toast, warm

coolheaded *adj* free from emotional or mental agitation — see CALM 2

coolish *adj* having a low or subnormal temperature — see COLD 1

coolness *n* **1** evenness of emotions or temper — see EQUANIMITY

2 the quality or state of being fashionable — see COOL 2

coop *n* an enclosure with an open framework for keeping animals — see CAGE

coop (up) *vb* to close or shut in by or as if by barriers — see ENCLOSE 1

cooperate *vb* **1** to participate or assist in a joint effort to accomplish an end ⟨Conservation groups *cooperated* with state authorities to find a humane way to manage the area's overpopulation of deer.⟩

syn band (together), collaborate, concert, concur, conjoin, conspire, join, league, team (up), unite

rel connive; affiliate, ally, associate, combine, confederate, hang together, interface

phrases make common cause, play ball, pull together

2 to form or enter into an association that furthers the interests of its members — see ALLY

cooperation *n* **1** the state of having shared interests or efforts (as in social or business matters) — see ASSOCIATION 1

2 the work and activity of a number of persons who individually contribute toward the efficiency of the whole — see TEAMWORK

cooperative *adj* used or done by a number of people as a group — see COLLECTIVE

coordinate *n* one that is equal to another in status, achievement, or value — see EQUAL

coordinate *vb* **1** to bring to a state free of conflicts, inconsistencies, or differences — see HARMONIZE 2

2 to form a pleasing relationship — see HARMONIZE 1

coordination *n* the work and activity of a number of persons who individually contribute toward the efficiency of the whole — see TEAMWORK

cop *n* a member of a force charged with law enforcement at the local level — see OFFICER 1

cop *vb*, *slang* to take physical control or possession of (something) suddenly or forcibly — see CATCH 1

copacetic *also* **copasetic** *or* **copesetic** *adj* being to one's liking — see SATISFACTORY 1

cope *n* something that covers or conceals like a piece of cloth — see CLOAK 1

cope *vb* to meet one's day-to-day needs — see GET ALONG 1

cope (with) *vb* to deal with (something) usually skillfully or efficiently — see HANDLE 1

copious *adj* pouring forth in great amounts — see PROFUSE

cop–out *n* the act or a means of getting or keeping away from something undesirable — see ESCAPE 2

cop out *vb* to break a promise or agreement — see RENEGE 1

coppice *n* a thick patch of shrubbery, small trees, or underbrush — see THICKET

copse *n* a thick patch of shrubbery, small trees, or underbrush — see THICKET

copulate *vb* to engage in sexual intercourse ⟨the time of year when deer in the wild are likely to *copulate*⟩
syn breed, mate, sleep
rel fornicate

copulation *n* sexual union involving penetration of the vagina by the penis — see SEXUAL INTERCOURSE

copy *n* something that is made to look exactly like something else ⟨a *copy* of the famous painting "Washington Crossing the Delaware"⟩
syn carbon copy, dummy, dupe, duplicate, duplication, facsimile, imitation, mock, reduplication, replica, replication, reproduction
rel counterfeit, fake, forgery, knockoff, phony (*also* phoney), rip-off, sham; miniature, mock-up, simulation; reconstruction, re-creation; image, likeness, semblance, shadow; impression, imprint, print; approximation, reincarnation; extra, reserve, spare
ant archetype, original, prototype

copy *vb* **1** to make an exact likeness of ⟨For the movie, set designers *copied* the Oval Office in the White House down to the smallest detail.⟩
syn copycat, duplicate, imitate, reduplicate, render, replicate, reproduce
rel counterfeit, fake, forge, knock off, rip off; mimic, simulate; reconstruct, re-create
near ant create, imagine, initiate, invent
ant originate
2 to use (someone or something) as the model for one's speech, mannerisms, or behavior — see IMITATE 1

copycat *n* a person who adopts the appearance or behavior of another especially in an obvious way ⟨Every pop star who makes it big soon has a whole cluster of *copycats*.⟩
syn aper, copyist, echo, follower, imitator
rel parrot; ape, emulator, impersonator, impressionist, mimic

copycat *vb* **1** to make an exact likeness of — see COPY 1
2 to use (someone or something) as the model for one's speech, mannerisms, or behavior — see IMITATE 1

copyist *n* **1** a person who adopts the appearance or behavior of another especially in an obvious way — see COPYCAT
2 one who writes from dictation or copies manuscripts — see SCRIBE 1

cord *n* **1** a length of braided, flexible material that is used for tying or connecting things ⟨a vacuum cleaner with an extra long *cord*⟩
syn cable, lace, lacing, line, rope, string, wire
rel guy, halyard, lanyard, stay; bungee cord, whipcord
2 a uniting or binding force or influence — see BOND 2

cordial *adj* **1** having or showing kindly feeling and sincere interest — see FRIENDLY 1
2 showing a natural kindness and courtesy especially in social situations — see GRACIOUS 1
3 having a renewing effect on the state of the body or mind — see TONIC 1

cordiality *n* kindly concern, interest, or support — see GOODWILL 1

core *n* **1** the seat of one's deepest thoughts and emotions ⟨In my very *core* I knew that an injustice was being committed.⟩
syn belly, blood, bone(s), bosom, breast, gut, heart, heartstrings, inside, quick, soul
rel conscience, mind
2 a thing or place that is of greatest importance to an activity or interest — see CENTER 1
3 the central part or aspect of something under consideration — see CRUX
4 the main or greater part of something as distinguished from its subordinate parts — see BODY 1
5 an area or point that is an equal distance from all points along an edge or outer surface — see CENTER 2

corker *n* something very good of its kind — see JIM-DANDY

corkscrew *adj* turning around an axis like the thread of a screw — see SPIRAL

corkscrew *vb* to follow a circular or spiral course — see WIND 1

corn *n* something (as a work of literature or music) that is too sentimental ⟨a story about a lost puppy that was pure *corn*⟩
syn mush, schmaltz (*also* schmalz), sludge, slush
rel claptrap, drivel, rubbish

corner *n* **1** a difficult, puzzling, or embarrassing situation from which there is no easy escape — see PREDICAMENT
2 a place where roads meet — see CROSSROAD 1
3 a point in a chain of events at which an important change (as in one's fortunes) occurs — see TURNING POINT

cornerstone *n* an immaterial thing upon which something else rests — see BASE 1

cornet *n* something shaped like a hollow cone and used as a container ⟨*cornets* of pastry dough that were baked and later filled with cream⟩
syn cornucopia, horn
rel funnel, tube

cornucopia *n* **1** an abundant source — see MINE 1
2 an amount or supply more than sufficient to meet one's needs — see PLENTY 1
3 something shaped like a hollow cone and used as a container — see CORNET

corny *adj* appealing to the emotions in an obvious and tiresome way ⟨*corny* violin music during the movie's love scenes⟩
syn gooey, maudlin, mawkish, mushy, saccharine, sappy, schmaltzy, sentimental, sloppy, slushy, sugarcoated, sudsy; flat, insipid, soft-boiled, tasteless, vapid, watery; cutesy
near ant unadulterated, unvarnished; anti-

---

sentimental, cynical, hard-boiled, hard-edged, hardheaded
ant unsentimental

corollary *n* 1 a condition or occurrence traceable to a cause — see EFFECT 1

2 something that is found along with something else — see ACCOMPANIMENT

coronet *n* a decorative band or wreath worn about the head as a symbol of victory or honor — see CROWN 1

corporal *adj* of or relating to the human body — see PHYSICAL 1

corporeal *adj* of or relating to the human body — see PHYSICAL 1

corps *n* the body of people in a profession or field of activity ⟨a reporter who is widely respected throughout the press *corps*⟩
syn brotherhood, community, fellowship, fraternity, sodality, vocation
rel calling, profession; association, club, federation, guild (*also* gild), organization, society

corpse *n* a dead body ⟨The startling discovery of a *corpse* required a call to the police.⟩
syn bones, cadaver, carcass, remains, stiff
rel mummy; carnage, carrion; ashes; deceased, decedent

corpulence *n* the condition of having an excess of body fat ⟨The doctor warned that the patient's *corpulence* was unhealthy.⟩
syn chubbiness, fat, fatness, fleshiness, grossness, obesity, plumpness, portliness, pudginess, rotundity, weight
rel bulkiness, heaviness; huskiness, stoutness; brawniness, burliness; endomorphy
near ant fitness, trimness; gauntness, scrawniness, skinniness, weediness
ant leanness, reediness, slenderness, slimness, svelteness, thinness

corpulent *adj* having an excess of body fat — see FAT 1

corral *n* an enclosure with an open framework for keeping animals — see CAGE

corral *vb* 1 to close or shut in by or as if by barriers — see ENCLOSE 1

2 to take physical control or possession of (something) suddenly or forcibly — see CATCH 1

3 to bring together in one body or place — see GATHER 1

correct *adj* 1 being in agreement with the truth or a fact or a standard ⟨a real brainteaser with only one *correct* solution to it⟩
syn accurate, exact, good, precise, proper, right, so, true, veracious
rel legitimate, logical, sound, valid; errorless, faultless, flawless, impeccable, inerrant, infallible, letter-perfect, perfect; rigorous, strict, stringent
phrases on target, on the money
near ant defective, faulty, flawed, imperfect
ant false, improper, inaccurate, incorrect, inexact, off, untrue, wrong

2 following the established traditions of refined society and good taste — see PROPER 1

3 marked by or showing careful attention to set forms and details — see CEREMONIOUS 1

correct *vb* 1 to remove errors, defects, deficiencies, or deviations from ⟨More time will be needed to *correct* the computer program.⟩
syn amend, debug, emend, rectify, reform, remedy
rel redraft, redraw, restyle, revise, rework, rewrite; cut, shorten; redress, right; ameliorate, better, improve; perfect, polish, touch up; fix, mend, repair; adjust, modulate, regulate; alter, change, modify
near ant damage, harm, hurt, impair, injure, mar, spoil; aggravate, worsen

2 to balance with an equal force so as to make ineffective — see OFFSET

3 to inflict a penalty on for a fault or crime — see PUNISH

correctable *adj* capable of being corrected — see REMEDIABLE

correcting *adj* inflicting, involving, or serving as punishment — see PUNITIVE

correction *n* 1 a change designed to correct or improve a written work ⟨The copy editor's *corrections* were marked in red.⟩
syn amendment, emendation
rel cut, deletion; addition, amplification, supplement; alteration, modification, revision; improvement, renovation; clarification, explanation, explication

2 suffering, loss, or hardship imposed in response to a crime or offense — see PUNISHMENT

correctional *adj* inflicting, involving, or serving as punishment — see PUNITIVE

corrective *adj* 1 serving to raise or adjust something to some standard or proper condition ⟨Eyeglasses are called *corrective* lenses by the department of motor vehicles.⟩
syn rectifying, remedial, remedying, reformative, reformatory
rel reparative, restorative; beneficial, helpful, salutary, wholesome; antidotal, counteractive, counterbalancing

2 inflicting, involving, or serving as punishment — see PUNITIVE

corrective *n* 1 a force or influence that makes an opposing force ineffective or less effective — see COUNTERBALANCE

2 something that corrects or counteracts something undesirable — see CURE 1

correctly *adv* in a manner suitable for the occasion or purpose — see PROPERLY

correlate *vb* to think of (something) in combination — see ASSOCIATE 2

correspond *vb* 1 to engage in an exchange of written messages ⟨old friends who have been *corresponding* for years⟩
syn write
rel communicate, intercommunicate; airmail, e-mail, telegraph; mail, post; answer, reply

2 to be in agreement on every point — see CHECK 1

correspond (to) *vb* 1 to be the exact counterpart of — see MATCH 1

2 to be the same in meaning or effect — see AMOUNT (TO) 2

correspondence *n* 1 a point which two or more things share in common — see SIMILARITY 2

2 the quality or state of having many qualities in common — see SIMILARITY 1

3 communications or parcels sent or carried through the postal system — see MAIL

correspondent *adj* having qualities in common — see ALIKE

correspondent *n* a person employed by a newspaper, magazine, or radio or television station to gather, write, or report news — see REPORTER

correspondent (with *or* **to)** *adj* not having or showing any apparent conflict — see CONSISTENT

corresponding *adj* having qualities in common — see ALIKE

correspondingly *adv* in like manner — see ALSO 1

corridor *n* 1 a broad geographical area — see REGION 2

2 a typically long narrow way connecting parts of a building — see HALL 2

corroborate *vb* 1 to give evidence or testimony to the truth or factualness of — see CONFIRM 1

2 to provide evidence or information for (as a claim or idea) — see SUPPORT 4

corroborating *adj* serving to give support to the truth or factualness of something — see CORROBORATIVE

corroboration *n* something presented in support of the truth or accuracy of a claim — see PROOF

corroborative *adj* serving to give support to the truth or factualness of something ⟨The results of the DNA fingerprinting were all the *corroborative* evidence the jury needed to convict.⟩

syn confirmatory, confirming, corroborating, corroboratory, substantiating, supporting, supportive, verifying, vindicating

rel auxiliary, supplementary; beneficial, helpful

near ant contradictory, contrary, counter, opposing

ant confuting, disproving, refuting

corroboratory *adj* serving to give support to the truth or factualness of something — see CORROBORATIVE

corrode *vb* to consume or wear away gradually — see EAT 2

corrosion *n* a gradual weakening, loss, or destruction ⟨the *corrosion* of family values that is often brought on by great wealth⟩

syn attrition, erosion, waste

rel breakdown, decay, decomposition, disintegration, dissolution

near ant gain, increase

ant buildup

corrupt *adj* having or showing lowered moral character or standards ⟨*corrupt* businessmen who are out to fleece the public⟩ ⟨*corrupt* business practices that should be investigated⟩

syn debased, debauched, decadent, degenerate, degraded, demoralized, depraved, dissipated, dissolute, libertine, loose, perverse, perverted, reprobate, sick, unclean, unwholesome, warped

rel crooked, cutthroat, dishonest, unethical, unprincipled, unscrupulous; contaminated, spoiled, tainted; bad, evil, immoral, iniquitous, miscreant, nefarious, sinful, vicious, wicked

near ant incorruptible; ethical, honest,

principled; good, moral, righteous, virtuous

ant pure, uncorrupt, uncorrupted

corrupt *vb* 1 to go through decomposition — see DECAY 1

2 to lower in character, dignity, or quality — see DEBASE 1

3 to influence someone with a bribe — see BRIBE

corrupted *adj* having undergone organic breakdown — see ROTTEN 1

corruptible *adj* open to improper influence and especially bribery — see VENAL

corruption *n* 1 the process by which dead organic matter separates into simpler substances ⟨The ancient Egyptians used special preservatives to spare their dead from complete *corruption*.⟩

syn breakdown, decay, decomposition, putrefaction, rot, spoilage

rel crumbling, disintegration, dissolution; curdling, moldering, souring

near ant growth, maturation, ripening

2 a sinking to a state of low moral standards and behavior ⟨The *corruption* of the upper classes eventually led to the fall of the Roman empire.⟩

syn corruptness, debasement, debauchery, decadence, degeneracy, degeneration, degradation, demoralization, depravity, dissipatedness, dissipation, dissoluteness, perversion

rel evil, immorality, sinfulness, villainy, wickedness; filth, gangrene, rot, squalor

near ant goodness, morality, righteousness, virtue

3 immoral conduct or practices harmful or offensive to society — see VICE 1

corruptness *n* a sinking to a state of low moral standards and behavior — see CORRUPTION 2

corsair *n* someone who engages in robbery of ships at sea — see PIRATE

cortege *also* **cortège** *n* 1 a body of employees or attendants who accompany and wait on a person ⟨The movie star's *cortege* included her stylist, personal assistant, and press agent.⟩

syn following, retinue, suite, train

rel crew, personnel, staff; court; assistant, attendant, helper, retainer

2 a body of individuals moving along in an orderly and often ceremonial way ⟨The funeral *cortege* of mourners stretched for three city blocks.⟩

syn parade, procession

rel progress; column, line, string, train

cosmetics *n pl* preparations intended to beautify the face — see MAKEUP 1

cosmic *also* **cosmical** *adj* unusually large — see HUGE

cosmopolitan *adj* having a wide and refined knowledge of the world especially from personal experience — see WORLDLY-WISE

cosmopolitan *n* a person with the outlook, experience, and manners thought to be typical of big city dwellers ⟨As someone who had lived in Paris for a year as an exchange student, she seemed very much the *cosmopolitan* to her old classmates.⟩

syn metropolitan, slicker, sophisticate

rel urbanite; worldling

---

ant bumpkin, hick, provincial, rustic, yokel

cosmos *n* the whole body of things observed or assumed — see UNIVERSE

cost *n* 1 a payment made in the course of achieving a result — see EXPENSE

2 the amount of money that is demanded as payment for something — see PRICE 1

3 the loss or penalty involved in achieving a goal — see PRICE 1

cost *vb* to have a price of ⟨The raffle tickets *cost* a dollar each.⟩

syn bring, fetch, go (for), run, sell (for)

rel list (for); amount (to), come (to), total; command, exact; ask, demand

costly *adj* commanding a large price ⟨Running is one sport that does not require a lot of *costly* equipment.⟩

syn dear, expensive, extravagant, high, precious, premium, valuable

rel exorbitant, overpriced, prohibitive, sky-high, steep, stiff, unaffordable, uneconomic (*or* uneconomical), unreasonable; deluxe, luxurious, sumptuous

near ant moderate, reasonable; valueless, worthless; discounted

ant cheap, inexpensive

costume *n* 1 clothing chosen as appropriate for a specific situation — see OUTFIT 1

2 clothing put on to hide one's true identity or imitate someone or something else — see DISGUISE 1

costume *vb* to outfit with clothes and especially fine or special clothes — see CLOTHE 1

coterie *n* a group of people sharing a common interest and relating together socially — see GANG 2

cotillion *also* **cotillon** *n* a social gathering for dancing — see DANCE

cottage *n* an often small house for recreational or seasonal use ⟨For a month every summer we rent a *cottage* on the ocean.⟩

syn cabin, camp, chalet, lodge

rel dacha; bungalow, cot; hut, shack, shanty

cottony *adj* 1 covered with or as if with hair — see HAIRY 1

2 smooth or delicate in appearance or feel — see SOFT 2

couch *n* a long upholstered piece of furniture designed for several sitters ⟨Find yourself a place on the *couch* and make yourself at home.⟩

syn davenport, divan, lounge, settee, sofa

rel lounger, love seat; daybed, sofa bed, studio couch; banquette, bench, ottoman

couch *vb* 1 to convey in appropriate or telling terms — see PHRASE

2 to lie low with the limbs close to the body — see CROUCH

cougar *n* a large tawny cat of the wild ⟨In many regions, suburban developments have encroached upon the habitat of the *cougar*.⟩

syn catamount, mountain lion, panther, puma

council *n* 1 a coming together of a number of persons for a specified purpose — see MEETING 1

2 a group of persons formally joined together for some common interest — see ASSOCIATION 2

3 a meeting featuring a group discussion — see FORUM 1

4 a local unit of an organization — see CHAPTER 1

5 an exchange of views for the purpose of exploring a subject or deciding an issue — see DISCUSSION 1

counsel *n* 1 a person whose profession is to conduct lawsuits for clients or to advise about legal rights and obligations — see LAWYER

2 an opinion suggesting a wise or proper course of action — see ADVICE

3 a person who gives advice especially professionally — see CONSULTANT

4 an exchange of views for the purpose of exploring a subject or deciding an issue — see DISCUSSION 1

counsel *vb* 1 to exchange viewpoints or seek advice for the purpose of finding a solution to a problem — see CONFER 2

2 to give advice and instruction to (someone) regarding the course or process to be followed — see GUIDE 1

3 to give advice to — see ADVISE 1

4 to put (something) forward as one's choice for a wise or proper course of action — see ADVISE 2

counselor *or* **counsellor** *n* 1 a person who gives advice especially professionally — see CONSULTANT

2 a person whose profession is to conduct lawsuits for clients or to advise about legal rights and obligations — see LAWYER

count *n* 1 a total number obtained or recorded by noting each thing as it was being added ⟨My *count* for the number of bird species and subspecies that visited the sanctuary that weekend was 43.⟩

syn tale, tally

rel score; amount, gross, sum, total, whole; recount

2 a formal claim of criminal wrongdoing against a person — see CHARGE 1

count *vb* 1 to find the sum of (a collection of things) by noting each one as it is being added ⟨*Count* the baseball gloves in the storage locker to see if there are enough to go around.⟩

syn enumerate, number, tell

rel add (up), tally, total; calculate, compute, reckon, table, tabulate; check, mark, tick (off); recount

2 to be of importance — see MATTER

3 to place reliance or trust — see DEPEND 2

4 to think of in a particular way — see CONSIDER 1

count (out) *vb* to prevent the participation, consideration, or inclusion of — see EXCLUDE

countenance *n* 1 facial appearance regarded as an indication of mood or feeling — see LOOK 1

2 the front part of the head — see FACE 1

3 evenness of emotions or temper — see EQUANIMITY

countenance *vb* 1 to have a favorable opinion of — see APPROVE (OF)

2 to put up with (something painful or difficult) — see BEAR 1

counter *adj* opposed to one's interests — see ADVERSE 1

counter *n* 1 a force or influence that

makes an opposing force ineffective or less effective — see COUNTERBALANCE

2 something that is as different as possible from something else — see OPPOSITE

counter *vb* to strive to reduce or eliminate — see FIGHT 2

counteract *vb* to balance with an equal force so as to make ineffective — see OFFSET

counteraction *n* a force or influence that makes an opposing force ineffective or less effective — see COUNTERBALANCE

counterattack *n* an attack made to counter an enemy's attack ⟨Suddenly the tide of battle turned, and the rebels, who had been falling back, made a furious *counterattack*.⟩

syn counteroffensive

rel sally, sortie; blitzkrieg, charge; assault, attack, offensive, onslaught

counterbalance *n* a force or influence that makes an opposing force ineffective or less effective ⟨The author's humor is a good *counterbalance* to the book's serious subject matter.⟩

syn balance, canceler (*or* canceller), corrective, counter, counteraction, counterpoise, counterweight, equipoise, neutralizer, offset

rel trade-off; ballast, weight

counterbalance *vb* to balance with an equal force so as to make ineffective — see OFFSET

counterfeit *adj* **1** being such in appearance only and made or manufactured with the intention of committing fraud ⟨*counterfeit* currency that had been passed all over town⟩

syn bogus, fake, false, forged, inauthentic, phony (*also* phoney), sham, spurious, unauthentic

rel artificial, factitious, imitation, man-made, mimic, mock, simulated, substitute, synthetic; dummy, nonfunctioning, ornamental; cultured, fabricated, manufactured; deceptive, delusive, misleading

near ant natural; actual, true, valid

ant authentic, bona fide, genuine, real, unfaked

2 not being or expressing what one appears to be or express — see INSINCERE

counterfeit *n* an imitation that is passed off as genuine — see FAKE 1

counterfeit *vb* **1** to imitate or copy especially in order to deceive — see FAKE 1

2 to present a false appearance of — see FEIGN

counteroffensive *n* an attack made to counter an enemy's attack — see COUNTERATTACK

counterpane *n* a decorative cloth used as a top covering for a bed ⟨a beautiful *counterpane* that was a family heirloom⟩

syn bedspread, coverlet, spread

rel comforter, puff, quilt; bedclothes, bedding, clothes

counterpart *n* **1** one that is equal to another in status, achievement, or value — see EQUAL

2 something or someone that strongly resembles another — see IMAGE 1

counterpoise *n* **1** a condition in which opposing forces are equal to one another — see BALANCE 1

2 a force or influence that makes an opposing force ineffective or less effective — see COUNTERBALANCE

counterpoise *vb* to balance with an equal force so as to make ineffective — see OFFSET

countersign *n* a word or phrase that must be spoken by a person in order to pass a guard — see PASSWORD

counterweight *n* a force or influence that makes an opposing force ineffective or less effective — see COUNTERBALANCE

countless *adj* too many to be counted ⟨I've told you *countless* times not to do that!⟩

syn innumerable, myriad, numberless, uncountable, uncounted, unnumbered, untold

rel endless, infinite, unlimited, vast; many, multitudinous, numerous

phrases beyond number

near ant finite, limited

ant countable, enumerable, numberable

country *adj* of, relating to, associated with, or typical of open areas with few buildings or people — see RURAL

country *n* **1** the land of one's birth, residence, or citizenship ⟨a great love for my *country*⟩

syn fatherland, home, homeland, motherland, sod

rel old country; community, neighborhood

2 the open rural area outside of big towns and cities ⟨out in the *country*, where the air is fresh and the rivers are clean⟩

syn boondocks, countryside, sticks

rel exurbia; backwater, backwoods, bush, frontier, hinterland, up-country; wild, wilderness

phrases middle of nowhere

near ant conurbation, megalopolis, urban sprawl

3 a body of people composed of one or more nationalities usually with its own territory and government — see NATION

countryman *n* **1** a person living in or originally from the same country as another — see COMPATRIOT 1

2 an awkward or simple person especially from a small town or the country — see HICK

countryside *n* the open rural area outside of big towns and cities — see COUNTRY 2

coup *n* a successful result brought about by hard work — see ACCOMPLISHMENT 1

couple *n* **1** a small number — see FEW

2 two things of the same or similar kind that match or are considered together — see PAIR

couple *vb* **1** to come together to form a single unit — see UNITE 1

2 to put or bring together so as to form a new and longer whole — see CONNECT 1

coupling *n* **1** a place where two or more things are united — see JOINT 1

2 the act or an instance of joining two or more things into one — see UNION 1

coupon *n* a small sheet of plastic, paper, or paperboard showing that the bearer has

---

syn synonym(s)   *rel* related words
ant antonym(s)   *near ant* near antonym(s)

a claim to something (as admittance) — see TICKET 1

courage n strength of mind to carry on in spite of danger ⟨the moral *courage* to speak out against injustice when no one else will⟩

syn bravery, courageousness, daring, dauntlessness, doughtiness, fearlessness, gallantry, greatheartedness, guts, hardihood, heart, heroism, intrepidity, intrepidness, nerve, stoutness, valor, virtue

rel backbone, fiber, fortitude, grit, mettle, pluck, pluckiness, spunk, temper; determination, perseverance, resolution; endurance, stamina, stomach, tenacity; audacity, boldness, brazenness, cheek, effrontery, gall, temerity

near ant cold feet, faintheartedness, fearfulness, mousiness, timidity, timorousness; feebleness, softness, weakness; impotence, ineffectualness; hesitation, indecision, indecisiveness, irresolution

ant cowardice, cowardliness, cravenness, dastardliness, poltroonery, spinelessness

courageous *adj* feeling or displaying no fear by temperament — see BRAVE 1

courageousness n strength of mind to carry on in spite of danger — see COURAGE

courier n one that carries a message or does an errand — see MESSENGER

course n 1 a way of acting or proceeding ⟨The president's usual *course* has been to obtain advice from several people and then make a decision.⟩

syn line, policy, procedure, program

rel blueprint, design, plan, scheme, strategy; intent, intention, purpose; approach, direction, method, path, pathway, tack

2 a series of lectures on a subject ⟨a *course* on American history from the colonial period to the present⟩

syn class

rel elective, refresher; clinic, institute, seminar, survey course; minicourse; core, curriculum

phrases course of study

3 a usually fixed or ordered series of actions or events leading to a result — see PROCESS 1

4 the direction along which something or someone moves — see PATH 1

5 an open man-made passageway for water — see CHANNEL 1

course vb 1 to go after or on the track of — see FOLLOW 2

2 to make one's way through, across, or over — see TRAVERSE

3 to proceed or move quickly — see HURRY 2

court n 1 the residence of a ruler ⟨Hampton *Court* was the imposing residence of King Henry VIII.⟩

syn palace

rel castle, château, estate, mansion, villa

2 an open space wholly or partly enclosed (as by buildings or walls) ⟨The art museum boasts a glass-sided *court* that is filled with an array of greenery and sculpture.⟩

syn close, courtyard, enclosure (*also* inclosure), patio, quadrangle, yard

rel atrium, galleria, peristyle; forecourt, place, plaza, square; gallery [*Southern & Midland*], porch, stoop; deck, sundeck

3 an assembly of persons for the administration of justice ⟨This *court* is now called to order.⟩

syn bar, bench, forum, tribunal

rel criminal court, judicatory, judicature, judiciary; high court, supreme court; court-martial, drumhead court-martial; inquisition, kangaroo court

phrases court of law

4 a public official having authority to decide questions of law — see JUDGE 2

court vb 1 to act so as to make (something) more likely ⟨You're *courting* disaster if you keep playing with matches.⟩

syn ask (for), invite, woo

rel angle (for), fish (for); hunt, search, seek; provoke, tempt

phrases look for

2 to go on dates that may eventually lead to marriage ⟨They *courted* for a year before getting married.⟩

syn date

rel attend, gallant, romance, spark, woo; escort, see, take out

phrases go steady, keep company, make love

courteous *adj* showing consideration, courtesy, and good manners — see POLITE 1

courteously *adv* with good reason or courtesy — see WELL 4

courteousness n speech or behavior that is a sign of good manners — see POLITENESS 1

courtesy n 1 an act of kind assistance — see FAVOR 1

2 an act or utterance that is a customary show of good manners — see CIVILITY 1

3 speech or behavior that is a sign of good manners — see POLITENESS 1

courting n the series of social engagements shared by a couple looking to get married — see COURTSHIP

courtliness n dignified or restrained beauty of form, appearance, or style — see ELEGANCE

courtly *adj* having or showing elegance — see ELEGANT 1

courtship n the series of social engagements shared by a couple looking to get married ⟨a long-married couple who look back on their whirlwind *courtship* with fondness and laughter⟩

syn courting, dating, suit

rel suit, wooing; affair (*also* affaire), love affair, romance; betrothal, engagement

courtyard n an open space wholly or partly enclosed (as by buildings or walls) — see COURT 2

cove n a part of a body of water that extends beyond the general shoreline — see GULF 1

covenant n 1 a formal agreement between two or more nations or peoples — see TREATY

2 a formal agreement to fulfill an obligation — see GUARANTEE 1

3 an arrangement about action to be taken — see AGREEMENT 2

covenant vb 1 to come to an arrangement as to a course of action — see AGREE 2

2 to make a solemn declaration of intent — see PROMISE 1

cover n 1 a piece placed over an open container to hold in, protect, or conceal its contents ⟨Where's the *cover* for the cookie jar?⟩

syn cap, lid, top

rel hood, roof; capsule, case, casing, covering, housing, jacket, sheath, shell

2 means or method of defending — see DEFENSE 1

3 something that encloses another thing especially to protect it — see ¹CASE 1

4 a raised covering over something for decoration or protection — see CANOPY

5 something that covers or conceals like a piece of cloth — see CLOAK 1

cover *vb* **1** to serve as a replacement usually for a time only ⟨A friend *covered* for me as a hospital volunteer while my family went on vacation.⟩

syn fill in, pinch-hit, stand in, sub, substitute, take over

rel understudy; relieve, spell; double (as)

2 to form a layer over ⟨By morning a foot of snow *covered* the ground.⟩

syn blanket, carpet, coat, overlay, overlie, overspread, sheet

rel enclose (*also* inclose), enshroud, envelop, enwrap, mantle, shawl, shroud, swathe, wrap; cloak, clothe, curtain, veil; circle, encircle, encompass

3 to place a protective layer over ⟨Better *cover* your skin with sunblock if you don't want a sunburn.⟩

syn screen, shield

rel cloak, clothe, veil; pall; canopy, cap, crown; disguise, mask, obscure

near ant bare, expose, uncover

4 to have (something) as a subject matter — see CONCERN 1

5 to keep secret or shut off from view — see ¹HIDE 2

6 to make one's way through, across, or over — see TRAVERSE

7 to pay continued close attention to (something) for a particular purpose — see MONITOR

8 to drive danger or attack away from — see DEFEND 1

cover (up) *vb* to keep from being publicly known — see SUPPRESS 1

coverage *n* the amount of something (as subject matter) included ⟨The biographical dictionary's *coverage* is limited to people no longer living.⟩

syn content

rel compass, gamut, range, scope, sweep; membership, participation

covering *n* **1** something that covers or conceals like a piece of cloth — see CLOAK 1

2 something that encloses another thing especially to protect it — see ¹CASE 1

coverlet *n* a decorative cloth used as a top covering for a bed — see COUNTERPANE

covert *adj* **1** screened or sequestered from view — see SECLUDED

2 undertaken or done so as to escape being observed or known by others — see SECRET 1

covert *n* **1** a place where a person goes to hide or to avoid others — see HIDEOUT

2 a thick patch of shrubbery, small trees, or underbrush — see THICKET

covet *vb* to have an earnest wish to own or enjoy — see DESIRE 1

coveting *adj* having or marked by an eager and often selfish desire especially for material possessions — see GREEDY 1

covetous *adj* **1** having or marked by an eager and selfish desire especially for material possessions — see GREEDY 1

2 having or showing mean resentment of another's possessions or advantages — see ENVIOUS

covetousness *n* **1** a painful awareness of another's possessions or advantages and a desire to have them too — see ENVY

2 an intense selfish desire for wealth or possessions — see GREED

cow *vb* to make timid or fearful by or as if by threats — see INTIMIDATE

coward *n* a person who shows a shameful lack of courage in the face of danger ⟨The soldiers who ran as soon as the first shots were fired were branded as *cowards*.⟩

syn chicken, craven, cur, dastard, funk, poltroon, recreant, sissy

rel defeatist, quitter; cream puff, milquetoast, pushover, weakling, wimp; snake, sneak

near ant daredevil

ant hero, stalwart, valiant

cowardice *n* a shameful lack of courage in the face of danger ⟨the *cowardice* shown by political leaders who were willing to give the Nazis whatever they wanted⟩

syn cowardliness, cravenness, dastardliness, spinelessness

rel diffidence, faintheartedness, fearfulness, timidity, timorousness; carefulness, cautiousness, wariness; bashfulness, shyness; feebleness, softness, weakness

near ant audacity, boldness, brazenness; backbone, fiber, fortitude, grit, mettle, pluck, spunk; determination, perseverance, resolution; endurance, stamina, tenacity

ant bravery, courage, courageousness, daring, dauntlessness, doughtiness, fearlessness, gallantry, greatheartedness, guts, hardihood, heart, heroism, intrepidity, intrepidness, nerve, stoutness, valiance, valor, virtue

cowardliness *n* a shameful lack of courage in the face of danger — see COWARDICE

cowardly *adj* having or showing a shameful lack of courage ⟨a *cowardly* bully who picks on the weak and defenseless⟩ ⟨vile charges that were made in a *cowardly*, unsigned letter⟩

syn chicken, chickenhearted, craven, dastardly, lily-livered, poltroon, pusillanimous, recreant, spineless, unheroic, yellow

rel diffident, fainthearted, fearful, timid, timorous; afraid, frightened, scared; careful, cautious, wary; bashful, coy, shy; feeble, soft, unmanly, weak

near ant audacious, bold, brazen, cheeky, nervy; plucky, spirited, spunky; determined, resolute

ant brave, courageous, daring, dauntless, doughty, fearless, gallant, greathearted,

---

syn synonym(s)   *rel* related words

ant antonym(s)   *near ant* near antonym(s)

gutsy, hardy, heroic (*also* heroical), intrepid, lionhearted, stalwart, stout, stouthearted, valiant, valorous

cowboy *n* a hired hand who tends cattle or horses at a ranch or on the range ⟨*Cowboys* were rounding up the cattle for branding.⟩

syn buckaroo (*also* buckeroo), cowhand, cowman, cowpoke, cowpuncher, wrangler

rel cowgirl; caballero [*chiefly Southwest*], gaucho, vaquero; horseman, horsewoman; cattleman, rancher, stockman; cowherd, drover, herder, herdsman

cower *vb* to draw back or crouch down in fearful submission ⟨After some time in the animal shelter, the rescued dog finally stopped *cowering* when approached.⟩

syn cringe, grovel, quail

rel flinch, recoil, shrink, squinch; blanch, blench, whiten; fawn, kowtow, toady

cowhand *n* a hired hand who tends cattle or horses at a ranch or on the range — see COWBOY

cowhide *vb* to strike repeatedly with something long and thin or flexible — see WHIP 1

cowman *n* a hired hand who tends cattle or horses at a ranch or on the range — see COWBOY

coworker *n* a fellow worker — see COLLEAGUE

cowpoke *n* a hired hand who tends cattle or horses at a ranch or on the range — see COWBOY

cowpuncher *n* a hired hand who tends cattle or horses at a ranch or on the range — see COWBOY

coy *adj* 1 affecting shyness or modesty ⟨Not wanting him to know that she was interested in him, she acted very *coy* at the dance.⟩

syn demure, kittenish

rel flirtatious, flirty, girlish; goody-goody, overmodest, priggish, prim, prudish

ant uncoy

2 not comfortable around people — see SHY 2

cozen *vb* 1 to cause to believe what is untrue — see DECEIVE

2 to rob by the use of trickery or threats — see FLEECE

cozener *n* a dishonest person who uses clever means to cheat others out of something of value — see TRICKSTER 1

cozy *adj* 1 enjoying physical comfort — see COMFORTABLE 2

2 providing physical comfort — see COMFORTABLE 1

crab *n* an irritable and complaining person — see GROUCH 1

crab *vb* 1 to express dissatisfaction, pain, or resentment usually tiresomely — see COMPLAIN

2 to reduce the soundness, effectiveness, or perfection of — see DAMAGE 1

crabby *adj* 1 easily irritated or annoyed — see IRRITABLE

2 given to complaining a lot — see FUSSY 1

crack *adj* having or showing exceptional knowledge, experience, or skill in a field of endeavor — see PROFICIENT

crack *n* 1 an irregular usually narrow break in a surface created by pressure ⟨A pebble struck the car's windshield and left a spidery *crack* in it.⟩

syn check, chink, cleft, cranny, crevice, fissure, rift, split

rel crevasse; craze, hairline; fracture, rupture; breach, gap, opening; cut, gash, incision, slit

2 a hard strike with a part of the body or an instrument — see ¹BLOW

3 a loud explosive sound — see CLAP 1

4 an effort to do or accomplish something — see ATTEMPT 1

5 something said or done to cause laughter — see JOKE 1

6 a person of odd or whimsical habits — see ECCENTRIC

crack *vb* 1 to break suddenly with an explosive sound ⟨The tree branch unexpectedly *cracked* under our weight.⟩

syn pop, snap

rel rend, rive, split; crackle, hiss, sizzle, sputter; burst, explode, shatter; clack, clatter, click

2 to yield to mental or emotional stress ⟨After hours of tough questioning the suspect finally *cracked* and blurted out a confession.⟩

syn break down, break up, freak (out)

rel choke

phrases blow one's cool, fall apart, go off the deep end, go to pieces, lose it

3 to change (as a secret message) from code into ordinary language — see DECODE 1

4 to deliver a blow to (someone or something) usually in a strong vigorous manner — see HIT 1

5 to find an answer for through reasoning — see SOLVE

6 to cause to go insane or as if insane — see CRAZE

crackbrain *n* a person of odd or whimsical habits — see ECCENTRIC

crack down (on) *vb* to put a stop to (something) by the use of force — see QUELL 1

crackerjack *adj* 1 having or showing exceptional knowledge, experience, or skill in a field of endeavor — see PROFICIENT

2 of the very best kind — see EXCELLENT

crackerjack *also* **crackajack** *n* 1 a person with a high level of knowledge or skill in a field — see EXPERT

2 something very good of its kind — see JIM-DANDY

crackpot *n* a person of odd or whimsical habits — see ECCENTRIC

crack-up *n* 1 a mental or nervous collapse — see BREAKDOWN 1

2 the violent coming together of two bodies into destructive contact — see CRASH 1

crack up *vb* 1 to declare enthusiastic approval of — see ACCLAIM

2 to praise or publicize lavishly and often excessively — see TOUT 1

3 to show mirth with an explosive vocal sound — see LAUGH 1

cradle *n* 1 a place of origin — see BIRTHPLACE

2 a point or place at which something is invented or perfected — see SOURCE 1

craft *n* 1 an occupation requiring skillful use of the hands ⟨The *craft* of cabinetmaking was much admired in colonial times.⟩

syn art, handcraft, handicraft, trade

rel skill; calling, occupation, profession, vocation

2 a small buoyant structure for travel on water — see BOAT 1

3 the inclination or practice of misleading others through lies or trickery — see DECEIT 1

4 skill in achieving one's ends through indirect, subtle, or underhanded means — see CUNNING 1

5 subtle or imaginative ability in inventing, devising, or executing something — see SKILL 1

craft *vb* to put (something) into proper and usually carefully worked out written form — see COMPOSE 1

craftiness *n* **1** skill in achieving one's ends through indirect, subtle, or underhanded means — see CUNNING 1

2 the inclination or practice of misleading others through lies or trickery — see DECEIT 1

craftsman *n* a person whose occupation requires skill with the hands — see ARTISAN

crafty *adj* clever at attaining one's ends by indirect and often deceptive means — see ARTFUL 1

crag *n* a steep wall of rock, earth, or ice — see CLIFF

craggy *adj* having an uneven edge or outline — see RAGGED 1

cram *vb* **1** to fit (people or things) into a tight space — see CROWD 1

2 to put into (something) as much as can be held or contained — see FILL 1

3 to fill with food to capacity — see GORGE 1

4 to swallow or eat greedily — see GOBBLE

crammed *adj* containing or seeming to contain the greatest quantity or number possible — see FULL 1

¹**cramp** *n* a painful sudden tightening of a muscle ⟨I was suddenly awakened by a *cramp* in my leg.⟩

syn charley horse, crick, spasm

rel contraction, jerk, pang, stitch, twinge, twitch

²**cramp** *n* something that makes movement or progress difficult — see ENCUMBRANCE

cramp *vb* to create difficulty for the work or activity of — see HAMPER

crane *vb* to move from a lower to a higher place or position — see RAISE 1

cranium *n* the case of bone that encloses the brain and supports the jaws of vertebrates — see SKULL

crank *n* **1** a person of odd or whimsical habits — see ECCENTRIC

2 an irritable and complaining person — see GROUCH 1

3 a sudden impulsive and apparently unmotivated idea or action — see WHIM

crank (up) *vb* to cause to function — see ACTIVATE

crankiness *n* readiness to show annoyance or impatience — see PETULANCE

cranky *adj* **1** difficult to use or operate especially because of size, weight, or design — see CUMBERSOME

---

2 easily irritated or annoyed — see IRRITABLE

3 given to complaining a lot — see FUSSY 1

4 different from the ordinary in a way that causes curiosity or suspicion — see ODD 2

cranny *n* an irregular usually narrow break in a surface created by pressure — see CRACK 1

crash *n* **1** the violent coming together of two bodies into destructive contact ⟨the fiery *crash* of two jumbo jets in midair⟩

syn collision, concussion, crack-up, smash, smashup, wreck

rel accident; demolition, destruction, ruin

2 a falling short of one's goals — see FAILURE 2

3 a loud explosive sound — see CLAP 1

4 a forceful coming together of two things — see IMPACT 1

crash *vb* **1** to cause to break with violence and much noise — see SMASH 1

2 to come into usually forceful contact with something — see HIT 2

3 to stop functioning — see FAIL 1

4 to force one's way — see ²PRESS 4

5 to go to a lower level especially abruptly — see DROP 2

6 *slang* to go to one's bed in order to sleep — see BED 1

7 *slang* to reside as a temporary guest — see VISIT 2

crass *adj* lacking in refinement or good taste — see COARSE 2

crassness *n* the quality or state of lacking refinement or good taste — see VULGARITY 1

crave *vb* to have an earnest wish to own or enjoy — see DESIRE 1

craven *adj* having or showing a shameful lack of courage — see COWARDLY

craven *n* a person who shows a shameful lack of courage in the face of danger — see COWARD

cravenness *n* a shameful lack of courage in the face of danger — see COWARDICE

craving *n* a strong wish for something — see DESIRE 1

crawl *vb* **1** to move slowly with the body close to the ground ⟨the time we had to *crawl* through a narrow passageway from one cave to another⟩

syn belly, creep, grovel, slide, slither, snake, worm, wriggle

rel crouch, squat; edge, inch, nose; skulk, sneak, steal, tiptoe

2 to move slowly ⟨The weekend traffic on the road to the beach just *crawled*.⟩

syn creep, drag, inch, limp, nose, ooze, plod, poke, slouch

rel lumber, shamble, shuffle, tramp, trudge

near ant float, glide, sail; hurry, tear

ant fly, race, speed, whiz (*or* whizz), zip

3 to move or act slowly — see DELAY 1

4 to be copiously supplied — see ABOUND

crawler *n* someone who moves slowly or more slowly than others — see SLOWPOKE

crawling *adj* moving or proceeding at less than the normal, desirable, or required speed — see SLOW 1

craze *n* a practice or interest that is very popular for a short time — see FAD

craze *vb* to cause to go insane or as if insane ⟨horses *crazed* by the stable fire⟩
syn crack, derange, frenzy, madden, unbalance, unhinge, unstring
rel agitate, bother, confuse, discompose, disquiet, distract, disturb, perturb, unsettle, upset; annoy, irritate, vex
near ant calm, quiet, relax, settle, soothe, tranquilize (*also* tranquillize)

crazy *adj* **1** conceived or made without regard for reason or reality — see FANTASTIC 1
2 showing urgent desire or interest — see EAGER
3 different from the ordinary in a way that causes curiosity or suspicion — see ODD 2
4 inclined or twisted to one side — see AWRY
5 marked by a long series of irregular curves — see CROOKED 1

crazy (about *or* **over)** *adj* filled with an intense or excessive love for — see ENAMORED (OF)

creak *n* a harsh grating sound — see RASP

cream *n* individuals carefully selected as being the best of a class — see ELITE 1

cream *vb* **1** to bring to a complete end the physical soundness, existence, or usefulness of — see DESTROY 1
2 to defeat by a large margin — see WHIP 2

crease *n* a small fold in a soft and otherwise smooth surface — see WRINKLE 1

crease *vb* to develop creases or folds — see WRINKLE 1

create *vb* to be the cause of (a situation, action, or state of mind) — see EFFECT

creation *n* **1** something (as a device) created for the first time through the use of the imagination — see INVENTION 1
2 the whole body of things observed or assumed — see UNIVERSE
3 a raising or a state of being raised to a higher rank or position — see ADVANCEMENT 1

creative *adj* **1** having the skill and imagination to create new things ⟨Thomas Edison's status as perhaps America's greatest *creative* genius⟩
syn clever, imaginative, ingenious, innovative, inventive, original
rel gifted, inspired, talented; resourceful; fecund, fertile, fruitful, generative, germinal, productive, prolific
near ant imitative, uninspired; infertile, unproductive; talentless
ant uncreative, unimaginative, uninventive, unoriginal
2 showing a noteworthy use of the imagination and creativity especially in inventing — see CLEVER 1

creativeness *n* the skill and imagination to create new things — see CREATIVITY 1

creativity *n* **1** the skill and imagination to create new things ⟨The arts and crafts fair showed the remarkable *creativity* of local artists and artisans.⟩
syn cleverness, creativeness, imagination, imaginativeness, ingeniousness, ingenuity, invention, inventiveness, originality
rel fecundity, fertility, fruitfulness, productiveness, productivity, prolificacy, prolificity, prolificness; resourcefulness; genius, giftedness, talent; fire, inspiration

near ant dryness, dullness (*also* dulness)
2 the ability to form mental images of things that either are not physically present or have never been conceived or created by others — see IMAGINATION 1

creator *n* **1** a person who establishes a whole new field of endeavor — see FATHER 2
2 *cap* the being worshipped as the creator and ruler of the universe — see DEITY 2

creature *n* **1** a member of the human race — see HUMAN
2 one of the lower animals as distinguished from human beings — see ANIMAL

credence *n* **1** firm belief in the integrity, ability, effectiveness, or genuineness of someone or something — see TRUST 1
2 mental conviction of the truth of some statement or the reality of some being or phenomenon — see BELIEF 1

credentials *n pl* a skill, an ability, or knowledge that makes a person able to do a particular job — see QUALIFICATION 1

credible *adj* worthy of being accepted as true or reasonable — see BELIEVABLE

credit *n* **1** the right to take possession of goods before paying for them ⟨Because of their reputation for not paying their bills, no store will extend the family *credit*.⟩
syn trust
rel installment plan, layaway; charge account, credit line
2 an asset that brings praise or renown — see GLORY 2
3 mental conviction of the truth of some statement or the reality of some being or phenomenon — see BELIEF 1
4 public acknowledgment or admiration for an achievement — see GLORY 1
5 the power to direct the thinking or behavior of others usually indirectly — see INFLUENCE 1

credit *vb* **1** to explain (something) as being the result of something else ⟨Hal has to *credit* his success in picking winning lottery numbers to pure luck.⟩
syn accredit, ascribe, attribute, impute, lay, put down
rel blame, charge, father (on), impute (to), pin (on); assign, refer; associate, attach, connect, link
2 to regard as right or true — see BELIEVE 1

creditable *adj* **1** deserving of high regard or great approval — see ADMIRABLE
2 worthy of being accepted as true or reasonable — see BELIEVABLE

credo *n* **1** a body of beliefs and practices regarding the supernatural and the worship of one or more deities — see RELIGION 1
2 the basic beliefs or guiding principles of a person or group — see CREED 1

credulity *n* readiness to believe the claims of others without sufficient evidence ⟨The quack pushing the phony medicine was taking advantage of the *credulity* of people hoping for miracle cures.⟩
syn credulousness, gullibility, naïveté (*also* naivete *or* naiveté), simpleness
rel artlessness, simplicity, unsophistication, unwariness, unworldliness; belief, credibility, faith, trust
near ant sophistication, worldliness; dis-

trust, mistrust, suspicion, suspiciousness, wariness; doubt, uncertainty

ant incredulity, skepticism

credulousness *n* readiness to believe the claims of others without sufficient evidence — see CREDULITY

creed *n* **1** the basic beliefs or guiding principles of a person or group ⟨Central to the *creed* of this organization of medical volunteers is the belief that health care is a basic human right.⟩

syn credo, doctrine, dogma, gospel, ideology (*also* idealogy), philosophy, testament

rel manifesto; metaphysic, theory; axiom, tenet, watchword

2 a body of beliefs and practices regarding the supernatural and the worship of one or more deities — see RELIGION 1

creek *n* **1** a natural body of running water smaller than a river ⟨the shallow *creek* that runs in back of our house⟩

syn brook, brooklet, rill, rivulet, run [*chiefly Midland*], streamlet

rel arroyo, fresh, freshet, runoff; coulee, slough (*also* slew *or* slue), stream, wash; canal, channel, cut, gut, kill, millrace, millstream, race, watercourse, waterway; affluent, branch, confluent, distributary, influent

2 *chiefly British* a part of a body of water that extends beyond the general shoreline — see GULF 1

creep *n* a person whose behavior is offensive to others — see JERK 1

creep *vb* **1** to advance gradually beyond the usual or desirable limits — see ENCROACH

2 to move or act slowly — see DELAY 1

3 to move slowly with the body close to the ground — see CRAWL 1

4 to move slowly — see CRAWL 2

creeping *adj* moving or proceeding at less than the normal, desirable, or required speed — see SLOW 1

creepy *adj* **1** fearfully and mysteriously strange or fantastic — see EERIE

2 marked by or causing agitation or uncomfortable feelings — see NERVOUS 2

crest *n* **1** the highest part or point — see HEIGHT 1

2 the line formed when two sloping surfaces come together along their topmost edge — see RIDGE

crestfallen *adj* feeling unhappiness — see SAD 1

crevice *n* an irregular usually narrow break in a surface created by pressure — see CRACK 1

crew *n* **1** a group involved in secret or criminal activities — see ¹RING 1

2 a group of people working together on a task — see GANG 1

crick *n* a painful sudden tightening of a muscle — see ¹CRAMP

crime *n* **1** activities that are in violation of the laws of the state ⟨a promise by the president to step up the war against *crime*⟩

syn criminality, lawbreaking, lawlessness

rel outlawry; gangsterism, hooliganism, racketeering; malfeasance, misconduct;

wrongdoing; evil, immorality, sin, wickedness; corruption, depravity; malefaction, misdeed, misdoing, offense (*or* offence), transgression, trespass

2 a regrettable or blameworthy act ⟨It's a *crime* to waste food, so give the rest of the pizza to me.⟩

syn disgrace, pity, shame, sin

rel outrage, scandal

3 a breaking of a moral or legal code — see OFFENSE 1

criminal *adj* contrary to or forbidden by law — see ILLEGAL 1

criminal *n* a person who has committed a crime ⟨car thieves, pickpockets, burglars, and other *criminals*⟩

syn crook, culprit, lawbreaker, malefactor, miscreant, offender

rel accomplice, principal; desperado, outlaw; convict, jailbird; perp, perpetrator; evildoer, gallows bird, misdoer, misfeasor, sinner, transgressor, trespasser, villain, wrongdoer; blackhander, gangster, hoodlum, hooligan, mobster, racketeer, thug; enforcer, gun, gunman, hit man, triggerman; backslider, recidivist, relapser, repeater; accused, arrestee, defendant, detainee, fish, suspect

near ant gangbuster

criminality *n* activities that are in violation of the laws of the state — see CRIME 1

crimp *n* **1** a small fold in a soft and otherwise smooth surface — see WRINKLE 1

2 something that makes movement or progress difficult — see ENCUMBRANCE

crimson *vb* to develop a rosy facial color (as from excitement or embarrassment) — see BLUSH

cringe *vb* **1** to draw back in fear, pain, or disgust — see FLINCH

2 to draw back or crouch down in fearful submission — see COWER

crinkle *n* a small fold in a soft and otherwise smooth surface — see WRINKLE 1

crinkle *vb* **1** to make small sounds usually by rubbing or moving ⟨a paper seat cover that *crinkles* with every move⟩

syn rustle

rel crackle, crepitate; creak, squeak; whoosh; babble, gurgle, murmur, sigh, whisper

2 to create (as by crushing) an irregular mass of creases in — see CRUMPLE 1

3 to develop creases or folds — see WRINKLE 1

cripple *vb* **1** to cause severe or permanent injury to — see MAIM

2 to reduce the soundness, effectiveness, or perfection of — see DAMAGE 1

3 to render powerless, ineffective, or unable to move — see PARALYZE 1

crisis *n* a time or state of affairs requiring prompt or decisive action — see EMERGENCY

crisp *adj* **1** having a texture that readily breaks into little pieces under pressure ⟨The bag of *crisp* cookies had a lot of crumbs on the bottom.⟩

syn brittle, crispy, crumbly, flaky (*also* flakey), friable, short

rel crackly, crisped, crispened, crunchy, crusty; breakable, delicate, fragile

near ant elastic, flexible, pliable, pliant, resilient; strong, sturdy, tough

---

syn synonym(s)   *rel* related words
ant antonym(s)   *near ant* near antonym(s)

2 being clean and in good order — see NEAT 1

3 marked by the use of few words to convey much information or meaning — see CONCISE

crisply *adv* in a few words — see SHORTLY 1

crispness *n* the quality or state of being marked by or using only few words to convey much meaning — see SUCCINCTNESS

crispy *adj* having a texture that readily breaks into little pieces under pressure — see CRISP 1

criterion *n* **1** something set up as an example against which others of the same type are compared — see STANDARD 1

2 something that sets apart an individual from others of the same kind — see CHARACTERISTIC

critic *n* **1** a person given to harsh judgments and to finding faults ⟨The president's hard-core *critics* are going to attack him no matter what he does.⟩

syn carper, castigator, caviler (*or* caviller), censurer, faultfinder, nitpicker

rel condemner (*or* condemnor), denouncer; belittler, decrier, denigrator, derider, detractor; crucifier; hairsplitter, pettifogger, quibbler; admonisher, haranguer, railer, ranter, rebuker, reproacher, reprover, scold, upbraider; bellyacher, complainer, crybaby, fusser, griper, grouch, grouser, grumbler, whiner

near ant commender, praiser

2 a person who makes or expresses a judgment on the quality of offerings in some field of endeavor ⟨The restaurant *critic* said that the fries at that fast-food outlet were the worst she'd ever eaten.⟩

syn reviewer

rel analyst, annotator, columnist, commentator; appraiser, evaluator, judge, referee

critical *adj* **1** given to making or expressing unfavorable judgments about things ⟨They are often *critical* of the mayor's policies.⟩

syn captious, carping, caviling (*or* cavilling), faultfinding, hypercritical, overcritical

rel discerning, discriminating, judicious; demanding, exacting, fastidious, finicky, fussy, nitpicky, particular, picky; pettifogging, quibbling; harsh, merciless, uncharitable, unforgiving

near ant undiscriminating; undemanding, unfussy; charitable, forgiving

ant uncritical

2 needing immediate attention — see ACUTE 2

3 of the greatest possible importance — see CRUCIAL

4 impossible to do without — see ESSENTIAL 1

criticism *n* an essay evaluating or analyzing something ⟨Every *criticism* of the movie has noted that there are major holes in its plot.⟩

syn notice, review

rel column, commentary, editorial, punditry; appraisal, assessment, evaluation; analysis, examination, opinion, outline, study, survey

criticize *vb* to express one's unfavorable opinion of the worth or quality of ⟨people who *criticize* every single idea that the principal has for improving the school⟩

syn blame, censure, condemn, denounce, fault, knock, pan, reprehend

rel skewer, tweak; assail, attack, blast, clobber, slam, slash; nick (at), snipe (at); beef, bellyache, carp, cavil, complain, crab, croak, fuss, gripe, grouse, growl, grumble, kick, kvetch, moan, murmur, mutter, quibble, whine; admonish, chide, drub, rebuke, reprimand, reproach, reprove; berate, castigate, crucify, excoriate, flay, gibbet, hammer, keelhaul, lambaste (*or* lambast), lash, pillory, scold, upbraid; bad-mouth, belittle, decry, deride, discommend, disparage, put down

phrases come down hard (on), find fault (with), take to task

near ant approve, commend, endorse (*also* indorse), recommend, sanction

ant extol (*also* extoll), laud, praise

critter *n* one of the lower animals as distinguished from human beings — see ANIMAL

croak *vb* **1** to express dissatisfaction, pain, or resentment usually tiresomely — see COMPLAIN

2 *slang* to stop living — see DIE 1

3 *slang* to deprive of life — see KILL 1

4 *slang* to put to death deliberately — see MURDER 1

croaking *adj* harsh and dry in sound — see HOARSE

crockery *n* articles made of baked clay ⟨a display of beautifully hand-painted *crockery* on the kitchen countertop⟩

syn earthenware, pottery, stoneware

rel ceramics; china, ironstone china, porcelain, redware

crony *n* **1** a person frequently seen in the company of another — see ASSOCIATE 1

2 a person who has a strong liking for and trust in another — see FRIEND 1

crook *n* **1** a person who has committed a crime — see CRIMINAL

2 something that curves or is curved — see BEND 1

crook *vb* **1** to cause to turn away from a straight line — see BEND 1

2 to turn away from a straight line or course — see CURVE 1

crooked *adj* **1** marked by a long series of irregular curves ⟨A long, *crooked* line of people had formed in front of the ticket booth.⟩

syn bending, crazy, curled, curling, curved, curving, devious, serpentine, sinuous, tortuous, twisted, twisting, winding, windy

rel zigzag, zigzagging; circling, coiled, coiling, corkscrew, looping, spiral, spiraling (*or* spiralling), swirling; circuitous, indirect, roundabout; rambling, wandering; irregular, jagged, uneven

near ant direct, linear

ant straight, straightaway

2 given to or marked by cheating and deception — see DISHONEST 2

3 inclined or twisted to one side — see AWRY

4 marked by, based on, or done by the use

of dishonest methods to acquire something of value — see FRAUDULENT 1

crookedness *n* the inclination or practice of misleading others through lies or trickery — see DECEIT 1

crop *n* **1** the quantity of an animal or vegetable product gathered at the end of a season ⟨The wheat *crop* is going to be exceptionally large this year.⟩

syn harvest

rel return, yield; cut, cutting

2 a usually small number of persons considered as a unit — see GROUP 2

crop *vb* **1** to look after or assist the growth of by labor and care — see GROW 1

2 to make (something) shorter or smaller with the use of a cutting instrument — see CLIP 1

crop (up) *vb* to come to one's attention especially gradually or unexpectedly — see ARISE 2

cropper *n* a falling short of one's goals — see FAILURE 2

croquette *n* a small usually rounded mass of minced food that has been fried — see CAKE 1

cross *adj* **1** being offspring produced by parents of different races, breeds, species, or genera — see MIXED 1

2 easily irritated or annoyed — see IRRITABLE

cross *n* **1** a test of faith, patience, or strength — see TRIAL 1

2 an offspring of parents with different genes especially when of different races, breeds, species, or genera — see HYBRID

cross *vb* **1** to be unfaithful or disloyal to — see BETRAY 1

2 to divide by passing through or across — see INTERSECT

3 to make one's way through, across, or over — see TRAVERSE

4 to enter the mind of — see OCCUR (TO)

cross (out) *vb* to show (something written) to be no longer valid by drawing a cross over or a line through it — see X (OUT)

crossbred *adj* being offspring produced by parents of different races, breeds, species, or genera — see MIXED 1

crossbred *n* an offspring of parents with different genes especially when of different races, breeds, species, or genera — see HYBRID

crossbreed *n* an offspring of parents with different genes especially when of different races, breeds, species, or genera — see HYBRID

cross fire *n* an often noisy or angry expression of differing opinions — see ARGUMENT 1

crossing *n* **1** a journey over water in a vessel — see SAIL

2 a place where roads meet — see CROSSROAD 1

crossness *n* readiness to show annoyance or impatience — see PETULANCE

crossroad *n* **1** *usually* **crossroads** *pl* a place where roads meet ⟨The fast-food chain has a restaurant at practically every *crossroads*.⟩

syn corner, crossing, intersection, junction

rel cloverleaf, interchange, overpass, underpass; circle, rotary, traffic circle

2 *usually* **crossroads** *pl* a time or state of affairs requiring prompt or decisive action — see EMERGENCY

cross section *n* a number of things selected from a group to stand for the whole — see SAMPLE 1

crossways *adv* in a line or direction running from corner to corner — see CROSSWISE

crosswise *adv* in a line or direction running from corner to corner ⟨First cut the sandwiches *crosswise* and then trim the crusts.⟩

syn athwart, bias, crossways, obliquely, transversely

rel across

phrases on the bias, on the diagonal

near ant lengthwise, longitudinally

crotchet *n* an odd or peculiar habit — see IDIOSYNCRASY

crotchetiness *n* readiness to show annoyance or impatience — see PETULANCE

crotchety *adj* easily irritated or annoyed — see IRRITABLE

crouch *vb* to lie low with the limbs close to the body ⟨The cat *crouched* in the bushes, waiting for the right moment to pounce on the chipmunk.⟩

syn couch, huddle, hunch, scrunch, squat, squinch

rel curl up

crow *vb* **1** to feel or express joy or triumph — see EXULT

2 to praise or express pride in one's own possessions, qualities, or accomplishments often to excess — see BOAST 1

crowd *n* **1** a great number of persons or creatures massed together ⟨A huge *crowd* of fans was on hand to greet the returning World Series champions.⟩

syn army, crush, drove, flock, herd, horde, host, legion, mass, mob, multitude, press, rout, swarm, throng

rel masses, rabble, rabblement, riffraff; gaggle; heap, mountain, pile; jam

2 a group of people sharing a common interest and relating together socially — see GANG 2

3 the body of the community as contrasted with the elite — see MASS 1

crowd *vb* **1** to fit (people or things) into a tight space ⟨*crowded* all the boats into the harbor before the storm struck⟩

syn cram, crush, jam, ram, sandwich, squeeze, stuff, wedge

rel fill, heap, jam-pack, load, pack

2 to move upon or fill (something) in great numbers ⟨Cars *crowded* the roads over the long holiday weekend.⟩

syn flock, mob, swarm, throng

rel beset, infest, invade, overrun; clog, dam, jam, obstruct, plug (up)

3 to gather into a closely packed group — see ²PRESS 3

crowded *adj* **1** containing or seeming to contain the greatest quantity or number possible — see FULL 1

2 having little space between items or parts — see CLOSE 1

---

syn synonym(s)   *rel* related words
ant antonym(s)   *near ant* near antonym(s)

crown *n* **1** a decorative band or wreath worn about the head as a symbol of victory or honor ⟨the *crown* of laurel leaves that is traditionally placed on the winner of the marathon⟩
syn coronet, diadem
rel tiara; garland, laurel
2 the position occupied by the one who comes in first in a competition ⟨his lifelong dream of someday winning the heavyweight boxing *crown*⟩
syn championship, title
3 the highest part or point — see HEIGHT 1
crown *vb* to bring to a triumphant conclusion ⟨The Olympic Games were *crowned* by spectacular closing ceremonies.⟩
syn cap (off), climax, culminate
rel complete, conclude, finish, round (off *or* out), terminate, wrap up
crucial *adj* of the greatest possible importance ⟨Water is *crucial* to our survival.⟩
syn critical, key, pivotal, vital
rel decisive, life-and-death (*also* life-or-death), weighty; basic, elementary, fundamental; essential, indispensable, necessary, requisite; pressing, urgent
near ant inconsequential, insignificant, minor, trivial, unimportant
crucible *n* a test of faith, patience, or strength — see TRIAL 1
crude *adj* **1** being such as found in nature and not altered by processing or refining ⟨A sizable spill of *crude* oil along a coastline is the worst kind of environmental disaster.⟩
syn native, natural, raw, rude, undressed, unprocessed, unrefined, untreated
rel undeveloped; semifinished, unfinished, unpolished; uncooked; impure, unfiltered
phrases in the raw, in the rough
near ant filtered, pure, purified
ant dressed, processed, refined, treated
2 belonging to or characteristic of an early level of skill or development — see PRIMITIVE 1
3 depicting or referring to sexual matters in a way that is unacceptable in polite society — see OBSCENE 1
4 lacking in refinement or good taste — see COARSE 2
5 hastily or roughly constructed — see RUDE 1
crudeness *n* **1** the quality or state of being obscene — see OBSCENITY
2 the quality or state of lacking refinement or good taste — see VULGARITY 1
cruel *adj* having or showing the desire to inflict severe pain and suffering on others ⟨a *cruel* dictator who imprisoned anyone who dared to speak out against him⟩ ⟨*Cruel* and unusual punishments are forbidden by the U.S. Constitution.⟩
syn atrocious, barbaric, barbarous, brutal, brute, fiendish, heartless, inhuman, inhumane, sadistic, savage, truculent, vicious, wanton
rel merciless, pitiless, ruthless, stonyhearted, unfeeling; fell, ferocious, grim; bloodthirsty, cutthroat, murderous, sanguinary, sanguine; catty, despiteful, hateful, malevolent, malicious, malign, malignant, mean, nasty, spiteful, vindictive; draconian, draconic, hardhanded, harsh, heavyhanded, oppressive

phrases red in tooth and claw
near ant tender, warm, warmhearted; charitable, clement, lenient, merciful, pitying; pacific, peaceable, peaceful
ant benign, benignant, compassionate, good-hearted, humane, kind, kindhearted, sympathetic, tenderhearted
2 difficult to endure — see HARSH 1
3 hard to accept or bear especially emotionally — see BITTER 2
4 having or showing a desire to cause someone pain or suffering for the sheer enjoyment of it — see HATEFUL
cruelty *n* disposition to willfully inflict pain and suffering on others ⟨Centuries after he ravaged Europe, Attila the Hun remains notorious for his *cruelty*.⟩
syn atrociousness, atrocity, barbarity, brutality, heartlessness, inhumanity, sadism, savageness, savagery, truculence, viciousness, wantonness
rel hard-heartedness, mercilessness, pitilessness, ruthlessness, unfeelingness; ferociousness, ferocity, fierceness, grimness; bloodlust, bloodthirstiness, murderousness, sanguineness, sanguinity; cattiness, hatefulness, malevolence, maliciousness, malignity, meanness, nastiness, spitefulness; hardhandedness, harshness, heavyhandedness, oppressiveness
near ant warmheartedness, warmness, warmth; charitableness, clemency, leniency, mercifulness, mercy, pity
ant compassion, good-heartedness, humanity, kindheartedness, kindness, sympathy
cruise *n* a journey over water in a vessel — see SAIL
cruise *vb* **1** to move about from place to place aimlessly — see WANDER 1
2 to move or proceed smoothly and readily — see FLOW 2
3 to travel on water in a vessel — see SAIL 1
crumb *n* **1** a very small amount — see PARTICLE 1
2 a very small piece — see BIT 1
crumble *vb* to become worse or of less value — see DETERIORATE 1
crumbly *adj* having a texture that readily breaks into little pieces under pressure — see CRISP 1
crummy *also* **crumby** *adj* falling short of a standard — see BAD 1
crumple *vb* **1** to create (as by crushing) an irregular mass of creases in ⟨*crumpled* the piece of paper and angrily threw it in the wastebasket⟩
syn crinkle, rumple, scrunch, wrinkle
rel corrugate, crease, crimp, fold, pleat, pucker, ruck; crisp, ripple, ruffle; contract, furrow, knit; mess (up), muss (up)
near ant even, iron, press, straighten; unfold; tidy
ant flatten, iron out, smooth, smoothen, uncrumple
2 to fall down or in as a result of physical pressure — see COLLAPSE 1
crunch *n* **1** a falling short of an essential or desirable amount or number — see DEFICIENCY
2 a time or state of affairs requiring prompt or decisive action — see EMERGENCY

crunch *vb* to press or strike against or together so as to make a scraping sound — see GRIND 2

crunch (on) *vb* to crush or grind with the teeth — see BITE (ON)

crusade *n* a series of activities undertaken to achieve a goal — see CAMPAIGN

crusader *n* one who is intensely or excessively devoted to a cause — see ZEALOT

crush *n* 1 a strong but often short-lived liking for another person ⟨Sue fondly remembers the *crush* that she had on a boy one summer long ago.⟩
syn infatuation, passion
rel fixation, obsession; affection, devotion, fondness, love; craze, fad, rage, vogue
2 a great number of persons or creatures massed together — see CROWD 1

crush *vb* 1 to cause to become a pulpy mass ⟨dark-colored grapes that will be *crushed* to make red wine⟩
syn mash, pulp, squash
rel press, squeeze; beat, pound, powder, pulverize
2 to put a stop to (something) by the use of force — see QUELL 1
3 to reduce to fine particles — see POWDER
4 to subject to incapacitating emotional or mental stress — see OVERWHELM 1
5 to apply external pressure on so as to force out the juice or contents of — see ²PRESS 2
6 to fit (people or things) into a tight space — see CROWD 1
7 to put one's arms around and press tightly — see EMBRACE 1

crusher *n* something (as a fact or argument) that is decisive or overwhelming — see CLINCHER

crusty *adj* being or characterized by direct, brief, and potentially rude speech or manner — see BLUNT 1

crux *n* the central part or aspect of something under consideration ⟨The *crux* of the problem is that the school's current budget is totally inadequate.⟩
syn core, essence, gist, heart, meat, net, nub, nubbin, nucleus, pith, pivot, point, root, sum
rel course, direction, drift, tenor; body, content, substance; hypothesis, proposition, purport, subject, theme, thesis
phrases sum and substance, the long and short (*or* the long and the short)

cry *n* 1 a loud vocal expression of strong emotion — see SHOUT
2 a natural vocal sound made by an animal — see CALL 1
3 an attention-getting word or phrase used to publicize something (as a campaign or product) — see SLOGAN
4 an earnest request — see PLEA 1
5 a sudden short emotional utterance — see EXCLAMATION

cry *vb* 1 to shed tears often while making meaningless sounds as a sign of pain or distress ⟨Some kids started to *cry* even before the doctor had given them their shot.⟩
syn bawl, blubber, sob, weep

rel grieve, keen, lament, mourn; howl, scream, squall, wail, yowl; mewl, pule, whimper, whine; sniffle, snivel; groan, moan, sigh
2 to utter one's distinctive animal sound ⟨We knew that we were getting very close to the ocean when we could hear sea gulls *crying*.⟩
syn call, sing
3 to speak so as to be heard at a distance — see CALL 1

cry (out) *vb* to utter with a sudden burst of strong feeling — see EXCLAIM

crybaby *n* a person who makes frequent complaints usually about little things ⟨car trips that were often spoiled by a couple of *crybabies* in the back seat⟩
syn baby, bellyacher, complainer, fusser, griper, grumbler, whiner
rel bawler, bleater, moaner, screamer, squawker, wailer, weeper; crab, grump, malcontent
near ant happy camper

cry down *vb* to express scornfully one's low opinion of — see DECRY 1

crying *adj* needing immediate attention — see ACUTE 2

crypt *n* an underground burial chamber ⟨The old church's *crypt* is the final resting place for the president and his beloved wife.⟩
syn catacomb(s), vault
rel mausoleum, sepulture, tomb

cryptic *adj* 1 being beyond one's powers to know, understand, or explain — see MYSTERIOUS 1
2 having an often intentionally veiled or uncertain meaning — see OBSCURE 1

crystalline *adj* easily seen through — see CLEAR 1

crystallize *also* **crystalize** *vb* to take on a definite form — see FORM 1

cub *n* 1 a person who is just starting out in a field of activity — see BEGINNER
2 a young person who is between infancy and adulthood — see CHILD 1

cubicle *n* one of the parts into which an enclosed space is divided — see COMPARTMENT

cuddle *vb* to lie close — see NUZZLE

cudgel *n* a heavy rigid stick used as a weapon or for punishment — see CLUB 1

¹cue *n* a slight or indirect pointing to something (as a solution or explanation) — see HINT 1

²cue *n* a series of persons or things arranged one behind another — see LINE 1

¹cuff *n* a hard strike with a part of the body or an instrument — see ¹BLOW

²cuff *n, usually* **cuffs** *pl* something that physically prevents free movement — see BOND 1

cuisine *n* the art or style of preparing food (as in a specified region) — see COOKERY

cull *n* something separated from a group or lot for not being as good as the others ⟨The unbruised apples will be packed in bags, and the *culls* will be used for cider.⟩
syn discard, reject, rejection, second
rel castaway, throwaway; hand-me-down, white elephant; rubbish, scrap, trash, waste

cull *vb* to decide to accept (someone or

---

syn synonym(s)   *rel* related words
ant antonym(s)   *near ant* near antonym(s)

something) from a group of possibilities — see CHOOSE 1

culminate *vb* to bring to a triumphant conclusion — see CROWN

culmination *n* the highest part or point — see HEIGHT 1

culpability *n* responsibility for wrongdoing or failure — see BLAME 1

culpable *adj* deserving reproach or blame — see BLAMEWORTHY

culprit *n* a person who has committed a crime — see CRIMINAL

cult *n* **1** a group of people showing intense devotion to a cause, person, or work (as a film) ⟨Long after it had gone off the air, the TV series continued to have a huge *cult*.⟩
syn following
rel discipleship; fandom
2 a body of beliefs and practices regarding the supernatural and the worship of one or more deities — see RELIGION 1

cultivate *vb* **1** to come to have gradually — see DEVELOP 2
2 to help the growth or development of — see FOSTER 1
3 to look after or assist the growth of by labor and care — see GROW 1
4 to work by plowing, sowing, and raising crops on — see FARM

cultivated *adj* having or showing a taste for the fine arts and gracious living ⟨The museum's annual gala for charity attracts not only a very wealthy, but also a very *cultivated* crowd.⟩
syn accomplished, civilized, cultured, genteel, polished, refined
rel cerebral, highbrow, high-toned, intellectual, intellectualist; bourgeois, middlebrow; educated, erudite, knowledgeable, learned, literate, scholarly, well-read; civil, courteous, mannerly, polite, well-bred; cosmopolitan, sophisticated, urbane; hypercivilized, overcivilized, oversophisticated
near ant ignorant, illiterate, uneducated, unlettered; lowbrow, unintelligent; coarse, ill-bred, ill-mannered; backwoods, provincial, rustic (*also* rustical); inelegant, polyester, unsophisticated; boorish, churlish, cloddish, clownish, crude, uncouth, vulgar
ant barbaric, barbarous, philistine, uncivilized, uncultured, ungenteel, unpolished, unrefined

cultivation *n* a high level of taste and enlightenment as a result of extensive intellectual training and exposure to the arts — see CULTURE 1

cultivator *n* a person who cultivates the land and grows crops on it — see FARMER

cultural *adj* of or relating to the fine arts ⟨With its many museums, theaters, and opera and ballet companies, the city is a *cultural* paradise.⟩
syn artistic
rel aesthetic (*also* esthetic *or* aesthetical *or* esthetical), tasteful
near ant nonaesthetic
ant nonartistic, noncultural

culture *n* **1** a high level of taste and enlightenment as a result of extensive intellectual training and exposure to the arts ⟨Because of its wide reputation as a place of *culture*, Boston became known as "the Athens of America."⟩

syn accomplishment, civilization, cultivation, polish, refinement
rel education, erudition, intellectualism, intellectuality, knowledge, learning, scholarship; cosmopolitanism, sophistication, urbanity; gentility, manners; class, elegance, grace, taste; civility, courteousness, courtesy, politeness
near ant ignorance, illiteracy; parochialism, provincialism, rusticity, unsophistication; boorishness, churlishness, clownishness, coarseness, crudeness, vulgarity
ant barbarianism, barbarism, philistinism
2 the way people live at a particular time and place — see CIVILIZATION 1

culture *vb* to look after or assist the growth of by labor and care — see GROW 1

cultured *adj* having or showing a taste for the fine arts and gracious living — see CULTIVATED

cumbersome *adj* difficult to use or operate especially because of size, weight, or design ⟨a long-handled wrench that is too *cumbersome* for tight spots, such as under the sink⟩
syn awkward, clumsy, cranky, cumbrous, ponderous, ungainly, unhandy, unwieldy
rel uncontrollable, unmanageable; bulky, elephantine, heavy, hulking, massive
near ant functional, practicable, practical, serviceable, useful
ant handy

cumbrous *adj* difficult to use or operate especially because of size, weight, or design — see CUMBERSOME

cummerbund *also* **cumberbund** *n* a strip of flexible material (as leather) worn around the waist — see ²BELT 1

cumulative *adj* produced by a series of additions of identical or similar things ⟨The *cumulative* scores will determine the winner.⟩
syn additive, incremental
rel gradual, step-by-step, stepwise; increscent, progressive; accruable, accrued, aggregated, amassed, built-up, compiled, conglomerated
near ant regressive

cunning *adj* **1** clever at attaining one's ends by indirect and often deceptive means — see ARTFUL 1
2 skillful with the hands — see DEXTEROUS 1

cunning *n* **1** skill in achieving one's ends through indirect, subtle, or underhanded means ⟨the *cunning* with which Tom Sawyer was able to get others to whitewash the fence for him⟩
syn artfulness, artifice, caginess (*also* cageyness), canniness, craft, craftiness, deviousness, foxiness, guile, slickness, slyness, sneakiness, subtleness, subtlety, wiliness
rel calculation, care, design; savvy, sharpness, shrewdness; cleverness, ingeniousness, ingenuity, inventiveness; ease, facility, finesse; deceitfulness, duplicity, shiftiness, underhandedness
2 subtle or imaginative ability in inventing, devising, or executing something — see SKILL 1
3 the inclination or practice of misleading others through lies or trickery — see DECEIT 1

cup *n* a round vessel equipped with a handle and designed for drinking ⟨a large *cup* that can hold almost a pint of hot chocolate⟩
  syn mug
  rel beaker, stein, tankard; chalice, goblet; demitasse, noggin; teacup
cupboard *n* **1** a built-in space for storage behind a door — see CLOSET 1
  2 a storage case typically having doors and shelves — see CABINET
cupidity *n* an intense selfish desire for wealth or possessions — see GREED
cur *n* **1** a person who shows a shameful lack of courage in the face of danger — see COWARD
  2 a person whose behavior is offensive to others — see JERK 1
curb *n* something that limits one's freedom of action or choice — see RESTRICTION 1
curb *vb* to keep from exceeding a desirable degree or level (as of expression) — see CONTROL 1
curdy *adj* having small pieces or lumps spread throughout — see CHUNKY 1
cure *n* **1** something that corrects or counteracts something undesirable ⟨A fun hobby is always a good *cure* for boredom.⟩
  syn corrective, remedy
  rel cure-all, elixir, panacea; answer, solution; aid, help, relief, succor; medicine, palliative
  2 a substance or preparation used to treat disease — see MEDICINE
cure *vb* **1** to bring about recovery from ⟨Do you have anything that will *cure* my headache?⟩
  syn heal, mend, remedy
  rel allay, alleviate, assuage, relieve; palliate, soothe; ease, lighten, moderate, temper; doctor, nurse; medicate, treat; diagnose
  near ant aggravate, worsen; misdiagnose, overdiagnose, underdiagnose
  2 to restore to a healthy condition — see HEAL 1
cure-all *n* something that cures all ills or problems ⟨Raising a young person's self-esteem is not the *cure-all* that some people think.⟩
  syn elixir, panacea
  rel magic bullet, silver bullet; corrective, cure, remedy; miracle drug, wonder drug
curio *n* **1** a small object displayed for its attractiveness or interest — see KNICKKNACK
  2 something strange or unusual that is an object of interest — see CURIOSITY 2
curiosity *n* **1** an eager desire to find out about things that are often none of one's business ⟨Our neighbor's *curiosity* about what we were doing last night was really offensive.⟩
  syn curiousness, inquisitiveness, nosiness
  rel attentiveness, concern, interest, regard, wonderment; inquiry, interrogation, prying, questioning; interference, intrusiveness, meddlesomeness, obtrusiveness, officiousness; eavesdropping, rubbernecking
  near ant apathy, disinterestedness, disregard, indifference, unconcern
  2 something strange or unusual that is an

object of interest ⟨The museum's *curiosities* include items constructed entirely out of toothpicks.⟩
  syn curio, exotic, oddity, oddment, rarity
  rel marvel, prodigy, rara avis, rare bird, wonder; abnormality, anomaly, freak, monster, monstrosity; malformation, mutant, mutation
  3 a small object displayed for its attractiveness or interest — see KNICKKNACK
  4 an odd or peculiar habit — see IDIOSYNCRASY
curious *adj* **1** interested in what is not one's own business ⟨*Curious* neighbors peered out of their windows as the new people moved in.⟩
  syn inquisitive, nosy (*or* nosey), prying, snoopy
  rel interfering, intrusive, meddlesome, meddling, obtrusive, officious; inquisitional, inquisitorial, questioning, quizzical; concerned, interested
  near ant apathetic, disinterested, indifferent, unconcerned, uninterested
  ant incurious, uncurious ·
  2 different from the ordinary in a way that causes curiosity or suspicion — see ODD 2
  3 noticeably different from what is generally found or experienced — see UNUSUAL 1
curiousness *n* an eager desire to find out about things that are often none of one's business — see CURIOSITY 1
curl *n* a length of hair that forms a loop or series of loops ⟨a little girl with beautiful shining *curls*⟩
  syn ringlet
  rel crimp, wave; perm, permanent, set; lock, tress
curl *vb* to follow a circular or spiral course — see WIND 1
curled *adj* **1** forming or styled into loops — see CURLY
  2 marked by a long series of irregular curves — see CROOKED 1
curling *adj* marked by a long series of irregular curves — see CROOKED 1
curl up *vb* to sit or recline comfortably or cozily — see SNUGGLE 1
curly *adj* forming or styled into loops ⟨the boy's naturally *curly* locks⟩
  syn curled
  rel crimped, crimpy, crisp, frizzled, frizzy, kinky, waved, wavy
  near ant lank, limp; straightened
  ant straight, uncurled
curmudgeon *n* an irritable and complaining person — see GROUCH 1
currency *n* something (as pieces of stamped metal or printed paper) customarily and legally used as a medium of exchange, a measure of value, or a means of payment — see MONEY
current *adj* accepted, used, or practiced by most people ⟨*Current* wisdom on parenting favors allowing children lots of self-expression.⟩
  syn conventional, customary, going, popular, prevailing, prevalent, standard, stock, usual
  rel average, common, everyday, normal, ordinary; regular, routine; ubiquitous, universal, widespread; accustomed, wonted; fashionable, in, modish, stylish

syn synonym(s) *rel* related words
ant antonym(s) *near ant* near antonym(s)

near ant abnormal, exceptional, extraordinary, uncommon

ant nonstandard, unconventional, unpopular, unusual

2 being or involving the latest methods, concepts, information, or styles — see MODERN

3 existing or in progress right now — see PRESENT 1

current *n* **1** a prevailing or general movement or inclination — see TREND 1

2 noticeable movement of air in a particular direction — see ¹WIND 1

currently *adv* at the present time — see NOW 1

curse *n* **1** a prayer that harm will come to someone ⟨uttered a *curse* upon his persecutor from the scaffold⟩

syn anathema, ban, execration, imprecation, malediction

rel censure, condemnation, damnation, denunciation, excommunication; hex, jinx, mojo, spell, voodoo; pox

near ant citation, commendation, endorsement (*also* indorsement)

ant benediction, benison, blessing

2 a source of harm or misfortune — see BANE 1

curse *vb* **1** to ask a divine power to send harm or evil upon ⟨I *curse* whoever had the idea of having annoying salespeople call up innocent people to sell them things they don't want.⟩

syn imprecate

rel condemn, damn, denounce, execrate, reprobate; hex, jinx, voodoo; darn (*also* durn), dash; cuss (out), fulminate (against), rail (against), revile

near ant applaud, commend, congratulate

ant bless

2 to cause persistent suffering to — see AFFLICT

3 to use offensive or indecent language — see SWEAR 1

4 to use profane or obscene language at or about — see DAMN 1

cursorily *adv* with excessive or careless speed — see HASTILY 1

cursory *adj* acting or done with excessive or careless speed — see HASTY 1

curt *adj* **1** being or characterized by direct, brief, and potentially rude speech or manner — see BLUNT 1

2 marked by the use of few words to convey much information or meaning — see CONCISE

curtail *vb* to make less in extent or duration — see SHORTEN

curtain *n* **1** something that covers or conceals like a piece of cloth — see CLOAK 1

2 curtains *pl* pieces of cloth hung to darken, decorate, or divide a room — see DRAPERY

3 curtains *pl* the permanent stopping of all the vital bodily activities — see DEATH 1

curtain *vb* to keep secret or shut off from view — see ¹HIDE 2

curvature *n* something that curves or is curved — see BEND 1

curve *n* something that curves or is curved — see BEND 1

curve *vb* **1** to turn away from a straight line or course ⟨After following a straight

path most of the way down the mountain, the ski trail abruptly *curves* to the right.⟩

syn arc, arch, bend, bow, crook, hook, round, sweep, swerve, trend, wheel

rel circle, coil, curlicue, curl, loop, spiral; turn, twist, wind; deviate, veer

ant straighten

2 to cause to turn away from a straight line — see BEND 1

curved *adj* marked by a long series of irregular curves — see CROOKED 1

curving *adj* marked by a long series of irregular curves — see CROOKED 1

cushion *n* something that serves as a protective barrier ⟨used a blanket as a *cushion* between the two tables in the moving van⟩

syn buffer, bumper, cocoon, fender, pad

rel baffle, muffler; padding; safeguard, shield; barricade, cordon

cushion *vb* to lessen the shock of ⟨A substantial nest egg helped to *cushion* the sudden loss of her job.⟩

syn buffer, gentle, soften

rel baffle, dampen, deaden, dull; moderate, modulate, temper; allay, alleviate, assuage, ease; lighten, mitigate, relieve

near ant heighten, intensify, sharpen

cushy *adj* providing physical comfort — see COMFORTABLE 1

cusp *n* **1** an interval of time just before the onset of something — see POINT 3

2 the last and usually sharp or tapering part of something long and narrow — see POINT 2

cuss *vb* to use offensive or indecent language — see SWEAR 1

custodian *n* **1** a person who takes care of a property sometimes for an absent owner ⟨The *custodian* made his usual rounds of the building to make sure that everything was OK.⟩

syn caretaker, guardian, janitor, keeper, warden, watchman

rel curator; sexton, steward

2 a person or group that watches over someone or something — see GUARD 1

3 someone that protects — see PROTECTOR

custody *n* responsibility for the safety and well-being of someone or something ⟨the government department having *custody* of all official state gifts⟩

syn care, guardianship, keeping, safekeeping, trust, ward

rel control, governorship, hand(s), management, superintendence, supervision

custom *adj* made or fitted to the needs or preferences of a specific customer — see CUSTOM-MADE

custom *n* **1** a usual manner of behaving or doing — see HABIT 1

2 an inherited or established way of thinking, feeling, or doing — see TRADITION 1

3 transactions or economic support provided by customers — see BUSINESS 1

customary *adj* **1** accepted, used, or practiced by most people — see CURRENT 1

2 based on customs usually handed down from a previous generation — see TRADITIONAL 1

customer *n* **1** a person who buys a product or uses a service from a business ⟨The store greatly values its regular *customers*.⟩

syn account, client, guest, patron

rel consumer, end user, user; buyer, correspondent, purchaser; browser, prospect, shopper, window-shopper; bargainer, haggler; regular

near ant merchant, seller, vendor (*also* vender); shopkeeper, tradesman; black marketeer (*or* black marketer), fence

2 a member of the human race — see HUMAN

customized *adj* made or fitted to the needs or preferences of a specific customer — see CUSTOM-MADE

custom–made *adj* made or fitted to the needs or preferences of a specific customer ⟨an odd-sized window that will require the purchase of *custom-made* curtains⟩

syn custom, customized, tailored, tailor-made

rel particular, special, specialized; custom-built; made-to-measure

ant mass-produced, ready-made

cut *n* **1** a piece that has been separated from the whole by cutting ⟨Choose *cuts* of meat that have very little visible fat.⟩

syn cutting, slice

rel chop, cutlet; length, part, portion, section, segment; chunk, hunk, lump; clipping, paring, shaving, sliver, snippet, splinter

2 an individual part of a process, series, or ranking — see DEGREE 1

3 something belonging to, due to, or contributed by an individual member of a group — see SHARE 1

4 an act or expression showing scorn and usually intended to hurt another's feelings — see INSULT

cut *vb* **1** to penetrate with a sharp edge (as a knife) ⟨I *cut* my hand on a piece of broken glass.⟩

syn gash, incise, rip, shear, slash, slice, slit

rel crosscut, hacksaw, saw, scissor; cleave, rive, split; pierce, stab; bruise, butcher, hack, haggle, lacerate, mangle; rend, tear; carve, chip, chisel, notch; anatomize, dissect, section; chop, dice, mince; amputate, cut off, sever

2 to fail to attend ⟨a warning that she had been *cutting* too many classes without valid excuses⟩

syn miss, skip

rel ignore, neglect, pass over

phrases absent oneself, play hooky

ant attend, show up (for)

3 to deliberately ignore or treat rudely — see SNUB 1

4 to make (something) shorter or smaller with the use of a cutting instrument — see CLIP 1

5 to shorten the standing leafy plant cover of — see MOW 1

6 to alter (something) for the worse with the addition of foreign or lower-grade substances — see ADULTERATE

7 to depart abruptly from a straight line or course — see SWERVE 1

8 to divide by passing through or across — see INTERSECT

9 to identify and examine the basic elements or parts of (something) especially for discovering interrelationships — see ANALYZE

cut (across) *vb* to make one's way through, across, or over — see TRAVERSE

cut (down) *vb* to bring down by cutting — see FELL 2

cut back *vb* **1** to make (something) shorter or smaller with the use of a cutting instrument — see CLIP 1

2 to make less in extent or duration — see SHORTEN

cute *adj* **1** clever at attaining one's ends by indirect and often deceptive means — see ARTFUL 1

2 making light of something usually regarded as serious or sacred — see FLIPPANT

3 very pleasing to look at — see BEAUTIFUL 1

cuteness *n* the qualities in a person or thing that as a whole give pleasure to the senses — see BEAUTY 1

cut in *vb* to cause a disruption in a conversation or discussion — see INTERRUPT

cutlet *n* a small usually rounded mass of minced food that has been fried — see CAKE 1

cut off *vb* **1** to bring (as an action or operation) to an immediate end — see STOP 1

2 to set or keep apart from others — see ISOLATE

cut out *vb* **1** to stop functioning — see FAIL 1

2 to bring (as an action or operation) to an immediate end — see STOP 1

3 to leave a place often for another — see GO 1

4 to take the place of — see REPLACE 1

cut–rate *adj* **1** costing little — see CHEAP 1

2 of low quality — see CHEAP 2

cutter *n* an instrument with a metal length that has a sharp edge for cutting — see KNIFE

cutthroat *adj* not guided by or showing a concern for what is right — see UNPRINCIPLED

cutthroat *n* a person who kills another person — see ASSASSIN

cutting *adj* **1** causing intense discomfort to one's skin ⟨a frigid day with a *cutting* wind that made it seem even colder⟩

syn biting, bitter, keen, penetrating, piercing, raw, sharp, shrewd, smarting, stinging

rel brisk, invigorating, nippy, snappy; needlelike, prickly, tingling; caustic

near ant balmy, gentle, mild, soothing

2 having an edge thin enough to cut or pierce something — see SHARP 1

3 marked by the use of wit that is intended to cause hurt feelings — see SARCASTIC

cutting *n* a piece that has been separated from the whole by cutting — see CUT 1

cut up *vb* to engage in attention-getting playful or boisterous behavior ⟨high-spirited cousins who *cut up* at every family gathering⟩

syn act up, clown (around), horse around, monkey (around), show off, skylark

rel carry on, misbehave; roughhouse; caper, cavort, disport, frisk, frolic, gambol, lark, rollick, romp; carouse, revel, roar, wassail

cycle *n* **1** a series of events or actions that

---

syn synonym(s)   *rel* related words
ant antonym(s)   *near ant* near antonym(s)

repeat themselves regularly and in the same order ⟨the *cycle* of birth, growth, decline, and death that is experienced by all life forms⟩

syn circle, round, wheel

rel pattern, syndrome; course, development, progression, run; beat, loop, ring; revolution, rotation, turn, turnover; chain, sequence, series, string, succession, train

2 a long or seemingly long period of time — see AGE 2

cynic *n* a person who distrusts other people and believes that everything is done for selfish reasons ⟨a *cynic* who believes that nobody does a good deed without expecting something in return⟩

syn misanthrope, pessimist

rel doubter, negativist, skeptic; belittler, critic, derider, detractor, scoffer; malcontent; defeatist, quitter

near ant optimist, Pollyanna, positivist; idealist, sentimentalist

cynical *adj* having or showing a deep distrust of human beings and their motives ⟨so *cynical* that he can't understand why anyone would volunteer to help out at a homeless shelter⟩

syn misanthropic, pessimistic

rel distrustful, mistrustful, negativist, negativistic, skeptical, suspicious; derisive, mocking, sardonic, scornful; defeatist, fatalistic, negative; ironic (*also* ironical), sarcastic; jaded, sophisticated, worldly-wise; hard-bitten, hard-boiled, hardcase, hard-edged, unsentimental

near ant trustful, trusting, unsuspicious; cheerful, optimistic, positive, positivist, positivistic, rose-colored; ingenuous, innocent, naive (*or* naïve), unsophisticated; impractical, romantic; maudlin, mushy, saccharine, sappy, sentimental

ant uncynical

cynosure *n* **1** a guiding or motivating purpose or principle — see COMPASS 1

2 a thing or place that is of greatest importance to an activity or interest — see CENTER 1

czar *also* **tsar** *or* **tzar** *n* a person of rank, power, or influence in a particular field — see MAGNATE

dab *n* **1** a quick thrust — see ¹POKE 1

2 a very small amount — see PARTICLE 1

3 a hard strike with a part of the body or an instrument — see ¹BLOW

dabbler *n* a person who regularly or occasionally engages in an activity as a pastime rather than as a profession — see AMATEUR 1

dad *n* a male human parent — see FATHER 1

daddy *n* **1** a male human parent — see FATHER 1

2 something belonging to an earlier time from which something else was later developed — see ANCESTOR 2

daffy *adj* showing or marked by a lack of good sense or judgment — see FOOLISH 1

daft *adj* showing or marked by a lack of good sense or judgment — see FOOLISH 1

daftness *n* lack of good sense or judgment — see FOOLISHNESS 1

daily *adj* occurring, done, produced, or appearing every day ⟨They made their *daily* stop at the coffee shop after work to relax before dinner.⟩

syn day-to-day, diurnal

rel alternate, cyclic (*or* cyclical), intermittent, periodic, recurrent, recurring, regular; ceaseless, continual, continuing, continuous, everlasting, frequent, incessant, perpetual, unbroken, unceasing, uninterrupted, unremitting

near ant monthly, weekly, yearly; erratic, infrequent, irregular; occasional, spasmodic, sporadic; interrupted

daintiness *n* the state or quality of having a delicate structure — see DELICACY 2

dainty *adj* **1** hard to please — see FINICKY

2 having qualities that appeal to a refined taste — see CHOICE 1

3 satisfying or pleasing because of fineness or mildness — see DELICATE 1

4 very pleasing to the sense of taste — see DELICIOUS 1

dainty *n* something that is pleasing to eat because it is rare or a luxury — see DELICACY 1

dais *n* a level usually raised surface — see PLATFORM

dale *n* an area of lowland between hills or mountains — see VALLEY

dalliance *n* activity engaged in to amuse oneself — see PLAY 1

dallier *n* someone who moves slowly or more slowly than others — see SLOWPOKE

dally *vb* **1** to engage in activity for amusement — see PLAY 1

2 to move or act slowly — see DELAY 1

3 to show a sexual attraction for someone just for fun — see FLIRT 1

4 to spend time doing nothing — see IDLE

dallying *adj* moving or proceeding at less than the normal, desirable, or required speed — see SLOW 1

dam *n* a bank of earth constructed to control water ⟨The river backed up behind the *dam* until it formed a new lake.⟩

syn dike, embankment, head, levee

rel breakwater, jetty, seawall; breastwork, bulwark, earthwork, rampart; canal, channel, ditch, gutter, trough; lock; barricade, barrier, block; floodgate, sluice; barrage, milldam, weir

dam *vb* **1** to prevent passage through by filling with something — see CLOG 1

2 to close up so that no empty spaces remain — see FILL 2

damage *n* 1 something that causes loss or pain — see INJURY 1

2 **damages** *pl* a sum of money to be paid as a punishment — see FINE

3 **damages** *pl* payment to another for a loss or injury — see COMPENSATION 1

4 the amount of money that is demanded as payment for something — see PRICE 1

damage *vb* 1 to reduce the soundness, effectiveness, or perfection of ⟨The burst pipe *damaged* the entire city's water supply.⟩

syn blemish, bloody, break, compromise, crab, cripple, deface, disfigure, flaw, harm, hurt, impair, injure, mar, spoil, vitiate

rel deteriorate, enervate, enfeeble, undermine, weaken; erode, scour, wash out, wear (away); tarnish; dent, ding, dint; botch, queer; lacerate, wound; disable, hamstring, lame, maim, mutilate, torment, torture; annihilate, bang up, bash, batter, clobber, crush, dash, decimate, demolish, desolate, destroy, devastate, do in, pulverize, raze, ruin, scourge, shatter, smash, tear down, total, waste, wipe out, wreck

near ant cure, heal, help, rectify, rehabilitate, remedy; edit, remodel, revise; ameliorate, better, enhance, enrich, improve, meliorate, perfect, refine

ant doctor, fix, mend, patch, rebuild, recondition, reconstruct, renovate, repair, revamp

2 to cause bodily damage to — see INJURE 1

damaging *adj* causing or capable of causing harm — see HARMFUL

dame *n* 1 a dignified usually elderly woman of some rank or authority — see MATRIARCH

2 a woman of high birth or social position — see GENTLEWOMAN

damn *vb* 1 to use profane or obscene language at or about ⟨*damned* the car for once again breaking down⟩

syn curse

rel imprecate, maledict; criticize, reprove; admonish, chide, rebuke, reprimand, reproach; blame, censure, reprehend, reprobate

near ant bless, extol (*also* extoll), glorify, laud, magnify, praise; acclaim, applaud, commend, compliment, hail, salute

2 to declare to be morally wrong or evil — see CONDEMN 1

3 to impose a judicial punishment on — see SENTENCE

damp *adj* 1 containing or characterized by an uncomfortable amount of moisture — see HUMID

2 slightly or moderately wet — see MOIST

damp *n* the amount of water suspended in the air in tiny droplets — see MOISTURE

damp *vb* 1 to deprive of emotional or intellectual vitality — see DEHYDRATE 1

2 to make or become slightly or moderately wet — see MOISTEN

3 to reduce or weaken in strength or feeling — see DULL 1

dampen *vb* 1 to make or become slightly or moderately wet — see MOISTEN

2 to reduce or weaken in strength or feeling — see DULL 1

3 to deprive of emotional or intellectual vitality — see DEHYDRATE 1

damper *n* a device on a musical instrument that deadens or softens its tone — see MUTE

dampness *n* the amount of water suspended in the air in tiny droplets — see MOISTURE

damsel *n* a young unmarried woman — see GIRL 1

dance *n* a social gathering for dancing ⟨Who are you taking to the *dance* on Saturday night?⟩

syn ball, cotillion (*also* cotillon), formal, hop, prom

rel blowout, celebration, event, festival, festivity, fete (*or* fête), gala, masquerade, mixer, party, reception, shindig, soiree (*or* soirée); hoedown, square dance

dance *vb* 1 to perform a series of usually rhythmic bodily movements to music ⟨She can't resist *dancing* to her favorite music.⟩

syn foot (it), hoof (it), step

rel prance, strut, trip; boogie (*also* boogy *or* boogey), bop, fox-trot, gavotte, jig, jitterbug, jive, mambo, polka, shag, shimmy, shuffle, tango, tap-dance, twist, waltz; tread

phrases shake a leg, trip the light fantastic

2 to make an irregular series of quick, sudden movements — see FLIT

dandle *vb* to treat with great or excessive care — see BABY

dandy *adj* of the very best kind — see EXCELLENT

dandy *n* 1 a man extremely interested in his clothing and personal appearance ⟨a *dandy* whose hair was always perfect⟩

syn beau, buck, dude, fop, gallant

rel blade, cavalier, dasher; clotheshorse, swell

near ant slob, sloven

2 something very good of its kind — see JIM-DANDY

danger *n* 1 the state of not being protected from injury, harm, or evil ⟨We were unaware of the *danger* that lay ahead.⟩

syn distress, endangerment, imperilment, jeopardy, peril, risk, trouble

rel exposure, liability, openness, vulnerability; precariousness, threat; susceptibility, susceptibleness; defenselessness, helplessness, weakness

near ant preservation, salvation; defense, protection; exemption, immunity, impunity, inviolability, invulnerableness

ant safeness, safety, secureness, security

2 something that may cause injury or harm ⟨willing to face the *dangers* of the Arctic in quest of the Northwest Passage⟩

syn hazard, menace, peril, pitfall, risk, threat, trouble

rel snare, trap; booby trap

near ant guard, protection, safeguard, shield, ward; asylum, harbor, haven, refuge, retreat, shelter

dangerous *adj* 1 involving potential loss or injury ⟨The soldiers were specially se-

---

syn synonym(s)   *rel* related words
ant antonym(s)   *near ant* near antonym(s)

lected to go on a *dangerous* mission behind enemy lines.⟩

syn grave, grievous, hazardous, jeopardizing, menacing, parlous, perilous, risky, serious, threatening, unhealthy, unsafe, venturesome

rel dicey, insecure, precarious, treacherous, uncertain; ultrahazardous; chance, haphazard, random; adverse, bad, baleful, baneful, deleterious, detrimental, evil, harmful, hurtful, ill, inimical, injurious, malignant, nasty, noxious, pernicious, pestilent; deadly, deathly, destructive, dire, fatal, fateful, lethal, mortal, murderous

near ant advantageous, beneficial, good; ultrasafe

ant harmless, innocent, innocuous, nonhazardous, nonthreatening, safe, unthreatening

2 causing or capable of causing harm — see HARMFUL

dangle *vb* to place on an elevated point without support from below — see HANG 1

dangling *adj* extending freely from a support from above — see DEPENDENT 1

dank *adj* slightly or moderately wet — see MOIST

dapper *adj* being strikingly neat and trim in style or appearance — see SMART 1

dapple *n* a small area that is different (as in color) from the main part — see SPOT 1

dapple *vb* to mark with small spots especially unevenly — see SPOT 1

dappled *also* **dapple** *adj* **1** marked with spots — see SPOTTED 1

2 having blotches of two or more colors — see PIED

dare *vb* **1** to invite (someone) to take part in a contest or to perform a feat — see CHALLENGE 2

2 to oppose (something hostile or dangerous) with firmness or courage — see FACE 2

daredevil *adj* **1** foolishly adventurous or bold — see FOOLHARDY 1

2 having or showing a lack of concern for the consequences of one's actions — see RECKLESS 1

daredevil *n* a person who seeks out very dangerous or foolhardy adventures with no apparent fear ⟨That little *daredevil* has broken an arm and an ankle this year alone.⟩

syn devil, madcap, madman

rel berserk (*or* berserker), cowboy

daring *adj* inclined or willing to take risks — see BOLD 1

daring *n* strength of mind to carry on in spite of danger — see COURAGE

dark *adj* **1** being without light or without much light ⟨It gets *dark* earlier in the winter.⟩

syn black, darkened, darkish, darkling, darksome, dim, dimmed, dusk, dusky, gloomy, murky, obscure, obscured, pitch-black, pitch-dark, pitchy, somber (*or* sombre)

rel crepuscular, twilit; moonless, starless; cloudy, dull, dulled, lackluster; shadowlike, shadowy, shady; gray (*also* grey), leaden, pale; beclouded, befogged, clouded, foggy, misty, smoggy, soupy

near ant ablaze, agleam, aglitter, alight, beaming, beamy, effulgent, glaring, glow-

ing, incandescent, lambent, radiant, relucent, resplendent, shining, sparkling; ultrabright; glossy, lustrous, shiny; floodlit (*also* floodlighted), highlighted, spotlighted (*or* spotlit); moonlit, moony, starlit, sunlit

ant bright, brightened, brilliant, illuminated, illumined, light, lightsome, lucent, lucid, luminous

2 causing or marked by an atmosphere lacking in cheer — see GLOOMY 1

3 given to keeping one's activities hidden from public observation or knowledge — see SECRETIVE

4 having an often intentionally veiled or uncertain meaning — see OBSCURE 1

5 lacking in education or the knowledge gained from books — see IGNORANT 1

6 not conforming to a high moral standard; morally unacceptable — see BAD 2

dark *n* **1** a time or place of little or no light ⟨I have a bad habit of running into tables in the *dark*.⟩

syn black, blackness, darkness, dusk, gloaming, gloom, murk, night, semidarkness, shade, shadows, twilight, umbra

rel midnight; blackout, brownout, dimout; shadiness, umbrage; dullness (*also* dulness), somberness; cloudiness, fogginess, haziness, mistiness, murkiness; dimness, faintness, gloominess, grayness, paleness; half-light

near ant moonlight, starlight, sunlight; effulgence, radiance, radiancy, shine, sunshine; incandescence, luminescence, luminosity

ant blaze, brightness, brilliance, day, daylight, glare, glow, light, lightness

2 the time from sunset to sunrise when there is no visible sunlight — see NIGHT 1

darken *vb* **1** to take on a gloomy or forbidding look ⟨His face slowly *darkened* as we told him the sad news.⟩

syn gloom, glower, lower (*also* lour)

rel frown, scowl; glare, stare; brood, mope, pet, pout, sulk; anger, bristle, fume, rage, steam, storm; intimidate, menace, threaten

ant brighten, cheer (up), lighten, perk (up)

2 to grow dark ⟨The sky *darkened* as a storm moved in.⟩

syn blacken, black out, dusk

rel dim, fade, wane; gloom, lower (*also* lour)

near ant dawn; beam, glow, radiate, shine

ant brighten, light, lighten

3 to make dark, dim, or indistinct — see CLOUD 1

4 to affect slightly with something morally bad or undesirable — see TAINT 1

darkened *adj* being without light or without much light — see DARK 1

darkening *adj* causing or marked by an atmosphere lacking in cheer — see GLOOMY 1

darkish *adj* being without light or without much light — see DARK 1

darkling *adj* being without light or without much light — see DARK 1

darkness *n* **1** a time or place of little or no light — see DARK 1

2 the quality or state of having a veiled or uncertain meaning — see OBSCURITY 1

3 the time from sunset to sunrise when there is no visible sunlight — see NIGHT 1

4 an overspreading element that produces an atmosphere of gloom — see CLOUD

darksome *adj* being without light or without much light — see DARK 1

darling *adj* 1 granted special treatment or attention 〈They poured gifts and affection on their *darling* child.〉

syn beloved, cherished, dear, favored, favorite, fond, loved, pet, precious, special, sweet

rel admired, adored, appreciated, esteemed, relished, revered; prized, treasured; preferred

near ant abhorred, abominated, despised, detested, disdained, disfavored, disliked, execrated, hated, loathed, unfavorite; abandoned, forgotten, ignored; alienated, estranged

ant unbeloved

2 having qualities that tend to make one loved — see LOVABLE

3 giving pleasure or contentment to the mind or senses — see PLEASANT 1

darling *n* 1 a person or thing that is preferred over others — see FAVORITE

2 a person with whom one is in love — see SWEETHEART

darn *n* the smallest amount or part imaginable — see LICK 1

darn *vb* to close up with a series of interlacing stitches — see SEW

dart *n* an act or expression showing scorn and usually intended to hurt another's feelings — see INSULT

dart *vb* to make an irregular series of quick, sudden movements — see FLIT

dash *n* active strength of body or mind — see VIGOR 1

dash *vb* 1 to go at a pace faster than a walk — see RUN 1

2 to proceed or move quickly — see HURRY 2

3 to send through the air especially with a quick forward motion of the arm — see THROW 1

4 to wet or soil by striking with something liquid or mushy — see SPLASH 2

5 to cause (something liquid or mushy) to move along in sheets — see SPLASH 1

6 to make sad — see DEPRESS 1

dashing *adj* inclined or willing to take risks — see BOLD 1

dashingly *adv* in a strikingly neat and trim manner — see SMARTLY

dastard *n* a person who shows a shameful lack of courage in the face of danger — see COWARD

dastardliness *n* a shameful lack of courage in the face of danger — see COWARDICE

dastardly *adj* having or showing a shameful lack of courage — see COWARDLY

date *n* 1 an agreement to be present at a specified time and place — see ENGAGEMENT 2

2 the period during which something exists, lasts, or is in progress — see DURATION 1

date *vb* 1 to go on a social engagement with 〈I don't want to *date* him—I'd rather just be friends.〉

syn take out

rel accompany, escort, see; court, woo

2 to go on dates that may eventually lead to marriage — see COURT 2

dated *adj* having passed its time of use or usefulness — see OBSOLETE

dateless *adj* 1 dating or surviving from the distant past — see ANCIENT 1

2 lasting forever — see EVERLASTING 1

3 having an existence or validity that does not change or diminish — see ABIDING

dating *n* the series of social engagements shared by a couple looking to get married — see COURTSHIP

datum *n* a single piece of information — see FACT 3

daub *vb* 1 to make dirty — see DIRTY

2 to rub an oily or sticky substance over — see SMEAR 1

daunt *vb* to lessen the courage or confidence of — see DISCOURAGE 1

dauntless *adj* feeling or displaying no fear by temperament — see BRAVE 1

dauntlessness *n* strength of mind to carry on in spite of danger — see COURAGE

davenport *n* a long upholstered piece of furniture designed for several sitters — see COUCH

dawdle *vb* 1 to move or act slowly — see DELAY 1

2 to spend time doing nothing — see IDLE

dawdler *n* someone who moves slowly or more slowly than others — see SLOWPOKE

dawdling *adj* moving or proceeding at less than the normal, desirable, or required speed — see SLOW 1

dawn *n* 1 the first appearance of light in the morning or the time of its appearance 〈We stayed up talking until *dawn*.〉

syn dawning, day, daybreak, daylight, light, morn, morning, sun, sunrise, sunup

rel daytime;

near ant dark, darkness, midnight, night, nighttime; midday; dusk, evening, eventide, gloaming, twilight

ant nightfall, sundown, sunset

2 the point at which something begins — see BEGINNING

dawn *vb* to come into existence — see BEGIN 2

dawn (on) *vb* to enter the mind of — see OCCUR (TO)

dawning *n* the first appearance of light in the morning or the time of its appearance — see DAWN 1

day *n* 1 the hours of light between one night and the next 〈During the *day*, we like to go play ball in the park.〉

syn daylight, daytime

rel light, sunlight, sunshine; dawn, dawning, daybreak, forenoon, morn, morning, sunrise; noon; dusk, evening, gloaming, nightfall, sundown, sunset, twilight

near ant black, blackness, dark, darkness

ant night, nighttime

2 an extent of time associated with a particular person or thing — see AGE 1

3 the first appearance of light in the morning or the time of its appearance — see DAWN 1

---

syn synonym(s)   **rel** related words

ant antonym(s)   **near ant** near antonym(s)

daybreak *n* the first appearance of light in the morning or the time of its appearance — see DAWN 1

daydream *n* a conception or image created by the imagination and having no objective reality — see FANTASY 1

daydreaming *n* the state of being lost in thought — see REVERIE

daylight *n* **1** the first appearance of light in the morning or the time of its appearance — see DAWN 1

2 the hours of light between one night and the next — see DAY 1

3 daylights *pl* the normal or healthy condition of the mental abilities — see MIND 2

daytime *n* the hours of light between one night and the next — see DAY 1

day-to-day *adj* occurring, done, produced, or appearing every day — see DAILY

daze *n* a state of mental confusion — see HAZE 2

daze *vb* **1** to make senseless or dizzy by a blow — see STUN 1

2 to overpower with light — see DAZZLE

dazed *adj* suffering from mental confusion — see DIZZY 2

dazzle *n* the quality or state of having or giving off light — see BRILLIANCE 1

dazzle *vb* to overpower with light ⟨Skiers were *dazzled* by the glare off of the slopes of freshly packed snow.⟩
syn bedazzle, blind, daze
rel confuse, overpower, overwhelm, stun

dazzling *adj* giving off or reflecting much light — see BRIGHT 1

deactivate *vb* to cause to stop functioning ⟨*Deactivate* the machine carefully, or you'll risk an electric shock.⟩
syn kill, shut off, turn off
rel flick (off); dismantle, mothball, phase out; arrest, brake, chock, cut off, draw up, halt, jam, stall, stick
near ant charge, electrify, energize, fire, fuel, generate, power, push; discharge, launch, release, switch, trip; reactivate
ant activate, actuate, crank (up), drive, move, propel, run, set off, spark, start, touch off, trigger, turn on

dead *adj* **1** no longer living ⟨I inherited this heirloom from my *dead* great-grandfather.⟩
syn breathless, cold, deceased, defunct, departed, fallen, gone, late, lifeless, low
rel extinct; dying, fading, moribund; stillborn; finished, lapsed, terminated; insensate, nonliving; done, done for
phrases bitten the dust
near ant animated; dynamic, lively, thriving, vibrant, vital, vivacious; active, functioning, operative, running
ant alive, animate, breathing, going, live, living, quick

2 lacking in gaiety, movement, or animation ⟨The store is often *dead* after 4:00 p.m.⟩
syn slow
rel lethargic, sluggish, torpid; dormant, fallow, free, idle, inactive, inert, inoperative, latent, off, vacant
near ant abounding, overflowing, swarming, teeming, thronging
ant alive, animated, astir, bustling, busy,

buzzing, flourishing, humming, lively, thriving, vibrant

3 depleted in strength, energy, or freshness — see WEARY 1

4 having no exceptions or restrictions — see ABSOLUTE 1

5 lacking in sensation or feeling — see NUMB 1

6 no longer existing — see EXTINCT

7 not being in a state of use, activity, or employment — see INACTIVE 2

8 of, relating to, or suggestive of death — see DEATHLY 1

9 producing inferior or only a small amount of vegetation — see BARREN 1

dead *adv* **1** in a direct line or course — see DIRECTLY 1

2 to a full extent or degree — see FULLY 1

dead *n* the state of being dead — see DEATH 2

deaden *vb* **1** to deprive of emotional or intellectual vitality — see DEHYDRATE 1

2 to reduce or weaken in strength or feeling — see DULL 1

dead heat *n* a situation in which neither participant in a contest, competition, or struggle comes out ahead of the other — see TIE 1

deadlock *n* a point in a struggle where neither side is capable of winning or willing to give in — see IMPASSE 1

deadly *adj* **1** likely to cause or capable of causing death ⟨The doctors were alarmed about the outbreak of the *deadly* new virus.⟩
syn baleful, deathly, fatal, kill, killer, lethal, mortal, murderous, pestilent, terminal, vital
rel baneful, deleterious, destructive, harmful, injurious, noxious, pernicious, truculent; infectious, infective, poisonous, sublethal, toxic, virulent; dangerous, grave, grievous, hazardous, jeopardizing, menacing, parlous, perilous, risky, serious, threatening, ugly, unhealthy, unsound; bloody, internecine, sanguinary, sanguine
near ant beneficial, restorative, salubrious, salutary; alleviative, corrective, remedial, tonic; advantageous, beneficial, useful; nonpoisonous, nontoxic, safe
ant healthful, healthy, nonfatal, nonlethal, wholesome

2 having no exceptions or restrictions — see ABSOLUTE 1

3 of, relating to, or suggestive of death — see DEATHLY 1

deadly *adv* to a great degree — see VERY 1

deadness *n* the state of being dead — see DEATH 2

deadpan *adj* not expressing any emotion — see BLANK 1

deadwood *n* discarded or useless material — see GARBAGE

deafening *adj* marked by a high volume of sound — see LOUD 1

¹deal *n* a considerable amount — see LOT 2

²deal *n* **1** an arrangement about action to be taken — see AGREEMENT 2

2 the transfer of ownership of something from one person to another for a price — see SALE

3 a formal agreement to fulfill an obligation — see GUARANTEE 1

4 position with regard to conditions and circumstances — see SITUATION 1

5 something bought or offered for sale at a desirable price — see BARGAIN 1

deal vb **1** to carry on the business of buying and selling goods or other property — see TRADE 1

2 to talk over or dispute the terms of a purchase — see BARGAIN 1

deal (in) vb to offer for sale to the public — see MARKET

deal (out) vb to give out (something) to appropriate individuals — see ADMINISTER 1

deal (with) vb **1** to behave toward in a stated way — see TREAT 1

2 to have (something) as a subject matter — see CONCERN 1

dealer n **1** a buyer and seller of goods for profit — see MERCHANT

2 the person in a business deal who hands over an item in exchange for money — see VENDOR

dealings n pl doings between individuals or groups — see RELATION 1

dean n the senior member of a group ⟨The *dean* of the Aspen ski instructors oversaw the training of the rescue team.⟩
syn elder, elder statesman, senior
rel better, superior; old hand, old-timer, vet, veteran
near ant inferior, subordinate, underling; beginner, colt, fledgling, freshman, greenhorn, neophyte, newbie, newcomer, novice, recruit, rookie, tenderfoot, tyro
ant baby, junior

dear adj **1** commanding a large price — see COSTLY

2 granted special treatment or attention — see DARLING 1

3 having qualities that tend to make one loved — see LOVABLE

dear n a person with whom one is in love — see SWEETHEART

dearth n **1** a falling short of an essential or desirable amount or number — see DEFICIENCY

2 the fact or state of being absent — see LACK 1

death n **1** the permanent stopping of all the vital bodily activities ⟨We were all saddened by the *death* of our dog.⟩
syn curtains, decease, demise, dissolution, doom, end, exit, expiration, fate, grave, passage, passing, quietus, sleep
rel casualty, fatality; martyrdom, self-destruction, self-murder, self-slaughter, suicide; annihilation, destruction, ending, extermination, ruin; assassination, execution, massacre, slaughter
near ant existence, life; creation, genesis, origination, rise
ant birth, nativity

2 the state of being dead ⟨*Death* is one of the few constants in the universe.⟩
syn dead, deadness, grave, lifelessness, sleep
rel mortality
near ant immortality; life span, lifetime
ant existence, life

3 the act of ceasing to exist ⟨the *death* of videotape⟩

syn demise, expiration, termination
rel dispersion, dissolution; cessation, close, conclusion, decease, discontinuance, doom, end, ending, finish, halt, lapse, passing, quietus, shutdown, shutoff, stop, stoppage, surcease; suicide; annihilation, destruction, ruin
near ant existence, persistence, prolongation; inauguration, initiation, institution, origination
ant alpha, beginning, birth, commencement, creation, dawn, genesis, inception, incipiency, launch, morning, onset, outset, start

4 something that is the cause of one's ultimate failure or loss of life — see DOWNFALL 1

5 the killing of a large number of people — see MASSACRE

deathless adj lasting forever — see EVERLASTING 1

deathly adj **1** of, relating to, or suggestive of death ⟨his *deathly* pallor⟩
syn dead, deadly, mortal
rel cadaverous; ghostlike, ghostly, phantom, spectral; inactive, inert, inoperative, lifeless, quiescent, still; macabre; baleful, fatal, fateful, fell, killer, lethal, murderous, pestilent
near ant active, alive, animate, breathing, live, living; animated, bouncing, brisk, energetic, frisky, jaunty, jazzy, lively, peppy, perky, pert, racy, snappy, spanking, sparky, spirited, sprightful, sprightly, springy, vigorous, vital, vivacious, zippy; able-bodied, chipper, fit, hale, healthy, hearty, robust, sound, well, whole, wholesome

2 likely to cause or capable of causing death — see DEADLY 1

debacle also **débâcle** n **1** a sudden violent event that brings about great loss or destruction — see DISASTER 1

2 something that has failed — see FAILURE 3

debar vb to prevent the participation, consideration, or inclusion of — see EXCLUDE

debark vb to go ashore from a ship — see DISEMBARK 1

debase vb **1** to lower in character, dignity, or quality ⟨We *debase* ourselves when we adopt the moral code and behavior of our despised enemies.⟩
syn abase, cheapen, corrupt, debauch, degrade, demean, demoralize, deprave, deteriorate, lessen, pervert, poison, profane, subvert, vitiate, warp
rel befoul, begrime, contaminate, defile, dilute, dirty, pollute, taint, thin, weaken; descend; disgrace, dishonor, humble, humiliate, shame, take down; blemish, damage, deface, destroy, flaw, harm, hurt, impair, mar, ruin, spoil, stain, tarnish, wreck; depreciate, downgrade
near ant dignify, exalt, honor; ameliorate, amend, better, enhance, enrich, improve, meliorate, perfect; clarify, clean, cleanse, purify, refine, restore; respect
ant elevate, ennoble, uplift

2 to reduce to a lower standing in one's own eyes or in others' eyes — see HUMBLE

debased adj having or showing lowered moral character or standards — see CORRUPT

---

debasement *n* a sinking to a state of low moral standards and behavior — see CORRUPTION 2

debatable *adj* **1** open to question or dispute ⟨It's always *debatable* which college football team is really number one, since there's more than one ranking system.⟩
syn disputable, doubtable, doubtful, moot, negotiable, questionable
rel contradictable, refutable; debated, disputed; dubious, iffy, inconclusive, indecisive, problematic (*also* problematical), shaky, uncertain; academic (*also* academical), hypothetical, speculative, theoretical (*also* theoretic); ambiguous, equivocal
near ant irrefutable; definite; unambiguous, unequivocal; absolute, clear, conclusive, decisive; uncontested, undisputed
ant accomplished, certain, incontestable, incontrovertible, indisputable, indubitable, positive, questionless, settled, sure, unanswerable, undebatable, undeniable, unquestionable
2 giving good reason for being doubted, questioned, or challenged — see DOUBTFUL 2

debate *n* **1** a careful weighing of the reasons for or against something — see CONSIDERATION 1
2 variance of opinion on a matter — see DISAGREEMENT 1
3 an exchange of views for the purpose of exploring a subject or deciding an issue — see DISCUSSION 1

debate *vb* **1** to give serious and careful thought to — see PONDER
2 to talk about (an issue) usually from various points of view and for the purpose of arriving at a decision or opinion — see DISCUSS

debater *n* a person who takes part in a dispute — see DISPUTANT

debauch *vb* to lower in character, dignity, or quality — see DEBASE 1

debauched *adj* having or showing lowered moral character or standards — see CORRUPT

debaucher *n* a person who has sunk below the normal moral standard — see DEGENERATE

debauchery *n* **1** immoral conduct or practices harmful or offensive to society — see VICE 1
2 a sinking to a state of low moral standards and behavior — see CORRUPTION 2

debilitate *vb* to diminish the physical strength of — see WEAKEN 1

debilitated *adj* lacking bodily strength — see WEAK 1

debilitation *n* **1** a gradual sinking and wasting away of mind or body — see DECLINE 1
2 the quality or state of lacking physical strength or vigor — see WEAKNESS 1

debility *n* the quality or state of lacking physical strength or vigor — see WEAKNESS 1

debonair *adj* **1** having or showing freedom from worries or troubles — see CAREFREE
2 having or showing very polished and worldly manners — see SUAVE

debris *n* **1** discarded or useless material — see GARBAGE

2 the portion or bits of something left over or behind after it has been destroyed — see REMAINS 1

debt *n* **1** something (as money) which is owed ⟨He filed for bankruptcy when his *debts* exceeded his assets.⟩
syn liability (*usually* liabilities), obligation, score
rel bond, delinquency; default, embarrassment
near ant quietus, quittance, repayment
2 a breaking of a moral or legal code — see OFFENSE 1

debug *vb* to remove errors, defects, deficiencies, or deviations from — see CORRECT 1

debunk *vb* **1** to prove to be false — see DISPROVE
2 to reveal the true nature of — see EXPOSE 1

decadence *n* **1** a change to a lower state or level — see DECLINE 2
2 a sinking to a state of low moral standards and behavior — see CORRUPTION 2

decadent *adj* **1** having lost forcefulness, courage, or spirit — see EFFETE 1
2 having or showing lowered moral character or standards — see CORRUPT

decadent *n* a person who has sunk below the normal moral standard — see DEGENERATE

decalogue *n* a collection or system of rules of conduct — see CODE

decamping *n* the act of leaving a place — see DEPARTURE 1

decampment *n* the act of leaving a place — see DEPARTURE 1

decapitate *vb* to cut off the head of ⟨Charles I of England was *decapitated* in 1649.⟩
syn behead, guillotine, head
rel prune, shorten, trim; scalp

decay *n* **1** a gradual sinking and wasting away of mind or body — see DECLINE 1
2 the process by which dead organic matter separates into simpler substances — see CORRUPTION 1

decay *vb* **1** to go through decomposition ⟨The logs *decayed* on the rain forest floor.⟩ ⟨The atom of plutonium *decayed* in the test chamber.⟩
syn break down, corrupt, decompose, disintegrate, fester, foul, molder, putrefy, rot, spoil
rel sour, turn; contaminate, defile, pollute, taint; addle, curdle, ferment, mortify; rust; crumble, decline, degenerate, descend, deteriorate, dilapidate, sink, wither
phrases fall apart, go to seed (*or* run to seed)
near ant age, develop, grow, mature, ripen; refresh, renew, restore; cleanse, purify; assemble, compose, integrate; ameliorate, better, improve, meliorate
2 to become worse or of less value — see DETERIORATE 1
3 to lose bodily strength or vigor — see WEAKEN 2

decayed *adj* **1** having lost forcefulness, courage, or spirit — see EFFETE 1
2 having undergone organic breakdown — see ROTTEN 1

decaying *n* a gradual sinking and wasting away of mind or body — see DECLINE 1

decease n the permanent stopping of all the vital bodily activities — see DEATH 1

deceased adj no longer living — see DEAD 1

deceit n 1 the inclination or practice of misleading others through lies or trickery ⟨a rise to power that was marked by treachery and *deceit*⟩

syn artifice, craft, craftiness, crookedness, cunning, deceitfulness, dishonesty, dissembling, dissimulation, double-dealing, duplicity, fakery, foxiness, fraud, guile, wiliness

rel equivocation, lying, mendacity, prevarication; chicanery, fraudulence, hanky-panky, skulduggery (*or* skullduggery); subterfuge, swindling, trickery, wile; falsehood, falsity, fib, untruth; hypocrisy, insincerity, sanctimoniousness, two-facedness; artfulness, caginess (*also* cageyness), deviousness, shrewdness; treacherousness, underhandedness, unscrupulousness; covertness, furtiveness, secrecy, shadiness, sneakiness, stealthiness; oiliness, shiftiness, slickness, slipperiness, slyness, smoothness

near ant candidness, candor, directness, frankness, openness, plainness; honesty, probity; dependability, reliability, reliableness, solidity, trustiness, trustworthiness; decency, goodness, incorruptibility, integrity, righteousness, truthfulness, uprightness, virtuousness

ant artlessness, forthrightness, good faith, guilelessness, ingenuousness, sincerity

2 the tendency to tell lies — see DISHONESTY 1

deceitful adj 1 marked by, based on, or done by the use of dishonest methods to acquire something of value — see FRAUDULENT 1

2 tending or having power to deceive — see DECEPTIVE 1

deceitfulness n 1 the inclination or practice of misleading others through lies or trickery — see DECEIT 1

2 the tendency to tell lies — see DISHONESTY 1

deceive vb to cause to believe what is untrue ⟨He went to great lengths to *deceive* his family about the nature of his new job at the mall.⟩

syn beguile, bluff, burn, catch, con, cozen, delude, dupe, fool, gaff, gull, have, hoax, hoodwink, humbug, misguide, misinform, mislead, snow, spoof, string along, take in, trick

rel kid, put on, tease; bleed, cheat, chisel, defraud, diddle, euchre, flam, fleece, hustle, mulct, rook, shortchange, skin, squeeze, stick, sting, swindle

phrases do a number on, lead one down the garden path (*also* lead one up the garden path), pull one's leg, pull the wool over one's eyes

near ant debunk, expose, reveal, show up, uncloak, uncover, unmask; disclose, divulge, tell, unveil; disabuse, disenchant, disillusion

ant undeceive

deceiving adj tending or having power to deceive — see DECEPTIVE 1

decelerate vb to cause to move or proceed at a less rapid pace — see SLOW

deceleration n a usually gradual decrease in the pace or level of activity of something — see SLOWDOWN

decency n 1 socially acceptable behavior ⟨The standards of basic *decency* called for them to help the older lady with her groceries.⟩

syn decorum, form, propriety

rel etiquette; civility, courteousness, courtesy, gentilesse, gentility, graciousness, mannerliness, politeness, politesse; dignity, grace, refinement; discretion, prudence; appropriateness, correctitude, correctness, decorousness, fitness, rightness, seemliness; attention, attentiveness, care, carefulness; character, goodness, high-mindedness, honesty, honor, integrity, morality, probity, rectitude, righteousness, straightness, uprightness, virtue, virtuousness

near ant coarseness, crudeness, gracelessness; discourtesy, impoliteness, incivility, vulgarity; imprudence, indiscretion; badness, evil, immorality, wickedness; debauchery, degeneracy, degradation, depravity, perversion; crookedness, dishonesty, underhandedness, unscrupulousness

ant impropriety, indecency

2 conduct that conforms to an accepted standard of right and wrong — see MORALITY 1

decent adj 1 conforming to a high standard of morality or virtue — see GOOD 2

2 following the accepted rules of moral conduct — see HONORABLE 1

3 following the established traditions of refined society and good taste — see PROPER 1

4 free from any trace of the coarse or indecent — see CHASTE 1

5 of a level of quality that meets one's needs or standards — see ADEQUATE 1

deceptive adj 1 tending or having power to deceive ⟨In his *deceptive* answer about the vehicle's history, the salesman said that the used car had never been hit by another car.⟩

syn beguiling, deceitful, deceiving, deluding, delusive, delusory, fallacious, false, misleading, specious

rel artful, crafty, cunning, devious, foxy, guileful, shady, shifty, slick, sly, sneaking, sneaky, subtile, subtle, trick, trickish, tricky, underhand, underhanded, wily; crooked, defrauding, dishonest, dissembling, double-dealing, faithless, fast, fraudulent, knavish, lying, mendacious, untrustworthy, untruthful; bogus, counterfeit, fake, feigned, forged, phony (*also* phoney), sham, spurious; insidious, perfidious, treacherous; artificial, backhanded, hypocritical, insincere, left-handed, two-faced

near ant candid, direct, foursquare, frank, free-spoken, open, openhearted, outspoken, plain, plainspoken, straight; clarifying, elucidative, explanatory; revealing, revelatory; honest, trustworthy, truthful

---

syn synonym(s) *rel* related words
ant antonym(s) *near ant* near antonym(s)

ant aboveboard, forthright, nondeceptive, straightforward

2 given to or marked by cheating and deception — see DISHONEST 2

decide *vb* **1** to come to a judgment about after discussion or consideration ⟨They *decided* to go out for pizza after the movie was over.⟩

syn choose, conclude, determine, figure, name, opt, resolve, settle (on *or* upon)

rel decree, rule; cull, elect, handpick, pick, prefer, select, single (out); adjudge, adjudicate, arbitrate, find, judge, referee, rule (on), umpire; chew over, cogitate, consider, contemplate, debate, deliberate, entertain, meditate, mull (over), ponder, question, ruminate, study, think (about *or* over), weigh

near ant abstain, decline, refuse, reject, turn down; delay, halt, hesitate, stall, temporize; shilly-shally, vacillate, waver

2 to give an opinion about (something at issue or in dispute) — see JUDGE 1

3 to come to an agreement or decision concerning the details of — see ARRANGE 1

4 to make final, definite, or beyond dispute — see CLINCH

5 to form an opinion or reach a conclusion through reasoning and information — see INFER 1

decided *adj* not subject to misinterpretation or more than one interpretation — see CLEAR 2

decidedness *n* firm or unwavering adherence to one's purpose — see DETERMINATION 1

decimate *vb* to bring to a complete end the physical soundness, existence, or usefulness of — see DESTROY 1

decimation *n* the state or fact of being rendered nonexistent, physically unsound, or useless — see DESTRUCTION 1

decipher *vb* **1** to change (as a secret message) from code into ordinary language — see DECODE 1

2 to have a clear idea of — see COMPREHEND 1

decision *n* **1** a position arrived at after consideration ⟨After much deliberation, we made a *decision* about what to have on our pizza.⟩

syn award, call, conclusion, deliverance, determination, diagnosis, judgment (*or* judgement), opinion, resolution, verdict

rel behest, charge, commandment, decree, dictate, directive, edict, instruction, mandate, order, word; last word, say-so; adjudication, disposition, doom, finding, ruling, sentence; choice, option, selection; consensus; belief, conviction, eye, feeling, mind, notion, persuasion, sentiment, view

near ant deadlock, draw, halt, stalemate, standoff, tie

2 firm or unwavering adherence to one's purpose — see DETERMINATION 1

decisive *adj* **1** fully committed to achieving a goal — see DETERMINED 1

2 having the power to persuade — see COGENT

3 serving to put an end to all debate or questioning — see CONCLUSIVE 1

decisiveness *n* firm or unwavering adherence to one's purpose — see DETERMINATION 1

deck *vb* to make more attractive by adding something that is beautiful or becoming — see DECORATE

declaim *vb* **1** to give a formal often extended talk on a subject — see TALK 1

2 to talk as if giving an important and formal speech — see ORATE 1

declamation *n* a usually formal discourse delivered to an audience — see SPEECH 1

declaration *n* a solemn and often public declaration of the truth or existence of something — see PROTESTATION

declare *vb* **1** to make known openly or publicly — see ANNOUNCE

2 to state as a fact usually forcefully — see CLAIM 1

3 to state clearly and strongly — see ASSERT 1

4 to make known (something abstract) through outward signs — see SHOW 1

declension *n* **1** a change to a lower state or level — see DECLINE 2

2 a downward slope — see DECLINE 3

decline *n* **1** a gradual sinking and wasting away of mind or body ⟨Doctors tried to slow the patient's *decline*.⟩

syn debilitation, decay, decaying, degeneration, descent, deterioration, ebbing, enfeeblement, weakening

rel exhaustion; drooping, flagging, limping; regression, relapse, setback

near ant invigoration, strengthening; progress; rejuvenation, rejuvenescence

ant comeback, improvement, rally, recovery, recuperation, rehabilitation, revitalization, snapback

2 a change to a lower state or level ⟨the *decline* of the Roman Empire⟩

syn decadence, declension, degeneracy, degeneration, degradation, descent, deterioration, downfall, downgrade, ebb, eclipse, fall

rel dark age, sunset; decay, rotting, spoiling; breakup, crumbling, decomposition, disintegration, dissolution; abasement, debasement; depreciation, lessening; decimation, demolishment, demolition, desolation, destruction, havoc, ruin, ruination; abatement, decrease, decrement, de-escalation, deflation, diminishment, diminution, dip, downslide, downtrend, downturn, drop, loss, lowering, reduction, sag, shrinkage, slip, slump

near ant advancement, development, evolution, growth; blossoming, flourishing, flowering; renewal, restoration, revitalization; heightening; accretion, accrual, addendum, addition, augmentation, boost, enhancement, gain, increase, increment, raise, supplement

ant ascent, rise, upswing

3 a downward slope ⟨The bicyclist lost control on the unexpectedly steep *decline*.⟩

syn declension, descent, dip, downgrade, fall, hang, hanging

rel basin, depression, hollow

near ant grade, gradient, hill, inclination, incline, lean, pitch, rake, tilt

ant acclivity, ascent, rise, upgrade, uphill, uprise

4 a loss of status — see COMEDOWN

5 the amount by which something is lessened — see DECREASE

decline *vb* **1** to show unwillingness to accept, do, engage in, or agree to ⟨He *declined* the invitation to the party.⟩ ⟨She *declined* to participate in the soccer game.⟩

syn disapprove, negative, pass, refuse, reject, reprobate, repudiate, spurn, throw out, turn down

rel disdain, rebuff, scorn, scout; overrule, veto; forbid, prohibit, proscribe; dismiss, ignore; abstain (from), forbear, refrain (from); deny, disavow, disclaim, dispute, gainsay; stick; abjure, recant, renounce, retract, take back, unsay, withdraw; avoid, bypass, detour; contradict, deny, disown, negate; disagree (with), disprove, dispute, rebut, refute; back down, back off, backtrack; disallow, recall, renege, revoke

phrases turn one's back on

near ant condone, countenance, swallow, tolerate; adopt, embrace, take, welcome; accede, acquiesce, agree, assent, consent; choose, handpick, select; espouse, support

ant accept, agree (to), approve

2 to be unwilling to grant — see DENY 2

3 to go to a lower level especially abruptly — see DROP 2

4 to become worse or of less value — see DETERIORATE 1

5 to grow less in scope or intensity especially gradually — see DECREASE 2

6 to lead or extend downward — see DESCEND 1

declined *adj* bending downward or forward — see NODDING

declining *adj* bending downward or forward — see NODDING

decode *vb* **1** to change (as a secret message) from code into ordinary language ⟨The agents worked into the night to *decode* the intercepted message from the enemy spy.⟩

syn break, crack, decipher

rel descramble, unscramble; render, translate; dope (out), figure out, puzzle (out), solve, unravel, work, work out

near ant garble, jumble (up), mix (up)

ant cipher, code, encipher, encode, encrypt

2 to have a clear idea of — see COMPREHEND 1

decolorize *vb* to make white or whiter by removing color — see WHITEN

decompose *vb* to go through decomposition — see DECAY 1

decomposed *adj* having undergone organic breakdown — see ROTTEN 1

decomposition *n* the process by which dead organic matter separates into simpler substances — see CORRUPTION 1

decorate *vb* to make more attractive by adding something that is beautiful or becoming ⟨*decorated* the mansion's hallways with priceless paintings and luxurious tapestries⟩

syn adorn, array, beautify, bedeck, bedizen, caparison, deck, do, doll up, dress, embellish, enrich, garnish, grace, ornament, trim

rel accessorize, dress up, trap, trick (out); brighten, freshen, smarten; boss, chase;

braid, embroider, feather, figure, filigree, fillet, flounce, frill, fringe, furbelow, garland, hang, lace, ribbon, swag, wreathe; appliqué, gild, paint

near ant simplify, streamline; bare, denude, dismantle, display, expose, reveal, strip, uncover; uglify

ant blemish, deface, disfigure, mar, scar, spoil

decoration *n* **1** something that decorates or beautifies ⟨Traditionally the family puts lots of *decorations* on and around the Christmas tree.⟩

syn adornment, caparison, embellishment, frill, garnish, ornament, trim

rel apparel, bells and whistles, blazonry, bric-a-brac, chichi, emblazonry, filigree, finery; flounce, flourish, furbelow, ruffle; enhancement, enrichment, improvement; appliqué, embossment, embroidery, fancywork; bedizenment, gilt, glitter; design, figure, pattern; furnishings, regalia, trappings

near ant blemish, defacement, disfigurement, scar; blot, spot, stain

2 something given in recognition of achievement — see AWARD 1

decorative *adj* serving to add beauty ⟨A necklace of *decorative* flowers was planted along the path to the cottage.⟩

syn adorning, beautifying, embellishing, ornamental

rel alluring, appealing, attractive, charming, delightful, glamorous (*also* glamourous), pleasing, prepossessing; beauteous, beautiful, comely, fair, gorgeous, handsome, lovely, pretty, stunning; detailed, elaborate, fancy, ornate

ant functional, utilitarian

decorous *adj* **1** following the established traditions of refined society and good taste — see PROPER 1

2 marked by or showing careful attention to set forms and details — see CEREMONIOUS 1

decorum *n* socially acceptable behavior — see DECENCY 1

decoy *n* something used to attract animals to a hook or into a trap — see BAIT 1

decoy *vb* to lead away from a usual or proper course by offering some pleasure or advantage — see LURE

decrease *n* the amount by which something is lessened ⟨The average *decrease* in the price of milk was five cents per gallon.⟩

syn abatement, decline, decrement, dent, depression, diminishment, diminution, drop, fall, loss, reduction, shrinkage

rel deduction, subtraction; downturn, slip, slump; curtailment, cut, cutback, retrenchment, shortening

near ant accretion, accrual, accumulation, addition, supplement; continuation, extension; upswing, uptrend, upturn

ant boost, enlargement, gain, increase, increment, raise, rise

decrease *vb* **1** to make smaller in amount, volume, or extent ⟨Workers *decreased* the volume of water flowing through the pipes in order to prevent an overflow.⟩

syn abate, de-escalate, dent, deplete, diminish, downsize, drop, dwindle, ease, knock down, lessen, lower, reduce

---

syn synonym(s)   *rel* related words
ant antonym(s)   *near ant* near antonym(s)

rel compress, condense, constrict, contract; abbreviate, abridge, clip, crop, curtail, cut, cut back, cut down, dock, nick, pare, prune, retrench, shorten, slash, trim, truncate, whittle; deflate, shrink; minimize; moderate, modify, modulate, qualify; deprive, strip

near ant blow up, dilate, distend, inflate, swell; elongate, extend, lengthen, prolong, protract; add (to), complement, supplement; enhance, heighten, intensify; redouble

ant aggrandize, amplify, augment, boost, enlarge, escalate, expand, increase, raise

2 to grow less in scope or intensity especially gradually ⟨The force of the wind slowly *decreased* until the flowers were standing upright again.⟩

syn abate, decline, de-escalate, diminish, dwindle, ease, ebb, fall, lessen, let up, lower, moderate, pall, recede, relent, remit, shrink, subside, taper, taper off, wane

rel compress, condense, constrict, contract; evaporate, fade (away), fritter (away), give out, melt (away), peter (out), tail (off), vanish; slacken, slow (down); alleviate, relax; flag, sink, weaken; cave (in), collapse, deflate

near ant appear, emerge, show up; blow up, distend, elongate, lengthen

ant accumulate, balloon, build, burgeon (*also* bourgeon), enlarge, escalate, expand, grow, increase, intensify, mount, mushroom, pick up, rise, snowball, soar, swell, wax

decree *n* **1** a statement of what to do that must be obeyed by those concerned — see COMMAND 1

2 an order publicly issued by an authority — see EDICT 1

decree *vb* to request the doing of by virtue of one's authority — see COMMAND 2

decrement *n* the amount by which something is lessened — see DECREASE

decry *vb* **1** to express scornfully one's low opinion of ⟨Scientists were quick to *decry* the claims of the psychic.⟩

syn bad-mouth, belittle, cry down, deprecate, depreciate, diminish, discount, dismiss, disparage, minimize, play down, put down, run down, write off

rel discommend; abuse, scold; disapprove (of), dislike; censure, condemn, criticize, denounce, reprehend, reprobate; asperse, defame, malign, rip, slander, slur, traduce, vilify; discredit, disgrace

phrases dump on

near ant approve, countenance, endorse (*also* indorse), favor, recommend, sanction; commend, compliment, eulogize

ant acclaim, applaud, exalt, extol (*also* extoll), glorify, laud, magnify, praise

2 to declare to be morally wrong or evil — see CONDEMN 1

decrying *adj* intended to make a person or thing seem of little importance or value — see DEROGATORY

dedicate *vb* to keep or intend for a special purpose — see DEVOTE 1

dedication *n* adherence to something to which one is bound by a pledge or duty — see FIDELITY

deduce *vb* to form an opinion or reach a

conclusion through reasoning and information — see INFER 1

deducible *adj* being or provable by reasoning in which the conclusion follows necessarily from given information — see DEDUCTIVE

deduct *vb* to take away (an amount or number) from a total — see SUBTRACT

deduction *n* **1** something that is or may be subtracted ⟨Contestants get a *deduction* from their scores for every incorrect guess.⟩

syn abatement, discount, reduction

rel giveback, kickback, rebate; dent, depreciation; decline, decrement, diminishment, diminution, drop, fall, loss; forfeit, forfeiture, penalty

near ant accretion, accrual, augmentation, boost, gain, increase, increment, raise, rise; appreciation

ant addition

2 the act or an instance of taking away from a total — see SUBTRACTION

3 an opinion arrived at through a process of reasoning — see CONCLUSION 1

deductive *adj* being or provable by reasoning in which the conclusion follows necessarily from given information ⟨a judgment reached through *deductive* logic⟩

syn deducible, derivable, inferable (*also* inferrible), reasoned

rel conjectural, hypothetical, purported, supposed, suppositional; logical, rational

near ant inducible, inductive; absolute, categorical (*also* categoric), definite, explicit, express; instinctive, intuitive; illogical, irrational

ant nondeductive

deed *n* **1** an act of notable skill, strength, or cleverness — see FEAT 1

2 something done by someone — see ACTION 1

deed *vb* to give over the legal possession or ownership of — see TRANSFER 1

deem *vb* to have as an opinion — see BELIEVE 2

deep *adj* **1** extending far downward ⟨lowered their bucket down a *deep* well⟩ ⟨The ax made a *deep* cut into the wood.⟩

syn abysmal, bottomless, profound

rel abyssal, unfathomable; boundless, endless, immeasurable, infinite, limitless, measureless, unlimited, vast

near ant depthless, two-dimensional; even, flat, flush, horizontal, level, plane, smooth; finite, limited, measured, restricted

ant shallow, shoal, skin-deep, superficial, surface

2 having a low musical pitch or range ⟨The tour guide had an impressively *deep* voice.⟩

syn bass, grave, low, throaty

rel boomy, tubby; gruff, hoarse, husky, rough, smoky (*also* smokey)

near ant squeaking, squeaky, squealing, thin; earsplitting, penetrating, piercing, strident; peeping, tinny

ant acute, high, high-pitched, piping, sharp, shrill, treble

3 being beyond one's powers to know, understand, or explain — see MYSTERIOUS 1

4 difficult for one of ordinary knowledge or intelligence to understand — see PROFOUND 1

5 having an often intentionally veiled or uncertain meaning — see OBSCURE 1
6 extreme in degree, power, or effect — see INTENSE 1
7 firmly established over time — see INVETERATE 1
8 having considerable extent — see EXTENSIVE
9 having the mind fixed on something — see ATTENTIVE 1
10 not close in time or space — see DISTANT 1

deep *n* **1** the most intense or characteristic phase of something — see THICK
2 the whole body of salt water that covers nearly three-fourths of the earth — see OCEAN 1
3 an immeasurable depth or space — see ABYSS

deepen *vb* to make markedly greater in measure or degree — see INTENSIFY

deep-rooted *adj* firmly established over time — see INVETERATE 1

deep-seated *adj* firmly established over time — see INVETERATE 1

de-escalate *vb* **1** to make smaller in amount, volume, or extent — see DECREASE 1
2 to grow less in scope or intensity especially gradually — see DECREASE 2

deface *vb* **1** to deliberately cause the damage or destruction of another's property — see VANDALIZE
2 to reduce the soundness, effectiveness, or perfection of — see DAMAGE 1

defacement *n* deliberate damaging or destroying of another's property — see VANDALISM

defacer *n* a person who damages or destroys property on purpose — see VANDAL

defamation *n* the making of false statements that damage another's reputation — see SLANDER

defamatory *adj* causing or intended to cause unjust injury to a person's good name — see LIBELOUS

defame *vb* to make untrue and harmful statements about — see SLANDER

defaming *n* the making of false statements that damage another's reputation — see SLANDER

default *n* the nonperformance of an assigned or expected action — see FAILURE 1

defeat *n* **1** failure to win a contest ⟨still getting over their *defeat* in the basketball game earlier that week⟩
syn beating, drubbing, licking, loss, lump, overthrow, rout, shellacking, trimming, trouncing, whipping
rel collapse, debacle (*also* débâcle), failure, fiasco, fizzle, flop, nonsuccess, setback, upset; lurch, shutout, washout, whitewash
near ant accomplishment, achievement; blowout, landslide, romp, sweep, walkaway, walkover
ant success, triumph, victory, win
2 a falling short of one's goals — see FAILURE 2

defeat *vb* to achieve a victory over — see BEAT 2

---

defeatist *adj* emphasizing or expecting the worst — see PESSIMISTIC 1

defeatist *n* one who emphasizes bad aspects or conditions and expects the worst — see PESSIMIST 1

defect *n* something that spoils the appearance or completeness of a thing — see BLEMISH

defect (from) *vb* to leave (a cause or party) often in order to take up another ⟨Soldiers *defected* from the rebel army en masse as the failure of their cause became apparent.⟩
syn desert, rat (on)
rel abandon, abdicate, abjure, apostatize, cut off, disown, forsake, quit, reject, renounce, repudiate, spurn; renege; depart, go, leave, withdraw
phrases go back on, jump ship, run out on, walk out on
near ant adhere (to), cling (to), stick (to *or* with); cherish, cultivate, foster

defective *adj* having a fault — see FAULTY

defector *n* a person who abandons a cause or organization usually without right — see RENEGADE

defend *vb* **1** to drive danger or attack away from ⟨a solemn oath to *defend* the mother country at any cost⟩
syn bulwark, cover, fence, guard, keep, protect, safeguard, screen, secure, shield, ward
rel avert, prevent; oppose, resist, withstand; battle, contend, fight, war; conserve, preserve, save
phrases stand up for
near ant bombard, storm; beset, besiege, overrun; capitulate, cave, submit, yield
ant assail, assault, attack
2 to continue to declare to be true or proper despite opposition or objections — see MAINTAIN 2

defendable *adj* **1** capable of being defended against physical attack — see TENABLE 1
2 capable of being defended with good reasoning against verbal attack — see TENABLE 2

defender *n* someone that protects — see PROTECTOR

defense *n* **1** means or method of defending ⟨Thorns are a rose's *defense* against grazing animals.⟩
syn aegis (*also* egis), ammunition, armor, cover, guard, protection, safeguard, screen, security, shield, wall, ward
rel arm, armament, munitions, weapon, weaponry; fastness, fort, fortress, palisade, stronghold
near ant aggression, assault, attack, offense (*or* offence), offensive
2 an explanation that frees one from fault or blame — see EXCUSE

defenseless *adj* lacking protection from danger or resistance against attack — see HELPLESS 1

defenselessness *n* the quality or state of having little resistance to some outside agent — see SUSCEPTIBILITY

defensible *adj* **1** capable of being defended against physical attack — see TENABLE 1
2 capable of being defended with good reasoning against verbal attack — see TENABLE 2

---

syn synonym(s)   *rel* related words
ant antonym(s)   *near ant* near antonyms(s)

defensive *adj* intended to resist or prevent attack or aggression ⟨a *defensive* alliance among the small nations against the aggressors⟩
syn protective
rel deterrent, preventive; safe, secure
near ant aggressive, bellicose, belligerent, combative, contentious, in-your-face, militant, pugnacious, quarrelsome, scrappy, truculent, warlike
ant offensive

defensive *n* a position of readiness to oppose actual or expected attack ⟨Their unexpectedly harsh words put him on the *defensive.*⟩
syn guard
rel alert, lookout, qui vive, watch
ant offensive

defer *vb* to assign to a later time — see POSTPONE

deference *n* a readiness or willingness to yield to the wishes of others — see COMPLIANCE 1

deferential *adj* marked by or showing proper regard for another's higher status — see RESPECTFUL

deferentially *adv* in a manner showing no signs of pride or self-assertion — see LOWLY

defiance *n* 1 refusal to obey — see DISOBEDIENCE
2 the inclination to resist — see RESISTANCE 1
3 an inclination to fight or quarrel — see BELLIGERENCE

defiant *adj* given to resisting authority or another's control — see DISOBEDIENT

deficiency *n* a falling short of an essential or desirable amount or number ⟨The disease may be caused by a nutritional *deficiency.*⟩
syn crunch, dearth, deficit, failure, famine, inadequacy, insufficiency, lack, paucity, pinch, poverty, scantiness, scarceness, scarcity, shortage, want
rel absence, omission; meagerness, poorness, skimpiness; necessity, need, privation
near ant bountifulness, copiousness; excess, overabundance, oversupply, surfeit, surplus
ant abundance, adequacy, amplitude, opulence, plenitude, plenty, sufficiency, wealth

deficient *adj* 1 lacking some necessary part — see INCOMPLETE
2 falling short of a standard — see BAD 1
3 not coming up to an expected measure or meeting a particular need — see SHORT 3

deficiently *adv* in an unsatisfactory way — see BADLY 1

deficit *n* a falling short of an essential or desirable amount or number — see DEFICIENCY

defile *n* a narrow opening between hillsides or mountains that can be used for passage — see CANYON

defile *vb* 1 to make unfit for use by the addition of something harmful or undesirable — see CONTAMINATE
2 to treat (a sacred place or object) shamefully or with great disrespect — see DESECRATE

defilement *n* 1 an act of great disrespect shown to God or to sacred ideas, people, or things — see BLASPHEMY
2 something that is or that makes impure — see IMPURITY 1

define *vb* 1 to draw or make apparent the outline of — see OUTLINE 1
2 to mark the limits of — see LIMIT 2
3 to point out the chief quality or qualities of an individual or group — see CHARACTERIZE 1
4 to give the rules about (something) clearly and exactly — see PRESCRIBE

defined *adj* having distinct or certain limits — see LIMITED 1

definite *adj* 1 having distinct or certain limits — see LIMITED 1
2 so clearly expressed as to leave no doubt about the meaning — see EXPLICIT
3 having no exceptions or restrictions — see ABSOLUTE 2

definitely *adv* without any question — see INDEED 1

definitive *adj* 1 being the most accurate and apparently thorough ⟨the *definitive* biography on the 16th president⟩
syn authoritative, classic, classical
rel conclusive, decisive; approved, official, sanctioned; accurate, correct; complete, comprehensive, exhaustive, thorough
2 serving to put an end to all debate or questioning — see CONCLUSIVE 1
3 so clearly expressed as to leave no doubt about the meaning — see EXPLICIT
4 constituting, serving as, or worthy of being a pattern to be imitated — see MODEL

deflect *vb* to change the course or direction of (something) — see TURN 2

deform *vb* to twist (something) out of a natural or normal shape or condition — see CONTORT

deformation *n* the twisting of something out of its natural or normal shape or condition — see CONTORTION

deformed *adj* badly or imperfectly formed — see MALFORMED

deformity *n* something that spoils the appearance or completeness of a thing — see BLEMISH

defraud *vb* to rob by the use of trickery or threats — see FLEECE

defrauder *n* a dishonest person who uses clever means to cheat others out of something of value — see TRICKSTER 1

defrauding *adj* marked by, based on, or done by the use of dishonest methods to acquire something of value — see FRAUDULENT 1

defrosted *adj* freed from a frozen state by exposure to warmth — see THAWED

deft *adj* 1 accomplished with trained ability — see SKILLFUL 1
2 skillful with the hands — see DEXTEROUS 1

deftness *n* 1 ease and grace in physical activity — see DEXTERITY 2
2 subtle or imaginative ability in inventing, devising, or executing something — see SKILL 1

defunct *adj* 1 no longer existing — see EXTINCT
2 no longer living — see DEAD 1

defy *vb* **1** to go against the commands, prohibitions, or rules of — see DISOBEY
2 to invite (someone) to take part in a contest or to perform a feat — see CHALLENGE 2
3 to oppose (something hostile or dangerous) with firmness or courage — see FACE 2
4 to refuse to give in to — see RESIST

degeneracy *n* **1** a change to a lower state or level — see DECLINE 2
2 a sinking to a state of low moral standards and behavior — see CORRUPTION 2

degenerate *adj* **1** having lost forcefulness, courage, or spirit — see EFFETE 1
2 having or showing lowered moral character or standards — see CORRUPT

degenerate *n* a person who has sunk below the normal moral standard ⟨a *degenerate* who is uninterested in anything but his own gratification⟩
syn backslider, debaucher, decadent, deviate, libertine, pervert, profligate, rake
rel bankrupt, delinquent, derelict, incorrigible; blackguard, cad, heel, knave, miscreant, rascal, reprobate, rogue, scoundrel, villain; lecher, playboy, playgirl
near ant saint

degenerate *vb* to become worse or of less value — see DETERIORATE 1

degeneration *n* **1** a change to a lower state or level — see DECLINE 2
2 a gradual sinking and wasting away of mind or body — see DECLINE 1
3 a sinking to a state of low moral standards and behavior — see CORRUPTION 2

degradation *n* **1** a change to a lower state or level — see DECLINE 2
2 a sinking to a state of low moral standards and behavior — see CORRUPTION 2

degrade *vb* **1** to bring to a lower grade or rank — see DEMOTE 1
2 to lower in character, dignity, or quality — see DEBASE 1
3 to reduce to a lower standing in one's own eyes or in others' eyes — see HUMBLE 1

degraded *adj* having or showing lowered moral character or standards — see CORRUPT

degrading *adj* intended to make a person or thing seem of little importance or value — see DEROGATORY

degree *n* **1** an individual part of a process, series, or ranking ⟨They worked on the project by *degrees* and eventually it got done.⟩
syn chapter, cut, grade, inch, notch, peg, phase, place, point, stage, step
rel angle, aspect, facet, side; amount, measure, plane; decrement, increment
2 the placement of someone or something in relation to others in a vertical arrangement — see RANK 1

dehydrate *vb* **1** to deprive of emotional or intellectual vitality ⟨a job that he claimed *dehydrated* his soul⟩
syn damp, dampen, deaden, enervate
rel burn out, debilitate, do in, drain, enfeeble, exhaust, fatigue, sap, tucker (out), undermine, weaken, wear, wear out; daunt, demoralize, discourage, dishearten, dispirit

near ant arouse, rouse, stir; charge, electrify, galvanize; excite, ferment, fire, foment, incite, inflame (*also* enflame), instigate, kindle, provoke, spark, trigger, whip (up); abet, boost, buoy, cheer, embolden, fortify, hearten, inspire, lift
ant brace, energize, enliven, invigorate, quicken, stimulate, vitalize, vivify
2 to make dry — see DRY 1

deification *n* excessive admiration of or devotion to a person — see WORSHIP

deify *vb* **1** to love or admire too much — see IDOLIZE
2 to offer honor or respect to (someone) as a divine power — see WORSHIP 1
3 to assign a high status or value to — see EXALT 1

deifying *adj* reflecting great admiration or devotion — see WORSHIPFUL

deign *vb* to descend to a level that is beneath one's dignity — see CONDESCEND 1

deity *n* **1** a being having superhuman powers and control over a particular part of life or the world ⟨To the ancient Greeks, Zeus was the *deity* who ruled over the sky and weather, and Poseidon was god of the sea.⟩
syn divinity, god
rel angel, demigod, demon (*or* daemon), devil, spirit, supernatural
2 *cap* the being worshipped as the creator and ruler of the universe ⟨We prayed to the *Deity* for guidance.⟩
syn Allah, Almighty, Author, Creator, Divinity, Everlasting, Father, God, Godhead, Jehovah, Maker, Providence, Supreme Being
3 the quality or state of being divine — see DIVINITY 1

dejected *adj* feeling unhappiness — see SAD 1

dejection *n* a state or spell of low spirits — see SADNESS

delay *n* an instance or period of being prevented from going about one's business ⟨There was a *delay* for our boarding while the airplane unloaded incoming passengers.⟩
syn detainment, holding pattern, holdup, wait
rel deferment, deferral, postponement; reprieve, respite; foot-dragging, hesitation, lag, pause, setback, slowdown
near ant haste, rush; dispatch, promptitude, promptness

delay *vb* to move or act slowly ⟨She ordered the kids to stop *delaying* and to get to bed.⟩
syn crawl, creep, dally, dawdle, dillydally, drag, lag, linger, loiter, mope, poke, shilly-shally, tarry
rel fiddle (around), monkey (around), play, potter (around), putter (around), trifle; idle, loaf, loll, lounge; ease, inch, lumber, plod, saunter, shuffle, stagger, stroll; decelerate, slow (down *or* up); filibuster, procrastinate, stall, temporize
phrases drag one's feet (*also* drag one's heels), drop behind, fall behind, hang fire, mark time, take one's time
near ant bowl, breeze, dart, hump, hurtle, hustle, scramble, stampede; gallop, jog, run, sprint, trot; accelerate, quicken,

---

speed (up); fast-forward, outpace, outrun, outstrip, overtake

ant barrel, bolt, career, course, dash, fly, hasten, hotfoot (it), hurry, race, rip, rocket, run, rush, scoot, scud, scurry, speed, tear, whirl, whisk, whiz (*or* whizz), zip

2 to assign to a later time — see POSTPONE

delectable *adj* 1 giving pleasure or contentment to the mind or senses — see PLEASANT 1

2 very pleasing to the sense of taste — see DELICIOUS 1

delectable *n* something that is pleasing to eat because it is rare or a luxury — see DELICACY 1

delectably *adv* in a pleasing way — see WELL 5

delectation *n* 1 a source of great satisfaction — see DELIGHT 1

2 the feeling experienced when one's wishes are met — see PLEASURE 1

delegate *n* 1 a person sent on a mission to represent another — see AMBASSADOR

2 a person who acts or does business for another — see AGENT 2

delegate *vb* 1 to appoint as one's representative ⟨He *delegated* his son to go pick up the tickets for him.⟩

syn commission, depute, deputize

rel assign, charge; appoint, designate, name

near ant abrogate; abdicate

2 to put (something) into the possession or safekeeping of another — see GIVE 2

delegation *n* 1 a body of persons chosen as representatives of a larger group — see CONTINGENT 1

2 the granting of power to perform various acts or duties — see COMMISSION 1

delete *vb* to show (something written) to be no longer valid by drawing a cross over or a line through it — see X (OUT)

deleterious *adj* causing or capable of causing harm — see HARMFUL

deletion *n* something left out — see OMISSION

deliberate *adj* 1 decided on as a result of careful thought ⟨The judge made a *deliberate* decision to impose the minimum sentence.⟩

syn advised, calculated, considered, knowing, measured, reasoned, studied, thoughtful, thought-out, weighed

rel aforethought, premeditated, prepense; educated, informed; intentional, purposeful; designed, intended, planned, projected; careful, meticulous; foresighted, forethoughtful, provident, prudent

near ant half-cocked, ill-advised; chance, haphazard, hit-or-miss, random; aimless, desultory, purposeless; hasty, hurried, rushed; abrupt, impetuous, sudden; automatic, extemporaneous, impromptu, instinctive, spontaneous

ant casual, unadvised, uncalculated, unconsidered, unstudied

2 made, given, or done with full awareness of what one is doing — see INTENTIONAL

deliberate *vb* to give serious and careful thought to — see PONDER

deliberately *adv* with full awareness of what one is doing — see INTENTIONALLY

deliberation *n* 1 a careful weighing of the reasons for or against something — see CONSIDERATION 1

2 an exchange of views for the purpose of exploring a subject or deciding an issue — see DISCUSSION 1

delicacy *n* 1 something that is pleasing to eat because it is rare or a luxury ⟨presented with a plate of national *delicacies* while they waited for the queen⟩

syn bit, dainty, delectable, goody (*or* goodie), tidbit (*also* titbit), treat, viand

rel morsel; dessert, junket, sweet, sweetmeat

2 the state or quality of having a delicate structure ⟨We never cease to marvel at the *delicacy* of a snowflake.⟩

syn daintiness, exquisiteness, fineness, fragility

rel diaphanousness, flimsiness, insubstantiality, wispiness; brittleness, crumbliness, friability

near ant firmness, solidity; strength

ant coarseness, crudeness, roughness, rudeness

3 the tendency to be or state of being squeamish ⟨The urgent need for blood prompted many people to overcome their habitual *delicacy* and become first-time donors.⟩

syn qualmishness, queasiness, squeamishness

rel daintiness, fastidiousness, finicalness, finickiness, fussiness

near ant boldness

ant indelicacy

4 the quality or state of being very accurate — see PRECISION

5 the quality or state of lacking physical strength or vigor — see WEAKNESS 1

6 the state or quality of being able to sense slight impressions or differences — see ACUITY

delicate *adj* 1 satisfying or pleasing because of fineness or mildness ⟨A heavy sauce would spoil the *delicate* flavor of this fish.⟩

syn airy, dainty, exquisite, refined, subtle

rel choice, elegant, extraordinary, incomparable, peerless, preeminent, prime, rare, select, superior, superlative, supreme, unsurpassed; picked, selected; fine, fragile, frail

near ant coarse, crude, rough; common, ordinary; average, fair, indifferent, mediocre, medium, middling, run-of-the-mill, second-rate

ant robust, strong, sturdy

2 able to sense slight impressions or differences — see ACUTE 1

3 accomplished with trained ability — see SKILLFUL 1

4 easily broken — see FRAGILE 1

5 easily injured without careful handling — see TENDER 1

6 hard to please — see FINICKY

7 having qualities that appeal to a refined taste — see CHOICE 1

8 lacking bodily strength — see WEAK 1

9 made or done with extreme care and accuracy — see FINE 2

10 meeting the highest standard of accuracy — see PRECISE 1

11 not harsh or stern especially in nature or effect — see GENTLE 1

12 requiring exceptional skill or caution in performance or handling — see TRICKY 1

delicious *adj* **1** very pleasing to the sense of taste ⟨The family sat down to a *delicious* Thanksgiving dinner.⟩

syn ambrosial, appetizing, dainty, delectable, flavorful, luscious, lush, palatable, savory (*also* savoury), scrumptious, succulent, tasteful, tasty, toothsome, yummy

rel digestible, eatable, edible; delightful, heavenly, pleasing; agreeable, gratifying, pleasant; satisfying; choice, delicate, exquisite, rare

near ant banal, boring, commonplace, tedious; noisome, smelly, stinky; noxious, unwholesome; miserable, wretched; abhorrent, abominable, awful, detestable, disagreeable, foul, horrid, nauseating, offensive, repellent (*also* repellant), repugnant, repulsive, sickening, unpleasant

ant distasteful, flat, flavorless, insipid, stale, tasteless, unappetizing, unpalatable, unsavory, yucky (*also* yukky)

2 giving pleasure or contentment to the mind or senses — see PLEASANT 1

deliciously *adv* in a pleasing way — see WELL 5

deliciousness *n* the quality of being delicious ⟨The fancy feast was *deliciousness* itself.⟩

syn lusciousness, palatability, savor (*also* savour), savoriness, tastiness

rel digestibility, edibility, edibleness; daintiness, delicacy

ant distastefulness, flatness, insipidity, staleness, tastelessness, unpalatability

delight *n* **1** a source of great satisfaction ⟨The opportunity for travel was one of the major *delights* of the couple's golden years.⟩

syn delectation, feast, joy, kick, manna, pleasure, treat

rel amusement, diversion, entertainment, fun, recreation; comfort, relief, solace; gratification, indulgence; ambrosia

2 someone or something that provides amusement or enjoyment — see FUN 1

3 the feeling experienced when one's wishes are met — see PLEASURE 1

delight *vb* **1** to feel or express joy or triumph — see EXULT

2 to give satisfaction to — see PLEASE 1

delight (in) *vb* to take pleasure in — see ENJOY 1

delighted *adj* experiencing pleasure, satisfaction, or delight — see GLAD 1

delightful *adj* **1** giving pleasure or contentment to the mind or senses — see PLEASANT 1

2 providing amusement or enjoyment — see FUN

delightfully *adv* in a pleasing way — see WELL 5

delimit *vb* to mark the limits of — see LIMIT 2

delineate *vb* **1** to draw or make apparent the outline of — see OUTLINE 1

2 to give a representation or account of in words — see DESCRIBE 1

delineated *adj* producing a mental picture

through clear and impressive description — see GRAPHIC 1

delineation *n* **1** a picture using lines to represent the chief features of an object or scene — see DRAWING

2 a vivid representation in words of someone or something — see DESCRIPTION 1

delinquency *n* **1** the nonperformance of an assigned or expected action — see FAILURE 1

2 the quality or state of being late — see LATENESS

delinquent *adj* not arriving, occurring, or settled at the due, usual, or proper time — see LATE 1

deliquesce *vb* to go from a solid to a liquid state — see LIQUEFY

delirious *adj* **1** feeling overwhelming fear or worry — see FRANTIC 1

2 marked by great and often stressful excitement or activity — see FURIOUS 1

delirium *n* a state of wildly excited activity or emotion — see FRENZY

deliver *vb* **1** to free from the penalties or consequences of sin — see SAVE 1

2 to remove from danger or harm — see SAVE 2

3 to give (something) over to the control or possession of another usually under duress — see SURRENDER 1

4 to put (something) into the possession of someone for use or consumption — see FURNISH 2

5 to put (something) into the possession or safekeeping of another — see GIVE 2

6 to turn out as planned or desired — see SUCCEED 1

7 to bring forth from the womb — see BEAR 1

8 to give (oneself) over to something especially unrestrainedly — see ABANDON 1

deliverance *n* **1** the saving from danger or evil — see SALVATION

2 a position arrived at after consideration — see DECISION 1

deliverer *n* **1** a person who delivers goods to customers usually over a regular local route — see DELIVERYMAN

2 one that saves from danger or destruction — see SAVIOR

delivery *n* **1** a freeing from an obligation or responsibility — see RELEASE 1

2 the act or process of giving birth to children — see CHILDBIRTH

deliveryman *n* a person who delivers goods to customers usually over a regular local route ⟨The *deliveryman* dropped off a package for us while we were at the store.⟩

syn deliverer

rel delivery boy; bearer, carrier, courier, go-between, liaison, messenger

delude *vb* to cause to believe what is untrue — see DECEIVE

deluding *adj* tending or having power to deceive — see DECEPTIVE 1

deluge *n* **1** a great flow of water or of something that overwhelms — see FLOOD

2 a steady falling of water from the sky in significant quantity — see RAIN 1

deluge *vb* to cover with a flood — see FLOOD

delusion *n* **1** a conception or image cre-

---

syn synonym(s)   *rel* related words
ant antonym(s)   *near ant* near antonym(s)

ated by the imagination and having no objective reality — see FANTASY 1

2 a false idea or belief — see FALLACY 1

delusive *adj* tending or having power to deceive — see DECEPTIVE 1

delusory *adj* tending or having power to deceive — see DECEPTIVE 1

deluxe *adj* showing obvious signs of wealth and comfort — see LUXURIOUS

delve (into) *vb* to search through or into — see EXPLORE 1

delving *n* a systematic search for the truth or facts about something — see INQUIRY 1

demagogue *also* **demagog** *n* a person who stirs up public feelings especially of discontent — see AGITATOR

demand *n* **1** something that someone insists upon having ⟨The store refused the customer's *demand* for a refund.⟩

syn claim, dun, requisition, ultimatum

rel desire, request, want, wish; drive, need, requirement, stipulation; basic, essential, must; imposition; condition, provision

2 the state of being sought after especially for purchase ⟨a steadily declining *demand* for film cameras⟩

syn call, market, request

rel bear market, bull market; buyer's market, seller's market

3 something necessary, indispensable, or unavoidable — see ESSENTIAL 1

demand *vb* **1** to ask for (something) earnestly or with authority ⟨The losing party *demanded* a recount of the votes cast in the election.⟩

syn call (for), claim, clamor (for), command, enjoin, exact, insist (on), press (for), quest, stipulate (for)

rel ask, plead (for), request, want; cry (for), necessitate, need, require, take, warrant; requisition; impose; badger, dun, hound

near ant give up, relinquish, surrender, yield

2 to have as a requirement — see NEED 1

3 to set or receive as a price — see CHARGE 1

demanding *adj* **1** requiring much time, effort, or careful attention ⟨The *demanding* assignment kept them working all night long.⟩

syn arduous, burdensome, challenging, exacting, grueling (*or* gruelling), laborious, onerous, taxing, toilsome

rel difficult, formidable, hard, herculean, rough, rugged, stiff, strenuous, tough; oppressive, trying; rigid, rigorous, severe, stern, strict, stringent

near ant easy, effortless, facile, simple, smooth

ant light, nondemanding, unchallenging, undemanding

2 hard to please — see FINICKY

3 requiring considerable physical or mental effort — see HARD 2

demarcate *vb* to mark the limits of — see LIMIT 2

demarcation *n* the state of being kept distinct — see SEPARATION 2

¹demean *vb* **1** to lower in character, dignity, or quality — see DEBASE 1

2 to reduce to a lower standing in one's own eyes or in others' eyes — see HUMBLE

²demean *vb* to manage the actions of (oneself) in a particular way — see BEHAVE

demeaning *adj* intended to make a person or thing seem of little importance or value — see DEROGATORY

demeanor *n* the way or manner in which one conducts oneself — see BEHAVIOR

demerit *n* a defect in character — see FAULT 1

demesne *n* **1** a part or portion having no fixed boundaries — see REGION 1

2 the area around and belonging to a building — see GROUND 1

demilitarization *n* the reduction or elimination of a country's armed forces or weapons — see DISARMAMENT

demilitarize *vb* to reduce the size and strength of the armed forces of — see DISARM 1

demise *n* **1** the permanent stopping of all the vital bodily activities — see DEATH 1

2 the act of ceasing to exist — see DEATH 3

3 a loss of status — see COMEDOWN

demise *vb* to stop living — see DIE 1

democracy *n* government in which the supreme power is held by the people and used by them directly or indirectly through representation ⟨Under our *democracy* the people have some control over their lives by being able to select their own political leaders.⟩

syn republic, self-government, self-rule

rel pure democracy; home rule, self-determination; autonomy, sovereignty (*also* sovranty)

near ant despotism, dictatorship, monarchy, monocracy, totalitarianism, tyranny

democratic *adj* of, relating to, or favoring political democracy ⟨The *democratic* system ensures that every citizen's voice is heard.⟩

syn popular, republican, self-governing, self-ruling

rel representative; libertarian, nontotalitarian

near ant autocratic (*also* autocratical), despotic, dictatorial, monarchal (*or* monarchial), monarchical (*also* monarchic), tyrannical (*also* tyrannic)

ant nondemocratic, undemocratic

demolish *vb* **1** to destroy (as a building) completely by knocking down or breaking to pieces ⟨Developers *demolished* the old warehouse to make room for the new shopping mall.⟩

syn level, raze, tear down

rel blow up; abolish, annihilate, crack up, crush, dash, decimate, destroy, devastate, devour, dissolve, do in, eradicate, extirpate, finish, flatten, obliterate, overturn, pulverize, ravage, ruin, scourge, smash, total, unmake, waste, wipe out, wreck

near ant build, construct, erect, put up, raise; rebuild, renew, renovate, restore; create, fabricate, fashion, forge, form, make, manufacture, shape

2 to bring to a complete end the physical soundness, existence, or usefulness of — see DESTROY 1

3 to cause to break open or into pieces by or as if by an explosive — see BLAST 1

demolishment *n* the state or fact of being rendered nonexistent, physically unsound, or useless — see DESTRUCTION 1

demolition *n* the state or fact of being rendered nonexistent, physically unsound, or useless — see DESTRUCTION 1

demon *or* **daemon** *n* **1** an evil spirit ⟨Only in rare cases is the ancient rite of exorcism performed to cast out a troublesome *demon.*⟩
syn devil, fiend, ghost, ghoul, imp
rel incubus, nightmare, succubus; genie, jinni (*or* jinn *also* djinni *or* djinn); apparition, banshee, bogey (*also* bogie *or* bogy), bugbear, familiar, genius, phantasm (*also* fantasm), phantom, poltergeist, shade, shadow, specter (*or* spectre), spirit, spook, vision, wraith; brownie, dwarf, elf, faerie (*also* faery), fairy, fay, gnome, goblin, gremlin, hobgoblin, kobold, leprechaun, pixie (*also* pixy), puck, sprite, troll; monster, ogre
near ant angel
2 a source of persistent emotional distress ⟨a man who was finally able to conquer the *demons* of his past⟩
syn affliction, terror, torment
rel bête noire, bogey (*also* bogie *or* bogy), bugaboo, bugbear, hobgoblin, ogre

demoniac *also* **demoniacal** *adj* of, relating to, or worthy of an evil spirit — see FIENDISH 1

demonic *also* **demonical** *adj* of, relating to, or worthy of an evil spirit — see FIENDISH 1

demonstrable *adj* capable of being proven as true or real — see VERIFIABLE

demonstrate *vb* **1** to gain full recognition or acceptance of — see ESTABLISH 1
2 to show the existence or truth of by evidence — see PROVE 1
3 to make known (something abstract) through outward signs — see SHOW 2
4 to make plain or understandable — see EXPLAIN 1
5 to show or make clear by using examples — see ILLUSTRATE 1

demonstration *n* **1** a mass meeting for the purpose of displaying or arousing support for a cause or person — see RALLY 2
2 an outward and often exaggerated indication of something abstract (as a feeling) for effect — see SHOW 1

demonstrative *adj* **1** showing feeling freely ⟨My grandmother was always very *demonstrative* when we visited, showering us with hugs and kisses.⟩
syn effusive, emotional, uninhibited, unreserved, unrestrained
rel dramatic, histrionic, hyperemotional, melodramatic, theatrical (*also* theatric); gushing, maudlin, mawkish, mushy, schmaltzy, sentimental; communicative, expansive; extroverted (*also* extraverted), outgoing; affectionate, feeling, intense, loving, passionate, sensitive, soulful, warm; blunt, candid, frank, outspoken, plain
near ant constrained; quiet, reticent, silent, taciturn; bashful, modest, retiring, shy; introverted, self-directed; aloof, detached, dispassionate, impassive, indifferent, phlegmatic, stolid, unconcerned, un-

feeling; chilly, cold, frigid, glacial, hard-boiled, hard-edged, icy, unfriendly
ant inhibited, reserved, restrained, undemonstrative, unemotional
2 having or expressing great depth of feeling — see FERVENT 1

demoralization *n* **1** a sinking to a state of low moral standards and behavior — see CORRUPTION 2
2 the state of being discouraged — see DISCOURAGEMENT

demoralize *vb* **1** to deprive of courage or confidence — see UNNERVE 1
2 to lessen the courage or confidence of — see DISCOURAGE 1
3 to lower in character, dignity, or quality — see DEBASE 1

demoralized *adj* having or showing lowered moral character or standards — see CORRUPT

demote *vb* to bring to a lower grade or rank ⟨The court-martial's decision was to *demote* the officer responsible for the failed mission.⟩
syn break, bust, degrade, downgrade, reduce
rel can, cashier, dismiss, downsize, fire, lay off, sack; abase, debase, demean, humble, humiliate, lower
near ant hire
ant advance, elevate, promote, raise

demount *vb* to take apart — see DISASSEMBLE 1

demur *n* a feeling or declaration of disapproval or dissent — see OBJECTION

demur *vb* to present an opposing opinion or argument — see OBJECT

demure *adj* **1** affecting shyness or modesty — see COY 1
2 not comfortable around people — see SHY 1
3 not having or showing any feelings of superiority, self-assertiveness, or showiness — see HUMBLE 1

demureness *n* the absence of any feelings of being better than others — see HUMILITY

den *n* **1** the shelter or resting place of a wild animal ⟨The foxes hid in their *den* until the bear finally left the area.⟩
syn burrow, hole, house, lair, lodge
rel nest; territory
2 a place where a person goes to hide or to avoid others — see HIDEOUT

denial *n* **1** an unwillingness to grant something asked for ⟨Our supervisor's *denial* of unpaid personal leave got mixed reactions from the staff.⟩
syn disallowance, nay, no, refusal, rejection
rel rebuff, repudiation, repulse, spurn; negative; ban, veto; deterrence, discouragement, repression, suppression
near ant acceptance, acquiescence, agreement, assent, authorization, clearance, concurrence, consent, leave, license (*or* licence), permission, sanction, sufferance; imprimatur, seal, stamp
ant allowance, approval, grant, OK (*or* okay)
2 a refusal to confirm the truth of a statement ⟨The senator issued a flat *denial* of the accusation against her.⟩

---

syn synonym(s)   *rel* related words
ant antonym(s)   *near ant* near antonym(s)

syn contradiction, disallowance, disavowal, disclaimer, negation, rejection, repudiation

rel disproof, rebuttal, refutation; negative

near ant concession, confession; affirmation, assertion, declaration; attestation, corroboration, documentation, substantiation, testament, testimony, validation

ant acknowledgment (*or* acknowledgement), admission, avowal, confirmation

denizen *n* **1** someone who regularly spends time in a particular place ⟨one of those muscular *denizens* of the gym⟩

syn familiar, frequenter, rat, regular

rel client, customer, guest, patron; addict, aficionado (*also* afficionado), buff, bug, devotee, enthusiast, fan, fanatic, fancier, fiend, freak, lover, maniac, nut

2 one who lives permanently in a place — see INHABITANT

denominate *vb* to give a name to — see NAME 1

denomination *n* a word or combination of words by which a person or thing is regularly known — see NAME 1

denotation *n* **1** a word or combination of words by which a person or thing is regularly known — see NAME 1

2 the idea that is conveyed or intended to be conveyed to the mind by language, symbol, or action — see MEANING 1

denotative *adj* indicating something — see INDICATIVE

denote *vb* **1** to communicate or convey (as an idea) to the mind — see MEAN 1

2 to serve as a sign or symptom of — see INDICATE 1

denoting *adj* indicating something — see INDICATIVE

denounce *vb* **1** to declare to be morally wrong or evil — see CONDEMN 1

2 to express one's unfavorable opinion of the worth or quality of — see CRITICIZE

3 to express public or formal disapproval of — see CENSURE 1

dense *adj* **1** having little space between items or parts — see CLOSE 1

2 not having or showing an ability to absorb ideas readily — see STUPID 1

denseness *n* the quality or state of lacking intelligence or quickness of mind — see STUPIDITY 1

density *n* **1** the degree to which a fluid can resist flowing — see CONSISTENCY

2 the quality or state of lacking intelligence or quickness of mind — see STUPIDITY 1

dent *n* **1** a sunken area forming a separate space — see HOLE 2

2 the amount by which something is lessened — see DECREASE

dent *vb* to make smaller in amount, volume, or extent — see DECREASE 1

dented *adj* curved inward — see HOLLOW

denuded *adj* lacking a usual or natural covering — see NAKED 2

denunciation *n* an often public or formal expression of disapproval — see CENSURE

deny *vb* **1** to declare not to be true ⟨The congressman *denied* all charges of wrongdoing.⟩

syn contradict, disallow, disavow, disclaim, disown, gainsay, negate, negative, refute, reject, repudiate

rel traverse; challenge, confute, disprove, rebut; disagree (with), dispute

near ant accept, adopt, embrace, espouse; affirm, announce, assert, aver, claim, declare, maintain, profess, submit; authenticate, corroborate, substantiate, validate, verify

ant acknowledge, admit, allow, avow, concede, confirm, own

2 to be unwilling to grant ⟨The director *denied* access to the top secret files to all but those with a need to know.⟩

syn decline, disallow, disapprove, negative, refuse, reject, reprobate, withhold

rel ban, enjoin, forbid, prohibit, proscribe, veto; rebuff, repel, spurn; check, constrain, curb, hold, keep, repress, restrain, restrict; hinder, impede, obstruct

near ant afford, furnish, give, provide, supply; authorize, commission, license (*also* licence); accede (to), acquiesce, agree (to), assent (to), consent (to), warrant; accord, sanction, vouchsafe

ant allow, concede, grant, let, OK (*or* okay), permit

3 to refuse to acknowledge as one's own or as one's responsibility — see DISCLAIM 1

depart *vb* **1** to leave a place often for another — see GO 2

2 to stop living — see DIE 1

departed *adj* **1** no longer existing — see EXTINCT

2 no longer living — see DEAD 1

departing *n* the act of leaving a place — see DEPARTURE 1

department *n* **1** a large unit of a governmental, business, or educational organization — see DIVISION 2

2 a region of activity, knowledge, or influence — see FIELD 2

departure *n* **1** the act of leaving a place ⟨His sudden *departure* left them wondering if they'd upset him.⟩

syn decamping, decampment, departing, exit, exiting, farewell, going, leave, leavetaking, lighting out, outgo, parting, quitting, walking out

rel flight, retirement, retreat, running away, withdrawal; diaspora, emigration, evacuation, exodus; embarkation, embarkment; disembarkation, egress; abandonment, forsaking, relinquishment

near ant coming; approach, entrance, ingress

ant advent, appearance, arrival

2 a turning away from a course or standard — see DIVERGENCE 2

depend *vb* **1** to be determined by, based on, or subject (to) ⟨Whether or not we play baseball will *depend* on how much rain we get.⟩

syn hang, hinge, ride, turn

rel base, establish, found, rest, stay; ground

2 to place reliance or trust ⟨I know I can always *depend* on you for help when I really need it.⟩

syn calculate, count, lean, reckon, rely

rel commit, entrust (*also* intrust), trust

phrases bank on, call on (*or* upon), figure on, look to, stand on

near ant distrust, mistrust, question, suspect

dependability *n* worthiness as the recipient of another's trust or confidence — see RELIABILITY

dependable *adj* worthy of one's trust ⟨They're seeking a *dependable* person to look after their summer home in the off-season.⟩

syn good, reliable, responsible, safe, secure, solid, steady, sure, tried, tried-and-true, true, trustworthy, trusty

rel constant, devoted, faithful, fast, loyal, staunch (*also* stanch), steadfast, true-blue; honest, sincere, single-minded; infallible, unerring; bedrock, firm, sound, strong; effective, telling; attested, authenticated, confirmed, proven, valid, validated, verified; blameless, faultless, guiltless, impeccable, inerrant, irreproachable, unimpeachable, unquestionable

near ant disloyal, faithless, false, fickle, inconstant, perfidious, recreant, traitorous, treacherous, unfaithful, untrue; deceitful, dishonest, lying, mendacious, untruthful

ant uncertain, undependable, unreliable, unsafe, untrustworthy

dependence *also* **dependance** *n* **1** the quality or state of needing something or someone ⟨a baby's total *dependence* upon his or her parents for every one of life's needs⟩

syn dependency, reliance

rel reciprocity, relativity; confidence, credence, faith, stock, trust

near ant autonomy, self-determination, sovereignty (*also* sovranty)

ant independence, self-reliance, self-sufficiency, self-support

2 something or someone to which one looks for support ⟨Ultimately rice became the chief *dependence* in that state.⟩

syn anchor, buttress, mainstay, pillar, reliance, standby

rel backbone, sinew(s), spine; right hand; bolsterer, crutch, stay; anchorage, harbor, refuge

dependency *n* the quality or state of needing something or someone — see DEPENDENCE 1

dependent *adj* **1** extending freely from a support from above ⟨The *dependent* willow branches swayed in the gentle breeze.⟩

syn dangling, hanging, pendent (*or* pendant), pendulous

rel drooping, flagging, lolling, sagging, wilting

2 determined by something else ⟨Our going to the movies tonight is *dependent* on whether or not we have any money left after we eat out.⟩

syn conditional, contingent (on *or* upon), subject (to), tentative

rel liable, open, susceptible; limited, modified, qualified, restricted; debatable, disputable, doubtable, doubtful, iffy, problematic (*also* problematical), questionable, shady, shaky, suspect, uncertain

near ant absolute, all-out, arrant, categorical (*also* categoric), complete, consummate, out-and-out, outright, perfect, simple, total,

ultimate, unadulterated, unalloyed, unconditional, unequivocal, unmitigated, unqualified, utter; basic, fundamental, primary

ant independent, unconditional

depict *vb* **1** to give a representation or account of in words — see DESCRIBE 1

2 to point out the chief quality or qualities of an individual or group — see CHARACTERIZE 1

3 to present a picture of — see PICTURE 1

depiction *n* a vivid representation in words of someone or something — see DESCRIPTION 1

deplete *vb* **1** to make complete use of ⟨Miners *depleted* the vein of copper ore after only a few months.⟩

syn absorb, burn, consume, devour, drain, exhaust, expend, play out, spend, use up

rel abate, decrease, de-escalate, diminish, downsize, dwindle, lessen, lower, reduce; eat, use; bankrupt, clean (out), impoverish; cripple, debilitate, disable, enfeeble, sap, undermine, weaken; dry up, empty; blow, dissipate, fritter (away), guzzle, lavish, misspend, run through, squander, throw away, waste

phrases run out of

near ant augment, enlarge, increase; bolster, enforce, fortify, strengthen; rebuild, repair, restore, revive; conserve, preserve, save

ant renew, replace

2 to make smaller in amount, volume, or extent — see DECREASE 1

deplorable *adj* **1** arousing or deserving of one's loathing and disgust — see CONTEMPTIBLE 1

2 of a kind to cause great distress — see REGRETTABLE

deplore *vb* **1** to feel or express sorrow for — see LAMENT 1

2 to feel sorry or dissatisfied about — see REGRET

deploring *adj* expressing or suggesting mourning — see MOURNFUL 1

deport *vb* **1** to force to leave a country — see BANISH 1

2 to manage the actions of (oneself) in a particular way — see BEHAVE

deportation *n* the forced removal from a homeland — see EXILE 1

deportee *n* a person forced to emigrate for political reasons — see ÉMIGRÉ 1

deportment *n* the way or manner in which one conducts oneself — see BEHAVIOR

depose *vb* **1** to remove from a position of prominence or power (as a throne) ⟨A military junta *deposed* the dictator after he had bankrupted the country.⟩

syn dethrone, displace, oust, uncrown, unmake, unseat, unthrone

rel can, cashier, discharge, dismiss, fire, muster out, remove, retire, sack; overthrow, subvert, supplant, topple, usurp; banish, boot (out), bounce, chase, drum (out), eject, expel, extrude, rout, run off, throw out

near ant baptize, inaugurate, induct, initiate, install, instate, invest; appoint, designate, elect

---

syn synonym(s) *rel* related words
ant antonym(s) *near ant* near antonym(s)

ant crown, enthrone, throne

2 to make a solemn declaration under oath for the purpose of establishing a fact — see TESTIFY

3 to arrange something in a certain spot or position — see PLACE 1

deposit *n* **1** matter that settles to the bottom of a body of liquid ⟨a *deposit* of silt on the river bed⟩

syn deposition, dregs, grounds, precipitate, sediment

rel lees; ooze, silt, sludge; dross, slag, waste

2 a collection of things kept available for future use or need — see STORE 1

3 a sum of money set aside for a particular purpose — see FUND 1

deposit *vb* **1** to put in an account ⟨We quickly *deposited* the check in a bank account.⟩

syn bank

rel cache, hoard, lay away, reserve, salt away, save, squirrel (away), stash, store, stow; invest

near ant remove, take out; disburse, expend, give, lay out, pay, spend

ant withdraw

2 to arrange something in a certain spot or position — see PLACE 1

deposition *n* matter that settles to the bottom of a body of liquid — see DEPOSIT 1

depository *n* a building for storing goods — see STOREHOUSE

depot *n* **1** a building for storing goods — see STOREHOUSE

2 a place where military arms are stored — see ARMORY

deprave *vb* to lower in character, dignity, or quality — see DEBASE 1

depraved *adj* having or showing lowered moral character or standards — see CORRUPT

depravedness *n* the state or quality of being utterly evil — see ENORMITY 1

depravity *n* **1** a sinking to a state of low moral standards and behavior — see CORRUPTION 2

2 immoral conduct or practices harmful or offensive to society — see VICE 1

3 the state or quality of being utterly evil — see ENORMITY 1

deprecate *vb* **1** to express scornfully one's low opinion of — see DECRY 1

2 to hold an unfavorable opinion of — see DISAPPROVE OF

deprecation *n* **1** refusal to accept as right or desirable — see DISAPPROVAL

2 the act of making a person or a thing seem little or unimportant — see DEPRECIATION

depreciate *vb* **1** to diminish the price or value of ⟨A faded finish will really *depreciate* your car when you decide to trade it in.⟩

syn break, cheapen, depress, downgrade, lower, mark down, reduce, sink, write off

rel debase, demonetize; underprice; abridge, compress, contract, de-escalate, deflate, downsize, dwindle, lessen, moderate, shrink

near ant bloat, blow up, inflate; overestimate, overprice, overrate, overvalue

ant appreciate, enhance, mark up, upgrade

2 to express scornfully one's low opinion of — see DECRY 1

depreciation *n* the act of making a person or a thing seem little or unimportant ⟨A *depreciation* of the role of minorities in the building of the nation was once a common feature of history books.⟩

syn belittlement, deprecation, detraction, diminishment, disparagement, put-down

rel aspersion, backbiting, calumny, defamation, libel, slander, vilification; derision, mockery, ridicule; abuse, invective, vituperation; censure, condemnation, criticism, denouncement, denunciation; de-emphasis, minimization, soft-pedaling

near ant acclaim, praise; approbation, approval, blessing, commendation; puffery

ant aggrandizement, ennoblement, exaltation, glorification, magnification

depreciative *adj* intended to make a person or thing seem of little importance or value — see DEROGATORY

depreciatory *adj* intended to make a person or thing seem of little importance or value — see DEROGATORY

depress *vb* **1** to make sad ⟨The thought of once again failing the bar exam *depressed* me.⟩

syn bum (out), burden, dash, oppress, sadden

rel ail, distress, trouble; afflict, torment, torture; daunt, demoralize, discourage, dishearten, dismay, dispirit, unnerve; agitate, bother, concern, discomfort, discompose, disquiet, disturb, freak (out), perturb, undo, unhinge, unsettle, upset, worry

near ant animate, enliven, invigorate; assure, comfort, console, reassure, solace, soothe; excite, inspire, stimulate; elate, exhilarate; encourage, hearten, delight, gratify, please; boost, elevate, lift, uplift

ant brighten, buoy, cheer (up), gladden, lighten, rejoice

2 to cause to fall intentionally or unintentionally — see DROP 1

3 to diminish the price or value of — see DEPRECIATE 1

4 to push steadily against with some force — see ²PRESS 1

depressed *adj* **1** curved inward — see HOLLOW

2 feeling unhappiness — see SAD 1

3 kept from having the necessities of life or a healthful environment — see DEPRIVED

depressing *adj* **1** causing or marked by an atmosphere lacking in cheer — see GLOOMY 1

2 causing unhappiness — see SAD 2

depression *n* **1** a period of decreased economic activity ⟨During the 1930s the U.S. suffered a great *depression*.⟩

syn recession, slump

rel bust, crash, panic; stagnation; downdraft, downswing, downtrend, downturn, slowdown

near ant development, growth; advancement, progress; rally, recovery

ant boom

2 a state or spell of low spirits — see SADNESS

3 a sunken area forming a separate space — see HOLE 2

4 the amount by which something is lessened — see DECREASE

deprivation *n* the state of being robbed of something normally enjoyed — see PRIVATION

deprived *adj* kept from having the necessities of life or a healthful environment ⟨a program to help *deprived* children⟩
syn depressed, disadvantaged, underprivileged
rel beggared, broke, destitute, impecunious, impoverished, indigent, needy, penniless, penurious, poor, poverty-stricken, unprivileged; bankrupt, bankrupted, insolvent; pinched, reduced, straitened
near ant blessed (*also* blest), fortunate, lucky; affluent, flush, loaded, moneyed (*also* monied), opulent, rich, wealthy, well-heeled, well-off, well-to-do; coddled, indulged, pampered, spoiled; comfortable, propertied, prosperous, successful; flourishing, prospering, thriving
ant advantaged, privileged

depth *n* 1 distance measured from the top to the bottom of something ⟨Be sure to check the *depth* of the water before diving off the dock.⟩
syn drop
rel lowness; draft, sounding
near ant shallowness; altitude, elevation, height, stature
2 the quality of being great in extent (as of insight) ⟨The *depth* of the poet's understanding of human nature has given his works a timeless appeal.⟩
syn profoundness, profundity
rel discernment, perception, perceptiveness, perceptivity, sagacity, sapience, sense, sensibility, wisdom; braininess, brightness, brilliance, intellect, intelligence, judgment (*or* judgement), reason, sense, smartness, wit; acuity, acuteness, keenness, penetration, perspicacity, sensitivity, sharpness
near ant shallowness, superficiality; brainlessness, idiocy, imbecility, mindlessness, simpleness, stupidity, witlessness; illogic, irrationality, unreasonableness, unsoundness
3 the most intense or characteristic phase of something — see THICK
4 the most extreme or advanced point — see HEIGHT 2

depthless *adj* lacking significant physical depth — see SHALLOW 1

depute *vb* to appoint as one's representative — see DELEGATE 1

deputize *vb* to appoint as one's representative — see DELEGATE 1

deputy *n* 1 a person who acts or does business for another — see AGENT 2
2 a person who helps a more skilled person — see HELPER

derange *vb* 1 to cause to go insane or as if insane — see CRAZE
2 to undo the proper order or arrangement of — see DISORDER

derangement *n* an act or instance of the order of things being disturbed — see UPSET

derelict *adj* 1 failing to give proper care and attention — see NEGLIGENT

2 left unoccupied or unused — see ABANDONED 1

dereliction *n* 1 the act of abandoning ⟨the *dereliction* of the cause by its leader⟩
syn abandonment, desertion, forsaking
rel defection; discard, dumping, jettisoning
near ant retention; recoupment, repossession, retrieval
ant reclamation
2 failure to take the care that a cautious person usually takes — see NEGLIGENCE 1
3 the nonperformance of an assigned or expected action — see FAILURE 1
4 a defect in character — see FAULT 1

deride *vb* to make (someone or something) the object of unkind laughter — see RIDICULE

derision *n* 1 a person or thing that is made fun of — see LAUGHINGSTOCK
2 the making of unkind jokes as a way of showing one's scorn for someone or something — see RIDICULE

derisive *adj* so foolish or pointless as to be worthy of scornful laughter — see RIDICULOUS 1

derisory *adj* 1 intended to make a person or thing seem of little importance or value — see DEROGATORY
2 so foolish or pointless as to be worthy of scornful laughter — see RIDICULOUS 1

derivable *adj* being or provable by reasoning in which the conclusion follows necessarily from given information — see DEDUCTIVE

derivative *adj* taken or created from something original or basic — see SECONDARY 1

derivative *n* something that naturally develops or is developed from something else ⟨The whole field of industrial robots is a *derivative* of technology developed for the space program.⟩
syn by-product, offshoot, outgrowth, spin-off
rel descendant (*also* descendent); aftermath, consequence, corollary, development, fruit, growth, issue, outcome, product, result, sequel, sequence, upshot; denouement (*also* dénouement), repercussion; aftereffect, side effect (*also* side reaction); copy, duplicate, facsimile, replica, reproduction
near ant archetype, original, prototype; antecedent, cause, determinant, occasion, reason
ant origin, root, source

derive *vb* to form an opinion or reach a conclusion through reasoning and information — see INFER 1

derogatory *adj* intended to make a person or thing seem of little importance or value ⟨The team's fans made *derogatory* remarks about their rivals.⟩
syn belittling, contemptuous, decrying, degrading, demeaning, depreciative, depreciatory, derisory, disdainful, disparaging, scornful, slighting, uncomplimentary
rel aspersing, defamatory, insulting, libelous (*or* libellous), maligning, slandering, slanderous, vilifying; abusive, opprobrious, scurrilous; catty, cruel, despiteful, hateful, malevolent, malicious, malign,

malignant, mean, nasty, spiteful, unkind, virulent; critical, denunciative, denunciatory; acrimonious, bitter, envious, jaundiced, jealous, rancorous, resentful; acrid, caustic, scathing, venomous

near ant admiring, adulatory, applauding, approving, friendly, positive; appreciative, respectful; kind, kindhearted, kindly, sympathetic, unmalicious, warm, warmhearted

ant commendatory, complimentary, laudative, laudatory

descant *vb* **1** to give a formal often extended talk on a subject — see TALK 1

2 to produce musical sounds with the voice — see SING 1

descend *vb* **1** to lead or extend downward ⟨The pathway *descends* to the river bank.⟩

syn decline, dip, drop, fall, plunge, sink

rel angle, cant, cock, heel, incline, lean, list, recline, slant, slope, tilt, tip

near ant even, flatten, level, plane, smooth, straighten

ant arise, ascend, climb, mount, rise, uprise, upsweep, upturn

2 to become worse or of less value — see DETERIORATE 1

3 to go to a lower level especially abruptly — see DROP 2

4 to come down from something (as a vehicle) — see ALIGHT 2

descend (on *or* upon) *vb* to take sudden, violent action against — see ATTACK 1

descendant *also* **descendent** *adj* bending downward or forward — see NODDING

descending *adj* bending downward or forward — see NODDING

descent *n* **1** the act or process of going to a lower level or altitude ⟨The airplane began its gradual *descent* to the landing field.⟩

syn dip, dive, down, drop, fall, nosedive, plunge

rel comedown, decline, downfall, downgrade; plummeting, sinking

near ant advance, headway, progress, progression; betterment, improvement

ant ascent, climb, rise, rising, soaring, upswing, upturn

2 a gradual sinking and wasting away of mind or body — see DECLINE 1

3 a change to a lower state or level — see DECLINE 2

4 a loss of status — see COMEDOWN

5 a sudden attack on and entrance into hostile territory — see RAID 1

6 the act or action of setting upon with force or violence — see ATTACK 1

7 the line of ancestors from whom a person is descended — see ANCESTRY

8 a downward slope — see DECLINE 3

describe *vb* **1** to give a representation or account of in words ⟨He tried to *describe* the dream he had last night as accurately as he could.⟩

syn delineate, depict, draw, image, paint, picture, portray, render, sketch

rel characterize, define, label, qualify, represent; demonstrate, illustrate; narrate, recite, recount, rehearse, relate, report, tell; display, exhibit, show; hint, suggest; draft, outline, silhouette, trace, vignette; summarize, sum up, touch off; redescribe, reimage

near ant color, distort, falsify, garble, misdescribe, misrepresent, misstate, pervert, twist, warp

2 to give an oral or written account of in some detail — see TELL 1

3 to point out the chief quality or qualities of an individual or group — see CHARACTERIZE 1

description *n* **1** a vivid representation in words of someone or something ⟨We immediately recognized the man from our cousin's *description* of him.⟩

syn delineation, depiction, picture, portrait, portrayal, sketch, vignette

rel account, anecdote, chronicle, narrative, report, story, tale, yarn; demonstration, exemplification, illustration; clarification, elucidation, explanation, explication, exposition

2 a number of persons or things that are grouped together because they have something in common — see SORT 1

descry *vb* **1** to come upon after searching, study, or effort — see FIND 1

2 to make note of (something) through the use of one's eyes — see SEE 1

desecrate *vb* to treat (a sacred place or object) shamefully or with great disrespect ⟨Vandals *desecrated* the tombstones with graffiti.⟩

syn defile, profane, violate

rel blaspheme, curse, swear; befoul, contaminate, foul, poison, pollute, soil, sully, taint; affront, defame, insult, offend, outrage

near ant bless, consecrate, dedicate, hallow, sanctify; honor, respect; cleanse, purge, purify

desecration *n* an act of great disrespect shown to God or to sacred ideas, people, or things — see BLASPHEMY

¹**desert** *n* land that is uninhabited or not fit for crops — see WASTELAND

²**desert** *n, usually* **deserts** *pl* suffering, loss, or hardship imposed in response to a crime or offense — see PUNISHMENT

desert *vb* **1** to leave (a cause or party) often in order to take up another — see DEFECT (FROM)

2 to cause to remain behind — see LEAVE 1

deserted *adj* left unoccupied or unused — see ABANDONED 1

deserter *n* a person who abandons a cause or organization usually without right — see RENEGADE

desertion *n* the act of abandoning — see DERELICTION 1

deserve *vb* to be or make worthy of (as a reward or punishment) — see EARN 2

deserved *adj* being what is called for by accepted standards of right and wrong — see JUST 1

deserving *adj* having sufficient worth or merit to receive one's honor, esteem, or reward — see WORTHY

desex *vb* to remove the sex organs of — see NEUTER

design *n* **1** a method worked out in advance for achieving some objective — see PLAN 1

2 a secret plan for accomplishing evil or unlawful ends — see PLOT 1

3 something that one hopes or intends to accomplish — see GOAL

4 a unit of decoration that is repeated all over something (as a fabric) — see PATTERN 1

5 the way in which the elements of something (as a work of art) are arranged — see COMPOSITION 3

design vb **1** to have in mind as a purpose or goal — see INTEND 1

2 to work out the details of (something) in advance — see PLAN 1

designate vb **1** to decide upon (the time or date for an event) usually from a position of authority — see APPOINT 1

2 to pick (someone) by one's authority for a specific position or duty — see APPOINT 1

3 to give a name to — see NAME 1

designation n **1** a word or combination of words by which a person or thing is regularly known — see NAME 1

2 the state or fact of being chosen for a position or duty — see APPOINTMENT 1

designedly adv with full awareness of what one is doing — see INTENTIONALLY

designer adj being or involving the latest methods, concepts, information, or styles — see MODERN

designer n one who creates or introduces something new — see INVENTOR

designing adj clever at attaining one's ends by indirect and often deceptive means — see ARTFUL 1

desirable adj suitable for bringing about a desired result under the circumstances — see EXPEDIENT

desire n **1** a strong wish for something ⟨A *desire* for adventure and excitement prompted him to move abroad.⟩

syn appetite, craving, drive, hankering, hunger, itch, longing, passion, pining, thirst, urge, yearning, yen

rel compulsion, impulse, impulsion, will, zeal; liking, love, taste, weakness; eagerness, impatience; want, wish; necessity, need, requirement; obsession; acquisitiveness, avarice, avariciousness, avidity, covetousness, cupidity, greed, greediness, rapaciousness, rapacity; mania

near ant abhorrence, abomination, allergy, averseness, aversion, disfavor, disgust, disinclination, dislike, disliking, distaste, hatred, loathing, nausea, repugnance, repulsion, revulsion; apathy, indifference, insouciance, nonchalance; unconcern

2 an earnest request — see PLEA 1

desire vb **1** to have an earnest wish to own or enjoy ⟨He greatly *desired* a new mountain bike for his next birthday.⟩

syn ache (for), covet, crave, die (for), hanker (for *or* after), hunger (for), itch (for), long (for), lust (for *or* after), pant (after), pine (for), repine (for), sigh (for), thirst (for), want, wish (for), yearn (for)

rel spoil (for); adore, delight (in), dig, enjoy, fancy, groove (on), like, love, relish, revel (in); favor, prefer; admire, appreciate, cherish, prize, treasure, value

phrases set one's heart on

near ant abhor, abominate, despise, detest, execrate, hate, loathe; decline, refuse, reject, spurn

2 to make a request for — see ASK (FOR) 1

desirous adj showing urgent desire or interest — see EAGER

desirousness n urgent desire or interest — see EAGERNESS

desist (from) vb to bring (as an action or operation) to an immediate end — see STOP 1

desk n a large unit of a governmental, business, or educational organization — see DIVISION 2

desolate adj **1** causing or marked by an atmosphere lacking in cheer — see GLOOMY 1

2 sad from lack of companionship or separation from others — see LONESOME 1

3 left unoccupied or unused — see ABANDONED 1

4 producing inferior or only a small amount of vegetation — see BARREN 1

desolate vb to bring to a complete end the physical soundness, existence, or usefulness of — see DESTROY 1

desolation n **1** a state or spell of low spirits — see SADNESS

2 land that is uninhabited or not fit for crops — see WASTELAND

3 the state of being unattended to or not cared for — see NEGLECT 1

4 the state or fact of being rendered nonexistent, physically unsound, or useless — see DESTRUCTION 1

despair n **1** utter loss of hope ⟨The endless drought drove the farmers to *despair*.⟩

syn desperation, despond, despondency, forlornness, hopelessness

rel blue devils, blues, dejection, depression, desolation, disconsolateness, dispiritedness, doldrums, dolor, downheartedness, dreariness, dumps, gloom, gloominess, joylessness, melancholy, mopes, oppression, sadness, sorrow, unhappiness; self-despair, self-pity; dolefulness, woefulness; agony, distress, pain; misery, woe, wretchedness; cynicism, pessimism; acceptance, resignation

phrases slough of despond

near ant cheer, cheerfulness, sunniness; optimism; gaiety (*also* gayety), glee, gleefulness, jollity, joviality, lightheartedness, merriment, mirth, mirthfulness; bliss, blissfulness, ecstasy, elation, euphoria, exhilaration, exuberance, exultation, gladness, happiness, joy, joyfulness, joyousness, jubilation, rapture, rapturousness

ant hopefulness

2 the state of being discouraged — see DISCOURAGEMENT

despair vb to lose all hope or confidence ⟨We *despaired* when we saw how little time we had left to complete our project.⟩

syn despond

rel give up, surrender, yield; darken, sadden; agonize, bleed, grieve, hurt, mourn, sorrow, suffer; discourage, dishearten, dispirit

phrases lose heart

near ant exult, rejoice; assure, encourage, hearten, reassure; hope

ant brighten, cheer (up), perk (up)

despairing adj **1** emphasizing or expecting the worst — see PESSIMISTIC 1

2 feeling or showing no hope — see DESPONDENT 1

---

syn synonym(s)　　*rel* related words
ant antonym(s)　　*near ant* near antonym(s)

desperation *n* utter loss of hope — see DESPAIR 1

despicable *adj* **1** arousing or deserving of one's loathing and disgust — see CONTEMPTIBLE 1

2 not following or in accordance with standards of honor and decency — see IGNOBLE 2

3 deserving pitying scorn (as for inadequacy) — see PITIFUL 1

despise *vb* **1** to dislike strongly — see HATE

2 to ignore in a disrespectful manner — see SCORN 2

despite *n* **1** open dislike for someone or something considered unworthy of one's concern or respect — see CONTEMPT

2 the desire to cause pain for the satisfaction of doing harm — see MALICE

3 the negative result caused by something that creates difficulty for achieving success — see DISADVANTAGE 2

despite *prep* without being prevented by ⟨We went to the party *despite* the bad weather outside.⟩
syn notwithstanding, with
phrases in defiance of, in despite of, in spite of

despiteful *adj* having or showing a desire to cause someone pain or suffering for the sheer enjoyment of it — see HATEFUL

despitefully *adv* in a mean or spiteful manner — see NASTILY

despitefulness *n* open dislike for someone or something considered unworthy of one's concern or respect — see CONTEMPT

despoil *vb* to search through with the intent of committing robbery — see RANSACK 1

despond *n* **1** a state or spell of low spirits — see SADNESS

2 utter loss of hope — see DESPAIR 1

despond *vb* to lose all hope or confidence — see DESPAIR

despondency *n* **1** a state or spell of low spirits — see SADNESS

2 the state of being discouraged — see DISCOURAGEMENT

3 utter loss of hope — see DESPAIR 1

despondent *adj* **1** feeling or showing no hope ⟨After four days and still no sign of the lost kitty, the boy grew *despondent*.⟩
syn despairing, forlorn, hopeless
rel blue, brokenhearted, crestfallen, dejected, depressed, disconsolate, doleful, down, downcast, downhearted, gloomy, glum, hangdog, heartbroken, heartsick, heartsore, inconsolable, joyless, low, low-spirited, melancholy, miserable, mournful, sad, saddened, sorrowful, sorry, unhappy, woebegone, woeful, wretched; disappointed, discouraged, disheartened, dispirited; accepting, resigned
near ant ecstatic, elated, enraptured, entranced, euphoric, exhilarated, exuberant, exultant; blithe, blithesome, jocund, jolly, jovial, lightsome, merry, mirthful; encouraged, heartened; animated, jaunty, lively, perky, sprightful, sprightly, vivacious; blissful, buoyant, cheerful, cheery, chipper, delighted, glad, gladdened, gladsome, gleeful, happy, joyful, joyous, jubilant, sunny, upbeat

ant hopeful, optimistic

2 feeling unhappiness — see SAD 1

despot *n* a person who uses power or authority in a cruel, unjust, or harmful way ⟨a *despot* who was finally overthrown⟩
syn dictator, oppressor, tyrannizer, tyrant
rel autarch, autocrat, monocrat; authoritarian, potentate, totalitarian; overlord, warlord; boss, captain, chief, dominator, kingpin, leader, master, overlord, ruler; king, monarch, prince, queen, sovereign (*also* sovran); baron, czar (*also* tsar *or* tzar), magnate, mogul, tycoon; disciplinarian, discipliner, enforcer, martinet, taskmaster
phrases man on horseback

despotic *adj* **1** exercising power or authority without interference by others — see ABSOLUTE 1

2 fond of ordering people around — see BOSSY

despotism *n* a system of government in which the ruler has unlimited power ⟨By the end of the 20th century many countries around the world had rejected *despotism* in favor of democracy.⟩
syn autocracy, dictatorship, totalitarianism, tyranny
rel monarchism, monarchy, monocracy; Communism, fascism, Nazism; domination, oppression
near ant democracy, self-government, self-rule; freedom, self-determination; autonomy, sovereignty (*also* sovranty)

destine *vb* to determine the fate of in advance ⟨His extreme height seemed to *destine* him for a career in basketball.⟩
syn doom, fate, foredoom, foreordain, ordain, predestine, predetermine, preordain
rel predestinate; augur, forecast, foretell, predict, presage, prognosticate, prophesy; preconceive, prejudge; condemn, sentence; bode, forebode (*also* forbode), portend; anticipate, divine, foreknow, foresee

destiny *n* a state or end that seemingly has been decided beforehand — see FATE 1

destitute *adj* **1** lacking money or material possessions — see POOR 1

2 utterly lacking in something needed, wanted, or expected — see DEVOID 1

destitution *n* the state of lacking sufficient money or material possessions — see POVERTY 1

de-stress *vb* to get rid of nervous tension or anxiety — see RELAX 1

destroy *vb* **1** to bring to a complete end the physical soundness, existence, or usefulness of ⟨They practically *destroyed* the safe in order to get at the money inside.⟩ ⟨Their poor scores on the final exam *destroyed* any chance they might have had to pass the course.⟩
syn annihilate, cream, decimate, demolish, desolate, devastate, do in, extinguish, pulverize, raze, rub out, ruin, shatter, smash, tear down, total, waste, wreck
rel beat, best, clobber, conquer, crush, defeat, drub, lick, master, overbear, overcome, overmatch, prevail (over), rout, scotch, skunk, subdue, surmount, thrash, trim, triumph (over), trounce, wallop, whip, win (against); blast, blow up, break, cripple, damage, deface, deteriorate,

disfigure, disintegrate, dissolve, harm, impair, injure, mangle, mar, mutilate, spoil, vitiate; erode, scour, wash out, wear (away); dilapidate, disassemble, dismantle, gut, take down, undo, unmake; blot out, efface, eradicate, expunge, exterminate, extirpate, liquidate, obliterate, remove, root (out), snuff (out), stamp (out), wipe out; despoil, havoc, loot, pillage, plunder, ravage, sack, trample, trash, vandalize

near ant doctor, fix, mend, patch, recondition, repair, revamp; create, invent; assemble, fabricate, fashion, forge, form, frame, make, manufacture, produce, shape; bring about, constitute, establish, father, found, institute, organize; conserve, preserve, protect, save; rebuild, reconstruct, remodel, renovate, restore

ant build, construct, erect, put up, raise, rear, set up

2 to bring destruction to (something) through violent action — see RAVAGE

3 to deprive of life — see KILL 1

destruction *n* **1** the state or fact of being rendered nonexistent, physically unsound, or useless ⟨The storm resulted in the *destruction* of their tree house.⟩

syn annihilation, decimation, demolishment, demolition, desolation, devastation, extermination, extinction, havoc, loss, obliteration, ruin, ruination, wastage, wreckage

rel depredation, despoilment, despoliation; breakup, collapse, disintegration, dissolution; assassination, execution, massacre, slaughter; dismantlement, effacement, eradication

near ant rescue, salvage, salvation, saving; conservation, preservation, protection; reclamation, reconstruction, re-creation, refurbishment, regeneracy, remodeling, renovation, restoration

ant building, construction, erection, raising

2 something that is the cause of one's ultimate failure or loss of life — see DOWNFALL 1

destructive *adj* **1** causing or tending to cause destruction ⟨The *destructive* storm blew down trees all over town.⟩

syn calamitous, cataclysmal (*or* cataclysmic), devastating, disastrous, ruinous

rel baleful, deadly, deathly, fatal, lethal, mortal, murderous, pestilent, poisonous, virulent, vital; deleterious, detrimental, harmful, pernicious

near ant preservative, protective; constructive, creative, formative, productive; harmless, innocent, innocuous, inoffensive; ameliorative, helpful, useful; healthful, healthy, nonfatal, nonlethal, salubrious, wholesome

ant nondestructive

2 bringing about ruin or misfortune — see FATAL 1

desultorily *adv* without definite aim, direction, rule, or method — see HIT OR MISS

desultory *adj* **1** lacking a definite plan, purpose, or pattern — see RANDOM

2 passing from one topic to another — see DISCURSIVE

detached *adj* **1** having or showing a lack of friendliness or interest in others — see COOL 1

2 not physically attached to another unit — see SEPARATE 2

detachment *n* **1** lack of favoritism toward one side or another ⟨The judge showed commendable *detachment* when deciding the controversial case.⟩

syn disinterestedness, equity, fairness, impartiality, justice, neutrality, objectivity

rel apathy, indifference, unconcern; broad-mindedness, open-mindedness, tolerance; straddling

near ant chauvinism, nepotism; subjectiveness, subjectivity; bent, inclination, leaning, penchant, predilection, predisposition, proclivity, propensity, tendency; preconception, prejudgment

ant bias, favor, favoritism, nonobjectivity, one-sidedness, partiality, partisanship, prejudice

2 a small military unit with a special task or function ⟨The general sent a *detachment* ahead to scout the enemy's position.⟩

syn detail

rel commando, firing squad, outpost, paratroops, patrol, picket, rear guard, sentry, watch; battalion, command, company, corps, division, regiment, squad, squadron, troop, wing

3 the absence of emotional involvement — see COOL 1

detail *n* **1** a separate part in a list, account, or series — see ITEM 1

2 a single piece of information — see FACT 3

3 a small military unit with a special task or function — see DETACHMENT 2

4 a specific task with which a person or group is charged — see MISSION

detail *vb* **1** to assign to a place or position — see ²POST

2 to pick (someone) by one's authority for a specific position or duty — see APPOINT 2

3 to specify one after another — see ENUMERATE 1

detailed *adj* **1** including many small descriptive features ⟨a *detailed* report on all the activities that their Scout troop had been involved in over the past year⟩

syn circumstantial, elaborate, full, minute, particular, particularized, thorough

rel enumerated, inventoried, itemized, listed, numerated; delineated, specific, specified; abundant, copious; comprehensive, encyclopedic, exhausting, exhaustive, inclusionary, inclusive, in-depth, omnibus, panoramic, thoroughgoing; distinct, explicit, sharp; mapped (out); descriptive, graphic (*also* graphical), picturesque, vivid

near ant brief, compact, concise, crisp, pithy, short, succinct, terse; ambiguous, indeterminate, nebulous, sketchy, vague; bird's-eye, broad, general, nonspecific, overall, unspecified

ant compendious, summary

2 made or done with great care or with much detail — see ELABORATE 1

detainment *n* an instance or period of being prevented from going about one's business — see DELAY

detect *vb* to come upon after searching, study, or effort — see FIND 1

detectable *adj* able to be perceived by a sense or by the mind — see PERCEPTIBLE

detection *n* the act or process of sighting or learning the existence of something for the first time — see DISCOVERY 1

detective *n* a person not on the police force who investigates criminal or illicit activity or searches for missing persons ⟨The code used by the serial killer in his letters to the police was actually cracked by an amateur *detective*.⟩

syn investigator, operative, sleuth

rel shadow, tail, tracer, tracker; fed, Federal, G-man, narc (*or* nark) [*slang*], plainclothesman

detector *n* a device that detects some physical quantity and responds usually with a transmitted signal — see SENSOR

deter *vb* to steer (a person) from an activity or course of action — see DISCOURAGE 2

detergent *n* a substance used for cleaning — see CLEANER

deteriorate *vb* 1 to become worse or of less value ⟨The garden slowly *deteriorated* after months of neglect.⟩

syn crumble, decay, decline, degenerate, descend, ebb, regress, retrograde, rot, sink, worsen

rel abate, de-escalate, diminish, downsize, dwindle, recede, wane; break down, corrupt, decompose, degrade, dilapidate, disintegrate, molder, putrefy; sour, spoil; lessen, lower, reduce; debilitate, undermine; droop, fail, fall, flag, lag, languish, run down, sag, slip, waste (away), weaken, wilt

phrases go to pot, go to seed (*or* run to seed)

near ant better, upgrade; enhance, enrich, fortify, heighten, intensify, strengthen; advance, develop, march, proceed, progress

ant ameliorate, improve, meliorate

2 to lower in character, dignity, or quality — see DEBASE 1

deterioration *n* 1 a gradual sinking and wasting away of mind or body — see DECLINE 1

2 a change to a lower state or level — see DECLINE 2

determinate *adj* 1 having been established and usually not subject to change — see FIXED 1

2 having distinct or certain limits — see LIMITED 1

determination *n* 1 firm or unwavering adherence to one's purpose ⟨a fierce *determination* to succeed⟩

syn decidedness, decision, decisiveness, firmness, granite, purposefulness, resoluteness, resolution, resolve

rel doggedness, obduracy, obstinacy, perseverance, persistence, persistency, stubbornness, tenaciousness, tenacity; certainty, certitude, confidence, sureness; alacrity, eagerness, gameness, readiness; backbone, fortitude, grit, iron, pluck, sand

near ant doubt, incertitude, indetermination, uncertainty; aversion, disinclination, indisposition, reluctance, unwillingness

ant hesitation, indecision, indecisiveness, irresoluteness, irresolution, vacillation

2 a position arrived at after consideration — see DECISION 1

3 an opinion arrived at through a process of reasoning — see CONCLUSION 1

determine *vb* 1 to give an opinion about (something at issue or in dispute) — see JUDGE 1

2 to come to a judgment about after discussion or consideration — see DECIDE 1

3 to come upon after searching, study, or effort — see FIND 1

4 to come to an end — see CEASE 1

5 to make final, definite, or beyond dispute — see CLINCH

determined *adj* 1 fully committed to achieving a goal ⟨His *determined* opponent would not be bluffed or shaken.⟩

syn bent (on *or* upon), bound, decisive, firm, hell-bent (on *or* upon), intent, out, purposeful, resolute, resolved, set, single-minded

rel bitter, vehement; certain, cocksure, confident, positive, sure; earnest, serious; steady, unfaltering, unhesitating, unswerving, unwavering; adamant, adamantine, dogged, hard, hardened, hardheaded, headstrong, immovable, implacable, inflexible, mulish, obdurate, persistent, pertinacious, perverse, pigheaded, rigid, self-willed, stubborn, tenacious, unbending, uncompromising, unrelenting, unyielding, willful (*or* wilful)

phrases on one's mettle

near ant distrustful, doubtful, dubious, mistrustful, skeptical, suspicious, uncertain, unconvinced, undecided, unsettled, unsure; disinclined, indisposed, loath (*also* loth *or* loathe), reluctant

ant faltering, hesitant, indecisive, irresolute, undetermined, unresolved, vacillating, wavering

2 showing no signs of slackening or yielding in one's purpose — see UNYIELDING 1

determinedly *adv* with great effort or determination — see HARD 1

deterrent *n* something that makes movement or progress difficult — see ENCUMBRANCE

detest *vb* to dislike strongly — see HATE

detestable *adj* not following or in accordance with standards of honor and decency — see IGNOBLE 2

dethrone *vb* to remove from a position of prominence or power (as a throne) — see DEPOSE 1

detonate *vb* to break open or into pieces usually because of internal pressure — see EXPLODE 1

detonation *n* the act or an instance of exploding — see EXPLOSION 1

detour *n* a turning away from a course or standard — see DIVERGENCE 2

detour *vb* 1 to avoid by going around ⟨We had to *detour* the construction zone in order to get to the stadium.⟩

syn bypass, circumnavigate, circumvent, skirt

rel leapfrog; avoid, dodge, duck, elude, escape, eschew, evade, flee, shake, shun

near ant confront, face, meet; accept, court, embrace, pursue, seek, welcome

2 to change one's course or direction — see TURN 3

detraction *n* the act of making a person or a thing seem little or unimportant — see DEPRECIATION

detriment *n* **1** something that causes loss or pain — see INJURY 1

2 the negative result caused by something that creates difficulty for achieving success — see DISADVANTAGE 2

detrimental *adj* causing or capable of causing harm — see HARMFUL

devastate *vb* **1** to bring destruction to (something) through violent action — see RAVAGE

2 to bring to a complete end the physical soundness, existence, or usefulness of — see DESTROY 1

3 to subject to incapacitating emotional or mental stress — see OVERWHELM 1

devastating *adj* causing or tending to cause destruction — see DESTRUCTIVE 1

devastation *n* the state or fact of being rendered nonexistent, physically unsound, or useless — see DESTRUCTION 1

develop *vb* **1** to gradually become clearer or more detailed ⟨The facts of what had happened slowly *developed* over the next few days.⟩
syn elaborate, evolve, unfold
rel advance, fare, forge, get along, get on, march, proceed, progress; blossom, grow, mature, ripen; materialize; emerge, play out

2 to come to have gradually ⟨The youngster *developed* a taste for green olives.⟩
syn acquire, cultivate, form
rel absorb, adopt, embrace, take in, take on; gain, get, obtain; achieve, attain, reach; foster, nourish, nurture, promote
near ant abandon, desert, forsake; cast, discard, ditch, dump, fling (off *or* away), jettison, junk, reject, scrap, shed, shuck (off), slough (*also* sluff), throw away, throw out, unload
ant lose

3 to become mature — see MATURE

4 to express more fully and in greater detail — see EXPAND 1

developed *adj* being far along in development — see ADVANCED

developer *n* one who creates or introduces something new — see INVENTOR

development *n* **1** the act or process of going from the simple or basic to the complex or advanced ⟨the *development* of an idea into a marketable product⟩
syn elaboration, evolution, expansion, growth, progress, progression
rel advancement, betterment, improvement, perfection, refinement; incubation, maturation, maturing, ripening; blossoming, flourishing, flowering; addition, augmentation, enhancement, supplementation; emergence, evolvement, metamorphosis
near ant backslide, lapse, relapse; decadence, decay, decaying, declension, decline, degeneracy, degeneration, degradation, descent, deterioration, devaluation; downfall, downgrade, ebbing, falling, weakening
ant regress, regression, retrogression, reversion

2 a condition or occurrence traceable to a cause — see EFFECT 1

3 the process of becoming mature — see MATURATION

deviant *adj* departing from some accepted standard of what is normal ⟨a study of *deviant* behavior⟩
syn aberrant, abnormal, anomalous, atypical, deviate, irregular, unnatural, untypical
rel unrepresentative; extraordinary, preternatural; rare, uncommon, uncustomary, unusual, unwonted; bizarre, curious, far-out, funny, kinky, odd, outlandish, out-of-the-way, quirky, remarkable, screwy, strange, wacky (*also* whacky), way-out, weird, wild; eccentric, freakish, idiosyncratic, nonconformist, unconventional, unorthodox; extraordinary, preternatural; rare, uncommon, uncustomary, unusual, unwonted; odd, peculiar, strange
near ant common, commonplace, everyday, familiar, ordinary, routine, run-of-the-mill, run-of-the-mine (*or* run-of-mine), unexceptional, unremarkable, workaday; customary, usual, wonted; archetypal (*also* archetypical), average, characteristic, representative
ant natural, normal, regular, standard, typical

deviant *n* a person who does not conform to generally accepted standards or customs — see NONCONFORMIST 1

deviate *adj* departing from some accepted standard of what is normal — see DEVIANT

deviate *n* a person who has sunk below the normal moral standard — see DEGENERATE

deviate *vb* to change one's course or direction — see TURN 3

device *n* **1** a clever often underhanded means to achieve an end — see TRICK 1

2 an article intended for use in work — see IMPLEMENT

3 devices *pl* a habitual attraction to some activity or thing — see INCLINATION 1

devil *n* **1** *cap* the supreme personification of evil often represented as the ruler of hell ⟨The *Devil* is traditionally seen as a being who relentlessly tempts people to commit evil.⟩
syn fiend, Lucifer, Satan, serpent
rel deuce, dickens; Mephistopheles

2 an evil spirit — see DEMON 1

3 a member of the human race — see HUMAN

4 an appealingly mischievous person — see SCAMP 1

5 a mean, evil, or unprincipled person — see VILLAIN

6 a person who seeks out very dangerous or foolhardy adventures with no apparent fear — see DAREDEVIL

devilfish *n* any of several extremely large rays ⟨They saw a *devilfish* when they went scuba diving in the Caribbean, but it swam away quickly.⟩
syn manta, manta ray, sea devil
rel ray, skate

devilish *adj* **1** going beyond a normal or acceptable limit in degree or amount — see EXCESSIVE

2 of, relating to, or worthy of an evil spirit — see FIENDISH 1

3 tending to or exhibiting reckless playfulness — see MISCHIEVOUS 1

devilishly *adv* beyond a normal or acceptable limit — see TOO 1

devilishness *n* playful, reckless behavior that is not intended to cause serious harm — see MISCHIEF 1

devil–may–care *adj* **1** having a relaxed, casual manner — see EASYGOING 1

2 having or showing a lack of concern for the consequences of one's actions — see RECKLESS 1

3 having or showing freedom from worries or troubles — see CAREFREE

devilment *n* playful, reckless behavior that is not intended to cause serious harm — see MISCHIEF 1

devilry or **deviltry** *n* **1** playful, reckless behavior that is not intended to cause serious harm — see MISCHIEF 1

2 the power to control natural forces through supernatural means — see MAGIC 1

devious *adj* **1** clever at attaining one's ends by indirect and often deceptive means — see ARTFUL 1

2 marked by a long series of irregular curves — see CROOKED 1

deviousness *n* skill in achieving one's ends through indirect, subtle, or underhanded means — see CUNNING 1

devise *vb* to create or think of by clever use of the imagination — see INVENT

deviser *n* one who creates or introduces something new — see INVENTOR

devoid *adj* **1** utterly lacking in something needed, wanted, or expected ⟨The so-called comedy is totally *devoid* of intelligence, originality, and even laughs.⟩

syn bankrupt, bare, barren, bereft, destitute, void

rel blank, empty, innocent, stark, vacant, wanting; deficient, fragmental, fragmentary, incomplete, insufficient, partial, short; absent, missing

near ant furnished, provided, supplied; brimming, bulging, bursting, chock-full (or chockful), crammed, crowded, fat, jammed, jam-packed, loaded, packed, saturated, stuffed; abounding, swarming, teeming, thick, thronging

ant filled, flush, fraught, full, replete, rife

2 lacking contents that could or should be present — see EMPTY 1

devote *vb* **1** to keep or intend for a special purpose ⟨I conscientiously *devote* several hours every weekend to playing with my dog.⟩

syn allocate, consecrate, dedicate, earmark, reserve, save

rel bless, hallow, sanctify; commit, consign, entrust (also intrust); apply, bestow, employ, use

phrases set apart, set aside

near ant ignore, neglect; misapply, misuse

2 to occupy (oneself) diligently or with close attention — see APPLY 2

devoted *adj* **1** feeling or showing love — see LOVING 1

2 firm in one's allegiance to someone or something — see FAITHFUL 1

devotedness *n* **1** a feeling of strong or constant regard for and dedication to someone — see LOVE 1

2 adherence to something to which one is bound by a pledge or duty — see FIDELITY

devotee *n* a person with a strong and habitual liking for something — see FAN

devotion *n* **1** a feeling of strong or constant regard for and dedication to someone — see LOVE 1

2 adherence to something to which one is bound by a pledge or duty — see FIDELITY

3 belief and trust in and loyalty to God — see FAITH 1

devotional *adj* of, relating to, or used in the practice or worship services of a religion — see RELIGIOUS 1

devour *vb* **1** to destroy all trace of — see CONSUME 1

2 to make complete use of — see DEPLETE 1

3 to swallow or eat greedily — see GOBBLE

devout *adj* **1** firm in one's allegiance to someone or something — see FAITHFUL 1

2 showing a devotion to God and to a life of virtue — see HOLY 1

devoutness *n* the quality or state of being spiritually pure or virtuous — see HOLINESS

dexterity *n* **1** mental skill or quickness ⟨the ambassador showed great *dexterity* in his handling of the touchy situation.⟩

syn adroitness, cleverness, finesse, sleight

rel faculty, knack, talent; competence, competency, efficiency, expertise, know-how, proficiency; ingeniousness, ingenuity, resourcefulness; savvy, sharpness, shrewdness; artfulness, artifice, caginess (also cageyness), canniness, craft, craftiness, cunning, deviousness, foxiness, guile, slickness, slyness, sneakiness, subtleness, wiliness

near ant inadequacy, incompetence, ineptitude, ineptness; brainlessness, denseness, density, doltishness, dopiness, dullness (also dulness), dumbness, fatuity, foolishness, mindlessness, obtuseness, senselessness, simpleness, slowness, stupidity, stupidness, witlessness

2 ease and grace in physical activity ⟨The juggler needed lots of *dexterity* in order to keep all five balls in the air at the same time.⟩

syn agility, deftness, nimbleness, sleight, spryness

rel coordination; flexibility, gracefulness, limberness, litheness, loose-jointedness, suppleness; handiness, sure-handedness; sure-footedness; adeptness, adroitness, finesse

near ant disability, inability, incapability, incapacity; debilitation, disablement, impairment, incapacitation; unhandiness

ant awkwardness, clumsiness, gaucheness, gawkiness, gawkishness, gracelessness, ham-handedness, heavy-handedness, klutziness, ungainliness

dexterous also **dextrous** *adj* **1** skillful with the hands ⟨The *dexterous* watchmaker was able to repair the antique watch's delicate gears and parts.⟩

syn clever, cunning, deft, handy

rel agile, flexible, graceful, limber, lissome (also lissom), lithe, lithesome, nimble, spry; coordinated; able, adept, capable, competent, expert, masterful, masterly, proficient, qualified, skilled, skillful, sure-handed; double-jointed, loose-jointed

near ant awkward, bungling, clumsy, fumbling, gauche, gawky, graceless, stiff, stilted, uncomfortable, uneasy, ungainly, ungraceful, wooden; incapable, incompetent, inept, inexpert, maladroit

ant handless, heavy-handed, unhandy

2 accomplished with trained ability — see SKILLFUL 1

diabolical *or* **diabolic** *adj* of, relating to, or worthy of an evil spirit — see FIENDISH 1

diabolicalness *n* the state or quality of being utterly evil — see ENORMITY 1

diadem *n* a decorative band or wreath worn about the head as a symbol of victory or honor — see CROWN 1

diagnosis *n* a position arrived at after consideration — see DECISION 1

diagonal *adj* running in a slanting direction ⟨The *diagonal* design ran up the wall all the way from the lower left to the upper right-hand corner.⟩

syn cant, canted, inclined, leaning, listing, oblique, pitched, slant, slanted, slantwise, sloped, sloping, tilted, tilting

near ant horizontal; level; plumb, up-and-down, vertical; parallel, perpendicular

diagonal *n* the degree to which something rises up from a position level with the horizon — see SLANT 1

diagram *n* something that visually explains or decorates a text — see ILLUSTRATION 1

dial *vb* to make a telephone call to — see CALL 2

dialect *n* the special terms or expressions of a particular group or field — see TERMINOLOGY

dialogue *also* **dialog** *n* **1** an exchange of views for the purpose of exploring a subject or deciding an issue — see DISCUSSION 1

2 talking or a talk between two or more people — see CONVERSATION

diametric *or* **diametrical** *adj* being as different as possible — see OPPOSITE

diarrhea *n* abnormally frequent intestinal evacuations with more or less fluid stools ⟨I was taken with severe *diarrhea* while attending the conference.⟩

syn flux, runs

rel dysentery; scour(s)

diatribe *n* a long angry speech or scolding — see TIRADE

dice *n* a small cube marked on each side with one to six spots and usually played in pairs in various games — see DIE

dice *vb* to cut into small pieces — see CHOP

dicker *n* a giving or taking of one thing of value in return for another — see EXCHANGE 1

dicker *vb* to talk over or dispute the terms of a purchase — see BARGAIN 1

dictate *n* a statement of what to do that must be obeyed by those concerned — see COMMAND 1

dictate *vb* to request the doing of by virtue of one's authority — see COMMAND 2

dictator *n* a person who uses power or authority in a cruel, unjust, or harmful way — see DESPOT

dictatorial *adj* **1** exercising power or authority without interference by others — see ABSOLUTE 1

2 fond of ordering people around — see BOSSY

3 having or showing a tendency to force one's will on others without any regard to fairness or necessity — see ARBITRARY 1

dictatorship *n* a system of government in which the ruler has unlimited power — see DESPOTISM

diction *n* **1** the clear and accurate pronunciation of words especially in public speaking ⟨Shakespearean actors with very good *diction*⟩

syn articulation, enunciation

rel elocution, expression, utterance; speech, wording

2 the way in which something is put into words — see WORDING 1

dictionary *n* a reference book giving information about the meanings, pronunciations, uses, and origins of words listed in alphabetical order ⟨Try to develop the habit of going to the *dictionary* whenever you encounter an unfamiliar word.⟩

syn lexicon, wordbook

rel gloss, glossary, thesaurus; vocabulary

die *n* a small cube marked on each side with one to six spots and usually played in pairs in various games ⟨He rolled the *die*, hoping for a six.⟩

syn bones, dice

die *vb* **1** to stop living ⟨The king *died* of old age after a long and fruitful reign.⟩

syn conk (out), croak [*slang*], demise, depart, drop, end, exit, expire, fall, go, pass (on), pass away, part, perish, succumb

rel predecease; consume, disappear, dry up, fade, fail

phrases bite the dust, buy it (*or* buy the farm), give up the ghost, kick the bucket

near ant come to, revive; linger; be, exist, subsist; flourish, prosper, thrive

ant breathe, live

2 to come to an end — see CEASE 1

3 to stop functioning — see FAIL 1

die (for) *vb* to have an earnest wish to own or enjoy — see DESIRE 1

differ *vb* **1** to be unlike; to not be the same ⟨My brother and I *differ* markedly in the way we handle money.⟩

syn contrast, vary

rel deviate, diverge, divide, fluctuate, separate

near ant accord, agree, conform, correspond

ant compare, match

2 to have a different opinion — see DISAGREE

difference *n* **1** the quality or state of being different ⟨the *difference* between right and wrong⟩

syn contrast, disagreement, discrepancy, disparateness, disparity, dissimilarity, distance, distinction, distinctiveness, distinctness, diverseness, diversity, unlikeness

rel deviance, divergence; differentiability, discriminability, distinguishability; change, modification, variation; variability, vari-

---

ance; anomalousness, incompatibility, incongruence, incongruity, incongruousness, nonconformity

near ant identicalness, identity; accordance, agreement, conformity, congruity, correspondence, parallelism, similitude; equality, equivalence, equivalency; homogeneity, homogeneousness, uniformity

ant alikeness, analogousness, analogy, community, likeness, resemblance, sameness, similarity

2 variance of opinion on a matter — see DISAGREEMENT 1

3 the act, process, or result of making different — see CHANGE 1

difference *vb* to understand or point out the difference in — see DISTINGUISH 1

different *adj* **1** being not of the same kind ⟨How are plantains *different* from bananas?⟩

syn disparate, dissimilar, distant, distinct, distinctive, distinguishable, diverse, other, unalike, unlike

rel divers, miscellaneous, mixed, several, sundry, variant, varied; differentiable, discriminable; alternate, alternative, individual, particular, peculiar, single; disproportionate, divergent, unequal

near ant equal, selfsame; equivalent, tantamount; akin, analogous, comparable, homological, homologous, related; homogeneous, homogenous, uniform

ant alike, identical, indistinguishable, kin, kindred, like, parallel, same, similar

2 not the same or shared — see SEPARATE 1

differential *adj* favoring, applying, or being unequal treatment of different classes of people — see DISCRIMINATORY

differentiate *vb* to understand or point out the difference in — see DISTINGUISH 1

differently *adv* in a different way — see OTHERWISE

difficult *adj* **1** requiring considerable physical or mental effort — see HARD 2

2 requiring exceptional skill or caution in performance or handling — see TRICKY 1

difficulty *n* **1** something that is a cause for suffering or special effort especially in the attainment of a goal ⟨the many *difficulties* that he encountered on the road from poor orphan to head of a major corporation⟩

syn adversity, asperity, hardness, hardship, rigor

rel discomfort, inconvenience, nuisance; affliction, trial, tribulation; knock, misfortune, mishap, tragedy; bar, catch, check, clog, crimp, embarrassment, handicap, hindrance, hitch, hurdle, impediment, interference, let, manacle, obstacle, obstruction, rub, shackle, snag, stop, trammel; block, chain, deterrent, encumbrance, fetter, inhibition; hump

near ant advantage, break, opportunity

2 something that makes a situation more complicated or difficult — see COMPLICATION 1

3 a feeling or declaration of disapproval or dissent — see OBJECTION

4 variance of opinion on a matter — see DISAGREEMENT 1

diffident *adj* not comfortable around people — see SHY 2

diffuse *adj* using or containing more words than necessary to express an idea — see WORDY 1

diffuseness *n* the use of too many words to express an idea — see VERBIAGE 1

dig *n* **1** a quick thrust — see ¹POKE 1

2 an act or expression showing scorn and usually intended to hurt another's feelings — see INSULT

3 digs *pl* a room or set of rooms in a private house or a block used as a separate dwelling place — see APARTMENT 1

dig *vb* **1** to hollow out or form (something) by removing earth ⟨A backhoe *dug* a hole in the backyard to make a swimming pool.⟩

syn excavate, shovel

rel dredge; burrow, claw, grub; dig in; scoop, spade; delve; mine, quarry

near ant fill (in); smooth (out *or* over)

2 to take pleasure in — see ENJOY 1

3 to have a clear idea of — see COMPREHEND 1

4 to urge or push forward with or as if with a pointed object — see PROD 1

dig (into) *vb* to search through or into — see EXPLORE 1

dig (through) *vb* to look through (as a place) carefully or thoroughly in an effort to find or discover something — see SEARCH 1

digest *n* **1** a short statement of the main points — see SUMMARY

2 a shortened version of a written work — see ABRIDGMENT

digest *vb* **1** to arrange or assign according to type — see CLASSIFY 1

2 to make into a short statement of the main points (as of a report) — see SUMMARIZE

diggings *n pl* the place where one lives — see HOME 1

digit *n* a character used to represent a mathematical value — see NUMBER 1

dignified *adj* having or showing a formal and serious or reserved manner ⟨assumed a *dignified* stance⟩ ⟨*dignified* funeral services for the fallen firefighters⟩

syn august, distinguished, imposing, portly, solemn, staid, stately

rel decorous, proper, seemly; grave, grim, sober, somber (*or* sombre); aristocratic, elegant, elevated, handsome, lordly, majestic, noble

near ant coarse, crass, crude, improper, indecent, uncouth, unseemly, vulgar

ant flighty, frivolous, giddy, goofy, silly, undignified

dignify *vb* to assign a high status or value to — see EXALT 1

dignity *n* high position within society — see RANK 2

digression *n* a departure from the subject under consideration — see TANGENT

digressive *adj* passing from one topic to another — see DISCURSIVE

dike *n* **1** a bank of earth constructed to control water — see DAM

2 a long narrow channel dug in the earth — see DITCH

dilapidated *adj* showing signs of advanced wear and tear and neglect — see SHABBY 1

dilapidation *n* the state of being unattended to or not cared for — see NEGLECT 1

dilatory *adj* moving or proceeding at less

than the normal, desirable, or required speed — see SLOW 1

dilemma *n* **1** a situation in which one has to choose between two or more equally unsatisfactory choices ⟨faced with a *dilemma* whether to cancel his vacation or miss the wedding⟩

syn quandary

rel deadlock, impasse, quagmire, stalemate, standoff; knot, problem; bind, difficulty, fix, hole, jam, pickle, pinch, plight, predicament, spot

near ant breeze, cinch, duck soup, snap

2 a difficult, puzzling, or embarrassing situation from which there is no easy escape — see PREDICAMENT

dilettante *adj* lacking or showing a lack of expert skill — see AMATEURISH

dilettante *n* a person who regularly or occasionally engages in an activity as a pastime rather than as a profession — see AMATEUR 1

diligence *n* attentive and persistent effort ⟨Through the *diligence* and ingenuity of a devoted group of citizens, the playground was reopened.⟩

syn assiduity, assiduousness, industriousness, industry

rel application, attentiveness, attention, care, concentration; doggedness, perseverance, persistence, tenacity, tirelessness; bother, effort, effortfulness, pains, painstaking, trouble

near ant carelessness, negligence, slackness; idleness, indolence, laziness

diligent *adj* involved in often constant activity — see BUSY 1

diligently *adv* with great effort or determination — see HARD 1

dillydally *vb* **1** to move or act slowly — see DELAY 1

2 to spend time doing nothing — see IDLE 1

dillydallying *adj* moving or proceeding at less than the normal, desirable, or required speed — see SLOW 1

dilute *adj* **1** not containing very much of some important element — see WEAK 3

2 containing foreign or lower-grade substances — see IMPURE 1

dilute *vb* to alter (something) for the worse with the addition of foreign or lower-grade substances — see ADULTERATE

diluted *adj* **1** not containing very much of some important element — see WEAK 3

2 containing foreign or lower-grade substances — see IMPURE 1

dim *adj* **1** being without light or without much light — see DARK 1

2 lacking a surface luster or gloss — see MATTE

3 not seen or understood clearly — see FAINT 1

dim *vb* to make dark, dim, or indistinct — see CLOUD 1

dimension *n* **1** the total amount of measurable space or surface occupied by something — see ¹SIZE

2 dimensions *pl* an area over which activity, capacity, or influence extends — see RANGE 2

diminish *vb* **1** to express scornfully one's low opinion of — see DECRY 1

2 to make smaller in amount, volume, or extent — see DECREASE 1

3 to grow less in scope or intensity especially gradually — see DECREASE 2

diminishment *n* **1** the act of making a person or a thing seem little or unimportant — see DEPRECIATION

2 the amount by which something is lessened — see DECREASE

diminution *n* the amount by which something is lessened — see DECREASE

diminutive *adj* of a size that is less than average — see SMALL 1

diminutive *n* a living thing much smaller than others of its kind — see DWARF 1

diminutiveness *n* the quality or state of being little in size — see SMALLNESS

dimmed *adj* being without light or without much light — see DARK 1

din *n* loud, confused, and usually inharmonious sound — see NOISE 1

din *vb* to say or state again — see REPEAT 1

dine *vb* **1** to take a meal ⟨They *dined* elegantly at the city's finest restaurant before taking in a show downtown.⟩

syn eat, fare, feed, partake, refresh

rel banquet, feast, repast; chow (down), dig in; glut, gorge, gormandize, overeat, overfeed, pig out; graze, nibble, nosh, pick, snack; board, mess, dine out; breakfast, lunch, sup; picnic

phrases break bread

near ant diet, fast

2 to entertain with a fancy meal — see FEAST 1

diner *n* a public establishment where meals are served to paying customers for consumption on the premises — see RESTAURANT

dinghy *n* a boat equipped with one or more sails — see SAILBOAT

dinginess *n* the state or quality of being dirty — see DIRTINESS

dingy *adj* not clean — see DIRTY 1

dinky *adj* of a size that is less than average — see SMALL 1

dinner *n* a large fancy meal often accompanied by ceremony or entertainment — see FEAST 1

dinnerware *n* dishes used for eating or serving food or drink — see TABLEWARE 2

dinning *adj* making loud, confused, and usually unharmonious sounds — see NOISY 1

dint *n* a sunken area forming a separate space — see HOLE 2

dip *n* **1** a downward slope — see DECLINE 3

2 the act or process of going to a lower level or altitude — see DESCENT 1

dip *vb* **1** to sink or push (something) briefly into or as if into a liquid ⟨First *dip* a paper towel in water.⟩ ⟨She *dipped* a hand into her pocket and pulled out a piece of candy.⟩

syn douse (*also* dowse), duck, dunk, immerse, souse, sop, submerge, submerse

rel bathe, moisten, soak, steep, wet; drench, drown, flood; dive, plunge, thrust

2 to lift out with something that holds liquid ⟨carefully *dipped* water from the bucket to the kettle⟩

syn bucket, lade, ladle, scoop, spoon

rel deplete, drain, eliminate, empty, exhaust; bleed, draw (off); dish; slop; decant, draw, pump, siphon (*also* syphon), suction

near ant pour; fill

3 to go to a lower level especially abruptly — see DROP 2

4 to lead or extend downward — see DESCEND 1

5 to take a quick or hasty look — see GLANCE 1

diplomacy *n* the ability to deal with others in touchy situations without offending them — see TACT

diplomatic *adj* having or showing tact — see TACTFUL

dipper *n* a utensil with a bowl and a handle that is used especially in cooking and serving food — see SPOON

dire *adj* 1 being or showing a sign of evil or calamity to come — see OMINOUS

2 causing fear — see FEARFUL 1

3 needing immediate attention — see ACUTE 2

4 causing or marked by an atmosphere lacking in cheer — see GLOOMY 1

direct *adj* 1 done or working without something else coming in between ⟨a zoologist whose works are based entirely on her *direct* observation of animals in the wild⟩ ⟨The virus was the *direct* cause of the disease.⟩

syn firsthand, immediate, primary

rel clinical, empirical (*also* empiric); efficient; hands-on

ant indirect, secondhand

2 free in expressing one's true feelings and opinions — see FRANK

3 going straight to the point clearly and firmly — see STRAIGHTFORWARD 1

4 free from irregularities or digressions in course — see STRAIGHT 1

direct *adv* in a direct line or course — see DIRECTLY 1

direct *vb* 1 to cause to move to a central point or along a restricted pathway — see CHANNEL

2 to issue orders to (someone) by right of authority — see COMMAND 1

3 to request the doing of by virtue of one's authority — see COMMAND 2

4 to look after and make decisions about — see CONDUCT 1

5 to point or turn (something) toward a target or goal — see AIM 1

6 to point out the way for (someone) especially from a position in front — see LEAD 1

direction *n* 1 a statement of what to do that must be obeyed by those concerned — see COMMAND 1

2 the act or activity of looking after and making decisions about something — see CONDUCT 1

3 a guiding or motivating purpose or principle — see COMPASS 1

4 a prevailing or general movement or inclination — see TREND 1

directive *n* 1 a statement of what to do that must be obeyed by those concerned — see COMMAND 1

2 an order publicly issued by an authority — see EDICT 1

3 a written communication giving information or directions — see MEMORANDUM 1

directly *adv* 1 in a direct line or course ⟨We went *directly* to the site without stopping to pick up extra supplies.⟩

syn dead, direct, due, plumb, plump, right, straight, straightway

phrases as the crow flies

near ant circuitously, deviously, veeringly

ant indirectly

2 in an honest and direct manner — see STRAIGHTFORWARD

3 in the same words — see VERBATIM

4 without delay — see IMMEDIATELY

5 at or within a short time — see SHORTLY 2

directness *n* the free expression of one's true feelings and opinions — see CANDOR 1

director *n* a person who manages or directs something — see EXECUTIVE

directorial *adj* suited for or relating to the directing of things — see EXECUTIVE

direful *adj* 1 being or showing a sign of evil or calamity to come — see OMINOUS

2 causing fear — see FEARFUL 1

dirge *n* a composition expressing one's grief over a loss — see LAMENT 2

dirt *n* 1 the loose surface material in which plants naturally grow ⟨Dig into the *dirt* to a depth of about three inches.⟩

syn clod, earth, ground, soil

rel blackland, clay, kaolin, muck, mud; dust, gravel, sand; humus, loam, topsoil; alluvium, colluvium, loess, marl, sediment, shingle, silt; mull; subsoil, substratum

2 the solid part of our planet's surface as distinguished from the sea and air — see EARTH 2

3 foul matter that mars the purity or cleanliness of something — see FILTH 1

4 solid matter discharged from an animal's alimentary canal — see DROPPING 1

dirtiness *n* the state or quality of being dirty ⟨The health inspector took the manager to task over the general *dirtiness* of the restaurant.⟩

syn dinginess, dustiness, filthiness, foulness, griminess, grubbiness, nastiness, smuttiness, soilage, squalidness, uncleanliness, uncleanness

rel discoloration, staining; impurity; messiness, mussiness, sloppiness, untidiness; insanitation, squalor; muddiness, sootiness

near ant purity

ant cleanliness, spotlessness

dirty *adj* 1 not clean ⟨After working in the factory all day, his clothes are very *dirty*.⟩

syn bedraggled, besmirched, black, blackened, dingy, dusty, filthy, foul, grimy, grubby, grungy, mucky, muddy, nasty, smutty, soiled, sordid, stained, sullied, unclean, uncleanly

rel contaminated, defiled, germy, impure, polluted, tainted; insanitary, uncleaned, unsanitary, unsterile, unsterilized, unwashed; greasy, gunky; littered, messed, messy, muddled, mussed, mussy, rumpled, scruffy, sloppy, slovenly, unkempt, untidy; raunchy, scuzzy [*slang*], shabby, sleazy, squalid

near ant clear, limpid, pure; cleaned, cleansed, combed, groomed, neat, ordered,

orderly, tidy; bleached, purified, whitened; bright, flawless, perfect, shiny, sparkling, unspotted, untouched; taintless, unblemished, undefiled, unpolluted, untainted, virgin, wholesome
ant clean, immaculate, spick-and-span (*or* spic-and-span), spotless, stainless, ultra-clean, unsoiled, unstained, unsullied
2 depicting or referring to sexual matters in a way that is unacceptable in polite society — see OBSCENE 1
3 marked by wet and windy conditions — see FOUL 1
4 not being in accordance with the rules or standards of what is fair in sport — see FOUL 2
5 not following or in accordance with standards of honor and decency — see IGNOBLE 2
6 arousing or deserving of one's loathing and disgust — see CONTEMPTIBLE 1
7 open to improper influence and especially bribery — see VENAL
dirty *vb* to make dirty ⟨She *dirtied* her new sneakers when she splashed in the puddle.⟩
syn befoul, begrime, besmirch, blacken, daub, foul, grime, mire, muck, muddy, smirch, smudge, soil, stain, sully
rel contaminate, defile, pollute, taint; discolor; confuse, disarrange, disarray, dishevel, disorder, draggle, jumble, mess, muddle
near ant decontaminate, purge, purify; disinfect, sanitize; brush, dry-clean, dust, mop, rinse, scour, scrub, sweep, wash, wipe; brighten, deodorize, freshen, renew; straighten (up)
ant clean, cleanse
disable *vb* **1** to cause severe or permanent injury to — see MAIM
2 to render powerless, ineffective, or unable to move — see PARALYZE 1
disabled *adj* deprived of the power to perform one or more natural bodily activities ⟨an entrance for *disabled* customers⟩
syn challenged, exceptional, impaired
rel special-needs; halt, paralyzed, quadriplegic; immobile, immobilized; ailing, diseased, ill, incapacitated, sick, unfit, unhealthy, unsound, unwell; blind, deaf, hard of hearing, mute
near ant bouncing, chipper, fit, hale, healthy, hearty, robust, sound, well, whole, wholesome
ant able-bodied, abled, nondisabled, unimpaired
disabuse *vb* to free from mistaken beliefs or foolish hopes — see DISILLUSION
disadvantage *n* **1** a feature of someone or something that creates difficulty for achieving success ⟨Their lack of height was a *disadvantage* on the basketball court.⟩
syn drawback, handicap, liability, minus, negative, strike
rel albatross, millstone, stranglehold; disability, impairment; failing, shortcoming; bar, catch, check, clog, crimp, embarrassment, hindrance, hitch, hurdle, impediment, interference, let, manacle, obstacle, obstruction, rub, shackle, stop, trammel

near ant vantage; head start, jump, lead, margin, start; ascendancy (*also* ascendency), better, command, control, drop, mastery, predominance, superiority, supremacy, transcendence, upper hand; prerogative, privilege; break, opportunity; aid, assistance, help
ant advantage, edge, plus
2 the negative result caused by something that creates difficulty for achieving success ⟨Intense pretrial publicity worked to our *disadvantage*.⟩
syn despite, detriment, disfavor, penalty
rel deficit, deprivation, expense, loss; damage, harm, hurt, injury; prejudice
near ant gain
ant advantage, favor
disadvantaged *adj* kept from having the necessities of life or a healthful environment — see DEPRIVED
disadvantageous *adj* opposed to one's interests — see ADVERSE 1
disaffect *vb* **1** to cause to change from friendly or loving to unfriendly or uncaring — see ESTRANGE
2 to make discontented — see DISCONTENT
disaffection *n* the loss of friendship or affection — see ESTRANGEMENT
disagree *vb* to have a different opinion ⟨The leader thought we were still headed north on the trail, but I *disagreed*.⟩
syn differ, dissent
rel clash, collide, conflict, contrast; counter, debate, object, oppose, protest, resist; contest, dispute; argue, bicker, fall out, quarrel
phrases take issue
near ant accede, accept, acquiesce, comply, consent, defer; affiliate, ally, associate, collaborate, come round, compromise, cooperate, get along, side
ant agree, assent, concur
disagree (with) *vb* to make an assertion that is contrary to one made by (another) — see CONTRADICT 1
disagreeable *adj* **1** having or showing a habitually bad temper — see ILL-TEMPERED
2 not giving pleasure to the mind or senses — see UNPLEASANT
disagreeing *adj* not being in agreement or harmony — see INCONSISTENT 1
disagreement *n* **1** variance of opinion on a matter ⟨There was some *disagreement* about what color the missing sweater actually was.⟩
syn controversy, debate, difference, difficulty, disputation, dispute, dissension (*also* dissention)
rel clash, collision, conflict, confliction, discord; combat, contention, strife, struggle; altercation, argument, bicker, falling-out, fight, kickup, misunderstanding, quarrel, set-to
near ant acceptance, compliance; concord, peace
ant accord, agreement, consensus, harmony, unanimity
2 an often noisy or angry expression of differing opinions — see ARGUMENT 1
3 the quality or state of being different — see DIFFERENCE 1
disallow *vb* **1** to declare not to be true — see DENY 1
2 to be unwilling to grant — see DENY 2

---

syn synonym(s)   *rel* related words
ant antonym(s)   *near ant* near antonym(s)

disallowance *n* 1 an unwillingness to grant something asked for — see DENIAL 1
2 a refusal to confirm the truth of a statement — see DENIAL 2

disappear *vb* to cease to be visible ⟨The stranger *disappeared* into the mists, never to be seen again.⟩
syn dissolve, evanesce, evaporate, fade, flee, fly, melt, sink, vanish
rel blank (out), clear, disperse, dissipate, dissolve, dry up; blur, dim
phrases drop out of sight
near ant arrive, break out, come out, emerge, issue, loom, show up
ant appear, materialize

disappoint *vb* to fall short in satisfying the expectation or hope of ⟨They were *disappointed* by the outcome of the big game.⟩
syn cheat, dissatisfy, fail, let down
rel bum (out), chagrin, discontent, disgruntle, displease, distress, upset; disenchant, disillusion; deceive, delude, mock
near ant fulfill (*or* fulfil); gladden
ant content, gratify, satisfy

disappointment *n* 1 the emotion felt when one's expectations are not met ⟨We felt keen *disappointment* when our offer on the house was rejected.⟩
syn dismay, dissatisfaction, frustration, letdown
rel crestfallenness, discontent, discontentedness, discontentment, disgruntlement; disenchantment, disillusionment; blues, dejectedness, dejection, depression, desolateness, desolation, despondency, disconsolateness, distress, doldrums, dolefulness, dolor, downheartedness, dreariness, dumps, gloom, gloominess, joylessness, melancholy, mopes, oppression, sadness, sorrow, unhappiness; chagrin, discomfiture
near ant fulfillment (*or* fulfilment); bliss, felicity, gladness, happiness, joy
ant content, contentedness, contentment, gratification, satisfaction
2 something that disappoints ⟨After all the publicity and high expectations, the sequel to the movie blockbuster was a huge *disappointment*.⟩
syn bummer, letdown
rel anticlimax, failure, fiasco, fizzle; lemon, loser
near ant success, winner; relief

disapprobation *n* refusal to accept as right or desirable — see DISAPPROVAL

disapproval *n* refusal to accept as right or desirable ⟨Thus far, every one of her choices for college has met with her parents' *disapproval*.⟩
syn deprecation, disapprobation, discountenance, disfavor, dislike, displeasure
rel distaste; rejection, thumbs-down; blame, censure, condemnation, criticism, denunciation, dispraise, opprobrium, reprehension, reproach, reprobation; antagonism, antipathy, hostility; belittlement, disparagement, objection, opposition
near ant acclaim, commendation, praise; endorsement (*also* indorsement), sanction, thumbs-up; empathy, sympathy
ant approbation, approval, favor

disapprove *vb* 1 to be unwilling to grant — see DENY 2

2 to show unwillingness to accept, do, engage in, or agree to — see DECLINE 1

disapprove (of) *vb* to hold an unfavorable opinion of ⟨My sister *disapproves of* my decision.⟩
syn deprecate, discountenance, disfavor, dislike, reprove, tsk-tsk
rel object (to), pooh-pooh (*also* pooh), reject, reprehend, reprobate, scorn; censure, condemn, criticize, denounce, discommend; chide, rebuke, reproach, scold
phrases look down one's nose (on)
near ant endorse (*also* indorse), sanction, support; adore, delight (in), dig, enjoy, fancy, groove (on), love, relish, revel (in)
ant approve, favor, like

disarm *vb* 1 to reduce the size and strength of the armed forces of ⟨The defeated nation was *disarmed* so that it would never again be a threat to international order.⟩
syn demilitarize
rel demobilize
near ant equip, reequip, weapon; embattle, mechanize, mobilize
ant arm, militarize
2 to lessen the anger or agitation of — see PACIFY 1

disarmament *n* the reduction or elimination of a country's armed forces or weapons ⟨The ambassador spoke at length about the possible unilateral *disarmament* of his country.⟩
syn demilitarization
rel demobilization
near ant equipment, reequipment; mobilization
ant armament, militarization

disarming *adj* 1 having qualities that tend to make one loved — see LOVABLE
2 likely or intended to win one's affection — see INGRATIATING
3 tending to lessen or avoid conflict or hostility — see PACIFIC 1

disarrange *vb* to undo the proper order or arrangement of — see DISORDER

disarranged *adj* lacking in order, neatness, and often cleanliness — see MESSY

disarrangement *n* a state in which everything is out of order — see CHAOS

disarray *n* a state in which everything is out of order — see CHAOS

disarray *vb* to undo the proper order or arrangement of — see DISORDER

disarrayed *adj* lacking in order, neatness, and often cleanliness — see MESSY

disassemble *vb* 1 to take apart ⟨You can *disassemble* the bookcase for easy storage.⟩
syn break down, demount, dismantle, dismember, knock down, take down
rel detach, disengage; break up, disaggregate, disarticulate, disconnect, disjoin, disjoint, dissever, disunite, divide, separate
near ant build, erect, pitch; combine, unite
ant assemble, construct
2 to go off in different directions and cease to exist as a body or unified whole — see DISPERSE 1

disaster *n* 1 a sudden violent event that brings about great loss or destruction ⟨Hurricanes are natural *disasters*.⟩
syn calamity, cataclysm, catastrophe, debacle (*also* débâcle), tragedy

rel collapse, crash, meltdown; Armageddon, doomsday, end-time; convulsion, paroxysm, upheaval; accident, casualty, fatality; misadventure, mischance, misfortune, mishap; blast, blow, double whammy, one-two (*or* one-two punch)

near ant godsend, manna, windfall

2 something that has failed — see FAILURE 3

disastrous *adj* **1** bringing about ruin or misfortune — see FATAL 1

2 causing or tending to cause destruction — see DESTRUCTIVE 1

disavow *vb* **1** to declare not to be true — see DENY 1

2 to refuse to acknowledge as one's own or as one's responsibility — see DISCLAIM 1

disavowal *n* a refusal to confirm the truth of a statement — see DENIAL 2

disband *vb* **1** to cease to exist or cause to cease to exist as a group or organization ⟨The university *disbanded* the committee after the report had been submitted.⟩ ⟨The rock group *disbanded* upon finishing their farewell tour.⟩

syn break up, disperse, dissolve

rel demobilize

near ant incorporate; consolidate; hang together

ant band, join, unite

2 to cause (members of a group) to move widely apart — see SCATTER 1

disbandment *n* an act or process in which something scatters or is scattered — see SCATTERING 1

disbelief *n* refusal to accept something as true ⟨Their story explaining their absence was met with *disbelief*.⟩

syn incredulity, unbelief

rel discredit, distrust, doubt, mistrust, skepticism, suspicion, uncertainty; denial, rejection, repudiation, unfaith

near ant acceptance, conviction, faith; trust

ant belief, credence, credit

disbelieve *vb* to think not to be true or real ⟨Many *disbelieved* the medium's claims that she could communicate with the spirits of the dead.⟩

syn discredit, negate

rel deny, reject, repudiate; distrust, doubt, mistrust, suspect; debunk, disprove, refute; deride, pooh-pooh (*also* pooh), scoff (at)

near ant trust

ant accept, believe, credit, swallow

disbeliever *n* a person who is always ready to doubt or question the truth or existence of something — see SKEPTIC

disbelieving *adj* inclined to doubt or question claims — see SKEPTICAL 1

disburden *vb* **1** to empty or rid of cargo — see UNLOAD 1

2 to set (a person or thing) free of something that encumbers — see RID

disburse *vb* to hand over or use up in payment — see SPEND 1

disbursement *n* **1** a payment made in the course of achieving a result — see EXPENSE

2 the act of offering money in exchange for goods or services — see PAYMENT 1

3 the act or process of giving out something to each member of a group — see DISTRIBUTION 1

discard *n* something separated from a group or lot for not being as good as the others — see CULL

discard *vb* to get rid of as useless or unwanted ⟨You should *discard* an old, torn sweater.⟩

syn cashier, cast (off), chuck, ditch, dump, fling (off *or* away), jettison, junk, lose, pitch, reject, scrap, shed, shuck (off), throw away, throw out, toss, unload

rel abandon, abdicate, desert, forsake; dismiss; abolish, annihilate, eliminate, eradicate, expunge, exterminate, extinguish, extirpate, liquidate, remove, root (out), stamp (out), wipe out

phrases dispose of, set aside

near ant adopt, embrace, take on; employ, use, utilize; hold, hold back, keep, retain

discarding *n* the getting rid of whatever is unwanted or useless — see DISPOSAL 1

discern *vb* **1** to make note of (something) through the use of one's eyes — see SEE 1

2 to understand or point out the difference in — see DISTINGUISH 1

3 to have a clear idea of — see COMPREHEND 1

discernible *also* **discernable** *adj* able to be perceived by a sense or by the mind — see PERCEPTIBLE

discerning *adj* having or showing deep understanding and intelligent application of knowledge — see WISE 1

discernment *n* the ability to understand inner qualities or relationships — see WISDOM 1

discharge *n* **1** a directed propelling of a missile by a firearm or artillery piece — see SHOT 1

2 a freeing from an obligation or responsibility — see RELEASE 1

3 the termination of the employment of an employee or a work force often temporarily — see LAYOFF

4 the doing of an action — see COMMISSION 2

discharge *vb* **1** to cause (a projectile) to be driven forward with force — see SHOOT 1

2 to empty or rid of cargo — see UNLOAD 1

3 to give what is owed for — see PAY 2

4 to release (as from slavery or confinement) — see FREE 1

5 to throw or give off — see EMIT 1

6 to cause a weapon to release a missile with great force — see SHOOT 2

7 to let go from office, service, or employment — see DISMISS 1

disciple *n* one who follows the opinions or teachings of another — see FOLLOWER 1

disciplinary *adj* inflicting, involving, or serving as punishment — see PUNITIVE

discipline *n* **1** a region of activity, knowledge, or influence — see FIELD 2

2 suffering, loss, or hardship imposed in response to a crime or offense — see PUNISHMENT

3 the checking of one's true feelings and

---

impulses when dealing with others — see
CONSTRAINT 1

discipline *vb* to inflict a penalty on for a
fault or crime — see PUNISH

disciplining *adj* inflicting, involving, or
serving as punishment — see PUNITIVE

disclaim *vb* 1 to refuse to acknowledge as
one's own or as one's responsibility ⟨He
disclaimed any part in the prank.⟩
syn deny, disavow, disown, repudiate
rel contradict, disallow, gainsay, negate,
negative, refuse, reject; challenge, confute, criticize, disprove, rebut, refute; dispute, question; abdicate, abjure, recant,
renounce, retract
phrases wash one's hands of
near ant accept, adopt, embrace, espouse;
admit, concede, confess, grant; affirm, announce, assert, aver, declare, maintain,
profess, submit; authenticate, confirm,
corroborate, substantiate, validate, verify
ant acknowledge, avow, claim, own, recognize
2 to declare not to be true — see DENY 1

disclaimer *n* 1 a document containing a
declaration of an intentional giving up of a
right, claim, or privilege — see WAIVER
2 a refusal to confirm the truth of a statement — see DENIAL 2

disclose *vb* to make known (as information
previously kept secret) — see REVEAL 1

disclosure *n* the act or an instance of
making known something previously unknown or concealed — see REVELATION

discombobulate *vb* to throw into a state
of mental uncertainty — see CONFUSE 1

discomfit *vb* 1 to prevent from achieving a
goal — see FRUSTRATE 1
2 to throw into a state of self-conscious
distress — see EMBARRASS 1

discomfiting *adj* causing embarrassment
— see AWKWARD 3

discomfiture *n* the emotional state of being made self-consciously uncomfortable
— see EMBARRASSMENT 1

discomfort *vb* to trouble the mind of; to
make uneasy — see DISTURB 1

discomforting *adj* 1 causing discomfort
— see UNCOMFORTABLE 1
2 causing worry or anxiety — see TROU-
BLESOME

discommode *vb* to cause discomfort to or
trouble for — see INCONVENIENCE

discommoding *adj* causing difficulty, discomfort, or annoyance — see INCONVE-
NIENT 1

discompose *vb* 1 to trouble the mind of;
to make uneasy — see DISTURB 1
2 to undo the proper order or arrangement of — see DISORDER

discomposing *adj* causing worry or anxiety — see TROUBLESOME

disconcert *vb* to throw into a state of self-
conscious distress — see EMBARRASS 1

disconcerting *adj* causing embarrassment — see AWKWARD 3

disconnect *vb* to set or force apart — see
SEPARATE 1

disconnected *adj* 1 not clearly or logically connected — see INCOHERENT 1
2 not physically attached to another unit
— see SEPARATE 2

disconsolate *adj* 1 causing or marked by

an atmosphere lacking in cheer — see
GLOOMY 1
2 feeling unhappiness — see SAD 1

disconsolateness *n* a state or spell of low
spirits — see SADNESS

discontent *adj* having a feeling that one
has been wronged or thwarted in one's
ambitions — see DISCONTENTED

discontent *n* the condition of being dissatisfied with one's life or situation ⟨The
rebels worked to stir up *discontent* among
the citizens.⟩
syn discontentedness, discontentment, disgruntlement, displeasure, dissatisfaction
rel bitterness, resentment; aggrievement,
disquiet, perturbation, uneasiness; blues,
dejection, depression, desolateness, desolation, despondency, disconsolateness,
doldrums, dolefulness, dolor, downheartedness, dreariness, dumps; misery, sadness, sorrow, unhappiness, wretchedness
near ant bliss, felicity, gladness, happiness, joy, lightheartedness; exultation, jubilation, triumph
ant contentedness, contentment, pleasure,
satisfaction

discontent *vb* to make discontented ⟨The
ongoing lack of decent food *discontented*
the soldiers in the rebel army.⟩
syn disaffect, disgruntle, displease, dissatisfy
rel alienate, estrange; aggrieve, agitate,
discompose, disquiet, disturb, perturb, upset; annoy, irk, irritate, nettle, peeve; depress, sadden
near ant delight, gladden, tickle; calm,
soothe, tranquilize (*also* tranquillize)
ant content, gratify, please, satisfy

discontented *adj* having a feeling that
one has been wronged or thwarted in
one's ambitions ⟨He was becoming increasingly *discontented* with his job.⟩
syn aggrieved, discontent, disgruntled,
displeased, dissatisfied, malcontent
rel disappointed, disenchanted, disillusioned, frustrated, unfulfilled; disquieted,
disturbed, perturbed, upset; dejected, depressed, despairing, despondent, disconsolate, doleful, down, downcast, downhearted, forlorn, hangdog, inconsolable, joyless,
low-spirited, miserable, mournful, sad,
sorrowful, unhappy
phrases out of joint
near ant blissful, delighted, glad, happy,
joyful, joyous; elated, exultant, jubilant,
triumphant
ant content, contented, gratified, pleased,
satisfied

discontentedness *n* the condition of being dissatisfied with one's life or situation
— see DISCONTENT

discontentment *n* the condition of being
dissatisfied with one's life or situation —
see DISCONTENT

discontinuance *n* the stopping of a process or activity — see END 1

discontinue *vb* 1 to bring (as an action or operation) to an immediate end — see STOP 1
2 to stop doing (something) permanently
— see QUIT 2
3 to come to an end — see CEASE 1

discontinuity *n* 1 an open space in a barrier (as a wall or hedge) — see GAP 1
2 a break in continuity — see GAP 2

discontinuous *adj* lacking in steadiness or regularity of occurrence — see FITFUL

discord *n* a lack of agreement or harmony ⟨The *discord* between two of the members threatened to tear our team of researchers apart.⟩

syn conflict, discordance, dissension (*also* dissention), dissent, dissidence, disunion, disunity, division, friction, schism, strife, variance, war, warfare

rel clash, collision, competition, contention; altercation, argument, bicker, brawl, debate, disagreement, dispute, divide, fissure; falling-out, fight, hassle, jar, mix-up, quarrel, row, run-in, scrap, spat, squabble, tiff, wrangle; incompatibility, incongruence, incongruity, incongruousness, inconsistence, inconsistency, inconsonance, inharmoniousness; animosity, antagonism, antipathy, cold war, enmity, hostility, ill will, rancor

near ant concurrence, cooperation

ant accord, agreement, concord, concordance, harmony, peace

discord *vb* to be out of harmony or agreement usually noticeably — see CLASH

discordance *n* **1** a lack of agreement or harmony — see DISCORD

2 loud, confused, and usually inharmonious sound — see NOISE 1

discordant *adj* **1** marked by or producing a harsh combination of sounds — see DISSONANT

2 making loud, confused, and usually unharmonious sounds — see NOISY 1

3 feeling or displaying eagerness to fight — see BELLIGERENT

4 not being in agreement or harmony — see INCONSISTENT 1

discount *n* something that is or may be subtracted — see DEDUCTION 1

discount *vb* **1** to dismiss as of little importance — see EXCUSE 1

2 to express scornfully one's low opinion of — see DECRY 1

discountenance *n* refusal to accept as right or desirable — see DISAPPROVAL

discountenance *vb* **1** to hold an unfavorable opinion of — see DISAPPROVE (OF)

2 to throw into a state of self-conscious distress — see EMBARRASS 1

discourage *vb* **1** to lessen the courage or confidence of ⟨I didn't let losing *discourage* me from trying again.⟩

syn chill, daunt, demoralize, dishearten, dismay, dispirit, frustrate, unnerve

rel browbeat, bully, cow, intimidate; depress, sadden, weigh; afflict, try; damp, dampen, deaden; distress, trouble; bother, irk, vex, worry; debilitate, enfeeble, undermine, weaken; frighten, horrify, scare

phrases throw cold water on

near ant buoy (up), cheer, gladden; animate, enliven, invigorate; enforce, fortify, strengthen; assure, reassure; boost, energize, excite, galvanize, inspire, lift, provoke, quicken, rally, stimulate, stir

ant embolden, encourage, hearten, nerve, steel

2 to steer (a person) from an activity or course of action ⟨The higher fines may help *discourage* drivers from speeding on the highway.⟩

syn deter, dissuade, inhibit

rel divert; unsell; repel

near ant egg (on), exhort, goad, prod, urge; impel, induce, prompt

ant encourage, persuade

discouragement *n* the state of being discouraged ⟨I tried desperately to avoid *discouragement* after failing the bar exam twice.⟩

syn demoralization, despair, despondency, disheartenment, dismay, dispiritedness

rel blues, dejection, depression, dumps, gloom, melancholy, mopes; defeatism, pessimism, resignation

near ant optimism, sanguinity

ant encouragement

discourse *n* talking or a talk between two or more people — see CONVERSATION

discourse *vb* **1** to give a formal often extended talk on a subject — see TALK 1

2 to talk as if giving an important and formal speech — see ORATE 1

discourteous *adj* showing a lack of manners or consideration for others — see IMPOLITE

discourteousness *n* rude behavior — see DISCOURTESY

discourtesy *n* rude behavior ⟨The courtiers shuddered at the *discourtesy* shown to the king.⟩

syn discourteousness, disrespect, impertinence, impoliteness, impudence, incivility, inconsiderateness, inconsideration, insolence, rudeness, ungraciousness

rel audacity, boldness, brashness, brassiness, forwardness, sauciness, shamelessness; boorishness, caddishness, churlishness, clownishness, crudeness, loutishness, vulgarity; abruptness, brusqueness, crustiness, curtness, gruffness, sharpness; crabbedness, crossness, disagreeableness, grumpiness, sullenness, surliness; impropriety, inappropriateness, incorrectness, indecency, unfitness, unsuitability; arrogance, conceit, conceitedness, presumption, pretense (*or* pretence), pretension, pretentiousness

near ant humility, meekness, modesty; deference, dutifulness, respectfulness, submissiveness; acceptability, appropriateness, correctness, decency, decorousness, fitness, goodness, propriety, respectability, respectableness, rightness, seemliness, suitability, suitableness; affability, cordiality, friendliness, geniality, hospitality, kindness; felicitousness, grace, gracefulness

ant civility, considerateness, consideration, courtesy, gentility, graciousness, politeness, politesse, thoughtfulness

discover *vb* **1** to come to an awareness of ⟨I was startled to *discover* that my keys were missing.⟩

syn ascertain, catch on (to), find out, hear, learn, realize, see, wise (up)

rel hit (on *or* upon), tumble (to); descry, detect, encounter, espy, see, spot; calculate, dope (out), figure out, find, puzzle

---

(out); discern, mind, note, observe, perceive; divine

phrases get wind of

near ant miss, overlook; disregard, ignore; forget, unlearn; blanket, blot out, cloak, conceal, cover, curtain, enshroud, hide, mask, occult, screen, shroud, veil

2 to come upon after searching, study, or effort — see FIND 1

3 to make known (as information previously kept secret) — see REVEAL 1

discovery *n* **1** the act or process of sighting or learning the existence of something for the first time ⟨the *discovery* of a new species of frog⟩

syn detection, finding, spotting, unearthing

rel awareness, espial, notice; disclosure, exposure, revelation, uncovering, unveiling; creation, invention; exploration; rediscovery

near ant disappearance, loss; concealment, hiding

2 something discovered ⟨His many zoological *discoveries* include several species of birds.⟩

syn find

rel pay dirt, strike; breakthrough

discredit *n* the state of having lost the esteem of others — see DISGRACE 1

discredit *vb* **1** to reduce to a lower standing in one's own eyes or in others' eyes — see HUMBLE

2 to think not to be true or real — see DISBELIEVE

3 to prove to be false — see DISPROVE

discreditable *adj* not respectable — see DISREPUTABLE

discreet *adj* **1** having or showing good judgment and restraint especially in conduct or speech ⟨He was very *discreet*, only saying what was necessary.⟩

syn intelligent, judicious, prudent

rel cautious, circumspect, cozy; forehanded, foresighted, foresightful, forethoughtful; discerning, discriminating, sage, sane, sapient, senseful, sensible, wise; canny, provident; astute, perspicacious, sagacious, shrewd

near ant careless, heedless, incautious, rash; improvident, shortsighted; foolish, unwise

ant imprudent, indiscreet, injudicious

2 not readily seen or noticed — see UNOBTRUSIVE

discreetness *n* the ability to make intelligent decisions especially in everyday matters — see COMMON SENSE

discrepancy *n* the quality or state of being different — see DIFFERENCE 1

discrepant *adj* not being in agreement or harmony — see INCONSISTENT 1

discrete *adj* not physically attached to another unit — see SEPARATE 2

discreteness *n* the state of being kept distinct — see SEPARATION 2

discretion *n* **1** the ability to make intelligent decisions especially in everyday matters — see COMMON SENSE

2 the power, right, or opportunity to choose — see CHOICE 2

3 the checking of one's true feelings and impulses when dealing with others — see CONSTRAINT 1

discretionary *adj* subject to one's freedom of choice — see OPTIONAL

discriminate *vb* to understand or point out the difference in — see DISTINGUISH 1

discriminating *adj* **1** favoring, applying, or being unequal treatment of different classes of people — see DISCRIMINATORY

2 serving to identify as belonging to an individual or group — see CHARACTERISTIC 1

discrimination *n* the state of being kept distinct — see SEPARATION 2

discriminative *adj* favoring, applying, or being unequal treatment of different classes of people — see DISCRIMINATORY

discriminatory *adj* favoring, applying, or being unequal treatment of different classes of people ⟨a company that was fined for its *discriminatory* practices⟩

syn differential, discriminating, discriminative

rel biased, inequitable, partial, partisan, prejudiced, prejudicial, unequal, unfair, unjust; clubby, selective; segregative

near ant equal, equitable, fair, just; impartial, neutral, objective, unbiased, uncolored, unprejudiced

ant nondiscriminatory

discursive *adj* passing from one topic to another ⟨The speaker's *discursive* style made it difficult to understand his point.⟩

syn desultory, digressive, leaping, maundering, rambling, wandering

rel circuitous, deviating, devious, indirect, roundabout

near ant coherent, consistent, logical; direct, focused (*also* focussed), straightforward, undeviating

discuss *vb* to talk about (an issue) usually from various points of view and for the purpose of arriving at a decision or opinion ⟨We *discussed* the new proposal for the school stadium.⟩

syn agitate, argue, bandy, canvass (*also* canvas), debate, dispute, moot, talk over

rel review, speak (about), talk (about); broach, introduce, propound, raise, stir up; forge, talk out, thrash (out); chew over, consider, deliberate, weigh

discussion *n* **1** an exchange of views for the purpose of exploring a subject or deciding an issue ⟨The *discussion* about the club budget went on for hours.⟩

syn argument, colloquy, conference, consult, council, counsel, debate, deliberation, dialogue (*also* dialog), give-and-take, palaver, parley, talk

rel bull session, chat room, forum, meeting, roundtable, seminar, skull session (*also* skull practice), symposium, talkathon; chat, conversation, rap, words; discourse; bargaining, consultancy, negotiation, pourparler

2 talking or a talk between two or more people — see CONVERSATION

disdain *n* open dislike for someone or something considered unworthy of one's concern or respect — see CONTEMPT

disdain *vb* to show contempt for — see SCORN 1

disdainful *adj* feeling or showing open dislike for someone or something regarded as undeserving of respect or concern — see CONTEMPTUOUS 1

2 having or displaying feelings of scorn for what is regarded as beneath oneself — see PROUD 1

3 intended to make a person or thing seem of little importance or value — see DEROGATORY

disease *n* an abnormal state that disrupts a plant's or animal's normal bodily functioning ⟨They caught a rare *disease* while they were traveling.⟩

syn ail, ailment, bug, complaint, complication, condition, disorder, fever, ill, illness, infirmity, malady, sickness, trouble

rel contagion, contagious disease; contagium, infection; attack, bout, fit, spell; debility, decrepitude, feebleness, frailness, lameness, sickliness, unhealthiness, unsoundness, unwellness, weakness; malaise, matter, pip; pest, pestilence, plague

near ant fitness, healthiness, heartiness, robustness, soundness, wholeness, wholesomeness; fettle, shape

ant health, wellness

disembark *vb* 1 to go ashore from a ship ⟨The cruise passengers *disembarked* as soon as they came to the terminal in Miami.⟩

syn debark, land

rel beach; anchor, dock, put in

near ant board, get (on); weigh (anchor)

ant embark

2 to come down from something (as a vehicle) — see ALIGHT 2

disembowel *vb* to take the internal organs out of — see GUT

disenchant *vb* to free from mistaken beliefs or foolish hopes — see DISILLUSION

disencumber *vb* 1 to empty or rid of cargo — see UNLOAD 1

2 to set (a person or thing) free of something that encumbers — see RID

disencumbered *adj* no longer burdened with something unpleasant or painful — see FREE 2

disengage *vb* to set free from entanglement or difficulty — see EXTRICATE

disentangle *vb* 1 to separate the various strands of — see UNRAVEL 1

2 to set free from entanglement or difficulty — see EXTRICATE

disfavor *n* 1 a strong feeling of not liking or approving — see DISLIKE 1

2 refusal to accept as right or desirable — see DISAPPROVAL

3 the negative result caused by something that creates difficulty for achieving success — see DISADVANTAGE 2

disfavor *vb* 1 to feel dislike for — see DISLIKE 1

2 to hold an unfavorable opinion of — see DISAPPROVE (OF)

disfigure *vb* to reduce the soundness, effectiveness, or perfection of — see DAMAGE 1

disfigurement *n* something that spoils the appearance or completeness of a thing — see BLEMISH

disgorge *vb* to violently throw out or off (something from within) — see ERUPT 1

disgrace *n* 1 the state of having lost the

esteem of others ⟨The students who cheated were in *disgrace* with their schoolmates.⟩

syn discredit, dishonor, disrepute, ignominy, infamy, odium, opprobrium, reproach, shame

rel scandal; contempt, despite, disdain, scorn; deprecation, disapprobation, disapproval, disfavor; abasement, debasement, debasing, degradation, dust, humbling, humiliation; blot, brand, shadow, slur, smirch, spot, stain, stigma, taint

near ant admiration, appreciation, estimation, regard; awe, fear, reverence; fame, glory, renown, repute

ant esteem, honor, respect

2 a cause of shame ⟨The exposure of his criminal record was a huge *disgrace* for the councilman.⟩

syn dishonor, opprobrium, reflection, reproach, scandal

rel blot, brand, slur, smirch, spot, stain, stigma, taint

near ant boast, glory, jewel, pride, treasure

ant credit, honor

3 a regrettable or blameworthy act — see CRIME 2

disgrace *vb* to reduce to a lower standing in one's own eyes or in others' eyes — see HUMBLE

disgraceful *adj* not respectable — see DISREPUTABLE

disgruntle *vb* 1 to cause to change from friendly or loving to unfriendly or uncaring — see ESTRANGE

2 to make discontented — see DISCONTENT

disgruntled *adj* having a feeling that one has been wronged or thwarted in one's ambitions — see DISCONTENTED

disgruntlement *n* 1 the condition of being dissatisfied with one's life or situation — see DISCONTENT

2 the loss of friendship or affection — see ESTRANGEMENT

disguise *n* 1 clothing put on to hide one's true identity or imitate someone or something else ⟨Mardi Gras revelers dressed in a colorful array of outlandish *disguises*.⟩

syn camouflage, costume, guise

rel domino, mask, veil, visor (*also* vizor), vizard; costumery, dress, getup, outfit, rig; coloring, makeup, paint

2 a display of emotion or behavior that is insincere or intended to deceive — see MASQUERADE

disguise *vb* 1 to change the dress or looks of so as to conceal true identity ⟨The spies *disguised* themselves as harmless tourists.⟩

syn camouflage, cloak, dress up, mask

rel blanket, blot out, conceal, cover, curtain, enshroud, hide, obscure, occult, screen, shroud, veil; affect, assume, counterfeit, dissemble, dissimulate, feign, pose, pretend, sham, simulate; act, fake, impersonate, masquerade, play; gild, gloss (over), varnish, whitewash

near ant display, exhibit, expose, flaunt, parade, show, uncloak, unclothe, uncover, undrape, unveil; bare, betray, disclose, discover, divulge, expose, reveal

ant unmask

2 to keep secret or shut off from view — see ¹HIDE 2

disgust *n* a dislike so strong as to cause

stomach upset or queasiness ⟨We turned from the grisly scene with *disgust*.⟩

syn aversion, distaste, horror, loathing, nausea, repugnance, repulsion, revulsion

rel abhorrence, abomination, antipathy, execration, hate, hatred; allergy, averseness, disapproval, disfavor, disinclination, dislike, disliking, displeasure

near ant appetite, bent, fancy, favor, fondness, like, liking, love, partiality, penchant, predilection, preference, propensity, relish, shine, taste, use

disgust *vb* to cause to feel disgust ⟨The smell of the greasy food *disgusted* me.⟩

syn nauseate, put off, repel, repulse, revolt, sicken, turn off

rel displease, distress; appall (*also* appal), disquiet, horrify; affront, insult, offend, outrage, shock

phrases turn one's stomach

near ant allure, attract, beguile, bewitch, captivate, charm, disarm, draw, enchant, entice, fascinate, lure, pull, seduce, tempt; delight, gratify, please, rejoice, tickle; enrapture, enthrall (*or* enthral); entrance; appeal (to), interest, intrigue

disgusted *adj* filled with disgust — see SICK 2

dish *n* 1 a usually circular utensil for holding something (as food) ⟨We threw all of the ingredients for the salsa into a *dish* and mixed them together.⟩

syn vessel

rel bowl, casserole, charger, cup, plate, platter, salver, saucer, server, tray, waiter

2 a physically attractive person — see DOLL 2

3 information or opinion that is widely disseminated without any authority or confirmation of accuracy — see RUMOR

dish *vb* to relate sometimes questionable or secret information of a personal nature — see GOSSIP

dishearten *vb* to lessen the courage or confidence of — see DISCOURAGE 1

disheartenment *n* the state of being discouraged — see DISCOURAGEMENT

dishevel *vb* to undo the proper order or arrangement of — see DISORDER

disheveled *or* **dishevelled** *adj* lacking in order, neatness, and often cleanliness — see MESSY

dishonest *adj* 1 telling or containing lies ⟨I think he is being *dishonest* about how much he knows.⟩ ⟨*dishonest* statements on the claims form⟩

syn lying, mendacious, untruthful

rel erroneous, fallacious, false, misleading, untrue; double-dealing, hypocrite, hypocritical, insincere, mealymouthed, smooth-tongued, two-faced; perjurious

near ant candid, open, plainspoken, straightforward; earnest, sincere, true; conscientious, moral, principled, scrupulous; dependable, reliable, trustworthy, trusty; decent, ethical, honorable, just, respectable, righteous, right-minded, straight, upright, upstanding, virtuous

ant honest, truthful, veracious

2 given to or marked by cheating and deception ⟨*dishonest* car dealers who roll back mileage gauges⟩ ⟨*dishonest* business deals that landed him in jail⟩

syn crooked, deceptive, double-dealing, fast, fraudulent, guileful, rogue, shady, sharp, shifty, underhand, underhanded

rel unconscionable, unethical, unprincipled, unscrupulous; deceitful, deceiving, deluding, delusive, delusory, false; artful, beguiling, cagey (*also* cagy), crafty, cunning, foxy, slick, sly, subtle, wily; defrauding, devious, furtive, slippery, sneaking, sneaky, trickish, tricky; insidious, perfidious, treacherous

near ant conscientious, decent, ethical, honorable, just, scrupulous, upright; forthright, straightforward

ant aboveboard, honest, straight

3 marked by, based on, or done by the use of dishonest methods to acquire something of value — see FRAUDULENT 1

dishonesty *n* 1 the tendency to tell lies ⟨If you gain a reputation for *dishonesty*, no one will believe you even when you're telling the truth.⟩

syn deceit, deceitfulness, falsehood, mendacity, untruthfulness

rel artifice, craft, craftiness, crookedness, cunning, dissembling, dissimulation, double-dealing, duplicity, fakery, foxiness, guile, insincerity, trickishness, wiliness; falseness; hypocrisy

near ant honor, incorruptibility; candidness, candor, frankness, good faith, sincerity, straightforwardness; dependability, reliability, reliableness, trustworthiness; accuracy, objectivity; authenticity, correctness, genuineness; credibility

ant honesty, integrity, probity, truthfulness, veraciousness, veracity, verity

2 the inclination or practice of misleading others through lies or trickery — see DECEIT 1

dishonor *n* 1 the state of having lost the esteem of others — see DISGRACE 1

2 a cause of shame — see DISGRACE 2

dishonor *vb* to reduce to a lower standing in one's own eyes or in others' eyes — see HUMBLE

dishonorable *adj* 1 not following or in accordance with standards of honor and decency — see IGNOBLE 2

2 not respectable — see DISREPUTABLE

disillusion *vb* to free from mistaken beliefs or foolish hopes ⟨We were *disillusioned* when we saw how the movie star acted in real life.⟩

syn disabuse, disenchant, undeceive

rel sophisticate; advise, apprise, clue (in), fill in, wise (up); debunk, expose, refute, show up, uncloak, uncover, unmask; disclose, divulge, spill, tell, unveil

near ant beguile, bluff, cozen, delude, dupe, fool, gull, hoax, hoodwink, kid, misguide, misinform, mislead, misrepresent, snow, take in, trick

disinclination *n* 1 a lack of willingness or desire to do or accept something — see RELUCTANCE

2 a strong feeling of not liking or approving — see DISLIKE 1

disinclined *adj* slow to begin or proceed with a course of action because of doubts or uncertainty — see HESITANT

disintegrate *vb* 1 to go through decomposition — see DECAY 1

2 to reduce to fine particles — see POWDER

disinter *vb* to remove from place of burial — see EXHUME

disinterested *adj* 1 having or showing a lack of interest or concern — see INDIFFERENT 1

2 marked by justice, honesty, and freedom from bias — see FAIR 2

disinterestedness *n* 1 lack of favoritism toward one side or another — see DETACHMENT 1

2 lack of interest or concern — see INDIFFERENCE

disjoin *vb* to set or force apart — see SEPARATE 1

disjoint *vb* 1 to set or force apart — see SEPARATE 1

2 to undo the proper order or arrangement of — see DISORDER

disjointed *adj* not clearly or logically connected — see INCOHERENT 1

dislike *n* 1 a strong feeling of not liking or approving ⟨I have a strong *dislike* for olives.⟩

syn allergy, averseness, aversion, disfavor, disinclination, disliking

rel disgust, distaste, loathing, nausea, repugnance, repulsion, revulsion; abhorrence, abomination, antipathy, execration, hate, hatred; deprecation, disapproval, displeasure, dissatisfaction; jaundice

near ant affection, attachment, devotedness, devotion, love, passion; bent, leaning, penchant, predilection, propensity, tendency

ant appetite, favor, fondness, like, liking, partiality, preference, relish, shine, taste, use

2 refusal to accept as right or desirable — see DISAPPROVAL

dislike *vb* 1 to feel dislike for ⟨The two dogs *disliked* each other the first time they met, and never did become friends.⟩

syn disfavor

rel abhor, abominate, detest, execrate, hate, loathe; condemn, despise, scorn; cringe (at), disapprove (of), mind, object (to), shy (from *or* away from)

near ant admire, appreciate, cherish, esteem, regard, respect; adore, deify, idolize, revere, reverence, venerate, worship; prize, treasure, value; savor (*also* savour); dote (on), idolize; favor, prefer

ant adore, cotton (to), delight (in), dig, enjoy, fancy, groove (on), like, love, relish, revel (in)

2 to hold an unfavorable opinion of — see DISAPPROVE (OF)

disliking *n* a strong feeling of not liking or approving — see DISLIKE 1

dislocate *vb* 1 to change the place or position of — see MOVE 1

2 to undo the proper order or arrangement of — see DISORDER

dislocation *n* an act or instance of the order of things being disturbed — see UPSET

disloyal *adj* not true in one's allegiance to someone or something — see FAITHLESS

disloyalty *n* 1 lack of faithfulness especially to one's husband or wife — see INFIDELITY 1

2 the act or fact of violating the trust or confidence of another — see BETRAYAL

dismal *adj* 1 causing or marked by an atmosphere lacking in cheer — see GLOOMY 1

2 causing unhappiness — see SAD 2

3 extremely unsatisfactory — see WRETCHED 1

dismantle *vb* to take apart — see DISASSEMBLE 1

dismay *n* 1 the emotion felt when one's expectations are not met — see DISAPPOINTMENT 1

2 the state of being discouraged — see DISCOURAGEMENT

dismay *vb* 1 to lessen the courage or confidence of — see DISCOURAGE 1

2 to trouble the mind of; to make uneasy — see DISTURB 1

dismember *vb* 1 to cause to separate into pieces usually suddenly or forcibly — see BREAK 1

2 to take apart — see DISASSEMBLE 1

dismiss *vb* 1 to let go from office, service, or employment ⟨Several employees were recently *dismissed*.⟩

syn bounce, can, cashier, discharge, fire, muster out, release, remove, retire, sack, terminate, turn off

rel downsize, excess, furlough, lay off, trim; boot (out), chuck (out), drum (out), throw out, unseat; separate

phrases send packing, show the door (one)

near ant keep; reemploy, rehire; contract, subcontract; recruit

ant employ, engage, hire, retain, take on

2 to drive or force out — see EJECT 1

3 to express scornfully one's low opinion of — see DECRY 1

dismissal *n* the termination of the employment of an employee or a work force often temporarily — see LAYOFF

disobedience *n* refusal to obey ⟨They gave up on training the dog to fetch because of his constant *disobedience*.⟩

syn contrariness, defiance, frowardness, insubordination, intractability, rebellion, rebelliousness, recalcitrance, refractoriness, unruliness, waywardness, willfulness

rel civil disobedience, noncooperation; discourteousness, disrespect, impertinence, impoliteness, impudence, inconsiderateness, inconsideration, insolence, rudeness, ungraciousness; doggedness, hardheadedness, mulishness, obduracy, obstinacy, peevishness, pertinaciousness, pertinacity, perversity, self-will, stubbornness, tenaciousness, tenacity; knavery, mischievousness, naughtiness

near ant amenability, amiability; submissiveness, subservience, subserviency; trainability; deference, docility, dutifulness

ant compliance, obedience, submission, subordinateness, subordination, tractability, tractableness

disobedient *adj* given to resisting authority or another's control ⟨The *disobedient* child refused to take a nap.⟩

syn balky, contrary, defiant, froward, insubordinate, intractable, obstreperous, rebel, rebellious, recalcitrant, refractory,

---

syn synonym(s)	*rel* related words
ant antonym(s)	*near ant* near antonym(s)

restive, ungovernable, unruly, untoward, wayward, willful (*or* wilful)

rel noncooperative, uncooperative; insurgent, mutinous; adamant, adamantine, dogged, hardheaded, headstrong, immovable, implacable, inflexible, mulish, obdurate, obstinate, opinionated, peevish, pertinacious, pigheaded, rigid, self-willed, stubborn, unbending, uncompromising, unrelenting, unyielding; fractious, restive, uncontrollable, unmanageable, wild; perverse, resistant, wrongheaded; bad, disorderly, errant, misbehaving, mischievous, naughty; undisciplined; discourteous, disrespectful, ill-bred, ill-mannered, ill-natured, impertinent, impolite, impudent, inconsiderate, insolent, ornery, rude, uncivil, uncouth, ungracious, unmannerly

near ant acquiescent, agreeable, amiable, cooperative, deferential, obliging; yielding; behaved, disciplined, well-bred; courteous, polite, respectful; kowtowing, obsequious, subservient; decorous, mannerly, orderly, proper; controllable, governable, manageable, trainable

ant amenable, compliant, conformable, docile, obedient, ruly, submissive, tractable

disobey *vb* to go against the commands, prohibitions, or rules of ⟨students who *disobey* their teachers and use cell phones in class⟩ ⟨drivers who consistently *disobey* traffic laws⟩

syn defy, mock, rebel (against)

rel disoblige; mutiny (against), revolt (against); disregard, ignore, overlook, overpass, pass over, tune out; brush off, dismiss, flout, pooh-pooh (*also* pooh), reject, scoff (at), scorn, shrug off, wink (at); breach, break, infringe, transgress, violate; buck, combat, contest, dispute, fight, oppose, resist, withstand

near ant capitulate (to), concede (to), defer (to), serve, stoop (to), submit (to), surrender (to), yield (to); cooperate (with); keep, observe; accede (to), acquiesce (to), agree (to), assent (to), oblige; attend, hear, heed, listen (to), mark, note, notice, regard, watch

ant comply (with), conform (to), follow, mind, obey

disoblige *vb* to cause discomfort to or trouble for — see INCONVENIENCE

disobliging *adj* causing difficulty, discomfort, or annoyance — see INCONVENIENT 1

disorder *n* **1** a state in which everything is out of order — see CHAOS

2 an abnormal state that disrupts a plant's or animal's normal bodily functioning — see DISEASE

disorder *vb* to undo the proper order or arrangement of ⟨Be careful not to *disorder* the carefully arranged contents of the dresser.⟩

syn confuse, derange, disarrange, disarray, discompose, dishevel, disjoint, dislocate, disorganize, disrupt, disturb, hash, jumble, mess (up), mix (up), muddle, muss, rumple, scramble, shuffle, tousle, tumble, upset

rel embroil, entangle, snarl, tangle; agitate, perturb, stir (up), unsettle; clutter

near ant align (*also* aline), line, line up, queue; classify, codify, methodize, systematize, systemize; adjust, fix; make up; unscramble

ant arrange, array, dispose, draw up, marshal (*also* marshall), order, organize, range, regulate, straighten (up), tidy

disordered *adj* lacking in order, neatness, and often cleanliness — see MESSY

disorderly *adj* **1** not restrained by or under the control of legal authority — see LAWLESS 1

2 lacking in order, neatness, and often cleanliness — see MESSY

disorganization *n* a state in which everything is out of order — see CHAOS

disorganize *vb* to undo the proper order or arrangement of — see DISORDER

disorient *vb* to throw into a state of mental uncertainty — see CONFUSE 1

disown *vb* **1** to declare not to be true — see DENY 1

2 to refuse to acknowledge as one's own or as one's responsibility — see DISCLAIM 1

disparage *vb* to express scornfully one's low opinion of — see DECRY 1

disparagement *n* the act of making a person or a thing seem little or unimportant — see DEPRECIATION

disparaging *adj* intended to make a person or thing seem of little importance or value — see DEROGATORY

disparate *adj* being not of the same kind — see DIFFERENT 1

disparateness *n* the quality or state of being different — see DIFFERENCE 1

disparity *n* the quality or state of being different — see DIFFERENCE 1

dispassionate *adj* marked by justice, honesty, and freedom from bias — see FAIR 2

dispatch *n* **1** a message on paper from one person or group to another — see ¹LETTER

2 a piece of conveyed information — see COMMUNICATION 1

dispatch *vb* **1** to cause to go or be taken from one place to another — see SEND

2 to deprive of life — see KILL 1

3 to put to death deliberately — see MURDER 1

4 to achieve a victory over — see BEAT 2

dispel *vb* to cause (members of a group) to move widely apart — see SCATTER 1

dispensable *adj* not needed by the circumstances or to accomplish an end — see UNNECESSARY

dispensation *n* the act or process of giving out something to each member of a group — see DISTRIBUTION 1

dispense *vb* to give out (something) to appropriate individuals — see ADMINISTER 1

dispersal *n* an act or process in which something scatters or is scattered — see SCATTERING

disperse *vb* **1** to go off in different directions and cease to exist as a body or unified whole ⟨The crowd *dispersed* once the show ended.⟩

syn disassemble, dissipate, dissolve, scatter

rel branch (out), break up, disband, diverge, divide, fork, separate, spill; clear,

disappear, evanesce, evaporate, fade, flee, go (away), melt
near ant congregate, gather, meet
2 to cause (members of a group) to move widely apart — see SCATTER 1
3 to cease to exist or cause to cease to exist as a group or organization — see DISBAND 1

dispersion *n* an act or process in which something scatters or is scattered — see SCATTERING 1

dispirit *vb* to lessen the courage or confidence of — see DISCOURAGE 1

dispiritedness *n* **1** a state or spell of low spirits — see SADNESS
2 the state of being discouraged — see DISCOURAGEMENT

displace *vb* **1** to change the place or position of — see MOVE 1
2 to force to leave a country — see BANISH 1
3 to take the place of — see REPLACE 1
4 to remove from a position of prominence or power (as a throne) — see DEPOSE 1

displacement *n* the forced removal from a homeland — see EXILE 1

display *n* **1** a public showing of objects of interest — see EXHIBITION 1
2 an outward and often exaggerated indication of something abstract (as a feeling) for effect — see SHOW 1

display *vb* **1** to present so as to invite notice or attention — see SHOW 1
2 to make known (something abstract) through outward signs — see SHOW 2

displease *vb* to make discontented — see DISCONTENT

displeased *adj* having a feeling that one has been wronged or thwarted in one's ambitions — see DISCONTENTED

displeasing *adj* not giving pleasure to the mind or senses — see UNPLEASANT

displeasure *n* **1** refusal to accept as right or desirable — see DISAPPROVAL
2 the condition of being dissatisfied with one's life or situation — see DISCONTENT

disport *vb* **1** to cause (someone) to pass the time agreeably occupied — see AMUSE
2 to engage in activity for amusement — see PLAY 1
3 to play and run about happily — see FROLIC 1
4 to present so as to invite notice or attention — see SHOW 1

disposal *n* **1** the getting rid of whatever is unwanted or useless ⟨Trash *disposal* is on Wednesday in our neighborhood.⟩
syn discarding, disposition, dumping, jettison, junking, removal, riddance, scrapping, throwing away
rel clearance, clearing, decimation, demolishment, demolition, destruction
near ant accumulation, acquirement, collection, deposit, gathering
2 the way objects in space or events in time are arranged or follow one another — see ORDER 1

dispose *vb* **1** to arrange something in a certain spot or position — see PLACE 1

2 to put into a particular arrangement — see ORDER 1

disposed *adj* having a desire or inclination (as for a specified course of action) — see WILLING 1

disposition *n* **1** one's characteristic attitude or mood ⟨He has a cheerful *disposition* and is very rarely depressed.⟩
syn grain, nature, temper, temperament
rel cheer, frame, habit, humor, inclination, mode, spirit; angle, mind-set, outlook, perspective, slant, standpoint, viewpoint; emotion, feeling, heart, passion, sentiment, spirit, strain; belief, conviction, judgment (*or* judgement), mind, notion, opinion, persuasion, view; expression, tone, vein; character, identity, individuality, makeup, mettle, personality, selfhood, self-identity, setup
2 a habitual attraction to some activity or thing — see INCLINATION 1
3 the getting rid of whatever is unwanted or useless — see DISPOSAL 1
4 the way objects in space or events in time are arranged or follow one another — see ORDER 1
5 an arrangement about action to be taken — see AGREEMENT 2

disproof *n* something (as an argument) that serves to disprove — see CONFUTATION

disprove *vb* to prove to be false ⟨Magellan's circumnavigation of the globe *disproved* any lingering notions that the earth is flat.⟩
syn belie, confound, confute, debunk, discredit, falsify, rebut, refute
rel overthrow, overturn; challenge, contest, query, question; doubt, mistrust; debate, discuss, hash (over), moot, talk over
phrases give the lie to
near ant document, evidence, evince, record, show, support, witness; back (up), buttress, corroborate, substantiate; adduce, attest, authenticate, certify, identify; demonstrate, display, illustrate, manifest
ant confirm, establish, prove, validate, verify

disputable *adj* **1** giving good reason for being doubted, questioned, or challenged — see DOUBTFUL 2
2 open to question or dispute — see DEBATABLE 1

disputant *n* a person who takes part in a dispute ⟨There were only three *disputants* in the argument, but they made enough noise for a dozen.⟩
syn arguer, bickerer, debater, disputer, fighter, quarreler (*or* quarreller), squabbler, wrangler
rel advocate, codefendant, defendant, plaintiff, pleader; challenger, contender, contestant, skirmisher; fusser, nitpicker, pettifogger, quibbler

disputation *n* variance of opinion on a matter — see DISAGREEMENT 1

disputatious *adj* **1** feeling or displaying eagerness to fight — see BELLIGERENT
2 given to arguing — see ARGUMENTATIVE 1

disputatiousness *n* an inclination to fight or quarrel — see BELLIGERENCE

dispute *n* **1** variance of opinion on a matter — see DISAGREEMENT 1

---

syn synonym(s)   *rel* related words
ant antonym(s)   *near ant* near antonym(s)

2 an often noisy or angry expression of differing opinions — see ARGUMENT 1

dispute *vb* **1** to demand proof of the truth or rightness of — see CHALLENGE 1

2 to express different opinions about something often angrily — see ARGUE 2

3 to talk about (an issue) usually from various points of view and for the purpose of arriving at a decision or opinion — see DISCUSS

disputer *n* a person who takes part in a dispute — see DISPUTANT

disquiet *n* **1** a disturbed or uneasy state — see UNREST

2 an uneasy state of mind usually over the possibility of an anticipated misfortune or trouble — see ANXIETY 1

disquiet *vb* to trouble the mind of; to make uneasy — see DISTURB 1

disquieting *adj* **1** causing worry or anxiety — see TROUBLESOME

2 marked by or causing agitation or uncomfortable feelings — see NERVOUS 2

disregard *n* lack of interest or concern — see INDIFFERENCE

disregard *vb* **1** to ignore in a disrespectful manner — see SCORN 2

2 to fail to give proper attention to — see NEGLECT 1

3 to dismiss as of little importance — see EXCUSE 1

disrepair *n* the state of being unattended to or not cared for — see NEGLECT 1

disreputable *adj* not respectable ⟨a *disreputable* Internet retailer that had a record of hundreds of complaints for shoddy merchandise and slow refunds⟩

syn discreditable, disgraceful, dishonorable, ignominious, infamous, notorious, shady, shameful, shoddy, shy

rel bad, criminal, immoral, seamy, sordid, unethical, unsavory, wicked; base, contemptible, despicable, detestable, dirty, low, mean, miserable, vile, wretched; evil, iniquitous, nefarious, rotten, sinful, unrighteous, vicious, villainous, wrong; corrupt, debased, debauched, degenerate, depraved, dissolute, gamy (*or* gamey), libertine, loose, perverted, reprobate

near ant decent, ethical, good, honest, just, moral, noble, principled, righteous, upright, upstanding; esteemed, prestigious, reputed, respected; authorized, legal, licensed, permissible, permitted; approved, endorsed (*also* indorsed), sanctioned; clean, correct, decorous, exemplary, proper, seemly

ant honorable, reputable, respectable

disrepute *n* the state of having lost the esteem of others — see DISGRACE 1

disrespect *n* rude behavior — see DISCOURTESY

disrespect *vb* **1** to cause hurt feelings or deep resentment in — see INSULT

2 to show contempt for — see SCORN 1

disrespectful *adj* showing a lack of manners or consideration for others — see IMPOLITE

disrobe *vb* to remove clothing from — see UNDRESS 1

disrobed *adj* lacking or shed of clothing — see NAKED 1

disrupt *vb* **1** to cause to separate into pieces usually suddenly or forcibly — see BREAK 1

2 to undo the proper order or arrangement of — see DISORDER

disruption *n* an act or instance of the order of things being disturbed — see UPSET

dissatisfaction *n* **1** the condition of being dissatisfied with one's life or situation — see DISCONTENT

2 the emotion felt when one's expectations are not met — see DISAPPOINTMENT 1

dissatisfactory *adj* falling short of a standard — see BAD 1

dissatisfied *adj* having a feeling that one has been wronged or thwarted in one's ambitions — see DISCONTENTED

dissatisfy *vb* **1** to fall short in satisfying the expectation or hope of — see DISAPPOINT

2 to make discontented — see DISCONTENT

dissect *vb* to identify and examine the basic elements or parts of (something) especially for discovering interrelationships — see ANALYZE

dissection *n* the separation and identification of the parts of a whole — see ANALYSIS 1

dissemble *vb* **1** to present a false appearance of — see FEIGN

2 to take on a false or deceptive appearance — see PRETEND 1

dissembling *n* **1** the inclination or practice of misleading others through lies or trickery — see DECEIT 1

2 the pretending of having virtues, principles, or beliefs that one in fact does not have — see HYPOCRISY

disseminate *vb* to cause to be known over a considerable area or by many people — see SPREAD 1

dissension *also* **dissention** *n* **1** a lack of agreement or harmony — see DISCORD

2 variance of opinion on a matter — see DISAGREEMENT 1

dissent *n* **1** a lack of agreement or harmony — see DISCORD

2 departure from a generally accepted theory, opinion, or practice — see HERESY

dissent *vb* to have a different opinion — see DISAGREE

dissenter *n* a person who believes, teaches, or advocates something opposed to accepted beliefs — see HERETIC 1

dissenting *adj* deviating from commonly accepted beliefs or practices — see HERETICAL

disservice *n* unfair or inadequate treatment of someone or something or an instance of this ⟨You do a great *disservice* to the professionals at the day-care center when you refer to them as "babysitters."⟩

syn inequity, injury, injustice, raw deal, shaft, unfairness, unjustness, wrong

rel affront, indignity, insult, offense (*or* offence), outrage, put-down, slight, slur; beef, complaint, grievance

near ant cricket

ant equitableness, equity, fairness, justice

dissever *vb* to set or force apart — see SEPARATE 1

dissidence *n* **1** a lack of agreement or harmony — see DISCORD

2 departure from a generally accepted theory, opinion, or practice — see HERESY

dissident *adj* deviating from commonly accepted beliefs or practices — see HERETICAL

dissident *n* a person who believes, teaches, or advocates something opposed to accepted beliefs — see HERETIC 1

dissimilar *adj* being not of the same kind — see DIFFERENT 1

dissimilarity *n* the quality or state of being different — see DIFFERENCE 1

dissimulate *vb* to take on a false or deceptive appearance — see PRETEND 1

dissimulation *n* **1** the inclination or practice of misleading others through lies or trickery — see DECEIT 1

2 the pretending of having virtues, principles, or beliefs that one in fact does not have — see HYPOCRISY

dissipate *vb* **1** to cause (members of a group) to move widely apart — see SCATTER 1

2 to use up carelessly — see WASTE 1

3 to go off in different directions and cease to exist as a body or unified whole — see DISPERSE 1

dissipated *adj* having or showing lowered moral character or standards — see CORRUPT

dissipatedness *n* a sinking to a state of low moral standards and behavior — see CORRUPTION 2

dissipation *n* **1** a sinking to a state of low moral standards and behavior — see CORRUPTION 2

2 an act or process in which something scatters or is scattered — see SCATTERING 1

dissociate *vb* to set or force apart — see SEPARATE 1

dissolute *adj* having or showing lowered moral character or standards — see CORRUPT

dissoluteness *n* a sinking to a state of low moral standards and behavior — see CORRUPTION 2

dissolution *n* **1** the act or process of a whole separating into two or more parts or pieces — see SEPARATION 1

2 the permanent stopping of all the vital bodily activities — see DEATH 1

dissolve *vb* **1** to cease to be visible — see DISAPPEAR

2 to cease to exist or cause to cease to exist as a group or organization — see DISBAND 1

3 to put an end to by formal action — see ABOLISH 1

4 to go off in different directions and cease to exist as a body or unified whole — see DISPERSE 1

dissonant *adj* marked by or producing a harsh combination of sounds ⟨A *dissonant* chorus of noises arose from the busy construction site.⟩

syn cacophonous, discordant, inharmonious, unmelodious, unmusical

rel blaring, clanging, clangorous, clashing, clattering, dinning, grating, harsh, jan-

gling, jangly, jarring, metallic, noisy, raspy, raucous, scratching, screeching, shrill, squeaky, strident; disagreeable, unpleasant, unpleasing; atonal, off-key, tuneless; resounding, sonorous; clamorous, uproarious

near ant euphonious, mellifluent, mellifluous, mellow, melodic, sweet, tuneful; resonant, sonorous; quavering, trilling, warbling; agreeable, appealing, pleasant; cadenced, lilting, lyric, lyrical, rhythmic (*or* rhythmical)

ant harmonious, harmonizing, melodious, musical

dissuade *vb* to steer (a person) from an activity or course of action — see DISCOURAGE 2

distance *n* **1** the space or amount of space between two points, lines, surfaces, or objects ⟨The *distance* between the earth and the sun is about 93 million miles.⟩

syn lead, length, remove, spacing, spread, stretch, way

rel altitude, area, breadth, depth, height, rise, space, volume, width; extension, extent; cast, range, reach, scope, shot, sweep, throw; drop, fall, flight, haul; berth, clearance

2 a wide space or area — see EXPANSE

3 the quality or state of being different — see DIFFERENCE 1

distant *adj* **1** not close in time or space ⟨The *distant* towers were barely visible in the fog.⟩

syn away, deep, far, faraway, far-flung, far-off, remote, removed

rel apart, devious, isolated, lonesome, obscure, odd, outlying, out-of-the-way, retired, secluded, secret, sequestered

near ant adjacent, adjoining, contiguous

ant close, near, nearby, nigh

2 having or showing a lack of friendliness or interest in others — see COOL 1

3 being not of the same kind — see DIFFERENT 1

distaste *n* a dislike so strong as to cause stomach upset or queasiness — see DISGUST

distasteful *adj* **1** disagreeable or disgusting to the sense of taste ⟨Cod-liver oil is so *distasteful* that it's worse than anything it cures.⟩

syn brackish, unappetizing, unpalatable, unsavory, yucky (*also* yukky)

rel abominable, awful, bad, filthy, foul, horrible, loathsome, nasty, nauseating, noisome, obnoxious, offensive, repellent (*also* repellant), repugnant, repulsive, revolting, shocking, sickening; bland, flat, flavorless, insipid, savorless, tasteless

near ant appealing, attractive, flavorful, piquant, rich

ant appetizing, delectable, delicious, palatable, savory (*also* savoury), tasty, toothsome, yummy

2 not giving pleasure to the mind or senses — see UNPLEASANT

3 causing intense displeasure, disgust, or resentment — see OFFENSIVE 1

distill *also* **distil** *vb* **1** to fall or let fall in or as if in drops — see DRIP

2 to remove usually visible impurities from — see CLARIFY 1

---

syn synonym(s)   *rel* related words
ant antonym(s)   *near ant* near antonym(s)

distinct *adj* **1** being not of the same kind — see DIFFERENT 1

2 not subject to misinterpretation or more than one interpretation — see CLEAR 2

3 of a particular or exact sort — see EXPRESS 1

4 serving to identify as belonging to an individual or group — see CHARACTERISTIC 1

distinction *n* **1** exceptionally high quality — see EXCELLENCE 1

2 a quality that gives something special worth — see EXCELLENCE 2

3 public acknowledgment or admiration for an achievement — see GLORY 1

4 the fact or state of being above others in rank or importance — see EMINENCE 1

5 something given in recognition of achievement — see AWARD 1

6 the quality or state of being different — see DIFFERENCE 1

7 the state of being kept distinct — see SEPARATION 1

distinctive *adj* **1** being not of the same kind — see DIFFERENT 1

2 serving to identify as belonging to an individual or group — see CHARACTERISTIC 1

distinctiveness *n* the quality or state of being different — see DIFFERENCE 1

distinctness *n* the quality or state of being different — see DIFFERENCE 1

distinguish *vb* **1** to understand or point out the difference in ⟨Even at such a young age, he could *distinguish* the calls of various birds.⟩

syn difference, differentiate, discern, discriminate, separate

rel contradistinguish; comprehend, grasp, know, understand; divide, part, sever; demarcate, set off

near ant confound, lump (together), mingle

ant confuse, mistake, mix (up)

2 to be an important feature of — see CHARACTERIZE 2

3 to find out or establish the identity of — see IDENTIFY 1

4 to make note of (something) through the use of one's eyes — see SEE 1

5 to arrange or assign according to type — see CLASSIFY 1

distinguishable *adj* **1** able to be perceived by a sense or by the mind — see PERCEPTIBLE

2 being not of the same kind — see DIFFERENT 1

distinguished *adj* **1** having or showing a formal and serious or reserved manner — see DIGNIFIED

2 standing above others in rank, importance, or achievement — see EMINENT

distinguishing *adj* serving to identify as belonging to an individual or group — see CHARACTERISTIC 1

distort *vb* **1** to change so much as to create a wrong impression or alter the meaning of — see GARBLE

2 to twist (something) out of a natural or normal shape or condition — see CONTORT

distorted *adj* badly or imperfectly formed — see MALFORMED

distortion *n* the twisting of something out of its natural or normal shape or condition — see CONTORTION

distract *vb* **1** to draw the attention or mind to something else ⟨We were *distracted* from our discussion by the noise outside.⟩

syn abstract, call off, divert

rel amuse, beguile, entertain; stray, wander

near ant concentrate, focus

2 to trouble the mind of; to make uneasy — see DISTURB 1

distracted *adj* **1** feeling overwhelming fear or worry — see FRANTIC 1

2 lost in thought and unaware of one's surroundings or actions — see ABSENT-MINDED 1

3 suffering from mental confusion — see DIZZY 2

distraction *n* **1** a state of mental uncertainty — see CONFUSION 1

2 a state of wildly excited activity or emotion — see FRENZY

3 the act or activity of providing pleasure or amusement especially for the public — see ENTERTAINMENT 1

4 someone or something that provides amusement or enjoyment — see FUN 1

distraught *adj* feeling overwhelming fear or worry — see FRANTIC 1

distress *n* **1** a state of great suffering of body or mind ⟨The upcoming bar exam is causing us considerable *distress*.⟩ ⟨The survivors were in extreme *distress* after having been stranded on the island for a week.⟩

syn affliction, agony, anguish, hurt, misery, pain, rack, strait(s), torment, torture, travail, tribulation, woe

rel discomfort; cross, crucible, trial; heartache, heartbreak, joylessness, sadness, sorrow, unhappiness; emergency, pinch; asperity, difficulty, hardship, rigor; ache, pang, smarting, soreness, stitch, throe, twinge; danger, jeopardy, trouble

near ant comfort, consolation, solace; alleviation, assuagement, ease, relief; peace, security; well-being

2 the state of not being protected from injury, harm, or evil — see DANGER 1

distress *vb* to trouble the mind of; to make uneasy — see DISTURB 1

distressful *adj* **1** marked by or causing agitation or uncomfortable feelings — see NERVOUS 2

2 of a kind to cause great distress — see REGRETTABLE

distressing *adj* **1** causing worry or anxiety — see TROUBLESOME

2 of a kind to cause great distress — see REGRETTABLE

3 marked by or causing agitation or uncomfortable feelings — see NERVOUS 2

distribute *vb* **1** to arrange or assign according to type — see CLASSIFY 1

2 to give as a share or portion — see ALLOT

3 to give out (something) to appropriate individuals — see ADMINISTER 1

distribution *n* **1** the act or process of giving out something to each member of a group ⟨Aid workers oversaw the *distribution* of medicine.⟩

syn allocation, allotment, apportionment, disbursement, dispensation, division, issuance

rel reallocation, reapportionment, redistribution, redivision, repartition; division, partition, separation

2 the way objects in space or events in time are arranged or follow one another — see ORDER 1

district n an area (as of a city) set apart for some purpose or having some special feature ⟨Independence Hall in Philadelphia's historic *district*⟩

syn neighborhood, quarter, section

rel belt, zone; department, division, part; ward; area, locality, place, region; barrio, enclave, ghetto, hood (or 'hood)

distrust n a feeling or attitude that one does not know the truth, truthfulness, or trustworthiness of someone or something — see DOUBT

distrust vb to have no trust or confidence in ⟨We instinctively *distrust* those phone calls that tell us we have won a free vacation or car.⟩

syn doubt, mistrust, question, suspect

rel disbelieve, discount, discredit, negate

near ant bank (on or upon), count (on or upon), depend (on or upon), rely (on or upon)

ant trust

distrustful adj **1** inclined to doubt or question claims — see SKEPTICAL 1

2 not feeling sure about the truth, wisdom, or trustworthiness of someone or something — see DOUBTFUL 1

distrustfully adv with distrust — see ASKANCE

distrustfulness n a feeling or attitude that one does not know the truth, truthfulness, or trustworthiness of someone or something — see DOUBT

disturb vb **1** to trouble the mind of; to make uneasy ⟨The news *disturbed* us.⟩

syn agitate, ail, alarm (also alarum), bother, concern, discomfort, discompose, dismay, disquiet, distract, distress, exercise, flurry, frazzle, freak (out), fuss, perturb, undo, unhinge, unsettle, upset, worry

rel aggravate, anger, annoy, bug, chafe, chivy (or chivvy), exasperate, fret, gall, get, grate, harry, irk, irritate, nettle, peeve, pester, pique, put off, put out, rile, vex; bedevil, haunt, plague; abash, confound, confuse, discomfit, disconcert, discountenance, embarrass, faze, fluster, jar, mortify, nonplus, rattle, shake up; daunt, demoralize, discourage, dishearten, dispirit, unnerve

near ant allay, alleviate, assuage; appease, conciliate, mollify, pacify, placate, propitiate

ant calm, compose, quiet, settle, soothe, tranquilize (also tranquillize)

2 to change the place or position of — see MOVE 1

3 to undo the proper order or arrangement of — see DISORDER

4 to thrust oneself upon (another) without invitation — see BOTHER 1

5 to cause discomfort to or trouble for — see INCONVENIENCE

disturbance n **1** a state of noisy, confused activity — see COMMOTION

2 an act or instance of the order of things being disturbed — see UPSET

3 the act of making unwelcome intrusions upon another — see ANNOYANCE 1

disturbing adj **1** causing annoyance — see ANNOYING

2 causing embarrassment — see AWKWARD 3

3 causing worry or anxiety — see TROUBLESOME

4 marked by or causing agitation or uncomfortable feelings — see NERVOUS 2

disunion n **1** a lack of agreement or harmony — see DISCORD

2 the act or process of a whole separating into two or more parts or pieces — see SEPARATION 1

disunite vb to set or force apart — see SEPARATE 1

disunited adj disagreeing with each other — see DIVIDED

disunity n a lack of agreement or harmony — see DISCORD

disuse n lack of use ⟨Since the car has experienced years of *disuse*, starting it up won't be easy.⟩

syn idleness, inactivity

rel abandonment, desertion, neglect; abeyance, dormancy, latency, quiescence

ant use

disused adj left unoccupied or unused — see ABANDONED 1

ditch n a long narrow channel dug in the earth ⟨After skidding on the ice, our car went right into the *ditch*.⟩

syn dike, gutter, trench, trough

rel culvert, drain, draw, gully (also gulley); ravine; drill, furrow

ditch vb **1** to end a usually intimate relationship with ⟨He *ditched* the band to start up a new one.⟩

syn dump, leave

rel brush (aside or off), cold-shoulder, cut, high-hat, slight, snub; abandon, desert, forsake, maroon, quit

phrases kiss good-bye

near ant hook up (with), take; befriend, latch (on or onto)

2 to get rid of as useless or unwanted — see DISCARD

dither n **1** a state of nervous or irritated concern — see FRET

2 a sense of panic or extreme nervousness — see JITTERS

dither vb to show uncertainty about the right course of action — see HESITATE

dithery adj feeling or showing uncomfortable feelings of uncertainty — see NERVOUS 1

ditty n a short musical composition for the human voice often with instrumental accompaniment — see SONG 1

diurnal adj occurring, done, produced, or appearing every day — see DAILY

divan n a long upholstered piece of furniture designed for several sitters — see COUCH

dive n **1** an act or instance of diving ⟨The penguin took a *dive* off of the ice sheet.⟩

syn pitch, plunge

rel dip, immersion, submersion; fall, plump, slip, spill, stumble, tumble; descent, drop; belly flop, jackknife, swan dive

---

syn synonym(s)   **rel** related words

ant antonym(s)   **near ant** near antonym(s)

near ant jump, leap

2 the act or process of going to a lower level or altitude — see DESCENT 1

dive *vb* **1** to cast oneself head first into deep water ⟨The children liked to *dive* off the dock.⟩

syn pitch, plunge, sound

rel dip, immerse, submerge; belly flop, plump, plunk (*or* plonk)

near ant surface

2 to go to a lower level especially abruptly — see DROP 2

diverge *vb* **1** to change one's course or direction — see TURN 3

2 to go or move in different directions from a central point — see SEPARATE 2

divergence *n* **1** a movement in different directions away from a common point ⟨a growing *divergence* of opinion⟩

syn separation

rel difference, disagreement, discrepancy, disparateness, disparity, dissidence, dissimilarity, distinction, distinctiveness, distinctness, diversity, unlikeness

phrases parting of the ways

near ant accord, agreement; likeness, similarity

ant convergence

2 a turning away from a course or standard ⟨Any *divergence* from the community's strict moral code was met with social ostracism.⟩

syn departure, detour, diversion

rel regression, retrogression, reversion

near ant adherence

divers *adj* being of many and various kinds — see MANIFOLD

diverse *adj* being not of the same kind — see DIFFERENT 1

diverseness *n* **1** the quality or state of being composed of many different elements or types — see VARIETY 1

2 the quality or state of being different — see DIFFERENCE 1

diversion *n* **1** someone or something that provides amusement or enjoyment — see FUN 1

2 the act or activity of providing pleasure or amusement especially for the public — see ENTERTAINMENT 1

3 a turning away from a course or standard — see DIVERGENCE 2

diversity *n* **1** the quality or state of being composed of many different elements or types — see VARIETY 1

2 the quality or state of being different — see DIFFERENCE 1

divert *vb* **1** to cause (someone) to pass the time agreeably occupied — see AMUSE

2 to change the course or direction of (something) — see TURN 2

3 to draw the attention or mind to something else — see DISTRACT 1

diverting *adj* providing amusement or enjoyment — see FUN

divide *vb* **1** to set or force apart — see SEPARATE 1

2 to go or move in different directions from a central point — see SEPARATE 2

divided *adj* disagreeing with each other ⟨The club members are sharply *divided* on the need for more fund-raising.⟩

syn disunited, split

rel balkanized, fractionalized, fractionated; cohesionless, factious

phrases at loggerheads, at odds

ant unanimous, undivided, united

dividend *n* something given in addition to what is ordinarily expected or owed — see BONUS

divider *n* something that divides, separates, or marks off — see DIVISION 1

divine *adj* **1** of the very best kind — see EXCELLENT

2 of, relating to, or being God — see HOLY 2

divine *vb* to realize or know about beforehand — see FORESEE

diviner *n* one who predicts future events or developments — see PROPHET 1

divinity *n* **1** the quality or state of being divine ⟨Henry David Thoreau felt the presence of *divinity* in every part of nature.⟩

syn deity, godhead, godhood

rel blessedness, godliness, holiness, piousness, saintliness

2 a being having superhuman powers and control over a particular part of life or the world — see DEITY 1

3 *cap* the being worshipped as the creator and ruler of the universe — see DEITY 2

divisible *adj* capable of being split into two or more parts or pieces — see SEPARABLE

division *n* **1** something that divides, separates, or marks off ⟨We poked our heads over the *division* between the yards to see what the fuss was about.⟩

syn divider, partition, separation

rel barrier, fence, wall; border, boundary, limit

2 a large unit of a governmental, business, or educational organization ⟨She was transferred to another *division* in the company.⟩

syn agency, arm, branch, bureau, department, desk, office, service

rel subdepartment, subdivision

3 one of the units into which a whole is divided on the basis of a common characteristic — see CLASS 2

4 the act or process of a whole separating into two or more parts or pieces — see SEPARATION 1

5 the act or process of giving out something to each member of a group — see DISTRIBUTION 1

6 a lack of agreement or harmony — see DISCORD

divorce *vb* to set or force apart — see SEPARATE 1

divulge *vb* to make known (as information previously kept secret) — see REVEAL 1

divulgence *n* the act or an instance of making known something previously unknown or concealed — see REVELATION

dizzy *adj* **1** having a feeling of being whirled about and in danger of falling down ⟨I felt very *dizzy* after I got off of the roller coaster.⟩

syn giddy, light-headed, reeling, whirling

rel faint, weak; addled, befuddled, confused, dazed, groggy

near ant clearheaded; stable, steady

2 suffering from mental confusion ⟨He felt *dizzy* from trying to remember all of the dates and names that were sure to be asked on the test.⟩

syn addled, befogged, befuddled, bewildered, confused, dazed, distracted, dopey (*also* dopy), shell-shocked, silly, stunned, stupefied

rel senseless, unconscious

phrases at sea, out of it

near ant alert, conscious

ant clearheaded

3 moving, proceeding, or acting with great speed — see FAST 1

4 lacking in seriousness or maturity — see GIDDY 1

do *n* **1** a social gathering — see PARTY 1

2 a statement of what to do that must be obeyed by those concerned — see COMMAND 1

do *vb* **1** to be fitting or proper ⟨That outfit just won't *do* for the wedding.⟩

syn befit, go, serve, suit

rel satisfy, suffice; function, work

phrases fill the bill (*or* fit the bill)

2 to be enough — see SERVE 2

3 to carry through (as a process) to completion — see PERFORM 1

4 to make more attractive by adding something that is beautiful or becoming — see DECORATE

5 to meet one's day-to-day needs — see GET ALONG 1

6 to be the cause of (a situation, action, or state of mind) — see EFFECT

7 to copy or exaggerate (someone or something) in order to make fun of — see MIMIC 1

8 to move forward along a course — see GO 1

9 to present a portrayal or performance of — see ACT 1

10 to rob by the use of trickery or threats — see FLEECE

11 to take place — see HAPPEN

doable *adj* capable of being done or carried out — see POSSIBLE 1

docile *adj* readily giving in to the command or authority of another — see OBEDIENT

docility *n* a readiness or willingness to yield to the wishes of others — see COMPLIANCE 1

dock *n* a structure used by boats and ships for taking on or landing cargo and passengers ⟨The boat remained tied up at the *dock* for a week, waiting for the weather to clear.⟩

syn float, jetty, landing, levee, pier, quay, wharf

rel berth, mooring, slip; dockyard, marina, quayage, shipyard, wharfage

¹**dock** *vb* **1** to make less in extent or duration — see SHORTEN

2 to make (something) shorter or smaller with the use of a cutting instrument — see CLIP 1

²**dock** *vb* to stop at or near a place along the shore — see LAND 1

docket *n* a listing of things to be presented or considered (as at a concert or play) — see PROGRAM 1

dockworker *n* one who loads and unloads ships at a port ⟨The *dockworkers* spent all afternoon taking crates off of the ship.⟩

syn longshoreman, stevedore

doctor *n* a person specially trained in healing human medical disorders ⟨We called a *doctor* as soon as we realized the baby was sick.⟩

syn medic, physician

rel family doctor, family physician, family practitioner, general practitioner; anesthesiologist, dermatologist, gynecologist, internist, neurologist, ob-gyn, obstetrician, ophthalmologist, orthopedist, pathologist, pediatrician (*also* pediatrist), physiatrist, podiatrist, radiologist, urologist; attending, clinician, hospitalist; specialist; plastic surgeon, surgeon; intern (*also* interne), resident; aidman, nurse, nurse-practitioner; EMT, paramedic (*also* paramedical); physical therapist, physiotherapist

ant nondoctor, nonphysician

doctor *vb* **1** to give medical treatment to ⟨a pledge to *doctor* the burn victims until they were whole again⟩

syn treat

rel cure, heal, mend, rehabilitate, remedy; attend, care (for), dose, drug, hospitalize, minister (to), nurse

2 to put into good shape or working order again — see MEND 1

3 to change (something) so as to make it suitable for a new use or situation — see ADAPT

doctrine *n* **1** a statement or body of statements concerning faith or morals proclaimed by a church ⟨the Catholic Church's *doctrine* on the Eucharist⟩

syn canon, dogma

rel canon law; belief, conviction, tenet; credo, creed, ideology (*also* idealogy), philosophy, theology; axiom, precept, principle; symbol

2 the basic beliefs or guiding principles of a person or group — see CREED 1

document *n* **1** a piece of paper with information written or to be written on it — see FORM 2

2 a written or printed paper giving information about or proof of something — see CERTIFICATE

document *vb* to show the existence or truth of by evidence — see PROVE 1

documentary *adj* restricted to or based on fact — see FACTUAL 1

documentation *n* something presented in support of the truth or accuracy of a claim — see PROOF

dodder *vb* to move forward while swaying from side to side — see STAGGER 1

dodge *n* a clever often underhanded means to achieve an end — see TRICK 1

dodge *vb* **1** to move suddenly aside or to and fro ⟨*dodging* through the crowd on his way to the exit⟩

syn duck, sidestep, weave, zigzag

rel avoid, elude, escape, evade, parry, shirk, skirt; deflect, turn; slide, slip

2 to avoid having to comply with (something) especially through cleverness — see CIRCUMVENT 1

3 to get or keep away from (as a responsibility) through cleverness or trickery — see ESCAPE 2

---

syn synonym(s)   **rel** related words
ant antonym(s)   **near ant** near antonym(s)

dodger *n* a dishonest person who uses clever means to cheat others out of something of value — see TRICKSTER 1

dodging *n* the act or a means of getting or keeping away from something undesirable — see ESCAPE 1

dodo *n* a stupid person — see IDIOT

doff *vb* to rid oneself of (a garment) — see REMOVE 1

dog *n* 1 a domestic mammal that is related to the wolves and foxes ⟨a *dog* who needs a loving home⟩
syn canine, doggy (*or* doggie), hound, pooch
rel cur, mongrel, mutt; bitch; lapdog, pup, puppy, puppy dog, whelp; bandog, bird dog, coonhound, courser, gundog, hunter, sheepdog, sled dog, watchdog, wolf dog, wolfhound; guide dog, police dog, working dog
2 a person whose behavior is offensive to others — see JERK 1

dog *vb* 1 to go after or on the track of — see FOLLOW 2
2 to subject (someone) to constant scoldings and sharp reminders — see NAG 1

dog-eared *adj* showing signs of advanced wear and tear and neglect — see SHABBY 1

dogged *adj* 1 continuing despite difficulties, opposition, or discouragement — see PERSISTENT
2 sticking to an opinion, purpose, or course of action in spite of reason, arguments, or persuasion — see OBSTINATE
3 showing no signs of slackening or yielding in one's purpose — see UNYIELDING 1

doggedness *n* a steadfast adherence to an opinion, purpose, or course of action in spite of reason, arguments, or persuasion — see OBSTINACY

dogging *n* the act of going after or in the tracks of another — see PURSUIT

doggy *or* **doggie** *n* a domestic mammal that is related to the wolves and foxes — see DOG 1

dogma *n* 1 a statement or body of statements concerning faith or morals proclaimed by a church — see DOCTRINE 1
2 the basic beliefs or guiding principles of a person or group — see CREED 1

do in *vb* 1 to bring to a complete end the physical soundness, existence, or usefulness of — see DESTROY 1
2 to deprive of life — see KILL 1
3 to put to death deliberately — see MURDER 1
4 to use up all the physical energy of — see EXHAUST 1
5 to rob by the use of trickery or threats — see FLEECE 1

doing *n* something done by someone — see ACTION 1

doldrums *n pl* 1 a state of temporary inactivity — see ABEYANCE
2 a state or spell of low spirits — see SADNESS
3 the state of being bored — see BOREDOM

dole *n* the giving of necessities and especially money to the needy — see CHARITY 1

doleful *adj* 1 expressing or suggesting mourning — see MOURNFUL 1
2 feeling unhappiness — see SAD 1

dolefulness *n* 1 a state or spell of low spirits — see SADNESS
2 deep sadness especially for the loss of someone or something loved — see SORROW

doll *n* 1 a small figure often of a human being used especially as a child's plaything ⟨There was a row of *dolls* along the shelf in the bedroom.⟩
syn action figure, dolly, puppet
rel rag doll; figure, figurine; handpuppet, marionette
2 a physically attractive person ⟨Her new boyfriend is a real *doll*!⟩
syn dish, fox, knockout
rel beauty, eyeful, goddess, lovely, stunner; beefcake, hunk, stud

doll up *vb* 1 to make more attractive by adding something that is beautiful or becoming — see DECORATE
2 to put on one's best or formal clothes — see DRESS UP 1

dolly *n* a small figure often of a human being used especially as a child's plaything — see DOLL 1

dolor *n* deep sadness especially for the loss of someone or something loved — see SORROW

dolorous *adj* expressing or suggesting mourning — see MOURNFUL 1

dolt *n* a stupid person — see IDIOT

doltish *adj* not having or showing an ability to absorb ideas readily — see STUPID 1

doltishness *n* the quality or state of lacking intelligence or quickness of mind — see STUPIDITY 1

domain *n* a region of activity, knowledge, or influence — see FIELD 2

domestic *adj* 1 of or relating to a household or family ⟨The surest way to maintain *domestic* peace and harmony is to have everyone pitch in on chores.⟩
syn familial, household
rel homelike, homely, homey (*also* homy); residential
ant nondomestic, nonfamilial
2 changed from the wild state so as to become useful and obedient to humans — see TAME 1
3 belonging to a particular place by birth or origin — see NATIVE 1

domestic *n* a person hired to perform household or personal services — see MAID 1

domesticated *adj* changed from the wild state so as to become useful and obedient to humans — see TAME 1

domicile *n* the place where one lives — see HOME 1

domicile *vb* to provide with living quarters or shelter — see HOUSE 1

dominance *n* 1 controlling power or influence over others — see SUPREMACY 1
2 the fact or state of being above others in rank or importance — see EMINENCE 1

dominant *adj* coming before all others in importance — see FOREMOST 1

dominate *vb* 1 to bring under one's control by force of arms — see CONQUER 1
2 to look down on — see OVERLOOK 1

dominating *n* the act or process of bringing someone or something under one's control — see CONQUEST

domination *n* 1 controlling power or influence over others — see SUPREMACY 1

2 the act or process of bringing someone or something under one's control — see CONQUEST

domineering *adj* fond of ordering people around — see BOSSY

dominion *n* 1 controlling power or influence over others — see SUPREMACY 1

2 the right or means to command or control others — see POWER 1

don *vb* to place on one's person — see PUT ON 1

donate *vb* to make a present of — see GIVE 1

donation *n* 1 a gift of money or its equivalent to a charity, humanitarian cause, or public institution —see CONTRIBUTION

2 something given to someone without expectation of a return — see GIFT 1

donator *n* one that helps another with gifts or money — see BENEFACTOR

done *adj* 1 brought or having come to an end — see COMPLETE 2

2 depleted in strength, energy, or freshness — see WEARY 1

3 no longer existing — see EXTINCT

donkey *n* 1 a sturdy and patient domestic mammal that is used especially to carry things ⟨We put our bags on the *donkey* and headed down the canyon.⟩

syn ass, burro, jackass

rel jack, jennet, jenny; hinny, mule; pack animal

2 a stupid person — see IDIOT

donor *n* one that helps another with gifts or money — see BENEFACTOR

doom *n* 1 a state or end that seemingly has been decided beforehand — see FATE 1

2 the permanent stopping of all the vital bodily activities — see DEATH 1

doom *vb* 1 to determine the fate of in advance — see DESTINE

2 to impose a judicial punishment on — see SENTENCE

door *n* 1 a barrier by which an entry is closed and opened ⟨We locked the *door* to the room so that no one could get in.⟩

syn gate, hatch, portal

rel double door, Dutch door, French door, lattice, portcullis, postern, revolving door, storm door, trapdoor, wicket

2 the opening through which one can enter or leave a structure ⟨a steady stream of visitors through the front *door*⟩

syn doorway, entrance, gate, gateway, way

rel hatch, hatchway

3 the means or right of entering or participating in — see ENTRANCE 1

doorkeeper *n* a person who tends a door ⟨The *doorkeeper* held the door open for us so we didn't have to put down our packages.⟩

syn doorman, gatekeeper

doorman *n* a person who tends a door — see DOORKEEPER

doorway *n* 1 the means or right of entering or participating in — see ENTRANCE 1

2 the opening through which one can enter or leave a structure — see DOOR 2

dope *n* 1 information not generally available to the public ⟨The stool pigeon gave us the *dope* on their deal.⟩

syn book, inside, lowdown, scoop, tip

rel dirt, dish, gossip, rumor, story; hint, pointer; information, intelligence, news, tidings, word

near ant ancient history, open secret

2 a stupid person — see IDIOT

dope (out) *vb* to find an answer for through reasoning — see SOLVE

dopey *also* **dopy** *adj* 1 not having or showing an ability to absorb ideas readily — see STUPID 1

2 suffering from mental confusion — see DIZZY 2

dopiness *n* the quality or state of lacking intelligence or quickness of mind — see STUPIDITY 1

do–rag *n* a scarf worn on the head — see BANDANNA

dork *n, slang* a stupid person, see IDIOT

dorky *adj, slang* not having or showing an ability to absorb ideas readily — see STUPID 1

dormancy *n* 1 a state of temporary inactivity — see ABEYANCE

2 lack of action or activity — see INACTION

dormant *adj* 1 being in a state of suspended consciousness — see ASLEEP 1

2 not being in a state of use, activity, or employment — see INACTIVE 2

dot *n* a small area that is different (as in color) from the main part — see SPOT 1

dot *vb* 1 to cover by or as if by scattering something over or on — see SCATTER 2

2 to mark with small spots especially unevenly — see SPOT 1

dote (on) *vb* to love or admire too much — see IDOLIZE

dotted *adj* marked with spots — see SPOTTED 1

dotty *adj* showing or marked by a lack of good sense or judgment — see FOOLISH 1

double *adj* 1 consisting of two members or parts that are usually joined ⟨an egg with a *double* yolk⟩

syn binary, bipartite, dual, duplex, twin, twofold

rel mated, paired

near ant unpaired

ant single

2 being twice as great or as many ⟨After it was ranked the best in the country, the college had *double* the usual number of applicants.⟩

syn twofold

3 not being or expressing what one appears to be or express — see INSINCERE

double *adv* to two times the amount or degree — see DOUBLY

double *n* something or someone that strongly resembles another — see IMAGE 1

double *vb* 1 to make twice as great or as many ⟨We *doubled* our investment in six months.⟩

syn duplicate, redouble

rel compound, multiply; accumulate, balloon, build (up), burgeon (*also* bourgeon), enlarge, escalate, expand, increase, mount, mushroom, proliferate, rise, snowball, swell, wax

---

syn synonym(s)   **rel** related words

ant antonym(s)   **near ant** near antonym(s)

2 to lay one part over or against another part of — see FOLD 1

double–cross *vb* to be unfaithful or disloyal to — see BETRAY 1

double cross *n* the act or fact of violating the trust or confidence of another — see BETRAYAL

double–crosser *n* one who betrays a trust or an allegiance — see TRAITOR

double–dealing *adj* 1 marked by, based on, or done by the use of dishonest methods to acquire something of value — see FRAUDULENT 1

2 not being or expressing what one appears to be or express — see INSINCERE

3 given to or marked by cheating and deception — see DISHONEST 2

double–dealing *n* the inclination or practice of misleading others through lies or trickery — see DECEIT 1

double–talk *n* 1 language marked by abstractions, jargon, euphemisms, and circumlocutions — see GIBBERISH 2

2 unintelligible or meaningless talk — see GIBBERISH 1

doubly *adv* to two times the amount or degree ⟨We did the test again to be *doubly* sure of the results.⟩

syn double, twice, twofold

doubt *n* a feeling or attitude that one does not know the truth, truthfulness, or trustworthiness of someone or something ⟨From the beginning I had my *doubts* about the investment scheme.⟩

syn distrust, distrustfulness, incertitude, misgiving, mistrust, mistrustfulness, query, reservation, skepticism, suspicion, uncertainty

rel disbelief, incredulity, unbelief; anxiety, concern, paranoia, wariness; compunction, qualm, scruple, tremor

near ant credence, faith

ant assurance, belief, certainty, certitude, confidence, conviction, sureness, surety, trust

doubt *vb* to have no trust or confidence in — see DISTRUST

doubtable *adj* 1 giving good reason for being doubted, questioned, or challenged — see DOUBTFUL 2

2 open to question or dispute — see DEBATABLE 1

doubter *n* a person who is always ready to doubt or question the truth or existence of something — see SKEPTIC

doubtful *adj* 1 not feeling sure about the truth, wisdom, or trustworthiness of someone or something ⟨He was *doubtful* about the decision to complete the project despite its mounting problems.⟩

syn distrustful, dubious, mistrustful, skeptical, suspicious, uncertain, unconvinced, undecided, unsettled, unsure

rel equivocal; diffident, insecure; halting, hesitant, indecisive, irresolute, vacillating, wavering; conflicted

phrases on the fence

near ant assured, confident, sanguine, self-assured; decisive, determined, resolute

ant certain, convinced, positive, sure

2 giving good reason for being doubted, questioned, or challenged ⟨The election results were highly *doubtful*, so an investigation was begun.⟩

syn debatable, disputable, doubtable, dubious, equivocal, fishy, problematic (*also* problematical), queer, questionable, shady, shaky, suspect, suspicious

rel alleged, so-called, supposed; moot; ambiguous, open, unclear; uncertain, undecided, undetermined; far-fetched, flimsy, improbable, unlikely, weak

near ant decisive, definitive; clear, obvious, open-and-shut, positive

ant certain, incontestable, indisputable, indubitable, questionless, sure, undeniable, undoubted, unproblematic, unquestionable

3 not likely to be true or to occur — see IMPROBABLE

4 open to question or dispute — see DEBATABLE 1

doubtfully *adv* with distrust — see ASKANCE

doubting *adj* inclined to doubt or question claims — see SKEPTICAL 1

doubtingly *adv* with distrust — see ASKANCE

doubtless *adj* having or showing a mind free from doubt — see CERTAIN 2

doubtless *adv* 1 without any question — see INDEED 1

2 by reasonable assumption — see PROBABLY

dough *n* something (as pieces of stamped metal or printed paper) customarily and legally used as a medium of exchange, a measure of value, or a means of payment — see MONEY

doughtiness *n* strength of mind to carry on in spite of danger — see COURAGE

doughty *adj* feeling or displaying no fear by temperament — see BRAVE 1

dour *adj* harsh and threatening in manner or appearance — see GRIM 1

¹**douse** *vb* to rid oneself of (a garment) — see REMOVE 1

²**douse** *also* **dowse** *vb* 1 to cause to cease burning — see EXTINGUISH 1

2 to make wet — see WET 1

3 to sink or push (something) briefly into or as if into a liquid — see DIP 1

doused *also* **dowsed** *adj* containing, covered with, or thoroughly penetrated by water — see WET 1

dove *n* 1 a person who opposes war or warlike policies ⟨The *doves* were in favor of using the surplus to improve the nation's schools and not its weapons systems.⟩

syn pacifist

rel peacemaker

near ant militarist; chauvinist, nationalist

ant hawk, jingo, warmonger

2 an innocent or gentle person — see LAMB

dovetail *vb* to be in agreement on every point — see CHECK 1

dowager *n* a dignified usually elderly woman of some rank or authority — see MATRIARCH

dowdily *adv* in a careless or unfashionable manner — see SLOPPILY

dowdy *adj* 1 lacking neatness in dress or person — see SLOPPY 1

2 marked by an obvious lack of style or good taste — see ¹TACKY 1

down *adj* **1** brought or having come to an end — see COMPLETE 2

2 directed down — see DOWNCAST 1

3 feeling unhappiness — see SAD 1

4 temporarily suffering from a disorder of the body — see SICK 1

5 not being in working order — see INOPERABLE 1

down *adv* **1** toward or in a lower position ⟨The stairs went *down* to the basement.⟩

syn below, downward (*or* downwards), over

rel facedown; low; downgrade, downstairs

near ant aloft

ant up, upward (*or* upwards), upwardly

2 from this or that place — see AWAY

¹**down** *n* a soft airy substance or covering — see FUZZ

²**down** *n* **1** something (as a situation or event) that is depressing — see DOWNER

2 the act or process of going to a lower level or altitude — see DESCENT 1

3 a loss of status — see COMEDOWN

³**down** *n, usually* **downs** *pl* a broad area of level or rolling treeless country — see PLAIN 1

down *vb* **1** to strike (someone) so forcefully as to cause a fall — see FELL 1

2 to take into the stomach through the mouth and throat — see SWALLOW 1

3 to reject by or as if by a vote — see NEGATIVE 1

downcast *adj* **1** directed down ⟨Her *downcast* gaze made us realize that she was shy.⟩

syn bowed, down, downward, lowered

near ant elevated, lifted, raised, uplifted, upward

2 feeling unhappiness — see SAD 1

downer *n* something (as a situation or event) that is depressing ⟨That story was a real *downer*.⟩

syn bummer, down

rel bore, drag; accident, fatality, mishap, woe; calamity, catastrophe, debacle (*also* débâcle), misfortune, tragedy

near ant pick-me-up, trip

ant upper

downfall *n* **1** something that is the cause of one's ultimate failure or loss of life ⟨An insatiable love of money would be their *downfall*.⟩

syn death, destruction, ruin, ruination

rel bane, curse, torment; Achilles' heel, tragic flaw

phrases kiss of death

2 a change to a lower state or level — see DECLINE 2

3 a loss of status — see COMEDOWN

4 a steady falling of water from the sky in significant quantity — see RAIN 1

downgrade *n* **1** a change to a lower state or level — see DECLINE 2

2 a downward slope — see DECLINE 3

downgrade *vb* **1** to bring to a lower grade or rank — see DEMOTE

2 to diminish the price or value of — see DEPRECIATE 1

downhearted *adj* feeling unhappiness — see SAD 1

downheartedness *n* a state or spell of low spirits — see SADNESS

downpour *n* a steady falling of water from the sky in significant quantity — see RAIN 1

downright *adj* **1** being or characterized by direct, brief, and potentially rude speech or manner — see BLUNT 1

2 having no exceptions or restrictions — see ABSOLUTE 2

downsize *vb* to make smaller in amount, volume, or extent — see DECREASE 1

down–to–earth *adj* **1** not having or showing any feelings of superiority, self-assertiveness, or showiness — see HUMBLE 1

2 willing to see things as they really are and deal with them sensibly — see REALISTIC 1

downward *adj* directed down — see DOWNCAST 1

downward *or* **downwards** *adv* toward or in a lower position — see DOWN 1

downwind *adj* being in the direction that the wind is blowing ⟨We were *downwind* of the deer, so it couldn't smell us.⟩

syn leeward

ant upwind, windward

downy *adj* smooth or delicate in appearance or feel — see SOFT 2

doze *n* a short sleep — see ¹NAP

doze *vb* **1** to be in a state of sleep — see SLEEP 1

2 to sleep lightly or briefly — see NAP 1

dozer *n* one who sleeps — see SLEEPER

dozing *adj* being in a state of suspended consciousness — see ASLEEP 1

dozing *n* a natural periodic loss of consciousness during which the body restores itself — see SLEEP 1

drab *adj* causing weariness, restlessness, or lack of interest — see BORING

draft *n* **1** a mass or quantity of something taken up and carried, conveyed, or transported — see LOAD 1

2 the portion of a serving of a beverage that is swallowed at one time — see DRINK 2

3 noticeable movement of air in a particular direction — see ¹WIND 1

draft *vb* **1** to pick especially for required military service ⟨My grandfather was *drafted* to fight in the war.⟩

syn conscript, levy

rel impress, press; enlist, enroll (*also* enrol), recruit; call up; sign up, volunteer

near ant discharge, muster out

2 to put (something) into proper and usually carefully worked out written form — see COMPOSE 1

3 to remove (liquid) gradually or completely — see DRAIN 1

draftee *n* a person forced or required to enroll in military service — see CONSCRIPT

drag *n* **1** someone or something boring ⟨That lecture was such a *drag* that half of the audience fell asleep.⟩

syn bore, drip

rel bummer, downer; pill

near ant blast, kick, rush, upper

2 a passage cleared for public vehicular travel — see WAY 1

3 something that makes movement or progress difficult — see ENCUMBRANCE

4 the portion of a serving of a beverage that is swallowed at one time — see DRINK 2

---

syn synonym(s) **rel** related words
ant antonym(s) **near ant** near antonym(s)

5 a person who spoils the pleasure of others — see KILLJOY

6 clothing chosen as appropriate for a specific situation — see OUTFIT 1

drag vb **1** to cause to follow by applying steady force on — see PULL 1

2 to move or act slowly — see DELAY 1

3 to move slowly — see CRAWL 2

dragger n someone who moves slowly or more slowly than others — see SLOWPOKE

dragging adj moving or proceeding at less than the normal, desirable, or required speed — see SLOW 1

drain vb **1** to remove (liquid) gradually or completely ⟨We *drained* the water from the tank before cleaning it.⟩
syn bleed, draft, draw (off), pump, siphon (*also* syphon), tap
rel suck; clear, empty, evacuate, exhaust, vacate, vacuate, void; decant; deplete; clean, flush, purge
near ant bathe, douse (*also* dowse), drench, soak, souse, wash, water, wet; deluge, drown, flood, inundate, overflow; submerge, swamp
ant fill

2 to make complete use of — see DEPLETE 1

3 to use up all the physical energy of — see EXHAUST 1

drained adj depleted in strength, energy, or freshness — see WEARY 1

drainpipe n a pipe or channel for carrying off water from a roof — see GUTTER 1

drama n **1** the public performance of plays ⟨He has been interested in *drama* from the first time he ever saw a play.⟩
syn dramatics, stage, theater (*or* theatre), theatricals
rel boards; acting, footlights; entertainment, showbiz, show business; amusement, distraction, diversion, recreation; exhibition, pageant, pageantry, presentation, production, show

2 a written work in which the story is told through speech and action that is intended to be acted out on stage — see PLAY 2

dramatic adj **1** having the general quality or effect of a stage performance ⟨the basketball player's *dramatic* announcement of his sudden retirement⟩
syn histrionic, melodramatic, theatrical (*also* theatric)
rel affected, emotional, emotionalistic, sensational; actorish, actorly, actressy, dramaturgic (*or* dramaturgical); ham; amazing, astonishing, astounding, awesome, exciting, eye-opening, fabulous, marvelous (*or* marvellous), surprising, wonderful, wondrous; overdramatic
near ant matter-of-fact, monotonous, uneventful, unexciting; uninspiring, unnewsworthy, unrewarding, unsensational, unspectacular; common, commonplace, ordinary, stale, unexceptional
ant undramatic

2 given to or marked by attention-getting behavior suggestive of stage acting — see THEATRICAL 1

3 likely to attract attention — see NOTICEABLE

dramatics n pl the public performance of plays — see DRAMA 1

dramatization n a written work in which the story is told through speech and action that is intended to be acted out on stage — see PLAY 2

drapery n pieces of cloth hung to darken, decorate, or divide a room ⟨The *drapery* for the picture window matched the color of the furniture in the center of the room.⟩
syn curtains, drapes
rel hanging(s), shade, tapestry, window shade

drapes n pl pieces of cloth hung to darken, decorate, or divide a room — see DRAPERY

draw n **1** a situation in which neither participant in a contest, competition, or struggle comes out ahead of the other — see TIE 1

2 something that attracts interest — see MAGNET

3 the act or an instance of applying force on something so that it moves in the direction of the force — see PULL 1

draw vb **1** to make a representation of by producing lines on a surface ⟨See if you can *draw* the bowl of fruit.⟩
syn picture
rel caricature, cartoon; crayon, pencil; outline, profile; scrawl, scribble, sketch

2 to cause to follow by applying steady force on — see PULL 1

3 to give a representation or account of in words — see DESCRIBE 1

4 to receive as return for effort — see EARN 1

5 to take away from a place or position — see REMOVE 2

6 to take the internal organs out of — see GUT

7 to shape with a hammer — see HAMMER 1

draw (off) vb to remove (liquid) gradually or completely — see DRAIN 1

drawback n a feature of someone or something that creates difficulty for achieving success — see DISADVANTAGE 1

drawing n a picture using lines to represent the chief features of an object or scene ⟨With an economy of lines, he created a vivid *drawing* of the tree.⟩
syn cartoon, delineation, sketch
rel contour, figure, outline, silhouette; caricature, illustration; depiction, image, likeness, portrait, representation; engraving, etch, etching; aquatint, charcoal, line drawing, pastel, watercolor; blueprint

drawing out n the act of making longer — see EXTENSION 1

draw on vb **1** to be the cause of (a situation, action, or state of mind) — see EFFECT

2 to come near or nearer — see APPROACH 1

draw out vb to make longer — see EXTEND 1

draw up vb **1** to bring (something) to a standstill — see ¹HALT 1

2 to put into a particular arrangement — see ORDER 1

3 to put (something) into proper and usually carefully worked out written form — see COMPOSE 1

dread adj causing fear — see FEARFUL 1

dread n **1** suspicion or fear of future harm or misfortune — see APPREHENSION 1

2 the emotion experienced in the presence or threat of danger — see FEAR 1

240   dreadful

3 something or someone that causes fear or dread especially without reason — see BOGEY 1

dreadful *adj* **1** causing fear — see FEARFUL 1

2 causing intense displeasure, disgust, or resentment — see OFFENSIVE 1

3 extremely disturbing or repellent — see HORRIBLE 1

4 extreme in degree, power, or effect — see INTENSE 1

5 having no exceptions or restrictions — see ABSOLUTE 2

dreadfulness *n* the quality of inspiring intense dread or dismay — see HORROR 1

dream *n* **1** a conception or image created by the imagination and having no objective reality — see FANTASY 1

2 something that one hopes or intends to accomplish — see GOAL

3 something very good of its kind — see JIM-DANDY

dream *vb* to form a mental picture of — see IMAGINE 1

dreamer *n* one whose conduct is guided more by the image of perfection than by the real world — see IDEALIST

dreamily *adv* in a pleasing way — see WELL 5

dreamy *adj* **1** giving pleasure or contentment to the mind or senses — see PLEASANT 1

2 tending to calm the emotions and relieve stress — see SOOTHING 1

drear *adj* causing or marked by an atmosphere lacking in cheer — see GLOOMY 1

dreariness *n* a state or spell of low spirits — see SADNESS

dreary *adj* **1** causing or marked by an atmosphere lacking in cheer — see GLOOMY 1

2 causing unhappiness — see SAD 2

3 causing weariness, restlessness, or lack of interest — see BORING

dredge *vb* to look through (as a place) carefully or thoroughly in an effort to find or discover something — see SEARCH 1

dredge (up) *vb* to come upon after searching, study, or effort — see FIND 1

dregs *n pl* matter that settles to the bottom of a body of liquid — see DEPOSIT 1

drench *vb* **1** to make wet — see WET

2 to wet thoroughly with liquid — see SOAK 1

drenched *adj* containing, covered with, or thoroughly penetrated by water — see WET 1

dress *adj* relating to or suitable for wearing to an event requiring elegant dress and manners ⟨The naval commander wore his *dress* uniform to the ball.⟩

syn dressy, formal

rel costume, costumey; chic, dapper, fashionable, in, modish, natty, sharp, smart, snappy, stylish; custom-made, fitted, tailored; black-tie, evening, white-tie; semiformal

near ant street; dowdy, outmoded, styleless, unfashionable, unstylish; frowsy (*or* frowzy), grungy, sloppy, sloven, slovenly, unkempt, untidy; disheveled (*or* dishevelled), messy, mussy, rumpled, wrinkled

ant casual, informal, sportif, sporty

dress *n* **1** a garment with a joined blouse and skirt usually worn by a woman or girl ⟨What a lovely *dress* you're wearing today!⟩

syn frock, gown

rel chemise, coatdress, granny dress, housedress, jumper, kimono, kirtle, minidress, Mother Hubbard, muumuu, overdress, sack, sheath, shift, shirtdress, shirtwaist, sundress, sweaterdress, tea gown

2 clothing chosen as appropriate for a specific situation — see OUTFIT 1

3 covering for the human body — see CLOTHING

4 the outward form of someone or something especially as indicative of a quality — see APPEARANCE 1

dress *vb* **1** to cover with a bandage — see BANDAGE

2 to make more attractive by adding something that is beautiful or becoming — see DECORATE

3 to make smooth or glossy usually by repeatedly applying surface pressure — see POLISH 1

4 to outfit with clothes and especially fine or special clothes — see CLOTHE 1

5 to put on one's best or formal clothes — see DRESS UP 1

6 to look after or assist the growth of by labor and care — see GROW 1

dress down *vb* to criticize (someone) severely or angrily especially for personal failings — see SCOLD

dressing *n* **1** a medicated covering used to heal an injury ⟨Nurses put a *dressing* over his cuts so they wouldn't get infected.⟩

syn plaster, poultice

rel cream, liniment, lotion, ointment, unguent

2 a savory fluid food used as a topping or accompaniment to a main dish — see SAUCE 1

dress up *vb* **1** to put on one's best or formal clothes ⟨We always like to *dress up* when going to parties.⟩

syn doll up, dress

rel preen, primp, prink, smarten (up); accessorize; apparel, array, attire, bedeck, bedizen, caparison, clothe, costume, deck, dude (up), garb, garment, invest, rig (out), robe, suit, tog (out *or* up)

2 to change the dress or looks of so as to conceal true identity — see DISGUISE 1

3 to outfit with clothes and especially fine or special clothes — see CLOTHE 1

dressy *adj* relating to or suitable for wearing to an event requiring elegant dress and manners — see DRESS

dribble *n* a very small piece — see BIT 1

dribble *vb* **1** to fall or let fall in or as if in drops — see DRIP

2 to flow in a broken irregular stream — see GURGLE

3 to let saliva or some other substance flow from the mouth — see DROOL 1

driblet *n* **1** a very small amount — see PARTICLE 1

2 the quantity of fluid that falls naturally in one rounded mass — see DROP 1

drift *n* **1** a pile or ridge of granular matter (as sand or snow) — see ²BANK

---

syn synonym(s)   *rel* related words
ant antonym(s)   *near ant* near antonym(s)

2 a prevailing or general movement or inclination — see TREND 1

3 the idea that is conveyed or intended to be conveyed to the mind by language, symbol, or action — see MEANING 1

drift *vb* **1** to move or proceed smoothly and readily — see FLOW 1

2 to rest or move along the surface of a liquid or in the air — see FLOAT 1

3 to move about from place to place aimlessly — see WANDER 1

drifter *n* a person who roams about without a fixed route or destination — see NOMAD

drill *n* **1** an established and often automatic or monotonous series of actions followed when engaging in some activity — see ROUTINE 1

2 something done over and over in order to develop skill — see EXERCISE 2

¹**drill** *vb* **1** to make a hole or series of holes in — see PERFORATE

2 to strike with a missile from a gun — see SHOOT 3

²**drill** *vb* to put or set into the ground to grow — see PLANT 1

drink *n* **1** a liquid suitable for drinking ⟨We went inside to have a *drink* after mowing the lawn.⟩

syn beverage, drinkable, libation, potable, quencher

rel potion; pop, soda, soda pop, soft drink; nectar; alcohol, brew, intoxicant, liquor, spirits; mix, mixer

2 the portion of a serving of a beverage that is swallowed at one time ⟨The thirsty soldier took a long *drink* from his canteen.⟩

syn belt, draft, drag, gulp, nip, quaff, shot, sip, slug, snort, sup, swallow, swig, swill

rel drop

3 a distilled beverage that can make a person drunk — see ALCOHOL

drink *vb* **1** to swallow in liquid form ⟨The doctor wants her to *drink* lots of water before the examination.⟩

syn gulp, guzzle, hoist, imbibe, quaff, sip, slurp, sup, swig, swill, toss (down *or* off)

rel lap, lick, suck; consume, down, kill, mouth (down); nip, tipple; pledge, toast, wine

2 to partake excessively of alcoholic beverages ⟨It's illegal to *drink* and drive.⟩

syn guzzle

rel carouse, revel; imbibe, nip

near ant abstain

3 to take in (something liquid) through small openings — see ABSORB 1

drinkable *adj* suitable for drinking — see POTABLE

drinkable *n* a liquid suitable for drinking — see DRINK 1

drip *n* **1** someone or something boring — see DRAG 1

2 the quantity of fluid that falls naturally in one rounded mass — see DROP 1

drip *vb* to fall or let fall in or as if in drops ⟨Water from the leaky roof was *dripping* all over the floor.⟩

syn distill (*also* distil), dribble, drop, trickle

rel drizzle, sprinkle; flow, pour, roll, run, stream; cascade, gutter, ripple; bleed, exude, ooze, seep, weep; discharge

near ant gush, spout, spurt

dripping *adj* containing, covered with, or thoroughly penetrated by water — see WET 1

drive *n* **1** a passage cleared for public vehicular travel — see WAY 1

2 a series of activities undertaken to achieve a goal — see CAMPAIGN

3 a strong wish for something — see DESIRE 1

4 active strength of body or mind — see VIGOR 1

5 readiness to engage in daring or difficult activity — see ENTERPRISE 2

drive *vb* **1** to urge, push, or force onward ⟨Cowboys *drove* the herd of cattle from San Antonio to San Francisco.⟩

syn herd, punch, run

rel shepherd; wrangle; exhort, flog, goad, hound, press, prick, prod, prompt, scourge, spur, whip

2 to travel by a motorized vehicle ⟨I'm going to *drive* across the country—want to come?⟩

syn automobile, motor, tool

rel roll, wheel; joyride; chauffeur, hack, taxi; ride; drag, race

3 to apply force to (someone or something) so that it moves in front of one — see PUSH 1

4 to cause (a person) to give in to pressure — see FORCE

5 to cause to function — see ACTIVATE

6 to set or keep in motion — see MOVE 2

7 to proceed or move quickly — see HURRY 2

drivel *n* **1** language, behavior, or ideas that are absurd and contrary to good sense — see NONSENSE 1

2 unintelligible or meaningless talk — see GIBBERISH 1

drivel *vb* to let saliva or some other substance flow from the mouth — see DROOL 1

2 to speak rapidly, inarticulately, and usually unintelligibly — see BABBLE 1

driver *n* a person who travels by automobile — see MOTORIST

drizzle *n* a light or fine rain ⟨The intermittent *drizzle* was just heavy enough to spoil all of our outdoor activities.⟩

syn mist, sprinkle

rel precipitation, rainfall, shower

near ant cloudburst, deluge, downpour, storm; rainstorm, thunderstorm; monsoon

droll *adj* causing or intended to cause laughter — see FUNNY 1

droll *n* a person (as a writer) noted for or specializing in humor — see HUMORIST

drollness *n* the amusing quality or element in something — see HUMOR 1

¹**drone** *n* a lazy person — see LAZYBONES

²**drone** *n* a monotonous sound like that of an insect in motion — see HUM

drone *vb* to fly, turn, or move rapidly with a fluttering or vibratory sound — see WHIR

drool *n* the fluid that is secreted into the mouth by certain glands — see SALIVA

drool *vb* **1** to let saliva or some other substance flow from the mouth ⟨The dog *drooled* when we put the steak down on the floor.⟩

syn dribble, drivel, salivate, slaver, slobber

rel water; expectorate, spit; foam, froth, splutter; sputter

2 to make an exaggerated display of affection or enthusiasm — see GUSH 2

3 to speak rapidly, inarticulately, and usually unintelligibly — see BABBLE 1

droop *n* the extent to which something hangs or dips below a straight line — see SAG

droop *vb* **1** to be limp from lack of water or vigor 〈The flowers *drooped* on their stalks in the blazing sun.〉

syn flag, hang, loll, sag, wilt

rel slouch, slump; cave (in), collapse, crumple, drop, fall, sink, subside, yield

near ant distend; rise, straighten, unbend, uncurl

2 to lose bodily strength or vigor — see WEAKEN 2

drooping *adj* bending downward or forward — see NODDING

droopy *adj* **1** bending downward or forward — see NODDING

2 not stiff in structure — see LIMP 1

3 feeling unhappiness — see SAD 1

drop *n* **1** the quantity of fluid that falls naturally in one rounded mass 〈A *drop* of water fell from the leaky faucet every few seconds.〉

syn blob, driblet, drip, droplet, glob, globule

rel gobbet; dewdrop, raindrop, tear, teardrop; spatter; dribble, trickle

2 distance measured from the top to the bottom of something — see DEPTH 1

3 the act or process of going to a lower level or altitude — see DESCENT 1

4 the amount by which something is lessened — see DECREASE

5 the more favorable condition or position in a competition — see ADVANTAGE 1

drop *vb* **1** to cause to fall intentionally or unintentionally 〈I *dropped* the fly ball.〉 〈*Drop* the anchor.〉

syn depress, lower, throw

rel flatten, floor, level; knock down, topple; plop, plunk down; bobble, bungle, foozle, fumble; immerse, sink, submerge

ant lift, pick up, raise

2 to go to a lower level especially abruptly 〈Although they start out high, prices for home electronics eventually *drop*.〉

syn crash, decline, descend, dip, dive, fall, lower, nose-dive, plummet, plunge, sink, tumble

rel abate, decrease, de-escalate, die (down), diminish, droop, dwindle, ebb, lessen, let up, moderate, subside, taper off, wane; recede, retreat

near ant accumulate, balloon, build, burgeon (*also* bourgeon), enlarge, escalate, expand, grow, increase, intensify, mushroom, pick up, snowball, swell, wax

ant arise, ascend, lift, mount, rise, soar, spike, up

3 to bring (as an action or operation) to an immediate end — see STOP 1

4 to stop doing (something) permanently — see QUIT 1

5 to lead or extend downward — see DESCEND 1

6 to put an end to (something planned or previously agreed to) — see CANCEL 1

7 to bring forth from the womb — see BEAR 1

8 to strike (someone) so forcefully as to cause a fall — see FELL 1

9 to fail to win, gain, or obtain — see LOSE 2

10 to fall or let fall in or as if in drops — see DRIP

11 to hand over or use up in payment — see SPEND 1

12 to make reference to or speak about briefly but specifically — see MENTION 1

13 to make smaller in amount, volume, or extent — see DECREASE 1

14 to stop living — see DIE 1

droplet *n* the quantity of fluid that falls naturally in one rounded mass — see DROP 1

dropping *n* **1** droppings *pl* solid matter discharged from an animal's alimentary canal 〈The only bad part about owning a rabbit was cleaning the *droppings* out of the litter box every night.〉

syn dirt, dung, excrement, excreta, feces, slops, waste

rel night soil, stool; dunghill, guano, manure, midden, muck; spoor; sewage, sewerage; coprolite

2 the act of putting an end to something planned or previously agreed to — see CANCELLATION

dross *n* discarded or useless material — see GARBAGE

droughty *adj* marked by little or no precipitation or humidity — see DRY 1

drove *n* **1** a great number of persons or creatures massed together — see CROWD 1

2 a group of domestic animals assembled or herded together — see HERD 1

drown *vb* **1** to cover with a flood — see FLOOD

2 to wet thoroughly with liquid — see SOAK 1

3 to make wet — see WET

drowse *n* a short sleep — see ¹NAP

drowse *vb* to sleep lightly or briefly — see NAP 1

drowsiness *n* the quality or state of desiring or needing sleep — see SLEEPINESS

drowsy *adj* **1** desiring or needing sleep — see SLEEPY 1

2 tending to cause sleep — see HYPNOTIC

drub *vb* **1** to strike repeatedly — see BEAT 1

2 to defeat by a large margin — see WHIP 2

drubbing *n* failure to win a contest — see DEFEAT 1

drudge *n* a person who does very hard or dull work 〈worked like a *drudge* at a low-paying job that had few benefits〉

syn drudger, grub, grubber, grunt, laborer, peon, plugger, slogger, toiler, worker

rel workhorse; serf

near ant shirker; drone, idler, lazybones, loafer, slouch, slug, sluggard

drudge *vb* to devote serious and sustained effort — see LABOR

drudger *n* a person who does very hard or dull work — see DRUDGE

drudgery *n* very hard or unpleasant work — see TOIL

drug *n* a substance or preparation used to treat disease — see MEDICINE

---

syn synonym(s) *rel* related words
ant antonym(s) *near ant* near antonyms(s)

druggist *n* a person who prepares drugs according to a doctor's prescription ⟨She got her prescription for antibiotics filled by the *druggist*.⟩

syn apothecary, pharmacist

rel pharmacologist

drugstore *n* a retail store where medicines and miscellaneous articles are sold ⟨We picked up her medicine and some toothpaste at the *drugstore*.⟩

syn apothecary, pharmacy

rel dispensary; sick bay

drum *n* a metal container in the shape of a cylinder — see CAN 1

drum *vb* to strike or cause to strike lightly and usually rhythmically — see ¹TAP

drum (out) *vb* to drive or force out — see EJECT 1

drunk *adj* being under the influence of alcohol ⟨a wedding guest who got a little *drunk*⟩

syn drunken, inebriate, inebriated, intoxicated

rel bleary-eyed; debauched, dissipated, dissolute; alcoholic, bibulous

near ant abstemious, abstinent, dry, temperate, teetotal; clearheaded, cool, level, steady

ant sober, straight

drunk *n* a person who makes a habit of getting drunk ⟨got a reputation as a *drunk*⟩

syn alcoholic, drunkard, inebriate

near ant teetotalist

drunkard *n* a person who makes a habit of getting drunk — see DRUNK

drunken *adj* being under the influence of alcohol — see DRUNK

dry *adj* 1 marked by little or no precipitation or humidity ⟨the *dry* climate of the American Southwest⟩

syn arid, droughty, sere (*also* sear), thirsty, waterless

rel air-dry; bone-dry, hyperarid, ultradry; baked, dehydrated, parched, sunbaked; rainless; desert

near ant awash, bathed, doused (*also* dowsed), drenched, dripping, saturated, soaked, soaking, sodden, soggy, sopping, soppy, soused, washed, watered, waterlogged, watery; deluged, drowned, flooded, inundated, overflowed; submerged, swamped; hydrated

ant damp, dank, humid, moist, wet

2 causing weariness, restlessness, or lack of interest — see BORING

3 having or showing a lack of friendliness or interest in others — see COOL 1

dry *vb* 1 to make dry ⟨The wind quickly *dried* their clothes.⟩

syn dehydrate, parch, scorch, sear

rel humidify; drain; evaporate; mummify, shrivel, wither, wizen; air-dry, bake

near ant bathe, deluge, douse (*also* dowse), drench, drown, flood, inundate, overflow, saturate, soak, sop, souse; damp, dampen, humidify, moisten; rehydrate; dip, dunk, submerge, swamp

ant hydrate, wash, water, wet

2 to lose liveliness, force, or freshness — see WITHER 1

dryad *n* a mythical goddess represented as a young woman and said to live outdoors — see NYMPH

dry run *n* a private performance or session in preparation for a public appearance — see REHEARSAL

dual *adj* consisting of two members or parts that are usually joined — see DOUBLE 1

dub *vb* 1 to give a name to — see NAME 1

2 to make or do (something) in a clumsy or unskillful way — see BOTCH

dubious *adj* 1 giving good reason for being doubted, questioned, or challenged — see DOUBTFUL 2

2 slow to begin or proceed with a course of action because of doubts or uncertainty — see HESITANT

3 not likely to be true or to occur — see IMPROBABLE

4 not feeling sure about the truth, wisdom, or trustworthiness of someone or something — see DOUBTFUL 1

dubiously *adv* with distrust — see ASKANCE

duck *n* a member of the human race — see HUMAN

duck *vb* 1 to get or keep away from (as a responsibility) through cleverness or trickery — see ESCAPE 2

2 to move suddenly aside or to and fro — see DODGE 1

3 to sink or push (something) briefly into or as if into a liquid — see DIP 1

ducking *n* the act or a means of getting or keeping away from something undesirable — see ESCAPE 2

duck soup *n* something that is easy to do — see CINCH

duct *n* a long hollow cylinder for carrying a substance (as a liquid or gas) — see PIPE 1

dud *n* 1 something that has failed — see FAILURE 3

2 **duds** *pl* covering for the human body — see CLOTHING

3 **duds** *pl* transportable items that one owns — see POSSESSION 2

dude *n* 1 a man extremely interested in his clothing and personal appearance — see DANDY 1

2 an adult male human being — see MAN 1

dudgeon *n* the feeling of being offended or resentful after a slight or indignity — see PIQUE

due *adj* 1 having reached the date at which payment is required ⟨The loan is *due* next April.⟩

syn mature

rel delinquent, outstanding, overdue, owed, owing, receivable, unpaid, unsettled; payable

near ant cleared, liquidated, paid (off *or* up), repaid, settled; prepaid

ant undue

2 being in accordance with the prescribed, normal, or logical course of events ⟨Their train is *due* to arrive in half an hour.⟩

syn anticipated, awaited, expected, scheduled, slated

near ant behind, behindhand, belated, delinquent, dilatory, late, latish, overdue, tardy; early, premature, untimely; unanticipated, unforeseen, unlooked-for

3 being what is called for by accepted standards of right and wrong — see JUST 1

due *adv* 1 as stated or indicated without the slightest difference — see EXACTLY 1

2 in a direct line or course — see DIRECT-LY 1

due (to) *adj* coming as a result — see RE-SULTANT

duel *n* an earnest effort for superiority or victory over another — see CONTEST 1

due to *prep* as the result of — see BECAUSE OF

dull *adj* 1 lacking sharpness of edge or point 〈The *dull* knife just bounced off the skin of the tomato without cutting it.〉

syn blunt, blunted, dulled, obtuse

rel dullish; rounded, smooth; even, flat, flattened, level

near ant jagged, needlelike, prickly, spiked, spikelike, spiky (*also* spikey), spiny; jabbing, lacerating, piercing, scratching, stabbing; ultrasharp

ant cutting, edged, edgy, ground, honed, keen, pointed, sharp, sharpened, whetted

2 causing weariness, restlessness, or lack of interest — see BORING

3 covered over by clouds — see OVERCAST

4 lacking a surface luster or gloss — see MATTE

5 lacking intensity of color — see PALE 1

6 not having or showing an ability to absorb ideas readily — see STUPID 1

7 not loud in pitch or volume — see SOFT 1

8 slow to move or act — see INACTIVE 1

dull *vb* 1 to reduce or weaken in strength or feeling 〈The aspirin *dulled* his headache and he was soon feeling better.〉

syn benumb, blunt, damp, dampen, deaden, numb

rel muffle, mute, tone (down); decrease, diminish, lessen, let up (on), lower, reduce, subdue; debilitate, enfeeble, weaken; dwindle, recede, subside, taper (off), wane; alleviate, ease, lighten; abate, moderate

near ant amplify, augment, beef (up), boost, consolidate, deepen, enhance, heighten, intensify, magnify, redouble, step up, strengthen; animate, arouse, stimulate

ant sharpen, whet

2 to make white or whiter by removing color — see WHITEN

dulled *adj* 1 lacking a surface luster or gloss — see MATTE

2 lacking intensity of color — see PALE 1

3 lacking sharpness of edge or point — see DULL 1

dullness *also* **dulness** *n* the quality or state of lacking intelligence or quickness of mind — see STUPIDITY 1

dumb *adj* 1 deliberately refraining from speech — see SILENT 1

2 not having or showing an ability to absorb ideas readily — see STUPID 1

3 tending not to speak frequently (as by habit or inclination) — see SILENT 2

dumbbell *n* a stupid person — see IDIOT

dumbfound *also* **dumfound** *vb* to make a strong impression on (someone) with something unexpected — see SURPRISE 1

dumbfounded *also* **dumfounded** *adj* affected with sudden and great wonder or surprise — see THUNDERSTRUCK

2 filled with amazement or wonder — see OPENMOUTHED

dumbfounding *also* **dumfounding** *adj* causing a strong emotional reaction because of unexpectedness — see SURPRISING 1

dumbness *n* 1 incapacity for or restraint from speaking — see SILENCE 1

2 the quality or state of lacking intelligence or quickness of mind — see STUPIDITY 1

dummy *adj* being such in appearance only and made with or manufactured from usually cheaper materials — see IMITATION

dummy *n* 1 a stupid person — see IDIOT

2 a three-dimensional representation of the human body used especially for displaying clothes — see MANNEQUIN 1

3 something that is made to look exactly like something else — see COPY

dump *n* 1 a place where discarded materials (as trash) are dumped 〈All of the used packaging eventually ends up in the *dump*.〉

syn landfill, sanitary landfill

rel dustbin, dustheap, junkyard, kitchen midden, midden; transfer station; mess, pigpen, pigsty, sty

2 a place where military arms are stored — see ARMORY

3 a dirty or messy place — see PIGPEN

dump *vb* 1 to end a usually intimate relationship with — see DITCH 1

2 to get rid of as useless or unwanted — see DISCARD

dumping *n* the getting rid of whatever is unwanted or useless — see DISPOSAL 1

dumps *n pl* a state or spell of low spirits — see SADNESS

dumpy *adj* 1 being compact and broad in build and often short in stature — see STOCKY

2 showing signs of advanced wear and tear and neglect — see SHABBY 1

dun *n* something that someone insists upon having — see DEMAND 1

dunce *n* a stupid person — see IDIOT

dung *n* solid matter discharged from an animal's alimentary canal — see DROPPING 1

dunk *vb* to sink or push (something) briefly into or as if into a liquid — see DIP 1

duo *n* two things of the same or similar kind that match or are considered together — see PAIR

¹dupe *n* one who is easily deceived or cheated 〈The swindler was able to escape with all of the *dupe's* money.〉

syn chump, gull, pigeon, pushover, sap, sucker, tool

rel mark, target, victim; butt, derision, laughingstock, mock, mockery; booby, dodo, fool, goose, half-wit, jackass, monkey, nincompoop, ninny, nitwit, simp, simpleton, turkey, yo-yo; loser; blockhead, dolt, dope, dumbbell, dummy, dunce, idiot, imbecile, moron

near ant cheat, cheater, cozener, defrauder, dodger, hoaxer, shark, sharper, slicker, swindler, trickster

²dupe *n* something that is made to look exactly like something else — see COPY

dupe *vb* to cause to believe what is untrue — see DECEIVE

---

syn synonym(s)   *rel* related words
ant antonym(s)   *near ant* near antonym(s)

duplex *adj* consisting of two members or parts that are usually joined — see DOUBLE 1

duplicate *adj* resembling another in every respect — see SAME 1

duplicate *n* 1 something or someone that strongly resembles another — see IMAGE 1
2 something that is made to look exactly like something else — see COPY

duplicate *vb* 1 to make an exact likeness of — see COPY 1
2 to make or do again — see REPEAT 4
3 to make twice as great or as many — see DOUBLE 1

duplication *n* 1 something or someone that strongly resembles another — see IMAGE 1
2 something that is made to look exactly like something else — see COPY
3 the act of saying or doing over again — see REPEAT

duplicity *n* the inclination or practice of misleading others through lies or trickery — see DECEIT 1

durability *n* uninterrupted or lasting existence — see CONTINUATION

duration *n* 1 the period during which something exists, lasts, or is in progress ⟨You should gradually increase the *duration* of your workout.⟩
syn continuance, date, life, life span, lifetime, run, standing, time
rel spell, stretch; span, tenure, term; hitch, tour, turn; half-life; age, longevity
2 uninterrupted or lasting existence — see CONTINUATION

duress *n* the use of power to impose one's will on another — see FORCE 2

during *prep* in the course of ⟨We took notes *during* class.⟩
syn amid (*or* amidst), by, over, pending, through, throughout

dusk *adj* being without light or without much light — see DARK 1

dusk *n* 1 the time from when the sun begins to set to the onset of total darkness ⟨We stopped playing at *dusk*, since it was getting too dark to see the ball.⟩
syn evening, eventide, gloaming, night, nightfall, sundown, sunset, twilight
rel dark, darkness, nighttime
near ant day, daytime, light; forenoon
ant dawn, dawning, daybreak, daylight, morn, morning, sunrise, sunup
2 a time or place of little or no light — see DARK 1
3 partial darkness due to the obstruction of light rays — see SHADE 1

dusk *vb* to grow dark — see DARKEN 2

dusky *adj* being without light or without much light — see DARK 1

dust *n* 1 discarded or useless material — see GARBAGE
2 the solid part of our planet's surface as

distinguished from the sea and air — see EARTH 2

dust *vb* to defeat by a large margin — see WHIP 2

dustiness *n* the state or quality of being dirty — see DIRTINESS

dusty *adj* 1 consisting of very small particles — see FINE 1
2 not clean — see DIRTY 1
3 causing weariness, restlessness, or lack of interest — see BORING

dutiful *adj* marked by or showing proper regard for another's higher status — see RESPECTFUL

duty *n* 1 a charge usually of money collected by the government from people or businesses for public use — see TAX
2 a piece of work that needs to be done regularly — see CHORE 1
3 something one must do because of prior agreement — see OBLIGATION 1

dwarf *n* 1 a living thing much smaller than others of its kind ⟨Shetland ponies are the *dwarfs* of the horse world.⟩
syn diminutive, midget, mite, peewee, pygmy (*also* pigmy), runt, scrub, shrimp
rel nubbin; mini, miniature; bantam; half-pint
near ant whale, whopper
ant behemoth, colossus, giant, jumbo, leviathan, mammoth, monster, titan
2 an imaginary being usually having a small human form and magical powers — see FAIRY

dwarf *vb* to hold back the normal growth of — see STUNT

dwarfish *adj* of a size that is less than average — see SMALL 1

dwell *vb* 1 to continue to be in a place for a significant amount of time — see ¹STAY 1
2 to have a home — see LIVE 1

dweller *n* one who lives permanently in a place — see INHABITANT

dwelling *n* the place where one lives — see HOME 1

dwindle *vb* 1 to make smaller in amount, volume, or extent — see DECREASE 1
2 to grow less in scope or intensity especially gradually — see DECREASE 2

dye *n* a substance used to color other materials — see PIGMENT

dye *vb* to give color or a different color to — see COLOR 1

dyestuff *n* a substance used to color other materials — see PIGMENT

dying *adj* nearly dead — see MORIBUND

dynamic *adj* 1 having active strength of body or mind — see VIGOROUS 1
2 marked by or uttered with forcefulness — see EMPHATIC 1

dynamically *adv* in a vigorous and forceful manner — see HARD 3

dyspeptic *adj* having or showing a habitually bad temper — see ILL-TEMPERED

each *adj* being one of a group ⟨*Each* park visitor receives a free souvenir.⟩
syn any, every
rel all; several; particular; respective, specific
phrases each and every
near ant neither

each *adv* for each one — see APIECE

eager *adj* showing urgent desire or interest ⟨Tom was *eager* to try out his new pair of skis.⟩
syn agog, anxious, ardent, athirst, avid, crazy, desirous, enthusiastic, excited, great, greedy, gung ho, hot, hungry, impatient, keen, nuts, raring, solicitous, thirsty, voracious, wild
rel engaged, interested; happy, hung up, obsessed; ambitious, appetent, covetous, craving, hankering, longing, pining; breathless, restive, restless; amenable, disposed, game, glad, inclined, ready, unreluctant, willing
phrases champing at the bit, chomping at the bit
near ant casual, incurious, insouciant, nonchalant, unconcerned, uninterested; aloof, detached, disinterested; impassive, stolid; halfhearted, lackadaisical, languid, languorous, lukewarm, spiritless; averse, disinclined, hesitant, loath (*also* loth *or* loathe); reluctant, unwilling
ant apathetic, indifferent, uneager, unenthusiastic

eagerness *n* urgent desire or interest ⟨students with an *eagerness* to learn⟩
syn appetite, ardor, avidity, desirousness, enthusiasm, excitement, hunger, impatience, keenness, lust, thirst
rel alacrity, quickness; ambition, zest; appetence, fervency, passion, warmth, zeal; amenability, readiness, willingness
near ant casualness, insouciance, nonchalance, unconcern; aloofness, detachment; impassivity, languor; halfheartedness, lukewarmness
ant apathy, indifference

ear *n* a state of being aware — see ATTENTION 2

earliest *adj* coming before all others in time or order — see FIRST 1

early *adj* **1** relating to or occurring near the beginning of a process, series, or time period ⟨*early* birds of the Jurassic period⟩
syn ancient, primal, primeval, primitive, primordial
rel embryonic, germinal, infant; aged, age-old, antediluvian, antiquated, antique, dateless, hoary, old, prehistoric (*also* prehistorical); obsolete, outmoded, out-of-date, passé
near ant advanced, complex, developed, evolved, high, higher; full-blown, full-fledged, full-scale
ant late
2 occurring before the usual or expected time ⟨We had an *early* dinner so as not to miss the concert.⟩

---

syn synonym(s)   **rel** related words
ant antonym(s)   **near ant** near antonym(s)

---

syn inopportune, precocious, premature, unseasonable, untimely
rel unanticipated, unexpected, unforeseen, unlooked-for; abrupt, sudden
near ant behindhand, belated, delinquent, latish, overdue, slow, tardy; anticipated, expected; delayed, detained, postponed
ant late

early *adv* before the usual or expected time ⟨That year spring arrived *early*.⟩
syn beforehand, inopportunely, precociously, prematurely, unseasonably
rel immediately, instantly, presently, promptly, pronto, punctually; apropos, betimes, seasonably
ant late, tardily

earmark *vb* to keep or intend for a special purpose — see DEVOTE 1

earn *vb* **1** to receive as return for effort ⟨I *earn* pocket money by mowing lawns.⟩
syn acquire, attain, bag, capture, carry, come by, draw, gain, garner, get, knock down, land, make, obtain, procure, realize, reap, secure, win
rel clear, gross, net; accomplish, achieve, notch (up), score; accumulate, amass, draw, rack up; catch, pick up; annex, occupy, take over; reacquire, reattain, recapture, regain, remake
near ant accord, give, grant, pay; give up, hand over, part (with), relinquish, surrender, yield
ant forfeit, lose
2 to be or make worthy of (as a reward or punishment) ⟨You've *earned* the afternoon off after all that hard work.⟩
rel deserve, merit, rate
near ant entitle, qualify

earnest *adj* not joking or playful in mood or manner — see SERIOUS 1

earnest *n* a mental state free of jesting or trifling — see EARNESTNESS

earnestness *n* a mental state free of jesting or trifling ⟨practiced the art of acting with great *earnestness*⟩
syn earnest, graveness, gravity, intentness, seriousness, soberness, sobriety, solemnity, staidness
rel gravitas, humorlessness; decisiveness, deliberation, determination, firmness, purposefulness, resoluteness, resolve; absorption, attentiveness, concentration, engrossment, enthrallment, immersion, intensity
near ant lightness, shallowness, superficiality; dalliance; cheerfulness, gaiety (*also* gayety), glee, high-spiritedness, merriment, mirth
ant facetiousness, flightiness, flippancy, frivolity, frivolousness, levity, lightheartedness, lightness, play, unseriousness

earnings *n pl* **1** an increase usually measured in money that comes from labor, business, or property — see INCOME 1
2 the amount of money left when expenses are subtracted from the total amount received — see PROFIT 1

earshot *n* range of hearing ⟨Babysitters should remain within *earshot* of young children.⟩

syn hail, hearing, sound

rel volume; distance, sight

earsplitting *adj* marked by a high volume of sound — see LOUD 1

earth *n* **1** the celestial body on which we live 〈environmentalists who are committed to preserving the *earth*〉

syn globe, planet, world

rel cosmos, creation, nature; universe; ball, orb, sphere; macrocosm, microcosm, microcosmos

2 the solid part of our planet's surface as distinguished from the sea and air 〈After the long flight, I was glad to feel the *earth* under my feet.〉

syn dirt, dust, ground, land, soil, terra firma

rel continent, zone; island, isthmus, mainland, peninsula

3 the loose surface material in which plants naturally grow — see DIRT 1

4 a very large amount of money — see FORTUNE 2

earthenware *n* articles made of baked clay — see CROCKERY

earthlike *adj* consisting or suggestive of earth — see EARTHY 1

earthly *adj* having to do with life on earth especially as opposed to that in heaven 〈*earthly* delights〉

syn carnal, fleshly, material, mundane, temporal, terrestrial, worldly

rel animal, bodily, corporal, corporeal, physical; daily, diurnal

near ant celestial, Elysian, empyreal, empyrean, supernal; metaphysical; devotional, divine, religious, sacred, spiritual, utopian; extraterrestrial; ethereal, supernatural

ant heavenly, nontemporal, unearthly, unworldly

earthquake *n* **1** a shaking of the earth 〈The San Andreas Fault is notorious for its *earthquakes*.〉

syn quake, shake, tremor

rel aftershock, foreshock, shock; cataclysm, convulsion, upheaval; seaquake

2 a violent disturbance (as of the political or social order) — see CONVULSION

earthy *adj* **1** consisting or suggestive of earth 〈the unmistakably *earthy* aroma of a greenhouse〉

syn earthlike, loamy

rel clayey, dusty, muddy, sandy, silty

2 willing to see things as they really are and deal with them sensibly — see REALISTIC 1

ease *n* **1** reduction of or freedom from pain 〈The sunburn medication brought me instant *ease*.〉

syn alleviation, comfort, release, relief

rel appeasement, assuagement, decrease, diminishment, mitigation, moderation, mollification; calming, salving, soothing

near ant discomfort, unrest; agony, anguish, misery, suffering, torment, torture; ache, pain, pang, prick, smart, sting, stitch, throe, tingle, twinge

2 carefree freedom from constraint — see ABANDON

3 freedom from activity or labor — see ¹REST 1

ease *vb* **1** to free from obstruction or difficulty 〈measures intended to *ease* the flow of traffic during rush hour〉

syn facilitate, grease, loosen (up), smooth, unclog

rel accelerate, expedite, hasten, hurry, quicken, rush, speed; advance, forward, further, promote; abet, aid, assist, help, improve; disentangle, straighten (out), untangle; simplify, streamline

phrases pave the way (for)

near ant hinder, impede; retard; aggravate, worsen; perplex, sophisticate

ant complicate

2 to make less taut — see SLACKEN 1

3 to make more bearable or less severe — see HELP 2

4 to make smaller in amount, volume, or extent — see DECREASE 1

5 to grow less in scope or intensity especially gradually — see DECREASE 2

easily *adv* **1** without difficulty 〈a skater who *easily* executes even the most difficult jumps〉

syn easy, effortlessly, facilely, fluently, freely, handily, lightly, painlessly, readily, smoothly, well

rel ably, adeptly, adroitly, competently, dexterously, efficiently, expertly, masterfully, proficiently, skillfully; instinctively, intuitively, naturally, spontaneously

phrases in a breeze, no sweat [*slang*], without ado, without a hitch

near ant awkwardly, clumsily, gracelessly, ham-handedly, ineptly, maladroitly, unskillfully; meticulously, painfully, painstakingly, thoroughly; assiduously, diligently, indefatigably, industriously, intensely, intently, mightily, sedulously, tirelessly

ant arduously, hardly, laboriously, strenuously

2 without any question — see INDEED 1

easy *adj* **1** involving minimal difficulty or effort 〈a minor problem with an *easy* solution〉

syn cheap, effortless, facile, fluent, fluid, light, painless, ready, royal, simple, smooth, snap, soft

rel idiotproof, mindless, quick, straightforward, unchallenging, uncomplicated; apparent, clear, clear-cut, distinct, evident, manifest, obvious, open-and-shut, palpable, patent, perspicuous, plain, transparent, unambiguous, unequivocal, unmistakable

near ant burdensome, exhausting, onerous, oppressive, painful, stressful, taxing, troublesome; abstruse, complex, complicated, intricate, involved, knotty, problematic (*also* problematical), recondite

ant arduous, demanding, difficult, exacting, formidable, grueling (*or* gruelling), hard, herculean, killer, labored, laborious, murderous, rough, severe, stiff, strenuous, toilful, toilsome, tough

2 readily taking advantage of 〈people who are *easy* prey for scam artists〉

syn exploitable, gullible (*also* gullable), naive (*or* naïve), susceptible, trusting, unwary, wide-eyed

rel credulous, overcredulous, trustful, uncritical, unsuspecting, unsuspicious; artless, genuine, guileless, innocent, simple, unsophisticated, unworldly; malleable, pliable, pliant; deceivable; acquiescent, agreeable, amiable, obliging; yielding *near ant* critical, cynical, mistrustful, skeptical, suspicious, wary; sophisticated; clear-sighted, hardheaded; shrewd, street-smart, streetwise

3 providing physical comfort — see COMFORTABLE 1

4 tolerant and kind in the judgment of and expectations for others — see INDULGENT 1

easy *adv* without difficulty — see EASILY 1

easygoing *adj* **1** having a relaxed, casual manner ⟨Counselors at the summer camp are pretty *easygoing*.⟩

syn affable, breezy, devil-may-care, happy-go-lucky, laid-back, low-pressure, mellow

rel carefree, casual, lackadaisical, nonchalant, unaffected, unconcerned, unfussy, unperturbed, untroubled, unworried; familiar, homey (*also* homy), informal; flexible, lax, lenient, permissive, pliable, pliant, soft; accessible, approachable; imperturbable, nerveless, unflappable, unshakable; amicable, companionable, comradely, cordial, genial, hail-fellow-well-met, hearty, neighborly, warm, warmhearted

near ant ceremonious, decorous, formal, rigid, strict; anxious, distressed, worried; jittery, jumpy, nervous, skittish, tense

ant high-strung, uptight

2 not bound by rigid standards ⟨Some people are pretty *easygoing* about housekeeping.⟩

syn flexible, lax, loose, relaxed, slack, unrestrained, unrestricted

rel careless, derelict, heedless, irresponsible, lazy, neglectful, negligent, remiss, slipshod, sloppy, sloven, slovenly, unfussy

near ant constrained, restrained, restricted, tight; careful, conscientious, exact, fussy, meticulous, painstaking, punctilious, scrupulous; implacable, inflexible

ant hard, harsh, rigid, rigorous, severe, stern, strict

eat *vb* **1** to take in as food ⟨Having gone all day without food, we greedily *ate* the hamburgers.⟩

syn consume, ingest, put down

rel digest, down, mouth (down), swallow; bolt, chow (down on), devour, glut (on), gobble (up *or* down), gorge, gulp, scoff, slop, snarf (down), swill, wolf; chew, gnaw (at *or* on), gum, lap, lick, nibble (on), nurse, pick (at); relish, savor (*also* savour), taste; banquet, dine, fare, feast, gormandize, pig out, regale; dispatch, polish off; breakfast, lunch, sup; munch, nosh, snack

2 to consume or wear away gradually ⟨The pot's protective coating was *eaten* away by the acid.⟩

syn bite (at), corrode, erode, fret, nibble

rel break down, break up, decompose, disintegrate, dissolve; decimate, destroy, devastate, ruin, waste, wreck

near ant freshen, recreate, refresh, refreshen, regenerate, rejuvenate, renew, restore, revitalize, revive

3 to take a meal — see DINE 1

4 to disturb the peace of mind of (someone) especially by repeated disagreeable acts — see IRRITATE 1

eat (up) *vb* **1** to receive or accept gladly or readily — see WELCOME

2 to destroy all trace of — see CONSUME 1

eatable *adj* suitable for use as food — see EDIBLE

eatables *n pl* substances intended to be eaten — see FOOD

eavesdrop (on) *vb* to listen to (another in private conversation) ⟨a nosy traveler who likes to *eavesdrop on* his fellow airline passengers⟩

syn listen in (on), overhear

rel bug, tap, wiretap; monitor, snoop, spy, surveil; attend, hear, hearken, heed, mind

eaves trough *n* a pipe or channel for carrying off water from a roof — see GUTTER 1

ebb *n* a change to a lower state or level — see DECLINE 2

ebb *vb* **1** to become worse or of less value — see DETERIORATE 1

2 to grow less in scope or intensity especially gradually — see DECREASE 1

ebbing *n* a gradual sinking and wasting away of mind or body — see DECLINE 1

ebony *adj* having the color of soot or coal — see BLACK 1

eccentric *adj* different from the ordinary in a way that causes curiosity or suspicion — see ODD 2

eccentric *n* a person of odd or whimsical habits ⟨an *eccentric* who designed his house to look like a Scottish castle⟩

syn character, codger, crack, crackbrain, crackpot, crank, flake, kook, nut, oddball, oddity, screwball, weirdo, zany

rel bohemian, maverick, nonconformist, quixote; coot, geezer; curio, rarity; freak

phrases odd duck, piece of work

near ant conformer, conformist, follower, sheep

eccentricity *n* an odd or peculiar habit — see IDIOSYNCRASY

ecclesiastic *adj* of or relating to a church — see ECCLESIASTICAL

ecclesiastical *adj* of or relating to a church ⟨*ecclesiastical* laws that have been in existence for centuries⟩

syn churchly, ecclesiastic

rel blessed (*also* blest), consecrated, divine, hallowed, holy, religious, sacramental, sacred, sacrosanct, sanctified; apostolic, canonical, clerical, episcopal, evangelical (*also* evangelic), ministerial, papal, pastoral, patriarchal, priestly, rabbinic (*or* rabbinical), sacerdotal

near ant lay, profane, secular, temporal; nonclerical; nondenominational, nonsectarian

ant nonchurch, nonecclesiastical

echelon *n* the placement of someone or something in relation to others in a vertical arrangement — see RANK 1

echo *n* **1** a person who adopts the appearance or behavior of another especially in an obvious way — see COPYCAT

2 a tiny often physical indication of something lost or vanished — see VESTIGE 1

echo *vb* **1** to continue or be repeated in a series of reflected sound waves — see REVERBERATE

2 to say after another — see REPEAT 3

---

syn synonym(s) *rel* related words

ant antonym(s) *near ant* near antonym(s)

eclectic *adj* consisting of many things of different sorts — see MISCELLANEOUS

eclipse *n* a change to a lower state or level — see DECLINE 2

eclipse *vb* to be greater, better, or stronger than — see SURPASS 1

economical *adj* careful in the management of money or resources — see FRUGAL

economize *vb* to avoid unnecessary waste or expense ⟨In tough times people learn how to *economize*.⟩

syn pinch, save, scrimp, skimp, spare

rel conserve, husband, maintain, manage, preserve; scrape; cut back, cut down, retrench; hoard, lay up

phrases pinch pennies

near ant blow, dissipate, fritter (away), lavish, misspend, run through, spend, squander, throw away; splurge

ant waste

economizing *adj* careful in the management of money or resources — see FRUGAL

economy *n* careful management of material resources ⟨People on fixed incomes are used to practicing *economy*.⟩

syn frugality, husbandry, parsimony, providence, scrimping, skimping, thrift

rel conservation, saving; miserliness, stinginess; belt-tightening, retrenchment; discretion, forehandedness, prudence; austerity, moderation, restraint, temperance

near ant extravagance, improvidence, lavishness, prodigality, squandering

ant wastefulness

ecstasy *n* a state of overwhelming usually pleasurable emotion ⟨Actors are typically in *ecstasy* upon winning an Oscar.⟩

syn elation, euphoria, exhilaration, heaven, high, intoxication, paradise, rapture, rhapsody, swoon, transport

rel exaltation; blessedness, bliss, blissfulness, delight, enchantment, felicity, gladness, happiness, joy, joyfulness, joyousness, pleasure; reverie, trance; inspiration; fervor, frenzy, madness, passion; cheer, cheerfulness, exuberance, glee, gleefulness, jubilance, jubilation, lightheartedness

near ant misery, sadness, unhappiness, woe, wretchedness; blues, dejection, desolation, despair, despondency, disconsolateness, disheartenment, dispiritedness, doldrums, downheartedness, dreariness, dumps, forlornness, gloom, gloominess, heartsickness, melancholy, mopes

ant depression

ecstatic *adj* experiencing or marked by overwhelming usually pleasurable emotion ⟨A football player who was *ecstatic* upon receiving a full athletic scholarship to the college of his choice⟩

syn elated, elevated, enraptured, entranced, euphoric, exhilarated, giddy, intoxicated, rapt, rapturous, rhapsodic (*also* rhapsodical)

rel enchanted, exultant, glorying, jubilant, rejoicing, triumphant; enthusiastic, excited, gung ho, thrilled; blissed-out, blissful, delighted, glad, gratified, happy, joyful, joyous, pleased, satisfied, tickled

phrases on cloud nine, over the moon

near ant blue, brokenhearted, crestfallen, dejected, despondent, disconsolate, disheartened, doleful, down, downcast, downhearted, forlorn, gloomy, glum, hangdog, heartbroken, heartsick, heartsore, inconsolable, joyless, low, low-spirited, melancholy, miserable, mournful, sad, saddened, sorrowful, sorry, unhappy, woebegone, woeful, wretched

ant depressed

Eden *n* an often imaginary place or state of utter perfection and happiness — see PARADISE 1

edge *n* 1 a harsh or sharp quality ⟨Her comments had a sarcastic *edge*.⟩

syn acidity, acidness, acridness, acrimoniousness, acrimony, acuteness, asperity, bite, bitterness, harshness, keenness, poignancy, pungency, roughness, sharpness, tartness

rel ginger, punch, spice; raucousness, severeness, severity, shrillness, virulence, vitriol; cattiness, maliciousness; pointedness, thorniness

near ant gentleness, kindliness

ant mildness, softness

2 the line or relatively narrow space that marks the outer limit of something — see BORDER 1

3 the more favorable condition or position in a competition — see ADVANTAGE 1

4 the power to produce a desired result — see EFFICACY

5 an interval of time just before the onset of something — see POINT 3

edge *vb* 1 to make sharp or sharper — see SHARPEN

2 to serve as a border for — see BORDER

edged *adj* having an edge thin enough to cut or pierce something — see SHARP 1

edgewise *adv* with one side faced forward — see SIDEWAYS 1

edginess *n* a state of nervousness marked by sudden jerky movements — see JUMPINESS

edgy *adj* 1 feeling or showing uncomfortable feelings of uncertainty — see NERVOUS 1

2 having an edge thin enough to cut or pierce something — see SHARP 1

3 serving or likely to arouse a strong reaction — see PROVOCATIVE

edible *adj* suitable for use as food ⟨*edible* plant products⟩

syn eatable, esculent

rel absorbable, chewable, digestible, ingestible, swallowable; nourishing, nutritious, nutritive; appetizing, delicious, flavorful, palatable, savory (*also* savoury), succulent, tasty, toothsome, toothy

near ant indigestible, nondigestible, nonnutritious, undigestible

ant inedible, nonedible, uneatable

edibles *n pl* substances intended to be eaten — see FOOD

edict *n* 1 an order publicly issued by an authority ⟨The school board's *edict* put a new student dress code into effect.⟩

syn bull, decree, directive, fiat, ruling

rel call, conclusion, decision, deliverance, determination, diagnosis, judgment (*or* judgement), opinion, resolution, verdict; announcement, declaration, dictum, manifesto, proclamation, pronouncement; canon, encyclical

2 a statement of what to do that must be obeyed by those concerned — see COMMAND 1

edifice *n* 1 a large, magnificent, or massive building ⟨The U.S. Capitol is one of our nation's most impressive *edifices*.⟩
syn hall, palace, tower
rel construction, erection, structure; castle, château, countryseat, estate, hacienda, manor, manor house, mansion, showplace, villa; mausoleum, memorial, monument
2 something built as a dwelling, shelter, or place for human activity — see BUILDING
3 the arrangement of parts that gives something its basic form — see FRAME 1

edify *vb* to provide (someone) with moral or spiritual understanding — see ENLIGHTEN 2

edit *vb* 1 to prepare for publication by correcting, rewriting, or updating ⟨The publisher *edited* a new version of its best-selling school dictionary.⟩
syn redraft, revamp, revise, rework
rel perfect, polish, touch up; copyedit, read; amend, annotate, correct, emend, rectify; fact-check; collect, compile; get out, issue, print, publish; abridge, redact
2 to change (something) so as to make it suitable for a new use or situation — see ADAPT

educate *vb* 1 to cause to acquire knowledge or skill in some field — see TEACH
2 to provide (someone) with moral or spiritual understanding — see ENLIGHTEN 2

educated *adj* 1 having or displaying advanced knowledge or education ⟨an *educated* work force⟩
syn erudite, knowledgeable, learned, literate, scholarly, well-read
rel civilized, cultivated, cultured; cerebral, highbrow, intellectual; polished, refined, well-bred; academic (*also* academical), bookish, didactic, didactical, inkhorn, pedantic, professorial; informed, instructed, schooled, skilled, trained; homeschooled; briefed, enlightened, informed, versed
near ant uncivilized, uncultivated, uncultured; lowbrow, semiliterate, unintellectual; ill-bred, unpolished, unrefined; uninformed, unknowledgeable; uninstructed, unschooled, untaught, untutored; semiliterate, undereducated
ant benighted, dark, ignorant, illiterate, uneducated, unlearned, unlettered, unscholarly
2 having or showing exceptional knowledge, experience, or skill in a field of endeavor — see PROFICIENT

education *n* 1 the act or process of imparting knowledge or skills to another ⟨a teacher who devoted herself to the *education* of children with special needs⟩
syn instruction, schooling, teaching, training, tutelage, tutoring
rel didactics, pedagogics, pedagogy; higher education, higher learning; coaching, conditioning, cultivation, preparation, readying; development, direction, guidance, nurturance, nurturing; edification, enlightenment, improvement; apprenticeship

2 the understanding and information gained from being educated ⟨a person whose extensive *education* was obvious to all who met him⟩
syn erudition, knowledge, learnedness, learning, scholarship
rel culture, edification, enlightenment; reading; bookishness, pedantry
near ant functional illiteracy
ant ignorance, illiteracy, illiterateness

educational *adj* 1 providing useful information or knowledge — see INFORMATIVE
2 of or relating to schooling or learning especially at an advanced level — see ACADEMIC 1

educative *adj* providing useful information or knowledge — see INFORMATIVE

educator *n* a person whose occupation is to give formal instruction in a school — see TEACHER

educe *vb* to draw out (something hidden, latent, or reserved) ⟨The gift of a puppy finally *educed* a response from the shy boy.⟩
syn elicit, evoke, inspire, raise
rel drag, dredge (up), extort, extract, pull, wangle, wrest, wring; coax (out), gain, get, obtain, procure, secure; bare, disclose, discover, divulge, evince, expose, reveal, uncloak, uncover, unmask, unveil
phrases call forth
near ant disregard, forget, ignore, miss, neglect, overlook, overpass, pass over

eerie *also* **eery** *adj* fearfully and mysteriously strange or fantastic ⟨*Eerie* noises would occasionally come from locked rooms in the castle.⟩
syn creepy, haunting, spooky, uncanny, unearthly, weird
rel ghastly, ghostlike, ghostly, ghoulish, spectral; bizarre, curious, odd, outlandish, outré, peculiar, quaint, quirky; unaccustomed, uncommon, unusual; metaphysical, preternatural, supernatural; enigmatic (*also* enigmatical), inscrutable, mysterious, puzzling
near ant common, commonplace, everyday, normal, ordinary, prosaic, routine, typical, unexceptional, unremarkable, usual; natural; expected, familiar, predictable

efface *vb* to destroy all traces of — see ANNIHILATE 1

effect *n* 1 a condition or occurrence traceable to a cause ⟨Better health is always one of the *effects* of improved hygiene.⟩
syn aftereffect, aftermath, child, conclusion, consequence, corollary, development, fate, fruit, issue, outcome, outgrowth, product, result, resultant, sequel, sequence, upshot
rel ramification; denouement (*also* dénouement), echo, implication, repercussion; afterclap, afterglow, aftershock; byproduct, fallout, offshoot, ripple, side effect (*also* side reaction), spin-off
phrases matter of course
near ant consideration, determinant, factor; base, basis, foundation, ground, groundwork; impetus, incentive, inspiration, instigation, stimulus; mother, origin, root, source, spring
ant antecedent, cause, occasion, reason
2 the power to bring about a result on

another ⟨Friendship has a profound *effect* on our lives.⟩

syn impact, influence, mark, repercussion, sway

rel authority, clout, prestige, pull, weight; command, domination, dominion, mastery; consequence, importance, significance; sovereignty (*also* sovranty), supremacy

near ant helplessness, impotence, impotency, powerlessness, weakness

3 effects *pl* transportable items that one owns — see POSSESSION 2

effect *vb* to be the cause of (a situation, action, or state of mind) ⟨classroom discussions designed to *effect* a change in racial attitudes⟩

syn beget, breed, bring, bring about, cause, create, do, draw on, effectuate, engender, generate, induce, make, occasion, produce, prompt, result (in), spawn, translate (into), work, yield

rel conduce (to), contribute (to); decide, determine; begin, establish, father, found, inaugurate, initiate, innovate, institute, introduce, launch, pioneer, set, set up, start; advance, cultivate, develop, encourage, forward, foster, further, nourish, nurture, promote; enact, render, turn out

phrases bring forth, give rise to

near ant impede, limit, restrict; clamp down (on), crack down (on), crush, dampen, put down, quash, quell, repress, smother, squash, squelch, stifle, subdue, suppress; arrest, check, control, curb, inhibit, rein (in), restrain, retard; abolish, demolish, destroy, extinguish, liquidate, quench

effective *adj* **1** producing or capable of producing a desired result ⟨an *effective* treatment of the once-dreaded disease⟩

syn effectual, efficacious, efficient, fruitful, operative, potent, productive

rel hyperefficient, ultraefficient; adequate, capable, competent; accomplished, adept, consummate, experienced, expert, masterly, practiced (*also* practised), proficient, skilled, skillful, versed, veteran, virtuoso; cogent, convincing, killer, sound, striking, telling, valid; active, dynamic; useful, working; applicable, feasible, functional, practicable, practical, realizable, usable (*also* useable), workable

near ant incapable, incompetent, inexperienced, inexpert, unqualified, unseasoned, unskilled, unskillful; abortive, bootless, futile, vain; empty, hollow, idle, pointless, unavailing, unprofitable, unsuccessful; inoperative, worthless

ant fruitless, ineffective, ineffectual, inefficient, inoperative, unfruitful, unproductive, useless

2 having the power to persuade — see COGENT

3 existing in fact and not merely as a possibility — see ACTUAL

effectiveness *n* **1** the capacity to persuade — see COGENCY 1

2 the power to produce a desired result — see EFFICACY

3 the quality of an utterance that provokes interest and produces an effect — see ¹PUNCH 1

effectual *adj* producing or capable of producing a desired result — see EFFECTIVE 1

effectualness *n* the power to produce a desired result — see EFFICACY

effectuate *vb* to be the cause of (a situation, action, or state of mind) — see EFFECT

effeminate *adj* of or relating to a man who has or displays qualities traditionally considered more suitable for women ⟨He had a high and somewhat *effeminate* voice.⟩

syn effete, womanish

rel feminine, girlish, girlie (*or* girly), womanlike, womanly; old-maidish, overnice, prissy, spinsterish; dandyish, dudish, foppish, sappy; camp, campy

ant manlike, manly, mannish, masculine, virile

effervescent *adj* joyously unrestrained — see EXUBERANT

effete *adj* **1** having lost forcefulness, courage, or spirit ⟨the soft, *effete* society that marked the final years of the Roman empire⟩

syn decadent, decayed, degenerate, overripe, washed-up

rel overrefined, precious; decaying, declining, dying, failing, waning; debilitated, enervate, enervated, enfeebled, feeble, frail, languid, sapped, soft, wasted, weak, weakened, wimpy; dissolute, immoral; debased, debauched, degraded, demoralized, depraved, dissipated, dissolute

ant undecadent

2 lacking bodily strength — see WEAK 1

3 lacking strength of will or character — see WEAK 2

4 of or relating to a man who has or displays qualities traditionally considered more suitable for women — see EFFEMINATE

efficacious *adj* producing or capable of producing a desired result — see EFFECTIVE 1

efficaciousness *n* the power to produce a desired result — see EFFICACY

efficacy *n* the power to produce a desired result ⟨We questioned the *efficacy* of the alarms in actually preventing auto theft.⟩

syn edge, effectiveness, effectualness, efficaciousness, efficiency, productiveness

rel ability, capability, capacity; potency, puissance, strength

near ant inability, inadequacy, incompetence

ant ineffectiveness, ineffectuality, ineffectualness, inefficiency

efficiency *n* the power to produce a desired result — see EFFICACY

efficient *adj* producing or capable of producing a desired result — see EFFECTIVE 1

effort *n* the active use of energy in producing a result ⟨The finished parade float was well worth the *effort*.⟩

syn elbow grease, exertion, expenditure, labor, pains, sweat, trouble, while, work

rel drudgery, grind, slog, strain, toil, travail; dint, energy; force, might, muscle, power, puissance; attempt, endeavor, essay, fling, go, pass, shot, stab, trial, try, whack

near ant adroitness, ease, facility, fluency, smoothness; dormancy, idleness, inaction, inactivity, indolence, inertia, languor, laziness, quiescence

effortless *adj* involving minimal difficulty or effort — see EASY 1

effortlessly *adv* without difficulty — see EASILY 1

effrontery *n* shameless boldness ⟨The little squirt had the *effrontery* to deny eating any cookies, even with the crumbs still on his lips.⟩

syn audacity, brashness, brass, brassiness, brazenness, cheek, cheekiness, chutzpah (*also* chutzpa *or* hutzpah *or* hutzpa), face, gall, nerve, nerviness, pertness, presumption, presumptuousness, sauce, sauciness, temerity

rel arrogance, assurance, cockiness, confidence, hardihood, overconfidence, sanguinity, self-assurance, self-confidence; discourteousness, disrespect, impertinence, impoliteness, impudence, incivility, inconsiderateness, inconsideration, insolence, rudeness, ungraciousness; back talk, sass; swagger, swash

near ant bashfulness, diffidence, faintheartedness, hesitancy, modesty, shyness, timidity, timidness, timorousness; civility, courteousness, courtesy, gentility, graciousness, mannerliness, manners

effulgence *n* the quality or state of having or giving off light — see BRILLIANCE 1

effulgent *adj* giving off or reflecting much light — see BRIGHT 1

effusive *adj* showing feeling freely — see DEMONSTRATIVE 1

egg (on) *vb* to try to persuade (someone) through earnest appeals to follow a course of action — see URGE

egghead *n* a person with strong intellectual interests — see INTELLECTUAL

ego *n* 1 a reasonable or justifiable sense of one's worth or importance — see PRIDE 1
2 an often unjustified feeling of being pleased with oneself or with one's situation or achievements — see COMPLACENCE 1

egocentric *adj* overly concerned with one's own desires, needs, or interests ⟨The novel's *egocentric* main character journeys to "find herself."⟩

syn egoistic (*also* egoistical), egotistic (*or* egotistical), self-centered, selfish, self-seeking

rel inner-directed; complacent, conceited, overweening, pompous, prideful, proud, self-complacent, self-conceited, self-contented, self-directed, self-glorifying, self-important, self-pleased, self-satisfied, smug, vain, vainglorious

near ant altruistic, beneficent, benevolent, charitable, generous, greathearted, humanitarian, magnanimous, philanthropic (*also* philanthropical), self-giving, self-sacrificing; other-directed; diffident, self-doubting; self-reflective

ant self-forgetful, self-forgetting, selfless, unselfish

egoism *n* excessive interest in oneself ⟨Because of her *egoism*, she never gave a thought to asking how the others felt.⟩

syn egotism, self-centeredness, self-interest, selfishness, self-regard

rel complacence, complacency, conceit, conceitedness, ego, pompousness, pride,

pridefulness, self-admiration, self-conceit, self-esteem, self-importance, self-indulgence, self-partiality, self-respect, self-satisfaction, self-sufficiency, smugness, vaingloriousness, vainglory, vainness, vanity; self-assumption, self-consequence, self-content, self-contentment, self-glorification

near ant altruism, generosity, magnanimity, self-sacrifice; detachment, disinterestedness, fairness, impartiality, neutrality, objectivity; self-flagellation; self-annihilation, self-immolation

ant self-abandonment, self-forgetfulness, selflessness, unselfishness

egoistic *also* **egoistical** *adj* 1 having too high an opinion of oneself — see CONCEITED
2 overly concerned with one's own desires, needs, or interests — see EGOCENTRIC

egotism *n* 1 an often unjustified feeling of being pleased with oneself or with one's situation or achievements — see COMPLACENCE 1
2 excessive interest in oneself — see EGOISM

egotistic *or* **egotistical** *adj* 1 having too high an opinion of oneself — see CONCEITED
2 overly concerned with one's own desires, needs, or interests — see EGOCENTRIC

egregious *adj* very noticeable especially for being incorrect or bad ⟨The student's theme was marred by a number of *egregious* errors in spelling.⟩

syn blatant, conspicuous, flagrant, glaring, gross, obvious, patent, pronounced, rank, striking

rel arresting, clear, distinct, dramatic, emphatic, evident, eye-catching, marked, notable, noticeable, outstanding, plain, prominent, remarkable, salient, showy, splashy; absolute, arrant, downright, outand-out, outright, sheer, stark, utter; detectable, discernible (*also* discernable), observable, perceptible, visible; abominable, atrocious, awful, deplorable, execrable, heinous, lousy, monstrous, outrageous

near ant imperceptible, inconspicuous, unnoticeable, unobtrusive; inconsequential, inconsiderable, insignificant, slight, small, trifling, trivial; concealed

egress *n* a place or means of going out — see EXIT 1

ejaculate *vb* to utter with a sudden burst of strong feeling — see EXCLAIM

ejaculation *n* a sudden short emotional utterance — see EXCLAMATION

eject *vb* 1 to drive or force out ⟨We summarily *ejected* the unwanted guest from our party.⟩

syn banish, boot (out), bounce, chase, dismiss, drum (out), expel, extrude, oust, out, rout, run off, throw out, turn out

rel deport, displace, evict, exile, expatriate, ostracize, read out, shut out; can, cashier, defenestrate, discharge, fire, muster out, release, remove, retire, sack, terminate

phrases give one the gate [*slang*], send packing

near ant accept, admit, take, take in;

---

welcome; entertain, harbor, house, lodge, shelter

2 to violently throw out or off (something from within) — see ERUPT 1

elaborate *adj* **1** made or done with great care or with much detail ⟨*elaborate* festivities for the 200th anniversary of the town's founding⟩

syn complex, complicated, detailed, fancy, intricate, involved, sophisticated

rel elegant, exquisite, grand, magnificent, ornate, splendid; chichi, extravagant, exuberant, fancified, flamboyant, frilly, gimmicked (up), grandiose, ostentatious, overwrought, showy, souped-up; Byzantine, convoluted, involute, involuted, labyrinthine

near ant modest, plain, uncomplicated; bald, bare, naked, unadorned, undecorated, unvarnished

ant simple, unfancy, unsophisticated

2 including many small descriptive features — see DETAILED 1

3 having many parts or aspects that are usually interrelated — see COMPLEX 1

elaborate *vb* to gradually become clearer or more detailed — see DEVELOP 1

elaborate (on) *vb* **1** to add to the interest of by including made-up details — see EMBROIDER

2 to express more fully and in greater detail — see EXPAND 1

elaborateness *n* the state or quality of having many interrelated parts or aspects — see COMPLEXITY 1

elaboration *n* **1** the act or process of going from the simple or basic to the complex or advanced — see DEVELOPMENT 1

2 the representation of something in terms that go beyond the facts — see EXAGGERATION

elapse *vb* to come to an end — see CEASE 1

elastic *adj* **1** able to revert to original size and shape after being stretched, squeezed, or twisted ⟨*elastic* rubber bands⟩

syn flexible, resilient, rubberlike, rubbery, springy, stretch, stretchable, supple

rel adaptable, ductile, kneadable, malleable, plastic, pliable, pliant; limber, lissome (*also* lissom), lithe, lithesome, willowy

near ant compact, firm, hard, solid, unyielding; brittle, crisp, crumbly, flaky (*also* flakey), friable, short

ant inelastic, inflexible, nonelastic, rigid, stiff

2 capable of being readily changed — see FLEXIBLE 1

elate *vb* to fill with great joy ⟨The winning of the state basketball championship *elated* the whole town.⟩

syn elevate, enrapture, exhilarate, intoxicate, transport

rel commove, excite, inspire, stimulate, uplift; content, delight, gladden, gratify, please, rejoice, satisfy, warm

near ant demoralize, discourage, dishearten, dispirit; distress, oppress, sadden

ant depress

elated *adj* experiencing or marked by overwhelming usually pleasurable emotion — see ECSTATIC

elation *n* a state of overwhelming usually pleasurable emotion — see ECSTASY

elbow *vb* to force one's way — see ²PRESS 4

elbow grease *n* the active use of energy in producing a result — see EFFORT

elder *n* **1** a person of advanced years — see SENIOR CITIZEN

2 one who is above another in rank, station, or office — see SUPERIOR

3 one who is older than another — see SENIOR 1

4 the senior member of a group — see DEAN

elderly *adj* being of advanced years and especially past middle age ⟨*Elderly* people who stay active are usually the healthiest and the happiest.⟩

syn aged, aging (*or* ageing), ancient, geriatric, long-lived, old, older, senior

rel centenarian, nonagenarian, octogenarian, septuagenarian, sexagenarian; oldish; adult, grown-up, mature, middle-aged; pensioned, retired, superannuated; venerable; decrepit, doddering, senile, tottery; overage (*also* overaged)

phrases long in the tooth, of a certain age

near ant ageless; youngish; adolescent, immature, juvenile, preteen, puerile; minor, underage; callow, green, inexperienced, raw; babyish, childish, childlike, infantile, infantine, kiddish

ant young, youthful

elder statesman *n* the senior member of a group — see DEAN

elect *adj* singled out from a number or group as more to one's liking — see SELECT 1

elect *n* individuals carefully selected as being the best of a class — see ELITE 1

elect *vb* to decide to accept (someone or something) from a group of possibilities — see CHOOSE 1

election *n* **1** the act or process of selecting — see SELECTION 1

2 the power, right, or opportunity to choose — see CHOICE 1

elective *adj* subject to one's freedom of choice — see OPTIONAL

electric *adj* causing great emotional or mental stimulation — see EXCITING 1

electrify *vb* to cause a pleasurable stimulation of the feelings of — see THRILL

electrifying *adj* causing great emotional or mental stimulation — see EXCITING 1

elegance *n* dignified or restrained beauty of form, appearance, or style ⟨the *elegance* of the hotel's French furnishings⟩

syn class, courtliness, elegancy, fineness, grace, gracefulness, handsomeness, majesty, refinement, stateliness

rel augustness, brilliance, gloriousness, glory, grandeur, grandness, lavishness, luxuriance, luxuriousness, luxury, magnificence, nobility, nobleness, opulence, ornateness, plushness, plushiness, resplendence, richness, splendor, sumptuousness; artfulness, chic, polish, sophistication, taste, tastefulness; classicism, dignity, exquisiteness, restraint, simplicity; affectedness, grandiosity, ostentation, ostentatiousness, pretentiousness, showiness

near ant coarseness, crudeness, flamboyance, flashiness, garishness, gaudiness, glitz, grotesqueness, grotesquerie (*also* grotesquery), kitsch, tastelessness, tawdriness, vulgarity

ant gracelessness, inelegance

elegancy n dignified or restrained beauty of form, appearance, or style — see ELEGANCE

elegant adj 1 having or showing elegance ⟨The bride's *elegant* gown received nothing but praise.⟩

syn classy, courtly, fine, graceful, handsome, majestic, refined, stately, tasteful

rel august, baronial, gallant, glorious, grand, heroic (*also* heroical), imposing, lavish, luxurious, magnificent, monumental, noble, ornate, proud, regal, rich, royal, splendid, superb; artful, genteel, polished, sophisticated; classic, conservative, exquisite, quiet, restrained, simple, understated; aristocratic, patrician; à la mode (*also* a la mode), chic, fashionable, in, modish, posh, sharp, sleek, smart, snappy, stylish, swagger, swank (*or* swanky); affected, grandiose, ostentatious, pretentious, recherché

near ant cheesy, coarse, crude, flamboyant, flashy, garish, gaudy, glitzy, grotesque, loud, raffish, splashy, tacky, tawdry, ticky-tacky (*also* ticky-tack); rough-edged, rude, trashy, uncouth, uncultivated, uncultured, unpolished, unrefined, vulgar

ant dowdy, graceless, inelegant, styleless, tasteless, unfashionable, unhandsome, unstylish

2 having qualities that appeal to a refined taste — see CHOICE 1

elegiac *also* **elegiacal** adj causing or marked by an atmosphere lacking in cheer — see GLOOMY 1

elegy n a composition expressing one's grief over a loss — see LAMENT 2

element n 1 one of the parts that make up a whole ⟨A free press is an essential *element* of a democracy.⟩

syn building block, component, constituent, factor, ingredient, member

rel basis, part and parcel; detail, item, particular, point; aspect, characteristic, facet, feature, trait; division, fragment, particle, partition, piece, portion, section, sector, segment; subcomponent

near ant aggregate, composite, compound, mass; sum, summation, total, totality; admixture, amalgam, amalgamation, blend, combination, intermixture, mix, mixture

ant whole

2 elements pl general or basic truths on which other truths or theories can be based — see PRINCIPLES 1

3 a region of activity, knowledge, or influence — see FIELD 2

elemental adj of or relating to the simplest facts or theories of a subject — see ELEMENTARY

elementary adj of or relating to the simplest facts or theories of a subject ⟨students who do not have even an *elementary* knowledge of geography⟩

syn basic, beginning, elemental, essential, fundamental, introductory, rudimentary, underlying

rel primal, primary, prime, simple; crude, primeval, primitive, primordial, rude, uncomplicated; preliminary, preparatory; crucial, important, key

near ant complex, sophisticated; complicated, convoluted, detailed, elaborate, extensive, intricate; developed, evolved, high, higher, refined

ant advanced

elephantine adj unusually large — see HUGE

elevate vb 1 to fill with great joy — see ELATE

2 to move from a lower to a higher place or position — see RAISE 1

3 to move higher in rank or position — see PROMOTE 1

4 to assign a high status or value to — see EXALT 1

elevated adj 1 being positioned above a surface ⟨an *elevated* monorail that transports visitors all over the theme park⟩

syn lifted, raised, uplifted, upraised

rel aerial; erect, perpendicular, standing, upright, upstanding, vertical

near ant low, low-lying, short, squat

ant sunken

2 very dignified in form, tone, or style ⟨the *elevated* language of Lincoln's Gettysburg Address⟩

syn eloquent, formal, high-flown, lofty, majestic, stately, towering

rel affected, bombastic, declamatory, florid, flowery, grandiloquent, grandiose, highfalutin (*also* hifalutin), oratorical, pompous, pretentious, rhetorical (*also* rhetoric), stilted; cultured, refined; classy, courtly, fine, graceful, tasteful; aristocratic, genteel, patrician; correct, educated, grammatical, proper; academic (*also* academical), bookish, learned, literary

near ant casual, colloquial, conversational, informal, nonformal, slangy, unbookish, unliterary, vernacular; coarse, common, crass, crude, gross, ill-bred, indecent, lowbred, lowbrow, rough, rude, tasteless, uncouth, uncultivated, uncultured, unpolished, unrefined, vulgar; incorrect, substandard, uneducated, unlearned

ant ineloquent, low, undignified

3 being at a higher level than average — see HIGH 2

4 having, characterized by, or arising from a dignified and generous nature — see NOBLE 2

5 located at a greater height than average or usual — see HIGH 3

6 experiencing or marked by overwhelming usually pleasurable emotion — see ECSTATIC

elevation n 1 a raising or a state of being raised to a higher rank or position — see ADVANCEMENT 1

2 an area of high ground — see HEIGHT 4

3 the distance of something or someone from bottom to top — see HEIGHT 3

4 the most extreme or advanced point — see HEIGHT 2

elf n an imaginary being usually having a small human form and magical powers — see FAIRY

elfin adj having an often mysterious or magical power to attract — see FASCINATING 1

elfish adj given to good-natured joking or teasing — see PLAYFUL

elicit vb to draw out (something hidden, latent, or reserved) — see EDUCE

---

syn synonym(s)   rel related words

ant antonym(s)   near ant near antonym(s)

eliminate *vb* to prevent the participation, consideration, or inclusion of — see EXCLUDE

elite *n* 1 individuals carefully selected as being the best of a class ⟨The winners of this science award represent the *elite* of our high schools.⟩
syn aristocracy, best, choice, cream, elect, fat, flower, pick, pride, prime, upper crust
rel establishment, gentry, nobility, quality, society, top, top drawer, upper class
phrases cream of the crop, Hall of Fame
near ant commoners, herd, masses, mob, multitude, rank and file, unwashed
2 the highest class in a society — see ARISTOCRACY 1

elixir *n* something that cures all ills or problems — see CURE-ALL

elocution *n* the art of speaking in public eloquently and effectively — see ORATORY 1

elongate *vb* to make longer — see EXTEND 1

elongate *or* **elongated** *adj* of great extent from end to end — see LONG 1

elongation *n* the act of making longer — see EXTENSION 1

eloquence *n* the art or power of speaking or writing in a forceful and convincing way ⟨the *eloquence* of Martin Luther King's "I Have a Dream" speech⟩
syn articulateness, poetry, rhetoric
rel expression, expressiveness; declamation, elocution, oratory; cogency, force, forcefulness, meaningfulness, persuasion, persuasiveness; ardor, emotion, fervency, fervidness, fervor, heat, intensity, passion, power, vehemence, warmth
phrases gift of gab
ant inarticulateness

eloquent *adj* 1 able to express oneself clearly and well — see ARTICULATE
2 clearly conveying a special meaning (as one's mood) — see EXPRESSIVE
3 very dignified in form, tone, or style — see ELEVATED 2

else *adj* resulting in an increase in amount or number — see ADDITIONAL

else *adv* in a different way — see OTHERWISE

elucidate *vb* to make plain or understandable — see EXPLAIN 1

elucidation *n* a statement that makes something clear — see EXPLANATION 1

elucidative *adj* serving to explain — see EXPLANATORY

elude *vb* to get or keep away from (as a responsibility) through cleverness or trickery — see ESCAPE 2

eluding *n* the act or a means of getting or keeping away from something undesirable — see ESCAPE 2

elusive *adj* hard to find, capture, or isolate ⟨The giant squid is one of the ocean's most *elusive* inhabitants.⟩
syn evasive, fugitive
rel cagey (*also* cagy), shifty; ephemeral, evanescent, fleeting, impermanent, momentary, passing, short-lived, temporary, transient, transitory; inaccessible, inconvenient, unapproachable, unattainable, unavailable, unobtainable, unreachable, untouchable
near ant accessible, approachable, attainable, available, convenient, obtainable, reachable

elvish *adj* tending to or exhibiting reckless playfulness — see MISCHIEVOUS 1

Elysium *n* 1 a dwelling place of perfect happiness for the soul after death — see HEAVEN 1
2 an often imaginary place or state of utter perfection and happiness — see PARADISE 1

emaciated *adj* suffering extreme weight loss as a result of hunger or disease ⟨As she recovered, she grew less *emaciated*.⟩
syn cadaverous, gaunt, haggard, skeletal, wasted
rel lank, lanky, rawboned, scraggy, scrawny, sinewy, skinny, spare, thin; starved, underfed, undernourished; famished, hungry, starving; shriveled (*or* shrivelled), withered, wizened
near ant beefy, brawny, burly, fit, hale, healthy, hearty, husky; chubby, corpulent, fat, fleshy, heavyset, obese, overweight, plump, portly, pudgy, roly-poly, rotund, stocky, thickset, tubby; flabby, soft

emancipate *vb* to release (as from slavery or confinement) — see FREE 1

emancipation *n* the act of setting free from slavery — see LIBERATION

emasculate *vb* to deprive of courage or confidence — see UNNERVE 1

embankment *n* a bank of earth constructed to control water — see DAM

embargo *n* an order that something not be done or used — see PROHIBITION 2

embark (on *or* **upon)** *vb* to take the first step in (a process or course of action) — see BEGIN 1

embarrass *vb* 1 to throw into a state of self-conscious distress ⟨The modest young soldier was *embarrassed* by the public praise for his heroism.⟩
syn abash, confound, confuse, discomfit, disconcert, discountenance, faze, fluster, mortify, nonplus, rattle
rel agitate, bother, chagrin, discomfort, discompose, dismay, disquiet, distress, disturb, perturb, put off, put out, unhinge, unsettle, upset; debase, degrade, demean, humble, humiliate, shame
near ant calm, comfort, console, relieve, soothe; buoy, cheer, embolden, encourage, hearten; assure, reassure
2 to create difficulty for the work or activity of — see HAMPER
3 to make complex or difficult — see COMPLICATE

embarrassing *adj* causing embarrassment — see AWKWARD 3

embarrassment *n* 1 the emotional state of being made self-consciously uncomfortable ⟨experienced the great *embarrassment* of tripping while on stage⟩
syn abashment, confusion, discomfiture, fluster, mortification
rel agitation, bother, chagrin, discomfort, discomposure, dismay, disquiet, distress, disturbance, perturbation, uneasiness, upset; disgrace, ignominy, shame; debasement, degradation, humiliation, mortification; humble pie
phrases egg on one's face
near ant aplomb, assurance, composure,

confidence, coolness, equanimity, poise, self-assurance, self-confidence, self-possession

2 something that makes movement or progress difficult — see ENCUMBRANCE

embed *also* **imbed** *vb* to set solidly in or as if in surrounding matter — see ENTRENCH

embellish *vb* **1** to add to the interest of by including made-up details — see EMBROIDER

2 to make more attractive by adding something that is beautiful or becoming — see DECORATE

embellishing *adj* serving to add beauty — see DECORATIVE

embellishment *n* **1** something that decorates or beautifies — see DECORATION 1

2 the representation of something in terms that go beyond the facts — see EXAGGERATION

embitter *vb* to implant bitter feelings in ⟨They refused to let the unfortunate incident *embitter* them.⟩

syn antagonize, envenom

rel aggravate, anger, enrage, incense, infuriate, madden; alienate, disaffect, disgruntle, estrange, set (against); curdle, sour

near ant endear, ingratiate; appease, assuage, mollify, pacify, placate, propitiate

embittered *adj* having or showing deep-seated resentment — see BITTER 1

emblem *n* a device, design, or figure used as an identifying mark ⟨The state uses a beehive as its *emblem*.⟩

syn ensign, hallmark, logo, symbol, trademark

rel attribute, icon (*also* ikon), pictograph; logogram, logograph; badge, coat of arms, cognizance, crest, insignia, monogram; colophon, stamp, token

emblematic *also* **emblematical** *adj* having the function or meaning of an object or figure that stands for something else — see SYMBOLIC

embodiment *n* a visible representation of something abstract (as a quality) ⟨Mother Theresa was often regarded as the *embodiment* of selfless devotion to others.⟩

syn abstract, epitome, genius, icon (*also* ikon), image, incarnation, manifestation, personification

rel concretization, exemplification, personalization, realization, substantiation; essence, quintessence, soul; archetype, exemplar, model, paradigm, pattern; reincarnation

embody *vb* **1** to make a part of a body or system ⟨They must *embody* their ideas in substantial institutions if they are to survive.⟩

syn absorb, assimilate, incorporate, integrate

rel amalgamate, blend, combine, commingle, fuse, intermingle, merge, mingle; acculturate, accustom, condition, enculturate, naturalize

2 to represent in visible form ⟨George Washington *embodied* so many of the virtues that Americans hold dear.⟩

syn body, epitomize, express, incarnate,

incorporate, manifest, materialize, personalize, personify, substantiate

rel actualize, concretize, realize; exemplify, illustrate, image, objectify, symbolize, typify

ant disembody

embolden *vb* to fill with courage or strength of purpose — see ENCOURAGE 1

emboldened *adj* inclined or willing to take risks — see BOLD 1

embosom *vb* to surround or cover closely — see ENFOLD 1

embower *vb* to surround or cover closely — see ENFOLD 1

embrace *vb* **1** to put one's arms around and press tightly ⟨Upon being finally reunited, the overjoyed father *embraced* his son.⟩

syn clasp, crush, enfold, grasp, hug, strain

rel clamp, cling, cradle, grab, grip, hold; bosom, embosom, encircle, entwine, envelop; fold, lock, twine, wrap; cuddle, fondle, nestle, nuzzle, pat, pet, snuggle, stroke

2 to surround or cover closely — see ENFOLD 1

3 to take for one's own use (something originated by another) — see ADOPT

4 to receive or accept gladly or readily — see WELCOME

5 to have as part of a whole — see INCLUDE 1

6 to form a circle around — see SURROUND

embroider *vb* to add to the interest of by including made-up details ⟨Dad likes to *embroider* his fishing stories.⟩

syn color, elaborate (on), embellish, exaggerate, magnify, pad, stretch

rel dress up; amplify, enhance, expand, flesh (out); fudge, hedge; overdo, overdraw, overemphasize, overplay, overstate; emphasize, stress; caricature; satirize

near ant belittle, minimize, play down, understate

embroidering *n* the representation of something in terms that go beyond the facts — see EXAGGERATION

embroidery *n* **1** decorative stitching done on cloth with the use of a needle — see NEEDLEWORK

2 the representation of something in terms that go beyond the facts — see EXAGGERATION

embroil *vb* to place in conflict or difficulties ⟨The town has been *embroiled* in controversy over the building of the huge shopping mall.⟩

syn bog (down), mire

rel enmesh (*also* immesh), ensnare, entangle, entrap, snare, tangle, trap

near ant emancipate, free, liberate, release

emend *vb* to remove errors, defects, deficiencies, or deviations from — see CORRECT 1

emendation *n* a change designed to correct or improve a written work — see CORRECTION 1

emerge *vb* to come to one's attention especially gradually or unexpectedly — see ARISE 2

emergency *n* a time or state of affairs requiring prompt or decisive action ⟨an alert, quick-thinking girl who is good to have around in an *emergency*⟩

---

syn synonym(s)   *rel* related words
ant antonym(s)   *near ant* near antonym(s)

syn clutch, crisis, crossroad(s), crunch, exigency, extremity, head, juncture, zero hour

rel contingency, possibility; climax, turning point; happening, landmark, milestone; condition, pass, situation, strait; deadlock, impasse, stalemate; corner, fix, hole, hot water, jam, last ditch, pinch, predicament, scrape, spot; eleventh hour, last minute

phrases moment of truth, point of no return

emigrant *n* one that leaves one place to settle in another ⟨a city with *emigrants* from many lands⟩

syn émigré (*also* emigré), immigrant, migrant, settler

rel defector, deportee, evacuee, exile, expatriate, refugee, relocatee, repatriate; alien, foreigner, illegal, noncitizen, nonnative; colonist, newcomer, squatter; migrator, pilgrim, pioneer, trekker

near ant aborigine, native; citizen, habitant, inhabitant, national, resident

ant nonimmigrant

émigré *also* **emigré** *n* **1** a person forced to emigrate for political reasons ⟨The revolution resulted in a flood of *émigrés* into neighboring countries.⟩

syn deportee, evacuee, exile, expatriate, refugee

rel alien, fugitive; castoff, outcast, pariah; loyalist, patriot

2 one that leaves one place to settle in another — see EMIGRANT

eminence *n* **1** the fact or state of being above others in rank or importance ⟨the *eminence* of the Nobel Prize in the field of awards and prizes⟩

syn distinction, dominance, noteworthiness, preeminence, primacy, superiority, supremacy, transcendence

rel celebrity, fame, famousness, glory, honor, renown, reputation, repute; megastardom, stardom, superstardom; greatness, illustriousness, nobleness, notableness; ascendancy (*also* ascendency), authority, domination, dominion; influence, power, prestige, weight; infamy, notoriety

near ant inferiority, mediocrity; obscureness, obscurity

2 an area of high ground — see HEIGHT 4

eminent *adj* standing above others in rank, importance, or achievement ⟨Many *eminent* surgeons are on the hospital's staff.⟩

syn astral, bright, distinguished, illustrious, luminous, noble, notable, noteworthy, outstanding, preeminent, prestigious, redoubtable, signal, star, superior

rel celebrated, exalted, famed, famous, glorious, honored, renowned, reputable; infamous, notorious; dominant, paramount, predominant

near ant insignificant, minor, unimportant; average, inferior, mediocre; obscure, uncelebrated, unsung

emissary *n* **1** a person sent on a mission to represent another — see AMBASSADOR

2 a person who tries secretly to obtain information for one country in the territory of another usually unfriendly country — see SPY

emit *vb* **1** to throw or give off ⟨nuclei that *emit* gamma rays⟩

syn cast, evolve, exhale, expel, give out, irradiate, issue, radiate, release, shoot, throw out, vent

rel eliminate, evacuate, excrete, exude, ooze, secrete; eject, erupt, gush, jet, pour, spew, spout, spray, spurt, squirt

near ant absorb, soak (up), sponge, suck (up), take up

2 to send forth using the vocal chords — see UTTER 1

emolument *n* the money paid regularly to a person for labor or services — see WAGE

emotion *n* **1** a subjective response to a person, thing, or situation — see FEELING 1

2 depth of feeling — see ARDOR 1

emotional *adj* **1** having or expressing great depth of feeling — see FERVENT 1

2 having the power to affect the feelings or sympathies — see MOVING

3 showing feeling freely — see DEMONSTRATIVE 1

emphasis *n* **1** a special notice or importance given to something ⟨a college with a long-established *emphasis* on sports⟩

syn accent, accentuation, stress, weight

rel attention, concentration, focus; consequence, import, moment, note, significance, value, worth; precedence, primacy, priority; consideration, heed, regard

near ant minimization, underemphasis; disregard, indifference

ant de-emphasis

2 the quality or state of being forceful (as in expression) — see VEHEMENCE 1

emphasize *vb* **1** to indicate the importance of by centering attention on ⟨supermarket tabloids that *emphasize* sensational news stories⟩

syn accent, accentuate, feature, highlight, illuminate, point (up), press, stress

rel focus, identify, pinpoint; advertise, boost, plug, promote, publicize; overplay

phrases bear down on, make much of

near ant tone (down), underemphasize, understate; belittle, discount, disparage, minimize

ant de-emphasize, play down

2 to make more apparent ⟨The long drapes *emphasize* the height of the ceiling.⟩

syn accentuate, stress, underline, underscore

rel amplify, beef (up), boost, strengthen; augment, deepen, enhance, enlarge, heighten, magnify, maximize, supplement; enliven, jazz (up)

near ant decrease, diminish, lessen, minimize, reduce, subdue, tone (down), understate, weaken

ant de-emphasize

emphatic *adj* **1** marked by or uttered with forcefulness ⟨The governor issued an *emphatic* denial of all charges.⟩

syn aggressive, assertive, dynamic, energetic, forceful, full-blooded, muscular, resounding, strenuous, vehement, vigorous, violent

rel decided, insistent, marked, pointed; absolute, categorical (*also* categoric), clear, plain, unambiguous, unequivocal; arresting, compelling, conspicuous, impelling, noticeable, striking *near ant* guarded, mild, weak, wishy-washy; ambiguous, equivocal, halting, hesitant; understated

ant nonassertive, nonemphatic, unemphatic

2 likely to attract attention — see NOTICE-ABLE

empire *n* a group of businesses or enterprises under one control — see CONGLOM-ERATE

empirical *also* **empiric** *adj* based on observation or experience ⟨guidelines for raising children that are based on *empirical* evidence⟩

syn experimental, objective, observational

rel actual, factual, genuine, hard, material, real; accepted, established, tried, tried-and-true; indisputable, undeniable; demonstrable, provable, verifiable

near ant conjectural, hypothetical, speculative; unproven, unsubstantiated; metaphysical, transcendentalist, visionary

ant nonempirical, theoretical (*also* theoretic), unempirical

2 capable of being proven as true or real — see VERIFIABLE

employ *n* the state of being provided with a paying job — see HIRE 1

employ *vb* 1 to provide with a paying job ⟨a new factory that will *employ* 500 people⟩

syn assume, engage, hire, pay, place, recruit, retain, take on

rel reemploy, reengage, rehire; apprentice, contract, job, partner, subcontract; enlist; advance, promote, upgrade; keep (on); headhunt, scout

near ant furlough, lay off, lock out

ant can, discharge, dismiss, fire, sack

2 to put into action or service — see USE 1

employable *adj* capable of or suitable for being used for a particular purpose — see USABLE 1

employed *adj* involved in often constant activity — see BUSY 1

employee *also* **employe** *n* one who works for another for wages or a salary ⟨an employer who was loved and admired by generations of *employees*⟩

syn hand, hireling, jobholder, retainer, worker

rel assistant, cog, flunky (*also* flunkey *or* flunkie), subordinate, underling, yes-man; drudge, grub, hack, jobber, laborer, toiler; nine-to-fiver, wage earner, wageworker, workingman, workingwoman, workman, workwoman; associate, colleague, coworker; temp, temporary

near ant boss, superior, supervisor

ant employer

employment *n* 1 the act or practice of employing something for a particular purpose — see USE 1

2 the activity by which one regularly makes a living — see OCCUPATION

3 the state of being provided with a paying job — see HIRE 1

emporium *n* an establishment where goods are sold to consumers — see SHOP 1

empower *vb* 1 to give official or legal power to — see AUTHORIZE 1

2 to make able or possible — see ENABLE 1

emptiness *n* 1 a need or desire for food — see HUNGER 1

2 empty space — see VACANCY 1

3 the quality or state of being empty — see VACANCY 2

empty *adj* 1 lacking contents that could or should be present ⟨The refrigerator is *empty*, so we'll have to eat out.⟩

syn bare, blank, clean, devoid, stark, vacant, vacuous, void

rel barren, hollow; available, clear, free, open; unfilled, unfurnished; unattended, uninhabited, unoccupied; abandoned, deserted, emptied, forsaken, vacated; depleted, drained, dry, exhausted

near ant complete; replete; furnished, provided, supplied; filled, occupied; flush, overflowing, packed, teeming

ant full

2 feeling a desire or need for food — see HUNGRY 1

3 having no meaning — see MEANINGLESS

4 having no usefulness — see WORTHLESS

5 producing no results — see FUTILE

6 not expressing any emotion — see BLANK 1

empty *vb* to remove the contents of ⟨*Empty* the room before starting to paint the ceiling.⟩

syn clear, evacuate, vacate, void

rel deplete, drain, eliminate, exhaust, waste; bleed, draw (off); clean, flush, purge, scour, sweep

ant fill, load

emulate *vb* 1 to be the same in meaning or effect — see AMOUNT (TO) 2

2 to use (someone or something) as the model for one's speech, mannerisms, or behavior — see IMITATE 1

emulative *adj* using or marked by the use of something else as a basis or model — see IMITATIVE 1

enable *vb* 1 to make able or possible ⟨My new glasses *enable* me to read the fine print.⟩

syn allow, empower, let, permit

rel fit, prepare, qualify, ready; approve, endorse (*also* indorse), sanction; condition, equip

near ant inhibit, preclude; disallow, enjoin, forbid, prohibit

ant prevent

2 to give official or legal power to — see AUTHORIZE 1

enact *vb* to put into effect through legislative or authoritative action ⟨Congress *enacts* all laws relating to foreign trade and immigration.⟩

syn constitute, lay down, legislate, make, ordain, pass

rel reenact, repass; bring about, effect; allow, authorize, permit, sanction; decree, dictate, proclaim; administer, execute; approve, confirm, ratify

near ant abolish, abrogate, annul, cancel, invalidate, kill, nullify; overturn, reverse, void

ant repeal, rescind, revoke

enactment *n* 1 a rule of conduct or action laid down by a governing authority and especially a legislature — see LAW 1

2 the doing of an action — see COMMIS-SION 2

---

syn synonym(s)   *rel* related words
ant antonym(s)   *near ant* near antonym(s)

enamored (of) *adj* filled with an intense or excessive love for ⟨I became completely *enamored* of the city and its people.⟩

syn crazy (about *or* over), enraptured (by), gone (on), infatuated (with), mad (about), nuts (about)

rel hung up (on), obsessed; foolish, silly, wild; bewitched, captivated, charmed, enchanted, entranced, fascinated

phrases stuck on, sweet on

near ant cool, detached, unenchanted, unimpressed; disenchanted, disillusioned; heart-free

encamp *vb* 1 to live in a camp or the outdoors — see CAMP (OUT)

2 to provide with living quarters or shelter — see HOUSE 1

encampment *n* a place where a group of people live for a short time in tents or cabins — see CAMP 1

encapsulate *vb* to make into a short statement of the main points (as of a report) — see SUMMARIZE

encapsulation *n* a short statement of the main points — see SUMMARY

encase *vb* to close or shut in by or as if by barriers — see ENCLOSE 1

enchain *vb* to confine or restrain with or as if with chains — see BIND 1

enchant *vb* 1 to attract or delight as if by magic — see CHARM 1

2 to cast a spell on — see BEWITCH 1

3 to hold the attention of as if by a spell — see ENTHRALL 1

enchanted *adj* being or appearing to be under a magic spell ⟨an *enchanted* isle of the South Pacific⟩

syn bewitched, charmed, entranced, magic, magical, spellbound

rel jinxed; dreamy, fairy, fairylike; fantastic (*also* fantastical), miraculous, utopian, wondrous; hypnotized, mesmerized; bedazzled, captivated, fascinated

enchanter *n* a person skilled in using supernatural forces — see MAGICIAN 1

enchanting *adj* having an often mysterious or magical power to attract — see FASCINATING 1

enchantment *n* 1 a spoken word or set of words believed to have magic power — see SPELL 1

2 the power of irresistible attraction — see CHARM 2

3 the power to control natural forces through supernatural means — see MAGIC 1

enchantress *n* 1 a woman believed to have often harmful supernatural powers — see WITCH 1

2 a woman whom men find irresistibly attractive — see SIREN

3 a lovely woman — see BEAUTY 2

encircle *vb* 1 to travel completely around ⟨communication satellites *encircling* the earth⟩

syn circle, circumnavigate, circumvent, compass, girdle, girth, orbit, ring, round

rel circumambulate, cross, traverse

2 to form a circle around — see SURROUND

enclose *also* **inclose** *vb* 1 to close or shut in by or as if by barriers ⟨dogs who spend the day *enclosed* in small cages⟩

syn cage, closet, coop (up), corral, encase, envelop, fence (in), hedge, house, immure, include, pen, wall (in)

rel bound, circumscribe, confine, contain, limit, restrict; encircle, encompass, enfold, enframe, frame, ring, surround; armor, cocoon, encapsulate, encapsule, encyst, ensheathe, ensphere, enwomb

2 to form a circle around — see SURROUND

3 to surround or cover closely — see ENFOLD 1

enclosure *also* **inclosure** *n* an open space wholly or partly enclosed (as by buildings or walls) — see COURT 2

encomium *n* a formal expression of praise ⟨the *encomiums* bestowed on a teacher at her retirement ceremonies⟩

syn accolade, citation, commendation, eulogy, homage, hymn, paean, panegyric, salutation, tribute

rel award, decoration, dedication, honor, prize; acclaim, acclamation, laudation; applause, plaudit(s); bravo; approval, cachet, compliment, recommendation

near ant censure, condemnation, denunciation, indictment, rebuke, reprimand, reproof; admonition, correction, harangue, lecture, sermon

encompass *vb* 1 to form a circle around — see SURROUND

2 to have as part of a whole — see INCLUDE 1

3 to surround or cover closely — see ENFOLD 1

encounter *n* a brief clash between enemies or rivals ⟨an *encounter* between fans of the rival teams⟩

syn brush, hassle, run-in, scrape, skirmish

rel argument, fight, quarrel, row, spat, squabble, tiff; battle, brawl, fray, wrangle

encounter *vb* 1 to come upon face-to-face or as if face-to-face — see MEET 1

2 to come upon unexpectedly or by chance — see HAPPEN (ON *or* UPON)

3 to enter into contest or conflict with — see ENGAGE 2

encourage *vb* 1 to fill with courage or strength of purpose ⟨a pep talk that *encouraged* the team to get out there and do their best⟩

syn buoy (up), cheer (up), embolden, hearten, inspire, steel

rel animate, enliven, invigorate; enforce, fortify, strengthen; assure, reassure; boost, energize, excite, galvanize, provoke, quicken, rally, stimulate, stir

near ant demoralize, depress, sadden; debilitate, enfeeble, hamstring, undermine, weaken; intimidate, psych (out)

ant daunt, discourage, dishearten, dispirit

2 to help the growth or development of — see FOSTER 1

3 to rouse to strong feeling or action — see PROVOKE 1

4 to try to persuade (someone) through earnest appeals to follow a course of action — see URGE

encouragement *n* something that arouses action or activity — see IMPULSE 1

encouraging *adj* 1 having qualities which inspire hope — see HOPEFUL 1

2 making one feel good inside — see HEARTWARMING

3 pointing toward a happy outcome — see FAVORABLE 2

encroach *vb* to advance gradually beyond the usual or desirable limits ⟨Each year the sea continues to *encroach* upon the island's beaches.⟩

syn creep, inch, worm

rel snake, sneak; entrench (*also* intrench), impinge, infringe, intrude, invade; overpass, overreach, overrun, overshoot, overstep

encrust *also* **incrust** *vb* to cover with a hardened layer ⟨My boots were *encrusted* with mud.⟩

syn cake, rime

rel besmear, coat, smear, spread; cover, daub; coagulate, congeal, harden

encumber *vb* **1** to create difficulty for the work or activity of — see HAMPER

2 to place a weight or burden on — see LOAD 1

encumbrance *n* something that makes movement or progress difficult ⟨Without the *encumbrance* of a heavy backpack, I could sprint along the trail.⟩

syn balk, bar, block, chain, clog, cramp, crimp, deterrent, drag, embarrassment, fetter, handicap, hindrance, hurdle, impediment, inhibition, interference, manacle, obstacle, obstruction, shackles, stop, stumbling block, trammel

rel catch, hitch, rub, snag; barrier, blockade, blockage, brick wall, stone wall; arrest, bit, brake, check, constraint, curb, hobble, rein, restraint; embargo, stoppage; delay, holdup, stall; burden, cumber, load; danger, hazard, peril, reef; adversity, difficulty, disadvantage, drawback, hardship

near ant catalyst, goad, impetus, incentive, spur, stimulant, stimulus; advantage, break, edge; aid, assistance, benefit, boost, help

encyclopedic *adj* covering everything or all important points ⟨a tour guide with an *encyclopedic* knowledge of New York City and its people⟩

syn compendious, complete, comprehensive, exhaustive, full, global, inclusive, indepth, omnibus, panoramic, thorough, universal

rel broad, encyclical, general, inclusionary, overall; cosmic (*also* cosmical), extensive, far, far-reaching, grand, large, vast, wide; blanket, unrestricted

near ant circumscribed, limited, narrow, restricted, specialized; exact, precise; individual, singular, specific; incomplete, patchy, sketchy

end *n* **1** the stopping of a process or activity ⟨got a drink at the *end* of practice⟩

syn arrest, cease, cessation, check, close, closure, conclusion, discontinuance, ending, expiration, finish, halt, lapse, offset, shutdown, shutoff, stay, stop, stoppage, surcease, termination

rel phaseout; abeyance, break, interruption; layoff, letup, moratorium, pause, standstill, suspension

near ant extension, persistence, prolongation

ant continuance, continuation

2 a real or imaginary point beyond which a person or thing cannot go — see LIMIT 1

3 an unused or unwanted piece or item typically of small size or value — see ¹SCRAP 1

4 something that one hopes or intends to accomplish — see GOAL

5 the last and usually sharp or tapering part of something long and narrow — see POINT 2

6 the last part of a process or action — see FINALE

7 the line or relatively narrow space that marks the outer limit of something — see BORDER 1

8 the permanent stopping of all the vital bodily activities — see DEATH 1

9 something belonging to, due to, or contributed by an individual member of a group — see SHARE 1

end *vb* **1** to bring (an event) to a natural or appropriate stopping point — see CLOSE 3

2 to bring (as an action or operation) to an immediate end — see STOP 1

3 to come to an end — see CEASE 1

4 to stop living — see DIE 1

endanger *vb* to place in danger ⟨a reckless use of fireworks that *endangered* the lives of many people⟩

syn adventure, compromise, gamble (with), hazard, imperil, jeopardize, menace, peril, risk, venture

rel intimidate, threaten; expose; subject; chance, wager

near ant guard, protect, shelter, shield; preserve, resume, save

endangered *adj* being in a situation where one is likely to meet with harm — see LIABLE 1

endangerment *n* the state of not being protected from injury, harm, or evil — see DANGER 1

endearing *adj* **1** having qualities that tend to make one loved — see LOVABLE

2 likely or intended to win one's affection — see INGRATIATING

endeavor *n* an effort to do or accomplish something — see ATTEMPT 1

endeavor *vb* **1** to devote serious and sustained effort — see LABOR

2 to make an effort to do — see ATTEMPT 1

ended *adj* brought or having come to an end — see COMPLETE 1

endemic *adj* belonging to a particular place by birth or origin — see NATIVE 1

ending *n* **1** the last part of a process or action — see FINALE

2 the stopping of a process or activity — see END 1

endless *adj* **1** being or seeming to be without limits — see INFINITE

2 lasting forever — see EVERLASTING 1

endorse *also* **indorse** *vb* to promote the interests or cause of — see SUPPORT 1

endow *vb* **1** to furnish freely or naturally with some power, quality, or attribute ⟨a young performer *endowed* with a great singing voice⟩

syn bless, endue (*or* indue), favor, gift, invest

rel equip, provide, supply; bestow (on *or* upon), clothe, confer (on), cover; accord,

---

syn synonym(s) *rel* related words
ant antonym(s) *near ant* near antonym(s)

award, grant; empower, enable, enhance, enrich, heighten; bequeath, will

near ant strip; deplete, drain, exhaust; skimp, stint

2 to furnish (as an institution) with a regular source of income ⟨a wealthy businessman who *endowed* several museums⟩

syn finance, fund, subsidize

rel establish, found, organize; bequeath, contribute, donate, support, underwrite; award, grant; back, promote, sponsor; capitalize, invest (in)

near ant draw; subsist

ant defund, disendow

3 to provide money for — see FINANCE 1

endowment *n* a special and usually inborn ability — see TALENT

endue *or* **indue** *vb* **1** to cause (as a person) to become filled or saturated with a certain quality or principle — see INFUSE

2 to furnish freely or naturally with some power, quality, or attribute — see ENDOW 1

endurable *adj* capable of being endured — see BEARABLE

endurance *n* uninterrupted or lasting existence — see CONTINUATION

endure *vb* **1** to come to a knowledge of (something) by living through it — see EXPERIENCE

2 to put up with (something painful or difficult) — see BEAR 2

3 to remain indefinitely in existence or in the same state — see CONTINUE 1

enduring *adj* having an existence or validity that does not change or diminish — see ABIDING

enemy *n* one that is hostile toward another ⟨a beloved minister with no known *enemies*⟩

syn adversary, antagonist, foe, hostile, opponent

rel archenemy, archfoe, nemesis; combatant, invader; competitor, emulator, rival

near ant buddy, chum, compadre, crony, fellow, hail-fellow, hail-fellow-well-met, hearty, hobnobber, mate, musketeer, pal; abettor (*also* abetter), accomplice, ally, collaborator, colleague, comrade, confederate, friendly, partner; adherent, disciple, follower; backer, benefactor, exponent, supporter, sympathizer, well-wisher

ant friend

energetic *adj* **1** having active strength of body or mind — see VIGOROUS 1

2 having much high-spirited energy and movement — see LIVELY 1

3 marked by or uttered with forcefulness — see EMPHATIC 1

energetically *adv* in a vigorous and forceful manner — see HARD 3

energize *vb* to give life, vigor, or spirit to — see ANIMATE

energized *adj* made or become fresh in spirits or vigor — see NEW 4

energy *n* **1** a spiritual force that is held to emanate from or give animation to living beings ⟨Many Eastern cultures believe in the significance of life *energy* in the healing process.⟩

syn aura, vibration(s)

rel inner light, light, nature, soul, spirit; élan vital, life, lifeblood

2 active strength of body or mind — see VIGOR 1

3 something with a usable capacity for doing work — see FUEL

4 the ability to exert effort for the accomplishment of a task — see POWER 2

enervate *vb* **1** to deprive of emotional or intellectual vitality — see DEHYDRATE 1

2 to diminish the physical strength of — see WEAKEN 1

enervated *adj* **1** lacking bodily energy or motivation — see LISTLESS

2 lacking bodily strength — see WEAK 1

enfeeble *vb* to diminish the physical strength of — see WEAKEN 1

enfeebled *adj* lacking bodily strength — see WEAK 1

enfeeblement *n* **1** a gradual sinking and wasting away of mind or body — see DECLINE 1

2 the quality or state of lacking physical strength or vigor — see WEAKNESS 1

enfold *vb* **1** to surround or cover closely ⟨Darkness began to *enfold* the house on the hill.⟩

syn bosom, cocoon, embosom, embower, embrace, enclose (*also* inclose), encompass, enshroud, envelop, enwrap, invest, involve, lap, mantle, muffle, shroud, swathe, veil, wrap

rel curtain; embed (*also* imbed), encase; swaddle; blanket, overlay, overspread; camouflage, cloak, disguise, mask; circle, encircle

near ant bare, denude, expose, strip

2 to put one's arms around and press tightly — see EMBRACE 1

enforce *vb* to carry out effectively ⟨The duty of the police is to *enforce* the law.⟩

syn administer, apply, execute, implement

rel bring about, effect, effectuate; discharge, fulfill (*or* fulfil), render; cite; enact, legislate; honor, observe, uphold; promulgate

near ant disregard, ignore, neglect

enfranchise *vb* to release (as from slavery or confinement) — see FREE 1

enfranchisement *n* **1** the act of setting free from slavery — see LIBERATION

2 the right to formally express one's position or will in an election — see VOTE 1

engage *vb* **1** to hold the attention of ⟨The challenging game *engaged* us all evening.⟩

syn absorb, bemuse, busy, engross, enthrall (*or* enthral), enwrap, fascinate, grip, immerse, interest, intrigue, involve, occupy

rel allure, attract, beguile, bewitch, captivate, charm, enchant, obsess; hypnotize, mesmerize; distract, preoccupy; hog, monopolize

phrases catch one's eye

near ant bore, jade, pall, tire, weary

2 to enter into contest or conflict with ⟨The troops were prepared to *engage* the enemy.⟩

syn battle, encounter, face, meet, take on

rel emulate, rival; contend, fight, oppose

near ant elude, escape, evade; retreat

3 to obligate by prior agreement — see PLEDGE 1

4 to provide with a paying job — see EMPLOY 1

5 to take or get the temporary use of (something) for a set sum — see HIRE 1

engaged *adj* **1** pledged in marriage ⟨The *engaged* couple make a charming pair.⟩

syn affianced, betrothed

rel committed

ant unattached

2 involved in often constant activity — see
BUSY 1

engagement *n* 1 the act or state of being
engaged to be married ⟨The fun couple
recently announced their *engagement*.⟩

syn betrothal, espousal

ant disengagement

2 an agreement to be present at a specified
time and place ⟨a lifelong practice of
marking all of my *engagements* on a weekly calendar⟩

syn appointment, date, rendezvous, tryst

rel arrangement; invitation; get-together,
meeting; call, visit; schedule

3 the state of being provided with a paying
job — see HIRE 1

engaging *adj* 1 having an often mysterious or magical power to attract — see
FASCINATING 1

2 holding the attention or provoking interest — see INTERESTING

engender *vb* 1 to be the cause of (a situation, action, or state of mind) — see EFFECT

2 to come into existence — see BEGIN 2

engine *n* a device that changes energy into
mechanical motion ⟨a car with a 200-horse-
power *engine*⟩

syn machine, motor

rel converter, transformer; appliance,
mechanism; equipment, tool; mill

engineer *n* a person who designs and
guides a plan or undertaking ⟨the *engineer*
of a movement to eradicate hunger⟩

syn mastermind

rel builder, maker, producer; captain, commander, director, handler, leader, manager, quarterback; contriver, designer, formulator, originator, spawner; arranger,
hatcher, organizer, planner, plotter, schemer; machinator, maneuverer; developer,
generator, inaugurator, initiator, inspirer,
instituter (*or* institutor), pioneer

engineer *vb* to plan out usually with subtle
skill or care ⟨The mayor *engineered* an
agreement to have a major league team
play in our city.⟩

syn contrive, finagle, finesse, frame,
machinate, maneuver, manipulate, mastermind, negotiate, wangle

rel arrange, concert, conclude, work out;
angle (for), compass, intrigue, plot,
scheme; connive; brew, concoct, cook
(up), hatch; captain, command, conduct,
direct, handle, manage, quarterback, run;
gerrymander

near ant blow, bobble, botch, bungle,
butcher, flub, fumble, louse up, mangle,
mess (up), mishandle, muff

engrave *vb* 1 to cut (as letters or designs)
on a hard surface ⟨*engraved* the birth and
death dates on the tombstone⟩

syn etch, grave, incise, inscribe

rel carve, chisel, sculpt, sculpture; chase,
groove, notch; score, trace; affix, impress

2 to produce a vivid impression of ⟨a scar
that forever *engraved* the killer's face in
the witness's mind⟩

syn brand, etch, impress, imprint, ingrain
(*also* engrain)

rel imbue, implant, inculcate, infuse; fix,
set, stamp

near ant blot out, expunge, obliterate

engross *vb* to hold the attention of — see
ENGAGE 1

engrossed *adj* having the mind fixed on
something — see ATTENTIVE 1

engrossing *adj* holding the attention or
provoking interest — see INTERESTING

engrossment *n* a focusing of the mind on
something — see ATTENTION 1

engulf *vb* to cover with a flood — see FLOOD

enhance *vb* 1 to make better — see IMPROVE

2 to make markedly greater in measure or
degree — see INTENSIFY

enhancement *n* an instance of notable
progress in the development of knowledge,
technology, or skill — see ADVANCE 2

enigma *n* something hard to understand
or explain — see MYSTERY

enigmatic *also* **enigmatical** *adj* 1 being
beyond one's powers to know, under-
stand, or explain — see MYSTERIOUS 1

2 having an often intentionally veiled or
uncertain meaning — see OBSCURE 1

enjoin *vb* 1 to ask for (something) earnestly or with authority — see DEMAND 1

2 to issue orders to (someone) by right of
authority — see COMMAND 1

3 to order not to do or use or to be done
or used — see FORBID

enjoining *n* the act of ordering that something not be done or used — see PROHIBI-
TION 1

enjoy *vb* 1 to take pleasure in ⟨We still *enjoy* seeing movies on the big screen.⟩

syn adore, delight (in), dig, fancy, groove
(on), like, love, relish, revel (in), savor
(*also* savour)

rel admire, appreciate, cherish, revere,
venerate, worship; prize, treasure, value;
devour, eat (up), feast (on); dote (on),
idolize; cotton (to), favor, prefer; indulge
(in), luxuriate (in), wallow (in)

phrases be partial to, get a kick out of (*or*
get a charge out of), go for, have a soft
spot for, take to

near ant abhor, abominate, detest, dislike,
hate, loathe; condemn, despise, scorn

2 to keep, control, or experience as one's
own — see HAVE 1

enjoyable *adj* 1 giving pleasure or contentment to the mind or senses — see
PLEASANT 1

2 providing amusement or enjoyment —
see FUN

enjoyment *n* 1 the fact or state of having
(something) at one's disposal — see POS-
SESSION 1

2 the feeling experienced when one's wishes are met — see PLEASURE 1

enlarge *vb* 1 to become greater in extent,
volume, amount, or number — see IN-
CREASE 2

2 to make greater in size, amount, or
number — see INCREASE 1

3 to release (as from slavery or confinement) — see FREE 1

enlighten *vb* 1 to give information to ⟨The
lecturer at the planetarium *enlightened* us
about the latest astronomical discoveries.⟩

---

syn synonym(s)   *rel* related words

ant antonym(s)   *near ant* near antonym(s)

syn acquaint, advise, apprise, brief, clear, clue (in), familiarize, fill in, hip, inform, instruct, tell, verse, wise (up)

rel advertise, alert, notify; announce (to), disclose (to); assure, certify, convince, reassure, warrant; educate, lecture, school, teach, tutor; disabuse, disenchant, disillusion, undeceive

phrases keep posted (one), let know (one)

near ant misinform, mislead

2 to provide (someone) with moral or spiritual understanding ⟨Many people around the world have been *enlightened* by the teachings of Gautama Buddha.⟩

syn edify, educate, illuminate, illumine, inspire, nurture

rel elevate, ennoble, enrich, ensoul, lift, uplift; better, improve, regenerate, renew, transform; exalt, glorify, transfigure

near ant confuse, perplex, puzzle; becloud, cloud, darken, obscure

enlist (in) *vb* to become a member of — see ENTER 2

enliven *vb* to give life, vigor, or spirit to — see ANIMATE

enmesh *also* **immesh** *vb* to catch or hold as if in a net — see ENTANGLE 2

enmity *n* a deep-seated ill will ⟨*Enmity* had existed between the two families for generations.⟩

syn animosity, antagonism, antipathy, bitterness, gall, grudge, hostility, jaundice, rancor

rel blood feud, feud, score, vendetta; hate, hatred, loathing; vindictiveness, virulence, vitriol; alienation, disaffection, estrangement; conflict, coolness, discord, friction, strain, tension; inhospitableness, unfriendliness; malice, malignancy, malignity, spite, spitefulness, venom

near ant amiability, amicability, civility, cordiality, friendliness, hospitality, neighborliness; comity, empathy, friendship, goodwill, sympathy, understanding

ant amity

ennoble *vb* to assign a high status or value to — see EXALT 1

ennui *n* the state of being bored — see BOREDOM

enormity *n* **1** the state or quality of being utterly evil ⟨the *enormity* of the crimes committed by the Nazis⟩

syn atrociousness, atrocity, badness, depravedness, depravity, diabolicalness, evilness, heinousness, hideousness, monstrosity, sinfulness, vileness, wickedness

rel accursedness, baseness, cursedness, devilishness, execrableness, hellishness; corruption, decadence, degeneracy, pervertedness; immorality; infamy, notoriety

near ant morality; chasteness, innocence, purity

ant goodness, righteousness, virtuousness

2 the quality or state of being very large — see IMMENSITY

enormous *adj* unusually large — see HUGE

enormously *adv* **1** to a great degree — see VERY 1

2 to a large extent or degree — see GREATLY 2

enormousness *n* the quality or state of being very large — see IMMENSITY

enough *adv* **1** in or to a degree or quantity that meets one's requirements or satisfaction ⟨The elevator is big *enough* to hold everyone.⟩

syn adequately, satisfactorily, sufficiently, suitably

rel acceptably, fairly, moderately, passably, tolerably; meetly, properly, rightly, seemly; agreeably, satisfyingly; abundantly, amply, optimally, plenteously, plentifully; commensurately, proportionately

ant inadequately, insufficiently, unsatisfactorily

2 to some degree or extent — see FAIRLY 1

3 to a full extent or degree — see FULLY 1

enrage *vb* to make angry — see ANGER

enraged *adj* feeling or showing anger — see ANGRY

enrapture *vb* **1** to fill with great joy — see ELATE

2 to fill with overwhelming emotion (as wonder or delight) — see ENTRANCE

enraptured *adj* experiencing or marked by overwhelming usually pleasurable emotion — see ECSTATIC

enraptured (by) *adj* filled with an intense or excessive love for — see ENAMORED (OF)

enrich *vb* **1** to make better — see IMPROVE

2 to make more attractive by adding something that is beautiful or becoming — see DECORATE

enroll *also* **enrol** *vb* **1** to add (a person) to a list or roll as a participant or member ⟨The community college will *enroll* anyone who has a GED or high school diploma.⟩

syn inscribe, list, matriculate, register

rel enlist, impanel, induct; conscript, draft, muster; book, schedule; check in

near ant check off; exclude, expel, expunge, reject; omit, overlook

2 to put (someone or something) on a list — see ¹LIST 2

enroll (in) *vb* to become a member of — see ENTER 2

enrollment *also* **enrolment** *n* the number of individuals registered — see REGISTRATION

ensconce *vb* **1** to establish or place comfortably or snugly ⟨The kids had contentedly *ensconced* themselves on the couch before the TV.⟩ ⟨happily *ensconced* in her new home⟩

syn install, lodge, nestle, perch, roost, settle

rel deploy, fix, locate, park, plant, position, set, situate, station; anchor, bivouac, camp, camp (out); burrow, curl up, dig in; harbor, house

2 to put into a hiding place — see ¹HIDE 1

enshrine *vb* to assign a high status or value to — see EXALT 1

enshroud *vb* **1** to keep secret or shut off from view — see ¹HIDE 2

2 to surround or cover closely — see ENFOLD 1

ensign *n* **1** a device, design, or figure used as an identifying mark — see EMBLEM

2 a piece of cloth with a special design that is used as an emblem or for signaling — see FLAG 1

enslavement *n* the state of being enslaved — see SLAVERY

ensnare *vb* to catch or hold as if in a net — see ENTANGLE 2

ensuing *adj* **1** being the one that comes immediately after another — see NEXT
2 being, occurring, or carried out at a time after something else — see SUBSEQUENT
ensure *vb* to make sure, certain, or safe ⟨regulations that *ensure* the wholesomeness of our food⟩
syn assure, cinch, guarantee, guaranty, insure, secure
rel attest, certify, vouch, warrant, witness; pledge, promise, swear
near ant enfeeble, undermine, weaken
entail *vb* to have as part of a whole — see INCLUDE 1
entangle *vb* **1** to twist together into a usually confused mass ⟨In the process of taking down the Christmas tree, we managed to *entangle* the string of lights into a hopeless mess of wires.⟩
syn interlace, intertwine, interweave, knot, snarl, tangle
rel jumble, scrabble, scramble; braid, entwine, entwist, plait, twine, weave, wind, wreathe, writhe
near ant unknot, unravel, unscramble
ant disentangle, unsnarl, untangle, untwine, untwist
2 to catch or hold as if in a net ⟨The swindler gradually became *entangled* in a web of lies.⟩
syn enmesh (*also* immesh), ensnare, entrap, mesh, net, snare, tangle, trap
rel bag, birdlime, capture, collar; embroil, implicate, involve, mire
near ant detach, disengage, extricate; clear, free, liberate
ant disentangle, untangle
3 to make complex or difficult — see COMPLICATE
entanglement *n* something that catches and holds — see WEB 1
enter *vb* **1** to go or come in or into ⟨The hikers *entered* the cave with considerable caution.⟩
syn access, penetrate, pierce
rel barge (in), breeze (in), burst (in *or* into), waltz (in); pop (in); stray (into), wander (into); crash, encroach, gate-crash, infiltrate, infringe, intrude, invade, trespass
phrases set foot in, step into
ant depart, exit, leave
2 to become a member of ⟨patriotic young men and women *entering* the armed services⟩ ⟨debutantes *entering* society⟩
syn enlist (in), enroll (in), join, sign on (for), sign up (for)
rel reenlist, reenroll, reenter, rejoin, re-up
near ant drop out, quit, withdraw
ant demit
3 to put (someone or something) on a list — see ¹LIST 2
4 to offer entrance (as to a place, school, or privilege) to — see ADMIT 2
enter (into *or* upon) *vb* to take the first step in (a process or course of action) — see BEGIN 1
enterprise *n* **1** a commercial or industrial activity or organization ⟨The booming economy witnessed the launch of many small *enterprises*.⟩

syn business, company, concern, establishment, firm, house, interest, outfit
rel conglomerate, corporation; association, cartel, chain, combine, syndicate, trust; agency, dealer, outlet
2 readiness to engage in daring or difficult activity ⟨the *enterprise* shown by the early developers and promoters of personal computers⟩
syn action, aggressiveness, ambition, drive, go, hustle, initiative
rel grit, pluck, snap, spirit, spunk, starch; killer instinct, overambitiousness; assertiveness, self-reliance; energy, hardihood, pep, vigor, vitality
near ant inactivity, inertia, passivity; diffidence, faintheartedness, timidity; hesitation, reluctance; indolence, laziness
3 a risky undertaking — see GAMBLE
enterprising *adj* **1** having or showing a bold forcefulness in the pursuit of a goal — see AGGRESSIVE 1
2 inclined or willing to take risks — see BOLD 1
entertain *vb* **1** to cause (someone) to pass the time agreeably occupied — see AMUSE
2 to give serious and careful thought to — see PONDER
3 to keep in one's mind or heart — see HARBOR 1
entertaining *adj* providing amusement or enjoyment — see FUN
entertainment *n* **1** the act or activity of providing pleasure or amusement especially for the public ⟨We didn't stay for the featured *entertainment* because we don't care for comedy acts.⟩ ⟨The film is purely for *entertainment* and not meant to be taken seriously.⟩
syn amusement, distraction, diversion, recreation
rel nightlife, show business; delectation, delight, enjoyment, joy, mirth; gratification, relaxation, relief, satisfaction; exhibition, performance, presentation, presentment, production, show; escapism
2 someone or something that provides amusement or enjoyment — see FUN 1
enthrall *or* **enthral** *vb* **1** to hold the attention of as if by a spell ⟨*Enthralled* by the flickering fire in the hearth, we lost all track of time.⟩
syn arrest, bedazzle, enchant, fascinate, grip, hypnotize, mesmerize, spellbind
rel enrapture, entrance, thrill; beguile, bewitch, charm; absorb, engage, engross, involve
2 to fill with overwhelming emotion (as wonder or delight) — see ENTRANCE
3 to hold the attention of — see ENGAGE 1
enthralled *adj* having the mind fixed on something — see ATTENTIVE 1
enthralling *adj* holding the attention or provoking interest — see INTERESTING
enthrallment *n* a focusing of the mind on something — see ATTENTION 1
enthrone *vb* to assign a high status or value to — see EXALT 1
enthuse *vb* to make an exaggerated display of affection or enthusiasm — see GUSH 2
enthusiasm *n* **1** a practice or interest that is very popular for a short time — see FAD

---

syn synonym(s)   *rel* related words
ant antonym(s)   *near ant* near antonym(s)

2 urgent desire or interest — see EAGER-NESS

3 depth of feeling — see ARDOR 1

enthusiast *n* a person with a strong and habitual liking for something — see FAN

enthusiastic *adj* showing urgent desire or interest — see EAGER

enthusiastically *adv* in an enthusiastic manner — see SKY-HIGH

entice *vb* to lead away from a usual or proper course by offering some pleasure or advantage — see LURE

enticement *n* **1** something that persuades one to perform an action for pleasure or gain — see LURE

2 the act or pressure of giving in to a desire especially when ill-advised — see TEMPTATION 1

entire *adj* **1** not divided or scattered among several areas of interest or concern — see WHOLE 1

2 not lacking any part or member that properly belongs to it — see COMPLETE 1

entirely *adv* to a full extent or degree — see FULLY 1

entitle *vb* **1** to give a right to ⟨The card *entitles* my grandmother to the discount for senior citizens.⟩

syn authorize, privilege, qualify

rel empower, enable, enfranchise, license (*also* licence); approve, endorse (*also* indorse); allow, let, permit; accredit, certificate, certify, ratify; legitimize, sanction, validate, warrant

near ant disable, disempower, disenfranchise; decertify; disallow, forbid, proscribe; delegitimize, invalidate, nullify

ant disqualify

2 to give a name to — see NAME 1

entity *n* one that has a real and independent existence ⟨the question of whether extrasensory perception will ever be a scientifically recognized *entity*⟩

syn being, existent, individual, individuality, integer, object, reality, something, substance, thing

rel body, subject; material, matter, quantity, stuff

near ant nonentity

entomb *vb* to place (a dead body) in the earth, a tomb, or the sea — see BURY 1

entombing *n* the act or ceremony of putting a dead body in its final resting place — see BURIAL 1

entombment *n* the act or ceremony of putting a dead body in its final resting place — see BURIAL 1

entrails *n pl* the internal organs of the body — see GUT 1

entrance *n* **1** the means or right of entering or participating in ⟨*Entrance* to the club is by invitation only.⟩

syn access, admission, admittance, door, doorway, entrée (*or* entree), entry, gateway, ingress, key, passport, ticket

rel approval, authorization, permission, qualification; open door, welcome mat

near ant discharge, dismissal, ejection, expulsion, ouster, rejection, removal

2 the opening through which one can enter or leave a structure — see DOOR 2

entrance *vb* to fill with overwhelming emotion (as wonder or delight) ⟨a production of *The Nutcracker* ballet that will *entrance* audiences⟩

syn carry away, enrapture, enthrall (*or* enthral), rap, rapture, ravish, transport

rel delight, gladden, gratify, please, satisfy; bewitch, captivate, charm, enchant, fascinate; elate, excite, exhilarate, stir

phrases knock dead, knock one's socks off

entranced *adj* **1** being or appearing to be under a magic spell — see ENCHANTED

2 experiencing or marked by overwhelming usually pleasurable emotion — see ECSTATIC

entrancing *adj* having an often mysterious or magical power to attract — see FASCINATING 1

entrap *vb* to catch or hold as if in a net — see ENTANGLE 2

entreat *vb* to make a request to (someone) in an earnest or urgent manner — see BEG

entreating *adj* asking humbly — see SUPPLIANT

entreaty *n* an earnest request — see PLEA 1

entrée *or* **entree** *n* the means or right of entering or participating in — see ENTRANCE 1

entrench *also* **intrench** *vb* to set solidly in or as if in surrounding matter ⟨a father who *entrenched* in our minds the belief that hard work pays off⟩

syn bed, embed (*also* imbed), fix, impact, implant, ingrain (*also* engrain), lodge, root

rel imbue, infuse; beat (into), drive (into); establish, place, put, settle, stick

near ant eliminate, eradicate; eject, expel; detach, disconnect, disengage, remove

ant dislodge, root (out), uproot

entrenched *also* **intrenched** *adj* firmly established over time — see INVETERATE 1

entrust *also* **intrust** *vb* **1** to give a task, duty, or responsibility to ⟨We *entrusted* our financial adviser with the investment of our savings.⟩

syn assign, charge, commission, task, trust

rel confer, impose; commit, consign, delegate, recommend, repose; allocate, allot; authorize, empower, invest

2 to put (something) into the possession or safekeeping of another — see GIVE 2

entry *n* **1** the entrance room of a building — see HALL 1

2 the means or right of entering or participating in — see ENTRANCE 1

entryway *n* the entrance room of a building — see HALL 1

entwine *vb* **1** to cause to twine about one another — see INTERTWINE 1

2 to follow a circular or spiral course — see WIND 1

enumerate *vb* **1** to specify one after another ⟨She proceeded to *enumerate* the reasons why she would be the best candidate.⟩

syn detail, itemize, list, numerate, recite, reel off, rehearse, tick (off)

rel outline; tabulate, tally; catalog (*or* catalogue), inventory; chart, diagram, graph; calculate, compute, estimate, figure, reckon; cite, mention, name

near ant generalize

2 to find the sum of (a collection of things) by noting each one as it is being added — see COUNT 1

3 to make a list of — see ¹LIST 1

enunciate *vb* **1** to utter clearly and distinctly — see ARTICULATE 1

2 to make known openly or publicly — see ANNOUNCE

3 to express (a thought or emotion) in words — see SAY 1

enunciation *n* the clear and accurate pronunciation of words especially in public speaking — see DICTION 1

envelop *vb* **1** to close or shut in by or as if by barriers — see ENCLOSE 1

2 to surround or cover closely — see ENFOLD 1

envenom *vb* to implant bitter feelings in — see EMBITTER

envenomed *adj* containing or contaminated with a substance capable of injuring or killing a living thing — see POISONOUS

envious *adj* having or showing mean resentment of another's possessions or advantages ⟨a family that is *envious* of their neighbors' big house⟩

   syn covetous, invidious, jaundiced, jealous, resentful

   rel begrudging, grudging; avaricious, grasping, greedy, rapacious; distrustful, suspicious; malicious, petty, spiteful

   phrases eating one's heart out, green with envy

   near ant generous, kind, kindhearted; altruistic, benevolent, charitable; well-meaning

   ant unenvious

enviousness *n* a painful awareness of another's possessions or advantages and a desire to have them too — see ENVY

environment *n* the circumstances, conditions, or objects by which one is surrounded ⟨the joys of growing up in the *environment* that a vibrant city offers⟩

   syn atmosphere, climate, environs, medium, milieu, setting, surround, surroundings

   rel location, place, position, space; backdrop, background; element; situation, status; habitat

environs *n pl* **1** the districts adjacent to a city ⟨The city and its *environs* total about a million in population.⟩

   syn outskirts, suburbia

   rel country, countryside, exurbia

   near ant downtown, inner city, midtown

2 an adjoining region or space ⟨You can get just about any kind of ethnic food in the *environs* of the university.⟩

   syn neighborhood

   rel environment, surround, surroundings

3 the circumstances, conditions, or objects by which one is surrounded — see ENVIRONMENT

envisage *vb* to form a mental picture of — see IMAGINE 1

envoy *n* **1** a person sent on a mission to represent another — see AMBASSADOR

2 a person who acts or does business for another — see AGENT 2

envy *n* a painful awareness of another's possessions or advantages and a desire to have them too ⟨Their exotic vacation inspired *envy* among their friends.⟩

   syn covetousness, enviousness, invidiousness, jealousy, resentment

rel animosity, enmity, hatred, ill will; malice, maliciousness, spitefulness

   near ant benevolence, goodwill, kindness, sympathy

enwrap *vb* **1** to hold the attention of — see ENGAGE 1

2 to surround or cover closely — see ENFOLD 1

eon *or* **aeon** *n* a long or seemingly long period of time — see AGE 2

ephemeral *adj* lasting only for a short time — see MOMENTARY

epicure *n* a person with refined tastes in food and wine ⟨an *epicure* who opened her own restaurant⟩

   syn epicurean, gourmand, gourmet

   rel connoisseur, dilettante; foodie

   near ant glutton, gorger, guzzler, hog, overeater, stuffer, swiller, trencherman

epicurean *n* a person with refined tastes in food and wine — see EPICURE

epigram *n* an often stated observation regarding something from common experience — see SAYING

epigrammatic *adj* marked by the use of few words to convey much information or meaning — see CONCISE

episode *n* something that happens — see EVENT 1

episodic *also* **episodical** *adj* **1** appearing in parts or numbers that follow regularly — see SERIAL

2 lacking in steadiness or regularity of occurrence — see FITFUL

epistle *n* a message on paper from one person or group to another — see [1]LETTER

epithet *n* **1** a descriptive or familiar name given instead of or in addition to the one belonging to an individual — see NICKNAME

2 an act or expression showing scorn and usually intended to hurt another's feelings — see INSULT

epitome *n* **1** a short statement of the main points — see SUMMARY

2 a visible representation of something abstract (as a quality) — see EMBODIMENT

3 the most perfect type or example — see QUINTESSENCE 1

epitomize *vb* **1** to make into a short statement of the main points (as of a report) — see SUMMARIZE

2 to represent in visible form — see EMBODY 2

epoch *n* an extent of time associated with a particular person or thing — see AGE 1

equable *adj* marked by temperatures that are neither too high nor too low — see CLEMENT 1

equal *adj* **1** marked by justice, honesty, and freedom from bias — see FAIR 2

2 resembling another in every respect — see SAME 1

3 having the required skills for an acceptable level of performance — see COMPETENT 1

4 free from emotional or mental agitation — see CALM 2

equal *n* one that is equal to another in status, achievement, or value ⟨a basketball player who truly has no *equal* in his sport⟩

   syn coequal, coordinate, counterpart,

---

   syn synonym(s)   *rel* related words

   ant antonym(s)   *near ant* near antonyms(s)

equivalent, fellow, like, match, parallel, peer, rival

rel analogue (*or* analog); double, half, mate, twin; associate, colleague, companion, copartner, partner; competitor

equal *vb* 1 to produce something equal to (as in quality or value) ⟨No one has *equaled* Shakespeare's plays.⟩

syn match, meet, tie

rel beat, better, eclipse, excel, outdistance, outdo, outshine, outstrip, overtop, surpass, top, transcend; amount (to), approach, touch; approximate, keep up, measure up (to), parallel, rival, stack up (against *or* with)

2 to be the same in meaning or effect — see AMOUNT (TO) 2

3 to be the exact counterpart of — see MATCH 1.

equality *n* the state or fact of being exactly the same in number, amount, status, or quality — see EQUIVALENCE

equalize *vb* to make equal in amount, degree, or status ⟨a plan to *equalize* educational opportunities for all the state's children, rich and poor alike⟩

syn balance, equate, even, level

rel equilibrate, equipoise; accommodate, adjust, compensate, fit; counterbalance; homogenize, normalize, regularize, standardize; democratize

near ant disequilibrate

equanimity *n* evenness of emotions or temper ⟨an Olympic diver who always displays remarkable *equanimity* on the platform⟩

syn aplomb, calmness, collectedness, composure, cool, coolness, countenance, equilibrium, imperturbability, placidity, repose, self-possession, serenity, tranquility (*or* tranquillity)

rel assurance, confidence, poise, self-assurance, self-confidence; easygoingness, laid-backness

near ant alarm (*also* alarum), anxiety, anxiousness, apprehension, apprehensiveness, care, concern, disquiet, solicitude, uneasiness, worry; excitability, excitableness, nervousness; disturbance

ant agitation, discomposure, perturbation

equate *vb* 1 to regard or represent as equal or comparable ⟨a value system that *equates* money with success⟩

syn compare, liken

rel associate, connect, correlate, identify, join, link, match, relate; group, lump (together); assort, categorize, class, classify, grade, group, sort

near ant differentiate, discern, discriminate, distinguish, separate

2 to describe as similar — see COMPARE 1

3 to make equal in amount, degree, or status — see EQUALIZE

equatorial *adj* being near the equator — see LOW 1

equilibrium *n* 1 a condition in which opposing forces are equal to one another — see BALANCE 1

2 evenness of emotions or temper — see EQUANIMITY

equine *n* a large hoofed domestic animal that is used for carrying or drawing loads and for riding — see HORSE

equip *vb* 1 to make competent (as by training, skill, or ability) for a particular office or function — see QUALIFY 2

2 to provide (someone) with what is needed for a task or activity — see FURNISH 1

equipage *n* a horse-drawn wheeled vehicle for carrying passengers — see CARRIAGE 1

equipment *n* items needed for the performance of a task or activity ⟨The *equipment* for the polar expedition included ships, instruments, sleds, dogs, and provisions.⟩

syn accoutrements (*or* accouterments), apparatus, gear, hardware, material(s), matériel (*or* materiel), outfit, paraphernalia, stuff, tackle

rel accessories, appurtenances, attachments, fittings; baggage, belongings, impedimenta; appliances, facilities, instruments, machinery, tools; apparel, attire, habiliments, raiment, trappings; armamentarium, armory, arsenal, battery; assets, resources

equipoise *n* 1 a condition in which opposing forces are equal to one another — see BALANCE 1

2 a force or influence that makes an opposing force ineffective or less effective — see COUNTERBALANCE

equitable *adj* marked by justice, honesty, and freedom from bias — see FAIR 2

equity *n* 1 lack of favoritism toward one side or another — see DETACHMENT 1

2 the practice of giving to others what is their due or an instance of this — see JUSTICE 1

equivalence *n* the state or fact of being exactly the same in number, amount, status, or quality ⟨moviegoers who mistakenly believe that there is an *equivalence* between the personality of an actor and that of his character⟩

syn equality, equivalency, par, parity, sameness

rel compatibility, correlation, correspondence; alikeness, community, likeness, parallelism, resemblance, similarity, similitude; exchangeability, interchangeability; identicalness, identity

near ant difference, disagreement, discrepancy, disparateness, disparity, distinction, distinctiveness, distinctness, divergence, diverseness, diversity; incompatibility; dissimilarity, unlikeness

ant imparity, inequality, nonequivalence

equivalency *n* the state or fact of being exactly the same in number, amount, status, or quality — see EQUIVALENCE

equivalent *n* one that is equal to another in status, achievement, or value — see EQUAL

equivocal *adj* 1 giving good reason for being doubted, questioned, or challenged — see DOUBTFUL 2

2 having an often intentionally veiled or uncertain meaning — see OBSCURE 1

equivocalness *n* the quality or state of having a veiled or uncertain meaning — see OBSCURITY 1

equivocate *vb* to avoid giving a definite answer or position ⟨The candidate *equivocated* as long as he could on controversial issues.⟩

syn fudge, hedge, pussyfoot

rel yo-yo; dodge, duck, elude, eschew, evade, shake, shirk, shun, sidestep, skirt; bypass, circumvent; cavil, quibble; straddle

phrases beat around the bush (*or* beat about the bush), hem and haw, straddle the fence

equivocation *n* 1 deliberate evasion in speech — see CIRCUMLOCUTION 1

2 the quality or state of having a veiled or uncertain meaning — see OBSCURITY 1

era *n* an extent of time associated with a particular person or thing — see AGE 1

eradicate *vb* to destroy all traces of — see ANNIHILATE 1

ere *prep* earlier than — see BEFORE 1

erect *adj* rising straight up ⟨a column still *erect* among the ancient ruins⟩

syn perpendicular, plumb, raised, standing, upright, upstanding, vertical

rel elevated, lifted, upended, upraised; semierect; freestanding, stand-alone

near ant prostrate, supine; diagonal, hanging, sagging, slant, slanted, slanting, slanty

ant flat, recumbent

erect *vb* 1 to fix in an upright position ⟨We need to *erect* our tent before the sun goes down.⟩

syn pitch, put up, raise, rear, set up, upend, upraise

rel brace, buttress, prop (up), shore (up), support; boost, crane, elevate, heave, heft, heighten, hike, hoist, jack (up), lift, perk (up), pick up, up, uphold, uplift

near ant demolish, flatten, knock down, level, raze, tear down

2 to form by putting together parts or materials — see BUILD

ergo *adv* for this or that reason — see THEREFORE

erode *vb* 1 to consume or wear away gradually — see EAT 2

2 to damage or diminish by continued friction — see ABRADE 1

erosion *n* a gradual weakening, loss, or destruction — see CORROSION

erotic *also* **erotical** *adj* of, relating to, exciting, or expressing sexual attraction or desire ⟨the *erotic* aspects of the fairy tale⟩

syn amatory, amorous, sexy

rel carnal, fleshly, sensual, sensuous; lascivious, lewd, lustful, obscene, prurient, suggestive, titillating; dirty, filthy, foul, gross, indecent, nasty, ribald, vulgar; fetishistic, perversive

near ant clean, decent, decorous, polite, proper, seemly; innocuous, inoffensive

err *vb* 1 to make a mistake ⟨We badly *erred* when we calculated the driving distance.⟩

syn blunder, flub, fluff, foul up, fumble, louse up, mess (up), screw up, stumble, trip

rel nod; bobble, botch, bungle, butcher, foozle, mangle, mishandle, muff, murder; miscalculate, misconceive, miscount, miscue, misdeem, misjudge, mistake; misconstrue, misinterpret, misunderstand

phrases drop the ball, lay an egg

2 to commit an offense — see OFFEND 1

errant *adj* 1 engaging in or marked by childish misbehavior — see NAUGHTY

2 traveling from place to place — see ITINERANT

erratic *adj* 1 lacking a definite plan, purpose, or pattern — see RANDOM

2 lacking in steadiness or regularity of occurrence — see FITFUL

3 not staying constant — see UNEVEN 2

4 different from the ordinary in a way that causes curiosity or suspicion — see ODD 2

erratically *adv* without definite aim, direction, rule, or method — see HIT OR MISS

erroneous *adj* not being in agreement with what is true — see FALSE 1

erroneously *adv* in a mistaken or inappropriate way — see WRONGLY

erroneousness *n* the quality or state of being false — see FALLACY 2

error *n* 1 an unintentional departure from truth or accuracy ⟨A report on the incident contained several unfortunate *errors*.⟩

syn blunder, bobble, fault, flub, fluff, fumble, gaff, gaffe, goof, inaccuracy, lapse, miscue, misstep, mistake, oversight, screwup, slip, slipup, stumble, trip

rel bloomer, blooper, boner, howler, pratfall; foul-up, snafu; misapprehension, miscomprehension, misconception, misconstruction, miscue, misdescription, misinterpretation, misjudgment, misreading, misstatement, misunderstanding

near ant accuracy, correctness, exactitude, exactness, preciseness, precision, strictness; inerrancy, infallibility, perfection

2 a breaking of a moral or legal code — see OFFENSE 1

3 a false idea or belief — see FALLACY 1

erstwhile *adj* having been such at some previous time — see FORMER 1

erudite *adj* 1 having or displaying advanced knowledge or education — see EDUCATED 1

2 suggestive of the vocabulary used in books — see BOOKISH

erudition *n* the understanding and information gained from being educated — see EDUCATION 2

erupt *vb* 1 to violently throw out or off (something from within) ⟨The volcano *erupted* clouds of poisonous gas and tons of hot ash.⟩

syn belch, disgorge, eject, expel, jet, spew, spout, spurt

rel gush, pour, squirt, stream, surge; exhale, issue, release, shoot, spit, spring, vent; discharge, emit, fire; cast, fling, heave, hurl, launch, pitch, toss

near ant bottle (up), contain, restrain, shut (in *or* up)

2 to develop suddenly and violently ⟨A fire *erupted*, and flames soon engulfed the room.⟩

syn break out, burst (forth), explode, flame, flare (up)

rel rocket, skyrocket; balloon, burgeon (*also* bourgeon), mount, multiply, mushroom, proliferate, snowball, swell, wax; blow up, detonate, touch off

eruption *n* 1 a sudden intense expression of strong feeling — see OUTBURST 1

2 the act or an instance of exploding — see EXPLOSION 1

escalate *vb* 1 to become greater in extent,

---

volume, amount, or number — see IN-CREASE 2

2 to make greater in size, amount, or number — see INCREASE 1

escalated *adj* being at a higher level than average — see HIGH 2

escapade *n* a playful or mischievous act intended as a joke — see PRANK

escape *n* **1** the act or an instance of getting free from danger or confinement ⟨a daring prison *escape*⟩
syn break, flight, getaway, lam, rout, slip
rel jailbreak; deliverance, liberation, redemption, release, rescue, salvation
near ant captivity, confinement, immurement, imprisonment, incarceration, internment; custody, hold, holding, retention; endangerment, hazard, imperilment, jeopardy, peril, risk, trouble

2 the act or a means of getting or keeping away from something undesirable ⟨the reading of science-fiction novels as an *escape* from reality⟩
syn avoidance, cop-out, dodging, ducking, eluding, evasion, out, shaking, shunning
rel bypassing, circumvention, runaround, sidestepping, skirting; averting, precluding, prevention
near ant abidance, endurance, submission, toleration

escape *vb* **1** to get free from a dangerous or confining situation ⟨Everyone managed to *escape* from the burning building in time.⟩
syn abscond, clear out, flee, fly, get out, lam, run away, run off
rel avoid, elude, evade, lose, shun; decamp, depart, elope, exit, go, leave, move, quit, sally (forth), shove (off), take off, walk out; disentangle, extricate; emancipate, enfranchise, free, liberate, loose, loosen, redeem, release, rescue, spring
phrases break free
near ant abide, dwell, hang around, linger, remain, stay, stick around, tarry; return

2 to get or keep away from (as a responsibility) through cleverness or trickery ⟨a judge who is determined not to let criminals *escape* punishment⟩
syn avoid, dodge, duck, elude, evade, finesse, get around, shake, shirk, shun
rel miss; avert, deflect, divert, obviate, parry, prevent, ward (off); ban, bar, debar, eliminate, except, exclude, preclude, rule out; bypass, circumvent, skirt; foil, fox, frustrate, outfox, outsmart, outwit, overreach, thwart
phrases fight shy of, keep clear of, stay clear of, steer clear of
near ant accept, court, embrace, pursue, seek, welcome; catch, contract, incur

escarpment *n* a steep wall of rock, earth, or ice — see CLIFF

escort *n* one that accompanies another for protection, guidance, or as a courtesy ⟨The mayor served as the senator's *escort* for her tour of the city.⟩
syn attendant, companion, guard, guide
rel chaperone (*or* chaperon), squire; shadow, sidekick; conductor, leader, pilot; convoy, courier, honor guard

escort *vb* to go along with in order to provide assistance, protection, or companionship — see ACCOMPANY 1

esculent *adj* suitable for use as food — see EDIBLE

esoteric *adj* **1** difficult for one of ordinary knowledge or intelligence to understand — see PROFOUND 1

2 not known or meant to be known by the general populace — see PRIVATE 1

especial *adj* **1** being out of the ordinary — see EXCEPTIONAL 1

2 of a particular or exact sort — see EXPRESS 1

especially *adv* **1** in the specific case of one person or thing as distinguished from others ⟨All employees, but *especially* the administrative assistants, will need to learn to use the new phone system.⟩
syn particularly
rel individually, personally; restrictively, selectively
phrases in especial, in particular
near ant broadly, widely
ant generally

2 to a great degree — see VERY 1

espionage *n* the secret gathering of information on others ⟨the acts of *espionage* on behalf of the Confederacy carried on by Belle Boyd and Rose Greenhow⟩
syn spying
rel counterespionage, counterintelligence, intelligence; cloak-and-dagger; observation, reconnaissance, surveillance; bugging, eavesdropping, wiretapping

espousal *n* **1** a ceremony in which two people are united in matrimony — see WEDDING

2 the act or state of being engaged to be married — see ENGAGEMENT 1

espouse *vb* **1** to give in marriage — see MARRY 2

2 to take as a spouse — see MARRY 3

3 to take for one's own use (something originated by another) — see ADOPT

esprit *n* active strength of body or mind — see VIGOR 1

espy *vb* to make note of (something) through the use of one's eyes — see SEE 1

essay *n* **1** a short piece of writing typically expressing a point of view ⟨school *essays* on what it means to be a patriot⟩
syn article, composition, paper, theme
rel column, commentary, editorial, feature, report, review, write-up; dissertation, thesis; tract, treatise; discourse, discussion, study

2 an effort to do or accomplish something — see ATTEMPT 1

3 a procedure or operation carried out to resolve an uncertainty — see EXPERIMENT

essay *vb* to make an effort to do — see ATTEMPT

essence *n* **1** the quality or qualities that make a thing what it is ⟨The belief that power ultimately rests with the people is the very *essence* of democracy.⟩
syn being, essentiality, nature, quintessence, soul, stuff, substance
rel heart, spirit; center, core, marrow, pith, seat; embodiment, epitome, incarnation, manifestation, personification; aspect, attribute, feature, property; gist, nub
phrases name of the game

2 the central part or aspect of something under consideration — see CRUX

essential *adj* 1 impossible to do without ⟨A well-stocked public library is *essential* for the well-being of a community.⟩

syn all-important, critical, imperative, indispensable, integral, necessary, needed, needful, required, requisite, vital

rel prerequisite; compulsory, mandatory, nonelective, obligatory; consequential, crucial, important, major, material, meaningful, momentous, significant, substantial, weighty; basic, central, fundamental, key, organic; insistent, persistent, pressing, urgent

phrases of the essence

near ant undesired, unwanted; inconsequential, insignificant, unimportant; excess, external, extra, extraneous, superfluous, surplus

ant dispensable, needless, nonessential, unessential, unnecessary, unneeded

2 of or relating to the simplest facts or theories of a subject — see ELEMENTARY

3 being a part of the innermost nature of a person or thing — see INHERENT

essential *n* 1 something necessary, indispensable, or unavoidable ⟨The *essentials* for success include a willingness to work and the right attitude.⟩

syn condition, demand, must, necessary, necessity, need, needful, requirement, requisite

rel precondition, prerequisite; advantage, edge, plus

near ant amenity, comfort, extra, extravagance, frill, indulgence, luxury, superfluity, surplus, surplusage

ant nonessential, nonnecessity

2 **essentials** *pl* general or basic truths on which other truths or theories can be based — see PRINCIPLES 1

essentiality *n* the quality or qualities that make a thing what it is — see ESSENCE 1

establish *vb* 1 to gain full recognition or acceptance of ⟨a first novel that *established* him as one of the most promising writers of his generation⟩

syn demonstrate, prove, show, substantiate

rel attest, authenticate, bear out, document, evidence, support, sustain, uphold; confirm, corroborate, justify, validate, verify

near ant confute, discredit, invalidate, rebut, refute

ant disprove

2 to show the existence or truth of by evidence — see PROVE 1

3 to be responsible for the creation and early operation or use of — see FOUND

establisher *n* a person who establishes a whole new field of endeavor — see FATHER 2

establishment *n* 1 a building, room, or suite of rooms occupied by a service business — see PLACE 2

2 a commercial or industrial activity or organization — see ENTERPRISE 1

3 a public organization with a particular purpose or function — see INSTITUTION 1

4 a structure that is designed and built for a particular purpose — see FACILITY

estate *n* 1 a large impressive residence — see MANSION

2 a state of being or fitness — see CONDITION 1

3 one of the segments of society into which people are grouped — see CLASS 1

4 a piece of land and its buildings used to grow crops or raise livestock — see FARM

esteem *n* a feeling of great approval and liking — see ADMIRATION 1

esteem *vb* 1 to think of in a particular way — see CONSIDER 1

2 to think very highly or favorably of — see ADMIRE

3 to have as an opinion — see BELIEVE 2

esteemed *adj* having a good reputation especially in a field of knowledge — see RESPECTABLE 1

estimate *n* 1 the act of placing a value on the nature, character, or quality of something ⟨What we owe our war veterans is beyond *estimate*.⟩

syn appraisal, appraisement, assessment, estimation, evaluation, reckoning, valuation

rel calculation, computation, measurement; audit, check, checkup, examination, inspection, review, scan, scrutiny, survey; reassessment, transvaluation; overestimation, overevaluation; underestimation

2 an opinion on the nature, character, or quality of something — see ESTIMATION 1

estimate *vb* 1 to make an approximate or tentative judgment regarding ⟨Experts *estimated* the value of the painting at a million dollars.⟩

syn appraise, assess, evaluate, rate, set, value

rel adjudge, deem, judge; ascertain, determine, discover, learn; price, prize; decide, settle; analyze, assay, survey, test; reappraise, reassess, reevaluate, rejudge, revalue; misesteem, misjudge, misprize

2 to decide the size, amount, number, or distance of (something) without actual measurement ⟨We *estimated* the snowfall to be about a foot.⟩

syn calculate, call, conjecture, figure, gauge (*also* gage), guess, judge, make, place, put, reckon, suppose

rel conclude, deduce, extrapolate, gather, infer, reason, understand

near ant calibrate, measure, scale; compute, work out

estimation *n* 1 an opinion on the nature, character, or quality of something ⟨The teacher's *estimation* of her student's scientific aptitude proved to be well-founded when he won a national science award.⟩

syn appraisal, appraisement, assessment, estimate, evaluation, fix, judgment (*or* judgement)

rel aperçu, feeling, impression, notion, perception; confidence, faith, stock, trust; belief, conviction, mind, persuasion, sentiment, view; conjecture, guess, hunch, hypothesis, surmise, theory

2 the act of placing a value on the nature, character, or quality of something — see ESTIMATE 1

3 a feeling of great approval and liking — see ADMIRATION 1

estrange *vb* to cause to change from friendly or loving to unfriendly or uncaring ⟨She *estranged* several of her coworkers when she let her promotion go to her head.⟩

syn alienate, disaffect, disgruntle, sour

rel antagonize, embitter, envenom; aggravate, anger, enrage, incense, inflame (*also* enflame), infuriate, madden, outrage, rankle, rile, roil; break up, dissociate, disunite, divide, separate, sever, split, sunder, uncouple, unlink, unyoke; disenchant, disillusion

near ant endear, ingratiate; appease, conciliate, disarm, mollify, pacify, placate, propitiate

ant reconcile

estrangement *n* the loss of friendship or affection ⟨After years of *estrangement*, the friends put their quarrel behind them.⟩

syn alienation, disaffection, disgruntlement, souring

rel antagonism, embitterment, envenoming; breach, breakup, divorce, rift, rupture, schism, separation, split; animosity, antagonism, antipathy, bitterness, hostility, jaundice, rancor; aggravation, furor, fury, incensing, indignation, infuriation, ire, outrage, rage, spleen, wrath; disenchantment, disillusionment

near ant endearment, ingratiation; appeasement, conciliation, mollification, pacification, propitiation

ant reconcilement, reconciliation

estuary *n* a part of a body of water that extends beyond the general shoreline — see GULF 1

etch *vb* 1 to cut (as letters or designs) on a hard surface — see ENGRAVE 1

2 to produce a vivid impression of — see ENGRAVE 2

eternal *adj* 1 having an existence or validity that does not change or diminish — see ABIDING

2 lasting forever — see EVERLASTING 1

eternally *adv* for all time — see EVER 1

eternity *n* 1 endless time ⟨the question whether the universe will end someday or continue to exist in *eternity*⟩

syn everlasting, infinity, perpetuity

rel boundlessness, endlessness, interminableness, limitlessness, permanence, permanency, timelessness

near ant temporariness, transitoriness

2 unending existence after death ⟨a firm belief in the *eternity* of the soul⟩

syn afterlife, beyond, hereafter, immortality

rel afterworld, otherworld

3 a long or seemingly long period of time — see AGE 2

ethereal *adj* 1 not composed of matter — see IMMATERIAL 1

2 resembling air in lightness — see AIRY 1

3 of, relating to, or suggesting heaven — see CELESTIAL

ethical *adj* 1 conforming to a high standard of morality or virtue — see GOOD 2

2 following the accepted rules of moral conduct — see HONORABLE 1

3 guided by or in accordance with one's sense of right and wrong — see CONSCIENTIOUS 1

ethics *n pl* the code of good conduct for an individual or group ⟨The *ethics* of scouting require scouts to be loyal, clean, and reverent.⟩

syn morality, morals, norms, principles, standards

rel customs, dictates, etiquette, manners, mores, values; beliefs, dogma, faith, tenets

ethnic *adj* of, relating to, or reflecting the traits exhibited by a group of people with a common ancestry and culture — see RACIAL

etiquette *n* personal conduct or behavior as evaluated by an accepted standard of appropriateness for a social or professional setting — see MANNER 1

eulogy *n* a formal expression of praise — see ENCOMIUM

euphonious *adj* 1 having a pleasantly flowing quality suggestive of music — see LYRIC 1

2 having a pleasing mixture of notes — see HARMONIOUS 1

euphoria *n* a state of overwhelming usually pleasurable emotion — see ECSTASY

euphoric *adj* experiencing or marked by overwhelming usually pleasurable emotion — see ECSTATIC

evacuate *vb* to remove the contents of — see EMPTY

evacuee *n* a person forced to emigrate for political reasons — see ÉMIGRÉ 1

evade *vb* to get or keep away from (as a responsibility) through cleverness or trickery — see ESCAPE 2

evaluate *vb* to make an approximate or tentative judgment regarding — see ESTIMATE 1

evaluation *n* 1 an opinion on the nature, character, or quality of something — see ESTIMATION 1

2 the act of placing a value on the nature, character, or quality of something — see ESTIMATE 1

evanesce *vb* to cease to be visible — see DISAPPEAR

evanescent *adj* lasting only for a short time — see MOMENTARY

evaporate *vb* to cease to be visible — see DISAPPEAR

evasion *n* the act or a means of getting or keeping away from something undesirable — see ESCAPE 2

evasive *adj* hard to find, capture, or isolate — see ELUSIVE

even *adj* 1 being neither more nor less than a certain amount, number, or extent ⟨The distance to town is an *even* mile.⟩

syn exact, flat, precise, round

near ant approximate, comparative, near, relative; imprecise

2 having a surface without bends, breaks, or irregularities — see LEVEL 1

3 resembling another in every respect — see SAME 1

4 not varying — see UNIFORM

even *adv* 1 not merely this but also ⟨The blue whale is a large, *even* enormous animal.⟩

syn indeed, nay, truly, verily, yea

rel assuredly, certainly, decidedly, definitely, doubtless, incontestably, incontrovertibly, indisputably, really, surely, truly, undeniably, undoubtedly, unquestionably

phrases in fact, in reality, in truth

2 to a full extent or degree — see FULLY 1

even vb 1 to make free from breaks, curves, or bumps ⟨*Even* the filling before adding the top layer of the cake.⟩
syn flatten, level, plane, smooth
rel clip, crop, pare, prune, shave, trim; lay, press, spread; card, comb, rake; surface
near ant coarsen, rumple, wrinkle; bend; dent, pit
ant rough, roughen
2 to make equal in amount, degree, or status — see EQUALIZE

evenhanded *adj* marked by justice, honesty, and freedom from bias — see FAIR 2

evening n 1 a later period of one's life — see AGE 3
2 the time from when the sun begins to set to the onset of total darkness — see DUSK 1

event n 1 something that happens ⟨Dinnertime was devoted to talking over the day's *events*.⟩
syn affair, circumstance, episode, happening, incident, occasion, occurrence, thing
rel coincidence, freak; landmark, milestone, page, phenomenon, turning point; adventure, experience, time; happenchance, happenstance; accident, crisis, emergency, juncture; achievement, deed, exploit, feat; news, tidings; circus, extravaganza, pageant
2 something that might happen ⟨In the *event* of rain, graduation ceremonies will be held indoors.⟩
syn case, contingency, contingent, eventuality, possibility
rel probability; accident, chance, hazard, risk
3 a competitive encounter between individuals or groups carried on for amusement, exercise, or in pursuit of a prize — see GAME 1
4 a social gathering — see PARTY 1

eventful *adj* having great meaning or lasting effect — see IMPORTANT 1

eventide n the time from when the sun begins to set to the onset of total darkness — see DUSK 1

eventuality n 1 something that can develop or become actual — see POTENTIAL
2 something that might happen — see EVENT 2

eventually *adv* at a later time — see YET 1

ever *adv* 1 for all time ⟨The name of Benedict Arnold will *ever* be linked with treason.⟩
syn always, aye (*also* ay), eternally, everlastingly, evermore, forever, forevermore, permanently, perpetually
rel enduringly, long, perennially
phrases for good (*also* for good and all), for keeps
ant ne'er, never, nevermore
2 in any way or respect — see AT ALL
3 on every relevant occasion — see ALWAYS 1
4 to a great degree — see VERY 1

everlasting *adj* 1 lasting forever ⟨Valentines typically express the giver's *everlasting* love and devotion.⟩
syn ceaseless, dateless, deathless, endless, eternal, immortal, permanent, perpetual, undying, unending

rel durable, enduring, lasting, long-lived, persistent, stubborn; imperishable, infeasible, indestructible, indissoluble, inexpungible; timeless; abiding, stable, standing, steadfast, steady, unfailing, unfaltering; continual, continuing, continuous, incessant, unbroken, unceasing, uninterrupted, unremitting
near ant ephemeral, evanescent, fleeting, fugitive, momentary, passing, short-lived, transitory; interim, provisional, short-term
ant impermanent, mortal, temporary, transient
2 having an existence or validity that does not change or diminish — see ABIDING

everlasting n 1 endless time — see ETERNITY 1
2 *cap* the being worshipped as the creator and ruler of the universe — see DEITY 2

everlastingly *adv* for all time — see EVER 1

evermore *adv* for all time — see EVER 1

every *adj* being one of a group — see EACH

everybody *pron* every person ⟨*Everybody* must do what his or her conscience dictates.⟩
syn all, everyone
rel anybody, anyone; somebody, someone
phrases each and everyone, one and all
ant nobody, none, no one

everyday *adj* 1 being of the type that is encountered in the normal course of events — see ORDINARY 1
2 having to do with the practical details of regular life — see MUNDANE 1
3 not designed to be worn only on special occasions — see CASUAL 1
4 often observed or encountered — see COMMON 1

everyone *pron* every person — see EVERYBODY

everyplace *adv* in every place or in all places — see EVERYWHERE

everywhere *adv* in every place or in all places ⟨Freedom and happiness are the goals of people *everywhere*.⟩
syn all over, everyplace, throughout
rel every which way; right and left
phrases all over the place (*or* map), far and near, in every corner (*or* quarter), on all hands (*or* on every hand)

evidence n something presented in support of the truth or accuracy of a claim — see PROOF

evident *adj* 1 appearing to be true on the basis of evidence that may or may not be confirmed — see APPARENT 1
2 not subject to misinterpretation or more than one interpretation — see CLEAR 2

evidently *adv* to all outward appearances — see APPARENTLY

evil *adj* 1 causing or capable of causing harm — see HARMFUL
2 not conforming to a high moral standard; morally unacceptable — see BAD 2
3 causing intense displeasure, disgust, or resentment — see OFFENSIVE 1

evil n that which is morally unacceptable ⟨Our free will allows us to choose between good and *evil*.⟩
syn bad, evildoing, ill, immorality, iniquity, sin, villainy, wrong

---

syn synonym(s)   *rel* related words
ant antonym(s)   *near ant* near antonym(s)

rel atrociousness, atrocity, badness, balefulness, darkness, depravedness, devilishness, diabolism, enormity, evilness, heinousness, satanism, sinfulness, vileness, wickedness; devilry (*or* deviltry); cancer, canker, decay, rot, squalor; corruption, debauchery, degeneracy, depravity, indecency, malefaction, perversion, pervertedness, scurrility, scurrilousness; abomination, anathema, taboo (*also* tabu)

near ant decency, goodness, honesty, integrity, probity, rectitude, uprightness; righteousness, virtuousness

ant good, morality, right, virtue

evildoer *n* 1 a person who commits moral wrongs ⟨If good people stand by and do nothing, *evildoers* will triumph.⟩

syn malefactor, sinner, wrongdoer

rel criminal, crook, felon, lawbreaker, miscreant, misdoer, misfeasor, offender, reprobate, transgressor, villain; corrupter (*also* corruptor)

near ant angel, innocent, saint

2 a mean, evil, or unprincipled person — see VILLAIN

evildoing *n* that which is morally unacceptable — see EVIL

evilness *n* the state or quality of being utterly evil — see ENORMITY 1

evince *vb* to make known (something abstract) through outward signs — see SHOW 2

eviscerate *vb* to take the internal organs out of — see GUT

evocative *adj* provoking a memory or mental association — see SUGGESTIVE 2

evoke *vb* to draw out (something hidden, latent, or reserved) — see EDUCE

evolution *n* the act or process of going from the simple or basic to the complex or advanced — see DEVELOPMENT 1

evolve *vb* 1 to gradually become clearer or more detailed — see DEVELOP 1

2 to throw or give off — see EMIT 1

evolved *adj* being far along in development — see ADVANCED

ewer *n* a handled container for holding and pouring liquids that usually has a lip or a spout — see PITCHER

exact *adj* 1 being in agreement with the truth or a fact or a standard — see CORRECT 1

2 being neither more nor less than a certain amount, number, or extent — see EVEN 1

3 following an original exactly — see FAITHFUL 2

4 made or done with extreme care and accuracy — see FINE 2

5 meeting the highest standard of accuracy — see PRECISE 1

exact *vb* 1 to ask for (something) earnestly or with authority — see DEMAND 1

2 to establish or apply as a charge or penalty — see IMPOSE

3 to get (as money) by the use of force or threats — see EXTORT

exacting *adj* 1 hard to please — see FINICKY

2 not allowing for any exceptions or loosening of standards — see RIGID 1

3 requiring considerable physical or mental effort — see HARD 2

4 requiring much time, effort, or careful attention — see DEMANDING 1

exactitude *n* the quality or state of being very accurate — see PRECISION

exactly *adv* 1 as stated or indicated without the slightest difference ⟨We will meet at *exactly* six o'clock.⟩

syn due, full, just, precisely, right, sharp, smack-dab, squarely

phrases on the button, on the nose

2 in the same manner — see JUST 1

3 in the same words — see VERBATIM

4 without any relaxation of standards or precision — see STRICTLY

5 to a full extent or degree — see FULLY 1

6 used to express agreement — see YES

exactness *n* the quality or state of being very accurate — see PRECISION

exaggerate *vb* 1 to add to the interest of by including made-up details — see EMBROIDER

2 to describe or express in too strong terms — see OVERSTATE

exaggeration *n* the representation of something in terms that go beyond the facts ⟨Their *exaggeration* was such that a rainstorm became a hurricane.⟩

syn caricature, coloring, elaboration, embellishment, embroidering, embroidery, hyperbole, magnification, overstatement, padding, stretching

rel amplification, enhancement; fabrication, misrepresentation; fudging, hedging; puffery; superlative

near ant belittlement, disparagement, minimizing, poor-mouthing

ant meiosis, understatement

exalt *vb* 1 to assign a high status or value to ⟨Popular support and media hype have *exalted* Super Bowl Sunday to the level of a national holiday.⟩

syn aggrandize, canonize, deify, dignify, elevate, ennoble, enshrine, enthrone, glorify, magnify

rel boost, lift, promote, raise, upgrade, uplift; heighten, intensify; idealize, romanticize, sanitize, sugarcoat; acclaim, extol (*also* extoll), honor, laud, praise

near ant belittle, decry, depreciate, disparage, minimize

ant abase, degrade, demean, humble, humiliate

2 to proclaim the glory of — see PRAISE 1

exam *n* a set of questions or problems designed to assess knowledge, skills, or intelligence — see EXAMINATION 1

examination *n* 1 a set of questions or problems designed to assess knowledge, skills, or intelligence ⟨Applicants to the prep school are required to take a demanding *examination*.⟩

syn exam, quiz, test

rel aptitude test, intelligence test, placement test; pretest, retest; board(s), midterm, midyear; catechism; audition; final; checkup, inspection, review

2 a systematic search for the truth or facts about something — see INQUIRY 1

3 a close look at or over someone or something in order to judge condition — see INSPECTION

examine *vb* 1 to put a series of questions to ⟨The defense attorney was eager to *examine* her star witness.⟩

syn grill, interrogate, pump, query, question, quiz

rel debrief; cross-examine, cross-question;

annoy, hound, pester; canvass (*also* canvas), poll

phrases give the third degree to, pick the brains of

2 to look over closely (as for judging quality or condition) — see INSPECT

3 to search through or into — see EXPLORE 1

example *n* one of a group or collection that shows what the whole is like ⟨a structure that is a fine *example* of contemporary architecture⟩

syn case, exemplar, illustration, instance, prototype, representative, sample, specimen

rel archetype, classic, locus classicus, paradigm; cross section, microcosm; evidence, indication, manifestation, sign

phrases case in point

exasperate *vb* to disturb the peace of mind of (someone) especially by repeated disagreeable acts — see IRRITATE 1

exasperating *adj* causing annoyance — see ANNOYING

exasperation *n* **1** something that is a source of irritation — see ANNOYANCE 3

2 the feeling of impatience or anger caused by another's repeated disagreeable acts — see ANNOYANCE 2

excavate *vb* to hollow out or form (something) by removing earth — see DIG 1

exceed *vb* **1** to go beyond the limit of ⟨The lawyers argued that the court had clearly *exceeded* its authority.⟩

syn break, outrun, overpass, overreach, overrun, overshoot, overstep, surpass, transcend

rel encroach, entrench (*also* intrench), infringe, invade, trespass; overdo, overutilize, overwork

2 to be greater, better, or stronger than — see SURPASS 1

exceeding *adj* being out of the ordinary — see EXCEPTIONAL 1

exceedingly *also* **exceeding** *adv* to a great degree — see VERY 1

excel *vb* to be greater, better, or stronger than — see SURPASS 1

excellence *n* **1** exceptionally high quality ⟨The annual awards honor *excellence* in children's literature.⟩

syn distinction, excellency, greatness, perfection, preeminence, superbness, superiority, supremacy

rel faultlessness, flawlessness, impeccability; goodness, value, worth; consequence, importance

near ant averageness, badness, crumminess, inferiority, mediocrity, ordinariness, worthlessness

2 a quality that gives something special worth ⟨The particular *excellence* of down in clothing and sleeping bags is its lightness.⟩

syn distinction, excellency, grace, merit, value, virtue

rel advantage, edge, plus, superiority

near ant blemish, defect, failing, fault, flaw; drawback, minus, negative

ant deficiency, demerit, disvalue

excellency *n* **1** a quality that gives something special worth — see EXCELLENCE 2

2 exceptionally high quality — see EXCELLENCE 1

excellent *adj* of the very best kind ⟨Fastfood fans rate this chain's fries as *excellent*.⟩

syn A1, awesome, bang-up, banner, beautiful, brave, bully, bumper, capital, choice, classic, cool [*slang*], crackerjack, dandy, divine, fabulous, famous, fantastic, fine, first-class, first-rate, grand, great, groovy, heavenly, hot, immense, jim-dandy, lovely, marvelous (*or* marvellous), mean, neat, nifty, noble, par excellence, prime, prize, quality, sensational, splendid, stellar, sterling, superb, superior, superlative, supernal, swell, terrific, tip-top, top, top-notch, top-of-the-line, unsurpassed, wonderful

rel acceptable, adequate, all right, decent, good, OK (*or* okay), passable, satisfactory, tolerable; better, exceptional, fancy, high-grade, high-test, premium, select, special, superfine; classical, standard, traditional

phrases out of this world, too much

near ant bad, inferior, low-grade, substandard, unsatisfactory; mediocre, middling, second-class, second-rate

ant atrocious, awful, execrable, lousy, pathetic, poor, rotten, terrible, vile, wretched

except *vb* **1** to present an opposing opinion or argument — see OBJECT

2 to prevent the participation, consideration, or inclusion of — see EXCLUDE

except *also* **excepting** *conj* if it were not for the fact that ⟨I'd go, *except* it's too far.⟩

syn but, only, saving, yet

except *also* **excepting** *prep* not including ⟨The store is open daily *except* Sundays.⟩

syn aside from, bar, barring, beside, besides, but, except for, excluding, exclusive of, other than, outside, outside of, save, saving

except for *prep* not including — see EXCEPT

exceptionable *adj* provoking or likely to provoke protest — see OBJECTIONABLE

exceptional *adj* **1** being out of the ordinary ⟨An *exceptional* amount of snow fell in March.⟩

syn aberrant, abnormal, anomalous, atypical, especial, exceeding, extraordinary, freak, odd, peculiar, phenomenal, rare, singular, uncommon, uncustomary, unique, unusual, unwonted

rel conspicuous, notable, noticeable, outstanding, prominent, remarkable, salient, striking; bizarre, deviant, eccentric, freakish, monstrous, oddball, outlandish, quaint, strange, weird; incomprehensible, inconceivable, incredible, unimaginable, unthinkable

near ant everyday, familiar, frequent

ant common, customary, normal, ordinary, typical, unexceptional, unextraordinary, usual

2 deprived of the power to perform one or more natural bodily activities — see DISABLED

3 having or showing quickness of mind — see INTELLIGENT 1

---

syn synonym(s) **rel** related words
ant antonym(s) **near ant** near antonym(s)

excerpt n a part taken from a longer work ⟨He'll read an *excerpt* from the novel at the book signing.⟩
syn extract, passage
rel clip, snippet, sound bite; citation, quotation; locus classicus; sample, selection

excess adj being over what is needed — see SPARE 1

excess n the state or an instance of going beyond what is usual, proper, or needed ⟨a new television season with an *excess* of sitcoms⟩
syn fat, overabundance, overage, overflow, overkill, overmuch, oversupply, redundancy, superabundance, superfluity, surfeit, surplus
rel abundance, bounty, plentitude, plenty, profusion, sufficiency; overproduction, overstock
near ant dearth, lack, scarcity, want
ant deficiency, deficit, insufficiency

excessive adj going beyond a normal or acceptable limit in degree or amount ⟨nerdy hackers who spend an *excessive* amount of time sitting in front of their computers⟩
syn devilish, exorbitant, extravagant, extreme, fancy, immoderate, inordinate, insane, intolerable, lavish, overdue, overmuch, overweening, steep, stiff, towering, unconscionable, undue, unmerciful
rel boundless, endless, immeasurable, infinite, limitless; unbearable, unjustifiable, unwarranted; improper, inappropriate, thick, unseemly; unrestrained
phrases a bit much, over the top
near ant deficient, inadequate, insufficient; minimal, minimum
ant middling, moderate, modest, reasonable, temperate

excessively adv beyond a normal or acceptable limit — see TOO 1

exchange n 1 a giving or taking of one thing or value in return for another ⟨*Exchanges* of commemorative pins are common among Olympic athletes.⟩
syn barter, commutation, dicker, swap, trade, trade-off, truck
rel replacement, substitution; reciprocation, recompense, requital; bargain, deal, horse trade, negotiation, transaction; bargaining, dealing, dickering, haggling, horse trading; logrolling
2 talking or a talk between two or more people — see CONVERSATION

exchange vb to give up (something) and take something else in return — see CHANGE 3

excitable adj easily excited by nature ⟨an *excitable* child who enjoys being outside⟩
syn flighty, fluttery, high-strung, hyperactive, jittery, jumpy, nervous, skittish, spasmodic, spooky
rel hot-blooded, mercurial, temperamental, unstable, volatile, volcanic; anxious, edgy, flibbertigibbety, nervy, tense, uptight; emotional, emotionalistic, hypersensitive, intense, sensitive, soulful
near ant calm, collected, cool, serene, tranquil; easy, easygoing, laid-back, relaxed
ant imperturbable, nerveless, unexcitable, unflappable, unshakable

excite vb 1 to cause a pleasurable stimulation of the feelings of — see THRILL

2 to rouse to strong feeling or action — see PROVOKE 1

excited adj 1 being in a state of increased activity or agitation — see FEVERISH 1
2 showing urgent desire or interest — see EAGER

excitement n 1 something that arouses a strong response from another — see PROVOCATION 1
2 urgent desire or interest — see EAGERNESS

exciter n a person who stirs up public feelings especially of discontent — see AGITATOR

exciting adj 1 causing great emotional or mental stimulation ⟨an *exciting*, come-from-behind victory for the underdogs in the last game of the World Series⟩
syn breathtaking, charged, electric, electrifying, exhilarating, galvanizing, hair-raising, inspiring, rip-roaring, rousing, stimulating, stirring, thrilling
rel arresting, interesting, intriguing, provocative, tantalizing, titillating; absorbing, engrossing, gripping, riveting; moving, poignant, touching; enchanting, enthralling, fascinating, spellbinding; dynamic, energetic, high-voltage, lively, lusty
near ant boring, tedious, tiresome; dreary, dull, humdrum, monotonous, uninteresting
ant unexciting
2 serving or likely to arouse a strong reaction — see PROVOCATIVE

exclaim vb to utter with a sudden burst of strong feeling ⟨The whole team *exclaimed* with one voice, "We won!"⟩
syn blurt (out), bolt, cry (out), ejaculate
rel blunder, leak; bellow, crow, holler, hoot, howl, roar, shout, whoop, yowl; aah (*also* ah), ooh; interject

exclamation n a sudden short emotional utterance ⟨The good news was greeted with a chorus of joyous *exclamations*.⟩
syn cry, ejaculation, interjection
rel aah (*also* ah), ooh; holler, hoot, howl, shout, whoop, yell, yelp, yowl; scream, screech, shriek, squall, squeak, squeal

exclude vb to prevent the participation, consideration, or inclusion of ⟨You can share files with some people on the network while *excluding* others.⟩
syn ban, bar, count (out), debar, eliminate, except, rule out, shut out
rel blackball, blacklist, excommunicate, ostracize; banish, deport, exile, expel, oust, throw out; obviate, preclude, prevent, prohibit; deter, stave off, ward (off); check off, disregard; comb (out), weed (out)
phrases close one's doors to
near ant accept, embrace, entertain, take in, welcome; unban
ant admit, include

excluding prep not including — see EXCEPT

exclusive adj 1 belonging only to the one person, unit, or group named — see SOLE 1
2 not divided or scattered among several areas of interest or concern — see WHOLE 1
3 being in the latest or current fashion — see STYLISH

exclusively adv for nothing other than — see SOLELY 1

exclusive of *prep* not including — see EX-CEPT

excoriate *vb* **1** to criticize harshly and usually publicly — see ATTACK 2

2 to make sore by continued rubbing — see CHAFE 1

excoriation *n* an often public or formal expression of disapproval — see CENSURE

excrement *n* solid matter discharged from an animal's alimentary canal — see DROPPING 1

excrescence *n* **1** an abnormal mass of tissue — see GROWTH 1

2 something that spoils the appearance or completeness of a thing — see BLEMISH

excreta *n pl* solid matter discharged from an animal's alimentary canal — see DROPPING 1

excruciating *adj* **1** intensely or unbearably painful ⟨He finally visited the doctor when the pain became *excruciating*.⟩

syn agonizing, harrowing, racking, tormenting, torturing, torturous, wrenching

rel acute, exquisite, extreme, fierce, intense, vehement, violent; biting, cutting, penetrating, piercing, sharp, shooting, smarting, stabbing, stinging, tearing, tiring

2 difficult to endure — see HARSH 1

3 hard to accept or bear especially emotionally — see BITTER 2

4 extreme in degree, power, or effect — see INTENSE 1

exculpate *vb* to free from a charge of wrongdoing ⟨I will present evidence that will *exculpate* my client.⟩

syn absolve, acquit, clear, exonerate, vindicate

rel atone (for), expiate; discharge, liberate, redeem, release, unburden; condone, excuse, whitewash; forgive, pardon, remit; avenge, redress, revenge

near ant accuse, arraign, charge, impeach, indict; convict

ant criminate, incriminate

exculpation *n* a setting free from a charge of wrongdoing — see ACQUITTAL

excursion *n* **1** a short trip for pleasure ⟨Our weekend *excursions* have encompassed virtually all parts of our home state.⟩

syn jaunt, junket, outing, ramble, sally, spin

rel journey, travel(s), voyage; tour; expedition, odyssey, safari; detour; hike, peregrination, trek, walk; pilgrimage

2 a departure from the subject under consideration — see TANGENT

excursionist *n* a person who travels for pleasure — see TOURIST

excusable *adj* worthy of forgiveness — see VENIAL

excuse *n* an explanation that frees one from fault or blame ⟨"A really important phone call" is no *excuse* for not paying proper attention to one's driving.⟩

syn alibi, defense, justification, plea, reason

rel color, guise, pretense (*or* pretence), pretext, rationale, rationalization, vindication, whitewash; cop-out, out; acknowledgment (*or* acknowledgement), atonement, confession; extenuation, palliation

excuse *vb* **1** to dismiss as of little importance ⟨More often than not, voters are willing to *excuse* a candidate's youthful indiscretion.⟩

syn brush (aside *or* off), condone, discount, disregard, forgive, gloss (over), gloze (over), ignore, overlook, overpass, pardon, pass over, remit, shrug off, whitewash, wink (at)

rel explain, justify, rationalize; absolve, acquit, clear, exculpate, exonerate, vindicate; waive, wave (aside *or* off)

phrases close one's eyes to, forgive and forget

near ant heed, mark, mind, note, object (to)

2 to be an acceptable reason for — see JUSTIFY 1

3 to make (something) seem less bad by offering excuses — see PALLIATE 1

execrable *adj* **1** extremely unsatisfactory — see WRETCHED 1

2 of low quality — see CHEAP 2

3 not following or in accordance with standards of honor and decency — see IGNOBLE 2

execrate *vb* **1** to declare to be morally wrong or evil — see CONDEMN 1

2 to dislike strongly — see HATE 1

execration *n* **1** a prayer that harm will come to someone — see CURSE 1

2 a very strong dislike — see HATE 1

3 something or someone that is hated — see HATE 2

execute *vb* **1** to carry out effectively — see ENFORCE

2 to carry through (as a process) to completion — see PERFORM 1

3 to put to death deliberately — see MURDER 1

execution *n* the doing of an action — see COMMISSION 2

executive *adj* suited for or relating to the directing of things ⟨the *executive* skills needed to manage a large business office⟩

syn administrative, directorial, managerial, supervisory

rel bureaucratic, governmental, ministerial, official, parliamentary; regulatory

ant nonmanagerial, nonsupervisory

executive *n* a person who manages or directs something ⟨a program that teaches company *executives* how to better manage their staffs⟩

syn administrator, director, manager, superintendent, supervisor

rel codirector, comanager, co-organizer; middle manager; boardman, officer, official; commissioner, minister; boss, chief, head, leader, president

exemplar *n* **1** one of a group or collection that shows what the whole is like — see EXAMPLE

2 someone of such unequaled perfection as to deserve imitation — see IDEAL 1

3 the most perfect type or example — see QUINTESSENCE 1

exemplary *adj* **1** constituting, serving as, or worthy of being a pattern to be imitated — see MODEL

2 serving as or offering a warning — see CAUTIONARY

exemplify *vb* to show or make clear by using examples — see ILLUSTRATE 1

---

syn synonym(s)   *rel* related words
ant antonym(s)   *near ant* near antonym(s)

exemption *n* freedom from punishment, harm, or loss — see IMPUNITY

exercise *n* **1** energetic movement of the body for the sake of physical fitness ⟨The doctor ordered plenty of fresh air and *exercise*.⟩

syn activity, conditioning, exertion

rel training, warm-up, workout; toning, trimming; aerobics, athletics, bodybuilding, calisthenics, gymnastics, isometrics, weight lifting

2 something done over and over in order to develop skill ⟨a young piano student dutifully going through the standard finger *exercises*⟩

syn drill, practice (*also* practise), routine, training, workout

rel assignment, homework, lesson; brush-up, refresher, review

3 the act or practice of employing something for a particular purpose — see USE 1

exercise *vb* **1** to bring to bear especially forcefully or effectively — see EXERT

2 to do over and over so as to become skilled — see PRACTICE

3 to put into action or service — see USE 1

4 to trouble the mind of; to make uneasy — see DISTURB 1

exert *vb* to bring to bear especially forcefully or effectively ⟨Parental involvement has consistently been shown to *exert* the most influence over a child's success in school.⟩

syn apply, exercise, ply, put out, wield

rel employ, use, utilize; abuse, misapply, misuse

exertion *n* **1** energetic movement of the body for the sake of physical fitness — see EXERCISE 1

2 the active use of energy in producing a result — see EFFORT

exfoliate *vb* to cast (a natural bodily covering or appendage) aside — see SHED 1

exhale *vb* **1** to let or force out of the lungs ⟨Before answering, the suspect *exhaled* a cloud of cigarette smoke.⟩

syn blow (out), breathe (out), expel, expire

rel expectorate

ant inbreathe, inspire

2 to throw or give off — see EMIT 1

exhaust *vb* **1** to use up all the physical energy of ⟨The long day at the county fair had *exhausted* everyone.⟩

syn break, burn out, bust, do in, drain, fatigue, frazzle, kill, outwear, tire, tucker (out), wash out, wear, wear out, weary

rel debilitate, enervate, enfeeble, sap, waste, weaken

phrases wear to a frazzle

near ant activate, energize, invigorate, rejuvenate, strengthen, vitalize; relax, rest, unwind

2 to make complete use of — see DEPLETE 1

exhausted *adj* depleted in strength, energy, or freshness — see WEARY 1

exhaustion *n* a complete depletion of energy or strength — see FATIGUE

exhaustive *adj* **1** trying all possibilities ⟨After an *exhaustive* search of our house, we still hadn't found the cat.⟩

syn all-out, clean, complete, comprehensive, full-scale, out-and-out, thorough, thoroughgoing, total

rel broad, extensive, far-reaching, in-depth, wide; general, global, inclusive, methodical (*also* methodic), systematic; no-holds-barred, unhampered, unrestrained

near ant aimless, desultory, haphazard, hit-or-miss, random; cursory, shallow, slipshod, superficial; limited, narrow, restricted

2 covering everything or all important points — see ENCYCLOPEDIC

exhaustively *adv* with attention to all aspects or details — see THOROUGHLY 1

exhibit *n* a public showing of objects of interest — see EXHIBITION 1

exhibit *vb* to present so as to invite notice or attention — see SHOW 1

exhibition *n* **1** a public showing of objects of interest ⟨an *exhibition* of valuable and fascinating artifacts from a recovered pirate ship⟩

syn display, exhibit, exposition, fair, show

rel demonstration, performance, presentation, production; pageant; auction, offering, presentment, sale

2 an outward and often exaggerated indication of something abstract (as a feeling) for effect — see SHOW 1

exhilarate *vb* **1** to cause a pleasurable stimulation of the feelings of — see THRILL

2 to fill with great joy — see ELATE

exhilarated *adj* experiencing or marked by overwhelming usually pleasurable emotion — see ECSTATIC

exhilarating *adj* causing great emotional or mental stimulation — see EXCITING 1

exhilaration *n* **1** a pleasurably intense stimulation of the feelings — see THRILL

2 a state of overwhelming usually pleasurable emotion — see ECSTASY

exhort *vb* to try to persuade (someone) through earnest appeals to follow a course of action — see URGE

exhume *vb* to remove from place of burial ⟨The remains of John Paul Jones were *exhumed* in Paris and transported with great ceremony to the U.S. Naval Academy.⟩

syn disinter, unearth

ant bury, entomb, inter, tomb

exigency *n* a time or state of affairs requiring prompt or decisive action — see EMERGENCY

exile *n* **1** the forced removal from a homeland ⟨The *exile* of French settlers from Nova Scotia resulted in the birth of the Cajun community in the U.S.⟩

syn banishment, deportation, displacement, expatriation, expulsion

rel ostracism; extradition; diaspora, dispersion, scattering; emigration, migration; evacuation; ethnic cleansing, transportation; dispossession, ejection, ouster

near ant repatriation, return; immigration

2 a person forced to emigrate for political reasons — see ÉMIGRÉ 1

exile *vb* to force to leave a country — see BANISH 1

exist *vb* to have life — see BE 1

existence *n* the fact of being or of being real ⟨The *existence* of UFO's is something that people continue to argue about.⟩

syn actuality, reality, subsistence

rel genuineness, realness; activity, animation, life; currency, presence, prevalence

near ant absence, dearth, lack, want; potentiality, virtuality

ant inexistence, nonbeing, nonexistence, unreality

existent *adj* **1** existing in fact and not merely as a possibility — see ACTUAL

2 having being at the present time — see EXTANT 1

existent *n* one that has a real and independent existence — see ENTITY

existing *adj* having being at the present time — see EXTANT 1

exit *n* **1** a place or means of going out ⟨All of the building's *exits* were clearly marked.⟩

syn egress, issue, outlet

rel escape, escape hatch, release; gate, mouth, opening, passage, vent

near ant access, entrée (*or* entree)

ant entrance, entry, entryway, ingress

2 the act of leaving a place — see DEPARTURE 1

3 the permanent stopping of all the vital bodily activities — see DEATH 1

exit *vb* **1** to leave a place often for another — see GO 2

2 to stop living — see DIE 1

exiting *n* the act of leaving a place — see DEPARTURE 1

exodus *n* a flowing or going out — see OUTFLOW

exonerate *vb* to free from a charge of wrongdoing — see EXCULPATE

exoneration *n* a setting free from a charge of wrongdoing — see ACQUITTAL

exorbitant *adj* going beyond a normal or acceptable limit in degree or amount — see EXCESSIVE

exorbitantly *adv* beyond a normal or acceptable limit — see TOO 1

exotic *adj* excitingly or mysteriously unusual ⟨the gradual disappearance of *exotic* lands in a culturally homogenized world⟩

syn fantastic (*also* fantastical), glamorous (*also* glamourous), marvelous (*or* marvellous), outlandish, romantic, strange

rel colorful, picture-book, picturesque, quaint; alien, foreign; dark, distant, faraway, remote; alluring, captivating, enchanting, fascinating, magical

ant familiar, nonexotic, nonglamorous, unexotic, unglamorous, unromantic

exotic *n* something strange or unusual that is an object of interest — see CURIOSITY 2

expand *vb* **1** to express more fully and in greater detail ⟨an article on the event that the author later *expanded* into a book⟩

syn amplify, develop, elaborate (on), flesh (out)

rel add (to), complement, supplement; discourse, expatiate, ramble, run on

near ant compress, contract; outline, summarize, sum up

ant abbreviate, abridge, condense, shorten

2 to make greater in size, amount, or number — see INCREASE 1

3 to arrange the parts of (something) over a wider area — see OPEN 3

4 to become greater in extent, volume, amount, or number — see INCREASE 2

expanse *n* a wide space or area ⟨the great

explorers who crossed the vast *expanses* of the seven seas in small ships⟩

syn breadth, distance, expansion, extent, field, length, plain, reach, sheet, spread, stretch, waste

rel domain, sphere, territory; compass, range, scope, sweep; gamut, scale, spectrum; depth, emptiness, void; extension, latitude, span; amplitude, immensity, magnitude

expansion *n* **1** something added (as by growth) — see INCREASE 1

2 the act or process of going from the simple or basic to the complex or advanced — see DEVELOPMENT 1

3 a wide space or area — see EXPANSE

expansive *adj* having considerable extent — see EXTENSIVE

expatiate *vb* to give a formal often extended talk on a subject — see TALK 1

expatriate *n* a person forced to emigrate for political reasons — see ÉMIGRÉ 1

expatriate *vb* to force to leave a country — see BANISH 1

expatriation *n* the forced removal from a homeland — see EXILE 1

expect *vb* to believe in the future occurrence of (something) ⟨We *expect* their arrival late this afternoon.⟩

syn anticipate, await, hope (for), watch (for)

rel bank on, count (on *or* upon), depend (on *or* upon), rely (on *or* upon), wait (for); envisage, foresee, foretell, predict, prophesy; assume, presume, presuppose; contemplate, eye, view

phrases look for, look forward to

near ant doubt, question

expectant *adj* **1** having or showing signs of eagerly awaiting something ⟨*Expectant* crowds gathered at the spot where the President was scheduled to make an appearance.⟩

syn agape, agog, anticipatory

rel open-eyed, openmouthed; alert, vigilant, watchful; anxious, athirst, breathless, eager, enthusiastic, raring; impatient, restive, restless

near ant apathetic, indifferent, unconcerned, unimpressed, uninterested, unmoved

2 containing unborn young within the body — see PREGNANT 1

expectant *n* one who seeks an office, honor, position, or award — see CANDIDATE

expected *adj* being in accordance with the prescribed, normal, or logical course of events — see DUE 2

expedient *adj* suitable for bringing about a desired result under the circumstances ⟨We made the *expedient* decision to sell the land to whomever offered the most money.⟩

syn advisable, desirable, judicious, politic, prudent, tactical, wise

rel advantageous, beneficial, profitable; useful, utilitarian; feasible, possible, practicable, practical; opportune, seasonable, timely; opportunistic, self-seeking

near ant impractical, profitless, unfeasible, unprofitable; inopportune, unseasonable, untimely

ant impolitic, imprudent, inadvisable, inexpedient, injudicious, unwise

---

syn synonym(s)   ***rel*** related words
ant antonym(s)   ***near ant*** near antonym(s)

expedient n **1** a temporary replacement — see MAKESHIFT

2 an action planned or taken to achieve a desired result — see MEASURE 1

3 something that one uses to accomplish an end especially when the usual means is not available — see RESOURCE 1

expedition n a going from one place to another usually of some distance — see JOURNEY

expeditious adj having or showing the ability to respond without delay or hesitation — see QUICK 1

expel vb **1** to drive or force out — see EJECT 1

2 to throw or give off — see EMIT 1

3 to violently throw out or off (something from within) — see ERUPT 1

4 to let or force out of the lungs — see EXHALE 1

expend vb **1** to hand over or use up in payment — see SPEND 1

2 to make complete use of — see DEPLETE 1

expenditure n **1** a payment made in the course of achieving a result — see EXPENSE

2 the active use of energy in producing a result — see EFFORT

expense n a payment made in the course of achieving a result ⟨They spared no *expense* in building the house of their dreams.⟩

syn charge, cost, disbursement, expenditure, outgo, outlay

rel overhead; outflow; pocket money, spending money; price, rate, tab, tariff, toll

expensive adj commanding a large price — see COSTLY

expensively adv in a luxurious manner — see HIGH

experience n **1** knowledge gained by actually doing or living through something ⟨The hospital is looking for nurses with operating-room *experience*.⟩

syn expertise, know-how, proficiency, savvy, skills

rel background; command, mastery; acquaintance, conversance, familiarity, intimacy

near ant ignorance, unawareness, unfamiliarity

ant inexperience

2 an exciting or noteworthy event that one experiences firsthand — see ADVENTURE 1

experience vb to come to a knowledge of (something) by living through it ⟨Have you ever *experienced* the loss of a pet?⟩

syn endure, feel, have, know, pass, see, suffer, sustain, taste, undergo, witness

rel encounter, meet; accept; assimilate, digest

phrases go through

experienced adj having or showing exceptional knowledge, experience, or skill in a field of endeavor — see PROFICIENT

experiment n a procedure or operation carried out to resolve an uncertainty ⟨Benjamin Franklin's famous *experiment* in which he flew a kite in a thunderstorm to see if lightning and electricity were identical⟩

syn essay, experimentation, test, trial

rel trial and error; dry run, shakedown; exercise, practice (*also* practise), rehears-

al, tryout, workout; crucible, ordeal; attempt, effort, try

experimental adj **1** made or done as an experiment ⟨an *experimental* procedure for patients suffering from hip pain⟩

syn pilot, trial

rel exploratory, investigative; preliminary, preparatory, provisional, temporary, tentative; conjectural, hypothetical, speculative, theoretical (*also* theoretic); untested, untried; unproved, unproven

near ant accepted, established, standard; tested, tried; advanced, developed; proved, proven; conclusive, decisive, definitive, final, permanent

2 based on observation or experience — see EMPIRICAL 1

experimentation n a procedure or operation carried out to resolve an uncertainty — see EXPERIMENT

expert adj **1** accomplished with trained ability — see SKILLFUL 1

2 having or showing exceptional knowledge, experience, or skill in a field of endeavor — see PROFICIENT

expert n a person with a high level of knowledge or skill in a field ⟨The book was written by an *expert* in the field.⟩

syn ace, adept, artist, authority, connoisseur, crackerjack (*also* crackajack), fiend, guru, hand, hotshot, maestro, master, past master, scholar, shark, virtuoso, whiz, wizard

rel pro, professional; consultant, hired gun, specialist; addict, aficionado (*also* afficionado), buff, devotee, enthusiast, fan; craftsman, journeyman; jack-of-all-trades, Renaissance man; mistress

near ant apprentice, beginner, neophyte, novice; dabbler, dilettante; nonprofessional

ant amateur, inexpert

expertise n knowledge gained by actually doing or living through something — see EXPERIENCE 1

expertly adv in a skillful or expert manner — see WELL 3

expiate vb to make up for (an offense) ⟨Yom Kippur is the holy day on which Jews are expected to *expiate* sins committed during the past year.⟩

syn atone (for), mend, redeem

rel compensate, recompense, reimburse, remunerate, repay; amend, correct, rectify, redress; propitiate

phrases make amends for, make good for

expiration n **1** the act of ceasing to exist — see DEATH 3

2 the stopping of a process or activity — see END 1

3 the permanent stopping of all the vital bodily activities — see DEATH 1

expire vb **1** to come to an end — see CEASE 1

2 to let or force out of the lungs — see EXHALE 1

3 to stop living — see DIE 1

expired adj no longer existing — see EXTINCT

explain vb **1** to make plain or understandable ⟨a pamphlet that *explains* the medical procedure in language that any layperson can understand⟩

syn clarify, clear (up), construe, demonstrate, elucidate, explicate, expound, get across, illuminate, illustrate, interpret, simplify, spell out

rel decipher, decode; analyze, break down; disentangle, undo, unravel, unscramble, untangle; resolve, solve; define, specify; annotate, commentate, gloss

near ant befog, cloud; confound, confuse

ant obscure

2 to give the reason for or cause of ⟨Can you *explain* why you're so early?⟩

syn account (for), attribute, explain away, rationalize

rel condone, excuse, forgive, justify; absolve, acquit, exculpate, exonerate, vindicate

explainable *adj* capable of having the reason for or cause of determined — see SOLVABLE

explain away *vb* 1 to give the reason for or cause of — see EXPLAIN 2

2 to make (something) seem less bad by offering excuses — see PALLIATE 1

explanation *n* 1 a statement that makes something clear ⟨an *explanation* of photosynthesis that most museum visitors will be able to understand⟩

syn clarification, construction, elucidation, explication, exposition, illumination, illustration, interpretation

rel paraphrase, restatement, translation; annotation, comment, commentary, epexegesis, gloss; deciphering, decoding; disentanglement, unscrambling; analysis; edification, enlightenment; meaning; demonstration, enactment; justification, rationale, rationalization, reasoning; caution, caveat, warning

2 a statement given to explain a belief or act — see REASON 1

explanatory *adj* serving to explain ⟨The *explanatory* section has as its heading "What the New Tax Changes Mean."⟩

syn elucidative, expository, illuminative, illustrative, interpretative, interpretive

rel analytic (*or* analytical), demonstrative, discursive; exculpatory, exonerative

explicable *adj* capable of having the reason for or cause of determined — see SOLVABLE

explicate *vb* to make plain or understandable — see EXPLAIN 1

explication *n* a statement that makes something clear — see EXPLANATION 1

explicit *adj* so clearly expressed as to leave no doubt about the meaning ⟨*explicit* instructions about what to do in an emergency⟩

syn clear-cut, definite, definitive, express, specific, unambiguous, unequivocal

rel avowed, declared, specified, stated; categorical (*also* categoric), complete, comprehensive, exhaustive, full; certain, sure, unmistakable; clear, distinct, lucid, well-defined; exact, precise; direct, literal, plain, simple, straightforward

near ant cryptic, dark, enigmatic (*also* enigmatical), obscure, unclear; imprecise, inaccurate, incorrect, inexact; incomprehensible, unintelligible

ant implicit, implied, inferred; ambiguous, circuitous; equivocal, indefinite, unspecific, vague

explicitness *n* 1 careful thoroughness of detail — see PARTICULARITY 1

2 clearness of expression — see SIMPLICITY 2

explode *vb* 1 to break open or into pieces usually because of internal pressure ⟨The container *exploded* when the liquid inside froze.⟩

syn blow, blow up, burst, detonate, go off, pop

rel fragment, shatter, smash, splinter; discharge, fire, shoot; balloon, burgeon (*also* bourgeon), mushroom

near ant collapse, fizzle

ant implode

2 to cause to break open or into pieces by or as if by an explosive — see BLAST 1

3 to develop suddenly and violently — see ERUPT 2

exploit *n* 1 an act of notable skill, strength, or cleverness — see FEAT 1

2 something done by someone — see ACTION 1

3 an exciting or noteworthy event that one experiences firsthand — see ADVENTURE 1

exploit *vb* 1 to take unfair advantage of ⟨the type of person who *exploits* a friend's good nature by constantly sponging off of him⟩

syn abuse, capitalize (on), cash in (on), impose (on *or* upon), play (on *or* upon), use, work

rel jerk around, manipulate, mistreat; bleed, cheat, fleece, overcharge, skin, soak, stick; commercialize, commodify

phrases trade on, walk on

2 to control or take advantage of by artful, unfair, or insidious means — see MANIPULATE 1

3 to put into action or service — see USE 1

exploitable *adj* 1 capable of or suitable for being used for a particular purpose — see USABLE 1

2 readily taken advantage of — see EASY 2

exploration *n* a systematic search for the truth or facts about something — see INQUIRY 1

explore *vb* 1 to search through or into ⟨Communities must *explore* new ways of raising money for their cultural institutions.⟩

syn delve (into), dig (into), examine, inquire (into), investigate, look (into), probe, research

rel inspect, sift, study, view; browse, cruise, peruse, scan, skim (through), surf, thumb (through)

phrases check into, check up on

2 to go into or range over for purposes of discovery ⟨We must continue to *explore* the depths of the ocean.⟩

syn hunt, probe, prospect, search

rel reconnoiter (*or* reconnoitre), scout; disclose, discover, reveal, unearth; fathom, plumb, sound

explosion *n* 1 the act or an instance of exploding ⟨the *explosion* of the first atomic bomb at Hiroshima⟩

syn blast, blowup, burst, bursting, detonation, eruption, outburst

---

syn synonym(s)   *rel* related words
ant antonym(s)   *near ant* near antonym(s)

rel discharge, firing, shooting; blowout, flare-up; bang, boom, pop; airburst, groundburst

ant implosion

2 a sudden intense expression of strong feeling — see OUTBURST 1

3 an outburst or display of excited anger — see TANTRUM

explosive *adj* **1** extreme in degree, power, or effect — see INTENSE 1

2 marked by bursts of destructive force or intense activity — see VIOLENT 1

exponent *n* **1** a person who actively supports or favors a cause ⟨*Exponents* of space exploration earnestly called for more missions to the outer reaches of the solar system.⟩

syn advocate, apostle, backer, booster, champion, friend, herald, paladin, promoter, proponent, supporter

rel loyalist, partisan (*also* partizan), stalwart; adherent, cohort, disciple, follower; applauder, cheerleader, encourager

near ant enemy, foe, rival; belittler, critic, faultfinder

ant adversary, antagonist, opponent

2 one who brings an art or science to full realization ⟨has long reigned as the nation's leading *exponent* of modern dance⟩

syn guru

rel dean, grand old man; ideologue (*also* idealogue), philosopher, theorist; advocate, apostle, backer, booster, champion, promoter, proponent, supporter

expose *vb* **1** to reveal the true nature of ⟨a well-researched article that *exposes* the UFO story as a hoax⟩

syn debunk, nail, show up, uncloak, uncover, undress, unmask

rel demolish, discredit, disprove; disclose, divulge, tell, unveil

phrases blow the whistle on

near ant conceal, hide, secrete, veil

ant camouflage, cloak, disguise, mask

2 to make known (as information previously kept secret) — see REVEAL 1

3 to make known (something abstract) through outward signs — see SHOW 2

4 to present so as to invite notice or attention — see SHOW 1

exposed *adj* **1** being in a situation where one is likely to meet with harm — see LIABLE 1

2 lacking a usual or natural covering — see NAKED 2

3 lacking protection from danger or resistance against attack — see HELPLESS 1

exposition *n* **1** a public showing of objects of interest — see EXHIBITION 1

2 a series of explanations or observations on something (as an event) — see COMMENTARY 1

3 a statement that makes something clear — see EXPLANATION 1

expository *adj* serving to explain — see EXPLANATORY

expostulation *n* a feeling or declaration of disapproval or dissent — see OBJECTION

exposure *n* **1** the state of being left without shelter or protection against something harmful ⟨Some people chronically avoid situations in which there is a high level of *exposure* to germs.⟩

syn liability, openness, vulnerability

rel predisposition, susceptibility; defenselessness, helplessness, weakness; danger, jeopardy, peril, risk

near ant protection, safeguarding, sheltering, shielding

2 the state or fact of facing a particular direction ⟨This plant will need to be in a room with a southern *exposure*.⟩

syn aspect

rel alignment (*also* alinement), arrangement

3 the act or an instance of making known something previously unknown or concealed — see REVELATION

expound *vb* **1** to make known (as an idea, emotion, or opinion) — see EXPRESS 1

2 to make plain or understandable — see EXPLAIN 1

express *adj* **1** of a particular or exact sort ⟨a trip to the supermarket with the *express* purpose of buying milk⟩

syn concrete, distinct, especial, peculiar, precise, set, special, specific

rel lone, only, separate, single, sole, solitary; distinctive, exclusive, individual, unique; limited, restricted; differentiated, specialized; given, specified

near ant general, generalized, generic, nonexclusive, universal

ant nonspecific

2 so clearly expressed as to leave no doubt about the meaning — see EXPLICIT

express *vb* **1** to make known (as an idea, emotion, or opinion) ⟨In a true democracy, a person can freely *express* his or her views.⟩

syn air, expound, give, look, raise, sound, state, vent, ventilate, voice

rel advertise, announce, declare, enunciate, proclaim, say; broadcast, circulate, disseminate, publish; describe, write, write up; sound off, speak out, speak up; chime in; communicate, convey, put across; offer, submit

phrases give air to, put forth

near ant censor, restrain, restrict

ant stifle, suppress

2 to apply external pressure on so as to force out the juice or contents of — see ²PRESS 2

3 to communicate or convey (as an idea) to the mind — see MEAN 1

4 to convey in appropriate or telling terms — see PHRASE

5 to represent in visible form — see EMBODY 2

expression *n* **1** an act, process, or means of putting something into words ⟨The poem is his *expression* of his wonder of nature.⟩

syn articulation, formulation, phrasing, statement, utterance, voice, wording

rel outlet, vent; observation, reflection, remark, thought; speech, tongue

2 facial appearance regarded as an indication of mood or feeling — see LOOK 1

3 a pronounceable series of letters having a distinct meaning especially in a particular field — see WORD 1

4 a sequence of words having a specific meaning — see PHRASE

expressionless *adj* not expressing any emotion — see BLANK 1

expressive *adj* clearly conveying a special meaning (as one's mood) ⟨The teacher's *expressive* sigh showed that she had heard that excuse many times before.⟩

syn eloquent, meaning, meaningful, pregnant, revealing, revelatory, significant, suggestive

rel graphic (*also* graphical), pictorial, vivid; evocative, redolent, reminiscent; weighty; flavorful, full-bodied, rich

ant unexpressive

expressway *n* a passage cleared for public vehicular travel — see WAY 1

expropriate *vb* 1 to take or make use of under a guise of authority but without actual right — see APPROPRIATE 1

2 to take ownership or control of (something) by right of one's authority — see CONFISCATE

expulsion *n* the forced removal from a homeland — see EXILE 1

expunge *vb* to destroy all traces of — see ANNIHILATE 1

expurgate *vb* to remove objectionable parts from — see CENSOR

exquisite *adj* 1 extreme in degree, power, or effect — see INTENSE 1

2 having qualities that appeal to a refined taste — see CHOICE 1

3 satisfying or pleasing because of fineness or mildness — see DELICATE 1

exquisiteness *n* the state or quality of having a delicate structure — see DELICACY 2

extant *adj* 1 having being at the present time ⟨a celebrated author who is generally regarded as America's greatest novelist *extant*⟩

syn alive, around, existent, existing, living

rel active, busy, flourishing, functioning, operating, working

near ant defunct, destroyed, exterminated; departed, gone, lost; nonexistent; idle, inactive, inert

ant dead, extinct

2 existing or in progress right now — see PRESENT 1

extemporaneous *adj* made or done without previous thought or preparation ⟨Caught by surprise, I had to make an *extemporaneous* speech at the awards banquet.⟩

syn ad-lib, extempore, impromptu, improvised, offhand, offhanded, snap, spur-of-the-moment, unconsidered, unplanned, unpremeditated, unprepared, unrehearsed, unstudied

rel unscripted; automatic, impulsive, instinctive, involuntary, spontaneous; casual, cursive, informal, unauthorized; half-baked, half-cocked, ill-advised

near ant deliberate, intended, intentional

ant considered, planned, premeditated, premeditative, prepared, rehearsed

extempore *adj* made or done without previous thought or preparation — see EXTEMPORANEOUS

extemporize *vb* to perform, make, or do without preparation — see IMPROVISE

extend *vb* 1 to make longer ⟨Our guests

from out of town *extended* their visit by a week.⟩

syn draw out, elongate, lengthen, outstretch, prolong, protract, stretch

rel amplify, enlarge, expand, increase; thin

near ant decrease, diminish, lessen, reduce; thicken

ant abbreviate, abridge, curtail, cut, cut back, shorten

2 to put before another for acceptance or consideration — see OFFER 1

3 to arrange the parts of (something) over a wider area — see OPEN 3

4 to be positioned along a certain course or in a certain direction — see RUN 3

5 to make greater in size, amount, or number — see INCREASE 1

6 to alter (something) for the worse with the addition of foreign or lower-grade substances — see ADULTERATE

extended *adj* 1 expressing one thing in terms normally used for another — see FIGURATIVE

2 having considerable extent — see EXTENSIVE

3 lasting for a considerable time — see LONG 2

4 of great extent from end to end — see LONG 1

extended family *n* those who live as a family in one house — see HOUSEHOLD

extension *n* 1 the act of making longer ⟨The board's *extension* of the school year drew howls of protest⟩

syn drawing out, elongation, lengthening, prolongation, prolonging, stretching

ant abbreviation, abridgment (*or* abridgement), curtailment, cutback, shortening

2 a smaller structure added to a main building — see ANNEX

extensive *adj* having considerable extent ⟨a rock hound whose *extensive* reading enables him to identify just about any rock or mineral⟩

syn broad, deep, expansive, extended, far-flung, far-reaching, rangy, wide, widespread

rel comprehensive, general, global, inclusive; boundless, endless, infinite, limitless, unlimited; capacious, commodious, roomy, spacious

near ant circumscribed, limited, restricted

ant narrow

extensively *adv* to a large extent or degree — see GREATLY 2

extent *n* 1 a real or imaginary point beyond which a person or thing cannot go — see LIMIT 1

2 a wide space or area — see EXPANSE

3 an area over which activity, capacity, or influence extends — see RANGE 2

4 the total amount of measurable space or surface occupied by something — see ¹SIZE

extenuate *vb* to make (something) seem less bad by offering excuses — see PALLIATE 1

exterior *adj* situated on the outside or farther out — see OUTER

exterior *n* an outer part or layer ⟨The *exterior* of the tooth consists of very hard enamel.⟩

syn face, outside, shell, skin, surface, veneer

---

syn synonym(s)   *rel* related words
ant antonym(s)   *near ant* near antonym(s)

rel facade (*also* façade), front, top; cover, covering, facing; appearance, disguise, guise, mask, semblance, show

ant inside, interior

exterminate *vb* to destroy all traces of — see ANNIHILATE 1

extermination *n* the state or fact of being rendered nonexistent, physically unsound, or useless — see DESTRUCTION 1

external *adj* 1 not being a vital part of or belonging to something — see EXTRINSIC

2 situated on the outside or farther out — see OUTER

extinct *adj* no longer existing ⟨A few overgrown ruins are all that remain of that once mighty but now *extinct* civilization.⟩

syn bygone, dead, defunct, departed, done, expired, gone, vanished

rel nonexistent; dying, faded, moribund; collapsed, fallen, overthrown; antiquated, dated, obsolete, passé; finished, lapsed, terminated; lost, missing

near ant active, dynamic, thriving, vibrant

ant alive, existent, existing, extant, living

extinction *n* the state or fact of being rendered nonexistent, physically unsound, or useless — see DESTRUCTION 1

extinguish *vb* 1 to cause to cease burning ⟨The fire in the skillet was quickly *extinguished* by slamming the lid on.⟩

syn blanket, douse (*also* dowse), put out, quench, snuff (out)

rel choke, smother, suffocate; blow out, rub out, snub (out), stamp (out), stub

ant fire, ignite, inflame (*also* enflame), kindle, light

2 to bring to a complete end the physical soundness, existence, or usefulness of — see DESTROY 1

extirpate *vb* to destroy all traces of — see ANNIHILATE 1

extol *also* **extoll** *vb* to proclaim the glory of — see PRAISE 1

extort *vb* to get (as money) by the use of force or threats ⟨He was arrested for *extorting* bribes.⟩

syn exact, wrest, wring

rel bleed, fleece, gouge, skin, squeeze; cheat, racketeer, swindle; coerce, compel, force

extortioner *n* a person who gets money from another by using force or threats — see RACKETEER

extortionist *n* a person who gets money from another by using force or threats — see RACKETEER

extra *adj* being over what is needed — see SPARE 1

extra *adv* to a great degree — see VERY 1

extra *n* 1 an interchangeable part or piece of equipment that is kept on hand for replacement of an original — see SPARE

2 something adding to pleasure or comfort but not absolutely necessary — see LUXURY 1

3 something given in addition to what is ordinarily expected or owed — see BONUS

extract *n* a part taken from a longer work — see EXCERPT

extract *vb* to draw out by force or with effort ⟨*extracted* a splinter from my hand⟩

syn prize, pry, pull, root (out), tear (out), uproot, wrest, wring, yank

rel mine, pluck, remove, take (out), withdraw; eke (out), scrounge

near ant implant, insert, install; cram, jam, ram, stuff, wedge

extraction *n* the line of ancestors from whom a person is descended — see ANCESTRY

extraneous *adj* 1 not being a vital part of or belonging to something — see EXTRINSIC

2 not having anything to do with the matter at hand — see IRRELEVANT

extraneousness *n* the quality or state of not having anything to do with the matter at hand — see IRRELEVANCE

extraordinary *adj* 1 being out of the ordinary — see EXCEPTIONAL 1

2 noticeably different from what is generally found or experienced — see UNUSUAL 1

extrapolate *vb* to form an opinion or reach a conclusion through reasoning and information — see INFER 1

extrasensory perception *n* the power of seeing or knowing about things that are not present to the senses — see CLAIRVOYANCE

extravagance *n* 1 the quality or fact of being free or wasteful in the expenditure of money ⟨Hollywood stars are famous for the *extravagance* of their parties.⟩

syn lavishness, prodigality, profusion, wastefulness

rel conspicuous consumption, splurge; bountifulness, generosity, liberality; improvidence, squandering; indulgence, overindulgence, self-indulgence; excess, overkill

near ant austerity, moderation, restraint, temperance

ant economy, frugality

2 an instance of spending money or resources without care or restraint — see WASTE 1

extravagant *adj* 1 given to spending money freely or foolishly — see PRODIGAL

2 going beyond a normal or acceptable limit in degree or amount — see EXCESSIVE

3 commanding a large price — see COSTLY

extravagantly *adv* in a luxurious manner — see HIGH

extreme *adj* 1 most distant from a center ⟨spacecraft that is specially designed to explore the *extreme* edge of our solar system⟩

syn farthermost, farthest, furthermost, furthest, outermost, outmost, remotest, ultimate, utmost

rel aftermost, rearmost, sternmost

near ant intermediate, medial, median, mid, middle, midmost

ant inmost, innermost, nearest

2 being very far from the center of public opinion ⟨Their *extreme* political views attracted only a small band of followers.⟩

syn extremist, fanatic (*or* fanatical), rabid, radical, revolutionary, revolutionist, ultra

rel subversive, violent, wild; reactionary

near ant conservative, moderate, temperate; conventional, orthodox, traditional; liberal, progressive

ant middle-of-the-road, nonrevolutionary, unrevolutionary

3 going beyond a normal or acceptable limit in degree or amount — see EXCESSIVE

extremely *adv* to a great degree — see VERY 1

extremist *adj* being very far from the center of public opinion — see EXTREME 2

extremist *n* a person who favors rapid and sweeping changes especially in laws and methods of government — see RADICAL

extremity *n* **1** a time or state of affairs requiring prompt or decisive action — see EMERGENCY

2 the most extreme or advanced point — see HEIGHT 2

extricate *vb* to set free from entanglement or difficulty ⟨You've woven such a web of lies that it's hard to see how you can *extricate* yourself now.⟩

syn clear, disengage, disentangle, free, liberate, release, untangle

rel deliver, redeem, rescue, save; disburden, disencumber, unburden; unravel, unsnarl, untie, untwine

phrases cut loose

near ant block, hamper, hinder, impede, obstruct; burden, encumber, load, weigh

ant embroil, entangle

extrinsic *adj* not being a vital part of or belonging to something ⟨The fact that the ring belonged to your grandmother is *extrinsic* to its value to a jeweler.⟩

syn accidental, alien, extraneous, external, foreign

rel exterior, outside; immaterial, inapplicable, insignificant, irrelevant; nonessential, unessential, unnecessary

near ant congenital, deep-seated, inborn, inbred; inside, interior, internal; basic, essential, necessary

ant inherent, innate, intrinsic

extroverted *also* **extraverted** *adj* likely to seek or enjoy the company of others — see CONVIVIAL

extrude *vb* to drive or force out — see EJECT 1

exuberance *n* the quality or state of having abundant or intense activity — see VITALITY 1

exuberant *adj* joyously unrestrained ⟨*Exuberant* crowds rushed to greet the returning national champions in collegiate basketball.⟩

syn bubbly, buoyant, effervescent, frolicsome, high-spirited, vivacious

rel extroverted (*also* extraverted), outgoing, uninhibited; carefree, happy-go-lucky, insouciant, joyful, lighthearted, lively, sprightly; boisterous, raucous, rollicking, rowdy; giddy, light-headed, over-exuberant, silly; ecstatic, euphoric, lyric, rapturous; audacious, bold, brash, brazen, impertinent, impudent, insolent, saucy

near ant constrained, inhibited, restrained, subdued; impassive, phlegmatic, stoic (*or* stoical), stolid; depressed, dour, glum, morose, surly

ant low-spirited, sullen

exuberantly *adv* in an enthusiastic manner — see SKY-HIGH

---

exude *vb* to flow forth slowly through small openings ⟨A sticky resin *exudes* from the bark of the tree.⟩

syn bleed, ooze, percolate, seep, strain, sweat, weep

rel dribble, drip, trickle; discharge, emit, give off, vent; flow, spring

near ant flood, gush, pour, stream, surge

exult *vb* to feel or express joy or triumph ⟨The winners of the Super Bowl spent the next week *exulting* in their victory.⟩

syn crow, delight, glory, joy, rejoice, triumph

rel gloat, preen, swell; boast, brag; flaunt, parade, show off, strut, swagger

phrases kick up one's heels

near ant bemoan, bewail, grieve, lament, regret, weep

exultant *adj* having or expressing feelings of joy or triumph ⟨the *exultant* winner of the award for best country artist of the year⟩

syn exulting, glorying, jubilant, prideful, proud, rejoicing, triumphant

rel ecstatic, elated, euphoric; arrogant, boastful, cocky; conquering, victorious, winning

near ant crestfallen, defeated, dejected, depressed, disconsolate, dispirited, downcast

exulting *adj* having or expressing feelings of joy or triumph — see EXULTANT

eye *n* **1** a circular strip — see ¹RING 2

2 a state of being aware — see ATTENTION 2

3 a thing or place that is of greatest importance to an activity or interest — see CENTER 1

4 an idea that is believed to be true or valid without positive knowledge — see OPINION 1

5 an instance of looking especially briefly — see LOOK 2

6 the ability to see — see EYESIGHT

7 a fixed intent look — see GAZE

eye *vb* **1** to keep one's eyes on — see WATCH 1

2 to make note of (something) through the use of one's eyes — see SEE 1

3 to give serious and careful thought to — see PONDER

eye-catching *adj* likely to attract attention — see NOTICEABLE

eyeless *adj* lacking the power of sight — see BLIND

eye-opening *adj* **1** causing a strong emotional reaction because of unexpectedness — see SURPRISING 1

2 causing wonder or astonishment — see MARVELOUS 1

eyesight *n* the ability to see ⟨the keen *eyesight* of a bird of prey⟩

syn eye, sight, vision

rel myopia, nearsightedness; farsightedness; astigmatism, diplopia, squint, strabismus; double vision

eyesore *n* something unpleasant to look at ⟨The old abandoned house was a neighborhood *eyesore*.⟩

syn fright, horror, mess, monstrosity, sight

rel eye-catcher; blot, smear, smudge, spot, stain

near ant vision

eyespot *n* a small area that is different (as in color) from the main part — see SPOT 1

fable *n* **1** a story intended to teach a basic truth or moral about life — see ALLEGORY
2 a traditional but unfounded story that gives the reason for a current custom, belief, or fact of nature — see MYTH 1
3 something that is the product of the imagination — see FICTION
4 a statement known by its maker to be untrue and made in order to deceive — see LIE

fabled *adj* based on, described in, or being a myth — see MYTHICAL 1

fabric *n* **1** a woven or knitted material (as of cotton or nylon) — see CLOTH
2 the arrangement of parts that gives something its basic form — see FRAME 1

fabricate *vb* **1** to bring into being by combining, shaping, or transforming materials — see MAKE 1
2 to create or think of by clever use of the imagination — see INVENT
3 to form by putting together parts or materials — see BUILD
4 to make a statement one knows to be untrue — see ¹LIE

fabrication *n* **1** a statement known by its maker to be untrue and made in order to deceive — see LIE
2 something that is the product of the imagination — see FICTION

fabricator *n* a person who tells lies — see LIAR

fabulous *adj* **1** based on, described in, or being a myth — see MYTHICAL 1
2 causing wonder or astonishment — see MARVELOUS 1
3 not real and existing only in the imagination — see IMAGINARY
4 of the very best kind — see EXCELLENT

facade *also* **façade** *n* **1** a forward part or surface — see FRONT 1
2 a display of emotion or behavior that is insincere or intended to deceive — see MASQUERADE
3 a deceptively attractive external appearance — see GLOSS 1

face *n* **1** the front part of the head ⟨His *face* is familiar.⟩
syn countenance, kisser [*slang*], mug, puss [*slang*], visage
rel appearance, aspect, features, lineaments, looks, mien, presence; expression, physiognomy
2 a forward part or surface — see FRONT 1
3 a twisting of the facial features in disgust or disapproval — see GRIMACE
4 an outer part or layer — see EXTERIOR
5 facial appearance regarded as an indication of mood or feeling — see LOOK 1
6 outward and often deceptive indication — see APPEARANCE 2
7 a member of the human race — see HUMAN
8 shameless boldness — see EFFRONTERY
9 a state of mind in which one is free from doubt — see CONFIDENCE 2

face *vb* **1** to stand or sit with the face or front toward ⟨The house *faces* the sparkling blue waters of the Pacific Ocean.⟩

syn front, look (toward), point (toward)
rel abut, adjoin, border, bound, fringe, margin, meet, neighbor, rim, skirt, touch; command, dominate, overlook; look down (on)
2 to oppose (something hostile or dangerous) with firmness or courage ⟨movie superheroes who are ever ready to *face* danger without blinking an eye⟩
syn beard, brave, brazen, breast, confront, dare, defy, outbrave
rel face up (to), front; affront; challenge; encounter, meet; accost, approach, corner; repel, resist, stand, withstand; battle, combat, contend (with), fight, oppose, square (off)
phrases stand up to
near ant avoid, eschew, shun; elude, escape, evade, shake
ant dodge, duck, funk, shirk, sidestep
3 to cover with something that protects — see SHEATHE
4 to enter into contest or conflict with — see ENGAGE 2

faceless *adj* not named or identified by a name — see NAMELESS 1

face–off *n* an earnest effort for superiority or victory over another — see CONTEST 1

face off *vb* to engage in a contest — see COMPETE

facet *n* a certain way in which something appears or may be regarded — see ASPECT 1

facetious *adj* **1** given to or marked by mature intelligent humor — see WITTY
2 making light of something usually regarded as serious or sacred — see FLIPPANT

facetiousness *n* a lack of seriousness often at an improper time — see FRIVOLITY

face–to–face *adv* in person and usually privately — see TÊTE-À-TÊTE

facile *adj* **1** having or showing a lack of depth of understanding or character — see SUPERFICIAL 2
2 involving minimal difficulty or effort — see EASY 1

facilely *adv* without difficulty — see EASILY 1

facilitate *vb* to free from obstruction or difficulty — see EASE 1

facility *n* a structure that is designed and built for a particular purpose ⟨The city is known for its medical *facilities*.⟩
syn complex, establishment, installation
rel building, edifice; institute, institution; business, company, concern, outfit

facsimile *n* **1** something or someone that strongly resembles another — see IMAGE 1
2 something that is made to look exactly like something else — see COPY

fact *n* **1** the quality of being actual ⟨Like other scientists, astronomers deal in the realm of *fact*, not speculation.⟩
syn actuality, factuality, materiality, reality
rel authenticity, genuineness, truth, verity
near ant fancy, fantasy (*also* phantasy), fiction, fictitiousness; dreaminess, surreality
ant irreality, unreality

2 something that actually exists ⟨Once considered a wild fantasy, the Internet is now a *fact* of everyday life.⟩

syn actuality, case, materiality, reality

rel certainty; circumstance, event, occurrence, phenomenon; element, item, particular, thing

near ant eventuality, possibility, potentiality, probability

ant fantasy (*also* phantasy), fiction, illusion

3 a single piece of information ⟨a book of little-known *facts* about famous people⟩

syn datum, detail, nicety, particular, particularity, point, specific

rel article, item; component, constituent, element, ingredient, member, part; aspect, circumstance, facet, factor; evidence, exhibit; database, information, knowledge

near ant error, fallacy, falsehood, inaccuracy, misconception, misstatement, myth

4 facts *pl* a collection of factual knowledge about something — see INFORMATION 1

faction *n* a group of people acting together within a larger group ⟨Several *factions* within the environmental movement have joined forces to save this wilderness area.⟩

syn bloc, block, body, coalition, party, sect, set, side, wing

rel splinter, split; crew, gang, pack, team; denomination, persuasion; caucus, movement

factitious *adj* lacking in natural or spontaneous quality — see ARTIFICIAL 1

factor *n* 1 a person who acts or does business for another — see AGENT 2

2 one of the parts that make up a whole — see ELEMENT 1

factory *n* a building or set of buildings for the manufacturing of goods ⟨The new *factory* will create hundreds of much-needed jobs.⟩

syn manufactory, mill, plant, shop, works, workshop

rel sweatshop; atelier, studio, workplace, workroom; yard

factual *adj* restricted to or based on fact ⟨a *factual* biography of George Washington that scoffs at the story about the cherry tree⟩

syn documentary, hard, historical, literal, matter-of-fact, nonfictional, objective, true

rel actual, authentic, bona fide, genuine, real, right; documented, established; confirmable, reliable, supportable, sustainable, verifiable; demonstrable, provable, incontestable, incontrovertible, indisputable, irrefutable, undeniable, unquestionable; plain, simple; certain, undoubted

near ant hypothetical, speculative, theoretical (*also* theoretic); apocryphal, unauthentic, undocumented; chimerical (*also* chimeric), fabulous, fanciful, fantastic (*also* fantastical), imaginary, imagined, invented, legendary, made-up, make-believe, mythical (*or* mythic), pretend; embroidered; insupportable, unsupportable

ant fictional, fictionalized, fictitious, non-

documentary, nonfactual, nonhistorical, unhistorical

2 existing in fact and not merely as a possibility — see ACTUAL

factuality *n* 1 agreement with fact or reality — see TRUTH

2 the quality of being actual — see FACT 1

faculty *n* 1 a natural ability of the mind or body — see POWER 3

2 a special and usually inborn ability — see TALENT

3 the physical or mental power to do something — see ABILITY

fad *n* a practice or interest that is very popular for a short time ⟨Once the *fad* for that kind of music had passed, nobody would have been caught dead listening to it.⟩

syn craze, enthusiasm, fashion, go, last word, latest, mode, rage, sensation, style, trend, vogue

rel nine days' wonder (*also* nine day wonder); new wave; crush, infatuation; fervor, passion; furor, fuss, hullabaloo, to-do, uproar; bandwagon, crusade, cult, movement; novelty, wrinkle; caprice, fancy, whim

near ant classic, standard

faddish *adj* enjoying widespread favor or approval — see POPULAR 1

faddy *adj* enjoying widespread favor or approval — see POPULAR 1

fade *vb* 1 to cease to be visible — see DISAPPEAR

2 to make white or whiter by removing color — see WHITEN

3 to lose bodily strength or vigor — see WEAKEN 2

faded *adj* lacking intensity of color — see PALE 1

faerie *also* **faery** *n* an imaginary being usually having a small human form and magical powers — see FAIRY

fail *vb* 1 to stop functioning ⟨My cell phone *failed* just as I was about to call you.⟩

syn break, break down, conk (out), crash, cut out, die, give out, stall

rel fizzle, sputter, wheeze; act up, malfunction; jam

ant start (up)

2 to be unsuccessful ⟨Despite all the publicity, the movie *failed* miserably at the box office.⟩

syn bomb, collapse, flop, flunk, fold, founder, miss, wash out

rel flounder, struggle; decline, sink, slip, slump, wane; crash, crumble, miscarry, misfire; go under; implode, self-destruct

phrases come a cropper, come to grief, come up empty, die on the vine, fall flat, fall on one's face, fall short, lay an egg

near ant cook, flourish, prosper, thrive; prevail, triumph, win

ant click, deliver, go, go over, pan out, succeed, work out

3 to fall short in satisfying the expectation or hope of — see DISAPPOINT

4 to lose bodily strength or vigor — see WEAKEN 2

5 to miss the opportunity or obligation — see NEGLECT 3

failing *n* a defect in character — see FAULT 1

---

syn synonym(s)   *rel* related words

ant antonym(s)   *near ant* near antonym(s)

failure *n* **1** the nonperformance of an assigned or expected action ⟨Your *failure* to check the batteries in the smoke detector could have tragic results.⟩

syn default, delinquency, dereliction, neglect, negligence, oversight

rel carelessness, heedlessness, inadvertence, inadvertency, laxity

near ant compliance, discharge, fulfillment (*or* fulfilment)

2 a falling short of one's goals ⟨The *failure* of the school's fund-raising drive was a big disappointment to all.⟩

syn collapse, crash, cropper, defeat, fizzle, nonsuccess

rel futility, uselessness; ineffectiveness, ineffectuality, ineffectualness, inefficaciousness, inefficacy; deficiency, inadequacy, insufficiency; disappointment, letdown, setback; insolvency, ruin

near ant victory, win

ant accomplishment, achievement, success

3 something that has failed ⟨The students' first attempt to build a homemade rocket was a disappointing *failure*.⟩

syn bomb, bummer, bust, catastrophe, debacle (*also* débâcle), disaster, dud, fiasco, fizzle, flop, frost, lemon, loser, miss, turkey, washout

rel also-ran, disappointment, dog; botch, hash, mess, muddle, shambles; nonevent; nonstarter

near ant corker, crackerjack (*also* crackajack), dandy, jim-dandy, phenomenon

ant blockbuster, hit, smash, success, winner

4 a falling short of an essential or desirable amount or number — see DEFICIENCY

faint *adj* **1** not seen or understood clearly ⟨After wandering in the woods for hours, we had only a *faint* idea of where we were.⟩

syn bleary, blurry, dim, foggy, fuzzy, gauzy, hazy, indefinite, indistinct, indistinguishable, misty, murky, nebulous, obscure, opaque, pale, shadowy, unclear, undefined, undetermined, vague

rel dark, dusky, gloomy; impalpable, inappreciable, intangible; incomprehensible, indiscernible, inexplicable, mysterious, puzzling

near ant bright, distinct, evident, obvious, plain; certain, firm, strong, sure

ant clear, definite, pellucid

2 lacking bodily strength — see WEAK 1

faint *n* a temporary state of unconsciousness ⟨Shocking news can cause a person to fall into a *faint*.⟩

syn blackout, insensibility, knockout, swim, swoon

rel daze, trance; drowsiness, narcosis, sleep, somnolence

faint *vb* to lose consciousness ⟨the kind of person who *faints* at the sight of blood⟩

syn black out, conk (out), pass out, swoon

rel break down, collapse; zonk (out)

ant come around, come round, come to, revive

fainthearted *adj* easily frightened — see SHY 1

faintheartedness *n* lack of willingness to assert oneself and take risks — see TIMIDITY

faintness *n* the quality or state of lacking physical strength or vigor — see WEAKNESS 1

fair *n* a public showing of objects of interest — see EXHIBITION 1

fair *adj* **1** not stormy or cloudy ⟨We prayed for *fair* weather during our vacation at the beach.⟩

syn bright, clear, cloudless, sunny, sunshiny, unclouded

rel balmy, clement, gentle, mild, moderate, temperate; calm, halcyon, peaceful, placid, serene, tranquil; fine, pleasant

near ant harsh, inclement, severe; blustering, blustery, breezy, gusty; foggy, hazy, misty, murky, soupy

ant bleak, cloudy, dirty, foul, nasty, overcast, rainy, raw, rough, squally, stormy, tempestuous, turbulent

2 marked by honesty, justice, and freedom from bias ⟨a commanding officer who enjoyed the respect of his soldiers because his decisions were always *fair*⟩

syn candid, disinterested, dispassionate, equal, equitable, evenhanded, impartial, indifferent, just, nonpartisan, objective, square, unbiased, unprejudiced

rel frank, forthright, open, straight, straightforward; balanced, rational, reasonable

near ant deceitful, deceptive, dishonest; arbitrary, unconscionable, unreasonable; jaundiced, unfriendly, unsympathetic; distorted, warped

ant biased, inequitable, nonobjective, one-sided, partial, partisan, prejudiced, unjust

3 following or according to the rules ⟨a hockey player who is respected for his *fair* play⟩

syn clean, legal, sportsmanlike, sportsmanly

rel just, law-abiding; ethical, moral, principled, scrupulous; honorable, irreproachable, unimpeachable

near ant immoral, unethical, unprincipled, unrighteous, unscrupulous, vicious, wrong

ant dirty, foul, nasty, unfair, unsportsmanlike

4 of light complexion ⟨*Fair* people tend to sunburn easily.⟩

syn light

rel ashen, ashy, pale, paled, palish, pallid, pasty, peaked, sallow, sallowish, wan, white

ant dark, swart

5 having qualities which inspire hope — see HOPEFUL 1

6 of a pale yellow or yellowish brown color — see BLOND

7 of average to below average quality — see MEDIOCRE 1

8 very pleasing to look at — see BEAUTIFUL 1

9 having no exceptions or restrictions — see ABSOLUTE 2

10 being what is called for by accepted standards of right and wrong — see JUST 1

11 free from dirt or stain — see CLEAN 1

fair *adv* according to the rules or the law — see FAIRLY 1

fairly *adv* **1** to some degree or extent ⟨For someone without professional training, she sings *fairly* well.⟩

syn enough, kind of, like, moderately, more or less, pretty, quite, rather, relatively, something, somewhat, sort of

rel acceptably, passably, tolerably; little; negligibly, nominally, slightly, vaguely; half, halfway, incompletely, part, partially, partly

phrases a bit, after a cent, a little, a mite, a tad, a touch, of sorts (*or* of a sort), to a degree

near ant awfully, beastly, deadly, especially, exceedingly (*also* exceeding), exceptionally, extremely, frightfully, greatly, heavily, highly, hugely, mightily, mortally, particularly, terribly, very; considerably, extensively, significantly, substantially

2 according to the rules or the law <Carson had acquired the land *fairly*.>

syn clean, fair

rel ethically, high-mindedly, morally, nobly; honorably

near ant ignobly, immorally, underhandedly, unethically; dishonorably

ant dirty, illegally

3 very close to but not completely — see ALMOST

fairness *n* **1** the qualities in a person or thing that as a whole give pleasure to the senses — see BEAUTY 1

2 lack of favoritism toward one side or another — see DETACHMENT 1

fairy *n* an imaginary being usually having a small human form and magical powers <*Fairies* are part of the folklore of many countries and cultures.>

syn brownie, dwarf, elf, faerie (*also* faery), gnome, goblin, gremlin, hobgoblin, leprechaun, pixie (*also* pixy), puck, sprite, troll

rel little people; changeling; imp; banshee, ghoul, hag, ogre

fairy tale *n* a statement known by its maker to be untrue and made in order to deceive — see LIE

faith *n* **1** belief and trust in and loyalty to God <a people who are known for their strong and steadfast *faith*>

syn devotion, piety, religion

rel devoutness, piousness, religiousness; adoration, reverence, veneration, worship; profession, protestation

near ant disbelief, doubt, unbelief, unfaith; agnosticism, know-nothingism

ant atheism, godlessness

2 a body of beliefs and practices regarding the supernatural and the worship of one or more deities — see RELIGION 1

3 adherence to something to which one is bound by a pledge or duty — see FIDELITY

4 firm belief in the integrity, ability, effectiveness, or genuineness of someone or something — see TRUST 1

5 mental conviction of the truth of some statement or the reality of some being or phenomenon — see BELIEF 1

faithful *adj* **1** firm in one's allegiance to someone or something <Fans of the Chicago Cubs are famously *faithful*.>

syn constant, devoted, devout, fast, good, loyal, pious, staunch (*also* stanch), steadfast, steady, true, true-blue

rel dependable, dutiful, reliable, responsible, solid, tried, tried-and-true, trustworthy, trusty; unfaltering, unhesitating, unwavering; determined, intent, resolute; confirmed, inveterate, sworn; ardent, avid, enthusiastic, fervent, fervid, gung ho, impassioned, passionate, serious

near ant irresponsible, undependable, unreliable, untrustworthy; faltering, hesitant, vacillating, wavering; dubious, irresolute, shaky, uncertain; apathetic, dispassionate, uninterested

ant disloyal, faithless, false, fickle, inconstant, perfidious, recreant, traitorous, treacherous, unfaithful, untrue

2 following an original exactly <a *faithful* filming of Robert Louis Stevenson's novel *Treasure Island*>

syn accurate, authentic, exact, precise, right, strict, true, veracious

rel lifelike, realistic; careful, conscientious, meticulous, punctilious, scrupulous; authoritative; bona fide, genuine, real

near ant careless, slack, slipshod, slovenly; erroneous, incorrect, invalid, off, unsound, untrue, untruthful, wrong

ant corrupt, corrupted, false, imprecise, inaccurate, inauthentic, inexact, loose, unfaithful

faithfulness *n* adherence to something to which one is bound by a pledge or duty — see FIDELITY

faithless *adj* not true in one's allegiance to someone or something <*faithless* friends who deserted him in his time of need>

syn disloyal, false, fickle, inconstant, perfidious, recreant, traitorous, treacherous, unfaithful, untrue

rel irresponsible, trustless, undependable, unreliable, untrustworthy; faltering, hesitant, vacillating, wavering; dubious, irresolute, uncertain; apathetic, dispassionate, uninterested

near ant dependable, dutiful, reliable, responsible, solid, tried, tried-and-true, trustworthy, trusty; unfaltering, unhesitating, unwavering; determined, intent, resolute; confirmed, inveterate, sworn; ardent, avid, enthusiastic, fervent, fervid, impassioned, passionate

ant constant, devoted, devout, faithful, fast, loyal, staunch (*also* stanch), steadfast, steady, true

faithlessness *n* **1** lack of faithfulness especially to one's husband or wife — see INFIDELITY 1

2 the act or fact of violating the trust or confidence of another — see BETRAYAL

fake *adj* **1** being such in appearance only and made with or manufactured from usually cheaper materials — see IMITATION

2 being such in appearance only and made or manufactured with the intention of committing fraud — see COUNTERFEIT 1

3 lacking in natural or spontaneous quality — see ARTIFICIAL 1

4 not being or expressing what one appears to be or express — see INSINCERE

fake *n* **1** an imitation that is passed off as genuine <Experts declared that one of the museum's prized paintings was actually a *fake*.>

---

syn counterfeit, forgery, hoax, humbug, phony (*also* phoney), sham

rel copycat, knockoff; copy, facsimile, replica, reproduction; dummy, mock-up; fraud, gaff, imposture, spoof, swindle; simulation, synthetic

near ant original

2 one who makes false claims of identity or expertise — see IMPOSTOR

fake *vb* **1** to imitate or copy especially in order to deceive ⟨Pranksters *faked* giant footprints and then claimed that they had seen Bigfoot.⟩

syn counterfeit, forge, phony

rel simulate; duplicate, reduplicate, replicate, reproduce; crib, plagiarize; adulterate, doctor, fudge, manipulate, tamper (with); concoct, cook (up), fabricate, invent

2 to present a false appearance of — see FEIGN

3 to perform, make, or do without preparation — see IMPROVISE

faker *n* one who makes false claims of identity or expertise — see IMPOSTOR

fakery *n* the inclination or practice of misleading others through lies or trickery — see DECEIT 1

fall *n* **1** the act of going down from an upright position suddenly and involuntarily ⟨a bad *fall* that resulted in several broken bones⟩

syn slip, spill, stumble, tumble

rel pratfall; misstep, trip; descent, dive, plunge, slide; free-fall

2 a change to a lower state or level — see DECLINE 2

3 a loss of status — see COMEDOWN

4 the act or process of going to a lower level or altitude — see DESCENT 1

5 the amount by which something is lessened — see DECREASE

6 *usually* **falls** *pl* a fall of water usually from a great height — see WATERFALL

7 a downward slope — see DECLINE 3

fall *vb* **1** to go down from an upright position suddenly and involuntarily ⟨Better sand that walkway before somebody *falls* on the ice.⟩

syn slip, stumble, topple, trip, tumble

rel collapse, crumple, drop, plop, plunk (*or* plonk), slump (over); crash, free-fall, nose-dive, plummet, plunge, precipitate, wipe out; slide

ant get up, rise, stand (up), uprise

2 to yield to the control or power of enemy forces ⟨The city *fell* to the enemy.⟩

syn capitulate, give up, knuckle under, submit, succumb, surrender

rel bow, buckle, cave (in), collapse, give (in); hand over, relinquish; lose; concede, fail, fold

near ant buck, defy, fight, oppose, repel, resist, withstand; beat, overcome, win; conquer, prevail, triumph

ant endure, stand

3 to go to a lower level especially abruptly — see DROP 2

4 to grow less in scope or intensity especially gradually — see DECREASE 2

5 to lead or extend downward — see DESCEND 1

6 to undergo defeat — see LOSE 3

7 to commit an offense — see OFFEND 1

8 to stop living — see DIE 1

fallacious *adj* **1** not using or following good reasoning — see ILLOGICAL

2 tending or having power to deceive — see DECEPTIVE 1

fallaciousness *n* the quality or state of being false — see FALLACY 2

fallacy *n* **1** a false idea or belief ⟨the once-common *fallacy* that the earth is flat⟩

syn delusion, error, falsehood, falsity, hallucination, illusion, misbelief, misconception, myth, old wives' tale, untruth

rel factoid; superstition; fiction, pretense (*or* pretence); distortion, inaccuracy, misapprehension, miscomprehension, misinterpretation, misjudgment, misperception, misunderstanding; misinformation, misreport, misrepresentation, misstatement; sophism, sophistry; fib, half-truth, lie, story, tale

ant truth, verity

2 the quality or state of being false ⟨The *fallacy* of the notion of spontaneous generation was demonstrated by the Dutch naturalist Leeuwenhoek.⟩

syn erroneousness, fallaciousness, falsehood, falseness, falsity, untruth

rel speciousness, spuriousness; delusion; inaccuracy, incorrectness; dishonesty, mendacity, untruthfulness

near ant accuracy, actuality, correctness, factuality, factualness, genuineness; credibility, honesty, trustworthiness, truthfulness, veracity

ant truth, verity

fall back *vb* to move back or away (as from something difficult, dangerous, or disagreeable) — see RETREAT 1

fallen *adj* no longer living — see DEAD 1

fall guy *n* a person or thing taking the blame for others — see SCAPEGOAT

falling-out *n* an often noisy or angry expression of differing opinions — see ARGUMENT 1

fall out *vb* **1** to express different opinions about something often angrily — see ARGUE 2

2 to come to be — see COME OUT 1

fallow *adj* not being in a state of use, activity, or employment — see INACTIVE 2

false *adj* **1** not in agreement with what is true ⟨Early reports about the explosion contained much *false* information.⟩

syn erroneous, inaccurate, incorrect, inexact, invalid, off, unsound, untrue, untruthful, wrong

rel counterfactual; specious, spurious; deceptive, delusive, delusory, distorted, fallacious, fictitious, illusory, misleading; amiss, askew, awry; deceitful, dishonest, fraudulent, lying, mendacious; unconfirmed, unproven, untested; fabricated, invented, made-up, trumped-up

phrases off base

near ant confirmed, demonstrated, established, proven, tested; faultless, flawless, impeccable, letter-perfect, perfect

ant accurate, correct, errorless, exact, factual, precise, proper, right, sound, true, valid, veracious

2 being such in appearance only and made with or manufactured from usually cheaper materials — see IMITATION

3 being such in appearance only and made or manufactured with the intention of committing fraud — see COUNTERFEIT 1

4 lacking in natural or spontaneous quality — see ARTIFICIAL 1

5 marked by, based on, or done by the use of dishonest methods to acquire something of value — see FRAUDULENT 1

6 not true in one's allegiance to someone or something — see FAITHLESS

7 tending or having power to deceive — see DECEPTIVE 1

falsehood *n* 1 a false idea or belief — see FALLACY 1

2 a statement known by its maker to be untrue and made in order to deceive — see LIE

3 the quality or state of being false — see FALLACY 2

4 the tendency to tell lies — see DISHONESTY 1

falseness *n* 1 lack of faithfulness especially to one's husband or wife — see INFIDELITY 1

2 the act or fact of violating the trust or confidence of another — see BETRAYAL

3 the quality or state of being false — see FALLACY 2

falsify *vb* 1 to change so much as to create a wrong impression or alter the meaning of — see GARBLE

2 to prove to be false — see DISPROVE

falsity *n* 1 a false idea or belief — see FALLACY 1

2 a statement known by its maker to be untrue and made in order to deceive — see LIE

3 lack of faithfulness especially to one's husband or wife — see INFIDELITY 1

4 the act or fact of violating the trust or confidence of another — see BETRAYAL

5 the quality or state of being false — see FALLACY 2

falter *vb* 1 to show uncertainty about the right course of action — see HESITATE

2 to swing unsteadily back and forth or from side to side — see TEETER 1

faltering *n* a state or an instance of temporary inaction because of uncertainty about the right course of action — see HESITATION

fame *n* the fact or state of being known to the public ⟨Many go to Hollywood in search of *fame* and fortune.⟩

syn celebrity, notoriety, renown

rel infamy; character, mark, name, report, reputability, reputation, repute; cachet, place, position, prestige, rank, standing, stature, status; megastardom, popularity, stardom, superstardom; distinction, eminence, glory, greatness, honor, illustriousness, note, preeminence, prominence, visibility; acclaim, accolade, acknowledgment (*or* acknowledgement), homage, laurels, praise, recognition; adoration, idolization

near ant disgrace, dishonor, disrepute, ignominy, odium, opprobrium, shame; inconspicuousness, invisibility; unpopularity

ant anonymity, oblivion, obscureness, obscurity

2 overall quality as seen or judged by people in general — see REPUTATION

famed *adj* widely known — see FAMOUS 1

familial *adj* of or relating to a household or family — see DOMESTIC 1

familiar *adj* 1 closely acquainted ⟨the little inside jokes that people who have long been *familiar* like to share⟩

syn bosom, chummy, close, friendly, intimate, thick, tight

rel clannish, close-knit, tight-knit; affable, boon, companionable, convivial, cordial, genial, gracious, hearty; gregarious, sociable, social; comfortable, cozy, easy, snug; amicable, neighborly; confidential, secretive; adoring, affectionate, dear, devoted, fond, loving, tender, tenderhearted, warm

near ant aloof, antisocial, cold, cool, detached, distant, frosty, remote, reserved, standoffish, unfriendly, unsociable, withdrawn

ant distant

2 having information especially as a result of study or experience ⟨book editors who are *familiar* with what is being taught in the schools⟩

syn abreast, acquainted, conversant, informed, knowledgeable, up, up-to-date, versed

rel alive, aware, cognizant, conscious, heedful, mindful, sensible, sentient

phrases at home, in the know

near ant insensible, unaware, unconscious, unmindful; blind, oblivious, unknowing, unwitting; inattentive, unheeding

ant ignorant, unacquainted, unfamiliar, uninformed, unknowledgeable

3 often observed or encountered — see COMMON 1

4 showing a lack of proper social reserve or modesty — see PRESUMPTUOUS 1

familiar *n* 1 someone who regularly spends time in a particular place — see DENIZEN 1

2 a person who has a strong liking for and trust in another — see FRIEND 1

familiarity *n* 1 the state of being in a very personal or private relationship ⟨The elderly couple enjoys a *familiarity* that is the result of many years of happy marriage.⟩

syn chumminess, closeness, inseparability, intimacy, nearness

rel immediacy; affinity, kinship; commitment, devotedness, devotion; affection, attachment, fondness, love, passion; constancy, faithfulness, fidelity; amity, fellowship, friendship, goodwill; affability, conviviality, cordiality, geniality; mutuality; cliquishness, clubbiness

near ant aloofness, coolness, remoteness, reserve

ant distance

2 a socially improper or unsuitable act or remark — see IMPROPRIETY 2

3 knowledge gained by personal experience — see ACQUAINTANCE

familiarize *vb* 1 to give information to — see ENLIGHTEN 1

2 to impart knowledge of a new thing or situation to — see ACQUAINT 1

family *n* 1 a group of persons who come from the same ancestor ⟨The Adams *family* made remarkable contributions to

---

syn synonym(s)   *rel* related words
ant antonym(s)   *near ant* near antonym(s)

American life for more than two centuries.⟩

syn blood, clan, folks, house, kin, kindred, kinfolk (*or* kinfolks), kinsfolk, line, lineage, people, race, stock, tribe

rel blended family, nuclear family; extended family, household, kith; brood; descendant (*also* descendent), issue, offspring, progeny, scion, seed; clansman, kinsman, kinswoman, relative; dynasty; nation, nationality

near ant ancestry, birth, descent, extraction, origin, pedigree

2 one of the units into which a whole is divided on the basis of a common characteristic — see CLASS 2

family tree *n* the line of ancestors from whom a person is descended — see ANCESTRY

famine *n* a falling short of an essential or desirable amount or number — see DEFICIENCY

famished *adj* **1** feeling a desire or need for food — see HUNGRY 1

2 lacking money or material possessions — see POOR 1

famishment *n* a need or desire for food — see HUNGER 1

famous *adj* **1** widely known ⟨a book about some of the most *famous* people of the last century⟩

syn celebrated, famed, noted, notorious, prominent, renowned, star, visible, well-known

rel fabled, fabulous, legendary; infamous; distinguished, eminent, exceptional, great, illustrious, leading, notable, noteworthy, outstanding, preeminent, prestigious, remarkable, supereminent, superior; important, significant; acknowledged, respected; favorite, popular, preferred

near ant insignificant, unimportant; inconspicuous; undistinguished, unexceptional; unpopular

ant anonymous, nameless, obscure, uncelebrated, unknown, unsung

2 of the very best kind — see EXCELLENT

fan *n* a person with a strong and habitual liking for something ⟨lifelong *fans* of country and western music⟩

syn addict, aficionado (*also* afficionado), buff, bug, devotee, enthusiast, fanatic, fancier, fiend, fool, freak, head, hound, junkie (*also* junky), lover, maniac, nut, sucker

rel groupie; admirer, amateur, collector, connoisseur, dilettante; authority, expert; adherent, convert, cultist, disciple, follower, hanger-on, votary; advocate, apostle, backer, champion, evangelist, exponent, friend, patron, promoter, proponent, supporter; partisan (*also* partizan), zealot; booster, rooter, well-wisher; faddist

near ant nonadmirer; belittler, carper, critic, detractor

ant nonfan

fan (out) *vb* **1** to arrange the parts of (something) over a wider area — see OPEN 3

2 to extend outwards from or as if from a central point — see RADIATE 1

fanatic *n* **1** a person with a strong and habitual liking for something — see FAN

2 one who is intensely or excessively devoted to a cause — see ZEALOT

fanatic *or* **fanatical** *adj* being very far from the center of public opinion — see EXTREME 2

fancier *n* a person with a strong and habitual liking for something — see FAN

fanciful *adj* **1** conceived or made without regard for reason or reality — see FANTASTIC 1

2 not real and existing only in the imagination — see IMAGINARY

fancy *adj* **1** made or done with great care or with much detail — see ELABORATE 1

2 going beyond a normal or acceptable limit in degree or amount — see EXCESSIVE

fancy *n* **1** a conception or image created by the imagination and having no objective reality — see FANTASY 1

2 a sudden impulsive and apparently unmotivated idea or action — see WHIM

3 positive regard for something — see LIKING

4 the ability to form mental images of things that either are not physically present or have never been conceived or created by others — see IMAGINATION 1

fancy *vb* **1** to form a mental picture of — see IMAGINE 1

2 to take pleasure in — see ENJOY 1

fanny *n* the part of the body upon which someone sits — see BUTTOCKS

fantastic *also* **fantastical** *adj* **1** conceived or made without regard for reason or reality ⟨a *fantastic* scheme for getting rich quick⟩

syn absurd, bizarre, crazy, fanciful, foolish, insane, nonsensical, preposterous, unreal, wild

rel implausible, inconceivable, incredible, unbelievable, unimaginable, unthinkable; extravagant, grotesque; curious, eccentric, far-out, funny, kinky, kooky (*also* kookie), odd, outlandish, out-of-the-way, peculiar, quaint, quirky, screwy, strange, wacky (*also* whacky), way-out, weird; farcical, laughable, ludicrous, ridiculous; nightmarish; dreamlike, surreal

phrases off the wall [*slang*]

ant realistic, reasonable

2 excitingly or mysteriously unusual — see EXOTIC

3 not real and existing only in the imagination — see IMAGINARY

4 too extraordinary or improbable to believe — see INCREDIBLE

5 fantastic of the very best kind — see EXCELLENT

fantasy *vb* to form a mental picture of — see IMAGINE 1

fantasy *also* **phantasy** *n* **1** a conception or image created by the imagination and having no objective reality ⟨a constant daydreamer who started to believe his own *fantasies*⟩

syn chimera, conceit, daydream, delusion, dream, fancy, figment, hallucination, illusion, nonentity, phantasm (*also* fantasm), pipe dream, unreality, vision

rel ignis fatuus, mirage, will-o'-the-wisp; idea; concoction, fable, fabrication, fiction, invention; envisaging, imaging, visualization; cloud-cuckoo-land, cloudland, utopia; daymare, nightmare

phrases castle in Spain, castle in the air
near ant actuality, fact, reality
2 the ability to form mental images of things that either are not physically present or have never been conceived or created by others — see IMAGINATION 1
3 something that is the product of the imagination — see FICTION

far *adj* **1** lasting for a considerable time — see LONG 2
2 not close in time or space — see DISTANT 1

far *adv* to a great degree — see VERY 1

faraway *adj* not close in time or space — see DISTANT 1

farce *n* **1** a poor, insincere, or insulting imitation of something — see MOCKERY 1
2 humorous entertainment — see COMEDY 1

farcical *adj* **1** causing or intended to cause laughter — see FUNNY 1
2 so foolish or pointless as to be worthy of scornful laughter — see RIDICULOUS 1

fare *n* substances intended to be eaten — see FOOD

fare *vb* **1** to meet one's day-to-day needs — see GET ALONG 1
2 to move forward along a course — see GO 1
3 to take a meal — see DINE 1

farewell *adj* given, taken, or performed at parting — see PARTING

farewell *n* **1** an expression of good wishes at parting — see GOOD-BYE
2 the act of leaving a place — see DEPARTURE 1
3 the act or process of two or more persons going off in different directions — see PARTING 1

far-fetched *adj* not likely to be true or to occur — see IMPROBABLE

far-flung *adj* **1** having considerable extent — see EXTENSIVE
2 not close in time or space — see DISTANT 1

farm *n* a piece of land and its buildings used to grow crops or raise livestock ⟨a *farm* that has been in the same family for five generations⟩
syn estate, farmstead, grange, ranch
rel farmland, farmyard; farmhouse, hacienda, homestead, manor, plantation, spread; garden, orchard

farm *vb* to work by plowing, sowing, and raising crops on ⟨We're planning on *farming* 50 acres the first year.⟩
syn cultivate, tend, till
rel crop, plant; harvest, reap; harrow, hoe; sharecrop

farmer *n* a person who cultivates the land and grows crops on it ⟨a young *farmer* whose family has been growing wheat for many generations⟩
syn agriculturist (*or* agriculturalist), agronomist, cultivator, grower, planter, tiller
rel farmhand, field hand, gleaner, harvester, plowman, reaper; workfolk (*or* workfolks); gentleman farmer, sharecropper, subsistence farmer, tenant farmer, yeoman; homesteader, nester [*West*]; granger; rancher, ranchero, ranchman
ant nonfarmer

farming *adj* engaged in or concerned with agriculture — see AGRICULTURAL

farming *n* the science or occupation of cultivating the soil, producing crops, and raising livestock — see AGRICULTURE

farmstead *n* a piece of land and its buildings used to grow crops or raise livestock — see FARM

far-off *adj* not close in time or space — see DISTANT 1

far-out *adj* different from the ordinary in a way that causes curiosity or suspicion — see ODD 2

far-reaching *adj* having considerable extent — see EXTENSIVE

farsighted *adj* having or showing awareness of and preparation for the future — see FORESIGHTED

farsightedness *n* concern or preparation for the future — see FORESIGHT 2

farther *adj* resulting in an increase in amount or number — see ADDITIONAL

farther *adv* at or to a greater distance or more advanced point ⟨They had traveled *farther* down the Colorado River than any previous explorers.⟩
syn beyond, further, yon, yonder

farthermost *adj* most distant from a center — see EXTREME 1

farthest *adj* most distant from a center — see EXTREME 1

fascinate *vb* **1** to attract or delight as if by magic — see CHARM 1
2 to hold the attention of as if by a spell — see ENTHRALL 1
3 to hold the attention of — see ENGAGE 1

fascinating *adj* having an often mysterious or magical power to attract ⟨The *fascinating* paintings of the Renaissance were on display at the museum.⟩
syn alluring, appealing, attractive, bewitching, captivating, charming, elfin, enchanting, engaging, entrancing, fetching, glamorous (*also* glamourous), luring, magnetic, seductive
rel absorbing, arresting, engrossing, enthralling, gripping, hypnotic, hypnotizing, mesmerizing, riveting, spellbinding; enticing, tantalizing, tempting; exciting, haunting, interesting, intriguing, titillating; beckoning, inviting, winning; darling, delightful, pleasant, pleasing
near ant boring, irksome, tedious, tiresome, wearisome; abhorrent, abominable, appalling, awful, distasteful, hideous, horrendous, horrible, horrid, invidious, loathsome, nauseating, noisome, obnoxious, odious, offensive, shocking, sickening; drab, dreary, dull, flat, humdrum, jading, leaden, monotonous, pedestrian, ponderous
ant repellent (*also* repellant), repelling, repugnant, repulsive, revolting, unalluring
2 holding the attention or provoking interest — see INTERESTING

fascination *n* the power of irresistible attraction — see CHARM 2

fashion *n* **1** a practice or interest that is very popular for a short time — see FAD
2 a distinctive way of putting ideas into words — see STYLE 1

3 a usual manner of behaving or doing — see HABIT 1

4 the means or procedure for doing something — see METHOD

5 high position within society — see RANK 2

6 the outward appearance of something as distinguished from its substance — see FORM 1

fashion *vb* **1** to change (something) so as to make it suitable for a new use or situation — see ADAPT

2 to bring into being by combining, shaping, or transforming materials — see MAKE 1

fashionable *adj* **1** being in the latest or current fashion — see STYLISH

2 enjoying widespread favor or approval — see POPULAR 1

fashionableness *n* **1** the state of enjoying widespread approval — see POPULARITY

2 the quality or state of being fashionable — see COOL 2

fast *adj* **1** moving, proceeding, or acting with great speed ⟨The *fast* pace of construction resulted in our new house being done ahead of schedule.⟩

syn blistering, breakneck, breathless, brisk, dizzy, fleet, fleet-footed, flying, hasty, hot, lightning, nippy, quick, rapid, rapid-fire, rattling, snappy, speedy, swift, whirlwind, zippy

rel expeditious, prompt, ready; accelerated, hastened, hurried, quickened, rushed; breathtaking; energetic, strenuous, strong, vigorous; high-speed; rush; ultrafast, ultrarapid

near ant crawling, dallying, dawdling, dilly-dallying, dragging, laggard, languid, lingering, plodding, poking, poky (*or* pokey), slowish, sluggish, unhurried; deliberate, leisurely, measured; dilatory, late, tardy; ultraslow

ant slow

2 firm in one's allegiance to someone or something — see FAITHFUL 1

3 firmly positioned in place and difficult to dislodge — see TIGHT 2

4 given to or marked by cheating and deception — see DISHONEST 2

5 marked by the ability to withstand stress without structural damage or distortion — see STABLE 1

6 not lasting for a considerable time — see SHORT 2

7 having or showing quickness of mind — see INTELLIGENT 1

fast *adv* **1** with great speed ⟨Run as *fast* as you can to get help.⟩

syn apace, briskly, fleetly, full tilt, hastily, hot, posthaste, presto, pronto, quick, quickly, rapidly, snappily, soon, speedily, swift, swiftly

rel immediately, promptly, readily; impetuously, impulsively, rashly, recklessly; abruptly, suddenly; energetically, vigorously

phrases a mile a minute, at full throttle, at full tilt, by leaps and bounds, in a hurry, in short order, like a shot, like gangbusters, like wildfire

near ant laggardly, lingeringly, ploddingly, sluggishly; deliberately, leisurely; tardily

ant slow, slowly

2 to a full extent or degree — see FULLY 1

fasten *vb* **1** to cause (something) to hold to another ⟨Use this paper clip to *fasten* your picture to the application form.⟩

syn affix, attach, bend, fix

rel adhere, bolt, cinch, clamp, clasp, clench, clinch, clip, glue, hang, harness, hasp, lace, lash, latch, nail, paste, pin, plaster, rivet, screw, shackle, staple, stick, strap, tack, tackle, tie, toggle, yoke; coapt, connect, join, link, unite; reaffix, reattach, refasten, refix, resecure; batten, belay, button

near ant break up, disconnect, disjoin, disjoint, dissever, dissociate, disunite, divide, divorce, part, separate, sever, split, sunder, uncouple, unlink, unyoke; loose, loosen; unbind, unfix, unlash, untie

ant detach, undo, unfasten, unhook

2 to put securely in place or in a desired position ⟨Don't forget to *fasten* all the lines on your tent.⟩

syn anchor, catch, clamp, fix, hitch, moor, secure, set

rel embed (*also* imbed), entrench (*also* intrench), implant, ingrain (*also* engrain), lodge, stuff, wedge

near ant extract, prize, pry, pull, root (out), tear (out), uproot, wrest, yank

ant loose, loosen, unfasten, unfix, unloose, unloosen

3 to fix (as one's attention) steadily toward a central objective — see CONCENTRATE 2

fastidious *adj* hard to please — see FINICKY

fastness *n* **1** a high rate of movement or performance — see SPEED 1

2 a structure or place from which one can resist attack — see FORT

3 adherence to something to which one is bound by a pledge or duty — see FIDELITY

fast–track *vb* to cause to move or proceed fast or faster — see HURRY 1

fat *n* **1** individuals carefully selected as being the best of a class — see ELITE 1

2 the state or an instance of going beyond what is usual, proper, or needed — see EXCESS

3 the condition of having an excess of body fat — see CORPULENCE

fat *adj* **1** having an excess of body fat ⟨the popular image of Santa Claus as a *fat* man in a red suit⟩

syn chubby, corpulent, fleshy, full, obese, overweight, plump, portly, pudgy, replete, roly-poly, rotund, round, tubby

rel beefy, bulky, chunky, heavy, heavyset, plumpish, stocky, stout, thick, thickset, weighty; brawny, burly, hefty, husky; dumpy, squat, stubby; hippy; flabby, soft

near ant angular, gaunt, lank, lanky, raw-boned, sinewy; cadaverous, emaciated, haggard, pinched, skeletal, wasted; puny, scraggy, scrawny, slight; rangy, reedy, spindling, spindly, stringy, svelte, sylphlike, twiggy, waspish, weedy, willowy; anorexic

ant lean, skinny, slender, slim, spare, thin

2 containing or seeming to contain the greatest quantity or number possible — see FULL 1

3 having a greater than usual measure across — see WIDE 1

4 having or being of relatively great depth or extent from one surface to its opposite — see THICK 1

5 producing abundantly — see FERTILE

6 yielding a profit — see PROFITABLE 1

fatal *adj* 1 bringing about ruin or misfortune ⟨I made the *fatal* mistake of sharing my secret with the office's biggest blabbermouth.⟩

syn calamitous, cataclysmal (*or* cataclysmic), catastrophic, destructive, disastrous, fateful, ruinous, unfortunate

rel hapless, ill-fated, ill-starred, luckless; adverse, baleful, baneful, damaging, deleterious, detrimental, evil, harmful, hurtful, ill, injurious, noxious, pernicious, prejudicial

near ant fluky (*also* flukey), fortuitous, fortunate, happy, lucky, providential; auspicious, bright, encouraging, fair, golden, heartening, hopeful, optimistic, promising, propitious, rose-colored, rosy, upbeat

2 likely to cause or capable of causing death — see DEADLY 1

fatality *n* a person or thing harmed, lost, or destroyed — see CASUALTY 1

fate *vb* to determine the fate of in advance — see DESTINE

fate *n* 1 a state or end that seemingly has been decided beforehand ⟨the belief that it was this country's *fate* to extend from sea to sea⟩

syn circumstance, destiny, doom, fortune, lot, portion

rel accident, chance, happenstance, hazard, luck; predestination; aftereffect, aftermath, conclusion, consequence, development, effect, fruit, issue, outcome, outgrowth, result, resultant, sequel, sequence, upshot

2 a condition or occurrence traceable to a cause — see EFFECT 1

3 the permanent stopping of all the vital bodily activities — see DEATH 1

fateful *adj* bringing about ruin or misfortune — see FATAL 1

fathead *n* a stupid person — see IDIOT

father *n* 1 a male human parent ⟨the special relationship that exists between *fathers* and sons⟩

syn dad, daddy, old man, pa, papa (*also* poppa), pop, sire

rel paterfamilias, patriarch; father figure, father image; stepfather

2 a person who establishes a whole new field of endeavor ⟨Sir Isaac Newton is regarded by many as the *father* of modern science.⟩

syn author, begetter, creator, establisher, founder, generator, inaugurator, initiator, instituter (*or* institutor), originator, sire

rel cocreator, cofounder; conceiver, contriver, designer, deviser, formulator, innovator, introducer, inventor, spawner; builder, maker, producer; developer, pioneer, researcher; organizer, promoter; encourager, galvanizer, inspiration, inspirer

near ant disciple, follower, pupil, student, supporter

3 a person who is several generations earlier in an individual's line of descent — see ANCESTOR 1

4 *cap* the being worshipped as the creator and ruler of the universe — see DEITY 2

father *vb* to become the father of ⟨Paul Revere somehow found room in his small house for the large family he had *fathered*.⟩

syn beget, get, sire

rel multiply, procreate, propagate, reproduce, spawn; bear, engender, gender, generate, produce

fatherland *n* the land of one's birth, residence, or citizenship — see COUNTRY 1

fathom *vb* to measure the depth of (as a body of water) typically with a weighted line — see ²SOUND 1

fatigue *vb* to use up all the physical energy of — see EXHAUST 1

fatigue *n* a complete depletion of energy or strength ⟨The day-long battle against the blaze left firefighters in a state of utter *fatigue*.⟩

syn burnout, collapse, exhaustion, frazzle, lassitude, prostration, tiredness, weariness

rel debilitation, debility, disablement, enfeeblement, faintness, feebleness, frailness, frailty, impotence, infirmity, weakness; overfatigue; languor, listlessness; sluggishness, slumber, torpidity; apathy, inertia, passiveness, passivity

near ant bounce, dash, drive, energy, ginger, go, liveliness, pep, punch, sap, snap, starch, verve, vigor, vim, vitality, zing, zip; might, muscle, potency, power, puissance, strength; briskness, jauntiness, spiritedness, sprightliness, vivaciousness, vivacity

ant refreshment, rejuvenation, rejuvenescence, revitalization

fatigued *adj* depleted in strength, energy, or freshness — see WEARY 1

fatness *n* the condition of having an excess of body fat — see CORPULENCE

fatty *adj* containing animal fat especially in unusual amounts ⟨*fatty* ground beef that was the cheapest available⟩

syn adipose

rel greasy; lardy, rich

near ant fibrous, gristly, stringy, tough; nonfat

ant defatted, lean

fatuity *n* 1 a foolish act or idea — see FOLLY 1

2 lack of good sense or judgment — see FOOLISHNESS 1

3 the quality or state of lacking intelligence or quickness of mind — see STUPIDITY 1

fatuous *adj* 1 not having or showing an ability to absorb ideas readily — see STUPID 1

2 showing or marked by a lack of good sense or judgment — see FOOLISH 1

faucet *n* a fixture for controlling the flow of a liquid ⟨Don't forget to turn off the *faucet*.⟩

syn cock, gate, spigot, stopcock, tap, valve

rel hydrant, spout; petcock

fault *vb* to express one's unfavorable opinion of the worth or quality of — see CRITICIZE

fault *n* 1 a defect in character ⟨the common *fault* of being quick to judge others⟩

syn demerit, dereliction, failing, foible, frailty, shortcoming, sin, vice, want, weakness

---

syn synonym(s) *rel* related words
ant antonym(s) *near ant* near antonym(s)

rel blot, spot, stain; blemish, deficiency, flaw, imperfection, minus, nit; Achilles' heel, soft spot; corruption, depravity, evil, immorality, sinfulness, wickedness
phrases feet of clay
near ant excellence, perfection; goodness, integrity, morality, probity, rectitude, righteousness
ant merit, virtue

2 an unintentional departure from truth or accuracy — see ERROR 1

3 responsibility for wrongdoing or failure — see BLAME 1

4 something that spoils the appearance or completeness of a thing — see BLEMISH

5 the state of being held as the cause of something that needs to be set right — see RESPONSIBILITY 1

faultfinder *n* a person given to harsh judgments and to finding faults — see CRITIC 1

faultfinding *adj* given to making or expressing unfavorable judgments about things — see CRITICAL 1

faultily *adv* in a mistaken or inappropriate way — see WRONGLY

faultless *adj* **1** being entirely without fault or flaw — see PERFECT 1

2 free from guilt or blame — see INNOCENT 2

faultlessly *adv* without any flaws or errors — see PERFECTLY 1

faultlessness *n* the quality or state of being free from guilt or blame — see INNOCENCE 1

faulty *adj* having a fault ⟨The cause of the power failure was traced to *faulty* wiring.⟩
syn amiss, bad, defective, flawed, imperfect
rel fallible; blemished, broken, crippled, damaged, defaced, disfigured, harmed, hurt, impaired, injured, marred, spoiled, vitiated; deficient, inadequate, incomplete, insufficient, wanting
phrases on the blink
near ant complete, entire, intact, whole; unblemished, undamaged, unimpaired, unspoiled
ant faultless, flawless, impeccable, perfect

faux *adj* being such in appearance only and made with or manufactured from usually cheaper materials — see IMITATION

favor *vb* **1** to do a service or favor for — see OBLIGE 1

2 to have a favorable opinion of — see APPROVE (OF)

3 to show partiality toward — see PREFER 1

4 to furnish freely or naturally with some power, quality, or attribute — see ENDOW 1

favor *n* **1** an act of kind assistance ⟨a good and generous friend who is always doing *favors* for others⟩
syn benevolence, boon, courtesy, grace, indulgence, kindness, mercy, service, turn
rel dispensation, waiver; advantage, benefit, blessing, godsend, manna; liberty, license (*or* licence), privilege
near ant hindrance, hurdle, impediment, interference, obstacle

2 a feeling of great approval and liking — see ADMIRATION 1

3 an acceptance of something as satisfactory — see APPROVAL

4 an attitude that always favors one way of feeling or acting especially without considering any other possibilities — see BIAS 1

5 positive regard for something — see LIKING

6 the state of enjoying widespread approval — see POPULARITY

favorable *adj* **1** expressing approval ⟨*Favorable* reviews for the movie were widespread.⟩
syn admiring, applauding, appreciative, approving, commendatory, complimentary, friendly, good, positive
rel accepting, warm; encomiastic, eulogistic, flattering, laudative, laudatory, panegyrical, praiseful; respectful, supportive, sympathetic; adoring, adulatory, idolizing, worshipful, worshipping (*also* worshiping); advisory, recommendatory
near ant captious, carping, caviling (*or* cavilling), censuring, critical, faultfinding, hypercritical, overcritical; belittling, contemptuous, disdainful, disparaging, scornful, slighting
ant adverse, depreciative, depreciatory, derogatory, disapproving, inappreciative, negative, unappreciative, uncomplimentary, unfavorable, unflattering, unfriendly

2 pointing toward a happy outcome ⟨*favorable* economic conditions for opening a new business⟩
syn auspicious, bright, encouraging, golden, heartening, hopeful, promising, propitious
rel fortuitous, fortunate, happy, lucky, providential; advantageous, beneficial, profitable, prosperous, salutary; idealistic, romantic, utopian, visionary
near ant unfortunate, unhappy, unlucky; calamitous, catastrophic, disastrous, fatal, ruinous; baleful, dark, dire, direful, doomy, foreboding, gloomy, ill, menacing, ominous, portentous, sinister, threatening
ant dim, discouraging, disheartening, futureless, hopeless, inauspicious, unfavorable, unpromising, unpropitious

3 promoting or contributing to personal or social well-being — see BENEFICIAL

favorably *adv* in a pleasing way — see WELL 5

favored *adj* **1** granted special treatment or attention — see DARLING 1

2 singled out from a number or group as more to one's liking — see SELECT 1

favorite *adj* **1** granted special treatment or attention — see DARLING 1

2 singled out from a number or group as more to one's liking — see SELECT 1

3 enjoying widespread favor or approval — see POPULAR 1

favorite *n* a person or thing that is preferred over others ⟨The youngest child was always Mother's *favorite*.⟩
syn darling, minion, pet, preference, speed
rel beloved, dear, sweetheart; jewel, prize, treasure
phrases cup of tea
near ant abomination, anathema, bête noire, bugbear

fawn *vb* to use flattery or the doing of favors in order to win approval especially from a superior ⟨a student who could not wait to *fawn* over the new teacher⟩

syn fuss, kowtow, suck (up), toady

rel drool, gush, slaver, slobber; endear, ingratiate; court, woo; adulate, idolize, worship; blandish, cajole, coax, flatter, overpraise, soft-soap; cower, cringe, grovel; abase, debase, demean; defer, submit, yield

phrases curry favor, kiss up to

near ant despise, disdain, scorn; gibe (*or* jibe), jeer, scoff; brave, challenge, defy

fawner *n* a person who flatters another in order to get ahead — see SYCOPHANT

fay *adj* given to good-natured joking or teasing — see PLAYFUL

faze *vb* to throw into a state of self-conscious distress — see EMBARRASS 1

fealty *n* adherence to something to which one is bound by a pledge or duty — see FIDELITY

fear *vb* to experience concern or anxiety — see WORRY 1

fear *n* **1** the emotion experienced in the presence or threat of danger ⟨The sight of the headless horseman filled the schoolmaster with *fear*.⟩

syn alarm (*also* alarum), anxiety, dread, fearfulness, fright, horror, panic, scare, terror, trepidation

rel phobia; creeps, jitters, nervousness, willies; pang, qualm, twinge; agitation, apprehension, consternation, discomposure, disquiet, funk, perturbation; concern, dismay, worry; cowardice, faintheartedness, timidity, timorousness

near ant aplomb, assurance, boldness, confidence, self-assurance, self-confidence; bravery, courage, courageousness, daring, dauntlessness, doughtiness, fearlessness, fortitude, gallantry, hardihood, intrepidity, intrepidness, stoutness, valor; audacity, guts, nerve

2 an uneasy state of mind usually over the possibility of an anticipated misfortune or trouble — see ANXIETY 1

fearful *adj* **1** causing fear ⟨the *fearful* roar of a lion⟩

syn alarming, dire, direful, dread, dreadful, fearsome, forbidding, formidable, frightening, frightful, ghastly, hair-raising, horrendous, horrible, horrifying, intimidating, redoubtable, scary, shocking, terrible, terrifying

rel daunting, demoralizing, disconcerting, discouraging, dismaying, disquieting, distressing, disturbing, perturbing, startling, threatening, troubling, trying, unnerving; creepy, eerie (*also* eery), weird; appalling, atrocious, awful, grisly, gruesome (*also* grewsome), hideous, horrid, macabre, monstrous, nightmarish

near ant calming, comforting, consoling, inviting, lulling, pacifying, quieting, reassuring, relaxing, soothing, tranquilizing (*also* tranquillizing); nonintimidating, nonthreatening

2 easily frightened — see SHY 1

3 extreme in degree, power, or effect — see INTENSE 1

4 filled with fear or dread — see AFRAID

fearfulness *n* the emotion experienced in the presence or threat of danger — see FEAR 1

fearless *adj* feeling or displaying no fear by temperament — see BRAVE 1

fearlessness *n* strength of mind to carry on in spite of danger — see COURAGE

fearsome *adj* **1** causing fear — see FEARFUL 1

2 extreme in degree, power, or effect — see INTENSE 1

3 easily frightened — see SHY 1

feasible *adj* capable of being done or carried out — see POSSIBLE 1

feast *n* **1** a large fancy meal often accompanied by ceremony or entertainment ⟨They celebrated their 50th wedding anniversary with a *feast* at a fancy banquet hall with their closest friends and family.⟩

syn banquet, dinner, feed, spread

rel chow, mess, repast, table; blowout, carnival, festival, fete (*or* fête), gala, party, shindig; festivity; barbecue (*also* barbeque), clambake, cookout, fry, luau, roast; buffet, luncheon

2 a source of great satisfaction — see DELIGHT 1

3 an amount or supply more than sufficient to meet one's needs — see PLENTY 1

feast *vb* **1** to entertain with a fancy meal ⟨The returning war heroes were *feasted* all over the country.⟩

syn banquet, dine, junket, regale

rel board, cater, feed, provision; fete (*or* fête), honor, recognize

2 to give satisfaction to — see PLEASE 1

feat *n* **1** an act of notable skill, strength, or cleverness ⟨Washington's legendary *feat* of tossing a silver dollar across the Rappahannock River⟩

syn deed, exploit, number, stunt, trick

rel accomplishment, achievement, attainment, coup, success, triumph; adventure; performance

2 something done by someone — see ACTION 1

feather *n* **1** a number of persons or things that are grouped together because they have something in common — see SORT 1

2 dressy clothing — see FINERY

3 a state of mind dominated by a particular emotion — see MOOD 1

featherbrained *adj* lacking in seriousness or maturity — see GIDDY 1

feathery *adj* having little weight — see ¹LIGHT 1

feature *n* something that sets apart an individual from others of the same kind — see CHARACTERISTIC

feature *vb* **1** to indicate the importance of by centering attention on — see EMPHASIZE 1

2 to form a mental picture of — see IMAGINE 1

feces *n pl* solid matter discharged from an animal's alimentary canal — see DROPPING 1

fecund *adj* producing abundantly — see FERTILE

federate *vb* to form or enter into an association that furthers the interests of its members — see ALLY

federation *n* an association of persons, parties, or states for mutual assistance and protection — see CONFEDERACY

fed up *adj* having one's patience, interest, or pleasure exhausted — see WEARY 2

fee *n* the amount of money that is demanded as payment for something — see PRICE 1

feeble *adj* lacking bodily strength — see WEAK 1

feebleness *n* the quality or state of lacking physical strength or vigor — see WEAKNESS 1

feed *n* 1 a large fancy meal often accompanied by ceremony or entertainment — see FEAST 1

2 food eaten or prepared for eating at one time — see MEAL

feed *vb* 1 to provide food or meals for ⟨a charity dedicated to *feeding* the hungry⟩
syn board, cater, provision, victual
rel serve, wait; nourish, nurture, sustain; banquet, dine, feast, regale; mess; batten, fatten, fill; force-feed, overfeed, surfeit; underfeed; hand-feed, spoon-feed; refeed, reprovision

2 to put (something) into the possession of someone for use or consumption — see FURNISH 2

3 to take a meal — see DINE 1

feed (**on, upon,** *or* **off**) *vb* to seize and eat (something) as prey — see PREY (ON *or* UPON)

feel *n* an indefinite physical response to a stimulus — see SENSATION 1

feel *vb* 1 to have a vague awareness of ⟨I *feel* trouble brewing in the town.⟩
syn perceive, scent, see, sense, smell, taste
rel behold, descry, discern, distinguish, espy, eye, look (at), note, notice, observe, perceive, regard, remark, sight, spy, view, witness; ascertain, catch on (to), discover, find out, hear, learn, realize; anticipate, divine, expect, foreknow, foresee; assume, conjecture, guess, presume, speculate, suppose, surmise, suspect

2 to come into bodily contact with (something) so as to perceive a slight pressure on the skin — see TOUCH 1

3 to come to a knowledge of (something) by living through it — see EXPERIENCE

4 to have as an opinion — see BELIEVE 2

5 to search for something blindly or uncertainly — see GROPE

6 to give the impression of being — see SEEM

feel (**for**) *vb* to have sympathy for — see PITY

feeling *n* 1 a subjective response to a person, thing, or situation ⟨an overall *feeling* of happiness about their new home⟩
syn emotion, passion, sentiment
rel impression, perception, sensation, sense; angle, outlook, perspective, standpoint, viewpoint; belief, conviction, judgment (*or* judgement), mind, notion, opinion, persuasion, verdict, view; receptiveness, receptivity, responsiveness, sensibility, sensitiveness, sensitivity
near ant insensitiveness, insensitivity, unfeelingness

2 **feelings** *pl* general emotional condition ⟨a remark that thoughtlessly hurt her *feelings*⟩
syn heartstrings, passions, sensibilities
rel cheer, frame, humor, mode, mood, spirit, temper

3 an idea that is believed to be true or valid without positive knowledge — see OPINION 1

4 an indefinite physical response to a stimulus — see SENSATION 1

5 sorrow or the capacity to feel sorrow for another's suffering or misfortune — see SYMPATHY 1

6 the capacity for feeling for another's unhappiness or misfortune — see HEART 1

feign *vb* to present a false appearance of ⟨I would never *feign* illness just to get out of a test.⟩
syn act, affect, assume, bluff, counterfeit, dissemble, fake, pretend, profess, put on, sham, simulate
rel dissimulate, impersonate, let on, masquerade, play, playact, pose; forge, imitate; camouflage, conceal, disguise, mask; feint; malinger
phrases make believe

feigned *adj* 1 lacking in natural or spontaneous quality — see ARTIFICIAL 1

2 not being or expressing what one appears to be or express — see INSINCERE

felicitate *vb* to express to (someone) admiration for his or her success or good fortune — see CONGRATULATE

felicitations *n pl* best wishes — see COMPLIMENT 2

felicitous *adj* 1 giving pleasure or contentment to the mind or senses — see PLEASANT 1

2 meeting the requirements of a purpose or situation — see FIT 1

felicitously *adv* in a pleasing way — see WELL 5

felicitousness *n* the quality or state of being especially suitable or fitting — see APPROPRIATENESS

felicity *n* 1 a feeling or state of well-being and contentment — see HAPPINESS 1

2 something that provides happiness or does good for a person or thing — see BLESSING 1

3 the quality or state of being especially suitable or fitting — see APPROPRIATENESS

feline *n* a small domestic animal known for catching mice — see CAT

feline *adj* moving easily — see GRACEFUL 1

fell *adj* 1 likely to cause or capable of causing death — see DEADLY 1

2 violently unfriendly or aggressive in disposition — see FIERCE 1

fell *vb* 1 to strike (someone) so forcefully as to cause a fall ⟨a boxer who was often *felled* in the first round⟩
syn bowl (down *or* over), down, drop, floor, knock down, level, mow (down), prostrate
rel kayo, KO; overthrow, topple; bang, bash, belt, bludgeon, clobber, hammer, hit, jab, paste, poke, pound, punch, slam, slap, slog, slug, smack, smite, sock, swat, swipe, thump, thwack, wallop, whack, whale

2 to bring down by cutting ⟨The settlers began the daunting task of *felling* the mighty trees that blanketed the island.⟩
syn chop (down), cut (down), hew, mow
rel bulldoze, demolish, flatten, level, raze, tear down

3 to deprive of life — see KILL 1

fellow n 1 a male romantic companion — see BOYFRIEND

2 a person frequently seen in the company of another — see ASSOCIATE 1

3 an adult male human being — see MAN 1

4 either of a pair matched in one or more qualities — see MATE 1

5 one that is equal to another in status, achievement, or value — see EQUAL

fellowship n 1 a friendly relationship marked by ready communication and mutual understanding — see RAPPORT

2 a group of persons formally joined together for some common interest — see ASSOCIATION 2

3 kindly concern, interest, or support — see GOODWILL 1

4 the body of people in a profession or field of activity — see CORPS

5 the feeling of closeness and friendship that exists between companions — see COMPANIONSHIP

felonious adj contrary to or forbidden by law — see ILLEGAL 1

female adj of, relating to, or marked by qualities traditionally associated with women — see FEMININE

female n an adult female human being — see WOMAN 1

feminine adj of, relating to, or marked by qualities traditionally associated with women ⟨a designer adding *feminine* touches to the clothing collection⟩

syn female, womanish, womanlike, womanly

rel girlie (*or* girly), girlish; effeminate, effete, unmanly; ladylike

near ant boyish, hoydenish, tomboyish; male, manlike, manly, mannish, masculine, virile; neuter; hairy-chested, hypermasculine

ant unfeminine, unwomanly

fen n spongy land saturated or partially covered with water — see SWAMP

fence n a physical object that blocks the way — see BARRIER

fence vb to drive danger or attack away from — see DEFEND 1

fence (in) vb to close or shut in by or as if by barriers — see ENCLOSE 1

fend (off) vb to drive back — see REPEL 1

fender n something that serves as a protective barrier — see CUSHION

feral adj living outdoors without taming or domestication by humans — see WILD 1

ferment n a disturbed or uneasy state — see UNREST

ferment vb to bring (something volatile or intense) into being — see INCITE 1

ferocious adj 1 extreme in degree, power, or effect — see INTENSE 1

2 marked by bursts of destructive force or intense activity — see VIOLENT 1

3 violently unfriendly or aggressive in disposition — see FIERCE 1

4 marked by great and often stressful excitement or activity — see FURIOUS 1

ferret (out) vb to come upon after searching, study, or effort — see FIND 1

ferry vb 1 to support and take from one place to another — see CARRY 1

2 to travel on water in a vessel — see SAIL 1

fertile adj producing abundantly ⟨The *fertile* mind of Leonardo da Vinci explored art, architecture, engineering, mathematics, and many other fields.⟩

syn fat, fecund, fruitful, lush, luxuriant, productive, prolific, rich

rel bearing, generative, producing, yielding; abounding, abundant, bountiful; copious, generous, liberal, plenteous, plentiful, plenitudinous; blooming, bursting, flourishing, swarming, teeming, thriving; creative, inventive, original

near ant meager (*or* meagre), scant, scanty, skimp, skimpy, spare, sparse

ant barren, dead, infertile, sterile, unfruitful, unproductive

fervency n depth of feeling — see ARDOR 1

fervent adj 1 having or expressing great depth of feeling ⟨a *fervent* speech that called for tolerance and compassion for those who are different⟩

syn ardent, blazing, burning, charged, demonstrative, emotional, fervid, feverish, fiery, flaming, glowing, hot-blooded, impassioned, incandescent, intense, passionate, red-hot, religious, torrid, vehement, warm, warm-blooded

rel gushing, maudlin, mawkish, mushy, saccharine, sappy, schmaltzy, sentimental, sloppy, sugary; histrionic, melodramatic; enthusiastic, gung ho, keen, zealous; enamored, infatuated, obsessed; uninhibited, unreserved, unrestrained; frenzied, orgiastic; overemotional, overexcited, overheated

phrases on fire

near ant detached, dry, impersonal, objective; reserved, undemonstrative

ant cold, cool, dispassionate, impassive, unemotional

2 having a notably high temperature — see HOT 1

fervid adj 1 having or expressing great depth of feeling — see FERVENT 1

2 having a notably high temperature — see HOT 1

fervidness n depth of feeling — see ARDOR 1

fervor n depth of feeling — see ARDOR 1

fester vb to go through decomposition — see DECAY 1

festival n a time or program of special events and entertainment in honor of something ⟨Tourists flock to the town for its annual strawberry *festival*.⟩

syn carnival, celebration, festivity, fete (*or* fête), fiesta, gala, jubilee

rel jamboree, merriment, merrymaking, rejoicing, revel, revelry; exhibit, exhibition, exposition, fair, show

festive adj indicative of or marked by high spirits or good humor — see MERRY

festivity n 1 a mood characterized by high spirits and amusement and often accompanied by laughter — see MIRTH

2 a time or program of special events and entertainment in honor of something — see FESTIVAL

3 joyful or festive activity — see MERRYMAKING

fetch vb to have a price of — see COST

fetching adj 1 having an often mysterious or magical power to attract — see FASCINATING 1

---

syn synonym(s)   **rel** related words
ant antonym(s)   **near ant** near antonym(s)

2 very pleasing to look at — see BEAUTIFUL 1

fetch up vb to bring (something) to a standstill — see ¹HALT 1

fete or **fête** n **1** a social gathering — see PARTY 1

2 a time or program of special events and entertainment in honor of something — see FESTIVAL

fete or **fête** vb to show appreciation, respect, or affection for (someone) with a public celebration — see HONOR

fetid adj having an unpleasant smell — see MALODOROUS

fetish also **fetich** n **1** something about which one is constantly thinking or concerned — see FIXATION

2 something worn or kept to bring good luck or keep away evil — see CHARM 1

fetter n **1** something that limits one's freedom of action or choice — see RESTRICTION 1

2 something that makes movement or progress difficult — see ENCUMBRANCE

3 something that physically prevents free movement — see BOND 1

fetter vb **1** to confine or restrain with or as if with chains — see BIND 1

2 to create difficulty for the work or activity of — see HAMPER

fettle n a state of being or fitness — see CONDITION 1

fever n **1** an abnormal state that disrupts a plant's or animal's normal bodily functioning — see DISEASE

2 a state of wildly excited activity or emotion — see FRENZY

feverish adj **1** being in a state of increased activity or agitation ⟨scary stories that were the product of a *feverish* imagination⟩
syn agitated, excited, frenzied, heated, hectic, hyperactive, overactive, overwrought
rel hyperexcited, overexcited; afire, aflutter, atingle; anxious, dithery, edgy, het up, high-strung, hyped-up, jittery, jumpy, nervous, nervy, perturbed, tense, troubled, uneasy, unquiet, upset, uptight, wired
phrases in a lather, keyed up
near ant calm, collected, composed, cool, coolheaded, placid, serene, tranquil, undisturbed, unperturbed, unshaken, untroubled, unworried

2 having or expressing great depth of feeling — see FERVENT 1

3 marked by great and often stressful excitement or activity — see FURIOUS 1

few n a small number ⟨A *few* of the songs on the album are good, but most are forgettable.⟩
syn couple, handful, scatter, scattering, smattering, sprinkle, sprinkling
rel fragment, iota, jot, modicum, particle, scrap, shred, tittle, whit
near ant majority, most; abundance, excess, plenty, surplus; deal, gobs, heap, lot, mass, much, peck, pile, plenitude, plenty, pot, profusion, quantity, raft, reams, slather, stack, wad, wealth
ant army, crowd, flock, horde, host, legion, loads, many, mountain, multitude, oodles, scads

fiancé n the person to whom one is engaged to be married — see BETROTHED

fiancée n the person to whom one is engaged to be married — see BETROTHED

fiasco n something that has failed — see FAILURE 3

fiat n an order publicly issued by an authority — see EDICT 1

fib n a statement known by its maker to be untrue and made in order to deceive — see LIE

fib vb to make a statement one knows to be untrue — see ¹LIE

fibber n a person who tells lies — see LIAR

fiber n **1** the strength of mind that enables a person to endure pain or hardship — see FORTITUDE

2 a thin, flexible structure that resembles a hair — see HAIR 2

fibrous adj resembling or having the texture of a mass of strings — see STRINGY

fickle adj **1** likely to change frequently, suddenly, or unexpectedly ⟨a *fickle* friendship that was on and off over the years⟩
syn capricious, changeable, changeful, flickery, fluctuating, fluid, inconsistent, inconstant, mercurial, mutable, skittish, temperamental, uncertain, unpredictable, unsettled, unstable, unsteady, variable, volatile
rel aimless, arbitrary, desultory, erratic, haphazard, hit-or-miss, irregular, random, scattered, slapdash, stray; hesitating, shaky, shilly-shally, shilly-shallying, vacillating, wavering; dicey, undependable, unreliable, untrustworthy; adaptable, mobile, protean, versatile
phrases up in the air
near ant equable, even, uniform; abiding, durable, lasting, permanent, persistent; dependable, reliable, sure, tried, tried-and-true, true, trustworthy, trusty
ant certain, changeless, constant, immutable, invariable, predictable, settled, stable, stationary, steady, unchangeable, unchanging, unvarying

2 not true in one's allegiance to someone or something — see FAITHLESS

fiction n something that is the product of the imagination ⟨Most stories about famous outlaws of the Old West are *fictions* that have little or nothing to do with fact.⟩
syn fable, fabrication, fantasy (also phantasy), figment, invention
rel anecdote, narrative, novel, story, tale, yarn; fairy tale, falsehood, falsity, fib, lie, mendacity, misrepresentation, prevarication, untruth, whopper; make-believe
near ant actuality, realness
ant fact, materiality, reality

fictional adj not real and existing only in the imagination — see IMAGINARY

fictitious adj not real and existing only in the imagination — see IMAGINARY

fiddle vb **1** to make jerky or restless movements — see FIDGET

2 to rob by the use of trickery or threats — see FLEECE

fiddle (around) vb to spend time in aimless activity ⟨We spent the snow day just *fiddling around*.⟩
syn goof (around), monkey (around), play, potter (around), putter (around), trifle
rel dally, dawdle, dillydally, idle, loaf, loll,

lounge; clown (around), horse around; diddle (with), tinker

near ant buckle (down), knuckle down, set (to), settle (down)

fiddle (with) *vb* to handle thoughtlessly, ignorantly, or mischievously — see TAMPER (WITH)

fidelity *n* adherence to something to which one is bound by a pledge or duty ⟨They have never wavered in their *fidelity* to the cause of freedom.⟩

syn adhesion, allegiance, attachment, commitment, constancy, dedication, devotedness, devotion, faith, faithfulness, fastness, fealty, loyalty, piety, steadfastness, troth

rel affection, fondness; determination, firmness, resolution; dependability, reliability, trustiness, trustworthiness

near ant alienation, disaffection, estrangement, separation

ant disloyalty, faithlessness, falseness, falsity, inconstancy, infidelity, perfidiousness, perfidy, treachery, unfaithfulness

fidget *vb* to make jerky or restless movements ⟨Small children are likely to *fidget* in church.⟩

syn fiddle, jerk, jig, jiggle, squirm, thrash, toss, twist, twitch, wiggle, wriggle, writhe

rel flit, flutter, twitter; quake, quiver, shake, shiver, shudder, tremble; pace

near ant relax, rest, unwind; calm (down), still

fidgets *n pl* a state of nervousness marked by sudden jerky movements — see JUMPINESS

fie *interj* how surprising, doubtful, or unbelievable — see NO

field *n* **1** a small area of usually open land ⟨a *field* that is the frequent site of neighborhood softball games⟩

syn clearing, ground, lot, parcel, plat, plot, tract

rel common(s); grass, green, greensward, lawn; glade, grassland, heathland, lea (*or* ley), meadow, moor, pasture, pastureland

2 a region of activity, knowledge, or influence ⟨the first woman to enter the *field* of medicine⟩

syn area, arena, business, circle, department, discipline, domain, element, firmament, front, game, line, province, realm, specialty, sphere, walk

rel frontier; study, subject; territory, turf; occupation, profession, pursuit, racket, vocation; ambit, amplitude, breadth, compass, confine, dimension(s), extent, ken, reach, scope, sweep, width; subfield, subspecialty

3 a part or portion having no fixed boundaries — see REGION 1

4 a place from which aircraft operate that usually has paved runways and a terminal — see AIRPORT

5 a wide space or area — see EXPANSE

6 active fighting during the course of a war — see COMBAT 1

field *vb* to deal with (something) usually skillfully or efficiently — see HANDLE 1

fiend *n* **1** a mean, evil, or unprincipled person — see VILLAIN

2 a person with a strong and habitual liking for something — see FAN

3 an evil spirit — see DEMON 1

4 the supreme personification of evil often represented as the ruler of hell — see DEVIL 1

5 a person with a high level of knowledge or skill in a field — see EXPERT

fiendish *adj* **1** of, relating to, or worthy of an evil spirit ⟨a *fiendish* delight in playing cruel tricks⟩

syn demoniac (*also* demoniacal), demonic (*also* demonical), devilish, diabolical (*or* diabolic), satanic

rel hellish; baleful, evil, sinister; malevolent, malicious, malignant; heinous, monstrous; immoral, iniquitous, nefarious, vicious, vile, villainous, wicked; barbarous, cruel, ferocious, inhuman, savage

near ant celestial, heavenly; beneficent, benevolent, benign, benignant; godly, holy, sainted, saintly; ethical, good, moral, righteous, virtuous

ant angelic (*or* angelical)

2 having or showing the desire to inflict severe pain and suffering on others — see CRUEL 1

fierce *adj* **1** violently unfriendly or aggressive in disposition ⟨The Vikings had a well-earned reputation for being *fierce* warriors.⟩

syn fell, ferocious, grim, savage, vicious

rel argumentative, bellicose, belligerent, combative, discordant, disputatious, gladiatorial, militant, pugnacious, scrappy, warlike; bare-knuckle (*or* bare-knuckled *or* bare-knuckles), in-your-face, take-no-prisoners; menacing, threatening; brute, inhuman, inhumane; barbaric, uncivilized, wild; heartless, implacable, merciless, pitiless, relentless, ruthless, unrelenting, wanton; bloodthirsty, bloody, homicidal, murdering, murderous, sanguinary, sanguine; rapacious, ravenous, voracious

near ant amicable, companionable, comradely, congenial, cordial, friendly, genial, hearty, warm, warmhearted; compliant, submissive, tame; benign, compassionate, kind, merciful; pacific, peaceable, peaceful; amiable, complaisant, obliging; human, humane; civilized, cultured

ant gentle, mild, unaggressive

2 extreme in degree, power, or effect — see INTENSE 1

3 harsh and threatening in manner or appearance — see GRIM 1

4 having or showing a bold forcefulness in the pursuit of a goal — see AGGRESSIVE 1

5 marked by bursts of destructive force or intense activity — see VIOLENT 1

6 marked by great and often stressful excitement or activity — see FURIOUS 1

fierceness *n* the quality or state of being forceful (as in expression) — see VEHEMENCE 1

fiery *adj* **1** being on fire — see ABLAZE 1

2 having a notably high temperature — see HOT 1

3 having or expressing great depth of feeling — see FERVENT 1

4 marked by a lively display of strong feeling — see SPIRITED 1

---

syn synonym(s) *rel* related words
ant antonym(s) *near ant* near antonym(s)

5 capable of catching or being set on fire — see COMBUSTIBLE

6 easily irritated or annoyed — see IRRITABLE

fiesta *n* a time or program of special events and entertainment in honor of something — see FESTIVAL

fight *n* **1** a physical dispute between opposing individuals or groups ⟨When he was young he got into one *fight* after another.⟩

syn battle, clash, combat, conflict, contest, fracas, fray, hassle, scrap, scrimmage, scuffle, skirmish, struggle, tussle

rel pitched battle; brawl, free-for-all, melee (*also* mêlée), mix-up, ruckus, ruction; blows, fistfight, fisticuffs, slugfest; confrontation, duel, face-off, joust; altercation, argument, contretemps, controversy, cross fire, disagreement, dispute, falling-out, kickup, misunderstanding, quarrel, row, spat, squabble, tangle, tiff, wrangle; catfight

near ant truce

2 a forceful effort to reach a goal or objective — see STRUGGLE 1

3 an inclination to fight or quarrel — see BELLIGERENCE

4 an often noisy or angry expression of differing opinions — see ARGUMENT 1

fight *vb* **1** to oppose (someone) in physical conflict ⟨a proud people who have fiercely *fought* all invaders of their homeland⟩

syn battle, clash (with), combat, scrimmage (with), skirmish (with), war (against)

rel duel, joust; bang, bash, bat, batter, beat, belt, bludgeon, bop, buffet, clobber, hammer, hit, knock, paste, pound, punch, slam, slap, slog, slug, smack, smite, sock, strike, swat, swipe, thump, thwack, wallop, whack, whale; box, spar; brawl; grapple, scuffle, tussle, wrestle; bump, collide

near ant give up, submit, surrender

2 to strive to reduce or eliminate ⟨a civil rights leader who · dedicated his life to *fighting* prejudice⟩

syn battle, combat, contend (with), counter, oppose

rel baffle, checkmate, foil, frustrate, resist, thwart, withstand; confront, defy, face, meet

near ant abide, bear, endure, suffer; advocate, back, champion, endorse (*also* indorse), support, uphold

ant advance, cultivate, encourage, forward, foster, further, nourish, nurture, promote

3 to engage in a contest — see COMPETE

4 to express different opinions about something often angrily — see ARGUE 2

5 to refuse to give in to — see RESIST

fighter *n* **1** a person engaged in military service — see SOLDIER

2 one that engages in the sport of fighting with the fists — see BOXER

3 a person who takes part in a dispute — see DISPUTANT

figment *n* **1** a conception or image created by the imagination and having no objective reality — see FANTASY 1

2 something that is the product of the imagination — see FICTION

figurative *adj* expressing one thing in terms normally used for another ⟨the *figu-*

rative use of "allergy" to mean "a feeling of dislike"⟩

syn extended, metaphoric (*or* metaphorical)

rel allegorical, emblematic (*also* emblematical), symbolic (*also* symbolical)

near ant literal; nonsymbolic

ant nonfigurative, nonmetaphorical

figure *n* **1** a character used to represent a mathematical value — see NUMBER 1

2 a line that traces the outer limits of an object or surface — see OUTLINE 1

3 a person who is widely known and usually much talked about — see CELEBRITY 1

4 a small statue — see FIGURINE

5 a three-dimensional representation of the human body used especially for displaying clothes — see MANNEQUIN 1

6 a unit of decoration that is repeated all over something (as a fabric) — see PATTERN 1

7 something that visually explains or decorates a text — see ILLUSTRATION 1

8 the amount of money that is demanded as payment for something — see PRICE 1

9 the outward appearance of something as distinguished from its substance — see FORM 1

10 the type of body that a person has — see PHYSIQUE

11 figures *pl* the act or process of performing mathematical operations to find a value — see CALCULATION

12 the outward form of someone or something especially as indicative of a quality — see APPEARANCE 1

figure *vb* **1** to come to a judgment about after discussion or consideration — see DECIDE 1

2 to decide the size, amount, number, or distance of (something) without actual measurement — see ESTIMATE 2

3 to determine (a value) by doing the necessary mathematical operations — see CALCULATE 1

4 to have as an opinion — see BELIEVE 2

figure out *vb* to find an answer for through reasoning — see SOLVE

figurine *n* a small statue ⟨His collection of *figurines* includes toy soldiers from every war that America has fought.⟩

syn figure, statuette

rel doll, dolly, hand puppet, marionette, puppet; bust, figurehead; carving, model, sculpture; dummy, form, manikin (*also* mannikin), mannequin

ant colossus

figuring *n* the act or process of performing mathematical operations to find a value — see CALCULATION

filch *vb* to take (something) without right and with an intent to keep — see STEAL 1

file *n* a series of persons or things arranged one behind another — see LINE 1

¹**file** *vb* to make smooth by friction — see GRIND 1

²**file** *vb* to move along with a steady regular step especially in a group — see MARCH 1

fill *n* soft material that is used to fill the hollow parts of something — see FILLING

fill *vb* **1** to put into (something) as much as can be held or contained ⟨*Fill* the basket with apples.⟩

syn brim, charge, cram, heap, jam, jam-pack, load, pack, stuff

rel drench, flood, glut, swamp; bloat, bulk; crowd, crush, mat, press, ram, shove, squash, squeeze; refill, refresh, reload, repack, replenish; overcharge, overfill, overflow, saturate; honeycomb, penetrate

near ant lighten; deplete, drain, eliminate, exhaust; bleed, draw (off); clean, flush, purge, scour, sweep

ant clear, empty, evacuate, vacate, void

2 to close up so that no empty spaces remain ⟨Before starting to paint, *fill* all the cracks with putty.⟩

syn block, bung, dam, pack, plug, stop, stuff

rel choke, clog, close (off), clot, congest, jam, obstruct, occlude; caulk, chink, seal; repack, restuff

near ant excavate, hollow (out), scoop (out), shovel

3 to do what is required by the terms of — see FULFILL 1

filled *adj* containing or seeming to contain the greatest quantity or number possible — see FULL 1

filler *n* soft material that is used to fill the hollow parts of something — see FILLING

fill in *vb* **1** to give information to — see ENLIGHTEN 1

2 to serve as a replacement usually for a time only — see COVER 1

filling *n* soft material that is used to fill the hollow parts of something ⟨The *filling* for the parka is goose down.⟩

syn fill, filler, padding, stuffing

rel packing; interlining, lining, quilting; buffer, bumper, cushion, fender, pad

film *n* **1** a story told by means of a series of continuously projected pictures and a sound track — see MOVIE 1

2 the art or business of making a movie — see MOVIE 2

filmy *adj* **1** being of a material lacking in sturdiness or substance — see FLIMSY 1

2 very thin and easy to see through — see SHEER 1

filter *vb* **1** to pass through a filter — see STRAIN 2

2 to remove usually visible impurities from — see CLARIFY 1

filth *n* **1** foul matter that mars the purity or cleanliness of something ⟨The *filth* in the restaurant's kitchen was unbelievable.⟩

syn dirt, grime, muck, smut, soil

rel scum, sewage, sewerage, slime, sludge, swill; dross, garbage, junk, litter, refuse, rubbish, scrap, trash, waste

near ant cleanliness, cleanness

2 the quality or state of being obscene — see OBSCENITY

filthiness *n* **1** the quality or state of being obscene — see OBSCENITY

2 the state or quality of being dirty — see DIRTINESS

filthy *adj* **1** depicting or referring to sexual matters in a way that is unacceptable in polite society — see OBSCENE 1

2 not clean — see DIRTY 1

filthy *adv* to a great degree — see VERY 1

finagle *vb* **1** to plan out usually with subtle skill or care — see ENGINEER

2 to use dishonest methods to achieve a goal — see CHEAT 1

final *adj* **1** following all others of the same kind in order or time — see LAST 1

2 having been established and usually not subject to change — see FIXED 1

finale *n* the last part of a process or action ⟨The *finale* to the festivities was a grand display of fireworks.⟩

syn close, closing, conclusion, consummation, end, ending, finis, finish, windup, wrap-up

rel acme, apex, climax, copestone, crown, culmination, high-water mark, meridian, peak, pinnacle, summit, tip-top, top, zenith; aftermath, anticlimax, coda, epilogue (*also* epilog), postscript; shank, tag end

near ant foreword, introduction, preamble, preface, prelude, prologue (*also* prolog)

ant beginning, dawn, opening, start

finalize *vb* **1** to bring (something) to a state where nothing remains to be done — see FINISH 1

2 to give official acceptance of as satisfactory — see APPROVE

finally *adv* at a later time — see YET 1

finance *vb* **1** to provide money for ⟨A local business kindly *financed* the high school band's trip to New York City.⟩

syn bankroll, capitalize, endow, fund, stake, subsidize, underwrite

rel grubstake; cofinance, refinance; advocate, aid, back, champion, endorse (*also* indorse), patronize, sponsor, support; maintain, nourish, provide (for); clear, defray, discharge, foot, liquidate, pay, pay off, pay up, quit, recompense, settle, spring (for), stand

ant defund

2 to furnish (as an institution) with a regular source of income — see ENDOW 2

finances *n pl* available money — see FUND 2

financial *adj* of or relating to money, banking, or investments ⟨The *financial* world was watching the stock market closely.⟩

syn fiscal, monetary, pecuniary, pocket

rel commercial

ant nonfinancial

find *n* something discovered — see DISCOVERY 2

find *vb* **1** to come upon after searching, study, or effort ⟨We finally *found* the information after searching dozens of Internet sites.⟩

syn ascertain, descry, detect, determine, discover, dredge (up), ferret (out), find out, get, hit (on *or* upon), hunt (down *or* up), learn, locate, root (out), rummage, run down, scare up, scout (up), track (down), turn up

rel espy, sight, spot; look for, search (for *or* out), seek

near ant lose, mislay, misplace, misset

ant miss, overlook, pass over

2 to come upon unexpectedly or by chance — see HAPPEN (ON *or* UPON)

finding *n* **1** a decision made by a court or tribunal regarding a case it has heard — see SENTENCE

---

syn synonym(s) *rel* related words

ant antonym(s) *near ant* near antonym(s)

2 the act or process of sighting or learning the existence of something for the first time — see DISCOVERY 1

find out *vb* **1** to come to an awareness of — see DISCOVER 1

2 to come upon after searching, study, or effort — see FIND 1

fine *adv* in a satisfactory way — see WELL 1

fine *adj* **1** consisting of very small particles ⟨the *fine* sand found on the island's beaches⟩

syn dusty, floury, powdery

rel smooth; filtered, pulverized, refined; superfine; ultrafine

near ant rough; unfiltered, unrefined; gravelly, gritty, sandy; pebbly, rocky, stony (*also* stoney); lumpy, mealy

ant coarse, grainy, granular, granulated

2 made or done with extreme care and accuracy ⟨the *fine* distinction between bravery and recklessness⟩

syn delicate, exact, hairline, hairsplitting, minute, nice, refined, subtle

rel nitpicking, quibbling; frivolous, inconsequential, inconsiderable, insignificant, negligible, petty, piddling, trifling, trivial; demanding, exacting, fastidious, finicky, fussy, meticulous, particular, picky

near ant apparent, clear, clear-cut, evident, manifest, obvious, open-and-shut, palpable, patent, perspicuous, plain, transparent, unambiguous, unequivocal, unmistakable; broad, indefinite; careless, heedless, incautious, slapdash, slipshod, sloppy

ant coarse, inexact, rough

3 being of less than usual width — see NARROW 1

4 being to one's liking — see SATISFACTORY 1

5 free from added matter — see PURE 1

6 meeting the highest standard of accuracy — see PRECISE 1

7 of a level of quality that meets one's needs or standards — see ADEQUATE 1

8 of a size that is less than average — see SMALL 1

9 of the very best kind — see EXCELLENT

10 having qualities that appeal to a refined taste — see CHOICE 1

11 able to sense slight impressions or differences — see ACUTE 1

12 having or showing elegance — see ELEGANT 1

fine *n* a sum of money to be paid as a punishment ⟨a $50 *fine* for speeding⟩

syn damages, forfeit, forfeiture, mulct, penalty

rel reparations; assessment, award, compensation; indemnity

¹**fine** *vb* to establish or apply as a charge or penalty — see IMPOSE

²**fine** *vb* to remove usually visible impurities from — see CLARIFY 1

fineness *n* **1** the quality or state of being little in size — see SMALLNESS

2 the quality or state of being very accurate — see PRECISION

3 the state or quality of having a delicate structure — see DELICACY 2

4 dignified or restrained beauty of form, appearance, or style — see ELEGANCE

finery *n* dressy clothing ⟨The guests arrived at the wedding in all their *finery*.⟩

syn array, best, bravery, caparison, feather, frippery, full dress, gaiety (*also* gayety), regalia

rel apparel, attire, costume, duds, habiliment(s), rags, raiment, rig, threads, togs, wear

phrases best bib and tucker

near ant tatters

finesse *n* mental skill or quickness — see DEXTERITY 1

finesse *vb* **1** to plan out usually with subtle skill or care — see ENGINEER

2 to get or keep away from (as a responsibility) through cleverness or trickery — see ESCAPE 2

finicky *adj* hard to please ⟨Cats have a reputation for being *finicky* eaters.⟩

syn choosy (*or* choosey), dainty, delicate, demanding, exacting, fastidious, fussy, nice, particular, picky

rel discerning, discriminating, selective; insightful, knowledgeable; captious, carping, caviling (*or* cavilling), critical, faultfinding, hypercritical, overcritical; careful, meticulous, painstaking, punctilious, scrupulous; queasy (*also* queazy), squeamish; peevish, petulant, prickly, touchy; prim, prissy

near ant affable, breezy, carefree, devilmay-care, happy-go-lucky, lackadaisical, laid-back, low-pressure, relaxed; flexible, lax, loose; lenient, permissive; uncritical; indiscriminating, undiscriminating

ant undemanding, unfastidious, unfussy

finis *n* the last part of a process or action — see FINALE

finish *n* **1** the last part of a process or action — see FINALE

2 the stopping of a process or activity — see END 1

finish *vb* **1** to bring (something) to a state where nothing remains to be done ⟨We should *finish* the painting of the house by tomorrow.⟩

syn complete, consummate, finalize, perfect, polish

rel stick out; accomplish, achieve, effect; carry out, carry through, discharge, do, execute, fulfill (*or* fulfil), perform; ameliorate, amend, better, enhance, enrich, improve, meliorate; machine, refine, round (off *or* out), shine, touch up

near ant abandon, desert, discontinue, drop, forsake, quit

2 to bring (an event) to a natural or appropriate stopping point — see CLOSE 3

3 to come to an end — see CEASE 1

finished *adj* brought or having come to an end — see COMPLETE 2

finite *adj* **1** having a limit ⟨Our nation's natural resources are abundant, but they are also *finite*.⟩

syn limited

rel circumscribed, restricted; definable, defined, definite, determinate, discrete; decided, established, fixed, set; exact, precise, specific; measurable, mensurable, numerable

near ant unconfined, unrestricted; immeasurable, indefinite, indeterminate, measureless, undefinable, undefined, unfathomable

ant boundless, endless, illimitable, infinite, limitless, unbounded, unlimited

2 having distinct or certain limits — see LIMITED 1

fire *n* 1 a destructive burning ⟨a number of suspicious *fires* in the neighborhood recently⟩
syn conflagration, holocaust, inferno
rel blaze, flare-up; backfire, bonfire, brush fire, campfire, forest fire, wildfire; arson
2 depth of feeling — see ARDOR 1
3 a test of faith, patience, or strength — see TRIAL 1

fire *vb* 1 to cause (a projectile) to be driven forward with force — see SHOOT 1
2 to cause a weapon to release a missile with great force — see SHOOT 2
3 to give life, vigor, or spirit to — see ANIMATE
4 to let go from office, service, or employment — see DISMISS 1
5 to send through the air especially with a quick forward motion of the arm — see THROW 1
6 to set (something) on fire — see BURN 2

fire (up) *vb* to rouse to strong feeling or action — see PROVOKE 1

firearm *n* a portable weapon from which a shot is discharged by gunpowder — see GUN 1

firebrand *n* a person who stirs up public feelings especially of discontent — see AGITATOR

firebug *n* a person who deliberately and unlawfully sets fire to a building or other property — see ARSONIST

fireproof *adj* incapable of being burned — see INCOMBUSTIBLE

fireside *n* the place where one lives — see HOME 1

fireworks *n pl* an outburst or display of excited anger — see TANTRUM

firing *n* a directed propelling of a missile by a firearm or artillery piece — see SHOT 1

firm *n* a commercial or industrial activity or organization — see ENTERPRISE 1

firm *adj* 1 not showing weakness or uncertainty ⟨a friendly fellow with a ready smile and a *firm* handshake⟩
syn forceful, hearty, iron, lusty, robust, solid, stout, strong, sturdy, vigorous
rel hard, ironclad, mighty, powerful, tough, unyielding; animated, brisk, energetic, frisky, jaunty, jazzy, lively, peppy, perky, spirited, sprightful, sprightly, springy, vital, vivacious, zippy; assured, certain, confident, sanguine, secure, sure
near ant feeble, fragile, frail; limp, listless, spiritless; diffident, insecure, self-doubting; characterless, effete, frail, spineless, weakened, wimpy, wishy-washy
ant uncertain, weak
2 having a consistency that does not easily yield to pressure ⟨cold butter that was too *firm* to spread⟩
syn compact, hard, rigid, solid, stiff, unyielding
rel compacted, compressed, hardened, indurated, stiffened, tempered; close, dense, heavy, thick, thickset; inelastic, inflexible, ramrod, unbending; compressed, condensed; adamantine, rocklike; sturdy, sub-

stantial; impenetrable, impermeable, nonporous
near ant loose, scattered, thin; bendable, elastic, flexible, malleable, pliable, pliant, supple; droopy, flaccid, floppy, lank, limp, slack; airy, light; permeable, porous; ultrasoft
ant flabby, soft, spongy, squashy, squishy
3 firmly positioned in place and difficult to dislodge — see TIGHT 2
4 fully committed to achieving a goal — see DETERMINED 1
5 having been established and usually not subject to change — see FIXED 1
6 marked by the ability to withstand stress without structural damage or distortion — see STABLE 1
7 based on sound reasoning or information — see GOOD 1

firm (up) *vb* to become physically firm or solid — see HARDEN 1

firmament *n* 1 the expanse of air surrounding the earth — see SKY 1
2 a region of activity, knowledge, or influence — see FIELD 2

firmly *adv* in a vigorous and forceful manner — see HARD 3

firmness *n* 1 firm or unwavering adherence to one's purpose — see DETERMINATION 1
2 the ability to withstand force or stress without being distorted, dislodged, or damaged — see STABILITY 1

first *adv* 1 as a substitute — see INSTEAD
2 by choice or preference — see RATHER 1

first *adj* 1 coming before all others in time or order ⟨the much-studied *first*—and last—voyage of the *Titanic*⟩
syn earliest, foremost, inaugural, initial, leadoff, maiden, original, pioneer, premier, virgin
rel ancient, early, primal, primary, prime, primeval, primitive, primordial; antecedent, preceding, previous
near ant advanced, late; consequent, ensuing, following, subsequent, succeeding, penultimate
ant final, last, latest, latter, terminal, terminating, ultimate
2 coming before all others in importance — see FOREMOST 1
3 highest in rank or authority — see HEAD

first–class *adj* of the very best kind — see EXCELLENT

firsthand *adj* done or working without something else coming in between — see DIRECT 1

firstly *adv* in the beginning — see ORIGINALLY

first–rate *adj* of the very best kind — see EXCELLENT

firth *n* a part of a body of water that extends beyond the general shoreline — see GULF 1

fiscal *adj* of or relating to money, banking, or investments — see FINANCIAL

fish *vb* to search for something blindly or uncertainly — see GROPE

fish *n* a member of the human race — see HUMAN

fishy *adj* giving good reason for being doubted, questioned, or challenged — see DOUBTFUL 2

fissure *n* an irregular usually narrow break in a surface created by pressure — see CRACK 1

fit *adj* 1 meeting the requirements of a purpose or situation ⟨clothing that is *fit* for horseback riding⟩

syn applicable, appropriate, apt, becoming, befitting, felicitous, fitted, fitting, good, happy, meet, pretty, proper, right, suitable

rel deserved, just, justified; needed, required, requisite; able, capable, competent, cut out, qualified, trained; pitch-perfect; acceptable, adequate, decent, kosher, satisfactory, serviceable, tolerable; correct, decorous, respectable, seemly; balanced, companionate, congruous, consonant, harmonious; rightful

phrases in order

near ant incapable, incompetent, inept, inexpert, unqualified, unskilled, unskillful, untrained; inadequate, intolerable, unacceptable, unsatisfactory; graceless, incorrect, indecorous; incompatible, uncongenial

ant improper, inapplicable, inappropriate, inapt, incongruous, indecent, infelicitous, misbecoming, unapt, unbecoming, unfit, unfitting, unhappy, unseemly, unsuitable, wrong

2 being in a state of fitness for some experience or action — see READY 1

3 capable of or suitable for being used for a particular purpose — see USABLE 1

4 enjoying health and vigor — see HEALTHY 1

5 having the required skills for an acceptable level of performance — see COMPETENT 1

fit *n* 1 a sudden experiencing of a physical or mental disorder — see ATTACK 2

2 a sudden intense expression of strong feeling — see OUTBURST 1

3 an outburst or display of excited anger — see TANTRUM

fit *vb* 1 to be in agreement on every point — see CHECK 1

2 to change (something) so as to make it suitable for a new use or situation — see ADAPT

3 to make competent (as by training, skill, or ability) for a particular office or function — see QUALIFY 2

4 to make or have room for — see ACCOMMODATE 1

5 to make ready in advance — see PREPARE 1

fit (in or **into)** *vb* to put among or between others — see INSERT

fit (out) *vb* to provide (someone) with what is needed for a task or activity — see FURNISH 1

fitful *adj* lacking in steadiness or regularity of occurrence ⟨A night of *fitful* sleep did not leave me feeling well rested the next morning.⟩

syn casual, catchy, choppy, discontinuous, episodic (*also* episodical), erratic, intermittent, irregular, occasional, spasmodic, sporadic, spotty, unsteady

rel convulsive, sudden, violent; broken, disconnected, fragmentary, interrupted; aimless, arbitrary, desultory, haphazard, hit-and-miss, hit-or-miss, odd, random,

scattered, slapdash, stray; capricious, changeful, changing, flickery, fluctuating, fluid, inconstant, mercurial, mutable, temperamental, uncertain, unpredictable, unsettled, unstable, varying, wavering; changeable, fickle, variable, volatile

near ant changeless, equable, even, stable, stationary, uniform; unchanging, unvarying, unwavering; methodical (*also* methodic), orderly, systematic; unrelenting, unremitting

ant constant, continuous, habitual, periodic, regular, repeated, steady

fitness *n* 1 the condition of being sound in body — see HEALTH 1

2 the quality or state of being especially suitable or fitting — see APPROPRIATENESS

fitted *adj* meeting the requirements of a purpose or situation — see FIT 1

fitting *adj* meeting the requirements of a purpose or situation — see FIT 1

fittingly *adv* in a manner suitable for the occasion or purpose — see PROPERLY

fittingness *n* the quality or state of being especially suitable or fitting — see APPROPRIATENESS

fix *n* 1 a difficult, puzzling, or embarrassing situation from which there is no easy escape — see PREDICAMENT

2 something given or promised in order to improperly influence a person's conduct or decision — see BRIBE

3 an opinion on the nature, character, or quality of something — see ESTIMATION 1

fix *vb* 1 to arrange something in a certain spot or position — see PLACE 1

2 to cause (something) to hold to another — see FASTEN 1

3 to come to an agreement or decision concerning the details of — see ARRANGE 1

4 to decide upon (the time or date for an event) usually from a position of authority — see APPOINT 1

5 to make ready in advance — see PREPARE 1

6 to put into good shape or working order again — see MEND 1

7 to put securely in place or in a desired position — see FASTEN 2

8 to set solidly in or as if in surrounding matter — see ENTRENCH

9 to remove the sex organs of — see NEUTER

10 to restore to a healthy condition — see HEAL 1

fixable *adj* capable of being corrected — see REMEDIABLE

fixation *n* something about which one is constantly thinking or concerned ⟨The band is my latest music *fixation*.⟩

syn fetish (*also* fetich), mania, obsession, preoccupation, prepossession

rel monomania; complex, problem, trip; appetite, compulsion, craving, desire, drive, enthusiasm, fascination, hankering, hunger, infatuation, itch, longing, lust, passion, pining, thirst, urge, yearning, yen; idiosyncrasy, quirk; bent, disposition, inclination, leaning, partiality, penchant, predilection, predisposition, proclivity, propensity, tendency *near ant* apathy, disinterestedness, disregard, indifference, insouciance, nonchalance, unconcern, unconcernedness

fixed *adj* 1 having been established and usually not subject to change ⟨The baseball card dealer's prices were *fixed*, so bargaining was not an option.⟩

syn certain, determinate, final, firm, flat, frozen, hard, hard-and-fast, set, settled, stable

rel nonadjustable, noncancelable, nonnegotiable, unchangeable; constant, steady, unchanging, uniform, unwavering; definite, exact, explicit, specific; given, stated, stipulated; dependable, good, reliable, responsible, safe, solid, sure, tried, tried-and-true, true, trustworthy, trusty

near ant adjustable, changeable, negotiable; indefinite, open-ended, unspecified; capricious, changeful, flickery, fluctuating, fluid, inconstant, mercurial, mutable, temperamental, uncertain, unpredictable, unsettled, unstable, unsteady, variable, volatile

2 not capable of changing or being changed — see INFLEXIBLE 1

fixedness *n* the state of continuing without change — see CONSTANCY 1

fizz *n* a sound similar to the speech sound \s\ stretched out — see HISS 1

fizz *vb* to make a sound like that of stretching out the speech sound \s\ — see HISS

fizzle *n* 1 a falling short of one's goals — see FAILURE 2

2 something that has failed — see FAILURE 3

fizzle *vb* to make a sound like that of stretching out the speech sound \s\ — see HISS

fjord *also* **fiord** *n* a part of a body of water that extends beyond the general shoreline — see GULF 1

flabbergast *vb* to make a strong impression on (someone) with something unexpected — see SURPRISE 1

flabbergasted *adj* 1 affected with sudden and great wonder or surprise — see THUNDERSTRUCK

2 filled with amazement or wonder — see OPENMOUTHED

flabbergasting *adj* causing a strong emotional reaction because of unexpectedness — see SURPRISING 1

flabby *adj* giving easily to the touch — see SOFT 3

flaccid *adj* not stiff in structure — see LIMP 1

¹**flag** *vb* 1 to be limp from lack of water or vigor — see DROOP 1

2 to lose bodily strength or vigor — see WEAKEN 1

²**flag** *vb* to direct or notify by a movement or gesture — see MOTION

flag *n* 1 a piece of cloth with a special design that is used as an emblem or for signaling ⟨The *flags* of both countries were prominently displayed at the treaty signing.⟩

syn banner, colors, ensign, guidon, jack, pennant, pennon, standard, streamer

rel bunting, gonfalon; black flag, Jolly Roger, tricolor, union jack, white flag; burgee, semaphore, signaler (*or* signaller)

2 an object intended to give public notice or warning — see SIGNAL 1

flagellate *vb* to strike repeatedly with something long and thin or flexible — see WHIP 1

flagon *n* a handled container for holding and pouring liquids that usually has a lip or a spout — see PITCHER

flagrant *adj* very noticeable especially for being incorrect or bad — see EGREGIOUS

flail *vb* 1 to move or cause to move with a striking motion — see FLAP

2 to strike repeatedly with something long and thin or flexible — see WHIP 1

flair *n* a special and usually inborn ability — see TALENT

¹**flake** *n* a small flat piece separated from a whole — see CHIP 1

²**flake** *n* a person of odd or whimsical habits — see ECCENTRIC

flaky *also* **flakey** *adj* having a texture that readily breaks into little pieces under pressure — see CRISP 1

flamboyance *n* excessive or unnecessary display — see OSTENTATION

flamboyant *adj* 1 likely to attract attention — see NOTICEABLE

2 excessively showy — see GAUDY

flame *n* a person with whom one is in love — see SWEETHEART

flame *vb* 1 to be on fire especially brightly — see BURN 1

2 to develop suddenly and violently — see ERUPT 1

3 to shine with a bright harsh light — see GLARE 1

4 to shoot forth bursts of light — see FLASH 1

flaming *adj* 1 being on fire — see ABLAZE 1

2 having or expressing great depth of feeling — see FERVENT 1

flammable *adj* capable of catching or being set on fire — see COMBUSTIBLE

flank *n* a place, space, or direction away from or beyond a central point or line — see SIDE 1

flank *vb* to be adjacent to — see ADJOIN 1

flanking *adj* having a border in common — see ADJACENT

flap *n* a state of wildly excited activity or emotion — see FRENZY

flap *vb* to move or cause to move with a striking motion ⟨the stirring sight of a huge flock of geese *flapping* their wings⟩

syn beat, flail, flop, flutter, whip

rel bang, batter, buffet, knock, pound, smack, spank, thump; flick, flicker, flit; fan, oscillate, sway, swing; undulate, wave; palpitate, pulse, throb

flapjack *n* a flat cake made from thin batter and cooked on both sides (as on a griddle) — see PANCAKE

flare *n* 1 a sudden and usually temporary growth of activity — see OUTBREAK 1

2 a sudden intense expression of strong feeling — see OUTBURST 1

3 the steady giving off of the form of radiation that makes vision possible — see LIGHT 1

flare *vb* to shine with a bright harsh light — see GLARE 1

flare (out) *vb* to arrange the parts of (something) over a wider area — see OPEN 3

---

flare (up) vb 1 to become very angry — see BLOW UP 1

2 to develop suddenly and violently — see ERUPT 2

flare–up n 1 a sudden and usually temporary growth of activity — see OUTBREAK 1

2 a sudden intense expression of strong feeling — see OUTBURST 1

flash adj lasting only for a short time — see MOMENTARY

flash n 1 a sudden and usually temporary growth of activity — see OUTBREAK 1

2 a sudden intense expression of strong feeling — see OUTBURST 1

3 a very small space of time — see INSTANT

4 something extraordinary or surprising — see WONDER 1

5 excessive or unnecessary display — see OSTENTATION

flash vb 1 to shoot forth bursts of light ⟨The actress's diamond necklace *flashed* as she hurried on stage to accept the award.⟩

syn flame, glance, gleam, glimmer, glint, glisten, glister, glitter, luster (*or* lustre), scintillate, shimmer, sparkle, twinkle, wink

rel beam, radiate, shine; bedazzle, blind, daze, dazzle; blaze, burn, flare, glare, glow

2 to present so as to invite notice or attention — see SHOW 1

3 to shine with light at regular intervals — see BLINK 1

4 to make known openly or publicly — see ANNOUNCE

flashiness n excessive or unnecessary display — see OSTENTATION

flashy adj 1 attractively eye-catching in style — see JAZZY 1

2 excessively showy — see GAUDY

flat adj 1 being neither more nor less than a certain amount, number, or extent — see EVEN 1

2 causing weariness, restlessness, or lack of interest — see BORING

3 having a surface without bends, breaks, or irregularities — see LEVEL 1

4 having been established and usually not subject to change — see FIXED 1

5 having no exceptions or restrictions — see ABSOLUTE 2

6 lacking a surface luster or gloss — see MATTE

7 lacking in qualities that make for spirit and character — see WISHY-WASHY 1

8 lacking in taste or flavor — see INSIPID 1

flat adv to a full extent or degree — see FULLY 1

flatten vb 1 to make free from breaks, curves, or bumps — see EVEN 1

2 to defeat by a large margin — see WHIP 2

flatter vb 1 to praise too much ⟨The billionaire has an army of assistants who are eager to *flatter* him at every opportunity.⟩

syn adulate, blarney, honey, overpraise, puff, soft-soap, stroke

rel blandish, cajole, coax, wheedle; fawn, kowtow, suck (up to), toady; idolize, worship; eulogize, extol (*also* extoll), laud, praise; applaud, commend, compliment; congratulate, felicitate; drool, gush, slaver, slobber; endear, ingratiate; court, romance, woo

near ant bad-mouth, belittle, decry, depreciate, disparage, put down

2 to think highly of (oneself) — see PRIDE

flattery n excessive praise ⟨a talk show host who is known for charming her guests with disingenuous *flattery*⟩

syn adulation, blarney, overpraise, soft soap

rel allurements, blandishments, endearments; caresses, compliments, congratulations, felicitations, greetings, regards, respects; adoration, idolatry, worship; fawning, sycophancy, toadying; cajolement, cajolery, ingratiation, smarm; acclaim, applause, commendation, praise

near ant bad-mouthing, belittlement, depreciation, detraction, disparagement, putdown

flatware n eating and serving utensils — see TABLEWARE 1

flaunt vb to present so as to invite notice or attention — see SHOW 1

flaunting n an outward and often exaggerated indication of something abstract (as a feeling) for effect — see SHOW 1

flavor n 1 a special quality or impression associated with something — see AURA 1

2 something (as an herb) that adds an agreeable or interesting taste to food — see SEASONING 1

3 the property of a substance that can be identified by the sense of taste — see TASTE 1

flavor vb to make more pleasant to the taste by adding something intensely flavored — see SEASON 1

flavorful adj very pleasing to the sense of taste — see DELICIOUS 1

flavoring n something (as an herb) that adds an agreeable or interesting taste to food — see SEASONING 1

flavorless adj lacking in taste or flavor — see INSIPID 1

flaw n something that spoils the appearance or completeness of a thing — see BLEMISH

flaw vb to reduce the soundness, effectiveness, or perfection of — see DAMAGE 1

flawed adj having a fault — see FAULTY

flawless adj being entirely without fault or flaw — see PERFECT 1

flawlessly adv without any flaws or errors — see PERFECTLY 1

flaxen adj of a pale yellow or yellowish brown color — see BLOND

flay vb 1 to criticize (someone) severely or angrily especially for personal failings — see SCOLD

2 to remove the natural covering of — see PEEL

fleck n 1 a small area that is different (as in color) from the main part — see SPOT 1

2 a very small piece — see BIT 1

fleck vb to mark with small spots especially unevenly — see SPOT 1

flecked adj marked with spots — see SPOTTED 1

fledgling n a person who is just starting out in a field of activity — see BEGINNER

flee vb 1 to cease to be visible — see DISAPPEAR

2 to get free from a dangerous or confining situation — see ESCAPE 1

3 to hasten away from something dangerous or frightening — see RUN 2

fleece *n* the hairy covering of a mammal especially when fine, soft, and thick — see FUR 1

fleece *vb* to rob by the use of trickery or threats ⟨swindlers who use the telephone to *fleece* senior citizens out of their savings⟩
syn beat, bleed, cheat, chisel, con, cozen, defraud, do, do in, fiddle, gaff, hustle, mulct, pluck, rip off, rook, screw, short, shortchange, skin, squeeze, stick, stiff, sting, swindle, victimize
rel extort, wrench, wrest, wring; clip, gouge, nick, overcharge, soak; exploit; deceive, dupe, fool, gull, trick; rope (in); betray, double-cross; fast-talk
phrases sell a bill of goods to, take for a ride, take to the cleaners

fleecy *adj* covered with or as if with hair — see HAIRY 1

fleet *adj* moving, proceeding, or acting with great speed — see FAST 1

fleet *n* a group of vehicles traveling together or under one management ⟨a *fleet* of buses rolling down the highway⟩
syn armada, caravan, cavalcade, line, motorcade, train
rel argosy, convoy, flotilla, navy; column, cortege (*also* cortège), parade, procession

fleet–footed *adj* moving, proceeding, or acting with great speed — see FAST 1

fleeting *adj* lasting only for a short time — see MOMENTARY

fleetly *adv* with great speed — see FAST 1

fleetness *n* a high rate of movement or performance — see SPEED 1

flesh *n* animal and especially mammal tissue used as food — see MEAT 1

flesh (out) *vb* to express more fully and in greater detail — see EXPAND 1

fleshiness *n* 1 the condition of having an excess of body fat — see CORPULENCE
2 the quality or state of being full of juice — see SUCCULENCE

fleshly *adj* 1 having to do with life on earth especially as opposed to that in heaven — see EARTHLY
2 of or relating to the human body — see PHYSICAL 1
3 pleasing to the physical senses — see SENSUAL

fleshy *adj* 1 full of juice — see JUICY
2 having an excess of body fat — see FAT 1

flexible *adj* 1 capable of being readily changed ⟨I'm lucky enough to have a very *flexible* work schedule.⟩
syn adaptable, adjustable, alterable, changeable, elastic, fluid, malleable, modifiable, pliable, variable
rel changing, fluctuating, inconstant, unstable, unsteady, varying, versatile
near ant constant, stable, steady, unchanging, uniform, unvarying
ant established, fixed, immutable, inelastic, inflexible, invariable, nonmalleable, ramrod, set, unadaptable, unalterable, unbudgeable, unchangeable
2 not bound by rigid standards — see EASYGOING 2
3 able to bend easily without breaking — see WILLOWY

4 able to revert to original size and shape after being stretched, squeezed, or twisted — see ELASTIC 1

flick *vb* to make an irregular series of quick, sudden movements — see FLIT

flick *n* a story told by means of a series of continuously projected pictures and a sound track — see MOVIE 1

flicker *vb* to make an irregular series of quick, sudden movements — see FLIT

flicker *n* 1 a story told by means of a series of continuously projected pictures and a sound track — see MOVIE 1
2 a sudden and usually temporary growth of activity — see OUTBREAK 1
3 an almost imperceptible sign of something — see HINT 2

flickery *adj* likely to change frequently, suddenly, or unexpectedly — see FICKLE 1

flier *also* **flyer** *n* 1 a risky undertaking — see GAMBLE
2 one who flies or is qualified to fly an aircraft or spacecraft — see PILOT

¹**flight** *n* travel through the air by the use of wings ⟨For centuries people have been fascinated by the *flight* of birds.⟩
syn flying
rel aviation; aeronautics; ballooning, gliding, hang gliding, paragliding, skydiving, soaring

²**flight** *n* the act or an instance of getting free from danger or confinement — see ESCAPE 1

flightiness *n* 1 a lack of seriousness often at an improper time — see FRIVOLITY
2 a state of nervousness marked by sudden jerky movements — see JUMPINESS

flighty *adj* 1 easily excited by nature — see EXCITABLE
2 lacking in seriousness or maturity — see GIDDY 1

flimsy *adj* 1 being of a material lacking in sturdiness or substance ⟨a *flimsy* scarf that was more for decoration than for warmth⟩
syn filmy, frothy, gauzy, gossamer, gossamery, insubstantial, sleazy, unsubstantial
rel dainty, delicate, fine; feeble, fragile, frail; sheer, transparent
near ant durable, knockabout, lasting, tough; coarse, heavy, rough, rude
ant sturdy, substantial
2 not likely to be true or to occur — see IMPROBABLE

flinch *vb* to draw back in fear, pain, or disgust ⟨There are some patients who *flinch* at the mere sight of a needle.⟩
syn blench, cringe, quail, recoil, shrink, squinch, wince
rel blanch, pale, whiten; quake, quiver, shake, shudder, tremble; crouch; jerk, start, twitch; recede, retire, retreat, withdraw; falter, hesitate, reel, waver
near ant advance, approach, near; beard, challenge, confront, defy, face

fling *n* 1 a time or instance of carefree fun ⟨Most families spend Labor Day weekend having one last summer *fling*.⟩
syn binge, frolic, gambol, idyll (*also* idyl), lark, revel, rollick, romp, spree
rel caper, escapade, prank; bender, bust, carouse, souse, toot; antic, monkeyshine(s), shenanigan(s); field day; festivity, merriment, merrymaking

---

syn synonym(s)   *rel* related words
ant antonym(s)   *near ant* near antonym(s)

2 an effort to do or accomplish something — see ATTEMPT 1

3 a brief romantic relationship — see AFFAIR 1

fling *vb* to send through the air especially with a quick forward motion of the arm — see THROW 1

fling (off *or* **away)** *vb* to get rid of as useless or unwanted — see DISCARD

flinty *adj* **1** given to exacting standards of discipline and self-restraint — see SEVERE 1

2 harsh and threatening in manner or appearance — see GRIM 1

flip *adj* making light of something usually regarded as serious or sacred — see FLIPPANT

flip *vb* **1** to turn over pages in an idle or cursory manner — see SKIM 1

2 to change the position of (an object) so that the opposite side or end is showing — see REVERSE 2

flippancy *n* a lack of seriousness often at an improper time — see FRIVOLITY

flippant *adj* making light of something usually regarded as serious or sacred ⟨He gave a *flippant* response to a serious question.⟩

syn cute, facetious, flip, pert, smart, smart-alecky, wise

rel flighty, frivolous; cheeky, cocky, fresh, impertinent, impish, impudent, mischievous, playful, roguish, sassy, saucy, waggish; disrespectful, rude; breezy, casual, glib, inappropriate, thoughtless

near ant grave, serious, sober, solemn, somber (*or* sombre)

ant earnest, sincere

flirt *vb* **1** to show a sexual attraction for someone just for fun ⟨The servers at that restaurant *flirt* with all the customers.⟩

syn dally, trifle

rel vamp; court, mash, woo; josh, kid, put on, razz, rib, tease; fool, lead on, string along; manipulate, play (with)

2 to make an irregular series of quick, sudden movements — see FLIT

flit *vb* to make an irregular series of quick, sudden movements ⟨Bargain hunters at the flea market *flitted* from table to table like hummingbirds in a garden.⟩

syn dance, dart, flick, flicker, flirt, flutter, zip

rel dash, fly, sail, shoot, speed, sprint, zing, zoom; scamper, scud, scurry, scuttle, skip, skitter; meander, ramble, roam, wander

near ant float, hang, hover

float *n* a structure used by boats and ships for taking on or landing cargo and passengers — see DOCK

float *vb* **1** to rest or move along the surface of a liquid or in the air ⟨a canoe *floating* down the river⟩ ⟨particles of dust *floating* in the air⟩

syn drift, glide, hang, hover, poise, ride, sail, swim, waft

rel bob, dangle, suspend; buoy; balloon, raft

near ant dive, plunge; dip, immerse, submerge, submerse

ant settle, sink

2 to move about from place to place aimlessly — see WANDER 1

flock *n* **1** a great number of persons or creatures massed together — see CROWD 1

2 a group of domestic animals assembled or herded together — see HERD 1

flock *vb* to move upon or fill (something) in great numbers — see CROWD 2

flog *vb* **1** to strike repeatedly with something long and thin or flexible — see WHIP 1

2 to strike repeatedly — see BEAT 1

flogger *n* a long thin or flexible tool for striking — see WHIP

flood *n* a great flow of water or of something that overwhelms ⟨A *flood* nearly wiped out the town.⟩ ⟨a *flood* of messages on my computer⟩

syn bath, cataclysm, cataract, deluge, flood tide, inundation, overflow, spate, torrent

rel current, river, stream, tide; cloudburst, discharge, flush, gush, outflow, outpouring; flux, inflow, influx; engulfment, washout; avalanche, blizzard; cascade, waterfall; excess, glut, overabundance, overage, overkill, overmuch, oversupply, superabundance, superfluity, surfeit, surplus

near ant dribble, drip, trickle

flood *vb* to cover with a flood ⟨The lowlands were completely *flooded*.⟩ ⟨Angry calls *flooded* the radio station.⟩

syn deluge, drown, engulf, gulf, inundate, overflow, overwhelm, submerge, submerse, swamp

rel avalanche, smother; overcome, overrun; flow, flush, gush, pour, sluice, spout, spurt, stream; douse (*also* dowse), drench, soak, wet

near ant dehydrate, dry, parch

ant drain

flood tide *n* a great flow of water or of something that overwhelms — see FLOOD

floor *n* the surface upon which a body of water lies — see BOTTOM 2

floor *vb* **1** to cause an unpleasant surprise for — see SHOCK 1

2 to make a strong impression on (someone) with something unexpected — see SURPRISE 1

3 to strike (someone) so forcefully as to cause a fall — see FELL 1

4 to subject to incapacitating emotional or mental stress — see OVERWHELM 1

flop *n* something that has failed — see FAILURE 3

flop *vb* **1** to throw or set down clumsily or casually ⟨They lazily *flopped* themselves onto the couch to watch the game.⟩ ⟨*flopped* the bag of groceries onto the counter⟩

syn plop, plump, plunk (*or* plonk)

rel fling, heave, sling, toss; ensconce, install, plant, settle

2 to be unsuccessful — see FAIL 2

3 to move or cause to move with a striking motion — see FLAP

floppy *adj* not stiff in structure — see LIMP 1

flora *n* green leaves or plants — see GREENERY

floral *adj* of or relating to flowers ⟨bedroom wallpaper with a *floral* pattern⟩

syn flowered, flowery

rel florid; abloom, blossomy, floriferous

florid *adj* **1** elaborately and often excessively decorated — see ORNATE 1

2 full of fine words and fancy expressions — see FLOWERY 1

3 having a healthy reddish skin tone — see RUDDY

floss *n* a soft airy substance or covering — see FUZZ

flounce *n* a strip of fabric gathered or pleated on one edge and used as trimming — see RUFFLE 1

flounder *vb* **1** to proceed or act clumsily or ineffectually ⟨unprepared singers who *floundered* helplessly through the musical number⟩
syn blunder, limp, lumber, plod, struggle, stumble, trudge
rel jog, shamble, shuffle; wallow, welter; falter, lurch, reel, stagger, sway, teeter, totter; fumble, muddle
near ant coast, fly, glide, kilt, sail, zip, zoom

2 to move heavily or clumsily — see LUMBER 1

flourish *vb* **1** to grow vigorously — see THRIVE 1

2 to reach a desired level of accomplishment — see SUCCEED 2

flourishing *adj* **1** having attained a desired end or state of good fortune — see SUCCESSFUL 2

2 marked by much life, movement, or activity — see ALIVE 2

3 marked by vigorous growth and well-being especially economically — see PROSPEROUS 1

floury *adj* consisting of very small particles — see FINE 1

flout *vb* to ignore in a disrespectful manner — see SCORN 2

flow *vb* **1** to move in a stream ⟨Water was *flowing* over the dam at a tremendous rate.⟩
syn pour, roll, run, stream
rel arise, issue, spring; course, race, rush; gush, spout, spurt; deluge, engulf, flood, inundate, overflow, overrun, swamp; cascade, dribble, drip, gutter, ripple, sheet, trickle; flush, wash out
near ant clot, coagulate, congeal, gel, harden, set
ant back up

2 to move or proceed smoothly and readily ⟨As everyone relaxed, the conversation really started to *flow*.⟩
syn bowl, breeze, brush, coast, cruise, drift, glide, roll, sail, skim, slide, slip, stream, sweep, whisk
rel fly, race, rush; speed
near ant limp, lumber, plod, stumble, trudge; shamble, shuffle; stamp, stomp, stump, tramp; labor, toil
ant flounder, struggle

flower *vb* to produce flowers — see BLOOM 1

flower *n* **1** the usually showy plant part that produces seeds ⟨*Flowers* are always a thoughtful gift.⟩
syn bloom, blossom
rel floret, flowerette (*also* flowerette); bouquet, nosegay, posy; arrangement, boutonniere, corsage, garland, lei, spray, wreath

2 a state or time of great activity, thriving, or achievement — see BLOOM 2

3 individuals carefully selected as being the best of a class — see ELITE 1

flowered *adj* of or relating to flowers — see FLORAL

flowery *adj* **1** full of fine words and fancy expressions ⟨the *flowery* verses that appear on valentines⟩
syn florid, grandiloquent, highfalutin (*also* hifalutin), high-flown, high-sounding, ornate, rhetorical (*also* rhetoric)
rel affected, fancy-pants, grandiose, pompous, pretentious, stilted; excessive, flattering, fulsome; boastful, bombastic; elevated, eloquent, lofty; bookish, inkhorn, learned
near ant prosaic, unpoetic; bald, direct, lean, matter-of-fact, plain, plainspoken, simple, spare, stark, straightforward, unadorned; natural, unaffected, unpretentious

2 of or relating to flowers — see FLORAL

flowing *adj* capable of moving like a liquid — see FLUID 1

flub *n* an unintentional departure from truth or accuracy — see ERROR 1

flub *vb* **1** to make or do (something) in a clumsy or unskillful way — see BOTCH

2 to make a mistake — see ERR 1

fluctuate *vb* to pass from one form, state, or level to another — see CHANGE 2

fluctuating *adj* **1** likely to change frequently, suddenly, or unexpectedly — see FICKLE 1

2 not staying constant — see UNEVEN 2

fluent *adj* **1** able to express oneself clearly and well — see ARTICULATE

2 capable of moving like a liquid — see FLUID 1

3 involving minimal difficulty or effort — see EASY 1

fluently *adv* without difficulty — see EASILY 1

fluff *n* **1** a soft airy substance or covering — see FUZZ

2 an unintentional departure from truth or accuracy — see ERROR 1

fluff *vb* **1** to make a mistake — see ERR 1

2 to make or do (something) in a clumsy or unskillful way — see BOTCH

fluffy *adj* resembling air in lightness — see AIRY 1

fluid *adj* **1** capable of moving like a liquid ⟨Warm the jam until it is *fluid*, then spread it over the cake.⟩
syn flowing, fluent, liquid
rel diluted, thin, watery, weak; semiliquid, semisolid
near ant clotted, coagulated, gelatinous, gelled, jelled, jellied, thick; gluey, glutinous, gooey, gummy, viscous
ant hard, nonliquid, solid

2 capable of being readily changed — see FLEXIBLE 1

3 involving minimal difficulty or effort — see EASY 1

4 likely to change frequently, suddenly, or unexpectedly — see FICKLE 1

fluky *also* **flukey** *adj* **1** coming or happening by good luck especially unexpectedly — see FORTUNATE 1

2 happening by chance — see ACCIDENTAL 1

flume *n* **1** a narrow opening between hillsides or mountains that can be used for passage — see CANYON

---

2 an open man-made passageway for water — see CHANNEL 1

flunk *vb* to be unsuccessful — see FAIL 2

flunky *also* **flunkey** *or* **flunkie** *n* a person who flatters another in order to get ahead — see SYCOPHANT

fluorescence *n* the steady giving off of the form of radiation that makes vision possible — see LIGHT 1

flurry *n* 1 a sudden and usually temporary growth of activity — see OUTBREAK 1
2 a sudden brief rush of wind — see GUST 1
3 a rapid or overwhelming outpouring of many things at once — see BARRAGE

flurry *vb* to trouble the mind of; to make uneasy — see DISTURB 1

flush *adj* 1 having a healthy reddish skin tone — see RUDDY
2 having a surface without bends, breaks, or irregularities — see LEVEL 1
3 having active strength of body or mind — see VIGOROUS 1
4 having goods, property, or money in abundance — see RICH 1
5 possessing or covered with great numbers or amounts of something specified — see RIFE
6 having a border in common — see ADJACENT

flush *n* 1 a rosy appearance (of the cheeks) — see BLOOM 2
2 a state or time of great activity, thriving, or achievement — see BLOOM 1
3 a sudden intense expression of strong feeling — see OUTBURST 1

flush *vb* 1 to pour liquid over or pour in order to cleanse ⟨Use this cleaner to *flush* the drain in the sink.⟩
syn irrigate, rinse, sluice, wash, wash out
rel deluge, engulf, flood, inundate, swamp; flow, gush, rush, stream; drench, saturate, soak; douse (*also* dowse), slosh, splash
2 to develop a rosy facial color (as from excitement or embarrassment) — see BLUSH

fluster *n* 1 a state of nervous or irritated concern — see FRET
2 the emotional state of being made self-consciously uncomfortable — see EMBARRASSMENT 1

fluster *vb* to throw into a state of self-conscious distress — see EMBARRASS 1

flustering *adj* causing embarrassment — see AWKWARD 3

flutter *n* a sudden and usually temporary growth of activity — see OUTBREAK 1

flutter *vb* 1 to make an irregular series of quick, sudden movements — see FLIT
2 to move or cause to move with a striking motion — see FLAP

fluttery *adj* easily excited by nature — see EXCITABLE

flux *n* 1 the frequent and usually sudden passing from one condition to another ⟨The English language is always in a state of *flux*.⟩
syn change, inconstancy, oscillation
rel metamorphosis, mutation, transformation, transmogrification, transmutation; vacillation, wavering
2 a flowing or coming in — see INFLUX
3 abnormally frequent intestinal evacuations with more or less fluid stools — see DIARRHEA

flux *vb* to go from a solid to a liquid state — see LIQUEFY

fly *vb* 1 to move through the air with or as if with outstretched wings ⟨The Wright brothers realized mankind's age-old wish to *fly*.⟩
syn glide, plane, soar, wing
rel drift, float, hang, hover, waft; coast, cruise, sail, sweep; dart, flit, flutter; catapult, jet, orbit, rocket; dive, stoop
2 to get free from a dangerous or confining situation — see ESCAPE 1
3 to proceed or move quickly — see HURRY 2
4 to hasten away from something dangerous or frightening — see RUN 2
5 to cease to be visible — see DISAPPEAR
6 to withstand scrutiny and gain acceptance or approval — see WASH 2

flying *adj* 1 acting or done with excessive or careless speed — see HASTY 1
2 moving, proceeding, or acting with great speed — see FAST 1

flying *n* travel through the air by the use of wings — see ¹FLIGHT

flyspeck *n* a very small piece — see BIT 1

foam *n* a light mass of fine bubbles formed in or on a liquid ⟨a steaming cup of hot cocoa with a sprinkling of marshmallows drifting through the *foam*⟩
syn froth, head, lather, spume, suds, surf
rel mousse; mist, spindrift, spray; scum

foam *vb* to be excited or emotionally stirred up with anger — see BOIL 1

foaming *adj* feeling or showing anger — see ANGRY

foamy *adj* covered with, consisting of, or resembling foam ⟨*foamy* milk shakes⟩
syn frothy, lathery, sudsy
rel bubbly, effervescent, fizzy, sparkling; soapy

focus *n* 1 a thing or place that is of greatest importance to an activity or interest — see CENTER 1
2 a guiding or motivating purpose or principle — see COMPASS 1

focus *vb* to fix (as one's attention) steadily toward a central objective — see CONCENTRATE 2

focused *also* **focussed** *adj* 1 having the mind fixed on something — see ATTENTIVE 1
2 not divided or scattered among several areas of interest or concern — see WHOLE 1

foe *n* 1 one that is hostile toward another — see ENEMY
2 one that takes a position opposite another in a competition or conflict — see OPPONENT 1

fog *n* 1 a state of mental confusion — see HAZE 2
2 an atmospheric condition in which suspended particles in the air rob it of its transparency — see HAZE 1
3 a state of mental uncertainty — see CONFUSION 1

fog *vb* 1 to make (something) unclear to the understanding — see CONFUSE 2
2 to make dark, dim, or indistinct — see CLOUD 1

foggy *adj* 1 filled with or dimmed by fine particles (as of dust or water) in suspension — see HAZY 1

2 not seen or understood clearly — see FAINT 1

fogy *also* **fogey** *n* a person with old-fashioned ideas ⟨old *fogies* who said that hip-hop would never last⟩

syn antediluvian, fossil, fuddy-duddy, reactionary, stick-in-the-mud

rel conservative, rightist, Tory; mandarin, old hand, old-timer, veteran; old maid

near ant liberal, progressive, radical

ant hipster, modern, trendy

foible *n* a defect in character — see FAULT 1

foil *vb* to prevent from achieving a goal — see FRUSTRATE 1

foist *vb* to offer (something fake, useless, or inferior) as genuine, useful, or valuable ⟨shopkeepers who *foist* shoddy souvenirs on unsuspecting tourists⟩

syn palm off, pass off, wish

rel entail, force, impose, inflict; counterfeit, fake, forge; distort, falsify, misrepresent

fold *n* a group of people sharing a common interest and relating together socially — see GANG 2

fold *vb* **1** to lay one part over or against another part of ⟨*Fold* the blanket so that it will fit inside the trunk.⟩

syn double

rel overlap, overlay, overlie; collapse; close, shut; plait, pleat

ant extend, open, spread, unfold, unroll

2 to be unsuccessful — see FAIL 2

folder *n* a short printed publication with no cover or with a paper cover — see PAMPHLET

foliage *n* green leaves or plants — see GREENERY

folk *n* **1** **folks** *pl* a group of persons who come from the same ancestor — see FAMILY 1

2 one of the segments of society into which people are grouped — see CLASS 1

3 **folks** *pl* human beings in general — see PEOPLE 1

folklore *n* the body of customs, beliefs, stories, and sayings associated with a people, thing, or place ⟨The Scottish Highlands are rich in *folklore*.⟩

syn legend, lore, myth, mythology, tradition

rel folklife; information, knowledge, wisdom; anecdote, fable, folktale, old wives' tale, tale, yarn

follow *vb* **1** to come after in time ⟨A wrap-up always *follows* the Super Bowl broadcast.⟩

syn postdate, succeed, supervene

rel displace, replace, supersede, supplant; ensue

ant antedate, precede, predate

2 to go after or on the track of ⟨Let's *follow* the boys to their hiding place.⟩

syn chase, course, dog, hound, pursue, run, shadow, tag, tail, trace, track, trail

rel accompany, chaperone (*or* chaperon), escort; hunt, search (for), seek; eye, observe, watch

phrases run after

near ant head

ant guide, lead, pilot

3 to act according to the commands of — see OBEY

4 to make one's way through, across, or over — see TRAVERSE

5 to take notice of and be guided by — see HEED 1

6 to keep one's eyes on — see WATCH 1

follower *n* **1** one who follows the opinions or teachings of another ⟨The *followers* of Gandhi have spread his philosophy of nonviolence all over the world.⟩

syn adherent, convert, disciple, partisan (*also* partizan), pupil, votary

rel apostle, missionary, proselytizer, soldier; faithful, loyalist; advocate, backer, champion, supporter; protégé, scholar, student; ideologist, ideologue (*also* idealogue), sectarian; admirer, cultist, devotee, enthusiast, fan, idolater (*or* idolator), worshipper (*or* worshiper), zealot; apparatchik, camp follower, flunky (*also* flunkey *or* flunkie), hanger-on, henchman, lackey, lickspittle, minion, stooge, sycophant, toady, yes-man

near ant apostate, defector, renegade, traitor, turncoat

ant leader

2 a person who adopts the appearance or behavior of another especially in an obvious way — see COPYCAT

following *adj* being the one that comes immediately after another — see NEXT

following *n* **1** a body of employees or attendants who accompany and wait on a person — see CORTEGE 1

2 a group of people showing intense devotion to a cause, person, or work (as a film) — see CULT 1

3 the act of going after or in the tracks of another — see PURSUIT

following *prep* subsequent to in time or order — see AFTER

folly *n* **1** a foolish act or idea ⟨The American purchase of Alaska was originally considered a grand *folly*.⟩

syn absurdity, asininity, fatuity, foolery, idiocy, imbecility, inanity, stupidity

rel absurdness, craziness, foolishness, inaneness, madness, senselessness, witlessness; monkeyshine(s), shenanigan(s), tomfoolery; drivel, humbug, nonsense, twaddle; blunder, bungle, flub, goof, howler

near ant discretion, forethought, prudence, sagacity, wisdom; brainstorm, inspiration

2 lack of good sense or judgment — see FOOLISHNESS 1

3 language, behavior, or ideas that are absurd and contrary to good sense — see NONSENSE 1

foment *vb* to bring (something volatile or intense) into being — see INCITE 1

fomenter *n* a person who stirs up public feelings especially of discontent — see AGITATOR

fond *adj* **1** having a liking or affection ⟨They discovered they were both *fond* of country music.⟩

syn affected, attached, inclined, partial

rel crazy (about *or* over), enamored, enraptured, gone (on), infatuated, mad (about), nuts (about); desirous, eager, enthusiastic, excited, gung ho, keen

---

syn synonym(s)   *rel* related words
ant antonym(s)   *near ant* near antonym(s)

phrases big on

near ant apathetic, cool, indifferent, uninterested; contemptuous, disdainful, scornful; antagonistic, antipathetic, hostile; alienated, disaffected, disenchanted, estranged

ant allergic, averse, disinclined

2 feeling or showing love — see LOVING 1

3 granted special treatment or attention — see DARLING 1

fondle *vb* to touch or handle in a tender or loving manner ⟨a cat who enjoys being *fondled* by his loving owners⟩

syn caress, gentle, love, pat, pet, stroke

rel bill, canoodle, cuddle, nestle, nose, nuzzle, snuggle, spoon; feel up, paw; cradle, embrace, enfold, hug; bounce, dandle, knead; baby, coddle, indulge, mollycoddle, pamper, spoil

fondness *n* 1 a feeling of strong or constant regard for and dedication to someone — see LOVE 1

2 positive regard for something — see LIKING

food *n* substances intended to be eaten ⟨a simple, little restaurant with excellent *food*⟩

syn bread, chow, chuck [*chiefly West*], eatables, edibles, fare, foodstuffs, grub, meat, provender, provisions, table, viands, victuals, vittles

rel commissary, rations, supplies; aliment, nutriment; diet, nurture; mess, pap; ensilage, feed, fodder, forage, silage, slop; swill; feast, meal, refreshments, regale, repast, spread; board; dish, plate, platter, serving; finger food, natural food

near ant bane, poison, toxin, venom

foodstuffs *n pl* substances intended to be eaten — see FOOD

fool *n* 1 a person who lacks good sense or judgment ⟨Only a *fool* would attempt to climb that mountain unprepared.⟩

syn booby, goose, half-wit, nincompoop, ninny, nitwit, simpleton, turkey, yo-yo

rel daredevil; madman, madwoman; blockhead, dodo, dolt, donkey, dope, dork [*slang*], dumbbell, dummy, dunce, fathead, gander, goon, half-wit, idiot, ignoramus, imbecile, know-nothing, moron, numskull (*or* numbskull), pinhead, stock; featherbrain; butt, dupe, laughingstock, mockery, monkey; chump, loser, schlemiel (*also* shlemiel); character, codger, crackbrain, crank, kook, oddball, screwball, weirdo; flibbertigibbet

near ant sage, thinker; brain, genius

2 a person formerly kept in a royal or noble household to amuse with jests and pranks ⟨A king's *fool* could get away with saying things that others in the palace couldn't.⟩

syn jester, motley

rel buffoon, clown, comedian, comedienne, comic, cutup, droll, harlequin, joker, jokester, madcap, merry-andrew, vice, wag, zany; mime, mummer

3 a person with a strong and habitual liking for something — see FAN

fool *adj* showing or marked by a lack of good sense or judgment — see FOOLISH 1

fool *vb* 1 to cause to believe what is untrue — see DECEIVE

2 to make jokes — see JOKE 1

fool (with) *vb* to handle thoughtlessly, ignorantly, or mischievously — see TAMPER (WITH)

foolery *n* 1 a foolish act or idea — see FOLLY 1

2 wildly playful or mischievous behavior — see HORSEPLAY

foolhardy *adj* 1 foolishly adventurous or bold ⟨hikers who were *foolhardy* enough to remain on the summit during a thunderstorm⟩

syn audacious, brash, daredevil, madcap, overbold, overconfident, reckless

rel adventuresome, adventurous, bold, daring, venturesome, venturous; hotheaded; impetuous, imprudent, impulsive, incautious, rash; brainless, foolish, harebrained, scatterbrained; careless, heedless, thoughtless; hasty, headlong, precipitate

near ant unadventurous, unambitious; fainthearted, fearful, mousy (*or* mousey); scary, shy, skittish, timid, timorous; calm, cool, levelheaded, sensible; chicken, chickenhearted, cowardly, craven, dastardly, lily-livered, pusillanimous, recreant, spineless, unheroic, yellow

ant careful, cautious, circumspect, guarded, heedful, prudent, safe, wary

2 having or showing a lack of concern for the consequences of one's actions — see RECKLESS 1

fooling *adj* marked by or expressive of mild or good-natured teasing — see QUIZZICAL

foolish *adj* 1 showing or marked by a lack of good sense or judgment ⟨*foolish* people who thought that the world would end in the year 2000⟩ ⟨a *foolish* scheme that was supposed to make us all rich⟩

syn absurd, asinine, balmy, brainless, cockeyed, daffy, daft, dotty, fatuous, fool, half-baked, harebrained, half-witted, inept, jerky, kooky (*also* kookie), nonsensical, nutty, preposterous, sappy, screwball, senseless, silly, simpleminded, stupid, unwise, wacky (*also* whacky), weak-minded, witless, zany

rel airheaded, chowderheaded, chuckleheaded, dense, dim, dim-witted, doltish, dopey (*also* dopy), dorky [*slang*], dull, dumb, dunderheaded, empty-headed, fatuous, feebleminded, idiotic (*also* idiotical), imbecile (*or* imbecilic), knuckleheaded, mindless, moronic, oafish, obtuse, opaque, simple, slow, slow-witted, soft, softheaded, thoughtless, thick, thickheaded, unintelligent, vacuous, witless; fallacious, illogical, invalid, irrational, unreasonable, unreasoning, unsound, weak; farcical, laughable, ludicrous, ridiculous; buffoonish, clownish; ill-advised, unconsidered, unreasoned

phrases out to lunch

near ant brainy, bright, clever, intelligent, smart; logical, rational, reasonable, valid; well-advised

ant judicious, prudent, sagacious, sage, sane, sapient, sensible, sound, wise

2 conceived or made without regard for reason or reality — see FANTASTIC 1

3 lacking importance — see UNIMPORTANT

foolishness *n* **1** lack of good sense or judgment ⟨the *foolishness* of going off to search for the fountain of youth⟩

syn absurdity, asininity, balminess, brainlessness, daftness, fatuity, folly, imbecility, inanity, madness, nonsensicalness, nuttiness, preposterousness, senselessness, silliness, simplicity, wackiness, witlessness, zaniness

rel denseness, doltishness, dopiness, dullness (*also* dulness), dumbness, feeblemindedness, idiocy, mindlessness, oafishness, obtuseness, simpleness, slowness, stupidity, stupidness, vacuity; fallacy, irrationality, unreasonableness; kookiness, weirdness; laughableness, ludicrousness, ridiculousness

near ant logicality, logicalness, rationality, rationalness, reasonability, reasonableness, validity; discernment, insight, perception

ant prudence, sagaciousness, sagacity, sageness, sanity, sapience, sensibleness, soundness, wisdom

2 language, behavior, or ideas that are absurd and contrary to good sense — see NONSENSE 1

3 the quality or state of lacking intelligence or quickness of mind — see STUPIDITY 1

foot *n* the lowest part, place, or point — see BOTTOM 3

foot *vb* to give what is owed for — see PAY 2

foot (it) *vb* **1** to go on foot — see WALK 1

2 to perform a series of usually rhythmic bodily movements to music — see DANCE 1

foot (up) *vb* to combine (numbers) into a single sum — see ADD 2

foothold *n* a place from which an advance (as for military operations) is made — see BASE 2

footing *n* **1** an immaterial thing upon which something else rests — see BASE 1

2 position with regard to conditions and circumstances — see SITUATION 1

3 the placement of someone or something in relation to others in a vertical arrangement — see RANK 1

footloose *adj* **1** not bound, confined, or detained by force — see FREE 3

2 not held back by rules, duties, or worries — see FREEWHEELING

footpath *n* a rough course or way formed by or as if by repeated footsteps — see TRAIL 1

footprint *n* the mark or impression made by a foot ⟨mysterious *footprints* along the beach⟩

syn footstep, step, trace, vestige

rel hoofprint; pug, spoor, track; tread

footstep *n* the mark or impression made by a foot — see FOOTPRINT

foozle *vb* to make or do (something) in a clumsy or unskillful way — see BOTCH

fop *n* a man extremely interested in his clothing and personal appearance — see DANDY 1

for *conj* for the reason that — see SINCE

forage *vb* to feed on grass or herbs — see ¹GRAZE

forage (for) *vb* to go in search of — see SEEK 1

foray *n* a sudden attack on and entrance into hostile territory — see RAID 1

foray (into) *vb* to enter for conquest or plunder — see INVADE

forbear *vb* to resist the temptation of ⟨She's old enough to make her own decisions, so we must *forbear* criticizing them.⟩

syn abjure, abstain (from), forgo (*also* forego), keep (from), refrain (from)

rel avoid, eschew, shun; check, constrain, curb, inhibit; deny, refuse, reject, repudiate; buck, combat, fight

near ant acquiesce (to), capitulate, concede (to), knuckle under (to)

ant bow (to), give in (to), submit (to), succumb (to), surrender (to), yield (to)

forbearance *n* **1** the capacity to endure what is difficult or disagreeable without complaining — see PATIENCE

2 kind, gentle, or compassionate treatment especially towards someone who is undeserving of it — see MERCY 1

forbearing *adj* accepting pains or hardships calmly or without complaint — see PATIENT 1

forbid *vb* to order not to do or use or to be done or used ⟨Smoking is *forbidden* throughout the building.⟩ ⟨We *forbid* you to see him.⟩

syn ban, bar, enjoin, interdict, outlaw, prohibit, proscribe

rel deter, discourage, dissuade; clamp down (on), crack down (on), crush, put down, quash, quell, repress, silence, snuff (out), squash, squelch, subdue, suppress; halt, preclude, prevent, stop; embargo, exclude, rule out, shut out; debar, disallow, reject, repudiate, veto; bridle, check, curb, inhibit, rein (in), restrain; block, hinder, impede, obstruct; illegalize

near ant approve, endorse (*also* indorse), sanction; authorize, license (*also* licence), warrant; abet, advance, cultivate, encourage, forward, further, nourish, nurture, promote, support; bid, command, order; abide, bear, brook, countenance, endure, tolerate

ant allow, let, permit, suffer

forbidden *adj* that may not be permitted — see IMPERMISSIBLE

forbidding *adj* **1** causing fear — see FEARFUL 1

2 harsh and threatening in manner or appearance — see GRIM 1

forbidding *n* the act of ordering that something not be done or used — see PROHIBITION 1

force *n* **1** a body of persons at work or available for work ⟨The entire *force* of the shipyard will be needed to get this government order done on time.⟩

syn help, manpower, personnel, pool, staff, workforce

rel labor, proletariat, rank and file; band, company, crew, gang, outfit, party, squad, team; employee (*also* employe), helper, hireling, worker

2 the use of power to impose one's will on another ⟨a cruel tyrant who disbanded the parliament and ruled by *force*⟩

syn coercion, compulsion, constraint, duress, pressure

---

syn synonym(s) *rel* related words
ant antonym(s) *near ant* near antonym(s)

rel browbeating, bulldozing, bullying; fear, intimidation, menace, sword, terror, terrorism, threat, violence; might, muscle, potency, puissance, strength; hardheadedness, self-will, willfulness; strain, stress

near ant agreement, approval, consent, permission; convincing, persuasion, reason, suasion

3 the ability to exert effort for the accomplishment of a task — see POWER 2

4 the capacity to persuade — see COGENCY 1

5 the quality of an utterance that provokes interest and produces an effect — see ¹PUNCH 1

6 the use of brute strength to cause harm to a person or property — see VIOLENCE 1

7 a body of officers of the law — see POLICE 2

8 the number of individuals or amount of something available at any given time — see SUPPLY

force *vb* to cause (a person) to give in to pressure ⟨I had to *force* myself to get up this morning.⟩ ⟨They were *forced* to sell at a lower price.⟩

syn coerce, compel, constrain, drive, impel, impress, make, muscle, obligate, oblige, press, pressure

rel browbeat, bulldoze, bully, cow, hector, intimidate; blackmail, high-pressure, menace, shame, terrorize, threaten; drag; badger, hound

phrases twist one's arm

near ant allow, let, permit; argue, convince, induce, move, persuade, prevail (on or upon), satisfy, talk (into), win (over)

forced *adj* **1** forcing one's compliance or participation in or as if by law — see MANDATORY

2 lacking in natural or spontaneous quality — see ARTIFICIAL 1

3 not made or done willingly or by choice — see INVOLUNTARY 1

forceful *adj* **1** having the power to persuade — see COGENT

2 marked by or uttered with forcefulness — see EMPHATIC 1

3 not showing weakness or uncertainty — see FIRM 1

4 having power over the minds or behavior of others — see INFLUENTIAL 1

forcefully *adv* in a vigorous and forceful manner — see HARD 3

forcefulness *n* **1** the capacity to persuade — see COGENCY 1

2 the quality of an utterance that provokes interest and produces an effect — see ¹PUNCH 1

3 the quality or state of being forceful (as in expression) — see VEHEMENCE 1

forcibly *adv* in a vigorous and forceful manner — see HARD 3

ford *n* a place where a body of water (as a sea or river) is shallow — see SHOAL

forearm *vb* to prepare (oneself) mentally or emotionally — see FORTIFY 1

forebear *also* **forebar** *n* a person who is several generations earlier in an individual's line of descent — see ANCESTOR 1

forebode *also* **forbode** *vb* to show signs of a favorable or successful outcome — see BODE

foreboding *adj* being or showing a sign of evil or calamity to come — see OMINOUS

foreboding *n* **1** a feeling that something bad will happen — see PREMONITION

2 something believed to be a sign or warning of a future event — see OMEN

3 suspicion or fear of future harm or misfortune — see APPREHENSION 1

forecast *n* a declaration that something will happen in the future — see PREDICTION

forecast *vb* to tell of or describe beforehand — see FORETELL

forecaster *n* one who predicts future events or developments — see PROPHET 1

forecasting *n* a declaration that something will happen in the future — see PREDICTION

foredoom *vb* to determine the fate of in advance — see DESTINE

forefather *n* a person who is several generations earlier in an individual's line of descent — see ANCESTOR 1

forefront *n* the leading or most important part of a movement ⟨a politician who was in the *forefront* of women's rights⟩

syn van, vanguard

rel spearhead; avant-garde

forego *vb* to go or come before in time — see PRECEDE

foregoer *n* **1** one that announces or indicates the later arrival of another — see FORERUNNER 1

2 something belonging to an earlier time from which something else was later developed — see ANCESTOR 2

foregoing *adj* going before another in time or order — see PREVIOUS

forehanded *adj* having or showing awareness of and preparation for the future — see FORESIGHTED

foreign *adj* **1** being, relating to, or characteristic of a country other than one's own ⟨More Americans should take an interest in *foreign* languages.⟩

syn alien, nonnative

rel imported, introduced, naturalized, transplanted; external, multicultural, multilateral; foreign-born, nonindigenous; distant, far-off, overseas, remote; bizarre, exotic, outlandish, strange

near ant endemic, local; aboriginal, indigenous

ant domestic, native

2 not being a vital part of or belonging to something — see EXTRINSIC

foreigner *n* a person who is not native to or known to a community — see STRANGER

foreknow *vb* to realize or know about beforehand — see FORESEE

foreknowledge *n* the special ability to see or know about events before they actually occur — see FORESIGHT 1

foreman *n* the person (as an employer or supervisor) who tells people and especially workers what to do — see BOSS

foremost *adj* **1** coming before all others in importance ⟨Albert Einstein is regarded by many as the *foremost* figure of the 20th century.⟩

syn arch, big, capital, cardinal, central, chief, dominant, first, grand, great, greatest, highest, key, leading, main, master, overbearing, paramount, predominant, preeminent, premier, primal, primary, principal, prior, sovereign (*also* sovran), supreme

rel distinguished, eminent, illustrious, noble, notable, noteworthy, outstanding, prestigious, signal, star, stellar, superior; high-level, senior, top; important, influential, major, mighty, momentous, significant; incomparable, matchless, unequaled (*or* unequalled), unparalleled, unsurpassed; celebrated, famed, famous, renowned

near ant inconsequential, inconsiderable, insignificant, minor, negligible, slight, trifling, trivial, unimportant; collateral, inferior, secondary, subordinate, subsidiary

ant last, least

2 highest in rank or authority — see HEAD

3 coming before all others in time or order — see FIRST 1

forename *n* a name that is placed before one's family name ⟨A long string of *forenames* was given to the latest addition to the royal family.⟩

syn Christian name, given name

rel appellation, denomination, designation; cognomen, denotation, epithet, handle, nickname, sobriquet (*also* soubriquet); title; alias, nom de plume, pen name, pseudonym; baptismal name

forenoon *n* the time from sunrise until noon — see MORNING 1

foreordain *vb* to determine the fate of in advance — see DESTINE

forepart *n* a forward part or surface — see FRONT 1

forerunner *n* **1** one that announces or indicates the later arrival of another ⟨The return of the swallows is traditionally regarded as a *forerunner* of spring.⟩

syn angel, foregoer, harbinger, herald, precursor

rel foreboder, foreshadower, foretaste, forewarning; advertiser, blazoner, crier, proclaimer; courier, messenger, runner; augury, auspice, boding, forebonding, foreshadowing, omen, portent, prefiguring, presage; mark, sign, symptom

2 something belonging to an earlier time from which something else was later developed — see ANCESTOR 2

foresee *vb* to realize or know about beforehand ⟨a freak accident that no one could possibly have *foreseen*⟩

syn anticipate, divine, foreknow

rel augur, forecast, foretell, predict, presage, prognosticate, prophesy; envisage, foreshadow, prefigure, visualize; alert, caution, foretoken, forewarn; preview; descry, discern, perceive; apprehend, dread, fear

foreseeing *adj* having or showing awareness of and preparation for the future — see FORESIGHTED

foreseer *n* one who predicts future events or developments — see PROPHET 1

foreshadow *vb* to give a slight indication of beforehand ⟨a series of small tremors that *foreshadowed* the massive earthquake the next day⟩

syn harbinger, herald, prefigure

rel anticipate, foreknow, foresee; forecast, foretell, predict, prognosticate, prophesy; forewarn; augur, bode, forebode (*also* forbode), portend, presage, promise; allude, connote, hint, imply, insinuate, intimate, suggest

foreshadowing *n* something believed to be a sign or warning of a future event — see OMEN

foresight *n* **1** the special ability to see or know about events before they actually occur ⟨a mysterious woman who claims to have the gift of *foresight*⟩

syn foreknowledge, prescience

rel foreboding, premonition, prenotion, presage, presentiment; clairvoyance, extrasensory perception, sixth sense; omniscience; augury, divination

2 concern or preparation for the future ⟨had the *foresight* to realize the global importance of the Internet⟩

syn farsightedness, foresightedness, forethought, prescience, providence, vision

rel premeditation; discernment, discretion, insight, perception, perceptiveness, prudence, sagaciousness, sagacity, sageness, sapience, wisdom

near ant hindsight

ant improvidence, myopia, shortsightedness

foresighted *adj* having or showing awareness of and preparation for the future ⟨the *foresighted* conservationists who worked to create the national park system⟩

syn farsighted, forehanded, foreseeing, forethoughtful, forward, prescient, proactive, provident, visionary

rel careful, cautious, heedful; discerning, insightful, perceptive, percipient, prudent, sagacious, sage, sapient, wise

near ant careless, heedless, incautious

ant half-baked, half-cocked, improvident, myopic, shortsighted

foresightedness *n* concern or preparation for the future — see FORESIGHT 2

forest *n* a dense growth of trees and shrubs covering a large area ⟨She owned a little cottage deep in the *forest*.⟩

syn timber, timberland, wood(s), woodland

rel brake, brushwood, chaparral, coppice, copse, covert, grove, scrubland, stand, thicket; greenwood, wildwood; woodlot; arboretum, plantation

forestall *vb* to keep from happening by taking action in advance — see PREVENT

forestallment *n* the act or practice of keeping something from happening — see PREVENTION

foretell *vb* to tell of or describe beforehand ⟨a 16th-century astrologer who, some claim, accurately *foretold* 20th-century events⟩

syn augur, call, forecast, predict, presage, prognosticate, prophesy, read

rel alert, caution, forewarn, warn; bode, forebode (*also* forbode), portend, promise; anticipate, divine, foreknow, foresee; announce, declare, herald, proclaim

near ant describe, narrate, recite, recount, relate, report, tell

---

syn synonym(s)   **rel** related words
ant antonym(s)   **near ant** near antonym(s)

foreteller *n* one who predicts future events or developments — see PROPHET 1

foretelling *n* a declaration that something will happen in the future — see PREDICTION

forethought *n* concern or preparation for the future — see FORESIGHT 2

forethoughtful *adj* having or showing awareness of and preparation for the future — see FORESIGHTED

forever *adv* 1 for all time — see EVER 1

2 on every relevant occasion — see ALWAYS 1

forever *n* a long or seemingly long period of time — see AGE 2

forevermore *adv* for all time — see EVER 1

forewarn *vb* to give notice to beforehand especially of danger or risk — see WARN

forewarning *n* the act or an instance of telling beforehand of danger or risk — see WARNING 1

foreword *n* a short section (as of a book) that leads to or explains the main part — see INTRODUCTION

forfeit *n* a sum of money to be paid as a punishment — see FINE

forfeiture *n* a sum of money to be paid as a punishment — see FINE

forgather *or* **foregather** *vb* to come together into one body or place — see ASSEMBLE 1

¹**forge** *vb* to move forward along a course — see GO 1

²**forge** *vb* 1 to imitate or copy especially in order to deceive — see FAKE 1

2 to shape with a hammer — see HAMMER 1

forged *adj* being such in appearance only and made or manufactured with the intention of committing fraud — see COUNTERFEIT 1

forgery *n* an imitation that is passed off as genuine — see FAKE 1

forget *vb* 1 to be unable to recall or think of ⟨I *forget* exactly on which street that the house is.⟩

syn unlearn

rel lose, miss; blank; misremember; disregard, ignore, neglect, overlook, overpass, pass over, slight, slur (over)

near ant remind

ant hark back (to), recall, recollect, remember, reminisce (about), think (of)

2 to fail to give proper attention to — see NEGLECT 1

3 to leave undone or unattended to especially through carelessness — see NEGLECT 2

4 to miss the opportunity or obligation — see NEGLECT 3

forgetful *adj* inclined to forget what one has learned or to do what one should ⟨We become more *forgetful* as we get older.⟩

syn absentminded

rel absent, abstracted, lost, oblivious, preoccupied, unmindful; amnesiac (*or* amnesic), senile; befogged, befuddled, bewildered, confused, dazed, muddled, scatterbrained, unfocused (*also* unfocussed); lax, neglectful, negligent, remiss, slack; careless, heedless, inconsiderate, thoughtless; inattentive, insensible, unaware, unconscious, unheeding, unknowing, unthinking

near ant alert, attentive, awake, keen, open-eyed, sharp, vigilant, watchful, wide-awake; careful, cautious, circumspect, conscientious, heedful, thoughtful, wary

ant retentive

forgetfulness *n* a state of being disregardful or unconscious of one's surroundings, concerns, or obligations — see OBLIVION

forgivable *adj* worthy of forgiveness — see VENIAL

forgive *vb* 1 to cease to have feelings of anger or bitterness toward ⟨It is not easy to *forgive* those who have hurt us.⟩

syn pardon

rel absolve, acquit, clear, exculpate, exonerate, vindicate; remit, shrive; condone, disregard, excuse, ignore, pass over, shrug off; discharge, liberate, redeem, release, unburden

near ant abhor, abominate, despise, detest, dislike, execrate, hate, loathe; avenge, redress, requite, retaliate, revenge; discipline, penalize, punish

2 to dismiss as of little importance — see EXCUSE 1

forgiveness *n* release from the guilt or penalty of an offense — see PARDON 1

forgo *also* **forego** *vb* to resist the temptation of — see FORBEAR

forgotten *adj* left unoccupied or unused — see ABANDONED 1

fork *vb* to go or move in different directions from a central point — see SEPARATE 2

forlorn *adj* 1 feeling unhappiness — see SAD 1

2 sad from lack of companionship or separation from others — see LONESOME 1

3 causing or marked by an atmosphere lacking in cheer — see GLOOMY 1

4 feeling or showing no hope — see DESPONDENT 1

forlornness *n* 1 a state or spell of low spirits — see SADNESS

2 utter loss of hope — see DESPAIR 1

form *vb* 1 to take on a definite form ⟨My ideas on the subject are just starting to *form*.⟩

syn crystallize (*also* crystalize), jell, shape (up), solidify

rel associate, coalesce, cohere, fuse; combine, conjoin, conjugate, connect, couple, join, link (up), unify, unite

near ant break down, decay, decompose, disintegrate

2 to be all the substance of — see CONSTITUTE 1

3 to bring into being by combining, shaping, or transforming materials — see MAKE 1

4 to come into existence — see BEGIN 2

5 to come to have gradually — see DEVELOP 2

form *n* 1 the outward appearance of something as distinguished from its substance ⟨The wood-carver carved the block of wood into the *form* of a duck.⟩

syn cast, configuration, conformation, fashion, figure, geometry, shape

rel contour, outline, profile, silhouette; frame, framework, shell, skeleton; arrangement, design, format, layout, make-up, organization, pattern, plan, setup *near ant* composition, material, matter, raw material, stuff, substance

2 a piece of paper with information written or to be written on it ⟨I filled out all the *forms* for applying to the school.⟩
syn blank, document, paper
rel instrument, writ; filing; sheet

3 personal conduct or behavior as evaluated by an accepted standard of appropriateness for a social or professional setting — see MANNER 1

4 a state of being or fitness — see CONDITION 1

5 a three-dimensional representation of the human body used especially for displaying clothes — see MANNEQUIN 1

6 an oft-repeated action or series of actions performed in accordance with tradition or a set of rules — see RITE

7 socially acceptable behavior — see DECENCY 1

8 the means or procedure for doing something — see METHOD

9 the type of body that a person has — see PHYSIQUE

10 the way in which the elements of something (as a work of art) are arranged — see COMPOSITION 3

formal *n* a social gathering for dancing — see DANCE

formal *adj* **1** following or agreeing with established form, custom, or rules ⟨a *formal* meeting of the board of directors⟩ ⟨a *formal* contract that was legally binding⟩
syn ceremonial, ceremonious, conventional, orthodox, regular, routine
rel authorized, official, sanctioned; accepted, correct, decorous, genteel, nice, polite, proper, respectable, seemly; formalistic, ritual, ritualistic; methodical (*also* methodic), orderly, systematic
near ant unauthorized, unofficial; graceless, improper, inappropriate, incorrect, indecorous, inept, infelicitous, unapt, unbecoming, unfit, unhappy, unseemly, unsuitable
ant casual, freewheeling, informal, irregular, unceremonious, unconventional, unorthodox

2 being something in name or form only — see NOMINAL 1

3 marked by or showing careful attention to set forms and details — see CEREMONIOUS 1

4 relating to or suitable for wearing to an event requiring elegant dress and manners — see DRESS

5 very dignified in form, tone, or style — see ELEVATED 2

formality *n* **1** an act or utterance that is a customary show of good manners — see CIVILITY 1

2 an oft-repeated action or series of actions performed in accordance with tradition or a set of rules — see RITE

formalize *vb* **1** to make agree with a single established standard or model — see STANDARDIZE

2 to give official acceptance of as satisfactory — see APPROVE

---

format *n* **1** the way in which something is sized, arranged, or organized ⟨The book's *format* is very user-friendly.⟩
syn arrangement, configuration, conformation, formation, layout, setup
rel design, plan, scheme; composition, constitution, getup, makeup; build, construction, structure

2 the way in which the elements of something (as a work of art) are arranged — see COMPOSITION 3

formation *n* the way in which something is sized, arranged, or organized — see FORMAT 1

formative *adj* having a role in deciding something's final form ⟨a teacher who was a *formative* influence on generations of students⟩
syn constructive, productive
rel causal, creative; consequential, influential
ant nonconstructive, nonproductive, unproductive

former *adj* **1** having been such at some previous time ⟨The coach is a *former* professional baseball player.⟩
syn erstwhile, late, old, onetime, other, past, sometime, whilom
rel bygone, dead, defunct, departed, expired, extinct, gone, long-ago, vanished
near ant contemporary, current, extant, ongoing, present, present-day; coming, future, prospective, unborn

2 going before another in time or order — see PREVIOUS

formidable *adj* **1** causing fear — see FEARFUL 1

2 requiring considerable physical or mental effort — see HARD 2

formless *adj* **1** having no definite or recognizable form ⟨a *formless* mass of clay that the potter transformed into an attractive bowl⟩
syn amorphous, shapeless, unformed, unshaped, unstructured
rel characterless; chaotic, disorganized, incoherent, systemless, unordered, unorganized; dim, fuzzy, hazy, indefinite, indeterminate, indistinct, indistinguishable, murky, nebulous, obscure, unclear, undefined, undetermined, vague
near ant coherent, ordered, orderly, organized; clear, decided, definite, distinct
ant formed, shaped, shapen, structured

2 not composed of matter — see IMMATERIAL 1

formulaic *adj* using or marked by the use of something else as a basis or model — see IMITATIVE 1

formulate *vb* **1** to convey in appropriate or telling terms — see PHRASE

2 to put (something) into proper and usually carefully worked out written form — see COMPOSE 1

formulation *n* an act, process, or means of putting something into words — see EXPRESSION 1

formulator *n* one who creates or introduces something new — see INVENTOR

forsake *vb* to cause to remain behind — see LEAVE 1

forsaken *adj* left unoccupied or unused — see ABANDONED 1

---

syn synonym(s)   *rel* related words
ant antonym(s)   *near ant* near antonym(s)

forsaking *n* the act of abandoning — see DERELICTION 1

fort *n* a structure or place from which one can resist attack ⟨a series of *forts* along the frontier⟩
syn bastion, castle, citadel, fastness, fortification, fortress, hold, stronghold
rel battlement, breastwork, bulwark, earthwork, embattlement, parapet, rampart; bunker, dugout; blockhouse, garrison house

forte *n* something for which a person shows a special talent ⟨Doing funny impressions of people has always been my *forte*.⟩
syn speciality, specialty, thing
rel area, arena, business, circle, demesne, department, discipline, domain, field, line, province, realm, sphere; element; aptitude, aptness, bent, faculty, flair, genius, gift, knack, talent; pursuit, racket, vocation; inclination, leaning, partiality, penchant, predilection, predisposition, proclivity, propensity, tendency

forth *adv* 1 toward a point ahead in space or time — see ONWARD 1
2 toward or at a point lying in advance in space or time — see ALONG

forthcoming *adj* 1 being soon to appear or take place ⟨Everyone's excited about the *forthcoming* company gala.⟩
syn approaching, coming, imminent, impending, nearing, oncoming, pending, upcoming
rel future; anticipated, awaited, expected, foreseen, predicted
phrases at hand, on hand, on tap, to come
near ant bygone, erstwhile, foregone, former, old, onetime, other, past, sometime, whilom
ant late, recent
2 free in expressing one's true feelings and opinions — see FRANK

forthright *adj* 1 free in expressing one's true feelings and opinions — see FRANK
2 going straight to the point clearly and firmly — see STRAIGHTFORWARD 1

forthrightly *adv* in an honest and direct manner — see STRAIGHTFORWARD

forthrightness *n* the free expression of one's true feelings and opinions — see CANDOR 1

forthwith *adv* without delay — see IMMEDIATELY

fortification *n* a structure or place from which one can resist attack — see FORT

fortify *vb* 1 to prepare (oneself) mentally or emotionally ⟨Kelly *fortified* herself for the basketball tournament with a series of confidence-boosting exercises.⟩
syn brace, forearm, nerve, poise, psych (up), ready, steel, strengthen
rel arm; harden, inure, season, toughen; bolster, boost, buoy (up), buttress, enforce, prop (up), support, sustain; cheer (up), comfort, embolden, encourage, hearten, inspire; rally, rouse, stir
near ant daunt, demoralize, discourage, dishearten, dispirit, psych (out), shake, unnerve; debilitate, enervate, enfeeble, prostrate, sap, soften, tire, undercut, undermine, weaken
2 to increase the ability of (as a muscle) to exert physical force — see STRENGTHEN 1

3 to make able to withstand physical hardship, strain, or exposure — see HARDEN 2

fortitude *n* the strength of mind that enables a person to endure pain or hardship ⟨It was only with the greatest *fortitude* that the Pilgrims were able to survive their first winter in Plymouth.⟩
syn backbone, constancy, fiber, grit, guts, pluck, spunk
rel determination, purposefulness, resoluteness, resolution; bravery, courage, courageousness, daring, dauntlessness, doughtiness, fearlessness, gallantry, greatheartedness, intrepidity, intrepidness, nerve, stoutness, valor; endurance, forbearance, stamina, sufferance, tolerance; heart, mettle, spirit; audacity, boldness, brass, cheek, effrontery, gall, hardihood, nerve, nerviness, temerity
near ant indecisiveness, irresoluteness, irresolution, vacillation; cowardice, cowardliness, cravenness, dastardliness, faintheartedness, pusillanimity, timidity, timorousness
ant spinelessness

fortress *n* a structure or place from which one can resist attack — see FORT

fortuitous *adj* 1 coming or happening by good luck especially unexpectedly — see FORTUNATE 1
2 happening by chance — see ACCIDENTAL 1

fortunate *adj* 1 coming or happening by good luck especially unexpectedly ⟨In a *fortunate* turn of events, the motel had one last vacancy.⟩
syn fluky (*also* flukey), fortuitous, happy, lucky, providential
rel convenient, opportune, seasonable, timely; unexpected, unforeseen, unlooked-for; accidental, chance, coincidental, serendipitous; auspicious, bright, encouraging, fair, heartening, hopeful, promising, propitious; benign, favorable, golden, good, halcyon; advantageous, beneficial, profitable
near ant inconvenient, inopportune, unseasonable, untimely; anticipated, expected, foreseen; deliberate, intentional, planned; inauspicious, unpromising; calamitous, catastrophic, disastrous
ant hapless, ill-fated, ill-starred, luckless, star-crossed, unfortunate, unhappy, unlucky
2 having good luck — see LUCKY 1

fortunateness *n* success that is partly the result of chance — see LUCK 1

fortune *n* 1 what is going to happen to someone in the time ahead ⟨The telephone psychic proceeded to tell me my *fortune*—at great length.⟩
syn future
rel circumstance, destiny, doom, fate, hap, lot, portion; futurities, outlook, prospect
near ant present
ant past
2 a very large amount of money ⟨The billionaire's huge mansion must have cost a *fortune*.⟩
syn bundle, earth, king's ransom, mint, pile, wad
rel heap, pot; bonanza, mine; assets, capital, means, property, riches, wealth,

wherewithal; bread [*slang*], cash, chips, currency, dough, gold, jack [*slang*], legal tender, lucre, pelf, tender, wampum

near ant petty cash, pin money, pocket money, spending money

ant mite, peanuts, pittance, song

3 a state or end that seemingly has been decided beforehand — see FATE 1

4 success that is partly the result of chance — see LUCK 1

5 the total of one's money and property — see WEALTH 1

fortune–teller *n* one who predicts future events or developments — see PROPHET 1

forty winks *n pl* a short sleep — see ¹NAP

forum *n* **1** a meeting featuring a group discussion ⟨a public *forum* called to find out how residents felt about a large discount store being built in their neighborhood⟩

syn colloquy, conference, council, panel, parley, roundtable, seminar, symposium

rel colloquium; caucus, town meeting; assembly, conclave, congregation, congress, consistory, convention, convocation, synod; debate, deliberation; brainstorming; chat room, newsgroup; medium, outlet, platform, venue

2 an assembly of persons for the administration of justice — see COURT 3

forward *adj* **1** showing a lack of proper social reserve or modesty — see PRESUMPTUOUS 1

2 being at or in the forward part or surface of something — see FRONT

3 being far along in development — see ADVANCED

4 having or showing awareness of and preparation for the future — see FORESIGHTED

forward *adv* **1** toward or at a point lying in advance in space or time — see ALONG

2 toward a point ahead in space or time — see ONWARD 1

forward *vb* to help the growth or development of — see FOSTER 1

forwards *adv* toward or at a point lying in advance in space or time — see ALONG

fossil *n* a person with old-fashioned ideas — see FOGY

foster *vb* **1** to help the growth or development of ⟨The head librarian firmly declared that it is indeed the duty of local government to *foster* learning and a love of reading.⟩

syn advance, cultivate, encourage, forward, further, incubate, nourish, nurse, nurture, promote

rel advocate, back, champion, endorse (*also* indorse), support, uphold; endow, finance, fund, patronize, stake, subsidize, underwrite; abet, aid, assist; advertise, boost, plug, publicize, tout; agitate (for), campaign (for), work (for)

near ant ban, bar, enjoin, forbid, interdict, outlaw, prevent, prohibit, proscribe; repress, snuff (out), squash, squelch, stifle, subdue, suppress; arrest, check, halt, retard; encumber, fetter, hobble, impede, interfere (with), manacle, obstruct, shackle

ant discourage, frustrate, hinder, inhibit

2 to bring to maturity through care and education — see BRING UP 1

foul *vb* **1** to make dirty — see DIRTY

2 to make unfit for use by the addition of something harmful or undesirable — see CONTAMINATE

3 to reduce to a lower standing in one's own eyes or in others' eyes — see HUMBLE

4 to go through decomposition — see DECAY 1

foul *adj* **1** marked by wet and windy conditions ⟨The *foul* weather brought out the windbreakers and rain slickers as everyone braced for a day of rough sailing.⟩

syn bleak, dirty, inclement, nasty, raw, rough, squally, stormy, tempestuous, turbulent

rel blowy, blustering, blustery, breezy, gusty, windblown, windswept; cloudy, overcast; rainy, snowy; foggy, hazy, misty, murky, soupy

near ant rainless; balmy, calm, halcyon, peaceful, placid, pleasant, serene

ant bright, clear, clement, cloudless, fair, sunny, sunshiny, unclouded

2 not being in accordance with the rules or standards of what is fair in sport ⟨an aggressive hockey player who is known for his *foul* play and readiness for a fight⟩

syn dirty, illegal, nasty, unfair, unsportsmanlike

rel dishonorable, shabby, shameful; ignoble, low, mean, ungentlemanly; immoral, rotten, unchivalrous, unethical, unjust, unprincipled, unrighteous, unscrupulous

phrases below the belt

near ant just, law-abiding; ethical, moral, principled, righteous, scrupulous; honorable, irreproachable, unimpeachable

ant clean, fair, legal, sportsmanlike, sportsmanly

3 causing intense displeasure, disgust, or resentment — see OFFENSIVE 1

4 depicting or referring to sexual matters in a way that is unacceptable in polite society — see OBSCENE 1

5 having an unpleasant smell — see MALODOROUS

6 not clean — see DIRTY 1

foulness *n* **1** the quality or state of being obscene — see OBSCENITY

2 the state or quality of being dirty — see DIRTINESS

foul play *n* **1** the taking of another person's life — see HOMICIDE 1

2 the use of brute strength to cause harm to a person or property — see VIOLENCE 1

foul-up *n* an instance of confusion ⟨There was a *foul-up* with our mail order, and not one item arrived as ordered.⟩

syn mix-up

rel bobble, botch, bungle, fumble; blunder, error, fault, flub, goof, inaccuracy, lapse, miscue, misstep, mistake, oversight, slip, slipup, stumble; chaos, confusion, disarrangement, disarray, disorder, disorganization, hash, jumble, mess, muddle, shambles

foul up *vb* **1** to make or do (something) in a clumsy or unskillful way — see BOTCH

2 to make a mistake — see ERR 1

found *vb* to be responsible for the creation and early operation or use of ⟨John Har-

---

syn synonym(s) **rel** related words
ant antonym(s) **near ant** near antonym(s)

vard did not actually *found* the university that now bears his name.⟩
syn begin, constitute, establish, inaugurate, initiate, innovate, institute, introduce, launch, pioneer, plant, set up, start
rel author, father, originate; conceive, concoct, contrive, cook (up), create, devise, fabricate, invent, make up, manufacture, produce, think (up); construct, put up; develop, enlarge, expand; endow, finance, fund, subsidize; arrange, organize, systematize
near ant abolish, annihilate, annul, nullify; end, finish, halt, stop, terminate; round (off *or* out), wind up, wrap up
ant phase out, shut (up)
foundation *n* 1 a public organization with a particular purpose or function — see INSTITUTION 1
2 an immaterial thing upon which something else rests — see BASE 1
founder *n* a person who establishes a whole new field of endeavor — see FATHER 2
founder *vb* 1 to be unsuccessful — see FAIL 2
2 to fall down or in as a result of physical pressure — see COLLAPSE 1
foursquare *adj* 1 free in expressing one's true feelings and opinions — see FRANK
2 going straight to the point clearly and firmly — see STRAIGHTFORWARD 1
3 having four equal sides and four right angles — see SQUARE 1
foursquare *adv* in an honest and direct manner — see STRAIGHTFORWARD
fox *n* a physically attractive person — see DOLL 1
fox *vb* 1 to throw into a state of mental uncertainty — see CONFUSE 1
2 to get the better of through cleverness — see OUTWIT
foxiness *n* 1 skill in achieving one's ends through indirect, subtle, or underhanded means — see CUNNING 1
2 the inclination or practice of misleading others through lies or trickery — see DECEIT 1
3 exceptional discernment and judgment especially in practical matters — see ACUMEN
foxy *adj* clever at attaining one's ends by indirect and often deceptive means — see ARTFUL 1
foyer *n* 1 a centrally located room in a building that serves as a gathering or waiting area or as a passageway into the interior ⟨Theatergoers crowded the *foyer* during the play's intermission.⟩
syn hall, lobby
rel entry, entryway, hallway, vestibule; concourse, corridor, gallery, passageway; antechamber, anteroom, chamber, waiting room
2 the entrance room of a building — see HALL 1
fracas *n* 1 a physical dispute between opposing individuals or groups — see FIGHT 1
2 a rough and often noisy fight usually involving several people — see BRAWL 1
fractionation *n* the act or process of a whole separating into two or more parts or pieces — see SEPARATION 1

fracture *vb* 1 to cause to separate into pieces usually suddenly or forcibly — see BREAK 1
2 to fail to keep — see VIOLATE 1
fragile *adj* 1 easily broken ⟨*fragile* flower petals⟩
syn breakable, delicate, frail
rel dainty, fine, gossamer; eggshell, flimsy, slight, tenuous; brittle, crisp, crispy, crumbly, crushable, embrittled, flaky (*also* flakey), friable, shaky, shivery, short; feeble, infirm, soft, spindly, tender, weak; inelastic, inflexible, stiff
near ant compact, firm, hard, rigid, solid, substantial, unyielding; elastic, flexible, resilient, rubberlike, rubbery, springy, stretch, stretchable, supple
ant nonbreakable, strong, sturdy, tough, unbreakable
2 easily injured without careful handling — see TENDER 1
3 small in degree — see REMOTE 1
fragility *n* 1 the state or quality of having a delicate structure — see DELICACY 2
2 the quality or state of lacking physical strength or vigor — see WEAKNESS 1
fragment *vb* to cause to separate into pieces usually suddenly or forcibly — see BREAK 1
fragment *n* a broken or irregular part of something that often remains incomplete ⟨*fragments* of broken glass⟩
syn bit, piece, scrap
rel shred, tatter; end, leftover, oddment, remainder, remnant, stub; portion, section, segment; chip, flake, shard, shatter, shiver, sliver, splinter; clipping, paring, shaving; atom, crumb, dribble, fleck, flyspeck, grain, granule, molecule, morsel, mote, nubbin, nugget, particle, patch, scruple, snip, snippet, speck, title
fragmental *adj* lacking some necessary part — see INCOMPLETE
fragmentary *adj* lacking some necessary part — see INCOMPLETE
fragrance *n* a sweet or pleasant smell ⟨the *fragrance* of lilac trees in full bloom⟩
syn aroma, bouquet, incense, perfume, redolence, scent, spice
rel essence, odor
ant reek, stench, stink
fragrant *adj* having a pleasant smell ⟨The balsam fir is a favorite as a Christmas tree because it is so *fragrant*.⟩
syn ambrosial, aromatic, perfumed, redolent, savory (*also* savoury), scented, sweet
rel flowery, fruity, pungent, spicy; odiferous, odored, odoriferous, odorous; clean, fresh, pure
near ant odorless, unscented, fusty, musty, stale; gamy (*or* gamey)
ant fetid, foul, malodorous, noisome, putrid, rank, reeking, reeky, skunky, smelly, stenchful, stenchy, stinking, stinky, strong
frail *adj* 1 easily broken — see FRAGILE 1
2 easily injured without careful handling — see TENDER 1
3 lacking bodily strength — see WEAK 1
4 lacking strength of will or character — see WEAK 2
5 small in degree — see REMOTE 1
frailness *n* 1 the quality or state of lacking

physical strength or vigor — see WEAKNESS 1

2 the quality or state of lacking strength of will or character — see WEAKNESS 2

frailty *n* **1** a defect in character — see FAULT 1

2 the quality or state of lacking physical strength or vigor — see WEAKNESS 1

3 the quality or state of lacking strength of will or character — see WEAKNESS 2

frame *vb* **1** to bring into being by combining, shaping, or transforming materials — see MAKE 1

2 to plan out usually with subtle skill or care — see ENGINEER

3 to put (something) into proper and usually carefully worked out written form — see COMPOSE 1

4 to work out the details of (something) in advance — see PLAN 1

5 to serve as a border for — see BORDER

frame *n* **1** the arrangement of parts that gives something its basic form ⟨Now that the *frame* has been built, we have a better idea of the size of our new house.⟩

syn configuration, edifice, fabric, framework, shell, skeleton, structure

rel cage, lattice, network; contour, figure, outline, profile, shape, silhouette; chassis

2 the type of body that a person has — see PHYSIQUE

3 the line or relatively narrow space that marks the outer limit of something — see BORDER 1

framework *n* the arrangement of parts that gives something its basic form — see FRAME 1

franchise *n* the right to formally express one's position or will in an election — see VOTE 1

frank *adj* free in expressing one's true feelings and opinions ⟨Our ballet teacher is very *frank* about telling her students whether she thinks they have the talent for a career in dance.⟩

syn candid, direct, forthcoming, forthright, foursquare, free-spoken, honest, open, openhearted, outspoken, plain, plainspoken, straight, straightforward, unguarded, unreserved

rel artless, earnest, guileless, ingenuous, innocent, naive (*or* naïve), natural, real, sincere, unaffected, undesigning, unpretending, unpretentious; outgoing, uninhibited, unrestrained; vocal, vociferous; abrupt, bluff, blunt, brusque (*also* brusk), crusty, curt, gruff, sharp; impertinent, impolite, inconsiderate, rude, tactless, thoughtless, uncivil, ungracious, unmannerly, unsubtle

near ant inhibited, reserved, restrained; close-mouthed, laconic, quiet, reticent, taciturn, tight-lipped, uncommunicative; diplomatic, politic, tactful; civil, considerate, courteous, polite

ant dissembling, uncandid, unforthcoming

frankly *adv* to tell the truth — see ACTUALLY 1

frankness *n* the free expression of one's true feelings and opinions — see CANDOR 1

frantic *adj* **1** feeling overwhelming fear or worry ⟨The *frantic* student searched all over the school for the lost notebook.⟩

syn agitated, delirious, distracted, distraught, frenzied, hysterical (*also* hysteric)

rel alarmed, anxious, disquieted, disturbed, nervous, perturbed, tense, troubled, upset, worried, wrought (up); berserk, demented, deranged, mad, maniacal (*also* maniac); nuclear; ranting, raving

phrases beside oneself

near ant calm, peaceful, placid, self-possessed, serene, tranquil; cool, coolheaded, undisturbed, unperturbed, unshaken, untroubled, unworried

ant collected, composed, self-collected, self-possessed, unhysterical

2 marked by great and often stressful excitement or activity — see FURIOUS 1

frantically *adv* in a confused and reckless manner — see HELTER-SKELTER 1

fraternal *adj* of, relating to, or befitting brothers ⟨There was a *fraternal* bond between the two boys all throughout their school years.⟩

syn brotherly

rel familial, sisterly; chummy, friendly, neighborly

fraternity *n* **1** a group of persons formally joined together for some common interest — see ASSOCIATION 2

2 the body of people in a profession or field of activity — see CORPS

fraternize *vb* **1** to come or be together as friends — see ASSOCIATE 1

2 to take part in social activities — see SOCIALIZE

fraud *n* **1** an instance of the use of dishonest methods to acquire something of value ⟨Thousands of people lost money when the investment scheme turned out to be a *fraud*.⟩

syn con, hustle, scam, sting, swindle

rel cross, fix; Ponzi scheme, pyramid scheme; racket, rip-off; thimblerig, three-card monte; device, dodge, gimmick, jig, ploy, scheme, sleight, stratagem, trick, wile; counterfeit, fake, forgery, hoax, humbug, phony (*also* phoney), sham

2 one who makes false claims of identity or expertise — see IMPOSTOR

3 the inclination or practice of misleading others through lies or trickery — see DECEIT 1

fraudulent *adj* **1** marked by, based on, or done by the use of dishonest methods to acquire something of value ⟨Hoping to get millions from the insurance company, the man made the *fraudulent* claim that he had been seriously injured in the accident.⟩

syn crooked, deceitful, defrauding, dishonest, double-dealing, false

rel beguiling, deceiving, deceptive, deluding, delusive, delusory, fallacious, misleading, specious; spurious

near ant legitimate, true, valid

ant aboveboard, honest, truthful

2 given to or marked by cheating and deception — see DISHONEST 2

fraught *adj* **1** possessing or covered with great numbers or amounts of something specified — see RIFE

2 marked by or causing agitation or uncomfortable feelings — see NERVOUS 2

fray *n* 1 a forceful effort to reach a goal or objective — see STRUGGLE 1

2 a physical dispute between opposing individuals or groups — see FIGHT 1

3 a rough and often noisy fight usually involving several people — see BRAWL 1

fray *vb* to damage or diminish by continued friction — see ABRADE 1

frayed *adj* worn or torn into or as if into rags — see RAGGED 2

frazzle *n* a complete depletion of energy or strength — see FATIGUE

frazzle *vb* 1 to damage or diminish by continued friction — see ABRADE 1

2 to use up all the physical energy of — see EXHAUST 1

3 to trouble the mind of; to make uneasy — see DISTURB 1

freak *adj* being out of the ordinary — see EXCEPTIONAL 1

freak *n* 1 a person, thing, or event that is far from normal ⟨That snowstorm in April was a *freak*, since our weather is usually much balmier by then.⟩

syn abnormality, anomaly, monster, monstrosity

rel abortion, malformation, miscreation, mutant, mutation; character, crackbrain, crackpot, crank, eccentric, kook, nut, oddball, screwball, weirdo; aberrant, deviant; individualist, maverick, nonconformist; curiosity, peculiarity, singularity; aberration, irregularity, oddity, rarity

near ant sample, specimen; commonplace, usual

ant average, norm, normal, par, standard

2 a person with a strong and habitual liking for something — see FAN

3 a sudden impulsive and apparently unmotivated idea or action — see WHIM

freak (out) *vb* 1 to trouble the mind of; to make uneasy — see DISTURB 1

2 to yield to mental or emotional stress — see CRACK 2

freckle *vb* to mark with small spots especially unevenly — see SPOT 1

freckled *adj* marked with spots — see SPOTTED 1

free *adj* 1 not being under the rule or control of another ⟨The country became *free* after many years under foreign control.⟩

syn autonomous, freestanding, independent, self-governing, self-ruling, separate, sovereign (*also* sovran)

rel freeborn; delivered, emancipated, freed, liberated, manumitted, redeemed, released; unconquered, unruled, unsupervised; empowered, enfranchised; democratic, republican

near ant bound, captive, conquered, enslaved, fettered, subdued, subjugated; inferior, subordinate, subservient

ant dependent, nonautonomous, non-self-governing, subject, unfree

2 no longer burdened with something unpleasant or painful ⟨After our son arrived home safely, we were grateful to be *free* from worry.⟩

syn disencumbered, quit, unburdened

rel delivered, freed, liberated, released; unhampered, unimpeded

near ant encumbered, handicapped, hindered, hobbled

3 not bound, confined, or detained by force ⟨All of the animals in the game preserve are *free* to roam all over its vast area.⟩

syn footloose, loose, unbound, unconfined, unrestrained

rel escaped; uncaged, unchained, unfettered, unleashed; uncaught; unanchored, unbolted, undone, unfastened, untied; clear, disengaged

phrases at large, at liberty

near ant caught; caged, chained, enclosed (*also* inclosed), immured, imprisoned, leashed, penned; anchored, bolted, fastened, fettered, manacled, shackled, tied; kidnapped (*also* kidnaped)

ant bound, restrained, unfree

4 not costing or charging anything ⟨Although the museum normally charges admission, on Wednesdays it is *free* to all.⟩

syn complimentary, gratis, gratuitous

rel nominal; bestowed, donated, given; pro bono; discretionary, freewill, optional, voluntary; uncompensated, unpaid

phrases on the house

near ant paid; costly, dear, expensive, high

5 allowing passage without obstruction — see OPEN 1

6 giving or sharing in abundance and without hesitation — see GENEROUS 1

7 not being in a state of use, activity, or employment — see INACTIVE 2

8 showing a lack of proper social reserve or modesty — see PRESUMPTUOUS 1

9 not physically attached to another unit — see SEPARATE 2

free *vb* 1 to release (as from slavery or confinement) ⟨A global crusade to *free* Nelson Mandela from a South African prison had emerged.⟩

syn discharge, emancipate, enfranchise, enlarge, liberate, loose, loosen, manumit, release, spring, unbind, uncage, unchain, unfetter

rel bail (out), deliver, parole, ransom, redeem, rescue, save; adrift, disencumber, disengage, disentangle, extricate; unshackle

phrases turn loose

near ant handcuff, manacle, shackle, trammel; commit, immure, imprison, incarcerate, intern, jail, lock (up); conquer, enslave, subdue, subjugate

ant bind, confine, enchain, fetter, restrain

2 to make passage through (something) possible by removing obstructions — see OPEN 2

3 to rid the surface of (as an area) from things in the way — see CLEAR 1

4 to set (a person or thing) free of something that encumbers — see RID

5 to set free from entanglement or difficulty — see EXTRICATE

freebie *or* **freebee** *n* something given to someone without expectation of a return — see GIFT 1

freebooter *n* someone who engages in robbery of ships at sea — see PIRATE

freedom *n* 1 the state of being free from the control or power of another ⟨We owe our *freedom* to the untold numbers of soldiers who have fought in our nation's wars since its founding.⟩

syn autonomy, independence, liberty, self-determination, self-government, sovereignty (*also* sovranty)

rel emancipation, enfranchisement, liberation, manumission, release

near ant captivity, enchainment, enslavement, immurement, imprisonment, incarceration, internment, subjugation

ant dependence (*also* dependance), heteronomy, subjection, unfreedom

2 the right to act or move freely ⟨The youngsters had full *freedom* of the park.⟩

syn authorization, free hand, latitude, license (*or* licence), run

rel authority, clutch, command, control, dominion, grip, hold, mandate, mastery, power, sway; range, room, space; blank check, carte blanche

free–for–all *adj* freely available for use or participation by all — see OPEN 2

free–for–all *n* **1** a rough and often noisy fight usually involving several people — see BRAWL 1

2 a state in which everything is out of order — see CHAOS

free hand *n* the right to act or move freely — see FREEDOM 2

freehanded *adj* giving or sharing in abundance and without hesitation — see GENEROUS 1

freeing *n* the act of setting free from slavery — see LIBERATION

freely *adv* **1** of one's own free will — see VOLUNTARILY

2 without difficulty — see EASILY 1

free–spoken *adj* free in expressing one's true feelings and opinions — see FRANK

freestanding *adj* **1** not physically attached to another unit — see SEPARATE 2

2 not being under the rule or control of another — see FREE 1

freeway *n* a passage cleared for public vehicular travel — see WAY 1

freewheeling *adj* not held back by rules, duties, or worries ⟨James Bond has long been the model of the *freewheeling* hero who encounters danger and excitement in every corner of the globe.⟩

syn footloose

rel affable, breezy, casual, devil-may-care, easygoing, happy-go-lucky, laid-back, nonchalant, relaxed; unattached, uncommitted; self-abandoned, unbridled, unrestrained; uninhibited; self-assured, self-confident, self-reliant

near ant attached, committed, pledged

ant tied

freewill *adj* done, made, or given with one's own free will — see VOLUNTARY 1

free will *n* the act or power of making one's own choices or decisions ⟨All of the workers at the animal shelter are unpaid and are there of their own *free will*.⟩

syn accord, autonomy, choice, self-determination, volition, will

rel election, preference, selection; bent, devices, disposition, inclination, leaning, partiality, penchant, predilection, predisposition, proclivity, propensity, tendency; alternative, discretion, option, pick, way

near ant coercion, compulsion, constraint, duress, force, pressure

freeze *n* a weather condition marked by low temperatures — see COLD

freeze *vb* to become physically firm or solid — see HARDEN 1

freezing *adj* having a low or subnormal temperature — see COLD 1

freight *n* **1** a mass or quantity of something taken up and carried, conveyed, or transported — see LOAD 1

2 the amount of money that is demanded as payment for something — see PRICE 1

freight *vb* to place a weight or burden on — see LOAD 1

frenetic *adj* marked by great and often stressful excitement or activity — see FURIOUS 1

frenzied *adj* **1** being in a state of increased activity or agitation — see FEVERISH 1

2 feeling overwhelming fear or worry — see FRANTIC 1

3 marked by great and often stressful excitement or activity — see FURIOUS 1

frenziedly *adv* in a confused and reckless manner — see HELTER-SKELTER 1

frenzy *n* a state of wildly excited activity or emotion ⟨In its *frenzy* to flee the danger, the herd thundered across the savannah.⟩

syn agitation, delirium, distraction, fever, flap, furor, furore, fury, hysteria, rage, rampage, uproar

rel chaos, confusion, disorder, havoc, pandemonium, turmoil; bedlam, bother, brouhaha, bustle, clamor, clatter, commotion, disturbance, fuss, hoo-ha (*also* hoohah), hubbub, hullabaloo, hurly-burly, ruckus, ruction, rumpus, shindy, squall, stew, stir, storm, tempest, to-do, tumult

near ant calm, calmness, peace, peacefulness, placidity, quiet, quietude, repose, restfulness, sereneness, serenity, still, stillness, tranquillity (*or* tranquility)

frenzy *vb* to cause to go insane or as if insane — see CRAZE

frequency *n* the fact or state of happening often ⟨The *frequency* of twins in that family is remarkable.⟩

syn commonness, frequentness, prevalence

rel constancy, regularity; appearance, incidence, occurrence

ant infrequence, infrequency, rareness, uncommonness, unusualness

frequent *adj* **1** appearing or occurring repeatedly from time to time — see REGULAR 1

2 often observed or encountered — see COMMON 1

frequent *vb* to go to or spend time in often ⟨Like their counterparts elsewhere, the town's teenagers like to *frequent* the local malls.⟩

syn haunt, resort (to), visit

rel patronize; attend, take in; infest, invade, overrun, swarm; call (on *or* upon), pop (in), run (in), stop (in *or* by); camp (out in), sojourn (at), stay (at), stop (over), tarry (in)

near ant dodge, duck, elude, escape, eschew, evade, shake

ant avoid, shun

frequenter *n* **1** a person who visits another — see GUEST 1

---

2 someone who regularly spends time in a particular place — see DENIZEN 1

frequently *adv* many times — see OFTEN

frequentness *n* the fact or state of happening often — see FREQUENCY

fresh *adj* **1** being in an original and unused or unspoiled state ⟨The restaurant uses only really *fresh* ingredients in all of its dishes.⟩

syn brand-new, mint, pristine, virgin, virginal

rel unaltered, unblemished, unbruised, uncontaminated, undamaged, undefiled, unharmed, unhurt, unimpaired, uninjured, unmarred, unpolluted, unsoiled, unspoiled, unsullied, untainted, untouched, unworn; new, spick-and-span (*or* spic-and-span)

near ant blemished, broken, bruised, damaged, defaced, defiled, disfigured, harmed, hurt, impaired, injured, marred, soiled, sullied, tainted; faded, shopworn, used, worn; contaminated, polluted, spoiled; hand-me-down, second hand

ant stale

2 displaying or marked by rude boldness — see NERVY 1

3 not known or experienced before — see NEW 2

4 resulting in an increase in amount or number — see ADDITIONAL

freshen *vb* to bring back to a former condition or vigor — see RENEW 1

freshened *adj* made or become fresh in spirits or vigor — see NEW 4

freshly *adv* not long ago — see NEWLY

freshman *n* a person who is just starting out in a field of activity — see BEGINNER

freshness *n* the quality or appeal of being new — see NOVELTY 1

fret *vb* **1** to consume or wear away gradually — see EAT 2

2 to damage or diminish by continued friction — see ABRADE 1

3 to experience concern or anxiety — see WORRY 1

4 to make sore by continued rubbing — see CHAFE 1

fret *n* a state of nervous or irritated concern ⟨One of my customers always gets into a *fret* if I'm so much as 5 minutes late delivering his pizza.⟩

syn dither, fluster, fuss, huff, lather, pother, stew, tizzy, twitter

rel bother, dudgeon, pique; alarm (*also* alarum), hand-wringing, panic; ado, agitation, delirium, distraction, furor, hysteria, uproar

friable *adj* having a texture that readily breaks into little pieces under pressure — see CRISP 1

friary *n* a residence for men under religious vows — see MONASTERY

friction *n* a lack of agreement or harmony — see DISCORD

frictionless *adj* having or marked by agreement in feeling or action — see HARMONIOUS 3

friend *n* **1** a person who has a strong liking for and trust in another ⟨really close *friends* who like to do everything together and are always sharing secrets⟩

syn alter ego, buddy, chum, compadre,

comrade, confidant, crony, familiar, intimate, pal

rel acquaintance; associate, cohort, colleague, companion, fellow, hearty, hobnobber, partner, peer, sport; blood brother, brother, main man, sister; abettor (*also* abetter), accomplice, ally, collaborator, confederate; pen pal; benefactor, supporter, sympathizer, well-wisher; friendly

near ant adversary, antagonist, competitor, opponent, rival; archenemy, nemesis

ant enemy, foe

2 a person who actively supports or favors a cause — see EXPONENT 1

friendliness *n* kindly concern, interest, or support — see GOODWILL 1

friendly *adj* **1** having or showing kindly feeling and sincere interest ⟨All of the people in my new department seem *friendly*.⟩ ⟨As a *friendly* gesture, we presented our new neighbors with a plate of homemade cookies.⟩

syn amicable, chummy, companionable, cordial, genial, hearty, neighborly, palsy, warm, warmhearted

rel affable, agreeable, approachable, good-natured, good-tempered, gracious, nice, sweet; clubby, convivial, gregarious, hospitable, sociable, social; jolly, jovial, merry; extroverted (*also* extraverted), outgoing; brotherly, fraternal, sisterly; close, familiar, intimate; adoring, affectionate, devoted, fond, loving, tender, tenderhearted

near ant alienated, estranged; chilly, cold, cold-blooded, cool, frigid, frosty, glacial, icy, wintry (*also* wintery); unsociable, unsocial; aggressive, argumentative, bellicose, belligerent, combative, contentious, disputatious, pugnacious, quarrelsome, scrappy, truculent; inhospitable, inimical

ant antagonistic, hostile, unfriendly

2 closely acquainted — see FAMILIAR 1

3 expressing approval — see FAVORABLE 1

4 willing to do a favor — see ACCOMMODATING

5 promoting or contributing to personal or social well-being — see BENEFICIAL

friendship *n* kindly concern, interest, or support — see GOODWILL 1

fright *n* **1** something unpleasant to look at — see EYESORE

2 the emotion experienced in the presence or threat of danger — see FEAR 1

fright *vb* to strike with fear — see FRIGHTEN

frighten *vb* to strike with fear ⟨Around the campfire the campers tried to *frighten* one another with ghostly legends and grisly tales.⟩

syn alarm (*also* alarum), fright, horrify, panic, scare, shock, spook, startle, terrify, terrorize

rel appall (*also* appal), dismay, floor, jolt, shake, shake up; amaze, astound, awe; chill, daunt, demoralize, dispirit, emasculate, psych (out), undo, unman, unnerve, unstring; discomfort, discompose, disconcert, disquiet, distract, distress, disturb, perturb, unsettle, upset, worry

phrases give one the creeps, make one's flesh creep (*or* crawl)

near ant assure, cheer, comfort, console,

solace, soothe; embolden, encourage, hearten, inspire, steel
ant reassure

frightened *adj* filled with fear or dread — see AFRAID

frightening *adj* causing fear — see FEARFUL 1

frightful *adj* **1** causing fear — see FEARFUL 1

2 extremely disturbing or repellent — see HORRIBLE 1

3 extreme in degree, power, or effect — see INTENSE 1

frightfully *adv* to a great degree — see VERY 1

frightfulness *n* the quality of inspiring intense dread or dismay — see HORROR 1

frigid *adj* **1** having a low or subnormal temperature — see COLD 1

2 lacking in friendliness or warmth of feeling — see COLD 2

frill *n* **1** a strip of fabric gathered or pleated on one edge and used as trimming — see RUFFLE 1

2 something adding to pleasure or comfort but not absolutely necessary — see LUXURY 1

3 something that decorates or beautifies — see DECORATION 1

fringe *n* the line or relatively narrow space that marks the outer limit of something — see BORDER 1

fringe *vb* **1** to be adjacent to — see ADJOIN 1

2 to serve as a border for — see BORDER

fringing *adj* having a border in common — see ADJACENT

frippery *n* dressy clothing — see FINERY

frisk *vb* to play and run about happily — see FROLIC 1

friskiness *n* a natural disposition for playful behavior — see PLAYFULNESS

frisky *adj* **1** given to good-natured joking or teasing — see PLAYFUL

2 having much high-spirited energy and movement — see LIVELY 1

fritter *n* a small usually rounded mass of minced food that has been fried — see CAKE 1

fritter (away) *vb* to use up carelessly — see WASTE 1

fritterer *n* someone who spends money freely or foolishly — see PRODIGAL

frivolity *n* a lack of seriousness often at an improper time ⟨The boys were scolded for joking during the funeral service, which was hardly the time for *frivolity*.⟩
syn facetiousness, flightiness, flippancy, frivolousness, levity, light-headedness, lightness, silliness
rel cheer, cheerfulness, festivity, gaiety (*also* gayety), glee, gleefulness, high-spiritedness, hilarity, joviality, lightheartedness, merriment, mirth, mirthfulness; childishness, goofiness, puerility; insignificance, littleness, slightness, smallness, triviality
near ant dejection, depression, despondency, dispiritedness, downheartedness, gloom, gloominess, heartsickness, joylessness, melancholy, mopes, moroseness, sadness, sullenness, unhappiness

ant earnestness, gravity, seriousness, soberness, solemnity

frivolous *adj* **1** lacking importance — see UNIMPORTANT

2 lacking in seriousness or maturity — see GIDDY 1

frivolousness *n* a lack of seriousness often at an improper time — see FRIVOLITY

frock *n* **1** a garment with a joined blouse and skirt usually worn by a woman or girl — see DRESS 1

2 a sleeveless garment worn so as to hang over the shoulders, arms, and back — see ¹CAPE

frolic *n* **1** a playful or mischievous act intended as a joke — see PRANK

2 a time or instance of carefree fun — see FLING 1

3 activity engaged in to amuse oneself — see PLAY 1

frolic *vb* **1** to play and run about happily ⟨Scores of swimmers were *frolicking* in the ocean surf along the beach.⟩
syn caper, cavort, disport, frisk, gambol, lark, rollick, romp, sport
rel bound, hop, leap, lope, skip, spring, trip, tumble; dance, prance; carouse, revel, roister; carry on, horse around; clown, cut up; joyride, roughhouse, skylark; kite
phrases cut capers, kick up one's heels
near ant mope, pout, stew, sulk

2 to engage in activity for amusement — see PLAY 1

frolicking *n* activity engaged in to amuse oneself — see PLAY 1

frolicsome *adj* **1** given to good-natured joking or teasing — see PLAYFUL

2 joyously unrestrained — see EXUBERANT

front *vb* to stand or sit with the face or front toward — see FACE 1

front *adj* being at or in the forward part or surface of something ⟨Visitors use the *front* door, but family knows to go around to the side entrance.⟩
syn anterior, forward
rel ventral
near ant dorsal
ant aft, after, hind, hinder, hindmost, posterior, rear, rearward

front *n* **1** a forward part or surface ⟨The *front* of the church features a magnificent stained-glass window.⟩
syn facade (*also* façade), face, forepart
rel outside, skin, surface, veneer
near ant innards, inside, interior
ant back, rear, rearward, reverse

2 a display of emotion or behavior that is insincere or intended to deceive — see MASQUERADE

3 a region of activity, knowledge, or influence — see FIELD 2

frontier *n* **1** a region along the dividing line between two countries ⟨the *frontier* on the U.S.-Mexico border⟩
syn border, borderland, march

2 a rural region that forms the edge of the settled or developed part of a country ⟨Alaska has been called America's last *frontier*.⟩
syn backwater, backwoods, bush, hinterland, up-country
rel boondocks, country, countryside, sticks
phrases (the) back of beyond

---

syn synonym(s)   *rel* related words
ant antonym(s)   *near ant* near antonym(s)

frontiersman *n* a person who settles in a new region ⟨The *frontiersmen* were willing to brave harsh living conditions in order to achieve a better life.⟩
syn colonist, colonizer, homesteader, pioneer, settler
rel explorer, pathfinder, trailblazer; bushranger, mountain man, woodsman

frost *n* 1 a covering of tiny ice crystals on a cold surface ⟨the wintertime routine of scraping the *frost* off the car's windshield every morning⟩
syn hoar, hoarfrost, rime
rel frostwork
2 something that has failed — see FAILURE 3

frost *vb* to disturb the peace of mind of (someone) especially by repeated disagreeable acts — see IRRITATE 1

frosty *adj* 1 having a low or subnormal temperature — see COLD 1
2 having or showing a lack of friendliness or interest in others — see COOL 1
3 lacking in friendliness or warmth of feeling — see COLD 2

froth *n* a light mass of fine bubbles formed in or on a liquid — see FOAM

frothy *adj* 1 covered with, consisting of, or resembling foam — see FOAMY
2 lacking in seriousness or maturity — see GIDDY 1
3 being of a material lacking in sturdiness or substance — see FLIMSY 1

froward *adj* 1 engaging in or marked by childish misbehavior — see NAUGHTY
2 given to resisting authority or another's control — see DISOBEDIENT
3 given to resisting control or discipline by others — see UNCONTROLLABLE

frowardness *n* refusal to obey — see DISOBEDIENCE

frown *n* a twisting of the facial features in disgust or disapproval — see GRIMACE

frown *vb* to look with anger or disapproval ⟨She was *frowning* when I arrived and I knew she was annoyed.⟩
syn glare, gloom, glower, lower (*also* lour), scowl
rel gape, gaze, ogle, stare; grimace, pout, sulk; growl, snarl, sneer, snigger
phrases look daggers (*or* stare daggers)
ant beam, grin, smile

frowsy *or* **frowzy** *adj* lacking neatness in dress or person — see SLOPPY 1

frozen *adj* 1 firmly positioned in place and difficult to dislodge — see TIGHT 2
2 having been established and usually not subject to change — see FIXED 1
3 lacking in friendliness or warmth of feeling — see COLD 2

frugal *adj* careful in the management of money or resources ⟨By being *frugal*, the family is able to stretch its monthly budget.⟩
syn economical, economizing, provident, scrimping, sparing, thrifty
rel conserving, preserving, saving; forehanded, foresighted, foresightful, prudent; penny-wise; cheap, close, closefisted, mean, niggard, niggardly, parsimonious, penurious, pinching, spare, stingy, stinting, tight, tightfisted
near ant improvident, shortsighted; boun-

tiful, charitable, freehanded, generous, liberal, munificent, openhanded, unselfish, unsparing; extravagant, indulgent, lavish
ant prodigal, profligate, spendthrift, squandering, thriftless, unthrifty, wasteful

frugality *n* careful management of material resources — see ECONOMY

fruit *n* 1 a condition or occurrence traceable to a cause — see EFFECT 1
2 something produced by physical or intellectual effort — see PRODUCT 1
3 the descendants of a person, animal, or plant — see OFFSPRING

fruitful *adj* 1 producing abundantly — see FERTILE
2 producing or capable of producing a desired result — see EFFECTIVE 1

fruition *n* the state of being actual or complete ⟨When she landed the lead in a Broadway play, a lifelong dream was brought to *fruition*.⟩
syn accomplishment, achievement, actuality, attainment, consummation, fulfillment (*or* fulfilment), pass, realization
rel success, triumph
near ant defeat, failure, fizzle, nonsuccess
ant naught (*also* nought), nonfulfillment

fruitless *adj* 1 producing no results — see FUTILE
2 not able to produce fruit or offspring — see STERILE 1

frustrate *vb* 1 to prevent from achieving a goal ⟨A multitude of conflicting opinions *frustrated* me in my attempt to find a computer that best suits my needs.⟩
syn baffle, balk, beat, checkmate, discomfit, foil, thwart
rel bar, block, clog, encumber, fetter, hamper, handicap, hinder, hobble, hold back, impede, inhibit, interfere (with), manacle, obstruct, shackle, tie up, trammel; arrest, check, halt, set back, short-circuit, stall, stop; avert, forestall, obviate, preclude, prevent; negate, neutralize, nullify; counteract, offset; conquer, defeat, overcome
near ant abet, aid, assist; ease, facilitate, smooth
ant advance, cultivate, encourage, forward, foster, further, nurture, promote
2 to lessen the courage or confidence of — see DISCOURAGE 1

frustrating *adj* causing annoyance — see ANNOYING

frustration *n* 1 something that is a source of irritation — see ANNOYANCE 3
2 the emotion felt when one's expectations are not met — see DISAPPOINTMENT 1
3 the feeling of impatience or anger caused by another's repeated disagreeable acts — see ANNOYANCE 2

fuddy–duddy *n* a person with old-fashioned ideas — see FOGY

fudge *n* language, behavior, or ideas that are absurd and contrary to good sense — see NONSENSE 1

fudge *vb* 1 to avoid giving a definite answer or position — see EQUIVOCATE
2 to use dishonest methods to achieve a goal — see CHEAT 1
3 to change so much as to create a wrong impression or alter the meaning of — see GARBLE

fuel *n* something with a usable capacity for doing work ⟨such nonrenewable *fuels* as coal, petroleum, and natural gas⟩
syn energy, power
rel kindling, propellant (*also* propellent); force

fugitive *adj* **1** hard to find, capture, or isolate — see ELUSIVE
2 lasting only for a short time — see MOMENTARY
3 traveling from place to place — see ITINERANT

fulfill *or* **fulfil** *vb* **1** to do what is required by the terms of ⟨The football player must remain with the team one more year to *fulfill* his contract.⟩
syn answer, complete, comply (with), fill, keep, meet, redeem, satisfy
rel conclude, consummate, finalize, finish, perfect; accomplish, achieve, bring about, carry out, effect; commit, compass, discharge, execute, make, perform
phrases abide by, make good (*or* make good on)
near ant default (on); disregard, forget, ignore, neglect, overlook, overpass, pass over, slight
ant breach, break, transgress, violate
2 to carry through (as a process) to completion — see PERFORM 1

fulfilling *adj* making one feel good inside — see HEARTWARMING

fulfillment *or* **fulfilment** *n* **1** the doing of an action — see COMMISSION 2
2 the state of being actual or complete — see FRUITION

full *adv* **1** to a full extent or degree — see FULLY 1
2 to a great degree — see VERY 1
3 as stated or indicated without the slightest difference — see EXACTLY 1

full *n* a complete amount of something — see WHOLE

full *adj* **1** containing or seeming to contain the greatest quantity or number possible ⟨At the start of the game everyone was *full* of energy and hope.⟩ ⟨The boy's bedroom is *full* of sports trophies and medals.⟩
syn brimful, brimming, bursting, chockfull (*or* chockful), crammed, crowded, fat, filled, jammed, jam-packed, loaded, packed, stuffed
rel overcrowded, overfilled, overflowing, overfull, overladen, overloaded, overstuffed; abounding, flush, fraught, replete, rife, swarming, teeming
near ant deficient, inadequate, incomplete, insufficient, short, shortish, shy, wanting; depleted, drained, exhausted
ant bare, blank, devoid, empty, stark, vacant, void
2 of the highest degree ⟨Even at the age of eighteen he hadn't reached his *full* height.⟩ ⟨a boat going at *full* speed⟩
syn greatest, maximum, top, topmost, utmost, utter
rel heightened, high
near ant lessened, low
ant least, littlest, lowest, minimal, minimum, slightest

3 having one's appetite completely satisfied ⟨Even the heartiest eaters are sure to be *full* when they leave that restaurant.⟩
syn replete, sated, satiate, satiated, stuffed, surfeited
rel glutted, gorged, overfed, overfull, overstuffed
near ant underfed, undernourished
ant empty, famished, hungry, starved, starving
4 covering everything or all important points — see ENCYCLOPEDIC
5 having an abundance of some characteristic quality (as flavor) — see FULL-BODIED
6 having an excess of body fat — see FAT 1
7 including many small descriptive features — see DETAILED 1
8 not lacking any part or member that properly belongs to it — see COMPLETE 1

full blast *adv* with all power or resources being used ⟨had the heat going *full blast*⟩
syn all out, full tilt, tooth and nail
rel completely, comprehensively, detailedly, exhaustively, fully, minutely, roundly, thoroughly, totally; extremely, utterly
phrases full steam ahead, in full career, like crazy, to the hilt

full-blooded *adj* **1** of unmixed ancestry — see PUREBRED
2 having a healthy reddish skin tone — see RUDDY
3 marked by or uttered with forcefulness — see EMPHATIC 1

full-blown *adj* fully grown or developed — see MATURE 1

full-bodied *adj* having an abundance of some characteristic quality (as flavor) ⟨After that huge Sunday brunch, everyone needed a *full-bodied* coffee.⟩
syn big, concentrated, full, lusty, muscular, plush, potent, rich, robust, strong
rel heavy; straight, undiluted, unmixed; high-octane, high-test; enriched, fortified; concentrated
near ant dilute, diluted, watered-down, watery
ant delicate, light, mild, thin, thinned, weak, weakened

full dress *n* dressy clothing — see FINERY

full-fledged *adj* fully grown or developed — see MATURE 1

full-scale *adj* trying all possibilities — see EXHAUSTIVE 1

full tilt *adv* **1** with all power or resources being used — see FULL BLAST
2 with great speed — see FAST 1

fully *adv* **1** to a full extent or degree ⟨The apartment comes *fully* furnished.⟩
syn all, all over, altogether, clean, completely, dead, enough, entirely, even, exactly, fast, flat, full, heartily, out, perfectly, plumb [*chiefly dialect*], quite, thoroughly, totally, utterly, well, wholly, wide
rel absolutely, categorically, cold, downright, plain, stone-cold, unqualifiedly; basically, by and large, chiefly, generally, largely, mainly, more or less, mostly, overall, predominantly, predominately, primarily, principally, substantially; abundantly, copiously, generously, greatly
phrases all the way, at length, down the

---

line, down to the ground, for fair, in whole, to bits, to pieces, to the hilt, to the max
near ant barely, hardly, just, kind of, marginally, minimally, scarcely, slightly, superficially; roughly, somewhat
ant half, halfway, incompletely, part, partially, partly
2 with attention to all aspects or details — see THOROUGHLY 1
fulminate *vb* to talk loudly and wildly — see RANT
fulmination *n* harsh insulting language — see ABUSE 1
fulsome *adj* **1** overly or insincerely flattering ⟨Not all of the players agreed with the captain's *fulsome* praise for the coach.⟩
syn adulatory, gushing, unctuous
rel drooling, slavering, slobbering; sickening; demonstrative, effusive, mushy, uninhibited, unreserved, unrestrained; artificial, backhanded, feigned, hypocritical, insincere, left-handed, mealymouthed, sanctimonious, two-faced; disarming, endearing, ingratiating, winning, winsome; extravagant, lavish, unrestrained; abundant, copious, profuse
near ant artless, earnest, genuine, honest, ingenuous, sincere, true, unaffected, unpretending, unpretentious
2 giving or sharing in abundance and without hesitation — see GENEROUS 1
3 causing intense displeasure, disgust, or resentment — see OFFENSIVE 1
fumble *n* an unintentional departure from truth or accuracy — see ERROR 1
fumble *vb* **1** to make or do (something) in a clumsy or unskillful way — see BOTCH
2 to search for something blindly or uncertainly — see GROPE
3 to make a mistake — see ERR 1
fumbled *adj* showing or marked by a lack of skill and tact (as in dealing with a situation) — see AWKWARD 2
fume *vb* **1** to be excited or emotionally stirred up with anger — see BOIL 1
2 to express one's anger usually violently — see RAGE 1
fuming *adj* feeling or showing anger — see ANGRY
fun *vb* to make jokes — see JOKE 1
fun *adj* providing amusement or enjoyment ⟨There were so many *fun* things to do at summer camp that the kids really hated to leave.⟩
syn amusing, delightful, diverting, enjoyable, entertaining, pleasurable
rel agreeable, beguiling, nice, pleasant, satisfying, welcome; recreational; antic, comic, comical, droll, farcical, funny, hilarious, humorous, laughable, ludicrous, ridiculous, riotous, risible, uproarious; blithesome, gleeful, happy, jocose, jocund, jolly, jovial, merry, mirthful, sunny; exciting, stimulating, thrilling
near ant disagreeable, displeasing, distasteful, uncongenial, unlovely, unpleasant, unpleasing, unwelcome
ant boring, drab, dreary, dull, flat, heavy, humdrum, jading, leaden, monotonous, pedestrian, pleasureless, ponderous, stodgy, stuffy, tedious, tiresome, tiring, uninteresting, wearisome, weary, wearying

fun *n* **1** someone or something that provides amusement or enjoyment ⟨Theme parks with their rides, shows, and games are great *fun* for the whole family.⟩
syn delight, distraction, diversion, entertainment, pleasure, recreation
rel escape, pastime, time killer; binge, fling, frolic, gambol, lark, revel, rollick, romp, spree; frolicking, rollicking; carousing, conviviality, festivity, gaiety (*also* gayety), hilarity, jollification, jollity, merrymaking, reveling (*or* revelling); revelry; picnic; laugh, riot, scream; activity, game
near ant killjoy, party pooper
ant bore, bummer, downer, drag
2 an attitude or manner not to be taken seriously ⟨Don't get mad: I was only saying it in *fun*.⟩
syn game, jest, play, sport
rel facetiousness, flightiness, flippancy, frivolity, frivolousness, levity, silliness
near ant earnestness, gravity, seriousness, soberness, sobriety, solemnity
ant earnest
3 activity engaged in to amuse oneself — see PLAY 1
4 a state of noisy, confused activity — see COMMOTION
function *n* **1** a social gathering — see PARTY 1
2 an assignment at which one regularly works for pay — see JOB 1
3 the action for which a person or thing is specially fitted or used or for which a thing exists — see ROLE
function *vb* to have a certain purpose ⟨The heart *functions* as a pump for the blood.⟩
syn act, perform, serve, work
rel operate, run; administer, carry on, control, direct, guide, handle, manage, oversee, regulate, supervise
functional *adj* **1** being in effective operation — see ACTIVE 1
2 capable of being put to use or account — see PRACTICAL 1
3 capable of or suitable for being used for a particular purpose — see USABLE 1
functionary *n* **1** a person who holds a public office — see OFFICIAL 1
2 a worker in a government agency — see BUREAUCRAT
functioning *adj* being in effective operation — see ACTIVE 1
fund *vb* **1** to furnish (as an institution) with a regular source of income — see ENDOW 2
2 to provide money for — see FINANCE 1
fund *n* **1** a sum of money set aside for a particular purpose ⟨Our club has a *fund* for parties—which we like to have as often as possible.⟩
syn account, budget, deposit, kitty, nest egg, pool
rel chest, coffer(s); assets, savings, savings account; bankroll, cache, collection, cushion, hoard, pocketbook, reserve, treasure; petty cash, pin money, pocket money, spending money
2 **funds** *pl* available money ⟨My *funds* were a little low, so I asked for a small advance on my paycheck.⟩
syn bankroll, coffers, finances, pocket, resources, wherewithal
rel shirt; bread [*slang*]; cash, chips, currency,

dough, gold, jack [*slang*], legal tender, lucre, pelf, scratch [*slang*], tender, wampum; assets, capital, deep pockets, fortune, means, opulence, riches, roll, substance, wealth; purse, treasury; cash flow; financing

near ant debts, liabilities

3 the number of individuals or amount of something available at any given time — see SUPPLY

fundamental *adj* of or relating to the simplest facts or theories of a subject — see ELEMENTARY

fundamentals *n pl* general or basic truths on which other truths or theories can be based — see PRINCIPLES 1

funeral *adj* expressing or suggesting mourning — see MOURNFUL 1

funeral director *n* a person who manages funerals and prepares the dead for burial or cremation ⟨The *funeral director* instructed the pallbearers on how to proceed.⟩

syn mortician, undertaker

rel embalmer

funereal *adj* causing or marked by an atmosphere lacking in cheer — see GLOOMY 1

¹**funk** *n* a strong unpleasant smell — see STINK 1

²**funk** *n* a person who shows a shameful lack of courage in the face of danger — see COWARD

funnel *vb* to cause to move to a central point or along a restricted pathway — see CHANNEL

funniness *n* the amusing quality or element in something — see HUMOR 1

funning *adj* marked by or expressive of mild or good-natured teasing — see QUIZZICAL

funny *n* **1** a series of drawings that tell a story or part of a story — see COMIC STRIP

2 something said or done to cause laughter — see JOKE 1

funny *adj* **1** causing or intended to cause laughter ⟨a very *funny* movie that had audiences rolling in the aisles⟩

syn antic, comic, comical, droll, farcical, hilarious, humorous, hysterical (*also* hysteric), laughable, ludicrous, ridiculous, riotous, risible, screaming, uproarious

rel amusing, diverting, entertaining; clownish, knockabout, slapstick, slapsticky, zany; facetious, flip, flippant, smart-alecky, snickery; jocular, playful, waggish; campy, jokey (*also* joky); rich, whimsical, witty, wry; blithesome, gleeful, jocose, jocund, jolly, jovial, laughing, merry, mirthful

near ant earnest, grave, no-nonsense, sedate, serious, severe, sober, sobersided, solemn, somber (*or* sombre), staid, unsmiling, weighty; affecting, moving, poignant, touching, tragic (*also* tragical); lachrymose, mournful, sad, sorrowful, tearful, woeful

ant humorless, lame, unamusing, uncomic, unfunny, unhumorous, unhysterical

2 different from the ordinary in a way that causes curiosity or suspicion — see ODD 2

3 noticeably different from what is generally found or experienced — see UNUSUAL 1

fur *n* **1** the hairy covering of a mammal especially when fine, soft, and thick ⟨The chinchilla is known for its exceptionally soft *fur*.⟩

syn coat, fleece, hair, jacket, pelage, pile, wool

rel undercoat, underfur; hide, leather, pelt, skin

2 a soft airy substance or covering — see FUZZ

3 the outer covering of an animal removed for its commercial value — see HIDE 1

furbelow *n* a strip of fabric gathered or pleated on one edge and used as trimming — see RUFFLE 1

furious *adj* **1** marked by great and often stressful excitement or activity ⟨Everyone worked at a *furious* pace in order to get the float ready for the parade.⟩

syn delirious, ferocious, feverish, fierce, frantic, frenetic, frenzied, mad, rabid, violent, wild

rel concentrated, high-pressured, intense, intensive, vehement; excessive, exorbitant, extravagant, extreme, immoderate, inordinate, lavish, overmuch, overweening, unconscionable, undue; demented, deranged, irrational, maniacal (*also* maniac)

near ant calm, peaceful, placid, quiet, serene, subdued, tranquil, undisturbed, unperturbed, untroubled; moderate, reasonable, temperate; casual, easygoing, low-pressure; balanced, sane, sound

ant relaxed

2 extreme in degree, power, or effect — see INTENSE 1

3 feeling or showing anger — see ANGRY

4 marked by bursts of destructive force or intense activity — see VIOLENT 1

furlough *n* the termination of the employment of an employee or a work force often temporarily — see LAYOFF

furnish *vb* **1** to provide (someone) with what is needed for a task or activity ⟨The art students were *furnished* with brushes, crayons, pencils, and various other art supplies.⟩

syn accoutre (*or* accouter), equip, fit (out), gird, outfit, provision, rig, supply

rel stock, store; bestow, contribute, donate, give, present; apportion, deal (out), dispense, distribute, mete (out), parcel (out), portion, prorate; allocate, allot, assign; arm, fortify, prepare

near ant strip

2 to put (something) into the possession of someone for use or consumption ⟨We'll gladly *furnish* the food for any out-of-town guests.⟩

syn deliver, feed, give, hand, hand over, provide, supply

rel ply (with); administer, allocate, apportion, deal (out), dispense, distribute, mete (out), parcel (out), portion, prorate; assign, cede, deed, make over, transfer

near ant conserve, keep up, maintain, preserve, save

ant hold (back), keep (back), reserve, retain, withhold

furnishings *n pl* the movable articles (such as tables and chairs) in a room — see FURNITURE

furniture *n* the movable articles (such as

---

tables and chairs) in a room ⟨We bought all new *furniture* for our new house.⟩
syn appointments, cabinetwork, furnishings, movables (*or* moveables)
rel belongings, chattels, effects, gear, goods, holdings, paraphernalia, possessions, things; case goods
near ant built-ins, fixtures

furor *n* 1 a state of noisy, confused activity — see COMMOTION

2 a state of wildly excited activity or emotion — see FRENZY

3 an intense emotional state of displeasure with someone or something — see ANGER

furore *n* 1 a state of noisy, confused activity — see COMMOTION

2 a state of wildly excited activity or emotion — see FRENZY

furrow *n* a small fold in a soft and otherwise smooth surface — see WRINKLE 1

furrow *vb* 1 to cut into and turn over the sod of (a piece of land) using a bladed implement — see PLOW 1

2 to develop creases or folds — see WRINKLE 1

furry *adj* 1 covered with or as if with hair — see HAIRY 1

2 made of or resembling hair — see HAIRY 1

further *adj* resulting in an increase in amount or number — see ADDITIONAL

further *adv* 1 at or to a greater distance or more advanced point — see FARTHER

2 in addition to what has been said — see MORE 1

further *vb* to help the growth or development of — see FOSTER 1

furtherance *n* forward movement in time or place — see ADVANCE 1

furthermore *adv* in addition to what has been said — see MORE 1

furthermost *adj* most distant from a center — see EXTREME 1

furthest *adj* most distant from a center — see EXTREME 1

furtive *adj* 1 given to acting in secret and to concealing one's intentions — see SNEAKY 1

2 undertaken or done so as to escape being observed or known by others — see SECRET 1

fury *n* 1 a bad-tempered scolding woman — see SHREW

2 a state of wildly excited activity or emotion — see FRENZY

3 an intense emotional state of displeasure with someone or something — see ANGER

fuse *vb* 1 to come together to form a single unit — see UNITE 1

2 to go from a solid to a liquid state — see LIQUEFY

3 to turn into a single mass or entity that is more or less the same throughout — see BLEND 1

fusillade *n* a rapid or overwhelming outpouring of many things at once — see BARRAGE

fusion *n* a distinct entity formed by the combining of two or more different things — see BLEND

fuss *n* 1 a feeling or declaration of disapproval or dissent — see OBJECTION

2 a state of nervous or irritated concern — see FRET

3 a state of noisy, confused activity — see COMMOTION

4 an expression of dissatisfaction, pain, or resentment — see COMPLAINT 1

fuss *vb* 1 to express dissatisfaction, pain, or resentment usually tiresomely — see COMPLAIN

2 to make an exaggerated display of affection or enthusiasm — see GUSH 2

3 to make often peevish criticisms or objections about matters that are minor, unimportant, or irrelevant — see QUIBBLE 1

4 to use flattery or the doing of favors in order to win approval especially from a superior — see FAWN

5 to experience concern or anxiety — see WORRY 1

6 to trouble the mind of; to make uneasy — see DISTURB 1

fusser *n* 1 a person who makes frequent complaints usually about little things — see CRYBABY

2 an irritable and complaining person — see GROUCH 1

fussy *adj* 1 given to complaining a lot ⟨Predictably, the kids riding in the back were *fussy* passengers, always asking "Are we there yet?"⟩
syn crabby, cranky, grouchy, grumpy, querulous
rel restive, restless, uneasy; discontented, disgruntled, displeased, dissatisfied; fretful, nervous, worrisome; cantankerous, choleric, cross, crotchety, irascible, irritable, ornery, peevish, perverse, pettish, petulant, quick-tempered, short-tempered, snappish, snappy, snippy, testy, waspish
near ant affable, agreeable, amiable, genial, good-humored, good-natured, good-tempered, gracious, well-disposed; accommodating, complaisant, obliging; easygoing, laid-back, relaxed
ant forbearing, long-suffering, patient, stoic (*or* stoical), tolerant, uncomplaining

2 hard to please — see FINICKY

3 taking, showing, or involving great care and effort — see PAINSTAKING

4 elaborately and often excessively decorated — see ORNATE 1

fusty *adj* having an unpleasant smell — see MALODOROUS

futile *adj* producing no results ⟨The prison is so well guarded that all attempts to escape have been *futile*.⟩
syn abortive, barren, bootless, empty, fruitless, ineffective, ineffectual, profitless, unavailing, unproductive, unprofitable, unsuccessful, useless, vain
rel hollow, idle, meaningless, pointless, valueless, worthless; hopeless, impossible, lost, no-win, unattainable; inadequate, insufficient, lacking, wanting
phrases in vain, no dice, not worth the candle, of no avail
near ant meaningful, worthwhile; adequate, sufficient; applicable, feasible, functional, practicable, practical, realizable, usable (*also* useable), workable
ant deadly, effective, effectual, efficacious, efficient, fruitful, potent, productive, profitable, successful, virtuous

future *adj* of a time after the present ⟨We must preserve our national parks in all their glory so that *future* generations can experience the majesty of nature.⟩

syn coming, unborn

rel approaching, forthcoming, imminent, impending, nearing, oncoming, pending, upcoming; after, ensuing, later, posterior, subsequent; anticipated, awaited, expected, planned, predicted, projected, prospective; eventual, final, last, ulterior, ultimate

near ant ancient, olden; antecedent, anterior, precedent, preceding, previous, prior

ant bygone, past

future *n* **1** time that is to come ⟨In the *future*, there may be medical discoveries that are beyond our fondest dreams.⟩

syn by-and-by, futurity, hereafter, offing

rel eventuality, finality; posterity

near ant yesterday, yesteryear; old, yore; moment, now, present, today

ant past

2 what is going to happen to someone in the time ahead — see FORTUNE 1

futurist *n* one who predicts future events or developments — see PROPHET 1

futurity *n* time that is to come — see FUTURE 1

fuzz *n* a soft airy substance or covering ⟨a comfortable old sweater with clumps of *fuzz* all over it⟩

syn down, floss, fluff, fur, lint, nap, pile

rel batting

fuzzy *adj* **1** made of or resembling hair — see HAIRY 2

2 not expressed in precise terms — see VAGUE 1

3 not seen or understood clearly — see FAINT 1

gab *vb* to engage in casual or rambling conversation — see CHAT 1

gab *n* friendly, informal conversation or an instance of this — see CHAT 1

gabble *n* unintelligible or meaningless talk — see GIBBERISH 1

gabble *vb* **1** to engage in casual or rambling conversation — see CHAT 1

2 to speak rapidly, inarticulately, and usually unintelligibly — see BABBLE 1

gabbler *n* a person who talks constantly — see CHATTERBOX

gabby *adj* fond of talking or conversation — see TALKATIVE

gabfest *n* friendly, informal conversation or an instance of this — see CHAT 1

gad (about) *vb* to move about from place to place aimlessly — see WANDER 1

gadabout *n* a person who roams about without a fixed route or destination — see NOMAD

gadfly *n* one who is obnoxiously annoying — see NUISANCE 1

gadget *n* an interesting and often novel device with a practical use ⟨She tried out a new *gadget* for weeding the garden.⟩

syn appliance, contraption, contrivance, gimmick, gizmo (*also* gismo), jigger

rel implement, instrument, tool, utensil; accessory (*also* accessary), adjunct; mechanism, trick; thingumajig

gaff *n* **1** a socially improper or unsuitable act or remark — see IMPROPRIETY 2

2 an unintentional departure from truth or accuracy — see ERROR 1

gaff *vb* **1** to cause to believe what is untrue — see DECEIVE

2 to rob by the use of trickery or threats — see FLEECE

gaffe *n* **1** a socially improper or unsuitable act or remark — see IMPROPRIETY 2

syn synonym(s)   *rel* related words
ant antonym(s)   *near ant* near antonym(s)

2 an unintentional departure from truth or accuracy — see ERROR 1

gag *n* **1** something said or done to cause laughter — see JOKE 1

2 a playful or mischievous act intended as a joke — see PRANK

gag *vb* **1** to discharge the contents of the stomach through the mouth — see VOMIT

2 to experience complete or partial blockage of the windpipe — see CHOKE 2

3 to make jokes — see JOKE 1

gage *n* something given or held to assure that the giver will keep a promise — see PLEDGE 1

gaiety *also* **gayety** *n* **1** dressy clothing — see FINERY

2 joyful or festive activity — see MERRYMAKING

3 a mood characterized by high spirits and amusement and often accompanied by laughter — see MIRTH

gaily *also* **gayly** *adv* **1** in a cheerful or happy manner ⟨We sat around the table, *gaily* joshing each other and laughing about the good old days.⟩

syn cheerfully, cheerily, happily, heartily, jocosely, jovially, merrily, mirthfully

rel amusedly, exuberantly, giddily, gigglingly, joyfully, joyously; blithely, blithesomely, breezily, gladly, laughingly, lightheartedly, sunnily; good-humoredly, good-naturedly, jocularly; hopefully, optimistically, sanguinely

near ant dejectedly, despondently, disconsolately, dispiritedly, wretchedly; forlornly, mournfully, sorrowfully; dourly, glumly, mirthlessly, sulkily, sullenly; dismally, drearily, gloomily, pessimistically

ant bleakly, cheerlessly, darkly, heavily, miserably, morosely, unhappily

2 in a quick and spirited manner ⟨children *gaily* running to the buses on the last day of school⟩

syn animatedly, animately, high-spiritedly, lively, pertly, spiritedly, sprightly, trippingly, vivaciously

rel friskily, gamesomely, playfully, skittishly, sportively; briskly, crisply, effervescently, energetically, springily; breezily, dapperly, dashingly, jauntily; agilely, nimbly, spryly

near ant halfheartedly, idly, indolently, lazily, lethargically, slothfully; heavily, inactively, listlessly, tiredly, wearily

ant dully, inanimately, sluggishly, tardily

gain *n* **1** something added (as by growth) — see INCREASE 1

2 the amount of money left when expenses are subtracted from the total amount received — see PROFIT 1

3 *usually* **gains** *pl* an increase usually measured in money that comes from labor, business, or property — see INCOME 1

gain *vb* **1** to gradually increase in ⟨Our hopes were raised as the movement *gained* strength.⟩

syn gather, grow (in), pick up

rel double (in), triple (in); accrue, accumulate, amass; excite, stimulate; enhance, enlarge, enrich, expand, extend, maximize; boost, elevate, jack (up), mount, ramp (up), step up

near ant abate, decline (in), diminish (in), dip, dwindle, fall (in), lessen, taper, taper off

ant decrease (in), lose

2 to receive as return for effort — see EARN 1

3 to become healthy and strong again after illness or weakness — see CONVALESCE

4 to become greater in extent, volume, amount, or number — see INCREASE 2

5 to obtain (as a goal) through effort — see ACHIEVE 1

6 to cause (someone) to agree with a belief or course of action by using arguments or earnest requests — see PERSUADE

gainful *adj* yielding a profit — see PROFITABLE 1

gainsay *vb* **1** to declare not to be true — see DENY 1

2 to make an assertion that is contrary to one made by (another) — see CONTRADICT 1

gal *n* a female romantic companion — see GIRLFRIEND

gala *n* a time or program of special events and entertainment in honor of something — see FESTIVAL

gale *n* a sudden intense expression of strong feeling — see OUTBURST 1

gall *n* **1** a deep-seated ill will — see ENMITY

2 shameless boldness — see EFFRONTERY

gall *vb* **1** to damage or diminish by continued friction — see ABRADE 1

2 to disturb the peace of mind of (someone) especially by repeated disagreeable acts — see IRRITATE 1

3 to make sore by continued rubbing — see CHAFE 1

gallant *adj* **1** feeling or displaying no fear by temperament — see BRAVE 1

2 having, characterized by, or arising from a dignified and generous nature — see NOBLE 2

3 large and impressive in size, grandeur, extent, or conception — see GRAND 1

gallant *n* **1** a man extremely interested in his clothing and personal appearance — see DANDY 1

2 a man who courts a woman usually with the goal of marrying her — see SUITOR 1

gallantly *adv* in a manner befitting a person of the highest character and ideals — see GREATLY 1

gallantry *n* strength of mind to carry on in spite of danger — see COURAGE

gallery *n* **1** a building or part of a building in which objects of interest are displayed — see MUSEUM

2 a typically long narrow way connecting parts of a building — see HALL 2

galling *adj* **1** causing annoyance — see ANNOYING

2 hard to accept or bear especially emotionally — see BITTER 2

gallivant *also* **galavant** *vb* to move about from place to place aimlessly — see WANDER 1

gallivanting *also* **galavanting** *adj* traveling from place to place — see ITINERANT

gallop *vb* to go at a pace faster than a walk — see RUN 1

galore *adj* **1** pouring forth in great amounts — see PROFUSE

2 being more than enough without being excessive — see PLENTIFUL

galvanize *vb* to cause a pleasurable stimulation of the feelings of — see THRILL

galvanizing *adj* causing great emotional or mental stimulation — see EXCITING 1

gamble *n* a risky undertaking ⟨It's a *gamble*, but I'm willing to take the risk.⟩

syn adventure, chance, enterprise, flier (*also* flyer), speculation, throw, venture

rel bet, hazard, stake, wager; liberty; dark horse, long shot, play

ant sure thing

gamble *vb* to risk (something) on the outcome of an uncertain event — see BET

gamble (on) *vb* to take a chance on — see RISK 1

gamble (with) *vb* to place in danger — see ENDANGER

gambler *n* one that bets (as on the outcome of a contest or sports event) — see BETTOR

gambol *n* a time or instance of carefree fun — see FLING 1

gambol *vb* to play and run about happily — see FROLIC 1

game *adj* having a desire or inclination (as for a specified course of action) — see WILLING 1

game *n* **1** a competitive encounter between individuals or groups carried on for amusement, exercise, or in pursuit of a prize ⟨decided he would indulge in a friendly basketball *game* with his friends before dinner⟩

syn bout, competition, contest, event, match, meet, sweepstakes (*also* sweepstake), tournament, tourney

rel athletics, sport; battle, conflict, scrimmage, skirmish, struggle, tug-of-war, tussle; championship, national('s); final, playoff, semifinal; derby, field day, open, outing; biathlon, decathlon, heptathlon, pentathlon, triathlon; marathon, race, ultramarathon; heat, round, run, set; rally, volley; rubber, runoff, sudden death; dead heat, photo finish, seesaw; classic

2 a method worked out in advance for achieving some objective — see PLAN 1

3 an attitude or manner not to be taken seriously — see FUN 2

4 the activity by which one regularly makes a living — see OCCUPATION

5 a region of activity, knowledge, or influence — see FIELD 2

gamut *n* the distance or extent between possible extremes — see RANGE 3

gander *n* an instance of looking especially briefly — see LOOK 2

gang *n* **1** a group of people working together on a task ⟨A *gang* of neighborhood residents spent the weekend cleaning up the park.⟩

syn army, band, company, crew, outfit, party, squad, team

rel battalion, corps, troop; force, host, stable, troupe; help, personnel, staff

2 a group of people sharing a common interest and relating together socially ⟨The whole *gang* went out for pizza.⟩ ⟨The school's gamers had their own little *gang*.⟩

syn body, bunch, circle, clan, clique, community, coterie, crowd, fold, lot, network, pack, ring, set

rel charmed circle, elite, in-group; club, college, fellowship, guild (*also* gild), league, organization, society; camp, faction, sect, side, tribe; mess, squad; brotherhood, fraternity, order, sisterhood, sodality, sorority; commune; alliance, bloc, coalition, confederation, congress, council, federation, union

3 a group involved in secret or criminal activities — see ¹RING 1

gangling *adj* being tall, thin and usually loose-jointed — see LANKY

gangly *adj* being tall, thin and usually loose-jointed — see LANKY

gangster *n* a violent, brutal person who is often a member of an organized gang — see HOODLUM

gap *n* **1** an open space in a barrier (as a wall or hedge) ⟨There were several visible *gaps* in the wall where the drywall had pulled away from the framing.⟩

syn breach, break, discontinuity, gulf, hiatus, hole, interstice, interval, opening, rent, rift, separation, void

rel chink, cleft, crack, cranny, crevice, fissure; notch, slit, split; interspace, pore; abyss, aperture, cavity, chasm, gape, orifice; fracture, rupture, severance

2 a break in continuity ⟨There was a 15-minute *gap* between the two televised sporting events.⟩

syn discontinuity, hiatus, interim, interlude, intermission, interruption, interstice, interval

rel interspace, lag, pause, space, time lag, window; bumper; adjournment, discontinuance, lapse, suspension; lull, recess, respite, rest; subinterval

near ant continuum, run, stretch; procession, progression

ant continuation

3 an incomplete or deficient area ⟨a *gap* in his understanding⟩

syn hiatus, hole, space, void

rel defectiveness, detriment, disability, failing, fault, impairment, weakness; deficiency, deficit, imperfection, inadequacy, incompleteness, insufficiency, insufficiency, lack, need, shortcoming, shortfall, want

4 a narrow opening between hillsides or mountains that can be used for passage — see CANYON

gape *n* a fixed intent look — see GAZE

gape *vb* to look long and hard in wonder or surprise ⟨stood *gaping* at the sight⟩

syn blink, gawk, gaze, goggle, peer, rubberneck, stare

rel glare, gloat, glower; consider, eye, fixate, observe, regard, watch; leer, ogle; peruse, pore (over), study; outstare, stare down

near ant glance, glimpse, peek, peep; browse, dip (into); scan; wink (at)

garb *n* **1** clothing chosen as appropriate for a specific situation — see OUTFIT 1

2 the outward form of someone or something especially as indicative of a quality — see APPEARANCE 1

garb *vb* to outfit with clothes and especially fine or special clothes — see CLOTHE 1

garbage *n* discarded or useless material ⟨The raccoons were looking for leftover food in the family's *garbage*.⟩

syn chaff, deadwood, debris, dross, dust, junk, litter, refuse, riffraff, rubbish, scrap, trash, truck, waste

rel sewage, slop, swill, wash; remains, rubble, ruins; dump, scrap heap; lumber, odds and ends, trumpery; jetsam, wreckage; castoff, cull, discard, hand-me-down, reject, throwaway

near ant catch, gem, goody (*or* goodie), jewel, pearl, plum, prize, treasure, trove, valuable; booty, find, salvage

garble *vb* to change so much as to create a wrong impression or alter the meaning of ⟨The candidate complained that his views had been deliberately *garbled* by his opponent.⟩

syn bend, color, cook, distort, falsify, fudge, misinterpret, misrepresent, misstate, pervert, slant, twist, warp

rel misdescribe, misspeak, mistranslate; belie, camouflage, disguise, dissemble, gloss (over), mask, veil, whitewash; censor; complicate, confound, confuse, mystify, obscure; equivocate, fib, lie, palter, prevaricate

near ant clarify, clear (up), explain, illuminate, illustrate, interpret, spell out; decipher

garden *n* a large room or building for enclosed public gatherings — see HALL 3

gargantuan *adj* unusually large — see HUGE

garish *adj* excessively showy — see GAUDY

garishness *n* excessive or unnecessary display — see OSTENTATION

garment *vb* to outfit with clothes and especially fine or special clothes — see CLOTHE 1

garments *n pl* covering for the human body — see CLOTHING

---

syn synonym(s)   *rel* related words
ant antonym(s)   *near ant* near antonym(s)

garner *vb* **1** to bring together in one body or place — see GATHER 1

2 to receive as return for effort — see EARN 1

garnish *n* something that decorates or beautifies — see DECORATION 1

garnish *vb* to make more attractive by adding something that is beautiful or becoming — see DECORATE

garrote *or* **garotte** *vb* to keep (someone) from breathing by exerting pressure on the windpipe — see CHOKE 1

garrulous *adj* **1** fond of talking or conversation — see TALKATIVE

2 using or containing more words than necessary to express an idea — see WORDY 1

gas *n* **1** boastful speech or writing — see BOMBAST 1

2 language that is impressive-sounding but not meaningful or sincere — see RHETORIC 1

3 active strength of body or mind — see VIGOR 1

gas *vb* to engage in casual or rambling conversation — see CHAT 1

gaseous *adj* marked by the use of impressive-sounding but mostly meaningless words and phrases — see RHETORICAL 1

gash *vb* to penetrate with a sharp edge (as a knife) — see CUT 1

gash *n* a long deep cut ⟨The hiker got a *gash* in his knee that required four stitches.⟩

syn incision, laceration, rent, rip, slash, slit, tear

rel abrasion, score, scrape, scratch; injury, wound; crack, fracture, rupture, snag

gasp *vb* to breathe hard, quickly, or with difficulty ⟨The runner was audibly *gasping* by the end of the marathon.⟩

syn blow, heave, hyperventilate, pant, puff, wheeze

rel choke, gag, gulp, huff; asphyxiate, smother, stifle, strangle; snore, snuffle; exhale, expire

phrases be out of breath

gate *n* **1** a barrier by which an entry is closed and opened — see DOOR 1

2 the opening through which one can enter or leave a structure — see DOOR 2

3 a fixture for controlling the flow of a liquid — see FAUCET

gatekeeper *n* a person who tends a door — see DOORKEEPER

gateway *n* **1** something that allows someone to achieve a desired goal — see PASSPORT 1

2 the means or right of entering or participating in — see ENTRANCE 1

3 the opening through which one can enter or leave a structure — see DOOR 2

gather *vb* **1** to bring together in one body or place ⟨He *gathered* the leftovers from the table and gave them to the dog.⟩ ⟨Let's *gather* the students and have them line up on the playground before going in from recess.⟩

syn accumulate, amass, assemble, collect, concentrate, congregate, corral, garner, group, lump, pick up, round up

rel ball, batch, bunch, cluster, huddle; heap, pile, stack; band, muster, raise, rally; flock, herd, hive, pack, press, swarm,

throng; combine, connect, join, link, merge, pool, unite; arrange, collate, compile, organize, systematize

phrases get together

near ant break up, disband, disintegrate, dissolve, separate, sever, split (up); dismiss, send

ant dispel, disperse, dissipate, scatter

2 to catch or collect (a crop or natural resource) for human use — see HARVEST

3 to come together into one body or place — see ASSEMBLE 1

4 to form an opinion or reach a conclusion through reasoning and information — see INFER 1

5 to gradually form into a layer, pile, or mass — see COLLECT 2

6 to gradually increase in — see GAIN 1

7 to call into being through the use of one's inner resources or powers — see SUMMON 2

gathering *n* **1** a body of people come together in one place ⟨The President spoke before the *gathering* of student leaders.⟩

syn assemblage, assembly, conference, congregation, convocation, meeting, muster

rel company, consort, coterie, gang, pack; caucus, forum, market, panel, rally, symposium, synod; gallery, grandstand, house; crowd, flock, horde, legion, multitude; press, swarm, throng; crush, mob, rabble

2 a coming together of a number of persons for a specified purpose — see MEETING 1

3 a mass or quantity that has piled up or that has been gathered over a period of time — see ACCUMULATION 1

gauche *adj* lacking social grace and assurance — see AWKWARD 1

gaud *n* a small object displayed for its attractiveness or interest — see KNICKKNACK

gaudiness *n* excessive or unnecessary display — see OSTENTATION

gaudy *adj* excessively showy ⟨gaudy decorations on all the doors and windows at festival time⟩

syn flamboyant, flashy, garish, glitzy, loud, noisy, ostentatious, splashy, swank (or swanky)

rel extravagant, fulsome, overdone, over-the-top, overwrought; bedizened, ornate; fancy, snazzy; blaring, bright, florid, glaring, glittery, overbright; graceless, inelegant, lurid, tacky, tasteless, tawdry, tinselly, vulgar

near ant inconspicuous, muted, restrained, subdued, toned (down), unobtrusive; elegant, graceful, tasteful; modest, plain, simple

ant conservative, quiet, understated, unflamboyant

gauge *also* **gage** *vb* **1** to decide the size, amount, number, or distance of (something) without actual measurement — see ESTIMATE 2

2 to find out the size, extent, or amount of — see MEASURE 1

gaunt *adj* suffering extreme weight loss as a result of hunger or disease — see EMACIATED

gauntlet *also* **gantlet** *n* a test of faith, patience, or strength — see TRIAL 1

gauzy *adj* **1** being of a material lacking in sturdiness or substance — see FLIMSY 1

2 very thin and easy to see through — see SHEER 1

3 not seen or understood clearly — see FAINT 1

gawk *n* a big clumsy often slow-witted person — see OAF 1

gawk *vb* to look long and hard in wonder or surprise — see GAPE

gawky *adj* having or showing an inability to move in a graceful manner — see CLUMSY 1

gaze *vb* to look long and hard in wonder or surprise — see GAPE

gaze *n* a fixed intent look ⟨her admiring *gaze* at the artwork⟩
syn eye, gape, regard, scrutiny, stare
rel glare, glower; contemplation, fixation; attention, observance, observation, surveillance, watch; examination, inspection, perusal, study, survey
near ant flash, glance, glimpse, peek, peep, sight; browse, scan

gazette *n* a publication that appears at regular intervals — see JOURNAL

gear *n* **1** items needed for the performance of a task or activity — see EQUIPMENT

2 transportable items that one owns — see POSSESSION 2

3 covering for the human body — see CLOTHING

gel *vb* to turn from a liquid into a substance resembling jelly — see COAGULATE

gem *n* **1** a usually valuable stone cut and polished for ornament ⟨a ring set with diamonds and other precious *gems*⟩
syn brilliant, gemstone, jewel, rock [*slang*]
rel bauble, bijou, trinket; birthstone; cameo, solitaire, teardrop; paste, rhinestone, zircon
near ant rough

2 someone or something unusually desirable — see PRIZE 1

gemstone *n* a usually valuable stone cut and polished for ornament — see GEM 1

genealogy *n* the line of ancestors from whom a person is descended — see ANCESTRY

general *adj* **1** belonging or relating to the whole ⟨a *general* increase in postage rates⟩ ⟨There's been a *general* improvement in the economy.⟩
syn blanket, common, generic, global, overall, universal
rel broad, broadscale, comprehensive, extensive, inclusionary, overarching, pervasive, ubiquitous, wholesale, wide, widespread; aggregate, collective, complete, full, plenary
near ant component, constituent; cross-sectional, divisional, fragmentary, partial; local, localized, regional, sectional
ant individual, particular

2 relating to the main elements and not to specific details ⟨She gave the *general* impression of being kindhearted.⟩ ⟨a *general* course of study in American history⟩
syn all-around (*also* all-round), bird's-eye, broad, nonspecific, overall
rel comprehensive, inclusive; absolute,

boundless, expansive, extensive, infinite, panoramic, vast, wide; nonspecific, unlimited, unrestricted, unspecified
near ant limited, restricted, specified; distinct, explicit, precise, sharp; comprehensive, elaborate, full, mapped (out), thorough; enumerated, inventoried, itemized, listed; individual, singular; particular
ant delineated, detailed, particularized, specific

3 held by or applicable to a majority of the people ⟨It was the *general* opinion that the politician was a liar.⟩ ⟨The *general* mood of the nation was one of hope and optimism.⟩
syn common, majority, overall, popular, prevailing, public, ruling, vulgar
rel unanimous, universal; pop; everyday, familiar, household, usual, well-known; dominant, predominant, preponderant; characteristic, typical; pandemic, pervasive, prevalent, rife, widespread; communal, shared
near ant rare, strange, unknown, unusual; distinctive, especial, idiosyncratic, peculiar, special, unique; individual, separate, singular
ant uncommon, unpopular

4 not limited or specialized in application or purpose ⟨a new kitchen tool of *general* usefulness⟩ ⟨a *general* education⟩
syn all-around (*also* all-round), all-purpose, unlimited, unqualified, unrestricted, unspecialized
rel mixed-use, multipurpose; broad, wide; nonspecific, unspecified, vague
near ant bounded, circumscribed, definite, demarcated, determinate, finite, qualified; selective
ant limited, restricted, specialized, technical

generality *n* **1** an idea or statement about all of the members of a group or all the instances of a situation — see GENERALIZATION

2 the main or greater part of something as distinguished from its subordinate parts — see BODY 1

3 the largest part or quantity of something — see MAJORITY 1

generalization *n* an idea or statement about all of the members of a group or all the instances of a situation ⟨made several sweeping *generalizations* about cities⟩
syn concept, conception, generality, notion, stereotype
rel cliché (*also* cliche), commonplace, platitude, truism; adage, proverb, saw, saying; oversimplification, simplification

generally *adv* **1** according to the usual course of things — see NATURALLY 2

2 for the most part — see CHIEFLY

generate *vb* to be the cause of (a situation, action, or state of mind) — see EFFECT

generator *n* a person who establishes a whole new field of endeavor — see FATHER 2

generic *adj* belonging or relating to the whole — see GENERAL 1

generosity *n* the quality or state of being generous — see LIBERALITY

generous *adj* **1** giving or sharing in abundance and without hesitation ⟨a civic

---

syn synonym(s)   *rel* related words
ant antonym(s)   *near ant* near antonym(s)

leader who is very *generous* with his money and time⟩

syn bounteous, bountiful, charitable, free, freehanded, fulsome, liberal, munificent, open, openhanded, unselfish, unsparing

rel extravagant, handsome, lavish, over-generous, profuse; altruistic, beneficent, benevolent, hospitable, humanitarian, philanthropic (*also* philanthropical); big, greathearted, largehearted, magnanimous, openhearted; compassionate, good-hearted, kind, kindly, sympathetic

near ant mean, petty, small; frugal, spare, sparing, thrifty; stinting; acquisitive, avaricious, avid, coveting, covetous, desirous, grasping, hoggish, mercenary, rapacious; begrudging, envious, grudging, resentful

ant cheap, close, closefisted, mingy, niggardly, parsimonious, penurious, selfish, stingy, stinting, tight, tightfisted, uncharitable

2 being more than enough without being excessive — see PLENTIFUL

generously *adv* in a generous manner — see WELL 2

genesis *n* the point at which something begins — see BEGINNING

genetic *also* **genetical** *adj* genetically passed or capable of being passed from parent to offspring — see HEREDITARY

genial *adj* **1** having an easygoing and pleasing manner especially in social situations — see AMIABLE

2 having or showing kindly feeling and sincere interest — see FRIENDLY 1

3 showing a natural kindness and courtesy especially in social situations — see GRACIOUS 1

4 marked by temperatures that are neither too high nor too low — see CLEMENT 1

geniality *n* the state or quality of having a pleasant or agreeable manner in socializing with others — see AMIABILITY 1

genius *n* **1** a very smart person ⟨The 16-year-old college graduate was considered to be a *genius*.⟩

syn brain, intellect, thinker, whiz, wizard

rel polymath, Renaissance man; blue, bluestocking, highbrow, intellectual; sage, savant; egghead, nerd; master, virtuoso

near ant ignoramus, illiterate, know-nothing, lowbrow; anti-intellectual, philistine; ass, donkey, fool, jackass; beast, boor, cad, churl, clown, creep, cur, heel, jerk, louse, lout, skunk, snake, stinker

ant blockhead, dodo, dolt, dope, dumbbell, dummy, dunce, fathead, goon, half-wit, hammerhead, idiot, imbecile, moron, nitwit, numskull (*or* numbskull), pinhead

2 a special and usually inborn ability — see TALENT

3 a habitual attraction to some activity or thing — see INCLINATION 1

4 the set of qualities that makes a person, a group of people, or a thing different from others — see NATURE 1

5 a visible representation of something abstract (as a quality) — see EMBODIMENT

gent *n* an adult male human being — see MAN 1

genteel *adj* **1** following the established traditions of refined society and good taste — see PROPER 1

2 having or showing a taste for the fine arts and gracious living — see CULTIVATED

3 of high birth, rank, or station — see NOBLE 1

4 showing consideration, courtesy, and good manners — see POLITE 1

gentile *n* a person who does not worship the God of the Bible — see HEATHEN 1

gentility *n* **1** speech or behavior that is a sign of good manners — see POLITENESS 1

2 the highest class in a society — see ARISTOCRACY 1

gentle *adj* **1** not harsh or stern especially in nature or effect ⟨Use a *gentle* detergent on that delicate silk blouse.⟩ ⟨her *gentle* ways⟩

syn balmy, benign, bland, delicate, light, mellow, mild, soft, soothing, tender

rel calm, pacific, peaceful, placid, quiet, serene, tranquil; clement, compassionate, easy, lenient, merciful; buffering, emollient, softening; sleek, slick, smooth

near ant exquisite, fierce, intense, powerful, severe; forceful, forcible, savage, violent; roughened, rugged, strong; abrading, irritating, roughening; grim, gruff, rude, stiff; heavy-handed, oppressive, pitiless, tyrannical (*also* tyrannic)

ant caustic, coarse, hard, harsh, rough, scathing, stern, ungentle

2 marked by temperatures that are neither too high nor too low — see CLEMENT 1

3 of high birth, rank, or station — see NOBLE 1

4 not loud in pitch or volume — see SOFT 1

gentle *vb* **1** to lessen the anger or agitation of — see PACIFY 1

2 to touch or handle in a tender or loving manner — see FONDLE

3 to lessen the shock of — see CUSHION

gentleman *n* **1** a man of high birth or social position ⟨Many of the signers of the Declaration of Independence were *gentlemen* who were risking everything.⟩

syn grandee, nobleman, peer

rel country gentleman, squire; cavalier, chevalier, knight; don, hidalgo, nabob, nawab; seigneur, seignior, sheikh (*or* sheik); baron, baronet, count, duke, earl, esquire, marchese, margrave, marquess (*or* marquis), master, prince, princelet, princeling, raja, viscount; lordship, sire [*archaic*]

near ant boor, churl, fellah, peasant, peon; commoner, pleb, plebeian; proletarian

2 an adult male human being — see MAN 1

3 an honorable and courteous man — see CAVALIER

gentlewoman *n* a woman of high birth or social position ⟨In the 19th century a number of American *gentlewomen* used their wealth and influence to further abolitionism, women's rights, and other worthy causes.⟩

syn dame, lady, noblewoman

rel baroness, countess, duchess, marchesa, marchioness, marquise, queen, viscountess; dowager, matriarch, matron, mistress; ladyship

gentry *n* **1** the highest class in a society — see ARISTOCRACY 1

2 one of the segments of society into which people are grouped — see CLASS 1

genuine *adj* **1** being exactly as appears or as claimed — see AUTHENTIC 1

2 free from any intent to deceive or impress others — see GUILELESS

3 existing in fact and not merely as a possibility — see ACTUAL

genuinely *adv* in actual fact — see VERY 2

geometry *n* the outward appearance of something as distinguished from its substance — see FORM 1

geriatric *adj* being of advanced years and especially past middle age — see ELDERLY

germane *adj* having to do with the matter at hand — see PERTINENT

germfree *adj* free from filth, infection, or dangers to health — see SANITARY

gestation *n* the state of containing unborn young within the body — see PREGNANCY

gesticulation *n* a movement of the body or limbs that expresses or emphasizes an idea or feeling — see GESTURE 1

gesture *vb* to direct or notify by a movement or gesture — see MOTION

gesture *n* **1** a movement of the body or limbs that expresses or emphasizes an idea or feeling ⟨She shrugged her shoulders in a *gesture* of indifference.⟩

syn gesticulation, mime, pantomime, sign, signal

rel beck, beckon, flourish, shrug, wave; body language, posture; indication, motion

2 an act or utterance that is a customary show of good manners — see CIVILITY 1

get *vb* **1** to acquire complete knowledge, understanding, or skill in — see LEARN 1

2 to become affected with (a disease or disorder) — see CONTRACT 1

3 to become the father of — see FATHER

4 to cause (someone) to agree with a belief or course of action by using arguments or earnest requests — see PERSUADE

5 to come upon after searching, study, or effort — see FIND 1

6 to disturb the peace of mind of (someone) especially by repeated disagreeable acts — see IRRITATE 1

7 to eventually have as a state or quality — see BECOME

8 to receive as return for effort — see EARN 1

9 to have a clear idea of — see COMPREHEND 1

10 to take physical control or possession of (something) suddenly or forcibly — see CATCH 1

11 to leave a place often for another — see GO 2

12 to achieve a victory over — see BEAT 2

13 to transmit information or requests to — see CONTACT

14 to put to death deliberately — see MURDER 1

15 to throw into a state of mental uncertainty — see CONFUSE 1

get *n* the descendants of a person, animal, or plant — see OFFSPRING

get across *vb* to make plain or understandable — see EXPLAIN 1

get along *vb* **1** to meet one's day-to-day needs ⟨Most college students can *get along* with just a few hours of sleep at night.⟩

syn cope, do, fare, get by, get on, make out, manage, shift

rel carry on, contrive, scrape (by *or* through), scrounge; last, survive; eke out, scrape (out), squeeze, wrest, wring; afford, swing

phrases fend for oneself, make do, make ends meet, make shift

near ant collapse, fail, fall short, fizzle, flounder; decline, peter (out), slump, wane; give up

2 to move forward along a course — see GO 1

get around *vb* **1** to achieve a victory over — see BEAT 2

2 to avoid having to comply with (something) especially through cleverness — see CIRCUMVENT 1

3 to become known — see GET OUT 1

4 to get or keep away from (as a responsibility) through cleverness or trickery — see ESCAPE 2

getaway *n* the act or an instance of getting free from danger or confinement — see ESCAPE 1

get by *vb* to meet one's day-to-day needs — see GET ALONG 1

get off *vb* **1** to leave a place often for another — see GO 2

2 to take the first step in (a process or course of action) — see BEGIN 1

get on *vb* **1** to meet one's day-to-day needs — see GET ALONG 1

2 to move forward along a course — see GO 1

get out *vb* **1** to become known ⟨News of the rock star's secret wedding *got out* to the news media.⟩

syn break, circulate, come out, get around, leak (out), out, spread

rel develop, transpire, unfold; disclose, reveal, spill, tell

near ant hush (up), suppress; conceal, disguise, hide, mask; secrete

2 to get free from a dangerous or confining situation — see ESCAPE 1

3 to produce and release for distribution in printed form — see PUBLISH 1

get–together *n* **1** a coming together of a number of persons for a specified purpose — see MEETING 1

2 a social gathering — see PARTY 1

getup *n* **1** clothing chosen as appropriate for a specific situation — see OUTFIT 1

2 the way in which the elements of something (as a work of art) are arranged — see COMPOSITION 3

get up *vb* **1** to leave one's bed — see ARISE 1

2 to outfit with clothes and especially fine or special clothes — see CLOTHE 1

3 to call into being through the use of one's inner resources or powers — see SUMMON 2

gewgaw *also* **geegaw** *n* a small object displayed for its attractiveness or interest — see KNICKKNACK

ghastliness *n* the quality of inspiring intense dread or dismay — see HORROR 1

ghastly *adj* **1** extremely disturbing or repellent — see HORRIBLE 1

2 extreme in degree, power, or effect — see INTENSE 1

3 causing fear — see FEARFUL 1

---

syn synonym(s)   *rel* related words
ant antonym(s)   *near ant* near antonym(s)

ghost *n* **1** the soul of a dead person thought of especially as appearing to living people ⟨We looked for *ghosts* in the graveyard on Halloween.⟩

syn apparition, bogey (*also* bogie *or* bogy), phantasm (*also* fantasm), phantom, poltergeist, shade, shadow, specter (*or* spectre), spirit, spook, sprite, vision, visitant, wraith

rel angel, familiar, genie, genius, jinni (*or* jinn *also* djinni *or* djinn); double, doppelgänger (*or* doppelganger); fetch; incubus, lamia, succubus, zombie (*also* zombi); demon (*or* daemon), devil, fiend, ghoul, imp

2 a tiny often physical indication of something lost or vanished — see VESTIGE 1

3 an evil spirit — see DEMON 1

ghoul *n* an evil spirit — see DEMON 1

giant *adj* unusually large — see HUGE

giant *n* something that is unusually large and powerful ⟨The Great Pyramids of Egypt are *giants* among the world's architectural wonders.⟩

syn behemoth, blockbuster, colossus, jumbo, leviathan, mammoth, monster, titan, whale, whopper

rel amazon, giantess; bulk, hulk; steamroller

near ant lightweight, weakling, wimp, wisp; nonentity, twerp, whippersnapper

ant diminutive, dwarf, half-pint, midget, mite, peewee, pygmy (*also* pigmy), runt, shrimp

gibber *vb* to speak rapidly, inarticulately, and usually unintelligibly — see BABBLE 1

gibber *n* unintelligible or meaningless talk — see GIBBERISH 1

gibberish *n* **1** unintelligible or meaningless talk ⟨The lad was so excited he could only talk *gibberish*.⟩

syn abracadabra, babble, blabber, doubletalk, drivel, gabble, gibber, jabber, jabberwocky, mumbo jumbo, nonsense, prattle

rel blah (*also* blah-blah), twaddle; chatter, gab, patter, prate, tattle, twitter; cackle, clack, clatter

2 language marked by abstractions, jargon, euphemisms, and circumlocutions ⟨All I got from the doctor's *gibberish* was that I had a sore throat, which I already knew.⟩

syn double-talk, gobbledygook (*also* gobbledegook), rigmarole (*also* rigamarole)

rel bureaucratese, computerese, educationese, governmentese, legalese, Pentagonese, psychobabble, technobabble; bombast, gas, grandiloquence, hot air, oratory, rhetoric, wind

gibe *or* **jibe** *vb* to make (someone or something) the object of unkind laughter — see RIDICULE

giddy *adj* **1** lacking in seriousness or maturity ⟨The *giddy* youngsters continued to laugh, joke, and make faces during the ceremonies.⟩

syn dizzy, featherbrained, flighty, frivolous, frothy, goofy, harebrained, lightheaded, puerile, scatterbrained, silly

rel fatuous, foolish, inane, nonsensical, witless; daffy, daft, fruity; flippant, fluttery, giggly, happy, light, lighthearted, playful; sappy, shallow, superficial

near ant grave, melancholy, somber (*or* sombre); thoughtful; dignified, heavy, nononsense, sedate, severe, solemn, staid

ant earnest, serious, serious-minded, sober

2 having a feeling of being whirled about and in danger of falling down — see DIZZY 1

3 experiencing or marked by overwhelming usually pleasurable emotion — see ECSTATIC

gift *n* **1** something given to someone without expectation of a return ⟨We gave him an unusual birthday *gift*.⟩

syn donation, freebie (*or* freebee), giveaway, lagniappe, largess (*also* largesse), present, presentation

rel alms, benefaction, beneficence, benevolence, charity, contribution, dole, handout, oblation, offering, philanthropy, tithe; grant, subsidy; remembrance, tribute, valentine; bonus, boon, windfall; courtesy, favor, generosity, sacrifice; gratuity, tip; award, prize, reward; dowry; bequest, legacy

near ant advance, loan; bribe, peace offering, sop

2 a special and usually inborn ability — see TALENT

gift *vb* to furnish freely or naturally with some power, quality, or attribute — see ENDOW 1

gigantic *adj* unusually large — see HUGE

giggle *n* an explosive sound that is a sign of amusement — see LAUGH 1

giggle *vb* to show mirth with an explosive vocal sound — see LAUGH 1

gimmick *n* **1** a clever often underhanded means to achieve an end — see TRICK 1

2 an interesting and often novel device with a practical use — see GADGET

3 a danger or difficulty that is hidden or not easily recognized — see PITFALL 1

ginger *n* active strength of body or mind — see VIGOR 1

gingerbread *adj* elaborately and often excessively decorated — see ORNATE 1

gingerly *adj* having or showing a close attentiveness to avoiding danger or trouble — see CAREFUL 1

gingery *adj* **1** having active strength of body or mind — see VIGOROUS 1

2 marked by a lively display of strong feeling — see SPIRITED 1

gird *vb* **1** to encircle or bind with or as if with a belt ⟨For the celebration of the heroes' return, well-wishers *girded* hundreds of trees with yellow ribbons.⟩ ⟨She *girded* her waist with a delicate sash.⟩

syn band, belt, girdle, girt, girth, wrap

rel tie up, truss; circle, enwreathe, loop, wind, wreathe; bandage, swathe; chain, cord, enchain, lash, rope, shackle, tape, wire

near ant unbind, unlash, unshackle, untie, unwind

ant ungird, unwrap

2 to provide (someone) with what is needed for a task or activity — see FURNISH 1

3 to form a circle around — see SURROUND

girdle *n* a strip of flexible material (as leather) worn around the waist — see ²BELT 1

girdle *vb* **1** to encircle or bind with or as if with a belt — see GIRD 1

2 to travel completely around — see EN-
CIRCLE 1

3 to form a circle around — see SUR-
ROUND

girl *n* 1 a young unmarried woman ⟨His
parents really like the *girl* he's engaged
to.⟩

syn damsel, maid, maiden, miss

rel virgin; deb, debutante, ingenue (*or* ingénue); lass, lassie, sister; colleen, mademoiselle, senorita (*or* señorita)

2 a female person who has not yet reached
adulthood ⟨When I was a *girl*, I wanted a
horse so badly.⟩

syn lass, lassie, miss

rel bobby-soxer, junior miss, schoolgirl,
teenybopper; gamine, hoyden, pixie (*also*
pixy), tomboy

3 a female romantic companion — see
GIRLFRIEND

girlfriend *n* a female romantic companion
⟨He proposed to his *girlfriend* of seven
years.⟩

syn gal, girl, lady, ladylove, old lady, woman

rel beloved, darling, dear, favorite, flame,
honey, love, lover, significant other,
sweet, sweetheart, valentine

girt *vb* to encircle or bind with or as if with
a belt — see GIRD 1

girth *n* the distance around a round body
— see CIRCUMFERENCE 1

girth *vb* 1 to encircle or bind with or as if
with a belt — see GIRD 1

2 to travel completely around — see EN-
CIRCLE 1

gist *n* the central part or aspect of something under consideration — see CRUX

give *vb* 1 to make a present of ⟨Math tu-
tors generously *give* their time to help students after school.⟩

syn bestow, contribute, donate, give
away, present, volunteer

rel chip in, kick in, pitch in, throw in;
award, confer, endow, endue (*or* indue),
render; furnish, provide; lavish, regale;
aid, assist, benefit, help; administer, dish
out, dispense, impart, issue, mete (out);
extend, offer, put up, tender; sacrifice

phrases give of

near ant hold, keep, pocket, retain, withhold; preserve, save; advance, lend, loan;
sell

2 to put (something) into the possession or
safekeeping of another ⟨I *gave* my camera
to my father to hold while I went swimming.⟩

syn commend, commit, consign, delegate,
deliver, entrust (*also* intrust), hand, hand
over, leave, pass, recommend, repose,
transfer, transmit, trust, turn over, vest

rel confer, grant; assign, deal (out), dispense, disperse, distribute, divide; hand in,
release, relinquish, submit, surrender,
turn in, yield; bequeath, hand down, hand
on, will; advance, lend, loan; furnish, supply

near ant detain, hold back, reserve, withhold; own, possess; accept, take in; occupy, take, take over

ant hold, keep, retain

3 to bring before the public in performance or exhibition — see PRESENT 1

4 to fall down or in as a result of physical
pressure — see COLLAPSE 1

5 to hand over or use up in payment —
see SPEND 1

6 to make known (as an idea, emotion, or
opinion) — see EXPRESS 1

7 to occupy (oneself) diligently or with
close attention — see APPLY 2

8 to produce as revenue — see YIELD 2

9 to put (something) into the possession of
someone for use or consumption — see
FURNISH 2

10 to put before another for acceptance
or consideration — see OFFER 1

11 to cause (something) to pass from one
to another — see COMMUNICATE 1

give–and–take *n* 1 an exchange of views
for the purpose of exploring a subject or
deciding an issue — see DISCUSSION 1

2 the act or practice of each side giving up
something in order to reach an agreement
— see CONCESSION 1

3 good-natured teasing or exchanging of
clever remarks — see BANTER

giveaway *n* something given to someone
without expectation of a return — see
GIFT 1

give away *vb* 1 to make known (something abstract) through outward signs —
see SHOW 2

2 to make a present of — see GIVE 1

give in *vb* 1 to give up and cease resistance
(as to a liking, temptation, or habit) — see
YIELD 1

2 to cease resistance (as to another's arguments, demands, or control) — see YIELD 3

given *adj* 1 being in the habit or custom
— see ACCUSTOMED

2 having a tendency to be or act in a certain way — see PRONE 1

3 known but not named — see CERTAIN 1

given *n* something taken as being true or
factual and used as a starting point for a
course of action or reasoning — see AS-
SUMPTION 1

given name *n* a name that is placed before
one's family name — see FORENAME

give out *vb* 1 to make known openly or
publicly — see ANNOUNCE

2 to throw or give off — see EMIT 1

3 to stop functioning — see FAIL 1

give up *vb* 1 to give (something) over to
the control or possession of another usually under duress — see SURRENDER 1

2 to stop doing (something) permanently
— see QUIT 2

3 to yield to the control or power of enemy forces — see FALL 2

4 to give (oneself) over to something especially unrestrainedly — see ABANDON 1

giving *n* the act of offering money in exchange for goods or services — see PAY-
MENT 1

gizmo *also* **gismo** *n* an interesting and often novel device with a practical use —
see GADGET

glacial *adj* 1 having a low or subnormal
temperature — see COLD 1

2 lacking in friendliness or warmth of feeling — see COLD 2

---

syn synonym(s)   **rel** related words
ant antonym(s)   **near ant** near antonym(s)

glad *adj* **1** experiencing pleasure, satisfaction, or delight ⟨The man was *glad* to see his old college buddies again, after so long an absence.⟩

syn blissful, delighted, gratified, happy, joyful, joyous, pleased, satisfied, thankful, tickled

rel blithe, blithesome, buoyant, cheerful, cheery, gladsome, lighthearted, sunny, upbeat; gleeful, jocund, jolly, jovial, merry, mirthful, smiling; beatific, ecstatic, elated, enraptured, euphoric, exhilarated, rapturous, rhapsodic (*also* rhapsodical); exuberant, exultant, jubilant, rapt, rejoicing, thrilled; hopeful, optimistic, rosy, sanguine

near ant aggrieved, anguished, blue, brokenhearted, dejected, depressed, despondent, disconsolate, disheartened, downcast, downhearted, forlorn, melancholy; doleful, dolorous, lachrymose, mournful, plaintive, sorrowful, sorry, woeful; black, dark, desolate, dispirited, gloomy, glum, grieved, heartbroken, heartsick, miserable, woebegone, wretched

ant displeased, dissatisfied, joyless, sad, unhappy, unpleased, unsatisfied

2 having a desire or inclination (as for a specified course of action) — see WILLING 1
3 serving to lift one's spirits — see CHEERFUL 2
4 feeling or expressing gratitude — see GRATEFUL 1

gladden *vb* to give satisfaction to — see PLEASE 1

gladdening *adj* making one feel good inside — see HEARTWARMING

gladiatorial *adj* feeling or displaying eagerness to fight — see BELLIGERENT

gladness *n* **1** a feeling or state of well-being and contentment — see HAPPINESS 1
2 the feeling experienced when one's wishes are met — see PLEASURE 1

gladsome *adj* having or showing a good mood or disposition — see CHEERFUL 1

glamorize *also* **glamourize** *vb* to represent or think of as better than reality would warrant — see IDEALIZE

glamorous *also* **glamourous** *adj* **1** excitingly or mysteriously unusual — see EXOTIC
2 having an often mysterious or magical power to attract — see FASCINATING 1

glamour *also* **glamor** *n* the power of irresistible attraction — see CHARM 2

glance *n* an instance of looking especially briefly — see LOOK 2

glance *vb* **1** to strike and fly off at an angle ⟨The basketball *glanced* off the rim.⟩ ⟨Her wild pitch *glanced* off my shoulder and landed in the dugout.⟩

syn bounce, carom, rebound, ricochet, skim, skip

rel brush, graze, nudge, rake, shave, sweep; bump, contact, hit, kiss, touch; sideswipe; reflect

2 to take a quick or hasty look ⟨I just *glanced* at the instructions before assembling the bike.⟩ ⟨He *glanced* over his shoulder to see if she was still there.⟩

syn browse, dip, glimpse, glint, peek, skim

rel peep; blink, squint; look over, peruse, scan

near ant examine, overlook, oversee,

question, survey; study, view; peer, pry; gawk, goggle, rubberneck; leer, ogle

ant gaze, stare

3 to shoot forth bursts of light — see FLASH 1

glare *n* the steady giving off of the form of radiation that makes vision possible — see LIGHT 1

glare *vb* **1** to shine with a bright harsh light ⟨The spotlight *glared* down on the suspect as the police questioned him relentlessly.⟩

syn beat, blaze, burn, flame, flare

rel beam, glow, radiate; flash, glance, gleam, glimmer, glint, glisten, glister, glitter, scintillate, shimmer, sparkle, twinkle; bedazzle, blind, daze, dazzle

2 to look with anger or disapproval — see FROWN

glaring *adj* very noticeable especially for being incorrect or bad — see EGREGIOUS

gleam *n* the steady giving off of the form of radiation that makes vision possible — see LIGHT 1

gleam *vb* to shoot forth bursts of light — see FLASH 1

glee *n* a mood characterized by high spirits and amusement and often accompanied by laughter — see MIRTH

glee club *n* an organized group of singers — see CHORUS 1

gleeful *adj* indicative of or marked by high spirits or good humor — see MERRY

gleefulness *n* a mood characterized by high spirits and amusement and often accompanied by laughter — see MIRTH

glide *vb* **1** to move or proceed smoothly and readily — see FLOW 2
2 to move through the air with or as if with outstretched wings — see FLY 1
3 to rest or move along the surface of a liquid or in the air — see FLOAT 1

glimmer *n* **1** a very small amount — see PARTICLE 1
2 an almost imperceptible sign of something — see HINT 2

glimmer *vb* to shoot forth bursts of light — see FLASH 1

glimpse *n* an instance of looking especially briefly — see LOOK 2

glimpse *vb* to take a quick or hasty look — see GLANCE 2

glint *vb* **1** to shoot forth bursts of light — see FLASH 1
2 to take a quick or hasty look — see GLANCE 2

glisten *vb* to shoot forth bursts of light — see FLASH 1

glistening *adj* having a shiny surface or finish — see GLOSSY

glister *vb* to shoot forth bursts of light — see FLASH 1

glitter *vb* to shoot forth bursts of light — see FLASH 1

glitz *n* excessive or unnecessary display — see OSTENTATION

glitzy *adj* excessively showy — see GAUDY

gloaming *n* **1** a time or place of little or no light — see DARK 1
2 the time from when the sun begins to set to the onset of total darkness — see DUSK 1

glob *n* **1** a small uneven mass — see LUMP 1
2 the quantity of fluid that falls naturally in one rounded mass — see DROP 1

global *adj* 1 belonging or relating to the whole — see GENERAL 1

2 covering everything or all important points — see ENCYCLOPEDIC

3 having every part of the surface the same distance from the center — see ROUND 1

globe *n* 1 a more or less round body or mass — see ¹BALL 1

2 the celestial body on which we live — see EARTH 1

globule *n* the quantity of fluid that falls naturally in one rounded mass — see DROP 1

gloom *n* 1 a state or spell of low spirits — see SADNESS

2 a time or place of little or no light — see DARK 1

gloom *vb* 1 to look with anger or disapproval — see FROWN

2 to take on a gloomy or forbidding look — see DARKEN 1

gloominess *n* a state or spell of low spirits — see SADNESS

gloomy *adj* 1 causing or marked by an atmosphere lacking in cheer ⟨The cold rain made for a *gloomy* day.⟩

syn black, bleak, cheerless, chill, cloudy, cold, comfortless, dark, darkening, depressing, desolate, dire, disconsolate, dismal, drear, dreary, elegiac (*also* elegiacal), forlorn, funereal, glum, godforsaken, gray (*also* grey), lonely, lonesome, lugubrious, miserable, morbid, morose, murky, saturnine, sepulchral, solemn, somber (*or* sombre), sullen, wretched

rel blue, dejected, depressed, despondent, disconsolate, down, droopy, hangdog, inconsolable, low, melancholy, mirthless, sad, unhappy, woebegone, woeful; dim, discomfiting, discouraging, disheartening, dismaying, dispiriting, distressful, distressing, upsetting; hopeless, pessimistic; lamentable, mournful, plaintive, sorrowful; colorless, drab, dull; dour, grim, lowering (*also* louring), lowery (*also* loury), menacing, oppressive, threatening

near ant blithe, blithesome, buoyant, jocund, jolly, joyful, joyous, merry, mirthful; encouraging, hopeful, optimistic; lighthearted, lightsome

ant bright, cheerful, cheering, cheery, comforting, cordial, festive, heartwarming, sunshiny

2 feeling unhappiness — see SAD 1

3 being without light or without enough light — see DARK 1

glorify *vb* 1 to assign a high status or value to — see EXALT 1

2 to offer honor or respect to (someone) as a divine power — see WORSHIP 1

3 to praise or publicize lavishly and often excessively — see TOUT 1

4 to proclaim the glory of — see PRAISE 1

5 to represent or think of as better than reality would warrant — see IDEALIZE

glorious *adj* large and impressive in size, grandeur, extent, or conception — see GRAND 1

gloriously *adv* in a pleasing way — see WELL 5

gloriousness *n* impressiveness of beauty on a large scale — see MAGNIFICENCE

glory *vb* to feel or express joy or triumph — see EXULT

glory *n* 1 public acknowledgment or admiration for an achievement ⟨The theater director gave the stage crew all the *glory* for the successful production.⟩

syn acclaim, accolade, applause, credit, distinction, homage, honor, laurels, sun

rel celebrity, fame, renown, repute; compliment, encomium, eulogy, panegyric, toast, tribute; acclamation, ovation, plaudit, praise, rave, rhapsody; citation, commendation, note, recommendation; enshrinement, enthronement, exaltation, glorification

2 an asset that brings praise or renown ⟨The new art museum has become the *glory* of the college campus.⟩

syn boast, credit, honor, jewel, pride, treasure

rel pièce de résistance, showpiece; attraction, feature, highlight; distinction, excellence, merit, value, virtue

phrases a feather in one's cap

near ant disgrace, dishonor; blemish, blot, defect, shame, slur, smirch, smudge, stain, stigma; eyesore, fright, horror, mess

3 impressiveness of beauty on a large scale — see MAGNIFICENCE

glorying *adj* having or expressing feelings of joy or triumph — see EXULTANT

gloss *n* 1 a deceptively attractive external appearance ⟨She used a computer to give her astrological predictions the *gloss* of real science.⟩

syn facade (*also* façade), veneer

rel fluff; fig leaf; charade, front, guise, masquerade, pose, semblance, show

2 brightness created by light reflected from a surface — see SHINE 1

gloss *vb* to make smooth or glossy usually by repeatedly applying surface pressure — see POLISH 1

gloss (over) *vb* 1 to make (something) seem less bad by offering excuses — see PALLIATE 1

2 to dismiss as of little importance — see EXCUSE 1

glossy *adj* having a shiny surface or finish ⟨the *glossy* finish on the gym floor⟩ ⟨a sports car with an interior upholstered with *glossy* leather⟩

syn buffed, burnished, glistening, lustrous, polished, rubbed, satin, satiny, sleek

rel brushed, eggshell, semigloss, semilustrous; silken, silky, slick, slippery; glassy, glazed, lacquered, shellacked, varnished; gleaming, glittering, reflective, shining

near ant lackluster; unvarnished

ant dim, dull, flat, lusterless, matte (*also* mat *or* matt)

glow *n* the steady giving off of the form of radiation that makes vision possible — see LIGHT 1

glow *vb* 1 to be on fire especially brightly — see BURN 1

2 to develop a rosy facial color (as from excitement or embarrassment) — see BLUSH

glower *vb* 1 to look with anger or disapproval — see FROWN

---

syn synonym(s)   *rel* related words
ant antonym(s)   *near ant* near antonym(s)

2 to take on a gloomy or forbidding look — see DARKEN 1

glowing *adj* **1** giving off or reflecting much light — see BRIGHT 1

2 having a healthy reddish skin tone — see RUDDY

3 having or being an outward sign of good feelings (as of love, confidence, or happiness) — see RADIANT 1

4 having or expressing great depth of feeling — see FERVENT 1

gloze (over) *vb* **1** to make (something) seem less bad by offering excuses — see PALLIATE 1

2 to dismiss as of little importance — see EXCUSE 1

glue *n* a substance used to stick things together 〈I used *glue* to stick the photo in the album.〉

syn adhesive, bond, cement, size

rel epoxy, epoxy resin, library paste, mucilage, paste, superglue, water glass; dope, gum

gluey *adj* tending to adhere to objects upon contact — see STICKY 1

glum *adj* **1** causing or marked by an atmosphere lacking in cheer — see GLOOMY 1

2 feeling unhappiness — see SAD 1

3 given to or displaying a resentful silence and often irritability — see SULKY

glut *vb* to fill with food to capacity — see GORGE 1

glutinous *adj* tending to adhere to objects upon contact — see STICKY 1

glutton *n* one who eats greedily or too much 〈He's such a *glutton* that he ate the whole cake.〉

syn gorger, gormandizer, gourmand, hog, overeater, pig, swiller

rel feaster, trencherman; muncher; guzzler

near ant dieter, nibbler, picker

gluttonous *adj* having a huge appetite — see VORACIOUS 1

gnash *vb* to press or strike against or together so as to make a scraping sound — see GRIND 2

gnaw (on) *vb* to crush or grind with the teeth — see BITE (ON)

gnome *n* an imaginary being usually having a small human form and magical powers — see FAIRY

go *adj* being in a state of fitness for some experience or action — see READY 1

go *n* **1** a practice or interest that is very popular for a short time — see FAD

2 active strength of body or mind — see VIGOR 1

3 an effort to do or accomplish something — see ATTEMPT 1

4 readiness to engage in daring or difficult activity — see ENTERPRISE 2

go *vb* **1** to move forward along a course 〈Everything is *going* according to our plans.〉

syn advance, come, come along, do, fare, forge, get along, get on, go off, march, pace, proceed, progress

rel accelerate, fast-forward, speed; approach, near; journey, pass, repair, run, travel, wend; actuate, drive, impel, propel, push; take out

phrases gain ground

near ant arrest, balk, block, check, detain, halt, hinder, hold back, impede, nip, obstruct, slow (down *or* up), stem; repress, retard, stunt, suppress; delay, interrupt, stall; cramp, hamper, inhibit; cease, let up, pause

ant remain, stand, stay, stop

2 to leave a place often for another 〈We will *go* on vacation at the end of the year.〉 〈She decided it would be better to *go* before it got any later.〉

syn bail out, begone, clear out, cut out, depart, exit, get, get off, go off, move, part, quit, sally (forth), shove (off), step (along), take off, walk out

rel start, strike out; abscond, decamp, escape, evacuate, flee, fly, get out, run away, scram, skip; light out; abandon, desert, forsake, vacate; emigrate; adjourn, remove, retire, retreat, withdraw

phrases beat it, hit the road, pull stakes (*or* pull up stakes), take a hike (*also* take a walk), take a powder

near ant abide, dwell, lodge, remain, settle, stay, tarry; approach, close, near; hit, land, reach

ant arrive, come, show up, turn up

3 to be fitting or proper — see DO 1

4 to be in agreement on every point — see CHECK 1

5 to be positioned along a certain course or in a certain direction — see RUN 3

6 to eventually have as a state or quality — see BECOME

7 to fall down or in as a result of physical pressure — see COLLAPSE 1

8 to have or be in a usual or proper place — see BELONG 1

9 to lose bodily strength or vigor — see WEAKEN 2

10 to make one's way through, across, or over — see TRAVERSE

11 to occur within a continuous range of variation — see RUN 4

12 to risk (something) on the outcome of an uncertain event — see BET

13 to come to an end — see CEASE 1

14 to have enough money for — see AFFORD

15 to put up with (something painful or difficult) — see BEAR 2

16 to stop living — see DIE 1

17 to turn out as planned or desired — see SUCCEED 1

go (for) *vb* to have a price of — see COST

go (to) *vb* to use or seek out as a source of aid, relief, or advantage — see RESORT (TO) 1

goad *n* something that arouses action or activity — see IMPULSE 1

goad *vb* **1** to try to persuade (someone) through earnest appeals to follow a course of action — see URGE

2 to urge or push forward with or as if with a pointed object — see PROD 1

goal *n* something that one hopes or intends to accomplish 〈Leaving the world a better place than I found it is one of my main *goals*.〉

syn aim, ambition, aspiration, design, dream, end, idea, ideal, intent, intention, mark, meaning, object, objective, plan, point, pretension, purpose, target, thing

rel grail, holy grail; plot, project, scheme;

desire, hope, mind, wish; destination, terminus

phrases name of the game

near ant means, method, way

goat *n* a person or thing taking the blame for others — see SCAPEGOAT

¹**gob** *n* **1** a small uneven mass — see LUMP 1
2 gobs *pl* a considerable amount — see LOT 2

²**gob** *n* one who operates or navigates a seagoing vessel — see SAILOR

gobbet *n* a small uneven mass — see LUMP 1

gobble *vb* to swallow or eat greedily ⟨They *gobbled* the sandwiches like they hadn't eaten for days.⟩

syn bolt, cram, devour, gorge, gormandize, gulp, scarf, scoff, wolf

rel overeat, pig out, swill

near ant nibble, peck, pick

gobbledygook *also* **gobbledegook** *n* language marked by abstractions, jargon, euphemisms, and circumlocutions — see GIBBERISH 2

go-between *n* **1** one that carries a message or does an errand — see MESSENGER
2 one who works with opposing sides in order to bring about an agreement — see MEDIATOR

goblin *n* an imaginary being usually having a small human form and magical powers — see FAIRY

god *n* **1** a being having superhuman powers and control over a particular part of life or the world — see DEITY 1
2 *cap* the being worshipped as the creator and ruler of the universe — see DEITY 2

goddess *n* a lovely woman — see BEAUTY 2

godforsaken *adj* causing or marked by an atmosphere lacking in cheer — see GLOOMY 1

godhead *n* **1** the quality or state of being divine — see DIVINITY 1
2 *cap* the being worshipped as the creator and ruler of the universe — see DEITY 2

godhood *n* the quality or state of being divine — see DIVINITY 1

godless *adj* lacking religious emotions, principles, or practices — see IRRELIGIOUS

godlike *adj* of, relating to, or being God — see HOLY 3

godliness *n* the quality or state of being spiritually pure or virtuous — see HOLINESS

godly *adj* **1** showing a devotion to God and to a life of virtue — see HOLY 1
2 of, relating to, or being God — see HOLY 3

godsend *n* something that provides happiness or does good for a person or thing — see BLESSING 2

Godspeed *n* an expression of good wishes at parting — see GOOD-BYE

go-getter *n* an ambitious person who eagerly goes after what is desired ⟨a *go-getter* with his sights set on the presidency⟩

syn hustler, live wire, powerhouse, rustler, self-starter

rel eager beaver; achiever, comer, doer, enterpriser; he-man, individualist; pistol

---

near ant dawdler, idler, loafer, lounger, putterer; goldbrick, malingerer, procrastinator, shirker, slacker; drone, lazybones, sluggard; dallier, laggard, lingerer, loiterer, slowpoke, stick-in-the-mud; daydreamer, dreamer; dropout, quitter

go-getting *adj* **1** having a strong desire for personal advancement — see AMBITIOUS 1
2 having or showing a bold forcefulness in the pursuit of a goal — see AGGRESSIVE 2

go-getting *n* eager desire for personal advancement — see AMBITION 1

goggle *vb* to look long and hard in wonder or surprise — see GAPE

going *adj* **1** accepted, used, or practiced by most people — see CURRENT 1
2 being in effective operation — see ACTIVE 1
3 having attained a desired end or state of good fortune — see SUCCESSFUL 1

going *n* **1** forward movement in time or place — see ADVANCE 1
2 the act of leaving a place — see DEPARTURE 1

gold *n* something (as pieces of stamped metal or printed paper) customarily and legally used as a medium of exchange, a measure of value, or a means of payment — see MONEY

golden *adj* **1** having qualities which inspire hope — see HOPEFUL 1
2 marked by conspicuously full and rich sounds or tones — see RESONANT
3 marked by vigorous growth and well-being especially economically — see PROSPEROUS 1
4 of a pale yellow or yellowish brown color — see BLOND
5 pointing toward a happy outcome — see FAVORABLE 2

golden-ager *n* a person of advanced years — see SENIOR CITIZEN

golden mean *n* a middle point between extremes — see MEAN 1

gone *adj* **1** no longer existing — see EXTINCT
2 no longer living — see DEAD 1
3 no longer possessed — see LOST
4 containing unborn young within the body — see PREGNANT 1

gone (on) *adj* filled with an intense or excessive love for — see ENAMORED (OF)

good *adv* in a satisfactory way — see WELL 1

good *n* **1** something that provides happiness or does good for a person or thing — see BLESSING 2
2 the state of doing well especially in relation to one's happiness or success — see WELFARE
3 goods *pl* products that are bought and sold in business — see MERCHANDISE
4 goods *pl* a skill, an ability, or knowledge that makes a person able to do a particular job — see QUALIFICATION 1
5 goods *pl* transportable items that one owns — see POSSESSION 2

good *adj* **1** based on sound reasoning or information ⟨We had enough information to make a *good* assessment of the situation.⟩

syn commonsense, firm, hard, informed,

---

just, justified, levelheaded, logical, rational, reasonable, sensible, sober, solid, valid, well-founded

rel actual, real, true; certain; sure; validated, verified; confirmed, corroborated, substantiated; cogent, convincing; colorable, credible, plausible

near ant unsubstantiated, unsupported, unwarranted; flimsy, implausible, unconvincing, weak; fallacious, false, misguided, misled

ant groundless, illogical, invalid, irrational, nonrational, nonsensical, nonvalid, unfounded, uninformed, unjustified, unreasonable, unreasoned, unsound

2 conforming to a high standard of morality or virtue ⟨a *good* person who seldom did wrong⟩ ⟨*Good* behavior will earn you the respect of others.⟩

syn all right, decent, ethical, honest, honorable, just, moral, nice, right, righteous, right-minded, straight, upright, virtuous

rel correct, decorous, proper, seemly; high-minded, noble, principled; commendable, creditable, exemplary, legitimate; esteemed, law-abiding, reputable, respected, upstanding, worthy; blameless, clean, guiltless, immaculate, incorrupt (*also* incorrupted), incorruptible, innocent, inoffensive, irreproachable, unobjectionable; angelic (*or* angelical), pure, scrupulous, spotless, uncorrupted, unerring; goody-goody, moralistic, pharisaical, rectitudinous, sanctimonious, self-righteous

near ant improper, incorrect, indecorous, naughty, unbecoming, unseemly; corrupt, debased, debauched, degenerate, depraved, dissolute, libertine, perverted, reprobate; unprincipled, unscrupulous; atrocious, infamous, villainous; base, low, mean, vicious, vile; blameworthy, objectionable, offensive; iniquitous, nefarious; errant, erring, fallen

ant bad, dishonest, dishonorable, evil, evil-minded, immoral, indecent, sinful, unethical, unrighteous, wicked, wrong

3 according to the rules of logic — see LOGICAL 1

4 being to one's liking — see SATISFACTORY 1

5 expressing approval — see FAVORABLE 1

6 firm in one's allegiance to someone or something — see FAITHFUL 1

7 giving pleasure or contentment to the mind or senses — see PLEASANT 1

8 having or showing exceptional knowledge, experience, or skill in a field of endeavor — see PROFICIENT

9 having sufficient worth or merit to receive one's honor, esteem, or reward — see WORTHY

10 having the required skills for an acceptable level of performance — see COMPETENT 1

11 meeting the requirements of a purpose or situation — see FIT 1

12 sufficiently large in size, amount, or number to merit attention — see CONSIDERABLE 1

13 worthy of one's trust — see DEPENDABLE

14 being in agreement with the truth or a fact or a standard — see CORRECT 1

15 very pleasing to look at — see BEAUTIFUL 1

16 beneficial to the health of body or mind — see HEALTHFUL

17 having or showing a concern for the welfare of others — see CHARITABLE 1

18 of a level of quality that meets one's needs or standards — see ADEQUATE

19 promoting or contributing to personal or social well-being — see BENEFICIAL

Good Book *n* a book made up of the writings accepted by Christians as coming from God — see BIBLE

good—bye *or* **good—by** *n* an expression of good wishes at parting ⟨We said our *good-byes* and headed for home.⟩

syn adieu, au revoir, bon voyage, farewell, Godspeed

rel leave-taking, send-off

near ant greeting(s), salutation, salute; welcome

ant hello

good—hearted *adj* having or marked by sympathy and consideration for others — see HUMANE 1

good—heartedness *n* the capacity for feeling for another's unhappiness or misfortune — see HEART 1

goodly *adj* **1** of a size greater than average of its kind — see LARGE

2 sufficiently large in size, amount, or number to merit attention — see CONSIDERABLE 1

3 very pleasing to look at — see BEAUTIFUL 1

good—natured *adj* having an easygoing and pleasing manner especially in social situations — see AMIABLE

good—naturedness *n* **1** a desire or disposition to please — see COMPLAISANCE

2 the state or quality of having a pleasant or agreeable manner in socializing with others — see AMIABILITY 1

goodness *n* conduct that conforms to an accepted standard of right and wrong — see MORALITY 1

good—tempered *adj* having an easygoing and pleasing manner especially in social situations — see AMIABLE

good—temperedness *n* the state or quality of having a pleasant or agreeable manner in socializing with others — see AMIABILITY 1

goodwill *n* **1** kindly concern, interest, or support ⟨the long tradition of *goodwill* that exists between the United States and Canada⟩.

syn amity, benevolence, brotherhood, charity, cordiality, fellowship, friendliness, friendship, kindliness, neighborliness

rel camaraderie, collegiality, community, companionship, company, comradeship; civility, comity, concord, harmony, rapport; charity, generosity; affinity, communion, empathy, kindness, sympathy, tolerance; altruism, philanthropy, selflessness, unselfishness

near ant disfavor; animosity, antagonism, antipathy, enmity, hate, hatred, hostility, incivility, malice, rancor; querulousness

ant ill will, malevolence, venom

2 cheerful readiness to do something — see ALACRITY

goody or **goodie** n something that is pleasing to eat because it is rare or a luxury — see DELICACY 1

gooey adj appealing to the emotions in an obvious and tiresome way — see CORNY

goof n 1 an unintentional departure from truth or accuracy — see ERROR 1

2 a stupid person — see IDIOT

goof (around) vb to spend time in aimless activity — see FIDDLE (AROUND)

goof (off) vb to spend time doing nothing — see IDLE

go off vb 1 to break open or into pieces usually because of internal pressure — see EXPLODE 1

2 to move forward along a course — see GO 1

3 to leave a place often for another — see GO 2

goofy adj lacking in seriousness or maturity — see GIDDY 1

goon n 1 a stupid person — see IDIOT

2 a violent, brutal person who is often a member of an organized gang — see HOODLUM

goose n a person who lacks good sense or judgment — see FOOL 1

goose egg n the numerical symbol 0 or the absence of number or quantity represented by it — see ZERO 1

go over vb to turn out as planned or desired — see SUCCEED 1

gore vb to penetrate or hold (something) with a pointed object — see IMPALE

gorge n a narrow opening between hillsides or mountains that can be used for passage — see CANYON

gorge vb 1 to fill with food to capacity ⟨We *gorged* ourselves on the four pies Aunt Martha had brought for Thanksgiving.⟩
syn cram, glut, sate, stuff, surfeit
rel gobble, gormandize, pig out; gulp, guzzle; cloy, fill; banquet, feast, regale
near ant diet, fast

2 to eat greedily or to excess ⟨The kids began *gorging* on Halloween candy the minute they got back from trick-or-treating.⟩
syn gormandize, overeat, pig out, swill
rel devour, glut, sate, stuff, surfeit, wolf; banquet, feast, regale; bolt, cram, gulp, guzzle
phrases load up on
near ant nibble, peck, pick, taste

3 to swallow or eat greedily — see GOBBLE

gorgeous adj very pleasing to look at — see BEAUTIFUL 1

gorgeousness n 1 the qualities in a person or thing that as a whole give pleasure to the senses — see BEAUTY 1

2 impressiveness of beauty on a large scale — see MAGNIFICENCE

gorger n one who eats greedily or too much — see GLUTTON

gormandize vb 1 to eat greedily or to excess — see GORGE 2

2 to swallow or eat greedily — see GOBBLE

gormandizer n one who eats greedily or too much — see GLUTTON

gory adj smeared or stained with blood — see BLOODY 1

gospel n the basic beliefs or guiding principles of a person or group — see CREED 1

gossamer adj 1 being of a material lacking in sturdiness or substance — see FLIMSY 1

2 resembling air in lightness — see AIRY 1

3 very thin and easy to see through — see SHEER 1

gossamery adj 1 being of a material lacking in sturdiness or substance — see FLIMSY 1

2 resembling air in lightness — see AIRY 1

3 very thin and easy to see through — see SHEER 1

gossip n 1 a person who habitually reveals personal or sensational facts about others ⟨Be careful what you say because he's a terrible *gossip*.⟩
syn talebearer, telltale
rel betrayer, blabbermouth, informant, informer, snitcher, squealer, stool pigeon, tattler, tattletale; libeler, scandalmonger

2 friendly, informal conversation or an instance of this — see CHAT 1

3 information or opinion that is widely disseminated without any authority or confirmation of accuracy — see RUMOR

gossip vb to relate sometimes questionable or secret information of a personal nature ⟨a neighbor who loves to *gossip* with others about everyone⟩
syn blab, dish, talk, tattle, wag
rel bandy (about), circulate, rumor; blabber, disclose, divulge, reveal, tell; hint, imply, insinuate, intimate, let on, suggest; inform, report, snitch, squeal, tip (off); babble, spill
phrases spill the beans
near ant clam up, shut up

gossipy adj having the style and content of everyday conversation — see CHATTY 1

gouge vb to charge (someone) too much for goods or services — see OVERCHARGE 1

gourmand n 1 a person with refined tastes in food and wine — see EPICURE

2 one who eats greedily or too much — see GLUTTON

gourmet n a person with refined tastes in food and wine — see EPICURE

govern vb 1 to exercise authority or power over ⟨The president is elected in order to *govern* the country.⟩
syn boss, captain, command, control, preside (over), rule
rel conduct, direct, head, lead; administer, manage, micromanage, oversee, regulate, superintend, supervise; dictate, dominate, domineer, lord (it over), master, oppress, reign (over), tyrannize; conquer, subdue, subjugate

2 to keep from exceeding a desirable degree or level (as of expression) — see CONTROL 1

3 to look after and make decisions about — see CONDUCT 1

governance n 1 lawful control over the affairs of a political unit (as a nation) — see RULE 2

2 the act or activity of looking after and making decisions about something — see CONDUCT 1

government n 1 lawful control over the affairs of a political unit (as a nation) — see RULE 2

---

syn synonym(s)　　*rel* related words
ant antonym(s)　　*near ant* near antonym(s)

2 the act or activity of looking after and making decisions about something — see CONDUCT 1

gown n **1** a garment with a joined blouse and skirt usually worn by a woman or girl — see DRESS 1

2 a loose pullover garment worn in bed — see NIGHTGOWN

gown vb to outfit with clothes and especially fine or special clothes — see CLOTHE 1

grab n an instance of theft — see THEFT 2

grab vb to take physical control or possession of (something) suddenly or forcibly — see CATCH 1

grace n **1** an act of kind assistance — see FAVOR 1

2 dignified or restrained beauty of form, appearance, or style — see ELEGANCE

3 a quality that gives something special worth — see EXCELLENCE 2

grace vb to make more attractive by adding something that is beautiful or becoming — see DECORATE

graceful adj **1** moving easily ⟨The graceful ballerina effortlessly leapt across the stage.⟩

syn agile, feline, light, light-footed (also light-foot), lightsome, lissome (also lissom), lithe, lithesome, nimble, spry

rel acrobatic, flexible, limber, loose-jointed, pliable, pliant, supple; adroit, deft, dexterous (also dextrous), light-fingered; fleet-footed, sure-footed; athletic, balletic, coordinated

near ant inflexible, rigid, stiff; bungling, inept, maladroit

ant awkward, clumsy, gawky, graceless, lumbering, ungainly, ungraceful

2 having or showing elegance — see ELEGANT 1

gracefulness n dignified or restrained beauty of form, appearance, or style — see ELEGANCE

graceless adj **1** lacking or showing a lack of nimbleness in using one's hands — see CLUMSY 1

2 lacking social grace and assurance — see AWKWARD 1

3 not appropriate for a particular occasion or situation — see INAPPROPRIATE

4 having or showing an inability to move in a graceful manner — see CLUMSY 2

5 showing poor judgment especially in personal relationships or social situations — see INDISCREET

gracious adj **1** showing a natural kindness and courtesy especially in social situations ⟨a gracious host who goes out of his way to make every guest feel welcome⟩

syn affable, cordial, genial, hospitable, sociable

rel agreeable, amiable, benign, benignant, congenial, convivial, friendly, kind, kindly, neighborly; accommodating, obliging, considerate, courteous, polite, thoughtful; cosmopolitan, sophisticated, urbane; approachable, attentive, outgoing

near ant boorish, churlish; abrupt, blunt, brusque (also brusk), curt, gruff, sharp, snippy; antisocial, disagreeable, discourteous, ill-mannered, impolite, rude, sullen, surly, uncivil, unfriendly, unkind, unmannerly; crabbed, crabby, cross, crusty, grumpy

ant inhospitable, ungenial, ungracious, unsociable

2 having an easygoing and pleasing manner especially in social situations — see AMIABLE

3 showing consideration, courtesy, and good manners — see POLITE 1

graciousness n **1** speech or behavior that is a sign of good manners — see POLITENESS 1

2 the state or quality of having a pleasant or agreeable manner in socializing with others — see AMIABILITY 1

gradational adj proceeding or changing by steps or degrees — see GRADUAL

gradationally adv by small steps or amounts — see GRADUALLY

grade n **1** an individual part of a process, series, or ranking — see DEGREE 1

2 degree of excellence — see QUALITY 1

3 one of the units into which a whole is divided on the basis of a common characteristic — see CLASS 2

4 something set up as an example against which others of the same type are compared — see STANDARD 1

5 the degree to which something rises up from a position level with the horizon — see SLANT 1

grade vb **1** to arrange or assign according to type — see CLASSIFY 1

2 to take or have a certain position within a group arranged in vertical classes — see RANK 1

gradient n the degree to which something rises up from a position level with the horizon — see SLANT 1

gradual adj proceeding or changing by steps or degrees ⟨A gradual drop in gas prices will take place over the next several months.⟩

syn gradational, incremental, phased, piecemeal, step-by-step

rel progressive, stepped, tapered; imperceptible, inching; decrescent, increscent

near ant acute, sharp; changeable, dynamic, meteoric, volatile

ant abrupt, sharp, sudden

gradually adv by small steps or amounts ⟨gradually worked his way down the class roster⟩ ⟨Add the sugar to the beaten egg whites gradually to make the meringue.⟩

syn gradationally, little by little, piece by piece, piecemeal

rel increasingly, progressively; fractionally, imperceptibly; slowly

phrases bit by bit, by degrees, inch by inch

near ant acutely, sharply, steeply; hastily, precipitously

ant abruptly, suddenly

graduation n a scheme of rank or order — see ³SCALE 1

grain n **1** a very small piece — see BIT 1

2 one's characteristic attitude or mood — see DISPOSITION 1

grainy adj made up of large particles — see COARSE 1

grand adj **1** large and impressive in size, grandeur, extent, or conception ⟨the grand ceremonies that typically mark the opening of the Olympic Games⟩

syn august, baronial, gallant, glorious,

grandiose, heroic (*also* heroical), imperial, imposing, magnificent, majestic, massive, monumental, noble, proud, regal, royal, splendid, stately

rel colossal, monstrous, prodigious, stupendous, tremendous; kingly, lordly, princely, queenly; awesome, awful, cosmic (*also* cosmical), sublime, wondrous; formidable, impressive, prepossessing, redoubtable; pompous; marvelous (*or* marvellous), superb, terrific, wonderful; extravagant, lavish, luxurious, opulent, palatial, palatine, sumptuous; gorgeous, resplendent, splendiferous; extraordinary, remarkable, sensational, striking; celestial, divine, heavenly

near ant lowly, modest, unprepossessing; average, common, mediocre, ordinary, run-of-the-mill, second-rate; mean, meretricious, shabby, sordid; insignificant, measly, paltry, petty, puny, trifling, trivial *ant* humble, unheroic, unimposing, unimpressive

2 coming before all others in importance — see FOREMOST 1

3 not lacking any part or member that properly belongs to it — see COMPLETE 1

4 of a size greater than average of its kind — see LARGE

5 of high birth, rank, or station — see NOBLE 1

6 of the very best kind — see EXCELLENT

7 unusually large — see HUGE

grandee *n* a man of high birth or social position — see GENTLEMAN 1

grandeur *n* impressiveness of beauty on a large scale — see MAGNIFICENCE

grandfather *n* a person who is several generations earlier in an individual's line of descent — see ANCESTOR 1

grandiloquence *n* **1** boastful speech or writing — see BOMBAST 1

2 language that is impressive-sounding but not meaningful or sincere — see RHETORIC 1

grandiloquent *adj* **1** full of fine words and fancy expressions — see FLOWERY 1

2 marked by the use of impressive-sounding but mostly meaningless words and phrases — see RHETORICAL 1

grandiose *adj* **1** large and impressive in size, grandeur, extent, or conception — see GRAND 1

2 self-consciously trying to present an appearance of grandeur or importance — see PRETENTIOUS 1

grandiosity *n* the quality or state of appearing or trying to appear more important or more valuable than is the case — see PRETENSE 1

grandly *adv* **1** in a luxurious manner — see HIGH

2 in a manner befitting a person of the highest character and ideals — see GREATLY 1

grandness *n* **1** impressiveness of beauty on a large scale — see MAGNIFICENCE

2 the quality or state of being large in size — see LARGENESS

grange *n* a piece of land and its buildings

used to grow crops or raise livestock — see FARM

granite *n* firm or unwavering adherence to one's purpose — see DETERMINATION 1

grant *n* a sum of money allotted for a specific use by official or formal action — see APPROPRIATION 1

grant *vb* **1** to accept the truth or existence of (something) usually reluctantly — see ADMIT 1

2 to give the ownership or benefit of (something) formally or publicly — see CONFER 1

granting *n* the approval by someone in authority for the doing of something — see PERMISSION

granular *adj* made up of large particles — see COARSE 1

granulated *adj* made up of large particles — see COARSE 1

granule *n* a very small piece — see BIT 1

graphic *n* something that visually explains or decorates a text — see ILLUSTRATION 1

graphic *also* **graphical** *adj* **1** producing a mental picture through clear and impressive description ⟨The report offered many *graphic* details about the earthquake.⟩

syn delineated, pictorial, picturesque, visual, vivid

rel depicted, descriptive, expressive; concrete, explicit, specific; faithful, lifelike, natural, photographic, realistic; fresh, incisive, sharp

near ant indeterminate, nebulous, obscure, sketchy, unclear, vague; bleary, blurry, dark, dim, faint, foggy, fuzzy, hazy, indefinite, indistinct, indistinguishable, muddy, murky, shadowlike, shadowy; ambiguous, cryptic, dark, enigmatic (*also* enigmatical), equivocal, inscrutable, mysterious

2 consisting of or relating to pictures — see PICTORIAL 1

grapple *n* **1** the act or manner of holding — see HOLD 1

2 an earnest effort for superiority or victory over another — see CONTEST 1

grapple *vb* **1** to seize and attempt to unbalance one another for the purpose of achieving physical mastery — see WRESTLE

2 to take physical control or possession of (something) suddenly or forcibly — see CATCH 1

grapple (with) *vb* to deal with (something) usually skillfully or efficiently — see HANDLE 1

grasp *n* **1** the ability to direct the course of something — see CONTROL 2

2 the act or manner of holding — see HOLD 1

3 the knowledge gained from the process of coming to know or understand something — see COMPREHENSION

grasp *vb* **1** to have a practical understanding of — see KNOW 1

2 to put one's arms around and press tightly — see EMBRACE 1

3 to reach for and take hold of by embracing with the fingers or arms — see TAKE 1

4 to have a clear idea of — see COMPREHEND 1

grasping *adj* having or marked by an ea-

---

syn synonym(s) *rel* related words
ant antonym(s) *near ant* near antonym(s)

ger and often selfish desire especially for material possessions — see GREEDY 1

graspingness *n* an intense selfish desire for wealth or possessions — see GREED

grassland *n* a broad area of level or rolling treeless country — see PLAIN 1

grate *vb* **1** to disturb the peace of mind of (someone) especially by repeated disagreeable acts — see IRRITATE 1

2 to pass roughly and noisily over or against a surface — see SCRAPE 1

3 to press or strike against or together so as to make a scraping sound — see GRIND 2

grateful *adj* **1** feeling or expressing gratitude ⟨She was *grateful* for her neighbor's help after she broke her foot.⟩

syn appreciative, glad, obliged, thankful

rel beholden, indebted; contented, delighted, gratified, pleased, satisfied, tickled; thanking

near ant inhospitable, rude, thoughtless, ungracious

ant inappreciative, thankless, unappreciative, ungrateful

2 giving pleasure or contentment to the mind or senses — see PLEASANT 1

gratefulness *n* acknowledgment of having received something good from another — see THANKS

gratification *n* the feeling experienced when one's wishes are met — see PLEASURE 1

gratified *adj* **1** experiencing pleasure, satisfaction, or delight — see GLAD 1

2 feeling that one's needs or desires have been met — see CONTENT

gratify *vb* **1** to give in to (a desire) — see INDULGE 1

2 to give satisfaction to — see PLEASE 1

gratifying *adj* **1** giving pleasure or contentment to the mind or senses — see PLEASANT 1

2 making one feel good inside — see HEARTWARMING

grating *adj* **1** disagreeable to one's aesthetic or artistic sense — see HARSH 1

2 harsh and dry in sound — see HOARSE

gratis *adj* not costing or charging anything — see FREE 4

gratitude *n* acknowledgment of having received something good from another — see THANKS

gratuitous *adj* **1** not costing or charging anything — see FREE 4

2 not needed by the circumstances or to accomplish an end — see UNNECESSARY

gratuity *n* **1** a small sum of money given for a service over and above what is due — see ²TIP 1

2 something given in addition to what is ordinarily expected or owed — see BONUS

grave *adj* **1** having a matter of importance as its topic — see SERIOUS 2

2 involving potential loss or injury — see DANGEROUS 1

3 not joking or playful in mood or manner — see SERIOUS 1

4 having a low musical pitch or range — see DEEP 2

grave *vb* to cut (as letters or designs) on a hard surface — see ENGRAVE 1

grave *n* **1** a final resting place for a dead person ⟨The boy put flowers on his grandmother's *grave*.⟩

syn burial, sepulture, tomb

rel catacomb, crypt, mausoleum, vault; cemetery, churchyard, potter's field

2 the permanent stopping of all the vital bodily activities — see DEATH 1

3 the state of being dead — see DEATH 2

gravel *adj* harsh and dry in sound — see HOARSE

gravelly *adj* harsh and dry in sound — see HOARSE

graveness *n* a mental state free of jesting or trifling — see EARNESTNESS

gravestone *n* a shaped stone laid over or erected near a grave and usually bearing an inscription to identify and preserve the memory of the deceased — see TOMBSTONE

graveyard *n* a piece of land used for burying the dead — see CEMETERY

gravid *adj* containing unborn young within the body — see PREGNANT 1

gravity *n* a mental state free of jesting or trifling — see EARNESTNESS

gravy *n* **1** a savory fluid food used as a topping or accompaniment to a main dish — see SAUCE 1

2 something given in addition to what is ordinarily expected or owed — see BONUS

gray *also* **grey** *adj* **1** of the color gray ⟨The *gray* sky portended snow.⟩

syn grayish, leaden, silver, silvery, slate, slaty (*also* slatey), steely

rel achromatic, colorless, neutral; dirty, dull, faded, sad, washed-out; ashen, ashy, chalky, livid, mousy (*or* mousey), pale, palish, white, whitish; chocolate, dun, sandy, sepia; grizzled, hoar, hoary

near ant ablaze, bright, deep, rich; colorful, motley, multicolored, polychromatic, polychrome, varicolored, variegated

2 causing or marked by an atmosphere lacking in cheer — see GLOOMY 1

grayish *adj* of the color gray — see GRAY 1

gray matter *n* the ability to learn and understand or to deal with problems — see INTELLIGENCE 1

¹**graze** *vb* to feed on grass or herbs ⟨cows *grazing* in the meadow⟩

syn browse, forage, pasture, rustle

rel eat, feed, nibble; range, stock; overgraze

²**graze** *vb* **1** to damage by rubbing against a sharp or rough surface — see SCRAPE 1

2 to pass lightly across or touch gently especially in passing — see ²BRUSH

graze *n* an area of skin roughened or worn away by harsh rubbing against another surface — see ABRASION

grease *vb* **1** to coat (something) with a slippery substance in order to reduce friction — see LUBRICATE

2 to free from obstruction or difficulty — see EASE 1

greased *adj* having or being a surface so smooth as to greatly reduce traction — see SLICK 1

greasy *adj* having or being a surface so smooth as to greatly reduce traction — see SLICK 1

great *adj* **1** having or showing exceptional knowledge, experience, or skill in a field of endeavor — see PROFICIENT

2 having, characterized by, or arising from a dignified and generous nature — see NOBLE 2

3 lasting for a considerable time — see LONG 2

4 of a size greater than average of its kind — see LARGE

5 of the very best kind — see EXCELLENT

6 showing urgent desire or interest — see EAGER

7 coming before all others in importance — see FOREMOST 1

8 of high birth, rank, or station — see NOBLE 1

great *adv* in a pleasing way — see WELL 5

greatcoat *n* a warm outdoor coat — see OVERCOAT

greatest *adj* **1** coming before all others in importance — see FOREMOST 1

2 of the highest degree — see FULL 2

greathearted *adj* **1** feeling or displaying no fear by temperament — see BRAVE 1

2 having, characterized by, or arising from a dignified and generous nature — see NOBLE 2

greatheartedness *n* strength of mind to carry on in spite of danger — see COURAGE

greatly *adv* **1** in a manner befitting a person of the highest character and ideals ⟨As commander of the Union army's first Black regiment, Robert Gould Shaw died as *greatly* as he had lived.⟩

syn gallantly, grandly, heroically, high-mindedly, honorably, magnanimously, nobly

rel loftily, venerably; magnificently, majestically; chivalrously; bravely

near ant abominably, contemptibly, despicably, detestably, hatefully, nastily, pitiably, sorrily, wretchedly; degenerately

ant basely, dishonorably, ignobly

2 to a large extent or degree ⟨Authorities have *greatly* increased the scope of their investigation into the matter.⟩

syn astronomically, broadly, colossally, considerably, enormously, extensively, highly, hugely, largely, massively, monstrously, much, sizably, staggeringly, stupendously, tremendously, utterly, vastly

rel appreciably, noticeably, significantly; abundantly, amply, copiously, healthily, plentifully

phrases a lot, by half, no end

near ant modestly; fractionally; imperceptibly, infinitesimally, insignificantly, invisibly, microscopically, minutely; barely, hardly, just, minimally, scarcely

ant little, negligibly, nominally, slightly

3 to a great degree — see VERY 1

greatness *n* **1** exceptionally high quality — see EXCELLENCE 1

2 the quality or state of being large in size — see LARGENESS

greed *n* an intense selfish desire for wealth or possessions ⟨Don't let *greed* for riches control you.⟩

syn acquisitiveness, avarice, avariciousness, avidity, covetousness, cupidity, graspingness, greediness, rapaciousness, rapacity

rel commercialism, materialism, possessiveness; piggishness; appetite, craving, desire, drive, hankering, hunger, itch, longing, lust, passion, pining, ravenousness, thirst, voracity, yearning, yen; egoism, egotism, self-centeredness, self-interest, selfishness, self-regard

near ant contentment, fulfillment (*or* fulfilment), gratification, satisfaction; bounteousness, bountifulness, bounty, charity, generosity, largesse (*also* largess), liberality, magnanimity, openhandedness, openheartedness, unselfishness; altruism, selflessness

greediness *n* an intense selfish desire for wealth or possessions — see GREED

greedy *adj* **1** having or marked by an eager and often selfish desire especially for material possessions ⟨a young rocker who was *greedy* for fame and riches⟩ ⟨the *greedy* exploitation of the land by developers⟩

syn acquisitive, avaricious, avid, coveting, covetous, grasping, mercenary, rapacious

rel commercialistic, materialistic, philistine; desirous, eager; hoggish, piggish, piggy, swinish; devouring, gluttonous, gobbling, ravenous, voracious; egocentric, egoistic (*also* egoistical), egotistic (*or* egotistical), self-centered, self-seeking; discontent, discontented, malcontent, unsatisfied; begrudging, grudging, resentful

near ant nonmaterialistic; altruistic, bounteous, bountiful, charitable, freehanded, generous, greathearted, handsome, liberal, magnanimous, munificent, openhanded, openhearted, selfless, unselfish, unsparing; controlled, moderate, restrained, temperate; content, sated, satisfied

2 having a huge appetite — see VORACIOUS 1

3 showing urgent desire or interest — see EAGER

green *adj* **1** covered with a thick, healthy natural growth — see LUSH 1

2 lacking in adult experience or maturity — see CALLOW

3 lacking in worldly wisdom or informed judgment — see NAIVE 1

green *n* **1** green leaves or plants — see GREENERY

2 something (as pieces of stamped metal or printed paper) customarily and legally used as a medium of exchange, a measure of value, or a means of payment — see MONEY

greenback *n* a piece of printed paper used as money in the United States — see ¹BILL 2

greenery *n* green leaves or plants ⟨Scottish highlands covered with lush greenery.⟩

syn flora, foliage, green, herbage, leafage, vegetation, verdure

rel grassland, prairie; underbrush, undergrowth

greenhorn *n* a person who is just starting out in a field of activity — see BEGINNER

greenhouse *n* a glass-enclosed building for growing plants — see CONSERVATORY

greeting *n* **1** an expression of goodwill upon meeting — see HELLO

2 greetings *pl* best wishes — see COMPLIMENT 2

---

gregarious *adj* likely to seek or enjoy the company of others — see CONVIVIAL

gregariousness *n* the quality or state of being social — see SOCIABILITY

gremlin *n* an imaginary being usually having a small human form and magical powers — see FAIRY

griddle cake *n* a flat cake made from thin batter and cooked on both sides (as on a griddle) — see PANCAKE

grief *n* **1** deep sadness especially for the loss of someone or something loved — see SORROW

2 the feeling of impatience or anger caused by another's repeated disagreeable acts — see ANNOYANCE 2

grievance *n* **1** a lingering ill will towards a person for a real or imagined wrong — see GRUDGE 1

2 an expression of dissatisfaction, pain, or resentment — see COMPLAINT 1

grieve *vb* to feel deep sadness or mental pain ⟨We all *grieved* over the lost cat.⟩

syn agonize, anguish, bleed, hurt, mourn, sorrow, suffer

rel ache, long (for), pine (away), sigh, smart; rack, torment, torture; bemoan, bewail, deplore, lament, rue; bawl, blubber, cry, groan, howl, keen, moan, sob, take on, wail, weep, yammer, yowl; languish; regret

phrases eat one's heart out, tear one's hair

near ant beam, cheer, crow, delight, exult, glory, joy, laugh, ravish, rejoice, triumph; assure, cheer, comfort, commiserate, console, reassure, solace, soothe, sympathize

grieve (for) *vb* to feel or express sorrow for — see LAMENT 1

grieving *adj* expressing or suggesting mourning — see MOURNFUL 1

grievous *adj* **1** difficult to endure — see HARSH 1

2 hard to accept or bear especially emotionally — see BITTER 2

3 involving potential loss or injury — see DANGEROUS 1

4 of a kind to cause great distress — see REGRETTABLE

grievously *adv* with feelings of bitterness or grief — see HARD 2

grill *n* a public establishment where meals are served to paying customers for consumption on the premises — see RESTAURANT

grill *vb* **1** to put a series of questions to — see EXAMINE 1

2 to put a question or questions to — see ASK 1

grim *adj* **1** harsh and threatening in manner or appearance ⟨a *grim* and desolate landscape⟩ ⟨a *grim* and short-tempered shopkeeper who didn't exactly invite friendly conversation⟩

syn austere, dour, fierce, flinty, forbidding, gruff, intimidating, lowering (*also* louring), rough, rugged, severe, stark, steely, stern, ungentle

rel bleak, cold, hostile, inhospitable, inimical, unfriendly, unsympathetic; adamant, bound, determined, firm, intent, purposeful, resolute, resolved, steadfast, unflinching; fixed, hard, hardened, hard-

headed, immovable, implacable, inflexible, ironhanded, mulish, obdurate, obstinate, rigid, self-willed, set, stiff, stubborn, unbending, uncompromising, unrelenting, unyielding, willful (*or* wilful); immutable, unchangeable; black, cheerless, dark, gloomy, glum, joyless, moody, morose, sulky, sullen, surly; brooding, grave, humorless, melancholy, serious, sober, sobersided, solemn, somber (*or* sombre), staid, unsmiling

near ant bland, meek, mellow, soft, soothing; easy, quiet, tranquil; agreeable, bright, cheerful, inviting, pleasant, pleasing, sweet; glad, happy, lighthearted, merry, mirthful, sunny; featherbrained, flighty, frivolous, giddy, goofy, harebrained, light-headed, playful, scatterbrained, silly

ant benign, benignant, gentle, mild, tender

2 difficult to endure — see HARSH 1

3 showing no signs of slackening or yielding in one's purpose — see UNYIELDING 1

4 violently unfriendly or aggressive in disposition — see FIERCE 1

grimace *vb* to distort one's face — see MUG 1

grimace *n* a twisting of the facial features in disgust or disapproval ⟨He made a *grimace* when he tasted the medicine.⟩

syn face, frown, lower (*also* lour), mouth, mug, pout, scowl

rel flinch, squinch, wince; growl, snarl; rictus, simper, smirk; scoff, sneer; glare, glower, look, stare

near ant grin, laugh, smile

grime *n* foul matter that mars the purity or cleanliness of something — see FILTH 1

grime *vb* to make dirty — see DIRTY

griminess *n* the state or quality of being dirty — see DIRTINESS

grimy *adj* not clean — see DIRTY 1

grin *vb* to express an emotion (as amusement) by curving the lips upward — see SMILE 1

grind *n* **1** a harsh grating sound — see RASP

2 a person devoted to intellectual or academic pursuits — see NERD 1

3 very hard or unpleasant work — see TOIL

4 an established and often automatic or monotonous series of actions followed when engaging in some activity — see ROUTINE 1

grind *vb* **1** to make smooth by friction ⟨After they are *ground* and polished, these stones can be used for jewelry.⟩

syn buff, file, hone, rasp, rub, sand

rel plane, scrape; sandblast, scour; burnish, dress, gloss, polish, shine, smooth; edge, hone, sharpen, strop, whet; regrind

near ant coarsen, rough (up), roughen, scuff

2 to press or strike against or together so as to make a scraping sound ⟨Everyone in the car winced when the driver *ground* the gears trying to switch into second.⟩

syn crunch, gnash, grate, grit, scrape, scrunch

rel creak, groan, moan, rasp, scratch, whine; clash, collide, jar

3 to make sharp or sharper — see SHARPEN

4 to make smooth or glossy usually by repeatedly applying surface pressure — see POLISH 1

5 to pass roughly and noisily over or against a surface — see SCRAPE 1

6 to reduce to fine particles — see POWDER

grinder *n* a large sandwich on a long split roll — see SUBMARINE

grip *n* **1** a bag designed to hold a traveler's clothing and personal articles — see TRAVELING BAG

2 the act or manner of holding — see HOLD 1

3 the knowledge gained from the process of coming to know or understand something — see COMPREHENSION

4 the right or means to command or control others — see POWER 1

5 a part by which an implement is held — see HANDLE 1

grip *vb* **1** to have or keep in one's hands — see HOLD 1

2 to hold the attention of as if by a spell — see ENTHRALL 1

3 to hold the attention of — see ENGAGE 1

4 to reach for and take hold of by embracing with the fingers or arms — see TAKE 1

gripe *n* an expression of dissatisfaction, pain, or resentment — see COMPLAINT 1

gripe *vb* **1** to disturb the peace of mind of (someone) especially by repeated disagreeable acts — see IRRITATE 1

2 to express dissatisfaction, pain, or resentment usually tiresomely — see COMPLAIN

griper *n* **1** a person who makes frequent complaints usually about little things — see CRYBABY

2 an irritable and complaining person — see GROUCH 1

gripping *adj* holding the attention or provoking interest — see INTERESTING

grisliness *n* the quality of inspiring intense dread or dismay — see HORROR 1

grisly *adj* extremely disturbing or repellent — see HORRIBLE 1

grit *n* the strength of mind that enables a person to endure pain or hardship — see FORTITUDE

grit *vb* to press or strike against or together so as to make a scraping sound — see GRIND 2

groan *n* **1** a crying out in grief — see LAMENT 1

2 a long low sound indicating pain or grief — see MOAN 1

groan *vb* to utter a moan — see MOAN 1

groomed *adj* being clean and in good order — see NEAT 1

groove *n* **1** an established and often automatic or monotonous series of actions followed when engaging in some activity — see ROUTINE 1

2 a situation or activity for which a person or thing is best suited — see NICHE 1

groove *vb* **1** to mark with or as if with a line or groove — see SCORE 1

2 to form a pleasing relationship — see HARMONIZE 1

groove (on) *vb* to take pleasure in — see ENJOY 1

groovy *adj* of the very best kind — see EXCELLENT

grope *vb* to search for something blindly or uncertainly ⟨She nervously *groped* for her car keys.⟩ ⟨*groping* for the right answer⟩
syn feel, fish, fumble, scrabble
rel grabble; cast about, hunt, look, reach, seek (out); capture, clutch, corral, get, grab, nab, nail, seize, snatch; comb, dig (through), dredge, rake, ransack, rifle, rummage, scour

gross *adj* **1** depicting or referring to sexual matters in a way that is unacceptable in polite society — see OBSCENE 1

2 lacking in refinement or good taste — see COARSE 2

3 very noticeable especially for being incorrect or bad — see EGREGIOUS

4 causing intense displeasure, disgust, or resentment — see OFFENSIVE 1

grossness *n* **1** the condition of having an excess of body fat — see CORPULENCE

2 the quality or state of being obscene — see OBSCENITY

3 the quality or state of lacking refinement or good taste — see VULGARITY 1

grot *n* a naturally formed underground chamber with an opening to the surface — see CAVE

grotesque *adj* **1** disagreeable to one's aesthetic or artistic sense — see HARSH 2

2 unpleasant to look at — see UGLY 1

grotesque *n* a strange or horrible and often frightening creature — see MONSTER 1

grotto *n* a naturally formed underground chamber with an opening to the surface — see CAVE

grouch *n* **1** an irritable and complaining person ⟨an uncle who is a real *grouch* when he's sick⟩
syn bear, bellyacher, complainer, crab, crank, curmudgeon, fusser, griper, grouser, growler, grumbler, grump, murmurer, mutterer, whiner
rel malcontent, sorehead; grinch, killjoy, party pooper, spoilsport; defeatist, pessimist; faultfinder, kicker, nagger, nitpicker, objector, quibbler, repiner; hypochondriac
near ant optimist, Pollyanna; happy camper

2 a state of resentful silence or irritability — see SULK

3 an expression of dissatisfaction, pain, or resentment — see COMPLAINT 1

grouch *vb* to express dissatisfaction, pain, or resentment usually tiresomely — see COMPLAIN

grouchiness *n* readiness to show annoyance or impatience — see PETULANCE

grouchy *adj* **1** easily irritated or annoyed — see IRRITABLE

2 given to complaining a lot — see FUSSY 1

ground *adj* having an edge thin enough to cut or pierce something — see SHARP 1

ground *n* **1** **grounds** *pl* the area around and belonging to a building ⟨an escorted tour of the White House and its surrounding *grounds*⟩
syn demesne, park, premises (*also* premisses), yard

---

rel acres, estate, land, lot, parcel, plot, property, real estate, realty; campus; churchyard, dooryard; close, enclosure (*also* inclosure), garden, plaza

2 grounds *pl* matter that settles to the bottom of a body of liquid — see DEPOSIT 1

3 grounds *pl* something (as a belief) that serves as the basis for another thing — see REASON 2

4 a small area of usually open land — see FIELD 1

5 an immaterial thing upon which something else rests — see BASE 1

6 the loose surface material in which plants naturally grow — see DIRT 1

7 the physical conditions or features that form the setting against which something is viewed — see BACKGROUND 1

8 the solid part of our planet's surface as distinguished from the sea and air — see EARTH 2

ground *vb* to find a basis — see BASE

grounded *adj* resting on the shore or bottom of a body of water — see AGROUND

groundless *adj* having no basis in reason or fact ⟨Please stop making *groundless* accusations against people you happen to dislike.⟩ ⟨Fears of a strike proved *groundless*.⟩

syn invalid, nonvalid, unfounded, unreasonable, unsubstantiated, unsupported, unwarranted

rel illogical, irrational, nonlogical, unconscionable; fallacious, false, misled, wrong; gratuitous, uncalled-for, unnecessary; flimsy, implausible, misleading, specious, unconvincing, untenable, weak; ill-advised, unreasoned; inconsistent; absurd, asinine, brainless, fatuous, foolish, half-witted, harebrained, meaningless, nonsensical, preposterous, senseless, silly, simpleminded, stupid, unwise; wacky (*also* whacky)

near ant validated, verified; confirmed, corroborated; informed, logical, rational; commonsense, sane, sensible, sober, wise; actual, genuine, real, true; certain, sure; clear, cogent, compelling, convincing, credible, persuasive, plausible, satisfying, solid, sound

ant good, hard, just, justified, reasonable, reasoned, substantiated, valid, well-founded

ground plan *n* a method worked out in advance for achieving some objective — see PLAN 1

ground rule *n* a statement spelling out the proper procedure or conduct for an activity — see RULE 1

groundwork *n* an immaterial thing upon which something else rests — see BASE 1

ground zero *n* a thing or place that is of greatest importance to an activity or interest — see CENTER 1

group *vb* **1** to arrange or assign according to type — see CLASSIFY 1

2 to bring together in one body or place — see GATHER 1

group *n* **1** a number of things considered as a unit ⟨Car buffs stood around admiring a *group* of classic cars in the parking lot.⟩

syn array, assemblage, band, bank, batch, battery, block, bunch, clot, clump, cluster, clutch, collection, grouping, huddle, knot, lot, muster, package, parcel, passel, set, suite

rel accumulation, aggregate, aggregation, conglomeration; agglomeration; assortment, hodgepodge, jumble, miscellany, mixture, odds and ends, sundries, variety; cycle, run, series, suit

phrases the whole kit and caboodle

near ant entity, item, single, unit

2 a usually small number of persons considered as a unit ⟨The next tour *group* was being seated for dinner.⟩

syn array, band, batch, battery, body, bunch, cluster, clutch, consort, crop, grouping, huddle, knot, lot, parcel, party, passel

rel assembly, collective, congregation, gathering, muster, organization; circle, clan, clique, coterie, fellowship, gang, ring, round, set; faction, guild (*also* gild), order, school, sect; crew, outfit, phalanx, task force, team; alliance, bloc, coalition, confederacy, confederation, federation, league, union; battalion, squadron; bevy, brood, covey

phrases the whole kit and caboodle

near ant individual, single

3 one of the units into which a whole is divided on the basis of a common characteristic — see CLASS 2

grouping *n* **1** a number of things considered as a unit — see GROUP 1

2 a usually small number of persons considered as a unit — see GROUP 2

grouse *vb* to express dissatisfaction, pain, or resentment usually tiresomely — see COMPLAIN

grouse *n* an expression of dissatisfaction, pain, or resentment — see COMPLAINT 1

grouser *n* an irritable and complaining person — see GROUCH 1

grovel *vb* **1** to draw back or crouch down in fearful submission — see COWER

2 to move slowly with the body close to the ground — see CRAWL 1

grow *vb* **1** to look after or assist the growth of by labor and care ⟨a dedicated home gardener who *grows* tomatoes in her small garden every summer⟩

syn crop, cultivate, culture, dress, promote, raise, rear, tend

rel breed, produce, propagate; plant, sow; gather, glean, harvest, reap; germinate, quicken, ripen, root

near ant kill; dig, extirpate, pick, pluck, pull (up), uproot; cut, hay, mow

2 to become mature — see MATURE

3 to eventually have as a state or quality — see BECOME

grow (in) *vb* to gradually increase in — see GAIN 1

grower *n* a person who cultivates the land and grows crops on it — see FARMER

growl *vb* **1** to express dissatisfaction, pain, or resentment usually tiresomely — see COMPLAIN

2 to make a long loud deep noise or cry — see ROAR 1

3 to make a low heavy rolling sound — see RUMBLE

growler *n* an irritable and complaining person — see GROUCH 1

grown-up *adj* relating to or typical of adults; displaying proper maturity — see ADULT 1

grown-up *n* a fully grown person — see ADULT

growth *n* 1 an abnormal mass of tissue ⟨The vet found a *growth* on the dog's neck under her collar.⟩
syn excrescence, lump, neoplasm, tumor
rel outgrowth; cancer, carcinoma, lymphoma, malignancy, melanoma, polyp; cyst, tubercle, wart
2 the act or process of going from the simple or basic to the complex or advanced — see DEVELOPMENT 1
3 the process of becoming mature — see MATURATION

grow up *vb* to become mature — see MATURE

grub *n* 1 substances intended to be eaten — see FOOD
2 a person who does very hard or dull work — see DRUDGE

grub *vb* to devote serious and sustained effort — see LABOR

grubber *n* a person who does very hard or dull work — see DRUDGE

grubbiness *n* the state or quality of being dirty — see DIRTINESS

grubby *adj* 1 not clean — see DIRTY 1
2 arousing or deserving of one's loathing and disgust — see CONTEMPTIBLE 1

grudge *n* 1 a lingering ill will towards a person for a real or imagined wrong ⟨He's had a *grudge* against her ever since she told on him.⟩
syn grievance, resentment, score
rel condemnation; offense (*or* offence), umbrage; complaint; dudgeon, huff, peeve, pique; despite, hatefulness, malevolence, malice, maliciousness, meanness, nastiness, spite, spitefulness, spleen, venom, viciousness; animosity, antagonism, antipathy, bitterness, enmity, hostility, rancor
2 a deep-seated ill will — see ENMITY

grueling *or* **gruelling** *adj* 1 requiring considerable physical or mental effort — see HARD 2
2 requiring much time, effort, or careful attention — see DEMANDING 1

gruesome *also* **grewsome** *n* extremely disturbing or repellent — see HORRIBLE 1

gruesomeness *n* the quality of inspiring intense dread or dismay — see HORROR 1

gruff *adj* 1 harsh and dry in sound — see HOARSE
2 harsh and threatening in manner or appearance — see GRIM 1

grumble *n* an expression of dissatisfaction, pain, or resentment — see COMPLAINT 1

grumble *vb* 1 to express dissatisfaction, pain, or resentment usually tiresomely — see COMPLAIN
2 to make a low heavy rolling sound — see RUMBLE

grumbler *n* 1 an irritable and complaining person — see GROUCH 1
2 a person who makes frequent complaints usually about little things — see CRYBABY

grump *n* an irritable and complaining person — see GROUCH 1

grump *vb* 1 to express dissatisfaction, pain, or resentment usually tiresomely — see COMPLAIN
2 to silently go about in a bad mood — see SULK

grumpiness *n* readiness to show annoyance or impatience — see PETULANCE

grumpy *adj* 1 easily irritated or annoyed — see IRRITABLE
2 given to complaining a lot — see FUSSY 1

grungy *adj* 1 not clean — see DIRTY 1
2 showing signs of advanced wear and tear and neglect — see SHABBY 1

grunt *n* 1 speech that is not clear enough to be understood — see MUMBLE
2 a person who does very hard or dull work — see DRUDGE

grunt *vb* to speak softly and unclearly — see MUMBLE

grunting *n* speech that is not clear enough to be understood — see MUMBLE

guarantee *vb* 1 to assume responsibility for the satisfactory quality or performance of — see WARRANT 1
2 to make sure, certain, or safe — see ENSURE
3 to state clearly and strongly — see ASSERT 1

guarantee *n* 1 a formal agreement to fulfill an obligation ⟨The contractors gave us a written *guarantee* that the work on the house would be done on time.⟩
syn bond, contract, covenant, deal, guaranty, surety, warranty
rel oath, pledge, troth, vow, word; accord, bargain, compact, concordat, convention, pact, treaty; assurance, insurance, seal; deposit, pawn, security
2 something given or held to assure that the giver will keep a promise — see PLEDGE 1

guarantor *n* a person who takes the responsibility for some other person or thing — see SPONSOR

guaranty *n* 1 a formal agreement to fulfill an obligation — see GUARANTEE 1
2 something given or held to assure that the giver will keep a promise — see PLEDGE 1

guaranty *vb* 1 to make sure, certain, or safe — see ENSURE
2 to assume responsibility for the satisfactory quality or performance of — see WARRANT 1

guard *n* 1 a person or group that watches over someone or something ⟨I checked in with the security *guard* at the gate.⟩
syn custodian, guardian, keeper, lookout, picket, sentinel, sentry, warden, warder, watch, watcher, watchman
rel patrol, spotter, surveillant, watchdog; bodyguard, convoy, defender, escort, honor guard; gatekeeper
2 a position of readiness to oppose actual or expected attack — see DEFENSIVE
3 a protective device (as on a weapon) to prevent accidental operation — see SAFETY 2
4 means or method of defending — see DEFENSE 1

---

syn synonym(s)   *rel* related words
ant antonym(s)   *near ant* near antonym(s)

5 one that accompanies another for protection, guidance, or as a courtesy — see ESCORT

6 someone that protects — see PROTECTOR

guard *vb* **1** to drive danger or attack away from — see DEFEND 1

2 to disallow entry into (a place) by means of a physical barrier at the entry point — see CLOSE (OFF)

guard (against) *vb* to be cautious of or on guard against — see BEWARE (OF)

guarded *adj* having or showing a close attentiveness to avoiding danger or trouble — see CAREFUL 1

guardian *n* **1** a person or group that watches over someone or something — see GUARD 1

2 a person who takes care of a property sometimes for an absent owner — see CUSTODIAN 1

3 someone that protects — see PROTECTOR

guardianship *n* responsibility for the safety and well-being of someone or something — see CUSTODY

guardrail *n* a protective barrier consisting of a horizontal bar and its supports — see RAILING

guardroom *n* a place of confinement for persons held in lawful custody — see JAIL

guess *n* an opinion or judgment based on little or no evidence — see CONJECTURE

guess *vb* **1** to form an opinion from little or no evidence ⟨Can you *guess* how many people were there?⟩

syn assume, conjecture, imagine, presume, speculate, suppose, surmise, suspect

rel conclude, deduce, gather, infer; hypothecate, theorize; believe, conceive, expect, judge, reckon [*chiefly dialect*]; take, think

near ant demonstrate, document, establish, prove, substantiate, validate; ascertain, determine, find out, learn

2 to decide the size, amount, number, or distance of (something) without actual measurement — see ESTIMATE 2

3 to have as an opinion — see BELIEVE 2

guest *n* **1** a person who visits another ⟨We invited the afternoon *guests* to stay for dinner.⟩

syn caller, frequenter, visitant, visitor

rel houseguest; company; invitee; crasher, hanger-on

near ant denizen, dweller, habitant, inhabitant, occupant, resident, resider; cohost, cohostess, host, hostess

2 a person who buys a product or uses a service from a business — see CUSTOMER 1

guffaw *n* an explosive sound that is a sign of amusement — see LAUGH 1

guidance *n* **1** an opinion suggesting a wise or proper course of action — see ADVICE

2 the act or activity of looking after and making decisions about something — see CONDUCT 1

3 the duty or function of watching or guarding for the sake of proper direction or control — see SUPERVISION 1

guide *n* one that accompanies another for protection, guidance, or as a courtesy — see ESCORT

guide *vb* **1** to give advice and instruction to (someone) regarding the course or process to be followed ⟨The pastry chef *guided* her through the creation of the wedding cake, showing her how to ice the layers, fashion the elaborate decorations, and assemble the whole shebang.⟩

syn coach, counsel, lead, mentor, pilot, shepherd, show, tutor

rel godfather; direct, engineer, steer, sway; accompany, attend, chaperone (*or* chaperon), convoy, escort, see, squire; oversee, superintend, supervise; drill, train; brief, enlighten, inform; instruct, school, teach, tutor; inculcate, indoctrinate; cultivate, foster, nurture

phrases walk through

2 to look after and make decisions about — see CONDUCT 1

3 to point out the way for (someone) especially from a position in front — see LEAD 1

guidon *n* a piece of cloth with a special design that is used as an emblem or for signaling — see FLAG 1

guild *also* **gild** *n* a group of persons formally joined together for some common interest — see ASSOCIATION 2

guile *n* **1** skill in achieving one's ends through indirect, subtle, or underhanded means — see CUNNING 1

2 the inclination or practice of misleading others through lies or trickery — see DECEIT 1

guileful *adj* **1** clever at attaining one's ends by indirect and often deceptive means — see ARTFUL 1

2 given to or marked by cheating and deception — see DISHONEST 2

guileless *adj* free from any intent to deceive or impress others ⟨She was an easygoing, *guileless* young woman who was comfortable just being herself.⟩

syn artless, genuine, honest, ingenuous, innocent, naive (*or* naïve), natural, real, simple, sincere, true, unaffected, unpretending, unpretentious

rel childlike, dewy-eyed, gee-whiz, impressionable, inexperienced, malleable, persuadable, persuasible, simpleminded, unsophisticated, unworldly, wide-eyed; spontaneous, unforced, unstudied; candid, direct, frank, free, free-spoken, open, openhearted, plain, plainspoken, single-minded, straight, straightforward, unguarded; trustful, trusting; exploitable, gullible (*also* gullable), susceptible, unwary

phrases on the level

near ant critical, cynical, mistrustful, skeptical, suspicious, wary; cosmopolitan, sophisticated, worldly, worldly-wise; civilized, cultivated, cultured, polished, refined; crooked, deceitful, deceptive, devious, double-dealing, hypocritical, manipulative, two-faced; arch, calculating, canny, crafty, cunning, designing, foxy, knavish, sharp, shifty, shrewd, slick, slippery, sly, subtle, tricky, underhanded, wily; flattering, mealymouthed, smooth, sycophantic, unctuous

ant affected, artful, artificial, assuming, dishonest, dissembling, dissimulating, fake, false, guileful, insincere, phony (*also* phoney), pretentious

guilelessly *adv* without any attempt to impress by deception or exaggeration — see NATURALLY 3

guilelessness *n* the quality or state of being simple and sincere — see NAÏVETÉ 1

guillotine *vb* to cut off the head of — see DECAPITATE

guilt *n* 1 a feeling of responsibility for wrongdoing ⟨He was wracked with *guilt* after he accidentally broke his sister's antique grandfather clock.⟩

syn contriteness, contrition, penitence, regret, remorse, remorsefulness, repentance, rue, self-reproach, shame

rel compunction, misgiving, prick, qualm, scruple; blame, culpability, fault; liability, rap, responsibility; chagrin, embarrassment; anguish, distress, grief, sadness, sorrow; bloodguilt, bloodguiltiness; excuses, hand-wringing, mea culpa

ant impenitence, remorselessness

2 responsibility for wrongdoing or failure — see BLAME 1

guiltless *adj* free from guilt or blame — see INNOCENT 2

guiltlessness *n* the quality or state of being free from guilt or blame — see INNOCENCE 1

guilty *adj* suffering from or expressive of a feeling of responsibility for wrongdoing ⟨She was burdened with a *guilty* conscience after stealing the newspaper from the newsstand.⟩

syn ashamed, shamed, shamefaced

rel apologetic, contrite, penitent, remorseful, repentant, sorry; regretful, rueful; penitential; blushing, chagrined, embarrassed, hangdog, sheepish; blamable, blameworthy, culpable

near ant impenitent, remorseless, unapologetic, unrepentant; brazen, cheeky, impudent; blameless, guiltless, innocent

ant shameless, unashamed

guise *n* 1 a display of emotion or behavior that is insincere or intended to deceive — see MASQUERADE

2 clothing chosen as appropriate for a specific situation — see OUTFIT 1

3 clothing put on to hide one's true identity or imitate someone or something else — see DISGUISE 1

4 outward and often deceptive indication — see APPEARANCE 2

gulch *n* a narrow opening between hillsides or mountains that can be used for passage — see CANYON

gulf *n* 1 a part of a body of water that extends beyond the general shoreline ⟨We dipped our feet in the warm waters of the *gulf*.⟩

syn arm, bay, bight, cove, creek [*chiefly British*], estuary, firth, fjord (*also* fiord), inlet, loch [*Scottish*]

rel harbor, port, road(s), roadstead; narrow, sound, strait; backwater, slough (*also* slew *or* slue)

2 an immeasurable depth or space — see ABYSS

3 a narrow opening between hillsides or mountains that can be used for passage — see CANYON

4 an open space in a barrier (as a wall or hedge) — see GAP 1

5 water moving rapidly in a circle with a hollow in the center — see WHIRLPOOL

gulf *vb* to cover with a flood — see FLOOD

gull *n* one who is easily deceived or cheated — see ¹DUPE

gull *vb* to cause to believe what is untrue — see DECEIVE

gullibility *n* readiness to believe the claims of others without sufficient evidence — see CREDULITY

gullible *also* **gullable** *adj* readily taken advantage of — see EASY 2

gulp *n* the portion of a serving of a beverage that is swallowed at one time — see DRINK 2

gulp *vb* 1 to swallow in liquid form — see DRINK 1

2 to swallow or eat greedily — see GOBBLE

gummy *adj* tending to adhere to objects upon contact — see STICKY 1

gun *vb* to strike with a missile from a gun — see SHOOT 3

gun *n* 1 a portable weapon from which a shot is discharged by gunpowder ⟨While her father preferred hunting with a crossbow, she preferred a *gun*.⟩

syn arm, firearm, piece, small arm

rel derringer, forty-five (*or* .45), gat [*slang*], handgun, revolver, rod [*slang*], sidearm, six-gun, six-shooter, zip gun; self-loader, semiautomatic; breechloader, culverin, fieldpiece, firelock, flintlock, harquebus (*or* arquebus), matchlock, musket, rifle, shotgun, smoothbore, twenty-two (*or* .22); AK-47, assault rifle, assault weapon, automatic, carbine, machine gun, machine pistol, repeater, submachine gun, tommy gun; speargun

2 **guns** *pl* large firearms (as cannon or rockets) — see ARTILLERY

gung ho *adj* showing urgent desire or interest — see EAGER

gurgle *vb* to flow in a broken irregular stream ⟨The tiny stream *gurgled* down the rocky slope and joined the larger river at the bottom of the hill.⟩

syn bubble, dribble, lap, plash, ripple, splash, trickle, wash

rel eddy, purl, swirl; swash, swish, whish; drip, drop; gush, jet, rush, spew, spout, spurt, squirt

near ant run

ant pour, roll, stream

guru *n* 1 a person with a high level of knowledge or skill in a field — see EXPERT

2 one who brings an art or science to full realization — see EXPONENT 2

gush *n* 1 a flowing or going out — see OUTFLOW

2 a sudden intense expression of strong feeling — see OUTBURST 1

gush *vb* 1 to flow out in great quantities or with force ⟨The dam cracked and water *gushed* from the break.⟩

syn jet, pour, rush, spew, spout, spurt, squirt

rel cascade, issue, roll, run, stream; plash, slosh, splash, wash; surge, swell; flush, sluice; deluge, drown, engulf, flood, inundate, overflow, overwhelm, submerge, submerse, swamp

near ant spatter, sprinkle; bleed, exude, leak, ooze, percolate, seep, strain, weep

ant dribble, drip, drop, trickle

2 to make an exaggerated display of affection or enthusiasm ⟨He *gushed* about his favorite basketball player, calling him "the best there ever was."⟩

syn drool, enthuse, fuss, rave, rhapsodize, slobber

rel dote (on), fawn; emote

gushing *adj* **1** overly or insincerely flattering — see FULSOME 1

2 pouring forth in great amounts — see PROFUSE

gust *n* **1** a sudden brief rush of wind ⟨A *gust* tore her umbrella from her grip and blew it down the street.⟩

syn blast, blow, flurry, williwaw

rel breeze, zephyr; current, draft; air, breath, waft; puff, whiff; bluster, gale, hurricane, squall, tempest, tornado, windstorm; northeaster, norther, northerly, northwester, southeaster, southwester, westerly

2 a sudden intense expression of strong feeling — see OUTBURST 1

gusty *adj* marked by strong wind or more wind than usual — see ¹WINDY 1

gut *n* **1** **guts** *pl* the internal organs of the body ⟨The student dissected the frog and looked at its *guts* with a mixture of fascination and disgust.⟩

syn entrails, innards, inside(s), viscera, vitals

rel bowel(s), intestine(s); chitterlings (*or* chitlins), giblet(s), variety meat

2 guts *pl* strength of mind to carry on in spite of danger — see COURAGE

3 guts *pl* the strength of mind that enables a person to endure pain or hardship — see FORTITUDE

4 the part of the body between the chest and the pelvis — see STOMACH 1

5 an enlarged or bulging abdomen — see POTBELLY

6 the seat of one's deepest thoughts and emotions — see CORE 1

gut *vb* to take the internal organs out of ⟨You'll need to *gut* the fish and wash it out before you can cook it.⟩

syn clean, disembowel, draw, eviscerate

rel bone, dress; cut, excise, extract, remove, withdraw, yank; transplant

gutsy *adj* **1** inclined or willing to take risks — see BOLD 1

2 feeling or displaying no fear by temperament — see BRAVE 1

gutter *n* **1** a pipe or channel for carrying off water from a roof ⟨One of his chores is to clean leaves and sticks out of the *gutters* before winter sets in.⟩

syn drainpipe, eaves trough, spout, trough, waterspout

rel drain, flume, sluice; conduit, duct; aqueduct

2 a long narrow channel dug in the earth — see DITCH

guy *n* **1** a member of the human race — see HUMAN

2 an adult male human being — see MAN 1

guzzle *vb* **1** to swallow in liquid form — see DRINK 1

2 to partake excessively of alcoholic beverages — see DRINK 2

gym *n* a building or room used for sports activities and exercising ⟨He decided to get up early and go to the *gym* to lift weights.⟩

syn gymnasium, spa

rel arena, bowl, coliseum, colosseum, stadium

gymnasium *n* a building or room used for sports activities and exercising — see GYM

gymnast *n* one who performs feats of physical strength, balance, and agility on special apparatus — see ACROBAT 1

gyrate *vb* to move in circles around an axis or center — see SPIN 1

gyration *n* a rapid turning about on an axis or central point — see SPIN 1

habit *n* **1** a usual manner of behaving or doing ⟨It was his *habit* to rise early.⟩

syn custom, fashion, pattern, practice (*also* practise), ritual, trick, way, wont

rel disposition; bent, inclination, proclivity, set, tendency, tenor, turn; bag, convention, form, mode, style; usage, use; deportment, manners, mores; drill, groove, jog trot, regime (*also* régime), regimen, rote, routine, rut; affectation, airs, pose; attribute, characteristic, mark, trait

2 the type of body that a person has — see PHYSIQUE

habitable *adj* suitable for living in — see LIVABLE

habitant *n* one who lives permanently in a place — see INHABITANT

habitat *n* the place where a plant or animal is usually or naturally found — see HOME 2

habitation *n* the place where one lives — see HOME 1

habitual *adj* **1** being such by habit and not likely to change ⟨She admits she's a *habitual* procrastinator, but she still manages to meet all her deadlines.⟩

syn chronic, confirmed, inveterate

rel incorrigible, unreconstructed, unregenerate; born, natural; persistent, regular, repeat, serial, steady, unchanging, unfailing; addicted; accustomed, habituated, used, wonted; deep-rooted, deep-seated, entrenched (*also* intrenched), inbred, inherent, innate, intrinsic; apt, inclined, prone *near ant* unaccustomed, unused; intermittent, occasional

2 appearing or occurring repeatedly from time to time — see REGULAR 1

habituated *adj* being in the habit or custom — see ACCUSTOMED

hacienda *n* a large impressive residence — see MANSION

hack *adj* used or heard so often as to be dull — see STALE 1

¹**hack** *n* **1** a V-shaped cut usually on an edge or a surface — see NOTCH 1

2 a hard strike with a part of the body or an instrument — see ¹BLOW

²**hack** *n* **1** an automobile that carries passengers for a fare usually determined by the distance traveled — see TAXICAB

2 a person who lacks experience and competence in an art or science — see AMATEUR 2

hack *vb* **1** to deal with (something) usually skillfully or efficiently — see HANDLE 1

2 to put up with (something painful or difficult) — see BEAR 2

hackney *adj* used or heard so often as to be dull — see STALE 1

hackney *vb* to use so much as to make less appealing ⟨Advertisers have *hackneyed* the word "revolutionary" so much that it now just means that a product is new.⟩
syn stereotype
rel bore, exhaust, overdo; coarsen; deplete, jade, tire, wear out; popularize

hackneyed *adj* used or heard so often as to be dull — see STALE 1

hag *n* a woman believed to have evil harmful supernatural powers — see WITCH 1

haggard *adj* suffering extreme weight loss as a result of hunger or disease — see EMACIATED

haggle *vb* to talk over or dispute the terms of a purchase — see BARGAIN 1

¹**hail** *n* **1** a heavy fall of objects — see RAIN 2

2 a rapid or overwhelming outpouring of many things at once — see BARRAGE

²**hail** *n* range of hearing — see EARSHOT

hail *vb* **1** to declare enthusiastic approval of — see ACCLAIM

2 to demand or request the presence or service of — see SUMMON 1

hair *n* **1** a very small distance or degree ⟨a race that was won by a *hair*⟩
syn ace, hairbreadth (*or* hairsbreadth), hairline, inch, step, stone's throw
rel bit, crumb, dab, iota, jot, minim, mite, particle, smidgen (*also* smidgeon *or* smidgin *or* smidge), trace, trifle
near ant infinity

2 a thin, flexible structure that resembles a hair ⟨discovered *hairs* on the plant's stem⟩
syn bristle, fiber, thread
rel microfiber; cord, rope, string, wire, yarn; fuzz, lint

3 the hairy covering of a mammal especially when fine, soft, and thick — see FUR 1

hairbreadth *adj* showing little difference in the standing of the competitors — see CLOSE 3

hairbreadth *or* **hairsbreadth** *n* a very small distance or degree — see HAIR 1

hairline *adj* **1** being of less than usual width — see NARROW 1

2 made or done with extreme care and accuracy — see FINE 2

3 meeting the highest standard of accuracy — see PRECISE 1

hairline *n* a very small distance or degree — see HAIR 1

hair–raising *adj* **1** causing fear — see FEARFUL 1

2 causing great emotional or mental stimulation — see EXCITING 1

hairsplitting *adj* made or done with extreme care and accuracy — see FINE 2

hairy *adj* **1** covered with or as if with hair ⟨a *hairy* spider⟩
syn bristly, cottony, fleecy, furry, hirsute, rough, shaggy, silky, unshorn, woolly (*also* wooly)
rel bearded, bewhiskered, mustachioed (*also* moustachioed), whiskered; stubbled, stubbly; downy, fluffy, fuzzy, linty, nappy
near ant beardless, shaved, shaven
ant bald, furless, glabrous, hairless, shorn, smooth

2 made of or resembling hair ⟨I found enough *hairy* clumps around the house to make another cat!⟩ ⟨a *hairy* mass of fiberglass insulation⟩
syn furry, fuzzy, rough, shaggy, woolly (*also* wooly)
rel downy, fluffy, nappy, puffy; hairlike

3 requiring exceptional skill or caution in performance or handling — see TRICKY 1

4 marked by or causing agitation or uncomfortable feelings — see NERVOUS 2

halcyon *adj* **1** free from storms or physical disturbance — see CALM 1

2 marked by vigorous growth and well-being especially economically — see PROSPEROUS 1

hale *adj* enjoying health and vigor — see HEALTHY 1

hale *vb* to cause to follow by applying steady force on — see PULL 1

half *adj* lacking some necessary part — see INCOMPLETE

half *adv* **1** in any way or respect — see AT ALL

2 in some measure or degree — see PARTLY

half *n* either of a pair matched in one or more qualities — see MATE 1

half–baked *adj* showing or marked by a lack of good sense or judgment — see FOOLISH 1

halfhearted *adj* showing little or no interest or enthusiasm — see TEPID 1

halfway *adj* **1** lacking some necessary part — see INCOMPLETE

2 occupying a position equally distant from the ends or extremes — see MIDDLE 1

halfway *adv* in some measure or degree — see PARTLY

half–wit *n* **1** a person who lacks good sense or judgment — see FOOL 1

2 a stupid person — see IDIOT

half–witted *adj* **1** not having or showing an ability to absorb ideas readily — see STUPID 1

2 showing or marked by a lack of good sense or judgment — see FOOLISH 1

hall *n* **1** the entrance room of a building

---

syn synonym(s)   *rel* related words
ant antonym(s)   *near ant* near antonyms(s)

⟨The dinner guests hung their coats in the *hall*.⟩

syn entry, entryway, foyer, hallway, lobby, vestibule

rel antechamber, anteroom, lounge, waiting room; door, doorway, entrance, portal, threshold

2 a typically long narrow way connecting parts of a building ⟨The bedroom is at the end of the *hall*.⟩

syn concourse, corridor, gallery, hallway, passageway

rel arcade, breezeway, cloister, loggia

3 a large room or building for enclosed public gatherings ⟨The concert *hall* was full.⟩

syn arena, auditorium, garden, theater (*or* theatre)

rel arena theater, music hall, odeum, playhouse, theater-in-the-round; ballroom; lyceum; chamber, house, senate

4 a centrally located room in a building that serves as a gathering or waiting area or as a passageway into the interior — see FOYER 1

5 a large impressive residence — see MANSION

6 a large, magnificent, or massive building — see EDIFICE 1

hallmark *n* **1** a device, design, or figure used as an identifying mark — see EMBLEM

2 something that sets apart an individual from others of the same kind — see CHARACTERISTIC

hallow *vb* **1** to make holy through prayers or ritual — see BLESS 1

hallowed *adj* **1** deserving honor and respect especially by reason of age — see VENERABLE 1

2 set apart or worthy of veneration by association with God — see HOLY 2

3 not to be violated, criticized, or tampered with — see SACRED 1

hallowing *n* the act of making something holy through religious ritual — see CONSECRATION

hallucination *n* **1** a conception or image created by the imagination and having no objective reality — see FANTASY 1

2 a false idea or belief — see FALLACY 1

hallway *n* **1** a typically long narrow way connecting parts of a building — see HALL 2

2 the entrance room of a building — see HALL 1

halt *n* **1** a point in a struggle where neither side is capable of winning or willing to give in — see IMPASSE 1

2 the stopping of a process or activity — see END 1

¹halt *vb* **1** to bring (something) to a standstill ⟨Traffic was *halted* by the parade.⟩

syn arrest, bring up, catch, check, draw up, fetch up, hold up, stall, stay, still, stop

rel baffle, balk, block, blockade, bottleneck, clog, dam, detain, hinder, hold, hold back, impede, obstruct, snag, stem; conclude, cut off, end, terminate; call, discontinue, suspend; choke off, rein (in), repress, squash, squelch, stanch (*or* staunch), stunt, suppress

near ant carry on, continue, keep (on), keep up, persist, run on; advance, fare, march, move, proceed, progress, wend; actuate, budge, drive, goad, impel, propel, push, spur, stir

2 to bring (as an action or operation) to an immediate end — see STOP 1

3 to come to an end — see CEASE 1

²halt *vb* **1** to walk while favoring one leg — see LIMP 1

2 to show uncertainty about the right course of action — see HESITATE

hammer *vb* **1** to shape with a hammer ⟨Medieval artisans *hammered* brass into various bowls and trays, which they then embossed with elaborate designs.⟩

syn beat, draw, forge, pound

rel chase, planish; fashion, form, knead, model, pat, work; mint, stamp; abate, boast, carve, chisel, cut, grave, hew, knap, sculpt, sculpture

2 to deliver a blow to (someone or something) usually in a strong vigorous manner — see HIT 1

3 to strike repeatedly — see BEAT 1

4 to criticize (someone) severely or angrily especially for personal failings — see SCOLD

hamper *vb* to create difficulty for the work or activity of ⟨Fallen branches *hampered* the hikers as they made their way along the narrow path.⟩

syn clog, cramp, embarrass, encumber, fetter, handcuff, handicap, hinder, hobble, hog-tie, hold back, hold up, impede, inhibit, interfere (with), manacle, obstruct, shackle, stymie, tie up, trammel

rel balk, check, constrain, curb, rein, restrain; bind, chain, halter, leash, tether, tie; arrest, brake, delay, retain, retard; barricade, block, blockade, roadblock; bog (down), mire; choke, smother, stifle, strangle, suffocate; baffle, foil, frustrate, stump, thwart; disrupt, sabotage; muzzle, repress, suppress; confine, hedge (in)

phrases cramp one's style, give a hard time

near ant clear, make way, open, unclog, unstop; free, liberate, release, untie; loosen, smooth; encourage, further, promote

ant aid, assist, facilitate, help

hams *n pl* the part of the body upon which someone sits — see BUTTOCKS

hamstring *vb* to render powerless, ineffective, or unable to move — see PARALYZE 1

hand *n* **1** a certain way in which something appears or may be regarded — see ASPECT 1

2 a place, space, or direction away from or beyond a central point or line — see SIDE 1

3 an arrow-shaped piece on a dial or scale for registering information — see POINTER 1

4 one who works for another for wages or a salary — see EMPLOYEE

5 the form or style of a particular person's writing — see HANDWRITING 1

6 *usually* **hands** *pl* the ability to direct the course of something — see CONTROL 2

7 **hands** *pl* the fact or state of having (something) at one's disposal — see POSSESSION 1

8 an act or instance of helping — see HELP 1

9 a person with a high level of knowledge or skill in a field — see EXPERT

hand *vb* **1** to put (something) into the possession of someone for use or consumption — see FURNISH 2

2 to shift possession of (something) from one person to another — see PASS 1

3 to put (something) into the possession or safekeeping of another — see GIVE 2

handbag *n* **1** a bag carried by hand and designed to hold a traveler's clothing and personal articles — see TRAVELING BAG

2 a container for carrying money and small personal items — see PURSE

handbook *n* a book used for instruction in a subject — see TEXTBOOK

handcraft *n* an occupation requiring skillful use of the hands — see CRAFT 1

handcuff *n, usually* **handcuffs** *pl* something that physically prevents free movement — see BOND 1

handcuff *vb* **1** to confine or restrain with or as if with chains — see BIND 1

2 to create difficulty for the work or activity of — see HAMPER

handful *n* a small number — see FEW

handicap *n* **1** a feature of someone or something that creates difficulty for achieving success — see DISADVANTAGE 1

2 something that makes movement or progress difficult — see ENCUMBRANCE

handicap *vb* to create difficulty for the work or activity of — see HAMPER

handicraft *n* an occupation requiring skillful use of the hands — see CRAFT 1

handicrafter *n* a person whose occupation requires skill with the hands — see ARTISAN

handily *adv* without difficulty — see EASILY 1

handiwork *n* something produced by physical or intellectual effort — see PRODUCT 1

handkerchief *n* a scarf worn on the head — see BANDANNA

handle *n* **1** a part by which an implement is held ⟨a set of steak knives with wooden *handles*⟩

syn grip

rel bar, handlebar; bow, loop; hilt, shaft; broomstick

2 a word or combination of words by which a person or thing is regularly known — see NAME 1

3 a descriptive or familiar name given instead of or in addition to the one belonging to an individual — see NICKNAME

handle *vb* **1** to deal with (something) usually skillfully or efficiently ⟨As host of a live TV talk show, she must *handle* any situation that comes up.⟩

syn address, contend (with), cope (with), field, grapple (with), hack, manage, maneuver, manipulate, negotiate, play, swing, take, treat

rel engineer, finesse, jockey; carry out, get off, pull; command, direct, guide, steer; control, micromanage, regulate, run; react (to), respond (to)

phrases come to grips with, have a grip on

near ant botch, bungle, foozle, fumble, louse up, mess (up), mishandle, muff, scamp

2 to behave toward in a stated way — see TREAT 1

3 to control the mechanical operation of — see OPERATE 1

---

4 to look after and make decisions about — see CONDUCT 1

5 to put up with (something painful or difficult) — see BEAR 2

6 to be in charge of — see BOSS 1

handling *n* the act or activity of looking after and making decisions about something — see CONDUCT 1

hand over *vb* **1** to give (something) over to the control or possession of another usually under duress — see SURRENDER 1

2 to put (something) into the possession of someone for use or consumption — see FURNISH 2

3 to put (something) into the possession or safekeeping of another — see GIVE 2

4 to shift possession of (something) from one person to another — see PASS 1

handpick *vb* to decide to accept (someone or something) from a group of possibilities — see CHOOSE 1

handsome *adj* **1** having or showing elegance — see ELEGANT 1

2 of a size greater than average of its kind — see LARGE

3 very pleasing to look at — see BEAUTIFUL 1

4 sufficiently large in size, amount, or number to merit attention — see CONSIDERABLE 1

handsomely *adv* in a generous manner — see WELL 2

handsomeness *n* **1** dignified or restrained beauty of form, appearance, or style — see ELEGANCE

2 the qualities in a person or thing that as a whole give pleasure to the senses — see BEAUTY 1

hand-to-mouth *adj* less plentiful than what is normal, necessary, or desirable — see MEAGER

handwriting *n* **1** the form or style of a particular person's writing ⟨She immediately recognized the *handwriting* on the envelope as that of her old college roommate.⟩

syn hand, penmanship, script

rel scratch, scrawl, scribble; cursive, print, running hand; autograph, John Henry

2 writing done by hand ⟨The columnist laments the decline of fine *handwriting*, as so few people write letters by hand anymore.⟩

syn calligraphy, longhand, manuscript, penmanship, script

rel lettering; shorthand, stenography

ant print, type, typewriting

handy *adj* **1** situated within easy reach — see CONVENIENT

2 skillful with the hands — see DEXTEROUS 1

hang *n* **1** a downward slope — see DECLINE 3

2 the extent to which something hangs or dips below a straight line — see SAG

hang *vb* **1** to place on an elevated point without support from below ⟨*Hang* your coats on the coat rack in the hall.⟩

syn dangle, sling, suspend, swing

rel hook, mount, pin, tack; garland, string; extend (out), jut, project, stick out; overhang, protrude; cascade, depend, fall; balance, poise

2 to be determined by, based on, or subject (to) — see DEPEND 1

---

syn synonym(s)   *rel* related words
ant antonym(s)   *near ant* near antonym(s)

3 to be limp from lack of water or vigor — see DROOP 1

4 to rest or move along the surface of a liquid or in the air — see FLOAT 1

5 to find a basis — see BASE

hang (over) vb to remain poised to inflict harm, danger, or distress on — see THREATEN

hang around vb to continue to be in a place for a significant amount of time — see ¹STAY 1

hang back vb to show uncertainty about the right course of action — see HESITATE

hangdog adj feeling unhappiness — see SAD 1

hanger–on n a person who is supported by or seeks support from another without making an adequate return — see LEECH

hanging adj **1** bending downward or forward — see NODDING

2 extending freely from a support from above — see DEPENDENT 1

hanging n a downward slope — see DECLINE 3

hangout n a place for spending time or for socializing ⟨A favorite *hangout* of the golden-agers is the local community center.⟩

syn haunt, rendezvous, resort

rel camp, canteen, club, clubhouse, country club, key club, service club, union; harbor, harborage, haven, nest, refuge, retreat, sanctuary

hanker (for or **after)** vb to have an earnest wish to own or enjoy — see DESIRE 1

hankering n a strong wish for something — see DESIRE 1

hanky–panky n the use of clever underhanded actions to achieve an end — see TRICKERY

haphazard adj lacking a definite plan, purpose, or pattern — see RANDOM

haphazard adv without definite aim, direction, rule, or method — see HIT OR MISS

haphazardly adv without definite aim, direction, rule, or method — see HIT OR MISS

hapless adj having, prone to, or marked by bad luck — see UNLUCKY 1

happen vb to take place ⟨Did anything exciting *happen* over the summer?⟩

syn be, befall, betide, chance, come, come about, cook, do, occur, pass, transpire

rel break, develop, rise, shape (up); arise, crop (up); materialize, spring (up); intervene; fall out, follow, result, turn out; go off, proceed

phrases come to pass

happen (on or **upon)** vb to come upon unexpectedly or by chance ⟨*happened on* the filming of a movie⟩

syn chance (upon), encounter, find, hit (upon), light (on or upon), meet, stumble (on or onto)

rel luck (out, on, onto, or into); confront, face; discover, strike, turn up

phrases bump into, come across, run across, run against, run into, run upon

happen (on or **upon)** vb to come upon face-to-face or as if face-to-face — see MEET 1

happening adj **1** being in the latest or current fashion — see STYLISH

2 marked by much life, movement, or activity — see ALIVE 2

3 enjoying widespread favor or approval — see POPULAR 1

happening n **1** an exciting or noteworthy event that one experiences firsthand — see ADVENTURE 1

2 something that happens — see EVENT 1

happily adv **1** in a cheerful or happy manner — see GAILY 1

2 in a manner suitable for the occasion or purpose — see PROPERLY

happiness n a feeling or state of well-being and contentment ⟨Her *happiness* was complete when she got her very own house.⟩

syn blessedness, bliss, blissfulness, felicity, gladness, joy

rel elation, exhilaration, exultation; ecstasy, euphoria, glory, heaven, paradise, rapture, rapturousness, ravishment, transport; delectation, delight, enjoyment, pleasure; cheer, cheerfulness, comfort, exuberance, gaiety (also gayety), gladsomeness, glee, gleefulness, jollity, joyfulness, joyousness, jubilance, jubilation, lightheartedness, merriness, mirth; content, contentedness, gratification, satisfaction

near ant anguish, desolation, joylessness, sorrow, woe, woefulness; blues, cheerlessness, dejection, depression, desolateness, despondency, disheartenment, dispiritedness, doldrums, downheartedness, gloom, gloominess, melancholy, plaintiveness

ant calamity, ill-being, misery, sadness, unhappiness, wretchedness

2 the feeling experienced when one's wishes are met — see PLEASURE 1

happy adj **1** coming or happening by good luck especially unexpectedly — see FORTUNATE 1

2 experiencing pleasure, satisfaction, or delight — see GLAD 1

3 feeling that one's needs or desires have been met — see CONTENT

4 having good luck — see LUCKY 1

5 meeting the requirements of a purpose or situation — see FIT 1

6 having extreme or relentless concern — see HUNG UP 1

happy–go–lucky adj **1** having a relaxed, casual manner — see EASYGOING 1

2 having or showing freedom from worries or troubles — see CAREFREE

harangue n **1** a long angry speech or scolding — see TIRADE

2 a usually formal discourse delivered to an audience — see SPEECH 1

harangue vb **1** to give a formal often extended talk on a subject — see TALK 1

2 to talk as if giving an important and formal speech — see ORATE 1

harassment n the act of making unwelcome intrusions upon another — see ANNOYANCE 1

harbinger n one that announces or indicates the later arrival of another — see FORERUNNER 1

harbinger vb to give a slight indication of beforehand — see FORESHADOW

harbor n **1** a part of a body of water protected and deep enough to be a place of safety for ships ⟨The tanker stayed in Boston *harbor* three days to undergo repairs.⟩

syn anchorage, harborage, haven, port

rel basin, dock, marina, moorage, mooring; arm, bay, bight, cove, estuary, firth, fjord (*also* fiord), gulf, inlet, lagoon, narrow, roads, roadstead; canal, channel, sound, strait; containerport, home port, seaport

2 something (as a building) that offers cover from the weather or protection from danger — see SHELTER

harbor *vb* **1** to keep in one's mind or heart ⟨He had long *harbored* a grudge against his old employer, who had high-handedly fired him without cause.⟩

syn bear, cherish, entertain, have, hold, nurse

rel cultivate, foster, nurture, support, sustain; carry, keep, maintain, preserve, remember, retain, treasure; cleave (to), cling (to), hug, stick (to); brood (about *or* over), fixate (on *or* upon), obsess (about *or* over)

phrases hang on to, hold on to

near ant disregard, drop, forget, ignore, neglect, overlook; abjure, decline, deny, disdain, refuse, reject, repudiate, scorn; abandon, desert, discard, forsake, give up, part (with), quit, renounce, throw out; expunge

2 to provide with living quarters or shelter — see HOUSE 1

3 to be or provide a shelter for — see SHELTER 1

harborage *n* **1** a part of a body of water protected and deep enough to be a place of safety for ships — see HARBOR 1

2 something (as a building) that offers cover from the weather or protection from danger — see SHELTER

hard *adj* **1** having or showing a lack of sympathy or tender feelings ⟨a *hard* man, who never had a kind word for anyone⟩

syn callous, cold-blooded, hard-boiled, heartless, inhuman, inhumane, insensate, insensitive, merciless, obdurate, pitiless, remorseless, ruthless, soulless, stony (*also* stoney), take-no-prisoners, thick-skinned, uncharitable, unfeeling, unmerciful, unsparing, unsympathetic

rel boorish, heedless, inconsiderate, thoughtless, uncaring, unfriendly, unloving, unthinking; grim, hard-bitten, harsh, heavy-handed, oppressive, rough, severe, sledge-hammer, stern, tough, ungentle; abusive, acrimonious, disagreeable, hateful, ill-natured, ill-tempered, malevolent, malicious, mean, rancorous, spiteful, surly, virulent; barbarous, brutal, cruel, evil-minded, savage, vicious; austere, cold, frosty

near ant benevolent, benignant, gentle, kind; clement, indulgent, lenient, mild; cordial, friendly, good-natured, good-tempered, gracious; tolerant, understanding; affectionate, fond, loving

ant charitable, compassionate, humane, kindhearted, kindly, merciful, sensitive, softhearted, sympathetic, tender, tenderhearted, warm, warmhearted

2 requiring considerable physical or mental effort ⟨Clearing land is *hard* work.⟩ ⟨a *hard* exam to pass⟩

syn arduous, challenging, demanding, difficult, exacting, formidable, grueling (*or* gruelling), heavy, herculean, killer, laborious, murderous, rigorous, rough, rugged, severe, stiff, strenuous, tall, toilsome, tough, uphill

rel abstract, abstruse, complex, complicated, elusive, hairy, insoluble, intricate, involved, knotty, opaque, problematic (*also* problematical), recondite, serious, spiny, stubborn, thorny, ticklish, tricky; bruising, burdensome, exhausting, labored, onerous, oppressive, stressful, taxing, tight, trying; annoying, bothersome, distressing, irksome, troublesome, vexatious; grievous, grim, strict, stringent; brutal, cruel, inhuman, painful

near ant achievable, clear, doable, elementary, manageable, uncomplicated; comforting, gentle, painless, relaxed, smooth, soothing; accessible, friendly, idiotproof, user-friendly

ant cheap, easy, effortless, facile, light, mindless, simple, soft, undemanding

3 able to withstand hardship, strain, or exposure — see HARDY 1

4 based on sound reasoning or information — see GOOD 1

5 difficult to endure — see HARSH 1

6 extreme in degree, power, or effect — see INTENSE 1

7 given to exacting standards of discipline and self-restraint — see SEVERE 1

8 having a consistency that does not easily yield to pressure — see FIRM 2

9 having been established and usually not subject to change — see FIXED 1

10 having or showing deep-seated resentment — see BITTER 1

11 sticking to an opinion, purpose, or course of action in spite of reason, arguments, or persuasion — see OBSTINATE

12 restricted to or based on fact — see FACTUAL 1

hard *adv* **1** with great effort or determination ⟨We took a much-needed break after working *hard* all week.⟩ ⟨a *hard*-won victory⟩

syn amain, arduously, assiduously, determinedly, diligently, hardly, industriously, intensely, intensively, intently, laboriously, mightily, purposefully, sedulously, strenuously

rel animatedly, briskly, dynamically, energetically, feverishly, spiritedly, vehemently, vigorously, zealously; continuously, ploddingly, steadfastly, steadily, unrelentingly, unremittingly; ardently, attentively, conscientiously, earnestly, exhaustively, meticulously, painstakingly, thoroughly; indefatigably, tirelessly, unflaggingly, untiringly, wearilessly; obstinately, stubbornly, willfully

near ant casually, desultorily, halfheartedly, indolently, lackadaisically, languidly, lazily, listlessly, shiftlessly, sluggishly, spiritlessly, tiredly, wearily

2 with feelings of bitterness or grief ⟨The boys took the news of their friend's moving away *hard*.⟩

syn agonizingly, bitterly, grievously, hardly, mournfully, painfully, regretfully, resentfully, ruefully, sadly, sorely, sorrowfully, unhappily, woefully, wretchedly

rel cheerlessly, dejectedly, despairingly,

despondently, disconsolately, dispiritedly, downheartedly, low-spiritedly; darkly, dismally, distressfully, distressingly, dourly, drearily, forlornly, gloomily, glumly, joylessly, mirthlessly, miserably, morosely, pessimistically, somberly, sullenly; acutely, harshly, keenly, piercingly, poignantly, severely, sharply; cruelly, hurtfully, rancorously

near ant cheerfully, cheerily, delightedly, gleefully, good-naturedly, lightheartedly, merrily, mirthfully, rejoicingly, sunnily; blithely, blithesomely, calmly, casually, dispassionately, easily, impassively, indifferently, lightly, nonchalantly, stoically, unconcernedly

ant blissfully, gladly, happily, joyfully, joyously

3 in a vigorous and forceful manner ⟨The batter hit the ball *hard*, causing it to soar out of bounds.⟩ ⟨The wind blew *hard* all day.⟩

syn dynamically, energetically, firmly, forcefully, forcibly, mightily, powerfully, roundly, stiffly, stoutly, strenuously, strongly, sturdily, vigorously

rel hammer and tongs, robustly, roughshod, sharply, vehemently, violently; animatedly, briskly, crisply, eagerly, gamely, heartily, lustily, snappily, spiritedly, spunkily, vivaciously; decidedly, determinedly, directly, emphatically, intensively, intently, purposefully, rigidly, smartly, solidly, squarely, steadfastly, steadily, sturdily, surely; aggressively, assertively, potently

phrases like gangbusters, to beat the band, with a vengeance, with might and main

near ant delicately, faintly, frailly, shakily; bloodlessly, halfheartedly, languidly, lazily, listlessly, spiritlessly; impotently, ineffectively, ineffectually, lamely, nervelessly, spinelessly, uncertainly

ant feebly, gently, softly, weakly

4 at, within, or to a short distance or time — see NEAR 1

5 in a manner so as to cause loss or suffering — see HARDLY 1

hard-and-fast *adj* **1** having been established and usually not subject to change — see FIXED 1

2 not capable of changing or being changed — see INFLEXIBLE 1

hard-bitten *adj* able to withstand hardship, strain, or exposure — see HARDY 1

hard-boiled *adj* **1** having or showing a lack of sympathy or tender feelings — see HARD 1

2 having or showing a practical cleverness or judgment — see SHREWD 1

hard-core *adj* firmly established over time — see INVETERATE 1

hard-driving *adj* having a strong desire for personal advancement — see AMBITIOUS 1

harden *vb* **1** to become physically firm or solid ⟨The glue begins to *harden* as soon as it is exposed to air.⟩

syn concrete, congeal, firm (up), freeze, set, solidify

rel cake, callus, encrust (*also* incrust); clot, coagulate, jell, jelly, thicken; calcify, crystallize (*also* crystalize), ossify, rigidify; anneal, case-harden, temper

near ant deliquesce, dissolve, flux, fuse, melt, smelt, thaw, unfreeze

ant liquefy (*also* liquify), soften

2 to make able to withstand physical hardship, strain, or exposure ⟨pioneer women who had been *hardened* by years of living on the plains⟩

syn fortify, inure, season, steel, strengthen, toughen

rel acclimate, acclimatize, adapt, adjust; anneal, temper; invigorate, vitalize; immunize; bolster, boost, brace, buttress, enforce, forearm, prop (up), support; break in, limber (up), train; accustom, condition, naturalize

near ant emasculate, enervate, enfeeble, exhaust, sap, weaken; cripple, debilitate, hamstring, incapacitate; sensitize

ant soften

3 to increase the ability of (as a muscle) to exert physical force — see STRENGTHEN 1

hardened *adj* **1** able to withstand hardship, strain, or exposure — see HARDY 1

2 sticking to an opinion, purpose, or course of action in spite of reason, arguments, or persuasion — see OBSTINATE

hardheaded *adj* **1** having or showing a practical cleverness or judgment — see SHREWD 1

2 sticking to an opinion, purpose, or course of action in spite of reason, arguments, or persuasion — see OBSTINATE

3 willing to see things as they really are and deal with them sensibly — see REALISTIC 1

hardheadedness *n* **1** a steadfast adherence to an opinion, purpose, or course of action in spite of reason, arguments, or persuasion — see OBSTINACY

2 exceptional discernment and judgment especially in practical matters — see ACUMEN

hardihood *n* **1** active strength of body or mind — see VIGOR 1

2 strength of mind to carry on in spite of danger — see COURAGE

hard-luck *adj* having, prone to, or marked by bad luck — see UNLUCKY 1

hardly *adv* **1** in a manner so as to cause loss or suffering ⟨The new judge vowed to deal *hardly* with repeat offenders.⟩

syn hard, harshly, ill, oppressively, roughly, severely, sternly, stiffly

rel callously, cold-bloodedly, hard-heartedly, heartlessly, inhumanely, inhumanly, insensitively, mercilessly, obdurately, pitilessly, ruthlessly, tyrannically, uncharitably, unfeelingly, unmercifully, unsparingly; abusively, brutishly, savagely, viciously; aggressively, assertively, decidedly, determinedly, firmly, grimly, strongly, toughly

near ant benevolently, benignantly, considerately, cordially, kindly, lovingly, tenderly; charitably, compassionately, humanely, mercifully, softheartedly, sympathetically, tolerantly, understandingly

ant clemently, gently, leniently, lightly, mildly, softly

2 certainly not ⟨The news is *hardly* surprising.⟩

syn ill, no, none, noway (*usually* no way), scarcely

rel near, never, nothing, nowise

phrases by no means, nothing doing, on no account

near ant awful, awfully, enormously, exceedingly (*also* exceeding), extremely, greatly, highly, hugely, mightily, mighty, most, quite, terribly, very; assuredly, perfectly, plainly, really, truly, unequivocally, unquestionably, utterly; doubtless, more or less, mostly, rather, slightly, somewhat

ant absolutely, certainly, completely, definitely, surely

3 by a very small margin — see JUST 2

4 with feelings of bitterness or grief — see HARD 2

5 with great effort or determination — see HARD 1

hardness *n* **1** something that is a cause for suffering or special effort especially in the attainment of a goal — see DIFFICULTY 1
2 the quality or state of being demanding or unyielding (as in discipline or criticism) — see SEVERITY

hardship *n* something that is a cause for suffering or special effort especially in the attainment of a goal — see DIFFICULTY 1

hard up *adj* lacking money or material possessions — see POOR 1

hardware *n* items needed for the performance of a task or activity — see EQUIPMENT

hardy *adj* **1** able to withstand hardship, strain, or exposure ⟨Chrysanthemums are *hardy* enough to survive a light frost.⟩
syn hard, hard-bitten, hardened, inured, rugged, stout, strong, sturdy, tough, toughened, vigorous
rel flinty, leathery, resilient, stalwart; durable, enduring, everlasting, immortal, imperishable, lasting, permanent, stable, staunch (*also* stanch), staying, tenacious, unyielding; flourishing, prospering, thriving; able-bodied, brawny, muscular; fit, fortified, hale, healthy, husky, lusty, red-blooded, robust, sound, strapping, virile; annealed, seasoned, tempered
near ant emasculated, enervated, enfeebled, exhausted, run-down, sapped, wasted, weakened, worn, worn-out; crippled, debilitated, diseased, incapacitated, infirm, unsound; fragile, frail, puny; resistless, sensitive, susceptible, unresistant, vulnerable, yielding
ant delicate, soft, tender, weak
2 inclined or willing to take risks — see BOLD 1

harebrained *adj* **1** lacking in seriousness or maturity — see GIDDY 1
2 showing or marked by a lack of good sense or judgment — see FOOLISH 1

hark *vb* to pay attention especially through the act of hearing — see LISTEN

hark back (to) *vb* to bring back to mind — see REMEMBER

harlequin *n* a comically dressed performer (as at a circus) who entertains with playful tricks and ridiculous behavior — see CLOWN 1

harm *n* something that causes loss or pain — see INJURY 1

harm *vb* **1** to cause bodily damage to — see INJURE 1
2 to reduce the soundness, effectiveness, or perfection of — see DAMAGE 1

harmful *adj* causing or capable of causing harm ⟨They use a pest control method that is not *harmful* to the environment.⟩
syn adverse, bad, baleful, baneful, damaging, dangerous, deleterious, detrimental, evil, hurtful, ill, injurious, mischievous, noxious, pernicious, prejudicial, wicked
rel hostile, inimical, unfriendly; contagious, deadly, infectious, infective, pestiferous, pestilent, poisonous, venomous; insidious, menacing, ominous, sinister, threatening; hazardous, imperiling (*or* imperilling), jeopardizing, perilous, risky, unsafe, unsound; nasty, noisome, unhealthful, unhealthy, unwholesome; destructive, fatal, killer, lethal, malignant, ruinous
near ant advantageous, beneficial, useful; favorable, good, propitious; healthful, healthy, helpful, palliative, remedial, salubrious, salutary, wholesome; secure, sound; benignant
ant benign, harmless, innocent, innocuous, inoffensive, safe

harmless *adj* not causing or being capable of causing injury or hurt ⟨a perfectly *harmless* little spider⟩
syn benign, innocent, innocuous, inoffensive, safe
rel healthful, healthy, salubrious, wholesome; benignant; sound, trustworthy; gentle, gracious, mild; nonthreatening, painless, unobjectionable
near ant poisonous, venomous; menacing, ominous, sinister, threatening; hazardous, imperiling (*or* imperilling), jeopardizing, perilous, risky, unsafe, unsound; nasty, noisome, unhealthful, unhealthy, unwholesome; offensive, painful, scathing, wounding; deadly, fatal, lethal, ruinous; destructive, insidious, malignant, noxious, pestilent, polluted, tainted
ant adverse, bad, baleful, baneful, damaging, dangerous, deleterious, detrimental, evil, harmful, hurtful, ill, injurious, mischievous, noxious, pernicious, prejudicial, wicked

harmonious *adj* **1** having a pleasing mixture of notes ⟨the naturally *harmonious* sounds of a forest glen in springtime⟩
syn euphonious, harmonizing, melodious, musical, symphonic, tuneful
rel blending, chiming, flowing, mellifluent, mellifluous; mellow, melodic, sweet; echoing, resonant, sonorous, quavering, trilling, warbling; agreeable, appealing, pleasant; cadenced, lilting, lyric, lyrical, rhythmic (*or* rhythmical), songful, songlike; chordal, homophonic, orchestral, polyphonic (*or* polyphonous), tonal
near ant blaring, clanging, clashing, clattering, grating, harsh, jangling, jarring, metallic, raspy, raucous, scratching, screeching, shrill, squeaky, strident; disagreeable, unpleasant, unpleasing; atonal, off-key
ant discordant, disharmonious, dissonant, inharmonious, tuneless, unmelodious, unmusical
2 having the parts agreeably related ⟨a

harmonious arrangement of archways and doorways in the palace courtyard⟩

syn balanced, congruous, consonant

rel even, proportioned, regular, symmetrical (*or* symmetric); aesthetic (*also* esthetic *or* aesthetical *or* esthetical); artistic, becoming, elegant, graceful, tasteful; agreeable, felicitous, pleasant, pleasing, satisfying; compatible, coordinated, matched, matching

near ant asymmetrical (*or* asymmetric), disordered, irregular, skewed, unequal, uneven, unsymmetrical; distasteful, graceless, inartistic, inelegant, tasteless, unaesthetic, unbecoming, ungraceful, unlovely; disagreeable, displeasing, dissatisfying, infelicitous, unfortunate, unpleasant, unsightly; clashing, conflicting, disunited, incompatible

ant disharmonic, disharmonious, incongruous, inharmonic, inharmonious, unbalanced

3 having or marked by agreement in feeling or action ⟨An unusually *harmonious* meeting among the leaders resulted in a quick peace agreement.⟩

syn agreeable, amicable, compatible, congenial, frictionless, kindred, unanimous, united

rel pacific, peaceable, peaceful; collaborating, cooperative, symbiotic, synergetic, synergic; sympathetic, tolerant, understanding; affable, amiable, cordial, friendly, genial, neighborly

near ant antagonistic, antipathetic, clashing, conflicting, hostile, inimical, unfriendly; belligerent, contentious, quarrelsome; contradicting, contradictory, contrary, opposing, opposite; competing, competitive, rivaling (*or* rivalling)

ant disagreeable, discordant, disharmonious, disunited, incompatible, inharmonious, uncongenial

4 not having or showing any apparent conflict — see CONSISTENT

harmonize *vb* **1** to form a pleasing relationship ⟨The color of the walls *harmonized* nicely with the blue tones in the carpet.⟩

syn agree, assort, blend, chime, chime in, conform, consort, coordinate, groove

rel accord, correlate, correspond, dovetail, hang together, match; meet, parallel; bond, coalesce, cohere, conjoin, fuse, merge, square, tally

near ant contradict, contrast, counter, differ, diverge, jar; cancel (out), counteract, negate, offset

ant clash, collide, conflict

2 to bring to a state free of conflicts, inconsistencies, or differences ⟨an attempt to *harmonize* the traditional stories about the event with the historical evidence⟩

syn accommodate, conciliate, conform, coordinate, key, reconcile

rel adapt, tune; blend, combine, connect, correlate, dovetail, fit, fuse, integrate, join, match, merge, orchestrate, pair, square, suit, synthesize, unify, unite; align (*also* aline), arrange, array, balance, equalize, even, order, proportion, regularize, standardize

near ant confuse, disarray, disorder, disorganize, disrupt, disturb, skew, upset; alienate, estrange

ant disharmonize

3 to be in agreement on every point — see CHECK 1

harmonizing *adj* having a pleasing mixture of notes — see HARMONIOUS 1

harmony *n* **1** a balanced, pleasing, or suitable arrangement of parts ⟨Her face had an angelic *harmony* that fascinated the leading painters of her day.⟩

syn balance, coherence, consonance, proportion, symmetry, symphony, unity

rel coordination, correlation, correspondence, equalization, equilibrium, evenness, order, orderliness, regularity, uniformity

near ant confusion, disorganization, disturbance, tension; disconnectedness, disjointedness, incompatibility; irregularity, unevenness

ant asymmetry, discordance, disproportion, disunity, imbalance, incoherence, violence

2 peaceful coexistence ⟨the apparent inability of the party's right and left wings to resolve their conflicts and live in *harmony* at least during the convention⟩

syn chime, comity, compatibility, concord, peace

rel amity, companionship, compatibleness, congeniality, fellowship, fraternization, friendship; collaboration, reciprocity, symbiosis; agreement, consensus, unanimity; cohesion, cohesiveness, unity; affinity, connection, empathy, kinship, oneness, rapport, solidarity, sympathy, understanding; peacefulness, sereneness, serenity, sweetness and light, tranquillity (*or* tranquility)

near ant antagonism, antipathy, enmity, hatred, hostility, unfriendliness; alienation, breach, divorce, estrangement, rupture, schism, severance; dissent, dissidence; anarchy, disorder, disturbance, strife, turmoil

ant conflict, discord, dissension (*also* dissention), variance

3 a state of consistency — see CONFORMITY 1

harness *vb* to put into action or service — see USE 1

harpoon *vb* to penetrate or hold (something) with a pointed object — see IMPALE

harrow *vb* to cause persistent suffering to — see AFFLICT

harrowing *adj* **1** hard to accept or bear especially emotionally — see BITTER 2

2 intensely or unbearably painful — see EXCRUCIATING 1

harrying *n* the act of making unwelcome intrusions upon another — see ANNOYANCE 1

harsh *adj* **1** difficult to endure ⟨a *harsh* winter⟩

syn bitter, brutal, burdensome, cruel, excruciating, grievous, grim, hard, heavy, inhuman, murderous, onerous, oppressive, rough, rugged, searing, severe, stiff, tough, trying

rel austere, bleak, comfortless, discomforting, forbidding, inhospitable, uncomfortable; rigorous, strict, stringent; agonizing, heartbreaking, heartrending, painful, wretched; crushing, grinding, overwhelming, wearing; insufferable, insupportable, intolerable, unbearable, unendurable; harrowing, tortuous; bad, disagreeable, hostile, unfriendly, unpleasant

near ant comfortable, cozy, luxurious, snug; agreeable, friendly, genial, hospitable, pleasant; peaceful, relaxing, reposeful, restful; bearable, endurable, painless, tolerable; balmy, calm, clement, gentle, mild, moderate, temperate
ant easy, light, soft

2 disagreeable to one's aesthetic or artistic sense ⟨The *harsh* lighting in the cafeteria makes the food look slightly off-color.⟩
syn grating, grotesque, jarring, unaesthetic
rel acid, flashy, garish, gaudy, loud, tawdry; tacky, tasteless, vulgar; inartistic, unartistic; artless, clumsy, crude, graceless, inelegant, rude; uncouth, uncultured, unrefined; gross, obscene, repugnant, repulsive, ugly; disagreeable, unpleasant, unpleasing; blaring, clashing, discordant, disharmonious, dissonant, inharmonious, jangling, off-key, ragged, raspy, raucous, unmelodious, unmusical
near ant artful, artistic; attractive, beautiful, becoming, comely; agreeable, appealing, felicitous, good, harmonious, harmonizing, pleasing, seemly; calming, comforting, soothing; softened, subdued; cultured, elegant, graceful, gracious, polished, refined, tasteful
ant aesthetic (*also* esthetic *or* aesthetical *or* esthetical)

3 causing discomfort — see UNCOMFORTABLE 1

4 given to exacting standards of discipline and self-restraint — see SEVERE 1

5 hard to accept or bear especially emotionally — see BITTER 2

6 not giving pleasure to the mind or senses — see UNPLEASANT

harshly *adv* in a manner so as to cause loss or suffering — see HARDLY 1

harshness *n* **1** a harsh or sharp quality — see EDGE 1

2 the quality or state of being demanding or unyielding (as in discipline or criticism) — see SEVERITY

harum–scarum *adj* having or showing a lack of concern for the consequences of one's actions — see RECKLESS 1

harum–scarum *adv* in a confused and reckless manner — see HELTER-SKELTER 1

harvest *n* the quantity of an animal or vegetable product gathered at the end of a season — see CROP 1

harvest *vb* to catch or collect (a crop or natural resource) for human use ⟨*harvest* salmon from nearby rivers⟩ ⟨Every year we *harvest* corn from our own garden.⟩
syn gather, pick, reap
rel fish, seal, shrimp, whale; accumulate, forage, garner; glean; cut, hay, mow; bag, capture, hunt, net, snare, trap; crop, grow, raise
near ant plant, seed, sow

hash *n* an unorganized collection or mixture of various things — see MISCELLANY 1

hash *vb* **1** to cut into small pieces — see CHOP

2 to undo the proper order or arrangement of — see DISORDER

hassle *n* **1** a brief clash between enemies or rivals — see ENCOUNTER

2 a physical dispute between opposing individuals or groups — see FIGHT 1

3 an often noisy or angry expression of differing opinions — see ARGUMENT 1

4 something that is a source of irritation — see ANNOYANCE 3

hassle *vb* **1** to attack repeatedly with mean put-downs or insults — see TEASE 2

2 to express different opinions about something often angrily — see ARGUE 2

haste *n* **1** a high rate of movement or performance — see SPEED 1

2 excited and often showy or disorderly speed — see HURRY 1

hasten *vb* **1** to cause to move or proceed fast or faster — see HURRY 1

2 to proceed or move quickly — see HURRY 2

hastily *adv* **1** with excessive or careless speed ⟨The *hastily* put together report contained a lot of errors.⟩
syn cursorily, headlong, hotfoot, hurriedly, pell-mell, precipitately, precipitously, rashly
rel headfirst, headily, hotheadedly, impatiently, impetuously, impulsively, recklessly, thoughtlessly; automatically, glancingly, haphazardly; impromptu, spontaneously; abruptly, suddenly; offhand, offhandedly
phrases on the spur of the moment
near ant calculatingly, circumspectly, designedly; falteringly, haltingly, hesitantly, hesitatingly, tentatively; leisurely, slowly
ant deliberately, studiedly

2 with great speed — see FAST 1

hastiness *n* excited and often showy or disorderly speed — see HURRY 1

hasty *adj* **1** acting or done with excessive or careless speed ⟨Anna later regretted her *hasty* decision to sell her car.⟩
syn cursory, hasty, headlong, helter-skelter, hurried, overhasty, pell-mell, precipitate, precipitous, rash, rushed
rel breakneck, breathtaking; headstrong, hotheaded, impatient, impetuous, impulsive, madcap, reckless, unadvised; quick, rapid, speedy, swift; horseback, impromptu, makeshift, offhand, offhanded, rush, slapdash, snap, spontaneous, spur-of-the-moment; abrupt, sudden
near ant calculated, calculating, measured; circumspect, foresighted, forethoughtful; drawn-out, extended, longterm, prolonged; faltering, hesitant, hesitating, tentative; dallying, dawdling, laggard, leisurely, poky (*or* pokey), shilly-shallying, slow
ant deliberate, unhurried, unrushed

2 moving, proceeding, or acting with great speed — see FAST 1

hat *n* a covering for the head usually having a shaped crown ⟨In those days, no properly dressed person left home without a *hat*.⟩
syn cap, headdress, headgear, headpiece, lid [*slang*]
rel baseball cap, beret, biretta, boater, bonnet, bowler, cloche, cocked hat, cowboy hat, cowl, derby, fedora, fez, hard hat,

helmet, high hat, homburg, hood, miter (or mitre), nightcap, panama, pillbox, porkpie hat, service cap, shako, silk hat, skullcap, sombrero, sou'wester, Stetson, stocking cap, stovepipe, sunbonnet, tam, tam-o'-shanter, ten-gallon hat, top hat, topper, toque, tricorne (or tricorn), turban, zucchetto

hatch *n* a barrier by which an entry is closed and opened — see DOOR 1

hatch *vb* to cover and warm eggs as the young inside develop — see SET 1

hate *n* 1 a very strong dislike ⟨*Hate* can sometimes be replaced with tolerance when people meet face to face.⟩

syn abhorrence, abomination, execration, hatred, loathing

rel cattiness, despite, despitefulness, hatefulness, invidiousness, malevolence, malice, maliciousness, malignancy, malignity, meanness, spite, spitefulness; aversion, disgust, distaste, horror, odium, repugnance, repulsion, revulsion; animosity, antagonism, antipathy, bitterness, contempt, disdain, enmity, grudge, hostility, jealousy, pique, resentment, scorn; bile, jaundice, rancor, spleen, venom, virulence, vitriol

near ant appetite, inclination, liking; admiration, adoration, veneration, worship; acceptance, tolerance; passion, relish, taste

ant affection, devotion, fondness, love

2 something or someone that is hated ⟨My one *hate* in gym is square dancing.⟩

syn abhorrence, abomination, anathema, antipathy, aversion, bête noire, execration

rel dread, horror, phobia; bogey (*also* bogie *or* bogy), bugaboo, bugbear; adversary, enemy; annoyance, grievance, hassle, nuisance, peeve

near ant beloved, darling, dear, honey, sweetheart; delight, enjoyment, felicity, joy, pleasure; favorite, like, preference; treasure

ant love

hate *vb* to dislike strongly ⟨I *hate* going out in the rain and cold.⟩

syn abhor, abominate, despise, detest, execrate, loathe

rel deplore, deprecate, disapprove (of), discountenance, disdain, disfavor, scorn

phrases have it in for

near ant desire, fancy, favor, like, prefer; enjoy, relish; admire, adore, approve (of), esteem, hallow, idolize, revere, venerate, worship; cherish, prize, treasure

ant love

hateful *adj* having or showing a desire to cause someone pain or suffering for the sheer enjoyment of it ⟨The most *hateful* comments were deleted from the website.⟩

syn catty, cruel, despiteful, malevolent, malicious, malign, malignant, mean, nasty, spiteful, vicious, virulent

rel devious, scoundrelly, scurvy, snakelike; acrimonious, bitter, envious, jaundiced, jealous, rancorous, resentful, vindictive; contemptuous, deprecating, derogatory, disdainful, disparaging, meanspirited, obnoxious, opprobrious, scornful, snide, unkind, unkindly, unloving;

baleful, baneful, evil; harsh, hostile, inimical; acrid, caustic, poisonous, scathing, venomous

near ant compassionate, good, goodhearted, kind, kindhearted, kindly, sympathetic, warm, warmhearted; affable, agreeable, amiable, cordial, friendly, genial, gracious, nice, pleasant; affectionate, amorous, sweet, tender, tenderhearted; humane; altruistic, high-minded, humanitarian, magnanimous, noble, philanthropic (*also* philanthropical)

ant benevolent, benign, benignant, loving, unmalicious

hatefully *adv* in a mean or spiteful manner — see NASTILY

hatefulness *n* the desire to cause pain for the satisfaction of doing harm — see MALICE

hatred *n* a very strong dislike — see HATE 1

haughtiness *n* an exaggerated sense of one's importance that shows itself in the making of excessive or unjustified claims — see ARROGANCE

haughty *adj* 1 having a feeling of superiority that shows itself in an overbearing attitude — see ARROGANT

2 having or displaying feelings of scorn for what is regarded as beneath oneself — see PROUD 1

haul *n* 1 the total amount collected or obtained especially at one time ⟨Our latest trip to collect shells at the beach resulted in quite a *haul*.⟩

syn bounty, catch, take, yield

rel bag; earnings, gain, gross, income, net, payoff, proceeds, profit, receipts, return, revenue, winnings; booty, loot, plunder, spoils, swag; appropriation, collection

near ant deduction, loss, subtraction

2 a mass or quantity of something taken up and carried, conveyed, or transported — see LOAD 1

3 the act or an instance of applying force on something so that it moves in the direction of the force — see PULL 1

haul *vb* 1 to cause to follow by applying steady force on — see PULL 1

2 to support and take from one place to another — see CARRY 1

haunches *n pl* the part of the body upon which someone sits — see BUTTOCKS

haunt *n* a place for spending time or for socializing — see HANGOUT

haunt *vb* to go to or spend time in often — see FREQUENT

haunting *adj* fearfully and mysteriously strange or fantastic — see EERIE

have *vb* 1 to keep, control, or experience as one's own ⟨My uncle *has* a sizable collection of baseball cards.⟩

syn command, enjoy, hold, own, possess, retain

rel keep, reserve, withhold; bear, carry; boast, show off, sport

phrases rejoice in

near ant abandon, cede, disclaim, disown, hand over, relinquish, renounce, surrender, yield; discard, dump; decline, reject, repudiate, spurn; need, require

ant lack, want

2 to agree to receive whether willingly or reluctantly — see TAKE 2

3 to bring forth from the womb — see BEAR 1

4 to cause to believe what is untrue — see DECEIVE

5 to come to a knowledge of (something) by living through it — see EXPERIENCE

6 to give permission for or to approve of — see ALLOW 1

7 to influence someone with a bribe — see BRIBE

8 to keep in one's mind or heart — see HARBOR 1

have (to) *vb* to be under necessity or obligation to — see NEED 2

haven *n* **1** a part of a body of water protected and deep enough to be a place of safety for ships — see HARBOR 1

2 something (as a building) that offers cover from the weather or protection from danger — see SHELTER

havoc *n* **1** a state in which everything is out of order — see CHAOS

2 the state or fact of being rendered nonexistent, physically unsound, or useless — see DESTRUCTION 1

hawk *n* one who urges or attempts to cause a war — see WARMONGER

hawk *vb* to sell from place to place usually in small quantities — see PEDDLE

hawker *n* one who sells things outdoors — see PEDDLER

hazard *n* **1** something that may cause injury or harm — see DANGER 2

2 the uncertain course of events — see CHANCE 1

hazard *vb* **1** to place in danger — see ENDANGER

2 to take a chance on — see RISK 1

hazardous *adj* involving potential loss or injury — see DANGEROUS 1

haze *n* **1** an atmospheric condition in which suspended particles in the air rob it of its transparency ⟨Jim could barely make out the tall buildings through the *haze*.⟩

syn fog, mist, murk, reek, smog, soup

rel bank, cloud, fume, miasma, smoke, smother, steam

2 a state of mental confusion ⟨He felt like he was in a *haze* from the jet lag.⟩

syn daze, fog, muddle, spin, swoon

rel reverie, trance; befuddlement, bewilderment, perplexity, puzzlement; delirium, malaise, paralysis; cloudiness, fogginess

near ant alertness, levelheadedness

¹**haze** *vb* to attack repeatedly with mean put-downs or insults — see TEASE 2

²**haze** *vb* to make dark, dim, or indistinct — see CLOUD 1

hazed *adj* covered over by clouds — see OVERCAST

hazy *adj* **1** filled with or dimmed by fine particles (as of dust or water) in suspension ⟨*Hazy* skies made it dangerous to fly.⟩ ⟨the *hazy* sunshine so common in August⟩

syn beclouded, befogged, clouded, cloudy, foggy, misty, murky, smoggy, soupy

rel overcast, rainy, stormy, thick; dirty, miry, mucky, muddy, slimy, slushy, turbid; smoky (*also* smokey), smudgy, sooty; filmy, milky, opaque

near ant bright, clean; clement, fair, sunny, sunshiny; translucent, transparent

ant clear, cloudless, limpid, pellucid, unclouded

2 covered over by clouds — see OVERCAST

3 not seen or understood clearly — see FAINT 1

head *adj* highest in rank or authority ⟨She was *head* editor of the magazine for 17 years.⟩

syn chief, commanding, first, foremost, high, lead, leading, preeminent, premier, presiding, primary, prime, principal, supreme, top

rel high-level, senior; controlling, directing, managing, officiating, overseeing, regnant, reigning, ruling, supervisory; main, major, paramount, predominant, predominate, sovereign (*also* sovran); ascendant (*also* ascendent), dominant, grand, superior, topmost, upmost, upper, uppermost

phrases in charge

near ant ancillary, inferior, last, less, lesser, lower, lowly, second, secondary, subordinate, subsidiary; assistant, assisting, coadjutor, deputy, junior, under

head *n* **1** the upper or front part of the body that contains the brain, the major sense organs, and the mouth ⟨I hit my *head* as I went through the low doorway.⟩

syn block [*slang*], noddle, noggin, pate, poll

rel cranium, crown, scalp, skull

2 the place of leadership or command ⟨Every year a different parent is placed at the *head* of the troop's cookie drive.⟩

syn chair, headship, helm, rein(s)

rel chieftainship, commandership, directorship; forefront, lead, vanguard; captainship, chairmanship, deanship, dictatorship, generalship, governorship, kingship, mastership, mastery, premiership, presidentship, superintendency; dominance, dominion, jurisdiction, sovereignty (*also* sovranty), sway, upper hand; eminence, height, pedestal, pinnacle, seat, throne, top

near ant ranks

3 a light mass of fine bubbles formed in or on a liquid — see FOAM

4 a member of the human race — see HUMAN

5 a time or state of affairs requiring prompt or decisive action — see EMERGENCY

6 the beginning part of a stream — see HEADWATER

7 the highest part or point — see HEIGHT 1

8 the normal or healthy condition of the mental abilities — see MIND 2

9 the part of a person that feels, thinks, perceives, wills, and especially reasons — see MIND 1

10 the person (as an employer or supervisor) who tells people and especially workers what to do — see BOSS

11 a bank of earth constructed to control water — see DAM

12 a room furnished with a fixture for flushing body waste — see TOILET

13 a person with a strong and habitual liking for something — see FAN

14 a word or series of words often in larger letters placed at the beginning of a pas-

syn synonym(s)   *rel* related words

ant antonym(s)   *near ant* near antonym(s)

sage or at the top of a page in order to introduce or categorize — see HEADING

15 a special and usually inborn ability — see TALENT

head *vb* **1** to go on a specified course or in a certain direction ⟨I turned around and *headed* for home.⟩

syn bear, make

rel aim, bend, direct, point, turn; beeline, light out, put, put out, set off, strike, take off; face, orient, steer; back, come about, come round, cut, incline, put about, reverse, swerve, tack, veer, wheel, yaw

2 to be at the front of — see LEAD 3

3 to be in charge of — see BOSS 1

4 to be positioned along a certain course or in a certain direction — see RUN 3

5 to point or turn (something) toward a target or goal — see AIM 1

6 to serve as leader of — see LEAD 2

7 to cut off the head of — see DECAPITATE

headache *n* **1** a dull, unpleasant, or difficult piece of work — see CHORE 2

2 something that is a source of irritation — see ANNOYANCE 3

headdress *n* a covering for the head usually having a shaped crown — see HAT

headgear *n* a covering for the head usually having a shaped crown — see HAT

heading *n* a word or series of words often in larger letters placed at the beginning of a passage or at the top of a page in order to introduce or categorize ⟨The recipe for turkey gumbo is under the *heading* "stews" rather than under "soups."⟩

syn caption, head, headline, rubric, title

rel banner, streamer; catch word, guide word, running head; greeting, salutation; superscript, superscription; subhead, subheading, subtitle

headland *n* **1** an area of high ground jutting out into a body of water beyond the line of the coast ⟨The lighthouse, situated on a narrow, rocky *headland*, commands an expansive view of the coast.⟩

syn point, promontory

rel cape, foreland, peninsula, spit; breakwater, jetty, levee

2 an area of land that juts out into a body of water — see ²CAPE

headline *n* a word or series of words often in larger letters placed at the beginning of a passage or at the top of a page in order to introduce or categorize — see HEADING

headlong *adj* acting or done with excessive or careless speed — see HASTY 1

headlong *adv* **1** with excessive or careless speed — see HASTILY 1

2 without delay — see IMMEDIATELY

headpiece *n* **1** a covering for the head usually having a shaped crown — see HAT

2 the ability to learn and understand or to deal with problems — see INTELLIGENCE 1

headquarters *n pl* **1** a place from which authority is exercised — see SEAT 1

2 the place from which a commander runs operations — see COMMAND 3

headship *n* **1** the duty or function of watching or guarding for the sake of proper direction or control — see SUPERVISION 1

2 the place of leadership or command — see HEAD 2

headstone *n* a shaped stone laid over or erected near a grave and usually bearing an inscription to identify and preserve the memory of the deceased — see TOMBSTONE

headstrong *adj* **1** given to resisting control or discipline by others — see UNCONTROLLABLE

2 sticking to an opinion, purpose, or course of action in spite of reason, arguments, or persuasion — see OBSTINATE

headwater *n, usually* **headwaters** *pl* the beginning part of a stream ⟨In the 1800s, Meriwether Lewis and William Clark explored the Missouri River from its mouth to its *headwaters*.⟩

syn head, source

rel geyser, headspring, hot spring, spring; branch

headway *n* forward movement in time or place — see ADVANCE 1

heal *vb* **1** to restore to a healthy condition ⟨This ointment will help *heal* the wound.⟩ ⟨*healed* the sick⟩

syn cure, fix, mend, rehabilitate, set up

rel attend (to), care (for), doctor, medicate, minister (to), nurse, physic, treat; fortify, rejuvenate, renew, resuscitate, revitalize, revive; alleviate, relieve, remedy, repair

near ant cripple, damage, disable, harm, hurt, impair, injure, lacerate, lame, maim, mangle, mutilate, wound; afflict, ail, debilitate, enervate, enfeeble, lay up, sap, sicken, waste, weaken

2 to become healthy and strong again after illness or weakness — see CONVALESCE

3 to bring about recovery from — see CURE 1

healing *n* the process or period of gradually regaining one's health and strength — see CONVALESCENCE

health *n* **1** the condition of being sound in body ⟨We nursed him back to *health*.⟩

syn fitness, healthiness, heartiness, robustness, sap, soundness, wellness, wholeness, wholesomeness

rel fettle, shape; cleanliness, hygiene; hardiness, lustiness, robustiousness, ruggedness, stamina, strength, toughness, vigor, vigorousness, vitality; bloom, flush, flushness; activeness, agility, liveliness, spryness; weal, welfare, well-being

near ant debility, decrepitude, feebleness, frailness, infirmity, lameness, sickliness, weakness; ailment, condition, disease, disorder, malady, trouble

ant illness, sickness, unhealthiness, unsoundness

2 a state of being or fitness — see CONDITION 1

healthful *adj* beneficial to the health of body or mind ⟨One of the most *healthful* forms of exercise is a brisk walk.⟩

syn good, healthy, restorative, salubrious, salutary, tonic, wholesome

rel alleviative, corrective, recuperative, refreshing, rehabilitative, rejuvenescent, remedial; advantageous, useful; aseptic, clean, hygienic, sanitary; nourishing, nutritional, nutritious

near ant damaging, deleterious, harmful, injurious, pernicious; infectious, poisonous, sickening, toxic; insanitary, unhygienic, unsanitary

ant noxious, unhealthful, unhealthy, unwholesome

healthiness *n* the condition of being sound in body — see HEALTH 1

healthy *adj* 1 enjoying health and vigor ⟨Always active, Grandma has remained *healthy* into her 80s.⟩

syn able-bodied, bouncing, fit, hale, hearty, robust, sound, well, whole, wholesome

rel hard, hardy, iron, lusty, rugged, stalwart, strong, sturdy, tough; active, agile, chipper, lively, sprightful, sprightly, spry, vigorous, vital; all right, good, right

phrases in fine fettle, in shape, in the pink

near ant decrepit, enfeebled, feeble, infirm, run-down, sickened, sickly, weak, weakened, weakly, worn-out; debilitated, halt, incapacitated, lame; delicate, fragile, frail; emaciated, gaunt, haggard, malnourished, undernourished; afflicted, troubled; bad, poorly

ant ailing, diseased, ill, sick, unfit, unhealthy, unsound, unwell

2 beneficial to the health of body or mind — see HEALTHFUL

3 sufficiently large in size, amount, or number to merit attention — see CONSIDERABLE 1

4 marked by vigorous growth and well-being especially economically — see PROSPEROUS 1

heap *n* 1 a considerable amount — see LOT 2

2 a quantity of things thrown or stacked on one another — see ¹PILE 1

heap *vb* 1 to give readily and in large quantities — see RAIN 2

2 to lay or throw on top of one another — see PILE 1

3 to put into (something) as much as can be held or contained — see FILL 1

hear *vb* 1 to come to an awareness of — see DISCOVER 1

2 to pay attention especially through the act of hearing — see LISTEN

hearing *n* range of hearing — see EARSHOT

hearken *vb* to pay attention especially through the act of hearing — see LISTEN

heart *n* 1 the capacity for feeling for another's unhappiness or misfortune ⟨She has a big *heart*.⟩

syn charity, commiseration, compassion, feeling, good-heartedness, humanity, kindheartedness, kindliness, kindness, mercy, pity, softheartedness, sympathy, warmheartedness

rel feelings, responsiveness, sensibility, sensitivity; affection, love, regard; empathy, rapport; altruism, benevolence, generosity, goodwill, humanism, humanitarianism, philanthropy; beneficence, benignancy

near ant callousness, indifference, unconcern; cruelty, harshness; animosity, antipathy, dislike, hatred, hostility

ant coldheartedness, hard-heartedness, inhumanity, mercilessness, pitilessness

2 a thing or place that is of greatest importance to an activity or interest — see CENTER 1

3 strength of mind to carry on in spite of danger — see COURAGE

4 the central part or aspect of something under consideration — see CRUX

5 the seat of one's deepest thoughts and emotions — see CORE 1

heartache *n* deep sadness especially for the loss of someone or something loved — see SORROW

heartbreak *n* deep sadness especially for the loss of someone or something loved — see SORROW

heartbreaking *adj* 1 causing unhappiness — see SAD 2

2 of a kind to cause great distress — see REGRETTABLE

3 deserving of one's pity — see PATHETIC 1

heartbroken *adj* 1 feeling unhappiness — see SAD 1

2 expressing or suggesting mourning — see MOURNFUL 1

hearten *vb* to fill with courage or strength of purpose — see ENCOURAGE 1

heartening *adj* 1 having qualities which inspire hope — see HOPEFUL 1

2 making one feel good inside — see HEARTWARMING

3 pointing toward a happy outcome — see FAVORABLE 1

hearth *n* the place where one lives — see HOME 1

hearthstone *n* the place where one lives — see HOME 1

heartily *adv* 1 in a cheerful or happy manner — see GAILY 1

2 to a full extent or degree — see FULLY 1

heartiness *n* the condition of being sound in body — see HEALTH 1

heartless *adj* 1 having or showing a lack of sympathy or tender feelings — see HARD 1

2 having or showing the desire to inflict severe pain and suffering on others — see CRUEL 1

heartlessness *n* disposition to willfully inflict pain and suffering on others — see CRUELTY

heartrending *adj* 1 causing unhappiness — see SAD 2

2 hard to accept or bear especially emotionally — see BITTER 2

3 of a kind to cause great distress — see REGRETTABLE

4 deserving of one's pity — see PATHETIC 1

heartsick *adj* feeling unhappiness — see SAD 1

heartsickness *n* a state or spell of low spirits — see SADNESS

heartsore *adj* feeling unhappiness — see SAD 1

heartstrings *n pl* 1 general emotional condition — see FEELING 2

2 the seat of one's deepest thoughts and emotions — see CORE 1

heartwarming *adj* making one feel good inside ⟨Sarah was deeply touched by the *heartwarming* welcome she received from her relatives in Israel.⟩

syn cheering, comforting, encouraging, fulfilling, gladdening, gratifying, heartening, rewarding, satisfying

---

syn synonym(s)   **rel** related words
ant antonym(s)   **near ant** near antonym(s)

rel affecting, inspiring, inspiriting, moving, poignant, stirring, touching; edifying, elevating, uplifting; sympathetic, tender; kind, kindly, loving, warm; animating, enlivening, exciting, exhilarating, invigorating, rousing, stimulating, thrilling; pleasing, pleasurable, welcoming

near ant cheerless, disappointing, disgruntling, displeasing, dissatisfying, heartbreaking, heartrending, saddening; discomforting, disconcerting, dismaying, distressing, disturbing, upsetting; cold, unfeeling, unfriendly, unkind, unloving, unpleasant

ant demoralizing, depressing, discouraging, disheartening, dispiriting

hearty *adj* **1** characterized by unqualified enthusiasm ⟨Their decision to marry at long last has the whole family's *hearty* approval.⟩

syn wholehearted

rel single-minded; ardent, avid, eager, enthusiastic, excited, exuberant, fervent, gung ho, impassioned, keen, mettlesome, passionate, raring, vehement, warm, zealous; animated, energetic, lively, spirited, vigorous; absolute, bona fide, earnest, genuine, sincere, unaffected, undisguised

near ant apathetic, disinterested, dispassionate, indifferent, uninterested; lackadaisical, listless, perfunctory, spiritless, uneager, unenthusiastic, unexcited; equivocal, hesitant, qualified, tentative, uncertain; delayed, dilatory, doubtful, hedging, hesitating; forced, reluctant, resistant, reticent, unwilling

ant grudging, halfhearted, lukewarm, tepid
2 enjoying health and vigor — see HEALTHY 1
3 having or showing kindly feeling and sincere interest — see FRIENDLY 1
4 not showing weakness or uncertainty — see FIRM 1

hearty *n* one who operates or navigates a seagoing vessel — see SAILOR

heat *n* **1** depth of feeling — see ARDOR 1
2 *slang* a body of officers of the law — see POLICE 2

heat *vb* **1** to cause to have or give off heat to a moderate degree — see WARM 1

heated *adj* **1** being in a state of increased activity or agitation — see FEVERISH 1
2 having or giving off heat to a moderate degree — see WARM 1

heathen *adj* not civilized — see UNCIVILIZED

heathen *n* **1** a person who does not worship the God of the Bible ⟨a belief held by *heathens*⟩

syn gentile, idolater (*or* idolator), pagan

rel atheist, nonbeliever, unbeliever; neopagan, polytheist

near ant Christian, Jew, Muslim
2 an uncivilized person ⟨considered the people to be *heathens*⟩

syn barbarian

rel Neanderthal, primitive

heathenish *adj* not civilized — see UNCIVILIZED

heave *vb* **1** to lift with effort ⟨I *heaved* my duffel bag into the bus's overhead compartment.⟩

syn boost, heft, hoist, jack (up)

rel elevate, hike, pick up, raise, rear, up, uplift, upraise, uprear

near ant depress, drop, lower; sink, submerge, submerse
2 to discharge the contents of the stomach through the mouth — see VOMIT
3 to move from a lower to a higher place or position — see RAISE 1
4 to send through the air especially with a quick forward motion of the arm — see THROW 1
5 to breathe hard, quickly, or with difficulty — see GASP

heaven *n* **1** a dwelling place of perfect happiness for the soul after death ⟨We prayed that the souls of the deceased would go to *heaven*.⟩

syn above, bliss, Elysium, kingdom come, paradise, sky

rel glory, promised land, Valhalla; afterlife, afterworld, hereafter, otherworld

phrases on high

near ant inferno; limbo, purgatory; hades, netherworld, underworld; abyss, pit

ant hell, Pandemonium, perdition
2 an often imaginary place or state of utter perfection and happiness — see PARADISE 1
3 a state of overwhelming usually pleasurable emotion — see ECSTASY
4 *usually* heavens *pl* the expanse of air surrounding the earth — see SKY 1

heavenly *adj* **1** of the very best kind — see EXCELLENT
2 of, relating to, or being God — see HOLY 3
3 of, relating to, or suggesting heaven — see CELESTIAL
4 giving pleasure or contentment to the mind or senses — see PLEASANT 1

heavily *adv* to a great degree — see VERY 1

heaviness *n* **1** the amount that something weighs — see WEIGHT 1
2 the state or quality of being heavy — see WEIGHTINESS 1

heavy *adj* **1** having great weight ⟨This trunk full of books is much too *heavy* for one person to lift.⟩

syn hefty, massive, ponderous, weighty

rel burdensome, leaden, lumpish; bulky, elephantine, massy, outsize (*also* outsized), voluminous; overweight, topheavy; solid, substantial; ultraheavy

near ant airy, ethereal, feathery, fluffy, gossamer, gossamery; flimsy, insubstantial, slight; lightweight, undersized (*also* undersize), underweight

ant light, weightless
2 causing weariness, restlessness, or lack of interest — see BORING
3 containing much seasoning, fat, or sugar — see RICH 2
4 covered over by clouds — see OVERCAST
5 difficult to endure — see HARSH 1
6 extreme in degree, power, or effect — see INTENSE 1
7 having a matter of importance as its topic — see SERIOUS 2
8 requiring considerable physical or mental effort — see HARD 2
9 having great power or influence — see IMPORTANT 2
10 containing unborn young within the body — see PREGNANT 1

heavy *n* **1** a mean, evil, or unprincipled person — see VILLAIN

2 one of high position or importance within a group — see BIG SHOT

heavy–handed *adj* **1** given to exacting standards of discipline and self-restraint — see SEVERE 1

2 lacking or showing a lack of nimbleness in using one's hands — see CLUMSY 1

heavyset *adj* being compact and broad in build and often short in stature — see STOCKY

heckle *vb* to attack repeatedly with mean put-downs or insults — see TEASE 2

heckler *n* a person who causes repeated emotional pain, distress, or annoyance to another — see TORMENTOR

hectic *adj* being in a state of increased activity or agitation — see FEVERISH 1

hectically *adv* in a confused and reckless manner — see HELTER-SKELTER 1

hector *n* a person who teases, threatens, or hurts more vulnerable persons — see BULLY

hector *vb* to make timid or fearful by or as if by threats — see INTIMIDATE

hedge *n* a physical object that blocks the way — see BARRIER

hedge *vb* **1** to avoid giving a definite answer or position — see EQUIVOCATE

2 to close or shut in by or as if by barriers — see ENCLOSE 1

heed *n* **1** a state of being aware — see ATTENTION 2

2 strict attentiveness to what one is doing — see CARE 1

heed *vb* **1** to take notice of and be guided by ⟨If we had *heeded* the ranger's advice, we might not have gotten lost.⟩

syn follow, listen (to), mind, note, observe, regard, watch

rel consider, contemplate, mull, ponder, weigh; comply (with), conform (to), keep, obey, respect; attend (to), hark (to), hear, hearken (to); mark, notice, see

near brush (aside *or* off), discount, dismiss, gloss (over), gloze (over), neglect, pass over, pooh-pooh (*also* pooh), scorn, shrug off; defy, flout; slight, snub

ant disregard, ignore, tune out

2 to pay attention especially through the act of hearing — see LISTEN

heedful *adj* having or showing a close attentiveness to avoiding danger or trouble — see CAREFUL 1

heedfulness *n* **1** a close attentiveness to avoiding danger — see CAUTION 1

2 strict attentiveness to what one is doing — see CARE 1

heedless *adj* not paying or showing close attention especially for the purpose of avoiding trouble — see CARELESS 1

heedlessness *n* failure to take the care that a cautious person usually takes — see NEGLIGENCE 1

heel *n* a person whose behavior is offensive to others — see JERK 1

heel *vb* to set or cause to be at an angle — see LEAN 1

heft *n* **1** the amount that something weighs — see WEIGHT 1

2 the power to direct the thinking or behavior of others usually indirectly — see INFLUENCE 1

heft *vb* **1** to lift with effort — see HEAVE 1

2 to move from a lower to a higher place or position — see RAISE 1

heftiness *n* **1** the quality or state of being large in size — see LARGENESS

2 the state or quality of being heavy — see WEIGHTINESS 1

hefty *adj* **1** having great weight — see HEAVY 1

2 of a size greater than average of its kind — see LARGE

3 strongly and heavily built — see ¹HUSKY 1

height *n* **1** the highest part or point ⟨Many regard the painting of the Sistine Chapel as the *height* of Michelangelo's career.⟩

syn acme, apex, climax, crest, crown, culmination, head, high noon, high-water mark, meridian, noon, noontime, peak, pinnacle, summit, tip-top, top, zenith

rel bloom, blossom, flood tide, flower, glory, heyday, prime; cap, ceiling, roof; extreme, extremity, tip, vertex; high, highlight, highspot

near ant abyss, base, foot; minimum

ant bottom, rock bottom

2 the most extreme or advanced point ⟨the *height* of arrogance⟩

syn depth, elevation, extremity, limit

rel consummation, epitome, quintessence, ultimate

3 the distance of something or someone from bottom to top ⟨The average *height* of the players on the volleyball team is well over six feet.⟩

syn altitude, elevation, inches, stature

rel rise; highness, loftiness, tallness

4 an area of high ground ⟨Gulliver, standing on a *height* near the shore, saw an island suspended above the sea.⟩

syn altitude(s), elevation, eminence, highland, hill, hump, mound, prominence, rise, upland

rel alp, mount, mountain, peak; butte, mesa, plateau, table, tableland; bluff, cliff, crag, precipice, steep, tor; ridge, sierra; sugarloaf; foothill, hillock, hummock, knob, knoll

near ant dale, dell, depression, dingle, glen, hollow, vale, valley; basin, bottom, bottomland, fen, flat, floodplain, plain, tidewater

ant lowland

5 the most intense or characteristic phase of something — see THICK

heighten *vb* **1** to make markedly greater in measure or degree — see INTENSIFY

2 to move from a lower to a higher place or position — see RAISE 1

heightened *adj* being at a higher level than average — see HIGH 3

heinousness *n* the state or quality of being utterly evil — see ENORMITY 1

heir *n* a person who has the right to inherit property ⟨Upon his death, Mr. Parkworth's property was divided evenly among his *heirs*, four sons and three daughters.⟩

syn inheritor, legatee

rel claimant; heir apparent, representative, succeeder, successor; coheir, coheir-

---

syn synonym(s)   *rel* related words
ant antonym(s)   *near ant* near antonym(s)

ess, heiress; beneficiary, devisee, grantee; descendant (*also* descendent), scion

heist *n* an instance of theft — see THEFT 2

heist *vb* to take (something) without right and with an intent to keep — see STEAL 1

helical *adj* turning around an axis like the thread of a screw — see SPIRAL

hell *n* 1 the place of punishment for the wicked after death ⟨condemned to *hell* for their sins⟩

syn Pandemonium, perdition

rel blazes, inferno; purgatory; hades, netherworld, shades, Tartarus, underworld; Sheol; abyss, pit; fire and brimstone, hellfire

near ant glory, promised land, Valhalla

ant bliss, elysian fields, Elysium, empyrean, heaven, kingdom come, paradise, sky

2 a situation or state that causes great suffering and unhappiness ⟨Pulling weeds under the hot summer sun was *hell*.⟩

syn agony, horror, misery, murder, nightmare, torment, torture

rel affliction, calvary, cross, curse, ordeal, trial, tribulation; calamity, misfortune, tragedy; gall, thorn; bummer, downer, drag

near ant delight, diversion, entertainment, fun, joy, pleasure, recreation; lark, picnic, riot

ant heaven, paradise

3 a state in which everything is out of order — see CHAOS

hell-bent (on *or* **upon)** *adj* fully committed to achieving a goal — see DETERMINED 1

hellion *n* an appealingly mischievous person — see SCAMP 1

hello *n* an expression of goodwill upon meeting ⟨We said our *hellos* and got right down to business.⟩

syn greeting, salutation, salute, welcome

rel ave, hail; amenities, civilities, pleasantries; regards, respects, wishes

ant adieu, bon voyage, farewell, Godspeed, good-bye (*or* good-by)

helm *n* the place of leadership or command — see HEAD 2

helm *vb* to operate or control the course of — see NAVIGATE 1

help *n* 1 an act or instance of helping ⟨I could use your *help* getting this tire back on the car.⟩

syn abetment, aid, assist, assistance, backing, boost, hand, lift, support

rel advancement, encouragement, facilitation, forwarding, furtherance, furthering, nurturance; benefaction, promotion; advice, care, counsel, guidance, mentoring; attendance, attention, hand-holding; assuagement, palliation, relief, succor

near ant constraint, frustration, inhibition, interference, obstruction, repression, restraint; deterrence, discouragement

ant hindrance

2 a thing that helps ⟨The blender is a great *help* for making smoothies.⟩

syn advantage, aid, benefit, boon

rel hand, lift, pick-me-up; support; blessing, godsend, windfall; recourse, refuge, resort, resource

near ant constraint, inhibitor, liability, obstacle, obstruction, restraint, stranglehold

ant disadvantage, drawback, encumbrance, hindrance, impediment, minus

3 a body of persons at work or available for work — see FORCE 1

help *vb* 1 to provide (someone) with what is useful or necessary to achieve an end ⟨We offered to *help* her when she moved into an apartment.⟩

syn abet, aid, assist, back, prop (up), support

rel advance, ease, facilitate, forward, foster, further, launch; champion, endorse (*also* indorse), patronize, promote, sponsor; attend, care (for), comfort, minister (to), succor; sustain; bolster, boost, buttress; advise, counsel, guide, mentor, nurture; bail out, deliver, rescue, save; embolden, encourage, hearten; benefit, favor, oblige, profit, serve

phrases bear a hand, to stand one in good stead

near ant balk, bar, block, constrain, hamper, handicap, hold back, impede, inhibit, obstruct, restrain, strangle; baffle, foil, frustrate, inconvenience, interfere, oppose, sabotage, thwart; desert, disappoint, fail, let down; discourage, dishearten; repress, retard, stifle, straiten, stunt; damage, harm, hurt, injure

ant hinder

2 to make more bearable or less severe ⟨The new ointment didn't *help* Josh's sunburn one bit.⟩

syn allay, alleviate, assuage, ease, mitigate, mollify, palliate, relieve, soothe

rel abate, lighten, moderate, soften, temper; cure, heal, remedy; amend, correct, emend, fix, mend, rectify, reform, repair; ameliorate, better, enhance, enrich, improve, meliorate, perfect, refine

near ant harm, hurt, impair, injure; heighten, intensify, sharpen

ant aggravate

3 to keep from happening by taking action in advance — see PREVENT

4 to provide with something useful or desirable — see BENEFIT

5 to make better — see IMPROVE

helper *n* a person who helps a more skilled person ⟨Over the summer Chris worked as a carpenter's *helper*.⟩

syn adjunct, adjutant, aid, aide, apprentice, assistant, coadjutor, deputy, helpmate, helpmeet, sidekick

rel attendant, servant; auxiliary, legman, subordinate, underling; employee (*also* employe), hand, help, hireling, laborer, worker; man Friday, right hand; aide-de-camp

helpful *adj* 1 providing service or assistance ⟨a website that I've always found to be *helpful* for finding information on common medical problems⟩

syn useful

rel advantageous, beneficial, efficacious, favorable, productive, profitable, salutary; accommodating, obliging

near ant ineffective, ineffectual; adverse, disadvantageous, inconvenient, profitless, unfavorable

ant unhelpful, useless

2 promoting or contributing to personal or social well-being — see BENEFICIAL

helpless *adj* 1 lacking protection from

danger or resistance against attack ⟨After the storm we found a *helpless* baby bird that had fallen out of its nest.⟩
syn defenseless, exposed, susceptible, undefended, unguarded, unprotected, unresistant, vulnerable
rel indefensible, untenable; uncovered, unsafe; overcome, preyed (on *or* upon); disarmed, passive, resistless, unarmed; feeble, frail, weak; abandoned, marooned
phrases in the lurch
near ant defensible; covered, fortified, safe, screened, secure, sheltered; armed, armored; immune, impenetrable, impregnable, invincible, strong, unassailable, unbeatable, unconquerable; almighty, omnipotent
ant guarded, invulnerable, protected, resistant, shielded
2 unable to act or achieve one's purpose — see POWERLESS

helpmate *n* a person who helps a more skilled person — see HELPER

helpmeet *n* a person who helps a more skilled person — see HELPER

helter–skelter *adj* **1** acting or done with excessive or careless speed — see HASTY 1
2 lacking a definite plan, purpose, or pattern — see RANDOM

helter–skelter *adv* **1** in a confused and reckless manner ⟨The sheep ran *helter-skelter* inside their pen when the coyote appeared in their midst.⟩
syn amok (*or* amuck), berserk, frantically, frenziedly, harum-scarum, hectically, madly, pell-mell, wild, wildly
rel agitatedly, confusedly, crazily, feverishly, haywire, skittishly, uncontrollably; heedlessly, hotheadedly, recklessly, wantonly; chaotically, riotously, tumultuously, turbulently; aimlessly, haphazard, haphazardly, hit-or-miss, topsy-turvy
near ant calmly, composedly, coolly (*also* cooly), imperturbably, peacefully, placidly, self-composedly, self-possessedly, serenely, unconcernedly; meekly, mildly, passively, tamely; methodically, orderly
2 without definite aim, direction, rule, or method — see HIT OR MISS

helter–skelter *n* a state of noisy, confused activity — see COMMOTION

hem *n* the line or relatively narrow space that marks the outer limit of something — see BORDER 1

hence *adv* **1** for this or that reason — see THEREFORE
2 from this or that place — see AWAY

henceforth *adv* from this point on ⟨*Henceforth*, there will be no more prolonged coffee breaks.⟩
syn henceforward, hereafter
rel afterward (*or* afterwards), later, subsequently; hereupon, thereupon

henceforward *adv* from this point on — see HENCEFORTH

henpeck *vb* to subject (someone) to constant scoldings and sharp reminders — see NAG 1

herald *n* **1** a person who actively supports or favors a cause — see EXPONENT 1

2 one that announces or indicates the later arrival of another — see FORERUNNER 1

herald *vb* **1** to give a slight indication of beforehand — see FORESHADOW
2 to make known openly or publicly — see ANNOUNCE

herbage *n* green leaves or plants — see GREENERY

herculean *adj* **1** requiring considerable physical or mental effort — see HARD 2
2 unusually large — see HUGE

herd *n* **1** a group of domestic animals assembled or herded together ⟨the great *herds* of cattle that cowboys once drove across the plains⟩
syn drove, flock
rel colony, covey, gaggle, pack, pod, school, swarm
2 the body of the community as contrasted with the elite — see MASS 1
3 a great number of persons or creatures massed together — see CROWD 1

herd *vb* to urge, push, or force onward — see DRIVE 1

herder *n* a tender of livestock ⟨The nomadic reindeer *herders* of Siberia live in reindeer-skin tents.⟩
syn herdsman
rel buckaroo (*also* buckeroo), cowboy, cowgirl, cowhand, cowherd, cowman, cowpoke, cowpuncher, gaucho, ranchero, vaquero; sheepherder, shepherd, shepherdess; goatherd; swineherd; wrangler; drover

herdsman *n* a tender of livestock — see HERDER

hereafter *adv* from this point on — see HENCEFORTH

hereafter *n* **1** time that is to come — see FUTURE 1
2 unending existence after death — see ETERNITY 2

hereditary *adj* genetically passed or capable of being passed from parent to offspring ⟨Eye and hair color are *hereditary*.⟩
syn genetic (*also* genetical), heritable, inborn, inheritable, inherited
rel congenital, inbred, inherent, innate, native, natural
near ant acquired
ant nonhereditary

heresy *n* departure from a generally accepted theory, opinion, or practice ⟨the *heresy* of asserting that Shakespeare was not a great writer⟩
syn dissent, dissidence, heterodoxy, nonconformity
rel error, fallacy, falsehood, misbelief, misconception, myth; apostasy, defection, infidelity, schism, separatism; deviance, iconoclasm, unconventionality; disagreement, discord, dissension (*also* dissention)
near ant agreement, conformation, conventionality
ant conformity, orthodoxy

heretic *n* **1** a person who believes, teaches, or advocates something opposed to accepted beliefs ⟨Galileo was condemned as a *heretic* for supporting Copernicus's thesis that the earth revolves around the sun and not vice versa.⟩
syn dissenter, dissident, nonconformist
rel apostate, defector, renegade; schismat-

ic, sectarian, separationist, separatist; disbeliever, infidel, misbeliever, unbeliever; bohemian, individualist

ant conformer, conformist

2 a person who does not conform to generally accepted standards or customs — see NONCONFORMIST 1

heretical *also* **heretic** *adj* deviating from commonly accepted beliefs or practices ⟨It would be *heretical* to suggest changing the long-standing company policy.⟩

syn dissenting, dissident, heterodox, maverick, nonconformist, nonorthodox, outthere, unconventional, unorthodox

rel free-spirited, freethinking, nontraditional; apostate, defecting, renegade; schismatic (*also* schismatical), sectarian, separatist

ant conforming, conformist, conventional, orthodox

heretofore *adv* up to this or that time — see HITHERTO

heritable *adj* genetically passed or capable of being passed from parent to offspring — see HEREDITARY

heritage *n* **1** an inherited or established way of thinking, feeling, or doing — see TRADITION 1

2 something that is or may be inherited — see INHERITANCE

hermit *n* a person who lives away from others — see RECLUSE

hermitage *n* **1** a place where a person goes to hide or to avoid others — see HIDEOUT

2 a residence for men under religious vows — see MONASTERY

hero *n* a large sandwich on a long split roll — see SUBMARINE

heroic *also* **heroical** *adj* **1** feeling or displaying no fear by temperament — see BRAVE 1

2 large and impressive in size, grandeur, extent, or conception — see GRAND 1

3 unusually large — see HUGE

heroically *adv* in a manner befitting a person of the highest character and ideals — see GREATLY 1

heroism *n* strength of mind to carry on in spite of danger — see COURAGE

hesitance *n* **1** a lack of willingness or desire to do or accept something — see RELUCTANCE

2 a state or an instance of temporary inaction because of uncertainty about the right course of action — see HESITATION

hesitancy *n* **1** a lack of willingness or desire to do or accept something — see RELUCTANCE

2 a state or an instance of temporary inaction because of uncertainty about the right course of action — see HESITATION

hesitant *adj* slow to begin or proceed with a course of action because of doubts or uncertainty ⟨He was *hesitant* about committing himself to the oversight of the project, which he knew would be long and difficult.⟩

syn cagey (*also* cagy), disinclined, dubious, indisposed, loath (*also* loth *or* loathe), reluctant, reticent

rel uneager, unenthusiastic; averse, unwilling; doubtful, faltering, halting, indecisive, infirm, irresolute, questioning, skep-

tical, uncertain, undecided, unsure, vacillating, wobbly (*also* wabbly); fainthearted, shy, timid

near ant eager, enthusiastic, glad, happy, keen; ready, willing; certain, decided, determined, resolute, sure, unquestioning

ant disposed, inclined

hesitate *vb* to show uncertainty about the right course of action ⟨I didn't *hesitate* to tell them that what they were doing was wrong and that I wanted no part of it.⟩

syn balance, dither, falter, halt, hang back, scruple, shilly-shally, stagger, teeter, vacillate, waver, wobble (*also* wabble)

rel haw, hem; dally, dawdle, dilly, linger, pause, procrastinate, wait; back down, chicken (out); consider, debate, deliberate, ponder, weigh; oscillate, sway; equivocate, hedge, pussyfoot

near ant decide; budge, stir; advance, continue

ant dive (in), plunge (in)

hesitation *n* a state or an instance of temporary inaction because of uncertainty about the right course of action ⟨Because of one moment's *hesitation*, I missed getting the picture of the elusive butterfly.⟩

syn faltering, hesitance, hesitancy, indecision, irresolution, pause, shilly-shally, shilly-shallying, vacillation, wavering, wobbling (*also* wabbling)

rel delay, hawing, procrastination, waiting; misgiving, second thought; consideration, debate, deliberation, doubt, incertitude, indecisiveness, indetermination, uncertainness, uncertainty; avoidance, equivocation; aversion, disinclination, indisposition, reluctance, unwillingness; faintheartedness, shyness, timidity, timidness

near ant certainty, certitude, confidence, decisiveness, determination, firmness, resoluteness, resolution, sureness; alacrity, eagerness, readiness

heterodox *adj* **1** deviating from commonly accepted beliefs or practices — see HERETICAL

2 not rigidly following established form, custom, or rules — see INFORMAL 1

heterodoxy *n* departure from a generally accepted theory, opinion, or practice — see HERESY

heterogeneous *adj* consisting of many things of different sorts — see MISCELLANEOUS

heterogeneousness *n* the quality or state of being composed of many different elements or types — see VARIETY 1

het up *adj* feeling or showing uncomfortable feelings of uncertainty — see NERVOUS 1

hew *vb* **1** to bring down by cutting — see FELL 2

2 to hold to something firmly as if by adhesion — see STICK 1

hew (to) *vb* to give steadfast support to — see ADHERE (TO) 1

hex *n* **1** a woman believed to have often harmful supernatural powers — see WITCH 1

2 something that brings bad luck — see JINX

3 a spoken word or set of words believed to have magic power — see SPELL 1

hex *vb* to cast a spell on — see BEWITCH 1

heyday *n* a state or time of great activity, thriving, or achievement — see BLOOM 1

hiatus *n* **1** an open space in a barrier (as a wall or hedge) — see GAP 1

2 an incomplete or deficient area — see GAP 3

3 a break in continuity — see GAP 2

hick *n* an awkward or simple person especially from a small town or the country ⟨I felt like a *hick* when I visited the city for the first time.⟩

syn bumpkin, churl, clodhopper, countryman, hillbilly, provincial, rustic, yokel

rel boor, clod, clown, gawk, lout, oaf; greenhorn, tenderfoot; backwoodsman, mountaineer

near ant slicker, smoothy (*or* smoothie); metropolitan, suburbanite, urbanite

ant cosmopolitan, sophisticate

hide *n* **1** the outer covering of an animal removed for its commercial value ⟨Seal *hides* are used by Inuits to make footwear, boats, shelters, bags, and clothing.⟩

syn fur, leather, pelt, skin

rel badger, beaver, chamois, chinchilla, ermine, fox, marten, mink, muskrat, otter, Persian lamb, rabbit, raccoon (*also* racoon), sable, seal; bearskin, buckskin, calfskin, coonskin, cowhide, deerskin, doeskin, goatskin, horsehide, kidskin, lambskin, pigskin, rawhide, sealskin, sharkskin, sheep, sheepskin, snakeskin; fleece, mouton; alligator, crocodile

2 the hairless natural covering of an animal prepared for use — see LEATHER 1

¹**hide** *vb* **1** to put into a hiding place ⟨The thief had *hidden* the stolen jewelry under the floorboards.⟩

syn bury, cache, conceal, ensconce, secrete

rel hoard, squirrel (away), stash; entomb, inter

near ant bare, expose, reveal, show, uncover, unmask, unveil, unwrap; flaunt, parade, show off; disinter, unearth

ant disclose, exhibit

2 to keep secret or shut off from view ⟨He tried to *hide* his criminal past.⟩ ⟨She *hid* the cat's litter box behind a screen.⟩

syn belie, blanket, blot out, cloak, conceal, cover, curtain, disguise, enshroud, mask, obscure, occult, screen, shroud, suppress, veil

rel bury, camouflage, cover (up); smother; gild, gloss (over), varnish, whitewash; becloud, bedim, befog, block, cloud, darken, eclipse, obstruct, occlude, overcast, overshadow, shade

near ant present; clarify, illuminate; advertise, air, broadcast, get out, proclaim, publicize, publish, spread

ant bare, disclose, display, divulge, expose, reveal, show, uncloak, uncover, unmask, unveil

3 to remain out of sight ⟨He *hid* in the closet during the game of hide-and-seek.⟩

syn lie, lurk, repose, skulk

rel slink, sneak; avoid, elude, evade

phrases lie low, sit tight

near ant come out, materialize, show up, turn up

ant appear

²**hide** *vb* **1** to strike repeatedly — see BEAT 1

2 to strike repeatedly with something long and thin or flexible — see WHIP 1

hideaway *n* a place where a person goes to hide or to avoid others — see HIDEOUT

hidebound *adj* tending to favor established ideas, conditions, or institutions — see CONSERVATIVE 1

hideous *adj* **1** causing intense displeasure, disgust, or resentment — see OFFENSIVE 1

2 extremely disturbing or repellent — see HORRIBLE 1

3 unpleasant to look at — see UGLY 1

hideousness *n* **1** the quality of inspiring intense dread or dismay — see HORROR 1

2 the state or quality of being utterly evil — see ENORMITY 1

hideout *n* a place where a person goes to hide or to avoid others ⟨Police found the stolen jewels under the floorboards in the thief's *hideout*, a cabin deep in the woods.⟩

syn concealment, covert, den, hermitage, hideaway, lair, nest

rel blind, cover, nook, recess; hangout, harbor, harborage, haunt, haven, refuge, retreat, shelter

hiding *n* the placing of something out of sight — see CONCEALMENT 1

hie *vb* to proceed or move quickly — see HURRY 2

higgledy–piggledy *adj* lacking in order, neatness, and often cleanliness — see MESSY

high *adj* **1** extending to a great distance upward ⟨Mount Everest is the *highest* mountain in the world.⟩

syn lofty, tall, towering

rel dominant, dominating, eminent, prominent; elevated, lifted, raised, uplifted, upswept; high-rise, statuesque

near ant flat, stubby, stumpy

ant low, low-lying, short, squat

2 being at a higher level than average ⟨Gasoline prices are *high* right now.⟩ ⟨a *high* fever⟩ ⟨people with *high* incomes⟩

syn elevated, escalated, heightened, increased, jacked (up), raised, up

rel extreme, full, maximized, maximum, peaked, sky-high, utmost; over, overfilled, overflowing, overfull, overlarge, overloaded, oversize (*or* oversized)

near ant decreased, depressed, dropped, receded, under

ant down, low

3 located at a greater height than average or usual ⟨an eagle's nest *high* on the cliff⟩ ⟨an old house with *high* ceilings⟩

syn airy, elevated

rel ascendant (*also* ascendent), ascending, soaring; overhead, overlooking, raised, upheld, uplifted, upraised; topmost, upmost, upper, uppermost, upward

near ant depressed, descendant (*also* descendent), descending, down, dropped, fallen, grounded, lowered, sunken; abreast, even, level

ant low, low-lying

4 being far along in development — see ADVANCED

5 commanding a large price — see COSTLY

6 having, characterized by, or arising from a dignified and generous nature — see NOBLE 2

7 highest in rank or authority — see HEAD

---

syn synonym(s) *rel* related words

ant antonym(s) *near ant* near antonym(s)

high *adv* in a luxurious manner ⟨After he had made a fortune, Philip lived pretty *high*.⟩
syn expensively, extravagantly, grandly, large, lavishly, luxuriously, opulently, palatially, richly, sumptuously
rel imposingly, impressively, magnificently, splendidly; grandiosely, ostentatiously, pompously, pretentiously; affluently, comfortably, fine, wealthily; immoderately, indulgently, intemperately, prodigally, wantonly, wastefully
near ant unpretentiously; cheaply, economically, frugally, inexpensively, meagerly, poorly, skimpily, sparely, sparingly, thriftily; conservatively, moderately, prudently, reasonably, restrainedly, sensibly, temperately
ant austerely, humbly, modestly, plainly, simply

high *n* 1 a state of overwhelming usually pleasurable emotion — see ECSTASY
2 the expanse of air surrounding the earth — see SKY 1

highborn *adj* of high birth, rank, or station — see NOBLE 1

highbrow *adj* much given to learning and thinking — see INTELLECTUAL 1

highbrow *n* a person with strong intellectual interests — see INTELLECTUAL

higher *adj* being far along in development — see ADVANCED

highest *adj* 1 being at a point or level higher than all others — see TOP 1
2 coming before all others in importance — see FOREMOST 1

highfalutin *also* **hifalutin** *adj* 1 full of fine words and fancy expressions — see FLOWERY 1
2 having a feeling of superiority that shows itself in an overbearing attitude — see ARROGANT
3 having or displaying feelings of scorn for what is regarded as beneath oneself — see PROUD 1
4 self-consciously trying to present an appearance of grandeur or importance — see PRETENTIOUS

high-flown *adj* 1 full of fine words and fancy expressions — see FLOWERY 1
2 very dignified in form, tone, or style — see ELEVATED 2

high-handed *adj* 1 having a feeling of superiority that shows itself in an overbearing attitude — see ARROGANT
2 having or showing a tendency to force one's will on others without any regard to fairness or necessity — see ARBITRARY 1

high-hat *adj* having a feeling of superiority that shows itself in an overbearing attitude — see ARROGANT

high-hat *vb* 1 to show contempt for — see SCORN 1
2 to deliberately ignore or treat rudely — see SNUB 1

high jinks *also* **hijinks** *n pl* wildly playful or mischievous behavior — see HORSEPLAY

highland *n* an area of high ground — see HEIGHT 4

highlight *vb* to indicate the importance of by centering attention on — see EMPHASIZE 1

highly *adv* 1 to a great degree — see VERY 1
2 to a large extent or degree — see GREATLY 2

high-minded *adj* 1 having, characterized by, or arising from a dignified and generous nature — see NOBLE 2
2 self-consciously trying to present an appearance of grandeur or importance — see PRETENTIOUS

high-mindedly *adv* in a manner befitting a person of the highest character and ideals — see GREATLY 1

high noon *n* 1 a state or time of great activity, thriving, or achievement — see BLOOM 1
2 the highest part or point — see HEIGHT 1
3 the middle of the day — see NOON 1

high-pitched *adj* having a high musical pitch or range — see SHRILL

high-pressure *adj* having or showing a bold forcefulness in the pursuit of a goal — see AGGRESSIVE 1

high-sounding *adj* full of fine words and fancy expressions — see FLOWERY 1

high-spirited *adj* 1 joyously unrestrained — see EXUBERANT
2 marked by a lively display of strong feeling — see SPIRITED 1

high-spiritedly *adv* in a quick and spirited manner — see GAILY 2

high-strung *adj* easily excited by nature — see EXCITABLE

high-water mark *n* the highest part or point — see HEIGHT 1

highway *n* a passage cleared for public vehicular travel — see WAY 1

hijack *also* **highjack** *vb* to take control of (a vehicle) by force — see COMMANDEER 1

hike *vb* 1 to travel by foot for exercise or pleasure ⟨She *hiked* along the trail around the pond.⟩
syn ramble, saunter, stroll, tramp, tromp
rel roam, rove, wander; peregrinate, traipse, traverse, trek, walk; march
2 to move from a lower to a higher place or position — see RAISE 1

hilarious *adj* causing or intended to cause laughter — see FUNNY 1

hilariousness *n* the amusing quality or element in something — see HUMOR 1

hilarity *n* a mood characterized by high spirits and amusement and often accompanied by laughter — see MIRTH 1

hill *n* 1 a quantity of things thrown or stacked on one another — see ¹PILE 1
2 an area of high ground — see HEIGHT 4
3 an upward slope — see ASCENT 2

hill *vb* to form into a pile or ridge of earth — see MOUND 1

hillbilly *n* an awkward or simple person especially from a small town or the country — see HICK

hind *adj* being at or in the part of something opposite the front part — see BACK

hinder *adj* being at or in the part of something opposite the front part — see BACK

hinder *vb* to create difficulty for the work or activity of — see HAMPER

hindmost *adj* 1 being at or in the part of something opposite the front part — see BACK
2 following all others of the same kind in order or time — see LAST 1

hindrance *n* something that makes movement or progress difficult — see ENCUMBRANCE

hinge *vb* to be determined by, based on, or subject (to) — see DEPEND 1

hint *n* **1** a slight or indirect pointing to something (as a solution or explanation) ⟨Can't you give me some *hint* as to where you're taking me?⟩

syn clue, cue, indication, inkling, intimation, lead, suggestion

rel breath, flicker, glimmer, glimpse, mention, scent, whiff, wind; hunch, idea, inspiration, notion; allusion, implication, inference; assistance, nod, prompt, tip, tip-off, wink; feeling, foreboding, intuition, premonition, presentiment, suspicion; augury, foreshadower, foretaste, harbinger, omen, portent, prefigurement, presage, symptom

near ant answer, solution

2 an almost imperceptible sign of something ⟨There was the slightest *hint* of impatience in her voice.⟩

syn breath, flicker, glimmer, suggestion, touch, trace, whiff

rel inkling, intimation, scent, wind; evidence, indication, mark, sign

near ant permeation, pervasion, saturation

3 a piece of advice or useful information especially from an expert — see ¹TIP 1

4 a very small amount — see PARTICLE 1

hint *vb* to convey an idea indirectly ⟨Fay kept *hinting* that she wouldn't mind an invitation to spend the weekend at their beach house.⟩

syn allude, imply, indicate, infer, insinuate, intimate, suggest

rel advert, mention, point, refer, signal, signalize, signify; smack (of), smell (of)

near ant announce, declare, proclaim; elucidate, explain, spell out; delineate, describe

hinterland *n* a rural region that forms the edge of the settled or developed part of a country — see FRONTIER 2

hip *adj* **1** being in the latest or current fashion — see STYLISH

2 having inside information — see WISE 2

hip *n* the quality or state of being fashionable — see COOL 2

hip *vb* to give information to — see ENLIGHTEN 1

hire *n* **1** the state of being provided with a paying job ⟨He spent most of his career in the *hire* of high-paying defense contractors.⟩

syn employ, employment, engagement

rel appointment, assignment, conscription, enlistment, recruitment; tenure; occupation, place, position, post, situation, work

near ant discharge, dismissal, firing, removal, sack, severance; suspension; furlough, layoff, leave, liberty, retirement

ant joblessness, nonemployment, unemployment

2 the money paid regularly to a person for labor or services — see WAGE

hire *vb* **1** to take or get the temporary use

of (something) for a set sum ⟨The Youngs *hired* a limousine for their daughter's wedding.⟩

syn charter, engage, lease, rent

rel sublease, sublet; arrange (for), bespeak, book, contract (for), order, reserve, sign up (for)

2 to provide with a paying job — see EMPLOY 1

hireling *n* one who works for another for wages or a salary — see EMPLOYEE

hirsute *adj* covered with or as if with hair — see HAIRY 1

hiss *n* **1** a sound similar to the speech sound \s\ stretched out ⟨the *hiss* of air escaping from a balloon⟩

syn fizz, sizzle, swish, whish, whiz (*or* whizz)

rel wheeze, whistle, whoosh, zip; sibilance, sibilant

2 a vocal sound made to express scorn or disapproval — see CATCALL

hiss *vb* to make a sound like that of stretching out the speech sound \s\ ⟨The frightened kitten *hissed* at us when we tried to pick it up.⟩

syn fizz, fizzle, sizzle, swish, whish, whiz (*or* whizz)

rel wheeze, whistle, whoosh, zip; bubble, effervesce; buzz, drone, hum

hissy fit *n* an outburst or display of excited anger — see TANTRUM

historian *n* a student or writer of history ⟨*Historians* are still trying to sort out fact from fiction in the story of Kateri Tekakwitha, the Lily of the Mohawks.⟩

syn chronicler

rel autobiographer, biographer; archivist, chronologist, genealogist, hagiographer

historical *adj* restricted to or based on fact — see FACTUAL 1

history *n* **1** an account of important events in the order in which they happened ⟨a *history* of the American Civil Rights Movement during the 1960s⟩

syn annals, chronicle, record

rel blog, commentary, journal, memoir, reminiscence(s); autobiography, biography, life; legend, narrative, saga, story, tale; archives, documentation, log, register, report; genealogy

2 a relating of events usually in the order in which they happened — see ACCOUNT 1

3 the events or experience of former times — see PAST

histrionic *adj* **1** given to or marked by attention-getting behavior suggestive of stage acting — see THEATRICAL 1

2 having the general quality or effect of a stage performance — see DRAMATIC 1

hit *n* **1** a person or thing that is successful ⟨The new babysitter turned out to be a *hit* with the kids.⟩

syn blockbuster, megahit, smash, success, winner

rel crackerjack (*also* crackajack), dandy, jim-dandy, pip, prizewinner; gem, jewel, treasure; marvel, natural, phenomenon, sensation, wonder; coup, triumph, victory

near ant disappointment, fizzle, lemon, loser

ant bomb, bummer, bust, catastrophe, debacle (*also* débâcle), dud, failure, fiasco, flop, misfire, turkey, washout

---

2 a hard strike with a part of the body or an instrument — see ¹BLOW

hit *vb* **1** to deliver a blow to (someone or something) usually in a strong vigorous manner ⟨A good carpenter *hits* a nail just two or three times to drive it in.⟩

syn bang, bash, bat, belt, bludgeon, bob, bop, box, bust, clap, clip, clobber, clock, clout, crack, hammer, knock, nail, paste, pound, punch, rap, slam, slap, slog, slug, smack, smite, sock, strike, swat, swipe, thump, thwack, wallop, whack, whale, zap *rel* batter, beat, buffet, bung, chop, cuff, drub, lace, lambaste (*or* lambast), lick, mangle, maul, pelt, pepper, pommel, pummel, rough; scuff; bunt, flick, stroke, tap; bump, butt, jab, kick, knee, poke, prod, push, shove, stamp; bowl (down *or* over), cream, deck, fell, floor, knock down, level; rabbit-punch, sucker punch; cane, club, cudgel, flail, flog, lash, sap, slash, sledge, sledgehammer, spear, stab, switch, thrash, whip; brain, conk, skull *phrases* hang one on

2 to come into usually forceful contact with something ⟨When she fell on the ice, she *hit* hard and badly bruised her elbow.⟩

syn bang, bash, bump, collide, crash, impact, impinge, knock, ram, slam, smash, strike, swipe, thud *rel* bounce, carom, clunk, glance, rebound, ricochet, skim, skip; contact, land, touch; brush, graze, kiss, nudge, scrape, shave, sweep; bulldoze, muscle, press, push *near ant* miss, skirt

3 to obtain (as a goal) through effort — see ACHIEVE 1

hit (on *or* **upon)** *vb* to come upon after searching, study, or effort — see FIND 1

hit (upon) *vb* to come upon unexpectedly or by chance — see HAPPEN (ON *or* UPON)

hitch *n* **1** a danger or difficulty that is hidden or not easily recognized — see PITFALL 1

2 a fixed period of time during which a person holds a job or position — see TERM 1

hitch *vb* **1** to move or cause to move with a sharp quick motion — see JERK 1

2 to put or bring together so as to form a new and longer whole — see CONNECT 1

3 to put securely in place or in a desired position — see FASTEN 2

4 to travel by securing free rides — see HITCHHIKE

hitcher *n* one who hitchhikes — see HITCHHIKER

hitchhike *vb* to travel by securing free rides ⟨a novel in which the hero undertakes a journey of self-discovery by *hitchhiking* around the country⟩ *syn* hitch, thumb *rel* bum; stow away

hitchhiker *n* one who hitchhikes ⟨*hitchhikers* whose car had broken down⟩ *syn* hitcher *rel* stowaway

hither *adj* being the less far of two — see NEAR 1

hitherto *adv* up to this or that time ⟨At the talent show Kyle revealed his *hitherto* unknown gift for doing impressions.⟩ *syn* heretofore, theretofore, yet

rel before, previously *phrases* so far, thus far *near ant* afterward (*or* afterwards), later, subsequently; hereupon, thereupon *ant* henceforth, henceforward, hereafter, thenceforth, thenceforward (*also* thenceforwards), thereafter

hit-or-miss *adj* lacking a definite plan, purpose, or pattern — see RANDOM

hit or miss *adv* without definite aim, direction, rule, or method ⟨I was learning Spanish *hit or miss*, mostly just by hearing my friends speak it.⟩

syn aimlessly, anyhow, anyway, anywise, desultorily, erratically, haphazard, haphazardly, helter-skelter, irregularly, randomly, willy-nilly *rel* arbitrarily, capriciously, carelessly, casually, indiscriminately, informally, offhand, offhandedly, promiscuously, whimsically; accidentally, fortuitously, inadvertently, unconsciously, unintentionally, unwittingly; disconnectedly, disjointedly, fitfully, intermittently, spottily, unpredictably; higgledy-piggledy, topsy-turvy *phrases* at random *near ant* carefully, formally, gingerly, meticulously, orderly, punctiliously; deliberately, intentionally, purposefully, purposely *ant* methodically

hoagie *also* **hoagy** *n* a large sandwich on a long split roll — see SUBMARINE

hoar *adj* dating or surviving from the distant past — see ANCIENT 1

hoar *n* a covering of tiny ice crystals on a cold surface — see FROST 1

hoard *n* **1** a supply stored up and often hidden away ⟨Dan keeps a *hoard* of empty yogurt containers in his basement workshop for storing whatnots.⟩ *syn* cache, stash, stockpile, store *rel* coffers, deposit, funds, nest egg, savings, sinking fund, treasure; inventory, pool, reserve, stock; provisions, resources; accumulation, assemblage, collection, gathering, harvest; repertory

2 a collection of things kept available for future use or need — see STORE 1

hoard *vb* to put (something of future use or value) in a safe or secret place ⟨He's been *hoarding* empty yogurt containers all winter, with the intention of using them to start seedlings in the spring.⟩ *syn* cache, lay away, lay up, put by, salt away, squirrel (away), stash, stockpile, store, stow, treasure *rel* accumulate, acquire, amass, assemble, collect, concentrate, garner, gather, pick up, round up, scrape (together); heap, pile, stack; conserve, husband, preserve; bank, coffer, deposit, hold, keep, reserve, retain, save, stock, withhold; bury, conceal, ensconce, secrete *phrases* set aside *near ant* cast, discard, ditch, dump, fling (off *or* away), jettison, throw away, throw out, unload; consume, squander, use up, waste; hand over, relinquish, surrender; blow, dissipate, fritter (away), lavish, misspend, run through, spend; deplete, exhaust, expend, impoverish; dispel, disperse, dissipate, scatter

hoarfrost *n* a covering of tiny ice crystals on a cold surface — see FROST 1

hoarse *adj* harsh and dry in sound ⟨The thirsty man spoke in a *hoarse* whisper.⟩
syn coarse, croaking, grating, gravel, gravelly, gruff, husky, rasping, raspy, scratchy, throaty
rel growling, growly, guttural; cacophonous, discordant, grinding, jarring, rough, scraping, scratching; cawing, raucous, screeching, strident; choked, cracked, strained, strangled; dissonant, inharmonious, unmelodious, unmusical
near ant gentle, gliding, golden, liquid, mellifluent, mellifluous, mellow, soothing, sweet, tender; satiny, silken, smooth, soft, velvety; euphonious, lyric, lyrical, melodic, melodious, musical

hoary *adj* dating or surviving from the distant past — see ANCIENT 1

hoax *n* an imitation that is passed off as genuine — see FAKE 1

hoax *vb* to cause to believe what is untrue — see DECEIVE

hoaxer *n* 1 a dishonest person who uses clever means to cheat others out of something of value — see TRICKSTER 1
2 one who makes false claims of identity or expertise — see IMPOSTOR

hob *n* playful, reckless behavior that is not intended to cause serious harm — see MISCHIEF 1

hobble *vb* 1 to create difficulty for the work or activity of — see HAMPER
2 to walk while favoring one leg — see LIMP 1

hobgoblin *n* 1 an imaginary being usually having a small human form and magical powers — see FAIRY
2 something or someone that causes fear or dread especially without reason — see BOGEY 1

hobnob *vb* 1 to come or be together as friends — see ASSOCIATE 1
2 to take part in social activities — see SOCIALIZE

hobnobber *n* a person frequently seen in the company of another — see ASSOCIATE 1

hobo *n* a homeless wanderer who may beg or steal for a living — see TRAMP

hock *vb* to leave as a guarantee of repayment of a loan — see PAWN

hodgepodge *n* an unorganized collection or mixture of various things — see MISCELLANY 1

hog *n* one who eats greedily or too much — see GLUTTON

hoggish *adj* having a huge appetite — see VORACIOUS 1

hogshead *n* an enclosed wooden vessel for holding beverages — see CASK

hog-tie *vb* to create difficulty for the work or activity of — see HAMPER

hogwash *n* language, behavior, or ideas that are absurd and contrary to good sense — see NONSENSE 1

hoist *vb* 1 to lift with effort — see HEAVE 1
2 to move from a lower to a higher place or position — see RAISE 1
3 to swallow in liquid form — see DRINK 1

hold *n* 1 the act or manner of holding ⟨Make sure you have a firm *hold* on the chain saw before you turn it on.⟩
syn clasp, clench, grapple, grasp, grip
rel anchorage, purchase; grab, seizure; foothold, footing, toehold; clinch, embrace, hug
near ant release, relinquishment
2 a structure or place from which one can resist attack — see FORT
3 the right or means to command or control others — see POWER 1
4 the state or fact of being able to exchange information regarding one's current situation — see TOUCH 1
5 the knowledge gained from the process of coming to know or understand something — see COMPREHENSION

hold *vb* 1 to have or keep in one's hands ⟨This casserole dish is too hot to *hold*, so grab a potholder.⟩
syn clench, cling (to), clutch, grip
rel bear, carry; bag, capture, catch, collar, corral, grab, grapple, hook, land, latch (on or onto), nab, nail, seize, snap (up), snare, snatch, take, trap; feel, handle, paw; clasp, embrace, grasp, hug; cradle
phrases hang on to, hold on to
near ant drop, give, hand, unclasp, unhand; cede, deliver, give up, hand over, release, relinquish, render, turn over, yield
2 to continue to have in one's possession or power — see KEEP 2
3 to have as an opinion — see BELIEVE 2
4 to have within — see CONTAIN 1
5 to keep in one's mind or heart — see HARBOR 1
6 to keep, control, or experience as one's own — see HAVE 1
7 to make or have room for — see ACCOMMODATE 1
8 to reach for and take hold of by embracing with the fingers or arms — see TAKE 1
9 to think of in a particular way — see CONSIDER 1
10 to keep from exceeding a desirable degree or level (as of expression) — see CONTROL 1
11 to point or turn (something) toward a target or goal — see AIM 1

hold back *vb* 1 to create difficulty for the work or activity of — see HAMPER
2 to refrain from openly showing or uttering — see SUPPRESS 2

holder *n* 1 one who has a legal or rightful claim to ownership — see PROPRIETOR
2 something into which a liquid or smaller objects can be put for storage or transportation — see CONTAINER

holding *n* 1 a decision made by a court or tribunal regarding a case it has heard — see SENTENCE
2 *usually* **holdings** *pl* transportable items that one owns — see POSSESSION 2

holding pattern *n* 1 a state of temporary inactivity — see ABEYANCE
2 an instance or period of being prevented from going about one's business — see DELAY

hold off (on) *vb* to assign to a later time — see POSTPONE

hold on *vb* 1 to remain indefinitely in existence or in the same state — see CONTINUE 1

2 to remain in place in readiness or expectation of something — see WAIT

hold out vb to continue to operate or to meet one's needs ⟨We hoped our supply of firewood would *hold out* until power was restored.⟩ ⟨Luckily, the old outboard motor *held out* till we made it to shore.⟩

syn hold up, keep up, last, prevail, survive

rel carry on, cope, endure, fare, get along, get by, get on, go, hang in, make out, manage, persevere; abide, continue, draw out, hang on, hold on, linger, persist, remain, run on, stretch

near ant break, break down, collapse, conk (out), crash, cut out, die, expire, stall, stop; run down, wane

ant fail, fizzle, give out, peter (out), run out

holdup n an instance or period of being prevented from going about one's business — see DELAY

hold up vb 1 to assign to a later time — see POSTPONE

2 to bring (something) to a standstill — see ¹HALT 1

3 to create difficulty for the work or activity of — see HAMPER

4 to continue to operate or to meet one's needs — see HOLD OUT

5 to remain indefinitely in existence or in the same state — see CONTINUE 1

6 to withstand scrutiny and gain acceptance or approval — see WASH 2

hole n 1 a place in a surface allowing passage into or through a thing ⟨Line up the pegs on section A with the *holes* in section B and press the two together.⟩

syn aperture, opening, orifice, perforation

rel loophole; breach, break, chink, cleft, crack, cranny, crevice, cut, fissure, gash, notch, rent, rift, rupture, slash, slit, split, tear; space; exit, mouth, outlet, pore, vent; entrance, inlet; pinhole, pinprick, punch, puncture; airhole, armhole, buttonhole, keyhole, knothole, peephole, pothole, wormhole

near ant fill, filler, filling, patch, plug, seal, stopper; barrier, blockage, obstacle, obstruction

2 a sunken area forming a separate space ⟨Dig a *hole* big enough to plant the tree.⟩

syn cavity, concavity, dent, depression, dint, hollow, indentation, pit, recess

rel burrow, cave, cavern, ditch, excavation, furrow, groove, gutter, trench, trough; basin, bowl, valley; alcove, cleft, niche, nook, opening, recess, socket; alveolus, dimple, gouge, impression, imprint, notch, pocket; borehole, chuckhole, crater, posthole, pothole, sinkhole, wallow, water hole, well; abyss, chasm, gulf, vacuity, vacuum, void

near ant hill, mound, rise; bump, bunch, hump, lump, swell, swelling, tumor

ant bulge, jut, projection, protrusion, protuberance

3 a difficult, puzzling, or embarrassing situation from which there is no easy escape — see PREDICAMENT

4 a dirty or messy place — see PIGPEN

5 an open space in a barrier (as a wall or hedge) — see GAP 1

6 the shelter or resting place of a wild animal — see DEN 1

7 an incomplete or deficient area — see GAP 3

hole vb to make a hole or series of holes in — see PERFORATE

holiness n the quality or state of being spiritually pure or virtuous ⟨Known throughout the world for his *holiness*, the prophet was visited daily by hundreds of pilgrims.⟩

syn blessedness, devoutness, godliness, piety, piousness, sainthood, saintliness, saintship, sanctity

rel asceticism, devotion, morality, prayerfulness, religiousness; priestliness; goodness, rectitude, righteousness, uprightness, virtue, virtuousness; consecration, sacredness

near ant blasphemousness, irreverence, sacrilegiousness; depravedness, depravity, evilness, heinousness, monstrosity, sinfulness, vileness, wickedness; hypocrisy, sanctimoniousness, sanctimony

ant godlessness, impiety, ungodliness, unholiness

holler n 1 a loud vocal expression of strong emotion — see SHOUT

2 an expression of dissatisfaction, pain, or resentment — see COMPLAINT 1

holler vb 1 to express dissatisfaction, pain, or resentment usually tiresomely — see COMPLAIN

2 to speak so as to be heard at a distance — see CALL 1

hollow adj curved inward ⟨There's a noticeably *hollow* spot in the mattress where he has been sleeping.⟩

syn concave, dented, depressed, indented, recessed, sunken

rel alveolar, cavernous, crescentic, cuplike, cupped, cuppy, recurved; dimpled, pockmarked; compressed, condensed, contracted, diminished, reduced

near ant ballooning, blown up, bulbous, enlarged, expanded, extended, jutting, projecting, puffy, risen; domed, global, round, rounded, spherical

ant bulging, cambered, convex, protruding, protrusive, protuberant

hollow n 1 a sunken area forming a separate space — see HOLE 2

2 an area of lowland between hills or mountains — see VALLEY

holocaust n 1 a destructive burning — see FIRE 1

2 the killing of a large number of people — see MASSACRE

holy adj 1 showing a devotion to God and to a life of virtue ⟨The *holy* monk spent many hours on his knees in prayer.⟩

syn devout, godly, pious, religious, sainted, saintly

rel ascetic (*also* ascetical), prayerful, reverent, reverential, spiritual, worshipful; pietistic, religiose; beatified, blessed (*also* blest), canonized, venerable; angelic (*or* angelical), cherubic; chaste, moral, pure, righteous, upright, virtuous

near ant blasphemous, desecrating, irreverent, profane, sacrilegious; nonreligious, secular, unspiritual, worldly; backsliding, unfaithful; evil, immoral, iniquitous, miscreant, sinful, sinning, unrighteous, wicked *ant* antireligious, faithless, godless, impious, irreligious, ungodly, unholy

2 set apart or worthy of veneration by association with God ⟨The Torah contains the *holy* writings of Judaism.⟩

syn blessed (*also* blest), consecrate, consecrated, hallowed, sacred, sacrosanct, sanctified

rel adored, enshrined, glorified, revered, venerated, worshipped (*also* worshiped); ceremonial, liturgical, priestly, religious, ritual, sacramental, spiritual; biblical, scriptural

near ant earthly, mundane, profane, secular, temporal, worldly

ant deconsecrated, desacralized, unconsecrated, unhallowed

3 of, relating to, or being God ⟨a *holy* relic⟩

syn blessed (*also* blest), divine, godlike, godly, heavenly, sacred, supernatural

rel eternal, everlasting, immortal; all-powerful, almighty, omnipotent, omniscient, supreme

near ant human, mortal, natural

4 not to be violated, criticized, or tampered with — see SACRED 1

Holy Writ *n* a book made up of the writings accepted by Christians as coming from God — see BIBLE

homage *n* **1** a formal expression of praise — see ENCOMIUM

2 public acknowledgment or admiration for an achievement — see GLORY 1

hombre *n* an adult male human being — see MAN 1

home *n* **1** the place where one lives ⟨As we entered his 34-room mansion, our host playfully exclaimed, "Welcome to our humble *home*!"⟩

syn abode, diggings, domicile, dwelling, fireside, habitation, hearth, hearthstone, house, lodging, pad, place, quarters, residence, roof

rel accommodations, housing, nest, shelter; bungalow, cabin, casita, chalet, cottage; duplex, ranch, ranch house, saltbox, split level, townhome, town house, tract house, triplex; apartment, apartment house, condominium, flat, tenement, tenement house, walk-up; penthouse, salon, suite; barracks, billet, boardinghouse, dorm, dormitory, lodging house, lodgment (*or* lodgement), room(s), rooming house; castle, château, countryseat, estate, hall, manor, manor house, mansion, palace, villa; farmhouse, grange, hacienda, homestead; hermitage, parsonage, rectory, vicarage; hovel, hut, hutch, shack, shanty

2 the place where a plant or animal is usually or naturally found ⟨the American South, the *home* of the armadillo⟩

syn habitat, niche, range, territory

rel element, environment, environs, haunt, locality, milieu, neighborhood, setting, surroundings

3 the land of one's birth, residence, or citizenship — see COUNTRY 1

4 those who live as a family in one house — see HOUSEHOLD

5 a place of origin — see BIRTHPLACE

homeland *n* the land of one's birth, residence, or citizenship — see COUNTRY 1

homely *adj* unpleasant to look at — see UGLY 1

homesteader *n* a person who settles in a new region — see FRONTIERSMAN

homicidal *adj* eager for or marked by the shedding of blood, extreme violence, or killing — see BLOODTHIRSTY

homicide *n* **1** the taking of another person's life ⟨the victim of a *homicide*⟩

syn blood, foul play, murder, slaying

rel manslaughter; bloodshed, butchery, carnage, decimation, destruction, massacre, slaughter; assassination, execution, hit; euthanasia, mercy killing; filicide, fratricide, matricide, parricide, patricide, regicide, uxoricide

2 a person who kills another person — see ASSASSIN

homily *n* **1** a public speech usually by a member of the clergy for the purpose of giving moral guidance or uplift — see SERMON

2 an idea or expression that has been used by many people — see COMMONPLACE

homogenize *vb* **1** to make agree with a single established standard or model — see STANDARDIZE

2 to turn into a single mass or entity that is more or less the same throughout — see BLEND 1

Homo sapiens *n* the human race — see MANKIND

hone *vb* **1** to make sharp or sharper — see SHARPEN

2 to make smooth by friction — see GRIND 1

honed *adj* having an edge thin enough to cut or pierce something — see SHARP 1

honest *adj* **1** being in the habit of telling the truth — see TRUTHFUL

2 conforming to a high standard of morality or virtue — see GOOD 2

3 following the accepted rules of moral conduct — see HONORABLE 1

4 free from any intent to deceive or impress others — see GUILELESS

5 free in expressing one's true feelings and opinions — see FRANK

6 guided by or in accordance with one's sense of right and wrong — see CONSCIENTIOUS 1

7 being exactly as appears or as claimed — see AUTHENTIC 1

honestly *adv* to tell the truth — see ACTUALLY 1

honesty *n* **1** devotion to telling the truth ⟨George Washington has gone down in history for his *honesty*.⟩

syn integrity, probity, truthfulness, veracity, verity

rel honor, honorableness, incorruptibility, rectitude, righteousness, right-mindedness, scrupulosity, scrupulousness, uprightness; artlessness, candidness, candor, forthrightness, frankness, good faith, guilelessness, ingenuousness, sincerity, straightforwardness; dependability, reliability, reliableness, trustiness, trustworthiness; accuracy, objectivity; authenticity, correctness, genuineness, truth; credibility

near ant artifice, crookedness, dissembling, dissimulation, double-dealing, duplicity,

---

fakery, falseness, falsity, fraudulentness, hypocrisy, insincerity, two-facedness; beguilement, craftiness, cunning, furtiveness, guile, indirection, insidiousness, oiliness, perfidy, slickness, slipperiness, slyness, smoothness, treacherousness, trickery, underhandedness, unscrupulousness, wiliness; equivocation, prevarication; exaggeration, inaccuracy

ant deceit, deceitfulness, dishonesty, lying, mendacity, untruthfulness

2 conduct that conforms to an accepted standard of right and wrong — see MORALITY 1

3 faithfulness to high moral standards — see HONOR 1

4 the free expression of one's true feelings and opinions — see CANDOR 1

honey *n* **1** a lovely woman — see BEAUTY 2

2 something very good of its kind — see JIM-DANDY

3 a person with whom one is in love — see SWEETHEART

honey *vb* to praise too much — see FLATTER 1

honor *n* **1** faithfulness to high moral standards ⟨The mayor, a man of *honor*, never broke a promise to the voters.⟩

syn honesty, integrity, probity, rectitude, righteousness, uprightness

rel blamelessness, character, conscientiousness, decency, fairness, high-mindedness, incorruptibility, justice, morality, nobility, reputability, respectability, right-mindedness, scrupulousness, virtue, virtuousness

near ant corruptibility, corruption, corruptness, debasement, debauchery, decadence, degeneracy, degradation, depravity, disgrace, disgracefulness, disreputableness, dissipatedness, dissipation, dissoluteness, perversion, pervertedness, profligacy, shamelessness, venality; criminality, crookedness, dishonesty, immorality, unrighteousness, unscrupulousness; meanness, reprehensibleness, rottenness, sinfulness, vileness, villainy, wickedness, wretchedness

ant baseness, dishonor, lowness

2 an asset that brings praise or renown — see GLORY 2

3 public acknowledgment or admiration for an achievement — see GLORY 1

4 something given in recognition of achievement — see AWARD 1

5 something granted as a special favor — see PRIVILEGE

honor *vb* to show appreciation, respect, or affection for (someone) with a public celebration ⟨The newlyweds were *honored* with a dinner given by the bride's grandmother.⟩

syn fete (*or* fête), recognize

rel acknowledge, cite, commend, compliment, credit, thank; extol (*also* extoll), glorify, laud, praise, tout; acclaim, applaud, cheer, hail, salute; celebrate, commemorate, memorialize, observe; congratulate, felicitate

near ant discredit, disgrace, dishonor, humble, humiliate, shame; bad-mouth, defame, libel, malign, slander; boo, hiss, hoot, jeer; censure, condemn, damn, denounce, reprobate; mock, put down, ridicule, slight

honorable *adj* **1** following the accepted rules of moral conduct ⟨The only *honorable* thing to do is to admit that you were wrong and apologize.⟩

syn decent, ethical, honest, just, noble, principled, respectable, righteous, upright, upstanding

rel blameless, guiltless, irreproachable, unassailable, unimpeachable; chivalrous, high-minded, right-minded; conscientious, fair, good, incorruptible, moral, reputable, respected, scrupulous, uncorrupted, virtuous

near ant bad, corrupt, criminal, crooked, evil, immoral, iniquitous, knavish, mean, nefarious, rascally, reprehensible, roguish, rotten, scoundrelly, sinful; unscrupulous, vile, villainous, wicked, wretched; blamable, blameworthy, censurable, culpable; debased, debauched, decadent, degenerate, degraded, demoralized, depraved, disgraceful, disreputable, dissipated, dissolute, libertine, perverse, perverted, profligate, reprobate, shameful, venal

ant base, dishonest, dishonorable, ignoble, low, unethical, unjust, unprincipled, unrighteous, unworthy

2 conforming to a high standard of morality or virtue — see GOOD 2

3 guided by or in accordance with one's sense of right and wrong — see CONSCIENTIOUS 1

honorably *adv* in a manner befitting a person of the highest character and ideals — see GREATLY 1

¹hood *n* a violent, brutal person who is often a member of an organized gang — see HOODLUM

²hood *n* something that covers or conceals like a piece of cloth — see CLOAK 1

hoodlum *n* a violent, brutal person who is often a member of an organized gang ⟨A couple of *hoodlums* held up the convenience store.⟩

syn gangster, goon, hood, hooligan, mobster, punk, roughneck, rowdy, ruffian, tough

rel cutthroat, scoundrel, villain; assassin, bandit, bravo, brigand, criminal, crook, desperado, felon, gunman, highwayman, lawbreaker, mafioso, malefactor, offender, outlaw, perp, perpetrator, pirate; pickpocket, racketeer, robber, swindler, thief, vandal

hoodwink *vb* to cause to believe what is untrue — see DECEIVE

hoof (it) *vb* **1** to go on foot — see WALK 1

2 to perform a series of usually rhythmic bodily movements to music — see DANCE 1

hook *n* a hard strike with a part of the body or an instrument — see ¹BLOW

hook *vb* **1** to cause to turn away from a straight line — see BEND 1

2 to put or bring together so as to form a new and longer whole — see CONNECT 1

3 to take (something) without right and with an intent to keep — see STEAL 1

4 to take physical control or possession of (something) suddenly or forcibly — see CATCH 1

5 to turn away from a straight line or course — see CURVE 1

hookup *n* the state of having shared interests or efforts (as in social or business matters) — see ASSOCIATION 1

hooligan *n* a violent, brutal person who is often a member of an organized gang — see HOODLUM

hoop *n* a circular strip — see ¹RING 2

hoosegow *n* a place of confinement for persons held in lawful custody — see JAIL

hoot *n* **1** a loud vocal expression of strong emotion — see SHOUT

2 a vocal sound made to express scorn or disapproval — see CATCALL

3 the smallest amount or part imaginable — see JOT

4 someone or something that is very funny — see SCREAM

hop *n* **1** a social gathering for dancing — see DANCE

2 an act of leaping into the air — see JUMP 1

hop *vb* **1** to move with a light springing step — see SKIP 1

2 to propel oneself upward or forward into the air — see JUMP 1

hope (for) *vb* to believe in the future occurrence of (something) — see EXPECT

hopeful *adj* **1** having qualities which inspire hope ⟨Economists are offering a *hopeful* forecast for a healthy economy in the coming year.⟩

syn auspicious, bright, encouraging, fair, golden, heartening, likely, optimistic, promising, propitious, rose-colored, rosy, upbeat

rel cheering, comforting, reassuring, soothing; assured, confident, decisive, doubtless, positive, sure, unhesitating; beamish, bullish; favorable, good

near ant cheerless, comfortless; doubtful, dubious, uncertain; bearish, grim, negative, unfavorable; funereal, glum, gray (*also* grey), miserable, wretched

ant bleak, dark, depressing, discouraging, disheartening, dismal, dreary, gloomy, hopeless, inauspicious, pessimistic, unencouraging, unlikely, unpromising, unpropitious

2 pointing toward a happy outcome — see FAVORABLE 2

hopeful *n* one who seeks an office, honor, position, or award — see CANDIDATE

hopeless *adj* **1** not capable of being cured or reformed ⟨a *hopeless* optimist who looked for the good in everyone and everything⟩

syn incorrigible, incurable, irrecoverable, irredeemable, irremediable, irretrievable, unrecoverable, unredeemable

rel irreparable, irreversible, uncorrectable; unencouraging, unpromising; impenitent, unreformed, unregenerate, unrepentant

near ant reversible; encouraging, promising; penitent, regretful, remorseful, repentant, rueful, sorry; correctable, fixable, rectifiable, repairable, reparable, salvable, salvageable

ant curable, reclaimable, recoverable, reformable, remediable, retrievable, savable (*or* saveable)

2 emphasizing or expecting the worst — see PESSIMISTIC 1

3 incapable of being solved or accomplished — see IMPOSSIBLE 1

4 feeling or showing no hope — see DESPONDENT 1

hopelessness *n* utter loss of hope — see DESPAIR 1

horde *n* a great number of persons or creatures massed together — see CROWD 1

horn *n* something shaped like a hollow cone and used as a container — see CORNET

horrendous *adj* **1** causing fear — see FEARFUL 1

2 causing intense displeasure, disgust, or resentment — see OFFENSIVE 1

3 extremely disturbing or repellent — see HORRIBLE 1

horrible *adj* **1** extremely disturbing or repellent ⟨a *horrible* car accident⟩

syn appalling, atrocious, awful, dreadful, frightful, ghastly, grisly, gruesome (*also* grewsome), hideous, horrendous, horrid, horrifying, lurid, macabre, monstrous, nightmare, nightmarish, shocking, terrible, terrific

rel alarming, bloodcurdling, dire, direful, fearful, fearsome, forbidding, formidable, frightening, gut-wrenching, hair-raising, intimidating, redoubtable, scary, terrifying; abhorrent, deplorable, disagreeable, distasteful, loathsome, nauseating, noisome, obnoxious, obscene, offensive, repugnant, repulsive, revolting, sickening; abominable, evil, foul, heinous, noxious, odious, unspeakable, vile; grotesque, ugly, unsightly

near ant agreeable, appealing, attractive, delectable, delicious, delightful, enjoyable, enticing, inviting, pleasant, pleasing, pleasurable, satisfying, welcome; cheering, comforting, soothing

2 causing fear — see FEARFUL 1

3 causing intense displeasure, disgust, or resentment — see OFFENSIVE 1

4 extremely unsatisfactory — see WRETCHED 1

horrid *adj* **1** causing intense displeasure, disgust, or resentment — see OFFENSIVE 1

2 extremely disturbing or repellent — see HORRIBLE 1

horridness *n* the quality of inspiring intense dread or dismay — see HORROR 1

horrified *adj* filled with fear or dread — see AFRAID

horrify *vb* to strike with fear — see FRIGHTEN

horrifying *adj* **1** causing fear — see FEARFUL 1

2 extremely disturbing or repellent — see HORRIBLE 1

horror *n* **1** the quality of inspiring intense dread or dismay ⟨It's difficult to even begin to comprehend the *horror* of the Holocaust.⟩

syn atrociousness, atrocity, awfulness, dreadfulness, frightfulness, ghastliness, grisliness, gruesomeness, hideousness, horridness, monstrosity, repulsiveness

rel badness, baseness, depravedness, depravity, diabolicalness, evil, evilness, foulness, heinousness, immorality, iniquity, invidiousness, sinfulness, ungodliness, viciousness, vileness, wickedness; deplorableness, despicableness, detestableness, execrableness, hatefulness, loathsomeness, reprehensibleness; creepiness, eeriness, fearfulness, fearsomeness, ghoulishness, scariness; agony, anguish, hellishness, misery, torment, torture

near ant agreeableness, delightfulness, pleasantness, pleasurableness; allurement, appeal, attraction, attractiveness

2 a situation or state that causes great suffering and unhappiness — see HELL 2

3 something unpleasant to look at — see EYESORE

4 the emotion experienced in the presence or threat of danger — see FEAR 1

5 a dislike so strong as to cause stomach upset or queasiness — see DISGUST

horse *n* a large hoofed domestic animal that is used for carrying or drawing loads and for riding ⟨The mounted police stable their *horses* in the city park.⟩

syn equine, nag, steed

rel colt, foal, gelding, mare, stallion; bronco, mustang, pony; charger, courser, galloper, hackney, mount, packhorse, prancer, quarter horse, racehorse, saddle horse, trotter, workhorse; bay, black, buckskin, dun, palomino, pinto, roan, skewbald, sorrel; cob, dobbin, jade, skate

horse around *vb* to engage in attention-getting playful or boisterous behavior — see CUT UP

horselaugh *n* an explosive sound that is a sign of amusement — see LAUGH 1

horseplay *n* wildly playful or mischievous behavior ⟨When he saw us spraying each other with the hose instead of washing the car, Dad yelled, "Cut out the *horseplay*!"⟩

syn clowning, foolery, high jinks (*also* hijinks), horsing around, monkeying, roughhouse, roughhousing, skylarking, tomfoolery

rel childishness, clownishness, foolishness, funning, jesting, joking, nonsense, silliness, waggery; boisterousness, rambunctiousness, rowdiness, rowdyism, devilry (*or* deviltry), impishness, knavery, mischief, mischievousness, prankishness, rascality, roguishness, trickery; cavorting, frivolity, frolicking, gamboling (*or* gambolling), merrymaking, playfulness, revelry, roistering, romping, sporting, sportiveness

horse sense *n* the ability to make intelligent decisions especially in everyday matters — see COMMON SENSE

horse–trade *vb* to talk over or dispute the terms of a purchase — see BARGAIN 1

horsewhip *vb* to strike repeatedly with something long and thin or flexible — see WHIP 1

horsing around *n* wildly playful or mischievous behavior — see HORSEPLAY

hose *n* a close-fitting covering for the foot and leg — see STOCKING

hospice *n* a place that provides rooms and usually a public dining room for overnight guests — see HOTEL

hospitable *adj* showing a natural kindness and courtesy especially in social situations — see GRACIOUS 1

host *n* **1** a great number of persons or creatures massed together — see CROWD 1

2 a large body of men and women organized for land warfare — see ARMY 1

hostel *n* a place that provides rooms and usually a public dining room for overnight guests — see HOTEL

hostelry *n* a place that provides rooms and usually a public dining room for overnight guests — see HOTEL

hostile *adj* **1** marked by opposition or ill will ⟨Her suggestions were given a *hostile* reception.⟩

syn adversary, antagonistic, antipathetic, inhospitable, inimical, jaundiced, mortal, negative, unfriendly, unsympathetic

rel adverse, argumentative, bellicose, belligerent, clashing, combative, conflicting, contentious, contrary, disputatious, militant, opposed, pugnacious, quarrelsome, resisting, scrappy, truculent; antisocial, cold, cool, disagreeable, disapproving, distant, frigid, icy; biased, prejudiced; acrimonious, bitter, despiteful, hateful, malevolent, malicious, malign, malignant, opprobrious, rancorous, spiteful, unloving, vindictive, virulent

near ant affable, amiable, amicable, civil, companionable, comradely, convivial, cordial, genial, good-natured, good-tempered, gracious, gregarious, neighborly, pleasant, sociable, social, warm; affectionate, devoted, kind, kindly, loving, nice, sweet; accepting, agreeable, approving, benign, empathetic, favorable, understanding, warmhearted, welcoming

ant friendly, hospitable, nonantagonistic, nonhostile, sympathetic

2 opposed to one's interests — see ADVERSE 1

hostile *n* one that is hostile toward another — see ENEMY

hostility *n* **1** a deep-seated ill will — see ENMITY

2 hostilities *pl* a state of armed violent struggle between states, nations, or groups — see WAR 1

hot *adj* **1** having a notably high temperature ⟨The casserole, just out of the oven, was too *hot* to eat.⟩

syn ardent, broiling, burning, fervent, fervid, fiery, piping hot, red, red-hot, roasting, scalding, scorching, searing, sultry, superheated, sweltering, torrid

rel blazing, glowing, seething, sizzling; heated, overheated, reheated, warmed; snug, toasty, warm; feverish, flushed, inflamed (*also* enflamed); muggy, steamy, summerlike, summery, tropical

near ant chill, chilly, cool, coolish, nippy, snappy; blizzardly, frosty, snowy, subfreezing, subzero, wintry (*also* wintery); chilled, cooled, refrigerated, unheated; benumbed, numb

ant arctic, bitter, cold, freezing, frigid, frozen, glacial, ice-cold, iced, icy

2 being or involving the latest methods, concepts, information, or styles — see MODERN

3 enjoying widespread favor or approval — see POPULAR 1

4 marked by bursts of destructive force or intense activity — see VIOLENT 1

5 showing urgent desire or interest — see EAGER

6 feeling or showing anger — see ANGRY

7 moving, proceeding, or acting with great speed — see FAST 1

8 of the very best kind — see EXCELLENT

hot *adv* with great speed — see FAST 1

hot air *n* **1** boastful speech or writing — see BOMBAST 1

2 language that is impressive-sounding but not meaningful or sincere — see RHETORIC 1

hot-blooded *adj* having or expressing great depth of feeling — see FERVENT 1

hotcake *n* a flat cake made from thin batter and cooked on both sides (as on a griddle) — see PANCAKE

hotchpotch *n* an unorganized collection or mixture of various things — see MISCELLANY 1

hotel *n* a place that provides rooms and usually a public dining room for overnight guests ⟨For their 50th anniversary they stayed at one of the finest *hotels* in San Francisco.⟩

syn hospice, hostel, hostelry, inn, lodge, public house, tavern

rel B and B, bed-and-breakfast, guesthouse; apartment hotel; accommodations, lodgings, rest; court, motel, motor court, motor inn, motor lodge, resort, spa, tourist court, youth hostel; camp, campground; bunkhouse, dorm, dormitory; boardinghouse, lodging house, rooming house

hotfoot *adv* with excessive or careless speed — see HASTILY 1

hotfoot (it) *vb* to proceed or move quickly — see HURRY 2

hothouse *n* a glass-enclosed building for growing plants — see CONSERVATORY

hotness *n* the state of enjoying widespread approval — see POPULARITY

hotshot *n* a person with a high level of knowledge or skill in a field — see EXPERT

hot war *n* a state of armed violent struggle between states, nations, or groups — see WAR 1

hound *n* **1** a domestic mammal that is related to the wolves and foxes — see DOG 1

2 a person with a strong and habitual liking for something — see FAN

3 a mean, evil, or unprincipled person — see VILLAIN

hound *vb* **1** to go after or on the track of — see FOLLOW 2

2 to subject (someone) to constant scoldings and sharp reminders — see NAG 1

hounding *n* the act of going after or in the tracks of another — see PURSUIT

house *n* **1** a commercial or industrial activity or organization — see ENTERPRISE 1

2 a group of persons who come from the same ancestor — see FAMILY 1

3 the place where one lives — see HOME 1

4 those who live as a family in one house — see HOUSEHOLD

5 the shelter or resting place of a wild animal — see DEN 1

house *vb* to provide with living quarters or shelter ⟨Some of the freshmen were temporarily *housed* in local motels while the new dorm was being finished.⟩

syn accommodate, bestow, billet, bivouac, board, bunk, camp, chamber, domicile, encamp, harbor, lodge, put up, quarter, roof, room, shelter, take in

rel ensconce, home, roost, secure, shed, stable, tent; barrack; bed (down)

near ant eject, evict

2 to close or shut in by or as if by barriers — see ENCLOSE 1

house cat *n* a small domestic animal known for catching mice — see CAT

household *adj* **1** of or relating to a household or family — see DOMESTIC 1

2 often observed or encountered — see COMMON 1

household *n* those who live as a family in one house ⟨a *household* that consists of a mom, two kids, and a grandmother⟩

syn extended family, home, house, ménage

rel blood, folks, kin, kindred, kinfolk (*or* kinfolks), kinsfolk, kith; brood; nuclear family; clan, community

housekeeper *n* a person hired to perform household or personal services — see MAID 1

housemaid *n* a person hired to perform household or personal services — see MAID 1

housing *n* something that encloses another thing especially to protect it — see [1]CASE 1

hovel *n* a small, simply constructed, and often temporary dwelling — see SHACK

hover *vb* to rest or move along the surface of a liquid or in the air — see FLOAT 1

hover (over) *vb* to remain poised to inflict harm, danger, or distress on — see THREATEN

howbeit *adv* in spite of that — see HOWEVER

howbeit *conj* in spite of the fact that — see ALTHOUGH

however *adv* in spite of that ⟨I'm all out of eggs; *however*, I can still make us a nice breakfast.⟩

syn howbeit, nevertheless, nonetheless, notwithstanding, still, though, withal, yet

rel after all, anyhow, regardless

phrases all the same (*or* just the same), at the same time

howl *n* **1** a crying out in grief — see LAMENT 1

2 a loud vocal expression of strong emotion — see SHOUT

3 a violent shouting — see CLAMOR 1

howl *vb* **1** to make a long loud mournful sound ⟨Several coyotes began *howling* close by as the sun went down.⟩ ⟨The wind *howled* on the open plain.⟩

syn bay, keen, wail, yowl

rel bawl, scream, screech, shriek, shrill, squall, squeal, yell, yelp

2 to cry out loudly and emotionally — see SCREAM 1

hub *n* a thing or place that is of greatest importance to an activity or interest — see CENTER 1

hubbub *n* **1** a state of noisy, confused activity — see COMMOTION

2 a violent shouting — see CLAMOR 1

huckster *n* one who sells things outdoors — see PEDDLER

huddle *n* **1** a coming together of a number

---

syn synonym(s)   *rel* related words
ant antonym(s)   *near ant* near antonym(s)

of persons for a specified purpose — see MEETING 1

2 a number of things considered as a unit — see GROUP 1

3 a usually small number of persons considered as a unit — see GROUP 2

huddle *vb* **1** to gather into a closely packed group — see ²PRESS 3

2 to lie low with the limbs close to the body — see CROUCH

hue *n* a property that becomes apparent when light falls on an object and by which things that are identical in form can be distinguished — see COLOR 1

hue and cry *n* a violent shouting — see CLAMOR 1

huff *n* **1** a state of nervous or irritated concern — see FRET

2 an outburst or display of excited anger — see TANTRUM

3 the feeling of being offended or resentful after a slight or indignity — see PIQUE

huff *vb* to talk loudly and wildly — see RANT

huffiness *n* **1** an exaggerated sense of one's importance that shows itself in the making of excessive or unjustified claims — see ARROGANCE

2 readiness to show annoyance or impatience — see PETULANCE

hug *vb* **1** to express to (someone) admiration for his or her success or good fortune — see CONGRATULATE

2 to put one's arms around and press tightly — see EMBRACE 1

huge *adj* unusually large ⟨The old stadium was replaced by a *huge* new one that seats 100,000 spectators.⟩

syn astronomical (*also* astronomic), bumper, colossal, cosmic (*also* cosmical), elephantine, enormous, gargantuan, giant, gigantic, grand, herculean, heroic (*also* heroical), immense, jumbo, king-size (*or* king-sized), leviathan, mammoth, massive, mighty, monster, monstrous, monumental, mountainous, oceanic, prodigious, super, titanic, tremendous, vast, vasty, whacking, whopping

rel big, bulky, considerable, extensive, good, goodly, great, gross, handsome, hefty, hulking, largish, major, outsize (*also* outsized), overgrown, oversize (*or* oversized), sizable (*or* sizeable), substantial, tidy, voluminous; august, formidable, grandiose, imposing, lofty, majestic; cavernous, monolithic, overwhelming, staggering, stupendous, towering; boundless, immeasurable, infinite

near ant little, mini, petite, pint-size (*or* pint-sized), puny, small, smallish, undersized (*also* undersize), dinky, dwarfish, half-pint

ant bantam, bitty, diminutive, infinitesimal, micro, microminiature, microscopic (*also* microscopical), midget, miniature, minuscule, minute, pocket, pygmy, teeny, teeny-weeny, tiny, wee

hugely *adv* **1** to a great degree — see VERY 1

2 to a large extent or degree — see GREATLY 2

hugeness *n* the quality or state of being very large — see IMMENSITY

hugger-mugger *adj* **1** lacking in order,

neatness, and often cleanliness — see MESSY

2 undertaken or done so as to escape being observed or known by others — see SECRET 1

hulk *n* a big clumsy often slow-witted person — see OAF 1

hulking *adj* **1** of a size greater than average of its kind — see LARGE

2 strongly and heavily built — see ¹HUSKY 1

hull *n* something that encloses another thing especially to protect it — see ¹CASE 1

hull *vb* to remove the natural covering of — see PEEL

hullabaloo *n* **1** a state of noisy, confused activity — see COMMOTION

2 a violent shouting — see CLAMOR 1

hum *n* a monotonous sound like that of an insect in motion ⟨We heard the *hum* of an outboard motor and a few minutes later the small craft came into sight.⟩

syn buzz, chirr, drone, purr, thrum, whir (*also* whirr), whiz (*or* whizz), zoom

rel babble, coo, gasp, gurgle, hiss, moan, murmur, rustle, sigh, whisper; whish, zing, zip

near ant bawl, howl, roar, scream, screech, shriek, squall, squeal, yelp, yell

hum *vb* **1** to be copiously supplied — see ABOUND

2 to fly, turn, or move rapidly with a fluttering or vibratory sound — see WHIR

human *adj* relating to or characteristic of human beings ⟨It's *human* nature to care about what people think of us.⟩

syn mortal, natural

rel hominid, humanlike, humanoid

near ant angelic (*or* angelical), divine, godlike, preternatural, superhuman, supernatural; immortal, omnipotent, omniscient; animal, beastly, brute; inhuman, robotic

ant nonhuman

human *n* a member of the human race ⟨*Humans* are not endowed with a natural defense against the elements, such as fur or a thick hide.⟩

syn being, bird, body, character, creature, customer, devil, duck, face, fish, guy, head, individual, life, man, mortal, party, person, personage, scout, sort, soul, specimen, stiff, thing, wight

rel hominid, humanoid; brother, fellow, fellowman, neighbor; celebrity, personality, somebody

phrases son of man

near ant animal, beast, brute, critter

humane *adj* **1** having or marked by sympathy and consideration for others ⟨*humane* guards who treated the prisoners decently⟩ ⟨The Geneva conventions spelled out standards for the *humane* treatment of prisoners of war.⟩

syn beneficent, benevolent, benignant, compassionate, good-hearted, kind, kindhearted, kindly, softhearted, sympathetic, tender, tenderhearted, warmhearted

rel considerate, solicitous, thoughtful; affable, amicable, benign, companionable, comradely, cordial, friendly, genial, gentle, good, good-natured, good-tempered, gracious, mild, neighborly, nice, pleasant, sweet, warm; clement, forbearing, forgiving, lenient, merciful, soft; patient, pitying, tolerant, understanding; altruistic, brotherly, charitable, freehanded, generous, greathearted, humanitarian, liberal, magnanimous, munificent, noble, openhearted, philanthropic (*also* philanthropical), selfless, unsparing

near ant merciless, pitiless, ruthless, stonyhearted; inconsiderate, insensitive, thoughtless, uncaring, unthinking; grim, hard-boiled, harsh, heavy-handed, severe, stern, tough, unsentimental; hateful, malevolent, malicious, malign, malignant, mean, nasty, spiteful, virulent; antihumanitarian, uncharitable

ant atrocious, barbaric, barbarous, brutal, brute, callous, cold-blooded, cruel, fiendish, heartless, inhuman, inhumane, insensate, sadistic, savage, truculent, uncompassionate, unfeeling, unkind, unkindly, unsympathetic, vicious, wanton

2 having or showing the capacity for sharing the feelings of another — see SYMPATHETIC 1

humanitarian *adj* having or showing a concern for the welfare of others — see CHARITABLE 1

humanity *n* **1** human beings in general — see PEOPLE 1

2 the capacity for feeling for another's unhappiness or misfortune — see HEART 1

3 the human race — see MANKIND

humankind *n* **1** human beings in general — see PEOPLE 1

2 the human race — see MANKIND

humble *adj* **1** not having or showing any feelings of superiority, self-assertiveness, or showiness ⟨a medical scientist who remained remarkably *humble* even after winning the Nobel Prize⟩

syn demure, down-to-earth, lowly, meek, modest, unassuming, unpretentious

rel acquiescent, compliant, deferential, resigned, submissive, unaggressive, unassertive, yielding; cowering, cringing, shrinking; ingenuous, naive (*or* naïve), plain, simple, unaffected; bashful, diffident, introverted, mousy (*or* mousey), overmodest, passive, quiet, reserved, retiring, sheepish, shy, subdued, timid, unobtrusive; self-deprecating, self-deprecatory

near ant aggressive, assertive, audacious, bold, brash, brassy, cheeky, forward, impertinent, impudent, saucy; cocksure, cocky, confident, hubristic, overconfident, self-confident; egocentric, egoistic (*also* egoistical), prideful, self-centered, self-complacent, self-conceited, self-congratulatory, self-important, self-satisfied, smug, stuck-up, swelled-headed; boastful, bombastic, braggy, swaggering, vain, vainglorious; condescending, disdainful, dominant, dominating, domineering, overbearing, patronizing, pontificating; flamboyant, ostentatious, showy; extroverted (*also* extraverted), immodest, outgoing, uninhibited, unreserved

ant arrogant, conceited, egotistic (*or* egotistical), haughty, highfalutin (*also* hifalutin), high-handed, high-hat, hoity-toity,

imperious, lordly, overweening, peremptory, pompous, presuming, presumptuous, pretentious, self-assertive, supercilious, superior, uppity

2 belonging to the class of people of low social or economic rank — see IGNOBLE 1

humble *vb* to reduce to a lower standing in one's own eyes or in others' eyes ⟨Philip was utterly *humbled* by a crushing defeat in the first round of the state chess tournament.⟩

syn abase, chasten, cheapen, debase, degrade, demean, discredit, disgrace, dishonor, foul, humiliate, lower, shame, sink, smirch, take down

rel abash, confound, confuse, discomfit, disconcert, discountenance, embarrass, faze, fluster, mortify, nonplus, rattle; belittle, castigate, criticize, cry down, decry, depreciate, diminish, discount, disparage, minimize, put down, ridicule, write off; bad-mouth, defame, defile, libel, malign, slander; affront, insult; censure, condemn, damn, denounce, execrate, reprehend, reprobate

near ant acclaim, applaud, boast, celebrate, cheer, cite, commend, compliment, congratulate, decorate, eulogize, extol (*also* extoll), hail, honor, laud, praise, salute, tout; acknowledge, recognize; highlight; dignify, ennoble, enshrine, enthrone, glorify, magnify; advance, boost, lift, promote, raise, upgrade, uplift; idealize, romanticize

ant aggrandize, canonize, deify, elevate, exalt

humbleness *n* the absence of any feelings of being better than others — see HUMILITY

humbly *adv* in a manner showing no signs of pride or self-assertion — see LOWLY

humbug *n* **1** an imitation that is passed off as genuine — see FAKE 1

2 language, behavior, or ideas that are absurd and contrary to good sense — see NONSENSE 1

3 one who makes false claims of identity or expertise — see IMPOSTOR

humbug *vb* to cause to believe what is untrue — see DECEIVE

humbuggery *n* language, behavior, or ideas that are absurd and contrary to good sense — see NONSENSE 1

humdrum *adj* causing weariness, restlessness, or lack of interest — see BORING

humdrum *n* a tedious lack of variety — see MONOTONY

humid *adj* containing or characterized by an uncomfortable amount of moisture ⟨The air was so *humid* that our beach towels hanging on the line never really got dry.⟩

syn damp, muggy, sticky, sultry

rel steamy, summerlike, summery, sweltering, torrid; semitropical (*also* semitropic), subhumid, subtropical (*also* subtropic), tropic, tropical; close, heavy, oppressive, smothering, stifling, stuffy, suffocating; dank, moist

near ant arid, baked, burned (*or* burnt), dehydrated, desert, droughty, dusty, parched, scorched, seared, semiarid, sere (*also* sear), sunbaked, thirsty, waterless

ant dry

---

syn synonym(s)   **rel** related words
ant antonym(s)   **near ant** near antonym(s)

humidity *n* the amount of water suspended in the air in tiny droplets — see MOISTURE

humiliate *vb* to reduce to a lower standing in one's own eyes or in others' eyes — see HUMBLE

humility *n* the absence of any feelings of being better than others ⟨Displaying genuine *humility*, the peace activist accepted the Nobel Prize on behalf of all who have worked to end the violence.⟩

syn demureness, humbleness, lowliness, meekness, modesty

rel acquiescence, compliance, deference, passivity, submission, submissiveness; ingenuousness, naïveté (*also* naivete *or* naïveté); directness, plainness, simpleness; bashfulness, diffidence, mousiness, quietness, reserve, reservedness, retiringness, sheepishness, shyness, timidity, timidness

near ant aggressiveness, assertiveness, boldness, brashness, brassiness, cheek, cheekiness, cockiness, forwardness, overconfidence, swagger, temerity; impertinence, impudence, insolence, nerve, sauciness; boastfulness, chest-thumping, self-centeredness, self-complacency, self-conceit, self-glorification, self-importance, self-satisfaction, vaingloriousness, vanity; condescension, disdain, scorn; flamboyance, ostentation, ostentatiousness, showiness

ant arrogance, assumption, conceit, egoism, egotism, haughtiness, huffiness, imperiousness, loftiness, lordliness, pompousness, presumptuousness, pretense (*or* pretence), pretension, pretentiousness, pride, pridefulness, superciliousness, superiority

humming *adj* marked by much life, movement, or activity — see ALIVE 2

humor *n* **1** the amusing quality or element in something ⟨We failed to see any *humor* in his lame jokes.⟩

syn comedy, comic, drollness, funniness, hilariousness, humorousness, richness

rel amusement, enjoyment, fun, pleasure; absurdity, irony, laughableness, ludicrousness, ridiculousness; whimsicality, wittiness, wryness; burlesque, caricature, farce, jest, lampoon, parody, satire, slapstick, spoof, takeoff; jocularity, jokiness, playfulness, waggishness

near ant agony, anguish, dolor, grief, heartache, heartbreak, misery, sorrow, torment, torture, tribulation, woe; gravity, seriousness, soberness, solemnity, somberness

ant pathos

2 humorous entertainment — see COMEDY 1

3 a state of mind dominated by a particular emotion — see MOOD 1

4 a sudden impulsive and apparently unmotivated idea or action — see WHIM

humor *vb* to give in to (a desire) — see INDULGE 1

humorist *n* a person (as a writer) noted for or specializing in humor ⟨Mark Twain is perhaps America's most beloved *humorist*.⟩

syn card, comedian, comic, droll, jester, joker, jokester, wag, wit

rel comedienne, entertainer; banterer, cutup, kidder, knockabout, practical joker, prankster, quipster, teaser, wisecracker; buffoon, clown, fool, harlequin, zany; caricaturist, lampooner, parodist, satirist

humorless *adj* not joking or playful in mood or manner — see SERIOUS 1

humorous *adj* **1** causing or intended to cause laughter — see FUNNY 1

2 given to or marked by mature intelligent humor — see WITTY

humorousness *n* the amusing quality or element in something — see HUMOR 1

hump *n* **1** an elevation of land higher than a hill — see MOUNTAIN 1

2 an area of high ground — see HEIGHT 4

hump *vb* **1** to devote serious and sustained effort — see LABOR

2 to proceed or move quickly — see HURRY 2

hunch *vb* to lie low with the limbs close to the body — see CROUCH

hung *adj* bending downward or forward — see NODDING

hunger *n* **1** a need or desire for food ⟨No degree of *hunger* would induce me to eat octopus.⟩

syn appetite, belly, emptiness, famishment, munchies, stomach

rel rapaciousness, rapacity, ravenousness, voraciousness, voracity; malnutrition, starvation, undernourishment; craving, sweet tooth; famine, fast, hunger strike; gourmandise, greed, hoggishness

near ant fill, glut, repleteness, repletion, satiation, satiety, satisfaction, surfeit

ant inappetence

2 a strong wish for something — see DESIRE 1

3 urgent desire or interest — see EAGERNESS

hunger (for) *vb* to have an earnest wish to own or enjoy — see DESIRE 1

hungry *adj* **1** feeling a desire or need for food ⟨John was still *hungry* after eating only a muffin for breakfast.⟩

syn empty, famished, starved, starving

rel rapacious, ravenous, voracious, wolfish; malnourished, underfed, undernourished; gluttonous, gormandizing, greedy, hoggish, piggish, piggy

near ant engorged, glutted, gorged, overfed, overfull, overstuffed, replete, stuffed, surfeited

ant full, sated, satiate, satiated, satisfied

2 showing urgent desire or interest — see EAGER

hung up *adj* **1** having extreme or relentless concern ⟨parents of a toddler who are already *hung up* about her getting into a good college⟩

syn happy, obsessed

rel absorbed, anxious, concerned, distracted, engaged, engrossed, full, involved, knee-deep, occupied, preoccupied, prepossessed, worried; ardent, crazy, dotty, fervent, fervid, feverish, foolish, impassioned, nuts, passionate, silly

near ant apathetic, casual, cool, detached, disinterested, dispassionate, incurious, indifferent, insouciant, nonchalant, unconcerned, uncurious, unenthusiastic, uninterested, uninvolved

390   hunk

2 feeling or showing uncomfortable feelings of uncertainty — see NERVOUS 1

hunk *n* a small uneven mass — see LUMP 1

hunt *n* an act or process of looking carefully or thoroughly for someone or something — see SEARCH

hunt *vb* **1** to seek out (game) for food or sport ⟨Native Americans of the plains *hunted* buffalo for food, clothing, and shelter.⟩

syn chase, stalk

rel capture, drag, net, snare, trap; dog, ferret, hawk, hound; course, pursue, run, run down, spoor, track, trail; gun (for), harpoon, kill, shoot; poach; cull

2 to go in search of — see SEEK 1

3 to go into or range over for purposes of discovery — see EXPLORE 2

hunt (down *or* **up)** *vb* to come upon after searching, study, or effort — see FIND 1

hunt (through) *vb* to look through (as a place) carefully or thoroughly in an effort to find or discover something — see SEARCH 1

hunter *n* a person who hunts game ⟨*Hunters* must have a license to shoot deer.⟩

syn huntsman

rel huntress, sportsman, sportswoman; archer, gunner; birder, falconer, fowler, hawker; hunter-gatherer, trapper; poacher

ant nonhunter

huntsman *n* a person who hunts game — see HUNTER

hurdle *n* something that makes movement or progress difficult — see ENCUMBRANCE

hurl *vb* **1** to discharge the contents of the stomach through the mouth — see VOMIT

2 to proceed or move quickly — see HURRY 2

3 to send through the air especially with a quick forward motion of the arm — see THROW 1

hurly–burly *n* a state of noisy, confused activity — see COMMOTION

hurried *adj* acting or done with excessive or careless speed — see HASTY 1

hurriedly *adv* with excessive or careless speed — see HASTILY 1

hurry *n* **1** excited and often showy or disorderly speed ⟨After all her *hurry* to get her report done on time, Elizabeth learned that it wasn't due till the following week.⟩

syn haste, hastiness, hustle, precipitation, precipitousness, rush

rel bustle, flurry, flutter, scurry, scuttle, stir, whirl; beeline, dash, scramble, stampede; hotheadedness, impetuosity, impetuousness, impulsiveness, impulsivity, rashness; expedition, expeditiousness, fastness, fleetness, quickness, rapidity, rapidness, speed, speediness, swiftness, velocity

near ant dilatoriness, lateness, pokiness, procrastination, slowness; languor, leisureliness, sluggishness; dormancy, inaction, inactivity, inertia, inertness, quiescence

ant deliberateness, deliberation

2 a high rate of movement or performance — see SPEED 1

hurry *vb* **1** to cause to move or proceed

---

syn synonym(s)   **rel** related words

ant antonym(s)   **near ant** near antonym(s)

---

fast or faster ⟨The new nurses were *hurried* through the orientation program because they were so desperately needed on the ward.⟩

syn accelerate, bundle, fast-track, hasten, quicken, rush, speed (up), whisk

rel drive, goad, prod, propel, push, race, spur, stir, urge; aid, dispatch, ease, encourage, expedite, facilitate

near ant delay, encumber, fetter, hamper, hinder, hobble, hold back, hold up, impede, interfere (with), manacle, rein (in), restrain, shackle, tie up, trammel; arrest, check, stall, stay, still, stop

ant brake, decelerate, retard, slow (down)

2 to proceed or move quickly ⟨If we *hurry*, we'll make the four o'clock train.⟩

syn barrel, belt, blast, blaze, blow, bolt, bowl, breeze, bundle, bustle, buzz, careen, career, chase, course, dash, drive, fly, hasten, hie, hotfoot (it), hump, hurl, hurtle, hustle, jet, jump, motor, nip, pelt, race, ram, rip, rocket, run, rush, rustle, scoot, scurry, scuttle, shoot, speed, step, tear, travel, trot, whirl, whisk, zip, zoom

rel dart, flit, scamper, scud, scuffle; stampede, streak, whiz (*or* whizz); gallop, jog, sprint; accelerate, quicken; fast-forward, outpace, outrun, outstrip, overtake

phrases beat it, get a move on, make tracks, shake a leg, step on it

near ant dally, dawdle, dillydally, drag, lag, linger, loiter, poke, tarry; lumber, plod, saunter, shuffle, stroll; decelerate, slow (down *or* up)

ant crawl, creep, poke

hurt *n* **1** a state of great suffering of body or mind — see DISTRESS 1

2 something that causes loss or pain — see INJURY 1

hurt *vb* **1** to feel or cause physical pain ⟨My head *hurts*.⟩ ⟨a bad sprain that really *hurts*⟩ ⟨I *hurt* all over.⟩

syn ache, pain, smart

rel bite, bleed, burn, chafe, cramp, fester, itch, nag, pinch, pound, rack, sting, swell, throb, tingle, twinge; agonize, anguish, suffer; afflict, harrow, torment, torture

2 to reduce the soundness, effectiveness, or perfection of — see DAMAGE 1

3 to cause bodily damage to — see INJURE 1

4 to feel deep sadness or mental pain — see GRIEVE

hurtful *adj* **1** causing or capable of causing harm — see HARMFUL

2 hard to accept or bear especially emotionally — see BITTER 2

hurting *adj* causing or feeling bodily pain — see PAINFUL 1

hurtle *vb* **1** to proceed or move quickly — see HURRY 2

2 to send through the air especially with a quick forward motion of the arm — see THROW 1

husband *n* a male partner in a marriage ⟨She and her *husband* just celebrated their 50th wedding anniversary.⟩

syn man, old man

rel better half, companion, consort, mate, partner, significant other, spouse; bridegroom; widower; househusband

husband *vb* to avoid the wasteful or destructive use of — see CONSERVE 1

husbandry *n* 1 careful management of material resources — see ECONOMY

2 the science or occupation of cultivating the soil, producing crops, and raising livestock — see AGRICULTURE

hush *n* 1 a state of freedom from storm or disturbance — see CALM 1

2 the near or complete absence of sound — see SILENCE 2

hush *vb* 1 to become still and orderly — see QUIET 1

2 to stop talking — see SHUT UP 1

3 to stop the noise or speech of — see SILENCE 1

hush (up) *vb* to keep from being publicly known — see SUPPRESS 1

hushed *adj* 1 free from disturbing noise or uproar — see QUIET 1

2 free from storms or physical disturbance — see CALM 1

3 mostly or entirely without sound — see SILENT 3

4 not known or meant to be known by the general populace — see PRIVATE 1

husk *n* something that encloses another thing especially to protect it — see ¹CASE 1

husk *vb* to remove the natural covering of — see PEEL

¹husky *adj* 1 strongly and heavily built ⟨a *husky* weight lifter⟩

syn beefy, brawny, burly, hefty, hulking

rel able-bodied, athletic, herculean, mighty, muscle-bound, muscular, powerful, robust, rugged, sinewy, stalwart, stout, strapping, strong, sturdy; chunky, compact, heavy, heavyset, solid, squat, stocky, thickset; chubby, portly, pudgy, roly-poly, tubby

near ant lean, light, lightweight, slender, slight, slim, svelte, sylphlike, thin, willowy; gangling, gangly, gaunt, gawky, lanky, reedy, scraggy, scrawny, skinny, spare, stringy, twiggy, waspish, weedy; spidery, wiry; debilitated, delicate, effete, emaciated, enervated, enfeebled, feeble, fragile, frail, infirm, puny, unathletic, weak, weakly, wimpy

2 of a size greater than average of its kind — see LARGE

²husky *adj* harsh and dry in sound — see HOARSE

hustle *n* 1 excited and often showy or disorderly speed — see HURRY 1

2 readiness to engage in daring or difficult activity — see ENTERPRISE 2

3 an instance of the use of dishonest methods to acquire something of value — see FRAUD 1

hustle *vb* 1 to devote serious and sustained effort — see LABOR

2 to proceed or move quickly — see HURRY 2

3 to rob by the use of trickery or threats — see FLEECE

hustler *n* an ambitious person who eagerly goes after what is desired — see GO-GETTER

hut *n* a small, simply constructed, and often temporary dwelling — see SHACK

hutch *n* 1 a small, simply constructed, and often temporary dwelling — see SHACK

2 a storage case typically having doors and shelves — see CABINET

3 an enclosure with an open framework for keeping animals — see CAGE

hybrid *adj* being offspring produced by parents of different races, breeds, species, or genera — see MIXED 1

hybrid *n* an offspring of parents with different genes especially when of different races, breeds, or genera ⟨A tangelo is a *hybrid* of the tangerine and the grapefruit.⟩

syn cross, crossbred, crossbreed, mongrel

rel mule; outcross; half-bred

near ant pureblood, purebred, thoroughbred

hygienic *adj* free from filth, infection, or dangers to health — see SANITARY

hymn *n* 1 a religious song ⟨Our Sunday church services always open with a *hymn*.⟩

syn anthem, canticle, carol, chorale, psalm, spiritual

rel dirge, lament, requiem; Gloria Patri, paean; mass, oratorio; processional, recessional

2 a formal expression of praise — see ENCOMIUM

hymn *vb* to proclaim the glory of — see PRAISE 1

hymnal *n* a book of hymns ⟨*Hymnals* are distributed among the congregation before the church service so everyone can join in the singing.⟩

syn hymnbook, psalmody

rel breviary, missal, Psalter; songbook, songster; antiphonal, antiphonary

hymnbook *n* a book of hymns — see HYMNAL

hyperactive *adj* 1 being in a state of increased activity or agitation — see FEVERISH 1

2 easily excited by nature — see EXCITABLE

hyperbole *n* the representation of something in terms that go beyond the facts — see EXAGGERATION

hypercritical *adj* given to making or expressing unfavorable judgments about things — see CRITICAL 1

hyperventilate *vb* to breathe hard, quickly, or with difficulty — see GASP

hypnosis *n* the art or act of inducing in a person a sleeplike state during which he or she readily follows suggestions ⟨With *hypnosis* there's some question as to just how involuntary the actions of the hypnotized person really are.⟩

syn hypnotism, mesmerism

rel autohypnosis, automatism, autosuggestion, self-hypnosis, self-suggestion; bewitchment, enchantment, spellbinding

hypnotic *adj* tending to cause sleep ⟨Her eyes soon grew heavy from the *hypnotic* rhythm of the train's wheels.⟩

syn drowsy, narcotic, opiate, slumberous (*or* slumbrous), somnolent

rel depressant, relaxant, sedative, tranquilizing (*also* tranquillizing); calming, comforting, lulling, pacifying, quieting, relaxing, restful, settling, soothing; analgesic, anesthetic, anesthetizing, benumbing, deadening, dulling, numbing; hypnotizing, mesmerizing, stupefying

near ant arousing, awakening, energizing, invigorating, rousing, stimulating, wakening, waking; bracing, refreshing, restorative, reviving, stimulative, stimulatory
ant stimulant

hypnotism *n* the art or act of inducing in a person a sleeplike state during which he or she readily follows suggestions — see HYPNOSIS

hypnotize *vb* to hold the attention of as if by a spell — see ENTHRALL 1

hypocrisy *n* the pretending of having virtues, principles, or beliefs that one in fact does not have ⟨the *hypocrisy* of people who claim to care about the environment but ride around in gas-guzzlers⟩
syn cant, dissembling, dissimulation, insincerity, piousness
rel deceit, deceitfulness, dishonesty, double-dealing, falsity, perfidy, two-facedness; affectation, affectedness, pretense (*or* pretence), pretension, pretentiousness, sanctimoniousness, self-righteousness, self-satisfaction; duplicity, fakery, falseness, fraudulentness, shamming; artificiality, glibness, oiliness, smoothness, unctuousness
near ant candor, directness, forthrightness, frankness, honesty, openheartedness, openness, probity, straightforwardness,

truthfulness; artlessness, guilelessness, naturalness, unaffectedness
ant genuineness, sincereness, sincerity

hypocritical *adj* not being or expressing what one appears to be or express — see INSINCERE

hypodermic *n* a slender hollow instrument by which material is put into or taken from the body through the skin — see NEEDLE 1

hypodermic needle *n* a slender hollow instrument by which material is put into or taken from the body through the skin — see NEEDLE 1

hypodermic syringe *n* a slender hollow instrument by which material is put into or taken from the body through the skin — see NEEDLE 1

hypothesis *n* an idea that is the starting point for making a case or conducting an investigation — see THEORY

hypothetical *adj* existing only as an assumption or speculation — see THEORETICAL 1

hysteria *n* a state of wildly excited activity or emotion — see FRENZY

hysterical *adj* **1** causing or intended to cause laughter — see FUNNY 1
2 feeling overwhelming fear or worry — see FRANTIC 1
3 filled with fear or dread — see AFRAID

I

ice–cold *adj* having a low or subnormal temperature — see COLD 1

icon *also* **ikon** *n* **1** a written or printed mark that is meant to convey information to the reader — see CHARACTER 1
2 a visible representation of something abstract (as a quality) — see EMBODIMENT
3 a person who is widely known and usually much talked about — see CELEBRITY 1
4 a two-dimensional design intended to look like a person or thing — see PICTURE 1

icy *adj* **1** having a low or subnormal temperature — see COLD 1
2 lacking in friendliness or warmth of feeling — see COLD 2

idea *n* **1** something imagined or pictured in the mind ⟨My *idea* of the perfect vacation spot is an uncrowded, unspoiled beach.⟩
syn concept, conception, image, impression, notion, picture, thought
rel apprehension, premonition, presentiment; preconception, prejudice, prepossession; delusion, hallucination, illusion, phantasm (*also* fantasm); caprice, conceit, fancy, vagary, whim; cognition, observation, perception, reflection; assumption, belief, conclusion, conviction; conjecture, guess, hunch, hypothesis, speculation, supposition, surmise, theory; brainstorm, brain wave, inspiration

near ant actuality, fact, reality
2 someone of such unequaled perfection as to deserve imitation — see IDEAL 1
3 something that one hopes or intends to accomplish — see GOAL

ideal *adj* **1** dealing with or expressing a quality or idea — see ABSTRACT 1
2 not real and existing only in the imagination — see IMAGINARY
3 being entirely without fault or flaw — see PERFECT 1

ideal *n* **1** someone of such unequaled perfection as to deserve imitation ⟨She's our *ideal* of the concerned, caring physician.⟩
syn beau ideal, classic, exemplar, idea, model, nonpareil, paragon
rel role model; embodiment, epitome, incarnation, manifestation, personification; archetype, example, mirror, paradigm, pattern; guideline, principle, rule; gauge (*also* gage), standard, touchstone; essence, quintessence; acme, apex, culmination, peak, pinnacle, summit, zenith; god, hero, icon (*also* ikon), idol
2 the most perfect type or example — see QUINTESSENCE 1
3 something that one hopes or intends to accomplish — see GOAL

idealist *n* one whose conduct is guided more by the image of perfection than by the real world ⟨An *idealist* sees the best in everyone, regardless of how they behave.⟩
syn dreamer, romantic, utopian, visionary
rel daydreamer, fantasizer, woolgatherer;

syn synonym(s) *rel* related words
ant antonym(s) *near ant* near antonym(s)

optimist, Pollyanna; do-gooder; reformer; perfectionist

near ant cynic, defeatist, pessimist

ant pragmatist, realist

idealize *vb* to represent or think of as better than reality would warrant ⟨He had a tendency to *idealize* his heroes and believe they could do no wrong.⟩

syn glamorize (*also* glamourize), glorify, romanticize

rel heroicize, heroize; soften; adulate, canonize, deify, idolize; aggrandize, dignify, ennoble, enshrine, enthrone, magnify

near ant belittle, decry, deprecate, disparage, minimize, put down

ant deglamorize

ideally *adv* without any flaws or errors — see PERFECTLY 1

identical *adj* 1 being one and not another — see SAME 2

2 resembling another in every respect — see SAME 1

identicalness *n* the state of being exactly alike — see IDENTITY 1

identify *vb* 1 to find out or establish the identity of ⟨There's sufficient forensic evidence to allow investigators to *identify* the perpetrator.⟩

syn distinguish, pinpoint, single (out)

rel diagnose; determine, find; locate, pick out, place, recognize, spot; check, examine, inspect, investigate, notice, observe, scrutinize; betray, disclose, discover, reveal

phrases put one's finger on

near ant camouflage, conceal, disguise, hide; counterfeit, feign, sham, simulate

2 to think of (something) in combination — see ASSOCIATE 2

identifying *adj* serving to identify as belonging to an individual or group — see CHARACTERISTIC 1

identity *n* 1 the state of being exactly alike ⟨Although the covers of the two paperback editions of the novel are different, there's a complete *identity* in the texts.⟩

syn identicalness, sameness

rel oneness, selfsameness; equality, equivalence; accordance, agreement, conformity, congruity, correspondence, likeness, resemblance, similarity

near ant alteration, change, modification, variation; distinction, distinctiveness, distinctness, individuality, separateness, uniqueness, unusualness; deviance, divergence; variance; incompatibility, incongruence, incongruity, incongruousness

ant difference, disagreement, discrepancy, disparateness, disparity, dissimilarity, unlikeness

2 the set of qualities that make a person different from other people — see INDIVIDUALITY 1

ideology *also* **idealogy** *n* the basic beliefs or guiding principles of a person or group — see CREED 1

idiocy *n* a foolish act or idea — see FOLLY 1

idiom *n* a sequence of words having a specific meaning — see PHRASE

idiosyncrasy *n* an odd or peculiar habit ⟨His only *idiosyncrasy* is his inveterate wearing of sneakers, even with business suits.⟩

syn crotchet, curiosity, eccentricity, mannerism, oddity, peculiarity, quirk, singularity, tic, trick, twist

rel affectation; airs; attribute, characteristic, mark, property, trait; custom, habit, pattern, practice (*also* practise), way, wont; abnormality, neuroticism, perversion, weirdness; disposition, genius, leaning, partiality; bent, inclination, penchant, predilection, predisposition, proclivity, propensity, tendency, turn; character, humor, identity, individuality, nature, personality, temperament

near ant conformity, sameness

idiot *n* a stupid person ⟨I really made an *idiot* of myself at the party.⟩

syn blockhead, dodo, dolt, donkey, dope, dork [*slang*], dumbbell, dummy, dunce, fathead, goof, goon, half-wit, ignoramus, imbecile, know-nothing, moron, nincompoop, ninny, nitwit, numskull (*or* numbskull), oaf, pinhead, simpleton, stock, turkey, yo-yo

rel booby, buffoon, fool, goose, zany; loser; gawk; featherbrain; beast, boor, cad, clown, creep, heel, jerk, skunk, snake, stinker, villain

near ant egghead, intellect, intellectual, sage, thinker, whiz, wizard

ant brain, genius

idle *adj* 1 not being in a state of use, activity, or employment — see INACTIVE 2

2 not easily aroused to action or work — see LAZY 1

idle *vb* to spend time doing nothing ⟨She likes to *idle* during the summer and recharge herself.⟩

syn bum, chill, dally, dawdle, dillydally, goof (off), kick back, lazy, loaf, loll, lounge

rel fiddle (around), fool, mess, monkey, muck, piddle, play, potter (around), putter (around), trifle; lag, linger, loiter, poke, relax, rest, tarry; mosey, saunter, stroll

phrases kill time, twiddle one's thumbs

near ant drudge, grind, grub, hump, hustle, labor, moil, peg, plod, plow, plug, sweat, toil, travail, work; apply, buckle (down); exert, put out

idleness *n* 1 an inclination not to do work or engage in activities — see LAZINESS

2 lack of action or activity — see INACTION

3 lack of use — see DISUSE

idler *n* a lazy person — see LAZYBONES

idolater *or* **idolator** *n* a person who does not worship the God of the Bible — see HEATHEN 1

idolatry *n* excessive admiration of or devotion to a person — see WORSHIP

idolization *n* excessive admiration of or devotion to a person — see WORSHIP

idolize *vb* to love or admire too much ⟨She blindly *idolized* her older sister, refusing to acknowledge her faults.⟩

syn adore, adulate, canonize, deify, dote (on), worship

rel appreciate, cherish, esteem, prize, treasure, value; fancy, favor, like, prefer; regard; hallow, respect, revere, venerate; approve, endorse (*also* indorse), support

near ant abhor, abominate, despise, detest, disdain, dislike, hate, loathe; belittle, deprecate, disparage, put down

idolizing *adj* reflecting great admiration or devotion — see WORSHIPFUL

idyll *also* **idyl** *n* a time or instance of carefree fun — see FLING 1

ignitable *also* **ignitible** *adj* capable of catching or being set on fire — see COMBUSTIBLE

ignite *vb* to set (something) on fire — see BURN 2

ignited *adj* being on fire — see ABLAZE 1

ignoble *adj* **1** belonging to the class of people of low social or economic rank ⟨an *ignoble* child who would one day grow up to be a prince among playwrights⟩
syn baseborn, common, humble, inferior, low, lower-class, lowly, mean, plebeian, proletarian, vulgar
rel bourgeois, middle-class; plain, poor, simple, working-class
near ant eminent, illustrious, notable, prominent
ant aristocratic, genteel, gentle, grand, great, high, highborn, lofty, noble, patrician, upper-class, wellborn
2 not following or in accordance with standards of honor and decency ⟨Such an *ignoble* act is completely unworthy of a military officer.⟩
syn base, contemptible, despicable, detestable, dirty, dishonorable, execrable, ignominious, low, mean, nasty, paltry, snide, sordid, vile, wretched
rel bad, evil, foul, immoral, iniquitous, miscreant, wicked, wrong; cruel, vicious; blamable, blameworthy, censurable, reprehensible; corrupt, debased, debauched, degenerate, depraved, dissolute, perverted; atrocious, villainous; unethical, unprincipled, unscrupulous; discreditable, disgraceful, disreputable, shameful, unworthy
near ant ethical, honest, just, principled, righteous, right-minded, scrupulous; commendable, excellent, exemplary, good, moral, right; decent, proper, reputable, respectable, seemly; blameless, guiltless; incorruptible, irreproachable; uncorrupted, unerring
ant high, high-minded, honorable, lofty, noble, straight, upright, venerable, virtuous

ignominious *adj* **1** not respectable — see DISREPUTABLE
2 not following or in accordance with standards of honor and decency — see IGNOBLE 2

ignominy *n* the state of having lost the esteem of others — see DISGRACE 1

ignoramus *n* a stupid person — see IDIOT

ignorance *n* **1** the state of being unaware or uninformed ⟨*Ignorance* of the law is no excuse.⟩
syn innocence, obliviousness, unawareness, unfamiliarity
rel callowness, greenness, inexperience, naïveté (*also* naivete *or* naïveté), rawness, simpleness, unsophistication
near ant experience, know-how; sophistication
ant acquaintance, awareness, cognizance, familiarity

2 the state of being unlearned ⟨"Our foe," said the educator, "is *ignorance*."⟩
syn illiteracy
rel functional illiteracy, innumeracy; brainlessness, dumbness, idiocy, imbecility, stupidity; philistinism; foolishness, mindlessness, senselessness, witlessness
near ant education, instruction, training; enlightenment, knowledge; erudition, scholarship
ant learning

ignorant *adj* **1** lacking in education or the knowledge gained from books ⟨They were *ignorant*, but not stupid.⟩
syn benighted, dark, illiterate, rude, simple, uneducated, uninstructed, unlearned, unlettered, unread, unschooled, untaught, untutored
rel functionally illiterate, innumerate, semiliterate, unknowledgeable; artless, lowbrow, philistine, uncultivated, uncultured; callow, green, inexperienced, innocent, naïve (*or* naïve); unsophisticated; raw, unskilled, untrained; brainless, dumb, idiotic (*also* idiotical), imbecile (*or* imbecilic), moronic, stupid, witless; foolish, senseless, silly
near ant brilliant, intelligent, smart; experienced, expert, trained; erudite, learned, scholarly; cultivated, cultured, highbrow, intellectual; sophisticated; acquainted, aware, familiar
ant educated, knowledgeable, literate, schooled, well-read

2 not informed about or aware of something ⟨He was *ignorant* of their wedding plans.⟩
syn innocent, insensible, oblivious, unacquainted, unaware, unconscious, uninformed, unknowing, unmindful, unwitting
rel uneducated, unschooled, untaught: absent, absentminded, abstracted, heedless, inattentive, inconscient
phrases in the dark
near ant hip, up-to-date; educated, knowledgeable, schooled, taught; heedful, observant; sensitive, sentient
ant acquainted, aware, cognizant, conscious, conversant, grounded, informed, knowing, mindful, witting

ignore *vb* **1** to fail to give proper attention to — see NEGLECT 1
2 to dismiss as of little importance — see EXCUSE 1

ilk *n* a number of persons or things that are grouped together because they have something in common — see SORT 1

ill *adj* **1** affected with nausea — see NAUSEOUS 1
2 causing or capable of causing harm — see HARMFUL
3 temporarily suffering from a disorder of the body — see SICK 1
4 falling short of a standard — see BAD 1
5 being or showing a sign of evil or calamity to come — see OMINOUS

ill *adv* **1** in a manner so as to cause loss or suffering — see HARDLY 1
2 certainly not — see HARDLY 2

ill *n* **1** an abnormal state that disrupts a plant's or animal's normal bodily functioning — see DISEASE
2 that which is morally unacceptable — see EVIL

---

syn synonym(s)   *rel* related words
ant antonym(s)   *near ant* near antonym(s)

3 bad luck or an example of this — see MISFORTUNE

ill–advised *adj* showing poor judgment especially in personal relationships or social situations — see INDISCREET

ill–bred *adj* **1** lacking in refinement or good taste — see COARSE 2

2 showing a lack of manners or consideration for others — see IMPOLITE

illegal *adj* **1** contrary to or forbidden by law ⟨It is *illegal* to import those birds into this country.⟩

syn criminal, felonious, illegitimate, illicit, lawless, unlawful, wrongful

rel bad, evil, immoral, shameful, sinful, unethical, wicked, wrong; blamable, blameworthy, censurable, reprehensible; banned, barred, contraband, criminalized, disallowed, discouraged, forbidden, interdicted, outlawed, prohibited, proscribed; bootleg, unauthorized, unlicensed, unsanctioned; under-the-counter, under-the-table; corrupt, unprincipled, unscrupulous, villainous

near ant ethical, good, just, principled, right, righteous, virtuous; allowed, permitted; authorized, licensed; approved, endorsed (*also* indorsed), sanctioned; abetted, encouraged, promoted, suggested, supported; correct, decent, decorous, proper, seemly

ant lawful, legal, legitimate

2 not being in accordance with the rules or standards of what is fair in sport — see FOUL 2

illegitimate *adj* **1** contrary to or forbidden by law — see ILLEGAL 1

2 not using or following good reasoning — see ILLOGICAL

ill–fated *adj* having, prone to, or marked by bad luck — see UNLUCKY 1

ill–favored *adj* unpleasant to look at — see UGLY 1

ill–humored *adj* having or showing a habitually bad temper — see ILL-TEMPERED

illicit *adj* contrary to or forbidden by law — see ILLEGAL 1

illimitable *adj* being or seeming to be without limits — see INFINITE

illiteracy *n* the state of being unlearned — see IGNORANCE 2

illiterate *adj* lacking in education or the knowledge gained from books — see IGNORANT 1

ill–mannered *adj* showing a lack of manners or consideration for others — see IMPOLITE

ill–natured *adj* having or showing a habitually bad temper — see ILL-TEMPERED

illness *n* **1** an abnormal state that disrupts a plant's or animal's normal bodily functioning — see DISEASE

2 the condition of not being in good health — see SICKNESS 1

illogical *adj* not using or following good reasoning ⟨the *illogical* claim that playing basketball makes people taller because one sees so many tall players⟩ ⟨*Illogical* people are likely to believe every sensational claim made online.⟩

syn fallacious, illegitimate, inconsequential, invalid, irrational, nonrational, unreasonable, unreasoning, unsound, weak

rel misleading, specious; half-baked, ill-advised, misguided, unconsidered, unreasoned; inconsistent; absurd, asinine, foolish, meaningless, nonsensical, preposterous, reasonless, senseless, silly; odd, peculiar, strange, surreal, unusual, weird; wacky (*also* whacky); disordered, disorganized, rambling, random; unconvincing; inexplicable, unaccountable, unexplainable

near ant commonsense, sane, sensible, sober, wise; enlightened, informed, just, justified, reasoned; ordered, organized; clear, cogent, compelling, convincing, credible, persuasive, plausible, satisfying, solid; certain, sure, true; confirmed, corroborated, demonstrated, established, substantiated, validated

ant logical, rational, reasonable, sound, valid, well-founded

ill–starred *adj* having, prone to, or marked by bad luck — see UNLUCKY 1

ill–tempered *adj* having or showing a habitually bad temper ⟨An *ill-tempered* cat will scratch with little provocation.⟩

syn acid, bearish, cantankerous, disagreeable, dyspeptic, ill-humored, ill-natured, ornery, splenetic, surly

rel choleric, crabby, cranky, crotchety, fussy, grouchy, grumpy, querulous; irascible, irritable, peevish, peppery, petulant, quick-tempered, short-tempered, snappish, snippy, testy, touchy; argumentative, contentious, contrary; angry, indignant, irate, mad, upset, uptight

near ant agreeable, amicable, congenial, friendly, pleasant; benign, gentle, kind, nice, sweet; bubbly, cheerful, cheery, effervescent, exuberant, high-spirited, joyful, lighthearted, lively, vivacious; content, glad, happy; calm, placid, serene; long-suffering, patient, tolerant

ant amiable, good-humored, good-natured, good-tempered

ill–treat *vb* to inflict physical or emotional harm upon — see ABUSE 1

illuminate *vb* **1** to supply with light ⟨A floor lamp *illuminates* a living room rather nicely.⟩

syn bathe, beacon, illumine, irradiate, light, lighten

rel brighten; beam, beat (down), radiate, shine; enhalo; floodlight; highlight; blaze, burn, fire, flame, glare, glow, ignite, incinerate, kindle; bedazzle, blind, daze, dazzle; gleam, glisten, glitter

near ant dim, dull, obscure; cover, shroud, veil; douse (*also* dowse), extinguish, put out, quench, snuff (out)

ant blacken, darken

2 to make plain or understandable — see EXPLAIN 1

3 to supplement with pictorial matter for the purpose of explanation or decoration — see ILLUSTRATE 2

4 to indicate the importance of by centering attention on — see EMPHASIZE 1

5 to provide (someone) with moral or spiritual understanding — see ENLIGHTEN 2

illuminated *adj* filled with much light — see BRIGHT 2

illumination *n* **1** a statement that makes something clear — see EXPLANATION 1

2 the quality or state of having or giving off light — see BRILLIANCE 1

3 the steady giving off of the form of radiation that makes vision possible — see LIGHT 1

illuminative *adj* serving to explain — see EXPLANATORY

illumine *vb* **1** to supply with light — see ILLUMINATE 1

2 to provide (someone) with moral or spiritual understanding — see ENLIGHTEN 2

illumined *adj* filled with much light — see BRIGHT 2

ill–use *vb* to inflict physical or emotional harm upon — see ABUSE 1

illusion *n* **1** a conception or image created by the imagination and having no objective reality — see FANTASY 1

2 a false idea or belief — see FALLACY 1

illusionist *n* one who practices tricks and illusions for entertainment — see MAGICIAN 2

illustrate *vb* **1** to show or make clear by using examples ⟨She *illustrated* her point with a story about her experiences as a field anthropologist.⟩

syn demonstrate, exemplify, instance

rel adduce, cite, mention, quote; name, specify; analyze, break down; clarify, clear (up), explain, explicate, expound; edify, elucidate, enlighten; illuminate; construe, interpret; simplify, spell out; detail, enumerate, list

near ant becloud, blur, cloud, darken, fog, muddy, obscure; confuse, perplex, puzzle

2 to supplement with pictorial material for the purpose of explanation or decoration ⟨lavishly *illustrated* the book on the artist Caravaggio with color plates⟩

syn illuminate

rel image, picture, visualize

3 to make plain or understandable — see EXPLAIN 1

illustration *n* **1** something that visually explains or decorates a text ⟨This book on birds has gorgeous *illustrations*.⟩

syn diagram, figure, graphic, plate, visual

rel art, artwork; drawing, illumination, image, pictogram, pictograph, picture; caption, key, legend; inset; depiction, pictorialization, portrait, portrayal, representation; clarification, elucidation, explanation, explication, exposition

2 a statement that makes something clear — see EXPLANATION 1

3 a two-dimensional design intended to look like a person or thing — see PICTURE 1

4 one of a group or collection that shows what the whole is like — see EXAMPLE

illustrative *adj* serving to explain — see EXPLANATORY

illustrious *adj* standing above others in rank, importance, or achievement — see EMINENT

image *vb* **1** to present a picture of — see PICTURE 1

2 to give a representation or account of in words — see DESCRIBE 1

3 to reproduce or show (an exact likeness) as a mirror would — see REFLECT 1

4 to form a mental picture of — see IMAGINE 1

image *n* **1** something or someone that strongly resembles another ⟨The girl is growing up to be the perfect *image* of her mother.⟩

syn alter ego, carbon copy, counterpart, double, duplicate, duplication, facsimile, likeness, match, picture, replica, ringer, spit, twin

rel effigy, portrait, portrayal; companion, fellow, mate; equal, equivalent; analogue (*or* analog), parallel

near ant antithesis, converse, opposite, reverse

2 a two-dimensional design intended to look like a person or thing — see PICTURE 1

3 something imagined or pictured in the mind — see IDEA 1

4 a visible representation of something abstract (as a quality) — see EMBODIMENT

imaginary *adj* not real and existing only in the imagination ⟨told by the psychologist that it was perfectly normal for their child to have an *imaginary* friend⟩

syn chimerical (*also* chimeric), fabulous, fanciful, fantastic (*also* fantastical), fictional, fictitious, ideal, imagined, invented, made-up, make-believe, mythical (*or* mythic), phantasmal, phantom, pretend, unreal, visionary

rel fabled, legendary, romantic; abstract, hypothetical, theoretical (*also* theoretic); unbelievable, unconvincing, unlikely; conceived, envisaged, envisioned, pictured, visualized; daydreamlike, deceptive, delusional, delusive, hallucinatory, illusory, phantasmagoric (*or* phantasmagorical); concocted, fabricated, feigned, fictive; inexistent, nonexistent

near ant authentic, genuine, true; factual, verifiable, verified; believable, convincing, realistic; corporeal, material, physical, solid, substantial; palpable, tangible

ant actual, existent, existing, real

imagination *n* **1** the ability to form mental images of things that either are not physically present or have never been conceived or created by others ⟨A cartoonist needs a fertile *imagination* in order to create interesting cartoons on demand.⟩

syn contrivance, creativity, fancy, fantasy (*also* phantasy), imaginativeness, invention, inventiveness, originality

rel brainstorm, brainstorming, inspiration; fecundity, fertility; ingenuity, resourcefulness; versatility; chimera, daydream, delusion, dream, figment, hallucination, illusion, mirage, phantasm (*also* fantasm), pipe dream; envisaging, visualization

near ant literality, literalness

2 the skill and imagination to create new things — see CREATIVITY 1

imaginative *adj* **1** having the skill and imagination to create new things — see CREATIVE 1

2 showing a noteworthy use of the imagination and creativity especially in inventing — see CLEVER 1

imaginativeness *n* **1** the ability to form mental images of things that either are not physically present or have never been conceived or created by others — see IMAGINATION 1

---

syn synonym(s)   *rel* related words
ant antonym(s)   *near ant* near antonym(s)

2 the skill and imagination to create new things — see CREATIVITY 1

imagine vb **1** to form a mental picture of ⟨She was determined to have the career that she had always *imagined*.⟩

syn conceive, conjure (up), dream, envisage, fancy, fantasy, feature, image, picture, see, vision, visualize

rel daydream, stargaze; hallucinate; re-create, reflect, relive, reminisce; contemplate, meditate, ponder, ruminate; concoct, fabricate, invent, make up, manufacture, plan, project; foresee, prefigure

2 to have as an opinion — see BELIEVE 2

3 to form an opinion from little or no evidence — see GUESS 1

imagined adj not real and existing only in the imagination — see IMAGINARY

imbecile n a stupid person — see IDIOT

imbecility n **1** a foolish act or idea — see FOLLY 1

2 lack of good sense or judgment — see FOOLISHNESS 1

imbibe vb **1** to swallow in liquid form — see DRINK 1

2 to take in (something liquid) through small openings — see ABSORB 1

imbue vb to cause (as a person) to become filled or saturated with a certain quality or principle — see INFUSE

imitate vb **1** to use (someone or something) as the model for one's speech, mannerisms, or behavior ⟨He's good at *imitating* his father.⟩

syn ape, copy, copycat, emulate, mime, mimic

rel ditto, echo, reecho, repeat; burlesque, caricature, lampoon, mock, parody, travesty; impersonate, perform, play; pantomime

2 to copy or exaggerate (someone or something) in order to make fun of — see MIMIC 1

3 to make an exact likeness of — see COPY 1

imitation n something that is made to look exactly like something else — see COPY

imitation adj being such in appearance only and made with or manufactured from usually cheaper materials ⟨The stage production uses only *imitation* diamonds, as real gems would be too expensive.⟩

syn artificial, bogus, dummy, fake, false, faux, imitative, man-made, mimic, mock, pretend, sham, simulated, substitute, synthetic

rel cultured, manufactured, process; unauthentic; adulterated, designer, doctored, engineered, fudged, juggled, manipulated, tampered (with); concocted, fabricated; counterfeit, deceptive, forged, fraudulent, misleading, phony (*also* phoney); affected, feigned, pinchbeck, pseudo, spurious

near ant authentic, bona fide, legitimate, true; premium, quality, valuable; pure, unadulterated

ant genuine, natural, real

imitative adj using or marked by the use of something else as a basis or model ⟨Your writing style tends to be *imitative* of whichever author you've recently read.⟩

syn apish, canned, emulative, formulaic, mimetic, mimic, unoriginal

rel copied, cribbed, plagiarized; artificial, bogus, factitious, fake, false, imitation, man-made, mock, sham, simulated, substitute, synthetic; duplicated, photocopied, reduplicated, reproduced, transcribed; backup; counterfeit, deceptive, forged, fraudulent, misleading; perfunctory, routine, uninspired

near ant authentic, bona fide, legitimate, true; genuine, natural, real; classic, ideal, model

ant archetypal (*also* archetypical), original

2 being such in appearance only and made with or manufactured from usually cheaper materials — see IMITATION

imitator n **1** a person who adopts the appearance or behavior of another especially in an obvious way — see COPYCAT

2 a person who imitates another's voice and mannerisms for comic effect — see MIMIC 1

immaculate adj **1** free from any trace of the coarse or indecent — see CHASTE 1

2 free from dirt or stain — see CLEAN 1

3 being entirely without fault or flaw — see PERFECT 1

immaterial adj **1** not composed of matter ⟨It is only possible to study *immaterial* forces like gravity by observing their effects on the physical world.⟩

syn bodiless, ethereal, formless, incorporeal, insubstantial, nonmaterial, nonphysical, spiritual, unsubstantial

rel metaphysical, supernatural; impalpable, insensible, intangible; airy, gaseous, gossamery, tenuous, thin, vaporous, wispish

near ant animal, carnal, fleshly; detectable, discernible (*also* discernable), noticeable, observable, palpable, sensible, tangible, visible; bulky, heavy, massive, solid

ant bodily, corporeal, material, physical, substantial

2 not having anything to do with the matter at hand — see IRRELEVANT

immature adj **1** being in the early stage of life, growth, or development — see YOUNG

2 having or showing the annoying qualities (as silliness) associated with children — see CHILDISH

3 lacking in adult experience or maturity — see CALLOW

immeasurable adj being or seeming to be without limits — see INFINITE

immediacy n the state or condition of being near — see PROXIMITY

immediate adj **1** done or occurring without any noticeable lapse in time — see INSTANTANEOUS

2 done or working without something else coming in between — see DIRECT 1

3 done, carried out, or given without delay — see PROMPT 1

4 not being distant in time, space, or significance — see CLOSE 2

5 existing or in progress right now — see PRESENT 1

immediately adv without delay ⟨If we don't leave *immediately*, we'll be late for the concert.⟩

syn bang, directly, forthwith, headlong, instantly, now, plumb, presently, promptly, pronto, right, right away, right now, straightaway, straightway

rel away, freely; anon, momentarily, shortly, soon; apace, briskly, fast, fleetly, full-tilt, posthaste, quick, quickly, rapidly, readily, snappily, speedily, swift, swiftly; abruptly, presto, suddenly, unexpectedly; hastily, impetuously, impulsively, rashly, recklessly; exactly, opportunely, punctually, seasonably

phrases at once, in no time, off the bat, on a dime, on the double, on the spot

near ant slowly; late, tardily

immemorial *adj* dating or surviving from the distant past — see ANCIENT 1

immense *adj* **1** unusually large — see HUGE

2 of the very best kind — see EXCELLENT

immenseness *n* the quality or state of being very large — see IMMENSITY

immensity *n* the quality or state of being very large ⟨The *immensity* of the mountain was awe-inspiring, especially up close.⟩

syn enormity, enormousness, hugeness, immenseness, magnitude, massiveness, vastness

rel bigness, extensiveness, greatness, largeness, sizableness, voluminousness, weightiness; awesomeness, grandness, stupendousness, tremendousness; boundlessness, limitlessness; ampleness, capaciousness, commodiousness, spaciousness; extravagance, extremeness, gaudiness, grandiosity

near ant littleness, puniness, smallness, triviality

ant diminutiveness, minuteness, tininess

immerse *vb* **1** to hold the attention of — see ENGAGE 1

2 to sink or push (something) briefly into or as if into a liquid — see DIP 1

immersed *adj* having the mind fixed on something — see ATTENTIVE 1

immersing *adj* holding the attention or provoking interest — see INTERESTING

immersion *n* a focusing of the mind on something — see ATTENTION 1

immigrant *n* one that leaves one place to settle in another — see EMIGRANT

imminent *adj* **1** giving signs of immediate occurrence ⟨Those clouds mean rain is *imminent*.⟩

syn impending, looming, pending, threatening

rel approaching, coming, forthcoming, future, near, nearing, oncoming, upcoming; brewing, gathering; likely, possible, probable; inevitable, unavoidable; lowering, menacing, ominous, portentous; anticipated, awaited, expected, foreseen, predicted

phrases around the corner

near ant distant, far-off, remote; eventual, ultimate; bygone, former, past; late, recent

2 being soon to appear or take place — see FORTHCOMING 1

immobile *adj* **1** fixed in a place or position — see STATIONARY 1

2 incapable of moving or being moved — see IMMOVABLE 1

immobilize *vb* to render powerless, ineffective, or unable to move — see PARALYZE 1

immoderate *adj* going beyond a normal or acceptable limit in degree or amount — see EXCESSIVE

immodest *adj* showing a lack of proper social reserve or modesty — see PRESUMPTUOUS 1

immolate *vb* to give up as an offering to a god — see SACRIFICE

immolation *n* something offered to a god — see SACRIFICE

immoral *adj* **1** not conforming to a high moral standard; morally unacceptable — see BAD 2

2 not guided by or showing a concern for what is right — see UNPRINCIPLED

immorality *n* **1** immoral conduct or practices harmful or offensive to society — see VICE 1

2 that which is morally unacceptable — see EVIL

immortal *adj* **1** lasting forever — see EVERLASTING 1

2 having an existence or validity that does not change or diminish — see ABIDING

immortality *n* unending existence after death — see ETERNITY 2

immortalize *vb* to give eternal or lasting existence to — see PERPETUATE

immovable *adj* **1** incapable of moving or being moved ⟨That boulder is *immovable*, even with a bulldozer.⟩

syn immobile, irremovable, nonmotile, nonmoving, unbudging, unmovable

rel motionless, moveless, static, stationary, still; fast, fixed, rooted, steadfast, stuck, wedged

near ant portable, removable (*also* removeable), transferable (*also* transferrable), transportable

ant mobile, motile, movable (*or* moveable), moving

2 sticking to an opinion, purpose, or course of action in spite of reason, arguments, or persuasion — see OBSTINATE

immunity *n* freedom from punishment, harm, or loss — see IMPUNITY

immure *vb* **1** to close or shut in by or as if by barriers — see ENCLOSE 1

2 to put in or as if in prison — see IMPRISON

immurement *n* the act of confining or the state of being confined — see INTERNMENT

immutability *n* the state of continuing without change — see CONSTANCY 1

immutable *adj* not capable of changing or being changed — see INFLEXIBLE 1

imp *n* **1** an appealingly mischievous person — see SCAMP 1

2 an evil spirit — see DEMON 1

impact *vb* **1** to act upon (a person or a person's feelings) so as to cause a response — see ¹AFFECT 1

2 to come into usually forceful contact with something — see HIT 2

3 to set solidly in or as if in surrounding matter — see ENTRENCH

impact *n* **1** a forceful coming together of two things ⟨The glass shattered immediately upon *impact* with the floor.⟩

syn bump, collision, concussion, crash,

---

syn synonym(s)   *rel* related words

ant antonym(s)   *near ant* near antonym(s)

jar, jolt, jounce, kick, shock, slam, smash, strike, wallop

rel blow, buffet, hit, knock, punch, rap, slap, thump; bashing, battering, bludgeoning, clobbering, hammering, lambasting, licking, pounding, pummeling (*also* pummelling), thrashing; contact, encounter, meeting, touch

2 the power to bring about a result on another — see EFFECT 2

3 the quality of an utterance that provokes interest and produces an effect — see ¹PUNCH 1

impair *vb* to reduce the soundness, effectiveness, or perfection of — see DAMAGE 1

impaired *adj* deprived of the power to perform one or more natural bodily activities — see DISABLED

impale *vb* to penetrate or hold (something) with a pointed object ⟨*Impale* a marshmallow or two on that stick and let's start toasting!⟩

syn gore, harpoon, jab, lance, peck, pick, pierce, puncture, run through, skewer, spear, spike, spit, stab, stick, transfix

rel spindle; perforate, riddle; bayonet, dirk, gimlet, pike, poniard, prong, quill; pinprick, poke, prick, punch, thrust; cut, knife, slice

impalpable *adj* **1** not capable of being perceived by the sense of touch — see INTANGIBLE

2 not perceptible by a sense or by the mind — see IMPERCEPTIBLE

impart *vb* to cause (something) to pass from one to another — see COMMUNICATE 1

impartial *adj* marked by justice, honesty, and freedom from bias — see FAIR 2

impartiality *n* lack of favoritism toward one side or another — see DETACHMENT 1

impassable *also* **impassible** *adj* impossible to get through or into — see IMPENETRABLE 1

impasse *n* **1** a point in a struggle where neither side is capable of winning or willing to give in ⟨Negotiations are at an *impasse*.⟩

syn deadlock, halt, stalemate, standoff, standstill

rel dead end; bind, bottleneck, corner, dilemma, fix, hole, jam, morass, pickle, pinch, plight, predicament, quagmire, quandary, spot; difficulty; problem

2 a difficult, puzzling, or embarrassing situation from which there is no easy escape — see PREDICAMENT

impassioned *adj* having or conveying great depth of feeling — see FERVENT 1

impassive *adj* **1** not feeling or showing emotion ⟨She remained *impassive* throughout the trial.⟩

syn apathetic, cold-blooded, numb, phlegmatic, stoic (*or* stoical), stolid, undemonstrative, unemotional

rel cold, cool, dispassionate, unmoved; calm, collected, composed; imperturbable, unflappable; reserved, reticent, taciturn; bland, blank, deadpan, dry, empty, expressionless, inexpressive, stone-faced, straight-faced, vacant, wooden; enigmatic (*also* enigmatical), impenetrable, inscrutable; aloof, bloodless, detached, indiffer-

ent, insensible, unconcerned, unsentimental; impersonal, objective, unresponsive; pitiless, unfeeling; inconsiderate, thoughtless

near ant blazing, burning, fiery, flaming, glowing, red-hot; ardent, enthusiastic, gung ho, warm-blooded, zealous; gushing, maudlin, mawkish, mushy, sentimental; dramatic, histrionic, melodramatic, overemotional, overheated; compassionate, responsive, sympathetic; reactive, sensitive

ant demonstrative, emotional, fervent, fervid, hot-blooded, impassioned, passionate, vehement

2 not expressing any emotion — see BLANK 1

impassivity *n* a lack of emotion or emotional expressiveness — see APATHY 1

impatience *n* urgent desire or interest — see EAGERNESS

impatient *adj* **1** showing urgent desire or interest — see EAGER

2 unable or unwilling to endure — see INTOLERANT 1

impeach *vb* **1** to make a claim of wrongdoing against — see ACCUSE

2 to demand proof of the truth or rightness of — see CHALLENGE 1

impeccability *n* the quality or state of being free from guilt or blame — see INNOCENCE 1

impeccable *adj* **1** being entirely without fault or flaw — see PERFECT 1

2 free from guilt or blame — see INNOCENT 2

3 free from sin — see INNOCENT 1

impeccably *adv* without any flaws or errors — see PERFECTLY 1

impecunious *adj* lacking money or material possessions — see POOR 1

impecuniousness *n* the state of lacking sufficient money or material possessions — see POVERTY 1

impede *vb* to create difficulty for the work or activity of — see HAMPER

impediment *n* something that makes movement or progress difficult — see ENCUMBRANCE

impel *vb* **1** to set or keep in motion — see MOVE 2

2 to cause (a person) to give in to pressure — see FORCE

impend *vb* to be about to happen — see LOOM

impend (over) *vb* to remain poised to inflict harm, danger, or distress on — see THREATEN

impending *adj* **1** being soon to appear or take place — see FORTHCOMING 1

2 giving signs of immediate occurrence — see IMMINENT 2

impenetrable *adj* **1** impossible to get through or into ⟨The ancient temple was surrounded by vast stretches of *impenetrable* jungle.⟩

syn impassable (*also* impassible), impermeable, impervious, impregnable

rel close, compact, dense, thick, tight; compressed, condensed; sturdy, substantial, tough; firm, frozen, hard, solid, stiff; inflexible, rigid, unbending, unyielding

near ant soft, squishy; bendable, elastic,

flexible, giving, malleable, pliable, yielding; absorbent, porous

ant negotiable, passable, penetrable, permeable

2 being beyond one's powers to know, understand, or explain — see MYSTERIOUS 1

3 impossible to understand — see INCOMPREHENSIBLE

4 not allowing penetration (as by gas, liquid, or light) — see TIGHT 1

impenitent *adj* not sorry for having done wrong — see REMORSELESS 1

imperative *adj* **1** forcing one's compliance or participation by or as if by law — see MANDATORY

2 impossible to do without — see ESSENTIAL 1

3 needing immediate attention — see ACUTE 2

imperative *n* **1** a statement of what to do that must be obeyed by those concerned — see COMMAND 1

2 something one must do because of prior agreement — see OBLIGATION 1

imperceptible *adj* not perceptible by a sense or by the mind ⟨a slight difference in hue between the two glasses that's *imperceptible* unless they're placed side by side⟩

syn impalpable, inappreciable, indistinguishable, insensible

rel inaudible, intangible; inconspicuous, indistinct, unnoticeable, unseeable, unseen; faint, insignificant, liminal, slender, slight, subtle, trivial; buried, concealed, covert, disguised, obscure, shrouded, unapparent, vague

near ant audible, observable, recognizable, tangible, visible; clear, conspicuous, evident, eye-catching, manifest, noticeable, obvious, plain, prominent, striking; apparent, distinct, significant, straightforward

ant appreciable, discernible (*also* discernable), palpable, perceptible, ponderable, sensible

imperfect *adj* having a fault — see FAULTY

imperfection *n* something that spoils the appearance or completeness of a thing — see BLEMISH

imperial *adj* large and impressive in size, grandeur, extent, or conception — see GRAND 1

imperil *vb* to place in danger — see ENDANGER

imperilment *n* the state of not being protected from injury, harm, or evil — see DANGER 1

imperious *adj* **1** fond of ordering people around — see BOSSY

2 having a feeling of superiority that shows itself in an overbearing attitude — see ARROGANT

3 having or showing a tendency to force one's will on others without any regard to fairness or necessity — see ARBITRARY 1

4 needing immediate attention — see ACUTE 2

imperiousness *n* an exaggerated sense of one's importance that shows itself in the

making of excessive or unjustified claims — see ARROGANCE

imperishable *adj* **1** impossible to destroy — see INDESTRUCTIBLE

2 having an existence or validity that does not change or diminish — see ABIDING

impermanent *adj* **1** intended to last, continue, or serve for a limited time — see TEMPORARY 1

2 lasting only for a short time — see MOMENTARY

impermeable *adj* **1** impossible to get through or into — see IMPENETRABLE 1

2 not allowing penetration (as by gas, liquid, or light) — see TIGHT 1

impermissible *adj* that may not be permitted ⟨Trial juries must be able to discern the difference between a permissible inference and *impermissible* speculation.⟩

syn banned, barred, forbidden, interdicted, outlawed, prohibited, proscribed, taboo (*also* tabu)

rel intolerable, unacceptable, unbearable, unendurable; illegal, illegitimate, illicit, improper, inappropriate, unauthorized, unlawful, unlicensed; ineffable, unmentionable; unseemly, unsuitable; objectionable; disallowed, disapproved, discouraged; refused, rejected, revoked, unsanctioned, vetoed; suppressed; precluded, prevented, stopped; excluded, ruled out, shut out; blocked, hindered, impeded, obstructed

near ant acceptable, bearable, endurable, tolerable; accepted, accredited, allowed, appropriate, approved, authorized, endorsed (*also* indorsed), lawful, legal, legitimate, licensed, OK (*or* okay), permitted, warranted; accorded, granted, sanctioned, vouchsafed; brooked, condoned, countenanced; encouraged, promoted, supported; commanded, mandatory, ordered, required; proper, seemly, suitable, tolerated, unobjectionable

ant allowable, permissible, permissive, sufferable

impersonate *vb* **1** to pretend to be (what one is not) in appearance or behavior ⟨He was arrested for *impersonating* a police officer.⟩

syn act, masquerade (as), play, pose (as)

rel ape, copy, imitate, mime, mimic, mock, monkey, parody, travesty; perform, portray

2 to present a portrayal or performance of — see ACT 1

impersonator *n* **1** a person who imitates another's voice and mannerisms for comic effect — see MIMIC 1

2 one who acts professionally (as in a play, movie, or television show) — see ACTOR 1

impertinence *n* **1** disrespectful or argumentative talk given in response to a command or request — see BACK TALK

2 rude behavior — see DISCOURTESY

3 the quality or state of not having anything to do with the matter at hand — see IRRELEVANCE

impertinent *adj* **1** displaying or marked by rude boldness — see NERVY 1

2 showing a lack of manners or consideration for others — see IMPOLITE

3 not having anything to do with the matter at hand — see IRRELEVANT

---

syn synonym(s)   **rel** related words
ant antonym(s)   **near ant** near antonym(s)

imperturbability *n* evenness of emotions or temper — see EQUANIMITY

imperturbable *adj* not easily panicked or upset — see UNFLAPPABLE

impervious *adj* **1** not allowing penetration (as by gas, liquid, or light) — see TIGHT 1

2 impossible to get through or into — see IMPENETRABLE 1

impetus *n* something that arouses action or activity — see IMPULSE 1

impiety *n* an act of great disrespect shown to God or to sacred ideas, people, or things — see BLASPHEMY

impinge *vb* to come into usually forceful contact with something — see HIT 2

impious *adj* not showing proper reverence for the holy or sacred — see IRREVERENT

impish *adj* tending to or exhibiting reckless playfulness — see MISCHIEVOUS 1

impishness *n* **1** a natural disposition for playful behavior — see PLAYFULNESS

2 playful, reckless behavior that is not intended to cause serious harm — see MISCHIEF 1

implacable *adj* **1** sticking to an opinion, purpose, or course of action in spite of reason, arguments, or persuasion — see OBSTINATE

2 showing no signs of slackening or yielding in one's purpose — see UNYIELDING 1

implant *vb* **1** to set permanently in the consciousness or mind-set ⟨a music teacher who strove to *implant* within his students a love of the classics⟩

syn breed, inculcate, plant, sow

rel drive, hammer, pound; embed (*also* imbed), entrench (*also* intrench), fix, lodge, root; imbue, infuse, ingrain (*also* engrain), inoculate, invest, steep, suffuse

2 to set solidly in or as if in surrounding matter — see ENTRENCH

implausible *adj* too extraordinary or improbable to believe — see INCREDIBLE

implement *vb* to carry out effectively — see ENFORCE

implement *n* an article intended for use in work ⟨gardening *implements* such as hoes, spades, and pruners⟩

syn device, instrument, tool, utensil

rel apparatus, appliance, mechanism; contraption, contrivance, gadget, gizmo (*also* gismo), jigger; accessory (*also* accessary), accoutrement (*or* accouterment), adjunct, appendage, attachment

implementation *n* the doing of an action — see COMMISSION 2

implicit *adj* **1** understood although not put into words ⟨The *implicit* agreement among members of the outing club is that everyone pays his or her own way on all trips.⟩

syn implied, tacit, unexpressed, unspoken, unvoiced, wordless

rel inferred, presumed; construed, interpreted; unannounced, undeclared, unsaid, untold; hinted, insinuated, intimated, suggested

near ant apparent, blatant, evident, manifest, obvious, plain, straightforward; unambiguous, unequivocal, unmistakable

ant explicit, express, expressed, spoken, stated, voiced

2 having or showing a mind free from doubt — see CERTAIN 2

3 existing only as a possibility and not in fact — see POTENTIAL

implied *adj* understood although not put into words — see IMPLICIT 1

implode *vb* to fall down or in as a result of physical pressure — see COLLAPSE 1

implore *vb* to make a request to (someone) in an earnest or urgent manner — see BEG

imploring *adj* asking humbly — see SUPPLIANT

imply *vb* to convey an idea indirectly — see HINT

impolite *adj* showing a lack of manners or consideration for others ⟨The librarian was shocked that anyone could be so *impolite* as to continue talking despite repeated warnings to be quiet.⟩

syn discourteous, disrespectful, ill-bred, ill-mannered, impertinent, inconsiderate, rude, thoughtless, uncalled-for, uncivil, ungracious, unhandsome, unmannerly

rel arch, audacious, bold, bold-faced, brash, brassy, brazen, cheeky, fresh, impudent, insolent, lippy, sassy, saucy, shameless; boorish, caddish, churlish, clownish, loutish, uncouth, vulgar; abrupt, blunt, brusque (*also* brusk), crusty, curt, gruff, sharp, snippety, snippy; antisocial, crabbed, cross, disagreeable, grumpy, sullen, surly; improper, incorrect, indecent, indecorous, unseemly; arrogant, conceited, haughty, high-handed, imperious, peremptory, pompous, presumptuous, pretentious, supercilious, superior

near ant humble, meek, modest, unassertive; deferential, dutiful, respectful, submissive, yielding; acceptable, appropriate, becoming, befitting, correct, decent, decorous, fit, fitting, good, meet, proper, respectable, right, seemly, suitable; affable, cordial, friendly, genial, hospitable, sociable; felicitous, graceful; chivalrous, courtly, gallant; ceremonious; elegant, refined

ant civil, considerate, courteous, genteel, gracious, mannerly, polite, thoughtful, well-bred

impoliteness *n* rude behavior — see DISCOURTESY

import *n* **1** the quality or state of being important — see IMPORTANCE

2 the idea that is conveyed or intended to be conveyed to the mind by language, symbol, or action — see MEANING 1

import *vb* **1** to be of importance — see MATTER

2 to communicate or convey (as an idea) to the mind — see MEAN 1

importance *n* the quality or state of being important ⟨A final exam has great *importance*.⟩

syn account, consequence, import, magnitude, moment, significance, weight, weightiness

rel celebrity, distinction, eminence, fame, note, noteworthiness, notoriety, preeminence, prominence, renown; store, substance, substantiveness, value, worth, worthiness; gravity, seriousness; authority, control, dominion, mastery, potency, power, sway; mark, name, report, reputation, repute; centrality, essentiality, essentialness; cachet, position, prestige, rank, standing, stature, status; glory, honor, illustriousness

near ant paltriness, valuelessness, worthlessness; discredit, disgrace, dishonor, disrepute, ignominy, infamy, odium, opprobrium, shame

ant littleness, puniness, slightness, smallness, triviality

important *adj* **1** having great meaning or lasting effect ⟨The discovery of penicillin was a very *important* event in the history of medicine.⟩

syn big, consequential, eventful, major, material, meaningful, momentous, monumental, much, significant, substantial, weighty

rel decisive, fatal, fateful, strategic; earnest, grave, heavy, serious, sincere; distinctive, exceptional, impressive, outstanding, prominent, remarkable; valuable, worthwhile, worthy; distinguished, eminent, great, illustrious, noble, notable, noteworthy, outstanding, preeminent, prestigious; famous, notorious, renowned; all-important, central, critical, crucial, essential, key, pivotal, seminal, vital

near ant paltry, petty, worthless; anonymous, nameless, obscure, uncelebrated, unknown

ant inconsequential, inconsiderable, insignificant, little, minor, negligible, slight, small, trifling, trivial, unimportant

2 having great power or influence ⟨Rachel Carson was an *important* figure in the environmental movement.⟩

syn heavy, influential, mighty, potent, powerful, puissant, significant, strong

rel high-level, senior, top; able, capable, competent, effective, efficient; celebrated, distinguished, dominant, eminent, famed, famous, great, illustrious, noble, notable, noteworthy, notorious, outstanding, preeminent, prestigious, prominent, renowned; dynamic, energetic, forceful, high-powered, robust, vigorous

near ant anonymous, nameless, obscure, uncelebrated, unknown; incapable, incompetent, ineffective, inept, inexpert, unfit, unqualified, unskilled, unskillful

ant helpless, impotent, insignificant, little, powerless, unimportant, weak

3 having a feeling of superiority that shows itself in an overbearing attitude — see ARROGANT

4 having too high an opinion of oneself — see CONCEITED

importune *vb* to make a request to (someone) in an earnest or urgent manner — see BEG

impose *vb* to establish or apply as a charge or penalty ⟨That state now *imposes* a fine for texting while driving.⟩

syn assess, charge, exact, fine, lay, levy, put

rel dock, excise, penalize, tax; extort, wrest, wring; bleed, fleece, gouge, skin, squeeze; coerce, compel, force; inflict, wreak

near ant abate, diminish, lessen; forgive, release; condone, disregard, excuse, gloss (over), gloze (over), ignore, pardon

ant remit

impose (on *or* **upon)** *vb* to take unfair advantage of — see EXPLOIT 1

imposing *adj* **1** having or showing a formal and serious or reserved manner — see DIGNIFIED

2 large and impressive in size, grandeur, extent, or conception — see GRAND 1

imposition *n* a charge usually of money collected by the government from people or businesses for public use — see TAX

impossible *adj* incapable of being solved or accomplished ⟨the seemingly *impossible* problem of world hunger⟩ ⟨Fitting everything in my backpack seemed an *impossible* task.⟩

syn hopeless, insoluble, insuperable, unattainable, unsolvable

rel impracticable, impractical, infeasible, unusable, unworkable; debatable, disputable, doubtable, doubtful, dubious, farfetched, fishy, improbable, problematic (*also* problematical), questionable, shady, shaky, suspect, suspicious, unfeasible, unlikely; implausible, inconceivable, incredible, unbelievable, unimaginable, unthinkable; futile, useless; absurd, fantastic (*also* fantastical), outlandish, preposterous, ridiculous

near ant applicable, functional, practicable, practical, reasonable, serviceable, usable (*also* useable), useful, working; likely, probable; acceptable, believable, conceivable, credible, plausible

ant achievable, attainable, doable, feasible, possible, realizable, resolvable, soluble, workable

impost *n* a charge usually of money collected by the government from people or businesses for public use — see TAX

impostor *or* **imposter** *n* one who makes false claims of identity or expertise ⟨The man who claimed to be a prince turned out to be an *impostor*.⟩

syn charlatan, fake, faker, fraud, hoaxer, humbug, mountebank, phony (*also* phoney), pretender, quack, ringer, sham

rel copycat, imitator, impersonator, mimic; actor, bluffer, counterfeiter, deceiver, dissembler, duper, feigner, misleader; operator, trickster; poseur; cozener, defrauder, dodger, sharper, sharpie (*or* sharpy), skinner, swindler

near ant ace, adept, authority, crackerjack (*also* crackajack), expert, maestro, master, past master, professional, virtuoso, whiz, wizard

impotence *n* the lack of sufficient ability, power, or means — see INABILITY

impotent *adj* **1** not able to produce fruit or offspring — see STERILE 1

2 unable to act or achieve one's purpose — see POWERLESS

impoverished *adj* **1** lacking money or material possessions — see POOR 1

2 producing inferior or only a small amount of vegetation — see BARREN 1

impoverishment *n* the state of lacking sufficient money or material possessions — see POVERTY 1

impracticable *adj* not capable of being put to use or account — see IMPRACTICAL

impractical *adj* not capable of being put to use or account ⟨The flimsy little toy

---

syn synonym(s)   **rel** related words
ant antonym(s)   **near ant** near antonym(s)

shovel was cute, but completely *impractical* for digging up tree stumps.⟩

syn impracticable, inoperable, nonpractical, unusable, unworkable, useless

rel unsuitable; inaccessible, unattainable, unavailable, unobtainable, unreachable; dead, dormant, fallow, free, idle, inactive, inert, inoperative, latent; arrested, interrupted; unrealistic

near ant accessible, acquirable, available, obtainable, procurable, reachable; all-around (*also* all-round), handy; active, alive, busy, employed, functioning, operating, operative, running, working

ant applicable, feasible, functional, operable, operational, practicable, practical, serviceable, usable (*also* useable), useful, utilizable, workable

imprecate *vb* to ask a divine power to send harm or evil upon — see CURSE 1

imprecation *n* a prayer that harm will come to someone — see CURSE 1

imprecise *adj* not precisely correct — see INEXACT 1

impregnable *adj* **1** incapable of being defeated, overcome, or subdued — see INVINCIBLE

2 impossible to get through or into — see IMPENETRABLE 1

impregnate *vb* to wet thoroughly with liquid — see SOAK 1

impress *n* a perceptible trace left by pressure — see PRINT 1

impress *vb* **1** to act upon (a person or a person's feelings) so as to cause a response — see ¹AFFECT 1

2 to produce a vivid impression of — see ENGRAVE 2

3 to cause (a person) to give in to pressure — see FORCE

impression *n* **1** a perceptible trace left by pressure — see PRINT 1

2 something imagined or pictured in the mind — see IDEA 1

impressionist *n* a person who imitates another's voice and mannerisms for comic effect — see MIMIC 1

impressive *adj* having the power to affect the feelings or sympathies — see MOVING

imprimatur *n* an acceptance of something as satisfactory — see APPROVAL

imprint *n* **1** a mark or series of marks left on a surface by something that has passed along it — see TRACK 1

2 a perceptible trace left by pressure — see PRINT 1

imprint *vb* to produce a vivid impression of — see ENGRAVE 2

imprison *vb* to put in or as if in prison ⟨In this society, we try to *imprison* criminals so that they can't do any more harm.⟩

syn commit, confine, immure, incarcerate, intern, jail, jug, lock (up)

rel constrain, limit, restrain, restrict, shut; bar, gate; apprehend, arrest, bust [*slang*], capture, catch, detain, nab, pick up, pinch, seize; impress, shanghai; hold, impound, keep; bind, enchain, fetter, handcuff, manacle, shackle, trammel

near ant emancipate, enfranchise, manumit, unbind, uncage, unchain, unfetter

ant discharge, free, liberate, release

imprisoned *adj* taken and held prisoner — see CAPTIVE

imprisonment *n* the act of confining or the state of being confined — see INTERNMENT

improbable *adj* not likely to be true or to occur ⟨It seems *improbable* that the two writers never met since they traveled in the same social circles.⟩

syn doubtful, dubious, far-fetched, flimsy, questionable, unapt, unlikely

rel implausible, impossible, inconceivable, incredible, unbelievable, unimaginable, unthinkable; absurd, bizarre, fantastic (*also* fantastical), foolish, nonsensical, odd, outlandish, preposterous, ridiculous, unreal, wild; outside, remote, slight

near ant believable, conceivable, credible, earthly, imaginable, plausible; possible, potential; liable

ant likely, probable

impromptu *adj* made or done without previous thought or preparation — see EXTEMPORANEOUS

improper *adj* not appropriate for a particular occasion or situation — see INAPPROPRIATE

improperly *adv* in a mistaken or inappropriate way — see WRONGLY

impropriety *n* **1** the quality or state of not being socially proper ⟨The *impropriety* of the song that the campers sang for the visitors was embarrassing.⟩

syn inappropriateness, incorrectness, indecency, indelicateness

rel coarseness, crudeness, vulgarity; immodesty, naughtiness; imprudence, indiscreetness, indiscretion; churlishness, discourteousness, disrespect, impertinence, impoliteness, impudence, incivility, inconsiderateness, inconsideration, insolence, rudeness, ungraciousness

near ant discretion, prudence; etiquette, form, manners, proprieties: considerateness, consideration, gentility, graciousness, thoughtfulness

ant appropriateness, correctness, decency, decorousness, decorum, fitness, propriety, rightness, seemliness, suitability, suitableness

2 a socially improper or unsuitable act or remark ⟨such *improprieties* as asking people how much money they make⟩

syn familiarity, gaff, gaffe, indiscretion, solecism

rel blunder, error, flub, fumble, goof, lapse, miscue, misstep, mistake, oversight, slip, slipup, stumble; discourtesy, incivility, offense (*or* offence); foul-up, muff; misapprehension, misconception, misjudgment, misstatement, misunderstanding

near ant form, manners, mores, proprieties

ant amenity, attention, civility, courtesy, formality, gesture, pleasantry

3 the quality or state of being unsuitable or unfitting — see INAPPROPRIATENESS 1

improve *vb* to make better ⟨A little salt would *improve* this bland food.⟩

syn ameliorate, amend, better, enhance, enrich, help, meliorate, perfect, refine, upgrade *rei* correct, emend, rectify, reform, remediate, remedy; edit, fine-tune, redraft, refurbish, rehab, rehabilitate, revamp, revise, rework; beef (up), fortify, intensify, strengthen; fine, hone, polish; retouch, touch up; sweeten

near ant damage, harm, hurt, impair, injure, spoil, tarnish, vitiate; blemish, deface, disfigure, flaw, mar; diminish, lessen, lower, reduce

ant worsen

improved *adj* being far along in development — see ADVANCED

improvement *n* an instance of notable progress in the development of knowledge, technology, or skill — see ADVANCE 2

improvident *adj* not thinking about and providing for the future ⟨the *improvident* view that you don't need to save for retirement⟩

syn myopic, shortsighted

rel careless, heedless, imprudent, incautious, injudicious, mindless, unguarded, unsafe, unwary, unwise; extravagant, prodigal, profligate, spendthrift, thriftless, unthrifty; indulgent, lavish, reckless, wasteful

near ant careful, judicious, prudent, sensible, wise; economical, economizing, frugal, scrimping, sparing, thrifty; conserving, preserving, saving

ant farsighted, forehanded, foreseeing, foresighted, forethoughtful, provident

improvise *vb* to perform, make, or do without preparation ⟨Since the award was a complete surprise, I *improvised* an acceptance speech.⟩

syn ad-lib, extemporize, fake

rel concoct, contrive, cook (up), devise, fabricate, hatch, invent, make up, manufacture, think (up); dash (off)

near ant arrange, lay, prepare, ready; consider, contemplate, ponder, study; exercise, practice (*also* practise), rehearse

improvised *adj* made or done without previous thought or preparation — see EXTEMPORANEOUS

imprudent *adj* showing poor judgment especially in personal relationships or social situations — see INDISCREET

impudence *n* 1 disrespectful or argumentative talk given in response to a command or request — see BACK TALK

2 rude behavior — see DISCOURTESY

impudent *adj* displaying or marked by rude boldness — see NERVY 1

impulse *n* 1 something that arouses action or activity ⟨The new auto factory was just the *impulse* that the local economy needed.⟩

syn boost, encouragement, goad, impetus, incentive, incitement, instigation, momentum, motivation, provocation, spur, stimulant, stimulus, yeast

rel inducement, invitation; antecedent, cause, consideration, grounds, motive, occasion, reason; catalyst, catalyzer, fuel, spark

phrases shot in the arm

ant counterincentive, disincentive

2 a habitual attraction to some activity or thing — see INCLINATION 1

impulsive *adj* 1 caused by or suggestive of an irresistible urge — see COMPULSIVE

2 prone to sudden illogical changes of mind, ideas, or actions — see WHIMSICAL

impulsiveness *n* an inclination to sudden illogical changes of mind, ideas, or actions — see WHIMSICALITY

impunity *n* freedom from punishment, harm, or loss ⟨She mistakenly believed that she could insult people with *impunity*.⟩

syn exemption, immunity

rel aegis (*also* egis), armor, cover, defense, guard, protection, safeguard, safety, security, shield; buffer, bumper, screen; absolution, absolving, dispensation, forgiveness

near ant exposure, liability, openness, susceptibility, susceptibleness, vulnerability

impure *adj* 1 containing foreign or lower-grade substances ⟨Be careful, because *impure* motor oil can damage your car's engine.⟩

syn adulterate, adulterated, alloyed, contaminated, dilute, diluted, polluted, tainted, thinned, weakened

rel unclarified, unfiltered, unrefined; besmirched, corrupted, debased, defiled, dirtied, fouled, soiled, spoiled, sullied; blended, commingled, incorporated, intermingled, intermixed, merged, mingled, mixed; coalesced, combined, compounded; cheapened, doctored

near ant clarified, filtered, purified, refined, ultrarefined; neat, plain, straight; concentrated; strong; uncombined; pasteurized; sterile, sterilized; clean, immaculate, spotless, stainless, unsoiled, unsullied

ant fine, pure, ultrapure, unadulterated, unalloyed, uncontaminated, uncut, undiluted, unmixed, unpolluted, untainted

2 depicting or referring to sexual matters in a way that is unacceptable in polite society — see OBSCENE 1

impurity *n* 1 something that is or that makes impure ⟨*Impurities* in the water made it cloudy.⟩

syn adulterant, contaminant, defilement, pollutant

rel blot, blotch, spot, stain, taint; dirt, filth, grime, muck, scum, sludge, smut, soil; blemish, defect, disfigurement, fault, flaw; abnormality, imperfection, irregularity

near ant clarifier, filter, purifier, refiner; cleanliness, immaculateness, purity

2 the quality or state of being obscene — see OBSCENITY

impute *vb* to explain (something) as being the result of something else — see CREDIT 1

in *adj* 1 being in the latest or current fashion — see STYLISH

2 enjoying widespread favor or approval — see POPULAR 1

3 being within the confines of a specified place — see PRESENT 2

in *adv* at, within, or to a short distance or time — see NEAR 1

in *n* the power to direct the thinking or behavior of others usually indirectly — see INFLUENCE 1

in *prep* using the means or agency of — see BY 2

---

syn synonym(s) *rel* related words
ant antonym(s) *near ant* near antonym(s)

inability *n* the lack of sufficient ability, power, or means ⟨the apparent *inability* of some young children to sit still⟩
syn impotence, inadequacy, incapability, incapacity, incompetence, ineptitude, insufficiency, powerlessness
rel disqualification, inaptitude; ineffectiveness, ineffectuality, ineffectualness, inefficaciousness, inefficacy, inefficiency
near ant aptitude, bent, endowment, flair, genius, gift, knack, talent; effectiveness, effectualness, efficaciousness, efficiency; fitness, suitability, suitableness; potency, power, puissance, sinew, strength
ant ability, adequacy, capability, capacity, competence, competency, potency

inaccessible *adj* hard or impossible to get to or get at ⟨The area is *inaccessible* by car.⟩
syn inconvenient, unapproachable, unattainable, unavailable, unobtainable, unreachable, untouchable
rel away, distant, far, faraway, far-off, remote, removed; apart, isolated, out-of-the-way, secluded
near ant close, immediate, near, nearby, neighboring, next-door, nigh
ant accessible, acquirable, approachable, attainable, convenient, getatable, handy, obtainable, procurable, reachable

inaccuracy *n* an unintentional departure from truth or accuracy — see ERROR 1

inaccurate *adj* 1 not being in agreement with what is true — see FALSE 1
2 not precisely correct — see INEXACT 1

inaccurately *adv* in a mistaken or inappropriate way — see WRONGLY

inaction *n* lack of action or activity ⟨As a result of the park department's *inaction*, the city's pools are not ready to open for the summer.⟩
syn dormancy, idleness, inactivity, inertness, nonaction, quiescence
rel indolence, inertia, languor, lassitude, laziness, listlessness, shiftlessness, sleepiness, sloth, sluggishness; dallying, loafing, lolling, lounging
near ant animateness, briskness, exuberance, jazziness, liveliness, peppiness, robustness, sprightliness, vibrancy, vivacity; assiduity, assiduousness, business, diligence, employment, industriousness, industry, occupation
ant action, activeness, activity

inactive *adj* 1 slow to move or act ⟨It's easiest to catch snakes early in the morning, while they're still cold and *inactive*.⟩
syn dull, inert, lethargic, quiescent, sleepy, sluggish, torpid
rel ambitionless, apathetic, indolent, languorous, lazy, lazyish, listless, shiftless, slack, slothful, sluggard, sluggardly; dormant, motionless, resting, sedentary, static, still; dead; dopey (*also* dopy), drugged; asleep, drowsy, somnambulant
near ant busy, engaged, occupied, working; animated, bouncing, dynamic, energetic, lively, peppy, perky, spirited, sprightly, springy, vigorous, vital, vivacious, zippy; assiduous, diligent, hardworking, industrious, sedulous
ant active
2 not being in a state of use, activity, or employment ⟨an *inactive* oil well⟩

syn dead, dormant, fallow, free, idle, inert, inoperative, latent, off, unused, vacant
rel abeyant, arrested, interrupted; unoccupied; asleep, lifeless, moribund, quiescent, sleepy; inoperable, unusable, unworkable, useless; dull, slow
phrases at rest, on the shelf, out of commission
near ant functional, operable, operational, workable; assiduous, industrious, sedulous; energetic, vigorous; feasible, practical, usable (*also* useable), useful, viable
ant active, alive, busy, employed, functioning, going, living, on, operating, operative, running, working

inactivity *n* 1 lack of action or activity — see INACTION
2 lack of use — see DISUSE

inadequacy *n* 1 a falling short of an essential or desirable amount or number — see DEFICIENCY
2 the lack of sufficient ability, power, or means — see INABILITY

inadequate *adj* not coming up to an expected measure or meeting a particular need — see SHORT 3

inadequately *adv* in an unsatisfactory way — see BADLY 1

inadvertent *adj* happening by chance — see ACCIDENTAL 1

inadvisable *adj* showing poor judgment especially in personal relationships or social situations — see INDISCREET

inane *adj* having no meaning — see MEANINGLESS

inanity *n* 1 a foolish act or idea — see FOLLY 1
2 lack of good sense or judgment — see FOOLISHNESS 1

inapplicability *n* the quality or state of not having anything to do with the matter at hand — see IRRELEVANCE

inapplicable *adj* not having anything to do with the matter at hand — see IRRELEVANT

inappreciable *adj* not perceptible by a sense or by the mind — see IMPERCEPTIBLE

inappropriate *adj* not appropriate for a particular occasion or situation ⟨He wore casual clothes that were *inappropriate* for the interview.⟩
syn amiss, graceless, improper, inapt, incongruous, incorrect, indecorous, inept, infelicitous, perverse, unapt, unbecoming, unfit, unhappy, unseemly, unsuitable, untoward, wrong
rel inopportune, unfortunate, unseasonable, untimely; extraneous, immaterial, inapplicable, irrelative, irrelevant; misbecoming, mismatched; incompatible, inconsistent, uncongenial; banned, barred, disallowed; forbidden, interdicted, outlawed, prohibited, proscribed; awkward, gauche, ungraceful; unacceptable, unsatisfactory
phrases out of place, out of the way
near ant fortunate, opportune, seasonable, timely; applicable, apposite, apropos, apt, germane, material, pat, pointed, relative, relevant; compatible, congenial, harmonious; allowed, authorized, permitted; approved, endorsed (*also* indorsed),

kosher, licensed, sanctioned; abetted, encouraged, promoted, supported; acceptable, adequate, all right, decent, fine, OK (or okay), passable, respectable, satisfactory, tolerable; balanced, companionate, congruous, consonant, harmonious

ant appropriate, becoming, befitting, correct, decorous, felicitous, fit, fitting, genteel, happy, meet, proper, right, seemly, suitable

inappropriately *adv* in a mistaken or inappropriate way — see WRONGLY

inappropriateness *n* **1** the quality or state of being unsuitable or unfitting ⟨I was angered by the *inappropriateness* of his comments.⟩

syn impropriety, inaptness, incorrectness, infelicity, unfitness, wrongness

rel extraneousness, inadequacy, inadmissibility, inapplicability, irrelevance, meaninglessness, pointlessness, senselessness; inauspiciousness, inexpedience, inexpediency, intolerability, undesirability, undesirableness, unsatisfactoriness, uselessness; unbecomingness

near ant admissibility, applicability, bearing, connection, materiality, pertinence, pointedness, relevance, relevancy

ant appropriateness, aptness, correctness, felicitousness, felicity, fitness, fittingness, propriety, rightness, seemliness, suitability, suitableness

2 the quality or state of not being socially proper — see IMPROPRIETY 1

inapt *adj* **1** not appropriate for a particular occasion or situation — see INAPPROPRIATE

2 lacking qualities (as knowledge, skill, or ability) required to do a job — see INCOMPETENT

inaptly *adv* in a mistaken or inappropriate way — see WRONGLY

inaptness *n* the quality or state of being unsuitable or unfitting — see INAPPROPRIATENESS 1

inarticulate *adj* unable to speak — see MUTE 1

inasmuch as *conj* for the reason that — see SINCE

inaugural *adj* coming before all others in time or order — see FIRST 1

inaugural *n* the process or an instance of being formally placed in an office or organization — see INSTALLATION 1

inaugurate *vb* **1** to be responsible for the creation and early operation or use of — see FOUND

2 to put into an office or welcome into an organization with special ceremonies — see INSTALL 1

inauguration *n* the process or an instance of being formally placed in an office or organization — see INSTALLATION 1

inaugurator *n* a person who establishes a whole new field of endeavor — see FATHER 2

inauspicious *adj* being or showing a sign of evil or calamity to come — see OMINOUS

inauthentic *adj* being such in appearance only and made or manufactured with the intention of committing fraud — see COUNTERFEIT 1

inborn *adj* **1** being a part of the innermost nature of a person or thing — see INHERENT

2 genetically passed or capable of being passed from parent to offspring — see HEREDITARY

inbred *adj* being a part of the innermost nature of a person or thing — see INHERENT

incandescence *n* the steady giving off of the form of radiation that makes vision possible — see LIGHT 1

incandescent *adj* **1** giving off or reflecting much light — see BRIGHT 1

2 having or expressing great depth of feeling — see FERVENT 1

incantation *n* a spoken word or set of words believed to have magic power — see SPELL 1

incapability *n* the lack of sufficient ability, power, or means — see INABILITY

incapable *adj* lacking qualities (as knowledge, skill, or ability) required to do a job — see INCOMPETENT

incapacitate *vb* **1** to render powerless, ineffective, or unable to move — see PARALYZE 1

2 to cause severe or permanent injury to — see MAIM

incapacity *n* the lack of sufficient ability, power, or means — see INABILITY

incarcerate *vb* to put in or as if in prison — see IMPRISON

incarcerated *adj* taken and held prisoner — see CAPTIVE

incarceration *n* the act of confining or the state of being confined — see INTERNMENT

incarnate *vb* to represent in visible form — see EMBODY 2

incarnation *n* a visible representation of something abstract (as a quality) — see EMBODIMENT

incautious *adj* not paying or showing close attention especially for the purpose of avoiding trouble — see CARELESS 1

incautiousness *n* failure to take the care that a cautious person usually takes — see NEGLIGENCE 1

incendiary *n* **1** a person who deliberately and unlawfully sets fire to a building or other property — see ARSONIST

2 a person who stirs up public feelings especially of discontent — see AGITATOR

incense *n* a sweet or pleasant smell — see FRAGRANCE

¹**incense** *vb* to make angry — see ANGER

²**incense** *vb* to fill or infuse with a pleasant odor or odor-releasing substance — see SCENT 1

incensed *adj* feeling or showing anger — see ANGRY

incentive *n* something that arouses action or activity — see IMPULSE 1

inception *n* the point at which something begins — see BEGINNING

incertitude *n* a feeling or attitude that one does not know the truth, truthfulness, or trustworthiness of someone or something — see DOUBT

---

syn synonym(s)   *rel* related words
ant antonym(s)   *near ant* near antonym(s)

incessant *adj* going on and on without any interruptions — see CONTINUOUS

incessantly *adv* on every relevant occasion — see ALWAYS 1

inch *n* 1 a very small distance or degree — see HAIR 1

2 an individual part of a process, series, or ranking — see DEGREE 1

3 **inches** *pl* the distance of something or someone from bottom to top — see HEIGHT 3

inch *vb* 1 to advance gradually beyond the usual or desirable limits — see ENCROACH

2 to move slowly — see CRAWL 2

incident *n* something that happens — see EVENT 1

incidental *adj* 1 happening by chance — see ACCIDENTAL 1

2 lacking importance — see UNIMPORTANT

incipiency *n* the point at which something begins — see BEGINNING

incise *vb* 1 to cut (as letters or designs) on a hard surface — see ENGRAVE 1

2 to penetrate with a sharp edge (as a knife) — see CUT 1

incision *n* a long deep cut — see GASH

incite *vb* 1 to bring (something volatile or intense) into being ⟨He was arrested for *inciting* a riot.⟩

syn abet, brew, ferment, foment, instigate, pick, provoke, raise, stir (up), whip (up)

rel advance, cultivate, encourage, forward, foster, further, nourish, nurture, promote, sow, stimulate; detonate, set, set off, trigger; excite, galvanize, inflame (*also* enflame), inspire, motivate, rouse; activate, energize, enliven, fire, invigorate, jazz (up), liven (up), pep (up), quicken, stimulate, vitalize

phrases set in motion

near ant bridle, check, constrain, curb, discourage, hold, inhibit, regulate, rein (in), restrain, tame; allay, calm, quiet, settle, soothe, still, subdue, tranquilize (*also* tranquillize)

2 to rouse to strong feeling or action — see PROVOKE 1

incitement *n* 1 something that arouses a strong response from another — see PROVOCATION 1

2 something that arouses action or activity — see IMPULSE 1

inciter *n* a person who stirs up public feelings especially of discontent — see AGITATOR

inciting *adj* serving or likely to arouse a strong reaction — see PROVOCATIVE

incivility *n* rude behavior — see DISCOURTESY

inclement *adj* marked by wet and windy conditions — see FOUL 1

inclination *n* 1 a habitual attraction to some activity or thing ⟨her natural *inclination* to help people in need⟩

syn affection, affinity, aptitude, bent, bias, bone, devices, disposition, genius, impulse, leaning, partiality, penchant, predilection, predisposition, proclivity, propensity, tendency, turn

rel favor, one-sidedness, partisanship, prejudice; endowment, faculty, flair, genius, gift, knack, talent; appetite, fancy,

fondness, like, liking, preference, taste; forte, speciality, specialty; convention, custom, habit, pattern, practice (*also* practise), routine, trick, way, wont; eccentricity, idiosyncrasy, oddity, peculiarity, quirk, singularity

near ant allergy, averseness, aversion, disfavor, disinclination, dislike, disliking, distaste; detachment, impartiality, neutrality, objectivity; apathy, disinterestedness, indifference, insouciance, nonchalance, unconcern

2 the act of positioning or an instance of being positioned at an angle — see TILT

3 the degree to which something rises up from a position level with the horizon — see SLANT 1

incline *n* the degree to which something rises up from a position level with the horizon — see SLANT 1

incline *vb* 1 to set or cause to be at an angle — see LEAN 1

2 to show a liking or proneness (for something) — see LEAN 2

inclined *adj* 1 having a desire or inclination (as for a specified course of action) — see WILLING 1

2 having a liking or affection — see FOND 1

3 having a tendency to be or act in a certain way — see PRONE 1

4 running in a slanting direction — see DIAGONAL

inclining *adj* bending downward or forward — see NODDING

include *vb* 1 to have as part of a whole ⟨The college application *included* some thought-provoking essay questions.⟩

syn carry, comprehend, contain, embrace, encompass, entail, involve, number, subsume, take in

rel comprise, consist (of); bracket; have, hold, own, possess; admit; compose, constitute, form, make; assimilate, embody, incorporate, integrate

near ant ban, bar, debar, preclude, prevent, prohibit; deny, refuse, reject; eliminate, except, rule out; lose, mislay, misplace

ant exclude, leave (out), omit

2 to close or shut in by or as if by barriers — see ENCLOSE 1

inclusive *adj* covering everything or all important points — see ENCYCLOPEDIC

inclusively *adv* with everyone or everything taken into account at the same time — see ALL AROUND

incognito *adj* not named or identified by a name — see NAMELESS 1

incoherent *adj* 1 not clearly or logically connected ⟨The thriller's *incoherent* plot left movie audiences wondering who did what.⟩

syn choppy, disconnected, disjointed, unconnected

rel baffling, bewildering, confounding, confused, confusing, disordered, disorderly, disorganized, muddled, perplexing, puzzling, unorganized; disconcerting, frustrating; fallacious, illogical, inconsistent, invalid, irrational, unsound; absurd, asinine, bizarre, curious, eccentric, foolish, odd, outlandish, outré, peculiar, screwy, strange, unreasonable, unusual, weird; inexplicable, unaccountable, unexplainable

near ant ordered, orderly, organized, systematic, systematized; logical, rational, reasonable, sensible, solid, sound, valid; cogent, compelling, convincing, persuasive, plausible, satisfying; clear, clear-cut, lucid, perspicuous, transparent, unambiguous, unequivocal, unmistakable

ant coherent, connected

2 consisting of particles that do not stick together — see LOOSE 2

incombustible *adj* incapable of being burned 〈We keep our important papers in an *incombustible* safe in the basement.〉

syn fireproof, noncombustible, nonflammable, noninflammable

rel nonexplosive

near ant ablaze, afire, aflame, blazing, burning, combusting, fiery, flaming, ignited, inflamed (*also* enflamed), kindled; consumable; explosive, incendiary, volcanic

ant burnable, combustible, flammable, ignitable (*also* ignitible), inflammable

income *n* **1** an increase usually measured in money that comes from labor, business, or property 〈Her summer job gave her some extra *income*.〉

syn earnings, gain(s), proceeds, profit, return, revenue, yield

rel windfall; salary, take-home pay, tips, wages; bankroll, capital, finances, funds, money, pocket, pocketbook, resources, wherewithal

near ant charge, cost, disbursement, expenditures, expenses, outgo, outlay

2 a flowing or coming in — see INFLUX

incommode *vb* to cause discomfort to or trouble for — see INCONVENIENCE

incommoding *adj* causing difficulty, discomfort, or annoyance — see INCONVENIENT 1

incommunicable *adj* beyond the power to describe — see INDESCRIBABLE

incomparable *adj* having no equal or rival for excellence or desirability — see ONLY 1

incompatible *adj* not being in agreement or harmony — see INCONSISTENT 1

incompetence *n* the lack of sufficient ability, power, or means — see INABILITY

incompetent *adj* lacking qualities (as knowledge, skill, or ability) required to do a job 〈An *incompetent* carpenter had built the deck, and the railings were loose already.〉

syn inapt, incapable, inept, inexpert, unfit, unqualified, unskilled, unskillful

rel ineffective, ineffectual, inefficient; amateurish, callow, green, inexperienced, raw, unprofessional; unequipped, unprepared, untrained; useless, worthless; disqualified, ineligible; wanting

near ant prepared, ready, trained; overqualified; accomplished, ace, adept, consummate, crack, experienced, practiced (*also* practised), seasoned, veteran, virtuoso; all-around (*also* all-round), protean, versatile

ant able, capable, competent, expert, fit, qualified, skilled, skillful, ultracompetent

incomplete *adj* lacking some necessary part 〈an *incomplete* puzzle that has several pieces missing〉

syn deficient, fragmental, fragmentary, half, halfway, partial

rel broken, damaged, flawed, impaired, imperfect, injured, marred, spoiled; sketchy, unassembled, uncompleted, unfinished

near ant flawless, unbroken, undamaged, unimpaired, uninjured, unmarred; completed, finished

ant complete, entire, full, intact, integral, perfect, whole

incompletely *adv* in some measure or degree — see PARTLY

incomprehensible *adj* impossible to understand 〈Rocket science is *incomprehensible* to most people.〉

syn impenetrable, unfathomable, unintelligible

rel abstruse, enigmatic (*also* enigmatical), esoteric, inscrutable, recondite, unsearchable; cryptic, darkling, deep, mysterious, mystic, oblique, obscure, occult, uncanny; unanswerable, unknowable; baffling, bewildering, confounding, confusing, mystifying, perplexing, puzzling; inconceivable, unimaginable, unthinkable

near ant basic, elemental, elementary, essential, fundamental, rudimentary, underlying; coherent, connected, ordered, orderly, organized, systematic, systematized; clear, cogent, compelling, convincing, lucid, pellucid, perspicuous, plain, straightforward

inconceivable *adj* too extraordinary or improbable to believe — see INCREDIBLE

incongruity *n* someone or something with qualities or features that seem to conflict with one another — see CONTRADICTION 1

incongruous *adj* **1** not appropriate for a particular occasion or situation — see INAPPROPRIATE

2 not being in agreement or harmony — see INCONSISTENT 1

inconsequential *adj* **1** lacking importance — see UNIMPORTANT

2 so small or unimportant as to warrant little or no attention — see NEGLIGIBLE 1

3 not using or following good reasoning — see ILLOGICAL

inconsiderable *adj* **1** lacking importance — see UNIMPORTANT

2 so small or unimportant as to warrant little or no attention — see NEGLIGIBLE 1

inconsiderate *adj* showing a lack of manners or consideration for others — see IMPOLITE

inconsiderateness *n* rude behavior — see DISCOURTESY

inconsideration *n* rude behavior — see DISCOURTESY

inconsistent *adj* **1** not being in agreement or harmony 〈*Inconsistent* theories make it difficult to settle on one explanation.〉

syn clashing, conflicting, disagreeing, discordant, discrepant, incompatible, incongruous, inharmonious, repugnant

rel irreconcilable; antagonistic, antipodal,

antipodean, antithetical, contradictory, contrary, diametric (or diametrical), opposing, opposite
phrases at odds, at variance
near ant akin, like, similar
ant agreeing, compatible, concordant, conformable (to), congruous, consistent, consonant, correspondent (with or ·to), harmonious, nonconflicting
2 likely to change frequently, suddenly, or unexpectedly — see FICKLE 1
inconsolable *adj* feeling unhappiness — see SAD 1
inconspicuous *adj* not readily seen or noticed — see UNOBTRUSIVE
inconstancy *n* 1 lack of faithfulness especially to one's husband or wife — see INFIDELITY 1
2 the frequent and usually sudden passing from one condition to another — see FLUX 1
inconstant *adj* 1 likely to change frequently, suddenly, or unexpectedly — see FICKLE 1
2 not true in one's allegiance to someone or something — see FAITHLESS
incontestable *adj* not capable of being challenged or proved wrong — see IRREFUTABLE
incontestably *adv* without any question — see INDEED 1
incontrovertible *adj* not capable of being challenged or proved wrong — see IRREFUTABLE
incontrovertibly *adv* without any question — see INDEED 1
inconvenience *n* something that is a source of irritation — see ANNOYANCE 3
inconvenience *vb* to cause discomfort to or trouble for ⟨He *inconvenienced* his sister by moving into her tiny apartment.⟩
syn discommode, disoblige, disturb, incommode, put out, trouble
rel burden, encumber, saddle, weigh; fetter, hamper, hamstring, handicap, hinder, hobble, hold back, hold up, impede, inhibit, interfere (with), manacle, obstruct, shackle, tie up, trammel; aggravate, anger, annoy, bother, bug, chafe, exasperate, gall, get, irk, nettle, peeve, pique, rile, vex; grate, inflame (also enflame), provoke; agitate, perturb, upset
near ant abet, aid, assist, help; ease, facilitate, smooth; appease, conciliate, disarm, mollify, pacify, placate; delight, gladden, gratify, please, satisfy; comfort, console, content
ant accommodate, favor, oblige
inconvenient *adj* 1 causing difficulty, discomfort, or annoyance ⟨The unexpected visitors showed up at an *inconvenient* time.⟩
syn awkward, discommoding, disobliging, incommoding
rel bothersome, burdensome, onerous, troublesome; annoying, disturbing, exasperating, frustrating, galling, irksome, irritating, maddening, riling, vexatious, vexing
near ant acceptable, bearable, endurable, sufferable, tolerable; advantageous, desirable, helpful
ant convenient, ultraconvenient
2 hard or impossible to get to or get at — see INACCESSIBLE

incorporate *vb* 1 to make a part of a body or system — see EMBODY 1
2 to turn into a single mass or entity that is more or less the same throughout — see BLEND 1
3 to represent in visible form — see EMBODY 2
incorporeal *adj* not composed of matter — see IMMATERIAL 1
incorrect *adj* 1 having an opinion that does not agree with truth or the facts ⟨You're *incorrect* about the date of the final exam—it's next Tuesday, not Wednesday.⟩
syn mistaken, wrong
rel confused, misguided, misinformed, misled; erroneous, false, inaccurate, inexact, untrue; deceived, deluded, duped, tricked
phrases all wet, full of it
near ant informed; accurate, exact, precise, true
ant correct, right
2 not appropriate for a particular occasion or situation — see INAPPROPRIATE
3 not being in agreement with what is true — see FALSE 1
incorrectly *adv* in a mistaken or inappropriate way — see WRONGLY
incorrectness *n* 1 the quality or state of being unsuitable or unfitting — see INAPPROPRIATENESS 1
2 the quality or state of not being socially proper — see IMPROPRIETY 1
incorrigible *adj* not capable of being cured or reformed — see HOPELESS 1
increase *n* 1 something added (as by growth) ⟨Shortly after he turned 12, he had a sudden height *increase*.⟩
syn accretion, accrual, addendum, addition, augmentation, boost, expansion, gain, increment, more, plus, proliferation, raise, rise, supplement
rel accumulation, assemblage, collection, gathering; complement; continuation, extension, uptrend, upturn; jump, run-up, spike
near ant deduction, subtraction
ant abatement, decline, decrease, decrement, diminishment, diminution, fall, lessening, loss, lowering, reduction, shrinkage
2 the act or process of becoming greater in number — see MULTIPLICATION
increase *vb* 1 to make greater in size, amount, or number ⟨We have to *increase* the number of season-ticket holders if the local sports franchise is to survive.⟩
syn accelerate, add (to), aggrandize, amplify, augment, boost, compound, enlarge, escalate, expand, extend, multiply, raise, swell, up
rel boom, jump, skyrocket, spike; bump (up), ratchet (up) (also rachet up); blow up, dilate, distend, inflate; draw out, elongate, flesh (out), lengthen, prolong, protract, stretch; develop, enhance, heighten, intensify, magnify; complement, supplement; beef (up), strengthen; maximize; accumulate, amass, collect; follow up, parlay
near ant abbreviate, abridge, curtail, shorten; compress, condense, constrict, contract; cut back, retrench
ant abate, decrease, de-escalate, diminish,

downsize, dwindle, lessen, lower, minify, reduce, subtract (from)

2 to become greater in extent, volume, amount, or number ⟨Traffic delays *increased* because of the construction.⟩

syn accelerate, accumulate, appreciate, balloon, boom, burgeon (*also* bourgeon), climb, enlarge, escalate, expand, gain, mount, multiply, mushroom, proliferate, rise, snowball, spread, swell, wax

rel jump, rocket, skyrocket, surge; heighten, intensify, redouble; blow up, bulk, distend, inflate, puff (up); crest, peak

ant contract, decrease, diminish, dwindle, lessen, recede, wane

increased *adj* being at a higher level than average — see HIGH 2

incredible *adj* too extraordinary or improbable to believe ⟨I find that an *incredible* coincidence.⟩

syn fantastic (*also* fantastical), implausible, inconceivable, incredulous, unbelievable, unconvincing, unimaginable, unthinkable

rel debatable, disputable, doubtable, doubtful, dubious, far-fetched, fishy, flimsy, questionable, shaky, suspect, suspicious, unlikely, unreasonable; hopeless, impossible; absurd, comical, farcical, laughable, ludicrous, outlandish, preposterous, ridiculous, risible, silly; indefensible, insupportable, untenable

phrases full of it

near ant likely, possible, probable; reasonable; certain, incontestable, indisputable, indubitable, questionless, sure, undeniable, undoubted, unquestionable

ant believable, cogitable, conceivable, convincing, credible, creditable, imaginable, plausible, supposable, thinkable

incredibly *adv* to a great degree — see VERY 1

incredulity *n* refusal to accept something as true — see DISBELIEF

incredulous *adj* **1** inclined to doubt or question claims — see SKEPTICAL 1

2 too extraordinary or improbable to believe — see INCREDIBLE

increment *n* something added (as by growth) — see INCREASE 1

incremental *adj* **1** proceeding or changing by steps or degrees — see GRADUAL

2 produced by a series of additions of identical or similar things — see CUMULATIVE

incriminate *vb* to make a claim of wrongdoing against — see ACCUSE

incubate *vb* **1** to cover and warm eggs as the young inside develop — see SET 1

2 to help the growth or development of — see FOSTER 1

inculcate *vb* **1** to cause (as a person) to become filled or saturated with a certain quality or principle — see INFUSE

2 to set permanently in the consciousness or mind-set — see IMPLANT 1

incumbent *adj* forcing one's compliance or participation by or as if by law — see MANDATORY

incurable *adj* not capable of being cured or reformed — see HOPELESS 1

incurious *adj* having or showing a lack of interest or concern — see INDIFFERENT 1

incursion *n* a sudden attack on and entrance into hostile territory — see RAID 1

indebted *adj* being under obligation for a favor or gift — see BEHOLDEN

indecency *n* **1** the quality or state of being obscene — see OBSCENITY

2 the quality or state of not being socially proper — see IMPROPRIETY 1

indecent *adj* depicting or referring to sexual matters in a way that is unacceptable in polite society — see OBSCENE 1

indecision *n* a state or an instance of temporary inaction because of uncertainty about the right course of action — see HESITATION

indecorous *adj* not appropriate for a particular occasion or situation — see INAPPROPRIATE

indeed *interj* how surprising, doubtful, or unbelievable — see NO

indeed *adv* **1** without any question ⟨I know that you can *indeed* do better than that!⟩

syn all right, alright, assuredly, certainly, definitely, doubtless, easily, incontestably, incontrovertibly, indisputably, plainly, really, so, sure, surely, truly, undeniably, undoubtedly, unquestionably

rel conceivably, likely, perhaps, possibly, probably; obviously, unmistakably

phrases by all means, by all odds, damn well, for certain, for sure

2 not merely this but also — see EVEN 1

3 to tell the truth — see ACTUALLY 1

indefatigable *adj* showing no signs of weariness even after long hard effort — see TIRELESS

indefensible *adj* too bad to be excused or justified — see INEXCUSABLE

indefinable *adj* beyond the power to describe — see INDESCRIBABLE

indefinite *adj* **1** being or seeming to be without limits — see INFINITE

2 not expressed in precise terms — see VAGUE 1

3 not seen or understood clearly — see FAINT 1

indelicacy *n* the quality or state of lacking refinement or good taste — see VULGARITY 1

indelicateness *n* **1** the quality or state of lacking refinement or good taste — see VULGARITY 1

2 the quality or state of not being socially proper — see IMPROPRIETY 1

indemnification *n* payment to another for a loss or injury — see COMPENSATION 1

indemnify *vb* to provide (someone) with a just payment for loss or injury — see COMPENSATE 1

indemnity *n* payment to another for a loss or injury — see COMPENSATION 1

indentation *n* **1** a sunken area forming a separate space — see HOLE 2

2 a V-shaped cut usually on an edge or a surface — see NOTCH 1

indented *adj* curved inward — see HOLLOW

independence *n* **1** the ability to care for one's self — see SELF-SUFFICIENCY

2 the state of being free from the control or power of another — see FREEDOM 1

---

syn synonym(s)   *rel* related words

ant antonym(s)   *near ant* near antonym(s)

independent *adj* **1** able to take care of oneself or itself without outside help — see SELF-SUFFICIENT

2 not being under the rule or control of another — see FREE 1

independently *adv* without aid or support — see ALONE 1

in-depth *adj* covering everything or all important points — see ENCYCLOPEDIC

indescribable *adj* beyond the power to describe ⟨the *indescribable* immensity of Mount Everest⟩
syn incommunicable, indefinable, ineffable, inexpressible, nameless, unspeakable, unutterable
rel unsayable; inconceivable, incredible, unbelievable, unimaginable, unthinkable; inexplicable, unexplainable; characterless
near ant conceivable, imaginable, thinkable
ant communicable, definable, expressible, speakable

indestructible *adj* impossible to destroy ⟨Diamonds are widely considered to be *indestructible* because they are one of the hardest known substances.⟩
syn imperishable, inextinguishable
rel incorruptible; deathless, immortal, perpetual, undying; indissoluble, ineffaceable, ineradicable, inexpungible; durable, enduring, everlasting, lasting, permanent, unbreakable; strong, sturdy, tough
near ant mortal; impermanent, transient, transitory; breakable, delicate, flimsy, fragile, frail
ant destructible, extinguishable, perishable

index *n* an arrow-shaped piece on a dial or scale for registering information — see POINTER 1

index *vb* to put (someone or something) on a list — see ¹LIST 2

indicate *vb* **1** to serve as a sign or symptom of ⟨His attitude seems to *indicate* that he has little interest in the project.⟩
syn bespeak, betoken, denote, mean, signify
rel bode, foreshow, foretell, presage

2 to convey an idea indirectly — see HINT 1

indication *n* a slight or indirect pointing to something (as a solution or explanation) — see HINT 1

indicative *adj* indicating something ⟨a wide-eyed look that is *indicative* of his constant curiosity⟩
syn denotative, denoting, reflective, significant, signifying, telltale
rel alluding, allusive, referring; characteristic, symptomatic; demonstrative, exhibiting, expressive; symbolic (*also* symbolical); connoting, hinting, implying, suggestive

indicator *n* an arrow-shaped piece on a dial or scale for registering information — see POINTER 1

indict *vb* to make a claim of wrongdoing against — see ACCUSE

indictment *n* a formal claim of criminal wrongdoing against a person — see CHARGE 1

indifference *n* lack of interest or concern ⟨It's a matter of complete *indifference* to me what you decide to do.⟩
syn apathy, casualness, complacence, dis-

interestedness, disregard, insouciance, nonchalance, unconcern
rel halfheartedness, lukewarmness; carelessness, heedlessness, recklessness, unawareness; listlessness; aloofness, cool, detachment; callosity, callousness, hardheartedness, hardness, insensitivity; bloodlessness, impassivity, phlegm, stoicism, stolidity
near ant attention, attentiveness, awareness, conscientiousness, curiosity, heedfulness, keenness; sensitivity; warmheartedness; bias, partiality, prejudice; ardor, desire, fervency, passion, vehemence, zeal
ant concern, interest, regard

indifferent *adj* **1** having or showing a lack of interest or concern ⟨*indifferent* about the result of the football game⟩
syn apathetic, casual, complacent, disinterested, incurious, insensible, insouciant, nonchalant, perfunctory, unconcerned, uncurious, uninterested
rel halfhearted, lukewarm, tepid; aloof, cold, numb, remote, unemotional; callous, insensitive, unfeeling; calm, cool, detached, dispassionate; careless, heedless, mindless; impassive, impervious, phlegmatic, stoic (*or* stoical), stolid; lethargic, listless; unimpressed
near ant attentive, aware, conscientious, heedful, mindful; caring, sensitive, warmhearted; ardent, fervent, keen, passionate, warm, zealous
ant concerned, interested

2 of average to below average quality — see MEDIOCRE 1

3 marked by justice, honesty, and freedom from bias — see FAIR 2

indigence *n* the state of lacking sufficient money or material possessions — see POVERTY 1

indigenous *adj* **1** belonging to a particular place by birth or origin — see NATIVE 1

2 being a part of the innermost nature of a person or thing — see INHERENT

indigent *adj* lacking money or material possessions — see POOR 1

indignant *adj* feeling or showing anger — see ANGRY

indignation *n* an intense emotional state of displeasure with someone or something — see ANGER

indignity *n* an act or expression showing scorn and usually intended to hurt another's feelings — see INSULT

indirect *adj* not straightforward or direct ⟨The cab driver took a very *indirect* route to the hotel.⟩ ⟨a long-winded, *indirect* answer to a very simple question⟩
syn circuitous, circular, roundabout
rel crooked, serpentine, sinuous, tortuous, twisting, winding; rambling, wandering; circumlocutory, long-winded, prolix, verbose; deceitful, deceptive, devious, dishonest, insidious, misleading, sneaky, underhand, underhanded; calculating, crafty, cunning, subtle, tricky
near ant candid, forthright, frank, honest, open, plain, unconcealed, undisguised
ant direct, straight, straightforward

indiscreet *adj* showing poor judgment especially in personal relationships or social

situations ⟨Telling a friend's secrets is *indiscreet*, and unkind as well.⟩
syn brash, graceless, ill-advised, imprudent, inadvisable, injudicious, tactless, unwise
rel dumb, idiotic (*also* idiotical), moronic, stupid; careless, heedless, inconsiderate, mindless, thoughtless; ill-mannered, improper, inappropriate, indecorous, unbecoming, uncivil, unseemly; foolish, harebrained, nonsensical, preposterous, senseless, silly
near ant intelligent, logical, rational, sensible, smart, sound; appropriate, becoming, civil, decorous, proper, seemly; sage, sane, sapient
ant advisable, discreet, judicious, prudent, tactful, wise

indiscretion *n* a socially improper or unsuitable act or remark — see IMPROPRIETY 2

indispensable *adj* impossible to do without — see ESSENTIAL 1

indisposed *adj* 1 slow to begin or proceed with a course of action because of doubts or uncertainty — see HESITANT
2 temporarily suffering from a disorder of the body — see SICK 1

indisposition *n* the condition of not being in good health — see SICKNESS 1

indisputable *adj* not capable of being challenged or proved wrong — see IRREFUTABLE

indisputably *adv* without any question — see INDEED 1

indistinct *adj* not seen or understood clearly — see FAINT 1

indistinguishable *adj* 1 not perceptible by a sense or by the mind — see IMPERCEPTIBLE
2 not seen or understood clearly — see FAINT 1
3 resembling another in every respect — see SAME 1

individual *n* 1 a member of the human race — see HUMAN
2 one that has a real and independent existence — see ENTITY

individual *adj* 1 of, relating to, or belonging to a single person ⟨Everyone has his or her own *individual* opinion about the subject, but you will have to work together.⟩
syn individualized, particular, peculiar, personal, personalized, private, privy, separate, singular, unique
rel characteristic, distinctive, intimate; identifying, idiosyncratic; especial, express, special, specific; independent, nonconformist, self-directed, self-sufficient; custom, customized, specialized
near ant broad, prevailing, prevalent, widespread; common, normal, regular, typical
ant general, generic, popular, public, shared, universal
2 not the same or shared — see SEPARATE 1
3 serving to identify as belonging to an individual or group — see CHARACTERISTIC 1

individualist *n* a person who does not conform to generally accepted standards or customs — see NONCONFORMIST 1

individuality *n* 1 the set of qualities that make a person different from other people ⟨Her *individuality* showed through in everything she did.⟩
syn character, identity, personality, selfhood, self-identity
rel distinctiveness, idiosyncrasy, oneness, peculiarity, separateness, singleness, singularity, uniqueness; disposition, humor, nature, temper, temperament; independence
near ant conformity, conventionality
2 one that has a real and independent existence — see ENTITY

individualized *adj* of, relating to, or belonging to a single person — see INDIVIDUAL 1

indoctrinate *vb* to cause to acquire knowledge or skill in some field — see TEACH

indolence *n* an inclination not to do work or engage in activities — see LAZINESS

indolent *adj* not easily aroused to action or work — see LAZY 1

indomitable *adj* incapable of being defeated, overcome, or subdued — see INVINCIBLE

indubitable *adj* not capable of being challenged or proved wrong — see IRREFUTABLE

induce *vb* 1 to be the cause of (a situation, action, or state of mind) — see EFFECT
2 to cause (someone) to agree with a belief or course of action by using arguments or earnest requests — see PERSUADE

inducement *n* the act of reasoning or pleading with someone to accept a belief or course of action — see PERSUASION 1

inducing *n* the act of reasoning or pleading with someone to accept a belief or course of action — see PERSUASION 1

induct *vb* to put into an office or welcome into an organization with special ceremonies — see INSTALL 1

inductee *n* a person forced or required to enroll in military service — see CONSCRIPT

induction *n* 1 the process or an instance of being formally placed in an office or organization — see INSTALLATION 1
2 an opinion arrived at through a process of reasoning — see CONCLUSION 1

indulge *vb* 1 to give in to (a desire) ⟨The grandparents *indulged* the child's wishes to an extent that they never did with their own children.⟩
syn cater (to), gratify, humor
rel bask, luxuriate, revel, wallow; coddle, mollycoddle, pamper, spoil; delight, please, pleasure; sate, satiate, satisfy
near ant bridle, check, constrain, curb, inhibit, restrain, stifle
2 to give (oneself) over to something especially unrestrainedly — see ABANDON 1
3 to treat with great or excessive care — see BABY

indulgence *n* 1 an act of kind assistance — see FAVOR 1
2 something adding to pleasure or comfort but not absolutely necessary — see LUXURY 1

indulgent *adj* 1 tolerant and kind in the judgment of and expectations for others ⟨She was perhaps a bit too *indulgent* with her children, who always seemed to get away with everything.⟩

syn synonym(s)   *rel* related words
ant antonym(s)   *near ant* near antonym(s)

syn charitable, clement, easy, soft

rel accommodating, acquiescent, amenable, obliging; easygoing, laid-back, undemanding

near ant demanding; uncharitable, unforgiving; inflexible, intolerant, unbending, uncompromising, unyielding

ant hard, harsh, severe, stern, strict

2 willing to do a favor — see ACCOMMODATING

industrious *adj* involved in often constant activity — see BUSY 1

industriously *adv* with great effort or determination — see HARD 1

industriousness *n* attentive and persistent effort — see DILIGENCE

industry *n* attentive and persistent effort — see DILIGENCE

inebriate *adj* being under the influence of alcohol — see DRUNK

inebriate *n* a person who makes a habit of getting drunk — see DRUNK

inebriated *adj* being under the influence of alcohol — see DRUNK

ineffable *adj* beyond the power to describe — see INDESCRIBABLE

ineffective *adj* **1** not producing the desired result ⟨an *ineffective* effort to reduce unemployment that only spurred inflation⟩

syn ineffectual, inefficient, inexpedient

rel abortive, bootless, fruitless, futile, nonproductive, pointless, profitless, unavailing, unproductive, unprofitable, unsuccessful, useless, worthless

near ant availing, beneficial, helpful, productive, profitable, successful, useful, worthwhile

ant effective, effectual, efficacious, efficient, expedient, operant, ultraefficient

2 producing no results — see FUTILE

ineffectual *adj* **1** not producing the desired result — see INEFFECTIVE 1

2 producing no results — see FUTILE

inefficient *adj* not producing the desired result — see INEFFECTIVE 1

inelegant *adj* **1** lacking social grace and assurance — see AWKWARD 1

2 marked by an obvious lack of style or good taste — see ¹TACKY 1

inept *adj* **1** lacking qualities (as knowledge, skill, or ability) required to do a job — see INCOMPETENT

2 not appropriate for a particular occasion or situation — see INAPPROPRIATE

3 showing or marked by a lack of skill and tact (as in dealing with a situation) — see AWKWARD 2

4 showing or marked by a lack of good sense or judgment — see FOOLISH 1

ineptitude *n* the lack of sufficient ability, power, or means — see INABILITY

inequity *n* **1** the state of being unfair or unjust — see INJUSTICE 1

2 unfair or inadequate treatment of someone or something or an instance of this — see DISSERVICE

inert *adj* **1** not being in a state of use, activity, or employment — see INACTIVE 2

2 slow to move or act — see INACTIVE 1

inertia *n* an inclination not to do work or engage in activities — see LAZINESS

inertness *n* lack of action or activity — see INACTION

inescapable *adj* impossible to avoid or evade — see INEVITABLE

inescapably *adv* because of necessity — see NEEDS

inevitable *adj* impossible to avoid or evade ⟨Getting wet is *inevitable* if you are going to try to give your dog a bath.⟩

syn certain, inescapable, necessary, sure, unavoidable, unescapable

rel decided, definite, settled; likely, possible, probable; destined, fated, foreordained, predestined, predetermined, preordained; inexorable, relentless, unremitting

phrases in the bag, in the cards (*also* on the cards)

near ant preventable (*also* preventible); doubtful, dubious, questionable, shaky, unclear; undecided, unsettled; undependable, unreliable; improbable, unlikely

ant avoidable, evadable, uncertain, unsure

inevitably *adv* because of necessity — see NEEDS

inexact *adj* **1** not precisely correct ⟨A thousand is an *inexact* figure for the number of islands in the St. Lawrence River.⟩

syn approximate, imprecise, inaccurate, loose

rel erroneous, false, incorrect, off, wrong; general, indefinable, indefinite, indeterminate, indistinct, undefined, undetermined, unsettled, vague; faulty, flawed, mistaken; specious; distorted, fallacious, misleading; doubtful, dubious, questionable, uncertain; inconclusive, indecisive, debatable, disputable; unconfirmed, unsubstantiated, unsupported

near ant certain, incontestable, indubitable, positive, sure, undeniable, unquestionable; correct, errorless, factual, right, sound, true, valid; clear-cut, decisive, definable, defined, definite; incontrovertible, indisputable, irrefutable; absolute, unqualified; confirmed, corroborated, determined, established, substantiated, supported, validated

ant accurate, dead, exact, precise, ultraprecise, veracious

2 not being in agreement with what is true — see FALSE 1

inexcusable *adj* too bad to be excused or justified ⟨Such rudeness is *inexcusable* and will be punished.⟩

syn indefensible, insupportable, unforgivable, unjustifiable, unpardonable, unwarrantable

rel insufferable, intolerable, unbearable, unendurable; abominable, atrocious, heinous, monstrous, outrageous, scandalous, shocking; egregious, flagrant, glaring, gross, rank; unacceptable, untenable; evil, iniquitous, vicious, wicked; base, contemptible, deplorable, despicable, dirty, execrable, ignoble, reprobate, vile, wretched; cruel, nasty; banned, barred, condemned, disallowed, forbidden, interdicted, outlawed, prohibited, proscribed

near ant acceptable, tolerable; authorized, legal, permissible; allowed, permitted, tolerated; approved, endorsed (*also* indorsed), sanctioned; abetted, encouraged, promoted, supported; ethical, moral, virtuous

ant defensible, excusable, forgivable, justifiable, pardonable, venial

inexhaustible *adj* showing no signs of weariness even after long hard effort — see TIRELESS

inexpedient *adj* not producing the desired result — see INEFFECTIVE 1

inexpensive *adj* costing little — see CHEAP 1

inexperienced *adj* **1** lacking in adult experience or maturity — see CALLOW

2 lacking or showing a lack of expert skill — see AMATEURISH

inexpert *adj* **1** lacking or showing a lack of expert skill — see AMATEURISH

2 lacking qualities (as knowledge, skill, or ability) required to do a job — see INCOMPETENT

3 showing or marked by a lack of skill and tact (as in dealing with a situation) — see AWKWARD 2

inexpert *n* a person who lacks experience and competence in an art or science — see AMATEUR 2

inexplicable *adj* impossible to explain ⟨an *inexplicable* desire for ice cream at two in the morning⟩

syn unaccountable, unexplainable

rel indefinable, indescribable, inexpressible, unsayable; cryptic, enigmatic (*also* enigmatical), impenetrable, incomprehensible, inscrutable, mysterious, unfathomable, unknowable; irrational, unreasonable, unsound; foolish, illogical, mindless, senseless; absurd, odd, peculiar, strange, unusual, weird

near ant logical, rational, reasonable, tenable; sane, sensible, wise; compelling, convincing, persuasive, plausible, satisfying; confirmed, corroborated, determined, established, explained, substantiated, validated

ant accountable, explainable, explicable

inexpressible *adj* beyond the power to describe — see INDESCRIBABLE

inexpressive *adj* not expressing any emotion — see BLANK 1

inextinguishable *adj* impossible to destroy — see INDESTRUCTIBLE

infallible *adj* **1** not being or likely to be wrong ⟨a teacher with an *infallible* memory for names⟩

syn unerring, unfailing

rel errorless, faultless, flawless, impeccable; certain, foolproof, inerrant, perfect, sure; dependable, reliable

near ant defective, faulty, flawed, imperfect; undependable, unreliable

ant fallible

2 not likely to fail ⟨an *infallible* cure for hiccups⟩

syn certain, sure, surefire, unfailing

rel dependable, reliable; deadly, unerring

near ant doubtful, questionable, uncertain

ant fallible

infamous *adj* not respectable — see DISREPUTABLE

infamy *n* the state of having lost the esteem of others — see DISGRACE 1

infant *n* a recently born person — see BABY 1

infantile *adj* having or showing the annoy-ing qualities (as silliness) associated with children — see CHILDISH

infatuated (with) *adj* filled with an intense or excessive love for — see ENAMORED (OF)

infatuation *n* a strong but often short-lived liking for another person — see CRUSH 1

infectious *adj* exciting a similar feeling or reaction in others — see CONTAGIOUS 2

infelicitous *adj* not appropriate for a particular occasion or situation — see INAPPROPRIATE

infelicity *n* the quality or state of being unsuitable or unfitting — see INAPPROPRIATENESS 1

infer *vb* **1** to form an opinion or reach a conclusion through reasoning and information ⟨He *inferred* that she had left because her coat was gone.⟩

syn conclude, decide, deduce, derive, extrapolate, gather, judge, make out, reason, understand

rel assume, suppose; conjecture, guess, speculate, surmise; construe, interpret, read; contemplate, philosophize, rationalize, think; ascertain, dope (out), find out

phrases draw a conclusion

2 to convey an idea indirectly — see HINT

inferable *also* **inferrible** *adj* being or provable by reasoning in which the conclusion follows necessarily from given information — see DEDUCTIVE

inference *n* an opinion arrived at through a process of reasoning — see CONCLUSION 1

inferior *n* one who is of lower rank and typically under the authority of another — see UNDERLING

inferior *adj* **1** situated lower down ⟨creatures that inhabit the dark, *inferior* depths of the ocean⟩

syn lower, nether

rel lowest; underlying

near ant highest, uppermost; overhanging, overhead

ant higher, superior, upper

2 of little or less value or merit ⟨a girl who has always felt *inferior* to her older sister⟩

syn mean, minor, secondary, second-class, second-rate

rel junior, lesser, lower, low-level, petty, smaller, subordinate, under; average, common, fair, middling, ordinary; amiss, bad, defective, unsatisfactory, wrong; deficient, inadequate, insufficient, unacceptable; littler, slighter, smaller; jerkwater, one-horse, small-time, two-bit

near ant major, more, primary, senior; choice, exceptional, first-class, first-rate, high-grade, premium, prime, select, selected; acceptable, adequate, sufficient

ant greater, higher, superior

3 belonging to the class of people of low social or economic rank — see IGNOBLE 1

4 falling short of a standard — see BAD 1

5 having not so great importance or rank as another — see LESSER

6 of low quality — see CHEAP 2

inferno *n* a destructive burning — see FIRE 1

infertile *adj* **1** not able to produce fruit or offspring — see STERILE 1

2 producing inferior or only a small amount of vegetation — see BARREN 1

---

syn synonym(s)   *rel* related words
ant antonym(s)   *near ant* near antonym(s)

infest *vb* to spread or swarm over in a troublesome manner ⟨In desperation, we called in an exterminator because the house was *infested* with ants.⟩

syn overrun

rel beset, overspread, overwhelm; abound, crawl, teem; annoy, pester, plague; contaminate, infect

infidelity *n* **1** lack of faithfulness especially to one's husband or wife ⟨warned the young couple of the high cost of dishonesty and *infidelity*⟩

syn disloyalty, faithlessness, falseness, falsity, inconstancy, unfaithfulness

rel adultery; betrayal, double-cross, double-dealing, duplicity, sellout, treachery, treason; deceit, lying

near ant staunchness, steadfastness; dependability, reliability; honesty, trustworthiness

ant allegiance, constancy, devotedness, devotion, faith, faithfulness, fealty, fidelity, loyalty

2 the act or fact of violating the trust or confidence of another — see BETRAYAL

3 a sexual encounter or relationship between a married person and someone other than their spouse — see ADULTERY

infiltrate *vb* to introduce in a gradual, secret, or clever way — see INSINUATE 1

infinite *adj* being or seeming to be without limits ⟨the *infinite* expanse of outer space⟩

syn bottomless, boundless, endless, illimitable, immeasurable, indefinite, limitless, measureless, unbounded, unfathomable, unlimited

rel abysmal; countless, incalculable, incomputable, innumerable, unmeasured; exhaustless, inexhaustible; extensive, far-flung, immense, vast

near ant measurable; depthless, shallow, superficial

ant bounded, circumscribed, definite, finite, limited, restricted

infinitesimal *adj* very small in size — see TINY

infinity *n* endless time — see ETERNITY 1

infirm *adj* lacking bodily strength — see WEAK 1

infirmity *n* **1** an abnormal state that disrupts a plant's or animal's normal bodily functioning — see DISEASE

2 the quality or state of lacking physical strength or vigor — see WEAKNESS 1

inflame *also* **enflame** *vb* **1** to make angry — see ANGER

2 to set (something) on fire — see BURN 2

inflamed *also* **enflamed** *adj* **1** being on fire — see ABLAZE 1

2 feeling or showing anger — see ANGRY

inflammable *adj* capable of catching or being set on fire — see COMBUSTIBLE

inflexibility *n* the quality or state of being demanding or unyielding (as in discipline or criticism) — see SEVERITY

inflexible *adj* **1** not capable of changing or being changed ⟨the *inflexible* law of gravity⟩

syn fixed, hard-and-fast, immutable, invariable, unalterable, unchangeable

rel changeless, constant, determinate, established, set, settled, stable, steadfast, steady, unaltered, unchanging, unvarying; immovable, unmovable

near ant adaptable, adjustable; fickle,

fluctuating, inconstant, uncertain, unsettled, unstable, varying; plastic, pliable, pliant, supple, willowy

ant alterable, changeable, elastic, flexible, mutable, variable

2 incapable of or highly resistant to bending — see STIFF 1

3 not allowing for any exceptions or loosening of standards — see RIGID 1

4 sticking to an opinion, purpose, or course of action in spite of reason, arguments, or persuasion — see OBSTINATE

inflow *n* a flowing or coming in — see INFLUX

influence *vb* to act upon (a person or a person's feelings) so as to cause a response — see ¹AFFECT 1

influence *n* **1** the power to direct the thinking or behavior of others usually indirectly ⟨a mayor who doesn't hesitate to use her *influence* to get business leaders behind civic improvements⟩

syn authority, clout, credit, heft, in, pull, sway, weight

rel counterinfluence; command, dominance, dominion, mastery, predominance, scepter, sovereignty (*also* sovranty), supremacy; consequence, eminence, importance, moment; impact, impress, impression, imprint, mark

near ant helplessness, impotence, impotency, powerlessness, weakness

2 the power to bring about a result on another — see EFFECT 2

influential *adj* **1** having power over the minds or behavior of others ⟨a highly *influential* writer⟩

syn authoritative, forceful, weighty

rel cogent, controlling, dominating, masterful; dominant, predominant, regnant, sovereign (*also* sovran); supreme; eminent, important, momentous

near ant helpless, impotent, powerless, weak; incapable

2 having great power or influence — see IMPORTANT 2

influx *n* a flowing or coming in ⟨a sudden *influx* of people into the exurbs⟩

syn flux, income, inflow, inrush

rel deluge, flood, flow, inundation, overflow, spate; torrent; rush, stampede; river, stream, tide

near ant emigration, exodus, flight

ant outflow, outpouring

inform *vb* **1** to give information (as to the authorities) about another's improper or unlawful activities — see SQUEAL 1

2 to give information to — see ENLIGHTEN 1

informal *adj* **1** not rigidly following established form, custom, or rules ⟨An *informal* meeting allowed everyone to get acquainted.⟩

syn heterodox, irregular, unceremonious, unconventional, unorthodox

rel unauthorized, unofficial; casual, easygoing, familiar, free and easy, lax, loose, offhand, relaxed

near ant correct, decorous, proper; constrained, inhibited, restrained, rigid, stiff, stuffy, uptight

ant ceremonial, ceremonious, conventional, formal, orthodox, regular, routine

2 not designed to be worn only on special occasions — see CASUAL 1

3 used in or suitable for speech and not formal writing — see COLLOQUIAL 1

informant *n* a person who provides information about another's wrongdoing — see INFORMER

information *n* **1** a collection of factual knowledge about something ⟨The network correspondent spent the entire day gathering *information* for her report on the brewing scandal.⟩

syn facts

rel findings, intelligence

2 a report of recent events or facts not previously known — see NEWS

informational *adj* providing useful information or knowledge — see INFORMATIVE

informative *adj* providing useful information or knowledge ⟨Some websites for family vacation resorts are very *informative* and some are practically useless.⟩

syn educational, educative, informational, instructional, instructive

rel comprehensive, copious, detailed, full; communicatory, edifying, elucidative, explanatory; chatty, gossipy, newsy; availing, beneficial, constructive, helpful, profitable

near ant impractical, unhelpful, unusable, useless

ant unenlightening, unilluminating, uninformative, uninstructive

informed *adj* **1** based on sound reasoning or information — see GOOD 1

2 having information especially as a result of study or experience — see FAMILIAR 2

informer *n* a person who provides information about another's wrongdoing ⟨The *informer* who told the police about that conspiracy has angered a lot of dangerous people.⟩

syn betrayer, informant, rat, snitch, snitcher, squealer, stool pigeon, talebearer, tattler, tattletale, telltale

rel collaborator; blabber, blabbermouth, gossip, leaker; snoop, snooper, spy; notifier

infraction *n* a failure to uphold the requirements of law, duty, or obligation — see BREACH 1

infrequent *adj* not often occurring or repeated ⟨a shut-in who made *infrequent* trips to the store⟩

syn isolated, occasional, odd, rare, sporadic

rel scarce, scattered, uncommon, unique, unusual; choppy, discontinuous, erratic, fitful, intermittent, irregular, spasmodic, spotty, unsteady

phrases few and far between

near ant daily, regular; common, ordinary, routine

ant frequent

infrequently *adv* not often — see SELDOM

infringement *n* a failure to uphold the requirements of law, duty, or obligation — see BREACH 1

infuriate *vb* to make angry — see ANGER

infuriate *adj* feeling or showing anger — see ANGRY

infuriated *adj* feeling or showing anger — see ANGRY

infuse *vb* to cause (as a person) to become filled or saturated with a certain quality or principle ⟨parents who *infuse* their children with a strong sense of responsibility to the community⟩

syn endue (or indue), imbue, inculcate, ingrain (*also* engrain), inoculate, invest, steep, suffuse

rel animate, charge, enliven, invigorate, leaven; implant, plant; impregnate, permeate, pervade, saturate; deluge, drown, fill, flood, inundate, overwhelm, submerge

near ant strip; clear, empty; eliminate, remove, take away

ingenious *adj* **1** having the skill and imagination to create new things — see CREATIVE 1

2 showing a noteworthy use of the imagination and creativity especially in inventing — see CLEVER 1

ingeniousness *n* the skill and imagination to create new things — see CREATIVITY 1

ingenuity *n* the skill and imagination to create new things — see CREATIVITY 1

ingenuous *adj* **1** free from any intent to deceive or impress others — see GUILELESS

2 lacking in worldly wisdom or informed judgment — see NAIVE 1

ingenuously *adv* without any attempt to impress by deception or exaggeration — see NATURALLY 1

ingenuousness *n* the quality or state of being simple and sincere — see NAÏVETÉ 1

ingest *vb* **1** to take in as food — see EAT 1

2 to take into the stomach through the mouth and throat — see SWALLOW 1

ingrain *also* **engrain** *vb* **1** to cause (as a person) to become filled or saturated with a certain quality or principle — see INFUSE

2 to produce a vivid impression of — see ENGRAVE 2

3 to set solidly in or as if in surrounding matter — see ENTRENCH

ingrain *adj* being a part of the innermost nature of a person or thing — see INHERENT

ingrained *also* **engrained** *adj* being a part of the innermost nature of a person or thing — see INHERENT

ingratiating *adj* likely or intended to win one's affection ⟨One of the children had a most *ingratiating* smile.⟩

syn disarming, endearing, winning, winsome

rel adorable, charming, likable (or likeable), lovable (*also* loveable); affecting, poignant, touching; adulatory, deferential, effusive, flattering, fulsome, groveling (or grovelling), kowtowing, obsequious, sycophantic; drooling, slavering, slobbering; saccharine, soapy, sugary, unctuous

near ant alienating, disaffecting, displeasing; repugnant, repulsive; arrogant, disdainful, haughty, insolent, proud, scornful

ant unendearing, uningratiating

ingredient *n* one of the parts that make up a whole — see ELEMENT 1

ingress *n* the means or right of entering or participating in — see ENTRANCE 1

inhabitable *adj* suitable for living in — see LIVABLE

inhabitant *n* one who lives permanently in

---

syn synonym(s)   *rel* related words

ant antonym(s)   *near ant* near antonym(s)

a place ⟨The *inhabitants* of the town don't like the tourists.⟩

syn denizen, dweller, habitant, occupant, resident, resider, tenant

rel aborigine, native; citizen, national, subject; colonist, émigré (*also* emigré), migrant, newcomer, settler; burgher, local, townie (*or* towny), villager

near ant alien, foreigner, nonresident; guest, tourist, visitor; defector, emigrant, escaper, evacuee, exile, expatriate, refugee
ant transient

inharmonious *adj* 1 not being in agreement or harmony — see INCONSISTENT 1

2 marked by or producing a harsh combination of sounds — see DISSONANT

inherent *adj* being a part of the innermost nature of a person or thing ⟨an *inherent* concept of justice⟩

syn constitutional, essential, inborn, inbred, indigenous, ingrain, ingrained (*also* engrained), innate, integral, intrinsic, native, natural

rel basic, deep-rooted, elemental, fundamental; congenital, hereditary, inherited, inmost, inner, interior; internal; characteristic, distinctive, peculiar; habitual, inveterate; normal, regular, typical

phrases in one's blood

near ant alien, foreign; accidental, coincidental, incidental; acquired; superficial, surface; exterior, external
ant adventitious, extraneous, extrinsic

inherently *adv* by natural character or ability — see NATURALLY 1

inheritable *adj* genetically passed or capable of being passed from parent to offspring — see HEREDITARY

inheritance *n* something that is or may be inherited ⟨A keen sense of humor was her *inheritance* from her mother.⟩

syn bequest, birthright, heritage, legacy, patrimony

rel heirloom; bestowal, gift, offering, present

inherited *adj* genetically passed or capable of being passed from parent to offspring — see HEREDITARY

inheritor *n* a person who has the right to inherit property — see HEIR

inhibit *vb* 1 to create difficulty for the work or activity of — see HAMPER

2 to keep from exceeding a desirable degree or level (as of expression) — see CONTROL 1

3 to steer (a person) from an activity or course of action — see DISCOURAGE 1

inhibition *n* 1 the checking of one's true feelings and impulses when dealing with others — see CONSTRAINT 1

2 something that makes movement or progress difficult — see ENCUMBRANCE

inhospitable *adj* marked by opposition or ill will — see HOSTILE 1

inhuman *adj* 1 difficult to endure — see HARSH 1

2 having or showing a lack of sympathy or tender feelings — see HARD 1

3 having or showing the desire to inflict severe pain and suffering on others — see CRUEL 1

inhumane *adj* 1 having or showing a lack of sympathy or tender feelings — see HARD 1

2 having or showing the desire to inflict severe pain and suffering on others — see CRUEL 1

inhumanity *n* disposition to willfully inflict pain and suffering on others — see CRUELTY

inimical *adj* 1 marked by opposition or ill will — see HOSTILE 1

2 opposed to one's interests — see ADVERSE 1

inimitable *adj* having no equal or rival for excellence or desirability — see ONLY 1

iniquitous *adj* not conforming to a high moral standard; morally unacceptable — see BAD 2

iniquity *n* 1 immoral conduct or practices harmful or offensive to society — see VICE 1

2 that which is morally unacceptable — see EVIL

initial *adj* coming before all others in time or order — see FIRST 1

initially *adv* in the beginning — see ORIGINALLY

initiate *vb* 1 to be responsible for the creation and early operation or use of — see FOUND

2 to impart knowledge of a new thing or situation to — see ACQUAINT 1

3 to put into an office or welcome into an organization with special ceremonies — see INSTALL 1

initiation *n* the process or an instance of being formally placed in an office or organization — see INSTALLATION 1

initiative *n* readiness to engage in daring or difficult activity — see ENTERPRISE 2

initiator *n* a person who establishes a whole new field of endeavor — see FATHER 2

inject *vb* to put among or between others — see INSERT

injudicious *adj* showing poor judgment especially in personal relationships or social situations — see INDISCREET

injure *vb* to cause bodily damage to ⟨Ted *injured* himself while skiing.⟩

syn damage, harm, hurt, wound

rel batter, bloody, blow out, bruise, contuse, cut, gash, gore, lacerate, scald, scar, scathe, strain, tear; crease, graze, nick; cripple, hamstring, lame, maim, mangle, mutilate; abuse, aggrieve, afflict, maltreat, torment, torture; lay up; blemish, impair, mar, scrape, spoil

near ant cure, fix, heal, mend, remedy

2 to reduce the soundness, effectiveness, or perfection of — see DAMAGE 1

injurious *adj* causing or capable of causing harm — see HARMFUL

injury *n* 1 something that causes loss or pain ⟨The harsh words were the worst *injury* that his father could inflict.⟩

syn affliction, damage, detriment, harm, hurt

rel disservice, injustice, outrage, wrong; affront, dart, indignity, insult, offense (*or* offence); beating, crippling, mayhem, mutilation; defacement, disability, disablement, disfigurement, impairment; lesion; rupture, strain; abrasion, chafe, scrape, scratch; bruise, contusion, swelling, wound; bump, concussion; cut, gash, laceration; burn, scald, scar, scathe, sear

near ant healing, recovery; cure, fix, remedy

2 unfair or inadequate treatment of someone or something or an instance of this — see DISSERVICE

injustice *n* **1** a state of being unfair or unjust ⟨The *injustice* of the coach's accusation that I'd been lazy frustrated and angered me.⟩

syn inequity, unfairness, unjustness

rel dirtiness, foulness

ant equity, fairness, justice

2 unfair or inadequate treatment of someone or something or an instance of this — see DISSERVICE

inkling *n* a slight or indirect pointing to something (as a solution or explanation) — see HINT 1

inlet *n* a part of a body of water that extends beyond the general shoreline — see GULF 1

inn *n* a place that provides rooms and usually a public dining room for overnight guests — see HOTEL

innards *n pl* **1** the internal organs of the body — see GUT 1

2 an interior or internal part — see INSIDE 1

innate *adj* being a part of the innermost nature of a person or thing — see INHERENT

innately *adv* by natural character or ability — see NATURALLY 1

inner *adj* **1** situated farther in ⟨an *inner* area of the national park that is some distance from the nearest road⟩

syn inside, interior, internal, inward

rel inmost, innermost; central, mid, middle, midmost

near ant outermost, outmost; surface

ant exterior, external, outer, outside, outward

2 of or relating to the mind — see MENTAL

innocence *n* **1** the quality or state of being free from guilt or blame ⟨The accused embezzler eventually proved her *innocence* and was released.⟩

syn blamelessness, faultlessness, guiltlessness, impeccability

rel decency, goodness, honesty, incorruptibility, integrity, law-abidingness, righteousness, uprightness, virtuousness; morality, virtue; chastity, purity, sinlessness; harmlessness, inoffensiveness

near ant blame, fault, responsibility; corruption, criminality, depravity, evil, immorality, reprehensibleness, sinfulness, wickedness; harmfulness, offensiveness

ant blameworthiness, culpability, guilt, guiltiness

2 the quality or state of being simple and sincere — see NAÏVETÉ 1

3 the state of being unaware or uninformed — see IGNORANCE 1

4 the quality or state of being morally pure — see CHASTITY

innocent *n* an innocent or gentle person — see LAMB

innocent *adj* **1** free from sin ⟨an *innocent* baby⟩

syn impeccable, pure

rel chaste, moral, virgin, virtuous; immaculate, spotless, unblemished, unstained,

unsullied; decent, ethical, good, honest, honorable, righteous, upright, virtuous; blameless, guiltless

near ant lascivious, lewd, lustful, oversexed, unchaste; evil, immoral, iniquitous, reprobate, unrighteous, virtueless, wicked; corrupt, debased, debauched, degenerate, depraved, dissolute, erring, fallen, lost, perverted; condemned, damned

ant impure, sinful, sinning

2 free from guilt or blame ⟨The robbery suspect was eventually found to be *innocent*.⟩

syn blameless, clear, faultless, guiltless, impeccable, irreproachable

rel absolved, acquitted, cleared, exonerated, vindicated; ethical, law-abiding, moral, righteous, upright, virtuous

phrases in the clear

near ant blamable, blameworthy, censurable, culpable, impeachable, indictable, punishable; accused, impeached, indicted; condemned, convicted; hangdog, shamed, shamefaced

ant guilty

3 free from any intent to deceive or impress others — see GUILELESS

4 lacking in worldly wisdom or informed judgment — see NAIVE 1

5 not causing or being capable of causing injury or hurt — see HARMLESS

6 not informed about or aware of something — see IGNORANT 2

innocently *adv* without any attempt to impress by deception or exaggeration — see NATURALLY 3

2 with purity of thought and deed — see PURELY 1

innocuous *adj* not causing or being capable of causing injury or hurt — see HARMLESS

innovate *vb* to be responsible for the creation and early operation or use of — see FOUND

innovation *n* something (as a device) created for the first time through the use of the imagination — see INVENTION 1

innovative *adj* **1** having the skill and imagination to create new things — see CREATIVE 1

2 showing a noteworthy use of the imagination and creativity especially in inventing — see CLEVER 1

innovator *n* one who creates or introduces something new — see INVENTOR

innumerable *adj* too many to be counted — see COUNTLESS

inoculate *vb* to cause (as a person) to become filled or saturated with a certain quality or principle — see INFUSE

inoffensive *adj* not causing or being capable of causing injury or hurt — see HARMLESS

inoperable *adj* **1** not being in working order ⟨We have several *inoperable* cars on the property.⟩

syn down, inoperative, malfunctioning, nonfunctional, nonfunctioning, nonoperating

rel broken; off; deactivated, deadlocked, ineffective, ineffectual, nonproductive, unproductive, unusable, unworkable, useless

phrases on the blink, on the fritz, out of commission

---

near ant effective, effectual, employable, performing, producing, productive, serving, usable (*also* useable), useful, viable, workable

ant functional, functioning, operable, operant, operating, operational, operative, running, working

2 not capable of being put to use or account — see IMPRACTICAL

inoperative *adj* **1** not being in a state of use, activity, or employment — see INACTIVE 2

2 not in working order — see INOPERABLE 1

3 having no legal or binding force — see NULL 1

inopportune *adj* occurring before the usual or expected time — see EARLY 2

inopportunely *adv* before the usual or expected time — see EARLY

inordinate *adj* going beyond a normal or acceptable limit in degree or amount — see EXCESSIVE

inordinately *adv* beyond a normal or acceptable limit — see TOO 1

input *n* an opinion suggesting a wise or proper course of action — see ADVICE

inquest *n* a systematic search for the truth or facts about something — see INQUIRY 1

inquire (into) *vb* to search through or into — see EXPLORE 1

inquire (of) *vb* to put a question or questions to — see ASK 1

inquiry *n* **1** a systematic search for the truth or facts about something ⟨an *inquiry* into the origins of the universe⟩

syn delving, examination, exploration, inquest, inquisition, investigation, probe, probing, research, study

rel quest; audit, check; checkup, diagnosis, inspection; hearing, interrogation, trial; feeler, query, question; poll, questionary, questionnaire, survey; challenge, cross-examination, grilling, quiz; rehearing, reinvestigation; self-exploration, self-reflection, self-scrutiny

2 an act or instance of asking for information — see QUESTION 2

inquisition *n* a systematic search for the truth or facts about something — see INQUIRY 1

inquisitive *adj* interested in what is not one's own business — see CURIOUS 1

inquisitiveness *n* an eager desire to find out about things that are often none of one's business — see CURIOSITY 1

inroad *n* a sudden attack on and entrance into hostile territory — see RAID 1

inrush *n* a flowing or coming in — see INFLUX

insane *adj* **1** conceived or made without regard for reason or reality — see FANTASTIC 1

2 going beyond a normal or acceptable limit in degree or amount — see EXCESSIVE

inscribe *vb* **1** to cut (as letters or designs) on a hard surface — see ENGRAVE 1

2 to add (a person) to a list or roll as a participant or member — see ENROLL 1

3 to put (someone or something) on a list — see ¹LIST 2

inscrutable *adj* **1** being beyond one's

powers to know, understand, or explain — see MYSTERIOUS 1

2 having an often intentionally veiled or uncertain meaning — see OBSCURE 1

insecure *adj* **1** not tightly fastened, tied, or stretched — see LOOSE 1

2 feeling or showing uncomfortable feelings of uncertainty — see NERVOUS 1

insecurity *n* the quality or state of not being firmly fixed in position — see INSTABILITY

insensate *adj* **1** lacking animate awareness or sensation ⟨the *insensate* stones⟩

syn insensible, senseless, unfeeling

rel lifeless; unconscious

near ant aware, cognizant, conscious; animated, lively, vibrant

ant animate, feeling, sensate, sensible, sensitive, sentient

2 having or showing a lack of sympathy or tender feelings — see HARD 1

insensibility *n* **1** a lack of emotion or emotional expressiveness — see APATHY 1

2 a temporary state of unconsciousness — see FAINT

insensible *adj* **1** having lost consciousness — see UNCONSCIOUS 1

2 not perceptible by a sense or by the mind — see IMPERCEPTIBLE

3 having or showing a lack of interest or concern — see INDIFFERENT 1

4 lacking animate awareness or sensation — see INSENSATE 1

5 lacking in refinement or good taste — see COARSE 2

6 not informed about or aware of something — see IGNORANT 2

insensitive *adj* **1** having or showing a lack of sympathy or tender feelings — see HARD 1

2 lacking in sensation or feeling — see NUMB 1

inseparability *n* the state of being in a very personal or private relationship — see FAMILIARITY 1

insert *vb* to put among or between others ⟨surreptitiously *inserted* the book in its proper place on the shelf⟩

syn fit (in *or* into), inject, insinuate, interject, interpolate, interpose, intersperse, introduce

rel cut in, inlay, inset, install; interfile, interline, lard, weave; cram, shove, thrust, wedge; add, append, attach

near ant eject, eliminate, exclude, expel, extract, withdraw; deduct, detach, subtract; reject

inside *adj* **1** not known or meant to be known by the general populace — see PRIVATE 1

2 situated farther in — see INNER 1

inside *n* **1** an interior or internal part ⟨The *inside* of the clock features an amazingly complex mechanism.⟩

syn innards, interior, within

rel belly, bowels, guts; stuffing; recesses; center, core, heart

near ant border, boundary, brim, edge, end, extremity, fringe, limit, margin, perimeter, periphery, rim; surface

ant exterior, outside

2 *usually* **insides** *pl* the internal organs of the body — see GUT 1

3 the seat of one's deepest thoughts and emotions — see CORE 1

4 information not generally available to the public — see DOPE 1

insight *n* the ability to understand inner qualities or relationships — see WISDOM 1

insightful *adj* having or showing deep understanding and intelligent application of knowledge — see WISE 1

insignificant *adj* **1** lacking importance — see UNIMPORTANT

2 so small or unimportant as to warrant little or no attention — see NEGLIGIBLE 1

insincere *adj* not being or expressing what one appears to be or express ⟨the *insincere* compliments of a spiteful gossip⟩

syn artificial, backhanded, counterfeit, double, double-dealing, fake, feigned, hypocritical, left-handed, mealy, mealy-mouthed, phony (*also* phoney), pretended, two-faced, unctuous

rel affected, assumed, claptrap, contrived, forced, mechanical, put-on, simulated, strained, unnatural; empty, hollow, meaningless; deceitful, devious, dishonest, false, untruthful; facile, glib, superficial; bogus, sham; facetious, jocular, tongue-in-cheek; canting, pharisaical, pious, sanctimonious, self-righteous, simon-pure

near ant direct, forthright, frank, heart-to-heart, open, plain, straightforward

ant artless, candid, genuine, honest, sincere, undesigning

insincerity *n* the pretending of having virtues, principles, or beliefs that one in fact does not have — see HYPOCRISY

insinuate *vb* **1** to introduce in a gradual, secret, or clever way ⟨Years were needed for the agent to *insinuate* himself into the criminal organization.⟩

syn infiltrate, slip, sneak, wind, worm, wriggle

rel creep, edge, wiggle; insert, interpolate, interpose, introduce

2 to convey an idea indirectly — see HINT

3 to put among or between others — see INSERT

insipid *adj* **1** lacking in taste or flavor ⟨an apple pie with a mushy, *insipid* filling that strongly resembled soggy cardboard⟩

syn flat, flavorless, savorless, tasteless, unsavory

rel bland, dilute, thin, watery, weak; plain, unflavored

near ant distasteful, loathsome, sickening, unappetizing, unpalatable; mawkish; appetizing, delectable, delicious, palatable, toothsome; keen, piquant, seasoned, spicy; flavored; heavy, rich

ant flavorful, sapid, savory (*also* savoury), tasteful, tasty

2 lacking in qualities that make for spirit and character — see WISHY-WASHY 1

insist *vb* to state as a fact usually forcefully — see CLAIM 1

insist (on) *vb* to ask for (something) earnestly or with authority — see DEMAND 1

insistence *n* a solemn and often public declaration of the truth or existence of something — see PROTESTATION

insistent *adj* continuing despite difficulties, opposition, or discouragement — see PERSISTENT

insolence *n* **1** disrespectful or argumentative talk given in response to a command or request — see BACK TALK

2 rude behavior — see DISCOURTESY

insolent *adj* displaying or marked by rude boldness — see NERVY 1

insoluble *adj* incapable of being solved or accomplished — see IMPOSSIBLE

insouciance *n* lack of interest or concern — see INDIFFERENCE

insouciant *adj* **1** having or showing freedom from worries or troubles — see CAREFREE

2 having or showing a lack of interest or concern — see INDIFFERENT 1

inspect *vb* to look over closely (as for judging quality or condition) ⟨*inspected* the collie before the dog show⟩

syn audit, check (out), con, examine, overlook, oversee, review, scan, scrutinize, survey, view

rel notice, observe, watch; comb, peruse, pore (over); analyze, dissect, parse; delve (into), explore, investigate, plumb, probe, research, study

phrases go over

near ant skim; glance (at *or* over); miss, overlook

inspection *n* a close look at or over someone or something in order to judge condition ⟨The recruits lined up for an *inspection*.⟩

syn audit, check, checkup, examination, review, scan, scrutiny, survey, view

rel analysis, assay, dissection; exploration, investigation, probe, research, study; inquisition, interrogation; once-over, perusal; observation, surveillance, watch; checkout, test-drive, trial run

inspire *vb* **1** to fill with courage or strength of purpose — see ENCOURAGE 1

2 to draw out (something hidden, latent, or reserved) — see EDUCE

3 to provide (someone) with moral or spiritual understanding — see ENLIGHTEN 1

inspiring *adj* causing great emotional or mental stimulation — see EXCITING 1

instability *n* the quality or state of not being firmly fixed in position ⟨The *instability* of the bridge became tragically apparent when it suddenly collapsed.⟩

syn insecurity, precariousness, shakiness, unsteadiness

rel insubstantiality, unsoundness; changeability, inconstancy, mutability; laxness, looseness, slackness

near ant firmness, soundness, substantiality

ant fastness, fixedness, security, stability, steadiness

install *vb* **1** to put into an office or welcome into an organization with special ceremonies ⟨*installed* her as the new principal of the high school⟩

syn baptize, inaugurate, induct, initiate, instate, invest, seat

rel swear in; consecrate, enshrine; accept, admit, take in; enlist, enroll (*also* enrol)

near ant can, discharge, fire, terminate; muster out

2 to establish or place comfortably or snugly — see ENSCONCE 1

---

syn synonym(s)   *rel* related words
ant antonym(s)   *near ant* near antonym(s)

installation *n* **1** the process or an instance of being formally placed in an office or organization ⟨The *installation* of a new president takes place once every four years.⟩
syn baptism, inaugural, inauguration, induction, initiation, installment (*also* instalment), investiture, investment
rel enlistment, enrollment (*also* enrolment); promotion
near ant discharge, removal
2 a structure that is designed and built for a particular purpose — see FACILITY

installment *also* **instalment** *n* the process or an instance of being formally placed in an office or organization — see INSTALLATION 1

instance *n* one of a group or collection that shows what the whole is like — see EXAMPLE

instance *vb* **1** to give as an example — see QUOTE 1
2 to make reference to or speak about briefly but specifically — see MENTION 1
3 to show or make clear by using examples — see ILLUSTRATE 1

instant *adj* **1** done or occurring without any noticeable lapse in time — see INSTANTANEOUS
2 needing immediate attention — see ACUTE 2
3 existing or in progress right now — see PRESENT 1

instant *n* a very small space of time ⟨It all happened in an *instant*.⟩
syn beat, flash, jiffy, minute, moment, second, shake, split second, trice, twinkle, twinkling, wink
rel snatch, spurt
near ant eon (*or* aeon), age, eternity, forever; infinity, lifetime

instantaneous *adj* done or occurring without any noticeable lapse in time ⟨The thunder following the flash of lightning was nearly *instantaneous*.⟩
syn immediate, instant, split-second, straightaway
rel summary; fast, hit-and-run, prompt, quick, rapid, speedy, swift
near ant dilatory, tardy; slow, sluggish; prolonged, protracted; deferred, delayed

instantly *adv* without delay — see IMMEDIATELY

instantly *conj* just at the moment that — see WHEN 2

instate *vb* to put into an office or welcome into an organization with special ceremonies — see INSTALL 1

instead *adv* as a substitute ⟨I was offered a ride, but I chose to walk *instead*.⟩
syn first, rather
rel alternately, alternatively
phrases in lieu

instigate *vb* **1** to bring (something volatile or intense) into being — see INCITE 1
2 to rouse to strong feeling or action — see PROVOKE 1

instigating *adj* serving or likely to arouse a strong reaction — see PROVOCATIVE

instigation *n* **1** something that arouses a strong response from another — see PROVOCATION 1
2 something that arouses action or activity — see IMPULSE 1

instigator *n* a person who stirs up public feelings especially of discontent — see AGITATOR

instinctive *adj* done instantly and without conscious thought or decision — see AUTOMATIC 1

instinctual *adj* done instantly and without conscious thought or decision — see AUTOMATIC 1

institute *n* **1** a group of persons formally joined together for some common interest — see ASSOCIATION 2
2 a public organization with a particular purpose or function — see INSTITUTION 1

institute *vb* to be responsible for the creation and early operation or use of — see FOUND

instituter *or* **institutor** *n* a person who establishes a whole new field of endeavor — see FATHER 2

institution *n* **1** a public organization with a particular purpose or function ⟨a charitable *institution* devoted to raising funds to feed the hungry⟩
syn establishment, foundation, institute
rel body, collective, group; corporation, enterprise; charity, philanthropy; think tank
2 a place where mentally ill people are cared for ⟨Their father was committed to an *institution* after his mental health began to rapidly deteriorate.⟩
syn asylum, bedlam
rel hospital; halfway house, home; hospice, sanatorium, sanitarium, sanitorium
3 a group of persons formally joined together for some common interest — see ASSOCIATION 2

instruct *vb* **1** to cause to acquire knowledge or skill in some field — see TEACH
2 to give information to — see ENLIGHTEN 1
3 to issue orders to (someone) by right of authority — see COMMAND 1

instruction *n* **1** a statement of what to do that must be obeyed by those concerned — see COMMAND 1
2 the act or process of imparting knowledge or skills to another — see EDUCATION 1

instructional *adj* providing useful information or knowledge — see INFORMATIVE

instructive *adj* providing useful information or knowledge — see INFORMATIVE

instructor *n* a person whose occupation is to give formal instruction in a school — see TEACHER

instrument *n* **1** a written or printed paper giving information about or proof of something — see CERTIFICATE
2 an article intended for use in work — see IMPLEMENT
3 something used to achieve an end — see AGENT 1
4 one that is or can be used to further the purposes of another — see ¹PAWN

instrumentalist *n* a person who plays a musical instrument — see MUSICIAN 1

instrumentality *n* something used to achieve an end — see AGENT 1

insubordinate *adj* given to resisting authority or another's control — see DISOBEDIENT

insubordination *n* refusal to obey — see DISOBEDIENCE

insubstantial *adj* 1 being of a material lacking in sturdiness or substance — see FLIMSY 1

2 not composed of matter — see IMMATERIAL 1

insufferable *adj* more than can be put up with — see UNBEARABLE

insufficiency *n* 1 a falling short of an essential or desirable amount or number — see DEFICIENCY

2 the lack of sufficient ability, power, or means — see INABILITY

insufficient *adj* not coming up to an expected measure or meeting a particular need — see SHORT 1

insular *adj* not broad or open in views or opinions — see NARROW 2

insulate *vb* to set or keep apart from others — see ISOLATE

insulation *n* the state of being alone or kept apart from others — see ISOLATION

insult *n* an act or expression showing scorn and usually intended to hurt another's feelings ⟨Panelists on that political talk show simply exchange *insults*, not ideas.⟩

syn affront, barb, cut, dart, dig, epithet, indignity, name, offense (*or* offence), outrage, personality, poke, put-down, sarcasm, slap, slight, slur

rel catcall, gibe (*or* jibe), jeer, mock, quip, sneer, taunt; abuse, invective, vituperation; disparage, opprobrium; disgrace, dishonor, shame; attack, criticism, knock, slam, swipe; torment, torture

near ant accolade, commendation, compliment; acclaim, applause, praise; adulation, flattery

insult *vb* to cause hurt feelings or deep resentment in ⟨*insulted* their hosts by casually remarking about the outdated look of their home⟩

syn affront, disrespect, offend, outrage, slap, slight, wound

rel cut, snub; displease, distress, disturb, hurt, pain, trouble, upset; jeer, mock, ridicule, sneer (at), taunt; defame, disparage, libel, malign, revile, slander, slur, smear; oppress, persecute, torment, torture

near ant acclaim, applaud, approve, hail; commend, compliment, eulogize, praise; adulate, flatter; exalt, glorify, honor; delight, gratify, please, satisfy

insuperable *adj* 1 incapable of being defeated, overcome, or subdued — see INVINCIBLE

2 incapable of being solved or accomplished — see IMPOSSIBLE

insupportable *adj* 1 more than can be put up with — see UNBEARABLE

2 too bad to be excused or justified — see INEXCUSABLE

insure *vb* to make sure, certain, or safe — see ENSURE

insurgency *n* open fighting against authority (as one's own government) — see REBELLION 1

insurgent *adj* taking part in a rebellion — see REBELLIOUS 1

insurgent *n* a person who rises up against authority — see REBEL

insurmountable *adj* incapable of being defeated, overcome, or subdued — see INVINCIBLE

insurrection *n* open fighting against authority (as one's own government) — see REBELLION 1

insurrectionary *adj* taking part in a rebellion — see REBELLIOUS 1

insurrectionary *n* a person who rises up against authority — see REBEL

insurrectionist *n* a person who rises up against authority — see REBEL

intact *adj* not lacking any part or member that properly belongs to it — see COMPLETE 1

intangible *adj* not capable of being perceived by the sense of touch ⟨*intangible* forces like gravity⟩

syn impalpable

rel bodiless, immaterial, incorporeal, insubstantial, unsubstantial; ethereal, spiritual, unreal

near ant corporeal, physical; embodied, material, real, solid, substantial

ant palpable, tactile, tangible, touchable

integer *n* 1 a character used to represent a mathematical value — see NUMBER 1

2 one that has a real and independent existence — see ENTITY

integral *adj* 1 being a part of the innermost nature of a person or thing — see INHERENT

2 impossible to do without — see ESSENTIAL 1

3 not lacking any part or member that properly belongs to it — see COMPLETE 1

integrate *vb* 1 to make a part of a body or system — see EMBODY 1

2 to turn into a single mass or entity that is more or less the same throughout — see BLEND 1

integrity *n* 1 conduct that conforms to an accepted standard of right and wrong — see MORALITY 1

2 devotion to telling the truth — see HONESTY 1

3 faithfulness to high moral standards — see HONOR 1

intellect *n* 1 a very smart person — see GENIUS 1

2 the ability to learn and understand or to deal with problems — see INTELLIGENCE 1

intellectual *adj* 1 much given to learning and thinking ⟨As the daughter of college professors, she's used to being around *intellectual* people.⟩

syn cerebral, highbrow, nerdy

rel cultivated, cultured; erudite, learned, literate, scholarly, well-read; academic (*also* academical), bookish, professorial; didactic, high-toned, hyperintellectual, pedantic; educated, schooled; brainy, bright, brilliant, clever, intelligent, quick-witted, smart

near ant uncultivated, uncultured; ignorant, illiterate, uneducated, unlettered, unread; dumb, foolish, idiotic (*also* idiotical), moronic, slow, stupid, unintelligent; benighted, unenlightened

ant anti-intellectual, lowbrow, nonintellectual, philistine

2 of or relating to the mind — see MENTAL 1

3 of or relating to schooling or learning

---

especially at an advanced level — see ACA-DEMIC 1

intellectual *n* a person with strong intellectual interests ⟨He discovered that in politics a reputation for being an *intellectual* was regarded as a liability.⟩

syn egghead, highbrow, nerd

rel bluestocking; Brahmin, mandarin, sage; brain, genius, intellect, thinker, whiz, wizard

near ant blockhead, dolt, dope, dumbbell, dummy, dunce, fathead, half-wit, imbecile, moron, nitwit, pinhead, simpleton

ant anti-intellectual, lowbrow, philistine

intellectuality *n* the ability to learn and understand or to deal with problems — see INTELLIGENCE 1

intelligence *n* **1** the ability to learn and understand or to deal with problems ⟨High scores on this test supposedly demonstrate great *intelligence*.⟩

syn brain(s), gray matter, headpiece, intellect, intellectuality, mentality, reason, sense

rel eggheadedness, highbrowism, intellectualism; braininess, brilliance; acumen, alertness, apprehension, astuteness, discernment, discriminability, insight, judgment (*or* judgement), perception, perspicacity; common sense, horse sense, mother wit; aptitude, talent; sagacity, sapience, wisdom, wit; head, mind, skull

near ant denseness, density, doltishness, dopiness, dullness (*also* dulness), dumbness, fatuity, feeblemindedness, foolishness, half-wittedness, idiocy, imbecility, senselessness, simpleness, slowness, stupidity

2 a report of recent events or facts not previously known — see NEWS

3 exceptional discernment and judgment especially in practical matters — see ACUMEN

intelligent *adj* **1** having or showing quickness of mind ⟨Proud parents typically insist that their children are *intelligent* way beyond their years.⟩ ⟨His *intelligent* response to the emergency averted a disaster.⟩

syn alert, brainy, bright, brilliant, clever, exceptional, fast, keen, nimble, quick, quick-witted, sharp, sharp-witted, smart

rel apt, ingenious, resourceful; acute, astute, discerning, insightful, knowing, perceptive, percipient, perspicacious, sagacious, sapient, savvy, wise; cerebral, erudite, genial, highbrow, knowledgeable, learned, literate, scholarly, well-read; creative, inventive, judicious, prudent, sage, sane, sapient, sensible, sound, wise; crafty, cunning, foxy, shrewd, wily; logical, rational, reasonable

near ant feebleminded, simpleminded; ignorant, illiterate, lowbrow, nonintellectual, unacademic, uneducated, uninformed, unintellectual, untaught, unthinking; absurd, asinine, balmy, cockeyed, daffy, daft, dotty, fool, half-baked, harebrained, nonsensical, preposterous, sappy, screwball, wacky (*also* whacky), zany

ant airheaded, boneheaded, brainless, bubbleheaded, chuckleheaded, dense, dim, dim-witted, doltish, dopey (*also* dopy), dorky [*slang*], dull, dumb, dunderheaded, empty-headed, fatuous, half-witted, knuckleheaded, mindless, obtuse, opaque, senseless, simple, slow, slow-witted, soft, softheaded, stupid, thick, thickheaded, thick-witted, unintelligent, vacuous, weak-minded, witless

2 having the ability to reason — see RATIONAL 1

3 having or showing good judgment and restraint especially in conduct or speech — see DISCREET 1

intemperate *adj* showing no signs of being under control — see RAMPANT 1

intend *vb* **1** to have in mind as a purpose or goal ⟨an aspiring entrepreneur who *intends* to revolutionize the biotech industry⟩

syn aim, aspire, calculate, contemplate, design, look, mean, meditate, plan, propose, purport, purpose

rel dream, hope, wish; consider, debate, mull (over), ponder; attempt, endeavor, strive, struggle, try; plot, scheme; accomplish, achieve, effect, execute, perform

phrases figure on

2 to communicate or convey (as an idea) to the mind — see MEAN 1

intended *n* the person to whom one is engaged to be married — see BETROTHED

intended *adj* made, given, or done with full awareness of what one is doing — see INTENTIONAL

intense *adj* **1** extreme in degree, power, or effect ⟨the *intense* cold of the polar regions⟩

syn acute, almighty, blistering, deep, dreadful, excruciating, explosive, exquisite, fearful, fearsome, ferocious, fierce, frightful, furious, ghastly, hard, heavy, intensive, keen, profound, terrible, vehement, vicious, violent

rel accentuated, concentrated, deepened; emphasized, enhanced, heightened, intensified, magnified; exhaustive, thorough; harsh, rigorous, severe

near ant feeble, weak; shallow, superficial; moderated, qualified; alleviated, eased, lightened, toned (down); abated, decreased, diminished, lessened, reduced, subdued

ant light, moderate, soft

2 having or expressing great depth of feeling — see FERVENT 1

intensely *adv* **1** with great effort or determination — see HARD 1

2 to a great degree — see VERY 1

intensify *vb* to make markedly greater in measure or degree ⟨*intensified* her efforts to preserve the town's historic buildings and landmarks⟩

syn accentuate, amplify, beef (up), boost, consolidate, deepen, enhance, heighten, magnify, redouble, step up, strengthen

rel broaden, enlarge, expand, extend, lengthen; accelerate, hasten, quicken; emphasize, point (up), sharpen, stress; augment, enforce, restrengthen, supplement; maximize; enliven, jazz (up); aggravate

near ant decrease, diminish, lessen, let up (on), reduce, subdue, tone (down), weaken; dwindle, recede, subside, taper (off), wane; alleviate, ease, lighten

ant abate, moderate

intensity *n* **1** depth of feeling — see ARDOR 1

2 the quality or state of being forceful (as in expression) — see VEHEMENCE 1

intensive *adj* extreme in degree, power, or effect — see INTENSE 1

intensively *adv* with great effort or determination — see HARD 1

intent *adj* **1** fully committed to achieving a goal — see DETERMINED 1
2 having the mind fixed on something — see ATTENTIVE 1

intent *n* **1** something that one hopes or intends to accomplish — see GOAL
2 the idea that is conveyed or intended to be conveyed to the mind by language, symbol, or action — see MEANING 1

intention *n* **1** something that one hopes or intends to accomplish — see GOAL
2 the idea that is conveyed or intended to be conveyed to the mind by language, symbol, or action — see MEANING 1

intentional *adj* made, given, or done with full awareness of what one is doing ⟨I'm fairly sure that your "accidental" cutting down of my rosebush was really *intentional*.⟩
syn conscious, deliberate, intended, knowing, purposeful, set, voluntary, willful (*or* wilful), witting
rel designed, planned; conscious; advised, calculated, considered, measured, reasoned, studied, thoughtful, weighed; premeditated, premeditative, prepense; discretionary, elective, optional, volunteer
near ant inadvertent, unwitting; accidental, chance, haphazard, hit-or-miss, incidental, random; aimless, desultory, purposeless; abrupt, impetuous, sudden; coerced, forced, involuntary; compulsory, mandatory, necessary, nonelective, obligatory, ordered, required; extemporaneous, impromptu, impulsive, instinctive, spontaneous, unforced, unpremeditated
ant nondeliberate, nonpurposive, unintentional

intentionally *adv* with full awareness of what one is doing ⟨The witness *intentionally* gave misleading answers to the questions.⟩
syn advisedly, consciously, deliberately, designedly, knowingly, purposefully, purposely, willfully, wittingly
rel calculatedly, studiedly; voluntarily, willingly; premeditatedly
phrases on purpose
near ant accidentally; haphazardly, randomly; involuntarily, unwillingly; impulsively, instinctively, spontaneously
ant inadvertently, unconsciously, unintentionally, unknowingly, unwittingly

intently *adv* with great effort or determination — see HARD 1

intentness *n* a mental state free of jesting or trifling — see EARNESTNESS

inter *vb* to place (a dead body) in the earth, a tomb, or the sea — see BURY 1

interaction *n* doings between individuals or groups — see RELATION 1

intercede *vb* to act as a go-between for opposing sides — see INTERVENE

intercessor *n* one who works with opposing sides in order to bring about an agreement — see MEDIATOR

intercommunicate *vb* to engage in an exchange of information or ideas — see COMMUNICATE 2

interconnect *vb* to put or bring together so as to form a new and longer whole — see CONNECT 1

intercourse *n* **1** doings between individuals or groups — see RELATION 1
2 sexual union involving penetration of the vagina by the penis — see SEXUAL INTERCOURSE

interdict *n* an order that something not be done or used — see PROHIBITION 2

interdict *vb* to order not to do or use or to be done or used — see FORBID

interdicted *adj* that may not be permitted — see IMPERMISSIBLE

interdicting *n* the act of ordering that something not be done or used — see PROHIBITION 1

interdiction *n* **1** an order that something not be done or used — see PROHIBITION 2
2 the act of ordering that something not be done or used — see PROHIBITION 1

interest *vb* to hold the attention of — see ENGAGE 1

interest *n* **1** a legal right to participation in the advantages, profits, and responsibility of something ⟨All of the workers at the food cooperative have an *interest* in it.⟩
syn claim, share, stake
rel co-ownership, ownership, part, partnership, possession, title
2 the state of doing well especially in relation to one's happiness or success — see WELFARE
3 a commercial or industrial activity or organization — see ENTERPRISE 1

interesting *adj* holding the attention or provoking interest ⟨This is one of the most *interesting* books I've read all year.⟩
syn absorbing, arresting, engaging, engrossing, enthralling, fascinating, gripping, immersing, intriguing, involving, riveting
rel breathtaking, electric, electrifying, exciting, exhilarating, galvanizing, inspiring, rousing, stimulating, stirring, thrilling; provocative, tantalizing; emphatic, showy, splashy, striking; curious, odd, unusual, weird; amazing, astonishing, astounding, eventful, eye-opening, fabulous, marvelous (*or* marvellous), surprising, wonderful, wondrous; amusing, entertaining
near ant tiresome, tiring, wearisome, wearying; sterile, unexciting; dreary, humdrum, pedestrian; demoralizing, discouraging, disheartening, dispiriting
ant boring, drab, dry, dull, heavy, monotonous, tedious, uninteresting

interfere *vb* to interest oneself in what is not one's concern ⟨a strong resentment of outsiders who attempted to *interfere* with their traditional ways of doing things⟩
syn butt in, intrude, meddle, mess, nose, obtrude, poke, pry, snoop
rel intercede, interpose, intervene; barge (in), chisel (in), encroach, infringe, invade, trespass; fiddle, fool, monkey, play, tamper
near ant avoid, eschew, shun; disregard, ignore, neglect, overlook

interfere (with) *vb* to create difficulty for the work or activity of — see HAMPER

interference *n* something that makes

syn synonym(s)   *rel* related words
ant antonym(s)   *near ant* near antonym(s)

movement or progress difficult — see EN-CUMBRANCE

interferer *n* a person who meddles in the affairs of others — see BUSYBODY

interfering *adj* thrusting oneself where one is not welcome or invited — see IN-TRUSIVE

interim *adj* 1 intended to last, continue, or serve for a limited time — see TEMPORARY 1

2 serving in a position for the time being — see ACTING

interim *n* a break in continuity — see GAP 2

interior *n* an interior or internal part — see INSIDE 1

interior *adj* 1 of or relating to the mind — see MENTAL

2 situated farther in — see INNER 1

interject *vb* to put among or between others — see INSERT

interjection *n* a sudden short emotional utterance — see EXCLAMATION

interlace *vb* 1 to cause to twine about one another — see INTERTWINE 1

2 to scatter or set here and there among other things — see THREAD 1

3 to twist together into a usually confused mass — see ENTANGLE 1

interloper *n* a person who meddles in the affairs of others — see BUSYBODY

interlude *n* a break in continuity — see GAP 2

intermediary *adj* occupying a position equally distant from the ends or extremes — see MIDDLE 1

intermediary *n* one who works with opposing sides in order to bring about an agreement — see MEDIATOR

intermediate *adj* 1 being about midway between extremes of amount or size — see MIDDLE 2

2 occupying a position equally distant from the ends or extremes — see MIDDLE 1

intermediate *n* one who works with opposing sides in order to bring about an agreement — see MEDIATOR

intermediate *vb* to act as a go-between for opposing sides — see INTERVENE

interment *n* the act or ceremony of putting a dead body in its final resting place — see BURIAL 1

intermingle *vb* to turn into a single mass or entity that is more or less the same throughout — see BLEND 1

intermission *n* a break in continuity — see GAP 2

intermittent *adj* 1 occurring or appearing at intervals ⟨*Intermittent* showers had me opening and closing my umbrella all day long.⟩

syn continual, periodic, periodical, recurrent, recurring

rel alternate, alternating, cyclic (*or* cyclical), rhythmic (*or* rhythmical), seasonal, serial; erratic, fitful, irregular, occasional, spasmodic, sporadic, spotty, unsteady

near ant eternal, everlasting, interminable, perpetual

ant constant, continuous, incessant, unceasing

2 lacking in steadiness or regularity of occurrence — see FITFUL

intermix *vb* to turn into a single mass or entity that is more or less the same throughout — see BLEND 1

intermixture *n* a distinct entity formed by the combining of two or more different things — see BLEND

intern *vb* to put in or as if in prison — see IMPRISON

internal *adj* 1 situated farther in — see INNER 1

2 of or relating to the mind — see MENTAL

interned *adj* taken and held prisoner — see CAPTIVE

internee *n* one that has been taken and held in confinement — see CAPTIVE

internment *n* the act of confining or the state of being confined ⟨The *internment* of Americans of Japanese descent during World War II is one of the more shameful chapters in United States history.⟩

syn captivity, confinement, immurement, imprisonment, incarceration, prison

rel bondage, enslavement, servitude; restraint, restriction; arrest, capture, entrapment; custody, detainment, house arrest; detention, hold

near ant emancipation, liberation, manumission, redemption, release; freedom, independence, liberty

interpenetrate *vb* to spread throughout — see PERMEATE

interpolate *vb* to put among or between others — see INSERT

interpose *vb* 1 to act as a go-between for opposing sides — see INTERVENE

2 to cause a disruption in a conversation or discussion — see INTERRUPT

3 to put among or between others — see INSERT

interposer *n* one who works with opposing sides in order to bring about an agreement — see MEDIATOR

interpret *vb* 1 to make plain or understandable — see EXPLAIN 1

2 to present a portrayal or performance of — see ACT 1

interpretation *n* 1 a statement that makes something clear — see EXPLANATION 1

2 a presentation of an artistic work (as a piece of music) from a particular point of view — see ACCOUNT 2

interpretative *adj* serving to explain — see EXPLANATORY

interpretive *adj* serving to explain — see EXPLANATORY

interring *n* the act or ceremony of putting a dead body in its final resting place — see BURIAL 1

interrogate *vb* 1 to put a question or questions to — see ASK 1

2 to put a series of questions to — see EXAMINE 1

interrupt *vb* to cause a disruption in a conversation or discussion ⟨It's rude to *interrupt* when someone is making an important point.⟩

syn break in, chime in, cut in, interpose, intrude

rel barge (in), bother, horn in; add, contribute, put in

interruption *n* 1 a break in continuity — see GAP 2

2 a momentary halt in an activity — see PAUSE 1

intersect *vb* to divide by passing through

or across ⟨A dry streambed *intersects* the trail at several points.⟩
syn bisect, cross, cut
rel crisscross

intersection *n* a place where roads meet — see CROSSROAD 1

intersperse *vb* 1 to scatter or set here and there among other things — see THREAD 1
2 to put among or between others — see INSERT

interstice *n* 1 a break in continuity — see GAP 2
2 an open space in a barrier (as a wall or hedge) — see GAP 1

intertwine *vb* 1 to cause to twine about one another ⟨*intertwined* two different colors of yarn⟩
syn entwine, interlace, interweave, lace, ply, twist, weave, wreathe, writhe
rel braid, plait, blend, fuse, join, link, mix
near ant disentangle, uncoil, untangle, untwine, unwind
2 to twist together into a usually confused mass — see ENTANGLE 1

interval *n* 1 a break in continuity — see GAP 2
2 an open space in a barrier (as a wall or hedge) — see GAP 1

intervene *vb* to act as a go-between for opposing sides ⟨I *intervened* in the argument before any real harm was done.⟩
syn intercede, intermediate, interpose, mediate
rel butt in, interfere, intrude, meddle, obtrude, pry, snoop; arbitrate, moderate, negotiate, referee; barge (in), bother; break (in), chime in, cut in; infringe, invade, trespass
near ant stand by; avoid, eschew, shun; disregard, ignore, overlook

interweave *vb* 1 to cause to twine about one another — see INTERTWINE 1
2 to scatter or set here and there among other things — see THREAD 1
3 to twist together into a usually confused mass — see ENTANGLE 1

intimacy *n* the state of being in a very personal or private relationship — see FAMILIARITY 1

intimate *adj* 1 closely acquainted — see FAMILIAR 1
2 not known or meant to be known by the general populace — see PRIVATE 1

intimate *n* a person who has a strong liking for and trust in another — see FRIEND 1

intimate *vb* to convey an idea indirectly — see HINT

intimation *n* a slight or indirect pointing to something (as a solution or explanation) — see HINT 1

intimidate *vb* to make timid or fearful by or as if by threats ⟨Refusing to be *intimidated* by the manager's harsh stare, I demanded my money back.⟩
syn browbeat, bulldoze, bully, cow, hector
rel bluster; affright, alarm (*also* alarum), frighten, horrify, scare, shock, spook, startle, terrify; menace, terrorize, threaten; badger, hound; bludgeon, coerce, compel, constrain, force, make, oblige,

press, pressure, push around; demoralize, psych (out), unman, unnerve; discompose, disconcert, disquiet, distress, disturb, perturb, upset
phrases pick on
near ant cheer, comfort, console, reassure, solace, soothe; embolden, encourage, hearten, steel; convince, persuade

intimidating *adj* 1 causing fear — see FEARFUL 1
2 harsh and threatening in manner or appearance — see GRIM 1

intimidator *n* a person who teases, threatens, or hurts more vulnerable persons — see BULLY

intolerable *adj* 1 more than can be put up with — see UNBEARABLE
2 going beyond a normal or acceptable limit in degree or amount — see EXCESSIVE

intolerant *adj* 1 unable or unwilling to endure ⟨*Intolerant* of fools, she is not an easy person to work for.⟩
syn impatient
rel uncompromising, unforgiving, unyielding; complaining, fussing, griping, grumbling, kvetching, protesting, whining
near ant accepting, forgiving, long-suffering, resigned, uncomplaining, willing; indulgent
ant abiding, enduring, forbearing, patient, tolerant
2 unwilling to grant other people social rights or to accept other viewpoints ⟨*intolerant* people who callously deny others the very rights that they take for granted⟩
syn bigoted, narrow, narrow-minded, prejudiced, small-minded
rel conservative, hidebound, old-fashioned, reactionary; blindfolded, blinkered, insular, parochial, provincial; biased, one-sided, partial, partisan
near ant extreme, progressive, radical; impartial, objective, unbiased
ant broad-minded, liberal, open-minded, tolerant, unprejudiced

intone *vb* to utter in musical or drawn out tones — see CHANT 1

intoxicant *n* a distilled beverage that can make a person drunk — see ALCOHOL

intoxicate *vb* 1 to cause a pleasurable stimulation of the feelings of — see THRILL
2 to fill with great joy — see ELATE

intoxicated *adj* 1 being under the influence of alcohol — see DRUNK
2 experiencing or marked by overwhelming usually pleasurable emotion — see ECSTATIC

intoxication *n* a state of overwhelming usually pleasurable emotion — see ECSTASY

intractability *n* refusal to obey — see DISOBEDIENCE

intractable *adj* 1 given to resisting authority or another's control — see DISOBEDIENT
2 given to resisting control or discipline by others — see UNCONTROLLABLE

intrepid *adj* feeling or displaying no fear by temperament — see BRAVE 1

intrepidity *n* strength of mind to carry on in spite of danger — see COURAGE

intrepidness *n* strength of mind to carry on in spite of danger — see COURAGE

intricacy *n* 1 something that makes a situ-

---

syn synonym(s)   **rel** related words
ant antonym(s)   **near ant** near antonym(s)

ation more complicated or difficult — see COMPLICATION 1

2 the state or quality of having many interrelated parts or aspects — see COMPLEXITY 1

intricate *adj* **1** having many parts or aspects that are usually interrelated — see COMPLEX 1

2 made or done with great care or with much detail — see ELABORATE 1

intrigue *n* a secret plan for accomplishing evil or unlawful ends — see PLOT 1

intrigue *vb* **1** to engage in a secret plan to accomplish evil or unlawful ends — see PLOT

2 to hold the attention of — see ENGAGE 1

intriguing *adj* holding the attention or provoking interest — see INTERESTING

intrinsic *adj* being a part of the innermost nature of a person or thing — see INHERENT

intrinsically *adv* by natural character or ability — see NATURALLY 1

introduce *vb* **1** to make (one person) known (to another) socially ⟨A friend *introduced* them, and they wound up getting married.⟩

syn acquaint, present

rel address, greet, hail, meet

2 to present or bring forward for discussion ⟨After about 20 minutes the moderator *introduced* a new topic for the debate.⟩

syn bring up, broach, moot, place, raise

rel allude (to), cite, mention, name, refer (to); offer, propose, suggest; air, express, speak (of), talk (about), vent, ventilate; interject, interrupt; debate, discuss, thrash (out *or* over)

near ant censor, hush (up), quiet, silence, suppress

3 to be responsible for the creation and early operation or use of — see FOUND

4 to impart knowledge of a new thing or situation to — see ACQUAINT 1

5 to put among or between others — see INSERT

introducer *n* one who creates or introduces something new — see INVENTOR

introduction *n* a short section (as of a book) that leads to or explains the main part ⟨A leading biologist wrote the *introduction* to that new textbook.⟩

syn foreword, preamble, preface, prelude, prologue (*also* prolog)

rel beginning, commencement, initiation, opening, origin, origination, outset, start

near ant postscript; aftermath; cessation, close, closing, conclusion, end, finale, finish, termination

ant epilogue (*also* epilog)

introductory *adj* **1** coming before the main part or item usually to introduce or prepare for what follows — see PRELIMINARY

2 of or relating to the simplest facts or theories of a subject — see ELEMENTARY

introverted *adj* not comfortable around people — see SHY 2

intrude *vb* **1** to cause a disruption in a conversation or discussion — see INTERRUPT

2 to interest oneself in what is not one's concern — see INTERFERE

intrude (upon) *vb* to thrust oneself upon (another) without invitation — see BOTHER 1

intruder *n* a person who meddles in the affairs of others — see BUSYBODY

intruding *adj* thrusting oneself where one is not welcome or invited — see INTRUSIVE

intrusive *adj* thrusting oneself where one is not welcome or invited ⟨She's that proverbially *intrusive* neighbor who never knocks before coming in.⟩

syn busy, interfering, intruding, meddlesome, meddling, nosy (*or* nosey), obtrusive, officious, presuming, presumptuous, prying, snoopy

rel bold, brazen, impertinent, impudent, insolent, rude; invading, trespassing; curious, inquisitive; annoying, harassing; overbearing

near ant hands-off; uninvolved; quiet, reclusive, reserved, reticent, retiring, silent, taciturn, withdrawn; inhibited, restrained, subdued

ant unobtrusive

inundate *vb* to cover with a flood — see FLOOD

inundation *n* a great flow of water or of something that overwhelms — see FLOOD

inure *vb* to make able to withstand physical hardship, strain, or exposure — see HARDEN 2

inured *adj* able to withstand hardship, strain, or exposure — see HARDY 1

invade *vb* to enter for conquest or plunder ⟨a superpower that had a tendency to *invade* and take over smaller and weaker countries⟩

syn foray (into), overrun, raid

rel despoil, loot, maraud, pillage, plunder, ransack, ravage, sack, strip; conquer, crush, dominate, overcome, overpower, overwhelm, subdue, subject, subjugate, vanquish; assail, assault, attack, beset, charge, rush, storm, strike; battle, clash (with), combat, fight, war (with); encroach, infringe, trespass; beleaguer, besiege, blockade, invest; garrison, occupy

near ant defend, guard, protect, safeguard, shield, ward; defy, oppose, repel, resist, withstand; capitulate (to), cede (to), submit (to), succumb (to), surrender (to), yield (to)

invader *n* one that starts armed conflict against another especially without reasonable cause — see AGGRESSOR

¹**invalid** *adj* chronically or repeatedly suffering from poor health — see SICKLY 1

²**invalid** *adj* **1** having no legal or binding force — see NULL 1

2 not being in agreement with what is true — see FALSE 1

3 not using or following good reasoning — see ILLOGICAL

4 having no basis in reason or fact — see GROUNDLESS

invalidate *vb* to put an end to by formal action — see ABOLISH 1

invariability *n* the state of continuing without change — see CONSTANCY 1

invariable *adj* not capable of changing or being changed — see INFLEXIBLE 1

invariably *adv* on every relevant occasion — see ALWAYS 1

invariant *adj* not varying — see UNIFORM

invasion *n* a sudden attack on and entrance into hostile territory — see RAID 1

invective *n* harsh insulting language — see ABUSE 1

invective *adj* marked by harsh insulting language — see ABUSIVE

invent *vb* to create or think of by clever use of the imagination ⟨They *invented* an explanation for the broken vase that would satisfy their grandmother.⟩

syn concoct, construct, contrive, cook (up), devise, fabricate, make up, manufacture, think (up)

rel design, hatch, produce; daydream, dream; conceive, envisage, imagine, picture, vision, visualize; ad-lib, extemporize, improvise

phrases come up with

near ant copy, copycat, duplicate, imitate, mimic, reduplicate, replicate, reproduce

invented *adj* not real and existing only in the imagination — see IMAGINARY

invention *n* **1** something (as a device) created for the first time through the use of the imagination ⟨His clever *invention* made people's lives easier.⟩

syn coinage, concoction, contrivance, creation, innovation, wrinkle

rel contraption, device, gadget, gizmo (*also* gismo), novelty; design, product, work; dream, fantasy (*also* phantasy), picture, vision; conception, imagining, origination

near ant carbon copy, copy, dupe, duplicate, duplication, facsimile, imitation, reduplication, replica, replication, reproduction

2 something that is the product of the imagination — see FICTION

3 the ability to form mental images of things that either are not physically present or have never been conceived or created by others — see IMAGINATION 1

4 the skill and imagination to create new things — see CREATIVITY 1

inventive *adj* **1** showing a noteworthy use of the imagination and creativity especially in inventing — see CLEVER 1

2 having the skill and imagination to create new things — see CREATIVE 1

inventiveness *n* **1** the ability to form mental images of things that either are not physically present or have never been conceived or created by others — see IMAGINATION 1

2 the skill and imagination to create new things — see CREATIVITY 1

inventor *n* one who creates or introduces something new ⟨the *inventor* of the electric light bulb⟩

syn contriver, designer, developer, deviser, formulator, innovator, introducer, originator

rel author, begetter, creator, establisher, father, founder, generator, inaugurator, initiator, instituter (*or* institutor), sire; groundbreaker, pioneer, planner; builder, maker, producer; dreamer

near ant aper, copier, copycat, duplicator, imitator, mimic

inventory *vb* to make a list of — see ¹LIST 1

inventory *n* the number of individuals or amount of something available at any given time — see SUPPLY

invert *vb* to change the position of (an ob-

ject) so that the opposite side or end is showing — see REVERSE 2

invertebrate *adj* lacking strength of will or character — see WEAK 2

invest *vb* **1** to cause (as a person) to become filled or saturated with a certain quality or principle — see INFUSE

2 to furnish freely or naturally with some power, quality, or attribute — see ENDOW 1

3 to give official or legal power to — see AUTHORIZE 1

4 to outfit with clothes and especially fine or special clothes — see CLOTHE 1

5 to put into an office or welcome into an organization with special ceremonies — see INSTALL 1

6 to surround (as a fortified place) with armed forces for the purpose of capturing or preventing commerce and communication — see BESIEGE 1

7 to surround and cover closely — see ENFOLD 1

investigate *vb* to search through or into — see EXPLORE 1

investigation *n* a systematic search for the truth or facts about something — see INQUIRY 1

investigator *n* a person not on the police force who investigates criminal or illicit activity or searches for missing persons — see DETECTIVE

investiture *n* the process or an instance of being formally placed in an office or organization — see INSTALLATION 1

investment *n* **1** the cutting off of an area by military means to stop the flow of people or supplies — see BLOCKADE

2 the process or an instance of being formally placed in an office or organization — see INSTALLATION 1

inveterate *adj* **1** firmly established over time ⟨He has an *inveterate* tendency to tell some very tall tales.⟩

syn confirmed, deep, deep-rooted, deepseated, entrenched (*also* intrenched), hard-core, rooted, settled

rel firm, fixed, frozen, hard, hard-and-fast, immutable, irradicable, set, unalterable, unchangeable; embedded (*also* imbedded), implanted, inculcated, instilled; inborn, inbred, ingrained (*also* engrained), inherent, innate, integral, intrinsic, natural; accustomed, chronic, customary, habitual, regular, typical, usual; abiding, enduring, lifelong, persistent, persisting

near ant brief, ephemeral, fleeting, impermanent, interim, momentary, provisional, short-lived, short-term, temporary, transient

2 being such by habit and not likely to change — see HABITUAL 1

invidious *adj* having or showing mean resentment of another's possessions or advantages — see ENVIOUS

invidiousness *n* a painful awareness of another's possessions or advantages and a desire to have them too — see ENVY

invigorate *vb* to give life, vigor, or spirit to — see ANIMATE

invigorated *adj* made or become fresh in spirits or vigor — see NEW 4

invigorating *adj* having a renewing effect on the state of the body or mind — see TONIC 1

invincible *adj* incapable of being defeated, overcome, or subdued ⟨an *invincible* wrestler who has never lost a match⟩
syn impregnable, indomitable, insuperable, insurmountable, invulnerable, unbeatable, unconquerable
rel inviolable, unassailable, unbreachable, untouchable; armored, defended, guarded, protected, safe, safeguarded, secure, shielded; unbeaten, unbowed, unconquered, undefeated, unsubdued
near ant exposed, imperiled (*or* imperilled), insecure, liable, open, susceptible, unguarded, unprotected, unsafe; defenseless, helpless, powerless, weak
ant superable, surmountable, vincible, vulnerable

inviolable *adj* not to be violated, criticized, or tampered with — see SACRED 1

invite *vb* **1** to request the presence or participation of ⟨She's *invited* only select friends to visit her new house.⟩
syn ask, bid
rel solicit; beckon, call, summon
2 to act so as to make (something) more likely — see COURT 1

invoice *n* a record of goods sold or services performed together with the costs due — see ¹BILL 1

involuntary *adj* **1** not made or done willingly or by choice ⟨My long stays on the sidelines during our football games were strictly *involuntary*.⟩
syn coerced, forced, unintended, unintentional, unwilling
rel accidental, unplanned, unpremeditated; automatic, impulsive, instinctive, spontaneous, unprompted; inadvertent, unconscious, unknowing, unwitting
near ant advised, conscious, considered, knowing, planned, premeditated, premeditative, purposeful; volitional; self-imposed, self-inflicted
ant deliberate, freewill, intentional, unforced, voluntary, willful (*or* wilful), willing
2 done instantly and without conscious thought or decision — see AUTOMATIC 1
3 forcing one's compliance or participation by or as if by law — see MANDATORY

involution *n* the state or quality of having many interrelated parts or aspects — see COMPLEXITY 2

involve *vb* **1** to be the business or affair of — see CONCERN 2
2 to have as part of a whole — see INCLUDE 1
3 to hold the attention of — see ENGAGE 1
4 to surround or cover closely — see ENFOLD 1

involved *adj* **1** having many parts or aspects that are usually interrelated — see COMPLEX 1
2 made or done with great care or with much detail — see ELABORATE 1

involving *adj* holding the attention or provoking interest — see INTERESTING

invulnerable *adj* incapable of being defeated, overcome, or subdued — see INVINCIBLE

inward *adj* situated farther in — see INNER 1

in-your-face *adj* having or showing a bold forcefulness in the pursuit of a goal — see AGGRESSIVE 1

iota *n* the smallest amount or part imaginable — see JOT

irascibility *n* readiness to show annoyance or impatience — see PETULANCE

irascible *adj* easily irritated or annoyed — see IRRITABLE

irate *adj* feeling or showing anger — see ANGRY

irateness *n* an intense emotional state of displeasure with someone or something — see ANGER

ire *n* an intense emotional state of displeasure with someone or something — see ANGER

ire *vb* to make angry — see ANGER

ireful *adj* feeling or showing anger — see ANGRY

irk *vb* to disturb the peace of mind of (someone) especially by repeated disagreeable acts — see IRRITATE 1

irk *n* something that is a source of irritation — see ANNOYANCE 3

irksome *adj* causing annoyance — see ANNOYING

iron *adj* not showing weakness or uncertainty — see FIRM 1

irons *n pl* something that physically prevents free movement — see BOND 1

irradiate *vb* **1** to supply with light — see ILLUMINATE 1
2 to throw or give off — see EMIT 1

irrational *adj* not using or following good reasoning — see ILLOGICAL

irrecoverable *adj* **1** not capable of being cured or reformed — see HOPELESS 1
2 not capable of being repaired, regained, or undone — see IRREPARABLE

irredeemable *adj* **1** not capable of being cured or reformed — see HOPELESS 1
2 not capable of being repaired, regained, or undone — see IRREPARABLE

irrefutable *adj* not capable of being challenged or proved wrong ⟨the *irrefutable* reply of "Because I like it!"⟩
syn accomplished, certain, incontestable, incontrovertible, indisputable, indubitable, positive, sure, unanswerable, undeniable, unquestionable
rel unambiguous, unequivocal; absolute, clear, conclusive, decisive, definite; uncontested, uncontradicted, undisputed, unquestioned
near ant debated, disputed; doubtful, dubious, iffy, inconclusive, indecisive, uncertain; ambiguous, equivocal; hypothetical, speculative, theoretical (*also* theoretic)
ant answerable, contradictable, debatable, disputable, doubtable, moot, negotiable, problematic (*also* problematical), questionable, refutable

irregular *adj* **1** departing from some accepted standard of what is normal — see DEVIANT
2 lacking in steadiness or regularity of occurrence — see FITFUL
3 not having a level or smooth surface — see UNEVEN 1
4 not rigidly following established form, custom, or rules — see INFORMAL 1
5 not staying constant — see UNEVEN 2

irregularly *adv* without definite aim, direction, rule, or method — see HIT OR MISS

irrelevance *n* the quality or state of not having anything to do with the matter at hand ⟨The *irrelevance* of the comment brought conversation to a standstill.⟩

syn extraneousness, impertinence, inapplicability

rel inappropriateness, inaptness, unfitness, unsuitability; inaneness, inanity, meaninglessness, pointlessness, uselessness

near ant appropriateness, aptness, fitness, suitability, suitableness; importance, significance; usefulness

ant applicability, bearing, connection, materiality, pertinence, relevance, relevancy

irrelevant *adj* not having anything to do with the matter at hand ⟨*irrelevant* questions that merely disrupted the classroom lesson⟩

syn extraneous, immaterial, impertinent, inapplicable

rel incidental, peripheral, tangent, tangential; dead, moot; inconsequential, insignificant, unimportant; empty, inane, meaningless, pointless, senseless, useless; inappropriate, inapt, unsuitable

phrases beside the point, neither here nor there

near ant important, meaningful, significant; sensible, useful; appropriate, apt, fit, suitable

ant applicable, apposite, apropos, germane, material, pertinent, pointed, relative, relevant

irreligious *adj* lacking religious emotions, principles, or practices ⟨raised in an *irreligious* family⟩

syn godless, nonreligious

rel churchless, unchurched; heathen, pagan, paganish, ungodly, unholy; agnostic, atheistic (*or* atheistical); unconsecrated, unhallowed; profane, secular, temporal, worldly

near ant devout, God-fearing, godly, holy, pious, prayerful, reverent, saintly, worshipful, worshipping (*also* worshiping); blessed (*also* blest), consecrated, hallowed, sacred, sacrosanct, sanctified; devotional, spiritual

ant religious

irremediable *adj* 1 not capable of being cured or reformed — see HOPELESS 1

2 not capable of being repaired, regained, or undone — see IRREPARABLE

irremovable *adj* incapable of moving or being moved — see IMMOVABLE 1

irreparable *adj* not capable of being repaired, regained, or undone ⟨*irreparable* damage to the car⟩

syn irrecoverable, irredeemable, irremediable, irretrievable, irreversible, unrecoverable, unredeemable

rel irreplaceable, irrevocable; unredeemed

near ant corrected, fixed, recovered, remedied, repaired

ant correctable, fixable, remediable, repairable, reparable, retrievable

irreproachable *adj* 1 free from guilt or blame — see INNOCENT 2

2 being entirely without fault or flaw — see PERFECT 1

irresolution *n* a state or an instance of temporary inaction because of uncertainty about the right course of action — see HESITATION

irresponsible *adj* having or showing a lack of concern for the consequences of one's actions — see RECKLESS 1

irretrievable *adj* 1 not capable of being cured or reformed — see HOPELESS 1

2 not capable of being repaired, regained, or undone — see IRREPARABLE

irreverence *n* an act of great disrespect shown to God or to sacred ideas, people, or things — see BLASPHEMY

irreverent *adj* not showing proper reverence for the holy or sacred ⟨*irreverent* behavior during church services⟩

syn blasphemous, impious, profane, sacrilegious

rel agnostic, atheistic (*or* atheistical); godless, heretical (*also* heretic), irreligious, nonreligious, religionless, secular; ungodly, unholy; unconsecrated, unhallowed; heathen, pagan, paganish

near ant devout, God-fearing, godly, holy, prayerful, religious, saintly, worshipful, worshipping (*also* worshiping); consecrated, hallowed, sacred, sacrosanct, sanctified

ant pious, reverent

irreversible *adj* not capable of being repaired, regained, or undone — see IRREPARABLE

irrigate *vb* to pour liquid over or through in order to cleanse — see FLUSH 1

irritability *n* readiness to show annoyance or impatience — see PETULANCE

irritable *adj* easily irritated or annoyed ⟨That *irritable* old man always yells at people to stay off of his lawn.⟩

syn choleric, crabby, cranky, cross, crotchety, fiery, grouchy, grumpy, irascible, peevish, perverse, pettish, petulant, prickly, quick-tempered, raspy, short-tempered, snappish, snappy, snippy, stuffy, testy, waspish

rel bearish, bilious, cantankerous, cross-grained, curmudgeonly, disagreeable, dyspeptic, ill-humored, ill-natured, ill-tempered, ornery, querulous, snarly, surly; argumentative, bellicose, belligerent, combative, contentious, disputatious, fractious, fretful, pugnacious, quarrelsome, scrappy, truculent; sensitive, short, sulky, sullen, touchy

phrases out of humor, out of sorts

near ant affable, companionable, cordial, extroverted (*also* extraverted), friendly, genial, gregarious, outgoing, sociable; agreeable, amiable, good-natured, good-tempered, sweet, well-disposed; carefree, easygoing, happy-go-lucky, relaxed; forbearing, long-suffering, obliging, patient, stoic (*or* stoical), tolerant, uncomplaining, understanding

irritableness *n* readiness to show annoyance or impatience — see PETULANCE

irritant *n* something that is a source of irritation — see ANNOYANCE 3

irritate *vb* 1 to disturb the peace of mind of (someone) especially by repeated disagreeable acts ⟨Constant chatter *irritated* the student, who was trying to concentrate on a hard assignment.⟩

---

syn synonym(s)   **rel** related words
ant antonym(s)   **near ant** near antonym(s)

syn aggravate, annoy, bother, bug, chafe, eat, exasperate, frost, gall, get, grate, gripe, irk, nettle, peeve, persecute, pique, put out, rasp, rile, ruffle, spite, vex

rel hassle, heckle; nag; inflame (*also* enflame), provoke, rouse; badger, bait, devil, hagride, harry, pester, plague, tease; anger, antagonize, enrage, incense, infuriate, madden, rankle, roil; agitate, discomfort, discompose, disquiet, distress, exercise, freak (out), fret, perturb, undo, unhinge, unsettle, upset, worry; affront, insult, offend, outrage; complicate, exacerbate, worsen

phrases get one's goat, get on one's nerves, get to, rub the wrong way, set one's teeth on edge, stick in one's craw, wear on

near ant appease, conciliate, mollify, oblige, pacify, placate, propitiate; delight, gladden, gratify, please, satisfy; assure, cheer, comfort, console, content, quiet, reassure, solace, soothe

2 to make sore by continued rubbing — see CHAFE 1

irritating *adj* **1** causing annoyance — see ANNOYING

2 causing an unpleasant tingling sensation — see SCRATCHY 2

irritation *n* the feeling of impatience or anger caused by another's repeated disagreeable acts — see ANNOYANCE 2

irruption *n* a sudden attack on and entrance into hostile territory — see RAID 1

island *n* a fairly small area of land completely surrounded by water ⟨The *island* of Hawaii is the largest in the Hawaiian archipelago.⟩

syn isle, islet

rel atoll, barrier reef, cay, coral reef, key

near ant continent, main, mainland

isle *n* a fairly small area of land completely surrounded by water — see ISLAND

islet *n* a fairly small area of land completely surrounded by water — see ISLAND

isolate *vb* to set or keep apart from others ⟨outlying villages that had been *isolated* from civilization⟩

syn cut off, insulate, seclude, segregate, separate, sequester

rel quarantine; confine, immure, incarcerate, intern, jail, lock (up), restrain, restrict; abstract, detach, disengage, remove; detain, hold, keep

near ant assimilate, associate, connect, join, link, unite; discharge, free, liberate, loose, release

ant desegregate, integrate, reintegrate

isolated *adj* **1** screened or sequestered from view — see SECLUDED

2 not often occurring or repeated — see INFREQUENT

isolation *n* the state of being alone or kept apart from others ⟨After the long book tour, the author looked forward to the *isolation* of his office.⟩

syn insulation, secludedness, seclusion, segregation, sequestration, solitariness, solitude

rel loneliness, lonesomeness; confinement, incarceration, internment, quarantine

near ant camaraderie, companionship, company, comradeship, fellowship, society

issuance *n* the act or process of giving out something to each member of a group — see DISTRIBUTION 1

issue *n* **1** a condition or occurrence traceable to a cause — see EFFECT 1

2 a place or means of going out — see EXIT 1

3 the descendants of a person, animal, or plant — see OFFSPRING

issue *vb* **1** to produce and release for distribution in printed form — see PUBLISH 1

2 to throw or give off — see EMIT 1

Italian sandwich *n* a large sandwich on a long split roll — see SUBMARINE

itch *n* a strong wish for something — see DESIRE 1

itch (for) *vb* to have an earnest wish to own or enjoy — see DESIRE 1

item *n* **1** a separate part in a list, account, or series ⟨I got all the *items* on my grocery list except cereal.⟩

syn detail, particular, point

rel article, object, stuff, thing; characteristic, component, constituent, element, factor, feature, member; ingredient; division, particle, partition, piece, portion, section, segment

near ant aggregate, composite, compound, conglomerate; sum, summation, total, totality, whole

2 a report of recent events or facts not previously known — see NEWS

itemize *vb* **1** to make a list of — see ¹LIST 1

2 to specify one after another — see ENUMERATE 1

itinerant *adj* traveling from place to place ⟨An *itinerant* musician can see a lot of the world.⟩

syn errant, fugitive, gallivanting (*also* galavanting), nomad, peripatetic, ranging, roaming, roving, vagabond, vagrant, wandering, wayfaring

rel drifting, footloose, rambling; sauntering, strolling, traipsing, walking; migrant, migratory

phrases on the move

near ant immobile, nonmoving, settled, standing, static, stationary; motionless, still

jab *n* a quick thrust — see ¹POKE 1

jab *vb* to penetrate or hold (something) with a pointed object — see IMPALE

jabber *n* unintelligible or meaningless talk — see GIBBERISH 1

jabber *vb* 1 to engage in casual or rambling conversation — see CHAT 1

2 to speak rapidly, inarticulately, and usually unintelligibly — see BABBLE 1

jabberer *n* a person who talks constantly — see CHATTERBOX

jabberwocky *n* unintelligible or meaningless talk — see GIBBERISH 1

jack *n* 1 *slang* something (as pieces of stamped metal or printed paper) customarily and legally used as a medium of exchange, a measure of value, or a means of payment — see MONEY

2 a piece of cloth with a special design that is used as an emblem or for signaling — see FLAG 1

3 one who operates or navigates a seagoing vessel — see SAILOR

4 the total of the bets at stake at one time — see POT 1

5 a person whose job is to cut down trees — see LUMBERJACK

jack (up) *vb* 1 to lift with effort — see HEAVE 1

2 to move from a lower to a higher place or position — see RAISE 1

jackass *n* a sturdy and patient domestic mammal that is used especially to carry things — see DONKEY 1

jacked (up) *adj* being at a higher level than average — see HIGH 2

jacket *n* 1 something that encloses another thing especially to protect it — see ¹CASE 1

2 the hairy covering of a mammal especially when fine, soft, and thick — see FUR 1

jackpot *n* the total of the bets at stake at one time — see POT 1

jack-tar *n* one who operates or navigates a seagoing vessel — see SAILOR

jade *vb* to make weary and restless by being dull or monotonous — see ²BORE

jaded *adj* 1 depleted in strength, energy, or freshness — see WEARY 1

2 having one's patience, interest, or pleasure exhausted — see WEARY 2

jading *adj* causing weariness, restlessness, or lack of interest — see BORING

jagged *adj* 1 having an uneven edge or outline — see RAGGED 1

2 not having a level or smooth surface — see UNEVEN 1

jail *n* a place of confinement for persons held in lawful custody ⟨sentenced to three years in *jail* for his crime⟩

syn brig, guardroom, hoosegow, jug, lockup, pen, penitentiary, prison, stockade

rel bull pen, cage, cell, hole; block, ward; guardhouse, hulk(s); concentration camp, labor camp, prison camp, work camp; dungeon, keep

near ant outside

jail *vb* to put in or as if in prison — see IMPRISON

jailbird *n* a person convicted as a criminal and serving a prison sentence — see CONVICT

jailed *adj* taken and held prisoner — see CAPTIVE

jam *n* 1 a crowded mass (as of cars) that impedes or blocks movement ⟨Thousands of cars trying to leave the stadium's parking lot at the same time are sure to create a *jam*.⟩

syn backup, bottleneck, snarl, tie-up

rel tangle; lock; congestion, traffic; crawl, delay, slowdown, stoppage

2 a difficult, puzzling, or embarrassing situation from which there is no easy escape — see PREDICAMENT

jam *vb* 1 to fit (people or things) into a tight space — see CROWD 1

2 to prevent passage through by filling with something — see CLOG 1

3 to put into (something) as much as can be held or contained — see FILL 1

4 to force one's way — see ²PRESS 4

jammed *adj* 1 containing or seeming to contain the greatest quantity or number possible — see FULL 1

2 firmly positioned in place and difficult to dislodge — see TIGHT 2

jam-pack *vb* to put into (something) as much as can be held or contained — see FILL 1

jam-packed *adj* 1 containing or seeming to contain the greatest quantity or number possible — see FULL 1

2 having little space between items or parts — see CLOSE 1

janitor *n* a person who takes care of a property sometimes for an absent owner — see CUSTODIAN 1

jar *n* 1 a forceful coming together of two things — see IMPACT 1

2 something that makes a strong impression because it is so unexpected — see SURPRISE 1

3 a harsh grating sound — see RASP

jar *vb* 1 to express different opinions about something often angrily — see ARGUE 1

2 to be out of harmony or agreement usually noticeably — see CLASH

jargon *n* the special terms or expressions of a particular group or field — see TERMINOLOGY

jarring *adj* 1 causing a strong emotional reaction because of unexpectedness — see SURPRISING 1

2 disagreeable to one's aesthetic or artistic sense — see HARSH 2

jaundice *n* a deep-seated ill will — see ENMITY

jaundiced *adj* 1 having or showing mean resentment of another's possessions or advantages — see ENVIOUS

2 marked by opposition or ill will — see HOSTILE 1

jaunt *n* a short trip for pleasure — see EXCURSION 1

jaunty *adj* having much high-spirited energy and movement — see LIVELY 1

javelin *n* a weapon with a long straight handle and sharp head or blade — see SPEAR

---

syn synonym(s) *rel* related words

ant antonym(s) *near ant* near antonym(s)

jaw *n* friendly, informal conversation or an instance of this — see CHAT 1

jaw *vb* **1** to criticize (someone) severely or angrily especially for personal failings — see SCOLD

2 to engage in casual or rambling conversation — see CHAT 1

jazz *n* language, behavior, or ideas that are absurd and contrary to good sense — see NONSENSE 1

jazz (up) *vb* to give life, vigor, or spirit to — see ANIMATE

jazziness *n* the quality or state of having abundant or intense activity — see VITALITY 1

jazzy *adj* **1** attractively eye-catching in style ⟨That's a *jazzy* bathing suit, with all those spangles.⟩

syn flashy, snazzy, splashy

rel cool, hip, neat; à la mode (*also* a la mode), chic, chichi; dapper, dashing, natty, sharp, smart, snappy, spruce; faddish, fashionable, in, modish, stylish, trendy; custom, designer; showy, striking; flamboyant, garish, gaudy, glittery, glitzy, loud, ostentatious, raffish, swank (*or* swanky), wild

near ant modest, plain, quiet, simple, unadorned; conservative, muted, restrained, subdued, toned-down, understated, unpretentious; styleless, unfashionable, unstylish

2 having much high-spirited energy and movement — see LIVELY 1

jealous *adj* **1** intolerant of rivalry or unfaithfulness ⟨a boyfriend who became *jealous* whenever she paid attention to anyone but him⟩

syn possessive

rel controlling, demanding, domineering, grasping; covetous, envious, invidious, jaundiced; distrustful, mistrustful, suspicious; overprotective, protective

near ant undemanding; permissive, tolerant, tolerating, trustful, trusting, understanding

2 having or showing mean resentment of another's possessions or advantages — see ENVIOUS

jealousy *n* a painful awareness of another's possessions or advantages and a desire to have them too — see ENVY

jeer *n* a vocal sound made to express scorn or disapproval — see CATCALL

jeer *vb* to make (someone or something) the object of unkind laughter — see RIDICULE

Jehovah *n* the being worshipped as the creator and ruler of the universe — see DEITY 2

jell *vb* **1** to take on a definite form — see FORM 1

2 to turn from a liquid into a substance resembling jelly — see COAGULATE

jelly *vb* to turn from a liquid into a substance resembling jelly — see COAGULATE

jeopardize *vb* to place in danger — see ENDANGER

jeopardizing *adj* involving potential loss or injury — see DANGEROUS 1

jeopardy *n* the state of not being protected from injury, harm, or evil — see DANGER 1

jerk *n* **1** a person whose behavior is offensive to others ⟨I know it's not fair, but you don't have to be such a *jerk* about it.⟩

syn beast, boor, cad, churl, clown, creep, cur, dog, heel, joker, louse, lout, pill, rat, scum, skunk, slob, snake, stinker, swine

rel barbarian, brute, caveman, Neanderthal, savage; loudmouth, vulgarian; lowlife, miscreant, rascal, rogue, roughneck, scab, scamp, scoundrel, villain, wretch; booby, fool, nincompoop, ninny, nitwit, nut; blockhead, dolt, dope, dork [*slang*], goon, halfwit, idiot, imbecile, moron, turkey

phrases son of a gun

near ant hero, heroine, role model; gentleman, lady; angel, saint

2 the act or an instance of applying force on something so that it moves in the direction of the force — see PULL 1

jerk *vb* **1** to move or cause to move with a sharp quick motion ⟨I *jerked* to one side to avoid getting hit.⟩ ⟨*jerked* the leash to get the dog's attention⟩

syn buck, hitch, jolt, twitch, yank

rel bump, jounce, lurch, pitch, stagger; jig, jiggle, jog, joggle, shake; drag, lug, pull, tug; pluck, tweak; grab, rip, snap (up); snatch, tear, wrench, wrest, wring

2 to make jerky or restless movements — see FIDGET

3 to make a series of small irregular or violent movements — see SHAKE 1

jerky *adj* **1** marked by a series of sharp quick motions ⟨made *jerky* progress walking with the new crutches⟩

syn bumpy, choppy, rough

rel erratic, fitful, irregular, spasmodic, unsteady; jagged, ragged, uneven

near ant calm, placid, smooth, steady, still

2 showing or marked by a lack of good sense or judgment — see FOOLISH 1

jerry-rigged *adj* hastily or roughly constructed — see RUDE 1

jest *n* **1** an attitude or manner not to be taken seriously — see FUN 2

2 something said or done to cause laughter — see JOKE 1

3 a playful or mischievous act intended as a joke — see PRANK

4 a person or thing that is made fun of — see LAUGHINGSTOCK

jest *vb* to make jokes — see JOKE 1

jester *n* **1** a person (as a writer) noted for or specializing in humor — see HUMORIST

2 a person formerly kept in a royal or noble household to amuse with jests and pranks — see FOOL 2

jesting *adj* marked by or expressive of mild or good-natured teasing — see QUIZZICAL

jesting *n* good-natured teasing or exchanging of clever remarks — see BANTER

jet *n* a usually forceful stream of fluid discharged from a narrow opening ⟨We bought a new showerhead that emits a superpowerful *jet* of water.⟩

syn spout, spurt, squirt

rel flush, gush, spew; spit, spray, spritz; geyser, spouter; blast, burst

jet *vb* **1** to flow out in great quantities or with force — see GUSH 1

2 to violently throw out or off (something from within) — see ERUPT 1

3 to proceed or move quickly — see HURRY 2

jettison *n* the getting rid of whatever is unwanted or useless — see DISPOSAL 1

jettison *vb* to get rid of as useless or unwanted — see DISCARD

jetty *n* a structure used by boats and ships for taking on or landing cargo and passengers — see DOCK

jewel *n* **1** a usually valuable stone cut and polished for ornament — see GEM 1

2 an asset that brings praise or renown — see GLORY 2

3 someone or something unusually desirable — see PRIZE 1

jibe *vb* to be in agreement on every point — see CHECK 1

jiffy *n* a very small space of time — see INSTANT

jig *n* a clever often underhanded means to achieve an end — see TRICK 1

jig *vb* to make jerky or restless movements — see FIDGET

jigger *n* an interesting and often novel device with a practical use — see GADGET

jiggle *vb* **1** to make a series of small irregular or violent movements — see SHAKE 1

2 to make jerky or restless movements — see FIDGET

jiggling *n* a series of slight movements by a body back and forth or from side to side — see VIBRATION 1

jim–dandy *n* something very good of its kind ⟨The brand new car was a *jim-dandy*.⟩

syn beauty, corker, crackerjack (*also* crackajack), dandy, dream, honey, knockout, nifty, pip, standout

rel marvel, phenomenon, prodigy, sensation, wonder; catch, diamond, gem, imperial, jewel, pearl, plum, treasure

phrases something else

near ant bust, disappointment, dud, failure, flop, lemon, letdown, loser, stinker, turkey

jim–dandy *adj* of the very best kind — see EXCELLENT

jimmy *vb* to raise, move, or pull apart with or as if with a lever — see ¹PRY 1

jingle *n* **1** a series of short high ringing sounds — see TINKLE

2 a short musical composition for the human voice often with instrumental accompaniment — see SONG 1

jingle *vb* to make a repeated sharp light ringing sound ⟨The bell on the kitten's collar *jingled* as she walked.⟩

syn chink, clink, tingle, tinkle

rel clang, clangor, clank, clash, crash; clack, clatter, rattle; chime, ding, ding-dong, gong, ping, plink, ring

jingo *n* **1** one who shows excessive favoritism towards his or her country — see NATIONALIST

2 one who urges or attempts to cause a war — see WARMONGER

jingoism *n* excessive favoritism towards one's own country — see CHAUVINISM

jinx *n* something that brings bad luck ⟨believed the broken mirror was a *jinx*⟩

syn hex

rel Jonah; curse, evil eye, pox, spell, voodoo; augury, omen, portent

near ant amulet, charm, fetish (*also* fetich), talisman

jinxed *adj* having, prone to, or marked by bad luck — see UNLUCKY 1

jitters *n pl* a sense of panic or extreme nervousness ⟨always got the *jitters* right before a test⟩

syn butterflies, dither, nerves, shakes, shivers, willies

rel cold sweat, creeps, fidgets, goose bumps; agitation, anxiety, fear, hysteria, uneasiness; frazzle; edginess, jumpiness, skittishness

near ant aplomb, calm, composure, equanimity, imperturbability, self-possession, tranquillity (*or* tranquility)

jittery *adj* **1** easily excited by nature — see EXCITABLE

2 feeling or showing uncomfortable feelings of uncertainty — see NERVOUS 1

jive *n* the special terms or expressions of a particular group or field — see TERMINOLOGY

jive *vb* **1** to make fun of in a good-natured way — see TEASE 1

2 to make jokes — see JOKE 1

job *n* **1** an assignment at which one regularly works for pay ⟨a high-paying *job* as a banker⟩

syn appointment, berth, billet, capacity, connection, function, place, position, post, situation

rel business, employ, employment, occupation, profession; work; office, spot; calling, pursuit, trade, vocation; line, racket; engagement, gig; livelihood, living; career, lifework, practice (*also* practise); duty, mission, posting, service, task

near ant joblessness, unemployment

2 a piece of work that needs to be done regularly — see CHORE 1

3 a specific task with which a person or group is charged — see MISSION

4 the action for which a person or thing is specially fitted or used or for which a thing exists — see ROLE

5 a dull, unpleasant, or difficult piece of work — see CHORE 2

jobholder *n* one who works for another for wages or a salary — see EMPLOYEE

jocose *adj* indicative of or marked by high spirits or good humor — see MERRY

jocosely *adv* in a cheerful or happy manner — see GAILY 1

jocular *adj* **1** given to or marked by mature intelligent humor — see WITTY

2 indicative of or marked by high spirits or good humor — see MERRY

jocund *adj* indicative of or marked by high spirits or good humor — see MERRY

jog *vb* **1** to go at a pace faster than a walk — see RUN 1

2 to make short up-and-down movements — see NOD

joggle *vb* to make a series of small irregular or violent movements — see SHAKE 1

join *n* a place where two or more things are united — see JOINT 1

join *vb* **1** to be adjacent to — see ADJOIN 1

2 to become a member of — see ENTER 2

3 to come together to form a single unit — see UNITE 1

4 to participate or assist in joint effort to accomplish an end — see COOPERATE 1

5 to put or bring together so as to form a new and longer whole — see CONNECT 1

---

syn synonym(s)   **rel** related words
ant antonym(s)   **near ant** near antonym(s)

joining *adj* having a border in common — see ADJACENT

joining *n* a place where two or more things are united — see JOINT 1

joint *adj* used or done by a number of people as a group — see COLLECTIVE

joint *n* 1 a place where two or more things are united ⟨The leak was found at a *joint* in the pipe.⟩

  syn connection, coupling, join, joining, junction, juncture

  rel link, tie; interconnection, intersection; abutment, articulation, attachment; seam; concourse, confluence, meeting; union

  near ant cleft, crack, crevice, fissure, gap, rift, separation

  2 a building, room, or suite of rooms occupied by a service business — see PLACE 1

jointly *adv* in or by combined action or effort — see TOGETHER 2

joke *n* 1 something said or done to cause laughter ⟨He was known for his hilarious *jokes*.⟩

  syn crack, funny, gag, jest, laugh, pleasantry, quip, rib, sally, waggery, wisecrack, witticism

  rel funning, joking, wisecracking; panic [*slang*], riot, scream; antic, caper, monkeyshine(s), practical joke, prank, trick; burlesque, caricature, lampoon, mock, mockery, parody, put-on, riff; comedy, humor, wit, wordplay

  2 a poor, insincere, or insulting imitation of something — see MOCKERY 1

  3 a person or thing that is made fun of — see LAUGHINGSTOCK

joke *vb* 1 to make jokes ⟨He was known for his ability to *joke* despite his lack of anything resembling a social life.⟩

  syn banter, chaff, fool, fun, gag, jest, jive, jolly, josh, kid, quip, wisecrack

  rel gibe (*or* jibe), haze, jeer, mock, rally, razz, rib, ridicule, tease; caricature, lampoon, parody, satirize; amuse, divert, entertain

  phrases crack wise

  2 to make fun of in a good-natured way — see TEASE 1

joker *n* 1 a person (as a writer) noted for or specializing in humor — see HUMORIST

  2 a person whose behavior is offensive to others — see JERK 1

  3 an adult male human being — see MAN 1

  4 a danger or difficulty that is hidden or not easily recognized — see PITFALL 1

jokester *n* a person (as a writer) noted for or specializing in humor — see HUMORIST

joking *adj* marked by or expressive of mild or good-natured teasing — see QUIZZICAL

jollification *n* joyful or festive activity — see MERRYMAKING

jollity *n* joyful or festive activity — see MERRYMAKING

jolly *adj* 1 indicative of or marked by high spirits or good humor — see MERRY

  2 giving pleasure or contentment to the mind or senses — see PLEASANT 1

jolly *adv* to a great degree — see VERY 1

jolly *vb* to make jokes — see JOKE 1

jolt *n* 1 a forceful coming together of two things — see IMPACT 1

  2 something that makes a strong impression because it is so unexpected — see SURPRISE 1

jolt *vb* 1 to make a series of small irregular or violent movements — see SHAKE 1

  2 to move or cause to move with a sharp quick motion — see JERK 1

  3 to cause an unpleasant surprise for — see SHOCK 1

josh *vb* 1 to make fun of in a good-natured way — see TEASE 1

  2 to make jokes — see JOKE 1

joshing *adj* marked by or expressive of mild or good-natured teasing — see QUIZZICAL

joshing *n* good-natured teasing or exchanging of clever remarks — see BANTER

jot *n* the smallest amount or part imaginable ⟨It's obvious that he doesn't have a *jot* of interest in history.⟩

  syn darn (*also* durn), hoot, iota, lick, modicum, rap, tittle, whit, whoop

  rel ace, bit, crumb, dab, driblet, glimmer, hint, little, mite, nip, ounce, particle, peanuts, pin, ray, scrap, scruple, semblance, shade, shadow, shred, smidgen (*also* smidgeon *or* smidgin *or* smidge), speck, spot, sprinkling, strain, streak, suspicion, touch, trace

jot (down) *vb* to make a written note of — see RECORD 1

jounce *n* a forceful coming together of two things — see IMPACT 1

jounce *vb* 1 to make a series of small irregular or violent movements — see SHAKE 1

  2 to make short up-and-down movements — see NOD

journal *n* a publication that appears at regular intervals ⟨a monthly scientific *journal*⟩

  syn bulletin, gazette, magazine, newspaper, organ, paper, periodical, review, serial

  rel annual, bimonthly, biweekly, daily, monthly, quarterly, semimonthly, semiweekly, triweekly, weekly, yearbook; digest, little magazine; fanzine; pictorial; slick; newsletter, newsmagazine, newsweekly

journalist *n* a person employed by a newspaper, magazine, or radio or television station to gather, write, or report news — see REPORTER

journey *n* a going from one place to another usually of some distance ⟨They were hungry and tired after their long *journey*.⟩

  syn expedition, passage, peregrination, travel(s), trek, trip

  rel commute, errand, excursion, flight, hop, jaunt, junket, outing, sally, sortie, tour; cruise, sail, voyage; drive, ride, spin; grand tour, odyssey, pilgrimage, progress, quest, safari; hike, slog, tramp, walk

journey *vb* to take a trip especially of some distance — see TRAVEL 1

jovial *adj* indicative of or marked by high spirits or good humor — see MERRY

joviality *n* a mood characterized by high spirits and amusement and often accompanied by laughter — see MIRTH

jovially *adv* in a cheerful or happy manner — see GAILY 1

joy *n* 1 a feeling or state of well-being and contentment — see HAPPINESS 1

  2 a source of great satisfaction — see DELIGHT 1

joy *vb* to feel or express joy or triumph — see EXULT

joyful *adj* experiencing pleasure, satisfaction, or delight — see GLAD 1

joyless *adj* feeling unhappiness — see SAD 1
joylessness *n* a state or spell of low spirits — see SADNESS
joyous *adj* experiencing pleasure, satisfaction, or delight — see GLAD 1
jubilant *adj* having or expressing feelings of joy or triumph — see EXULTANT
jubilee *n* a time or program of special events and entertainment in honor of something — see FESTIVAL
judge *n* **1** a person who impartially decides or resolves a dispute or controversy ⟨played the role of *judge* in their disagreement⟩
syn arbiter, arbitrator, referee, umpire
rel jurist, justice, magistrate; intermediary, intermediate, mediator, moderator, negotiator; conciliator, go-between, peacemaker, reconciler, troubleshooter; decider
2 a public official having authority to decide questions of law ⟨The *judge* gave the defendant a suspended sentence.⟩
syn bench, court, jurist, justice, magistrate
rel chief justice, circuit judge, justice of the peace, squire; auditor, master
judge *vb* **1** to give an opinion about (something at issue or in dispute) ⟨The committee will *judge* the case solely on the evidence.⟩
syn adjudge, adjudicate, arbitrate, decide, determine, referee, rule (on), settle, umpire
rel consider, deem, deliberate, hear, ponder, weigh; size up; mediate, moderate, negotiate; try; find (for *or* against); conclude, resolve
near ant equivocate, hedge, pussyfoot, skirt
2 to decide the size, amount, number, or distance of (something) without actual measurement — see ESTIMATE 2
3 to form an opinion or reach a conclusion through reasoning and information — see INFER 1
4 to have as an opinion — see BELIEVE 2
judgment *or* **judgement** *n* **1** a decision made by a court or tribunal regarding a case it has heard — see SENTENCE
2 a position arrived at after consideration — see DECISION 1
3 an idea that is believed to be true or valid without positive knowledge — see OPINION 1
4 an opinion on the nature, character, or quality of something — see ESTIMATION 1
judicious *adj* **1** having or showing good judgment and restraint especially in conduct or speech — see DISCREET 1
2 suitable for bringing about a desired result under the circumstances — see EXPEDIENT
jug *n* **1** a place of confinement for persons held in lawful custody — see JAIL
2 a handled container for holding and pouring liquids that usually has a lip or a spout — see PITCHER
jug *vb* to put in or as if in prison — see IMPRISON
jugglery *n* the use of clever underhanded actions to achieve an end — see TRICKERY
juiciness *n* the quality or state of being full of juice — see SUCCULENCE
juicy *adj* full of juice ⟨She bit into the *juicy* orange.⟩

syn fleshy, pulpy, succulent
rel sappy, watery
near ant dehydrated, desiccated, dry, sere (*also* sear), shriveled (*or* shrivelled), withered
ant juiceless, sapless
jumble *n* **1** a state in which everything is out of order — see CHAOS
2 an unorganized collection or mixture of various things — see MISCELLANY 1
jumble *vb* to undo the proper order or arrangement of — see DISORDER
jumbled *adj* lacking in order, neatness, and often cleanliness — see MESSY
jumbo *adj* unusually large — see HUGE
jumbo *n* something that is unusually large and powerful — see GIANT
jump *n* **1** an act of leaping into the air ⟨She took a small *jump* forward to avoid stepping in the puddle.⟩
syn bound, hop, leap, spring, vault
rel bounce, lope, skip; caper, gambol; attack, pounce; dive, pitch, plunge
2 the more favorable condition or position in a competition — see ADVANTAGE 1
jump *vb* **1** to propel oneself upward or forward into the air ⟨Jared *jumped* across the ditch.⟩
syn bound, hop, leap, spring, vault
rel bounce, hurdle, leapfrog, lope, skip; buck; caper, capriole, cavort, frolic, gambol, romp; attack, pounce; shoot, skyrocket
2 to move suddenly and sharply (as in surprise) — see START 1
3 to proceed or move quickly — see HURRY 2
jump (on) *vb* **1** to take sudden, violent action against — see ATTACK 1
2 to criticize harshly and usually publicly — see ATTACK 2
jumpiness *n* a state of nervousness marked by sudden jerky movements ⟨The police detective interpreted the suspect's *jumpiness* as a sign of guilt.⟩
syn edginess, fidgets, flightiness, restiveness, skittishness
rel agitation, anxiety, anxiousness, apprehension, apprehensiveness, disquiet, restlessness, trepidation, uneasiness, upset, worry; nerves, tenseness, tension; butterflies, dither, jitters, shakes, shivers, willies
near ant confidence, self-assurance, self-confidence, sureness; control, self-control, aplomb, calm, calmness, collectedness, composure, coolness, ease, easiness, equanimity, equilibrium, imperturbability, poise, repose, self-possession, tranquillity (*or* tranquility)
jumpy *adj* **1** easily excited by nature — see EXCITABLE
2 feeling or showing uncomfortable feelings of uncertainty — see NERVOUS 1
junction *n* **1** a place where two or more things are united — see JOINT 1
2 the act or an instance of joining two or more things into one — see UNION 1
3 a place where roads meet — see CROSSROAD 1
juncture *n* **1** a particular and often important moment in time — see POINT 1
2 a place where two or more things are united — see JOINT 1
3 a time or state of affairs requiring prompt or decisive action — see EMERGENCY

---

syn synonym(s)   *rel* related words
ant antonym(s)   *near ant* near antonym(s)

junior *adj* having not so great importance or rank as another — see LESSER

junior *n* one who is of lower rank and typically under the authority of another — see UNDERLING

junk *n* **1** that which is of low quality or worth ⟨I couldn't believe that such *junk* was chosen to be read for the book club.⟩ ⟨My car is *junk*—it spends more time in the shop than on the road!⟩
syn rubbish, trash
rel claptrap, humbug, nonsense; bomb, dud, lemon, stinker, turkey; mess, muddle, shambles
2 discarded or useless material — see GARBAGE

junk *vb* to get rid of as useless or unwanted — see DISCARD

junket *n* a short trip for pleasure — see EXCURSION 1

junket *vb* to entertain with a fancy meal — see FEAST 1

junkie *also* **junky** *n* a person with a strong and habitual liking for something — see FAN

junking *n* the getting rid of whatever is unwanted or useless — see DISPOSAL 1

junky *adj* **1** having no usefulness — see WORTHLESS
2 of low quality — see CHEAP 2

jurisdiction *n* lawful control over the affairs of a political unit (as a nation) — see RULE 2

jurist *n* a public official having authority to decide questions of law — see JUDGE 2

just *adj* **1** being what is called for by accepted standards of right and wrong ⟨A *just* punishment should fit the crime.⟩
syn competent, deserved, due, fair, justified, merited, right, rightful, warranted
rel applicable, appropriate, apt, fit, fitting, meet, proper, requisite, suitable; lawful, legal, legitimate; accurate, correct, true; strict, stringent, uncompromising; equitable, impartial
near ant incoherent, incorrect, irrelative, irrelevant; improper, inapplicable, inappropriate, inapt, indefensible, unjustifiable, unreasonable, unsuitable; biased, inequitable, partial, unequal; arbitrary, despotic; illegitimate, unlawful
ant undeserved, undue, unfair, unjust, unjustified, unmerited, unwarranted
2 based on sound reasoning or information — see GOOD 1
3 conforming to a high standard of morality or virtue — see GOOD 2
4 following the accepted rules of moral conduct — see HONORABLE 1
5 guided by or in accordance with one's sense of right and wrong — see CONSCIENTIOUS 1
6 marked by justice, honesty, and freedom from bias — see FAIR 2

just *adv* **1** in the same manner ⟨You can do it *just* the way they do.⟩
syn exactly, precisely
rel even, expressly, faultlessly, perfectly; identically, uniformly; alike, likewise, similarly
phrases to a T
near ant slightly, somewhat, vaguely; differently, variably

2 by a very small margin ⟨I was *just* over the minimum height requirement for the amusement park ride.⟩
syn barely, hardly, marginally, scarcely, slightly
rel minimally, minutely, scantly; almost, closely, more or less, nearly, partly, roughly, somewhat
phrases by the skin of one's teeth
near ant definitely, easily, plainly, quite, unquestionably; abundantly, completely, copiously, fully, generously, greatly
ant considerably, significantly, substantially, vastly, well
3 nothing more than ⟨I was *just* kidding!⟩
syn but, merely, only, purely, simply
4 as stated or indicated without the slightest difference — see EXACTLY 1
5 for nothing other than — see SOLELY 1
6 not long ago — see NEWLY

justice *n* **1** the practice of giving to others what is their due or an instance of this ⟨They felt that *justice* was done in court.⟩
syn equity, right
rel equitability, equitableness, fairness, impartiality; goodness, righteousness, virtue; honor, integrity, uprightness
near ant bias, one-sidedness, partiality, prejudice; unfairness, unjustness, wrongfulness; corruption, impropriety; crime, offense (or offence), wrongdoing; disservice, harm
ant inequity, injustice, raw deal, wrong
2 a public official having authority to decide questions of law — see JUDGE 2
3 lack of favoritism toward one side or another — see DETACHMENT 1

justifiable *adj* capable of being defended with good reasoning against verbal attack — see TENABLE 1

justification *n* an explanation that frees one from fault or blame — see EXCUSE

justified *adj* **1** based on sound reasoning or information — see GOOD 1
2 being what is called for by accepted standards of right and wrong — see JUST 1

justify *vb* **1** to be an acceptable reason for ⟨He tried to *justify* his behavior by saying everyone else was doing it too.⟩
syn excuse
rel account (for), explain, explain away, rationalize; brush (aside *or* off), condone, disregard, forgive, gloss (over), gloze (over), ignore, pardon, pass over, remit, shrug off, wink (at)
2 to continue to declare to be true or proper despite opposition or objections — see MAINTAIN 1

jut *n* a part that sticks out from the general mass of something — see BULGE 1

jut *vb* to extend outward beyond a usual point — see BULGE 1

juvenile *adj* **1** being in the early stage of life, growth, or development — see YOUNG
2 having or showing the annoying qualities (as silliness) associated with children — see CHILDISH
3 lacking in adult experience or maturity — see CALLOW

juvenile *n* a young person who is between infancy and adulthood — see CHILD 1

juxtaposed *adj* having a border in common — see ADJACENT

keelhaul *vb* to criticize (someone) severely or angrily especially for personal failings — see SCOLD

keen *adj* **1** able to sense slight impressions or differences — see ACUTE 1

2 causing intense discomfort to one's skin — see CUTTING 1

3 having an edge thin enough to cut or pierce something — see SHARP 1

4 having or showing quickness of mind — see INTELLIGENT 1

5 showing urgent desire or interest — see EAGER

6 extreme in degree, power, or effect — see INTENSE 1

keen *n* a crying out in grief — see LAMENT 1

keen *vb* to make a long loud mournful sound — see HOWL 1

keenness *n* **1** a harsh or sharp quality — see EDGE 1

2 urgent desire or interest — see EAGERNESS

3 exceptional discernment and judgment especially in practical matters — see ACUMEN

4 the state or quality of being able to sense slight impressions or differences — see ACUITY

keep *vb* **1** to mark with an appropriate practice, rite, or ceremony ⟨*kept* the Sabbath by not working⟩

syn celebrate, commemorate, observe

rel bless, consecrate, sanctify, solemnize; fete (*or* fête), honor, laud, praise; memorialize, remember

near ant disregard, forget, ignore, neglect, overlook

ant break, transgress, violate

2 to continue to have in one's possession or power ⟨The money is yours to *keep*.⟩ ⟨*Keep* my secret and don't tell it to anyone!⟩

syn hold, reserve, retain, withhold

rel conserve, guard, preserve, protect, save; boast, enjoy, have, own, possess; command, control, detain, direct, manage, rule; bear, harbor; cherish, cling (to), hug, treasure

phrases hang on to, hold on to

near ant abandon, cede, drop; contribute, donate, give; discard, dump; decline, reject, repudiate, spurn; lose

ant give up, hand over, release, relinquish, surrender, yield

3 to do what is required by the terms of — see FULFILL 1

4 to place somewhere for safekeeping or ready availability — see STORE 1

5 to pay the living expenses of — see SUPPORT 2

6 to look after and make decisions about — see CONDUCT 1

7 to keep from exceeding a desirable degree or level (as of expression) — see CONTROL 1

8 to drive danger or attack away from — see DEFEND 1

keep (from) *vb* to resist the temptation of — see FORBEAR

keep (to) *vb* to give steadfast support to — see ADHERE (TO) 1

keeper *n* **1** a person or group that watches over someone or something — see GUARD 1

2 a person who takes care of a property sometimes for an absent owner — see CUSTODIAN 1

keeping *n* **1** responsibility for the safety and well-being of someone or something — see CUSTODY

2 the fact or state of having (something) at one's disposal — see POSSESSION 1

3 the following of a custom, rule, or law — see OBSERVANCE 1

4 a state of being or fitness — see CONDITION 1

keepsake *n* something that serves to keep alive the memory of a person or event — see MEMORIAL

keep up *vb* **1** to continue to operate or to meet one's needs — see HOLD OUT 1

2 to keep in good condition — see MAINTAIN 1

3 to remain indefinitely in existence or in the same state — see CONTINUE 1

keg *n* an enclosed wooden vessel for holding beverages — see CASK

kerchief *n* a scarf worn on the head — see BANDANNA

kerf *n* a V-shaped cut usually on an edge or a surface — see NOTCH 1

key *adj* **1** coming before all others in importance — see FOREMOST 1

2 of the greatest possible importance — see CRUCIAL

key *n* **1** an explanatory list of the symbols on a map or chart — see LEGEND 1

2 something that allows someone to achieve a desired goal — see PASSPORT 1

3 the means or right of entering or participating in — see ENTRANCE 1

key *vb* to bring to a state free of conflicts, inconsistencies, or differences — see HARMONIZE 2

keystone *n* an immaterial thing upon which something else rests — see BASE 1

kibitzer *also* **kibbitzer** *n* a person who meddles in the affairs of others — see BUSYBODY

kick *n* **1** a pleasurably intense stimulation of the feelings — see THRILL

2 a source of great satisfaction — see DELIGHT 1

3 a feeling or declaration of disapproval or dissent — see OBJECTION

4 a forceful coming together of two things — see IMPACT 1

kick *vb* to express dissatisfaction, pain, or resentment usually tiresomely — see COMPLAIN

kick back *vb* **1** to refrain from labor or exertion — see REST 1

2 to spend time doing nothing — see IDLE

kick in *vb* to make a donation as part of a group effort — see CONTRIBUTE 1

kick off *vb* to take the first step in (a process or course of action) — see BEGIN 1

kid *n* a young person who is between infancy and adulthood — see CHILD 1

---

syn synonym(s)   *rel* related words

ant antonym(s)   *near ant* near antonym(s)

kid *vb* **1** to make fun of in a good-natured way — see TEASE 1

2 to make jokes — see JOKE 1

kidding *adj* marked by or expressive of mild or good-natured teasing — see QUIZZICAL

kiddish *adj* having or showing the annoying qualities (as silliness) associated with children — see CHILDISH

kiddo *n* a young person who is between infancy and adulthood — see CHILD 1

kidnap *vb* to carry away (as a person) forcibly or unlawfully ⟨The wealthy industrialist was *kidnapped* and held for ransom.⟩

syn abduct

rel capture, impress, seize, shanghai, waylay; abscond (*with*), snatch, spirit; hijack (*also* highjack); catch, steal, take

phrases make away with, make off with, run off with

near ant deliver, ransom, redeem, rescue; restore, return

kill *vb* **1** to deprive of life ⟨During the war more soldiers were *killed* by disease than anything else.⟩

syn claim, croak [*slang*], destroy, dispatch, do in, fell, slay, take

rel butcher, cut down, finish, get, murder, rub out, scrag, take out, waste; annihilate, blot out, decimate, kill off, massacre, mow, slaughter, smite; execute, martyr, terminate

phrases do away with, make away with

near ant raise, restore, resurrect, resuscitate, revive; nurture

ant animate

2 to reject by or as if by a vote — see NEGATIVE 1

3 to show (something written) to be no longer valid by drawing a cross over or a line through it — see X (OUT)

4 to use up all the physical energy of — see EXHAUST 1

5 to attract or delight as if by magic — see CHARM 1

6 to cause to stop functioning — see DEACTIVATE

killer *adj* **1** likely to cause or capable of causing death — see DEADLY 1

2 requiring considerable physical or mental effort — see HARD 2

killer *n* **1** a dull, unpleasant, or difficult piece of work — see CHORE 2

2 a person who kills another person — see ASSASSIN

killjoy *n* a person who spoils the pleasure of others ⟨His perpetually negative attitude made him a real *killjoy* when others were trying to have fun.⟩

syn drag, spoilsport, wet blanket

rel fuddy-duddy, goody-goody, Goody Two-shoes, old maid, stick-in-the-mud; defeatist, pessimist; complainer, crab, cynic, grouch, grump, sorehead, whiner; bore, downer, drip

near ant cutup, jester, live wire; carouser, celebrant, celebrator, merrymaker, rejoicer, reveler (*or* reveller), roisterer

kilter *n* a state of being or fitness — see CONDITION 1

kin *n* **1** a group of persons who come from the same ancestor — see FAMILY 1

2 a person connected with another by blood or marriage — see RELATIVE

kind *adj* **1** given to or made with heedful anticipation of the needs and happiness of others — see THOUGHTFUL 1

2 having or marked by sympathy and consideration for others — see HUMANE 1

kind *n* **1** a number of persons or things that are grouped together because they have something in common — see SORT 1

2 one of the units into which a whole is divided on the basis of a common characteristic — see CLASS 2

kindhearted *adj* having or marked by sympathy and consideration for others — see HUMANE 1

kindheartedness *n* the capacity for feeling for another's unhappiness or misfortune — see HEART 1

kindle *vb* to set (something) on fire — see BURN 2

kindled *adj* being on fire — see ABLAZE 1

kindliness *n* **1** kindly concern, interest, or support — see GOODWILL 1

2 the capacity for feeling for another's unhappiness or misfortune — see HEART 1

kindly *adj* **1** having or marked by sympathy and consideration for others — see HUMANE 1

2 promoting or contributing to personal or social well-being — see BENEFICIAL

kindly *adv* with good reason or courtesy — see WELL 4

kindness *n* **1** an act of kind assistance — see FAVOR 1

2 the capacity for feeling for another's unhappiness or misfortune — see HEART 1

kind of *adv* to some degree or extent — see FAIRLY 1

kindred *adj* **1** having a close connection like that between family members — see RELATED

2 having or marked by agreement in feeling or action — see HARMONIOUS 3

kindred *n* a group of persons who come from the same ancestor — see FAMILY 1

kinfolk *or* **kinfolks** *n pl* a group of persons who come from the same ancestor — see FAMILY 1

king *n* a person of rank, power, or influence in a particular field — see MAGNATE

kingdom come *n* a dwelling place of perfect happiness for the soul after death — see HEAVEN 1

kingly *adj* fit for or worthy of a royal ruler — see MONARCHICAL

kingpin *n* **1** one of high position or importance within a group — see BIG SHOT

2 the person (as an employer or supervisor) who tells people and especially workers what to do — see BOSS

king-size *or* **king-sized** *adj* **1** unusually large — see HUGE

2 of great extent from end to end — see LONG 1

king's ransom *n* a very large amount of money — see FORTUNE 2

kinsfolk *n pl* a group of persons who come from the same ancestor — see FAMILY 1

kinship *n* the fact or state of having something in common — see CONNECTION 1

kinsman *n* a person connected with another by blood or marriage — see RELATIVE

kirk *n, chiefly Scottish* a building for public

worship and especially Christian worship
— see CHURCH 1

kiss *vb* **1** to touch one another with the lips
as a sign of love ⟨It's traditional for couples to *kiss* under the mistletoe at Christmastime.⟩

syn smooch

rel buss, French-kiss, osculate, smack; canoodle, make out, pet, spoon; nestle, snuggle

2 to pass lightly across or touch gently especially in passing — see ²BRUSH

kisser *n, slang* **1** the front part of the head
— see FACE 1

2 the opening through which food passes
into the body of an animal — see MOUTH 1

kittenish *adj* affecting shyness or modesty
— see COY 1

¹**kitty** *n* a small domestic animal known for
catching mice — see CAT

²**kitty** *n* a sum of money set aside for a particular purpose — see FUND 1

knack *n* **1** a clever often underhanded
means to achieve an end — see TRICK 1

2 a special and usually inborn ability —
see TALENT

knapsack *n* a soft-sided case designed for
carrying belongings especially on the back
— see PACK 1

knave *n* a mean, evil, or unprincipled person — see VILLAIN

knavery *n* **1** a playful or mischievous act
intended as a joke — see PRANK

2 playful, reckless behavior that is not intended to cause serious harm — see MISCHIEF 1

knavish *adj* tending to or exhibiting reckless playfulness — see MISCHIEVOUS 1

knell *vb* to make the clear sound heard
when metal vibrates — see ²RING

knickknack *also* **nicknack** *n* a small object displayed for its attractiveness or interest ⟨A variety of pretty porcelain *knickknacks* adorned the mantel.⟩

syn bauble, curio, curiosity, gaud, gewgaw
(*also* geegaw), novelty, ornamental, trinket
rel bagatelle, trifle; figurine, ornament;
keepsake, memento, souvenir; conversation piece; collectible (*or* collectable), collector's item

knife *n* an instrument with a metal length
that has a sharp edge for cutting ⟨Be careful in using the *knife* to split open the cardboard box.⟩

syn blade, cutter

rel cleaver, hack; bayonet, bodkin, bolo,
bowie knife, cutlass, dagger, dirk, jackknife,
machete, pocketknife, poniard, sheath knife,
stiletto, stylet, switchblade, yataghan; rapier,
saber (*or* sabre), steel, sword; scalpel

knob *n* a small uneven mass — see LUMP 1

knock *n* **1** a hard strike with a part of the
body or an instrument — see ¹BLOW

2 bad luck or an example of this — see
MISFORTUNE

3 a change in status for the worse usually
temporarily — see REVERSE 1

knock *vb* **1** to come into usually forceful
contact with something — see HIT 2

2 to deliver a blow to (someone or something) usually in a strong vigorous manner
— see HIT 1

3 to express one's unfavorable opinion of
the worth or quality of — see CRITICIZE

knock (about) *vb* to move about from
place to place aimlessly — see WANDER 1

knockabout *adj* being rough or noisy in a
high-spirited way — see BOISTEROUS

knock down *vb* **1** to receive as return for
effort — see EARN 1

2 to take apart — see DISASSEMBLE 1

3 to strike (someone) so forcefully as to
cause a fall — see FELL 1

4 to make smaller in amount, volume, or
extent — see DECREASE 1

knock off *vb* **1** to bring (as an action or
operation) to an immediate end — see
STOP 1

2 to stop doing (something) permanently
— see QUIT 2

3 to take away (an amount or number)
from a total — see SUBTRACT

knockout *adj* very pleasing to look at —
see BEAUTIFUL 1

knockout *n* **1** a lovely woman — see BEAUTY 2

2 a temporary state of unconsciousness —
see FAINT

3 something very good of its kind — see JIM-DANDY

4 a physically attractive person — see DOLL 2

knot *n* **1** a number of things considered as
a unit — see GROUP 1

2 a small rounded mass of swollen tissue
— see BUMP 1

3 a uniting or binding force or influence
— see BOND 2

4 a usually small number of persons considered as a unit — see GROUP 2

5 something that requires thought and
skill for resolution — see PROBLEM 1

knot *vb* to twist together into a usually
confused mass — see ENTANGLE 1

knotty *adj* **1** having many parts or aspects
that are usually interrelated — see COMPLEX 1

2 requiring exceptional skill or caution in
performance or handling — see TRICKY 1

know *vb* **1** to have a practical understanding of ⟨a career diplomat who *knows* several languages⟩

syn comprehend, grasp, understand

rel appreciate, apprehend, fathom, follow,
perceive; have, possess; catch on (to), pick
up

near ant misapprehend, misconceive, misinterpret, misknow, misunderstand

2 to come to a knowledge of (something)
by living through it — see EXPERIENCE

3 to have a clear idea of — see COMPREHEND 1

know–how *n* knowledge gained by actually doing or living through something —
see EXPERIENCE 1

knowing *adj* **1** having inside information
— see WISE 2

2 having or showing a practical cleverness
or judgment — see SHREWD 1

3 made, given, or done with full awareness
of what one is doing — see INTENTIONAL

---

4 decided on as a result of careful thought — see DELIBERATE 1

knowingly *adv* with full awareness of what one is doing — see INTENTIONALLY

knowledge *n* **1** a body of facts learned by study or experience ⟨The forest ranger shared some of his vast *knowledge* of the woods with us.⟩

syn lore, science, wisdom

rel dope, information, intelligence, know, lowdown, news; evidence, facts; acquaintance, awareness, familiarity; erudition, learning, scholarship; expertise, know-how

near ant ignorance, inexperience, innocence, unfamiliarity

2 the understanding and information gained from being educated — see EDUCATION 2

3 a state of being aware — see ATTENTION 2

knowledgeable *adj* **1** having information especially as a result of study or experience — see FAMILIAR 2

2 having or displaying advanced knowledge or education — see EDUCATED 1

know–nothing *n* a stupid person — see IDIOT

knuckle under *vb* **1** to cease resistance (as to another's arguments, demands, or control) — see YIELD 3

2 to yield to the control or power of enemy forces — see FALL 2

kook *n* a person of odd or whimsical habits — see ECCENTRIC

kooky *also* **kookie** *adj* **1** different from the ordinary in a way that causes curiosity or suspicion — see ODD 2

2 showing or marked by a lack of good sense or judgment — see FOOLISH 1

kowtow *vb* to use flattery or the doing of favors in order to win approval especially from a superior — see FAWN

label *n* a slip (as of paper or cloth) that is attached to something to identify or describe it ⟨On its frame the painting had a *label* with its title and the name of the artist.⟩

syn marker, tag, ticket

rel caption, legend; brand, emblem, hallmark, logo, mark, symbol, trademark; badge, decal, plaque, seal, stamp, sticker

label *vb* **1** to attach an identifying slip to ⟨He *labeled* all of the poisonous materials with the familiar skull and crossbones.⟩

syn mark, tag, ticket

rel caption, earmark, hallmark, stamp; call, designate, identify, name, tab; entitle, style, term, title; brand, stigmatize

2 to give a name to — see NAME 1

labor *n* **1** a dull, unpleasant, or difficult piece of work — see CHORE 2

2 the active use of energy in producing a result — see EFFORT

3 very hard or unpleasant work — see TOIL

4 the act or process of giving birth to children — see CHILDBIRTH

5 something produced by physical or intellectual effort — see PRODUCT 1

labor *vb* to devote serious and sustained effort ⟨He *labored* most of the day over the difficult legal brief.⟩

syn drudge, endeavor, grub, hump, hustle, moil, peg (away), plod, plow, plug, slog, strain, strive, struggle, sweat, toil, travail, tug, work

rel apply (oneself), buckle (down), dig in, hammer (away), knuckle down, pitch in; attack, drive; essay, try; exercise, exert, overexert, overwork; eke out, grind (out), put out, scrabble, scratch; trudge, wade

phrases sweat blood

near ant break, ease (up), let up, slacken; bum, chill, dally, dillydally, goof (off), idle, loaf, lounge, shirk, slack (off); bask, loll, relax, repose, rest, unwind; dabble, goof

(around), hang, monkey (around), play, potter (around), putter (around), trifle

laborer *n* a person who does very hard or dull work — see DRUDGE

laborious *adj* **1** involved in often constant activity — see BUSY 1

2 requiring considerable physical or mental effort — see HARD 2

3 requiring much time, effort, or careful attention — see DEMANDING 1

laboriously *adv* with great effort or determination — see HARD 1

laborsaving *adj* designed to replace or decrease human labor and especially physical labor ⟨A new *laborsaving* device let us clean the house in half the time.⟩

syn automated, automatic, robotic, self-acting

rel mechanical, motorized, nonmanual; computerized; aiding, helping; easing, relieving; time-saving; semiautomatic

ant nonautomated, nonautomatic

labyrinth *n* a confusing and complicated arrangement of passages — see MAZE

labyrinthine *adj* having many parts or aspects that are usually interrelated — see COMPLEX 1

lace *n* **1** a length of braided, flexible material that is used for tying or connecting things — see CORD 1

2 a length of something formed of three or more strands woven together — see BRAID

lace *vb* **1** to cause to twine about one another — see INTERTWINE 1

2 to scatter or set here and there among other things — see THREAD 1

3 to strike repeatedly — see BEAT 1

4 to make more pleasant to the taste by adding something intensely flavored — see SEASON 1

5 to alter (something) for the worse with the addition of foreign or lower-grade substances — see ADULTERATE

laceration *n* a long deep cut — see GASH

lachrymose *adj* given to expressing strong emotion (as sorrow) by readily shedding tears — see TEARFUL 1

lacing *n* 1 a length of braided, flexible material that is used for tying or connecting things — see CORD 1

2 a length of something formed of three or more strands woven together — see BRAID

lack *n* 1 the fact or state of being absent ⟨The *lack* of news about the situation was frustrating.⟩

syn absence, dearth, want

rel deficiency, deficit, failure, famine, inadequacy, insufficiency, meagerness, paucity, poverty, scantiness, scantness, scarceness, scarcity, shortage, skimpiness; deprivation, loss, necessity, need, needfulness, omission

near ant abundance, amplitude, bounty, plenitude, plenteousness, plentifulness, plentitude, plenty, wealth; adequacy, sufficiency; excess, overabundance, oversupply, superabundance, surfeit, surplus; deluge, flood; bushel, deal, gobs, heap, loads, lot, mass, mountain, much, oodles, peck, pile, pot, quantity, raft, reams, scads, stack, volume, wad

ant presence

2 a falling short of an essential or desirable amount or number — see DEFICIENCY

3 a state of being without something necessary, desirable, or useful — see NEED 1

lackadaisical *adj* lacking bodily energy or motivation — see LISTLESS

lacking *adj* 1 not coming up to an expected measure or meeting a particular need — see SHORT 3

2 not present or in evidence — see ABSENT 2

laconic *adj* 1 marked by the use of few words to convey much information or meaning — see CONCISE

2 tending not to speak frequently (as by habit or inclination) — see SILENT 2

laconically *adv* in a few words — see SHORTLY 1

lad *n* 1 a male person who has not yet reached adulthood — see BOY 1

2 an adult male human being — see MAN 1

ladder *n* a scheme of rank or order — see ³SCALE 1

laddie *n* a male person who has not yet reached adulthood — see BOY 1

lade *vb* 1 to lift out with something that holds liquid — see DIP 2

2 to place a weight or burden on — see LOAD 1

lading *n* a mass or quantity of something taken up and carried, conveyed, or transported — see LOAD 1

ladle *n* a utensil with a bowl and a handle that is used especially in cooking and serving food — see SPOON

ladle *vb* to lift out with something that holds liquid — see DIP 2

lady *n* 1 an adult female human being — see WOMAN 1

2 a female partner in a marriage — see WIFE

3 a woman of high birth or social position — see GENTLEWOMAN

4 a female romantic companion — see GIRLFRIEND

ladylove *n* a female romantic companion — see GIRLFRIEND

lag *adj* following all others of the same kind in order or time — see LAST 1

lag *vb* 1 to lose bodily strength or vigor — see WEAKEN 2

2 to move or act slowly — see DELAY 1

laggard *adj* moving or proceeding at less than the normal, desirable, or required speed — see SLOW 1

laggard *n* someone who moves slowly or more slowly than others — see SLOWPOKE

laggardly *adv* at a pace that is less than usual, desirable, or expected — see SLOW

lagger *n* someone who moves slowly or more slowly than others — see SLOWPOKE

lagging *adj* moving or proceeding at less than the normal, desirable, or required speed — see SLOW 1

lagniappe *n* 1 something given in addition to what is ordinarily expected or owed — see BONUS

2 something given to someone without expectation of a return — see GIFT 1

laid-back *adj* having a relaxed, casual manner — see EASYGOING 1

lair *n* 1 a place where a person goes to hide or to avoid others — see HIDEOUT

2 the shelter or resting place of a wild animal — see DEN 1

lam *n* the act or an instance of getting free from danger or confinement — see ESCAPE 1

lam *vb* to get free from a dangerous or confining situation — see ESCAPE 1

lamb *n* an innocent or gentle person ⟨The new guys at football camp were *lambs* who hardly knew what awaited them.⟩

syn angel, dove, innocent, sheep

rel babe, colt, cub, fledgling, greenhorn, ingenue (*or* ingénue), naif (*or* naif), newbie, tenderfoot, virgin; cherub, saint; mollycoddle, sissy, softy (*or* softie), weakling, wimp; dupe, pigeon, sap, sucker

near ant bully, roughneck, rowdy, tough; beast, boor, cad, churl, clown, creep, cur, heel, jerk, joker, louse, lout, slob; shark, skunk, snake, stinker; devil, knave, miscreant, no-good, rapscallion, rascal, reprobate, rogue, scalawag (*or* scallywag), scamp, scoundrel, varlet, villain

ant wolf

lambaste *or* **lambast** *vb* 1 to criticize (someone) severely or angrily especially for personal failings — see SCOLD

2 to criticize harshly and usually publicly — see ATTACK 2

lambent *adj* giving off or reflecting much light — see BRIGHT 1

lame *adj* 1 arousing or deserving of one's loathing and disgust — see CONTEMPTIBLE 1

2 falling short of a standard — see BAD 1

lame *vb* to cause severe or permanent injury to — see MAIM

lamella *n* a small thin piece of material that resembles an animal scale — see ²SCALE

lament *n* 1 a crying out in grief ⟨the na-

---

tional *lament* that was heard when President Kennedy was assassinated⟩

syn groan, howl, keen, lamentation, moan, plaint, wail

rel cry, sob, tears; agonizing, grieving, mourning, sorrowing, suffering, weeping; hand-wringing, regret; anguish, dolor, grief, heartache, heartbreak, sorrow, woe

near ant cheering, laughing, smiling

ant exultation, rejoicing

2 a composition expressing one's grief over a loss ⟨a poem that is her *lament* for her late grandmother⟩

syn dirge, elegy, requiem

near ant encomium, eulogy, paean, panegyric

3 an expression of dissatisfaction, pain, or resentment — see COMPLAINT 1

lament *vb* **1** to feel or express sorrow for ⟨She *lamented* her friend's decision to move across the country.⟩

syn bemoan, bewail, deplore, grieve (for), mourn, wail (for)

rel elegize; cry (for), keen, moan, weep; regret, rue; bawl, blubber, sob; agonize, bleed, hurt, sorrow, suffer

near ant beam, cheer, grin, laugh, smile

ant delight, exult (in), glory (in), joy

2 to feel sorry or dissatisfied about — see REGRET

lamentable *adj* **1** expressing or suggesting mourning — see MOURNFUL 1

2 of a kind to cause great distress — see REGRETTABLE

lamentation *n* a crying out in grief — see LAMENT 1

lamina *n* a small thin piece of material that resembles an animal scale — see ²SCALE

lamp *n* something that provides illumination — see LIGHT 2

lampoon *n* a creative work that uses sharp humor to point up the foolishness of a person, institution, or human nature in general — see SATIRE

lance *n* a weapon with a long straight handle and sharp head or blade — see SPEAR

lance *vb* to penetrate or hold (something) with a pointed object — see IMPALE

land *n* **1** a body of people composed of one or more nationalities usually with its own territory and government — see NATION

2 a broad geographical area — see REGION 2

3 the solid part of our planet's surface as distinguished from the sea and air — see EARTH 2

land *vb* **1** to stop at or near a place along the shore ⟨The Pilgrims *landed* at Plymouth after exploring Cape Cod Bay.⟩

syn anchor, dock

rel berth, moor, tie up; beach, ground; harbor; arrive, reach, show up, turn up; debark, disembark

phrases make port

near ant embark, launch, sail

2 to get to a destination — see COME 2

3 to go ashore from a ship — see DISEMBARK 1

4 to come to rest after descending from the air — see ALIGHT 1

5 to receive as return for effort — see EARN 1

6 to take physical control or possession of

(something) suddenly or forcibly — see CATCH 1

landfill *n* a place where discarded materials (as trash) are dumped — see DUMP 1

landing *n* a structure used by boats and ships for taking on or landing cargo and passengers — see DOCK

landlord *n* the owner of land or housing that is rented to another ⟨We agreed to pay the *landlord* the rent on the first Monday of each month.⟩

syn lessor, letter, renter

rel landlady; laird, landholder, landowner; proprietor; slumlord

ant lodger, roomer, tenant

landmark *n* a point in a chain of events at which an important change (as in one's fortunes) occurs — see TURNING POINT

language *n* **1** the stock of words, pronunciation, and grammar used by a people as their basic means of communication ⟨Great Britain, the United States, Australia, and other countries where English is the dominant *language*⟩

syn lingo, mother tongue, speech, tongue, vocabulary

rel argot, cant, colloquial, dialect, idiolect, idiom, jargon, parlance, patois, patter, pidgin, slang, slanguage, vernacular; colloquialism, localism, provincialism, regionalism, shibboleth, vernacularism; terminology; coinage, modernism, neologism

2 the special terms or expressions of a particular group or field — see TERMINOLOGY

3 the way in which something is put into words — see WORDING 1

languid *adj* **1** lacking bodily energy or motivation — see LISTLESS

2 lacking bodily strength — see WEAK 1

3 moving or proceeding at less than the normal, desirable, or required speed — see SLOW 1

languish *vb* to lose bodily strength or vigor — see WEAKEN 2

languishing *adj* lacking bodily energy or motivation — see LISTLESS

languor *n* the quality or state of lacking physical strength or vigor — see WEAKNESS 1

languorous *adj* lacking bodily energy or motivation — see LISTLESS

lank *adj* not stiff in structure — see LIMP 1

lanky *adj* being tall, thin and usually loose-jointed ⟨The *lanky* basketball star was great at slam-dunking.⟩

syn gangling, gangly, rangy, spindling, spindly

rel angular, gaunt, lank, rawboned, scraggy, scrawny, skinny; lean, slender, slim, spare, thin; racy, reedy, spidery, stringy, twiggy, waspish, weedy, willowy, wiry

near ant beefy, bulky, chubby, chunky, heavyset, pudgy, squat, stocky, stout, stubby, sturdy, sturdy, thickset, weighty; muscle-bound; corpulent, fat, fleshy, full, gross, obese, overweight, plump, portly, roly-poly, rotund, round, tubby

lap *n* a portion of a trip — see LEG 2

¹lap *vb* **1** to flow along or against — see WASH 1

2 to flow in a broken irregular stream — see GURGLE

3 to move with a splashing motion — see SLOSH 1

²lap vb **1** to lie over parts of one another — see OVERLAP

2 to surround or cover closely — see ENFOLD 1

lapping n a partial covering of one thing by an adjoining member — see OVERLAP

lapse n **1** a change in status for the worse usually temporarily — see REVERSE 1

2 an unintentional departure from truth or accuracy — see ERROR 1

3 the stopping of a process or activity — see END 1

lapse vb to come to an end — see CEASE 1

larceny n the unlawful taking and carrying away of property without the consent of its owner — see THEFT 1

large adj of a size greater than average of its kind ⟨He was hungry, so he ordered the *large* pizza.⟩

syn big, bulky, considerable, goodly, grand, great, handsome, hefty, hulking, husky, largish, outsize (*also* outsized), oversize (*or* oversized), sizable (*or* sizeable), substantial, tidy, voluminous

rel astronomical (*also* astronomic), bumper, cavernous, colossal, cosmic (*also* cosmical), elephantine, enormous, gargantuan, gigantic, gross, herculean, heroic (*also* heroical), Himalayan, huge, immense, jumbo, king-size (*or* king-sized), leviathan, major, mammoth, massive, monolithic, monstrous, monumental, mountainous, prodigious, staggering, stupendous, super, super-duper, titanic, tremendous, vast, vasty, whacking, whopping; bloated

near ant diminutive, half-pint, infinitesimal, little-bitty, microscopic (*also* microscopical), mini, miniature, minuscule, minute, pint-size (*or* pint-sized), pocket-size (*also* pocket-sized), pygmy, teeny, teeny-weeny, tiny, wee

ant bantam, dinky, dwarf, dwarfish, little, puny, small, smallish, undersized (*also* undersize)

large adv in a luxurious manner — see HIGH

largely adv **1** for the most part — see CHIEFLY

2 to a large extent or degree — see GREATLY 2

largeness n the quality or state of being large in size ⟨I was impressed by the *largeness* of the portions at the new restaurant.⟩

syn bigness, bulkiness, grandness, greatness, heftiness, voluminousness

rel enormity, enormousness, extensiveness, hugeness, immenseness, immensity, magnitude, massiveness, mightiness, mountainousness, stupendousness, vastness; extravagance, extremeness; abundance, ampleness, bountifulness, copiousness, generosity, liberality

near ant diminutiveness, minuteness, tininess; slightness; meagerness, poorness, scantiness, scarceness, scarcity, skimpiness, slenderness, slimness, spareness, sparseness, sparsity, stinginess; deficiency, inadequacy

ant fineness, littleness, puniness, smallness

largess *also* **largesse** n **1** something given to someone without expectation of a return — see GIFT 1

2 the quality or state of being generous — see LIBERALITY

largish adj **1** of a size greater than average of its kind — see LARGE

2 sufficiently large in size, amount, or number to merit attention — see CONSIDERABLE 1

lariat n a rope or long leather thong with a noose used especially for catching livestock — see LASSO

lark n a time or instance of carefree fun — see FLING 1

lark vb to play and run about happily — see FROLIC 1

lascivious adj **1** depicting or referring to sexual matters in a way that is unacceptable in polite society — see OBSCENE 1

2 having a strong sexual desire — see LUSTFUL

lasciviousness n the quality or state of being obscene — see OBSCENITY

lash n **1** a hard strike with a part of the body or an instrument — see ¹BLOW

2 a long thin or flexible tool for striking — see WHIP

lash vb **1** to strike repeatedly with something long and thin or flexible — see WHIP 1

2 to strike repeatedly — see BEAT 1

lass n a female person who has not yet reached adulthood — see GIRL 2

lassie n a female person who has not yet reached adulthood — see GIRL 2

lassitude n a complete depletion of energy or strength — see FATIGUE

lasso n a rope or long leather thong with a noose used especially for catching livestock ⟨The cowpuncher skillfully tossed the *lasso* around the calf's neck.⟩

syn lariat, reata, riata

last adj **1** following all others of the same kind in order or time ⟨*Last* one in the pool is a rotten egg!⟩

syn closing, concluding, final, hindmost, lag, latest, latter, rearmost, terminal, terminating, ultimate

rel consequent, ensuing, eventual, following, succeeding; conclusive, crowning, decisive, definitive; farthermost, farthest, furthermost, furthest, remotest; lowest; endmost, extreme, outermost, outmost, utmost; penultimate

near ant eminent, premier, superior

ant beginning, earliest, first, foremost, inaugural, initial, leadoff, maiden, opening, original, pioneer, primary, starting

2 serving to put an end to all debate or questioning — see CONCLUSIVE 1

3 of the greatest or highest degree or quantity — see ULTIMATE 1

last vb **1** to continue to operate or to meet one's needs — see HOLD OUT

2 to remain indefinitely in existence or in the same state — see CONTINUE 1

lasting adj having an existence or validity that does not change or diminish — see ABIDING

last word n a practice or interest that is very popular for a short time — see FAD

late adj **1** not arriving, occurring, or settled

---

syn synonym(s)   **rel** related words

ant antonym(s)   **near ant** near antonym(s)

at the due, usual, or proper time ⟨I ran as fast as I could, but was still *late* for class.⟩
syn behind, behindhand, belated, delinquent, latish, overdue, tardy
rel delayed, detained, postponed; dallying, dawdling, dilatory, dillydallying, dragging, laggard, lagging, poky (*or* pokey), slow, sluggish, unhurried
near ant opportune, seasonable, timely; prompt, punctual
ant early, inopportune, precocious, premature, unseasonable, untimely
2 having been such at some previous time — see FORMER 1
3 no longer living — see DEAD 1
4 being far along in development — see ADVANCED
late *adv* **1** after the due, usual, or proper time ⟨She has a bad habit of arriving *late*.⟩
syn tardily
rel afterward (*or* afterwards), anon, eventually, later, latterly, subsequently, thereafter; dilatorily, laggardly, slow, slowly, sluggishly
near ant immediately, promptly, punctually; pronto, quickly, rapidly, snappily, speedily, swiftly
ant beforehand, early, inopportunely, precociously, prematurely, unseasonably
2 not long ago — see NEWLY
lately *adv* not long ago — see NEWLY
latency *n* a state of temporary inactivity — see ABEYANCE
lateness *n* the quality or state of being late ⟨We were unable to get into the movie due to our *lateness* in arriving.⟩
syn belatedness, delinquency, tardiness
rel dilatoriness, sluggishness
near ant promptitude, promptness, punctuality
ant earliness, prematureness, prematurity
latent *adj* not being in a state of use, activity, or employment — see INACTIVE 1
later *adj* being, occurring, or carried out at a time after something else — see SUBSEQUENT
later *adv* following in time or place — see AFTER
lateral *adj* of, relating to, or located on one side — see SIDE
latest *adj* following all others of the same kind in order or time — see LAST 1
latest *n* a practice or interest that is very popular for a short time — see FAD
lather *n* **1** a light mass of fine bubbles formed in or on a liquid — see FOAM
2 a state of nervous or irritated concern — see FRET
lathery *adj* covered with, consisting of, or resembling foam — see FOAMY
latish *adj* not arriving, occurring, or settled at the due, usual, or proper time — see LATE 1
latitude *n* **1** an allowable margin of freedom or variation — see SLACK 1
2 the right to act or move freely — see FREEDOM 2
latrine *n* a room furnished with a fixture for flushing body waste — see TOILET
latter *adj* following all others of the same kind in order or time — see LAST 1
laud *vb* **1** to declare enthusiastic approval of — see ACCLAIM
2 to proclaim the glory of — see PRAISE 1

laudable *adj* deserving of high regard or great approval — see ADMIRABLE
laugh *n* **1** an explosive sound that is a sign of amusement ⟨The child's frown turned into a *laugh* when he saw the clown.⟩
syn cackle, chortle, chuckle, giggle, guffaw, horselaugh, laughter, snicker, snigger, titter, twitter
rel crow, whoop; grin, simper, smile, smirk
near ant cry, groan, moan, sob, wail; face, frown, grimace, lower (*also* lour), mouth, pout, scowl
2 someone or something that is very funny — see SCREAM
3 something said or done to cause laughter — see JOKE 1
laugh *vb* **1** to show mirth with an explosive vocal sound ⟨Everyone *laughed* when the clown dramatically slipped and fell.⟩
syn break up, cackle, chortle, chuckle, crack up, giggle, roar, scream, snicker, titter, twitter
rel grin, smile
phrases split one's sides
near ant bawl, blubber, cry, sob, weep; howl, scream, squall, wail; yowl; pule, whimper, whine; sniffle, snivel; groan, moan, sigh
2 to express scornful amusement by means of facial contortions — see SNEER
laugh (at) *vb* to make (someone or something) the object of unkind laughter — see RIDICULE
laughable *adj* **1** causing or intended to cause laughter — see FUNNY 1
2 so foolish or pointless as to be worthy of scornful laughter — see RIDICULOUS 1
laughing *adj* indicative of or marked by high spirits or good humor — see MERRY
laughingstock *n* a person or thing that is made fun of ⟨The team has become the *laughingstock* of the league.⟩
syn butt, derision, jest, joke, mark, mock, mockery, sport, target
rel chump, dupe, fall guy, fool, gull, monkey, pigeon, sap, sucker, victim
near ant darling, favorite, pet
laughter *n* an explosive sound that is a sign of amusement — see LAUGH 1
launch *n* the point at which something begins — see BEGINNING
launch *vb* **1** to be responsible for the creation and early operation or use of — see FOUND
2 to take the first step in (a process or course of action) — see BEGIN 1
3 to send through the air especially with a quick forward motion of the arm — see THROW 1
laurels *n pl* public acknowledgment or admiration for an achievement — see GLORY 1
lavatory *n* a room furnished with a fixture for flushing body waste — see TOILET
lave *vb* to flow along or against — see WASH 1
lavish *adj* **1** going beyond a normal or acceptable limit in degree or amount — see EXCESSIVE
2 pouring forth in great amounts — see PROFUSE
3 showing obvious signs of wealth and comfort — see LUXURIOUS

lavish *vb* **1** to give readily and in large quantities — see RAIN 2

2 to use up carelessly — see WASTE 1

lavishly *adv* **1** in a generous manner — see WELL 2

2 in a luxurious manner — see HIGH

lavishness *n* the quality or fact of being free or wasteful in the expenditure of money — see EXTRAVAGANCE 1

law *n* **1** a rule of conduct or action laid down by a governing authority and especially a legislature ⟨A record number of *laws* were passed in that legislative session.⟩

syn act, bill, constitution, enactment, ordinance, statute

rel command, commandment, decree, dictate, directive, edict, fiat, ruling; bylaw, ground rule, regulation, rule; amendment, legislation; common law, martial law; prohibition, proscription, restriction

near higher law

2 a collection or system of rules of conduct — see CODE

3 the department of government that keeps order, fights crime, and enforces statutes — see POLICE 1

law–abiding *adj* readily giving in to the command or authority of another — see OBEDIENT

lawbreaker *n* a person who has committed a crime — see CRIMINAL

lawbreaking *adj* not restrained by or under the control of legal authority — see LAWLESS 1

lawbreaking *n* **1** a breaking of a moral or legal code — see OFFENSE 1

2 activities that are in violation of the laws of the state — see CRIME 1

lawful *adj* permitted by law — see LEGAL 1

lawfulness *n* the quality or state of being legal — see LEGALITY

lawgiver *n* a member of an organized body of persons having the authority to make laws — see LEGISLATOR

lawless *adj* **1** not restrained by or under the control of legal authority ⟨a *lawless* mob⟩

syn anarchic (*also* anarchical), disorderly, lawbreaking, unruly

rel defiant, insubordinate, mutinous, rebellious, refractory, riotous; undisciplined; criminal, felonious, illegal, illegitimate, illicit, unlawful, wrongful; disobedient, froward, intractable, recalcitrant

near ant lawful, legal, legalized, legitimate; amenable, compliant, docile, obedient, submissive, tractable

ant law-abiding, orderly

2 contrary to or forbidden by law — see ILLEGAL 1

lawlessness *n* **1** a state in which there is widespread wrongdoing and disregard for rules and authority — see ANARCHY

2 activities that are in violation of the laws of the state — see CRIME 1

lawmaker *n* a member of an organized body of persons having the authority to make laws — see LEGISLATOR

lawsuit *n* a court case for enforcing a right or claim ⟨The homeowner filed a *lawsuit* against the moving company that was refusing to be held responsible for damaging her furniture.⟩

syn action, proceeding, suit

rel litigation; case, cause, complaint; counterclaim, countersuit, cross action, cross-claim

lawyer *n* a person whose profession is to conduct lawsuits for clients or to advise about legal rights and obligations ⟨Their *lawyers* told them that they couldn't use the park for the concert without permission from the city.⟩

syn advocate, attorney, counsel, counselor (*or* counsellor)

rel cocounsel; district attorney, prosecuting attorney, prosecutor, solicitor; criminal lawyer, public defender, trial lawyer; solicitor; jurist; lawgiver, lawmaker, legislator, solon

lax *adj* **1** failing to give proper care and attention — see NEGLIGENT

2 not bound by rigid standards — see EASYGOING 2

3 not tightly fastened, tied, or stretched — see LOOSE 1

laxness *n* failure to take the care that a cautious person usually takes — see NEGLIGENCE 1

lay *n* **1** a rhythmic series of musical tones arranged to give a pleasing effect — see MELODY

2 a short musical composition for the human voice often with instrumental accompaniment — see SONG 1

lay *vb* **1** to arrange something in a certain spot or position — see PLACE 1

2 to cause to come to rest at the bottom (as of a liquid) — see SETTLE 1

3 to establish or apply as a charge or penalty — see IMPOSE

4 to make ready in advance — see PREPARE 1

5 to put a layer of on a surface — see SPREAD 2

6 to risk (something) on the outcome of an uncertain event — see BET

7 to explain (something) as being the result of something else — see CREDIT 1

8 to place (a dead body) in the earth, a tomb, or the sea — see BURY 1

lay away *vb* to put (something of future use or value) in a safe or secret place — see HOARD

lay down *vb* **1** to put into effect through legislative or authoritative action — see ENACT

2 to state clearly and strongly — see ASSERT 1

3 to give the rules about (something) clearly and exactly — see PRESCRIBE

4 to give (something) over to the control or possession of another usually under duress — see SURRENDER 1

layoff *n* the termination of the employment of an employee or a work force often temporarily ⟨Even senior employees lost their jobs in the massive *layoff*.⟩

syn discharge, dismissal, furlough

rel pink slip; bum's rush, downsizing, firing, heave-ho, sack; closing, shutdown; shakeout, shake-up

---

syn synonym(s)   *rel* related words
ant antonym(s)   *near ant* near antonym(s)

near ant callback, recall, reemployment, rehire

lay off *vb* to bring (as an action or operation) to an immediate end — see STOP 1

lay off (of) *vb* to stop doing (something) permanently — see QUIT 2

layout *n* **1** the way in which something is sized, arranged, or organized — see FORMAT 1

2 the way in which the elements of something (as a work of art) are arranged — see COMPOSITION 3

lay over **1** to hand over or use up in payment — see SPEND 1

2 to work out the details of (something) in advance — see PLAN 1

3 to put into a particular arrangement — see ORDER 1

4 to present so as to invite notice or attention — see SHOW 1

layover *n* a brief halt in a journey — see STOP 1

lay up *vb* to put (something of future use or value) in a safe or secret place — see HOARD

laziness *n* an inclination not to do work or engage in activities ⟨If not for my *laziness*, I could have gotten more done over the weekend.⟩

syn idleness, indolence, inertia, shiftlessness, sloth

rel apathy, languor, lassitude, listlessness, sluggishness; dallying, loafing, lolling, lounging

near ant ambition, enterprise, go, hustle, initiative; assiduity, assiduousness, diligence, perseverance; animation, briskness, energy, exuberance, jazziness, liveliness, lustiness, pep, peppiness, robustness, sprightliness, vibrancy, vigor, vim, vitality, vivacity

ant drive, industriousness, industry

lazy *adj* **1** not easily aroused to action or work ⟨The *lazy* dog just wanted to lie on the couch all day and sleep.⟩

syn idle, indolent, shiftless, slothful

rel apathetic, drowsy, inert, languorous, lethargic, listless, quiescent, sleepy, sluggish, torpid

near ant ambitious, diligent, enterprising, zealous; active, animated, bouncing, brisk, dynamic, energetic, exuberant, frisky, jaunty, jazzy, lively, peppy, perky, pert, snappy, spirited, sprightly, springy, vigorous, vivacious, zippy

ant industrious

2 failing to give proper care and attention — see NEGLIGENT

lazy *vb* to spend time doing nothing — see IDLE

lazybones *n pl* a lazy person ⟨He's a *lazybones* who is never willing to do any work.⟩

syn drone, idler, loafer, slouch, slug, sluggard

rel bum; crawler, creeper, dawdler, laggard, putterer, slowpoke, snail, stick-in-the-mud, straggler; malingerer, shirker, slacker; dallier, lingerer, loiterer, loller, lounger, saunterer; delayer, procrastinator

near ant achiever, comer; live wire, powerhouse

ant doer, go-ahead, go-getter, hummer, hustler, rustler, self-starter

lea *or* **ley** *n* **1** a broad area of level or rolling treeless country — see PLAIN 1

2 open land over which livestock may roam and feed — see RANGE 1

lead *adj* highest in rank or authority — see HEAD

lead *n* **1** the person who has the most important role in a play, movie, or TV show — see STAR 2

2 the space or amount of space between two points, lines, surfaces, or objects — see DISTANCE 1

3 a piece of advice or useful information especially from an expert — see ¹TIP 1

4 a slight or indirect pointing to something (as a solution or explanation) — see HINT 1

lead *vb* **1** to point out the way for (someone) especially from a position in front ⟨An enthusiastic docent *led* our group through the art museum.⟩

syn conduct, direct, guide, marshal (*also* marshall), pilot, route, show, steer, usher

rel precede; accompany, attend, chaperone (*or* chaperon), convoy, escort, see; control, manage

near ant dog, hound, shadow, tail, tailgate

ant follow, trail

2 to serve as leader of ⟨A senior programmer is *leading* the team that is developing the new accounting software.⟩

syn boss, captain, command, head, spearhead

rel control, dominate; direct, govern, handle, manage, oversee, regulate, run, superintend, supervise

near ant bow (to), comply (with), defer (to), follow, obey, serve, submit (to), yield (to)

3 to be at the front of ⟨The local high school's marching band *led* the parade.⟩

syn head

rel precede; announce, herald; accompany, attend, escort, usher

near ant conclude, end, finish, stop, terminate; tail, tailgate; dog, follow, trail

4 to be positioned along a certain course or in a certain direction — see RUN 3

5 to give advice and instruction to (someone) regarding the course or process to be followed — see GUIDE 1

leaden *adj* **1** causing weariness, restlessness, or lack of interest — see BORING

2 of the color gray — see GRAY 1

leader *n* **1** a long hollow cylinder for carrying a substance (as a liquid or gas) — see PIPE 1

2 the person (as an employer or supervisor) who tells people and especially workers what to do — see BOSS

leading *adj* **1** coming before all others in importance — see FOREMOST 1

2 highest in rank or authority — see HEAD

leadoff *adj* coming before all others in time or order — see FIRST 1

lead on *vb* to lead away from a usual or proper course by offering some pleasure or advantage — see LURE

leafage *n* green leaves or plants — see GREENERY

leaflet *n* a short printed publication with no cover or with a paper cover — see PAMPHLET

leafy *adj* covered with a thick, healthy natural growth — see LUSH 1

league *n* **1** a group of persons formally joined together for some common interest — see ASSOCIATION 2

2 an association of persons, parties, or states for mutual assistance and protection — see CONFEDERACY

3 one of the units into which a whole is divided on the basis of a common characteristic — see CLASS 2

league *vb* **1** to form or enter into an association that furthers the interests of its members — see ALLY

2 to participate or assist in a joint effort to accomplish an end — see COOPERATE 1

leak (out) *vb* to become known — see GET OUT 1

lean *adj* having a noticeably small amount of body fat — see THIN 1

lean *n* the degree to which something rises up from a position level with the horizon — see SLANT 1

lean *vb* **1** to set or cause to be at an angle ⟨Just *lean* the ladder against the tree and climb up it.⟩

syn angle, cant, cock, heel, incline, list, pitch, slant, slope, tilt, tip

rel bank; bend, deviate, swerve, veer; decline, descend, recline, retreat

near ant even, flatten, level, straighten

2 to show a liking or preference for (something) ⟨The family's diet *leans* toward vegetarian.⟩

syn incline, run, tend, trend

rel go, gravitate; indicate, point, suggest

near ant avoid, shun, shy (from *or* away from)

3 to place reliance or trust — see DEPEND 1

leaning *adj* running in a slanting direction — see DIAGONAL

leaning *n* **1** a prevailing or general movement or inclination — see TREND 1

2 a habitual attraction to some activity or thing — see INCLINATION 1

leap *n* an act of leaping into the air — see JUMP 1

leap *vb* to propel oneself upward or forward into the air — see JUMP 1

leaping *adj* passing from one topic to another — see DISCURSIVE

learn *vb* **1** to acquire complete knowledge, understanding, or skill in ⟨After months of trying, he finally *learned* the dance steps.⟩

syn get, master, pick up

rel apprehend, comprehend, grasp, know, understand; absorb, assimilate, digest, imbibe; major (in), study; memorize

phrases get the hang of

near ant forget; misunderstand; miss, overlook; disregard, ignore, neglect

ant unlearn

2 to come to an awareness of — see DISCOVER 1

3 to come upon after searching, study, or effort — see FIND 1

4 to commit to memory — see MEMORIZE

learned *adj* **1** having or displaying advanced knowledge or education — see EDUCATED 1

2 suggestive of the vocabulary used in books — see BOOKISH

learnedness *n* the understanding and information gained from being educated — see EDUCATION 2

learning *n* the understanding and information gained from being educated — see EDUCATION 2

lease *vb* **1** to give the possession and use of (something) in return for periodic payment — see RENT 1

2 to take or get the temporary use of (something) for a set sum — see HIRE 1

leather *n* **1** the hairless natural covering of an animal prepared for use ⟨The company claims to use only the finest *leathers* for its shoes and handbags.⟩

syn hide, skin

rel coat, fleece, fur, pelt; alligator, antelope, buckskin, calfskin, chamois, cordovan, cowhide, crocodile, deerskin, doeskin, goatskin, horsehide, kid, kidskin, lambskin, morocco, ostrich, pigskin, seal, sharkskin, sheepskin, snakeskin; nubuck, patent leather, suede

2 the outer covering of an animal removed for its commercial value — see HIDE 1

leather *vb* to strike repeatedly with something long and thin or flexible — see WHIP 1

leathery *adj* not easily chewed — see TOUGH 1

leave *n* **1** a period during which the usual routine of school or work is suspended — see VACATION

2 the approval by someone in authority for the doing of something — see PERMISSION

3 the act of leaving a place — see DEPARTURE 1

leave *vb* **1** to cause to remain behind ⟨You can *leave* your lunch in the refrigerator while we're outside.⟩ ⟨starry-eyed lovers who promise never to *leave* one another⟩

syn abandon, desert, forsake, maroon, quit, strand

rel discard, ditch, dump, fling, jettison, junk, scrap, shed, shuck (off), throw away, throw out; deliver, give up, hand over, relinquish, surrender, yield; escape, retreat (from), take off (from), vacate, withdraw (from); abjure, cut off, disown, reject, renounce, repudiate, separate (from)

phrases walk away from, walk out on

near ant harbor, have, hold, keep, own, possess, reserve, retain, withhold; redeem, rescue, save

ant reclaim

2 to give by means of a will ⟨I'm going to *leave* all of my possessions to my children.⟩

syn bequeath, will

rel deed; hand down, hand on, pass (down); devise

3 to give up (a job or office) — see QUIT 1

4 to put (something) into the possession or safekeeping of another — see GIVE 2

5 to end a usually intimate relationship with — see DITCH 1

6 to give permission to — see ALLOW 2

leave off *vb* **1** to bring (as an action or operation) to an immediate end — see STOP 1

2 to come to an end — see CEASE 1

leave–taking *n* **1** the act of leaving a place — see DEPARTURE 1

2 the act or process of two or more persons going off in different directions — see PARTING 1

---

syn synonym(s)   *rel* related words
ant antonym(s)   *near ant* near antonym(s)

leavings *n pl* a remaining group or portion — see REMAINDER 1

lecture *vb* 1 to criticize (someone) severely or angrily especially for personal failings — see SCOLD

2 to give a formal often extended talk on a subject — see TALK 1

leech *n* a person who is supported by or seeks support from another without making an adequate return ⟨Whenever we go out for pizza, that *leech* always has an excuse for not paying his fair share.⟩

syn hanger-on, moocher, parasite, sponge, sponger

rel dependent; idler; flunky (*also* flunkey *or* flunkie), henchman, lackey; cheapskate, miser, niggard, piker, scrooge, skinflint, tightwad

near ant benefactor, philanthropist, supporter

leer (at) *vb* to look at in a flirtatious or desiring way — see OGLE

leeward *adj* being in the direction that the wind is blowing — see DOWNWIND

left *n* a political belief stressing progress, the essential goodness of humankind, and individual freedom — see LIBERALISM

left-handed *adj* 1 lacking or showing a lack of nimbleness in using one's hands — see CLUMSY 1

2 not being or expressing what one appears to be or express — see INSINCERE

leftover *n* 1 an unused or unwanted piece or item typically of small size or value — see ¹SCRAP 1

2 **leftovers** *pl* a remaining group or portion — see REMAINDER 1

leg *n* 1 a lower limb of an animal ⟨He broke his *leg* when he accidentally stepped in that gopher hole.⟩

syn pin

rel member; foreleg, forelimb; calf, drumstick, ham, shank, shin, thigh

2 a portion of a trip ⟨On the first *leg* of the cruise they went south to the Caribbean.⟩

syn lap, stage

rel layover, stopover

leg (it) *vb* to go on foot — see WALK 1

legacy *n* something that is or may be inherited — see INHERITANCE

legal *adj* 1 permitted by law ⟨Is it *legal* to build a campfire in the park?⟩

syn lawful, legitimate

rel allowable, authorized, noncriminal, permissible; justifiable, warrantable; constitutional; de jure, regulation, statutory; good, innocent, just, proper, right

near ant bad, corrupt, evil, immoral, iniquitous, reprobate, sinful, wicked, wrong; banned, criminal, forbidden, guilty, impermissible, outlawed, prohibited, unauthorized, unjust; under-the-counter, under-the-table; nonconstitutional, unconstitutional

ant illegal, illegitimate, illicit, lawless, unlawful, wrongful

2 following or according to the rules — see FAIR 3

legality *n* the quality or state of being legal ⟨The senator questioned the *legality* of the proposed espionage operation.⟩

syn lawfulness, legitimacy

rel rightfulness, rightness; permissibility, permissibleness

near ant badness, immorality, iniquity, sinfulness, unjustness, wickedness, wrongness; criminality, unconstitutionality

ant illegality, illegitimacy, unlawfulness, wrongfulness

legal tender *n* something (as pieces of stamped metal or printed paper) customarily and legally used as a medium of exchange, a measure of value, or a means of payment — see MONEY

legate *n* a person sent on a mission to represent another — see AMBASSADOR

legatee *n* a person who has the right to inherit property — see HEIR

legend *n* 1 an explanatory list of the symbols on a map or chart ⟨The *legend* indicated that a large circle represented a major city, while a small circle stood for a small town.⟩

syn key

rel scale; caption; guide, table

2 an explanation or description accompanying a pictorial illustration — see CAPTION 1

3 a traditional but unfounded story that gives the reason for a current custom, belief, or fact of nature — see MYTH 1

4 the body of customs, beliefs, stories, and sayings associated with a people, thing, or place — see FOLKLORE

legendary *adj* based on, described in, or being a myth — see MYTHICAL 1

legerdemain *n* 1 the art or skill of performing tricks or illusions for entertainment — see MAGIC 2

2 the use of clever underhanded actions to achieve an end — see TRICKERY

legion *adj* being of a large but indefinite number — see MANY

legion *n* 1 a large body of men and women organized for land warfare — see ARMY 1

2 a great number of persons or creatures massed together — see CROWD 1

legionary *n* a person engaged in military service — see SOLDIER

legionnaire *n* a person engaged in military service — see SOLDIER

legislate *vb* to put into effect through legislative or authoritative action — see ENACT

legislator *n* a member of an organized body of persons having the authority to make laws ⟨The *legislators* met in an all-night session to hammer out the details of the bill.⟩

syn lawgiver, lawmaker, solon

rel assemblyman, assemblywoman; congressman, congresswoman; senator

legitimacy *n* the quality or state of being legal — see LEGALITY

legitimate *adj* permitted by law — see LEGAL 1

lei *n* an ornamental chain or string (as of beads) worn around the neck — see NECKLACE

leisure *n* freedom from activity or labor — see ¹REST 1

leisurely *adj* moving or proceeding at less than the normal, desirable, or required speed — see SLOW 1

leisurely *adv* at a pace that is less than usual, desirable, or expected — see SLOW

lemon *n* something that has failed — see FAILURE 3

lend *vb* to give to another for temporary use with the understanding that it or a like thing will be returned ⟨I can *lend* you my copy of the textbook until the weekend.⟩ ⟨Can you *lend* me five dollars?⟩

syn advance, loan

rel furnish, give, grant; lease, rent

near ant take

ant borrow

length *n* **1** a wide space or area — see EXPANSE

2 the space or amount of space between two points, lines, surfaces, or objects — see DISTANCE 1

lengthen *vb* to make longer — see EXTEND 1

lengthening *n* the act of making longer — see EXTENSION 1

lengthy *adj* **1** of great extent from end to end — see LONG 1

2 lasting for a considerable time — see LONG 2

lenience *n* kind, gentle, or compassionate treatment especially towards someone who is undeserving of it — see MERCY 1

leniency *n* kind, gentle, or compassionate treatment especially towards someone who is undeserving of it — see MERCY 1

lenity *n* kind, gentle, or compassionate treatment especially towards someone who is undeserving of it — see MERCY 1

leprechaun *n* an imaginary being usually having a small human form and magical powers — see FAIRY

less *adj* having not so great importance or rank as another — see LESSER

lessen *vb* **1** to make smaller in amount, volume, or extent — see DECREASE 1

2 to grow less in scope or intensity especially gradually — see DECREASE 2

3 to lower in character, dignity, or quality — see DEBASE 1

lesser *adj* having not so great importance or rank as another ⟨It was the *lesser* evil of the two choices.⟩

syn inferior, junior, less, lower, minor, smaller, subordinate

rel little, mean, small; minute, petty; jerkwater, one-horse, second-class, secondrate, two-bit; associate, auxiliary, secondary, subsidiary

near ant choice, exceptional, first-class, first-rate

ant greater, higher, major, more, primary, prime, senior, superior

lesson *n* something assigned to be read or studied ⟨Your *lesson* for tonight will be the chapter on chemical reactions.⟩

syn assignment, reading

rel homework, schoolwork; lecture; drill, exercise, practice (*also* practise), étude, study

lessor *n* the owner of land or housing that is rented to another — see LANDLORD

let *vb* **1** to give permission to — see ALLOW 2

2 to make able or possible — see ENABLE 1

3 to fail to prevent (some behavior on someone's part) especially from neglect or indifference — see ALLOW 3

letdown *n* **1** the emotion felt when one's

expectations are not met — see DISAPPOINTMENT 1

2 something that disappoints — see DISAPPOINTMENT 2

let down *vb* to fall short in satisfying the expectation or hope of — see DISAPPOINT

lethal *adj* likely to cause or capable of causing death — see DEADLY 1

lethargic *adj* slow to move or act — see INACTIVE 1

let on *vb* to take on a false or deceptive appearance — see PRETEND 1

¹**letter** *n* a message on paper from one person or group to another ⟨He faithfully wrote her a *letter* every week they were apart.⟩

syn dispatch, epistle, memo, memorandum, missive, note

rel billet-doux, open letter; airmail, card, electronic mail, e-mail, junk mail, mail, postal card, postcard; communication, report; encyclical

²**letter** *n* the owner of land or housing that is rented to another — see LANDLORD

letter carrier *n* a person who delivers mail ⟨We like to leave a little gift in the mailbox around Christmas for our *letter carrier*.⟩

syn mail carrier, mailman, postman

rel courier, messenger; postmaster, postmistress

letter-perfect *adj* being entirely without fault or flaw — see PERFECT 1

letup *n* a usually gradual decrease in the pace or level of activity of something — see SLOWDOWN

let up *vb* **1** to come to an end — see CEASE 1

2 to grow less in scope or intensity especially gradually — see DECREASE 2

levee *n* **1** a bank of earth constructed to control water — see DAM

2 a structure used by boats and ships for taking on or landing cargo and passengers — see DOCK

level *adj* **1** having a surface without bends, breaks, or irregularities ⟨looked for a *level* place to land the plane⟩

syn even, flat, flush, plane, smooth

rel exact, uniform; aligned (*also* alined), regular, true; horizontal, tabular; plumb, straight, vertical

near ant inexact, irregular, unaligned, warped; undulating, undulatory, wavy; pitted, pockmarked

ant bumpy, coarse, lumpy, rough, uneven, unsmoothed

2 free from emotional or mental agitation — see CALM 2

level *n* the placement of someone or something in relation to others in a vertical arrangement — see RANK 1

level *vb* **1** to make equal in amount, degree, or status — see EQUALIZE

2 to make free from breaks, curves, or bumps — see EVEN 1

3 to point or turn (something) toward a target or goal — see AIM 1

4 to strike (someone) so forcefully as to cause a fall — see FELL 1

5 to destroy (as a building) completely by knocking down or breaking to pieces — see DEMOLISH 1

levelheaded *adj* based on sound reasoning or information — see GOOD 1

levelheadedness *n* the ability to make

---

syn synonym(s)   *rel* related words

ant antonym(s)   *near ant* near antonym(s)

intelligent decisions especially in everyday matters — see COMMON SENSE

lever *vb* to raise, move, or pull apart with or as if with a lever — see ¹PRY 1

leviathan *adj* unusually large — see HUGE

leviathan *n* something that is unusually large and powerful — see GIANT

levity *n* a lack of seriousness often at an improper time — see FRIVOLITY

levy *n* a charge usually of money collected by the government from people or businesses for public use — see TAX

levy *vb* 1 to pick especially for required military service — see DRAFT 1
2 to establish or apply as a charge or penalty — see IMPOSE

lewd *adj* 1 depicting or referring to sexual matters in a way that is unacceptable in polite society — see OBSCENE 1
2 having a strong sexual desire — see LUSTFUL
3 hinting at or intended to call to mind matters regarded as indecent — see SUGGESTIVE 1

lewdness *n* the quality or state of being obscene — see OBSCENITY

lexical *adj* of or relating to words or language — see VERBAL 1

lexicon *n* a reference book giving information about the meanings, pronunciations, uses, and origins of words listed in alphabetical order — see DICTIONARY

liability *n* 1 a feature of someone or something that creates difficulty for achieving success — see DISADVANTAGE 1
2 the state of being held as the cause of something that needs to be set right — see RESPONSIBILITY 1
3 the state of being left without shelter or protection against something harmful — see EXPOSURE 1
4 the quality or state of being likely to occur — see PROBABILITY 1
5 *usually* **liabilities** *pl* something (as money) which is owed — see DEBT 1

liable *adj* 1 being in a situation where one is likely to meet with harm ⟨Because of his frail constitution, he's *liable* to diseases.⟩
syn endangered, exposed, open, sensitive, subject (to), susceptible, vulnerable
rel likely, prone; uncovered, undefended, unguarded, unprotected, unscreened, unsecured
phrases at risk, in deep water, in jeopardy
near ant covered, guarded, protected, safeguarded, screened, secured, sheltered, shielded, warded
ant insusceptible, invulnerable, unexposed, unsusceptible
2 being the one who must meet an obligation or suffer the consequences for failing to do so — see RESPONSIBLE 1

liaison *n* 1 the fact or state of having something in common — see CONNECTION 1
2 the state of having shared interests or efforts (as in social or business matters) — see ASSOCIATION 1

liar *n* a person who tells lies ⟨She knew he was a *liar* when he started claiming that he was an astronaut.⟩
syn fabricator, fibber, prevaricator, storyteller

rel exaggerator; calumniator, defamer, libeler, libelist, slanderer; perjurer; distorter, falsifier; equivocator, palterer; gossip, talebearer; charlatan, cheat, cheater, counterfeiter, cozener, deceiver, defrauder, dissembler, dissimulator, fraud, hustler, knave, mountebank, operator, pretender
near ant square shooter

libation *n* a liquid suitable for drinking — see DRINK 1

libel *n* the making of false statements that damage another's reputation — see SLANDER

libel *vb* to make untrue and harmful statements about — see SLANDER

libeling *or* **libelling** *n* the making of false statements that damage another's reputation — see SLANDER

libelous *or* **libellous** *adj* causing or intended to cause unjust injury to a person's good name ⟨*libelous* statements about a celebrity for which the tabloid was sued⟩
syn defamatory, scandalous, slanderous
rel erroneous, false, inaccurate, incorrect, inexact, invalid, untrue, wrong; depreciative, depreciatory, derogatory, disparaging, uncomplimentary, unfavorable, unflattering; invidious, objectionable; maligning, traducing, vilifying; hateful, malevolent, malicious, spiteful
near ant appreciative, complimentary, favorable; adulatory, commendatory, eulogistic, laudatory; accurate, correct, errorless, factual, right, sound, true, valid

liberal *adj* 1 not bound by traditional ways or beliefs ⟨parents who take a very *liberal* attitude toward letting their children stay out late⟩
syn broad-minded, nonconventional, nonorthodox, nontraditional, open-minded, progressive, radical, unconventional, unorthodox
rel advanced, contemporary, modern; forbearing, indulgent, large-minded, lenient, permissive, tolerant; extreme; impartial, objective, unbiased
near ant hard, rigid, strict; doctrinal; bigoted, blinkered, intolerant, narrow-minded; reactionary, unreconstructed
ant conservative, conventional, hidebound, nonprogressive, old-fashioned, orthodox, stodgy, traditional
2 being more than enough without being excessive — see PLENTIFUL
3 giving or sharing in abundance and without hesitation — see GENEROUS 1

liberalism *n* a political belief stressing progress, the essential goodness of humankind, and individual freedom ⟨*Liberalism* had always claimed to stand for the greatest social good.⟩
syn left
rel neoliberalism; radicalism, socialism
near ant neoconservatism
ant right

liberality *n* the quality or state of being generous ⟨Already known for his *liberality*, the billionaire continued to give away record amounts of money.⟩
syn bountifulness, bounty, generosity, largess (*also* largesse), openhandedness, openheartedness, philanthropy, unselfishness

rel beneficence, charity, kindliness, self-lessness; kindness; gift, gratuity, lagniappe; tribute; extravagance, improvidence, lavishness, prodigality, wastefulness; spendthrift; dissipating, squandering

near ant conserving, economizing, economy, frugality, husbandry, providence, scrimping, skimping, thrift; conservation, saving; husbanding, managing; scraping; cutting back

ant cheapness, closeness, meanness, miserliness, parsimony, penuriousness, pinching, selfishness, stinginess, tightness, ungenerosity

liberally *adv* in a generous manner — see WELL 2

liberate *vb* 1 to release (as from slavery or confinement) — see FREE 1
2 to set free from entanglement or difficulty — see EXTRICATE

liberation *n* the act of setting free from slavery ⟨The *liberation* of enslaved people was one of the key results of the Civil War.⟩
syn emancipation, enfranchisement, freeing, manumission
rel deliverance, redemption, salvation; autonomy, freedom, independence, liberty, self-government, sovereignty (*also* sovranty)
near ant bondage, serfdom, servitude, yoke; captivity, imprisonment, incarceration, internment; conquest, subjugation
ant enslavement

libertine *adj* having or showing lowered moral character or standards — see CORRUPT

libertine *n* a person who has sunk below the normal moral standard — see DEGENERATE

liberty *n* 1 the power, right, or opportunity to choose — see CHOICE 1
2 the state of being free from the control or power of another — see FREEDOM 1

library *n* 1 a place where books, periodicals, and records are kept for use but not for sale ⟨I went to the *library* to do some research for my report.⟩
syn archive
2 an organized group of objects acquired and maintained for study, exhibition, or personal pleasure — see COLLECTION 1

license *also* **licence** *vb* to give official or legal power to — see AUTHORIZE 1

license *or* **licence** *n* 1 the approval by someone in authority for the doing of something — see PERMISSION
2 the granting of power to perform various acts or duties — see COMMISSION 1
3 the right to act or move freely — see FREEDOM 2

licentious *adj* having a strong sexual desire — see LUSTFUL

licentiousness *n* immoral conduct or practices harmful or offensive to society — see VICE 1

lick *n* 1 a hard strike with a part of the body or an instrument — see ¹BLOW
2 a very small amount — see PARTICLE 1
3 the smallest amount or part imaginable — see JOT

lick *vb* 1 to strike repeatedly — see BEAT 1
2 to achieve a victory over — see BEAT 2

licking *n* failure to win a contest — see DEFEAT 1

lid *n* 1 a piece placed over an open container to hold in, protect, or conceal its contents — see COVER 1
2 *slang* a covering for the head usually having a shaped crown — see HAT

lie *n* a statement known by its maker to be untrue and made in order to deceive ⟨He wanted to deny the accusation, but he couldn't tell a *lie*.⟩
syn fable, fabrication, fairy tale, falsehood, falsity, fib, mendacity, prevarication, story, tale, untruth, whopper
rel distortion, exaggeration, half-truth; ambiguity, equivocation; defamation, libel, slander; perjury; bluff, fiction, pose, pretense (*or* pretence); fallacy, misconception, myth; falsification, misinformation, misreport, misrepresentation, misstatement; deceit, deceitfulness, dishonesty, duplicity, fraudulence
near ant fact, truism, verity; honesty, truthfulness, veracity; authentication, confirmation, substantiation, validation, verification
ant truth

¹**lie** *vb* to make a statement one knows to be untrue ⟨Would I *lie* to you about that?⟩
syn fabricate, fib, prevaricate
rel perjure; equivocate, fudge, palter; beguile, cozen, deceive, delude, dupe, fool, gull, hoax, hoodwink, kid, take in, trick; defame, libel, slander, traduce; falsify, misreport, misrepresent, misstate; distort, garble; dissemble, dissimulate; misguide, misinform, mislead
near ant assert, swear, testify; authenticate, confirm, substantiate, validate, verify

²**lie** *vb* 1 to be positioned along a certain course or in a certain direction — see RUN 3
2 to occupy a place or location — see STAND 1
3 to remain out of sight — see ¹HIDE 3

lie detector *n* an instrument for detecting physical signs of the tension that goes with lying ⟨hooked the suspect up to a *lie detector* before interrogating him⟩
syn polygraph

life *n* 1 a history of a person's life — see BIOGRAPHY
2 a member of the human race — see HUMAN
3 active strength of body or mind — see VIGOR 1
4 the period during which something exists, lasts, or is in progress — see DURATION 1
5 the way people live at a particular time and place — see CIVILIZATION 1

lifeless *adj* no longer living — see DEAD 1

lifelessness *n* the state of being dead — see DEATH 2

lifelike *adj* closely resembling the object imitated — see NATURAL 2

life span *n* the period during which something exists, lasts, or is in progress — see DURATION 1

lifestyle *n* the way people live at a particular time and place — see CIVILIZATION 1

lifetime *n* the period during which some-

---

thing exists, lasts, or is in progress — see DURATION 1

lift *n* 1 an act or instance of helping — see HELP 1

2 a means of getting to a destination in a vehicle driven by another — see RIDE

lift *vb* 1 to move from a lower to a higher place or position — see RAISE 1

2 to move or extend upward — see ASCEND

3 to take (something) without right and with an intent to keep — see STEAL 1

lifted *adj* being positioned above a surface — see ELEVATED 1

ligature *n* 1 something that physically prevents free movement — see BOND 1

2 a uniting or binding force or influence — see BOND 2

light *n* 1 the steady giving off of the form of radiation that makes vision possible 〈He read poetry to her by the *light* of the moon.〉
syn blaze, flare, fluorescence, glare, gleam, glow, illumination, incandescence, luminescence, radiance, shine
rel flash, glimmer, glint, glitter, scintillation, shimmer, sparkle, twinkle; daylight, moonlight, sunlight, sunshine; afterglow, aurora, beam, ray, shaft, streak, stream, sunbeam; glisten, gloss, luster (*or* lustre), polish, reflection, sheen
near ant blackness, dark, darkness, dimness, dusk, duskiness, gloom, night, shadow
2 something that provides illumination 〈Please turn off the *light* when you go to bed.〉
syn beacon, lamp
rel arc lamp (*also* arc light), candelabra, candelabrum, candle, chandelier, flare, flash, flashlight, floodlight, fluorescent lamp, gaslight, headlight, incandescent lamp, klieg light (*or* kleig light), lantern, light bulb, lighting, sconce, streetlight, sun lamp
3 a person who is widely known and usually much talked about — see CELEBRITY 1
4 the first appearance of light in the morning or the time of its appearance — see DAWN 1

¹**light** *adj* 1 having little weight 〈The suitcase was as *light* as a feather after all the clothes were removed.〉
syn feathery, lightweight, underweight, weightless
rel bantam, diminutive, little, minute, puny, small, smallish, tiny, undersized (*also* undersize), wee; flimsy, fragile, insubstantial; petite, slender, slight, slim, thin
near ant big, considerable, extensive, goodly, great, handsome, huge, hulking, jumbo, king-size (*or* king-sized), large, largish, massive, overscale (*or* overscaled), oversize (*or* oversized), sizable (*or* sizeable), substantial, super, voluminous, whacking; bulky, cumbersome, unwieldy
ant heavy, hefty, leaden, overweight, ponderous, weighty
2 involving minimal difficulty or effort — see EASY 1
3 less plentiful than what is normal, necessary, or desirable — see MEAGER
4 moving easily — see GRACEFUL 1
5 not harsh or stern especially in nature or effect — see GENTLE 1
6 resembling air in lightness — see AIRY 1

²**light** *adj* 1 filled with much light — see BRIGHT 2
2 lacking intensity of color — see PALE 1
3 of light complexion — see FAIR 4

¹**light** *vb* 1 to set (something) on fire — see BURN 2
2 to supply with light — see ILLUMINATE 1

²**light** *vb* 1 to come to rest after descending from the air — see ALIGHT 1
2 to come down from something (as a vehicle) — see ALIGHT 2

light (on *or* **upon)** *vb* to come upon unexpectedly or by chance — see HAPPEN (ON *or* UPON)

¹**lighten** *vb* to become glad or hopeful — see CHEER (UP) 1

²**lighten** *vb* to supply with light — see ILLUMINATE 1

light–footed *also* **light–foot** *adj* moving easily — see GRACEFUL 1

light–headed *adj* 1 having a feeling of being whirled about and in danger of falling down — see DIZZY 1
2 lacking in seriousness or maturity — see GIDDY 1

light–headedness *n* a lack of seriousness often at an improper time — see FRIVOLITY

lighthearted *adj* having or showing freedom from worries or troubles — see CAREFREE

lightheartedness *n* carefree freedom from constraint — see ABANDON

lighting out *n* the act of leaving a place — see DEPARTURE 1

lightly *adv* without difficulty — see EASILY 1

¹**lightness** *n* 1 the state or quality of having little weight 〈The first thing I noticed about the little bird was its *lightness*; I could hardly tell I was holding it in my hand.〉
syn slightness, weightlessness
rel airiness, delicacy, ethereality, etherealness; flimsiness, fluffiness, insubstantiality
near ant solidity, solidness, substantiality
ant heaviness, heftiness, massiveness, ponderousness, weightiness
2 a lack of seriousness often at an improper time — see FRIVOLITY

²**lightness** *n* the quality or state of having or giving off light — see BRILLIANCE 1

lightning *adj* moving, proceeding, or acting with great speed — see FAST 1

¹**lightsome** *adj* filled with much light — see BRIGHT 2

²**lightsome** *adj* 1 having or showing a good mood or disposition — see CHEERFUL 1
2 having or showing freedom from worries or troubles — see CAREFREE
3 moving easily — see GRACEFUL 1

lightweight *adj* having little weight — see ¹LIGHT 1

lightweight *n* a person of no importance or influence — see NOBODY

¹**like** *n* 1 a number of persons or things that are grouped together because they have something in common — see SORT 1
2 one that is equal to another in status, achievement, or value — see EQUAL

²**like** *n* positive regard for something — see LIKING

like *adj* having qualities in common — see ALIKE

like *adv* to some degree or extent — see FAIRLY 1

like *conj* the way it would be or one would do if — see AS IF

like *vb* **1** to wish to have ⟨I'd *like* another slice of pizza, please.⟩

syn care (for), want

rel adore, delight (in), dig, enjoy, fancy, groove (on), love, relish, revel (in), welcome; covet, crave, desire, die (for), hanker (for *or* after), wish (for), yearn (for)

phrases feel like

2 to show partiality toward — see PREFER 1

3 to take pleasure in — see ENJOY 1

4 to see fit — see CHOOSE 2

likelihood *n* the quality or state of being likely to occur — see PROBABILITY 1

likely *adj* **1** having a high chance of occurring ⟨It's *likely* we'll see them at the party.⟩

syn probable

rel conceivable, earthly, imaginable, possible, potential, supposable; apt, bound, certain, doubtless, imminent, inescapable, inevitable, liable, necessary, sure, unavoidable

near ant impossible, inconceivable, unimaginable

ant doubtful, dubious, improbable, questionable, unlikely

2 having qualities which inspire hope — see HOPEFUL 1

3 worthy of being accepted as true or reasonable — see BELIEVABLE

likely *adv* by reasonable assumption — see PROBABLY

liken *vb* **1** to describe as similar — see COMPARE 1

2 to regard or represent as equal or comparable — see EQUATE 1

likeness *n* **1** a two-dimensional design intended to look like a person or thing — see PICTURE 1

2 something or someone that strongly resembles another — see IMAGE 1

3 the quality or state of having many qualities in common — see SIMILARITY 1

likewise *adv* **1** in addition to what has been said — see MORE 1

2 in like manner — see ALSO 1

liking *n* positive regard for something ⟨I have a *liking* for dark chocolate.⟩

syn appetite, fancy, favor, fondness, like, love, love affair, partiality, preference, relish, shine, taste, use

rel craving, desire, hankering, longing, thirst, yen; enthusiasm, interest, passion; bias, prejudice; bent, inclination, leaning, propensity, tendency; tooth; palate; weakness

near ant apathy, disinclination; indifference, unconcern

ant aversion, disfavor, disgust, dislike, distaste, hatred, loathing

lily-livered *adj* having or showing a shameful lack of courage — see COWARDLY

limb *n* a major outgrowth from the main stem of a woody plant — see BRANCH 1

limber *adj* able to bend easily without breaking — see WILLOWY

limit *n* **1** a real or imaginary point beyond

which a person or thing cannot go ⟨There was no *limit* to the number of challenges they faced.⟩

syn bound, boundary, cap, ceiling, confines, end, extent, limitation, line, termination

rel extremity, terminus; border, brim, edge, margin, rim, verge; outside; bar, barrier, fence, hedge, restraint, stop, wall

2 the most extreme or advanced point — see HEIGHT 2

limit *vb* **1** to set bounds or an upper limit for ⟨You should *limit* the note to a few words.⟩

syn cap, circumscribe, confine, restrict

rel bar, block, hamper, hinder, impede, obstruct; constrict, contract, lessen, narrow, pinch, squeeze, quell, repress, suppress; number; modify, qualify

near ant broaden, expand, widen; overextend, overreach

ant exceed

2 to mark the limits of ⟨Adjectives *limit* the meanings of nouns.⟩

syn bound, circumscribe, define, delimit, demarcate, terminate

rel control, determine, govern; delineate, describe

limitation *n* **1** a real or imaginary point beyond which a person or thing cannot go — see LIMIT 1

2 something that limits one's freedom of action or choice — see RESTRICTION 1

3 the act or practice of keeping something (as an activity) within certain boundaries — see RESTRICTION 2

limited *adj* having distinct or certain limits ⟨To avoid overcrowding, the number of tickets to the outdoor concerts is *limited*.⟩

syn bounded, circumscribed, defined, definite, determinate, finite, measured, narrow, restricted

rel modified, qualified; detailed, exact, precise, specific; constricted, moderate, modest; minute, puny, small, tiny; determined, fixed, settled

near ant bottomless, countless, incalculable, inexhaustible, innumerable, unfathomable; unqualified, unreserved; general, indeterminate, nebulous, vague; enlarged, escalated, expanded; copious, plenitudinous, plentiful

ant boundless, dimensionless, endless, illimitable, immeasurable, indefinite, infinite, limitless, measureless, unbounded, undefined, unlimited, unmeasured

2 having a limit — see FINITE 1

limitless *adj* being or seeming to be without limits — see INFINITE

limp *adj* **1** not stiff in structure ⟨His broken arm was *limp* as he held it against his side.⟩

syn droopy, flaccid, floppy, lank, yielding

rel flabby, mushy, semisoft, soft, squashy, squishy; delicate, flimsy, insubstantial; elastic, flexible, lax, loose, pliant, relaxed, resilient, springy, stretchy; supple

near ant firm, hard, indurated, solid, sound, strong; brittle, crisp; compact, dense, substantial

ant inflexible, resilient, rigid, stiff, sturdy, tense

2 depleted in strength, energy, or freshness — see WEARY 1

---

syn synonym(s)   **rel** related words
ant antonym(s)   **near ant** near antonym(s)

3 lacking bodily energy or motivation — see LISTLESS

limp *vb* **1** to walk while favoring one leg ⟨She *limped* all day after stubbing her toe on the lawn sprinkler.⟩

syn halt, hobble

rel hitch; blunder, falter, flounder, lurch, shamble, shuffle, stagger, stumble, teeter, totter, waver, wobble (*also* wabble); dodder

near ant breeze, glide, sail

ant stride

2 to proceed or act clumsily or ineffectually — see FLOUNDER 1

3 to move slowly — see CRAWL 2

limpid *adj* **1** easily seen through — see CLEAR 1

2 free from emotional or mental agitation — see CALM 2

limpidity *n* the state or quality of being easily seen through — see CLARITY 1

limpidness *n* the state or quality of being easily seen through — see CLARITY 1

line *n* **1** a series of persons or things arranged one behind another ⟨The *line* for tickets stretched around the block.⟩

syn column, cue, file, queue, range, string, train

rel echelon, rank, row; chain, progression, sequence, succession; array

2 a way of acting or proceeding — see COURSE 1

3 the activity by which one regularly makes a living — see OCCUPATION

4 a region of activity, knowledge, or influence — see FIELD 2

5 a real or imaginary point beyond which a person or thing cannot go — see LIMIT 1

6 a hollow cylinder for carrying a substance (as a liquid or gas) — see PIPE 1

7 a length of braided, flexible material that is used for tying or connecting things — see CORD 1

8 a group of vehicles traveling together or under one management — see FLEET 1

9 the direction along which something or someone moves — see PATH 1

10 a group of persons who come from the same ancestor — see FAMILY 1

11 the line of ancestors from whom a person is descended — see ANCESTRY

lineage *n* **1** the line of ancestors from whom a person is descended — see ANCESTRY

2 a group of persons who come from the same ancestor — see FAMILY 1

linear *adj* free from irregularities or digressions in course — see STRAIGHT 1

linger *vb* to move or act slowly — see DELAY 1

lingerer *n* someone who moves slowly or more slowly than others — see SLOWPOKE

lingo *n* **1** the stock of words, pronunciation, and grammar used by a people as their basic means of communication — see LANGUAGE 1

2 the special terms or expressions of a particular group or field — see TERMINOLOGY

linguistic *also* **linguistical** *adj* of or relating to words or language — see VERBAL 1

link *n* **1** a rod-shaped portion of seasoned ground meat in a casing — see SAUSAGE

2 a uniting or binding force or influence — see BOND 2

link *vb* **1** to put or bring together so as to form a new and longer whole — see CONNECT 1

2 to think of (something) in combination — see ASSOCIATE 2

link (up) *vb* to come together to form a single unit — see UNITE 1

linkage *n* the fact or state of having something in common — see CONNECTION 1

linking *n* the act or an instance of joining two or more things into one — see UNION 1

linkup *n* the state of having shared interests or efforts (as in social or business matters) — see ASSOCIATION 1

lint *n* a soft airy substance or covering — see FUZZ

lionhearted *adj* feeling or displaying no fear by temperament — see BRAVE 1

liquefy *also* **liquify** *vb* to go from a solid to a liquid state ⟨The steel *liquefied* in the intense heat of the forge.⟩

syn deliquesce, flux, fuse, melt, run, thaw

rel dissolve, render; soften, thin

near ant clot, coagulate, congeal, gel, jell, jelly, thicken

ant harden, set, solidify

liquid *adj* **1** capable of moving like a liquid — see FLUID 1

2 easily seen through — see CLEAR 1

liquidate *vb* **1** to destroy all traces of — see ANNIHILATE 1

2 to put to death deliberately — see MURDER 1

3 to give what is owed for — see PAY 2

liquor *n* a distilled beverage that can make a person drunk — see ALCOHOL

lissome *also* **lissom** *adj* **1** moving easily — see GRACEFUL 1

2 able to bend easily without breaking — see WILLOWY

¹**list** *n* a record of a series of items (as names or titles) usually arranged according to some system ⟨We put eggs, sour cream, tomatoes, roast beef, and cheddar cheese on the shopping *list*.⟩

syn canon, catalog (*or* catalogue), checklist, listing, menu, register, registry, roll, roster, schedule, table

rel agenda, bibliography, compilation, directory, docket, enumeration, glossary, index, inventory, manifest, payroll; calendar, timetable

²**list** *n* the act of positioning or an instance of being positioned at an angle — see TILT

³**list** *n* a long narrow piece of material — see STRIP 1

¹**list** *vb* **1** to make a list of ⟨The coach *listed* the people on the team.⟩

syn enumerate, inventory, itemize, numerate

rel count, mark, number; check (off), tick (off)

2 to put (someone or something) on a list ⟨Her number isn't *listed* in the phone book.⟩

syn catalog (*or* catalogue), enroll (*also* enrol), enter, index, inscribe, put down, record, register, schedule, slate

rel book, card, file, note; classify, compile, tabulate, tally; reschedule

near ant delete

3 to add (a person) to a list or roll as a participant or member — see ENROLL 1

4 to specify one after another — see ENUMERATE 1

²list *vb* to set or cause to be at an angle — see LEAN 1

listen *vb* to pay attention especially through the act of hearing ⟨Would you *listen* to what I have to say?⟩

syn attend, hark, hear, hearken, heed, mind

phrases prick up one's ears

near ant discount, disregard

ant ignore, tune out

listen (to) *vb* to take notice of and be guided by — see HEED 1

listen (in on) *vb* to listen to (another in private conversation) — see EAVESDROP (ON)

listing *adj* **1** inclined or twisted to one side — see AWRY

2 running in a slanting direction — see DIAGONAL

listing *n* a record of a series of items (as names or titles) usually arranged according to some system — see ¹LIST

listless *adj* lacking bodily energy or motivation ⟨When I had the flu, I felt *listless* and worn-out.⟩

syn enervated, lackadaisical, languid, languishing, languorous, limp, spiritless

rel indolent, lazy, slothful; dull, lethargic, logy (*also* loggy), sleepy, sluggish, torpid; exhausted, tired, weary; feeble, frail, weak; apathetic, impassive, indifferent, phlegmatic, stolid; inactive, inert

near ant active, dynamic, industrious; avid, eager, enthusiastic, keen, lively, vivacious; cheerful, chipper, perky, up; agog, alert, awake, open-eyed, sleepless, vigilant, watchful, wide-awake

ant ambitious, animated, energetic, enterprising, motivated

listlessness *n* **1** the state of being bored — see BOREDOM

2 the quality or state of lacking physical strength or vigor — see WEAKNESS 1

literal *adj* restricted to or based on fact — see FACTUAL 1

literary *adj* suggestive of the vocabulary used in books — see BOOKISH

literate *adj* having or displaying advanced knowledge or education — see EDUCATED 1

lithe *adj* **1** able to bend easily without breaking — see WILLOWY

2 moving easily — see GRACEFUL 1

3 having a noticeably small amount of body fat — see THIN 1

lithesome *adj* **1** able to bend easily without breaking — see WILLOWY

2 moving easily — see GRACEFUL 1

litter *n* **1** an unorganized collection or mixture of various things — see MISCELLANY 1

2 discarded or useless material — see GARBAGE

littered *adj* lacking in order, neatness, and often cleanliness — see MESSY

little *adj* **1** having relatively little height — see SHORT 1

2 lacking importance — see UNIMPORTANT

3 not broad or open in views or opinions — see NARROW 2

4 not lasting for a considerable time — see SHORT 2

5 of a size that is less than average — see SMALL 1

little *adv* **1** in a very small quantity or degree ⟨We had *little* more than we needed to survive in the wilderness.⟩

syn negligibly, nominally, slightly

rel meagerly, scantily; barely, hardly, just, marginally, minimally, scarcely

phrases a bit, a trifle

near ant completely, entirely, purely, thoroughly, totally, utterly; exceptionally; appreciably, discernibly, noticeably, palpably; abundantly, plentifully; generously, handsomely, liberally; grandly, hugely, monstrously

ant awfully, beastly, considerably, deadly, especially, exceedingly (*also* exceeding), extensively, extra, extremely, far, frightfully, full, greatly, heavily, highly, mightily, mighty, mortally, most, much, particularly, rattling, real, right, significantly, so, substantially, super, terribly, too, very, whacking

2 not often — see SELDOM

little *n* a very small amount — see PARTICLE 1

little by little *adv* by small steps or amounts — see GRADUALLY

littleness *n* the quality or state of being little in size — see SMALLNESS

littlest *adj* being the least in amount, number, or size possible — see MINIMAL

livable *also* **liveable** *adj* suitable for living in ⟨After we added some furniture and painted the walls, the apartment was *livable*.⟩

syn habitable, inhabitable

rel comfortable, cozy, homelike, homey (*also* homy), intimate, snug; acceptable, bearable, endurable, sufferable, supportable, sustainable, tolerable

near ant uncomfortable; humble; insupportable, intolerable, unacceptable, unbearable, unendurable

ant uninhabitable, unlivable

live *adj* **1** being in effective operation — see ACTIVE 1

2 having or showing life — see ALIVE 1

live *vb* **1** to have a home ⟨He *lives* next door to the hospital.⟩

syn abide, dwell, reside

rel lodge, settle, stay; frequent, haunt, visit; cohabit, inhabit, occupy; people; lease, rent, sublet, tenant

2 to have life — see BE 1

liveliness *n* the quality or state of having abundant or intense activity — see VITALITY 1

lively *adv* in a quick and spirited manner — see GAILY 2

lively *adj* **1** having much high-spirited energy and movement ⟨The *lively* puppy was racing around the dining room floor chasing after people's shoelaces.⟩

syn active, airy, animate, animated, bouncing, brisk, energetic, frisky, jaunty, jazzy, mettlesome, peppy, perky, pert, racy, snappy, spanking, sparky, spirited, sprightly, springy, vital, vivacious, zippy

rel dapper, dashing, spiffy; agog, alert, awake, open-eyed, up, wide-awake; agile, nimble, spry; bright, buoyant, cheerful, chipper, chirpy, effervescent, sparkly, upbeat; eager, enthusiastic, keen; frolicsome, impish, pixieish, playful; boisterous, bubbly, ebullient, exuberant, high-spirited

phrases on the go

near ant indolent, lazy, unambitious; inert, lethargic, sleepy, sluggish, tired, torpid, weary; apathetic, impassive, phlegmatic, stolid; boring, dull, irksome, tedious

ant dead, inactive, lackadaisical, languid, languishing, languorous, leaden, lifeless, limp, listless, spiritless, vapid

2 marked by much life, movement, or activity — see ALIVE 2

liven (up) *vb* to give life, vigor, or spirit to — see ANIMATE

livery *n* the distinctive clothing worn by members of a particular group — see UNIFORM

live wire *n* an ambitious person who eagerly goes after what is desired — see GO-GETTER

livid *adj* **1** feeling or showing anger — see ANGRY

2 lacking a healthy skin color — see PALE 2

living *adj* **1** being in effective operation — see ACTIVE 1

2 having being at the present time — see EXTANT 1

3 having or showing life — see ALIVE 1

4 closely resembling the object imitated — see NATURAL 2

load *n* **1** a mass or quantity of something taken up and carried, conveyed, or transported ⟨hoisted a *load* of grain on the truck going to Florida⟩

syn burden, cargo, draft, freight, haul, lading, loading, payload, weight

rel consignment; boatload, shipload, trainload, truckload, wagonload; ballast, deadweight; overload, surcharge; bale, bundle, pack, package, packet, parcel, shipment; manifest; body, bulk, mass

2 loads *pl* a considerable amount — see LOT 2

load *vb* **1** to place a weight or burden on ⟨students complaining that their teachers were *loading* them with work⟩

syn burden, encumber, freight, lade, lumber, saddle, weight

rel clog, clutter, fill, pack; heap, mound, pile, stack; press, weigh; strain, tax; overburden, overload, overtax, surcharge; hamper, handicap; afflict, oppress

near ant alleviate, ease, lighten, relieve

ant disburden, discharge, disencumber, unburden, unlade, unload

2 to put into (something) as much as can be held or contained — see FILL 1

loaded *adj* **1** containing or seeming to contain the greatest quantity or number possible — see FULL 1

2 having goods, property, or money in abundance — see RICH 1

loading *n* a mass or quantity of something taken up and carried, conveyed, or transported — see LOAD 1

loaf *vb* to spend time doing nothing — see IDLE

loafer *n* a lazy person — see LAZYBONES

loamy *adj* consisting or suggestive of earth — see EARTHY 1

loan *vb* to give to another for temporary use with the understanding that it or a like thing will be returned — see LEND

loath *also* **loth** *or* **lothe** *adj* slow to begin or proceed with a course of action because of doubts or uncertainty — see HESITANT

loathe *vb* to dislike strongly — see HATE

loathing *n* **1** a dislike so strong as to cause stomach upset or queasiness — see DISGUST

2 a very strong dislike — see HATE 1

loathsome *adj* causing intense displeasure, disgust, or resentment — see OFFENSIVE 1

lob *vb* to send through the air especially with a quick forward motion of the arm — see THROW 1

lobby *n* **1** a centrally located room in a building that serves as a gathering or waiting area or as a passageway into the interior — see FOYER 1

2 the entrance room of a building — see HALL 1

local *n* **1** a local unit of an organization — see CHAPTER 1

2 a usually longtime resident of a locality — see NATIVE

locale *n* **1** the area or space occupied by or intended for something — see PLACE 1

2 the place and time in which the action for a portion of a dramatic work (as a movie) is set — see SCENE 1

locality *n* the area or space occupied by or intended for something — see PLACE 1

locate *vb* to come upon after searching, study, or effort — see FIND 1

location *n* the area or space occupied by or intended for something — see PLACE 1

loch *n*, *Scottish* a part of a body of water that extends beyond the general shoreline — see GULF 1

lock (up) *vb* to put in or as if in prison — see IMPRISON

locker *n* **1** a covered rectangular container for storing or transporting things — see CHEST

2 a storage case typically having doors and shelves — see CABINET

lockup *n* a place of confinement for persons held in lawful custody — see JAIL

locus *n* **1** a thing or place that is of greatest importance to an activity or interest — see CENTER 1

2 the area or space occupied by or intended for something — see PLACE 1

locution *n* a distinctive way of putting ideas into words — see STYLE 1

lodestone *also* **loadstone** *n* something that attracts interest — see MAGNET

lodge *n* **1** a place that provides rooms and usually a public dining room for overnight guests — see HOTEL

2 an often small house for recreational or seasonal use — see COTTAGE

3 the meeting place of an organization — see CLUB 2

4 the shelter or resting place of a wild animal — see DEN 1

lodge *vb* **1** to provide with living quarters or shelter — see HOUSE 1

2 to establish or place comfortably or snugly — see ENSCONCE 1

3 to set solidly in or as if in surrounding matter — see ENTRENCH

lodged *adj* firmly positioned in place and difficult to dislodge — see TIGHT 2

lodger *n* one who rents a room or apartment in another's house — see TENANT 1

lodging *n* 1 the place where one lives — see HOME 1

2 **lodgings** *pl* a room or set of rooms in a private house or a block used as a separate dwelling place — see APARTMENT 1

3 a place to sleep and related amenities for the temporary use of a tourist or traveler — see ACCOMMODATION 1

loft *vb* to send through the air especially with a quick forward motion of the arm — see THROW 1

loftiest *adj* being at a point or level higher than all others — see TOP 1

loftiness *n* an exaggerated sense of one's importance that shows itself in the making of excessive or unjustified claims — see ARROGANCE

lofty *adj* 1 extending to a great distance upward — see HIGH 1

2 having a feeling of superiority that shows itself in an overbearing attitude — see ARROGANT

3 having or displaying feelings of scorn for what is regarded as beneath oneself — see PROUD 1

4 having, characterized by, or arising from a dignified and generous nature — see NOBLE 2

5 very dignified in form, tone, or style — see ELEVATED 2

log *vb* 1 to make a written note of — see RECORD 1

2 to obtain (as a goal) through effort — see ACHIEVE 1

logger *n* a person whose job is to cut down trees — see LUMBERJACK

logic *n* the thought processes that have been established as leading to valid solutions to problems ⟨I tried to use *logic* to figure out the solution to the puzzle.⟩
syn reason, reasoning, sense
rel cogency, coherence, logicality, logicalness, rationality, rationalness; persuasiveness; syllogism; analysis, dissection; deduction, induction; disputation
near ant illogic, incoherence; absurdity, brainlessness, insanity, irrationality, nonsensicalness, preposterousness, senselessness

logical *adj* 1 according to the rules of logic ⟨The lawyer won the case with a *logical* argument about the motives of the suspect.⟩
syn analytic (*or* analytical), coherent, consequent, good, rational, reasonable, sensible, sound, valid, well-founded
rel cognitive, empirical (*also* empiric); defendable, defensible, justifiable, maintainable, supportable, sustainable, tenable
near ant fallacious, misleading, sophistic (*or* sophistical), specious; unarticulated; unscientific; absurd, cockeyed, daffy, fatuous, half-baked, half-witted, harebrained, nonsensical, preposterous, simpleminded, stupid, weak-minded, witless; senseless, thoughtless; unconvincing
ant illegitimate, illogical, incoherent, in-

consequential, invalid, irrational, unreasonable, unsound, weak

2 based on sound reasoning or information — see GOOD 1

logo *n* a device, design, or figure used as an identifying mark — see EMBLEM

logy *also* **loggy** *adj* depleted in strength, energy, or freshness — see WEARY 1

loiter *vb* to move or act slowly — see DELAY 1

loiterer *n* someone who moves slowly or more slowly than others — see SLOWPOKE

loll *vb* 1 to be limp from lack of water or vigor — see DROOP 1

2 to refrain from labor or exertion — see REST 1

3 to spend time doing nothing — see IDLE

lone *adj* 1 being the one or ones of a class with no other members — see ONLY 2

2 not being in the company of others — see ALONE 1

lonely *adj* 1 not being in the company of others — see ALONE 1

2 sad from lack of companionship or separation from others — see LONESOME 1

3 causing or marked by an atmosphere lacking in cheer — see GLOOMY 1

lonesome *adj* 1 sad from lack of companionship or separation from others ⟨a *lonesome* kitten left at the pound⟩
syn desolate, forlorn, lonely, lorn
rel friendless; abandoned, deserted, forgotten, forsaken, neglected, rejected; alone, lone, solitary, solo, unaccompanied; only, sole
near ant accompanied, attended, escorted

2 not being in the company of others — see ALONE 1

3 causing or marked by an atmosphere lacking in cheer — see GLOOMY 1

lone wolf *n* a person who does not conform to generally accepted standards or customs — see NONCONFORMIST 1

long *adj* 1 of great extent from end to end ⟨Giraffes have *long* necks to help them reach leaves on tall trees.⟩
syn elongate (*or* elongated), extended, king-size (*or* king-sized), lengthy
rel extensive, far-reaching, longish, outstretched; oblong, rectangular; big, considerable, hefty, hulking, jumbo, large, largish, overscale (*or* overscaled), oversize (*or* oversized), sizable (*or* sizeable), substantial, super
near ant abbreviated, abridged, curtailed, diminished, shortened; bitty, diminutive, little, miniature, minute, puny, small, smallish, teeny, tiny, undersized (*also* undersize), wee
ant brief, curt, short, shortish

2 lasting for a considerable time ⟨If it's boring, even a movie with a running time of 90 minutes can seem *long*.⟩
syn extended, far, great, lengthy, long-lived, long-term
rel endless, everlasting, interminable, persistent; longish, overlong, prolonged, protracted; permanent; all-day, all-night; multiday, multiyear
near ant abrupt, sudden; abbreviated, condensed, curtailed, shortened; ephemeral, fleeting, momentary, transient, transitory; impermanent; short-range

---

syn synonym(s)　*rel* related words
ant antonym(s)　*near ant* near antonym(s)

ant brief, little, mini, short, shortish, short-lived, short-term

long *n* a long or seemingly long period of time — see AGE 2

long (for) *vb* to have an earnest wish to own or enjoy — see DESIRE 1

longhand *n* writing done by hand — see HANDWRITING 2

longing *n* a strong wish for something — see DESIRE 1

long-lived *adj* **1** being of advanced years and especially past middle age — see EL-DERLY

2 lasting for a considerable time — see LONG 2

longshoreman *n* one who loads and unloads ships at a port — see DOCKWORKER

long-suffering *adj* accepting pains or hardships calmly or without complaint — see PATIENT 1

long-suffering *n* the capacity to endure what is difficult or disagreeable without complaining — see PATIENCE

long-term *adj* lasting for a considerable time — see LONG 2

long-winded *adj* using or containing more words than necessary to express an idea — see WORDY 1

long-windedness *n* the use of too many words to express an idea — see VERBIAGE 1

look *n* **1** facial appearance regarded as an indication of mood or feeling ⟨You should have seen the *look* on your face when we yelled "Surprise!"⟩

syn cast, countenance, expression, face, visage

rel frown, grimace, lower (*also* lour), mouth, pout, scowl; grin, smile; air, appearance, aspect, bearing, demeanor, manner, mien, presence

2 an instance of looking especially briefly ⟨She gave the junk mail a quick *look* before throwing it in the wastebasket.⟩

syn cast, eye, gander, glance, glimpse, peek, peep, regard, sight, view

rel gape, gaze, glare, leer, ogle, stare

3 the outward form of someone or something especially as indicative of a quality — see APPEARANCE 1

4 looks *pl* the qualities in a person or thing that as a whole give pleasure to the senses — see BEAUTY 1

look *vb* **1** to give the impression of being — see SEEM

2 to make known (as an idea, emotion, or opinion) — see EXPRESS 1

3 to have in mind as a purpose or goal — see INTEND 1

look (at) *vb* to make note of (something) through the use of one's eyes — see SEE 1

look (into) *vb* to search through or into — see EXPLORE 1

look (toward) *vb* to stand or sit with the face or front toward — see FACE 1

looking glass *n* a smooth or polished surface that forms images by reflection — see MIRROR

lookout *n* **1** a high place or structure from which a wide view is possible ⟨We went up to the *lookout* on the top of the hill to watch the fireworks.⟩

syn observatory, outlook, overlook

rel aerie, crow's nest, tower, watchtower

2 all that can be seen from a certain point — see VIEW 1

3 a person or group that watches over someone or something — see GUARD 1

look up *vb* **1** to go in search of — see SEEK 1

2 to become glad or hopeful — see CHEER (UP) 1

loom *vb* to be about to happen ⟨He could tell that a storm was *looming* when the sky suddenly darkened.⟩

syn brew, impend

rel advance, approach, draw on, gather, near; hang, hover, lower (*also* lour), menace, overhang, threaten

near ant abate, decline, de-escalate, die down, diminish, disappear, dwindle, ebb, fade, fall, lessen, let up, lower, moderate, recede, relent, remit, shrink, subside, taper, taper off, vanish, wane; fall back, pass, recede, retreat, withdraw

looming *adj* giving signs of immediate occurrence — see IMMINENT 1

loop *n* a circular strip — see ¹RING 2

loose *adj* **1** not tightly fastened, tied, or stretched ⟨Secure your neckerchief with a *loose* knot.⟩

syn insecure, lax, loosened, relaxed, slack, slackened, unsecured

rel detached, free, unattached, unbound, undone, unfastened, untied; baggy, blousy, saggy

near ant constrained, restrained; attached, bound, fastened, tied; fast, firm, jammed, snug, stuck, wedged

ant taut, tense, tight

2 consisting of particles that do not stick together ⟨The car wheels slipped on the *loose* gravel in the driveway.⟩

syn incoherent, unconsolidated

rel nonadhesive, nonviscous; disconnected, disjointed, separate, unconnected; coarse, granular, rough

near ant connected, solid; compacted, compressed; adhesive, gelatinous, gluey, glutinous, gooey, gummy, sticky, viscid, viscous

ant coherent, compact, dense, packed

3 not bound by rigid standards — see EASYGOING 2

4 not bound, confined, or detained by force — see FREE 3

5 not precisely correct — see INEXACT 1

6 having or showing lowered moral character or standards — see CORRUPT

loose *vb* **1** to cause (a projectile) to be driven forward with force — see SHOOT 1

2 to find emotional release for — see TAKE OUT 1

3 to release (as from slavery or confinement) — see FREE 1

4 to set free (from a state of being held in check) — see RELEASE 1

loosen *vb* **1** to make less taut — see SLACKEN 1

2 to release (as from slavery or confinement) — see FREE 1

3 to set free (from a state of being held in check) — see RELEASE 1

loosen (up) *vb* to free from obstruction or difficulty — see EASE 1

loosened *adj* not tightly fastened, tied, or stretched — see LOOSE 1

loot *n* valuables stolen or taken by force

⟨The burglar was caught when he foolishly stopped to examine the *loot* from the robbery.⟩
syn booty, pillage, plunder, spoil, swag
rel prize; catch, haul, take, treasure; pilferage; windfall
loot *vb* to search through with the intent of committing robbery — see RANSACK 1
lop (off) *vb* to make (something) shorter or smaller with the use of a cutting instrument — see CLIP 1
lope *vb* to move with a light springing step — see SKIP 1
lopsided *adj* inclined or twisted to one side — see AWRY
loquacious *adj* fond of talking or conversation — see TALKATIVE
lord (it over) *vb* to assume or treat with an air of superiority — see CONDESCEND 2
lordliness *n* an exaggerated sense of one's importance that shows itself in the making of excessive or unjustified claims — see ARROGANCE
lordly *adj* 1 having a feeling of superiority that shows itself in an overbearing attitude — see ARROGANT
2 having or displaying feelings of scorn for what is regarded as beneath oneself — see PROUD 1
3 having, characterized by, or arising from a dignified and generous nature — see NOBLE 2
lore *n* 1 a body of facts learned by study or experience — see KNOWLEDGE 1
2 the body of customs, beliefs, stories, and sayings associated with a people, thing, or place — see FOLKLORE
lorn *adj* sad from lack of companionship or separation from others — see LONESOME 1
lose *vb* 1 to be unable to find or have at hand ⟨I always *lose* my keys.⟩
syn mislay, misplace
rel forget, miss, overlook, pass over
near ant enjoy, have, hold, keep, occupy, own, possess, retain; descry, detect, find, locate, run down, scare up, scout (up), track (down)
2 to fail to win, gain, or obtain ⟨If the team *loses* this game, they're out of the playoffs.⟩
syn drop
rel forfeit
near ant conquer, prevail (over), triumph (over)
ant nail (down), win
3 to undergo defeat ⟨She really hates to *lose* at anything.⟩
syn fall
rel falter; throw; forfeit; bomb, collapse, crack (up), fail, flop, flunk, fold, founder, miss, strike out, wash out
phrases take the count
near ant flourish, prosper, succeed, thrive
ant conquer, prevail, triumph, win
4 to get rid of as useless or unwanted — see DISCARD
5 to use up carelessly — see WASTE 1
loser *n* something that has failed — see FAILURE 3

loss *n* 1 the act or an instance of not having or being able to find ⟨He was upset over the *loss* of his wedding ring.⟩
syn mislaying, misplacement
rel deprivation, dispossession, privation; forfeit, forfeiture, penalty; sacrifice; bereavement; absence, lack, need, want
near ant control, hands, having, keeping, possession
ant gain
2 a person or thing harmed, lost, or destroyed — see CASUALTY 1
3 failure to win a contest — see DEFEAT 1
4 the amount by which something is lessened — see DECREASE
5 the state of being robbed of something normally enjoyed — see PRIVATION
6 the state or fact of being rendered nonexistent, physically unsound, or useless — see DESTRUCTION 1
lost *adj* no longer possessed ⟨We searched all over the house for the *lost* keys.⟩
syn gone, mislaid, misplaced, missing
rel absent, castaway; irrecoverable, irretrievable; forgotten, unknown
near ant cherished, loved, prized, protected, treasured, valued
ant owned, retained
lot *n* 1 a small piece of land that is developed or available for development ⟨The softball team often plays in the vacant *lot* down at the end of the street.⟩
syn parcel, plat, plot, property, tract
rel patch; lease; development; real estate
2 a considerable amount ⟨You'll need to do a *lot* of studying for the test.⟩ ⟨You sure bought a *lot* of clothing.⟩
syn abundance, barrel, boatload, bucket, bunch, bundle, bushel, chunk, deal, gobs, heap, loads, mass, mess, mountain, much, multiplicity, myriad, oodles, pack, passel, peck, pile, plenitude, plentitude, plenty, pot, profusion, quantity, raft, reams, scads, sight, spate, stack, store, volume, wad, wealth, yard
rel plague, rash; bonanza, embarrassment, excess, overabundance, overage, overkill, overmuch, oversupply, redundancy, superabundance, superfluity, surfeit, surplus; deluge, flood, overflow; army, bevy, cram, crowd, crush, drove, flock, herd, horde, host, legion, mob, multitude, press, score, sea, swarm, throng
phrases all kinds (of), quite a bit
near ant atom, crumb, dot, fleck, flyspeck, fragment, grain, granule, iota, jot, modicum, molecule, mote, nubbin, particle, ray, scrap, shred, tittle, whit; smattering
ant ace, bit, dab, driblet, glimmer, handful, hint, lick, little, mite, mouthful, nip, ounce, peanuts, pinch, pittance, scruple, shade, shadow, smidgen (*also* smidgeon *or* smidgin *or* smidge), speck, spot, sprinkle, sprinkling, strain, streak, tad, touch, trace
3 a small area of usually open land — see FIELD 1
4 a number of things considered as a unit — see GROUP 1
5 a state or end that seemingly has been decided beforehand — see FATE 1
6 a group of people sharing a common interest and relating together socially — see GANG 2

---

7 a usually small number of persons considered as a unit — see GROUP 2

lot *vb* **1** to give as a share or portion — see ALLOT

loud *adj* **1** marked by a high volume of sound ⟨*loud* music that could be heard all over the neighborhood⟩
syn blaring, blasting, booming, clamorous, clangorous, deafening, earsplitting, piercing, resounding, roaring, sonorous, stentorian, thunderous
rel brazen, dinning, discordant, noisy, obstreperous, raucous, rip-roaring, vociferous; grating, harsh, overloud, sharp, shrill, squealing, strident
near ant dead, quiet, silent, still, stilly, ultraquiet; calm, dreamy, peaceful, restful, serene, soothing, tranquil; hushed, muffled, muted, softened, toned (down)
ant gentle, low, soft

2 excessively showy — see GAUDY

lounge *n* a long upholstered piece of furniture designed for several sitters — see COUCH

lounge *vb* **1** to refrain from labor or exertion — see REST 1

2 to spend time doing nothing — see IDLE

louse *n* a person whose behavior is offensive to others — see JERK 1

louse up *vb* **1** to make a mistake — see ERR 1

2 to make or do (something) in a clumsy or unskillful way — see BOTCH

lousy *adj* **1** arousing or deserving of one's loathing and disgust — see CONTEMPTIBLE 1

2 falling short of a standard — see BAD 1

3 extremely unsatisfactory — see WRETCHED 1

4 of low quality — see CHEAP 2

5 possessing or covered with great numbers or amounts of something specified — see RIFE

lout *n* **1** a big clumsy often slow-witted person — see OAF 1

2 a person whose behavior is offensive to others — see JERK 1

loutish *adj* having or showing crudely insensitive or impolite manners — see CLOWNISH

lovable *also* **loveable** *adj* having qualities that tend to make one loved ⟨She was a *lovable* child, always helpful and kind.⟩
syn adorable, darling, dear, disarming, endearing, precious, sweet, winning, winsome
rel embraceable, kissable; beloved, cherished, favored, favorite, loved, treasured; attractive, beautiful, desirable, lovely; alluring, appealing, captivating, charming, enchanting, engaging, entrancing, fascinating, fetching; admirable, likable (*or* likeable), reputable, respectable; affable, agreeable, cheerful, cordial, friendly, genial, good-natured, good-tempered, gracious, kind, nice, pleasant; delightful, pleasing
near ant unloved; contemptible, disagreeable, distasteful, heinous, horrible, lousy, nasty, offensive, unlikable, unpleasant, wretched; frightful, grotesque, hideous, ill-favored, monstrous, repellent (*also* repellant); repugnant, repulsive; ugly, unattractive, unsightly, vile; appalling, awful, dreadful, foul, horrendous, horrid, nauseating, noisome, obnoxious, obscene, revolting, shocking, sickening
ant abhorrent, abominable, detestable, hateful, loathsome, odious, unlovable

love *n* **1** a feeling of strong or constant regard for and dedication to someone ⟨Her *love* for her children was truly selfless.⟩
syn affection, attachment, devotedness, devotion, fondness, passion
rel appetite, fancy, favor, like, liking, partiality, preference, relish, taste; craving, crush, desire, infatuation, longing, lust, yearning, zeal; appreciation, esteem, estimation, regard, respect; allegiance, faithfulness, fealty, fidelity, loyalty, steadfastness
near ant animosity, antagonism, antipathy, aversion, disfavor, dislike, enmity, hostility; abhorrence, disgust, repugnance, repulsion, revulsion
ant abomination, hate, hatred, loathing, rancor

2 a person with whom one is in love — see SWEETHEART

3 positive regard for something — see LIKING

4 a brief romantic relationship — see AFFAIR 1

love *vb* **1** to hold dear ⟨patriots who *loved* their country well enough to die for it⟩
syn appreciate, cherish, prize, treasure, value
rel delight (in), dig, enjoy, groove (on), like, relish, revel (in); admire, apprize, esteem, regard, respect, revere, reverence, venerate; enshrine, memorialize; adore, caress, dote (on), idolize, worship
phrases set store by (*or* set store on)
near ant abhor, abominate, despise, detest, execrate, hate, loathe; disdain, scorn, slight, sniff (at), snub; bad-mouth, belittle, cry down, decry, deprecate, depreciate, disparage, minimize, put down, write off
ant disvalue

2 to feel passion, devotion, or tenderness for ⟨a husband who *loves* his wife more than anything⟩
syn adore, cherish, worship
rel adulate, canonize, deify, idealize, idolize; revere, reverence, venerate; delight (in), dote (on)
phrases carry a torch for (*or* carry the torch for), fall for, lose one's heart (to)
near ant antagonize, displease; disapprove (of), disfavor, dislike; disgust, nauseate, repel, repulse, revolt, sicken, turn off
ant abhor, abominate, despise, detest, execrate, hate, loathe

3 to take pleasure in — see ENJOY 1

4 to touch or handle in a tender or loving manner — see FONDLE

love affair *n* **1** a brief romantic relationship — see AFFAIR 1

2 positive regard for something — see LIKING

loved *adj* granted special treatment or attention — see DARLING 1

loveliness *n* the qualities in a person or thing that as a whole give pleasure to the senses — see BEAUTY 1

lovely *adj* **1** of the very best kind — see EXCELLENT

2 very pleasing to look at — see BEAUTIFUL 1

lover *n* a person with a strong and habitual liking for something — see FAN

loving *adj* **1** feeling or showing love ⟨They were a *loving* family, supporting each other when times were bad.⟩

syn adoring, affectionate, devoted, fond, tender, tenderhearted

rel caring, compassionate, considerate, cordial, doting, forgiving, kind, understanding, warmhearted; ardent, fervent, impassioned, passionate, warm; enamored, infatuated, lovesick; mushy, romantic, sappy, sentimental; brotherly, fatherly, motherly, sisterly

near ant aloof, antisocial, cool, detached, distant, dry, frosty, indifferent, pitiless, remote, reserved, standoffish, unbending, uncaring, unfeeling; disaffected, unconcerned, uninvolved; cold, frigid, unfriendly; callous, cold-blooded, heartless, pitiless, ruthless, unromantic, unsentimental

ant unloving

2 taking, showing, or involving great care and effort — see PAINSTAKING

low *adj* **1** being near the equator ⟨We took a cruise to the *low* northern latitudes.⟩

syn equatorial, tropical

rel semitropical (*also* semitropic), subtropical (*also* subtropic)

near ant temperate

ant polar

2 belonging to or characteristic of an early level of skill or development — see PRIMITIVE 1

3 belonging to the class of people of low social or economic rank — see IGNOBLE 1

4 feeling unhappiness — see SAD 1

5 having a low musical pitch or range — see DEEP 2

6 having relatively little height — see SHORT 1

7 lacking bodily strength — see WEAK 1

8 lacking in refinement or good taste — see COARSE 2

9 not following or in accordance with standards of honor and decency — see IGNOBLE 2

10 not loud in pitch or volume — see SOFT 1

11 costing little — see CHEAP 1

12 of, relating to, or located at the bottom — see BOTTOM

13 not coming up to an expected measure or meeting a particular need — see SHORT 3

14 no longer living — see DEAD 1

lowbred *adj* lacking in refinement or good taste — see COARSE 2

lowbrow *adj* lacking in refinement or good taste — see COARSE 2

lowbrow *n* a person who is chiefly interested in material comfort and is hostile or indifferent to art and culture — see PHILISTINE

lowdown *n* information not generally available to the public — see DOPE 1

lower *adj* **1** having not so great importance or rank as another — see LESSER

2 situated lower down — see INFERIOR 1

¹**lower** *vb* **1** to cause to fall intentionally or unintentionally — see DROP 1

2 to go to a lower level especially abruptly — see DROP 2

3 to make smaller in amount, volume, or extent — see DECREASE 1

4 to grow less in scope or intensity especially gradually — see DECREASE 2

5 to reduce to a lower standing in one's own eyes or in others' eyes — see HUMBLE 1

6 to diminish the price or value of — see DEPRECIATE 1

²**lower** *also* **lour** *vb* **1** to take on a gloomy or forbidding look — see DARKEN 1

2 to look with anger or disapproval — see FROWN

lower *also* **lour** *n* a twisting of the facial features in disgust or disapproval — see GRIMACE

lower–class *adj* belonging to the class of people of low social or economic rank — see IGNOBLE 1

lowered *adj* directed down — see DOWNCAST 1

lowering *also* **louring** *adj* **1** covered over by clouds — see OVERCAST

2 harsh and threatening in manner or appearance — see GRIM 1

lowest *adj* being the least in amount, number, or size possible — see MINIMAL

low–grade *adj* of low quality — see CHEAP 2

lowliness *n* the absence of any feelings of being better than others — see HUMILITY

lowly *adj* **1** belonging to the class of people of low social or economic rank — see IGNOBLE 1

2 not having or showing any feelings of superiority, self-assertiveness, or showiness — see HUMBLE 1

lowly *adv* **1** in a manner showing no signs of pride or self-assertion ⟨*Lowly* bowing before his king, he accepted his knighthood.⟩

syn deferentially, humbly, meanly, meekly, modestly, sheepishly, submissively

rel obsequiously, servilely, subserviently; fearfully, timidly; bashfully, diffidently, self-deprecatingly, shyly, timorously; courteously, politely, respectfully

phrases cap in hand

near ant discourteously, disdainfully, disrespectfully, impertinently, rashly, recklessly, saucily; impolitely, impudently, rudely, ungraciously

ant arrogantly, audaciously, brashly, brazenly, contemptuously, haughtily, huffily, imperiously, loftily, pompously, presumptuously, pretentiously, pridefully, proudly, scornfully

low–lying *adj* having relatively little height — see SHORT 1

lowness *n* **1** the quality or state of lacking refinement or good taste — see VULGARITY 1

2 the quality or state of lacking physical strength or vigor — see WEAKNESS 1

low–pressure *adj* having a relaxed, casual manner — see EASYGOING 1

low–spirited *adj* feeling unhappiness — see SAD 1

loyal *adj* firm in one's allegiance to someone or something — see FAITHFUL 1

loyalist *n* a person who loves his or her

loyalty *n* adherence to something to which one is bound by a pledge or duty — see FIDELITY

lozenge *n* a small mass containing medicine to be taken orally — see PILL 1

lubber *n* a big clumsy often slow-witted person — see OAF 1

lubricate *vb* to coat (something) with a slippery substance in order to reduce friction ⟨It's not a good idea to use olive oil to *lubricate* the gears in an appliance.⟩
syn grease, oil, slick, wax
rel bathe, douse (*also* dowse), drench, soak, souse, wash, water, wet
near ant coarsen, rough, roughen; dehydrate, dry, parch, sear

lubricated *adj* having or being a surface so smooth as to greatly reduce traction — see SLICK 1

lucent *adj* 1 easily seen through — see CLEAR 1
2 giving off or reflecting much light — see BRIGHT 1

lucid *adj* 1 giving off or reflecting much light — see BRIGHT 1
2 having full use of one's mind and control over one's actions — see SANE
3 not subject to misinterpretation or more than one interpretation — see CLEAR 2

lucidity *n* clearness of expression — see SIMPLICITY 2

lucidness *n* clearness of expression — see SIMPLICITY 2

Lucifer *n* the supreme personification of evil often represented as the ruler of hell — see DEVIL 1

luck *n* 1 success that is partly the result of chance ⟨Some people have all the *luck*.⟩
syn fortunateness, fortune, luckiness
rel blessing, boon, godsend, hit, serendipity, strike, windfall; break, chance, opportunity; coup, stroke
near ant knock, misadventure, mishap; adversity, curse, debacle (*also* débâcle), sorrow, tragedy, trouble; calamity, cataclysm, catastrophe, disaster; defeat, failure; accident, casualty; disappointment, lapse, letdown, reversal, reverse, setback, slipup; destiny, doom, fate, lot, portion; hex, jinx
ant mischance, misfortune, unluckiness
2 the uncertain course of events — see CHANCE 1

luckiness *n* success that is partly the result of chance — see LUCK 1

luckless *adj* having, prone to, or marked by bad luck — see UNLUCKY 1

lucky *adj* 1 having good luck ⟨The *lucky* contestant finished the game show with $10,000.⟩
syn fortunate, happy
rel blessed (*also* blest), favored, gifted, privileged; fair, golden, promising; hot
near ant disadvantaged
ant hapless, ill-fated, ill-starred, luckless, star-crossed, unfortunate, unhappy, unlucky
2 coming or happening by good luck especially unexpectedly — see FORTUNATE 1

lucrative *adj* yielding a profit — see PROFITABLE 1

lucre *n* 1 something (as pieces of stamped metal or printed paper) customarily and legally used as a medium of exchange, a measure of value, or a means of payment — see MONEY
2 the amount of money left when expenses are subtracted from the total amount received — see PROFIT 1

ludicrous *adj* 1 causing or intended to cause laughter — see FUNNY 1
2 so foolish or pointless as to be worthy of scornful laughter — see RIDICULOUS 1

lug *n* a big clumsy often slow-witted person — see OAF 1

lug *vb* 1 to cause to follow by applying steady force on — see PULL 1
2 to support and take from one place to another — see CARRY 1

lugubrious *adj* 1 causing or marked by an atmosphere lacking in cheer — see GLOOMY 1
2 expressing or suggesting mourning — see MOURNFUL 1

lukewarm *adj* 1 having or giving off heat to a moderate degree — see WARM 1
2 showing little or no interest or enthusiasm — see TEPID 1

lukewarmness *n* the quality or state of being moderate in temperature — see WARMTH 1

lull *n* a momentary halt in an activity — see PAUSE 1

lull *vb* to free from distress or disturbance — see CALM 1

lulling *adj* tending to calm the emotions and relieve stress — see SOOTHING 1

lumber *n* tree logs as prepared for human use — see WOOD 1

lumber *vb* 1 to move heavily or clumsily ⟨The elephant *lumbered* through the jungle.⟩
syn barge, clump, flounder, lump, plod, pound, scuff, scuffle, shamble, shuffle, slog, slough, stamp, stomp, stumble, stump, tramp, tromp, trudge
rel drag, flop, haul; blunder, careen, dodder, lurch, reel, stagger, sway, teeter, totter, waddle, weave, wobble (*also* wabble)
near ant drift, float, hang, hover, poise, waft
ant breeze, coast, glide, slide, waltz, whisk
2 to proceed or act clumsily or ineffectually — see FLOUNDER 1
3 to make a low heavy rolling sound — see RUMBLE
4 to place a weight or burden on — see LOAD 1

lumberjack *n* a person whose job is to cut down trees ⟨The sawmill gets most of its business from the *lumberjacks* up north.⟩
syn jack, logger
rel lumberer; sawyer; forester

luminary *n* 1 a ball-shaped gaseous celestial body that shines by its own light — see STAR 1
2 a person who is widely known and usually much talked about — see CELEBRITY 1

luminescence *n* the steady giving off of the form of radiation that makes vision possible — see LIGHT 1

luminosity *n* the quality or state of having or giving off light — see BRILLIANCE 1

luminous *adj* 1 giving off or reflecting much light — see BRIGHT 1

2 standing above others in rank, importance, or achievement — see EMINENT

3 not subject to misinterpretation or more than one interpretation — see CLEAR 2

lump *n* **1** a small uneven mass ⟨She dumped a *lump* of clay on the table and started to sculpt.⟩

syn blob, chunk, clod, clot, clump, glob, gob, gobbet, hunk, knob, knob, nub, nubble, nugget, wad

rel drop, globule; block, body, bulk; particle, piece, portion; bit, chip, crumb, granule, morsel, nubbin, patch, scrap

2 a small rounded mass of swollen tissue — see BUMP 1

3 an abnormal mass of tissue — see GROWTH 1

4 failure to win a contest — see DEFEAT 1

5 a big clumsy often slow-witted person — see OAF 1

lump *vb* **1** to bring together in one body or place — see GATHER 1

2 to move heavily or clumsily — see LUMBER 1

lumpy *adj* **1** having small pieces or lumps spread throughout — see CHUNKY 1

2 not having a level or smooth surface — see UNEVEN 1

lurch *vb* **1** to make a series of unsteady side-to-side motions — see ROCK 1

2 to move forward while swaying from side to side — see STAGGER 1

lure *n* **1** something that persuades one to perform an action for pleasure or gain ⟨The promise of easy money is always the *lure* for some people to try get-rich-quick schemes.⟩

syn allurement, bait, enticement, temptation, turn-on

rel appeal, call; attraction, encouragement, goad, impetus, impulse, incentive, inducement, motivation, persuasion, seducement, seduction, spur, stimulus; decoy, snare, trap

near ant alarm (*also* alarum), alert, caution, forewarning, notice, warning

2 something used to attract animals to a hook or into a trap — see BAIT 1

3 the act or pressure of giving in to a desire especially when ill-advised — see TEMPTATION 1

lure *vb* to lead away from a usual or proper course by offering some pleasure or advantage ⟨*lured* the bear out of its den⟩

syn allure, bait, beguile, betray, decoy, entice, lead on, seduce, solicit, tempt

rel draw in, inveigle, persuade, rope (in); snow; catch, enmesh (*also* immesh), ensnare, entrap, mesh, snare, tangle, trap; bewitch, captivate, charm, enchant, fascinate, magnetize, wile

near ant alert, caution, forewarn, ward (off), warn; drive (away *or* off), repulse

lurid *adj* **1** extremely disturbing or repellent — see HORRIBLE 1

2 lacking a healthy skin color — see PALE 2

3 arousing a strong and usually superficial interest or emotional reaction — see SENSATIONAL 1

luring *adj* having an often mysterious or

magical power to attract — see FASCINATING 1

lurk *vb* **1** to move about in a sly or secret manner — see SNEAK 1

2 to remain out of sight — see ¹HIDE 3

lurker *n* someone who acts in a sly and secret manner — see SNEAK

luscious *adj* **1** very pleasing to the sense of taste — see DELICIOUS 1

2 pleasing to the physical senses — see SENSUAL

3 giving pleasure or contentment to the mind or senses — see PLEASANT 1

lusciousness *n* the quality of being delicious — see DELICIOUSNESS

lush *adj* **1** covered with a thick, healthy natural growth ⟨They loved to go for picnics in the *lush* woodlands.⟩

syn green, leafy, luxuriant, overgrown, verdant

rel fat, fecund, fertile, fruitful, productive, prolific, rich; dense

near ant bleak, depleted, impoverished, infertile, poor, stark, unproductive; arid, dead, desert, dry, parched, sere (*also* sear), waterless

ant barren, leafless

2 growing thickly and vigorously — see RANK 1

3 very pleasing to the sense of taste — see DELICIOUS 1

4 marked by vigorous growth and well-being especially economically — see PROSPEROUS 1

5 pleasing to the physical senses — see SENSUAL

6 producing abundantly — see FERTILE

lust *n* **1** intense sexual desire ⟨was filled with *lust*⟩

syn ardor, passion

rel lasciviousness, lewdness, libidinousness, licentiousness, salaciousness, wantonness

near ant frigidity

2 urgent desire or interest — see EAGERNESS

lust (**for** *or* **after**) *vb* to have an earnest wish to own or enjoy — see DESIRE 1

luster *or* **lustre** *n* **1** brightness created by light reflected from a surface — see SHINE 1

2 the quality or state of having or giving off light — see BRILLIANCE 1

luster *or* **lustre** *vb* to shoot forth bursts of light — see FLASH 1

lusterless *adj* lacking a surface luster or gloss — see MATTE

lustful *adj* having a strong sexual desire ⟨had a *lustful* dream⟩

syn lascivious, lewd, licentious, passionate, wanton

rel aroused, excited; easy, fast, loose, promiscuous; dissipated, dissolute, libertine; corrupt, debased, debauched, decadent, degenerate, degraded, demoralized, depraved, dissipated, dissolute, immoral, indecent

near ant celibate, chaste, decent, immaculate, modest, moral, pure, virtuous; maidenly, virginal; innocent; priggish, prim, prudish, puritanical, straitlaced (*or* straightlaced)

ant frigid

lustiness *n* the quality or state of having

abundant or intense activity — see VITAL-ITY 1

lustrous *adj* 1 giving off or reflecting much light — see BRIGHT 1

2 having a shiny surface or finish — see GLOSSY

lusty *adj* 1 having active strength of body or mind — see VIGOROUS 1

2 not showing weakness or uncertainty — see FIRM 1

3 having an abundance of some characteristic quality (as flavor) — see FULL-BODIED

luxuriant *adj* 1 covered with a thick, healthy natural growth — see LUSH 1

2 growing thickly and vigorously — see RANK 1

3 producing abundantly — see FERTILE

4 showing obvious signs of wealth and comfort — see LUXURIOUS

luxurious *adj* showing obvious signs of wealth and comfort ⟨The *luxurious* apartment was filled with the latest electronic gadgets and fine works of art.⟩

syn deluxe, lavish, luxuriant, luxury, opulent, palatial, plush, sumptuous

rel costly, dear, expensive, precious, premium, rich; extravagant, grandiose, ostentatious, pretentious, showy; august, awesome, baronial, beautiful, gorgeous, grand, imposing, impressive, kingly, magnificent, majestic, monumental, noble, regal, royal, splendid, stately

near ant economical, frugal, meager (*or* meagre), spare, stingy, thrifty

ant ascetic (*also* ascetical), austere, humble

luxuriously *adv* in a luxurious manner — see HIGH

luxury *adj* showing obvious signs of wealth and comfort — see LUXURIOUS

luxury *n* 1 something adding to pleasure or comfort but not absolutely necessary ⟨A private yacht is a *luxury*.⟩

syn amenity, comfort, extra, frill, indulgence, superfluity

rel extravagance, nonessential; delicacy, nicety, treat; accessory (*also* accessary), accoutrement (*or* accouterment), bells and whistles, option

ant basic, essential, fundamental, must, necessity, requirement

2 something that adds to one's ease of living — see COMFORT 2

lying *adj* telling or containing lies — see DISHONEST 1

lynx-eyed *adj* having unusually keen vision — see SHARP-EYED

lyric *adj* 1 having a pleasantly flowing quality suggestive of music ⟨They performed a slow, *lyric* dance for the audience.⟩

syn euphonious, lyrical, mellifluous, mellow, melodic, melodious, musical

rel golden, sweet

near ant disconnected, staccato; discordant, dissonant, grating, harsh, inharmonious, jarring, strident, unmelodious, unmusical

ant unlyrical

2 having qualities suggestive of poetry — see POETIC

lyric *n* 1 a composition using rhythm and often rhyme to create a lyrical effect — see POEM

2 a short musical composition for the human voice often with instrumental accompaniment — see SONG 1

lyrical *adj* 1 having a pleasantly flowing quality suggestive of music — see LYRIC 1

2 having qualities suggestive of poetry — see POETIC

ma *n* a female human parent — see MOTHER

macabre *adj* extremely disturbing or repellent — see HORRIBLE 1

Machiavellian *adj* not guided by or showing a concern for what is right — see UNPRINCIPLED

machinate *vb* 1 to engage in a secret plan to accomplish evil or unlawful ends — see PLOT

2 to plan out usually with subtle skill or care — see ENGINEER

machination *n* a secret plan for accomplishing evil or unlawful ends — see PLOT 1

machine *n* 1 a device that changes energy into mechanical motion — see ENGINE

2 a self-propelled passenger vehicle on four wheels — see CAR

machinery *n* something used to achieve an end — see AGENT 1

macrocosm *n* the whole body of things observed or assumed — see UNIVERSE

mad *adj* 1 feeling or showing anger — see ANGRY

2 marked by great and often stressful excitement or activity — see FURIOUS 1

mad *n* an intense emotional state of displeasure with someone or something — see ANGER

mad (about) *adj* filled with an intense or excessive love for — see ENAMORED (OF)

madcap *adj* foolishly adventurous or bold — see FOOLHARDY 1

madcap *n* a person who seeks out very dangerous or foolhardy adventures with no apparent fear — see DAREDEVIL

madden *vb* 1 to cause to go insane or as if insane — see CRAZE

2 to make angry — see ANGER

maddening *adj* causing annoyance — see ANNOYING

made-up *adj* not real and existing only in the imagination — see IMAGINARY

madhouse *n* a place of uproar or confusion ⟨Our house is always a *madhouse* on school mornings, with five kids and two dogs running around.⟩

syn babel, bedlam, circus, three-ring circus

rel bustle, commotion, pandemonium, racket, ruckus, tumult, turmoil; brouhaha, clamor, clatter, din, hubbub, noise; chaos, confusion, disarrangement, disarray, disorder, havoc, hell, mess, muss, shambles

near ant arcadia, heaven, paradise, utopia; calm, lull, peace, respite; hush, quiet, silence, stillness

madly *adv* 1 in a confused and reckless manner — see HELTER-SKELTER 1

2 in an enthusiastic manner — see SKY-HIGH

madman *n* a person who seeks out very dangerous or foolhardy adventures with no apparent fear — see DAREDEVIL

madness *n* 1 lack of good sense or judgment — see FOOLISHNESS 1

2 an intense emotional state of displeasure with someone or something — see ANGER

maelstrom *n* water moving rapidly in a circle with a hollow in the center — see WHIRLPOOL

maestro *n* a person with a high level of knowledge or skill in a field — see EXPERT

Mafia *n* a group involved in secret or criminal activities — see ¹RING 1

magazine *n* 1 a building for storing goods — see STOREHOUSE

2 a place where military arms are stored — see ARMORY

3 a publication that appears at regular intervals — see JOURNAL

magic *adj* 1 being or appearing to be under a magic spell — see ENCHANTED

2 having seemingly supernatural qualities or powers — see MYSTIC 1

magic *n* 1 the power to control natural forces through supernatural means ⟨He claimed that he could summon a storm through *magic*.⟩

syn bewitchment, conjuring, devilry (*or* deviltry), enchantment, mojo, necromancy, sorcery, witchcraft, witchery, wizardry

rel abracadabra, amulet, charm, fetish (*also* fetich), mascot, talisman; conjuration, incantation, spell; curse, hex, jinx; augury, crystal gazing, divining, forecasting, foreknowing, foreseeing, foretelling, fortune-telling, predicting, presaging, prognosticating, prophesying, soothsaying; occultism, spiritualism; augur, omen; exorcism; alchemy

near ant science

2 the art or skill of performing tricks or illusions for entertainment ⟨The couple hired an entertainer to perform *magic* for their child's 10th birthday party.⟩

syn conjuring, legerdemain, prestidigitation

rel trickery

phrases sleight of hand

3 the power of irresistible attraction — see CHARM 2

magical *adj* 1 being or appearing to be under a magic spell — see ENCHANTED

2 being so extraordinary or abnormal as to suggest powers which violate the laws of nature — see SUPERNATURAL 2

---

3 having seemingly supernatural qualities or powers — see MYSTIC 1

magician *n* 1 a person skilled in using supernatural forces ⟨The *magician* was able to summon the birds of the air and the beasts of the field with a simple spell.⟩

syn conjurer (*or* conjuror), enchanter, necromancer, sorcerer, witch, wizard

rel enchantress, hag, hex, sorceress; warlock; occultist; medicine man, shaman, shamanist, witch doctor; crystal gazer, diviner, foreseer, fortune-teller, prognosticator, prophesier, prophet, seer, soothsayer; medium; exorciser, exorcist

2 one who practices tricks and illusions for entertainment ⟨The famous *magician's* signature trick was pulling a rabbit out of a hat.⟩

syn conjurer (*or* conjuror), illusionist, prestidigitator, trickster

rel enchanter, enchantress

magistrate *n* a public official having authority to decide questions of law — see JUDGE 2

magnanimous *adj* having, characterized by, or arising from a dignified and generous nature — see NOBLE 2

magnanimously *adv* in a manner befitting a person of the highest character and ideals — see GREATLY 1

magnate *n* a person of rank, power, or influence in a particular field ⟨a studio *magnate* who had the biggest stars in Hollywood at his beck and call⟩

syn baron, captain, czar (*also* tsar *or* tzar), king, mogul, monarch, prince, tycoon

rel big shot, bigwig, figure, nabob, notable, personage; celebrity, personality, star, superstar; deity, demigod, god

near ant lightweight, small-timer; inferior, subordinate, underling; nobody, nothing, zero

magnet *n* something that attracts interest ⟨The giant theme park is a *magnet* for tourists to the area.⟩

syn attraction, draw, lodestone (*also* loadstone)

rel capital, center, cynosure, mecca, pole; allure, allurement, bait, enticement, fascination, lure, temptation, turn-on; appeal, call; incentive, inducement, persuasion, spur, stimulus; curiosity, sight(s)

magnetic *adj* having an often mysterious or magical power to attract — see FASCINATING 1

magnetism *n* the power of irresistible attraction — see CHARM 1

magnetize *vb* to attract or delight as if by magic — see CHARM 1

magnification *n* the representation of something in terms that go beyond the facts — see EXAGGERATION

magnificence *n* impressiveness of beauty on a large scale ⟨The *magnificence* of the great castle hallway is beyond description.⟩

syn augustness, brilliance, gloriousness, glory, gorgeousness, grandeur, grandness, majesty, nobility, nobleness, resplendence, splendor, stateliness, stupendousness, sublimeness, superbness

rel awesomeness, formidability, marvelousness, wonderfulness, wondrousness;

---

dignity, elegance, grace; lavishness, luxuriance, luxuriousness, luxury, opulence; princeliness, richness, sumptuousness; grandiosity, ostentation, pretentiousness; elaborateness, flashiness, gaudiness, ornateness, poshness, ritziness, showiness, swankiness; extraordinariness, remarkableness

magnificent *adj* large and impressive in size, grandeur, extent, or conception — see GRAND 1

magnify *vb* 1 to add to the interest of by including made-up details — see EMBROIDER

2 to assign a high status or value to — see EXALT 1

3 to make markedly greater in measure or degree — see INTENSIFY

4 to proclaim the glory of — see PRAISE 1

magnitude *n* 1 the quality or state of being important — see IMPORTANCE

2 the quality or state of being very large — see IMMENSITY

3 the total amount of measurable space or surface occupied by something — see ¹SIZE

magnum opus *n* something (as a work of art) that is a great achievement and often its creator's greatest achievement — see MASTERPIECE

maid *n* 1 a person hired to perform household or personal services ⟨hired a *maid* to take care of the house⟩

syn charwoman, domestic, housekeeper, housemaid, maidservant

rel attendant, chambermaid; nursemaid; menial

2 a young unmarried woman — see GIRL 1

maiden *adj* coming before all others in time or order — see FIRST 1

maiden *n* a young unmarried woman — see GIRL 1

maidservant *n* a person hired to perform household or personal services — see MAID 1

mail *n* communications or parcels sent or carried through the postal system ⟨Jed began receiving lots of *mail* after he became known as a frequent donor to charities.⟩

syn correspondence, matter, parcel post, snail mail

rel airmail, airpost, certified mail, registered mail, rural delivery, rural free delivery, special delivery, special handling; direct mail, junk mail, mailer; card, dispatch, epistle, letter, message, missive, note, postal card, postcard, printed matter

mail *vb* to send through the postal system ⟨If you don't *mail* that letter soon, it's going to arrive late.⟩

syn post

rel airmail, frank; address, consign; direct, dispatch, forward, remit, route, ship, transmit, transport; register

near ant get

mail carrier *n* a person who delivers mail — see LETTER CARRIER

mailman *n* a person who delivers mail — see LETTER CARRIER

maim *vb* to cause severe or permanent injury to ⟨On-the-job accidents *maim* far too many workers every year.⟩

syn cripple, disable, incapacitate, lame, mutilate

rel dismember, hamstring, hobble, paralyze; batter, bruise, mangle, maul, rough (up); gore, lacerate, wing, wound; disfigure, scar; kneecap; break, damage, harm, hurt, impair, injure; bash, beat, belt, bludgeon, buffet, drub, hammer, lace, lambaste (*or* lambast), lick, paste, pelt, pommel, pound, pummel, thump; bang, box, hit, punch, slap, smack, smash, sock, spank, swat, swipe, thrash, thwack, whack; flog, lash, wallop, whip; kill, murder; torment, torture

near ant cure, heal, rehabilitate, remedy; doctor, fix, mend, patch; rejuvenate, renew, repair, restore

main *adj* coming before all others in importance — see FOREMOST 1

main *n* 1 muscular strength — see MUSCLE 1

2 one of the great divisions of land on the globe or the main part of such a division — see MAINLAND

3 the main or greater part of something as distinguished from its subordinate parts — see BODY 1

mainland *n* one of the great divisions of land on the globe or the main part of such a division ⟨The boat back to the *mainland* leaves once every two days.⟩

syn continent, main

rel subcontinent, supercontinent

near ant island, isle, islet; atoll, barrier reef, cay, coral reef, key; cape, headland, peninsula, promontory

mainly *adv* for the most part — see CHIEFLY

mainstay *n* someone or something to which one looks for support — see DEPENDENCE 2

maintain *vb* 1 to keep in good condition ⟨He repairs and *maintains* antique cars as a hobby.⟩

syn conserve, keep up, preserve, save

rel service; support, sustain; cure (for), husband, manage; defend, guard, protect, safeguard, screen, shield; cure, fix, heal, remedy; mend, patch, rebuild, reconstruct, rehabilitate, rejuvenate, restore

near ant disregard, ignore, neglect; break, damage, destroy, harm, hurt, impair, injure, ruin, wreck

2 to continue to declare to be true or proper despite opposition or objections ⟨Part of debating is learning to *maintain* your position in the face of harsh challenges.⟩

syn defend, justify, support, uphold

rel advocate, champion, espouse; confirm, vindicate, warrant; affirm, assert, aver, avouch, avow, claim, contend, insist, plead, proclaim, profess, protest, state; argue, debate, discuss; emphasize, stress, underline, underscore

phrases stand up for, stick up for

near ant abandon, abjure, forswear, recant, retract, take back, withdraw; reverse, switch; disprove, rebut, refute

3 to pay the living expenses of — see SUPPORT 2

4 to state (something) as a reason in support of or against something under consideration — see ARGUE 1

5 to state as a fact usually forcefully — see CLAIM 1

maintainable *adj* capable of being defended

with good reasoning against verbal attack — see TENABLE 2

maintenance *n* the act or activity of keeping something in an existing and usually satisfactory condition ⟨I was hired to perform basic *maintenance* until the property could be sold.⟩

syn conservation, conserving, preservation, preserving, upkeep

rel support, sustaining; care, custody, guardianship; defense, guarding, protection, safeguarding, safekeeping

near ant dereliction, disregard, ignoring, inattention, neglect, negligence; damage, demolition, destruction, harm, hurt, injury, ruin, ruination

majestic *adj* 1 having or showing elegance — see ELEGANT 1

2 large and impressive in size, grandeur, extent, or conception — see GRAND 1

3 very dignified in form, tone, or style — see ELEVATED 2

majesty *n* 1 a dignified bearing or appearance befitting someone of royal status ⟨Even as a child, the princess possessed a certain *majesty* that would later serve her well.⟩

syn augustness, stateliness

rel high-mindedness, magnanimity, nobility, nobleness; haughtiness, lordliness, pompousness; dignity, poise; gloriousness, grandeur, grandness, greatness, impressiveness, magnificence, resplendence, splendor; class, elegance, grace

2 dignified or restrained beauty of form, appearance, or style — see ELEGANCE

3 impressiveness of beauty on a large scale — see MAGNIFICENCE

major *adj* 1 sufficiently large in size, amount, or number to merit attention — see CONSIDERABLE 1

2 having great meaning or lasting effect — see IMPORTANT 1

majority *adj* held by or applicable to a majority of the people — see GENERAL 3

majority *n* 1 the largest part or quantity of something ⟨A vast *majority* of the town's residents support the proposed tax reduction.⟩

syn bulk, generality, mass

rel plurality; maximum, most; abundance, heap, loads, lot, much, oodles, plenty, profusion, reams, scads, wealth

near ant couple, few, handful, smattering, sprinkling; least, minimum

2 the state of being fully grown or developed — see MATURITY

make *vb* 1 to bring into being by combining, shaping, or transforming materials ⟨Will you help me *make* the dough for the cookies?⟩

syn fabricate, fashion, form, frame, manufacture, produce

rel assemble, build, construct, erect, make up, put up, raise, rear, set up, structure, throw up; craft, handcraft; hew; forge, shape; patch (together), throw up; prefabricate; create, invent, mint, originate; establish, father, institute, organize; concoct, contrive, cook (up), design, devise, imagine, think (up); conceive, envisage,

picture, visualize; refashion, remake, remanufacture

phrases put together

near ant disassemble, dismantle, take apart; break up, dismember; flatten, pulverize, raze, ruin, shatter, smash, wreck; blow up, explode

2 to obtain (as a goal) through effort — see ACHIEVE 1

3 to be the cause of (a situation, action, or state of mind) — see EFFECT

4 to carry through (as a process) to completion — see PERFORM 1

5 to cause (a person) to give in to pressure — see FORCE

6 to decide the size, amount, number, or distance of (something) without actual measurement — see ESTIMATE 2

7 to form by putting together parts or materials — see BUILD

8 to give the impression of being — see SEEM

9 to go on a specified course or in a certain direction — see HEAD 1

10 to put into effect through legislative or authoritative action — see ENACT

11 to receive as return for effort — see EARN 1

12 to have a clear idea of — see COMPREHEND 1

make–believe *adj* not real and existing only in the imagination — see IMAGINARY 1

make out *vb* 1 to meet one's day-to-day needs — see GET ALONG 1

2 to have a clear idea of — see COMPREHEND 1

3 to take on a false or deceptive appearance — see PRETEND 1

4 to form an opinion or reach a conclusion through reasoning and information — see INFER 1

make over *vb* 1 to change in form, appearance, or use — see CONVERT 2

2 to give over the legal possession or ownership of — see TRANSFER 1

3 to make different in some way — see CHANGE 1

Maker *n* the being worshipped as the creator and ruler of the universe — see DEITY 2

makeshift *adj* taking the place of one that came before — see NEW 1

makeshift *n* a temporary replacement ⟨When his belt broke, he was forced to use string as a *makeshift*.⟩

syn expedient, stopgap

rel quick fix; recourse, refuge, resort; alternate, backup, standby, stand-in, substitute, understudy

makeup *n* 1 preparations intended to beautify the face ⟨She never left the house without applying her *makeup* and arranging her jewelry.⟩

syn cosmetics, paint

rel greasepaint; camo, camouflage; cold cream, cream, eye shadow, kohl, lipstick, lotion, mascara, oil, powder, rouge, vanishing cream

2 the way in which the elements of something (as a work of art) are arranged — see COMPOSITION 3

make up *vb* 1 to be all the substance of — see CONSTITUTE 1

---

syn synonym(s)   *rel* related words
ant antonym(s)   *near ant* near antonym(s)

2 to create or think of by clever use of the imagination — see INVENT

3 to form by putting together parts or materials — see BUILD

make up (for) *vb* to balance with an equal force so as to make ineffective — see OFFSET

making *n, often pl* **makings** the basic elements from which something can be developed ⟨She has all the *makings* of an excellent leader, but she needs some experience first.⟩

syn material, raw material, stuff, substance

rel possibility, potential, potentiality; matter, metal

maladroit *adj* **1** lacking or showing a lack of nimbleness in using one's hands — see CLUMSY 1

2 showing or marked by a lack of skill and tact (as in dealing with a situation) — see AWKWARD 2

malady *n* an abnormal state that disrupts a plant's or animal's normal bodily functioning — see DISEASE

malcontent *adj* having a feeling that one has been wronged or thwarted in one's ambitions — see DISCONTENTED

male *adj* of, relating to, or marked by qualities traditionally associated with men — see MASCULINE

male *n* an adult male human being — see MAN 1

malediction *n* a prayer that harm will come to someone — see CURSE 1

malefaction *n* a breaking of a moral or legal code — see OFFENSE 1

malefactor *n* **1** a person who commits moral wrongs — see EVILDOER 1

2 a person who has committed a crime — see CRIMINAL

malevolence *n* the desire to cause pain for the satisfaction of doing harm — see MALICE

malevolent *adj* having or showing a desire to cause someone pain or suffering for the sheer enjoyment of it — see HATEFUL

malevolently *adv* in a mean or spiteful manner — see NASTILY

malfeasance *n* improper or illegal behavior — see MISCONDUCT

malformed *adj* badly or imperfectly formed ⟨a dog with a *malformed* tail⟩

syn deformed, distorted, misshapen, monstrous, shapeless

rel defaced, disfigured; aberrant, abnormal, freakish, mutant; asymmetrical (*or* asymmetric), crooked, disproportionate, irregular, lopsided, nonsymmetrical, overbalanced, unbalanced, unequal; horrible, terrible; ugly, unattractive

near ant shapely; flawless, perfect

ant undeformed

malfunctioning *adj* not being in working order — see INOPERABLE 1

malice *n* the desire to cause pain for the satisfaction of doing harm ⟨She claimed that her criticisms were without *malice*.⟩

syn cattiness, despite, hatefulness, malevolence, maliciousness, malignancy, malignity, meanness, nastiness, spite, spitefulness, spleen, venom, viciousness

rel abusiveness, cruelty; abhorrence, abomination, execration, hate, hatred, loathing; animosity, antagonism, antipathy, bitterness, enmity, grudge, hostility, ill will, jaundice, mean-spiritedness, rancor, resentment; despicableness, invidiousness; vengefulness, vindictiveness; aversion, disgust, distaste, horror, repugnance, repulsion, revulsion; contempt, disdain; jealousy, pique, resentment, scorn; bile, rancor, virulence, vitriol

near ant devotion, love, passion; amiability, amicability, amity, civility, cordiality, friendliness, hospitality; adoration, ardor, infatuation, veneration, worship; affection, charity, kindliness, kindness; comity, empathy, friendship, goodwill, sympathy, understanding

malicious *adj* having or showing a desire to cause someone pain or suffering for the sheer enjoyment of it — see HATEFUL

maliciously *adv* in a mean or spiteful manner — see NASTILY

maliciousness *n* the desire to cause pain for the satisfaction of doing harm — see MALICE

malign *adj* having or showing a desire to cause someone pain or suffering for the sheer enjoyment of it — see HATEFUL

malign *vb* to make untrue and harmful statements about — see SLANDER

malignancy *n* the desire to cause pain for the satisfaction of doing harm — see MALICE

malignant *adj* having or showing a desire to cause someone pain or suffering for the sheer enjoyment of it — see HATEFUL

malignantly *adv* in a mean or spiteful manner — see NASTILY

maligning *n* the making of false statements that damage another's reputation — see SLANDER

malignity *n* the desire to cause pain for the satisfaction of doing harm — see MALICE

malleability *n* the quality or state of being easily molded — see PLASTICITY

malleable *adj* **1** capable of being easily molded or modeled — see PLASTIC 1

2 capable of being readily changed — see FLEXIBLE 1

malodorous *adj* having an unpleasant smell ⟨The cellar will need to be cleared of several *malodorous* piles of garbage.⟩

syn fetid, foul, fusty, musty, noisome, rank, reeking, reeky, ripe, smelly, stinking, stinky, strong

rel putrid, skunky, stale; bad, offensive, repulsive, revolting, vile; decayed, decaying, decomposed, decomposing, rotted, rotten, rotting, spoiled, spoiling; dirty, filthy, nasty, noxious; odiferous, odoriferous, odorous

near ant flowery, fruity, spicy, woodsy

ant ambrosial, aromatic, fragrant, perfumed, redolent, savory (*also* savoury), scented, sweet

maltreat *vb* **1** to inflict physical or emotional harm upon — see ABUSE 1

2 to abuse physically — see MANHANDLE 1

mama *also* **mamma** *or* **momma** *n* a female human parent — see MOTHER

mammoth *adj* unusually large — see HUGE

mammoth *n* something that is unusually large and powerful — see GIANT

mammy *n* a female human parent — see MOTHER

man *n* **1** an adult male human being ⟨Several *men* will be needed to dig up the old tree stump in the backyard.⟩

syn buck, dude, fellow, gent, gentleman, guy, hombre, joker, lad, male

rel sir; buddy, buster

2 a male romantic companion — see BOYFRIEND

3 a member of the human race — see HUMAN

4 the human race — see MANKIND

5 a male partner in a marriage — see HUSBAND

manacle *n* **1** *usually* **manacles** *pl* something that physically prevents free movement — see BOND 1

2 something that makes movement or progress difficult — see ENCUMBRANCE

manacle *vb* **1** to confine or restrain with or as if with chains — see BIND 1

2 to create difficulty for the work or activity of — see HAMPER

manage *vb* **1** to deal with (something) usually skillfully or efficiently — see HANDLE 1

2 to look after and make decisions about — see CONDUCT 1

3 to meet one's day-to-day needs — see GET ALONG 1

management *n* the act or activity of looking after and making decisions about something — see CONDUCT 1

manager *n* a person who manages or directs something — see EXECUTIVE

managerial *adj* suited for or relating to the directing of things — see EXECUTIVE

man-at-arms *n* a person engaged in military service — see SOLDIER

mandate *n* the granting of power to perform various acts or duties — see COMMISSION 1

mandate *vb* to request the doing of by virtue of one's authority — see COMMAND 2

mandatory *adj* forcing one's compliance or participation by or as if by law ⟨The tests are *mandatory* for all students wishing to graduate.⟩

syn compulsory, forced, imperative, incumbent, involuntary, necessary, nonelective, obligatory, peremptory, required

rel all-important, essential, indispensable, needed, requisite; insistent, persistent, pressing, urgent; demanded, enforced; coercive

near ant chosen, discretionary; dispensable, unnecessary, unneeded, unwanted; inconsequential, insignificant, nonessential, unimportant

ant elective, optional, voluntary

maneuver *vb* **1** to deal with (something) usually skillfully or efficiently — see HANDLE 1

2 to plan out usually with subtle skill or care — see ENGINEER

manful *adj* feeling or displaying no fear by temperament — see BRAVE 1

mangle *vb* to make or do (something) in a clumsy or unskillful way — see BOTCH

mangy *adj* showing signs of advanced wear and tear and neglect — see SHABBY 1

manhandle *vb* **1** to abuse physically ⟨charges that the police *manhandled* peaceful protesters⟩

syn maltreat, maul, mishandle, rough (up)

rel abuse, ill-treat, ill-use, mistreat, misuse; roughhouse, wrestle; bash, batter, beat, buffet, drub, lambaste (*or* lambast), lick, pommel, pound, pummel, slap, thrash; harm, hurt, injure, wound; oppress, persecute, wrong; ambush, assail, attack; clobber, fight, gang up (on), hit, jump, knock; torment, torture

near ant caress, fondle, pet; coddle, mollycoddle, pamper; care (for), foster, nurture

2 to inflict physical or emotional harm upon — see ABUSE 1

manhood *n* the set of qualities traditionally considered appropriate for or characteristic of men — see VIRILITY

mania *n* something about which one is constantly thinking or concerned — see FIXATION

maniac *n* a person with a strong and habitual liking for something — see FAN

manifest *adj* not subject to misinterpretation or more than one interpretation — see CLEAR 1

manifest *vb* **1** to make known (something abstract) through outward signs — see SHOW 2

2 to represent in visible form — see EMBODY 2

manifestation *n* a visible representation of something abstract (as a quality) — see EMBODIMENT

manifold *adj* being of many and various kinds ⟨The *manifold* attractions of that state make it an ideal destination for a family vacation.⟩

syn divers, multifarious, myriad

rel multiform, multiple, multiplex, multitudinous; heterogeneous, heterogenous, miscellaneous, mixed, sundry; different, diverse, unlike, varied

near ant homogeneous, homogenous, monolithic, unmixed, unvaried; alike, identical, same; distinct, distinctive, individual, separate; alone, lone, only, sole, solitary; singular, unique

manikin *also* **mannikin** *n* **1** a three-dimensional representation of the human body used especially for displaying clothes — see MANNEQUIN 1

2 a person who poses with or wears merchandise (as clothes) often for pictorial advertising — see MODEL 2

manipulate *vb* **1** to control or take advantage of by artful, unfair, or insidious means ⟨The con man would slyly *manipulate* the emotions of his marks in order to win their sympathy and trust.⟩

syn exploit, play (upon)

rel engineer, finagle, jockey, maneuver; beguile, bluff, cozen, deceive, delude, dupe, fool, gull, hoax, hoodwink, kid, shanghai, snow, take in, trick; intrigue, machinate, plot, scheme; arrange, contrive, devise, finesse, mastermind; cheat, chisel, con, defraud, fleece, hustle, swindle

2 to deal with (something) usually skillfully or efficiently — see HANDLE 1

---

syn synonym(s)   *rel* related words
ant antonym(s)   *near ant* near antonym(s)

3 to plan out usually with subtle skill or care — see ENGINEER

mankind *n* the human race ⟨All of *mankind* stands to gain if world peace is ever achieved.⟩

syn Homo sapiens, humanity, humankind, man

rel being, body, creature, fellowman, human, individual, mortal, party, person

manliness *n* the set of qualities traditionally considered appropriate for or characteristic of men — see VIRILITY

manly *adj* of, relating to, or marked by qualities traditionally associated with men — see MASCULINE

man–made *adj* **1** being such in appearance only and made with or manufactured from usually cheaper materials — see IMITATION

2 produced by humans rather than natural processes — see SYNTHETIC 1

manna *n* **1** a source of great satisfaction — see DELIGHT 1

2 something that provides happiness or does good for a person or thing — see BLESSING 2

mannequin *n* **1** a three-dimensional representation of the human body used especially for displaying clothes ⟨The *mannequin* over there looks so real.⟩

syn dummy, figure, form, manikin (*also* mannikin)

rel doll

2 a person who poses with or wears merchandise (as clothes) often for pictorial advertising — see MODEL 2

manner *n* **1** manners *pl* personal conduct or behavior as evaluated by an accepted standard of appropriateness for a social or professional setting ⟨The young man's impeccable *manners* are an unmistakable sign of a good upbringing.⟩

syn etiquette, form, mores, proprieties

rel amenities, civilities, pleasantries; bearing, demeanor, deportment, mien; courtesy, decorum, mannerliness, politeness; formalities, protocol, rules; air, carriage, poise, polish, pose, posture, presence

2 a distinctive way of putting ideas into words — see STYLE 1

3 a number of persons or things that are grouped together because they have something in common — see SORT 1

4 the means or procedure for doing something — see METHOD

mannerism *n* an odd or peculiar habit — see IDIOSYNCRASY

mannerliness *n* speech or behavior that is a sign of good manners — see POLITENESS 1

mannerly *adj* showing consideration, courtesy, and good manners — see POLITE 1

mannish *adj* **1** of, relating to, or marked by qualities traditionally associated with men — see MASCULINE

2 having qualities or traits that are traditionally considered inappropriate for a girl or woman — see UNFEMININE

manor *n* a large impressive residence — see MANSION

manor house *n* a large impressive residence — see MANSION

manpower *n* a body of persons at work or available for work — see FORCE 1

mansion *n* a large impressive residence ⟨If I ever win the lottery, I'm going to buy a *mansion* in the hills.⟩

syn castle, château, estate, hacienda, hall, manor, manor house, palace, villa

rel showplace; abode, domicile, dwelling, habitation, hearth, home, house, lodging(s), pad, place; housing, nest, quarter(s), roof; great house; country house, countryseat; aerie, penthouse; salon, suite, town house

man–size *or* **man–sized** *adj* of, relating to, or marked by qualities traditionally associated with men — see MASCULINE

manta *n* any of several extremely large rays — see DEVILFISH

manta ray *n* any of several extremely large rays — see DEVILFISH

mantilla *n* a scarf worn on the head — see BANDANNA

mantle *n* **1** a sleeveless garment worn so as to hang over the shoulders, arms, and back — see ¹CAPE

2 something that covers or conceals like a piece of cloth — see CLOAK 1

mantle *vb* to surround or cover closely — see ENFOLD 1

manual *n* a book used for instruction in a subject — see TEXTBOOK

manufactory *n* a building or set of buildings for the manufacturing of goods — see FACTORY

manufacture *vb* **1** to bring into being by combining, shaping, or transforming materials — see MAKE 1

2 to create or think of by clever use of the imagination — see INVENT

manumission *n* the act of setting free from slavery — see LIBERATION

manumit *vb* to release (as from slavery or confinement) from — see FREE 1

manuscript *n* writing done by hand — see HANDWRITING 2

many *adj* being of a large but indefinite number ⟨A journey of *many* miles begins with a single step.⟩

syn legion, multiple, multiplex, multitudinous, numerous

rel countless, innumerable, numberless, uncountable, unnumbered, untold; several, some; miscellaneous, mixed, sundry; divers, manifold, multifarious, myriad

phrases all kinds of, quite a few

near ant countable, limited

ant few

map *n* an illustration of certain features of a geographical area ⟨a wall *map* of the United States⟩

syn chart

rel ground plan, plan, plat, plot; relief map

map (out) *vb* to work out the details of (something) in advance — see PLAN 1

mar *n* something that spoils the appearance or completeness of a thing — see BLEMISH

mar *vb* **1** to affect slightly with something morally bad or undesirable — see TAINT 1

2 to reduce the soundness, effectiveness, or perfection of — see DAMAGE 1

maraud *vb* to search through with the intent of committing robbery — see RANSACK 1

marble *vb* to mark with small spots especially unevenly — see SPOT 1

marbled *adj* having blotches of two or more colors — see PIED

¹march *n* a region along the dividing line between two countries — see FRONTIER 1

²march *n* forward movement in time or place — see ADVANCE 1

march *vb* **1** to move along with a steady regular step especially in a group ⟨The band had to practice for hours to be able to *march* in perfect step.⟩

syn file, pace, parade, stride

rel goose-step; step, traipse, tread; hike, tramp; lumber, plod, stamp, stomp, stride, trudge

near ant meander, ramble, stroll, wander

2 to move forward along a course — see GO 1

margin *n* the line or relatively narrow space that marks the outer limit of something — see BORDER 1

margin *vb* to serve as a border for — see BORDER

marginally *adv* by a very small margin — see JUST 2

marine *adj* **1** of or relating to the sea ⟨He loves collecting little *marine* creatures while at the beach.⟩

syn maritime, oceanic, pelagic

rel abyssal, deepwater, saltwater; benthic; nautical, naval; undersea, underwater; hydrographic, oceanographic (*also* oceanographical)

2 of or relating to navigation of the sea ⟨a collection of *marine* instruments, including a sextant⟩

syn maritime, nautical, navigational

rel naval; oceangoing, seafaring, seagoing; hydrographic, oceanographic (*also* oceanographical)

mariner *n* one who operates or navigates a seagoing vessel — see SAILOR

marital *adj* of or relating to marriage ⟨Neither of them ever forgot their *marital* vows, no matter how hard things sometimes got.⟩

syn conjugal, connubial, married, matrimonial, nuptial, wedded

rel espoused, matched, mated; bridal, prenuptial; spousal, wifely; affianced, betrothed, committed, engaged, pledged, promised

ant nonmarital

maritime *adj* **1** of or relating to navigation of the sea — see MARINE 2

2 of or relating to the sea — see MARINE 1

mark *n* **1** a person or thing that is made fun of — see LAUGHINGSTOCK

2 a person or thing that is the object of abuse, criticism, or ridicule — see TARGET 1

3 overall quality as seen or judged by people in general — see REPUTATION

4 something set up as an example against which others of the same type are compared — see STANDARD 1

5 something that one hopes or intends to accomplish — see GOAL

6 something that sets apart an individual from others of the same kind — see CHARACTERISTIC

7 something that spoils the appearance or completeness of a thing — see BLEMISH

8 the power to bring about a result on another — see EFFECT 2

mark *vb* **1** to attach an identifying slip to — see LABEL 1

2 to be an important feature of — see CHARACTERIZE 2

3 to make a written note of — see RECORD 1

mark down *vb* to diminish the price or value of — see DEPRECIATE 1

marked *adj* likely to attract attention — see NOTICEABLE

marker *n* **1** a slip (as of paper or cloth) that is attached to something to identify or describe it — see LABEL

2 something that sets apart an individual from others of the same kind — see CHARACTERISTIC

market *n* the state of being sought after especially for purchase — see DEMAND 2

market *vb* to offer for sale to the public ⟨Local farmers *market* their garden-fresh produce at roadside stands all over the valley.⟩

syn deal (in), merchandise (*also* merchandize), put up, retail, sell, vend

rel presell, wholesale; hawk, peddle; barter, distribute, exchange, export, handle, trade, traffic (in); advertise, ballyhoo, boost, plug, promote, tout; auction; provide, supply; carry, keep, stock

ant buy, purchase

marketable *adj* **1** fit to be offered for sale ⟨Bob realized that the birdhouses he enjoyed making were *marketable* and began selling them at craft fairs.⟩

syn salable (*or* saleable)

rel commercial, profitable; costly, fancy, fine, high-grade, precious, premium, prime, valuable

near ant damaged, shopworn; cheap, useless, worthless; bad, inferior, low-grade, substandard, unsatisfactory

ant nonsalable, unmarketable, unsalable, unsellable

2 fit or likely to be sold especially on a large scale — see COMMERCIAL

marketplace *n* the buying and selling of goods especially on a large scale and between different places — see COMMERCE 1

marksman *n* a person skilled in shooting at a target ⟨Only the best *marksmen* can hit the bull's-eye at 500 feet.⟩

syn sharpshooter, shooter, shot

rel sniper; rifleman; trapshooter; gun, gunman, gunner; markswoman

maroon *vb* to cause to remain behind — see LEAVE 1

marriage *n* **1** a union representing a special kind of social and legal partnership between two people ⟨They have a very happy *marriage*.⟩

syn match, matrimony, wedlock

rel monogamy; bigamy, polyandry, polygamy, polygyny; intermarriage, miscegenation, mixed marriage, remarriage; cohabitation, common-law marriage; civil union, domestic partnership; attachment, commitment, relationship; betrothal, engagement, espousal, hand, pledge, promise, proposal, troth

near ant divorce, separation

2 a ceremony in which two people are united in matrimony — see WEDDING

---

syn synonym(s)   *rel* related words
ant antonym(s)   *near ant* near antonym(s)

married *adj* of or relating to marriage — see MARITAL

marry *vb* **1** to perform the ceremony of marriage for ⟨They chose a priest who was a family friend to *marry* them.⟩
syn wed
rel match, mate; conjoin, connect, unite; affiance

2 to give in marriage ⟨Once they *marry* off me and my siblings, my parents are selling their house.⟩
syn espouse, match, wed
rel affiance, engage; affiance, betroth, pledge, promise

3 to take as a spouse ⟨He *married* his girlfriend three years ago, and they've been happy ever since.⟩
syn espouse, wed
rel affiance, betroth, engage, propose; remarry
near ant separate (from)
ant divorce

4 to take a spouse ⟨She had always believed she would never *marry*, but fate proved her wrong.⟩
syn wed
rel couple, mate; pair off, remarry
phrases tie the knot
near ant divorce, separate

5 to come together to form a single unit — see UNITE 1

marsh *n* spongy land saturated or partially covered with water — see SWAMP

marshal *also* **marshall** *vb* **1** to assemble and make ready for action — see MOBILIZE

2 to point out the way for (someone) especially from a position in front — see LEAD 1

3 to put into a particular arrangement — see ORDER 1

marshaling *or* **marshalling** *n* an act of gathering forces together to renew or attempt an effort — see RALLY 1

marshland *n* spongy land saturated or partially covered with water — see SWAMP

martial *adj* of, relating to, or suitable for war or a warrior ⟨The marching band played "The Battle Hymn of the Republic" and several other *martial* airs.⟩
syn military, soldierly
rel aggressive, bellicose, combative, contentious, guerrilla, pugnacious, quarrelsome, scrappy, truculent, warlike; belligerent, militant, militarist, militaristic, warring
near ant civil, civilian, nonmilitary; conciliatory, nonviolent, pacific, peaceable, peaceful; affable, amiable, amicable, benevolent, complaisant, cordial, easygoing, friendly, genial, good-natured, obliging
ant unsoldierly

2 of or relating to the armed services — see MILITARY 1

marvel *n* something extraordinary or surprising — see WONDER 1

marveling *or* **marvelling** *adj* filled with amazement or wonder — see OPEN-MOUTHED

marvelous *or* **marvellous** *adj* **1** causing wonder or astonishment ⟨The sheer immensity of the ancient ruin known as Stonehenge is *marvelous* to behold.⟩
syn amazing, astonishing, astounding, awesome, awful, eye-opening, fabulous, miraculous, portentous, prodigious, staggering, stunning, stupendous, sublime, surprising, wonderful, wondrous
rel incomprehensible, inconceivable, incredible, unbelievable, unimaginable, unthinkable; extraordinary, phenomenal, rare, sensational; singular, uncommon, unique, unusual, unwonted; conspicuous, notable, noticeable, outstanding, remarkable; impressive, smashing, striking; alluring, attracting, attractive, beguiling, bewitching, captivating, charming, enchanting, enthralling, fascinating, interesting
near ant unimpressive, uninspiring, unremarkable; boring, dull, jading, monotonous, tedious, tiring, uninspired, uninteresting, wearisome, weary, wearying; common, customary, mundane, normal, ordinary, typical, unexceptional, usual

2 excitingly or mysteriously unusual — see EXOTIC

3 of the very best kind — see EXCELLENT

mascot *n* something worn or kept to bring good luck or keep away evil — see CHARM 1

masculine *adj* of, relating to, or marked by qualities traditionally associated with men ⟨Some people consider a deep voice to be a particularly appealing *masculine* trait.⟩
syn male, manly, mannish, man-size (*or* man-sized), virile
rel ultramasculine; boyish, hoydenish, tomboyish
near ant effeminate, girlish; feminine, womanish, womanlike, womanly; emasculated, impotent, weakened; neuter
ant unmanly, unmasculine

masculinity *n* the set of qualities traditionally considered appropriate for or characteristic of men — see VIRILITY

mash *vb* **1** to apply external pressure on so as to force out the juice or contents of — see ²PRESS 2

2 to cause to become a pulpy mass — see CRUSH 1

mask *n* **1** a cover or partial cover for the face used to disguise oneself ⟨an elaborate *mask* that would be suitable for a fancy masquerade ball⟩
syn vizard
rel camouflage, costume, disguise, guise; bill, cloak, domino, hood, veil, visor (*also* vizor)

2 something that covers or conceals like a piece of cloth — see CLOAK 1

mask *vb* **1** to change the dress or looks of so as to conceal true identity — see DISGUISE 1

2 to keep secret or shut off from view — see ¹HIDE 2

masquerade *n* a display of emotion or behavior that is insincere or intended to deceive ⟨Although she was deeply bored, she maintained a *masquerade* of polite interest as her guest droned on.⟩
syn act, airs, charade, disguise, facade (*also* façade), front, guise, pose, pretense (*or* pretence), put-on, semblance, show
rel impersonation, performance, portrayal; image, persona; appearance, color, gloss; camouflage, cloak; affectation, deceit, dissembling, dissimulation, double-dealing, duplicity, fakery, fraud, guile; betrayal, double cross, faithlessness, falseness, falsity,

infidelity, perfidy, treachery, treason, unfaithfulness; excuse, pretext

near ant candidness, candor, directness, forthrightness, frankness, openheartedness, outspokenness, straightforwardness; artlessness, genuineness, naïveté (*also* naiveté *or* naïveté)

masquerade (as) *vb* to pretend to be (what one is not) in appearance or behavior — see IMPERSONATE 1

mass *n* 1 **masses** *pl* the body of the community as contrasted with the elite ⟨The *masses* demanded the elimination of tax breaks for the rich.⟩

syn commoners, crowd, herd, mob, multitude, people, plebeians, populace, public, rank and file

rel cattle, proletariat, rabble, riffraff, rout, trash, unwashed

near ant gentry, nobility, patriciate, peerage, society

ant A-list, aristocracy, best, choice, cream, elect, elite, fat, flower, pick, pride, upper crust

2 a considerable amount — see LOT 2

3 a distinct and separate portion of matter — see BODY 2

4 the main or greater part of something as distinguished from its subordinate parts — see BODY 1

5 the largest part or quantity of something — see MAJORITY 1

6 a great number of persons or creatures massed together — see CROWD 1

mass *vb* to gradually form into a layer, pile, or mass — see COLLECT 2

massacre *n* the killing of a large number of people ⟨the infamous *massacre* of more than 200 Lakota at Wounded Knee, South Dakota⟩

syn butchery, carnage, death, holocaust, slaughter

rel bloodletting, bloodshed, foul play, homicide, manslaughter, murder, slaying; annihilation, decimation, eradication, extermination; genocide, pogrom

massacre *vb* to kill on a large scale ⟨The country's rival ethnic groups began *massacring* one another.⟩

syn butcher, mow (down), slaughter

rel dispatch, do in, execute, fell, murder, slay, smite; annihilate, blot out, decimate, eradicate, exterminate, waste, wipe out

massive *adj* 1 having great weight — see HEAVY 1

2 unusually large — see HUGE

3 large and impressive in size, grandeur, extent, or conception — see GRAND 1

massively *adv* to a large extent or degree — see GREATLY 1

massiveness *n* 1 the quality or state of being very large — see IMMENSITY

2 the state or quality of being heavy — see WEIGHTINESS 1

mass–produced *adj* made beforehand in large numbers — see READY-MADE

master *adj* 1 coming before all others in importance — see FOREMOST 1

2 having or showing exceptional knowledge, experience, or skill in a field of endeavor — see PROFICIENT

master *n* 1 a person with a high level of knowledge or skill in a field — see EXPERT

2 one that defeats an enemy or opponent — see VICTOR 1

3 the person (as an employer or supervisor) who tells people and especially workers what to do — see BOSS

master *vb* 1 to achieve a victory over — see BEAT 2

2 to acquire complete knowledge, understanding, or skill in — see LEARN 1

masterful *adj* 1 accomplished with trained ability — see SKILLFUL 1

2 fond of ordering people around — see BOSSY

3 having a feeling of superiority that shows itself in an overbearing attitude — see ARROGANT

4 having or showing exceptional knowledge, experience, or skill in a field of endeavor — see PROFICIENT

masterfully *adv* in a skillful or expert manner — see WELL 3

masterfulness *n* 1 subtle or imaginative ability in inventing, devising, or executing something — see SKILL 1

2 an exaggerated sense of one's importance that shows itself in the making of excessive or unjustified claims — see ARROGANCE

masterly *adj* 1 accomplished with trained ability — see SKILLFUL 1

2 having or showing exceptional knowledge, experience, or skill in a field of endeavor — see PROFICIENT

masterly *adv* in a skillful or expert manner — see WELL 3

mastermind *n* a person who designs and guides a plan or undertaking — see ENGINEER

mastermind *vb* to plan out usually with subtle skill or care — see ENGINEER

masterpiece *n* something (as a work of art) that is a great achievement and often its creator's greatest achievement ⟨Michelangelo's frescoes in the Sistine Chapel are often considered to be his *masterpieces*.⟩

syn classic, magnum opus

rel masterstroke, pièce de résistance, showpiece; blockbuster, megahit, smash, success, winner; gem, jewel, prize, treasure

near ant bomb, catastrophe, debacle (*also* débâcle), disaster, dud, failure, fiasco, fizzle, flop, loser, turkey, washout

mastership *n* a highly developed skill in or knowledge of something — see COMMAND 2

mastery *n* 1 a highly developed skill in or knowledge of something — see COMMAND 2

2 the right or means to command or control others — see POWER 1

masticate *vb* to crush or grind with the teeth — see BITE 1

match *n* 1 a competitive encounter between individuals or groups carried on for amusement, exercise, or in pursuit of a prize — see GAME 1

2 a union representing a special kind of social and legal partnership between two people — see MARRIAGE 1

---

syn synonym(s)   **rel** related words

ant antonym(s)   **near ant** near antonym(s)

3 either of a pair matched in one or more qualities — see MATE 1

4 one that is equal to another in status, achievement, or value — see EQUAL

5 something or someone that strongly resembles another — see IMAGE 1

6 an earnest effort for superiority or victory over another — see CONTEST 1

match *vb* **1** to be the exact counterpart of ⟨Your socks don't *match*.⟩ ⟨the rare blood type that exactly *matched* that of the transplant recipient⟩

syn correspond (to), equal, parallel

rel blend (with), conform (to), coordinate (with), go (with), harmonize (with); complement, supplement; counterbalance, counterpoise; echo, image, mirror, repeat; add up (to), amount (to), approach, come (to), near; measure (up), rival, suggest

2 to give in marriage — see MARRY 2

3 to produce something equal to (as in quality or value) — see EQUAL 1

matching *adj* having qualities in common — see ALIKE

matchless *adj* having no equal or rival for excellence or desirability — see ONLY 1

mate *n* **1** either of a pair matched in one or more qualities ⟨Have you seen the *mate* to this glove anywhere?⟩

syn companion, fellow, half, match, twin

rel coordinate; coequal, counterpart, equal, equivalent, like, parallel, peer, rival; carbon copy, double, duplicate, facsimile, identical twin, likeness, replica, ringer; analogue (*or* analog), similarity

near ant antipode, antithesis, contrary, converse, opposite, reverse

2 a person frequently seen in the company of another — see ASSOCIATE 1

3 the person to whom another is married — see SPOUSE

mate *vb* to engage in sexual intercourse — see COPULATE

material *adj* **1** relating to or composed of matter ⟨There's no *material* evidence that a crime has been committed.⟩

syn concrete, physical, substantial

rel bodily, carnal, corporal, corporeal, embodied, fleshly; apparent, appreciable, detectable, discernible (*also* discernable), noticeable, observable, palpable, perceptible, seeable, sensible, tangible, touchable, visible; objective, phenomenal; bulky, heavy, hefty, massive, ponderous, solid, weighty

near ant bodiless, disembodied, formless, incorporeal; ethereal, insubstantial, unsubstantial; impalpable, imperceptible, insensible, intangible, unnoticeable; metaphysical, spiritual

ant immaterial, nonmaterial, nonphysical

2 having great meaning or lasting effect — see IMPORTANT 1

3 having to do with life on earth especially as opposed to that in heaven — see EARTHLY

4 having to do with the matter at hand — see PERTINENT

5 of or relating to the human body — see PHYSICAL 1

material *n* **1** the basic elements from which something can be developed — see MAKING

2 *usually* **materials** *pl* items needed for the performance of a task or activity — see EQUIPMENT

materialist *n* a person who is chiefly interested in material comfort and is hostile or indifferent to art and culture — see PHILISTINE

materiality *n* **1** something that actually exists — see FACT 2

2 the fact or state of being pertinent — see PERTINENCE

3 the quality of being actual — see FACT 1

materialize *vb* **1** to come into existence — see BEGIN 2

2 to come into view — see APPEAR 1

3 to come to one's attention especially gradually or unexpectedly — see ARISE 2

4 to represent in visible form — see EMBODY 2

matériel *or* **materiel** *n* items needed for the performance of a task or activity — see EQUIPMENT

maternal *adj* of, relating to, or characteristic of a mother — see MOTHERLY

maternity *n* motherly character or qualities ⟨She had such *maternity* at such a young age that all her classmates went to her for comfort.⟩

syn motherliness

rel nurturance; fertility, fruitfulness

mathematical *adj* meeting the highest standard of accuracy — see PRECISE 1

matriarch *n* a dignified usually elderly woman of some rank or authority ⟨Even though she was 87, the *matriarch* of the family knew everything that was going on.⟩

syn dame, dowager, matron

rel grandam (*or* grandame); headmistress, mistress

matriculate *vb* to add (a person) to a list or roll as a participant or member — see ENROLL 1

matrimonial *adj* of or relating to marriage — see MARITAL

matrimony *n* a union representing a special kind of social and legal partnership between two people — see MARRIAGE 1

matron *n* a dignified usually elderly woman of some rank or authority — see MATRIARCH

matte *also* **mat** *or* **matt** *adj* lacking a surface luster or gloss ⟨I chose a paint with a *matte* finish so the walls wouldn't be too shiny.⟩

syn dim, dull, dulled, flat, lusterless

rel tarnished, unpolished; cloudy, dingy, dirty, drab, lackluster, mousy (*or* mousey), muddy; gray (*also* grey), leaden, pale, palish; black, dark, darkened, darkish, dimmed, dusky, gloomy, murky, obscure

near ant buffed, burnished, glazed, lacquered, polished, rubbed, shellacked, varnished; satin, satiny; silken, silky; gleaming, glimmering, glinting, glistening, glittering, scintillating, shimmering, shining, sparkling, twinkling; beaming, bedazzling, bright, brightened, brilliant, dazzling, effulgent, glowing, incandescent, lambent, lucent, lucid, luminous, radiant, refulgent, resplendent

ant glossy, lustrous, shiny, sleek

matter *n* **1** a major object of interest or concern (as in a discussion or artistic composition) ⟨That is not relevant to the *matter* under discussion.⟩

syn content, motif, motive, question, subject, theme, topic

rel subject matter; talking point; count, idea, point, purpose; consideration, issue, problem; body, bulk, burden, core, crux, essence, fundamental, generality, gist, grist, heart, main, marrow, mass, net, nub, nubbin, nucleus, pith, pivot, purport, quick, staple, substance, sum

near ant digression, excursion, interjection, parenthesis, tangent

2 something to be dealt with ⟨We must take care of this *matter* before it becomes a real problem.⟩

syn affair, business, thing

rel consideration, issue, problem; crisis, crossroad(s), crunch, emergency, exigency, head, juncture, strait, zero hour; concern, trouble, worry; care, lookout, responsibility; corner, fix, hole, jam, pickle, pinch, predicament, scrape, spot

phrases ball of wax

3 communications or parcels sent or carried through the postal system — see MAIL

4 something that requires thought and skill for resolution — see PROBLEM 1

5 an approximate amount, extent, or degree — see NEIGHBORHOOD 1

matter *vb* to be of importance ⟨She believes that doing well in school really does *matter*.⟩

syn count, import, mean, signify, weigh

rel affect, concern, influence, sway; add up (to), amount (to)

phrases carry weight, cut ice

matter-of-fact *adj* **1** restricted to or based on fact — see FACTUAL 1

2 willing to see things as they really are and deal with them sensibly — see REALISTIC 1

maturation *n* the process of becoming mature ⟨A flower's *maturation* from bud to full bloom can take weeks.⟩

syn development, growth, maturing, ripening

rel blossoming, flourishing, flowering; mellowing, softening; evolution, evolvement, expansion, progression; coming-of-age, maturity

near ant decadence, decay, decaying, declension, decline, declining, degeneration, descent, deterioration; ebbing, fading, shriveling (*or* shrivelling), waning, wilting, withering; death, decease, demise, dying, end, exit, expiration; regression, retrogression, reversion

mature *adj* **1** fully grown or developed ⟨I like pears when they're still hard, before they're *mature*.⟩

syn adult, full-blown, full-fledged, matured, ripe, ripened

rel aged, aging (*or* ageing), long-lived, old, older; golden, mellow

near ant blooming, blossoming, burgeoning, flourishing, flowering; undeveloped, unfinished, unfledged, unformed

ant adolescent, green, immature, juvenile, unripe, unripened, young, youngish, youthful

2 having reached the date at which payment is required — see DUE 1

3 relating to or typical of adults; displaying proper maturity — see ADULT 1

mature *vb* to become mature ⟨A young figure skater whose talent is still *maturing*⟩

syn age, develop, grow, grow up, progress, ripen

rel mellow, soften; bloom, blossom, burgeon (*also* bourgeon), flourish, flower; open, unfold; advance, evolve; get along, get on, gray (*also* grey)

near ant decay, decline, degenerate, deteriorate, sink, worsen; droop, dry, fade, flag, sag, shrivel, wane, waste (away), weaken, wilt, wither; regress, retrogress, revert; backslide, lapse, return

matured *adj* fully grown or developed — see MATURE 1

maturing *n* the process of becoming mature — see MATURATION

maturity *n* the state of being fully grown or developed ⟨People are legally considered to have reached *maturity* at the age of 18 in the United States.⟩

syn adulthood, majority

rel manhood; bloom, flush, heyday, prime; middle age, midlife

near ant babyhood, infancy, toddlerhood; childhood, youth

ant immaturity

maudlin *adj* appealing to the emotions in an obvious and tiresome way — see CORNY

maul *vb* **1** to abuse physically — see MANHANDLE 1

2 to strike repeatedly — see BEAT 1

maunder *vb* **1** to move about from place to place aimlessly — see WANDER 1

2 to talk at length without sticking to a topic or getting to a point — see RAMBLE 1

maundering *adj* passing from one topic to another — see DISCURSIVE

maverick *adj* deviating from commonly accepted beliefs or practices — see HERETICAL

maverick *n* a person who does not conform to generally accepted standards or customs — see NONCONFORMIST 1

mawkish *adj* appealing to the emotions in an obvious and tiresome way — see CORNY

mawkishness *n* the state or quality of having an excess of tender feelings (as of love, nostalgia, or compassion) — see SENTIMENTALITY

maxim *n* an often stated observation regarding something from common experience — see SAYING

maximum *adj* **1** of the greatest or highest degree or quantity — see ULTIMATE 1

2 of the highest degree — see FULL 2

maximum *n* the greatest amount, number, or part — see MOST

maybe *adv* it is possible — see PERHAPS

mayhap *adv* it is possible — see PERHAPS

maze *n* a confusing and complicated arrangement of passages ⟨The mansion had a beautifully landscaped *maze* that was constructed of tall cypresses.⟩

syn labyrinth

rel meander; jungle, quagmire; catacomb, cat's cradle, knot, snarl, tangle, web; entanglement, entrapment, snare, trap

---

syn synonym(s)   *rel* related words
ant antonym(s)   *near ant* near antonym(s)

maze *vb* to throw into a state of mental uncertainty — see CONFUSE 1

meager *or* **meagre** *adj* less plentiful than what is normal, necessary, or desirable ⟨Everyday he eats a *meager* breakfast of toast and coffee.⟩

syn hand-to-mouth, light, niggardly, poor, scant, scanty, scarce, skimpy, slender, slim, spare, sparing, sparse, stingy

rel deficient, inadequate, insufficient, lacking, short, wanting; bare, bare-bones; least, littlest, lowest, mere, minimal, slightest

phrases thin on the ground

near ant adequate, enough, satisfactory, sufficient, tolerable; fat, fecund, fertile, fruitful, prolific, rich; lavish, luxuriant; excess, extra, surplus

ant abundant, ample, bountiful, copious, generous, liberal, plenteous, plentiful

meal *n* food eaten or prepared for eating at one time ⟨All she wants to do is sit quietly after the large Thanksgiving *meal*.⟩

syn chow, feed, menu, mess, repast, table

rel board; breakfast, buffet, collation, dinner, lunch, luncheon, refreshments, snack, supper, tea; banquet, feast, regale, spread; bake, barbecue (*also* barbeque), clambake, cookout, fry, luau, picnic, potluck, roast

mealy *adj* 1 lacking a healthy skin color — see PALE 2

2 not being or expressing what one appears to be or express — see INSINCERE

mealymouthed *adj* not being or expressing what one appears to be or express — see INSINCERE

¹mean *adj* 1 being about midway between extremes of amount or size — see MIDDLE 2

²mean *adj* 1 belonging to the class of people of low social or economic rank — see IGNOBLE 1

2 giving or sharing as little as possible — see STINGY 1

3 having or showing a desire to cause someone pain or suffering for the sheer enjoyment of it — see HATEFUL

4 not following or in accordance with standards of honor and decency — see IGNOBLE 2

5 of little or less value or merit — see INFERIOR 2

6 of the very best kind — see EXCELLENT

7 showing signs of advanced wear and tear and neglect — see SHABBY 1

8 arousing or deserving of one's loathing and disgust — see CONTEMPTIBLE 1

mean *n* 1 a middle point between extremes ⟨That candidate's moderate views were seen as the *mean* that voters were looking for.⟩

syn golden mean, medium, middle, midpoint

rel arithmetic mean, average; median, norm, par, standard

phrases middle of the road

near ant maximum, utmost; minimum

2 means *pl* an action planned or taken to achieve a desired result — see MEASURE 1

3 means *pl* something used to achieve an end — see AGENT 1

4 means *pl* the total of one's money and property — see WEALTH 1

mean *vb* 1 to communicate or convey (as

an idea) to the mind ⟨The national anthem *means* various things to various people.⟩

syn denote, express, import, intend, signify, spell

rel connote, imply, suggest; hint, infer, insinuate, intimate; embody, epitomize, personify, represent, symbol, symbolize; advert, allude (to), cite, instance, mention, refer (to), specify, touch (on *or* upon); designate, indicate, signal

2 to be of importance — see MATTER

3 to have in mind as a purpose or goal — see INTEND 1

4 to serve as a sign or symptom of — see INDICATE 1

meander *vb* to move about from place to place aimlessly — see WANDER 1

meaning *adj* clearly conveying a special meaning (as one's mood) — see EXPRESSIVE

meaning *n* 1 the idea that is conveyed or intended to be conveyed to the mind by language, symbol, or action ⟨the unmistakable *meaning* of the skier's upraised arms as he finished his spectacular run⟩

syn content, denotation, drift, import, intent, intention, purport, sense, significance, signification

rel connotation; clue, cue, hint, implication, indication, inkling, intimation, suggestion; message, tenor, theme; bottom, essence, essentiality, nature, soul, spirit, stuff; acceptance, acceptation; burden, crux, gist; core, heart, marrow, nub, nucleus, pith, point, quick

2 something that one hopes or intends to accomplish — see GOAL

meaningful *adj* 1 clearly conveying a special meaning (as one's mood) — see EXPRESSIVE

2 having great meaning or lasting effect — see IMPORTANT 1

meaningless *adj* having no meaning ⟨This argument over seating arrangements is an utterly *meaningless* bit of nonsense.⟩

syn empty, inane, pointless, senseless

rel frivolous, inconsequential, inconsiderable, insignificant, minor, negligible, slight, trifling, trivial, unimportant; absurd, asinine, balmy, brainless, empty-headed, fatuous, foolish, half-witted, harebrained, mindless, nonsensical, preposterous, stupid, unintelligent, unwise, weak-minded, witless, zany; irrational, unreasonable; aimless, haphazard, purposeless

near ant eloquent, expressive, pregnant, revealing, suggestive, telling; logical, rational, reasonable, valid; consequential, eventful, important, key, major, momentous, substantial, weighty

ant meaningful, significant

meanly *adv* 1 in a manner showing no signs of pride or self-assertion — see LOWLY

2 in a mean or spiteful manner — see NASTILY

meanness *n* the desire to cause pain for the satisfaction of doing harm — see MALICE

measly *adj* so small or unimportant as to warrant little or no attention — see NEGLIGIBLE 1

measure *n* 1 an action planned or taken to achieve a desired result ⟨such new

security *measures* as metal detectors at all the entrances⟩
syn expedient, means, move, shift, step
rel act, action, deed, doing, feat, thing; course, procedure, proceeding, process; activity, affair, business, dealing, enterprise, event; attempt, crack, endeavor, essay, fling, go, initiative, operation, pass, shot, stab, trial, try, undertaking, whack; effort, exertion, labor, pains, trouble, while, work; project, proposal, proposition; makeshift, resort, resource, stopgap; countermeasure, countermove, counterstep
2 a given or particular mass or aggregate of matter — see AMOUNT
3 something set up as an example against which others of the same type are compared — see STANDARD 1
4 the recurrent pattern formed by a series of sounds having a regular rise and fall in intensity — see RHYTHM
5 the total amount of measurable space or surface occupied by something — see ¹SIZE
measure *vb* **1** to find out the size, extent, or amount of ⟨For this experiment, you need to carefully *measure* all the chemicals before you mix them together.⟩
syn gauge (*also* gage), scale, span
rel weigh; calibrate, caliper; quantify, quantitate; lay off; calculate, cipher, compute, figure, reckon, work out; appraise, assess, conjecture, estimate, evaluate, guess, judge, suppose, value; add up, sum, tally, total
2 to keep from exceeding a desirable degree or level (as of expression) — see CONTROL 1
measured *adj* **1** decided on as a result of careful thought — see DELIBERATE 1
2 having distinct or certain limits — see LIMITED 1
3 marked by or occurring with a noticeable regularity in the rise and fall of sound — see RHYTHMIC
measureless *adj* being or seeming to be without limits — see INFINITE
measurement *n* the total amount of measurable space or surface occupied by something — see ¹SIZE
measure up (to) *vb* to come near or nearer to in character or quality — see APPROXIMATE
meat *n* **1** animal and especially mammal tissue used as food ⟨We need to go shopping: there's only enough *meat* in the freezer for one more dinner.⟩
syn flesh
rel game, poultry, red meat, variety meat
2 substances intended to be eaten — see FOOD
3 the central part or aspect of something under consideration — see CRUX
mecca *n* a thing or place that is of greatest importance to an activity or interest — see CENTER 1
mechanical *adj* **1** done instantly and without conscious thought or decision — see AUTOMATIC 1

2 lacking in natural or spontaneous quality — see ARTIFICIAL 1
medal *n* a piece of metal given in honor of a special event, a person, or an achievement ⟨The display case held an impressive array of military *medals* from World War II.⟩
syn medallion, order
rel decoration, honor; crown, insignia, laurel, ribbon, title; bronze, gold, silver; badge, button, chevron, clasp, cockade, color, ensign, rosette, star; distinction; award, prize; citation, commendation
medallion *n* a piece of metal given in honor of a special event, a person, or an achievement — see MEDAL
meddle *vb* to interest oneself in what is not one's concern — see INTERFERE
meddler *n* a person who meddles in the affairs of others — see BUSYBODY
meddlesome *adj* thrusting oneself where one is not welcome or invited — see INTRUSIVE
meddling *adj* thrusting oneself where one is not welcome or invited — see INTRUSIVE
medial *adj* occupying a position equally distant from the ends or extremes — see MIDDLE 1
median *adj* **1** being about midway between extremes of amount or size — see MIDDLE 2
2 occupying a position equally distant from the ends or extremes — see MIDDLE 1
mediate *adj* occupying a position equally distant from the ends or extremes — see MIDDLE 1
mediate *vb* to act as a go-between for opposing sides — see INTERVENE
mediator *n* one who works with opposing sides in order to bring about an agreement ⟨If you two cannot resolve this argument on your own, we'll have to bring in a *mediator*.⟩
syn buffer, conciliator, go-between, intercessor, intermediary, intermediate, interposer, middleman, peacemaker
rel troubleshooter; moderator; bargainer, negotiant, negotiator; appeaser, pacificator, pacifier, reconciler; agent, attorney, deputy, factor, procurator, proxy; liaison, medium; arbiter, arbitrator, judge, referee, umpire; adviser (*also* advisor), counselor (*or* counsellor)
medic *n* a person specially trained in healing human medical disorders — see DOCTOR
medication *n* a substance or preparation used to treat disease — see MEDICINE
medicine *n* a substance or preparation used to treat disease ⟨If you don't take all the doses of your *medicine*, you might get sick again.⟩
syn cure, drug, medication, pharmaceutical, physic, remedy, specific
rel cure-all, panacea; botanical, patent medicine, prescription drug; cordial, potion, tonic; miracle drug, wonder drug; cap, capsule, pill, tablet; injection, shot; embrocation, liniment, lotion, ointment, potion, poultice; antibiotic, serum; cathartic, purgative
mediocre *adj* **1** of average to below aver-

---

syn synonym(s)   **rel** related words
ant antonym(s)   **near ant** near antonym(s)

age quality ⟨The entree was good, but the dessert was just *mediocre*.⟩

syn common, fair, indifferent, medium, middling, ordinary, passable, second-class, second-rate, so-so

rel acceptable, adequate, all right, alright, decent, OK (*or* okay), reasonable, satisfactory, sufficient, sufficing, tolerable; moderate, modest; presentable, respectable; minimal, unexceptional

near ant A1, capital, distinguished, excellent, exceptional, fine, first-class, first-rate, grand, great, matchless, maximum, number one (*also* No. 1), optimal, optimum, outstanding, par excellence, peerless, preeminent, prime, sensational, special, splendid, stellar, sterling, superb, superior, superlative, supreme, swell, terrific, tip-top, top, top-notch; unmatched, unparalleled, unsurpassed; deficient, inadequate, insufficient, lacking, unacceptable, unsatisfactory, wanting

2 of low quality — see CHEAP 2

meditate *vb* **1** to give serious and careful thought to — see PONDER

2 to have in mind as a purpose or goal — see INTEND 1

meditation *n* long or deep thinking about spiritual matters — see CONTEMPLATION

meditative *adj* given to or marked by long, quiet thinking — see CONTEMPLATIVE

medium *adj* **1** being about midway between extremes of amount or size — see MIDDLE 2

2 occupying a position equally distant from the ends or extremes — see MIDDLE 1

3 of average to below average quality — see MEDIOCRE 1

medium *n* **1** a middle point between extremes — see MEAN 1

2 something used to achieve an end — see AGENT 1

3 the circumstances, conditions, or objects by which one is surrounded — see ENVIRONMENT

medley *n* an unorganized collection or mixture of various things — see MISCELLANY 1

meek *adj* not having or showing any feelings of superiority, self-assertiveness, or showiness — see HUMBLE 1

meekly *adv* in a manner showing no signs of pride or self-assertion — see LOWLY

meekness *n* the absence of any feelings of being better than others — see HUMILITY

meet *adj* meeting the requirements of a purpose or situation — see FIT 1

meet *n* a competitive encounter between individuals or groups carried on for amusement, exercise, or in pursuit of a prize — see GAME 1

meet *vb* **1** to come upon face-to-face or as if face-to-face ⟨We never once *met* another car on that lonely country road.⟩

syn catch, chance (upon), encounter, happen (upon), stumble (upon)

rel accost, confront; face, greet, salute; collide (with), crash (into); crisscross, cross, pass; hit (upon), light (upon), tumble (to); reencounter, remeet

phrases bump into, cross paths (with), run across, run into, run upon

near ant avoid, dodge, duck, elude, escape, evade, shake, shun

2 to come together into one body or place — see ASSEMBLE 1

3 to come upon unexpectedly or by chance — see HAPPEN (ON *or* UPON)

4 to do what is required by the terms of — see FULFILL 1

5 to enter into contest or conflict with — see ENGAGE 2

6 to produce something equal to (as in quality or value) — see EQUAL 1

7 to put up with (something painful or difficult) — see BEAR 2

8 to give what is owed for — see PAY 2

meeting *n* **1** a coming together of a number of persons for a specified purpose ⟨There will be another committee *meeting* next week to discuss fundraising.⟩

syn assembly, congress, convention, convocation, council, gathering, get-together, huddle

rel clinic, workshop; caucus, conclave, synod; demonstration, rally; conversation, dialogue (*also* dialog), discourse, discussion, palaver; talk; negotiation, parley, summit; conference, forum, roundtable, seminar, symposium; session

2 a body of people come together in one place — see GATHERING 1

3 the coming together of two or more things to the same point — see CONVERGENCE

meetly *adv* in a manner suitable for the occasion or purpose — see PROPERLY

megahit *n* a person or thing that is successful — see HIT 1

megalopolis *n* a thickly settled, highly populated area — see CITY

melancholy *adj* **1** causing unhappiness — see SAD 2

2 feeling unhappiness — see SAD 1

3 given to or marked by long, quiet thinking — see CONTEMPLATIVE

melancholy *n* a state or spell of low spirits — see SADNESS

mélange *n* an unorganized collection or mixture of various things — see MISCELLANY 1

meld *n* a distinct entity formed by the combining of two or more different things — see BLEND

meld *vb* to turn into a single mass or entity that is more or less the same throughout — see BLEND 1

melee *n* a rough and often noisy fight usually involving several people — see BRAWL 1

meliorate *vb* to make better — see IMPROVE

mellifluous *adj* having a pleasantly flowing quality suggestive of music — see LYRIC 1

mellow *adj* **1** having a pleasantly flowing quality suggestive of music — see LYRIC 1

2 not harsh or stern especially in nature or effect — see GENTLE 1

3 having an easygoing and pleasing manner especially in social situations — see AMIABLE

4 having a relaxed, casual manner — see EASYGOING 1

melodic *adj* having a pleasantly flowing quality suggestive of music — see LYRIC 1

melodious *adj* **1** having a pleasantly flowing quality suggestive of music — see LYRIC 1

2 having a pleasing mixture of notes — see HARMONIOUS 1

melodramatic *adj* **1** given to or marked by attention-getting behavior suggestive of stage acting — see THEATRICAL 1

2 having the general quality or effect of a stage performance — see DRAMATIC 1

melody *n* a rhythmic series of musical tones arranged to give a pleasing effect ⟨This week, we'll learn to play a more complicated *melody* on the saxophone.⟩

syn air, lay, song, strain, tune, warble

rel descant (*also* discant); cadence, measure, meter, rhythm; ballad, ditty, hymn, lyric, madrigal

melt *vb* **1** to cease to be visible — see DISAPPEAR

2 to go from a solid to a liquid state — see LIQUEFY

member *n* **1** one of the parts that make up a whole — see ELEMENT 1

2 one of the pieces from which something is designed to be assembled — see PART 1

memento *n* something that serves to keep alive the memory of a person or event — see MEMORIAL

memo *n* **1** a message on paper from one person or group to another — see ¹LETTER

2 a usually brief written reminder — see NOTE 1

3 a written communication giving information or directions — see MEMORANDUM 1

memoir *n* a history of a person's life — see BIOGRAPHY

memorandum *n* **1** a written communication giving information or directions ⟨I'm waiting for the *memorandum* that will explain the new vacation policy.⟩

syn directive, memo, notice

rel announcement, bulletin, declaration, notification, posting, proclamation, pronouncement, release; dispatch, report; charge, command, dictate; directions, instructions, orders, word

2 a message on paper from one person or group to another — see ¹LETTER

3 a usually brief written reminder — see NOTE 1

memorial *adj* serving to preserve the memory of a person, thing, or an event — see COMMEMORATIVE

memorial *n* something that serves to keep alive the memory of a person or event ⟨The Vietnam War *Memorial* is a starkly beautiful testimonial to the bravery of the soldiers who served in Vietnam.⟩

syn commemorative, keepsake, memento, monument, remembrance, reminder, souvenir, token

rel memorabilia; relic, vestige; cairn, landmark, marker; tribute; cenotaph

memorialize *vb* to be a memorial of — see COMMEMORATE

memorializing *adj* serving to preserve the memory of a person, thing, or an event — see COMMEMORATIVE

memorize *vb* to commit to memory ⟨Everyone has to *memorize* a poem for next week's class.⟩

syn con, learn, study

rel hark back (to), recall, recollect, relive, remember, reminisce (about), retain, think (of); accept, apprehend, comprehend, grasp, know, understand; absorb, digest

near ant forget, misremember; disregard, ignore, neglect, overlook, overpass, pass over, slight, slur (over)

ant unlearn

memory *n* **1** the power or process of recalling what has been previously learned or experienced ⟨A photographic *memory* makes taking tests entirely too easy.⟩

syn mind, recollection, remembrance, reminiscence

rel contemplation, meditation, reflection, retrospection, thinking; awareness, cognizance; apprehension, comprehension, grasp, grip, perception, understanding

near ant amnesia, repression; forgetfulness

2 a particular act or instance of recalling or the thing remembered ⟨I have only the vaguest *memory* of the family vacation we took the year I turned three.⟩

syn recall, recollection, remembrance, reminiscence

rel flashback; memento, memorial, reminder, souvenir; association

menace *n* something that may cause injury or harm — see DANGER 2

menace *vb* **1** to place in danger — see ENDANGER

2 to remain poised to inflict harm, danger, or distress on — see THREATEN

menacing *adj* **1** being or showing a sign of evil or calamity to come — see OMINOUS

2 involving potential loss or injury — see DANGEROUS 1

ménage *n* those who live as a family in one house — see HOUSEHOLD

mend *vb* **1** to put into good shape or working order again ⟨That shirt will be as good as new when I finished *mending* it.⟩

syn doctor, fix, patch, recondition, renovate, repair, revamp

rel fix up, overhaul, rebuild, reconstruct, refurbish; aid, cure, heal, help; condition, prepare, ready; care (for), maintain, service; freshen, refresh, refreshen, regenerate, rejuvenate, renew, restore, revitalize, revive; ameliorate, better, enhance, enrich, improve, meliorate

near ant blemish, break, damage, deface, disfigure, flaw, harm, hurt, impair, injure, mar, ruin, spoil, vandalize, wreck; cripple, disable, maim, mangle, mutilate

2 to become healthy and strong again after illness or weakness — see CONVALESCE

3 to restore to a healthy condition — see HEAL 1

4 to make up for (an offense) — see EXPIATE

5 to change one's behavior or character for the better — see REFORM 2

6 to bring about recovery from — see CURE 1

mendacious *adj* telling or containing lies — see DISHONEST 1

---

syn synonym(s)   *rel* related words
ant antonym(s)   *near ant* near antonym(s)

mendacity *n* 1 a statement known by its maker to be untrue and made in order to deceive — see LIE

2 the tendency to tell lies — see DISHONESTY 1

mendicant *n* a person who lives by public begging — see BEGGAR

mending *n* the process or period of gradually regaining one's health and strength — see CONVALESCENCE

menstruation *n* an occurrence of menstruating — see PERIOD 1

mental *adj* of or relating to the mind ⟨A funny *mental* image made him laugh out loud.⟩

syn cerebral, inner, intellectual, interior, internal, psychological (*also* psychologic)

rel cognitive, conscious; telepathic; brainy, clever, intelligent, quick-witted, rational, reasoning, sharp, sharp-witted, smart, thinking

near ant bodily, carnal, corporal, corporeal, fleshly, physical; unconscious; brainless, doltish, half-witted, mindless, obtuse, simple, slow-witted, stupid, thickheaded, unintelligent, weak-minded, witless

ant nonmental

mentality *n* the ability to learn and understand or to deal with problems — see INTELLIGENCE 1

mention *n* a formal recognition of an achievement or praiseworthy deed — see COMMENDATION 1

mention *vb* 1 to make reference to or speak about briefly but specifically ⟨You only *mentioned* in passing some of your accomplishments.⟩

syn advert (to), cite, drop, instance, name, note, notice, quote, refer (to), specify, touch (on *or* upon)

rel allude (to), hint (at), imply, infer, intend, intimate, suggest; point (out), signal, signify; denominate, designate; indicate; bring up, broach, interject, interpolate, interpose, introduce; infiltrate, insinuate, worm; advertise, announce, broadcast, declare, proclaim, pronounce, publicize, publish, sound

near ant disregard, forget, ignore, neglect, overlook, overpass, pass over, slight

2 to give as an example — see QUOTE 1

mentor *vb* to give advice and instruction to (someone) regarding the course or process to be followed — see GUIDE 1

menu *n* 1 a list of foods served at or available for a meal ⟨The *menu* at the fancy restaurant listed many dishes that I had never heard of.⟩

syn card

rel chow, chuck [*chiefly West*], cuisine, fare, grub, provender, table

phrases bill of fare

2 a record of a series of items (as names or titles) usually arranged according to some system — see ¹LIST

3 food eaten or prepared for eating at one time — see MEAL

mercenary *adj* having or marked by an eager and often selfish desire especially for material possessions — see GREEDY 1

merchandise *n* products that are bought and sold in business ⟨We stock only the finest-quality *merchandise* in this store.⟩

syn goods, wares

rel line; export, import; inventory, staples, stock, stuff, supply; job lot; domestics, durables (*also* durable goods), hard goods

merchandise *also* **merchandize** *vb* to offer for sale to the public — see MARKET

merchandiser *n* 1 a buyer and seller of goods for profit — see MERCHANT

2 the person in a business deal who hands over an item in exchange for money — see VENDOR

merchant *n* a buyer and seller of goods for profit ⟨free trade agreements that are favored by *merchants* on both sides of the border⟩

syn dealer, merchandiser, trader, tradesman, trafficker

rel businessman, enterpriser, entrepreneur; buyer, marketer, purchaser; hawker, huckster, hustler, peddler (*also* pedlar); retailer, seller, shopkeeper, storekeeper, vendor (*also* vender); jobber, middleman, wholesaler; distributor, provider, provisioner, purveyor, supplier

mercifulness *n* kind, gentle, or compassionate treatment especially towards someone who is undeserving of it — see MERCY 1

merciless *adj* having or showing a lack of sympathy or tender feelings — see HARD 1

mercurial *adj* likely to change frequently, suddenly, or unexpectedly — see FICKLE 1

mercy *n* 1 kind, gentle, or compassionate treatment especially towards someone who is undeserving of it ⟨Always show your enemies *mercy*, because it makes you a better person.⟩

syn charity, clemency, forbearance, lenience, leniency, lenity, mercifulness, quarter

rel humanitarianism, philanthropy; empathy, pity, sympathy, understanding; commiseration, favor, grace; benevolence, care, compassion, gentleness, goodness, goodwill, kindliness, kindness; altruism, generosity, magnanimity, nobility

near ant hard-heartedness, mercilessness, pitilessness, ruthlessness, uncharitableness; reprisal, requital, retaliation, retribution, revenge, vengeance; venom, vindictiveness, virulence, vitriol; atrocity, barbarity, brutality, cruelty, sadism, savageness, savagery, truculence, viciousness, violence, wantonness; castigation, chastisement, discipline, punishment, scolding; abhorrence, abomination, execration, hate, hatred, loathing

2 an act of kind assistance — see FAVOR 1

3 the capacity for feeling for another's unhappiness or misfortune — see HEART 1

mere *adj* being this and no more ⟨His voice did not rise above a *mere* whisper.⟩

syn bare, very

rel absolute, all-out, arrant, out-and-out, outright, pure, sheer, simple, stark, total, unadulterated, unalloyed, unmitigated, unqualified, utter; alone, lone, only, singular, sole, solitary, solo, unique

merely *adv* nothing more than — see JUST 3

merge *vb* to turn into a single mass or entity that is more or less the same throughout — see BLEND 1

merging *n* the act or an instance of joining two or more things into one — see UNION 1

meridian *n* the highest part or point — see HEIGHT 1

merit *n* **1** a quality that gives something special worth — see EXCELLENCE 2

2 the relative usefulness or importance of something as judged by specific qualities — see WORTH 1

merit *vb* to be or make worthy of (as a reward or punishment) — see EARN 2

merited *adj* being what is called for by accepted standards of right and wrong — see JUST 1

meritorious *adj* **1** deserving of high regard or great approval — see ADMIRABLE

2 having sufficient worth or merit to receive one's honor, esteem, or reward — see WORTHY

merrily *adv* in a cheerful or happy manner — see GAILY 1

merriment *n* **1** a mood characterized by high spirits and amusement and often accompanied by laughter — see MIRTH

2 joyful or festive activity — see MERRYMAKING

merriness *n* a mood characterized by high spirits and amusement and often accompanied by laughter — see MIRTH

merry *adj* indicative of or marked by high spirits or good humor ⟨the traditional depiction of Santa Claus as a rotund man with *merry*, twinkling blue eyes⟩
syn blithesome, festive, gleeful, jocose, jocular, jocund, jolly, jovial, laughing, mirthful, sunny
rel amused, beaming, chuckling, giggling, smiling; bright, buoyant, carefree, cheerful, cheery, chipper, lighthearted, lightsome, upbeat; animated, bouncing, frisky, jaunty, lively, peppy, perky, spirited, sprightful, sprightly, vivacious, zippy; blessed (*also* blest), blissful, delighted, ecstatic, elated, enraptured, entranced, euphoric, exhilarated, transported; exultant, gladsome, happy, high, joyful, joyous, jubilant, overjoyed, radiant, rapturous, ravished, thrilled, tickled; amusing, facetious, flippant, frolicsome, funny, hilarious, jesting, joking, joshing, playful, sportive, witty
near ant aggrieved, anguished, blue, brokenhearted, crestfallen, dejected, depressed, despondent, disconsolate, disheartened, dispirited, downcast, downhearted, forlorn, glum, heartbroken, heartsick, low-spirited, melancholy, sad, saddened, sorrowful, unhappy; crying, groaning, moaning, sobbing, wailing, weeping; discontented, disgruntled, moody

merrymaker *n* one who engages in merrymaking especially in honor of a special occasion — see CELEBRANT

merrymaking *n* joyful or festive activity ⟨The Fourth of July is always an occasion of much *merrymaking* at our home.⟩
syn conviviality, festivity, gaiety (*also* gayety), jollification, jollity, merriment, rejoicing, reveling (*or* revelling), revelry
rel carousal, carouse; delight, diversion, entertainment, fun, mischief, pleasure,

recreation; cheer, cheerfulness, cheeriness, glee, gleefulness, hilarity, joviality, merriness, mirth, mirthfulness; carnival, celebration, festival, party, revel; frolicking, gamboling (*or* gambolling), rollicking, romping; binge, fling, frolic, gambol, lark, rollick, romp, spree; frivolity, funning, jesting, jocularity, joking, joshing, levity, lightheartedness, playfulness, zaniness
near ant dolefulness, dolor, gloom, gloominess, grief, heartache, heartbreak, heartsickness, misery, mourning, woe, wretchedness; dejection, depression, despondency, disconsolateness, dispiritedness, doldrums, downheartedness, forlornness, joylessness, melancholy, sorrow, unhappiness

mesa *n* a broad flat area of elevated land — see PLATEAU

mesh *n* **1** *usually* **meshes** *pl* something that catches and holds — see WEB 1

2 a fabric made of strands loosely twisted, knotted, or woven together at regular intervals — see ¹NET 1

mesh *vb* to catch or hold as if in a net — see ENTANGLE 2

mesmerism *n* the art or act of inducing in a person a sleeplike state during which he or she readily follows suggestions — see HYPNOSIS

mesmerize *vb* to hold the attention of as if by a spell — see ENTHRALL 1

mess *n* **1** a state in which everything is out of order — see CHAOS

2 food eaten or prepared for eating at one time — see MEAL

3 something unpleasant to look at — see EYESORE

4 a considerable amount — see LOT 2

mess *vb* to interest oneself in what is not one's concern — see INTERFERE

mess (up) *vb* **1** to make or do (something) in a clumsy or unskillful way — see BOTCH

2 to undo the proper order or arrangement of — see DISORDER

3 to make a mistake — see ERR 1

4 to strike repeatedly — see BEAT 1

mess (with) *vb* to handle thoughtlessly, ignorantly, or mischievously — see TAMPER (WITH)

message *n* a piece of conveyed information — see COMMUNICATION 1

messed *adj* lacking in order, neatness, and often cleanliness — see MESSY

messenger *n* one that carries a message or does an errand ⟨The *messenger* comes by twice a day to pick up packages.⟩
syn courier, go-between, page, runner
rel forerunner, harbinger, herald; agent, ambassador, delegate, deputy, emissary, envoy, representative; bearer, carrier, deliveryman, letter carrier, mail carrier, mailman

messiness *n* a state in which everything is out of order — see CHAOS

messy *adj* lacking in order, neatness, and often cleanliness ⟨a *messy* room⟩
syn chaotic, cluttered, confused, disarranged, disarrayed, disheveled (*or* dishevelled), disordered, disorderly, higgledy-piggledy, hugger-mugger, jumbled, littered, messed, muddled, mussed, mussy, pell-mell,

---

syn synonym(s)   **rel** related words
ant antonym(s)   **near ant** near antonym(s)

rumpled, sloppy, topsy-turvy, tousled, tumbled, unkempt, untidy, upside-down

rel bedraggled, besmirched, blackened, dingy, dirty, filthy, foul, grimy, grubby, grungy, mucky, nasty, soiled, spotted, squalid, stained, sullied, unclean, uncleanly; dowdy, frowsy (*or* frowzy), shaggy, slatternly, sloven, slovenly

phrases at sixes and sevens, out of joint

near ant clean, cleaned, hygienic, immaculate, sparkling, spick-and-span (*or* spic-and-span), spotless, stainless, unsoiled, unsullied; methodical (*also* methodic), regular, systematic, systematized; careful, fastidious, finicky, fussy, meticulous; combed, groomed, manicured; taintless, undefiled, unpolluted, untainted, wholesome

ant crisp, neat, neatened, ordered, orderly, organized, shipshape, snug, tidied, tidy, trim, uncluttered, well-ordered

metamorphose *vb* to change in form, appearance, or use — see CONVERT 2

metamorphosis *n* a change in form, appearance, or use — see CONVERSION 1

metaphor *n* an elaborate or fanciful way of expressing something — see CONCEIT 1

metaphoric *or* **metaphorical** *adj* expressing one thing in terms normally used for another — see FIGURATIVE

metaphysical *adj* 1 dealing with or expressing a quality or idea — see ABSTRACT 1

2 of, relating to, or being part of a reality beyond the observable physical universe — see SUPERNATURAL 1

mete (out) *vb* to give out (something) to appropriate individuals — see ADMINISTER 1

meter *n* the recurrent pattern formed by a series of sounds having a regular rise and fall in intensity — see RHYTHM

method *n* the means or procedure for doing something ⟨The city council is stuck in the last century and needs to adopt more modern *methods* for doing things.⟩

syn approach, fashion, form, manner, strategy, style, system, tack, tactics, technique, way

rel mode, modus operandi; blueprint, design, game, ground plan, intrigue, layout, line, model, plan, plot, program, route, scheme; expedient, move, shift, step; practice (*also* practise), process, routine; policy

methodical *also* **methodic** *adj* following a set method, arrangement, or pattern ⟨a *methodical* study plan that included lists of points to memorize⟩

syn neat, orderly, organized, regular, systematic, systematized

rel ordered, regularized, standardized, structured; accurate, clocklike, correct, exact, precise; detailed, specific

near ant chaotic, disordered, disorderly

ant disorganized, haphazard, hit-or-miss, immethodical, irregular, nonsystematic, patternless, planless, systemless, unsystematic

meticulous *adj* taking, showing, or involving great care and effort — see PAINSTAKING

meticulousness *n* strict attentiveness to what one is doing — see CARE 1

metrical *or* **metric** *adj* marked by or occurring with a noticeable regularity in the rise and fall of sound — see RHYTHMIC

metropolis *n* a thickly settled, highly populated area — see CITY

metropolitan *n* a person with the outlook, experience, and manners thought to be typical of big city dwellers — see COSMOPOLITAN

mettlesome *adj* 1 having much high-spirited energy and movement — see LIVELY 1

2 marked by a lively display of strong feeling — see SPIRITED 1

mewl *vb* to utter feeble plaintive cries — see WHIMPER 1

microscopic *also* **microscopical** *adj* very small in size — see TINY

mid *adj* occupying a position equally distant from the ends or extremes — see MIDDLE 1

mid *prep* in or into the middle of — see AMONG

midday *n* the middle of the day — see NOON 1

middle *adj* 1 occupying a position equally distant from the ends or extremes ⟨You must mark the exact *middle* point of each of these lines in order to solve the problem.⟩

syn central, halfway, intermediary, intermediate, medial, median, mediate, medium, mid, midmost

rel equidistant; inmost, inner, innermost, nearest; betwixt and between, gray (*also* grey), in-between

near ant outer, peripheral

ant extreme, farthest, farthermost, furthermost, furthest, outermost, outmost, remotest, utmost

2 being about midway between extremes of amount or size ⟨a house that is *middle*-sized for that neighborhood⟩ ⟨a man of *middle* height⟩

syn average, intermediate, mean, median, medium, middling, moderate, modest

rel reasonable; common, commonplace, conventional, normal, popular, regular, routine, standard, typical, usual; adequate, passable, tolerable

near ant excessive, extreme; exceptional, rare, strange, uncommon, unusual; distinctive, idiosyncratic, special, unique; individual, peculiar, private

middle *n* 1 a middle point between extremes — see MEAN 1

2 an area or point that is an equal distance from all points along an edge or outer surface — see CENTER 2

3 the middle region of the human torso — see MIDRIFF

4 the most intense or characteristic phase of something — see THICK

middleman *n* one who works with opposing sides in order to bring about an agreement — see MEDIATOR

middle-of-the-road *adj* avoiding major social change or extreme political ideas — see MODERATE 1

middling *adj* 1 being about midway between extremes of amount or size — see MIDDLE 2

2 of average to below average quality — see MEDIOCRE 1

midget *n* a living thing much smaller than others of its kind — see DWARF 1

midmost *adj* occupying a position equally distant from the ends or extremes — see MIDDLE 1

midpoint *n* **1** a middle point between extremes — see MEAN 1

2 an area or point that is an equal distance from all points along an edge or outer surface — see CENTER 2

midriff *n* the middle region of the human torso ⟨*Midriff*-baring tops are popular this summer.⟩

syn middle, waist, waistline

rel trunk; abdomen, belly, gut, stomach

midst *n* **1** an area or point that is an equal distance from all points along an edge or outer surface — see CENTER 2

2 the most intense or characteristic phase of something — see THICK

midst *prep* in or into the middle of — see AMONG

mien *n* the outward form of someone or something especially as indicative of a quality — see APPEARANCE 1

might *n* the ability to exert effort for the accomplishment of a task — see POWER 2

mightily *adv* **1** to a great degree — see VERY 1

2 with great effort or determination — see HARD 1

3 in a vigorous and forceful manner — see HARD 3

mighty *adj* **1** having great power or influence — see IMPORTANT 2

2 unusually large — see HUGE

mighty *adv* to a great degree — see VERY 1

migrant *adj* having a way of life that involves moving from one region to another typically on a seasonal basis — see MIGRATORY

migrant *n* one that leaves one place to settle in another — see EMIGRANT

migratory *adj* having a way of life that involves moving from one region to another typically on a seasonal basis ⟨Most of the apple crop is picked by *migratory* workers.⟩ ⟨*migratory* birds heading south for the winter⟩

syn migrant, mobile

rel errant, fugitive, itinerant, peripatetic, ranging, roaming, roving, traveling (*or* travelling), vagabond, vagrant, wandering, wayfaring; drifting, fiddle-footed, footloose, gadabout, gallivanting (*also* galavanting), rambling, sauntering, strolling, traipsing

near ant immobile, stationary; established, fast, fixed, rooted, sedentary, set, settled

ant nonmigrant, nonmigratory, resident

mild *adj* **1** marked by temperatures that are neither too high nor too low — see CLEMENT 1

2 not harsh or stern especially in nature or effect — see GENTLE 1

milestone *n* a point in a chain of events at

which an important change (as in one's fortunes) occurs — see TURNING POINT

milieu *n* the circumstances, conditions, or objects by which one is surrounded — see ENVIRONMENT

militancy *n* an inclination to fight or quarrel — see BELLIGERENCE

militant *adj* **1** feeling or displaying eagerness to fight — see BELLIGERENT

2 having or showing a bold forcefulness in the pursuit of a goal — see AGGRESSIVE 1

militant *n* one who is intensely or excessively devoted to a cause — see ZEALOT

militarist *n* one who urges or attempts to cause a war — see WARMONGER

military *adj* **1** of or relating to the armed services ⟨The colonel testified that revealing any more information would have required giving away *military* secrets.⟩

syn martial, service

rel naval; GI, gladiatorial, mercenary, soldierly; militant, militarist, militaristic, warlike; enlisted, regular; paramilitary

near ant civil, civilian

ant nonmilitary

2 of, relating to, or suitable for war or a warrior — see MARTIAL 1

military *n* the combined army, air force, and navy of a nation — see ARMED FORCES

mill *n* a building or set of buildings for the manufacturing of goods — see FACTORY

mill *vb* to reduce to fine particles — see POWDER

mime *n* **1** an actor in a story performed silently and entirely by body movements ⟨an internationally renowned *mime*⟩

syn mimic, mummer, pantomime, pantomimist

rel entertainer, performer, player, trouper; aper, imitator, impersonator, impressionist; clown, pantaloon

2 a movement of the body or limbs that expresses or emphasizes an idea or feeling — see GESTURE 1

mime *vb* to use (someone or something) as the model for one's speech, mannerisms, or behavior — see IMITATE 1

mimetic *adj* using or marked by the use of something else as a basis or model — see IMITATIVE 1

mimic *adj* **1** being such in appearance only and made with or manufactured from usually cheaper materials — see IMITATION

2 using or marked by the use of something else as a basis or model — see IMITATIVE 1

mimic *n* **1** a person who imitates another's voice and mannerisms for comic effect ⟨a gifted *mimic* who can do a terrific imitation of anyone's voice⟩

syn imitator, impersonator, impressionist

rel burlesquer, caricaturist, lampooner, mocker, parodist, satirist; mime, mimer, mummer, pantomime, pantomimist; actor, player, trouper; ape, copycat, echo, parrot

2 an actor in a story performed silently and entirely by body movements — see MIME 1

mimic *vb* **1** to copy or exaggerate (someone or something) in order to make fun of ⟨The comedian was famous for *mimicking* the President's distinctive way of speaking.⟩

---

syn synonym(s)   *rel* related words
ant antonym(s)   *near ant* near antonym(s)

syn burlesque, caricature, do, imitate, mock, parody, spoof, travesty

rel lampoon, satirize; deride, gibe (*or* jibe), ridicule; ape, copycat, monkey, parrot; duplicate, emulate, replicate, reproduce; act, counterfeit, dissemble, fake, feign, pretend, sham, simulate; elaborate, embellish, embroider, exaggerate, magnify, pad, stretch; amplify, enhance, expand, flesh (out), overdraw, overstate, put on; mime, pantomime; impersonate, perform, play

2 to use (someone or something) as the model for one's speech, mannerisms, or behavior — see IMITATE 1

mince *vb* to cut into small pieces — see CHOP

mind *n* **1** the part of a person that feels, thinks, perceives, wills, and especially reasons ⟨I went for a walk to clear my *mind*.⟩

syn brain, cerebrum, head, psyche, thinker

rel gray matter, intellect, intelligence, reason, skull; acumen, alertness, astuteness, brilliance, insight, mentality, perception, perspicacity, sagacity, sapience, wisdom, wit

2 the normal or healthy condition of the mental abilities ⟨That noise is driving me out of my *mind*.⟩

syn daylights, head, reason, saneness, sanity, wit(s)

rel rationality, reasonableness, sense; clearheadedness, lucidity, lucidness, soundness; wisdom

near ant delusion, hallucination; delirium, frenzy, hysteria

ant dementia, unreason

3 an idea that is believed to be true or valid without positive knowledge — see OPINION 1

4 the power or process of recalling what has been previously learned or experienced — see MEMORY 1

mind *vb* **1** to pay attention especially through the act of hearing — see LISTEN

2 to act according to the commands of — see OBEY

3 to be cautious of or on guard against — see BEWARE 1

4 to have an interest or concern for — see CARE

5 to take charge of especially on behalf of another — see ²TEND 1

6 to take notice of and be guided by — see HEED 1

minded *adj* having a desire or inclination (as for a specified course of action) — see WILLING 1

mindful *adj* having specified facts or feelings actively impressed on the mind — see CONSCIOUS 1

mindless *adj* **1** not having or showing an ability to absorb ideas readily — see STUPID 1

2 not paying or showing close attention especially for the purpose of avoiding trouble — see CARELESS 1

mindlessness *n* the quality or state of lacking intelligence or quickness of mind — see STUPIDITY 1

mine *n* **1** an abundant source ⟨a baseball fanatic who is a *mine* of fascinating trivia about the game⟩

syn cornucopia

rel repository, store, storehouse; cache, hoard, stash; bonanza

2 a usually concealed explosive device designed to go off when disturbed — see BOOBY TRAP 1

mingle *vb* **1** to turn into a single mass or entity that is more or less the same throughout — see BLEND 1

2 to take part in social activities — see SOCIALIZE

miniature *adj* very small in size — see TINY

miniature *n* an exact representation of something in greatly reduced size — see MODEL 1

minimal *adj* being the least in amount, number, or size possible ⟨The repairs were made with *minimal* disruption to the workday.⟩

syn littlest, lowest, minimum, slightest

rel fewer, lesser, low, minor, modest, slight, small, smaller; infinitesimal, micro, subminiature, ultramicro; irreducible

near ant highest

ant biggest, full, greatest, hugest, largest, maximum, most, top, topmost, utmost

minimize *vb* to express scornfully one's low opinion of — see DECRY 1

minimum *adj* being the least in amount, number, or size possible — see MINIMAL

minion *n* a person or thing that is preferred over others — see FAVORITE

minister *n* a person sent on a mission to represent another — see AMBASSADOR

minister (to) *vb* to attend to the needs and comforts of — see NURSE 1

ministerial *adj* of, relating to, or characteristic of the clergy — see CLERICAL

minor *adj* **1** having not so great importance or rank as another — see LESSER

2 of little or less value or merit — see INFERIOR 2

3 lacking importance — see UNIMPORTANT

minstrel *n* a person who writes poetry — see POET

minstrelsy *n* writing that uses rhythm, vivid language, and often rhyme to evoke an emotional response — see POETRY 1

mint *adj* being in an original and unused or unspoiled state — see FRESH 1

mint *n* a very large amount of money — see FORTUNE 2

minus *n* a feature of someone or something that creates difficulty for achieving success — see DISADVANTAGE 1

minus *prep* not having — see WITHOUT 1

minuscule *adj* very small in size — see TINY

minute *adj* **1** including many small descriptive features — see DETAILED 1

2 lacking importance — see UNIMPORTANT

3 so small or unimportant as to warrant little or no attention — see NEGLIGIBLE 1

4 made or done with extreme care and accuracy — see FINE 2

5 very small in size — see TINY

minute *n* a very small space of time — see INSTANT

minutely *adv* with attention to all aspects or details — see THOROUGHLY 1

miracle *n* something extraordinary or surprising — see WONDER 1

miraculous *adj* **1** being so extraordinary or abnormal as to suggest powers which violate the laws of nature — see SUPERNATURAL 2

2 causing wonder or astonishment — see MARVELOUS 1

mire *n* **1** soft wet earth — see MUD

2 spongy land saturated or partially covered with water — see SWAMP

3 a difficult, puzzling, or embarrassing situation from which there is no easy escape — see PREDICAMENT

mire *vb* **1** to make dirty — see DIRTY

2 to place in conflict or difficulties — see EMBROIL

mirror *n* a smooth or polished surface that forms images by reflection ⟨Breaking a *mirror* is supposed to bring seven years of bad luck.⟩

syn looking glass

rel cheval glass, hand glass, pier glass

mirror *vb* to reproduce or show (an exact likeness) as a mirror would — see REFLECT 1

mirth *n* a mood characterized by high spirits and amusement and often accompanied by laughter ⟨Her unexpected visit provided much *mirth* in the office.⟩

syn cheer, cheerfulness, cheeriness, festivity, gaiety (*also* gayety), glee, gleefulness, hilarity, joviality, merriment, merriness, mirthfulness

rel frivolity, levity; jollification, jollity, reveling (*or* revelling), revelry; brightness, buoyancy, good-humoredness, good-naturedness, humor, sunniness; gamesomeness, insouciance, lightheartedness, playfulness, sportiveness; clownishness, flippancy, funning, jest, jesting, jocoseness, jocosity, jocularity, joking, joshing; frolicking, gamboling (*or* gambolling), rollicking, romping

near ant blues, dejection, depression, forlornness, sadness, sorrow, unhappiness; dolefulness, dolorousness, joylessness, plaintiveness, woe, woefulness; blackness, darkness, gloominess; desolateness, desolation; heartbreak, misery, mourning, wretchedness

mirthful *adj* indicative of or marked by high spirits or good humor — see MERRY

mirthfully *adv* in a cheerful or happy manner — see GAILY 1

mirthfulness *n* a mood characterized by high spirits and amusement and often accompanied by laughter — see MIRTH

miry *adj* full of or covered with soft wet earth — see MUDDY 1

misadventure *n* bad luck or an example of this — see MISFORTUNE

misanthrope *n* a person who distrusts other people and believes that everything is done for selfish reasons — see CYNIC

misanthropic *adj* having or showing a deep distrust of human beings and their motives — see CYNICAL

misapplication *n* incorrect or improper use — see MISUSE

misapply *vb* to put to a bad or improper use ⟨You've *misapplied* the theorem to certain problems that require a different formula.⟩ ⟨public funds that were *misapplied*⟩

syn abuse, misuse, pervert, profane

rel degrade, twist; mismanage; corrupt, debase, desecrate

near ant apply, employ, use, utilize; respect

misapprehend *vb* to fail to understand the true or actual meaning of — see MISUNDERSTAND

misapprehension *n* **1** a failure to understand correctly — see MISUNDERSTANDING 1

2 a wrong judgment — see MISTAKE 1

misappropriate *vb* to take (something) without right and with an intent to keep — see STEAL 1

misbehave *vb* to behave badly ⟨scolded the children for *misbehaving*⟩

syn act out, act up, carry on

rel misconduct; disobey, rebel; clown (around), cut up, horse around, kid (around); show off; roughhouse

phrases raise Cain (*or* raise hell), run riot

near ant obey; acquit, act, bear, comport, conduct, demean, deport, quit; comply, conform; check, collect, compose, constrain, contain, control, curb, handle, inhibit, move, quiet, repress, restrain

misbehaving *adj* engaging in or marked by childish misbehavior — see NAUGHTY

misbehavior *n* improper or illegal behavior — see MISCONDUCT

misbelief *n* a false idea or belief — see FALLACY 1

miscalculate *vb* to make an incorrect judgment regarding ⟨They *miscalculated* how difficult the mountainous trek would be.⟩

syn misconceive, misjudge, mistake

rel misapprehend, misconstrue, misinterpret, misunderstand; overestimate, overrate, overvalue; discount, misreckon

miscarry *vb* to go wrong ⟨The plan *miscarried* and we had to start all over.⟩

syn misfire

rel miss; break down, bust, come (out), crash, die, fail, founder, stall; bomb, fizzle, flame out, flop, flunk, fold, wash out; flounder, struggle; decline, slip, slump, wane

phrases come a cropper, come to grief, fall flat, fall short

near ant prevail, succeed; flourish, prosper, thrive

miscellaneous *adj* consisting of many things of different sorts ⟨The bottom of the drawer was always a *miscellaneous* accumulation of odds and ends.⟩

syn assorted, eclectic, heterogeneous, mixed, motley, patchwork, promiscuous, ragtag, varied

rel manifold, multifarious; multiple, multiplex, myriad; disparate, divergent, diverse, sundry; amalgamated, blended, combined, commingled, commixed, conglomerated, fused, incorporated, intermingled, intermixed, merged, mingled; composite, conglomerate, hybrid; unclassified, unsorted

near ant monolithic, uniform; alike, iden-

---

tical, like, same; distinct, distinctive, individual, separate

ant homogeneous

miscellaneousness *n* the quality or state of being composed of many different elements or types — see VARIETY 1

miscellany *n* 1 an unorganized collection or mixture of various things ⟨The box from the attic contained a *miscellany* of old records, family photo albums, and long-forgotten love letters.⟩

syn agglomerate, agglomeration, assortment, clutter, hash, hodgepodge, hotchpotch, jumble, litter, medley, mélange, mishmash, motley, muddle, patchwork, potpourri, ragbag, rummage, scramble, shuffle, tumble, variety, welter

rel notions, oddments, odds and ends, sundries; admixture, amalgam, blend, combination, commixture, composite, compound, fusion, intermixture, mix-up; mess, morass, shambles

2 a collection of writings — see ANTHOLOGY

mischance *n* 1 a chance and usually sudden event bringing loss or injury — see ACCIDENT 1

2 bad luck or an example of this — see MISFORTUNE

mischief *n* 1 playful, reckless behavior that is not intended to cause serious harm ⟨They are always up to some kind of *mischief*.⟩

syn devilishness, devilment, devilry (*or* deviltry), hob, impishness, knavery, mischievousness, rascality, roguishness

rel diabolicalness, misbehavior, misconduct, naughtiness, troublemaking; friskiness, playfulness, sportiveness; chicanery, trickery; goings-on, hanky-panky, high jinks (*also* hijinks), monkeying, skylarking, tomfoolery; horseplay, roughhousing; antic, caper, practical joke, trick

near ant gravity, seriousness, solemnity

2 a natural disposition for playful behavior — see PLAYFULNESS

3 an appealingly mischievous person — see SCAMP 1

mischievous *adj* 1 tending to or exhibiting reckless playfulness ⟨The children had been so *mischievous* that we had to pay the babysitter extra to clean up the mess.⟩

syn arch, devilish, elvish, impish, knavish, pixieish, prankish, rascally, roguish, sly, waggish

rel antic, coltish, coy, frisky, frolicsome, kittenish, playful, sportive; happy, lighthearted, whimsical; energetic, lively, spirited, sprightly; artful, crafty, cunning, trickish, tricky, wily; misbehaving, naughty, troublemaking; pestering, riling, teasing

near ant grave, grim, sedate, sober, solemn, staid, stern

2 engaging in or marked by childish misbehavior — see NAUGHTY

3 causing or capable of causing harm — see HARMFUL

mischievousness *n* 1 a natural disposition for playful behavior — see PLAYFULNESS

2 playful, reckless behavior that is not intended to cause serious harm — see MISCHIEF 1

misconceive *vb* to make an incorrect judgment regarding — see MISCALCULATE

misconception *n* a false idea or belief — see FALLACY 1

misconduct *n* improper or illegal behavior ⟨Some rough play got the hockey player fined for *misconduct* on the ice.⟩

syn malfeasance, misbehavior, misdoing, wrongdoing

rel crime, malefaction, misdeed, misdemeanor, sin, transgression, trespass, wrong; malpractice; goings-on, hanky-panky; familiarity, impropriety, indiscretion; blunder, flub, fumble, goof, lapse, miscue, misstep, mistake, slip, slipup, stumble

misconduct *vb* to manage badly — see MISMANAGE

misconstruction *n* a failure to understand correctly — see MISUNDERSTANDING 1

misconstrue *vb* to fail to understand the true or actual meaning of — see MISUNDERSTAND

misconstruing *n* a failure to understand correctly — see MISUNDERSTANDING 1

miscreant *n* 1 a mean, evil, or unprincipled person — see VILLAIN

2 a person who has committed a crime — see CRIMINAL

miscue *n* an unintentional departure from truth or accuracy — see ERROR 1

misdeed *n* a breaking of a moral or legal code — see OFFENSE 1

misdoing *n* 1 a breaking of a moral or legal code — see OFFENSE 1

2 improper or illegal behavior — see MISCONDUCT

miser *n* a mean grasping person who is usually stingy with money ⟨The *miser* liked to sit and play with his money.⟩

syn cheapskate, niggard, piker, scrooge, skinflint, tightwad

rel hoarder, pack rat, saver

near ant prodigal, profligate, spender, spendthrift, squanderer, waster, wastrel

miserable *adj* 1 causing or marked by an atmosphere lacking in cheer — see GLOOMY 1

2 feeling unhappiness — see SAD 1

3 of low quality — see CHEAP 2

4 showing signs of advanced wear and tear and neglect — see SHABBY 1

5 deserving of one's pity — see PATHETIC 1

6 deserving pitying scorn (as for inadequacy) — see PITIFUL 1

miserliness *n* the quality or practice of being overly sparing with money — see PARSIMONY 1

misery *n* 1 a situation or state that causes great suffering and unhappiness — see HELL 2

2 a state of great suffering of body or mind — see DISTRESS 1

misfire *vb* to go wrong — see MISCARRY

misfortune *n* bad luck or an example of this ⟨Through sheer *misfortune* our car got a flat tire and we were late for the ceremony.⟩ ⟨Our *misfortunes* of the last year included the loss of a beloved pet.⟩

syn adversity, ill, knock, misadventure, mischance, mishap, tragedy

rel calamity, cataclysm, catastrophe, disaster; affliction, hardship, trial, tribulation, woe; distress, misery, suffering, unhappiness; defeat, failure, fizzle, nonsuccess; curse, evil, sorrow, trouble; accident, casualty; blow, body blow, disappointment, letdown, setback; circumstance, destiny, doom, fate, lot, portion

near ant break, chance, godsend, hit, opportunity, strike, stroke, windfall; accomplishment, achievement, success

ant fortune, luck, serendipity

misgiving *n* **1** a feeling or attitude that one does not know the truth, truthfulness, or trustworthiness of someone or something — see DOUBT

2 an uneasy feeling about the rightness of what one is doing or going to do — see QUALM

3 suspicion or fear of future harm or misfortune — see APPREHENSION 1

misgovern *vb* to manage badly — see MISMANAGE

misguide *vb* to cause to believe what is untrue — see DECEIVE

mishandle *vb* **1** to inflict physical or emotional harm upon — see ABUSE 1

2 to abuse physically — see MANHANDLE 1

3 to manage badly — see MISMANAGE

mishap *n* **1** a chance and usually sudden event bringing loss or injury — see ACCIDENT 1

2 bad luck or an example of this — see MISFORTUNE

mishmash *n* an unorganized collection or mixture of various things — see MISCELLANY 1

misinform *vb* to cause to believe what is untrue — see DECEIVE

misinterpret *vb* **1** to change so much as to create a wrong impression or alter the meaning of — see GARBLE

2 to fail to understand the true or actual meaning of — see MISUNDERSTAND

misinterpretation *n* a failure to understand correctly — see MISUNDERSTANDING 1

misjudge *vb* to make an incorrect judgment regarding — see MISCALCULATE

misjudging *n* a wrong judgment — see MISTAKE 1

misjudgment *n* a wrong judgment — see MISTAKE 1

mislaid *adj* no longer possessed — see LOST

mislay *vb* to be unable to find or have at hand — see LOSE 1

mislaying *n* the act or an instance of not having or being able to find — see LOSS 1

mislead *vb* to cause to believe what is untrue — see DECEIVE

misleading *adj* tending or having power to deceive — see DECEPTIVE 1

mismanage *vb* to manage badly ⟨The business was *mismanaged* so seriously that it eventually had to declare bankruptcy.⟩

syn misconduct, misgovern, mishandle, misrule

rel abuse, ill-treat, ill-use, maltreat, mistreat, misuse; damage, harm, hurt, violate; botch, bungle

---

syn synonym(s)   *rel* related words
ant antonym(s)   *near ant* near antonym(s)

near ant govern, handle, husband, manage, rule; care (for), nurture; aid, help, protect, rescue

misplace *vb* to be unable to find or have at hand — see LOSE 1

misplaced *adj* no longer possessed — see LOST

misplacement *n* the act or an instance of not having or being able to find — see LOSS 1

misread *vb* to fail to understand the true or actual meaning of — see MISUNDERSTAND

misreading *n* a failure to understand correctly — see MISUNDERSTANDING 1

misrepresent *vb* **1** to change so much as to create a wrong impression or alter the meaning of — see GARBLE

2 to give a misleading impression of — see BELIE 1

misrule *n* a state in which there is widespread wrongdoing and disregard for rules and authority — see ANARCHY

misrule *vb* to manage badly — see MISMANAGE

¹**miss** *n* **1** a female person who has not yet reached adulthood — see GIRL 2

2 a young unmarried woman — see GIRL 1

²**miss** *n* something that has failed — see FAILURE 3

miss *vb* **1** to fail to attend — see CUT 2

2 to fail to understand the true or actual meaning of — see MISUNDERSTAND

3 to be unsuccessful — see FAIL 2

misshapen *adj* badly or imperfectly formed — see MALFORMED

missing *adj* **1** no longer possessed — see LOST

2 not present or in evidence — see ABSENT 2

3 not at a certain place — see ABSENT 1

mission *n* a specific task with which a person or group is charged ⟨Your *mission* is to clean up the house before company arrives.⟩

syn assignment, brief, business, charge, detail, job, operation, post

rel burden, chore, duty, need, obligation, office, requirement, responsibility; errand, labor, work; commitment, pledge, promise; appointment, commission, designation, nomination; compulsion, constraint, restraint

missive *n* a message on paper from one person or group to another — see ¹LETTER

misspend *vb* to use up carelessly — see WASTE 1

misstate *vb* to change so much as to create a wrong impression or alter the meaning of — see GARBLE

misstep *n* **1** a wrong judgment — see MISTAKE 1

2 an unintentional departure from truth or accuracy — see ERROR 1

mist *n* **1** a light or fine rain — see DRIZZLE

2 an atmospheric condition in which suspended particles in the air rob it of its transparency — see HAZE 1

mist *vb* to make dark, dim, or indistinct — see CLOUD 1

mistake *n* **1** a wrong judgment ⟨I made a *mistake* when I believed him.⟩

syn misapprehension, misjudging, misjudgment, misstep, slip, slipup

rel blunder, errancy, error, fault, flub, fumble, gaffe, goof, inaccuracy, lapse, miscue, stumble, trip; foul-up, muff; misstatement; misconception, misconstruction, misconstruing, misinterpretation, misunderstanding

2 an unintentional departure from truth or accuracy — see ERROR 1

mistake *vb* **1** to fail to understand the true or actual meaning of — see MISUNDERSTAND

2 to make an incorrect judgment regarding — see MISCALCULATE

3 to fail to differentiate (a thing) from something similar or related — see CONFUSE 3

mistaken *adj* having an opinion that does not agree with truth or the facts — see INCORRECT 1

mistakenly *adv* in a mistaken or inappropriate way — see WRONGLY

mistreat *vb* to inflict physical or emotional harm upon — see ABUSE 1

mistrust *n* a feeling or attitude that one does not know the truth, truthfulness, or trustworthiness of someone or something — see DOUBT

mistrust *vb* to have no trust or confidence in — see DISTRUST

mistrustful *adj* **1** inclined to doubt or question claims — see SKEPTICAL 1

2 not feeling sure about the truth, wisdom, or trustworthiness of someone or something — see DOUBTFUL 1

mistrustfully *adv* with distrust — see ASKANCE

mistrustfulness *n* a feeling or attitude that one does not know the truth, truthfulness, or trustworthiness of someone or something — see DOUBT

misty *adj* **1** filled with or dimmed by fine particles (as of dust or water) in suspension — see HAZY 1

2 not seen or understood clearly — see FAINT 1

misunderstand *vb* to fail to understand the true or actual meaning of ⟨You *misunderstood* that poem because you took everything so literally.⟩

syn misapprehend, misconstrue, misinterpret, misread, miss, mistake

rel misconceive, misjudge; mishear

ant appreciate, apprehend, catch, comprehend, conceive, fathom, get, grasp, know, make out, penetrate, perceive, see, seize, take in, understand

misunderstanding *n* **1** a failure to understand correctly ⟨People once thought that there were canals on Mars because of a common *misunderstanding* of a report by an Italian astronomer.⟩

syn misapprehension, misconstruction, misconstruing, misinterpretation, misreading

rel misconception, misperception, mistake

near ant appreciation, apprehension, comprehension, conception, grasp, knowledge, perception, understanding; awareness, realization

2 an often noisy or angry expression of differing opinions — see ARGUMENT 1

misusage *n* incorrect or improper use — see MISUSE

misuse *n* incorrect or improper use ⟨The warranty for this dryer is null and void if you subject the product to deliberate *misuse.*⟩

syn abuse, misapplication, misusage, perversion

rel mishandling, mismanagement, mismanaging; ill-treatment, ill-usage, maltreatment, mistreatment; damage, destruction, ruin, spoiling, wrecking; corruption, debasement, desecration, prostitution

near ant application, employment, use, utilization

misuse *vb* **1** to put to a bad or improper use — see MISAPPLY

2 to inflict physical or emotional harm upon — see ABUSE 1

mite *n* **1** a very small sum of money ⟨I have only a *mite* left to buy lunch for the rest of the week.⟩

syn peanuts, pittance, shoestring, song

rel petty cash, pocket money, spending money

near ant bankroll, capital, funds, means, wherewithal; opulence, riches, treasure, wealth; bonanza, mine, treasury

ant bundle, fortune, mint, wad

2 a living thing much smaller than others of its kind — see DWARF 1

3 a very small amount — see PARTICLE 1

mitigate *vb* to make more bearable or less severe — see HELP 2

mix *n* a distinct entity formed by the combining of two or more different things — see BLEND

mix *vb* **1** to turn into a single mass or entity that is more or less the same throughout — see BLEND 1

2 to take part in social activities — see SOCIALIZE

mix (up) *vb* **1** to fail to differentiate (a thing) from something similar or related — see CONFUSE 3

2 to undo the proper order or arrangement of — see DISORDER

mixed *adj* **1** being offspring produced by parents of different races, breeds, species, or genera ⟨Our *mixed* dog has a greyhound's body but the features of a collie.⟩

syn cold-blooded (*or* coldblood), cross, crossbred, hybrid, mongrel

rel grade, half-bred; crossed, hybridized, interbred, outcrossed

near ant pedigreed (*or* pedigree); inbred, linebred, straightbred

ant full-blooded, purebred, thoroughbred

2 consisting of many things of different sorts — see MISCELLANEOUS

mixture *n* a distinct entity formed by the combining of two or more different things — see BLEND

mix–up *n* an instance of confusion — see FOUL-UP

moan *n* **1** a long low sound indicating pain or grief ⟨She uttered an agonized *moan* and clutched her stomach.⟩

syn groan, wail

rel blubbering, crying, sniveling, sobbing, weeping, whimpering, whining, yammering; keen, lament, lamentation, plaint;

bawl, cry, howl, shriek, squall, whimper, whine, yelp, yowl

near ant cackle, chortle, chuckle, giggle, guffaw, laugh, snicker, snigger, titter, twitter

2 a crying out in grief — see LAMENT 1

3 an expression of dissatisfaction, pain, or resentment — see COMPLAINT 1

moan *vb* **1** to utter a moan ⟨The child *moaned* and cried when it was discovered that his favorite toy was lost.⟩

syn groan, wail

rel blubber, cry, sob, weep; sniff, snivel, whimper, whine; bemoan, bewail, deplore, keen, lament, rue; agonize, anguish, bleed, grieve, hurt, mourn, sorrow, suffer; bawl, howl, shriek, squall, yammer, yelp, yowl

near ant cackle, chortle, chuckle, crack up, giggle, guffaw, laugh, snicker, titter, twitter

2 to express dissatisfaction, pain, or resentment usually tiresomely — see COMPLAIN

mob *n* **1** a great number of persons or creatures massed together — see CROWD 1

2 a group involved in secret or criminal activities — see RING 1

3 the body of the community as contrasted with the elite — see MASS 1

mob *vb* to move upon or fill (something) in great numbers — see CROWD 2

mobile *adj* **1** capable of being moved especially with ease — see MOVABLE

2 having a way of life that involves moving from one region to another typically on a seasonal basis — see MIGRATORY

mobilization *n* an act of gathering forces together to renew or attempt an effort — see RALLY 1

mobilize *vb* to assemble and make ready for action ⟨We are prepared to *mobilize* the troops on very short notice.⟩

syn marshal (*also* marshall), muster, rally

rel arrange, group, line up, order, organize; call (up), convene, summon; activate; collect, round up

near ant disarrange, disorder, disorganize; disrupt, disturb; deactivate, dismiss; break up, disband, dissolve, split (up)

ant demobilize

mobster *n* a violent, brutal person who is often a member of an organized gang — see HOODLUM

mock *adj* **1** being such in appearance only and made with or manufactured from usually cheaper materials — see IMITATION

2 lacking in natural or spontaneous quality — see ARTIFICIAL 1

mock *n* **1** a person or thing that is made fun of — see LAUGHINGSTOCK

2 something that is made to look exactly like something else — see COPY

mock *vb* **1** to copy or exaggerate (someone or something) in order to make fun of — see MIMIC 1

2 to make (someone or something) the object of unkind laughter — see RIDICULE

3 to go against the commands, prohibitions, or rules of — see DISOBEY

mocker *n* a person who causes repeated emotional pain, distress, or annoyance to another — see TORMENTOR

mockery *n* **1** a poor, insincere, or insulting imitation of something ⟨He argued that a failure to charge white-collar criminals makes a *mockery* of the rule of law.⟩

syn caricature, cartoon, farce, joke, parody, sham, travesty

rel burlesque, comedy; lampoon, takeoff; counterfeit, fake, feigning, forgery, hoax, humbug, knockoff, phony (*also* phoney), pretense (*or* pretence)

near ant homage, tribute

2 a person or thing that is made fun of — see LAUGHINGSTOCK

3 the making of unkind jokes as a way of showing one's scorn for someone or something — see RIDICULE

mod *adj* being or involving the latest methods, concepts, information, or styles — see MODERN

¹mode *n* **1** a distinctive way of putting ideas into words — see STYLE 1

2 a state of mind dominated by a particular emotion — see MOOD 1

²mode *n* a practice or interest that is very popular for a short time — see FAD

model *adj* constituting, serving as, or worthy of being a pattern to be imitated ⟨the university's *model* program⟩

syn archetypal (*also* archetypical), classic, definitive, exemplary, paradigmatic, quintessential, textbook

rel ideal, nonpareil, special, unique; absolute, flawless, impeccable, perfect; A1, bang-up, banner, capital, choice, crackerjack, dandy, excellent, fabulous, fantastic, fine, first-class, first-rate, grand, great, marvelous (*or* marvellous), nifty, par excellence, prime, sensational, splendid, stellar, sterling, superb, superior, superlative, swell, terrific, tip-top, top, top-notch, unsurpassed, wonderful

near ant bad, low-grade, poor, substandard, unsatisfactory; atrocious, execrable, vile, wretched; deficient, disappointing, failed, inadequate, inferior; average, normal, ordinary, representative, typical; mediocre, second-class, second-rate

model *n* **1** an exact representation of something in greatly reduced size ⟨The dollhouse was a tiny, perfect *model* of the family's actual house.⟩

syn miniature

rel carbon copy, copy, dummy, dupe, duplicate, duplication, facsimile, imitation, mock, reduplication, replica, replication, reproduction; dwarf, midget, mini, pocket edition, pygmy (*also* pigmy)

near ant archetype, original, prototype; blowup, enlargement

2 a person who poses with or wears merchandise (as clothes) often for pictorial advertising ⟨The most famous *models* can earn thousands of dollars an hour.⟩

syn manikin (*also* mannikin), mannequin

rel spokesmodel, supermodel

3 someone of such unequaled perfection as to deserve imitation — see IDEAL 1

moderate *adj* **1** avoiding extremes in behavior or expression ⟨a *moderate* coffee drinker⟩

---

syn synonym(s)   *rel* related words
ant antonym(s)   *near ant* near antonym(s)

syn temperate

rel controlled, curbed, disciplined, inhibited, restrained, self-controlled, self-disciplined; calculated, deliberate, measured; levelheaded, rational, reasonable, sensible; average, mediocre, medium, modest, run-of-the-mill, so-so; normal, ordinary, regular, routine, typical, usual

near ant excessive, extreme, inordinate, radical; irrational, unreasonable, unreasoning; extremist, fanatic (or fanatical), rabid; unbridled, unchecked, uncontrolled, unrestrained

ant immoderate, intemperate

2 avoiding major social change or extreme political ideas ⟨The candidate attracts more *moderate* voters.⟩

syn central, middle-of-the-road

rel conventional, nonrevolutionary, orthodox, traditional; levelheaded, rational, reasonable, sensible; neutral

near ant excessive; conservative, reactionary, rightist; leftist, liberal, progressive; fanatic (or fanatical), rabid, subversive, violent; agitating, exciting, fomenting, incendiary, inciting, instigating, provocative, provoking; rabble-rousing; dissenting

ant extremist, radical, revolutionary, revolutionist; ultra

3 being about midway between extremes of amount or size — see MIDDLE 2

4 marked by temperatures that are neither too high nor too low — see CLEMENT 1

moderate *vb* to grow less in scope or intensity especially gradually — see DECREASE 1

moderately *adv* to some degree or extent — see FAIRLY 1

moderateness *n* an avoidance of extremes in one's actions, beliefs, or habits — see TEMPERANCE

moderation *n* an avoidance of extremes in one's actions, beliefs, or habits — see TEMPERANCE

moderator *n* a person in charge of a meeting — see CHAIR 1

modern *adj* being or involving the latest methods, concepts, information, or styles ⟨changed the furniture for a more *modern* look⟩

syn contemporary, current, designer, hot, mod, modernistic, new, newfangled, newfashioned, present-day, red-hot, space-age, ultramodern, up-to-date

rel fashionable, happening, in, modish, now, stylish; last; latest; modernized, updated; futuristic, high-tech (also hi-tech); latter-day, recent

near ant anachronistic; aged, age-old, ancient, antediluvian, hoary, old, venerable; bygone, former, late, olden, past; antique, historical; retro, retrograde; obsolete, outmoded, outworn, unmodernized; old-world; discarded, disused, moth-eaten, forgotten, remote

ant antiquated, archaic, dated, fusty, musty, oldfangled, old-fashioned, old-time, out-of-date, passé

modern *n* a person with very modern ideas ⟨considers himself a *modern* when it comes to certain issues⟩

syn ultramodernist

rel leftist, lefty, liberal, progressive; extremist, radical, reformer, reformist, revolutionary, revolutionist; bohemian

near ant conservative, rightist, right-winger, standpatter, Tory; old hand, old-timer, veteran; conformist; Bourbon, diehard; square

ant antediluvian, dodo, fogy (also fogey), fossil, fuddy-duddy, reactionary, stick-in-the-mud

modernistic *adj* being or involving the latest methods, concepts, information, or styles — see MODERN

modest *adj* **1** being about midway between extremes of amount or size — see MIDDLE 2

2 free from any trace of the coarse or indecent — see CHASTE 1

3 not comfortable around people — see SHY 2

4 not having or showing any feelings of superiority, self-assertiveness, or showiness — see HUMBLE 1

modestly *adv* **1** in a manner showing no signs of pride or self-assertion — see LOWLY

2 with purity of thought and deed — see PURELY 1

modesty *n* **1** the absence of any feelings of being better than others — see HUMILITY

2 the quality or state of being morally pure — see CHASTITY

modicum *n* the smallest amount or part imaginable — see JOT

modifiable *adj* capable of being readily changed — see FLEXIBLE 1

modification *n* the act, process, or result of making different — see CHANGE 1

modify *vb* **1** to limit the meaning of (as a noun) — see QUALIFY 1

2 to make different in some way — see CHANGE 1

modish *adj* **1** being in the latest or current fashion — see STYLISH

2 enjoying widespread favor or approval — see POPULAR 1

modishness *n* **1** the quality or state of being fashionable — see COOL 2

2 the state of enjoying widespread approval — see POPULARITY

mogul *n* a person of rank, power, or influence in a particular field — see MAGNATE

moil *vb* to devote serious and sustained effort — see LABOR

moist *adj* slightly or moderately wet ⟨Luckily, my new suede shoes are only a bit *moist* after I accidentally wore them in the rain.⟩

syn damp, dank

rel semimoist; dewy, misty; humid, muggy, sticky; sultry, summery, sweltering, torrid, tropical; awash, bathed, doused (also dowsed), drenched, dripping, saturate, saturated, soaked, soaking, sodden, soggy, sopping, soppy, soused, steeped, washed, watered, waterlogged

near ant arid, dry, waterless; baked, bone-dry, burned (or burnt), dehydrated, desert, droughty, dusty, parched, scorched, seared, sere (also sear), sunbaked

moisten *vb* to make or become slightly or moderately wet ⟨*Moisten* the cloth before cleaning with it.⟩

syn damp, dampen

rel bathe, lave; douse (*also* dowse), drench, impregnate, saturate, soak, souse, steep, wash, water, wet; humidify; dip, dunk, immerge, immerse; flush, irrigate, rinse, sluice; refresh, rehydrate, remoisten

near ant dehumidify, dehydrate, parch, scorch, sear

ant dry

moisture *n* the amount of water suspended in the air in tiny droplets ⟨Dew is really just *moisture* from the air that condenses and collects when the temperature drops at night.⟩

syn damp, dampness, humidity

rel mugginess, stickiness, stuffiness; sultriness; clamminess, dankness, soddenness, sogginess, wetness

near ant aridity, dryness

mojo *n* **1** something worn or kept to bring good luck or keep away evil — see CHARM 1

2 the power to control natural forces through supernatural means — see MAGIC 1

molder *vb* to go through decomposition — see DECAY 1

molecule *n* a very small piece — see BIT 1

mollify *vb* **1** to lessen the anger or agitation of — see PACIFY 1

2 to make more bearable or less severe — see HELP 2

mollifying *adj* tending to avoid conflict or hostility — see PACIFIC 1

mollycoddle *vb* to treat with great or excessive care — see BABY

molt *vb* to cast (a natural bodily covering or appendage) aside — see SHED 1

mom *n* a female human parent — see MOTHER

moment *n* **1** a particular point at which an event takes place — see OCCASION 1

2 the quality or state of being important — see IMPORTANCE

3 a very small space of time — see INSTANT

4 the time currently existing or in progress — see ¹PRESENT

momentarily *adv* at or within a short time — see SHORTLY 2

momentary *adj* lasting only for a short time ⟨The pain of the flu shot was only *momentary*.⟩

syn brief, ephemeral, evanescent, flash, fleeting, fugitive, impermanent, passing, short-lived, temporary, transient, transitory

rel little, short, shortish; acting, interim, provisional, short-term

near ant lifelong; continuing, durable, persistent; imperishable, indestructible

ant ceaseless, dateless, deathless, endless, enduring, eternal, everlasting, immortal, lasting, long-lived, permanent, perpetual, timeless, undying, unending

momentous *adj* having great meaning or lasting effect — see IMPORTANT 1

momentum *n* something that arouses action or activity — see IMPULSE 1

monarch *n* **1** one who rules over a people with a sole, supreme, and usually hereditary authority ⟨The ruling *monarch* of Britain at that time was Queen Elizabeth I.⟩

syn autocrat, potentate, ruler, sovereign (*also* sovran)

rel coruler; Caesar, czar (*also* tsar *or* tzar), emir (*or* amir *also* ameer), emperor, empress, kaiser, khan, king, mogul, prince, queen, satrap, shah, sultan, suzerain; authoritarian, despot, dictator, führer (*or* fuehrer), monocrat, overlord, tyrant

2 a person of rank, power, or influence in a particular field — see MAGNATE

monarchal *or* **monarchial** *adj* fit for or worthy of a royal ruler — see MONARCHICAL

monarchical *also* **monarchic** *adj* fit for or worthy of a royal ruler ⟨Guests who stay in the hotel's most expensive suite live in *monarchical* splendor.⟩

syn kingly, monarchal (*or* monarchial), princely, queenly, regal, royal

rel aristocratic, baronial, imperial, lordly, noble, patrician; grandiose, heroic (*also* heroical), imposing, magnificent, majestic, monumental, splendid, stately

monastery *n* a residence for men under religious vows ⟨Gregory Mendel worked out his concepts of genetics by doing breeding experiments using pea plants in the *monastery's* garden.⟩

syn abbey, cloister, friary, hermitage, priory

rel house; convent, nunnery; lamasery

monetary *adj* of or relating to money, banking, or investments — see FINANCIAL

money *n* something (as pieces of stamped metal or printed paper) customarily and legally used as a medium of exchange, a measure of value, or a means of payment ⟨Are you sure you have enough *money* to buy all that?⟩

syn bread [*slang*], bucks, cash, change, chips, currency, dough, gold, green, jack [*slang*], legal tender, lucre, pelf, tender, wampum

rel coinage, specie; paper money, scrip; cashier's check, check, draft, money order, note, promissory note; bill, greenback; bankroll, capital, finances, funds, wad; mite, peanuts, pittance, shoestring; bundle, fortune, king's ransom, mint, pile, pot; opulence, riches, treasure, wealth; resources, wherewithal; petty cash, pin money, pocket money, spending money

moneyed *also* **monied** *adj* having goods, property, or money in abundance — see RICH 1

mongrel *adj* being offspring produced by parents of different races, breeds, species, or genera — see MIXED 1

mongrel *n* an offspring of parents with different genes especially when of different races, breeds, species, or genera — see HYBRID

monitor *vb* to pay continued close attention to (something) for a particular purpose ⟨Police regularly *monitor* that road to record traffic density and to catch speeders.⟩

syn cover, watch

rel surveil; eye; behold, espy, look, note, notice, observe, regard, see, sight, spy, view, witness; gape, gawk, gaze, glare, goggle, peer, rubberneck, stare; glance, glimpse, peek, peep

phrases keep an eye on

---

monkey *n* an appealingly mischievous person — see SCAMP 1

monkey (around) *vb* 1 to engage in attention-getting playful or boisterous behavior — see CUT UP

2 to spend time in aimless activity — see FIDDLE (AROUND)

monkey (with) *vb* to handle thoughtlessly, ignorantly, or mischievously — see TAMPER (WITH)

monkeying *n* wildly playful or mischievous behavior — see HORSEPLAY

monochromatic *adj* 1 having or consisting of a single color ⟨Although marble and bronze sculptures are *monochromatic*, they can be amazingly lifelike.⟩

syn solid

rel achromatic, neutral

near ant dappled (*also* dapple), marbled, shaded; mottled, parti-color (*or* parti-colored), piebald, pied, pinto, skewbald; barred, brindled (*or* brindle), streaked, striated; checkered, dotted, patterned, plaid, striped; flecked, speckled, spotted; bicolored (*or* bicolor), dichromatic, two-tone

ant colorful, motley, multicolored, polychromatic, polychrome, varicolored, varied, variegated

2 causing weariness, restlessness, or lack of interest — see BORING

monopolize *vb* to have complete control over ⟨It is illegal in the United States to *monopolize* an entire industry.⟩ ⟨You shouldn't *monopolize* the exercise equipment while others are waiting to use it.⟩

syn sew up

rel corner, hog; absorb, consume, engross; have, hold, own, possess; command, control, direct, govern, manage, reign (over), rule

monotonous *adj* causing weariness, restlessness, or lack of interest — see BORING

monotonousness *n* a tedious lack of variety — see MONOTONY

monotony *n* a tedious lack of variety ⟨The *monotony* of the cafeteria's selections was as bad as the quality.⟩

syn humdrum, monotonousness, sameness

rel uniformity; blahs, boredom, drabness, dullness (*also* dulness), ennui, restlessness, tediousness, tedium, tiresomeness, weariness, wearisomeness

near ant diversity, multiplicity, variety; variability, variation; absorption, engagement, engrossment, enthrallment, fascination, grip, interest, involvement; animation, enlivenment, invigoration, stimulation

monster *adj* unusually large — see HUGE

monster *n* 1 a strange or horrible and often frightening creature ⟨Both children insisted that their parents check under the bed for *monsters* every night.⟩

syn grotesque, monstrosity, ogre

rel ogress; Frankenstein; banshee, bogeyman (*also* bogyman), demon (*or* daemon), devil, fiend, fright, imp, incubus; horror, terror; abomination, anathema; abnormality, freak; mutant, mutation

2 a person, thing, or event that is far from normal — see FREAK 1

3 a mean, evil, or unprincipled person — see VILLAIN

4 something that is unusually large and powerful — see GIANT

monstrosity *n* 1 a person, thing, or event that is far from normal — see FREAK 1

2 a strange or horrible and often frightening creature — see MONSTER 1

3 something unpleasant to look at — see EYESORE

4 the quality of inspiring intense dread or dismay — see HORROR 1

5 the state or quality of being utterly evil — see ENORMITY 1

monstrous *adj* 1 badly or imperfectly formed — see MALFORMED

2 extremely disturbing or repellent — see HORRIBLE 1

3 unusually large — see HUGE

4 unpleasant to look at — see UGLY 1

monstrously *adv* 1 beyond a normal or acceptable limit — see TOO 1

2 to a large extent or degree — see GREATLY 2

monument *n* 1 a shaped stone laid over or erected near a grave and usually bearing an inscription to identify and preserve the memory of the deceased — see TOMBSTONE

2 something that serves to keep alive the memory of a person or event — see MEMORIAL

monumental *adj* 1 large and impressive in size, grandeur, extent, or conception — see GRAND 1

2 unusually large — see HUGE

3 having great meaning or lasting effect — see IMPORTANT 1

mooch *vb* 1 to move about in a sly or secret manner — see SNEAK 1

2 to move about from place to place aimlessly — see WANDER 1

moocher *n* a person who is supported by or seeks support from another without making an adequate return — see LEECH

mood *n* 1 a state of mind dominated by a particular emotion ⟨Losing my favorite sweater left me in a bad *mood* for the rest of the day.⟩

syn cheer, feather, humor, mode, spirit, temper

rel angle, mind-set, outlook, perspective, slant, standpoint, viewpoint; emotion, feeling, heart, passion, sentiment; strain; expression, tone, vein; character, disposition, identity, individuality, makeup, mettle, personality, temper, temperament

phrases frame of mind

2 a special quality or impression associated with something — see AURA 1

moody *adj* frequently influenced by moods and especially bad moods ⟨a brilliant but *moody* artist⟩

syn temperamental

rel capricious, changeable, changeful, fickle, fluctuating, fluid, freakish, impulsive, inconstant, mercurial, mutable, uncertain, unsettled, unstable, unsteady, variable, volatile, whimsical; sulky; choleric, crabby, cranky, cross, crotchety, grouchy, grumpy, irascible, irritable, peevish, petulant, quick-tempered, short-tempered, snappish, snippety, snippy, testy, waspish

near ant equable, even; immutable, inflexible, invariable, unalterable, unchangeable; changeless, constant, settled, stable, steady, unchanging

moon *n* a long or seemingly long period of time — see AGE 2

moonshine *n* **1** illegally produced liquor ⟨During Prohibition, *moonshine* and "bathtub gin" were made secretly.⟩
syn bootleg
rel bathtub gin, red-eye, rotgut; alcohol, booze, drink, firewater, grog, rum, spirits
2 a distilled beverage that can make a person drunk — see ALCOHOL
3 language, behavior, or ideas that are absurd and contrary to good sense — see NONSENSE 1

moor *n* **1** a broad area of level or rolling treeless country — see PLAIN 1
2 spongy land saturated or partially covered with water — see SWAMP

moor *vb* to put securely in place or in a desired position — see FASTEN 2

moot *adj* open to question or dispute — see DEBATABLE 1

moot *vb* **1** to present or bring forward for discussion — see INTRODUCE 2
2 to talk about (an issue) usually from various points of view and for the purpose of arriving at a decision or opinion — see DISCUSS

mope *vb* **1** to move or act slowly — see DELAY 1
2 to silently go about in a bad mood — see SULK

mopes *n pl* a state or spell of low spirits — see SADNESS

moppet *n* a young person who is between infancy and adulthood — see CHILD 1

moral *adj* **1** conforming to a high standard of morality or virtue — see GOOD 2
2 guided by or in accordance with one's sense of right and wrong — see CONSCIENTIOUS 1

moralist *n* a person who is greatly concerned with seemly behavior and morality especially regarding sexual matters — see PRUDE

morality *n* **1** conduct that conforms to an accepted standard of right and wrong ⟨He has a reputation for unswerving *morality*.⟩
syn character, decency, goodness, honesty, integrity, probity, rectitude, righteousness, rightness, uprightness, virtue, virtuousness
rel high-mindedness, honor, incorruptibility, right-mindedness, scrupulosity, scrupulousness; appropriateness, correctness, decorousness, decorum, etiquette, fitness, propriety, seemliness; ethics, morals
near ant impropriety, indecency, indiscretion; debauchery, degeneracy, degradation, depravity, perversion, pervertedness, sinfulness; crookedness, dishonesty, underhandedness, unscrupulousness; lowness, meanness, viciousness, vileness; corruption
ant badness, evil, evildoing, immorality, iniquity, sin, villainy, wickedness
2 the code of good conduct for an individual or group — see ETHICS

morally *adv* with purity of thought and deed — see PURELY 1

morals *n pl* the code of good conduct for an individual or group — see ETHICS

morass *n* **1** something that catches and holds — see WEB 1
2 spongy land saturated or partially covered with water — see SWAMP

moratorium *n* a state of temporary inactivity — see ABEYANCE

morbid *adj* causing or marked by an atmosphere lacking in cheer — see GLOOMY 1

mordant *adj* marked by the use of wit that is intended to cause hurt feelings — see SARCASTIC

more *adj* resulting in an / increase in amount or number — see ADDITIONAL

more *adv* **1** in addition to what has been said ⟨The sci-fi movie was totally unbelievable and, what's *more*, it was boring.⟩
syn additionally, again, also, besides, further, furthermore, likewise, moreover, then, too, withal, yet
phrases as well, for good measure, in addition to, into the bargain (*also* in the bargain), on top of, to boot, what's more
2 to a greater or higher extent ⟨The boxers for this bout are *more* evenly matched than the last two were.⟩
syn better

more *n* something added (as by growth) — see INCREASE 1

more or less *adv* **1** very close to but not completely — see ALMOST
2 to some degree or extent — see FAIRLY 1

moreover *adv* in addition to what has been said — see MORE 1

mores *n pl* personal conduct or behavior as evaluated by an accepted standard of appropriateness for a social or professional setting — see MANNER 1

moribund *adj* nearly dead ⟨With its rundown look and empty aisles, the grocery store appeared *moribund*.⟩
syn dying
rel expiring, fading, passing away, sinking; decadent, declining, deteriorating; dead, deceased, defunct, departed, fallen, gone, lifeless, passed away; terminal
phrases at death's door
near ant alive, animate, live, living, quick; being, breathing, existing, subsisting, surviving; booming, flourishing, prospering, roaring, thriving; animated, bouncing, energetic, frisky, jazzy, lively, peppy, perky, spirited, sprightful, sprightly, springy, vital, vivacious, zippy

morn *n* **1** the first appearance of light in the morning or the time of its appearance — see DAWN 1
2 the time from sunrise until noon — see MORNING 1

morning *n* **1** the time from sunrise until noon ⟨After working in the fields all *morning*, we were ready for a hearty lunch.⟩
syn forenoon, morn
rel dawn, dawning, daybreak, daylight; cockcrow, sunrise, sunup; day, daytime, light
near ant dark, darkness, night, nighttime, twilight; dusk, evening, nightfall, sundown, sunset
2 the first appearance of light in the morn-

---

syn synonym(s)   *rel* related words
ant antonym(s)   *near ant* near antonym(s)

ing or the time of its appearance — see DAWN 1

3 the point at which something begins — see BEGINNING

moron *n* a stupid person — see IDIOT

morose *adj* causing or marked by an atmosphere lacking in cheer — see GLOOMY 1

morsel *n* **1** a small piece or quantity of food ⟨The chef's cuisine is so good that diners will want to savor every *morsel*.⟩

syn bite, mouthful, nibble, nugget, taste, tidbit (*also* titbit)

rel nosh, snack; appetizer, canapé, hors d'oeuvre; bit, chew, crumb, dab, dribble, driblet, fleck, hint, mote, nubbin, particle, pinch, scrap, scruple, shred, smidgen (*also* smidgeon *or* smidgin *or* smidge), snip, snippet, speck, spot, sprinkling, suspicion, tittle, touch, trace

2 a very small piece — see BIT 1

mortal *adj* **1** likely to cause or capable of causing death — see DEADLY 1

2 of, relating to, or suggestive of death — see DEATHLY 1

3 relating to or characteristic of human beings — see HUMAN

4 marked by opposition or ill will — see HOSTILE 1

mortal *n* a member of the human race — see HUMAN

mortally *adv* to a great degree — see VERY 1

mortician *n* a person who manages funerals and prepares the dead for burial or cremation — see FUNERAL DIRECTOR

mortification *n* the emotional state of being made self-consciously uncomfortable — see EMBARRASSMENT 1

mortify *vb* to throw into a state of self-conscious distress — see EMBARRASS 1

¹**most** *adv* to a great degree — see VERY 1

²**most** *adv* very close to but not completely — see ALMOST

most *adj* of the greatest or highest degree or quantity — see ULTIMATE 1

most *n* the greatest amount, number, or part ⟨This room will accommodate 50 people at the *most*.⟩

syn maximum, outside

rel best, ultimate, utmost; extreme

ant least, minimum

mostly *adv* for the most part — see CHIEFLY 1

mote *n* a very small piece — see BIT 1

moth–eaten *adj* **1** having passed its time of use or usefulness — see OBSOLETE

2 showing signs of advanced wear and tear and neglect — see SHABBY 1

3 used or heard so often as to be dull — see STALE 1

mother *adj* of, relating to, or characteristic of a mother — see MOTHERLY

mother *n* a female human parent ⟨He dreaded telling his *mother* that he'd put a dent in her car.⟩

syn ma, mama (*also* mamma *or* momma), mammy, mom, old lady

rel matriarch, matron; stepmother; supermom, superwoman

mother *vb* **1** to bring forth from the womb — see BEAR 1

2 to attend to the needs and comforts of — see NURSE 1

motherland *n* **1** a place of origin — see BIRTHPLACE

2 the land of one's birth, residence, or citizenship — see COUNTRY 1

motherliness *n* motherly character or qualities — see MATERNITY

motherly *adj* of, relating to, or characteristic of a mother ⟨She showed a sweet *motherly* tenderness toward the tiny kitten she was taking care of.⟩

syn maternal, mother

rel parental; female, feminine, womanish, womanlike, womanly; matriarchal, matronly; caring, giving, nurturing

mother tongue *n* the stock of words, pronunciation, and grammar used by a people as their basic means of communication — see LANGUAGE 1

motif *n* **1** a major object of interest or concern (as in a discussion or artistic composition) — see MATTER 1

2 a unit of decoration that is repeated all over something (as a fabric) — see PATTERN 1

motion *n* the act or an instance of changing position — see MOVEMENT 1

motion *vb* to direct or notify by a movement or gesture ⟨The referee *motioned* the team captains to confer with him on the sideline.⟩

syn beckon, flag, gesture, signal, wave

rel nod; gesticulate, mime, pantomime, sign; signalize; acquaint, advise, inform, relate, tell; flourish, shrug

motionlessly *adv* without motion — see STILL 1

motion picture *n* **1** a story told by means of a series of continuously projected pictures and a sound track — see MOVIE 1

2 motion pictures *pl* the art or business of making a movie — see MOVIE 2

motivation *n* something that arouses action or activity — see IMPULSE 1

motive *n* **1** a major object of interest or concern (as in a discussion or artistic composition) — see MATTER 1

2 a unit of decoration that is repeated all over something (as a fabric) — see PATTERN 1

3 something (as a belief) that serves as the basis for another thing — see REASON 2

motley *adj* **1** consisting of many things of different sorts — see MISCELLANEOUS

2 marked by a variety of usually vivid colors — see COLORFUL

motley *n* **1** a person formerly kept in a royal or noble household to amuse with jests and pranks — see FOOL 2

2 an unorganized collection or mixture of various things — see MISCELLANY 1

motor *n* **1** a device that changes energy into mechanical motion — see ENGINE

2 a self-propelled passenger vehicle on four wheels — see CAR

motor *vb* **1** to proceed or move quickly — see HURRY 2

2 to travel by a motorized vehicle — see DRIVE 2

motorboat *n* a boat equipped with a motor ⟨*Motorboats* are banned on the lake because they are a hazard to swimmers.⟩

syn powerboat, speedboat

rel cabin cruiser, cruiser, hydrofoil, motor sailer, runabout, sedan

motorcade *n* a group of vehicles traveling

together or under one management — see
FLEET

motorcar *n* a self-propelled passenger vehicle on four wheels — see CAR

motor home *n* a motor vehicle that is specially equipped for living while traveling — see CAMPER

motorist *n* a person who travels by automobile ⟨Environmental organizations suggest that *motorists* get together and carpool to avoid adding to pollution levels.⟩
syn automobilist, driver
rel operator; codriver; chauffeur; carpooler
ant nondriver

motor vehicle *n* a self-propelled passenger vehicle on four wheels — see CAR

mottle *n* a small area that is different (as in color) from the main part — see SPOT 1

mottle *vb* to mark with small spots especially unevenly — see SPOT 1

mottled *adj* 1 having blotches of two or more colors — see PIED
2 marked with spots — see SPOTTED 1

mound *n* 1 a pile or ridge of granular matter (as sand or snow) — see ²BANK
2 a quantity of things thrown or stacked on one another — see ¹PILE 1
3 an area of high ground — see HEIGHT 4

mound *vb* 1 to form into a pile or ridge of earth ⟨First, *mound* the mulch around the plants.⟩
syn bank, hill
rel heap, pile, pyramid, stack; embank; bunch, bundle, clump, lump, mass, wad; accumulate, amass, assemble, collect, conglomerate, gather, group
2 to lay or throw on top of one another — see PILE 1

¹mount *n* an elevation of land higher than a hill — see MOUNTAIN 1

²mount *n* a structure that holds up or serves as a foundation for something else — see SUPPORT 1

mount *vb* 1 to become greater in extent, volume, amount, or number — see INCREASE 2
2 to bring before the public in performance or exhibition — see PRESENT 1
3 to move or extend upward — see ASCEND

mountain *n* 1 an elevation of land higher than a hill ⟨My cousin likes to climb *mountains* just because she can.⟩
syn alp, hump, mount, peak
rel cordillera, mountain range, range, sierra; inselberg, knob, seamount; aiguille, horn, mountaintop, pinnacle, summit
near ant basin, bowl, depression, hollow, vale, valley
2 a considerable amount — see LOT 2
3 a quantity of things thrown or stacked on one another — see ¹PILE 1

mountain lion *n* a large tawny cat of the wild — see COUGAR

mountainous *adj* unusually large — see HUGE

mounteebank *n* one who makes false claims of identity or expertise — see IMPOSTOR

mounting *n* a structure that holds up or

serves as a foundation for something else — see SUPPORT 1

mourn *vb* 1 to feel deep sadness or mental pain — see GRIEVE
2 to feel or express sorrow for — see LAMENT 1

mournful *adj* 1 expressing or suggesting mourning ⟨She had such a *mournful* expression that we wondered what could be wrong.⟩
syn aching, anguished, bemoaning, bewailing, bitter, deploring, doleful, dolorous, funeral, grieving, heartbroken, lamentable, lugubrious, plaintive, regretful, rueful, sorrowful, sorry, wailing, weeping, woeful
rel elegiac (*also* elegiacal), melancholy; dejected, depressed, despondent, disconsolate, dispirited, downcast, downhearted, heartsick, heartsore, inconsolable, tearful; brokenhearted, careworn, crestfallen, downcast, downhearted, forlorn, gloomy, glum, low-spirited, miserable, sad, triste, unhappy, woebegone; bawling, crying, groaning, howling, keening, moaning, yammering; black, bleak, cheerless, comfortless, dark, darkening, desolate, dismal, dreary, funereal, gloomy, glum, gray (*also* grey), joyless, low, miserable, moody, morbid, morose, pathetic, pessimistic, piteous, saturnine, somber (*or* sombre), sullen
near ant delighted, exulting, glorying, happy, joyful, rejoicing, triumphant; bright, cheerful, cheering, cheery, laughing, smiling; blissful, blithe, blithesome, buoyant, jocund, jolly, joyous, lighthearted, merry, mirthful; encouraging, hopeful, optimistic; ecstatic, elated, euphoric, exhilarated, giddy, rapturous, rhapsodic (*also* rhapsodical)
2 feeling unhappiness — see SAD 1
3 causing unhappiness — see SAD 1

mournfully *adv* with feelings of bitterness or grief — see HARD 2

mouse *vb* to move about in a sly or secret manner — see SNEAK 1

mousy *or* **mousey** *adj* easily frightened — see SHY 1

mouth *n* 1 the opening through which food passes into the body of an animal ⟨The baby chicks opened their *mouths* very wide and chirped piteously when their mother came back with worms.⟩
syn kisser [*slang*], mug
rel countenance, face, puss [*slang*], visage
2 a twisting of the facial features in disgust or disapproval — see GRIMACE
3 disrespectful or argumentative talk given in response to a command or request — see BACK TALK

mouth *vb* 1 to distort one's face — see MUG 1
2 to speak softly and unclearly — see MUMBLE

mouth (off) *vb* to talk as if giving an important and formal speech — see ORATE 1

mouthful *n* a small piece or quantity of food — see MORSEL 1

mouthpiece *n* a person who speaks for another or for a group — see SPOKESPERSON

movable *or* **moveable** *adj* capable of be-

---

syn synonym(s)   **rel** related words
ant antonym(s)   **near ant** near antonym(s)

ing moved especially with ease ⟨Any furniture that is not *movable* will be covered with protective cloths by the painters.⟩

syn mobile, portable

rel adjustable, flexible, modular; removable (*also* removeable), transferable (*also* transferrable), transportable; motile, moving; unbalanced, unstable, unsteady; manageable

near ant nonmotile, nonmoving; motionless, moveless, standing, static, stationary, still, stuck, wedged; fast, fixed, rooted, steadfast

ant immobile, immovable, irremovable, nonmobile, unmovable

movables *or* **moveables** *n pl* **1** the movable articles (such as tables and chairs) in a room — see FURNITURE

2 transportable items that one owns — see POSSESSION 2

move *n* **1** an action planned or taken to achieve a desired result — see MEASURE 1

2 the act or an instance of changing position — see MOVEMENT 1

move *vb* **1** to change the place or position of ⟨I need you to *move* all your books off that chair before company gets here.⟩

syn budge, dislocate, displace, disturb, remove, shift, transfer, transpose

rel bear, carry, cart, convey, drive, haul, lug, tote, transmit, transplant, transport; replace, supersede, supplant; alter, make over, modify, redo, refashion, remake, remodel, revamp, revise, rework, vary

near ant anchor, fix, freeze, moor, secure, set, stabilize; embed (*also* imbed), entrench (*also* intrench), implant, ingrain (*also* engrain), lodge, root

2 to set or keep in motion ⟨The hands of the wall clock are *moved* by battery.⟩

syn actuate, drive, impel, propel, work

rel activate, motivate, provoke; abet, ferment, foment, incite, raise, stir (up), whip (up); set off, trigger, trip; arouse, excite, fire (up), galvanize, inflame (*also* enflame), inspire, instigate, rouse, stimulate

near ant bridle, check, constrain, contain, control, curb, inhibit, regulate, rein (in), restrain

3 to change one's position ⟨Don't *move* while I'm trying to draw your portrait.⟩

syn budge, shift, stir

rel fiddle, fidget, jiggle, squiggle, squirm, toss, twitch, wiggle, wriggle, writhe; rouse

near ant hang around, remain, stay, stick around, tarry; stabilize

ant freeze, still

4 to act upon (a person or a person's feelings) so as to cause a response — see ¹AFFECT 1

5 to rouse to strong feeling or action — see PROVOKE 1

6 to cause (someone) to agree with a belief or course of action by using arguments or earnest requests — see PERSUADE

7 to cause to function — see ACTIVATE

8 to leave a place often for another — see GO 2

movement *n* **1** the act or an instance of changing position ⟨A sudden *movement* in the far corner of the room made her turn in that direction.⟩

syn motion, move, shift, shifting, stir, stirring

rel dislocation, migration, relocation; locomotion, mobility, motility, motivity; fidgeting, squirm, squirming, twitching, wriggling, writhing; flailing, flapping, waving

near ant immobility; inertia, inertness, stillness; cessation, discontinuance, ending, expiration, finish, halt, lapse, pause, shutdown, shutoff, stop, stoppage, surcease, termination

ant motionlessness

2 a series of activities undertaken to achieve a goal — see CAMPAIGN

movie *n* **1** a story told by means of a series of continuously projected pictures and a sound track ⟨There was much excitement when it was announced that the popular children's book would be turned into a *movie*.⟩

syn film, flick, flicker, motion picture, moving picture, picture

rel animated cartoon, cartoon, docudrama, documentary, feature; silent, talkie

2 movies *pl* the art or business of making a movie ⟨Many a small-town girl has gone to Hollywood, dreaming of making it big in the *movies*.⟩

syn cinema, film, motion pictures, pictures, screen

rel showbiz, show business

moving *adj* having the power to affect the feelings or sympathies ⟨He gave a truly *moving* graduation speech that had some graduates in tears.⟩

syn affecting, emotional, impressive, poignant, stirring, touching

rel eloquent, expressive, meaningful, significant; demonstrative, excitable, feeling, passionate, responsive, sensitive; exciting, inspirational, provoking, rousing, stimulating; dramatic, histrionic, melodramatic, theatrical (*also* theatric); cathartic

near ant cold, cool, detached, dispassionate; deadpan

ant unaffecting, unemotional, unimpressive

moving picture *n* a story told by means of a series of continuously projected pictures and a sound track — see MOVIE 1

mow *vb* **1** to shorten the standing leafy plant cover of ⟨You really should *mow* the lawn before it gets much higher.⟩

syn cut

rel clip, crop, curtail, cut back, dock, hack, lop, manicure, nip, pare, prune, trim; bob, shave, shear, snip

2 to bring down by cutting — see FELL 2

mow (down) *vb* **1** to kill on a large scale — see MASSACRE

2 to strike (someone) so forcefully as to cause a fall — see FELL 1

much *adj* having great meaning or lasting effect — see IMPORTANT 1

much *adv* **1** to a great degree — see VERY 1

2 to a large extent or degree — see GREATLY 2

3 very close to but not completely — see ALMOST

4 many times — see OFTEN

much *n* a considerable amount — see LOT 2

muck *n* **1** foul matter that mars the purity or cleanliness of something — see FILTH 1

2 soft wet earth — see MUD

muck *vb* to make dirty — see DIRTY

mucky *adj* **1** full of or covered with soft wet earth — see MUDDY 1

2 not clean — see DIRTY 1

mud *n* soft wet earth ⟨We cannot play softball today because the field turned to *mud* after last night's heavy rain.⟩

syn mire, muck, ooze, slime, slop, sludge, slush

rel gumbo, silt; clay, dirt, gravel, humus, loam, sand, soil; glop, slop, swill

muddle *n* **1** a state in which everything is out of order — see CHAOS

2 a state of mental confusion — see HAZE 2

3 a state of mental uncertainty — see CONFUSION 1

4 an unorganized collection or mixture of various things — see MISCELLANY 1

muddle *vb* **1** to throw into a state of mental uncertainty — see CONFUSE 1

2 to undo the proper order or arrangement of — see DISORDER

muddled *adj* lacking in order, neatness, and often cleanliness — see MESSY

muddy *adj* **1** full of or covered with soft wet earth ⟨Please do not walk in the house with *muddy* boots on, as you will get the carpet dirty.⟩

syn miry, mucky, oozy, slimy, sludgy, slushy

rel clayey, loamy, silty; bedraggled; dirty, filthy, foul, grimy, grubby, grungy, gunky, impure, smutty, soiled, squalid, stained, sullied, unclean, uncleanly

near ant clean, immaculate, pristine, sparkling, spick-and-span (*or* spic-and-span), spotless, unsoiled, unstained, unsullied

2 having visible particles in liquid suspension — see CLOUDY 1

3 not clean — see DIRTY 1

muddy *vb* **1** to throw into a state of mental uncertainty — see CONFUSE 1

2 to make (something) unclear to the understanding — see CONFUSE 2

3 to make dirty — see DIRTY

muff *vb* to make or do (something) in a clumsy or unskillful way — see BOTCH

muffle *vb* **1** to deaden the sound of ⟨The walls *muffled* their conversation so that only a low murmur was heard.⟩

syn mute, stifle

rel insulate, soundproof; pad; dampen, mellow, soften, subdue, tone (down); baffle; smother

near ant amplify, boost, deepen, enhance, heighten, increase, magnify, step up, strengthen

ant unmuffle

2 to surround or cover closely — see ENFOLD 1

mug *n* **1** a round vessel equipped with a handle and designed for drinking — see CUP

2 the front part of the head — see FACE 1

3 the opening through which food passes into the body of an animal — see MOUTH 1

4 a twisting of the facial features in disgust or disapproval — see GRIMACE

mug *vb* **1** to distort one's face ⟨Every time their picture was snapped, both children *mugged* by sticking out their tongues or scrunching up their faces.⟩

syn grimace, mouth

rel pout; contort, deform, twist, warp; frown, glare, gloom, glower, lower (*also* lour); scowl; gape, gaze, ogle, stare; growl, snarl, sneer; simper, smirk

phrases make a face (*or* make faces), pull a face

near ant beam, grin, smile

2 to take a photograph of — see PHOTOGRAPH

muggy *adj* containing or characterized by an uncomfortable amount of moisture — see HUMID

mulct *n* a sum of money to be paid as a punishment — see FINE

mulct *vb* to rob by the use of trickery or threats — see FLEECE

mulish *adj* sticking to an opinion, purpose, or course of action in spite of reason, arguments, or persuasion — see OBSTINATE

mulishness *n* a steadfast adherence to an opinion, purpose, or course of action in spite of reason, arguments, or persuasion — see OBSTINACY

mull (over) *vb* to give serious and careful thought to — see PONDER

multicolored *adj* marked by a variety of usually vivid colors — see COLORFUL

multifarious *adj* being of many and various kinds — see MANIFOLD

multiple *adj* **1** used or done by a number of people as a group — see COLLECTIVE

2 being of a large but indefinite number — see MANY

multiplex *adj* being of a large but indefinite number — see MANY

multiplication *n* the act or process of becoming greater in number ⟨There's been a steady *multiplication* in our attic of old equipment since the revolution in consumer electronics.⟩

syn accumulating, accumulation, addition, increase, proliferation

rel doubling, quadrupling, tripling; creep, growth, rise, spread; enlargement, escalation, expansion; amplification; distension (*or* distention); accretion, accrual, augmentation; extension, lengthening; boost, gain, hike, increment, rise

near ant abatement, compressing, compression, condensation, constriction, contraction, diminishing, diminishment, diminution, drop, fall, lessening, lowering, reduction, shrinkage, shrinking; retrenching, retrenchment, shortening

ant decrease

multiplicity *n* **1** a considerable amount — see LOT 2

2 the quality or state of being composed of many different elements or types — see VARIETY 1

multiply *vb* **1** to bring forth offspring — see PROCREATE

2 to make greater in size, amount, or number — see INCREASE 1

3 to become greater in extent, volume, amount, or number — see INCREASE 1

multitude *n* **1** a great number of persons or creatures massed together — see CROWD 1

2 the body of the community as contrasted with the elite — see MASS 1

---

syn synonym(s)　　*rel* related words
ant antonym(s)　　*near ant* near antonym(s)

multitudinous *adj* being of a large but indefinite number — see MANY

mum *adj* deliberately refraining from speech — see SILENT 1

mumble *n* speech that is not clear enough to be understood ⟨He spoke in a *mumble*.⟩
syn grunt, grunting, murmur, murmuring, mutter, muttering
rel rumor, undertone, whisper; babble, babbling, blab, blabbing, chatter, chattering, drivel, driveling (*or* drivelling), gabble, gabbling, jabber, jabbering, maundering, prattle, prattling, rambling

mumble *vb* to speak softly and unclearly ⟨I can't understand you if you *mumble*.⟩
syn grunt, mouth, murmur, mutter
rel babble, blab, chatter, drivel, gabble, gibber, jabber, maunder, prattle, ramble; breathe, gasp, pant, whisper; buzz
near ant articulate, enunciate
ant speak out, speak up

mumbo jumbo *n* unintelligible or meaningless talk — see GIBBERISH 1

mummer *n* 1 an actor in a story performed silently and entirely by body movements — see MIME 1
2 one who acts professionally (as in a play, movie, or television show) — see ACTOR 1

munchies *n pl* a need or desire for food — see HUNGER 1

mundane *adj* 1 having to do with the practical details of regular life ⟨They didn't want to be bothered with *mundane* concerns like doing the dishes while on vacation.⟩
syn everyday, prosaic, terrestrial, workaday
rel earthly, temporal, worldly; average, common, commonplace, customary, familiar, garden, generic, normal, ordinary, plain, popular, routine, run-of-the-mill, standard, typical, unexceptional, unremarkable, usual; frequent, habitual, regular
near ant high-minded, lofty, noble, sublime; aberrant, abnormal, atypical; exceptional, extraordinary, freak, peculiar, phenomenal, rare, singular, special, uncommon, uncustomary, unique, unusual, unwonted; bizarre, curious, far-out, odd, outlandish, out-of-the-way, quirky, remarkable, screwy, strange, weird, wild
2 having to do with life on earth especially as opposed to that in heaven — see EARTHLY

municipality *n* a thickly settled, highly populated area — see CITY

munificent *adj* giving or sharing in abundance and without hesitation — see GENEROUS 1

munificently *adv* in a generous manner — see WELL 3

murder *n* 1 a situation or state that causes great suffering and unhappiness — see HELL 2
2 the taking of another person's life — see HOMICIDE 1

murder *vb* 1 to put to death deliberately ⟨It is illegal to *murder* someone.⟩
syn croak [*slang*], dispatch, do in, execute, get, liquidate, rub out, slay, terminate
rel shoot; blot out, claim, cut down, destroy, fell, kill, smite, zap; butcher, massacre, mow (down), slaughter; annihilate, eliminate, eradicate, exterminate, wipe out
phrases do away with
near ant animate, raise, restore, resurrect, resuscitate, revive
2 to make or do (something) in a clumsy or unskillful way — see BOTCH

murderer *n* a person who kills another person — see ASSASSIN

murdering *adj* eager for or marked by the shedding of blood, extreme violence, or killing — see BLOODTHIRSTY

murderous *adj* 1 difficult to endure — see HARSH 1
2 requiring considerable physical or mental effort — see HARD 2
3 likely to cause or capable of causing death — see DEADLY 1
4 eager for or marked by the shedding of blood, extreme violence, or killing — see BLOODTHIRSTY

murk *n* 1 a time or place of little or no light — see DARK 1
2 an atmospheric condition in which suspended particles in the air rob it of its transparency — see HAZE 1

murkiness *n* the quality or state of having a veiled or uncertain meaning — see OBSCURITY 1

murky *adj* 1 being without light or without much light — see DARK 1
2 causing or marked by an atmosphere lacking in cheer — see GLOOMY 1
3 filled with or dimmed by fine particles (as of dust or water) in suspension — see HAZY 1
4 having an often intentionally veiled or uncertain meaning — see OBSCURE 1
5 not seen or understood clearly — see FAINT 1

murmur *n* 1 an expression of dissatisfaction, pain, or resentment — see COMPLAINT 1
2 speech that is not clear enough to be understood — see MUMBLE

murmur *vb* 1 to express dissatisfaction, pain, or resentment usually tiresomely — see COMPLAIN
2 to speak softly and unclearly — see MUMBLE

murmurer *n* an irritable and complaining person — see GROUCH 1

murmuring *n* speech that is not clear enough to be understood — see MUMBLE

muscle *n* 1 muscular strength ⟨I'm going to need someone with real *muscle* to help me move all this furniture.⟩
syn beef, brawn, main
rel force, might, potency, power, puissance, sinew; energy, vigor
near ant impotence, impotency, weakness; debilitation, debility, enfeeblement, faintness, feebleness, frailness, frailty, infirmity
2 the ability to exert effort for the accomplishment of a task — see POWER 2

muscle *vb* 1 to cause (a person) to give in to pressure — see PRESSURE
2 to force one's way — see ²PRESS 4

muscular *adj* 1 marked by a well-developed musculature ⟨Olympic runners tend to have very *muscular* legs.⟩

syn brawny, sinewy

rel wiry; powerful, strong; beefy, burly, hefty, hulking, husky; able-bodied, athletic, herculean, mighty, robust, rugged, stalwart, stout, strapping, sturdy; muscle-bound; sculpted

near ant nonathletic; debilitated, delicate, effete, enervated, enfeebled, feeble, fragile, frail, weak, weakened, weakly, wimpy; light, lightweight, slight; lean, slender, slim, svelte, sylphlike, thin, willowy; emaciated, gaunt, lank, rawboned, scraggy, spare

ant scrawny, skinny

2 having muscles capable of exerting great physical force — see STRONG 1

3 marked by or uttered with forcefulness — see EMPHATIC 1

4 having an abundance of some characteristic quality (as flavor) — see FULL-BODIED

museum *n* a building or part of a building in which objects of interest are displayed ⟨a trip to the *Museum* of Natural History⟩

syn gallery, salon

rel archives, assemblage, collection, library; display, exhibition; studio

mush *n* **1** something (as a work of literature or music) that is too sentimental — see CORN

2 the state or quality of having an excess of tender feelings (as of love, nostalgia, or compassion) — see SENTIMENTALITY

mushroom *vb* to become greater in extent, volume, amount, or number — see INCREASE 2

mushy *adj* **1** appealing to the emotions in an obvious and tiresome way — see CORNY

2 giving easily to the touch — see SOFT 3

musical *adj* **1** having a pleasantly flowing quality suggestive of music — see LYRIC 1

2 having a pleasing mixture of notes — see HARMONIOUS 1

musicale *n* an entertainment featuring singing or the playing of musical instruments — see CONCERT

musician *n* **1** a person who plays a musical instrument ⟨The violinist was a famous and exquisitely talented *musician*.⟩

syn instrumentalist, player

rel minstrel; artist, performer; maestro, virtuoso; accompanist, recitalist, soloist, symphonist; accordionist, bassoonist, clarinetist (*or* clarinettist), cornetist (*or* cornettist), drummer, fiddler, flautist, flutist, guitarist, harpist, hornist, keyboardist, oboist, organ-grinder, organist, percussionist, pianist, picker, piper, reedman, saxophonist, trombonist, trumpeter, violinist, violist

2 a person who writes musical compositions — see COMPOSER

muskeg *n* spongy land saturated or partially covered with water — see SWAMP

muss *n* a state in which everything is out of order — see CHAOS

muss *vb* to undo the proper order or arrangement of — see DISORDER

mussed *adj* lacking in order, neatness, and often cleanliness — see MESSY

mussy *adj* lacking in order, neatness, and often cleanliness — see MESSY

must *n* something necessary, indispensable, or unavoidable — see ESSENTIAL 1

must *vb* to be under necessity or obligation to — see NEED 2

muster *n* **1** a body of people come together in one place — see GATHERING 1

2 a number of things considered as a unit — see GROUP 1

muster *vb* **1** to assemble and make ready for action — see MOBILIZE

2 to bring together in assembly by or as if by command — see CONVOKE

3 to be made up of — see COMPRISE 1

muster out *vb* to let go from office, service, or employment — see DISMISS 1

musty *adj* **1** having an unpleasant smell — see MALODOROUS

2 used or heard so often as to be dull — see STALE 1

mutable *adj* likely to change frequently, suddenly, or unexpectedly — see FICKLE 1

mutate *vb* to pass from one form, state, or level to another — see CHANGE 2

mute *adj* **1** unable to speak ⟨The child is both deaf and *mute*.⟩

syn inarticulate, speechless, voiceless

rel closemouthed, laconic, reserved, reticent, taciturn, tight-lipped, uncommunicative; mum, nonspeaking, quiet, silent, wordless

near ant blabby, chatty, communicative, expansive, gabby, garrulous, loquacious, talkative, talky, vocal; expatiating, speaking out, speaking up; articulating, speaking, talking; articulate, eloquent, fluent, voluble

2 deliberately refraining from speech — see SILENT 1

mute *n* a device on a musical instrument that deadens or softens its tone ⟨I was practicing my trumpet at three in the morning when the *mute* fell out, and I managed to wake everyone up.⟩

syn damper

rel muffler, quieter, softener, soft pedal

mute *vb* **1** to stop the noise or speech of — see SILENCE 1

2 to deaden the sound of — see MUFFLE 1

muted *adj* **1** mostly or entirely without sound — see SILENT 3

2 not excessively showy — see QUIET 2

3 deliberately refraining from speech — see SILENT 1

muteness *n* incapacity for or restraint from speaking — see SILENCE 1

mutilate *vb* to cause severe or permanent injury to — see MAIM

mutineer *n* a person who rises up against authority — see REBEL

mutinous *adj* taking part in a rebellion — see REBELLIOUS 1

mutiny *n* open fighting against authority (as one's own government) — see REBELLION 1

mutiny *vb* to rise up against established authority — see REBEL

mutter *n* speech that is not clear enough to be understood — see MUMBLE

mutter *vb* **1** to express dissatisfaction, pain, or resentment usually tiresomely — see COMPLAIN

---

syn synonym(s) *rel* related words
ant antonym(s) *near ant* near antonym(s)

2 to speak softly and unclearly — see MUMBLE

mutterer *n* an irritable and complaining person — see GROUCH 1

muttering *n* speech that is not clear enough to be understood — see MUMBLE

mutual *adj* used or done by a number of people as a group — see COLLECTIVE

myopic *adj* **1** able to see near things more clearly than distant ones — see NEAR-SIGHTED

2 not thinking about and providing for the future — see IMPROVIDENT

myriad *adj* **1** being of many and various kinds — see MANIFOLD

2 too many to be counted — see COUNTLESS

myriad *n* a considerable amount — see LOT 2

mysterious *adj* **1** being beyond one's powers to know, understand, or explain ⟨The huge stone statues on Easter Island are ancient, *mysterious*, and haunting.⟩

syn cryptic, deep, enigmatic (*also* enigmatical), impenetrable, inscrutable, mystic, occult, uncanny

rel dark, darkling, fuzzy, murky, obscure, shadowy, vague; ambiguous, equivocal; imponderable, incomprehensible, unfathomable, unintelligible, unsearchable; inexplicable, unaccountable, unexplainable; unanswerable, unknowable; metaphysical, mystical, numinous, supernatural; abstruse, esoteric, recondite; baffling, befuddling, bewildering, confounding, confusing, mystifying, perplexing, puzzling

near ant apparent, clear, evident, manifest, obvious, open-and-shut, palpable, patent, perspicuous, plain, straightforward, transparent, unambiguous, unequivocal, unmistakable

2 having an often intentionally veiled or uncertain meaning — see OBSCURE 1

mystery *n* something hard to understand or explain ⟨The cause of the disease is still a *mystery* to scientists.⟩

syn conundrum, enigma, mystification, puzzle, puzzlement, riddle, secret

rel brainteaser, case, challenge, knot, matter, perplexity, poser, problem, stumper, trouble

mystic *adj* **1** having seemingly supernatural qualities or powers ⟨The notion that a cat has nine lives is based upon the belief that nine is a *mystic* number.⟩

syn magic, magical, occult, weird

rel bewitched, enchanted, spellbound; bewitching, charming, conjuring, enchanting, wiling; amazing, astonishing, astounding, awesome, extraordinary, fabulous, marvelous (*or* marvellous), miraculous, portentous, stunning, stupendous, sublime, wondrous; divining, forecasting, foreknowing, foreseeing, foretelling, predicting, presaging, prognosticating, prophesying, soothsaying; metaphysical, preternatural, unearthly

near ant commonplace, everyday, normal, ordinary, prosaic, routine, run-of-the-mill, unexceptional, unremarkable, usual, workaday

2 being beyond one's powers to know, understand, or explain — see MYSTERIOUS 1

3 having an often intentionally veiled or uncertain meaning — see OBSCURE 1

mystification *n* **1** a state of mental uncertainty — see CONFUSION 1

2 something hard to understand or explain — see MYSTERY

mystify *vb* to throw into a state of mental uncertainty — see CONFUSE 1

myth *n* **1** a traditional but unfounded story that gives the reason for a current custom, belief, or fact of nature ⟨According to an ancient Greek *myth*, humans acquired fire from Prometheus, a Titan who had stolen it from heaven.⟩

syn fable, legend

rel allegory, parable; fabrication, fantasy (*also* phantasy), fiction, figment, invention; narrative, saga, story, tale, yarn

2 the body of customs, beliefs, stories, and sayings associated with a people, thing, or place — see FOLKLORE

3 a false idea or belief — see FALLACY 1

mythical *or* **mythic** *adj* **1** based on, described in, or being a myth ⟨For years the Spanish conquistadors searched for the *mythical* El Dorado, a place of unimaginable riches.⟩

syn fabled, fabulous, legendary

rel famed, romanticized, storied; chimerical (*also* chimeric), fabricated, fantastic (*also* fantastical), fictional, fictitious; fanciful, imaginary, imagined, invented, made-up, make-believe, pretend, unreal; allegorical, mythological (*also* mythologic); semilegendary

near ant actual, existent, real, real-world; historical; factual, true; attested, authenticated, confirmed, established, proven, substantiated, validated, verified; authentic, bona fide, genuine, real-life

2 not real and existing only in the imagination — see IMAGINARY

mythology *n* the body of customs, beliefs, stories, and sayings associated with a people, thing, or place — see FOLKLORE

nab *vb* **1** to take or keep under one's control by authority of law — see ARREST 1

2 to take physical control or possession of (something) suddenly or forcibly — see CATCH 1

nabob *n* one of high position or importance within a group — see BIG SHOT

nag *n* a large hoofed domestic animal that is used for carrying or drawing loads and for riding — see HORSE

nag *vb* **1** to subject (someone) to constant scoldings and sharp reminders ⟨My parents are always *nagging* me about my homework.⟩

syn dog, henpeck, hound, needle

rel carp (at), fuss (about *or* over), nitpick; annoy, badger, bait, bother, bug, chivy (*or* chivvy), harry, hassle, irk, pester, plague, ride, vex, yap (at); goad, incite, prod, prompt, spur, urge; exhort, insist, press, pressure, push; blandish, cajole, coax, wheedle; beg, importune, plead

phrases pick at

near ant compliment; commend, laud, praise, recommend, tout; acclaim, applaud, eulogize, extol (*also* extoll)

2 to express dissatisfaction, pain, or resentment usually tiresomely — see COMPLAIN

naiad *n* a mythical goddess represented as a young woman and said to live outdoors — see NYMPH

nail *vb* **1** to deliver a blow to (someone or something) usually in a strong vigorous manner — see HIT 1

2 to make final, definite, or beyond dispute — see CLINCH

3 to reveal the true nature of — see EXPOSE 1

4 to take or keep under one's control by authority of law — see ARREST 1

5 to take physical control or possession of (something) suddenly or forcibly — see CATCH 1

naive *or* **naïve** *adj* **1** lacking in worldly wisdom or informed judgment ⟨a first-time buyer who was so *naive* that he believed the salesman's spiel and paid good money for the rusty and broken-down car⟩

syn green, ingenuous, innocent, simple, simpleminded, uncritical, unknowing, unsophisticated, unsuspecting, unsuspicious, unwary, unworldly, wide-eyed

rel callow, childish, immature, inexperienced, raw; childlike, impractical, unrealistic; believing, credulous, gullible (*also* gullable), susceptible, trustful, trusting, unguarded; beguiled, duped, gulled, tricked; careless, heedless, thoughtless

near ant critical, cynical, doubting, incredulous, skeptical, suspecting, suspicious, unconvinced; careful, cautious, guarded, leery (*also* leary), wary, watchful; down-to-earth, hardheaded, pragmatic (*also* pragmatical), realistic, sober; street-smart, streetwise

ant cosmopolitan, experienced, knowing, sophisticated, worldly, worldly-wise

2 free from any intent to deceive or impress others — see GUILELESS

3 readily taken advantage of — see EASY 2

naively *or* **naïvely** *adv* without any attempt to impress by deception or exaggeration — see NATURALLY 3

naïveté *also* **naivete** *or* **naiveté** *n* **1** the quality or state of being simple and sincere ⟨Her *naïveté* led her to leave her new car unlocked while she shopped at the mall.⟩

syn artlessness, guilelessness, ingenuousness, innocence, naturalness, simpleness, simplicity, unsophistication, unworldliness

rel candor, frankness, genuineness, honesty, openness, sincerity, straightforwardness, unaffectedness, unpretentiousness; callowness, childishness, inexperience, rawness; insularity, parochialism, provincialism; carelessness, heedlessness, thoughtlessness; ignorance, obliviousness, unawareness; credulity, credulousness, gullibility, impressionability; idealism, impracticality, optimism

near ant affectedness, artificiality, pretentiousness; deviousness, dishonesty, insincerity; disbelief, doubtfulness, incredulity, suspiciousness; carefulness, caution, wariness; pessimism, skepticism; maturity

ant artfulness, cynicism, sophistication, worldliness

2 readiness to believe the claims of others without sufficient evidence — see CREDULITY

naked *adj* **1** lacking or shed of clothing ⟨I had recurrent nightmares about being *naked* in public.⟩

syn bare, disrobed, nude, stripped, unclad, unclothed, undressed

rel denuded; peeled

phrases in the altogether (*or* in the buff *or* the nude *or* one's birthday suit *or* in the raw), stark naked

near ant covered, veiled; arrayed, caparisoned, decked (out), rigged (out), tricked (out); vested; decent

ant appareled (*or* apparelled), attired, clothed, dressed, garbed, invested, robed, suited

2 lacking a usual or natural covering ⟨The winter trees now look so *naked* without their colorful fall foliage.⟩

syn bald, bare, denuded, exposed, open, peeled, stripped, uncovered

rel displayed, revealed; hairless, shaven; disrobed, unclad, unclothed, undressed; furless, skinned; divested; unprotected

near ant mantled; overgrown, overrun, overspread; bearded, hairy

ant covered

3 free from all additions or embellishment — see PLAIN 1

name *adj* having a good reputation especially in a field of knowledge — see RESPECTABLE 1

name *n* **1** a word or combination of words by which a person or thing is regularly

---

syn synonym(s)   *rel* related words

ant antonym(s)   *near ant* near antonym(s)

known ⟨The guy introduced himself and then asked what my *name* was.⟩

syn appellation, cognomen, denomination, denotation, designation, handle, title

rel baptismal name, Christian name, forename, given name; maiden name, middle name; diminutive, epithet, nickname, sobriquet (*also* soubriquet); banner, rubric, tag; alias, nom de plume, pen name, pseudonym; binomial, monomial; trivial name, vernacular; misnomer; brand name, label, trademark, trade name

2 an act or expression showing scorn and usually intended to hurt another's feelings — see INSULT

3 outward and often deceptive indication — see APPEARANCE 2

4 overall quality as seen or judged by people in general — see REPUTATION

5 a person who is widely known and usually much talked about — see CELEBRITY 1

name *vb* **1** to give a name to ⟨Amy decided to *name* her new puppy "Bubbles."⟩

syn baptize, call, christen, denominate, designate, dub, entitle, label, style, term, title

rel brand, stigmatize, tag; denote, specify; miscall, misname, mistitle; nickname

2 to make reference to or speak about briefly but specifically — see MENTION 1

3 to pick (someone) by one's authority for a specific position or duty — see APPOINT 1

4 to decide to accept (someone or something) from a group of possibilities — see CHOOSE 1

5 to decide upon (the time or date for an event) usually from a position of authority — see APPOINT 1

6 to come to a judgment about after discussion or consideration — see DECIDE 1

nameless *adj* **1** not named or identified by a name ⟨The victim of the crime will remain *nameless* to protect his privacy.⟩ ⟨those *nameless* editors who write the synopses for TV shows in the newspaper⟩

syn anonymous, faceless, incognito, unbaptized, unchristened, unidentified, unnamed, untitled

rel undetermined, unspecified; obscure, uncelebrated, unheard-of, unheralded, unknown, unsung; unexceptional, unremarkable

near ant denominated, designated, specified; labeled (*or* labelled), tabbed, titled; celebrated, famed, famous, known, notable, noted, noteworthy, remarkable, renowned, well-known; exceptional

ant baptized, christened, dubbed, named, termed

2 beyond the power to describe — see INDESCRIBABLE

3 not widely known — see OBSCURE 2

namer *n* someone with the right or responsibility for making a selection — see SELECTOR

nanny *also* **nannie** *n* a person employed to care for a young child or children — see NURSE

¹**nap** *n* a short sleep ⟨so tired that she needed to take a refreshing *nap* before soccer practice⟩

syn catnap, doze, drowse, forty winks, siesta, snooze, wink

rel repose, rest; slumber; bed

²**nap** *n* a soft airy substance or covering — see FUZZ

nap *vb* **1** to sleep lightly or briefly ⟨decided to let the kids *nap* for a few more minutes before waking them⟩

syn catnap, doze, drowse, slumber, snooze

rel relax, repose, rest; couch, lay, lie, roost; lull

near ant arise, arouse, awake, awaken, get up, rise, rouse, uprise, wake (up), waken

2 to be in a state of sleep — see SLEEP 1

napping *adj* being in a state of suspended consciousness — see ASLEEP 1

napping *n* a natural periodic loss of consciousness during which the body restores itself — see SLEEP 1

narcotic *adj* tending to cause sleep — see HYPNOTIC

narcotic *n* something that soothes, calms, or induces passivity or a sense of security — see OPIATE

narrate *vb* to give an oral or written account of in some detail — see TELL 1

narration *n* a relating of events usually in the order in which they happened — see ACCOUNT 1

narrative *n* **1** a relating of events usually in the order in which they happened — see ACCOUNT 1

2 a work with imaginary characters and events that is shorter and usually less complex than a novel — see STORY 1

narrow *adj* **1** being of less than usual width ⟨The cat found a *narrow* opening in the fence that he was able to squeeze through.⟩

syn fine, hairline, needlelike, skinny, slender, slim, thin

rel attenuated, elongate (*or* elongated), linear; bottleneck, close, compressed, condensed, constricted, contracted, squeezed, tight, tightened; lanky, rangy, reedy, shoestring, spindly, stalky, stringy, twiggy, willowy, wispy; lank, spare

near ant chunky, squat, stocky, stumpy, thick, thickset; bulky, massive, voluminous; thickish, widish

ant broad, fat, wide

2 not broad or open in views or opinions ⟨a *narrow* person with outdated ideas⟩

syn insular, little, narrow-minded, parochial, petty, picayune, provincial, sectarian, small, small-minded

rel inflexible, ironbound, obdurate, obstinate, rigid, set, stubborn, unyielding, wrongheaded; bigoted, intolerant; biased, jaundiced, one-sided, partial, partisan, prejudiced; brass bound, hidebound, old-fashioned, reactionary, stodgy, straitlaced (*or* straightlaced), stuffy; opinionated

near ant impartial, nonpartisan, objective, unbiased, unprejudiced; freethinking

ant broad-minded, cosmopolitan, liberal, open, open-minded, receptive, tolerant

3 having distinct or certain limits — see LIMITED 1

4 showing little difference in the standing of the competitors — see CLOSE 3

5 unwilling to grant other people social

rights or to accept other viewpoints — see INTOLERANT 2

narrow-minded *adj* **1** unwilling to grant other people social rights or to accept other viewpoints — see INTOLERANT 2

2 not broad or open in views or opinions — see NARROW 2

narrows *n pl* a narrow body of water between two land masses — see CHANNEL 2

nastily *adv* in a mean or spiteful manner ⟨He *nastily* stuck his foot out and tripped the front runner, simply because he couldn't stand to see her win.⟩

syn cattily, despitefully, hatefully, malevolently, maliciously, malignantly, meanly, spitefully, viciously, villainously, virulently, wickedly

rel contemptuously, deprecatingly, disdainfully, scornfully; acrimoniously, hostilely, invidiously, obnoxiously, rancorously, venomously, vindictively, vituperatively; bitterly, enviously, jealously, resentfully; callously, cruelly, hard-heartedly, heartlessly, inhumanely, kindlessly, mercilessly, pitilessly, ruthlessly, soullessly, unfeelingly; disagreeably, ill, ungraciously, unkindly; ill-naturedly, inconsiderately, insensitively, thoughtlessly

near ant affably, agreeably, amiably, cordially, genially, good-naturedly, nicely, pleasantly; altruistically, humanely; considerately, feelingly, lovingly, mercifully, sensitively, softheartedly, solicitously, thoughtfully; compassionately, sympathetically

ant benevolently, benignantly, good-heartedly, kindheartedly, kindly

nastiness *n* **1** the desire to cause pain for the satisfaction of doing harm — see MALICE

2 the quality or state of being obscene — see OBSCENITY

3 the state or quality of being dirty — see DIRTINESS

nasty *adj* **1** arousing or deserving of one's loathing and disgust — see CONTEMPTIBLE 1

2 causing intense displeasure, disgust, or resentment — see OFFENSIVE 1

3 causing or feeling bodily pain — see PAINFUL 1

4 depicting or referring to sexual matters in a way that's unacceptable in polite society — see OBSCENE 1

5 having or showing a desire to cause someone pain or suffering for the sheer enjoyment of it — see HATEFUL

6 marked by wet and windy conditions — see FOUL 1

7 not clean — see DIRTY 1

8 not giving pleasure to the mind or senses — see UNPLEASANT

9 causing worry or anxiety — see TROUBLESOME

10 not being in accordance with the rules or standards of what is fair in sport — see FOUL 2

11 not following or in accordance with standards of honor and decency — see IGNOBLE 2

12 requiring exceptional skill or caution

in performance or handling — see TRICKY 1

nation *n* a body of people composed of one or more nationalities usually with its own territory and government ⟨The American people became one *nation* when they adopted the Constitution in 1789.⟩

syn commonwealth, country, land, sovereignty (*also* sovranty), state

rel city-state, ministate, nation-state; domain, dominion, empire, realm, republic; democracy, dictatorship, monarchy, monocracy, oligarchy, sovereign (*also* sovran), theocracy; fatherland, homeland, motherland; great power, power, sea power, superpower, world power

national *adj* of or relating to a nation ⟨played the home team's *national* anthem before the start of the soccer game⟩

syn civil, public

rel civic, federal, municipal; government, governmental; democratic, republican; nationwide

near ant global; alien, external, foreign

ant nonnational

national *n* a person who owes allegiance to a government and is protected by it — see CITIZEN 1

nationalism *n* **1** excessive favoritism towards one's own country — see CHAUVINISM

2 love and support for one's country — see PATRIOTISM

nationalist *adj* **1** having or showing excessive favoritism towards one's own country ⟨a politician with a xenophobic, *nationalist* platform⟩

syn chauvinist, nationalistic

rel loyal, patriotic; antiforeign, anti-immigrant, nativist, nativistic, xenophobic

near ant internationalist

2 having or showing love and support for one's country — see PATRIOTIC

nationalist *n* one who shows excessive favoritism towards his or her country ⟨a staunch *nationalist* who favored any policy that would give the country more power in the international arena⟩

syn chauvinist, jingo

rel loyalist, patriot; hawk, warmonger; nativist

near ant internationalist; neutralist

nationalistic *adj* **1** having or showing love and support for one's country — see PATRIOTIC

2 having or showing excessive favoritism towards one's own country — see NATIONALIST 1

native *adj* **1** belonging to a particular place by birth or origin ⟨Though she now lived in the Northeast, she was a *native* Midwesterner.⟩

syn aboriginal, born, domestic, endemic, indigenous

rel local, regional; original

near ant imported, introduced, transplanted; alien, foreign, strange; expatriate, immigrant

ant nonindigenous, nonnative

2 being such as found in nature and not altered by processing or refining — see CRUDE 1

3 being a part of the innermost nature of a person or thing — see INHERENT

native *n* a usually longtime resident of a locality ⟨The *natives* seem to resent the summer tourists even though they depend upon them for their livelihood.⟩

syn local, townie (*or* towny)

rel denizen, dweller, habitant, inhabitant, occupant, resident, resider

near ant excursionist, sightseer, traveler (*or* traveller); holidayer, vacationer, vacationist

nativity *n* the act or instance of being born — see BIRTH 1

nattily *adv* in a strikingly neat and trim manner — see SMARTLY

natty *adj* being strikingly neat and trim in style or appearance — see SMART 1

natural *adj* **1** being such from birth or by nature ⟨From his first visits to the wading pool, we could tell that our little boy loved water and was a *natural* swimmer.⟩

syn born, congenital

rel chronic, confirmed, habitual, incorrigible, ingrained (*also* engrained), inveterate, proper, regular, unreconstructed, unregenerate; constitutional, consummate; elemental, elementary, essential; connate, hereditary, inborn, inherent, innate, intimate, intrinsic, native; instinctual, intuitive

near ant cultivated, developed, trained; alien, foreign, unnatural

2 closely resembling the object imitated ⟨The diorama featuring stuffed birds and plastic plants actually looked very *natural*.⟩

syn lifelike, living, near, realistic

rel alike, like, matching, similar, verisimilar; akin, analogous, approximate, comparable, resembling; accurate, close, faithful, true; compelling, convincing; expressive, graphic (*also* graphical), vivid

near ant dissimilar, off, unalike, unlike; incomparable, unmatched; contrasted, contrasting, different, disparate; fake, mock, phony (*also* phoney), sham

ant nonrealistic, unnatural, unrealistic

3 being such by blood and not by adoption or marriage ⟨an adult adoptee who has decided to search for his *natural* parents⟩

syn birth

ant adopted, adoptive, nonbiological

4 being a part of the innermost nature of a person or thing — see INHERENT

5 being such as found in nature and not altered by processing or refining — see CRUDE 1

6 existing without human habitation or cultivation — see WILD 2

7 free from any intent to deceive or impress others — see GUILELESS

8 relating to or characteristic of human beings — see HUMAN

naturally *adv* **1** by natural character or ability ⟨tour guides who are *naturally* outgoing and can easily approach and converse with strangers⟩

syn constitutionally, inherently, innately, intrinsically

rel basically, elementally, essentially, fundamentally; instinctively, intuitively

near ant artificially, unnaturally

2 according to the usual course of things ⟨We *naturally* like to be as comfortable as possible.⟩

syn commonly, generally, normally, ordinarily, typically, usually

rel customarily, habitually, regularly, routinely; familiarly; conventionally, traditionally

phrases as a rule, needless to say, of course, on the whole

near ant funnily, oddly, peculiarly, queerly, strangely, weirdly; anomalously, irregularly; radically

ant abnormally, atypically, extraordinarily, untypically, unusually

3 without any attempt to impress by deception or exaggeration ⟨a boy trying to act *naturally* around the girl he has a crush on⟩

syn artlessly, guilelessly, ingenuously, innocently, naively (*or* naïvely), sincerely, unaffectedly, unfeignedly, unpretentiously

rel genuinely, honestly, simply, truly; freely, openheartedly, openly; candidly, frankly, matter-of-factly; casually, coolly (*also* cooly), nonchalantly

near ant cannily, deceitfully, deceptively, deviously, dishonestly, falsely; calculatingly, craftily, cunningly, furtively, insidiously, sharply, slickly, slyly (*also* slily), underhand, underhanded, underhandedly; flatteringly, unctuously

ant affectedly, artificially, hypocritically, insincerely, pretentiously, unnaturally

naturalness *n* **1** carefree freedom from constraint — see ABANDON

2 the quality or state of being simple and sincere — see NAÏVETÉ 1

nature *n* **1** the set of qualities that makes a person, a group of people, or a thing different from others ⟨His books have a humorous *nature*.⟩ ⟨Her *nature* was such that lying was never an option for her.⟩ ⟨The stoic *nature* of these people enables them to endure one calamity after another.⟩

syn character, colors, complexion, constitution, genius, personality, tone

rel distinctiveness, distinctness, individuality, singularity, uniqueness; attribute, characteristic, earmark, essentiality, feature, flavor, hallmark, mark, point, property, savor (*also* savour), stamp, trait; disposition, grain, sort, temper, temperament; composition, makeup; essence, essentiality, interior, interiority, soul, spirit; metal, stuff, substance; habit, way

2 that part of the physical world that is removed from human habitation ⟨Bill needed to get out of the office and back to *nature* in order to clear his head.⟩

syn open, open air, outdoors, out-of-doors, wild, wilderness

rel backwoods, bush, country, frontier, hinterland, sticks, up-country; outside, without; badland, barren, desert, waste, wasteland

3 a number of persons or things that are grouped together because they have something in common — see SORT 1

4 one's characteristic attitude or mood — see DISPOSITION 1

5 the quality or qualities that make a thing what it is — see ESSENCE 1

6 the whole body of things observed or assumed — see UNIVERSE

naught *also* **nought** *n* the numerical symbol 0 or the absence of number or quantity represented by it — see ZERO 1

naughty *adj* engaging in or marked by childish misbehavior ⟨The children were *naughty* at school today.⟩

syn bad, contrary, errant, froward, misbehaving, mischievous

rel defiant, disrespectful, ill-mannered, ill-natured, impolite, improper, impudent, indecorous, insolent, rude, uncouth, unmannerly; disobedient, headstrong, intractable, obstreperous, recalcitrant, refractory, transgressing, unruly, untoward, willful (*or* wilful); balky, restive, uncontrollable, ungovernable, wayward, wild; elfish, impish, knavish, monkeying, monkeyish, ornery, pixieish, prankish, rascally, roguish, waggish; disorderly, rowdy; babyish, childish, immature, infantile, juvenile, kiddish, puerile

near ant acquiescent, compliant, complying, dutiful, obedient, submissive; considerate, courteous, kindly, mannerly, polite, thoughtful; angelic (*or* angelical), cherubic, divine, heavenly; amenable, docile, governable, tractable; amiable, complaisant, good-natured, obliging, pleasant; discreet, modest; adult, grown-up, mature

ant behaved, behaving, nice, orderly

nausea *n* **1** a disturbed condition of the stomach in which one feels like vomiting ⟨Symptoms include fever accompanied by a loss of appetite and *nausea*.⟩

syn qualmishness, queasiness, queerness, sickness, squeamishness

rel qualm; airsickness, altitude sickness, car sickness, morning sickness, motion sickness, mountain sickness, seasickness

2 a dislike so strong as to cause stomach upset or queasiness — see DISGUST

nauseate *vb* to cause to feel disgust — see DISGUST

nauseated *adj* **1** affected with nausea — see NAUSEOUS 1

2 filled with disgust — see SICK 2

nauseating *adj* causing intense displeasure, disgust, or resentment — see OFFENSIVE 1

nauseous *adj* **1** affected with nausea ⟨After eating the last four pieces of the two-week-old pizza, he was feeling a little *nauseous*.⟩

syn ill, nauseated, qualmish, queasy (*also* queazy), queer, queerish, sick, sickish, squeamish

rel green, peaked, sickly; unsettled, upset

near ant settled; healthy, well

2 causing intense displeasure, disgust, or resentment — see OFFENSIVE 1

nautical *adj* of or relating to navigation of the sea — see MARINE 2

navigable *adj* capable of being traveled on — see PASSABLE 1

navigate *vb* **1** to operate or control the course of ⟨the hours of training that are required before a student pilot is allowed to *navigate* an airplane solo⟩

syn helm, pilot, steer

rel commandeer, hijack (*also* highjack)

2 to travel on water in a vessel — see SAIL 1

3 to make one's way through, across, or over — see TRAVERSE

navigational *adj* of or relating to navigation of the sea — see MARINE 2

navigator *n* one who operates or navigates a seagoing vessel — see SAILOR

nay *adv* not merely this but also — see EVEN 1

nay *n* **1** a vote or decision against something — see NO 1

2 an unwillingness to grant something asked for — see DENIAL 1

Neanderthal *n* a big clumsy often slow-witted person — see OAF 1

Neanderthal *or* **Neandertal** *adj* not civilized — see UNCIVILIZED

near *adj* **1** being the less far of two ⟨Grab the comforter from the *near* side of the bed and fold it in half.⟩

syn closer, hither, nigher, this

rel forward, front, inside

near ant distant, remote, remoter; back, outside

ant far, farther, further, opposite, other

2 being such only when compared to something else — see COMPARATIVE

3 closely resembling the object imitated — see NATURAL 2

4 not being distant in time, space, or significance — see CLOSE 2

near *adv* **1** at, within, or to a short distance or time ⟨As the campers grew cold, they gravitated *nearer* to the campfire.⟩ ⟨As summer draws *near*, we usually start planning our annual vacation.⟩

syn around, by, close, hard, in, nearby, nigh

rel hereabouts (*or* hereabout), thereabouts (*also* thereabout); along, alongside; accessibly, conveniently, handily

phrases at close quarters, at hand, on one's doorstep, within call

2 to a close degree ⟨Copy the artist's drawing into your own sketchbook as *near* as you can.⟩

syn closely, nearly

near ant distantly, remotely

3 very close to but not completely — see ALMOST

near *prep* close to — see AROUND 1

near *vb* **1** to come near or nearer — see APPROACH 1

2 to move closer — see COME 1

nearby *adj* not being distant in time, space, or significance — see CLOSE 2

nearby *adv* at, within, or to a short distance or time — see NEAR 1

nearing *adj* being soon to appear or take place — see FORTHCOMING 1

nearly *adv* **1** to a close degree — see NEAR 2

2 very close to but not completely — see ALMOST

nearness *n* **1** the state of being in a very personal or private relationship — see FAMILIARITY 1

2 the state or condition of being near — see PROXIMITY

nearsighted *adj* able to see near things more clearly than distant ones ⟨I am a little *nearsighted* and need to wear glasses to drive.⟩

syn myopic, shortsighted

rel astigmatic; purblind

ant farsighted

neat *adj* **1** being clean and in good order ⟨Keep the kitchen *neat* so the cook doesn't have to work around piles of dirty dishes.⟩

syn crisp, groomed, orderly, shipshape, snug, tidied, tidy, trim, uncluttered

rel dapper, natty, saucy, smart, spiffy, spruce; immaculate, spick-and-span (*or* spic-and-span), spotless; sleek, streamlined, taut; organized; straight, systematic

near ant scruffy, seedy, shabby, slipshod, sloppy; dirty, filthy, foul, nasty, sordid, squalid; dowdy, frowsy (*or* frowzy), rumpled, tousled, tumbled; disorganized, unsystematic

ant disheveled (*or* dishevelled), disordered, disorderly, messy, mussed, mussy, sloven, slovenly, unkempt, untidy

2 free from added matter — see PURE 1

3 of the very best kind — see EXCELLENT

4 following a set method, arrangement, or pattern — see METHODICAL

nebulous *adj* **1** having an often intentionally veiled or uncertain meaning — see OBSCURE 1

2 not seen or understood clearly — see FAINT 1

nebulousness *n* the quality or state of having a veiled or uncertain meaning — see OBSCURITY 1

necessarily *adv* because of necessity — see NEEDS

necessary *adj* **1** forcing one's compliance or participation by or as if by law — see MANDATORY

2 impossible to avoid or evade — see INEVITABLE

3 impossible to do without — see ESSENTIAL 1

necessary *n* something necessary, indispensable, or unavoidable — see ESSENTIAL 1

necessitate *vb* to have as a requirement — see NEED 1

necessity *n* **1** something necessary, indispensable, or unavoidable — see ESSENTIAL 1

2 the state of lacking sufficient money or material possessions — see POVERTY 1

neck and neck *adj* showing little difference in the standing of the competitors — see CLOSE 3

necklace *n* an ornamental chain or string (as of beads) worn around the neck ⟨found a lovely *necklace* to match the bracelet and ring her mother had given her⟩

syn choker, collar, lei

rel torque (*or* torc); beads, carcanet [*archaic*], rivière; rope, strand; bangle, lavaliere (*also* lavalliere), locket, pendant (*also* pendent)

necromancer *n* a person skilled in using supernatural forces — see MAGICIAN 1

necromancy *n* the power to control natural forces through supernatural means — see MAGIC 1

need *n* **1** a state of being without something

necessary, desirable, or useful ⟨When it came time to wrap the presents, he found he was in *need* of adhesive tape.⟩

syn absence, lack, needfulness, want

rel deficiency, deficit, inadequacy, insufficiency; dearth, meagerness, paucity, poverty, scantiness, scarceness, scarcity, shortage, skimpiness; defect, minus; deprivation, privation; demand, essential, necessity, requirement, requisite

near ant adequacy, enough, sufficiency; fund, pool, stock, supply; excess, fill, overabundance, oversupply, plenty, surfeit, surplus; hoard, stockpile

2 something necessary, indispensable, or unavoidable — see ESSENTIAL 1

3 something one must do because of prior agreement — see OBLIGATION 1

4 the state of lacking sufficient money or material possessions — see POVERTY 1

need *vb* **1** to have as a requirement ⟨a national crisis that *needs* a strong leader to solve it⟩

syn bear, challenge, claim, demand, necessitate, require, take, want, warrant

rel entail, involve; ask, beg, claim, clamor (for), cry (for); hurt (for), lack; command, enjoin, exact, insist, press, quest, stipulate

phrases call for

near ant own, possess

ant have, hold

2 to be under necessity or obligation to ⟨You *need* not stand when she enters the room.⟩

syn have (to), must, ought (to), shall, should

rel will

needed *adj* impossible to do without — see ESSENTIAL 1

needful *adj* **1** impossible to do without — see ESSENTIAL 1

2 lacking money or material possessions — see POOR 1

needful *n* something necessary, indispensable, or unavoidable — see ESSENTIAL 1

needfulness *n* a state of being without something necessary, desirable, or useful — see NEED 1

neediness *n* the state of lacking sufficient money or material possessions — see POVERTY 1

needle *n* **1** a slender hollow instrument by which material is put into or taken from the body through the skin ⟨The nurse inserted the *needle* into his vein and collected some blood for testing.⟩

syn hypodermic, hypodermic needle, hypodermic syringe, syringe

2 an arrow-shaped piece on a dial or scale for registering information — see POINTER 1

needle *vb* **1** to attack repeatedly with mean put-downs or insults — see TEASE 2

2 to subject (someone) to constant scoldings and sharp reminders — see NAG 1

needlelike *adj* being of less than usual width — see NARROW 1

needler *n* a person who causes repeated emotional pain, distress, or annoyance to another — see TORMENTOR

needless *adj* not needed by the circumstances or to accomplish an end — see UNNECESSARY

needlework *n* decorative stitching done on cloth with the use of a needle ⟨a visit to the art museum to see an exhibition of 18th-century *needlework*⟩

syn embroidery

rel crewel, cross-stitch, needlepoint; hemstitch, smocking; fancywork

needs *adv* because of necessity ⟨The dangers of global warming must *needs* be recognized—and recognized soon—by the industrialized nations of the world.⟩

syn inescapably, inevitably, necessarily, perforce, unavoidably

rel involuntarily

ant unnecessarily

needy *adj* lacking money or material possessions — see POOR 1

ne'er *adv* at no time — see NEVER 1

nefarious *adj* not conforming to a high moral standard; morally unacceptable — see BAD 2

negate *vb* 1 to declare not to be true — see DENY 1

2 to put an end to by formal action — see ABOLISH 1

3 to think not to be true or real — see DISBELIEVE

negation *n* a refusal to confirm the truth of a statement — see DENIAL 2

negative *adj* 1 marked by opposition or ill will — see HOSTILE 1

2 opposed to one's interests — see ADVERSE 1

negative *n* 1 a vote or decision against something — see NO 1

2 something that is as different as possible from something else — see OPPOSITE

3 a feature of someone or something that creates difficulty for achieving success — see DISADVANTAGE 1

negative *vb* 1 to reject by or as if by a vote ⟨Although the rebuttal was very eloquent, the jury *negatived* it in favor of the prosecution's argument.⟩ ⟨We promptly *negatived* the idea of having pizza again for dinner, noting that we had already had it for three nights that week.⟩

syn blackball, down, kill, veto

rel decline, disallow, disapprove, dismiss, refuse; blacklist

near ant admit, allow, approve, assent (to), pass, sanction; elect, support

ant confirm, ratify

2 to declare not to be true — see DENY 1

3 to show unwillingness to accept, do, engage in, or agree to — see DECLINE 1

4 to be unwilling to grant — see DENY 2

neglect *n* 1 the state of being unattended to or not cared for ⟨For years the barn sat in *neglect* until one day it finally fell down.⟩

syn desolation, dilapidation, disrepair, seediness

rel inattention, negligence; abandonment, desertion; decay, decrepitude, dereliction, deterioration, disintegration, dumpiness, ruin, ruination

near ant conservation, preservation, upkeep

ant keeping, repair

2 the nonperformance of an assigned or expected action — see FAILURE 1

neglect *vb* 1 to fail to give proper attention to ⟨The news media *neglected* the real issues of the campaign and focused on personalities.⟩

syn bypass, disregard, forget, ignore, overlook, overpass, pass over, slight, slur (over)

rel fail; miss, omit; brush (aside *or* off), reject, shrug off; disdain, pooh-pooh (*also* pooh), scorn; scant, skimp

near ant appreciate, cherish, prize, treasure, value; cultivate, foster, nurse, nurture; pamper; remember; listen (to), watch; follow, mark, note, notice, observe, remark

ant attend (to), heed, mind, regard, tend (to)

2 to leave undone or unattended to especially through carelessness ⟨I've *neglected* my garden, and now it's overgrown with weeds.⟩

syn forget, shirk

rel slack (off)

near ant carry out, do, execute, perform; accomplish, achieve; keep up, maintain

ant attend (to), remember

3 to miss the opportunity or obligation ⟨Conveniently, the salesman *neglected* to mention that the car had been through a flood.⟩

syn fail, forget, omit

rel disregard, ignore, overlook, overpass, pass over, slight; slide, slip; default; skip

phrases miss out on

near ant heed, mind, remember; keep, observe; carry out, do, execute, perform, practice (*also* practise); discharge, fulfill (*or* fulfil), meet, satisfy; comply (with)

neglected *adj* showing signs of advanced wear and tear and neglect — see SHABBY 1

neglectful *adj* failing to give proper care and attention — see NEGLIGENT

neglecting *adj* failing to give proper care and attention — see NEGLIGENT

negligence *n* 1 failure to take the care that a cautious person usually takes ⟨The accident was caused by the driver's *negligence*.⟩

syn carelessness, dereliction, heedlessness, incautiousness, laxness, slackness

rel foolhardiness, rashness, recklessness, wildness; neglect, omission; delinquency, irresponsibility, irresponsibleness, malfeasance, malpractice, misconduct; misdirection, mishandling, mismanagement; forgetfulness, inadvertence, inattention, inattentiveness, obliviousness, shortsightedness, unwariness

near ant alertness, attention, attentiveness, awareness; circumspection, observance, vigilance, watchfulness; responsibility, responsibleness

ant care, carefulness, caution, cautiousness, heedfulness

2 the nonperformance of an assigned or expected action — see FAILURE 1

negligent *adj* failing to give proper care and attention ⟨The youngster has been woefully *negligent* in taking care of the vacationing neighbor's dog, repeatedly forgetting to feed the poor animal.⟩

---

syn careless, derelict, lax, lazy, neglectful, neglecting, remiss, slack

rel heedless, incautious, irresponsible, reckless, wild; unguarded, unwary; forgetful; disregarding, inattentive, oblivious, thoughtless, unheeding, unmindful, unthinking; apathetic, indifferent, unconcerned, uninterested

near ant meticulous, painstaking, punctilious; cautious, circumspect, gingerly, guarded; alert, heedful, heeding, mindful, observant, regardful, regarding, vigilant, wary, watchful; foresighted, forethoughtful, provident, responsible; thinking, thoughtful; concerned, interested

ant attentive, careful, conscientious, nonnegligent

negligible *adj* 1 so small or unimportant as to warrant little or no attention ⟨The two cents in change was such a *negligible* sum that she left the store without bothering to take it.⟩

syn inconsequential, inconsiderable, insignificant, measly, minute, nominal, paltry, petty, picayune, piddling, slight, trifling, trivial

rel inferior, mean; imperceptible, inappreciable; little, puny, tiny; hairsplitting, nitpicking, pettifogging, quibbling; one-horse, penny-ante, two-bit

near ant serious, substantial, weighty; eventful, momentous, pivotal; conspicuous, noteworthy, outstanding, prominent, remarkable, striking; appreciable, discernible (*also* discernable), measurable

ant big, consequential, considerable, important, material, significant

2 lacking importance — see UNIMPORTANT

3 small in degree — see REMOTE 1

negligibly *adv* in a very small quantity or degree — see LITTLE 1

negotiable *adj* 1 capable of being traveled on — see PASSABLE 1

2 open to question or dispute — see DEBATABLE 1

negotiate *vb* 1 to bring about through discussion and compromise ⟨Ava wanted to *negotiate* a higher salary before she accepted the job offer.⟩

syn arrange, bargain, concert, conclude

rel settle (on or upon); chaffer, deal, dicker, haggle, horse-trade, palter; agree; contract, covenant; argue, debate, discuss, hash (over); reason, talk, talk over, work out; renegotiate

2 to deal with (something) skillfully or efficiently — see HANDLE 1

3 to plan out usually with subtle skill or care — see ENGINEER

4 to talk over or dispute the terms of a purchase — see BARGAIN 1

5 to carry through (as a process) to completion — see PERFORM 1

negotiation *n* the act or practice of each side giving up something in order to reach an agreement — see CONCESSION 1

neigh *vb* to make the cry typical of a horse ⟨The horses *neighed* when the rider came into the barn.⟩

syn nicker, whinny

neighbor *vb* to be adjacent to — see ADJOIN 1

neighborhood *n* 1 an approximate amount, extent, or degree ⟨a movie that's said to have cost in the *neighborhood* of 100 million dollars⟩

syn matter, tune

rel nearness, proximity

2 an area (as of a city) set apart for some purpose or having some special feature — see DISTRICT

3 the people living in a particular area — see COMMUNITY 1

4 an adjoining region or space — see ENVIRONS 2

neighboring *adj* 1 having a border in common — see ADJACENT

2 not being distant in time, space, or significance — see CLOSE 2

neighborliness *n* kindly concern, interest, or support — see GOODWILL 1

neighborly *adj* having or showing kindly feeling and sincere interest — see FRIENDLY 1

nemesis *n* 1 one who inflicts punishment in return for an injury or offense ⟨Batman is the Joker's main *nemesis* and always foils his wicked plots.⟩

syn avenger, castigator, chastiser, punisher, scourge, vigilante

rel revenger; redresser, righter; requiter

near ant ransomer, redeemer, vindicator

2 suffering, loss, or hardship imposed in response to a crime or offense — see PUNISHMENT

3 a source of harm or misfortune — see BANE 1

neophyte *n* 1 a person who has recently been persuaded to join a religious sect — see CONVERT 1

2 a person who is just starting out in a field of activity — see BEGINNER

neoplasm *n* an abnormal mass of tissue — see GROWTH 1

nerd *n* 1 a person devoted to intellectual or academic pursuits ⟨The candidate accepted being characterized as a *nerd* and branded herself as smart and hardworking.⟩

syn bookworm, grind

rel egghead, highbrow, intellectual; brain, genius; academic, scholar

near ant slacker, underachiever; lowbrow

2 a person with strong intellectual interests — see INTELLECTUAL

nerdy *adj* much given to learning and thinking — see INTELLECTUAL 1

nerve *n* 1 shameless boldness — see EFFRONTERY

2 strength of mind to carry on in spite of danger — see COURAGE

3 **nerves** *pl* a sense of panic or extreme nervousness — see JITTERS

nerve *vb* to prepare (oneself) mentally or emotionally — see FORTIFY 1

nerved *adj* inclined or willing to take risks — see BOLD 1

nerveless *adj* 1 lacking strength of will or character — see WEAK 1

2 not easily panicked or upset — see UNFLAPPABLE

nerviness *n* shameless boldness — see EFFRONTERY

nervous *adj* 1 feeling or showing uncomfortable feelings of uncertainty ⟨He was *nervous* about how he would do at the varsity basketball tryouts.⟩

syn aflutter, anxious, dithery, edgy, het up, hung up, insecure, jittery, jumpy, nervy, perturbed, queasy (*also* queazy), tense, troubled, uneasy, unquiet, upset, uptight, worried

rel aggrieved, concerned, disquieted, distraught, distressed, disturbed, freaked, freaked-out, shook-up; foreboding, hesitant, misgiving; fretful, fretting, stewing; flustered, twittered, undone, unnerved, unstrung; obsessed, preoccupied, restless; flighty, fluttery, high-strung, skittish, spooky; annoyed, put out

phrases keyed up, on edge, on pins and needles, on tenterhooks

near ant confident, self-assured, self-confident, sure; controlled, self-controlled

ant calm, collected, cool, easy, happy-go-lucky, nerveless, relaxed

2 marked by or causing agitation or uncomfortable feelings ⟨A *nervous* silence filled the room as the teacher handed out the graded exams.⟩

syn agitating, anxious, creepy, disquieting, distressful, distressing, disturbing, fraught, hairy, restless, tense, uneasy, unnerving, unsettling, worrisome

rel bothersome, troublesome; foreboding, misgiving; discouraging, disheartening, strained; restive, restless, unrestful; awkward, embarrassing

near ant restful; pacific

ant calming, comfortable, easy, peaceful, quiet, quieting, tranquil

3 easily excited by nature — see EXCITABLE

nervousness *n* an uneasy state of mind usually over the possibility of an anticipated misfortune or trouble — see ANXIETY 1

nervy *adj* **1** displaying or marked by rude boldness ⟨The *nervy* waiter held up the small tip and called out to the departing customers, "Hope it doesn't break the bank!"⟩

syn audacious, bold, bold-faced, brash, brassy, brazen, cheeky, cocksure, cocky, fresh, impertinent, impudent, insolent, sassy, saucy, wise

rel assertive, forward, obtrusive; audacious, defiant, disrespectful; shameless, unabashed, unblushing; bluff, blunt, curt; cute, facetious, flip, flippant, pert, smart, smart-alecky; lippy

near ant demure, humble, modest; courteous, genteel, mannerly, polite, proper; deferential, respectful; abashed, ashamed, blushing, embarrassed, shamefaced; gentle, mild; inconspicuous, unobtrusive

ant meek, mousy (*or* mousey), retiring, shy, timid

2 inclined or willing to take risks — see BOLD 1

3 feeling or showing uncomfortable feelings of uncertainty — see NERVOUS 1

nest *n* a place where a person goes to hide or to avoid others — see HIDEOUT

nest egg *n* a sum of money set aside for a particular purpose — see FUND 1

nestle *vb* **1** to lie close — see NUZZLE

2 to sit or recline comfortably or cozily — see SNUGGLE 1

3 to establish or place comfortably or snugly — see ENSCONCE 1

¹**net** *n* **1** a fabric made of strands loosely twisted, knotted, or woven together at regular intervals ⟨The basketball didn't go into the basket—it just hit the *net*.⟩

syn mesh, netting, network

rel web, webbing; grille (*also* grill), lattice, screen, screening, wirework; filigree, fishnet, lace

2 a device or scheme for capturing another by surprise — see TRAP 2

3 something that catches and holds — see WEB 1

²**net** *n* **1** the amount of money left when expenses are subtracted from the total amount received — see PROFIT 1

2 the central part or aspect of something under consideration — see CRUX

¹**net** *vb* **1** to catch or hold as if in a net — see ENTANGLE 2

2 to take physical control or possession of (something) suddenly or forcibly — see CATCH 1

²**net** *vb* to receive after charges and deductions have been made ⟨The entrepreneur *netted* millions on that deal.⟩

syn clear

rel earn, gain, garner, get, make, realize; cash in (on), rake (in); clean up

near ant gross

nether *adj* situated lower down — see INFERIOR 1

netting *n* a fabric made of strands loosely twisted, knotted, or woven together at regular intervals — see ¹NET 1

nettle *vb* to disturb the peace of mind of (someone) especially by repeated disagreeable acts — see IRRITATE 1

nettling *adj* causing annoyance — see ANNOYING

network *n* **1** a fabric made of strands loosely twisted, knotted, or woven together at regular intervals — see ¹NET 1

2 something made up of many interdependent or related parts — see SYSTEM 1

3 a group of people sharing a common interest and relating together socially — see GANG 2

neuter *vb* to remove the sex organs of ⟨He agreed to let the children have the dog on the condition that they have her *neutered*.⟩

syn alter, desex, fix

rel emasculate, geld; spay; sterilize

neutral *adj* not favoring or joined to either side in a quarrel, contest, or war ⟨Sweden remained *neutral* during World War II, refusing to join either side in the conflict.⟩

syn nonpartisan

rel nonaligned; hands-off, noninterventionist; autonomous, independent, sovereign (*also* sovran), unaffiliated; nonbelligerent; individualistic; disinterested, evenhanded, fair, impartial, indifferent, unbiased, uninfluenced, unprejudiced; bipartisan

phrases on the fence

near ant biased, partial, partisan, prejudiced, unfair; affiliated, associated, federated; belligerent

ant allied, confederate

neutrality *n* lack of favoritism toward one side or another — see DETACHMENT 1

neutralize *vb* to balance with an equal force so as to make ineffective — see OFFSET

neutralizer *n* a force or influence that makes an opposing force ineffective or less effective — see COUNTERBALANCE

never *adv* **1** at no time ⟨I have *never* been out of the country.⟩
syn ne'er
rel nevermore; not; infrequently, little, rarely, seldom
near ant eternally, everlastingly, evermore, invariably; frequently, often, recurrently, repeatedly
ant always, constantly, continuously, endlessly, ever, forever, perpetually
2 not in any degree, way, or under any condition ⟨Though she turned down his offer of marriage twice, he was *never* convinced that she did not love him.⟩
syn no, none, nothing, noway (*or* noways), nowise
rel nowhere near
phrases by no means, in no wise, nothing doing, on no account
near ant completely, extremely, full, fully, par excellence, right, very; altogether, exactly; somehow, someway (*also* someways); out
ant anyhow, anyway, anywise, at all, ever, half, however

nevertheless *adv* in spite of that — see HOWEVER

new *adj* **1** taking the place of one that came before ⟨After my bike was stolen, my scooter became my *new* mode of transportation.⟩
syn makeshift, substitute
rel alternate, alternative, pinch; different, other, separate; extra, spare; improvised, jury; another, second; utility; successive; equivalent
near ant first, former; equal, identical, same; lasting, permanent
ant original
2 not known or experienced before ⟨Spanish was a *new* course of study for her.⟩ ⟨I like to visit *new* places.⟩
syn fresh, novel, original, strange, unaccustomed, unfamiliar, unheard-of, unknown, unprecedented
rel innovative, unique; nontraditional, unconventional, untried, unused, unworn; pathbreaking, pioneering, trailblazing
near ant conventional, established, traditional, tried, tried-and-true; derivative, imitative
ant familiar, hackneyed, old, time-honored, tired, warmed-over
3 recently made and never used before ⟨That unique scent is the telltale sign of a *new* car.⟩
syn brand-new, spick-and-span (*or* spic-and-span), unused
rel clean, fresh, mint, pristine, unspoiled; untouched; newfangled, new-fashioned; natural, raw, unprocessed, untreated, unworked, virgin
near ant dirty, soiled, spoiled, stale; aged, old, shabby, shopworn, well-handled, worn
ant hand-me-down, second hand, used

4 made or become fresh in spirits or vigor ⟨A little rest made him a *new* man after the exhausting basketball game.⟩
syn energized, freshened, invigorated, newborn, reanimated, recreated, reenergized, refreshed, regenerated, renewed, resuscitated, revived
rel animated, enlivened, exhilarated, jazzed (up); resurrected; rested, untired, unwearied
near ant tired, weary; dampened, deadened; emasculated; demoralized, disheartened, dispirited
ant drained, enervate, enervated, exhausted, weakened
5 being or involving the latest methods, concepts, information, or styles — see MODERN

new *adv* not long ago — see NEWLY

newbie *n* a person who is just starting out in a field of activity — see BEGINNER

newborn *adj* made or become fresh in spirits or vigor — see NEW 4

newborn *n* a recently born person — see BABY 1

newcomer *n* a person who is just starting out in a field of activity — see BEGINNER

newfangled *adj* being or involving the latest methods, concepts, information, or styles — see MODERN

new–fashioned *adj* being or involving the latest methods, concepts, information, or styles — see MODERN

newly *adv* not long ago ⟨a *newly* married couple still getting to know one another⟩
syn freshly, just, late, lately, new, now, only, recently
rel latterly
phrases of late
near ant before, early, erstwhile, previously; heretofore, hitherto
ant anciently

newness *n* the quality or appeal of being new — see NOVELTY 1

news *n pl* a report of recent events or facts not previously known ⟨I heard the good *news* about your promotion.⟩
syn information, intelligence, item, story, tidings, word
rel announcement, bulletin, communication, correspondence, dispatch, message, reportage; dope, lowdown, scoop, tidbit (*also* titbit), tip; gossip, rumor, tale, tattle; feedback; disinformation, propaganda

newsman *n* a person employed by a newspaper, magazine, or radio or television station to gather, write, or report news — see REPORTER

newspaper *n* a publication that appears at regular intervals — see JOURNAL

newsy *adj* having the style and content of everyday conversation — see CHATTY 1

next *adj* being the one that comes immediately after another ⟨My house is the *next* one.⟩ ⟨Turn at the *next* street, not this one.⟩ ⟨She was *next* in line for concert tickets.⟩
syn coming, ensuing, following, succeeding
rel consecutive, sequential, successive; posterior, subsequent; immediate; second
phrases on deck
near ant anterior, former; past; last

ant antecedent, foregoing, precedent, preceding, previous, prior

next–door *adj* not being distant in time, space, or significance — see CLOSE 2

next to *adv* very close to but not completely — see ALMOST

next to *prep* **1** close to — see AROUND 1

2 subsequent to in time or order — see AFTER

nib *n* **1** the jaws of a bird together with their hornlike covering — see BEAK 1

2 the last and usually sharp or tapering part of something long and narrow — see POINT 2

nibble *n* a small piece or quantity of food — see MORSEL 1

nibble *vb* **1** to eat reluctantly and in small bites ⟨Having no real appetite at all, I just *nibbled* during the party.⟩

syn peck, pick

rel graze, nosh, snack; taste

near ant gorge, gormandize, overeat, pig out, swill

2 to crush or grind with the teeth — see BITE (ON)

3 to consume or wear away gradually — see EAT 2

nice *adj* **1** following the established traditions of refined society and good taste — see PROPER 1

2 giving pleasure or contentment to the mind or senses — see PLEASANT 1

3 hard to please — see FINICKY

4 having an easygoing and pleasing manner especially in social situations — see AMIABLE

5 made or done with extreme care and accuracy — see FINE 2

6 conforming to a high standard of morality or virtue — see GOOD 2

nicely *adv* **1** in a pleasing way — see WELL 5

2 in a satisfactory way — see WELL 1

3 with good reason or courtesy — see WELL 4

niceness *n* the state or quality of having a pleasant or agreeable manner in socializing with others — see AMIABILITY 1

nicety *n* **1** a single piece of information — see FACT 3

2 something that adds to one's ease of living — see COMFORT 2

3 the quality or state of being very accurate — see PRECISION

niche *n* **1** a hollowed-out space in a wall ⟨Statues of various saints occupy the *niches* lining the abbey's many corridors.⟩

syn alcove, nook, recess

rel corner, cranny, cubbyhole; cubicle, dent, embrasure, indentation

2 a situation or activity for which a person or thing is best suited ⟨After several false starts, she finally found her *niche* in the restaurant business.⟩

syn groove, place

rel appointment, berth, billet, capacity, function, job, position, post; rank, standing, station, status; forte, speciality, specialty, thing

3 the place where a plant or animal is usually or naturally found — see HOME 2

nick *n* a V-shaped cut usually on an edge or a surface — see NOTCH 1

nicker *vb* to make the cry typical of a horse — see NEIGH

nickname *n* a descriptive or familiar name given instead of or in addition to the one belonging to an individual ⟨His wavy hair earned him the *nickname* "Curly" early in life.⟩

syn alias, cognomen, epithet, handle, sobriquet (*also* soubriquet)

rel appellation, denomination, denotation, designation, label, tag, title; anonym, nom de plume, pen name, pseudonym

nifty *adj* of the very best kind — see EXCELLENT

nifty *n* something very good of its kind — see JIM-DANDY

niggard *adj* giving or sharing as little as possible — see STINGY 1

niggard *n* a mean grasping person who is usually stingy with money — see MISER

niggardly *adj* **1** giving or sharing as little as possible — see STINGY 1

2 less plentiful than what is normal, necessary, or desirable — see MEAGER

nigh *adj* not being distant in time, space, or significance — see CLOSE 2

nigh *adv* **1** at, within, or to a short distance or time — see NEAR 1

2 very close to but not completely — see ALMOST

nigh *prep* close to — see AROUND 1

nigh *vb* **1** to come near or nearer — see APPROACH 1

2 to move closer to — see COME 1

nigher *adj* being the less far of two — see NEAR 1

night *adj* of, relating to, or occurring in the night — see NOCTURNAL

night *n* **1** the time from sunset to sunrise when there is no visible sunlight ⟨The couple loved to sit outside at *night* and watch the stars.⟩

syn dark, darkness, nighttime

rel dusk, evening, gloaming, nightfall, twilight; midnight

near ant dawn, daybreak, sunrise, sunup; forenoon, morning; high noon, midday, noon, noonday, noontide, noontime

ant day, daytime

2 a time or place of little or no light — see DARK 1

3 the time from when the sun begins to set to the onset of total darkness — see DUSK 1

nightclub *n* a bar or restaurant offering special nighttime entertainment (as music, dancing, or comedy acts) ⟨We decided to go dancing at a local *nightclub* after the long dinner and movie.⟩

syn cabaret, café (*also* cafe), club, roadhouse

rel disco; barroom, saloon, tavern; dive, honky-tonk, speakeasy

nightdress *n* a loose pullover garment worn in bed — see NIGHTGOWN

nightfall *n* the time from when the sun begins to set to the onset of total darkness — see DUSK 1

nightgown *n* a loose pullover garment worn in bed ⟨decided to buy a flannel *nightgown* instead of pajamas⟩

---

syn gown, nightdress, nightshirt

rel nightclothes; pajamas, pj's; nightcap; lingerie, negligee (*also* negligé), nightie (*or* nighty)

nightly *adj* of, relating to, or occurring in the night — see NOCTURNAL

nightmare *adj* extremely disturbing or repellent — see HORRIBLE 1

nightmare *n* a situation or state that causes great suffering and unhappiness — see HELL 2

nightmarish *adj* extremely disturbing or repellent — see HORRIBLE 1

nightshirt *n* a loose pullover garment worn in bed — see NIGHTGOWN

nightstick *n* a heavy rigid stick used as a weapon or for punishment — see CLUB 1

nighttime *adj* of, relating to, or occurring in the night — see NOCTURNAL

nighttime *n* the time from sunset to sunrise when there is no visible sunlight — see NIGHT 1

nil *n* the numerical symbol 0 or the absence of number or quantity represented by it — see ZERO 1

nimble *adj* 1 having or showing quickness of mind — see INTELLIGENT 1

2 moving easily — see GRACEFUL 1

nimbleness *n* ease and grace in physical activity — see DEXTERITY 2

nincompoop *n* 1 a person who lacks good sense or judgment — see FOOL 1

2 a stupid person — see IDIOT

ninny *n* 1 a person who lacks good sense or judgment — see FOOL 1

2 a stupid person — see IDIOT

¹**nip** *n* 1 the quality or state of being stimulating to the mind or senses — see PIQUANCY

2 a very small amount — see PARTICLE 1

3 an uncomfortable degree of coolness — see CHILL

²**nip** *n* the portion of a serving of a beverage that is swallowed at one time — see DRINK 2

nip *vb* 1 to make (something) shorter or smaller with the use of a cutting instrument — see CLIP 1

2 to squeeze tightly between two surfaces, edges, or points — see PINCH 1

3 to take (something) without right and with an intent to keep — see STEAL 1

4 to proceed or move quickly — see HURRY 2

nip and tuck *adj* showing little difference in the standing of the competitors — see CLOSE 3

nipper *n* a male person who has not yet reached adulthood — see BOY 1

nipping *adj* 1 having a low or subnormal temperature — see COLD 1

2 uncomfortably cool — see CHILLY 1

nippy *adj* 1 having a low or subnormal temperature — see COLD 1

2 having a powerfully stimulating odor or flavor — see SHARP 2

3 moving, proceeding, or acting with great speed — see FAST 1

4 uncomfortably cool — see CHILLY 1

nitpick *vb* to make often peevish criticisms or objections about matters that are minor, unimportant, or irrelevant — see QUIBBLE 1

nitpicker *n* a person given to harsh judgments and to finding faults — see CRITIC 1

nitwit *n* 1 a person who lacks good sense or judgment — see FOOL 1

2 a stupid person — see IDIOT

no *adv* 1 not in any degree, way, or under any condition — see NEVER 2

2 certainly not — see HARDLY 1

no *interj* how surprising, doubtful, or unbelievable ⟨*No*—you can't possibly mean that I failed that test! I studied for days!⟩

syn ah, aha, fie, indeed, pshaw, well, what, why

rel gee, gee whiz, hello, lo, oh; fiddlesticks, pooh; there; oops (*or* whoops *also* woops); egad, gad, the devil, the dickens

no *n* 1 a vote or decision against something ⟨Though I wanted spaghetti for dinner, the consensus was a decisive *no*.⟩

syn nay, negative

rel con; blackball, veto; denial, negation, refusal

near ant pro; acceptance, approval, grace

ant positive, yea, yes

2 an unwillingness to grant something asked for — see DENIAL 1

nobility *n* 1 impressiveness of beauty on a large scale — see MAGNIFICENCE

2 the highest class in a society — see ARISTOCRACY 1

noble *adj* 1 of high birth, rank, or station ⟨Despite his *noble* background, the prince is known for his unpretentious way with common people.⟩

syn aristocratic, genteel, gentle, grand, great, highborn, patrician, upper-class, wellborn

rel high, lofty, superior; elevated, ennobled, exalted; gentlemanly, kingly, knightly, ladylike, lordly, princely, queenly, regal, royal; high-level, senior

near ant inferior, mean; ordinary, plain; abased, degraded; junior, subordinate

ant baseborn, common, humble, ignoble, low, lower-class, lowly, mean, nonaristocratic, plebeian, ungenteel

2 having, characterized by, or arising from a dignified and generous nature ⟨The factory owner had a kind, *noble* disposition that showed in his unstinting generosity toward the poor.⟩ ⟨Our country was founded on the *noble* ideas that are put forth in the Founding Fathers' writings.⟩

syn big, chivalrous, elevated, gallant, great, greathearted, high, high-minded, lofty, lordly, magnanimous, sublime

rel ennobled, exalted, glorified; heroic (*also* heroical), honorable, valiant, venerable, worthy; knightly, princely, regal; inspiring, moving, uplifting; august, magnificent, majestic

near ant sordid, squalid, vile, wretched; abominable, contemptible, despicable, detestable, hateful, offensive, repulsive, ugly, vicious; dastardly, dirty, lousy, sorry; little, mean, narrow, small-minded

ant base, debased, degenerate, degraded, ignoble, low

3 following the accepted rules of moral conduct — see HONORABLE 1

4 large and impressive in size, grandeur, extent, or conception — see GRAND 1

5 of the very best kind — see EXCELLENT

6 standing above others in rank, importance, or achievement — see EMINENT

nobleman *n* a man of high birth or social position — see GENTLEMAN 1

nobleness *n* impressiveness of beauty on a large scale — see MAGNIFICENCE

noblewoman *n* a woman of high birth or social position — see GENTLEWOMAN

nobly *adv* in a manner befitting a person of the highest character and ideals — see GREATLY 1

nobody *n* a person of no importance or influence ⟨Tired of feeling like a *nobody*, she decided to launch her own business.⟩
syn cipher, lightweight, nonentity, nothing, pip-squeak, pygmy (*also* pigmy), shrimp, twerp, whippersnapper, zero, zilch
rel noncelebrity; figurehead, puppet; nonperson
near ant chief, head, lead, leader; celebrity, luminary, notable, personality, star, superstar
ant big shot, bigwig, eminence, figure, kingpin, magnate, nabob, personage, somebody, VIP

nobody *pron* no person ⟨There is *nobody* home.⟩ ⟨*Nobody* wants to clean up that mess.⟩
syn none, no one
near ant anybody, anyone; somebody, someone
ant everybody, everyone

nocturnal *adj* of, relating to, or occurring in the night ⟨He bought a new telescope so he could pursue his favorite *nocturnal* hobby of astronomy.⟩
syn night, nightly, nighttime
rel late; midnight, overnight
near ant noon
ant daily, diurnal

nod *vb* to make short up-and-down movements ⟨Though she couldn't see the rain, she knew it had started because she could see the flowers *nod* as raindrops hit them.⟩
syn bob, bobble, jog, jounce, pump, seesaw, wag
rel jerk, jiggle, shake, wiggle, wobble (*also* wabble); oscillate, rock, sway, swing, undulate; drop, duck

nodding *adj* bending downward or forward ⟨Some students, with *nodding* heads, were helplessly falling asleep during the boring lecture.⟩
syn bowed, bowing, declined, declining, descendant (*also* descendent), descending, drooping, droopy, hanging, hung, inclining, pendulous, sagging, stooping, weeping
rel floppy, limp; dangling, falling, pendent (*or* pendant); dipping, sinking, slumping
near ant erect, inflexible, rigid, stiff; elevated, raised, upraised
ant unbending, upright

noddle *n* the upper or front part of the body that contains the brain, the major sense organs, and the mouth — see HEAD 1

node *n* a small rounded mass of swollen tissue — see BUMP 1

nodule *n* a small rounded mass of swollen tissue — see BUMP 1

Noel *n* the season celebrating Christmas — see YULETIDE

noggin *n* the upper or front part of the body that contains the brain, the major sense organs, and the mouth — see HEAD 1

no-good *adj* having no usefulness — see WORTHLESS

no-good *n* a mean, evil, or unprincipled person — see VILLAIN

noise *n* **1** loud, confused, and usually inharmonious sound ⟨The incessant *noise* of traffic on Fifth Avenue made normal conversation impossible.⟩
syn babel, blare, bluster, cacophony, chatter, clamor, clangor, din, discordance, racket, rattle, roar
rel discord; commotion, furor, hubbub, hullabaloo, hurly-burly, rumpus, tumult, uproar; clatter; bang, blast, boom, clap, crack, crash
near ant calm, hush, lull; quietude, serenity, tranquillity (*or* tranquility)
ant quiet, silence, silentness, still, stillness
2 a violent shouting — see CLAMOR 1

noiseless *adj* mostly or entirely without sound — see SILENT 3

noisome *adj* **1** bad for the well-being of the body — see UNHEALTHY 1
2 causing intense displeasure, disgust, or resentment — see OFFENSIVE 1
3 having an unpleasant smell — see MALODOROUS

noisy *adj* **1** making loud, confused, and usually unharmonious sounds ⟨The *noisy* crowd marched up the street, shouting ever louder as they approached the palace.⟩
syn clangorous, dinning, discordant
rel cacophonous, dissonant; resounding, sonorous; clamorous, uproarious; blatant, obstreperous, strident, vociferous; blaring, booming, brassy, brazen, clanging, earsplitting, jangly
near ant calm, hushed
ant noiseless, quiet, silent, soundless, still
2 full of or characterized by the presence of noise ⟨The crowded auditorium was *noisy*, packed with excited theatergoers eager for the show to start.⟩ ⟨The manufacturing plant was a decidedly *noisy* place, so we wore ear protection while we toured it.⟩
syn clamorous, clangorous, clattering, clattery, resounding, uproarious
rel resonant, sonorous; buzzing, humming, murmuring; blustery, boisterous, raucous, rip-roaring, roaring, roistering, romping, rowdy; tumultuous, woolly (*also* wooly); obstreperous, vociferous
near ant calm, peaceful, serene, tranquil
ant hushed, noiseless, quiet, silent, soundless, stilled, stilly
3 excessively showy — see GAUDY
4 likely to attract attention — see NOTICEABLE

nomad *adj* traveling from place to place — see ITINERANT

nomad *n* a person who roams about without a fixed route or destination ⟨After college she became quite the *nomad*, backpacking through Europe with no particular destination.⟩
syn drifter, gadabout, rambler, roamer,

rover, stroller, vagabond, wanderer, way-farer

rel laggard, straggler; lingerer, loiterer, sojourner; bum, hobo, tramp; sightseer, traveler (*or* traveller); migrant, transient, vagrant; saunterer; hiker

near ant homebody; denizen, dweller, habitant, inhabitant, resident, settler

nominal *adj* **1** being something in name or form only ⟨He was the *nominal* head of state—everyone knew the country was actually run by one of his advisers.⟩

syn formal, paper, titular

rel so-called; phantom, virtual; apparent, assumed, evident, ostensible, presumed, seeming, supposed

near ant actual, real, true

2 so small or unimportant as to warrant little or no attention — see NEGLIGIBLE 1

nominally *adv* in a very small quantity or degree — see LITTLE 1

nonaction *n* lack of action or activity — see INACTION

nonbinding *adj* having no legal or binding force — see NULL 1

nonchalance *n* lack of interest or concern — see INDIFFERENCE

nonchalant *adj* having or showing a lack of interest or concern — see INDIFFERENT 1

noncombustible *adj* incapable of being burned — see INCOMBUSTIBLE

nonconflicting *adj* not having or showing any apparent conflict — see CONSISTENT

nonconformist *adj* deviating from commonly accepted beliefs or practices — see HERETICAL

nonconformist *n* **1** a person who does not conform to generally accepted standards or customs ⟨Always the *nonconformist*, she insisted on wearing red on St. Patrick's Day and not green like everyone else.⟩

syn bohemian, deviant, heretic, individualist, lone wolf, maverick

rel freethinker; character, codger, crackbrain, crackpot, crank, eccentric, freak, kook, nut, oddball, screwball, weirdo; eight ball, misfit, outsider

near ant adherent, follower, supporter; sheep

ant conformer, conformist

2 a person who believes, teaches, or advocates something opposed to accepted beliefs — see HERETIC 1

nonconformity *n* departure from a generally accepted theory, opinion, or practice — see HERESY

nonconventional *adj* not bound by traditional ways or beliefs — see LIBERAL 1

none *adv* **1** certainly not — see HARDLY 1

2 not in any degree, way, or under any condition — see NEVER 2

none *pron* no person — see NOBODY

nonelective *adj* forcing one's compliance or participation by or as if by law — see MANDATORY

nonentity *n* **1** a conception or image created by the imagination and having no objective reality — see FANTASY 1

2 a person of no importance or influence — see NOBODY

nonessential *adj* not needed by the circumstances or to accomplish an end — see UNNECESSARY

nonetheless *adv* in spite of that — see HOWEVER

nonexistent *adj* not present or in evidence — see ABSENT 2

nonfictional *adj* restricted to or based on fact — see FACTUAL 1

nonflammable *adj* incapable of being burned — see INCOMBUSTIBLE

nonfunctional *adj* not being in working order — see INOPERABLE 1

nonfunctioning *adj* not being in working order — see INOPERABLE 1

noninflammable *adj* incapable of being burned — see INCOMBUSTIBLE

nonliterary *adj* used in or suitable for speech and not formal writing — see COLLOQUIAL 1

nonmaterial *adj* not composed of matter — see IMMATERIAL 1

nonmotile *adj* incapable of moving or being moved — see IMMOVABLE 1

nonmoving *adj* **1** fixed in a place or position — see STATIONARY 1

2 incapable of moving or being moved — see IMMOVABLE 1

nonnative *adj* being, relating to, or characteristic of a country other than one's own — see FOREIGN 1

nonnative *n* a person who is not native to or known to a community — see STRANGER

nonobjective *adj* using elements of form (as color, line, or texture) with little or no attempt at creating a realistic picture — see ABSTRACT 2

no-nonsense *adj* not joking or playful in mood or manner — see SERIOUS 1

nonoperating *adj* not being in working order — see INOPERABLE 1

nonorthodox *adj* **1** deviating from commonly accepted beliefs or practices — see HERETICAL

2 not bound by traditional ways or beliefs — see LIBERAL 1

nonpareil *adj* having no equal or rival for excellence or desirability — see ONLY 1

nonpareil *n* someone of such unequaled perfection as to deserve imitation — see IDEAL 1

nonpartisan *adj* **1** marked by justice, honesty, and freedom from bias — see FAIR 2

2 not favoring or joined to either side in a quarrel, contest, or war — see NEUTRAL

nonphysical *adj* not composed of matter — see IMMATERIAL 1

nonplus *vb* to throw into a state of self-conscious distress — see EMBARRASS 1

nonpractical *adj* not capable of being put to use or account — see IMPRACTICAL

nonprofessional *adj* lacking or showing a lack of expert skill — see AMATEURISH

nonprofessional *n* a person who regularly or occasionally engages in an activity as a pastime rather than as a profession — see AMATEUR 1

nonpublic *adj* not known or meant to be known by the general populace — see PRIVATE 1

nonrational *adj* not using or following good reasoning — see ILLOGICAL

nonrealistic *adj* using elements of form (as color, line, or texture) with little or no attempt at creating a realistic picture — see ABSTRACT 2

nonreligious *adj* **1** lacking religious emotions, principles, or practices — see IRRELIGIOUS

2 not involving religion or religious matters — see PROFANE 1

nonresistant *adj* receiving or enduring without offering resistance — see PASSIVE

nonsense *n* **1** language, behavior, or ideas that are absurd and contrary to good sense ⟨told him to stop his mischievous *nonsense* and start behaving properly⟩ ⟨The discussion about building a time machine was complete *nonsense*.⟩ ⟨A hundred years ago, the idea that man could walk on the moon was regarded as impractical *nonsense*.⟩

syn blarney, bull [*slang*], bunk, claptrap, drivel, folly, foolishness, fudge, hogwash, humbug, humbuggery, jazz, moonshine, piffle, rot, rubbish, senselessness, silliness, stupidity, trash, trumpery, twaddle

rel absurdity, asininity, foolery, idiocy, imbecility, inaneness, inanity, kookiness; absurdness, craziness, madness, senselessness, witlessness; monkeyshine(s), shenanigan(s), tomfoolery; gas, hot air, rigmarole (*also* rigamarole); double-talk

near ant levelheadedness, rationality, reasonability, reasonableness, sensibleness; common sense, horse sense, sense; discernment, judgment (*or* judgement), wisdom

2 unintelligible or meaningless talk — see GIBBERISH 1

nonsensical *adj* **1** conceived or made without regard for reason or reality — see FANTASTIC 1

2 showing or marked by a lack of good sense or judgment — see FOOLISH 1

nonsensicalness *n* lack of good sense or judgment — see FOOLISHNESS 1

nonspecific *adj* relating to the main elements and not to specific details — see GENERAL 2

nonsuccess *n* a falling short of one's goals — see FAILURE 2

nontraditional *adj* not bound by traditional ways or beliefs — see LIBERAL 1

nonvalid *adj* **1** having no basis in reason or fact — see GROUNDLESS

2 having no legal or binding force — see NULL 1

nonviolent *adj* not involving violence or force — see PEACEFUL 2

nook *n* a hollowed-out space in a wall — see NICHE 1

noon *n* **1** the middle of the day ⟨We eat a big lunch around *noon* then have dinner in the evening.⟩

syn high noon, midday, noonday, noontide, noontime

rel forenoon, morning; evening

2 the highest part or point — see HEIGHT 1

noonday *n* the middle of the day — see NOON 1

no one *pron* no person — see NOBODY

noontide *n* the middle of the day — see NOON 1

noontime *n* **1** the highest part or point — see HEIGHT 1

2 the middle of the day — see NOON 1

norm *n* **1** what is typical of a group, class, or series — see AVERAGE

2 norms *pl* the code of good conduct for an individual or group — see ETHICS

normal *adj* **1** being of the type that is encountered in the normal course of events — see ORDINARY 1

2 having full use of one's mind and control over one's actions — see SANE

3 having or showing the qualities associated with the members of a particular group or kind — see TYPICAL 1

normal *n* what is typical of a group, class, or series — see AVERAGE

normalcy *n* the state or fact of being the way things usually are — see NORMALITY

normality *n* the state or fact of being the way things usually are ⟨The county slowly has returned to *normality* after a week of flash flooding.⟩

syn normalcy, status quo

rel groove, routine, rut; currency, prevalence; conventionality; harmony, orderliness, peace

near ant irregularity, uncommonness, unusualness; disruptiveness; disruption, disturbance; anomalousness, deviance; exceptionalness, extraordinariness, noteworthiness, remarkableness

ant abnormality

normalize *vb* to make agree with a single established standard or model — see STANDARDIZE

normally *adv* according to the usual course of things — see NATURALLY 2

nose *n* **1** the part of the face bearing the nostrils and nasal cavity ⟨With that *nose*, the baby sure looks like his father.⟩

syn beak

rel snout, pugnose

2 the last and usually sharp or tapering part of something long and narrow — see POINT 2

nose *vb* **1** to become aware of by means of the sense organs in the nose — see SMELL 1

2 to interest oneself in what is not one's concern — see INTERFERE

3 to move slowly — see CRAWL 2

nosedive *n* the act or process of going to a lower level or altitude — see DESCENT 1

nose–dive *vb* to go to a lower level especially abruptly — see DROP 2

nosegay *n* a bunch of flowers — see BOUQUET 1

nosiness *n* an eager desire to find out about things that are often none of one's business — see CURIOSITY 1

nosy *or* **nosey** *adj* **1** interested in what is not one's own business — see CURIOUS 1

2 thrusting oneself where one is not welcome or invited — see INTRUSIVE

notable *adj* **1** standing above others in rank, importance, or achievement — see EMINENT

2 worth remembering or mentioning — see NOTEWORTHY 1

notable *n* a person who is widely known and usually much talked about — see CELEBRITY 1

notation *n* a usually brief written reminder — see NOTE 1

notch *n* **1** a V-shaped cut usually on an edge or a surface ⟨lifted up the fence rail

---

syn synonym(s)   *rel* related words
ant antonym(s)   *near ant* near antonym(s)

and positioned it in the *notch* cut into the post⟩

syn chip, hack, indentation, kerf, nick

rel groove, score, undercut; slit

2 a narrow opening between hillsides or mountains that can be used for passage — see CANYON

3 an individual part of a process, series, or ranking — see DEGREE 1

notch (up) *vb* to obtain (as a goal) through effort — see ACHIEVE 1

note *n* **1** a usually brief written reminder ⟨I'll make a *note* to myself so I don't forget to pick up some milk on the way home.⟩

syn memo, memorandum, notation

rel memoir, memorial, minutes, protocol, report; line; document, writing

2 a message on paper from one person or group to another — see ¹LETTER

3 a natural vocal sound made by an animal — see CALL 1

4 a piece of printed paper used as money in the United States — see ¹BILL 2

5 a special quality or impression associated with something — see AURA 1

6 overall quality as seen or judged by people in general — see REPUTATION

7 a briefly expressed opinion — see REMARK

8 a state of being aware — see ATTENTION 2

9 something that sets apart an individual from others of the same kind — see CHARACTERISTIC

note *vb* **1** to make a statement of one's opinion — see REMARK 1

2 to make a written note of — see RECORD 1

3 to make note of (something) through the use of one's eyes — see SEE 1

4 to make reference to or speak about briefly but specifically — see MENTION 1

5 to take notice of and be guided by — see HEED 1

noted *adj* widely known — see FAMOUS 1

notepad *n* a number of sheets of writing paper glued together at one edge — see PAD 1

noteworthiness *n* the fact or state of being above others in rank or importance — see EMINENCE 1

noteworthy *adj* **1** worth remembering or mentioning ⟨Nothing *noteworthy* happened while you were gone.⟩

syn notable, observable, remarkable

rel quotable, repeatable; newsworthy

near ant average, ordinary, prosaic, routine, run-of-the-mill, standard, unexceptional

ant forgettable, unmemorable, unremarkable

2 standing above others in rank, importance, or achievement — see EMINENT

nothing *adv* not in any degree, way, or under any condition — see NEVER 2

nothing *n* **1** a person of no importance or influence — see NOBODY

2 something of little importance — see TRIFLE

3 the numerical symbol 0 or the absence of number or quantity represented by it — see ZERO 1

notice *n* **1** a published statement informing the public of a matter of general interest — see ANNOUNCEMENT

2 a state of being aware — see ATTENTION 2

3 a written communication giving information or directions — see MEMORANDUM 1

4 an essay evaluating or analyzing something — see CRITICISM

5 the act or an instance of telling beforehand of danger or risk — see WARNING 1

notice *vb* **1** to make note of (something) through the use of one's eyes — see SEE 1

2 to make reference to or speak about briefly but specifically — see MENTION 1

noticeable *adj* likely to attract attention ⟨The stain on the new carpet was quite *noticeable*, and nothing we did made it any lighter.⟩

syn arresting, bold, brilliant, catchy, commanding, conspicuous, dramatic, emphatic, eye-catching, flamboyant, marked, noisy, prominent, pronounced, remarkable, showy, splashy, striking

rel detectable, discernible (*also* discernable), observable, perceptible, recognizable, visible; outstanding, salient; distinguished, eminent, impressive, notable, noteworthy; highlighted, spotlighted; flagrant, glaring, howling, screaming; flashy, garish, gaudy, glitzy, jazzy, loud, meretricious, swank (*or* swanky); tawdry; highfalutin (*also* hifalutin), ostentatious, pretentious; extravagant, fancy, florid, glittery; opulent, ornate, overdone, overwrought

near ant subtle; concealed, shrouded; dim, faint, obscure; insignificant, undistinguished, unimportant; modest, unaffected, unassuming, unpretentious; conservative, plain, quiet, simple, understated; muted, restrained, subdued, toned-down

ant inconspicuous, unemphatic, unflamboyant, unnoticeable, unobtrusive, unremarkable, unshowy

notification *n* a published statement informing the public of a matter of general interest — see ANNOUNCEMENT

notion *n* **1 notions** *pl* small useful items ⟨The fabric store had a wide variety of thread, pins, buttons, and other *notions*.⟩

syn novelties, odds and ends, sundries

rel baubles, bric-a-brac, gewgaws (*also* geegaws), knickknacks (*also* nicknacks), trinkets; gadgets, gimmicks, jiggers

2 a sudden impulsive and apparently unmotivated idea or action — see WHIM

3 an idea that is believed to be true or valid without positive knowledge — see OPINION 1

4 something imagined or pictured in the mind — see IDEA 1

5 an idea or statement about all of the members of a group or all the instances of a situation — see GENERALIZATION

notoriety *n* **1** a person who is widely known and usually much talked about — see CELEBRITY 1

2 the fact or state of being known to the public — see FAME 1

notorious *adj* **1** not respectable — see DISREPUTABLE

2 widely known — see FAMOUS 1

notwithstanding *adv* in spite of that — see HOWEVER

notwithstanding *conj* in spite of the fact that — see ALTHOUGH

notwithstanding *prep* without being prevented by — see DESPITE

nourish *vb* **1** to help the growth or development of — see FOSTER 1

2 to supply with nourishment — see SUSTAIN 1

3 to bring to maturity through care and education — see BRING UP 1

nourishing *adj* providing the substances necessary for health and bodily growth — see NUTRITIOUS

novel *adj* not known or experienced before — see NEW 2

novelette *n* a work with imaginary characters and events that is shorter and usually less complex than a novel — see STORY 1

novella *n* a work with imaginary characters and events that is shorter and usually less complex than a novel — see STORY 1

novelty *n* **1** the quality or appeal of being new ⟨The *novelty* of having a cat wore off after the first time I had to change the litter box.⟩

syn freshness, newness, originality

rel bizarreness, strangeness, unfamiliarity, unusualness; progressiveness; currentness, recentness, up-to-dateness; departure, divergence, innovation, offshoot, shoot

near ant banality, commonness, familiarity; outdatedness, staleness

2 novelties *pl* small useful items — see NOTION 1

3 a small object displayed for its attractiveness or interest — see KNICKKNACK

novice *n* a person who is just starting out in a field of activity — see BEGINNER

now *adv* **1** at the present time ⟨That company doesn't make those toys *now* because they are unsafe.⟩

syn anymore, currently, nowadays, presently, right now, today

rel here

phrases at present, for the time being

near ant away, far, farthest, remotest; heretofore, hitherto, since; previously

ant before, long, then

2 not long ago — see NEWLY

3 on some occasions — see SOMETIMES

4 without delay — see IMMEDIATELY

now *conj* for the reason that — see SINCE

now *n* the time currently existing or in progress — see ¹PRESENT

nowadays *adv* at the present time — see NOW 1

noway *adv* **1** *or* **noways** not in any degree, way, or under any condition — see NEVER 2

2 *usually* **no way** certainly not — see HARDLY 2

nowise *adv* not in any degree, way, or under any condition — see NEVER 2

noxious *adj* **1** bad for the well-being of the body — see UNHEALTHY 1

2 causing or capable of causing harm — see HARMFUL

3 causing intense displeasure, disgust, or resentment — see OFFENSIVE 1

nth *adj* of the greatest or highest degree or quantity — see ULTIMATE 1

nub *n* **1** a small uneven mass — see LUMP 1

2 the central part or aspect of something under consideration — see CRUX

nubbin *n* **1** a very small piece — see BIT 1

2 the central part or aspect of something under consideration — see CRUX

nubble *n* a small uneven mass — see LUMP 1

nubbly *adj* having small pieces or lumps spread throughout — see CHUNKY 1

nubby *adj* having small pieces or lumps spread throughout — see CHUNKY 1

nucleus *n* **1** a thing or place that is of greatest importance to an activity or interest — see CENTER 1

2 the central part or aspect of something under consideration — see CRUX

nude *adj* lacking or shed of clothing — see NAKED 1

nudge *vb* **1** to pass lightly across or touch gently especially in passing — see ²BRUSH

2 to try to persuade (someone) through earnest appeals to follow a course of action — see URGE

nugget *n* **1** a small piece or quantity of food — see MORSEL 1

2 a small uneven mass — see LUMP 1

3 a very small piece — see BIT 1

nuisance *n* **1** one who is obnoxiously annoying ⟨The new neighbor is threatening to become a *nuisance*, dropping in on us several times a day.⟩

syn annoyance, annoyer, bother, gadfly, pain, persecutor, pest, tease, teaser

rel headache; harrier, heckler, interrupter (*also* interruptor); hassle, plague; molester, tormentor (*also* tormenter); torturer

phrases pain in the neck

near ant charmer, smoothy (*or* smoothie); comforter, solacer, soother

2 something that is a source of irritation — see ANNOYANCE 3

null *adj* **1** having no legal or binding force ⟨The contract was *null* because I forgot to sign it.⟩

syn bad, inoperative, invalid, nonbinding, nonvalid, null and void, void

rel illegal; useless, worthless; ineffective, ineffectual

near ant legal; working

ant binding, good, valid

2 having no usefulness — see WORTHLESS 1

null *vb* to put an end to by formal action — see ABOLISH 1

null and void *adj* having no legal or binding force — see NULL 1

nullify *vb* to put an end to by formal action — see ABOLISH 1

numb *adj* **1** lacking in sensation or feeling ⟨I've been sitting in the same position for too long and now my feet are *numb*.⟩

syn asleep, benumbed, dead, insensitive, numbed, torpid, unfeeling

rel chilled, nipped; anesthetized, deadened, drugged, stupefied; blunted, dulled; insensible, senseless, unconscious; insensate

near ant awake

ant feeling, sensible, sensitive

2 not expressing any emotion — see BLANK 1

---

syn synonym(s)   *rel* related words
ant antonym(s)   *near ant* near antonym(s)

3 not feeling or showing emotion — see IMPASSIVE 1

numb *vb* to reduce or weaken in strength or feeling — see DULL 1

numbed *adj* lacking in sensation or feeling — see NUMB 1

number *n* **1** a character used to represent a mathematical value ⟨asked him to write out the equation in *numbers*, not letters⟩

syn digit, figure, integer, numeral, whole number

rel decimal; cipher; symbol

2 a literary, musical, or artistic production — see COMPOSITION 1

3 a performance regularly presented by an individual or group — see ACT 1

4 an act of notable skill, strength, or cleverness — see FEAT 1

5 **numbers** *pl* the act or process of performing mathematical operations to find a value — see CALCULATION

number *vb* **1** to find the sum of (a collection of things) by noting each one as it is being added — see COUNT 1

2 to have a total of — see AMOUNT (TO) 1

3 to have as part of a whole — see INCLUDE 1

number crunching *n* the act or process of performing mathematical operations to find a value — see CALCULATION

numberless *adj* too many to be counted — see COUNTLESS

numbing *adj* **1** causing weariness, restlessness, or lack of interest — see BORING

2 having a low or subnormal temperature — see COLD 1

numbness *n* a lack of emotion or emotional expressiveness — see APATHY 1

numeral *n* a character used to represent a mathematical value — see NUMBER 1

numerate *vb* **1** to make a list of — see ¹LIST 1

2 to specify one after another — see ENUMERATE 1

numerous *adj* being of a large but indefinite number — see MANY

numskull or **numbskull** *n* a stupid person — see IDIOT

nuptial *adj* of or relating to marriage — see MARITAL

nuptial *n*, *usually* **nuptials** *pl* a ceremony in which two people are united in matrimony — see WEDDING

nurse *n* a person employed to care for a young child or children ⟨In *Peter Pan*, the Darling children's *nurse*, Nana, was actually a large dog.⟩

syn babysitter, nanny (*also* nannie), nursemaid, sitter

rel duenna, governess

nurse *vb* **1** to attend to the needs and comforts of ⟨Jim willingly lent a hand to *nurse* his grandmother in her final years, helping her get from one room to the other and making sure she was warm.⟩

syn care (for), minister (to), mother

rel cure, heal, remedy; doctor, treat; aid, conserve, preserve, provide (for), support; baby, coddle, mollycoddle, pamper, spoil; cater (to), humor; indulge

phrases look after, look out for, look to, see to, take care of, wait on (*also* wait upon)

near ant brush (aside *or* off), forget, ignore, neglect, overlook, slight

2 to keep in one's mind or heart — see HARBOR 1

3 to treat with great or excessive care — see BABY

4 to bring to maturity through care and education — see BRING UP 1

5 to help the growth or development of — see FOSTER 1

6 to use or give out in stingy amounts — see SPARE 1

nursemaid *n* a person employed to care for a young child or children — see NURSE

nurture *vb* **1** to help the growth or development of — see FOSTER 1

2 to provide (someone) with moral or spiritual understanding — see ENLIGHTEN 1

3 to supply with nourishment — see SUSTAIN 1

nut *n* **1** a person of odd or whimsical habits — see ECCENTRIC

2 a person with a strong and habitual liking for something — see FAN

nutrient *adj* providing the substances necessary for health and bodily growth — see NUTRITIOUS

nutritional *adj* providing the substances necessary for health and bodily growth — see NUTRITIOUS

nutritious *adj* providing the substances necessary for health and bodily growth ⟨Kate opted for a *nutritious* snack and bought an apple instead of a candy bar.⟩

syn nourishing, nutrient, nutritional, nutritive

rel enriched, fortified; dietary, dietetic; beneficial, healthful, healthy, restorative, salubrious, salutary, wholesome

near ant unhealthful, unhealthy, unwholesome

ant nonnutritious, nonnutritive

nutritive *adj* providing the substances necessary for health and bodily growth — see NUTRITIOUS

nuts *adj* showing urgent desire or interest — see EAGER

nuts (about) *adj* filled with an intense or excessive love for — see ENAMORED (OF)

nuttiness *n* lack of good sense or judgment — see FOOLISHNESS 1

nutty *adj* showing or marked by a lack of good sense or judgment — see FOOLISH 1

nuzzle *vb* to lie close ⟨newborn puppies *nuzzling* against their mother to stay warm⟩

syn cuddle, nestle, snuggle

rel curl up; crouch, huddle

near ant blench, flinch, quail, recoil, shrink, shy, start, wince

nymph *n* a mythical goddess represented as a young woman and said to live outdoors ⟨She bought the book of fairy tales for the beautiful engravings of *nymphs* and fairies featured between the stories.⟩

syn dryad, naiad, oread

rel mermaid, Nereid, Oceanid, sea-maid (*or* sea-maiden), siren, water nymph

oaf *n* **1** a big clumsy often slow-witted person ⟨It's not nice to call your brother an *oaf*.⟩

syn clod, clodhopper, gawk, hulk, lout, lubber, lug, lump, Neanderthal

rel chump, turkey; blockhead, bonehead, dolt, dope, dork [*slang*], dumbbell, dumbhead, dum-dum, dummy, dunce, dunderhead, fathead, galoot [*slang*], goof, goon, half-wit, hammerhead, hardhead, idiot, ignoramus, imbecile, know-nothing, lump, meathead, moron, nincompoop, ninny, numskull (*or* numbskull), pinhead, schnook [*slang*], simpleton, thickhead, woodenhead, yo-yo; boor, brute, cad, churl, clown, creep, cur, heel, louse, skunk, snake, stinker; fool, goose; klutz

near ant brain, egghead, genius, intellectual, sage, thinker, whiz, wizard

2 a stupid person — see IDIOT

oafish *adj* not having or showing an ability to absorb ideas readily — see STUPID 1

oafishness *n* the quality or state of lacking intelligence or quickness of mind — see STUPIDITY 1

oar *n* a person who drives a boat forward by means of oars — see OARSMAN

oar *vb* to move a boat by means of oars — see ¹ROW

oarsman *n* a person who drives a boat forward by means of oars ⟨the only *oarsman* in a rowboat designed for two⟩

syn oar, rower, sculler

rel bowman, oarswoman; coxswain, crewman; puller; kayaker

oath *n* a person's solemn declaration that he or she will do or not do something — see PROMISE

obduracy *n* a steadfast adherence to an opinion, purpose, or course of action in spite of reason, arguments, or persuasion — see OBSTINACY

obdurate *adj* **1** having or showing a lack of sympathy or tender feelings — see HARD 1

2 sticking to an opinion, purpose, or course of action in spite of reason, arguments, or persuasion — see OBSTINATE

obedience *n* **1** a bending to the authority or control of another ⟨The drill sergeant demanded complete and unquestioning *obedience* from the recruits.⟩

syn compliance, submission, subordination

rel abidance, amenability, tractability, trainability; acquiescence, capitulation, obeisance, obsequiousness, submissiveness, surrender, yielding; deference, docility, dutifulness, humility, meekness, modesty, servility, subordinateness, subservience; inhibition, repression, restraint, suppression; control, discipline, order

near ant disrespect, impudence, insolence, rudeness; insurgency, insurrection, mutiny, outbreak, revolt; hardheadedness, mulishness, mutinousness, obstinacy, perversity,

stubbornness; misbehavior, mischievousness, naughtiness; dissent, dissidence

ant contrariness, contumacy, defiance, disobedience, frowardness, insubordination, intractability, noncompliance, rebelling, rebellion, rebelliousness, recalcitrance, refractoriness, self-will, unruliness, waywardness, willfulness

2 a readiness or willingness to yield to the wishes of others — see COMPLIANCE 1

3 the following of a custom, rule, or law — see OBSERVANCE 1

obedient *adj* readily giving in to the command or authority of another ⟨That boy is so *obedient* that he does everything the first time he is asked.⟩

syn amenable, compliant, conformable, docile, law-abiding, submissive, tractable

rel acquiescent, agreeable, amiable, dutiful, obliging, placable; fawning, kowtowing, obeisant, obsequious, subordinate, subservient; decorous, disciplined, mannerly, orderly; controllable, disciplinable, governable, handleable, manageable, tame, teachable, trainable; gentle, meek, mild

near ant insurgent, mutinous; dogged, hardheaded, headstrong, mulish, obdurate, obstinate, peevish, pigheaded, self-willed, stubborn, unyielding; uncontrollable, unmanageable, wild; perverse, resistant; disorderly, errant, misbehaving, mischievous, naughty; ill-bred, undisciplined; dissident, nonconformist; disrespectful, ill-mannered, impolite, impudent, insolent, rude

ant balky, contrary, defiant, disobedient, froward, insubordinate, intractable, noncompliant, obstreperous, rebel, rebellious, recalcitrant, refractory, restive, unamenable, ungovernable, unruly, untoward, wayward, willful (*or* wilful)

obese *adj* having an excess of body fat — see FAT 1

obesity *n* the condition of having an excess of body fat — see CORPULENCE

obey *vb* to act according to the commands of ⟨She taught her dog to *obey* her when she said "Sit!"⟩ ⟨Most people *obey* the law and wear their seat belts.⟩

syn adhere (to), comply (with), conform (to), follow, mind, observe

rel defer (to), submit (to), surrender (to), yield (to); accede (to), acquiesce (to), agree (to), assent (to); attend, hear, heed, listen (to), mark, note, notice, regard, take, watch

phrases abide by, fall in with, keep to

near ant disoblige; challenge, dare; refuse, renounce, repudiate; brush off, disregard, ignore, overlook, overpass, pass over, tune out, wink (at); dismiss, pooh-pooh (*also* pooh), shrug off; breach, break, infringe, transgress, violate; deride, flout, mock, scoff (at), scorn; mutiny (against), revolt (against); buck, combat, contest, dispute, fight, oppose, resist, withstand

ant defy, disobey, rebel (against)

object *n* **1** something material that can be perceived by the senses ⟨I kept tripping

---

syn synonym(s)   **rel** related words
ant antonym(s)   **near ant** near antonym(s)

over countless little *objects* scattered about the darkened room.⟩
syn thing
rel article, item, piece; being, entity, substance; good; thingummy
2 one that has a real and independent existence — see ENTITY
3 something that one hopes or intends to accomplish — see GOAL

object *vb* to present an opposing opinion or argument ⟨They *objected* to the conductor's insistence that their train tickets were not valid.⟩
syn demur, except, protest, remonstrate (with)
rel cavil, quibble; challenge, dare, defy, fight; conflict, debate, dispute, hassle, quarrel, squabble, wrangle; beef, bellyache, carp, complain, crab, croak, fuss, gripe, grouch, grouse, growl, grumble, grump, holler, keen, moan, murmur, mutter, nag, repine, scream, squawk, squeal, wail, whimper, whine, yammer, yowl; balk, gag, stick; censure, criticize, denounce; disobey, rebel, withstand; demonstrate
phrases take exception, take issue
near ant approve, sanction; accept; accede, acquiesce, agree, assent; adhere, comply, conform, follow, mind, obey, observe; advocate, champion, defend, maintain, support, sustain, uphold; applaud, cheer, commend

objection *n* a feeling or declaration of disapproval or dissent ⟨Pardon me, but I have an *objection* to any plan that requires staying out all night.⟩
syn challenge, complaint, demur, difficulty, expostulation, fuss, kick, protest, question, remonstrance, stink
rel compunction, doubt, misgiving, qualm, scruple; cavil, quibble; argument, conflict, debate, dispute, quarrel, squabble; censure, criticism; defiance, disobedience, rebellion; distrust, distrustfulness, incertitude, indetermination, mistrust, mistrustfulness, reservation, skepticism, suspicion, uncertainty; qualmishness, uneasiness; reluctance, unwillingness
near ant willingness; approval, sanction; acceptance, acquiescence, agreement, assent; compliance, obedience

objectionable *adj* provoking or likely to provoke protest ⟨found nothing *objectionable* about the TV show⟩
syn censurable, exceptionable, obnoxious, offensive, reprehensible
rel unacceptable, undesirable, unwanted, unwelcome; disagreeable, displeasing, distasteful, unpleasant; bad, execrable, lousy, miserable, terrible, unspeakable, wretched; atrocious, infamous; abhorrent, gross, loathsome, repellent (*also* repellant), repugnant, repulsive, revolting, sickening, vile; debasing, perverted, profane; off, racy, salty, suggestive; indecent, indecorous, unbecoming; earthy, unprintable; bawdy, coarse, crude, dirty, filthy, foul, gross, lewd, nasty, obscene, smutty, vulgar; lascivious, pornographic, ribald, scurrilous
near ant acceptable, agreeable, blessed (*also* blest), congenial, delectable, deli-

cious, delightful, enjoyable, felicitous, good, grateful, gratifying, nice, palatable, pleasant, pleasing, pleasurable, satisfying, welcome; approved, endorsed (*also* indorsed), sanctioned; becoming, correct, decent, decorous, exemplary, proper, respectable, seemly; blameless, commendable, creditable; immaculate, perfect, pure, spotless; politically correct
ant inoffensive, unobjectionable

objective *adj* 1 based on observation or experience — see EMPIRICAL 1
2 marked by justice, honesty, and freedom from bias — see FAIR 2
3 restricted to or based on fact — see FACTUAL 1

objective *n* something that one hopes or intends to accomplish — see GOAL

objectivity *n* lack of favoritism toward one side or another — see DETACHMENT 1

obligate *vb* to cause (a person) to give in to pressure — see FORCE

obligated *adj* being under obligation for a favor or gift — see BEHOLDEN

obligation *n* 1 something one must do because of prior agreement ⟨Their financial *obligations* keep them from giving to charities as much as they would like.⟩
syn burden, charge, commitment, duty, imperative, need, office, responsibility
rel oath, pledge, promise, vow, word; arrangement, prearrangement, setup; compact, contract, covenant, pact, trust; debt, payment, tribute; compulsion, constraint, restraint; must, requirement; coercion, duress, force; appointment, engagement, reservation; burden
near ant grace, postponement, stay; discharge, ease, exemption, release, relief, waiver; loophole; alternative, choice, option, pick, preference, selection
2 something (as money) which is owed — see DEBT 1

obligatory *adj* forcing one's compliance or participation by or as if by law — see MANDATORY

oblige *vb* 1 to do a service or favor for ⟨I would appreciate it greatly if you could *oblige* me by bringing a dessert to the party.⟩
syn accommodate, favor
rel humor, indulge; coddle, mollycoddle, pamper; appease, conciliate, mollify, pacify, placate; delight, gladden, gratify, please, satisfy; abet, aid, assist, help, support; attend, care (for), comfort, minister (to), relieve, succor
near ant bother, discommode, disturb, incommode, inconvenience, trouble; burden, encumber, saddle, weigh; desert, disappoint, fail, let down; constrain, hamper, hamstring, hinder, hobble, hold back, impede, obstruct, restrain; frustrate, oppose, sabotage, thwart
ant disoblige
2 to cause (a person) to give in to pressure — see FORCE

obliged *adj* 1 being under obligation for a favor or gift — see BEHOLDEN
2 feeling or expressing gratitude — see GRATEFUL 1

obliging *adj* willing to do a favor — see ACCOMMODATING

oblique adj 1 inclined or twisted to one side — see AWRY

2 running in a slanting direction — see DIAGONAL

obliquely adv in a line or direction running from corner to corner — see CROSSWISE

obliterate vb to destroy all traces of — see ANNIHILATE 1

obliteration n the state or fact of being rendered nonexistent, physically unsound, or useless — see DESTRUCTION 1

oblivion n a state of being disregardful or unconscious of one's surroundings, concerns, or obligations ⟨For two weeks each year the stressed-out couple enjoys the blissful *oblivion* that comes with a vacation at the beach.⟩

syn forgetfulness, obliviousness

rel ignorance, innocence, insensibility, unawareness, unconsciousness, unfamiliarity; absentmindedness, absorption, inattention, inattentiveness, preoccupation

near ant memory, recall, recollection, remembrance; alertness, awareness, cognizance

oblivious adj not informed about or aware of something — see IGNORANT 2

obliviousness n 1 a state of being disregardful or unconscious of one's surroundings, concerns, or obligations — see OBLIVION

2 the state of being unaware or uninformed — see IGNORANCE 1

obnoxious adj 1 causing intense displeasure, disgust, or resentment — see OFFENSIVE 1

2 provoking or likely to provoke protest — see OBJECTIONABLE

obscene adj 1 depicting or referring to sexual matters in a way that is unacceptable in polite society ⟨an inappropriate and *obscene* gesture⟩

syn bawdy, blue, coarse, crude, dirty, filthy, foul, gross, impure, indecent, lascivious, lewd, nasty, ribald, smutty, vulgar, wanton

rel broad, coarse-grained, gamy (*or* gamey), off, racy, salty, suggestive; earthy, scatological; immodest, indecorous, low, unbecoming; depraved, kinky, naughty, perverse, perverted, wicked; exceptionable, objectionable, unacceptable, undesirable, unwanted, unwelcome; abhorrent, debasing, loathsome, offensive, repellent (*also* repellant), repugnant, repulsive, revolting; distasteful, obnoxious, unpleasant; abusive, scurrilous

near ant priggish, prim, prudish, puritanical, staid, straitlaced (*or* straightlaced); correct, decorous, genteel, nice, polite, proper, respectable, seemly; innocuous, inoffensive; appropriate, becoming, fit, meet, suitable; immaculate, perfect, pure, spotless, virginal

ant clean, decent, nonobscene, wholesome

2 causing intense displeasure, disgust, or resentment — see OFFENSIVE 1

obscenity n the quality or state of being obscene ⟨arrested on *obscenity* charges⟩

syn bawdiness, coarseness, crudeness, filth, filthiness, foulness, grossness, impurity, indecency, lasciviousness, lewdness, nastiness, ribaldry, smut, smuttiness, vulgarity, wantonness

rel broadness, earthiness, gaminess, raciness, saltiness, suggestiveness; immodesty, indelicacy, indelicateness, lowness, unbecomingness; lechery; depravedness, depravity, kinkiness, naughtiness, perverseness, perversion, perversity, pervertedness, wickedness; abusiveness, scurrilousness; loathsomeness, offensiveness, repellency, repugnance, repulsiveness; distastefulness, obnoxiousness, unpleasantness

near ant priggery, priggishness, primness, prudery, prudishness, puritanism; correctness, decency, decorousness, decorum, seemliness; immaculateness, perfection, purity, spotlessness

obscure adj 1 having an often intentionally veiled or uncertain meaning ⟨a fantasy writer who likes to put lots of *obscure* references and images in her tales of wizards and warlocks⟩

syn ambiguous, cryptic, dark, deep, enigmatic (*also* enigmatical), equivocal, inscrutable, murky, mysterious, mystic, nebulous, occult, opaque

rel abstruse, esoteric, recondite; cloaked, concealed, disguised, masked, shrouded; cloudy, dim, faint, foggy, fuzzy, hazy, indistinct, indistinguishable, misty, muddy, shaded, shadowlike, shadowy, sphinxlike; indefinite, inexact, noncommittal, questionable, unclear, uncertain, undefined, undetermined, vague; impenetrable, incomprehensible, inexplicable, eerie (*also* eery), uncanny, weird; baffling, bewildering, confounding, confusing, mystifying, perplexing, puzzling, unfathomable; circuitous, indirect, roundabout

near ant knowable, pellucid; bright, distinct, evident, self-explanatory; certain, firm, strong, sure; defined, determined; direct, straightforward; definite, exact, explicit

ant accessible, clear, obvious, plain, unambiguous, unequivocal

2 not widely known ⟨He's an *obscure* artist now, but he's sure to be famous someday.⟩

syn nameless, uncelebrated, unknown, unsung

rel insignificant, minor, unimportant; undistinguished, unexceptional, unremarkable; unpopular; anonymous, faceless, unnoticeable, unrecognizable; unnoticed; forgotten, unremembered

near ant fabled, fabulous, legendary; infamous; distinguished, eminent, exceptional, great, illustrious, notable, outstanding, prestigious, remarkable; honorable, reputable, respectable; important, influential, leading, major, newsworthy, noteworthy, significant; favorite, popular, preferred

ant celebrated, famed, famous, noted, notorious, prominent, renowned, well-known

3 being without light or without much light — see DARK 1

4 not seen or understood clearly — see FAINT 1

obscure vb 1 to keep secret or shut off from view — see ¹HIDE 2

2 to make dark, dim, or indistinct — see CLOUD 1

obscured adj being without light or without much light — see DARK 1

obscurity n 1 the quality or state of having a veiled or uncertain meaning ⟨The 16th-century astrologer's predictions are so filled with *obscurity* that people can interpret them any way they want.⟩

syn ambiguity, ambiguousness, darkness, equivocalness, equivocation, murkiness, nebulousness, opacity

rel mystery, reconditeness; cloudiness, dimness, faintness, fogginess, fuzziness, haziness, indefiniteness, indistinctness, mistiness, shade, shadow, uncertainty, vagueness; incomprehensibility, incomprehensibleness; depth, profoundness; inscrutability

near ant comprehensibility, intelligibility, legibility; brightness, distinctness, self-evidence; certainty, surety; definiteness, exactness, explicitness, incision, incisiveness, lucidity, lucidness, perspicuity, perspicuousness; directness, forthrightness, straightforwardness

ant clarity, clearness, obviousness, plainness

2 the quality or state of being mostly or completely unknown ⟨The singer languished in relative *obscurity* for years before becoming famous.⟩

syn anonymity, silence

rel oblivion; inconspicuousness, invisibility, invisibleness; unpopularity

near ant mark, name, note, report, reputation, repute; favor, popularity; importance, significance; distinction, eminence, glory, greatness, honor, illustriousness, note, preeminence, prominence; position, prestige, rank, standing, stature; acclaim, acknowledgment (*or* acknowledgement), praise, recognition; adoration, idolization

ant celebrity, fame, notoriety, renown

observable adj 1 capable of being seen — see VISIBLE 1

2 worth remembering or mentioning — see NOTEWORTHY 1

observance n 1 the following of a custom, rule, or law ⟨The *observance* of this family tradition would make your grandmother very happy.⟩ ⟨*observance* of the smoking ban in public buildings⟩

syn abidance, adherence, compliance, conformity, keeping, obedience, observation

rel deference, honor, regard, respect, upholding; acquiescence, submission, surrender; attendance, attention, heed, notice

near ant brush-off, disregard, ignoring; delinquency, dereliction, forgetting, neglect, overlooking; challenge, defiance, flouting, rebellion

ant breach, infraction, infringement, nonobservance, transgression, trespass, violation

2 an oft-repeated action or series of actions performed in accordance with tradition or a set of rules — see RITE

3 a state of being aware — see ATTENTION 2

observant adj 1 paying close attention usually for the purpose of anticipating approaching danger or opportunity — see ALERT 1

2 having the mind fixed on something — see ATTENTIVE 1

observation n 1 a state of being aware — see ATTENTION 2

2 the following of a custom, rule, or law — see OBSERVANCE 1

observational adj based on observation or experience — see EMPIRICAL 1

observatory n a high place or structure from which a wide view is possible — see LOOKOUT 1

observe vb 1 to act according to the commands of — see OBEY

2 to mark with an appropriate practice, rite, or ceremony — see KEEP 1

3 to keep one's eyes on — see WATCH 1

4 to make a statement of one's opinion — see REMARK 1

5 to make note of (something) through the use of one's eyes — see SEE 1

6 to take notice of and be guided by — see HEED 1

obsessed adj having extreme or relentless concern — see HUNG UP 1

obsession n something about which one is constantly thinking or concerned — see FIXATION

obsessive adj caused by or suggestive of an irresistible urge — see COMPULSIVE

obsolete adj having passed its time of use or usefulness ⟨I was told my old printer is *obsolete* and I can't get replacement parts.⟩

syn antiquated, archaic, dated, moth-eaten, outdated, outmoded, out-of-date, outworn, passé, superannuated

rel aging (*or* ageing), obsolescent; discarded, disused, inoperable, unusable, unworkable, useless; dead, defunct, expired, extinct, vanished; dormant, fallow, idle, inactive, inert, inoperative, latent; ancient, antediluvian, antique, dateless, fusty, musty, old; oldfangled, old-fashioned, old-time, retro; aged, age-old, hoary, venerable; bygone, erstwhile, former, late, old-world, past

near ant contemporary, current, mod, modern, new, newfangled, new-fashioned, present-day, recent, ultramodern, up-to-date; fresh; modernized, refurbished, remodeled, renewed; functional, operable, operational, workable; active, alive, busy, employed, functioning, operating, operative

obstacle n something that makes movement or progress difficult — see ENCUMBRANCE

obstinacy n a steadfast adherence to an opinion, purpose, or course of action in spite of reason, arguments, or persuasion ⟨The *obstinacy* of the parties made negotiating a compromise difficult.⟩

syn bullheadedness, doggedness, hardheadedness, mulishness, obduracy, pertinaciousness, pertinacity, self-will, stubbornness, willfulness

rel perverseness, perversity, waywardness, wrongheadedness; adamancy (*also* adamance), determination, implacability, inexorability, inflexibility, inveteracy, perseverance, persistence, persistency, relentlessness, resolve, single-mindedness, steadfastness, tenaciousness, tenacity; firmness, hardness, rigor, rigorousness, sternness, strictness; rigidity, rigidness; cantankerousness, contrariness, cussedness; defiance, disobedience, frowardness, insubordination, intractability, rebelliousness, recalcitrance, refractoriness, unruliness

near ant broad-mindedness, open-mindedness, reasonability, reasonableness, receptiveness, receptivity; acceptance, acquiescence, flexibility, pliability; compliance, docility, obedience, subordinateness, subordination; submission, surrender, willingness, yielding; subservience, subserviency

obstinate *adj* sticking to an opinion, purpose, or course of action in spite of reason, arguments, or persuasion ⟨The child was *obstinate* about wanting that specific toy, despite being offered several others.⟩

syn adamant, dogged, hard, hardened, hardheaded, headstrong, immovable, implacable, inflexible, mulish, obdurate, opinionated, ossified, pat, pertinacious, perverse, pigheaded, self-willed, stubborn, unbending, uncompromising, unrelenting, unyielding, willful (*or* wilful)

rel obsessive; wayward, wrongheaded; determined, hell-bent, inexorable, persistent, relentless, resolved, set, single-minded, steadfast, stouthearted, tenacious, unflinching; firm, hard-line, iron, severe, stern, strict; hidebound, narrow-minded, rigid; cantankerous; contrary; disobedient, froward, insubordinate, intractable, recalcitrant, refractory, uncooperative, ungovernable, unmanageable, unruly; defiant, insurgent, mutinous; indomitable, invincible, unconquerable; confirmed, inveterate, unregenerate; demanding, exacting; dogmatic

near ant docile, obedient, placable, submissive, tractable; accepting, persuadable, receptive, responsive, willing; governable, manageable, reasonable, temperate; subservient

ant acquiescent, agreeable, amenable, compliant, complying, flexible, pliable, pliant, relenting, yielding

obstreperous *adj* **1** engaging in or marked by loud and insistent cries especially of protest — see VOCIFEROUS

2 given to resisting authority or another's control — see DISOBEDIENT

obstruct *vb* **1** to create difficulty for the work or activity of — see HAMPER

2 to prevent passage through by filling with something — see CLOG 1

obstruction *n* something that makes movement or progress difficult — see ENCUMBRANCE

obtain *vb* to receive as return for effort — see EARN 1

obtainable *adj* possible to get — see AVAILABLE 1

obtrude *vb* to interest oneself in what is not one's concern — see INTERFERE

obtrusive *adj* thrusting oneself where one is not welcome or invited — see INTRUSIVE

obtuse *adj* **1** lacking sharpness of edge or point — see DULL 1

2 not having or showing an ability to absorb ideas readily — see STUPID 1

obtuseness *n* the quality or state of lacking intelligence or quickness of mind — see STUPIDITY 1

obviate *vb* to keep from happening by taking action in advance — see PREVENT

obvious *adj* **1** not subject to misinterpretation or more than one interpretation — see CLEAR 2

2 very noticeable especially for being incorrect or bad — see EGREGIOUS

occasion *n* **1** a particular point at which an event takes place ⟨On that *occasion*, I met your father.⟩

syn moment, time

rel flash, instant, jiffy, minute, second, shake, split second, trice, twinkle, wink; bit, space, spell, stretch, while

2 a favorable combination of circumstances, time, and place — see OPPORTUNITY

3 someone or something responsible for a result — see CAUSE 1

4 something that happens — see EVENT 1

occasion *vb* to be the cause of (a situation, action, or state of mind) — see EFFECT

occasional *adj* **1** lacking in steadiness or regularity of occurrence — see FITFUL

2 not often occurring or repeated — see INFREQUENT

occasionally *adv* on some occasions — see SOMETIMES

occlude *vb* to prevent passage through by filling with something — see CLOG 1

occult *adj* **1** being beyond one's powers to know, understand, or explain — see MYSTERIOUS 1

2 having an often intentionally veiled or uncertain meaning — see OBSCURE 1

3 having seemingly supernatural qualities or powers — see MYSTIC 1

occult *vb* to keep secret or shut off from view — see ¹HIDE 2

occupant *n* one who lives permanently in a place — see INHABITANT

occupation *n* the activity by which one regularly makes a living ⟨My primary *occupation* is stockbroker, but I'm a drummer in a rock band on the weekends.⟩

syn calling, employment, game, line, profession, trade, vocation, work

rel call, lifework; business, enterprise, field, livelihood, living, racket [*slang*]; assignment, engagement, gig, mission; art, craft, handcraft, handicraft; appointment, berth, billet, office, place, position, post, situation; duty, function, job, load, task, workload

near ant pursuit

occupied *adj* involved in often constant activity — see BUSY 1

occupy *vb* to hold the attention of — see ENGAGE 1

occur *vb* to take place — see HAPPEN

occur (to) *vb* to enter the mind of ⟨It didn't *occur* to me to ask until much later.⟩

syn come (to), cross, dawn (on), strike

rel recall, recollect, remember, reminisce;

---

con, learn, memorize; appear, arrive, emerge, materialize

near ant forget, unlearn; disregard, ignore, neglect, overlook

occurrence *n* something that happens — see EVENT 1

ocean *n* **1** the whole body of salt water that covers nearly three-fourths of the earth ⟨The *ocean* still holds mysteries that we are only beginning to unravel.⟩

syn blue, brine, deep, sea, seven seas

rel blue water, high seas, main, waters; basin; Davy Jones's locker, depths

2 an immeasurable depth or space — see ABYSS

oceanic *adj* **1** of or relating to the sea — see MARINE 1

2 unusually large — see HUGE

ocular *adj* of, relating to, or used in vision — see VISUAL 1

odd *adj* **1** being one of a pair or set without a corresponding mate ⟨Somehow, there's always at least one *odd* sock that comes out of the dryer.⟩

syn unmatched, unpaired

rel alone, lone, only, single, singular, sole, solitary

ant matched, paired

2 different from the ordinary in a way that causes curiosity or suspicion ⟨There's something *odd* about his explanation.⟩

syn bizarre, cranky, crazy, curious, eccentric, erratic, far-out, funny, kooky (*also* kookie), offbeat, outlandish, out-of-the-way, peculiar, quaint, queer, queerish, quirky, remarkable, screwy, strange, wacky (*also* whacky), way-out, weird, wild

rel aberrant, abnormal, addlepated, flaky; extraordinary, fantastic (*also* fantastical), freak, freakish, freaky, phenomenal; atypical, rare, singular, uncommon, uncustomary, unique, unusual, unwonted; conspicuous, notable, noticeable, outstanding, prominent, salient, striking; atrocious, outrageous, shocking; out-there, unconventional, unorthodox; baffling, bewildering, confounding, mystifying, perplexing, puzzling

near ant average, commonplace, everyday, garden, normal, ordinary, prosaic, routine, run-of-the-mill, standard, typical, unexceptional, unremarkable, usual, workaday; conformist, conservative, conventional; expected, familiar, predictable; common, customary, frequent, habitual, regular, wonted

3 being out of the ordinary — see EXCEPTIONAL 1

4 noticeably different from what is generally found or experienced — see UNUSUAL 1

5 not often occurring or repeated — see INFREQUENT

oddball *n* a person of odd or whimsical habits — see ECCENTRIC

oddity *n* **1** an odd or peculiar habit — see IDIOSYNCRASY

2 something strange or unusual that is an object of interest — see CURIOSITY 2

3 something that is different from what is ordinary or expected — see ANOMALY 1

4 a person of odd or whimsical habits — see ECCENTRIC

oddment *n* **1** an unused or unwanted

piece or item typically of small size or value — see ¹SCRAP 1

2 something that is different from what is ordinary or expected — see ANOMALY 1

3 something strange or unusual that is an object of interest — see CURIOSITY 2

odds *n pl* a measure of how often an event will occur instead of another — see PROBABILITY 2

odds and ends *n pl* **1** small useful items — see NOTION 1

2 a remaining group or portion — see REMAINDER 1

odious *adj* causing intense displeasure, disgust, or resentment — see OFFENSIVE 1

odium *n* the state of having lost the esteem of others — see DISGRACE 1

odor *n* **1** a special quality or impression associated with something — see AURA 1

2 the quality of a thing that makes it perceptible to the sense organs in the nose — see SMELL 1

3 overall quality as seen or judged by people in general — see REPUTATION

of *prep* **1** earlier than — see BEFORE 1

2 having to do with — see ABOUT 1

off *adj* **1** falling short of a standard — see BAD 1

2 not being in a state of use, activity, or employment — see INACTIVE 2

3 not being in agreement with what is true — see FALSE 1

4 small in degree — see REMOTE 1

off *adv* from this or that place — see AWAY

offbeat *adj* **1** different from the ordinary in a way that causes curiosity or suspicion — see ODD 2

2 noticeably different from what is generally found or experienced — see UNUSUAL 1

offend *vb* **1** to commit an offense ⟨Since this is the first time you've *offended*, we'll let you off lightly.⟩

syn err, fall, sin, transgress, trespass, wander

rel breach, break, infringe, violate; backslide, lapse; mess up

phrases break the law, fall from grace

near ant forgive, justify, pardon; regret, repent, rue

2 to cause hurt feelings or deep resentment in — see INSULT

3 to fail to keep — see VIOLATE 1

offender *n* a person who has committed a crime — see CRIMINAL

offense *or* **offence** *n* **1** a breaking of a moral or legal code ⟨was fined for a minor *offense*⟩

syn breach, crime, debt, error, lawbreaking, malefaction, misdeed, misdoing, sin, transgression, trespass, violation, wrongdoing

rel felony, misconduct, misdemeanor, misfeasance; fault, foible, peccadillo; break, infringement; immorality, iniquity, sinfulness, vice, wickedness; corruption, debauchery, depravity, licentiousness; abuse, criminality, illegality, lawlessness, unlawfulness; descent, downfall, fall

near ant blamelessness, faultlessness, guiltlessness, impeccability, innocence; goodness, morality, righteousness, virtue, virtuousness

ant noncrime

2 the act or action of setting upon with force or violence — see ATTACK 1

3 an act or expression showing scorn and usually intended to hurt another's feelings — see INSULT

4 the feeling of being offended or resentful after a slight or indignity — see PIQUE

offensive *adj* **1** causing intense displeasure, disgust, or resentment ⟨I find your disrespectful attitude toward your grandparents very *offensive*.⟩ ⟨The smell of rotting food is quite *offensive*.⟩

syn abhorrent, abominable, appalling, awful, distasteful, dreadful, evil, foul, fulsome, gross, hideous, horrendous, horrible, horrid, loathsome, nasty, nauseating, nauseous, noisome, noxious, obnoxious, obscene, odious, repellent (*also* repellant), repugnant, repulsive, revolting, scandalous, shocking, sickening, ugly

rel exceptionable, objectionable; disagreeable, dislikable (*also* dislikeable); unpleasant; contemptible, despicable, detestable, hard, hateful; unhealthy, unsavory, unwholesome; execrable, lousy, miserable; shocking, sick, sickish, sickly, terrible, unspeakable, vile; off-putting, undesirable, unwanted, unwelcome; distressing, disturbing, upsetting

near ant acceptable, agreeable, alluring, appealing, attractive, blessed (*also* blest), desirable, enjoyable, felicitous, gratifying, heavenly, inviting, likable (*or* likeable), luscious, nice, palatable, pleasant, pleasing, pleasurable, satisfying, savory (*also* savoury), sweet, welcome; unexceptionable, unobjectionable

ant innocuous, inoffensive

2 provoking or likely to provoke protest — see OBJECTIONABLE

offensive *n* the act or action of setting upon with force or violence — see ATTACK 1

offer *n* **1** an effort to do or accomplish something — see ATTEMPT 1

2 something which is presented for consideration — see PROPOSAL

offer *vb* **1** to put before another for acceptance or consideration ⟨I *offered* my boss an alternative to the original plan, which would have required me to work overtime.⟩

syn extend, give, proffer, tender

rel pose, propose; hold out; give in, submit; volunteer

phrases run by (*or* run past)

near ant accept, take; accredit, approbate, approve, authorize, clear, confirm, finalize, formalize, OK (*or* okay), ratify, sanction, warrant; decline, deny, disallow, disapprove, rebut, negative, reject, turn down, veto; rebuff, rebut, refuse, spurn; retract, withdraw; disregard, ignore, neglect, overlook

2 to set before the mind for consideration — see PROPOSE 1

3 to bring before the public in performance or exhibition — see PRESENT 1

4 to give up as an offering to a god — see SACRIFICE

offering *n* something offered to a god — see SACRIFICE

offhand *adj* made or done without previous thought or preparation — see EXTEMPORANEOUS

offhanded *adj* made or done without previous thought or preparation — see EXTEMPORANEOUS

office *n* **1** a large unit of a governmental, business, or educational organization — see DIVISION 2

2 something one must do because of prior agreement — see OBLIGATION 1

officeholder *n* a person who holds a public office — see OFFICIAL

officer *n* **1** a member of a force charged with law enforcement at the local level ⟨If you are ever lost, find the nearest *officer* and ask for help.⟩

syn cop, policeman, police officer

rel patrolman, policewoman; detective, inspector, investigator, plainclothesman, sleuth; marshal (*also* marshall), sheriff, trooper; peace officer; captain, sergeant; constabulary, heat [*slang*], police, police force; operative

near ant civilian

2 a person who holds a public office — see OFFICIAL

official *adj* ordered or allowed by those in authority ⟨The *official* languages for those Olympic Games were French and English.⟩

syn authorized, sanctioned

rel lawful, legal, legitimate, permissible, regulation; approved, endorsed (*also* indorsed); abetted, encouraged, promoted, suggested, supported; licensed; authoritative, canonical, ex officio; semiofficial

near ant illegal, illegitimate, illicit, impermissible, lawless, unlawful, wrongful; unapproved, unlicensed

ant nonofficial, unauthorized, unofficial, unsanctioned

official *n* a person who holds a public office ⟨Some of our best public *officials* do their jobs quietly and are never in the news.⟩

syn functionary, officeholder, officer, public servant

rel bureaucrat; administrator, commissioner, director, executive, head, manager, regulator, superintendent, supervisor; chair, chairman; flunky (*also* flunkey *or* flunkie), minion, underling; co-official

officious *adj* thrusting oneself where one is not welcome or invited — see INTRUSIVE

offing *n* time that is to come — see FUTURE 1

offset *n* **1** a force or influence that makes an opposing force ineffective or less effective — see COUNTERBALANCE

2 the stopping of a process or activity — see END 1

offset *vb* to balance with an equal force so as to make ineffective ⟨If you get a high grade on this quiz, it will *offset* the D from your last one.⟩

syn annul, cancel (out), compensate (for), correct, counteract, counterbalance, counterpoise, make up (for), neutralize

rel invalidate, negate, neuter, nullify; atone (for); outbalance, outweigh, redeem; redress, relieve, remedy; override, overrule

---

syn synonym(s)   *rel* related words
ant antonym(s)   *near ant* near antonym(s)

offshoot *n* 1 a branch of a main stem especially of a plant ⟨We knew the rosebush had survived the harsh winter when it began producing *offshoots* and turning green again.⟩

syn outgrowth, shoot

rel excrescence, growth; bough, branchlet, limb; floret; spray, sprig, spur

2 something that naturally develops or is developed from something else — see DERIVATIVE

offspring *n* the descendants of a person, animal, or plant ⟨The racehorse's *offspring* all proved to be very good racers as well.⟩ ⟨The couple celebrated their 50th wedding anniversary surrounded by three generations of *offspring*.⟩

syn fruit, get, issue, posterity, progeny, seed, spawn

rel brood, hatch, litter, young; child, scion; family, kin; lineage, stock

near ant ancestor, antecedent, father, forebear (*also* forbear), forefather, grandfather, parent

oft *adv* many times — see OFTEN

often *adv* many times ⟨I seem to stumble *often* when I try to walk in high heels.⟩

syn constantly, continually, frequently, much, oft, oftentimes (*or* ofttimes), repeatedly

rel always, consistently, continuously, continuously, perpetually, unceasingly, uninterruptedly; afresh, again, anew; commonly, habitually, ordinarily, regularly, routinely; intermittently, periodically, recurrently; generally, usually; consecutively

phrases a lot, time after time, time and again

near ant now, occasionally, sometimes, sporadically; ne'er, never

ant infrequently, little, rarely, seldom

oftentimes *or* **ofttimes** *adv* many times — see OFTEN

ogle *vb* to look at in a flirtatious or desiring way ⟨I do wish you two would stop *ogling* each other during class.⟩

syn leer (at)

rel eye, gape, gawk, gaze, glare, goggle, peer, rubberneck, stare

phrases make eyes (at)

ogre *n* 1 a strange or horrible and often frightening creature — see MONSTER 1

2 something or someone that causes fear or dread especially without reason — see BOGEY 1

oh *n* the numerical symbol 0 or the absence of number or quantity represented by it — see ZERO 1

oil *n* a picture created with oil paint — see PAINTING

oil *vb* to coat (something) with a slippery substance in order to reduce friction — see LUBRICATE

oiled *adj* having or being a surface so smooth as to greatly reduce traction — see SLICK 1

oil painting *n* a picture created with oil paint — see PAINTING

oilskin *n* a coat made of water-resistant material — see RAINCOAT

OK *or* **okay** *adj* 1 being to one's liking — see SATISFACTORY 1

2 of a level of quality that meets one's needs or standards — see ADEQUATE

OK *or* **okay** *adv* 1 in a satisfactory way — see WELL 1

2 used to express agreement — see YES

OK *or* **okay** *n* an acceptance of something as satisfactory — see APPROVAL

OK *or* **okay** *vb* 1 to give official acceptance of as satisfactory — see APPROVE

2 to have a favorable opinion of — see APPROVE (OF)

old *adj* 1 being of advanced years and especially past middle age — see ELDERLY

2 dating or surviving from the distant past — see ANCIENT 1

3 having been such at some previous time — see FORMER 1

4 causing weariness, restlessness, or lack of interest — see BORING

older *adj* being of advanced years and especially past middle age — see ELDERLY

oldfangled *adj* pleasantly reminiscent of an earlier time — see OLD-FASHIONED 1

old-fashioned *adj* 1 pleasantly reminiscent of an earlier time ⟨an elegant, *old-fashioned* bun that was held in place with pearl hairpins⟩

syn antique, oldfangled, old-time, old-world, quaint, retro

rel antiquated, moldy, obsolete; historical, olden, traditional; old hat, outdated, outmoded, out-of-date, outworn, passé, superannuated; dated, fusty, moth-eaten, musty, stodgy; aged, age-old, ancient, antediluvian, hoary, venerable; bygone, erstwhile, former, late, past; forgotten, remote; anachronistic

near ant fresh, new; chic, designer, fashionable, smart, stylish; modernized, refurbished, remodeled, renewed, updated; last, latest; futuristic, high-tech (*also* hi-tech), latter-day, nontraditional; recent

ant contemporary, current, hot, mod, modern, modernistic, new age, newfangled, new-fashioned, present-day, red-hot, space-age, ultramodern, up-to-date

2 tending to favor established ideas, conditions, or institutions — see CONSERVATIVE 1

old hand *n* a person with long experience in a specified area — see VETERAN

old lady *n* 1 a female human parent — see MOTHER

2 a female partner in a marriage — see WIFE

3 a female romantic companion — see GIRLFRIEND

old man *n* 1 a male human parent — see FATHER 1

2 a male partner in a marriage — see HUSBAND

3 a male romantic companion — see BOYFRIEND

oldster *n* a person of advanced years — see SENIOR CITIZEN

old-time *adj* pleasantly reminiscent of an earlier time — see OLD-FASHIONED 1

old-timer *n* 1 a person of advanced years — see SENIOR CITIZEN

2 a person with long experience in a specified area — see VETERAN

old wives' tale *n* a false idea or belief — see FALLACY 1

old–world *adj* pleasantly reminiscent of an earlier time — see OLD-FASHIONED 1

omen *n* something believed to be a sign or warning of a future event ⟨Some people still believe that a black cat crossing your path is a bad *omen*.⟩

syn augury, auspice, boding, foreboding, foreshadowing, portent, prefiguring, presage

rel forerunner, harbinger, herald, precursor; foretaste, hint, inkling, intimation, suggestion; forewarning; forecast, foretelling, prediction, prognostication, prophecy (*also* prophesy)

phrases straw in the wind

ominous *adj* being or showing a sign of evil or calamity to come ⟨That comment about downsizing from the company president sounded *ominous*.⟩

syn baleful, dire, direful, foreboding, ill, inauspicious, menacing, portentous, sinister, threatening

rel black, bleak, cheerless, chill, cold, comfortless, dark, darkening, depressing, desolate, dim, disconsolate, dismal, drear, dreary, forlorn, funereal, gloomy, glum, godforsaken, gray (*also* grey), lonely, lonesome, lugubrious, miserable, morbid, morose, murky, saturnine, sepulchral, somber (*or* sombre), sullen, wretched; discouraging, disheartening, hopeless, unfavorable, unpromising, unpropitious; ill-fated, ill-starred, star-crossed, troubled, unfortunate, unlucky; evil, malign, malignant

near ant auspicious, benign, bright, encouraging, favorable, golden, heartening, hopeful, promising, propitious, prosperous

ant unthreatening

omission *n* something left out ⟨The disk contains a selection of deleted scenes, and a couple of the *omissions* greatly add to the intelligibility of the movie's plot.⟩

syn deletion

rel elimination; blank, skip; lapse, slip; deduction, reduction, subtraction; default, delinquency, dereliction, failure, neglect, negligence, oversight, pretermission; abbreviation, condensation

near ant inclusion; accretion, accrual, addendum, addition, augmentation, boost, expansion, gain, increase, increment

omit *vb* to miss the opportunity or obligation — see NEGLECT 3

omnibus *adj* covering everything or all important points — see ENCYCLOPEDIC

omnipotent *adj* having unlimited power or authority ⟨the belief that God is *omnipotent* and omniscient⟩

syn all-powerful, almighty

rel great, sovereign (*also* sovran), supreme, towering; authoritative, majestic, master, masterful; mighty, potent, powerful, puissant, strong; divine, godlike; able, capable, competent, effective, efficient; authoritarian, autocratic (*also* autocratical), despotic, dictatorial, tyrannical (*also* tyrannic)

near ant helpless, impotent, powerless;

limited, restricted; paralyzed, weak; incapable, incompetent, ineffective, ineffectual, inept, unfit, useless; feeble, frail, infirm

omnipresent *adj* present in all places and at all times ⟨seeking some much-needed relief from the *omnipresent* noise of the big city⟩

syn ubiquitous, universal

rel boundless, endless, horizonless, illimitable, immeasurable, indefinite, infinite, limitless, measureless, unbounded, unfathomable, unlimited; extensive, farflung, widespread

near ant bounded, circumscribed, finite, limited, measured, narrow, restricted

on *adj* being in effective operation — see ACTIVE 1

on *adv* 1 toward a point ahead in space or time — see ONWARD 1

2 toward or at a point lying in advance in space or time — see ALONG

on *prep* 1 having to do with — see ABOUT 1

2 in or into contact with — see AGAINST

oncoming *adj* being soon to appear or take place — see FORTHCOMING 1

one *adj* 1 being the one or ones of a class with no other members — see ONLY 2

2 known but not named — see CERTAIN 1

one–dimensional *adj* having or showing a lack of depth of understanding or character — see SUPERFICIAL 2

onerous *adj* 1 difficult to endure — see HARSH 1

2 requiring much time, effort, or careful attention — see DEMANDING 1

one–sided *adj* inclined to favor one side over another — see PARTIAL 1

one–sidedness *n* an attitude that always favors one way of feeling or acting especially without considering any other possibilities — see BIAS 1

onetime *adj* having been such at some previous time — see FORMER 1

ongoing *adj* 1 being in progress or development ⟨We do seem to be making some headway on that *ongoing* project.⟩ ⟨the ever *ongoing* quest for knowledge by men and women of science⟩

syn afoot, proceeding

rel functioning, happening, operating, working; alive, going; advancing, continuing, gaining

near ant receding, regressing, retrogressing

ant arrested, ended, halted, stalled, stopped

2 existing or in progress right now — see PRESENT 1

3 having an existence or validity that does not change or diminish — see ABIDING

only *adj* 1 having no equal or rival for excellence or desirability ⟨The *only* way to really appreciate the beauty of the forest is to walk through it.⟩

syn incomparable, inimitable, matchless, nonpareil, peerless, unequaled (*or* unequalled), unexampled, unmatched, unparalleled, unrivaled (*or* unrivalled), unsurpassable, unsurpassed

rel alone, singular, unique; exceptional; extraordinary, rare, uncommon, unusual; awesome, beautiful, brave, capital, choice, classic, dandy, divine, excellent, fabulous,

---

fantastic, fine, first-class, first-rate, grand, great, lovely, marvelous (*or* marvellous), par excellence, quality, sensational, splendid, stellar, sterling, superb, superior, superlative, swell, terrific, tip-top, top, topnotch, wonderful; better, preferred; exceptional, fancy, high-grade, special
phrases out of sight
near ant common, commonplace, everyday, familiar, frequent, normal, ordinary, routine, ubiquitous, usual; inferior, lesser, worse, worst; deficient, dissatisfactory, lame, lousy, low, lower, off, paltry, poor, punk, substandard, unacceptable, unsatisfactory, wanting; low-grade, substandard; mediocre, second-class, second-rate; atrocious, awful, execrable, pathetic, rotten, terrible, vile, wretched

2 being the one or ones of a class with no other members ⟨That is the *only* possible right answer.⟩ ⟨We were the *only* passengers on the tour bus.⟩
syn alone, lone, one, singular, sole, solitary, special, unique
rel single, solo, unaccompanied, unattended; incomparable, inimitable, matchless, peerless, unequaled (*or* unequalled), unmatched, unparalleled, unrivaled (*or* unrivalled), unsurpassable, unsurpassed; distinct, distinctive, individual, separate; nonce
near ant divers, manifold, multifarious, myriad; assorted, heterogeneous, miscellaneous, mixed, motley, patchwork, promiscuous, varied; popular, prevailing, prevalent, rampant; perennial, recurrent, repeated

only *adv* **1** for nothing other than — see SOLELY 1
2 not long ago — see NEWLY
3 nothing more than — see JUST 3
only *conj* if it were not for the fact that — see EXCEPT
onrush *n* forward movement in time or place — see ADVANCE 1
onset *n* **1** the act or action of setting upon with force or violence — see ATTACK 1
2 the point at which something begins — see BEGINNING
onslaught *n* the act or action of setting upon with force or violence — see ATTACK 1
onward *also* **onwards** *adv* **1** toward a point ahead in space or time ⟨We must continue to move *onward*, or we will not get there in time.⟩
syn ahead, forth, forward, on
near ant backward (*or* backwards)
2 toward or at a point lying in advance in space or time — see ALONG
oodles *n pl* a considerable amount — see LOT 2
ooze *n* soft wet earth — see MUD
ooze *vb* **1** to flow forth slowly through small openings — see EXUDE
2 to move slowly — see CRAWL 2
oozy *adj* full of or covered with soft wet earth — see MUDDY 1
opacity *n* the quality or state of having a veiled or uncertain meaning — see OBSCURITY 1
opaque *adj* **1** having an often intentionally veiled or uncertain meaning — see OBSCURE 1

2 not seen or understood clearly — see FAINT 1
3 not having or showing an ability to absorb ideas readily — see STUPID 1
open *adj* **1** allowing passage without obstruction ⟨Thank you for clearing out the hallway so that it's *open* again.⟩
syn clear, cleared, free, unclogged, unclosed, unobstructed, unstopped
rel enterable, navigable, passable; emptied, empty, unoccupied, vacant; exposed, revealed; gaping, wide, yawning; unbarred, unbolted, unclasped, unfastened, unlatched, unlocked, unsealed
near ant impassable (*also* impassible); constricted, cramped, encumbered, hampered, hindered, impeded, interfered (with), trammeled (*or* trammelled); barricaded, blockaded, dammed, gated
ant blocked, clogged, closed, jammed, obstructed, plugged, shut, stopped, stuffed, uncleared

2 freely available for use or participation by all ⟨The lanes at the bowling alley will be *open* during the afternoon, but will be available only for league play in the evening.⟩
syn free-for-all, public, unrestricted
rel collective, common, communal, shared; accessible, available, free; unregulated, unreserved
near ant limited; inaccessible, unavailable
ant closed, exclusive, off-limits, private, restricted

3 being in a situation where one is likely to meet with harm — see LIABLE 1
4 free in expressing one's true feelings and opinions — see FRANK
5 lacking a usual or natural covering — see NAKED 2
6 not known by only a select few — see PUBLIC 1
7 not yet settled or decided — see PENDING 1
8 willing to consider new or different ideas — see OPEN-MINDED 1
9 giving or sharing in abundance and without hesitation — see GENEROUS 1
open *n* that part of the physical world that is removed from human habitation — see NATURE 2
open *vb* **1** to change from a closed to an open position ⟨Please *open* the door to let the cat out.⟩
syn unclose
rel unbar, unbolt, unclasp, unfasten, unlatch, unlock; unbutton, unclench, unfold, unzip; disengage, release, slip
near ant bar, bolt, clasp, fasten, latch, lock; button (up), zip (up)
ant close, shut

2 to make passage through (something) possible by removing obstructions ⟨We need to *open* this drain that's clogged with hair.⟩
syn clear, free, unclog, unstop
rel ease, facilitate, loosen (up), smooth
near ant constrict, encumber, hamper, hinder, impede, interfere (with), obstruct, trammel; barricade, blockade
ant block, clog (up), close, dam (up), plug (up), stop
3 to arrange the parts of (something) over

a wider area ⟨When we got too close, the cardinal *opened* its wings and flew to a higher branch.⟩

syn expand, extend, fan (out), flare (out), outspread, outstretch, spread (out), stretch (out), unfold

rel overspread

near ant compact, compress, condense, reduce

ant close, contract, fold

4 to rid the surface of (as an area) from things in the way — see CLEAR 1

5 to take the first step in (a process or course of action) — see BEGIN 1

open-air *adj* of, relating to, or held in the open air — see OUTDOOR

open air *n* that part of the physical world that is removed from human habitation — see NATURE 2

open-and-shut *adj* not subject to misinterpretation or more than one interpretation — see CLEAR 2

open-eyed *adj* paying close attention usually for the purpose of anticipating approaching danger or opportunity — see ALERT 1

openhanded *adj* giving or sharing in abundance and without hesitation — see GENEROUS 1

openhandedly *adv* in a generous manner — see WELL 2

openhandedness *n* the quality or state of being generous — see LIBERALITY

openhearted *adj* free in expressing one's true feelings and opinions — see FRANK

openheartedness *n* **1** the free expression of one's true feelings and opinions — see CANDOR 1

2 the quality or state of being generous — see LIBERALITY

opening *n* **1** a favorable combination of circumstances, time, and place — see OPPORTUNITY

2 a place in a surface allowing passage into or through a thing — see HOLE 1

3 an open space in a barrier (as a wall or hedge) — see GAP 1

open-minded *adj* **1** willing to consider new or different ideas ⟨All I ask is that you try to be *open-minded* when we present our suggestions.⟩

syn broad-minded, open, receptive

rel impartial, neutral, objective, unbiased, unprejudiced; easygoing, nonjudgmental, tolerant; calm, detached, dispassionate; amenable, compliant; impressionable, suggestible, susceptible; persuadable, persuasible

near ant biased, narrow, one-sided, partial, partisan, prejudiced; bigoted, intolerant

ant narrow-minded, unreceptive

2 not bound by traditional ways or beliefs — see LIBERAL 1

openmouthed *adj* filled with amazement or wonder ⟨The stunning view from the mountaintop left us *openmouthed* and at a loss for words.⟩

syn amazed, astonished, astounded, awed, awestruck (*also* awestricken), dumb-

founded (*also* dumbfounded), flabbergasted, marveling (*or* marvelling), wondering

rel startled, surprised (*also* surprized); bewildered, puzzled; overwhelmed, staggered, stunned, stupefied

near ant unimpressed; disinterested, incurious, indifferent, unconcerned, uninterested; dispassionate, impassive, unemotional; bored, jaded

openness *n* **1** the free expression of one's true feelings and opinions — see CANDOR 1

2 the state of being left without shelter or protection against something harmful — see EXPOSURE 1

open sesame *n* something that allows someone to achieve a desired goal — see PASSPORT 1

operable *adj* capable of or suitable for being used for a particular purpose — see USABLE 1

operate *vb* **1** to control the mechanical operation of ⟨Do not *operate* heavy machinery, including cars, after taking this medication.⟩

syn handle, run, work

rel use; maneuver, manipulate, ply, wield; command, control, direct, drive, guide, pilot, steer

2 to look after and make decisions about — see CONDUCT 1

3 to produce a desired effect — see ACT 2

4 to put into action or service — see USE 1

operating *adj* being in effective operation — see ACTIVE 1

operation *n* **1** a specific task with which a person or group is charged — see MISSION

2 a usually fixed or ordered series of actions or events leading to a result — see PROCESS 1

3 the act or activity of looking after and making decisions about something — see CONDUCT 1

4 the act or practice of employing something for a particular purpose — see USE 1

operational *adj* being in effective operation — see ACTIVE 1

operative *adj* **1** being in effective operation — see ACTIVE 1

2 producing or capable of producing a desired result — see EFFECTIVE 1

operative *n* **1** a person who tries secretly to obtain information for one country in the territory of another usually unfriendly country — see SPY

2 a person not on the police force who investigates criminal or illicit activity or searches for missing persons — see DETECTIVE

opiate *adj* tending to cause sleep — see HYPNOTIC

opiate *n* something that soothes, calms, or induces passivity or a sense of security ⟨a cultural critic who argues that the Internet has now joined television as an *opiate* of the American people⟩

syn narcotic

rel pacifier, palliative; hypnotic, sedative, tranquilizer (*also* tranquillizer)

opine *vb* to make a statement of one's opinion — see REMARK 1

opinion *n* **1** an idea that is believed to be true or valid without positive knowledge

---

syn synonym(s)   **rel** related words
ant antonym(s)   **near ant** near antonym(s)

⟨In my *opinion*, it's the best car on the market.⟩

syn belief, conviction, eye, feeling, judgment (*or* judgement), mind, notion, persuasion, sentiment, verdict, view

rel say; impression, perception, take; assumption, presumption, presupposition; conclusion, decision, determination; deliverance, estimate, estimation; credence, credit, faith; concept, conception, idea, thought; position, stance, stand; comment, observation, reflection, remark; conjecture, guess, hunch, hypothesis, surmise, theory; advice, input, recommendation, suggestion; angle, outlook, perspective, shoes, slant, standpoint, viewpoint; counterview

near ant fact, truth

2 a position arrived at after consideration — see DECISION 1

opinionated *adj* sticking to an opinion, purpose, or course of action in spite of reason, arguments, or persuasion — see OBSTINATE

opponent *n* **1** one that takes a position opposite another in a competition or conflict ⟨In martial arts, before the match begins, always bow to your *opponent*.⟩

syn adversary, antagonist, foe, rival

rel equal, match; enemy; archenemy, nemesis; competitor, contestant, combatant

near ant accomplice, ally, confederate, partner; advocate, champion, exponent, proponent, supporter, sympathizer

2 one that is hostile toward another — see ENEMY

opportune *adj* especially suitable for a certain time — see TIMELY 1

opportunist *n* **1** a person who dexterously and expediently changes or adopts opinions — see ACROBAT 2

2 one who does things only for his own benefit and with little regard for right and wrong — see SELF-SEEKER

opportunity *n* a favorable combination of circumstances, time, and place ⟨This art school could be a wonderful *opportunity* for you to finally develop your talent for painting.⟩

syn break, chance, occasion, opening, room, shot

rel play, way; juncture, pass

oppose *vb* **1** to refuse to give in to — see RESIST

2 to strive to reduce or eliminate — see FIGHT 2

opposite *adj* being as different as possible ⟨Those two are fundamentally *opposite*—she being loquacious and outgoing where he is quiet and reserved.⟩

syn antipodal, antipodean, antithetical, contradictory, contrary, diametric (*or* diametrical), polar

rel adverse, negative, unfavorable; antagonistic, antipathetic, counter, cross, hostile; converse, inverse, reverse; alien, disparate, dissimilar, divergent, unalike, unlike

near ant alike, analogous, like, similar; equivalent, identical, same; synonymous

ant noncontradictory

opposite *n* something that is as different as possible from something else ⟨No matter what I say, you insist on the *opposite*.⟩

syn antipode, antithesis, contrary, counter, negative, reverse

rel negation; antonym; counterpoint; converse, inverse

near ant synonym; analogue (*or* analog), counterpart; carbon copy, copy, duplicate, replica

opposition *n* the inclination to resist — see RESISTANCE 1

oppress *vb* **1** to make sad — see DEPRESS 1

2 to subject to incapacitating emotional or mental stress — see OVERWHELM 1

oppression *n* a state or spell of low spirits — see SADNESS

oppressive *adj* difficult to endure — see HARSH 1

oppressively *adv* in a manner so as to cause loss or suffering — see HARDLY 1

oppressor *n* a person who uses power or authority in a cruel, unjust, or harmful way — see DESPOT

opprobrious *adj* marked by harsh insulting language — see ABUSIVE

opprobrium *n* **1** a cause of shame — see DISGRACE 2

2 the state of having lost the esteem of others — see DISGRACE 1

opt *vb* to come to a judgment about after discussion or consideration — see DECIDE 1

opt (for) *vb* to decide to accept (someone or something) from a group of possibilities — see CHOOSE 1

optic *adj* of, relating to, or used in vision — see VISUAL 1

optical *adj* of, relating to, or used in vision — see VISUAL 1

optimism *n* an inclination to believe in the most favorable outcome ⟨your perpetual *optimism* even when things look bleak⟩

syn sanguinity

rel brightness, cheerfulness, perkiness, sunniness; hope, hopefulness, rosiness; idealism

near ant skepticism; apprehension, caution, concern; cynicism; despair, desperation, discouragement, disheartenment, hopelessness; bleakness, cheerlessness, dreariness, gloominess; pragmatism

ant bearishness, pessimism

optimistic *adj* having qualities which inspire hope — see HOPEFUL 1

option *n* **1** something that is not necessary in itself but adds to the convenience or performance of the main piece of equipment — see ACCESSORY 1

2 the power, right, or opportunity to choose — see CHOICE 1

optional *adj* subject to one's freedom of choice ⟨At the resort all recreational activities are *optional*, and you may choose to participate in none of them.⟩

syn discretionary, elective, voluntary

rel alternate, alternative, chosen; dispensable, unnecessary, unneeded, unwanted

near ant essential, indispensable, necessary, requisite

ant compulsory, mandatory, nonelective, nonvoluntary, obligatory, required

opulence *n* the total of one's money and property — see WEALTH 1

opulent *adj* **1** having goods, property, or money in abundance — see RICH 1

2 showing obvious signs of wealth and comfort — see LUXURIOUS

opulently *adv* in a luxurious manner — see HIGH

opus *n* a literary, musical, or artistic production — see COMPOSITION 1

oral *adj* 1 expressed or communicated by voice — see VOCAL

2 made or carried on through speaking rather than in writing — see VERBAL 2

orate *vb* 1 to talk as if giving an important and formal speech ⟨Given the opportunity, many politicians will *orate* at considerable length on just about any subject.⟩

syn declaim, discourse, harangue, mouth (off)

rel rant, rave; lecture, preach, sermonize; advertise, announce, broadcast, declare, proclaim, pronounce; speak, speechify, talk

2 to give a formal often extended talk on a subject — see TALK 1

oration *n* a usually formal discourse delivered to an audience — see SPEECH 1

oratorical *adj* marked by the use of impressive-sounding but mostly meaningless words and phrases — see RHETORICAL 1

oratory *n* 1 the art of speaking in public eloquently and effectively ⟨a presidential hopeful with a gift for *oratory* and a highly charismatic personality⟩

syn elocution

rel bombast, grandiloquence; eloquence, rhetoric; discourse, speech, talk

2 language that is impressive-sounding but not meaningful or sincere — see RHETORIC 1

orb *n* a more or less round body or mass — see ¹BALL 1

orbit *vb* to travel completely around — see ENCIRCLE 1

orchestra *n* a usually large group of musicians playing together — see ²BAND 1

ordain *vb* 1 to determine the fate of in advance — see DESTINE

2 to request the doing of by virtue of one's authority — see COMMAND 2

3 to put into effect through legislative or authoritative action — see ENACT

ordeal *n* a test of faith, patience, or strength — see TRIAL 1

order *n* 1 the way objects in space or events in time are arranged or follow one another ⟨You always keep your books in perfect alphabetical *order*.⟩ ⟨We haven't found out the *order* of the speeches yet.⟩

syn arrangement, array, disposal, disposition, distribution, ordering, sequence, setup

rel precedence, priority; chain, procession, progression, succession; series; aligning (*also* alining), alignment (*also* alinement), lining up; design, layout, pattern, structure, system

near ant confusion, disorder, disorganization, disruption, upset; disconnection, disjointedness

2 a group of persons formally joined together for some common interest — see ASSOCIATION 2

3 a number of persons or things that are grouped together because they have something in common — see SORT 1

4 a piece of metal given in honor of a special event, a person, or an achievement — see MEDAL

5 a state of being or fitness — see CONDITION 1

6 a statement of what to do that must be obeyed by those concerned — see COMMAND 1

7 one of the segments of society into which people are grouped — see CLASS 1

8 one of the units into which a whole is divided on the basis of a common characteristic — see CLASS 2

order *vb* 1 to put into a particular arrangement ⟨I've *ordered* all of my books according to subject matter.⟩ ⟨He likes to *order* his life so that there are few surprises.⟩

syn arrange, array, classify, codify, dispose, draw up, lay out, marshal (*also* marshall), organize, range, systematize

rel make up, straighten (up); unscramble; align (*also* aline), cue, line, line up, queue; alphabetize, file, prioritize, sequence; place, set; display, map (out)

ant derange, disarrange, disarray, disorder, mess (up), muss (up), rumple, upset

2 to give a request or demand for ⟨The players *ordered* hamburgers for lunch.⟩

syn ask (for), request, requisition

rel commission, solicit; charter, hire, license (*also* licence)

phrases call for

3 to request the doing of by virtue of one's authority — see COMMAND 1

4 to issue orders to (someone) by right of authority — see COMMAND 1

ordering *n* 1 a scheme of rank or order — see ³SCALE 1

2 the way objects in space or events in time are arranged or follow one another — see ORDER 1

orderly *adj* 1 being clean and in good order — see NEAT 1

2 following a set method, arrangement, or pattern — see METHODICAL

ordinance *n* a rule of conduct or action laid down by a governing authority and especially a legislature — see LAW 1

ordinarily *adv* according to the usual course of things — see NATURALLY 2

ordinary *adj* 1 being of the type that is encountered in the normal course of events ⟨It was a perfectly *ordinary* and undistinguished shirt.⟩

syn average, common, commonplace, everyday, normal, prosaic, routine, run-of-the-mill, standard, unexceptional, unremarkable, usual, workaday

rel regular, typical, unextraordinary; familiar, homely, plain, popular, vulgar; natural; customary, wonted; insignificant, trivial, unimportant; frequent, habitual; expected, predictable

phrases par for the course

near ant curious, funny, peculiar, quaint, queer; aberrant, anomalous, atypical, irregular, untypical; rare, scarce; fantastic (*also* fantastical), phenomenal; bizarre, far-out, outrageous, wacky (*also* whacky),

---

syn synonym(s)   *rel* related words
ant antonym(s)   *near ant* near antonym(s)

way-out, weird, wild; eccentric, idiosyncratic, kooky (*also* kookie), nonconformist, oddball, offbeat, unconventional, unorthodox; freak, freakish; conspicuous, notable, outstanding, prominent, salient, signal, striking, unexampled, unprecedented; singular, unique, unparalleled

ant abnormal, exceptional, extraordinary, odd, out-of-the-way, strange, unusual

2 of average to below average quality — see MEDIOCRE 1

3 often observed or encountered — see COMMON 1

ordnance *n* large firearms (as cannon or rockets) — see ARTILLERY

oread *n* a mythical goddess represented as a young woman and said to live outdoors — see NYMPH

organ *n* **1** a publication that appears at regular intervals — see JOURNAL

2 something used to achieve an end — see AGENT 1

organization *n* a group of persons formally joined together for some common interest — see ASSOCIATION 2

organize *vb* **1** to put into a particular arrangement — see ORDER 1

2 to work out the details of (something) in advance — see PLAN 1

organized *adj* following a set method, arrangement, or pattern — see METHODICAL

orient *vb* to impart knowledge of a new thing or situation to — see ACQUAINT 1

orientate *vb* to impart knowledge of a new thing or situation to — see ACQUAINT 1

orifice *n* a place in a surface allowing passage into or through a thing — see HOLE 1

origin *n* **1** a point or place at which something is invented or provided — see SOURCE 1

2 the source from which something grows or develops — see SEED 1

3 the line of ancestors from whom a person is descended — see ANCESTRY

original *adj* **1** coming before all others in time or order — see FIRST 1

2 having the skill and imagination to create new things — see CREATIVE 1

3 not known or experienced before — see NEW 2

original *n* something from which copies are made ⟨Please make copies to hand out, but keep the *original*.⟩

syn archetype, prototype

rel source; example, paradigm, pattern; beau ideal, classic, exemplar, ideal, model, nonpareil, paragon; blueprint, draft

near ant copy, imitation, replica, reproduction; counterfeit, fake, forgery, sham

originality *n* **1** the quality or appeal of being new — see NOVELTY 1

2 the skill and imagination to create new things — see CREATIVITY 1

3 the ability to form mental images of things that either are not physically present or have never been conceived or created by others — see IMAGINATION 1

originally *adv* in the beginning ⟨We *originally* planned to go out tonight, but we changed our minds.⟩

syn firstly, initially, primarily

rel incipiently; primitively

phrases at first, to start with

near ant finally, lastly, ultimately

originate *vb* to come into existence — see BEGIN 2

originator *n* **1** one who creates or introduces something new — see INVENTOR

2 a person who establishes a whole new field of endeavor — see FATHER 2

orison *n* an address to God or a deity — see PRAYER 1

ornament *n* something that decorates or beautifies — see DECORATION 1

ornament *vb* to make more attractive by adding something that is beautiful or becoming — see DECORATE

ornamental *adj* serving to add beauty — see DECORATIVE

ornamental *n* a small object displayed for its attractiveness or interest — see KNICK-KNACK

ornate *adj* **1** elaborately and often excessively decorated ⟨an *ornate* gambling casino that is designed to look like an Italian palace⟩

syn bedizened, florid, fussy, gingerbread, overdecorated, overwrought

rel arabesque, rococo; extravagant, flamboyant, splashy; bedaubed, flashy, garish, gaudy, glitzy, loud, ostentatious, pretentious, showy, swank (*or* swanky); tawdry; elaborate, extreme; adorned, arrayed, beautified, bedecked, decorated, dressed, embellished, enriched, garnished, ornamented, trimmed; flowery, frilly, lacy; bejeweled (*or* bejewelled), bossed, chased, emblazoned, embossed, embroidered, flounced, fringed, garlanded, gilded (*or* gilt), laced, sequined (*or* sequinned), wreathed

near ant bare, denuded, exposed, naked, stripped, uncovered; modest, simple, unassuming, unpretentious; conservative, muted, quiet, restrained, subdued, tasteful, toned-down, understated, unobtrusive

ant austere, plain, severe, stark, unadorned

2 full of fine words and fancy expressions — see FLOWERY 1

ornery *adj* having or showing a habitually bad temper — see ILL-TEMPERED

orthodox *adj* **1** following or agreeing with established form, custom, or rules — see FORMAL 1

2 tending to favor established ideas, conditions, or institutions — see CONSERVATIVE 1

oscillation *n* **1** the frequent and usually sudden passing from one condition to another — see FLUX 1

2 a series of slight movements by a body back and forth or from side to side — see VIBRATION 1

ossified *adj* sticking to an opinion, purpose, or course of action in spite of reason, arguments, or persuasion — see OBSTINATE

ostensible *adj* appearing to be true on the basis of evidence that may or may not be confirmed — see APPARENT 1

ostensibly *adv* to all outward appearances — see APPARENTLY

ostentation *n* excessive or unnecessary display ⟨The sheer *ostentation* of the rock star's mansion was overwhelming.⟩

syn flamboyance, flash, flashiness, garishness, gaudiness, glitz, ostentatiousness, pretentiousness, showiness, swank

rel pretense (*or* pretence); pageant, parade, show; dazzle, fanfare, pageantry, pomp, razzmatazz; adornment, decoration, dressing, embellishment, garnishment, trimming; extravagance, fanciness, luxuriance, luxuriousness, magnificence, opulence, richness, sumptuousness; luridness; meretriciousness, tawdriness, vulgarity

near ant moderation, modesty, restraint, simplicity, understatement; elegance, gracefulness, tastefulness; minimalism

ant austerity, plainness, severity

ostentatious *adj* **1** excessively showy — see GAUDY

2 self-consciously trying to present an appearance of grandeur or importance — see PRETENTIOUS 1

ostentatiousness *n* excessive or unnecessary display — see OSTENTATION

other *adj* **1** being not of the same kind — see DIFFERENT 1

2 resulting in an increase in amount or number — see ADDITIONAL

3 having been such at some previous time — see FORMER 1

other than *prep* not including — see EXCEPT

otherwise *adv* in a different way ⟨The candidate was gracious in his defeat, though he clearly wished the election had gone *otherwise*.⟩

syn differently, else

rel dissimilarly, diversely, variously

near ant similarly

ant likewise

ought (to) *vb* to be under necessity or obligation to — see NEED 2

ounce *n* a very small amount — see PARTICLE 1

oust *vb* **1** to drive or force out — see EJECT 1

2 to remove from a position of prominence or power (as a throne) — see DEPOSE 1

out *adj* **1** fully committed to achieving a goal — see DETERMINED 1

2 not at a certain place — see ABSENT 1

out *adv* **1** in or into the open air — see OUTDOORS

2 with one's normal voice speaking the words — see ALOUD

3 to a full extent or degree — see FULLY 1

4 from this or that place — see AWAY

out *n* the act or a means of getting or keeping away from something undesirable — see ESCAPE 2

out *vb* **1** to become known — see GET OUT 1

2 to drive or force out — see EJECT 1

out-and-out *adj* **1** having no exceptions or restrictions — see ABSOLUTE 2

2 trying all possibilities — see EXHAUSTIVE 1

outbrave *vb* to oppose (something hostile or dangerous) with firmness or courage — see FACE 1

outbreak *n* **1** a sudden and usually temporary growth of activity ⟨There was an immediate *outbreak* of paper shuffling and a pretense of work when the supervisor passed through the room.⟩

syn burst, flare, flare-up, flash, flicker, flurry, flutter, outburst, spurt

rel recrudescence, recurrence, renewal; binge, jag, spree; boost, increase, pickup, upswing, upturn; eruption, explosion, paroxysm; deluge, flood, rush, spate, surge, volley; commotion, furor, uproar

near ant calm, doldrums, slump

2 open fighting against authority (as one's own government) — see REBELLION 1

outburst *n* **1** a sudden intense expression of strong feeling ⟨The judge directed the courtroom spectators to refrain from any *outbursts* when the verdict was read.⟩

syn agony, blaze, burst, eruption, explosion, fit, flare, flare-up, flash, flush, gale, gush, gust, paroxysm, spasm, storm

rel blowup, grouch, rage, tantrum; ecstasy, rapture, transport; delirium, frenzy, furor

2 a sudden and usually temporary growth of activity — see OUTBREAK 1

3 the act or an instance of exploding — see EXPLOSION 1

outcast *n* one who is cast out or rejected by society ⟨The professor is something of an *outcast* in the halls of academe now that his former support of a dictatorial regime has become public.⟩

syn castaway, castoff, pariah, reject

rel untouchable; outsider; deportee, exile

near ant insider

outclass *vb* to be greater, better, or stronger than — see SURPASS 1

outcome *n* a condition or occurrence traceable to a cause — see EFFECT 1

outcry *n* a violent shouting — see CLAMOR 1

outdated *adj* having passed its time of use or usefulness — see OBSOLETE

outdistance *vb* to be greater, better, or stronger than — see SURPASS 1

outdo *vb* to be greater, better, or stronger than — see SURPASS 1

outdoor *also* **outdoors** *adj* of, relating to, or held in the open air ⟨An *outdoor* picnic is always at the mercy of the weather, of course.⟩

syn open-air, out-of-door (*or* out-of-doors)

rel airy; exterior, external, outer, outside, outward; outermost, outmost

near ant inner, inside, interior, internal, inward; inmost, innermost

ant indoor

outdoors *adv* in or into the open air ⟨I can't wait to get *outdoors* and into the sunshine.⟩

syn out, outside

rel without

near ant in, inside, within

ant indoors

outdoors *n* that part of the physical world that is removed from human habitation — see NATURE 2

outer *adj* situated on the outside or farther out ⟨The *outer* edge of the blade of your figure skate always wears out faster than the inner because you use it more.⟩

---

syn synonym(s)　　*rel* related words
ant antonym(s)　　*near ant* near antonym(s)

syn exterior, external, outside, outward

rel outermost, outlying, outmost; superficial, surface

near ant inmost, innermost; mid, middle, midmost

ant inner, inside, interior, internal, inward

outermost *adj* most distant from a center
— see EXTREME 1

outfit *n* **1** clothing chosen as appropriate for a specific situation ⟨The restaurant provides its waitstaff with themed *outfits*.⟩ ⟨Do you want to buy a new *outfit* for the Halloween party?⟩

syn costume, drag, dress, garb, getup, guise, togs

rel apparel, attire, clothes, duds, habiliment(s), raiment; fashion, mode, style; array, caparison

2 a commercial or industrial activity or organization — see ENTERPRISE 1

3 a group of people working together on a task — see GANG 1

4 items needed for the performance of a task or activity — see EQUIPMENT

5 the distinctive clothing worn by members of a particular group — see UNIFORM

outfit *vb* to provide (someone) with what is needed for a task or activity — see FURNISH 1

outflow *n* a flowing or going out ⟨Over the last year the state experienced an unprecedented brain drain as the *outflow* of highly educated professionals exceeded the inflow.⟩

syn exodus, gush, outpouring

rel drain, flow; ebb, reflux, reflux; rush, stampede; diaspora, emigration, flight; discharge, effluence, emanation, emission

near ant deluge, flood, inundation, overflow, spate, torrent; river, stream, tide

ant flux, inflow, influx, inrush

outfox *vb* to get the better of through cleverness — see OUTWIT

outgo *n* **1** a payment made in the course of achieving a result — see EXPENSE

2 the act of leaving a place — see DEPARTURE 1

outgoing *adj* likely to seek or enjoy the company of others — see CONVIVIAL

outgrowth *n* **1** a branch of a main stem especially of a plant — see OFFSHOOT 1

2 a condition or occurrence traceable to a cause — see EFFECT 1

3 something that naturally develops or is developed from something else — see DERIVATIVE

outing *n* a short trip for pleasure — see EXCURSION 1

outlander *n* a person who is not native to or known to a community — see STRANGER

outlandish *adj* **1** different from the ordinary in a way that causes curiosity or suspicion — see ODD 2

2 excitingly or mysteriously unusual — see EXOTIC

outlast *vb* to last longer than ⟨I truly hope this car will *outlast* our previous one.⟩ ⟨Your work will probably *outlast* you.⟩

syn outlive, outwear

rel survive; outstay; abide (beyond), endure (past), hold (past), hold out (past), last (beyond), persist (beyond); draw out, perpetuate; succeed

outlaw *vb* to order not to do or use or to be done or used — see FORBID

outlawed *adj* that may not be permitted — see IMPERMISSIBLE

outlawing *n* the act of ordering that something not be done or used — see PROHIBITION 1

outlay *n* a payment made in the course of achieving a result — see EXPENSE

outlay *vb* to hand over or use up in payment — see SPEND 1

outlet *n* a place or means of going out — see EXIT 1

outline *n* **1** a line that traces the outer limits of an object or surface ⟨Place your hand on the paper and draw an *outline* around it.⟩

syn contour, figure, silhouette

rel delineation, sketch; profile, skyline; cast, configuration, conformation, form, geometry, shape; framework, skeleton

2 a short statement of the main points — see SUMMARY

outline *vb* **1** to draw or make apparent the outline of ⟨She carefully *outlined* the tree before she started drawing in the leaves.⟩

syn define, delineate, silhouette, sketch, trace

rel line; bound, fringe, margin, skirt; edge, hem, rim, trim; frame; circle, compass, encircle, girdle, girth, loop, ring, round, surround; chart, diagram, draw, map (out)

2 to make into a short statement of the main points (as of a report) — see SUMMARIZE

outlive *vb* to last longer than — see OUTLAST

outlook *n* **1** a high place or structure from which a wide view is possible — see LOOKOUT 1

2 a way of looking at or thinking about something — see PERSPECTIVE 1

3 all that can be seen from a certain point — see VIEW 1

out loud *adv* with one's normal voice speaking the words — see ALOUD

outmaneuver *vb* to get the better of through cleverness — see OUTWIT

outmoded *adj* having passed its time of use or usefulness — see OBSOLETE

outmost *adj* most distant from a center — see EXTREME 1

out-of-date *adj* having passed its time of use or usefulness — see OBSOLETE

out-of-door *or* **out-of-doors** *adj* of, relating to, or held in the open air — see OUTDOOR

out-of-doors *n* that part of the physical world that is removed from human habitation — see NATURE 2

out-of-the-way *adj* **1** different from the ordinary in a way that causes curiosity or suspicion — see ODD 2

2 noticeably different from what is generally found or experienced — see UNUSUAL 1

outpouring *n* a flowing or going out — see OUTFLOW

output *n* something produced by physical or intellectual effort — see PRODUCT 1

outrage *n* **1** an act or expression showing scorn and usually intended to hurt another's feelings — see INSULT

2 an intense emotional state of displeasure with someone or something — see ANGER
outrage vb **1** to cause hurt feelings or deep resentment in — see INSULT
2 to make angry — see ANGER
outraged adj feeling or showing anger — see ANGRY
outrank vb to be greater in importance than — see OUTWEIGH
outright adj having no exceptions or restrictions — see ABSOLUTE 2
outrun vb to go beyond the limit of — see EXCEED 1
outset n the point at which something begins — see BEGINNING
outshine vb to be greater, better, or stronger than — see SURPASS 1
outside adj **1** situated on the outside or farther out — see OUTER
2 small in degree — see REMOTE 1
3 of the greatest or highest degree or quantity — see ULTIMATE 1
outside adv in or into the open air — see OUTDOORS
outside n **1** an outer part or layer — see EXTERIOR
2 the greatest amount, number, or part — see MOST
3 the outward form of someone or something especially as indicative of a quality — see APPEARANCE 1
outside prep **1** not including — see EXCEPT
2 out of the reach or sphere of — see BEYOND 2
outside of prep **1** not including — see EXCEPT
2 out of the reach or sphere of — see BEYOND 2
outsider n a person who is not native to or known to a community — see STRANGER
outsize also **outsized** adj of a size greater than average of its kind — see LARGE
outskirts n pl the districts adjacent to a city — see ENVIRONS 1
outsmart vb to get the better of through cleverness — see OUTWIT
outspoken adj free in expressing one's true feelings and opinions — see FRANK
outspokenness n the free expression of one's true feelings and opinions — see CANDOR 1
outspread vb to arrange the parts of (something) over a wider area — see OPEN 3
outstanding adj **1** not yet paid ⟨There are several *outstanding* bills left, but at least we paid the rest.⟩
syn overdue, owed, owing, payable, unpaid, unsettled
rel due, mature
near ant prepaid
ant cleared, liquidated, paid (off *or* up), repaid, settled
2 standing above others in rank, importance, or achievement — see EMINENT
outstretch vb **1** to arrange the parts of (something) over a wider area — see OPEN 3
2 to make longer — see EXTEND 1
outstrip vb to be greater, better, or stronger than — see SURPASS 1

out–there adj deviating from commonly accepted beliefs or practices — see HERETICAL
outward adj situated on the outside or farther out — see OUTER
outward n outward and often deceptive indication — see APPEARANCE 2
outwear vb **1** to last longer than — see OUTLAST
2 to use up all the physical energy of — see EXHAUST 1
outweigh vb to be greater in importance than ⟨In most elections the state of the economy *outweighs* all other issues.⟩
syn outrank, overbalance, overshadow, overweigh
rel count, import, matter, mean, signify, weigh; dwarf; exceed, outstrip, surpass, transcend
outwit vb to get the better of through cleverness ⟨a plan to *outwit* their opponents at their own game⟩
syn fox, outfox, outmaneuver, outsmart, overreach
rel outguess, second-guess; baffle, balk, circumvent, foil, frustrate, thwart; cozen, deceive, dupe, fool, gull, trick; conquer, defeat, lick, overcome
outworn adj having passed its time of use or usefulness — see OBSOLETE
oval adj having the shape of an egg ⟨the *Oval* Office in the White House⟩
syn ovate, ovoid (*also* ovoidal)
ovate adj having the shape of an egg — see OVAL
ovation n enthusiastic and usually public expression of approval — see APPLAUSE 1
over adj brought or having come to an end — see COMPLETE 2
over adv **1** from one side to the other of an intervening space ⟨Let's swim *over* to that island.⟩
syn across, athwart, through
rel clear
2 yet another time — see AGAIN 1
3 to or in a higher place — see ABOVE
4 from beginning to end — see THROUGH 1
5 toward or in a lower position — see DOWN 1
over prep **1** higher than — see ABOVE
2 in the course of — see DURING
3 on or to the farther side of — see BEYOND 1
4 to the opposite side of — see ACROSS 1
5 in random positions within the boundaries of — see AROUND 2
overabundance n the state or an instance of going beyond what is usual, proper, or needed — see EXCESS
overactive adj being in a state of increased activity or agitation — see FEVERISH 1
overage n the state or an instance of going beyond what is usual, proper, or needed — see EXCESS
overall adj **1** belonging or relating to the whole — see GENERAL 1
2 relating to the main elements and not to specific details — see GENERAL 2
3 held by or applicable to a majority of the people — see GENERAL 3
overall adv **1** with everyone or everything taken into account at the same time — see ALL AROUND
2 for the most part — see CHIEFLY

---

syn synonym(s)   *rel* related words
ant antonym(s)   *near ant* near antonym(s)

over and above *prep* in addition to — see BESIDES 1

overbalance *vb* to be greater in importance than — see OUTWEIGH

overbear *vb* to achieve a victory over — see BEAT 2

overbearing *adj* 1 coming before all others in importance — see FOREMOST 1
2 fond of ordering people around — see BOSSY

overbold *adj* foolishly adventurous or bold — see FOOLHARDY 1

overburden *vb* to fill or load to excess — see OVERLOAD

overcast *adj* covered over by clouds ⟨The dark, *overcast* sky made the whole day seem depressing.⟩
syn beclouded, clouded, cloudy, dull, hazed, hazy, heavy, lowering (*also* louring), overclouded
rel bedimmed, befogged, blackened, darkened, dim, dimmed, dulled, dusky, misty, murky, obscure, obscured, overshadowed; black, bleak, cheerless, dark, desolate, dismal, dreary, funereal, gloomy, glum, gray (*also* grey), somber (*or* sombre), sullen
near ant sunlit, sunny, sunshiny; brightened, brilliant, dazzling, illuminated, illumined, lightened, radiant, shiny
ant clear, cloudless

overcast *vb* to make dark, dim, or indistinct — see CLOUD 1

overcharge *vb* 1 to charge (someone) too much for goods or services ⟨I think that store may have *overcharged* us for the shoes, which were supposed to be on sale.⟩
syn gouge, soak, sting, surcharge
rel cheat, defraud, stick; clip, fleece, skin; mischarge
ant undercharge
2 to fill or load to excess — see OVERLOAD

overcloud *vb* to make dark, dim, or indistinct — see CLOUD 1

overclouded *adj* covered over by clouds — see OVERCAST

overcoat *n* a warm outdoor coat ⟨Put your *overcoat* on—it's freezing out there!⟩
syn greatcoat, surcoat, topcoat
rel chesterfield, frock coat, mackinaw, ulster; jacket, parka, surtout; oilskin, raincoat, sou'wester; wrap
near ant undercoat

overcome *vb* 1 to achieve a victory over — see BEAT 2
2 to subject to incapacitating emotional or mental stress — see OVERWHELM 1

overconfident *adj* foolishly adventurous or bold — see FOOLHARDY 1

overcritical *adj* given to making or expressing unfavorable judgments about things — see CRITICAL 1

overdecorated *adj* elaborately and often excessively decorated — see ORNATE 1

overdo *vb* to describe or express in too strong terms — see OVERSTATE

overdraw *vb* to describe or express in too strong terms — see OVERSTATE

overdue *adj* 1 not arriving, occurring, or settled at the due, usual, or proper time — see LATE 1
2 not yet paid — see OUTSTANDING 1
3 going beyond a normal or acceptable

limit in degree or amount — see EXCESSIVE

overeat *vb* to eat greedily or to excess — see GORGE 2

overeater *n* one who eats greedily or too much — see GLUTTON

overestimate *vb* to place too high a value on ⟨The contractors *overestimated* their ability to do the work on such short notice.⟩
syn overrate, overvalue
rel appreciate, cherish, prize, treasure, value; admire, esteem, regard, respect; adore, idolize, revere, reverence, venerate, worship
near ant minimize, play down, soft-pedal; belittle, decry, depreciate, disparage; despise, disdain, scorn; abhor, abominate, detest, loathe

overfamiliar *adj* showing a lack of proper social reserve or modesty — see PRESUMPTUOUS 1

overfill *vb* 1 to fill or load to excess — see OVERLOAD
2 to flow over the brim or top of — see OVERFLOW 1

overflow *n* 1 a great flow of water or of something that overwhelms — see FLOOD 1
2 the state or an instance of going beyond what is usual, proper, or needed — see EXCESS

overflow *vb* 1 to flow over the brim or top of ⟨While the waiter stood there gawking at the nearby celebrity, my coffee was *overflowing* its cup and pouring onto our table.⟩
syn overfill
rel boil over, run over, spill, well (up); flow, flush, gush, pour, sluice, spout, spurt, stream; deluge, drown, engulf, flood, inundate, overwhelm, submerge, submerse, swamp; wash (over); brim, cascade, slop, slosh
near ant recede
2 to cover with a flood — see FLOOD 2
3 to be copiously supplied — see ABOUND

overgrown *adj* covered with a thick, healthy natural growth — see LUSH 1

overhang *n* a part that sticks out from the general mass of something — see BULGE 1

overhang *vb* 1 to extend outward beyond a usual point — see BULGE 1
2 to remain poised to inflict harm, danger, or distress on — see THREATEN

overhasty *adj* acting or done with excessive or careless speed — see HASTY 1

overhaul *vb* to move fast enough to get even with — see OVERTAKE

overhead *adv* to or in a higher place — see ABOVE

overhear *vb* to listen to (another in private conversation) — see EAVESDROP (ON)

overkill *n* the state or an instance of going beyond what is usual, proper, or needed — see EXCESS

overlap *n* a partial covering of one thing by an adjoining another ⟨The orthodontist will try to fix that *overlap* of two of your upper incisors.⟩
syn lapping
rel shingling; overlaying, overlying, overspreading

overlap *vb* to lie over parts of one another

⟨The brochures on the display table should *overlap* but not so much that the titles are obscured.⟩
syn lap, overlay, overlie, overspread
rel shingle

overlay *vb* **1** to form a layer over — see COVER 2
2 to lie over parts of one another — see OVERLAP

overlie *vb* **1** to lie over parts of one another — see OVERLAP
2 to form a layer over — see COVER 2

overload *vb* to fill or load to excess ⟨Try not to *overload* your backpack, or you could end up with back problems.⟩
syn overburden, overcharge, overfill
rel stuff; burden, charge, encumber, lade, load, lumber, saddle, weight
near ant lighten, unburden, unload

overlook *n* a high place or structure from which a wide view is possible — see LOOK-OUT 1

overlook *vb* **1** to look down on ⟨The fortress *overlooks* the city.⟩
syn command, dominate
rel face, front
2 to fail to give proper attention to — see NEGLECT 1
3 to be in charge of — see BOSS 1
4 to cast a spell on — see BEWITCH 1
5 to look over closely (as for judging quality or condition) — see INSPECT
6 to dismiss as of little importance — see EXCUSE 1
7 to look after and make decisions about — see CONDUCT 1

overly *adv* beyond a normal or acceptable limit — see TOO 1

overmatch *vb* to achieve a victory over — see BEAT 2

overmuch *adj* going beyond a normal or acceptable limit in degree or amount — see EXCESSIVE

overmuch *adv* beyond a normal or acceptable limit — see TOO 1

overmuch *n* the state or an instance of going beyond what is usual, proper, or needed — see EXCESS

overpass *vb* **1** to dismiss as of little importance — see EXCUSE 1
2 to go beyond the limit of — see EXCEED 1
3 to fail to give proper attention to — see NEGLECT 1

overpower *vb* **1** to bring under one's control by force of arms — see CONQUER 1
2 to subject to incapacitating emotional or mental stress — see OVERWHELM 1

overpowering *n* the act or process of bringing someone or something under one's control — see CONQUEST

overpraise *n* excessive praise — see FLATTERY

overpraise *vb* to praise too much — see FLATTER 1

overrate *vb* to place too high a value on — see OVERESTIMATE

overreach *vb* **1** to get the better of through cleverness — see OUTWIT
2 to go beyond the limit of — see EXCEED 1

overripe *adj* having lost forcefulness, courage, or spirit — see EFFETE 1

overrun *vb* **1** to enter for conquest or plunder — see INVADE
2 to go beyond the limit of — see EXCEED 1
3 to spread or swarm over in a troublesome manner — see INFEST

oversee *vb* **1** to look after and make decisions about — see CONDUCT 1
2 to be in charge of — see BOSS 1
3 to take charge of especially on behalf of another — see ²TEND 1
4 to look over closely (as for judging quality or condition) — see INSPECT

overshadow *vb* **1** to make dark, dim, or indistinct — see CLOUD 1
2 to be greater in importance than — see OUTWEIGH

overshoot *vb* to go beyond the limit of — see EXCEED 1

oversight *n* **1** the act or activity of looking after and making decisions about something — see CONDUCT 1
2 an unintentional departure from truth or accuracy — see ERROR 1
3 the duty or function of watching or guarding for the sake of proper direction or control — see SUPERVISION 1
4 the nonperformance of an assigned or expected action — see FAILURE 1

oversize *or* **oversized** *adj* of a size greater than average of its kind — see LARGE

overspread *vb* **1** to form a layer over — see COVER 2
2 to lie over parts of one another — see OVERLAP

overstate *vb* to describe or express in too strong terms ⟨It appears you've somewhat *overstated* your computer skills, if you can't find the "on" button!⟩
syn exaggerate, overdo, overdraw, put on
rel color, elaborate, embellish, embroider, magnify, pad, stretch; fudge, hedge; overemphasize, overplay, sensationalize
near ant belittle, minimize, play down
ant understate

overstatement *n* the representation of something in terms that go beyond the facts — see EXAGGERATION

overstep *vb* to go beyond the limit of — see EXCEED 1

oversupply *n* the state or an instance of going beyond what is usual, proper, or needed — see EXCESS

overtake *vb* to move fast enough to get even with ⟨She had to hurry to *overtake* her friends, who had forgotten their umbrellas.⟩ ⟨The thunderstorm *overtook* them suddenly.⟩
syn catch, catch up (with), overhaul
rel chase, pursue; gain, reach; pass, surpass
near ant fall short

overthrow *n* failure to win a contest — see DEFEAT 1

overtop *vb* to be greater, better, or stronger than — see SURPASS 1

overturn *vb* to turn on one's side or upside down — see CAPSIZE

overvalue *vb* to place too high a value on — see OVERESTIMATE

overweening *adj* **1** having too high an opinion of oneself — see CONCEITED

---

syn synonym(s)   **rel** related words
ant antonym(s)   **near ant** near antonym(s)

2 going beyond a normal or acceptable limit in degree or amount — see EXCESSIVE

3 having a feeling of superiority that shows itself in an overbearing attitude — see ARROGANT

overweigh *vb* to be greater in importance than — see OUTWEIGH

overweight *adj* having an excess of body fat — see FAT 1

overwhelm *vb* **1** to subject to incapacitating emotional or mental stress ⟨Just the thought of how much work there is to do *overwhelms* me.⟩

syn crush, devastate, floor, oppress, overcome, overpower, prostrate, snow under, swamp, whelm

rel deluge, drown, sink; confute, defeat, refute; break, demoralize, distress, disturb, rock, shatter, stagger, throw, unman, unnerve, upset

2 to cover with a flood — see FLOOD

overwrought *adj* **1** being in a state of increased activity or agitation — see FEVERISH 1

2 elaborately and often excessively decorated — see ORNATE 1

ovoid *adj* having the shape of an egg — see OVAL

owed *adj* not yet paid — see OUTSTANDING 1

owing *adj* not yet paid — see OUTSTANDING 1

owing to *prep* as the result of — see BECAUSE OF

own *vb* to keep, control, or experience as one's own — see HAVE 1

own (up to) *vb* to accept the truth or existence of (something) usually reluctantly — see ADMIT 1

owner *n* one who has a legal or rightful claim to ownership — see PROPRIETOR

pa *n* a male human parent — see FATHER 1

pace *vb* **1** to move along with a steady regular step especially in a group — see MARCH 1

2 to move forward along a course — see GO 1

pacific *adj* **1** tending to lessen or avoid conflict or hostility ⟨As a *pacific* gesture, we invited our feuding neighbors to our backyard barbecue.⟩

syn appeasing, conciliating, conciliatory, disarming, mollifying, pacifying, peacemaking, placating, propitiatory

rel endearing, ingratiating, winning, winsome; peaceable, peaceful; nonbelligerent, unaggressive, unassertive; calming, comforting, lulling, quieting, relaxing, soothing, tranquilizing (*also* tranquillizing); obliging, satisfying; affable, agreeable, amiable, amicable, benevolent, genial, gentle, good-natured, good-tempered, kind, kindly; passive, submissive, yielding

near ant aggravating, annoying, chafing, exasperating, frustrating, galling, irksome, irritating, nettling, provoking, rankling, riling, vexing; incensing, infuriating, maddening; antagonistic, antipathetic, hostile, inhospitable, inimical, unfriendly, unsympathetic; aggressive, agonistic, argumentative, assertive, bellicose, belligerent, combative, contentious, pugnacious, quarrelsome, scrappy, truculent; martial, militant, militaristic, warlike

ant antagonizing

2 inclined to live in peace and to avoid war — see PEACEFUL 1

pacifist *n* a person who opposes war or warlike policies — see DOVE 1

pacifist *or* **pacifistic** *adj* inclined to live in peace and to avoid war — see PEACEFUL 1

pacify *vb* **1** to lessen the anger or agitation of ⟨I tried to *pacify* the crying child.⟩

syn appease, assuage, conciliate, disarm, gentle, mollify, placate, propitiate

rel calm, comfort, console, content, hush, quiet, soothe, tranquilize (*also* tranquillize); endear (to), ingratiate; delight, gladden, gratify, please; cater (to), humor, indulge; blandish, cajole, coax, wheedle; baby, coddle, mollycoddle, pamper, spoil

near ant aggravate, annoy, antagonize, bother, bug, chafe, cross, exasperate, gall, get, grate, irk, irritate, nettle, peeve, pique, put out, rankle, rile, roil, ruffle, vex; provoke, rouse; harry, persecute, pester; agitate, discomfort, distress, disturb, fret, perturb, unhinge, unsettle, upset, worry; affront, insult, offend, slight

ant anger, enrage, incense, inflame (*also* enflame), infuriate, ire, madden, outrage

2 to bring under one's control by force of arms — see CONQUER 1

pacifying *adj* **1** tending to calm the emotions and relieve stress — see SOOTHING 1

2 tending to lessen or avoid conflict or hostility — see PACIFIC 1

pack *n* **1** a soft-sided case designed for carrying belongings especially on the back ⟨Part of basic training is becoming accustomed to taking very long hikes with an 80-pound *pack*.⟩

syn backpack, knapsack, rucksack

rel haversack; carryall, grip, handbag, suitcase, traveling bag, fanny pack, school bag, seabag; overnight bag, overnight case, weekend bag

2 a wrapped or sealed case containing an item or set of items — see PACKAGE 1

3 a considerable amount — see LOT 2

4 a group of people sharing a common interest and relating together socially — see GANG 2

pack *vb* **1** to close up so that no empty spaces remain — see FILL 2

2 to put into (something) as much as can be held or contained — see FILL 1

3 to support and take from one place to another — see CARRY 1

4 to wear or have on one's person — see CARRY 2

pack (off) *vb* to cause to go or be taken from one place to another — see SEND

package *n* **1** a wrapped or sealed case containing an item or set of items ⟨Bill got a job sorting *packages* in the mail room.⟩

syn bundle, pack, packet, parcel

rel bag, poke [*chiefly Southern & Midland*], pouch, sack; bale; box, container, crate

2 a number of things considered as a unit — see GROUP 1

packed *adj* **1** containing or seeming to contain the greatest quantity or number possible — see FULL 1

2 having little space between items or parts — see CLOSE 1

packet *n* a wrapped or sealed case containing an item or set of items — see PACKAGE 1

pact *n* **1** a formal agreement between two or more nations or peoples — see TREATY

2 an arrangement about action to be taken — see AGREEMENT 2

pad *n* **1** a number of sheets of writing paper glued together at one edge ⟨We'll need to buy a new *pad* for telephone messages soon.⟩

syn notepad, tablet

rel scratch pad; album, notebook, scrapbook; booklet, pamphlet

2 a place set aside for sleeping — see BED 1

3 something that serves as a protective barrier — see CUSHION

4 the place where one lives — see HOME 1

¹**pad** *vb* to add to the interest of by including made-up details — see EMBROIDER

²**pad** *vb* to go on foot — see WALK 1

padding *n* **1** soft material that is used to fill the hollow parts of something — see FILLING

2 the representation of something in terms that go beyond the facts — see EXAGGERATION

paddle *vb* **1** to move a boat by means of oars — see ¹ROW

2 to strike repeatedly — see BEAT 1

paean *n* a formal expression of praise — see ENCOMIUM

pagan *n* a person who does not worship the God of the Bible — see HEATHEN 1

page *n* one that carries a message or does an errand — see MESSENGER

pageant *n* a staged presentation often with music that consists of a procession of narrated or enacted scenes ⟨We always put on a Christmas *pageant* every year.⟩

syn cavalcade

rel tableau; kaleidoscope, montage, panorama; drama, dramatization, play; demonstration, performance, presentation, production; exhibition, show; parade, procession, progress

pail *n* a round container that is open at the top and outfitted with a handle ⟨Fetch me a *pail* full of water, please.⟩

syn bucket

rel cauldron, kettle, pot; canteen, flagon,

jar, jug, pitcher; hod; tub, vat; holder, receptacle, vessel

pain *n* **1** a sharp unpleasant sensation usually felt in some specific part of the body ⟨The child was crying because of a *pain* in her knee.⟩

syn ache, pang, prick, shoot, smart, sting, stitch, throe, tingle, twinge

rel discomfort, distress, soreness; affliction, agony, anguish, misery, sufferance, suffering, torment, torture; inflammation, sore, swelling; damage, detriment, harm, hurt, injury; backache, bellyache, charley horse, colic, complaint, earache, gripe, headache, stomachache, toothache

near ant comfort, ease, easiness

2 a state of great suffering of body or mind — see DISTRESS 1

3 pains *pl* strict attentiveness to what one is doing — see CARE 1

4 pains *pl* the active use of energy in producing a result — see EFFORT

5 one who is obnoxiously annoying — see NUISANCE 1

pain *vb* to feel or cause physical pain — see HURT 1

painful *adj* **1** causing or feeling bodily pain ⟨Her broken arm was too *painful* for her to go on the trip.⟩

syn aching, achy, hurting, nasty, sore

rel agonizing, excruciating, torturous; damaging, deleterious, detrimental, harmful, hurtful, injurious, noxious, pernicious; raw, tender; bleeding, burning, chafing, cramping; itching, pinching, pricking, prickling, smarting, stinging; inflamed (*also* enflamed); grievous, severe, threatening, wounding

near ant healing, helping, remedial

ant indolent, painless

2 hard to accept or bear especially emotionally — see BITTER 2

painfully *adv* with feelings of bitterness or grief — see HARD 2

painkiller *n* something (as a drug) that relieves pain ⟨I took an over-the-counter *painkiller* for my headache.⟩

syn analgesic, anesthetic

rel sedative, tranquilizer (*also* tranquillizer); narcotic, opiate

painless *adj* involving minimal difficulty or effort — see EASY 1

painlessly *adv* without difficulty — see EASILY 1

painstaking *adj* taking, showing, or involving great care and effort ⟨She was always *painstaking* about her work.⟩

syn careful, conscientious, fussy, loving, meticulous, scrupulous

rel assiduous, diligent, indefatigable, persevering, sedulous; exhaustive, thorough, thoroughgoing; alert, attentive, observant, vigilant, watchful; accurate, exact, precise, strict; critical, demanding, discriminating, exacting, fastidious, finicky, particular; cautious, circumspect, gingerly, guarded, heedful, mindful, wary; deliberate, plodding, slow; studied, thoughtful; all-out, determined, dogged, intensive, patient, tenacious, tireless, zealous

near ant cursory, halfhearted; heedless, inattentive, incautious, mindless, unguarded, unsafe, unwary; lax, neglectful,

---

syn synonym(s)　　**rel** related words
ant antonym(s)　　**near ant** near antonym(s)

negligent, slipshod, sloppy, slovenly; imprecise; inaccurate, uncritical, undemanding, undiscriminating; bold, impetuous, rash, reckless; apathetic, indifferent, lackadaisical, lazy

ant careless

paint *n* preparations intended to beautify the face — see MAKEUP 1

paint *vb* 1 to give a representation or account of in words — see DESCRIBE 1

2 to give color or a different color to — see COLOR 1

painting *n* a picture created with oil paint ⟨The *Mona Lisa* is a haunting *painting* of a woman with a most mysterious smile.⟩

syn canvas (*also* canvass), oil, oil painting *rel* fresco, mural, panorama; diptych, triptych; drawing, etching, finger painting, pastel, sketch, tempera; masterpiece; pièce de résistance, showpiece

pair *n* two things of the same or similar kind that match or are considered together ⟨a *pair* of blue socks⟩ ⟨The cheerleader and the computer nerd make quite a *pair* together.⟩

syn brace, couple, duo, twain, twosome *rel* span, yoke; partnership, team; companion, complement, doublet, fellow, half, match, mate, twin; coordinate, counterpart, equal, equivalent, like, parallel, peer, rival

pal *n* a person who has a strong liking for and trust in another — see FRIEND 1

pal (around) *vb* to come or be together as friends — see ASSOCIATE 1

palace *n* 1 a large impressive residence — see MANSION

2 a large, magnificent, or massive building — see EDIFICE 1

3 the residence of a ruler — see COURT 1

paladin *n* a person who actively supports or favors a cause — see EXPONENT 1

palatability *n* the quality of being delicious — see DELICIOUSNESS

palatable *adj* 1 being to one's liking — see SATISFACTORY 1

2 giving pleasure or contentment to the mind or senses — see PLEASANT 1

3 very pleasing to the sense of taste — see DELICIOUS 1

palatial *adj* showing obvious signs of wealth and comfort — see LUXURIOUS

palatially *adv* in a luxurious manner — see HIGH

palaver *n* 1 an exchange of views for the purpose of exploring a subject or deciding an issue — see DISCUSSION 1

2 friendly, informal conversation or an instance of this — see CHAT 1

palaver *vb* 1 to engage in casual or rambling conversation — see CHAT 1

2 to get (someone) to do something by gentle urging, special attention, or flattery — see COAX

pale *adj* 1 lacking intensity of color ⟨We chose a very *pale* pink for the walls of the room.⟩

syn dull, dulled, faded, light, pastel, washed-out

rel flat, lackluster, lusterless, matte (*also* mat *or* matt); dim, faint; dirty, muddy; achromatic, colorless, uncolored, undyed, unpainted, unstained; blanched, bleached,

washed, white, whitened; gray (*also* grey), indistinct, neutral

near ant bright, brilliant, vibrant, vivid; dyed, painted, stained, tinged, tinted; colorful, motley, multicolored, polychromatic, polychrome, varicolored, variegated; flashy, garish, gaudy, loud, showy, splashy

ant dark, deep, rich

2 lacking a healthy skin color ⟨After a week with the flu, she was deathly *pale* and noticeably thinner.⟩

syn ashen, ashy, blanched, cadaverous, livid, lurid, mealy, paled, pallid, pasty, peaked, wan

rel sallow, sallowish, sick, sickly, waxen; white, whitened; anemic, bloodless; untanned; whey-faced, white-faced

near ant blushing, flushed

ant blooming, florid, flush, full-blooded, glowing, red, rosy, rubicund, ruddy, sanguine

3 not seen or understood clearly — see FAINT 1

pale *vb* to make white or whiter by removing color — see WHITEN

paled *adj* lacking a healthy skin color — see PALE 2

palisade *n* a steep wall of rock, earth, or ice — see CLIFF

pall *n* 1 a boxlike container for holding a dead body — see COFFIN

2 an overspreading element that produces an atmosphere of gloom — see CLOUD

3 something that covers or conceals like a piece of cloth — see CLOAK 1

pall *vb* to grow less in scope or intensity especially gradually — see DECREASE 2

palliate *vb* 1 to make (something) seem less bad by offering excuses ⟨Don't try to *palliate* your constant lying by claiming that everybody lies.⟩

syn excuse, explain away, extenuate, gloss (over), gloze (over), whitewash

rel sugarcoat, varnish; apologize, atone, confess; account (for), explain, justify, rationalize; minimize, play down, soft-pedal; alleviate, ease, lessen, lighten, mitigate, moderate, soften, temper; absolve, acquit, clear, exculpate, exonerate, vindicate

2 to make more bearable or less severe — see HELP 2

pallid *adj* lacking a healthy skin color — see PALE 2

palm off *vb* to offer (something fake, useless, or inferior) as genuine, useful, or valuable — see FOIST

palmy *adj* 1 having attained a desired end or state of good fortune — see SUCCESSFUL 1

2 marked by vigorous growth and well-being especially economically — see PROSPEROUS 1

palpable *adj* 1 able to be perceived by a sense or by the mind — see PERCEPTIBLE

2 capable of being perceived by the sense of touch — see TANGIBLE

3 not subject to misinterpretation or more than one interpretation — see CLEAR 2

palpitate *vb* to expand and contract in a rhythmic manner — see PULSATE

palpitation *n* a rhythmic expanding and contracting — see PULSATION

palsy *adj* having or showing kindly feeling and sincere interest — see FRIENDLY 1

palsy *n* complete or partial loss of physical function (as motion or sensation) in a part of the body — see PARALYSIS

palter *vb* to talk over or dispute the terms of a purchase — see BARGAIN 1

paltry *adj* 1 arousing or deserving of one's loathing and disgust — see CONTEMPTIBLE 1

2 falling short of a standard — see BAD 1

3 not following or in accordance with standards of honor and decency — see IGNOBLE 2

4 so small or unimportant as to warrant little or no attention — see NEGLIGIBLE 1

pamper *vb* to treat with great or excessive care — see BABY

pamphlet *n* a short printed publication with no cover or with a paper cover ⟨*pamphlets* about common safety precautions that we all can put into use⟩

syn booklet, brochure, circular, folder, leaflet

rel dodger, flysheet, handbill, handout, throwaway; advertisement, catalog (*or* catalogue), shopper; tract; paperback, paperbound, pocket book; guidebook, handbook, how-to, instructions, manual

pan *vb* to express one's unfavorable opinion of the worth or quality of — see CRITICIZE

panacea *n* something that cures all ills or problems — see CURE-ALL

pancake *n* a flat cake made from thin batter and cooked on both sides (as on a griddle) ⟨Every Sunday morning, we have *pancakes* and bacon for breakfast.⟩

syn flapjack, griddle cake, hotcake, slapjack

rel oatcake, wheat cake; blin, blintze (*or* blintz), crepe (*or* crêpe)

pandemonium *n* 1 a state of noisy, confused activity — see COMMOTION

2 *cap* the place of punishment for the wicked after death — see HELL 1

panegyric *n* a formal expression of praise — see ENCOMIUM

panel *n* 1 a meeting featuring a group discussion — see FORUM 1

2 a select group of persons assigned to consider or take action on some matter — see COMMITTEE

pang *n* a sharp unpleasant sensation usually felt in some specific part of the body — see PAIN 1

panhandler *n* a person who lives by public begging — see BEGGAR

panic *n* the emotion experienced in the presence or threat of danger — see FEAR 1

panic *vb* to strike with fear — see FRIGHTEN

panorama *n* all that can be seen from a certain point — see VIEW 1

panoramic *adj* covering everything or all important points — see ENCYCLOPEDIC

pan out *vb* 1 to come to be — see COME OUT 1

2 to turn out as planned or desired — see SUCCEED 1

pant *vb* to breathe hard, quickly, or with difficulty — see GASP

pant (after) *vb* to have an earnest wish to own or enjoy — see DESIRE 1

pantaloons *n pl* an outer garment covering each leg separately from waist to ankle — see PANTS

panther *n* a large tawny cat of the wild — see COUGAR

pantomime *n* 1 a movement of the body or limbs that expresses or emphasizes an idea or feeling — see GESTURE 1

2 an actor in a story performed silently and entirely by body movements — see MIME 1

pantomimist *n* an actor in a story performed silently and entirely by body movements — see MIME 1

pants *n pl* an outer garment covering each leg separately from waist to ankle ⟨You'll need a nice pair of *pants* for the job interview.⟩

syn breeches, britches, pantaloons, slacks, trousers

rel baggies, bell-bottoms, blue jeans; cargo pants, cords, corduroys, denims, jeans; hose, legging (*or* leggin); sweatpants; pants suit, pantsuit; bloomers, knee breeches, knickerbockers

papa *also* **poppa** *n* a male human parent — see FATHER 1

paper *adj* being something in name or form only — see NOMINAL 1

paper *n* 1 a piece of paper with information written or to be written on it — see FORM 2

2 a publication that appears at regular intervals — see JOURNAL

3 a short piece of writing done as a school exercise — see COMPOSITION 2

4 a short piece of writing typically expressing a point of view — see ESSAY 1

par *n* 1 something set up as an example against which others of the same type are compared — see STANDARD 1

2 the state or fact of being exactly the same in number, amount, status, or quality — see EQUIVALENCE

3 what is typical of a group, class, or series — see AVERAGE

parable *n* a story intended to teach a basic truth or moral about life — see ALLEGORY

parade *n* a body of individuals moving along in an orderly and often ceremonial way — see CORTEGE 2

parade *vb* 1 to move along with a steady regular step especially in a group — see MARCH 1

2 to present so as to invite notice or attention — see SHOW 1

paradigmatic *adj* constituting, serving as, or worthy of being a pattern to be imitated — see MODEL

paradise *n* 1 an often imaginary place or state of utter perfection and happiness ⟨an idealist who trotted the globe looking for *paradise*⟩

syn Eden, Elysium, heaven, promised land, utopia

rel arcadia; dreamland, dreamworld, fairyland, wonderland

phrases Garden of Eden

near ant fool's paradise

ant hell

---

syn synonym(s)   *rel* related words
ant antonym(s)   *near ant* near antonym(s)

2 a dwelling place of perfect happiness for the soul after death — see HEAVEN 1

3 a state of overwhelming usually pleasurable emotion — see ECSTASY

paradox *n* someone or something with qualities or features that seem to conflict with one another — see CONTRADICTION 1

paragon *n* someone of such unequaled perfection as to deserve imitation — see IDEAL 1

parallel *adj* having qualities in common — see ALIKE

parallel *n* **1** a point which two or more things share in common — see SIMILARITY 2

2 one that is equal to another in status, achievement, or value — see EQUAL

parallel *vb* to be the exact counterpart of — see MATCH 1

parallelism *n* the quality or state of having many qualities in common — see SIMILARITY 1

paralysis *n* complete or partial loss of physical function (as motion or sensation) in a part of the body ⟨a tick bite that can result in a dog's *paralysis*⟩

syn palsy

rel cerebral palsy, multiple sclerosis, poliomyelitis; debilitation, debility, decrepitude, enfeeblement, feebleness, frailness, frailty, weakness; infirmity, lameness; disability, impairment; paraplegia, paresis, quadriplegia, spastic paralysis

near ant mobility, motility, sensation

paralytic *adj* affected with paralysis ⟨Animals with rabies eventually enter a *paralytic* stage.⟩

syn paralyzed

rel challenged, crippled, disabled, maimed, mutilated; halt, hobbled, lame, lamed; impaired, incapacitated; paraplegic, paretic, quadriplegic; debilitated, decrepit, enfeebled, feeble, frail, infirm, wasted, weak, weakened

near ant able-bodied; fit, hale, healthy, hearty, robust, sound, well, whole

paralyze *vb* **1** to render powerless, ineffective, or unable to move ⟨A blizzard *paralyzed* the city for two days.⟩

syn cripple, disable, hamstring, immobilize, incapacitate, prostrate

rel debilitate, enervate, enfeeble, sap, tire, undercut, undermine, weaken; hobble, lame; maim, mutilate

near ant energize, galvanize, invigorate, vitalize; fortify, strengthen; empower; freshen, refresh, refreshen, regenerate, rejuvenate, restore, revitalize, revive

2 to deprive of courage or confidence — see UNNERVE 1

paralyzed *adj* **1** affected with paralysis — see PARALYTIC

2 unable to act or achieve one's purpose — see POWERLESS 1

paramount *adj* **1** coming before all others in importance — see FOREMOST 1

2 of the greatest or highest degree or quantity — see ULTIMATE 1

paraphernalia *n* **1** items needed for the performance of a task or activity — see EQUIPMENT

2 transportable items that one owns — see POSSESSION 2

paraphrase *n* an instance of expressing something in different words ⟨Your essays on human rights should have some original thought and not be simply a *paraphrase* of what's in the textbook.⟩

syn rephrasing, restatement, restating, rewording, translating, translation

rel rehash; abstract, recap, recapitulation, reiteration, summary

near ant copy, transcript, transcription

ant quotation, quote

paraphrase *vb* to express something (as a text or statement) in different words ⟨Could you *paraphrase* your diagnosis of my medical condition, using simpler language?⟩

syn rephrase, restate, reword, translate

rel recapitulate, reiterate, summarize, sum up

near ant echo, repeat; copy, reproduce, transcribe

ant quote

parasite *n* a person who is supported by or seeks support from another without making an adequate return — see LEECH

parboil *vb* to cook in a liquid heated to the point that it gives off steam — see BOIL 2

parcel *n* **1** a number of things considered as a unit — see GROUP 1

2 a small area of usually open land — see FIELD 1

3 a small piece of land that is developed or available for development — see LOT 1

4 a usually small number of persons considered as a unit — see GROUP 2

5 a wrapped or sealed case containing an item or set of items — see PACKAGE 1

parcel (out) *vb* to give out (something) to appropriate individuals — see ADMINISTER 1

parcel post *n* communications or parcels sent or carried through the postal system — see MAIL

parch *vb* to make dry — see DRY 1

pardon *n* release from the guilt or penalty of an offense ⟨The criminal is hoping for a presidential *pardon*.⟩

syn absolution, amnesty, forgiveness, remission, remittal

rel parole; acquittal, exculpation, exoneration, vindication; condonation; exemption, immunity, impunity, indemnity; commutation, commuting, reprieve; clemency, leniency, mercy

near ant conviction, sentence; assessment, charge, fine, imposition, levying; castigation, chastening, chastisement, condemnation

ant penalty, punishment, retribution

pardon *vb* **1** to cease to have feelings of anger or bitterness toward — see FORGIVE 1

2 to dismiss as of little importance — see EXCUSE 1

pardonable *adj* worthy of forgiveness — see VENIAL

pare *vb* to make (something) shorter or smaller with the use of a cutting instrument — see CLIP 1

parentage *n* the line of ancestors from whom a person is descended — see ANCESTRY

parenthood *n* the caring for a child by its parents — see PARENTING

parenting *n* the caring for a child by its

parents ⟨As the big day approaches, the expectant couple are starting to get worried about their readiness for *parenting*.⟩
syn parenthood
rel raising, rearing, upbringing; fatherhood, fathering, paternity; maternity, motherhood, mothering; caregiving, caretaking

par excellence *adj* of the very best kind — see EXCELLENT

pariah *n* one who is cast out or rejected by society — see OUTCAST

parity *n* the state or fact of being exactly the same in number, amount, status, or quality — see EQUIVALENCE

park *n* the area around and belonging to a building — see GROUND 1

parley *n* **1** a meeting featuring a group discussion — see FORUM 1
2 an exchange of views for the purpose of exploring a subject or deciding an issue — see DISCUSSION 1

parley *vb* to exchange viewpoints or seek advice for the purpose of finding a solution to a problem — see CONFER 2

parliament *n* the highest lawmaking body of a political unit — see CONGRESS 1

parlor *n* a building, room, or suite of rooms occupied by a service business — see PLACE 2

parlous *adj* involving potential loss or injury — see DANGEROUS 1

parochial *adj* not broad or open in views or opinions — see NARROW 2

parody *n* **1** a work that imitates and exaggerates another work for comic effect ⟨The musical is a *parody* of every biblical epic ever made.⟩
syn burlesque, caricature, put-on, spoof, takeoff, travesty
rel lampoon, mockery, satire; comedy, farce, humor, sketch, slapstick, squib; distortion, exaggeration; imitation, impersonation, mimicking
2 a poor, insincere, or insulting imitation of something — see MOCKERY 1

parody *vb* to copy or exaggerate (someone or something) in order to make fun of — see MIMIC 1

paroxysm *n* **1** a sudden intense expression of strong feeling — see OUTBURST 1
2 a violent disturbance (as of the political or social order) — see CONVULSION 1

parrot *vb* to say after another — see REPEAT 3

parsimonious *adj* giving or sharing as little as possible — see STINGY 1

parsimony *n* **1** the quality or practice of being overly sparing with money ⟨Her *parsimony* was so extreme that she'd walk five miles to the store to save a few cents on gas.⟩
syn cheapness, closeness, miserliness, penuriousness, pinching, stinginess, tightness
rel conserving, economizing, economy, frugality, husbandry, providence, scrimping, skimping, thrift; conservation, saving; husbanding, managing
near ant bountifulness, bounty, generosi-

ty, largesse (*also* largess), liberality, open-handedness, openheartedness, philanthropy, unselfishness; extravagance, lavishness; dissipation, improvidence, prodigality, squandering, wastefulness
2 careful management of material resources — see ECONOMY

part *adv* in some measure or degree — see PARTLY

part *n* **1** one of the pieces from which something is designed to be assembled ⟨The model car came in several small *parts* that had to be put together.⟩
syn member, partition, portion, section, segment
rel component, constituent, element, factor, ingredient, parcel; bit, fragment, particle, scrap
near ant whole; aggregate, composite, compound, sum, total, totality
2 something belonging to, due to, or contributed by an individual member of a group — see SHARE 1
3 the action for which a person or thing is specially fitted or used or for which a thing exists — see ROLE
4 *usually* **parts** *pl* a broad geographical area — see REGION 2

part *vb* **1** to go or move in different directions from a central point — see SEPARATE 2
2 to leave a place often for another — see GO 2
3 to set or force apart — see SEPARATE 1
4 to stop living — see DIE 1

partake *vb* **1** to take a share or part ⟨We should all *partake* of the city's rich cultural offerings while we have the opportunity.⟩
syn participate, share
rel endure, experience, feel, know, see, taste, undergo; encounter, meet; accept
2 to take a meal — see DINE 1

partaker *n* one who takes part in something — see PARTICIPANT

partial *adj* **1** inclined to favor one side over another ⟨That judge is always *partial* to the defense, so be careful.⟩
syn biased, one-sided, partisan, prejudiced
rel hostile, inimical, jaundiced, unfriendly, unsympathetic; distorted, misrepresented, shaded, warped
near ant open, open-minded, persuasible, receptive; aloof, detached, dispassionate, hardheaded, impersonal, unemotional; cold, distant, remote; apathetic, incurious, indifferent, unconcerned, uncurious, unenthusiastic, uninterested
ant disinterested, equal, equitable, even-handed, fair, impartial, neutral, nonpartisan, objective, unbiased, unprejudiced
2 having a liking or affection — see FOND 1
3 lacking some necessary part — see INCOMPLETE

partiality *n* **1** an attitude that always favors one way of feeling or acting especially without considering any other possibilities — see BIAS 1
2 a habitual attraction to some activity or thing — see INCLINATION 1
3 positive regard for something — see LIKING

partially *adv* in some measure or degree — see PARTLY

participant *n* one who takes part in something ⟨He seemed to be a willing *participant* in the prank.⟩

syn actor, partaker, participator, party, player, sharer

rel accessory (*also* accessary), aide, assistant, helper; colleague, partner

near ant looker-on, watcher

ant nonparticipant

participate *vb* to take a share or part — see PARTAKE 1

participator *n* one who takes part in something — see PARTICIPANT

particle *n* 1 a very small amount ⟨There was not a *particle* of truth in what she said.⟩

syn ace, bit, crumb, dab, driblet, glimmer, hint, lick, little, mite, nip, ounce, peanuts, ray, scruple, shade, shadow, shred, smack, smidgen (*also* smidgeon *or* smidgin *or* smidge), snap, spark, spatter, speck, splash, spot, sprinkling, strain, streak, suspicion, tad, touch, trace

rel hoot, iota, jot, minim, minimum, modicum, semblance, tittle, vestige, whit; atom, dot, fleck, flyspeck, grain, granule, molecule, morsel, mote, nubbin, patch, scrap; dash, drop, pinch; part, portion, section; bite, nibble, taste; handful, scattering, smattering; dose, shot

phrases drop in the bucket

near ant abundance, barrel, boatload, bucket, bundle, bushel, deal, gobs, heaps, loads, lot, mass, mess, mountain, much, oodles, passel, peck, pile, plenty, potful, profusion, quantity, raft, reams, scads, stack, wad, wealth; volume; chunk, hunk, lump, slab

2 a very small piece — see BIT 1

particular *adj* 1 hard to please — see FINICKY

2 of, relating to, or belonging to a single person — see INDIVIDUAL 1

3 tending to select carefully — see SELECTIVE

4 including many small descriptive features — see DETAILED 1

particular *n* 1 a separate part in a list, account, or series — see ITEM 1

2 a single piece of information — see FACT 1

particularity *n* 1 careful thoroughness of detail ⟨With great *particularity* she described the scene.⟩

syn explicitness, specificity

rel attentiveness, care, carefulness, conscientiousness, finicalness, finickiness, fussiness, meticulousness, meticulosity; alertness, cautiousness, circumspection, heedfulness, scrupulousness; discrimination, selectivity; accuracy, definitude, exactitude, exactness, fineness, preciseness, precision

near ant imprecision, inaccuracy, inexactness; indistinctness, vagueness

ant generality

2 a single piece of information — see FACT 1

3 something that sets apart an individual from others of the same kind — see CHARACTERISTIC

particularized *adj* including many small descriptive features — see DETAILED 1

particularly *adv* 1 in the specific case of one person or thing as distinguished from others — see ESPECIALLY 1

2 to a great degree — see VERY 1

parting *adj* given, taken, or performed at parting ⟨She gave him a *parting* gift to remember her by.⟩

syn farewell, valedictory

rel closing, concluding, final, last, ultimate; departing, leaving

parting *n* 1 the act or process of two or more persons going off in different directions ⟨Although their *parting* was sad, they knew they would see each other again.⟩

syn farewell, leave-taking, separation

rel departure, exit, exiting, exodus, going, leaving, quitting, running away; decamping, decampment, flight, withdrawal; abandonment, desertion, forsaking

near ant reunion; arrival, greeting, salutation, welcome; gathering, joining, meeting

2 the act of leaving a place — see DEPARTURE 1

partisan *adj* inclined to favor one side over another — see PARTIAL 1

partisan *also* **partizan** *n* 1 one who follows the opinions or teachings of another — see FOLLOWER 1

2 one who is intensely or excessively devoted to a cause — see ZEALOT

3 one who stubbornly or intolerantly adheres to his or her own opinions and prejudices — see BIGOT

partisanship *n* an attitude that always favors one way of feeling or acting especially without considering any other possibilities — see BIAS 1

partition *n* 1 one of the pieces from which something is designed to be assembled — see PART 1

2 something that divides, separates, or marks off — see DIVISION 1

3 the act or process of a whole separating into two or more parts or pieces — see SEPARATION 1

partly *adv* in some measure or degree ⟨You're only *partly* right.⟩

syn half, halfway, incompletely, part, partially

rel fairly, kind of, like, moderately, more or less, pretty, quite, rather, relatively, somewhat, sort of

phrases in part

near ant absolutely, dead, downright, plain; especially, exceedingly (*also* exceeding), exceptionally, extremely, greatly, highly, hugely, particularly, very

ant all, altogether, completely, entirely, fully, perfectly, quite, totally, utterly, wholly

partner *n* the person to whom another is married — see SPOUSE

partnership *n* the state of having shared interests or efforts (as in social or business matters) — see ASSOCIATION 1

parturition *n* the act or process of giving birth to children — see CHILDBIRTH

party *n* 1 a social gathering ⟨We're all invited to the big *party* to celebrate the end of the year.⟩

syn affair, bash, binge, blast, blowout, do, event, fete (*or* fête), function, get-together, reception, shindig *rel* benefit, fund-raiser; celebration, gala, occasion; bake, clambake, cocktail party, hen party, house party, housewarming, icebreaker, meet and greet, mixer, salon, shower, social, soiree (*or* soirée), supper, symposium, tea, tea party

2 a group of people acting together within a larger group — see FACTION

3 a group of people working together on a task — see GANG 1

4 a member of the human race — see HUMAN

5 a usually small number of persons considered as a unit — see GROUP 2

6 one who takes part in something — see PARTICIPANT

¹**pass** *n* **1** a narrow opening between hillsides or mountains that can be used for passage — see CANYON

2 a passage cleared for public vehicular travel — see WAY 1

²**pass** *n* **1** a small sheet of plastic, paper, or paperboard showing that the bearer has a claim to something (as admittance) — see TICKET 1

2 an effort to do or accomplish something — see ATTEMPT 1

3 the state of being actual or complete — see FRUITION

pass *vb* **1** to shift possession of (something) from one person to another ⟨Could you please *pass* me the phone?⟩

syn buck, hand, hand over, reach, transfer

rel relay; bear, carry; handle, paw; cede, deliver, give, give up, release, relinquish, render, surrender, turn over; yield

2 to come to an end — see CEASE 1

3 to put (something) into the possession or safekeeping of another — see GIVE 2

4 to put into effect through legislative or authoritative action — see ENACT

5 to take place — see HAPPEN

6 to come to a knowledge of (something) by living through it — see EXPERIENCE

7 to express (a thought or emotion) in words — see SAY 1

8 to show unwillingness to accept, do, engage in, or agree to — see DECLINE 1

9 to withstand scrutiny and gain acceptance or approval — see WASH 2

pass (on) *vb* to stop living — see DIE 1

pass (over) *vb* to make one's way through, across, or over — see TRAVERSE

passable *adj* **1** capable of being traveled on ⟨After the snowstorm ends, the roads might not be *passable* for the morning ride to school.⟩

syn navigable, negotiable

rel clear, cleared, free, open, unclogged, unclosed, unobstructed, unstopped

near ant blocked, choked, clogged, closed, congested, dammed, jammed, obstructed, plugged (up), stopped (up), stuffed; barricaded, blockaded

ant impassable (*also* impassible), unnegotiable, unpassable

2 capable of being passed into or through — see PENETRABLE

3 of a level of quality that meets one's needs or standards — see ADEQUATE

syn synonym(s)   *rel* related words
ant antonym(s)   *near ant* near antonym(s)

4 of average to below average quality — see MEDIOCRE 1

passably *adv* in a satisfactory way — see WELL 1

passage *n* **1** an established course for traveling from one place to another ⟨the long *passage* down the Atlantic seaboard, around Cape Horn, and up the Pacific Coast to California⟩

syn approach, avenue, path, route, way

rel bypath, byway, lane; artery, boulevard, bypass, drive, expressway, freeway, highway, pass, passageway, pike, road, roadway, row, street, thoroughfare, turnpike; walk, walkway; trace, track, trail; airway; bikeway; channel, gat, watercourse, waterway; door

2 a going from one place to another usually of some distance — see JOURNEY

3 a journey over water in a vessel — see SAIL

4 a part taken from a longer work — see EXCERPT

5 forward movement in time or place — see ADVANCE 1

6 the permanent stopping of all the vital bodily activities — see DEATH 1

passageway *n* a typically long narrow way connecting parts of a building — see HALL 2

pass away *vb* to stop living — see DIE 1

passé *adj* having passed its time of use or usefulness — see OBSOLETE

passel *n* **1** a number of things considered as a unit — see GROUP 1

2 a usually small number of persons considered as a unit — see GROUP 2

3 a considerable amount — see LOT 2

passing *adj* lasting only for a short time — see MOMENTARY

passing *adv* to a great degree — see VERY 1

passing *n* the permanent stopping of all the vital bodily activities — see DEATH 1

passion *n* **1** a feeling of strong or constant regard for and dedication to someone — see LOVE 1

2 a strong but often short-lived liking for another person — see CRUSH 1

3 a strong wish for something — see DESIRE 1

4 a subjective response to a person, thing, or situation — see FEELING 1

5 depth of feeling — see ARDOR 1

6 passions *pl* general emotional condition — see FEELING 2

7 intense sexual desire — see LUST 1

passionate *adj* **1** having a strong sexual desire — see LUSTFUL

2 having or expressing great depth of feeling — see FERVENT 1

passive *adj* receiving or enduring without offering resistance ⟨The union rank and file were surprisingly *passive* about the givebacks in the new labor contract.⟩

syn acquiescent, nonresistant, resigned, tolerant, tolerating, unresistant, yielding

rel forbearing, impassive, long-suffering, patient, stoic (*or* stoical), uncomplaining; agreeable, amenable, compliant, complying, docile, guidable, obedient, pliable, pliant, subordinate, tractable, willing; obeisant, submissive, surrendering; amiable, obliging; subservient; disciplined, governable, manageable; apathetic, uncaring, unresponsive

near ant defiant; contrary, disobedient, froward, insubordinate, insurgent, intractable, rebellious, recalcitrant, refractory, restive, uncontrollable, ungovernable, unruly, untoward; balky, perverse, wayward, wrongheaded; headstrong, willful (*or* wilful); indomitable; undisciplined, unmanageable; dissident, nonconformist

ant protesting, resistant, resisting, unyielding

pass off *vb* to offer (something fake, useless, or inferior) as genuine, useful, or valuable — see FOIST

pass out *vb* to lose consciousness — see FAINT

pass over *vb* **1** to fail to give proper attention to — see NEGLECT 1
2 to dismiss as of little importance — see EXCUSE 1

passport *n* **1** something that allows someone to achieve a desired goal ⟨Meeting that movie director could be your *passport* to a big acting career.⟩
syn gateway, key, open sesame, secret, ticket
rel password; accomplishment, achievement, attainment, coup, success, triumph; blueprint, design, ground plan, plan, program, scheme, strategy
2 the means or right of entering or participating in — see ENTRANCE 1

password *n* a word or phrase that must be spoken by a person in order to pass a guard ⟨No one gets in without the *password*.⟩
syn countersign, watchword, word
rel shibboleth, sign; signal; hint, indication; parole

past *adj* having been such at some previous time — see FORMER 1

past *n* the events or experience of former times ⟨We spent a pleasant evening recalling the *past* together.⟩
syn auld lang syne, history, yesterday, yesteryear, yore
rel bygone; flashback; annals, chronicle, record; memoir; long ago
near ant by-and-by, future, futurity, hereafter, offing; moment, now, present, today

past *prep* **1** on or to the farther side of — see BEYOND 1
2 subsequent to in time or order — see AFTER

paste *vb* **1** to defeat by a large margin — see WHIP 2
2 to deliver a blow to (someone or something) usually in a strong vigorous manner — see HIT 1

pastel *adj* lacking intensity of color — see PALE 1

past master *n* a person with a high level of knowledge or skill in a field — see EXPERT

pastoral *adj* **1** of, relating to, associated with, or typical of open areas with few buildings or people — see RURAL
2 of, relating to, or characteristic of the clergy — see CLERICAL

pasturage *n* open land over which livestock may roam and feed — see RANGE 1

pasture *n* open land over which livestock may roam and feed — see RANGE 1

pasture *vb* to feed on grass or herbs — see ¹GRAZE

pasty *adj* lacking a healthy skin color — see PALE 2

pat *adj* sticking to an opinion, purpose, or course of action in spite of reason, arguments, or persuasion — see OBSTINATE

pat *adv* without any flaws or errors — see PERFECTLY 1

pat *vb* to touch or handle in a tender or loving manner — see FONDLE

patch *n* **1** a small area that is different (as in color) from the main part — see SPOT 1
2 a very small piece — see BIT 1

patch *vb* to put into good shape or working order again — see MEND 1

patchwork *adj* consisting of many things of different sorts — see MISCELLANEOUS

patchwork *n* an unorganized collection or mixture of various things — see MISCELLANY 1

pate *n* the upper or front part of the body that contains the brain, the major sense organs, and the mouth — see HEAD 1

patent *adj* **1** not subject to misinterpretation or more than one interpretation — see CLEAR 2
2 very noticeable especially for being incorrect or bad — see EGREGIOUS

path *n* **1** the direction along which something or someone moves ⟨Try to stay out of the *path* of the golf balls while playing.⟩ ⟨I tripped over a rock directly in my *path*.⟩
syn course, line, pathway, route, steps, track, way
rel circle, loop, orbit; arc, flight path, trajectory; ascent, descent
2 a rough course or way formed by or as if by repeated footsteps — see TRAIL 1
3 an established course for traveling from one place to another — see PASSAGE 1

pathetic *adj* **1** deserving of one's pity ⟨The plight of the homeless animals was quite *pathetic*.⟩
syn heartbreaking, heartrending, miserable, piteous, pitiable, pitiful, poor, rueful, sorry, wretched
rel deplorable, lamentable, regrettable; emotional, impressive, inspiring; affecting, moving, poignant, stirring, touching; distressing, disturbing, upsetting; grievous, mournful, sad, sorrowful, woeful
near ant unimpressive, uninspiring
2 causing unhappiness — see SAD 2
3 deserving pitying scorn (as for inadequacy) — see PITIFUL 1
4 so foolish or pointless as to be worthy of scornful laughter — see RIDICULOUS 1

pathway *n* **1** a rough course or way formed by or as if by repeated footsteps — see TRAIL 1
2 the direction along which something or someone moves — see PATH 1

patience *n* the capacity to endure what is difficult or disagreeable without complaining ⟨I don't have the *patience* to stand in line for so long.⟩
syn forbearance, long-suffering, sufferance, tolerance
rel acquiescence, resignation; passiveness, passivity; amenability, compliance, conformism, docility, obedience, subordination,

tractability, willingness; discipline, self-control; submission, submissiveness

near ant defiance; contrariness, disobedience, insubordination, intractability, recalcitrance, resistance, willfulness

ant impatience

patient *adj* 1 accepting pains or hardships calmly or without complaint ⟨You were very *patient* about having to wait for me for so long.⟩

syn forbearing, long-suffering, stoic (*or* stoical), tolerant, uncomplaining

rel lenient; acquiescent, passive, resigned, unresistant, yielding; agreeable, amenable, compliant, complying, docile, obedient, placable, submissive, subordinate, tractable, willing; subservient; amiable, obliging; collected, composed; restrained; disciplined, self-contained, self-controlled

near ant defiant, resistant; contrary, disobedient, insubordinate, intractable, rebellious, recalcitrant, refractory, ungovernable, unmanageable, unruly

ant complaining, fed up, impatient, protesting

2 continuing despite difficulties, opposition, or discouragement — see PERSISTENT

patient *n* an individual awaiting or under medical care and treatment ⟨The nurse asked the *patient* to change into a paper gown.⟩

syn case

rel inpatient, outpatient; rehabilitant; sufferer, victim; convalescent, nursling

patio *n* an open space wholly or partly enclosed (as by buildings or walls) — see COURT 2

patois *n* the special terms or expressions of a particular group or field — see TERMINOLOGY

patrician *adj* of high birth, rank, or station — see NOBLE 1

patrimony *n* something that is or may be inherited — see INHERITANCE

patriot *n* a person who loves his or her country and supports its interests and policies ⟨the contention that true *patriots* would be willing to do anything for their country⟩

syn loyalist

rel chauvinist; nationalist, superpatriot; compatriot, countryman

near ant collaborator, quisling, spy, traitor; betrayer, deserter, recreant; renegade

patriotic *adj* having or showing love and support for one's country ⟨Hanging a flag outside one's home is a *patriotic* gesture.⟩

syn nationalist, nationalistic

rel chauvinist; superpatriotic; constant, devoted, faithful, loyal, staunch (*also* stanch), steadfast, steady, true; ardent, fervent, fervid, impassioned, passionate

near ant traitorous, treasonous; disaffected, disloyal, faithless, false, fickle, inconstant, perfidious, recreant, treacherous, unfaithful

ant unpatriotic

patriotism *n* love and support for one's country ⟨Her *patriotism* was so heartfelt

that she quit her job to work for the war effort.⟩

syn nationalism

rel chauvinism; jingoism; allegiance, constancy, devotion, faithfulness, fealty, loyalty, staunchness, steadfastness; fervency, fervidness, passion

near ant desertion, treason; disaffection, disloyalty, faithlessness, falseness, fickleness, inconstancy, perfidiousness, treachery, unfaithfulness

patron *n* 1 a person who buys a product or uses a service from a business — see CUSTOMER 1

2 a person who takes the responsibility for some other person or thing — see SPONSOR

3 one that helps another with gifts or money — see BENEFACTOR

patronize *vb* 1 to assume or treat with an air of superiority — see CONDESCEND 2

2 to promote the interests or cause of — see SUPPORT 1

patter *n* 1 friendly, informal conversation or an instance of this — see CHAT 1

2 the special terms or expressions of a particular group or field — see TERMINOLOGY

patter *vb* to engage in casual or rambling conversation — see CHAT 1

pattern *n* 1 a unit of decoration that is repeated all over something (as a fabric) ⟨a coverlet with a nosegay of tiny pink roses as the *pattern*⟩

syn design, figure, motif, motive

rel scheme; device; adornment, caparison, decoration, embellishment, frill, garnish, ornament, trim

2 a usual manner of behaving or doing — see HABIT 1

3 an established and often automatic or monotonous series of actions followed when engaging in some activity — see ROUTINE 1

4 the way in which the elements of something (as a work of art) are arranged — see COMPOSITION 3

patty *also* **pattie** *n* a small usually rounded mass of minced food that has been fried — see CAKE 1

paucity *n* a falling short of an essential or desirable amount or number — see DEFICIENCY

paunch *n* an enlarged or bulging abdomen — see POTBELLY

pauperism *n* the state of lacking sufficient money or material possessions — see POVERTY 1

pause *n* 1 a momentary halt in an activity ⟨There was a brief *pause* for applause in her speech.⟩

syn break, breath, breather, interruption, lull, recess

rel interim, interlude, intermission, interval, respite, rest; cessation, discontinuance, ending, expiration, finishing, hitch, lapse, stoppage, stopping, termination; abeyance, moratorium, surcease, suspension; discontinuity, gap, hiatus

near ant continuation, endurance, persistence, progress, progression; extension, prolongation

2 a state or an instance of temporary inaction because of uncertainty about the right course of action — see HESITATION

pause *vb* to come to a temporary halt in one's activity 〈He *paused* for a moment to regain his composure.〉

syn break

rel hesitate; break in, interrupt; cease, discontinue, end, finish, stop, terminate; knock off, lay off, quit; lapse, let up

phrases catch one's breath, hold one's horses

near ant continue, persist; advance, progress; extend, prolong, stretch

¹**pawn** *n* one that is or can be used to further the purposes of another 〈Though he liked to play up his influence with city hall, he was really just another *pawn* of the political bosses.〉

syn instrument, puppet, tool

rel chump, dupe, foil, gull, sucker, victim; minion, stooge; lap dog, yes-man

²**pawn** *n* something given or held to assure that the giver will keep a promise — see PLEDGE 1

pawn *vb* to leave as a guarantee of repayment of a loan 〈He *pawned* his antique watch in order to pay off his debt.〉

syn hock, pledge

rel deposit; bond

near ant buy (back), redeem, win (back)

pay *n* 1 the money paid regularly to a person for labor or services — see WAGE

2 something (as money) that is given or received in return for goods or services — see PAYMENT 2

pay *vb* 1 to give (someone) the sum of money owed for goods or services received 〈We need to *pay* the cashier and then we can leave.〉

syn compensate, recompense, remunerate

rel refund, reimburse, repay, requite; remit; pay off, pay up, prepay

near ant repudiate

2 to give what is owed for 〈You ought to *pay* that bill before it's overdue.〉

syn balance, clear, discharge, foot, liquidate, meet, pay off, pay up, quit, recompense, settle, spring (for), stand

ant repudiate

3 to hand over or use up in payment — see SPEND 1

4 to produce as revenue — see YIELD 2

5 to provide with a paying job — see EMPLOY 1

payable *adj* not yet paid — see OUTSTANDING 1

paying *adj* yielding a profit — see PROFITABLE 1

paying *n* the act of offering money in exchange for goods or services — see PAYMENT 1

payload *n* a mass or quantity of something taken up and carried, conveyed, or transported — see LOAD 1

payment *n* 1 the act of offering money in exchange for goods or services 〈They are very prompt in the *payment* of their credit card bills.〉

syn compensation, disbursement, giving, paying, remittance, remuneration

rel tendering; reimbursement, repayment; paying off, paying up, prepayment; overpayment

near ant underpayment

ant nonpayment

2 something (as money) that is given or received in return for goods or services 〈Our *payment* for all the work we did barely covered our expenses.〉 〈We finally mailed our last car *payment* last week.〉

syn compensation, consideration, pay, recompense, remittance, remuneration, requital

rel salary, stipend, wage(s); disbursement, expenditure, outlay; rebate, refund; indemnity, recoupment, redress, reparation, restitution; settlement; deposit; reimbursement, repayment; prepayment; overpayment; rent, rental

3 the money paid regularly to a person for labor or services — see WAGE

payoff *n* the amount of money left when expenses are subtracted from the total amount received — see PROFIT 1

pay off *vb* 1 to give what is owed for — see PAY 2

2 to influence someone with a bribe — see BRIBE

pay up *vb* to give what is owed for — see PAY 2

peace *n* 1 a state without war 〈After a long and bitter war, the troubled region finally achieved *peace*.〉

syn peacefulness

rel accord, amity, concord, harmony; calm, quiet, serenity, tranquillity (*or* tranquility); order, stability; pacification

near ant conflict, contention, discord, dissidence, strife, trouble; tumult, turmoil, unrest, upheaval; fighting, warfare; action, battle, combat

ant war

2 freedom from disquieting or oppressive thoughts or emotions 〈a light, humorous novel that is good for putting my mind at *peace* right before I go to sleep〉

syn calm, calmness, peacefulness, placidity, sereneness, serenity, tranquillity (*or* tranquility)

rel content, contentment, ease; comfort, consolation, relief, solace; quiet, quietude, repose

near ant care, concern, perturbation; strain, stress, tenseness, tension; consternation, desperateness, desperation, dis-comfort, discomposure, dismay, distraction, distress, disturbance, edginess, jitters, jumpiness, nervousness; fear, fearfulness, torment, upset; doubt, dread, foreboding, incertitude, misgiving, presentiment, suspense, uncertainty

ant agitation, alarm (*also* alarum), anguish, anxiety, anxiousness, apprehension, apprehensiveness, uneasiness, vexation, worry

3 a state of freedom from storm or disturbance — see CALM 1

4 peaceful coexistence — see HARMONY 2

peaceable *adj* 1 inclined to live in peace and to avoid war — see PEACEFUL 1

2 not involving violence or force — see PEACEFUL 2

peaceful *adj* 1 inclined to live in peace and to avoid war 〈a *peaceful* country that remained neutral during World War 2〉

syn pacific, pacifist (*or* pacifistic), peaceable

rel irenic, nonaggressive, nonbelligerent, noncombative, unaggressive, unwarlike; antimilitarist, antimilitaristic, antiviolence, antiwar; calm, mild, neutral, quiet, relaxed, serene, tranquil; affable, amiable, amicable, benevolent, genial, gentle, kind, kindly; submissive, yielding

near ant militarist, militaristic; aggressive, bellicose, belligerent, combative, contentious, discordant, pugnacious, quarrelsome, scrappy, truculent; antagonistic, argumentative, fierce, gladiatorial, hostile, hot-tempered

ant bloodthirsty, hawkish, martial, warlike

2 not involving violence or force ⟨UN officials struggled to find a *peaceful* solution to the troublesome conflict.⟩

syn nonviolent, peaceable

rel bloodless; conciliatory, irenic, pacific; peacemaking; nonbelligerent, unaggressive, unassertive; appeasing, conciliating, mollifying, pacifying, placating; calming, quieting, soothing

near ant armed, martial, militant, military, warlike; aggressive, assertive, bellicose, belligerent, combative, contentious, quarrelsome; antagonistic, argumentative, fierce, gladiatorial, hostile; tempestuous, volcanic

ant forced, violent

3 free from disturbing noise or uproar — see QUIET 1

4 free from storms or physical disturbance — see CALM 1

5 free from emotional or mental agitation — see CALM 2

peacefulness *n* **1** a state of freedom from storm or disturbance — see CALM 1

2 a state without war — see PEACE 1

3 freedom from disquieting or oppressive thoughts or emotions — see PEACE 2

peacemaker *n* one who works with opposing sides in order to bring about an agreement — see MEDIATOR

peacemaking *adj* tending to lessen or avoid conflict or hostility — see PACIFIC 1

peak *n* **1** an elevation of land higher than a hill — see MOUNTAIN 1

2 the highest part or point — see HEIGHT 1

3 the projecting front part of a hat or cap — see VISOR

¹**peaked** *adj* tapering to a thin tip — see POINTED 1

²**peaked** *adj* **1** lacking a healthy skin color — see PALE 2

2 temporarily suffering from a disorder of the body — see SICK 1

peal *vb* to make the clear sound heard when metal vibrates — see ²RING

peanuts *n pl* **1** a very small amount — see PARTICLE 1

2 a very small sum of money — see MITE 1

pearl *n* someone or something unusually desirable — see PRIZE 1

pebbly *adj* not having a level or smooth surface — see UNEVEN 1

peck *n* a considerable amount — see LOT 2

peck *vb* **1** to eat reluctantly and in small bites — see NIBBLE 1

2 to penetrate or hold (something) with a pointed object — see IMPALE

peculiar *adj* **1** being out of the ordinary — see EXCEPTIONAL 1

2 different from the ordinary in a way that causes curiosity or suspicion — see ODD 2

3 noticeably different from what is generally found or experienced — see UNUSUAL 1

4 of, relating to, or belonging to a single person — see INDIVIDUAL 1

5 serving to identify as belonging to an individual or group — see CHARACTERISTIC 1

6 of a particular or exact sort — see EXPRESS 1

peculiarity *n* **1** an odd or peculiar habit — see IDIOSYNCRASY

2 something that sets apart an individual from others of the same kind — see CHARACTERISTIC

pecuniary *adj* of or relating to money, banking, or investments — see FINANCIAL

pedagogue *n* a person whose occupation is to give formal instruction in a school — see TEACHER

peddle *vb* to sell from place to place usually in small quantities ⟨They *peddled* fruits and vegetables out of their truck.⟩

syn hawk

rel retail, wholesale; deal (in), distribute, high-pressure, hustle, market, merchandise (*also* merchandize), trade (in), vend

peddler *also* **pedlar** *n* one who sells things outdoors ⟨the *peddler* on the street corner selling baseball caps⟩

syn hawker, huckster

rel dealer, merchandiser, merchant, seller, vendor (*also* vender); concessionaire; black marketer (*or* black marketeer), bootlegger, fence, fencer, hustler, pusher, smuggler, trader

near ant buyer, purchaser; consumer, end user, user

pedestrian *adj* causing weariness, restlessness, or lack of interest — see BORING

pedigree *n* the line of ancestors from whom a person is descended — see ANCESTRY

pedigreed *or* **pedigree** *adj* of unmixed ancestry — see PUREBRED

peek *n* an instance of looking especially briefly — see LOOK 2

peek *vb* to take a quick or hasty look — see GLANCE 2

peel *vb* to remove the natural covering of ⟨She *peels* apples with lightning speed.⟩

syn bark, denude, flay, hull, husk, shell, shuck, skin

rel bare, denude, expose, scale, strip; pare

peel (off) *vb* to rid oneself of (a garment) — see REMOVE 1

peeled *adj* lacking a usual or natural covering — see NAKED 2

peep *n* an instance of looking especially briefly — see LOOK 2

peep *vb* to make a short sharp sound like a small bird — see CHIRP

peer *n* **1** a man of high birth or social position — see GENTLEMAN 1

2 one that is equal to another in status, achievement, or value — see EQUAL

peer *vb* to look long and hard in wonder or surprise — see GAPE

peerless *adj* having no equal or rival for excellence or desirability — see ONLY 1

peeve *n* 1 something that is a source of irritation — see ANNOYANCE 3

2 the feeling of being offended or resentful after a slight or indignity — see PIQUE

peeve *vb* to disturb the peace of mind of (someone) especially by repeated disagreeable acts — see IRRITATE 1

peeving *adj* causing annoyance — see ANNOYING

peevish *adj* easily irritated or annoyed — see IRRITABLE

peevishness *n* readiness to show annoyance or impatience — see PETULANCE

peewee *n* a living thing much smaller than others of its kind — see DWARF 1

peg *n* an individual part of a process, series, or ranking — see DEGREE 1

peg *vb* 1 to arrange or assign according to type — see CLASSIFY 1

2 to send through the air especially with a quick forward motion of the arm — see THROW 1

peg (away) *vb* to devote serious and sustained effort — see LABOR

pelage *n* the hairy covering of a mammal especially when fine, soft, and thick — see FUR 1

pelagic *adj* of or relating to the sea — see MARINE 1

pelf *n* something (as pieces of stamped metal or printed paper) customarily and legally used as a medium of exchange, a measure of value, or a means of payment — see MONEY

pellet *n* a usually round or cone-shaped little piece of lead made to be fired from a firearm — see BULLET

pell-mell *adj* 1 acting or done with excessive or careless speed — see HASTY 1

2 lacking in order, neatness, and often cleanliness — see MESSY

pell-mell *adv* 1 in a confused and reckless manner — see HELTER-SKELTER 1

2 with excessive or careless speed — see HASTILY 1

pellucid *adj* 1 easily seen through — see CLEAR 1

2 not subject to misinterpretation or more than one interpretation — see CLEAR 2

¹**pelt** *n* a hard strike with a part of the body or an instrument — see ¹BLOW

²**pelt** *n* the outer covering of an animal removed for its commercial value — see HIDE 1

pelt *vb* 1 to proceed or move quickly — see HURRY 2

2 to send through the air especially with a quick forward motion of the arm — see THROW 1

3 to strike repeatedly — see BEAT 1

¹**pen** *n* a place of confinement for persons held in lawful custody — see JAIL

²**pen** *n* an enclosure with an open framework for keeping animals — see CAGE

³**pen** *n* a person who creates a written work — see AUTHOR 1

¹**pen** *vb* to close or shut in by or as if by barriers — see ENCLOSE 1

²**pen** *vb* to compose and set down on paper the words of — see WRITE 1

penal *adj* inflicting, involving, or serving as punishment — see PUNITIVE

penalize *vb* to inflict a penalty on for a fault or crime — see PUNISH

penalizing *adj* inflicting, involving, or serving as punishment — see PUNITIVE

penalty *n* 1 a sum of money to be paid as a punishment — see FINE

2 suffering, loss, or hardship imposed in response to a crime or offense — see PUNISHMENT

3 the negative result caused by something that creates difficulty for achieving success — see DISADVANTAGE 2

penchant *n* a habitual attraction to some activity or thing — see INCLINATION 1

pendant *also* **pendent** *n* an ornament worn on a chain around the neck or wrist ⟨Navajo necklaces with *pendants* finely crafted in genuine sky-blue turquoise⟩

syn bangle, charm

rel locket, teardrop

pendent *or* **pendant** *adj* extending freely from a support from above — see DEPENDENT 1

pending *adj* 1 not yet settled or decided ⟨A decision is *pending* about whether to buy computers or sports equipment with this money.⟩

syn open, undecided, undetermined, unresolved, unsettled

rel hanging; debatable, disputable, moot, uncertain, unsure

phrases in hand

near ant confirmed, established; certain, sure

ant decided, determined, resolved, settled

2 being soon to appear or take place — see FORTHCOMING 1

3 giving signs of immediate occurrence — see IMMINENT 1

pending *prep* in the course of — see DURING

pendulous *adj* 1 bending downward or forward — see NODDING

2 extending freely from a support from above — see DEPENDENT 1

penetrable *adj* capable of being passed into or through ⟨Unfortunately, our netting proved to be a rather *penetrable* barrier that allowed in our cabin a steady stream of mosquitoes.⟩

syn passable, permeable, porous

rel absorbent; breathable

near ant airtight, watertight; close, compact, dense, thick

ant impassable (*also* impassible), impenetrable, impermeable, impervious, nonporous

penetrate *vb* to go or come in or into — see ENTER 1

penetrating *adj* causing intense discomfort to one's skin — see CUTTING 1

peninsula *n* an area of land that juts out into a body of water — see ²CAPE

penitence *n* a feeling of responsibility for wrongdoing — see GUILT 1

penitent *adj* feeling sorrow for a wrong that one has done — see CONTRITE

penitentiary *n* a place of confinement for persons held in lawful custody — see JAIL

penman *n* 1 a person who creates a written work — see AUTHOR 1

2 one who writes from dictation or copies manuscripts — see SCRIBE 1

penmanship n **1** the form or style of a particular person's writing — see HANDWRITING 1

2 writing done by hand — see HANDWRITING 2

pennant n a piece of cloth with a special design that is used as an emblem or for signaling — see FLAG 1

penniless adj lacking money or material possessions — see POOR 1

pennon n a piece of cloth with a special design that is used as an emblem or for signaling — see FLAG 1

pensive adj given to or marked by long, quiet thinking — see CONTEMPLATIVE

penstock n a long hollow cylinder for carrying a substance (as a liquid or gas) — see PIPE 1

penthouse n a smaller structure added to a main building — see ANNEX

penumbra n partial darkness due to the obstruction of light rays — see SHADE 1

penurious adj **1** giving or sharing as little as possible — see STINGY 1

2 lacking money or material possessions — see POOR 1

penuriousness n **1** the quality or practice of being overly sparing with money — see PARSIMONY 1

2 the state of lacking sufficient money or material possessions — see POVERTY 1

penury n the state of lacking sufficient money or material possessions — see POVERTY 1

peon n a person who does very hard or dull work — see DRUDGE

people n pl **1** human beings in general ⟨Despite the horrors she witnessed, Anne Frank never lost her faith in *people*.⟩
syn folks, humanity, humankind, public, world
rel community, society; crowd, masses, mob, populace, proletariat, rabble, riffraff

2 the body of the community as contrasted with the elite — see MASS 1

3 a group of persons who come from the same ancestor — see FAMILY 1

people vb to supply with inhabitants — see SETTLE 2

pep n active strength of body or mind — see VIGOR 1

pep (up) vb to give life, vigor, or spirit to — see ANIMATE

pepper vb **1** to cover by or as if by scattering something over or on — see SCATTER 2

2 to mark with small spots especially unevenly — see SPOT 1

peppery adj marked by a lively display of strong feeling — see SPIRITED 1

peppiness n the quality or state of having abundant or intense activity — see VITALITY 1

peppy adj **1** having active strength of body or mind — see VIGOROUS 1

2 having much high-spirited energy and movement — see LIVELY 1

per adv for each one — see APIECE

per prep using the means or agency of — see BY 2

perambulation n a relaxed journey on foot for exercise or pleasure — see WALK 1

per capita adv for each one — see APIECE

perceive vb **1** to have a vague awareness of — see FEEL 1

2 to make note of (something) through the use of one's eyes — see SEE 1

3 to have a clear idea of — see COMPREHEND 1

percentage n a measure of how often an event will occur instead of another — see PROBABILITY 2

perceptible adj able to be perceived by a sense or by the mind ⟨You should note a *perceptible* temperature change when you add the second element.⟩
syn appreciable, detectable, discernible (*also* discernable), distinguishable, palpable, sensible
rel audible, observable, tangible, visible; clear, conspicuous, evident, eye-catching, manifest, noticeable, obvious, plain, ponderable, prominent, striking; apparent, distinct, identifiable, significant
near ant inaudible, intangible; inconspicuous, indistinct, unnoticeable, unobtrusive; faint, insignificant, slight, trivial; buried, concealed, covert, disguised, obscure, shrouded, vague
ant impalpable, imperceptible, inappreciable, indistinguishable, insensible, undetectable

perception n **1** the ability to understand inner qualities or relationships — see WISDOM 1

2 the knowledge gained from the process of coming to know or understand something — see COMPREHENSION

perceptive adj **1** able to sense slight impressions or differences — see ACUTE 1

2 having or showing deep understanding and intelligent application of knowledge — see WISE 1

perceptiveness n **1** the ability to understand inner qualities or relationships — see WISDOM 1

2 the state or quality of being able to sense slight impressions or differences — see ACUITY

perch vb **1** to come to rest after descending from the air — see ALIGHT 1

2 to establish or place comfortably or snugly — see ENSCONCE 1

perchance adv it is possible — see PERHAPS

percolate vb to flow forth slowly through small openings — see EXUDE

percolate (into) vb to spread throughout — see PERMEATE

perdition n the place of punishment for the wicked after death — see HELL 1

peregrinate vb **1** to make one's way through, across, or over — see TRAVERSE

2 to take a trip especially of some distance — see TRAVEL 1

peregrination n a going from one place to another usually of some distance — see JOURNEY

peremptory adj **1** fond of ordering people around — see BOSSY

2 forcing one's compliance or participation by or as if by law — see MANDATORY

syn synonym(s)   **rel** related words
ant antonym(s)   **near ant** near antonym(s)

3 having a feeling of superiority that shows itself in an overbearing attitude — see ARROGANT

4 having or showing a tendency to force one's will on others without any regard to fairness or necessity — see ARBITRARY 1

perennial *adj* having an existence or validity that does not change or diminish — see ABIDING

perfect *adj* **1** being entirely without fault or flaw ⟨A stunningly *perfect* performance—not the slightest mistake—won her the gold medal in women's figure skating.⟩

syn absolute, faultless, flawless, ideal, immaculate, impeccable, irreproachable, letter-perfect, picture-perfect, unblemished

rel consummate, expert, masterly; classic, excellent, fabulous, fine, first-class, first-rate, grand, great, superb, superior, superlative, terrific, top, top-notch, unsurpassed; mint, unbruised, undamaged, unimpaired, uninjured, unmarred, unspoiled; exceptional, fancy, high-grade, special; inerrant, infallible, unerring, unfailing

near ant deficient, inadequate, insufficient, wanting; fallible; blemished, blighted, broken, damaged, defaced, disfigured, impaired, injured, malformed, marred, misshapen

ant amiss, bad, censurable, defective, faulty, flawed, imperfect, reproachable

2 having no exceptions or restrictions — see ABSOLUTE 2

3 not lacking any part or member that properly belongs to it — see COMPLETE 1

perfect *vb* **1** to bring (something) to a state where nothing remains to be done — see FINISH 1

2 to make better — see IMPROVE

perfection *n* **1** exceptionally high quality — see EXCELLENCE 1

2 the most perfect type or example — see QUINTESSENCE 1

3 the quality or state of being very accurate — see PRECISION

perfectly *adv* **1** without any flaws or errors ⟨You did that handspring *perfectly* on your first try.⟩

syn faultlessly, flawlessly, ideally, impeccably, pat

rel excellently, finely, grandly, greatly, marvelously, superbly, superiorly, superlatively, terrifically; exceptionally, fancily

phrases to a nicety, to a T, to a turn, to the nines

near ant deficiently, inadequately, incompletely, insufficiently; fallibly; atrociously, execrably, wretchedly

ant badly, defectively, faultily, imperfectly

2 to a full extent or degree — see FULLY 1

perfidious *adj* not true in one's allegiance to someone or something — see FAITHLESS

perfidy *n* the act or fact of violating the trust or confidence of another — see BETRAYAL

perforate *vb* to make a hole or series of holes in ⟨He *perforated* the sheet with his pencil and put it in his binder.⟩

syn bore, drill, hole, pierce, punch, puncture, riddle

rel broach, tap; poke, prick, prickle; pen-

etrate; burrow (into), excavate, gouge, groove, hollow; break, cut, gash, notch, rend, rupture, slash, slit, split

near ant fill, patch, plug, seal

perforation *n* **1** a mark or small hole made by a pointed instrument — see PRICK 1

2 a place in a surface allowing passage into or through a thing — see HOLE 1

perforce *adv* because of necessity — see NEEDS

perform *vb* **1** to carry through (as a process) to completion ⟨She *performed* the task quickly and expertly.⟩

syn accomplish, achieve, carry out, commit, compass, do, execute, fulfill (*or* fulfil), make, negotiate

rel bring about, effect, effectuate, implement; ace, nail; engage (in), practice (*also* practise); work (at); reduplicate, reenact, repeat; actualize, attain, realize; complete, end, finish, wind up

phrases go through

near ant fail; skimp, slight, slur

2 to have a certain purpose — see FUNCTION

3 to present a portrayal or performance of — see ACT 1

4 to produce a desired effect — see ACT 2

performance *n* **1** a presentation of an artistic work (as a piece of music) from a particular point of view — see ACCOUNT 2

2 the doing of an action — see COMMISSION 2

perfume *n* a sweet or pleasant smell — see FRAGRANCE

perfume *vb* to fill or infuse with a pleasant odor or odor-releasing substance — see SCENT 1

perfumed *adj* having a pleasant smell — see FRAGRANT

perfunctory *adj* having or showing a lack of interest or concern — see INDIFFERENT 1

perhaps *adv* it is possible ⟨*Perhaps* we will not have to take this exam, but I doubt it.⟩

syn conceivably, maybe, mayhap, perchance, possibly

rel likely, probably; certainly, doubtless, sure, surely, undoubtedly; presumably, presumedly, supposably, supposedly

peril *n* **1** something that may cause injury or harm — see DANGER 2

2 the state of not being protected from injury, harm, or evil — see DANGER 1

peril *vb* to place in danger — see ENDANGER

perilous *adj* involving potential loss or injury — see DANGEROUS 1

perimeter *n* the line or relatively narrow space that marks the outer limit of something — see BORDER 1

period *n* **1** an occurrence of menstruating ⟨began getting her *period*⟩

syn menstruation

rel menses

2 an extent of time associated with a particular person or thing — see AGE 1

periodic *adj* **1** appearing or occurring repeatedly from time to time — see REGULAR 1

2 occurring or appearing at intervals — see INTERMITTENT 1

periodical *adj* **1** appearing in parts or

numbers that follow regularly — see SE-RIAL

2 occurring or appearing at intervals — see INTERMITTENT 1

3 appearing or occurring repeatedly from time to time — see REGULAR 1

periodical *n* a publication that appears at regular intervals — see JOURNAL

peripatetic *adj* traveling from place to place — see ITINERANT

peripheral *adj* available to supply something extra when needed — see AUXILIARY

periphery *n* the line or relatively narrow space that marks the outer limit of something — see BORDER 1

perish *vb* to stop living — see DIE 1

perk (up) *vb* **1** to become glad or hopeful — see CHEER (UP) 1

2 to move from a lower to a higher place or position — see RAISE 1

perky *adj* having much high-spirited energy and movement — see LIVELY 1

permanent *adj* lasting forever — see EVERLASTING 1

permanently *adv* for all time — see EVER 1

permeable *adj* capable of being passed into or through — see PENETRABLE

permeate *vb* to spread throughout ⟨The smell of freshly baked bread *permeated* the house.⟩

syn interpenetrate, percolate (into), pervade, riddle, suffuse, transfuse

rel diffuse (through), impregnate, pass (into), penetrate; fill (up); drench, imbue, infuse, saturate, soak, steep; flood, glut

permissible *adj* that may be permitted ⟨a *permissible* level of noise⟩

syn admissible, allowable

rel acceptable, bearable, endurable, tolerable; accredited, allowed, authorized, endorsed (*also* indorsed), licensed, OK (*or* okay), permitted, sanctioned, warranted; lawful, legal; mandatory, ordered, required

near ant intolerable, unacceptable, unbearable, unendurable; objectionable; denied, disallowed, refused, rejected, vetoed; suppressed; outlawed

ant banned, barred, forbidden, impermissible, inadmissible, interdicted, prohibited, proscribed

permission *n* the approval by someone in authority for the doing of something ⟨She asked for *permission* to have a piece of candy.⟩ ⟨The President granted *permission* for the foreign diplomats to have special quarters.⟩

syn allowance, authorization, clearance, concurrence, consent, granting, leave, license (*or* licence), sanction, sufferance, warrant

rel imprimatur, seal, stamp; accreditation; liberty, pass; concession, patent, permit; tolerance, toleration; acceptance, acquiescence, agreement, assent, OK (*or* okay); accord, grant

near ant denial, refusal, rejection, revocation; veto; deterrence, discouragement

repression, suppression; ban, embargo, exclusion

ant interdiction, prohibition, proscription

permit *vb* **1** to give permission for or to approve of — see ALLOW 1

2 to give permission to — see ALLOW 2

3 to make able or possible — see ENABLE 1

4 to fail to prevent (some behavior on someone's part) especially from neglect or indifference — see ALLOW 3

pernicious *adj* causing or capable of causing harm — see HARMFUL

perpendicular *adj* rising straight up — see ERECT

perpetration *n* the doing of an action — see COMMISSION 2

perpetual *adj* **1** going on and on without any interruptions — see CONTINUOUS

2 having an existence or validity that does not change or diminish — see ABIDING

3 lasting forever — see EVERLASTING 1

perpetually *adv* **1** for all time — see EVER 1

2 on every relevant occasion — see ALWAYS 1

perpetuate *vb* to give eternal or lasting existence to ⟨We hope to *perpetuate* this holiday tradition.⟩

syn immortalize

rel commemorate, memorialize; celebrate, enshrine, honor; conserve, keep up, maintain, preserve, support, sustain; defend, guard, protect, safeguard

near ant extinguish, put out, snuff (out); annihilate, crush, decimate, demolish, destroy, devastate; eradicate, expunge, extirpate, obliterate, wipe out

perpetuity *n* endless time — see ETERNITY 1

perplex *vb* **1** to make complex or difficult — see COMPLICATE

2 to throw into a state of mental uncertainty — see CONFUSE 1

perplexity *n* a state of mental uncertainty — see CONFUSION 1

perquisite *n* **1** a small sum of money given for a service over and above what is due — see ²TIP 1

2 something given in addition to what is ordinarily expected or owed — see BONUS

persecute *vb* **1** to cause persistent suffering to — see AFFLICT

2 to disturb the peace of mind of (someone) especially by repeated disagreeable acts — see IRRITATE 1

persecutor *n* **1** a person who causes repeated emotional pain, distress, or annoyance to another — see TORMENTOR

2 one who is obnoxiously annoying — see NUISANCE 1

persevere *vb* to continue despite difficulties, opposition, or discouragement ⟨Although he was frustrated by the lack of financial resources and support, he *persevered* in his scientific research.⟩

syn carry on, persist

rel dig in, hang on, keep up; knuckle down

phrases gut it out, hang in there

near ant give up, knock off, quit; bow, give in, submit, succumb, surrender, yield; falter, hang back, hesitate, shilly-shally, vacillate, waver

persevering *adj* continuing despite diffi-

culties, opposition, or discouragement —
see PERSISTENT

persist vb **1** to continue despite difficulties, opposition, or discouragement — see PERSEVERE

2 to remain indefinitely in existence or in the same state — see CONTINUE 1

persistence n uninterrupted or lasting existence — see CONTINUATION

persistent adj continuing despite difficulties, opposition, or discouragement ⟨Although his first attempts were unsuccessful, he was *persistent* in his pursuit of a career in music.⟩

syn dogged, insistent, patient, persevering, pertinacious, tenacious

rel assured, certain, determined, firm, hell-bent, intent, positive, resolute, resolved, single-minded, sure; adamant, dogged, hardened, hardheaded, headstrong, implacable, mulish, obdurate, obstinate, opinionated, peevish, pertinacious, perverse, pigheaded, self-willed, stiff-necked, stubborn, unregenerate, unyielding, willful (*or* wilful); unfaltering, unhesitating, unwavering; resistant, wayward, wrongheaded; constant, devoted, faithful, good, loyal, staunch (*also* stanch), steadfast, steady, true; indomitable, unconquerable; hard, inflexible, relentless, stern, unbending, unflinching, unrelenting

near ant quitting, surrendering, yielding; faltering, hesitant, hesitating, irresolute, vacillating, wavering; disloyal, faithless, false, fickle, inconstant, perfidious, traitorous, treacherous

person n a member of the human race — see HUMAN

personableness n the state or quality of having a pleasant or agreeable manner in socializing with others — see AMIABILITY 1

personage n **1** a member of the human race — see HUMAN

2 a person who is widely known and usually much talked about — see CELEBRITY 1

personal adj of, relating to, or belonging to a single person — see INDIVIDUAL 1

personality n **1** a person who is widely known and usually much talked about — see CELEBRITY 1

2 the set of qualities that make a person different from other people — see INDIVIDUALITY 1

3 the set of qualities that makes a person, a group of people, or a thing different from others — see NATURE 1

4 an act or expression showing scorn and usually intended to hurt another's feelings — see INSULT

personalize vb to represent in visible form — see EMBODY 2

personalized adj of, relating to, or belonging to a single person — see INDIVIDUAL 1

personally adv in person and usually privately — see TÊTE-À-TÊTE

personalty n transportable items that one owns — see POSSESSION 2

personification n a visible representation of something abstract (as a quality) — see EMBODIMENT

personify vb to represent in visible form — see EMBODY 2

personnel n a body of persons at work or available for work — see FORCE 1

perspective n **1** a way of looking at or thinking about something ⟨Whether she was being rude or candid was all a matter of *perspective*.⟩

syn angle, outlook, shoes, slant, standpoint, viewpoint

rel interpretation, spin; belief, conviction, eye, feeling, judgment (*or* judgement), mind, mind-set, notion, opinion, perception, persuasion, sentiment, verdict, view; impression, take

phrases frame of reference, point of view

2 all that can be seen from a certain point — see VIEW 1

perspicuity n clearness of expression — see SIMPLICITY 2

perspicuous adj not subject to misinterpretation or more than one interpretation — see CLEAR 2

perspicuousness n clearness of expression — see SIMPLICITY 2

persuade vb to cause (someone) to agree with a belief or course of action by using arguments or earnest requests ⟨He *persuaded* his teachers to grant an extension.⟩

syn argue, bring, convert, convince, gain, get, induce, move, prevail (on *or* upon), satisfy, talk (into), win (over)

rel blandish, blarney, cajole, coax, entreat, exhort, fast-talk, urge, wheedle; allure, beguile, lead on, lure, seduce, snow, tempt; brainwash, overpersuade; incline, influence, move, prompt, sell, sway; reason (with)

near ant deter, discourage, dissuade, unsell

persuading n the act of reasoning or pleading with someone to accept a belief or course of action — see PERSUASION 1

persuasion n **1** the act of reasoning or pleading with someone to accept a belief or course of action ⟨the suffragists' gradual *persuasion* of the American people that voting rights had to be extended to women⟩

syn conversion, convincing, inducement, inducing, persuading, suasion

rel blandishment, cajolement, cajolery, coaxing, entreaty, exhortation, urging, wheedling; seduction, tempting; influencing, prompting, swaying; lobbying, pressuring; brainwashing, overpersuasion

2 a body of beliefs and practices regarding the supernatural and the worship of one or more deities — see RELIGION 1

3 an idea that is believed to be true or valid without positive knowledge — see OPINION 1

4 the capacity to persuade — see COGENCY 1

persuasive adj having the power to persuade — see COGENT

persuasiveness n the capacity to persuade — see COGENCY 1

pert adj **1** having much high-spirited energy and movement — see LIVELY 1

2 making light of something usually regarded as serious or sacred — see FLIPPANT

3 sharp and pleasantly stimulating to the mind or senses — see PIQUANT

pertain *vb* 1 to be the property of a person or group of persons — see BELONG 2

2 to have a relation or connection — see APPLY 1

pertain (to) *vb* to have (something) as a subject matter — see CONCERN 1

pertinacious *adj* 1 continuing despite difficulties, opposition, or discouragement — see PERSISTENT

2 sticking to an opinion, purpose, or course of action in spite of reason, arguments, or persuasion — see OBSTINATE

pertinaciousness *n* a steadfast adherence to an opinion, purpose, or course of action in spite of reason, arguments, or persuasion — see OBSTINACY

pertinacity *n* a steadfast adherence to an opinion, purpose, or course of action in spite of reason, arguments, or persuasion — see OBSTINACY

pertinence *n* the fact or state of being pertinent ⟨Job applicants should question the *pertinence* of any questions about their personal lives.⟩

syn applicability, bearing, connection, materiality, relevance, relevancy

rel appropriateness, aptness, felicitousness, fitness, fittingness, rightness, seemliness, suitability, suitableness; importance, significance; usefulness

near ant inappropriateness, inaptness, infelicity, unfitness, unsuitability; meaninglessness, pointlessness, uselessness

ant extraneousness, inapplicability, irrelevance, irrelevancy

pertinent *adj* having to do with the matter at hand ⟨He impressed the jury with his concise, *pertinent* answers to the attorney's questions.⟩

syn applicable, apposite, apropos, germane, material, pointed, relative, relevant

rel appropriate, apt, fit, fitting, suitable; important, meaningful, significant; sensible, useful; admissible, allowable

phrases to the point

near ant frivolous, inconsequential, insignificant, little, minor, negligible, slight, trifling, trivial, unimportant; meaningless, purposeless, senseless, useless; inappropriate, inapt, unsuitable; inadmissible

ant extraneous, immaterial, impertinent, inapplicable, irrelative, irrelevant, pointless

pertly *adv* in a quick and spirited manner — see GAILY 2

pertness *n* shameless boldness — see EFFRONTERY

perturb *vb* to trouble the mind of; to make uneasy — see DISTURB 1

perturbed *adj* feeling or showing uncomfortable feelings of uncertainty — see NERVOUS 1

perturbing *adj* causing worry or anxiety — see TROUBLESOME

peruse *vb* to go over and mentally take in the content of — see READ 1

pervade *vb* to spread throughout — see PERMEATE

perverse *adj* 1 easily irritated or annoyed — see IRRITABLE

2 having or showing lowered moral character or standards — see CORRUPT

3 sticking to an opinion, purpose, or course of action in spite of reason, arguments, or persuasion — see OBSTINATE

4 not appropriate for a particular occasion or situation — see INAPPROPRIATE

perverseness *n* readiness to show annoyance or impatience — see PETULANCE

perversion *n* 1 a sinking to a state of low moral standards and behavior — see CORRUPTION 2

2 incorrect or improper use — see MISUSE

perversity *n* readiness to show annoyance or impatience — see PETULANCE

pervert *n* a person who has sunk below the normal moral standard — see DEGENERATE

pervert *vb* 1 to change so much as to create a wrong impression or alter the meaning of — see GARBLE

2 to lower in character, dignity, or quality — see DEBASE 1

3 to put to a bad or improper use — see MISAPPLY

perverted *adj* having or showing lowered moral character or standards — see CORRUPT

pessimist *n* 1 one who emphasizes bad aspects or conditions and expects the worst ⟨She's such a *pessimist* that she's convinced she'll fail every test.⟩

syn defeatist

rel cynic, fatalist, nihilist; hardnose, pragmatist, realist; worrier, worrywart

near ant dreamer, idealist, idealizer, romantic, romanticist, utopian, visionary; sentimentalist

ant optimist, Pollyanna

2 a person who distrusts other people and believes that everything is done for selfish reasons — see CYNIC

pessimistic *adj* 1 emphasizing or expecting the worst ⟨With that *pessimistic* attitude, it's no wonder you're depressed!⟩

syn bearish, defeatist, despairing, hopeless

rel cynical, fatalistic, nihilist, nihilistic; discouraging, disheartening, inauspicious, unlikely, unpromising; bleak, cheerless, comfortless, depressing, desolate, dismal, dreary, funereal, gloomy, morose, saturnine, sepulchral, somber (*or* sombre), sullen; grim; contrary, hostile, negative

near ant auspicious, bright, encouraging, fair, golden, heartening, likely, promising, propitious; cheering, comforting, reassuring; favorable, good, positive; idealist, romantic, utopian, visionary; cheerful, cheery, chipper, sunny

ant hopeful, optimistic, rose-colored, rosy, upbeat

2 having or showing a deep distrust of human beings and their motives — see CYNICAL

pest *n* 1 a widespread disease resulting in a high rate of death — see PLAGUE

2 one who is obnoxiously annoying — see NUISANCE 1

3 something that is a source of irritation — see ANNOYANCE 3

pester *vb* to thrust oneself upon (another) without invitation — see BOTHER 1

pestering *n* the act of making unwelcome

---

syn synonym(s)   *rel* related words
ant antonym(s)   *near ant* near antonym(s)

intrusions upon another — see ANNOYANCE 1

pestiferous *adj* causing annoyance — see ANNOYING

pestilence *n* a widespread disease resulting in a high rate of death — see PLAGUE

pestilent *adj* 1 capable of being passed by physical contact from one person to another — see CONTAGIOUS 1

2 causing annoyance — see ANNOYING

3 likely to cause or capable of causing death — see DEADLY 1

pesty *adj* causing annoyance — see ANNOYING

pet *adj* granted special treatment or attention — see DARLING 1

¹**pet** *n* a person or thing that is preferred over others — see FAVORITE

²**pet** *n* a state of resentful silence or irritability — see SULK

pet *vb* to touch or handle in a tender or loving manner — see FONDLE

petition *n* an earnest request — see PLEA 1

petition *vb* to make a request to (someone) in an earnest or urgent manner — see BEG

petitioner *n* one who asks earnestly for a favor or gift — see SUPPLICANT

pettish *adj* easily irritated or annoyed — see IRRITABLE

pettishness *n* readiness to show annoyance or impatience — see PETULANCE

petty *adj* 1 not broad or open in views or opinions — see NARROW 2

2 so small or unimportant as to warrant little or no attention — see NEGLIGIBLE 1

petulance *n* readiness to show annoyance or impatience ⟨I do not appreciate your *petulance* and eagerness to argue.⟩

syn crankiness, crossness, crotchetiness, grouchiness, grumpiness, huffiness, irascibility, irritability, irritableness, peevishness, perverseness, perversity, pettishness, testiness, waspishness

rel cantankerousness, crustiness, curmudgeonliness, disagreeableness, dyspepsia, fretfulness, orneriness, sulkiness, surliness; aggression, aggressiveness, bellicosity, belligerence, combativeness, contentiousness, contrariness, disputatiousness, pugnacity, scrappiness, truculence, truculency; fussiness, querulousness, rudeness; oversensitiveness, sensitivity, touchiness; animosity, antagonism, antipathy, fierceness, hostility, jaundice, rancor, unfriendliness; anger, exasperation, fury, indignation, wrath; hot-bloodedness, passion

near ant forbearance, long-suffering, patience, tolerance, understanding; affability, agreeableness, amenity, amicability, cordiality, friendliness, geniality, sociability; amiability, amiableness, good-humoredness, good-naturedness, good-temperedness; coolness, serenity, tranquillity (*or* tranquility); easygoingness, gentleness, kindliness, mildness

petulant *adj* easily irritated or annoyed — see IRRITABLE

phantasm *n* also **fantasm** *n* 1 a conception or image created by the imagination and having no objective reality — see FANTASY 1

2 the soul of a dead person thought of especially as appearing to living people — see GHOST 1

phantasmal *adj* not real and existing only in the imagination — see IMAGINARY

phantom *adj* not real and existing only in the imagination — see IMAGINARY

phantom *n* the soul of a dead person thought of especially as appearing to living people — see GHOST 1

pharmaceutical *n* a substance or preparation used to treat disease — see MEDICINE

pharmacist *n* a person who prepares drugs according to a doctor's prescription — see DRUGGIST

pharmacy *n* a retail store where medicines and miscellaneous articles are sold — see DRUGSTORE

phase *n* 1 a certain way in which something appears or may be regarded — see ASPECT 1

2 an individual part of a process, series, or ranking — see DEGREE 1

phased *adj* proceeding or changing by steps or degrees — see GRADUAL

phenomenal *adj* 1 being out of the ordinary — see EXCEPTIONAL 1

2 being so extraordinary or abnormal as to suggest powers which violate the laws of nature — see SUPERNATURAL 2

phenomenon *n* something extraordinary or surprising — see WONDER 1

philanthropic *also* **philanthropical** *adj* having or showing a concern for the welfare of others — see CHARITABLE 1

philanthropy *n* 1 a gift of money or its equivalent to a charity, humanitarian cause, or public institution — see CONTRIBUTION

2 the giving of necessities and especially money to the needy — see CHARITY 1

3 the quality or state of being generous — see LIBERALITY

philharmonic *n* a usually large group of musicians playing together — see ²BAND 1

philistine *n* a person who is chiefly interested in material comfort and is hostile or indifferent to art and culture ⟨the town's *philistines* who think that spending on the arts is a waste of taxpayers' money⟩

syn lowbrow, materialist

rel boor, bounder, cad, churl, clown, creep, heel, jerk, joker, louse, lout, rat, rotter, scum

near ant highbrow; middlebrow; egghead, intellectual, sage, thinker; brain, genius

philosophy *n* the basic beliefs or guiding principles of a person or group — see CREED 1

phlegm *n* a lack of emotion or emotional expressiveness — see APATHY 1

phlegmatic *adj* not feeling or showing emotion — see IMPASSIVE 1

phone *vb* to make a telephone call to — see CALL 2

phony *also* **phoney** *adj* 1 being such in appearance only and made or manufactured with the intention of committing fraud — see COUNTERFEIT 1

2 lacking in natural or spontaneous quality — see ARTIFICIAL 1

3 not being or expressing what one appears to be or express — see INSINCERE

phony *also* **phoney** *n* 1 an imitation that is passed off as genuine — see FAKE 1

2 one who makes false claims of identity or expertise — see IMPOSTOR

phony *vb* to imitate or copy especially in order to deceive — see FAKE 1

photo *n* a picture created from an image recorded on a light-sensitive surface by a camera — see PHOTOGRAPH

photo *vb* to take a photograph of — see PHOTOGRAPH

photograph *n* a picture created from an image recorded on a light-sensitive surface by a camera ⟨The old *photograph* was faded but still clear enough to make out.⟩
syn photo, print, shot, snap, snapshot
rel blowup, enlargement, still; telephoto; daguerreotype, tintype

photograph *vb* to take a photograph of ⟨We've been *photographing* the baby virtually nonstop.⟩
syn mug, photo, shoot, snap
rel image, picture, rephotograph, retake; film, videotape

photographer *n* one who takes photographs ⟨We'll need to choose a *photographer* for the wedding.⟩
syn shooter, shutterbug
rel cinematographer

phrase *n* a sequence of words having a specific meaning ⟨kids drawing literal representations of the *phrase* "to rain cats and dogs"⟩
syn expression, idiom
rel cliché (*also* clichè); locution, term; epithet, expletive, name; byword, cry, motto, shibboleth, slogan, watchword; archaism, colloquialism, euphemism, modernism, neologism, provincialism, vulgarism
phrases figure of speech

phrase *vb* to convey in appropriate or telling terms ⟨He had trouble thinking of how to *phrase* his question for the visiting dignitary.⟩
syn articulate, clothe, couch, express, formulate, put, say, state, word
rel craft, frame; hint, imply, insinuate, intimate, suggest; paraphrase, rephrase, restate, reword, summarize, translate; communicate, disclose, speak, talk, tell, utter, verbalize; describe, render, write up

phraseology *n* 1 a distinctive way of putting ideas into words — see STYLE 1
2 the way in which something is put into words — see WORDING 1

phrasing *n* 1 an act, process, or means of putting something into words — see EXPRESSION 1
2 the way in which something is put into words — see WORDING 1

phylactery *n* something worn or kept to bring good luck or keep away evil — see CHARM 1

physic *n* a substance or preparation used to treat disease — see MEDICINE

physical *adj* 1 of or relating to the human body ⟨*physical* sensations such as heat and pain⟩
syn animal, bodily, carnal, corporal, corporeal, fleshly, material, somatic
rel anatomic (*or* anatomical), physiological (*or* physiologic); sensual, sensuous; hand-to-hand
near ant cerebral, inner, intellectual, mental, psychological (*also* psychologic); bodiless, immaterial, incorporeal, insubstantial, spiritual; ethereal, metaphysical
ant nonmaterial, nonphysical
2 relating to or composed of matter — see MATERIAL 1

physician *n* a person specially trained in healing human medical disorders — see DOCTOR

physique *n* the type of body that a person has ⟨exercise equipment that can be adjusted to suit the user's *physique*⟩
syn build, constitution, figure, form, frame, habit, shape
rel structure

picayune *adj* 1 not broad or open in views or opinions — see NARROW 2
2 so small or unimportant as to warrant little or no attention — see NEGLIGIBLE 1

picayune *n* something of little importance — see TRIFLE

pick *n* 1 a person or thing that is chosen — see CHOICE 2
2 individuals carefully selected as being the best of a class — see ELITE 1
3 the power, right, or opportunity to choose — see CHOICE 1

pick *vb* 1 to catch or collect (a crop or natural resource) for human use — see HARVEST
2 to decide to accept (someone or something) from a group of possibilities — see CHOOSE 1
3 to bring (something volatile or intense) into being — see INCITE 1
4 to eat reluctantly and in small bites — see NIBBLE 1
5 to penetrate or hold (something) with a pointed object — see IMPALE

picked *adj* singled out from a number or group as more to one's liking — see SELECT 1

picker *n* someone with the right or responsibility for making a selection — see SELECTOR

picket *n* a person or group that watches over someone or something — see GUARD 1

picking *n* the act or process of selecting — see SELECTION 1

pickle *n* a difficult, puzzling, or embarrassing situation from which there is no easy escape — see PREDICAMENT

pick up *vb* 1 to acquire complete knowledge, understanding, or skill in — see LEARN 1
2 to bring together in one body or place — see GATHER 1
3 to get possession of (something) by giving money in exchange for — see BUY 1
4 to gradually increase in — see GAIN 1
5 to move from a lower to a higher place or position — see RAISE 1
6 to take or keep under one's control by authority of law — see ARREST 1
7 to make a place neat and orderly by removing extraneous stuff — see CLEAN (UP) 1
8 to begin again or return to after an interruption — see RESUME

picky *adj* 1 hard to please — see FINICKY
2 tending to select carefully — see SELECTIVE

---

syn synonym(s)   **rel** related words
ant antonym(s)   **near ant** near antonym(s)

picnic *n* something that is easy to do — see CINCH

pictorial *adj* **1** consisting of or relating to pictures ⟨That photojournalist is planning to do a primarily *pictorial* report on the wildlife sanctuaries in Africa.⟩
syn graphic (*also* graphical), visual
rel photographic, video; drawn, painted, represented; illustrational, illustrative
2 producing a mental picture through clear and impressive description — see GRAPHIC 1

picture *n* **1** a two-dimensional design intended to look like a person or thing ⟨Using only watercolors, she produced a strikingly lifelike *picture* of her mother.⟩
syn icon (*also* ikon), illustration, image, likeness
rel delineation, depiction, representation, resemblance, view; portrait; daub, drawing, finger painting; etching, silhouette, sketch, watercolor; caricature, cartoon; montage, photograph; hieroglyph, hieroglyphic, ideogram, ideograph; pictograph; diagram
2 a story told by means of a series of continuously projected pictures and a sound track — see MOVIE 1
3 a vivid representation in words of someone or something — see DESCRIPTION 1
4 position with regard to conditions and circumstances — see SITUATION 1
5 something or someone that strongly resembles another — see IMAGE 1
6 something imagined or pictured in the mind — see IDEA 1
7 **pictures** *pl* the art or business of making a movie — see MOVIE 2

picture *vb* **1** to present a picture of ⟨the famous painting that *pictures* the Founding Fathers signing the Declaration of Independence⟩
syn depict, image, portray, represent
rel delineate, describe, document, render; outline, silhouette, sketch; illustrate, show; diagram; caricature
2 to form a mental picture of — see IMAGINE 1
3 to give a representation or account of in words — see DESCRIBE 1
4 to make a representation by producing lines on a surface — see DRAW 1

picture-perfect *adj* being without any fault or flaw — see PERFECT 1

picturesque *adj* producing a mental picture through clear and impressive description — see GRAPHIC 1

piddling *adj* so small or unimportant as to warrant little or no attention — see NEGLIGIBLE 1

piebald *adj* having blotches of two or more colors — see PIED

piece *n* **1** a broken or irregular part of something that often remains incomplete — see FRAGMENT
2 a literary, musical, or artistic production — see COMPOSITION 1
3 a portable weapon from which a shot is discharged by gunpowder — see GUN 1
4 something belonging to, due to, or contributed by an individual member of a group — see SHARE 1

piece *vb* to form by putting together parts or materials — see BUILD

piece by piece *adv* by small steps or amounts — see GRADUALLY

piecemeal *adj* proceeding or changing by steps or degrees — see GRADUAL

piecemeal *adv* **1** by small steps or amounts — see GRADUALLY
2 into parts or pieces — see APART

pied *adj* having blotches of two or more colors ⟨Although the mother's was pure black, the foal's coat was *pied.*⟩
syn blotched, dappled (*also* dapple), marbled, mottled, piebald, pinto, splotched, spotted
rel shaded; checkered, motley, multicolored, polychromatic, polychrome, varicolored, variegated; blotted, brindled (*or* brindle); calico, speckled, streaked; colorful, pigmented; dotted, peppered, sprinkled; stippled
near ant monochromatic, solid

pier *n* **1** a structure used by boats and ships for taking on or landing cargo and passengers — see DOCK
2 an upright shaft that supports an overhead structure — see PILLAR 1

pierce *vb* **1** to go or come in or into — see ENTER 1
2 to make a hole or series of holes in — see PERFORATE
3 to penetrate or hold (something) with a pointed object — see IMPALE

piercing *adj* **1** causing intense discomfort to one's skin — see CUTTING 1
2 marked by a high volume of sound — see LOUD 1

piety *n* **1** belief and trust in and loyalty to God — see FAITH 1
2 the quality or state of being spiritually pure or virtuous — see HOLINESS
3 adherence to something to which one is bound by a pledge or duty — see FIDELITY

piffle *n* language, behavior, or ideas that are absurd and contrary to good sense — see NONSENSE 1

pig *n* one who eats greedily or too much — see GLUTTON

pigeon *n* one who is easily deceived or cheated — see ¹DUPE

piggish *adj* having a huge appetite — see VORACIOUS 1

pigheaded *adj* sticking to an opinion, purpose, or course of action in spite of reason, arguments, or persuasion — see OBSTINATE

pigment *n* a substance used to color other materials ⟨I'm running out of the black *pigment.*⟩
syn color, coloring, dye, dyestuff, stain
rel tint, toner; cast, hue, shade, tinge
pigment *vb* to give color or a different color to — see COLOR 1

pig out *vb* to eat greedily or to excess — see GORGE 2

pigpen *n* a dirty or messy place ⟨Your room is a *pigpen*—so clean it up!⟩
syn dump, hole, pigsty, shambles, sty
rel chaos, confusion, disarrangement, disarray, disorder, disorganization, mess, muddle, muss; havoc, hell; clutter, jumble, litter, mishmash, welter

pigsty *n* a dirty or messy place — see PIGPEN

¹pike *n* a passage cleared for public vehicular travel — see WAY 1

²pike *n* a weapon with a long straight handle and sharp head or blade — see SPEAR

³pike *n* the last and usually sharp or tapering part of something long and narrow — see POINT 2

piker *n* a mean grasping person who is usually stingy with money — see MISER

pikestaff *n* a weapon with a long straight handle and sharp head or blade — see SPEAR

pilaster *n* an upright shaft that supports an overhead structure — see PILLAR 1

¹pile *n* 1 a quantity of things thrown or stacked on one another ⟨a large *pile* of newspapers that needed to be disposed of⟩
syn cock, heap, hill, mound, mountain, stack
rel bank, bar, drift, embankment; bed, layer; mow, pyramid, rick; barrow, cairn, pyre; accumulation, aggregate, array, assemblage, collection, conglomeration, gathering, grouping, hoard, huddle, jumble, knot
2 a considerable amount — see LOT 2
3 a very large amount of money — see FORTUNE 2

²pile *n* 1 a soft airy substance or covering — see FUZZ
2 the hairy covering of a mammal especially when fine, soft, and thick — see FUR 1

pile *vb* 1 to lay or throw on top of one another ⟨*piled* all the clothes on the chair before putting them away⟩
syn heap, mound, stack
rel bank; layer; pyramid; accumulate, amass, assemble, collect, concentrate, garner, gather, group, mass; bunch, clump, lump
ant unpile
2 to gather into a closely packed group — see ²PRESS 3

pile (up) *vb* to gradually form into a layer, pile, or mass — see COLLECT 2

pilfer *vb* to take (something) without right and with an intent to keep — see STEAL 1

pilgrimage *vb* to take a trip especially of some distance — see TRAVEL 1

pill *n* 1 a small mass containing medicine to be taken orally ⟨You'll have to take one of these *pills* every six hours for your flu.⟩
syn cap, capsule, lozenge, tablet
rel cure, drug, medication, pharmaceutical, physic, remedy, specific; miracle drug, wonder drug; potion, preparation; dosage, dose
2 a person whose behavior is offensive to others — see JERK 1

pillage *n* valuables stolen or taken by force — see LOOT

pillage *vb* to search through with the intent of committing robbery — see RANSACK 1

pillar *n* 1 an upright shaft that supports an overhead structure ⟨The ancient Greek temple boasted graceful marble *pillars* with richly ornamented tops.⟩
syn column, pier, pilaster, post, stanchion
rel caryatid, pedestal; buttress, flying buttress; needle, obelisk; pile, piling
2 something or someone to which one looks for support — see DEPENDENCE 2

pilot *adj* made or done as an experiment — see EXPERIMENTAL 1

pilot *n* one who flies or is qualified to fly an aircraft or spacecraft ⟨The airline is seeking experienced *pilots* to fly the new airplane.⟩
syn airman, aviator, birdman, flier (*also* flyer)
rel ace, barnstormer, bush pilot, copilot, flyboy, test pilot; captain, skipper

pilot *vb* 1 to give advice and instruction to (someone) regarding the course or process to be followed — see GUIDE 1
2 to point out the way for (someone) especially from a position in front — see LEAD 1
3 to operate or control the course of — see NAVIGATE 1

pin *n* a lower limb of an animal — see LEG 1

pinch *n* 1 an instance of theft — see THEFT 1
2 the act of taking into one's control by authority of law — see ARREST 1
3 a falling short of an essential or desirable amount or number — see DEFICIENCY

pinch *vb* 1 to squeeze tightly between two surfaces, edges, or points ⟨The zipper on those jeans always *pinches* me.⟩
syn nip
rel crimp, tweak; clasp, clutch, grasp, grip, hold, take
near ant drop, free, loose, loosen, release, spring
2 to take (something) without right and with an intent to keep — see STEAL 1
3 to take or keep under one's control by authority of law — see ARREST 1
4 to avoid unnecessary waste or expense — see ECONOMIZE

pincher *n* one who steals — see THIEF

pinch–hit *vb* to serve as a replacement usually for a time only — see COVER 1

pinch hitter *n* a person or thing that takes the place of another — see SUBSTITUTE

pinching *n* the quality or practice of being overly sparing with money — see PARSIMONY 1

pine (for) *vb* to have an earnest wish to own or enjoy — see DESIRE 1

pinhead *n* a stupid person — see IDIOT

pinhole *n* a mark or small hole made by a pointed instrument — see PRICK 1

pining *n* a strong wish for something — see DESIRE 1

pinnacle *n* the highest part or point — see HEIGHT 1

pinpoint *adj* meeting the highest standard of accuracy — see PRECISE 1

pinpoint *vb* 1 to find out or establish the identity of — see IDENTIFY 1
2 to point or turn (something) toward a target or goal — see AIM 1

pinprick *n* a mark or small hole made by a pointed instrument — see PRICK 1

---

syn synonym(s)   *rel* related words
ant antonym(s)   *near ant* near antonym(s)

pinto adj having blotches of two or more colors — see PIED

pint-size or **pint-sized** adj of a size that is less than average — see SMALL 1

pioneer adj coming before all others in time or order — see FIRST 1

pioneer n a person who settles in a new region — see FRONTIERSMAN

pioneer vb to be responsible for the creation and early operation or use of — see FOUND

pious adj 1 firm in one's allegiance to someone or something — see FAITHFUL 1
2 showing a devotion to God and to a life of virtue — see HOLY 1

piousness n 1 the pretending of having virtues, principles, or beliefs that one in fact does not have — see HYPOCRISY
2 the quality or state of being spiritually pure or virtuous — see HOLINESS

¹**pip** n a small area that is different (as in color) from the main part — see SPOT 1

²**pip** n something very good of its kind — see JIM-DANDY

pip n to make a short sharp sound like a small bird — see CHIRP

pipe n 1 a long hollow cylinder for carrying a substance (as a liquid or gas) ⟨The plumber came and fixed the water *pipe* that was leaking.⟩
syn channel, conduit, duct, leader, line, penstock, trough, tube
rel drain, drainpipe, funnel, hydrant, main, smokestack, spout, standpipe, stovepipe, tile, waste pipe, waterspout; pipage (or pipeage), pipeline, piping
2 an enclosed vessel for holding beverages — see CASK

pipe vb 1 to cause to move to a central point or along a restricted pathway — see CHANNEL
2 to make a short sharp sound like a small bird — see CHIRP

pipe down vb 1 to become still and orderly — see QUIET 1
2 to stop talking — see SHUT UP 1

pipe dream n a conception or image created by the imagination and having no objective reality — see FANTASY 1

pipeline n a direct way of passing along information or supplies ⟨A roadie serves as the columnist's *pipeline* for news about the band.⟩ ⟨The enemy destroyed our *pipeline* for resupply.⟩
syn channel
rel avenue, conduit, route; grapevine, outlet; origin, source; supplier; connection, contact

piping adj having a high musical pitch or range — see SHRILL

piping hot adj having a notably high temperature — see HOT 1

pip-squeak n a person of no importance or influence — see NOBODY

piquancy n the quality or state of being stimulating to the mind or senses ⟨a talk show host known for the quickness and *piquancy* of his wit⟩ ⟨I appreciated the *piquancy* of the peppers in the sauce.⟩
syn nip, pungency, spice, zest, zing
rel raciness, spiciness; fieriness, hotness; acuteness, keenness, sharpness; provocativeness; excitement, invigoration, stimu-

lant, stimulation, stimulus, thrill; flavor, redolence, savor (also savour), savoriness, tastiness
near ant flatness, tastelessness; dullness (also dulness), insipidity, monotonousness, monotony, predictability, tediousness; blandness, thinness, weakness
ant insipidity

piquant adj sharp and pleasantly stimulating to the mind or senses ⟨a *piquant* tidbit of information about the new neighbors⟩ ⟨The *piquant* cuisine of India boasts some highly spiced dishes.⟩
syn pert, poignant, pungent, salty, savory (also savoury), zesty
rel racy, spicy; fiery, gingery, hot, peppery, vinegary; acute, keen; biting, bitter, cutting, mordant, trenchant; animating, energizing, exciting, galvanizing, invigorating, piquing, provocative, provoking; ambrosial, appetizing, delectable, delicious, luscious, palatable, scrumptious, toothsome; flavorful, savorous, tasty
near ant flat, flavorless, savorless, tasteless; arid, banal, barren, boring, colorless, drab, dreary, dry, dull, flat, humdrum, leaden, monotonous, numbing, pedestrian, ponderous, stale, stodgy, tedious, tiring, wearisome; bland, dilute, thin, watery, weak
ant insipid, zestless

pique n the feeling of being offended or resentful after a slight or indignity ⟨After a moment of *pique*, she responded calmly to the accusation.⟩
syn dudgeon, huff, offense (or offence), peeve, resentment, umbrage
rel aggravation, anger, annoyance, bother, discomfort, exasperation, frustration, irritation, vexation; agitation, angriness, displeasure, distress, disturbance, indignation, irateness, ire, outrage, upset; dander, temper; fit, pouts, sulk(s); tantrum, tizzy; affront, barb, dig, indignity, insult, putdown, slap, slight, slur
near ant satisfaction; appeasement, mollification, pacification; contentment, delight, gratification, happiness, pleasure

pique vb 1 to disturb the peace of mind of (someone) especially by repeated disagreeable acts — see IRRITATE 1
2 to rouse to strong feeling or action — see PROVOKE 1

piquing adj serving or likely to arouse a strong reaction — see PROVOCATIVE

piracy n the act or pursuit of robbing ships at sea ⟨Many countries have harsh penalties for *piracy* now.⟩
syn pirating
rel depredation, despoilment, despoliation, looting, marauding, pillaging, plunder, plundering, raiding, robbery, sacking; privateering

pirate n someone who engages in robbery of ships at sea ⟨Sir Francis Drake was a British *pirate* who preyed on Spanish ships with the connivance of Elizabeth I.⟩
syn buccaneer, corsair, freebooter, rover
rel despoiler, looter, marauder, pillager, plunderer, raider, robber; privateer

pirate vb to take or make use of under a guise of authority but without actual right — see APPROPRIATE 1

pirating *n* the act or pursuit of robbing ships at sea — see PIRACY

pirouette *n* a rapid turning about on an axis or central point — see SPIN 1

pirouette *vb* to move in circles around an axis or center — see SPIN 1

pit *n* a sunken area forming a separate space — see HOLE 2

pit-a-pat *vb* to expand and contract in a rhythmic manner — see PULSATE

pitch *n* 1 an act or instance of diving — see DIVE 1

2 the degree to which something rises up from a position level with the horizon — see SLANT 1

pitch *vb* 1 to fix in an upright position — see ERECT 1

2 to cast oneself head first into deep water — see DIVE 1

3 to make a series of unsteady side-to-side motions — see ROCK 1

4 to send through the air especially with a quick forward motion of the arm — see THROW 1

5 to get rid of as useless or unwanted — see DISCARD

6 to provide publicity for — see PUBLICIZE 1

7 to set or cause to be at an angle — see LEAN 1

pitch-black *adj* 1 being without light or without much light — see DARK 1

2 having the color of soot or coal — see BLACK 1

pitch-dark *adj* 1 being without light or without much light — see DARK 1

2 having the color of soot or coal — see BLACK 1

pitched *adj* 1 inclined or twisted to one side — see AWRY

2 running in a slanting direction — see DIAGONAL

pitcher *n* a handled container for holding and pouring liquids that usually has a lip or a spout ⟨Please bring me the *pitcher* of lemonade from the table.⟩

syn ewer, flagon, jug

rel carafe, decanter; bucket, pail, pot; bottle, canteen, cup, fiasco, flask, jorum, mug, stein, stoup, tankard; kettle, teakettle

pitch in *vb* to make a donation as part of a group effort — see CONTRIBUTE 1

pitchy *adj* 1 being without light or without much light — see DARK 1

2 having the color of soot or coal — see BLACK 1

piteous *adj* deserving of one's pity — see PATHETIC 1

pitfall *n* 1 a danger or difficulty that is hidden or not easily recognized ⟨Buying a house can be full of *pitfalls* for the unwary.⟩

syn booby trap, catch, gimmick, hitch, joker, snag

rel snare, trap, trip wire, web; hazard, peril, risk; bomb, bombshell, kicker, surprise (*also* surprize); bait, decoy, lure

2 something that may cause injury or harm — see DANGER 2

pith *n* the central part or aspect of something under consideration — see CRUX

pithily *adv* in a few words — see SHORTLY 1

pithiness *n* the quality or state of being marked by or using only few words to convey much meaning — see SUCCINCTNESS

pithy *adj* marked by the use of few words to convey much information or meaning — see CONCISE

pitiable *adj* 1 arousing or deserving of one's loathing and disgust — see CONTEMPTIBLE 1

2 deserving pitying scorn (as for inadequacy) — see PITIFUL 1

3 deserving of one's pity — see PATHETIC 1

pitiful *adj* 1 deserving pitying scorn (as for inadequacy) ⟨That piece of junk is a *pitiful* excuse for a car.⟩

syn contemptible, despicable, miserable, pathetic, pitiable, sad, sorry, wretched

rel deplorable, discreditable, disgraceful, disreputable, ignominious, infamous, misbegotten, notorious, shameful; abhorrent, abominable, beastly, detestable, hateful, lousy, odious, stinking; bad, inferior, lame, poor; dishonorable, shameful; meritless, unworthy, worthless

near ant admirable, commendable, creditable, laudable, meritorious, praiseworthy, redoubtable; notable, noteworthy, noticeable, outstanding, reputable, worthy; excellent; flawless, perfect; honorable, noble

ant decent, presentable, respectable

2 arousing or deserving of one's loathing and disgust — see CONTEMPTIBLE 1

3 deserving of one's pity — see PATHETIC 1

pitiless *adj* having or showing a lack of sympathy or tender feelings — see HARD 1

pittance *n* a very small sum of money — see MITE 1

pitter-patter *vb* to expand and contract in a rhythmic manner — see PULSATE

pity *n* 1 a regrettable or blameworthy act — see CRIME 1

2 the capacity for feeling for another's unhappiness or misfortune — see HEART 1

pity *vb* to have sympathy for ⟨I always *pity* the people who have to work in this freezing weather.⟩

syn ache (for), bleed (for), commiserate (with), condole (with), feel (for), sympathize (with), yearn (over)

rel care (for); grieve (for), sorrow (for); love; empathize (with), identify (with); tolerate, understand

near ant disregard, ignore, neglect, overlook; dislike, hate, scorn

pivot *n* the central part or aspect of something under consideration — see CRUX

pivot *vb* to move (something) in a curved or circular path on or as if on an axis — see TURN 1

pivotal *adj* of the greatest possible importance — see CRUCIAL

pixie *also* **pixy** *n* an imaginary being usually having a small human form and magical powers — see FAIRY

pixieish *adj* tending to or exhibiting reckless playfulness — see MISCHIEVOUS 1

placard *n* a sheet bearing an announcement for posting in a public place — see POSTER

placard *vb* 1 to affix (as a notice) to or on a suitable place — see ¹POST 1

2 to make known openly or publicly — see ANNOUNCE

placate *vb* to lessen the anger or agitation of — see PACIFY 1

placating *adj* tending to lessen or avoid conflict or hostility — see PACIFIC 1

place *n* 1 the area or space occupied by or intended for something ⟨the *place* chosen for the picnic⟩ ⟨There's the *place* where I left my umbrella.⟩

syn locale, locality, location, locus, point, position, site, spot, where

rel scene; region, section, sector; here, there

2 a building, room, or suite of rooms occupied by a service business ⟨We're going to our favorite *place* to eat.⟩

syn establishment, joint, parlor, salon

rel spot, station; facility, installation; club, house; den, dive, hole

3 an assignment at which one regularly works for pay — see JOB 1

4 an extent or area available for or used up by some activity or thing — see ROOM 1

5 the action for which a person or thing is specially fitted or used or for which a thing exists — see ROLE

6 the place where one lives — see HOME 1

7 the placement of someone or something in relation to others in a vertical arrangement — see RANK 1

8 a situation or activity for which a person or thing is best suited — see NICHE 2

9 an individual part of a process, series, or ranking — see DEGREE 1

place *vb* 1 to arrange something in a certain spot or position ⟨He carefully *placed* the flowers in a vase.⟩

syn depose, deposit, dispose, fix, lay, position, put, set, set up, situate, stick

rel move, rearrange, reorder, shift; orient; establish, locate, plant, settle; clap, flop, plop, plump, plunk (*or* plonk); put down, slap; ensconce, niche; assemble, collect; carry; berth, park; affix, anchor, lock, lodge, wedge; array, lay out, line up, queue, rank; set down

near ant remove, take; banish; dislodge, displace, replace, supersede, supplant

2 to arrange or assign according to type — see CLASSIFY 1

3 to decide the size, amount, number, or distance of (something) without actual measurement — see ESTIMATE 2

4 to take or have a certain position within a group arranged in vertical classes — see RANK 1

5 to pick (someone) by one's authority for a specific position or duty — see APPOINT 2

6 to present or bring forward for discussion — see INTRODUCE 2

7 to provide with a paying job — see EMPLOY 1

placid *adj* 1 free from emotional or mental agitation — see CALM 2

2 free from storms or physical disturbance — see CALM 1

3 free from disturbing noise or uproar — see QUIET 1

placidity *n* 1 a state of freedom from storm or disturbance — see CALM 1

2 evenness of emotions or temper — see EQUANIMITY

3 freedom from disquieting or oppressive thoughts or emotions — see PEACE 1

plague *n* a widespread disease resulting in a high rate of death ⟨The Black Death was a *plague* that killed about one third of Europe's population in the Middle Ages.⟩

syn pest, pestilence

rel pandemic; affection, affliction, ailment, contagion, illness, infection, infirmity, malady, sickness; curse, scourge

plague *vb* to cause persistent suffering to — see AFFLICT

plain *adj* 1 free from all additions or embellishment ⟨I like my hamburgers *plain*, with no ketchup or relish.⟩ ⟨Just give us the *plain* facts.⟩

syn bald, bare, naked, simple, unadorned, undecorated, unvarnished

rel denuded, divested, stripped; au naturel, earthy, elemental, homely, natural, unsophisticated; clean; austere, bleak, severe, stark; minimalist; inconspicuous, muted, restrained, sober, subdued, toned (down), unobtrusive; conservative, quiet, understated; no-frills

near ant flamboyant, flashy, garish, gaudy, glittery, glitzy, loud, ostentatious, showy, splashy, swank (*or* swanky), tawdry; bedizened, florid, lurid, ornate; overdecorated, overdone, overwrought; elaborate, extravagant, ornate, rococo; apparelled (*or* apparelled), arrayed, bedecked, decked-out, dressed, embroidered, garnished, trimmed

ant adorned, decorated, embellished, fancy, ornamented

2 free from added matter — see PURE 1

3 free in expressing one's true feelings and opinions — see FRANK

4 going straight to the point clearly and firmly — see STRAIGHTFORWARD 1

5 not subject to misinterpretation or more than one interpretation — see CLEAR 2

plain *adv* in an honest and direct manner — see STRAIGHTFORWARD

plain *n* 1 a broad area of level or rolling treeless country ⟨The first settlers in that area lived on the vast *plains* in lonely log cabins.⟩

syn down(s), grassland, lea (*or* ley), moor, prairie, savanna (*also* savannah), steppe, tundra, veld (*or* veldt)

rel field, meadow; floodplain; bottom, bottomland, flat, lowland; plateau, table, tableland, upland

2 a wide space or area — see EXPANSE

plainly *adv* 1 in an honest and direct manner — see STRAIGHTFORWARD

2 without any question — see INDEED 1

plainness *n* 1 the free expression of one's true feelings and opinions — see CANDOR 1

2 the quality or state of having a form or

structure of few parts or elements — see SIMPLICITY 1

plainspoken *adj* free in expressing one's true feelings and opinions — see FRANK

plaint *n* **1** a crying out in grief — see LAMENT 1

2 an expression of dissatisfaction, pain, or resentment — see COMPLAINT 1

plaintiff *n* the person in a legal proceeding who makes a charge of wrongdoing against another — see COMPLAINANT

plaintive *adj* expressing or suggesting mourning — see MOURNFUL 1

plait *n* a length of something formed of three or more strands woven together — see BRAID

plait *vb* to form into a braid — see BRAID

plan *n* **1** a method worked out in advance for achieving some objective ⟨There is a contingency *plan* in the office for handling almost any emergency.⟩

syn arrangement, blueprint, design, game, ground plan, program, project, scheme, strategy, system

rel collusion, conspiracy, plot; contrivance, device, maneuver, ruse, stratagem, subterfuge, trick; counterplan, counterstrategy; means, tactic, technique, way; procedure, protocol; conception, idea, projet, proposal, specific(s), specification(s); aim, intent, intention, purpose; diagram, formula, layout, map, pattern, platform, policy, setup

2 something that one hopes or intends to accomplish — see GOAL

plan *vb* to work out the details of (something) in advance ⟨We *planned* the school dance down to the smallest detail.⟩

syn arrange, blueprint, budget, calculate, chart, design, frame, lay out, map (out), organize, prepare, project, scheme (out), shape

rel conspire, contrive, devise, intrigue, machinate, plot, put up; concert, get up; draft, outline, sketch; aim, figure, have on, intend, mean; contemplate, meditate, premeditate

2 to have in mind as a purpose or goal — see INTEND 1

plane *adj* having a surface without bends, breaks, or irregularities — see LEVEL 1

plane *n* a vehicle for traveling through the air that has fixed wings for lift — see AIRPLANE

¹plane *vb* to make free from breaks, curves, or bumps — see EVEN 1

²plane *vb* to move through the air with or as if with outstretched wings — see FLY 1

planet *n* the celestial body on which we live — see EARTH 1

plant *n* a building or set of buildings for the manufacturing of goods — see FACTORY

plant *vb* **1** to put or set into the ground to grow ⟨I'll *plant* the marigold seeds in the spring.⟩

syn drill, put in, seed, sow

rel bed; replant, transplant; broadcast, scatter; pot; overseed, reseed

near ant gather, harvest, reap

2 to be responsible for the creation and early operation or use of — see FOUND

3 to set permanently in the consciousness or mind-set — see IMPLANT 1

plantation *n* a settlement in a new country or region — see COLONY 1

planter *n* a person who cultivates the land and grows crops on it — see FARMER

plash *vb* **1** to flow in a broken irregular stream — see GURGLE

2 to move with a splashing motion — see SLOSH 1

3 to wet or soil by striking with something liquid or mushy — see SPLASH 2

plaster *n* a medicated covering used to heal an injury — see DRESSING 1

plastic *adj* **1** capable of being easily molded or modeled ⟨Silly Putty is famous for being very *plastic*.⟩

syn malleable

rel adaptable; bendable, ductile, pliable, pliant, supple, willowy; elastic, flexible, limber, resilient, workable; bending, giving, kneadable, tractable, yielding

near ant inflexible, intractable, rigid, stiff

2 lacking in natural or spontaneous quality — see ARTIFICIAL 1

plasticity *n* the quality or state of being easily molded ⟨We chose that type of clay for its greater *plasticity*.⟩

syn malleability

rel adaptability; ductility, pliability, pliableness, pliancy, pliantness, suppleness; elasticity, flexibility, limberness, resilience, workability, workableness

near ant inflexibility, rigidity, stiffness

¹plat *n* a length of something formed of three or more strands woven together — see BRAID

²plat *n* **1** a small area of usually open land — see FIELD 1

2 a small piece of land that is developed or available for development — see LOT 1

plat *vb* to form into a braid — see BRAID

plate *n* **1** a small thin piece of material that resembles an animal scale — see ²SCALE

2 something that visually explains or decorates a text — see ILLUSTRATION 1

plateau *n* a broad flat area of elevated land ⟨Indigenous peoples have inhabited the *plateau* for centuries.⟩

syn mesa, table, tableland

rel butte, height, highland; upland

platform *n* a level usually raised surface ⟨You'll have to stand up there on the *platform* for your speech.⟩

syn dais, podium, rostrum, stage, stand

rel altar, pulpit; riser, scaffold; gallery

platitude *n* an idea or expression that has been used by many people — see COMMONPLACE

plaudit *n, usually* **plaudits** *pl* enthusiastic and usually public expression of approval — see APPLAUSE 1

plausible *adj* worthy of being accepted as true or reasonable — see BELIEVABLE

play *n* **1** activity engaged in to amuse oneself ⟨It's such a delight to watch the children in their *play*.⟩

syn dalliance, frolic, frolicking, fun, recreation, relaxation, rollicking, sport

rel gamboling (*or* gambolling); romping; amusement, diversion, entertainment; pas-

---

syn synonym(s) *rel* related words
ant antonym(s) *near ant* near antonym(s)

time; friskiness, playfulness, sportiveness, wantonness; knavery, mischief, mischievousness, rascality, roguishness, waggery; binge, fling, kick, lark, revel, rollick, spree; hilarity, merriment, merrymaking, revelry; high jinks (*also* hijinks), horseplay, tomfoolery; avocation, pursuit

near ant drudgery, labor, work; duty, obligation, responsibility

2 a written work in which the story is told through speech and action that is intended to be acted out on stage ⟨We'll be putting on a school *play* using that stage.⟩

syn drama, dramatization

rel interlude, playlet; comedy, docudrama, melodrama, musical, musical comedy, tragedy, tragicomedy; magnum opus, opus, work

3 an attitude or manner not to be taken seriously — see FUN 2

4 the act or practice of employing something for a particular purpose — see USE 1

5 a clever often underhanded means to achieve an end — see TRICK 1

play *vb* **1** to engage in activity for amusement ⟨He needed some time to run and *play* in the yard after his hard work.⟩

syn dally, disport, frolic, recreate, rollick, skylark, sport

rel cavort, frisk, gambol, romp; dabble, trifle; amuse, divert, entertain; delight, please; fiddle (around), putter (around); bum (around), dawdle, idle, loaf, lounge (around *or* about), relax, rest, screw around, slack (off); jest, joke, tease

near ant drudge, labor, plod, plug (away), strain, strive, struggle, sweat, toil, work

2 to present a portrayal or performance of — see ACT 1

3 to pretend to be (what one is not) in appearance or behavior — see IMPERSONATE 1

4 to spend time in aimless activity — see FIDDLE (AROUND)

5 to deal with (something) usually skillfully or efficiently — see HANDLE 1

6 to risk (something) on the outcome of an uncertain event — see BET

play (on *or* upon) *vb* to take unfair advantage of — see EXPLOIT 1

play (upon) *vb* to control or take advantage of by artful, unfair, or insidious means — see MANIPULATE 1

play (with) *vb* to handle thoughtlessly, ignorantly, or mischievously — see TAMPER (WITH)

play down *vb* to express scornfully one's low opinion of — see DECRY 1

played out *adj* depleted in strength, energy, or freshness — see WEARY 1

player *n* **1** a person who plays a musical instrument — see MUSICIAN 1

2 one who acts professionally (as in a play, movie, or television show) — see ACTOR 1

3 one who takes part in something — see PARTICIPANT

playful *adj* given to good-natured joking or teasing ⟨The little girl was lighthearted and *playful*.⟩

syn antic, coltish, elfish, fay, frisky, frolicsome, rollicking, sportive

rel coy, kittenish; happy, lighthearted,

whimsical; energetic, frolic, jocund, lively, merry, spirited, sprightly, spunky, vivacious; devilish, impish, knavish, mischievous, pixie (*also* pixy), rascally, roguish; amusing, diverting, enjoyable, entertaining, fun, pleasurable; dabbling, frivolous, goofy, silly, trifling; jesting, jocose, jocular, joking, prankish, teasing

near ant dutiful, responsible; grave, grim, serious, solemn, somber (*or* sombre), stern, stolid; no-nonsense, priggish, starchy, stuffy; decorous, formal, proper, sedate, staid; guarded, inhibited, restrained

ant earnest, serious-minded, sober, sobersided

playfulness *n* a natural disposition for playful behavior ⟨The *playfulness* of the kitten can be quite amusing.⟩

syn friskiness, impishness, mischief, mischievousness, prankishness, sportiveness

rel coyness, kittenishness; archness, devilment, devilry (*or* deviltry), hob, rascality, roguishness, waggery; devilishness, diabolicalness, knavery; frivolousness; energy, liveliness, spiritedness, sprightliness, spunkiness, vivaciousness, vivacity; gaiety (*also* gayety), jocularity, lightheartedness, mirthfulness, whimsicality

near ant graveness, grimness, seriousness, solemnity, sternness; priggishness, starchiness, stuffiness; constraint, restraint, self-control

ant earnestness, soberness

playhouse *n* a building or part of a building where movies are shown — see THEATER 1

play out *vb* to make complete use of — see DEPLETE 1

plea *n* **1** an earnest request ⟨a *plea* for donations⟩

syn appeal, cry, desire, entreaty, petition, pleading, prayer, solicitation, suit, supplication

rel application, requisition; call, claim, demand, insistence

2 an explanation that frees one from fault or blame — see EXCUSE

plead *vb* to state (something) as a reason in support of or against something under consideration — see ARGUE 1

plead (for) *vb* to make a request for — see ASK (FOR) 1

plead (to) *vb* to make a request to (someone) in an earnest or urgent manner — see BEG

pleader *n* one who asks earnestly for a favor or gift — see SUPPLICANT

pleading *adj* asking humbly — see SUPPLIANT

pleading *n* an earnest request — see PLEA 1

pleasant *adj* **1** giving pleasure or contentment to the mind or senses ⟨The massage was extremely *pleasant* and relaxing.⟩

syn agreeable, blessed (*also* blest), congenial, darling, delectable, delicious, delightful, dreamy, enjoyable, felicitous, good, grateful, gratifying, heavenly, jolly, luscious, nice, palatable, pleasing, pleasurable, pretty, satisfying, savory (*also* savoury), sweet, tasty, welcome

rel alluring, attractive, desirable, enviable,

inviting, relishable, tempting; charming, enchanting, fascinating; calming, comforting, soothing; amusing, diverting, entertaining, recreative; affable, amiable, cheerful, cheery, comfortable, genial, goodly, good-natured, gracious, hospitable, kindly, personable; glad, happy, joyous; elating, exhilarating; ecstatic, euphoric, rapturous

near ant abominable, ghastly, god-awful, hellish, horrid, miserable, wretched; distasteful, obnoxious, offensive, repellent (*also* repellant), repugnant, repulsive, unsavory, vile, yucky (*also* yukky); abhorrent, detestable, hateful, odious; displeasing, dissatisfying; depressing, disheartening, dismal, dreary, gloomy, heartbreaking, heartrending, joyless, sad, unhappy; deplorable, doleful, dolorous, lamentable, lugubrious, mournful, regrettable, sorrowful, tragic (*also* tragical); aggravating, annoying, exasperating, irritating, peeving, perturbing, vexing; forbidding; hostile, intimidating; angering, enraging, incensing, inflaming (*also* enflaming), infuriating, maddening, outraging, rankling, riling; distressing, disturbing, upsetting

ant disagreeable, unpalatable, unpleasant, unwelcome

2 having an easygoing and pleasing manner especially in social situations — see AMIABLE

pleasantly *adv* in a pleasing way — see WELL 5

pleasantness *n* the state or quality of having a pleasant or agreeable manner in socializing with others — see AMIABILITY 1

pleasantry *n* **1** an act or utterance that is a customary show of good manners — see CIVILITY 1

2 something said or done to cause laughter — see JOKE 1

please *vb* **1** to give satisfaction to ⟨Fresh flowers *please* me greatly.⟩

syn content, delight, feast, gladden, gratify, rejoice, satisfy, suit, warm

rel appease, mollify, pacify, placate, soothe; assuage, quench, sate, satiate; excite, tickle, titillate; amuse, divert, entertain, treat; captivate, charm, galvanize, thrill; calm, comfort; cater (to), humor, indulge; coddle, mollycoddle, pamper, spoil

near ant aggravate, annoy, bother, chafe, cross, exasperate, gall, grate, irk, irritate, nettle, peeve, perturb, pique, ruffle, vex; anger, enrage, incense, inflame (*also* enflame), infuriate, madden, outrage, rankle, rile, roil; provoke, rouse; agitate, distress, disturb, fret, upset; harry, pester

ant displease

2 to see fit — see CHOOSE 2

pleased *adj* **1** experiencing pleasure, satisfaction, or delight — see GLAD 1

2 feeling that one's needs or desires have been met — see CONTENT

pleasing *adj* giving pleasure or contentment to the mind or senses — see PLEASANT 1

pleasingly *adv* in a pleasing way — see WELL 5

pleasurable *adj* **1** giving pleasure or contentment to the mind or senses — see PLEASANT 1

2 providing amusement or enjoyment — see FUN

pleasure *n* **1** the feeling experienced when one's wishes are met ⟨Nothing gives me more *pleasure* than a hot meal after a long day.⟩

syn content, contentedness, contentment, delectation, delight, enjoyment, gladness, gratification, happiness, relish, satisfaction

rel afterglow; bliss, felicity, glee, gleefulness, joy; amusement, diversion, entertainment; elation, exhilaration, exultation, intoxication; ecstasy, euphoria, heaven, rapture; cheer, cheerfulness, exuberance, gaiety (*also* gayety), jollity, joyfulness, jubilation; comfort, ease, restfulness

near ant misery, sadness, unhappiness, wretchedness; anguish, desolation, joylessness, sorrow, woe; dejection, depression, despondency, dispiritedness, gloom, melancholy; aggravation, annoyance, exasperation, irritation, pique, vexation; anger, fury, rage; agitation, distress, disturbance, upset; discomfort, restlessness, uneasiness

ant discontent, discontentedness, discontentment, displeasure, dissatisfaction, unhappiness

2 a source of great satisfaction — see DELIGHT 1

3 someone or something that provides amusement or enjoyment — see FUN 1

pleat *vb* to form into a braid — see BRAID

plebeian *adj* belonging to the class of people of low social or economic rank — see IGNOBLE 1

plebeians *n pl* the body of the community as contrasted with the elite — see MASS 1

pledge *n* **1** something given or held to assure that the giver will keep a promise ⟨I was required to leave my keys as a *pledge* that I would bring the car back.⟩

syn gage, guarantee, guaranty, pawn, security

rel bond; deposit, down payment, earnest; surety, warranty; assurance, oath, promise, troth, word; commitment, compact, contract, covenant; recognizance

2 a person's solemn declaration that he or she will do or not do something — see PROMISE

pledge *vb* **1** to obligate by prior agreement ⟨I would love to go to dinner with you, but I've *pledged* myself to a play with my parents that night.⟩

syn commit, engage, troth

rel affiance, betroth, plight, promise, swear, vow; contract, enlist, enroll (*also* enrol), sign on, sign up; overcommit

near ant renege

2 to leave as a guarantee of repayment of a loan — see PAWN

3 to make a solemn declaration of intent — see PROMISE 1

plenary *adj* not lacking any part or member that properly belongs to it — see COMPLETE 1

---

syn synonym(s)   *rel* related words
ant antonym(s)   *near ant* near antonym(s)

plenitude *n* 1 a considerable amount — see LOT 2

2 an amount or supply more than sufficient to meet one's needs — see PLENTY 1

plenteous *adj* being more than enough without being excessive — see PLENTIFUL

plentiful *adj* being more than enough without being excessive ⟨a *plentiful* amount of strawberries that will be more than enough for a couple of pies⟩

syn abundant, ample, bounteous, bountiful, comfortable, galore, generous, liberal, plenteous, plenty

rel extra, supernumerary, surplus; abounding, blooming, overflowing, plump, replete, rich, rife, teeming, wealthy; adequate, enough, sufficient; fat, fecund, fertile, fruitful, luxuriant, prodigal, prolific; copious, fulsome, lavish, profuse

phrases all kinds of, thick on the ground

near ant deficient, inadequate, insufficient, lacking, wanting; meager (*or* meagre), niggardly, stingy; skimpy; least, minimum; light, slight, small; barren, infertile, sterile, unfruitful, unproductive

ant bare, minimal, scant, spare

plentitude *n* 1 a considerable amount — see LOT 2

2 an amount or supply more than sufficient to meet one's needs — see PLENTY 1

plenty *adj* being more than enough without being excessive — see PLENTIFUL

plenty *n* 1 an amount or supply more than sufficient to meet one's needs ⟨You'll have *plenty* of time to make your connecting flight.⟩

syn abundance, cornucopia, feast, plenitude, plentitude, superabundance, wealth

rel adequacy, competence, competency, sufficiency; ampleness, amplitude, liberality; excess, overdose, overflow, overkill, oversupply, redundancy, superfluity, superfluousness, surfeit, surplus; copiousness, fecundity, fertility, fruitfulness, opulence, richness; lavishness, luxuriance

phrases embarrassment of riches

near ant paucity, poverty, scarcity; barrenness, infertility, sterility

ant deficiency, inadequacy, insufficiency

2 a considerable amount — see LOT 2

pliable *adj* 1 able to bend easily without breaking — see WILLOWY

2 capable of being readily changed — see FLEXIBLE 1

pliant *adj* able to bend easily without breaking — see WILLOWY

plod *vb* 1 to devote serious and sustained effort — see LABOR

2 to proceed or act clumsily or ineffectually — see FLOUNDER 1

3 to move slowly — see CRAWL 2

4 to move heavily or clumsily — see LUMBER 1

plop *vb* to throw or set down clumsily or casually — see FLOP 1

plot *n* 1 a secret plan for accomplishing evil or unlawful ends ⟨They hatched a *plot* to steal the famous painting.⟩

syn conspiracy, design, intrigue, machination, scheme

rel counterconspiracy, counterplot; frame-up; manipulation, subterfuge, trickery; artifice, contrivance, dodge, draft, maneuver, stratagem, trick; cabal, confederacy, ring; game, gimmick, racket; ground plan, program, strategy, system; collusion, complicity, connivance, conniving, conspiration

2 a small area of usually open land — see FIELD 1

3 a small piece of land that is developed or available for development — see LOT 1

4 the unfolding of events in a dramatic or literary work — see ACTION 2

plot *vb* to engage in a secret plan to accomplish evil or unlawful ends ⟨He *plotted* his revenge.⟩

syn connive, conspire, contrive, intrigue, machinate, put up, scheme

rel counterplot; brew, concoct, cook (up), devise, hatch; engineer, jockey, maneuver, manipulate; design, frame, lay out, map, plan, shape

plow *vb* 1 to cut into and turn over the sod of (a piece of land) using a bladed implement ⟨We'll have to get out there and *plow* and plant both fields before it rains.⟩

syn break, furrow

rel cultivate, till; fallow; harrow, hoe, list, rake, rototill

2 to devote serious and sustained effort — see LABOR

ploy *n* a clever often underhanded means to achieve an end — see TRICK 1

pluck *n* 1 the act or an instance of applying force on something so that it moves in the direction of the force — see PULL 1

2 the strength of mind that enables a person to endure pain or hardship — see FORTITUDE

pluck *vb* to rob by the use of trickery or threats — see FLEECE

plug *vb* 1 to close up so that no empty spaces remain — see FILL 2

2 to devote serious and sustained effort — see LABOR

3 to provide publicity for — see PUBLICIZE 1

plug (up) *vb* to prevent passage through by filling with something — see CLOG 1

plugger *n* a person who does very hard or dull work — see DRUDGE

plum *n* someone or something unusually desirable — see PRIZE 1

plumb *adj* 1 having no exceptions or restrictions — see ABSOLUTE 2

2 rising straight up — see ERECT

plumb *adv* 1 in a direct line or course — see DIRECTLY 1

2 *chiefly dialect* to a full extent or degree — see FULLY 1

3 without delay — see IMMEDIATELY

plumb *vb* to measure the depth of (as a body of water) typically with a weighted line — see ²SOUND 1

plume *n* something given in recognition of achievement — see AWARD 1

plume *vb* to think highly of (oneself) — see PRIDE

plummet *vb* to go to a lower level especially abruptly — see DROP 2

plump *adj* having an excess of body fat — see FAT 1

plump *adv* in a direct line or course — see DIRECTLY 1

plump *n* a hard strike with a part of the body or an instrument — see ¹BLOW

plump *vb* to throw or set down clumsily or casually — see FLOP 1

plump (for) *vb* to promote the interests or cause of — see SUPPORT 1

plumpness *n* the condition of having an excess of body fat — see CORPULENCE

plunder *n* valuables stolen or taken by force — see LOOT

plunder *vb* to search through with the intent of committing robbery — see RANSACK 1

plunge *n* **1** an act or instance of diving — see DIVE 1

2 the act or process of going to a lower level or altitude — see DESCENT 1

plunge *vb* **1** to cast oneself head first into deep water — see DIVE 1

2 to go to a lower level especially abruptly — see DROP 2

3 to lead or extend downward — see DESCEND 1

plunk *or* **plonk** *vb* to throw or set down clumsily or casually — see FLOP 1

plus *n* something added (as by growth) — see INCREASE 1

plush *adj* **1** having an abundance of some characteristic quality (as flavor) — see FULL-BODIED

2 showing obvious signs of wealth and comfort — see LUXURIOUS

ply *n* an attitude that always favors one way of feeling or acting especially without considering any other possibilities — see BIAS 1

¹ply *vb* to bring to bear especially forcefully or effectively — see EXERT

²ply *vb* to cause to twine about one another — see INTERTWINE 1

poach *vb* to cook in a liquid heated to the point that it gives off steam — see BOIL 2

po'boy *also* **poor boy** *n* a large sandwich on a long split roll — see SUBMARINE

pocket *adj* **1** of a size that is less than average — see SMALL 1

2 of or relating to money, banking, or investments — see FINANCIAL

pocket *n* available money — see FUND 2

pocket *vb* **1** to refrain from openly showing or uttering — see SUPPRESS 1

2 to take (something) without right and with an intent to keep — see STEAL 1

3 to put up with (something painful or difficult) — see BEAR 2

pocketbook *n* a container for carrying money and small personal items — see PURSE

pocket–size *also* **pocket–sized** *adj* of a size that is less than average — see SMALL 1

pockmark *n* something that spoils the appearance or completeness of a thing — see BLEMISH

pod *n* something that encloses another thing especially to protect it — see ¹CASE 1

podium *n* a level usually raised surface — see PLATFORM

poem *n* a composition using rhythm and often rhyme to create a lyrical effect

〈Your assignment is to write two *poems* about springtime.〉

syn lyric, song, verse

rel ballad, lay; anacreontic, clerihew, eclogue, elegy, English sonnet, epigram, epode, epopee, epos, georgic, idyll (*also* idyl), jingle, lament, limerick, madrigal, ode, pastoral, pastorale, psalm, rondeau, rondel (*or* rondelle), rondelet, sonnet, triolet, villanelle; haiku, senryu, tanka; blank verse, free verse, minstrelsy, poesy, poetry, versification, vers libre

poet *n* a person who writes poetry 〈Emily Dickinson is famous as the *poet* who rarely left the house but often journeyed to the depths of the human heart.〉

syn bard, minstrel, versifier

rel poetess; poet laureate; epigrammatist, lyricist, rhymer, sonneteer

poetic *adj* having qualities suggestive of poetry 〈Your description of the sun setting over the Grand Canyon was a particularly *poetic* piece of writing.〉

syn bardic, lyric, lyrical, poetical

rel metrical (*or* metric), rhyming (*also* riming), rhythmic (*or* rhythmical); rhapsodic (*also* rhapsodical); florid, flowery, grandiloquent, highfalutin (*also* hifalutin), high-flown, ornate; glamorized (*also* glamourized), idealized, romanticized; figurative, metaphoric (*or* metaphorical), symbolic (*also* symbolical)

near ant factual, literal, matter-of-fact

ant prosaic, prose, unlyrical, unpoetic

poetical *adj* having qualities suggestive of poetry — see POETIC

poetry *n* **1** writing that uses rhythm, vivid language, and often rhyme to provoke an emotional response 〈Not all *poetry* has to rhyme.〉

syn minstrelsy, song, verse

rel blank verse, free verse

ant prose

2 the art or power of speaking or writing in a forceful and convincing way — see ELOQUENCE

poignancy *n* a harsh or sharp quality — see EDGE 1

poignant *adj* **1** having the power to affect the feelings or sympathies — see MOVING

2 sharp and pleasantly stimulating to the mind or senses — see PIQUANT

point *n* **1** a particular and often important moment in time 〈It was at that *point* that I had to stop and check on the experiment.〉

syn juncture

rel beat, crack, flash, instant, jiffy, minute, moment, nanosecond, second, split second, tick, trice, twinkle, wink; bit, spell, stretch, while; cusp, nick, threshold, verge; crisis, crunch time

phrases moment of truth

2 the last and usually sharp or tapering part of something long and narrow 〈Be careful with the *point* on that umbrella, or you could hurt someone.〉

syn apex, cusp, end, nib, nose, pike, tip

rel pinpoint; prong, tine; barb, jag, prickle, snag, spike, sticker

3 an interval of time just before the onset of something 〈Dan was at the *point* of accepting the new job when he realized he didn't want to leave his old one.〉

---

syn synonym(s)   *rel* related words
ant antonym(s)   *near ant* near antonym(s)

syn cusp, edge, threshold, verge

rel nick

4 a separate part in a list, account, or series — see ITEM 1

5 a single piece of information — see FACT 3

6 a small area that is different (as in color) from the main part — see SPOT 1

7 an area of high ground jutting out into a body of water beyond the line of the coast — see HEADLAND 1

8 an area of land that juts out into a body of water — see ²CAPE

9 an individual part of a process, series, or ranking — see DEGREE 1

10 something that sets apart an individual from others of the same kind — see CHARACTERISTIC

11 the area or space occupied by or intended for something — see PLACE 1

12 the quality of an utterance that provokes interest and produces an effect — see ¹PUNCH 1

13 something that one hopes or intends to accomplish — see GOAL

14 the central part or aspect of something under consideration — see CRUX

point (toward) *vb* to stand or sit with the face or front toward — see FACE 1

point (up) *vb* to indicate the importance of by centering attention on — see EMPHASIZE 1

pointed *adj* **1** tapering to a thin tip ⟨The sansevieria's long *pointed* leaves make it an easily recognized houseplant.⟩

syn peaked, sharp, tipped

rel needlelike, spiny; jagged, pronged, spiked, spikelike, spiky (*also* spikey); bladelike, knifelike

near ant dull, rounded

ant blunt

2 having to do with the matter at hand — see PERTINENT

pointer *n* **1** an arrow-shaped piece on a dial or scale for registering information ⟨The *pointer* on the scale indicated the pumpkin weighed eight pounds.⟩

syn hand, index, indicator, needle

rel dial, face, gauge (*also* gage)

2 a piece of advice or useful information especially from an expert — see ¹TIP 1

pointless *adj* having no meaning — see MEANINGLESS

poise *n* **1** a condition in which opposing forces are equal to one another — see BALANCE 1

2 a general way of holding the body — see POSTURE 1

poise *vb* **1** to prepare (oneself) mentally or emotionally — see FORTIFY 1

2 to rest or move along the surface of a liquid or in the air — see FLOAT 1

poison *adj* containing or contaminated with a substance capable of injuring or killing a living thing — see POISONOUS

poison *n* a substance that by chemical action can kill or injure a living thing ⟨The only way to get rid of rats is to leave out *poison*.⟩

syn bane, toxin, venom

rel cancer, contagion, disease, virus; fungicide, germicide, herbicide, insecticide, pesticide

near ant antivenin, antivenom; cure, cureall, elixir, panacea

poison *vb* **1** to affect slightly with something morally bad or undesirable — see TAINT 1

2 to make unfit for use by the addition of something harmful or undesirable — see CONTAMINATE

3 to lower in character, dignity, or quality — see DEBASE 1

4 to cause to have often negative opinions formed without sufficient knowledge — see PREJUDICE

poisoned *adj* containing or contaminated with a substance capable of injuring or killing a living thing — see POISONOUS

poisonous *adj* containing or contaminated with a substance capable of injuring or killing a living thing ⟨Don't eat those mushrooms—they're *poisonous*.⟩

syn envenomed, poison, poisoned, toxic, venomous

rel contagious, infectious, infective, pathogenic, pestilent; baneful, deleterious, harmful, hurtful, injurious, malignant, noxious, virulent; unhealthful, unhealthy, unwholesome

near ant beneficial, healthful, healthy, helpful, palliative, remedial, salubrious, salutary, wholesome; benign, harmless, innocuous, inoffensive; nonfatal, nonlethal

ant nonpoisonous, nontoxic, nonvenomous

¹**poke** *n* **1** a quick thrust ⟨A *poke* at the fire sent sparks flying.⟩

syn dab, dig, jab

rel punch; stab, stick; push, shove; jam, jerk, jog, nudge

2 a hard strike with a part of the body or an instrument — see ¹BLOW

3 an act or expression showing scorn and usually intended to hurt another's feelings — see INSULT

²**poke** *n, chiefly Southern & Midland* a container made of a flexible material (as paper or plastic) — see BAG 1

poke *vb* **1** to extend outward beyond a usual point — see BULGE 1

2 to interest oneself in what is not one's concern — see INTERFERE

3 to move or act slowly — see DELAY 1

4 to move slowly — see CRAWL 2

poking *adj* moving or proceeding at less than the normal, desirable, or required speed — see SLOW 1

poky *or* **pokey** *adj* moving or proceeding at less than the normal, desirable, or required speed — see SLOW 1

polar *adj* **1** being as different as possible — see OPPOSITE

2 having a low or subnormal temperature — see COLD 1

police *n* **1** the department of government that keeps order, fights crime, and enforces statutes ⟨If you have something to report, call the *police*.⟩

syn law

rel judiciary, jurisprudence, justice

2 a body of officers of the law ⟨*Police* blockaded the street for the parade.⟩

syn constabulary, force, heat [*slang*], police force

rel bobby [*British*], constable, cop, gendarme, officer, policeman, police officer, policewoman, shamus [*slang*], trooper

police force *n* a body of officers of the law — see POLICE 2

policeman *n* a member of a force charged with law enforcement at the local level — see OFFICER 1

police officer *n* a member of a force charged with law enforcement at the local level — see OFFICER 1

policy *n* **1** a way of acting or proceeding — see COURSE 1

2 the ability to make intelligent decisions especially in everyday matters — see COMMON SENSE

polish *n* **1** a high level of taste and enlightenment as a result of extensive intellectual training and exposure to the arts — see CULTURE 1

2 brightness created by light reflected from a surface — see SHINE 1

polish *vb* **1** to make smooth or glossy usually by repeatedly applying surface pressure ⟨You'll need to *polish* your shoes with a clean rag before the performance.⟩

syn buff, burnish, dress, gloss, grind, rub, shine, smooth

rel sleek, slick; coat, glaze, japan, lacquer, varnish; face, finish, veneer; brighten; file, rasp, sand, sandblast, sandpaper, scour, scrape, scrub; bob, bone, lap

near ant rough (up), roughen, ruffle, scuff (up)

2 to bring (something) to a state where nothing remains to be done — see FINISH 1

polished *adj* **1** having a shiny surface or finish — see GLOSSY

2 having or showing a taste for the fine arts and gracious living — see CULTIVATED

polite *adj* **1** showing consideration, courtesy, and good manners ⟨It's only *polite* to hold the door for the person behind you.⟩

syn civil, courteous, genteel, gracious, mannerly, well-bred

rel attentive, careful, considerate, nice, solicitous, thoughtful; chivalrous, civilized, courtly, gallant, gentlemanlike, gentlemanly, ladylike; ceremonial, ceremonious, red-carpet; couth, formal, smooth, suave, unctuous, urbane; elegant, refined; deferential, dutiful, respectful, submissive, yielding; affable, cordial, friendly, genial, hospitable, pleasant, sociable; felicitous, graceful; demure, humble, meek, modest

near ant heedless, inconsiderate, thoughtless; audacious, bold, bold-faced, brash, brassy, disrespectful, impertinent, impudent, insolent, lippy, saucy, shameless; boorish, churlish, clownish, loutish, uncouth, vulgar; arrogant, conceited, presuming, presumptuous, pretentious

ant discourteous, ill-bred, ill-mannered, impolite, inconsiderate, mannerless, rude, thoughtless, uncivil, ungenteel, ungracious, unmannerly

2 following the established traditions of refined society and good taste — see PROPER 1

politeness *n* **1** speech or behavior that is a sign of good manners ⟨The little girl's *politeness* greatly impressed her teacher.⟩

syn civility, courteousness, courtesy, gentility, graciousness, mannerliness

rel attentiveness, consideration, thoughtfulness; chivalrousness, chivalry, courtliness, gallantry, gentlemanliness, knightliness; breeding, manners; suaveness, unctuousness, urbanity; elegance, refinement; deference, respect; decency, decorousness, decorum, polish, propriety, respectability, seemliness; affability, cordiality, friendliness, geniality, hospitality, sociability; felicitousness, gracefulness; humility, meekness, modesty, shyness

near ant audacity, boldness, brashness, brassiness, disrespect, impertinence, impudence, insolence, sauciness, shamelessness; boorishness, churlishness, clownishness, loutishness, vulgarity; inconsiderateness, inconsideration, thoughtlessness; arrogance, conceit, presumption, pretentiousness

ant discourteousness, discourtesy, impoliteness, incivility, rudeness, surliness, ungraciousness

2 an act or utterance that is a customary show of good manners — see CIVILITY 1

politic *adj* **1** having or showing tact — see TACTFUL

2 suitable for bringing about a desired result under the circumstances — see EXPEDIENT

poll *n* the upper or front part of the body that contains the brain, the major sense organs, and the mouth — see HEAD 1

poll *vb* **1** to go around and approach (people) with a request for opinions or information — see CANVASS 1

2 to make (something) shorter or smaller with the use of a cutting instrument — see CLIP 1

pollutant *n* something that is or that makes impure — see IMPURITY 1

pollute *vb* to make unfit for use by the addition of something harmful or undesirable — see CONTAMINATE

polluted *adj* containing foreign or lower-grade substances — see IMPURE 1

poltergeist *n* the soul of a dead person thought of especially as appearing to living people — see GHOST 1

poltroon *adj* having or showing a shameful lack of courage — see COWARDLY

poltroon *n* a person who shows a shameful lack of courage in the face of danger — see COWARD

polychromatic *adj* marked by a variety of usually vivid colors — see COLORFUL

polychrome *adj* marked by a variety of usually vivid colors — see COLORFUL

polygraph *n* an instrument for detecting physical signs of the tension that goes with lying — see LIE DETECTOR

pommel *vb* to strike repeatedly — see BEAT 1

pompous *adj* **1** having a feeling of superiority that shows itself in an overbearing attitude — see ARROGANT

2 having too high an opinion of oneself — see CONCEITED

3 self-consciously trying to present an appearance of grandeur or importance — see PRETENTIOUS 1

pompousness *n* **1** an exaggerated sense

of one's importance that shows itself in the making of excessive or unjustified claims — see ARROGANCE

2 an often unjustified feeling of being pleased with oneself or with one's situation or achievements — see COMPLACENCE 1

ponder *vb* to give serious and careful thought to ⟨I'm *pondering* whether or not I should join another committee.⟩

syn chew over, cogitate, consider, contemplate, debate, deliberate, entertain, eye, meditate, mull (over), pore (over), question, revolve, ruminate, study, think (about *or* over), turn, weigh

rel muse (upon), reflect (on *or* upon), reminisce; analyze, explore, review; conclude, reason; second-guess, speculate (about); brood (about *or* over), fixate (on *or* upon), fret (about *or* over), obsess (about *or* over); believe, conceive, opine; absorb, assimilate, digest

phrases beat one's brains out (about), chew on, cudgel one's brains (about), look at

near ant disregard, ignore, overlook, slight; dismiss, pooh-pooh (*also* pooh), reject

ponderous *adj* 1 causing weariness, restlessness, or lack of interest — see BORING

2 having great weight — see HEAVY 1

3 difficult to use or operate especially because of size, weight, or design — see CUMBERSOME

ponderousness *n* the state or quality of being heavy — see WEIGHTINESS 1

pooch *n* a domestic mammal that is related to the wolves and foxes — see DOG 1

¹**pool** *n* a small often deep body of water ⟨a secluded *pool* that has long been a locally favored spot for cooling off⟩

syn puddle, well

rel basin, hole, sinkhole; swimming pool; lake, pond, water hole

²**pool** *n* 1 a body of persons at work or available for work — see FORCE 1

2 the number of individuals or amount of something available at any given time — see SUPPLY

3 a sum of money set aside for a particular purpose — see FUND 1

4 the total of the bets at stake at one time — see POT 1

pooled *adj* used or done by a number of people as a group — see COLLECTIVE

poor *adj* 1 lacking money or material possessions ⟨Every year, we make up a basket of food at Thanksgiving for a *poor* family in the neighborhood.⟩

syn beggared, broke, destitute, famished, hard up, impecunious, impoverished, indigent, needful, needy, penniless, penurious, poverty-stricken

rel deprived, disadvantaged, dispossessed, underprivileged; bankrupt, bankrupted, bust (*or* busted), insolvent; possessionless; depressed, distressed, hand-to-mouth, pinched, reduced, straitened; cash-strapped, low, short

phrases down on one's luck, out at elbows (*or* out at the elbows), out of pocket

near ant comfortable, prosperous

ant affluent, deep-pocketed, fat, fat-cat, flush, moneyed (*also* monied), opulent,

rich, wealthy, well-heeled, well-off, well-to-do

2 producing inferior or only a small amount of vegetation — see BARREN 1

3 less plentiful than what is normal, necessary, or desirable — see MEAGER

4 falling short of a standard — see BAD 1

5 of low quality — see CHEAP 2

6 deserving of one's pity — see PATHETIC 1

poorly *adj* temporarily suffering from a disorder of the body — see SICK 1

poorly *adv* in an unsatisfactory way — see BADLY 1

poorness *n* the state of lacking sufficient money or material possessions — see POVERTY 1

pop *adj* enjoying widespread favor or approval — see POPULAR 1

¹**pop** *n* a loud explosive sound — see CLAP 1

²**pop** *n* a male human parent — see FATHER 1

pop *vb* 1 to break open or into pieces usually because of internal pressure — see EXPLODE 1

2 to break suddenly with an explosive sound — see CRACK 1

3 to cause to break open or into pieces by or as if by an explosive — see BLAST 1

pop (in) *vb* to make a brief visit — see CALL 3

populace *n* the body of the community as contrasted with the elite — see MASS 1

popular *adj* 1 enjoying widespread favor or approval ⟨an actor who was *popular* in the 1990s⟩

syn big, faddish, faddy, fashionable, favorite, happening, hot, in, modish, pop, popularized, red-hot, vogue

rel semipopular; preferred, selected; desirable, liked, wanted; celebrated, famed, famous, noted, notorious, prominent, renowned, well-known; fabled, fabulous, legendary; leading, notable, outstanding, prominent, remarkable

near ant washed-up; despised, detested, disliked, hated, rejected; anonymous, nameless, obscure, unknown; inconspicuous

ant out, unfashionable, unpopular

2 accepted, used, or practiced by most people — see CURRENT 1

3 held by or applicable to a majority of people — see GENERAL 3

4 of, relating to, or favoring political democracy — see DEMOCRATIC

5 being within the financial means of most people — see ACCESSIBLE 1

6 costing little — see CHEAP 1

popularity *n* the state of enjoying widespread approval ⟨the *popularity* of low-heeled shoes this season⟩

syn fashionableness, favor, hotness, modishness, vogue

rel craze, fad, mode, rage, style, trend; bandwagon, boom; fame, notoriety, prominence, renown; enthusiasm, fervor, passion

near ant oblivion, obscurity

ant disfavor, unpopularity

popularized *adj* enjoying widespread favor or approval — see POPULAR 1

pore (over) *vb* 1 to give serious and careful thought to — see PONDER

2 to go over and mentally take in the content of — see READ 1

porous *adj* capable of being passed into or through — see PENETRABLE

port *n* a part of a body of water protected and deep enough to be a place of safety for ships — see HARBOR 1

portable *adj* capable of being moved especially with ease — see MOVABLE

portal *n* a barrier by which an entry is closed and opened — see DOOR 1

portent *n* **1** something believed to be a sign or warning of a future event — see OMEN

2 something extraordinary or surprising — see WONDER 1

portentous *adj* **1** being or showing a sign of evil or calamity to come — see OMINOUS

2 causing wonder or astonishment — see MARVELOUS 1

portion *n* **1** a state or end that seemingly has been decided beforehand — see FATE 1
2 one of the pieces from which something is designed to be assembled — see PART 1
3 something belonging to, due to, or contributed by an individual member of a group — see SHARE 1

portion *vb* to give out (something) to appropriate individuals — see ADMINISTER 1

portliness *n* the condition of having an excess of body fat — see CORPULENCE

portly *adj* **1** having an excess of body fat — see FAT 1
2 having or showing a formal and serious or reserved manner — see DIGNIFIED

portmanteau *n* a bag carried by hand and designed to hold a traveler's clothing and personal articles — see TRAVELING BAG

portrait *n* a vivid representation in words of someone or something — see DESCRIPTION 1

portray *vb* **1** to give a representation or account of in words — see DESCRIBE 1
2 to point out the chief quality or qualities of an individual or group — see CHARACTERIZE 1
3 to present a picture of — see PICTURE 1
4 to present a portrayal or performance of — see ACT 1

portrayal *n* a vivid representation in words of someone or something — see DESCRIPTION 1

pose *n* a display of emotion or behavior that is insincere or intended to deceive — see MASQUERADE

pose *vb* to set before the mind for consideration — see PROPOSE 1

pose (as) *vb* to pretend to be (what one is not) in appearance or behavior — see IMPERSONATE 1

position *n* **1** an assignment at which one regularly works for pay — see JOB 1
2 the action for which a person or thing is specially fitted or used or for which a thing exists — see ROLE
3 the area or space occupied by or intended for something — see PLACE 1
4 the place where someone is assigned to stand or remain — see STATION 1

5 the placement of someone or something in relation to others in a vertical arrangement — see RANK 1

position *vb* to arrange something in a certain spot or position — see PLACE 1

positive *adj* **1** expressing approval — see FAVORABLE 1
2 having or showing a mind free from doubt — see CERTAIN 2
3 not capable of being challenged or proved wrong — see IRREFUTABLE

positiveness *n* a state of mind in which one is free from doubt — see CONFIDENCE 2

possess *vb* to keep, control, or experience as one's own — see HAVE 1

possession *n* **1** the fact or state of having (something) at one's disposal ⟨The university has several old manuscripts in its *possession*.⟩

syn control, enjoyment, hands, keeping
rel ownership, proprietorship; authority, command, dominion, mastery, power; repossession, retention; claiming, collaring, confiscation, procurement
near ant dispossession, relinquishment, surrendering, transferal
ant nonpossession

2 possessions *pl* transportable items that one owns ⟨We packed up all of our *possessions* and excitedly moved into a new house.⟩

syn chattels, duds, effects, gear, goods, holdings, movables (*or* moveables), paraphernalia, personalty, stuff, things
rel treasures, valuables; appointments, fixtures, furnishings; estate, property, tangibles; collateral
near ant immovables, real estate

possessive *adj* intolerant of rivalry or unfaithfulness — see JEALOUS 1

possessor *n* one who has a legal or rightful claim to ownership — see PROPRIETOR

possibility *n* **1** something that can develop or become actual — see POTENTIAL
2 something that might happen — see EVENT 2

possible *adj* **1** capable of being done or carried out ⟨I think that building the entire set in two days is *possible*, albeit difficult.⟩
syn achievable, attainable, doable, feasible, practicable, realizable, viable, workable
rel practical, reasonable, sensible; contingent, likely, probable; acceptable, believable, conceivable, creditable, plausible, thinkable; available, usable (*also* useable)
near ant impractical, unrealistic; doubtful, dubious, far-fetched, improbable, unlikely; implausible, inconceivable, incredible, unbelievable; futile, useless, vain; absurd, fantastic (*also* fantastical), outlandish, preposterous, ridiculous; unthinkable
ant hopeless, impossible, impracticable, infeasible, nonviable, unattainable, unfeasible, unviable, unworkable

2 existing only as a possibility and not in fact — see POTENTIAL

possibly *adv* it is possible — see PERHAPS

¹**post** *n* **1** a specific task with which a person or group is charged — see MISSION
2 the place where someone is assigned to stand or remain — see STATION 1

---

3 an assignment at which one regularly works for pay — see JOB 1

²**post** *n* an upright shaft that supports an overhead structure — see PILLAR 1

¹**post** *vb* **1** to affix (as a notice) to or on a suitable place ⟨The student organizations generally *post* their announcements on the campus bulletin board.⟩

syn placard

rel nail, plaster, tack (up); advertise, announce, bill, blaze, broadcast, call, declare, proclaim, promulgate, publicize, publish

near ant remove, take down

2 to make known openly or publicly — see ANNOUNCE

²**post** *vb* to assign to a place or position ⟨The police are planning to *post* an officer outside the hospital room of the witness.⟩

syn detail, station

rel set; appoint; place, position

³**post** *vb* to send through the postal system — see MAIL

postdate *vb* to come after in time — see FOLLOW 1

poster *n* a sheet bearing an announcement for posting in a public place ⟨We put up a hundred *posters* announcing the concert.⟩

syn bill, placard

rel billboard, sign, signboard; broadside, handbill, handout, playbill, show bill; ad, advertisement, announcement, bulletin, dispatch, release

posterior *adj* **1** being at or in the part of something opposite the front part — see BACK

2 being, occurring, or carried out at a time after something else — see SUBSEQUENT

posterior *n* the part of the body upon which someone sits — see BUTTOCKS

posterity *n* the descendants of a person, animal, or plant — see OFFSPRING

posthaste *adv* with great speed — see FAST 1

posthumous *adj* occurring after one's death ⟨The soldier was awarded a *posthumous* medal for valor.⟩

syn postmortem

rel belated, delayed, late

posting *n* a published statement informing the public of a matter of general interest — see ANNOUNCEMENT

postman *n* a person who delivers mail — see LETTER CARRIER

postmortem *adj* occurring after one's death — see POSTHUMOUS

postmortem *n* examination of a dead body especially to find out the cause of death — see AUTOPSY

postmortem examination *n* examination of a dead body especially to find out the cause of death — see AUTOPSY

postpone *vb* to assign to a later time ⟨We'll have to *postpone* a decision until we have all the information.⟩

syn defer, delay, hold off (on), hold up, put off, remit, shelve

rel suspend; hesitate, pause, stay; detain, retard, slow; extend, lengthen, prolong, protract, stretch (out); wait

near ant act, deal (with), decide (upon), do, work (on)

postulate *n* something taken as being true

or factual and used as a starting point for a course of action or reasoning — see ASSUMPTION 1

postulate *vb* to take as true or as a fact without actual proof — see ASSUME 2

posture *n* **1** a general way of holding the body ⟨A good upright *posture* will prevent backaches.⟩

syn carriage, poise, stance, station

rel attention; body language; pose, seat; bearing, behavior, conduct, demeanor, deportment; air, poise, presence; aspect, look, mien

2 position with regard to conditions and circumstances — see SITUATION 1

posy *n* a bunch of flowers — see BOUQUET 1

pot *n* **1** the total of the bets at stake at one time ⟨Everyone got a bit nervous when the *pot* grew to more than a hundred dollars.⟩

syn jack, jackpot, pool

rel fund, kitty; bet, stake, wager

2 a considerable amount — see LOT 2

potable *adj* suitable for drinking ⟨Around here, the only *potable* water comes from wells.⟩

syn drinkable

rel clean, fresh, pure, uncontaminated, unpolluted; nonpoisonous

near ant contaminated, dirty, foul, polluted; poison, poisonous, toxic; unhealthful, unhealthy, unwholesome

ant undrinkable

potable *n* a liquid suitable for drinking — see DRINK 1

potbelly *n* an enlarged or bulging abdomen ⟨an image of the Laughing Buddha with his *potbelly*⟩

syn beer belly, belly, gut, paunch

rel breadbasket [*slang*], stomach, tummy

potency *n* the ability to exert effort for the accomplishment of a task — see POWER 2

potent *adj* **1** having an abundance of some characteristic quality (as flavor) — see FULL-BODIED

2 having great power or influence — see IMPORTANT 1

3 producing or capable of producing a desired result — see EFFECTIVE 1

potentate *n* one who rules over a people with a sole, supreme, and usually hereditary authority — see MONARCH 1

potential *adj* existing only as a possibility and not in fact ⟨I can see a few *potential* problems with co-owning a beach house with another couple.⟩

syn implicit, possible

rel conceivable, imaginable, plausible, thinkable; likely, probable; conjectural, hypothetical, suppositional, theoretical (*also* theoretic); alleged, assumed, purported, reputed, supposed; achievable, attainable, doable, feasible, practicable, viable, workable

near ant authenticated, confirmed, demonstrated, established, proven, substantiated; authentic, bona fide, genuine, true

ant actual, existent, factual, real

potential *n* something that can develop or become actual ⟨a time when cloning was merely a *potential* and the stuff of science fiction⟩

syn capability, eventuality, possibility, potentiality, prospect

rel likelihood, probability; latency, potency

near ant actuality, reality; certainty

potentiality *n* something that can develop or become actual — see POTENTIAL

pother *n* **1** a state of nervous or irritated concern — see FRET

2 a state of noisy, confused activity — see COMMOTION

potpourri *n* an unorganized collection or mixture of various things — see MISCELLANY 1

potter (around) *vb* to spend time in aimless activity — see FIDDLE (AROUND)

potterer *n* a person who regularly or occasionally engages in an activity as a pastime rather than as a profession — see AMATEUR 1

potter's field *n* a piece of land used for burying the dead — see CEMETERY

pottery *n* articles made of baked clay — see CROCKERY

potty *n* a room furnished with a fixture for flushing body waste — see TOILET

pouch *n* a container made of a flexible material (as paper or plastic) — see BAG 1

pouch *vb* to extend outward beyond a usual point — see BULGE 1

poultice *n* a medicated covering used to heal an injury — see DRESSING 1

pounce (on *or* **upon)** *vb* to take sudden, violent action against — see ATTACK 1

¹pound *n* a hard strike with a part of the body or an instrument — see ¹BLOW

²pound *n* an enclosure with an open framework for keeping animals — see CAGE

pound *vb* **1** to move heavily or clumsily — see LUMBER 1

2 to deliver a blow to (someone or something) usually in a strong vigorous manner — see HIT 1

3 to strike repeatedly — see BEAT 1

4 to shape with a hammer — see HAMMER 1

5 to reduce to fine particles — see POWDER

pour *vb* **1** to cause to flow in a stream ⟨She lifted the teakettle and *poured* some hot water from the spout.⟩

syn stream

rel ladle, spoon; cascade, trickle; deluge, flood, inundate, overflow

2 to move in a stream — see FLOW 1

3 to flow out in great quantities or with force — see GUSH 1

4 to fall as water in a continuous stream of drops from the clouds — see RAIN 1

5 to give readily and in large quantities — see RAIN 2

pouring *adj* marked by or abounding with rain — see RAINY

pout *n* **1** a twisting of the facial features in disgust or disapproval — see GRIMACE

2 pouts *pl* a state of resentful silence or irritability — see SULK

pout *vb* **1** to extend outward beyond a usual point — see BULGE 1

2 to silently go about in a bad mood — see SULK

pouting *adj* given to or displaying a resentful silence and often irritability — see SULKY

poverty *n* **1** the state of lacking sufficient money or material possessions ⟨He dreamed of finding a good job and working his way out of *poverty* and debt.⟩

syn beggary, destitution, impecuniousness, impoverishment, indigence, necessity, need, neediness, pauperism, penuriousness, penury, poorness, want

rel gutter, misery, woe, wretchedness; exigency; emergency; austerity, deprivation, privation

near ant luxury, prosperity

ant opulence, richness, wealth, wealthiness

2 a falling short of an essential or desirable amount or number — see DEFICIENCY

poverty–stricken *adj* lacking money or material possessions — see POOR 1

powder *vb* to reduce to fine particles ⟨You have to *powder* the antibiotic tablet and mix it with food.⟩

syn atomize, beat, crush, disintegrate, grind, mill, pound, pulverize

rel grate; crumble, crunch; break, bust, dash, fracture, fragment; shatter, smash, splinter

powdery *adj* consisting of very small particles — see FINE 1

power *n* **1** the right or means to command or control others ⟨The emir has nearly complete *power* over the emirate.⟩

syn arm, authority, clutch, command, control, dominion, grip, hold, mastery, rein(s), sway

rel clout, influence, pull, voice, weight; jurisdiction; direction, management; dominance, imperium, predominance, sovereignty (*also* sovranty), supremacy; prerogative, privilege, right

near ant helplessness, weakness

ant impotence, impotency, powerlessness

2 the ability to exert effort for the accomplishment of a task ⟨The corporation has the *power* to accomplish almost anything.⟩ ⟨You'll need to build a bit more *power* in order to be a star pitcher.⟩

syn energy, force, might, muscle, potency, puissance, sinew, strength, vigor

rel aptitude, capability, capacity, competence, competency; adequacy, effectiveness, effectualness, usefulness

near ant disability, inability, inaptitude, incapability, incapableness, incapacity, incompetence; ineffectiveness, ineffectuality, ineffectualness, inefficaciousness, inefficacy, uselessness; helplessness, paralysis

ant impotence, impotency, powerlessness, weakness

3 a natural ability of the mind or body ⟨Dogs have a very highly developed *power* of smell.⟩

syn faculty

rel function; capability, capacity; aptitude, endowment, flair, genius, gift, instinct, knack, talent

near ant inability, incapability, incapacity; inaptitude, inaptness, ineptness

4 something with a usable capacity for doing work — see FUEL

powerboat *n* a boat equipped with a motor — see MOTORBOAT

powerful *adj* having great power or influence — see IMPORTANT 2

powerfully *adv* in a vigorous and forceful manner — see HARD 3

powerhouse *n* an ambitious person who eagerly goes after what is desired — see GO-GETTER

powerless *adj* unable to act or achieve one's purpose ⟨I wish I could help you, but I am *powerless* in this situation.⟩
syn helpless, impotent, paralyzed, weak
rel incapable, incompetent, ineffective, ineffectual, inept, unfit, useless; feeble, frail, infirm, passive, spineless, supine, unaggressive
near ant able, capable, competent, effective, efficient; authoritarian, autocratic (*also* autocratical), despotic, dictatorial, tyrannical (*also* tyrannic); dominant, dynamic, energetic, forceful, robust, sturdy, tough, vigorous
ant mighty, potent, powerful, puissant, strong

powerlessness *n* the lack of sufficient ability, power, or means — see INABILITY

practicable *adj* 1 capable of being done or carried out — see POSSIBLE 1
2 capable of being put to use or account — see PRACTICAL 1
3 capable of or suitable for being used for a particular purpose — see USABLE 1

practical *adj* 1 capable of being put to use or account ⟨a *practical* and simple solution for the town's waste disposal⟩ ⟨She has some *practical* information on sightseeing in San Francisco.⟩
syn applicable, functional, practicable, serviceable, usable (*also* useable), useful, workable, working
rel down-to-earth, pragmatic (*also* pragmatical), utilitarian; accessible, available, obtainable, reachable; all-around (*also* all-round), handy; active, alive, busy, employed, functioning, operating, operative
near ant abstract, academic (*also* academical), armchair, theoretical (*also* theoretic); inaccessible, unattainable, unavailable, unobtainable, unreachable; unsuitable
ant impracticable, impractical, inapplicable, nonpractical, unusable, unworkable, useless
2 willing to see things as they really are and deal with them sensibly — see REALISTIC 1

practical joke *n* a playful or mischievous act intended as a joke — see PRANK

practically *adv* very close to but not completely — see ALMOST

practice *also* **practise** *n* 1 a private performance or session in preparation for a public appearance — see REHEARSAL
2 a usual manner of behaving or doing — see HABIT 1
3 something done over and over in order to develop skill — see EXERCISE 2

practice *also* **practise** *vb* to do over and over so as to become skilled ⟨In order to play the guitar well, you need to *practice* fingering every single day.⟩
syn exercise, rehearse, run over
rel groove, perfect, refine; point (for), prepare (for), train (with); drill, repeat; work (at *or* on); review, study

practiced *also* **practised** *adj* 1 having or showing exceptional knowledge, experience, or skill in a field of endeavor — see PROFICIENT
2 accomplished with trained ability — see SKILLFUL 1

pragmatic *also* **pragmatical** *adj* willing to see things as they really are and deal with them sensibly — see REALISTIC 1

prairie *n* a broad area of level or rolling treeless country — see PLAIN 1

praise *vb* 1 to proclaim the glory of ⟨hymns that *praise* God⟩
syn bless, carol, celebrate, exalt, extol (*also* extoll), glorify, hymn, laud, magnify, resound
rel adore, belaud, deify, idolize, worship; acclaim, applaud, commend, compliment, hail, renown, salute; chant, cheer, eulogize, rhapsodize
near ant blame, censure, reprehend, reprobate; criticize, reprove; admonish, chide, keelhaul, rebuke, reprimand, reproach; castigate, lambaste (*or* lambast)
2 to declare enthusiastic approval of — see ACCLAIM

praiseworthy *adj* deserving of high regard or great approval — see ADMIRABLE

prance *vb* to walk with exaggerated arm and leg movements — see STRUT 1

prank *n* a playful or mischievous act intended as a joke ⟨As a *prank*, several students managed to change all the classroom clocks to different times.⟩
syn antic, caper, escapade, frolic, gag, jest, knavery, practical joke, trick, waggery
rel skylarking; high jinks (*also* hijinks), horseplay, play, roughhousing, rowdyism; shenanigan(s), tomfoolery; joking, kidding, teasing; hoax, maneuver, ploy; caprice, conceit, fancy, vagary, whim, whimsy (*also* whimsey); fraud, hanky-panky, hoodwinking, ruse, sham, stratagem, subterfuge, trickery, wile

prankish *adj* tending to or exhibiting reckless playfulness — see MISCHIEVOUS 1

prankishness *n* a natural disposition for playful behavior — see PLAYFULNESS

prate *vb* to engage in casual or rambling conversation — see CHAT 1

prattle *n* unintelligible or meaningless talk — see GIBBERISH 1

prattle *vb* 1 to engage in casual or rambling conversation — see CHAT 1
2 to speak rapidly, inarticulately, and usually unintelligibly — see BABBLE 1

prattler *n* a person who talks constantly — see CHATTERBOX

pray *vb* to make a request to (someone) in an earnest or urgent manner — see BEG

prayer *n* 1 an address to God or a deity ⟨He always said a *prayer* before going to sleep.⟩
syn orison
rel collect, grace, litany, thanksgiving; evensong, matins, vespers; appeal, begging, beseeching, entreaty, imploring, petition, pleading, request, soliciting, suit, supplication
2 an earnest request — see PLEA 1

preamble *n* 1 a performance, activity, or

event that precedes and sets the stage for the main event — see PRELUDE 1

2 a short section (as of a book) that leads to or explains the main part — see INTRODUCTION

precariousness *n* the quality or state of not being firmly fixed in position — see INSTABILITY

precautionary *adj* concerned with or serving to keep something from happening — see PREVENTIVE

precede *vb* to go or come before in time ⟨There are two speeches which will *precede* yours.⟩

syn antedate, forego, predate

ant follow, postdate, succeed

precedence *n* the right to one's attention before other things considered less important — see PRIORITY

precedent *adj* going before another in time or order — see PREVIOUS

preceding *adj* going before another in time or order — see PREVIOUS

preceptor *n* a person whose occupation is to give formal instruction in a school — see TEACHER

precious *adj* **1** commanding a large price — see COSTLY

2 granted special treatment or attention — see DARLING 1

3 having qualities that tend to make one loved — see LOVABLE

precipice *n* a steep wall of rock, earth, or ice — see CLIFF

precipitate *adj* acting or done with excessive or careless speed — see HASTY 1

precipitate *n* matter that settles to the bottom of a body of liquid — see DEPOSIT 1

precipitate *vb* to fall as water in a continuous stream of drops from the clouds — see RAIN 1

precipitately *adv* with excessive or careless speed — see HASTILY 1

precipitating *adj* marked by or abounding with rain — see RAINY

precipitation *n* excited and often showy or disorderly speed — see HURRY 1

precipitous *adj* **1** acting or done with excessive or careless speed — see HASTY 1

2 having an incline approaching the perpendicular — see STEEP 1

precipitously *adv* with excessive or careless speed — see HASTILY 1

precipitousness *n* excited and often showy or disorderly speed — see HURRY 1

précis *n* a short statement of the main points — see SUMMARY

precise *adj* **1** meeting the highest standard of accuracy ⟨a machine which takes very *precise* measurements⟩

syn accurate, close, delicate, exact, fine, hairline, mathematical, pinpoint, refined, rigorous

rel correct, right, strict, true; definite, definitive; nice, subtle; careful, fastidious, finicky, meticulous

near ant approximate, round; false, incorrect, untrue, wrong; careless, loose; indefinite, unclear, vague; doubtful, dubious, questionable, unreliable, untrustworthy

ant coarse, imprecise, inaccurate, inexact, rough

2 being in agreement with the truth or a fact or a standard — see CORRECT 1

3 being neither more nor less than a certain amount, number, or extent — see EVEN 1

4 following an original exactly — see FAITHFUL 2

5 of a particular or exact sort — see EXPRESS 1

precisely *adv* **1** as stated or indicated without the slightest difference — see EXACTLY 1

2 in the same manner — see JUST 1

3 without any relaxation of standards or precision — see STRICTLY

preciseness *n* the quality or state of being very accurate — see PRECISION

precision *n* the quality or state of being very accurate ⟨The company that measures TV ratings prides itself on the *precision* of its calculations.⟩

syn accuracy, closeness, delicacy, exactitude, exactness, fineness, nicety, perfection, preciseness, rigor, rigorousness, veracity

rel correctness, fidelity, rightness, strictness, truth; definiteness, definitiveness, definitude, determinacy; nicety, subtlety; care, carefulness, fastidiousness, meticulousness, persnicketiness

near ant approximation, roundness; falseness, falsity, incorrectness, wrongness; carelessness, guesswork, looseness; indefiniteness, vagueness

ant coarseness, impreciseness, imprecision, inaccuracy, inexactitude, inexactness, roughness

preclude *vb* to keep from happening by taking action in advance — see PREVENT

precluding *n* the act or practice of keeping something from happening — see PREVENTION

precocious *adj* occurring before the usual or expected time — see EARLY 2

precociously *adv* before the usual or expected time — see EARLY

preconception *n* an attitude, belief, or impression formed in advance of actual experience of something — see PREPOSSESSION 2

precursor *n* **1** one that announces or indicates the later arrival of another — see FORERUNNER 1

2 something belonging to an earlier time from which something else was later developed — see ANCESTOR 2

predaceous *or* **predacious** *adj* living by killing and eating other animals — see PREDATORY

predate *vb* to go or come before in time — see PRECEDE

predatory *adj* living by killing and eating other animals ⟨Hawks are *predatory* and pose a danger to rabbits and other pets.⟩

syn predaceous (*or* predacious), rapacious

rel carnivorous; aggressive, deadly, ferocious, fierce, savage, violent; untamed, wild

near ant herbivorous, vegetarian; gentle, submissive, tame

predecessor *n* something belonging to an

---

syn synonym(s)   *rel* related words

ant antonym(s)   *near ant* near antonym(s)

earlier time from which something else was later developed — see ANCESTOR 2

predestine *vb* to determine the fate of in advance — see DESTINE

predetermine *vb* to determine the fate of in advance — see DESTINE

predicament *n* a difficult, puzzling, or embarrassing situation from which there is no easy escape ⟨If you had told the truth in the first place, we wouldn't be in this *predicament*.⟩

syn bind, corner, dilemma, fix, hole, impasse, jam, mire, pickle, quagmire, spot

rel difficulty, node; hot water, soup; pinch, plight, quandary, scrape, trouble; deadlock, halt, stalemate, standstill; clutch, crisis, crossroad, emergency, exigency, juncture, strait

phrases kettle of fish

predicate *vb* to find a basis — see BASE

predict *vb* to tell of or describe beforehand — see FORETELL

predicting *n* a declaration that something will happen in the future — see PREDICTION

prediction *n* a declaration that something will happen in the future ⟨We were all amazed when the fortune-teller's *predictions* turned out to be true.⟩

syn auguring, augury, cast, forecast, forecasting, foretelling, predicting, presaging, prognosis, prognostication, prophecy (*also* prophesy), soothsaying

rel foreboding, harbinger, omen, portent, prospectus, sign; foreknowledge; foresight; conjecture, guess, surmise

predictive *adj* being a sign of a later course of events — see PROPHETIC

predilection *n* a habitual attraction to some activity or thing — see INCLINATION 1

predisposition *n* a habitual attraction to some activity or thing — see INCLINATION 1

predominance *n* controlling power or influence over others — see SUPREMACY 1

predominant *adj* coming before all others in importance — see FOREMOST 1

predominantly *adv* for the most part — see CHIEFLY

preeminence *n* 1 exceptionally high quality — see EXCELLENCE 1

2 controlling power or influence over others — see SUPREMACY 1

3 the fact or state of being above others in rank or importance — see EMINENCE 1

preeminent *adj* 1 coming before all others in importance — see FOREMOST 1

2 highest in rank or authority — see HEAD

3 standing above others in rank, importance, or achievement — see EMINENT

preempt *vb* to take or make use of under a guise of authority but without actual right — see APPROPRIATE 1

preface *n* a short section (as of a book) that leads to or explains the main part — see INTRODUCTION

prefer *vb* 1 to show partiality toward ⟨I generally *prefer* chocolate ice cream over vanilla.⟩

syn care (for), favor, like

rel adore, cotton (to), delight (in), dig, enjoy, fancy, groove (on), relish, revel (in); choose, cull, handpick, name, pick, select, single (out); take; covet, crave, desire,

hanker (for *or* after), want, wish (for); incline (toward), tend (to)

phrases be partial to, go in for

near ant disfavor, dislike; abhor, abominate, detest, hate, loathe; decline, refuse, reject, turn down; discard, jettison, throw away, throw out

2 to decide to accept (someone or something) from a group of possibilities — see CHOOSE 1

preferably *adv* by choice or preference — see RATHER 1

preference *n* 1 a person or thing that is preferred over others — see FAVORITE

2 positive regard for something — see LIKING

3 the power, right, or opportunity to choose — see CHOICE 1

4 a raising or a state of being raised to a higher rank or position — see ADVANCEMENT 1

preferment *n* a raising or a state of being raised to a higher rank or position — see ADVANCEMENT 1

preferred *adj* singled out from a number or group as more to one's liking — see SELECT 1

prefigure *vb* to give a slight indication of beforehand — see FORESHADOW

prefiguring *n* something believed to be a sign or warning of a future event — see OMEN

pregnancy *n* the state of containing unborn young within the body ⟨An elephant's *pregnancy* can last almost two years.⟩

syn gestation

rel conception; begetting, breeding, generation, procreation, siring, spawning

near ant barrenness, infertility

pregnant *adj* 1 containing unborn young within the body ⟨We only realized that our cat had been *pregnant* when she unexpectedly delivered three kittens.⟩

syn big, expectant, gone, gravid, heavy

rel parturient, prenatal; childbearing, gestational; brooding; conceiving, impregnated

phrases with child, with young

near ant barren, infertile; aborting, miscarrying; delivered

ant nonpregnant

2 clearly conveying a special meaning (as one's mood) — see EXPRESSIVE

prejudgment *n* an attitude, belief, or impression formed in advance of actual experience of something — see PREPOSSESSION 1

prejudice *n* 1 an attitude that always favors one way of feeling or acting especially without considering any other possibilities — see BIAS 1

2 hatred of or discrimination against a person or persons based on their race — see RACISM

prejudice *vb* to cause to have often negative opinions formed without sufficient knowledge ⟨All the bad stories I had heard about the incoming CEO *prejudiced* me against him even before the first meeting.⟩

syn bias, poison, turn

rel dispose, incline, predispose; influence, prepossess; convince, persuade, suggest

prejudiced *adj* **1** inclined to favor one side over another — see PARTIAL 1

2 unwilling to grant other people social rights or to accept other viewpoints — see INTOLERANT 2

prejudicial *adj* **1** causing or capable of causing harm — see HARMFUL

2 opposed to one's interests — see ADVERSE 1

preliminary *adj* coming before the main part or item usually to introduce or prepare for what follows ⟨We need to do some *preliminary* research in order to properly focus the experiment.⟩

syn beginning, introductory, preparatory, primary

rel introducing, prefacing, preparing, readying; premonitory, warning; basic, elementary, fundamental

near ant following, subsequent

preliminary *n* a performance, activity, or event that precedes and sets the stage for the main event — see PRELUDE 1

prelude *n* **1** a performance, activity, or event that precedes and sets the stage for the main event ⟨Appetizers were offered as a *prelude* to dinner.⟩

syn preamble, preliminary, prologue (*also* prolog)

rel lead-in; start

2 a short section (as of a book) that leads to or explains the main part — see INTRODUCTION

premature *adj* occurring before the usual or expected time — see EARLY 2

prematurely *adv* before the usual or expected time — see EARLY

premier *adj* **1** coming before all others in time or order — see FIRST 1

2 highest in rank or authority — see HEAD

3 coming before all others in importance — see FOREMOST 1

premise *also* **premiss** *n* **1** something taken as being true or factual and used as a starting point for a course of action or reasoning — see ASSUMPTION 1

2 premises *pl* the area around and belonging to a building — see GROUND 1

premise *vb* to take as true or as a fact without actual proof — see ASSUME 1

premium *adj* commanding a large price — see COSTLY

premium *n* something given in recognition of achievement — see AWARD 1

premonition *n* a feeling that something bad will happen ⟨She had a *premonition* that her cat would somehow get hurt that day.⟩

syn foreboding, presage, presentiment, prognostication

rel foreknowledge; feel, insight, intuition; augury, omen, portent, sign; agitation, alarm (*also* alarum), anxiety, anxiousness, apprehension, apprehensiveness, care, concern, disquiet, doubt, dread, fear, misgiving, nervousness, uneasiness, worry; foresight, prescience

premonitory *adj* serving as or offering a warning — see CAUTIONARY

preoccupation *n* something about which one is constantly thinking or concerned — see FIXATION

preoccupied *adj* lost in thought and unaware of one's surroundings or actions — see ABSENTMINDED 1

preordain *vb* to determine the fate of in advance — see DESTINE

preparatory *adj* coming before the main part or item usually to introduce or prepare for what follows — see PRELIMINARY

prepare *vb* **1** to make ready in advance ⟨I think I have *prepared* myself well for this challenge.⟩ ⟨We *prepared* the classroom for the important visitors by getting rid of some unsightly clutter.⟩

syn fit, fix, fix, ready

rel brace, fortify, gird, steel; batten, gear up, mount; educate, indoctrinate, instruct, school, train, tutor; boot (up), prime; arrange, set, spread; arm, equip, forearm, furnish, outfit, provide, supply; draft, draw up, frame

2 to make competent (as by training, skill, or ability) for a particular office or function — see QUALIFY 2

3 to put (something) into proper and usually carefully worked out written form — see COMPOSE 1

4 to work out the details of (something) in advance — see PLAN 1

prepared *adj* being in a state of fitness for some experience or action — see READY 1

prepossession *n* **1** an attitude, belief, or impression formed in advance of actual experience of something ⟨The foreign tourists' *prepossessions* about life in the U.S. had been formed by many hours of American TV shows.⟩

syn preconception, prejudgment

rel bias, favor, partiality, prejudice; assumption, conjecture, hypothesis, imagining, predetermination, presumption, presupposition, speculation, supposition, theory, thesis; concept, conception, image, notion, picture, thought

near ant detachment, impartiality, neutrality, objectivity, open-mindedness, unbiasedness

2 something about which one is constantly thinking or concerned — see FIXATION

preposterous *adj* **1** conceived or made without regard for reason or reality — see FANTASTIC 1

2 showing or marked by a lack of good sense or judgment — see FOOLISH 1

3 so foolish or pointless as to be worthy of scornful laughter — see RIDICULOUS 1

preposterousness *n* lack of good sense or judgment — see FOOLISHNESS 1

prerogative *n* something to which one has a just claim — see RIGHT 1

presage *n* **1** a feeling that something bad will happen — see PREMONITION

2 something believed to be a sign or warning of a future event — see OMEN

presage *vb* to tell of or describe beforehand — see FORETELL

presaging *n* a declaration that something will happen in the future — see PREDICTION

prescience *n* **1** the special ability to see or know about events before they actually occur — see FORESIGHT 1

2 concern or preparation for the future — see FORESIGHT 2

prescient *adj* having or showing awareness of and preparation for the future — see FORESIGHTED

prescribe *vb* to give the rules about (something) clearly and exactly ⟨In chess, you can move the various pieces only in certain *prescribed* ways.⟩

syn define, lay down, specify

rel decree, dictate, ordain; assign, direct, fix, set, settle; arrange, order; choose, select; bid, charge, command, enjoin, instruct, tell; conduct, control, govern, lead, manage; coerce, compel, constrain, force; obligate, oblige, require

presence *n* 1 a position within view ⟨The will was signed in the *presence* of two witnesses.⟩

syn company, sight

rel closeness, contiguity, immediacy, nearness, proximity

2 the outward form of someone or something especially as indicative of a quality — see APPEARANCE 1

present *adj* 1 existing or in progress right now ⟨I am very busy at the *present* moment.⟩

syn current, extant, immediate, instant, ongoing, present-day

rel contemporary, modern, modernistic, new, newfangled, new-fashioned, recent, red-hot, space-age, ultramodern, up-to-date; breathing, existent, living

near ant coming, future, unborn; completed, concluded, done, ended, finished, over, terminated, through, up; ancient, antediluvian, antiquated, antique, archaic, dated, fusty, musty, obsolete, old, oldfangled, old-fashioned, old-time, out-of-date, outworn, passé; bygone, erstwhile, former, past

2 being within the confines of a specified place ⟨All of you are required to be *present* for every meeting.⟩

syn attending, in

rel accompanying, observing, participating; available; abounding; latent; breathing, existent, existing, extant, live

phrases at hand, in attendance, on hand

near ant departed, gone, retired; nonexistent; AWOL, truant; dead, deceased, defunct; lost, vanished; belated, delayed, late, tardy

ant absent, away, missing, out

¹**present** *n* the time currently existing or in progress ⟨I cannot talk to you at *present*, but perhaps in a few minutes.⟩

syn moment, now, today

rel phase, stage, state

near ant history, past, yesterday, yesteryear, yore; by-and-by, future, futurity, hereafter, offing

²**present** *n* something given to someone without expectation of a return — see GIFT 1

present *vb* 1 to bring before the public in performance or exhibition ⟨We will *present* a performance of *Our Town* tomorrow evening.⟩

syn carry, give, mount, offer, stage

rel display, exhibit, expose, parade, show, show off, unveil; preview; act, impersonate, perform, play, portray; depict, dramatize, enact, render, represent; extend, proffer, tender

phrases come out with

2 to make (one person) known (to another) socially — see INTRODUCE 1

3 to make a present of — see GIVE 1

presentation *n* something given to someone without expectation of a return — see GIFT 1

present-day *adj* 1 being or involving the latest methods, concepts, information, or styles — see MODERN

2 existing or in progress right now — see PRESENT 1

presentiment *n* a feeling that something bad will happen — see PREMONITION

presently *adv* 1 at or within a short time — see SHORTLY 2

2 at the present time — see NOW 1

3 without delay — see IMMEDIATELY

preservation *n* 1 the act or activity of keeping something in an existing and usually satisfactory condition — see MAINTENANCE

2 the careful maintaining and protection of something valuable especially in its natural or original state — see CONSERVATION 1

preserve *vb* to keep in good condition — see MAINTAIN 1

preserving *n* the act or activity of keeping something in an existing and usually satisfactory condition — see MAINTENANCE

preside (over) *vb* 1 to exercise authority or power over — see GOVERN 1

2 to look after and make decisions about — see CONDUCT 1

president *n* a person in charge of a meeting — see CHAIR 1

presiding *adj* highest in rank or authority — see HEAD

press *n* 1 a built-in space for storage behind a door — see CLOSET 1

2 a great number of persons or creatures massed together — see CROWD 1

3 a storage case typically having doors and shelves — see CABINET

¹**press** *vb* to take or make use of under a guise of authority but without actual right — see APPROPRIATE 1

²**press** *vb* 1 to push steadily against with some force ⟨an old doorbell that requires you to *press* the button hard⟩

syn bear (down on), depress, shove, weigh (on or upon)

rel compress, mash, punch, squash, squeeze, squish; compel, force, pressure; lean (on or against); muscle; drive, propel, thrust; compact, condense, constrict, contract, crush, scrunch, wring; cram, jam, jam-pack, pack, stuff, wedge

2 to apply external pressure on so as to force out the juice or contents of ⟨My family will only drink juice from freshly *pressed* oranges.⟩

syn crush, express, mash, squeeze

rel pulp, puree (or purée); extract, extrude

3 to gather into a closely packed group ⟨Everyone *pressed* around me to see the pictures.⟩

syn bunch, cluster, crowd, huddle, pile

rel assemble, collect, concentrate, congregate, convene, converge, flock, forgather (*or* foregather), herd, swarm, throng; encircle, mob, surround; embrace, hug

near ant break up, disband, disperse, split (up)

4 to force one's way ⟨We continued to *press* deeper and deeper into the tangled rain forest.⟩

syn bore, bull, bulldoze, crash, elbow, jam, muscle, push, shoulder, squeeze

rel ram, shove, thrust

5 to cause (a person) to give in to pressure — see FORCE

6 to try to persuade (someone) through earnest appeals to follow a course of action — see URGE

7 to indicate the importance of by centering attention on — see EMPHASIZE 1

press (for) *vb* to ask for (something) earnestly or with authority — see DEMAND 1

pressing *adj* needing immediate attention — see ACUTE 2

pressure *n* **1** the burden on one's emotional or mental well-being created by demands on one's time — see STRESS 1

2 the use of power to impose one's will on another — see FORCE 2

pressure *vb* to cause (a person) to give in to pressure — see FORCE

prestidigitation *n* the art or skill of performing tricks or illusions for entertainment — see MAGIC 2

prestidigitator *n* one who practices tricks and illusions for entertainment — see MAGICIAN 2

prestigious *adj* **1** having a good reputation especially in a field of knowledge — see RESPECTABLE 1

2 standing above others in rank, importance, or achievement — see EMINENT

presto *adv* with great speed — see FAST 1

presumably *adv* **1** to all outward appearances — see APPARENTLY

2 by reasonable assumption — see PROBABLY

presume *vb* **1** to form an opinion from little or no evidence — see GUESS 1

2 to take as true or as a fact without actual proof — see ASSUME 2

presumed *adj* appearing to be true on the basis of evidence that may or may not be confirmed — see APPARENT 1

presuming *adj* **1** having a feeling of superiority that shows itself in an overbearing attitude — see ARROGANT

2 showing a lack of proper social reserve or modesty — see PRESUMPTUOUS 1

3 thrusting oneself where one is not welcome or invited — see INTRUSIVE

presumption *n* **1** shameless boldness — see EFFRONTERY

2 something taken as being true or factual and used as a starting point for a course of action or reasoning — see ASSUMPTION 1

presumptuous *adj* **1** showing a lack of proper social reserve or modesty ⟨It's a little *presumptuous* of you to assume that I'm your new best friend just because I invited you along.⟩

syn bold, familiar, forward, free, immodest, overfamiliar, presuming

syn synonym(s)   *rel* related words
ant antonym(s)   *near ant* near antonym(s)

rel arrogant, complacent, conceited, egoistic (*also* egoistical), egotistic (*or* egotistical), highfalutin (*also* hifalutin), highhat, hoity-toity, important, overweening, pompous, prideful, proud, self-assertive, self-complacent, self-conceited, self-important, self-satisfied, smug, uppity, vain, vainglorious; cavalier, disdainful, haughty, lordly, pretentious, stuck-up, supercilious, superior; audacious, bold-faced, brash, brassy, brazen, cheeky, cocky, fresh, impertinent, impudent, insolent, overbold, pert, sassy, saucy; confident, self-assured, self-confident, sure; boastful, braggart, bragging; domineering, high-handed, imperious

near ant demure, down-to-earth, humble, lowly, meek, unassertive, unpretentious; bashful, mousy (*or* mousey), retiring, shy, timid, timorous; diffident, self-doubting

ant modest, unassuming

2 having a feeling of superiority that shows itself in an overbearing attitude — see ARROGANT

3 thrusting oneself where one is not welcome or invited — see INTRUSIVE

presumptuousness *n* **1** an exaggerated sense of one's importance that shows itself in the making of excessive or unjustified claims — see ARROGANCE

2 shameless boldness — see EFFRONTERY

presuppose *vb* to take as true or as a fact without actual proof — see ASSUME 2

presupposition *n* something taken as being true or factual and used as a starting point for a course of action or reasoning — see ASSUMPTION 1

pretend *adj* **1** being such in appearance only and made with or manufactured from usually cheaper materials — see IMITATION

2 not real and existing only in the imagination — see IMAGINARY

pretend *vb* **1** to take on a false or deceptive appearance ⟨I *pretended* that I didn't care what other people had to say about me.⟩

syn dissemble, dissimulate, let on, make out

rel act, impersonate, masquerade, play, playact, pose; affect, assume, counterfeit, fake, feign, profess, put on, sham, simulate; camouflage, conceal, disguise, mask; bluff, feint

phrases make a pretense, make a show, make believe, put on an act, put up a front

2 to present a false appearance of — see FEIGN

pretended *adj* **1** lacking in natural or spontaneous quality — see ARTIFICIAL 1

2 not being or expressing what one appears to be or express — see INSINCERE

pretender *n* one who makes false claims of identity or expertise — see IMPOSTOR

pretense *or* **pretence** *n* **1** the quality or state of appearing or trying to appear more important or more valuable than is the case ⟨She seemed to be a very down-to-earth woman who was completely free of *pretense*.⟩

syn affectation, affectedness, grandiosity, pretension, pretentiousness

rel arrogance, complacency, conceit, egotism, imperiousness, pompousness, presumptuousness, pride, self-aggrandizement, self-assertion, self-assumption, self-conceit, self-consequence, self-glorification, self-importance, self-satisfaction, smugness, vaingloriousness, vainglory, vainness, vanity; disdain, haughtiness, lordliness, snobbery, snobbishness, superciliousness, superiority; confidence, presumption, self-assurance, self-confidence, sureness; grandiloquence; flamboyance, flashiness, garishness, gaudiness, glitz, mummery, ostentation, ostentatiousness, show, showiness

near ant demureness, humbleness, humility, lowliness, meekness, modesty; bashfulness, diffidence, shyness, timidity; naturalness, sincerity

2 a display of emotion or behavior that is insincere or intended to deceive — see MASQUERADE

3 an entitlement to something — see CLAIM 1

4 an exaggerated sense of one's importance that shows itself in the making of excessive or unjustified claims — see ARROGANCE

pretension *n* **1** an entitlement to something — see CLAIM 1

2 an exaggerated sense of one's importance that shows itself in the making of excessive or unjustified claims — see ARROGANCE

3 the quality or state of appearing or trying to appear more important or more valuable than is the case — see PRETENSE 1

4 something that one hopes or intends to accomplish — see GOAL

pretentious *adj* self-consciously trying to present an appearance of grandeur or importance ⟨That *pretentious* couple always serves caviar at their parties, even though they themselves dislike it.⟩

syn affected, grandiose, highfalutin (*also* hifalutin), high-minded, ostentatious, pompous, snippy

rel airy, grandiloquent, high-flown, high-sounding, high-toned; arrogant, complacent, conceited, egoistic (*also* egoistical), egotistic (*or* egotistical), high-handed, high-hat, hoity-toity, imperious, important, overweening, presumptuous, prideful, proud, self-centered, self-complacent, self-conceited, self-important, self-obsessed, self-pleased, self-satisfied, smug, uppity, vain, vainglorious; self-aggrandizing, self-dramatizing, self-glorifying, self-promoting; cavalier, disdainful, haughty, lordly, stuck-up, supercilious, superior; flamboyant, flashy, flaunting, garish, gaudy, glitzy, showy, splashy

near ant demure, down-to-earth, homely, humble, lowly, meek, retiring, unassertive, unassuming; bashful, diffident, mousy (*or* mousey), overmodest, passive, quiet, reserved, shy, timid

ant modest, unpretentious

2 having a feeling of superiority that shows itself in an overbearing attitude — see ARROGANT

pretentiousness *n* **1** an exaggerated sense of one's importance that shows itself in the making of excessive or unjustified claims — see ARROGANCE

2 excessive or unnecessary display — see OSTENTATION

3 the quality or state of appearing or trying to appear more important or more valuable than is the case — see PRETENSE 1

preternatural *adj* **1** of, relating to, or being part of a reality beyond the observable physical universe — see SUPERNATURAL 1

2 being so extraordinary or abnormal as to suggest powers which violate the laws of nature — see SUPERNATURAL 2

prettiness *n* the qualities in a person or thing that as a whole give pleasure to the senses — see BEAUTY 1

pretty *adj* **1** giving pleasure or contentment to the mind or senses — see PLEASANT 1

2 meeting the requirements of a purpose or situation — see FIT 1

3 very pleasing to look at — see BEAUTIFUL 1

pretty *adv* to some degree or extent — see FAIRLY 1

prevail *vb* **1** to achieve victory (as in a contest) — see WIN 1

2 to continue to operate or to meet one's needs — see HOLD OUT

prevail (on *or* **upon)** *vb* to cause (someone) to agree with a belief or course of action by using arguments or earnest requests — see PERSUADE

prevail (over) *vb* to achieve a victory over — see BEAT 2

prevailing *adj* **1** accepted, used, or practiced by most people — see CURRENT 1

2 held by or applicable to a majority of the people — see GENERAL 3

prevalence *n* the fact or state of happening often — see FREQUENCY

prevalent *adj* accepted, used, or practiced by most people — see CURRENT 1

prevaricate *vb* to make a statement one knows to be untrue — see ¹LIE

prevarication *n* a statement known by its maker to be untrue and made in order to deceive — see LIE

prevaricator *n* a person who tells lies — see LIAR

prevent *vb* to keep from happening by taking action in advance ⟨A lot of problems would have been *prevented* if we'd just prepared better.⟩

syn avert, forestall, help, obviate, preclude, stave off

rel anticipate, provide; negate, neutralize, nullify; save; baffle, balk, checkmate, deter, foil, frustrate, thwart; bar, block, hamper, hinder, impede, interfere (with), retard, stall; deflect, fend (off), stop, ward (off); avoid, circumvent, dodge, duck, elude, escape, eschew, evade, shake, shirk, shun; forbid, inhibit, prohibit; arrest, check, halt, stop; compensate (for), counteract, counterbalance, make up (for), offset

near ant abet, aid, assist; ease, facilitate, smooth, unclog; advance, cultivate, encourage, forward, foster, further, nurture, promote; allow, leave, let, permit

preventative *adj* concerned with or serving to keep something from happening — see PREVENTIVE

prevention *n* the act or practice of keeping something from happening ⟨Good hygiene is crucial to the *prevention* of illness.⟩

syn averting, forestalling, precluding

rel avoidance, circumvention; negation, neutralization; determent, deterrence, foiling, frustration, thwarting; barring, enjoining, forbidding, interdicting, interdiction, outlawing, prohibiting, prohibition, proscribing, proscription

near ant aid, assistance, backing, support; facilitation; advancement, cultivation, encouragement, nurture, promotion

preventive *adj* concerned with or serving to keep something from happening ⟨If you start taking this *preventive* medicine now, you may not get sick after all.⟩

syn precautionary, preventative

rel deterrent, deterring; negating, neutralizing, nullifying; baffling, balking, foiling, frustrating, thwarting; blocking, hampering, hindering, impeding

near ant abetting, aiding, assisting; easing, facilitating, smoothing; encouraging, forwarding, fostering, furthering, nurturing, promoting

previous *adj* going before another in time or order ⟨The new instructor should consult with the *previous* teacher about the lesson plans.⟩ ⟨The *previous* math problem also included a reference to store discounts.⟩

syn antecedent, anterior, foregoing, former, precedent, preceding, prior

rel advance, early, premature; earliest, first, inaugural, initial, maiden, original, pioneer; preexisting; introductory, preliminary; erstwhile, whilom

near ant advanced, late; closing, concluding, final, last, latest, latter, terminal, ultimate

ant after, ensuing, following, later, posterior, subsequent, succeeding

previously *adv* so as to precede something in order of time — see AHEAD 1

previous to *prep* earlier than — see BEFORE 1

prey *n* 1 an animal that is hunted or killed ⟨Rabbits are common *prey* for owls and hawks.⟩

syn chase, quarry

rel game; kill, victim; beast, brute, creature, critter; target

near ant chaser, hunter, pursuer

2 a person or thing harmed, lost, or destroyed — see CASUALTY 1

3 a person or thing that is the object of abuse, criticism, or ridicule — see TARGET 1

prey (on *or* upon) *vb* to seize and eat (something) as prey ⟨A fox has been *preying on* the chickens.⟩

syn feed (on, upon, *or* off)

rel chase, hunt, pursue, stalk; destroy, dispatch, do in, fell, kill, slay

price *n* 1 the amount of money that is demanded as payment for something ⟨I really wanted to buy that shirt, but the *price* was more money than I had.⟩

syn charge, cost, damage, fee, figure, freight

rel market value, valuation, value; asking price, list price, sticker price; price point, rate, tariff, unit price; carrying charge, overcharge, service charge (*also* service fee), surcharge; account, bill, check, invoice, tab

2 the loss or penalty involved in achieving a goal ⟨I finished the project, but the *price* was losing a night's sleep.⟩

syn cost

rel expense, toll; damages, forfeit, forfeiture, mulct, sacrifice; risk

3 something offered or given in return for a service performed — see REWARD

prick *n* 1 a mark or small hole made by a pointed instrument ⟨The immunization shot left a *prick* on my arm that turned into a bruise.⟩

syn perforation, pinhole, pinprick, punch, puncture, stab

rel gouge, groove, hollow; break, cut, gash, incision, laceration, notch, rent, rip, rupture, slash, slit, tear

2 a sharp unpleasant sensation usually felt in some specific part of the body — see PAIN 1

prickly *adj* 1 causing an unpleasant tingling sensation — see SCRATCHY 2

2 easily irritated or annoyed — see IRRITABLE

3 having leaves or branches which are likely to cause a scratch — see SCRATCHY 1

4 requiring exceptional skill or caution in performance or handling — see TRICKY 1

pride *n* 1 a reasonable or justifiable sense of one's worth or importance ⟨Finishing that survival course gave me a real sense of *pride* and confidence in my abilities.⟩

syn ego, pridefulness, self-esteem, self-regard, self-respect

rel aplomb, assurance, confidence, self-assurance, self-confidence, self-pride, self-worth; dignity, face, honor, prestige

near ant discredit, disgrace, dishonor, disrepute, humiliation, ignominy, infamy, odium, opprobrium, shame; demureness, humbleness, humility, modesty; diffidence, meekness, shyness, timidity, timidness

2 an asset that brings praise or renown — see GLORY 2

3 an often unjustified feeling of being pleased with oneself or with one's situation or achievements — see COMPLACENCE 1

4 individuals carefully selected as being the best of a class — see ELITE 1

pride *vb* to think highly of (oneself) ⟨He *prides* himself on the quality of his writing.⟩

syn flatter, plume

rel boast, brag, crow, swagger; congratulate, felicitate

prideful *adj* 1 having or displaying feelings of scorn for what is regarded as beneath oneself — see PROUD 1

2 having too high an opinion of oneself — see CONCEITED

3 having or expressing feelings of joy or triumph — see EXULTANT

pridefulness *n* 1 a reasonable or justifiable sense of one's worth or importance — see PRIDE 1

---

syn synonym(s)   **rel** related words
ant antonym(s)   **near ant** near antonym(s)

2 an often unjustified feeling of being pleased with oneself or with one's situation or achievements — see COMPLACENCE 1

priestly *adj* of, relating to, or characteristic of the clergy — see CLERICAL

prim *adj* given to or marked by very conservative standards regarding personal behavior or morals — see STRAITLACED

primacy *n* the fact or state of being above others in rank or importance — see EMINENCE 1

primal *adj* **1** coming before all others in importance — see FOREMOST 1
2 relating to or occurring near the beginning of a process, series, or time period — see EARLY 1

primarily *adv* **1** in the beginning — see ORIGINALLY
2 for the most part — see CHIEFLY

primary *adj* **1** coming before all others in importance — see FOREMOST 1
2 done or working without something else coming in between — see DIRECT 1
3 highest in rank or authority — see HEAD
4 coming before the main part or item usually to introduce or prepare for what follows — see PRELIMINARY

prime *adj* **1** highest in rank or authority — see HEAD
2 of the very best kind — see EXCELLENT

prime *n* **1** a state or time of great activity, thriving, or achievement — see BLOOM 1
2 individuals carefully selected as being the best of a class — see ELITE 1

primer *n* a book used for instruction in a subject — see TEXTBOOK

primeval *adj* relating to or occurring near the beginning of a process, series, or time period — see EARLY 1

primitive *adj* **1** belonging to or characteristic of an early level of skill or development ⟨*Primitive* wooden tools were used before the Iron Age.⟩
syn crude, low, rude, rudimentary
rel basic, simple, uncomplicated; homely, unsophisticated; early, embryonic, primeval, primordial; backward, underdeveloped, undeveloped; aged, ancient, antediluvian, antiquated, antique, dated, fusty, hoary, musty, obsolete, old, oldfangled, old-fashioned, old-time, out-of-date, outworn, passé, past, quaint, unmodernized
near ant complex, complicated, intricate, involved, sophisticated; full-blown, mature, matured, perfected, ripe, ripened; civilized, cultivated, enlightened, refined; contemporary, current, latest, mod, modern, modernistic, new, newfangled, newfashioned, novel, now, present-day, spaceage, state-of-the-art, supermodern, ultramodern, up-to-date
ant advanced, developed, evolved, high, higher, late
2 relating to or occurring near the beginning of a process, series, or time period — see EARLY 1

primordial *adj* relating to or occurring near the beginning of a process, series, or time period — see EARLY 1

prince *n* a person of rank, power, or influence in a particular field — see MAGNATE

princely *adj* fit for or worthy of a royal ruler — see MONARCHICAL

principal *adj* **1** coming before all others in importance — see FOREMOST 1
2 highest in rank or authority — see HEAD

principal *n* the person who has the most important role in a play, movie, or TV show — see STAR 2

principally *adv* for the most part — see CHIEFLY

principled *adj* **1** following the accepted rules of moral conduct — see HONORABLE 1
2 guided by or in accordance with one's sense of right and wrong — see CONSCIENTIOUS 1

principles *n pl* **1** general or basic truths on which other truths or theories can be based ⟨If you don't learn the *principles* of algebra now, you won't understand much later on.⟩
syn basics, elements, essentials, fundamentals, rudiments
rel basis, bedrock, cornerstone, foundation, groundwork, keystone, underpinning; belief, canon, doctrine, dogma, faith, philosophy; axiom, law, precept, tenet; rule, standard; theorem
near ant details, trivia
2 the code of good conduct for an individual or group — see ETHICS

print *n* **1** a perceptible trace left by pressure ⟨One telltale sign that I had been napping was the *print* left by the chenille bedspread on my cheek.⟩
syn impress, impression, imprint, stamp
rel dent, hollow, indentation; mark, sign
2 a picture created from an image recorded on a light-sensitive surface by a camera — see PHOTOGRAPH

print *vb* to produce and release for distribution in printed form — see PUBLISH 1

prior *adj* **1** coming before all others in importance — see FOREMOST 1
2 going before another in time or order — see PREVIOUS

priority *n* the right to one's attention before other things considered less important ⟨The committee has decided to give your request *priority*, so you'll have a meeting early tomorrow morning.⟩
syn precedence, right-of-way
rel preference; urgency; ascendancy (*also* ascendency), preeminence, primacy, supremacy; transcendence, transcendency; order, progression, sequence, succession; front burner
near ant back burner

prior to *prep* earlier than — see BEFORE 1

priory *n* a residence for men under religious vows — see MONASTERY

prison *n* **1** a place of confinement for persons held in lawful custody — see JAIL
2 the act of confining or the state of being confined — see INTERNMENT

prisoner *n* one that has been taken and held in confinement — see CAPTIVE

pristine *adj* **1** being in an original and unused or unspoiled state — see FRESH 1
2 free from dirt or stain — see CLEAN 1

private *adj* **1** not known or meant to be known by the general populace ⟨That he is planning to retire is *private* information until he makes a public announcement.⟩

syn confidential, esoteric, hushed, inside, intimate, nonpublic, privy, secret

rel classified, restricted, top secret; silent, unadvertised, unannounced, undisclosed, unmentioned, unsaid, untold; clandestine, closet, collusive, conspiratorial, covert; furtive, hugger-mugger, occult, sneak, sneaking, sneaky, stealthy, surreptitious, undercover, underground, underhand, underhanded; personal; closeted, concealed; silenced, stifled, suppressed; backstage, offscreen, offstage

near ant well-known; advertised, aired, announced, blazed, broadcast, declared, disclosed, divulged, enunciated, heralded, proclaimed, professed, promulgated, publicized, published, reported, spotlighted

ant common, open, public

2 undertaken or done so as to escape being observed or known by others — see SECRET 1

3 of, relating to, or belonging to a single person — see INDIVIDUAL 1

privation *n* the state of being robbed of something normally enjoyed ⟨The constant *privation* of sleep was starting to affect my work.⟩

syn deprivation, loss

rel absence, dearth, lack, need, want; dispossession; denial, forfeit, forfeiture, penalty, sacrifice; bereavement; deficiency, inadequacy, insufficiency, paucity, poverty, scarcity, shortage

near ant control, ownership, possession; accumulation, acquiring, gain

privilege *n* something granted as a special favor ⟨The town's oldest resident will have the *privilege* of leading the parade kicking off the Heritage Celebration.⟩

syn boon, concession, honor

rel courtesy; claim, right; birthright; perquisite, prerogative; charter, grant, patent; exemption, immunity, waiver

near ant burden, duty, obligation, responsibility

privilege *vb* to give a right to — see ENTITLE 1

privy *adj* **1** not known or meant to be known by the general populace — see PRIVATE 1

2 undertaken or done so as to escape being observed or known by others — see SECRET 1

3 of, relating to, or belonging to a single person — see INDIVIDUAL 1

prize *adj* of the very best kind — see EXCELLENT

prize *n* **1** someone or something unusually desirable ⟨The picture would be the *prize* of any museum's collection.⟩

syn catch, gem, jewel, pearl, plum, treasure

rel blessing, find, godsend, goody (*or* goodie), valuable, windfall; booty, loot, plunder, spoil, swag; brass ring; glory, pride; gold, jackpot, prize money

near ant lemon, loser

2 something given in recognition of achievement — see AWARD 1

¹**prize** *vb* **1** to draw out by force or with effort — see EXTRACT

2 to raise, move, or pull apart with or as if with a lever — see ¹PRY 1

²**prize** *vb* to hold dear — see LOVE 1

prizefighter *n* one that engages in the sport of fighting with the fists — see BOXER

proactive *adj* having or showing awareness of and preparation for the future — see FORESIGHTED

probability *n* **1** the quality or state of being likely to occur ⟨The plot of the movie thriller was exciting and surprising but woefully lacking in *probability*.⟩

syn liability, likelihood

rel credibility, plausibility, plausibleness; feasibility, possibility, potentiality, reasonability, reasonableness, viability

near ant doubtfulness, dubiousness; impracticability, impracticality; implausibility, incredibility, incredibleness

ant improbability, unlikelihood, unlikeliness

2 a measure of how often an event will occur instead of another ⟨The *probability* of flipping a coin and getting heads 50 times in a row is not good.⟩

syn chance, odds, percentage

rel outlook, prospect; contingency, possibility, potential, potentiality; conditional probability

probable *adj* **1** worthy of being accepted as true or reasonable — see BELIEVABLE

2 having a high chance of occurring — see LIKELY 1

probably *adv* by reasonable assumption ⟨We would *probably* win that bet.⟩

syn doubtless, likely, presumably

rel maybe, mayhap, perchance, perhaps, possibly; conceivably, imaginably, plausibly, practically, reasonably; potentially; assuredly, certainly, conclusively, decisively, definitely, definitively, indisputably, indubitably, really, surely, truly, undeniably, undoubtedly, unquestionably; presumedly, supposably, supposedly

phrases as like as not (*or* like as not)

near ant implausibly, inconceivably, incredibly, unbelievably, unthinkably

ant improbably

probe *n* a systematic search for the truth or facts about something — see INQUIRY 1

probe *vb* **1** to search through or into — see EXPLORE 1

2 to go into or range over for purposes of discovery — see EXPLORE 2

probing *n* a systematic search for the truth or facts about something — see INQUIRY 1

probity *n* **1** conduct that conforms to an accepted standard of right and wrong — see MORALITY 1

2 devotion to telling the truth — see HONESTY 1

3 faithfulness to high moral standards — see HONOR 1

problem *n* **1** something that requires thought and skill for resolution ⟨the *problem* of habitat loss⟩

syn case, challenge, knot, matter, trouble

rel issue, question; corner, fix, hole, hot water, jam, mire, pickle, predicament, quagmire, spot; crux, toughie (*also* toughy); dilemma, quandary; catch, glitch, hitch, pitfall, snag; conundrum, enigma, mystery,

---

syn synonym(s)   *rel* related words
ant antonym(s)   *near ant* near antonym(s)

puzzle, puzzlement, riddle; brainteaser, poser, stumper

near ant magic bullet, silver bullet; cure-all, panacea

ant answer, solution

2 an interrogative expression often used to test knowledge — see QUESTION 1

problematic *also* **problematical** *adj* **1** requiring exceptional skill or caution in performance or handling — see TRICKY 1

2 giving good reason for being doubted, questioned, or challenged — see DOUBTFUL 2

procedure *n* **1** a usually fixed or ordered series of actions or events leading to a result — see PROCESS 1

2 a way of acting or proceeding — see COURSE 1

proceed *vb* to move forward along a course — see GO 1

proceed (along) *vb* to make one's way through, across, or over — see TRAVERSE 1

proceeding *adj* being in progress or development — see ONGOING 1

proceeding *n* **1** a court case for enforcing a right or claim — see LAWSUIT

2 a usually fixed or ordered series of actions or events leading to a result — see PROCESS 1

proceeds *n pl* **1** an increase usually measured in money that comes from labor, business, or property — see INCOME 1

2 the amount of money left when expenses are subtracted from the total amount received — see PROFIT 1

process *n* **1** a usually fixed or ordered series of actions or events leading to a result ⟨the *process* by which the elastic fibers spun by silkworms are turned into soft, lustrous cloth⟩

syn course, operation, procedure, proceeding

rel drill, routine; fashion, form, manner, method, mode, style, system, technique, way; approach, arrangement, blueprint, design, formula, ground plan, layout, plan, plot, program, project, scheme, strategy

2 forward movement in time or place — see ADVANCE 1

procession *n* **1** a body of individuals moving along in an orderly and often ceremonial way — see CORTEGE 2

2 forward movement in time or place — see ADVANCE 1

proclaim *vb* to make known openly or publicly — see ANNOUNCE

proclivity *n* a habitual attraction to some activity or thing — see INCLINATION 1

procreate *vb* to bring forth offspring ⟨Animals have a natural instinct to *procreate*.⟩

syn breed, multiply, propagate, reproduce

rel bear, beget, engender, gender, generate, get, have, mother, parent, produce, sire; hatch, spawn

procurable *adj* possible to get — see AVAILABLE 1

procurator *n* a person who acts or does business for another — see AGENT 2

procure *vb* to receive as return for effort — see EARN 1

prod *vb* **1** to urge or push forward with or as if with a pointed object ⟨The boy kept *prodding* the sheep with a staff to get them to move along faster.⟩

syn dig, goad, spur

rel chuck, jab, jog, knock, nudge, poke; bore, drill, perforate, pierce, prick, punch, puncture, stab, stick; drive, hale, propel

2 to try to persuade (someone) through earnest appeals to follow a course of action — see URGE

prodigal *adj* given to spending money freely or foolishly ⟨The *prodigal* child always spent her allowance the minute she got it.⟩

syn extravagant, profligate, spendthrift, squandering, thriftless, unthrifty, wasteful

rel improvident, myopic, shortsighted; unselfish, unsparing; careless, heedless, imprudent, incautious, injudicious, unwise; indulgent, reckless, splurging, wanton

near ant cheap, close, closefisted, mean, niggardly, parsimonious, penurious, pinching, spare, sparing, stingy, stinting, tight, tightfisted; careful, judicious, prudent, sensible, wise; farsighted, forehanded, foreseeing, foresighted, provident

ant conserving, economical, economizing, frugal, scrimping, skimping, thrifty

prodigal *n* someone who spends money freely or foolishly ⟨The million-dollar lottery winner was such a *prodigal* that his windfall was exhausted after only a few years.⟩

syn fritterer, profligate, spender, spendthrift, squanderer, waster, wastrel

rel dissipate

near ant cheapskate, miser, niggard, piker, scrooge, skinflint, tightwad; conserver, saver

ant economizer

prodigality *n* **1** an instance of spending money or resources without care or restraint — see WASTE 1

2 the quality or fact of being free or wasteful in the expenditure of money — see EXTRAVAGANCE 1

prodigious *adj* **1** causing wonder or astonishment — see MARVELOUS 1

2 unusually large — see HUGE

prodigy *n* something extraordinary or surprising — see WONDER 1

produce *n* something produced by physical or intellectual effort — see PRODUCT 1

produce *vb* **1** to be the cause of (a situation, action, or state of mind) — see EFFECT

2 to bring forth from the womb — see BEAR 1

3 to bring into being by combining, shaping, or transforming materials — see MAKE 1

4 to present so as to invite notice or attention — see SHOW 1

product *n* **1** something produced by physical or intellectual effort ⟨That biography is the *product* of years of work.⟩ ⟨a rebuilt car which is the *product* of several people's labor⟩

syn affair, fruit, handiwork, labor, output, produce, production, thing, work, yield

rel article, entry, object; goods, line, merchandise, wares; handcraft, handicraft; aftereffect, aftermath, conclusion, consequence, corollary, development, effect, issue, outcome, result, resultant, sequel, sequence, upshot; by-product, derivative, offshoot, offspring, outgrowth, residual, side effect (*also* side reaction), spin-off

2 a condition or occurrence traceable to a cause — see EFFECT 1

production *n* something produced by physical or intellectual effort — see PRODUCT 1

productive *adj* 1 having a role in deciding something's final form — see FORMATIVE

2 producing abundantly — see FERTILE

3 producing or capable of producing a desired result — see EFFECTIVE 1

productiveness *n* the power to produce a desired result — see EFFICACY

profane *adj* 1 not involving religion or religious matters ⟨It was hard to juggle the requirements of church and our more *profane* duties.⟩

syn nonreligious, secular, temporal

rel atheistic, godless, irreligious, pagan, paganish, religionless; lay, nonclerical; nondenominational, nonsectarian; earthly, mundane, worldly; material, physical, substantial; bodily, carnal, corporal, fleshly; blasphemous, impious, irreverent, sacrilegious; unconsecrated, unhallowed

near ant divine, spiritual; consecrated, hallowed, holy, sacrosanct, sanctified; churchly, devout, godly, pious, prayerful, reverent, worshipful; ethereal, insubstantial, metaphysical, unsubstantial

ant religious, sacred

2 not showing proper reverence for the holy or sacred — see IRREVERENT

profane *vb* 1 to lower in character, dignity, or quality — see DEBASE 1

2 to put to a bad or improper use — see MISAPPLY

3 to treat (a sacred place or object) shamefully or with great disrespect — see DESECRATE

profess *vb* 1 to present a false appearance of — see FEIGN

2 to state clearly and strongly — see ASSERT 1

3 to state as a fact usually forcefully — see CLAIM 1

profession *n* 1 a solemn and often public declaration of the truth or existence of something — see PROTESTATION

2 the activity by which one regularly makes a living — see OCCUPATION

proffer *n* something which is presented for consideration — see PROPOSAL

proffer *vb* 1 to put before another for acceptance or consideration — see OFFER 1

2 to set before the mind for consideration — see PROPOSE 1

proficiency *n* 1 a highly developed skill in or knowledge of something — see COMMAND 2

2 knowledge gained by actually doing or living through something — see EXPERIENCE 1

proficient *adj* having or showing exceptional knowledge, experience, or skill in a field of endeavor ⟨She is quite *proficient* at

computer repair.⟩ ⟨a *proficient* rendition of a difficult piano piece.⟩

syn accomplished, ace, adept, complete, consummate, crack, crackerjack, educated, experienced, expert, good, great, master, masterful, masterly, practiced (*also* practised), skilled, skillful, versed, veteran, virtuoso

rel adroit, clever, deft, dexterous (*also* dextrous), handy, sure-handed; gifted, talented; polished, refined; effective, effectual, efficient, workmanlike; able, capable, competent, fit, fitted, qualified; educated, knowledgeable, schooled, taught, trained, tutored; all-around (*also* all-round), well-rounded; multiskilled, multitalented

near ant incapable, incompetent, inept, unfit, unqualified, weak; artless, crude, rude; ineffective, ineffectual, inefficient; talentless, ungifted, untalented; ignorant, unschooled, untaught, untrained, untutored; beginning, green, inexperienced, new, raw, unseasoned, untested, untried, would-be; primitive, rough, unpolished; awkward, clumsy, heavy-handed

ant amateur, amateurish, inexperienced, inexpert, unprofessional, unseasoned, unskilled, unskillful

proficiently *adv* in a skillful or expert manner — see WELL 3

profit *n* 1 the amount of money left when expenses are subtracted from the total amount received ⟨After we deducted the cost of sugar, lemons, and paper cups, the *profit* from a day of lemonade sales was about $20.⟩

syn earnings, gain, lucre, net, payoff, proceeds, return

rel cleanup, windfall; gross, sales; compensation, emolument, income, pay, payment, remittal, requital, salary, wages; interest, return, revenue, yield

near ant charge, cost, disbursement, expenditure, expense, loss, outgo, outlay

2 an increase usually measured in money that comes from labor, business, or property — see INCOME 1

profit *vb* to provide with something useful or desirable — see BENEFIT

profitable *adj* 1 yielding a profit ⟨Selling real estate on the side turned out to be a *profitable* venture.⟩

syn fat, gainful, lucrative, paying, remunerative

rel advantageous, beneficial, favorable, rewarding, useful, worthwhile; bankable

near ant disadvantageous, unfavorable

ant unprofitable

2 promoting or contributing to personal or social well-being — see BENEFICIAL

profitless *adj* producing no results — see FUTILE

profligacy *n* immoral conduct or practices harmful or offensive to society — see VICE 1

profligate *adj* given to spending money freely or foolishly — see PRODIGAL

profligate *n* 1 someone who spends money freely or foolishly — see PRODIGAL

2 a person who has sunk below the normal moral standard — see DEGENERATE

profound *adj* 1 difficult for one of ordinary knowledge or intelligence to under-

---

syn synonym(s)   *rel* related words
ant antonym(s)   *near ant* near antonym(s)

stand ⟨a *profound* observation about good and evil that few listeners fully grasped⟩
syn abstruse, deep, esoteric, recondite
rel erudite, learned, scholarly; academic (*also* academical), pedantic; complex, complicated, hard; darkling, enigmatic (*also* enigmatical), inscrutable, mysterious, mystic, mystical, uncanny; impenetrable, incomprehensible, unfathomable, unintelligible; ambiguous, cryptic; unanswerable, unknowable; baffling, bewildering, confounding, confusing, disorienting, mystifying, perplexing, puzzling
near ant easy, facile, simple, straightforward; apparent, clear, clear-cut, distinct, evident, lucid, manifest, obvious, perspicuous, plain, transparent
ant shallow, superficial
2 extreme in degree, power, or effect — see INTENSE 1
3 having no exceptions or restrictions — see ABSOLUTE 2
4 extending far downward — see DEEP 1
profoundness *n* the quality of being great in extent (as of insight) — see DEPTH 2
profundity *n* the quality of being great in extent (as of insight) — see DEPTH 2
profuse *adj* pouring forth in great amounts ⟨We received *profuse* thanks for our efforts.⟩ ⟨a *profuse* rush of water from the collapsing dike⟩
syn copious, galore, gushing, lavish, riotous
rel abounding, abundant, ample, bounteous, bountiful, liberal, plenteous, plentiful; extravagant, luxuriant; fat, fecund, fertile; free, munificent, openhanded, unsparing; excessive, immoderate, redundant; adequate, enough, sufficient
near ant meager (*or* meagre), niggardly, poor, scant, scanty, spare, sparse, stingy; deficient, inadequate, incomplete, insufficient, lacking, scarce, unsatisfactory, wanting; bare, mere, minimal
ant dribbling, trickling
profusion *n* **1** a considerable amount — see LOT 2
2 the quality or fact of being free or wasteful in the expenditure of money — see EXTRAVAGANCE 1
progeny *n* the descendants of a person, animal, or plant — see OFFSPRING
prognosis *n* a declaration that something will happen in the future — see PREDICTION
prognosticate *vb* to tell of or describe beforehand — see FORETELL
prognostication *n* **1** a declaration that something will happen in the future — see PREDICTION
2 a feeling that something bad will happen — see PREMONITION
prognosticator *n* one who predicts future events or developments — see PROPHET 1
program *n* **1** a listing of things to be presented or considered (as at a concert or play) ⟨The *program* will tell us the scheduled order of musical numbers.⟩
syn agenda, calendar, docket, schedule, timetable
rel card, dance card, exercises, plate; arrangement, order, ordering, organization, sequence, setup
phrases bill of fare

2 a method worked out in advance for achieving some objective — see PLAN 1
3 a way of acting or proceeding — see COURSE 1
progress *n* **1** forward movement in time or place — see ADVANCE 1
2 the act or process of going from the simple or basic to the complex or advanced — see DEVELOPMENT 1
progress *vb* **1** to become mature — see MATURE
2 to move forward along a course — see GO 1
progression *n* **1** a series of things linked together — see CHAIN 1
2 forward movement in time or place — see ADVANCE 1
3 the act or process of going from the simple or basic to the complex or advanced — see DEVELOPMENT 1
progressive *adj* **1** being far along in development — see ADVANCED
2 not bound by traditional ways or beliefs — see LIBERAL 1
prohibit *vb* to order not to do or use or to be done or used — see FORBID
prohibited *adj* that may not be permitted — see IMPERMISSIBLE
prohibiting *n* the act of ordering that something not be done or used — see PROHIBITION 1
prohibition *n* **1** the act of ordering that something not be done or used ⟨The principal's *prohibition* against the use of cell phones in the school building met with unanimous approval by the teachers.⟩
syn banning, barring, enjoining, forbidding, interdicting, interdiction, outlawing, prohibiting, proscribing, proscription
rel bidding, charging, decreeing, dictation, direction, instruction; deterrence, discouragement, dissuading; repression, suppression; coercion, compulsion, constraint, force
near ant allowance, permission, sufferance, toleration; approval, endorsement (*also* indorsement); authorization, clearance, license (*or* licence), sanction; encouragement, promotion, support; compliance, obedience, submission
2 an order that something not be done or used ⟨The city issued a *prohibition* against parking on the street during snowstorms.⟩
syn ban, embargo, interdict, interdiction, proscription, veto
rel no-no, taboo (*also* tabu); constraint, inhibition, limitation, restraint, restriction; deterrent, discouragement; repression, suppression; prevention; denial, disallowance, negation, refusal, rejection; objection, protest; caveat, warning; commandment, decree, dictate, edict, mandate
near ant sufferance, tolerance, toleration; allowance, allowing, authorization, clearance, consent, granting, leave, letting, license (*or* licence), licensing (*also* licencing), permission, permitting, sanction, sanctioning; approbation, approval, blessing, endorsement (*also* indorsement), imprimatur, OK (*or* okay); enabling, encouragement, facilitation, promotion, support; compliance, obedience, submission; acquiescence, agreement, assent

project *n* a method worked out in advance for achieving some objective — see PLAN 1

project *vb* 1 to extend outward beyond a usual point — see BULGE 1

2 to work out the details of (something) in advance — see PLAN 1

projection *n* a part that sticks out from the general mass of something — see BULGE 1

proletarian *adj* belonging to the class of people of low social or economic rank — see IGNOBLE 1

proletariat *n* people looked down upon as ignorant and of the lowest class — see RABBLE

proliferate *vb* to become greater in extent, volume, amount, or number — see INCREASE 2

proliferation *n* 1 something added (as by growth) — see INCREASE 1

2 the act or process of becoming greater in number — see MULTIPLICATION

prolific *adj* producing abundantly — see FERTILE

prolix *adj* using or containing more words than necessary to express an idea — see WORDY 1

prolixity *n* the use of too many words to express an idea — see VERBIAGE 1

prologue *also* **prolog** *n* 1 a performance, activity, or event that precedes and sets the stage for the main event — see PRELUDE 1

2 a short section (as of a book) that leads to or explains the main part — see INTRODUCTION

prolong *vb* to make longer — see EXTEND 1

prolongation *n* the act of making longer — see EXTENSION 1

prolonging *n* the act of making longer — see EXTENSION 1

prom *n* a social gathering for dancing — see DANCE

prominence *n* an area of high ground — see HEIGHT 4

prominent *adj* 1 likely to attract attention — see NOTICEABLE

2 widely known — see FAMOUS 1

promiscuous *adj* consisting of many things of different sorts — see MISCELLANEOUS

promise *n* a person's solemn declaration that he or she will do or not do something ⟨He made a *promise* to arrive on time.⟩
syn oath, pledge, troth, vow, word
rel appointment, arrangement, commitment, engagement, obligation; agreement, compact, contract, covenant; assurance, guarantee, guaranty, undertaking; bond, deposit, gage, pawn, security, token, warranty

promise *vb* 1 to make a solemn declaration of intent ⟨They *promised* to keep in touch with us after they moved away.⟩
syn covenant, pledge, swear, vow
rel affiance, betroth, plight, troth; accede, agree, assent, consent; contract, engage, ensure, guarantee, undertake; affirm, assert, aver, avouch, avow, declare, insist, warrant
phrases give one's word

2 to show signs of a favorable or successful outcome — see BODE

promised land *n* an often imaginary place or state of utter perfection and happiness — see PARADISE 1

promising *adj* 1 having qualities which inspire hope — see HOPEFUL 1

2 pointing toward a happy outcome — see FAVORABLE 2

promontory *n* 1 an area of high ground jutting out into a body of water beyond the line of the coast — see HEADLAND 1

2 an area of land that juts out into a body of water — see ²CAPE

promote *vb* 1 to move higher in rank or position ⟨The navy *promoted* her to captain for her record of outstanding performance.⟩
syn advance, elevate, raise, upgrade
rel forward, further; aggrandize, boost, heighten, improve, lift, uplift; commission, ennoble, knight; acclaim, applaud, celebrate, cite, commend, compliment, congratulate, decorate; eulogize, exalt, extol (*also* extoll), glorify, hail, honor, laud, praise, salute
phrases kick upstairs
near ant depose, dethrone, dismiss, expel, impeach, oust, overthrow, remove, unmake, unseat; demean, disgrace, dishonor, humble, humiliate, mortify, shame, take down; censure, condemn, denounce
ant abase, degrade, demote, downgrade, lower, reduce

2 to help the growth or development of — see FOSTER 1

3 to look after or assist the growth of by labor and care — see GROW 1

4 to provide publicity for — see PUBLICIZE 1

promoter *n* a person who actively supports or favors a cause — see EXPONENT 1

promotion *n* a raising or a state of being raised to a higher rank or position — see ADVANCEMENT 1

prompt *adj* 1 done, carried out, or given without delay ⟨*Prompt* treatment of snakebites is always advisable.⟩
syn immediate, punctual, speedy, timely
rel apt, quick, ready, swift, willing; opportune, seasonable; early
near ant delinquent, latish, overdue; behind, behindhand, delayed, detained; dilatory, laggard, slow
ant belated, late, tardy

2 having or showing the ability to respond without delay or hesitation — see QUICK 1

prompt *vb* 1 to be the cause of (a situation, action, or state of mind) — see EFFECT

2 to try to persuade (someone) through earnest appeals to follow a course of action — see URGE

promptitude *n* the quality or habit of arriving or being ready on time ⟨His chronic tardiness has put him in poor standing with his boss, who values hustle and *promptitude*.⟩
syn promptness, punctuality, timeliness
rel alacrity, aptness, quickness, readiness, willingness; earliness, prematurity
near ant belatedness, lateness; slowness
ant tardiness, unpunctuality

promptly *adv* without delay — see IMMEDIATELY

promptness *n* the quality or habit of arriving or being ready on time — see PROMPTITUDE

promulgate *vb* to make known openly or publicly — see ANNOUNCE

prone *adj* **1** having a tendency to be or act in a certain way ⟨He was *prone* to emotional outbursts under stress.⟩
syn apt, given, inclined, tending
rel choosing, preferring; disposed, liable, likely, minded, predisposed, willing
near ant averse, disinclined, indisposed, loath (*also* loth *or* loathe), unwilling
2 lying with the face downwards ⟨He was in a *prone* position on the floor.⟩
syn prostrate
rel flat, recumbent; reclining, reposing; horizontal
near ant erect, raised, standing, upright, upstanding, vertical
ant supine

proneness *n* an established pattern of behavior — see TENDENCY 1

pronounced *adj* **1** likely to attract attention — see NOTICEABLE
2 very noticeable especially for being incorrect or bad — see EGREGIOUS

pronto *adv* **1** with great speed — see FAST 1
2 without delay — see IMMEDIATELY

proof *n* something presented in support of the truth or accuracy of a claim ⟨She presented *proof* that she had not cheated.⟩
syn attestation, confirmation, corroboration, documentation, evidence, substantiation, testament, testimony, validation, witness
rel (the) goods; certificate, document, exhibit; demonstration, illustration; authentication, identification, manifestation, verification
near ant rebuttal, refutation; accusation, allegation, charge; assumption, conjecture, guess, presumption, surmise, suspicion
ant disproof

prop (up) *vb* **1** to hold up or serve as a foundation for — see SUPPORT 3
2 to provide (someone) with what is useful or necessary to achieve an end — see HELP 1

propagate *vb* **1** to bring forth offspring — see PROCREATE
2 to cause to be known over a considerable area or by many people — see SPREAD 1

propel *vb* **1** to apply force to (someone or something) so that it moves in front of one — see PUSH 1
2 to set or keep in motion — see MOVE 2

propensity *n* **1** an established pattern of behavior — see TENDENCY 1
2 a habitual attraction to some activity or thing — see INCLINATION 1

proper *adj* **1** following the established traditions of refined society and good taste ⟨The formal ball called for *proper* attire—tuxedos and full-length gowns only.⟩
syn befitting, correct, decent, decorous, genteel, nice, polite, respectable, seemly
rel acceptable, adequate, satisfactory, tolerable; dress, dressy, formal; dignified, elegant, gracious; priggish, prim, stiff, stuffy; apt, material, relevant; allowed, authorized, kosher, permitted
near ant intolerable, unacceptable, unsatisfactory; casual, grungy, informal; seedy, shabby, tacky; banned, barred, disallowed; forbidden, interdicted, outlawed, prohibited, proscribed
ant improper, inappropriate, incorrect, indecent, indecorous, unbecoming, ungenteel, unseemly
2 being in agreement with the truth or a fact or a standard — see CORRECT 1
3 marked by or showing careful attention to set forms and details — see CEREMONIOUS 1
4 meeting the requirements of a purpose or situation — see FIT 1
5 serving to identify as belonging to an individual or group — see CHARACTERISTIC 1

properly *adv* in a manner suitable for the occasion or purpose ⟨The scouts were *properly* dressed for a week of camping.⟩
syn appropriately, congruously, correctly, fittingly, happily, meetly, right, rightly, suitably
rel well; acceptably, adequately, passably, satisfactorily, tolerably; decorously
near ant unacceptably, unsatisfactorily; inopportunely, unfortunately, unseasonably
ant improperly, inappropriately, incongruously, incorrectly, unseemly, unsuitably, wrongly

property *n* **1** a small piece of land that is developed or available for development — see LOT 1
2 something that sets apart an individual from others of the same kind — see CHARACTERISTIC

prophecy *also* **prophesy** *n* a declaration that something will happen in the future — see PREDICTION

prophesier *n* one who predicts future events or developments — see PROPHET 1

prophesy *vb* to tell of or describe beforehand — see FORETELL

prophet *n* **1** one who predicts future events or developments ⟨an economist who is regarded by many as a reliable *prophet* of future developments in the global economy⟩
syn augur, diviner, forecaster, foreseer, foreteller, fortune-teller, futurist, prognosticator, prophesier, seer, soothsayer, visionary
rel prophetess, sibyl; mystic, oracle
2 a person who speaks for another or for a group — see SPOKESPERSON

prophetic *also* **prophetical** *adj* being a sign of a later course of events ⟨In retrospect, those lower-than-expected sales numbers were a *prophetic* indicator of the financial trouble the company would soon be in.⟩
syn predictive
rel baleful, dire, foreboding, menacing, portentous, sinister, threatening; inauspicious, unpromising; oracular; revelatory, telling

near ant auspicious, promising, propitious, rosy

propitiate *vb* to lessen the anger or agitation of — see PACIFY 1

propitiatory *adj* tending to lessen or avoid conflict or hostility — see PACIFIC 1

propitious *adj* 1 having qualities which inspire hope — see HOPEFUL 1

2 pointing toward a happy outcome — see FAVORABLE 2

proponent *n* a person who actively supports or favors a cause — see EXPONENT 1

proportion *n* 1 a balanced, pleasing, or suitable arrangement of parts — see HARMONY 1

2 something belonging to, due to, or contributed by an individual member of a group — see SHARE 1

3 the relationship in quantity, amount, or size between two or more things — see RATIO

4 the total amount of measurable space or surface occupied by something — see ¹SIZE

proportional *adj* corresponding in size, amount, extent, or degree ⟨The website's popularity increased exponentially, resulting in a *proportional* increase in advertising revenue.⟩

syn commensurate, proportionate

rel balanced, symmetrical (*or* symmetric); reciprocal; contingent, dependent, relative; akin, comparable, similar

phrases in proportion

near ant asymmetrical (*or* asymmetric), distorted, irregular, lopsided, nonsymmetrical, twisted, unsymmetrical; unbalanced

ant disproportionate

proportionate *adj* corresponding in size, amount, extent, or degree — see PROPORTIONAL

proposal *n* something which is presented for consideration ⟨The city council is accepting *proposals* for ways to use that land.⟩

syn offer, proffer, proposition, suggestion

rel counteroffer, counterproposal, countersuggestion; feeler; motion; advancement, nomination, recommendation; bid, presentation, submission, submittal, tender; arrangement, game, ground plan, layout, line, plan, plot, project, strategy, system; conception, idea, notion, theory, thought

propose *vb* 1 to set before the mind for consideration ⟨He *proposed* that we go for a walk this afternoon.⟩

syn advance, bounce, offer, pose, proffer, propound, suggest, vote

rel move; recommend; present, submit, tender; file, lay, lodge; arrange, calculate, chart, contrive, cover, frame, map, plan, plot, shape

phrases put forth, put forward

2 to have in mind as a purpose or goal — see INTEND 1

proposition *n* 1 an idea that is the starting point for making a case or conducting an investigation — see THEORY

2 something which is presented for consideration — see PROPOSAL

propound *vb* to set before the mind for consideration — see PROPOSE 1

proprietor *n* one who has a legal or rightful claim to ownership ⟨the *proprietor* of a used-car dealership⟩

syn holder, owner, possessor

rel co-owner, coproprietor; landlord, landowner

near ant squatter; renter, tenant

propriety *n* 1 socially acceptable behavior — see DECENCY 1

2 **proprieties** *pl* personal conduct or behavior as evaluated by an accepted standard of appropriateness for a social or professional setting — see MANNER 1

3 the quality or state of being especially suitable or fitting — see APPROPRIATENESS

prorate *vb* to give out (something) to appropriate individuals — see ADMINISTER 1

prosaic *adj* 1 being of the type that is encountered in the normal course of events — see ORDINARY 1

2 having to do with the practical details of regular life — see MUNDANE 1

proscribe *vb* to order not to do or use or to be done or used — see FORBID

proscribed *adj* that may not be permitted — see IMPERMISSIBLE

proscribing *n* the act of ordering that something not be done or used — see PROHIBITION 1

proscription *n* 1 the act of ordering that something not be done or used — see PROHIBITION 1

2 an order that something not be done or used — see PROHIBITION 2

proselyte *n* a person who has recently been persuaded to join a religious sect — see CONVERT 1

proselyte *vb* to persuade to change to one's religious faith — see CONVERT 1

proselytize *vb* to persuade to change to one's religious faith — see CONVERT 1

prospect *n* 1 all that can be seen from a certain point — see VIEW 1

2 one who seeks an office, honor, position, or award — see CANDIDATE

3 something that can develop or become actual — see POTENTIAL

prospect *vb* to go into or range over for purposes of discovery — see EXPLORE 2

prosper *vb* 1 to grow vigorously — see THRIVE 1

2 to reach a desired level of accomplishment — see SUCCEED 2

prospering *adj* marked by vigorous growth and well-being especially economically — see PROSPEROUS 1

prosperous *adj* 1 marked by vigorous growth and well-being especially economically ⟨a *prosperous* business that will soon be expanding⟩

syn booming, flourishing, golden, halcyon, healthy, lush, palmy, prospering, roaring, successful, thriving

rel affluent, moneyed (*also* monied), opulent, rich, substantial, wealthy, well-heeled, well-off, well-to-do; comfortable

near ant declining, dying, failing, floundering, languishing, struggling; bankrupt, bankrupted, insolvent

ant depressed, unprosperous, unsuccessful

---

syn synonym(s)   *rel* related words
ant antonym(s)   *near ant* near antonym(s)

2 having attained a desired end or state of good fortune — see SUCCESSFUL 1

3 growing thickly and vigorously — see RANK 1

prostrate *adj* **1** depleted in strength, energy, or freshness — see WEARY 1

2 lacking bodily strength — see WEAK 1

3 lying with the face downwards — see PRONE 2

prostrate *vb* **1** to diminish the physical strength of — see WEAKEN 1

2 to render powerless, ineffective, or unable to move — see PARALYZE 1

3 to subject to incapacitating emotional or mental stress — see OVERWHELM 1

4 to strike (someone) so forcefully as to cause a fall — see FELL 1

prostrated *adj* lacking bodily strength — see WEAK 1

prostration *n* a complete depletion of energy or strength — see FATIGUE

protean *adj* able to do many different kinds of things — see VERSATILE

protect *vb* to drive danger or attack away from — see DEFEND 1

protection *n* **1** means or method of defending — see DEFENSE 1

2 someone that protects — see PROTECTOR

3 the state of not being exposed to danger — see SAFETY 1

protective *adj* intended to resist or prevent attack or aggression — see DEFENSIVE

protector *n* someone that protects ⟨saw his older brother as his *protector*⟩
syn custodian, defender, guard, guardian, protection
rel bodyguard, champion; lookout, sentinel, sentry, warden, warder, watch, watchdog, watchman; conserver, harborer, keeper, preserver, saver

protest *n* a feeling or declaration of disapproval or dissent — see OBJECTION

protest *vb* **1** to state as a fact usually forcefully — see CLAIM 1

2 to present an opposing opinion or argument — see OBJECT

protestation *n* a solemn and often public declaration of the truth or existence of something ⟨The governor went on television to make a passionate *protestation* of his innocence in the bribery scandal.⟩
syn affirmation, assertion, avouchment, avowal, claim, declaration, insistence, profession
rel allegation; announcement, proclamation, pronouncement; argument, justification, rationalization, reason; confirmation, reaffirmation, reconfirmation, vindication
near ant disclaimer; challenge, dispute, question; confutation, disproof, rebuttal, refutation; contradiction, denial, negation
ant disavowal

prototype *n* **1** one of a group or collection that shows what the whole is like — see EXAMPLE

2 something belonging to an earlier time from which something else was later developed — see ANCESTOR 2

3 something from which copies are made — see ORIGINAL

protract *vb* to make longer — see EXTEND 1

protrude *vb* to extend outward beyond a usual point — see BULGE 1

protrusion *n* a part that sticks out from the general mass of something — see BULGE 1

protuberance *n* a part that sticks out from the general mass of something — see BULGE 1

proud *adj* **1** having or displaying feelings of scorn for what is regarded as beneath oneself ⟨She was too *proud* to accept help from her family.⟩
syn disdainful, haughty, highfalutin (*also* hifalutin), lofty, lordly, prideful, superior
rel complacent, conceited, egoistic, egotistic (*also* egotistical), important, self-assertive, self-conceited, self-contented, self-important, self-satisfied, smug, uppity, vain, vainglorious; arrogant, pretentious, stuck-up, supercilious; cavalier, overbearing, overweening, peremptory, swaggering; high-sounding, pompous; condescending, patronizing; cocky, overconfident, presuming, presumptuous; boastful, bombastic, self-glorifying; audacious, bold, brash, brassy, cheeky, cocksure, forward, impertinent, impudent, saucy; confident, presuming, self-assured, self-confident, sure; bossy, domineering, high-handed, imperious; egocentric, self-centered, selfish
near ant demure, meek, unassuming, unpretentious; bashful, retiring, shy, timid; diffident, self-doubting; acquiescent, compliant, deferential, resigned, submissive, unassertive, yielding; cowering, cringing, shrinking; passive, quiet, reserved, subdued, unobtrusive
ant humble, lowly, modest

2 having too high an opinion of oneself — see CONCEITED

3 large and impressive in size, grandeur, extent, or conception — see GRAND 1

4 having or expressing feelings of joy or triumph — see EXULTANT

provable *adj* capable of being proven as true or real — see VERIFIABLE

prove *vb* **1** to show the existence or truth of by evidence ⟨The defense attorney used DNA evidence to *prove* the defendant's innocence.⟩
syn demonstrate, document, establish, substantiate, validate
rel back (up), buttress, corroborate; evidence, evince, record, support, uphold, witness; adduce, attest, authenticate, certify, identify; confirm, sustain, verify, vouch; clinch, nail, settle
near ant challenge, dispute, object; allege, assume, conjecture, guess, presume, surmise, suspect
ant disprove, rebut, refute

2 to come to be — see COME OUT 1

3 to gain full recognition or acceptance of — see ESTABLISH 1

provender *n* substances intended to be eaten — see FOOD

proverb *n* an often stated observation regarding something arising from common experience — see SAYING

provide *vb* to put (something) into the

possession of someone for use or consumption — see FURNISH 2

provide (for) *vb* to pay the living expenses of — see SUPPORT 2

providence *n* **1** careful management of material resources — see ECONOMY

2 concern or preparation for the future — see FORESIGHT 2

3 *cap* the being worshipped as the creator and ruler of the universe — see DEITY 2

provident *adj* **1** careful in the management of money or resources — see FRUGAL

2 having or showing awareness of and preparation for the future — see FORESIGHTED

providential *adj* coming or happening by good luck especially unexpectedly — see FORTUNATE 1

province *n* a region of activity, knowledge, or influence — see FIELD 2

provincial *adj* not broad or open in views or opinions — see NARROW 2

provincial *n* an awkward or simple person especially from a small town or the country — see HICK

provision *n* **1** something upon which the carrying out of an agreement or offer depends — see CONDITION 2

2 provisions *pl* substances intended to be eaten — see FOOD

provision *vb* **1** to provide (someone) with what is needed for a task or activity — see FURNISH 1

2 to provide food or meals for — see FEED 1

provisional *adj* **1** intended to last, continue, or serve for a limited time — see TEMPORARY 1

2 serving in a position for the time being — see ACTING

proviso *n* something upon which the carrying out of an agreement or offer depends — see CONDITION 2

provocation *n* **1** something that arouses a strong response from another ⟨a patient person who gets angry only when the greatest of *provocations*⟩

syn excitement, incitement, instigation

rel encouragement, goad, incentive, inducement, jog, prod, spur, stimulant, stimulation, stimulus; enticement, lure; induction, inspiration, motivation; aggravation, annoyance, bother, frustration, hassle, headache, irritant, nuisance, peeve, pest

near ant subduing

2 something that arouses action or activity — see IMPULSE 1

provocative *adj* serving or likely to arouse a strong reaction ⟨a *provocative* editorial that sparked a heated discussion⟩

syn charged, edgy, exciting, inciting, instigating, piquing, provoking, stimulating

rel explosive, fiery, incendiary, triggering; inducing, inspirational, inspiring, motivating, motivational, motivative; jeering, taunting, teasing; activating, energizing, galvanizing, quickening, vitalizing; angering, enraging, maddening, upsetting; aggravating, annoying, bothersome, exasperat-

ing, galling, irksome, irritating, vexatious, vexing

near ant subduing

ant noninflammatory

provoke *vb* **1** to rouse to strong feeling or action ⟨The remarks finally *provoked* them to anger.⟩ ⟨Bees generally will not sting unless they are *provoked*.⟩

syn arouse, encourage, excite, fire (up), incite, instigate, move, pique, spark, stimulate, stir

rel fan, ignite, inflame (*also* enflame), kindle, trigger; activate, animate, drive, energize, galvanize, induce, inspire, key (up), motivate, quicken, set off, vitalize; abet, ferment, foment, raise, whip (up); anger, enrage, madden, upset; jeer, taunt, tease; annoy, bother, exasperate, gall, irritate, vex

phrases build a fire under

near ant calm, soothe, subdue, tranquilize (*also* tranquillize); appease, mollify, pacify, placate

2 to bring (something volatile or intense) into being — see INCITE 1

provoking *adj* serving or likely to arouse a strong reaction — see PROVOCATIVE

proximity *n* the state or condition of being near ⟨The *proximity* of the curtains to the fireplace was a cause of concern for the safety inspector.⟩

syn closeness, contiguity, immediacy, nearness

rel abutment, juxtaposition

ant distance, remoteness

proxy *n* a person who acts or does business for another — see AGENT 2

prude *n* a person who is greatly concerned with seemly behavior and morality especially regarding sexual matters ⟨too much of a *prude* to enjoy the movie⟩

syn moralist, puritan

rel moralizer; goody-goody, Goody Two-shoes; fuddy-duddy, old maid, prig

near ant libertarian, libertine; misbehaver

prudence *n* **1** a close attentiveness to avoiding danger — see CAUTION 1

2 the ability to make intelligent decisions especially in everyday matters — see COMMON SENSE

prudent *adj* **1** having or showing good judgment and restraint especially in conduct or speech — see DISCREET 1

2 suitable for bringing about a desired result under the circumstances — see EXPEDIENT

3 having or showing deep understanding and intelligent application of knowledge — see WISE 1

prudery *n* a tendency to care a great deal about seemly behavior and morals especially in sexual matters ⟨the well-known *prudery* of the Victorians⟩

syn prudishness, puritanism

rel priggery, priggishness, primness

near ant lechery, prurience, pruriency; libertinage; libertarianism

prudish *adj* given to or marked by very conservative standards regarding personal behavior or morals — see STRAITLACED

prudishness *n* a tendency to care a great deal about seemly behavior and morals especially in sexual matters — see PRUDERY

---

syn synonym(s)   **rel** related words

ant antonym(s)   **near ant** near antonym(s)

prune *vb* to make (something) shorter or smaller with the use of a cutting instrument — see CLIP 1

¹pry *vb* **1** to raise, move, or pull apart with or as if with a lever ⟨It took some effort to *pry* up the trap door.⟩
syn jimmy, lever, prize
rel elevate, hoist, lift, uplift; break up, detach, disengage, disjoin, divide, part, pull, separate
near ant connect, join
2 to draw out by force or with effort — see EXTRACT

²pry *vb* to interest oneself in what is not one's concern — see INTERFERE

prying *adj* **1** interested in what is not one's own business — see CURIOUS 1
2 thrusting oneself where one is not welcome or invited — see INTRUSIVE

psalm *n* a religious song — see HYMN 1
psalmody *n* a book of hymns — see HYMNAL

pseudo *adj* lacking in natural or spontaneous quality — see ARTIFICIAL 1

pseudonym *n* a fictitious or assumed name ⟨The most notorious serial killer of the 19th century remains known only by the *pseudonym* of Jack the Ripper.⟩
syn alias
rel nom de plume, pen name; appellation, designation; epithet, nickname, sobriquet (*also* soubriquet)

pshaw *interj* how surprising, doubtful, or unbelievable — see NO

psych (up) *vb* to prepare (oneself) mentally or emotionally — see FORTIFY 1

psyche *n* **1** an immaterial force within a human being thought to give the body life, energy, and power — see SOUL 1
2 the part of a person that feels, thinks, perceives, wills, and especially reasons — see MIND 1

psychological *also* **psychologic** *adj* of or relating to the mind — see MENTAL

pub *n* a place of business where alcoholic beverages are sold to be consumed on the premises — see BARROOM

public *adj* **1** not known by only a select few ⟨information that is *public* knowledge⟩
syn open
rel general, popular; nonclassified, unclassified, well-known; advertised, aired, announced, broadcast, declared, disclosed, divulged, heralded, posted, proclaimed, promulgated, publicized, published, spotlighted; reported, reputed, rumored
phrases on record
near ant classified; unadvertised, unannounced, undisclosed; clandestine, collusive, conspiratorial, covert; surreptitious, undercover, underhand, underhanded; intimate, personal; concealed, reserved, silenced, stifled, suppressed, withheld; recanted, retracted, revoked
ant confidential, private, privy, secret
2 freely available for use or participation by all — see OPEN 2
3 of or relating to a nation — see NATIONAL
4 held by or applicable to a majority of the people — see GENERAL 3
5 used or done by a number of people as a group — see COLLECTIVE

public *n* **1** human beings in general — see PEOPLE 1
2 the body of the community as contrasted with the elite — see MASS 1

public house *n* a place that provides rooms and usually a public dining room for overnight guests — see HOTEL

publicity *n* information released to the media that is designed to gain public attention or support for a person, business, or cause ⟨An endless flow of *publicity* for our charity event resulted in a great turnout.⟩
syn ballyhoo
rel ad, advertisement, commercial, message, plug, promotion, spot, word; advertising, marketing, propaganda; pronouncement, publication, release; broadcast, bulletin, dispatch, report, story; write-up

publicize *vb* **1** to provide publicity for ⟨The movie studios widely *publicized* their summer blockbusters.⟩
syn ballyhoo, pitch, plug, promote, tout
rel advertise, bark, merchandise (*also* merchandize), sell; push; acclaim, hail, laud, praise; endorse (*also* indorse), plump (for), plunk (for) *or* plonk (for); recommend, review; announce, broadcast, publish
phrases beat the drum (for)
2 to make known openly or publicly — see ANNOUNCE

public servant *n* **1** a person who holds a public office — see OFFICIAL
2 a worker in a government agency — see BUREAUCRAT

publish *vb* **1** to produce and release for distribution in printed form ⟨Our local animal shelter *publishes* a newsletter.⟩
syn get out, issue, print, put out
rel copublish; reissue, reprint, republish; serialize; contribute, edit, syndicate; distribute, market
phrases come out with
near ant censor, suppress
2 to make known openly or publicly — see ANNOUNCE

puck *n* an imaginary being usually having a small human form and magical powers — see FAIRY

puddle *n* a small often deep body of water — see ¹POOL

pudginess *n* the condition of having an excess of body fat — see CORPULENCE

pudgy *adj* having an excess of body fat — see FAT 1

puerile *adj* **1** having or showing the annoying qualities (as silliness) associated with children — see CHILDISH
2 lacking in adult experience or maturity — see CALLOW
3 lacking in seriousness or maturity — see GIDDY 1

puff *n* a slight or gentle movement of air — see BREEZE 1

puff *vb* **1** to breathe hard, quickly, or with difficulty — see GASP
2 to praise too much — see FLATTER 1

pugilist *n* one that engages in the sport of fighting with the fists — see BOXER

pugnacious *adj* feeling or displaying eagerness to fight — see BELLIGERENT

pugnacity *n* an inclination to fight or quarrel — see BELLIGERENCE

puissance *n* the ability to exert effort for the accomplishment of a task — see POWER 2

puissant *adj* having great power or influence — see IMPORTANT 2

puke *vb* to discharge the contents of the stomach through the mouth — see VOMIT

pule *vb* to utter feeble plaintive cries — see WHIMPER 1

pull *n* **1** the act or an instance of applying force on something so that it moves in the direction of the force ⟨I gave the door such a *pull* that when it suddenly opened, I nearly fell backwards.⟩
syn draw, haul, jerk, pluck, tug, wrench, yank
rel drag, tow; hitch, twitch; grab, snatch
near ant heave, shove, thrust
ant push
2 the power to direct the thinking or behavior of others usually indirectly — see INFLUENCE 1
3 the more favorable condition or position in a competition — see ADVANTAGE 1

pull *vb* **1** to cause to follow by applying steady force on ⟨a team of horses *pulling* a heavy wagon⟩
syn drag, draw, hale, haul, lug, tow, tug
rel attract; heave, jerk, yank; carry, convey, ferry, move, transport
near ant shove, thrust
ant drive, propel, push
2 to draw out by force or with effort — see EXTRACT
3 to injure by overuse, misuse, or pressure — see STRAIN 1

pulp *vb* to cause to become a pulpy mass — see CRUSH 1

pulpiness *n* the quality or state of being full of juice — see SUCCULENCE

pulpy *adj* full of juice — see JUICY
2 giving easily to the touch — see SOFT 3

pulsate *vb* to expand and contract in a rhythmic manner ⟨The heart muscle *pulsates* regularly to pump blood.⟩
syn beat, palpitate, pit-a-pat, pitter-patter, pulse, throb
rel fluctuate, oscillate, vibrate; quiver, tremble

pulsation *n* a rhythmic expanding and contracting ⟨You should press against the artery in your wrist and count the *pulsations* to calculate your heart rate.⟩
syn beat, beating, palpitation, pulse, throb
rel oscillation, vibration; quiver, tremble, tremor

pulse *n* a rhythmic expanding and contracting — see PULSATION

pulse *vb* to expand and contract in a rhythmic manner — see PULSATE

pulverize *vb* **1** to bring to a complete end the physical soundness, existence, or usefulness of — see DESTROY 1
2 to reduce to fine particles — see POWDER

puma *n* a large tawny cat of the wild — see COUGAR

pummel *vb* to strike repeatedly — see BEAT 1

pump *vb* **1** to make short up-and-down movements — see NOD
2 to put a series of questions to — see EXAMINE 1
3 to remove (liquid) gradually or completely — see DRAIN 1

¹punch *n* **1** the quality of an utterance that provokes interest and produces an effect ⟨The real *punch* of the speech came in its closing lines.⟩
syn cogency, effectiveness, force, forcefulness, impact, point
rel payoff; importance; appeal, attraction, charm, fascination
2 active strength of body or mind — see VIGOR 1
3 a hard strike with a part of the body or an instrument — see ¹BLOW

²punch *n* a mark or small hole made by a pointed instrument — see PRICK 1

punch *vb* **1** to deliver a blow to (someone or something) usually in a strong vigorous manner — see HIT 1
2 to make a hole or series of holes in — see PERFORATE
3 to urge, push, or force onward — see DRIVE 1

puncheon *n* an enclosed wooden vessel for holding beverages — see CASK

punctilious *adj* marked by or showing careful attention to set forms and details — see CEREMONIOUS 1

punctual *adj* done, carried out, or given without delay — see PROMPT 1

punctuality *n* the quality or habit of arriving or being ready on time — see PROMPTITUDE

puncture *n* a mark or small hole made by a pointed instrument — see PRICK 1

puncture *vb* **1** to make a hole or series of holes in — see PERFORATE
2 to penetrate or hold (something) with a pointed object — see IMPALE

pungency *n* **1** a harsh or sharp quality — see EDGE 1
2 the quality or state of being stimulating to the mind or senses — see PIQUANCY

pungent *adj* **1** having a powerfully stimulating odor or flavor — see SHARP 2
2 marked by the use of wit that is intended to cause hurt feelings — see SARCASTIC
3 sharp and pleasantly stimulating to the mind or senses — see PIQUANT

puniness *n* the quality or state of being little in size — see SMALLNESS

punish *vb* to inflict a penalty on for a fault or crime ⟨The child was *punished* for breaking the rules.⟩ ⟨If caught, the thief will be severely *punished*.⟩
syn castigate, chasten, chastise, correct, discipline, penalize
rel assess, charge, dock, fine, impose, levy, mulct; convict, sentence; condemn, damn, denounce; criticize, keelhaul, rebuke, reprimand, reprove; wreak
near ant forfeit; get off, ransom, release; commute, reprieve; absolve, acquit, exculpate, exonerate, vindicate
ant excuse, pardon, spare

punisher *n* one who inflicts punishment in return for an injury or offense — see NEMESIS 1

punishment *n* suffering, loss, or hardship

---

imposed in response to a crime or offense ⟨He is serving five years in prison as *punishment* for his crime.⟩

syn castigation, chastisement, correction, desert(s), discipline, nemesis, penalty, wrath

rel reprisal, retaliation, retribution, revenge, vengeance; assessment, charge, fine, mulct; example, sentence; confinement, imprisonment, incarceration; condemnation, damnation, denouncement; censure, criticism, rebuke, reprimand, reproof

near ant amnesty, indemnity, pardon, parole; acquittal, exculpation, exoneration, vindication; exemption, immunity, impunity; release; commutation, reprieve; absolution, forgiveness, remission, remitment; condonation, disregard, overlooking

punitive *adj* inflicting, involving, or serving as punishment ⟨Any misbehavior was immediately met with a *punitive* response.⟩ ⟨The company had to pay a million dollars in *punitive* damages.⟩

syn castigating, chastening, chastising, correcting, correctional, corrective, disciplinary, disciplining, penal, penalizing

rel retaliative, retaliatory, retributive, retributory, revengeful; vengeful, wrathful

near ant compensatory; acquitting, exculpating, exculpatory, exonerating, vindicating; absolving, condoning, pardoning, remitting; commuting, reprieving

ant nonpunitive

punk *adj* **1** falling short of a standard — see BAD 1

2 extremely unsatisfactory — see WRETCHED 1

3 temporarily suffering from a disorder of the body — see SICK 1

punk *n* **1** a person who is just starting out in a field of activity — see BEGINNER

2 a violent, brutal person who is often a member of an organized gang — see HOODLUM

puny *adj* of a size that is less than average — see SMALL 1

pupil *n* **1** one who attends a school — see STUDENT

2 one who follows the opinions or teachings of another — see FOLLOWER 1

puppet *n* **1** a small figure often of a human being used especially as a child's plaything — see DOLL 1

2 one that is or can be used to further the purposes of another — see ¹PAWN

purchase *vb* to get possession of (something) by giving money in exchange for — see BUY 1

pure *adj* **1** free from added matter ⟨I'm allergic to any jewelry that isn't *pure* silver.⟩ ⟨The solution must be kept *pure* for the experiment to work.⟩

syn absolute, fine, neat, plain, purified, refined, straight, unadulterated, unalloyed, undiluted, unmixed

rel clarified, filtered; clean, fresh, taintless, uncontaminated, uncorrupted, undefiled, unpolluted, untainted; rendered, tried; concentrated, full-bodied, strong; uncombined

near ant besmirched, contaminated, corrupted, debased, defiled, fouled, polluted,

soiled, spoiled, sullied, tainted; unclarified; cheapened, doctored, watered-down

ant adulterated, alloyed, diluted, impure, mixed

2 free from any trace of the coarse or indecent — see CHASTE 1

3 free from sin — see INNOCENT 1

4 having no exceptions or restrictions — see ABSOLUTE 2

purebred *adj* of unmixed ancestry ⟨That horse is a *purebred* Arabian.⟩

syn full-blooded, pedigreed (*or* pedigree), thoroughbred

rel well-bred; inbred

near ant crossbred, crossed, half-blood (*or* half-blooded), half-bred, hybridized, interbred, outcrossed

ant hybrid, mixed, mongrel

purely *adv* **1** with purity of thought and deed ⟨vowed to live *purely* and in the service of God⟩

syn chastely, innocently, modestly, morally, righteously, virtuously

rel decorously, properly; priggishly, primly, prudishly

near ant indecently, obscenely, vulgarly; lasciviously, lewdly, lustfully

ant evilly, immorally, impurely, sinfully, wickedly

2 for nothing other than — see SOLELY 1

3 nothing more than — see JUST 3

purge *vb* to free from moral guilt or blemish especially ceremonially — see PURIFY 1

purification *n* the act or fact of freeing from sin or moral guilt ⟨Some people must undergo a ritual *purification* after certain activities.⟩

syn cleansing, sanctification

rel rebirth, regeneration, restoration; grace, redemption, salvation; absolution, forgiveness, remission; acquittal, clearance, clearing, exoneration, vindication; atonement, expiation

near ant blasphemy, defilement, desecration, violation; corruption, debasement, perversion; pollution, sullying, tarnishing

purified *adj* free from added matter — see PURE 1

purify *vb* **1** to free from moral guilt or blemish especially ceremonially ⟨She believed she could be *purified* through prayer.⟩

syn cleanse, purge, sanctify

rel amend, improve, refine; heal, regenerate, restore; elevate, ennoble, uplift; absolve, acquit, clear, exonerate, vindicate

near ant corrupt, debase, debauch, defile, degrade, demean, deprave, pervert, stain, warp; poison, profane; sully, tarnish

2 to remove usually visible impurities from — see CLARIFY 1

puritan *n* a person who is greatly concerned with seemly behavior and morality especially regarding sexual matters — see PRUDE

puritanical *adj* given to or marked by very conservative standards regarding personal behavior or morals — see STRAITLACED

puritanism *n* a tendency to care a great deal about seemly behavior and morals especially in sexual matters — see PRUDERY

purity *n* the quality or state of being morally pure — see CHASTITY

purloin *vb* to take (something) without right and with an intent to keep — see STEAL 1

purloiner *n* one who steals — see THIEF

purport *n* the idea that is conveyed or intended to be conveyed to the mind by language, symbol, or action — see MEANING 1

purport *vb* **1** to have in mind as a purpose or goal — see INTEND 1

2 to state as a fact usually forcefully — see CLAIM 1

purpose *n* **1** something that one hopes or intends to accomplish — see GOAL

2 the action for which a person or thing is specially fitted or used or for which a thing exists — see ROLE

purpose *vb* to have in mind as a purpose or goal — see INTEND 1

purposeful *adj* **1** fully committed to achieving a goal — see DETERMINED 1

2 made, given, or done with full awareness of what one is doing — see INTENTIONAL

purposefully *adv* **1** with full awareness of what one is doing — see INTENTIONALLY

2 with great effort or determination — see HARD 1

purposefulness *n* firm or unwavering adherence to one's purpose — see DETERMINATION 1

purposely *adv* with full awareness of what one is doing — see INTENTIONALLY

purr *n* a monotonous sound like that of an insect in motion — see HUM

purse *n* a container for carrying money and small personal items ⟨I left my *purse* at home, so I can't buy anything after all.⟩

syn bag, handbag, pocketbook

rel clutch, clutch bag; billfold; poke, pouch, sack; shoulder bag

pursuance *n* the doing of an action — see COMMISSION 2

pursue *vb* **1** to go after or on the track of — see FOLLOW 2

2 to go in search of — see SEEK 1

pursuing *n* the act of going after or in the tracks of another — see PURSUIT

pursuit *n* the act of going after or in the tracks of another ⟨The cat ran down the street with a pair of dogs in *pursuit*.⟩

syn chase, chasing, dogging, following, hounding, pursuing, shadowing, tagging, tailing, tracing, tracking, trailing

rel hot pursuit; tagging along; path, track, trail; search, seeking

push *n* a series of activities undertaken to achieve a goal — see CAMPAIGN

push *vb* **1** to apply force to (someone or something) so that it moves in front of one ⟨I had to *push* my damaged bike all the way home.⟩

syn drive, propel, shove, thrust

rel impel, move; bear (down), compress, depress, jam, pressure, squash, squeeze, weigh (upon); bulldoze, compel, force, lean (on *or* against), muscle, ram

2 to force one's way — see ²PRESS 4

pushover *n* **1** a person without strength of character — see WEAKLING 2

2 one who is easily deceived or cheated — see ¹DUPE

3 something that is easy to do — see CINCH

pusillanimous *adj* having or showing a shameful lack of courage — see COWARDLY

¹**puss** *n, slang* the front part of the head — see FACE 1

²**puss** *n* a small domestic animal known for catching mice — see CAT

pussy *n* a small domestic animal known for catching mice — see CAT

pussyfoot *vb* **1** to avoid giving a definite answer or position — see EQUIVOCATE

2 to move about in a sly or secret manner — see SNEAK 1

put *vb* **1** to arrange something in a certain spot or position — see PLACE 1

2 to convey in appropriate or telling terms — see PHRASE

3 to decide the size, amount, number, or distance of (something) without actual measurement — see ESTIMATE 2

4 to establish or apply as a charge or penalty — see IMPOSE

5 to change (something) so as to make it suitable for a new use or situation — see ADAPT

6 to risk (something) on the outcome of an uncertain event — see BET

put by *vb* to put (something of future use or value) in a safe or secret place — see HOARD

put-down *n* **1** an act or expression showing scorn and usually intended to hurt another's feelings — see INSULT

2 the act of making a person or a thing seem little or unimportant — see DEPRECIATION

put down *vb* **1** to express scornfully one's low opinion of — see DECRY 1

2 to make a written note of — see RECORD 1

3 to put (someone or something) on a list — see ¹LIST 1

4 to put a stop to (something) by the use of force — see QUELL 1

5 to explain (something) as being the result of something else — see CREDIT 1

6 to take in as food — see EAT 1

put in *vb* to put or set into the ground to grow — see PLANT 1

put off *vb* **1** to assign to a later time — see POSTPONE

2 to rid oneself of (a garment) — see REMOVE 1

3 to cause to feel disgust — see DISGUST

put-on *adj* lacking in natural and spontaneous quality — see ARTIFICIAL 1

put-on *n* **1** a display of emotion or behavior that is insincere or intended to deceive — see MASQUERADE

2 a work that imitates and exaggerates another work for comic effect — see PARODY 1

put on *vb* **1** to place on one's person ⟨I put *on* a coat and shoes to go outside.⟩

syn don, slip (on *or* into), throw (on)

rel apparel, array, attire, bedeck, bedizen, bundle up, caparison, clothe, doll up, dress, garb, rig, robe, suit, trick, uniform; overdress

near ant disrobe, strip, undress

ant doff, remove, take off

2 to describe or express in too strong terms — see OVERSTATE

---

3 to present a false appearance of — see FEIGN

put out *vb* **1** to bring to bear especially forcefully or effectively — see EXERT

2 to cause to cease burning — see EXTINGUISH 1

3 to disturb the peace of mind of (someone) especially by repeated disagreeable acts — see IRRITATE 1

4 to cause discomfort to or trouble for — see INCONVENIENCE

5 to produce and release for distribution in printed form — see PUBLISH 1

putrefaction *n* the process by which dead organic matter separates into simpler substances — see CORRUPTION 1

putrefied *adj* having undergone organic breakdown — see ROTTEN 1

putrefy *vb* to go through decomposition — see DECAY 1

putrid *adj* having undergone organic breakdown — see ROTTEN 1

putter (around) *vb* to spend time in aimless activity — see FIDDLE (AROUND)

putterer *n* a person who regularly or occasionally engages in an activity as a pastime rather than as a profession — see AMATEUR 1

put up *vb* **1** to fix in an upright position — see ERECT 1

2 to form by putting together parts or materials — see BUILD

3 to offer for sale to the public — see MARKET

4 to provide with living quarters or shelter — see HOUSE 1

5 to engage in a secret plan to accomplish evil or unlawful ends — see PLOT

6 to place somewhere for safekeeping or ready availability — see STORE 1

puzzle *n* something hard to understand or explain — see MYSTERY

puzzle *vb* to throw into a state of mental uncertainty — see CONFUSE 1

puzzle (out) *vb* to find an answer for through reasoning — see SOLVE

puzzlement *n* **1** a state of mental uncertainty — see CONFUSION 1

2 something hard to understand or explain — see MYSTERY

pygmy *adj* of a size that is less than average — see SMALL 1

pygmy *also* **pigmy** *n* **1** a living thing much smaller than others of its kind — see DWARF 1

2 a person of no importance or influence — see NOBODY

quack *n* one who makes false claims of identity or expertise — see IMPOSTOR

quadrangle *n* an open space wholly or partly enclosed (as by buildings or walls) — see COURT 2

quaff *n* the portion of a serving of a beverage that is swallowed at one time — see DRINK 2

quaff *vb* to swallow in liquid form — see DRINK 1

quagmire *n* **1** a difficult, puzzling, or embarrassing situation from which there is no easy escape — see PREDICAMENT

2 something that catches and holds — see WEB 1

quail *vb* **1** to draw back in fear, pain, or disgust — see FLINCH

2 to draw back or crouch down in fearful submission — see COWER

quaint *adj* **1** different from the ordinary in a way that causes curiosity or suspicion — see ODD 2

2 pleasantly reminiscent of an earlier time — see OLD-FASHIONED 1

quake *n* a shaking of the earth — see EARTHQUAKE 1

quake *vb* to make a series of small irregular or violent movements — see SHAKE 1

quaking *adj* marked by or given to small uncontrollable bodily movements — see SHAKY 1

qualification *n* **1** a skill, an ability, or knowledge that makes a person able to do a particular job ⟨The fashion firm was looking for an applicant who could list superior sewing skills among his or her *qualifications*.⟩

syn capability, credentials, goods, stuff

rel command, expertise, know-how, mastership, mastery, proficiency; ability, capacity, competence, competency, facility, faculty; aptitude, endowment, flair, genius, gift, knack, talent; forte, specialty; fitness, suitability, suitableness; makings, potentiality

2 something upon which the carrying out of an agreement or offer depends — see CONDITION 2

qualified *adj* having the required skills for an advanced level of performance — see COMPETENT 1

qualify *vb* **1** to limit the meaning of (as a noun) ⟨*Qualifying* the noun "adventure" in the title of your story with a descriptive adjective would make it more attention-grabbing.⟩

syn modify

rel alter, color, distort, misrepresent, misstate, pervert, twist, warp; narrow

near ant broaden, expand, widen

2 to make competent (as by training, skill, or ability) for a particular office or function ⟨Her career as a defense attorney has *qualified* her to be a legal analyst for the news show.⟩

syn equip, fit, prepare, ready, season, train

rel accustom, adapt, adjust, condition, shape, tailor; authorize, entitle; empower, enable; educate, indoctrinate, instruct, school, teach, tutor

3 to give a right to — see ENTITLE 1

4 to give official or legal power to — see AUTHORIZE 1

quality *adj* of the very best kind — see EXCELLENT

quality *n* **1** degree of excellence ⟨We expect a high *quality* of service in such a fancy restaurant.⟩

syn caliber (*or* calibre), class, grade, rate

rel hallmark; mark; footing, place, position, rank, standing, stature, status; benchmark, criterion, measure, par, standard, touchstone, yardstick

2 high position within society — see RANK 2

3 something that sets apart an individual from others of the same kind — see CHARACTERISTIC

qualm *n* an uneasy feeling about the rightness of what one is doing or going to do ⟨She has no *qualms* about downloading pirated movies from the Internet.⟩

syn compunction, misgiving, scruple

rel conscience; distrust, doubt, incertitude, mistrust, reservation, skepticism, suspicion, uncertainness, uncertainty; qualmishness, uneasiness; reluctance, unwillingness; demur, fuss, objection, protest, question, remonstrance; aversion, disinclination, indisposition, reluctance, unwillingness; guilt, regret, remorse, self-reproach, shame

near ant aplomb, assurance, certainty, certitude, confidence, conviction, self-assurance, self-confidence, sureness

qualmish *adj* affected with nausea — see NAUSEOUS 1

qualmishness *n* **1** a disturbed condition of the stomach in which one feels like vomiting — see NAUSEA 1

2 the tendency to or state of being squeamish — see DELICACY 3

quandary *n* a situation in which one has to choose between two or more equally unsatisfactory choices — see DILEMMA 1

quantity *n* **1** a considerable amount — see LOT 2

2 a given or particular mass or aggregate of matter — see AMOUNT

quarrel *n* an often noisy or angry expression of differing opinions — see ARGUMENT 1

quarrel *vb* to express different opinions about something often angrily — see ARGUE 2

quarreler *or* **quarreller** *n* a person who takes part in a dispute — see DISPUTANT

quarrelsome *adj* **1** feeling or displaying eagerness to fight — see BELLIGERENT

2 given to arguing — see ARGUMENTATIVE 1

quarry *n* an animal that is hunted or killed — see PREY 1

quarter *n* **1** an area (as of a city) set apart for some purpose or having some special feature — see DISTRICT

2 kind, gentle, or compassionate treatment especially towards someone who is undeserving of it — see MERCY 1

3 the place where someone is assigned to stand or remain — see STATION 1

4 quarters *pl* the place where one lives — see HOME 1

quarter *vb* to provide with living quarters or shelter — see HOUSE 1

¹**quash** *vb* to put a stop to (something) by the use of force — see QUELL 1

²**quash** *vb* to put an end to by formal action — see ABOLISH 1

quaver *vb* to sing with the alternation of two musical tones — see WARBLE

quavery *adj* marked by or given to small uncontrollable bodily movements — see SHAKY 1

quay *n* a structure used by boats and ships for taking on or landing cargo and passengers — see DOCK

queasiness *n* **1** a disturbed condition of the stomach in which one feels like vomiting — see NAUSEA 1

2 the tendency to or state of being squeamish — see DELICACY 3

queasy *also* **queazy** *adj* **1** affected with nausea — see NAUSEOUS 1

2 feeling or showing uncomfortable feelings of uncertainty — see NERVOUS 1

queen *n* a lovely woman — see BEAUTY 2

queenly *adj* fit for or worthy of a royal ruler — see MONARCHICAL

queer *adj* **1** affected with nausea — see NAUSEOUS 1

2 different from the ordinary in a way that causes curiosity or suspicion — see ODD 2

3 noticeably different from what is generally found or experienced — see UNUSUAL 1

4 giving good reason for being doubted, questioned, or challenged — see DOUBTFUL 2

queerish *adj* **1** affected with nausea — see NAUSEOUS 1

2 different from the ordinary in a way that causes curiosity or suspicion — see ODD 2

queerness *n* a disturbed condition of the stomach in which one feels like vomiting — see NAUSEA 1

quell *vb* **1** to put a stop to (something) by the use of force ⟨The National Guard was called in to help *quell* the late-night disturbances downtown.⟩

syn clamp down (on), crack down (on), crush, put down, quash, repress, silence, snuff (out), squash, squelch, subdue, suppress

rel douse (*also* dowse), extinguish, put out, quench; smother, stifle, strangle, throttle; annihilate, decimate, demolish, desolate, destroy, devastate, rub out, ruin, smash, waste, wreck; exterminate, obliterate, wipe out; conquer, dominate, overcome, overpower, overwhelm, subdue, subjugate, vanquish

phrases sit on

near ant abet, aid, assist, back, help, prop up, support; foment, incite, instigate, provoke, stir, whip (up); advance, cultivate, encourage, forward, foster, further, nourish, nurture, promote

2 to stop the noise or speech of — see SILENCE 1

quench *vb* **1** to cause to cease burning — see EXTINGUISH 1

---

syn synonym(s)   *rel* related words
ant antonym(s)   *near ant* near antonym(s)

2 to put a complete end to (a physical need or desire) — see SATISFY 1

quencher *n* a liquid suitable for drinking — see DRINK 1

querulous *adj* given to complaining a lot — see FUSSY 1

query *n* **1** a feeling or attitude that one does not know the truth, truthfulness, or trustworthiness of someone or something — see DOUBT 1

2 an act or instance of asking for information — see QUESTION 2

query *vb* **1** to demand proof of the truth or rightness of — see CHALLENGE 1

2 to put a question or questions to — see ASK 1

3 to put a series of questions to — see EXAMINE 1

quest *n* an act or process of looking carefully or thoroughly for someone or something — see SEARCH

quest *vb* **1** to ask for (something) earnestly or with authority — see DEMAND 1

2 to go in search of — see SEEK 1

3 to make a request for — see ASK (FOR) 1

question *n* **1** an interrogative expression often used to test knowledge ⟨Because I have missed so many classes, I had a hard time answering every *question* on today's surprise quiz.⟩

syn problem

rel brainteaser, conundrum, poser, puzzle, quiz, riddle, stickler, stumper, toughie (*also* toughy)

near ant answer, response, solution

2 an act or instance of asking for information ⟨After reading the brief statement to the reporters, the lawyer ended the press conference by saying, "No more *questions*, please!"⟩ ⟨the dozens of *questions* researched by the reference librarians⟩

syn call, inquiry, query, request

rel interrogatory; poll, questionnaire, survey; inquisition, interrogating, interrogation, questioning; examination, exploration, inquest, investigation, probe, probing, research, study

near ant answer, reply, response

3 a feeling or declaration of disapproval or dissent — see OBJECTION

4 a major object of interest or concern (as in a discussion or artistic composition) — see MATTER 1

question *vb* **1** to demand proof of the truth or rightness of — see CHALLENGE 1

2 to give serious and careful thought to — see PONDER

3 to have no trust or confidence in — see DISTRUST

4 to put a question or questions to — see ASK 1

5 to put a series of questions to — see EXAMINE 1

questionable *adj* **1** giving good reason for being doubted, questioned, or challenged — see DOUBTFUL 2

2 not likely to be true or to occur — see IMPROBABLE

3 open to question or dispute — see DEBATABLE 1

questioner *n* a person who is always ready to doubt or question the truth or existence of something — see SKEPTIC

questioning *adj* inclined to doubt or question claims — see SKEPTICAL 1

queue *n* a series of persons or things arranged one behind another — see LINE 1

quibble *vb* **1** to make often peevish criticisms or objections about matters that are minor, unimportant, or irrelevant ⟨He spent the entire evening *quibbling* about the historical inaccuracies in the television series on World War II.⟩

syn carp, cavil, fuss, nitpick

rel criticize, fault; beef, bellyache, complain, crab, gripe, grouse, growl, grumble, kick, moan, squawk, squeal, wail, whine, yammer, yowl

phrases split hairs

near ant applaud, commend, compliment, praise, recommend; approve, back, champion, endorse (*also* indorse), support

2 to express different opinions about something often angrily — see ARGUE 2

quick *adj* **1** having or showing the ability to respond without delay or hesitation ⟨She's a *quick* wit, always ready with a pun or joke when the moment calls for one.⟩

syn alacritous, alert, expeditious, prompt, ready, willing

rel receptive, responsive; immediate, instant, instantaneous, summary; breakneck, breathless, brisk, fast, fleet, fleet-footed, hit-and-run, lightning, rapid, rapid-fire, rattling, snappy, speedy, swift, whirlwind; eager, keen, sharp; apt, clever, quick, quick-witted, ready-witted, sharp-witted, smart

near ant unresponsive; crawling, creeping, dallying, dawdling, dilatory, dillydallying, dragging, laggard, lagging, lazy, lazyish, leisurely, logy (*also* loggy), poking, poky (*or* pokey), slothful, slow, slowish, sluggish, tardy, unhurried; dormant, idle, inactive, inert

2 having or showing quickness of mind — see INTELLIGENT 1

3 moving, proceeding, or acting with great speed — see FAST 1

4 having or showing life — see ALIVE 1

5 able to sense slight impressions or differences — see ACUTE 1

quick *adv* with great speed — see FAST 1

quick *n* the seat of one's deepest thoughts and emotions — see CORE 1

quicken *vb* **1** to cause to move or proceed fast or faster — see HURRY 1

2 to give life, vigor, or spirit to — see ANIMATE

quickly *adv* with great speed — see FAST 1

quickness *n* a high rate of movement or performance — see SPEED 1

quick-tempered *adj* easily irritated or annoyed — see IRRITABLE

quick-witted *adj* having or showing quickness of mind — see INTELLIGENT 1

quiescence *n* **1** a state of temporary inactivity — see ABEYANCE

2 lack of action or activity — see INACTION

quiescent *adj* slow to move or act — see INACTIVE 1

quiet *adj* **1** free from disturbing noise or uproar ⟨We left the din of the concert and went to a *quiet* restaurant where we could hear one another talk.⟩

syn calm, hushed, peaceful, placid, restful, serene, still, stilly, tranquil

rel noiseless, silent, soundless; mute, speechless, wordless; dead, motionless, quiescent; muffled, muted, quieted; dull, gentle, low, soft; ultraquiet

near ant tempestuous, wild; blaring, blasting, booming, earsplitting, piercing, roaring, thunderous

ant boisterous, clamorous, clattery, deafening, loud, noisy, raucous, rip-roaring, roistering, romping, rowdy, tumultuous, unquiet, uproarious

2 not excessively showy ⟨She decided that it would be best to wear a *quiet* business suit to the job interview.⟩

syn conservative, muted, restrained, sober, subdued, toned-down, understated, unpretentious

rel appropriate, becoming, fit, fitting, proper, suitable; modest, plain, simple, unadorned, undecorated; inconspicuous, unnoticeable, unobtrusive; graceful, handsome, refined, tasteful; drab, mousy (*or* mousey); practical, sensible

near ant meretricious; graceless, inelegant, tacky, tasteless, tawdry, trashy, vulgar; fancy, frilly, gilded (*or* gilt), ornate, rococo; overdecorated, overdone, overwrought

ant flamboyant, flashy, garish, gaudy, glitzy, loud, noisy, ostentatious, splashy, swank (*or* swanky)

3 free from storms or physical disturbance — see CALM 1

4 screened or sequestered from view — see SECLUDED

5 mostly or entirely without sound — see SILENT 3

6 not loud in pitch or volume — see SOFT 1

quiet *adv* without motion — see STILL 1

quiet *n* **1** a state of freedom from storm or disturbance — see CALM 1

2 the near or complete absence of sound — see SILENCE 2

quiet *vb* **1** to become still and orderly ⟨The museum docent told the rowdy youngsters to *quiet* down for the tour.⟩

syn calm (down), chill out [*slang*], hush, pipe down, settle (down)

rel dry up; relax, tranquilize (*also* tranquillize), unwind, zone out

phrases cool it

near ant clown (around), horse around, monkey (around), show off, skylark

ant act up, carry on, cut up

2 to free from distress or disturbance — see CALM 1

3 to stop the noise or speech of — see SILENCE 1

quiet (down) *vb* to stop talking — see SHUT UP 1

quieted *adj* mostly or entirely without sound — see SILENT 3

quieting *adj* tending to calm the emotions and relieve stress — see SOOTHING 1

quietly *adv* without motion — see STILL 1

quietness *n* **1** a state of freedom from storm or disturbance — see CALM 1

2 the near or complete absence of sound — see SILENCE 2

quietude *n* **1** a state of freedom from storm or disturbance — see CALM 1

2 the near or complete absence of sound — see SILENCE 2

quietus *n* **1** a freeing from an obligation or responsibility — see RELEASE 1

2 the permanent stopping of all the vital bodily activities — see DEATH 1

quintessence *n* **1** the most perfect type or example ⟨The Parthenon in Greece was considered the *quintessence* of the perfectly proportioned building.⟩

syn acme, beau ideal, byword, classic, epitome, exemplar, ideal, perfection

rel archetype, model, prototype; paradigm, standard; nonpareil, paragon; abstract, embodiment, incarnation, manifestation, personification; height, meridian, ultimate, zenith; benchmark, criterion, touchstone, yardstick

2 the quality or qualities that make a thing what it is — see ESSENCE 1

quintessential *adj* constituting, serving as, or worthy of being a pattern to be imitated — see MODEL

quip *n* something said or done to cause laughter — see JOKE 1

quip *vb* to make jokes — see JOKE 1

quirk *n* an odd or peculiar habit — see IDIOSYNCRASY

quirky *adj* different from the ordinary in a way that causes curiosity or suspicion — see ODD 2

quisling *n* one who betrays a trust or an allegiance — see TRAITOR

quit *adj* no longer burdened with something unpleasant or painful — see FREE 2

quit *vb* **1** to give up (a job or office) ⟨He decided to *quit* his job at the fast-food restaurant.⟩

syn bag, chuck, leave, resign (from), retire (from), step down (from)

rel abandon, vacate; drop out (of), throw up

phrases give notice

near ant hire (out *or* on)

ant stay (at)

2 to stop doing (something) permanently ⟨Her doctor told her it was high time she *quit* smoking.⟩

syn abandon, discontinue, drop, give up, knock off, lay off (of)

rel break off, break up, cease, close, conclude, end, expire, finish, halt, leave off, shut off; pause, taper off; throw up; round (off *or* out), terminate, wind up, wrap up

phrases hang it up, have done (with)

near ant go, run on; hang in, hang on, hold on, persevere, persist; renew, reopen, restart, resume; preserve, stay; begin, commence, start

ant carry on, continue, keep, keep up, maintain

3 to bring (an action or operation) to an immediate end — see STOP 1

4 to cause to remain behind — see LEAVE 1

5 to cease resistance (as to another's arguments, demands, or control) — see YIELD 3

6 to come to an end — see CEASE 1

---

syn synonym(s)   *rel* related words
ant antonym(s)   *near ant* near antonym(s)

7 to give what is owed for — see PAY 2

8 to leave a place often for another — see GO 2

9 to manage the actions of (oneself) in a particular way — see BEHAVE

quite *adv* **1** to a full extent or degree — see FULLY 1

2 to some degree or extent — see FAIRLY 1

quittance *n* **1** a freeing from an obligation or responsibility — see RELEASE 1

2 payment to another for a loss or injury — see COMPENSATION 1

quitting *n* the act of leaving a place — see DEPARTURE 1

quiver *n* an instance of shaking involuntarily with fear or cold — see SHIVER 1

quiver *vb* to make a series of small irregular or violent movements — see SHAKE 1

quivering *adj* marked by or given to small uncontrollable bodily movements — see SHAKY 1

quivering *n* a series of slight movements by a body back and forth or from side to side — see VIBRATION 1

quiz *n* **1** a person who causes repeated emotional pain, distress, or annoyance to another — see TORMENTOR

2 a set of questions or problems designed to assess knowledge, skills, or intelligence — see EXAMINATION 1

quiz *vb* **1** to put a question or questions to — see ASK 1

2 to put a series of questions to — see EXAMINE 1

quizzical *adj* marked by or expressive of mild or good-natured teasing ⟨My puns are usually greeted with loud *quizzical* groans by my so-called friends.⟩

syn bantering, chaffing, fooling, funning, jesting, joking, joshing, kidding, rallying, razzing, ribbing

rel bandying, quipping; baiting, deriding, derisive, derisory, hassling, heckling, jeering, mocking, needling, ridiculing, taunting; contemptuous, disdainful, sarcastic, scornful

quota *n* something belonging to, due to, or contributed by an individual member of a group — see SHARE 1

quotation *n* a passage referred to, repeated, or offered as an example ⟨The beautiful autumn day brought to mind this *quotation* from Thoreau: "So live in each season as it passes; breathe the air, drink the drink, taste the fruit, and resign yourself to the influences of each."⟩

syn citation, quote

rel allusion, reference; excerpt, extract; line, part, section; snippet

quote *n* a passage referred to, repeated, or offered as an example — see QUOTATION

quote *vb* **1** to give as an example ⟨I could *quote* to you a hundred instances in the past when you've lied to me.⟩

syn adduce, cite, instance, mention

rel exemplify, represent; advert (to), illustrate, instance, name, refer (to), specify, touch (on *or* upon); bear out, corroborate, document, substantiate, validate; reference, source

2 to make reference to or speak about briefly but specifically — see MENTION 1

3 to say after another — see REPEAT 3

rabble *n* people looked down upon as ignorant and of the lowest class ⟨The crown prince was reminded that even the *rabble* of the realm deserved his attention and compassion.⟩

syn proletariat, riffraff, rout, scum, trash

rel dregs; commoners, herd, masses, mob, multitude, people, plebeians, populace, public, rank and file; bourgeoisie, middle class, working class

near ant elect, establishment; nobility, peerage

ant aristocracy, elite, gentry, society, upper class, upper crust

rabble–rouser *n* a person who stirs up public feelings especially of discontent — see AGITATOR

rabid *adj* **1** being very far from the center of public opinion — see EXTREME 2

2 feeling or showing anger — see ANGRY

3 marked by bursts of destructive force or intense activity — see VIOLENT 1

4 marked by great and often stressful excitement or activity — see FURIOUS 1

race *n* a group of persons who come from the same ancestor — see FAMILY 1

race *vb* **1** to engage in a contest — see COMPETE

2 to proceed or move quickly — see HURRY 2

raceway *n* an open man-made passageway for water — see CHANNEL 1

racial *adj* of, relating to, or reflecting the traits exhibited by a group of people with a common ancestry and culture ⟨an optional question about *racial* identity⟩

syn ethnic, tribal

rel familial; folk; kin, kindred; cultural, multicultural, national

ant nonracial

racism *n* hatred of or discrimination against a person or persons based on their race ⟨The 1963 bombing of the Sixteenth Street Baptist Church in Birmingham, Alabama, was one of the most deplorable incidents of *racism* that occurred during the Civil Rights Movement of the 1960s.⟩

syn prejudice

rel race-baiting; apartheid, jim crow, segregation, separatism; narrowness

near ant antidiscrimination, antiracism, antisegregation; assimilationism

rack *n* **1** a place set aside for sleeping — see BED 1

2 a state of great suffering of body or mind — see DISTRESS 1

rack *vb* **1** to cause persistent suffering to — see AFFLICT

2 to injure by overuse, misuse, or pressure — see STRAIN 1

racket *n* loud, confused, and usually inharmonious sound — see NOISE 1

racketeer *n* a person who gets money from another by using force or threats ⟨a *racketeer* serving time in prison⟩

syn blackmailer, extortioner, extortionist

rel blackhander, gangster, hoodlum, mafioso, mobster; bully, ruffian, thug; gouger, hustler, profiteer, shark, sharper, sharpie (*or* sharpy), swindler

racking *adj* intensely or unbearably painful — see EXCRUCIATING 1

rack up *vb* **1** to gain (as points or runs in a game) as credit towards one's total number of points — see SCORE 2

2 to obtain (as a goal) through effort — see ACHIEVE 1

racy *adj* **1** having much high-spirited energy and movement — see LIVELY 1

2 hinting at or intended to call to mind matters regarded as indecent — see SUGGESTIVE 1

radiance *n* **1** the quality or state of having or giving off light — see BRILLIANCE 1

2 the steady giving off of the form of radiation that makes vision possible — see LIGHT 1

radiant *adj* **1** having or being an outward sign of good feelings (as of love, confidence, or happiness) ⟨She left the interview with a *radiant* smile on her face, confident she had gotten the job.⟩ ⟨a *radiant* bride⟩

syn aglow, beaming, bright, glowing, sunny

rel brilliant, dazzling, effulgent, gleaming, luminous, refulgent, shining, starry; blithe, blithesome, bright, cheerful, cheery, chipper, gladsome, lightsome, merry, mirthful, optimistic, upbeat; jocund, jovial, laughing, smiling; blooming, rosy; blissful, delighted, gratified, happy, joyful, joyous

near ant blank, flat, listless, stoic (*or* stoical), unemotional; black, dark, darkening, depressing, dismal, gloomy, glum, gray (*also* grey), melancholy, sullen; frowning, glaring, glowering, lowering (*also* louring), scowling

2 giving off or reflecting much light — see BRIGHT 1

radiate *vb* **1** to extend outwards from or as if from a central point ⟨the heat *radiating* from the fire⟩ ⟨The spokes of a bicycle wheel *radiate* from the hub towards the rim.⟩

syn branch, fan (out), ray

rel diffuse, dispel, disperse, dissipate; fork, stem; diverge, divide, part, ramify, separate, split, uncouple, unlink, unyoke; scatter, splay, spread

near ant approach, close in (on), near; center (on), centralize; connect, couple, join, link, unite

ant concentrate, converge, focus, funnel, meet

2 to emit rays of light — see SHINE 1

3 to throw or give off — see EMIT 1

radical *adj* **1** being very far from the center of public opinion — see EXTREME 2

2 not bound by traditional ways or beliefs — see LIBERAL 1

radical *n* a person who favors rapid and sweeping changes especially in laws and methods of government ⟨He was a *radical* in his youth, but now he's pretty moderate.⟩

syn extremist, revolutionary, revolutionist

rel young Turk; leftist, lefty, red; progressive, reformer, reformist; anarchist, subversive; agitator, insurgent, insurrectionist, rebel; secessionist, separationist, separatist

near ant conservative, fuddy-duddy, reactionary, rightist, standpatter, Tory

ant moderate

raffish *adj* lacking in refinement or good taste — see COARSE 2

raffishness *n* the quality or state of lacking in refinement or good taste — see VULGARITY 1

raft *n* a considerable amount — see LOT 2

ragbag *n* an unorganized collection or mixture of various things — see MISCELLANY 1

rage *n* **1** a state of wildly excited activity or emotion — see FRENZY

2 an intense emotional state of displeasure with someone or something — see ANGER

3 a practice or interest that is very popular for a short time — see FAD

rage *vb* **1** to express one's anger usually violently ⟨The bad call prompted the coach to *rage* about the refereeing.⟩

syn bristle, fume, storm

rel blow up, flare (up); bluster, carry on, fulminate, rampage, rant, rave, take on; burn, foam, seethe, smolder (*or* smoulder); steam; chafe, fret, stew

phrases make a scene, run amok (*or* run amuck)

near ant allay, appease, pacify, soothe; check, choke (back), collect, compose, contain, curb, pocket, rein, repress, restrain, smother, stifle, strangle, subdue, suppress, swallow; moderate, temper, tone (down); ease, let up, relax; calm, cool, hush, quell, quiet, settle, still

2 to be excited or emotionally stirred up with anger — see BOIL 1

ragged *adj* **1** having an uneven edge or outline ⟨The Rocky Mountains cut an angular, *ragged* profile against the sky, in contrast to the rounded silhouette of the rolling, green Adirondack Mountains.⟩

syn broken, craggy, jagged, scraggly, scraggy

rel saw-toothed, serrate, serrated; harsh, rough, roughened, rugged; bumpy, coarse, irregular, nonuniform

near ant regular, uniform; flat, flush, level, plane

ant clean, even, smooth, soft, unbroken

2 worn or torn into or as if into rags ⟨We finally convinced her to throw away her favorite pair of jeans, *ragged* from decades of yard work.⟩

syn frayed, raggedy, ratty, seedy, shabby, tattered, threadbare, worn-out

rel dowdy, scruffy, tatterdemalion; dingy, faded; lacerate (*or* lacerated), shredded; holey, patchy; broken-down, decrepit, dilapidated, dog-eared, grungy, mangy, moth-eaten, run-down, scuzzy [*slang*], tacky

near ant brand-new, new, spick-and-span (*or* spic-and-span), unused

3 not having a level or smooth surface — see UNEVEN 1

4 wearing torn or worn-out clothes — see TATTERED 1

raggedy *adj* **1** wearing torn or worn-out clothes — see TATTERED 1

2 worn or torn into or as if into rags — see RAGGED 2

ragtag *adj* **1** consisting of many things of different sorts — see MISCELLANEOUS

2 wearing torn or worn-out clothes — see TATTERED 1

raid *n* **1** a sudden attack on and entrance into hostile territory ⟨Repeated Viking *raids* wore down the defenses of the seaside village.⟩

syn descent, foray, incursion, inroad, invasion, irruption

rel pillage, plunder; aggression, assault, offense (*or* offence), offensive, onset, onslaught, rush, siege, storm, strike; charge, sally, sortie; ambuscade, ambush, surprise (*also* surprize), trap; air raid, blitz, blitzkrieg, bombardment; counterattack, counteroffensive

2 the act or action of setting upon with force or violence — see ATTACK 1

raid *vb* **1** to enter for conquest or plunder — see INVADE

2 to take sudden, violent action against — see ATTACK 1

raider *n* one that starts armed conflict against another especially without reasonable cause — see AGGRESSOR

rail *n* **1** a protective barrier consisting of a horizontal bar and its supports — see RAILING

2 a roadway overlaid with parallel steel rails over which trains travel — see RAILROAD

rail (at *or* **against)** *vb* to criticize (someone) severely or angrily especially for personal failings — see SCOLD

railing *n* a protective barrier consisting of a horizontal bar and its supports ⟨They had to put a childproof *railing* on the balcony when the baby started walking.⟩

syn balustrade, banister (*also* bannister), guardrail, rail

rel handrail; taffrail; fender

raillery *n* good-natured teasing or exchanging of clever remarks — see BANTER

railroad *n* a roadway overlaid with parallel steel rails over which trains travel ⟨That *railroad* hasn't been used for passenger trains for decades.⟩

syn rail, railway, road

rel el, elevated, elevated railroad; monorail

railway *n* a roadway overlaid with parallel steel rails over which trains travel — see RAILROAD

raiment *n* covering for the human body — see CLOTHING

rain *n* **1** a steady falling of water from the sky in significant quantity ⟨The *rain* continued for most of the day.⟩

syn cloudburst, deluge, downfall, downpour, rainfall, rainstorm, storm, wet

rel precipitation, shower; thundershower, thunderstorm, weather

near ant drizzle, mist, scud, sprinkle

2 a heavy fall of objects ⟨The Norman invaders fled when the castle's defenders threw a *rain* of stones down upon them.⟩

syn hail, shower, storm

rel barrage, bombardment, broadside, cannonade, fusillade, salvo, volley; flood, gush, rush, spate, torrent; eruption, outbreak, outburst

rain *vb* **1** to fall as water in a continuous stream of drops from the clouds ⟨It started *raining* early this morning and hasn't let up since.⟩

syn pour, precipitate, storm

rel shower; hail, squall; deluge, drown, engulf, flood, inundate, swamp

phrases rain cats and dogs

near ant drizzle, mist, sprinkle

2 to give readily and in large quantities ⟨She *rained* praise upon her graduating students.⟩ ⟨The squadron *rained* bombs on the enemy's fortifications.⟩

syn heap, lavish, pour, shower

rel gush, stream; flood, inundate, overflow, overwhelm, swamp; bombard, hail

near ant hold back, keep, reserve, retain, withhold

raincoat *n* a coat made of water-resistant material ⟨I grabbed my umbrella and *raincoat* before going out in the thunderstorm.⟩

syn oilskin, slicker

rel rain gear, rainwear; poncho, sou'wester, trench, trench coat

rainfall *n* a steady falling of water from the sky in significant quantity — see RAIN 1

rainstorm *n* a steady falling of water from the sky in significant quantity — see RAIN 1

rainy *adj* marked by or abounding with rain ⟨found that the cold, *rainy* weather made his joints swell and ache⟩

syn pouring, precipitating, stormy, wet

rel drizzling, drizzly, misty, sprinkling

near ant dry

raise *n* something added (as by growth) — see INCREASE 1

raise *vb* **1** to move from a lower to a higher place or position ⟨He asked members of the audience to *raise* their hands if they had been to his show before.⟩

syn boost, crane, elevate, heave, heft, heighten, hike, hoist, jack (up), lift, perk (up), pick up, take up, up, uphold, uplift, upraise

rel ascend, mount, rise; rear, upend

near ant descend, dip, fall, pitch, plunge, slip; bear, depress, press, push; sink, submerge

ant drop, lower

2 to bring to maturity through care and education — see BRING UP 1

3 to bring (something volatile or intense) into being — see INCITE 1

4 to draw out (something hidden, latent, or reserved) — see EDUCE

5 to fix in an upright position — see ERECT 1

6 to form by putting together parts or materials — see BUILD

7 to look after or assist the growth of by labor and care — see GROW 1

8 to make greater in size, amount, or number — see INCREASE 1

9 to move higher in rank or position — see PROMOTE 1

10 to present or bring forward for discussion — see INTRODUCE 2

11 to make known (as an idea, emotion, or opinion) — see EXPRESS 1

raised *adj* **1** being at a higher level than average — see HIGH 2

2 being positioned above a surface — see ELEVATED 1

3 rising straight up — see ERECT

¹**rake** *n* a person who has sunk below the normal moral standard — see DEGENERATE

²**rake** *n* the degree to which something rises up from a position level with the horizon — see SLANT 1

rake *vb* **1** to look through (as a place) carefully or thoroughly in an effort to find or discover something — see SEARCH 1

¹**rally** *vb* **1** to assemble and make ready for action — see MOBILIZE

2 to become healthy and strong again after illness or weakness — see CONVALESCE

3 to regain a former or normal state — see RECOVER 2

²**rally** *vb* to make fun of in a good-natured way — see TEASE 1

rally *n* **1** an act of gathering forces together to renew or attempt an effort ⟨In a state-wide *rally* the community was able to provide aid to everyone affected by the storm.⟩

syn marshaling (*also* marshalling), mobilization, rallying

rel call, call-up, summons; convening, convocation, muster, mustering

phrases call to arms

2 a mass meeting for the purpose of displaying or arousing support for a cause or person ⟨a huge *rally* for the candidate on the eve of the election⟩

syn demonstration

rel assembly, conference, congress, convention, convocation, council, gathering; march; protest, sit-down, sit-in, strike; counterdemonstration, counterprotest, counterrally

3 the process or period of gradually regaining one's health and strength — see CONVALESCENCE

rallying *adj* marked by or expressive of mild or good-natured teasing — see QUIZZICAL

rallying *n* an act of gathering forces together to renew or attempt an effort — see RALLY 1

ram *vb* **1** to come into usually forceful contact with something — see HIT 2

2 to fit (people or things) into a tight space — see CROWD 1

3 to proceed or move quickly — see HURRY 2

ramble *n* **1** a short trip for pleasure — see EXCURSION 1

2 a relaxed journey on foot for exercise or pleasure — see WALK 1

ramble *vb* **1** to talk at length without sticking to a topic or getting to a point ⟨The teenagers sat around the pizza parlor, *rambling* on about dating, homework, movies, and the local football team.⟩

syn maunder, rattle, run on

rel deviate, digress, stray, wander; sidetrack; blab, blabber, chat, chatter, drivel, drool, gab, gibber, jabber, patter, prate, prattle

phrases run one's mouth

2 to move about from place to place aimlessly — see WANDER 1

3 to travel by foot for exercise or pleasure — see HIKE 1

rambler *n* a person who roams about without a fixed route or destination — see NOMAD

rambling *adj* **1** passing from one topic to another — see DISCURSIVE

2 using or containing more words than necessary to express an idea — see WORDY 1

rambunctious *adj* being rough or noisy in a high-spirited way — see BOISTEROUS

ramify *vb* to set or force apart — see SEPARATE 1

rampage *n* a state of wildly excited activity or emotion — see FRENZY

rampant *adj* **1** showing no signs of being under control ⟨Rumors of their engagement ran *rampant*.⟩

syn abandoned, intemperate, raw, unbounded, unbridled, unchecked, uncontrolled, unhampered, unhindered, unrestrained

rel uncontrollable, ungovernable; barbaric, hog wild, riotous, uninhibited, wild

near ant moderate, tempered

ant bridled, checked, constrained, controlled, curbed, governed, hampered, hindered, restrained, temperate

2 growing thickly and vigorously — see RANK 1

ramrod *adj* given to exacting standards of discipline and self-restraint — see SEVERE 1

ranch *n* a piece of land and its buildings used to grow crops or raise livestock — see FARM

rancor *n* a deep-seated ill will — see ENMITY

rancorous *adj* having or showing deep-seated resentment — see BITTER 1

random *adj* lacking a definite plan, purpose, or pattern ⟨Since we were new in town, our choice of a vet for our dog was entirely *random*.⟩

syn aimless, arbitrary, desultory, erratic, haphazard, helter-skelter, hit-or-miss, scattered, slapdash, stray

rel accidental, casual, chance, chancy, contingent, fluky (*also* flukey), fortuitous, inadvertent, incidental, lucky, unconsidered, unintended, unintentional, unplanned, unpremeditated; scattershot, shotgun; irregular, odd, sporadic, spot; directionless, objectless, purposeless; unsystematic; undirected; disorderly, disorganized; undiscriminating, unselective

near ant established, fixed, regular, set, stable, steady; constant, continuous, even; arranged, managed, orchestrated, ordered, planned; aware, conscious, deliberate, purposeful, thoughtful, willful (*or* wilful)

---

syn synonym(s)   *rel* related words
ant antonym(s)   *near ant* near antonym(s)

ant methodical (*also* methodic), nonrandom, orderly, organized, regular, systematic, systematized

randomly *adv* without definite aim, direction, rule, or method — see HIT OR MISS

range *n* **1** open land over which livestock may roam and feed ⟨knew exactly how many head of cattle were turned out on the *range* that morning to graze⟩
syn lea (*or* ley), pasturage, pasture
rel ranch, station; feedlot, stockyard, yard; grassland, pampas, prairie, savanna (*also* savannah), steppe

2 an area over which activity, capacity, or influence extends ⟨I didn't know she had such a wide *range* of knowledge until I talked to her.⟩
syn amplitude, breadth, compass, confines, dimension(s), extent, reach, realm, scope, sweep, width
rel gamut, spectrum, spread; circle, demesne, department, discipline, domain, element, field, province, region, specialty, sphere; frontier; horizon, panorama

3 the distance or extent between possible extremes ⟨an actor who can go through the full *range* of emotion, from joy to sorrow, in mere minutes⟩
syn gamut, scale, spectrum, spread, stretch
rel measure, pitch, scale; ambit, amplitude, compass, dimension(s); extent, reach, realm, scope, sweep, width

4 a relaxed journey on foot for exercise or pleasure — see WALK 1

5 a series of persons or things arranged one behind another — see LINE 1

6 an appliance that prepares food for consumption by heating it — see COOKER 1

7 the place where a plant or animal is usually or naturally found — see HOME 2

range *vb* **1** to arrange or assign according to type — see CLASSIFY 1

2 to move about from place to place aimlessly — see WANDER 1

3 to occur within a continuous range of variation — see RUN 4

4 to put into a particular arrangement — see ORDER 1

ranging *adj* traveling from place to place — see ITINERANT

rangy *adj* **1** being tall, thin and usually loose-jointed — see LANKY

2 having considerable extent — see EXTENSIVE

rank *adj* **1** growing thickly and vigorously ⟨The wall was covered with trumpet vines so *rank* you couldn't see the trellis beneath them.⟩
syn lush, luxuriant, prosperous, rampant, weedy
rel lavish, profuse; overgrown, overrun, verdant; close, dense, thick
near ant dormant; blighted, stunted
ant sparse

2 having an unpleasant smell — see MALODOROUS

3 very noticeable especially for being incorrect or bad — see EGREGIOUS

4 having no exceptions or restrictions — see ABSOLUTE 2

rank *n* **1** the placement of someone or something in relation to others in a vertical arrangement ⟨attained the highest *rank* in the Freemasons⟩
syn degree, echelon, footing, level, place, position, ranking, reach(es), situation, standing, station, status, stratum
rel condition, estate, order, walk; capacity, function; rating

2 high position within society ⟨remembered as a woman of *rank* who socialized only with other members of the elite⟩
syn class, dignity, fashion, quality, standing, state
rel gentility, gentleness, nobility, nobleness; grandness, highness, loftiness; distinction, dominance, precedence, preeminence, primacy, superiority; caste, station, status; preferment
near ant debasement, degradation; subordinateness, subordination; baseness, commonness, inferiority, lowliness, lowness

3 a series of people or things arranged side by side — see ¹ROW 1

4 *usually* **ranks** *pl* one of the units into which a whole is divided on the basis of a common characteristic — see CLASS 2

rank *vb* **1** to take or have a certain position within a group arranged in vertical classes ⟨My favorite pitcher *ranks* first in the league for number of consecutive outs.⟩
syn be, grade, place, rate, stand
rel seed; count; categorize, class, classify, codify, group, separate, set, sort; install, instate

2 to arrange or assign according to type — see CLASSIFY 1

rank and file *n* the body of the community as contrasted with the elite — see MASS 1

ranking *n* **1** a scheme of rank or order — see ³SCALE 1

2 the placement of someone or something in relation to others in a vertical arrangement — see RANK 1

rankle *vb* **1** to be excited or emotionally stirred up with anger — see BOIL 1

2 to make angry — see ANGER

rankled *adj* feeling or showing anger — see ANGRY

rankling *adj* causing annoyance — see ANNOYING

ransack *vb* **1** to search through with the intent of committing robbery ⟨It was clear that the thieves who had *ransacked* the museum were professionals—they bypassed most of the exhibits and went straight for the vaults.⟩
syn despoil, loot, maraud, pillage, plunder, sack
rel break in, burglarize, rip off, steal (from); comb, hunt, rake, rifle, rummage; harry, raid; ravish

2 to look through (a place) carefully or thoroughly in an effort to find or discover something — see SEARCH 1

ransom *vb* to free from captivity or punishment by paying a price ⟨The prince emptied the treasury to *ransom* his son from the kidnappers.⟩
syn redeem
rel deliver, rescue, save; emancipate, liberate; recover, regain, retrieve; release; buy; salvage

rant *n* **1** a long angry speech or scolding — see TIRADE

2 boastful speech or writing — see BOM-BAST 1

rant *vb* to talk loudly and wildly ⟨When the salesclerk gave him incorrect change, he began *ranting* about the poor service.⟩
syn bluster, fulminate, huff, rave, spout
rel sound off, speak out, speak up; blare, blurt (out), bolt; declaim, harangue, mouth (off), orate, pontificate; carry on, rage, storm, take on
near ant grunt, murmur, mutter, slur; breathe, whisper

¹**rap** *n* 1 a formal claim of criminal wrong-doing against a person — see CHARGE 1
2 a hard strike with a part of the body or an instrument — see ¹BLOW
3 responsibility for wrongdoing or failure — see BLAME 1

²**rap** *n* friendly, informal conversation or an instance of this — see CHAT 1

³**rap** *n* the smallest amount or part imaginable — see JOT

¹**rap** *vb* 1 to deliver a blow to (someone or something) usually in a strong vigorous manner — see HIT 1
2 to strike or cause to strike lightly and usually rhythmically — see ¹TAP

²**rap** *vb* to engage in casual or rambling conversation — see CHAT 1

³**rap** *vb* 1 to fill with overwhelming emotion (as wonder or delight) — see ENTRANCE 1
2 to take physical control or possession of (something) suddenly or forcibly — see CATCH 1

rapacious *adj* 1 having a huge appetite — see VORACIOUS 1
2 living by killing and eating other animals — see PREDATORY
3 having or marked by an eager and often selfish desire especially for material possessions — see GREEDY 1

rapaciousness *n* an intense selfish desire for wealth or possessions — see GREED

rapacity *n* an intense selfish desire for wealth or possessions — see GREED

rapid *adj* moving, proceeding, or acting with great speed — see FAST 1

rapid-fire *adj* moving, proceeding, or acting with great speed — see FAST 1

rapidity *n* a high rate of movement or performance — see SPEED 1

rapidly *adv* with great speed — see FAST 1

rapidness *n* a high rate of movement or performance — see SPEED 1

rapport *n* a friendly relationship marked by ready communication and mutual understanding ⟨His good *rapport* with his students was one of the reasons why the school board named him Teacher of the Year.⟩
syn communion, fellowship, rapprochement
rel accord, agreement, concord, harmony; oneness, solidarity, unity; affinity, empathy, sympathy, understanding; amity, chumminess, companionship, friendliness, friendship; reciprocity, symbiosis
near ant alienation, disaffection, disgruntlement, estrangement; cold shoulder, distance, iciness; animosity, antagonism, an-

tipathy, bitterness, enmity, hostility, jaundice, rancor, spite

rapprochement *n* a friendly relationship marked by ready communication and mutual understanding — see RAPPORT

rapscallion *n* 1 a mean, evil, or unprincipled person — see VILLAIN
2 an appealingly mischievous person — see SCAMP 1

rapt *adj* 1 experiencing or marked by overwhelming usually pleasurable emotion — see ECSTATIC
2 having the mind fixed on something — see ATTENTIVE 1

rapture *n* a state of overwhelming usually pleasurable emotion — see ECSTASY

rapture *vb* to fill with overwhelming emotion (as wonder or delight) — see EN-TRANCE

rapturous *adj* experiencing or marked by overwhelming usually pleasurable emotion — see ECSTATIC

rare *adj* 1 being out of the ordinary — see EXCEPTIONAL 1
2 having qualities that appeal to a refined taste — see CHOICE 1
3 not often occurring or repeated — see INFREQUENT
4 noticeably different from what is generally found or experienced — see UNUSUAL 1

rarely *adv* not often — see SELDOM

raring *adj* showing urgent desire or interest — see EAGER

rarity *n* 1 something strange or unusual that is an object of interest — see CURIOSITY 2
2 something that is different from what is ordinary or expected — see ANOMALY 1

rascal *n* 1 a mean, evil, or unprincipled person — see VILLAIN
2 an appealingly mischievous person — see SCAMP 1

rascality *n* playful, reckless behavior that is not intended to cause serious harm — see MISCHIEF 1

rascally *adj* tending to or exhibiting reckless playfulness — see MISCHIEVOUS 1

rash *adj* acting or done with excessive or careless speed — see HASTY 1

rashly *adv* with excessive or careless speed — see HASTILY 1

rasp *n* a harsh grating sound ⟨The rusted lock opened with a *rasp*.⟩
syn creak, grind, jar, scrape
rel clang, clangor, clank, clash; scuff; croak, gargle; blast, bray, screech

rasp *vb* 1 to make smooth by friction — see GRIND 1
2 to pass roughly and noisily over or against a surface — see SCRAPE 1
3 to disturb the peace of mind of (someone) especially by repeated disagreeable acts — see IRRITATE 1
4 to damage or diminish by continued friction — see ABRADE 1

raspberry *n* a vocal sound made to express scorn or disapproval — see CATCALL

rasping *adj* harsh and dry in sound — see HOARSE

raspy *adj* 1 easily irritated or annoyed — see IRRITABLE
2 harsh and dry in sound — see HOARSE

rat *n* 1 a person who provides information

---

about another's wrongdoing — see IN-FORMER

2 someone who regularly spends time in a particular place — see DENIZEN 1

3 a person whose behavior is offensive to others — see JERK 1

rat (on) vb **1** to give information (as to the authorities) about another's improper or unlawful activities — see SQUEAL 1

2 to leave (a cause or party) often in order to take up another — see DEFECT (FROM)

¹**rate** vb **1** to be or make worthy of (as a reward or punishment) — see EARN 2

2 to make an approximate or tentative judgment regarding — see ESTIMATE 1

3 to take or have a certain position within a group arranged in vertical classes — see RANK 1

4 to think of in a particular way — see CONSIDER 1

²**rate** vb to criticize (someone) severely or angrily especially for personal failings — see SCOLD

rate n **1** degree of excellence — see QUAL-ITY 1

2 the relationship in quantity, amount, or size between two or more things — see RATIO

rather adv **1** by choice or preference ⟨I would *rather* go to the movies than stay at home.⟩

syn first, preferably, readily, soon, will-ingly

rel alternately, alternatively, instead; de-sirably, gladly, wishfully; obligingly, vol-untarily

near ant reluctantly; forcibly, willy-nilly

ant involuntarily, unwillingly

2 as a substitute — see INSTEAD

3 to some degree or extent — see FAIRLY 1

ratify vb to give official acceptance of as satisfactory — see APPROVE

ratio n the relationship in quantity, amount, or size between two or more things ⟨The *ratio* of students to teachers in the school is nine to one.⟩

syn proportion, rate

rel average; frequency; correspondence; percentage

near ant disproportion

ration vb to give as a share or portion — see ALLOT

rational adj **1** having the ability to reason ⟨Human beings are *rational* creatures.⟩

syn intelligent, reasonable, reasoning, thinking

rel analytic (or analytical), logical; brainy, cerebral, highbrow, intellectual; cogni-tional, cognitive, mental; levelheaded, prac-tical, sane, sensible, sober

near ant brainless, dense, doltish, dopey (also dopy), dull, dumb, fatuous, half-wit-ted, mindless, obtuse, senseless, slow, stu-pid, thickheaded; fallacious, groundless, illogical, invalid, nonsensical

ant irrational, nonrational, nonthinking, unintelligent, unreasonable, unreasoning, unthinking

2 according to the rules of logic — see LOGICAL 1

3 based on sound reasoning or informa-tion — see GOOD 1

rationale n a statement given to explain a belief or act — see REASON 1

rationalize vb to give the reason for or cause of — see EXPLAIN 2

rattle n loud, confused, and usually inhar-monious sound — see NOISE 1

rattle vb **1** to make a series of short sharp noises ⟨The children tromped through the kitchen, making the plates on the shelf *rattle*.⟩

syn clack, clatter

rel chink, chirp, clank, click, clink; clang, clash, crash; spatter, sputter; racket

2 to engage in casual or rambling conver-sation — see CHAT 1

3 to talk at length without sticking to a topic or getting to a point — see RAMBLE 1

4 to throw into a state of self-conscious distress — see EMBARRASS 1

rattling adj moving, proceeding, or acting with great speed — see FAST 1

ratty adj **1** showing signs of advanced wear and tear and neglect — see SHABBY 1

2 worn or torn into or as if into rags — see RAGGED 2

raucous adj being rough or noisy in a high-spirited way — see BOISTEROUS

ravage vb to bring destruction to (some-thing) through violent action ⟨The forest was *ravaged* by fire.⟩

syn destroy, devastate, ruin, scourge

rel despoil, foray, harry, loot, maraud, pil-lage, plunder, sack, strip; annihilate, deso-late, eradicate, expunge, extinguish, extir-pate, obliterate, rub out, shatter, smash, total, waste, wipe out, wreck; decimate, mow; demolish, raze; crush, overpower, overrun, overthrow, overwhelm

near ant recondition, recover, redeem, re-habilitate, restore; fix, mend, patch, re-pair, revamp

rave vb **1** to make an exaggerated display of affection or enthusiasm — see GUSH 2

2 to talk loudly and wildly — see RANT

rave n, often **raves** pl enthusiastic and usually public expression of approval — see APPLAUSE 1

ravel (out) vb to separate the various strands of — see UNRAVEL 1

raven adj having the color of soot or coal — see BLACK 1

ravenous adj having a huge appetite — see VORACIOUS 1

ravine n a narrow opening between hill-sides or mountains that can be used for passage — see CANYON

ravish vb to fill with overwhelming emo-tion (as wonder or delight) — see EN-TRANCE

ravishing adj very pleasing to look at — see BEAUTIFUL 1

raw adj **1** not cooked ⟨You should wash your hands after handling *raw* chicken.⟩

syn uncooked

rel unheated; rare; half-baked, underdone

near ant well-done; overdone; baked, boiled, braised, broiled, fried, grilled, heated, roasted, sautéed (also sauteed); burned (or burnt), charred, scorched

ant cooked

2 being such as found in nature and not altered by processing or refining — see CRUDE 1

3 lacking in adult experience or maturity — see CALLOW

4 marked by wet and windy conditions — see FOUL 1

5 uncomfortably cool — see CHILLY 1

6 causing intense discomfort to one's skin — see CUTTING 1

7 showing no signs of being under control — see RAMPANT 1

raw deal *n* unfair or inadequate treatment of someone or something or an instance of this — see DISSERVICE

raw material *n* the basic elements from which something can be developed — see MAKING

rawness *n* **1** an uncomfortable degree of coolness — see CHILL

2 the quality or state of lacking refinement or good taste — see VULGARITY 1

ray *n* **1** a narrow sharply defined line of light radiating from an object — see SHAFT 1

2 a very small amount — see PARTICLE 1

ray *vb* **1** to emit rays of light — see SHINE 1

2 to extend outwards from or as if from a central point — see RADIATE 1

raze *vb* **1** to bring to a complete end the physical soundness, existence, or usefulness of — see DESTROY 1

2 to destroy (as a building) completely by knocking down or breaking to pieces — see DEMOLISH 1

razz *vb* to make fun of in a good-natured way — see TEASE 1

razzing *adj* marked by or expressive of mild or good-natured teasing — see QUIZZICAL

reach *n* **1** a wide space or area — see EXPANSE

2 an area over which activity, capacity, or influence extends — see RANGE 2

3 *usually* **reaches** *pl* the placement of someone or something in relation to others in a vertical arrangement — see RANK 1

reach *vb* **1** to shift possession of (something) from one person to another — see PASS 1

2 to transmit information or requests to — see CONTACT

3 to act upon (a person or a person's feelings) so as to cause a response — see ¹AFFECT 1

reachable *adj* situated within easy reach — see CONVENIENT

reacquire *vb* to get again in one's possession — see RECOVER 1

react *vb* to act or behave in response (as to a stimulus or influence) ⟨It was my first touchdown, and I didn't know how to *react* to the cheers of the crowd.⟩

syn reply, respond

rel answer, return; retaliate; construe, interpret, read, take, understand; contend (with), cope (with), grapple (with), handle, manage, negotiate

near ant act, behave; affect, cause, draw, effect

reaction *n* action or behavior that is done in return to other action or behavior ⟨Their *reaction* to the news was positive.⟩

syn answer, reply, response, take

rel backlash, kickback; rebound; recoil, reflex; revulsion, rise; counterreaction, counterresponse

near ant action, behavior; cause, effect

reactionary *adj* tending to favor established ideas, conditions, or institutions — see CONSERVATIVE 1

reactionary *n* **1** a person whose political beliefs are centered on tradition and keeping things the way they are — see CONSERVATIVE

2 a person with old-fashioned ideas — see FOGY

read *vb* **1** to go over and mentally take in the content of ⟨He always *reads* the newspaper in the morning as he eats breakfast.⟩

syn peruse, pore (over)

rel browse, dip (into), leaf (through), scan, skim, spread (through), thumb (through), turn over; devour, gobble (up), slog (through), wade (through); reread; proofread; decipher; review, study; apprehend, comprehend, grasp, make, make out, perceive, understand

2 to tell of or describe beforehand — see FORETELL

readdress *vb* to consider again especially with the possibility of change or reversal — see RECONSIDER

readily *adv* **1** by choice or preference — see RATHER 1

2 without difficulty — see EASILY 1

reading *n* **1** a presentation of an artistic work (as a piece of music) from a particular point of view — see ACCOUNT 2

2 something assigned to be read or studied — see LESSON

ready *adj* **1** being in a state of fitness for some experience or action ⟨After studying for months, she felt *ready* for the bar exam.⟩

syn fit, go, prepared, set

rel conditioned, primed, ripe; armed, braced, fortified, steeled; qualified, trained

near ant unqualified, untrained

ant half-baked, half-cocked, underprepared, unprepared, unready

2 having a desire or inclination (as for a specified course of action) — see WILLING 1

3 having or showing the ability to respond without delay or hesitation — see QUICK 1

4 involving minimal difficulty or effort — see EASY 1

ready *vb* **1** to make competent (as by training, skill, or ability) for a particular office or function — see QUALIFY 2

2 to make ready in advance — see PREPARE 1

3 to prepare (oneself) mentally or emotionally — see FORTIFY 1

ready–made *adj* made beforehand in large numbers ⟨The store carries mostly inexpensive *ready-made* clothing.⟩

syn mass-produced, store

rel ready-to-wear; prefabricated

near ant homemade

ant custom, customized, custom-made, tailored, tailor-made

real *adj* **1** being exactly as appears or as claimed — see AUTHENTIC 1

---

syn synonym(s)   *rel* related words
ant antonym(s)   *near ant* near antonym(s)

reasoned 609

2 existing in fact and not merely as a possibility — see ACTUAL

3 free from any intent to deceive or impress others — see GUILELESS

real *adv* to a great degree — see VERY 1

realistic *adj* **1** willing to see things as they really are and deal with them sensibly ⟨high schoolers who need to be more *realistic* in their career choices, as so few people end up as pro athletes⟩

syn down-to-earth, earthy, hardheaded, matter-of-fact, practical, pragmatic (*also* pragmatical)

rel idealless, philistine, utilitarian; grounded, levelheaded, logical, no-nonsense, rational, reasonable, sane, sensible, sober, sobersided, sound; bottom-line, hard, hardboiled, hard-edged, tough-minded, unromantic, unsentimental

near ant fanciful, fantastic (*also* fantastical), imaginative; romantic, sentimental; cheerful, optimistic, rose-colored; trustful, trusting, unsuspicious; half-baked, illogical, irrational, unreasonable; theoretical (*also* theoretic)

ant blue-sky, impractical, unrealistic, utopian, visionary

2 closely resembling the object imitated — see NATURAL 2

reality *n* **1** something that actually exists — see FACT 1

2 the fact of being or of being real — see EXISTENCE

3 the quality of being actual — see FACT 1

4 one that has a real and independent existence — see ENTITY

realizable *adj* capable of being done or carried out — see POSSIBLE 1

realization *n* the state of being actual or complete — see FRUITION

realize *vb* **1** to come to an awareness of — see DISCOVER 1

2 to receive as return for effort — see EARN 1

really *adv* **1** in actual fact — see VERY 2

2 to tell the truth — see ACTUALLY 1

3 without any question — see INDEED 1

4 to a great degree — see VERY 1

realm *n* **1** a region of activity, knowledge, or influence — see FIELD 2

2 an area over which activity, capacity, or influence extends — see RANGE 2

reams *n pl* a considerable amount — see LOT 2

reanalyze *vb* to consider again especially with the possibility of change or reversal — see RECONSIDER

reanimate *vb* to bring back to life, practice, or activity — see REVIVE 1

reanimated *adj* made or become fresh in spirits or vigor — see NEW 4

reanimation *n* the act or an instance of bringing something back to life, public attention, or vigorous activity — see REVIVAL

reap *vb* **1** to catch or collect (a crop or natural resource) for human use — see HARVEST

2 to receive as return for effort — see EARN 1

reappraisal *n* a usually critical look at a past event — see REVIEW 1

rear *adj* being at or in the part of something opposite the front part — see BACK

rear *n* **1** a behind part or surface ⟨The *rear* of the car was sleekly designed.⟩

syn back, reverse, tail

ant face, forehead, forepart, front

2 the part of the body upon which someone sits — see BUTTOCKS

rear *vb* **1** to bring to maturity through care and education — see BRING UP 1

2 to fix in an upright position — see ERECT 1

3 to form by putting together parts or materials — see BUILD

4 to look after or assist the growth of by labor and care — see GROW 1

rearmost *adj* following all others of the same kind in order or time — see LAST 1

rearward *adj* **1** being at or in the part of something opposite the front part — see BACK

2 directed, turned, or done toward the back — see BACKWARD 1

rearward *also* **rearwards** *adv* toward the back — see BACKWARD 1

reason *n* **1** a statement given to explain a belief or act ⟨She gave a good *reason* for her seemingly suspicious behavior.⟩

syn account, argument, case, explanation, rationale

rel alibi, apologia, defense, excuse, justification, vindication; appeal, plea; guise, pretense (*or* pretence), pretext, rationalization

2 something (as a belief) that serves as the basis for another thing ⟨A firm belief that we are here on earth to help others is the *reason* for her tireless volunteer work.⟩

syn account, authority, grounds, motive, subject, wherefore, why

rel antecedent, cause, consideration, impetus, incentive, inspiration, instigation, occasion, stimulus

3 an explanation that frees one from fault or blame — see EXCUSE

4 someone or something responsible for a result — see CAUSE 1

5 the ability to learn and understand or to deal with problems — see INTELLIGENCE 1

6 the normal or healthy condition of the mental abilities — see MIND 2

7 the thought processes that have been established as leading to valid solutions to problems — see LOGIC

reason *vb* **1** to form an opinion or reach a conclusion through reasoning and information — see INFER 1

2 to state (something) as a reason in support of or against something under consideration — see ARGUE 1

reasonable *adj* **1** according to the rules of logic — see LOGICAL 1

2 based on sound reasoning or information — see GOOD 1

3 costing little — see CHEAP 1

4 having the ability to reason — see RATIONAL 1

reasonably *adv* with good reason or courtesy — see WELL 4

reasoned *adj* **1** based on sound reasoning or information — see GOOD 1

2 being or provable by reasoning in which

the conclusion follows necessarily from given information — see DEDUCTIVE

3 decided on as a result of careful thought — see DELIBERATE 1

reasoning *adj* having the ability to reason — see RATIONAL 1

reasoning *n* the thought processes that have been established as leading to valid solutions to problems — see LOGIC

reassure *vb* to ease the grief or distress of — see COMFORT

reata *n* a rope or long leather thong with a noose used especially for catching livestock — see LASSO

rebel *adj* given to resisting authority or another's control — see DISOBEDIENT

rebel *n* a person who rises up against authority ⟨The *rebel* would not submit peacefully, even after he was captured.⟩

syn insurgent, insurrectionary, insurrectionist, mutineer, red, revolter, revolutionary, revolutionist

rel challenger, defier, insubordinate, oppositionist, resister; anarchist; discontent, extremist, malcontent, radical

near ant loyalist, patriot, supporter; counterinsurgent, counterrevolutionary, counterrevolutionist

rebel *vb* to rise up against established authority ⟨The colonists *rebelled* in the wake of an onslaught of abuses.⟩

syn mutiny, revolt

rel defy, disobey, mock; revolutionize; buck, combat, contest, fight, oppose, resist, withstand

near ant comply (with), follow, mind, obey, submit; attend, serve

rebel (against) *vb* to go against the commands, prohibitions, or rules of — see DISOBEY

rebellion *n* **1** open fighting against authority (as one's own government) ⟨The *rebellion* would have failed if not for the aid sent by other countries.⟩

syn insurgency, insurrection, mutiny, outbreak, revolt, revolution, rising, uprising

rel coup, coup d'état (*or* coup d'etat), overthrow; sedition, treachery, treason; subversion

near ant counterinsurgency, counterrevolution

2 refusal to obey — see DISOBEDIENCE

rebellious *adj* **1** taking part in a rebellion ⟨The *rebellious* troops fought a pitched battle with divisions still loyal to the government.⟩

syn insurgent, insurrectionary, mutinous, revolutionary

rel traitorous, treacherous, treasonous; agitating, demagogic, rabble-rousing; defiant, disobedient, insubordinate, intractable, recalcitrant, refractory, restive, ungovernable, unruly

near ant constant, devoted, loyal, staunch (*also* stanch), steadfast, true, true-blue; compliant, obedient, submissive, tractable

2 given to resisting authority or another's control — see DISOBEDIENT

rebelliousness *n* refusal to obey — see DISOBEDIENCE

rebirth *n* the act or an instance of bringing something back to life, public attention, or vigorous activity — see REVIVAL

rebound *vb* **1** to regain a former or normal state — see RECOVER 2

2 to strike and fly off at an angle — see GLANCE 1

rebuff *n* treatment that is deliberately unfriendly — see COLD SHOULDER

rebuke *n* an often public or formal expression of disapproval — see CENSURE

rebuke *vb* **1** to criticize (someone) so as to correct a fault ⟨The father was forced to *rebuke* his son for the spendthrift ways he had adopted since arriving at college.⟩

syn admonish, chide, reprimand, reproach, reprove

rel berate, castigate, chew out, dress down, flay, harangue, jaw, keelhaul, lambaste (*or* lambast), lecture, rail (at *or* against), rate, scold, score, upbraid; abuse, assail, attack, bad-mouth, blame, blast, censure, condemn, criticize, crucify, denounce, excoriate, reprehend, slam; mock, put down; deride, ridicule, scoff, scorn

phrases burn one's ears, get after, get on

near ant approve, endorse (*also* indorse), OK (*or* okay), sanction; applaud, extol (*also* extoll), hail, laud, praise, salute, tout

2 to criticize (someone) severely or angrily especially for personal failings — see SCOLD

3 to express public or formal disapproval of — see CENSURE 1

rebut *vb* **1** to drive back — see REPEL 1

2 to prove to be false — see DISPROVE

rebuttal *n* something (as an argument) that serves to disprove — see CONFUTATION

recalcitrance *n* refusal to obey — see DISOBEDIENCE

recalcitrant *adj* **1** given to resisting authority or another's control — see DISOBEDIENT

2 given to resisting control or discipline by others — see UNCONTROLLABLE

recall *n* **1** a particular act or instance of recalling or the thing remembered — see MEMORY 2

2 the act of putting an end to something planned or previously agreed to — see CANCELLATION

recall *vb* **1** to bring back to mind — see REMEMBER

2 to put an end to (something planned or previously agreed to) — see CANCEL 1

recant *vb* to solemnly or formally reject or go back on (as something formerly adhered to) — see ABJURE 1

recap *n* a short statement of the main points — see SUMMARY

recap *vb* to make into a short statement of the main points (as of a report) — see SUMMARIZE

recapitulate *vb* to make into a short statement of the main points (as of a report) — see SUMMARIZE

recapitulation *n* a short statement of the main points — see SUMMARY

recapture *n* the act or process of getting something back — see RECOVERY 1

recapture *vb* to get again in one's possession — see RECOVER 1

---

syn synonym(s)   *rel* related words
ant antonym(s)   *near ant* near antonym(s)

recast *vb* to make different in some way — see CHANGE 1

recede *vb* **1** to grow less in scope or intensity especially gradually — see DECREASE 2

2 to move back or away (as from something difficult, dangerous, or disagreeable) — see RETREAT 1

recently *adv* not long ago — see NEWLY

receptacle *n* something into which a liquid or smaller objects can be put for storage or transportation — see CONTAINER

reception *n* a social gathering — see PARTY 1

receptive *adj* willing to consider new or different ideas — see OPEN-MINDED 1

recess *n* **1** a hollowed-out space in a wall — see NICHE 1

2 a period during which the usual routine of school or work is suspended — see VACATION

3 a momentary halt in an activity — see PAUSE 1

4 a sunken area forming a separate space — see HOLE 2

recess *vb* to bring to a formal close for a period of time — see ADJOURN

recessed *adj* curved inward — see HOLLOW

recession *n* **1** a period of decreased economic activity — see DEPRESSION 1

2 an act of moving away especially from something difficult, dangerous, or disagreeable — see RETREAT 1

reciprocal *adj* related to each other in such a way that one completes the other — see COMPLEMENTARY

recite *vb* **1** to give an oral or written account of in some detail — see TELL 1

2 to give from memory — see REPEAT 2

3 to specify one after another — see ENUMERATE 1

reckless *adj* having or showing a lack of concern for the consequences of one's actions ⟨The *reckless* skiers were making everyone nervous by schussing down the mountainside at lightning speed.⟩

syn daredevil, devil-may-care, foolhardy, harum-scarum, irresponsible

rel adventurous, audacious, bold, daring, venturesome; hasty, headlong, hotheaded, impetuous, precipitate, rash, wild; blithe, carefree, happy-go-lucky, madcap, slaphappy; nonchalant, unconcerned, unworried; careless, freewheeling, heedless, inattentive, incautious, mindless, regardless, unheeding, unmindful; inconsiderate, thoughtless, unthinking

near ant careful, cautious, circumspect, heedful; overcareful, overcautious, timid

ant responsible

2 foolishly adventurous or bold — see FOOLHARDY 1

reckon *vb* **1** to decide the size, amount, number, or distance of (something) without actual measurement — see ESTIMATE 1

2 *chiefly dialect* to have as an opinion — see BELIEVE 2

3 to determine (a value) by doing the necessary mathematical operations — see CALCULATE 1

4 to place reliance or trust — see DEPEND 2

5 to think of in a particular way — see CONSIDER 1

reckoning *n* **1** the act of placing a value on the nature, character, or quality of something — see ESTIMATE 1

2 the act or process of performing mathematical operations to find a value — see CALCULATION

reclaim *vb* **1** to get again in one's possession — see RECOVER 1

2 to make better in behavior or character — see REFORM 1

3 to obtain (a raw material) by separating it from a by-product or waste product — see RECYCLE

reclamation *n* the act or process of getting something back — see RECOVERY 1

recluse *n* a person who lives away from others ⟨He was sick of cities and crowds, so he decided to go live by himself in the woods as a *recluse*.⟩

syn hermit, solitary

rel homebody, shut-in

near ant socialite; socializer

recognize *vb* **1** to have a clear idea of — see COMPREHEND 1

2 to show appreciation, respect, or affection for (someone) with a public celebration — see HONOR

recoil *vb* to draw back in fear, pain, or disgust — see FLINCH

recollect *vb* to bring back to mind — see REMEMBER

re–collect *vb* **1** to gain emotional or mental control of — see COLLECT 1

2 to get again in one's possession — see RECOVER 1

recollection *n* **1** a particular act or instance of recalling or the thing remembered — see MEMORY 2

2 the power or process of recalling what has been previously learned or experienced — see MEMORY 1

recommend *vb* **1** to put (something) into the possession or safekeeping of another — see GIVE 2

2 to put (something) forward as one's choice for a wise or proper course of action — see ADVISE 2

recompense *n* **1** payment to another for a loss or injury — see COMPENSATION 1

2 something (as money) that is given or received in return for goods or services — see PAYMENT 2

recompense *vb* **1** to give (someone) the sum of money owed for goods or services received — see PAY 1

2 to give what is owed for — see PAY 2

3 to provide (someone) with a just payment for loss or injury — see COMPENSATE 1

reconceive *vb* to consider again especially with the possibility of change or reversal — see RECONSIDER

reconcile *vb* to bring to a state free of conflicts, inconsistencies, or differences — see HARMONIZE 2

recondite *adj* difficult for one of ordinary knowledge or intelligence to understand — see PROFOUND 1

recondition *vb* to put into good shape or working order again — see MEND 1

reconsider *vb* to consider again especially

with the possibility of change or reversal ⟨The new intelligence forced the general to *reconsider* his plan of attack.⟩

syn readdress, reanalyze, reconceive, re-evaluate, reexamine, rethink, review, reweigh

rel rehear; reconceptualize, reenvision, reimagine; reappraise, reassess, reinvestigate, restudy; amend, correct, emend, rectify, reform, remedy, revise

phrases change one's mind (about), go over, think better of

near ant assert, defend, maintain, uphold

reconsideration *n* a usually critical look at a past event — see REVIEW 1

record *n* 1 a relating of events usually in the order in which they happened — see ACCOUNT 1

2 an account of important events in the order in which they happened — see HISTORY 1

record *vb* 1 to make a written note of ⟨The reporter *recorded* the events of the evening in her tablet for later reference.⟩

syn jot (down), log, mark, note, put down, register, report, set down, take down

rel chronicle, minute, transcribe; enter, inscribe; chalk (up), notch, score

2 to put (someone or something) on a list — see ¹LIST 2

recount *vb* to give an oral or written account of in some detail — see TELL 1

recoup *vb* 1 to get again in one's possession — see RECOVER 1

2 to provide (someone) with a just payment for loss or injury — see COMPENSATE 1

3 to become healthy and strong again after illness or weakness — see CONVALESCE

recoupment *n* 1 payment to another for a loss or injury — see COMPENSATION 1

2 the act or process of getting something back — see RECOVERY 1

recourse *n* something that one uses to accomplish an end especially when the usual means is not available — see RESOURCE 1

recover *vb* 1 to get again in one's possession ⟨After fishing around in the garbage for 10 minutes, I was able to *recover* my lost keys.⟩

syn reacquire, recapture, reclaim, re-collect, recoup, regain, repossess, retake, retrieve

rel recruit, replenish; redeem, repurchase; rescue

near ant lose, mislay, misplace

2 to regain a former or normal state ⟨After a disastrous first half, the team was able to *recover* and pull off a victory.⟩

syn bounce (back), rally, rebound, snap back

rel reanimate, revitalize, revive

phrases make (or stage) a comeback

near ant decline, fail, worsen

3 to become healthy and strong again after illness or weakness — see CONVALESCE

4 to obtain (a raw material) by separating it from a by-product or waste product — see RECYCLE

recovery *n* 1 the act or process of getting something back ⟨The *recovery* of the sunken boat took over a week.⟩

syn recapture, reclamation, recoupment, repossession, retrieval

rel recruitment, replenishment; redemption, rescue

near ant loss, misplacement

2 the process or period of gradually regaining one's health and strength — see CONVALESCENCE

recreant *adj* 1 having or showing a shameful lack of courage — see COWARDLY

2 not true in one's allegiance to someone or something — see FAITHLESS

recreant *n* 1 a person who abandons a cause or organization usually without right — see RENEGADE

2 a person who shows a shameful lack of courage in the face of danger — see COWARD

3 one who betrays a trust or an allegiance — see TRAITOR

recreate *vb* 1 to bring back to a former condition or vigor — see RENEW 1

2 to engage in activity for amusement — see PLAY 1

recreated *adj* made or become fresh in spirits or vigor — see NEW 4

recreation *n* 1 activity engaged in to amuse oneself — see PLAY 1

2 someone or something that provides amusement or enjoyment — see FUN 1

3 the act or activity of providing pleasure or amusement especially for the public — see ENTERTAINMENT 1

recreational vehicle *n* a motor vehicle that is specially equipped for living while traveling — see CAMPER

recruit *n* a person who is just starting out in a field of activity — see BEGINNER

recruit *vb* to provide with a paying job — see EMPLOY 1

rectify *vb* to remove errors, defects, deficiencies, or deviations from — see CORRECT 1

rectifying *adj* serving to raise or adjust something to some standard or proper condition — see CORRECTIVE 1

rectitude *n* 1 conduct that conforms to an accepted standard of right and wrong — see MORALITY 1

2 faithfulness to high moral standards — see HONOR 1

recuperate *vb* to become healthy and strong again after illness or weakness — see CONVALESCE

recuperation *n* the process or period of gradually regaining one's health and strength — see CONVALESCENCE

recurrent *adj* occurring or appearing at intervals — see INTERMITTENT 1

recurring *adj* occurring or appearing at intervals — see INTERMITTENT 1

recycle *vb* to obtain (a raw material) by separating it from a by-product or waste product ⟨*Recycling* the aluminum from soft drink cans is environmentally sound.⟩

syn reclaim, recover

rel reuse; process, reprocess

red *adj* 1 having a healthy reddish skin tone — see RUDDY

2 having a notably high temperature — see HOT 1

---

syn synonym(s)   *rel* related words
ant antonym(s)   *near ant* near antonym(s)

red *n* a person who rises up against authority — see REBEL

red–blooded *adj* having active strength of body or mind — see VIGOROUS 1

redden *vb* to develop a rosy facial color (as from excitement or embarrassment) — see BLUSH

redeem *vb* 1 to do what is required by the terms of — see FULFILL 1

2 to free from captivity or punishment by paying a price — see RANSOM

3 to free from the penalties or consequences of sin — see SAVE 1

4 to make better in behavior or character — see REFORM 1

5 to make up for (an offense) — see EXPIATE

redeemer *n* one that saves from danger or destruction — see SAVIOR

red–hot *adj* 1 being or involving the latest methods, concepts, information, or styles — see MODERN

2 having a notably high temperature — see HOT 1

3 having or expressing great depth of feeling — see FERVENT 1

4 enjoying widespread favor or approval — see POPULAR 1

redo *n* the act of saying or doing over again — see REPEAT

redo *vb* 1 to make different in some way — see CHANGE 1

2 to make or do again — see REPEAT 4

redoing *n* the act, process, or result of making different — see CHANGE 1

redolence *n* 1 a sweet or pleasant smell — see FRAGRANCE

2 the quality of a thing that makes it perceptible to the sense organs in the nose — see SMELL 1

redolent *adj* having a pleasant smell — see FRAGRANT

redouble *vb* 1 to make markedly greater in measure or degree — see INTENSIFY

2 to make twice as great or as many — see DOUBLE 1

redoubtable *adj* 1 causing fear — see FEARFUL 1

2 standing above others in rank, importance, or achievement — see EMINENT

redraft *vb* to prepare for publication by correcting, rewriting, or updating — see EDIT 1

redress *n* payment to another for a loss or injury — see COMPENSATION 1

redress *vb* to punish in kind the wrongdoer responsible for — see AVENGE

reduce *vb* 1 to bring to a lower grade or rank — see DEMOTE

2 to make smaller in amount, volume, or extent — see DECREASE 1

3 to diminish the price or value of — see DEPRECIATE 1

reduction *n* 1 something that is or may be subtracted — see DEDUCTION 1

2 the amount by which something is lessened — see DECREASE

3 the act or an instance of bringing to a lower grade or rank — see BUMP 2

redundancy *n* 1 the use of too many words to express an idea — see VERBIAGE 1

2 the state or an instance of going beyond what is usual, proper, or needed — see EXCESS

redundant *adj* being over what is needed — see SPARE 1

reduplicate *vb* 1 to make an exact likeness of — see COPY 1

2 to make or do again — see REPEAT 4

reduplication *n* 1 something that is made to look exactly like something else — see COPY

2 the act of saying or doing over again — see REPEAT

reecho *vb* 1 to continue or be repeated in a series of reflected sound waves — see REVERBERATE

2 to say after another — see REPEAT 3

reek *n* 1 a strong unpleasant smell — see STINK 1

2 an atmospheric condition in which suspended particles in the air rob it of its transparency — see HAZE 1

reek *vb* to give off an extremely unpleasant smell — see STINK

reeking *adj* having an unpleasant smell — see MALODOROUS

reeky *adj* having an unpleasant smell — see MALODOROUS

reel *n* a rapid turning about on an axis or central point — see SPIN 1

reel *vb* 1 to be in a confused state as if from being twirled around — see SPIN 2

2 to move forward while swaying from side to side — see STAGGER 1

reeling *adj* having a feeling of being whirled about and in danger of falling down — see DIZZY 1

reel off *vb* 1 to give from memory — see REPEAT 2

2 to specify one after another — see ENUMERATE 1

reenergized *adj* made or become fresh in spirits or vigor — see NEW 4

reevaluate *vb* to consider again especially with the possibility of change or reversal — see RECONSIDER

reexamination *n* a usually critical look at a past event — see REVIEW 1

reexamine *vb* to consider again especially with the possibility of change or reversal — see RECONSIDER

refashion *vb* to make different in some way — see CHANGE 1

refashioning *n* the act, process, or result of making different — see CHANGE 1

refer *vb* to have a relation or connection — see APPLY 1

refer (to) *vb* 1 to make reference to or speak about briefly but specifically — see MENTION 1

2 to use or seek out as a source of aid, relief, or advantage — see RESORT (TO) 1

referee *n* a person who impartially decides or resolves a dispute or controversy — see JUDGE 1

referee *vb* to give an opinion about (something at issue or in dispute) — see JUDGE 1

reference *n* 1 something mentioned in a text as providing related and especially supporting information ⟨The author's argument is interesting, but the lack of *references* makes me wonder if it can be proven.⟩

syn authority, source

rel citation, excerpt, extract, quotation; caption, cross-reference, footnote, note

2 relation to or concern with something specified — see RESPECT 1

refine *vb* to make better — see IMPROVE

refined *adj* **1** being far along in development — see ADVANCED

2 free from added matter — see PURE 1

3 having or showing a taste for the fine arts and gracious living — see CULTIVATED

4 having or showing elegance — see ELEGANT 1

5 made or done with extreme care and accuracy — see FINE 2

6 satisfying or pleasing because of fineness or mildness — see DELICATE 1

7 meeting the highest standard of accuracy — see PRECISE 1

refinement *n* **1** an instance of notable progress in the development of knowledge, technology, or skill — see ADVANCE 2

2 a high level of taste and enlightenment as a result of extensive intellectual training and exposure to the arts — see CULTURE 1

3 dignified or restrained beauty of form, appearance, or style — see ELEGANCE

reflect *vb* **1** to reproduce or show (an exact likeness) as a mirror would ⟨Her face was *reflected* in the waters of the still pond.⟩

syn image, mirror

rel copy, duplicate, imitate, reduplicate, repeat, replicate, reproduce

2 to make a statement of one's opinion — see REMARK 1

reflection *n* **1** a briefly expressed opinion — see REMARK

2 a cause of shame — see DISGRACE 2

3 a careful weighing of the reasons for or against something — see CONSIDERATION 1

reflective *adj* **1** given to or marked by long, quiet thinking — see CONTEMPLATIVE

2 indicating something — see INDICATIVE

reform *vb* **1** to make better in behavior or character ⟨an effort to *reform* repeat offenders⟩

syn reclaim, redeem, regenerate, rehabilitate

rel reeducate; amend, improve, refine; cleanse, purify, restore

near ant abase, canker, corrupt, debauch, degrade, demean, demoralize, deprave, lower, pervert, poison, profane, subvert, warp

2 to change one's behavior or character for the better ⟨a cheating athlete who *reformed* after getting caught⟩

syn amend, mend

rel behave, regenerate; better, improve

phrases clean up one's act

near ant backslide, regress

3 to remove errors, defects, deficiencies, or deviations from — see CORRECT 1

reformative *adj* serving to raise or adjust something to some standard or proper condition — see CORRECTIVE 1

reformatory *adj* serving to raise or adjust something to some standard or proper condition — see CORRECTIVE 1

refractoriness *n* refusal to obey — see DISOBEDIENCE

refractory *adj* **1** given to resisting authority or another's control — see DISOBEDIENT

2 given to resisting control or discipline by others — see UNCONTROLLABLE

refrain *n* a part of a song or hymn that is repeated every so often — see CHORUS 2

refrain (from) *vb* to resist the temptation of — see FORBEAR

refresh *vb* **1** to bring back to a former condition or vigor — see RENEW 1

2 to take a meal — see DINE 1

refreshed *adj* made or become fresh in spirits or vigor — see NEW 4

refreshen *vb* to bring back to a former condition or vigor — see RENEW 1

refreshing *adj* having a renewing effect on the state of the body or mind — see TONIC 1

refrigerate *vb* to cause to lose heat — see COOL

refuge *n* something (as a building) that offers cover from the weather or protection from danger — see SHELTER

refuge *vb* to be or provide a shelter for — see SHELTER 1

refugee *n* a person forced to emigrate for political reasons — see ÉMIGRÉ 1

refulgence *n* the quality or state of having or giving off light — see BRILLIANCE 1

refulgent *adj* giving off or reflecting much light — see BRIGHT 1

refund *vb* to make a return payment to — see REPAY

refusal *n* an unwillingness to grant something asked for — see DENIAL 1

refuse *n* discarded or useless material — see GARBAGE

refuse *vb* **1** to be unwilling to grant — see DENY 2

2 to show unwillingness to accept, do, engage in, or agree to — see DECLINE 1

refutation *n* something (as an argument) that serves to disprove — see CONFUTATION

refute *vb* **1** to declare not to be true — see DENY 1

2 to prove to be false — see DISPROVE

regain *vb* to get again in one's possession — see RECOVER 1

regal *adj* **1** fit for or worthy of a royal ruler — see MONARCHICAL

2 large and impressive in size, grandeur, extent, or conception — see GRAND 1

regale *vb* **1** to cause (someone) to pass the time agreeably occupied — see AMUSE

2 to entertain with a fancy meal — see FEAST 1

regalia *n* dressy clothing — see FINERY

regard *n* **1** a feeling of great approval and liking — see ADMIRATION 1

2 an instance of looking especially briefly — see LOOK 2

3 relation to or concern with something specified — see RESPECT 1

4 regards *pl* best wishes — see COMPLIMENT 2

5 a fixed intent look — see GAZE

---

regard vb **1** to make note of (something) through the use of one's eyes — see SEE 1
2 to take notice of and be guided by — see HEED 1
3 to think of in a particular way — see CONSIDER 1
4 to think very highly or favorably of — see ADMIRE

regardful adj marked by or showing proper regard for another's higher status — see RESPECTFUL

regarding prep having to do with — see ABOUT 1

regardless adv in spite of everything ⟨The weather looked bad, but they were resolved to go on with their picnic *regardless*.⟩
syn anyhow, anyway
rel after all, however, nevertheless; always
phrases at all events, at any rate, in any case, in any event, no matter, whether or no (*or* whether or not)

regenerate vb **1** to bring back to a former condition or vigor — see RENEW 1
2 to bring back to life, practice, or activity — see REVIVE 1
3 to make better in behavior or character — see REFORM 1

regenerated adj made or become fresh in spirits or vigor — see NEW 4

regeneration n the act or an instance of bringing something back to life, public attention, or vigorous activity — see REVIVAL

regime *also* **régime** n lawful control over the affairs of a political unit (as a nation) — see RULE 2

regimen n lawful control over the affairs of a political unit (as a nation) — see RULE 2

region n **1** a part or portion having no fixed boundaries ⟨If you look in the upper left *region* of the sky, you can see the constellation Orion.⟩
syn area, demesne, field, zone
rel corner, section; locale, locality, location, locus, place, point, position, site, space, spot
2 a broad geographical area ⟨Corn is mostly grown in the central *regions* of the country.⟩
syn belt, corridor, land, part(s), tract, zone
rel district, domain, latitude(s), range, realm, territory; neighborhood

¹**register** n an official whose job is to keep records — see CLERK 1

²**register** n a record of a series of items (as names or titles) usually arranged according to some system — see ¹LIST

register vb **1** to add (a person) to a list or roll as a participant or member — see ENROLL 1
2 to make a written note of — see RECORD 1
3 to put (someone or something) on a list — see ¹LIST 2
4 to have a clear idea of — see COMPREHEND 1

registrar n an official whose job is to keep records — see CLERK 1

registration n the number of individuals registered ⟨There was a large *registration*

for the popular swim classes at the community center.⟩
syn enrollment (*also* enrolment), registry
rel class, roster; count, membership

registry n **1** a record of a series of items (as names or titles) usually arranged according to some system — see ¹LIST
2 the number of individuals registered — see REGISTRATION

regress vb **1** to go back to a previous and usually lower state or level ⟨In extreme circumstances, people sometimes *regress* to the behavior they exhibited in childhood.⟩
syn retrogress, return, revert
rel backslide, lapse, relapse; throw back; ebb; decline, degenerate, drop, fall, retrograde, worsen
near ant grow, mature, ripen
ant advance, develop, evolve, progress
2 to become worse or of less value — see DETERIORATE 1

regression n the act or an instance of going back to an earlier and lower level especially of intelligence or behavior ⟨*regression* to childish behavior⟩
syn retrogression, reversion
rel backslide, lapse, relapse; atavism, return; nondevelopment; decline, degeneration
near ant gestation, growth, maturation, ripening
ant advancement, development, evolution, progression

regret n a feeling of responsibility for wrongdoing — see GUILT 1

regret vb to feel sorry or dissatisfied about ⟨We *regret* any inconvenience that we may have caused you.⟩
syn bemoan, deplore, lament, repent, rue
rel ache (for), bewail, grieve (for), mourn, sorrow (for)
near ant delight (in), enjoy, relish, revel (in), savor (*also* savour)

regretful adj **1** expressing or suggesting mourning — see MOURNFUL 1
2 feeling sorrow for a wrong that one has done — see CONTRITE

regretfully adv with feelings of bitterness or grief — see HARD 2

regrettable adj of a kind to cause great distress ⟨The explorers forged ahead despite the *regrettable* loss of some of their companions.⟩
syn deplorable, distressful, distressing, grievous, heartbreaking, heartrending, lamentable, tragic (*also* tragical), unfortunate, unlucky, woeful
rel troublesome, vexatious; affecting, doleful, moving, piteous, poignant, ruthful, touching; awful, dire, dreadful, fearful, severe, terrible; alarming, disturbing, perturbing, traumatic, unsettling; crushing, excruciating, harrowing, horrible, horrifying, intolerable, overwhelming, shocking, sickening, unbearable; miserable, pitiful, sad, wretched; calamitous, disastrous
near ant gratifying, pleasing, ¹rewarding, satisfying; comforting, encouraging, heartening; cheering, heartwarming, inspiring; fortunate, happy, lucky

regular adj **1** appearing or occurring

repeatedly from time to time ⟨What with one or another of our pets having problems, we've been *regular* visitors at the animal hospital.⟩

syn constant, frequent, habitual, periodic, periodical, repeated, steady

rel continual, intermittent, recurrent, recurring; cyclic (*or* cyclical); around-the-clock, round-the-clock; chronic, confirmed, inveterate; expected, usual

near ant episodic (*also* episodical), occasional; unexpected, unusual

ant inconstant, infrequent, irregular

2 following a set method, arrangement, or pattern — see METHODICAL

3 following or agreeing with established form, custom, or rules — see FORMAL 1

4 having no exceptions or restrictions — see ABSOLUTE 2

5 having or showing the qualities associated with the members of a particular group or kind — see TYPICAL 1

regular *n* **1** a person engaged in military service — see SOLDIER

2 someone who regularly spends time in a particular place — see DENIZEN 1

regularize *vb* to make agree with a single established standard or model — see STANDARDIZE

regulate *vb* **1** to keep from exceeding a desirable degree or level (as of expression) — see CONTROL 1

2 to look after and make decisions about — see CONDUCT 1

regulation *n* **1** a statement spelling out the proper procedure or conduct for an activity — see RULE 1

2 the act or activity of looking after and making decisions about something — see CONDUCT 1

3 the duty or function of watching or guarding for the sake of proper direction or control — see SUPERVISION 1

regulator *n* a mechanism for adjusting the operation of a device, machine, or system — see CONTROL 1

rehabilitate *vb* **1** to make better in behavior or character — see REFORM 1

2 to restore to a healthy condition — see HEAL 1

rehabilitation *n* the process or period of gradually regaining one's health and strength — see CONVALESCENCE

rehearsal *n* a private performance or session in preparation for a public appearance ⟨We made a few mistakes in *rehearsal*, but we were pretty sure that we'd be OK on opening night.⟩

syn dry run, practice (*also* practise), trial

rel dress rehearsal; preview; drill, exercise

rehearse *vb* **1** to do over and over so as to become skilled — see PRACTICE

2 to give an oral or written account of in some detail — see TELL 1

3 to say or state again — see REPEAT 1

4 to specify one after another — see ENUMERATE 1

reimburse *vb* to make a return payment to — see REPAY

rein *n* **1** *usually* **reins** *pl* the place of leadership or command — see HEAD 2

2 the act or practice of keeping something (as an activity) within certain boundaries — see RESTRICTION 2

3 *usually* **reins** *pl* the right or means to command or control others — see POWER 1

rein (in) *vb* to keep from exceeding a desirable degree or level (as of expression) — see CONTROL 1

reiterate *vb* **1** to make or do again — see REPEAT 4

2 to say or state again — see REPEAT 1

reiteration *n* the act of saying or doing over again — see REPEAT

reiterative *adj* marked by repetition — see REPETITIVE

reject *n* **1** one who is cast out or rejected by society — see OUTCAST

2 something separated from a group or lot for not being as good as the others — see CULL

reject *vb* **1** to be unwilling to grant — see DENY 2

2 to declare not to be true — see DENY 1

3 to get rid of as useless or unwanted — see DISCARD

4 to show unwillingness to accept, do, engage in, or agree to — see DECLINE 1

rejected *adj* left unoccupied or unused — see ABANDONED 1

rejection *n* **1** a refusal to confirm the truth of a statement — see DENIAL 2

2 an unwillingness to grant something asked for — see DENIAL 1

3 something separated from a group or lot for not being as good as the others — see CULL

rejoice *vb* **1** to feel or express joy or triumph — see EXULT

2 to give satisfaction to — see PLEASE 1

rejoicing *adj* having or expressing feelings of joy or triumph — see EXULTANT

rejoicing *n* joyful or festive activity — see MERRYMAKING

rejoin *vb* to speak or write in reaction to a question or to another reaction — see ANSWER 1

rejoinder *n* something spoken or written in reaction especially to a question — see ANSWER 1

rejuvenate *vb* **1** to bring back to a former condition or vigor — see RENEW 1

2 to bring back to life, practice, or activity — see REVIVE 1

rejuvenation *n* the act or an instance of bringing something back to life, public attention, or vigorous activity — see REVIVAL

rekindle *vb* to bring back to life, practice, or activity — see REVIVE 1

relate *vb* **1** to form a close personal relationship — see COMMUNE

2 to give an oral or written account of in some detail — see TELL 1

3 to have a relation or connection — see APPLY 1

4 to think of (something) in combination — see ASSOCIATE 2

related *adj* having a close connection like that between family members ⟨the *related* fields of anthropology and archaeology⟩

---

syn synonym(s)   **rel** related words
ant antonym(s)   **near ant** near antonym(s)

syn affiliated, akin, allied, kindred

rel associated, connected, interconnected, interrelated, joined; alike, analogous, cognate, comparable, connate, correspondent, corresponding, matching, parallel, resemblant, resembling, similar, suchlike; apropos, cogent, germane, material, pertinent, relevant

near ant different, disparate, dissimilar, distinct, distinctive, diverse, other, unalike, unlike; discriminable, distinguishable

ant unrelated

relation *n* **1 relations** *pl* doings between individuals or groups ⟨*Relations* between the rival newspapers remained friendly despite their competition for the same stories.⟩

syn commerce, dealings, interaction, intercourse

rel interrelationship; cross-fertilization, cross-pollination; companionship, company

ant nonintercourse

2 a person connected with another by blood or marriage — see RELATIVE

3 the fact or state of having something in common — see CONNECTION 1

4 the state of having shared interests or efforts (as in social or business matters) — see ASSOCIATION 1

5 relations *pl* sexual union involving penetration of the vagina by the penis — see SEXUAL INTERCOURSE

relationship *n* **1** the fact or state of having something in common — see CONNECTION 1

2 the state of having shared interests or efforts (as in social or business matters) — see ASSOCIATION 1

relative *adj* **1** being such only when compared to something else — see COMPARATIVE

2 having to do with the matter at hand — see PERTINENT

relative *n* a person connected with another by blood or marriage ⟨It's always fun to see all your *relatives* at a big family gathering.⟩

syn kin, kinsman, relation

rel in-law; kinswoman; blood, clan, family, folk, house, kinfolk (*or* kinfolks), kinsfolk, line, lineage, people, race, stock, tribe

ant nonrelative

relatively *adv* to some degree or extent — see FAIRLY 1

relax *vb* **1** to get rid of nervous tension or anxiety ⟨She took deep breaths to *relax* before going on stage.⟩

syn chill, chill out [*slang*], de-stress, unwind

rel unbend; bask, kick back, loll, lounge, repose, rest; bum, dally, dawdle, dillydally, drone, footle, goof (off), idle, loaf, vegetate, zone out; alleviate, comfort, ease, relieve; calm, compose, cool, quiet, settle

phrases hang loose

ant tense (up)

2 to make less taut — see SLACKEN 1

3 to refrain from labor or exertion — see REST 1

relaxation *n* **1** activity engaged in to amuse oneself — see PLAY 1

2 freedom from activity or labor — see ¹REST 1

relaxed *adj* **1** enjoying physical comfort — see COMFORTABLE 2

2 not bound by rigid standards — see EASYGOING 2

3 not tightly fastened, tied, or stretched — see LOOSE 1

relaxing *adj* tending to calm the emotions and relieve stress — see SOOTHING 1

release *n* **1** a freeing from an obligation or responsibility ⟨Because they had legally declared bankruptcy, they received *release* from their debt.⟩

syn delivery, discharge, quietus, quittance

rel dispensation, exemption, immunity, waiver

2 a document containing a declaration of an intentional giving up of a right, claim, or privilege — see WAIVER

3 a published statement informing the public of a matter of general interest — see ANNOUNCEMENT

4 reduction of or freedom from pain — see EASE 1

release *vb* **1** to set free (from a state of being held in check) ⟨The losing player *released* his anger with a great yell of frustration.⟩

syn loose, loosen, uncork, unleash, unlock, unloose, unloosen

rel discharge, emancipate, enfranchise, free, liberate, manumit, spring, unbind, uncage, unchain, unfetter, unmoor, unshackle; air, express, vent

phrases let go

near ant handcuff, manacle, shackle, trammel; bind, confine, enchain, fetter; halter, hamper

ant bridle, check, constrain, contain, control, curb, govern, hold, inhibit, regulate, rein (in), restrain, smother, tame

2 to find emotional release for — see TAKE OUT 1

3 to release (as from slavery or confinement) — see FREE 1

4 to set free from entanglement or difficulty — see EXTRICATE

5 to throw or give off — see EMIT 1

6 to make known openly or publicly — see ANNOUNCE

7 to let go from office, service, or employment — see DISMISS 1

relent *vb* **1** to cease resistance (as to another's arguments, demands, or control) — see YIELD 3

2 to grow less in scope or intensity especially gradually — see DECREASE 2

relentless *adj* showing no signs of slackening or yielding in one's purpose — see UNYIELDING 1

relevance *n* the fact or state of being pertinent — see PERTINENCE

relevancy *n* the fact or state of being pertinent — see PERTINENCE

relevant *adj* having to do with the matter at hand — see PERTINENT

reliability *n* worthiness as the recipient of another's trust or confidence ⟨We never had reason to question the *reliability* of the park rangers in the event of an emergency.⟩

syn dependability, reliableness, responsibility, solidity, solidness, sureness, trustworthiness *rel* inerrancy, infallibility; credibility, creditability, creditableness

near ant doubtfulness, dubiousness, questionableness, shakiness, uncertainness

ant unreliability

reliable *adj* worthy of one's trust — see DEPENDABLE

reliableness *n* worthiness as the recipient of another's trust or confidence — see RELIABILITY

reliance *n* **1** something or someone to which one looks for support — see DEPENDENCE 2

2 the quality or state of needing something or someone — see DEPENDENCE 1

relic *n* **1** a tiny often physical indication of something lost or vanished — see VESTIGE 1

2 something belonging to or surviving from an earlier period — see ANTIQUE

relief *n* **1** a feeling of ease from grief or trouble — see COMFORT 1

2 a person or thing that takes the place of another — see EASE 1

3 reduction of or freedom from pain — see EASE 1

relieve *vb* **1** to make more bearable or less severe — see HELP 2

2 to set (a person or thing) free of something that encumbers — see RID

3 to take the place of — see REPLACE 1

religion *n* **1** a body of beliefs and practices regarding the supernatural and the worship of one or more deities ⟨The Jewish *religion* has followers in many parts of the globe.⟩

syn credo, creed, cult, faith, persuasion

rel church, communion, denomination, sect; doctrine, dogma, theology; deism, heathenism, monotheism, paganism, pantheism, polytheism, theism

near ant agnosticism, know-nothingism; atheism, godlessness, secularism

2 belief and trust in and loyalty to God — see FAITH 1

religious *adj* **1** of, relating to, or used in the practice or worship services of a religion ⟨Johann Sebastian Bach wrote some of the most beautiful *religious* music in the world.⟩

syn devotional, sacred, spiritual

rel blessed (*also* blest), consecrated, hallowed, holy, sacrosanct, sanctified; solemn; liturgical, ritual, sacramental; semireligious, semisacred

near ant earthly, mundane, terrestrial, worldly

ant nonreligious, profane, secular

2 showing a devotion to God and to a life of virtue — see HOLY 1

3 having or expressing great depth of feeling — see FERVENT 1

relinquish *vb* **1** to give (something) over to the control or possession of another usually under duress — see SURRENDER 1

2 to give up (as a position of authority) formally — see ABDICATE

relinquishment *n* the usually forced yielding of one's person or possessions to the control of another — see SURRENDER

relish *n* **1** positive regard for something — see LIKING

2 the feeling experienced when one's wishes are met — see PLEASURE 1

relish *vb* to take pleasure in — see ENJOY 1

reluctance *n* a lack of willingness or desire to do or accept something ⟨The mice showed an odd *reluctance* to eat the cheese we had put out for them.⟩

syn disinclination, hesitance, hesitancy, reticence, unwillingness

rel faltering, hesitation, indecision, irresolution, shilly-shallying, staggering, vacillation, wavering, wobbling (*also* wabbling); distrust, distrustfulness, doubt, incertitude, misgiving, mistrust, mistrustfulness, skepticism, suspicion, uncertainness, uncertainty

near ant assurance, assuredness, certainty, certitude, conviction, positiveness, sureness, surety

ant inclination, willingness

reluctant *adj* slow to begin or proceed with a course of action because of doubts or uncertainty — see HESITANT

rely *vb* to place reliance or trust — see DEPEND 2

remain *vb* **1** to continue to be in a place for a significant amount of time — see ¹STAY 1

2 to remain indefinitely in existence or in the same state — see CONTINUE 1

remainder *n* **1** a remaining group or portion ⟨The *remainder* of the water was saved in case it was needed later.⟩

syn balance, leavings, leftovers, odds and ends, remains, remnant, residue, rest

rel fragment, scrap, vestige; butt, oddment, scraping(s), stub, stump; excess, fat, overabundance, overage, overflow, overkill, overmuch, oversupply, superabundance, superfluity, surfeit, surplus

near ant body, bulk, main, mass, most, weight

2 an unused or unwanted piece or item typically of small size or value — see ¹SCRAP 1

remains *n pl* **1** the portion or bits of something left over or behind after it has been destroyed ⟨The *remains* of the tree ripped apart by the tornado littered the street for weeks afterward.⟩

syn ashes, debris, residue, rubble, ruins, wreck, wreckage

rel jetsam, leavings, remnant; chaff, deadwood, dross, dust, garbage, junk, litter, refuse, riffraff, rubbish, scrap, trash, waste

2 a dead body — see CORPSE

3 a remaining group or portion — see REMAINDER 1

remake *vb* **1** to make different in some way — see CHANGE 1

2 to make or do again — see REPEAT 4

remaking *n* the act, process, or result of making different — see CHANGE 1

remark *n* a briefly expressed opinion ⟨The director made some short *remarks* about the new museum before officially opening the doors to visitors.⟩

syn comment, note, reflection

rel analysis, commentary, exposition; belief, conviction, eye, feeling, judgment (*or* judgement), mind, notion, persuasion, sentiment, verdict, view; advice, input

remark *vb* **1** to make a statement of one's

---

syn synonym(s)   *rel* related words
ant antonym(s)   *near ant* near antonym(s)

opinion ⟨The mayor *remarked* on how quickly the building project was progressing.⟩

syn allow, comment, note, observe, opine, reflect

rel commentate; articulate, express, say, speak, state, talk, tell, utter, verbalize, vocalize; conjecture, guess, speculate, suppose, surmise

2 to make note of (something) through the use of one's eyes — see SEE 1

remarkable *adj* **1** different from the ordinary in a way that causes curiosity or suspicion — see ODD 2

2 likely to attract attention — see NOTICEABLE

3 worth remembering or mentioning — see NOTEWORTHY

remediable *adj* capable of being corrected ⟨The problems with the local transportation system were severe but still *remediable*.⟩

syn correctable, fixable, repairable, reparable

rel amendable, emendable, improvable, resolvable; reversible, reformable, regenerable; corrected, fixed, remedied, repaired

near ant irretrievable, unrecoverable; irreplaceable, irreversible, irrevocable

ant incorrigible, irrecoverable, irredeemable, irremediable, irreparable, unredeemable

remedial *adj* serving to raise or adjust something to some standard or proper condition — see CORRECTIVE 1

remedy *n* **1** a substance or preparation used to treat disease — see MEDICINE

2 something that corrects or counteracts something undesirable — see CURE 1

remedy *vb* **1** to bring about recovery from — see CURE 1

2 to remove errors, defects, deficiencies, or deviations from — see CORRECT 1

remedying *adj* serving to raise or adjust something to some standard or proper condition — see CORRECTIVE 1

remember *vb* to bring back to mind ⟨I *remember* very clearly the fun we had that long-ago summer, but I can't *remember* what I had for lunch yesterday.⟩

syn hark back (to), recall, recollect, reminisce (about), think (of)

rel recapture, recur; educe, elicit, evoke, extract, raise, remind; relive; represent

near ant misremember; disregard, ignore, neglect, overlook; lose, miss; blank (out)

ant forget, unlearn

remembrance *n* **1** a particular act or instance of recalling or the thing remembered — see MEMORY 2

2 something that serves to keep alive the memory of a person or event — see MEMORIAL

3 the power or process of recalling what has been previously learned or experienced — see MEMORY 1

reminder *n* something that serves to keep alive the memory of a person or event — see MEMORIAL

reminisce (about) *vb* to bring back to mind — see REMEMBER

reminiscence *n* **1** a particular act or instance of recalling or the thing remembered — see MEMORY 2

2 the power or process of recalling what has been previously learned or experienced — see MEMORY 1

reminiscent *adj* provoking a memory or mental association — see SUGGESTIVE 2

remiss *adj* failing to give proper care and attention — see NEGLIGENT

remissible *adj* worthy of forgiveness — see VENIAL

remission *n* release from the guilt or penalty of an offense — see PARDON

remit *vb* **1** to grow less in scope or intensity especially gradually — see DECREASE 2

2 to dismiss as of little importance — see EXCUSE 1

3 to assign to a later time — see POSTPONE

remitment *n* the act of offering money in exchange for goods or services — see PAYMENT 1

remittable *adj* worthy of forgiveness — see VENIAL

remittal *n* release from the guilt or penalty of an offense — see PARDON

remittance *n* **1** something (as money) that is given or received in return for goods or services — see PAYMENT 2

2 the act of offering money in exchange for goods or services — see PAYMENT 1

remnant *n* **1** a remaining group or portion — see REMAINDER 1

2 an unused or unwanted piece or item typically of small size or value — see ¹SCRAP 1

remodel *vb* to make different in some way — see CHANGE 1

remodeling *n* the act, process, or result of making different — see CHANGE 1

remonstrance *n* a feeling or declaration of disapproval or dissent — see OBJECTION

remonstrate (with) *vb* to present an opposing opinion or argument — see OBJECT

remorse *n* a feeling of responsibility for wrongdoing — see GUILT 1

remorseful *adj* feeling sorrow for a wrong that one has done — see CONTRITE

remorsefulness *n* a feeling of responsibility for wrongdoing — see GUILT 1

remorseless *adj* **1** not sorry for having done wrong ⟨The *remorseless* criminal was sentenced to life in prison without chance of parole.⟩

syn impenitent, shameless, unashamed, unrepentant

rel cruel, merciless, pitiless, ruthless, unmerciful; evil, immoral, iniquitous, nefarious, reprobate, unregenerate, vicious, vile, villainous, wicked; callous, cold-blooded, heartless, inhuman, inhumane, soulless, unfeeling

near ant hangdog, shamefaced; charitable, compassionate, humane, merciful, sensitive, softhearted, sympathetic, tender, tenderhearted, warm, warmhearted

ant apologetic, ashamed, contrite, guilty, penitent, regretful, remorseful, repentant, rueful, shamed, sorry

2 having or showing a lack of sympathy or tender feelings — see HARD 1

remote *adj* **1** small in degree ⟨There's a *remote* chance that it'll rain today, so I brought an umbrella.⟩

syn fragile, frail, negligible, off, outside, slight, slim, small

rel minimal, minor; little, tiny

near ant great, large; distinct, significant; considerable, goodly, healthy, largish, respectable, significant, sizable (*or* sizeable), substantial, tidy

ant good

2 having or showing a lack of friendliness or interest in others — see COOL 1

3 screened or sequestered from view — see SECLUDED

4 not close in time or space — see DISTANT 1

remotest *adj* most distant from a center — see EXTREME 1

removal *n* the getting rid of whatever is unwanted or useless — see DISPOSAL 1

remove *n* the space or amount of space between two points, lines, surfaces, or objects — see DISTANCE 1

remove *vb* **1** to rid oneself of (a garment) ⟨I *removed* my coat as soon as I got inside.⟩

syn doff, douse, peel (off), put off, shrug off, take off

rel husk, shed; kick (off); disrobe, strip, undress

near ant wear; apparel, array, attire, bedeck, clothe, dress, garb, rig, robe, suit

ant don, put on, slip (into), throw (on)

2 to take away from a place or position ⟨He carefully *removed* the old manuscript from the shelf.⟩

syn clear, draw, take out, withdraw

rel demount, dislodge; abstract, cut, draw off, draw out, extract, pull; budge, dislocate, displace, disturb, move, shift, transfer, transpose

near ant mount; anchor, clamp, fix, hitch, moor, secure, set; embed (*also* imbed), entrench (*also* intrench), implant, ingrain (*also* engrain), lodge, root; set up, site, situate, stick

ant place, position, put

3 to change the place or position of — see MOVE 1

4 to let go from office, service, or employment — see DISMISS 1

removed *adj* not close in time or space — see DISTANT 1

remunerate *vb* **1** to give (someone) the sum of money owed for goods or services received — see PAY 1

2 to provide (someone) with a just payment for loss or injury — see COMPENSATE 1

remuneration *n* **1** the act of offering money in exchange for goods or services — see PAYMENT 1

2 payment to another for a loss or injury — see COMPENSATION 1

3 something (as money) that is given or received in return for goods or services — see PAYMENT 2

remunerative *adj* yielding a profit — see PROFITABLE 1

rend *vb* to cause (something) to separate into jagged pieces by violently pulling at it — see TEAR 1

render *vb* **1** to give (something) over to the control or possession of another usually under duress — see SURRENDER 1

2 to make an exact likeness of — see COPY 1

3 to give a representation or account of in words — see DESCRIBE 1

rendezvous *n* **1** a place for spending time or for socializing — see HANGOUT

2 an agreement to be present at a specified time and place — see ENGAGEMENT 2

rendezvous *vb* to come together into one body or place — see ASSEMBLE 1

renegade *n* a person who abandons a cause or organization usually without right ⟨a band of *renegades* who had deserted their infantry units⟩

syn apostate, defector, deserter, recreant

rel betrayer, double-crosser, quisling, traitor, traitress (*or* traitoress), turncoat; abandoner, dropout, leaver; defier, insurgent, insurrectionary, insurrectionist, mutineer, rebel, red, revolter, revolutionary, revolutionist; discontent, malcontent

near ant adherent, disciple, follower, supporter; fanatic, militant, partisan (*also* partizan), zealot

ant loyalist

renege *vb* **1** to break a promise or agreement ⟨My so-called best friend promised to help me move, only to *renege* come Saturday morning.⟩

syn back down, back off, cop out

rel chicken (out), wimp out; backpedal, backtrack; disavow, recall, recant, repudiate, retract, take back, unsay, withdraw; beg off

phrases go back on

near ant adhere (to); comply (with), fulfill (*or* fulfil), honor, keep, satisfy

2 to solemnly or formally reject or go back on (as something formerly adhered to) — see ABJURE 1

renew *vb* **1** to bring back to a former condition or vigor ⟨The trip to New York *renewed* our enthusiasm for travel.⟩

syn freshen, recreate, refresh, refreshen, regenerate, rejuvenate, repair, restore, resuscitate, revitalize, revive

rel make over, overhaul, reclaim, recondition, reconstitute, redesign, redevelop, redo, reengineer, refurbish, rehab, rehabilitate, remake, remodel, renovate; refill, replenish, resupply

2 to begin again or return to after an interruption — see RESUME

3 to bring back to life, practice, or activity — see REVIVE 1

4 to make or do again — see REPEAT 4

renewal *n* **1** the act of saying or doing over again — see REPEAT

2 the act or an instance of bringing something back to life, public attention, or vigorous activity — see REVIVAL

renewed *adj* made or become fresh in spirits or vigor — see NEW 4

renounce *vb* **1** to give up (as a position of authority) formally — see ABDICATE

2 to solemnly or formally reject or go back on (as something formerly adhered to) — see ABJURE 1

renouncement *n* the act or practice of giving up or rejecting something once enjoyed or desired — see RENUNCIATION

---

syn synonym(s)   *rel* related words
ant antonym(s)   *near ant* near antonym(s)

renovate vb to put into good shape or working order again — see MEND 1

renown n the fact or state of being known to the public — see FAME 1

renowned adj widely known — see FAMOUS 1

rent n 1 a long deep cut — see GASH

2 an open space in a barrier (as a wall or hedge) — see GAP 1

rent vb 1 to give the possession and use of (something) in return for periodic payment ⟨We *rented* the apartment to a college student for $500 a month.⟩

syn lease

rel charter, engage, hire; lodge; sublease, sublet

2 to take or get the temporary use of (something) for a set sum — see HIRE 1

renter n 1 one who rents a room or apartment in another's house — see TENANT 1

2 the owner of land or housing that is rented to another — see LANDLORD

renunciation n the act or practice of giving up or rejecting something once enjoyed or desired ⟨His sudden *renunciation* of his smoking habit pleased his whole family.⟩

syn renouncement, repudiation, self-denial

rel denial, refusal; relinquishment, resignation, surrender; self-abnegation, self-renunciation

near ant acceptance; adoption, embrace, embracement, espousal

ant indulgence, self-indulgence

reopen vb to begin again or return to after an interruption — see RESUME

rep n a person who acts or does business for another — see AGENT 2

repair n a state of being or fitness — see CONDITION 1

repair vb 1 to bring back to a former condition or vigor — see RENEW 1

2 to put into good shape or working order again — see MEND 1

repairable adj capable of being corrected — see REMEDIABLE

reparable adj capable of being corrected — see REMEDIABLE

reparation n payment to another for a loss or injury — see COMPENSATION 1

repartee n 1 a quick witty response — see RETORT 1

2 good-natured teasing or exchanging of clever remarks — see BANTER

repast n food eaten or prepared for eating at one time — see MEAL

repay vb to make a return payment to ⟨I *repaid* my friend the $20 he had lent me.⟩

syn refund, reimburse

rel give back, render (to); compensate, recompense, remunerate; liquidate, pay down, pay off, pay up, quit, satisfy, settle; reciprocate, requite

phrases pay back

repeal n the act of putting an end to something planned or previously agreed to — see CANCELLATION

repeal vb 1 to put an end to (something planned or previously agreed to) — see CANCEL 1

2 to put an end to by formal action — see ABOLISH 1

3 to solemnly or formally reject or go back on (as something formerly adhered to) — see ABJURE 1

repeat n the act of saying or doing over again ⟨If we don't want a *repeat* of last year's disastrous celebration, we had better do some more planning.⟩

syn duplication, redo, reduplication, reiteration, renewal, repetition, replication

rel rebroadcast, rerun; recitation, rehearsal

repeat vb 1 to say or state again ⟨I *repeated* the address over and over until I had it memorized.⟩

syn chime, din, rehearse, reiterate

rel paraphrase, reword; echo, reecho; mouth, parrot; abstract, encapsulate, epitomize, outline, recap, recapitulate, summarize, sum up

phrases come again

2 to give from memory ⟨Kate *repeated* correctly all the verses she had memorized.⟩

syn recite, reel off, say

rel con, learn, memorize, study; declaim, mouth, orate, speak

near ant read

3 to say after another ⟨Now *repeat* the oath after me.⟩

syn echo, parrot, quote, reecho

rel mouth; ape, copy, copycat, emulate, imitate, mime, mimic

4 to make or do again ⟨Try not to *repeat* your mistakes.⟩

syn duplicate, redo, reduplicate, reiterate, remake, renew, replicate

rel recreate, reenact, reinvent

repeated adj appearing or occurring repeatedly from time to time — see REGULAR 1

repeatedly adv many times — see OFTEN

repel vb 1 to drive back ⟨The defenders *repelled* the attacking army after several hours of fierce fighting.⟩

syn fend (off), rebut, repulse, stave off

rel defy, fight, hold off, oppose, resist, stand off, withstand; deflect, ward (off); rebuff, snub, spurn

near ant embrace, hail, welcome

2 to cause to feel disgust — see DISGUST

3 to refuse to give in to — see RESIST

repelled adj filled with disgust — see SICK 2

repellent also **repellant** adj causing intense displeasure, disgust, or resentment — see OFFENSIVE 1

repent vb to feel sorry or dissatisfied about — see REGRET

repentance n a feeling of responsibility for wrongdoing — see GUILT 1

repentant adj feeling sorrow for a wrong that one has done — see CONTRITE

repercussion n the power to bring about a result on another — see EFFECT 2

repetition n the act of saying or doing over again — see REPEAT

repetitious adj marked by repetition — see REPETITIVE

repetitive adj marked by repetition ⟨the *repetitive* lyrics of so many rock songs⟩

syn reiterative, repetitious

rel redundant

rephrase vb to express something (as a text or statement) in different words — see PARAPHRASE

rephrasing n an instance of expressing

something in different words — see PARA-PHRASE

repine (for) *vb* to have an earnest wish to own or enjoy — see DESIRE 1

replace *vb* **1** to take the place of ⟨The old street lights were *replaced* by more energy-efficient models.⟩
syn cut out, displace, relieve, substitute, supersede, supplant
rel preempt, usurp
2 to bring, send, or put back to a former or proper place — see RETURN 1

replacement *n* a person or thing that takes the place of another — see SUBSTITUTE

replete *adj* **1** having an excess of body fat — see FAT 1
2 possessing or covered with great numbers or amounts of something specified — see RIFE
3 having one's appetite completely satisfied — see FULL 3

replica *n* **1** something or someone that strongly resembles another — see IMAGE 1
2 something that is made to look exactly like something else — see COPY

replicate *vb* **1** to make an exact likeness of — see COPY 1
2 to make or do again — see REPEAT 4

replication *n* **1** something that is made to look exactly like something else — see COPY
2 the act of saying or doing over again — see REPEAT

reply *n* **1** action or behavior that is done in return to other action or behavior — see REACTION
2 something spoken or written in reaction especially to a question — see ANSWER 1

reply *vb* **1** to act or behave in response (as to a stimulus or influence) — see REACT
2 to speak or write in reaction to a question or to another reaction — see ANSWER 1

report *n* **1** a loud explosive sound — see CLAP 1
2 a relating of events usually in the order in which they happened — see ACCOUNT 1
3 overall quality as seen or judged by people in general — see REPUTATION
4 information or opinion that is widely disseminated without any authority or confirmation of accuracy — see RUMOR

report *vb* **1** to give an oral or written account of in some detail — see TELL 1
2 to make a written note of — see RECORD 1

reporter *n* a person employed by a newspaper, magazine, or radio or television station to gather, write, or report news ⟨The *reporter* was careful to ask as many questions as possible without annoying anyone.⟩
syn correspondent, journalist, newsman
rel broadcaster, newspaperman, newswoman; anchor, anchorman, anchorperson, anchorwoman; columnist, commentator; copyreader, editor; muckraker, photojournalist, police reporter, sportswriter

repose *n* **1** a natural periodic loss of consciousness during which the body restores itself — see SLEEP 1

2 a state of freedom from storm or disturbance — see CALM 1
3 freedom from activity or labor — see ¹REST 1
4 evenness of emotions or temper — see EQUANIMITY

¹repose *vb* **1** to remain out of sight — see ¹HIDE 3
2 to refrain from labor or exertion — see ¹REST 1

²repose *vb* to put (something) into the possession or safekeeping of another — see GIVE 2

repository *n* a building for storing goods — see STOREHOUSE

repossess *vb* to get again in one's possession — see RECOVER 1

repossession *n* the act or process of getting something back — see RECOVERY 1

reprehend *vb* **1** to declare to be morally wrong or evil — see CONDEMN 1
2 to express one's unfavorable opinion of the worth or quality of — see CRITICIZE

reprehensible *adj* **1** deserving reproach or blame — see BLAMEWORTHY
2 provoking or likely to provoke protest — see OBJECTIONABLE

represent *vb* **1** to point out the chief quality or qualities of an individual or group — see CHARACTERIZE 1
2 to present a picture of — see PICTURE 1
3 to serve as a material counterpart of — see SYMBOLIZE

representative *adj* **1** having or showing the qualities associated with the members of a particular group or kind — see TYPICAL 1
2 having the function or meaning of an object or figure that stands for something else — see SYMBOLIC

representative *n* **1** a person who acts or does business for another — see AGENT 2
2 a person sent on a mission to represent another — see AMBASSADOR
3 one of a group or collection that shows what the whole is like — see EXAMPLE

repress *vb* **1** to put a stop to (something) by the use of force — see QUELL 1
2 to refrain from openly showing or uttering — see SUPPRESS 2

repression *n* the checking of one's true feelings and impulses when dealing with others — see CONSTRAINT 1

reprimand *n* an often public or formal expression of disapproval — see CENSURE

reprimand *vb* **1** to criticize (someone) severely or angrily especially for personal failings — see SCOLD
2 to criticize (someone) so as to correct a fault — see REBUKE 1
3 to express public or formal disapproval of — see CENSURE

reprisal *n* **1** *usually* **reprisals** *pl* payment to another for a loss or injury — see COMPENSATION 1
2 the act or an instance of responding to an injury with an injury — see REVENGE

reproach *n* **1** a cause of shame — see DISGRACE 2
2 an often public or formal expression of disapproval — see CENSURE
3 the state of having lost the esteem of others — see DISGRACE 1

reproach *vb* **1** to criticize (someone) severely or angrily especially for personal failings — see SCOLD

2 to criticize (someone) so as to correct a fault — see REBUKE 1

3 to express public or formal disapproval of — see CENSURE 1

reproachable *adj* deserving reproach or blame — see BLAMEWORTHY

reprobate *adj* having or showing lowered moral character or standards — see CORRUPT

reprobate *n* a mean, evil, or unprincipled person — see VILLAIN

reprobate *vb* **1** to be unwilling to grant — see DENY 2

2 to show unwillingness to accept, do, engage in, or agree to — see DECLINE 1

3 to declare to be morally wrong or evil — see CONDEMN 1

reproduce *vb* **1** to bring forth offspring — see PROCREATE

2 to make an exact likeness of — see COPY 1

reproduction *n* something that is made to look exactly like something else — see COPY

reproof *n* an often public or formal expression of disapproval — see CENSURE

reprove *vb* **1** to criticize (someone) so as to correct a fault — see REBUKE 1

2 to express public or formal disapproval of — see CENSURE 1

3 to hold an unfavorable opinion of — see DISAPPROVE (OF)

republic *n* government in which the supreme power is held by the people and used by them directly or indirectly through representation — see DEMOCRACY

republican *adj* of, relating to, or favoring political democracy — see DEMOCRATIC

repudiate *vb* **1** to declare not to be true — see DENY 1

2 to refuse to acknowledge as one's own or as one's responsibility — see DISCLAIM 1

3 to show unwillingness to accept, do, engage in, or agree to — see DECLINE 1

4 to solemnly or formally reject or go back on (as something formerly adhered to) — see ABJURE 1

repudiation *n* **1** a refusal to confirm the truth of a statement — see DENIAL 2

2 the act or practice of giving up or rejecting something once enjoyed or desired — see RENUNCIATION

repugnance *n* a dislike so strong as to cause stomach upset or queasiness — see DISGUST

repugnant *adj* **1** causing intense displeasure, disgust, or resentment — see OFFENSIVE 1

2 not being in agreement or harmony — see INCONSISTENT 1

repulse *n* treatment that is deliberately unfriendly — see COLD SHOULDER

repulse *vb* **1** to cause to feel disgust — see DISGUST

2 to drive back — see REPEL 1

repulsed *adj* filled with disgust — see SICK 2

repulsion *n* a dislike so strong as to cause stomach upset or queasiness — see DISGUST

repulsive *adj* causing intense displeasure, disgust, or resentment — see OFFENSIVE 1

repulsiveness *n* the quality of inspiring intense dread or dismay — see HORROR 1

reputable *adj* having a good reputation especially in a field of knowledge — see RESPECTABLE 1

reputation *n* overall quality as seen or judged by people in general ⟨The college's athletic department has a good *reputation*, but the school's science facilities are a bit lacking.⟩

syn character, fame, mark, name, note, odor, report, repute

rel credit, honor; celebrity, notoriety, renown; image, persona; admiration, regard, reverence

near ant discredit, disgrace, dishonor, disrepute, ignominy, infamy, odium, opprobrium, reproach, shame

repute *n* overall quality as seen or judged by people in general — see REPUTATION

reputed *adj* **1** appearing to be true on the basis of evidence that may or may not be confirmed — see APPARENT 1

2 having a good reputation especially in a field of knowledge — see RESPECTABLE 1

request *n* **1** an act or instance of asking for information — see QUESTION 2

2 the state of being sought after especially for purchase — see DEMAND 2

request *vb* **1** to give a request or demand for — see ORDER 2

2 to make a request for — see ASK (FOR) 1

3 to make a request of — see ASK 2

requiem *n* a composition expressing one's grief over a loss — see LAMENT 2

require *vb* to have as a requirement — see NEED 1

required *adj* **1** forcing one's compliance or participation by or as if by law — see MANDATORY

2 impossible to do without — see ESSENTIAL 1

requirement *n* something necessary, indispensable, or unavoidable — see ESSENTIAL 1

requisite *adj* impossible to do without — see ESSENTIAL 1

requisite *n* something necessary, indispensable, or unavoidable — see ESSENTIAL 1

requisition *n* something that someone insists upon having — see DEMAND 1

requisition *vb* to give a request or demand for — see ORDER 2

requital *n* **1** payment to another for a loss or injury — see COMPENSATION 1

2 something (as money) that is given or received in return for goods or services — see PAYMENT 2

3 the act or an instance of responding to an injury with an injury — see REVENGE

requite *vb* **1** to provide (someone) with a just payment for loss or injury — see COMPENSATE 1

2 to punish in kind the wrongdoer responsible for — see AVENGE

rescind *vb* **1** to put an end to (something planned or previously agreed to) — see CANCEL 1

2 to put an end to by formal action — see ABOLISH 1

rescission *n* the act of putting an end to something planned or previously agreed to — see CANCELLATION

rescue *n* the saving from danger or evil — see SALVATION

rescue *vb* to remove from danger or harm — see SAVE 2

rescuer *n* one that saves from danger or destruction — see SAVIOR

research *n* a systematic search for the truth or facts about something — see INQUIRY 1

research *vb* to search through or into — see EXPLORE 1

resemblance *n* **1** a point which two or more things share in common — see SIMILARITY 2

2 the quality or state of having many qualities in common — see SIMILARITY 1

resembling *adj* having qualities in common — see ALIKE

resentful *adj* **1** having or showing deep-seated resentment — see BITTER 1

2 having or showing mean resentment of another's possessions or advantages — see ENVIOUS

resentfully *adv* with feelings of bitterness or grief — see HARD 2

resentment *n* **1** a lingering ill will towards a person for a real or imagined wrong — see GRUDGE 1

2 a painful awareness of another's possessions or advantages and a desire to have them too — see ENVY

3 the feeling of being offended or resentful after a slight or indignity — see PIQUE

reservation *n* **1** a feeling or attitude that one does not know the truth, truthfulness, or trustworthiness of someone or something — see DOUBT

2 something upon which the carrying out of an agreement or offer depends — see CONDITION 2

reserve *n* **1** the checking of one's true feelings and impulses when dealing with others — see CONSTRAINT 1

2 a collection of things kept available for future use or need — see STORE 1

3 a person or thing that takes the place of another — see SUBSTITUTE

4 an interchangeable part or piece of equipment that is kept on hand for replacement of an original — see SPARE

reserve *vb* **1** to arrange to have something (as a hotel room) held for one's future use ⟨We made sure to *reserve* a kennel for our dog several months before the start of the family vacation.⟩
syn bespeak, book
rel earmark; contract, engage, hire, retain
2 to continue to have in one's possession or power — see KEEP 2
3 to keep or intend for a special purpose — see DEVOTE 1

reserved *adj* inclined not to speak frequently (as by habit or inclination) — see SILENT 2

reside *vb* to have a home — see LIVE 1

residence *n* the place where one lives — see HOME 1

resident *n* one who lives permanently in a place — see INHABITANT

resider *n* one who lives permanently in a place — see INHABITANT

residue *n* **1** the portion or bits of something left over or behind after it has been destroyed — see REMAINS 1

2 a remaining group or portion — see REMAINDER 1

resign *vb* to give up (as a position of authority) formally — see ABDICATE

resign (from) *vb* to give up (a job or office) — see QUIT 1

resigned *adj* receiving or enduring without offering resistance — see PASSIVE

resilient *adj* able to revert to original size and shape after being stretched, squeezed, or twisted — see ELASTIC 1

resist *vb* to refuse to give in to ⟨It is important to *resist* the temptation to run away from your problems.⟩
syn buck, defy, fight, oppose, repel, withstand
rel battle, combat, contend (with); challenge, contest, contradict, dispute; baffle, balk, foil, frustrate, thwart; check, counter, hinder, obstruct, stem
ant bow (to), capitulate (to), give in (to), knuckle under (to), stoop (to), submit (to), succumb (to), surrender (to), yield (to)

resistance *n* **1** the inclination to resist ⟨After some initial *resistance*, the city council warmed up to the proposed development plan.⟩
syn defiance, opposition
rel demur, objection, protest, remonstrance; compunction, misgiving, reservation; disobedience, noncompliance, recalcitrance; contrariety, contrariness
near ant compliance, obedience; acceptance, approval
ant acquiescence
2 a secret organization in a conquered country fighting against enemy forces ⟨Soldiers from the *resistance* were captured after a skirmish outside the foreign ministry.⟩
syn underground
rel cabal, conspiracy

resolute *adj* fully committed to achieving a goal — see DETERMINED 1

resoluteness *n* firm or unwavering adherence to one's purpose — see DETERMINATION 1

resolution *n* **1** a position arrived at after consideration — see DECISION 1

2 firm or unwavering adherence to one's purpose — see DETERMINATION 1

resolvable *adj* capable of having the reason for or cause of determined — see SOLVABLE

resolve *n* firm or unwavering adherence to one's purpose — see DETERMINATION 1

resolve *vb* **1** to come to a judgment about after discussion or consideration — see DECIDE 1

2 to find an answer for through reasoning — see SOLVE

3 to set or force apart — see SEPARATE 1

resolved *adj* fully committed to achieving a goal — see DETERMINED 1

resonant *adj* marked by conspicuously

---

syn synonym(s)   **rel** related words
ant antonym(s)   **near ant** near antonym(s)

full and rich sounds or tones ⟨The orator's *resonant* voice filled the hall.⟩

syn golden, resounding, reverberant, reverberating, rotund, round, sonorous, vibrant

rel deep, full, mellifluous, mellow, rich; loud, powerful, stentorian, thunderous

near ant cavernous, hollow; faint, low, murmurous, muted, smothered, soft, weak; thin, tinny

resonate *vb* to continue or be repeated in a series of reflected sound waves — see REVERBERATE

resort *n* 1 a place for spending time or for socializing — see HANGOUT

2 something that one uses to accomplish an end especially when the usual means is not available — see RESOURCE 1

resort (to) *vb* 1 to use or seek out as a source of aid, relief, or advantage ⟨He had to *resort* to asking his parents for money.⟩

syn consult, go (to), refer (to), turn (to)

rel employ, use, utilize; depend (on), rely (on)

phrases fall back on

2 to go to or spend time in often — see FREQUENT

resound *vb* 1 to proclaim the glory of — see PRAISE 1

2 to continue or be repeated in a series of reflected sound waves — see REVERBERATE

resounding *adj* 1 full of or characterized by the presence of noise — see NOISY 2

2 marked by a high volume of sound — see LOUD 1

3 marked by conspicuously full and rich sounds or tones — see RESONANT

4 marked by or uttered with forcefulness — see EMPHATIC 1

resource *n* 1 something that one uses to accomplish an end especially when the usual means is not available ⟨We used every possible *resource* to raise the funds needed to save our town's oldest house.⟩

syn expedient, recourse, resort

rel hope, opportunity, possibility; relief; makeshift, replacement, stopgap, substitute

2 **resources** *pl* available money — see FUND 2

respect *n* 1 relation to or concern with something specified ⟨with *respect* to your application⟩

syn reference, regard

2 a feeling of great approval and liking — see ADMIRATION

3 **respects** *pl* best wishes — see COMPLIMENT 2

respect *vb* to think very highly or favorably of — see ADMIRE

respectable *adj* 1 having a good reputation especially in a field of knowledge ⟨No *respectable* dietician would advise people to eat just one kind of food.⟩

syn esteemed, name, prestigious, reputable, reputed, respected

rel honorable, venerable, worthy; creditable, good, praiseworthy; celebrated, distinguished, famed, famous, honored, illustrious, notable, prominent, redoubtable, renowned, well-known

near ant seedy, shadowy, shady; obscure, undistinguished, unknown

ant disreputable

2 following the accepted rules of moral conduct — see HONORABLE 1

3 following the established traditions of refined society and good taste — see PROPER 1

4 of a level of quality that meets one's needs or standards — see ADEQUATE

5 sufficiently large in size, amount, or number to merit attention — see CONSIDERABLE 1

respected *adj* having a good reputation especially in a field of knowledge — see RESPECTABLE 1

respectful *adj* marked by or showing proper regard for another's higher status ⟨The children were remarkably *respectful* while in the president's office.⟩

syn deferential, dutiful, regardful

rel reverent, reverential, venerating, worshipful; fawning, groveling (*or* grovelling), kowtowing, obsequious, subservient, sycophantic, toadying; civil, courteous, gracious, polite

near ant abusive, insulting, offensive; belittling, demeaning, depreciative, depreciatory, derogatory, disparaging; contemptuous, impudent, irreverent, scornful; discourteous, insolent, rude, uncivil

ant disrespectful, undutiful

respecting *prep* having to do with — see ABOUT 1

respective *adj* not the same or shared — see SEPARATE 1

respire *vb* to inhale and exhale air — see BREATHE 1

resplendence *n* impressiveness of beauty on a large scale — see MAGNIFICENCE

respond *vb* 1 to act or behave in response (as to a stimulus or influence) — see REACT

2 to speak or write in reaction to a question or to another reaction — see ANSWER 1

response *n* 1 action or behavior that is done in return to other action or behavior — see REACTION

2 something spoken or written in reaction especially to a question — see ANSWER 1

responsibility *n* 1 the state of being held as the cause of something that needs to be set right ⟨*Responsibility* for the accident lies with the driver who was speeding.⟩

syn blame, fault, liability

rel accountability, answerability

2 something one must do because of prior agreement — see OBLIGATION 1

3 worthiness as the recipient of another's trust or confidence — see RELIABILITY

responsible *adj* 1 being the one who must meet an obligation or suffer the consequences for failing to do so ⟨The state laws hold pet owners *responsible* for any damage or injury done by improperly restrained animals.⟩

syn accountable, amenable, answerable, liable

rel beholden, indebted, obligated, obliged

near ant exempt, immune

ant irresponsible, nonaccountable, unaccountable

2 worthy of one's trust — see DEPEND-ABLE

¹rest *n* **1** freedom from activity or labor ⟨The coming weekend will provide some much needed *rest.*⟩

syn ease, leisure, relaxation, repose

rel catnapping, dozing, lazing, napping, resting, sleep, slumber, slumbering, snoozing; quiet, silence, stillness; calm, peace, peacefulness, placidity, respite, restfulness, sereneness, serenity, tranquillity (*or* tranquility)

near ant pressure, strain, stress, tenseness, tension

ant exertion, labor, toil, work

2 a natural periodic loss of consciousness during which the body restores itself — see SLEEP 1

²rest *n* a remaining group or portion — see REMAINDER 1

rest *vb* **1** to refrain from labor or exertion ⟨a beach resort that caters to fitness enthusiasts and adventurers as well as vacationers who just want to *rest*⟩

syn bask, kick back, loll, lounge, relax, repose

rel bum, hang, hang around, idle, loaf, slack (off)

near ant drudge, grub, hump, hustle, labor, moil, peg (away), plod, plow, plug, slog, strain, strive, struggle, sweat, toil, travail, work; exercise, work out

2 to be in a state of sleep — see SLEEP 1

3 to find a basis — see BASE

restart *vb* to begin again or return to after an interruption — see RESUME

restate *vb* to express something (as a text or statement) in different words — see PARAPHRASE

restatement *n* an instance of expressing something in different words — see PARAPHRASE

restating *n* an instance of expressing something in different words — see PARAPHRASE

restaurant *n* a public establishment where meals are served to paying customers for consumption on the premises ⟨When we get sick of cooking dinner at home, we like to go out to eat at a nice *restaurant.*⟩

syn café (*also* cafe), diner, grill

rel cafeteria, lunch counter, luncheonette, lunchroom, snack bar; pizzeria; coffeehouse, coffee shop, teahouse, tearoom; bar, barroom, inn, tavern

restful *adj* free from disturbing noise or uproar — see QUIET 1

restfulness *n* a state of freedom from storm or disturbance — see CALM 1

resting *adj* being in a state of suspended consciousness — see ASLEEP 1

resting *n* a natural periodic loss of consciousness during which the body restores itself — see SLEEP 1

restitution *n* payment to another for a loss or injury — see COMPENSATION 1

restive *adj* **1** given to resisting authority or another's control — see DISOBEDIENT

2 lacking or denying rest — see RESTLESS 1

restiveness *n* **1** a disturbed or uneasy state — see UNREST

2 a state of nervousness marked by sudden jerky movements — see JUMPINESS

restless *adj* **1** lacking or denying rest ⟨The worried mother spent a *restless* night, tossing and turning in bed for hours.⟩

syn restive, uneasy, unquiet, unrestful

rel agitated, distressed, disturbed, perturbed, troubled, unsettled; aflutter, anxious, dithery, edgy, het up, hung up, jittery, jumpy, nervous, nervy, tense, upset, uptight, worried

near ant calm, easy, peaceful, quiet, relaxing, tranquil

ant restful

2 marked by or causing agitation or uncomfortable feelings — see NERVOUS 2

restlessness *n* **1** a disturbed or uneasy state — see UNREST

2 the state of being bored — see BOREDOM

restorative *adj* **1** beneficial to the health of body or mind — see HEALTHFUL

2 having a renewing effect on the state of the body or mind — see TONIC 1

restore *vb* **1** to bring back to a former condition or vigor — see RENEW 1

2 to bring, send, or put back to a former or proper place — see RETURN 1

restrain *vb* **1** to keep from exceeding a desirable degree or level (as of expression) — see CONTROL 1

2 to take or keep under one's control by authority of law — see ARREST 1

restrained *adj* not excessively showy — see QUIET 2

restraint *n* **1** the checking of one's true feelings and impulses when dealing with others — see CONSTRAINT 1

2 something that limits one's freedom of action or choice — see RESTRICTION 1

3 the power to control one's actions, impulses, or emotions — see WILL 1

restrict *vb* to set bounds or an upper limit for — see LIMIT 1

restricted *adj* having distinct or certain limits — see LIMITED 1

restriction *n* **1** something that limits one's freedom of action or choice ⟨The logging company decided to relocate to another state where there would be fewer *restrictions* on its operations.⟩

syn check, condition, constraint, curb, fetter, limitation, restraint

rel proviso, qualification, reservation, stipulation, strings; ban, prohibition, proscription

near ant freedom, latitude

2 the act or practice of keeping something (as an activity) within certain boundaries ⟨The *restriction* of surfing to the southern end of the beach rankled some surfers.⟩

syn confinement, limitation, rein, stint

rel constraint, restraint; containment, isolation, segregation

result *n* **1** a condition or occurrence traceable to a cause — see EFFECT 1

2 something attained by mental effort and especially by computation — see ANSWER 2

result (in) *vb* to be the cause of (a situation, action, or state of mind) — see EFFECT

resultant *adj* coming as a result ⟨She de-

---

syn synonym(s)　　**rel** related words
ant antonym(s)　　**near ant** near antonym(s)

serves credit for the increase in sales and the *resultant* increase in profit.⟩

syn attendant, consequent, consequential, due (to)

rel accompanying, coincident, concomitant

near ant causal

resultant *n* a condition or occurrence traceable to a cause — see EFFECT 1

resume *vb* to begin again or return to after an interruption ⟨We *resumed* the game as soon as the rain had passed.⟩

syn continue, pick up, renew, reopen, restart

rel resuscitate, revive

near ant complete, conclude, consummate, end, finalize, finish; belay, break, can [*slang*], cease, check, cut, desist, discontinue, drop, halt, knock off, leave off, quit, scuttle, shut off, stay, stop, terminate

résumé *or* **resume** *also* **resumé** *n* a short statement of the main points — see SUMMARY

resurgence *n* the act or an instance of bringing something back to life, public attention, or vigorous activity — see REVIVAL

resurrect *vb* to bring back to life, practice, or activity — see REVIVE 1

resurrection *n* the act or an instance of bringing something back to life, public attention, or vigorous activity — see REVIVAL

resuscitate *vb* **1** to bring back to a former condition or vigor — see RENEW 1

2 to bring back to life, practice, or activity — see REVIVE 1

resuscitated *adj* made or become fresh in spirits or vigor — see NEW 4

resuscitation *n* the act or an instance of bringing something back to life, public attention, or vigorous activity — see REVIVAL

retail *vb* to offer for sale to the public — see MARKET

retain *vb* **1** to continue to have in one's possession or power — see KEEP 2

2 to keep, control, or experience as one's own — see HAVE 1

3 to provide with a paying job — see EMPLOY 1

retainer *n* one who works for another for wages or a salary — see EMPLOYEE

retake *vb* to get again in one's possession — see RECOVER 1

retaliate *vb* to punish in kind the wrongdoer responsible for — see AVENGE

retaliation *n* the act or an instance of responding to an injury with an injury — see REVENGE

retard *vb* to cause to move or proceed at a less rapid pace — see SLOW

retardation *n* a usually gradual decrease in the pace or level of activity of something — see SLOWDOWN

retch *vb* to discharge the contents of the stomach through the mouth — see VOMIT

rethink *vb* to consider again especially with the possibility of change or reversal — see RECONSIDER

reticence *n* a lack of willingness or desire to do or accept something — see RELUCTANCE

reticent *adj* **1** given to keeping one's activities hidden from public observation or knowledge — see SECRETIVE

2 tending not to speak frequently (as by habit or inclination) — see SILENT 2

3 slow to begin or proceed with a course of action because of doubts or uncertainty — see HESITANT

retinue *n* a body of employees or attendants who accompany and wait on a person — see CORTEGE 1

retire *vb* **1** to go to one's bed in order to sleep — see BED 1

2 to let go from office, service, or employment — see DISMISS 1

3 to move back or away (as from something difficult, dangerous, or disagreeable) — see RETREAT 1

retire (from) *vb* to give up (a job or office) — see QUIT 1

retired *adj* screened or sequestered from view — see SECLUDED

retirement *n* an act of moving away especially from something difficult, dangerous, or disagreeable — see RETREAT 1

retiring *adj* not comfortable around people — see SHY 2

retort *n* **1** a quick witty response ⟨She responded to the heckler with a scathing but hilarious *retort* that instantly won over the audience.⟩

syn comeback, repartee, riposte

rel squelch; back talk; crack, quip, sally, wisecrack, witticism, zinger; cut, insult, put-down

2 something spoken or written in reaction especially to a question — see ANSWER 1

retort *vb* to speak or write in reaction to a question or to another reaction — see ANSWER 1

retract *vb* to solemnly or formally reject or go back on (as something formerly adhered to) — see ABJURE 1

retreat *n* **1** an act of moving away especially from something difficult, dangerous, or disagreeable ⟨We made a strategic *retreat* when we realized that we were outnumbered.⟩

syn recession, retirement, withdrawal

rel rout; flinch, recoil, revulsion, shrinking; disengagement, disentanglement

ant advance, advancement

2 something (as a building) that offers cover from the weather or protection from danger — see SHELTER

retreat *vb* **1** to move back or away (as from something difficult, dangerous, or disagreeable) ⟨We *retreated* to the safety of the cellar at the first sign of the tornado.⟩

syn back away, fall back, recede, retire, withdraw

rel flee, fly; flinch, recoil, shrink; chicken (out); back down, backpedal, backtrack, climb down; detach, disengage, disentangle, pull away; abandon, depart, evacuate, go, leave, quit, vacate

phrases give ground, give way, lose ground

near ant beard, brave, brazen, breast, confront, dare, defy, face, outbrave

ant advance

2 to hasten away from something dangerous or frightening — see RUN 2

retribution *n* the act or an instance of

responding to an injury with an injury —
see REVENGE

retrieval *n* the act or process of getting
something back — see RECOVERY 1

retrieve *vb* to get again in one's possession
— see RECOVER 1

retro *adj* pleasantly reminiscent of an earlier time — see OLD-FASHIONED 1

retrograde *adj* directed, turned, or done
toward the back — see BACKWARD 1

retrograde *vb* to become worse or of less
value — see DETERIORATE 1

retrogress *vb* to go back to a previous and
usually lower state or level — see RE-
GRESS 1

retrogression *n* the act or an instance of
going back to an earlier and lower level
especially of intelligence or behavior —
see REGRESSION

retrospect *n* a usually critical look at a
past event — see REVIEW 1

retrospection *n* a usually critical look at a
past event — see REVIEW 1

return *n* 1 something spoken or written in
reaction especially to a question — see
ANSWER 1

2 an increase usually measured in money
that comes from labor, business, or property — see INCOME 1

3 the amount of money left when expenses are subtracted from the total amount
received — see PROFIT 1

return *vb* 1 to bring, send, or put back to a
former or proper place ⟨When I'm done
reading a book, I always *return* it to the
very shelf I got it from.⟩

syn replace, restore

rel reconvey

near ant remove, take

2 to produce as revenue — see YIELD 2

3 to speak or write in reaction to a question
or to another reaction — see ANSWER 1

4 to go back to a previous and usually
lower state or level — see REGRESS 1

revamp *vb* 1 to make different in some
way — see CHANGE 1

2 to prepare for publication by correcting,
rewriting, or updating — see EDIT 1

3 to put into good shape or working order
again — see MEND 1

revamping *n* the act, process, or result of
making different — see CHANGE 1

reveal *vb* 1 to make known (as information previously kept secret) ⟨At the end of
the book, the detective *reveals* the identity
of the mysterious stranger.⟩

syn bare, disclose, discover, divulge, expose, spill, tell, unbosom, uncloak, uncover, unmask, unveil

rel share; debunk, show up; unclothe, undrape; advertise, announce, blaze, broadcast, declare, placard, post, proclaim, promulgate, publicize, publish, sound; betray,
blab, give away, leak; inform, squeal, talk;
communicate, impart, relate; disinter,
rake up, smoke out, unearth

phrases bring to light, go public (with),
let the cat out of the bag (about), spill the
beans (about)

near ant camouflage, disguise; gild, gloss

(over), varnish, whitewash; becloud, bedim, befog, cloud, darken, eclipse, obscure,
overcast, overshadow, shade

ant cloak, conceal, cover (up), enshroud,
hide, mask, shroud, veil

2 to make known (something abstract)
through outward signs — see SHOW 2

revealing *adj* clearly conveying a special
meaning (as one's mood) — see EXPRES-
SIVE

revel *n* a time or instance of carefree fun
— see FLING 1

revel (in) *vb* to take pleasure in — see EN-
JOY 1

revelation *n* the act or an instance of making known something previously un-
known or concealed ⟨the *revelation* of the
movie star's secret marriage by the tab-
loids⟩ ⟨a new biography of the former
president that contains several shocking
revelations⟩

syn disclosure, divulgence, exposure

rel bombshell, kick, kicker, surprise (*also*
surprize); acknowledgment (*or* acknowledgement), admission, avowal, concession, confession

near ant concealment

revelatory *adj* clearly conveying a special
meaning (as one's mood) — see EXPRES-
SIVE

reveler *or* **reveller** *n* one who engages in
merrymaking especially in honor of a special occasion — see CELEBRANT

reveling *or* **revelling** *n* joyful or festive
activity — see MERRYMAKING

revelry *n* joyful or festive activity — see
MERRYMAKING

revenge *n* the act or an instance of responding to an injury with an injury ⟨Both
sides were determined to get *revenge* for
perceived wrongs and showed little interest in ending the feud.⟩

syn reprisal, requital, retaliation, retribution, vengeance

rel counter, counterattack, counteroffensive; castigation, chastisement, correction;
desert(s), discipline, nemesis, penalty, punishment, wrath

near ant clemency, grace, leniency, lenity,
mercy; forgiveness, pardon, remission

revenge *vb* to punish in kind the wrongdoer responsible for — see AVENGE

revengeful *adj* likely to seek revenge —
see VINDICTIVE

revenue *n* an increase usually measured in
money that comes from labor, business, or
property — see INCOME 1

reverberant *adj* marked by conspicuously
full and rich sounds or tones — see RESO-
NANT

reverberate *vb* to continue or be repeated
in a series of reflected sound waves ⟨The
sound of thunder *reverberated* from one
end of the mountain pass to the other.⟩

syn echo, reecho, resonate, resound,
sound

rel ring, roll

near ant damp, dampen, deaden, dull,
quiet

reverberating *adj* marked by conspicuously full and rich sounds or tones — see
RESONANT

---

syn synonym(s) *rel* related words

ant antonym(s) *near ant* near antonym(s)

---

revere *vb* to offer honor or respect to

(someone) as a divine power — see WOR-
SHIP 1

revered *adj* deserving honor and respect
especially by reason of age — see VENER-
ABLE 1

reverence *vb* to offer honor or respect to
(someone) as a divine power — see WOR-
SHIP 1

reverend *adj* deserving honor and respect
especially by reason of age — see VENER-
ABLE 1

reverie *also* **revery** *n* the state of being
lost in thought ⟨I was lost in *reverie* and
didn't realize my flight was boarding until
it was almost too late.⟩

syn daydreaming, study, trance, woolgathering

rel contemplation, meditation; absentmindedness, absorption, preoccupation;
chimera, conceit, daydream, delusion,
dream, fancy, fantasy (*also* phantasy), figment, hallucination, illusion, phantasm
(*also* fantasm), pipe dream

reversal *n* a change in status for the worse
usually temporarily — see REVERSE 1

reverse *n* 1 a change in status for the
worse usually temporarily ⟨The party has
suffered some major *reverses* as a result of
the corruption scandal.⟩

syn knock, lapse, reversal, setback

rel disappointment, frustration, letdown;
comedown, decline, descent, down, downfall, fall; recession, regression, retrogression, reversion; relapse; breakdown, collapse, crash, meltdown, ruin

near ant status quo

2 something that is as different as possible
from something else — see OPPOSITE

3 a behind part or surface — see REAR 1

reverse *vb* 1 to change (as an opinion) to
the contrary ⟨The appeals court *reversed*
the district court's decision.⟩

syn switch

rel abrogate, annul, overturn, repeal, rescind,
revoke; backtrack, countermand, revert

near ant maintain, support, uphold

2 to change the position of (an object) so
that the opposite side or end is showing
⟨When one side of the cleaning cloth gets
dirty, just *reverse* it.⟩ ⟨You can *reverse* the
jacket for a whole new look.⟩

syn flip, invert, turn over

rel transpose; exchange, interchange,
shift, switch; overturn, upset

reversion *n* the act or an instance of going
back to an earlier and lower level especially of intelligence or behavior — see
REGRESSION

revert *vb* to go back to a previous and usually lower state or level — see REGRESS 1

review *n* 1 a usually critical look at a past
event ⟨A *review* of yesterday's football
game gave us a lot of good ideas on how to
improve for the next one.⟩

syn reappraisal, reconsideration, reexamination, retrospect, retrospection

rel recap, recapitulation, rehash

near ant preview

2 a close look at or over someone or something in order to judge condition — see
INSPECTION

3 a publication that appears at regular intervals — see JOURNAL

4 an essay evaluating or analyzing something — see CRITICISM

5 the act, process, or result of making different — see CHANGE 1

review *vb* 1 to consider again especially
with the possibility of change or reversal
— see RECONSIDER

2 to look over closely (as for judging quality or condition) — see INSPECT

reviewer *n* a person who makes or expresses a judgment on the quality of offerings in some field of endeavor — see
CRITIC 2

revise *n* the act, process, or result of making different — see CHANGE 1

revise *vb* 1 to make different in some way
— see CHANGE 1

2 to prepare for publication by correcting,
rewriting, or updating — see EDIT 1

revision *n* the act, process, or result of
making different — see CHANGE 1

revitalization *n* the act or an instance of
bringing something back to life, public attention, or vigorous activity — see RE-
VIVAL

revitalize *vb* 1 to bring back to a former
condition or vigor — see RENEW 1

2 to bring back to life, practice, or activity
— see REVIVE 1

revival *n* the act or an instance of bringing
something back to life, public attention,
or vigorous activity ⟨There was a *revival* of
interest in the author's classic horror stories after a film version of his best-known
tale was released.⟩

syn reanimation, rebirth, regeneration,
rejuvenation, renewal, resurgence, resurrection, resuscitation, revitalization

rel renascence; reinvention; reactivation;
rally, recovery, recuperation; restoral, restoration

near ant death, expiration, extinction

revive *vb* 1 to bring back to life, practice,
or activity ⟨an effort to *revive* the once-
common custom of celebrating May 1 as a
springtime festival of games and dances⟩

syn reanimate, regenerate, rejuvenate, rekindle, renew, resurrect, resuscitate, revitalize

rel kick-start; reactivate, restart; reinvent;
refresh, refreshen

near ant extinguish, kill, quench, suppress

2 to bring back to a former condition or
vigor — see RENEW 1

3 to gain consciousness again — see COME
TO

revived *adj* made or become fresh in spirits or vigor — see NEW 4

reviving *adj* having a renewing effect on the
state of the body or mind — see TONIC 1

revocation *n* the act of putting an end to
something planned or previously agreed to
— see CANCELLATION

revoke *vb* to put an end to (something
planned or previously agreed to) — see
CANCEL 1

revolt *n* open fighting against authority (as
one's own government) — see REBELLION 1

revolt *vb* 1 to cause to feel disgust — see
DISGUST

2 to rise up against established authority
— see REBEL

revolted *adj* filled with disgust — see SICK 2

revolter *n* a person who rises up against authority — see REBEL

revolting *adj* causing intense displeasure, disgust, or resentment — see OFFENSIVE 1

revolution *n* **1** a rapid turning about on an axis or central point — see SPIN 1
2 open fighting against authority (as one's own government) — see REBELLION 1

revolutionary *adj* **1** being very far from the center of public opinion — see EXTREME 2
2 taking part in a rebellion — see REBELLIOUS 1

revolutionary *n* **1** a person who favors rapid and sweeping changes especially in laws and methods of government — see RADICAL
2 a person who rises up against authority — see REBEL

revolutionist *adj* being very far from the center of public opinion — see EXTREME 2

revolutionist *n* **1** a person who favors rapid and sweeping changes especially in laws and methods of government — see RADICAL
2 a person who rises up against authority — see REBEL

revolve *vb* **1** to move (something) in a curved or circular path on or as if on an axis — see TURN 1
2 to move in circles around an axis or center — see SPIN 1
3 to give serious and careful thought to — see PONDER

revulsion *n* a dislike so strong as to cause stomach upset or queasiness — see DISGUST

reward *n* something offered or given in return for a service performed ⟨There was a *reward* of $50 for the return of the missing cat.⟩
syn bounty, price
rel bonus, lagniappe, premium; bonanza, jackpot; award, decoration, distinction, honor, prize; gratuity, tip; desert(s), wages

reward *vb* to give something as a token of gratitude or admiration for a service or achievement ⟨The firefighters were *rewarded* by the city for their heroic actions.⟩
syn award
rel cite, decorate, honor, remember; compensate, pay, recompense, requite; reimburse, repay; acclaim, applaud, commend, compliment, hail, praise, salute

rewarding *adj* making one feel good inside — see HEARTWARMING

reweigh *vb* to consider again especially with the possibility of change or reversal — see RECONSIDER

reword *vb* to express something (as a text or statement) in different words — see PARAPHRASE

rewording *n* an instance of expressing something in different words — see PARAPHRASE

rework *vb* **1** to make different in some way — see CHANGE 1
2 to prepare for publication by correcting, rewriting, or updating — see EDIT 1

reworking *n* the act, process, or result of making different — see CHANGE 1

rhapsodic *also* **rhapsodical** *adj* experiencing or marked by overwhelming usually pleasurable emotion — see ECSTATIC

rhapsodically *adv* in an enthusiastic manner — see SKY-HIGH

rhapsodize *vb* to make an exaggerated display of affection or enthusiasm — see GUSH 2

rhapsody *n* a state of overwhelming usually pleasurable emotion — see ECSTASY

rhetoric *n* **1** language that is impressive-sounding but not meaningful or sincere ⟨The mayor's promise was just *rhetoric*, since there was no money in the city budget to fulfill it.⟩
syn bombast, gas, grandiloquence, hot air, oratory, verbiage, wind
rel claptrap, drivel, gibberish, hogwash, humbug, jabberwocky, jazz, moonshine, nonsense; affectedness, floweriness, grandiosity, loftiness, pretension, pretentiousness; verboseness, verbosity, windiness, wordiness
2 the art or power of speaking or writing in a forceful and convincing way — see ELOQUENCE

rhetorical *also* **rhetoric** *adj* **1** marked by the use of impressive-sounding but mostly meaningless words and phrases ⟨You can skip over the *rhetorical* passages and still get the gist of the essay.⟩
syn bombastic, gaseous, grandiloquent, oratorical, windy
rel elevated, florid, flowery, grandiose, high-falutin (*also* hifalutin), high-flown, high-sounding, lofty, ornate, pompous, pretentious; overdone, verbose, wordy
near ant eloquent, well-spoken; bald, direct, matter-of-fact, plain, plainspoken, simple, stark, straightforward, unadorned, unaffected, unpretentious
ant unrhetorical
2 full of fine words and fancy expressions — see FLOWERY 1
3 of or relating to words or language — see VERBAL 1

rhythm *n* the recurrent pattern formed by a series of sounds having a regular rise and fall in intensity ⟨the steady *rhythm* of the rain falling on the roof⟩
syn beat, cadence, measure, meter
rel accent, accentuation, emphasis, stress; backbeat; drum, throb; lilt, movement, sway, swing; hexameter, pentameter, tetrameter, trimeter

rhythmic *or* **rhythmical** *adj* marked by or occurring with a noticeable regularity in the rise and fall of sound ⟨lulled to sleep by the *rhythmic* sound of her mother's voice reading the beloved childhood classic⟩
syn cadenced, measured, metrical (*or* metric)
rel even, regular, steady, uniform; lilting, musical, swaying
ant arrhythmic, nonmetrical, unmeasured, unrhythmic

riata *n* a rope or long leather thong with a noose used especially for catching livestock — see LASSO

rib *n* something said or done to cause laughter — see JOKE 1

---

syn synonym(s)   *rel* related words
ant antonym(s)   *near ant* near antonym(s)

rib *vb* to make fun of in a good-natured way — see TEASE 1

ribald *adj* 1 depicting or referring to sexual matters in a way that is unacceptable in polite society — see OBSCENE 1

2 hinting at or intended to call to mind matters regarded as indecent — see SUGGESTIVE 1

ribaldry *n* the quality or state of being obscene — see OBSCENITY

ribbing *adj* marked by or expressive of mild or good-natured teasing — see QUIZZICAL

ribbon *n* a long narrow piece of material — see STRIP 1

rich *adj* 1 having goods, property, or money in abundance ⟨You would have to be quite *rich* to be able to afford a home in that neighborhood.⟩

syn affluent, flush, loaded, moneyed (*also* monied), opulent, wealthy, well-fixed, well-heeled, well-off, well-to-do

rel better-off, comfortable, propertied, prosperous, substantial, successful; flourishing, prospering, thriving; advantaged, blessed (*also* blest), privileged

phrases in the chips

near ant unaffluent; deprived, disadvantaged, hand-to-mouth, underprivileged; bankrupt, bankrupted, beggared, broke, indebted, insolvent; depressed, pinched, reduced, straitened; low, short

ant destitute, impecunious, impoverished, indigent, needy, penniless, penurious, poor, poverty-stricken

2 containing much seasoning, fat, or sugar ⟨Stay away from *rich* foods before you sleep.⟩

syn heavy

rel buttery, fat, fatty, greasy; caloric, calorific, fattening; oversweet; filling, overfilling, satiating, sating; spicy, sugary, sweet; creamy, sauced

near ant natural, plain, simple; unseasoned; diet, nonfattening, slimming; nonfat

ant light, lite

3 having an abundance of some characteristic quality (as flavor) — see FULL-BODIED

4 producing abundantly — see FERTILE

riches *n pl* the total of one's money and property — see WEALTH 1

richly *adv* in a luxurious manner — see HIGH

richness *n* the amusing quality or element in something — see HUMOR 1

ricochet *vb* to strike and fly off at an angle — see GLANCE 1

rid *vb* to set (a person or thing) free of something that encumbers ⟨worked two jobs to *rid* himself of debt⟩

syn clear, disburden, disencumber, free, relieve, unburden

rel discharge, emancipate, enfranchise, liberate, loose, loosen, manumit, release, spring, unbind, uncage, unchain, unfetter; bail (out), deliver, redeem, rescue; disengage, disentangle, extricate

near ant bog (down), fetter, hamper, restrain, shackle, subject, weight (down)

ant burden, encumber, saddle

riddance *n* the getting rid of whatever is unwanted or useless — see DISPOSAL 1

riddle *n* something hard to understand or explain — see MYSTERY

riddle *vb* 1 to make a hole or series of holes in — see PERFORATE

2 to spread throughout — see PERMEATE

ride *n* a means of getting to a destination in a vehicle driven by another ⟨an organization that provides *rides* for senior citizens⟩

syn lift, transportation

rel drive, spin, turn; joyride; conveyance, passage, transport

ride *vb* 1 to attack repeatedly with mean put-downs or insults — see TEASE 2

2 to make fun of in a good-natured way — see TEASE 1

3 to rest or move along the surface of a liquid or in the air — see FLOAT 1

4 to be determined by, based on, or subject (to) — see DEPEND 1

ride (out) *vb* to come safely through — see SURVIVE 1

ridge *n* the line formed when two sloping surfaces come together along their topmost edge ⟨pigeons roosting along the *ridge* of the roof⟩

syn crest

rel divide; backbone, ridgepole, spine; eminence, peak, prominence, promontory, rise

ridicule *n* the making of unkind jokes as a way of showing one's scorn for someone or something ⟨Though initially an object of *ridicule*, the theory turned out to be correct.⟩

syn derision, mockery, sport

rel contempt, disdain, scorn; belittlement, deprecation, disparagement; catcall, insult, put-down; laughter, snickering; burlesque, caricature, mimicry, satire

near ant applause, approval, commendation, praise

ridicule *vb* to make (someone or something) the object of unkind laughter ⟨The term "big bang theory" was originally coined to *ridicule* the belief that the universe was created by a giant explosion.⟩

syn deride, gibe (*or* jibe), jeer, laugh (at), mock, scout, skewer

rel scoff (at), scorn, sneer (at); bad-mouth, belittle, decry, disparage, pooh-pooh (*also* pooh), put down; jive, josh, kid, quiz, razz, rib, ride, tease, tweak, twit; bait, bug, catcall, harry, hassle, heckle, needle, pester, target, taunt, torment; ape, burlesque, caricature, imitate, lampoon, mimic, parody, parrot, pillory, satirize, take off (on), travesty

phrases make fun of, make sport of, poke fun at, rag on

near ant applaud, approve, commend, endorse (*also* indorse), sanction

ridiculer *n* a person who causes repeated emotional pain, distress, or annoyance to another — see TORMENTOR

ridiculous *adj* 1 so foolish or pointless as to be worthy of scornful laughter ⟨a movie thriller with such a *ridiculous* plot that it gets only guffaws from audiences⟩

syn absurd, comical, derisive, derisory, farcical, laughable, ludicrous, pathetic, preposterous, risible, silly

rel asinine, brainless, dumb, fatuous, foolish, half-baked, half-witted, harebrained, idiotic (*also* idiotical), imbecile (*or* imbecilic), inane, jerky, moronic, nonsensical, simpleminded, stupid, unwise, weak-minded, witless; balmy, cockeyed, daffy, daft, dotty, kooky (*also* kookie), screwball, senseless, wacky (*also* whacky); fantastic (*also* fantastical), far-fetched, inconceivable, incredible, unbelievable, unreal, unrealistic, unreasonable; illogical, irrational
phrases for the birds
near ant earnest, serious, solemn; believable, conceivable, credible, logical, rational, realistic, reasonable, sensible
2 causing or intended to cause laughter — see FUNNY 1

rife *adj* possessing or covered with great numbers or amounts of something specified ⟨The school was *rife* with rumors.⟩
syn abounding, abundant, awash, flush, fraught, lousy, replete, swarming, teeming, thick, thronging
rel brimming, bulging, bursting, chockfull (*or* chockful), crammed, crowded, fat, filled, full, jammed, jam-packed, loaded, packed, saturated, stuffed; clogged, congested, overcrowded, overfilled, overflowing, overfull, overladen, overloaded, overstuffed, surfeited; alive, animated, astir, bustling, busy, buzzing, humming, lively
near ant bare, barren, blank, devoid, empty, stark, vacant, void; depleted, drained, exhausted; deficient, incomplete, insufficient, short

riffraff *n* **1** discarded or useless material — see GARBAGE
2 people looked down upon as ignorant and of the lowest class — see RABBLE

rifle *vb* to look through (as a place) carefully or thoroughly in an effort to find or discover something — see SEARCH 1

rift *n* **1** an irregular usually narrow break in a surface created by pressure — see CRACK 1
2 an open space in a barrier (as a wall or hedge) — see GAP 1

rig *n* **1** a horse-drawn wheeled vehicle for carrying passengers — see CARRIAGE 1
2 covering for the human body — see CLOTHING
rig *vb* to provide (someone) with what is needed for a task or activity — see FURNISH 1

rig (out) *vb* to outfit with clothes and especially fine or special clothes — see CLOTHE 1

right *adj* **1** following an original exactly — see FAITHFUL 2
2 being exactly as appears or as claimed — see AUTHENTIC 1
3 being in agreement with the truth or a fact or a standard — see CORRECT 1
4 being what is called for by accepted standards of right and wrong — see JUST 1
5 conforming to a high standard of morality or virtue — see GOOD 2
6 free from irregularities or digressions in course — see STRAIGHT 1
7 having full use of one's mind and control over one's actions — see SANE

8 meeting the requirements of a purpose or situation — see FIT 1
right *adv* **1** as stated or indicated without the slightest difference — see EXACTLY 1
2 in a direct line or course — see DIRECTLY 1
3 to a great degree — see VERY 1
4 without delay — see IMMEDIATELY
5 in a manner suitable for the occasion or purpose — see PROPERLY

right *n* **1** something to which one has a just claim ⟨Everyone has the *right* to life, liberty, and the pursuit of happiness.⟩
syn birthright, prerogative
rel call, due, perquisite, pretense (*or* pretense), pretension, privilege
2 an entitlement to something — see CLAIM 1
3 the practice of giving to others what is their due or an instance of this — see JUSTICE 1

right away *adv* without delay — see IMMEDIATELY

righteous *adj* **1** conforming to a high standard of morality or virtue — see GOOD 2
2 following the accepted rules of moral conduct — see HONORABLE 1

righteously *adv* with purity of thought and deed — see PURELY 1

righteousness *n* **1** conduct that conforms to an accepted standard of right and wrong — see MORALITY 1
2 faithfulness to high moral standards — see HONOR 1

rightful *adj* being what is called for by accepted standards of right and wrong — see JUST 1

rightist *n* a person whose political beliefs are centered on tradition and keeping things the way they are — see CONSERVATIVE

rightly *adv* in a manner suitable for the occasion or purpose — see PROPERLY

right-minded *adj* conforming to a high standard of morality or virtue — see GOOD 2

rightness *n* **1** conduct that conforms to an accepted standard of right and wrong — see MORALITY 1
2 the quality or state of being especially suitable or fitting — see APPROPRIATENESS

right now *adv* **1** at the present time — see NOW 1
2 without delay — see IMMEDIATELY

right-of-way *n* the right to one's attention before other things considered less important — see PRIORITY

rigid *adj* **1** not allowing for any exceptions or loosening of standards ⟨*rigid* enforcement of drug laws⟩
syn exacting, inflexible, rigorous, strict, stringent, uncompromising
rel close, conscientious, exact, fussy, meticulous, painstaking, punctilious, scrupulous, undeviating; adamant, adamantine, determined, dogged, firm, relentless, resolved, single-minded, steadfast, stubborn, tenacious, unbending, unflinching; immovable, implacable, unappeasable, unrelenting, unsparing, unyielding; austere, demanding, flinty, grim, hard, hardened, harsh, severe, stern, tough

---

syn synonym(s)　*rel* related words
ant antonym(s)　*near ant* near antonym(s)

near ant acquiescent, compliant, compromising, pliable, pliant, relenting, yielding; easy, easygoing, gentle, indulgent, kindly, lenient, merciful, mild, pampering, soft, spoiling, tolerant; neglectful, negligent, remiss, slipshod, sloppy, slovenly, unfussy
ant flexible, lax, loose, relaxed, slack
2 given to exacting standards of discipline and self-restraint — see SEVERE 1
3 having a consistency that does not easily yield to pressure — see FIRM 2
4 incapable of or highly resistant to bending — see STIFF 1
5 stretched with little or no give — see TAUT

rigidity *n* the quality or state of being demanding or unyielding (as in discipline or criticism) — see SEVERITY

rigidly *adv* without any relaxation of standards or precision — see STRICTLY

rigidness *n* the quality or state of being demanding or unyielding (as in discipline or criticism) — see SEVERITY

rigmarole *also* **rigamarole** *n* language marked by abstractions, jargon, euphemisms, and circumlocutions — see GIBBERISH 2

rigor *n* **1** something that is a cause for suffering or special effort especially in the attainment of a goal — see DIFFICULTY 1
2 the quality or state of being demanding or unyielding (as in discipline or criticism) — see SEVERITY
3 the quality or state of being very accurate — see PRECISION

rigorous *adj* **1** given to exacting standards of discipline and self-restraint — see SEVERE 1
2 meeting the highest standard of accuracy — see PRECISE 1
3 not allowing for any exceptions or loosening of standards — see RIGID 1
4 requiring considerable physical or mental effort — see HARD 2

rigorously *adv* without any relaxation of standards or precision — see STRICTLY

rigorousness *n* **1** the quality or state of being demanding or unyielding (as in discipline or criticism) — see SEVERITY
2 the quality or state of being very accurate — see PRECISION

rile *vb* **1** to disturb the peace of mind of (someone) especially by repeated disagreeable acts — see IRRITATE 1
2 to make angry — see ANGER

riled *adj* feeling or showing anger — see ANGRY

riling *adj* causing annoyance — see ANNOYING

rill *n* a natural body of running water smaller than a river — see CREEK 1

rim *n* the line or relatively narrow space that marks the outer limit of something — see BORDER 1

rim *vb* to serve as a border for — see BORDER

rime *n* a covering of tiny ice crystals on a cold surface — see FROST 1

rime *vb* to cover with a hardened layer — see ENCRUST

¹ring *n* **1** a group involved in secret or criminal activities ⟨a *ring* of counterfeiters passing phony $20 bills⟩

syn cabal, conspiracy, crew, gang, Mafia, mob, syndicate
rel bunch, circle, clan, clique, coterie, crowd, galère, lot, network, pack, set; junta, oligarchy
2 a circular strip ⟨A metal *ring* encircled the barrel.⟩
syn band, circle, eye, hoop, loop, round
rel belt, cincture, collar, girdle; wreath; annulet, becket, coil, curl, furl, hank, spiral, spire, twirl, whorl
3 a group of people sharing a common interest and relating together socially — see GANG 1
4 something with a perfectly round circumference — see CIRCLE 1

²ring *n* a communication by telephone — see CALL 3

¹ring *vb* **1** to form a circle around — see SURROUND
2 to travel completely around — see ENCIRCLE 1

²ring *vb* to make the clear sound heard when metal vibrates ⟨I didn't hear the doorbell *ring*.⟩
syn chime, knell, peal, toll
rel chink, clang, clank, clash, clink, ding, ding-dong, gong, jingle, ping, plink, plunk (*or* plonk), tingle, tinkle; echo, resonate, resound, reverberate

ringer *n* **1** one who makes false claims of identity or expertise — see IMPOSTOR
2 something or someone that strongly resembles another — see IMAGE 1

ringlet *n* a length of hair that forms a loop or series of loops — see CURL

rinse *vb* to pour liquid over or through in order to cleanse — see FLUSH 1

riot *n* someone or something that is very funny — see SCREAM

riotous *adj* **1** causing or intended to cause laughter — see FUNNY 1
2 pouring forth in great amounts — see PROFUSE

rip *n* a long deep cut — see GASH

rip *vb* **1** to cause (something) to separate into jagged pieces by violently pulling at it — see TEAR 1
2 to penetrate with a sharp edge (as a knife) — see CUT 1
3 to proceed or move quickly — see HURRY 2
4 to separate or remove by forceful pulling — see TEAR 2

ripe *adj* **1** fully grown or developed — see MATURE 1
2 having an unpleasant smell — see MALODOROUS

ripen *vb* to become mature — see MATURE

ripened *adj* fully grown or developed — see MATURE 1

ripening *n* the process of becoming mature — see MATURATION

rip-off *n* an instance of theft — see THEFT 2

rip off *vb* **1** to remove valuables from (a place) unlawfully — see ROB
2 to take (something) without right and with an intent to keep — see STEAL 1
3 to rob by the use of trickery or threats — see FLEECE

riposte *n* a quick witty response — see RETORT 1

riposte *vb* to speak or write in reaction to a question or to another reaction — see ANSWER 1

ripple *vb* to flow in a broken irregular stream — see GURGLE

rip–roaring *adj* causing great emotional or mental stimulation — see EXCITING 1

rise *n* **1** a raising or a state of being raised to a higher rank or position — see ADVANCEMENT 1
2 an area of high ground — see HEIGHT 4
3 an upward slope — see ASCENT 2
4 something added (as by growth) — see INCREASE 1
5 the act or an instance of rising or climbing up — see ASCENT 1

rise *vb* **1** to become greater in extent, volume, amount, or number — see INCREASE 2
2 to leave one's bed — see ARISE 1
3 to move or extend upward — see ASCEND

risible *adj* **1** causing or intended to cause laughter — see FUNNY 1
2 so foolish or pointless as to be worthy of scornful laughter — see RIDICULOUS 1

rising *n* **1** open fighting against authority (as one's own government) — see REBELLION 1
2 the act or an instance of rising or climbing up — see ASCENT 1

risk *n* **1** something that may cause injury or harm — see DANGER 2
2 the state of not being protected from injury, harm, or evil — see DANGER 1

risk *vb* **1** to take a chance on ⟨Colette didn't want to *risk* running out of food for her party, so she bought twice what she thought she would actually need.⟩
syn adventure, chance, gamble (on), hazard, tempt, venture
rel beard, brave, brazen, breast, challenge, confront, dare, defy, face, outbrave; compromise, endanger, imperil, jeopardize, menace; expose, subject; bet (on), wager
phrases run the risk of
2 to place in danger — see ENDANGER

risky *adj* involving potential loss or injury — see DANGEROUS 1

rite *n* an oft-repeated action or series of actions performed in accordance with tradition or a set of rules ⟨the annual summer *rite* of loading up the car for the big family vacation⟩
syn ceremonial, ceremony, form, formality, observance, ritual, solemnity
rel amenities, civility, decorum, etiquette, graces, proprieties; protocol; convention, custom, habit, manners, mores, practice (*also* practise), standard, tradition, way; celebration, service

ritual *n* **1** a usual manner of behaving or doing — see HABIT 1
2 an oft-repeated action or series of actions performed in accordance with tradition or a set of rules — see RITE

rival *n* **1** one that is equal to another in status, achievement, or value — see EQUAL
2 one that takes a position opposite another in a competition or conflict — see OPPONENT 1

3 one who strives for the same thing as another — see COMPETITOR

rival *vb* to engage in a contest — see COMPETE

rivalry *n* an earnest effort for superiority or victory over another — see CONTEST 1

rive *vb* **1** to cause to separate into pieces usually suddenly or forcibly — see BREAK 1
2 to cause (something) to separate into jagged pieces by violently pulling at it — see TEAR 1

rivet *vb* to fix (as one's attention) steadily toward a central objective — see CONCENTRATE 2

riveting *adj* holding the attention or provoking interest — see INTERESTING

rivulet *n* a natural body of running water smaller than a river — see CREEK 1

road *n* **1** a passage cleared for public vehicular travel — see WAY 1
2 a roadway overlaid with parallel steel rails over which trains travel — see RAILROAD

roadhouse *n* a bar or restaurant offering special nighttime entertainment (as music, dancing, or comedy acts) — see NIGHTCLUB

roadway *n* a passage cleared for public vehicular travel — see WAY 1

roam *vb* to move about from place to place aimlessly — see WANDER 1

roamer *n* a person who roams about without a fixed route or destination — see NOMAD

roaming *adj* traveling from place to place — see ITINERANT

roar *n* **1** a violent shouting — see CLAMOR 1
2 loud, confused, and usually inharmonious sound — see NOISE 1

roar *vb* **1** to make a long loud deep noise or cry ⟨The car's engine *roared* as it sped away.⟩
syn bellow, boom, growl, thunder
rel grumble, roll, rumble; bang, blare, blast, peal, scream, screech, shriek, squall; bawl, call, cry, holler, hoot, shout, whoop, yell; howl, wail, yowl
near ant grunt, mouth, mumble, murmur, mutter, whisper; mewl, pule, squeak, whimper
2 to speak so as to be heard at a distance — see CALL 1
3 to show mirth with an explosive vocal sound — see LAUGH 1

roaring *adj* **1** marked by a high volume of sound — see LOUD 1
2 marked by vigorous growth and well-being especially economically — see PROSPEROUS 1

roaring *adv* to a great degree — see VERY 1

roast *vb* to make fun of in a good-natured way — see TEASE 1

roasting *adj* having a notably high temperature — see HOT 1

rob *vb* to remove valuables from (a place) unlawfully ⟨in jail for *robbing* a bank⟩
syn burglarize, rip off, steal (from)
rel ransack, rifle; despoil, loot, pillage, plunder, ravish, sack, spoil, strip; bleed, break in, cheat, chisel, cozen, defraud, exploit, fleece, hustle, mulct, pluck, rook, shortchange, skin, squeeze, stick, sting, swindle; hold up, mug, roll, stick up

---

syn synonym(s)   *rel* related words
ant antonym(s)   *near ant* near antonym(s)

robber *n* one who steals — see THIEF

robbery *n* the unlawful taking and carrying away of property without the consent of its owner — see THEFT 1

robe *n* something that covers or conceals like a piece of cloth — see CLOAK 1

robe *vb* to outfit with clothes and especially fine or special clothes — see CLOTHE 1

robotic *adj* 1 designed to replace or decrease human labor and especially physical labor — see LABORSAVING

2 done instantly and without conscious thought or decision — see AUTOMATIC 1

robust *adj* 1 enjoying health and vigor — see HEALTHY 1

2 having active strength of body or mind — see VIGOROUS 1

3 having an abundance of some characteristic quality (as flavor) — see FULL-BODIED

4 not showing weakness or uncertainty — see FIRM 1

robustness *n* 1 the condition of being sound in body — see HEALTH 1

2 the quality or state of having abundant or intense activity — see VITALITY 1

rock *n, slang* a usually valuable stone cut and polished for ornament — see GEM 1

rock *vb* 1 to make a series of unsteady side-to-side motions ⟨The boat was *rocking* so much that several passengers felt seasick.⟩
syn careen, lurch, pitch, roll, seesaw, sway, toss, wobble (*also* wabble)
rel blunder, buck, dodder, falter, flounder, halt, hitch, hobble, jerk, jolt, reel, shake, stagger, stumble, teeter, toddle, totter, tumble, vacillate, vibrate, waddle, waver, weave; oscillate, undulate, wag, waggle

2 to swing unsteadily back and forth or from side to side — see TEETER 1

3 to make senseless or dizzy by a blow — see STUN 1

4 to make a strong impression on (someone) with something unexpected — see SURPRISE 1

rock bottom *n* the lowest part, place, or point — see BOTTOM 3

rocket *vb* 1 to proceed or move quickly — see HURRY 2

2 to rise abruptly and rapidly — see SKYROCKET

rod *n* 1 a heavy rigid stick used as a weapon or for punishment — see CLUB 1

2 a straight piece (as of wood or metal) that is longer than it is wide — see BAR 1

rogue *adj* given to or marked by cheating and deception — see DISHONEST 2

rogue *n* 1 a mean, evil, or unprincipled person — see VILLAIN

2 an appealingly mischievous person — see SCAMP 1

roguish *adj* tending to or exhibiting reckless playfulness — see MISCHIEVOUS 1

roguishness *n* playful, reckless behavior that is not intended to cause serious harm — see MISCHIEF 1

roil *vb* 1 to be in a state of violent rolling motion — see SEETHE 1

2 to make angry — see ANGER

roiled *adj* 1 feeling or showing anger — see ANGRY

2 having visible particles in liquid suspension — see CLOUDY 1

roisterer *n* one who engages in merrymaking especially in honor of a special occasion — see CELEBRANT

role *also* **rôle** *n* the action for which a person or thing is specially fitted or used or for which a thing exists ⟨studying the *role* of sunlight in the body's production of vitamin D⟩
syn business, capacity, function, job, part, place, position, purpose, task, work
rel affair, concern, hand, involvement, participation; niche, office, post, situation; calling, occupation, pursuit, vocation; activity, assignment, charge, commission, duty, employ, mission, responsibility, service, use

¹**roll** *n* a record of a series of items (as names or titles) usually arranged according to some system — see ¹LIST

²**roll** *n* a rapid turning about on an axis or central point — see SPIN 1

roll *vb* 1 to form into a round compact mass — see WAD

2 to make a low heavy rolling sound — see RUMBLE

3 to make a series of unsteady side-to-side motions — see ROCK 1

4 to move (something) in a curved or circular path on or as if on an axis — see TURN 1

5 to move in a stream — see FLOW 1

6 to move in circles around an axis or center — see SPIN 1

7 to move or proceed smoothly and readily — see FLOW 2

rollick *n* a time or instance of carefree fun — see FLING 1

rollick *vb* 1 to engage in activity for amusement — see PLAY 1

2 to play and run about happily — see FROLIC 1

rollicking *adj* 1 being rough or noisy in a high-spirited way — see BOISTEROUS

2 given to good-natured joking or teasing — see PLAYFUL

rollicking *n* activity engaged in to amuse oneself — see PLAY 1

roly-poly *adj* having an excess of body fat — see FAT 1

romance *n* a brief romantic relationship — see AFFAIR 1

romantic *adj* excitingly or mysteriously unusual — see EXOTIC

romantic *n* one whose conduct is guided more by the image of perfection than by the real world — see IDEALIST

romanticize *vb* to represent or think of as better than reality would warrant — see IDEALIZE

romp *n* a time or instance of carefree fun — see FLING 1

romp *vb* to play and run about happily — see FROLIC 1

roof *n* 1 a raised covering over something for decoration or protection — see CANOPY

2 the place where one lives — see HOME 1

roof *vb* to provide with living quarters or shelter — see HOUSE 1

rook *vb* to rob by the use of trickery or threats — see FLEECE

rookie *n* a person who is just starting out in a field of activity — see BEGINNER

room *n* **1** an extent or area available for or used up by some activity or thing ⟨I need more *room* to do a cartwheel.⟩ ⟨They made *room* for him on the bench.⟩

syn place, space, way

rel capacity, compass, range, scope; berth, clearance, freedom, latitude, play

2 an area within a building that has been set apart from surrounding space by a wall ⟨Tim finally had a *room* to himself when his older brother went off to college.⟩

syn apartment, cell, chamber, closet

rel accommodation, bay, berth, booth, cabin, compartment, cubicle; alcove, niche, nook, recess; snuggery [*chiefly British*]

3 a favorable combination of circumstances, time, and place — see OPPORTUNITY

room *vb* to provide with living quarters or shelter — see HOUSE 1

roomer *n* one who rents a room or apartment in another's house — see TENANT 1

roomy *adj* more than adequate or average in capacity — see SPACIOUS

roost *vb* **1** to come to rest after descending from the air — see ALIGHT 1

2 to establish or place comfortably or snugly — see ENSCONCE 1

root *n* **1** a point or place at which something is invented or provided — see SOURCE 1

2 the source from which something grows or develops — see SEED 1

3 an immaterial thing upon which something else rests — see BASE 1

4 the central part or aspect of something under consideration — see CRUX

root *vb* to set solidly in or as if in surrounding matter — see ENTRENCH

root (out) *vb* **1** to destroy all traces of — see ANNIHILATE 1

2 to draw out by force or with effort — see EXTRACT

3 to come upon after searching, study, or effort — see FIND 1

rooted *adj* firmly established over time — see INVETERATE 1

rope *n* a length of braided, flexible material that is used for tying or connecting things — see CORD 1

ropy *also* **ropey** *adj* being of a consistency that resists flow — see THICK 2

rose–colored *adj* having qualities which inspire hope — see HOPEFUL 1

roster *n* a record of a series of items (as names or titles) usually arranged according to some system — see ¹LIST

rostrum *n* a level usually raised surface — see PLATFORM

rosy *adj* **1** having a healthy reddish skin tone — see RUDDY

2 having qualities which inspire hope — see HOPEFUL 1

rot *n* **1** language, behavior, or ideas that are absurd and contrary to good sense — see NONSENSE 1

2 the process by which dead organic matter separates into simpler substances — see CORRUPTION 1

rot *vb* **1** to become worse or of less value — see DETERIORATE 1

2 to go through decomposition — see DECAY 1

rotate *vb* **1** to move (something) in a curved or circular path on or as if on an axis — see TURN 1

2 to move in circles around an axis or center — see SPIN 1

rotation *n* a rapid turning about on an axis or central point — see SPIN 1

rote *n* an established and often automatic or monotonous series of actions followed when engaging in some activity — see ROUTINE 1

rotten *adj* **1** having undergone organic breakdown ⟨*rotten*, smelly meat that should have been thrown out⟩

syn addled, bad, corrupted, decayed, decomposed, putrefied, putrid, spoiled

rel curdled, fermented, off, rank, sour, soured, turned; contaminated, defiled, fouled, impure, polluted, tainted; corroded, crumbled, degenerated, deteriorated, disintegrated; decaying, decomposing, disintegrating, mildewy, moldering, moldy, putrefying, putrescent, rotting; gangrenous

near ant fresh, good, sweet; preserved, pristine, uncontaminated, undefiled, unpolluted, unspoiled, untainted, untouched

ant undecomposed

2 not conforming to a high moral standard; morally unacceptable — see BAD 2

3 not giving pleasure to the mind or senses — see UNPLEASANT

4 extremely unsatisfactory — see WRETCHED 1

5 of low quality — see CHEAP 2

rotund *adj* **1** having an excess of body fat — see FAT 1

2 marked by conspicuously full and rich sounds or tones — see RESONANT

rotundity *n* the condition of having an excess of body fat — see CORPULENCE

rough *adj* **1** covered with or as if with hair — see HAIRY 1

2 marked by bursts of destructive force or intense activity — see VIOLENT 1

3 marked by wet and windy conditions — see FOUL 1

4 not having a level or smooth surface — see UNEVEN 1

5 requiring considerable physical or mental effort — see HARD 2

6 difficult to endure — see HARSH 1

7 harsh and threatening in manner or appearance — see GRIM 1

8 hastily or roughly constructed — see RUDE 1

9 lacking in refinement or good taste — see COARSE 1

10 made of or resembling hair — see HAIRY 1

11 marked by a series of sharp quick motions — see JERKY 1

12 marked by turmoil or disturbance especially of natural elements — see WILD 3

rough (up) *vb* **1** to strike repeatedly — see BEAT 1

2 to abuse physically — see MANHANDLE 1

---

syn synonym(s)   *rel* related words
ant antonym(s)   *near ant* near antonym(s)

roughened *adj* not having a level or smooth surface — see UNEVEN 1

roughhouse *n* wildly playful or mischievous behavior — see HORSEPLAY

roughhousing *n* wildly playful or mischievous behavior — see HORSEPLAY

roughly *adv* in a manner so as to cause loss or suffering — see HARDLY 1

roughneck *adj* lacking in refinement or good taste — see COARSE 2

roughneck *n* a violent, brutal person who is often a member of an organized gang — see HOODLUM

roughness *n* 1 a harsh or sharp quality — see EDGE 1

2 the quality or state of lacking refinement or good taste — see VULGARITY 1

round *adj* 1 having every part of the surface the same distance from the center ⟨*round* ping pong balls⟩ ⟨The earth is not perfectly *round*.⟩

syn global, spherical

rel annular, circular, discoid, discoidal, disklike, ringlike; curved, looped, spiral; bulbous, rotund, rounded, roundish; cylindrical (*also* cylindric), oblong, oval, ovate, ovoid (*also* ovoidal)

ant nonspherical

2 having an excess of body fat — see FAT 1

3 marked by conspicuously full and rich sounds or tones — see RESONANT

4 being neither more nor less than a certain amount, number, or extent — see EVEN 1

round *adv* 1 from beginning to end — see THROUGH 1

2 on all sides or in every direction — see AROUND 1

3 toward the opposite direction — see AROUND 2

round *n* 1 a circular strip — see ¹RING 2

2 a series of events or actions that repeat themselves regularly and in the same order — see CYCLE 1

3 something with a perfectly round circumference — see CIRCLE 1

round *prep* in random positions within the boundaries of — see AROUND 2

round *vb* 1 to form into a round compact mass — see WAD

2 to travel completely around — see ENCIRCLE 1

3 to turn away from a straight line or course — see CURVE 1

round (off *or* **out)** *vb* 1 to bring (an event) to a natural or appropriate stopping point — see CLOSE 3

2 to serve as a completing element to — see COMPLEMENT

roundabout *adj* not straightforward or direct — see INDIRECT

roundly *adv* 1 in a vigorous and forceful manner — see HARD 3

2 with attention to all aspects or details — see THOROUGHLY 1

roundtable *n* a meeting featuring a group discussion — see FORUM 1

roundup *n* a short statement of the main points — see SUMMARY

round up *vb* to bring together in one body or place — see GATHER 1

rouse *vb* 1 to cause to stop sleeping — see WAKE 1

2 to cease to be asleep — see WAKE 2

rousing *adj* 1 causing great emotional or mental stimulation — see EXCITING 1

2 marked by much life, movement, or activity — see ALIVE 2

¹**rout** *n* 1 a great number of persons or creatures massed together — see CROWD 1

2 people looked down upon as ignorant and of the lowest class — see RABBLE

²**rout** *n* 1 failure to win a contest — see DEFEAT 1

2 the act or an instance of getting free from danger or confinement — see ESCAPE 1

rout *vb* 1 to defeat by a large margin — see WHIP 2

2 to drive or force out — see EJECT 1

route *n* 1 a passage cleared for public vehicular travel — see WAY 1

2 an established course for traveling from one place to another — see PASSAGE 1

3 the direction along which something or someone moves — see PATH 1

route *vb* to point out the way for (someone) especially from a position in front — see LEAD 1

routine *adj* 1 being of the type that is encountered in the normal course of events — see ORDINARY 1

2 following or agreeing with established form, custom, or rules — see FORMAL 1

3 often observed or encountered — see COMMON 1

routine *n* 1 an established and often automatic or monotonous series of actions followed when engaging in some activity ⟨Part of my morning *routine* is drinking a cup of coffee while reading the news.⟩

syn drill, grind, groove, pattern, rote, rut, treadmill

rel regimen; custom, fashion, habit, practice (*also* practise), trick, wont; approach, manner, method, procedure, strategy, style, tack, technique, way

2 something done over and over in order to develop skill — see EXERCISE 2

3 a performance regularly presented by an individual or group — see ACT 1

rove *vb* to move about from place to place aimlessly — see WANDER 1

rover *n* 1 a person who roams about without a fixed route or destination — see NOMAD

2 someone who engages in robbery of ships at sea — see PIRATE

roving *adj* traveling from place to place — see ITINERANT

¹**row** *n* 1 a series of people or things arranged side by side ⟨stood in a *row* to have their picture taken⟩ ⟨Three *rows* of eight jelly beans equals 24 jelly beans.⟩

syn bank, rank

rel chain, column, cue, file, line, procession, queue, range, string, train; echelon; sequence

2 a passage cleared for public vehicular travel — see WAY 1

²**row** *n* 1 a rough and often noisy fight usually involving several people — see BRAWL 1

2 a state of noisy, confused activity — see COMMOTION

3 an often noisy or angry expression of differing opinions — see ARGUMENT 1

¹**row** *vb* to move a boat by means of oars ⟨*rowed* around the lake⟩
  syn oar, paddle, scull
  rel canoe, kayak; pole, punt; feather, pull

²**row** *vb* to express different opinions about something often angrily — see ARGUE 2

rowdy *adj* being rough or noisy in a high-spirited way — see BOISTEROUS

rowdy *n* a violent, brutal person who is often a member of an organized gang — see HOODLUM

rower *n* a person who drives a boat forward by means of oars — see OARSMAN

royal *adj* **1** fit for or worthy of a royal ruler — see MONARCHICAL
  2 large and impressive in size, grandeur, extent, or conception — see GRAND 1
  3 involving minimal difficulty or effort — see EASY 1

rub *n* something that is a source of irritation — see ANNOYANCE 3

rub *vb* **1** to damage or diminish by continued friction — see ABRADE 1
  2 to make smooth by friction — see GRIND 1
  3 to make smooth or glossy usually by repeatedly applying surface pressure — see POLISH 1

rubbed *adj* having a shiny surface or finish — see GLOSSY

rubberlike *adj* able to revert to original size and shape after being stretched, squeezed, or twisted — see ELASTIC 1

rubberneck *n* a person who travels for pleasure — see TOURIST

rubberneck *vb* to look long and hard in wonder or surprise — see GAPE

rubbery *adj* able to revert to original size and shape after being stretched, squeezed, or twisted — see ELASTIC 1

rubbish *n* **1** discarded or useless material — see GARBAGE
  2 that which is of low quality or worth — see JUNK 1
  3 language, behavior, or ideas that are absurd and contrary to good sense — see NONSENSE 1

rubbishy *adj* of low quality — see CHEAP 1

rubble *n* the portion or bits of something left over or behind after it has been destroyed — see REMAINS 1

rubicund *adj* having a healthy reddish skin tone — see RUDDY

rub out *vb* **1** to bring to a complete end the physical soundness, existence, or usefulness of — see DESTROY 1
  2 to put to death deliberately — see MURDER 1
  3 to destroy all traces of — see ANNIHILATE 1

rubric *n* **1** a word or series of words often in larger letters placed at the beginning of a passage or at the top of a page in order to introduce or categorize — see HEADING
  2 an inherited or established way of thinking, feeling, or doing — see TRADITION 1
  3 one of the units into which a whole is divided on the basis of a common characteristic — see CLASS 2

rucksack *n* a soft-sided case designed for carrying belongings especially on the back — see PACK 1

ruckus *n* **1** a rough and often noisy fight usually involving several people — see BRAWL 1
  2 a state of noisy, confused activity — see COMMOTION

ruction *n* **1** a rough and often noisy fight usually involving several people — see BRAWL 1
  2 a state of noisy, confused activity — see COMMOTION

ruddy *adj* having a healthy reddish skin tone ⟨*Ruddy* complexions run in the family.⟩
  syn blooming, florid, flush, full-blooded, glowing, red, rosy, rubicund, sanguine
  rel bronzed, brown, suntanned, tanned; bloomy, blushing, flushed, warm; cherubic
  near ant waxen; blanched, white, whitened; anemic, sick, sickly; white-faced
  ant ashen, ashy, livid, lurid, mealy, pale, paled, palish, pallid, pasty, peaked, sallow, sallowish, wan

rude *adj* **1** hastily or roughly constructed ⟨a *rude* shelter built from unfinished logs by some forgotten pioneer⟩
  syn artless, clumsy, crude, jerry-rigged, rough, unrefined
  rel defective, faulty, flawed, imperfect; imprecise, inexact; inartistic, undressed, unfinished, unpolished, unworked; amateur, amateurish, inexpert, unprofessional, unskilled, unskillful; primitive, rudimentary; unshaped, unshapen
  near ant faultless, finished, flawless, meticulous, perfect, perfected, polished, well-done; adept, adroit, dexterous (*also* dextrous), expert, masterful, masterly, neat, practiced (*also* practised), skillful, workmanlike; artful, artistic, sophisticated; exact, precise
  ant refined
  2 belonging to or characteristic of an early level of skill or development — see PRIMITIVE 1
  3 lacking in refinement or good taste — see COARSE 2
  4 not civilized — see UNCIVILIZED
  5 showing a lack of manners or consideration for others — see IMPOLITE
  6 lacking in education or the knowledge gained from books — see IGNORANT 1
  7 being such as found in nature and not altered by processing or refining — see CRUDE 1

rudeness *n* **1** rude behavior — see DISCOURTESY
  2 the quality or state of lacking refinement or good taste — see VULGARITY 1

rudimentary *adj* **1** belonging to or characteristic of an early level of skill or development — see PRIMITIVE 1
  2 of or relating to the simplest facts or theories of a subject — see ELEMENTARY

rudiments *n pl* general or basic truths on which other truths or theories can be based — see PRINCIPLES 1

rue *n* a feeling of responsibility for wrong-doing — see GUILT 1

rue *vb* to feel sorry or dissatisfied about — see REGRET

---

syn synonym(s)   **rel** related words
ant antonym(s)   **near ant** near antonym(s)

rueful *adj* 1 expressing or suggesting mourning — see MOURNFUL 1

2 feeling sorrow for a wrong that one has done — see CONTRITE

3 deserving of one's pity — see PATHETIC 1

ruefully *adv* with feelings of bitterness or grief — see HARD 2

ruffian *n* a violent, brutal person who is often a member of an organized gang — see HOODLUM

ruffle *n* 1 a strip of fabric gathered or pleated on one edge and used as trimming ⟨likes lace curtains without *ruffles* and chintz curtains with *ruffles*⟩

syn flounce, frill, furbelow

rel border, fringe, trim; plait, pleat, ruff; bunting, skirting

2 something that is a source of irritation — see ANNOYANCE 3

ruffle *vb* to disturb the peace of mind of (someone) especially by repeated disagreeable acts — see IRRITATE 1

rugged *adj* 1 able to withstand hardship, strain, or exposure — see HARDY 1

2 difficult to endure — see HARSH 1

3 harsh and threatening in manner or appearance — see GRIM 1

4 having muscles capable of exerting great physical force — see STRONG 1

5 not having a level or smooth surface — see UNEVEN 1

6 requiring considerable physical or mental effort — see HARD 2

7 marked by turmoil or disturbance especially of natural elements — see WILD 3

8 lacking in refinement or good taste — see COARSE 2

ruin *n* 1 the state or fact of being rendered nonexistent, physically unsound, or useless — see DESTRUCTION 1

2 **ruins** *pl* the portion or bits of something left over or behind after it has been destroyed — see REMAINS 1

3 something that is the cause of one's ultimate failure or loss of life — see DOWNFALL 1

ruin *vb* 1 to cause to lose one's fortune and become unable to pay one's debts ⟨After he was *ruined* by the Great Chicago Fire of 1871, the industrialist was forced to sell his mansion and start all over again.⟩

syn bankrupt, break, bust

rel beggar, impoverish, pauperize; reduce, straiten; clean (out), wipe out

near ant enrich, richen

2 to bring destruction to (something) through violent action — see RAVAGE

3 to bring to a complete end the physical soundness, existence, or usefulness of — see DESTROY 1

ruination *n* 1 something that is the cause of one's ultimate failure or loss of life — see DOWNFALL 1

2 the state or fact of being rendered nonexistent, physically unsound, or useless — see DESTRUCTION 1

ruinous *adj* 1 bringing about ruin or misfortune — see FATAL 1

2 causing or tending to cause destruction — see DESTRUCTIVE 1

rule *n* 1 a statement spelling out the proper procedure or conduct for an activity ⟨Read the *rules* that are posted before you use the pool.⟩

syn bylaw, ground rule, regulation

rel code, constitution, decalogue, directory; act, law, ordinance, statute; behest, charge, command, commandment, decree, dictate, direction, directive, edict, fiat, instruction, order; axiom, fundamental, maxim, precept; moral, principle, value; ban, interdiction, prohibition, proscription, restriction; blueprint, canon, formula, guide, guideline, standard

2 lawful control over the affairs of a political unit (as a nation) ⟨the years during which Russia was under Communist *rule*⟩

syn administration, authority, governance, government, jurisdiction, regime (*also* régime), regimen

rel dominion, power, sovereignty (*also* sovranty), supremacy, sway; command, leadership; direction, management, regulation, superintendence, supervision; autocracy, dictatorship, mastery, oppression, subjugation, tyranny

3 an inherited or established way of thinking, feeling, or doing — see TRADITION 1

rule *vb* 1 to exercise authority or power over — see GOVERN 1

2 to keep from exceeding a desirable degree or level (as of expression) — see CONTROL 1

rule (on) *vb* to give an opinion about (something at issue or in dispute) — see JUDGE 1

rule out *vb* to prevent the participation, consideration, or inclusion of — see EXCLUDE

ruler *n* one who rules over a people with a sole, supreme, and usually hereditary authority — see MONARCH 1

ruling *adj* held by or applicable to a majority of the people — see GENERAL 3

ruling *n* 1 a decision made by a court or tribunal regarding a case it has heard — see SENTENCE

2 an order publicly issued by an authority — see EDICT 1

rumble *vb* to make a low heavy rolling sound ⟨When thunder *rumbled* in the distant sky, we wisely began packing up our picnic.⟩

syn growl, grumble, lumber, roll

rel boom, drum, thunder; bellow

ruminant *adj* given to or marked by long, quiet thinking — see CONTEMPLATIVE

ruminate *vb* to give serious and careful thought to — see PONDER

rummage *n* an unorganized collection or mixture of various things — see MISCELLANY 1

rummage *vb* 1 to come upon after searching, study, or effort — see FIND 1

2 to look through (as a place) carefully or thoroughly in an effort to find or discover something — see SEARCH 1

rumor *n* information or opinion that is widely disseminated without any authority or confirmation of accuracy ⟨*Rumor* has it that she's planning to shut down the company.⟩

syn buzz, dish, gossip, report, talk, tattle, word

rel tale, whisper, whispering; hint, intimation, rumbling; propaganda; dirt, scandal

rumor *vb* to make (as a piece of information) the subject of common talk without any authority or confirmation of accuracy ⟨For years people have been *rumoring* the CEO's imminent retirement.⟩

syn bruit (about), circulate, whisper

rel bandy (about), blab, gossip, tattle; bare, disclose, divulge, expose, report, reveal, spill, tell; hint, imply, insinuate, intimate, suggest; broadcast, proclaim, propagate, publicize, spread

rump *n* the part of the body upon which someone sits — see BUTTOCKS

rumple *vb* **1** to create (as by crushing) an irregular mass of creases in — see CRUMPLE 1

2 to develop creases or folds — see WRINKLE 1

3 to undo the proper order or arrangement of — see DISORDER

rumpled *adj* lacking in order, neatness, and often cleanliness — see MESSY

rumpus *n* a state of noisy, confused activity — see COMMOTION

run *n* **1** a prevailing or general movement or inclination — see TREND 1

2 *chiefly Midland* a natural body of running water smaller than a river — see CREEK 1

3 the period during which something exists, lasts, or is in progress — see DURATION 1

4 the right to act or move freely — see FREEDOM 2

5 runs *pl* abnormally frequent intestinal evacuations with more or less fluid stools — see DIARRHEA

run *vb* **1** to go at a pace faster than a walk ⟨We *ran* all the way to the bus stop, but still missed the bus.⟩

syn dash, gallop, jog, sprint, trip, trot

rel bound, canter, leap, lope, skip, spring; barrel, belt, blast, blaze, blow, bolt, bowl, breeze, bustle, buzz, careen, course, foot (it), hasten, hie, hoof (it), hotfoot (it), hump, hurl, hurry, hurtle, hustle, jet, leg (it), pelt, race, ram, rip, rocket, rush, rustle, shoot, speed, tear, whirl, whisk, zip, zoom; scoot, scurry, scuttle, step (along)

near ant saunter, shamble, shuffle, stroll; crawl, creep, dally, dawdle, dillydally, drag, lag, linger, loiter, poke, tarry; lumber, plod, trudge; hobble, limp

2 to hasten away from something dangerous or frightening ⟨Rather than *run* from a black bear, it's better to hold your ground and make lots of noise.⟩

syn bolt, break, flee, fly, retreat, run away, run off

rel abscond, clear out, decamp, elope, escape, get (away), get out, light out, make off, scram, skip (out), skirr

phrases beat a retreat, beat it, make tracks, turn tail

near ant beard, brave, confront, dare, defy, face; abide, dwell, hang around, linger, remain, stay, stick around, tarry

3 to be positioned along a certain course or in a certain direction ⟨The road *runs* along the river for a while.⟩

syn bear, extend, go, head, lead, lie

rel cross, cut, pass; course, follow, span, traverse

4 to occur within a continuous range of variation ⟨The electric bill *runs* between 30 and 50 dollars a month.⟩

syn go, range, vary

rel alternate, fluctuate, move, shift; change, mutate; extend, reach, stretch, sweep

5 to move in a stream — see FLOW 1

6 to proceed or move quickly — see HURRY 2

7 to show a liking or proneness (for something) — see LEAN 2

8 to urge, push, or force onward — see DRIVE 1

9 to control the mechanical operation of — see OPERATE 1

10 to eventually have as a state or quality — see BECOME

11 to go from a solid to a liquid state — see LIQUEFY

12 to look after and make decisions about — see CONDUCT 1

13 to cause to function — see ACTIVATE

14 to have a price of — see COST

15 to come or be together as friends — see ASSOCIATE 1

16 to go after or on the track of — see FOLLOW 2

run away *vb* **1** to get free from a dangerous or confining situation — see ESCAPE 1

2 to hasten away from something dangerous or frightening — see RUN 2

run–down *adj* **1** showing signs of advanced wear and tear and neglect — see SHABBY 1

2 temporarily suffering from a disorder of the body — see SICK 1

run down *vb* **1** to come upon after searching, study, or effort — see FIND 1

2 to express scornfully one's low opinion of — see DECRY 1

run–in *n* a brief clash between enemies or rivals — see ENCOUNTER

runner *n* one that carries a message or does an errand — see MESSENGER

running *adj* **1** being in effective operation — see ACTIVE 1

2 going on and without any interruptions — see CONTINUOUS

running *n* the act or activity of looking after and making decisions about something — see CONDUCT 1

runny *adj* having an overly soft liquid consistency ⟨*runny* scrambled eggs⟩

syn soupy, watery

rel flowing, fluent, fluid, liquefied; dilute, diluted, thin, thinned, watered-down, weak, weakened; sloshy, slushy, soggy, waterlogged, wet

near ant ropy (*also* ropey), syrupy, viscid, viscous; creamy, heavy, thick, thickened, thickish; gelatinous, gluey, glutinous, gooey, gummy, sticky

run off *vb* **1** to drive or force out — see EJECT 1

2 to get free from a dangerous or confining situation — see ESCAPE 1

3 to hasten away from something dangerous or frightening — see RUN 2

---

syn synonym(s)   **rel** related words
ant antonym(s)   **near ant** near antonym(s)

run–of–the–mill *adj* being of the type that is encountered in the normal course of events — see ORDINARY 1

run on *vb* **1** to engage in casual or rambling conversation — see CHAT 1

2 to remain indefinitely in existence or in the same state — see CONTINUE 1

3 to talk at length without sticking to a topic or getting to a point — see RAMBLE 1

run over *vb* to do over and over so as to become skilled — see PRACTICE

runt *n* a living thing much smaller than others of its kind — see DWARF 1

run through *vb* **1** to penetrate or hold (something) with a pointed object — see IMPALE

2 to use up carelessly — see WASTE 1

rural *adj* of, relating to, associated with, or typical of open areas with few buildings or people ⟨grew up in a *rural* community where more than half the people were farmers⟩ ⟨a painter noted for his *rural* landscapes⟩
syn bucolic, country, pastoral, rustic (*also* rustical)
rel backwoods, backwoodsy, countrified (*also* countryfied); provincial; agrarian, agricultural; nonurban, semirural
near ant citified, urbanized; metropolitan, municipal; nonagricultural, nonfarm
ant urban

rush *n* **1** excited and often showy or disorderly speed — see HURRY 1

2 the act or action of setting upon with force or violence — see ATTACK 1

rush *vb* **1** to cause to move or proceed fast or faster — see HURRY 1

2 to flow out in great quantities or with force — see GUSH 1

3 to proceed or move quickly — see HURRY 2

4 to take sudden, violent action against — see ATTACK 1

rushed *adj* acting or done with excessive or careless speed — see HASTY 1

rustic *n* an awkward or simple person especially from a small town or the country — see HICK

rustic *also* **rustical** *adj* **1** lacking social grace and assurance — see AWKWARD 1

2 of, relating to, associated with, or typical of open areas with few buildings or people — see RURAL

rustle *vb* **1** to feed on grass or herbs — see ¹GRAZE

2 to proceed or move quickly — see HURRY 2

3 to make small sounds usually by rubbing or moving — see CRINKLE 1

rustler *n* an ambitious person who eagerly goes after what is desired — see GO-GETTER

rut *n* an established and often automatic or monotonous series of actions followed when engaging in some activity — see ROUTINE 1

ruthless *adj* having or showing a lack of sympathy or tender feelings — see HARD 1

RV *n* a motor vehicle that is specially equipped for living while traveling — see CAMPER

sable *adj* having the color of soot or coal — see BLACK 1

saccharine *adj* appealing to the emotions in an obvious and tiresome way — see CORNY

sacerdotal *adj* of, relating to, or characteristic of the clergy — see CLERICAL

sack *n* **1** a container made of a flexible material (as paper or plastic) — see BAG 1

2 a place set aside for sleeping — see BED 1

¹sack *vb* to let go from office, service, or employment — see DISMISS 1

²sack *vb* to search through with the intent of committing robbery — see RANSACK 1

sacred *adj* **1** not to be violated, criticized, or tampered with ⟨the *sacred* trust that exists between elected officials and the electorate⟩
syn hallowed, holy, inviolable, sacrosanct, unassailable, untouchable
rel inviolate, pure; privileged, protected, secure, shielded; exempt, immune
near ant blasphemous, irreverent, profane, sacrilegious

2 of, relating to, or being God — see HOLY 3

3 of, relating to, or used in the practice or worship services of a religion — see RELIGIOUS 1

4 set apart or worthy of veneration by association with God — see HOLY 2

5 deserving honor and respect especially by reason of age — see VENERABLE 1

sacrifice *n* something offered to a god ⟨The herders selected their best lamb as a *sacrifice* in order to receive blessings from their god.⟩
syn immolation, offering, victim
rel libation, propitiation; holocaust; contribution, donation

sacrifice *vb* to give up as an offering to a god ⟨an ancient ritual that involved *sacrificing* an animal⟩
syn immolate, offer
rel consecrate, dedicate, devote; give, hand over, surrender, yield

sacrilege *n* an act of great disrespect shown to God or to sacred ideas, people, or things — see BLASPHEMY

sacrilegious *adj* not showing proper reverence for the holy or sacred — see IRREVERENT

sacristy *n* a room in a church building for sacred furnishings (as vestments) ⟨Our choir robes were stored in the *sacristy*.⟩
syn vestry
rel cloakroom

sacrosanct *adj* **1** not to be violated, criticized, or tampered with — see SACRED 1

2 set apart or worthy of veneration by association with God — see HOLY 2

sad *adj* **1** feeling unhappiness ⟨Movies in which the hero dies always make us feel *sad*.⟩

syn bad, blue, brokenhearted, crestfallen, dejected, depressed, despondent, disconsolate, doleful, down, downcast, downhearted, droopy, forlorn, gloomy, glum, hangdog, heartbroken, heartsick, heartsore, inconsolable, joyless, low, low-spirited, melancholy, miserable, mournful, saddened, sorrowful, sorry, unhappy, woebegone, woeful, wretched

rel aggrieved, distressed, troubled, uneasy, upset, worried; despairing, hopeless, sunk; disappointed, discouraged, disheartened, dispirited; suicidal; dolorous, lachrymose, lugubrious, plaintive, tearful; regretful, rueful; anguished, grieving, wailing, weeping; black, bleak, cheerless, comfortless, dark, darkening, depressing, desolate, dismal, dreary, elegiac (*also* elegiacal), funereal, gray (*also* grey), morbid, morose, saturnine, somber (*or* sombre), sullen

near ant ecstatic, elated, enraptured, entranced, euphoric, exhilarated, exuberant, exultant, overjoyed, rapturous, rhapsodic (*also* rhapsodical); blithe, blithesome, jocose, jocular, jocund, jolly, jovial, lightsome, merry, mirthful; excited, thrilled; hopeful, optimistic, rosy, sanguine; encouraged, heartened; animated, bouncing, energetic, frisky, jaunty, lively, peppy, perky, spirited, sprightly, springy, vital, vivacious, zippy; content, gratified, pleased, satisfied; beaming, grinning, laughing, smiling

ant blissful, buoyant, buoyed, cheerful, cheery, chipper, delighted, glad, gladdened, gladsome, gleeful, happy, joyful, joyous, jubilant, sunny, upbeat

2 causing unhappiness ⟨The *sad* news about our uncle's death made my father cry.⟩

syn depressing, dismal, dreary, heartbreaking, heartrending, melancholy, mournful, pathetic, saddening, sorry, tearful, teary

rel deplorable, distressful, grievous, lamentable, unfortunate, woeful; discomforting, discomposing, disquieting, distressing, disturbing, perturbing; discouraging, disheartening, dispiriting

near ant heartening, heartwarming, inspiring, stimulating, stirring, uplifting; agreeable, delightful, enjoyable, pleasant, pleasing, pleasurable, satisfying, welcome; exhilarating, thrilling

ant cheering, cheery, glad, happy

3 deserving pitying scorn (as for inadequacy) — see PITIFUL 1

sadden *vb* to make sad — see DEPRESS 1

saddened *adj* feeling unhappiness — see SAD 1

saddening *adj* causing unhappiness — see SAD 2

saddle *vb* to place a weight or burden on — see LOAD 1

sadism *n* disposition to willfully inflict

pain and suffering on others — see CRUELTY

sadistic *adj* having or showing the desire to inflict severe pain and suffering on others — see CRUEL 2

sadly *adv* with feelings of bitterness or grief — see HARD 2

sadness *n* a state or spell of low spirits ⟨She was filled with *sadness* at the thought of having to leave her family.⟩

syn blues, dejection, depression, desolation, despond, despondency, disconsolateness, dispiritedness, doldrums, dolefulness, downheartedness, dreariness, dumps, forlornness, gloom, gloominess, heartsickness, joylessness, melancholy, mopes, oppression, unhappiness

rel melancholia, self-pity; anguish, dolor, grief, mourning, somberness, sorrow, woefulness; agony, distress, pain; misery, woe, wretchedness; discouragement, disheartenment; moodiness; despair, desperation, hopelessness; dismalness, morbidness, moroseness

near ant gaiety (*also* gayety), glee, gleefulness, humor, jollity, joviality, lightheartedness, merriment, mirth, mirthfulness; cheer, cheerfulness, cheeriness, hopefulness, optimism, sunniness; contentedness, contentment, satisfaction; delight, gratification

ant bliss, blissfulness, ecstasy, elation, euphoria, exhilaration, exuberance, exultation, felicity, gladness, happiness, joy, joyfulness, joyousness, jubilation, rapture, rapturousness

safe *adj* **1** not exposed to the threat of loss or injury ⟨The minute the rain started, we looked for a place where we would be *safe* from a drenching downpour.⟩

syn all right, alright, secure

rel hale, healthy, intact, sound, well, whole; unharmed, unhurt, uninjured, unscathed

near ant damaged, harmed, hurt, injured, scathed, wounded

ant endangered, exposed, imperiled (*or* imperilled), insecure, liable, open, subject (to), susceptible, threatened, unsafe, violable, vulnerable

2 providing safety ⟨We tried to find a *safe* place to hide our valuables while we went swimming.⟩

syn secure, snug

rel guarding, protecting, safeguarding, sheltering, shielding; defended, guarded, protected, sheltered, shielded; impregnable, inviolable, invulnerable, unassailable, unconquerable

near ant menacing, perilous, threatening; undefended, unguarded, unprotected, vulnerable; precarious, treacherous, uncertain

ant dangerous, hazardous, insecure, risky, unsafe

3 having or showing a close attentiveness to avoiding danger or trouble — see CAREFUL 1

4 not causing or being capable of causing injury or hurt — see HARMLESS

5 worthy of one's trust — see DEPENDABLE

safe *n* a specially reinforced container to

---

syn synonym(s)   *rel* related words
ant antonym(s)   *near ant* near antonym(s)

keep valuables safe ⟨The hotel recommended that we keep all our valuables in its *safe* during our stay.⟩

syn coffer, safe-deposit box, strongbox

rel vault; locker, storeroom, treasury; box, caddy, case, casket, chest, footlocker, locker, trunk

safe–deposit box *n* a specially reinforced container to keep valuables safe — see SAFE

safeguard *n* means or method of defending — see DEFENSE 1

safeguard *vb* to drive danger or attack away from — see DEFEND 1

safekeeping *n* responsibility for the safety and well-being of someone or something — see CUSTODY

safeness *n* the state of not being exposed to danger — see SAFETY 1

safety *n* 1 the state of not being exposed to danger ⟨We were lucky to make it to *safety* just as the lions broke loose from their cage at the zoo.⟩

syn protection, safeness, security

rel aegis (*also* egis), cover, defense, guardianship, ward; guard, safeguard, screen, shield; asylum, harbor, haven, refuge, retreat, shelter; impregnability, impregnableness, invincibility, invincibleness, inviolability, inviolableness, invulnerability, invulnerableness

near ant hazard, risk, threat; instability, precariousness; exposure, liability, openness, violability, vulnerability, vulnerableness; susceptibility, susceptibleness

ant danger, distress, endangerment, imperilment, jeopardy, peril, trouble

2 a protective device (as on a weapon) to prevent accidental operation ⟨The gun couldn't be fired as long as the *safety* was on.⟩

syn guard

rel lock; defense, protection, safeguard, shield

sag *vb* 1 to be limp from lack of water or vigor — see DROOP 1

2 to decline gradually from a standard level — see SLIP 1

3 to lose bodily strength or vigor — see WEAKEN 2

sag *n* the extent to which something hangs or dips below a straight line ⟨If there's too much *sag* in the rod, the curtains will drag on the floor.⟩

syn droop, hang, slack, slackness

rel floppiness, laxity, laxness, limpness, looseness

near ant rigidity, rigidness, tautness, tenseness, tension, tightness

sagacious *adj* having or showing deep understanding and intelligent application of knowledge — see WISE 1

sagaciousness *n* the ability to understand inner qualities or relationships — see WISDOM 1

sagacity *n* the ability to understand inner qualities or relationships — see WISDOM 1

sage *adj* having or showing deep understanding and intelligent application of knowledge — see WISE 1

sage *n* a person of deep wisdom or learning ⟨The young prince made a pilgrimage to the *sage*, hoping to learn the meaning of life.⟩

syn savant, scholar

rel seer, wise man; brain, egghead, genius, highbrow, intellect, intellectual, thinker, whiz, wizard; rabbi; master, mentor, teacher

near ant blockhead, dodo, dolt, dope, dumbbell, dummy, dunce, fool, goon, half-wit, idiot, ignoramus, imbecile, know-nothing, moron, nincompoop, ninny, nitwit, numskull (*or* numbskull), pinhead, simpleton

sageness *n* the ability to understand inner qualities or relationships — see WISDOM 1

sagging *adj* bending downward or forward — see NODDING

sail *n* a journey over water in a vessel ⟨We went for a brief *sail* on the bay to relax.⟩

syn crossing, cruise, passage, voyage

sail *vb* 1 to travel on water in a vessel ⟨I can't *sail* when there's any breeze at all because I get seasick easily.⟩

syn boat, cruise, ferry, navigate, voyage

rel canoe, kayak, yacht; coast

phrases make sail, take ship

2 to move or proceed smoothly and readily — see FLOW 2

3 to rest or move along the surface of a liquid or in the air — see FLOAT 1

sailboat *n* a boat equipped with one or more sails ⟨We were stuck in the *sailboat* for an hour until the wind came up and we could move again.⟩

syn bark, dinghy, windjammer

rel brigantine, caravel, catamaran, catboat, clipper, corvette, cutter, frigate, galleon, galley, junk, keelboat, ketch, knockabout, lugger, outrigger, schooner, ship, sloop, square-rigger, xebec, yacht, yawl; bottom, craft, vessel

sailor *n* one who operates or navigates a seagoing vessel ⟨The *sailors* were glad to be arriving in port after their long voyage.⟩

syn gob, hearty, jack, jack-tar, mariner, navigator, salt, sea dog, seafarer, seaman, swab, tar

rel crewman, deckhand, shipmate; able-bodied seaman, able seaman, lubber

sainted *adj* showing a devotion to God and to a life of virtue — see HOLY 1

sainthood *n* the quality or state of being spiritually pure or virtuous — see HOLINESS

saintliness *n* the quality or state of being spiritually pure or virtuous — see HOLINESS

saintly *adj* showing a devotion to God and to a life of virtue — see HOLY 1

saintship *n* the quality or state of being spiritually pure or virtuous — see HOLINESS

salable *or* **saleable** *adj* 1 fit or likely to be sold especially on a large scale — see COMMERCIAL

2 fit to be offered for sale — see MARKETABLE 1

salary *n* the money paid regularly to a person for labor or services — see WAGE

sale *n* the transfer of ownership of something from one person to another for a price ⟨My neighbor tried to make a *sale*, but no one was interested in buying his old car.⟩

syn deal, trade, transaction

rel auction, haggle, horse-trading, negotiation; bargain, buy, steal; purchase; clearance, closeout, fire sale; fair; rummage sale

salesclerk *n* a person employed to sell goods or services especially in a store — see SALESPERSON

salesman *n* a person employed to sell goods or services especially in a store — see SALESPERSON

salesperson *n* a person employed to sell goods or services especially in a store ⟨We asked the *salesperson* to see if there were any shoes in our size in the stockroom.⟩

syn clerk, salesclerk, salesman

rel salespeople; salesgirl, saleslady, saleswoman, shopgirl; pitchman, pitchwoman; floorwalker

saline *adj* of, relating to, or containing salt — see SALTY 1

salinity *n* the quality or state of being salty — see SALTINESS

saliva *n* the fluid that is secreted into the mouth by certain glands ⟨Our mouths filled with *saliva* when we smelled the delicious dinner.⟩

syn drool, slaver, slobber, spit, spittle

rel foam, froth; expectoration, salivation, sputum

salivate *vb* to let saliva or some other substance flow from the mouth — see DROOL 1

sally *n* 1 a short trip for pleasure — see EXCURSION 1

2 something said or done to cause laughter — see JOKE 1

sally (forth) *vb* to leave a place often for another — see GO 2

salon *n* 1 a building or part of a building in which objects of interest are displayed — see MUSEUM

2 a building, room, or suite of rooms occupied by a service business — see PLACE 2

saloon *n* a place of business where alcoholic beverages are sold to be consumed on the premises — see BARROOM

salt *adj* of, relating to, or containing salt — see SALTY 1

salt *n* one who operates or navigates a sea-going vessel — see SAILOR

salt *vb* to scatter or set here and there among other things — see THREAD 1

salt away *vb* to put (something of future use or value) in a safe or secret place — see HOARD

saltiness *n* the quality or state of being salty ⟨the *saltiness* of the pretzels⟩

syn brininess, salinity, saltness

near ant freshness, purity; sweetness

saltness *n* the quality or state of being salty — see SALTINESS

salty *adj* 1 of, relating to, or containing salt ⟨*Salty* sea water is safe to swim in, but you really shouldn't swallow it.⟩

syn brackish, briny, saline, salt

rel hard

near ant sweet; clear, pure; freshwater

ant nonsaline

2 hinting at or intended to call to mind matters regarded as indecent — see SUGGESTIVE 1

---

3 sharp and pleasantly stimulating to the mind or senses — see PIQUANT

salubrious *adj* beneficial to the health of body or mind — see HEALTHFUL

salutary *adj* 1 promoting or contributing to personal or social well-being — see BENEFICIAL

2 beneficial to the health of body or mind — see HEALTHFUL

salutation *n* 1 a formal expression of praise — see ENCOMIUM

2 an expression of goodwill upon meeting — see HELLO

salute *n* an expression of goodwill upon meeting — see HELLO

salute *vb* to declare enthusiastic approval of — see ACCLAIM

salvation *n* the saving from danger or evil ⟨We hoped that rain would bring *salvation* from the heat wave.⟩

syn deliverance, rescue

rel ransom, recovery, redemption; extrication; defense, guard, protection, safeguard, safeguarding, security; conservation, guardianship, preservation, safekeeping

salvo *n* a rapid or overwhelming outpouring of many things at once — see BARRAGE

same *adj* 1 resembling another in every respect ⟨I bought the *same* shirt online for five dollars less.⟩

syn coequal, duplicate, equal, even, identical, indistinguishable

rel akin, alike, analogous, comparable, coordinate, correspondent, corresponding, equivalent, like, matching, parallel, similar, such, suchlike, synonymous, tantamount

near ant divers, miscellaneous, sundry, varied

ant different, disparate, dissimilar, distant, distinct, distinctive, distinguishable, diverse, other, unlike, unlike

2 being one and not another ⟨That's the *same* guy I saw down at the beach yesterday.⟩

syn identical, selfsame, very

near ant disparate, dissimilar, distinct, distinctive, distinguishable, diverse, unalike, unlike, varied

ant another, different, other

sameness *n* 1 a tedious lack of variety — see MONOTONY

2 the state of being exactly alike — see IDENTITY 1

3 the state or fact of being exactly the same in number, amount, status, or quality — see EQUIVALENCE

sample *vb* to put (something) to a test — see TRY (OUT)

sample *n* 1 a number of things selected from a group to stand for the whole ⟨Based on a *sample* of the menu items, we decided that this was the best restaurant in town.⟩

syn cross section, selection, slice

rel case, example, exemplar, exemplification, illustration, instance, representative, specimen; archetype, classic, paradigm, prototype; microcosm

2 one of a group or collection that shows what the whole is like — see EXAMPLE

sanctification *n* 1 the act of making

---

something holy through religious ritual —
see CONSECRATION

2 the act or fact of freeing from sin or
moral guilt — see PURIFICATION

sanctified *adj* set apart or worthy of veneration by association with God — see
HOLY 2

sanctify *vb* **1** to free from moral guilt or
blemish especially ceremonially — see PU-
RIFY 1

2 to make holy through prayers or ritual
— see BLESS 1

sanction *n* the approval by someone in
authority for the doing of something —
see PERMISSION

sanction *vb* to give official acceptance of
as satisfactory — see APPROVE

sanctioned *adj* ordered or allowed by
those in authority — see OFFICIAL

sanctity *n* the quality or state of being
spiritually pure or virtuous — see HOLI-
NESS

sanctuary *n* **1** a place that is considered
sacred (as within a religion) — see SHRINE

2 something (as a building) that offers
cover from the weather or protection
from danger — see SHELTER

sanctum *n* **1** a place that is considered sacred (as within a religion) — see SHRINE

2 something (as a building) that offers
cover from the weather or protection
from danger — see SHELTER

sand *vb* to make smooth by friction — see
GRIND 1

sand *n, often* **sands** *pl* the usually sandy
or gravelly land bordering a body of water
— see BEACH

sandwich *vb* to fit (people or things) into
a tight space — see CROWD 1

sandy *adj* of a pale yellow or yellowish
brown color — see BLOND

sane *adj* having full use of one's mind and
control over one's actions ⟨The court
ruled that the woman was indeed *sane*
when she made out her will.⟩

syn balanced, clearheaded, lucid, normal,
right, stable

rel analytic (*or* analytical), clear, coherent,
logical, rational, reasonable; even-keeled,
judicious, levelheaded, sensible, wise;
healthy, sound, unneurotic; well-adjusted,
well-balanced

near ant daft, wacky (*also* whacky); foolish, senseless, witless; irrational, unreasonable; distracted, distraught, frantic, frenzied; fixated, obsessed

ant insane, unsound

saneness *n* the normal or healthy condition of the mental abilities — see MIND 2

sanguinary *adj* eager for or marked by
the shedding of blood, extreme violence,
or killing — see BLOODTHIRSTY

sanguine *adj* **1** eager for or marked by the
shedding of blood, extreme violence, or
killing — see BLOODTHIRSTY

2 having a healthy reddish skin tone — see
RUDDY

3 having or showing a mind free from
doubt — see CERTAIN 2

sanguinity *n* an inclination to believe in
the most favorable outcome — see OPTI-
MISM

sanitary *adj* free from filth, infection, or

dangers to health ⟨The nurse made sure
that everything in the room was *sanitary*
so that the baby wouldn't get sick.⟩

syn aseptic, germfree, hygienic, sterile

rel germproof; antibacterial, antibiotic,
germicidal, microbicidal; clean, immaculate, pristine, spick-and-span (*or* spic-and-
span), spotless, stainless, unsoiled, unstained, unsullied; pure, taintless, undefiled,
unpolluted, untainted; bleached, cleansed,
purified, scrubbed, washed, whitened

near ant infectious, pathogenic, poisonous, sickening, toxic; bedraggled, besmirched, dingy, dirty, dusty, filthy, foul,
grimy, grubby, grungy, mucky, muddy,
nasty, smirched, soiled, sordid, stained,
sullied, unclean, uncleanly, unwashed; defiled, polluted, tainted, unsterilized

ant germy, insanitary, unhygienic, unsanitary, unsterile

sanitary landfill *n* a place where discarded materials (as trash) are dumped — see
DUMP 1

sanity *n* the normal or healthy condition
of the mental abilities — see MIND 2

sans *prep* not having — see WITHOUT 1

sap *n* **1** active strength of body or mind —
see VIGOR 1

2 one who is easily deceived or cheated —
see ¹DUPE

3 the condition of being sound in body —
see HEALTH 1

sap *vb* to diminish the physical strength of
— see WEAKEN 1

sapience *n* the ability to understand inner
qualities or relationships — see WISDOM 1

sapient *adj* having or showing deep understanding and intelligent application of
knowledge — see WISE 1

sapped *adj* lacking bodily strength — see
WEAK 1

sappiness *n* the state or quality of having
an excess of tender feelings (as of love,
nostalgia, or compassion) — see SENTI-
MENTALITY

sappy *adj* **1** appealing to the emotions in
an obvious and tiresome way — see
CORNY

2 showing or marked by a lack of good
sense or judgment — see FOOLISH 1

sarcasm *n* an act or expression showing
scorn and usually intended to hurt another's feelings — see INSULT

sarcastic *adj* marked by the use of wit
that is intended to cause hurt feelings
⟨Her *sarcastic* comments didn't do anything to help the situation.⟩

syn acid, acidic, acrid, biting, caustic, cutting, mordant, pungent, sardonic, satiric
(*or* satirical), scalding, scathing, sharp,
smart-alecky, tart

rel brisk, cross, sharp-tongued, sour, spiky
(*also* spikey), tartish; incisive, keen, poignant, trenchant; cynical, dry, ironic (*also*
ironical), wry; facetious, flippant, tongue-
in-cheek; acrimonious, bitter, resentful;
harsh, rough, severe, stringent; abrupt,
blunt, brusque (*also* brusk), concise, crisp,
curt, gruff, pithy, snippety, snippy, succinct, terse; backhanded, insincere

near ant amusing, droll, merry, playful,
sportive, waggish; gentle, mild; bland;

good-humored, good-natured; diplomatic, polite, smooth, suave, urbane; affable, cordial, genial, gracious, hospitable, sociable

sardonic *adj* marked by the use of wit that is intended to cause hurt feelings — see SARCASTIC

sash *n* a strip of flexible material (as leather) worn around the waist — see ²BELT 1

sass *n* disrespectful or argumentative talk given in response to a command or request — see BACK TALK

sassy *adj* displaying or marked by rude boldness — see NERVY 1

Satan *n* the supreme personification of evil often represented as the ruler of hell — see DEVIL 1

satanic *adj* of, relating to, or worthy of an evil spirit — see FIENDISH 1

sate *vb* 1 to fill with food to capacity — see GORGE 1

2 to put a complete end to (a physical need or desire) — see SATISFY 1

sated *adj* having one's appetite completely satisfied — see FULL 3

satiate *adj* having one's appetite completely satisfied — see FULL 3

satiate *vb* to put a complete end to (a physical need or desire) — see SATISFY 1

satiated *adj* having one's appetite completely satisfied — see FULL 3

satin *adj* 1 having a shiny surface or finish — see GLOSSY

2 smooth or delicate in appearance or feel — see SOFT 2

satiny *adj* 1 having a shiny surface or finish — see GLOSSY

2 smooth or delicate in appearance or feel — see SOFT 2

satire *n* a creative work that uses sharp humor to point up the foolishness of a person, institution, or human nature in general ⟨a *satire* about the music industry in which a handsome but untalented youth is turned into a rock star⟩

syn lampoon

rel burlesque, caricature, parody, spoof, takeoff; comedy, farce, sketch, skit, slapstick, squib; derision, ridicule; cartoon, mockery, travesty

satiric *or* **satirical** *adj* marked by the use of wit that is intended to cause hurt feelings — see SARCASTIC

satisfaction *n* 1 the feeling experienced when one's wishes are met — see PLEASURE 1

2 payment to another for a loss or injury — see COMPENSATION 1

3 a state of mind in which one is free from doubt — see CONFIDENCE 2

satisfactorily *adv* 1 in a satisfactory way — see WELL 1

2 in or to a degree or quantity that meets one's requirements or satisfaction — see ENOUGH 1

satisfactoriness *n* the quality or state of meeting one's needs adequately — see SUFFICIENCY

satisfactory *adj* 1 being to one's liking ⟨We found the meal most *satisfactory*.⟩

syn agreeable, all right, alright, copacetic (*also* copasetic *or* copesetic), fine, good, OK (*or* okay), palatable

rel delectable, delicious, delightful, dreamy, felicitous, gratifying, nice, pleasant, pleasing, scrumptious, welcome; acceptable, adequate, decent, passable, tolerable

near ant bad, deficient, inferior, lousy, poor, punk, substandard, unacceptable, wanting, wretched; mediocre, middling, second-class, second-rate

ant disagreeable, unsatisfactory

2 of a level of quality that meets one's needs or standards — see ADEQUATE

satisfied *adj* 1 experiencing pleasure, satisfaction, or delight — see GLAD 1

2 feeling that one's needs or desires have been met — see CONTENT

satisfy *vb* 1 to put a complete end to (a physical need or desire) ⟨The players *satisfied* their hunger after the game with a big pasta dinner.⟩

syn assuage, quench, sate, satiate

rel cater (to), gratify, humor, indulge; alleviate, lighten, relieve; cloy, saturate, surfeit

near ant arouse, excite, pique, stimulate; tantalize, tease

2 to cause (someone) to agree with a belief or course of action by using arguments or earnest requests — see PERSUADE

3 to do what is required by the terms of — see FULFILL 1

4 to give satisfaction to — see PLEASE 1

5 to provide (someone) with a just payment for loss or injury — see COMPENSATE 1

satisfying *adj* 1 giving pleasure or contentment to the mind or senses — see PLEASANT 1

2 having the power to persuade — see COGENT

3 making one feel good inside — see HEARTWARMING

satisfyingly *adv* in a pleasing way — see WELL 5

saturate *vb* to wet thoroughly with liquid — see SOAK 1

saturate *adj* containing, covered with, or thoroughly penetrated by water — see WET 1

saturated *adj* containing, covered with, or thoroughly penetrated by water — see WET 1

saturnine *adj* causing or marked by an atmosphere lacking in cheer — see GLOOMY 1

sauce *n* 1 a savory fluid food used as a topping or accompaniment to a main dish ⟨The chef poured *sauce* over the meat just before he served it.⟩

syn dressing, gravy

rel condiment, relish, seasoning; fixing(s), garnish, topping; dip, marinade

2 disrespectful or argumentative talk given in response to a command or request — see BACK TALK

3 shameless boldness — see EFFRONTERY

sauciness *n* shameless boldness — see EFFRONTERY

saucy *adj* displaying or marked by rude boldness — see NERVY 1

saunter *n* a relaxed journey on foot for exercise or pleasure — see WALK 1

syn synonym(s)   *rel* related words
ant antonym(s)   *near ant* near antonyms(s)

saunter *vb* to travel by foot for exercise or pleasure — see HIKE 1

sausage *n* a rod-shaped portion of seasoned ground meat in a casing ⟨A couple of *sausages* and eggs make a good breakfast.⟩
syn link
rel bologna, frank, frankfurter, kielbasa, knockwurst (*also* knackwurst), liver sausage (*also* liver pudding), liverwurst, pepperoni, salami, Vienna sausage, weenie, wiener (*also* weiner), wienerwurst; blood sausage (*also* blood pudding)

savage *n* a mean, evil, or unprincipled person — see VILLAIN

savage *adj* 1 having or showing the desire to inflict severe pain and suffering on others — see CRUEL 1
2 living outdoors without taming or domestication by humans — see WILD 1
3 violently unfriendly or aggressive in disposition — see FIERCE 1

savage *vb* to criticize harshly and usually publicly — see ATTACK 2

savageness *n* disposition to willfully inflict pain and suffering on others — see CRUELTY

savagery *n* disposition to willfully inflict pain and suffering on others — see CRUELTY

savanna *also* **savannah** *n* a broad area of level or rolling treeless country — see PLAIN 1

savant *n* a person of deep wisdom or learning — see SAGE

save *prep* not including — see EXCEPT

save *vb* 1 to free from the penalties or consequences of sin ⟨believes the Lord will *save* him⟩
syn deliver, redeem
rel reclaim, reform; forgive, pardon, remit, shrive; bless, hallow; consecrate, purify, sanctify
2 to remove from danger or harm ⟨The firefighters managed to *save* the family's dogs.⟩
syn bail out, deliver, rescue
rel salvage; emancipate, free, liberate, release; disentangle, extricate; recover
ant adventure, compromise, endanger, gamble (with), hazard, imperil, jeopardize, peril, risk, venture
3 to avoid unnecessary waste or expense — see ECONOMIZE
4 to keep in good condition — see MAINTAIN 1
5 to keep or intend for a special purpose — see DEVOTE 1

saver *n* one that saves from danger or destruction — see SAVIOR

saving *conj* if it were not for the fact that — see EXCEPT

saving *prep* not including — see EXCEPT

savior *or* **saviour** *n* one that saves from danger or destruction ⟨The highway patrol officer proved to be our *savior*, arriving on the scene just as the car broke down.⟩
syn deliverer, redeemer, rescuer, saver
rel custodian, defender, guard, guardian, keeper, lookout, protector, sentinel, sentry, warden, warder, watch, watcher, watchman; ransomer; salvager

savor *also* **savour** *n* 1 the property of a substance that can be identified by the sense of taste — see TASTE 1
2 the quality of being delicious — see DELICIOUSNESS

savor *also* **savour** *vb* 1 to make more pleasant to the taste by adding something intensely flavored — see SEASON 1
2 to take pleasure in — see ENJOY 1

savoriness *n* the quality of being delicious — see DELICIOUSNESS

savorless *adj* lacking in taste or flavor — see INSIPID 1

savory *also* **savoury** *adj* 1 having a pleasant smell — see FRAGRANT
2 very pleasing to the sense of taste — see DELICIOUS 1
3 giving pleasure or contentment to the mind or senses — see PLEASANT 1
4 sharp and pleasantly stimulating to the mind or senses — see PIQUANT

savvy *n* knowledge gained by actually doing or living through something — see EXPERIENCE 1

savvy *adj* having or showing a practical cleverness or judgment — see SHREWD 1

savvy *vb* to have a clear idea of — see COMPREHEND 1

saw *n* an often stated observation regarding something from common experience — see SAYING

saw-toothed *adj* notched or toothed along the edge — see SERRATED

say *n* the right to express a wish, choice, or opinion — see VOICE 1

say *vb* 1 to express (a thought or emotion) in words ⟨Why don't you just *say* what's on your mind?⟩
syn articulate, enunciate, pass, speak, state, talk, tell, utter, verbalize, vocalize
rel air, discuss, share, sound, vent, ventilate, voice; blabber, blurt, get off, shoot; advertise, announce, blaze, broadcast, declare, post, proclaim, promulgate, publicize, publish; affirm, allege, assert, aver, avouch, avow; breathe, chirp, drawl, gasp, mouth, murmur, purr, shout, spout, whisper; clothe, couch, formulate, phrase, word; comment, pipe up (with), remark
phrases put into words
near ant stifle, suppress
2 to convey in appropriate or telling terms — see PHRASE
3 to give from memory — see REPEAT 2
4 to take as true or as a fact without actual proof — see ASSUME 2

saying *n* an often stated observation regarding something from common experience ⟨There's an old *saying* that you should let sleeping dogs lie.⟩
syn adage, aphorism, byword, epigram, maxim, proverb, saw, word
rel cliché (*also* cliche), commonplace, platitude, wheeze; expression, felicity; axiom, motto, precept, truism, truth; formula; comment, note, reflection, remark

say-so *n* the right to express a wish, choice, or opinion — see VOICE 1

scabby *adj* arousing or deserving of one's loathing and disgust — see CONTEMPTIBLE 1

scads *n pl* a considerable amount — see LOT 2

scalawag *or* **scallywag** *n* a mean, evil, or unprincipled person — see VILLAIN

scalding *adj* **1** having a notably high temperature — see HOT 1
2 marked by the use of wit that is intended to cause hurt feelings — see SARCASTIC

¹**scale** *n* a device for measuring weight ⟨The vet had a special *scale* for weighing the biggest dogs.⟩
syn balance
rel gravimeter

²**scale** *n* a small thin piece of material that resembles an animal scale ⟨*Scales* of mica were embedded in the granite.⟩
syn lamella, lamina, plate
rel chip, flake, sliver, splint, splinter; sheet, slice

³**scale** *n* **1** a scheme of rank or order ⟨a student who scored very highly on a standard intelligence *scale*⟩
syn graduation, ladder, ordering, ranking
rel food chain, pecking order (*also* peck order); arrangement, array, disposal, disposition, sequence, series, setup; degree, echelon, footing, level, place, position, reaches, situation, spot, standing, station, status
2 the distance or extent between possible extremes — see RANGE 3

scale *vb* to find out the size, extent, or amount of — see MEASURE 1

scaly *adj* composed of or covered with scales ⟨The snake's *scaly* skin was dry to the touch.⟩
syn squamous
rel scalelike
near ant smooth
ant scaleless

scam *n* an instance of the use of dishonest methods to acquire something of value — see FRAUD 1

scamp *n* **1** an appealingly mischievous person ⟨Those little *scamps* are always getting into trouble, but no one has the heart to punish them.⟩
syn devil, hellion, imp, mischief, monkey, rapscallion, rascal, rogue, urchin
rel cutup, madcap, skylarker; brat, nuisance; juvenile delinquent; gamin, gamine
near ant beast, boor, cad, churl, clown, creep, cur, heel, joker, louse, lout, skunk, snake, stinkard, stinker; knave, miscreant, reprobate, scalawag (*or* scallywag), scoundrel, varlet, villain
2 a mean, evil, or unprincipled person — see VILLAIN

scan *n* a close look at or over someone or something in order to judge condition — see INSPECTION

scan *vb* to look over closely (as for judging quality or condition) — see INSPECT

scandal *n* a cause of shame — see DISGRACE 2

scandalous *adj* **1** causing intense displeasure, disgust, or resentment — see OFFENSIVE 1
2 causing or intended to cause unjust injury to a person's good name — see LIBELOUS

scant *adj* less plentiful than what is normal, necessary, or desirable — see MEAGER

scant *vb* to use or give out in stingy amounts — see SPARE 1

scantiness *n* a falling short of an essential or desirable amount or number — see DEFICIENCY

scanty *adj* less plentiful than what is normal, necessary, or desirable — see MEAGER

scapegoat *n* a person or thing taking the blame for others ⟨Companies often use the economy as a *scapegoat* to avoid taking responsibility for dropping sales.⟩
syn fall guy, goat, whipping boy
rel victim; butt, dupe, fool, laughingstock, mark, mockery, monkey; excuse

¹**scar** *n* something that spoils the appearance or completeness of a thing — see BLEMISH

²**scar** *n* a steep wall of rock, earth, or ice — see CLIFF

scarce *adj* **1** less plentiful than what is normal, necessary, or desirable — see MEAGER
2 not coming up to an expected measure or meeting a particular need — see SHORT 3

scarcely *adv* **1** by a very small margin — see JUST 2
2 certainly not — see HARDLY 2

scarceness *n* a falling short of an essential or desirable amount or number — see DEFICIENCY

scarcity *n* a falling short of an essential or desirable amount or number — see DEFICIENCY

scare *vb* to strike with fear — see FRIGHTEN

scare *n* the emotion experienced in the presence or threat of danger — see FEAR 1

scared *adj* filled with fear or dread — see AFRAID

scare up *vb* to come upon after searching, study, or effort — see FIND 1

scarf *vb* to swallow or eat greedily — see GOBBLE

scarp *n* a steep wall of rock, earth, or ice — see CLIFF

scary *adj* **1** causing fear — see FEARFUL 1
2 easily frightened — see SHY 1
3 filled with fear or dread — see AFRAID

scathe *vb* to criticize harshly and usually publicly — see ATTACK 2

scathing *adj* marked by the use of wit that is intended to cause hurt feelings — see SARCASTIC

scatter *n* a small number — see FEW

scatter *vb* **1** to cause (members of a group) to move widely apart ⟨The noise of the backfiring car *scattered* the pigeons.⟩
syn clear out, disband, dispel, disperse, dissipate, squander
rel break up, isolate, part, segregate, separate, split (up); diffuse, disseminate, diverge, spread
near ant agglutinate, conglomerate; unify, unite
ant assemble, cluster, collect, concentrate, congregate, gather, mughter
2 to cover by or as if by scattering something over or on ⟨The hillside was *scattered* with boulders deposited by the last ice age.⟩
syn bestrew, dot, pepper, sow, spray, sprinkle, strew

---

syn synonym(s)   **rel** related words
ant antonym(s)   **near ant** near antonym(s)

rel blanket, drizzle, dust; stud; dapple, fleck, speckle, stipple; bespatter, spatter

3 to go off in different directions and cease to exist as a body or unified whole — see DISPERSE 1

scatterbrained *adj* lacking in seriousness or maturity — see GIDDY 1

scattered *adj* lacking a definite plan, purpose, or pattern — see RANDOM

scattering *n* **1** an act or process in which something scatters or is scattered ⟨the *scattering* of the leaves by the wind⟩
syn disbandment, dispersal, dispersion, dissipation
rel diffusion, dissemination; breakup, dissolution, disunion, separation, split
near ant assembly, collection, concentration, gathering

2 a small number — see FEW

scenario *n* the written form of a story prepared for film production — see SCREENPLAY

scene *n* **1** the place and time in which the action for a portion of a dramatic work (as a movie) is set ⟨The first *scene* was the kitchen of a fancy restaurant during dinner.⟩
syn background, locale, setting
rel backdrop, scenery, set; tableau

2 an outburst or display of excited anger — see TANTRUM

3 position with regard to conditions and circumstances — see SITUATION 1

4 the array of painted backgrounds and furnishings used to establish the setting in a stage production — see SCENERY

scenery *n* the array of painted backgrounds and furnishings used to establish the setting in a stage production ⟨The musical was worth seeing just for the elaborate *scenery*.⟩
syn scene, set
rel backdrop, drop; background; set piece; property

scent *n* **1** a sweet or pleasant smell — see FRAGRANCE

2 the quality of a thing that makes it perceptible to the sense organs in the nose — see SMELL 1

scent *vb* **1** to fill or infuse with a pleasant odor or odor-releasing substance ⟨fancy bars of soap *scented* with lavender⟩
syn incense, perfume
near ant deodorize
ant stink up

2 to become aware of by means of the sense organs in the nose — see SMELL 1

3 to have a vague awareness of — see FEEL 1

scented *adj* having a pleasant smell — see FRAGRANT

schedule *n* **1** a listing of things to be presented or considered (as at a concert or play) — see PROGRAM 1

2 a record of a series of items (as names or titles) usually arranged according to some system — see ¹LIST

schedule *vb* to put (someone or something) on a list — see ¹LIST 2

scheduled *adj* being in accordance with the prescribed, normal, or logical course of events — see DUE 2

scheme *n* **1** a clever often underhanded means to achieve an end — see TRICK 1

2 a secret plan for accomplishing evil or unlawful ends — see PLOT 1

3 a method worked out in advance for achieving some objective — see PLAN 1

scheme *vb* to engage in a secret plan to accomplish evil or unlawful ends — see PLOT

scheme (out) *vb* to work out the details of (something) in advance — see PLAN 1

schism *n* **1** a lack of agreement or harmony — see DISCORD

2 the act or process of a whole separating into two or more parts or pieces — see SEPARATION 1

schmaltz *also* **schmalz** *n* something (as a work of literature or music) that is too sentimental — see CORN

schmaltzy *adj* appealing to the emotions in an obvious and tiresome way — see CORNY

schmooze *n* friendly, informal conversation or an instance of this — see CHAT 1

schmooze *or* **shmooze** *vb* to engage in casual or rambling conversation — see CHAT 1

scholar *n* **1** a person of deep wisdom or learning — see SAGE

2 a person with a high level of knowledge or skill in a field — see EXPERT

3 one who attends a school — see STUDENT

scholarly *adj* **1** having or displaying advanced knowledge or education — see EDUCATED 1

2 of or relating to schooling or learning especially at an advanced level — see ACADEMIC 1

scholarship *n* the understanding and information gained from being educated — see EDUCATION 2

scholastic *adj* of or relating to schooling or learning especially at an advanced level — see ACADEMIC 1

school *vb* to cause to acquire knowledge or skill in some field — see TEACH

school *n* a place or establishment for teaching and learning ⟨one of the first *schools* in the country to offer online courses⟩
syn academy, seminary
rel boarding school, preparatory school, prep school; elementary school, grammar school, high school, junior high school, kindergarten, middle school, primary school, public school, secondary school, senior high school, trade school, training school; charter school, magnet school, minischool

schooling *n* the act or process of imparting knowledge or skills to another — see EDUCATION 1

schoolteacher *n* a person whose occupation is to give formal instruction in a school — see TEACHER

science *n* a body of facts learned by study or experience — see KNOWLEDGE 1

scintillate *vb* **1** to give off sparks — see SPARK 1

2 to shoot forth bursts of light — see FLASH 1

scoff *vb* to swallow or eat greedily — see GOBBLE

scold *vb* to criticize (someone) severely or angrily especially for personal failings ⟨He *scolded* the kids for not cleaning up the mess they had made in the kitchen.⟩

syn bawl out, berate, castigate, chastise, chew out, dress down, flay, hammer, jaw, keelhaul, lambaste (*or* lambast), lecture, rail (at *or* against), rate, rebuke, reprimand, reproach, score, upbraid

rel admonish, chide, remonstrate (with), reprove; abuse, assail, attack, bad-mouth, blame, blast, censure, condemn, criticize, crucify, denounce, dis (*also* diss) [*slang*], excoriate, fault, harangue, knock, lace (into), lash, pan, reprehend, revile, scourge, slam, vituperate; belittle, disparage, mock, put down; ridicule, scoff, scorn

phrases lay into, read the riot act (to), take to task

near ant approve, endorse (*also* indorse), sanction; extol (*also* extoll), laud, praise

scoop *n* 1 a utensil with a bowl and a handle that is used especially in cooking and serving food — see SPOON

2 information not generally available to the public — see DOPE 1

scoop *vb* to lift out with something that holds liquid — see DIP 2

scoot *vb* to proceed or move quickly — see HURRY 2

scope *n* an area over which activity, capacity, or influence extends — see RANGE 2

scorch *vb* 1 to burn on the surface ⟨The picnickers kept *scorching* their marshmallows, deliberately sticking their skewers into the licking flames of the campfire.⟩

syn char, sear, singe

rel fire, ignite, inflame (*also* enflame); kindle, light; bake, cremate, incinerate; scald, scathe

2 to make dry — see DRY 1

scorching *adj* having a notably high temperature — see HOT 1

score *n* 1 a lingering ill will towards a person for a real or imagined wrong — see GRUDGE 1

2 something (as money) which is owed — see DEBT 1

score *vb* 1 to mark with or as if with a line or groove ⟨The glassblower *scored* the glass rod first so that it would break cleanly.⟩

syn groove, scribe, seam

rel abrade, file, graze, mill, rasp, scarify, scratch; bevel, chamfer, flute

2 to gain (as points or runs in a game) as credit towards one's total number of points ⟨He *scored* the winning goal in the final minute of play.⟩

syn rack up, tally

rel triumph, win; best, defeat

near ant lose

3 to obtain (as a goal) through effort — see ACHIEVE 1

4 to criticize (someone) severely or angrily especially for personal failings — see SCOLD

scorn *n* open dislike for someone or something considered unworthy of one's concern or respect — see CONTEMPT

scorn *vb* 1 to show contempt for ⟨*scorned* the traditions of their ancestors⟩

syn disdain, disrespect, high-hat, slight, sniff (at), snub

rel scout; abhor, abominate, despise, detest, execrate, hate, loathe; belittle, deplore, deprecate, disparage; disapprove (of), discountenance, disfavor

phrases look down one's nose (at), sneeze at, thumb one's nose (at), walk over

near ant cherish, prize, treasure, value; admire, esteem, lionize; hallow, revere, venerate, worship; accept, appreciate, approve (of), care (for), countenance, favor, OK (*or* okay), subscribe (to)

ant honor, respect

2 to ignore in a disrespectful manner ⟨She *scorned* the advice of her ophthalmologist and had the laser eye surgery anyway.⟩

syn despise, disregard, flout

rel dismiss, forget, neglect, overlook, overpass, pass over, slur (over); belittle, deprecate, disparage, slight

near ant accept, approve; use

scornful *adj* 1 feeling or showing open dislike for someone or something regarded as undeserving of respect or concern — see CONTEMPTUOUS 1

2 intended to make a person or thing seem of little importance or value — see DEROGATORY

scoundrel *n* a mean, evil, or unprincipled person — see VILLAIN

scour *vb* to look through (as a place) carefully or thoroughly in an effort to find or discover something — see SEARCH 1

scourge *n* 1 a long thin or flexible tool for striking — see WHIP

2 one who inflicts punishment in return for an injury or offense — see NEMESIS 1

3 a source of harm or misfortune — see BANE 1

scourge *vb* 1 to bring destruction to (something) through violent action — see RAVAGE

2 to strike repeatedly with something long and thin or flexible — see WHIP 1

scout *n* a member of the human race — see HUMAN

scout *vb* to make (someone or something) the object of unkind laughter — see RIDICULE

scout (up) *vb* to come upon after searching, study, or effort — see FIND 1

scowl *n* a twisting of the facial features in disgust or disapproval — see GRIMACE

scowl *vb* to look with anger or disapproval — see FROWN

scrabble *n* a forceful effort to reach a goal or objective — see STRUGGLE 1

scrabble *vb* 1 to move (as up or over something) often with the help of the hands in holding or pulling — see CLIMB 1

2 to search for something blindly or uncertainly — see GROPE

scraggly *adj* having an uneven edge or outline — see RAGGED 1

scraggy *adj* 1 having an uneven edge or outline — see RAGGED 1

2 not having a level or smooth surface — see UNEVEN 1

scramble *n* an unorganized collection or mixture of various things — see MISCELLANY 1

scramble *vb* 1 to move (as up or over something) often with the help of the hands in holding or pulling — see CLIMB 1

2 to undo the proper order or arrangement of — see DISORDER

¹**scrap** n **1** an unused or unwanted piece or item typically of small size or value ⟨Only a *scrap* of silk was left on the sewing table after they had finished the project.⟩

syn end, leftover, oddment, remainder, remnant, stub

rel leavings, odds and ends, pickings, refuse, remains, residual, residue, scraping(s), stump, vestige; balance, rest; chip, flake, fragment, piece, sliver, splinter; ribbon(s), shred, tatter

near ant whole

2 a broken or irregular part of something that often remains incomplete — see FRAGMENT

3 a very small piece — see BIT 1

4 discarded or useless material — see GARBAGE

²**scrap** n **1** an often noisy or angry expression of differing opinions — see ARGUMENT 1

2 a physical dispute between opposing individuals or groups — see FIGHT 1

¹**scrap** vb to express different opinions about something often angrily — see ARGUE 2

²**scrap** vb **1** to get rid of as useless or unwanted — see DISCARD

2 to put an end to (something planned or previously agreed to) — see CANCEL 1

scrape n **1** a brief clash between enemies or rivals — see ENCOUNTER

2 a harsh grating sound — see RASP

3 an area of skin roughened or worn away by harsh rubbing against another surface — see ABRASION

scrape vb **1** to pass roughly and noisily over or against a surface ⟨The rusty old gate *scrapes* against the pavement whenever anyone opens it.⟩

syn grate, grind, rasp, scratch

rel rub; groan, whine

near ant glide, skate, slide

2 to damage by rubbing against a sharp or rough surface ⟨She *scraped* her knee when she fell down.⟩

syn abrade, graze, scratch, scuff

rel bark; skin; chafe, fret, gall; claw, cut, lacerate; bruise, contuse

near ant polish, smooth, soften, wax

3 to press or strike against or together so as to make a scraping sound — see GRIND 1

scrappiness n an inclination to fight or quarrel — see BELLIGERENCE

scrapping n the getting rid of whatever is unwanted or useless — see DISPOSAL 1

scrappy adj **1** feeling or displaying eagerness to fight — see BELLIGERENT

2 given to arguing — see ARGUMENTATIVE 1

scratch vb **1** to damage by rubbing against a sharp or rough surface — see SCRAPE 2

2 to pass roughly and noisily over or against a surface — see SCRAPE 1

3 to write or draw hastily or carelessly — see SCRIBBLE 1

scratch (out) vb **1** to compose and set down on paper the words of — see WRITE 1

2 to show (something written) to be no longer valid by drawing a cross over or a line through it — see X (OUT)

scratchy adj **1** having leaves or branches which are likely to cause a scratch ⟨*scratchy* shrubbery that's intended to keep his dogs in the yard⟩

syn brambly, prickly, thistly, thorny

rel burred; bristly, coarse, jagged, rough

2 causing an unpleasant tingling sensation ⟨The wool pants are so *scratchy* that I can't stand to wear them.⟩

syn irritating, prickly

rel coarse, harsh, rough

near ant silken, silky, soft, soothing

3 harsh and dry in sound — see HOARSE

scrawl vb to write or draw hastily or carelessly — see SCRIBBLE 1

scream n someone or something that is very funny ⟨That new comedy is a *scream*!⟩

syn hoot, laugh, riot

rel crack, gag, jest, joke, pleasantry, quip, sally, waggery, wisecrack, witticism; caution, sight

near ant bummer, downer

scream vb **1** to cry out loudly and emotionally ⟨We *screamed* when the roller coaster began its 30-foot plunge.⟩

syn howl, screech, shriek, shrill, squall, squeal, yell, yelp

rel bay, keen, squawk, wail, yowl; bawl, call, cry, holler, shout, thunder, vociferate

near ant murmur, mutter, whisper

2 to show mirth with an explosive vocal sound — see LAUGH 1

3 to express dissatisfaction, pain, or resentment usually tiresomely — see COMPLAIN

screaming adj **1** arousing a strong and usually superficial interest or emotional reaction — see SENSATIONAL 1

2 causing or intended to cause laughter — see FUNNY 1

screech vb to cry out loudly and emotionally — see SCREAM 1

screeching adj having a high musical pitch or range — see SHRILL

screen n **1** the art or business of making a movie — see MOVIE 2

2 means or method of defending — see DEFENSE 1

screen vb **1** to drive danger or attack away from — see DEFEND 1

2 to keep secret or shut off from view — see ¹HIDE 2

3 to pass through a filter — see STRAIN 2

4 to place a protective layer over — see COVER 3

screenplay n the written form of a story prepared for film production ⟨Each actor will be given a copy of the *screenplay* to study.⟩

syn scenario, script

rel story, text

screw vb **1** to twist (something) out of a natural or normal shape or condition — see CONTORT

2 to rob by the use of trickery or threats — see FLEECE

screwball adj showing or marked by a lack of good sense or judgment — see FOOLISH 1

screwball n a person of odd or whimsical habits — see ECCENTRIC

screwing n the twisting of something out of its natural or normal shape or condition — see CONTORTION

screwlike adj turning around an axis like the thread of a screw — see SPIRAL

screwup n 1 an unintentional departure from truth or accuracy — see ERROR 1

2 someone who bungles an effort — see BUTCHER

screw up vb 1 to make a mistake — see ERR 1

2 to make or do (something) in a clumsy or unskillful way — see BOTCH

screwy adj different from the ordinary in a way that causes curiosity or suspicion — see ODD 2

scribble vb 1 to write or draw hastily or carelessly ⟨She *scribbled* a quick note on the pad by the door before leaving.⟩
syn scratch, scrawl
rel jot (down); inscribe, letter, pen, pencil, print, write

2 to compose and set down on paper the words of — see WRITE 1

scribe n 1 one who writes from dictation or copies manuscripts ⟨Variations between the different manuscripts attest to the fallibility of the *scribes* who transmitted them.⟩
syn copyist, penman

2 an official whose job is to keep records — see CLERK 1

3 a person who creates a written work — see AUTHOR 1

scribe vb to mark with or as if with a line or groove — see SCORE 1

scrimmage n a physical dispute between opposing individuals or groups — see FIGHT 1

scrimmage (with) vb to oppose (someone) in physical conflict — see FIGHT 1

scrimp vb to avoid unnecessary waste or expense — see ECONOMIZE

scrimping adj careful in the management of money or resources — see FRUGAL

scrimping n careful management of material resources — see ECONOMY

script n 1 the form or style of a particular person's writing — see HANDWRITING 1

2 the written form of a story prepared for film production — see SCREENPLAY

3 writing done by hand — see HANDWRITING 2

Scripture n a book made up of the writings accepted by Christians as coming from God — see BIBLE

scrooge n a mean grasping person who is usually stingy with money — see MISER

scrub n a living thing much smaller than others of its kind — see DWARF 1

scrub vb to put an end to (something planned or previously agreed to) — see CANCEL 1

scruffy adj showing signs of advanced wear and tear and neglect — see SHABBY 1

scrumptious adj very pleasing to the sense of taste — see DELICIOUS 1

scrunch vb 1 to create (as by crushing) an irregular mass of creases in — see CRUMPLE 1

2 to lie low with the limbs close to the body — see CROUCH

3 to press or strike against or together so as to make a scraping sound — see GRIND 2

¹**scruple** n 1 a very small amount — see PARTICLE 1

2 a very small piece — see BIT 1

²**scruple** n an uneasy feeling about the rightness of what one is doing or going to do — see QUALM

scruple vb to show uncertainty about the right course of action — see HESITATE

scrupulous adj 1 guided by or in accordance with one's sense of right and wrong — see CONSCIENTIOUS 1

2 taking, showing, or involving great care and effort — see PAINSTAKING

scrupulousness n strict attentiveness to what one is doing — see CARE 1

scrutinize vb to look over closely (as for judging quality or condition) — see INSPECT

scrutiny n 1 a close look at or over someone or something in order to judge condition — see INSPECTION

2 a fixed intent look — see GAZE

scuff vb 1 to damage by rubbing against a sharp or rough surface — see SCRAPE 2

2 to move heavily or clumsily — see LUMBER 1

scuffle n a physical dispute between opposing individuals or groups — see FIGHT 1

scuffle vb 1 to move heavily or clumsily — see LUMBER 1

2 to seize and attempt to unbalance one another for the purpose of achieving physical mastery — see WRESTLE

scull vb to move a boat by means of oars — see ¹ROW

sculler n a person who drives a boat forward by means of oars — see OARSMAN

sculpt vb to create a three-dimensional representation of (something) using solid material ⟨The colossal statue was *sculpted* from a single block of marble.⟩
syn carve, sculpture
rel chisel, engrave, etch, grave, incise, inscribe; knap; cast, form, model, shape

sculpture vb to create a three-dimensional representation of (something) using solid material — see SCULPT

scum n 1 people looked down upon as ignorant and of the lowest class — see RABBLE

2 a person whose behavior is offensive to others — see JERK 1

scummy adj arousing or deserving of one's loathing and disgust — see CONTEMPTIBLE 1

scurrilous adj marked by harsh insulting language — see ABUSIVE

scurry vb to proceed or move quickly — see HURRY 2

scurvy adj arousing or deserving of one's loathing and disgust — see CONTEMPTIBLE 1

scuttle vb to proceed or move quickly — see HURRY 2

sea n the whole body of salt water that covers nearly three-fourths of the earth — see OCEAN 1

sea devil n any of several extremely large rays — see DEVILFISH

---

syn synonym(s)   *rel* related words
ant antonym(s)   *near ant* near antonym(s)

sea dog *n* one who operates or navigates a seagoing vessel — see SAILOR

seafarer *n* one who operates or navigates a seagoing vessel — see SAILOR

seam *vb* to mark with or as if with a line or groove — see SCORE 1

seaman *n* one who operates or navigates a seagoing vessel — see SAILOR

sear *vb* 1 to burn on the surface — see SCORCH 1

2 to make dry — see DRY 1

search *n* an act or process of looking carefully or thoroughly for someone or something ⟨The *search* for the missing hikers lasted several days.⟩

syn hunt, quest

rel shakedown; sweep; chase, pursuit; reconnaissance, scout; canvass (*also* canvas), survey; exploration, probe, forage

search *vb* 1 to look through (as a place) carefully or thoroughly in an effort to find or discover something ⟨Archaeologists have begun to *search* the southern end of the valley, where they believe the underground tombs are located.⟩

syn comb, dig (through), dredge, hunt (through), rake, ransack, rifle, rummage, scour

rel frisk, pat down; audit, check (out), examine, inspect, investigate, review, scan, scrutinize, survey; ascertain, descry, detect, determine, discover, ferret (out), find, find out, get, hit (on *or* upon), learn, locate, run down, scare up, track (down); grub (about), poke (around); explore, probe, snoop; browse, glance (over), look over; peruse, study

near ant hide; abandon, lose; ignore, neglect

2 to go into or range over for purposes of discovery — see EXPLORE 2

search (for *or* out) *vb* to go in search of — see SEEK 1

searing *adj* 1 having a notably high temperature — see HOT 1

2 difficult to endure — see HARSH 1

season *vb* 1 to make more pleasant to the taste by adding something intensely flavored ⟨The chef *seasoned* the vegetables as soon as they came out of the oven.⟩

syn flavor, lace, savor (*also* savour), spice

rel enhance, enrich, sauce; pepper, salt; aromatize, perfume

2 to bring to a proper or desired state of fitness — see CONDITION 1

3 to make able to withstand physical hardship, strain, or exposure — see HARDEN 2

4 to make competent (as by training, skill, or ability) for a particular office or function — see QUALIFY 2

seasonable *adj* especially suitable for a certain time — see TIMELY 1

seasoning *n* 1 something (as an herb) that adds an agreeable or interesting taste to food ⟨The stew was too bland before they added the *seasoning*.⟩

syn flavor, flavoring, spice

rel sauce

2 something used to enhance the flavor of cooked or prepared food — see CONDIMENT

seat *n* 1 a place from which authority is exercised ⟨All applications had to be submitted at the county *seat* for proper processing.⟩

syn command, headquarters

rel high command; center, home; capital

2 the part of the body upon which someone sits — see BUTTOCKS

3 a thing or place that is of greatest importance to an activity or interest — see CENTER 1

seat *vb* 1 to cause to sit down ⟨The usher *seated* them in the third row.⟩

syn set down, sit

rel ensconce, settle; lay, lie, rest; place, put; recline, repose

2 to put into an office or welcome into an organization with special ceremonies — see INSTALL 1

seclude *vb* to set or keep apart from others — see ISOLATE

secluded *adj* screened or sequestered from view ⟨We stayed in a *secluded* resort, far away from the regular tourist crowds.⟩

syn cloistered, covert, isolated, quiet, remote, retired, secret, sheltered

rel lone, lonely, lonesome, reclusive, solitary; private

near ant obvious, visible; exposed

secludedness *n* the state of being alone or kept apart from others — see ISOLATION

seclusion *n* the state of being alone or kept apart from others — see ISOLATION

¹**second** *n* a very small space of time — see INSTANT

²**second** *n* something separated from a group or lot for not being as good as the others — see CULL

secondary *adj* 1 taken or created from something original or basic ⟨History textbooks are *secondary* sources for historical information and do not represent original research.⟩

syn derivative, secondhand

rel unoriginal; consequent, resultant

near ant fundamental, nonderivative; first, primary

ant basic, original

2 of little or less value or merit — see INFERIOR 2

second–class *adj* 1 of little or less value or merit — see INFERIOR 2

2 of average to below average quality — see MEDIOCRE 1

secondhand *adj* taken or created from something original or basic — see SECONDARY 1

second–rate *adj* 1 of average to below average quality — see MEDIOCRE 1

2 of little or less value or merit — see INFERIOR 2

3 of low quality — see CHEAP 2

secrecy *n* the practice or habit of keeping secrets or keeping one's affairs secret ⟨She swore him to *secrecy*.⟩

syn closeness, secretiveness

rel confidentiality; discreetness, discretion, prudence; circumspection, wariness; reserve, reticence, silence, taciturnity; furtiveness, shiftiness, slyness, sneakiness, underhandedness; concealment, covertness, subterfuge

near ant candor, frankness, honesty, openness; imprudence, indiscretion

secret adj 1 undertaken or done so as to escape being observed or known by others ⟨a *secret* operation to rescue captive soldiers behind enemy lines⟩

syn clandestine, covert, furtive, huggermugger, private, privy, sneak, sneaking, sneaky, stealthy, surreptitious, undercover, underground, underhand, underhanded

rel off-the-record; classified, confidential, restricted, top secret, undisclosed; concealed, secreted

near ant acknowledged, avowed; aboveboard, straightforward, unconcealed, undisguised; unclassified, unrestricted; clear, evident, manifest, obvious, patent, plain
ant open, overt, public

2 working on missions in which one's objectives, activities, or true identity are not publicly revealed ⟨*secret* agents whose wartime exploits were known only by top government officials⟩

syn undercover
rel covert, private, secretive
near ant overt

3 screened or sequestered from view — see SECLUDED

4 not known or meant to be known by the general populace — see PRIVATE 1

secret n 1 information shared only with another or with a select few ⟨You didn't really expect him to keep a *secret* from me, did you?⟩

syn confidence
rel dope, lowdown
near ant open secret

2 something hard to understand or explain — see MYSTERY

3 something that allows someone to achieve a desired goal — see PASSPORT 1

secretary n an official whose job is to keep records — see CLERK 1

secrete vb to put into a hiding place — see ¹HIDE 1

secretion n the placing of something out of sight — see CONCEALMENT 1

secretive adj given to keeping one's activities hidden from public observation or knowledge ⟨The intelligence agency remained *secretive* despite the media's demands for more openness in government.⟩

syn close, closemouthed, dark, reticent, uncommunicative

rel quiet, reserved, silent, taciturn, tightlipped; discreet, prudent; clandestine, covert, furtive, hugger-mugger, secret, sneak, sneaky, stealthy, surreptitious, undercover, underhand, underhanded

near ant candid, frank, honest; blunt, outspoken, tactless
ant communicative, open

secretiveness n the practice or habit of keeping secrets or keeping one's affairs secret — see SECRECY

sect n a group of people acting together within a larger group — see FACTION

sectarian adj not broad or open in views or opinions — see NARROW 2

sectarian n one who stubbornly or intolerantly adheres to his or her own opinions and prejudices — see BIGOT

section n 1 an area (as of a city) set apart for some purpose or having some special feature — see DISTRICT

2 one of the pieces from which something is designed to be assembled — see PART 1

secular adj not involving religion or religious matters — see PROFANE 1

secure adj 1 having or showing great faith in oneself or one's abilities — see CONFIDENT 1

2 not exposed to the threat of loss or injury — see SAFE 1

3 providing safety — see SAFE 2

4 worthy of one's trust — see DEPENDABLE

secure vb 1 to drive danger or attack away from — see DEFEND 1

2 to make sure, certain, or safe — see ENSURE

3 to put securely in place or in a desired position — see FASTEN 2

4 to receive as return for effort — see EARN 1

security n 1 means or method of defending — see DEFENSE 1

2 something given or held to assure that the giver will keep a promise — see PLEDGE 1

3 the state of not being exposed to danger — see SAFETY 1

sedate adj 1 not joking or playful in mood or manner — see SERIOUS 1

2 free from emotional or mental agitation — see CALM 2

sedative adj tending to calm the emotions and relieve stress — see SOOTHING 1

sediment vb to cause to come to rest at the bottom (as of a liquid) — see SETTLE 1

sediment n matter that settles to the bottom of a body of liquid — see DEPOSIT 1

seduce vb to lead away from a usual or proper course by offering some pleasure or advantage — see LURE

seducer n one that tries to get a person to give in to a desire — see TEMPTER

seduction n the act or pressure of giving in to a desire, especially when ill-advised — see TEMPTATION 1

seductive adj having an often mysterious or magical power to attract — see FASCINATING 1

seductiveness n the power of irresistible attraction — see CHARM 2

seductress n a woman whom men find irresistibly attractive — see SIREN

sedulous adj involved in often constant activity — see BUSY 1

sedulously adv with great effort or determination — see HARD 1

see vb 1 to make note of (something) through the use of one's eyes ⟨Out of the corner of my eye I *saw* the deer run into the woods.⟩

syn behold, catch, descry, discern, distinguish, espy, eye, look (at), note, notice, observe, perceive, regard, remark, sight, spot, spy, view, witness

rel identify, make out, pick out, pick up; attend (to), consider, heed, mark, mind; study, watch; examine, inspect, scan, scrutinize, survey; glance (at), glimpse, peer (at)

phrases get a load of [*slang*], lay eyes on, set eyes on

---

syn synonym(s)   **rel** related words
ant antonym(s)   **near ant** near antonym(s)

near ant disregard, ignore, neglect, overpass, pass over; miss, overlook
2 to come to a knowledge of (something) by living through it — see EXPERIENCE
3 to come to an awareness of — see DISCOVER 1
4 to have a vague awareness of — see FEEL 1
5 to make a social call upon — see VISIT 1
6 to have a clear idea of — see COMPREHEND 1
7 to go along with in order to provide assistance, protection, or companionship — see ACCOMPANY 1
8 to form a mental picture of — see IMAGINE 1
seeable *adj* capable of being seen — see VISIBLE 1
seed *n* **1** the source from which something grows or develops ⟨Ancient Greece provided the *seed* for much of Western civilization's political and philosophical thought.⟩
syn origin, root
rel spring, well, wellhead; beginning, birth, commencement, dawn, genesis, inception, incipiency, launch, morning, onset, outset, start, threshold; creation, inauguration, origination
2 the descendants of a person, animal, or plant — see OFFSPRING
seed *vb* to put or set into the ground to grow — see PLANT 1
seediness *n* the state of being unattended to or not cared for — see NEGLECT 1
seedy *adj* **1** showing signs of advanced wear and tear and neglect — see SHABBY 1
2 worn or torn into or as if into rags — see RAGGED 2
seeing *conj* for the reason that — see SINCE
seek *vb* **1** to go in search of ⟨Henry Hudson was set adrift by mutinous crewmen while *seeking* the Northwest Passage to the Pacific Ocean.⟩
syn cast about (for), cast around (for), forage (for), hunt, look up, pursue, quest, search (for *or* out)
rel ferret (out), root (out)
phrases look for
near ant hide, lose; ignore, neglect
2 to make a request for — see ASK (FOR) 1
3 to make an effort to do — see ATTEMPT
seeker *n* one who seeks an office, honor, position, or award — see CANDIDATE
seem *vb* to give the impression of being ⟨I tried to cheer them up because they *seemed* depressed.⟩
syn act, appear, feel, look, make, sound
rel dissemble, pretend; recall, resemble, suggest; hint, imply, insinuate
seeming *adj* appearing to be true on the basis of evidence that may or may not be confirmed — see APPARENT 1
seeming *n* outward and often deceptive indication — see APPEARANCE 2
seemingly *adv* to all outward appearances — see APPARENTLY
seemliness *n* the quality or state of being especially suitable or fitting — see APPROPRIATENESS
seemly *adj* **1** following the established traditions of refined society and good taste — see PROPER 1

2 very pleasing to look at — see BEAUTIFUL 1
seep *vb* to flow forth slowly through small openings — see EXUDE
seer *n* one who predicts future events or developments — see PROPHET 1
seesaw *vb* **1** to make a series of unsteady side-to-side motions — see ROCK 1
2 to make short up-and-down movements — see NOD
seethe *vb* **1** to be in a state of violent rolling motion ⟨The water *seethed* with schools of feeding piranha.⟩
syn boil, churn, roil
rel reel, spin, swirl, whirl; agitate, stir
near ant abate, calm, subside
2 to be excited or emotionally stirred up with anger — see BOIL 1
segment *n* one of the pieces from which something is designed to be assembled — see PART 1
segregate *vb* to set or keep apart from others — see ISOLATE
segregation *n* the state of being alone or kept apart from others — see ISOLATION
seize *vb* **1** to have a clear idea of — see COMPREHEND 1
2 to take or keep under one's control by authority of law — see ARREST 1
3 to take physical control or possession of (something) suddenly or forcibly — see CATCH 1
4 to take or make use of under a guise of authority but without actual right — see APPROPRIATE 1
seizure *n* **1** a sudden experiencing of a physical or mental disorder — see ATTACK 2
2 the unlawful taking or withholding of something from the rightful owner under a guise of authority — see APPROPRIATION 2
seldom *adv* not often ⟨We *seldom* go to the theater downtown because its prices are so high.⟩
syn infrequently, little, rarely
rel ne'er, never; irregularly, occasionally, sometimes, sporadically
phrases once in a blue moon
near ant customarily, generally, habitually, ordinarily, routinely, usually; always, constantly, continually, continuously, endlessly, eternally, ever, everlastingly, evermore, forever, invariably, perennially, perpetually, unceasingly; chronically, recurrently, repeatedly
ant frequently, oft, often, oftentimes (*or* ofttimes)
select *vb* to decide to accept (someone or something) from a group of possibilities — see CHOOSE 1
select *adj* **1** singled out from a number or group as more to one's liking ⟨The company claims to use only *select* beans to make its coffee.⟩
syn choice, chosen, elect, favored, favorite, picked, preferred, selected
rel fashionable; exclusive; culled, picked over, screened, weeded (out), winnowed (out)
phrases of choice
near ant average, common, commonplace, ordinary, run-of-the-mill

2 having qualities that appeal to a refined taste — see CHOICE 1

selected *adj* singled out from a number or group as more to one's liking — see SELECT 1

selecting *n* the act or process of selecting — see SELECTION 1

selection *n* **1** the act or process of selecting ⟨Her *selection* of a running mate was a long, tedious affair.⟩

syn choice, choosing, election, picking, selecting

rel option; appointment, assignment, designation, naming, nomination; decision

2 a person or thing that is chosen — see CHOICE 2

3 the power, right, or opportunity to choose — see CHOICE 1

4 a number of things selected from a group to stand for the whole — see SAMPLE 1

selective *adj* tending to select carefully ⟨We were highly *selective* about the music we listened to.⟩

syn choosy (*or* choosey), particular, picky

rel nice; fastidious, finicky, fussy; discerning, discriminating, judicious

near ant indiscriminating

ant nonselective, unselective

selector *n* someone with the right or responsibility for making a selection ⟨the librarians who are the *selectors* of the annual award for best children's book⟩

syn chooser, namer, picker

rel elector, voter; nominator; decider

self–acting *adj* designed to replace or decrease human labor and especially physical labor — see LABORSAVING

self–admiration *n* an often unjustified feeling of being pleased with oneself or with one's situation or achievements — see COMPLACENCE 1

self–assertive *adj* **1** having or showing a bold forcefulness in the pursuit of a goal — see AGGRESSIVE 1

2 having a feeling of superiority that shows itself in an overbearing attitude — see ARROGANT

self–assurance *n* great faith in oneself or one's abilities — see CONFIDENCE 1

self–assured *adj* having or showing great faith in oneself or one's abilities — see CONFIDENT 1

self–centered *adj* overly concerned with one's own desires, needs, or interests — see EGOCENTRIC

self–centeredness *n* excessive interest in oneself — see EGOISM

self–conceit *n* an often unjustified feeling of being pleased with oneself or with one's situation or achievements — see COMPLACENCE 1

self–conceited *adj* having too high an opinion of oneself — see CONCEITED

self–confidence *n* great faith in oneself or one's abilities — see CONFIDENCE 1

self–confident *adj* having or showing great faith in oneself or one's abilities — see CONFIDENT 1

self–containment *n* the power to control

one's actions, impulses, or emotions — see WILL 1

self–control *n* **1** the power to control one's actions, impulses, or emotions — see WILL 1

2 the checking of one's true feelings and impulses when dealing with others — see CONSTRAINT 1

self–denial *n* the act or practice of giving up or rejecting something once enjoyed or desired — see RENUNCIATION

self–destruction *n* the act of deliberately killing oneself — see SUICIDE

self–determination *n* **1** the act or power of making one's own choices or decisions — see FREE WILL

2 the state of being free from the control or power of another — see FREEDOM 1

self–discipline *n* the power to control one's actions, impulses, or emotions — see WILL 1

self–esteem *n* **1** a reasonable or justifiable sense of one's worth or importance — see PRIDE 1

2 an often unjustified feeling of being pleased with oneself or with one's situation or achievements — see COMPLACENCE 1

3 great faith in oneself or one's abilities — see CONFIDENCE 1

self–governing *adj* **1** not being under the rule or control of another — see FREE 1

2 of, relating to, or favoring political democracy — see DEMOCRATIC

self–government *n* **1** government in which the supreme power is held by the people and used by them directly or indirectly through representation — see DEMOCRACY

2 the power to control one's actions, impulses, or emotions — see WILL 1

3 the state of being free from the control or power of another — see FREEDOM 1

selfhood *n* the set of qualities that make a person different from other people — see INDIVIDUALITY 1

self–identity *n* the set of qualities that make a person different from other people — see INDIVIDUALITY 1

self–importance *n* an exaggerated sense of one's importance that shows itself in the making of excessive or unjustified claims — see ARROGANCE

2 an often unjustified feeling of being pleased with oneself or with one's situation or achievements — see COMPLACENCE 1

self–important *adj* having too high an opinion of oneself — see CONCEITED

self–imposed *adj* done, made, or given with one's own free will — see VOLUNTARY 1

self–interest *n* excessive interest in oneself — see EGOISM

selfish *adj* overly concerned with one's own desires, needs, or interests — see EGOCENTRIC

selfishness *n* excessive interest in oneself — see EGOISM

self–possessed *adj* free from emotional or mental agitation — see CALM 2

self–possession *n* **1** evenness of emotions or temper — see EQUANIMITY

2 the power to control one's actions, impulses, or emotions — see WILL 1

---

syn synonym(s)   *rel* related words
ant antonym(s)   *near ant* near antonym(s)

self–regard *n* **1** excessive interest in oneself — see EGOISM

2 a reasonable or justifiable sense of one's worth or importance — see PRIDE 1

self–reliance *n* the ability to care for one's self — see SELF-SUFFICIENCY

self–reliant *adj* able to take care of oneself or itself without outside help — see SELF-SUFFICIENT

self–reproach *n* a feeling of responsibility for wrongdoing — see GUILT 1

self–respect *n* a reasonable or justifiable sense of one's worth or importance — see PRIDE 1

self–restraint *n* **1** the power to control one's actions, impulses, or emotions — see WILL 1

2 the checking of one's true feelings and impulses when dealing with others — see CONSTRAINT 1

self–rule *n* government in which the supreme power is held by the people and used by them directly or indirectly through representation — see DEMOCRACY

self–ruling *adj* **1** of, relating to, or favoring political democracy — see DEMOCRATIC

2 not being under the rule or control of another — see FREE 1

selfsame *adj* being one and not another — see SAME 2

self–satisfaction *n* an often unjustified feeling of being pleased with oneself or with one's situation or achievements — see COMPLACENCE 1

self–satisfied *adj* having too high an opinion of oneself — see CONCEITED

self–seeker *n* one who does things only for his own benefit and with little regard for right and wrong ⟨He's a *self-seeker* who is nice only to people who can do him favors.⟩

syn opportunist, temporizer

rel egocentric; conniver, machinator, plotter, schemer; hanger-on, leech

near ant altruist

self–seeking *adj* **1** having a strong desire for personal advancement — see AMBITIOUS 1

2 overly concerned with one's own desires, needs, or interests — see EGOCENTRIC

self–starter *n* an ambitious person who eagerly goes after what is desired — see GO-GETTER

self–sufficiency *n* the ability to care for one's self ⟨*Self-sufficiency* is a goal that all teenagers should work towards.⟩

syn independence, self-reliance, self-support

rel autonomy, freedom, self-determination; potency, power, resilience, strength

near ant helplessness, impotence, impotency, inadequacy, weakness

ant dependence (*also* dependance), reliance

self–sufficient *adj* able to take care of oneself or itself without outside help ⟨The college student worked nights so that he would be *self-sufficient*.⟩

syn independent, self-reliant, self-supporting

rel autonomous, free, self-determining; potent, powerful, resilient, strong

near ant helpless, inadequate, incompetent, insufficient; impotent, weak

ant dependent, reliant

self–support *n* the ability to care for one's self — see SELF-SUFFICIENCY

self–supporting *adj* able to take care of oneself or itself without outside help — see SELF-SUFFICIENT

self–will *n* a steadfast adherence to an opinion, purpose, or course of action in spite of reason, arguments, or persuasion — see OBSTINACY

self–willed *adj* sticking to an opinion, purpose, or course of action in spite of reason, arguments, or persuasion — see OBSTINATE

sell *vb* to offer for sale to the public — see MARKET

sell (for) *vb* to have a price of — see COST

sell (out) *vb* to be unfaithful or disloyal to — see BETRAY 1

seller *n* the person in a business deal who hands over an item in exchange for money — see VENDOR

sellout *n* the act or fact of violating the trust or confidence of another — see BETRAYAL

semblance *n* **1** a display of emotion or behavior that is insincere or intended to deceive — see MASQUERADE

2 outward and often deceptive indication — see APPEARANCE 2

semidarkness *n* a time or place of little or no light — see DARK 1

seminar *n* a meeting featuring a group discussion — see FORUM 1

seminary *n* a place or establishment for teaching and learning — see SCHOOL

send *vb* to cause to go or be taken from one place to another ⟨They promised to *send* the package in the morning.⟩

syn consign, dispatch, pack (off), ship, shoot, transfer, transmit, transport

rel convey, deliver, hand over, pass, render; advance, drop, launch; address, forward; export, import; bestow, contribute, donate, give, present; resend, return

near ant acquire, draw, earn, gain, garner, get, obtain, procure, secure

ant accept

senior *adj* being of advanced years and especially past middle age — see ELDERLY

senior *n* **1** one who is older than another ⟨Since the man next door is my *senior* by a number of years, I always address him as "Mr. Barton."⟩

syn elder

rel ancestor, forerunner, predecessor

near ant contemporary, peer; descendant (*also* descendent), successor

ant junior

2 one who is above another in rank, station, or office — see SUPERIOR

3 the senior member of a group — see DEAN

4 a person of advanced years — see SENIOR CITIZEN

senior citizen *n* a person of advanced years ⟨More and more *senior citizens* are living active, rewarding lives.⟩

syn ancient, elder, golden-ager, oldster, old-timer, senior *rel* graybeard, patriarch; beldam (*or* beldame), dowager, grandam (*or* grandame); adult, grown-up

near ant adolescent, minor; child, cub, juvenile, kid

ant youngster, youth

sensation *n* **1** an indefinite physical response to a stimulus ⟨We felt just the smallest *sensation* of warmth when we leaned against the radiator.⟩

syn feel, feeling, sense

rel impression, perception; hint, suggestion, touch

2 a practice or interest that is very popular for a short time — see FAD

3 something extraordinary or surprising — see WONDER 1

sensational *adj* **1** arousing a strong and usually superficial interest or emotional reaction ⟨The *sensational* news story caused a stir, but after a few days everyone forgot about it.⟩

syn lurid, screaming

rel catchy; colorful, juicy, racy, suggestive; dramatic, histrionic, melodramatic, theatrical (*also* theatric); coarse, vulgar; gory, shocking

near ant innocuous, inoffensive, tame; dignified, formal, proper, restrained

ant nonsensational

2 of or relating to physical sensation or the senses — see SENSORY

3 of the very best kind — see EXCELLENT

sense *n* **1** an indefinite physical response to a stimulus — see SENSATION 1

2 the ability to learn and understand or to deal with problems — see INTELLIGENCE 1

3 the ability to make intelligent decisions especially in everyday matters — see COMMON SENSE

4 the idea that is conveyed or intended to be conveyed to the mind by language, symbol, or action — see MEANING 1

5 the thought processes that have been established as leading to valid solutions to problems — see LOGIC

sense *vb* **1** to have a vague awareness of — see FEEL 1

2 to have a clear idea of — see COMPREHEND 1

senseless *adj* **1** having lost consciousness — see UNCONSCIOUS 1

2 having no meaning — see MEANINGLESS

3 not having or showing an ability to absorb ideas readily — see STUPID 1

4 showing or marked by a lack of good sense or judgment — see FOOLISH 1

5 lacking animate awareness or sensation — see INSENSATE 1

senselessness *n* **1** lack of good sense or judgment — see FOOLISHNESS 1

2 language, behavior, or ideas that are absurd and contrary to good sense — see NONSENSE 1

3 the quality or state of lacking intelligence or quickness of mind — see STUPIDITY 1

sensibilities *n pl* general emotional condition — see FEELING 2

sensible *adj* **1** able to be perceived by a sense or by the mind — see PERCEPTIBLE

2 according to the rules of logic — see LOGICAL 1

3 based on sound reasoning or information — see GOOD 1

4 having revealed facts or feelings actively impressed on the mind — see CONSCIOUS 1

sensibleness *n* the ability to make intelligent decisions especially in everyday matters — see COMMON SENSE

sensitive *adj* **1** able to sense slight impressions or differences — see ACUTE 1

2 being in a situation where one is likely to meet with harm — see LIABLE 1

3 easily injured without careful handling — see TENDER 1

4 of or relating to physical sensation or the senses — see SENSORY

5 requiring exceptional skill or caution in performance or handling — see TRICKY 1

sensitiveness *n* the state or quality of being able to sense slight impressions or differences — see ACUITY

sensitivity *n* the state or quality of being able to sense slight impressions or differences — see ACUITY

sensor *n* a device that detects some physical quantity and responds usually with a transmitted signal ⟨The thief accidentally triggered the motion *sensor*, which set off the alarm.⟩

syn detector

rel eye; electric eye, photoelectric cell; alarm (*also* alarum), trigger

sensory *adj* of or relating to physical sensation or the senses ⟨Trying to listen to music while watching the TV and eating dinner caused a sort of *sensory* overload.⟩

syn sensational, sensitive, sensuous

rel afferent, receptive; sensate, sensual

near ant extrasensory, intuitional

sensual *adj* pleasing to the physical senses ⟨the *sensual* feel of a velvet shirt against the skin⟩

syn carnal, fleshly, luscious, lush, sensuous, voluptuous

rel bodily, corporeal; agreeable, delectable, delicious, delightful, dreamy, gratifying, palatable, pleasant, pleasing, pleasurable, scrumptious; epicurean, luxurious

near ant harsh, painful, uncomfortable; foul, hideous

sensuous *adj* **1** of or relating to physical sensation or the senses — see SENSORY

2 pleasing to the physical senses — see SENSUAL

sentence *n* a decision made by a court or tribunal regarding a case it has heard ⟨Because it was a first offense, the defendant was given a suspended *sentence*.⟩

syn finding, holding, judgment (*or* judgement), ruling

rel inquest, verdict; authority; decree, edict, order; declaration, deliverance, dictum, pronouncement; conclusion, decision, determination, opinion, resolution; discipline, penalty, punishment

sentence *vb* to impose a judicial punishment on ⟨The judge *sentenced* him to a fine and time served.⟩

syn condemn, damn, doom

rel adjudge, judge; castigate, censure, chasten, chastise, correct, discipline, pe-

---

nalize, punish; conclude, decide, decree, determine, find, opine, resolve, rule
near ant pardon, reprieve

sentient *adj* having specified facts or feelings actively impressed on the mind — see CONSCIOUS 1

sentiment *n* **1** a subjective response to a person, thing, or situation — see FEELING 1
2 an idea that is believed to be true or valid without positive knowledge — see OPINION 1

sentimental *adj* appealing to the emotions in an obvious and tiresome way — see CORNY

sentimentalism *n* the state or quality of having an excess of tender feelings (as of love, nostalgia, or compassion) — see SENTIMENTALITY

sentimentality *n* the state or quality of having an excess of tender feelings (as of love, nostalgia, or compassion) ⟨The *sentimentality* of the story of star-crossed lovers only made it even more popular with moviegoers.⟩
syn mawkishness, mush, sappiness, sentimentalism, sloppiness
rel emotion; sentiment; corn, corniness, hokeyness (*or* hokiness), schmaltz (*also* schmalz)
near ant cynicism, hardheadedness, hardheartedness

sentinel *n* a person or group that watches over someone or something — see GUARD 1

sentry *n* a person or group that watches over someone or something — see GUARD 1

separable *adj* capable of being split into two or more parts or pieces ⟨the outdated belief that the atom is the smallest particle of matter and is not *separable*⟩
syn divisible
rel detachable
near ant combinable, joinable
ant indivisible

separate *adj* **1** not the same or shared ⟨We stayed in *separate* apartments on our vacation.⟩
syn different, individual, respective
rel disparate, dissimilar, distinct, distinctive, distinguishable, divergent, diverse, unalike, varied
near ant identical, selfsame, very
ant same
2 not physically attached to another unit ⟨The housing development has 200 *separate* homes, each with its own enclosed yard.⟩
syn detached, disconnected, discrete, free, freestanding, single, unattached, unconnected
rel independent, self-contained; individual, private
near ant adjoining
ant attached, connected, joined, linked
3 not being under the rule or control of another — see FREE 1
4 of, relating to, or belonging to a single person — see INDIVIDUAL 1

separate *vb* **1** to set or force apart ⟨We tried to *separate* the gluey pages, but they were stuck tight.⟩
syn break up, disconnect, disjoin, disjoint, dissever, dissociate, disunite, divide, divorce, part, ramify, resolve, sever, split, sunder, uncouple, unlink, unyoke

rel break down, decompose, disassemble, disintegrate, dissolve; bisect, cleave, dissect, halve, partition, quarter, segment, subdivide, trisect; break, fracture, pull, rend, rift, rip, rive, rupture, tear; cut off, insulate, isolate, seclude, segregate, sequester; detach, disengage, disentangle, unravel, untie
near ant assemble, associate, blend, combine, mingle, mix; connect, couple; accumulate, agglutinate, attach, bind, cement, close, fasten, fuse, knit, stick, weld
ant join, link, unify, unite
2 to go or move in different directions from a central point ⟨The searchers *separated* in order to cover more ground.⟩
syn branch (out), diverge, divide, fork, part, spread
rel bestrew, break up, broadcast, clear out, disband, dispel, disperse, dissipate, distribute, scatter, sow; distance, recede, retreat
near ant assemble, gather, meet
ant converge, join
3 to arrange or assign according to type — see CLASSIFY 1
4 to set or keep apart from others — see ISOLATE
5 to understand or point out the difference in — see DISTINGUISH 1

separation *n* **1** the act or process of a whole separating into two or more parts or pieces ⟨the *separation* of Norway and Sweden into two independent nations in 1905⟩
syn breakup, dissolution, disunion, division, fractionation, partition, schism, split
rel breach, rupture; divorce, severance; decomposition, disassembly, dismemberment, segmentation, subdivision; diffusion, dispersal, dispersion, scattering; administration, apportionment, distribution; isolation, seclusion, segregation, sequestration
near ant assemblage, association; attachment, conjunction, connection, link, linkage, linkup; aggregation, combination, consolidation, fusion
ant unification, union
2 the state of being kept distinct ⟨The *separation* of church and state is an important concept in the United States.⟩
syn demarcation, discreteness, discrimination, distinction
rel differentiation; isolation, segregation
near ant blurring, confusion
3 a movement in different directions away from a common point — see DIVERGENCE 1
4 an open space in a barrier (as a wall or hedge) — see GAP 1
5 the act or process of two or more persons going off in different directions — see PARTING 1
6 something that divides, separates, or marks off — see DIVISION 1

sepulchral *adj* causing or marked by an atmosphere lacking in cheer — see GLOOMY 1

sepulture *n* **1** a final resting place for a dead person — see GRAVE 1
2 the act or ceremony of putting a dead body in its final resting place — see BURIAL 1

sequel *n* a condition or occurrence traceable to a cause — see EFFECT 1

sequence *n* **1** a condition or occurrence traceable to a cause — see EFFECT 1

2 a series of things linked together — see CHAIN 1

3 the way objects in space or events in time are arranged or follow one another — see ORDER 1

sequential *adj* following one after another without others coming in between — see CONSECUTIVE

sequester *vb* **1** to set or keep apart from others — see ISOLATE

2 to take ownership or control of (something) by right of one's authority — see CONFISCATE

sequestration *n* the state of being alone or kept apart from others — see ISOLATION

sere *also* **sear** *adj* marked by little or no precipitation or humidity — see DRY 1

serene *adj* **1** free from disturbing noise or uproar — see QUIET 1

2 free from emotional or mental agitation — see CALM 2

3 free from storms or physical disturbance — see CALM 1

sereneness *n* **1** a state of freedom from storm or disturbance — see CALM 1

2 freedom from disquieting or oppressive thoughts or emotions — see PEACE 2

serenity *n* **1** a state of freedom from storm or disturbance — see CALM 1

2 evenness of emotions or temper — see EQUANIMITY

3 freedom from disquieting or oppressive thoughts or emotions — see PEACE 2

serial *adj* appearing in parts or numbers that follow regularly ⟨"The Count of Monte Cristo" first appeared as a *serial* novel from 1844 to 1846.⟩

syn episodic (*also* episodical), periodical

rel sequential; successive; periodic, recurrent, recurring, regular

serial *n* a publication that appears at regular intervals — see JOURNAL

serious *adj* **1** not joking or playful in mood or manner ⟨I'm *serious* when I say that you need to be aware of your surroundings when driving.⟩

syn earnest, grave, humorless, no-nonsense, sedate, severe, sober, solemn, staid, uncomic, unsmiling, weighty

rel harsh, stern, strict; businesslike, professional; dignified, distinguished, elevated, serious-minded; gloomy, grim

near ant antic, comic, comical, droll, farcical, funny, hilarious, hysterical (*also* hysteric), laughable, light, light-headed, ludicrous, ridiculous, riotous, risible, screaming, uproarious; featherbrained, flighty, frivolous, goofy, harebrained, lighthearted, puerile, scatterbrained

ant facetious, flip, flippant, humorous, jesting, jocular, joking, playful

2 having a matter of importance as its topic ⟨a very *serious* film that deals with our justice system⟩

syn grave, heavy, weighty

rel big, consequential, eventful, important, major, material, meaningful, momentous, portentous, significant, solid, substantial

near ant frivolous, insignificant, little, minor, silly, slight, small, trivial, unimportant

ant light, unserious

3 involving potential loss or injury — see DANGEROUS 1

seriousness *n* a mental state free of jesting or trifling — see EARNESTNESS

sermon *n* a public speech usually by a member of the clergy for the purpose of giving moral guidance or uplift ⟨a *sermon* whose message was that we should love our neighbors as much as we love ourselves⟩

syn homily

rel address, lecture, speech, talk; exhortation; lesson

serpent *n* **1** a limbless reptile with a long body — see SNAKE 1

2 the supreme personification of evil often represented as the ruler of hell — see DEVIL 1

3 one who betrays a trust or an allegiance — see TRAITOR

serpentine *adj* marked by a long series of irregular curves — see CROOKED 1

serrate *adj* notched or toothed along the edge — see SERRATED

serrated *adj* notched or toothed along the edge ⟨You should use a *serrated* knife when cutting bread, so you don't squash the loaf.⟩

syn saw-toothed, serrate

rel serried; jagged, ragged; wavy

near ant flat, smooth

serve *vb* **1** to be an employee for ⟨a butler who *served* several prime ministers⟩

syn work (for)

rel attend, minister (to), tend (to)

phrases wait on (*also* wait upon)

2 to be enough ⟨They made the pasta *serve* for eight guests.⟩

syn do, suffice

rel answer, suit; assuage, content, quench, sate, satiate, satisfy

3 to be fitting or proper — see DO 1

4 to behave toward in a stated way — see TREAT 1

5 to have a certain purpose — see FUNCTION

6 to provide with something useful or desirable — see BENEFIT

server *n* a person who serves food or drink ⟨We had barely finished ordering when the *server* brought our salads.⟩

syn waiter, waitperson

rel waitress; barkeep (*also* barkeeper), bartender; sommelier; steward, stewardess; headwaiter

service *adj* of or relating to the armed services — see MILITARY 1

service *n* **1** an act of kind assistance — see FAVOR 1

2 the capacity for being useful for some purpose — see USE 2

3 the combined army, air force, and navy of a nation — see ARMED FORCES

4 a large unit of a governmental, business, or educational organization — see DIVISION 2

serviceability *n* the capacity for being useful for some purpose — see USE 2

---

syn synonym(s)   *rel* related words
ant antonym(s)   *near ant* near antonym(s)

serviceable *adj* **1** capable of being put to use or account — see PRACTICAL 1

2 capable of or suitable for being used for a particular purpose — see USABLE 1

3 of a level of quality that meets one's needs or standards — see ADEQUATE

serviceableness *n* the capacity for being useful for some purpose — see USE 2

serviceman *n* a person engaged in military service — see SOLDIER

servility *n* the state of being enslaved — see SLAVERY

servitude *n* the state of being enslaved — see SLAVERY

set *adj* **1** being in a state of fitness for some experience or action — see READY 1

2 firmly positioned in place and difficult to dislodge — see TIGHT 2

3 fully committed to achieving a goal — see DETERMINED 1

4 having been established and usually not subject to change — see FIXED 1

5 of a particular or exact sort — see EXPRESS 1

6 made, given, or done with full awareness of what one is doing — see INTENTIONAL

set *n* **1** a group of people acting together within a larger group — see FACTION

2 a group of people sharing a common interest and relating together socially — see GANG 2

3 a number of things considered as a unit — see GROUP 1

4 one of the units into which a whole is divided on the basis of a common characteristic — see CLASS 1

5 the array of painted backgrounds and furnishings used to establish the setting in a stage production — see SCENERY

set *vb* **1** to cover and warm eggs as the young inside develop ⟨The hen *set* for days.⟩

syn brood, hatch, incubate, sit

rel lay, spawn

2 to decide upon (the time or date for an event) usually from a position of authority — see APPOINT 1

3 to make an approximate or tentative judgment regarding — see ESTIMATE 1

4 *chiefly dialect* to rest on the buttocks or haunches — see SIT 1

5 to point or turn (something) toward a target or goal — see AIM 1

6 to come to an agreement or decision concerning the details of — see ARRANGE 1

7 to put securely in place or in a desired position — see FASTEN 2

8 to turn from a liquid into a substance resembling jelly — see COAGULATE

9 to arrange something in a certain spot or position — see PLACE 1

10 to become physically firm or solid — see HARDEN 1

setback *n* a change in status for the worse usually temporarily — see REVERSE 1

set down *vb* **1** to cause to sit down — see SEAT 1

2 to make a written note of — see RECORD 1

3 to think of in a particular way — see CONSIDER 1

set in *vb* to come into existence — see BEGIN 2

set off *vb* to cause to function — see ACTIVATE

settee *n* a long upholstered piece of furniture designed for several sitters — see COUCH

setting *n* **1** the circumstances, conditions, or objects by which one is surrounded — see ENVIRONMENT

2 the place and time in which the action for a portion of a dramatic work (as a movie) is set — see SCENE 1

settle *vb* **1** to cause to come to rest at the bottom (as of a liquid) ⟨The light rain will *settle* the dust in the air.⟩ ⟨Allowing a few moments of rest will *settle* the grounds in the coffee.⟩

syn lay, sediment

rel filter, screen, sieve, sift, strain; clarify, clear; resettle

near ant agitate, disturb, mix, stir

ant raise

2 to supply with inhabitants ⟨The region was originally *settled* by farmers.⟩

syn people

rel inhabit; move (to), relocate (to)

ant depopulate

3 to give an opinion about (something at issue or in dispute) — see JUDGE 1

4 to come to an agreement or decision concerning the details of — see ARRANGE 1

5 to come to rest after descending from the air — see ALIGHT 1

6 to establish or place comfortably or snugly — see ENSCONCE 1

7 to free from distress or disturbance — see CALM 1

8 to gain emotional or mental control of — see COLLECT 1

9 to give what is owed for — see PAY 2

10 to make final, definite, or beyond dispute — see CLINCH

11 to stop the noise or speech of — see SILENCE 1

settle (down) *vb* to become still and orderly — see QUIET 1

settle (on *or* upon) *vb* to come to a judgment about after discussion or consideration — see DECIDE 1

settled *adj* **1** firmly established over time — see INVETERATE 1

2 having been established and usually not subject to change — see FIXED 1

settlement *n* an arrangement about action to be taken — see AGREEMENT 2

settler *n* **1** a person who settles in a new region — see FRONTIERSMAN

2 one that leaves one place to settle in another — see EMIGRANT

setup *n* **1** the way in which something is sized, arranged, or organized — see FORMAT 1

2 the way objects in space or events in time are arranged or follow one another — see ORDER 1

set up *vb* **1** to arrange something in a certain spot or position — see PLACE 1

2 to be responsible for the creation and early operation or use of — see FOUND

3 to fix in an upright position — see ERECT 1

4 to form by putting together parts or materials — see BUILD

5 to restore to a healthy condition — see HEAL 1

seven seas *n pl* the whole body of salt water that covers nearly three-fourths of the earth — see OCEAN 1

sever *vb* to set or force apart — see SEPARATE 1

severe *adj* **1** given to exacting standards of discipline and self-restraint ⟨a *severe*, uncompromising teacher who closed the classroom door precisely when the bell rang and let no one in afterward⟩

syn austere, authoritarian, flinty, hard, harsh, heavy-handed, ramrod, rigid, rigorous, stern, strict, tough

rel demanding, exacting; uncharitable, unforgiving; adamant, callous, hardened, hard-line, immovable, implacable, inflexible, merciless, pitiless, relentless, rock-ribbed, stiff, unbending, uncompromising, unrelenting, unsparing, unyielding; dour, gruff; ascetic (*also* ascetical), monastic, monkish; browbeating, bullying

near ant easy, easygoing, laid-back, undemanding; charitable, kind, merciful, mild, patient, soft, softhearted; accepting, compromising, yielding; responsive, willing; acquiescent, agreeable, amenable, complaisant, compliant, flexible, pliable, pliant

ant clement, forbearing, gentle, indulgent, lax, lenient, tolerant

2 harsh and threatening in manner or appearance — see GRIM 1

3 not joking or playful in mood or manner — see SERIOUS 1

4 difficult to endure — see HARSH 1

5 requiring considerable physical or mental effort — see HARD 2

severely *adv* **1** in a manner so as to cause loss or suffering — see HARDLY 1

2 to a great degree — see VERY 1

severity *n* the quality or state of being demanding or unyielding (as in discipline or criticism) ⟨Even though no one expected the film to be a hit with the critics, the director was taken aback by the *severity* of the criticism.⟩

syn hardness, harshness, inflexibility, rigidity, rigidness, rigor, rigorousness, sternness, strictness

rel callousness, hard-heartedness, implacability, obduracy, pitilessness; dourness, gruffness; asceticism, austereness, austerity, monasticism; determination, firmness, resolve, steadfastness

near ant forbearance, indulgence, kindness, lenience, patience, softness, tolerance; responsiveness, willingness

ant flexibility, gentleness, laxness, mildness

sew *vb* to close up with a series of interlacing stitches ⟨Luckily, I was able to *sew* the tear so skillfully that my pants looked as good as new.⟩

syn darn, stitch

rel mend, patch, repair; baste, ease, fell, finish, overcast; cross-stitch, embroider; crochet, knit

near ant unsew

---

syn synonym(s) *rel* related words
ant antonym(s) *near ant* near antonym(s)

sew up *vb* to have complete control over — see MONOPOLIZE

sex *n* sexual union involving penetration of the vagina by the penis — see SEXUAL INTERCOURSE

sexual intercourse *n* sexual union involving penetration of the vagina by the penis ⟨had a talk with his son about *sexual intercourse*⟩

syn coitus, copulation, intercourse, relations, sex, sexual relations

rel fornication; safe sex; sexuality; breeding, insemination

phrases making love

sexual relations *n pl* sexual union involving penetration of the vagina by the penis — see SEXUAL INTERCOURSE

sexy *adj* of, relating to, exciting, or expressing sexual attraction or desire — see EROTIC

shabby *adj* **1** showing signs of advanced wear and tear and neglect ⟨*shabby* wallpaper that was peeling from the walls⟩

syn dilapidated, dog-eared, dumpy, grungy, mangy, mean, miserable, moth-eaten, neglected, ratty, run-down, scruffy, seedy, tacky, threadbare, tumbledown

rel abandoned, uncared-for, unkept; desolate, forlorn, godforsaken; broken-down, decrepit, tired, worn-out; bedraggled, dingy, ragged, tattered; decaying, deteriorated, deteriorating, ramshackle, rattletrap, rickety; broken, damaged, harmed, hurt, impaired, injured, wrecked

phrases gone to seed

near ant brand-new, fresh, new; kept-up, maintained; mended, patched, rebuilt, reconstructed; smart, spiffy, spruce

2 worn or torn into or as if into rags — see RAGGED 2

shack *n* a small, simply constructed, and often temporary dwelling ⟨a farmer's *shack* out in the fields that's used for lambing and as a shelter from storms⟩

syn cabin, camp, hovel, hut, hutch, shanty

rel lean-to, shed; cot, cottage, lodge; cabana; bungalow, chalet; hogan, wickiup, wigwam; tent

shackle *n* **1** something that physically prevents free movement — see BOND 1

2 shackles *pl* something that makes movement or progress difficult — see ENCUMBRANCE

shackle *vb* **1** to confine or restrain with or as if with chains — see BIND 1

2 to create difficulty for the work or activity of — see HAMPER

shade *n* **1** partial darkness due to the obstruction of light rays ⟨It was hard to see in the *shade* after being in the brilliant sunlight.⟩ ⟨The trees cast *shade*.⟩

syn dusk, penumbra, shadiness, shadow, umbra

rel blackness, dimness, duskiness, gloom, gloominess, murkiness, obscurity, semidarkness, somberness; cloudiness

near ant brightness, brilliance, effulgence, illumination, incandescence, light, lightness, lucidity, lucidness, luminosity, radiance, radiancy

2 a time or place of little or no light — see DARK 1

3 a property that becomes apparent when

light falls on an object and by which things that are identical in form can be distinguished — see COLOR 1

4 a very small amount — see PARTICLE 1

5 the soul of a dead person thought of especially as appearing to living people — see GHOST 1

shade *vb* to shelter (something) from light and heat ⟨The trees *shaded* us quite nicely from the noonday sun.⟩
syn shadow
rel cloud, darken, dim, dull, overcast, overshadow; canopy, cover, protect, screen
near ant illuminate, light, lighten; expose

shaded *adj* protected from the sun's rays — see SHADY 1

shadiness *n* partial darkness due to the obstruction of light rays — see SHADE 1

shadow *n* **1** partial darkness due to the obstruction of light rays — see SHADE 1

2 shadows *pl* a time or place of little or no light — see DARK 1

3 a tiny often physical indication of something lost or vanished — see VESTIGE 1

4 a very small amount — see PARTICLE 1

5 the soul of a dead person thought of especially as appearing to living people — see GHOST 1

6 an overspreading element that produces an atmosphere of gloom — see CLOUD

shadow *vb* **1** to go after or on the track of — see FOLLOW 2

2 to make dark, dim, or indistinct — see CLOUD 1

3 to shelter (something) from light and heat — see SHADE

shadowed *adj* protected from the sun's rays — see SHADY 1

shadowing *n* the act of going after or in the tracks of another — see PURSUIT

shadowy *adj* **1** not seen or understood clearly — see FAINT 1

2 protected from the sun's rays — see SHADY 1

shady *adj* **1** protected from the sun's rays ⟨a lovely *shady* spot in the park that was pleasantly cool⟩
syn shaded, shadowed, shadowy
rel canopied, covered, sheltered; cloudy; dark, darkened, darkish, darkling, darksome, dim, dimmed, dusky, gloomy, inky, moonless, murky, obscure, obscured, penumbral, pitch-black, pitch-dark, somber (*or* sombre)
near ant bedazzling, bright, brightened, brilliant, dazzling, effulgent, illuminated, illumined, incandescent, light, lucent, lucid, luminary, luminous; beaming, lambent, radiant, shining; lustrous
ant exposed, shadeless, sunny

2 given to or marked by cheating and deception — see DISHONEST 2

3 giving good reason for being doubted, questioned, or challenged — see DOUBTFUL 2

4 given to acting in secret and to concealing one's intentions — see SNEAKY 1

5 not respectable — see DISREPUTABLE

shaft *n* **1** a narrow sharply defined line of light radiating from an object ⟨*Shafts* of late-afternoon sunlight pierced the blinds and streaked the floor.⟩
syn beam, ray

rel moonbeam, sunbeam, sunburst; laser

2 a weapon with a long straight handle and sharp head or blade — see SPEAR

3 unfair or inadequate treatment of someone or something or an instance of this — see DISSERVICE

shaggy *adj* **1** covered with or as if with hair — see HAIRY 1

2 made of or resembling hair — see HAIRY 2

shake *n* **1** a very small space of time — see INSTANT

2 shakes *pl* a sense of panic or extreme nervousness — see JITTERS

3 a shaking of the earth — see EARTHQUAKE 1

shake *vb* **1** to make a series of small irregular or violent movements ⟨The bus rattled and *shook* as it barreled down a rutted road.⟩
syn agitate, convulse, jerk, jiggle, joggle, jolt, jounce, quake, quiver, shudder, vibrate, wobble (*also* wabble)
rel rock, sway, swing; chatter, quaver, shiver, thrill, tremble; twitch; dodder, waver; flicker, fluctuate, flutter, oscillate, undulate, wave; beat, palpitate, pit-a-pat, pitter-patter, pulsate, pulse, throb

2 to get or keep away from (as a responsibility) through cleverness or trickery — see ESCAPE 1

shake up *vb* to cause an unpleasant surprise for — see SHOCK 1

shakiness *n* the quality or state of not being firmly fixed in position — see INSTABILITY

shaking *adj* marked by or given to small uncontrollable bodily movements — see SHAKY 1

shaking *n* **1** a series of slight movements by a body back and forth or from side to side — see VIBRATION 1

2 the act or a means of getting or keeping away from something undesirable — see ESCAPE 2

shaky *adj* **1** marked by or given to small uncontrollable bodily movements ⟨The old man's hands were so *shaky* that I was afraid he'd drop the glass.⟩
syn quaking, quavery, quivering, shaking, shuddering, shuddery, tottery, trembling, tremulous, wobbling (*also* wabbling), wobbly (*also* wabbly)
rel convulsive, shivery; rocky, unstable, unsteady, wavering, wavery; palpitating, pulsating, throbbing
near ant controlled, firm, settled, stable, steady

2 giving good reason for being doubted, questioned, or challenged — see DOUBTFUL 2

shall *vb* to be under necessity or obligation to — see NEED 2

shallow *n*, *usually* **shallows** *pl* a place where a body of water (as a sea or river) is shallow — see SHOAL

shallow *adj* **1** lacking significant physical depth ⟨The dog quickly dug a *shallow* hole that was barely deep enough to accommodate his bone.⟩
syn depthless, shoal
rel skin-deep, superficial, surface; measur-

able; finite, limited, measured, restricted; even, flat, flush, horizontal, level, plane, smooth; two-dimensional

near ant abysmal, abyssal, bottomless, boundless, endless, immeasurable, infinite, limitless, measureless, profound, unfathomable, unlimited, vast; navigable
ant deep

2 having or showing a lack of depth of understanding or character — see SUPERFICIAL 2

sham *adj* **1** being such in appearance only and made with or manufactured from usually cheaper materials — see IMITATION

2 being such in appearance only and made or manufactured with the intention of committing fraud — see COUNTERFEIT 1

3 lacking in natural or spontaneous quality — see ARTIFICIAL 1

sham *n* **1** a poor, insincere, or insulting imitation of something — see MOCKERY 1

2 an imitation that is passed off as genuine — see FAKE 1

3 one who makes false claims of identity or expertise — see IMPOSTOR

sham *vb* to present a false appearance of — see FEIGN

shamble *vb* to move heavily or clumsily — see LUMBER 1

shambles *n pl* **1** a dirty or messy place — see PIGPEN

2 a state in which everything is out of order — see CHAOS

shame *n* **1** a feeling of responsibility for wrongdoing — see GUILT 1

2 a regrettable or blameworthy act — see CRIME 2

3 the state of having lost the esteem of others — see DISGRACE 1

shame *vb* to reduce to a lower standing in one's own eyes or in others' eyes — see HUMBLE

shamed *adj* suffering from or expressive of a feeling of responsibility for wrongdoing — see GUILTY

shamefaced *adj* suffering from or expressive of a feeling of responsibility for wrongdoing — see GUILTY

shameful *adj* not respectable — see DISREPUTABLE

shameless *adj* **1** not embarrassed or ashamed — see UNABASHED

2 not sorry for having done wrong — see REMORSELESS 1

shanty *n* a small, simply constructed, and often temporary dwelling — see SHACK

shape *n* **1** a state of being or fitness — see CONDITION 1

2 the outward appearance of something as distinguished from its substance — see FORM 1

3 the type of body that a person has — see PHYSIQUE

shape *vb* **1** to change (something) so as to make it suitable for a new use or situation — see ADAPT

2 to work out the details of (something) in advance — see PLAN 1

shape (up) *vb* to take on a definite form — see FORM 1

shapeless *adj* **1** badly or imperfectly formed — see MALFORMED

2 having no definite or recognizable form — see FORMLESS 1

share *vb* to take a share or part — see PARTAKE 1

share *n* **1** something belonging to, due to, or contributed by an individual member of a group ⟨My *share* of the lottery winnings is over a million dollars.⟩ ⟨Her *share* of the bill comes to $13.44.⟩

syn allotment, allowance, cut, end, part, piece, portion, proportion, quota, slice, take

rel lot, ration; commission, percentage; member, partition, section, segment

near ant aggregate, composite, compound, pool, sum, total, totality; whole

2 a legal right to participation in the advantages, profits, and responsibility of something — see INTEREST 1

shared *adj* used or done by a number of people as a group — see COLLECTIVE

sharer *n* one who takes part in something — see PARTICIPANT

shark *n* **1** a dishonest person who uses clever means to cheat others out of something of value — see TRICKSTER 1

2 a person with a high level of knowledge or skill in a field — see EXPERT

sharp *adv* as stated or indicated without the slightest difference — see EXACTLY 1

sharp *adj* **1** having an edge thin enough to cut or pierce something ⟨Be careful, as that knife is *sharp* enough to slice off a finger.⟩

syn cutting, edged, edgy, ground, honed, keen, sharpened, stropped, trenchant, whetted

rel clawlike, daggerlike, knifelike; jabbing, jagged, lacerating, piercing, scratching, stabbing; pointed, spiky (*also* spikey)

near ant rounded, smooth; soft

ant blunt, blunted, dull, dulled, obtuse

2 having a powerfully stimulating odor or flavor ⟨a *sharp* cheese⟩

syn nippy, pungent, strong, tangy

rel acid, acidic; acrid, bitter, harsh; gingery, hot, peppery, piquant, spicy, tart, zesty; putrid, rank, skunky; appetizing, delectable, delicious, palatable, toothsome; flavorful, savory (*also* savoury), tasty; aromatic, redolent

near ant aged, mellow, ripe; gentle, soft; flat, flavorless, insipid; savorless, tasteless, zestless; dilute, thin, watery, weak

ant bland, mild, smooth

3 tapering to a thin tip — see POINTED 1

4 being in the latest or current fashion — see STYLISH

5 being strikingly neat and trim in style or appearance — see SMART 1

6 causing intense discomfort to one's skin — see CUTTING 1

7 given to or marked by cheating and deception — see DISHONEST 2

8 having or showing a practical cleverness or judgment — see SHREWD 1

9 having or showing quickness of mind — see INTELLIGENT 1

10 marked by the use of wit that is intended to cause hurt feelings — see SARCASTIC

---

syn synonym(s)   *rel* related words
ant antonym(s)   *near ant* near antonym(s)

11 able to sense slight impressions or differences — see ACUTE 1

12 uncomfortably cool — see CHILLY 1

sharpen *vb* to make sharp or sharper ⟨You need to *sharpen* your penknife's blade frequently in order to be able to whittle properly.⟩
syn edge, grind, hone, strop, whet
rel file
near ant buff, burnish, gloss, polish, round, smooth
ant blunt, dull

sharpened *adj* having an edge thin enough to cut or pierce something — see SHARP 1

sharper *n* a dishonest person who uses clever means to cheat others out of something of value — see TRICKSTER 1

sharp–eyed *adj* having unusually keen vision ⟨A very *sharp-eyed* child found the last Easter egg, which was hidden in the flower arrangement.⟩
syn clear-sighted, lynx-eyed
rel sighted; alert, attentive, aware, observant, observing, vigilant, watchful
near ant blind, eyeless, sightless, stone-blind; astigmatic, myopic, nearsighted, shortsighted; purblind

sharply *adv* in a strikingly neat and trim manner — see SMARTLY

sharpness *n* 1 a harsh or sharp quality — see EDGE 1

2 an uncomfortable degree of coolness — see CHILL

3 exceptional discernment and judgment especially in practical matters — see ACUMEN

4 the state or quality of being able to sense slight impressions or differences — see ACUITY

sharpshooter *n* a person skilled in shooting at a target — see MARKSMAN

sharp–witted *adj* 1 having or showing a practical cleverness or judgment — see SHREWD 1

2 having or showing quickness of mind — see INTELLIGENT 1

shatter *vb* 1 to bring to a complete end the physical soundness, existence, or usefulness of — see DESTROY 1

2 to cause to break open or into pieces by or as if by an explosive — see BLAST 1

3 to cause to break with violence and much noise — see SMASH 1

shave *vb* 1 to make (something) shorter or smaller with the use of a cutting instrument — see CLIP 1

2 to pass lightly across or touch gently especially in passing — see ²BRUSH

shaver *n* a male person who has not yet reached adulthood — see BOY 1

shear *vb* 1 to make (something) shorter or smaller with the use of a cutting instrument — see CLIP 1

2 to penetrate with a sharp edge (as a knife) — see CUT 1

sheath *n* something that encloses another thing especially to protect it — see ¹CASE 1

sheathe *also* **sheath** *vb* to cover with something that protects ⟨Sometimes shipbuilders *sheathe* a ship's bottom with copper for extra protection from barnacles and other threats.⟩
syn face

rel apparel, array, clothe, dress, garb, robe; encase, enclose (*also* inclose), enshroud, envelop, enwrap, invest, lap, mantle, shroud, surround, swathe, veil, wrap; blanket, overlay, overspread
near ant bare, denude, expose, strip; unswathe

shed *vb* 1 to cast (a natural bodily covering or appendage) aside ⟨A snake's skin doesn't grow as the snake does, so every so often the snake will *shed* its old skin.⟩
syn exfoliate, molt, slip, slough (*also* sluff)
rel flake, peel, scale; chuck, discard, ditch, fling (off *or* away), jettison, junk, scrap, shuck (off), throw away, throw out, unload

2 to get rid of as useless or unwanted — see DISCARD

sheen *n* brightness created by light reflected from a surface — see SHINE 1

sheep *n* an innocent or gentle person — see LAMB

sheepish *adj* not comfortable around people — see SHY 2

sheepishly *adv* in a manner showing no signs of pride or self-assertion — see LOWLY

sheer *vb* 1 to change one's course or direction — see TURN 3

2 to depart abruptly from a straight line or course — see SWERVE 1

sheer *adj* 1 very thin and easy to see through ⟨We had to get window shades because passersby could see right through our *sheer* curtains.⟩
syn filmy, gauzy, gossamer, gossamery, transparent
rel clear, crystalline, limpid, liquid, lucent, pellucid; lucid, translucent; dainty, delicate, flimsy, fragile, frail, insubstantial, unsubstantial; colorless, uncolored
near ant opaque; cloudy, foggy, hazy, misty, murky, nebulous, smoky (*also* smokey); drab, dull, lackluster, lusterless

2 having no exceptions or restrictions — see ABSOLUTE 2

3 having an incline approaching the perpendicular — see STEEP 1

sheet *vb* to form a layer over — see COVER 2

sheet *n* a wide space or area — see EXPANSE

shell *n* 1 something that encloses another thing especially to protect it — see ¹CASE 1

2 the arrangement of parts that gives something its basic form — see FRAME 1

3 an outer part or layer — see EXTERIOR

shell *vb* 1 to remove the natural covering of — see PEEL

2 to use bombs or artillery against — see BOMBARD 1

shellacking *n* failure to win a contest — see DEFEAT 1

shell–shocked *adj* 1 suffering from high levels of physical and especially psychological stress — see STRESSED-OUT

2 suffering from mental confusion — see DIZZY 2

shelter *n* something (as a building) that offers cover from the weather or protection from danger ⟨The sudden fierce storm forced us to run to the nearest *shelter*.⟩
syn asylum, harbor, harborage, haven, refuge, retreat, sanctuary, sanctum

rel oasis; anchorage, mooring, port; cover, screen; housing, lodging, quarters, residence, rest, roof; cloister, closet, covert, den, hermitage, hideaway, hideout, lair; lean-to, lee, shed, windbreak

shelter *vb* **1** to be or provide a shelter for ⟨The abandoned barn *shelters* a colony of stray cats.⟩

syn harbor, refuge

rel cover, defend, protect, safeguard, screen, secure, shield, ward; domicile, house, place, quarter; shade, shadow

near ant expose

2 to provide with living quarters or shelter — see HOUSE 1

sheltered *adj* screened or sequestered from view — see SECLUDED

shelve *vb* to assign to a later time — see POSTPONE

shepherd *vb* to give advice and instruction to (someone) regarding the course or process to be followed — see GUIDE 1

shibboleth *n* **1** an attention-getting word or phrase used to publicize something (as a campaign or product) — see SLOGAN

2 an idea or expression that has been used by many people — see COMMONPLACE

shield *n* means or method of defending — see DEFENSE 1

shield *vb* **1** to drive danger or attack away from — see DEFEND 1

2 to place a protective layer over — see COVER 3

shift *n* **1** an action planned or taken to achieve a desired result — see MEASURE 1

2 the act or an instance of changing position — see MOVEMENT 1

shift *vb* **1** to change the place or position of — see MOVE 1

2 to change one's position — see MOVE 3

3 to pass from one form, state, or level to another — see CHANGE 2

4 to give up (something) and take something else in return — see CHANGE 3

5 to meet one's day-to-day needs — see GET ALONG 1

shifting *n* the act or an instance of changing position — see MOVEMENT 1

shiftless *adj* not easily aroused to action or work — see LAZY 1

shiftlessness *n* an inclination not to do work or engage in activities — see LAZINESS

shifty *adj* **1** given to acting in secret and to concealing one's intentions — see SNEAKY 1

2 given to or marked by cheating and deception — see DISHONEST 2

shillelagh *also* **shillalah** *n* a heavy rigid stick used as a weapon or for punishment — see CLUB 1

shilly–shally *vb* **1** to show uncertainty about the right course of action — see HESITATE

2 to move or act slowly — see DELAY 1

shilly–shally *n* a state or an instance of temporary inaction because of uncertainty about the right course of action — see HESITATION

shilly–shallying *n* a state or an instance of temporary inaction because of uncertainty about the right course of action — see HESITATION

shimmer *vb* to shoot forth bursts of light — see FLASH 1

shindig *n* a social gathering — see PARTY 1

shindy *n* a state of noisy, confused activity — see COMMOTION

shine *n* **1** brightness created by light reflected from a surface ⟨The troop inspector insisted on nothing less than a dazzling *shine* from every pair of shoes in the line of review.⟩

syn burnish, gloss, luster (*or* lustre), polish, sheen

rel glare, gleam, glimmer, glint, glisten, glow, shimmer; blink, flicker, sparkle, twinkle; illumination, irradiation; iridescence, luminescence; brilliance, luminosity, radiance, radiancy, refulgence; finish, glaze

near ant dimness, dinginess, dirtiness, drabness, dullness (*also* dulness), flatness; grayness, paleness; cloudiness, gloom, murkiness, obscureness, obscurity, somberness

2 the steady giving off of the form of radiation that makes vision possible — see LIGHT 1

3 positive regard for something — see LIKING

shine *vb* **1** to emit rays of light ⟨The sun appears to *shine* particularly brightly in summer because that is when it's closest to the Earth.⟩

syn beam, radiate, ray

rel blaze, burn, fire, flame, gleam, glimmer, glint, glisten, glister, glitter, glow, luminesce, sheen, shimmer; blink, flare, flash, flicker, luster (*or* lustre), scintillate, sparkle, twinkle; beat (down), glare; brighten, illuminate, illumine, irradiate, light, lighten; bedazzle, blind, daze, dazzle

near ant blacken, darken; lower (*also* lour)

2 to make smooth or glossy usually by repeatedly applying surface pressure — see POLISH 1

shining *adj* giving off or reflecting much light — see BRIGHT 1

shiny *adj* giving off or reflecting much light — see BRIGHT 1

ship *n* a large craft for travel by water ⟨a cruise *ship* plying the warm waters of the Caribbean⟩

syn boat, vessel

rel aircraft carrier, argosy, barge, containership, corvette, cruiser, cutter, destroyer, ferryboat, flagship, freighter, icebreaker, ironclad, lightship, liner, man-of-war (*also* man-o'-war), merchantman, merchant ship, motor ship, packet, steamer, steamship, superliner, supertanker, tanker, trader, tramp, transport, warship; bark (*or* barque), brig, brigantine, caravel, clipper, junk, ketch, sailboat, schooner, squarerigger, tall ship, windjammer, xebec, yacht

ship *vb* to cause to go or be taken from one place to another — see SEND

shippable *adj* capable of being taken from one place to another by public carrier ⟨Only boxes of five pounds and under are *shippable* by the postal service.⟩

syn transferable (*also* transferrable), transmittable, transportable

---

syn synonym(s)   *rel* related words
ant antonym(s)   *near ant* near antonym(s)

rel addressable; mailable

ant nontransferable, receivable

shipshape *adj* being clean and in good order — see NEAT 1

shipwreck *n* the destruction or loss of a ship ⟨The *shipwreck* of much of the Spanish Armada ended Spain's plans for invading England.⟩

syn shipwrecking, wreck, wreckage, wrecking

rel beaching, grounding, stranding; foundering, sinking; scuttling

near ant recovery, salvage, salvaging

shipwreck *vb* to cause irreparable damage to (a ship) by running aground or sinking ⟨The yachtsman fell asleep at the wheel and *shipwrecked* his ketch on the rocks.⟩

syn strand, wreck

rel beach; founder; scuttle

near ant recover, salvage

shipwrecking *n* the destruction or loss of a ship — see SHIPWRECK

shirk *vb* 1 to get or keep away from (as a responsibility) through cleverness or trickery — see ESCAPE 1

2 to leave undone or unattended to especially through carelessness — see NEGLECT 2

3 to move about in a sly or secret manner — see SNEAK 1

shirker *n* one who deliberately avoids work or duty — see SLACKER

shiver *n* 1 an instance of shaking involuntarily with fear or cold ⟨experienced a sudden *shiver* when the wind blew the door open⟩

syn quiver, shudder, tremble

rel agitation, convulsing, jolt, quake, shake, tremor, vibration, wobble (*also* wabble); flutter, oscillation, wave; beat, palpitation, pulsation, pulse, throb

2 shivers *pl* a sense of panic or extreme nervousness — see JITTERS

shivery *adj* having a low or subnormal temperature — see COLD 1

shoal *adj* lacking significant physical depth — see SHALLOW 1

shoal *n* a place where a body of water (as a sea or river) is shallow ⟨The *shoals* off Nantucket Island are famous as the final resting places of many ill-fated ships.⟩

syn ford, shallow(s)

rel bank, bar, sandbank, sandbar, towhead

near ant trench; abyss, deep, depth, gulf

shock *n* 1 a forceful coming together of two things — see IMPACT 1

2 the state of being strongly impressed by something unexpected or unusual — see SURPRISE 2

shock *vb* 1 to cause an unpleasant surprise for ⟨Mom was *shocked* by the news that her coworker had been fired.⟩ ⟨I was *shocked* to find out that I was the victim of identity theft.⟩

syn appall (*also* appal), floor, jolt, shake up

rel astonish, dumbfound (*also* dumfound), flabbergast, freak (out), stun, stupefy; affright, alarm (*also* alarum), dismay, fright, frighten, horrify, panic, scare, scarify, spook, startle, terrify, terrorize; disgust, nauseate, repel, revolt, sicken, turn off; displease, offend, outrage, scandalize; amaze, astound, awe; chill, daunt, demoralize, dispirit, emasculate, undo, unman, unnerve, unstring; discomfort, discompose, disconcert, disquiet, distress, disturb, perturb, shake, unsettle, upset; crush, overpower, overwhelm

phrases knock for a loop

near ant buffer, cushion; delight, gratify, please, rejoice, tickle; charm, entice, tempt; assure, cheer, comfort, console, solace, soothe; reassure

2 to make a strong impression on (someone) with something unexpected — see SURPRISE 1

3 to strike with fear — see FRIGHTEN

shocked *adj* 1 affected with sudden and great wonder or surprise — see THUNDERSTRUCK

2 filled with disgust — see SICK 2

3 filled with fear or dread — see AFRAID

shocking *adj* 1 causing a strong emotional reaction because of unexpectedness — see SURPRISING 1

2 causing fear — see FEARFUL 1

3 causing intense displeasure, disgust, or resentment — see OFFENSIVE 1

4 extremely disturbing or repellent — see HORRIBLE 1

shoddy *adj* 1 of low quality — see CHEAP 2

2 not respectable — see DISREPUTABLE

shoes *n pl* a way of looking at or thinking about something — see PERSPECTIVE 1

shoestring *n* a very small sum of money — see MITE 1

shoot *n* 1 a branch of a main stem especially of a plant — see OFFSHOOT 1

2 a sharp unpleasant sensation usually felt in some specific part of the body — see PAIN 1

shoot *vb* 1 to cause (a projectile) to be driven forward with force ⟨BB guns *shoot* small round metal pellets.⟩

syn blast, discharge, fire, loose

rel launch, project; blaze (at), snipe (at); cast, catapult, fling, heave, hurl, hurtle, lob, pelt, pitch, sling, throw, toss

2 to cause a weapon to release a missile with great force ⟨Soldiers train extensively to learn to *shoot* accurately and quickly.⟩

syn blast, discharge, fire

rel blaze, pepper; plink, snipe

3 to strike with a missile from a gun ⟨Hunters can *shoot* turkeys only during the legally specified open season.⟩

syn drill, gun

rel bring down, drop; blaze, pepper, snipe (at); blast (at), fire (at); shotgun; machine-gun, tommy-gun

4 to proceed or move quickly — see HURRY 2

5 to take a photograph of — see PHOTOGRAPH

6 to throw or give off — see EMIT 1

7 to voice one's opinions freely with force — see SPEAK UP

8 to cause to go or be taken from one place to another — see SEND

shoot (up) *vb* to rise abruptly and rapidly — see SKYROCKET

shooter *n* 1 a person skilled in shooting at a target — see MARKSMAN

2 one who takes photographs — see PHOTOGRAPHER

shop *n* **1** *also* **shoppe** an establishment where goods are sold to consumers ⟨The only *shop* that has that video game in stock is halfway across the state.⟩

syn bazaar, emporium, store

rel market, marketplace, outlet, showroom; boutique, chain store, department store, dime store, exchange, five-and-ten (*also* five-and-dime), mart, thrift shop, variety store

2 a building or set of buildings for the manufacturing of goods — see FACTORY

3 the special terms or expressions of a particular group or field — see TERMINOLOGY

shopworn *adj* used or heard so often as to be dull — see STALE 1

shore *n* a structure that holds up or serves as a foundation for something else — see SUPPORT 1

shore (up) *vb* **1** to hold up or serve as a foundation for — see SUPPORT 3

2 to provide evidence or information for (as a claim or idea) — see SUPPORT 4

short *adj* **1** having relatively little height ⟨He is *short* for his age.⟩

syn little, low, low-lying

rel dwarf, dwarfish; compact, petite, slight; diminutive, half-pint, pint-size (*or* pint-sized), pocket, pocket-size (*also* pocket-sized), pygmy, small, smallish; bantam, bitty, dinky, mini, miniature, minute, puny, teeny, teeny-weeny, tiny, undersized (*also* undersize), wee; stubby, stumpy, stunted

near ant elevated, lifted, raised, uplifted, upswept; high-rise, statuesque; gangling, gangly, lanky, rangy; big, bulky, hefty, hulking, large, largish, outsize (*also* outsized), oversize (*or* oversized), sizable (*or* sizeable), voluminous

ant high, lofty, tall, towering

2 not lasting for a considerable time ⟨Fortunately for those of us in the hot sun, the graduation speech was *short* and to the point.⟩

syn brief, fast, little

rel shortish; abbreviated, abridged, curtailed, cut-back, shortened, syncopated; compact, condensed; abrupt, sudden; ephemeral, fleeting, momentary, short-lived, transient, transitory; impermanent; compendious, concise, pithy, succinct, summary, terse; short-range, short-term

near ant endless, everlasting, interminable, persistent, unending; longish, overlong, prolonged, protracted; permanent; enlarged, expanded, supplemented; long-range, long-term

ant extended, far, great, lengthy, long, long-lived

3 not coming up to an expected measure or meeting a particular need ⟨Regrettably, the art supplies are *short* this year, so you'll have to share.⟩

syn deficient, inadequate, insufficient, lacking, low, scarce, shy, wanting

rel substandard, unacceptable, unsatisfactory; hand-to-mouth, lean, light, meager (*or* meagre), poor, scant, scanty, skimp,

skimpy, slender, slim, spare, sparse, stingy; bare, minimum; slight, small

near ant abundant, ample, bounteous, bountiful, copious, generous, liberal, plenteous, plentiful; enlarged, expanded, supplemented; abounding, overflowing, teeming; satisfactory, tolerable; big, considerable, hefty, jumbo, king-size (*or* king-sized), large, largish, oversize (*or* oversized), sizable (*or* sizeable)

ant adequate, enough, sufficient

4 having a texture that readily breaks into little pieces under pressure — see CRISP 1

5 being or characterized by direct, brief, and potentially rude speech or manner — see BLUNT 1

short *adv* with great suddenness ⟨The bicyclist ahead of me unexpectedly pulled up *short* and I almost plowed into him.⟩

syn abruptly, suddenly

rel surprisingly, unexpectedly; directly, immediately, instantly, promptly, pronto, right, right away, straightaway; fast, full-tilt, posthaste, quick, quickly, rapidly, readily, snappily, speedily, swift, swiftly; hastily, impetuously, impulsively, rashly, recklessly

phrases all of a sudden (*also* on a sudden)

near ant gradually, slowly; hesitantly

short *vb* to rob by the use of trickery or threats — see FLEECE

shortage *n* a falling short of an essential or desirable amount or number — see DEFICIENCY

shortchange *vb* to rob by the use of trickery or threats — see FLEECE

shortcoming *n* a defect in character — see FAULT 1

shorten *vb* to make less in extent or duration ⟨We decided to *shorten* the distance we had to walk home by cutting across the neighbor's lawn.⟩ ⟨If Grandma has to go shopping today, you'll need to *shorten* your visit.⟩

syn abbreviate, abridge, curtail, cut back, dock, truncate

rel abstract, digest, encapsulate, epitomize, recapitulate, summarize, sum up; abate, compress, constrict, contract, cut, cut down, pare, prune, trim; decrease, de-escalate, deflate, diminish, downsize, dwindle, lessen, lower, moderate, modify, reduce, retrench, shrink, slash, subtract (from), taper

near ant enlarge, expand, supplement; add, aggrandize, amplify, augment, balloon, boost, dilate, escalate, heighten, increase, maximize, raise; blow up, distend, inflate, swell

ant elongate, extend, lengthen, prolong, protract

short–lived *adj* lasting only for a short time — see MOMENTARY

shortly *adv* **1** in a few words ⟨The sudden closing of the restaurant was announced only with a *shortly* worded sign: "Out of Business."⟩

syn briefly, compactly, concisely, crisply, laconically, pithily, succinctly, summarily, tersely

rel exactly, precisely; abruptly, bluffly, bluntly, brusquely

phrases in a nutshell, in a word, in brief, in short, in sum

---

syn synonym(s)   **rel** related words
ant antonym(s)   **near ant** near antonym(s)

near ant redundantly, repetitiously

ant diffusely, long-windedly, verbosely, wordily

2 at or within a short time ⟨The meeting will begin *shortly*, so don't go too far away.⟩

syn anon, directly, momentarily, presently, soon

rel forthwith, immediately, instantly, now, promptly, pronto, right away, right now, straightaway, straightway

shortness *n* the condition of being short — see BREVITY 1

shortsighted *adj* **1** able to see near things more clearly than distant ones — see NEARSIGHTED

2 not thinking about and providing for the future — see IMPROVIDENT

short story *n* a work with imaginary characters and events that is shorter and usually less complex than a novel — see STORY 1

short–tempered *adj* easily irritated or annoyed — see IRRITABLE

short–term *adj* intended to last, continue, or serve for a limited time — see TEMPORARY 1

shot *n* **1** a directed propelling of a missile by a firearm or artillery piece ⟨Cannon operators often had to use several *shots* to figure out the range of their targets.⟩

syn blasting, discharge, firing

rel barrage, blitz, blitzkrieg, bombardment, broadside, burst, cannonade, fusillade, hail, salvo, shower, storm, volley

2 an effort to do or accomplish something — see ATTEMPT 1

3 a picture created from an image recorded on a light-sensitive surface by a camera — see PHOTOGRAPH

4 a person skilled in shooting at a target — see MARKSMAN

5 the portion of a serving of a beverage that is swallowed at one time — see DRINK 2

6 an opinion or judgment based on little or no evidence — see CONJECTURE

7 a favorable combination of circumstances, time, and place — see OPPORTUNITY

should *vb* to be under necessity or obligation to — see NEED 2

shoulder *vb* **1** to take to or upon oneself — see ASSUME 1

2 to force one's way — see ²PRESS 4

shout *vb* to speak so as to be heard at a distance — see CALL 1

shout *n* a loud vocal expression of strong emotion ⟨I gave a sudden *shout* of surprise when the shower abruptly turned ice-cold.⟩

syn cry, holler, hoot, howl, whoop, yell, yowl

rel ejaculation, interjection; scream, screech, shriek, shrill, squall, squeak, squeal, yelp; bawl, bellow, clamor, outcry, roar; wail

near ant mumble, murmur, mutter; gasp, whimper, whisper

shove *vb* **1** to apply force to (someone or something) so that it moves in front of one — see PUSH 1

2 to push steadily against with some force — see ²PRESS 1

shove (off) *vb* to leave a place often for another — see GO 2

shovel *vb* to hollow out or form (something) by removing earth — see DIG 1

show *n* **1** an outward and often exaggerated indication of something abstract (as a feeling) for effect ⟨The children made a *show* of disgust when confronted with asparagus.⟩

syn demonstration, display, exhibition, flaunting

rel act, charade, facade (*also* façade), front, guise, pretense (*or* pretence), put-on, semblance, simulation; affectation, pose, sham; betrayal, disclosure

2 a display of emotion or behavior that is insincere or intended to deceive — see MASQUERADE

3 outward and often deceptive indication — see APPEARANCE 2

4 a public showing of objects of interest — see EXHIBITION 1

show *vb* **1** to present so as to invite notice or attention ⟨Fishing for compliments, the neighbors *showed* their new car to everyone on the block.⟩

syn display, disport, exhibit, expose, flash, flaunt, lay out, parade, produce, show off, sport, strut, unveil

rel brandish, flourish, wave; advertise, air, announce, blaze, broadcast, herald, placard, post, proclaim, publicize, sound, trumpet; divulge, talk (about); bare, discover, reveal, uncleak, uncover, unmask

near ant camouflage, disguise, mask; conceal, cover, curtain, enshroud, hide, obscure, occlude, occult, shroud, veil

2 to make known (something abstract) through outward signs ⟨The actor's expressive face *shows* his every thought and emotion clearly.⟩

syn bespeak, betray, communicate, declare, demonstrate, display, evince, expose, give away, manifest, reveal

rel bare, disclose, unclock, uncover; advertise, air, announce, blaze, broadcast, placard, proclaim, publicize, sound, trumpet; project

near ant belie, misrepresent; distort, falsify, garble, twist; camouflage, disguise; gild, gloss (over), varnish, whitewash; conceal, counterfeit, cover, hide, mask, obscure, occlude, veil

3 to gain full recognition or acceptance of — see ESTABLISH 1

4 to give advice and instruction to (someone) regarding the course or process to be followed — see GUIDE 1

5 to point out the way for (someone) especially from a position in front — see LEAD 1

6 to come into view — see APPEAR 1

shower *n* **1** a heavy fall of objects — see RAIN 2

2 a rapid or overwhelming outpouring of many things at once — see BARRAGE

shower *vb* to give readily and in large quantities — see RAIN 2

showiness *n* excessive or unnecessary display — see OSTENTATION

show off *vb* **1** to engage in attention-getting playful or boisterous behavior — see CUT UP

2 to present so as to invite notice or attention — see SHOW 1

show up vb **1** to come into view — see APPEAR 1

2 to get to a destination — see COME 2

3 to reveal the true nature of — see EXPOSE 1

showy adj likely to attract attention — see NOTICEABLE

shred n a very small amount — see PARTICLE 1

shred vb to cause (something) to separate into jagged pieces by violently pulling at it — see TEAR 1

shrew n a bad-tempered scolding woman ⟨the famous Shakespearean play about a *shrew* and the suitor who reforms her⟩

syn fury, virago

rel gorgon; carper, faultfinder, nitpicker, scold

shrewd adj **1** having or showing a practical cleverness or judgment ⟨a *shrewd* used car dealer who knew how to make the best possible deal⟩ ⟨*shrewd* investments that paid off big⟩

syn astute, canny, clear-sighted, hardboiled, hardheaded, knowing, savvy, sharp, sharp-witted, smart

rel artful, cagey (*also* cagy), crafty, cunning, devious, foxy, guileful, slick, sly, subtle, tricky, wily; discerning, insightful, perceptive, percipient, perspicacious, sagacious, sage, sapient, wise; agile, alert, brainy, bright, brilliant, clever, intelligent, keen, nimble, quick, quick-witted, sharp-eyed; apt, ingenious, resourceful; calculating

near ant artless, guileless, ingenuous, innocent, naive (*or* naïve); exploitable, gullible (*also* gullable); dense, dull, obtuse; brainless, dim-witted, dopey (*also* dopy), dumb, empty-headed, feebleminded, half-witted, knuckleheaded, simple, slow, slow-witted, softheaded, stupid, thickheaded, thick-witted, unintelligent, weak-minded; foolish, idiotic (*also* idiotical), imbecile (*or* imbecilic), moronic, silly, thoughtless, witless; ignorant, uninformed

ant unknowing

2 causing intense discomfort to one's skin — see CUTTING 1

3 clever at attaining one's ends by indirect and often deceptive means — see ARTFUL 1

shrewdness n exceptional discernment and judgment especially in practical matters — see ACUMEN

shriek vb to cry out loudly and emotionally — see SCREAM 1

shrieking adj having a high musical pitch or range — see SHRILL

shrill vb to cry out loudly and emotionally — see SCREAM 1

shrill adj having a high musical pitch or range ⟨the *shrill* sound of a policeman's whistle⟩

syn high-pitched, piping, screeching, shrieking, squeaking, squeaky, treble, whistling

rel peeping, thin, tinny; earsplitting, nasal,

penetrating, piercing, sharp, strident; squealing, whining, whiny (*also* whiney), yapping, yelping

near ant gruff, hoarse, husky, rough, smoky (*also* smokey)

ant bass, deep, grave, low, throaty

shrimp n **1** a living thing much smaller than others of its kind — see DWARF 1

2 a person of no importance or influence — see NOBODY

shrine n a place that is considered sacred (as within a religion) ⟨For centuries pilgrims have traveled to the *shrine* of Saint Thomas à Becket in Canterbury, England.⟩

syn sanctuary, sanctum

rel reliquary

shrink vb **1** to become smaller in size or volume through the drawing together of particles of matter — see CONTRACT 2

2 to draw back in fear, pain, or disgust — see FLINCH

3 to grow less in scope or intensity especially gradually — see DECREASE 2

shrinkage n the amount by which something is lessened — see DECREASE

shroud n something that covers or conceals like a piece of cloth — see CLOAK 1

shroud vb **1** to keep secret or shut off from view — see ¹HIDE 2

2 to make dark, dim, or indistinct — see CLOUD 1

3 to surround or cover closely — see ENFOLD 1

shrug off vb **1** to dismiss as of little importance — see EXCUSE 1

2 to rid oneself of (a garment) — see REMOVE 1

shuck n, usually **shucks** pl something of little importance — see TRIFLE

shuck vb to remove the natural covering of — see PEEL

shuck (off) vb to get rid of as useless or unwanted — see DISCARD

shudder n an instance of shaking involuntarily with fear or cold — see SHIVER 1

shudder vb to make a series of small irregular or violent movements — see SHAKE 1

shuddering adj marked by or given to small uncontrollable bodily movements — see SHAKY 1

shuddering n a series of slight movements by a body back and forth or from side to side — see VIBRATION 1

shuddery adj marked by or given to small uncontrollable bodily movements — see SHAKY 1

shuffle n **1** an unorganized collection or mixture of various things — see MISCELLANY 1

2 deliberate evasion in speech — see CIRCUMLOCUTION 1

shuffle vb **1** to move heavily or clumsily — see LUMBER 1

2 to undo the proper order or arrangement of — see DISORDER

shun vb to get or keep away from (as a responsibility) through cleverness or trickery — see ESCAPE 2

shunning n the act or a means of getting or keeping away from something undesirable — see ESCAPE 2

---

syn synonym(s)   *rel* related words
ant antonym(s)   *near ant* near antonym(s)

shush *vb* to stop the noise or speech of — see SILENCE 1

shut *vb* **1** to position (something) so as to prevent passage through an opening — see CLOSE 1

2 to stop the operations of — see CLOSE 2

shutdown *n* the stopping of a process or activity — see END 1

shutoff *n* the stopping of a process or activity — see END 1

shut off *vb* **1** to bring (as an action or operation) to an immediate end — see STOP 1

2 to cause to stop functioning — see DEACTIVATE

shut out *vb* to prevent the participation, consideration, or inclusion of — see EXCLUDE

shutterbug *n* one who takes photographs — see PHOTOGRAPHER

shut up *vb* **1** to stop talking ⟨You have no right to tell the rest of us to *shut up*.⟩

syn clam up, hush, pipe down, quiet (down)

rel calm (down), cool (down), settle (down)

phrases hold one's tongue (*or* hold one's peace)

near ant sound off, speak out, speak up, spout (off)

ant speak, talk

2 to stop the noise or speech of — see SILENCE 1

shy *adj* **1** easily frightened ⟨a *shy* cat who hid under the bed every time she heard any loud noise⟩

syn fainthearted, fearful, fearsome, mousy (*or* mousey), scary, skittish, timid, timorous, tremulous

rel chicken, chickenhearted, cowardly, craven, dastardly, lily-livered, spineless, yellow; jittery, jumpy, spooky; anxious, nervous; afraid, alarmed, horrified, panicked, panicky, panic-stricken, scared, shocked, spooked, startled, terrified, terrorized, unnerved

near ant brave, courageous, dauntless, doughty, fearless, gallant, greathearted, heroic (*also* heroical), intrepid, lionhearted, stalwart, stout, stouthearted, undaunted, valiant, valorous; assured, confident, self-assured, self-confident; determined, firm, game, plucky, resolute, undeterred, unflinching, unswerving; mettlesome, spirited, spunky

ant adventuresome, adventurous, audacious, bold, daring, dashing, gutsy, hardy, venturesome, venturous

2 not comfortable around people ⟨a *shy* person who finds talking to anyone but a close friend to be an awkward and unpleasant experience⟩

syn backward, bashful, coy, demure, diffident, introverted, modest, retiring, sheepish, withdrawn

rel antisocial, unsociable, unsocial; awkward, embarrassed, self-conscious, unadventurous, unassertive, unenterprising; inhibited, reserved, uneasy, uptight

near ant boon, companionable, convivial, gregarious, sociable, social; bold, dashing, forceful; brash, forward, overbold, uninhibited, unreserved

ant extroverted (*also* extraverted), immodest, outgoing

3 not coming up to an expected measure or meeting a particular need — see SHORT 3

4 not respectable — see DISREPUTABLE

sick *adj* **1** temporarily suffering from a disorder of the body ⟨He is at home *sick* in bed.⟩

syn ailing, bad, down, ill, indisposed, peaked, poorly, punk, run-down, sickened, unhealthy, unsound, unwell

rel lousy, sickish; nauseated, nauseous, qualmish, queasy (*also* queazy), squeamish; airsick, carsick, seasick; dizzy, lightheaded, shaky; achy, feverish; diseased, disordered; decrepit, feeble, fragile, frail, infirm, invalid, sickly, weak, weakly; afflicted, troubled; challenged, debilitated, disabled, halt, incapacitated, lame; hypochondriac, hypochondriacal

phrases out of sorts, under the weather

near ant able-bodied, conditioned, fit; cured; better, convalescing, improved, mending, recovering, recuperating, rehabilitated; hardy, hearty, lusty, robust, rugged, stalwart, strong, tough; blooming, bouncing, chipper, flourishing, flush, thriving

ant hale, healthful, healthy, sound, well, whole, wholesome

2 filled with disgust ⟨It makes me *sick* to think of someone hurting a helpless animal.⟩

syn disgusted, nauseated, repelled, repulsed, revolted, shocked, sickened

rel fed up, weary; angered, angry, displeased, enraged, fuming, furious, incensed, indignant, infuriated, irate, livid, mad, outraged, rankled, riled, roiled, sore, steaming, upset, worked up, wrought (up)

near ant delighted, gratified, pleased, satisfied, thankful, thrilled, tickled; beguiled, bewitched, captivated, charmed, enchanted, enthralled, entranced, fascinated, mesmerized, spellbound

3 affected with nausea — see NAUSEOUS 1

4 having one's patience, interest, or pleasure exhausted — see WEARY 2

5 having or showing lowered moral character or standards — see CORRUPT

sicken *vb* to cause to feel disgust — see DISGUST

sicken (with) *vb* to become affected with (a disease or disorder) — see CONTRACT 1

sickened *adj* **1** temporarily suffering from a disorder of the body — see SICK 1

2 filled with disgust — see SICK 2

sickening *adj* causing intense displeasure, disgust, or resentment — see OFFENSIVE 1

sickish *adj* affected with nausea — see NAUSEOUS 1

sickly *adj* **1** chronically or repeatedly suffering from poor health ⟨a *sickly* foal that seemed to catch everything that the other horses had⟩

syn ailing, invalid, weakly

rel bedfast, bedridden; delicate, fragile, frail; dying, fading, incurable, moribund; challenged, debilitated, incapacitated, lame; decrepit, enfeebled, feeble, infirm, weak, weakened, worn-out; ill, indisposed, peaked, poorly, run-down, sick, unhealthy, unsound, unwell

near ant able-bodied, fit, hale, hearty, sound, whole, wholesome
ant healthy, well
2 bad for the well-being of the body — see UNHEALTHY 1

sickness *n* **1** the condition of not being in good health ⟨She was plagued by *sickness* most of her adult life.⟩
syn illness, indisposition, unhealthiness, unsoundness
rel malaise; affliction, ailment, condition, disease, disorder, dysfunction (*also* dysfunction), malady, trouble, upset; debility, decrepitude, feebleness, frailness, infirmity, invalidism, weakness; hypochondria
near ant comeback, convalescence, healing, mending, rally, recovery, recuperation, rehab, rehabilitation, snapback; fettle, fitness, shape; hardiness, heartiness, lustiness, robustness, ruggedness, stamina, strength, toughness, vigor, vigorousness, vitality; bloom, flush, flushness; weal, welfare, well-being
ant health, healthiness, soundness, wellness, wholeness, wholesomeness
2 an abnormal state that disrupts a plant's or animal's normal bodily functioning — see DISEASE
3 a disturbed condition of the stomach in which one feels like vomiting — see NAUSEA 1

side *adj* of, relating to, or located on one side ⟨Please bring all deliveries to the *side* door.⟩
syn lateral
rel left, right; one-sided

side *n* **1** a place, space, or direction away from or beyond a central point or line ⟨Will everyone who wants to sign up for volleyball please stand off to this *side* of the gym?⟩
syn flank, hand
rel outside; face, top; bottom, foot, underbelly, underbody, underpart, underside, undersurface; lee, leeward, windward; left, right
near ant center, inside, interior, middle, midway
2 a certain way in which something appears or may be regarded — see ASPECT 1
3 a group of people acting together within a larger group — see FACTION

sideboard *n* a storage case typically having doors and shelves — see CABINET

sidekick *n* a person who helps a more skilled person — see HELPER

sidestep *vb* **1** to avoid having to comply with (something) especially through cleverness — see CIRCUMVENT 1
2 to move suddenly aside or to and fro — see DODGE 1

sideways *adv* **1** with one side faced forward ⟨I had to walk *sideways* to get between the two towering piles of boxes.⟩
syn broadside, edgewise, sidewise
rel aslant, indirectly, obliquely; laterally, sideward (*or* sidewards)
near ant direct, right, straight
2 with distrust — see ASKANCE

sidewise *adv* with one side faced forward — see SIDEWAYS 1

---

syn synonym(s) *rel* related words
ant antonym(s) *near ant* near antonym(s)

siege *n* **1** a sudden experiencing of a physical or mental disorder — see ATTACK 2
2 the cutting off of an area by military means to stop the flow of people or supplies — see BLOCKADE

siesta *n* a short sleep — see ¹NAP

sigh (for) *vb* to have an earnest wish to own or enjoy — see DESIRE 1

sight *n* **1** a position within view — see PRESENCE 1
2 an instance of looking especially briefly — see LOOK 2
3 something unpleasant to look at — see EYESORE
4 the ability to see — see EYESIGHT
5 a considerable amount — see LOT 2

sight *vb* to make note of (something) through the use of one's eyes — see SEE 1

sightless *adj* lacking the power of sight — see BLIND

sightliness *n* the qualities in a person or thing that as a whole give pleasure to the senses — see BEAUTY 1

sightly *adj* very pleasing to look at — see BEAUTIFUL 1

sightseer *n* a person who travels for pleasure — see TOURIST

sign *n* **1** a movement of the body or limbs that expresses or emphasizes an idea or feeling — see GESTURE 1
2 a written or printed mark that is meant to convey information to the reader — see CHARACTER 1

sign *vb* to write one's name on (as a document) ⟨You'll have to *sign* the contract for it to be legal.⟩
syn autograph
rel sign up; cosign, countersign, endorse (*also* indorse), register, sign on; inscribe; author, pen, pencil (in), scratch (out), scrawl, scribble; notarize

signal *adj* standing above others in rank, importance, or achievement — see EMINENT

signal *vb* to direct or notify by a movement or gesture — see MOTION

signal *n* **1** an object intended to give public notice or warning ⟨Stop signs are *signals* for vehicles to come to a full stop.⟩
syn flag, tocsin
rel red light; knell
2 a movement of the body or limbs that expresses or emphasizes an idea or feeling — see GESTURE 1

significance *n* **1** the idea that is conveyed or intended to be conveyed to the mind by language, symbol, or action — see MEANING 1
2 the quality or state of being important — see IMPORTANCE

significant *adj* **1** clearly conveying a special meaning (as one's mood) — see EXPRESSIVE
2 indicating something — see INDICATIVE
3 having great meaning or lasting effect — see IMPORTANT 1
4 having great power or influence — see IMPORTANT 2
5 sufficiently large in size, amount, or number to merit attention — see CONSIDERABLE 1

signification *n* the idea that is conveyed or intended to be conveyed to the mind by language, symbol, or action — see MEANING 1

signify *vb* **1** to be of importance — see MATTER

2 to communicate or convey (as an idea) to the mind — see MEAN 1

3 to serve as a sign or symptom of — see INDICATE 1

signifying *adj* indicating something — see INDICATIVE

sign on (for) *vb* to become a member of — see ENTER 2

sign up (for) *vb* to become a member of — see ENTER 2

silence *n* **1** incapacity for or restraint from speaking ⟨The violinist expects complete *silence* from the audience during his concerts.⟩

syn dumbness, muteness, speechlessness, stillness

rel reserve, reticence, reticency, taciturnity

near ant communication, speaking, talking; eloquence, fluency, volubility; chattiness, loquaciousness, loquacity, talkativeness; verboseness, verbosity, windiness, wordiness

2 near or complete absence of sound ⟨The *silence* of the garden was refreshing after the din of the party inside.⟩

syn hush, quiet, quietness, quietude, still, stillness

rel calm, lull, peace, peacefulness, tranquillity (*or* tranquility)

near ant cacophony, chatter, clamor, clangor, din, hubbub, racket, rattle, roar, tumult, uproar

ant noise, sound

3 the quality or state of being mostly or completely unknown — see OBSCURITY 1

silence *vb* **1** to stop the noise or speech of ⟨The instructor quickly *silenced* anyone who tried to interrupt.⟩ ⟨We need to have a repairman come and *silence* that door alarm.⟩

syn hush, mute, quell, quiet, settle, shush, shut up, squelch, still

near ant agitate, stir

2 to put a stop to (something) by the use of force — see QUELL 1

silent *adj* **1** deliberately refraining from speech ⟨The suddenly *silent* child had to be prompted to say hello.⟩

syn dumb, mum, mute, muted, speechless, uncommunicative, wordless

rel inarticulate, tongue-tied; nonvocal, voiceless; sulking, sulky, sullen

near ant articulate, eloquent, fluent, voluble, well-spoken; gabby, garrulous, loquacious, talkative, talky; outspoken, unreserved, vocal; facile, glib, smooth-tongued

ant communicative, speaking, talking

2 tending not to speak frequently (as by habit or inclination) ⟨A naturally *silent* boy, he was often overshadowed by his louder siblings.⟩

syn closemouthed, dumb, laconic, reserved, reticent, taciturn, tight-lipped, uncommunicative

rel aloof, inhibited, introverted, reserved, restrained; sedate, self-contained, sober, staid; backward, bashful, coy, demure, diffident, modest, retiring, sheepish

near ant free-spoken, outspoken, vocal;

long-winded, prolix, rambling, verbose, windy, wordy; extroverted (*also* extraverted), gregarious, outgoing, sociable

ant blabby, chatty, gabby, garrulous, loquacious, talkative, talky, unreserved

3 mostly or entirely without sound ⟨The room was so *silent* that you could have heard the proverbial pin drop.⟩

syn hushed, muted, noiseless, quiet, quieted, soundless, still, stilly

rel calm, peaceable, peaceful, serene, tranquil

near ant boisterous, clamorous, clangorous, clattering, clattery, raucous, rip-roaring, roaring, roistering, tumultuous

ant noisy, unquiet, uproarious

silent treatment *n* treatment that is deliberately unfriendly — see COLD SHOULDER

silhouette *n* a line that traces the outer limits of an object or surface — see OUTLINE 1

silhouette *vb* to draw or make apparent the outline of — see OUTLINE 1

silken *adj* smooth or delicate in appearance or feel — see SOFT 2

silky *adj* **1** smooth or delicate in appearance or feel — see SOFT 2

2 covered with or as if with hair — see HAIRY 1

silliness *n* **1** lack of good sense or judgment — see FOOLISHNESS 1

2 language, behavior, or ideas that are absurd and contrary to good sense — see NONSENSE 1

3 a lack of seriousness often at an improper time — see FRIVOLITY

silly *adj* **1** lacking in seriousness or maturity — see GIDDY 1

2 showing or marked by a lack of good sense or judgment — see FOOLISH 1

3 so foolish or pointless as to be worthy of scornful laughter — see RIDICULOUS 1

4 suffering from mental confusion — see DIZZY 2

silver *adj* of the color gray — see GRAY 1

silver *n* eating and serving utensils — see TABLEWARE 1

silverware *n* eating and serving utensils — see TABLEWARE 1

silvery *adj* of the color gray — see GRAY 1

similar *adj* having qualities in common — see ALIKE

similarity *n* **1** the quality or state of having many qualities in common ⟨The *similarity* between the two essays is too great to be coincidental—one author virtually copied the other.⟩

syn alikeness, community, correspondence, likeness, parallelism, resemblance, similitude

rel semblance; affinity, analogousness; equation, equivalence, equivalency, par, parity; identicalness, identity, sameness; correlation, relationship; exchangeability, interchangeability; accordance, agreement, compatibility, conformity, congruity

near ant inequality; conflict; incompatibility, incongruence, incongruity, incongruousness, nonconformity; disproportion, imbalance, inequality, nonequivalence

ant difference, disagreement, discrepancy,

disparateness, disparity, dissimilarity, distinctiveness, distinctness, unlikeness

2 a point which two or more things share in common ⟨The only *similarity* between this project and the last one is that both will involve some lab work.⟩

syn congruity, correspondence, parallel, resemblance, similitude

rel counterpart, equal, equivalent; analogy; homology

near ant difference, discrepancy; deviance, divergence, incongruence, incongruity; change, modification, variation

ant dissimilarity

similarly *adv* in like manner — see ALSO 1

similitude *n* **1** the quality or state of having many qualities in common — see SIMILARITY 1

2 a point which two or more things share in common — see SIMILARITY 2

simmer *vb* to cook in a liquid heated to the point that it gives off steam — see BOIL 2

simple *adj* **1** free from all additions or embellishment — see PLAIN 1

2 free from any intent to deceive or impress others — see GUILELESS

3 having no exceptions or restrictions — see ABSOLUTE 2

4 involving minimal difficulty or effort — see EASY 1

5 lacking in worldly wisdom or informed judgment — see NAIVE 1

6 lacking in education or the knowledge gained from books — see IGNORANT 1

7 not having or showing an ability to absorb ideas readily — see STUPID 1

simpleminded *adj* **1** lacking in worldly wisdom or informed judgment — see NAIVE 1

2 showing or marked by a lack of good sense or judgment — see FOOLISH 1

simpleness *n* **1** the quality or state of being simple and sincere — see NAÏVETÉ 1

2 the quality or state of lacking intelligence or quickness of mind — see STUPIDITY 1

3 readiness to believe the claims of others without sufficient evidence — see CREDULITY

simpleton *n* **1** a person who lacks good sense or judgment — see FOOL 1

2 a stupid person — see IDIOT

simplicity *n* **1** the quality or state of having a form or structure of few parts or elements ⟨The *simplicity* of this machine should ensure ease of use by almost anyone.⟩

syn plainness, unsophistication

rel homogeneity, homogeneousness, uniformity, unity

ant complexity, complicacy, complicatedness, complication, elaborateness, intricacy, sophistication

2 clearness of expression ⟨The *simplicity* of this poem is beautiful.⟩

syn clarity, explicitness, lucidity, lucidness, perspicuity, perspicuousness

rel incision, incisiveness; directness, forthrightness, openness, straightforwardness; comprehensibility, intelligibility, legibility

near ant ambiguity, ambiguousness, equivocalness, equivocation, obliquity, opacity; incomprehensibility, incomprehensibleness, unintelligibility, unintelligibleness; circuitousness, deviousness, indirectness, indistinctness; dimness, disjointedness, incoherence; faintness, fuzziness, muddiness, nebulousness, vagueness

ant obscureness, obscurity, unclarity

3 lack of good sense or judgment — see FOOLISHNESS 1

4 the quality or state of being simple and sincere — see NAÏVETÉ 1

simplify *vb* **1** to make less complex ⟨You need to *simplify* this process somewhat or you'll never finish it today.⟩

syn streamline

rel dumb down, oversimplify; prune, strip (down), trim; purify, refine

near ant elaborate

ant complex, complicate, perplex, sophisticate

2 to make plain or understandable — see EXPLAIN 1

simply *adv* **1** for nothing other than — see SOLELY 1

2 nothing more than — see JUST 3

simulate *vb* to present a false appearance of — see FEIGN

simulated *adj* **1** being such in appearance only and made with or manufactured from usually cheaper materials — see IMITATION

2 lacking in natural or spontaneous quality — see ARTIFICIAL 1

simultaneous *adj* existing or occurring at the same period of time — see CONTEMPORARY 1

simultaneously *adv* at one and the same time — see TOGETHER 1

sin *n* **1** a breaking of a moral or legal code — see OFFENSE 1

2 that which is morally unacceptable — see EVIL

3 immoral conduct or practices harmful or offensive to society — see VICE 1

4 a regrettable or blameworthy act — see CRIME 2

5 a defect in character — see FAULT 1

sin *vb* to commit an offense — see OFFEND 1

since *conj* for the reason that ⟨*Since* you are already here, we might as well get the meeting started.⟩

syn as, because, for, inasmuch as, now, seeing, whereas

sincere *adj* free from any intent to deceive or impress others — see GUILELESS

sincerely *adv* without any attempt to impress by deception or exaggeration — see NATURALLY 3

sinew *n* the ability to exert effort for the accomplishment of a task — see POWER 2

sinewy *adj* **1** having muscles capable of exerting great physical force — see STRONG 1

2 marked by a well-developed musculature — see MUSCULAR 1

sinful *adj* not conforming to a high moral standard; morally unacceptable — see BAD 2

---

syn synonym(s)   *rel* related words
ant antonym(s)   *near ant* near antonym(s)

sinfulness *n* the state or quality of being utterly evil — see ENORMITY 1

sing *vb* 1 to produce musical sounds with the voice ⟨It's relatively rare to find actors who can also *sing* well.⟩
syn carol, chant, descant, vocalize
rel belt; crooner, harmonize, hum, lilt, quaver, trill, warble, yodel; serenade
2 to utter in musical or drawn out tones — see CHANT 1
3 to utter one's distinctive animal sound — see CRY 2
4 to give information (as to the authorities) about another's improper or unlawful activities — see SQUEAL 1

singe *vb* to burn on the surface — see SCORCH 1

singer *n* one who sings ⟨A famous opera *singer* will be performing at the gala opening of the arts center.⟩
syn caroler (*or* caroller), songster, vocalist, vocalizer, voice
rel belter; crooner, harmonizer, hummer, warbler, yodeler; serenader; cantor, chanter, chorister; songstress; bard, troubadour

single *adj* 1 not married ⟨posted his status as *single*⟩
syn unattached, unmarried, unwed
rel fancy-free, footloose; marriageable, unpaired; divorced, separated
near ant mated, paired; affianced, betrothed, committed, engaged, pledged, promised; remarried
ant attached, espoused, hitched, married, wedded (*also* wed)
2 belonging only to the one person, unit, or group named — see SOLE 1
3 not physically attached to another unit — see SEPARATE 2
4 not being in the company of others — see ALONE 1

single (out) *vb* 1 to decide to accept (someone or something) from a group of possibilities — see CHOOSE 1
2 to find out or establish the identity of — see IDENTIFY 1

single–handedly *adv* without aid or support — see ALONE 1

single–minded *adj* fully committed to achieving a goal — see DETERMINED 1

singly *adv* without aid or support — see ALONE 1

singular *adj* 1 being out of the ordinary — see EXCEPTIONAL 1
2 noticeably different from what is generally found or experienced — see UNUSUAL 1
3 of, relating to, or belonging to a single person — see INDIVIDUAL 1
4 being the one or ones of a class with no other members — see ONLY 2

singularity *n* an odd or peculiar habit — see IDIOSYNCRASY

sinister *adj* being or showing a sign of evil or calamity to come — see OMINOUS

sink *vb* 1 to become worse or of less value — see DETERIORATE 1
2 to go to a lower level especially abruptly — see DROP 2
3 to cease to be visible — see DISAPPEAR
4 to diminish the price or value of — see DEPRECIATE 1
5 to reduce to a lower standing in one's own eyes or in others' eyes — see HUMBLE 1

6 to lead or extend downward — see DESCEND 1
7 to lose bodily strength or vigor — see WEAKEN 1

sinner *n* a person who commits moral wrongs — see EVILDOER 1

sinuous *adj* marked by a long series of irregular curves — see CROOKED 1

sip *vb* to swallow in liquid form — see DRINK 1

sip *n* the portion of a serving of a beverage that is swallowed at one time — see DRINK 2

siphon *also* **syphon** *vb* 1 to remove (liquid) gradually or completely — see DRAIN 1
2 to cause to move to a central point or along a restricted pathway — see CHANNEL

sire *vb* to become the father of — see FATHER

sire *n* 1 a male human parent — see FATHER 1
2 a person who establishes a whole new field of endeavor — see FATHER 2

siren *n* a woman whom men find irresistibly attractive ⟨In addition to being a brilliant writer, Anaïs Nin had a reputation as a *siren*.⟩
syn enchantress, seductress, temptress
rel beguiler, charmer, seducer, vamp

sissy *n* a person who shows a shameful lack of courage in the face of danger — see COWARD

sit *vb* 1 to rest on the buttocks or haunches ⟨Everybody needs to *sit* down, or no one will be able to see the movie.⟩
syn set [*chiefly dialect*]
rel perch; lounge, slouch, sprawl, squat, straddle
near ant arise, get up, rise, stand
2 to cause to sit down — see SEAT 1
3 to cover and warm eggs as the young inside develop — see SET 1
4 to occupy a place or location — see STAND 1

site *n* the area or space occupied by or intended for something — see PLACE 1

sitter *n* a person employed to care for a young child or children — see NURSE

sitting duck *n* a person or thing that is the object of abuse, criticism, or ridicule — see TARGET 1

situate *vb* to arrange something in a certain spot or position — see PLACE 1

situation *n* 1 position with regard to conditions and circumstances ⟨The school's *situation* is improving with additional financial help.⟩
syn deal, footing, picture, posture, scene, status, story
rel rank, standing; place, spot, state; score, status quo
2 an assignment at which one regularly works for pay — see JOB 1
3 the placement of someone or something in relation to others in a vertical arrangement — see RANK 1

sixth sense *n* the power of seeing or knowing about things that are not present to the senses — see CLAIRVOYANCE

sizable *or* **sizeable** *adj* 1 of a size greater than average of its kind — see LARGE
2 sufficiently large in size, amount, or number to merit attention — see CONSIDERABLE 1

sizably *adv* to a large extent or degree — see GREATLY 2

¹**size** *n* the total amount of measurable space or surface occupied by something ⟨We worried that the immense *size* of the sofa would make getting it through the doorway impossible.⟩

syn bulk, dimension, extent, magnitude, measure, measurement, proportion

rel area; capaciousness, commodiousness, roominess, spaciousness; ampleness, amplitude, bigness, bulkiness, enormousness, heftiness, hugeness, immenseness, immensity, largeness, mass, massiveness, monstrousness, stupendousness, tremendousness, vastness, volume, voluminousness

²**size** *n* a substance used to stick things together — see GLUE

sizzle *n* a sound similar to the speech sound \s\ stretched out — see HISS 1

sizzle *vb* 1 to make a sound like that of stretching out the speech sound \s\ — see HISS

2 to be excited or emotionally stirred up with anger — see BOIL 1

skeletal *adj* suffering extreme weight loss as a result of hunger or disease — see EMACIATED

skeleton *n* the arrangement of parts that gives something its basic form — see FRAME 1

skeptic *n* a person who is always ready to doubt or question the truth or existence of something ⟨the demand by *skeptics* that believers in Bigfoot produce some hard evidence of that hairy humanoid⟩

syn disbeliever, doubter, questioner, unbeliever

rel agnostic; cynic, misanthrope, pessimist; derider, ridiculer, scoffer

near ant chump, dupe, gull, pigeon, sucker

skeptical *adj* 1 inclined to doubt or question claims ⟨It's good to be *skeptical* about what you see on TV.⟩

syn disbelieving, distrustful, doubting, incredulous, mistrustful, questioning, suspecting, suspicious, unbelieving

rel paranoid (*also* paranoidal); critical, puzzled, quizzical; careful, cautious, guarded, gun-shy, leery (*also* leary), wary, watchful; cynical, experienced, knowing, sophisticated, worldly, worldly-wise; curious, inquiring, inquisitive, nosy (*or* nosey), snoopy; uncertain, unconvinced, undecided, undetermined, unsettled, unsure; hesitant

near ant ingenuous, innocent, naive (*or* naïve), simple, simpleminded, unknowing, unsophisticated, unworldly, wide-eyed; certain, confident, positive, sure; deceived, duped, gulled, tricked; careless, heedless, unsuspecting, unsuspicious, unwary

ant credulous, gullible (*also* gullable), trustful, trusting, uncritical, unquestioning

2 not feeling sure about the truth, wisdom, or trustworthiness of someone or something — see DOUBTFUL 1

---

skeptically *adv* with distrust — see ASKANCE

skepticism *n* a feeling or attitude that one does not know the truth, truthfulness, or trustworthiness of someone or something — see DOUBT

sketch *n* 1 a picture using lines to represent the chief features of an object or scene — see DRAWING

2 a vivid representation in words of someone or something — see DESCRIPTION 1

sketch *vb* 1 to draw or make apparent the outline of — see OUTLINE 1

2 to give a representation or account of in words — see DESCRIBE 1

skewed *adj* inclined or twisted to one side — see AWRY

skewer *vb* 1 to penetrate or hold (something) with a pointed object — see IMPALE

2 to make (someone or something) the object of unkind laughter — see RIDICULE

skill *n* 1 subtle or imaginative ability in inventing, devising, or executing something ⟨With unbelievable *skill*, the expert in origami transformed a few sheets of paper into a menagerie of exotic animals.⟩

syn adeptness, adroitness, art, artfulness, artifice, artistry, cleverness, craft, cunning, deftness, masterfulness, skillfulness

rel dexterity, ease, finesse, handiness; experience, expertise, expertness, know-how, proficiency; creativity, ingenuity, inventiveness, knowledge, learning; aptitude, bent, flair, gift, knack, talent

near ant awkwardness, clumsiness, klutziness; inability, inadequacy, incapability, incapacity, incompetence, ineffectiveness, ineffectuality, ineffectualness, inefficacy, inefficiency

ant artlessness, ineptitude, ineptness, maladroitness

2 **skills** *pl* knowledge gained by actually doing or living through something — see EXPERIENCE 1

skilled *adj* having or showing exceptional knowledge, experience, or skill in a field of endeavor — see PROFICIENT

skillful *adj* 1 accomplished with trained ability ⟨The ice skater performed a *skillful* and graceful series of jumps.⟩

syn adroit, artful, deft, delicate, dexterous (*also* dextrous), expert, masterful, masterly, practiced (*also* practised), virtuoso, workmanlike

rel facile, smooth; artistic, creative, fancy, ingenious, neat; adept, clever, cunning; able, adequate, capable, competent

near ant awkward, clumsy, crude; ineffective, ineffectual; incompetent, inept

ant amateur, amateurish, artless, rude, unprofessional, unskillful

2 having or showing exceptional knowledge, experience, or skill in a field of endeavor — see PROFICIENT

skillfully *adv* in a skillful or expert manner — see WELL 3

skillfulness *n* subtle or imaginative ability in inventing, devising, or executing something — see SKILL 1

skim *vb* 1 to turn over pages in an idle or cursory manner ⟨I'll just *skim* through a few styling magazines and see if something interesting catches my eye.⟩

---

syn synonym(s)   *rel* related words
ant antonym(s)   *near ant* near antonym(s)

syn flip, thumb

rel browse, dip; glance (at), look over, scan

near ant pore (over); study

2 to move or proceed smoothly and readily — see FLOW 2

3 to pass lightly across or touch gently especially in passing — see ²BRUSH

4 to strike and fly off at an angle — see GLANCE 1

5 to take a quick or hasty look — see GLANCE 2

skimp *vb* to avoid unnecessary waste or expense — see ECONOMIZE

skimp (on) *vb* to use or give out in stingy amounts — see SPARE 1

skimping *n* careful management of material resources — see ECONOMY

skimpy *adj* less plentiful than what is normal, necessary, or desirable — see MEAGER

skin *n* **1** an outer part or layer — see EXTERIOR

2 the outer covering of an animal removed for its commercial value — see HIDE 1

3 the hairless natural covering of an animal prepared for use — see LEATHER 1

skin *vb* **1** to remove the natural covering of — see PEEL

2 to rob by the use of trickery or threats — see FLEECE

3 to defeat by a large margin — see WHIP 2

skin–deep *adj* **1** lying on or affecting only the outer layer of something — see SUPERFICIAL 1

2 having or showing a lack of depth of understanding or character — see SUPERFICIAL 2

skinflint *n* a mean grasping person who is usually stingy with money — see MISER

skinny *adj* **1** being of less than usual width — see NARROW 1

2 having a noticeably small amount of body fat — see THIN 1

skip *vb* **1** to move with a light springing step ⟨children *skipping* along the woodland path⟩

syn bounce, bound, hop, lope, trip

rel caper, frisk, gambol, romp; skim, skitter; jump, leap, vault

near ant lumber, plod, trudge

2 to fail to attend — see CUT 2

3 to strike and fly off at an angle — see GLANCE 1

skipper *n* a person in overall command of a ship — see CAPTAIN 1

skirmish *n* **1** a brief clash between enemies or rivals — see ENCOUNTER

2 a physical dispute between opposing individuals or groups — see FIGHT 1

skirmish (with) *vb* to oppose (someone) in physical conflict — see FIGHT 1

skirt *n* the line or relatively narrow space that marks the outer limit of something — see BORDER 1

skirt *vb* **1** to avoid by going around — see DETOUR 1

2 to avoid having to comply with (something) especially through cleverness — see CIRCUMVENT 1

3 to be adjacent to — see ADJOIN 1

4 to serve as a border for — see BORDER

skirting *adj* having a border in common — see ADJACENT

skirting *n* the line or relatively narrow space that marks the outer limit of something — see BORDER 1

skittish *adj* **1** easily excited by nature — see EXCITABLE

2 easily frightened — see SHY 1

3 likely to change frequently, suddenly, or unexpectedly — see FICKLE 1

skittishness *n* a state of nervousness marked by sudden jerky movements — see JUMPINESS

skulduggery *or* **skullduggery** *n* the use of clever underhanded actions to achieve an end — see TRICKERY

skulk *vb* **1** to move about in a sly or secret manner — see SNEAK 1

2 to remain out of sight — see ¹HIDE 3

skulk *n* someone who acts in a sly and secret manner — see SNEAK

skulker *n* someone who acts in a sly and secret manner — see SNEAK

skull *n* the case of bone that encloses the brain and supports the jaws of vertebrates ⟨Paleoanthropologists recently found the *skull* of a prehistoric man in a remote area of the desert.⟩

syn cranium

rel braincase; death's-head; head, noddle, noggin, pate, poll; crown, scalp

skunk *n* a person whose behavior is offensive to others — see JERK 1

skunk *vb* **1** to defeat by a large margin — see WHIP 2

2 to achieve a victory over — see BEAT 2

sky *n* **1** the expanse of air surrounding the earth ⟨The *sky* usually looks deep blue on a bright clear day.⟩

syn blue, firmament, heaven(s), high

rel midair; horizon, skyline

2 a dwelling place of perfect happiness for the soul after death — see HEAVEN 1

sky–high *adv* in an enthusiastic manner ⟨Some reviewers had praised the movie *sky-high*, but we thought that it was just a so-so comedy.⟩

syn enthusiastically, exuberantly, madly, rhapsodically

rel avidly, eagerly, excitedly, impatiently, keenly; fanatically, rabidly, warmly, zealously

near ant aloofly, disinterestedly, impassively, incuriously; hesitantly, reluctantly, unwillingly

ant apathetically, indifferently, lukewarmly, perfunctorily

skylark *vb* **1** to engage in attention-getting playful or boisterous behavior — see CUT UP

2 to engage in activity for amusement — see PLAY 1

skylarking *n* wildly playful or mischievous behavior — see HORSEPLAY

skyrocket *vb* to rise abruptly and rapidly ⟨The crisis has caused oil prices to *skyrocket*.⟩

syn rocket, shoot (up), soar, zoom

rel accumulate, appreciate, balloon, burgeon (*also* bourgeon), enlarge, escalate, expand, increase, mount, multiply, mushroom, proliferate, snowball, swell, wax; crest, peak, surge; heighten, intensify

near ant collapse, fall; contract, decrease, diminish, drop, lessen, wane *ant* nose-dive, plummet, plunge, slump, tumble

slack *adj* **1** failing to give proper care and attention — see NEGLIGENT

2 not bound by rigid standards — see EASYGOING 2

3 not tightly fastened, tied, or stretched — see LOOSE 1

slack *n* **1** an allowable margin of freedom or variation 〈Our boss doesn't cut us any *slack* when it comes to being back from lunch on time.〉

syn latitude, space

rel license (*or* licence), rein, swing

2 the extent to which something hangs or dips below a straight line — see SAG

3 slacks *pl* an outer garment covering each leg separately from waist to ankle — see PANTS

slack *vb* to make less taut — see SLACKEN 1

slacken *vb* **1** to make less taut 〈You'll need to *slacken* the rope a bit to get it free of that post.〉

syn ease, loosen, relax, slack

rel detach, free, unbind, undo, unfasten, untie

near ant attach, bind, fasten, tie; constrain, restrain

ant strain, stretch, tense, tension

2 to cause to move or proceed at a less rapid pace — see SLOW

slackened *adj* not tightly fastened, tied, or stretched — see LOOSE 1

slacker *n* one who deliberately avoids work or duty 〈There will be no *slackers* tolerated in this group—anyone who doesn't do their share will be booted out.〉

syn shirker

rel malingerer; dropout, quitter; drone, idler, lazybones, loafer, slouch, slug, sluggard; dallier, lingerer, loiterer, lounger, saunterer; dawdler, laggard, putterer, slowpoke; bum, derelict, ne'er-do-well, no-good

near ant live wire, powerhouse; doer, gogetter, hustler, rustler, self-starter

slackness *n* **1** failure to take the care that a cautious person usually takes — see NEGLIGENCE 1

2 the extent to which something hangs or dips below a straight line — see SAG

slam *n* **1** a hard strike with a part of the body or an instrument — see ¹BLOW

2 a loud explosive sound — see CLAP 1

3 a forceful coming together of two things — see IMPACT 1

slam *vb* **1** to shove into a closed position with force and noise 〈Please don't *slam* the door every time you step out.〉

syn bang

rel close, shut, stop; bar, batten (down), bolt, chain, fasten, latch, lock, seal, secure

near ant open; unbar, unbolt, unfasten, unlatch, unlock, unseal

2 to deliver a blow to (someone or something) usually in a strong vigorous manner — see HIT 1

3 to come into usually forceful contact with something — see HIT 2

4 to criticize harshly and usually publicly — see ATTACK 2

slander *n* the making of false statements that damage another's reputation 〈Instead of resorting to *slander*, the candidates should be outlining their plans for the future.〉

syn aspersing, blackening, defamation, defaming, libel, libeling (*or* libelling), maligning, smearing, traducing, vilification, vilifying

rel aspersion, smear; backbiting, detraction; abuse, invective, vituperation; attack, censure, criticism, denunciation; contempt, disdain, scorn; belittlement, disparagement; hatefulness, malevolence, malice, maliciousness, malignancy, malignity, meanness, nastiness, spite, spitefulness, spleen, venom, viciousness

near ant acclaim, accolade, applause, commendation, praise; esteem, honor, respect; adulation, flattery; adoration, reverence, veneration, worship

slander *vb* to make untrue and harmful statements about 〈For some reason, that newspaper seems determined to *slander* one particular celebrity.〉

syn asperse, blacken, defame, libel, malign, smear, traduce, vilify

rel belittle, disparage; discredit, disgrace, dishonor, shame; abase, debase, degrade, humble, humiliate; disdain, scorn

near ant exalt, glorify, honor; acclaim, applaud, commend, praise; esteem, respect; admire, regard; adore, revere, venerate, worship

slanderous *adj* causing or intended to cause unjust injury to a person's good name — see LIBELOUS

slang *n* the special terms or expressions of a particular group or field — see TERMINOLOGY

slant *adj* running in a slanting direction — see DIAGONAL

slant *n* **1** the degree to which something rises up from a position level with the horizon 〈The road has just enough of a *slant* to make bicycling up it a little strenuous.〉

syn cant, diagonal, grade, gradient, inclination, incline, lean, pitch, rake, slope, upgrade

rel ascent, bank, climb, rise

near ant declension, decline, descent, dip, downgrade, fall, hang, hanging, receding

2 a way of looking at or thinking about something — see PERSPECTIVE 1

slant *vb* **1** to change so much as to create a wrong impression or alter the meaning of — see GARBLE

2 to set or cause to be at an angle — see LEAN 1

slanted *adj* **1** inclined or twisted to one side — see AWRY

2 running in a slanting direction — see DIAGONAL

slanting *adj* inclined or twisted to one side — see AWRY

slantways *adv* so as to slant — see SLANTWISE

slantwise *adj* **1** inclined or twisted to one side — see AWRY

2 running in a slanting direction — see DIAGONAL

slantwise *adv* so as to slant 〈Be careful

not to lay the first boards *slantwise*, or the whole bookcase will be crooked.⟩

syn slantways

rel down, downward (*or* downwards), up, upward (*or* upwards)

slap *n* 1 a hard strike with a part of the body or an instrument — see ¹BLOW

2 an act or expression showing scorn and usually intended to hurt another's feelings — see INSULT

slap *vb* 1 to deliver a blow to (someone or something) usually in a strong vigorous manner — see HIT 1

2 to cause hurt feelings or deep resentment in — see INSULT

slapdash *adj* lacking a definite plan, purpose, or pattern — see RANDOM

slapjack *n* a flat cake made from thin batter and cooked on both sides (as on a griddle) — see PANCAKE

slapstick *n* humorous entertainment — see COMEDY 1

slash *n* a long deep cut — see GASH

slash *vb* 1 to penetrate with a sharp edge (as a knife) — see CUT 1

2 to strike repeatedly with something long and thin or flexible — see WHIP 1

slate *adj* of the color gray — see GRAY 1

¹**slate** *vb* to put (someone or something) on a list — see ¹LIST 2

²**slate** *vb* to strike repeatedly — see BEAT 1

slated *adj* being in accordance with the prescribed, normal, or logical course of events — see DUE 2

slaty *also* **slatey** *adj* of the color gray — see GRAY 1

slaughter *n* the killing of a large number of people — see MASSACRE

slaughter *vb* to kill on a large scale — see MASSACRE

slaver *vb* to let saliva or some other substance flow from the mouth — see DROOL 1

slaver *n* the fluid that is secreted into the mouth by certain glands — see SALIVA

slavery *n* the state of being enslaved ⟨discovered the stories of ancestors who had endured *slavery*.⟩

syn bondage, enslavement, servility, servitude, thrall, thralldom (*or* thraldom), yoke

rel peonage, serfdom; dependence (*also* dependance); subjection, subjugation; captivity, enchainment, imprisonment, incarceration

near ant emancipation, enfranchisement, liberation, manumission; autonomy, independence, self-government, sovereignty (*also* sovranty)

ant freedom, liberty

slay *vb* 1 to deprive of life — see KILL 1

2 to put to death deliberately — see MURDER 1

slaying *n* the taking of another person's life — see HOMICIDE 1

sleazy *adj* 1 of low quality — see CHEAP 2

2 being of a material lacking in sturdiness or substance — see FLIMSY 1

sleek *adj* having a shiny surface or finish — see GLOSSY

sleep *n* 1 a natural periodic loss of consciousness during which the body restores itself ⟨Neither of them has been getting much *sleep* since the baby was born.⟩

syn bed, catnapping, dozing, napping, repose, rest, resting, slumber, slumbering, snoozing

rel catnap, doze, drowse, forty winks, nap, siesta, snooze, wink; oversleeping; dreaming, rapid eye movement

2 the state of being dead — see DEATH 2

3 the permanent stopping of all the vital bodily activities — see DEATH 1

sleep *vb* 1 to be in a state of sleep ⟨The baby *slept* for the entire length of the car trip.⟩

syn catnap, doze, nap, rest, slumber, snooze

rel drop off, drowse (off), nod off; oversleep, sleep in; dream, hibernate

near ant arise, arouse, awake, rise, wake

2 to engage in sexual intercourse — see COPULATE

sleeper *n* one who sleeps ⟨She's a light *sleeper* and usually wakes up when I get in late.⟩

syn dozer, slumberer

rel nodder

near ant riser, waker

sleepiness *n* the quality or state of desiring or needing sleep ⟨The truck driver keeps a thermos of coffee with him to stave off *sleepiness*.⟩

syn drowsiness, somnolence

rel fatigue, tiredness, weariness; lassitude, sluggishness, torpidity; dozing, resting, sleeping, slumbering; oversleeping

near ant awareness

sleeping *adj* being in a state of suspended consciousness — see ASLEEP 1

sleepless *adj* not sleeping or able to sleep — see WAKEFUL

sleepy *adj* 1 desiring or needing sleep ⟨The *sleepy* children were carried up to bed.⟩

syn drowsy, slumberous (*or* slumbrous), somnolent

rel asleep, dormant, dozing, resting, sleeping, slumbering; nodding, yawning

near ant restive, restless, sleepless

ant alert, awake, conscious, wakeful, wide-awake

2 slow to move or act — see INACTIVE 1

sleight *n* 1 a clever often underhanded means to achieve an end — see TRICK 1

2 mental skill or quickness — see DEXTERITY 1

3 ease and grace in physical activity — see DEXTERITY 2

slender *adj* 1 being of less than usual width — see NARROW 1

2 having a noticeably small amount of body fat — see THIN 1

3 less plentiful than what is normal, necessary, or desirable — see MEAGER

sleuth *n* a person not on the police force who investigates criminal or illicit activity or searches for missing persons — see DETECTIVE

slice *vb* 1 to cut into long slender pieces — see SLIVER

2 to penetrate with a sharp edge (as a knife) — see CUT 1

slice *n* 1 a number of things selected from a group to stand for the whole — see SAMPLE 1

2 a piece that has been separated from the whole by cutting — see CUT 1

3 something belonging to, due to, or contributed by an individual member of a group — see SHARE 1

slick vb to coat (something) with a slippery substance in order to reduce friction — see LUBRICATE

slick adj **1** having or being a surface so smooth as to greatly reduce traction ⟨Roads are often *slick* during the first hour of a rainstorm.⟩

syn greased, greasy, lubricated, oiled, slicked, slippery, slithery

rel brushed, buffed, burnished, glossed, ground, polished, rubbed, shined; coated, glazed, waxed; soapy; rasped, sandblasted, sanded, sandpapered, scoured, scraped, scrubbed

near ant coarsened, rough, roughened, scuffed, uneven

2 clever at attaining one's ends by indirect and often deceptive means — see ARTFUL 1

slicked adj having or being a surface so smooth as to greatly reduce traction — see SLICK 1

slicker n **1** a coat made of water-resistant material — see RAINCOAT

2 a person with the outlook, experience, and manners thought to be typical of big city dwellers — see COSMOPOLITAN

slickness n skill in achieving one's ends through indirect, subtle, or underhanded means — see CUNNING 1

slide vb **1** to move about in a sly or secret manner — see SNEAK 1

2 to move or proceed smoothly and readily — see FLOW 2

3 to move slowly with the body close to the ground — see CRAWL 1

slight adj **1** lacking bodily strength — see WEAK 1

2 lacking importance — see UNIMPORTANT

3 of a size that is less than average — see SMALL 1

4 so small or unimportant as to warrant little or no attention — see NEGLIGIBLE 1

5 small in degree — see REMOTE 1

slight n an act or expression showing scorn and usually intended to hurt another's feelings — see INSULT

slight vb **1** to cause hurt feelings or deep resentment in — see INSULT

2 to deliberately ignore or treat rudely — see SNUB 1

3 to show contempt for — see SCORN 1

4 to fail to give proper attention to — see NEGLECT 1

slightest adj being the least in amount, number, or size possible — see MINIMAL 1

slighting adj intended to make a person or thing seem of little importance or value — see DEROGATORY

slightly adv **1** by a very small margin — see JUST 1

2 in a very small quantity or degree — see LITTLE 1

slightness n **1** the quality or state of being little in size — see SMALLNESS

2 the state or quality of having little weight — see ¹LIGHTNESS 1

slim adj **1** being of less than usual width — see NARROW 1

2 having a noticeably small amount of body fat — see THIN 1

3 less plentiful than what is normal, necessary, or desirable — see MEAGER

4 small in degree — see REMOTE 1

slime n soft wet earth — see MUD

slimy adj full of or covered with soft wet earth — see MUDDY 1

¹sling vb to place on an elevated point without support from below — see HANG 1

²sling vb to send through the air especially with a quick forward motion of the arm — see THROW 1

slink vb to move about in a sly or secret manner — see SNEAK 1

¹slip n a long narrow piece of material — see STRIP 1

²slip n **1** an unintentional departure from truth or accuracy — see ERROR 1

2 the act of going down from an upright position suddenly and involuntarily — see FALL 1

3 the act or an instance of getting free from danger or confinement — see ESCAPE 1

4 a wrong judgment — see MISTAKE 1

slip vb **1** to decline gradually from a standard level ⟨The store's quality of service began to *slip* after the new owners took over.⟩

syn sag

rel drop, fall, slump; flag, sink, slacken, slow (down), weaken; abate, contract, decrease, de-escalate, die (down), diminish, dwindle, ebb, lessen, let up, lower, moderate, recede, relent, shrink, subside, taper, taper off, wane

near ant rocket, shoot (up), soar; balloon, burgeon (*also* bourgeon), enlarge, escalate, expand, increase, mount, multiply, mushroom, proliferate, snowball, swell, wax; crest, peak, surge

2 to go down from an upright position suddenly and involuntarily — see FALL 1

3 to introduce in a gradual, secret, or clever way — see INSINUATE 1

4 to move about in a sly or secret manner — see SNEAK 1

5 to move or proceed smoothly and readily — see FLOW 2

6 to cast (a natural bodily covering or appendage) aside — see SHED 1

slip (on *or* **into)** vb to place on one's person — see PUT ON 1

slippery adj **1** given to acting in secret and to concealing one's intentions — see SNEAKY 1

2 having or being a surface so smooth as to greatly reduce traction — see SLICK 1

slipup n **1** an unintentional departure from truth or accuracy — see ERROR 1

2 a wrong judgment — see MISTAKE 1

slit n a long deep cut — see GASH

slit vb to penetrate with a sharp edge (as a knife) — see CUT 1

slither vb to move slowly with the body close to the ground — see CRAWL 1

slithery adj having or being a surface so smooth as to greatly reduce traction — see SLICK 1

---

syn synonym(s)   *rel* related words
ant antonym(s)   *near ant* near antonym(s)

sliver *n* a small flat piece separated from a whole — see CHIP 1

sliver *vb* to cut into long slender pieces ⟨carefully *slivered* the rattan stems into strips for basketry⟩

syn slice, splinter

rel chip, chop, dice, hash, julienne, mince; saw, scissor; cleave, rive, split; gash, incise, rip, slash, slit

slob *n* 1 a dirty or sloppy person ⟨a *slob* of a professor whose office was littered with a decade's worth of notes and student papers⟩

syn sloven

ant neatnik

2 a person whose behavior is offensive to others — see JERK 1

slobber *n* the fluid that is secreted into the mouth by certain glands — see SALIVA

slobber *vb* 1 to let saliva or some other substance flow from the mouth — see DROOL 1

2 to make an exaggerated display of affection or enthusiasm — see GUSH 2

slobby *adj* lacking neatness in dress or person — see SLOPPY 1

slog *vb* 1 to deliver a blow to (someone or something) usually in a strong vigorous manner — see HIT 1

2 to devote serious and sustained effort — see LABOR

3 to strike repeatedly — see BEAT 1

4 to move heavily or clumsily — see LUMBER 1

slogan *n* an attention-getting word or phrase used to publicize something (as a campaign or product) ⟨Within days, virtually everyone was familiar with the newest advertising *slogan* for that brand of soda.⟩

syn banner, cry, shibboleth, watchword

rel expression, idiom; catchword, cliché (*also* cliche); maxim, motto; battle cry, war cry

slogger *n* a person who does very hard or dull work — see DRUDGE

slop *n* 1 soft wet earth — see MUD

2 **slops** *pl* solid matter discharged from an animal's alimentary canal — see DROPPING 1

slop *vb* to cause (something liquid or mushy) to move along in sheets — see SPLASH 1

slope *n* the degree to which something rises up from a position level with the horizon — see SLANT 1

slope *vb* to set or cause to be at an angle — see LEAN 1

sloped *adj* running in a slanting direction — see DIAGONAL

sloping *adj* running in a slanting direction — see DIAGONAL

sloppily *adv* in a careless or unfashionable manner ⟨a *sloppily* arranged desk⟩

syn dowdily, slovenly

rel slatternly; messily, untidily; shabbily, sleazily; dingily, dirtily, filthily, foully

near ant neatly, orderly, tidily; fashionably, modishly; carefully, fastidiously, fussily, meticulously; spotlessly

ant nattily, sharply, smart, smartly, sprucely

sloppiness *n* the state or quality of having an excess of tender feelings (as of love, nostalgia, or compassion) — see SENTIMENTALITY

sloppy *adj* 1 lacking neatness in dress or person ⟨a *sloppy* child who always seems to have spilled something on his clothes⟩

syn dowdy, frowsy (*or* frowzy), slobby, slovenly, unkempt, untidy

rel slatternly; chaotic, cluttered, confused, disarranged, disheveled (*or* dishevelled), disordered, messed, messy, muddled, mussed, mussy, rumpled, shaggy, uncombed, wrinkled; shabby, sleazy; besmirched, blackened, dingy, dirty, filthy, foul, grimy, grubby, grungy, mucky, nasty, soiled, spotted, squalid, stained, sullied, unclean, uncleanly

near ant chic, fashionable, modish, stylish; combed, groomed; neat, ordered, orderly, tidy; careful, fastidious, fussy, meticulous; clean, cleaned, immaculate, spotless, stainless, unsoiled, unsullied

ant dapper, dashing, dolled up, sharp, smart, spruce

2 lacking in order, neatness, and often cleanliness — see MESSY

3 appealing to the emotions in an obvious and tiresome way — see CORNY

slosh *vb* 1 to move with a splashing motion ⟨The baby gurgled contentedly as the water *sloshed* gently around him in the bathtub.⟩

syn lap, plash, splash, swash

rel babble, bubble, gurgle, ripple

2 to cause (something liquid or mushy) to move along in sheets — see SPLASH 1

sloth *n* an inclination to do work or engage in activities — see LAZINESS

slothful *adj* not easily aroused to action or work — see LAZY 1

slouch *n* a lazy person — see LAZYBONES

slouch *vb* to move slowly — see CRAWL 2

slough *also* **slew** *or* **slue** *n* spongy land saturated or partially covered with water — see SWAMP

¹**slough** *vb* to move heavily or clumsily — see LUMBER 1

²**slough** *also* **sluff** *vb* to cast (a natural bodily covering or appendage) aside — see SHED 1

sloven *n* a dirty or sloppy person — see SLOB 1

slovenly *adj* lacking neatness in dress or person — see SLOPPY 1

slovenly *adv* in a careless or unfashionable manner — see SLOPPILY

slow *adj* 1 moving or proceeding at less than the normal, desirable, or required speed ⟨Because of the holiday, traffic to the beach was particularly *slow*.⟩ ⟨*slow* readers⟩

syn crawling, creeping, dallying, dawdling, dilatory, dillydallying, dragging, laggard, lagging, languid, leisurely, poking, poky (*or* pokey), sluggish, tardy, unhurried

rel deliberate, measured; inactive, inert, lethargic; lingering, loitering, tarrying; ambling, heavy-footed, inching, plodding, shuffling, slow-footed, strolling; decelerating, slowing; procrastinating, stalling

near ant expeditious, prompt, ready; accelerated, hastened, quickened; hurried, rushed *ant* barreling, bolting, breakneck, breath-less, brisk, careering, dizzy, fast, fleet, fly-ing, hasty, hurrying, lightning, meteoric, quick, racing, rapid, rocketing, running, rushing, speeding, speedy, swift, warp-speed, whirling, whirlwind, whisking, zip-ping

2 not having or showing an ability to ab-sorb ideas readily — see STUPID 1

3 lacking in gaiety, movement, or anima-tion — see DEAD 2

4 causing weariness, restlessness, or lack of interest — see BORING

slow *adv* at a pace that is less than usual, desirable, or expected ⟨You need to go *slow* with this experiment, or you'll make mistakes.⟩

syn laggardly, leisurely, slowly, sluggishly, tardily

rel carefully, cautiously, deliberately, pur-posefully; heavily, ploddingly

near ant immediately, posthaste, presto, promptly, pronto, readily, soon; impetu-ously, impulsively, rashly, recklessly; abruptly, suddenly

ant apace, briskly, fast, fleetly, full tilt, hastily, quick, quickly, rapidly, snappily, speedily, swift, swiftly

slow *vb* to cause to move or proceed at a less rapid pace ⟨If you don't *slow* your de-livery down a bit, your speech will be over too soon.⟩

syn brake, decelerate, retard, slacken

rel halt, stop; encumber, hamper, handi-cap, hinder, hobble, hold back, hold up, impede, inhibit, obstruct, set back, tie up; arrest, check, constrain, curb, rein, re-strain; baffle, foil, frustrate, thwart

near ant drive, encourage, goad, propel, push, spur, stir, urge; advance, aid, dis-patch, ease, expedite, facilitate, forward, further, help

ant accelerate, hasten, hurry, quicken, rush, speed (up), step up

slowdown *n* a usually gradual decrease in the pace or level of activity of something ⟨Disease experts are encouraged by the re-cent *slowdown* in the spread of the virus.⟩

syn braking, deceleration, letup, retarda-tion

rel decline, drop, slump; ebb, remission, retreat, wane; flagging, weakening; arrest, check, halt, stoppage; collapse, crash, fall, plunge

ant acceleration, hastening, quickening

slowly *adv* at a pace that is less than usual, desirable, or expected — see SLOW

slowness *n* the quality or state of lacking intelligence or quickness of mind — see STUPIDITY 1

slowpoke *n* someone who moves slowly or more slowly than others ⟨Quit being such a *slowpoke* this morning, or you'll be late.⟩

syn crawler, dallier, dawdler, dragger, lag-gard, lagger, lingerer, loiterer, snail, strag-gler

rel latecomer; idler, lazybones, loafer, lounger, slouch, slug, sluggard; delayer, procrastinator

near ant go-getter, hustler, scrambler; hurrier, rusher, speeder

ant speedster

sludge *n* **1** soft wet earth — see MUD

2 something (as a work of literature or music) that is too sentimental — see CORN

sludgy *adj* full of or covered with soft wet earth — see MUDDY 1

¹**slug** *n* a hard strike with a part of the body or an instrument — see ¹BLOW

²**slug** *n* **1** a lazy person — see LAZYBONES

2 the portion of a serving of a bever-age that is swallowed at one time — see DRINK 2

slug *vb* to deliver a blow to (someone or something) usually in a strong vigorous manner — see HIT 1

sluggard *n* a lazy person — see LAZY-BONES

sluggish *adj* **1** moving or proceeding at less than the normal, desirable, or re-quired speed — see SLOW 1

2 slow to move or act — see INACTIVE 1

sluggishly *adv* at a pace that is less than usual, desirable, or expected — see SLOW

sluice *vb* to pour liquid over or through in order to cleanse — see FLUSH 1

slumber *n* a natural periodic loss of con-sciousness during which the body restores itself — see SLEEP 1

slumber *vb* **1** to be in a state of sleep — see SLEEP 1

2 to sleep lightly or briefly — see NAP 1

slumberer *n* one who sleeps — see SLEEP-ER

slumbering *adj* being in a state of sus-pended consciousness — see ASLEEP 1

slumbering *n* a natural periodic loss of consciousness during which the body re-stores itself — see SLEEP 1

slumberous *or* **slumbrous** *adj* **1** desiring or needing sleep — see SLEEPY 1

2 tending to cause sleep — see HYPNOTIC

slump *n* a period of decreased economic activity — see DEPRESSION 1

slur *n* **1** an act or expression showing scorn and usually intended to hurt anoth-er's feelings — see INSULT

2 a mark of guilt or disgrace — see STAIN 1

slur (over) *vb* to fail to give proper atten-tion to — see NEGLECT 1

slurp *vb* to swallow in liquid form — see DRINK 1

slush *n* **1** soft wet earth — see MUD

2 something (as a work of literature or music) that is too sentimental — see CORN

slushy *adj* **1** full of or covered with soft wet earth — see MUDDY 1

2 appealing to the emotions in an obvious and tiresome way — see CORNY

sly *adj* **1** clever at attaining one's ends by indirect and often deceptive means — see ARTFUL 1

2 given to acting in secret and to conceal-ing one's intentions — see SNEAKY 1

3 tending to or exhibiting reckless playful-ness — see MISCHIEVOUS 1

slyness *n* skill in achieving one's ends through indirect, subtle, or underhanded means — see CUNNING 1

¹**smack** *n* a very small amount — see PAR-TICLE 1

²**smack** *n* a hard strike with a part of the body or an instrument — see ¹BLOW

smack *vb* to deliver a blow to (someone or something) usually in a strong vigorous manner — see HIT 1

smack–dab *adv* as stated or indicated without the slightest difference — see EXACTLY 1

small *adj* 1 of a size that is less than average ⟨a *small* cat who never weighed more than five pounds⟩
syn bantam, diminutive, dinky, dwarfish, fine, little, pint-size (*or* pint-sized), pocket, pocket-size (*also* pocket-sized), puny, pygmy, slight, smallish, undersized (*also* undersize)
rel dwarf; runtish, runty, scrubby, stunted; bitty, infinitesimal, micro, microscopic (*also* microscopical), mini, miniature, miniaturized, minuscule, minute, teeny, teeny-weeny, tiny, wee
near ant bulky, hefty, hulking, massive, voluminous; cavernous, colossal, elephantine, enormous, gargantuan, giant, gigantic, gross, herculean, heroic (*also* heroical), huge, immense, jumbo, mammoth, monstrous, monumental, mountainous, prodigious, staggering, stupendous, titanic, tremendous, vast
ant big, considerable, goodly, grand, great, handsome, husky, king-size (*or* king-sized), large, largish, outsize (*also* outsized), overscale (*or* overscaled), oversize (*or* oversized), sizable (*or* sizeable), substantial, tidy, whacking, whopping
2 small in degree — see REMOTE 1
3 lacking importance — see UNIMPORTANT
4 not broad or open in views or opinions — see NARROW 2

small arm *n* a portable weapon from which a shot is discharged by gunpowder — see GUN 1

smaller *adj* having not so great importance or rank as another — see LESSER

small–fry *adj* lacking importance — see UNIMPORTANT

smallish *adj* of a size that is less than average — see SMALL 1

small–minded *adj* 1 unwilling to grant other people social rights or to accept other viewpoints — see INTOLERANT 2
2 not broad or open in views or opinions — see NARROW 2

smallness *n* the quality or state of being little in size ⟨My grandmother was surprised by the *smallness* of the latest electronic devices.⟩
syn diminutiveness, fineness, littleness, puniness, slightness
rel petiteness; minuteness, tininess; meagerness, poorness, scantiness, scantness, scarceness, scarcity, skimpiness, slenderness, slimness, spareness, sparseness
near ant enormity, enormousness, grossness, hugeness, immenseness, immensity, mountainousness, stupendousness; extensiveness, vastness; heaviness, heftiness, weightiness; bulkiness, massiveness, voluminousness
ant bigness, grandness, greatness, largeness, magnitude

small talk *n* friendly, informal conversation or an instance of this — see CHAT 1

smart *n* a sharp unpleasant sensation usually felt in some specific part of the body — see PAIN 1

smart *vb* to feel or cause physical pain — see HURT 1

smart *adj* 1 being strikingly neat and trim in style or appearance ⟨Dressed in their *smart* new uniforms, the cadets proudly paraded around the grounds of the military school.⟩
syn dapper, natty, sharp, snappy, spruce
rel dolled up, dressy, elegant, formal, spiffed-up; orderly, tidy; à la mode (*also* a la mode), chic, fashionable, in, modish, stylish; careful, fastidious, fussy, meticulous; combed, groomed
near ant messy, mussed, rumpled, uncombed, untidy, wrinkled; shabby, sleazy; dowdy, inelegant, unfashionable, unstylish
ant disheveled (*or* dishevelled), frowsy (*or* frowzy), sloppy, slovenly, unkempt
2 being in the latest or current fashion — see STYLISH
3 given to or marked by mature intelligent humor — see WITTY
4 making light of something usually regarded as serious or sacred — see FLIPPANT
5 having or showing a practical cleverness or judgment — see SHREWD 1
6 having or showing quickness of mind — see INTELLIGENT 1
7 having a wide and refined knowledge of the world especially from personal experience — see WORLDLY-WISE

smart aleck *also* **smart alec** *n* a person who likes to show off in a clever but annoying way ⟨Some *smart aleck* in the audience kept shouting clever insults at the nervous speaker.⟩
syn smarty (*or* smartie), wiseacre, wise guy
rel know-it-all; wisecracker; hotshot, show-off

smart–alecky *adj* 1 making light of something usually regarded as serious or sacred — see FLIPPANT
2 marked by the use of wit that is intended to cause hurt feelings — see SARCASTIC

smarting *adj* causing intense discomfort to one's skin — see CUTTING 1

smartly *adv* in a strikingly neat and trim manner ⟨The *smartly* dressed scouts marched at the head of the Memorial Day parade.⟩
syn dashingly, nattily, sharply, snappily, sprucely
rel neatly, orderly, tidily, trimly; elegantly, fashionably, modishly, stylishly, swankily
near ant dowdily, inelegantly; slatternly; messily, untidily
ant sloppily, slovenly

smarty *or* **smartie** *n* a person who likes to show off in a clever but annoying way — see SMART ALECK

smash *n* 1 a forceful coming together of two things — see IMPACT 1
2 the violent coming together of two bodies into destructive contact — see CRASH 1
3 a hard strike with a part of the body or an instrument — see ¹BLOW
4 a loud explosive sound — see CLAP 1
5 a person or thing that is successful — see HIT 1

smash *vb* **1** to cause to break with violence and much noise ⟨The ball *smashed* the window.⟩

syn break down, crash, shatter

rel bust, demolish, fragment; bash, demolish, destroy, devastate, pulverize, ruin, tear down, total, waste, wreck; shiver, splinter, split; crack, crunch, crush, snap

2 to cause to break open or into pieces by or as if by an explosive — see BLAST 1

3 to bring to a complete end the physical soundness, existence, or usefulness of — see DESTROY 1

4 to come into usually forceful contact with something — see HIT 2

smashup *n* the violent coming together of two bodies into destructive contact — see CRASH 1

smattering *n* a small number — see FEW

smear *vb* **1** to rub an oily or sticky substance over ⟨The toddler gleefully *smeared* her hair and face with maple syrup.⟩

syn anoint, bedaub, besmear, daub

rel coat, paint, plaster; grease, oil; gum, lard, pitch, tar; befoul, begrime, besmirch, blacken, dirty, foul, grime, mire, muck, muddy, smirch, smudge, soil, stain, sully

2 to make untrue and harmful statements about — see SLANDER

smearing *n* the making of false statements that damage another's reputation — see SLANDER

smell *n* **1** the quality of a thing that makes it perceptible to the sense organs in the nose ⟨The *smell* of vanilla is supposed to be very soothing.⟩

syn aroma, odor, redolence, scent, sniff

rel whiff; bouquet, fragrance, perfume; ambrosia, lusciousness, savor (*also* savour), savoriness, spice; acridness, fetidness, foulness, gaminess, noisomeness, rancidity, rankness, reek, stench, stink

2 a special quality or impression associated with something — see AURA 1

smell *vb* **1** to become aware of by means of the sense organs in the nose ⟨We *smelled* the aroma of freshly baked cookies as soon as we walked in the house.⟩

syn nose, sniff, whiff

rel breathe, respire; snort, snuffle; savor (*also* savour)

2 to have a vague awareness of — see FEEL 1

smelly *adj* having an unpleasant smell — see MALODOROUS

smidgen *also* **smidgeon** *or* **smidgin** *or* **smidge** *n* a very small amount — see PARTICLE 1

smile *vb* **1** to express an emotion (as amusement) by curving the lips upward ⟨The soldier *smiled* in pleasure when he saw the giant sign welcoming him home.⟩

syn beam, grin

rel laugh, simper; smirk, sneer

near ant grimace; frown, glare, gloom, glower, lower (*also* lour); scowl; pout, sulk

2 to express scornful amusement by means of facial contortions — see SNEER

smirch *n* a mark of guilt or disgrace — see STAIN 1

smirch *vb* **1** to make dirty — see DIRTY

2 to reduce to a lower standing in one's own eyes or in others' eyes — see HUMBLE

smite *vb* to deliver a blow to (someone or something) usually in a strong vigorous manner — see HIT 1

smog *n* an atmospheric condition in which suspended particles in the air rob it of its transparency — see HAZE 1

smoggy *adj* filled with or dimmed by fine particles (as of dust or water) in suspension — see HAZY 1

smooch *vb* to touch one another with the lips as a sign of love — see KISS 1

smooth *adj* **1** having or showing very polished and worldly manners — see SUAVE

2 involving minimal difficulty or effort — see EASY 1

3 having a surface without bends, breaks, or irregularities — see LEVEL 1

4 free from emotional or mental agitation — see CALM 2

smooth *vb* **1** to free from obstruction or difficulty — see EASE 1

2 to make free from breaks, curves, or bumps — see EVEN 1

3 to make smooth or glossy usually by repeatedly applying surface pressure — see POLISH 1

smoothly *adv* without difficulty — see EASILY 1

smother *vb* **1** to be or cause to be killed by lack of breathable air ⟨Children should never play inside discarded appliances because they could become entrapped and *smother*.⟩

syn choke, stifle, strangle, suffocate

rel garrote (*or* garotte), throttle; asphyxiate

near ant breathe, exhale, expire, inspire; resuscitate, revive

2 to refrain from openly showing or uttering — see SUPPRESS 2

smudge *vb* to make dirty — see DIRTY

smudge *n* a mark of guilt or disgrace — see STAIN 1

smug *adj* having too high an opinion of oneself — see CONCEITED

smugness *n* an often unjustified feeling of being pleased with oneself or with one's situation or achievements — see COMPLACENCE 1

smut *n* **1** foul matter that mars the purity or cleanliness of something — see FILTH 1

2 the quality or state of being obscene — see OBSCENITY

smuttiness *n* **1** the quality or state of being obscene — see OBSCENITY

2 the state or quality of being dirty — see DIRTINESS

smutty *adj* **1** depicting or referring to sexual matters in a way that is unacceptable in polite society — see OBSCENE 1

2 not clean — see DIRTY 1

snag *n* a danger or difficulty that is hidden or not easily recognized — see PITFALL 1

snag *vb* to take physical control or possession of (something) suddenly or forcibly — see CATCH 1

snail *n* someone who moves slowly or more slowly than others — see SLOWPOKE

snail mail *n* communications or parcels sent or carried through the postal system — see MAIL

---

syn synonym(s)   **rel** related words

ant antonym(s)   **near ant** near antonym(s)

snake *vb* **1** to move about in a sly or secret manner — see SNEAK 1

2 to move slowly with the body close to the ground — see CRAWL 1

snake *n* **1** a limbless reptile with a long body ⟨*Snakes* are cold-blooded, so they regulate their body temperature by alternately basking in sunlight and seeking shade.⟩

syn serpent, viper

rel adder, anaconda, asp, blacksnake, boa, bull snake, bushmaster, cobra, constrictor, copperhead, coral snake, cottonmouth moccasin, diamondback rattlesnake, fer-de-lance, garter snake, gopher snake, green snake, hognose snake, indigo snake, king cobra, king snake, krait, mamba, milk snake, moccasin, pit viper, puff adder, python, racer, rat snake, rattlesnake, sea serpent, sidewinder, water moccasin, water snake

2 a person whose behavior is offensive to others — see JERK 1

3 one who betrays a trust or an allegiance — see TRAITOR

snap *adj* **1** involving minimal difficulty or effort — see EASY 1

2 made or done without previous thought or preparation — see EXTEMPORANEOUS

snap *n* **1** a loud explosive sound — see CLAP 1

2 a picture created from an image recorded on a light-sensitive surface by a camera — see PHOTOGRAPH

3 active strength of body or mind — see VIGOR 1

4 a weather condition marked by low temperatures — see COLD

5 a very small amount — see PARTICLE 1

6 something that is easy to do — see CINCH

snap *vb* **1** to speak sharply or irritably ⟨The shopkeeper finally *snapped* at one customer who couldn't seem to make up his mind.⟩

syn bark, snarl

rel growl, grumble; roar, scream, shout, shriek, yell; fulminate, rage, rant, rave, sputter, storm, tee off, vent, vituperate; blow up, explode, flare (up)

near ant calm (down), simmer down

2 to break suddenly with an explosive sound — see CRACK 1

3 to take a photograph of — see PHOTOGRAPH

4 to pass from one form, state, or level to another — see CHANGE 2

snap (up) *vb* to take physical control or possession of (something) suddenly or forcibly — see CATCH 1

snapback *n* the process or period of gradually regaining one's health and strength — see CONVALESCENCE

snap back *vb* **1** to become healthy and strong again after illness or weakness — see CONVALESCE

2 to regain a former or normal state — see RECOVER 2

snappily *adv* **1** with great speed — see FAST 1

2 in a strikingly neat and trim manner — see SMARTLY

snappish *adj* easily irritated or annoyed — see IRRITABLE

snappy *adj* **1** being in the latest or current fashion — see STYLISH

2 easily irritated or annoyed — see IRRITABLE

3 having a low or subnormal temperature — see COLD 1

4 having much high-spirited energy and movement — see LIVELY 1

5 moving, proceeding, or acting with great speed — see FAST 1

6 being strikingly neat and trim in style or appearance — see SMART 1

snapshot *n* a picture created from an image recorded on a light-sensitive surface by a camera — see PHOTOGRAPH

snare *n* **1** a device or scheme for capturing another by surprise — see TRAP 1

2 something that catches and holds — see WEB 1

snare *vb* **1** to catch or hold as if in a net — see ENTANGLE 2

2 to take physical control or possession of (something) suddenly or forcibly — see CATCH 1

¹**snarl** *vb* **1** to speak sharply or irritably — see SNAP 1

²**snarl** *vb* to twist together into a usually confused mass — see ENTANGLE 1

snarl *n* a crowded mass (as of cars) that impedes or blocks movement — see JAM 1

snatch *vb* to take physical control or possession of (something) suddenly or forcibly — see CATCH 1

snatching *n* an instance of theft — see THEFT 2

snazzy *adj* attractively eye-catching in style — see JAZZY 1

sneak *adj* undertaken or done so as to escape being observed or known by others — see SECRET 1

sneak *n* someone who acts in a sly and secret manner ⟨"Why, you little *sneak*," the mother exclaimed, "you made my birthday present right under my nose!"⟩

syn lurker, skulk, skulker

rel skunk, snake; sharper, slicker, swindler; snoop, snooper, spy; stalker

sneak *vb* **1** to move about in a sly or secret manner ⟨The little kids *sneak* around upstairs when they're supposed to be in bed.⟩

syn lurk, mooch, mouse, pussyfoot, shirk, skulk, slide, slink, slip, snake, steal

rel crawl, creep, inch, worm; pad, tiptoe

2 to introduce in a gradual, secret, or clever way — see INSINUATE 1

sneakiness *n* skill in achieving one's ends through indirect, subtle, or underhanded means — see CUNNING 1

sneaking *adj* **1** given to acting in secret and to concealing one's intentions — see SNEAKY 1

2 undertaken or done so as to escape being observed or known by others — see SECRET 1

3 arousing or deserving of one's loathing and disgust — see CONTEMPTIBLE 1

sneaky *adj* **1** given to acting in secret and to concealing one's intentions ⟨His opponent's *sneaky* campaign manager was clearly up to something.⟩

syn furtive, shady, shifty, slippery, sly, sneaking, stealthy

rel artful, crafty, cunning, devious, foxy,

guileful, slick, wily; close, closemouthed, reticent, secretive; clandestine, covert, dark; deceitful, deceiving, deceptive, devious, trickish, tricky, underhand, underhanded; crooked, defrauding, dishonest, dissembling, double-dealing, knavish, two-faced; lying, mendacious, untrustworthy, untruthful; insidious, perfidious, serpentine, treacherous

near ant aboveboard, forthright, plainspoken, straightforward; candid, direct, foursquare, frank, open, plain; honest, trustworthy, truthful

2 undertaken or done so as to escape being observed or known by others — see SECRET 1

sneer *vb* to express scornful amusement by means of facial contortions ⟨She *sneered* at me in disgust.⟩

syn laugh, smile, snicker, snigger

rel sniff, snort; catcall, deride, gibe (*or* jibe), hoot, insult, jeer, mock, ridicule; decry, despise, disdain; scoff (at), scorn; badmouth, belittle, disparage, pooh-pooh (*also* pooh), put down; heckle, jive, razz, rib, ride, taunt, tease, torment

snicker *n* an explosive sound that is a sign of amusement — see LAUGH 1

snicker *vb* **1** to express scornful amusement by means of facial contortions — see SNEER

2 to show mirth with an explosive vocal sound — see LAUGH 1

snide *adj* not following or in accordance with standards of honor and decency — see IGNOBLE 2

sniff *n* the quality of a thing that makes it perceptible to the sense organs in the nose — see SMELL 1

sniff *vb* to become aware of by means of the sense organs in the nose — see SMELL 1

sniff (at) *vb* to show contempt for — see SCORN 1

snigger *n* an explosive sound that is a sign of amusement — see LAUGH 1

snigger *vb* to express scornful amusement by means of facial contortions — see SNEER

snip *vb* to make (something) shorter or smaller with the use of a cutting instrument — see CLIP 1

snip *n* a very small piece — see BIT 1

snippet *n* a very small piece — see BIT 1

snippy *adj* **1** being or characterized by direct, brief, and potentially rude speech or manner — see BLUNT 1

2 easily irritated or annoyed — see IRRITABLE

3 self-consciously trying to present an appearance of grandeur or importance — see PRETENTIOUS 1

¹**snitch** *vb* to give information (as to the authorities) about another's improper or unlawful activities — see SQUEAL 1

²**snitch** *vb* to take (something) without right and with an intent to keep — see STEAL 1

snitch *n* a person who provides information about another's wrongdoing — see INFORMER

snitcher *n* a person who provides information about another's wrongdoing — see INFORMER

snoop *vb* to interest oneself in what is not one's concern — see INTERFERE

snoopy *adj* **1** interested in what is not one's own business — see CURIOUS 1

2 thrusting oneself where one is not welcome or invited — see INTRUSIVE

snooze *n* a short sleep — see ¹NAP

snooze *vb* **1** to be in a state of sleep — see SLEEP 1

2 to sleep lightly or briefly — see NAP 1

snoozing *n* a natural periodic loss of consciousness during which the body restores itself — see SLEEP 1

snort *n* **1** a vocal sound made to express scorn or disapproval — see CATCALL

2 the portion of a serving of a beverage that is swallowed at one time — see DRINK 2

snow *vb* to cause to believe what is untrue — see DECEIVE

snowball *vb* to become greater in extent, volume, amount, or number — see INCREASE 2

snow under *vb* **1** to defeat by a large margin — see WHIP 2

2 to subject to incapacitating emotional or mental stress — see OVERWHELM 1

snub *n* treatment that is deliberately unfriendly — see COLD SHOULDER

snub *vb* **1** to deliberately ignore or treat rudely ⟨The *snob* in town always *snubbed* anyone she thought was beneath her.⟩

syn cold-shoulder, cut, high-hat, slight

rel isolate, ostracize; brush (aside *or* off), disdain, rebuff, reject, repel, repulse, scorn, spurn; disregard, forget, neglect, overlook, shrug off

2 to show contempt for — see SCORN 1

snuff (out) *vb* **1** to cause to cease burning — see EXTINGUISH 1

2 to destroy all traces of — see ANNIHILATE 1

3 to put a stop to (something) by the use of force — see QUELL 1

snug *adj* **1** being clean and in good order — see NEAT 1

2 providing physical comfort — see COMFORTABLE 1

3 enjoying physical comfort — see COMFORTABLE 2

4 firmly positioned in place and difficult to dislodge — see TIGHT 3

5 providing safety — see SAFE 2

snug *vb* to sit or recline comfortably or cozily — see SNUGGLE 1

snuggle *vb* **1** to sit or recline comfortably or cozily ⟨It's particularly nice to *snuggle* next to the fire on a snowy day.⟩

syn curl up, nestle, snug

rel burrow; couch, crouch, huddle, hunch, scrunch, squat, squinch

2 to lie close — see NUZZLE

so *adj* being in agreement with the truth or a fact or a standard — see CORRECT 1

so *adv* **1** for this or that reason — see THEREFORE

2 in like manner — see ALSO 1

3 to a great degree — see VERY 1

4 without any question — see INDEED 1

soak *vb* **1** to wet thoroughly with liquid

---

syn synonym(s)   *rel* related words
ant antonym(s)   *near ant* near antonym(s)

⟨We ran for home as soon as the rain started, but our clothes still ended up *soaked*.⟩
syn drench, drown, impregnate, saturate, sop, souse, steep
rel marinate, seethe; presoak; dip, immerse, inundate, submerge; swamp; bathe, douse (*also* dowse), hydrate, swill, wash, water; infiltrate, penetrate, permeate; damp, dampen, humidify, moisten
near ant dehydrate, dry, parch, sear; drain, empty, void; dehumidify
ant wring (out)

2 to charge (someone) too much for goods or services — see OVERCHARGE 1

3 to make up — see WET

soak (up) *vb* to take in (something liquid) through small openings — see ABSORB 1

soaked *adj* containing, covered with, or thoroughly penetrated by water — see WET 1

soaking *adj* containing, covered with, or thoroughly penetrated by water — see WET 1

soap *n* a substance used for cleaning — see CLEANER

soar *n* the act or an instance of rising or climbing up — see ASCENT 1

soar *vb* 1 to move or extend upward — see ASCEND

2 to move through the air with or as if with outstretched wings — see FLY 1

3 to rise abruptly and rapidly — see SKYROCKET

sob *vb* to shed tears often while making meaningless sounds as a sign of pain or distress — see CRY 1

sober *adj* 1 not having one's mind affected by alcohol ⟨was *sober* to drive home⟩
syn clearheaded, straight
rel abstemious, abstinent, dry, temperate; cool, level, steady
near ant alcoholic, bibulous; maudlin; befuddled, besotted, dopey (*also* dopy); debauched, dissipated, dissolute
ant drunk, drunken, high, inebriate, inebriated, intoxicated, soused, tipsy

2 based on sound reasoning or information — see GOOD 1

3 not joking or playful in mood or manner — see SERIOUS 1

4 not excessively showy — see QUIET 2

5 given to or marked by restraint in the satisfaction of one's appetites — see ABSTEMIOUS

soberness *n* a mental state free of jesting or trifling — see EARNESTNESS

sobriety *n* a mental state free of jesting or trifling — see EARNESTNESS

sobriquet *also* **soubriquet** *n* a descriptive or familiar name given instead of or in addition to the one belonging to an individual — see NICKNAME

sociability *n* the quality or state of being social ⟨Her *sociability* was called into question when she said she hated parties.⟩
syn conviviality, gregariousness
rel amiability, cordiality, folksiness, friendliness, neighborliness; camaraderie, companionship, fellowship
near ant bashfulness, coyness, diffidence, shyness, timidity, timidness; introversion; modesty, retiringness
ant unsociability, unsociableness

sociable *adj* 1 likely to seek or enjoy the company of others — see CONVIVIAL

2 showing a natural kindness and courtesy especially in social situations — see GRACIOUS 1

social *adj* likely to seek or enjoy the company of others — see CONVIVIAL

socialize *vb* to take part in social activities ⟨He likes to *socialize* with his coworkers after work ends.⟩
syn associate, fraternize, hobnob, mingle, mix
rel carouse, party, revel; circulate
phrases rub elbows (*or* rub shoulders)
near ant avoid, eschew, shun; slight, snub

society *n* 1 a group of persons formally joined together for some common interest — see ASSOCIATION 2

2 the feeling of closeness and friendship that exists between companions — see COMPANIONSHIP

3 the way people live at a particular time and place — see CIVILIZATION 1

¹**sock** *n* a close-fitting covering for the foot and leg — see STOCKING

²**sock** *n* a hard strike with a part of the body or an instrument — see ¹BLOW

sock *vb* to deliver a blow to (someone or something) usually in a strong vigorous manner — see HIT 1

sod *n* the land of one's birth, residence, or citizenship — see COUNTRY 1

sodality *n* 1 a group of persons formally joined together for some common interest — see ASSOCIATION 2

2 the body of people in a profession or field of activity — see CORPS

sodden *adj* containing, covered with, or thoroughly penetrated by water — see WET 1

sofa *n* a long upholstered piece of furniture designed for several sitters — see COUCH

soft *adj* 1 not loud in pitch or volume ⟨*Soft* music played in the background while we ate.⟩
syn dull, gentle, low, quiet
rel dead, silent, still; calm, dreamy, hushed, peaceful, restful, serene, soothing, stilly, tranquil; muffled, muted, softened, toned (down)
near ant brazen, dinning, discordant, noisy, obstreperous, raucous, rip-roaring, vociferous; grating, harsh, shrill, squealing, strident; clarion, clear, trumpetlike
ant blaring, blasting, booming, clamorous, clangorous, deafening, earsplitting, loud, overloud, piercing, resounding, ringing, roaring, sonorous, stentorian, thunderous

2 smooth or delicate in appearance or feel ⟨I like this sweater the best because it is so *soft* and comfortable.⟩
syn cottony, downy, satin, satiny, silken, silky, velvety
rel creamy; chiffon, delicate, fine, slick; ultrasoft
near ant bumpy, irregular, jagged, lumpy, pebbly; broken, jagged, ragged, roughened, rugged, scraggy; grainy, granular, gritty
ant coarse, harsh, rough, scratchy

3 giving easily to the touch ⟨*Soft* mattresses make it very easy to fall asleep, but they have a tendency to get lumpy.⟩
syn flabby, mushy, pulpy, spongy, squashy, squishy

rel fleshy; droopy, flaccid, floppy, lank, limp, slack, yielding; bendable, compressible, crushable, elastic, flexible, kneadable, malleable, pliable, pliant, resilient, supple, willowy, workable; airy, light

near ant inelastic, inflexible, rigid, stiff, tense, unbending, unyielding; resistant, sound, strong, sturdy, tough; hardened, indurated, stiffened, tempered; compacted, compressed, condensed; adamantine, rock, rocklike; sturdy, substantial

ant firm, hard, solid

4 involving minimal difficulty or effort — see EASY 1

5 lacking bodily strength — see WEAK 1

6 lacking strength of will or character — see WEAK 2

7 not harsh or stern especially in nature or effect — see GENTLE 1

8 providing physical comfort — see COMFORTABLE 1

9 tolerant and kind in the judgment of and expectations for others — see INDULGENT 1

10 marked by temperatures that are neither too high nor too low — see CLEMENT 1

soften *vb* **1** to diminish the physical strength of — see WEAKEN 1

2 to lessen the shock of — see CUSHION 1

softened *adj* lacking bodily strength — see WEAK 1

softhearted *adj* having or marked by sympathy and consideration for others — see HUMANE 1

softheartedness *n* the capacity for feeling for another's unhappiness or misfortune — see HEART 1

softness *n* the quality or state of lacking strength of will or character — see WEAKNESS 2

soft–soap *vb* **1** to get (someone) to do something by gentle urging, special attention, or flattery — see COAX

2 to praise too much — see FLATTER 1

soft soap *n* excessive praise — see FLATTERY

softy *or* **softie** *n* a person lacking in physical strength — see WEAKLING 1

soggy *adj* containing, covered with, or thoroughly penetrated by water — see WET 1

¹**soil** *n* foul matter that mars the purity or cleanliness of something — see FILTH 1

²**soil** *n* **1** the loose surface material in which plants naturally grow — see DIRT 1

2 the solid part of our planet's surface as distinguished from the sea and air — see EARTH 2

soil *vb* to make dirty — see DIRTY

soilage *n* the state or quality of being dirty — see DIRTINESS

soiled *adj* not clean — see DIRTY 1

sojourn *n* a temporary residing as another's guest — see VISIT 1

sojourn *vb* to reside as a temporary guest — see VISIT 2

solace *n* **1** a feeling of ease from grief or trouble — see COMFORT 1

2 the giving of hope and strength in times of grief, distress, or suffering — see CONSOLATION 1

solace *vb* **1** to ease the grief or distress of — see COMFORT

2 to cause (someone) to pass the time agreeably occupied — see AMUSE

solacing *n* the giving of hope and strength in times of grief, distress, or suffering — see CONSOLATION 1

solar plexus *n* the part of the body between the chest and the pelvis — see STOMACH 1

soldier *n* a person engaged in military service ⟨a platoon of *soldiers*⟩

syn fighter, legionary, legionnaire, man-at-arms, regular, serviceman, warrior

rel servicewoman; cavalier, cavalryman, cuirassier; doughboy, footman, foot soldier, infantryman; commando, raider; marine, ranger; artilleryman, cannoneer, gunner, musketeer, rifleman; GI, guardsman, militiaman, minuteman; conscript, draftee, enrollee, recruit; reservist

ant civilian

soldierly *adj* of, relating to, or suitable for war or a warrior — see MARTIAL 1

sole *adj* **1** belonging only to the one person, unit, or group named ⟨The landowner has *sole* rights to the property, so he can do whatever he wants to with it.⟩

syn exclusive, single, unshared

rel proprietary; personal, private

near ant common, communal, conjoint, cooperative, joint, multiple, mutual, pooled, public, shared, united

ant nonexclusive

2 being the one or ones of a class with no other members — see ONLY 2

solecism *n* a socially improper or unsuitable act or remark — see IMPROPRIETY 2

solely *adv* **1** for nothing other than ⟨The promotion was based *solely* on merit.⟩

syn alone, exclusively, just, only, purely, simply

rel basically, by and large, chiefly, generally, largely, mainly, mostly, predominantly, primarily, principally, substantially

near ant additionally, also, besides, likewise

2 without aid or support — see ALONE 1

solemn *adj* **1** having or showing a formal and serious or reserved manner — see DIGNIFIED

2 not joking or playful in mood or manner — see SERIOUS 1

3 causing or marked by an atmosphere lacking in cheer — see GLOOMY 1

solemnity *n* **1** a mental state free of jesting or trifling — see EARNESTNESS

2 an oft-repeated action or series of actions performed in accordance with tradition or a set of rules — see RITE

solicit *vb* **1** to go around and approach (people) with a request for opinions or information — see CANVASS 1

2 to make a request for — see ASK (FOR) 1

3 to make a request of — see ASK 2

4 to make a request to (someone) in an earnest or urgent manner — see BEG

5 to lead away from a usual or proper course by offering some pleasure or advantage — see LURE

solicitation *n* an earnest request — see PLEA 1

soliciting *adj* asking humbly — see SUPPLIANT

---

syn synonym(s)   *rel* related words
ant antonym(s)   *near ant* near antonym(s)

solicitor n 1 one that tries to get a person to give in to a desire — see TEMPTER

2 one who asks earnestly for a favor or gift — see SUPPLICANT

solicitous adj 1 given to or made with heedful anticipation of the needs and happiness of others — see THOUGHTFUL 1

2 showing urgent desire or interest — see EAGER

solicitude n 1 an uneasy state of mind usually over the possibility of an anticipated misfortune or trouble — see ANXIETY 1

2 attention accompanied by protectiveness and responsibility — see CARE 2

solid adj 1 based on sound reasoning or information — see GOOD 1

2 having a consistency that does not easily yield to pressure — see FIRM 2

3 having or consisting of a single color — see MONOCHROMATIC 1

4 not showing weakness or uncertainty — see FIRM 1

5 worthy of one's trust — see DEPENDABLE

solidify vb 1 to become physically firm or solid — see HARDEN 1

2 to take on a definite form — see FORM 1

solidity n worthiness as the recipient of another's trust or confidence — see RELIABILITY

solidness n worthiness as the recipient of another's trust or confidence — see RELIABILITY

solitariness n the state of being alone or kept apart from others — see ISOLATION

solitary adj 1 being the one or ones of a class with no other members — see ONLY 2

2 not being in the company of others — see ALONE 1

solitary n a person who lives away from others — see RECLUSE

solitude n the state of being alone or kept apart from others — see ISOLATION

solo adv not being in the company of others — see ALONE 1

solon n a member of an organized body of persons having the authority to make laws — see LEGISLATOR

soluble adj capable of having the reason for or cause of determined — see SOLVABLE

solution n something attained by mental effort and especially by computation — see ANSWER 2

solvable adj capable of having the reason for or cause of determined ⟨I'm sure that the mystery of what happened to the missing pizza is *solvable*.⟩

syn answerable, explainable, explicable, resolvable, soluble

rel analyzable, decipherable; feasible, workable

near ant difficult, inextricable, knotty; impossible, insuperable; absurd, fantastic (*also* fantastical), outlandish, preposterous, ridiculous

ant hopeless, inexplicable, insoluble, unexplainable, unresolvable, unsolvable

solve vb to find an answer for through reasoning ⟨It took me half an hour to *solve* the logic puzzle.⟩

syn answer, break, crack, dope (out), fig-

ure out, puzzle (out), resolve, unravel, work, work out

rel conclude, decide, deduce, gather, infer, judge, reason; clear (up), iron out, straighten (out), unscramble, untangle, untie; assume, conjecture, divine, guess, presume, speculate; decipher, decode

somatic adj of or relating to the human body — see PHYSICAL 1

somber *or* **sombre** adj 1 being without light or without much light — see DARK 1

2 causing or marked by an atmosphere lacking in cheer — see GLOOMY 1

some adj known but not named — see CERTAIN 1

somebody n a person who is widely known and usually much talked about — see CELEBRITY 1

someday adv at a later time — see YET 1

something adv to some degree or extent — see FAIRLY 1

something n one that has a real and independent existence — see ENTITY

sometime adj having been such at some previous time — see FORMER 1

sometime adv at a later time — see YET 1

sometimes adv on some occasions ⟨*Sometimes* I like to go skiing, and *sometimes* I prefer to stay inside where it's warm.⟩

syn now, occasionally

rel intermittently, off and on, periodically, recurrently; infrequently, little, rarely, seldom; irregularly, sporadically, variously

phrases at times, every now and then (*or* every now and again *or* every so often), from time to time, once in a while, on occasion

near ant frequently, much, oft, often, oftentimes (*or* ofttimes); commonly, ordinarily, regularly, routinely, usually; always, consistently, constantly, invariably; continually, continuingly, continuously, incessantly, perpetually, unceasingly, uninterruptedly; endlessly, ever, interminably

somewhat adv to some degree or extent — see FAIRLY 1

somnolence n the quality or state of desiring or needing sleep — see SLEEPINESS

somnolent adj 1 desiring or needing sleep — see SLEEPY 1

2 tending to cause sleep — see HYPNOTIC

song n 1 a short musical composition for the human voice often with instrumental accompaniment ⟨She sang a little-known *song* for the talent show.⟩

syn ballad, ditty, jingle, lay, lyric, vocal

rel anthem, cantata, canticle, carol, chorale, hymn, noel, psalm, spiritual; dirge, lament, requiem, threnody; paean; aria, barcarole (*or* barcarolle), chant, chantey (*or* chanty *or* shanty), folk song, glee, madrigal, motet, part-song, round, roundelay, serenade

2 a composition using rhythm and often rhyme to create a lyrical effect — see POEM

3 a rhythmic series of musical tones arranged to give a pleasing effect — see MELODY

4 a very small sum of money — see MITE 1

5 writing that uses rhythm, vivid language,

and often rhyme to provoke an emotional response — see POETRY 1

songster *n* one who sings — see SINGER

sonny *n* a male person who has not yet reached adulthood — see BOY 1

sonorous *adj* **1** marked by a high volume of sound — see LOUD 1

2 marked by conspicuously full and rich sounds or tones — see RESONANT

soon *adv* **1** at or within a short time — see SHORTLY 2

2 by choice or preference — see RATHER 1

3 with great speed — see FAST 1

soothe *vb* **1** to ease the grief or distress of — see COMFORT

2 to free from distress or disturbance — see CALM 1

3 to make more bearable or less severe — see HELP 2

soothing *adj* **1** tending to calm the emotions and relieve stress ⟨The *soothing* music eventually put the entire yoga class in the proper mood.⟩

syn calming, comforting, dreamy, lulling, pacifying, quieting, relaxing, sedative, tranquilizing (*also* tranquillizing)

rel analgesic, anesthetic, deadening, depressant, numbing

near ant painful, stressful, tiresome, troubling, trying, unsettling, worrisome; energizing, invigorating, stimulant, stimulating; aggravating, annoying, bothersome, disturbing, exasperating, frustrating, galling, grating, harassing, irksome, irritating, maddening, troublesome, vexatious, vexing

2 not harsh or stern especially in nature or effect — see GENTLE 1

soothsayer *n* one who predicts future events or developments — see PROPHET 1

soothsaying *n* a declaration that something will happen in the future — see PREDICTION

sop *n* something given or promised in order to improperly influence a person's conduct or decision — see BRIBE

sop *vb* **1** to wet thoroughly with liquid — see SOAK 1

2 to make wet — see WET

3 to sink or push (something) briefly into or as if into a liquid — see DIP 1

sophisticate *n* a person with the outlook, experience, and manners thought to be typical of big city dwellers — see COSMOPOLITAN

sophisticate *vb* **1** to make complex or difficult — see COMPLICATE

2 to alter (something) for the worse with the addition of foreign or lower-grade substances — see ADULTERATE

sophisticated *adj* **1** having a wide and refined knowledge of the world especially from personal experience — see WORLDLY-WISE

2 having many parts or aspects that are usually interrelated — see COMPLEX 1

3 having or showing very polished and worldly manners — see SUAVE

4 made or done with great care or with much detail — see ELABORATE 1

sophistication *n* the state or quality of having many interrelated parts or aspects — see COMPLEXITY 1

sopping *adj* containing, covered with, or thoroughly penetrated by water — see WET 1

soppy *adj* containing, covered with, or thoroughly penetrated by water — see WET 1

sorcerer *n* a person skilled in using supernatural forces — see MAGICIAN 1

sorceress *n* a woman believed to have often harmful supernatural powers — see WITCH 1

sorcery *n* the power to control natural forces through supernatural means — see MAGIC 1

sordid *adj* **1** not clean — see DIRTY 1

2 not following or in accordance with standards of honor and decency — see IGNOBLE 2

sore *adj* **1** causing or feeling bodily pain — see PAINFUL 1

2 feeling or showing anger — see ANGRY

3 having or showing deep-seated resentment — see BITTER 1

sore *adv* to a great degree — see VERY 1

sorely *adv* **1** with feelings of bitterness or grief — see HARD 2

2 to a great degree — see VERY 1

sorrow *vb* to feel deep sadness or mental pain — see GRIEVE

sorrow *n* deep sadness especially for the loss of someone or something loved ⟨He felt great *sorrow* at the loss of his beloved dog.⟩

syn affliction, anguish, dolefulness, dolor, grief, heartache, heartbreak, woe

rel agony, distress, pain, suffering, torment; blues, dejection, depression, desolateness, desolation, despair, despondency, disconsolateness, dispiritedness, distress, doldrums, downheartedness, dreariness, dumps, forlornness, gloom, gloominess, heartsickness, joylessness, melancholy, misery, mopes, oppression, unhappiness, woefulness, wretchedness; contrition, guilt, regret, remorse, rue, self-reproach, shame; melancholia, self-pity

near ant gaiety (*also* gayety), humor, jollity, joviality, lightheartedness, merriment, merrymaking, mirth, mirthfulness; hopefulness, optimism, sunniness; enjoyment; content, contentedness, contentment

ant bliss, blissfulness, cheer, cheerfulness, cheeriness, delight, ecstasy, elation, euphoria, exhilaration, exuberance, exultation, gladness, gladsomeness, glee, gleefulness, happiness, joy, joyfulness, joyousness, jubilation, pleasure, rapture, rapturousness

sorrowful *adj* **1** expressing or suggesting mourning — see MOURNFUL 1

2 feeling unhappiness — see SAD 1

sorrowfully *adv* with feelings of bitterness or grief — see HARD 2

sorry *adj* **1** arousing or deserving of one's loathing and disgust — see CONTEMPTIBLE 1

2 causing unhappiness — see SAD 2

3 deserving pitying scorn (as for inadequacy) — see PITIFUL 1

4 feeling sorrow for a wrong that one has done — see CONTRITE

---

syn synonym(s)   *rel* related words
ant antonym(s)   *near ant* near antonym(s)

5 feeling unhappiness — see SAD 1

6 expressing or suggesting mourning — see MOURNFUL 1

7 deserving of one's pity — see PATHETIC 1

sort *n* **1** a number of persons or things that are grouped together because they have something in common ⟨I prefer jackets with zippers to the *sort* that close with buttons.⟩

syn breed, class, description, feather, ilk, kind, like, manner, nature, order, species, strain, stripe, type, variety

rel model; sample; specimen; bracket, bunch, category, division, family, grade, group, grouping, lot, persuasion, rank(s), set, suite

2 a member of the human race — see HUMAN

sort *vb* **1** to come or be together as friends — see ASSOCIATE 1

2 to be in agreement on every point — see CHECK 1

3 to arrange or assign according to type — see CLASSIFY 1

sort of *adv* to some degree or extent — see FAIRLY 1

so–so *adj* of average to below average quality — see MEDIOCRE 1

so–so *adv* in a satisfactory way — see WELL 1

soul *n* **1** an immaterial force within a human being thought to give the body life, energy, and power ⟨Many religions teach that the *soul* is immortal.⟩

syn psyche, spirit

rel life, vitality; being, essence, quintessence

near ant body, flesh

2 a member of the human race — see HUMAN

3 the quality or qualities that make a thing what it is — see ESSENCE 1

4 the seat of one's deepest thoughts and emotions — see CORE 1

soulless *adj* having or showing a lack of sympathy or tender feelings — see HARD 1

¹**sound** *vb* **1** to continue or be repeated in a series of reflected sound waves — see REVERBERATE

2 to give the impression of being — see SEEM

3 to make known (as an idea, emotion, or opinion) — see EXPRESS 1

4 to make known openly or publicly — see ANNOUNCE

²**sound** *vb* **1** to measure the depth of (as a body of water) typically with a weighted line ⟨The pilot *sounded* the river to make sure we weren't in any danger of running aground.⟩

syn fathom, plumb

rel gauge (*also* gage), scale, span; remeasure, replumb

2 to cast oneself head first into deep water — see DIVE 1

¹**sound** *n* range of hearing — see EARSHOT

²**sound** *n* a narrow body of water between two land masses — see CHANNEL 2

sound *adj* **1** according to the rules of logic — see LOGICAL 1

2 enjoying health and vigor — see HEALTHY 1

3 marked by the ability to withstand stress without structural damage or distortion — see SILENT 3

soundless *adj* mostly or entirely without sound — see SILENT 3

soundness *n* **1** the ability to withstand force or stress without being distorted, dislodged, or damaged — see STABILITY 1

2 the condition of being sound in body — see HEALTH 1

sound off *vb* **1** to voice one's opinions freely with force — see SPEAK UP

2 to speak so as to be heard at a distance — see CALL 1

soup *n* an atmospheric condition in which suspended particles in the air rob it of its transparency — see HAZE 1

soupy *adj* **1** filled with or dimmed by fine particles (as of dust or water) in suspension — see HAZY 1

2 having an overly soft liquid consistency — see RUNNY

sour *vb* to cause to change from friendly or loving to unfriendly or uncaring — see ESTRANGE

sour *adj* **1** causing or characterized by the one of the basic taste sensations that is produced chiefly by acids ⟨The *sour* candy made our mouths all wrinkly inside.⟩

syn acid, acidic, tart, vinegary

rel dry, soured, unsweetened; pungent, sharp, tangy, zestful, zesty; astringent, puckery; hyperacid

near ant sweet; bland, smooth; flat, flavorless, insipid, savorless, tasteless, zestless; dilute, thin, watery, weak

2 not giving pleasure to the mind or senses — see UNPLEASANT

3 falling short of a standard — see BAD 1

source *n* **1** a point or place at which something is invented or provided ⟨We were uncertain as to the *source* of the rumors.⟩ ⟨a *source* of inspiration⟩

syn cradle, origin, root, spring, well

rel beginning, commencement, dawn, genesis, inception, launch, onset, outset, start, threshold; ground zero, square one

2 the beginning part of a stream — see HEADWATER

3 something mentioned in a text as providing related and especially supporting information — see REFERENCE 1

souring *n* the loss of friendship or affection — see ESTRANGEMENT

souse *vb* **1** to make wet — see WET

2 to sink or push (something) briefly into or as if into a liquid — see DIP 1

3 to wet thoroughly with liquid — see SOAK 1

soused *adj* containing, covered with, or thoroughly penetrated by water — see WET 1

souvenir *n* something that serves to keep alive the memory of a person or event — see MEMORIAL

sovereign *also* **sovran** *adj* **1** coming before all others in importance — see FOREMOST 1

2 not being under the rule or control of another — see FREE 1

sovereign *also* **sovran** *n* one who rules over a people with a sole, supreme, and usually hereditary authority — see MONARCH 1

sovereignty *also* **sovranty** *n* **1** the state of being free from the control or power of another — see FREEDOM 1

2 a body of people composed of one or more nationalities usually with its own territory and government — see NATION

3 controlling power or influence over others — see SUPREMACY 1

sow *vb* **1** to cover by or as if by scattering something over or on — see SCATTER 2

2 to put or set into the ground to grow — see PLANT 1

3 to set permanently in the consciousness or mind-set — see IMPLANT 1

spa *n* a building or room used for sports activities and exercising — see GYM

space *n* **1** an extent or area available for or used up by some activity or thing — see ROOM 1

2 an indefinite but usually short period of time — see WHILE 1

3 an incomplete or deficient area — see GAP 3

4 an allowable margin of freedom or variation — see SLACK 1

space–age *adj* being or involving the latest methods, concepts, information, or styles — see MODERN

spacing *n* the space or amount of space between two points, lines, surfaces, or objects — see DISTANCE 1

spacious *adj* more than adequate or average in capacity ⟨Almost all of the guests were able to fit into the *spacious* living room.⟩

syn ample, capacious, commodious, roomy

rel cavernous, voluminous; broad; wide; big, bulky, considerable, generous, goodly, grand, great, handsome, hefty, hulking, large, largish, outsize (*also* outsized), overscale (*or* overscaled), oversize (*or* oversized), sizable (*or* sizeable), substantial, tidy; expansive, extended, extensive, vast; boundless, limitless, unbounded

near ant cramped, incommodious, limited, narrow, restricted; small, snug, tight, tiny

span *vb* to find out the size, extent, or amount of — see MEASURE 1

spank *n* a hard strike with a part of the body or an instrument — see ¹BLOW

spanking *adj* having much high-spirited energy and movement — see LIVELY 1

spanking *adv* to a great degree — see VERY 1

spare *adj* **1** being over what is needed ⟨I had some *spare* time to kill, so I cleaned up my cubicle a bit.⟩

syn excess, extra, redundant, superfluous, supernumerary, surplus

rel accessory, additional, supplemental, supplementary; dispensable, extraneous, gratuitous, needless, nonessential, uncalled-for, unessential, unnecessary, unneeded, unwanted; abundant, ample, bountiful, copious, plenteous, plentiful

near ant deficient, inadequate, insufficient, meager (*or* meagre); niggardly, poor, scant, scanty, scarce, short, skimpy, sparse

2 giving or sharing as little as possible — see STINGY 1

3 having a noticeably small amount of body fat — see THIN 1

4 less plentiful than what is normal, necessary, or desirable — see MEAGER

spare *n* an interchangeable part or piece of equipment that is kept on hand for replacement of an original ⟨We promptly replaced the burnt-out lightbulb with a *spare*.⟩

syn extra, reserve

rel backup, substitute; stock; carbon copy, copy, double, dummy, dupe, duplicate, replacement, replica, replication, reproduction

near ant archetype, original, prototype

spare *vb* **1** to give or give out in stingy amounts ⟨I'll have a banana split—and don't *spare* the whipped cream!⟩

syn nurse, scant, skimp (on), stint (on)

rel mete (out), portion (out), ration (out); pinch, shortchange; conserve, preserve

near ant heap, lavish, pour, rain, shower

2 to avoid unnecessary waste or expense — see ECONOMIZE

sparing *adj* **1** careful in the management of money or resources — see FRUGAL

2 giving or sharing as little as possible — see STINGY 1

3 less plentiful than what is normal, necessary, or desirable — see MEAGER

spark *n* a very small amount — see PARTICLE 1

spark *vb* **1** to give off sparks ⟨The broken radio *sparked* and smoked the instant it was plugged in.⟩

syn scintillate, sparkle

rel flash, shine, twinkle; blaze, burn, combust, flame, flare (up), glow, light (up), radiate, scintillate

2 to cause to function — see ACTIVATE

3 to rouse to strong feeling or action — see PROVOKE 1

sparkle *vb* **1** to give off sparks — see SPARK 1

2 to shoot forth bursts of light — see FLASH 1

sparky *adj* having much high-spirited energy and movement — see LIVELY 1

sparse *adj* less plentiful than what is normal, necessary, or desirable — see MEAGER

spasm *n* **1** a painful sudden tightening of a muscle — see ¹CRAMP

2 a sudden intense expression of strong feeling — see OUTBURST 1

spasmodic *adj* **1** lacking in steadiness or regularity of occurrence — see FITFUL

2 easily excited by nature — see EXCITABLE

spat *n* an often noisy or angry expression of differing opinions — see ARGUMENT 1

spat *vb* to express different opinions about something often angrily — see ARGUE 2

spate *n* **1** a great flow of water or of something that overwhelms — see FLOOD

2 a considerable amount — see LOT 2

spatter *vb* **1** to cause (something liquid or mushy) to move along in sheets — see SPLASH 1

2 to wet or soil by striking with something liquid or mushy — see SPLASH 2

---

syn synonym(s)   **rel** related words
ant antonym(s)   **near ant** near antonym(s)

spatter *n* a very small amount — see PARTICLE 1

spawn *n* the descendants of a person, animal, or plant — see OFFSPRING

spawn *vb* to be the cause of (a situation, action, or state of mind) — see EFFECT

speak *vb* 1 to express (a thought or emotion) in words — see SAY 1

2 to give a formal often extended talk on a subject — see TALK 1

speak (to *or* **with)** *vb* to communicate with by means of spoken words — see TALK (TO)

speaker *n* 1 a person in charge of a meeting — see CHAIR 1

2 a person who speaks for another or for a group — see SPOKESPERSON

speak out *vb* to voice one's opinions freely with force — see SPEAK UP

speak up *vb* to voice one's opinions freely with force ⟨She's never been afraid to *speak up* at town meetings.⟩

syn shoot, sound off, speak out, spout (off)

rel bawl, bay, bellow, call, cry, holler, roar, shout, sing (out), thunder, vociferate, yell; articulate, enunciate

phrases speak one's mind

near ant clam up, dummy up, hush, shut up, suppress; quiet

spear *vb* to penetrate or hold (something) with a pointed object — see IMPALE

spear *n* a weapon with a long straight handle and sharp head or blade ⟨The Roman gladiator thrust his *spear* triumphantly into the lion's side.⟩

syn javelin, lance, pike, pikestaff, shaft

rel dart, spike; gaff, halberd (*also* halbert), harpoon, trident

spearhead *vb* to serve as leader of — see LEAD 2

special *adj* 1 being the one or ones of a class with no other members — see ONLY 2

2 granted special treatment or attention — see DARLING 1

3 of a particular or exact sort — see EXPRESS 1

speciality *n* something for which a person shows a special talent — see FORTE

specialized *adj* used by or intended for experts in a particular field of knowledge — see TECHNICAL

specialty *n* 1 a region of activity, knowledge, or influence — see FIELD 2

2 something for which a person shows a special talent — see FORTE

species *n* 1 one of the units into which a whole is divided on the basis of a common characteristic — see CLASS 2

2 a number of persons or things that are grouped together because they have something in common — see SORT 1

specific *adj* 1 of a particular or exact sort — see EXPRESS 1

2 so clearly expressed as to leave no doubt about the meaning — see EXPLICIT

specific *n* 1 a substance or preparation used to treat disease — see MEDICINE

2 a single piece of information — see FACT 3

3 something that sets apart an individual from others of the same kind — see CHARACTERISTIC

specificity *n* careful thoroughness of detail — see PARTICULARITY 1

specify *vb* 1 to give the rules about (something) clearly and exactly — see PRESCRIBE

2 to make reference to or speak about briefly but specifically — see MENTION 1

specimen *n* 1 a member of the human race — see HUMAN

2 one of a group or collection that shows what the whole is like — see EXAMPLE

specious *adj* tending or having power to deceive — see DECEPTIVE 1

speck *n* 1 a small area that is different (as in color) from the main part — see SPOT 1

2 a very small amount — see PARTICLE 1

3 a very small piece — see BIT 1

speck *vb* to mark with small spots especially unevenly — see SPOT 1

speckle *n* a small area that is different (as in color) from the main part — see SPOT 1

speckle *vb* to mark with small spots especially unevenly — see SPOT 1

speckled *adj* marked with spots — see SPOTTED 1

specter *or* **spectre** *n* the soul of a dead person thought of especially as appearing to living people — see GHOST 1

spectrum *n* the distance or extent between possible extremes — see RANGE 3

speculate *vb* to form an opinion from little or no evidence — see GUESS 1

speculation *n* a risky undertaking — see GAMBLE

speculative *adj* existing only as an assumption or speculation — see THEORETICAL 1

speech *n* 1 a usually formal discourse delivered to an audience ⟨The guest of honor gave a short *speech* in appreciation of the award.⟩

syn address, declamation, harangue, oration, talk

rel diatribe, rant, tirade; eulogy, panegyric, tribute; keynote address (*or* keynote speech), lecture, salutatory; homily, sermon; monologue (*also* monolog), soliloquy; pitch, presentation, spiel

2 the stock of words, pronunciation, and grammar used by a people as their basic means of communication — see LANGUAGE 1

speechless *adj* 1 deliberately refraining from speech — see SILENT 1

2 unable to speak — see MUTE 1

speechlessness *n* incapacity for or restraint from speaking — see SILENCE 1

speed *n* 1 a high rate of movement or performance ⟨We dashed off the remaining paperwork with as much *speed* as possible so we could leave for the long weekend.⟩

syn celerity, fastness, fleetness, haste, hurry, quickness, rapidity, rapidness, speediness, swiftness, velocity

rel clip, gait, pace, rate, tempo; drive, hustle; acceleration, hastiness, precipitation, precipitousness, rush; alacrity, dispatch, expedition, expeditiousness, promptitude, promptness

near ant languor, leisureliness, torpidity; deliberateness, deliberation; dilatoriness, lateness, pokiness, procrastination

ant slowness, sluggishness

2 a person or thing that is preferred over others — see FAVORITE

speed *vb* to proceed or move quickly — see HURRY 2

speed (up) *vb* to cause to move or proceed fast or faster — see HURRY 1

speedboat *n* a boat equipped with a motor — see MOTORBOAT

speedily *adv* with great speed — see FAST 1

speediness *n* a high rate of movement or performance — see SPEED 1

speedy *adj* moving, proceeding, or acting with great speed — see FAST 1

2 done, carried out, or given without delay — see PROMPT 1

spell *vb* **1** to cast a spell on — see BEWITCH 1

2 to communicate or convey (as an idea) to the mind — see MEAN 1

spell *n* **1** a spoken word or set of words believed to have magic power ⟨The witch cast a *spell* that turned the prince into a toad.⟩

syn abracadabra, bewitchment, charm, conjuration, enchantment, hex, incantation

rel curse, jinx; conjuring, magic, mojo, necromancy, sorcery, voodoo, voodooism, witchcraft, witchery, wizardry; amulet, charm, fetish (*also* fetich), phylactery, talisman

2 a sudden experiencing of a physical or mental disorder — see ATTACK 2

3 an indefinite but usually short period of time — see WHILE 1

spellbind *vb* to hold the attention of as if by a spell — see ENTHRALL 1

spellbound *adj* being or appearing to be under a magic spell — see ENCHANTED

spell out *vb* to make plain or understandable — see EXPLAIN 1

spend *vb* **1** to hand over or use up in payment ⟨I always end up *spending* too much money at the store.⟩

syn disburse, drop, expend, give, lay out, outlay, pay

rel lavish, rain; blow, dissipate, fritter (away), run through, squander, throw away, waste

near ant cache, hoard, lay up, save; acquire, earn, gain, garner, make, procure, realize, secure, win

2 to make complete use of — see DEPLETE 1

3 to use up carelessly — see WASTE 1

spender *n* someone who spends money freely or foolishly — see PRODIGAL

spendthrift *adj* given to spending money freely or foolishly — see PRODIGAL

spendthrift *n* someone who spends money freely or foolishly — see PRODIGAL

spent *adj* depleted in strength, energy, or freshness — see WEARY 1

spew *vb* **1** to flow out in great quantities or with force — see GUSH 1

2 to violently throw out or off (something from within) — see ERUPT 1

3 to discharge the contents of the stomach through the mouth — see VOMIT

sphere *n* **1** a more or less round body or mass — see ¹BALL 1

2 a region of activity, knowledge, or influence — see FIELD 2

3 a ball-shaped gaseous celestial body that shines by its own light — see STAR 1

spherical *adj* having every part of the surface the same distance from the center — see ROUND 1

spice *n* **1** a sweet or pleasant smell — see FRAGRANCE

2 something (as an herb) that adds an agreeable or interesting taste to food — see SEASONING 1

3 the quality or state of being stimulating to the mind or senses — see PIQUANCY

spice *vb* to make more pleasant to the taste by adding something intensely flavored — see SEASON 1

spick-and-span *or* **spic-and-span** *adj* **1** free from dirt or stain — see CLEAN 1

2 recently made and never used before — see NEW 3

spicy *adj* hinting at or intended to call to mind matters regarded as indecent — see SUGGESTIVE 1

spigot *n* a fixture for controlling the flow of a liquid — see FAUCET

spike *vb* **1** to penetrate or hold (something) with a pointed object — see IMPALE

2 to give life, vigor, or spirit to — see ANIMATE

spill *n* the act of going down from an upright position suddenly and involuntarily — see FALL 1

spill *vb* to make known (as information previously kept secret) — see REVEAL 1

spin *n* **1** a rapid turning about on an axis or central point ⟨The ice skater moved into a tight *spin* at the end of her routine.⟩

syn gyration, pirouette, reel, revolution, roll, rotation, twirl, wheel, whirl

rel circulation, ring, round; coil, curl, curve, spiral, twist, whorl; circle, orbit; eddy, swirl

2 a state of mental confusion — see HAZE 2

3 a short trip for pleasure — see EXCURSION 1

spin *vb* **1** to move in circles around an axis or center ⟨*Spinning* on its axis, the Earth makes one complete rotation every 23 hours 56 minutes 4 seconds.⟩

syn gyrate, pirouette, revolve, roll, rotate, turn, twirl, wheel, whirl

rel coil, curl, curve, round, spiral, swirl, twine, twist, wind; circle, circulate, encircle, orbit, ring; pivot

2 to be in a confused state as if from being twirled around ⟨My head *spun* as I contemplated all the possible problems this restructuring could cause.⟩

syn reel, swim, turn, whirl

rel swirl

near ant calm, collect; settle, steady

3 to move (something) in a curved or circular path or as if on an axis — see TURN 1

spinal column *n* a column of bones supporting the trunk of a vertebrate animal — see SPINE

spindling *adj* being tall, thin and usually loose-jointed — see LANKY

spindly *adj* being tall, thin and usually loose-jointed — see LANKY

---

syn synonym(s)   *rel* related words
ant antonym(s)   *near ant* near antonym(s)

spine *n* a column of bones supporting the trunk of a vertebrate animal 〈He hurt his *spine* in the accident, but the doctor says he'll be walking again in no time.〉

syn backbone, chine, spinal column, vertebral column

rel back, spinal cord, vertebra

spineless *adj* 1 lacking strength of will or character — see WEAK 2

2 having or showing a shameful lack of courage — see COWARDLY

spinelessness *n* 1 the quality or state of lacking strength of will or character — see WEAKNESS 2

2 a shameful lack of courage in the face of danger — see COWARDICE

spin–off *n* something that naturally develops or is developed from something else — see DERIVATIVE

spiny *adj* requiring exceptional skill or caution in performance or handling — see TRICKY 1

spiral *vb* to follow a circular or spiral course — see WIND 1

spiral *adj* turning around an axis like the thread of a screw 〈A *spiral* staircase takes visitors up into the Statue of Liberty.〉

syn coiling, corkscrew, helical, screwlike, winding

rel circular; curling, curving, swirly, twisting

near ant lineal, linear, right, straight

spirit *n* 1 an immaterial force within a human being thought to give the body life, energy, and power — see SOUL 1

2 a state of mind dominated by a particular emotion — see MOOD 1

3 the soul of a dead person thought of especially as appearing to living people — see GHOST 1

4 **spirits** *pl* a distilled beverage that can make a person drunk — see ALCOHOL

spirited *adj* marked by a lively display of strong feeling 〈The town meeting featured a *spirited* debate about the proposed ban on skateboarding in the plaza downtown.〉

syn fiery, gingery, high-spirited, mettlesome, peppery, spunky

rel aggressive, ambitious, assertive, high-pressure, in-your-face, militant; animate, animated, bouncing, brisk, energetic, frisky, jaunty, jazzy, peppy, perky, pert, racy, scrappy, snappy, spanking, sparky, sprightly, springy, vital, vivacious, zippy; ardent, fervent, impassioned, passionate; emphatic, obtrusive

near ant bloodless, boring, dull, lifeless; dead, lackadaisical, languid, languorous, limp, listless; inert, lethargic, sleepy, sluggish, tired, torpid; low-pressure, nonassertive, unaggressive, unambitious, unassertive, unenterprising

ant halfhearted, leaden, spiritless

2 having much high-spirited energy and movement — see LIVELY 1

spiritedly *adv* in a quick and spirited manner — see GAILY 2

spiritless *adj* lacking bodily energy or motivation — see LISTLESS

spiritual *adj* 1 not composed of matter — see IMMATERIAL 1

2 of, relating to, or used in the practice or worship services of a religion — see RELIGIOUS 1

spiritual *n* a religious song — see HYMN 1

¹**spit** *n* an area of land that juts out into a body of water — see ²CAPE

²**spit** *n* 1 something or someone that strongly resembles another — see IMAGE 1

2 the fluid that is secreted into the mouth by certain glands — see SALIVA

spit *vb* to penetrate or hold (something) with a pointed object — see IMPALE

spite *n* the desire to cause pain for the satisfaction of doing harm — see MALICE

spite *vb* to disturb the peace of mind of (someone) especially by repeated disagreeable acts — see IRRITATE 1

spiteful *adj* having or showing a desire to cause someone pain or suffering for the sheer enjoyment of it — see HATEFUL

spitefully *adv* in a mean or spiteful manner — see NASTILY

spitefulness *n* the desire to cause pain for the satisfaction of doing harm — see MALICE

spittle *n* the fluid that is secreted into the mouth by certain glands — see SALIVA

spit up *vb* to discharge the contents of the stomach through the mouth — see VOMIT

splash *n* a very small amount — see PARTICLE 1

splash *vb* 1 to cause (something liquid or mushy) to move along in sheets 〈rowdy teenagers *splashing* water at each other in the community pool〉

syn dash, slop, slosh, spatter, swash

rel dabble, lap, plash, wash; spray, sprinkle, spritz; squirt

2 to wet or soil by striking with something liquid or mushy 〈The bus *splashed* us as it barreled through the puddles.〉

syn bespatter, dash, plash, spatter, splatter

rel drench, drown, impregnate, saturate, soak, sop, souse, steep; bathe, douse (*also* dowse), wash, water; slop, slush, spray, sprinkle, squirt

3 to flow along or against — see WASH 1

4 to flow in a broken irregular stream — see GURGLE

5 to move with a splashing motion — see SLOSH 1

splashy *adj* 1 likely to attract attention — see NOTICEABLE

2 attractively eye-catching in style — see JAZZY 1

3 excessively showy — see GAUDY

splatter *vb* to wet or soil by striking with something liquid or mushy — see SPLASH 2

spleen *n* 1 an intense emotional state of displeasure with someone or something — see ANGER

2 the desire to cause pain for the satisfaction of doing harm — see MALICE

splendid *adj* 1 large and impressive in size, grandeur, extent, or conception — see GRAND 1

2 of the very best kind — see EXCELLENT

3 giving off or reflecting much light — see BRIGHT 1

splendidly *adv* in a pleasing way — see WELL 5

splendor *n* 1 impressiveness of beauty on a large scale — see MAGNIFICENCE

2 the quality or state of having or giving off light — see BRILLIANCE 1

3 something extraordinary or surprising — see WONDER 1

splenetic *adj* having or showing a habitually bad temper — see ILL-TEMPERED

splint *n* a small flat piece separated from a whole — see CHIP 1

splinter *n* a small flat piece separated from a whole — see CHIP 1

splinter *vb* to cut into long slender pieces — see SLIVER

split *adj* disagreeing with each other — see DIVIDED

split *n* **1** an irregular usually narrow break in a surface created by pressure — see CRACK 1

2 the act or process of a whole separating into two or more parts or pieces — see SEPARATION 1

split *vb* to set or force apart — see SEPARATE 1

split–second *adj* done or occurring without any noticeable lapse in time — see INSTANTANEOUS

split second *n* a very small space of time — see INSTANT

splotch *n* a small area that is different (as in color) from the main part — see SPOT 1

splotch *vb* to mark with small spots especially unevenly — see SPOT 1

splotched *adj* having blotches of two or more colors — see PIED

splotchy *adj* marked with spots — see SPOTTED 1

spoil *n* valuables stolen or taken by force — see LOOT

spoil *vb* **1** to affect slightly with something morally bad or undesirable — see TAINT 1

2 to go through decomposition — see DECAY 1

3 to reduce the soundness, effectiveness, or perfection of — see DAMAGE 1

4 to treat with great or excessive care — see BABY

spoilage *n* the process by which dead organic matter separates into simpler substances — see CORRUPTION 1

spoiled *adj* having undergone organic breakdown — see ROTTEN 1

spoilsport *n* a person who spoils the pleasure of others — see KILLJOY

spoken *adj* **1** made or carried on through speaking rather than in writing — see VERBAL 2

2 expressed or communicated by voice — see VOCAL

spokesman *n* a person who speaks for another or for a group — see SPOKESPERSON

spokesperson *n* a person who speaks for another or for a group ⟨The *spokesperson* for the protesting students presented their demands to the administration.⟩

syn mouthpiece, prophet, speaker, spokesman

rel spokesmodel, spokeswoman; front, promoter; communicator, sayer, talker; agent, ambassador, delegate, emissary, envoy, representative

sponge *n* a person who is supported by or seeks support from another without making an adequate return — see LEECH

sponge *vb* to take in (something liquid) through small openings — see ABSORB 1

sponger *n* a person who is supported by or seeks support from another without making an adequate return — see LEECH

spongy *adj* **1** giving easily to the touch — see SOFT 3

2 able to soak up liquids especially readily — see ABSORBENT

sponsor *n* a person who takes the responsibility for some other person or thing ⟨You'll need a *sponsor* to recommend you in order to get into the exclusive country club.⟩

syn backer, guarantor, patron, surety

rel chaperone (*or* chaperon); advocate, champion, supporter; angel, benefactor, underwriter; coach, mentor, teacher; co-sponsor

spontaneity *n* carefree freedom from constraint — see ABANDON

spontaneous *adj* done instantly and without conscious thought or decision — see AUTOMATIC 1

spontaneousness *n* carefree freedom from constraint — see ABANDON

spoof *n* a work that imitates and exaggerates another work for comic effect — see PARODY 1

spoof *vb* **1** to copy or exaggerate (someone or something) in order to make fun of — see MIMIC 1

2 to cause to believe what is untrue — see DECEIVE

spook *n* **1** a person who tries secretly to obtain information for one country in the territory of another usually unfriendly country — see SPY

2 the soul of a dead person thought of especially as appearing to living people — see GHOST 1

spook *vb* to strike with fear — see FRIGHTEN

spooked *adj* filled with fear or dread — see AFRAID

spooky *adj* **1** easily excited by nature — see EXCITABLE

2 fearfully and mysteriously strange or fantastic — see EERIE

spoon *vb* to lift out with something that holds liquid — see DIP 2

spoon *n* a utensil with a bowl and a handle that is used especially in cooking and serving food ⟨An assortment of metal and wooden *spoons* should be part of every cook's culinary arsenal.⟩

syn dipper, ladle, scoop

rel skimmer; dessertspoon, soupspoon, tablespoon, teaspoon

sporadic *adj* **1** lacking in steadiness or regularity of occurrence — see FITFUL

2 not often occurring or repeated — see INFREQUENT

sport *n* **1** activity engaged in to amuse oneself — see PLAY 1

2 an attitude or manner not to be taken seriously — see FUN 2

3 the making of unkind jokes as a way of showing one's scorn for someone or something — see RIDICULE

4 a person or thing that is made fun of — see LAUGHINGSTOCK

---

syn synonym(s)   *rel* related words

ant antonym(s)   *near ant* near antonym(s)

sport *vb* 1 to engage in activity for amusement — see PLAY 1

2 to play and run about happily — see FROLIC 1

3 to present so as to invite notice or attention — see SHOW 1

sportive *adj* given to good-natured joking or teasing — see PLAYFUL

sportiveness *n* a natural disposition for playful behavior — see PLAYFULNESS

sportsmanlike *adj* following or according to the rules — see FAIR 3

sportsmanly *adj* following or according to the rules — see FAIR 3

spot *n* 1 a small area that is different (as in color) from the main part ⟨In summer the white coat of the snow leopard is studded with brownish black *spots*.⟩

syn blotch, dapple, dot, eyespot, fleck, mottle, patch, pip, point, speck, speckle, splotch

rel birthmark, freckle, mole; blob, blot, smear, smudge, stain; spatter, splash; polka dot

2 a difficult, puzzling, or embarrassing situation from which there is no easy escape — see PREDICAMENT

3 a mark of guilt or disgrace — see STAIN 1

4 a very small amount — see PARTICLE 1

5 the area or space occupied by or intended for something — see PLACE 1

spot *vb* 1 to mark with small spots especially unevenly ⟨To give the effect of sunlight on water, the artist *spotted* the lake in his painting with flecks of gold paint.⟩

syn blotch, dapple, dot, fleck, freckle, marble, mottle, pepper, speck, speckle, splotch, sprinkle, stipple

rel blot, dye, stain; band, bar, streak, stripe; intersperse, set, stud; bespatter, spatter

2 to make note of (something) through the use of one's eyes — see SEE 1

spotless *adj* free from dirt or stain — see CLEAN 1

spotted *adj* 1 marked with spots ⟨The *spotted* tablecloth clashed with the stripes on the wallpaper.⟩

syn dappled (*also* dapple), dotted, flecked, freckled, mottled, speckled, splotchy, spotty, stippled, variegated

rel spangled; marbled, moiré (*or* moire), veined; colorful, motley, multicolored, polychromatic, polychrome, varicolored, variegated; blotched, piebald, pinto, roan

near ant solid

ant unspotted

2 having blotches of two or more colors — see PIED

spotting *n* the act or process of sighting or learning the existence of something for the first time — see DISCOVERY 1

spotty *adj* 1 lacking in steadiness or regularity of occurrence — see FITFUL

2 marked with spots — see SPOTTED 1

spouse *n* the person to whom another is married ⟨Employees and their *spouses* are covered by the health plan.⟩

syn better half, consort, mate, partner

rel soul mate; bridegroom, husband, man, old man; bride, helpmate, helpmeet, lady, wife

near ant ex; single; bachelor; bachelorette, maid, maiden, spinster

spout *n* 1 a pipe or channel for carrying off water from a roof — see GUTTER 1

2 a usually forceful stream of fluid discharged from a narrow opening — see JET

spout *vb* 1 to flow out in great quantities or with force — see GUSH 1

2 to talk loudly and wildly — see RANT

3 to violently throw out or off (something from within) — see ERUPT 1

spout (off) *vb* to voice one's opinions freely with force — see SPEAK UP

spray *vb* to cover by or as if by scattering something over or on — see SCATTER 2

spread *n* 1 a decorative cloth used as a top covering for a bed — see COUNTERPANE

2 a large fancy meal often accompanied by ceremony or entertainment — see FEAST 1

3 a wide space or area — see EXPANSE

4 the distance or extent between possible extremes — see RANGE 3

5 the space or amount of space between two points, lines, surfaces, or objects — see DISTANCE 1

spread *vb* 1 to cause to be known over a considerable area or by many people ⟨*Spread* the news!⟩

syn broadcast, circulate, disseminate, propagate

rel radiate, sprawl; diffuse, dispense, disperse, dissipate, scatter, sow; communicate, convey, impart, pass (on), transmit

near ant cloak, conceal, enshroud, hide, mask, obscure, secrete, shroud, veil; contain, limit, restrict

2 to put a layer of on a surface ⟨We *spread* the fertilizer over the lawn evenly until it was fully covered.⟩

syn apply, lay

rel anoint, bedaub, besmear, dab, daub, plaster, slather, smear; blanket, carpet, coat, cover, layer, mantle, overlay, overspread, sheet, surface

near ant bare, expose, peel, strip, uncover

3 to become known — see GET OUT 1

4 to cause (something) to pass from one to another — see COMMUNICATE 1

5 to go or move in different directions from a central point — see SEPARATE 2

6 to become greater in extent, volume, amount, or number — see INCREASE 2

spread (out) *vb* to arrange the parts of (something) over a wider area — see OPEN 3

spreading *adj* exciting a similar feeling or reaction in others — see CONTAGIOUS 2

spree *n* a time or instance of carefree fun — see FLING 1

sprightliness *n* the quality or state of having abundant or intense activity — see VITALITY 1

sprightly *adj* having much high-spirited energy and movement — see LIVELY 1

sprightly *adv* in a quick and spirited manner — see GAILY 2

spring *n* 1 an act of leaping into the air — see JUMP 1

2 a point or place at which something is invented or provided — see SOURCE 1

spring *vb* 1 to come into existence — see BEGIN 2

2 to propel oneself upward or forward into the air — see JUMP 1

3 to release (as from slavery or confinement) — see FREE 1

spring (for) *vb* to give what is owed for — see PAY 2

spring (up) *vb* to come to one's attention especially gradually or unexpectedly — see ARISE 2

springy *adj* **1** able to revert to original size and shape after being stretched, squeezed, or twisted — see ELASTIC 1

2 having much high-spirited energy and movement — see LIVELY 1

sprinkle *n* **1** a light or fine rain — see DRIZZLE

2 a small number — see FEW

sprinkle *vb* **1** to cover by or as if by scattering something over or on — see SCATTER 2

2 to mark with small spots especially unevenly — see SPOT 1

sprinkling *n* **1** a small number — see FEW

2 a very small amount — see PARTICLE 1

sprint *vb* to go at a pace faster than a walk — see RUN 1

sprite *n* **1** an imaginary being usually having a small human form and magical powers — see FAIRY

2 the soul of a dead person thought of especially as appearing to living people — see GHOST 1

spruce *adj* being strikingly neat and trim in style or appearance — see SMART 1

sprucely *adv* in a strikingly neat and trim manner — see SMARTLY

spry *adj* moving easily — see GRACEFUL 1

spryness *n* ease and grace in physical activity — see DEXTERITY 2

spume *n* a light mass of fine bubbles formed in or on a liquid — see FOAM

spunk *n* the strength of mind that enables a person to endure pain or hardship — see FORTITUDE

spunky *adj* marked by a lively display of strong feeling — see SPIRITED 1

spur *n* **1** something that arouses action or activity — see IMPULSE 1

2 a structure that holds up or serves as a foundation for something else — see SUPPORT 1

spur *vb* to urge or push forward with or as if with a pointed object — see PROD 1

spurious *adj* being such in appearance only and made or manufactured with the intention of committing fraud — see COUNTERFEIT 1

spurn *vb* to show unwillingness to accept, do, engage in, or agree to — see DECLINE 1

spur-of-the-moment *adj* made or done without previous thought or preparation — see EXTEMPORANEOUS

spurt *n* **1** a sudden and usually temporary growth of activity — see OUTBREAK 1

2 a usually forceful stream of fluid discharged from a narrow opening — see JET

spurt *vb* **1** to flow out in great quantities or with force — see GUSH 1

2 to violently throw out or off (something from within) — see ERUPT 1

---

sputter *vb* to speak rapidly, inarticulately, and usually unintelligibly — see BABBLE 1

spy *vb* to make note of (something) through the use of one's eyes — see SEE 1

spy *n* a person who tries secretly to obtain information for one country in the territory of another usually unfriendly country ⟨The government *spy* risked his life every day.⟩

syn agent, emissary, operative, spook

rel courier; counterspy; infiltrator, informer, stool pigeon

phrases secret agent, undercover agent

spying *n* the secret gathering of information on others — see ESPIONAGE

squabble *n* an often noisy or angry expression of differing opinions — see ARGUMENT 1

squabble *vb* to express different opinions about something often angrily — see ARGUE 2

squabbler *n* a person who takes part in a dispute — see DISPUTANT

squad *n* a group of people working together on a task — see GANG 1

squalidness *n* the state or quality of being dirty — see DIRTINESS

squall *n* **1** a disturbance of the atmosphere accompanied by wind and often by precipitation (as rain or snow) — see STORM 1

2 a state of noisy, confused activity — see COMMOTION

squall *vb* to cry out loudly and emotionally — see SCREAM 1

squally *adj* **1** marked by wet and windy conditions — see FOUL 1

2 marked by strong wind or more wind than usual — see WINDY 1

squamous *adj* composed of or covered with scales — see SCALY

squander *vb* **1** to use up carelessly — see WASTE 1

2 to cause (members of a group) to move widely apart — see SCATTER 1

squanderer *n* someone who spends money freely or foolishly — see PRODIGAL

squandering *adj* given to spending money freely or foolishly — see PRODIGAL

square *adj* **1** having four equal sides and four right angles ⟨a *square* room⟩

syn foursquare

rel blocky, boxlike, boxy, cubic, cubical; squarish; rectangular

2 marked by justice, honesty, and freedom from bias — see FAIR 2

square *vb* **1** to be in agreement on every point — see CHECK 1

2 to influence someone with a bribe — see BRIBE

squarely *adv* as stated or indicated without the slightest difference — see EXACTLY 1

squash *vb* **1** to cause to become a pulpy mass — see CRUSH 1

2 to put a stop to (something) by the use of force — see QUELL 1

squashy *adj* giving easily to the touch — see SOFT 3

squat *adj* being compact and broad in build and often short in stature — see STOCKY

---

syn synonym(s)   *rel* related words

ant antonym(s)   *near ant* near antonym(s)

squat vb to lie low with the limbs close to the body — see CROUCH

squatty adj being compact and broad in build and often short in stature — see STOCKY

squawk n an expression of dissatisfaction, pain, or resentment — see COMPLAINT 1

squawk vb to express dissatisfaction, pain, or resentment usually tiresomely — see COMPLAIN

squeaking adj having a high musical pitch or range — see SHRILL

squeaky adj having a high musical pitch or range — see SHRILL

squeal vb 1 to give information (as to the authorities) about another's improper or unlawful activities ⟨That stool pigeon *squealed* to the police about the whole operation.⟩

syn inform, rat (on), sing, snitch, talk, tell (on)

rel betray, give away, turn in; cross, double-cross, sell (out); blab, tattle; tip (off)

2 to cry out loudly and emotionally — see SCREAM 1

3 to express dissatisfaction, pain, or resentment usually tiresomely — see COMPLAIN

squealer n a person who provides information about another's wrongdoing — see INFORMER

squeamish adj affected with nausea — see NAUSEOUS 1

squeamishness n 1 a disturbed condition of the stomach in which one feels like vomiting — see NAUSEA 1

2 the tendency to be or state of being squeamish — see DELICACY 3

squeeze vb 1 to apply external pressure on so as to force out the juice or contents of — see ²PRESS 2

2 to fit (people or things) into a tight space — see CROWD 1

3 to reduce in size or volume by or as if by pressing parts or members together — see COMPRESS 1

4 to rob by the use of trickery or threats — see FLEECE

5 to force one's way — see ²PRESS 4

squeeze n 1 the act or process of reducing the size or volume of something by or as if by pressing — see COMPRESSION

2 *slang* a person with whom one is in love — see SWEETHEART

squeezing n the act or process of reducing the size or volume of something by or as if by pressing — see COMPRESSION

squelch vb 1 to put a stop to (something) by the use of force — see QUELL 1

2 to stop the noise or speech of — see SILENCE 1

squinch vb 1 to lie low with the limbs close to the body — see CROUCH

2 to twist (something) out of a natural or normal shape or condition — see CONTORT

3 to draw back in fear, pain, or disgust — see FLINCH

squinching n the twisting of something out of its natural or normal shape or condition — see CONTORTION

squire vb to go along with in order to provide assistance, protection, or companionship — see ACCOMPANY 1

squirm vb to make jerky or restless movements — see FIDGET

squirrel (away) vb to put (something of future use or value) in a safe or secret place — see HOARD

squirt vb to flow out in great quantities or with force — see GUSH 1

squirt n 1 a usually forceful stream of fluid discharged from a narrow opening — see JET

2 a young person who is between infancy and adulthood — see CHILD 1

squishy adj giving easily to the touch — see SOFT 3

stab n 1 a mark or small hole made by a pointed instrument — see PRICK 1

2 an effort to do or accomplish something — see ATTEMPT 1

stab vb to penetrate or hold (something) with a pointed object — see IMPALE

stability n 1 the ability to withstand force or stress without being distorted, dislodged, or damaged ⟨The bridge was designed with such great *stability* that it supposedly will not collapse even under the harshest weather conditions.⟩

syn firmness, soundness, strength, sturdiness

rel dependability, durability, reliability; solidity, solidness; cohesion, toughness

near ant insubstantiality, unsoundness, unsubstantiality; weakness

ant insecurity, instability, precariousness, shakiness, unsteadiness

2 the state of continuing without change — see CONSTANCY 1

stable adj 1 marked by the ability to withstand stress without structural damage or distortion ⟨The observation tower is *stable* enough to withstand the strongest winds without collapsing.⟩

syn fast, firm, sound, strong, sturdy

rel dependable, durable, reliable; unbreakable; beefy, solid; cohesive, tough

near ant infirm, insecure, weak; shaky, tottery, unbalanced, wobbly (*also* wably); unsubstantial

ant rickety, unsound, unstable, unsteady

2 having been established and usually not subject to change — see FIXED 1

3 having full use of one's mind and control over one's actions — see SANE

4 not undergoing a change in condition — see CONSTANT 1

stack n 1 a considerable amount — see LOT 2

2 a quantity of things thrown or stacked on one another — see ¹PILE 1

stack vb to lay or throw on top of one another — see PILE 1

stack up (against or **with)** vb to come near or nearer to in character or quality — see APPROXIMATE

stadium n a large usually roofless building for sporting events with tiers of seats for spectators ⟨The football game will be held at the new *stadium*, which seats 100,000 people.⟩

syn bowl, circus, coliseum, colosseum

rel park; gym, gymnasium, spa; arena, hippodrome

staff n 1 a body of persons at work or available for work — see FORCE 1

2 a heavy rigid stick used as a weapon or for punishment — see CLUB 1

stage *n* 1 a level usually raised surface — see PLATFORM

2 a portion of a trip — see LEG 2

3 an individual part of a process, series, or ranking — see DEGREE 1

4 the public performance of plays — see DRAMA 1

stage *vb* to bring before the public in performance or exhibition — see PRESENT 1

stagger *vb* 1 to move forward while swaying from side to side ⟨I was so tired last night that I just *staggered* upstairs to bed without eating dinner.⟩

syn careen, dodder, lurch, reel, teeter, totter, waddle

rel rock, roll, seesaw, swag, sway, waver, weave, wobble (*also* wabble); clomp, clump, flounder, lumber, lump, pound, scuffle, shamble, shuffle, stamp, stomp, stumble, tramp, tromp

2 to show uncertainty about the right course of action — see HESITATE

staggering *adj* causing wonder or astonishment — see MARVELOUS 1

staggeringly *adv* to a large extent or degree — see GREATLY 2

staid *adj* 1 not joking or playful in mood or manner — see SERIOUS 1

2 having or showing a formal and serious or reserved manner — see DIGNIFIED

staidness *n* a mental state free of jesting or trifling — see EARNESTNESS

stain *vb* 1 to affect slightly with something morally bad or undesirable — see TAINT 1

2 to give color or a different color to — see COLOR 1

3 to make dirty — see DIRTY

stain *n* 1 a mark of guilt or disgrace ⟨The *stain* of this cowardly act would haunt him for the rest of his career.⟩

syn blot, brand, slur, smirch, smudge, spot, stigma, taint

rel discredit, disgrace, dishonor, disrepute, guilt, ignominy, infamy, odium, opprobrium, reproach, shame; corruption, depravity, immorality, iniquity, sin, vice

near ant award, credit, honor; chasteness, chastity, modesty, purity, stainlessness; honesty, integrity, probity, rectitude, uprightness; goodness, righteousness, virtuousness; fame

2 a substance used to color other materials — see PIGMENT

stained *adj* not clean — see DIRTY 1

stainless *adj* free from dirt or stain — see CLEAN 1

stake *n* 1 a legal right to participation in the advantages, profits, and responsibility of something — see INTEREST 1

2 the money or thing risked on the outcome of an uncertain event — see BET 1

stake *vb* 1 to provide money for — see FINANCE 1

2 to risk (something) on the outcome of an uncertain event — see BET

stale *adj* 1 used or heard so often as to be dull ⟨Viewers were bored by the *stale* story lines of the new crop of sitcoms.⟩

syn banal, cliché, commonplace, hack, hackney, hackneyed, moth-eaten, musty, shopworn, stereotyped, threadbare, tired, trite

rel twice-told; canned, derivative, imitative, tried-and-true, unimaginative, uninspired, unoriginal; boring, colorless, drab, dreary, dry, dull, dusty, flat, heavy, humdrum, leaden, monotonous, numbing, old, pedestrian, ponderous, prosaic, stodgy, stuffy, tame, tedious, tiresome, tiring, uninteresting, vapid, wearisome, weary, wearying

near ant animating, energizing, enlivening, exciting, galvanizing, invigorating, stimulating; absorbing, engaging, engrossing, gripping, interesting, intriguing, involving, riveting; pathbreaking, pioneering, trailblazing

ant fresh, new, novel, original

2 causing weariness, restlessness, or lack of interest — see BORING

stalemate *n* 1 a point in a struggle where neither side is capable of winning or willing to give in — see IMPASSE 1

2 a situation in which neither participant in a contest, competition, or struggle comes out ahead of the other — see TIE 1

stalk *vb* 1 to seek out (game) for food or sport — see HUNT 1

2 to walk with exaggerated arm and leg movements — see STRUT 1

stall *vb* 1 to bring (something) to a standstill — see ¹HALT 1

2 to stop functioning — see FAIL 1

stalwart *adj* 1 feeling or displaying no fear by temperament — see BRAVE 1

2 having muscles capable of exerting great physical force — see STRONG 1

stamp *n* 1 a perceptible trace left by pressure — see PRINT 1

2 something that sets apart an individual from others of the same kind — see CHARACTERISTIC

stamp *vb* 1 to move heavily or clumsily — see LUMBER 1

2 to tread on heavily so as to crush or injure — see TRAMPLE

stamp (out) *vb* to destroy all traces of — see ANNIHILATE 1

stance *n* a general way of holding the body — see POSTURE 1

stanchion *n* an upright shaft that supports an overhead structure — see PILLAR 1

stand *n* a level usually raised surface — see PLATFORM

stand *vb* 1 to occupy a place or location ⟨The monument *stands* in the middle of the town plaza.⟩

syn be, be, lie, sit

rel command, overlook; hang around, remain, rest, stay, stick around, tarry; await, wait; post, station; dwell, reside

2 to put up with (something painful or difficult) — see BEAR 1

3 to give what is owed for — see PAY 2

4 to take or have a certain position within a group arranged in vertical classes — see RANK 1

standard *adj* 1 being of the type that is encountered in the normal course of events — see ORDINARY 1

2 having or showing the qualities associated with the members of a particular group or kind — see TYPICAL 1

3 accepted, used, or practiced by most people — see CURRENT 1

standard *n* **1** something set up as an example against which others of the same type are compared ⟨The animation in that movie set the *standard* against which all later animated cartoons were judged.⟩

syn bar, benchmark, criterion, grade, mark, measure, par, touchstone, yardstick

rel case, example, instance; average, norm, rule; acme, apex, meridian, peak, pinnacle, summit, zenith

near ant aberration, abnormality

2 a piece of cloth with a special design that is used as an emblem or for signaling — see FLAG 1

3 what is typical of a group, class, or series — see AVERAGE

4 **standards** *pl* the code of good conduct for an individual or group — see ETHICS

standardize *vb* to make agree with a single established standard or model ⟨The plan is to *standardize* the test for reading comprehension so that we can see how students across the state compare.⟩

syn formalize, homogenize, normalize, regularize

rel codify, marshal (*also* marshall), methodize, order, organize, systematize, systemize; average, equalize, even; square; accredit, certify; control, govern, regulate, rule; conciliate, conform, coordinate, harmonize, integrate, reconcile, synthesize

near ant customize, individualize, tailor

standby *n* something or someone to which one looks for support — see DEPENDENCE 2

stand by *vb* to give steadfast support to — see ADHERE (TO) 1

stand-in *n* a person or thing that takes the place of another — see SUBSTITUTE

stand in *vb* to serve as a replacement usually for a time only — see COVER 1

standing *adj* rising straight up — see ERECT

standing *n* **1** high position within society — see RANK 2

2 the period during which something exists, lasts, or is in progress — see DURATION 1

3 the placement of someone or something in relation to others in a vertical arrangement — see RANK 1

standoff *n* **1** a situation in which neither participant in a contest, competition, or struggle comes out ahead of the other — see TIE 1

2 a point in a struggle where neither side is capable of winning or willing to give in — see IMPASSE 1

standoffish *adj* having or showing a lack of friendliness or interest in others — see COOL 1

standout *n* **1** a person who is widely known and usually much talked about — see CELEBRITY 1

2 something very good of its kind — see JIM-DANDY

stand out *vb* to extend outward beyond a usual point — see BULGE 1

standpoint *n* a way of looking at or thinking about something — see PERSPECTIVE 1

standstill *n* a point in a struggle where neither side is capable of winning or willing to give in — see IMPASSE 1

staple *n* the main or greater part of something as distinguished from its subordinate parts — see BODY 1

star *adj* **1** of or relating to the stars — see STELLAR 1

2 standing above others in rank, importance, or achievement — see EMINENT

3 widely known — see FAMOUS 1

star *n* **1** a ball-shaped gaseous celestial body that shines by its own light ⟨It's difficult to see the *stars* at night in the middle of the city because of all the streetlights.⟩

syn luminary, sphere, sun

rel cluster; binary star, brown dwarf, dwarf, fixed star, giant star, neutron star, nova, pulsar, quasar, red dwarf, red giant, red star, supergiant, supernova, variable star, white dwarf

2 the person who has the most important role in a play, movie, or TV show ⟨When the *star* of the school play came down with the flu on opening night, her understudy got to go on.⟩

syn lead, principal

rel leading lady, leading man; superstar; ingenue (*or* ingénue), starlet

near ant extra, supernumerary

3 a person who is widely known and usually much talked about — see CELEBRITY 1

starch *n* active strength of body or mind — see VIGOR 1

starchy *adj* marked by or showing careful attention to set forms and details — see CEREMONIOUS 1

star-crossed *adj* having, prone to, or marked by bad luck — see UNLUCKY 1

stare *vb* to look long and hard in wonder or surprise — see GAPE

stare *n* a fixed intent look — see GAZE

stark *adj* **1** harsh and threatening in manner or appearance — see GRIM 1

2 having no exceptions or restrictions — see ABSOLUTE 1

3 lacking contents that could or should be present — see EMPTY 1

4 producing inferior or only a small amount of vegetation — see BARREN 1

starry *adj* of or relating to the stars — see STELLAR 1

start *n* the point at which something begins — see BEGINNING

start *vb* **1** to move suddenly and sharply (as in surprise) ⟨I *started* from my chair when I heard the sudden scream.⟩

syn bolt, jump, startle

rel jerk, jolt, twitch; blench, cringe, flinch, quail, recoil, shrink, spook, squinch, wince; bound, leap, spring; react, respond

2 to be responsible for the creation and early operation or use of — see FOUND

3 to cause to function — see ACTIVATE

4 to come into existence — see BEGIN 2

5 to extend outward beyond a usual point — see BULGE 1

6 to take the first step in (a process or course of action) — see BEGIN 1

startle *vb* **1** to make a strong impression

702   startling

on (someone) with something unexpected
— see SURPRISE 1
2 to move suddenly and sharply (as in surprise) — see START 1
3 to strike with fear — see FRIGHTEN

startling *adj* causing a strong emotional reaction because of unexpectedness — see SURPRISING 1

starved *adj* feeling a desire or need for food — see HUNGRY 1

starving *adj* feeling a desire or need for food — see HUNGRY 1

stash *n* a supply stored up and often hidden away — see HOARD 1

stash *vb* to put (something of future use or value) in a safe or secret place — see HOARD

stashing *n* the placing of something out of sight — see CONCEALMENT 1

state *n* **1** a body of people composed of one or more nationalities usually with its own territory and government — see NATION 1
2 high position within society — see RANK 2

state *vb* **1** to convey in appropriate or telling terms — see PHRASE
2 to express (a thought or emotion) in words — see SAY 1
3 to make known (as an idea, emotion, or opinion) — see EXPRESS 1

statehouse *n* the building in which a state legislature meets — see CAPITOL

stateliness *n* **1** a dignified bearing or appearance befitting someone of royal status — see MAJESTY 1
2 dignified or restrained beauty of form, appearance, or style — see ELEGANCE
3 impressiveness of beauty on a large scale — see MAGNIFICENCE

stately *adj* **1** having or showing a formal and serious or reserved manner — see DIGNIFIED
2 having or showing elegance — see ELEGANT 1
3 large and impressive in size, grandeur, extent, or conception — see GRAND 1
4 very dignified in form, tone, or style — see ELEVATED 2

statement *n* **1** a record of goods sold or services performed together with the costs due — see ¹BILL 1
2 an act, process, or means of putting something into words — see EXPRESSION 1
3 something that is said — see WORD 2

static *adj* fixed in a place or position — see STATIONARY 1

station *vb* to assign to a place or position — see ²POST

station *n* **1** the place where someone is assigned to stand or remain ⟨The soldiers remained at their *station* even though a huge enemy force was approaching.⟩
syn position, post, quarter
rel assignment, brief, business, charge, detail, job, operation
2 a regular stopping place ⟨The historic house was once a *station* on the Underground Railroad, the network that helped Africans escaping enslavement reach freedom in the North.⟩
syn stop, way station

---

syn synonym(s)   *rel* related words
ant antonym(s)   *near ant* near antonym(s)

rel depot, terminal; layover, stopover
3 the placement of someone or something in relation to others in a vertical arrangement — see RANK 1
4 a general way of holding the body — see POSTURE 1

stationary *adj* **1** fixed in a place or position ⟨A *stationary* bicycle is good for exercise, but you won't enjoy the scenery very much.⟩
syn immobile, nonmoving, static
rel immovable, irremovable, nonmotile, unmovable; frozen, motionless, moveless, stagnant, still; stuck, unbudging, wedged; fast, rooted, steadfast
phrases in place
near ant motile; adjustable, flexible, modular; displaceable, portable, removable (*also* removeable), transferable (*also* transferrable), transportable; unbalanced, unstable, unsteady
ant mobile, movable (*or* moveable), moving, nonstationary
2 not undergoing a change in condition — see CONSTANT 1

statuette *n* a small statue — see FIGURINE
stature *n* the distance of something or someone from bottom to top — see HEIGHT 3

status *n* **1** position with regard to conditions and circumstances — see SITUATION 1
2 the placement of someone or something in relation to others in a vertical arrangement — see RANK 1

status quo *n* the state or fact of being the way things usually are — see NORMALITY

statute *n* a rule of conduct or action laid down by a governing authority and especially a legislature — see LAW 1

staunch *also* **stanch** *adj* firm in one's allegiance to someone or something — see FAITHFUL 1

stave off *vb* **1** to drive back — see REPEL 1
2 to keep from happening by taking action in advance — see PREVENT

¹stay *n* **1** a temporary residing as another's guest — see VISIT 1
2 the stopping of a process or activity — see END 1

²stay *n* a structure that holds up or serves as a foundation for something else — see SUPPORT 1

¹stay *vb* **1** to continue to be in a place for a significant amount of time ⟨Let's *stay* inside this pavilion until it stops raining.⟩
syn abide, dwell, hang around, remain, stick around, tarry
rel await, hang on, hold on, wait; dally, dawdle, linger, loiter; outstay, overstay
near ant abscond, decamp, escape, evacuate, flee, fly, get out, run away, scram, skip; abandon, desert, forsake, vacate
ant bail out, clear out, cut out, depart, exit, get off, go, go off, leave, move, quit, shove (off), take off, walk out
2 to bring (something) to a standstill — see ¹HALT 1
3 to remain in place in readiness or expectation of something — see WAIT
4 to reside as a temporary guest — see VISIT 2

²stay *vb* to hold up or serve as a foundation for — see SUPPORT 3

stead *n* the more favorable condition or position in a competition — see ADVANTAGE 1

steadfast *adj* firm in one's allegiance to someone or something — see FAITHFUL 1

steadfastness *n* adherence to something to which one is bound by a pledge or duty — see FIDELITY

steadiness *n* the state of continuing without change — see CONSTANCY 1

steady *adj* **1** firm in one's allegiance to someone or something — see FAITHFUL 1

2 appearing or occurring repeatedly from time to time — see REGULAR 1

3 not undergoing a change in condition — see CONSTANT 1

4 not varying — see UNIFORM

5 worthy of one's trust — see DEPENDABLE

steal *n* something bought or offered for sale at a desirable price — see BARGAIN 1

steal *vb* **1** to take (something) without right and with an intent to keep ⟨The guy who tried to *steal* my car was sentenced to a year in jail.⟩

syn appropriate, filch, heist, hook, lift, misappropriate, nip, pilfer, pinch, pocket, purloin, rip off, snitch, swipe, thieve

rel burglarize, rob; loot, pillage, plunder, sack; carjack, hijack (*also* highjack); pick, rifle; poach, rustle, shoplift; collar, grab, grasp, nail, seize, snatch, take; mooch, sponge

phrases make away with, make off with, run off with, walk off with

near ant buy, purchase; bestow, contribute, donate, give, hand over, present

2 to move about in a sly or secret manner — see SNEAK 1

steal (from) *vb* to remove valuables from (a place) unlawfully — see ROB

stealer *n* one who steals — see THIEF

stealing *n* the unlawful taking and carrying away of property without the consent of its owner — see THEFT 1

stealthy *adj* **1** given to acting in secret and to concealing one's intentions — see SNEAKY 1

2 undertaken or done so as to escape being observed or known by others — see SECRET 1

steam *vb* to be excited or emotionally stirred up with anger — see BOIL 1

steaming *adj* feeling or showing anger — see ANGRY

steed *n* a large hoofed domestic animal that is used for carrying or drawing loads and for riding — see HORSE

steel *n* a hand weapon with a length of metal sharpened on one or both sides and usually tapered to a sharp point — see SWORD

steel *vb* **1** to fill with courage or strength of purpose — see ENCOURAGE 1

2 to make able to withstand physical hardship, strain, or exposure — see HARDEN 2

3 to prepare (oneself) mentally or emotionally — see FORTIFY 1

steely *adj* **1** harsh and threatening in manner or appearance — see GRIM 1

2 of the color gray — see GRAY 1

steep *adj* **1** having an incline approaching the perpendicular ⟨a very *steep* rock face that is nearly impossible to climb⟩

syn abrupt, bold, precipitous, sheer

rel perpendicular, plumb, straight, vertical; craggy, hillocky, hilly, mountainous, scarped; angled, canted, cocked, heeled, inclined, listed, slanted, sloped, tilted, tipped

near ant gentle, gradual, moderate, soft; even, flat, flush, horizontal, level, plane

ant easy

2 going beyond a normal or acceptable limit in degree or amount — see EXCESSIVE

steep *vb* **1** to cause (as a person) to become filled or saturated with a certain quality or principle — see INFUSE

2 to wet thoroughly with liquid — see SOAK 1

steer *vb* **1** to point out the way for (someone) especially from a position in front — see LEAD 1

2 to operate or control the course of — see NAVIGATE 1

stellar *adj* **1** of or relating to the stars ⟨Humankind's dream of *stellar* navigation is hampered by the vast distances between the stars, even in our own galaxy.⟩

syn astral, star, starry

rel celestial, empyrean, heavenly; intergalactic, interstellar; astronomical (*also* astronomic), astrophysical; astronautic (*or* astronautical); starlike, star-spangled

2 of the very best kind — see EXCELLENT

stench *n* a strong unpleasant smell — see STINK 1

stentorian *adj* marked by a high volume of sound — see LOUD 1

step *n* **1** an action planned or taken to achieve a desired result — see MEASURE 1

2 an individual part of a process, series, or ranking — see DEGREE 1

3 the mark or impression made by a foot — see FOOTPRINT

4 steps *pl* the direction along which something or someone moves — see PATH 1

5 a very small distance or degree — see HAIR 1

step *vb* **1** to go on foot — see WALK 1

2 to perform a series of usually rhythmic bodily movements to music — see DANCE 1

3 to proceed or move quickly — see HURRY 2

step (along) *vb* to leave a place often for another — see GO 2

step-by-step *adj* proceeding or changing by steps or degrees — see GRADUAL

step down (from) *vb* **1** to give up (a job or office) — see QUIT 1

2 to give up (as a position of authority) formally — see ABDICATE

steppe *n* a broad area of level or rolling treeless country — see PLAIN 1

step up *vb* to make markedly greater in measure or degree — see INTENSIFY

stereotype *n* an idea or statement about all of the members of a group or all the instances of a situation — see GENERALIZATION

stereotype *vb* to use so much as to make less appealing — see HACKNEY

stereotyped *adj* used or heard so often as to be dull — see STALE 1

sterile *adj* **1** not able to produce fruit or offspring ⟨*Sterile* couples sometimes choose to adopt needy children.⟩ ⟨The apple tree turned out to be *sterile*, never yielding a crop of apples.⟩

syn barren, fruitless, impotent, infertile, unfruitful

rel altered, desexed, neutered, sterilized; castrated, emasculated, gelded; spayed; unproductive

near ant fecund, luxuriant, productive, prolific; enriched, fertilized, rich; impregnated, pregnant; potent; bearing, producing, yielding; blooming, bursting, flourishing, swarming, teeming

ant fat, fertile, fruitful

2 free from filth, infection, or dangers to health — see SANITARY

sterling *adj* of the very best kind — see EXCELLENT

stern *adj* **1** given to exacting standards of discipline and self-restraint — see SEVERE 1

2 harsh and threatening in manner or appearance — see GRIM 1

sternly *adv* in a manner so as to cause loss or suffering — see HARDLY 1

sternness *n* the quality or state of being demanding or unyielding (as in discipline or criticism) — see SEVERITY

stevedore *n* one who loads and unloads ships at a port — see DOCKWORKER

stew *n* **1** a state of nervous or irritated concern — see FRET

2 a state of noisy, confused activity — see COMMOTION

stew *vb* **1** to cook in a liquid heated to the point that it gives off steam — see BOIL 2

2 to experience concern or anxiety — see WORRY 1

steward *vb* to look after and make decisions about — see CONDUCT 1

stewardship *n* **1** the act or activity of looking after and making decisions about something — see CONDUCT 1

2 the duty or function of watching or guarding for the sake of proper direction or control — see SUPERVISION 1

stick *vb* **1** to hold to something firmly as if by adhesion ⟨Those magnets are strong enough to *stick* to the refrigerator without any problems.⟩

syn adhere, cleave, cling, hew

rel bind, cohere, fasten, fuse, glue, unite

near ant loosen; drop, fall

2 to arrange something in a certain spot or position — see PLACE 1

3 to penetrate or hold (something) with a pointed object — see IMPALE

4 to rob by the use of trickery or threats — see FLEECE

stick (to *or* **with)** *vb* to give steadfast support to — see ADHERE (TO) 1

stick around *vb* to continue to be in a place for a significant amount of time — see ¹STAY 1

stick-in-the-mud *n* a person with old-fashioned ideas — see FOGY

stick out *vb* **1** to extend outward beyond a usual point — see BULGE 1

2 to put up with (something painful or difficult) — see BEAR 2

sticks *n pl* the open rural area outside of big towns and cities — see COUNTRY 2

sticky *adj* **1** tending to adhere to objects upon contact ⟨Both sides of the tape are *sticky*, making it a little tricky to work with.⟩

syn adherent, adhesive, gluey, glutinous, gummy, tacky, tenacious, viscid

rel gelatinous, gooey, ropy (*also* ropey), syrupy, viscous; pitchy, tarry

near ant nonviscous

ant nonadhesive

2 containing or characterized by an uncomfortable amount of moisture — see HUMID

3 requiring exceptional skill or caution in performance or handling — see TRICKY 1

stiff *adj* **1** incapable of or highly resistant to being bent ⟨Use a *stiff* piece of paper for the project.⟩

syn inflexible, rigid, stiffened, unyielding

rel inelastic; firm, hard, solid, sound, strong; nonelastic, nonmalleable

near ant elastic, resilient, springy, stretchy, workable; malleable, plastic; droopy, flabby, flaccid, mushy, semisoft, soft, squashy, squishy; lank, limber, limp, lissome (*also* lissom), lithe, lithesome, willowy

ant flexible, floppy, pliable, pliant, supple, yielding

2 difficult to endure — see HARSH 1

3 going beyond a normal or acceptable limit in degree or amount — see EXCESSIVE

4 having a consistency that does not easily yield to pressure — see FIRM 2

5 lacking social grace and assurance — see AWKWARD 1

6 requiring considerable physical or mental effort — see HARD 2

7 marked by or showing careful attention to set forms and details — see CEREMONIOUS 1

stiff *n* **1** a dead body — see CORPSE

2 a member of the human race — see HUMAN

stiff *vb* to rob by the use of trickery or threats — see FLEECE

stiffened *adj* incapable of or highly resistant to bending — see STIFF 1

stiffly *adv* **1** in a manner so as to cause loss or suffering — see HARDLY 1

2 in a vigorous and forceful manner — see HARD 3

stifle *vb* **1** to be or cause to be killed by lack of breathable air — see SMOTHER 1

2 to refrain from openly showing or uttering — see SUPPRESS 2

3 to deaden the sound of — see MUFFLE 1

stifling *adj* lacking fresh air — see STUFFY 1

stigma *n* a mark of guilt or disgrace — see STAIN 1

still *adj* **1** free from disturbing noise or uproar — see QUIET 1

2 free from storms or physical disturbance — see CALM 1

3 mostly or entirely without sound — see SILENT 3

still *n* **1** a state of freedom from storm or disturbance — see CALM 1

2 the near or complete absence of sound — see SILENCE 2

---

syn synonym(s)   *rel* related words
ant antonym(s)   *near ant* near antonym(s)

still *vb* **1** to bring (something) to a standstill — see ¹HALT 1

2 to free from distress or disturbance — see CALM 1

3 to stop the noise or speech of — see SILENCE 1

still *adv* **1** without motion ⟨The cat sat absolutely *still*, watching as the mouse began to make its way across the floor.⟩

syn motionlessly, quiet, quietly

rel immovably; inactively

near ant movably

2 in spite of that — see HOWEVER

stillness *n* **1** a state of freedom from storm or disturbance — see CALM 1

2 incapacity for or restraint from speaking — see SILENCE 1

3 the near or complete absence of sound — see SILENCE 2

stilly *adj* **1** free from disturbing noise or uproar — see QUIET 1

2 free from storms or physical disturbance — see CALM 1

3 mostly or entirely without sound — see SILENT 3

stilted *adj* **1** lacking social grace and assurance — see AWKWARD 1

2 marked by or showing careful attention to set forms and details — see CEREMONIOUS 1

stimulant *n* something that arouses action or activity — see IMPULSE 1

stimulate *vb* **1** to give life, vigor, or spirit to — see ANIMATE

2 to rouse to strong feeling or action — see PROVOKE 1

stimulating *adj* **1** causing great emotional or mental stimulation — see EXCITING 1

2 having a renewing effect on the state of the body or mind — see TONIC 1

3 serving or likely to arouse a strong reaction — see PROVOCATIVE

stimulative *adj* having a renewing effect on the state of the body or mind — see TONIC 1

stimulus *n* something that arouses action or activity — see IMPULSE 1

sting *vb* **1** to charge (someone) too much for goods or services — see OVERCHARGE 1

2 to rob by the use of trickery or threats — see FLEECE

sting *n* **1** an instance of the use of dishonest methods to acquire something of value — see FRAUD 1

2 a sharp unpleasant sensation usually felt in some specific part of the body — see PAIN 1

stinger *n* a hard strike with a part of the body or an instrument — see ¹BLOW

stinginess *n* the quality or practice of being overly sparing with money — see PARSIMONY 1

stinging *adj* causing intense discomfort to one's skin — see CUTTING 1

stingy *adj* **1** giving or sharing as little as possible ⟨Until his redemption, Ebenezer Scrooge is the classic example of a very *stingy*, heartless miser.⟩

syn cheap, close, closefisted, mean, niggard, niggardly, parsimonious, penurious, spare, sparing, stinting, tight, tightfisted, uncharitable

rel careful, conserving, economical, economizing, frugal, saving, scrimping, skimp-

ing, thrifty; acquisitive, avaricious, covetous, grasping, greedy, hoggish, mercenary, rapacious; begrudging, envious, grudging, resentful; inhospitable

near ant altruistic, selfless, unselfish; extravagant, lavish, overgenerous, profuse; beneficent, benevolent, hospitable, humanitarian, philanthropic (*also* philanthropical); compassionate, good-hearted, greathearted, kindly, magnanimous, openhearted; thriftless, unthrifty; dissipating, frittering, prodigal, profligate, spendthrift, splurging, squandering, wasteful, wasting

ant bounteous, bountiful, charitable, freehanded, generous, liberal, munificent, openhanded, unsparing

2 less plentiful than what is normal, necessary, or desirable — see MEAGER

stink *n* **1** a strong unpleasant smell ⟨The *stink* of burned plastic lingered in the kitchen for days after we accidentally melted a spatula on the stove.⟩

syn funk, reek, stench

rel acridness, fetidness, foulness, fustiness, malodorousness, mustiness, rancidity, rankness, staleness; badness, vileness; dirtiness, filthiness, nastiness; odor, redolence, scent

near ant floweriness, lusciousness, savoriness, spiciness, sweetness

ant aroma, fragrance, perfume

2 a feeling or declaration of disapproval or dissent — see OBJECTION

stink *vb* to give off an extremely unpleasant smell ⟨The dog *stinks* because she tangled with a skunk again.⟩

syn reek

rel exhale, savor (*also* savour), smell; decay, decompose, rot, spoil; disgust, offend, repulse, revolt

stinker *n* a person whose behavior is offensive to others — see JERK 1

stinking *adj* having an unpleasant smell — see MALODOROUS

stinky *adj* having an unpleasant smell — see MALODOROUS

stint *n* **1** a fixed period of time during which a person holds a job or position — see TERM 1

2 the act or practice of keeping something (as an activity) within certain boundaries — see RESTRICTION 2

stint (on) *vb* to use or give out in stingy amounts — see SPARE 1

stinting *adj* giving or sharing as little as possible — see STINGY 1

stipend *n* the money paid regularly to a person for labor or services — see WAGE

stipple *vb* to mark with small spots especially unevenly — see SPOT 1

stippled *adj* marked with spots — see SPOTTED 1

stipulate (for) *vb* to ask for (something) earnestly or with authority — see DEMAND 1

stipulation *n* something upon which the carrying out of an agreement or offer depends — see CONDITION 2

stir *n* **1** a state of noisy, confused activity — see COMMOTION

2 the act or an instance of changing position — see MOVEMENT 1

stir *vb* **1** to cause (as a liquid) to move

about in a circle especially repeatedly ⟨The recipe says to *stir* the mixture carefully until it's properly blended.⟩

syn agitate, churn, swirl, wash, whirl

rel beat, paddle, whip, whisk; reel, shake, wheel

2 to change one's position — see MOVE 3

3 to rouse to strong feeling or action — see PROVOKE 1

stir (up) *vb* to bring (something volatile or intense) into being — see INCITE 1

stirring *adj* **1** causing great emotional or mental stimulation — see EXCITING 1

2 having the power to affect the feelings or sympathies — see MOVING

3 marked by much life, movement, or activity — see ALIVE 2

stirring *n* the act or an instance of changing position — see MOVEMENT 1

stitch *n* a sharp unpleasant sensation usually felt in some specific part of the body — see PAIN 1

stitch *vb* to close up with a series of interlacing stitches — see SEW

stock *adj* accepted, used, or practiced by most people — see CURRENT 1

stock *n* **1** a group of persons who come from the same ancestor — see FAMILY 1

2 a stupid person — see IDIOT

3 firm belief in the integrity, ability, effectiveness, or genuineness of someone or something — see TRUST 1

4 the line of ancestors from whom a person is descended — see ANCESTRY

5 the number of individuals or amount of something available at any given time — see SUPPLY

stockade *n* a place of confinement for persons held in lawful custody — see JAIL

stocking *n* a close-fitting covering for the foot and leg ⟨thick wool *stockings* designed to be worn with hiking boots⟩

syn hose, sock

rel hosiery; support hose; anklet, bobby socks, bootee

stockpile *n* a supply stored up and often hidden away — see HOARD 1

stockpile *vb* to put (something of future use or value) in a safe or secret place — see HOARD

stocky *adj* being compact and broad in build and often short in stature ⟨The *stocky* boxer's strength and speed more than make up for his opponent's longer reach.⟩

syn chunky, dumpy, heavyset, squat, squatty, stout, stubby, stumpy, thickset

rel beefy, brawny, bulky, burly, husky, sturdy, thick, thickish, weighty; chubby, heavy, plump, portly, pudgy, roly-poly, rotund, round, tubby

near ant delicate, fragile, frail, puny; lean, skinny, slender, slim, spare, thin; angular, gaunt, lank, lanky, rawboned, sinewy; scraggy, scrawny, slight; spindly, twiggy, waspish, weedy, willowy, wiry

stodgy *adj* causing weariness, restlessness, or lack of interest — see BORING

stoic *or* **stoical** *adj* **1** accepting pains or hardships calmly or without complaint — see PATIENT 1

2 not feeling or showing emotion — see IMPASSIVE 1

stolid *adj* **1** not expressing any emotion — see BLANK 1

2 not feeling or showing emotion — see IMPASSIVE 1

stomach *vb* to put up with (something painful or difficult) — see BEAR 2

stomach *n* **1** the part of the body between the chest and the pelvis ⟨Please don't lean on my *stomach*—I just had a big meal!⟩

syn abdomen, belly, breadbasket [*slang*], gut, solar plexus, tummy

rel middle, midriff, waist; paunch, potbelly; thorax

2 a need or desire for food — see HUNGER 1

stomachache *n* abdominal pain especially when focused in the digestive organs ⟨All that fried food gave me a *stomachache*.⟩

syn bellyache

rel colic, cramps, gripes

stomp *vb* **1** to move heavily or clumsily — see LUMBER 1

2 to tread on heavily so as to crush or injure — see TRAMPLE

stone–blind *adj* lacking the power of sight — see BLIND

stone's throw *n* a very small distance or degree — see HAIR 1

stoneware *n* articles made of baked clay — see CROCKERY

stony *also* **stoney** *adj* having or showing a lack of sympathy or tender feelings — see HARD 1

stool pigeon *n* a person who provides information about another's wrongdoing — see INFORMER

stoop *vb* to descend to a level that is beneath one's dignity — see CONDESCEND 1

stooping *adj* bending downward or forward — see NODDING

stop *n* **1** a brief halt in a journey ⟨Our guide called for a *stop* at the trail hut so we could eat and rest a bit.⟩

syn layover, stopover

rel break, pause, rest

2 a regular stopping place — see STATION 2

3 something that makes movement or progress difficult — see ENCUMBRANCE

4 the stopping of a process or activity — see END 1

stop *vb* **1** to bring (as an action or operation) to an immediate end ⟨The manufacturer will *stop* selling the toy and will immediately recall all the units that have already been sold.⟩

syn break, break off, break up, can [*slang*], cease, cut off, cut out, desist (from), discontinue, drop, end, halt, knock off, lay off, leave off, quit, shut off

rel complete, conclude, finish; deactivate; block, blockade, dam, delay, detain, hinder, hold, hold back, impede, kibosh, obstruct, stem; call, suspend; arrest, brake, check, clamp down, rein (in), squash, squelch, stamp, stanch (*or* staunch), stunt, suppress; pause, stay, suspend

phrases have done with, put the kibosh on

near ant carry on, continue, keep up, run on; advance, proceed, progress

2 to bring (something) to a standstill — see ¹HALT 1

---

3 to close up so that no empty spaces remain — see FILL 2

4 to come to an end — see CEASE 1

stop (by or in) *vb* to make a brief visit — see CALL 3

stop (up) *vb* to prevent passage through by filling with something — see CLOG 1

stopcock *n* a fixture for controlling the flow of a liquid — see FAUCET

stopgap *n* a temporary replacement — see MAKESHIFT

stopover *n* a brief halt in a journey — see STOP 1

stoppage *n* the stopping of a process or activity — see END 1

storage *n* a building for storing goods — see STOREHOUSE

store *adj* made beforehand in large numbers — see READY-MADE

store *n* **1** a collection of things kept available for future use or need ⟨He has a *store* of old magazines that he has been collecting for years.⟩

syn cache, deposit, hoard, reserve

rel budget, fund, nest egg; armory, arsenal, bank, pool, stock, stockpile, supply; accumulation, assemblage, collection, gathering

2 a supply stored up and often hidden away — see HOARD 1

3 an establishment where goods are sold to consumers — see SHOP 1

4 a considerable amount — see LOT 2

store *vb* **1** to place somewhere for safekeeping or ready availability ⟨We decided to *store* the lawn mower in the shed instead of the garage.⟩

syn keep, put up, stow

rel cellar, garage, hangar, house, warehouse; file, pack, shelve

2 to put (something of future use or value) in a safe or secret place — see HOARD

storehouse *n* a building for storing goods ⟨The company has a large *storehouse* filled with lumber for manufacturing its line of furniture.⟩

syn depository, depot, magazine, repository, storage, warehouse

rel cache, stockroom, storeroom; bank, bin, container, locker, safe-deposit box, strongbox; arsenal, dump; stowage

storm *vb* **1** to express one's anger usually violently — see RAGE 1

2 to fall as water in a continuous stream of drops from the clouds — see RAIN 1

3 to take sudden, violent action against — see ATTACK 1

4 to be excited or emotionally stirred up with anger — see BOIL 1

storm *n* **1** a disturbance of the atmosphere accompanied by wind and often by precipitation (as rain or snow) ⟨a winter *storm* bringing about six inches of snow⟩

syn squall, tempest

rel blizzard, ice storm, snowstorm; cloudburst, hailstorm, rainstorm, thundershower, thunderstorm, weather, windstorm; northeaster (*or* nor'easter), norther, southeaster, southwester; cyclone, hurricane, typhoon; sandstorm

2 a heavy fall of objects — see RAIN 2

3 a rapid or overwhelming outpouring of many things at once — see BARRAGE

4 a state of noisy, confused activity — see COMMOTION

5 a steady falling of water from the sky in significant quantity — see RAIN 1

6 a sudden intense expression of strong feeling — see OUTBURST 1

7 a violent disturbance (as of the political or social order) — see CONVULSION

stormy *adj* **1** marked by bursts of destructive force or intense activity — see VIOLENT 1

2 marked by or abounding with rain — see RAINY

3 marked by sudden or violent disturbance — see CONVULSIVE 1

4 marked by turmoil or disturbance especially of natural elements — see WILD 3

5 marked by wet and windy conditions — see FOUL 1

story *n* **1** a work with imaginary characters and events that is shorter and usually less complex than a novel ⟨He's a talented writer, but his quirky *stories* will never find a wide readership.⟩

syn narrative, novelette, novella, short story, tale, yarn

rel bedtime story; exemplum, fable, parable; anecdote, joke; fairy tale, folktale, legend, myth, romance; account, annals, chronicle, history, record, report

2 a brief account of something interesting that happened especially to one personally ⟨Grandpa is always telling *stories* about what it was like growing up on a farm.⟩

syn anecdote, tale, yarn

rel episode, event, happening, incident, occurrence; recital, recitation

3 a report of recent events or facts not previously known — see NEWS

4 a relating of events usually in the order in which they happened — see ACCOUNT 1

5 a rumor or report of a personal or sensational nature — see TALE 1

6 a statement known by its maker to be untrue and made in order to deceive — see LIE

7 the unfolding of events in a dramatic or literary work — see ACTION 2

8 position with regard to conditions and circumstances — see SITUATION 1

storyteller *n* a person who tells lies — see LIAR

stout *adj* **1** able to withstand hardship, strain, or exposure — see HARDY 1

2 being compact and broad in build and often short in stature — see STOCKY

3 feeling or displaying no fear by temperament — see BRAVE 1

4 having muscles capable of exerting great physical force — see STRONG 1

5 not showing weakness or uncertainty — see FIRM 1

stouthearted *adj* feeling or displaying no fear by temperament — see BRAVE 1

stoutly *adv* in a vigorous and forceful manner — see HARD 3

stoutness *n* strength of mind to carry on in spite of danger — see COURAGE

stow *vb* **1** to place somewhere for safekeeping or ready availability — see STORE 1

2 to put (something of future use or value) in a safe or secret place — see HOARD

straggler *n* someone who moves slowly or more slowly than others — see SLOWPOKE

straight *adv* **1** in a direct line or course — see DIRECTLY 1

2 in an honest and direct manner — see STRAIGHTFORWARD

straight *adj* **1** free from irregularities or digressions in course ⟨In the wide, open spaces of the West some rural roads are incredibly *straight*.⟩

syn direct, linear, right, straightaway, straightforward

rel unbent, uncurled, untwisted; undeviating, unswerving

near ant bowed, rounded; entwined, kinked, swirled, turned, turning, twined, twining, twisted, twisting, veering, warped; bending, coiled, coiling, corkscrew, curled, curling, curved, curving, looped, looping, spiral, spiraling (*or* spiralling), wavy, winding; devious, serpentine, sinuous; crooked, zigzag, zigzagging

2 conforming to a high standard of morality or virtue — see GOOD 2

3 free from added matter — see PURE 1

4 free in expressing one's true feelings and opinions — see FRANK

5 going straight to the point clearly and firmly — see STRAIGHTFORWARD 1

6 not having one's mind affected by alcohol — see SOBER 1

7 following one after another without others coming in between — see CONSECUTIVE

straightaway *adj* **1** done or occurring without any noticeable lapse in time — see INSTANTANEOUS

2 free from irregularities or digressions in course — see STRAIGHT 1

straightaway *adv* without delay — see IMMEDIATELY

straighten *vb* to cause to follow a line that is without bends or curls ⟨*Straighten* that extension cord—it should be just long enough to reach the wall outlet.⟩

syn unbend, uncurl

rel uncoil, unroll, unwind; disentangle, untangle, untwine, untwist

near ant arc, bend, bow, hook, round; entwine, swirl, turn, twine, twist; coil, loop, spiral, wind

ant bend, crook, curl, curve

straightforward *adj* **1** going straight to the point clearly and firmly ⟨a *straightforward* account of the football game with no digressions or personal comments⟩

syn direct, forthright, foursquare, plain, straight

rel aboveboard, candid, frank, free-spoken, honest, open, openhearted, outspoken, plainspoken, unguarded, unreserved; artless, earnest, sincere; uninhibited, unrestrained; abrupt, bluff, blunt, brusque (*also* brusk), curt, gruff, point-blank, sharp; impolite, inconsiderate, rude, tactless

near ant circumlocutory, long-winded, prolix, verbose, wordy; inhibited, reserved, restrained; civil, courteous, polite, tactful; ambiguous, equivocal, evasive,

misleading; double-dealing, hypocritical, two-faced

ant circuitous, indirect, roundabout

2 free from irregularities or digressions in course — see STRAIGHT 1

3 free in expressing one's true feelings and opinions — see FRANK

4 not subject to misinterpretation or more than one interpretation — see CLEAR 2

straightforward *also* **straightforwards** *adv* in an honest and direct manner ⟨She finally told him *straightforward* that he wasn't going to get the job.⟩

syn directly, forthrightly, foursquare, plain, plainly, straight, straightforwardly

rel candidly, frankly, honestly, openheartedly, openly, unguardedly, unreservedly; artlessly, earnestly, simply, sincerely; abruptly, bluntly, brusquely, gruffly, point-blank, sharply; impolitely, inconsiderately, rudely, tactlessly

near ant long-windedly, verbosely, wordily; civilly, courteously, diplomatically, politely, tactfully; ambiguously, circuitously, equivocally, evasively, indirectly

straightforwardly *adv* in an honest and direct manner — see STRAIGHTFORWARD

straightforwardness *n* the free expression of one's true feelings and opinions — see CANDOR 1

straightway *adv* **1** without delay — see IMMEDIATELY

2 in a direct line or course — see DIRECTLY 1

¹**strain** *n* **1** the line of ancestors from whom a person is descended — see ANCESTRY

2 a rhythmic series of musical tones arranged to give a pleasing effect — see MELODY

3 a very small amount — see PARTICLE 1

4 a number of persons or things that are grouped together because they have something in common — see SORT 1

²**strain** *n* the burden on one's emotional or mental well-being brought by demands on one's time — see STRESS 1

strain *vb* **1** to injure by overuse, misuse, or pressure ⟨In order to lift something heavy, squat down and lift with your legs, or you'll *strain* your back.⟩

syn pull, rack, stretch, wrench

rel fray, tax, weaken; damage, harm, hurt, impair, wound; batter, bruise, tear; cripple, lame, mangle, mutilate

2 to pass through a filter ⟨Better *strain* that coffee thoroughly to get all the grounds out.⟩

syn filter, screen

rel leach, percolate

3 to devote serious and sustained effort — see LABOR

4 to flow forth slowly through small openings — see EXUDE

5 to subject (a personal quality or faculty) to often excessive stress — see TRY 1

6 to put one's arms around and press tightly — see EMBRACE 1

strained *adj* lacking in natural or spontaneous quality — see ARTIFICIAL 1

strait *n* **1** a narrow body of water between two land masses — see CHANNEL 2

2 *often* **straits** *pl* a state of great suffering of body or mind — see DISTRESS 1

---

syn synonym(s)   *rel* related words
ant antonym(s)   *near ant* near antonym(s)

straitlaced *or* **straightlaced** *adj* given to or marked by very conservative standards regarding personal behavior or morals ⟨In the movie, she plays a teacher whose forthrightness with her students shocks her more *straitlaced* colleagues.⟩

syn prim, prudish, puritanical

rel priggish, staid, stuffy; genteel, proper, refined; decent, honest, moral, right, righteous, upright, virtuous

near ant liberated, permissive; bad, immoral, improper, indecent, lax, loose, prurient, wicked; slatternly, sleazy; debauched, degenerate, degraded, depraved, perverted

strand *n* the usually sandy or gravelly land bordering a body of water — see BEACH

strand *vb* **1** to cause irreparable damage to (a ship) by running aground or sinking — see SHIPWRECK

2 to cause to remain behind — see LEAVE 1

stranded *adj* resting on the shore or bottom of a body of water — see AGROUND

strange *adj* **1** different from the ordinary in a way that causes curiosity or suspicion — see ODD 2

2 excitingly or mysteriously unusual — see EXOTIC

3 not known or experienced before — see NEW 2

4 noticeably different from what is generally found or experienced — see UNUSUAL 1

stranger *n* a person who is not native to or known to a community ⟨The people of the island are quick to make *strangers* feel at home.⟩

syn foreigner, nonnative, outlander, outsider

rel alien, nonresident; outcast, pariah; drifter, transient, wanderer

near ant buddy, chum, comrade, confidant, crony, familiar, friend, intimate, pal; acquaintance, associate, cohort, colleague, companion, fellow, hearty, hobnobber, mate, partner, peer; citizen, habitant, inhabitant, resident

ant native

strangle *vb* **1** to be or cause to be killed by lack of breathable air — see SMOTHER 1

2 to keep (someone) from breathing by exerting pressure on the windpipe — see CHOKE 1

3 to refrain from openly showing or uttering — see SUPPRESS 2

stratagem *n* a clever often underhanded means to achieve an end — see TRICK 1

strategy *n* **1** a method worked out in advance for achieving some objective — see PLAN 1

2 the means or procedure for doing something — see METHOD

stratum *n* **1** one of the segments of society into which people are grouped — see CLASS 1

2 the placement of someone or something in relation to others in a vertical arrangement — see RANK 1

straw *adj* of a pale yellow or yellowish brown color — see BLOND

stray *adj* lacking a definite plan, purpose, or pattern — see RANDOM

streak *n* **1** a line or long narrow section

differing in color from the background — see ¹STRIPE 1

2 a very small amount — see PARTICLE 1

streak *vb* to make stripes on — see STRIPE

streaked *adj* having stripes — see STRIPED

stream *vb* **1** to cause to flow in a stream — see POUR 1

2 to move in a stream — see FLOW 1

3 to move or proceed smoothly and readily — see FLOW 2

streamer *n* a piece of cloth with a special design that is used as an emblem or for signaling — see FLAG 1

streamlet *n* a natural body of running water smaller than a river — see CREEK 1

streamline *vb* to make less complex — see SIMPLIFY 1

street *n* a passage cleared for public vehicular travel — see WAY 1

strength *n* **1** the ability to exert effort for the accomplishment of a task — see POWER 2

2 the ability to withstand force or stress without being distorted, dislodged, or damaged — see STABILITY 1

strengthen *vb* **1** to increase the ability of (as a muscle) to exert physical force ⟨Lifting weights every day will eventually *strengthen* your muscles.⟩ ⟨The army makes new recruits run for miles in order to *strengthen* them.⟩

syn beef (up), fortify, harden, toughen

rel anneal, temper; firm (up), tone (up); energize, invigorate, vitalize; restrengthen

near ant cripple, incapacitate, paralyze; damage, harm, hurt, impair, injure; break down, wear out; sap, undercut, undermine

ant debilitate, enervate, enfeeble, weaken

2 to make able to withstand physical hardship, strain, or exposure — see HARDEN 2

3 to make markedly greater in measure or degree — see INTENSIFY

4 to prepare (oneself) mentally or emotionally — see FORTIFY 1

strenuous *adj* **1** marked by or uttered with forcefulness — see EMPHATIC 1

2 requiring considerable physical or mental effort — see HARD 2

strenuously *adv* **1** in a vigorous and forceful manner — see HARD 3

2 with great effort or determination — see HARD 1

stress *n* **1** the burden on one's emotional or mental well-being created by demands on one's time ⟨With a full-time job and her college courses, the young woman is under a lot of *stress* right now.⟩

syn pressure, strain, tension

rel load, weight; anxiety, concern, uneasiness, worry; aggravation, anger, annoyance, exasperation, irritation, persecution, trouble

near ant comfort, consolation

2 a special notice or importance given to something — see EMPHASIS 1

stress *vb* **1** to experience concern or anxiety — see WORRY 1

2 to make more apparent — see EMPHASIZE 2

3 to indicate the importance of by centering attention on — see EMPHASIZE 1

stressed–out *adj* suffering from high levels of physical and especially psychological

stress ⟨The demands of this job are enough to make anyone *stressed-out*.⟩
syn shell-shocked
rel burned-out (*or* burnt-out), exhausted, tired, worn-out; undone, unnerved, unstrung; edgy, nervous, tense, uneasy
near ant laid-back, relaxed, rested; carefree, devil-may-care, happy-go-lucky, lighthearted, unconcerned

stretch *adj* able to revert to original size and shape after being stretched, squeezed, or twisted — see ELASTIC 1

stretch *n* **1** a wide space or area — see EXPANSE
2 an indefinite but usually short period of time — see WHILE 1
3 the distance or extent between possible extremes — see RANGE 3
4 the space or amount of space between two points, lines, surfaces, or objects — see DISTANCE 1

stretch *vb* **1** to add to the interest of by including made-up details — see EMBROIDER
2 to injure by overuse, misuse, or pressure — see STRAIN 1
3 to make longer — see EXTEND 1
4 to subject (a personal quality or faculty) to often excessive stress — see TRY 1

stretch (out) *vb* to arrange the parts of (something) over a wider area — see OPEN 3
stretchable *adj* able to revert to original size and shape after being stretched, squeezed, or twisted — see ELASTIC 1
stretching *n* **1** the act of making longer — see EXTENSION 1
2 the representation of something in terms that go beyond the facts — see EXAGGERATION

strew *vb* to cover by or as if by scattering something over or on — see SCATTER 2
strict *adj* **1** following an original exactly — see FAITHFUL 2
2 given to exacting standards of discipline and self-restraint — see SEVERE 1
3 not allowing for any exceptions or loosening of standards — see RIGID 1

strictly *adv* without any relaxation of standards or precision ⟨*Strictly* speaking, Columbus did not discover America—the people living there had long known about it.⟩ ⟨The rules must be *strictly* obeyed.⟩
syn exactly, precisely, rigidly, rigorously
rel carefully, conscientiously, meticulously, scrupulously
ant imprecisely, inexactly, loosely

strictness *n* the quality or state of being demanding or unyielding (as in discipline or criticism) — see SEVERITY
stricture *n* an often public or formal expression of disapproval — see CENSURE
stride *vb* to move along with a steady regular step especially in a group — see MARCH 1
strife *n* **1** a lack of agreement or harmony — see DISCORD
2 an earnest effort for superiority or victory over another — see CONTEST 1
strike *n* **1** a work stoppage by a body of workers intended to force an employer to

meet their demands ⟨The nurses will go on *strike* tomorrow unless they're finally given a pay raise.⟩
syn walkout
rel sit-down, sit-in, slowdown; lockout
2 the act or action of setting upon with force or violence — see ATTACK 1
3 a feature of someone or something that creates difficulty for achieving success — see DISADVANTAGE 1
4 a forceful coming together of two things — see IMPACT 1

strike *vb* **1** to refuse to work in order to force an employer to meet demands ⟨The union is calling for its members to *strike* until the mining company agrees to meet safety standards.⟩
syn walk, walk out
rel sit in; lock out
2 to act upon (a person or a person's feelings) so as to cause a response — see ¹AFFECT 1
3 to enter the mind of — see OCCUR (TO)
4 to come into usually forceful contact with something — see HIT 2
5 to deliver a blow to (someone or something) usually in a strong vigorous manner — see HIT 1
6 to take sudden, violent action against — see ATTACK 1

strike (into) *vb* to take the first step in (a process or course of action) — see BEGIN 1
strike (out) *vb* to show (something written) to be no longer valid by drawing a cross over or a line through it — see X (OUT)
striking *adj* **1** likely to attract attention — see NOTICEABLE
2 very noticeable especially for being incorrect or bad — see EGREGIOUS

string *n* **1** a length of braided, flexible material that is used for tying or connecting things — see CORD 1
2 a series of persons or things arranged one behind another — see LINE 1
3 a series of things linked together — see CHAIN 1

string *vb* to put together into a series by means of or as if by means of a thread — see THREAD 2
string along *vb* to cause to believe what is untrue — see DECEIVE
stringent *adj* not allowing for any exceptions or loosening of standards — see RIGID 1

stringy *adj* resembling or having the texture of a mass of strings ⟨*stringy* hair that clearly needs a good washing⟩
syn fibrous
rel knotty, ropy (*also* ropey), thready; sinewy, wiry

strip *vb* to remove clothing from — see UNDRESS 1
strip *n* **1** a long narrow piece of material ⟨Now tear the paper into *strips* and fold them up carefully.⟩
syn list, ribbon, slip
rel slat; band, bandage, belt, binding, girth, strap, swatch, swath (*or* swathe), tape
2 a series of drawings that tell a story or part of a story — see COMIC STRIP
¹**stripe** *n* **1** a line or long narrow section differing in color from the background ⟨The United States flag has seven red *stripes*.⟩

syn band, bar, streak

rel blaze, crossbar, pinstripe

2 a number of persons or things that are grouped together because they have something in common — see SORT 1

²**stripe** *n* a hard strike with a part of the body or an instrument — see ¹BLOW

stripe *vb* to make stripes on ⟨The children carefully *striped* the paper with red and blue paint.⟩

syn band, bar, streak

rel blaze

striped *adj* having stripes ⟨The zebra is a black-and-white *striped* animal.⟩

syn barred, streaked

rel corded, tabby

stripling *n* a male person who has not yet reached adulthood — see BOY 1

stripped *adj* lacking a usual or natural covering — see NAKED 2

2 lacking or shed of clothing — see NAKED 1

strive *vb* **1** to devote serious and sustained effort — see LABOR

2 to make an effort to do — see ATTEMPT

stroke *n* a hard strike with a part of the body or an instrument — see ¹BLOW

stroke *vb* **1** to touch or handle in a tender or loving manner — see FONDLE

2 to praise too much — see FLATTER 1

stroke (out) *vb* to show (something written) to be no longer valid by drawing a cross over or a line through it — see X (OUT)

stroll *n* a relaxed journey on foot for exercise or pleasure — see WALK 1

stroll *vb* to travel by foot for exercise or pleasure — see HIKE 1

stroller *n* a person who roams about without a fixed route or destination — see NOMAD

strong *adj* **1** having muscles capable of exerting great physical force ⟨I need some *strong* people to help me move furniture.⟩

syn brawny, muscular, rugged, sinewy, stalwart, stout

rel forceful, forcible, mighty, potent, powerful, puissant; able-bodied, athletic, fit, trim; beefy, burly, husky, strapping; masculine, virile; hard, inured, strengthened, sturdy, tough, toughened; energetic, energized, invigorated, lusty, red-blooded, robust, vigorous, vitalized; hale, healthy, hearty, sound

near ant challenged, disabled, incapacitated, paralyzed; impotent, powerless; puny, slight, small, unathletic, unfit, unhealthy

ant delicate, feeble, frail, weak, weakling, wimpy

2 able to withstand hardship, strain, or exposure — see HARDY 1

3 having a powerfully stimulating odor or flavor — see SHARP 2

4 having an abundance of some characteristic quality (as flavor) — see FULL-BODIED

5 having an unpleasant smell — see MALODOROUS

6 having great power or influence — see IMPORTANT 2

7 having the power to persuade — see COGENT

8 marked by the ability to withstand stress

without structural damage or distortion — see STABLE 1

9 not showing weakness or uncertainty — see FIRM 1

strongbox *n* a specially reinforced container to keep valuables safe — see SAFE

stronghold *n* a structure or place from which one can resist attack — see FORT

strongly *adv* in a vigorous and forceful manner — see HARD 3

strop *vb* to make sharp or sharper — see SHARPEN

stropped *adj* having an edge thin enough to cut or pierce something — see SHARP 1

structure *n* **1** something built as a dwelling, shelter, or place for human activity — see BUILDING

2 something put together by arranging or connecting an array of parts — see CONSTRUCTION 1

3 the arrangement of parts that gives something its basic form — see FRAME 1

struggle *n* **1** a forceful effort to reach a goal or objective ⟨the child's determined *struggle* to make straight A's in school⟩

syn battle, fight, fray, scrabble, throes

rel effort, exertion, labor, pains, trouble, work; drudgery, grind, sweat, toil, travail; combat, conflict, contest, strife, tussle, war, warfare; attempt, endeavor, essay, try

2 a physical dispute between opposing individuals or groups — see FIGHT 1

3 an earnest effort for superiority or victory over another — see CONTEST 1

struggle *vb* **1** to proceed or act clumsily or ineffectually — see FLOUNDER 1

2 to devote serious and sustained effort — see LABOR

strut *vb* **1** to walk with exaggerated arm and leg movements ⟨The cat *strutted* proudly onto the porch with a bird in its mouth.⟩

syn prance, stalk, swagger

rel flounce, mince, traipse; pussyfoot, tiptoe; sweep; parade; pad, step, tread; pace, stride; lumber, lurch, pound, shamble, shuffle, stagger

2 to present so as to invite notice or attention — see SHOW 1

stub *n* an unused or unwanted piece or item typically of small size or value — see ¹SCRAP 1

stubborn *adj* sticking to an opinion, purpose, or course of action in spite of reason, arguments, or persuasion — see OBSTINATE

stubbornness *n* a steadfast adherence to an opinion, purpose, or course of action in spite of reason, arguments, or persuasion — see OBSTINACY

stubby *adj* being compact and broad in build and often short in stature — see STOCKY

stuck *adj* firmly positioned in place and difficult to dislodge — see TIGHT 2

stuck-up *adj* having too high an opinion of oneself — see CONCEITED

student *n* one who attends a school ⟨a straight-A *student* at the local high school⟩

syn pupil, scholar

rel schoolboy, schoolchild, schoolgirl; schoolfellow, schoolmate; coed, collegian,

postgraduate, undergraduate; high schooler, kindergartner (*also* kindergartener), middle schooler; freshman, junior, senior, sophomore; underclassman, undergrad, upperclassman; exchange student
ant nonstudent

studied *adj* decided on as a result of careful thought — see DELIBERATE 1

study *n* 1 a systematic search for the truth or facts about something — see INQUIRY 1
2 the state of being lost in thought — see REVERIE
3 a careful weighing of the reasons for or against something — see CONSIDERATION 1

study *vb* 1 to use the mind to acquire knowledge ⟨You'll have to *study* hard and learn all about the Revolutionary War in order to pass the history test.⟩
syn bone (up)
rel cram; analyze, deduce, find out; con, learn, memorize, read; research, restudy; apprehend, comprehend, grasp, know, understand; absorb, digest
phrases go over, go through
2 to commit to memory — see MEMORIZE
3 to give serious and careful thought to — see PONDER

stuff *n* 1 a skill, an ability, or knowledge that makes a person able to do a particular job — see QUALIFICATION 1
2 the basic elements from which something can be developed — see MAKING
3 the quality or qualities that make a thing what it is — see ESSENCE 1
4 transportable items that one owns — see POSSESSION 2
5 items needed for the performance of a task or activity — see EQUIPMENT

stuff *vb* 1 to close up so that no empty spaces remain — see FILL 2
2 to fill with food to capacity — see GORGE 1
3 to fit (people or things) into a tight space — see CROWD 1
4 to prevent passage through by filling with something — see CLOG 1
5 to put into (something) as much as can be held or contained — see FILL 1

stuffed *adj* 1 containing or seeming to contain the greatest quantity or number possible — see FULL 1
2 having one's appetite completely satisfied — see FULL 3

stuffing *n* soft material that is used to fill the hollow parts of something — see FILLING

stuffy *adj* 1 lacking fresh air ⟨The house was very *stuffy* after being closed up for a month.⟩
syn breathless, close, stifling, suffocating
rel airless, unventilated; heavy, oppressive, thick
near ant bracing, brisk, invigorating, refreshed, refreshing, restorative, reviving, sweet
ant airy, breezy, unstuffy
2 causing weariness, restlessness, or lack of interest — see BORING
3 easily irritated or annoyed — see IRRITABLE

stumble *n* 1 an unintentional departure from truth or accuracy — see ERROR 1
2 the act of going down from an upright position suddenly and involuntarily — see FALL 1

stumble *vb* 1 to go down from an upright position suddenly and involuntarily — see FALL 1
2 to proceed or act clumsily or ineffectually — see FLOUNDER 1
3 to move heavily or clumsily — see LUMBER 1
4 to make a mistake — see ERR 1

stumble (on *or* **onto)** *vb* to come upon unexpectedly or by chance — see HAPPEN (ON *or* UPON)

stumble (upon) *vb* to come upon face-to-face or as if face-to-face — see MEET 1

stumbling block *n* something that makes movement or progress difficult — see ENCUMBRANCE

stump *vb* 1 to move heavily or clumsily — see LUMBER 1
2 to invite (someone) to take part in a contest or to perform a feat — see CHALLENGE 2

stumpy *adj* being compact and broad in build and often short in stature — see STOCKY

stun *vb* 1 to make senseless or dizzy by a blow ⟨A powerful uppercut to the jaw *stunned* the boxer and sent him crashing to the canvas.⟩
syn daze, rock
rel deaden, paralyze; benumb, numb, stupefy; knock down; bang, bash, belt, bludgeon, clobber, clout, hammer, hit, paste, pound, punch, rap, slam, slap, slug, smack, smite, sock, strike, swat, thump, thwack, wallop, whack, whale; batter, beat, buffet, bung, chop, cuff, drub, pelt, pummel
phrases knock for a loop, knock silly
2 to make a strong impression on (someone) with something unexpected — see SURPRISE 1

stunned *adj* 1 affected with sudden and great wonder or surprise — see THUNDERSTRUCK
2 suffering from mental confusion — see DIZZY 2

stunner *n* 1 a lovely woman — see BEAUTY 2
2 something that makes a strong impression because it is so unexpected — see SURPRISE 1

stunning *adj* 1 causing a strong emotional reaction because of unexpectedness — see SURPRISING 1
2 causing wonder or astonishment — see MARVELOUS 1
3 very pleasing to look at — see BEAUTIFUL 1

stunt *n* an act of notable skill, strength, or cleverness — see FEAT 1

stunt *vb* to hold back the normal growth of ⟨Unfortunately, an unusually dry summer seems to have permanently *stunted* the tree.⟩
syn dwarf, suppress
rel arrest, catch, check, halt, hold up, stall, stay, still, stop; balk, block, hold back, impede, obstruct, stem; diminish, downsize, shrink

---

syn synonym(s)   *rel* related words
ant antonym(s)   *near ant* near antonym(s)

near *ant* advance, boost, encourage, forward, foster, nourish, nurture, promote

stupefied *adj* **1** affected with sudden and great wonder or surprise — see THUNDERSTRUCK

2 suffering from mental confusion — see DIZZY 2

stupefy *vb* to make a strong impression on (someone) with something unexpected — see SURPRISE 1

stupefying *adj* causing a strong emotional reaction because of unexpectedness — see SURPRISING 1

stupendous *adj* causing wonder or astonishment — see MARVELOUS 1

stupendously *adv* to a large extent or degree — see GREATLY 2

stupendousness *n* impressiveness of beauty on a large scale — see MAGNIFICENCE

stupid *adj* **1** not having or showing an ability to absorb ideas readily ⟨The instructor assured us that there are no *stupid* questions.⟩

syn brainless, dense, doltish, dopey (*also* dopy), dorky [*slang*], dull, dumb, fatuous, half-witted, mindless, oafish, obtuse, opaque, senseless, simple, slow, thick, thick-headed, unintelligent, vacuous, weak-minded, witless

rel feebleminded, simpleminded; foolish, idiotic, imbecile (*or* imbecilic); moronic; ignorant, illiterate, lowbrow, uneducated, uninformed, unintellectual, untaught, unthinking; absurd, asinine, balmy, cockeyed, daffy, daft, half-baked, harebrained, nonsensical, wacky, zany; imperceptive, unwise

near *ant* ingenious, resourceful; acute, astute, discerning, insightful, keen, knowing, perceptive, sagacious, sage, sapient, savvy, wise; cerebral, erudite, highbrow, intellectual, knowledgeable, learned, literate, scholarly, thinking, well-read; crafty, cunning, foxy, shrewd, wily; judicious, prudent, sane, sensible, sound

ant apt, brainy, bright, brilliant, clever, fast, intelligent, keen, nimble, quick, quick-witted, sharp, sharp-witted, smart

2 causing weariness, restlessness, or lack of interest — see BORING

3 showing or marked by a lack of good sense or judgment — see FOOLISH 1

stupidity *n* **1** the quality or state of lacking intelligence or quickness of mind ⟨The *stupidity* of the dialogue between the two romantic leads had movie audiences giggling uncontrollably.⟩

syn brainlessness, denseness, density, doltishness, dopiness, dullness (*also* dulness), dumbness, fatuity, foolishness, mindlessness, oafishness, obtuseness, senselessness, simpleness, slowness, stupidness, thickness, vacuity, witlessness

rel feeblemindedness; absurdity, asininity, balminess, daftness, folly, idiocy, inaneness, inanity, madness, nonsensicalness, nuttiness, preposterousness, silliness, wackiness, zaniness

near *ant* acumen, alertness, astuteness, discernment, insight, judgment (*or* judgement), perception; sagacity, sageness, sapience, wisdom, wit; logicalness, rationality, reasonableness, soundness, validity

ant braininess, brightness, brilliance, cleverness, intelligence, quick-wittedness, smartness

2 a foolish act or idea — see FOLLY 1

3 language, behavior, or ideas that are absurd and contrary to good sense — see NONSENSE 1

stupidness *n* the quality or state of lacking intelligence or quickness of mind — see STUPIDITY 1

sturdily *adv* in a vigorous and forceful manner — see HARD 3

sturdiness *n* the ability to withstand force or stress without being distorted, dislodged, or damaged — see STABILITY 1

sturdy *adj* **1** able to withstand hardship, strain, or exposure — see HARDY 1

2 marked by the ability to withstand stress without structural damage or distortion — see STABLE 1

3 not showing weakness or uncertainty — see FIRM 1

sty *n* a dirty or messy place — see PIGPEN

style *vb* to give a name to — see NAME 1

style *n* **1** a distinctive way of putting ideas into words ⟨I correctly identified the quotation because I recognized Mark Twain's inimitable *style*.⟩

syn fashion, locution, manner, mode, phraseology, tone, vein

rel address, delivery, elocution; archaism, colloquialism, regionalism; acceptation, connotation, denotation, expression, idiom

2 the means or procedure for doing something — see METHOD

3 a practice or interest that is very popular for a short time — see FAD

styleless *adj* marked by an obvious lack of style or good taste — see ¹TACKY 1

stylish *adj* being in the latest or current fashion ⟨a pretty, *stylish* dress⟩

syn à la mode (*also* a la mode), chic, cool [*slang*], exclusive, fashionable, happening, hip, in, modish, sharp, smart, snappy, supercool, swell, trendy

rel dapper, dashing, dressy, natty, sassy, saucy, spiffy, spruce; chichi, classy, nobby, posh, swank (*or* swanky); elegant, graceful, handsome, majestic, refined, sophisticated, stately, tasteful, understated; flashy, gallant; dandyish, dudish, foppish

near *ant* cheesy, tacky, unattractive, unbecoming; graceless, inelegant, tasteless, trashy; frowsy (*or* frowzy), sloppy, slovenly, unkempt, untidy; disheveled (*or* dishevelled), messy, mussy, rumpled, wrinkled; shabby, sleazy

ant dowdy, out, outmoded, styleless, unfashionable, unstylish

stymie *vb* to create difficulty for the work or activity of — see HAMPER

suasion *n* the act of reasoning or pleading with someone to accept a belief or course of action — see PERSUASION 1

suave *adj* having or showing very polished and worldly manners ⟨The *suave* gentleman charmed everyone who attended parties at the embassy.⟩

syn debonair, smooth, sophisticated, urbane

rel cavalier, glib, slick, unctuous; civilized, couth, cultivated, cultured, genteel, graceful, gracious, poised, polished, refined, well-bred; cosmopolitan, metropolitan, smart, worldly-wise; assured, calm, collected, composed, confident, cool, placid, secure, self-assured, self-confident, self-possessed, serene, tranquil, undisturbed, unperturbed

near ant awkward, clumsy, gauche, graceless, stiff, stilted, uncomfortable, uneasy, ungraceful, wooden; hick, parochial, provincial, rustic (*also* rustical); uncivilized, uncultured, unrefined; unsophisticated, unworldly; gawky, lubberly, stodgy, ungainly; diffident, insecure

ant boorish, churlish, classless, clownish, loutish, uncouth

¹sub *n* a large sandwich on a long split roll — see SUBMARINE

²sub *n* a person or thing that takes the place of another — see SUBSTITUTE

sub *vb* to serve as a replacement usually for a time only — see COVER 1

subdue *vb* 1 to achieve a victory over — see BEAT 2

2 to bring under one's control by force of arms — see CONQUER 1

3 to put a stop to (something) by the use of force — see QUELL 1

subdued *adj* not excessively showy — see QUIET 1

subduer *n* one that defeats an enemy or opponent — see VICTOR 1

subduing *n* the act or process of bringing someone or something under one's control — see CONQUEST

subject *n* 1 a major object of interest or concern (as in a discussion or artistic composition) — see MATTER 1

2 a person who owes allegiance to a government and is protected by it — see CITIZEN 1

3 something (as a belief) that serves as the basis for another thing — see REASON 2

subject *vb* to bring under one's control by force of arms — see CONQUER 1

subject (to) *adj* 1 determined by something else — see DEPENDENT 2

2 being in a situation where one is likely to meet with harm — see LIABLE 1

subjecting *n* the act or process of bringing someone or something under one's control — see CONQUEST

subjection *n* the act or process of bringing someone or something under one's control — see CONQUEST

subjugate *vb* to bring under one's control by force of arms — see CONQUER 1

subjugating *n* the act or process of bringing someone or something under one's control — see CONQUEST

subjugation *n* the act or process of bringing someone or something under one's control — see CONQUEST

sublime *adj* 1 causing wonder or astonishment — see MARVELOUS 1

2 having, characterized by, or arising from a dignified and generous nature — see NOBLE 2

sublimeness *n* impressiveness of beauty on a large scale — see MAGNIFICENCE

submarine *adj* living, lying, or occurring below the surface of the water — see UNDERWATER

submarine *n* a large sandwich on a long split roll ⟨always orders a roast beef *submarine* with the works⟩

syn grinder, hero, hoagie (*also* hoagy), Italian sandwich, po'boy (*also* poor boy), sub

submerge *vb* 1 to cover with a flood — see FLOOD

2 to sink or push (something) briefly into or as if into a liquid — see DIP 1

3 to refrain from openly showing or uttering — see SUPPRESS 2

submerged *adj* living, lying, or occurring below the surface of the water — see UNDERWATER

submerse *vb* 1 to cover with a flood — see FLOOD

2 to sink or push (something) briefly into or as if into a liquid — see DIP 1

submission *n* 1 a bending to the authority or control of another — see OBEDIENCE 1

2 the usually forced yielding of one's person or possessions to the control of another — see SURRENDER

submissive *adj* readily giving in to the command or authority of another — see OBEDIENT

submissively *adv* in a manner showing no signs of pride or self-assertion — see LOWLY

submissiveness *n* a readiness or willingness to yield to the wishes of others — see COMPLIANCE 1

submit *vb* 1 to cease resistance (as to another's arguments, demands, or control) — see YIELD 3

2 to give up and cease resistance (as to a liking, temptation, or habit) — see YIELD 1

3 to yield to the control or power of enemy forces — see FALL 2

submitting *n* the usually forced yielding of one's person or possessions to the control of another — see SURRENDER

subordinate *adj* having not so great importance or rank as another — see LESSER

subordinate *n* one who is of lower rank and typically under the authority of another — see UNDERLING

subordinate *vb* to bring under one's control by force of arms — see CONQUER 1

subordination *n* a bending to the authority or control of another — see OBEDIENCE 1

subscribe (to) *vb* to have a favorable opinion of — see APPROVE (OF)

subsequent *adj* being, occurring, or carried out at a time after something else ⟨I'll do the first problem as an example, but all *subsequent* efforts must be done on your own.⟩

syn after, ensuing, later, posterior

rel behind, belated, delayed, late, slow; closing, concluding, eventual, final, last, latest, latter, terminal, ultimate; following

near ant advance, advanced, early, premature

ant antecedent, anterior, foregoing, former, precedent, preceding, previous, prior

---

syn synonym(s)   *rel* related words
ant antonym(s)   *near ant* near antonym(s)

subsequently *adv* following in time or place — see AFTER

subside *vb* to grow less in scope or intensity especially gradually — see DECREASE 2

subsidize *vb* 1 to furnish (as an institution) with a regular source of income — see ENDOW 2

2 to provide money for — see FINANCE 1

subsidy *n* a sum of money allotted for a specific use by official or formal action — see APPROPRIATION 1

subsist *vb* to have life — see BE 1

subsistence *n* 1 the fact of being or of being real — see EXISTENCE

2 uninterrupted or lasting existence — see CONTINUATION

substance *n* 1 the basic elements from which something can be developed — see MAKING

2 the quality or qualities that make a thing what it is — see ESSENCE 1

3 the total of one's money and property — see WEALTH 1

4 one that has a real and independent existence — see ENTITY

substandard *adj* falling short of a standard — see BAD 1

substantial *adj* 1 having great meaning or lasting effect — see IMPORTANT 1

2 of a size greater than average of its kind — see LARGE

3 relating to or composed of matter — see MATERIAL 1

4 sufficiently large in size, amount, or number to merit attention — see CONSIDERABLE 1

substantially *adv* for the most part — see CHIEFLY

substantiate *vb* 1 to gain full recognition or acceptance of — see ESTABLISH 1

2 to give evidence or testimony to the truth or factualness of — see CONFIRM 1

3 to represent in visible form — see EMBODY 2

4 to show the existence or truth of by evidence — see PROVE 1

5 to provide evidence or information for (as a claim or idea) — see SUPPORT 4

substantiating *adj* serving to give support to the truth or factualness of something — see CORROBORATIVE

substantiation *n* something presented in support of the truth or accuracy of a claim — see PROOF

substitute *adj* 1 being such in appearance only and made with or manufactured from usually cheaper materials — see IMITATION

2 taking the place of one that came before — see NEW 1

substitute *vb* 1 to give up (something) and take something else in return — see CHANGE 3

2 to serve as a replacement usually for a time only — see COVER 1

3 to take the place of — see REPLACE 1

substitute *n* a person or thing that takes the place of another ⟨You'll be getting a *substitute* until your regular teacher is feeling better.⟩ ⟨If you like, you can use nuts as a *substitute* for coconut in that recipe.⟩

syn backup, pinch hitter, relief, replacement, reserve, stand-in, sub

rel alternate, understudy; makeshift, stopgap; agent, attorney, commissary, delegate, deputy, envoy, factor, proxy, representative, surrogate; assistant, reliever, second; successor, superseder

subsume *vb* to have as part of a whole — see INCLUDE 1

subterfuge *n* the use of clever underhanded actions to achieve an end — see TRICKERY

subtle *adj* 1 clever at attaining one's ends by indirect and often deceptive means — see ARTFUL 1

2 made or done with extreme care and accuracy — see FINE 2

3 satisfying or pleasing because of fineness or mildness — see DELICATE 1

subtleness *n* skill in achieving one's ends through indirect, subtle, or underhanded means — see CUNNING 1

subtlety *n* skill in achieving one's ends through indirect, subtle, or underhanded means — see CUNNING 1

subtract *vb* to take away (an amount or number) from a total ⟨If you *subtract* 10 from 23, you get 13.⟩ ⟨You can *subtract* the amount you spent on groceries from the total you owe for room and board.⟩

syn abate, deduct, knock off, take off

rel decrease, diminish, discount, downsize, dwindle, knock down, lessen, lower, reduce; abbreviate, abridge, clip, crop, curtail, cut, cut back, cut down, dock, pare, prune, retrench, shorten, slash, trim, truncate, whittle

near ant adjoin, annex, append; complement, supplement; enhance, heighten, intensify, magnify; aggrandize, amplify, augment, beef (up), boost, compound, enlarge, escalate, expand, increase, multiply

ant add, tack (on)

subtraction *n* the act or an instance of taking away from a total ⟨The restaurant may not have raised the price, but there's definitely been a *subtraction* in the number of fries in a side order.⟩

syn deduction

rel discount, kickback, rebate; abatement, decline, diminishment, diminution, drop, fall, loss, reduction, shrinkage; curtailment, cut, cutback

near ant boost, enlargement, gain, increase, increment, raise, rise; accretion, accrual, accumulation, addendum, augmentation, supplement, supplementation

ant addition

suburbia *n* the districts adjacent to a city — see ENVIRONS 1

subvert *vb* to lower in character, dignity, or quality — see DEBASE 1

succeed *vb* 1 to turn out as planned or desired ⟨The advertising campaign that finally *succeeded* used humor to sell the product.⟩

syn click, deliver, go, go over, pan out, work out

rel catch on; flourish, prosper, thrive; cook, percolate

phrases bear fruit, catch fire, deliver the goods, do the trick, go like clockwork *near ant* languish; flounder, struggle; decline, sink, slip, slump, wane; crash, crumble, flame out; choke, crack up, miscarry, misfire; fall down, go under; implode, self-destruct

ant bomb, collapse, fail, flop, flunk, fold, founder, miss, strike out, wash out

2 to reach a desired level of accomplishment 〈If you want to *succeed* in show business, you have to feel comfortable in front of an audience.〉

syn arrive, flourish, prosper, thrive

rel prevail, triumph, win; excel

phrases come into one's own, cut it, cut the mustard, get ahead, get somewhere, get there, hack it, hit it big, make good, make it, make one's mark, make the grade

near ant flounder, struggle

ant fail

3 to come after in time — see FOLLOW 1

succeeding *adj* **1** being the one that comes immediately after another — see NEXT

2 following one after another without others coming in between — see CONSECUTIVE

success *n* **1** a person or thing that is successful — see HIT 1

2 a successful result brought about by hard work — see ACCOMPLISHMENT 1

successful *adj* **1** having attained a desired end or state of good fortune 〈The play had a *successful* run on Broadway.〉

syn flourishing, going, palmy, prosperous, thriving, triumphant

rel coming, promising; booming, growing, roaring, robust

phrases in clover (*also* in the clover)

near ant futureless, hopeless, inauspicious, no-good, unpromising; collapsing, failing, flopping, flunking, folding, washing-out; declining, slipping, slumping, waning; destroyed, wrecked

ant failed, unsuccessful

2 marked by vigorous growth and well-being especially economically — see PROSPEROUS 1

successional *adj* following one after another without others coming in between — see CONSECUTIVE

successive *adj* following one after another without others coming in between — see CONSECUTIVE

succinct *adj* marked by the use of few words to convey much information or meaning — see CONCISE

succinctly *adv* in a few words — see SHORTLY 1

succinctness *n* the quality or state of being marked by or using only few words to convey much meaning 〈Caesar's observation, "I came, I saw, I conquered," is famous for its *succinctness*.〉

syn brevity, briefness, compactness, conciseness, crispness, pithiness, terseness

rel abruptness, brusqueness, curtness, shortness

near ant redundancy, repetitiousness, repetitiveness, tautology

ant diffuseness, long-windedness, prolixity, verbosity, wordiness

succulence *n* the quality or state of being full of juice 〈The *succulence* of the apple was such that the first bite sent juice running down my chin.〉

syn fleshiness, juiciness, pulpiness

rel sap, sappiness

near ant dryness

succulent *adj* **1** full of juice — see JUICY

2 very pleasing to the sense of taste — see DELICIOUS 1

succumb *vb* **1** to cease resistance (as to another's arguments, demands, or control) — see YIELD 3

2 to give up and cease resistance (as to a liking, temptation, or habit) — see YIELD 1

3 to stop living — see DIE 1

4 to yield to the control or power of enemy forces — see FALL 2

such *adj* having qualities in common — see ALIKE

such *adv* to a great degree — see VERY 1

suchlike *adj* having qualities in common — see ALIKE

suck (up) *vb* **1** to use flattery or the doing of favors in order to win approval especially from a superior — see FAWN

2 to take in (something liquid) through small openings — see ABSORB 1

sucker *n* **1** one who is easily deceived or cheated — see [1]DUPE

2 a person with a strong and habitual liking for something — see FAN

sudden *adj* not expected — see UNEXPECTED

suddenly *adv* **1** with great suddenness — see SHORT

2 without warning — see UNAWARES

suds *n pl* a light mass of fine bubbles formed in or on a liquid — see FOAM

sudsy *adj* covered with, consisting of, or resembling foam — see FOAMY

sue (for) *vb* to make a request for — see ASK (FOR) 1

suffer *vb* **1** to come to a knowledge of (something) by living through it — see EXPERIENCE

2 to feel deep sadness or mental pain — see GRIEVE

3 to give permission for or to approve of — see ALLOW 1

4 to fail to prevent (some behavior on someone's part) especially from neglect or indifference — see ALLOW 3

sufferable *adj* capable of being endured — see BEARABLE

sufferance *n* **1** the approval by someone in authority for the doing of something — see PERMISSION

2 the capacity to endure what is difficult or disagreeable without complaining — see PATIENCE

suffice *vb* to be enough — see SERVE 2

sufficiency *n* the quality or state of meeting one's needs adequately 〈The *sufficiency* of the portions is such that you will leave the restaurant with a full stomach but without doggie bags.〉

syn acceptability, adequacy, satisfactoriness

rel bountifulness, copiousness; excess, overabundance, oversupply, surfeit, surplus; abundance, amplitude, opulence,

---

syn synonym(s)   *rel* related words
ant antonym(s)   *near ant* near antonym(s)

plenitude, plenteousness, plentifulness, plentitude, plenty

near ant lack, want; crunch, dearth, deficit, famine, lack, shortage; meagerness, paucity, poorness, poverty, rareness, rarity, scantiness, scantness, scarceness, scarcity, skimpiness; necessity, need, privation

ant inadequacy, insufficiency, unsatisfactoriness

sufficiently *adv* **1** in or to a degree or quantity that meets one's requirements or satisfaction — see ENOUGH 1

2 in a satisfactory way — see WELL 1

suffocate *vb* **1** to be or cause to be killed by lack of breathable air — see SMOTHER 1

2 to keep (someone) from breathing by exerting pressure on the windpipe — see CHOKE 1

3 to experience complete or partial blockage of the windpipe — see CHOKE 2

suffocating *adj* lacking fresh air — see STUFFY 1

suffrage *n* the right to formally express one's position or will in an election — see VOTE 1

suffuse *vb* **1** to cause (as a person) to become filled or saturated with a certain quality or principle — see INFUSE

2 to spread throughout — see PERMEATE

sugarcoated *adj* appealing to the emotions in an obvious and tiresome way — see CORNY

sugary *adj* appealing to the emotions in an obvious and tiresome way — see CORNY

suggest *vb* **1** to convey an idea indirectly — see HINT

2 to put (something) forward as one's choice for a wise or proper course of action — see ADVISE 2

3 to set before the mind for consideration — see PROPOSE 1

suggestion *n* **1** a slight or indirect pointing to something (as a solution or explanation) — see HINT 1

2 something which is presented for consideration — see PROPOSAL

3 an almost imperceptible sign of something — see HINT 1

suggestive *adj* **1** hinting at or intended to call to mind matters regarded as indecent ⟨was offended by the *suggestive* comment⟩

syn bawdy, lewd, racy, ribald, salty, spicy

rel leering; coarse, crude, earthy, foul, gross, vulgar; dirty, filthy, lascivious, nasty, obscene, pornographic, prurient, smutty; immodest, indecorous, naughty

near ant clean, decent; innocuous, inoffensive; priggish, prim, prudish, puritanical, staid, straitlaced (*or* straightlaced); correct, decorous, genteel, proper, respectable, seemly

2 provoking a memory or mental association ⟨a haunting and *suggestive* song about a long-lost love⟩

syn evocative, reminiscent

rel eloquent, expressive, meaningful, pregnant, revealing, significant; affecting, emotional, impressive, moving, poignant, stirring, touching; exciting, provocative, provoking, rousing, stimulating

3 clearly conveying a special meaning (as one's mood) — see EXPRESSIVE

suicide *n* the act of deliberately killing oneself ⟨a *suicide* hotline⟩

syn self-destruction

rel martyrdom; homicide, murder, slaying; dispatch, manslaughter; assassination, execution; euthanasia, mercy killing

suit *n* **1** a court case for enforcing a right or claim — see LAWSUIT

2 an earnest request — see PLEA 1

3 the series of social engagements shared by a couple looking to get married — see COURTSHIP

suit *vb* **1** to be fitting or proper — see DO 1

2 to give satisfaction to — see PLEASE 1

3 to outfit with clothes and especially fine or special clothes — see CLOTHE 1

4 to change (something) so as to make it suitable for a new use or situation — see ADAPT

suitability *n* the quality or state of being especially suitable or fitting — see APPROPRIATENESS

suitable *adj* **1** having the required skills for an acceptable level of performance — see COMPETENT 1

2 meeting the requirements of a purpose or situation — see FIT 1

suitableness *n* the quality or state of being especially suitable or fitting — see APPROPRIATENESS

suitably *adv* **1** in a manner suitable for the occasion or purpose — see PROPERLY

2 in or to a degree or quantity that meets one's requirements or satisfaction — see ENOUGH 1

suitcase *n* a bag carried by hand and designed to hold a traveler's clothing and personal articles — see TRAVELING BAG

suite *n* **1** a body of employees or attendants who accompany and wait on a person — see CORTEGE 1

2 a number of things considered as a unit — see GROUP 1

3 a room or set of rooms in a private house or a block used as a separate dwelling place — see APARTMENT 1

suitor *n* **1** a man who courts a woman usually with the goal of marrying her ⟨My sister married her *suitor* of six years on Sunday.⟩

syn gallant, swain, wooer

rel beau, boyfriend, fellow, man, old man, squeeze [*slang*]; admirer, crush, steady; beloved, darling, dear, favorite, flame, honey, love, lover, sweetheart, valentine; date, escort; fiancé, intended

2 one who asks earnestly for a favor or gift — see SUPPLICANT

sulk *n* a state of resentful silence or irritability ⟨a child sitting in a *sulk* over a minor disagreement⟩

syn grouch, pet, pouts, sulkiness, sullenness

rel blues, dumps, mopes; surliness; biliousness, crankiness, crossness, crotchetiness, grouchiness, grumpiness, huffiness, irascibility, irritability, irritableness, peevishness, perverseness, perversity, pettishness, petulance, surliness, testiness, waspishness; cantankerousness, disagreeableness, fretfulness, orneriness

near ant cheerfulness, gaiety (*also* gayety), gladsomeness, high-spiritedness, lightheartedness, perkiness; affability, agreeableness, amenity, amicability, cordiality, friendliness, geniality, graciousness, pleasantness, sociability, sociality; amiability, amiableness, good-humoredness, good-naturedness, good-temperedness

sulk *vb* to silently go about in a bad mood ⟨The toddler would *sulk* for hours whenever he didn't get his way.⟩

syn grump, mope, pout

rel brood, dwell (on), mull (over), muse (over), ponder; frown, glower, lower (*also* lour), scowl

sulkiness *n* a state of resentful silence or irritability — see SULK

sulky *adj* given to or displaying a resentful silence and often irritability ⟨The cancellation of the trip made him *sulky*.⟩

syn glum, pouting, sullen, surly

rel dour, gloomy, morose; choleric, crabby, cranky, cross, crotchety, grouchy, grumpy, irascible, irritable, peevish, perverse, pettish, petulant, prickly, quick-tempered, short-tempered, snappish, snappy, snippety, snippy, testy, waspish; brooding, moping; bilious, cantankerous, disagreeable, dyspeptic, ill-humored, ill-natured, ill-tempered, ornery; temperamental, touchy

near ant sociable; cheerful, cheery, gladsome, good-humored, good-natured, good-tempered, perky, sunny; carefree, easygoing, happy-go-lucky, relaxed

sullen *adj* **1** causing or marked by an atmosphere lacking in cheer — see GLOOMY 1

2 given to or displaying a resentful silence and often irritability — see SULKY

sullenness *n* a state of resentful silence or irritability — see SULK

sullied *adj* not clean — see DIRTY 1

sully *vb* to make dirty — see DIRTY

sultry *adj* **1** containing or characterized by an uncomfortable amount of moisture — see HUMID

2 having a notably high temperature — see HOT 1

sum *n* **1** a complete amount of something — see WHOLE

2 a short statement of the main points — see SUMMARY

3 the central part or aspect of something under consideration — see CRUX

sum *vb* to combine (numbers) into a single sum — see ADD 2

sum (to *or* **into)** *vb* to have a total of — see AMOUNT (TO) 1

summarily *adv* in a few words — see SHORTLY 1

summarization *n* a short statement of the main points — see SUMMARY

summarize *vb* to make into a short statement of the main points (as of a report) ⟨The closing moments of the newscast *summarizes* the main story of the day.⟩

syn abstract, digest, encapsulate, epitomize, outline, recap, recapitulate, sum up, wrap up

rel abridge, condense, curtail, cut back, shorten; downsize, shrink; concentrate, consolidate; simplify, streamline

near ant elongate, extend, lengthen, prolong, protract; amplify, elaborate (on *or* upon), expand, supplement

summary *adj* marked by the use of few words to convey much information or meaning — see CONCISE

summary *n* a short statement of the main points ⟨Many book reports choose to begin with a *summary* of the book.⟩

syn abstract, brief, digest, encapsulation, epitome, outline, précis, recap, recapitulation, résumé (*or* resume *also* resumé), round-up, sum, summarization, synopsis, wrap-up

rel abbreviation, abridgment (*or* abridgement), compend, condensation, curtailment, shortening; simplification, streamlining; rehash; conclusion, epilogue (*also* epilog)

near ant amplification, enlargement, expansion; addendum, supplement

summation *n* a complete amount of something — see WHOLE

summit *n* the highest part or point — see HEIGHT 1

summon *vb* **1** to demand or request the presence or service of ⟨Without explanation, the managing editor *summoned* me to his office.⟩

syn call, hail

rel cite, subpoena; assemble, call out, call up, convene, convoke, muster; ask, bid, invite; command, order, request, requisition; beckon, demand; buzz, knell, page, ring, whistle

phrases send for

near ant dismiss, send (away); banish, boot (out), drum (out), eject, expel, oust, out, rout, run off, throw out

2 to call into being through the use of one's inner resources or powers ⟨She managed to *summon* a bright smile despite the gloomy day.⟩

syn conjure (up), gather, get up

rel educe, elicit, evoke, raise

3 to bring together in assembly by or as if by command — see CONVOKE

sumptuous *adj* showing obvious signs of wealth and comfort — see LUXURIOUS

sumptuously *adv* in a luxurious manner — see HIGH

sum up *vb* to make into a short statement of the main points (as of a report) — see SUMMARIZE

sun *n* **1** the light given off by the star around which the planet Earth revolves ⟨Be sure to wear sunscreen if you plan to spend more than a few minutes in the *sun*.⟩

syn sunlight, sunshine

rel sunburst; daylight; glare, shine

near ant cloudiness; penumbra, shade, shadiness, shadow, umbra

2 a ball-shaped gaseous celestial body that shines by its own light — see STAR 1

3 the first appearance of light in the morning or the time of its appearance — see DAWN 1

4 public acknowledgment or admiration for an achievement — see GLORY 1

sunder *vb* to set or force apart — see SEPARATE 1

sundown *n* the time from when the sun begins to set to the onset of total darkness — see DUSK 1

---

sundries *n pl* small useful items — see NOTION 1

sunken *adj* 1 curved inward — see HOLLOW

2 living, lying, or occurring below the surface of the water — see UNDERWATER

sunlight *n* the light given off by the star around which the planet Earth revolves — see SUN 1

sunny *adj* 1 having or being an outward sign of good feelings (as of love, confidence, or happiness) — see RADIANT 1

2 having or showing a good mood or disposition — see CHEERFUL 1

3 indicative of or marked by high spirits or good humor — see MERRY

4 not stormy or cloudy — see FAIR 1

sunrise *n* the first appearance of light in the morning or the time of its appearance — see DAWN 1

sunset *n* the time from when the sun begins to set to the onset of total darkness — see DUSK 1

sunshine *n* the light given off by the star around which the planet Earth revolves — see SUN 1

sunshiny *adj* not stormy or cloudy — see FAIR 1

sunup *n* the first appearance of light in the morning or the time of its appearance — see DAWN 1

sup *n* the portion of a serving of a beverage that is swallowed at one time — see DRINK 2

sup *vb* to swallow in liquid form — see DRINK 1

super *adj* unusually large — see HUGE

super *adv* to a great degree — see VERY 1

superabundance *n* 1 an amount or supply more than sufficient to meet one's needs — see PLENTY 1

2 the state or an instance of going beyond what is usual, proper, or needed — see EXCESS

superannuated *adj* having passed its time of use or usefulness — see OBSOLETE

superb *adj* of the very best kind — see EXCELLENT

superbness *n* 1 exceptionally high quality — see EXCELLENCE 1

2 impressiveness of beauty on a large scale — see MAGNIFICENCE

supercilious *adj* having a feeling of superiority that shows itself in an overbearing attitude — see ARROGANT

superciliousness *n* an exaggerated sense of one's importance that shows itself in the making of excessive or unjustified claims — see ARROGANCE

supercool *adj* being in the latest or current fashion — see STYLISH

superficial *adj* 1 lying on or affecting only the outer layer of something ⟨a *superficial* scratch that barely even broke the skin⟩

syn skin-deep, surface

rel depthless, shallow, shoal; two-dimensional; external

near ant deep, deep-seated

2 having or showing a lack of depth of understanding or character ⟨a *superficial* analysis of how the violence in video games affects young people⟩

syn facile, one-dimensional, shallow, skin-deep

rel cursory, hasty, oversimple, passing, sketchy; aimless, desultory, haphazard, hit-or-miss, random; limited, narrow, restricted

near ant discerning, penetrating; broad, complete, comprehensive, exhaustive, extensive, far-reaching, wide; general, global, inclusive; detailed, in-depth; critical

ant deep, profound

superfluity *n* 1 something adding to pleasure or comfort but not absolutely necessary — see LUXURY 1

2 the state or an instance of going beyond what is usual, proper, or needed — see EXCESS

superfluous *adj* being over what is needed — see SPARE 1

superheated *adj* having a notably high temperature — see HOT 1

superhuman *adj* being so extraordinary or abnormal as to suggest powers which violate the laws of nature — see SUPERNATURAL 2

superintend *vb* 1 to be in charge of — see BOSS 1

2 to look after and make decisions about — see CONDUCT 1

3 to take charge of especially on behalf of another — see ²TEND 1

superintendence *n* 1 the act or activity of looking after and making decisions about something — see CONDUCT 1

2 the duty or function of watching or guarding for the sake of proper direction or control — see SUPERVISION 1

superintendency *n* 1 the duty or function of watching or guarding for the sake of proper direction or control — see SUPERVISION 1

2 the act or activity of looking after and making decisions about something — see CONDUCT 1

superintendent *n* a person who manages or directs something — see EXECUTIVE

superior *adj* 1 having a feeling of superiority that shows itself in an overbearing attitude — see ARROGANT

2 having or displaying feelings of scorn for what is regarded as beneath oneself — see PROUD 1

3 of the very best kind — see EXCELLENT

4 standing above others in rank, importance, or achievement — see EMINENT

superior *n* one who is above another in rank, station, or office ⟨If a customer is rude to you, report it to your *superior* and she'll handle it.⟩

syn better, elder, senior

rel boss, chief, head, leader, master

near ant assistant, deputy

ant inferior, subordinate, underling

superiority *n* 1 an exaggerated sense of one's importance that shows itself in the making of excessive or unjustified claims — see ARROGANCE

2 exceptionally high quality — see EXCELLENCE 1

3 the fact or state of being above others in rank or importance — see EMINENCE 1

superlative *adj* of the very best kind — see EXCELLENT

supernal *adj* **1** of the very best kind — see EXCELLENT

2 of, relating to, or suggesting heaven — see CELESTIAL

supernatural *adj* **1** of, relating to, or being part of a reality beyond the observable physical universe ⟨The man believes in ghosts, guardian angels, and other *supernatural* beings.⟩

syn metaphysical, preternatural, unearthly

rel mystic, mystical, occult; extrasensory; celestial, divine, ethereal, heavenly, spiritual, unworldly

near ant earthly, mundane

ant natural

2 being so extraordinary or abnormal as to suggest powers which violate the laws of nature ⟨He seems to read books with *supernatural* speed.⟩

syn magical, miraculous, phenomenal, preternatural, superhuman, uncanny, unearthly

rel bizarre, curious, eerie (*also* eery), far-out, grotesque, outlandish, out-of-the-way, outrageous, outré, peculiar, quaint, queer, quirky, screwy, strange, wacky (*also* whacky), way-out, weird, wild; baffling, bewildering, confounding, mystifying, perplexing, puzzling, shocking; aberrant, atypical, fantastic (*also* fantastical), flaky, freak, freakish, idiosyncratic, marvelous (*or* marvellous), prodigious, rare, singular, uncommon, unique, unnatural, unusual

near ant average, commonplace, everyday, ordinary, prosaic, routine, run-of-the-mill, typical, unexceptional, unremarkable, usual, workaday; expected, familiar, predictable; common, customary, frequent, habitual, regular, wonted

3 of, relating to, or being God — see HOLY 3

supernumerary *adj* being over what is needed — see SPARE 1

supersede *vb* to take the place of — see REPLACE 1

superstar *n* a person who is widely known and usually much talked about — see CELEBRITY 1

supervene *vb* to come after in time — see FOLLOW 1

supervise *vb* **1** to be in charge of — see BOSS 1

2 to look after and make decisions about — see CONDUCT 1

3 to take charge of especially on behalf of another — see ²TEND 1

supervision *n* **1** the duty or function of watching or guarding for the sake of proper direction or control ⟨One of your responsibilities will be the *supervision* of all fund-raising activities for the club.⟩

syn care, charge, guidance, headship, oversight, regulation, stewardship, superintendence, superintendency, surveillance

rel monitoring, observance, observing, policing; administration, control, direction, generalship, hand(s), management, running; leadership, piloting, shepherding,

steering; government, rule; aegis (*also* egis), auspices, guardianship, protection, trusteeship, tutelage

2 the act or activity of looking after and making decisions about something — see CONDUCT 1

supervisor *n* a person who manages or directs something — see EXECUTIVE

supervisory *adj* suited for or relating to the directing of things — see EXECUTIVE

supplant *vb* to take the place of — see REPLACE 1

supple *adj* **1** able to bend easily without breaking — see WILLOWY

2 able to revert to original size and shape after being stretched, squeezed, or twisted — see ELASTIC 1

supplement *n* **1** something added (as by growth) — see INCREASE 1

2 something that serves to complete or make up for a deficiency in something else — see COMPLEMENT 1

3 a part added at the end of a book or periodical — see ADDENDUM 1

supplemental *adj* **1** available to supply something extra when needed — see AUXILIARY

2 related to each other in such a way that one completes the other — see COMPLEMENTARY

supplementary *adj* **1** available to supply something extra when needed — see AUXILIARY

2 related to each other in such a way that one completes the other — see COMPLEMENTARY

suppliant *n* one who asks earnestly for a favor or gift — see SUPPLICANT

suppliant *adj* asking humbly ⟨The *suppliant* thief pleaded for a second chance.⟩

syn beseeching, entreating, imploring, pleading, soliciting, supplicant, supplicating

rel begging, insistent, persistent

supplicant *adj* asking humbly — see SUPPLIANT

supplicant *n* one who asks earnestly for a favor or gift ⟨The new governor soon had to deal with a long line of *supplicants* asking for jobs and other political favors.⟩

syn petitioner, pleader, solicitor, suitor, suppliant

rel beggar, mendicant, panhandler

supplicate *vb* to make a request to (someone) in an earnest or urgent manner — see BEG

supplicating *adj* asking humbly — see SUPPLIANT

supplication *n* an earnest request — see PLEA 1

supply *vb* **1** to provide (someone) with what is needed for a task or activity — see FURNISH 1

2 to put (something) into the possession of someone for use or consumption — see FURNISH 2

supply *n* the number of individuals or amount of something available at any given time ⟨The *supply* of parents willing to coach youth soccer seems to be shrinking.⟩

syn budget, force, fund, inventory, pool, stock

rel reserve, resource; cache, hoard, stock-

---

syn synonym(s)   *rel* related words
ant antonym(s)   *near ant* near antonym(s)

pile; refill, renewal, replacement; kitty, nest egg, pot, purse; mine, source, spring, well

support n 1 a structure that holds up or serves as a foundation for something else ⟨If you don't add a couple more *supports* to that tower of blocks, it's going to fall down.⟩

syn brace, buttress, mount, mounting, shore, spur, stay, underpinning

rel shoring; column, pedestal, pilaster, pillar; arch, bolster, bracket, cantilever, girder; bearing; crutch, peg, post, stake, stanchion, stand, stilt, strut, truss; base, foundation, frame

2 an act or instance of helping — see HELP 1

support vb 1 to promote the interests or cause of ⟨Though childless themselves, they *support* the local schools both by volunteering and by fiercely opposing funding cuts.⟩

syn advocate, back, champion, endorse (*also* indorse), patronize, plump (for)

rel adopt, embrace, espouse; abet, aid, assist, help, prop (up), second, side (with); bolster, boost, buttress; advance, forward, further; plug, preach

phrases go in for, go to bat for, hold a brief for, stand up for, stick up for

near ant baffle, foil, frustrate, interfere, oppose, sabotage, thwart; desert, disappoint, fail, let down

2 to pay the living expenses of ⟨They have three children to *support*.⟩

syn keep, maintain, provide (for)

rel finance, fund, patronize, set up, sponsor, stake, underwrite

phrases foot the bill (for), take care of

3 to hold up or serve as a foundation for ⟨pillars *supporting* the bridge⟩

syn bear, bolster, brace, buttress, carry, prop (up), shore (up), stay, sustain, underpin, uphold

rel steady, truss, underlie

4 to provide evidence or information for (as a claim or idea) ⟨studies that *support* the claim that eating dark chocolate lowers the risk of cardiovascular disease⟩

syn back, bolster, buttress, corroborate, shore (up), substantiate

rel confirm, establish, prove, verify; affirm, avouch, validate

near ant undercut, undermine, weaken

5 to continue to declare to be true or proper despite opposition or objections — see MAINTAIN 2

6 to give evidence or testimony to the truth or factualness of — see CONFIRM 1

7 to provide (someone) with what is useful or necessary to achieve an end — see HELP 1

8 to put up with (something painful or difficult) — see BEAR 2

supportable adj 1 capable of being defended with good reasoning against verbal attack — see TENABLE 1

2 capable of being endured — see BEARABLE

3 capable of being proven as true or real — see VERIFIABLE

supporter n 1 a person who actively supports or favors a cause — see EXPONENT 1

2 someone associated with another to give assistance or moral support — see ALLY

supporting adj serving to give support to the truth or factualness of something — see CORROBORATIVE

supportive adj serving to give support to the truth or factualness of something — see CORROBORATIVE

suppose vb 1 to decide the size, amount, number, or distance of (something) without actual measurement — see ESTIMATE 2

2 to form an opinion from little or no evidence — see GUESS 1

3 to have as an opinion — see BELIEVE 2

4 to take as true or as a fact without actual proof — see ASSUME 2

supposed adj appearing to be true on the basis of evidence that may or may not be confirmed — see APPARENT 1

supposedly adv to all outward appearances — see APPARENTLY

supposition n 1 an idea that is the starting point for making a case or conducting an investigation — see THEORY

2 an opinion or judgment based on little or no evidence — see CONJECTURE

3 something taken as being true or factual and used as a starting point for a course of action or reasoning — see ASSUMPTION 1

suppositional adj existing only as an assumption or speculation — see THEORETICAL 1

suppress vb 1 to keep from being publicly known ⟨The governor tried to *suppress* the news.⟩

syn cover (up), hush (up)

rel black out, censor, gag, muzzle, silence; quash, repress, smother, spike, squash, squelch, stifle, strangle, throttle

near ant debunk, expose, reveal, show up, uncloak, uncover, unmask; blab, disclose, divulge, spill, tell, unveil; broadcast, circulate, publish, spread; describe, narrate, recite, recount, rehearse, relate, report

2 to refrain from openly showing or uttering ⟨He managed to *suppress* a laugh.⟩ ⟨*suppressed* her anger⟩

syn choke (back), hold back, pocket, repress, smother, stifle, strangle, submerge, swallow

rel control, govern, manage; bridle, check, curb, quash, quell; bottle up, contain; muffle, squelch

near ant express, loose, release, take out, unleash, vent

3 to hold back the normal growth of — see STUNT

4 to put a stop to (something) by the use of force — see QUELL 1

5 to keep secret or shut off from view — see ¹HIDE 2

suppression n the checking of one's true feelings and impulses when dealing with others — see CONSTRAINT 1

supremacy n 1 controlling power or influence over others ⟨The Roman empire had *supremacy* over the entire Mediterranean world.⟩

syn ascendancy (*also* ascendency), dominance, domination, dominion, predominance, preeminence, sovereignty (*also* sovranty)

rel primacy, superiority; lordship, scepter; arm, authority, choke hold, clutch, command, control, grip, hold, mastery, sway; direction, management; clout, might, pull, weight; eminence, importance, moment; prerogative, privilege, right

near ant helplessness, weakness; impotence, impotency, powerlessness

2 exceptionally high quality — see EXCELLENCE 1

3 the fact or state of being above others in rank or importance — see EMINENCE 1

supreme *adj* **1** highest in rank or authority — see HEAD

2 coming before all others in importance — see FOREMOST 1

3 of the greatest or highest degree or quantity — see ULTIMATE 1

Supreme Being *n* the being worshiped as the creator and ruler of the universe — see DEITY 1

supremely *adv* to a great degree — see VERY 1

surcease *n* the stopping of a process or activity — see END 1

surcharge *vb* to charge (someone) too much for goods or services — see OVERCHARGE 1

surcoat *n* a warm outdoor coat — see OVERCOAT

sure *adj* **1** having or showing a mind free from doubt — see CERTAIN 2

2 impossible to avoid or evade — see INEVITABLE

3 not likely to fail — see INFALLIBLE 2

4 worthy of one's trust — see DEPENDABLE

5 not capable of being challenged or proved wrong — see IRREFUTABLE

sure *adv* without any question — see INDEED 1

surefire *adj* not likely to fail — see INFALLIBLE 2

surely *adv* without any question — see INDEED 1

sureness *n* **1** a state of mind in which one is free from doubt — see CONFIDENCE 2

2 worthiness as the recipient of another's trust or confidence — see RELIABILITY

surety *n* **1** a formal agreement to fulfill an obligation — see GUARANTEE 1

2 a person who takes the responsibility for some other person or thing — see SPONSOR

3 a state of mind in which one is free from doubt — see CONFIDENCE 2

surf *n* a light mass of fine bubbles formed in or on a liquid — see FOAM

surface *adj* lying on or affecting only the outer layer of something — see SUPERFICIAL 1

surface *n* an outer part or layer — see EXTERIOR

surface *vb* **1** to come to one's attention especially gradually or unexpectedly — see ARISE 2

2 to penetrate the surface (as of water) from below — see BROACH 1

surfeit *n* the state or an instance of going beyond what is usual, proper, or needed — see EXCESS

surfeit *vb* to fill with food to capacity — see GORGE 1

surfeited *adj* having one's appetite completely satisfied — see FULL 3

surge *n* a moving ridge on the surface of water — see WAVE

surly *adj* **1** given to or displaying a resentful silence and often irritability — see SULKY

2 having or showing a habitually bad temper — see ILL-TEMPERED

surmise *n* an opinion or judgment based on little or no evidence — see CONJECTURE

surmise *vb* to form an opinion from little or no evidence — see GUESS 1

surmount *vb* to achieve a victory over — see BEAT 2

surpass *vb* **1** to be greater, better, or stronger than ⟨She always tried to *surpass* her older brother at anything he did.⟩

syn beat, better, eclipse, exceed, excel, outclass, outdistance, outdo, outshine, outstrip, overtop, top, transcend

rel outpace, outrun, overpass; best, clobber, conquer, crush, defeat, drub, lick, master, overcome, overmatch, prevail (over), rout, shame, skunk, subdue, surmount, thrash, trim, triumph (over), trounce, wallop, whip, win (against), worst; outbalance, outweigh, overbear, overshadow, trump

phrases go one better, run circles around (*or* run rings around)

near ant lose (to)

2 to go beyond the limit of — see EXCEED 1

surplus *adj* being over what is needed — see SPARE 1

surplus *n* the state or an instance of going beyond what is usual, proper, or needed — see EXCESS

surprise *also* **surprize** *n* **1** something that makes a strong impression because it is so unexpected ⟨The anniversary party was such a complete *surprise* that the couple was speechless for a moment.⟩

syn bombshell, jar, jolt, stunner

rel shock, thunderclap; eye-opener, revelation, shocker; amazement, marvel, wonder

phrases bolt from the blue (*also* bolt out of the blue)

2 the state of being strongly impressed by something unexpected or unusual ⟨stared in utter *surprise* at the deer in his cabin⟩

syn amazement, astonishment, shock

rel awe, wonder, wonderment; startle; bewilderment, confusion, consternation, discomfiture, dismay

3 a setup in which hidden attackers lie in wait — see AMBUSH 1

surprise *also* **surprize** *vb* **1** to make a strong impression on (someone) with something unexpected ⟨I was very *surprised* when my parents offered to pay the down payment on our house.⟩

syn amaze, astonish, astound, dumbfound (*also* dumfound), flabbergast, floor, rock, shock, startle, stun, stupefy

rel befuddle, bewilder, confound, confuse, daze, discomfit, disconcert, dismay, jar, muddle, nonplus, perplex, shake up

phrases knock for a loop, take aback, take by surprise

---

2 to lie in wait for and attack by surprise
— see AMBUSH

surprising *adj* **1** causing a strong emotional reaction because of unexpectedness ⟨The *surprising* news that they were going to have a baby had them rushing to buy nursery furniture.⟩

syn amazing, astonishing, astounding, dumbfounding (*also* dumfounding), eye-opening, flabbergasting, jarring, shocking, startling, stunning, stupefying

rel unannounced, unanticipated, unexpected, unforeseen; awesome, awful, breathtaking, fabulous, marvelous (*or* marvellous), miraculous, portentous, prodigious, staggering, stupendous, sublime, wonderful, wondrous; befuddling, bewildering, confounding, confusing, disconfiting, disconcerting, dismaying, flustering, muddling, nonplussing (*also* nonplusing), perplexing, upsetting; incomprehensible, inconceivable, incredible, unbelievable, unimaginable, unlikely, unthinkable

near ant common, customary, normal, ordinary, typical, unexceptional, unremarkable, usual

ant unsurprising

2 causing wonder or astonishment — see MARVELOUS 1

surrender *n* the usually forced yielding of one's person or possessions to the control of another ⟨*surrendered* the territory to the invaders⟩

syn capitulating, capitulation, relinquishment, submission, submitting

rel acceptance, acquiescence, concession; compromise; appeasement, conciliation; reconcilement, reconciliation; capture, fall

near ant resistance

surrender *vb* **1** to give (something) over to the control or possession of another usually under duress ⟨The toddler *surrendered* the doll to her mother after a brief struggle.⟩ ⟨The commander *surrendered* the garrison without having fired a single shot.⟩

syn cede, deliver, give up, hand over, lay down, relinquish, render, turn in, turn over, yield

rel commit, consign, entrust (*also* intrust), transfer; forfeit, release, waive; abnegate, renounce, resign; abandon, desert, discard, forsake, part (with), shed

near ant keep, retain, withhold

2 to cease resistance (as to another's argument, demands, or control) — see YIELD 3

3 to give up (as a position of authority) formally — see ABDICATE

4 to give up and cease resistance (as to a liking, temptation, or habit) — see YIELD 1

5 to yield to the control or power of enemy forces — see FALL 2

6 to give (oneself) over to something especially unrestrainedly — see ABANDON 1

surreptitious *adj* undertaken or done so as to escape being observed or known by others — see SECRET 1

surround *n* the circumstances, conditions, or objects by which one is surrounded — see ENVIRONMENT

surround *vb* to form a circle around ⟨She

was *surrounded* by cheering fans within moments of scoring the winning goal.⟩

syn circle, compass, embrace, encircle, enclose (*also* inclose), encompass, gird, girdle, ring, wreathe

rel circumscribe, cordon (off), fence (in), wall; beset, besiege, entrench (*also* intrench), invest, swarm

surroundings *n pl* the circumstances, conditions, or objects by which one is surrounded — see ENVIRONMENT

surveillance *n* the duty or function of watching or guarding for the sake of proper direction or control — see SUPERVISION 1

survey *n* a close look at or over someone or something in order to judge condition — see INSPECTION

survey *vb* **1** to go around and approach (people) with a request for opinions or information — see CANVASS 1

2 to look over closely (as for judging quality or condition) — see INSPECT

survive *vb* **1** to come safely through ⟨The cat miraculously *survived* a two-story fall.⟩

syn ride (out), outlive, wear out; pull through; abide, continue, endure, hang on, hold on, hold out, hold up, last, lead, persist, stand, stick out, withstand; be, breathe, exist, live, subsist; flourish, prosper, thrive

phrases make it (through)

near ant decease, depart, die, expire, pass (on), pass away, perish, succumb; disappear, evaporate, fade, vanish; cease, end, stop

2 to continue to operate or to meet one's needs — see HOLD OUT

susceptibility *n* the quality or state of having little resistance to some outside agent ⟨His aunt's unfortunate *susceptibility* to viruses meant that she nearly always sick.⟩ ⟨a country doctor who had a well-known *susceptibility* to anyone with a hard-luck story⟩

syn defenselessness, vulnerability, weakness

rel helplessness, powerlessness; passiveness, passivity; feebleness, frailness, frailty, infirmity; exposure, liability, openness, predisposition, proneness, sensitivity; receptiveness, receptivity

near ant immunity; indomitability, indomitableness, invincibility

ant invulnerability

susceptible *adj* **1** being in a situation where one is likely to meet with harm — see LIABLE 1

2 lacking protection from danger or resistance against attack — see HELPLESS 1

3 readily taken advantage of — see EASY 2

suspect *adj* giving good reason for being doubted, questioned, or challenged — see DOUBTFUL 2

suspect *vb* **1** to form an opinion from little or no evidence — see GUESS 1

2 to have no trust or confidence in — see DISTRUST

suspecting *adj* inclined to doubt or question claims — see SKEPTICAL 1

suspend *vb* **1** to bring to a formal close for a period of time — see ADJOURN

2 to place on an elevated point without support from below — see HANG 1

suspense *n* a state of temporary inactivity — see ABEYANCE

suspension *n* a state of temporary inactivity — see ABEYANCE

suspicion *n* **1** a feeling or attitude that one does not know the truth, truthfulness, or trustworthiness of someone or something — see DOUBT

2 a very small amount — see PARTICLE 1

suspicious *adj* **1** giving good reason for being doubted, questioned, or challenged — see DOUBTFUL 2

2 inclined to doubt or question claims — see SKEPTICAL 1

3 not feeling sure about the truth, wisdom, or trustworthiness of someone or something — see DOUBTFUL 1

suspiciously *adv* with distrust — see ASKANCE

sustain *vb* **1** to supply with nourishment ⟨A granola bar should *sustain* you long enough to last until lunch.⟩

syn nourish, nurture

rel sate, satiate, satisfy; nurse; cloy, fill, surfeit; fortify, replenish, strengthen; feed; board, cater, provision, victual

2 to come to a knowledge of (something) by living through it — see EXPERIENCE

3 to put up with (something painful or difficult) — see BEAR 2

4 to hold up or serve as a foundation for — see SUPPORT 3

sustainable *adj* **1** capable of being defended with good reasoning against verbal attack — see TENABLE 2

2 capable of being proven as true or real — see VERIFIABLE

3 capable of being endured — see BEARABLE

svelte *adj* having a noticeably small amount of body fat — see THIN 1

swab *n* one who operates or navigates a seagoing vessel — see SAILOR

swag *n* valuables stolen or taken by force — see LOOT

swagger *vb* **1** to praise or express pride in one's own possessions, qualities, or accomplishments often to excess — see BOAST 1

2 to walk with exaggerated arm and leg movements — see STRUT 1

swaggerer *n* someone who boasts — see BRAGGART

swain *n* **1** a male romantic companion — see BOYFRIEND

2 a man who courts a woman usually with the goal of marrying her — see SUITOR 1

swallow *n* the portion of a serving of a beverage that is swallowed at one time — see DRINK 1

swallow *vb* **1** to take into the stomach through the mouth and throat ⟨Try not to *swallow* the toothpaste.⟩

syn down, ingest

rel drink, guzzle, imbibe, sip; bolt, devour, gobble (up *or* down), gulp; consume, eat, mouth (down); sup; gorge, scarf, scoff, wolf; chew, gnaw (at *or* on), lap, lick, munch, nibble (on); dispatch, finish, polish off

2 to refrain from openly showing or uttering — see SUPPRESS 2

3 to regard as right or true — see BELIEVE 1

swamp *vb* **1** to cover with a flood — see FLOOD

2 to subject to incapacitating emotional or mental stress — see OVERWHELM 1

swamp *n* spongy land saturated or partially covered with water ⟨You can't build there because the area is mostly *swamp*.⟩

syn bog, fen, marsh, marshland, mire, moor, morass, muskeg, slough (*also* slew *or* slue), swampland, wash

rel swale; quagmire

swampland *n* spongy land saturated or partially covered with water — see SWAMP

swank *n* excessive or unnecessary display — see OSTENTATION

swank *or* **swanky** *adj* excessively showy — see GAUDY

swap *n* a giving or taking of one thing of value in return for another — see EXCHANGE 1

swap *vb* to give up (something) and take something else in return — see CHANGE 3

swarm *n* a great number of persons or creatures massed together — see CROWD 1

¹**swarm** *vb* **1** to move upon or fill (something) in great numbers — see CROWD 2

2 to be copiously supplied — see ABOUND

²**swarm** *vb* to move (as up or over something) often with the help of the hands in holding or pulling — see CLIMB 1

swarming *adj* possessing or covered with great numbers or amounts of something specified — see RIFE

swash *vb* **1** to move with a splashing motion — see SLOSH 1

2 to cause (something liquid or mushy) to move along in sheets — see SPLASH 1

swat *n* a hard strike with a part of the body or an instrument — see ¹BLOW

swat *vb* to deliver a blow to (someone or something) usually in a strong vigorous manner — see HIT 1

swathe *vb* **1** to surround or cover closely — see ENFOLD 1

2 to cover with a bandage — see BANDAGE

sway *n* **1** the power to bring about a result on another — see EFFECT 2

2 the power to direct the thinking or behavior of others usually indirectly — see INFLUENCE 1

3 the right or means to command or control others — see POWER 1

sway *vb* **1** to act upon (a person or a person's feelings) so as to cause a response — see ¹AFFECT 1

2 to make a series of unsteady side-to-side motions — see ROCK 1

swear *vb* **1** to use offensive or indecent language ⟨No one is allowed to *swear* in this house.⟩

syn blaspheme, curse, cuss

rel confound, damn, execrate, imprecate; fulminate, rail, rant, revile

2 to make a solemn declaration of intent — see PROMISE 1

3 to make a solemn declaration under oath for the purpose of establishing a fact — see TESTIFY

sweat *n* **1** the active use of energy in producing a result — see EFFORT

---

2 very hard or unpleasant work — see TOIL

3 an uneasy state of mind usually over the possibility of an anticipated misfortune or trouble — see ANXIETY 1

sweat vb **1** to devote serious and sustained effort — see LABOR

2 to experience concern or anxiety — see WORRY 1

3 to flow forth slowly through small openings — see EXUDE

sweat out vb **1** to put up with (something painful or difficult) — see BEAR 2

sweep n an area over which activity, capacity, or influence extends — see RANGE 2

sweep vb **1** to move or proceed smoothly and readily — see FLOW 2

2 to turn away from a straight line or course — see CURVE 1

sweepstakes also **sweep-stake** n pl **1** an earnest effort for superiority or victory over another — see CONTEST 1

2 a competitive encounter between individuals or groups carried on for amusement, exercise, or in pursuit of a prize — see GAME 1

sweet adj **1** granted special treatment or attention — see DARLING 1

2 having a pleasant smell — see FRAGRANT

3 having an easygoing and pleasing manner especially in social situations — see AMIABLE

4 having qualities that tend to make one loved — see LOVABLE

5 giving pleasure or contentment to the mind or senses — see PLEASANT 1

sweet n **1** a food having a high sugar content ⟨Remember to brush your teeth after eating *sweets*.⟩
syn confection, sweetmeat
rel confectionery, dessert, pastry

2 a person with whom one is in love — see SWEETHEART

sweetheart n a person with whom one is in love ⟨I married my high-school *sweetheart* as soon as we both finished college.⟩
syn beloved, darling, dear, flame, honey, love, squeeze [*slang*], sweet
rel beau, boy, boyfriend, fellow, man, swain; gal, girl, ladyfriend, ladylove, lass; amour, lover, paramour; date, escort, steady; admirer, gallant, suitor, wooer; husband; bride, wife; fiancé, intended; crush, heartthrob

sweetmeat n a food having a high sugar content — see SWEET 1

sweetness n the state or quality of having a pleasant or agreeable manner in socializing with others — see AMIABILITY 1

swell adj **1** of the very best kind — see EXCELLENT

2 being in the latest or current fashion — see STYLISH

swell vb **1** to become greater in extent, volume, amount, or number — see INCREASE 2

2 to make greater in size, amount, or number — see INCREASE 1

3 to extend outward beyond a usual point — see BULGE 1

swell n **1** a part that sticks out from the general mass of something — see BULGE 1

2 a moving ridge on the surface of water — see WAVE

swelling n a small rounded mass of swollen tissue — see BUMP 1

sweltering adj having a notably high temperature — see HOT 1

swerve vb **1** to depart abruptly from a straight line or course ⟨The car *swerved* sharply to avoid the squirrel in the road.⟩
syn break, cut, sheer, veer, yaw
rel skew; arc, arch, bend, bow, crook, curve, hook, round, sweep, wheel; pivot; circle, coil, curl, loop, spiral; turn, twist, wind; weave, zigzag; deviate, stray, wander, waver
ant straighten

2 to turn away from a straight line or course — see CURVE 1

3 to cause to turn away from a straight line — see BEND 1

4 to change one's course or direction — see TURN 3

swift adj moving, proceeding, or acting with great speed — see FAST 1

swift adv with great speed — see FAST 1

swiftly adv with great speed — see FAST 1

swiftness n a high rate of movement or performance — see SPEED 1

swig n the portion of a serving of a beverage that is swallowed at one time — see DRINK 1

swig vb to swallow in liquid form — see DRINK 1

swill n the portion of a serving of a beverage that is swallowed at one time — see DRINK 1

swill vb **1** to eat greedily or to excess — see GORGE 2

2 to swallow in liquid form — see DRINK 1

swiller n one who eats greedily or too much — see GLUTTON

swim vb **1** to be in a confused state as if from being twirled around — see SPIN 2

2 to rest or move along the surface of a liquid or in the air — see FLOAT 1

swim n a temporary state of unconsciousness — see FAINT

swimmingly adv in a pleasing way — see WELL 5

swindle n an instance of the use of dishonest methods to acquire something of value — see FRAUD 1

swindle vb to rob by the use of trickery or threats — see FLEECE

swindler n a dishonest person who uses clever means to cheat others out of something of value — see TRICKSTER 1

swine n a person whose behavior is offensive to others — see JERK 1

swing vb **1** to change one's course or direction — see TURN 3

2 to change the course or direction of (something) — see TURN 2

3 to deal with (something) usually skillfully or efficiently — see HANDLE 1

4 to move (something) in a curved or circular path on or as if on an axis — see TURN 1

5 to place on an elevated point without support from below — see HANG 1

6 to have enough money for — see AFFORD

swinish *adj* having a huge appetite — see VORACIOUS 1

swipe *n* a hard strike with a part of the body or an instrument — see ¹BLOW

swipe *vb* **1** to come into usually forceful contact with something — see HIT 2

2 to deliver a blow to (someone or something) usually in a strong vigorous manner — see HIT 1

3 to take (something) without right and with an intent to keep — see STEAL 1

swiping *n* an instance of theft — see THEFT 2

swirl *vb* **1** to cause (as a liquid) to move about in a circle especially repeatedly — see STIR 1

2 to move (something) in a curved or circular path on or as if on an axis — see TURN 1

swish *n* **1** a sound similar to the speech sound \s\ stretched out — see HISS 1

2 a quick jerky movement from side to side or up and down — see ¹WAG

swish *vb* **1** to make a sound like that of stretching out the speech sound \s\ — see HISS

2 to move from side to side or up and down with quick jerky motions — see WAG 1

switch *n* **1** a long thin or flexible tool for striking — see WHIP

2 a quick jerky movement from side to side or up and down — see ¹WAG

3 a hard strike with a part of the body or an instrument — see ¹BLOW

switch *vb* **1** to give up (something) and take something else in return — see CHANGE 3

2 to move from side to side or up and down with quick jerky motions — see WAG 1

3 to strike repeatedly with something long and thin or flexible — see WHIP 1

4 to change (as an opinion) to the contrary — see REVERSE 1

5 to strike repeatedly — see BEAT 1

swoon *vb* to lose consciousness — see FAINT

swoon *n* **1** a state of mental confusion — see HAZE 2

2 a temporary state of unconsciousness — see FAINT

3 a state of overwhelming usually pleasurable emotion — see ECSTASY

sword *n* a hand weapon with a length of metal sharpened on one or both sides and usually tapered to a sharp point ⟨Once upon a time dueling with *swords* was the gentlemanly way to settle a point of honor.⟩

syn blade, brand, steel

rel broadsword, cutlass, rapier, saber (*or* sabre), scimitar, smallsword

sycophant *n* a person who flatters another in order to get ahead ⟨When her career was riding high, the self-deluded actress often mistook *sycophants* for true friends.⟩

syn fawner, flunky (*also* flunkey *or* flunkie), toady

rel yes-man; hanger-on, leech, parasite,

sponge, sponger; henchman, lackey, minion, stooge; groveler, idolater (*or* idolator), worshiper (*or* worshipper), zealot; adherent, convert, disciple, follower, partisan (*also* partizan), pupil, votary

symbol *n* **1** a device, design, or figure used as an identifying mark — see EMBLEM

2 a written or printed mark that is meant to convey information to the reader — see CHARACTER 1

symbolic *also* **symbolical** *adj* having the function or meaning of an object or figure that stands for something else ⟨The butterfly in the poem is *symbolic* of the impermanence of youth.⟩

syn emblematic (*also* emblematical), representative

rel figurative, metaphoric (*or* metaphorical); allegorical

near ant actual, literal

ant nonsymbolic

symbolize *vb* to serve as a material counterpart of ⟨The flag *symbolizes* our country.⟩

syn represent

rel embody, epitomize, incarnate, manifest, materialize, objectify, personalize, personify; exemplify, illustrate

phrases stand for

symmetry *n* a balanced, pleasing, or suitable arrangement of parts — see HARMONY 1

sympathetic *adj* **1** having or showing the capacity for sharing the feelings of another ⟨a *sympathetic* smile⟩ ⟨She needed a *sympathetic* listener who would understand her problem.⟩

syn compassionate, humane, understanding

rel feeling, perceptive, sensitive; considerate, gentle, softhearted, tender, tenderhearted, warm, warmhearted; benevolent, benignant, charitable, kind, kindhearted, kindly, magnanimous; clement, lenient, merciful, tolerant; pitying

near ant inconsiderate, insensitive, thoughtless, unthinking; aloof, cool, indifferent, uncaring, uninterested; unaffectionate, unfriendly, unloving; merciless, pitiless, ruthless; bigoted, narrow-minded, small-minded; brutal, grim, harsh, oppressive, rough, severe, stern, tough, unrelenting; abusive, acrimonious, hateful, hostile, ill-natured, ill-tempered, malevolent, malicious, mean, rancorous, spiteful, surly, unkind, virulent

ant callous, cold-blooded, coldhearted, hard, heartless, inhuman, inhumane, obdurate, unfeeling, unsympathetic

2 having or marked by sympathy and consideration for others — see HUMANE 1

sympathize (with) *vb* to have sympathy for — see PITY

sympathizer *n* someone associated with another to give assistance or moral support — see ALLY

sympathy *n* **1** sorrow or the capacity to feel sorrow for another's suffering or misfortune ⟨Since losing her own brother, the nurse has had greater *sympathy* for families going through the same agony.⟩

syn commiseration, compassion, feeling

rel condolence, regret; humanity, kind-

---

heartedness, kindliness, kindness, mercy, pity, softheartedness, warmheartedness; affinity, empathy, rapport, sensitivity, understanding; altruism, benevolence, charity, generosity, goodwill, humanitarianism, largesse (*also* largess), magnanimity
near ant indifference, insensitivity, unconcern; cruelty, harshness, inhumanity; animosity, antipathy, dislike, hatred, hostility
ant callousness, coldheartedness, hardheartedness, heartlessness
2 the capacity for feeling for another's unhappiness or misfortune — see HEART 1
symphonic *adj* having a pleasing mixture of notes — see HARMONIOUS 1
symphony *n* 1 a balanced, pleasing, or suitable arrangement of parts — see HARMONY 1
2 a usually large group of musicians playing together — see ²BAND 1
symphony orchestra *n* a usually large group of musicians playing together — see ²BAND 1
symposium *n* a meeting featuring a group discussion — see FORUM 1
symptomatic *adj* serving to identify as belonging to an individual or group — see CHARACTERISTIC 1
synchronous *adj* existing or occurring at the same period of time — see CONTEMPORARY 1
syndicate *n* 1 a group involved in secret or criminal activities — see ¹RING 1
2 a number of businesses or enterprises united for commercial advantage — see CARTEL
synopsis *n* a short statement of the main points — see SUMMARY

synthetic *adj* 1 produced by humans rather than natural processes ⟨That organic farm doesn't use any pesticides or *synthetic* fertilizers.⟩
syn artificial, man-made
rel fabricated, manufactured; cultivated, processed, refined; industrial, mechanical; faux, imitation
near ant crude, raw
ant natural
2 being such in appearance only and made with or manufactured from usually cheaper materials — see IMITATION
syringe *n* a slender hollow instrument by which material is put into or taken from the body through the skin — see NEEDLE 1
syrupy *adj* being of a consistency that resists flow — see THICK 2
system *n* 1 something made up of many interdependent or related parts ⟨The national highway *system* allows travel from one end of the country to the other.⟩ ⟨the democratic *system* of checks and balances in government⟩
syn complex, network
rel interlacement, mesh, meshwork, net, plexus, web; aggregate, conglomerate, totality, whole; sequence, series
2 a method worked out in advance for achieving some objective — see PLAN 1
3 the means or procedure for doing something — see METHOD
systematic *adj* following a set method, arrangement, or pattern — see METHODICAL
systematize *vb* to put into a particular arrangement — see ORDER 1
systematized *adj* following a set method, arrangement, or pattern — see METHODICAL

tab *n* 1 a record of goods sold or services performed together with the costs due — see ¹BILL 1
2 the amount owed at a bar or restaurant or the slip of paper stating the amount — see CHECK 1
tabernacle *n* a building for public worship and especially Christian worship — see CHURCH 1
table *n* 1 a leg-mounted piece of furniture with a broad flat top designed for the serving of food ⟨We sat at the kitchen *table*, playing cards for hours on end.⟩
syn board
rel coffee table, refectory table, tea table; bar, counter; buffet, sideboard, side table; bed table, card table
2 food eaten or prepared for eating at one time — see MEAL
3 a broad flat area of elevated land — see PLATEAU
4 a record of a series of items (as names or titles) usually arranged according to some system — see ¹LIST
5 substances intended to be eaten — see FOOD

tableland *n* a broad flat area of elevated land — see PLATEAU
tablet *n* 1 a number of sheets of writing paper glued together at one edge — see PAD 1
2 a small mass containing medicine to be taken orally — see PILL 1
table talk *n* friendly, informal conversation or an instance of this — see CHAT 1
tableware *n* 1 eating and serving utensils ⟨During the party we ran short of *tableware*, so I went next door and borrowed some forks and knives.⟩
syn flatware, silver, silverware
rel place setting, setting, setup; silver plate; cutlery; chopstick, fork, knife, spoon, tablespoon, teaspoon
2 dishes used for eating or serving food or drink ⟨The couple would take out their good *tableware* only on special occasions.⟩
syn dinnerware
rel place setting, setting, setup; china, chinaware, crockery, earthenware, porcelain, pottery, stoneware; glassware; plate,

saucer; cup, demitasse, goblet, mug, teacup; bowl, casserole, charger, platter, tureen

taboo also **tabu** adj that may not be permitted — see IMPERMISSIBLE

tacit adj understood although not put into words — see IMPLICIT 1

taciturn adj tending not to speak frequently (as by habit or inclination) — see SILENT 2

tack n the means or procedure for doing something — see METHOD

tack (on) vb to join (something) to a mass, quantity, or number so as to bring about an overall increase — see ADD 1

tackle n items needed for the performance of a task or activity — see EQUIPMENT

tackle vb to start work on energetically — see ATTACK 3

¹**tacky** adj 1 marked by an obvious lack of style or good taste 〈It was *tacky* to wear sneakers to the wedding.〉 〈*tacky* plastic flowers〉

syn cheesy, dowdy, inelegant, styleless, tasteless, trashy, unfashionable, unstylish

rel graceless, inappropriate, incorrect, unbecoming, unseemly, unsuitable, wrong; coarse, crude, unrefined, vulgar; cheap, common, inferior, junky, lousy, low-grade, second-rate, shoddy, sleazy, tawdry; flashy, garish, gaudy, glitzy, grotesque, loud, ostentatious, showy, splashy

near ant appropriate, becoming, correct, fitting, proper, right, seemly, suitable; conservative, genteel, handsome, quiet, refined, restrained, simple, understated

ant chic, classic, classy, elegant, exquisite, fashionable, fine, posh, smart, sophisticated, stylish, tasteful

2 showing signs of advanced wear and tear and neglect — see SHABBY 1

²**tacky** adj tending to adhere to objects upon contact — see STICKY 1

tact n the ability to deal with others in touchy situations without offending them 〈With supreme *tact*, Isabel suggested to her neighbor that her flower garden was probably not the best place for his dog to use as a bathroom.〉

syn diplomacy, tactfulness

rel considerateness, consideration, courteousness, courtesy, delicacy, graciousness, sensitivity, thoughtfulness; civility, etiquette, mannerliness, manners, politeness; charm, gallantry, gentility, gracefulness, poise, suaveness, suavity; adroitness, deftness, dexterity, finesse; deference, regard, respect

near ant discourteousness, discourtesy, impoliteness, inconsiderateness, inconsideration, indelicacy, thoughtlessness, ungraciousness; impoliteness, incivility; boorishness, brashness, brassiness, loutishness; awkwardness, gaucheness, gracelessness, maladroitness; disrespect, impertinence, impudence, insolence, rudeness

ant clumsiness, insensitivity, tactlessness

tactful adj having or showing tact 〈Amy tried to be *tactful* when asked to critique her friend's singing.〉

syn diplomatic, politic

rel considerate, courteous, delicate, graceful, gracious, thoughtful; civil, mannerly, polite; charming, gallant, genteel, suave; affable, cordial, friendly, genial, kind, kindhearted

near ant discourteous, inconsiderate, thoughtless, ungracious; ill-bred, ill-mannered, impolite, uncalled-for, uncivil, unmannerly; boorish, brash, brassy, caddish, churlish, clownish, loutish, uncouth; disrespectful, impertinent, impudent, insolent, rude

ant gauche, impolitic, tactless, untactful

tactfulness n the ability to deal with others in touchy situations without offending them — see TACT

tactical adj suitable for bringing about a desired result under the circumstances — see EXPEDIENT

tactics n pl the means or procedure for doing something — see METHOD

tactless adj showing poor judgment especially in personal relationships or social situations — see INDISCREET

tad n **1** a very small amount — see PARTICLE 1

2 a male person who has not yet reached adulthood — see BOY 1

tag n a slip (as of paper or cloth) that is attached to something to identify or describe it — see LABEL

tag vb **1** to attach an identifying slip to — see LABEL 1

2 to go after or on the track of — see FOLLOW 2

tagging n the act of going after or in the tracks of another — see PURSUIT

tail n **1** the part of the body upon which someone sits — see BUTTOCKS

2 a behind part or surface — see REAR 1

tail vb to go after or on the track of — see FOLLOW 2

tailing n the act of going after or in the tracks of another — see PURSUIT

tailor vb to change (something) so as to make it suitable for a new use or situation — see ADAPT

tailored adj made or fitted to the needs or preferences of a specific customer — see CUSTOM-MADE

tailor–made adj made or fitted to the needs or preferences of a specific customer — see CUSTOM-MADE

taint n a mark of guilt or disgrace — see STAIN 1

taint vb **1** to affect slightly with something morally bad or undesirable 〈criticism of her sister's singing that was *tainted* by envy〉 〈A tendency toward conceitedness *taints* that athlete's status as a role model.〉

syn blemish, darken, mar, poison, spoil, stain, tarnish, touch, vitiate

rel begrime, besmear, besmirch, blacken, blur, cloud, dirty, discolor, pollute, smear, smirch, smudge, soil, sully, tar; abase, cheapen, debase, degrade, demean, discredit, disgrace, dishonor, foul, lower, shame, sink; bastardize, corrupt, debauch, demoralize, deprave, pervert, subvert

near ant cleanse, purify; dignify, elevate, ennoble, enshrine, glorify, hallow, magnify, uplift

---

syn synonym(s)   **rel** related words
ant antonym(s)   **near ant** near antonym(s)

2 to make unfit for use by the addition of something harmful or undesirable — see CONTAMINATE

tainted *adj* containing foreign or lower-grade substances — see IMPURE 1

take *n* 1 action or behavior that is done in return to other action or behavior — see REACTION

2 the total amount collected or obtained especially at one time — see HAUL 1

3 something belonging to, due to, or contributed by an individual member of a group — see SHARE 1

take *vb* 1 to reach for and take hold of by embracing with the fingers or arms ⟨*Take* my hand, or we'll get separated in this crowd.⟩

syn clasp, grasp, grip, hold

rel clench, cling (to), clutch, hold on (to); catch, nab, seize, snatch

phrases hang on to, lay hold of

near ant discharge, drop, free, liberate, release; deliver, entrust (*also* intrust), give, hand, hand over, pass, relinquish, transfer, transmit, turn over, unhand

2 to agree to receive whether willingly or reluctantly ⟨Will you *take* that call?⟩ ⟨Ed *took* a cut in pay.⟩

syn accept, have

rel accede (to), assent (to), concede (to), confirm, consent (to), OK (*or* okay), ratify, sanction, warrant; acquiesce (to), capitulate (to), give in (to), submit (to), succumb (to), surrender (to), yield (to); abide, bear, brook, countenance, endure, shoulder, stand, stick out, stomach, support, sustain, swallow, sweat out, tolerate; adopt, embrace, welcome

near ant dissent (to), object (to), oppose, protest; hold off, resist, withstand; combat, contest, fight

ant decline, deny, disallow, disapprove, negative, refuse, reject, spurn, turn down, veto

3 to become affected with (a disease or disorder) — see CONTRACT 1

4 to decide to accept (someone or something) from a group of possibilities — see CHOOSE 1

5 to get possession of (something) by giving money in exchange for — see BUY 1

6 to have as a requirement — see NEED 1

7 to make or have room for — see ACCOMMODATE 1

8 to produce a desired effect — see ACT 2

9 to put up with (something painful or difficult) — see BEAR 2

10 to regard as right or true — see BELIEVE 1

11 to achieve a victory over — see BEAT 2

12 to deal with (something) usually skillfully or efficiently — see HANDLE 1

13 to offer entrance (as to a place, school, or privilege) to — see ADMIT 2

14 to deprive of life — see KILL 1

take back *vb* to solemnly or formally reject or go back on (as something formerly adhered to) — see ABJURE 1

take down *vb* 1 to reduce to a lower standing in one's own eyes or in others' eyes — see HUMBLE

2 to take apart — see DISASSEMBLE 1

3 to make a written note of — see RECORD 1

take in *vb* 1 to cause to believe what is untrue — see DECEIVE

2 to have as part of a whole — see INCLUDE 1

3 to provide with living quarters or shelter — see HOUSE 1

take-no-prisoners *adj* having or showing a lack of sympathy or tender feelings — see HARD 1

takeoff *n* a work that imitates and exaggerates another work for comic effect — see PARODY 1

take off *vb* 1 to leave a place often for another — see GO 2

2 to rid oneself of (a garment) — see REMOVE 1

3 to take away (an amount or number) from a total — see SUBTRACT

take on *vb* 1 to enter into contest or conflict with — see ENGAGE 1

2 to provide with a paying job — see EMPLOY 1

3 to take for one's own use (something originated by another) — see ADOPT

take out *vb* 1 to find emotional release for ⟨He *took out* his frustrations by splitting a cord of firewood.⟩

syn loose, release, unleash, vent

rel act out; air, express, state, ventilate, voice

phrases give way (to)

near ant control, govern, handle, manage; bridle, check, constrain, curb, hold back, quell, rein (in), restrain, smother, tame; allay, lull, quiet, soothe, still; choke, inhibit, muffle, pocket, repress, stifle, strangle, swallow

ant bottle (up), repress, suppress

2 to go on a social engagement with — see DATE 1

3 to take away from a place or position — see REMOVE 2

take over *vb* 1 to serve as a replacement usually for a time only — see COVER 1

2 to take to or upon oneself — see ASSUME 1

3 to take or make use of under a guise of authority but without actual right — see APPROPRIATE 1

take up *vb* 1 to move from a lower to a higher place or position — see RAISE 1

2 to take in (something liquid) through small openings — see ABSORB 1

3 to take for one's own use (something originated by another) — see ADOPT

taking *adj* very pleasing to look at — see BEAUTIFUL 1

tale *n* 1 a rumor or report of a personal or sensational nature ⟨Don't believe the *tales* you hear about our neighbor's kid.⟩

syn story, whisper

rel dirt, gossip, talebearing, talk, tattle; defamation, libel, slander; fable, fabrication, fairy tale, falsehood, falsity, fib, lie, mendacity, prevarication, untruth, whopper

2 a brief account of something interesting that happened especially to one personally — see STORY 2

3 a statement known by its maker to be untrue and made in order to deceive — see LIE

4 a work with imaginary characters and

events that is shorter and usually less complex than a novel — see STORY 1

5 a total number obtained or recorded by noting each thing as it was being added — see COUNT 1

talebearer *n* **1** a person who habitually reveals personal or sensational facts about others — see GOSSIP 1

2 a person who provides information about another's wrongdoing — see INFORMER

talent *n* a special and usually inborn ability ⟨Liza's musical *talent* was already apparent by the time she was five.⟩ ⟨a *talent* for coming up with really funny answers to stupid questions⟩

syn aptitude, bent, endowment, faculty, flair, genius, gift, head, knack

rel affinity, bias, disposition, impulse, inclination, leaning, partiality, penchant, predilection, predisposition, proclivity, propensity, tendency, turn; ear, eye, mind, nose; feel, hang, instinct, touch, way; capability, competence, facility, proficiency, skill; capacity, potential, power; forte, specialty

near ant disability, handicap, inability, incapacity; shortcoming, weakness

talisman *n* something worn or kept to bring good luck or keep away evil — see CHARM 1

talk *n* **1** a usually formal discourse delivered to an audience — see SPEECH 1

2 an exchange of views for the purpose of exploring a subject or deciding an issue — see DISCUSSION 1

3 friendly, informal conversation or an instance of this — see CHAT 1

4 information or opinion that is widely disseminated without any authority or confirmation of accuracy — see RUMOR

talk *vb* **1** to give a formal often extended talk on a subject ⟨The fire chief often *talks* at school assemblies about fire safety.⟩

syn declaim, descant, discourse, expatiate, harangue, lecture, orate, speak

rel recite, soliloquize; expound, pontificate; mouth, spout; filibuster

phrases hold forth, take the floor

2 to engage in casual or rambling conversation — see CHAT 1

3 to express (a thought or emotion) in words — see SAY 1

4 to give information (as to the authorities) about another's improper or unlawful activities — see SQUEAL 1

5 to relate sometimes questionable or secret information of a personal nature — see GOSSIP

talk (into) *vb* to cause (someone) to agree with a belief or course of action by using arguments or earnest requests — see PERSUADE

talk (to) *vb* to communicate with by means of spoken words ⟨I had never *talked to* a real live cowboy before.⟩

syn chat (with), converse (with), speak (to *or* with)

rel accost, address, board, greet, hail, herald; inform, notify, tell

phrases engage in conversation

talkative *adj* fond of talking or conversation ⟨A *talkative* outgoing tour guide showed our school group around the city.⟩

syn blabby, chatty, conversational, gabby, garrulous, loquacious, talky

rel communicative, expansive; demonstrative, effusive, gushing; free-spoken, outspoken, unreserved, vocal; articulate, fluent, glib, voluble, well-spoken; gossipy, talebearing, tale-telling; long-winded, prolix, rambling, verbose, windy, wordy; extroverted (*also* extraverted), gregarious, outgoing, sociable

near ant quiet, shy; mum, mute, silent, speechless, tongue-tied, wordless; evasive, nonvocal, secretive, self-contained; aloof, indrawn, inhibited, introverted, retiring, unsociable, withdrawn

ant closemouthed, laconic, reserved, reticent, taciturn, tight-lipped, uncommunicative

talk down (to) *vb* to assume or treat with an air of superiority — see CONDESCEND 2

talker *n* a person who talks constantly — see CHATTERBOX

talk over *vb* to talk about (an issue) usually from various points of view and for the purpose of arriving at a decision or opinion — see DISCUSS

talky *adj* fond of talking or conversation — see TALKATIVE

tall *adj* **1** extending to a great distance upward — see HIGH 1

2 requiring considerable physical or mental effort — see HARD 2

tally *n* a total number obtained or recorded by noting each thing as it was being added — see COUNT 1

tally *vb* **1** to be in agreement on every point — see CHECK 1

2 to gain (as points or runs in a game) as credit towards one's total number of points — see SCORE 2

tame *adj* **1** changed from the wild state so as to become useful and obedient to humans ⟨Every evening, a wild Canada goose is at the food trough with our *tame* geese.⟩

syn domestic, domesticated, tamed

rel housebroken, trained; docile, gentle, semidomesticated; subdued, submissive

near ant unbroken, untrained

ant feral, undomesticated, untamed, wild

2 causing weariness, restlessness, or lack of interest — see BORING

tame *vb* to keep from exceeding a desirable degree or level (as of expression) — see CONTROL 1

tamed *adj* changed from the wild state so as to become useful and obedient to humans — see TAME 1

tamper (with) *vb* to handle thoughtlessly, ignorantly, or mischievously ⟨Someone has *tampered with* my computer files.⟩

syn fiddle (with), fool (with), mess (with), monkey (with), play (with), tinker (with)

rel abuse, alter, doctor, manhandle, manipulate, mistreat, misuse; butt in, interfere, intrude, meddle

tan *vb* to strike repeatedly — see BEAT 1

tangent *n* a departure from the subject under consideration ⟨In the middle of her de-

scription of her dog's symptoms, she went off on a *tangent* about its cute behavior.⟩
syn digression, excursion
rel circuitousness, circumlocution, diffuseness, prolixity, verbosity, windiness, wordiness

tangible *adj* capable of being perceived by the sense of touch ⟨a firm belief in the existence of the soul, even though it is not at all *tangible*⟩
syn palpable, touchable
rel tactile; corporeal, physical; actual, concrete, embodied, existent, material, real, substantial; appreciable, detectable, discernible (*also* discernable), noticeable, observable, perceptible, seeable, sensible, visible
near ant bodiless, formless, immaterial, incorporeal, insubstantial, nonmaterial, nonphysical, unsubstantial; abstract, ethereal, spiritual, unreal, virtual; imperceptible, insensible
ant impalpable, intangible

tangle *n* a state of mental uncertainty — see CONFUSION 1

tangle *vb* 1 to catch or hold as if in a net — see ENTANGLE 2
2 to twist together into a usually confused mass — see ENTANGLE 1

tangy *adj* having a powerfully stimulating odor or flavor — see SHARP 2

tantrum *n* an outburst or display of excited anger ⟨Billy had a *tantrum* when he found his little sister using his model paints.⟩
syn blowup, explosion, fireworks, fit, hissy fit, huff, scene
rel eruption, flare-up, outburst, storm, uproar; agitation, delirium, distraction, frenzy, furor, furore, fury, hysteria, rage, rampage; convulsion(s), paroxysm, seizure, spasm, upheaval; angriness, indignation, irateness, ire, spleen, wrath, wrathfulness; reaction, rise; dander, temper; pet, pouts, sulk(s), sulkiness, sullenness

¹**tap** *vb* 1 to strike or cause to strike lightly and usually rhythmically ⟨Meg *tapped* her foot in time to the music.⟩ ⟨kept *tapping* the desk with his pencil⟩
syn beat, drum, rap
rel bang, bash, bat, bop, hammer, hit, knock, paste, pound, slam, smack, sock, strike, swat, thud, thump, thwack, wallop, whack; pat, pit-a-pat, pitter-patter

²**tap** *vb* to remove (liquid) gradually or completely — see DRAIN 1

tap *n* a fixture for controlling the flow of a liquid — see FAUCET

taper *vb* to grow less in scope or intensity especially gradually — see DECREASE 2

taper off *vb* to grow less in scope or intensity especially gradually — see DECREASE 2

tar *n* one who operates or navigates a seagoing vessel — see SAILOR

tardily *adv* 1 after the due, usual, or proper time — see LATE 1
2 at a pace that is less than usual, desirable, or expected — see SLOW

tardiness *n* the quality or state of being late — see LATENESS

tardy *adj* 1 moving or proceeding at less than the normal, desirable, or required speed — see SLOW 1

2 not arriving, occurring, or settled at the due, usual, or proper time — see LATE 1

target *n* 1 a person or thing that is the object of abuse, criticism, or ridicule ⟨The hapless vice president quickly became the favorite *target* of late-night comedians.⟩
syn butt, mark, prey, sitting duck, victim
rel laughingstock, mockery; fall guy, goat, scapegoat, whipping boy
near ant defamer, libeler, libelist, traducer; baiter, heckler, needler, ribber, taunter, tease, teaser, tormentor (*also* tormenter), torturer; derider, insulter, mocker, ridiculer, scoffer, scorner; caricaturist, lampooner, parodist, satirist
2 a person or thing that is made fun of — see LAUGHINGSTOCK
3 something that one hopes or intends to accomplish — see GOAL

tarnish *vb* to affect slightly with something morally bad or undesirable — see TAINT 1

tarry *vb* 1 to continue to be in a place for a significant amount of time — see STAY 1
2 to move or act slowly — see DELAY 1
3 to reside as a temporary guest — see VISIT 2

tart *adj* 1 causing or characterized by the one of the basic taste sensations that is produced chiefly by acids — see SOUR 1
2 marked by the use of wit that is intended to cause hurt feelings — see SARCASTIC

tartness *n* 1 a harsh or sharp quality — see EDGE 1
2 biting sharpness of feeling or expression — see ACRIMONY 1

task *n* 1 a piece of work that needs to be done regularly — see CHORE 1
2 the action for which a person or thing is specially fitted or used or for which a thing exists — see ROLE

task *vb* to give a task, duty, or responsibility to — see ENTRUST 1

taskmaster *n* the person (as an employer or supervisor) who tells people and especially workers what to do — see BOSS

taste *n* 1 the property of a substance that can be identified by the sense of taste ⟨I can't stand the *taste* of cherry-flavored cough syrup.⟩
syn flavor, savor (*also* savour)
rel relish, smack; savoriness, tastiness; aftertaste
near ant tastelessness
2 a small piece or quantity of food — see MORSEL 1
3 positive regard for something — see LIKING

taste *vb* 1 to come to a knowledge of (something) by living through it — see EXPERIENCE
2 to have a vague awareness of — see FEEL 1

tasteful *adj* 1 having or showing elegance — see ELEGANT 1
2 very pleasing to the sense of taste — see DELICIOUS 1

tasteless *adj* 1 lacking in refinement or good taste — see COARSE 2
2 lacking in taste or flavor — see INSIPID 1
3 marked by an obvious lack of style or good taste — see ¹TACKY 1

tastelessness *n* the quality or state of

lacking refinement or good taste — see VULGARITY 1

tastiness *n* the quality of being delicious — see DELICIOUSNESS

tasty *adj* **1** giving pleasure or contentment to the mind or senses — see PLEASANT 1

2 very pleasing to the sense of taste — see DELICIOUS 1

tatter *vb* to cause (something) to separate into jagged pieces by violently pulling at it — see TEAR 1

tattered *adj* **1** wearing torn or worn-out clothes ⟨arrived at the refugee camp *tattered* and exhausted⟩

syn ragged, raggedy, ragtag

rel bedraggled, scruffy, shabby, threadbare

near ant decked (out), dolled up, dressed up; spiffy

2 worn or torn into or as if into rags — see RAGGED 2

tattle *n* information or opinion that is widely disseminated without any authority or confirmation of accuracy — see RUMOR

tattle *vb* to relate sometimes questionable or secret information of a personal nature — see GOSSIP

tattler *n* a person who provides information about another's wrongdoing — see INFORMER

tattletale *n* a person who provides information about another's wrongdoing — see INFORMER

taunt *vb* to attack repeatedly with mean put-downs or insults — see TEASE 2

taunter *n* a person who causes repeated emotional pain, distress, or annoyance to another — see TORMENTOR

taut *adj* stretched with little or no give ⟨a *taut* clothesline⟩

syn rigid, tense, tight

rel firm, inflexible, stiff, tightened, unrelaxed, unyielding

near ant drooping, droopy, flaccid, floppy, hanging, lank, limp, loosened, relaxed, sagging, slackened, yielding; elastic, flexible, pliant, resilient, springy, stretchy, supple

ant lax, loose, slack

tavern *n* **1** a place of business where alcoholic beverages are sold to be consumed on the premises — see BARROOM

2 a place that provides rooms and usually a public dining room for overnight guests — see HOTEL

tawny *adj* of a pale yellow or yellowish brown color — see BLOND

tax *n* a charge usually of money collected by the government from people or businesses for public use ⟨The state sales *tax* boosted the final cost of my new computer.⟩

syn assessment, duty, imposition, impost, levy

rel direct tax, personal tax; capitation, custom(s), excise, hidden tax, income tax, poll tax, property tax, sales tax, single tax, sin tax, tariff, toll, tribute, value-added tax, withholding tax; supertax, surcharge, surtax

tax *vb* to subject (a personal quality or faculty) to often excessive stress — see TRY 1

taxi *n* an automobile that carries passengers for a fare usually determined by the distance traveled — see TAXICAB

taxicab *n* an automobile that carries passengers for a fare usually determined by the distance traveled ⟨took a *taxicab* to the airport⟩

syn cab, hack, taxi

rel hackney; limousine; rickshaw (*also* ricksha)

taxing *adj* requiring much time, effort, or careful attention — see DEMANDING 1

teach *vb* to cause to acquire knowledge or skill in some field ⟨*taught* us about the basics of organic gardening⟩

syn educate, indoctrinate, instruct, school, train, tutor

rel coach, mentor; drill, fit, ground, prepare, prime, qualify; direct, guide, lead, rear; lecture, moralize, preach; implant, inculcate; homeschool; edify, enlighten; brief, familiarize, impart (to), inform, verse; initiate, introduce, show; reeducate, reschool, reteach, retrain

teacher *n* a person whose occupation is to give formal instruction in a school ⟨a young man who ardently wants to become a *teacher* and teach first grade⟩

syn educator, instructor, pedagogue (*also* pedagog), preceptor, schoolteacher

rel headmaster, master, rector, schoolmaster; headmistress, schoolmarm (*or* schoolma'am), schoolmistress; coach, guide, guru, preparer, trainer; mentor, tutor; dean, doctor, don, professor; governess, homeschooler

teaching *n* the act or process of imparting knowledge or skills to another — see EDUCATION 1

team *n* a group of people working together on a task — see GANG 1

team (up) *vb* to participate or assist in a joint effort to accomplish an end — see COOPERATE 1

teamwork *n* the work and activity of a number of persons who individually contribute toward the efficiency of the whole ⟨It takes *teamwork* to pull off a successful fund-raiser.⟩

syn collaboration, cooperation, coordination

rel fellowship, partnership; community, mutualism, reciprocity, symbiosis; synergism; communion, cooperativeness, kinship, oneness, solidarity, togetherness, unity

ant noncooperation

tear *n* a long deep cut — see GASH

tear *vb* **1** to cause (something) to separate into jagged pieces by violently pulling at it ⟨angrily *tore* the letter to shreds⟩

syn rend, rip, rive, shred, tatter

rel break, cleave, rupture, split; cut, gash, incise, lacerate, slash; butcher, dismember, dissect, hack, mangle

2 to separate or remove by forceful pulling ⟨*tore* the book from his hand⟩

syn rip, wrench, wrest, yank

rel grab, nab, seize, snap (up), snatch; lop (off), nip; amputate, cut (off), dissever,

---

sever; extract, force, jerk, prize, pry, pull, root (out), uproot

near ant reattach

3 to proceed or move quickly — see HUR-RY 2

tear (out) *vb* to draw out by force or with effort — see EXTRACT

tear down *vb* **1** to bring to a complete end the physical soundness, existence, or usefulness of — see DESTROY 1

2 to destroy (as a building) completely by knocking down or breaking to pieces — see DEMOLISH 1

tearful *adj* **1** given to expressing strong emotion (as sorrow) by readily shedding tears ⟨a *tearful* woman who can be counted on to cry at every wedding, anniversary, and funeral⟩

syn lachrymose, teary

rel demonstrative, effusive, emotional; maudlin, mawkish, sentimental; bawling, blubbering, crying, keening, sniffling, sniveling, sobbing, wailing, weeping, whimpering; bemoaning, bewailing; doleful, grieving, mournful, plaintive; brokenhearted, dejected, depressed, despondent, disconsolate, downcast, downhearted, heartbroken, heartsick, inconsolable, miserable, sad, sorrowful, woebegone, woeful, wretched

near ant beaming, laughing, smiling; blithe, blithesome, cheerful, cheery, happy, jocose, jovial, lighthearted, lightsome, merry, mirthful, sunny

2 causing unhappiness — see SAD 2

teary *adj* **1** causing unhappiness — see SAD 2

2 given to expressing strong emotion (as sorrow) by readily shedding tears — see TEARFUL 1

tease *n* **1** a person who causes repeated emotional pain, distress, or annoyance to another — see TORMENTOR

2 one who is obnoxiously annoying — see NUISANCE 1

tease *vb* **1** to make fun of in a good-natured way ⟨Pam likes to *tease* her twin brother about his seemingly endless string of girlfriends.⟩

syn chaff, jive, joke, josh, kid, rally, razz, rib, ride, roast

rel banter; fool, fun, string along; jest, quip, wisecrack

2 to attack repeatedly with mean put-downs or insults ⟨He was *teased* for being so tall at such a young age.⟩

syn bait, hassle, haze, heckle, needle, ride, taunt

rel deride, gibe (*or* jibe), jeer, mock, ridicule; annoy, bother, bug, chafe, fret, frost, gall, get, gnaw (at), grate, gripe, irk, irritate, nettle, peeve, pester, pique, put out, rasp, rile, ruffle, spite, trouble, vex; aggravate, exasperate, goad, test, try; aggrieve, agitate, bedevil, beleaguer, discomfort, disturb, perturb; badger, dog, hound; browbeat, bully, hector; harry, persecute, plague, terrorize, torment, torture

phrases make game of, pick on

teaser *n* **1** a person who causes repeated emotional pain, distress, or annoyance to another — see TORMENTOR

2 one who is obnoxiously annoying — see NUISANCE 1

teasing *n* the act of making unwelcome intrusions upon another — see ANNOYANCE 1

technical *adj* used by or intended for experts in a particular field of knowledge ⟨Although the owner's manual was supposedly written for the average consumer, it's filled with *technical* language.⟩

syn specialized

rel esoteric, limited, narrow, peculiar, restricted, special, specific, unique; authoritative, expert, professional, specialist (*or* specialistic)

near ant common, generalized, generic, nonexclusive, nonspecific, ordinary, overall, universal; inexpert, lay, nonprofessional, unprofessional; self-explanatory, straightforward

ant general, nontechnical, untechnical

technique *n* the means or procedure for doing something — see METHOD

tedious *adj* causing weariness, restlessness, or lack of interest — see BORING

tedium *n* the state of being bored — see BOREDOM

teem *vb* to be copiously supplied — see ABOUND

teeming *adj* possessing or covered with great numbers or amounts of something specified — see RIFE

teeny *adj* very small in size — see TINY

teeny–weeny *adj* very small in size — see TINY

teeter *vb* **1** to swing unsteadily back and forth or from side to side ⟨He nervously *teetered* at the edge of the pool.⟩

syn falter, rock, totter, waver, wobble (*also* wabble)

rel flounder, lurch, stumble, toddle; quake, quaver, quiver, shake, shudder, tremble, vibrate; careen, reel, stagger, weave

2 to move forward while swaying from side to side — see STAGGER 1

3 to show uncertainty about the right course of action — see HESITATE

telephone *vb* to make a telephone call to — see CALL 2

tell *vb* **1** to give an oral or written account of in some detail ⟨They *told* the story of how they had met.⟩

syn chart, chronicle, describe, narrate, recite, recount, rehearse, relate, report

rel deliver, give, reel off, state, utter, voice; detail, enumerate, itemize, particularize; bare, disclose, divulge, expose, reveal; delineate, depict, express, render, sketch

phrases set forth

2 to express (a thought or emotion) in words — see SAY 1

3 to find the sum of (a collection of things) by noting each one as it is being added — see COUNT 1

4 to give information to — see ENLIGHTEN 1

5 to issue orders to (someone) by right of authority — see COMMAND 1

6 to make known (as information previously kept secret) — see REVEAL 1

tell (on) *vb* **1** to act upon (a person or a person's feelings) so as to cause a response — see ¹AFFECT 1

2 to give information (as to the authorities) about another's improper or unlawful activities — see SQUEAL 1

telling *adj* having the power to persuade — see COGENT

telltale *adj* indicating something — see INDICATIVE

telltale *n* **1** a person who habitually reveals personal or sensational facts about others — see GOSSIP 1

2 a person who provides information about another's wrongdoing — see INFORMER

temerity *n* shameless boldness — see EFFRONTERY

temper *n* **1** a special quality or impression associated with something — see AURA 1

2 a state of mind dominated by a particular emotion — see MOOD 1

3 one's characteristic attitude or mood — see DISPOSITION 1

temperament *n* one's characteristic attitude or mood — see DISPOSITION 1

temperamental *adj* **1** frequently influenced by moods and especially bad moods — see MOODY

2 likely to change frequently, suddenly, or unexpectedly — see FICKLE 1

temperance *n* an avoidance of extremes in one's actions, beliefs, or habits ⟨My father attributes his ripe old age to *temperance* in all things, especially eating and drinking.⟩

syn moderateness, moderation, temperateness

rel constraint, control, discipline, restraint, self-control, self-discipline; asceticism, austerity, frugality, mortification, sacrifice, self-containment, self-denial; abnegation, abstention, avoidance, eschewal, forbearance; rationality, reasonableness, reasonableness, sensibility, sensibleness; soberness, sobriety

near ant unrestraint; extremism, radicalness; irrationality, unreasonableness

temperate *adj* **1** avoiding extremes in behavior or expression — see MODERATE 1

2 marked by temperatures that are neither too high nor too low — see CLEMENT 1

3 given to or marked by restraint in the satisfaction of one's appetites — see ABSTEMIOUS

temperateness *n* an avoidance of extremes in one's actions, beliefs, or habits — see TEMPERANCE

tempest *n* **1** a disturbance of the atmosphere accompanied by wind and often by precipitation (as rain or snow) — see STORM 1

2 a violent disturbance (as of the political or social order) — see CONVULSION

tempestuous *adj* **1** marked by bursts of destructive force or intense activity — see VIOLENT 1

2 marked by sudden or violent disturbance — see CONVULSIVE 1

3 marked by turmoil or disturbance especially of natural elements — see WILD 3

4 marked by wet and windy conditions — see FOUL 1

temple *n* a building for public worship and especially Christian worship — see CHURCH 1

temporal *adj* **1** having to do with life on earth especially as opposed to that in heaven — see EARTHLY

2 not involving religion or religious matters — see PROFANE 2

temporary *adj* **1** intended to last, continue, or serve for a limited time ⟨summer workers looking for *temporary* accommodations in private homes⟩

syn impermanent, interim, provisional, short-term

rel acting; alternate, proxy, substitute; expedient, improvised, makeshift; intermediary, intermediate, transitional; ephemeral, fleeting, fugitive, short-lived, transitory; conditional, contingent, limited, qualified, short-range, tentative; replaceable, terminable, terminate

near ant final, fixed, set, settled; extended, lasting, long-range, standing; dateless, deathless, endless, enduring, eternal, everlasting, immortal, perpetual, timeless, undying, unending

ant long-term, permanent

2 lasting only for a short time — see MOMENTARY

3 serving in a position for the time being — see ACTING

temporizer *n* **1** a person who dexterously and expediently changes or adopts opinions — see ACROBAT 2

2 one who does things only for his own benefit and with little regard for right and wrong — see SELF-SEEKER

tempt *vb* **1** to lead away from a usual or proper course by offering some pleasure or advantage — see LURE 1

2 to take a chance on — see RISK 1

temptation *n* **1** the act or pressure of giving in to a desire especially when ill-advised ⟨He felt the *temptation* to go sailing, but did his chores instead.⟩

syn allurement, enticement, lure, seduction

rel allure, appeal, attraction, attractiveness, charm, enchantment, glamour (*also* glamor); beckoning, invitation; bait, inducement, influence, persuasion, power, sway

2 something that persuades one to perform an action for pleasure or gain — see LURE 1

tempter *n* one that tries to get a person to give in to a desire ⟨There is no greater *tempter* to put off studying than my dog when he wants to play.⟩

syn baiter, seducer, solicitor

rel beguiler, enchantress, siren, temptress; tantalizer; briber, inducer, inveigler, persuader; corrupter (*also* corruptor), debaser, debaucher, degrader, perverter, undoer

temptress *n* a woman whom men find irresistibly attractive — see SIREN

tenable *adj* **1** capable of being defended against physical attack ⟨The soldiers' encampment on the open plain was not *tenable*, so they retreated to higher ground.⟩

syn defendable, defensible

rel defended, guarded, protected, safeguarded, secure, secured, shielded; im-

---

syn synonym(s)   *rel* related words
ant antonym(s)   *near ant* near antonym(s)

pregnable, indomitable, invincible, inviolable, invulnerable, unassailable, unbeatable, unconquerable, untouchable

near ant vincible, vulnerable; assailable, exposed, imperiled (*or* imperilled), insecure, liable, open, susceptible, undefended, unguarded, unprotected, unsecured; defenseless, helpless, powerless, weak

ant indefensible, untenable

2 capable of being defended with good reasoning against verbal attack ⟨the *tenable* theory that a giant meteor strike set off a chain of events resulting in the demise of the dinosaurs⟩

syn defendable, defensible, justifiable, maintainable, supportable, sustainable

rel rational, reasonable, sensible; acceptable, admissible, allowable, legitimate, passable, unobjectionable, viable, warrantable; confirmable, provable, verifiable; explainable, explicable

near ant absurd, illogical, irrational, ridiculous, unsound; extreme, outrageous, unreasonable; groundless, objectionable, unacceptable, unfounded; inexplicable, unexplainable

ant indefensible, insupportable, unjustifiable, unsustainable, untenable

tenacious *adj* **1** continuing despite difficulties, opposition, or discouragement — see PERSISTENT

2 tending to adhere to objects upon contact — see STICKY 1

tenant *n* **1** one who rents a room or apartment in another's house ⟨The laundry in the basement is for *tenants* only.⟩

syn boarder, lodger, renter, roomer

rel roommate (*also* roomie); occupant, occupier, resident, resider

near ant landholder, landowner, proprietor; landlady; slumlord

ant landlord, lessor, letter

2 one who lives permanently in a place — see INHABITANT

¹**tend** *vb* to show a liking or proneness (for something) — see LEAN 2

²**tend** *vb* **1** to take charge of especially on behalf of another ⟨*Tend* the store while I run an errand.⟩

syn attend, care (for), mind, oversee, superintend, supervise, watch

rel conduct, control, direct, govern, guide, manage, operate, preside (over), regulate, run, steward; guard, patrol, protect, safeguard, shield; baby, babysit, chaperone (*or* chaperon), mother, shepherd

phrases look after, see after, see to, take care of

near ant abandon, disregard, forget, ignore, neglect, pass over

2 to look after or assist the growth of by labor and care — see GROW 1

3 to work by plowing, sowing, and raising crops on — see FARM

4 to look after and make decisions about — see CONDUCT 1

tendency *n* **1** an established pattern of behavior ⟨a *tendency* to drop things⟩ ⟨a *tendency* to make snap judgments⟩

syn aptness, proneness, propensity, way

rel affinity, aptitude, bent, disposition, inclination, leaning, partiality, penchant, predilection, predisposition, proclivity,

turn; custom, habit, pattern, practice (*also* practise), routine, wont; eccentricity, idiosyncrasy, oddity, peculiarity, quirk, singularity, trick

near ant averseness, disinclination, dislike, indisposition

2 a prevailing or general movement or inclination — see TREND 1

3 a habitual attraction to some activity or thing — see INCLINATION 1

tender *adj* **1** easily injured without careful handling ⟨a *tender* wound⟩ ⟨*tender* plants that cannot take the cold⟩ ⟨*tender* pride that got bruised⟩

syn delicate, fragile, frail, sensitive

rel breakable, brittle, crushable, friable; feeble, flimsy, puny, slight, soft, tenuous, weak; perishable, resistless, susceptible, unresistant, vulnerable, yielding

near ant durable, firm, flinty, hard, hardy, resistant, robust, rugged, solid, sound, stiff, stout, strong, sturdy, substantial; infrangible, nonbreakable, unbreakable; hardened, inured, strengthened, tempered, toughened

ant tough

2 feeling or showing love — see LOVING 1

3 having or marked by sympathy and consideration for others — see HUMANE 1

4 lacking bodily strength — see WEAK 1

5 not harsh or stern especially in nature or effect — see GENTLE 1

tender *n* something (as pieces of stamped metal or printed paper) customarily and legally used as a medium of exchange, a measure of value, or a means of payment — see MONEY

tender *vb* to put before another for acceptance or consideration — see OFFER 1

tenderfoot *n* a person who is just starting out in a field of activity — see BEGINNER

tenderhearted *adj* **1** feeling or showing love — see LOVING 1

2 having or marked by sympathy and consideration for others — see HUMANE 1

tending *adj* having a tendency to be or act in a certain way — see PRONE 1

tenement *n* a room or set of rooms in a private house or a block used as a separate dwelling place — see APARTMENT 1

tense *adj* **1** feeling or showing uncomfortable feelings of uncertainty — see NERVOUS 1

2 marked by or causing agitation or uncomfortable feelings — see NERVOUS 2

3 stretched with little or no give — see TAUT

tension *n* the burden on one's emotional or mental well-being created by demands on one's time — see STRESS 1

tent *n* a raised covering over something for decoration or protection — see CANOPY

tentative *adj* determined by something else — see DEPENDENT 2

tenure *n* a fixed period of time during which a person holds a job or position — see TERM 1

tepid *adj* **1** showing little or no interest or enthusiasm ⟨The proposed table tennis club met with only a *tepid* response.⟩

syn halfhearted, lukewarm, uneager, unenthusiastic

rel apathetic, disinterested, dispassionate,

impassive, indifferent, neutral, uncaring, uninterested; lackadaisical, languid, listless, perfunctory, undemonstrative, unemotional, unresponsive; unfeeling, unsympathetic; chill, chilly, cold, cool, frigid, frosty, glacial, icy, unfriendly, wintry (*also* wintery)

near ant agog, ardent, avid, exuberant, fervid, feverish, fiery, gung ho, hot-blooded, impassioned, intense, raring, red-hot, vehement; engaged, engrossed, interested; ready, willing; cordial, friendly, genial, warmhearted

ant eager, enthusiastic, hearty, keen, passionate, warm, wholehearted

2 having or giving off heat to a moderate degree — see WARM 1

term *n* **1** a fixed period of time during which a person holds a job or position ⟨elected for a two-year *term* as mayor⟩

syn hitch, stint, tenure, tour

rel shift, watch; go, turn; duration, standing, time; cycle, span, spell, stretch; life, life span, lifetime, run

2 a pronounceable series of letters having a distinct meaning especially in a particular field — see WORD 1

term *vb* to give a name to — see NAME 1

terminal *adj* **1** following all others of the same kind in order or time — see LAST 1

2 likely to cause or capable of causing death — see DEADLY 1

terminate *vb* **1** to bring (an event) to a natural or appropriate stopping point — see CLOSE 3

2 to come to an end — see CEASE 1

3 to mark the limits of — see LIMIT 2

4 to put to death deliberately — see MURDER 1

5 to let go from office, service, or employment — see DISMISS 1

terminated *adj* brought or having come to an end — see COMPLETE 2

terminating *adj* following all others of the same kind in order or time — see LAST 1

termination *n* **1** a real or imaginary point beyond which a person or thing cannot go — see LIMIT 1

2 the act of ceasing to exist — see DEATH 3

3 the stopping of a process or activity — see END 1

terminology *n* the special terms or expressions of a particular group or field ⟨the *terminology* favored by sportscasters⟩ ⟨medical *terminology* that can be hard for the patient to understand⟩

syn argot, cant, dialect, jargon, jive, language, lingo, patois, patter, shop, slang, vocabulary

rel colloquialism, idiom, localism, parlance, pidgin, provincialism, regionalism, speech, vernacular; journalese

terra firma *n* the solid part of our planet's surface as distinguished from the sea and air — see EARTH 2

terrestrial *adj* **1** having to do with life on earth especially as opposed to that in heaven — see EARTHLY

2 having to do with the practical details of regular life — see MUNDANE 1

terrible *adj* **1** causing fear — see FEARFUL 1

2 extreme in degree, power, or effect — see INTENSE 1

3 extremely disturbing or repellent — see HORRIBLE 1

4 extremely unsatisfactory — see WRETCHED 1

5 of low quality — see CHEAP 2

terribly *adv* to a great degree — see VERY 1

terrific *adj* **1** of the very best kind — see EXCELLENT

2 extremely disturbing or repellent — see HORRIBLE 1

terrified *adj* filled with fear or dread — see AFRAID

terrify *vb* to strike with fear — see FRIGHTEN

terrifying *adj* causing fear — see FEARFUL 1

territory *n* the place where a plant or animal is usually or naturally found — see HOME 2

terror *n* **1** a source of persistent emotional distress — see DEMON 2

2 the emotion experienced in the presence or threat of danger — see FEAR 1

terrorize *vb* to strike with fear — see FRIGHTEN

terrorized *adj* filled with fear or dread — see AFRAID

terse *adj* marked by the use of few words to convey much information or meaning — see CONCISE

tersely *adv* in a few words — see SHORTLY 1

terseness *n* the quality or state of being marked by or using only few words to convey much meaning — see SUCCINCTNESS

test *n* **1** a procedure or operation carried out to resolve an uncertainty — see EXPERIMENT

2 a set of questions or problems designed to assess knowledge, skills, or intelligence — see EXAMINATION 1

test *vb* **1** to put (something) to a test — see TRY (OUT)

2 to subject (a personal quality or faculty) to often excessive stress — see TRY 1

testament *n* **1** something presented in support of the truth or accuracy of a claim — see PROOF

2 the basic beliefs or guiding principles of a person or group — see CREED 1

testify *vb* to make a solemn declaration under oath for the purpose of establishing a fact ⟨Several witnesses *testified* that they had seen the accused in the vicinity of the crime scene.⟩

syn attest, depose, swear, witness

rel verify; vouch; promise, vow

phrases bear witness

testify (to) *vb* to declare (something) to be true or genuine — see CERTIFY 1

testimony *n* something presented in support of the truth or accuracy of a claim — see PROOF

testiness *n* readiness to show annoyance or impatience — see PETULANCE

testy *adj* easily irritated or annoyed — see IRRITABLE

tête–à–tête *adv* in person and usually privately ⟨met *tête-à-tête* with the student's parents to discuss his academic progress⟩

---

syn synonym(s)   *rel* related words

ant antonym(s)   *near ant* near antonym(s)

syn face-to-face, personally

rel familiarly; directly, immediately

phrases in private, in secret

near ant distantly, indirectly; openly, publicly

tête-à-tête *n* friendly, informal conversation or an instance of this — see CHAT 1

text *n* a book used for instruction in a subject — see TEXTBOOK

textbook *adj* constituting, serving as, or worthy of being a pattern to be imitated — see MODEL

textbook *n* a book used for instruction in a subject ⟨One shelf in my bookcase is crammed full of my old college *textbooks*.⟩

syn handbook, manual, primer, text

rel schoolbook; grammar, speller; tract, treatise; dictionary, lexicon, vocabulary, wordbook; casebook, encyclopedia, reference; bible, guide, guidebook

textile *n* a woven or knitted material (as of cotton or nylon) — see CLOTH

thankful *adj* 1 experiencing pleasure, satisfaction, or delight — see GLAD 1

2 feeling or expressing gratitude — see GRATEFUL 1

thankfulness *n* acknowledgment of having received something good from another — see THANKS

thankless *adj* 1 not showing gratitude ⟨a *thankless* boss who seems oblivious to the extra effort his subordinates have made⟩

syn unappreciative, ungrateful

rel rude, thoughtless, ungracious

near ant beholden, indebted; gratified, pleased; courteous, gracious, thoughtful

ant appreciative, grateful, obliged, thankful

2 not likely to be appreciated by those who benefit ⟨the *thankless* job of cleaning up after a party⟩

syn unappreciated, ungrateful

rel uncredited, underappreciated, underrated, undervalued, unnoticed, unrewarded, unsung, unvalued

near ant credited, esteemed, honored, prized, regarded, rewarded, valued; creditable, meritorious, praiseworthy

ant appreciated

thanks *n pl* acknowledgment of having received something good from another ⟨To express our *thanks*, we'd like to present you with this plaque.⟩

syn appreciation, appreciativeness, gratefulness, gratitude, thankfulness

rel thanksgiving; gratification, satisfaction; acknowledgment (*or* acknowledgement), recognition, tribute

ant unappreciation

thaw *vb* to go from a solid to a liquid state — see LIQUEFY

thawed *adj* freed from a frozen state by exposure to warmth ⟨recommends cooking *thawed* fish within 24 hours⟩

syn defrosted, unfrozen

rel liquefied, melted, molten; deiced; heated, warmed

near ant chilled, iced, refrigerated; quick-frozen, refrozen, supercooled; congealed, glaciated, semisolid; frostbitten, frosty, icy

ant frozen

theater *or* **theatre** *n* 1 a building or part of a building where movies are shown ⟨There's still one *theater* in town that shows independent films.⟩

syn cinema, playhouse

rel nickelodeon; megaplex, multiplex

2 the public performance of plays — see DRAMA 1

3 a large room or building for enclosed public gatherings — see HALL 3

theatrical *also* **theatric** *adj* 1 given to or marked by attention-getting behavior suggestive of stage acting ⟨After stepping out of their hired limousine, the prom couple made a *theatrical* entrance in their evening clothes.⟩

syn dramatic, histrionic, melodramatic

rel overacted, overdone, sensational, staged; conspicuous, elaborate, flamboyant, grandiose, ostentatious, showy; affected, artificial, mannered, pretentious, self-conscious, studied, unnatural

near ant nondramatic, nontheatrical, unaffected, underplayed, unpretentious; muted, restrained, subdued, toned (down); conservative, discreet, inconspicuous; modest, plain, quiet, simple

ant undramatic

2 having the general quality or effect of a stage performance — see DRAMATIC 1

theatricals *n pl* the public performance of plays — see DRAMA 1

theft *n* 1 the unlawful taking and carrying away of property without the consent of its owner ⟨While violent crime in the city has decreased dramatically, the rate of *theft* has risen slightly.⟩

syn larceny, robbery, stealing, thievery

rel burglary, housebreaking; embezzlement, embezzling, graft, misapplication, misappropriation; filching, pilferage, pilfering, purloining, shoplifting; carjacking, hijacking (*also* highjacking), shanghaiing

2 an instance of theft ⟨The police found the stolen car an hour after the *theft* was reported.⟩

syn grab, heist, pinch, rip-off, snatching, swiping

rel break-in, burglary, holdup, mugging, stickup

theme *n* 1 a major object of interest or concern (as in a discussion or artistic composition) — see MATTER 1

2 a short piece of writing done as a school exercise — see COMPOSITION 2

3 a short piece of writing typically expressing a point of view — see ESSAY 1

then *adv* in addition to what has been said — see MORE 1

theoretical *also* **theoretic** *adj* 1 existing only as an assumption or speculation ⟨The merits of the new testing procedures are purely *theoretical*, since no one has ever used them before.⟩

syn academic (*also* academical), conjectural, hypothetical, speculative, suppositional

rel alleged, assumed, presumed, presupposed, proposed, supposed, unproved, unproven, untested; debatable, moot; abstract, conceptual, intellectual, metaphysical; nonclinical, nonpractical; nonempirical

near ant clinical, practical; concrete, defined, definite, distinct; attested, authenti-

738   theory

cated, confirmed, demonstrated, established, proven, substantiated, tested, time-tested, validated, verified; empirical (*also* empiric), nonspeculative, nontheoretical, observational

ant actual, factual, real

2 dealing with or expressing a quality or idea — see ABSTRACT 1

theory *n* an idea that is the starting point for making a case or conducting an investigation ⟨She set out to prove her *theory* that people can't really taste any difference between colas, so they buy according to the product's image.⟩

syn hypothesis, proposition, supposition, thesis

rel assumption, concession, premise (*also* premiss), presumption, presupposition, theorem; conjecture, generalization, guess, guesswork, inference, speculation, surmise; proffer, proposal, suggestion; feeling, hunch, impression, inkling, notion, suspicion; concept, conception, construct

near ant assurance, certainty, fact, knowledge

thereafter *adv* following in time or place — see AFTER

therefore *adv* for this or that reason ⟨It's snowing hard; *therefore* I think we should stay home.⟩

syn accordingly, consequently, ergo, hence, so, thereupon, thus

phrases in consequence

theretofore *adv* up to this or that time — see HITHERTO

thereupon *adv* for this or that reason — see THEREFORE

thesis *n* **1** an idea or opinion that is put forth in a discussion or debate — see CONTENTION 1

2 an idea that is the starting point for making a case or conducting an investigation — see THEORY

thick *adj* **1** having or being of relatively great depth or extent from one surface to its opposite ⟨A *thick* board was laid across the pit.⟩

syn chunky, fat

rel blockish, blocky, bulky, dense, hefty, thickish; broad, deep, wide

near ant narrow, shallow

ant skinny, slender, slim, thin

2 being of a consistency that resists flow ⟨*thick* maple syrup for pancakes⟩

syn ropy (*also* ropey), syrupy, viscid, viscous

rel creamy, heavy, slushy, thickened, thickish, turbid, undiluted; semifluid, semiliquid; gluey, glutinous, sticky; gelatinous, gooey, gummy, jellylike; concentrated, condensed

near ant flowing, fluid; dilute, diluted, liquid, watered-down, weak

ant runny, soupy, thin, watery

3 closely acquainted — see FAMILIAR 1

4 having a greater than usual measure across — see WIDE 1

5 having little space between items or parts — see CLOSE 1

6 not having or showing an ability to absorb ideas readily — see STUPID 1

7 possessing or covered with great numbers or amounts of something specified — see RIFE

thick *n* the most intense or characteristic phase of something ⟨In the *thick* of winter many Northerners are dreaming of tropical islands.⟩

syn deep, depth, height, middle, midst

rel center, heart

thicket *n* a thick patch of shrubbery, small trees, or underbrush ⟨flushed a pheasant from a *thicket* of willows⟩

syn brake, brushwood, chaparral, coppice, copse, covert

rel canebrake; brush, bush, scrub, scrubland; bramble, jungle, tangle; grove, hedge, stand, woodlot; forest, greenwood, wildwood, wood, woodland

thickheaded *adj* not having or showing an ability to absorb ideas readily — see STUPID 1

thickness *n* **1** the degree to which a fluid can resist flowing — see CONSISTENCY

2 the quality or state of lacking intelligence or quickness of mind — see STUPIDITY 1

thickset *adj* being compact and broad in build and often short in stature — see STOCKY

thick–skinned *adj* having or showing a lack of sympathy or tender feelings — see HARD 1

thief *n* one who steals ⟨A *thief* has been stealing wallets and valuables from the lockers at the gym.⟩

syn pincher, purloiner, robber, stealer

rel burglar, cat burglar, housebreaker, safecracker; embezzler, grafter; kleptomaniac; pickpocket, pilferer, shoplifter; abductor, carjacker, hijacker, kidnapper (*also* kidnaper), skyjacker

thieve *vb* to take (something) without right and with an intent to keep — see STEAL 1

thievery *n* the unlawful taking and carrying away of property without the consent of its owner — see THEFT 1

thin *adj* **1** having a noticeably small amount of body fat ⟨After her bout with pneumonia, she looked *thinner*.⟩

syn lean, lithe, skinny, slender, slim, spare, svelte

rel clean-limbed, trim; sylphlike, willowy; angular, rawboned, scraggy, scrawny, sinewy, wiry; lank, lanky, rangy, reedy, spindling, spindly, stringy, twiggy, waspish, weedy; anorexic, cadaverous, emaciated, gaunt, haggard, pinched, skeletal, wasted, wizened; meager (*or* meagre), puny, slight

near ant beefy, bulky, chunky, fleshy, heavy, heavyset, stocky, stout, thick, thickset, weighty; brawny, burly, husky, pudgy, roly-poly, squat, stubby; flabby, soft; full, hippy, round

ant chubby, corpulent, fat, obese, overweight, plump, portly, rotund, tubby

2 being of less than usual width — see NARROW 1

3 not containing very much of some important element — see WEAK 3

thin *vb* to alter (something) for the worse with the addition of foreign or lower-grade substances — see ADULTERATE

---

syn synonym(s)   *rel* related words
ant antonym(s)   *near ant* near antonym(s)

thing *n* **1** a member of the human race — see HUMAN

2 one that has a real and independent existence — see ENTITY

3 something done by someone — see ACTION 1

4 something material that can be perceived by the senses — see OBJECT 1

5 something produced by physical or intellectual effort — see PRODUCT 1

6 something that happens — see EVENT 1

7 something that one hopes or intends to accomplish — see GOAL

8 something to be dealt with — see MATTER 2

9 things *pl* transportable items that one owns — see POSSESSION 2

10 something for which a person shows a special talent — see FORTE

think *vb* to have as an opinion — see BELIEVE 2

think (about *or* **over)** *vb* to give serious and careful thought to — see PONDER

think (of) *vb* to bring back to mind — see REMEMBER

think (up) *vb* to create or think of by clever use of the imagination — see INVENT

thinker *n* **1** a very smart person — see GENIUS 1

2 the part of a person that feels, thinks, perceives, wills, and especially reasons — see MIND 1

thinking *adj* having the ability to reason — see RATIONAL 1

thinned *adj* **1** containing foreign or lower-grade substances — see IMPURE 1

2 not containing very much of some important element — see WEAK 3

thirst *n* **1** a strong wish for something — see DESIRE 1

2 urgent desire or interest — see EAGERNESS

thirst (for) *vb* to have an earnest wish to own or enjoy — see DESIRE 1

thirsty *adj* **1** marked by little or no precipitation or humidity — see DRY 1

2 showing urgent desire or interest — see EAGER

3 able to soak up liquids especially readily — see ABSORBENT

this *adj* being the less far of two — see NEAR 1

thistly *adj* having leaves or branches which are likely to cause a scratch — see SCRATCHY 1

thorn *n* something that is a source of irritation — see ANNOYANCE 3

thorny *adj* **1** having leaves or branches which are likely to cause a scratch — see SCRATCHY 1

2 requiring exceptional skill or caution in performance or handling — see TRICKY 1

thorough *adj* **1** having no exceptions or restrictions — see ABSOLUTE 2

2 including many small descriptive features — see DETAILED 1

3 trying all possibilities — see EXHAUSTIVE 1

4 covering everything or all important points — see ENCYCLOPEDIC

thoroughbred *adj* of unmixed ancestry — see PUREBRED

thoroughfare *n* a passage cleared for public vehicular travel — see WAY 1

thoroughgoing *adj* **1** having no exceptions or restrictions — see ABSOLUTE 2

2 trying all possibilities — see EXHAUSTIVE 1

thoroughly *adv* **1** with attention to all aspects or details ⟨They searched the grounds *thoroughly* for any sign of the intruder.⟩

syn completely, comprehensively, exhaustively, fully, minutely, roundly, totally

rel meticulously, microscopically; all-out, full blast, intensively; broadly, encyclopedically, extensively, generally, globally, widely; conclusively, definitely, perfectly

phrases at length, from stem to stern, from the ground up, in detail

near ant aimlessly, desultorily, haphazardly, hit-or-miss, randomly; cursorily, imperfectly, inadequately, shallowly, summarily, superficially; indeterminately, nebulously, vaguely

2 to a full extent or degree — see FULLY 1

though *adv* in spite of that — see HOWEVER

though *conj* in spite of the fact that — see ALTHOUGH

thought *n* **1** a careful weighing of the reasons for or against something — see CONSIDERATION 1

2 something imagined or pictured in the mind — see IDEA 1

thoughtful *adj* **1** given to or made with heedful anticipation of the needs and happiness of others ⟨a *thoughtful* offer to watch the neighbors' children on moving day⟩ ⟨a *thoughtful* manager who understands that people's families should be more important than their jobs⟩

syn attentive, considerate, kind, solicitous

rel brotherly, good, good-hearted, helpful, hospitable, kindhearted, kindly, neighborly, nice; caring, compassionate, sympathetic, tender; chivalrous, courteous, courtly, gallant, gracious, polite; diplomatic, tactful; deferential, dutiful, obliging, regardful, respectful; altruistic, beneficent, benevolent, benignant, humane, selfless, unselfish; charitable, generous, magnanimous

near ant inattentive, uncaring, unheeding; inhospitable, unkind, unkindly; ill-bred, ill-mannered, impolite, rude, uncivil, unmannerly; unhelpful; malevolent, malicious, mean, spiteful

ant heedless, inconsiderate, thoughtless, unthinking

2 decided on as a result of careful thought — see DELIBERATE 1

3 given to or marked by long, quiet thinking — see CONTEMPLATIVE

thoughtfully *adv* with good reason or courtesy — see WELL 4

thoughtless *adj* showing a lack of manners or consideration for others — see IMPOLITE

thought–out *adj* decided on as a result of careful thought — see DELIBERATE 1

thrall *n* the state of being enslaved — see SLAVERY

thralldom *or* **thraldom** *n* the state of being enslaved — see SLAVERY

thrash *vb* **1** to defeat by a large margin — see WHIP 2

2 to strike repeatedly with something long and thin or flexible — see WHIP 1

3 to strike repeatedly — see BEAT 1

4 to make jerky or restless movements — see FIDGET

thread *n* **1** a thin, flexible structure that resembles a hair — see HAIR 2

2 threads *pl* covering for the human body — see CLOTHING

thread *vb* **1** to scatter or set here and there among other things ⟨This history book *threads* excerpts from the diaries of pioneer women into its account of the settlement of the West.⟩

syn interlace, intersperse, interweave, lace, salt, weave, wreathe

rel insert, intermingle, mingle, mix; alternate, juxtapose; amalgamate, assimilate, blend, combine, commingle, embody, fuse, incorporate, integrate, merge

2 to put together into a series by means of or as if by means of a thread ⟨The reporter *threaded* his newspaper articles about the basketball team into a book that was essentially a chronicle of their championship season.⟩

syn concatenate, string

rel chain, connect, join, link, unite; interlace, intersperse, intertwine, interweave, lace, weave, wreathe

threadbare *adj* **1** showing signs of advanced wear and tear and neglect — see SHABBY 1

2 used or heard so often as to be dull — see STALE 1

3 worn or torn into or as if into rags — see RAGGED 2

threat *n* something that may cause injury or harm — see DANGER 2

threaten *vb* to remain poised to inflict harm, danger, or distress on ⟨The powerful hurricane continues to *threaten* the southern coastline.⟩

syn hang (over), hover (over), impend (over), menace, overhang

rel endanger, hazard, imperil, jeopardize, peril

threatening *adj* **1** giving signs of immediate occurrence — see IMMINENT 1

2 being or showing a sign of evil or calamity to come — see OMINOUS

3 involving potential loss or injury — see DANGEROUS 1

threefold *adj* having three units or parts — see TRIPLE

three–ring circus *n* a place of uproar or confusion — see MADHOUSE

threesome *n* a group of three ⟨The *threesome* has been playing music together since all three were in high school.⟩

syn triad, trinity, trio, triple, triplet, triumvirate

rel trilogy, triptych; triple crown; triplicate; triplex

threshold *n* **1** an interval of time just before the onset of something — see POINT 3

2 the point at which something begins — see BEGINNING

thrift *n* careful management of material resources — see ECONOMY

thriftless *adj* given to spending money freely or foolishly — see PRODIGAL

thrifty *adj* careful in the management of money or resources — see FRUGAL

thrill *n* a pleasurably intense stimulation of the feelings ⟨Everyone gets a real *thrill* out of the Independence Day fireworks.⟩

syn bang, charge, exhilaration, kick, titillation, wallop

rel jolt, shock, surprise (*also* surprize); delectation, delight, enjoyment, joy, lift, pleasure; amusement, diversion, entertainment, fun, treat

thrill *vb* to cause a pleasurable stimulation of the feelings of ⟨I was *thrilled* to hear that you got the promotion that you'd been so desperately wanting.⟩

syn charge, electrify, excite, exhilarate, galvanize, intoxicate, titillate, turn on

rel arouse, incite, inspire, provoke, stimulate; bewitch, captivate, charm, delight, enchant, enthrall (*or* enthral), hypnotize, mesmerize, rivet, spellbind; interest, intrigue, tantalize

near ant bore, jade, pall, tire, weary; demoralize, discourage, dishearten, dispirit

thrilling *adj* causing great emotional or mental stimulation — see EXCITING 1

thrive *vb* **1** to grow vigorously ⟨These plants *thrive* with relatively little sunlight.⟩

syn burgeon (*also* bourgeon), flourish, prosper

rel luxuriate, overgrow, proliferate, shoot up; germinate, root; bloom, flower, fruit, produce, propagate, regenerate, seed

2 to reach a desired level of accomplishment — see SUCCEED 2

thriving *adj* **1** having attained a desired end or state of good fortune — see SUCCESSFUL 1

2 marked by much life, movement, or activity — see ALIVE 2

3 marked by vigorous growth and well-being especially economically — see PROSPEROUS 1

throaty *adj* **1** harsh and dry in sound — see HOARSE

2 having a low musical pitch or range — see DEEP 2

throb *n* a rhythmic expanding and contracting — see PULSATION

throb *vb* to expand and contract in a rhythmic manner — see PULSATE

throe *n* **1** a sharp unpleasant sensation usually felt in some specific part of the body — see PAIN 1

2 throes *pl* a forceful effort to reach a goal or objective — see STRUGGLE 1

throng *n* a great number of persons or creatures massed together — see CROWD 1

throng *vb* to move upon or fill (something) in great numbers — see CROWD 2

thronging *adj* possessing or covered with great numbers or amounts of something specified — see RIFE

throttle *vb* to keep (someone) from breathing by exerting pressure on the windpipe — see CHOKE 1

through *adj* brought or having come to an end — see COMPLETE 2

---

syn synonym(s)   *rel* related words
ant antonym(s)   *near ant* near antonym(s)

through *adv* 1 from beginning to end ⟨I read the letter *through* twice.⟩ ⟨never once missed class the whole year *through*⟩
syn around, over, round, throughout
2 from one side to the other of an intervening space — see OVER 1
through *prep* 1 in or into the middle of — see AMONG
2 in random positions within the boundaries of — see AROUND 2
3 in the course of — see DURING
4 to the opposite side of — see ACROSS 1
5 along the way of — see BY 1
6 as the result of — see BECAUSE OF
7 using the means or agency of — see BY 2
throughout *adv* 1 from beginning to end — see THROUGH 1
2 in every place or in all places — see EVERYWHERE
throughout *prep* 1 in random positions within the boundaries of — see AROUND 2
2 in the course of — see DURING
throw *n* a risky undertaking — see GAMBLE
throw *vb* 1 to send through the air especially with a quick forward motion of the arm ⟨She *threw* a life preserver to the drowning man.⟩
syn cast, catapult, chuck, dash, fire, fling, heave, hurl, hurtle, launch, lob, loft, peg, pelt, pitch, sling, toss
rel bowl, dart, flip, gun, hook, pass, roll, shoot; buck, eject, impel, precipitate, project, propel, rifle, thrust
phrases let fly
2 to cause to fall intentionally or unintentionally — see DROP 1
throw (on) *vb* to place on one's person — see PUT ON 1
throw away *vb* 1 to get rid of as useless or unwanted — see DISCARD
2 to use up carelessly — see WASTE 1
throwing away *n* the getting rid of whatever is unwanted or useless — see DISPOSAL 1
throw out *vb* 1 to drive or force out — see EJECT 1
2 to get rid of as useless or unwanted — see DISCARD
3 to throw or give off — see EMIT 1
4 to show unwillingness to accept, do, engage in, or agree to — see DECLINE 1
throw up *vb* to discharge the contents of the stomach through the mouth — see VOMIT
thrum *n* a monotonous sound like that of an insect in motion — see HUM
thrust *vb* 1 to apply force to (someone or something) so that it moves in front of one — see PUSH 1
2 to move or extend upward — see ASCEND
thud *n* a hard strike with a part of the body or an instrument — see ¹BLOW
thud *vb* to come into usually forceful contact with something — see HIT 2
thumb *vb* 1 to travel by securing free rides — see HITCHHIKE
2 to turn over pages in an idle or cursory manner — see SKIM 1
thump *n* a hard strike with a part of the body or an instrument — see ¹BLOW
thump *vb* 1 to deliver a blow to (someone

or something) usually in a strong vigorous manner — see HIT 1
2 to strike repeatedly — see BEAT 1
thunder *vb* 1 to make a long loud deep noise or cry — see ROAR 1
2 to speak so as to be heard at a distance — see CALL 1
thunderclap *n* a loud explosive sound — see CLAP 1
thunderous *adj* marked by a high volume of sound — see LOUD 1
thunderstruck *adj* affected with sudden and great wonder or surprise ⟨She was *thunderstruck* to learn that she had been adopted.⟩
syn amazed, astonished, astounded, awestruck (*also* awestricken), bowled over, dumbfounded (*also* dumfounded), flabbergasted, shocked, stunned, stupefied
rel blindsided, startled, surprised (*also* surprized); aghast, appalled, dismayed, horrified; bewildered, confused, dazed, overwhelmed; agape, awed, awesome, openmouthed, wide-eyed, widemouthed
near ant blasé (*also* blase), casual, nonchalant, unruffled
thus *adv* for this or that reason — see THEREFORE
thwack *n* 1 a hard strike with a part of the body or an instrument — see ¹BLOW
2 a loud explosive sound — see CLAP 1
thwack *vb* to deliver a blow to (someone or something) usually in a strong vigorous manner — see HIT 1
thwart *vb* to prevent from achieving a goal — see FRUSTRATE 1
tic *n* an odd or peculiar habit — see IDIOSYNCRASY
tick (off) *vb* to specify one after another — see ENUMERATE 1
ticket *n* 1 a small sheet of plastic, paper, or paperboard showing that the bearer has a claim to something (as admittance) ⟨Only people with *tickets* will be allowed past the front gates.⟩
syn check, coupon, pass
rel certificate, note, token
2 a slip (as of paper or cloth) that is attached to something to identify or describe it — see LABEL
3 the means or right of entering or participating in — see ENTRANCE 1
4 something that allows someone to achieve a desired goal — see PASSPORT 1
ticket *vb* to attach an identifying slip to — see LABEL 1
tickled *adj* experiencing pleasure, satisfaction, or delight — see GLAD 1
ticklish *adj* 1 easily offended — see TOUCHY 1
2 requiring exceptional skill or caution in performance or handling — see TRICKY 1
tidbit *also* **titbit** *n* 1 something that is pleasing to eat because it is rare or a luxury — see DELICACY 1
2 a small piece or quantity of food — see MORSEL 1
tide *n* a prevailing or general movement or inclination — see TREND 1
tidied *adj* being clean and in good order — see NEAT 1
tidings *n pl* a report of recent events or facts not previously known — see NEWS

tidy *adj* **1** being clean and in good order — see NEAT 1

2 of a size greater than average of its kind — see LARGE

3 sufficiently large in size, amount, or number to merit attention — see CONSIDERABLE 1

tie *n* **1** a situation in which neither participant in a contest, competition, or struggle comes out ahead of the other ⟨The competition for first place in the dessert division ended in a *tie* between the chocolate pecan pie and the walnut fudge tart.⟩
syn dead heat, draw, stalemate, standoff
rel deadlock, impasse; seesaw; photo finish; toss-up

2 a uniting or binding force or influence — see BOND 2

tie *vb* **1** to gather into a tight mass by means of a line or cord ⟨*tied* the newspapers into a bundle⟩
syn band, bind, truss
rel cinch, cord, rope, strap, thread, wire; gird, girt; lash, leash, tether; interlace, intertwine, interweave, lace; entangle, knot, snarl, tangle, twist; coil, wind
near ant undo, unfasten, unlace, unlash, unloose, unloosen, unstrap, unstring, unthread; unleash, untether; disentangle, unravel, unsnarl, untangle, untwine, untwist; uncoil, unspool, unwind
ant unbind, untie

2 to produce something equal to (as in quality or value) — see EQUAL 1

tie-up *n* **1** a crowded mass (as of cars) that impedes or blocks movement — see JAM 1

2 the state of having shared interests or efforts (as in social or business matters) — see ASSOCIATION 1

tie up *vb* to create difficulty for the work or activity of — see HAMPER

tiff *n* an often noisy or angry expression of differing opinions — see ARGUMENT 1

tiff *vb* to express different opinions about something often angrily — see ARGUE 1

tight *adj* **1** not allowing penetration (as by gas, liquid, or light) ⟨The lid forms a *tight* seal with the canister that will keep the spices fresh.⟩
syn impenetrable, impermeable, impervious
rel close, compact, dense, snug, thick; airtight, hermetic (*also* hermetical), watertight; lightproof, soundproof, waterproof
near ant absorbent, leaky, porous, unsealed
ant penetrable, permeable

2 firmly positioned in place and difficult to dislodge ⟨a *tight* screw that won't come loose⟩ ⟨a jar with a *tight* lid⟩
syn fast, firm, frozen, jammed, lodged, set, snug, stuck, wedged
rel bonded, cemented, glued; anchored, clamped; embedded (*also* imbedded), entrenched (*also* intrenched), impacted, implanted; attached, bound, fastened, secured; immovable, unyielding
near ant detached, dislodged, freed, loosened, unattached, unbound, undone, unfastened, unsecured; movable (*or* moveable), yielding
ant insecure, loose

3 giving or sharing as little as possible — see STINGY 1

4 having little space between items or parts — see CLOSE 1

5 showing little difference in the standing of the competitors — see CLOSE 3

6 stretched with little or no give — see TAUT

7 closely acquainted — see FAMILIAR 1

tightfisted *adj* giving or sharing as little as possible — see STINGY 1

tight-lipped *adj* tending not to speak frequently (as by habit or inclination) — see SILENT 2

tightness *n* the quality or practice of being overly sparing with money — see PARSIMONY 1

tightwad *n* a mean grasping person who is usually stingy with money — see MISER

till *vb* to work by plowing, sowing, and raising crops on — see FARM

tiller *n* a person who cultivates the land and grows crops on it — see FARMER

tilt *n* the act of positioning or an instance of being positioned at an angle ⟨Kate indicated her approval with a slight *tilt* of her head.⟩
syn angling, bend, cock, inclination, list, tip
rel turn, twist, veer; bow, dip, nod

tilt *vb* to set or cause to be at an angle — see LEAN 1

tilted *adj* **1** inclined or twisted to one side — see AWRY

2 running in a slanting direction — see DIAGONAL

tilting *adj* running in a slanting direction — see DIAGONAL

timber *n* **1** a dense growth of trees and shrubs covering a large area — see FOREST

2 tree logs as prepared for human use — see WOOD 1

timberland *n* a dense growth of trees and shrubs covering a large area — see FOREST

time *n* **1** a particular point at which an event takes place — see OCCASION 1

2 an exciting or noteworthy event that one experiences firsthand — see ADVENTURE 1

3 an extent of time associated with a particular person or thing — see AGE 1

4 the period during which something exists, lasts, or is in progress — see DURATION 1

timeless *adj* having an existence or validity that does not change or diminish — see ABIDING

timeliness *n* the quality or habit of arriving or being ready on time — see PROMPTITUDE

timely *adj* especially suitable for a certain time ⟨a *timely* invitation to lunch that came just as I was starting to feel hungry⟩
syn opportune, seasonable
rel appropriate, apt, fit, fitting, meet, pat, proper, suitable; pertinent, relative, relevant; fortunate, lucky, propitious; anticipated, expected; prompt, punctual
near ant improper, inappropriate, irrelative, irrelevant, unfit, unseemly, unsuitable; unfortunate, unlucky; behind, be-

---

syn synonym(s)   *rel* related words
ant antonym(s)   *near ant* near antonym(s)

hindhand, belated, delayed, delinquent, late, latish, overdue, postponed, slow, tardy; anticipatory, early, precocious, premature; abrupt, sudden, unanticipated, unexpected

ant inopportune, unseasonable, untimely
2 done, carried out, or given without delay — see PROMPT 1

timepiece *n* a device to measure time ⟨The only *timepiece* she used at the cabin was a garden sundial.⟩
syn chronometer, clock, timer
rel alarm clock, atomic clock, cuckoo clock, grandfather clock, time clock; hourglass, sandglass, sundial, water clock; chronograph, stopwatch, watch

timer *n* a device to measure time — see TIMEPIECE

timetable *n* a listing of things to be presented or considered (as at a concert or play) — see PROGRAM 1

timid *adj* easily frightened — see SHY 1

timidity *n* lack of willingness to assert oneself and take risks ⟨None of the scouts showed the least *timidity* about rappeling down the cliff.⟩
syn faintheartedness, timidness, timorousness
rel bashfulness, constraint, embarrassment, inhibition, restraint, shyness, skittishness; hesitation, indecision, indecisiveness, irresoluteness, irresolution; cowardice, cowardliness, cravenness, spinelessness
near ant assurance, confidence, self-assertiveness, self-assurance, self-confidence; composure, coolness, insouciance, nonchalance, unconcern; backbone, decisiveness, determination, firmness, fortitude, grit, mettle, resoluteness, resolution, spunk; bravery, courage, courageousness, daring, dauntlessness, doughtiness, fearlessness, intrepidity, intrepidness, valor; brazenness, effrontery, gall, temerity
ant audacity, boldness, nerve

timidness *n* lack of willingness to assert oneself and take risks — see TIMIDITY

timorous *adj* easily frightened — see SHY 1

timorousness *n* lack of willingness to assert oneself and take risks — see TIMIDITY

tin *n* a metal container in the shape of a cylinder — see CAN 1

tincture *n* a property that becomes apparent when light falls on an object and by which things that are identical in form can be distinguished — see COLOR 1

tincture *vb* to give color or a different color to — see COLOR 1

tinge *n* a property that becomes apparent when light falls on an object and by which things that are identical in form can be distinguished — see COLOR 1

tinge *vb* to give color or a different color to — see COLOR 1

tingle *n* a sharp unpleasant sensation usually felt in some specific part of the body — see PAIN 1

tingle *vb* to make a repeated sharp light ringing sound — see JINGLE

tinker (with) *vb* to handle thoughtlessly, ignorantly, or mischievously — see TAMPER (WITH)

tinkle *n* a series of short high ringing sounds ⟨the soothing *tinkle* of the wind chime on the back porch⟩
syn chime(s), jingle, tintinnabulation
rel clatter, rattle; chink, clang, clank, clink, ding-dong, ping, ring; chirr, ripple, trill, warble

tinkle *vb* to make a repeated sharp light ringing sound — see JINGLE

tint *n* a property that becomes apparent when light falls on an object and by which things that are identical in form can be distinguished — see COLOR 1

tint *vb* to give color or a different color to — see COLOR 1

tintinnabulation *n* a series of short high ringing sounds — see TINKLE

tiny *adj* very small in size ⟨The forest ranger showed us how every square foot of forest is alive with *tiny* creatures.⟩
syn atomic, bitty, infinitesimal, microscopic (*also* microscopical), miniature, minuscule, minute, teeny, teeny-weeny, wee
rel baby, diminutive, dwarf, elfin, half-pint, little, micro, model, petite, pocket, pocket-size (*also* pocket-sized), pygmy, small, smallish; dinky, dwarfish, insignificant, pint-size (*or* pint-sized), puny, scrubby, undersized (*also* undersize)
near ant big, bulky, bumper, considerable, extensive, good, goodly, grand, great, gross, handsome, hefty, hulking, jumbo, king-size (*or* king-sized), large, largish, major, outsize (*also* outsized), overgrown, overscale (*or* overscaled), oversize (*or* oversized), sizable (*or* sizeable), substantial, super, whacking, whopping
ant astronomical (*also* astronomic), colossal, cosmic, elephantine, enormous, giant, gigantic, herculean, heroic, huge, immense, mammoth, massive, monster, monstrous, monumental, mountainous, prodigious, titanic, tremendous

¹tip *n* **1** a piece of advice or useful information especially from an expert ⟨I got some *tips* from a horticulturist on how to get my violets to bloom.⟩
syn hint, lead, pointer
rel advisement, assistance, counsel, guidance, recommendation, suggestion; caution, cautioning, sign, signal, telltale, tip-off, warning; brief, direction, feedback, instruction
2 information not generally available to the public — see DOPE 1

²tip *n* **1** a small sum of money given for a service over and above what is due ⟨We gave our waiter an extra large *tip* for such fantastic service.⟩
syn gratuity, perquisite
rel donation, gift, lagniappe, largesse (*also* largess); present; bonus, favor, reward; contribution, offering
2 something given in addition to what is ordinarily expected or owed — see BONUS

³tip *n* the act of positioning or an instance of being positioned at an angle — see TILT

⁴tip *n* the last and usually sharp or tapering part of something long and narrow — see POINT 2

tip *vb* to set or cause to be at an angle — see LEAN 1

tip–off *n* something that tells of approaching danger or risk — see WARNING 2

tipped *adj* tapering to a thin tip — see POINTED 1

tipping *adj* inclined or twisted to one side — see AWRY

tip–top *adj* of the very best kind — see EXCELLENT

tip–top *n* the highest part or point — see HEIGHT 1

tirade *n* a long angry speech or scolding ⟨After the inspection by the health department, we had to listen to the manager's *tirade* about keeping the restaurant's kitchen clean.⟩
syn diatribe, harangue, rant
rel assault, attack, broadside, invective, lambasting, lashing, tongue-lashing, vituperation; berating, chewing out, rebuke, reprimand, reproach, reproof; abuse, castigation, censure, condemnation, denunciation; excoriation, execration, revilement; admonishment, admonition, lecture, sermon
near ant encomium, eulogy, panegyric, rhapsody, tribute; acclaim, acclamation, accolade, citation, homage, honor, praise; approval, blessing, commendation, endorsement (*also* indorsement), sanction; ovation, plaudit, rave

tire *vb* 1 to diminish the physical strength of — see WEAKEN 1
2 to make weary and restless by being dull or monotonous — see ²BORE
3 to use up all the physical energy of — see EXHAUST 1

tired *adj* 1 depleted in strength, energy, or freshness — see WEARY 1
2 having one's patience, interest, or pleasure exhausted — see WEARY 1
3 used or heard so often as to be dull — see STALE 1

tiredness *n* a complete depletion of energy or strength — see FATIGUE

tireless *adj* showing no signs of weariness even after long hard effort ⟨a *tireless* advocate for human rights⟩
syn indefatigable, inexhaustible, unflagging, untiring, weariless
rel assiduous, conscientious, diligent, meticulous, painstaking, sedulous; determined, dogged, patient, persevering, persistent, pertinacious, plodding, relentless, steadfast, steady, stubborn, tenacious, unabated, unfailing, unfaltering, unflinching, unrelenting, unremitting, unwavering; industrious, intense, laborious, strenuous
near ant indolent, lackadaisical, laggard, lazy, listless, shiftless, slothful, sluggish; apathetic, casual, desultory, languid, spiritless; beat, broken, burned-out (*or* burnt-out), done in, drained, enervated, jaded, overtaxed, overworked, played out, sapped, spent, tuckered (out), wearied, worn-out

tiresome *adj* causing weariness, restlessness, or lack of interest — see BORING

tiring *adj* causing weariness, restlessness, or lack of interest — see BORING

titan *n* something that is unusually large and powerful — see GIANT

titanic *adj* unusually large — see HUGE

titillate *vb* to cause a pleasurable stimulation of the feelings of — see THRILL

titillation *n* a pleasurably intense stimulation of the feelings — see THRILL

title *n* 1 a word or combination of words by which a person or thing is regularly known — see NAME 1
2 a word or series of words often in larger letters placed at the beginning of a passage or at the top of a page in order to introduce or categorize — see HEADING
3 the position occupied by the one who comes in first in a competition — see CROWN 2

title *vb* to give a name to — see NAME 1

titter *n* an explosive sound that is a sign of amusement — see LAUGH 1

titter *vb* to show mirth with an explosive vocal sound — see LAUGH 1

tittle *n* 1 a very small piece — see BIT 1
2 the smallest amount or part imaginable — see JOT

titular *adj* being something in name or form only — see NOMINAL 1

tizzy *n* a state of nervous or irritated concern — see FRET

to *prep* earlier than — see BEFORE 1

toady *n* a person who flatters another in order to get ahead — see SYCOPHANT

toady *vb* to use flattery or the doing of favors in order to win approval especially from a superior — see FAWN

toast *vb* to cause to have or give off heat to a moderate degree — see WARM 1

toasty *adj* having or giving off heat to a moderate degree — see WARM 1

tocsin *n* 1 an object intended to give public notice or warning — see SIGNAL 1
2 something that tells of approaching danger or risk — see WARNING 2

today *adv* at the present time — see NOW 1

today *n* the time currently existing or in progress — see ¹PRESENT

to–do *n* a state of noisy, confused activity — see COMMOTION

together *adv* 1 at one and the same time ⟨The two packages, although sent on different days, arrived *together*.⟩
syn coincidentally, coincidently, concurrently, contemporaneously, simultaneously
rel close, immediately, near
phrases at once, in unison
near ant apart, independently, individually, singly
ant separately
2 in or by combined action or effort ⟨Working *together*, we can get this project done on time.⟩
syn conjointly, jointly
rel collectively, mutually, reciprocally, unanimously, unitedly; cooperatively, symbiotically
phrases in concert
ant apart, independently, individually, separately, severally, single-handedly, singly, solely, unaided, unassisted, unilaterally
3 with everyone or everything taken into account at the same time — see ALL AROUND

togs *n pl* 1 clothing chosen as appropriate for a specific situation — see OUTFIT 1

---

syn synonym(s)   *rel* related words
ant antonym(s)   *near ant* near antonym(s)

2 covering for the human body — see CLOTHING

toil *n* very hard or unpleasant work ⟨After years of *toil* in a sweatshop, Kim was finally able to start her own business.⟩

syn drudgery, grind, labor, sweat, travail

rel spadework; effort, exertion, pains, struggle, trouble; chore, duty, job, obligation, responsibility; routine, tedium, treadmill

near ant decompression, ease, leisure, relaxation, repose, rest; amusement, dalliance, diversion, entertainment, recreation, sport; dormancy, idleness, inactivity, inertia, inertness; dallying, goldbricking, loafing, lolling, lounging

ant fun, play

toil *vb* to devote serious and sustained effort — see LABOR

toiler *n* a person who does very hard or dull work — see DRUDGE

toilet *n* a room furnished with a fixture for flushing body waste ⟨We were directed to the *toilets* in the church basement.⟩

syn bath, bathroom, head, latrine, lavatory, potty, washroom, water closet

rel commode; outhouse, privy

toilsome *adj* **1** requiring considerable physical or mental effort — see HARD 2

2 requiring much time, effort, or careful attention — see DEMANDING 1

token *n* something that serves to keep alive the memory of a person or event — see MEMORIAL

tolerable *adj* **1** capable of being endured — see BEARABLE

2 of a level of quality that meets one's needs or standards — see ADEQUATE

tolerably *adv* in a satisfactory way — see WELL 1

tolerance *n* the capacity to endure what is difficult or disagreeable without complaining — see PATIENCE

tolerant *adj* **1** accepting pains or hardships calmly or without complaint — see PATIENT 1

2 receiving or enduring without offering resistance — see PASSIVE

tolerate *vb* **1** to fail to prevent (some behavior on someone's part) especially from neglect or indifference — see ALLOW 3

2 to put up with (something painful or difficult) — see BEAR 2

tolerating *adj* receiving or enduring without offering resistance — see PASSIVE

toll *vb* to make the clear sound heard when metal vibrates — see ²RING

tomb *n* a final resting place for a dead person — see GRAVE 1

tomboyish *adj* having qualities or traits that are traditionally considered inappropriate for a girl or woman — see UNFEMININE

tombstone *n* a shaped stone laid over or erected near a grave and usually bearing an inscription to identify and preserve the memory of the deceased ⟨The historic cemetery's many *tombstones* marking the graves of children are telling reminders of the harshness of pioneer life.⟩

syn gravestone, headstone, monument

rel cross, marker, plaque, table, tablet; monolith, obelisk, pillar; memorial, shrine; burial, sepulture, tomb

tome *n* a set of printed sheets of paper bound together between covers and forming a work of fiction or nonfiction — see BOOK 1

tomfoolery *n* wildly playful or mischievous behavior — see HORSEPLAY

tone *n* **1** a distinctive way of putting ideas into words — see STYLE 1

2 a property that becomes apparent when light falls on an object and by which things that are identical in form can be distinguished — see COLOR 1

3 the set of qualities that makes a person, a group of people, or a thing different from others — see NATURE 1

toned–down *adj* not excessively showy — see QUIET 2

tongue *n* the stock of words, pronunciation, and grammar used by a people as their basic means of communication — see LANGUAGE 1

tonic *adj* **1** having a renewing effect on the state of the body or mind ⟨Never underestimate the *tonic* power of humor on a sick person.⟩

syn bracing, cordial, invigorating, refreshing, restorative, reviving, stimulating, stimulative, vital, vitalizing

rel conditioning, strengthening; animating, exhilarating, quickening, sharp; corrective, curing, rectifying, recuperative, rehabilitative, remedial, remedying, reparative; beneficial, healthful, healthy, helpful, salubrious, salutary, wholesome; healing, medicinal

near ant deadening, debilitating, draining, enervating, enfeebling, exhausting, numbing, sapping, weakening, wearying; deleterious, injurious, pernicious; noxious, unhealthful, unhealthy, unwholesome

2 beneficial to the health of body or mind — see HEALTHFUL

too *adv* **1** beyond a normal or acceptable limit ⟨Ticket prices for the concert are simply *too* high.⟩

syn devilishly, excessively, exorbitantly, inordinately, monstrously, overly, overmuch, unacceptably, unduly

rel extravagantly, immoderately, intemperately; inexcusably, obscenely, unbearably, unconscionably, unreasonably; improperly, inappropriately; abnormally, extraordinarily, freakishly, singularly, unusually; astronomically, considerably, especially, exceedingly (*also* exceeding), exceptionally, extra, extremely, greatly, highly, hugely, incredibly, mightily, remarkably, significantly, substantially, super, terribly, very

phrases to a fault, to death, with a vengeance

near ant acceptably, moderately, modestly, reasonably, temperately; barely, hardly, just, marginally, meagerly, minimally, scantily, scarcely, slightly

ant deficiently, inadequately, insufficiently

2 in addition to what has been said — see MORE 1

3 to a great degree — see VERY 1

tool *n* **1** an article intended for use in work — see IMPLEMENT

2 one that is or can be used to further the purposes of another — see ¹PAWN

3 one who is easily deceived or cheated — see ¹DUPE

tool *vb* to travel by a motorized vehicle — see DRIVE 2

tooth and nail *adv* with all power or resources being used — see FULL BLAST

toothsome *adj* very pleasing to the sense of taste — see DELICIOUS 1

top *adj* **1** being at a point or level higher than all others ⟨an office in the *top* story of the building⟩ ⟨the *top* student in our graduating class⟩

syn highest, loftiest, topmost, upmost, uppermost

rel higher, loftier, upper; consummate, maximal, maximized, maximum, peaked, supreme, utmost, uttermost; chief, dominant, first, foremost, head, leading, predominant, preeminent, premier, principal; dominant, dominating, eminent, prominent, towering

near ant below, lower, nether, under, underneath; low, lowered, low-lying, sunken

ant lowest

2 of the greatest or highest degree or quantity — see ULTIMATE 1

3 of the highest degree — see FULL 2

4 of the very best kind — see EXCELLENT

5 highest in rank or authority — see HEAD

top *n* **1** a piece placed over an open container to hold in, protect, or conceal its contents — see COVER 1

2 the highest part or point — see HEIGHT 1

top *vb* to be greater, better, or stronger than — see SURPASS 1

topcoat *n* a warm outdoor coat — see OVERCOAT

topic *n* a major object of interest or concern (as in a discussion or artistic composition) — see MATTER 1

topmost *adj* **1** being at a point or level higher than all others — see TOP 1

2 of the highest degree — see FULL 2

top-notch *adj* of the very best kind — see EXCELLENT

top-of-the-line *adj* of the very best kind — see EXCELLENT

topper *n* something (as a fact or argument) that is decisive or overwhelming — see CLINCHER

topple *vb* to go down from an upright position suddenly and involuntarily — see FALL 1

topsy-turvy *adj* lacking in order, neatness, and often cleanliness — see MESSY

torment *n* **1** a situation or state that causes great suffering and unhappiness — see HELL 2

2 a state of great suffering of body or mind — see DISTRESS 1

3 a source of persistent emotional distress — see DEMON 1

torment *vb* to cause persistent suffering to — see AFFLICT

tormenting *adj* **1** hard to accept or bear especially emotionally — see BITTER 2

2 intensely or unbearably painful — see EXCRUCIATING 1

tormentor *also* **tormenter** *n* a person who causes repeated emotional pain, distress, or annoyance to another ⟨He was shocked to learn that his childhood *tormentor* had written a book about the dangers of bullying.⟩

syn baiter, heckler, mocker, needler, persecutor, quiz, ridiculer, taunter, tease, teaser, torturer

rel belittler, derider, detractor, giber (*or* jiber), insulter, jeerer, scoffer, scorner; smart aleck (*also* smart alec), smarty (*or* smartie), smarty-pants, wiseacre, wiseguy; kidder, lampooner, satirist; bother, disturber, pest

near ant defender, deliverer, guard, protector, rescuer, savior (*or* saviour); comforter, solace, soother; bodyguard, champion

torpid *adj* **1** slow to move or act — see INACTIVE 1

2 lacking in sensation or feeling — see NUMB 1

torrent *n* a great flow of water or of something that overwhelms — see FLOOD

torrid *adj* **1** having a notably high temperature — see HOT 1

2 having or expressing great depth of feeling — see FERVENT 1

tortuous *adj* marked by a long series of irregular curves — see CROOKED 1

torture *n* **1** a situation or state that causes great suffering and unhappiness — see HELL 2

2 a state of great suffering of body or mind — see DISTRESS 1

torture *vb* **1** to cause persistent suffering to — see AFFLICT

2 to twist (something) out of a natural or normal shape or condition — see CONTORT

torturer *n* a person who causes repeated emotional pain, distress, or annoyance to another — see TORMENTOR

torturing *adj* intensely or unbearably painful — see EXCRUCIATING 1

torturing *n* the twisting of something out of its natural or normal shape or condition — see CONTORTION

torturous *adj* **1** hard to accept or bear especially emotionally — see BITTER 2

2 intensely or unbearably painful — see EXCRUCIATING 1

Tory *n* a person whose political beliefs are centered on tradition and keeping things the way they are — see CONSERVATIVE

toss *vb* **1** to make a series of unsteady side-to-side motions — see ROCK 1

2 to make jerky or restless movements — see FIDGET

3 to send through the air especially with a quick forward motion of the arm — see THROW 1

4 to get rid of as useless or unwanted — see DISCARD

toss (down *or* **off)** *vb* to swallow in liquid form — see DRINK 1

total *adj* **1** having no exceptions or restrictions — see ABSOLUTE 2

2 not lacking any part or member that properly belongs to it — see COMPLETE 1

3 trying all possibilities — see EXHAUSTIVE 1

total *n* a complete amount of something — see WHOLE

---

syn synonym(s)   *rel* related words
ant antonym(s)   *near ant* near antonym(s)

total *vb* **1** to have a total of — see AMOUNT (TO) 1

2 to combine (numbers) into a single sum — see ADD 2

3 to bring to a complete end the physical soundness, existence, or usefulness of — see DESTROY 1

totalitarianism *n* a system of government in which the ruler has unlimited power — see DESPOTISM

totality *n* a complete amount of something — see WHOLE

totally *adv* **1** to a full extent or degree — see FULLY 1

2 with attention to all aspects or details — see THOROUGHLY 1

tote *vb* to support and take from one place to another — see CARRY 1

totter *vb* **1** to move forward while swaying from side to side — see STAGGER 1

2 to swing unsteadily back and forth or from side to side — see TEETER 1

tottery *adj* marked by or given to small uncontrollable bodily movements — see SHAKY 1

touch *n* **1** the state or fact of being able to exchange information regarding one's current situation ⟨Everyone promised to keep in *touch* over the summer.⟩

syn communication, contact, hold

rel commerce, communion, intercommunication, intercourse

2 a very small amount — see PARTICLE 1

3 something that sets apart an individual from others of the same kind — see CHARACTERISTIC

4 an almost imperceptible sign of something — see HINT 1

touch *vb* **1** to come into bodily contact with (something) so as to perceive a slight pressure on the skin ⟨Be careful not to *touch* this pan—it's still hot!⟩

syn feel

rel caress, embrace, fondle, hug, kiss, nose, nudge, nuzzle, paw, rub, stroke; palp, palpate; brush, graze, shave, skim; clasp, clench, cling (to), clutch, grasp, grip, handle, hold; chuck, clap, dab, flick, pat, tag, tap, tip; hit, knock, pound, rap, whack

2 to act upon (a person or a person's feelings) so as to cause a response — see [1]AFFECT 1

3 to affect slightly with something morally bad or undesirable — see TAINT 1

4 to be adjacent to — see ADJOIN 1

5 to be the business or affair of — see CONCERN 2

touch (on *or* upon) *vb* to make reference to or speak about briefly but specifically — see MENTION 1

touchable *adj* capable of being perceived by the sense of touch — see TANGIBLE

touch down *vb* to come to rest after descending from the air — see ALIGHT 1

touching *adj* **1** having a border in common — see ADJACENT

2 having the power to affect the feelings or sympathies — see MOVING

touching *prep* having to do with — see ABOUT 1

touch off *vb* to cause to function — see ACTIVATE

touchstone *n* something set up as an example against which others of the same type are compared — see STANDARD 1

touchy *adj* **1** easily offended ⟨Watch what you say around him, as he's very *touchy* about every little thing.⟩

syn ticklish

rel hypersensitive, oversensitive, sensitive, supersensitive, tender; choleric, crabby, cranky, cross, crotchety, grouchy, grumpy, irascible, irritable, peevish, perverse, pettish, petulant, prickly, quick-tempered, short-tempered, snappish, snappy, snippy, stuffy, testy, waspish; bearish, bilious, cantankerous, curmudgeonly, disagreeable, dyspeptic, ill-humored, ill-natured, ill-tempered, ornery, querulous, surly

near ant agreeable, amiable, good-natured, good-tempered, well-disposed; carefree, easygoing, happy-go-lucky, relaxed, unconcerned; forbearing, long-suffering, obliging, understanding

ant thick-skinned

2 requiring exceptional skill or caution in performance or handling — see TRICKY 1

3 capable of catching or being set on fire — see COMBUSTIBLE

tough *adj* **1** not easily chewed ⟨Her steak was so *tough* that she suggested the waiter use it as a hockey puck.⟩

syn chewy, leathery

rel fibrous, gristly, sinewy, stringy; brittle, crunchy, hard

near ant mushy, soft

ant tender

2 able to withstand hardship, strain, or exposure — see HARDY 1

3 difficult to endure — see HARSH 1

4 requiring considerable physical or mental effort — see HARD 2

5 requiring exceptional skill or caution in performance or handling — see TRICKY 1

6 given to exacting standards of discipline and self-restraint — see SEVERE 1

tough *n* a violent, brutal person who is often a member of an organized gang — see HOODLUM

toughen *vb* **1** to increase the ability of (as a muscle) to exert physical force — see STRENGTHEN 1

2 to make able to withstand physical hardship, strain, or exposure — see HARDEN 2

toughened *adj* able to withstand hardship, strain, or exposure — see HARDY 1

tour *n* a fixed period of time during which a person holds a job or position — see TERM 1

tour *vb* to take a trip especially of some distance — see TRAVEL 1

tourist *n* a person who travels for pleasure ⟨*Tourists* from all over like to take pictures of the alligators in the bayou.⟩

syn excursionist, rubberneck, sightseer, traveler (*or* traveller)

rel holidayer, vacationer, vacationist; guest, hosteler (*or* hosteller); visitor; transient; journeyer, pilgrim, wayfarer

tournament *n* a competitive encounter between individuals or groups carried on for amusement, exercise, or in pursuit of a prize — see GAME 1

tourney *n* a competitive encounter between

individuals or groups carried on for amusement, exercise, or in pursuit of a prize — see GAME 1

tousle *vb* to undo the proper order or arrangement of — see DISORDER

tousled *adj* lacking in order, neatness, and often cleanliness — see MESSY

tout *vb* 1 to praise or publicize lavishly and often excessively ⟨a new cleaning agent *touted* as the only product a homeowner needs for all his or her cleaning chores⟩
syn ballyhoo, crack up, glorify, trumpet
rel acclaim, applaud, extol (*also* extoll), laud, magnify; commend, compliment, eulogize; advance, advertise, announce, blare, blaze, boost, herald, offer, plug, promote, publicize; assert, aver, claim, declare, lay down, make out, proclaim, pronounce
2 to declare enthusiastic approval of — see ACCLAIM
3 to provide publicity for — see PUBLICIZE 1

tow *vb* to cause to follow by applying steady force on — see PULL 1

toward *or* **towards** *prep* having to do with — see ABOUT 1

tower *n* a large, magnificent, or massive building — see EDIFICE 1

towering *adj* 1 extending to a great distance upward — see HIGH 1
2 going beyond a normal or acceptable limit in degree or amount — see EXCESSIVE
3 very dignified in form, tone, or style — see ELEVATED 2

town *n* a thickly settled, highly populated area — see CITY

townie *or* **towny** *n* 1 a usually longtime resident of a locality — see NATIVE
2 a person who lives in a town on a permanent basis — see BURGHER

toxic *adj* containing or contaminated with a substance capable of injuring or killing a living thing — see POISONOUS

toxin *n* a substance that by chemical action can kill or injure a living thing — see POISON

trace *n* 1 a mark or series of marks left on a surface by something that has passed along it — see TRACK 1
2 a passage cleared for public vehicular travel — see WAY 1
3 a rough course or way formed by or as if by repeated footsteps — see TRAIL 1
4 a tiny often physical indication of something lost or vanished — see VESTIGE 1
5 a very small amount — see PARTICLE 1
6 an almost imperceptible sign of something — see HINT 2
7 the mark or impression made by a foot — see FOOTPRINT

trace *vb* 1 to draw or make apparent the outline of — see OUTLINE 1
2 to go after or on the track of — see FOLLOW 2

tracing *n* the act of going after or in the tracks of another — see PURSUIT

track *n* 1 a mark or series of marks left on a surface by something that has passed along it ⟨a muddy *track* across the kitchen floor⟩
syn imprint, trace, trail
rel footprint, footstep, hoofprint, path, rut, step, tread; artifact, leavings, relic, remain(s), remainder, remnant, residual, residue, sign, spoor, token, vestige; clue, cue, hint, indication, inkling, intimation, lead, suggestion; scent, shadow, whiff
2 a rough course or way formed by or as if by repeated footsteps — see TRAIL 1
3 the direction along which something or someone moves — see PATH 1

track *vb* 1 to go after or on the track of — see FOLLOW 2
2 to make one's way through, across, or over — see TRAVERSE

track (down) *vb* to come upon after searching, study, or effort — see FIND 1

tracking *n* the act of going after or in the tracks of another — see PURSUIT

tract *n* 1 a broad geographical area — see REGION 2
2 a small area of usually open land — see FIELD 1
3 a small piece of land that is developed or available for development — see LOT 1

tractable *adj* readily giving in to the command or authority of another — see OBEDIENT

trade *n* 1 a giving or taking of one thing of value in return for another — see EXCHANGE 1
2 an occupation requiring skillful use of the hands — see CRAFT 1
3 the activity by which one regularly makes a living — see OCCUPATION
4 the buying and selling of goods especially on a large scale and between different places — see COMMERCE 1
5 the transfer of ownership of something from one person to another for a price — see SALE

trade *vb* 1 to carry on the business of buying and selling goods or other property ⟨The U.S. agreed to *trade* with China.⟩
syn deal, traffic
rel bargain, barter, horse-trade, negotiate, transact; auction, exchange, merchandise (*also* merchandize), rebuy, resell, swap; buy, pick up, purchase, take; distribute, market, peddle, retail, sell, supply, vend, wholesale; bootleg, fence, smuggle; corner, monopolize, undersell; invest, speculate
near ant blackball, boycott
2 to give up (something) and take something else in return — see CHANGE 3

trademark *n* 1 a device (as a word) identifying the maker of a piece of merchandise and legally reserved for the exclusive use of that person or company ⟨"Kleenex" is a *trademark* for a cleansing tissue.⟩
syn brand
rel brand name, trade name; collective mark, emblem, hallmark, imprint, label, logo, mark, service mark, stamp; copyright, patent
2 a device, design, or figure used as an identifying mark — see EMBLEM

trade–off *n* a giving or taking of one thing of value in return for another — see EXCHANGE 1

---

trader n a buyer and seller of goods for profit — see MERCHANT

tradesman n 1 a buyer and seller of goods for profit — see MERCHANT

2 a person whose occupation requires skill with the hands — see ARTISAN

tradition n 1 an inherited or established way of thinking, feeling, or doing ⟨the town *tradition* of having the oldest resident ride at the head of the parade⟩

syn convention, custom, heritage, rubric, rule

rel ethic, form, mode, mores, norm, principles, standards, values; birthright, inheritance, legacy; folklore, lore, superstition; culture, lifestyle

2 the body of customs, beliefs, stories, and sayings associated with a people, thing, or place — see FOLKLORE

traditional adj 1 based on customs usually handed down from a previous generation ⟨a *traditional* Passover meal at his grandparents' house⟩

syn classical, conventional, customary

rel authentic, established, fixed, historical; common, habitual, orthodox, usual; ancestral, antediluvian, old-world; aged, age-old, ancient, antediluvian, hoary, old, venerable; ageless, dateless, immemorial, timeless

near ant contemporary, current, modern, modernized, new, new-age, present-day, updated, up-to-date; futuristic, high-tech (*also* hi-tech), hot, latest, mod, modernistic, newfangled, new-fashioned, red-hot, space-age, state-of-the-art, supermodern, ultramodern; nonconformist, nonorthodox, original, progressive, revolutionary, unorthodox, unprecedented, unusual

ant nontraditional, unconventional, uncustomary, untraditional

2 tending to favor established ideas, conditions, or institutions — see CONSERVATIVE 1

traduce vb 1 to fail to keep — see VIOLATE 1

2 to make untrue and harmful statements about — see SLANDER

traducing n the making of false statements that damage another's reputation — see SLANDER

traffic n the buying and selling of goods especially on a large scale and between different places — see COMMERCE 1

traffic vb to carry on the business of buying and selling of goods or other property — see TRADE 1

trafficker n a buyer and seller of goods for profit — see MERCHANT

tragedy n 1 a sudden violent event that brings about great loss or destruction — see DISASTER 1

2 bad luck or an example of this — see MISFORTUNE

tragic also **tragical** adj of a kind to cause great distress — see REGRETTABLE

trail n 1 a rough course or way formed by or as if by repeated footsteps ⟨We took a *trail* through the woods to get to the main road.⟩

syn footpath, path, pathway, trace, track

rel bridle path; towpath; alley, alleyway, bypath, byroad, bystreet, byway, passageway, walkway; shortcut; lane, pass, passage, road, roadway, route, row, run, runway, street, thoroughfare

2 a mark or series of marks left on a surface by something that has passed along it — see TRACK 1

trail vb to go after or on the track of — see FOLLOW 2

trailer n a motor vehicle that is specially equipped for living while traveling — see CAMPER

trailing n the act of going after or in the tracks of another — see PURSUIT

train n 1 a body of employees or attendants who accompany and wait on a person — see CORTEGE 1

2 a group of vehicles traveling together or under one management — see FLEET

3 a series of persons or things arranged one behind another — see LINE 1

4 a series of things linked together — see CHAIN 1

train vb 1 to bring to a proper or desired state of fitness — see CONDITION 1

2 to cause to acquire knowledge or skill in some field — see TEACH

3 to fix (as one's attention) steadily toward a central objective — see CONCENTRATE 2

4 to point or turn (something) toward a target or goal — see AIM 1

5 to make competent (as by training, skill, or ability) for a particular office or function — see QUALIFY 1

trainer n a person who trains performers or athletes — see COACH

training n 1 something done over and over in order to develop skill — see EXERCISE 2

2 the act or process of imparting knowledge or skills to another — see EDUCATION 1

traipse vb 1 to go on foot — see WALK 1

2 to move about from place to place aimlessly — see WANDER 1

trait n something that sets apart an individual from others of the same kind — see CHARACTERISTIC

traitor n one who betrays a trust or an allegiance ⟨accused by her family of being a *traitor* when she sold their traditionally animal-friendly business to a competitor known to use animals for testing its products⟩

syn apostate, betrayer, double-crosser, quisling, recreant, serpent, snake, turncoat

rel collaborationist, collaborator, subversive, subverter; cocospirator, conspirator, intriguer, plotter, schemer; defector, deserter, renegade; informant, informer, rat, snitch, snitcher, squealer, stool pigeon, talebearer, tattler, tattletale

traitorous adj not true in one's allegiance to someone or something — see FAITHLESS

trammel n something that makes movement or progress difficult — see ENCUMBRANCE

trammel vb 1 to confine or restrain with or as if with chains — see BIND 1

2 to create difficulty for the work or activity of — see HAMPER

tramp n a homeless wanderer who may beg or steal for a living ⟨The police encouraged the *tramps* who were sleeping in the park to spend the bitterly cold night in the homeless shelter.⟩

syn bum, hobo, vagabond, vagrant

rel drifter, roamer, transient; beggar, derelict, mendicant, panhandler; dodger, malingerer, shirker, slacker; gamine, ragamuffin, urchin, waif

tramp *vb* **1** to move heavily or clumsily — see LUMBER 1

2 to tread on heavily so as to crush or injure — see TRAMPLE

3 to travel by foot for exercise or pleasure — see HIKE 1

trample *vb* to tread on heavily so as to crush or injure ⟨Isabel looked out her window and beheld the neighbor's Labrador retriever *trampling* her begonias.⟩

syn stamp, stomp, tromp, tramp

rel override, run down, run over, step (on); mash, pulp, smash, squash, squelch; hoof, kick

trance *n* the state of being lost in thought — see REVERIE

tranquil *adj* **1** free from disturbing noise or uproar — see QUIET 1

2 free from emotional or mental agitation — see CALM 2

3 free from storms or physical disturbance — see CALM 1

tranquilize *also* **tranquillize** *vb* to free from distress or disturbance — see CALM 1

tranquilizing *also* **tranquillizing** *adj* tending to calm the emotions and relieve stress — see SOOTHING 1

tranquillity *or* **tranquility** *n* **1** a state of freedom from storm or disturbance — see CALM 1

2 evenness of emotions or temper — see EQUANIMITY

3 freedom from disquieting or oppressive thoughts or emotions — see PEACE 2

transaction *n* the transfer of ownership of something from one person to another for a price — see SALE

transcend *vb* **1** to be greater, better, or stronger than — see SURPASS 1

2 to go beyond the limit of — see EXCEED 1

transcendence *n* the fact or state of being above others in rank or importance — see EMINENCE 1

transfer *vb* **1** to give over the legal possession or ownership of ⟨Claire's grandfather agreed to *transfer* certain stocks to her when she turned 18.⟩

syn alienate, assign, cede, convey, deed, make over

rel bequeath, hand down, leave, pass (down), will; bestow, commend, commit, confer, contribute, deliver, donate, grant, hand over, move, pass, present, release, relinquish, surrender, transmit, turn in, turn over, vest, yield; consign, entrust (*also* intrust), trust; lease, lend, loan, rent

phrases dispose of

near ant expropriate

2 to cause (something) to pass from one to another — see COMMUNICATE 1

3 to cause to go or be taken from one place to another — see SEND

4 to change the place or position of — see MOVE 1

5 to put (something) into the possession or safekeeping of another — see GIVE 2

6 to shift possession of (something) from one person to another — see PASS 1

transferable *also* **transferrable** *adj* capable of being taken from one place to another by public carrier — see SHIPPABLE

transfiguration *n* a change in form, appearance, or use — see CONVERSION 1

transfigure *vb* to change in form, appearance, or use — see CONVERT 2

transfix *vb* to penetrate or hold (something) with a pointed object — see IMPALE

transform *vb* to change in form, appearance, or use — see CONVERT 2

transformation *n* a change in form, appearance, or use — see CONVERSION 1

transfuse *vb* **1** to cause (something) to pass from one to another — see COMMUNICATE 1

2 to spread throughout — see PERMEATE

transgress *vb* **1** to commit an offense — see OFFEND 1

2 to fail to keep — see VIOLATE 1

transgression *n* **1** a breaking of a moral or legal code — see OFFENSE 1

2 a failure to uphold the requirements of law, duty, or obligation — see BREACH 1

transient *adj* lasting only for a short time — see MOMENTARY

transitory *adj* lasting only for a short time — see MOMENTARY

translate *vb* to express something (as a text or statement) in different words — see PARAPHRASE

translate (into) *vb* to be the cause of (a situation, action, or state of mind) — see EFFECT

translating *n* an instance of expressing something in different words — see PARAPHRASE

translation *n* an instance of expressing something in different words — see PARAPHRASE

transmit *vb* **1** to cause (something) to pass from one to another — see COMMUNICATE 1

2 to cause to go or be taken from one place to another — see SEND

3 to put (something) into the possession or safekeeping of another — see GIVE 2

transmittable *adj* **1** capable of being passed by physical contact from one person to another — see CONTAGIOUS 1

2 capable of being taken from one place to another by public carrier — see SHIPPABLE

transparency *n* the state or quality of being easily seen through — see CLARITY 1

transparent *adj* **1** easily seen through — see CLEAR 1

2 not subject to misinterpretation or more than one interpretation — see CLEAR 2

3 very thin and easy to see through — see SHEER 1

transpire *vb* to take place — see HAPPEN

transport *n* **1** a state of overwhelming usually pleasurable emotion — see ECSTASY

2 something used to carry goods or passengers — see CONVEYANCE

transport *vb* **1** to cause to go or be taken from one place to another — see SEND

---

syn synonym(s)   **rel** related words

ant antonym(s)   **near ant** near antonym(s)

2 to fill with great joy — see ELATE

3 to fill with overwhelming emotion (as wonder or delight) — see ENTRANCE

4 to force to leave a country — see BANISH 1

5 to support and take from one place to another — see CARRY 1

transportable *adj* capable of being taken from one place to another by public carrier — see SHIPPABLE

transportation *n* **1** a means of getting to a destination in a vehicle driven by another — see RIDE

2 something used to carry goods or passengers — see CONVEYANCE

transpose *vb* to change the place or position of — see MOVE 1

transversely *adv* in a line or direction running from corner to corner — see CROSSWISE

trap *n* **1** a device or scheme for capturing another by surprise ⟨Undercover agents devised a *trap* to catch the counterfeiters.⟩ ⟨a bear *trap*⟩

syn ambush, net, snare, web

rel entanglement, entrapment, envelopment; booby trap, catch, hazard, land mine, pitfall, snag; artifice, cheat, double-dealing, duplicity, ploy, ruse, subterfuge, trick

2 a setup in which hidden attackers lie in wait — see AMBUSH 1

3 something that catches and holds — see WEB 1

trap *vb* **1** to catch or hold as if in a net — see ENTANGLE 2

2 to take physical control or possession of (something) suddenly or forcibly — see CATCH 1

trash *n* **1** discarded or useless material — see GARBAGE

2 language, behavior, or ideas that are absurd and contrary to good sense — see NONSENSE 1

3 people looked down upon as ignorant and of the lowest class — see RABBLE

4 that which is of low quality or worth — see JUNK 1

trashy *adj* **1** marked by an obvious lack of style or good taste — see ¹TACKY 1

2 of low quality — see CHEAP 2

travail *n* **1** a state of great suffering of body or mind — see DISTRESS 1

2 very hard or unpleasant work — see TOIL

3 the act or process of giving birth to children — see CHILDBIRTH

travail *vb* to devote serious and sustained effort — see LABOR

travel *n, often* **travels** *pl* a going from one place to another usually of some distance — see JOURNEY

travel *vb* **1** to take a trip especially of some distance ⟨The couple loves to *travel* and has been to 34 countries.⟩

syn journey, peregrinate, pilgrimage, tour, trek, voyage

rel gallivant (*also* galavant), hop, jaunt, knock (about), ramble, roam, rove, traipse, wander; migrate, road-trip; cab, coach, cruise, drive, fly, gig, jet, motor, navigate, ride, roll, sail, trundle; barnstorm

2 to make one's way through, across, or over — see TRAVERSE

3 to proceed or move quickly — see HURRY 2

4 to come or be together as friends — see ASSOCIATE 1

traveler *or* **traveller** *n* a person who travels for pleasure — see TOURIST

traveling bag *n* a bag carried by hand and designed to hold a traveler's clothing and personal articles ⟨*traveling bags* made of lightweight but tough fabrics⟩

syn carryall, grip, handbag, portmanteau, suitcase

rel overnight bag (*also* overnight case); carpetbag, duffel bag, kit; backpack, haversack, knapsack, rucksack; attaché, attaché case, briefcase, valise; baggage, bags, luggage

traverse *vb* to make one's way through, across, or over ⟨The spider *traversed* the wall from end to end.⟩

syn course, cover, cross, cut (across), follow, go, navigate, pass (over), peregrinate, proceed (along), track, travel

rel hike, traipse, tramp, tread, walk; ride, run; crisscross

travesty *n* **1** a poor, insincere, or insulting imitation of something — see MOCKERY 1

2 a work that imitates and exaggerates another work for comic effect — see PARODY 1

travesty *vb* to copy or exaggerate (someone or something) in order to make fun of — see MIMIC 1

treacherous *adj* not true in one's allegiance to someone or something — see FAITHLESS

treachery *n* the act or fact of violating the trust or confidence of another — see BETRAYAL

tread *vb* to go on foot — see WALK 1

treadmill *n* an established and often automatic or monotonous series of actions followed when engaging in some activity — see ROUTINE 1

treason *n* the act or fact of violating the trust or confidence of another — see BETRAYAL

treasure *n* **1** an asset that brings praise or renown — see GLORY 2

2 someone or something unusually desirable — see PRIZE 1

treasure *vb* **1** to hold dear — see LOVE 1

2 to put (something of future use or value) in a safe or secret place — see HOARD

treat *n* **1** a source of great satisfaction — see DELIGHT 1

2 something that is pleasing to eat because it is rare or a luxury — see DELICACY 1

treat *vb* **1** to behave toward in a stated way ⟨She tries to *treat* all of her students fairly and equally, regardless of her personal feelings toward them.⟩

syn act (toward), be (to), deal (with), handle, serve, use

rel consider, esteem, rate, reckon, regard, view; engage (with), react (to), respond (to)

phrases do by

2 to deal with (something) usually skillfully or efficiently — see HANDLE 1

3 to exchange viewpoints or seek advice

for the purpose of finding a solution to a problem — see CONFER 2

4 to give medical treatment to — see DOCTOR 1

treat (of) *vb* to have (something) as a subject matter — see CONCERN 1

treaty *n* a formal agreement between two or more nations or peoples ⟨In accordance with a *treaty* between the United States and the tribes of the Pacific Northwest, commercial fishing of certain kinds of salmon is limited to Indigenous people.⟩

syn accord, alliance, compact, convention, covenant, pact

rel entente; bargain, bond, charter, concord, contract, deal, settlement, understanding

treble *adj* **1** having a high musical pitch or range — see SHRILL

2 having three units or parts — see TRIPLE

trek *n* a going from one place to another usually of some distance — see JOURNEY

trek *vb* to take a trip especially of some distance — see TRAVEL 1

tremble *n* an instance of shaking involuntarily with fear or cold — see SHIVER 1

trembling *adj* marked by or given to small uncontrollable bodily movements — see SHAKY 1

trembling *n* a series of slight movements by a body back and forth or from side to side — see VIBRATION 1

tremendous *adj* unusually large — see HUGE

tremendously *adv* to a large extent or degree — see GREATLY 2

tremor *n* a shaking of the earth — see EARTHQUAKE 1

tremulous *adj* **1** easily frightened — see SHY 1

2 marked by or given to small uncontrollable bodily movements — see SHAKY 1

trench *n* a long narrow channel dug in the earth — see DITCH

trenchant *adj* having an edge thin enough to cut or pierce something — see SHARP 1

trend *n* **1** a prevailing or general movement or inclination ⟨According to the survey, there's a growing *trend* for companies to offer flexible hours.⟩

syn current, direction, drift, leaning, run, tendency, tide, wind

rel curve, shift, swing, turn, upside; custom, habit, propensity, tenor, way; countercurrent, countertrend; undercurrent, undertow

2 a practice or interest that is very popular for a short time — see FAD

trend *vb* **1** to show a liking or proneness (for something) — see LEAN 2

2 to turn away from a straight line or course — see CURVE 1

trendy *adj* being in the latest or current fashion — see STYLISH

trepidation *n* the emotion experienced in the presence or threat of danger — see FEAR 1

trespass *n* **1** a breaking of a moral or legal code — see OFFENSE 1

2 a failure to uphold the requirements of law, duty, or obligation — see BREACH 1

trespass *vb* to commit an offense — see OFFEND 1

triad *n* a group of three — see THREESOME

triadic *adj* having three units or parts — see TRIPLE

trial *adj* made or done as an experiment — see EXPERIMENTAL 1

trial *n* **1** a test of faith, patience, or strength ⟨Living with her insufferable relatives was a real *trial*.⟩

syn cross, crucible, fire, gauntlet (*also* gantlet), ordeal

rel baptism, initiation; adversity, affliction, asperity, misadventure, mischance, misfortune, mishap, privation, tragedy, tribulation, trouble, vicissitude, woe; challenge, complication, difficulty, hardship, rigor; annoyance, discomfort, inconvenience, nuisance

phrases baptism of fire

2 a private performance or session in preparation for a public appearance — see REHEARSAL

3 a procedure or operation carried out to resolve an uncertainty — see EXPERIMENT

4 an effort to do or accomplish something — see ATTEMPT 1

5 something that is a source of irritation — see ANNOYANCE 3

tribal *adj* of, relating to, or reflecting the traits exhibited by a group of people with a common ancestry and culture — see RACIAL

tribe *n* a group of persons who come from the same ancestor — see FAMILY 1

tribulation *n* a state of great suffering of body or mind — see DISTRESS 1

tribunal *n* an assembly of persons for the administration of justice — see COURT 3

tribute *n* a formal expression of praise — see ENCOMIUM

trice *n* a very small space of time — see INSTANT

trick *n* **1** a clever often underhanded means to achieve an end ⟨He used every *trick* in the book to get out of appearing in the charity's fashion show.⟩

syn artifice, device, dodge, gimmick, jig, knack, play, ploy, scheme, sleight, stratagem, wile

rel bluff, feint; chicanery, craft, cunning, duplicity, fakery, jugglery, legerdemain, skulduggery (*or* skullduggery); subterfuge, swindling, trickery; fraud, hoax, sham, swindle; blind, front, smoke screen

phrases sleight of hand

2 a playful or mischievous act intended as a joke — see PRANK

3 a usual manner of behaving or doing — see HABIT 1

4 an act of notable skill, strength, or cleverness — see FEAT 1

5 an odd or peculiar habit — see IDIOSYNCRASY

trick *vb* to cause to believe what is untrue — see DECEIVE

trickery *n* the use of clever underhanded actions to achieve an end ⟨Delia resorted to *trickery*—even loading up the fishing equipment—to induce her dog into the car for his vet appointment.⟩

syn artifice, chicanery, hanky-panky, jugglery, legerdemain, skulduggery (*or* skullduggery), subterfuge, wile

rel artlessness, caginess (*also* cageyness), craftiness, cunning, deviousness, foxiness, oiliness, shadiness, sharpness, shiftiness, shrewdness, slickness, slipperiness, slyness, sneakiness, treachery, underhandedness, williness; crookedness, deceit, deceitfulness, dishonesty, dissimulation, double-dealing, duplicity, guile, hypocrisy, insincerity; fakery, humbuggery, imposture, quackery; design, plotting

near ant artlessness, forthrightness, guilelessness, ingenuousness, sincerity; candidness, candor, directness, openness, plainness

trickle *vb* 1 to fall or let fall in or as if in drops — see DRIP

2 to flow in a broken irregular stream — see GURGLE

trickster *n* 1 a dishonest person who uses clever means to cheat others out of something of value ⟨A heartless *trickster* swindled the elderly woman out of her life savings.⟩

syn cheat, cheater, cozener, defrauder, dodger, hoaxer, shark, sharper, swindler

rel double-crosser; bluffer, charlatan, fake, faker, humbug, impostor (*or* imposter), mountebank, phony (*also* phoney), pretender, quack, ringer, sham; adventurer, fox, knave, prankster, rascal, rogue; slicker, smoothy (*or* smoothie), wheeler-dealer; plotter, schemer, sneak

2 one who practices tricks and illusions for entertainment — see MAGICIAN 2

tricky *adj* 1 requiring exceptional skill or caution in performance or handling ⟨a *tricky* musical passage for the woodwind section⟩

syn catchy, delicate, difficult, hairy, knotty, nasty, prickly, problematic (*also* problematical), sensitive, spiny, sticky, thorny, ticklish, touchy, tough

rel abstract, abstruse, complex, complicated, hard, intricate, involved, recondite, serious; problem, troublesome, troublous, vexatious, vexing, worrisome; burdensome, demanding, exacting, inconvenient, onerous, oppressive, painful, stressful

near ant easy, effortless, manageable, simple, straightforward, uncomplicated, undemanding

2 clever at attaining one's ends by indirect and often deceptive means — see ARTFUL 1

tried *adj* worthy of one's trust — see DEPENDABLE

tried–and–true *adj* worthy of one's trust — see DEPENDABLE

trifle *n* something of little importance ⟨Let us not speak of *trifles* when our nation may be going to war.⟩

syn child's play, nothing, picayune, shuck(s), triviality

rel naught (*also* nought), smoke, zero; peanuts, pittance, song, straw, two bits; bunk, claptrap, drivel, folly, fudge, hogwash, humbug, humbuggery, nonsense, piffle, rot, trash

trifle *vb* 1 to show a sexual attraction for someone just for fun — see FLIRT 1

2 to spend time in aimless activity — see FIDDLE (AROUND)

trifle (away) *vb* to use up carelessly — see WASTE 1

trifling *adj* 1 lacking importance — see UNIMPORTANT

2 so small or unimportant as to warrant little or no attention — see NEGLIGIBLE 1

trigger *vb* to cause to function — see ACTIVATE

trill *vb* to sing with the alternation of two musical tones — see WARBLE

trim *adj* being clean and in good order — see NEAT 1

trim *n* 1 a state of being or fitness — see CONDITION 1

2 something that decorates or beautifies — see DECORATION 1

trim *vb* 1 to achieve a victory over — see BEAT 2

2 to defeat by a large margin — see WHIP 1

3 to make (something) shorter or smaller with the use of a cutting instrument — see CLIP 1

4 to make more attractive by adding something that is beautiful or becoming — see DECORATE

trimmer *n* one that defeats an enemy or opponent — see VICTOR 1

trimming *n* failure to win a contest — see DEFEAT 1

trinity *n* a group of three — see THREESOME

trinket *n* a small object displayed for its attractiveness or interest — see KNICK-KNACK

trio *n* a group of three — see THREESOME

trip *n* 1 a going from one place to another usually at some distance — see JOURNEY

2 an unintentional departure from truth or accuracy — see ERROR 1

trip *vb* 1 to go at a pace faster than a walk — see RUN 1

2 to go down from an upright position suddenly and involuntarily — see FALL 1

3 to move with a light springing step — see SKIP 1

4 to make a mistake — see ERR 1

tripartite *adj* having three units or parts — see TRIPLE

triple *adj* having three units or parts ⟨a *triple* scoop of chocolate ice cream⟩

syn threefold, treble, triadic, tripartite, triplex

rel triplicate

triple *n* a group of three — see THREESOME

triplet *n* a group of three — see THREESOME

triplex *adj* having three units or parts — see TRIPLE

trippingly *adv* in a quick and spirited manner — see GAILY 2

trite *adj* used or heard so often as to be dull — see STALE 1

triumph *n* 1 a successful result brought about by hard work — see ACCOMPLISHMENT 1

2 an instance of defeating an enemy or opponent — see VICTORY

triumph *vb* 1 to achieve victory (as in a contest) — see WIN 1

2 to feel or express joy or triumph — see EXULT

triumph (over) *vb* to achieve a victory over — see BEAT 2

triumphant *adj* **1** having attained a desired end or state of good fortune — see SUCCESSFUL 1

2 having or expressing feelings of joy or triumph — see EXULTANT

triumvirate *n* a group of three — see THREESOME

trivial *adj* **1** lacking importance — see UNIMPORTANT

2 so small or unimportant as to warrant little or no attention — see NEGLIGIBLE 1

triviality *n* something of little importance — see TRIFLE

troll *n* an imaginary being usually having a small human form and magical powers — see FAIRY

tromp *vb* **1** to move heavily or clumsily — see LUMBER 1

2 to tread on heavily so as to crush or injure — see TRAMPLE

3 to travel by foot for exercise or pleasure — see HIKE 1

troop *n* **1** an organized group of stage performers — see COMPANY 1

2 **troops** *pl* the combined army, air force, and navy of a nation — see ARMED FORCES

tropical *adj* being near the equator — see LOW 1

trot *vb* **1** to go at a pace faster than a walk — see RUN 1

2 to proceed or move quickly — see HURRY 2

troth *n* **1** a person's solemn declaration that he or she will or will not do something — see PROMISE

2 adherence to something to which one is bound by a pledge or duty — see FIDELITY

troth *vb* to obligate by prior agreement — see PLEDGE 1

trouble *n* **1** an abnormal state that disrupts a plant's or animal's normal bodily functioning — see DISEASE

2 something that may cause injury or harm — see DANGER 2

3 something that requires thought and skill for resolution — see PROBLEM 1

4 the active use of energy in producing a result — see EFFORT

5 the state of not being protected from injury, harm, or evil — see DANGER 1

trouble *vb* **1** to experience concern or anxiety — see WORRY 1

2 to cause discomfort to or trouble for — see INCONVENIENCE

troubled *adj* feeling or showing uncomfortable feelings of uncertainty — see NERVOUS 1

troublesome *adj* causing worry or anxiety ⟨the *troublesome* news that there will be more cuts in the school budget⟩

syn discomforting, discomposing, disquieting, distressing, disturbing, nasty, perturbing, troubling, troublous, unsettling, upsetting, worrisome

rel daunting, demoralizing, discomfiting, disconcerting, discouraging, disheartening, dismaying, dispiriting; chilling, frightening, scary; alarming, dire, direful, dread, dreadful, fearful, fearsome, forbidding, formidable, frightening, frightful, ghastly, hair-raising, horrendous, horrible, horrifying, intimidating, scary, shocking, terrible, terrifying

near ant calming, quieting, settling, soothing; comforting, consoling, lulling, narcotic, pacifying, relaxing, sedative, tranquilizing (*also* tranquillizing)

ant reassuring

troubling *adj* causing worry or anxiety — see TROUBLESOME

troublous *adj* causing worry or anxiety — see TROUBLESOME

trough *n* **1** a long hollow cylinder for carrying a substance (as a liquid or gas) — see PIPE 1

2 a long narrow channel dug in the earth — see DITCH

3 a pipe or channel for carrying off water from a roof — see GUTTER 1

trounce *vb* to defeat by a large margin — see WHIP 2

trouncing *n* failure to win a contest — see DEFEAT 1

troupe *n* an organized group of stage performers — see COMPANY 1

trouper *n* one who acts professionally (as in a play, movie, or television show) — see ACTOR 1

trousers *n pl* an outer garment covering each leg separately from waist to ankle — see PANTS

truce *n* a temporary stopping of fighting ⟨Both sides agreed to a 24-hour *truce* beginning at midnight on Christmas Eve.⟩

syn armistice, cease-fire

rel accord, reconcilement, reconciliation; détente (*or* detente); peace, peacetime

near ant conflict, hostilities, hot war, war

truck *n* **1** a giving or taking of one thing of value in return for another — see EXCHANGE 1

2 discarded or useless material — see GARBAGE

truculence *n* **1** an inclination to fight or quarrel — see BELLIGERENCE

2 disposition to willfully inflict pain and suffering on others — see CRUELTY

truculent *adj* **1** feeling or displaying eagerness to fight — see BELLIGERENT

2 marked by harsh insulting language — see ABUSIVE

3 having or showing the desire to inflict severe pain and suffering on others — see CRUEL 1

trudge *vb* **1** to move heavily or clumsily — see LUMBER 1

2 to proceed or act clumsily or ineffectually — see FLOUNDER 1

true *adj* **1** being exactly as appears or as claimed — see AUTHENTIC 1

2 being in agreement with the truth or a fact or a standard — see CORRECT 1

3 existing in fact and not merely as a possibility — see ACTUAL

4 firm in one's allegiance to someone or something — see FAITHFUL 1

---

syn synonym(s)   *rel* related words
ant antonym(s)   *near ant* near antonym(s)

5 following an original exactly — see FAITHFUL 2

6 free from any intent to deceive or impress others — see GUILELESS

7 restricted to or based on fact — see FACTUAL 1

8 worthy of one's trust — see DEPENDABLE

9 having or showing the qualities associated with the members of a particular group or kind — see TYPICAL 1

true–blue *adj* firm in one's allegiance to someone or something — see FAITHFUL 1

truism *n* an idea or expression that has been used by many people — see COMMONPLACE

truly *adv* **1** not merely this but also — see EVEN 1

2 to tell the truth — see ACTUALLY 1

3 without any question — see INDEED 1

4 in actual fact — see VERY 2

trumpery *adj* of low quality — see CHEAP 2

trumpery *n* language, behavior, or ideas that are absurd and contrary to good sense — see NONSENSE 1

trumpet *vb* **1** to make known openly or publicly — see ANNOUNCE

2 to praise or publicize lavishly and often excessively — see TOUT 1

truncate *vb* to make less in extent or duration — see SHORTEN

truncheon *n* a heavy rigid stick used as a weapon or for punishment — see CLUB 1

trunk *n* a covered rectangular container for storing or transporting things — see CHEST

truss *vb* to gather into a tight mass by means of a line or cord — see TIE 1

trust *n* **1** firm belief in the integrity, ability, effectiveness, or genuineness of someone or something ⟨a relationship of mutual *trust* between lawyer and client⟩
syn confidence, credence, faith, stock
rel acceptance, assurance, assuredness, certainty, certitude, conviction, positiveness, sureness, surety; credit, dependence (*also* dependance), hope, reliance
near ant disbelief, incredulity, unbelief; distrustfulness, doubt, dubiousness, incertitude, misgiving, mistrustfulness, nonconfidence, skepticism, suspicion, uncertainness, uncertainty; disenchantment, disillusion, disillusionment
ant distrust, mistrust

2 a number of businesses or enterprises united for commercial advantage — see CARTEL

3 responsibility for the safety and well-being of someone or something — see CUSTODY

4 the right to take possession of goods before paying for them — see CREDIT 1

trust *vb* **1** to give a task, duty, or responsibility to — see ENTRUST 1

2 to put (something) into the possession or safekeeping of another — see GIVE 2

3 to regard as right or true — see BELIEVE 1

trustful *adj* having or showing trust in another — see TRUSTING 1

trusting *adj* **1** having or showing trust in another ⟨Delia couldn't look into her dog's *trusting* eyes as she drove him to the vet.⟩
syn confiding, trustful

rel artless, childlike, credulous, guileless, gullible (*also* gullable), innocent, naive (*or* naïve), simple, unsophisticated; dependent, hopeful, reliant; accepting, believing, certain, confident, convinced, overconfident, secure, sure, unquestioning, unsuspecting, unsuspicious, unwary
near ant disbelieving, incredulous, unbelieving, unconvinced, undecided, unpersuaded; dubious, hesitant, leery (*also* leary), oversuspicious, skeptical, suspicious, uncertain, unsure, wary
ant distrustful, doubtful, doubting, mistrustful, trustless, untrusting

2 readily taken advantage of — see EASY 2

trustworthiness *n* worthiness as the recipient of another's trust or confidence — see RELIABILITY

trustworthy *adj* worthy of one's trust — see DEPENDABLE

trusty *adj* worthy of one's trust — see DEPENDABLE

truth *n* agreement with fact or reality ⟨There is no *truth* to the rumor that the business is moving to another state.⟩
syn factuality, verity
rel accuracy, actuality, authenticity, correctness; credibility, honesty, trustiness, trustworthiness, truthfulness, veracity; dependability, reliability
near ant erroneousness, fallaciousness, fallacy; falsehood, fiction, half-truth, lie; impreciseness, imprecision, inaccuracy, incorrectness, inexactitude, inexactness; deceit, dishonesty, equivocation, lying, mendacity, prevarication, untruthfulness
ant falseness, falsity, untruth

truthful *adj* being in the habit of telling the truth ⟨a *truthful* youngster who wouldn't just make up a story like that⟩
syn honest, veracious
rel candid, direct, forthcoming, forthright, foursquare, frank, free-spoken, open, openhearted, out-front, outspoken, plain, plainspoken; believable, credible, true, veritable; artless, earnest, genuine, guileless, unaffected, unpretending, unpretentious; conscientious, moral, principled, scrupulous; aboveboard, dependable, reliable, trustworthy, trusty
near ant fallacious, false, untrue; unbelievable, undependable, unreliable, unscrupulous, untrustworthy; bluffing, dissembling, dissimulating, equivocating, hypocritical, insincere, posing, pretending; artful, deceitful, deceptive, devious, evasive, slick, slippery, sly, sneaky, treacherous, tricky, underhanded, wily
ant dishonest, fibbing, lying, mendacious, prevaricating, untruthful

truthfully *adv* to tell the truth — see ACTUALLY 1

truthfulness *n* devotion to telling the truth — see HONESTY 1

try *n* an effort to do or accomplish something — see ATTEMPT 1

try *vb* **1** to subject (a personal quality or faculty) to often excessive stress ⟨You're *trying* my patience!⟩
syn strain, stretch, tax, test
rel demand, exact, importune, press, pressure, push; aggravate, agitate, annoy, bother, exasperate, gall, get (to), gnaw

(at), grate, harry, hassle, irk, irritate, nettle, pain, peeve, pester, rile, spite, vex

2 to make an effort to do — see ATTEMPT

try (out) *vb* to put (something) to a test ⟨Want to *try out* my new skateboard?⟩ ⟨*tried out* his skill at archery⟩
syn sample, test
rel check (out), examine, experiment (with), explore, feel (out), investigate, research, study; resample, retest

trying *adj* difficult to endure — see HARSH 1

tryst *n* an agreement to be present at a specified time and place — see ENGAGEMENT 2

tsk–tsk *vb* to hold an unfavorable opinion of — see DISAPPROVE (OF)

tubby *adj* having an excess of body fat — see FAT 1

tube *n* a long hollow cylinder for carrying a substance (as a liquid or gas) — see PIPE 1

tucker (out) *vb* to use up all the physical energy of — see EXHAUST 1

tuckered (out) *adj* depleted in strength, energy, or freshness — see WEARY 1

tug *n* the act or an instance of applying force on something so that it moves in the direction of the force — see PULL 1

tug *vb* **1** to cause to follow by applying steady force on — see PULL 1

2 to devote serious and sustained effort — see LABOR

tug-of-war *n* an earnest effort for superiority or victory over another — see CONTEST 1

tumble *n* **1** an unorganized collection or mixture of various things — see MISCELLANY 1

2 the act of going down from an upright position suddenly and involuntarily — see FALL 1

3 a state in which everything is out of order — see CHAOS

tumble *vb* **1** to go down from an upright position suddenly and involuntarily — see FALL 1

2 to go to a lower level especially abruptly — see DROP 2

3 to undo the proper order or arrangement of — see DISORDER

4 to fall down or in as a result of physical pressure — see COLLAPSE 1

tumble (to) *vb* to have a clear idea of — see COMPREHEND 1

tumbled *adj* lacking in order, neatness, and often cleanliness — see MESSY

tumbledown *adj* showing signs of advanced wear and tear and neglect — see SHABBY 1

tummy *n* the part of the body between the chest and the pelvis — see STOMACH 1

tumor *n* an abnormal mass of tissue — see GROWTH 1

tumult *n* **1** a state of noisy, confused activity — see COMMOTION

2 a violent disturbance (as of the political or social order) — see CONVULSION

3 a violent shouting — see CLAMOR 1

tumultuous *adj* **1** marked by sudden or violent disturbance — see CONVULSIVE 1

2 marked by turmoil or disturbance especially of natural elements — see WILD 3

3 marked by bursts of destructive force or intense activity — see VIOLENT 1

tundra *n* a broad area of level or rolling treeless country — see PLAIN 1

tune *n* **1** a rhythmic series of musical tones arranged to give a pleasing effect — see MELODY

2 a state of consistency — see CONFORMITY 1

3 an approximate amount, extent, or degree — see NEIGHBORHOOD 1

tuneful *adj* having a pleasing mixture of notes — see HARMONIOUS 1

turbid *adj* having visible particles in liquid suspension — see CLOUDY 1

turbulent *adj* **1** marked by bursts of destructive force or intense activity — see VIOLENT 1

2 marked by turmoil or disturbance especially of natural elements — see WILD 3

3 marked by wet and windy conditions — see FOUL 1

4 marked by sudden or violent disturbance — see CONVULSIVE 1

turkey *n* **1** a person who lacks good sense or judgment — see FOOL 1

2 a stupid person — see IDIOT

3 something that has failed — see FAILURE 3

turmoil *n* **1** a disturbed or uneasy state — see UNREST

2 a state of noisy, confused activity — see COMMOTION

turn *n* **1** a relaxed journey on foot for exercise or pleasure — see WALK 1

2 an act of kind assistance — see FAVOR 1

3 a habitual attraction to some activity or thing — see INCLINATION 1

4 something that curves or is curved — see BEND 1

5 a sudden experiencing of a physical or mental disorder — see ATTACK 2

6 a performance regularly presented by an individual or group — see ACT 1

turn *vb* **1** to move (something) in a curved or circular path on or as if on an axis ⟨*turned* the doorknob as quietly as possible⟩
syn pivot, revolve, roll, rotate, spin, swing, swirl, twirl, twist, wheel, whirl
rel screw, unscrew; twiddle; coil, crank, reel, wind; circulate

2 to change the course or direction of (something) ⟨The dog *turned* the stampeding flock of sheep around.⟩ ⟨He *turned* his cart uphill.⟩
syn deflect, divert, swing, veer, wheel, whip
rel avert, deviate, move, rechannel, shift, shunt, sidetrack, swerve, switch, transfer; twist, whirl, zigzag; bend, curve, sway; reverse

3 to change one's course or direction ⟨We *turned* left at the light.⟩ ⟨The storm unexpectedly *turned* south and missed our area.⟩
syn detour, deviate, diverge, sheer, swerve, swing, turn off, veer, wheel
rel tack, zigzag; double (back)

4 to eventually have as a state or quality — see BECOME

---

syn synonym(s)   **rel** related words
ant antonym(s)   **near ant** near antonym(s)

5 to move in circles around an axis or center — see SPIN 1

6 to give serious and careful thought to — see PONDER

7 to be determined by, based on, or subject (to) — see DEPEND 1

8 to be in a confused state as if from being twirled around — see SPIN 2

9 to cause to have often negative opinions formed without sufficient knowledge — see PREJUDICE

turn (to) *vb* to use or seek out as a source of aid, relief, or advantage — see RESORT (TO) 1

turncoat *n* one who betrays a trust or an allegiance — see TRAITOR

turn down *vb* to show unwillingness to accept, do, engage in, or agree to — see DECLINE 1

turn in *vb* **1** to give (something) over to the control or possession of another usually under duress — see SURRENDER 1

2 to go to one's bed in order to sleep — see BED 1

turning point *n* a point in a chain of events at which an important change (as in one's fortunes) occurs ⟨The *turning point* came when Victor finally admitted he was a werewolf.⟩

syn climax, corner, landmark, milestone
rel break, clincher, crusher, highlight, topper; conversion, metamorphosis, transfiguration, transformation; clutch, crisis, crossroad(s), crunch, emergency, head, juncture, zero hour

turn off *vb* **1** to cause to feel disgust — see DISGUST

2 to change one's course or direction — see TURN 3

3 to let go from office, service, or employment — see DISMISS 1

4 to cause to stop functioning — see DEACTIVATE

turn-on *n* something that persuades one to perform an action for pleasure or gain — see LURE 1

turn on *vb* **1** to cause a pleasurable stimulation of the feelings of — see THRILL

2 to cause to function — see ACTIVATE

turn out *vb* **1** to leave one's bed — see ARISE 1

2 to remove the dirt from — see CLEAN 1

3 to drive or force out — see EJECT 1

4 to come to be — see COME OUT 1

turn over *vb* **1** to give (something) over to the control or possession of another usually under duress — see SURRENDER 1

2 to put (something) into the possession or safekeeping of another — see GIVE 2

3 to turn on one's side or upside down — see CAPSIZE

4 to change the position of (an object) so that the opposite side or end is showing — see REVERSE 1

turnpike *n* a passage cleared for public vehicular travel — see WAY 1

turn up *vb* **1** to come into view — see APPEAR 1

2 to get to a destination — see COME 2

3 to come upon after searching, study, or effort — see FIND 1

tussle *n* a physical dispute between opposing individuals or groups — see FIGHT 1

tussle *vb* to seize and attempt to unbalance one another for the purpose of achieving physical mastery — see WRESTLE

tutelage *n* the act or process of imparting knowledge or skills to another — see EDUCATION 1

tutor *vb* **1** to cause to acquire knowledge or skill in some field — see TEACH

2 to give advice and instruction to (someone) regarding the course or process to be followed — see GUIDE 1

tutoring *n* the act or process of imparting knowledge or skills to another — see EDUCATION 1

twaddle *n* language, behavior, or ideas that are absurd and contrary to good sense — see NONSENSE 1

twain *n* two things of the same or similar kind that match or are considered together — see PAIR

tweet *vb* to make a short sharp sound like a small bird — see CHIRP

twerp *n* a person of no importance or influence — see NOBODY

twice *adv* to two times the amount or degree — see DOUBLY 1

twilight *n* **1** a time or place of little or no light — see DARK 1

2 the time from when the sun begins to set to the onset of total darkness — see DUSK 1

twin *adj* consisting of two members or parts that are usually joined — see DOUBLE 1

twin *n* **1** either of a pair matched in one or more qualities — see MATE 1

2 something or someone that strongly resembles another — see IMAGE 1

twine *vb* to follow a circular or spiral course — see WIND 1

twinge *n* a sharp unpleasant sensation usually felt in some specific part of the body — see PAIN 1

twinkle *n* a very small space of time — see INSTANT

twinkle *vb* **1** to shine with light at regular intervals — see BLINK 1

2 to shoot forth bursts of light — see FLASH 1

twinkling *n* a very small space of time — see INSTANT

twirl *n* a rapid turning about on an axis or central point — see SPIN 1

twirl *vb* **1** to turn (something) in a curved or circular path on or as if on an axis — see TURN 1

2 to move in circles around an axis or center — see SPIN 1

twist *n* **1** a forceful rotating or pulling motion for the purpose of dislodging something — see WRENCH 1

2 an odd or peculiar habit — see IDIOSYNCRASY

twist *vb* **1** to change so much as to create a wrong impression or alter the meaning of — see GARBLE

2 to follow a circular or spiral course — see WIND 1

3 to move (something) in a curved or circular path on or as if on an axis — see TURN 1

4 to move by or as if by a forceful rotation — see WRENCH 1

758   twisted

5 to make jerky or restless movements — see FIDGET

6 to cause to twine about one another — see INTERTWINE 1

twisted *adj* marked by a long series of irregular curves — see CROOKED 1

twisting *adj* marked by a long series of irregular curves — see CROOKED 1

twisting *n* a forceful rotating or pulling motion for the purpose of dislodging something — see WRENCH 1

twitch *vb* **1** to make jerky or restless movements — see FIDGET

2 to move or cause to move with a sharp quick motion — see JERK 1

twitching *n* a series of slight movements by a body back and forth or from side to side — see VIBRATION 1

twitter *n* **1** a state of nervous or irritated concern — see FRET

2 an explosive sound that is a sign of amusement — see LAUGH 1

twitter *vb* **1** to engage in casual or rambling conversation — see CHAT 1

2 to make a short sharp sound like a small bird — see CHIRP

3 to show mirth with an explosive vocal sound — see LAUGH 1

two-faced *adj* not being or expressing what one appears to be or express — see INSINCERE

twofold *adj* **1** being twice as great or as many — see DOUBLE 2

2 consisting of two members or parts that are usually joined — see DOUBLE 1

twofold *adv* to two times the amount or degree — see DOUBLY

twosome *n* two things of the same or similar kind that match or are considered together — see PAIR

tycoon *n* a person of rank, power, or influence in a particular field — see MAGNATE

type *n* **1** a number of persons or things that are grouped together because they have something in common — see SORT 1

2 one of the units into which a whole is divided on the basis of a common characteristic — see CLASS 2

type *vb* to arrange or assign according to type — see CLASSIFY 1

typical *adj* **1** having or showing the qualities associated with the members of a particular group or kind ⟨*typical* behavior for a two-year-old⟩

syn archetypal (*also* archetypical), average, characteristic, normal, regular, representative, standard, true

rel common, commonplace, conventional, customary, everyday, ordinary, usual, wonted, workaday; classic, textbook; expected, familiar, habitual, predictable, routine, unexceptional, unremarkable; predominant, preponderant

near ant uncommon, unconventional, uncustomary, unusual, unwonted; distinctive, especial, exceptional, extraordinary, infrequent, noteworthy, rare, remarkable, singular, special, unexpected, unfamiliar, unique, unpredictable; eccentric, idiosyncratic, peculiar, unorthodox; curious, odd, oddball, offbeat, outlandish, quirky, screwy, strange, wacky (*also* whacky), way-out; bizarre, fantastic (*also* fantastical), far-out, freak, freakish, kooky (*also* kookie), out-of-the-way, outrageous, rare, unnatural, weird, wild

ant aberrant, abnormal, anomalous, atypical, deviant, irregular, nonrepresentative, nontypical, untypical

2 serving to identify as belonging to an individual or group — see CHARACTERISTIC 1

typically *adv* according to the usual course of things — see NATURALLY 2

tyrannical *also* **tyrannic** *adj* **1** exercising power or authority without interference by others — see ABSOLUTE 1

2 fond of ordering people around — see BOSSY

tyrannizer *n* a person who uses power or authority in a cruel, unjust, or harmful way — see DESPOT

tyrannous *adj* **1** exercising power or authority without interference by others — see ABSOLUTE 1

2 fond of ordering people around — see BOSSY

tyranny *n* a system of government in which the ruler has unlimited power — see DESPOTISM

tyrant *n* a person who uses power or authority in a cruel, unjust, or harmful way — see DESPOT

tyro *n* a person who is just starting out in a field of activity — see BEGINNER

ubiquitous *adj* **1** often observed or encountered — see COMMON 1

2 present in all places and at all times — see OMNIPRESENT

ugly *adj* **1** unpleasant to look at ⟨Her first attempt at painting was pretty *ugly*—a portrait of her sister that was not at all flattering.⟩

syn grotesque, hideous, homely, ill-favored, monstrous, unappealing, unattractive, unbeautiful, unhandsome, unlovely, unpleasing, unpretty, unsightly, vile

rel abhorrent, abominable, appalling, awful, distasteful, dreadful, gross, horrible, horrid, loathsome, nauseating, nauseous, noisome, repellent (*also* repellant), repugnant, repulsive, revolting, sickening

near ant shapely; imposing, impressive, prepossessing

ant aesthetic (*also* esthetic *or* aesthetical *or* esthetical), attractive, beauteous, beautiful, bonny (*also* bonnie) [*chiefly British*], comely, cute, fair, fetching, goodly, gorgeous,

---

syn synonym(s)   *rel* related words
ant antonym(s)   *near ant* near antonym(s)

handsome, knockout, lovely, pretty, ravishing, seemly, sightly, stunning, taking

2 causing intense displeasure, disgust, or resentment — see OFFENSIVE 1

ultimate *adj* **1** of the greatest or highest degree or quantity ⟨the *ultimate* speed yet attained by a land-based vehicle⟩

syn consummate, last, maximum, most, nth, outside, paramount, supreme, top, utmost, uttermost

rel unequaled (*or* unequalled), unmatched, unparalleled, unrivaled (*or* unrivalled), unsurpassed; biggest, hugest, largest; topmost, upmost, uppermost

near ant littlest; lowest

ant least, minimal, minimum, slightest

2 following all others of the same kind in order or time — see LAST 1

3 most distant from a center — see EXTREME 1

ultimately *adv* at a later time — see YET 1

ultimatum *n* something that someone insists upon having — see DEMAND 1

ultra *adj* being very far from the center of public opinion — see EXTREME 2

ultramodern *adj* being or involving the latest methods, concepts, information, or styles — see MODERN

ultramodernist *n* a person with very modern ideas — see MODERN

umbra *n* **1** a time or place of little or no light — see DARK 1

2 partial darkness due to the obstruction of light rays — see SHADE 1

umbrage *n* the feeling of being offended or resentful after a slight or indignity — see PIQUE 1

umpire *n* a person who impartially decides or resolves a dispute or controversy — see JUDGE 1

umpire *vb* to give an opinion about (something at issue or in dispute) — see JUDGE 1

unabashed *adj* not embarrassed or ashamed ⟨*Unabashed* by their booing and hissing, he continued with his musical performance.⟩

syn shameless, unashamed, unblushing, unembarrassed

rel prideful, proud; bold, brassy, brazen, cheeky, impudent, insolent, saucy; unapologetic, undaunted, undeterred, undismayed; unblinking, unflinching; impenitent, remorseless, unrepentant

near ant confused, discomfited, disconcerted, discountenanced, fazed, flustered, mortified, rattled; apologetic, contrite, penitent, remorseful, repentant, sorry

ant abashed, ashamed, embarrassed, hangdog, shamed, shamefaced, sheepish

unacceptable *adj* falling short of a standard — see BAD 1

unacceptably *adv* **1** beyond a normal or acceptable limit — see TOO 1

2 in an unsatisfactory way — see BADLY 1

unacclimated *adj* not having acquired a habit or tolerance — see UNUSED 1

unaccompanied *adj* not being in the company of others — see ALONE 1

unaccountable *adj* impossible to explain — see INEXPLICABLE

unaccustomed *adj* **1** not having acquired a habit or tolerance — see UNUSED 1

2 not known or experienced before — see NEW 2

3 noticeably different from what is generally found or experienced — see UNUSUAL 1

unacquainted *adj* not informed about or aware of something — see IGNORANT 2

unadapted *adj* not having acquired a habit or tolerance — see UNUSED 1

unadjusted *adj* not having acquired a habit or tolerance — see UNUSED 1

unadorned *adj* free from all additions or embellishment — see PLAIN 1

unadulterated *adj* **1** free from added matter — see PURE 1

2 having no exceptions or restrictions — see ABSOLUTE 2

unaesthetic *adj* disagreeable to one's aesthetic or artistic sense — see HARSH 1

unaffected *adj* free from any intent to deceive or impress others — see GUILELESS

unaffectedly *adv* without any attempt to impress by deception or exaggeration — see NATURALLY 3

unaided *adv* without aid or support — see ALONE 1

unalike *adj* being not of the same kind — see DIFFERENT 1

unalloyed *adj* **1** free from added matter — see PURE 1

2 having no exceptions or restrictions — see ABSOLUTE 2

unalterable *adj* not capable of changing or being changed — see INFLEXIBLE 1

unambiguous *adj* **1** not subject to misinterpretation or more than one interpretation — see CLEAR 2

2 so clearly expressed as to leave no doubt about the meaning — see EXPLICIT

unanimity *n* the state of being of one opinion about something — see AGREEMENT 1

unanimous *adj* having or marked by agreement in feeling or action — see HARMONIOUS 3

unanswerable *adj* not capable of being challenged or proved wrong — see IRREFUTABLE

unanticipated *adj* not expected — see UNEXPECTED

unappealing *adj* unpleasant to look at — see UGLY 1

unappeasable *adj* showing no signs of slackening or yielding in one's purpose — see UNYIELDING 1

unappetizing *adj* disagreeable or disgusting to the sense of taste — see DISTASTEFUL 1

unappreciated *adj* not likely to be appreciated by those who benefit — see THANKLESS 2

unappreciative *adj* not showing gratitude — see THANKLESS 1

unapproachable *adj* hard or impossible to get to or get at — see INACCESSIBLE

unapt *adj* **1** not appropriate for a particular occasion or situation — see INAPPROPRIATE

2 not likely to be true or to occur — see IMPROBABLE

unashamed *adj* **1** not embarrassed or ashamed — see UNABASHED

2 not sorry for having done wrong — see REMORSELESS 1

unasked *adj* not searched or asked for — see UNSOUGHT

unassailable *adj* not to be violated, criticized, or tampered with — see SACRED 1

unassisted *adv* without aid or support — see ALONE 1

unassuming *adj* not having or showing any feelings of superiority, self-assertiveness, or showiness — see HUMBLE 1

unattached *adj* **1** not married — see SINGLE 1
2 not physically attached to another unit — see SEPARATE 2

unattainable *adj* **1** hard or impossible to get to or get at — see INACCESSIBLE
2 incapable of being solved or accomplished — see IMPOSSIBLE

unattractive *adj* unpleasant to look at — see UGLY 1

unauthentic *adj* being such in appearance only and made or manufactured with the intention of committing fraud — see COUNTERFEIT 1

unavailable *adj* hard or impossible to get to or get at — see INACCESSIBLE

unavailing *adj* producing no results — see FUTILE

unavoidable *adj* impossible to avoid or evade — see INEVITABLE

unavoidably *adv* because of necessity — see NEEDS

unaware *adj* not informed about or aware of something — see IGNORANT 2

unaware *adv* without warning — see UNAWARES

unawareness *n* the state of being unaware or uninformed — see IGNORANCE 1

unawares *adv* without warning ⟨The thunderstorm caught us *unawares*, and we scrambled to get off the ridge as lightning started to flash.⟩
syn aback, suddenly, unaware, unexpectedly
rel abruptly, short; amazingly, astoundingly, surprisingly
phrases all of a sudden, off base
near ant laggardly, leisurely, slowly, sluggishly, tardily; obviously

unbalance *vb* to cause to go insane or as if insane — see CRAZE

unbalanced *adj* not being in or able to maintain a state of balance — see UNSTABLE 1

unbaptized *adj* not named or identified by a name — see NAMELESS 1

unbearable *adj* more than can be put up with ⟨This heat is *unbearable*—when are we going to get air-conditioning?⟩
syn insufferable, insupportable, intolerable, unendurable, unsupportable
rel unacceptable; crushing, overwhelming; comfortless, hard, harsh, painful, uncomfortable; appalling, dreadful, excruciating, gruesome (*also* gruesome), harrowing, horrendous, horrible, horrid, horrifying, nightmarish, shocking, terrible, tormenting, torturous, vile, wretched
near ant livable (*also* liveable); acceptable; adequate, admissible, allowable, reasonable, satisfactory

ant endurable, sufferable, supportable, sustainable, tolerable

unbeatable *adj* incapable of being defeated, overcome, or subdued — see INVINCIBLE

unbeautiful *adj* unpleasant to look at — see UGLY 1

unbecoming *adj* not appropriate for a particular occasion or situation — see INAPPROPRIATE

unbeknownst *also* **unbeknown** *adj* happening or existing without one's knowledge — see UNKNOWN 1

unbelief *n* refusal to accept something as true — see DISBELIEF

unbelievable *adj* too extraordinary or improbable to believe — see INCREDIBLE

unbeliever *n* a person who is always ready to doubt or question the truth or existence of something — see SKEPTIC

unbelieving *adj* inclined to doubt or question claims — see SKEPTICAL 1

unbend *vb* to cause to follow a line that is without bends or curls — see STRAIGHTEN

unbending *adj* **1** having or showing a lack of friendliness or interest in others — see COOL 1
2 sticking to an opinion, purpose, or course of action in spite of reason, arguments, or persuasion — see OBSTINATE

unbiased *adj* marked by justice, honesty, and freedom from bias — see FAIR 2

unbidden *also* **unbid** *adj* not searched or asked for — see UNSOUGHT

unbind *vb* **1** to disengage the knotted parts of — see UNTIE
2 to release (as from slavery or confinement) — see FREE 1

unblemished *adj* being entirely without fault or flaw — see PERFECT 1

unblock *vb* to rid the surface of (as an area) from things in the way — see CLEAR 1

unblushing *adj* not embarrassed or ashamed — see UNABASHED

unborn *adj* of a time after the present — see FUTURE

unbosom *vb* to make known (as information previously kept secret) — see REVEAL 1

unbound *adj* not bound, confined, or detained by force — see FREE 3

unbounded *adj* **1** being or seeming to be without limits — see INFINITE
2 showing no signs of being under control — see RAMPANT 1

unbraid *vb* to separate the various strands of — see UNRAVEL 1

unbridled *adj* showing no signs of being under control — see RAMPANT 1

unbroken *adj* **1** going on and on without any interruptions — see CONTINUOUS
2 living outdoors without taming or domestication by humans — see WILD 1

unbudging *adj* incapable of moving or being moved — see IMMOVABLE 1

unburden *vb* **1** to empty or rid of cargo — see UNLOAD 1
2 to set (a person or thing) free of something that encumbers — see RID

unburdened *adj* no longer burdened with something unpleasant or painful — see FREE 2

---

uncage *vb* to release (as from slavery or confinement) — see FREE 1

uncalled–for *adj* 1 not needed by the circumstances or to accomplish an end — see UNNECESSARY

2 showing a lack of manners or consideration for others — see IMPOLITE

uncanny *adj* 1 being beyond one's powers to know, understand, or explain — see MYSTERIOUS 1

2 being so extraordinary or abnormal as to suggest powers which violate the laws of nature — see SUPERNATURAL 2

3 fearfully and mysteriously strange or fantastic — see EERIE

uncataloged *adj* not appearing on a list — see UNLISTED

unceasing *adj* going on and on without any interruptions — see CONTINUOUS

uncelebrated *adj* not widely known — see OBSCURE 2

unceremonious *adj* 1 being or characterized by direct, brief, and potentially rude speech or manner — see BLUNT 1

2 not rigidly following established form, custom, or rules — see INFORMAL 1

uncertain *adj* 1 likely to change frequently, suddenly, or unexpectedly — see FICKLE 1

2 not feeling sure about the truth, wisdom, or trustworthiness of someone or something — see DOUBTFUL 1

uncertainty *n* a feeling or attitude that one does not know the truth, truthfulness, or trustworthiness of someone or something — see DOUBT

unchain *vb* to release (as from slavery or confinement) — see FREE 1

unchangeable *adj* not capable of changing or being changed — see INFLEXIBLE 1

unchangeableness *n* the state of continuing without change — see CONSTANCY 1

unchanging *adj* 1 not undergoing a change in condition — see CONSTANT 1

2 not varying — see UNIFORM

uncharitable *adj* 1 giving or sharing as little as possible — see STINGY 1

2 having or showing a lack of sympathy or tender feelings — see HARD 1

unchecked *adj* showing no signs of being under control — see RAMPANT 1

unchristened *adj* not named or identified by a name — see NAMELESS 1

uncivil *adj* 1 not civilized — see UNCIVILIZED

2 showing a lack of manners or consideration for others — see IMPOLITE

uncivilized *adj* not civilized ⟨Inaccurately characterized as *uncivilized* by early historians, the Indigenous peoples of the region had a sophisticated and advanced culture.⟩

syn barbarian, barbaric, barbarous, heathen, heathenish, Neanderthal (*or* Neandertal), rude, uncivil, uncultivated, wild

rel coarse, crude, primitive, rough; uncouth, uncultured

near ant cultured, enlightened, humane, sophisticated; genteel, polished, polite, refined, urbane, well-bred; semicivilized

ant civilized

unclad *adj* lacking or shed of clothing — see NAKED 1

unclean *adj* 1 having or showing lowered moral character or standards — see CORRUPT

2 not clean — see DIRTY 1

uncleanliness *n* the state or quality of being dirty — see DIRTINESS

uncleanly *adj* not clean — see DIRTY 1

uncleanness *n* the state or quality of being dirty — see DIRTINESS

unclear *adj* 1 not expressed in precise terms — see VAGUE 1

2 not seen or understood clearly — see FAINT 1

uncloak *vb* 1 to make known (as information previously kept secret) — see REVEAL 1

2 to reveal the true nature of — see EXPOSE 1

unclog *vb* 1 to make passage through (something) possible by removing obstructions — see OPEN 2

2 to free from obstruction or difficulty — see EASE 1

unclogged *adj* allowing passage without obstruction — see OPEN 1

unclose *vb* to change from a closed to an open position — see OPEN 1

unclosed *adj* allowing passage without obstruction — see OPEN 1

unclothe *vb* to remove clothing from — see UNDRESS 1

unclothed *adj* lacking or shed of clothing — see NAKED 1

unclouded *adj* not stormy or cloudy — see FAIR 1

uncluttered *adj* being clean and in good order — see NEAT 1

uncolored *adj* lacking an addition of color — see COLORLESS 1

uncomfortable *adj* 1 causing discomfort ⟨Unfortunately, dressing up for the dance meant wearing an *uncomfortable* shirt.⟩

syn comfortless, discomforting, harsh

rel aching, hurting, miserable, nasty, painful, sore; agonizing, excruciating, torturous; distressing, disturbing, upsetting; awkward, cumbersome, inconvenient, ungainly; uneasy; chafing, cramping, itching, pinching, pricking, prickling, smarting, stinging

near ant easy, soothing; cozy, cushy, snug, soft; easeful, relaxing, reposeful, restful

ant comfortable

2 causing embarrassment — see AWKWARD 3

3 lacking social grace and assurance — see AWKWARD 1

uncomic *adj* not joking or playful in mood or manner — see SERIOUS 1

uncommon *adj* 1 being out of the ordinary — see EXCEPTIONAL 1

2 noticeably different from what is generally found or experienced — see UNUSUAL 1

uncommunicative *adj* 1 deliberately refraining from speech — see SILENT 1

2 given to keeping one's activities hidden from public observation or knowledge — see SECRETIVE

3 tending not to speak frequently (as by habit or inclination) — see SILENT 2

uncomplaining *adj* accepting pains or hardships calmly or without complaint — see PATIENT 1

uncomplimentary *adj* intended to make a person or thing seem of little importance or value — see DEROGATORY

uncompromising *adj* **1** not allowing for any exceptions or loosening of standards — see RIGID 1

2 sticking to an opinion, purpose, or course of action in spite of reason, arguments, or persuasion — see OBSTINATE

unconcern *n* lack of interest or concern — see INDIFFERENCE

unconcerned *adj* **1** having or showing freedom from worries or troubles — see CAREFREE

2 having or showing a lack of interest or concern — see INDIFFERENT 1

unconditional *adj* having no exceptions or restrictions — see ABSOLUTE 2

unconfined *adj* not bound, confined, or detained by force — see FREE 3

uncongenial *adj* not giving pleasure to the mind or senses — see UNPLEASANT

unconnected *adj* **1** not clearly or logically connected — see INCOHERENT 1

2 not physically attached to another unit — see SEPARATE 2

unconquerable *adj* incapable of being defeated, overcome, or subdued — see INVINCIBLE

unconscionable *adj* **1** going beyond a normal or acceptable limit in degree or amount — see EXCESSIVE

2 not guided by or showing a concern for what is right — see UNPRINCIPLED

unconscious *adj* **1** having lost consciousness ⟨The guard was knocked *unconscious* by a blow to the head.⟩

syn cold, insensible, senseless

rel semiconscious; anesthetized; collapsed

near ant alert, awake, aware, up; resuscitated, revived

ant conscious

2 not informed about or aware of something — see IGNORANT 2

unconsidered *adj* made or done without previous thought or preparation — see EXTEMPORANEOUS

unconsolidated *adj* consisting of particles that do not stick together — see LOOSE 2

uncontrollable *adj* given to resisting control or discipline by others ⟨The *uncontrollable* child kept throwing tantrums in public and creating scenes.⟩

syn froward, headstrong, intractable, recalcitrant, refractory, ungovernable, unmanageable, unruly, untoward, wayward, willful (*or* wilful)

rel contrary, difficult, hardheaded, incorrigible, mulish, obdurate, obstinate, opinionated, perverse, pigheaded, self-willed, stiff, stiff-necked, stubborn; undisciplined, unpunished; uncontrolled, wild; boisterous, irrepressible, rambunctious, rowdy; disobedient, insubordinate, rebellious

phrases out of hand

near ant docile, obedient, well-behaved; compliant, placable, pliable, submissive, yielding; accepting, persuadable, receptive, responsive, willing; reasonable, temperate, trainable

ant controllable, governable, manageable, tractable

uncontrolled *adj* showing no signs of being under control — see RAMPANT 1

unconventional *adj* **1** deviating from commonly accepted beliefs or practices — see HERETICAL

2 not bound by traditional ways or beliefs — see LIBERAL 1

3 not rigidly following established form, custom, or rules — see INFORMAL 1

unconvinced *adj* not feeling sure about the truth, wisdom, or trustworthiness of someone or something — see DOUBTFUL 1

unconvincing *adj* too extraordinary or improbable to believe — see INCREDIBLE

uncooked *adj* not cooked — see RAW 1

uncork *vb* to set free (from a state of being held in check) — see RELEASE 1

uncountable *adj* too many to be counted — see COUNTLESS

uncounted *adj* too many to be counted — see COUNTLESS

uncouple *vb* to set or force apart — see SEPARATE 1

uncouth *adj* **1** having or showing crudely insensitive or impolite manners — see CLOWNISH

2 lacking in refinement or good taste — see COARSE 2

uncover *vb* **1** to make known (as information previously kept secret) — see REVEAL 1

2 to reveal the true nature of — see EXPOSE 1

uncovered *adj* lacking a usual or natural covering — see NAKED 2

uncritical *adj* lacking in worldly wisdom or informed judgment — see NAIVE 1

uncrown *vb* to remove from a position of prominence or power (as a throne) — see DEPOSE 1

unctuous *adj* **1** not being or expressing what one appears to be or express — see INSINCERE

2 overly or insincerely flattering — see FULSOME 1

uncultivated *adj* **1** existing without human habitation or cultivation — see WILD 2

2 lacking in refinement or good taste — see COARSE 2

3 not civilized — see UNCIVILIZED

uncultured *adj* lacking in refinement or good taste — see COARSE 2

uncurious *adj* having or showing a lack of interest or concern — see INDIFFERENT 1

uncurl *vb* to cause to follow a line that is without bends or curls — see STRAIGHTEN

uncustomary *adj* **1** being out of the ordinary — see EXCEPTIONAL 1

2 noticeably different from what is generally found or experienced — see UNUSUAL 1

undaunted *adj* feeling or displaying no fear by temperament — see BRAVE 1

undeceive *vb* to free from mistaken beliefs or foolish hopes — see DISILLUSION

undecided *adj* **1** not yet settled or decided — see PENDING 1

2 not feeling sure about the truth, wisdom, or trustworthiness of someone or something — see DOUBTFUL 1

---

syn synonym(s)   *rel* related words
ant antonym(s)   *near ant* near antonym(s)

undecorated *adj* free from all additions or embellishment — see PLAIN 1

undefended *adj* lacking protection from danger or resistance against attack — see HELPLESS 1

undefined *adj* not seen or understood clearly — see FAINT 1

undemonstrative *adj* not feeling or showing emotion — see IMPASSIVE 1

undeniable *adj* not capable of being challenged or proved wrong — see IRREFUTABLE

undeniably *adv* without any question — see INDEED 1

under *adv* in or to a lower place — see BELOW 1

under *prep* in a lower position than — see BELOW 1

underbelly *n* **1** the side or part facing downward from something — see BOTTOM 1

2 a vulnerable point — see ACHILLES' HEEL

underbody *n* the side or part facing downward from something — see BOTTOM 1

underclothes *n pl* clothing intended to be worn underneath other clothing — see UNDERWEAR

underclothing *n* clothing intended to be worn underneath other clothing — see UNDERWEAR

undercover *adj* **1** undertaken or done so as to escape being observed or known by others — see SECRET 1

2 working on missions in which one's objectives, activities, or true identity are not publicly revealed — see SECRET 2

undergarments *n pl* clothing intended to be worn underneath other clothing — see UNDERWEAR

undergo *vb* to come to a knowledge of (something) by living through it — see EXPERIENCE

underground *adj* undertaken or done so as to escape being observed or known by others — see SECRET 1

underground *n* a secret organization in a conquered country fighting against enemy forces — see RESISTANCE 2

underhand *adj* **1** given to or marked by cheating and deception — see DISHONEST 2

2 undertaken or done so as to escape being observed or known by others — see SECRET 1

underhanded *adj* **1** given to or marked by cheating and deception — see DISHONEST 2

2 undertaken or done so as to escape being observed or known by others — see SECRET 1

underline *vb* to make more apparent — see EMPHASIZE 2

underling *n* one who is of lower rank and typically under the authority of another ⟨The real estate tycoon has a whole army of *underlings* to attend to the details.⟩

syn inferior, junior, subordinate

rel attendant, follower, retainer; domestic, menial, steward; flunky (*also* flunkey *or* flunkie), henchman, lackey, minion; adjutant, aid, aide, assistant, coadjutor, deputy, second, second fiddle; helpmate, helpmeet, mate, sidekick

near ant boss, captain, chief, foreman, head, headman, helmsman, kingpin, leader, master, taskmaster

ant senior, superior

underlying *adj* of or relating to the simplest facts or theories of a subject — see ELEMENTARY

underneath *adv* in or to a lower place — see BELOW 1

underpart *n* the side or part facing downward from something — see BOTTOM 1

underpin *vb* to hold up or serve as a foundation for — see SUPPORT 3

underpinning *n* **1** an immaterial thing upon which something else rests — see BASE 1

2 a structure that holds up or serves as a foundation for something else — see SUPPORT 1

underprivileged *adj* kept from having the necessities of life or a healthful environment — see DEPRIVED

underscore *vb* to make more apparent — see EMPHASIZE 2

underside *n* the side or part facing downward from something — see BOTTOM 1

undersized *also* **undersize** *adj* of a size that is less than average — see SMALL 1

understand *vb* **1** to form an opinion or reach a conclusion through reasoning and information — see INFER 1

2 to have a practical understanding of — see KNOW 1

3 to have a clear idea of — see COMPREHEND 1

understanding *adj* having or showing the capacity for sharing the feelings of another — see SYMPATHETIC 1

understanding *n* **1** an arrangement about action to be taken — see AGREEMENT 2

2 the knowledge gained from the process of coming to know or understand something — see COMPREHENSION

understated *adj* not excessively showy — see QUIET 2

undersurface *n* the side or part facing downward from something — see BOTTOM 1

undertake *vb* to take to or upon oneself — see ASSUME 1

undertaker *n* a person who manages funerals and prepares the dead for burial or cremation — see FUNERAL DIRECTOR

underwater *adj* living, lying, or occurring below the surface of the water ⟨*Underwater* plants don't require as much light to grow as surface plants.⟩ ⟨a vessel designed for *underwater* exploration⟩

syn aquatic, submarine, submerged, sunken

rel oceanic; undersea; abysmal, abyssal, deep, deepwater

underwear *n* clothing intended to be worn underneath other clothing ⟨*Underwear* has got to be the most boring thing that one could ever receive as a birthday present!⟩

syn underclothes, underclothing, undergarments, undies

rel lingerie; panties; slip, underskirt; boxers, boxer shorts, briefs, drawers, long johns, pants, shorts, underdrawers, underpants, undershirt, undershorts, union suit;

nightdress, nightgown, nightshirt, pajamas, pj's

near ant outerwear

underweight *adj* having little weight — see ¹LIGHT 1

underwrite *vb* to provide money for — see FINANCE 1

undetermined *adj* **1** not seen or understood clearly — see FAINT 1

2 not yet settled or decided — see PENDING 1

undeviating *adj* not varying — see UNIFORM

undies *n pl* clothing intended to be worn underneath other clothing — see UNDERWEAR

undiluted *adj* free from added matter — see PURE 1

undisturbed *adj* free from emotional or mental agitation — see CALM 2

undivided *adj* not divided or scattered among several areas of interest or concern — see WHOLE 1

undo *vb* **1** to deprive of courage or confidence — see UNNERVE 1

2 to disengage the knotted parts of — see UNTIE

3 to trouble the mind of; to make uneasy — see DISTURB 1

undomesticated *adj* living outdoors without taming or domestication by humans — see WILD 1

undoubtedly *adv* without any question — see INDEED 1

undress *vb* **1** to remove clothing from ⟨I quickly *undressed* myself and pulled on a set of dry clothes.⟩

syn disrobe, strip, unclothe

rel bare, denude, expose, uncover, undrape, unveil; bark, flay, peel, skin

near ant apparel, array, attire, caparison, clothe, costume, cover, deck, dress, feather, garb, garment, invest, rig (out), vest; cloak, mantle; swaddle, swathe; accoutre (*or* accouter); equip, furnish, outfit

ant dress, gown, robe

2 to reveal the true nature of — see EXPOSE 1

undressed *adj* **1** being such as found in nature and not altered by processing or refining — see CRUDE 1

2 lacking or shed of clothing — see NAKED 1

undue *adj* going beyond a normal or acceptable limit in degree or amount — see EXCESSIVE

unduly *adv* beyond a normal or acceptable limit — see TOO 1

undyed *adj* lacking an addition of color — see COLORLESS 1

undying *adj* **1** having an existence or validity that does not change or diminish — see ABIDING

2 lasting forever — see EVERLASTING 1

uneager *adj* showing little or no interest or enthusiasm — see TEPID 1

unearth *vb* to remove from place of burial — see EXHUME

unearthing *n* the act or process of sighting or learning the existence of something for the first time — see DISCOVERY 1

unearthly *adj* **1** being so extraordinary or abnormal as to suggest powers which violate the laws of nature — see SUPERNATURAL 2

2 fearfully and mysteriously strange or fantastic — see EERIE

3 of, relating to, or being part of a reality beyond the observable physical universe — see SUPERNATURAL 1

uneasiness *n* **1** a disturbed or uneasy state — see UNREST

2 an uneasy state of mind usually over the possibility of an anticipated misfortune or trouble — see ANXIETY 1

uneasy *adj* **1** feeling or showing uncomfortable feelings of uncertainty — see NERVOUS 1

2 lacking or denying rest — see RESTLESS 1

3 lacking social grace and assurance — see AWKWARD 1

4 marked by or causing agitation or uncomfortable feelings — see NERVOUS 2

uneducated *adj* lacking in education or the knowledge gained from books — see IGNORANT 1

unembarrassed *adj* not embarrassed or ashamed — see UNABASHED

unemotional *adj* not feeling or showing emotion — see IMPASSIVE 1

unending *adj* lasting forever — see EVERLASTING 1

unendurable *adj* more than can be put up with — see UNBEARABLE

unenthusiastic *adj* showing little or no interest or enthusiasm — see TEPID 1

unequal *adj* not staying constant — see UNEVEN 2

unequaled *or* **unequalled** *adj* having no equal or rival for excellence or desirability — see ONLY 1

unequivocal *adj* **1** not subject to misinterpretation or more than one interpretation — see CLEAR 2

2 so clearly expressed as to leave no doubt about the meaning — see EXPLICIT

unerring *adj* not being or likely to be wrong — see INFALLIBLE 1

unescapable *adj* impossible to avoid or evade — see INEVITABLE

unessential *adj* not needed by the circumstances or to accomplish an end — see UNNECESSARY

unethical *adj* **1** not conforming to a high moral standard; morally unacceptable — see BAD 2

2 not guided by or showing a concern for what is right — see UNPRINCIPLED

uneven *adj* **1** not having a level or smooth surface ⟨The driveway is *uneven* and collects water in several large puddles whenever it rains.⟩

syn broken, bumpy, coarse, irregular, jagged, lumpy, pebbly, ragged, rough, roughened, rugged, scraggy

rel lopsided, unbalanced; inexact, unaligned; rutted, rutty, undulating, wavy; pitted, pocked; knobby, knurled, knurly, nubbly, nubby; burred, harsh, sandpapery, scraggly, scratchy

near ant exact, uniform; aligned (*also* alined), regular, true; horizontal, tabular; plumb, straight, vertical; flush

---

ant even, flat, level, plane, smooth

2 not staying constant ⟨The level of attendance at the ballpark has been very *uneven* this season.⟩

syn changing, erratic, fluctuating, irregular, unequal, unstable, unsteady, varying

rel capricious, changeable, changeful, choppy, fickle, fluid, inconsistent, inconstant, mercurial, mutable, uncertain, unsettled, variable, volatile

near ant regular

ant changeless, constant, stable, steady, unchanging, unvarying

3 inclined or twisted to one side — see AWRY

unexampled *adj* having no equal or rival for excellence or desirability — see ONLY 1

unexceptional *adj* being of the type that is encountered in the normal course of events — see ORDINARY 1

unexpected *adj* not expected ⟨The failure of the backup generator was *unexpected* and a contingency for which we weren't prepared.⟩

syn abrupt, sudden, unanticipated, unforeseen, unlooked-for

rel unintended, unplanned; improbable, unlikely; startling, surprising

near ant predicted, prophesied; unsurprising

ant anticipated, expected, foreseen

unexpectedly *adv* without warning — see UNAWARES

unexplainable *adj* impossible to explain — see INEXPLICABLE

unexpressed *adj* understood although not put into words — see IMPLICIT 1

unfailing *adj* **1** not being or likely to be wrong — see INFALLIBLE 1

2 not likely to fail — see INFALLIBLE 2

unfailingly *adv* on every relevant occasion — see ALWAYS 1

unfair *adj* not being in accordance with the rules or standards of what is fair in sport — see FOUL 2

unfairness *n* **1** a state of being unfair or unjust — see INJUSTICE 1

2 unfair or inadequate treatment of someone or something or an instance of this — see DISSERVICE

unfaithful *adj* not true in one's allegiance to someone or something — see FAITHLESS

unfaithfulness *n* **1** lack of faithfulness especially to one's husband or wife — see INFIDELITY 1

2 the act or fact of violating the trust or confidence of another — see BETRAYAL

3 a sexual encounter or relationship between a married person and someone other than their spouse — see ADULTERY

unfamiliar *adj* not known or experienced before — see NEW 2

unfamiliarity *n* the state of being unaware or uninformed — see IGNORANCE 1

unfashionable *adj* marked by an obvious lack of style or good taste — see ¹TACKY 1

unfasten *vb* to disengage the knotted parts of — see UNTIE

unfathomable *adj* **1** being or seeming to be without limits — see INFINITE

2 impossible to understand — see INCOMPREHENSIBLE

unfavorable *adj* opposed to one's interests — see ADVERSE 1

unfeeling *adj* **1** having or showing a lack of sympathy or tender feelings — see HARD 1

2 lacking in sensation or feeling — see NUMB 1

3 lacking animate awareness or sensation — see INSENSATE 1

unfeignedly *adv* without any attempt to impress by deception or exaggeration — see NATURALLY 3

unfeminine *adj* having qualities or traits that are traditionally considered inappropriate for a girl or woman ⟨In bygone days pants were considered *unfeminine*, and even women bicycling were expected to wear skirts.⟩

syn mannish, tomboyish, unladylike

rel gentlemanly, male, manly, masculine

near ant effeminate, girlish, sissified, sissy, unmanly, unmasculine, womanish, womanlike; distaff, petticoat

ant female, feminine, ladylike, womanly

unfetter *vb* to release (as from slavery or confinement) — see FREE 1

unfit *adj* **1** lacking qualities (as knowledge, skill, or ability) required to do a job — see INCOMPETENT

2 not appropriate for a particular occasion or situation — see INAPPROPRIATE

unfitness *n* the quality or state of being unsuitable or unfitting — see INAPPROPRIATENESS 1

unflagging *adj* showing no signs of weariness even after long hard effort — see TIRELESS

unflappable *adj* not easily panicked or upset ⟨The *unflappable* teacher never even blinked when the whiteboard came crashing down.⟩

syn imperturbable, nerveless, unshakable

rel calm, collected, composed, cool, coolheaded, icy, nonchalant, placid, self-collected, self-possessed, serene, steely, tranquil, undisturbed, unperturbed, unruffled, unshaken, untroubled, unworried

near ant panicky; aflutter, anxious, dithery, edgy, het up, hung up, jittery, jumpy, nervous, nervy, perturbed, shaky, tense, troubled, uneasy, upset, uptight, worried

ant perturbable, shakable (*or* shakeable)

unfledged *adj* lacking in adult experience or maturity — see CALLOW

unflinching *adj* showing no signs of slackening or yielding in one's purpose — see UNYIELDING 1

unfold *vb* **1** to arrange the parts of (something) over a wider area — see OPEN 3

2 to gradually become clearer or more detailed — see DEVELOP 1

3 to produce flowers — see BLOOM 1

4 to come into view — see APPEAR 1

unforced *adj* done, made, or given with one's own free will — see VOLUNTARY 1

unforeseen *adj* not expected — see UNEXPECTED

unforgivable *adj* too bad to be excused or justified — see INEXCUSABLE

unformed *adj* **1** having no definite or recognizable form — see FORMLESS 1

2 lacking in adult experience or maturity — see CALLOW

unfortunate *adj* **1** bringing about ruin or misfortune — see FATAL 1

2 having, prone to, or marked by bad luck — see UNLUCKY 1

3 of a kind to cause great distress — see REGRETTABLE

unfounded *adj* having no basis in reason or fact — see GROUNDLESS

unfriendly *adj* **1** lacking in friendliness or warmth of feeling — see COLD 2

2 marked by opposition or ill will — see HOSTILE 1

3 opposed to one's interests — see ADVERSE 1

unfrozen *adj* freed from a frozen state by exposure to warmth — see THAWED

unfruitful *adj* not able to produce fruit or offspring — see STERILE 1

ungainly *adj* **1** difficult to use or operate especially because of size, weight, or design — see CUMBERSOME

2 having or showing an inability to move in a graceful manner — see CLUMSY 2

ungentle *adj* harsh and threatening in manner or appearance — see GRIM 1

ungovernable *adj* **1** given to resisting authority or another's control — see DISOBEDIENT

2 given to resisting control or discipline by others — see UNCONTROLLABLE

ungraceful *adj* lacking social grace and assurance — see AWKWARD 1

ungracious *adj* showing a lack of manners or consideration for others — see IMPOLITE

ungraciousness *n* rude behavior — see DISCOURTESY

ungrateful *adj* **1** not likely to be appreciated by those who benefit — see THANKLESS 2

2 not showing gratitude — see THANKLESS 1

unguarded *adj* **1** free in expressing one's true feelings and opinions — see FRANK

2 lacking protection from danger or resistance against attack — see HELPLESS 1

3 not paying or showing close attention especially for the purpose of avoiding trouble — see CARELESS 1

unhampered *adj* showing no signs of being under control — see RAMPANT 1

unhandsome *adj* **1** unpleasant to look at — see UGLY 1

2 showing a lack of manners or consideration for others — see IMPOLITE

unhandy *adj* **1** difficult to use or operate especially because of size, weight, or design — see CUMBERSOME

2 lacking or showing a lack of nimbleness in using one's hands — see CLUMSY 1

unhappily *adv* with feelings of bitterness or grief — see HARD 2

unhappiness *n* a state or spell of low spirits — see SADNESS

unhappy *adj* **1** feeling unhappiness — see SAD 1

2 having, prone to, or marked by bad luck — see UNLUCKY 1

3 not appropriate for a particular occasion or situation — see INAPPROPRIATE

unhealthful *adj* bad for the well-being of the body — see UNHEALTHY 1

unhealthiness *n* the condition of not being in good health — see SICKNESS 1

unhealthy *adj* **1** bad for the well-being of the body ⟨We knew that the junk food at the carnival was *unhealthy*, but it tasted so good!⟩

syn noisome, noxious, sickly, unhealthful, unwholesome

rel germy, insanitary, unhygienic, unsanitary; nonnutritious; poisonous, toxic; fatal, lethal, mortal

near ant hygienic, sanitary; nutritious

ant healthful, healthy

2 involving potential loss or injury — see DANGEROUS 1

3 temporarily suffering from a disorder of the body — see SICK 1

unheard–of *adj* not known or experienced before — see NEW 2

unheroic *adj* having or showing a shameful lack of courage — see COWARDLY

unhindered *adj* showing no signs of being under control — see RAMPANT 1

unhinge *vb* **1** to cause to go insane or as if insane — see CRAZE

2 to trouble the mind of; to make uneasy — see DISTURB 1

unhurried *adj* moving or proceeding at less than the normal, desirable, or required speed — see SLOW 1

unidentified *adj* **1** known but not named — see CERTAIN 1

2 not named or identified by a name — see NAMELESS 1

unification *n* the act or an instance of joining two or more things into one — see UNION 1

uniform *adj* not varying ⟨Using cookie cutters will make the cookies *uniform* in size.⟩

syn even, invariant, steady, unchanging, undeviating, unvarying, unwavering

rel fixed, immutable, invariable, set, unalterable, unchangeable

ant changing, deviating, nonuniform, unsteady, varying

uniform *n* the distinctive clothing worn by members of a particular group ⟨The band *uniform* was brown with red and white stripes.⟩

syn livery, outfit

rel fatigues, full dress, regimentals; costume, finery, regalia

unify *vb* **1** to bring (something) to a central point or under a single control — see CENTRALIZE

2 to come together to form a single unit — see UNITE 1

unimaginable *adj* too extraordinary or improbable to believe — see INCREDIBLE

unimportant *adj* lacking importance ⟨We figured that the details were *unimportant* as long as we got the basic design correct.⟩

syn foolish, frivolous, incidental, inconsequential, inconsiderable, insignificant, little, minor, minute, negligible, slight, small, small-fry, trifling, trivial

rel jerkwater, one-horse; nickel-and-dime, paltry, petty, small-time, worthless; anon-

ymous, nameless, obscure, uncelebrated, unknown
phrases neither here nor there
near ant decisive, fatal, fateful; chief, dominant, overbearing, overmastering, principal; distinctive, exceptional, impressive, outstanding, prominent, remarkable; valuable, worthwhile, worthy; distinguished, eminent, great, illustrious, preeminent, prestigious; famous, notorious, renowned; all-important, basic, essential, fundamental, key
ant big, consequential, eventful, important, major, material, meaningful, momentous, significant, substantial, unfrivolous, weighty

uninformed *adj* not informed about or aware of something — see IGNORANT 2

uninhibited *adj* showing feeling freely — see DEMONSTRATIVE 1

uninstructed *adj* lacking in education or the knowledge gained from books — see IGNORANT 1

unintelligent *adj* not having or showing an ability to absorb ideas readily — see STUPID 1

unintelligible *adj* impossible to understand — see INCOMPREHENSIBLE

unintended *adj* 1 happening by chance — see ACCIDENTAL 1
2 not made or done willingly or by choice — see INVOLUNTARY 1

unintentional *adj* 1 happening by chance — see ACCIDENTAL 1
2 not made or done willingly or by choice — see INVOLUNTARY 1

uninterested *adj* having or showing a lack of interest or concern — see INDIFFERENT 1

uninteresting *adj* causing weariness, restlessness, or lack of interest — see BORING

uninterrupted *adj* going on and on without any interruptions — see CONTINUOUS

uninvited *adj* not searched or asked for — see UNSOUGHT

union *n* 1 the act or an instance of joining two or more things into one ⟨The *union* of the two smaller student groups provided new opportunities for collaboration.⟩
syn combination, combining, connecting, connection, consolidation, coupling, junction, linking, merging, unification
rel agglomeration, amalgamation, blend, coalescence, commingling, compounding, fusion, intermingling, intermixture, mingling, mix, mixture; reunification, reunion
near ant detachment, divorcement, separation, severance
ant breakup, disconnection, dissolution, disunion, division, parting, partition, schism, scission, split
2 an association of persons, parties, or states for mutual assistance and protection — see CONFEDERACY
3 the state of having shared interests or efforts (as in social or business matters) — see ASSOCIATION 1

unique *adj* 1 of, relating to, or belonging to a single person — see INDIVIDUAL 1
2 being out of the ordinary — see EXCEPTIONAL 1
3 being the one or ones of a class with no other members — see ONLY 2

4 noticeably different from what is generally found or experienced — see UNUSUAL 1

unison *n* the state of being of one opinion about something — see AGREEMENT 1

unite *vb* 1 to come together to form a single unit ⟨Using the microscope, we watched the water droplets *unite* into a single pool.⟩
syn associate, coalesce, combine, conjoin, conjugate, connect, couple, fuse, join, link (up), marry, unify
rel mate, yoke; ally, confederate, league; chain, compound, hitch, hook, splice; assemble, cluster, congregate, convene, gather, meet; recombine, reconnect, rejoin, reunify, reunite
near ant detach, disaffiliate, disconnect, disjoin, disjoint, dissociate, disunite, divide, divorce, fractionate, isolate, resolve, uncouple, unyoke; disband, disperse, scatter
ant break up, dissever, part, section, separate, sever, split, sunder, unlink
2 to bring (something) to a central point or under a single control — see CENTRALIZE
3 to form or enter into an association that furthers the interests of its members — see ALLY
4 to participate or assist in a joint effort to accomplish an end — see COOPERATE 1

united *adj* 1 having or marked by agreement in feeling or action — see HARMONIOUS 3
2 used or done by a number of people as a group — see COLLECTIVE

unity *n* a balanced, pleasing, or suitable arrangement of parts — see HARMONY 1

universal *adj* 1 able to do many different kinds of things — see VERSATILE
2 belonging or relating to the whole — see GENERAL 1
3 covering everything or all important points — see ENCYCLOPEDIC
4 present in all places and at all times — see OMNIPRESENT

universe *n* the whole body of things observed or assumed ⟨questioning the theory that the *universe* is constantly expanding⟩
syn cosmos, creation, macrocosm, nature, world
rel existence, reality
near ant void

unjustifiable *adj* too bad to be excused or justified — see INEXCUSABLE

unjustness *n* 1 the state of being unfair or unjust — see INJUSTICE 1
2 unfair or inadequate treatment of someone or something or an instance of this — see DISSERVICE

unkempt *adj* 1 lacking in order, neatness, and often cleanliness — see MESSY
2 lacking neatness in dress or person — see SLOPPY 1

unknowing *adj* 1 lacking in worldly wisdom or informed judgment — see NAIVE 1
2 not informed about or aware of something — see IGNORANT 2

unknown *adj* 1 happening or existing without one's knowledge ⟨*Unknown* to me was the fact that while I was out, my family was hurriedly preparing a surprise birthday party.⟩

syn unbeknownst (*also* unbeknown)
rel unperceived, unsuspected; unaware, unconscious, unmindful; unknowing, unsuspecting, unwitting; ignorant, unacquainted, unfamiliar
2 not known or experienced before — see NEW 2
3 not widely known — see OBSCURE 1

unlade *vb* to empty or rid of cargo — see UNLOAD 1

unladylike *adj* having qualities or traits that are traditionally considered inappropriate for a girl or woman — see UNFEMININE

unlash *vb* to disengage the knotted parts of — see UNTIE

unlawful *adj* **1** contrary to or forbidden by law — see ILLEGAL 1
2 not conforming to a high moral standard; morally unacceptable — see BAD 2

unlearn *vb* to be unable to recall or think of — see FORGET 1

unlearned *adj* lacking in education or the knowledge gained from books — see IGNORANT 1

unleash *vb* **1** to set free (from a state of being held in check) — see RELEASE 1
2 to find emotional release for — see TAKE OUT 1

unlettered *adj* lacking in education or the knowledge gained from books — see IGNORANT 1

unlike *adj* being not of the same kind — see DIFFERENT 1

unlikely *adj* not likely to be true or to occur — see IMPROBABLE

unlikeness *n* the quality or state of being different — see DIFFERENCE 1

unlimited *adj* **1** being or seeming to be without limits — see INFINITE
2 not limited or specialized in application or purpose — see GENERAL 4

unlink *vb* to set or force apart — see SEPARATE 1

unlisted *adj* not appearing on a list ⟨She kept her phone number *unlisted* so as to reduce the number of unwanted calls.⟩
syn uncataloged, unrecorded, unregistered
rel unwritten; unidentified; unspecified; undisclosed, unknown, unrevealed
ant cataloged (*or* catalogued), listed, recorded, registered

unliterary *adj* used in or suitable for speech and not formal writing — see COLLOQUIAL 1

unload *vb* **1** to empty or rid of cargo ⟨The dockworkers *unloaded* the ship.⟩
syn disburden, discharge, disencumber, unburden, unlade, unpack
rel free, lighten, relieve; clear, empty, evacuate, vacate, void
near ant charge, cram, fill, heap, jam, jam-pack, stuff
ant load, pack
2 to get rid of as useless or unwanted — see DISCARD

unlock *vb* to set free (from a state of being held in check) — see RELEASE 1

unlooked–for *adj* not expected — see UNEXPECTED

unloose *vb* to set free (from a state of being held in check) — see RELEASE 1

unloosen *vb* to set free (from a state of being held in check) — see RELEASE 1

unlovely *adj* **1** not giving pleasure to the mind or senses — see UNPLEASANT
2 unpleasant to look at — see UGLY 1

unlucky *adj* **1** having, prone to, or marked by bad luck ⟨The *unlucky* campers had rain all week.⟩ ⟨I'm so *unlucky* I don't bother to play the lottery.⟩ ⟨an *unlucky* throw of the dice⟩
syn hapless, hard-luck, ill-fated, ill-starred, jinxed, luckless, star-crossed, unfortunate, unhappy
rel adverse, ill, inauspicious, unfavorable, unpromising, untoward; calamitous, catastrophic, disastrous; damned, tragic (*also* tragical)
near ant blessed (*also* blest), favored, gifted, privileged; auspicious, fair, favorable, golden, promising, propitious
ant fortunate, happy, lucky
2 of a kind to cause great distress — see REGRETTABLE

unmake *vb* to remove from a position of prominence or power (as a throne) — see DEPOSE 1

unmanageable *adj* given to resisting control or discipline by others — see UNCONTROLLABLE

unmannerly *adj* showing a lack of manners or consideration for others — see IMPOLITE

unmarried *adj* not married — see SINGLE 1

unmask *vb* **1** to make known (as information previously kept secret) — see REVEAL 1
2 to reveal the true nature of — see EXPOSE 1

unmatched *adj* **1** being one of a pair or set without a corresponding mate — see ODD 1
2 having no equal or rival for excellence or desirability — see ONLY 1

unmelodious *adj* marked by or producing a harsh combination of sounds — see DISSONANT

unmerciful *adj* **1** going beyond a normal or acceptable limit in degree or amount — see EXCESSIVE
2 having or showing a lack of sympathy or tender feelings — see HARD 1

unmindful *adj* not informed about or aware of something — see IGNORANT 2

unmistakable *adj* not subject to misinterpretation or more than one interpretation — see CLEAR 2

unmitigated *adj* having no exceptions or restrictions — see ABSOLUTE 2

unmixed *adj* free from added matter — see PURE 1

unmovable *adj* incapable of moving or being moved — see IMMOVABLE 1

unmusical *adj* marked by or producing a harsh combination of sounds — see DISSONANT

unnamed *adj* **1** known but not named — see CERTAIN 1
2 not named or identified by a name — see NAMELESS 1

unnatural *adj* **1** departing from some accepted standard of what is normal — see DEVIANT

---

syn synonym(s)   *rel* related words
ant antonym(s)   *near ant* near antonym(s)

2 lacking in natural or spontaneous quality — see ARTIFICIAL 1

unnecessary *adj* not needed by the circumstances or to accomplish an end ⟨That large suitcase is *unnecessary*—we are only going to be away for a couple of days!⟩

syn dispensable, gratuitous, needless, nonessential, uncalled-for, unessential, unwarranted

rel discretionary, elective, optional; extra, extraneous, irrelative, irrelevant, redundant, superfluous

near ant all-important, crucial, important, vital; imperative, pressing, urgent

ant essential, indispensable, necessary, needed, needful, required

unnerve *vb* 1 to deprive of courage or confidence ⟨The riding accident so *unnerved* me that for a while I was afraid to get back on a horse.⟩

syn demoralize, emasculate, paralyze, undo, unstring

rel debilitate, enervate, enfeeble, neuter, weaken; prostrate, sap, soften, tire, waste; frighten, intimidate, psych (out), scare, terrify, terrorize; daunt, discourage, dishearten, dismay, dispirit; craze, derange, madden, unbalance, unhinge; discompose, disquiet, disturb, faze, perturb, unsettle, upset

near ant fortify, strengthen; embolden, encourage, hearten

ant nerve

2 to lessen the courage or confidence of — see DISCOURAGE 1

unnerving *adj* marked by or causing agitation or uncomfortable feelings — see NERVOUS 2

unnoticeable *adj* not readily seen or noticed — see UNOBTRUSIVE

unnumbered *adj* too many to be counted — see COUNTLESS

unobstructed *adj* allowing passage without obstruction — see OPEN 1

unobtainable *adj* hard or impossible to get to or get at — see INACCESSIBLE

unobtrusive *adj* not readily seen or noticed ⟨The notice that an 18% tip would be automatically added was so *unobtrusive* we almost didn't see it at the bottom of the menu.⟩

syn discreet, inconspicuous, unnoticeable

rel unnoticed, unremarked, unseen; impalpable, imperceptible, inappreciable, indistinguishable, insensible; faint, indistinct, obscure; concealed

near ant arresting, eye-catching, showy, striking; flashy, loud, noisy; apparent, clear, discernible (*also* discernable), distinct, evident, manifest, obvious, patent, plain, prominent, unmistakable; blatant, flagrant, glaring, gross, screaming

ant conspicuous, noticeable, visible

unoriginal *adj* using or marked by the use of something else as a basis or model — see IMITATIVE 1

unorthodox *adj* 1 deviating from commonly accepted beliefs or practices — see HERETICAL

2 not bound by traditional ways or beliefs — see LIBERAL 1

3 not rigidly following established form, custom, or rules — see INFORMAL 1

unpack *vb* to empty or rid of cargo — see UNLOAD 1

unpaid *adj* not yet paid — see OUTSTANDING 1

unpainted *adj* lacking an addition of color — see COLORLESS 1

unpaired *adj* being one of a pair or set without a corresponding mate — see ODD 1

unpalatable *adj* 1 disagreeable or disgusting to the sense of taste — see DISTASTEFUL 1

2 not giving pleasure to the mind or senses — see UNPLEASANT

unparalleled *adj* having no equal or rival for excellence or desirability — see ONLY 1

unpardonable *adj* too bad to be excused or justified — see INEXCUSABLE

unperturbed *adj* free from emotional or mental agitation — see CALM 2

unplanned *adj* 1 happening by chance — see ACCIDENTAL 1

2 made or done without previous thought or preparation — see EXTEMPORANEOUS

unpleasant *adj* not giving pleasure to the mind or senses ⟨The burnt pot roast had a very *unpleasant* odor.⟩

syn bad, bitter, disagreeable, displeasing, distasteful, harsh, nasty, rotten, sour, uncongenial, unlovely, unpalatable, unpleasing, unsavory, unwelcome, wicked, yucky (*also* yukky)

rel abhorrent, abominable, appalling, awful, beastly, bilious, dreadful, foul, ghastly, hideous, horrendous, horrible, horrid, invidious, loathsome, nauseating, nauseous, noisome, obnoxious, obscene, odious, offensive, repellent (*also* repellant), repugnant, repulsive, revolting, scandalous, seamy, shocking, sick, sickening, ugly, vile, villainous; aggravating, annoying, galling, irritating, vexing; crummy (*also* crumby), lousy, miserable, wretched

near ant delectable, delicious, delightful, dreamy, felicitous; amiable, charming, cheery, friendly, jolly, kindly, sweet

ant agreeable, congenial, good, grateful, gratifying, nice, palatable, pleasant, pleasing, pleasurable, satisfying, welcome

unpleasing *adj* 1 not giving pleasure to the mind or senses — see UNPLEASANT

2 unpleasant to look at — see UGLY 1

unpolished *adj* lacking in refinement or good taste — see COARSE 2

unprecedented *adj* not known or experienced before — see NEW 2

unpredictable *adj* likely to change frequently, suddenly, or unexpectedly — see FICKLE 1

unprejudiced *adj* marked by justice, honesty, and freedom from bias — see FAIR 2

unpremeditated *adj* 1 happening by chance — see ACCIDENTAL 1

2 made or done without previous thought or preparation — see EXTEMPORANEOUS

unprepared *adj* made or done without previous thought or preparation — see EXTEMPORANEOUS

unpretending *adj* free from any intent to deceive or impress others — see GUILELESS

unpretentious *adj* 1 free from any intent

to deceive or impress others — see GUILE-
LESS

2 not excessively showy — see QUIET 2

3 not having or showing any feelings of
superiority, self-assertiveness, or showiness — see HUMBLE 1

unpretentiously *adv* without any attempt
to impress by deception or exaggeration
— see NATURALLY 3

unpretty *adj* unpleasant to look at — see
UGLY 1

unprincipled *adj* not guided by or showing a concern for what is right ⟨an *unprincipled* businessman who made a lot of
money—and didn't care how he did it⟩

syn cutthroat, immoral, Machiavellian,
unconscionable, unethical, unscrupulous

rel merciless, pitiless, remorseless, ruthless; crooked, deceitful, dishonest, knavish; corrupt, debased, debauched, decadent, degenerate, degraded, demoralized,
depraved, dissipated, libertine, licentious,
profligate; dog-eat-dog, opportunistic; calculating, sharp

near ant conscientious, good, honorable,
just, noble, righteous, virtuous

ant ethical, moral, principled, scrupulous

unprocessed *adj* being such as found in
nature and not altered by processing or
refining — see CRUDE 1

unproductive *adj* **1** producing inferior or
only a small amount of vegetation — see
BARREN 1

2 producing no results — see FUTILE

unprofessional *adj* lacking or showing a
lack of expert skill — see AMATEURISH

unprofitable *adj* producing no results —
see FUTILE

unprogressive *adj* tending to favor established ideas, conditions, or institutions —
see CONSERVATIVE 1

unprotected *adj* lacking protection from
danger or resistance against attack — see
HELPLESS 1

unqualified *adj* **1** having no exceptions or
restrictions — see ABSOLUTE 2

2 lacking qualities (as knowledge, skill, or
ability) required to do a job — see INCOM-
PETENT

3 not limited or specialized in application
or purpose — see GENERAL 4

unquestionable *adj* not capable of being
challenged or proved wrong — see IRRE-
FUTABLE

unquestionably *adv* without any question
— see INDEED 1

unquiet *adj* **1** feeling or showing uncomfortable feelings of uncertainty — see
NERVOUS 1

2 lacking or denying rest — see REST-
LESS 1

unravel *vb* **1** to separate the various strands
of ⟨It took us forever to *unravel* the jumbled mass of Christmas tree lights.⟩

syn disentangle, ravel (out), unbraid, unsnarl, untangle, untwine, untwist

rel fray, fret; smooth, straighten (out); uncoil, undo, unknot, unlace, unroll, unstring, unthread, untie, unwind

near *ant* braid, knot, lace, plait, ply,
splice, tie, wind

ant entangle, snarl, tangle

2 to find an answer for through reasoning
— see SOLVE

unreachable *adj* hard or impossible to get
to or get at — see INACCESSIBLE

unread *adj* lacking in education or the
knowledge gained from books — see IG-
NORANT 1

unreal *adj* **1** conceived or made without
regard for reason or reality — see FAN-
TASTIC 1

2 not real and existing only in the imagination — see IMAGINARY

unreality *n* a conception or image created
by the imagination and having no objective reality — see FANTASY 1

unreasonable *adj* **1** having no basis in
reason or fact — see GROUNDLESS

2 not using or following good reasoning
— see ILLOGICAL

unreasoning *adj* not using or following
good reasoning — see ILLOGICAL

unrecorded *adj* not appearing on a list —
see UNLISTED

unrecoverable *adj* **1** not capable of being
cured or reformed — see HOPELESS 1

2 not capable of being repaired, regained,
or undone — see IRREPARABLE

unredeemable *adj* **1** not capable of being
cured or reformed — see HOPELESS 1

2 not capable of being repaired, regained,
or undone — see IRREPARABLE

unrefined *adj* **1** being such as found in nature and not altered by processing or refining — see CRUDE 1

2 hastily or roughly constructed — see
RUDE 1

3 lacking in refinement or good taste —
see COARSE 2

unregistered *adj* not appearing on a list
— see UNLISTED

unrehearsed *adj* made or done without
previous thought or preparation — see
EXTEMPORANEOUS

unrelenting *adj* **1** sticking to an opinion,
purpose, or course of action in spite of
reason, arguments, or persuasion — see
OBSTINATE

2 showing no signs of slackening or yielding in one's purpose — see UNYIELDING 1

unremarkable *adj* being of the type that is
encountered in the normal course of
events — see ORDINARY 1

unremitting *adj* going on and on without
any interruptions — see CONTINUOUS

unrepentant *adj* not sorry for having
done wrong — see REMORSELESS 1

unreserved *adj* **1** free in expressing one's
true feelings and opinions — see FRANK

2 showing feeling freely — see DEMON-
STRATIVE 1

unresistant *adj* **1** lacking protection from
danger or resistance against attack — see
HELPLESS 1

2 receiving or enduring without offering
resistance — see PASSIVE

unresolved *adj* not yet settled or decided
— see PENDING 1

unrest *n* a disturbed or uneasy state ⟨a period of civil *unrest*⟩ ⟨His stomach *unrest*
was just a sign of stage fright.⟩

---

syn synonym(s)   **rel** related words
ant antonym(s)   **near ant** near antonym(s)

syn disquiet, ferment, restiveness, restlessness, turmoil, uneasiness

rel fidgets; agitation, commotion, confusion, excitement, hubbub, stir, storm, trouble, tumult, tumultuousness, turbulence, upheaval, uproar, unsettlement; disruption, perturbation; agitation, anxiety, inquietude, queasiness, tension; anarchy, chaos, disorder, welter

near ant order, orderliness

ant calm, ease, peace, peacefulness, quiet, tranquillity (*or* tranquility)

unrestful *adj* lacking or denying rest — see RESTLESS 1

unrestrained *adj* **1** not bound by rigid standards — see EASYGOING 2

2 not bound, confined, or detained by force — see FREE 3

3 showing feeling freely — see DEMONSTRATIVE 1

4 showing no signs of being under control — see RAMPANT 1

unrestraint *n* carefree freedom from constraint — see ABANDON

unrestricted *adj* **1** freely available for use or participation by all — see OPEN 2

2 not bound by rigid standards — see EASYGOING 2

3 not limited or specialized in application or purpose — see GENERAL 4

unrighteous *adj* not conforming to a high moral standard; morally unacceptable — see BAD 2

unripe *adj* lacking in adult experience or maturity — see CALLOW

unripened *adj* lacking in adult experience or maturity — see CALLOW

unrivaled *or* **unrivalled** *adj* having no equal or rival for excellence or desirability — see ONLY 1

unruffled *adj* free from emotional or mental agitation — see CALM 2

unruliness *n* refusal to obey — see DISOBEDIENCE

unruly *adj* **1** given to resisting authority or another's control — see DISOBEDIENT

2 given to resisting control or discipline by others — see UNCONTROLLABLE

3 not restrained by or under the control of legal authority — see LAWLESS 1

unsafe *adj* **1** involving potential loss or injury — see DANGEROUS 1

2 not paying or showing close attention especially for the purpose of avoiding trouble — see CARELESS 1

unsatisfactorily *adv* in an unsatisfactory way — see BADLY 1

unsatisfactory *adj* falling short of a standard — see BAD 1

unsavory *adj* **1** disagreeable or disgusting to the sense of taste — see DISTASTEFUL 1

2 not conforming to a high moral standard; morally unacceptable — see BAD 2

3 not giving pleasure to the mind or senses — see UNPLEASANT

4 lacking in taste or flavor — see INSIPID 1

unsay *vb* to solemnly or formally reject or go back on (as something formerly adhered to) — see ABJURE 1

unschooled *adj* lacking in education or the knowledge gained from books — see IGNORANT 1

unscrupulous *adj* not guided by or showing a concern for what is right — see UNPRINCIPLED

unseasonable *adj* occurring before the usual or expected time — see EARLY 2

unseasonably *adv* before the usual or expected time — see EARLY

unseat *vb* to remove from a position of prominence or power (as a throne) — see DEPOSE 1

unsecured *adj* not tightly fastened, tied, or stretched — see LOOSE 1

unseemly *adj* not appropriate for a particular occasion or situation — see INAPPROPRIATE

unselfish *adj* giving or sharing in abundance and without hesitation — see GENEROUS 1

unselfishness *n* the quality or state of being generous — see LIBERALITY

unsettle *vb* to trouble the mind of; to make uneasy — see DISTURB 1

unsettled *adj* **1** likely to change frequently, suddenly, or unexpectedly — see FICKLE 1

2 not yet paid — see OUTSTANDING 1

3 not yet settled or decided — see PENDING 1

4 not feeling sure about the truth, wisdom, or trustworthiness of someone or something — see DOUBTFUL 1

unsettling *adj* **1** causing worry or anxiety — see TROUBLESOME

2 marked by or causing agitation or uncomfortable feelings — see NERVOUS 2

unshakable *adj* not easily panicked or upset — see UNFLAPPABLE

unshaken *adj* free from emotional or mental agitation — see CALM 2

unshaped *adj* having no definite or recognizable form — see FORMLESS 1

unshared *adj* belonging only to the one person, unit, or group named — see SOLE 1

unshorn *adj* covered with or as if with hair — see HAIRY 1

unsightly *adj* unpleasant to look at — see UGLY 1

unskilled *adj* **1** lacking or showing a lack of expert skill — see AMATEURISH

2 lacking qualities (as knowledge, skill, or ability) required to do a job — see INCOMPETENT

unskillful *adj* **1** lacking qualities (as knowledge, skill, or ability) required to do a job — see INCOMPETENT

2 lacking or showing a lack of expert skill — see AMATEURISH

unsmiling *adj* not joking or playful in mood or manner — see SERIOUS 1

unsnarl *vb* to separate the various strands of — see UNRAVEL 1

unsociable *adj* having or showing a lack of friendliness or interest in others — see COOL 1

unsoiled *adj* free from dirt or stain — see CLEAN 1

unsolicited *adj* not searched or asked for — see UNSOUGHT

unsolvable *adj* incapable of being solved or accomplished — see IMPOSSIBLE

unsophisticated *adj* lacking in worldly wisdom or informed judgment — see NAIVE 1

unsophistication *n* **1** the quality or state

of being simple and sincere — see NAÏVETÉ 1

2 the quality or state of having a form or structure of few parts or elements — see SIMPLICITY 1

unsought *adj* not searched or asked for ⟨The meddling neighbor insisted on giving us *unsought* advice.⟩

syn unasked, unbidden (*also* unbid), uninvited, unsolicited

rel undesired, unwanted, unwelcome; objectionable, offensive, unacceptable, undesirable; uncalled-for, unnecessary

near ant needed, needed, required; desired, wanted, welcome

ant requested, solicited

unsound *adj* **1** not being in agreement with what is true — see FALSE 1

2 not using or following good reasoning — see ILLOGICAL

3 temporarily suffering from a disorder of the body — see SICK 1

unsoundness *n* the condition of not being in good health — see SICKNESS 1

unsparing *adj* **1** giving or sharing in abundance and without hesitation — see GENEROUS 1

2 having or showing a lack of sympathy or tender feelings — see HARD 1

unspeakable *adj* beyond the power to describe — see INDESCRIBABLE

unspecialized *adj* not limited or specialized in application or purpose — see GENERAL 4

unspecified *adj* known but not named — see CERTAIN 1

unspoken *adj* understood although not put into words — see IMPLICIT 1

unsportsmanlike *adj* not being in accordance with the rules or standards of what is fair in sport — see FOUL 2

unstable *adj* **1** not being in or able to maintain a state of balance ⟨The minute we put the books down on the *unstable* desk, the whole stack went crashing to the floor.⟩

syn unbalanced, unsteady

rel rocky, shaky, tippy, tipsy, wavery, wobbly (*also* wabbly); infirm, insecure, precarious, unsound; doddering, doddery, jiggling, jiggly, rickety, teetering, tottery; askew, awry, cockeyed, lopsided, uneven

near ant even, level, straight; sound, sturdy, substantial

ant balanced, equilibrated, stabilized, stable, steady

2 likely to change frequently, suddenly, or unexpectedly — see FICKLE 1

3 not staying constant — see UNEVEN 2

unstained *adj* **1** free from dirt or stain — see CLEAN 1

2 lacking an addition of color — see COLORLESS 1

unsteadiness *n* the quality or state of not being firmly fixed in position — see INSTABILITY

unsteady *adj* **1** lacking in steadiness or regularity of occurrence — see FITFUL 2

2 likely to change frequently, suddenly, or unexpectedly — see FICKLE 1

3 not being in or able to maintain a state of balance — see UNSTABLE 1

4 not staying constant — see UNEVEN 2

unstintingly *adv* in a generous manner — see WELL 2

unstop *vb* to make passage through (something) possible by removing obstructions — see OPEN 1

unstopped *adj* allowing passage without obstruction — see OPEN 1

unstring *vb* **1** to cause to go insane or as if insane — see CRAZE

2 to deprive of courage or confidence — see UNNERVE 1

unstructured *adj* having no definite or recognizable form — see FORMLESS 1

unstudied *adj* made or done without previous thought or preparation — see EXTEMPORANEOUS

unstylish *adj* marked by an obvious lack of style or good taste — see ¹TACKY 1

unsubstantial *adj* **1** not composed of matter — see IMMATERIAL 1

2 being of a material lacking in sturdiness or substance — see FLIMSY 1

3 lacking bodily strength — see WEAK 1

unsubstantiated *adj* having no basis in reason or fact — see GROUNDLESS

unsuccessful *adj* producing no results — see FUTILE

unsuitable *adj* not appropriate for a particular occasion or situation — see INAPPROPRIATE

unsuitably *adv* in a mistaken or inappropriate way — see WRONGLY

unsullied *adj* free from dirt or stain — see CLEAN 1

unsung *adj* not widely known — see OBSCURE 2

unsupportable *adj* more than can be put up with — see UNBEARABLE

unsupported *adj* having no basis in reason or fact — see GROUNDLESS

unsure *adj* not feeling sure about the truth, wisdom, or trustworthiness of someone or something — see DOUBTFUL 1

unsurpassable *adj* having no equal or rival for excellence or desirability — see ONLY 1

unsurpassed *adj* **1** having no equal or rival for excellence or desirability — see ONLY 1

2 of the very best kind — see EXCELLENT

unsuspecting *adj* lacking in worldly wisdom or informed judgment — see NAIVE 1

unsuspicious *adj* lacking in worldly wisdom or informed judgment — see NAIVE 1

unsympathetic *adj* **1** having or showing a lack of sympathy or tender feelings — see HARD 1

2 lacking in friendliness or warmth of feeling — see COLD 2

3 marked by opposition or ill will — see HOSTILE 1

4 opposed to one's interests — see ADVERSE 1

untamed *adj* **1** existing without human habitation or cultivation — see WILD 2

2 living outdoors without taming or domestication by humans — see WILD 1

untangle *vb* **1** to separate the various strands of — see UNRAVEL 1

2 to set free from entanglement or difficulty — see EXTRICATE

---

syn synonym(s)   *rel* related words
ant antonym(s)   *near ant* near antonym(s)

untaught *adj* lacking in education or the knowledge gained from books — see IGNORANT 1

unthinkable *adj* too extraordinary or improbable to believe — see INCREDIBLE

unthrifty *adj* given to spending money freely or foolishly — see PRODIGAL

unthrone *vb* to remove from a position of prominence or power (as a throne) — see DEPOSE 1

untidy *adj* **1** lacking in order, neatness, and often cleanliness — see MESSY
2 lacking neatness in dress or person — see SLOPPY 1

untie *vb* to disengage the knotted parts of ⟨She always makes sure to *untie* her shoelaces before removing her shoes.⟩
syn unbind, undo, unfasten, unlash
rel unbraid, unlace; disentangle, ravel, unravel, unsnarl, untangle, unwind; loose, loosen
near ant braid, interlace, interweave, lace, wind; entangle, snarl, tangle
ant bind, fasten, knot, lash, tie

untimely *adj* occurring before the usual or expected time — see EARLY 2

untiring *adj* showing no signs of weariness even after long hard effort — see TIRELESS

untitled *adj* not named or identified by a name — see NAMELESS 1

untold *adj* too many to be counted — see COUNTLESS

untouchable *adj* **1** hard or impossible to get to or get at — see INACCESSIBLE
2 not to be violated, criticized, or tampered with — see SACRED 1

untoward *adj* **1** given to resisting authority or another's control — see DISOBEDIENT
2 given to resisting control or discipline by others — see UNCONTROLLABLE
3 opposed to one's interests — see ADVERSE 1
4 not appropriate for a particular occasion or situation — see INAPPROPRIATE

untreated *adj* being such as found in nature and not altered by processing or refining — see CRUDE 1

untroubled *adj* **1** free from emotional or mental agitation — see CALM 2
2 free from storms or physical disturbance — see CALM 1

untrue *adj* **1** not being in agreement with what is true — see FALSE 1
2 not true in one's allegiance to someone or something — see FAITHLESS

untruth *n* **1** a false idea or belief — see FALLACY 1
2 a statement known by its maker to be untrue and made in order to deceive — see LIE
3 the quality or state of being false — see FALLACY 2

untruthful *adj* **1** not being in agreement with what is true — see FALSE 1
2 telling or containing lies — see DISHONEST 1

untruthfulness *n* the tendency to tell lies — see DISHONESTY 1

untutored *adj* lacking in education or the knowledge gained from books — see IGNORANT 1

untwine *vb* to separate the various strands of — see UNRAVEL 1

untwist *vb* to separate the various strands of — see UNRAVEL 1

untypical *adj* departing from some accepted standard of what is normal — see DEVIANT

unusable *adj* not capable of being put to use or account — see IMPRACTICAL

unused *adj* **1** not having acquired a habit or tolerance ⟨The runner's performance suffered because he was *unused* to running at such high elevations.⟩
syn unacclimated, unaccustomed, unadapted, unadjusted
rel unseasoned
near ant unaffected, uninfluenced
ant acclimated, accustomed, adapted, adjusted, habituated, used
2 recently made and never used before — see NEW 3
3 not being in a state of use, activity, or employment — see INACTIVE 2

unusual *adj* **1** noticeably different from what is generally found or experienced ⟨We found some *unusual* shells by the high-tide mark while combing the beach.⟩
syn curious, extraordinary, funny, odd, offbeat, out-of-the-way, peculiar, queer, rare, singular, strange, unaccustomed, uncommon, uncustomary, unique, weird
rel bizarre, eccentric, far-out, kooky (*also* kookie), oddball, outlandish, way-out; aberrant, abnormal, atypical, exceptional, irregular; newsworthy, notable, noteworthy, noticeable, particular, remarkable, special
near ant unexceptional; expected, predictable; familiar, normal, regular, typical
ant common, ordinary, plain, usual
2 being out of the ordinary — see EXCEPTIONAL 1

unutterable *adj* beyond the power to describe — see INDESCRIBABLE

unvarnished *adj* free from all additions or embellishment — see PLAIN 1

unvarying *adj* **1** not undergoing a change in condition — see CONSTANT 1
2 not varying — see UNIFORM

unveil *vb* **1** to make known (as information previously kept secret) — see REVEAL 1
2 to present so as to invite notice or attention — see SHOW 1

unvoiced *adj* understood although not put into words — see IMPLICIT 1

unwarrantable *adj* too bad to be excused or justified — see INEXCUSABLE

unwarranted *adj* **1** not needed by the circumstances or to accomplish an end — see UNNECESSARY
2 having no basis in reason or fact — see GROUNDLESS

unwary *adj* **1** lacking in worldly wisdom or informed judgment — see NAIVE 1
2 not paying or showing close attention especially for the purpose of avoiding trouble — see CARELESS 1
3 readily taken advantage of — see EASY 2

unwavering *adj* not varying — see UNIFORM

unwed *adj* not married — see SINGLE 1

unwelcome *adj* not giving pleasure to the mind or senses — see UNPLEASANT

unwell *adj* temporarily suffering from a disorder of the body — see SICK 1

unwholesome *adj* 1 bad for the well-being of the body — see UNHEALTHY 1
2 having or showing lowered moral character or standards — see CORRUPT

unwieldy *adj* difficult to use or operate especially because of size, weight, or design — see CUMBERSOME

unwilling *adj* not made or done willingly or by choice — see INVOLUNTARY 1

unwillingness *n* a lack of willingness or desire to do or accept something — see RELUCTANCE

unwind *vb* to get rid of nervous tension or anxiety — see RELAX 1

unwise *adj* 1 showing or marked by a lack of good sense or judgment — see FOOLISH 1
2 showing poor judgment especially in personal relationships or social situations — see INDISCREET

unwitting *adj* 1 happening by chance — see ACCIDENTAL 1
2 not informed about or aware of something — see IGNORANT 2

unwonted *adj* being out of the ordinary — see EXCEPTIONAL 1

unworkable *adj* not capable of being put to use or account — see IMPRACTICAL

unworldliness *n* the quality or state of being simple and sincere — see NAÏVETÉ 1

unworldly *adj* lacking in worldly wisdom or informed judgment — see NAIVE 1

unworried *adj* free from emotional or mental agitation — see CALM 2

unwritten *adj* made or carried on through speaking rather than in writing — see VERBAL 2

unyielding *adj* 1 showing no signs of slackening or yielding in one's purpose ⟨The pioneers faced the challenge of settling the frontier with *unyielding* courage.⟩
syn determined, dogged, grim, implacable, relentless, unappeasable, unflinching, unrelenting
rel persevering, persistent, tenacious; hard, hardheaded, headstrong, intractable, mulish, obdurate, opinionated, peevish, pertinacious, perverse, pigheaded, self-willed, stubborn, uncooperative, willful (*or* wilful); merciless, ruthless, unforgiving; inextinguishable, insatiable
near ant slackening, softening, yielding; impotent, invertebrate, slack, spineless, weak; complaisant, obliging, pliable, pliant
2 having a consistency that does not easily yield to pressure — see FIRM 1
3 incapable of or highly resistant to bending — see STIFF 1
4 sticking to an opinion, purpose, or course of action in spite of reason, arguments, or persuasion — see OBSTINATE 1

unyoke *vb* to set or force apart — see SEPARATE 1

up *adj* 1 being at a higher level than average — see HIGH 2
2 brought or having come to an end — see COMPLETE 2
3 having information especially as a result of study or experience — see FAMILIAR 2

up *vb* 1 to make greater in size, amount, or number — see INCREASE 1
2 to move from a lower to a higher place or position — see RAISE 1
3 to move or extend upward — see ASCEND

upbeat *adj* 1 having or showing a good mood or disposition — see CHEERFUL 1
2 having qualities which inspire hope — see HOPEFUL 1

upbraid *vb* to criticize (someone) severely or angrily especially for personal failings — see SCOLD

upcoming *adj* being soon to appear or take place — see FORTHCOMING 1

up–country *n* a rural region that forms the edge of the settled or developed part of a country — see FRONTIER 2

upend *vb* 1 to achieve a victory over — see BEAT 2
2 to fix in an upright position — see ERECT 1

upgrade *n* 1 an upward slope — see ASCENT 2
2 a raising or a state of being raised to a higher rank or position — see ADVANCEMENT 1
3 the degree to which something rises up from a position level with the horizon — see SLANT 1

upgrade *vb* 1 to move higher in rank or position — see PROMOTE 1
2 to make better — see IMPROVE

upheaval *n* a violent disturbance (as of the political or social order) — see CONVULSION

uphill *adj* requiring considerable physical or mental effort — see HARD 2

uphill *n* an upward slope — see ASCENT 2

uphold *vb* 1 to continue to declare to be true or proper despite opposition or objections — see MAINTAIN 1
2 to hold up or serve as a foundation for — see SUPPORT 3
3 to move from a lower to a higher place or position — see RAISE 1

upkeep *n* the act or activity of keeping something in an existing and usually satisfactory condition — see MAINTENANCE

upland *n* an area of high ground — see HEIGHT 4

uplift *vb* to move from a lower to a higher place or position — see RAISE 1

uplifted *adj* being positioned above a surface — see ELEVATED 1

upmost *adj* being at a point or level higher than all others — see TOP 1

upon *prep* in or into contact with — see AGAINST

upper–class *adj* of high birth, rank, or station — see NOBLE 1

upper class *n* the highest class in a society — see ARISTOCRACY 1

upper crust *n* 1 individuals carefully selected as being the best of a class — see ELITE 1
2 the highest class in a society — see ARISTOCRACY 1

upper hand *n* the more favorable condition or position in a competition — see ADVANTAGE 1

uppermost *adj* being at a point or level higher than all others — see TOP 1

uppish *adj* having a feeling of superiority

---

syn synonym(s)   **rel** related words
ant antonym(s)   **near ant** near antonym(s)

that shows itself in an overbearing attitude — see ARROGANT

uppity *adj* having a feeling of superiority that shows itself in an overbearing attitude — see ARROGANT

upraise *vb* **1** to move from a lower to a higher place or position — see RAISE 1

2 to fix in an upright position — see ERECT 1

upraised *adj* being positioned above a surface — see ELEVATED 1

upright *adj* **1** conforming to a high standard of morality or virtue — see GOOD 2

2 following the accepted rules of moral conduct — see HONORABLE 1

3 rising straight up — see ERECT

uprightness *n* **1** conduct that conforms to an accepted standard of right and wrong — see MORALITY 1

2 faithfulness to high moral standards — see HONOR 1

uprise *n* an upward slope — see ASCENT 2

uprise *vb* **1** to leave one's bed — see ARISE 1

2 to move or extend upward — see ASCEND

uprising *n* open fighting against authority (as one's own government) — see REBELLION 1

uproar *n* **1** a state of noisy, confused activity — see COMMOTION

2 a state of wildly excited activity or emotion — see FRENZY

3 a violent disturbance (as of the political or social order) — see CONVULSION

4 a violent shouting — see CLAMOR 1

uproarious *adj* **1** causing or intended to cause laughter — see FUNNY 1

2 full of or characterized by the presence of noise — see NOISY 1

uproot *vb* to draw out by force or with effort — see EXTRACT

upset *adj* feeling or showing uncomfortable feelings of uncertainty — see NERVOUS 1

upset *n* an act or instance of the order of things being disturbed ⟨The move to a new town is just the latest in a series of *upsets* for my family over the last year.⟩

syn derangement, dislocation, disruption, disturbance

rel convulsion, revolution, unsettledness, unsettlement, upheaval

upset *vb* **1** to trouble the mind of; to make uneasy — see DISTURB 1

2 to turn on one's side or upside down — see CAPSIZE

3 to undo the proper order or arrangement of — see DISORDER

upsetting *adj* causing worry or anxiety — see TROUBLESOME

upshot *n* a condition or occurrence traceable to a cause — see EFFECT 1

upside-down *adj* lacking in order, neatness, and often cleanliness — see MESSY

upstanding *adj* **1** following the accepted rules of moral conduct — see HONORABLE 1

2 rising straight up — see ERECT

uptight *adj* feeling or showing uncomfortable feelings of uncertainty — see NERVOUS 1

up-to-date *adj* **1** being or involving the latest methods, concepts, information, or styles — see MODERN

2 having information especially as a result of study or experience — see FAMILIAR 2

upturn *vb* to move or extend upward — see ASCEND

urbane *adj* having or showing very polished and worldly manners — see SUAVE

urbanize *vb* to accustom to the ways of the city — see CITIFY

urchin *n* an appealingly mischievous person — see SCAMP 1

urge *n* a strong wish for something — see DESIRE 1

urge *vb* to try to persuade (someone) through earnest appeals to follow a course of action ⟨The public service announcement *urges* pet owners to spay or neuter their pets.⟩

syn egg (on), encourage, exhort, goad, nudge, press, prod, prompt

rel drive, propel, spur, stimulate; hurry, hustle, push, rush; adjure, beseech, implore, importune; blandish, cajole, coax, soft-soap, wheedle; high-pressure, nag, needle, pressure; foment, incite, instigate, provoke, stir (up)

near ant deter, discourage, dissuade; brake, check, constrain, curb; hold back, inhibit, restrain

urgent *adj* needing immediate attention — see ACUTE 2

usable *also* **useable** *adj* **1** capable of or suitable for being used for a particular purpose ⟨Although the spade is *usable* as a snow shovel, it doesn't do a very good job.⟩

syn available, employable, exploitable, fit, functional, operable, practicable, serviceable, useful

rel applicable, relevant; doable, feasible, viable, workable; reusable

ant impracticable, inoperable, nonfunctional, unavailable, unemployable, unusable

2 capable of being put to use or account — see PRACTICAL 1

usage *n* the act or practice of employing something for a particular purpose — see USE 1

use *n* **1** the act or practice of employing something for a particular purpose ⟨The *use* of cell phones is strictly prohibited in the doctor's office.⟩

syn application, employment, exercise, operation, play, usage

rel exertion; reuse

near ant disuse, nonuse

2 the capacity for being useful for some purpose ⟨The broken grill isn't going to be of much *use* in cooking the hamburgers.⟩

syn account, avail, service, serviceability, serviceableness, usefulness, utility

rel advantage, benefit, gain; aid, assistance, help; applicability, appropriateness, fitness, relevance; profit, value, worth

near ant inapplicability, inappropriateness

ant uselessness, worthlessness

3 positive regard for something — see LIKING

use *vb* **1** to put into action or service ⟨I will need to *use* the large hammer for this project.⟩

syn apply, employ, exercise, exploit, harness, operate, utilize

rel handle, manipulate, wield; direct, run, work; cannibalize, recycle, reuse

phrases bring to bear, draw on (*or* upon), make use of

near ant ignore, neglect; misapply, misuse

2 to behave toward in a stated way — see TREAT 1

3 to take unfair advantage of — see EXPLOIT 1

used *adj* being in the habit or custom — see ACCUSTOMED

useful *adj* **1** capable of being put to use or account — see PRACTICAL 1

2 capable of or suitable for being used for a particular purpose — see USABLE 1

3 providing service or assistance — see HELPFUL 1

usefulness *n* the capacity for being useful for some purpose — see USE 2

useless *adj* **1** not capable of being put to use or account — see IMPRACTICAL

2 producing no results — see FUTILE

user *n* a person who regularly uses drugs especially illegally — see ADDICT 1

use up *vb* to make complete use of — see DEPLETE 1

usher *vb* to point out the way for (someone) especially from a position in front — see LEAD 1

usual *adj* **1** accepted, used, or practiced by most people — see CURRENT 1

2 being of the type that is encountered in the normal course of events — see ORDINARY 1

3 often observed or encountered — see COMMON 1

usually *adv* according to the usual course of things — see NATURALLY 1

usurp *vb* to take or make use of under a guise of authority but without actual right — see APPROPRIATE 1

utensil *n* an article intended for use in work — see IMPLEMENT

utility *n* the capacity for being useful for some purpose — see USE 2

utilize *vb* to put into action or service — see USE 1

utmost *adj* **1** most distant from a center — see EXTREME 1

2 of the greatest or highest degree or quantity — see ULTIMATE 1

3 of the highest degree — see FULL 2

utopia *n* an often imaginary place or state of utter perfection and happiness — see PARADISE 1

utopian *n* one whose conduct is guided more by the image of perfection than by the real world — see IDEALIST

utter *adj* **1** having no exceptions or restrictions — see ABSOLUTE 2

2 of the highest degree — see FULL 2

utter *vb* **1** to send forth using the vocal chords ⟨She tried not to *utter* a sound as the doctor gave her a flu shot.⟩

syn emit

rel deliver; blurt (out), ejaculate, exclaim; gasp, groan, heave, hoot, moan, pant, quaver, snarl, sob, sputter, squawk, squeak, squeal, stammer, stutter, whimper, yowl; mouth, whisper

2 to express (a thought or emotion) in words — see SAY 1

utterance *n* **1** an act, process, or means of putting something into words — see EXPRESSION 1

2 something that is said — see WORD 2

uttered *adj* expressed or communicated by voice — see VOCAL

utterly *adv* **1** to a full extent or degree — see FULLY 1

2 to a large extent or degree — see GREATLY 2

uttermost *adj* of the greatest or highest degree or quantity — see ULTIMATE 1

vacancy *n* **1** empty space ⟨the vast *vacancy* that exists between our solar system and the nearest star having its own orbiting planets⟩

syn blank, blankness, emptiness, vacuity, void

rel inane, vacuum; air, open, waste; bareness, barrenness, bleakness, desolateness, hollowness; cavity, gap, hole, hollow

near ant repleteness

2 the quality or state of being empty ⟨The *vacancy* of the gymnasium was apparent to me as I shot baskets alone.⟩

syn bareness, emptiness, vacuity

rel hollowness; blankness, vacuum, void; barrenness, bleakness, desolateness; availability, clearness, openness; dryness, exhaustion

near ant abundance, fatness, repleteness

vacant *adj* **1** lacking contents that could or should be present — see EMPTY 1

2 not being in a state of use, activity, or employment — see INACTIVE 2

3 not expressing any emotion — see BLANK 1

4 left unoccupied or unused — see ABANDONED 1

vacate *vb* **1** to put an end to by formal action — see ABOLISH 1

2 to remove the contents of — see EMPTY

vacated *adj* left unoccupied or unused — see ABANDONED 1

vacation *n* a period during which the usual routine of school or work is suspended ⟨Area schools are on *vacation* that week in February so local ski resorts do a booming business.⟩

syn break, leave, recess

rel sabbatical; furlough, liberty; breather, relaxation, respite, rest; interim, intermis-

---

syn synonym(s)   *rel* related words
ant antonym(s)   *near ant* near antonym(s)

sion, interval; feast, holy day, legal holiday; idling, loafing, lounging, slacking; downtime

vacillate *vb* to show uncertainty about the right course of action — see HESITATE

vacillation *n* a state or an instance of temporary inaction because of uncertainty about the right course of action — see HESITATION

vacuity *n* 1 empty space — see VACANCY 1

2 the quality or state of being empty — see VACANCY 2

3 the quality or state of lacking intelligence or quickness of mind — see STUPIDITY 1

vacuous *adj* 1 lacking contents that could or should be present — see EMPTY 1

2 not having or showing an ability to absorb ideas readily — see STUPID 1

vagabond *adj* traveling from place to place — see ITINERANT

vagabond *n* 1 a homeless wanderer who may beg or steal for a living — see TRAMP

2 a person who roams about without a fixed route or destination — see NOMAD

vagary *n* a sudden impulsive and apparently unmotivated idea or action — see WHIM

vagrant *adj* traveling from place to place — see ITINERANT

vagrant *n* a homeless wanderer who may beg or steal for a living — see TRAMP

vague *adj* 1 not expressed in precise terms ⟨He gave as *vague* a reply as he could, hoping not to give away the surprise.⟩

syn fuzzy, indefinite, unclear

rel ambiguous, cryptic, dark, enigmatic (*also* enigmatical), equivocal, murky, nebulous, obscure, unintelligible; bleary, blurry, dim, faint, foggy, gauzy, hazy, misty; indeterminate, indistinct, indistinguishable, uncertain, undefinable, undefined, undetermined; inexplicable, inscrutable, mysterious; baffling, bewildering, confounding, confusing, mystifying, obfuscatory, perplexing, puzzling, unfathomable

near ant candid, direct, forthright, foursquare, frank, honest, open, openhearted, outspoken, plainspoken, straight, straightforward, unguarded; obvious, plain, unambiguous, unequivocal; defined, distinct, well-defined; blatant, patent, unmistakable

ant clear, definite, explicit, specific

2 not seen or understood clearly — see FAINT 1

vain *adj* 1 having too high an opinion of oneself — see CONCEITED

2 producing no results — see FUTILE

3 having no usefulness — see WORTHLESS

vainglorious *adj* having too high an opinion of oneself — see CONCEITED

vaingloriousness *n* an often unjustified feeling of being pleased with oneself or with one's situation or achievements — see COMPLACENCE 1

vainglory *n* an often unjustified feeling of being pleased with oneself or with one's situation or achievements — see COMPLACENCE 1

vainness *n* an often unjustified feeling of being pleased with oneself or with one's

situation or achievements — see COMPLACENCE 1

vale *n* an area of lowland between hills or mountains — see VALLEY

valedictory *adj* given, taken, or performed at parting — see PARTING

valiant *adj* feeling or displaying no fear by temperament — see BRAVE 1

valid *adj* 1 according to the rules of logic — see LOGICAL 1

2 based on sound reasoning or information — see GOOD 1

validate *vb* 1 to give evidence or testimony to the truth or factualness of — see CONFIRM 1

2 to show the existence or truth of by evidence — see PROVE 1

validation *n* something presented in support of the truth or accuracy of a claim — see PROOF

valley *n* an area of lowland between hills or mountains ⟨The *valley* will be the first to flood if the river rises.⟩

syn dale, hollow, vale

rel canyon (*also* cañon), dell, depression, dingle, glen, gorge, gulch, gully (*also* gulley), ravine, rift valley; basin, bowl

near ant alp, mount, mountain, peak; height, mountaintop, pinnacle, summit; plateau, tableland

valor *n* strength of mind to carry on in spite of danger — see COURAGE

valorous *adj* feeling or displaying no fear by temperament — see BRAVE 1

valuable *adj* commanding a large price — see COSTLY

valuation *n* 1 the act of placing a value on the nature, character, or quality of something — see ESTIMATE 1

2 the amount of money for which something will find a buyer — see VALUE 1

3 the relative usefulness or importance of something as judged by specific qualities — see WORTH 1

value *n* 1 the amount of money for which something will find a buyer ⟨The real *value* of that house is close to a million dollars.⟩

syn valuation, worth

rel charge, cost, fee, figure, price, rate; appraisal, assessment, estimate, estimation, evaluation; face value, list price, unit price

2 a quality that gives something special worth — see EXCELLENCE 2

3 the relative usefulness or importance of something as judged by specific qualities — see WORTH 1

value *vb* 1 to hold dear — see LOVE 1

2 to make an approximate or tentative judgment regarding — see ESTIMATE 1

valueless *adj* having no usefulness — see WORTHLESS

valve *n* a fixture for controlling the flow of a liquid — see FAUCET

van *n* the leading or most important part of a movement — see FOREFRONT

vandal *n* a person who damages or destroys property on purpose ⟨A group of *vandals* broke several gravestones in the cemetery.⟩

syn defacer

rel graffitist, tagger; demolisher, desecrater (*or* desecrator), despoiler, destroyer, ravager, ruiner, saboteur, waster, wrecker; depredator, looter, marauder, pillager, plunderer, ransacker, sacker, spoiler, spoliator

near ant conserver, preserver, protector, saver; conservator, preservationist

vandalism *n* deliberate damaging or destroying of another's property ⟨Anyone guilty of *vandalism* to university property will be expelled.⟩

syn defacement

rel demolishing, demolishment, desecrating, desecration, destruction, ravage, ravaging, ruin, ruination, wrecking; sabotage; depredation, despoiling, despoilment, looting, marauding, pillage, pillaging, plunder, plundering, predation, ransacking, sacking, spoliation

near ant conservation, preservation, protection, salvage, saving

vandalize *vb* to deliberately cause the damage or destruction of another's property ⟨My car was *vandalized* in the parking lot.⟩

syn deface

rel desecrate, violate; graffiti, tag; bang up, break, damage, harm, hurt, impair, mar, shatter, spoil; annihilate, demolish, destroy, devastate, ravage, raven, raze, ruin, scourge, smash, tear down, total, waste, wipe out, wreck; sabotage; depredate, despoil, loot, marauad, pillage, plunder, ransack, sack, spoliate

near ant conserve, preserve, protect, save; salvage; build, rebuild

vanguard *n* the leading or most important part of a movement — see FOREFRONT

vanish *vb* to cease to be visible — see DISAPPEAR

vanished *adj* no longer existing — see EXTINCT

vanity *n* an often unjustified feeling of being pleased with oneself or with one's situation or achievements — see COMPLACENCE 1

vanquish *vb* to bring under one's control by force of arms — see CONQUER 1

vanquisher *n* one that defeats an enemy or opponent — see VICTOR 1

vanquishing *n* the act or process of bringing someone or something under one's control — see CONQUEST

vantage *n* the more favorable condition or position in a competition — see ADVANTAGE 1

variable *adj* **1** capable of being readily changed — see FLEXIBLE 1

2 likely to change frequently, suddenly, or unexpectedly — see FICKLE 1

variance *n* a lack of agreement or harmony — see DISCORD

variation *n* the act, process, or result of making different — see CHANGE 1

varicolored *adj* marked by a variety of usually vivid colors — see COLORFUL

varied *adj* **1** consisting of many things of different sorts — see MISCELLANEOUS

2 marked by a variety of usually vivid colors — see COLORFUL

variegated *adj* **1** marked by a variety of usually vivid colors — see COLORFUL

2 marked with spots — see SPOTTED 1

variety *n* **1** the quality or state of being composed of many different elements or types ⟨The sheer *variety* of the city's restaurants was dazzling.⟩

syn assortment, diverseness, diversity, heterogeneousness, miscellaneousness, multiplicity, variousness

rel disparateness, disparity, dissimilarity, distinction, distinctiveness, distinctness, unlikeness

near ant homogeneity, homogeneousness, likeness, sameness, similarity; fewness, paucity

2 an unorganized collection or mixture of various things — see MISCELLANY 1

3 a number of persons or things that are grouped together because they have something in common — see SORT 1

variousness *n* the quality or state of being composed of many different elements or types — see VARIETY 1

varlet *n* a mean, evil, or unprincipled person — see VILLAIN

vary *vb* **1** to be unlike; to not be the same — see DIFFER 1

2 to make different in some way — see CHANGE 1

3 to occur within a continuous range of variation — see RUN 4

4 to pass from one form, state, or level to another — see CHANGE 2

varying *adj* not staying constant — see UNEVEN 2

vast *adj* unusually large — see HUGE

vastly *adv* **1** to a great degree — see VERY 1

2 to a large extent or degree — see GREATLY 2

vastness *n* the quality or state of being very large — see IMMENSITY

vasty *adj* unusually large — see HUGE

¹vault *n* an underground burial chamber — see CRYPT

²vault *n* an act of leaping into the air — see JUMP 1

vault *vb* to propel oneself upward or forward into the air — see JUMP 1

veer *vb* **1** to change one's course or direction — see TURN 3

2 to change the course or direction of (something) — see TURN 2

3 to depart abruptly from a straight line or course — see SWERVE 1

vegetation *n* green leaves or plants — see GREENERY

vehemence *n* **1** the quality or state of being forceful (as in expression) ⟨The *vehemence* in her voice when she insisted that she never gossiped surprised me.⟩

syn aggressiveness, assertiveness, emphasis, fierceness, forcefulness, intensity, vigorousness, violence

rel potency, power, strength; eloquence; ardor, fervency, fervidness, fervor, insistence, passion, warmth; stridency, vociferousness; clearness, directness, incision, incisiveness, plainness, straightforwardness, vividness

near ant ambiguity, equivocation; delicacy, lightness, subtlety

ant feebleness, mildness, weakness

2 depth of feeling — see ARDOR 1

---

vehement adj 1 marked by or uttered with forcefulness — see EMPHATIC 1
2 extreme in degree, power, or effect — see INTENSE 1
3 having or expressing great depth of feeling — see FERVENT 1

vehicle n 1 something used to achieve an end — see AGENT 1
2 something used to carry goods or passengers — see CONVEYANCE

veil n something that covers or conceals like a piece of cloth — see CLOAK 1

veil vb 1 to keep secret or shut off from view — see ¹HIDE 2
2 to surround or cover closely — see ENFOLD 1

vein n a distinctive way of putting ideas into words — see STYLE 1

veld or **veldt** n a broad area of level or rolling treeless country — see PLAIN 1

velocity n a high rate of movement or performance — see SPEED 1

velvety adj smooth or delicate in appearance or feel — see SOFT 2

venal adj open to improper influence and especially bribery ⟨That judge is known for being *venal* and easily bought.⟩
syn bribable, corruptible, dirty
rel temptable; hack, mercenary; crooked, cutthroat, dishonest, Machiavellian, unethical, unmoral, unprincipled, unscrupulous; corrupt, corrupted, debased, debauched, defiled, degenerate, degraded, demoralized, depraved, dissipated, dissolute, perverse, perverted, reprobate, sleazy, vitiated, warped; bad, evil, immoral, iniquitous, nefarious, sinful, vicious, wicked
near ant ethical, honest, principled, scrupulous; good, moral, righteous, upright, virtuous
ant incorruptible

vend vb to offer for sale to the public — see MARKET

vendor also **vender** n the person in a business deal who hands over an item in exchange for money ⟨We're thinking of making a deal with that other software *vendor*.⟩
syn dealer, merchandiser, seller
rel merchant, trader, tradesman; auctioneer, concessionaire; black marketer (or black marketeer), bootlegger, fence, fencer, hustler, scalper, smuggler, trafficker; discounter, distributor, e-tailer, exporter, jobber, reseller, retailer, wholesaler; chapman [British], hawker, huckster, peddler (also pedlar); salesclerk, salesman, salesperson, saleswoman, shopgirl; bargainer, haggler, horse trader, palterer
near ant consumer, end user, user
ant buyer, purchaser

veneer n 1 a deceptively attractive external appearance — see GLOSS 1
2 an outer part or layer — see EXTERIOR

venerable adj 1 deserving honor and respect especially by reason of age ⟨The *venerable* old man was a cherished source of advice and wisdom for the villagers.⟩
syn hallowed, revered, reverend, sacred, venerated
rel honorable, reputable, respectable; considered, esteemed, honored, respected, reverenced; admirable, distinguished, redoubtable, worthy; good, moral, noble, righteous
near ant bad, discreditable, disgraceful, dishonorable, disreputable, ignominious, infamous, loose, notorious, shameful; immoral, seamy, shadowy, shady, sordid, unsavory, vile, wicked; base, contemptible, despicable, detestable, dirty, low, mean, wretched
2 dating or surviving from the distant past — see ANCIENT 1

venerate vb to offer honor or respect to (someone) as a divine power — see WORSHIP 1

venerated adj deserving honor and respect especially by reason of age — see VENERABLE 1

vengeance n the act or an instance of responding to an injury with an injury — see REVENGE

vengeful adj likely to seek revenge — see VINDICTIVE

venial adj worthy of forgiveness ⟨Taking the restaurant's menu as a souvenir seems like a *venial* offense.⟩
syn excusable, forgivable, pardonable, remissible, remittable
rel justifiable; allowable, permissible; insignificant, minor, petty, trifling, trivial, unimportant; harmless, ignorable, tolerable
near ant abominable, criminal, evil, heinous; sinful, vile, wicked
ant indefensible, inexcusable, mortal, unforgivable, unjustifiable, unpardonable

venom n 1 a substance that by chemical action can kill or injure a living thing — see POISON
2 the desire to cause pain for the satisfaction of doing harm — see MALICE

venomous adj containing or contaminated with a substance capable of injuring or killing a living thing — see POISONOUS

vent vb 1 to find emotional release for — see TAKE OUT 1
2 to make known (as an idea, emotion, or opinion) — see EXPRESS 1
3 to throw or give off — see EMIT 1

ventilate vb to make known (as an idea, emotion, or opinion) — see EXPRESS 1

venture n a risky undertaking — see GAMBLE

venture vb 1 to place in danger — see ENDANGER
2 to take a chance on — see RISK 1

venturesome adj 1 inclined or willing to take risks — see BOLD 1
2 involving potential loss or injury — see DANGEROUS 1

venturous adj inclined or willing to take risks — see BOLD 1

veracious adj 1 being in the habit of telling the truth — see TRUTHFUL
2 following an original exactly — see FAITHFUL 2
3 being in agreement with the truth or a fact or a standard — see CORRECT 1

veracity n 1 devotion to telling the truth — see HONESTY 1
2 the quality or state of being very accurate — see PRECISION

verbal adj 1 of or relating to words or language ⟨The child didn't yet have the *verbal*

skills needed to tell the doctor about the pain he was experiencing.⟩
syn lexical, linguistic (*also* linguistical), rhetorical (*also* rhetoric), wordy
rel communicative, conversational
ant nonlexical, nonlinguistic, nonverbal
2 made or carried on through speaking rather than in writing ⟨A *verbal* agreement carries less force than a written contract.⟩
syn oral, spoken, unwritten
rel consensual, implicit, informal; articulated, verbalized; given, pronounced, sounded, stated, told, voiced
near ant explicit, formal
ant paper, written
verbalize *vb* to express (a thought or emotion) in words — see SAY 1
verbatim *adv* in the same words ⟨You can't just copy the encyclopedia article *verbatim* for your report—that's plagiarism!⟩
syn directly, exactly, word for word
rel accurately, precisely; identically; literally
near ant basically, essentially, virtually; carelessly, freely, imprecisely, inaccurately, loosely
ant inexactly
verbiage *n* **1** the use of too many words to express an idea ⟨Teachers discourage the *verbiage* that students resort to in order to lengthen their reports.⟩
syn circumlocution, diffuseness, longwindedness, prolixity, redundancy, verboseness, verbosity, windiness, wordiness
rel circuitousness, circularity, digressiveness; pleonasm, tautology; reiteration, repetition, repetitiousness, repetitiveness; embellishment, embroidering, exaggeration, hyperbole, overstatement
near ant brevity, briefness, compactness, conciseness, crispness, pithiness, succinctness, terseness
2 language that is impressive-sounding but not meaningful or sincere — see RHETORIC 1
3 the way in which something is put into words — see WORDING 1
verbose *adj* using or containing more words than necessary to express an idea — see WORDY 1
verboseness *n* the use of too many words to express an idea — see VERBIAGE 1
verbosity *n* the use of too many words to express an idea — see VERBIAGE 1
verdant *adj* covered with a thick, healthy natural growth — see LUSH 1
verdict *n* **1** a position arrived at after consideration — see DECISION 1
2 an idea that is believed to be true or valid without positive knowledge — see OPINION 1
verdure *n* green leaves or plants — see GREENERY
verge *n* **1** an interval of time just before the onset of something — see POINT 3
2 the line or relatively narrow space that marks the outer limit of something — see BORDER 1
verge (on) *vb* **1** to be adjacent to — see ADJOIN 1

2 to come very close to being — see BORDER (ON) 1
verging *adj* having a border in common — see ADJACENT
verifiable *adj* capable of being proven as true or real ⟨We're not sure whether that's a *verifiable* hypothesis.⟩ ⟨You need a *verifiable* letter from your doctor to file a claim for short-term disability.⟩
syn confirmable, demonstrable, empirical (*also* empiric), provable, supportable, sustainable
rel documentable, well-founded; defensible, excusable, justifiable, vindicable, warrantable; alleged, assumed, conjectured, guessed, presumed, surmised, suspected
near ant debatable, disprovable, disputable, refutable
ant indemonstrable, insupportable, unprovable, unsupportable, unsustainable, unverifiable
verify *vb* to give evidence or testimony to the truth or factualness of — see CONFIRM 1
verifying *adj* serving to give support to the truth or factualness of something — see CORROBORATIVE
verily *adv* **1** to tell the truth — see ACTUALLY 1
2 not merely this but also — see EVEN 1
veritably *adv* in actual fact — see VERY 2
verity *n* **1** agreement with fact or reality — see TRUTH
2 devotion to telling the truth — see HONESTY 1
vernacular *adj* used in or suitable for speech and not formal writing — see COLLOQUIAL 1
versatile *adj* able to do many different kinds of things ⟨A *versatile* baseball player can play any position.⟩ ⟨This tool is *versatile* enough to serve as a wrench or pliers.⟩
syn adaptable, all-around (*also* all-round), protean, universal
rel mixed-use, multipurpose; well-rounded; able, ace, adept, experienced, expert, masterful, proficient, skilled, skillful; adjustable, alterable, changeable, elastic, flexible, fluid, malleable, modifiable, plastic, pliable, pliant, supple, variable
near ant limited; amateur, inexperienced
verse *n* **1** a composition using rhythm and often rhyme to create a lyrical effect — see POEM
2 writing that uses rhythm, vivid language, and often rhyme to provoke an emotional response — see POETRY 1
verse *vb* to give information to — see ENLIGHTEN 1
versed *adj* **1** having information especially as a result of study or experience — see FAMILIAR 2
2 having or showing exceptional knowledge, experience, or skill in a field of endeavor — see PROFICIENT
versifier *n* a person who writes poetry — see POET
vertebral column *n* a column of bones supporting the trunk of a vertebrate animal — see SPINE
vertical *adj* rising straight up — see ERECT
verve *n* active strength of body or mind — see VIGOR 1

---

very *adj* **1** being one and not another — see SAME 2

2 being this and no more — see MERE

3 existing in fact and not merely as a possibility — see ACTUAL

4 having no exceptions or restrictions — see ABSOLUTE 2

very *adv* **1** to a great degree ⟨That was a *very* brave thing to do.⟩

syn almighty, awful, awfully, badly, beastly, bone, colossally, deadly, enormously, especially, ever, exceedingly (*also* exceeding), extra, extremely, far, filthy, frightfully, full, greatly, heavily, highly, hugely, incredibly, intensely, jolly, mightily, mighty, mortally, most, much, particularly, passing, real, really, right, roaring, severely, so, sore, sorely, spanking, such, super, supremely, terribly, too, vastly, way, whacking, wicked, wildly

rel absolutely, altogether, completely, downright, entirely, fully, purely, radically, thoroughly, totally, utterly, wholly; deeply, profoundly; exceptionally, remarkably; considerably, extensively, significantly, substantially; appreciably, discernibly, markedly, noticeably, obviously, palpably, plainly, visibly; abundantly, plentifully; astronomically, grandly, monstrously; excessively, obscenely, overmuch; amazingly, astonishingly, staggeringly

phrases a lot, as all get-out, good and

near ant meagerly, scantily; barely, hardly, just, marginally, minimally, scarcely

ant little, negligibly, nominally, slightly, somewhat

2 in actual fact ⟨The *very* same thing happened to me.⟩

syn actually, authentically, genuinely, really, truly, veritably

rel accurately, exactly, just, precisely, right, sharp, smack-dab, squarely; almost, nearly, practically, virtually; literally, simply

phrases in actuality, in reality, in truth

near ant apparently, ostensibly, outwardly, plausibly, seemingly

ant professedly, supposedly

vessel *n* **1** a large craft for travel by water — see SHIP

2 a small buoyant structure for travel on water — see BOAT 1

3 a usually circular utensil for holding something (as food) — see DISH 1

4 something into which a liquid or small objects can be put for storage or transportation — see CONTAINER

vest *vb* **1** to give official or legal power to — see AUTHORIZE 1

2 to put (something) into the possession or safekeeping of another — see GIVE 2

3 to give the ownership or benefit of (something) formally or publicly — see CONFER 1

vestibule *n* the entrance room of a building — see HALL 1

vestige *n* **1** a tiny often physical indication of something lost or vanished ⟨A few strange words carved on a tree were the only *vestige* of the lost colony of Roanoke.⟩

syn echo, ghost, relic, shadow, trace

rel memento, remembrance, reminder; artifact; afterimage, aftertaste; balance, corpse, hangover, leftover, oddment, remainder, remnant, scrap; dreg(s), leavings, remain(s), residual, residue, rest

2 the mark or impression made by a foot — see FOOTPRINT

vestry *n* a room in a church building for sacred furnishings (as vestments) — see SACRISTY

vet *n* a person with long experience in a specified area — see VETERAN

veteran *adj* having or showing exceptional knowledge, experience, or skill in a field of endeavor — see PROFICIENT

veteran *n* a person with long experience in a specified area ⟨As a *veteran* of overseas travel, she gave us solid advice about planning our trip.⟩

syn old hand, old-timer, vet

rel doyenne; adept, dab hand [*chiefly British*], expert, guru, hand, master, past master, pro, professional

near ant apprentice, cub; amateur, dilettante; learner, student, trainee; candidate, entrant, probationer

ant beginner, colt, fledgling, freshman, greenhorn, neophyte, newbie, newcomer, novice, recruit, rookie, tenderfoot, tyro

veto *n* an order that something not be done or used — see PROHIBITION 2

veto *vb* to reject by or as if by a vote — see NEGATIVE 1

vex *vb* **1** to disturb the peace of mind of (someone) especially by repeated disagreeable acts — see IRRITATE 1

2 to throw into a state of mental uncertainty — see CONFUSE 1

vexation *n* **1** the act of making unwelcome intrusions upon another — see ANNOYANCE 1

2 the feeling of impatience or anger caused by another's repeated disagreeable acts — see ANNOYANCE 2

3 something that is a source of irritation — see ANNOYANCE 3

vexatious *adj* causing annoyance — see ANNOYING

vexing *adj* causing annoyance — see ANNOYING

via *prep* **1** along the way of — see BY 1

2 using the means or agency of — see BY 2

viable *adj* capable of being done or carried out — see POSSIBLE 1

viand *n* **1** something that is pleasing to eat because it is rare or a luxury — see DELICACY 1

2 viands *pl* substances intended to be eaten — see FOOD

vibrancy *n* the quality or state of having abundant or intense activity — see VITALITY 1

vibrant *adj* **1** marked by much life, movement, or activity — see ALIVE 2

2 marked by conspicuously full and rich sounds or tones — see RESONANT

vibrate *vb* to make a series of slight irregular or violent movements — see SHAKE 1

vibration *n* a series of slight movements by a body back and forth or from side to side ⟨the *vibration* of the floor caused by thundering feet in the hallway⟩

syn jiggling, oscillation, quivering, shaking, shuddering, trembling, twitching

rel juddering [*chiefly British*], quaking, rocking; jiggle, palpitation, quiver, shake, shiver, shudder, tremble, tremor, twitch

2 *often* **vibrations** *pl* a spiritual force that is held to emanate from or give animation to living beings — see ENERGY 1

3 *usually* **vibrations** *pl* a special quality or impression associated with something — see AURA 1

vice *n* **1** immoral conduct or practices harmful or offensive to society ⟨a unit in the police department assigned to focus on *vice*⟩

syn corruption, debauchery, depravity, immorality, iniquity, licentiousness, profligacy, sin

rel bad, badness, evil, evildoing, ill, villainy, wickedness, wrong; atrociousness, evilness, heinousness, sinfulness, unscrupulousness, viciousness, vileness, villainousness; devilry (*or* deviltry); corruptness, debasement, degeneracy, degeneration, depravedness, dissoluteness, dissolution; indecency, lasciviousness, lechery, lewdness, looseness, perversion, pervertedness, wantonness; abomination, anathema, taboo (*also* tabu); criminality, reprehensibleness; baseness, despicableness, dirtiness, lowness, meanness; lousiness, wretchedness

near ant good, right; honesty, honor, integrity, legitimacy, probity, rectitude, scrupulosity, scrupulousness, uprightness; goodness, righteousness, virtuousness; blamelessness, chastity, innocence, perfection, pureness, purity, spotlessness; cleanness, correctness, decency, decorousness, propriety, rightness, seemliness

ant morality, virtue

2 a defect in character — see FAULT 1

vicious *adj* **1** extreme in degree, power, or effect — see INTENSE 1

2 having or showing the desire to inflict severe pain and suffering on others — see CRUEL 1

3 not conforming to a high moral standard; morally unacceptable — see BAD 2

4 violently unfriendly or aggressive in disposition — see FIERCE 1

5 having or showing a desire to cause someone pain or suffering for the sheer enjoyment of it — see HATEFUL

viciously *adv* in a mean or spiteful manner — see NASTILY

viciousness *n* **1** the desire to cause pain for the satisfaction of doing harm — see MALICE

2 disposition to willfully inflict pain and suffering on others — see CRUELTY

victim *n* **1** a person or thing harmed, lost, or destroyed — see CASUALTY 1

2 a person or thing that is the object of abuse, criticism, or ridicule — see TARGET 1

3 something offered to a god — see SACRIFICE

victimize *vb* to rob by the use of trickery or threats — see FLEECE

victor *n* **1** one that defeats an enemy or

opponent ⟨The computer is usually the *victor* in a chess match against a human opponent.⟩

syn beater, conqueror, master, subduer, trimmer, vanquisher, whipper, winner

rel champ, champion, finalist, placer; dominator, overdog, ruler, subjugator, top dog

near ant punching bag, pushover, quitter; failure, flop, washout; underdog

ant loser

2 the person who comes in first in a competition — see CHAMPION 1

victory *n* an instance of defeating an enemy or opponent ⟨With great effort, our team managed an upset *victory* in the final moments.⟩

syn triumph, win

rel capture, conquest, mastery, subjugation, vanquishing; blowout, landslide, laugher, romp, shutout, sweep, walkaway, walkover; squeaker; success

near ant upset; collapse, debacle (*also* débâcle), disaster, failure, fizzle, flop, nonsuccess, washout; decline, slip, slump, wane; lurch, setback

ant beating, defeat, drubbing, licking, loss, overthrow, rout, shellacking, trimming, whipping

victual *vb* to provide food or meals for — see FEED 1

victuals *n pl* substances intended to be eaten — see FOOD

vie *vb* to engage in a contest — see COMPETE

view *n* **1** all that can be seen from a certain point ⟨The *view* of the mountains from the inn's porch is spectacular.⟩

syn command, lookout, outlook, panorama, perspective, prospect, vista

rel scene, scenery; ken; sight; visual field

2 an idea that is believed to be true or valid without positive knowledge — see OPINION 1

3 an instance of looking especially briefly — see LOOK 2

4 a close look at or over someone or something in order to judge condition — see INSPECTION

view *vb* **1** to look over closely (as for judging quality or condition) — see INSPECT

2 to make note of (something) through the use of one's eyes — see SEE 1

3 to think of in a particular way — see CONSIDER 1

viewpoint *n* a way of looking at or thinking about something — see PERSPECTIVE 1

vigilance *n* the state of being constantly attentive and responsive to signs of opportunity, activity, or danger ⟨Eternal *vigilance* is the price of freedom.⟩

syn alert, alertness, attentiveness, watch, watchfulness

rel aliveness, awareness, receptiveness, receptivity, sensitivity; care, carefulness, cautiousness, chariness, heedfulness, wariness; preparation, readiness; vigil

near ant absentmindedness, daydreaming, daze, distraction; absorption, engrossment, obliviousness, preoccupation; unawareness, unconsciousness; carelessness, heedlessness, inattention, inattentiveness, inobservance; unwariness

vigilant *adj* paying close attention usually

---

syn synonym(s) *rel* related words
ant antonym(s) *near ant* near antonym(s)

for the purpose of anticipating approaching danger or opportunity — see ALERT 1

vigilante *n* one who inflicts punishment in return for an injury or offense — see NEMESIS 1

vignette *n* a vivid representation in words of someone or something — see DESCRIPTION 1

vigor *n* **1** active strength of body or mind ⟨She was picked to lead the volunteer group because of her *vigor* and enthusiasm.⟩

syn bounce, dash, drive, energy, esprit, gas, ginger, go, hardihood, life, pep, punch, sap, snap, starch, verve, vim, vitality, zing, zip

rel animal spirits, animation, briskness, jauntiness, liveliness, snappiness, spirit, spiritedness, sprightliness, spunk, spunkiness, vibrancy, vivaciousness, vivacity; ardor, élan, fervor, fire, passion, zeal; main, metal, mettle, might, muscle, potency, power, puissance, stamina, strength; brawniness, fitness, hardiness, huskiness, sturdiness, virility; health, healthiness, soundness, verdure, wellness

near ant indolence, laziness; debilitation, debility, delicacy, disablement, enfeeblement, faintness, feebleness, frailness, frailty, impotence, impotency, infirmity, powerlessness, puniness, slightness, softness, weakness; exhaustion, inanition, prostration

ant listlessness, sluggishness, torpidity

2 the ability to exert effort for the accomplishment of a task — see POWER 2

vigorous *adj* **1** having active strength of body or mind ⟨He remains healthy and *vigorous* despite being over 80 years old.⟩

syn dynamic, energetic, flush, gingery, lusty, peppy, red-blooded, robust, vital

rel animated, brisk, dashing, lively, spirited, sprightly, vivacious; energized, enlivened, invigorated, vitalized; firm, fortified, mettlesome, mighty, powerful, puissant, strong; refreshed, rejuvenated, revitalized; able-bodied, athletic, beefy, brawny, burly, fit, hardy, husky, muscular, robustious, rugged, stalwart, stout, strapping, sturdy, tough, virile; hale, healthy, hearty, sound; capable, competent

near ant delicate, effete, enervated, faint, feeble, frail, infirm, wan, weak, weakened; impotent, powerless, prostrate, prostrated, sapped, tired; indolent, lackadaisical, languid, lazy; invertebrate, nerveless, soft, spineless, wimpy; ill, unhealthy, unsound, unwell; broken-down, debilitated, decrepit, disabled, wasted, worn-out

ant dull, lethargic, listless, sluggish, torpid

2 able to withstand hardship, strain, or exposure — see HARDY 1

3 marked by or uttered with forcefulness — see EMPHATIC 1

4 not showing weakness or uncertainty — see FIRM 1

vigorously *adv* in a vigorous and forceful manner — see HARD 1

vigorousness *n* **1** the quality or state of being forceful (as in expression) — see VEHEMENCE 1

2 the quality or state of having abundant or intense activity — see VITALITY 1

vile *adj* **1** not conforming to a high moral standard; morally unacceptable — see BAD 2

2 not following or in accordance with standards of honor and decency — see IGNOBLE 2

3 unpleasant to look at — see UGLY 1

vileness *n* the state or quality of being utterly evil — see ENORMITY 1

vilification *n* the making of false statements that damage another's reputation — see SLANDER

vilify *vb* to make untrue and harmful statements about — see SLANDER

vilifying *n* the making of false statements that damage another's reputation — see SLANDER

villa *n* a large impressive residence — see MANSION

villager *n* a person who lives in a town on a permanent basis — see BURGHER

villain *n* a mean, evil, or unprincipled person ⟨Only a heartless *villain* would do something so cruel.⟩

syn beast, brute, devil, evildoer, fiend, heavy, hound, knave, miscreant, monster, no-good, rapscallion, rascal, reprobate, rogue, savage, scalawag (*or* scallywag), scamp, scoundrel, varlet, wretch

rel villainess; blackguard; criminal, crook, culprit, felon, lawbreaker, malefactor, offender, perp, perpetrator, transgressor; sinner, trespasser, wrongdoer; cad, heel, serpent, snake, viper; bandit, bravo, desperado, outlaw; con, convict, jailbird; assassin, cutthroat, gangster, goon, gunman, hoodlum, hooligan, racketeer, ruffian, thug; rough, rowdy, tough; loser, lowlife, stinker, trash

near ant angel, innocent, saint; hero

villainous *adj* not conforming to a high moral standard; morally unacceptable — see BAD 2

villainously *adv* in a mean or spiteful manner — see NASTILY

villainy *n* that which is morally unacceptable — see EVIL

vim *n* active strength of body or mind — see VIGOR 1

vindicate *vb* **1** to free from a charge of wrongdoing — see EXCULPATE

2 to give evidence or testimony to the truth or factualness of — see CONFIRM 1

vindicating *adj* serving to give support to the truth or factualness of something — see CORROBORATIVE

vindication *n* a setting free from a charge of wrongdoing — see ACQUITTAL

vindictive *adj* likely to seek revenge ⟨Be careful not to annoy the *vindictive* old woman who lives down the street.⟩

syn revengeful, vengeful

rel avenging, retaliatory; resentful, uncharitable, unforgiving; catty, cruel, despiteful, hateful, malevolent, malicious, malign, malignant, mean, nasty, sadistic, spiteful, venomous, vicious, viperish, virulent; narrow-minded, petty, small-minded; grim, implacable, merciless, pitiless, relentless, unrelenting; baleful, baneful, evil, harsh, hostile, inimical, wrathful

near ant charitable, forgiving, merciful, relenting; benevolent, benign, benignant, loving; brotherly, compassionate, good, good-hearted, kind, kindhearted, kindly, sympathetic, warm, warmhearted; altruistic, humane, humanitarian, philanthropic (*also* philanthropical); sweet, tender, tenderhearted; high-minded, magnanimous, noble

vinegary *adj* causing or characterized by the one of the basic taste sensations that is produced chiefly by acids — see SOUR 1

violate *vb* **1** to fail to keep ⟨You've *violated* the company's new rule against smoking on the premises.⟩

syn breach, break, fracture, offend, traduce, transgress

rel disobey, rebel; brush (off), disregard, flout, ignore, neglect, overpass, pass over, slight, tune out, wink (at); dismiss, pooh-pooh (*also* pooh), scorn, shrug off; defy, resist, withstand

near ant defer (to), serve, submit (to), surrender (to), yield (to); attend, hear, heed, listen (to), mark, note, notice, regard, watch

ant comply (with), conform (to), follow, mind, obey, observe

2 to treat (a sacred place or object) shamefully or with great disrespect — see DESECRATE

violation *n* **1** a breaking of a moral or legal code — see OFFENSE 1

2 a failure to uphold the requirements of law, duty, or obligation — see BREACH 1

violence *n* **1** the use of brute strength to cause harm to a person or property ⟨They settled their disagreement without resorting to *violence*.⟩

syn force, foul play

rel coercion, compulsion, constraint, duress, pressure; barbarity, brutality, savagery; damage, detriment, harm, hurt, impairment, injury; crippling, maiming, mayhem, mutilation; assault, attack, bashing, battering, battery, beating, belting, bludgeoning, buffeting, clubbing, cudgeling (*or* cudgelling), drubbing, flogging, hammering, lacing, licking, mauling, paddling, pelting, pommeling (*or* pommelling), pounding, pummeling (*also* pummelling), smashing, socking, thrashing, tromping, whaling, whipping; frenzy, fury, onslaught, outbreak, outrage, paroxysm, rage, rampage, revolt, riot, rupture, shock, storm, terror, threat, tumult, turbulence, upheaval, uproar; browbeating, bulldozing, bullying, hectoring, strong-arming

near ant pacificism, pacifism

ant nonviolence

2 the quality or state of being forceful (as in expression) — see VEHEMENCE 1

3 depth of feeling — see ARDOR 1

violent *adj* **1** marked by bursts of destructive force or intense activity ⟨the volcano's *violent* eruptions⟩

syn convulsive, explosive, ferocious, fierce, furious, hot, rabid, rough, stormy, tempestuous, tumultuous, turbulent, volcanic

rel barbarous, brutal, savage, vicious; antagonistic, hostile; aggressive, assertive,

bellicose, belligerent, combative, contentious, gladiatorial, pugnacious, quarrelsome, truculent; combustible, volatile; agitated, frantic, frenzied, mad; cataclysmal (*or* cataclysmic), destructive, ruinous

near ant calm, halcyon, pacific, serene, tranquil; nonbelligerent, unaggressive

ant nonviolent, peaceable, peaceful

2 extreme in degree, power, or effect — see INTENSE 1

3 marked by great and often stressful excitement or activity — see FURIOUS 1

4 marked by or uttered with forcefulness — see EMPHATIC 1

VIP *n* a person who is widely known and usually much talked about — see CELEBRITY 1

viper *n* a limbless reptile with a long body — see SNAKE 1

virago *n* a bad-tempered scolding woman — see SHREW

virgin *adj* **1** never having had sexual relations ⟨young people who are *virgin*⟩

syn virginal

rel chaste, modest, pure, vestal; innocent, untouched; abstinent, celibate, continent; unmarried, unwed

ant deflowered

2 being in an original and unused or unspoiled state — see FRESH 1

3 free from any trace of the coarse or indecent — see CHASTE 1

4 existing without human habitation or cultivation — see WILD 2

5 coming before all others in time or order — see FIRST 1

virginal *adj* **1** being in an original and unused or unspoiled state — see FRESH 1

2 never having had sexual relations — see VIRGIN 1

3 free from any trace of the coarse or indecent — see CHASTE 1

virile *adj* of, relating to, or marked by qualities traditionally associated with men — see MASCULINE

virility *n* the set of qualities traditionally considered appropriate for or characteristic of men ⟨an actor known for playing roles evincing *virility*⟩

syn manhood, manliness, masculinity

rel maleness; boyishness, mannishness, tomboyishness

near ant girlishness; girlhood, maidenhood; effeminacy, effeteness; emasculation

ant muliebrity

virtually *adv* very close to but not completely — see ALMOST

virtue *n* **1** a quality that gives something special worth — see EXCELLENCE 2

2 conduct that conforms to an accepted standard of right and wrong — see MORALITY 1

3 strength of mind to carry on in spite of danger — see COURAGE

virtuoso *adj* **1** accomplished with trained ability — see SKILLFUL 1

2 having or showing exceptional knowledge, experience, or skill in a field of endeavor — see PROFICIENT

virtuoso *n* a person with a high level of knowledge or skill in a field — see EXPERT

virtuous *adj* conforming to a high standard of morality or virtue — see GOOD 2

---

syn synonym(s)   *rel* related words
ant antonym(s)   *near ant* near antonym(s)

virtuously *adv* with purity of thought and deed — see PURELY 1

virtuousness *n* conduct that conforms to an accepted standard of right and wrong — see MORALITY 1

virulence *n* biting sharpness of feeling or expression — see ACRIMONY 1

virulent *adj* having or showing a desire to cause someone pain or suffering for the sheer enjoyment of it — see HATEFUL

virulently *adv* in a mean or spiteful manner — see NASTILY

visage *n* 1 facial appearance regarded as an indication of mood or feeling — see LOOK 1

2 the front part of the head — see FACE 1

viscera *n pl* the internal organs of the body — see GUT 1

viscid *adj* 1 being of a consistency that resists flow — see THICK 2

2 tending to adhere to objects upon contact — see STICKY 1

viscosity *n* the degree to which a fluid can resist flowing — see CONSISTENCY

viscous *adj* being of a consistency that resists flow — see THICK 2

visible *adj* 1 capable of being seen ⟨The *visible* light spectrum runs from red to violet.⟩

syn apparent, observable, seeable, visual

rel viewable; detectable, discernible (*also* discernable), noticeable, perceptible; clear, conspicuous, evident, eye-catching, manifest, obvious, overt, patent, perceivable, plain, prominent, striking; exposed, external, outer, outward, superficial

near ant disappeared, dissolved, evanesced, evaporated, melted, vanished, vaporized; imperceptible, indiscernible, indistinct, unnoticeable, unobservable; faint, inconspicuous, insignificant, slight, unobtrusive, vague; buried, concealed, covert, disguised, latent, obscure, shrouded

ant sightless, viewless

2 widely known — see FAMOUS 1

vision *n* 1 a conception or image created by the imagination and having no objective reality — see FANTASY 1

2 the ability to see — see EYESIGHT

3 the soul of a dead person thought of especially as appearing to living people — see GHOST 1

4 concern or preparation for the future — see FORESIGHT 2

vision *vb* to form a mental picture of — see IMAGINE 1

visionary *adj* 1 not real and existing only in the imagination — see IMAGINARY 1

2 having or showing awareness of and preparation for the future — see FORESIGHTED

visionary *n* 1 one who predicts future events or developments — see PROPHET 1

2 one whose conduct is guided more by the image of perfection than by the real world — see IDEALIST

visit *n* 1 a temporary residing as another's guest ⟨My aunt always looks forward to her weeklong annual *visit* with her mother.⟩

syn sojourn, stay

rel field trip, homestay, sleepover; layover, stop, stopover

2 a coming to see another briefly for social or business reasons — see CALL 2

visit *vb* 1 to make a social call upon ⟨The community leaders make a point of *visiting* everyone who moves into the neighborhood.⟩

syn call (on *or* upon), see

rel look up, seek (out)

near ant brush (aside *or* off), cold-shoulder, ignore, snub

2 to reside as a temporary guest ⟨an old friend who comes to *visit* for a month every summer⟩

syn crash [*slang*], sojourn, stay, tarry

rel come by, stop (by); frequent, haunt; inhabit, occupy

near ant abide, dwell, live, reside

3 to engage in casual or rambling conversation — see CHAT 1

4 to go to or spend time in often — see FREQUENT

5 to make a brief visit — see CALL 3

visitant *n* 1 a person who visits another — see GUEST 1

2 the soul of a dead person thought of especially as appearing to living people — see GHOST 1

visitation *n* a coming to see another briefly for social or business reasons — see CALL 2

visitor *n* a person who visits another — see GUEST 1

visor *also* **vizor** *n* the projecting front part of a hat or cap ⟨The *visor* on your baseball cap should provide adequate shade for your eyes.⟩

syn bill, brim, peak

rel shade

vista *n* all that can be seen from a certain point — see VIEW 1

visual *adj* 1 of, relating to, or used in vision ⟨The eyes are the primary *visual* organs in humans.⟩

syn ocular, optic, optical

rel seeing, sighted; focusing (*also* focussing)

ant nonvisual

2 capable of being seen — see VISIBLE 1

3 consisting of or relating to pictures — see PICTORIAL 1

4 producing a mental picture through clear and impressive description — see GRAPHIC 1

visual *n* something that visually explains or decorates a text — see ILLUSTRATION 1

visualize *vb* to form a mental picture of — see IMAGINE 1

vital *adj* 1 having active strength of body or mind — see VIGOROUS 1

2 having much high-spirited energy and movement — see LIVELY 1

3 impossible to do without — see ESSENTIAL 1

4 likely to cause or capable of causing death — see DEADLY 1

5 of the greatest possible importance — see CRUCIAL

6 having a renewing effect on the state of the body or mind — see TONIC 1

vitality *n* 1 the quality or state of having abundant or intense activity ⟨a city known for the *vitality* of its music scene⟩

syn animation, briskness, exuberance,

jazziness, liveliness, lustiness, peppiness, robustness, sprightliness, vibrancy, vigorousness

rel buoyancy, jauntiness, springiness; brightness, cheer, cheerfulness, chirpiness, effervescence, friskiness, sparkle, spirit, verve, vivaciousness, vivacity; eagerness, ebullience, ebulliency, enthusiasm, keenness, spiritedness; friskiness, impishness, pertness, playfulness

near ant indolence, laziness; anemia, bloodlessness; languor, limpness, listlessness, sleepiness, sluggishness, spiritlessness, torpidity, weariness; apathy, impassivity; dullness (*also* dulness), pallidness, tediousness, tedium, vapidity, vapidness

ant inactivity, lifelessness

2 active strength of body or mind — see VIGOR 1

vitalize *vb* to give life, vigor, or spirit to — see ANIMATE

vitalizing *adj* having a renewing effect on the state of the body or mind — see TONIC 1

vitals *n pl* the internal organs of the body — see GUT 1

vitiate *vb* 1 to affect slightly with something morally bad or undesirable — see TAINT 1

2 to reduce the soundness, effectiveness, or perfection of — see DAMAGE 1

3 to lower in character, dignity, or quality — see DEBASE 1

vitriol *n* 1 biting sharpness of feeling or expression — see ACRIMONY 1

2 harsh insulting language — see ABUSE 1

vittles *n pl* substances intended to be eaten — see FOOD

vituperate *vb* to criticize harshly and usually publicly — see ATTACK 2

vituperation *n* harsh insulting language — see ABUSE 1

vivacious *adj* 1 having much high-spirited energy and movement — see LIVELY 1

2 joyously unrestrained — see EXUBERANT

vivaciously *adv* in a quick and spirited manner — see GAILY 2

vivid *adj* producing a mental picture through clear and impressive description — see GRAPHIC 1

vivify *vb* to give life, vigor, or spirit to — see ANIMATE

vizard *n* a cover or partial cover for the face used to disguise oneself — see MASK 1

vocabulary *n* 1 the special terms or expressions of a particular group or field — see TERMINOLOGY

2 the stock of words, pronunciation, and grammar used by a people as their basic means of communication — see LANGUAGE 1

vocal *adj* expressed or communicated by voice ⟨Our cat is given to making strange *vocal* noises in the dead of night.⟩

syn oral, spoken, uttered, voiced

rel articulated, enunciated, pronounced, sonant; breathed, chirped, drawled, gasped, intoned, mouthed, mumbled, murmured, muttered, purred, shouted, spluttered, sputtered, squeaked, whispered

near ant inarticulate; mute, quiet, silent; unexpressed, unsaid, unspoken, unuttered, unvoiced; surd, voiceless

ant nonvocal

vocal *n* a short musical composition for the human voice often with instrumental accompaniment — see SONG 1

vocalist *n* one who sings — see SINGER

vocalize *vb* 1 to express (a thought or emotion) in words — see SAY 1

2 to produce musical sounds with the voice — see SING 1

vocalizer *n* one who sings — see SINGER

vocation *n* 1 the activity by which one regularly makes a living — see OCCUPATION

2 the body of people in a profession or field of activity — see CORPS

vociferate *vb* to speak so as to be heard at a distance — see CALL 1

vociferous *adj* engaging in or marked by loud and insistent cries especially of protest ⟨*Vociferous* opponents of the bill protested angrily outside the chambers of the legislature.⟩

syn blatant, clamorous, obstreperous

rel clangorous, dinning, discordant, noisy; loudmouthed, outspoken, vocal; boisterous, raucous, robustious, rowdy, uproarious; cacophonous, dissonant, earsplitting, grating, shrill, strident; blaring, blustering, booming, brassy, brazen

near ant noiseless, quiet, silent, soundless, still; calm, hushed, subdued

vogue *adj* enjoying widespread favor or approval — see POPULAR 1

vogue *n* 1 a practice or interest that is very popular for a short time — see FAD

2 the state of enjoying widespread approval — see POPULARITY

voice *n* 1 the right to express a wish, choice, or opinion ⟨Everyone will have a *voice* in the decision of where to go for our vacation.⟩

syn say, say-so, vote

rel part, role (*also* rôle), share; ballot, enfranchisement, franchise, suffrage; belief, conviction, judgment (*or* judgement), opinion, sentiment, view

2 an act, process, or means of putting something into words — see EXPRESSION 1

3 one who sings — see SINGER

voice *vb* to make known (as an idea, emotion, or opinion) — see EXPRESS 1

voiced *adj* expressed or communicated by voice — see VOCAL

voiceless *adj* unable to speak — see MUTE 1

void *adj* 1 having no legal or binding force — see NULL 1

2 lacking contents that could or should be present — see EMPTY 1

3 utterly lacking in something needed, wanted, or expected — see DEVOID 1

4 left unoccupied or unused — see ABANDONED 1

void *n* 1 an incomplete or deficient area — see GAP 3

2 empty space — see VACANCY 1

3 an open space in a barrier (as a wall or hedge) — see GAP 1

void *vb* 1 to put an end to by formal action — see ABOLISH 1

2 to remove the contents of — see EMPTY

---

syn synonym(s)   *rel* related words
ant antonym(s)   *near ant* near antonym(s)

volatile *adj* likely to change frequently, suddenly, or unexpectedly — see FICKLE 1

volcanic *adj* marked by bursts of destructive force or intense activity — see VIOLENT 1

volition *n* 1 the act or power of making one's own choices or decisions — see FREE WILL

2 the power, right, or opportunity to choose — see CHOICE 1

volitional *adj* done, made, or given with one's own free will — see VOLUNTARY 1

volley *n* a rapid or overwhelming outpouring of many things at once — see BARRAGE

volume *n* 1 a considerable amount — see LOT 2

2 a given or particular mass or aggregate of matter — see AMOUNT

3 a set of printed sheets of paper bound together between covers and forming a work of fiction or nonfiction — see BOOK 1

4 the largest number or amount that something can hold — see CAPACITY 1

voluminous *adj* of a size greater than average of its kind — see LARGE

voluminousness *n* the quality or state of being large in size — see LARGENESS

voluntarily *adv* of one's own free will ⟨You took part in this *voluntarily*, so you have no cause to complain.⟩

syn freely, willingly

rel consciously, deliberately, intentionally, knowingly, wittingly; acquiescently, consentingly; electively, optionally

phrases of one's own accord

near ant unconsciously, unintentionally, unknowingly, unwittingly; reluctantly

ant involuntarily, unwillingly

voluntary *adj* 1 done, made, or given with one's own free will ⟨a *voluntary* contribution to the school's fund-raising drive⟩

syn freewill, self-imposed, unforced, volitional, volunteer, willing

rel discretionary, elective, optional; impulsive, instinctive, spontaneous, unpremeditated; conscious, deliberate, intentional, knowing, willful (*or* wilful)

near ant compulsory, enforced, mandatory, necessary, nonelective, obligatory, ordered, required

ant coerced, compelled, forced, involuntary, nonvoluntary, unwilled

2 subject to one's freedom of choice — see OPTIONAL

3 made, given, or done with full awareness of what one is doing — see INTENTIONAL

volunteer *adj* done, made, or given with one's own free will — see VOLUNTARY 1

volunteer *vb* to make a present of — see GIVE 1

voluptuous *adj* pleasing to the physical senses — see SENSUAL

vomit *vb* to discharge the contents of the stomach through the mouth ⟨The children with the flu *vomited* every time they tried to eat something.⟩

syn barf, gag, heave, hurl, puke, retch, spew, spit up, throw up

rel disgorge, regurgitate; eject, expel; nauseate

phrases lose one's lunch [*slang*], toss one's cookies

voracious *adj* 1 having a huge appetite ⟨It seemed like the *voracious* kitten was eating her weight in food every day.⟩

syn gluttonous, greedy, hoggish, piggish, rapacious, ravenous, swinish

rel hearty, wolfish; devouring, gobbling, gorging, gormandizing, gulping; empty, famished, hungry, starved, starving; malnourished, underfed, undernourished

near ant content, full, glutted, sated, satiated, satisfied, stuffed

2 showing urgent desire or interest — see EAGER

vortex *n* water moving rapidly in a circle with a hollow in the center — see WHIRLPOOL

votary *n* one who follows the opinions or teachings of another — see FOLLOWER 1

vote *n* 1 the right to formally express one's position or will in an election ⟨In the United States, women were granted the *vote* by the 19th Amendment in 1920.⟩

syn ballot, enfranchisement, franchise, suffrage

rel say, say-so, voice

ant disenfranchisement

2 a piece of paper indicating a person's preferences in an election — see BALLOT 1

3 the right to express a wish, choice, or opinion — see VOICE 1

vote *vb* to set before the mind for consideration — see PROPOSE 1

vouch (for) *vb* to declare (something) to be true or genuine — see CERTIFY 1

vow *n* a person's solemn declaration that he or she will do or not do something — see PROMISE

vow *vb* to make a solemn declaration of intent — see PROMISE 1

voyage *n* a journey over water in a vessel — see SAIL

voyage *vb* 1 to take a trip especially of some distance — see TRAVEL 1

2 to travel on water in a vessel — see SAIL 1

vulgar *adj* 1 belonging to the class of people of low social or economic rank — see IGNOBLE 1

2 depicting or referring to sexual matters in a way that is unacceptable in polite society — see OBSCENE 1

3 held by or applicable to a majority of the people — see GENERAL 3

4 lacking in refinement or good taste — see COARSE 2

5 used in or suitable for speech and not formal writing — see COLLOQUIAL 1

vulgarity *n* 1 the quality or state of lacking refinement or good taste ⟨Our cousins' general *vulgarity* and poor manners irritate me.⟩

syn coarseness, commonness, crassness, crudeness, grossness, indelicacy, indelicateness, lowness, raffishness, rawness, roughness, rudeness, tastelessness

rel boorishness, churlishness, clownishness, loutishness, rowdiness, rusticity, uncouthness; artlessness, gracelessness, inelegance, unsophistication; insensitiveness, insensitivity, thoughtlessness; kitsch, tackiness

near ant courtliness, urbanity; elegance, grace, graciousness; consideration, sensitivity, thoughtfulness *ant* cultivation, gentility, polish, refinement, tastefulness

2 the quality or state of being obscene — see OBSCENITY

vulnerability *n* 1 the quality or state of having little resistance to some outside agent — see SUSCEPTIBILITY

2 the state of being left without shelter or protection against something harmful — see EXPOSURE 1

vulnerable *adj* 1 being in a situation where one is likely to meet with harm — see LIABLE 1

2 lacking protection from danger or resistance against attack — see HELPLESS 1

wackiness *n* lack of good sense or judgment — see FOOLISHNESS 1

wacky *also* **whacky** *adj* 1 different from the ordinary in a way that causes curiosity or suspicion — see ODD 2

2 showing or marked by a lack of good sense or judgment — see FOOLISH 1

wad *n* 1 a considerable amount — see LOT 2

2 a small uneven mass — see LUMP 1

3 a very large amount of money — see FORTUNE 2

wad *vb* to form into a round compact mass ⟨Disgusted, she *wadded* up the paper and threw it in the wastebasket.⟩

syn agglomerate, ball, roll, round

rel bunch, clump, lump; pearl, pellet, pelletize; sphere

near ant flatten, open, smooth, spread, unfold

ant unroll

waddle *vb* to move forward while swaying from side to side — see STAGGER 1

waft *n* a slight or gentle movement of air — see BREEZE 1

waft *vb* to rest or move along the surface of a liquid or in the air — see FLOAT 1

¹**wag** *n* a quick jerky movement from side to side or up and down ⟨The dog gave its tail a single *wag* before it flopped back down.⟩

syn swish, switch, waggle, whisk

rel oscillation, rock, sway, swing, waver; flap, flutter, wave, whip; flick, jerk, jolt, snap, twitch; jiggle, shake, wiggle; bob, nod

²**wag** *n* a person (as a writer) noted for or specializing in humor — see HUMORIST

wag *vb* 1 to move from side to side or up and down with quick jerky motions ⟨The cat's tail *wagged* back and forth in annoyance.⟩

syn swish, switch, waggle

rel oscillate, rock, sway, swing, waver; beat, flail, flap, flop, lash, whip; flick, flicker, flutter, wave; jerk, jolt; jig, jiggle, joggle, shake, twitch, wiggle; bob, jog, nod

2 to relate sometimes questionable or secret information of a personal nature — see GOSSIP

3 to make short up-and-down movements — see NOD

wage *n*, *often* **wages** *pl* the money paid regularly to a person for labor or services ⟨The *wage* you earn is more than enough to support us comfortably.⟩

syn emolument, hire, pay, payment, salary, stipend

rel living wage, minimum wage, nominal wages, take-home pay; double time, overtime, time and a half; compensation, recompense, remittance, remuneration, requital, return; recoupment, redress, reparation, restitution; reimbursement, repayment; earnings, profit, takings, yield

wager *n* the money or thing risked on the outcome of an uncertain event — see BET 1

wager *vb* to risk (something) on the outcome of an uncertain event — see BET

wagerer *n* one that bets (as on the outcome of a contest or sports event) — see BETTOR

waggery *n* 1 something said or done to cause laughter — see JOKE 1

2 a playful or mischievous act intended as a joke — see PRANK

waggish *adj* tending to or exhibiting reckless playfulness — see MISCHIEVOUS 1

waggle *n* a quick jerky movement from side to side or up and down — see ¹WAG 1

waggle *vb* to move from side to side or up and down with quick jerky motions — see WAG 1

wagon *n* a wheeled usually horse-drawn vehicle used for hauling — see CART

wail *n* 1 a crying out in grief — see LAMENT 1

2 a long low sound indicating pain or grief — see MOAN 1

3 an expression of dissatisfaction, pain, or resentment — see COMPLAINT 1

wail *vb* 1 to express dissatisfaction, pain, or resentment usually tiresomely — see COMPLAIN

2 to make a long loud mournful sound — see HOWL 1

3 to utter a moan — see MOAN 1

wail (for) *vb* to feel or express sorrow for — see LAMENT 1

wailing *adj* expressing or suggesting mourning — see MOURNFUL 1

wain *n* a wheeled usually horse-drawn vehicle used for hauling — see CART

waist *n* the middle region of the human torso — see MIDRIFF

waistline *n* the middle region of the human torso — see MIDRIFF

wait *n* an instance or period of being prevented from going about one's business — see DELAY

wait *vb* to remain in place in readiness or

expectation of something ⟨Please *wait* here, and we'll seat you shortly.⟩

syn await, bide, hold on, stay

rel hang around, linger, remain, stick around, tarry; stand by; anticipate, expect, watch (for)

phrases bide one's time, cool one's heels, hold one's breath, sit tight

waiter *n* a person who serves food or drink — see SERVER

waitperson *n* a person who serves food or drink — see SERVER

waiver *n* a document containing a declaration of an intentional giving up of a right, claim, or privilege ⟨Before you can participate in the athletic program, you have to sign a *waiver* in which you give up your right to sue.⟩

syn disclaimer, release

rel dispensation, exemption, indemnity; abdication, relinquishment, renouncement; renunciation, surrender

wake *vb* 1 to cause to stop sleeping ⟨My banging around in the kitchen *woke* my wife.⟩

syn arouse, awake, awaken, rouse, waken

rel roust, raise; revive, reawaken; agitate, bestir, disturb, excite, provoke, stimulate, stir

near ant hypnotize, mesmerize

ant lull

2 to cease to be asleep ⟨I *woke* with a start when the door slammed.⟩

syn arouse, awake, awaken, rouse, waken

rel arise, get up, rise, turn out, uprise; watch; revive; reawaken; shift, stir

near ant catnap, conk (off *or* out), doze, drop off, nap, nod, rest, sleep, slumber, snooze; bed (down), couch, flop, retire, sack out, turn in; lie up, sleep in; oversleep

3 to give notice to beforehand especially of danger or risk — see WARN

wakeful *adj* not sleeping or able to sleep ⟨The mother remained *wakeful* until her child returned home.⟩

syn awake, sleepless, wide-awake

rel aroused, awakened, roused, rousted, wakened; about, astir, up; aware, conscious; revived; reawakened

near ant drowsy, nodding, sleepy, slumberous (*or* slumbrous), somnolent; dreaming; hypnotized, mesmerized

ant asleep, dormant, dozing, napping, resting, sleeping, slumbering, unawakened

waken *vb* 1 to cause to stop sleeping — see WAKE 1

2 to cease to be asleep — see WAKE 2

wake–up call *n* something that tells of approaching danger or risk — see WARNING 2

walk *n* 1 a relaxed journey on foot for exercise or pleasure ⟨We went for a long *walk* tonight because it was such a nice night.⟩

syn constitutional, perambulation, ramble, range, saunter, stroll, turn, wander

rel parade, paseo; expedition, hike, march, peregrination, traipse, tramp, travel, traversal, traverse, trek, trip, walkabout; excursion, jaunt, junket, outing, sally, spin, tour; pilgrimage, progress, safari

2 a region of activity, knowledge, or influence — see FIELD 2

walk *vb* 1 to go on foot ⟨I *walked* slowly to school.⟩

syn foot (it), hoof (it), leg (it), pad, step, traipse, tread

rel parade; march, pace, stride, troop; power walk; hike, peregrinate, trek; mosey, ramble, saunter, stroll, wander; clump, stomp, stump, tramp, trample, tromp; footslog, plod, trudge; gimp, hobble, limp; mince, prance, pussyfoot, tiptoe; bounce, stalk, strut, swagger; falter, lumber, lurch, pound, scuff, shamble, shuffle, stagger, stumble, toddle, waddle; nip, tap, trip, trot

2 to refuse to work in order to force an employer to meet demands — see STRIKE 1

walking out *n* the act of leaving a place — see DEPARTURE 1

walkout *n* a work stoppage by a body of workers intended to force an employer to meet their demands — see STRIKE 1

walk out *vb* 1 to leave a place often for another — see GO 2

2 to refuse to work in order to force an employer to meet demands — see STRIKE 1

wall *n* 1 a physical object that blocks the way — see BARRIER

2 means or method of defending — see DEFENSE 1

wall (in) *vb* to close or shut in by or as if by barriers — see ENCLOSE 1

wallop *n* 1 a forceful coming together of two things — see IMPACT 1

2 a hard strike with a part of the body or an instrument — see ¹BLOW

3 a pleasurably intense stimulation of the feelings — see THRILL

wallop *vb* 1 to strike repeatedly — see BEAT 1

2 to defeat by a large margin — see WHIP 2

3 to deliver a blow to (someone or something) usually in a strong vigorous manner — see HIT 1

wampum *n* something (as pieces of stamped metal or printed paper) customarily and legally used as a medium of exchange, a measure of value, or a means of payment — see MONEY

wan *adj* lacking a healthy skin color — see PALE 2

wander *n* a relaxed journey on foot for exercise or pleasure — see WALK 1

wander *vb* 1 to move about from place to place aimlessly ⟨We just went outside and *wandered* around until it was time to go.⟩

syn bat, cruise, drift, float, gad (about), gallivant (*also* galavant), knock (about), maunder, meander, mooch, ramble, range, roam, rove, traipse

rel saunter, stroll; dawdle, mope; hobo, tramp, vagabond; mill (about *or* around); straggle, stray

2 to commit an offense — see OFFEND 1

wanderer *n* a person who roams about without a fixed route or destination — see NOMAD

wandering *adj* 1 passing from one topic to another — see DISCURSIVE

2 traveling from place to place — see ITINERANT

wane *vb* to grow less in scope or intensity especially gradually — see DECREASE 2

wangle *vb* to plan out usually with subtle skill or care — see ENGINEER

want *n* **1** the fact or state of being absent — see LACK 1

2 a falling short of an essential or desirable amount or number — see DEFICIENCY

3 a state of being without something necessary, desirable, or useful — see NEED 1

4 the state of lacking sufficient money or material possessions — see POVERTY 1

5 a defect in character — see FAULT 1

want *vb* **1** to have an earnest wish to own or enjoy — see DESIRE 1

2 to have as a requirement — see NEED 1

3 to see fit — see CHOOSE 2

4 to wish to have — see LIKE 1

wanting *adj* **1** falling short of a standard — see BAD 1

2 not coming up to an expected measure or meeting a particular need — see SHORT 3

3 not present or in evidence — see ABSENT 2

wanting *prep* not having — see WITHOUT 1

wanton *adj* **1** depicting or referring to sexual matters in a way that is unacceptable in polite society — see OBSCENE 1

2 having a strong sexual desire — see LUSTFUL

3 having or showing the desire to inflict severe pain and suffering on others — see CRUEL 1

wantonness *n* **1** disposition to willfully inflict pain and suffering on others — see CRUELTY

2 the quality or state of being obscene — see OBSCENITY

war *n* **1** a state of armed violent struggle between states, nations, or groups ⟨The *war* was the result of ethnic tensions that had been building in the region for decades.⟩

syn conflagration, conflict, hostilities, hot war

rel civil war, cold war, holy war, limited war, police action, world war; action, battle, engagement, skirmish; combat, fighting, warfare

near ant demilitarization, demobilization, disarmament; pacification; cease-fire, truce; calm, peacefulness, tranquillity (*or* tranquility)

ant peace

2 a lack of agreement or harmony — see DISCORD

3 an earnest effort for superiority or victory over another — see CONTEST 1

war (against) *vb* to oppose (someone) in physical conflict — see FIGHT 1

warble *n* a rhythmic series of musical tones arranged to give a pleasing effect — see MELODY

warble *vb* to sing with the alternation of two musical tones ⟨The skylark *warbled* prettily outside our window.⟩

syn quaver, trill

rel slur; yodel; belt, carol, chant, chorus, croon, descant, harmonize, troll, vocalize; lilt

ward *n* **1** means or method of defending — see DEFENSE 1

2 responsibility for the safety and well-being of someone or something — see CUSTODY

ward *vb* to drive danger or attack away from — see DEFEND 1

warden *n* **1** a person or group that watches over someone or something — see GUARD 1

2 a person who takes care of a property sometimes for an absent owner — see CUSTODIAN 1

warder *n* a person or group that watches over someone or something — see GUARD 1

warehouse *n* a building for storing goods — see STOREHOUSE

wares *n pl* products that are bought and sold in business — see MERCHANDISE

warfare *n* **1** a lack of agreement or harmony — see DISCORD

2 an earnest effort for superiority or victory over another — see CONTEST 1

wariness *n* a close attentiveness to avoiding danger — see CAUTION 1

warlike *adj* feeling or displaying eagerness to fight — see BELLIGERENT

warm *adj* **1** having or giving off heat to a moderate degree ⟨The pan was still *warm*, but no longer too hot to touch.⟩

syn heated, lukewarm, tepid, toasty, warmed

rel thawed; broiling, burning, fiery, hot, piping hot, red-hot, roasting, scalding, scorching, searing, steamy, sultry, sweltering, torrid; overheated, roasted, superheated, sweltering; blazing, glowing, molten, sizzling; reheated, rewarmed, warmed-over

near ant arctic, bitter, bleak, chill, chilly, cold, freezing, frigid, frosty, glacial, ice-cold, iced, icy, nippy, polar, raw, sharp, snappy, snowy, subfreezing, subzero, ultracold, winterly, wintry (*also* wintery); frosted; benumbed, nipped, numb

ant chilled, cool, cooled, coolish, refrigerated, unheated

2 having or expressing great depth of feeling — see FERVENT 1

3 having or showing kindly feeling and sincere interest — see FRIENDLY 1

warm *vb* **1** to cause to have or give off heat to a moderate degree ⟨You'll need to *warm* the food in the microwave.⟩

syn heat, toast

rel overheat, superheat; reheat, rewarm; thaw; bake, cook, roast; burn, char, fire, parch, scald, scorch, sear

near ant freeze, frost, supercool

ant chill, cool, refrigerate

2 to give satisfaction to — see PLEASE 1

warm–blooded *adj* having or expressing great depth of feeling — see FERVENT 1

warmed *adj* having or giving off heat to a moderate degree — see WARM 1

warmhearted *adj* **1** having or marked by sympathy and consideration for others — see HUMANE 1

2 having or showing kindly feeling and sincere interest — see FRIENDLY 1

warmheartedness *n* the capacity for feeling for another's unhappiness or misfortune — see HEART 1

warmness *n* the quality or state of being moderate in temperature — see WARMTH 1

warmonger *n* one who urges or attempts

---

syn synonym(s)   **rel** related words
ant antonym(s)   **near ant** near antonym(s)

to cause a war ⟨The *warmongers* met with overwhelming opposition.⟩
syn hawk, jingo, militarist
rel agitator, firebrand, fomenter, instigator, rabble-rouser; belligerent, combatant, militant; chauvinist
near ant peacemaker; peacekeeper
ant dove, pacifist

warmth *n* **1** the quality or state of being moderate in temperature ⟨The cozy *warmth* of the inn's parlor was a welcome relief from the wintry weather outside.⟩
syn lukewarmness, warmness
rel balminess, mildness, temperateness; glow, radiance, radiancy; heat, hotness, stuffiness, sultriness, torridity, torridness
near ant bitterness, bleakness, cold, frigidity, frigidness, frostiness, iciness, rawness, sharpness; frost
ant chill, chilliness, coolness
2 depth of feeling — see ARDOR 1

warn *vb* **1** to give notice to beforehand especially of danger or risk ⟨The lifeguard *warned* the boys that if they continued playing so rough, someone was sure to get hurt.⟩
syn advise, alert, caution, forewarn, wake
rel augur, forecast, foretell, harbinger, predict, presage, prognosticate, prophesy; apprise, inform, notify, tip (off); admonish; bode, forebode (*also* forbode), foreshadow, foretoken, portend
near ant imperil, risk

warning *adj* serving as or offering a warning — see CAUTIONARY

warning *n* **1** the act or an instance of telling beforehand of danger or risk ⟨She delivered a strict *warning* that anyone who was caught stealing would be fired.⟩
syn admonishment, admonition, alarm (*also* alarum), alert, caution, forewarning, notice
rel auguring, augury, forecasting, foretelling, predicting, prediction, premonition, presaging, prognosticating, prophecy (*also* prophesy), prophesying; apprising, informing, notification, notifying, tip-off; advice, counsel, guidance, recommendation, suggestion; tip; announcement, declaration
2 something that tells of approaching danger or risk ⟨The ominously darkening sky was a *warning* that a storm was approaching.⟩
syn caution, tip-off, tocsin, wake-up call
rel omen, portent, premonition, presage; notice, notification; buoy, indicator, knell, sign, signal; foretaste, foretoken; announcement, declaration
phrases handwriting on the wall
near ant all clear

warp *n* an immaterial thing upon which something else rests — see BASE 1

warp *vb* **1** to change so much as to create a wrong impression or alter the meaning of — see GARBLE
2 to lower in character, dignity, or quality — see DEBASE 1
3 to twist (something) out of a natural or normal shape or condition — see CONTORT

warped *adj* having or showing lowered moral character or standards — see CORRUPT

warping *n* the twisting of something out of its natural or normal shape or condition — see CONTORTION

warrant *n* the approval by someone in authority for the doing of something — see PERMISSION

warrant *vb* **1** to assume responsibility for the satisfactory quality or performance of ⟨The computer company unconditionally *warrants* all of its products for one full year.⟩
syn guarantee, guaranty
rel attest, authenticate, avouch, certify, testify (to), vouch (for), witness; assure, bond, contract, covenant; pledge, plight, stipulate, swear, undertake, vow; adhere, assert, aver, avow, declare, insist; insure
2 to give official acceptance of as satisfactory — see APPROVE
3 to have as a requirement — see NEED 1
4 to state as a fact usually forcefully — see CLAIM 1
5 to give official or legal power to — see AUTHORIZE 1

warranted *adj* being what is called for by accepted standards of right and wrong — see JUST 1

warranty *n* a formal agreement to fulfill an obligation — see GUARANTEE 1

warrior *n* a person engaged in military service — see SOLDIER

wary *adj* having or showing a close attentiveness to avoiding danger or trouble — see CAREFUL 1

wash *n* spongy land saturated or partially covered with water — see SWAMP

wash *vb* **1** to flow along or against ⟨Crystal-clear waters gently *wash* the island's unspoiled beaches.⟩
syn bathe, lap, lave, splash
rel bubble, gurgle, plash, ripple, slosh
2 to withstand scrutiny and gain acceptance or approval ⟨The employee's story about missing the bus didn't *wash* with her manager.⟩
syn fly, hold up, pass
rel go down, go over, go through, play, take, work
phrases hold water, pass muster
3 to flow in a broken irregular stream — see GURGLE
4 to make wet — see WET
5 to pour liquid over or through in order to cleanse — see FLUSH 1
6 to cause (as a liquid) to move about in a circle especially repeatedly — see STIR 1

washed *adj* containing, covered with, or thoroughly penetrated by water — see WET 1

washed–out *adj* **1** lacking intensity of color — see PALE 1
2 depleted in strength, energy, or freshness — see WEARY 1

washed–up *adj* having lost forcefulness, courage, or spirit — see EFFETE 1

washout *n* something that has failed — see FAILURE 3

wash out *vb* **1** to be unsuccessful — see FAIL 2
2 to make white or whiter by removing color — see WHITEN
3 to use up all the physical energy of — see EXHAUST 1

4 to pour liquid over or through in order to cleanse — see FLUSH 1

washroom *n* a room furnished with a fixture for flushing body waste — see TOILET

waspish *adj* easily irritated or annoyed — see IRRITABLE

waspishness *n* readiness to show annoyance or impatience — see PETULANCE

wassail *vb* to take part in drunken revelry — see CAROUSE

wastage *n* the state or fact of being rendered nonexistent, physically unsound, or useless — see DESTRUCTION 1

waste *adj* producing inferior or only a small amount of vegetation — see BARREN 1

waste *n* **1** an instance of spending money or resources without care or restraint ⟨It seems like a *waste* to spend my entire paycheck on a bigger TV.⟩

syn extravagance, prodigality

rel indulgence, luxury, splurge; loss, wastage; dissipation, profligacy, profusion, squandering, wastefulness; overindulgence, self-indulgence; excess, overkill

near ant necessity; belt-tightening, conservation, economizing, economy, frugality, parsimony, saving, scrimping, skimping, thrift; austerity, moderation, restraint, temperance, temperateness

2 discarded or useless material — see GARBAGE

3 land that is uninhabited or not fit for crops — see WASTELAND

4 solid matter discharged from an animal's alimentary canal — see DROPPING 1

5 a wide space or area — see EXPANSE

6 a gradual weakening, loss, or destruction — see CORROSION

waste *vb* **1** to use up carelessly ⟨He *wasted* his lottery winnings on more lottery tickets that were worthless.⟩

syn blow, dissipate, fritter (away), lavish, lose, misspend, run through, spend, squander, throw away, trifle (away)

rel splurge; consume, deplete, exhaust, impoverish, overspend, shoot; indulge, overindulge; disburse, expend, lay out

phrases play ducks and drakes with (*or* make ducks and drakes of)

near ant economize, scrimp, skimp; preserve, protect, save; hoard, lay up

ant conserve

2 to bring to a complete end the physical soundness, existence, or usefulness of — see DESTROY 1

3 to diminish the physical strength of — see WEAKEN 1

waste (away) *vb* to lose bodily strength or vigor — see WEAKEN 2

wasted *adj* **1** lacking physical strength — see WEAK 1

2 suffering extreme weight loss as a result of hunger or disease — see EMACIATED

wasteful *adj* given to spending money freely or foolishly — see PRODIGAL

wastefulness *n* the quality or fact of being free or wasteful in the expenditure of money — see EXTRAVAGANCE 1

wasteland *n* land that is uninhabited or

not fit for crops ⟨With proper irrigation and fertilizer, they turned the desert *wasteland* into a fertile plain.⟩

syn barren, desert, desolation, waste

rel badland; brush, bush; dust bowl; open, open air, outdoors, out-of-doors; nature, wild, wilderness

waster *n* someone who spends money freely or foolishly — see PRODIGAL

wastrel *n* someone who spends money freely or foolishly — see PRODIGAL

watch *n* **1** a person or group that watches over someone or something — see GUARD 1

2 the state of being constantly attentive and responsive to signs of opportunity, activity, or danger — see VIGILANCE

watch *vb* **1** to keep one's eyes on ⟨I turned my head to continue *watching* the bird as it flew away.⟩

syn eye, follow, observe

rel behold, look, perceive, regard, see, view; gape, gawk, gaze, glare, goggle, look on, peer, rubberneck, stare; guard, wake, ward; monitor, study, spy; espy, glance, glimpse, peek, peep

phrases have one's eye on

near ant blink, wink

2 to take notice of and be guided by — see HEED 1

3 to pay continued close attention to (something) for a particular purpose — see MONITOR

4 to have an interest or concern for — see CARE

5 to take charge of especially on behalf of another — see ²TEND 1

watch (for) *vb* to believe in the future occurrence of (something) — see EXPECT

watcher *n* a person or group that watches over someone or something — see GUARD 1

watchful *adj* paying close attention usually for the purpose of anticipating approaching danger or opportunity — see ALERT 1

watchfulness *n* the state of being constantly attentive and responsive to signs of opportunity, activity, or danger — see VIGILANCE

watchman *n* **1** a person or group that watches over someone or something — see GUARD 1

2 a person who takes care of a property sometimes for an absent owner — see CUSTODIAN 1

watch out (for) *vb* to be cautious of or on guard against — see BEWARE (OF)

watchword *n* **1** a word or phrase that must be spoken by a person in order to pass a guard — see PASSWORD

2 an attention-getting word or phrase used to publicize something (as a campaign or product) — see SLOGAN

water *vb* to make wet — see WET

water closet *n* a room furnished with a fixture for flushing body waste — see TOILET

watercourse *n* an open man-made passageway for water — see CHANNEL 1

watercraft *n* a small buoyant structure for travel on water — see BOAT 1

watered *adj* containing, covered with, or thoroughly penetrated by water — see WET 1

---

syn synonym(s)   **rel** related words

ant antonym(s)   **near ant** near antonym(s)

waterfall *n* a fall of water usually from a great height ⟨I used to like to throw sticks in the stream and watch them go over the *waterfall*.⟩

syn cascade, cataract, fall(s)

rel flume; chute (*also* shute), rapid(s), shoot; white water

waterless *adj* marked by little or no precipitation or humidity — see DRY 1

waterlogged *adj* containing, covered with, or thoroughly penetrated by water — see WET 1

waterproof *adj* made of or treated with material that does not allow water to penetrate ⟨Luckily, my backpack is *waterproof*, so my clothes didn't get wet.⟩

syn waterproofed

rel rainproof; water-repellent, water-resistant; staunch (*also* stanch), watertight; nonabsorbent, nonporous; weatherproof

near ant absorbent, porous; leaky

waterproofed *adj* made of or treated with material that does not allow water to penetrate — see WATERPROOF

waterspout *n* a pipe or channel for carrying off water from a roof — see GUTTER 1

waterway *n* an open man-made passageway for water — see CHANNEL 1

watery *adj* 1 containing, covered with, or thoroughly penetrated by water — see WET 1

2 having an overly soft liquid consistency — see RUNNY

3 not containing very much of some important element — see WEAK 3

4 lacking in qualities that make for spirit and character — see WISHY-WASHY 1

wave *n* a moving ridge on the surface of water ⟨The toddler was almost knocked down by the *waves* created by the speedboat.⟩

syn billow, surge, swell

rel sea(s); surf; breaker, whitecap; comber, curl; ripple, wavelet; ground swell, roller; tidal wave, tsunami

wave *vb* to direct or notify by a movement or gesture — see MOTION

waver *vb* 1 to show uncertainty about the right course of action — see HESITATE

2 to swing unsteadily back and forth or from side to side — see TEETER 1

wavering *n* a state or an instance of temporary inaction because of uncertainty about the right course of action — see HESITATION

¹**wax** *vb* 1 to coat (something) with a slippery substance in order to reduce friction — see LUBRICATE

2 *slang* to defeat by a large margin — see WHIP 2

²**wax** *vb* 1 to become greater in extent, volume, amount, or number — see INCREASE 1

2 to eventually have as a state or quality — see BECOME

way *adv* to a great degree — see VERY 1

way *n* 1 a passage cleared for public vehicular travel ⟨The town honored the local sports hero by naming after him a short *way* connecting two shopping centers.⟩

syn artery, avenue, boulevard, drag, drive, expressway, freeway, highway, pass, pike, road, roadway, route, row, street, thoroughfare, trace, turnpike

rel causeway; autoroute, interstate, superhighway; beltway, bypass, parkway; corniche, switchback; through street; Main Street; backstreet, branch, bystreet, byway, crossroad, secondary road, shunpike, side road, side street; alley, alleyway; circle, lane, place; cul-de-sac, dead end; corridor; track, trail; promenade, walk

2 a usual manner of behaving or doing — see HABIT 1

3 an established course for traveling from one place to another — see PASSAGE 1

4 an established pattern of behavior — see TENDENCY 1

5 an extent or area available for or used up by some activity or thing — see ROOM 1

6 the direction along which something or someone moves — see PATH 1

7 the means or procedure for doing something — see METHOD

8 the opening through which one can enter or leave a structure — see DOOR 2

9 the power, right, or opportunity to choose — see CHOICE 1

10 the space or amount of space between two points, lines, surfaces, or objects — see DISTANCE 1

wayfarer *n* a person who roams about without a fixed route or destination — see NOMAD

wayfaring *adj* traveling from place to place — see ITINERANT

waylay *vb* to lie in wait for and attack by surprise — see AMBUSH

way–out *adj* different from the ordinary in a way that causes curiosity or suspicion — see ODD 2

way station *n* a regular stopping place — see STATION 2

wayward *adj* 1 given to resisting authority or another's control — see DISOBEDIENT

2 given to resisting control or discipline by others — see UNCONTROLLABLE

waywardness *n* refusal to obey — see DISOBEDIENCE

weak *adj* 1 lacking bodily strength ⟨The little boy was simply too *weak* to lift the box.⟩

syn debilitated, delicate, effete, enervated, enfeebled, faint, feeble, frail, infirm, languid, low, prostrate, prostrated, sapped, slight, soft, softened, tender, unsubstantial, wasted, weakened, wimpy

rel challenged, disabled, incapacitated, invalid; paralyzed; broken-down, decrepit; impotent, powerless; breakable, flimsy, fragile; dizzy, groggy, rocky, unsteady; drained, exhausted, flagging, tired, weary, worn-out; damaged, harmed, hurt, impaired, injured, lame, unsound; resistless, susceptible, unresistant, vulnerable, yielding

near ant able-bodied, athletic, beefy, brawny, fit, husky, muscular, sinewy, strapping, virile; hard, hardy, lusty, red-blooded, robust, sturdy, tough; fortified, hardened, inured, strengthened, toughened; energetic, energized, invigorated, vigorous, vitalized; hale, healthy, sound; capable, competent; convalescing, recovering, recuperating *ant* mighty, powerful, rugged, stalwart, stout, strong

2 lacking strength of will or character ⟨He proved to be a *weak* leader.⟩

syn characterless, effete, frail, invertebrate, nerveless, soft, spineless, weakened, weakling, wimpy, wishy-washy

rel flabby, flaccid, forceless, ineffective, ineffectual; impotent, powerless; emasculated, unnerved; lamblike, meek, pliable, submissive; corrupt, dastardly, unprincipled, unscrupulous, villainous; cowardly, craven, fainthearted, lily-livered, nebbishy, poltroon, pusillanimous, sissy, timid; infirm, irresolute, vacillating

near ant ethical, good, moral, principled, right, righteous, upright, virtuous; determined, mettlesome, resolute, unrelenting; courageous, stalwart, stouthearted

ant backboned, firm, hard, strong, tough

3 not containing very much of some important element ⟨The coffee came out too *weak* because I didn't use enough ground beans.⟩

syn dilute, diluted, thin, thinned, watery, weakened

rel adulterated, watered-down

near ant enriched, fortified; concentrated, condensed, evaporated

ant full-bodied, rich, strong

4 not using or following good reasoning — see ILLOGICAL

5 unable to act or achieve one's purpose — see POWERLESS

weaken *vb* **1** to diminish the physical strength of ⟨Weeks of hardship in the desert had greatly *weakened* them.⟩

syn debilitate, enervate, enfeeble, prostrate, sap, soften, tire, waste

rel cripple, disable, hamstring, incapacitate; deplete, depress, exhaust, impoverish, unman, wash out; damage, harm, hurt, impair, injure, invalid, lay up; break down, wear down, wear out; paralyze

near ant energize, invigorate, recruit, rejuvenate, vitalize; harden, season, toughen

ant beef (up), fortify, strengthen

2 to lose bodily strength or vigor ⟨The bodybuilder *weakened* once she eased off on her workouts.⟩

syn decay, droop, fade, fail, flag, go, lag, languish, sag, sink, waste (away), wilt, wither

rel break down, wear out; yield; degenerate, deteriorate, rot, run down

near ant convalesce, rally, rebound, recover, recuperate; gain

3 to alter (something) for the worse with the addition of foreign or lower-grade substances — see ADULTERATE

weakened *adj* **1** containing foreign or lower-grade substances — see IMPURE 1

2 lacking bodily strength — see WEAK 1

3 lacking strength of will or character — see WEAK 2

4 not containing very much of some important element — see WEAK 3

weakening *n* a gradual sinking and wasting away of mind or body — see DECLINE 1

weakling *adj* lacking strength of will or character — see WEAK 2

weakling *n* **1** a person lacking in physical strength ⟨a puppy that was the *weakling* of the litter⟩

syn softy (*or* softie), wimp

rel pushover; milksop, mollycoddle, sissy

ant powerhouse

2 a person without strength of character ⟨Only a *weakling* would be willing to lie to save himself from punishment.⟩

syn pushover, wimp

rel coward, milquetoast, mouse, nebbish, nervous Nellie (*or* nervous Nelly); sheep

near ant mensch

ant stalwart

weakly *adj* chronically or repeatedly suffering from poor health — see SICKLY 1

weak–minded *adj* **1** not having or showing an ability to absorb ideas readily — see STUPID 1

2 showing or marked by a lack of good sense or judgment — see FOOLISH 1

weakness *n* **1** the quality or state of lacking physical strength or vigor ⟨The flu left me with such overwhelming *weakness* that I could hardly stand.⟩

syn debilitation, debility, delicacy, enfeeblement, faintness, feebleness, fragility, frailness, frailty, infirmity, languor, listlessness, lowness

rel decay, decrepitude; breakdown, collapse, prostration; exhaustion, fatigue, lassitude, weariness; defenselessness, helplessness, impotence, impuissance, powerlessness; effeteness, softness; disablement, incapacitation, invalidism; damage, harm, hurt, impairment, injury

near ant energy, vitality; brawniness, fitness, heftiness, huskiness, lustiness, muscularity, virility; hardness, ruggedness, stoutness, sturdiness, toughness; health, healthiness, soundness, wellness

ant hardihood, hardiness, robustness, strength, vigor

2 the quality or state of lacking strength of will or character ⟨In a moment of *weakness* he told them the secret.⟩

syn frailness, frailty, softness, spinelessness

rel collapse; failing, flaw, foible, peccadillo; evil, immorality, wickedness; corruption, corruptness

near ant discipline, self-discipline; goodness, integrity, morality, rectitude, righteousness, rightness, uprightness, virtuousness

ant backbone, chutzpah (*also* chutzpa *or* hutzpah *or* hutzpa), firmness, fortitude, hardihood, mettle, nerve, resoluteness, strength, toughness

3 a defect in character — see FAULT 1

4 the quality or state of having little resistance to some outside agent — see SUSCEPTIBILITY 1

weal *n* the state of doing well especially in relation to one's happiness or success — see WELFARE

wealth *n* **1** the total of one's money and property ⟨Her *wealth* increased to the point where she could afford several luxurious homes.⟩

syn capital, fortune, means, opulence, riches, substance, wherewithal, worth *rel* belongings, chattels, effects, holdings, paraphernalia, possessions, things; bankroll, deep pockets, finances, funds, money; abundance, prosperity, success; treasure, valuables; personalty, property; nest egg, reserve, resources, savings, treasury

near ant debts, liabilities

2 a considerable amount — see LOT 2

3 an amount or supply more than sufficient to meet one's needs — see PLENTY 1

wealthy *adj* having goods, property, or money in abundance — see RICH 1

wear *n* **1** the result of long and hard use ⟨After several years, the carpet was finally showing *wear*.⟩

syn wear and tear

rel abrasion, corrosion, erosion; decomposition, deterioration, disintegration; fatigue

near ant fixing, mending, patching, rebuilding, reconditioning, reconstruction, renovation, repair, revamping

2 covering for the human body — see CLOTHING

wear *vb* **1** to use up all the physical energy of — see EXHAUST 1

2 to damage or diminish by continued friction — see ABRADE 1

wear and tear *n* the result of long and hard use — see WEAR 1

wearied *adj* **1** depleted in strength, energy, or freshness — see WEARY 1

2 having one's patience, interest, or pleasure exhausted — see WEARY 2

weariless *adj* showing no signs of weariness even after long hard effort — see TIRELESS

weariness *n* **1** a complete depletion of energy or strength — see FATIGUE

2 the state of being bored — see BOREDOM

wearisome *adj* causing weariness, restlessness, or lack of interest — see BORING

wear out *vb* to use up all the physical energy of — see EXHAUST 1

weary *adj* **1** depleted in strength, energy, or freshness ⟨I am just too *weary* to do any more work tonight.⟩

syn beat, bleary, burned-out (*or* burntout), bushed, dead, done, drained, exhausted, fatigued, jaded, limp, logy (*also* loggy), played out, prostrate, spent, tired, tuckered (out), washed-out, wearied, worn, worn-out

rel overfatigued, overtaxed, overworked; broken-down, run-down; debilitated, enervate, enervated, enfeebled, sapped, weakened; drowsy, heavy, sleepy; lethargic, sluggish

phrases worn to a frazzle

near ant fresh, refreshed, rejuvenated, relaxed, rested, revitalized; active, energetic, invigorated, peppy, strengthened, strong, tireless, vitalized, weariless

ant unwearied

2 having one's patience, interest, or pleasure exhausted ⟨I am totally *weary* of this constant bickering.⟩

syn bored, fed up, jaded, sick, tired, wearied

rel apathetic, disinterested, uninterested; glutted, sated, satiated, surfeited; dejected, demoralized, discouraged, disheartened,

dispirited; beat, burned-out (*or* burntout), bushed, done in, drained, enervated, exhausted, fatigued, limp, played out, tuckered (out), worn-out; frustrated; disgusted, nauseated, repulsed; blasé (*also* blase), world-weary

near ant animated, energized, enlivened, excited, galvanized, invigorated, stimulated, vitalized; amused, entertained; beguiled, bewitched, captivated, charmed, enchanted, enthralled, fascinated, hypnotized, mesmerized; delighted, pleased, thrilled

ant absorbed, engaged, engrossed, interested, intrigued, rapt

3 causing weariness, restlessness, or lack of interest — see BORING

weary *vb* **1** to make weary and restless by being dull or monotonous — see ²BORE

2 to use up all the physical energy of — see EXHAUST 1

wearying *adj* causing weariness, restlessness, or lack of interest — see BORING

weather *vb* to come safely through — see SURVIVE 1

weave *vb* **1** to cause to twine about one another — see INTERTWINE 1

2 to scatter or set here and there among other things — see THREAD 1

3 to move suddenly aside or to and fro — see DODGE 1

web *n* **1** something that catches and holds ⟨He was caught in the *web* of branches.⟩ ⟨She was trapped by her own *web* of lies.⟩

syn entanglement, mesh(es), morass, net, quagmire, snare, trap

rel knot, snarl, tangle; cat's cradle, labyrinth, maze; cobweb, spiderweb

2 a device or scheme for capturing another by surprise — see TRAP 1

wed *vb* **1** to give in marriage — see MARRY 2

2 to perform the ceremony of marriage for — see MARRY 1

3 to take a spouse — see MARRY 4

4 to take as a spouse — see MARRY 3

wedded *adj* of or relating to marriage — see MARITAL

wedding *n* a ceremony in which two people are united in matrimony ⟨The couple chose to have a garden *wedding*.⟩

syn bridal, espousal, marriage, nuptial(s)

rel match, matrimony, wedlock; union

wedge *vb* to fit (people or things) into a tight space — see CROWD 1

wedged *adj* firmly positioned in place and difficult to dislodge — see TIGHT 2

wedlock *n* a union representing a special kind of social and legal partnership between two people — see MARRIAGE 1

wee *adj* very small in size — see TINY

weedy *adj* growing thickly and vigorously — see RANK 1

weep *vb* **1** to flow forth slowly through small openings — see EXUDE

2 to shed tears often while making meaningless sounds as a sign of pain or distress — see CRY 1

weeping *adj* **1** bending downward or forward — see NODDING

2 expressing or suggesting mourning — see MOURNFUL 1

weigh *vb* **1** to be of importance — see MATTER

2 to give serious and careful thought to — see PONDER

weigh (on *or* upon) *vb* to push steadily against with some force — see ²PRESS 1

weighed *adj* decided on as a result of careful thought — see DELIBERATE 1

weight *n* **1** the amount that something weighs ⟨Because of a back condition, I'm not allowed to lift anything with a *weight* of over 10 pounds.⟩

syn avoirdupois, heaviness, heft

rel bulk, mass; poundage, tonnage; dead-weight; heftiness, massiveness, ponderousness, weightiness; solidity, solidness, substantiality, substantialness

2 the quality or state of being important — see IMPORTANCE

3 a mass or quantity of something taken up and carried, conveyed, or transported — see LOAD 1

4 a special notice or importance given to something — see EMPHASIS 1

5 the main or greater part of something as distinguished from its subordinate parts — see BODY 1

6 the power to direct the thinking or behavior of others usually indirectly — see INFLUENCE 1

7 the condition of having an excess of body fat — see CORPULENCE

weight *vb* to place a weight or burden on — see LOAD 1

weightiness *n* **1** the state or quality of being heavy ⟨the *weightiness* of the bookcase made it difficult to move⟩

syn heaviness, heftiness, massiveness, ponderousness

rel overweight; solidity, solidness, substantiality, substantialness; bulk, bulkiness, hugeness; cumbersomeness

near ant airiness, delicacy, ethereality, etherealness; flimsiness, fluffiness, insubstantiality, slightness

ant lightness, weightlessness

2 the quality or state of being important — see IMPORTANCE

weightless *adj* having little weight — see ¹LIGHT 1

weightlessness *n* the state or quality of having little weight — see ¹LIGHTNESS 1

weighty *adj* **1** having a matter of importance as its topic — see SERIOUS 2

2 having great meaning or lasting effect — see IMPORTANT 1

3 having great weight — see HEAVY 1

4 not joking or playful in mood or manner — see SERIOUS 1

5 having power over the minds or behavior of others — see INFLUENTIAL 1

weird *adj* **1** different from the ordinary in a way that causes curiosity or suspicion — see ODD 2

2 fearfully and mysteriously strange or fantastic — see EERIE

3 having seemingly supernatural qualities or powers — see MYSTIC 1

4 noticeably different from what is generally found or experienced — see UNUSUAL 1

weirdo *n* a person of odd or whimsical habits — see ECCENTRIC

welcome *adj* giving pleasure or contentment to the mind or senses — see PLEASANT 1

welcome *n* an expression of goodwill upon meeting — see HELLO

welcome *vb* to receive or accept gladly or readily ⟨The eager recruits *welcomed* every new project with which they were presented.⟩

syn eat (up), embrace

rel adopt, espouse, take up; greet, hail; enjoy, like, prefer; choose, cull, decide (on), elect, handpick, name, opt (for), pick, select, single (out), take

near ant decline, refuse, reject, spurn, turn down; demur (to), object (to)

welfare *n* the state of doing well especially in relation to one's happiness or success ⟨I have your *welfare* at heart.⟩

syn good, interest, weal, well-being

rel fortune, prosperity, prosperousness, success, successfulness; fitness, health, healthiness, robustness, soundness, wellness, wholeness, wholesomeness; bliss, felicity, happiness, joy; advantage, benefit, gain, sake; content, contentedness, gratification, satisfaction

near ant unhealthiness, unsoundness; misery, sadness, suffering, unhappiness, wretchedness

ant ill-being

well *adj* enjoying health and vigor — see HEALTHY 1

well *adv* **1** in a satisfactory way ⟨Our current system for dividing household chores works *well*, so let's keep it.⟩

syn acceptably, adequately, all right, alright, fine, good, nicely, OK (*or* okay), passably, satisfactorily, so-so, sufficiently, tolerably

rel appropriately, aptly, congruously, correctly, decorously, felicitously, fittingly, happily, meetly, rightly, seemly, suitably; satisfyingly; effectively, effectually, efficiently, neatly, tidily

near ant unbearably; inappropriately, incorrectly, indecently, unsuitably; awfully, deplorably, disastrously, dreadfully, horrendously, horribly, horridly, miserably, terribly

ant bad, badly, deficiently, ill, inadequately, insufficiently, poorly, unacceptably, unsatisfactorily

2 in a generous manner ⟨a warm and gracious host who always treats guests *well*⟩

syn amply, bountifully, generously, handsomely, lavishly, liberally, munificently, openhandedly, unstintingly

rel considerately, courteously, hospitably, kindly, nicely, reasonably, thoughtfully; affably, amiably, cheerfully, cheerily, congenially, cordially, friendlily, genially, good-heartedly, good-naturedly; selflessly, ungrudgingly, unselfishly; altruistically, beneficently, benevolently, bigheartedly, charitably, humanely, kindheartedly, magnanimously, philanthropically

near ant contemptuously, disdainfully, rudely, scornfully; obnoxiously, provocatively; coldly, coolly (*also* cooly), frigidly, hostilely; angrily, belligerently; begrudgingly, grudgingly

ant parsimoniously, stingily, ungenerously

---

3 in a skillful or expert manner ⟨She plays the piano very *well*.⟩

syn ably, adeptly, adroitly, capably, competently, expertly, masterfully, masterly, proficiently, skillfully

rel aptly, fluently; cleverly, dexterously, neatly, nimbly; easily, facilely, handily

near ant inaptly; awkwardly, clumsily, crudely

ant amateurishly, artlessly, incapably, incompetently, inefficiently, ineptly, inexpertly, poorly, unskillfully

4 with good reason or courtesy ⟨We cannot *well* refuse the invitation.⟩

syn considerately, courteously, kindly, nicely, reasonably, thoughtfully

rel pleasantly; excusably, fairly, justifiably, validly; discreetly, judiciously, prudently, sensibly, wisely; chivalrously, decorously, deferentially, gallantly, politely, respectfully, solicitously; compassionately, humanely, kindheartedly, sympathetically

near ant contemptuously, disdainfully, disrespectfully, impolitely, rudely, scornfully, snootily; cruelly, heartlessly, nastily, viciously; shabbily, unfairly

ant discourteously, inconsiderately, thoughtlessly

5 in a pleasing way ⟨The day went *well*, despite the rough beginning.⟩

syn agreeably, delectably, deliciously, delightfully, dreamily, favorably, felicitously, gloriously, great, nicely, pleasantly, pleasingly, satisfyingly, splendidly, swimmingly

rel finely, grandly, magnificently; advantageously, helpfully, blessedly, fortunately, happily, luckily; excellently, superbly, marvelously, sensationally, wonderfully; attractively, beautifully, handsomely; appealingly, appetizingly, enticingly, invitingly, temptingly

near ant abominably, appallingly, awfully, dreadfully, horrendously, horribly, horridly, shockingly, sickeningly, terribly, vilely; annoyingly, disgustingly, distressingly, irritatingly, vexingly

ant badly, disagreeably, ill, unpleasantly

6 to a full extent or degree — see FULLY 1

7 without difficulty — see EASILY 1

well *interj* how surprising, doubtful, or unbelievable — see NO

well *n* **1** a point or place at which something is invented or provided — see SOURCE 1

2 a small often deep body of water — see ¹POOL

well–being *n* the state of doing well especially in relation to one's happiness or success — see WELFARE

wellborn *adj* of high birth, rank, or station — see NOBLE 1

well–bred *adj* showing consideration, courtesy, and good manners — see POLITE 1

well–disposed *adj* having an easygoing and pleasing manner especially in social situations — see AMIABLE

well–fixed *adj* having goods, property, or money in abundance — see RICH 1

well–founded *adj* **1** according to the rules of logic — see LOGICAL 1

2 based on sound reasoning or information — see GOOD 1

well–heeled *adj* having goods, property, or money in abundance — see RICH 1

well–known *adj* widely known — see FAMOUS 1

wellness *n* the condition of being sound in body — see HEALTH 1

well–nigh *adv* very close to but not completely — see ALMOST

well–off *adj* having goods, property, or money in abundance — see RICH 1

well–read *adj* having or displaying advanced knowledge or education — see EDUCATED 1

well–spoken *adj* able to express oneself clearly and well — see ARTICULATE

well–to–do *adj* having goods, property, or money in abundance — see RICH 1

welter *n* **1** a state of noisy, confused activity — see COMMOTION

2 an unorganized collection or mixture of various things — see MISCELLANY 1

3 a state in which everything is out of order — see CHAOS

wet *adj* **1** containing, covered with, or thoroughly penetrated by water ⟨I left the car windows open while it rained, and the seats got all *wet*.⟩

syn awash, bathed, bedraggled, doused (*also* dowsed), drenched, dripping, saturate, saturated, soaked, soaking, sodden, soggy, sopping, soppy, soused, washed, watered, waterlogged, watery

rel deluged, drowned, flooded, inundated, overflowed; submerged, swamped; hydrated; dipped, dunked, splashed; aqueous, steeped; flushed, irrigated, laved, rinsed, sluiced; damp, dank, humid, moist, semimoist; boggy, miry, seepy, sloppy, squashy

near ant bone-dry, hyperarid, ultradry; waterproof, water-repellent, water-resistant, watertight; baked, dehydrated, freeze-dried; droughty, parched, sere (*also* sear), sunbaked, thirsty; wrung

ant arid, dry, unwatered, waterless

2 marked by or abounding with rain — see RAINY

3 appealing to the emotions in an obvious and tiresome way — see CORNY

wet *n* a steady falling of water from the sky in significant quantity — see RAIN 1

wet *vb* to make wet ⟨You need to *wet* your hair thoroughly first.⟩

syn bathe, douse (*also* dowse), drench, drown, soak, sop, souse, wash, water

rel asperse, damp, dampen, drizzle, humidify, hydrate, mist, moisten, moisturize, shower, sprinkle; deluge, flood, hose (down), inundate, overflow; submerge, swamp; splash; impregnate, saturate, steep; flush, irrigate, lave, rinse, slosh, sluice; dip, duck, dunk; rehydrate, rewash, rewet

near ant dewater, evaporate, freeze-dry; drip-dry, wring; dehumidify

ant dehydrate, dry, parch, scorch, sear

wet blanket *n* a person who spoils the pleasure of others — see KILLJOY

whack *n* **1** an effort to do or accomplish something — see ATTEMPT 1

2 a hard strike with a part of the body or an instrument — see ¹BLOW

3 a loud explosive sound — see CLAP 1

whack *vb* to deliver a blow to (someone or

something) usually in a strong vigorous manner — see HIT 1

whacking *adj* unusually large — see HUGE

whacking *adv* to a great degree — see VERY 1

whale *n* something that is unusually large and powerful — see GIANT

whale *vb* 1 to deliver a blow to (someone or something) usually in a strong vigorous manner — see HIT 1

2 to strike repeatedly with something long and thin or flexible — see WHIP 1

3 to strike repeatedly — see BEAT 1

wharf *n* a structure used by boats and ships for taking on or landing cargo and passengers — see DOCK

what *interj* how surprising, doubtful, or unbelievable — see NO

wheedle *vb* to get (someone) to do something by gentle urging, special attention, or flattery — see COAX

wheel *n* 1 a rapid turning about on an axis or central point — see SPIN 1

2 one of high position or importance within a group — see BIG SHOT

3 a series of events or actions that repeat themselves regularly and in the same order — see CYCLE 1

4 **wheels** *pl, slang* a self-propelled passenger vehicle on four wheels — see CAR

wheel *vb* 1 to change the course or direction of (something) — see TURN 2

2 to move (something) in a curved or circular path on or as if on an axis — see TURN 1

3 to move in circles around an axis or center — see SPIN 1

4 to turn away from a straight line or course — see CURVE 1

5 to change one's course or direction — see TURN 3

wheeze *vb* to breathe hard, quickly, or with difficulty — see GASP

whelm *vb* to subject to incapacitating emotional or mental stress — see OVERWHELM 1

whelp *n* a young person who is between infancy and adulthood — see CHILD 1

when *conj* 1 at or during the time that ⟨She complained that no one was paying attention to her *when* she gave her speech.⟩

syn as, while

near ant after

2 just at the moment that ⟨You should say hello *when* you answer the phone.⟩

syn instantly

near ant after, since

3 in spite of the fact that — see ALTHOUGH

where *adv* at, in, or to what place ⟨*Where* will you be tonight?⟩

syn whereabouts (*also* whereabout), whither

rel wherever

near ant whence

where *n* the area or space occupied by or intended for something — see PLACE 1

whereabouts *also* **whereabout** *adv* at, in, or to what place — see WHERE

whereas *conj* 1 for the reason that — see SINCE

2 in spite of the fact that — see ALTHOUGH

wherefore *n* something (as a belief) that serves as the basis for another thing — see REASON 2

wherewithal *n* 1 available money — see FUND 2

2 the total of one's money and property — see WEALTH 1

whet *vb* to make sharp or sharper — see SHARPEN

whetted *adj* having an edge thin enough to cut or pierce something — see SHARP 1

whiff *n* an almost imperceptible sign of something — see HINT 2

whiff *vb* to become aware of by means of the sense organs in the nose — see SMELL 1

while *conj* 1 at or during the time that — see WHEN 1

2 in spite of the fact that — see ALTHOUGH

while *n* 1 an indefinite but usually short period of time ⟨We stayed at the fair for a *while* longer.⟩

syn bit, space, spell, stretch

rel lapse; season, span; day, epoch, era; beat, flash, instant, jiffy, minute, moment, nanosecond, New York minute, second, shake, split second, spurt, trice, twinkle, twinkling, wink; eon (*or* aeon), age, eternity, infinity, perpetuity; interim, interlude, intermission, interval

2 the active use of energy in producing a result — see EFFORT

whilom *adj* having been such at some previous time — see FORMER 1

whim *n* a sudden impulsive and apparently unmotivated idea or action ⟨On a *whim*, we stopped at the roadside stand to get ice cream.⟩

syn caprice, crank, fancy, freak, humor, notion, vagary, whimsy (*also* whimsey)

rel capriciousness, fancifulness, fantasy (*also* phantasy), freakishness, impetuosity, whimsicality; conceit; concept, conception, image, impression, picture, thought; brainstorm, inspiration

phrases bee in one's bonnet

whimper *n* an expression of dissatisfaction, pain, or resentment — see COMPLAINT 1

whimper *vb* to utter feeble plaintive cries ⟨The dog *whimpered* to be let in.⟩

syn mewl, pule

rel fuss, sniffle, snivel, snuffle, whine; bawl, blubber, cry, sob, weep; peep, squeak; yelp; mumble, murmur, mutter; groan, moan, sigh

near ant scream, screech, shriek, squeal; howl, squall, wail, yowl; call, squawk; bellow, roar

2 to express dissatisfaction, pain, or resentment usually tiresomely — see COMPLAIN

whimsical *adj* prone to sudden illogical changes of mind, ideas, or actions ⟨It's hard to make plans with such a *whimsical* best friend.⟩

syn capricious, impulsive

rel impetuous, mercurial, moody, temperamental, volatile; crankish, eccentric, flaky, quirky; arbitrary, erratic, fickle, inconstant, irregular, shaky, willful (*or* willful); impractical, quixotical, romantic, unrealistic, utopian, visionary

near ant equable; down-to-earth, earthy, hard-boiled, hardheaded, levelheaded, matter-of-fact, practical, pragmatic (*also* pragmatical), reasonable, sensible, tough-minded; grounded, logical, no-nonsense, rational, sane, sober, sobersided, sound; fast, fixed, hard-and-fast, immutable, inflexible, invariable, unalterable, unbending, unchangeable, uncompromising, unrelenting, unyielding; changeless, constant, established, set, settled, stable, steadfast, steady, unchanging, unvarying

whimsicality *n* an inclination to sudden illogical changes of mind, ideas, or actions ⟨His *whimsicality* made him an unpredictable companion.⟩

syn caprice, capriciousness, impulsiveness

rel mercurialness, moodiness, unpredictability, willfulness; eccentricity, flakiness; arbitrariness, fickleness, inconstancy, irregularity, volatileness, volatility; changeability, flexibility, mutability, variability, variableness

near ant levelheadedness, practicality, reasonableness; fastness, firmness, fixedness, immovability, immovableness, immutability, inflexibility, invariability; changelessness, constancy, stability, steadfastness, steadiness

whimsy *also* **whimsey** *n* a sudden impulsive and apparently unmotivated idea or action — see WHIM

whine *n* an expression of dissatisfaction, pain, or resentment — see COMPLAINT 1

whine *vb* to express dissatisfaction, pain, or resentment usually tiresomely — see COMPLAIN

whiner *n* **1** a person who makes frequent complaints usually about little things — see CRYBABY

2 an irritable and complaining person — see GROUCH 1

whinny *vb* to make the cry typical of a horse — see NEIGH

whip *n* a long thin or flexible tool for striking ⟨The vacuum cleaner's cord rewound suddenly and hit him on the leg like a *whip*.⟩

syn flogger, lash, scourge, switch

rel birch, blacksnake, bullwhip, cat-o'-nine-tails, cowhide, crop, hickory, knout, quirt, rattan, rawhide, strap; bastinado (*or* bastinade), bat, billy, billy club, bludgeon, cane, club, cudgel, flail, nightstick, staff

whip *vb* **1** to strike repeatedly with something long and thin or flexible ⟨a jockey *whipping* his horse with a riding crop⟩

syn birch, cowhide, flagellate, flail, flog, hide, horsewhip, lash, leather, scourge, slash, switch, thrash, whale

rel knout, quirt, strap; cut; flick, touch up; cane, club, cudgel, fustigate; pistol-whip; bang, bop, box, bust, clap, clip, clobber, clout, crack, cuff, hit, knock, lam, paste, punch, slap, slug, smack, smite, sock, spank, swat, swipe, thwack, wallop, whack; bash, baste, bat, batter, beat, belabor, belt, bludgeon, buffet, bung, drub, hammer, lace, lambaste (*or* lambast), lath-

er, lick, mangle, maul, paddle, pelt, pommel, pound, pummel, rough, slate, slog, thump, tromp

2 to defeat by a large margin ⟨We *whipped* them 13-0 in the last game.⟩

syn annihilate, bomb, bury, clobber, cream, drub, dust, flatten, paste, rout, skin, skunk, snow under, thrash, trim, trounce, wallop, wax [*slang*]

rel sweep, upset; beat, best, conquer, dispatch, hurdle, lick, master, overbear, overcome, overmatch, prevail (over), subdue, surmount, take, throw, triumph (over), win (against), worst; crush, knock off, overpower, overthrow, overwhelm, subjugate, upend, vanquish; ace (out), better, eclipse, exceed, outdistance, outdo, outfight, outshine, outstrip, overtop, surpass, top, transcend; edge (out); cap, excel, flourish, score, succeed; break, destroy, do in, finish, sink, slaughter

phrases beat the pants off, eat alive, run circles around (*or* run rings around), wipe the floor with (*or* wipe the ground with)

3 to change the course or direction of (something) — see TURN 2

4 to move or cause to move with a striking motion — see FLAP

5 to strike repeatedly — see BEAT 1

whip (up) *vb* to bring (something volatile or intense) into being — see INCITE 1

whipper *n* one that defeats an enemy or opponent — see VICTOR 1

whippersnapper *n* a person of no importance or influence — see NOBODY

whipping *n* failure to win a contest — see DEFEAT 1

whipping boy *n* a person or thing taking the blame for others — see SCAPEGOAT

whir *also* **whirr** *n* a monotonous sound like that of an insect in motion — see HUM

whir *also* **whirr** *vb* to fly, turn, or move rapidly with a fluttering or vibratory sound ⟨The hummingbird *whirred* as it hovered over a flower.⟩ ⟨Our tires *whirred* as we traveled over the rough road.⟩

syn buzz, drone, hum, whish, whiz (*or* whizz), zip, zoom

rel chirr; thrum; fizz, hiss, murmur, purr, rustle, sigh, sizzle, swish, whisper; coo, curr; wheeze, whistle, whoosh

whirl *n* **1** a rapid turning about on an axis or central point — see SPIN 1

2 a state of mental uncertainty — see CONFUSION 1

3 a state of noisy, confused activity — see COMMOTION

4 an effort to do or accomplish something — see ATTEMPT 1

whirl *vb* **1** to cause (as a liquid) to move about in a circle especially repeatedly — see STIR 1

2 to move (something) in a curved or circular path on or as if on an axis — see TURN 1

3 to move in circles around an axis or center — see SPIN 1

4 to proceed or move quickly — see HURRY 2

5 to be in a confused state as if from being twirled around — see SPIN 2

whirling *adj* having a feeling of being

whirled about and in danger of falling down — see DIZZY 1

whirlpool *n* water moving rapidly in a circle with a hollow in the center ⟨In *The Odyssey*, Ulysses is trapped between the six-headed monster Scylla and Charybdis, a deadly *whirlpool* that threatens to suck in his ship.⟩

syn gulf, maelstrom, vortex

rel tourbillion (*or* tourbillon); eddy, swirl, whirl

whirlwind *adj* moving, proceeding, or acting with great speed — see FAST 1

whish *n* a sound similar to the speech sound \s\ stretched out — see HISS 1

whish *vb* **1** to fly, turn, or move rapidly with a fluttering or vibratory sound — see WHIR

2 to make a sound like that of stretching out the speech sound \s\ — see HISS

whisk *n* a quick jerky movement from side to side or up and down — see ¹WAG

whisk *vb* **1** to cause to move or proceed fast or faster — see HURRY 1

2 to move or proceed smoothly and readily — see FLOW 2

3 to proceed or move quickly — see HURRY 2

whisper *n* a rumor or report of a personal or sensational nature — see TALE 1

whisper *vb* to make (as a piece of information) the subject of common talk without any authority or confirmation of accuracy — see RUMOR

whistling *adj* having a high musical pitch or range — see SHRILL

whit *n* the smallest amount or part imaginable — see JOT

white *adj* lacking an addition of color — see COLORLESS 1

whiten *vb* to make white or whiter by removing color ⟨Years of sunlight had almost completely *whitened* the flag.⟩

syn blanch, bleach, blench, decolorize, dull, fade, pale, wash out

rel brighten, lighten; dim, mat (*also* matte *or* matt); whitewash; frost, silver

near ant blacken; blotch, checker, dapple, daub, discolor, fleck, marble, mottle, pattern, polychrome, shade, speck, speckle, splotch, spot, streak, striate, stripe, tarnish, variegate; color, dye, paint, pigment, stain, tincture, tinge, tint; burnish, polish, shine

ant darken, deepen, embrown

whitewash *vb* **1** to dismiss as of little importance — see EXCUSE 1

2 to make (something) seem less bad by offering excuses — see PALLIATE 1

whither *adv* at, in, or to what place — see WHERE

¹**whiz** *or* **whizz** *n* **1** a sound similar to the speech sound \s\ stretched out — see HISS 1

2 a monotonous sound like that of an insect in motion — see HUM

²**whiz** *n* **1** a person with a high level of knowledge or skill in a field — see EXPERT

2 a very smart person — see GENIUS 1

whiz *or* **whizz** *vb* **1** to make a sound like that of stretching out the speech sound \s\ — see HISS

2 to fly, turn, or move rapidly with a fluttering or vibratory sound — see WHIR

whole *adj* **1** not divided or scattered among several areas of interest or concern ⟨You'll need to put your *whole* effort into this project.⟩

syn all, concentrated, entire, exclusive, focused (*also* focussed), undivided

rel absolute, complete, full, lump, teetotal, thorough, total, unadulterated, unalloyed, unqualified, utter; comprehensive, intact, integral, perfect, unbroken; entireness, wholeness

near ant deficient, fragmental, fragmentary, halfway, incomplete, partial

ant diffuse, divided, scattered

2 enjoying health and vigor — see HEALTHY 1

3 not lacking any part or member that properly belongs to it — see COMPLETE 1

whole *n* a complete amount of something ⟨The landlord eventually refunded the *whole* of our deposit.⟩

syn aggregate, full, sum, summation, total, totality

rel gross; comprehensiveness, cumulativeness; bulk, mass; enchilada, schmear

phrases grand total, the whole bit, the whole kit and caboodle, the whole nine yards, the whole shebang

near ant net

wholehearted *adj* characterized by unqualified enthusiasm — see HEARTY 1

wholeness *n* the condition of being sound in body — see HEALTH 1

whole number *n* a character used to represent a mathematical value — see NUMBER 1

wholesome *adj* **1** enjoying health and vigor — see HEALTHY 1

2 beneficial to the health of body or mind — see HEALTHFUL

wholesomeness *n* the condition of being sound in body — see HEALTH 1

wholly *adv* to a full extent or degree — see FULLY 1

whoop *n* **1** a loud vocal expression of strong emotion — see SHOUT

2 the smallest amount or part imaginable — see JOT

whopper *n* **1** a statement known by its maker to be untrue and made in order to deceive — see LIE

2 something that is unusually large and powerful — see GIANT

whopping *adj* unusually large — see HUGE

why *interj* how surprising, doubtful, or unbelievable — see NO

why *n* something (as a belief) that serves as the basis for another thing — see REASON 2

wicked *adj* **1** not conforming to a high moral standard; morally unacceptable — see BAD 2

2 not giving pleasure to the mind or senses — see UNPLEASANT

3 causing or capable of causing harm — see HARMFUL

wicked *adv* to a great degree — see VERY 1

wickedly *adv* in a mean or spiteful manner — see NASTILY

wickedness *n* the state or quality of being utterly evil — see ENORMITY 1

---

wide *adj* **1** having a greater than usual measure across ⟨The river is so *wide* that building a bridge across it would be impractical.⟩
syn broad, fat, thick
rel expansive, extensive; commodious, roomy, spacious; outsize (*also* outsized), oversize (*or* oversized), sizable (*or* sizeable), substantial, tidy, voluminous
near ant fine, hairlike, reedlike; elongate (*or* elongated), needlelike; bottleneck, close, compressed, condensed, constricted, contracted, squeezed, tight, tightened; attenuated; small, smallish, undersized (*also* undersize)
ant hairline, narrow, skinny, slender, slim, thin
2 having considerable extent — see EXTENSIVE
wide *adv* to a full extent or degree — see FULLY 1
wide-awake *adj* **1** not sleeping or able to sleep — see WAKEFUL
2 paying close attention usually for the purpose of anticipating approaching danger or opportunity — see ALERT 1
wide-eyed *adj* **1** lacking in worldly wisdom or informed judgment — see NAIVE 1
2 readily taken advantage of — see EASY 2
widespread *adj* having considerable extent — see EXTENSIVE
width *n* an area over which activity, capacity, or influence extends — see RANGE 2
wield *vb* to bring to bear especially forcefully or effectively — see EXERT
wife *n* a female partner in a marriage ⟨I was pleased to meet your *wife*⟩
syn lady, old lady
rel bride; better half, companion, consort, mate, partner, significant other, soul mate, spouse; dowager; matron; hausfrau, homemaker, housewife; widow
wiggle *vb* to make jerky or restless movements — see FIDGET
wight *n* a member of the human race — see HUMAN
wild *adj* **1** living outdoors without taming or domestication by humans ⟨*Wild* animals can be shy or aggressive when confronted by humans.⟩
syn feral, savage, unbroken, undomesticated, untamed
rel uncontrolled, undocile, unsubdued, untrained; brutal, brute; barbarous, uncivilized
near ant controlled, docile, familiar, semidomesticated, subdued, submissive; halterbroken, housebroken, trained; civilized, semicivilized, socialized
ant broken, domestic, domesticated, gentled, tame, tamed
2 existing without human habitation or cultivation ⟨That land has been completely *wild* since the owners abandoned it.⟩
syn natural, uncultivated, untamed, virgin
rel uninhabited, unpeopled, unsettled; overgrown, spontaneous, untended; waste; undeveloped; desolate, forlorn, howling
near ant inhabited; developed; seminatural
ant cultivated, tamed
3 marked by turmoil or disturbance especially of natural elements ⟨a *wild* night, full of wind and rain⟩
syn rough, rugged, stormy, tempestuous, tumultuous, turbulent
rel blustering, blustery, violent; brutal, harsh, severe; roily, unquiet, unsettled; bleak, inclement, nasty, raw, squally
near ant calm, halcyon, peaceful, placid, quiet, serene, tranquil; bright, clear, clement, cloudless, fair, sunny, sunshiny, unclouded
4 conceived or made without regard for reason or reality — see FANTASTIC 1
5 different from the ordinary in a way that causes curiosity or suspicion — see ODD 2
6 marked by great and often stressful excitement or activity — see FURIOUS 1
7 not civilized — see UNCIVILIZED
8 showing urgent desire or interest — see EAGER
wild *adv* in a confused and reckless manner — see HELTER-SKELTER 1
wild *n* that part of the physical world that is removed from human habitation — see NATURE 2
wilderness *n* that part of the physical world that is removed from human habitation — see NATURE 2
wildly *adv* **1** in a confused and reckless manner — see HELTER-SKELTER 1
2 to a great degree — see VERY 1
wile *n* **1** a clever often underhanded means to achieve an end — see TRICK 1
2 the use of clever underhanded actions to achieve an end — see TRICKERY
wile *vb* to attract or delight as if by magic — see CHARM 1
wiliness *n* **1** skill in achieving one's ends through indirect, subtle, or underhanded means — see CUNNING 1
2 the inclination or practice of misleading others through lies or trickery — see DECEIT 1
will *n* **1** the power to control one's actions, impulses, or emotions ⟨She kept her face still by sheer force of *will*.⟩
syn restraint, self-containment, self-control, self-discipline, self-government, self-possession, self-restraint, willpower
rel self-abnegation, self-denial; moderateness, moderation, temperance, temperateness; determination, nerve; command, control, discipline, mastery; abnegation, abstinence, abstention, avoidance, eschewal, forbearance; soberness, sobriety; aplomb, assurance, composure, confidence, coolness, equanimity, poise, self-confidence; discretion
near ant gratification, indulgence, self-indulgence; overindulgence; demerit, failing, fault, feebleness, foible, frailty, shortcoming, vice, weakness; indiscipline, unrestraint
2 the act or power of making one's own choices or decisions — see FREE WILL
will *vb* **1** to give by means of a will — see LEAVE 2
2 to see fit — see CHOOSE 2
willful *or* **wilful** *adj* **1** given to resisting authority or another's control — see DISOBEDIENT
2 given to resisting control or discipline by others — see UNCONTROLLABLE

3 having or showing a tendency to force one's will on others without any regard to fairness or necessity — see ARBITRARY 1

4 made, given, or done with full awareness of what one is doing — see INTENTIONAL

5 sticking to an opinion, purpose, or course of action in spite of reason, arguments, or persuasion — see OBSTINATE

willfully *adv* with full awareness of what one is doing — see INTENTIONALLY

willfulness *n* **1** a steadfast adherence to an opinion, purpose, or course of action in spite of reason, arguments, or persuasion — see OBSTINACY

2 refusal to obey — see DISOBEDIENCE

willies *n pl* a sense of panic or extreme nervousness — see JITTERS

willing *adj* **1** having a desire or inclination (as for a specified course of action) ⟨I'm a little confused, but perfectly *willing* to do as you ask.⟩

syn amenable, disposed, game, glad, inclined, minded, ready

rel predisposed, prone; accommodating, agreeable, compliant, cooperative, obedient, obliging, submissive; favorable, receptive; prepared, prompt, quick, responsive, swift; desirous, eager, enthusiastic, excited

near ant averse, loath (*also* loth *or* loathe), reluctant, reticent

ant disinclined, unamenable, unwilling

2 having or showing the ability to respond without delay or hesitation — see QUICK 1

3 done, made, or given with one's own free will — see VOLUNTARY 1

willingly *adv* **1** by choice or preference — see RATHER 1

2 of one's own free will — see VOLUNTARILY

willingness *n* cheerful readiness to do something — see ALACRITY

williwaw *n* **1** a state of noisy, confused activity — see COMMOTION

2 a sudden brief rush of wind — see GUST 1

willowy *adj* able to bend easily without breaking ⟨The rattan's stems are split into *willowy* staves that are woven together to produce exquisite baskets.⟩

syn flexible, limber, lissome (*also* lissom), lithe, lithesome, pliable, pliant, supple

rel adaptable, ductile, elastic, fluid, kneadable, malleable, modifiable, plastic, variable, yielding; droopy, flaccid, floppy, limp; semiflexible

near ant inelastic, nonmalleable, unyielding; breakable, brittle, fragile

ant inflexible, rigid, stiff, stiffened

willpower *n* the power to control one's actions, impulses, or emotions — see WILL 1

willy-nilly *adv* without definite aim, direction, rule, or method — see HIT OR MISS

wilt *vb* **1** to be limp from lack of water or vigor — see DROOP 1

2 to lose bodily strength or vigor — see WEAKEN 2

3 to lose liveliness, force, or freshness — see WITHER 1

wily *adj* clever at attaining one's ends by indirect and often deceptive means — see ARTFUL 1

wimp *n* **1** a person lacking in physical strength — see WEAKLING 1

2 a person without strength of character — see WEAKLING 2

wimpy *adj* **1** lacking bodily strength — see WEAK 1

2 lacking strength of will or character — see WEAK 2

win *n* an instance of defeating an enemy or opponent — see VICTORY

win *vb* **1** to achieve victory (as in a contest) ⟨the kind of person who always has to *win*—even if the game is just for fun⟩

syn conquer, prevail, triumph

rel overcome, sweep; squeak, squeeze; contend, vie; succeed; breeze, romp

phrases carry the day; kick butt

near ant collapse, fail, flop, fold, wash out; flounder, struggle; decline, slip, slump, wane

ant lose

2 to receive as return for effort — see EARN 1

3 to obtain (as a goal) through effort — see ACHIEVE 1

win (against) *vb* to achieve a victory over — see BEAT 2

win (over) *vb* to cause (someone) to agree with a belief or course of action by using arguments or earnest requests — see PERSUADE

wince *vb* to draw back in fear, pain, or disgust — see FLINCH

¹**wind** *n* **1** noticeable movement of air in a particular direction ⟨There's a *wind* coming from underneath the front door.⟩

syn current, draft

rel blast, blow, flurry, gale, gust, headwind, squall, tailwind, tempest, tornado, windstorm; breath, breeze, puff, waft, zephyr

2 a prevailing or general movement or inclination — see TREND 1

3 language that is impressive-sounding but not meaningful or sincere — see RHETORIC 1

²**wind** *n* something that curves or is curved — see BEND 1

wind *vb* **1** to follow a circular or spiral course ⟨Flowering vines *wind* around the porch's graceful columns.⟩

syn coil, corkscrew, curl, entwine, spiral, twine, twist

rel arc, arch, bend, crook, curve, hook, sweep, swerve, turn, veer, wheel; swirl, whirl; circle, encircle, loop; interlace, intertwine, lace; bow, bulge; meander, weave, zigzag

near ant straighten

2 to introduce in a gradual, secret, or clever way — see INSINUATE 1

windbag *n* a person who talks constantly — see CHATTERBOX

windfall *n* something that provides happiness or does good for a person or thing — see BLESSING 2

windiness *n* the use of too many words to express an idea — see VERBIAGE 1

winding *adj* **1** marked by a long series of irregular curves — see CROOKED 1

2 turning around an axis like the thread of a screw — see SPIRAL

windjammer *n* a boat equipped with one or more sails — see SAILBOAT

---

windup *n* the last part of a process or action — see FINALE

wind up *vb* **1** to bring (an event) to a natural or appropriate stopping point — see CLOSE 3

2 to come to an end — see CEASE 1

¹**windy** *adj* **1** marked by strong wind or more wind than usual ⟨One particularly *windy* day should shake the last of the autumn leaves from the trees.⟩

syn blowy, blustery, breezy, gusty, squally

rel drafty; stormy, tempestuous

near ant breathless, calm, motionless, still

2 marked by the use of impressive-sounding but mostly meaningless words and phrases — see RHETORICAL 1

3 using or containing more words than necessary to express an idea — see WORDY 1

²**windy** *adj* marked by a long series of irregular curves — see CROOKED 1

wing *n* a group of people acting together within a larger group — see FACTION

wing *vb* to move through the air with or as if with outstretched wings — see FLY 1

wink *n* **1** a short sleep — see ¹NAP

2 a very small space of time — see INSTANT

wink *vb* **1** to rapidly open and close one's eyes ⟨She *winked* several times to get the dust and grit out of her eyes.⟩

syn blink

rel bat, flutter; squint

2 to shine with light at regular intervals — see BLINK 1

3 to shoot forth bursts of light — see FLASH 1

4 to secretly sympathize with or pretend ignorance of something improper or unlawful — see CONNIVE 1

wink (at) *vb* to dismiss as of little importance — see EXCUSE 1

winner *n* **1** a person or thing that is successful — see HIT 1

2 one that defeats an enemy or opponent — see VICTOR 1

3 the person who comes in first in a competition — see CHAMPION 1

winning *adj* **1** having qualities that tend to make one loved — see LOVABLE

2 likely or intended to win one's affection — see INGRATIATING

winsome *adj* **1** having or showing a good mood or disposition — see CHEERFUL 1

2 likely or intended to win one's affection — see INGRATIATING

3 having qualities that tend to make one loved — see LOVABLE

wintry *also* **wintery** *adj* **1** having a low or subnormal temperature — see COLD 1

2 lacking in friendliness or warmth of feeling — see COLD 2

wipe out *vb* to destroy all traces of — see ANNIHILATE 1

wire *n* a length of braided, flexible material that is used for tying or connecting things — see CORD 1

wisdom *n* **1** the ability to understand inner qualities or relationships ⟨With age and experience comes *wisdom*—hopefully.⟩ ⟨Neither book learning nor simple intelligence should be confused with *wisdom*.⟩

syn discernment, insight, perception, perceptiveness, sagaciousness, sagacity, sageness, sapience

rel acuity, acumen, astuteness, keenness, penetration, perspicacity, sensitivity, understanding; appreciation, apprehension, comprehension, grasp; brain(s), braininess, brightness, brilliance, canniness, cleverness, gray matter, intellect, intelligence, judgment (*or* judgement), mentality, power, reason, sense, smartness, wit; discrimination, foresight, foresightedness, prudence, sanity; logic, rationality

near ant density, dullness (*also* dulness), obtuseness; brainlessness, folly, foolishness, idiocy, imbecility, mindlessness, silliness, simpleness, stupidity, witlessness; illogic, irrationality, unreasonableness, unsoundness; preposterousness, senselessness, silliness, zaniness

2 a body of facts learned by study or experience — see KNOWLEDGE 1

3 the ability to make intelligent decisions especially in everyday matters — see COMMON SENSE

wise *adj* **1** having or showing deep understanding and intelligent application of knowledge ⟨a respected and *wise* old judge famous for her sensible rulings⟩

syn discerning, insightful, perceptive, prudent, sagacious, sage, sapient

rel acute, penetrating, percipient, perspicacious; experienced; discriminating, discriminative; brainy, bright, brilliant, clever, intelligent, keen, nimble, quick, quick-witted, smart; cerebral, erudite, knowledgeable, learned, literate, scholarly; astute, clearheaded, piercing, sharp, shrewd; contemplative, reflective, thoughtful

near ant dense, dull, obtuse, purblind, woodenheaded; brainless, dumb, feebleminded, foolish, idiotic (*also* idiotical), imbecile (*or* imbecilic), knuckleheaded, moronic, silly, simple, slow, slow-witted, stupid, thoughtless, unintelligent, witless; undiscriminating

ant unwise

2 having inside information ⟨They fooled everyone else, but I'd heard them talking and was *wise* to their true intentions.⟩

syn hip, knowing

rel alerted, aware, clued (in), forewarned, informed, prepared, ready, warned; observant, observing, sharp, sharp-eyed; alert, attentive, open-eyed, vigilant, watchful; plugged-in, with-it

phrases in the know

near ant oblivious, unaware, unconscious, uninformed, unwitting; heedless, unmindful; unprepared, unready, unwary

ant unknowing

3 suitable for bringing about a desired result under the circumstances — see EXPEDIENT

4 making light of something usually regarded as serious or sacred — see FLIPPANT

5 displaying or marked by rude boldness — see NERVY 1

wise (up) *vb* **1** to give information to — see ENLIGHTEN 1

2 to come to an awareness of — see DISCOVER 1

wiseacre *n* a person who likes to show off in a clever but annoying way — see SMART ALECK

wisecrack *n* something said or done to cause laughter — see JOKE 1

wisecrack *vb* to make jokes — see JOKE 1

wise guy *n* a person who likes to show off in a clever but annoying way — see SMART ALECK

wish *vb* **1** to offer (something fake, useless, or inferior) as genuine, useful, or valuable — see FOIST

2 to see fit — see CHOOSE 2

wish (for) *vb* to have an earnest wish to own or enjoy — see DESIRE 1

wishy–washy *adj* **1** lacking in qualities that make for spirit and character ⟨This story is too *wishy-washy*; you need to add some verve to it.⟩

syn banal, flat, insipid, watery

rel unexciting, uninspiring, unrewarding; bland, boring, drab, dreary, dry, dull, heavy, humdrum, jading, leaden, lifeless, monotonous, pedestrian, ponderous, tedious, tiresome, tiring, uninteresting, vapid, wearisome, weary, wearying; inane, innocuous, inoffensive; mild, soft, subdued, tame, weak; common, commonplace, ordinary, stale, unexceptional

near ant piquant, poignant, pungent, racy, spicy; meaty, substantial; entertaining, exciting, galvanizing, inspiring, invigorating, thrilling

2 lacking strength of will or character — see WEAK 2

wit *n* **1** a person (as a writer) noted for or specializing in humor — see HUMORIST

2 the ability to make intelligent decisions especially in everyday matters — see COMMON SENSE

3 *usually pl* **wits** *pl* the normal or healthy condition of the mental abilities — see MIND 2

4 exceptional discernment and judgment especially in practical matters — see ACUMEN

witch *n* **1** a woman believed to have often harmful supernatural powers ⟨The 17th-century house had once belonged to a woman who was hanged as a *witch*.⟩

syn enchantress, hag, hex, sorceress

rel charmer, conjurer (*or* conjuror), enchanter, necromancer; magician, sorcerer, warlock, wizard

2 a person skilled in using supernatural forces — see MAGICIAN 1

witchcraft *n* the power to control natural forces through supernatural means — see MAGIC 1

witchery *n* **1** the power of irresistible attraction — see CHARM 2

2 the power to control natural forces through supernatural means — see MAGIC 1

with *prep* **1** as the result of — see BECAUSE OF

2 using the means or agency of — see BY 2

3 without being prevented by — see DESPITE

withal *adv* **1** in addition to what has been said — see MORE 1

2 in spite of that — see HOWEVER

withdraw *vb* **1** to move back or away (as from something difficult, dangerous, or disagreeable) — see RETREAT 1

2 to solemnly or formally reject or go back on (as something formerly adhered to) — see ABJURE 1

3 to take away from a place or position — see REMOVE 2

withdrawal *n* an act of moving away especially from something difficult, dangerous, or disagreeable — see RETREAT 1

withdrawn *adj* not comfortable around people — see SHY 2

wither *vb* **1** to lose liveliness, force, or freshness ⟨Shortly after the moon landing, interest in the space program *withered*.⟩ ⟨The old man seemed to *wither* suddenly upon turning 80.⟩

syn dry, wilt

rel mummify, shrivel, wizen; decline, fade, wane; decrease, diminish, lessen

near ant freshen, revive; bloom, flourish, prosper, thrive; develop, grow, increase, wax; crest, peak, surge

2 to lose bodily strength or vigor — see WEAKEN 2

withhold *vb* **1** to be unwilling to grant — see DENY 2

2 to continue to have in one's possession or power — see KEEP 2

within *n* an interior or internal part — see INSIDE 1

without *prep* **1** not having ⟨spent two days *without* food⟩

syn absent, minus, sans, wanting

2 out of the reach or sphere of — see BEYOND 2

withstand *vb* to refuse to give in to — see RESIST

witless *adj* **1** not having or showing an ability to absorb ideas readily — see STUPID 1

2 showing or marked by a lack of good sense or judgment — see FOOLISH 1

witlessness *n* **1** lack of good sense or judgment — see FOOLISHNESS 1

2 the quality or state of lacking intelligence or quickness of mind — see STUPIDITY 1

witness *n* something presented in support of the truth or accuracy of a claim — see PROOF

witness *vb* **1** to declare (something) to be true or genuine — see CERTIFY 1

2 to make note of (something) through the use of one's eyes — see SEE 1

3 to make a solemn declaration under oath for the purpose of establishing a fact — see TESTIFY

4 to come to a knowledge of (something) by living through it — see EXPERIENCE

witticism *n* something said or done to cause laughter — see JOKE 1

witting *adj* **1** having specified facts or feelings actively impressed on the mind — see CONSCIOUS 1

2 made, given, or done with full awareness of what one is doing — see INTENTIONAL

wittingly *adv* with full awareness of what one is doing — see INTENTIONALLY

witty *adj* given to or marked by mature intelligent humor ⟨a witty and sardonic blogger who never fails to amuse her legion of readers⟩ ⟨He's well-known for his *witty* retorts.⟩

---

syn synonym(s)   *rel* related words
ant antonym(s)   *near ant* near antonym(s)

syn clever, facetious, humorous, jocular, smart

rel cerebral, highbrow, intellectual; bantering, frivolous, jesting, joking, joshing, teasing; antic, comic, comical, droll, farcical, funny, hysterical, laughable, ludicrous, ridiculous, riotous, risible, rollicking, screaming, uproarious; amusing, diverting, entertaining; mischievous, playful, prankish; jocose, jocund, jolly, jovial, laughing, merry, mirthful, sunny; scintillating, sparkling; flip, flippant, pert, smartalecky, waggish; whimsical

near ant brainless, lowbrow, stupid, witless; corny, hackney, hackneyed, lame; humorless, unamusing, uncomic, unfunny; earnest, grave, serious, serious-minded, sober, solemn, somber (*or* sombre); doleful, dolorous, lachrymose, plaintive, sorry, tearful, woeful

wizard *n* 1 a person skilled in using supernatural forces — see MAGICIAN 1

2 a person with a high level of knowledge or skill in a field — see EXPERT

3 a very smart person — see GENIUS 1

wizardry *n* the power to control natural forces through supernatural means — see MAGIC 1

wobble *also* **wabble** *vb* 1 to make a series of small irregular or violent movements — see SHAKE 1

2 to make a series of unsteady side-to-side motions — see ROCK 1

3 to show uncertainty about the right course of action — see HESITATE

4 to swing unsteadily back and forth or from side to side — see TEETER 1

wobbling *also* **wabbling** *adj* marked by or given to small uncontrollable bodily movements — see SHAKY 1

wobbling *also* **wabbling** *n* a state or an instance of temporary inaction because of uncertainty about the right course of action — see HESITATION

wobbly *also* **wabbly** *adj* marked by or given to small uncontrollable bodily movements — see SHAKY 1

woe *n* 1 a state of great suffering of body or mind — see DISTRESS 1

2 deep sadness especially for the loss of someone or something loved — see SORROW

woebegone *adj* feeling unhappiness — see SAD 1

woeful *adj* 1 expressing or suggesting mourning — see MOURNFUL 1

2 feeling unhappiness — see SAD 1

3 of a kind to cause great distress — see REGRETTABLE

woefully *adv* with feelings of bitterness or grief — see HARD 2

wolf *vb* to swallow or eat greedily — see GOBBLE

woman *n* 1 an adult female human being ⟨the first *woman* to become governor of the state⟩

syn female, lady

rel dame, gentlewoman; madame, senora (*or* señora); beauty, belle, damsel, gal, girl, ingenue (*or* ingénue), lass, lassie, mademoiselle, maid, maiden, miss, senorita (*or* señorita)

2 a female romantic companion — see GIRLFRIEND

womanish *adj* 1 of or relating to a man who has or displays qualities traditionally considered more suitable for women — see EFFEMINATE

2 of, relating to, or marked by qualities traditionally associated with women — see FEMININE

womanlike *adj* of, relating to, or marked by qualities traditionally associated with women — see FEMININE

womanly *adj* of, relating to, or marked by qualities traditionally associated with women — see FEMININE

wonder *n* 1 something extraordinary or surprising ⟨The cunningly crafted miniature of our house is a *wonder*, perfect in every detail.⟩

syn caution, flash, marvel, miracle, phenomenon, portent, prodigy, sensation, splendor

rel curiosity, sight; beauty, corker, crackerjack (*also* crackajack), dandy, jim-dandy, knockout; apparition, appearance

2 the rapt attention and deep emotion caused by the sight of something extraordinary ⟨When we first saw the pyramids of Egypt, we gazed with openmouthed *wonder*.⟩

syn admiration, amazement, astonishment, awe, wonderment

rel dread; fear; respect, reverence, veneration; curiosity, interest; shock, surprise; disbelief, incredulity; beguilement, bewitchment, captivation, enchantment, fascination; animation, enlightenment, enlivenment, excitement, invigoration, stimulation; absorption, engagement, engrossment, enthrallment, immersion, involvement

near ant apathy, indifference, unconcern; boredom, doldrums, ennui, listlessness, restlessness, tedium, tiredness, weariness, weltschmerz; cheerlessness, dispiritedness, joylessness, melancholy

wonderful *adj* 1 causing wonder or astonishment — see MARVELOUS 1

2 of the very best kind — see EXCELLENT

wondering *adj* filled with amazement or wonder — see OPENMOUTHED

wonderment *n* the rapt attention and deep emotion caused by the sight of something extraordinary — see WONDER 2

wondrous *adj* causing wonder or astonishment — see MARVELOUS 1

wont *adj* being in the habit or custom — see ACCUSTOMED

wont *n* a usual manner of behaving or doing — see HABIT 1

woo *vb* to act so as to make (something) more likely — see COURT 1

wood *n* 1 tree logs as prepared for human use ⟨a huge load of *wood* outside the furniture maker's factory⟩

syn lumber, timber

rel beam, brace, pile, post, ridgepole, sill, splint, stake, stave, stick; bar, billet, block; cordwood, firewood

2 *often* **woods** *pl* a dense growth of trees and shrubs covering a large area — see FOREST

wooden *adj* lacking social grace and assurance — see AWKWARD 1

woodland *n* a dense growth of trees and shrubs covering a large area — see FOREST

wooer *n* a man who courts a woman usually with the goal of marrying her — see SUITOR 1

wool *n* the hairy covering of a mammal especially when fine, soft, and thick — see FUR 1

woolgathering *n* the state of being lost in thought — see REVERIE

woolly *also* **wooly** *adj* **1** made of or resembling hair — see HAIRY 2

2 covered with or as if with hair — see HAIRY 1

word *n* **1** a pronounceable series of letters having a distinct meaning especially in a particular field ⟨My doctor used all of these medical *words* that I didn't understand.⟩

syn expression, term

rel linguistic form, monosyllable, morpheme, speech form; polysyllable; collocation, idiom, locution, phrase; archaism, coinage, colloquialism, euphemism, loanword, modernism, neologism, vernacularism

2 something that is said ⟨I agreed with every *word* she said.⟩

syn statement, utterance

rel communication, message; announcement, declamation, declaration, manifesto, proclamation, pronouncement; verbalization, vocalization

3 a report of recent events or facts not previously known — see NEWS

4 a person's solemn declaration that he or she will do or not do something — see PROMISE

5 a statement of what to do that must be obeyed by those concerned — see COMMAND 1

6 information or opinion that is widely disseminated without any authority or confirmation of accuracy — see RUMOR

7 a word or phrase that must be spoken by a person in order to pass a guard — see PASSWORD

8 an often stated observation regarding something from common experience — see SAYING

word *vb* to convey in appropriate or telling terms — see PHRASE

wordbook *n* a reference book giving information about the meanings, pronunciations, uses, and origins of words listed in alphabetical order — see DICTIONARY

word for word *adv* in the same words — see VERBATIM

wordiness *n* the use of too many words to express an idea — see VERBIAGE 1

wording *n* **1** the way in which something is put into words ⟨It's important to get the *wording* of this law precisely correct.⟩

syn diction, language, phraseology, phrasing, verbiage

rel expression, formulation, locution; enunciation, phrase, speech, style, utterance, voice

2 an act, process, or means of putting something into words — see EXPRESSION 1

---

syn synonym(s)   *rel* related words
ant antonym(s)   *near ant* near antonym(s)

wordless *adj* **1** deliberately refraining from speech — see SILENT 1

2 understood although not put into words — see IMPLICIT 1

wordy *adj* **1** using or containing more words than necessary to express an idea ⟨Her writing style is far too *wordy* for my tastes.⟩

syn circuitous, circumlocutory, diffuse, garrulous, long-winded, prolix, rambling, verbose, windy

rel chatty, communicative, conversational, gabby, loquacious, talkative, talky, voluble; periphrastic; redundant, repetitious, tautological, tautologous; embellished, embroidered; bombastic, gaseous, gassy, grandiloquent, highfalutin (*also* hifalutin)

near ant brief, short; aphoristic, epigrammatic; compendious, summary; abbreviated, abridged, condensed, shortened; abrupt, blunt, brusque (*also* brusk), curt, laconic, snippy

ant compact, concise, crisp, pithy, succinct, terse

2 of or relating to words or language — see VERBAL 1

work *n* **1** a literary, musical, or artistic production — see COMPOSITION 1

2 something produced by physical or intellectual effort — see PRODUCT 1

3 the action for which a person or thing is specially fitted or used or for which a thing exists — see ROLE

4 the active use of energy in producing a result — see EFFORT

5 the activity by which one regularly makes a living — see OCCUPATION

6 works *pl* a building or set of buildings for the manufacturing of goods — see FACTORY

work *vb* **1** to be the cause of (a situation, action, or state of mind) — see EFFECT

2 to find an answer for through reasoning — see SOLVE

3 to have a certain purpose — see FUNCTION

4 to produce a desired effect — see ACT 2

5 to set or keep in motion — see MOVE 2

6 to control the mechanical operation of — see OPERATE 1

7 to devote serious and sustained effort — see LABOR

8 to take unfair advantage of — see EXPLOIT 1

work (for) *vb* to be an employee for — see SERVE 1

workable *adj* **1** capable of being done or carried out — see POSSIBLE 1

2 capable of being put to use or account — see PRACTICAL 1

workaday *adj* **1** being of the type that is encountered in the normal course of events — see ORDINARY 1

2 having to do with the practical details of regular life — see MUNDANE 1

3 not designed to be worn only on special occasions — see CASUAL 1

worker *n* **1** a person who does very hard or dull work — see DRUDGE

2 one who works for another for wages or a salary — see EMPLOYEE

workforce *n* a body of persons at work or available for work — see FORCE 1

working *adj* **1** being in effective operation — see ACTIVE 1

2 capable of being put to use or account — see PRACTICAL 1

3 involved in often constant activity — see BUSY 1

workmanlike *adj* accomplished with trained ability — see SKILLFUL 1

workout *n* something done over and over in order to develop skill — see EXERCISE 2

work out *vb* **1** to find an answer for through reasoning — see SOLVE

2 to turn out as planned or desired — see SUCCEED 1

3 to determine (a value) by doing the necessary mathematical operations — see CALCULATE 1

workshop *n* a building or set of buildings for the manufacturing of goods — see FACTORY

world *n* **1** human beings in general — see PEOPLE 1

2 the celestial body on which we live — see EARTH 1

3 the whole body of things observed or assumed — see UNIVERSE

worldly *adj* **1** having a wide and refined knowledge of the world especially from personal experience — see WORLDLY-WISE

2 having to do with life on earth especially as opposed to that in heaven — see EARTHLY

worldly-wise *adj* having a wide and refined knowledge of the world especially from personal experience ⟨Her long career as a globe-trotting journalist has made her very *worldly-wise* and even a little jaded.⟩

syn cosmopolitan, smart, sophisticated, worldly

rel suave, urbane; civilized, cultivated, cultured, polished, refined; experienced, knowing, practiced, schooled, seasoned; bored, cynical, jaded, skeptical; down-to-earth, pragmatic (*also* pragmatical), realistic, sober

near ant callow, green, inexperienced, raw; parochial, provincial, rustic (*also* rustical); philistine, uncivilized, uncultured, unrefined; childlike, simple, simpleminded; impractical; uncritical, unknowing

ant guileless, ingenuous, innocent, naive (*or* naïve), unsophisticated, untutored, unworldly, wide-eyed

worm *vb* **1** to advance gradually beyond the usual or desirable limits — see ENCROACH

2 to introduce in a gradual, secret, or clever way — see INSINUATE 1

3 to move slowly with the body close to the ground — see CRAWL 1

worn *adj* depleted in strength, energy, or freshness — see WEARY 1

worn-out *adj* **1** depleted in strength, energy, or freshness — see WEARY 1

2 worn or torn into or as if into rags — see RAGGED 2

worried *adj* feeling or showing uncomfortable feelings of uncertainty — see NERVOUS 1

worrisome *adj* **1** causing worry or anxiety — see TROUBLESOME

2 marked by or causing agitation or uncomfortable feelings — see NERVOUS 2

worry *n* an uneasy state of mind usually over the possibility of an anticipated misfortune or trouble — see ANXIETY 1

worry *vb* **1** to experience concern or anxiety ⟨They *worried* for days about whether the loan would be approved.⟩

syn bother, fear, fret, fuss, stew, stress, sweat, trouble

rel agonize; long, pine, yearn; chafe; despair

phrases give a hang (*or* care a hang), sweat blood

near ant accept; abide, bear, endure, stick out, stomach, sustain, take, tolerate

2 to trouble the mind of; to make uneasy — see DISTURB 1

worsen *vb* to become worse or of less value — see DETERIORATE 1

worship *n* excessive admiration of or devotion to a person ⟨the *worship* of professional athletes who often turn out to be all too fallible⟩

syn adulation, deification, idolatry, idolization, worshipping (*also* worshiping)

rel adoration, deference, glorification, reverence, veneration; idealization, romanticization; affection, fancy, favor, fondness, like, liking, love; appreciation, esteem, regard, respect; approval

near ant condemnation, disapproval, disfavor, dislike, dismissal, disregard, hatred, loathing, scorn

worship *vb* **1** to offer honor or respect to (someone) as a divine power ⟨The ancient Greeks *worshipped* many different gods.⟩

syn adore, deify, glorify, revere, reverence, venerate

rel admire, honor, love, regard, respect; apotheosize, canonize, dignify, exalt, lionize, magnify; extol (*also* extoll), laud, praise; delight, gratify, please, satisfy

near ant blaspheme, desecrate, profane, violate; affront, dishonor, disrespect, insult, offend, outrage, pique, ridicule, scorn, slight; displease; defame, disparage, libel, malign, slander, slur, smear

2 to feel passion, devotion, or tenderness for — see LOVE 2

3 to love or admire too much — see IDOLIZE

worshipful *adj* reflecting great admiration or devotion ⟨a movie fan's *worshipful* stare upon finally meeting her idol⟩ ⟨a teacher surrounded by *worshipful* little children⟩

syn adoring, adulatory, deifying, idolizing, worshipping (*also* worshiping)

rel glorifying, reverent, reverential, venerating; hagiographic (*also* hagiographical); affectionate, fond, loving; appreciative, deferential, respectful; approving

near ant condemning, contemptuous, disapproving, hateful, loathing, scornful

worshipping *also* **worshiping** *adj* reflecting great admiration or devotion — see WORSHIPFUL

worshipping *also* **worshiping** *n* excessive admiration of or devotion to a person — see WORSHIP

worst *vb* to achieve a victory over — see BEAT 2

worth *n* **1** the relative usefulness or impor-

tance of something as judged by specific qualities ⟨Money alone cannot determine the true *worth* of some things.⟩
syn account, merit, valuation, value
rel assessment, estimation, evaluation; excellence, greatness, perfection; consequence, importance, significance, weight
near ant emptiness, valuelessness, worthlessness; baseness, cheapness, crumminess, inferiority, lousiness, meanness, paltriness, poorness; deficiency, inadequacy, insufficiency, unacceptability
2 the amount of money for which something will find a buyer — see VALUE 1
3 the total of one's money and property — see WEALTH 1
worthless *adj* having no usefulness ⟨That expensive toy is *worthless* now that it's broken.⟩
syn empty, junky, no-good, null, vain, valueless
rel base, cheap, inferior, lousy, low-grade, second-rate; bad, defective, dud, flawed, imperfect, substandard, unsatisfactory; deficient, inadequate, insufficient, unacceptable
near ant precious; cherished, esteemed, prized, treasured; choice, exceptional, fancy, high-grade, special
ant useful, valuable, worthy
worthy *adj* having sufficient worth or merit to receive one's honor, esteem, or reward ⟨made charitable contributions to the American Red Cross and other *worthy* causes⟩ ⟨a *worthy* opponent in a tennis match⟩
syn deserving, good, meritorious
rel admirable, commendable, creditable, laudable, praiseworthy; cherished, prized, treasured; choice, excellent, exceptional, fancy, high-grade, primary, prime, special
near ant base, cheap, inferior, secondrate, substandard; bad, defective, flawed, imperfect; deficient, inadequate, insufficient, unacceptable, unsatisfactory
ant no-good, undeserving, valueless, worthless
wound *vb* **1** to cause bodily damage to — see INJURE 1
2 to cause hurt feelings or deep resentment in — see INSULT
wraith *n* the soul of a dead person thought of especially as appearing to living people — see GHOST 1
wrangle *n* an often noisy or angry expression of differing opinions — see ARGUMENT 1
wrangle *vb* to express different opinions about something often angrily — see ARGUE 2
wrangler *n* **1** a hired hand who tends cattle or horses at a ranch or on the range — see COWBOY
2 a person who takes part in a dispute — see DISPUTANT
wrap *vb* **1** to encircle or bind with or as if with a belt — see GIRD 1
2 to surround or cover closely — see ENFOLD 1
wraps *n pl* something that covers or conceals like a piece of cloth — see CLOAK 1

wrap–up *n* **1** a short statement of the main points — see SUMMARY
2 the last part of a process or action — see FINALE
wrap up *vb* **1** to bring (an event) to a natural or appropriate stopping point — see CLOSE 3
2 to make into a short statement of the main points (as of a report) — see SUMMARIZE
wrath *n* **1** an intense emotional state of displeasure with someone or something — see ANGER
2 suffering, loss, or hardship imposed in response to a crime or offense — see PUNISHMENT
wrathful *adj* feeling or showing anger — see ANGRY
wrathfulness *n* an intense emotional state of displeasure with someone or something — see ANGER
wreathe *vb* **1** to cause to twine about one another — see INTERTWINE 1
2 to scatter or set here and there among other things — see THREAD 1
3 to form a circle around — see SURROUND
wreck *n* **1** the portion or bits of something left over or behind after it has been destroyed — see REMAINS 1
2 the destruction or loss of a ship — see SHIPWRECK
3 the violent coming together of two bodies into destructive contact — see CRASH 1
wreck *vb* **1** to cause irreparable damage to (a ship) by running aground or sinking — see SHIPWRECK
2 to bring to a complete end the physical soundness, existence, or usefulness of — see DESTROY 1
wreckage *n* **1** the state or fact of being rendered nonexistent, physically unsound, or useless — see DESTRUCTION 1
2 the portion or bits of something left over or behind after it has been destroyed — see REMAINS 1
3 the destruction or loss of a ship — see SHIPWRECK
wrecking *n* the destruction or loss of a ship — see SHIPWRECK
wrench *n* **1** a forceful rotating or pulling motion for the purpose of dislodging something ⟨With a sharp *wrench* of the hammer I pulled the nail from the board.⟩
syn twist, twisting, wrenching, wresting, wringing
rel draft, draw, extraction, pull, tug, yank; dislocation, displacement
2 the act or an instance of applying force on something so that it moves in the direction of the force — see PULL 1
wrench *vb* **1** to move by or as if by a forceful rotation ⟨With one last sharp yank, he *wrenched* the lid off the bottle of ketchup.⟩
syn twist, wrest, wring
rel draw, dredge (up), extract, jerk, lug, pluck, pull, tug, tweak, yank; jimmy, lever, pry; budge, dislocate, displace, disturb, remove; shift, transfer, transpose
2 to injure by overuse, misuse, or pressure — see STRAIN 1
3 to separate or remove by forceful pulling — see TEAR 2

---

syn synonym(s)   *rel* related words
ant antonym(s)   *near ant* near antonym(s)

wrenching *adj* intensely or unbearably painful — see EXCRUCIATING 1

wrenching *n* a forceful rotating or pulling motion for the purpose of dislodging something — see WRENCH 1

wrest *vb* 1 to draw out by force or with effort — see EXTRACT

2 to get (as money) by the use of force or threats — see EXTORT

3 to move by or as if by a forceful rotation — see WRENCH 1

4 to separate or remove by forceful pulling — see TEAR 2

wresting *n* a forceful rotating or pulling motion for the purpose of dislodging something — see WRENCH 1

wrestle *vb* to seize and attempt to unbalance one another for the purpose of achieving physical mastery ⟨The young sisters *wrestled* on the floor over the toy.⟩

syn grapple, scuffle, tussle

rel battle, clash (with), combat, contend, duel, fight, war (against); bash, batter, beat, buffet, hit, punch, slug, strike; box, spar; brawl, skirmish

wretch *n* a mean, evil, or unprincipled person — see VILLAIN

wretched *adj* 1 extremely unsatisfactory ⟨This report is simply *wretched*—you'll have to rewrite it.⟩

syn atrocious, awful, dismal, execrable, horrible, lousy, punk, rotten, terrible

rel bad, deficient, inferior, off, poor, substandard, wanting; contemptible, miserable, shameful; defective, faulty, flawed; low-grade, mediocre, reprehensible, second-rate; bum, useless, valueless, worthless; inadequate, insufficient, lacking; abominable, fiendish, odious, vile

near ant choice, excellent, exceptional, first-class, first-rate, premium, prime, superior; adequate, sufficient; acceptable, satisfactory

ant great, marvelous (*or* marvellous), wonderful

2 arousing or deserving of one's loathing and disgust — see CONTEMPTIBLE 1

3 causing or marked by an atmosphere lacking in cheer — see GLOOMY 1

4 falling short of a standard — see BAD 1

5 feeling unhappiness — see SAD 1

6 not following or in accordance with standards of honor and decency — see IGNOBLE 2

7 of low quality — see CHEAP 2

8 deserving of one's pity — see PATHETIC 1

9 deserving pitying scorn (as for inadequacy) — see PITIFUL 1

wretchedly *adv* 1 in an unsatisfactory way — see BADLY 1

2 with feelings of bitterness or grief — see HARD 2

wriggle *vb* 1 to make jerky or restless movements — see FIDGET

2 to move slowly with the body close to the ground — see CRAWL 1

3 to introduce in a gradual, secret, or clever way — see INSINUATE 1

wring *vb* 1 to get (as money) by the use of force or threats — see EXTORT

2 to move by or as if by a forceful rotation — see WRENCH 1

3 to draw out by force or with effort — see EXTRACT

wringing *n* a forceful rotating or pulling motion for the purpose of dislodging something — see WRENCH 1

wrinkle *n* 1 a small fold in a soft and otherwise smooth surface ⟨The old woman's face creased into *wrinkles* as she smiled.⟩ ⟨The curtains cascaded onto the floor in ripples and *wrinkles*.⟩

syn crease, crimp, crinkle, furrow

rel corrugation, layer, loop, plait, pleat, ply, pucker, seam, tuck; crow's-foot

2 something (as a device) created for the first time through the use of the imagination — see INVENTION 1

wrinkle *vb* 1 to develop creases or folds ⟨If you don't fold clothes promptly after drying, they'll *wrinkle*.⟩

syn crease, crinkle, furrow, rumple

rel collapse, crumple, double, fold

2 to create (as by crushing) an irregular mass of creases in — see CRUMPLE 1

write *vb* 1 to compose and set down on paper the words of ⟨A staunch supporter of the old school, he prefers to *write* all of his letters by hand.⟩

syn author, pen, scratch (out), scribble

rel cast, compose, craft, draft, draw up, formulate, frame, prepare; recast, redraft, revise, rewrite; letter, print, type, typewrite; record, take down, transcribe; autograph, pencil (in), register, sign; couch, express, phrase, put, word

2 to engage in an exchange of written messages — see CORRESPOND 1

write off *vb* 1 to express scornfully one's low opinion of — see DECRY 1

2 to diminish the price or value of — see DEPRECIATE 1

writer *n* a person who creates a written work — see AUTHOR 1

writhe *vb* 1 to twine about one another — see INTERTWINE 1

2 to make jerky or restless movements — see FIDGET

wrong *adj* 1 falling short of a standard — see BAD 1

2 having an opinion that does not agree with truth or the facts — see INCORRECT 1

3 not appropriate for a particular occasion or situation — see INAPPROPRIATE

4 not being in agreement with what is true — see FALSE 1

5 not conforming to a high moral standard; morally unacceptable — see BAD 2

wrong *adv* off the desired or intended path or course ⟨All of our carefully laid plans have gone *wrong*.⟩

syn afield, amiss, astray, awry

rel badly; faultily, improperly, inappropriately, incorrectly, mistakenly, wrongly; inadequately, insufficiently, unpromisingly

near ant perfectly; auspiciously, favorably, promisingly; correctly, properly, rightly; appropriately, fittingly, suitably

ant right, well

wrong *n* 1 that which is morally unacceptable — see EVIL

2 unfair or inadequate treatment of someone or something or an instance of this — see DISSERVICE

wrongdoer *n* a person who commits moral wrongs — see EVILDOER 1

wrongdoing *n* **1** a breaking of a moral or legal code — see OFFENSE 1

2 improper or illegal behavior — see MISCONDUCT

wrongful *adj* contrary to or forbidden by law — see ILLEGAL 1

wrongly *adv* in a mistaken or inappropriate way ⟨You have *wrongly* interpreted this line of the poem.⟩

syn amiss, erroneously, faultily, improperly, inaccurately, inappropriately, inaptly, incorrectly, mistakenly, unsuitably

rel misguidedly; fallibly, imperfectly; extraneously, irrelevantly, meaninglessly, pointlessly, senselessly; inadequately, insufficiently; undesirably, unsatisfactorily; foolishly, unwisely

near ant infallibly, perfectly; germanely, meaningfully, pertinently, relevantly, sensibly; acceptably, adequately, satisfactorily, sufficiently; prudently, sagely, wisely

ant appropriately, aptly, correctly, fittingly, properly, right, rightly, suitably, well

wrongness *n* the quality or state of being unsuitable or unfitting — see INAPPROPRIATENESS 1

wroth *adj* feeling or showing anger — see ANGRY

x (out) *vb* to show (something written) to be no longer valid by drawing a cross over or a line through it ⟨You can *x out* the names of the people who have already left.⟩

syn cancel, cross (out), delete, kill, scratch (out), strike (out), stroke (out)

rel blot out, efface, eradicate, expunge, obliterate, root (out), rub out, wipe out; bleep, blip, clip, cut, excise, remove; censor, clean (up), expurgate, redact; abbreviate, crop, shorten; black out, repress, silence, suppress

near ant stet

yammer *n* an expression of dissatisfaction, pain, or resentment — see COMPLAINT 1

yammer *vb* to express dissatisfaction, pain, or resentment usually tiresomely — see COMPLAIN

yank *n* the act or an instance of applying force on something so that it moves in the direction of the force — see PULL 1

yank *vb* **1** to move or cause to move with a sharp quick motion — see JERK 1

2 to draw out by force or with effort — see EXTRACT

3 to separate or remove by forceful pulling — see TEAR 2

¹**yard** *n* **1** an open space wholly or partly enclosed (as by buildings or walls) — see COURT 2

2 the area around and belonging to a building — see GROUND 1

²**yard** *n* a considerable amount — see LOT 2

yardstick *n* something set up as an example against which others of the same type are compared — see STANDARD 1

yarn *n* **1** a brief account of something interesting that happened especially to one personally — see STORY 2

2 a work with imaginary characters and events that is shorter and usually less complex than a novel — see STORY 1

yaw *vb* to depart abruptly from a straight line or course — see SWERVE 1

yea *adv* **1** not merely this but also — see EVEN 1

2 used to express agreement — see YES

yea *n* a vote or decision for something — see YES

yeah *adv* used to express agreement — see YES

yearn (for) *vb* to have an earnest wish to own or enjoy — see DESIRE 1

yearn (over) *vb* to have sympathy for — see PITY

yearning *n* a strong wish for something — see DESIRE 1

yeast *n* something that arouses action or activity — see IMPULSE 1

yell *n* a loud vocal expression of strong emotion — see SHOUT

yell *vb* **1** to cry out loudly and emotionally — see SCREAM 1

2 to speak so as to be heard at a distance — see CALL 1

yellow *adj* having or showing a shameful lack of courage — see COWARDLY

yelp *vb* to cry out loudly and emotionally — see SCREAM 1

yen *n* a strong wish for something — see DESIRE 1

yes *adv* used to express agreement ⟨*Yes*, I'll be ready for the test tomorrow.⟩

syn all right, alright, aye (*also* ay), exactly, OK (*or* okay), yea, yeah

rel absolutely, assuredly, certainly, indeed, disputably, undoubtedly, unquestionably

ant nay, no, no way, scarcely

---

syn synonym(s)   *rel* related words

ant antonym(s)   *near ant* near antonym(s)

yes *n* a vote or decision for something ⟨The bill passed with 50 "*yeses*" and 12 "noes."⟩

syn yea

rel pro; acceptance, acquiescence, agreement, approval, assent, concurrence, consent, permission, sanction

near ant con; blackball, veto; denial, disallowance, negation, refusal, rejection

ant nay, negative, no, non placet

yesterday *n* the events or experience of former times — see PAST

yesteryear *n* the events or experience of former times — see PAST

yet *adv* **1** at a later time ⟨We may *yet* figure it out.⟩

syn eventually, finally, someday, sometime, ultimately

rel anon, directly, imminently, momentarily, presently, shortly, soon; forthwith, immediately, promptly, pronto, right away, right now, straightaway, straightway

phrases at last (*or* at long last), at length, in the end, in the fullness of time, in time

near ant ne'er, never, nevermore

2 in addition to what has been said — see MORE 1

3 in spite of that — see HOWEVER

4 up to this or that time — see HITHERTO

yet *conj* if it were not for the fact that — see EXCEPT

yield *n* **1** an increase usually measured in money that comes from labor, business, or property — see INCOME 1

2 something produced by physical or intellectual effort — see PRODUCT 1

3 the total amount collected or obtained especially at one time — see HAUL 1

yield *vb* **1** to give up and cease resistance (as to a liking, temptation, or habit) ⟨I finally *yielded* to temptation and had a bowl of ice cream.⟩

syn bow, cave (in), give in, submit, succumb, surrender

rel cater (to), gratify, indulge, wallow; acquiesce (to), concede (to); buckle (under), knuckle under; give over (to)

near ant battle, breast, combat, confront, counter, defy, face, fight, meet, object, oppose, repel; thwart, withstand; reject; bridle, check, constrain, curb, inhibit, restrain, stifle

ant hold off, resist

2 to produce as revenue ⟨I expect that stock to *yield* at least 14% profit this year.⟩

syn bear, give, pay, return

rel net; afford, furnish, provide, supply; pay off

3 to cease resistance (as to another's arguments, demands, or control) ⟨After initially balking at the order, the soldier *yielded* when the commanding officer threatened a formal charge of insubordination.⟩

syn blink, bow, budge, capitulate, concede, give in, knuckle under, quit, relent, submit, succumb, surrender

rel acquiesce; defer

phrases say uncle, throw in the towel (*also* throw in the sponge)

near ant contend, fight, hold off; battle, breast, combat, confront, counter, defy,

face, meet, object, oppose, repel; thwart, withstand

ant resist

4 to be the cause of (a situation, action, or state of mind) — see EFFECT

5 to fall down or in as a result of physical pressure — see COLLAPSE 1

6 to give (something) over to the control or possession of another usually under duress — see SURRENDER 1

7 to give (oneself) over to something especially unrestrainedly — see ABANDON 1

yielding *adj* **1** receiving or enduring without offering resistance — see PASSIVE

2 not stiff in structure — see LIMP 1

yoke *n* the state of being enslaved — see SLAVERY

yoke *vb* to put or bring together so as to form a new and longer whole — see CONNECT 1

yokel *n* an awkward or simple person especially from a small town or the country — see HICK

yon *adv* at or to a greater distance or more advanced point — see FARTHER

yonder *adv* at or to a greater distance or more advanced point — see FARTHER

yore *n* the events or experience of former times — see PAST

young *adj* being in the early stage of life, growth, or development ⟨A *young* cat requires more food than an older one.⟩ ⟨a *young* tree that will eventually reach 50 feet tall⟩

syn adolescent, immature, juvenile, youngish, youthful

rel ephebic, minor, preteen, subadult, teenage (*or* teenaged), underage; embryonic; callow, green, inexperienced, puerile, raw; babyish, childish, childlike, infantile, infantine, kiddish; undeveloped, unfinished, unfledged, unformed, unripe, unripened; blooming, blossoming, burgeoning, flourishing, flowering

near ant aged, aging (*or* ageing), ancient, elderly, geriatric, long-lived, old, older, oldish, senior; full-blown, full-fledged; golden, mellow, ripe, ripened; middle-aged; anile, decrepit, doddering, over-the-hill, senile, spavined, tottery

ant adult, grown-up, mature, matured

youngish *adj* being in the early stage of life, growth, or development — see YOUNG

youngster *n* a young person who is between infancy and adulthood — see CHILD 1

youth *n* **1** a male person who has not yet reached adulthood — see BOY 1

2 a young person who is between infancy and adulthood — see CHILD 1

3 the state or time of being a child — see CHILDHOOD

youthful *adj* being in the early stage of life, growth, or development — see YOUNG

yowl *n* a loud vocal expression of strong emotion — see SHOUT

yowl *vb* **1** to express dissatisfaction, pain, or resentment usually tiresomely — see COMPLAIN

2 to make a long loud mournful sound — see HOWL 1

yo–yo *n* **1** a person who lacks good sense or judgment — see FOOL 1

2 a stupid person — see IDIOT

yucky *also* **yukky** *adj* **1** disagreeable or disgusting to the sense of taste — see DISTASTEFUL 1

2 not giving pleasure to the mind or senses — see UNPLEASANT

yuletide *n* the season celebrating Christmas ⟨These days, as far as the stores are concerned, *yuletide* starts in September.⟩

syn Christmastide, Christmastime, Noel

rel Advent; Christmas, nativity, Xmas, yule

yummy *adj* very pleasing to the sense of taste — see DELICIOUS 1

zaniness *n* lack of good sense or judgment — see FOOLISHNESS 1

zany *adj* showing or marked by a lack of good sense or judgment — see FOOLISH 1

zany *n* **1** a comically dressed performer (as at a circus) who entertains with playful tricks and ridiculous behavior — see CLOWN 1

2 a person of odd or whimsical habits — see ECCENTRIC

zap *vb* to deliver a blow to (someone or something) usually in a strong vigorous manner — see HIT 1

zealot *n* one who is intensely or excessively devoted to a cause ⟨*Zealots* on both sides of the issue resorted to name-calling and scare tactics.⟩

syn crusader, fanatic, militant, partisan (*also* partizan)

rel activist; dreamer, idealist, visionary; cultist, disciple, follower, hanger-on, idolizer, votary; addict, aficionado (*also* afficionado), buff, bug, devotee, enthusiast, fan, fancier, fiend, fool, freak, head, hound, junkie (*also* junky), lover, maniac, nut, sucker; advocate, apostle, backer, champion, evangelist, patron, promoter, stalwart, supporter; booster, rooter, well-wisher; faddist

near ant dabbler, dilettante

ant nonmilitant

zenith *n* the highest part or point — see HEIGHT 1

zephyr *n* a slight or gentle movement of air — see BREEZE 1

zero *n* **1** the numerical symbol 0 or the absence of number or quantity represented by it ⟨Anything multiplied by *zero* comes out to *zero*.⟩

syn aught, cipher, goose egg, naught (*also* nought), nil, nothing, oh, zilch, zip

rel blank, void

2 a person of no importance or influence — see NOBODY

zero hour *n* a time or state of affairs requiring prompt or decisive action — see EMERGENCY

zest *n* the quality or state of being stimulating to the mind or senses — see PIQUANCY

zesty *adj* sharp and pleasantly stimulating to the mind or senses — see PIQUANT

zigzag *vb* to move suddenly aside or to and fro — see DODGE 1

zilch *n* **1** a person of no importance or influence — see NOBODY

2 the numerical symbol 0 or the absence of number or quantity represented by it — see ZERO 1

zing *n* **1** active strength of body or mind — see VIGOR 1

2 the quality or state of being stimulating to the mind or senses — see PIQUANCY

¹**zip** *n* active strength of body or mind — see VIGOR 1

²**zip** *n* the numerical symbol 0 or the absence of number or quantity represented by it — see ZERO 1

zip *vb* **1** to fly, turn, or move rapidly with a fluttering or vibratory sound — see WHIR

2 to make an irregular series of quick, sudden movements — see FLIT

3 to proceed or move quickly — see HURRY 2

zip (up) *vb* to give life, vigor, or spirit to — see ANIMATE

zippy *adj* **1** having much high-spirited energy and movement — see LIVELY 1

2 moving, proceeding, or acting with great speed — see FAST 1

zone *n* **1** a broad geographical area — see REGION 2

2 a part or portion having no fixed boundaries — see REGION 1

zoom *n* a monotonous sound like that of an insect in motion — see HUM

zoom *vb* **1** to fly, turn, or move rapidly with a fluttering or vibratory sound — see WHIR

2 to proceed or move quickly — see HURRY 2

3 to rise abruptly and rapidly — see SKYROCKET
